# INFORMATION
# PLEASE
# ALMANAC
## Atlas and Yearbook
## 1962

# INFORMATION PLEASE ALMANAC

# Atlas and Yearbook

# 1962

★

*Planned and Supervised by*

DAN GOLENPAUL ASSOCIATES

SIMON AND SCHUSTER · New York City

**Library of Congress Catalog Card No. 47–845**

*Printed in the U. S. A.*

© COPYRIGHT NOVEMBER 1961 BY DAN GOLENPAUL ASSOCIATES

PREVIOUS EDITIONS COPYRIGHT 1947, 1948, 1949, 1950, 1951, 1952, 1953, 1954, 1955, 1956, 1957, 1958, 1959, 1960 BY DAN GOLENPAUL ASSOCIATES

# FOREWORD

*By*

## DAN GOLENPAUL

### Editor

This is the sixteenth edition of the INFORMATION PLEASE ALMANAC and the second edition of our current format which combines the best elements of an almanac, atlas and yearbook.

We adopted the new format with the 1961 edition as something of an experiment. The verdict of our readers encouraged us to continue the experiment with improvements, of course.

The new format enables us to provide an enduring record of the American contemporary scene of each year. When you read the *Headline Stories of 1961* they will refer you to related photos, maps, and tabular material included in this edition. We suggest that you read the *News Roundup of Major Events of 1961* for an example of how we integrated the various sections of our book.

No other single volume published gives you this scope which is what makes the INFORMATION PLEASE ALMANAC, ATLAS AND YEARBOOK an essential tool for students and everybody who wants to be informed and acquire a better understanding of events today.

We would like to believe that we have developed a technique that has increased the usefulness of our book. We would be very happy to receive opinions from our readers on our new format with some expression of their favorite sections and material.

We are confident that our book contains few, if any, errors, but we submit that "to err is human." Although all of our material is checked at least 10 times by different people, things can happen. Sometimes an error will turn up. If we haven't found it, you may; and we invite you to bring to our attention any error if you find it. We hasten to add that your only reward will be the satisfaction of being more alert than our staff.

Whatever degree of success we may achieve with our 1962 edition we owe to many individuals: our contributors, associate editors, and our loyal, hardworking, harassed office staff who not only met every challenge and requirement, but did it with pride and respect for the editor's objectives.

While you are looking for the errors, we will start working on the 1963 edition. "Time and tide stayeth for no man" nor for any annual book.

# TABLE OF CONTENTS

# ADDENDA

The INFORMATION PLEASE ALMANAC is designed for study, reading and reference. Since students need the use of this book for part of the fall term, we made it available in early December. To accomplish this, we print some sections before December and, therefore, it became necessary to add changes at the latest possible date. Listed here are some of the additions for various sections indicated by the page numbers.

## AVIATION (page 227)

Air Force Major Robert White flew the X-15 to a height of 215,000 feet, reached a speed of 3,477 mph., to break the altitude record for winged, man-controlled flight by 8¾ miles. (Oct. 11)

## AWARDS (page 451)

The Nobel Prize for Medicine was awarded to Hungarian-born Dr. Georg von Bekesy of Harvard for his "discoveries concerning the physical mechanism of stimulation within the cochlea"—a division of the labyrinth of the ear (Oct. 19).

The Nobel Prize for Peace was awarded, posthumously for the first time, to Dag Hammarskjöld (Oct. 23). The prize money will be given to Hammarskjöld's estate.

## IRELAND (EIRE) (page 715)

In the general elections (Oct. 4) in Ireland to the Dáil (parliament) the Fianna Fail party won only 70 seats, leaving it 3 short of the number necessary to control the government. The Fine Gael, opposition party, gained 6 seats for a total of 47. Sean Lemass was re-elected Prime Minister.

## SOUTH AFRICA, REPUBLIC OF (page 751)

Prime Minister Verwoerd won a new 5-year term in the elections of Oct. 18.

## TURKEY (page 762)

Elections to a new Parliament (Oct. 15) were held for the first time since a military coalition overthrew Premier Adnan Menderes' administration in May, 1960. Results indicated no one party had won a majority in either the Assembly or the Senate.

## UGANDA (page 644)

London announced on Oct. 9 that Uganda will achieve full independence on Oct. 9, 1962, and elections will follow in mid-April, 1963.

(Addenda continued on page 911)

# LIGHT AND SERIOUS TOUCHES

## By Marcus Duffield

### JANUARY 1961

The new young President of the United States emulated the mountain goat that leaped from crag to crag. At the inaugural ball, Kennedy wanted to greet the VIP's in the boxes, but the connecting aisles were impassibly jammed. So he leaped from box to box, thereby throwing into a state of jitters the less athletic Secret Service men assigned to guard him. . . . Inaugural gowns were featured in a Washington department-store window at $595, but the more expensive ones were inside. Forty bucks would buy a chap a presentable silk topper. . . . When Kennedy made Bobby the Attorney General, the word in Washington was: "Little Brother Is Watching You." . . . The outgoing Republicans were sniffing for jobs. One who landed on his feet was Jim Hagerty, press aide to Eisenhower, who just about doubled his salary with $50,000 a year at the American Broadcasting Co. . . . Things were looking up all over. People in Texas were enjoying their Christmas gifts—matching airplanes labeled "His" and "Hers," which cost only $200,000 a pair. For the common folk there was a dehydrated beer (awaiting government approval), which you would buy and add water, just like canned orange juice. The dehydrated martini cocktail was at that time just a dream in somebody's eye.

### FEBRUARY 1961

These bold Kennedy men had a word for it. The economy was in a "recession," and had been for months. The Eisenhower men never used that naughty word, although they must have suspected something, with over five million unemployed, the highest since 1941. Now another phrase popped into the news. Maybe, just maybe, the recession was "bottoming out." Or, to put it in a more refined way, maybe it was "saucering out." Undaunted, the New York B. Altman store on Fifth Avenue held its spring fashion show for dogs. Their doggy duds were tailored from tail to paw. Red trench coats sold at $15 per pup. If you wanted to go in for canine coats of mink it would cost you $110. . . . There was good news for skiers. No lack of snow from New England down to Virginia. Snow machines ($15,000 each) spewed water, atomized by compressed-air blast, above ski trails, and it came down snow. . . . Up to the fringe of outer space, the United States shot the nearest thing to man— Ham, the chimpanzee, who grinned from ear to ear when he came home and reached for an apple. . . . Much more astonished than Ham were the 580 humans crossing the Atlantic on the Portuguese luxury liner *Santa Maria*. They thought piracy in the Caribbean had gone out of fashion 300 years ago, but they were fooled. They and their whole ship were kidnaped by Portuguese rebels, who wandered about and finally wound up in the port of Recife, Brazil, where nobody wanted to go. Captain Kidd never did things on such a grand scale.

## MARCH 1961

CULTURAL NOTES—Carillons, which for centuries have chimed from church steeples, went heathen. An ingenious Pennsylvania firm now sells them to banks, department stores, and a brewery to improve their "image." . . . Not to be outdone by the secular, the Trappistine nuns were developing a booming business in selling their luxury candies (caramels and butternut munches) all over the country. . . . The runaway best-selling book of the month was 13 years in the making—an entirely new translation of the New Testament in modern language. . . . In the music field, the surprising development was the boom in player pianos for the family rumpus room. Manufacturing of them had stopped in 1928—too old-fashioned—and now it began turning new-fashioned in a big way. . . . In the nonalcoholic field, coffee houses were spreading throughout the country and getting more and more ambitious. New York's "Phase 2" offered a half-hour review called "Pass the Nuts." Hollywood's "Renaissance" put out its own newsletter and held art classes. In St. Louis the "Laughing Buddha" went in for folk songs. . . . And while all this was going on, the serious side of mankind was anxious about the chaotic Congo, where African tribal warriors were fighting United Nations troops sent there to stamp down turbulence. . . . In the United States, there was the mightiest flood of words from the White House since the beginning of the New Deal, 28 years ago. Message after Kennedy message suggested to Congress what it might do about missiles, houses, the new Peace Corps, etc., etc., etc.

## APRIL 1961

Far too much news this month. Why can't we space things out? Big headlines: ADOLF EICHMANN ON TRIAL IN ISRAEL FOR SLAUGHTERING 6 MILLION JEWS IN WORLD WAR II! And: RUSSIA ROCKETS FIRST MAN INTO ORBIT AROUND THE WORLD! And: ANTI-CASTRO INVASION OF CUBA FAILS DESPITE U.S. HELP! And: FRANCE ESCAPES CIVIL WAR OVER ALGERIA! Our nerves were edgy as we wondered: What next? . . . But there was one optimistic note: The American tear-gas industry had its best year, what with so much trouble afoot all around the world. A small example: Police used eight tear-gas bombs to break up a demonstration of a few thousand Harvard University students. Seems they were outraged at the university's decree that diplomas henceforth will be printed in English instead of Latin. . . . Another cheerful note: A drug company put on the market a planned-parenthood pill for dogs. . . . Women were now able to limber up their toes. The extremely pointed shoe was on the way out, thanks to Christian Dior. On the way in—a snub-nosed, square-toed shoe that looked somewhat like the bill of a platypus. . . . Weirdest hobby of this spring: Do-it-yourself helicopters. You buy the pieces for $3,000, including an overgrown motorcycle engine, and put the contraption together. Then you fly it straight up a mile or more, or forward at 65 miles an hour, and finally land it on your driveway.

## MAY 1961

Obviously, the woman of the month was Mrs. John T. Heges, owner of a tavern on the bank of the Potomac River. It was raining buckets, and three wet, muddy-shoed men came in. She threw out them tramps. Them tramps, on a hike, were Supreme Court Justice William O. Douglas, Secretary of the Interior Stewart L. Udall, and Senator Paul H. Douglas of Illinois. . . . Treasury Secretary Dillon, who was not on the hike, announced that the recession is really over. But nearly six million Americans still were unemployed, largely because of automation. Undaunted was the Los Angeles Turf Club, whose stock was selling at around $70,000 a share. . . . A problem running into billions of dollars was tossed into the lap of the Du Pont Company. The Supreme Court told it to get rid of 63 million shares of General Motors to break up a monopoly—biggest divorce in the business world in many a year. . . . A problem that could not be solved by money haunted 20,248 eager youths who strove to get into the eight Ivy League colleges, and were turned down. The fortunate ones who were accepted numbered 13,311. . . . One fortunate American, Alan B. Shepard, Jr., took a little ride—only 15 minutes. A rocket took him up 115 miles into space at a maximum speed of 5,000 miles an hour. He was plucked from the ocean, and he sneezed. . . . In the calm life down on earth, frantic publishers kept putting out new magazines, called by names such as "Caterpillar," and "Monocle."

## JUNE 1961

Summer cometh in, complete with bathing suits. One little swim costume for sale in New York was nylon satin splashed with mauve, and it wound up with slender bloomers. One-piece suit: $135. If you wanted a skirt to match, that nicked you another $125. Or, if you wanted a tricky swim suit, there was one that was transparent—until you put it on, at which time it became opaque in deference to old-time modesty. . . . Of course, you didn't need to go into the water. There was a new thing called "Floater-Loafer." This was a lounge chair that floated in your pool, or any other calm chunk of water. It was made of expanded polystyrene, in case you're curious why it floats. . . . Such was the progress of modern science that you could walk on water, as well as sit on it. A type of plastic foam was being made for water shoes, with which the wearer could shuffle across a lake at three miles an hour, average walking speed. . . . For the most elegant and expensive dunking (ladies only, please), you could go to the Revlon beauty parlor on Fifth Avenue, New York City, which installed a sunken Roman bath (bubble, spa, or sea water) with a warmed towel and a $10 massage afterward. . . . Returning to solid ground, the most currently famous vehicle was a rocking chair hitherto manufactured in complete obscurity by the tiny P. & P. Chair Company in Asheboro, North Carolina. It was made of oak with a specially curved back. Now this chair suddenly rocked and creaked all over the nation, and the little factory gasped at its orders. The chair was being rocked in by President Kennedy in the White House.

## JULY 1961

The name of a place—Berlin—became a symbol for a world crisis. Khrushchev made threats, and East Germany restricted traffic into West Berlin; but President Kennedy stood firm, and England and France prepared for an emergency. . . . Speaking from the White House, President Kennedy asked for 270,000 more men for the Armed Forces, and $3.457 billion for the defense budget to meet Soviet threats. . . . The name of a man—Virgil Grissom—made Americans cheer. He was the second astronaut to ride into space more than 100 miles above the earth and land safely. (Unfortunately, his space capsule was lost in the Atlantic Ocean.) . . . What's in a name? The name of President Lincoln was deleted from a television show sponsored by a car manufacturer, a producer testified before the Federal Communications Commission, because Lincoln was the name of a car made by a competitor. . . . When one American family does something, all American families want to do the same thing. The new vogue was a mass movement of campers returning to the "wilderness." A total of 16,500,000 men, women, and children were reported headed for the camping grounds. Were they really copying Henry David Thoreau and returning to nature? Could be. But at many national park camping sites, campers found hot and cold running water, plumbing facilities done in the city fashion, cocktail lounges, automatic laundries, television, and hairdressers. . . . Texas joined the national boating boom in the usual Texas manner—determined to become the leading boating state in the United States. In the nation, one family out of twelve owns a boat. In Texas, it is one out of eight. Added Texas touch: On the stern of one fifty-foot craft, a mink-lined doghouse has been secured for a pink toy poodle.

## AUGUST 1961

Outside of comic opera, playing at war is very dangerous. In Berlin they seemed to be playing at war, and the world became tense and worried. American tanks moved within ten feet of the Red Berlin border to shield West Berliners. Not many yards away on the East Berlin side, a water-gun car moved up and splashed water on GIs. Later, the water cannon was aimed at three United States Generals. . . . The Russians announced with glee that Comrade Cosmonaut Titov had taken a 17,750 mph. ride in space, circling the globe 17½ times, making a journey as far as the moon and back. . . . The unrelenting desire for progress and keeping up with modern times was also reflected in the opening of Matsubuya, a new, glittering geisha establishment in Tokyo. Matsubuya proudly announced membership in the Diners' Club. . . . The heat and humidity reached sweltering heights in August. For those who felt guilty about doing less work in the hot weather, the *National Geographic* had these comforting words: "The ant—bane of the sluggards—does not work all the time. The ant takes long rests, sometimes remaining motionless for hours. An anthill seems to be bustling because nappers hide from sight." . . . In France a deaf dog was in the news. A band of thieves stole eight Cézanne paintings—including "The Card Players"—from a museum in Aix-en-Provence. While the burglaring deed was being done, the custodian dozed, and the watchdog—a deaf terrier—heard nothing. . . . Women were being rediscovered in fashion for 1962. The good word from Paris was that the accent would be on the shape, and there would be curves, nothing but curves. Even fabrics were body-conscious: They draped, spiraled, clung closer, hugged the midriff—the key to the 1962 silhouette.

## SEPTEMBER 1961

Nikita Khrushchev announced to the world that the Soviet Union intended to resume nuclear testing, and did—exploding bombs all through September. Reaction of the people of the United States was sadness and worry. Some showed their concern in extremes. Public officials in Chicago received calls from women who were afraid their hair curlers were radioactive. Men inquired whether the olives in their martinis were safe. . . . Some Americans apparently have entered a here-today-gone-tomorrow phase. They want to rent everything. People now rent mink stoles for $35 a night, five dozen highball glasses for a party for $7.50, fine crystal goblets at $24 a dozen, contemporary paintings from the New York Circulating Library of Paintings, and artificial grass. There is even a place to rent a kitchen sink. One can rent an elephant for $5 a day. . . . A Philadelphia judge worried about the excuse the attorney for Butler Young gave when the defendant did not appear in court on a drunken driving charge. "Mr. Young is sitting with a sick elephant," the attorney said. He wasn't pulling the judge's leg. Mr. Young works at the Philadelphia zoo. . . . Senators probing gambling in the United States learned that a special magnet worth $150 can be worn inside the trousers by one gambler. When gambler No. 2, working as a partner, tosses the dice in which metal dust has been forced into the painted number spots, gambler No. 1, standing at the other end of the table, controls the turn of the dice by slight body movements that go unnoticed by bettors around the table concentrating on the roll. . . . Capping teeth is used by dentists to give Hollywood stars a beautiful mouth. Now it seems cows like to be beautiful, too. A veterinarian found that cows gain weight and give more milk when their teeth are capped.

## OCTOBER 1961

Creepiness about the danger of war was overtaking us, and President Kennedy said no wonder: "We happen to live in the most dangerous time in the history of the human race." . . . One company making air raid shelters found its business jumping to 600 orders a week, and it charged up to $2,900 for each shelter. Sears, Roebuck started to offer cheaper ones, only $700. One smart company peddled a combination fall-out shelter and swimming pool so you couldn't lose if the war failed to show up. A moral argument arose. People were putting revolvers in their shelters to shoot their shelterless neighbors if they started rushing in. Was this chummy? . . . People were spending their money so fast that savings banks, desperate for deposits, were offering prizes such as travel clocks, blankets, chicken-fryers if you opened a $25 account. To make spending easier, the S. H. Kress variety store in New York, once famous for its five-and-dime items, opened a department to sell diamonds up to $99. . . . Yes, there was money around. The musical *My Fair Lady* broke all Broadway records by grossing $18 million, and broke all Hollywood records by snaring $5½ million for the film rights. Even the little off-Broadway intimate revues were catching the popular fancy; three of them had sketches built around the end of the world. . . . Sad that the world should end just when we shook off the last need for exercise—the new electric toothbrush did the work. Detachable bristles, one set for each member of the family.

# NEWS ROUNDUP OF MAJOR EVENTS OF 1961

This 1961 was a year of anxiety lest mankind be headed down the road to nuclear suicide. The Soviet Union was responsible for the world's fear.

Russia announced on Aug. 30 that it would break its promise of 1958 to abstain from nuclear testing. This had brought a voluntary moratorium by the United States and Britain, too. Now in 1961, Russia far surpassed its 1958 pre-ban string of tests in the atmosphere, distributing radioactive fallout all over the world. Early in September President Kennedy announced that the United States, having a duty not to lag in defense, would resume tests, too— deep underground in order not to pollute the atmosphere with radioactivity. (*See* table "Nuclear Tests, 1961," page 60.)

The Russian blasts were doubly ominous inasmuch as the Soviet Union had kept the world on tenterhooks during the year with its threats against West Berlin. (*See* "Headline Story," page 18, and map, page 133.) Premier Khrushchev said he would sign a separate peace treaty with East Germany, giving it control of the West's access to West Berlin and the power to block such access. Aggravating the situation, the Communists erected a wall between

East Berlin and West Berlin, cutting the city in two. (*See* photographs, pages 101–103.)

In the September elections in West Germany, eighty-five-year-old Chancellor Adenauer's Christian Democratic party lost ground. Previously it had held majority control of Parliament, but no longer. The opposition Social Democrats gained, and so did the small third party, the Free Democrats. With the latter party Adenauer had to form a coalition government.

## Southeast Asia

On the other side of the world, the Communists (in this case Red China as well as the Soviet Union) were committing aggression in the hope of seizing control of Southeast Asia. The United States was so perturbed by the Communist-inspired civil war in Laos (*see* maps on pages 133 and 144) that the U.S. 7th Fleet moved into the vicinity in March with its warplanes within striking distance. A 14-nation East-West conference met for months in Geneva to draw up rules for guarding the independence of Laos, which was enjoying a temporary truce during the conference. Not until Oct. 8 did the Laotians themselves agree on a supposedly neutralist coalition government combining three factions: Communist, neutralist, and pro-West. But the "neutralist" Premier they chose, Prince Souvanna Phouma, was on very friendly terms with his half-brother, Prince Souphanouvong, the leader of the Laos Communists.

Adjoining Laos is South Vietnam, another of the little countries that gained independence after the French left Indochina. Also like Laos, South Vietnam was invaded by Communist guerrillas from the Red-dominated northern half of the country, known as North Vietnam.

President Kennedy was deeply concerned lest the pro-West government of President Ngo Dinh Diem of South Vietnam be overthrown. In October he dispatched his White House military adviser, Gen. Maxwell D. Taylor, to Saigon, the capital, to investigate the situation. One of the possibilities was that the United States would send a contingent of troops to South Vietnam to stand in reserve in case of a crisis.

## Cuba, the Dominican Republic, and Brazil

The Communists were busy in the Western Hemisphere also. They were behind the Cuban dictator, Fidel Castro, in his anti-United States actions. The United States broke diplomatic relations with Cuba, and gave preparatory training to Cuban exiles who invaded Cuba in an attempt to overthrow Castro. The invasion was a failure. (*See* "Headline Story," page 21, map, page 139.)

Elsewhere in the Western Hemisphere there was peace, although marred occasionally by unpleasant episodes.

In the Dominican Republic, the dictator for thirty-one years, Generalissimo Rafael Leonidas Trujillo, was slain by a gunshot from ambush. During his dictatorship it was estimated that he was responsible for having put to death more than 1,000 of his countrymen.

Brothers and sons of Trujillo clung to positions of power. The Organization of American States, hoping to check the Trujillo influence, investigated conditions there and recommended diplomatic sanctions. The United States already had broken off diplomatic relations.

Brazil surprisingly lost a President. (*See* map, page 138.) Janio Quadros had been elected by a landslide in South America's largest nation and had taken office less than seven months before, but he resigned the Presidency on Aug. 25 and left the new capital, Brasilia, to disappear abroad. He said he was disgusted with the tactics of his political foes. Brazil's Vice-President, João Goulart, was called home from Hong Kong where he had just emerged from a trip to Red China. Suspecting him of Leftism, the armed forces in Brazil prevented his taking office for twelve days. By that time the constitution had been amended to center executive power in a Premier instead of the President.

## France

Turning back to the European scene, we find France the most uneasy country of Europe in 1961. In this case the Communists, although numerous and powerful in France, were not the original trouble-makers, but were ready to take whatever advantage they could.

The French province of Algeria had been in revolt for nearly seven years at great cost in lives on both sides. President de Gaulle had decided to settle the matter by allowing the Algerian Moslems to vote on their political future. He offered them the choice of autonomy under continued union with France, or complete independence. This was to be determined in a plebiscite. But the rebels were suspicious of his terms and continued their revolt. (*See* map, page 130.)

The further de Gaulle carried his negotiations with the rebels, the more alarmed became the million French who had settled in Algeria. They feared being driven out if independence were achieved. They were backed by Rightist generals commanding the large French army in Algeria. (*See* photographs, page 125.)

On April 22, the military cabal revolted against the de Gaulle government at Paris and seized the capital, Algiers. They were determined to halt Algerian independence even if it meant civil war in continental France and an attempt to seize Paris.

De Gaulle proclaimed a state of emergency, giving him powers of a dictator, and ordered the loyal army in France to liquidate the Algerian insurrection, by force of arms if necessary. The Navy remained loyal and blockaded the mutineers, depriving them of food and ammunition. Police in Algeria joined some loyal army units in seizing key points from the insurrectionists. In a few days the insurrection collapsed. France remained, however, in a state of tension.

To add to France's troubles, a former colony, now independent, next door to Algeria, was kicking up its heels. President Habib Bourguiba of Tunisia demanded that France agree to the principle of abandoning and moving out of its naval base of Tunisia at Bizerte, one of its biggest and most strategically placed naval bases. He set no deadline.

## The United Arab Republic

A dream of President Nasser of Egypt was to create a vast Arab state reaching from the Atlantic all across northern Africa to the Persian Gulf. Three years ago he absorbed Syria into what he then termed the United Arab Republic. This was to have been a first step. In September, 1961, Nasser's dream blew up.

Syria revolted and cast off Egyptian rule. The United Arab Repubic was no more. The revolt was almost bloodless, but so conclusive that Nasser accepted the result without a struggle. (*See* map, page 142.)

## The Congo

Two thousand miles to the south in Africa, in mid-continent, the newly independent Congo nation was struggling to bring order out of chaos, aided by troops of the United Nations stationed there. Amid tribal fighting and regional quarrels it succeeded in forming a central government at Léopold-ville. (*See* map, page 129.)

But there was one hold-out, the rich province of Katanga, which refused to join the central Congo nation and insisted on independence. Belgian influence and enormous Belgian investments were a factor there. The U.N. authorized its forces in Katanga to eliminate Belgian officers and soldiers from the Katanga army.

In trying to do so, the U.N. troops were successfully resisted by Katanga warriors, and there was bloody fighting with deaths on both sides. More than 100 U.N. soldiers from Ireland were captured. U.N. Secretary-General Dag Hammarskjöld flew to the Congo to try to arrange a truce with President Moise Tshombe of Katanga. In the short, final leg of Hammarskjöld's flight, his plane crashed and he was killed. (*See* "Headline Story," page 20; photographs, pages 104–107.)

## The United States

The United States watched how its new President, John F. Kennedy, would fare with Congress. He did fairly well, but did not get all the legislation he wanted.

Congress co-operated with the President in creating an entirely new organization, the Peace Corps. Its mission was to send specially trained young men and women to underdeveloped nations abroad and share their skills. They were to work on such things as road-building, irrigation projects, medical improvements.

Congress followed the President's recommendation in increasing the minimum wage to $1.00 and $1.15. Area redevelopment, including slum clearance, was put on the statute books for the first time.

On the defeated list of Kennedy-proposed legislation were measures for broad Federal aid to education; medical care for the aged; and a new Cabinet post headed by a Secretary for Urban Affairs.

No new legislation was involved in the field of racial integration, but progress was noted under previous laws and court decisions. Opening of schools to Negroes on at least a token basis spread to the Deep South in such states as Georgia and Texas. (*See* photographs, pages 112–113.) Nine Negro students entered higher schools in Atlanta with no disturbances. Atlanta eating places, including department and drug stores, were opened to Negroes.

In politics, news was made by former Vice-President Nixon, the defeated Republican candidate for the Presidency. He announced that he would enter the race for Governor of California in 1962. He said he would keep on serving, if elected, and would not be a candidate for the Presidency in 1964.

On the whole, it was a prosperous year for the country. The year had started with the tail end of a recession inherited from 1960. The recession gradually wore off. By August, shares traded in Wall Street reached the highest level in history and the Dow-Jones ticker reached a high of 713.94.

However, more than five million persons remained unemployed. This was attributed in part to the effects of automation—reduction of jobs because of scientific advances in industry.

The United States sent two men into space. Still we were behind the Soviet Union, which sent two men into orbit. (*See* "Space Age News," pages 52–62.)

The Americans were Navy Cmdr. Alan B. Shepard, Jr., who was sent up by *Redstone* rocket on May 5, and Air Force Capt. Virgil I. Grissom. Shepard went up 116.5 miles in his space cabin from Cape Canaveral, Fla., in a flight that lasted 15 minutes. Grissom went up 118 miles. In both cases the men were parachuted to the sea at the end of their flights and were recovered in good health. (*See* photographs, pages 115–119.)

The two Russian astronauts were Yuri Y. Gagarin, who orbited the earth in one hour, forty-eight minutes, and Gherman S. Titov, who circled the earth repeatedly in a flight of twenty-five hours, eighteen minutes. Both landed safely. (*See* photographs, page 114.)

# HEADLINE STORIES OF 1961
## KENNEDY'S TRIPS

As a candidate for office, John F. Kennedy tended to belittle the many foreign trips made by President Dwight D. Eisenhower. "The duty of the chief executive," said candidate Kennedy, "is to stay at the helm in Washington." (*See* photographs beginning page 97.)

But after assuming the Presidency, Mr. Kennedy apparently discovered that personal contact with other heads of state might be fairly important. Before he had been in office five months, he had visited Canada and Europe for conferences with Prime Minister Diefenbaker, President De Gaulle, Premier Khrushchev, and Prime Minister Macmillan. Following are some of the results of his travels:

OTTAWA, Canada: The two leaders agreed that Communist Cuba constituted a threat to the peaceful and democratic evolution of Latin American peoples. Whereas Mr. Kennedy urged Canada to join the Organization of

American States and to give more economic aid to Latin America, Mr. Diefenbaker made no definite commitments. But the general feeling was that the American proposals had gained at least a measure of support as a result of the Kennedy visit.

PARIS, France: The meetings between Presidents Kennedy and de Gaulle were apparently highly successful. As expected, the two men agreed that a firm stand should be taken against the Soviets on Berlin and that all efforts should be made to establish an independent, neutral Laos. Although there was no announced agreement on two questions which had plagued relations between France and the United States—more French support for NATO and French control of nuclear weapons on French soil—two subsequent moves indicated that a compromise of sorts had been reached: de Gaulle ordered two divisions and an air wing home from Algeria to bolster European forces; and two squadrons of American fighter-bombers, which left France because of French insistence on control over their nuclear weapons, returned to France—although without the weapons. But it was a beginning. And officials in both capitals indicated that de Gaulle and Kennedy saw eye-to-eye on most international problems as a result of their personal contacts.

VIENNA, Austria: Here President Kennedy met dictator Khrushchev. The official communiqué described their talks as "useful," "frank," and "courteous," but it was obvious that they would not lead to any immediate relaxation of tension between the two nations. Mr. Khrushchev was blunt and adamant. Mr. Kennedy conceded nothing. But at least the two leaders had an opportunity to come to know each other during two days of conferences and to keep the door open for further talks if necessary. From the President's point of view, he and his Administration now had a personal knowledge of what they were up against in adopting future policy.

LONDON, England: Prime Minister Macmillan was apparently not prepared to take as firm a stand on Berlin as Presidents Kennedy and de Gaulle, but the communiqué still stressed the necessity of maintaining the Allied position in Berlin. The English-speaking leaders also agreed on the need for a cease-fire in Laos.

Whatever the accomplishments of the European trip—or lack of them—it was at least evident that Premier Khrushchev had failed to drive any wedge into, or create any division among, the Western allies. And the President's public appearances, along with those of his wife, had considerably enhanced his personal prestige both here and abroad.

## BERLIN

The Berlin crisis continued to bubble along during 1961 and threatened to come to a boil, involving the Western democracies and the U.S.S.R. more seriously than ever before. (*See* photographs beginning page 101; maps beginning page 132.)

West Berlin is a thorn in the side of the Communist bloc. It is a showcase of prosperous democratic plenty in the midst of Communist poverty. Its radio stations disseminate facts which controvert Communist propaganda.

Until last year it was also an escape hatch for East Germans wishing to flee from Communist dictatorship. Although the city was divided into four zones —American, British, French, and Russian—subways and elevated trains moved freely from one to the other. The one drawback was that its lines of communications with West Germany—by air, highway, and railroad—were under Soviet control.

To put an end to democratic activities in West Berlin, and to try to force the West to recognize East Germany as a sovereign state, Premier Nikita Khrushchev threatened to sign a peace treaty with East Germany and turn over control of the access routes to the East German regime. The Western point of view was that the Allies were in West Berlin, and had the right of access to it, by virtue of a four-power, wartime agreement which the Soviet Union could not void unilaterally; that the East German administration was not sovereign but a puppet government kept in office by the Red Army.

The continued Russian threats prompted fears that the Communists might soon do something to cut off the escape route from East Germany to the west. The flood of refugees into West Berlin started to increase until, for the first time since the abortive anti-Communist uprisings in 1953, it surpassed 2,000 a day. The fears were soon justified. The Red regime suddenly made Berlin a divided city on Aug. 13, 1961. Barbed-wire barricades appeared in streets constituting the border between West and East zones, soon to be replaced by more permanent concrete-block walls topped by broken glass. Doors and walls of buildings situated in the East zone, but fronting on West Berlin streets, were bricked up. Transportation between the two zones was completely shut down. Men and women who worked in the West and lived in the East, or vice-versa, were barred from crossing the frontier. Then to make the possibility of escape even more remote, buildings along the dividing line were razed, and deep trenches ten feet wide were dug along the devastated area. The wall surrounding East Berlin soon resembled the outside of a Nazi concentration camp. Residents in frontier buildings were forcibly moved out.

Nor was this total division limited to Berlin. Whole villages along the frontier between East and West Germany were evacuated. Families were separated. The result was inhuman but successful. The flood of refugees dropped off to a mere trickle. A few escaped by jumping off buildings into nets held by West Berlin firemen. Others desperately crashed through the barriers in trucks and cars. But in large measure the escape hatch was sealed.

The United States announced it would not retreat from Berlin. President Kennedy sent, as his personal representative to West Berlin, Gen. Lucius Clay, hailed by free Germans because he had commanded U.S. forces in West Germany when the famous air lift broke the Russian blockade of West Berlin in 1948–49. A token reinforcement of American troops was sent to the former German capital.

In the autumn of 1961, Soviet Foreign Minister Gromyko and Secretary of State Rusk held a series of talks in New York regarding Berlin. These were climaxed by a two-hour talk in the White House between President Kennedy and Gromyko. The purpose was to find out whether fruitful negotiations with Russia could be held at the level of a formal conference of the Foreign Ministers of the big powers.

## HAMMARSKJÖLD AND THE UNITED NATIONS

"They thought they could crush me. But . . ." With these words Dag Hammarskjöld, Secretary-General of the United Nations, indicated to a colleague in early September that he was weathering well the vehement and acrimonious opposition of the Soviet Union which had even led Russian delegates to call him a "murderer" on the floor of the General Assembly. But two weeks later, the Swede who was the world's foremost international civil service chief lay in an African mortuary, killed in an airplane crash in Northern Rhodesia on Sept. 17 while on a mission to try to bring peace to the war-torn Congo (Léopoldville). With his death, the U.N. faced an even worse crisis. (*See* photographs beginning page 104; map, page 131.)

The U.S.S.R. had originally backed U.N. intervention in the former Belgian colony when the new independent regime proved incapable of maintaining order. After all, a leftist, Patrice Lumumba, was the Premier, and if the U.N. helped keep a friend of the U.S.S.R. in office, so much the better. But Mr. Lumumba was soon overthrown by the Army chief, Col. Mobutu, who promptly kicked out all Communist diplomats. The Soviet Union reversed its stand and bitterly assailed Mr. Hammarskjöld for continuing to maintain the 16,700-man international force in the Congo although the original U.N. resolution had authorized the Secretary-General to take whatever steps might be necessary to end the chaos in that new African republic. Mr. Lumumba was subsequently shot while trying to escape from Katanga tribesmen.

Although the Soviets had the veto power in the Security Council, they decided that what they also needed was an additional veto power in the Secretariat of the U.N. They began ignoring Mr. Hammarskjöld, addressing all communications simply to "The Secretariat" instead of to him as Secretary-General and, with an eye to the expiration of his term in April, 1963, began propagandizing for a three-man administration, one each for the West, the Communists, and the neutrals, and with each to have the power of a veto. The proposal was received coolly by most non-Communist delegates, and matters would not have come to a head until 1963 had it not been for the untimely death of Mr. Hammarskjöld. (*See* photograph, page 107.)

The Russians immediately proposed an interim three-man Secretariat. The West turned down the proposal just as promptly. Among the member nations, sentiment began to crystallize in favor of the neutral Burmese delegate, U Thant, as interim Secretary-General to fill out the unexpired term. Russia suggested three under-secretaries to help him but with the suggestion that all act unanimously, a tacit recognition of the veto power. The counterproposal was for five under-secretaries without any veto power representing the West, the Communists, Africa, Western Europe, and Latin America. The

U.S.S.R. retorted with a request for a sixth under-secretary representing Eastern Europe. It seemed for the time being, at least, that the veto demand had been dropped.

In the meantime, the Communists had managed to create another crisis. Outer Mongolia (*see* map, page 147), a Soviet satellite, had applied for membership, and Nationalist China, on the basis of ancient claims to suzerainty, had threatened to veto the application in the Security Council. The U.S.S.R. in turn promised to veto the application of another new African nation, Mauritania. (*See* map, page 130.) This led the other newly independent African nations to blame Nationalist China for Mauritania's predicament. They indicated they might well vote to seat Red China and to oust the Formosa administration from its permanent seat on the Security Council if and when the matter came to a vote.

In Africa, the Congolese crisis abated. The numerous political parties had come to a compromise agreement on a civilian administration, backed by the Parliament, in which almost all were represented. Only Premier Tshombe, of the secessionist Katanga province, held aloof. U.N. troops moved into the province and clashed with the Premier's Belgian-led army. It was an attempt to bring about a cease-fire in talks with Mr. Tshombe and to unify the country which brought Mr. Hammarskjöld flying to Central Africa and to death.

In the meantime, President Kennedy appeared before the General Assembly. In a forceful speech in which he also proposed sweeping disarmament and said the United States had the will and the weapons to meet the Soviet challenge in Berlin, he rejected the "troika" proposal for a U.N. executive. The U.N., he said, was not divided into three forces—Communist, democratic, and neutral—but into two groups: those who wanted to make the organization work as it was intended and those who wanted to undermine it with veto powers. Even the three horses of the troika did not have three drivers, he added, but only one, and so must the U.N. executive. (*See* photograph, page 107.)

Soon thereafter Soviet Foreign Minister Andrei Gromyko, who had arrived for the Assembly session, traveled to Washington to confer with the President. He returned to New York to confer with U.N. Ambassador Adlai Stevenson and they went on to London for talks with Prime Minister Harold Macmillan. Mr. Gromyko dropped the demand for a troika, leaving the number and nationality of the under-secretaries the only issue. The United States indicated it would ask the General Assembly to act if no agreement could be reached in the Security Council.

## CUBA

On the third day of 1961 the United States took the drastic step of breaking diplomatic relations with Premier Castro's Cuban government. The basic reason was that Cuba had moved so close to the Russian Communist orbit that, in the words of a subsequent State Department paper, the Castro regime "offers a clear and present danger." Also, the regime seized about a billion dollars' worth of American property in Cuba and had promised compensation but not paid it.

The technical reason for the break, as cited by President Eisenhower, was that Cuba had demanded that all United States diplomatic representatives except eleven be withdrawn from Cuba. The 3,000 Americans in Cuba were urged by the State Department to leave, and travel to Cuba was forbidden later except for urgent reasons.

The next major development came on April 17 when an army of anti-Castro Cuban exiles attempted an invasion of Cuba that failed utterly. The United States did not play a military role in the invasion itself, but did play an active role in preparing for it. In the eyes of the world, the United States suffered a blow to its prestige because of the connection. (*See* map, page 139.)

The Cuban troops taking part in the invasion had been trained by Americans, primarily representatives of the Central Intelligence Agency, in Central America. They had landed on the southern coast of Cuba and had expected anti-Castro partisans on the island to stage a simultaneous insurrection. The CIA had also counted on a complete absence of air cover for the defending forces.

The invasion planners were wrong on all counts. Expecting the invasion, Castro had rounded up all dissidents and potential insurrectionists. He did have enough planes to give his army air cover, whereas the invaders had none. The result was a fiasco; virtually all the 1,400-man force surrendered.

A month later, Castro sarcastically told a television rally that he would trade 1,200 invasion prisoners for 500 bulldozers and tractors with caterpillar treads. The offer was immediately taken up by a group of private citizens in the United States, with government sanction, but came to nothing when Castro seemed to increase his demands. But throughout the world the proposed exchange was denounced and compared with Nazi Germany's proposal to trade Jews for trucks during World War II.

In the meantime, Castro was trying to "export" his revolutionary movement to other Latin American countries, and both foreign and local Communists were doing their best to turn increased nationalism in the Western Hemisphere into a crusade against "Yanqui imperialism."

Apart from this, South American government officials had long complained that the bulk of American foreign aid was going to Europe and Asia, with very little in our own back yard. It was against this background that an Inter-American Economic and Social Council met in Uruguay and with United States assistance drafted an "Alliance for Progress." The United States agreed to furnish long-term development loans which could mean the total expenditure of $20 billion south of the Rio Grande, at least half of it to come from South American governments or private capital. Some of the objects to be attained from this expenditure were more schooling for children, more and better low-cost housing, price stabilization for basic exports, a broadening of the economic base of all one-crop countries, more realistic tax reforms, wider distribution of national wealth, and better health programs.

It was a large order, but one which would ward off revolutionary Communist designs if properly put into effect.

# HIJACK

Desperate refugees, seeking to escape from Communist dictatorships in Europe, had occasionally succeeded in hijacking airplanes, locomotives, and smaller vessels to flee to freedom. But it was not until communism had approached the shores of the United States by gaining a foothold in Cuba, with less than 100 miles separating the oppressed victims from liberty, that the business of taking over common carriers by pistol-wielding passengers really reached its zenith. And then the practice spread not only from legitimate political refugees to criminals and crackpots, but from small craft to intercontinental jet planes and transatlantic ocean liners.

The most dramatic of these stories during 1961 was the 11-day cruise to nowhere of the 20,906-ton Portuguese liner *Santa Maria*. On Jan. 20, the vessel left La Guaira, Venezuela, on a regular crossing to Curacão, Port Everglades, Fla., and Lisbon. Aboard her, unbeknownst to the authorities and crew members, were 70 rebels dedicated to the overthrow of Portuguese Premier and dictator Salazar. On Jan. 22, after the liner had left the popular cruise stop of Curacão in the Netherlands Antilles, the rebels took over the ship under the leadership of Capt. Henrique Galvão. Casualties among the crew were one dead and one wounded. The wounded man was put ashore in the British Antilles, and the *Santa Maria* then headed for the open Atlantic. According to broadcasts from Capt. Galvão, the seizure constituted the beginning of an uprising against Premier Salazar, and he indicated the liner was bound for Angola, a Portuguese possession on the west coast of Africa, where a full-fledged revolution against the Lisbon regime was already in progress.

Warships and airplanes of both the United States and Great Britain searched the high seas. The interest of the United States was prompted by concern for the American passengers aboard. The vessel was finally located and followed. Since, unfortunately for Capt. Galvão, no corresponding revolution had broken out in Portugal, and Angola authorities had the situation well in hand as far as its coastal towns were concerned, he had no friendly port to head for. After a mid-ocean conference with U. S. Navy officers and and offer of political asylum from Brazilian officials, he and his band of revolutionaries finally put in at the port of Recife, and the jittery passengers swarmed ashore on Feb. 2. The ship itself was turned back to its Portuguese owners.

While the hijacking of the *Santa Maria* was a one-shot affair, the theft of Cuban air liners and other planes had been going on since April, 1959. Up until Oct. 28, 1960, ten freight or passenger planes and four crop dusters had been seized by refugees and flown to the United States, and were then returned to Cuba. But on Oct. 29, a hijacked air liner was seized and sold under court order to satisfy a legal debt judgment against the Havana government. Creditors were quick to act after that, and by July, 1961, ten more Cuban planes had been seized and sold. This began to hurt the Havana regime. Although a National Airlines Convair hijacked on May 1 was returned to the United States the same day, an Eastern Air Lines Electra forced to land in Havana in July by a Castro supporter was seized by Cuba. Eventually it was exchanged for a Cuban patrol boat, which arrived in Miami with refugees a month later.

But by now the publicity surrounding the armed seizures of aircraft began to give ideas to persons other than pro-Castro or anti-Castro partisans. In August, an American ex-convict and his son took over a Continental Airlines jet en route from Phoenix to El Paso, and ordered the pilot to fly to Havana. When the pilot claimed he could not reach Cuba without extra fuel, the father-son combination allowed the plane to land at El Paso, keeping the crew and four passengers on board as hostages. When the hijackers ordered it to take off again, law enforcement officials riddled the tires with bullets, eventually overpowered the air pirates.

Only a week later, an Algerian boarded a Pan American World Airways jet flying from Mexico City to Guatemala City and forced its diversion to Havana. Before it became known that the hijacker was not a Cuban, a terrific hue and cry arose in Washington, with some Congressmen demanding that the marines land in Cuba to insure return of seized American aircraft. The furore, insofar as it was directed against the Havana regime, quickly died down for two reasons: the revelation of the hijacker's nationality, and the fact that the airplane was quickly returned to the United States. A probable reason for the prompt Cuban action: the presence on board the craft of Dr. Julio Cesar Turbay Ayala, Foreign Minister of Columbia.

The theft of the American planes brought demands that their pilots be armed, that passengers be searched for arms, that baggage be X-rayed. What Congress did was to pass a bill creating a new class of crime—air piracy—and making it a Federal offense punishable by death.

# NEWS CHRONOLOGY OF 1961

### (For Space Age News Chronology, see page 58)

## JANUARY 1961

1 U.S. calls for Southeast Asia Treaty Organization meeting on Communist invasion of Laos.
   (Jan. 6—SEATO takes no action.)
3 U.S. breaks diplomatic relations with Cuba.
5 U.N. Security Council refuses to act on Cuban complaint about U.S. aggression.
8 De Gaulle referendum backs his Algerian policy.
10 2 Negroes—first in 175 years—enter University of Georgia under Federal court order.
12 President-elect Kennedy sells all stocks to avoid conflict of interest; buys bonds.
14 U.S. orders citizens to sell gold held abroad.
15 Texas Tower off New Jersey collapses, killing 28.
16 Eisenhower budget is $80.9 billion, peacetime record.

20 John F. Kennedy inaugurated as 35th President.
22 Portuguese luxury liner *Santa Maria* seized in Caribbean by armed rebels against Portuguese dictator Salazar.
25 Russia frees 2 U.S. flyers held as spies. Kennedy discloses it at first press conference.
30 Gloomy Kennedy State-of-Union message sees perils at home and abroad.
31 U.S. chimpanzee named Ham is shot to edge of outer space and recovered alive and cheerful.

## FEBRUARY 1961

1 Minuteman solid-fuel rocket succeeds in first test.
2 600 passengers of hijacked Portuguese liner *Santa Maria* landed at Recife, Brazil.
6 7 executives of leading U.S. electrical

manufacturing companies sent to jail for 30 days for antitrust-law violations.

7 Britain holds 5—2 Americans included —as spies for Russia.

9 Kennedy asks hospital care for elderly in Social Security.

12 Russia fires rocket toward Venus from orbiting Sputnik.

13 Katanga Province, Congo, says Lumumba was slain by tribesmen while escaping from prison.

14 Russia announces boycott of U.N. Secretary General Hammarskjöld over Lumumba slaying.

15 73 killed in New York–Brussels plane crash in Belgium, including U.S. skating team of 18.

17 West Germany offers aid of $1 billion a year to underdeveloped countries, easing U.S. gold outflow.

20 U.N. votes use of force in Congo to prevent civil war. Defeats Soviet proposal to withdraw.

20 Kennedy offers $5.6-billion plan to aid education.

23 6-day strike halting major U.S. airlines ends.

27 King Mohammed V of Morocco dies; son becomes King Hassan II.

28 Kennedy urges higher truck taxes to pay for interstate super-highway system.

## MARCH 1961

1 Kennedy sets up U.S. Peace Corps; youths to aid underdeveloped countries.

2 Gov. Rockefeller of N.Y. and wife climb down ladder to escape fire in Albany executive mansion.

5 U.N. forces driven out of key port of Matadi by Congolese.

6 Kennedy sets up new machinery to curb racial bias in industry.

8 First U.S. nuclear submarine, *Patrick Henry*, bases at Holy Loch, Scotland, after record 66 days, 22 hours under water.

11 Congo chiefs agree on loose confederation instead of central government.

13 Kennedy proposes 10-year plan to raise Latin American living standards.

15 Union of South Africa decides to leave British Commonwealth.

17 New college basketball scandal in fixing of games.

19 U.S. investigates price-fixing in meat, milk, and drugs.

22 U.S. rushes planes and arms to save Laos from Soviet domination.

24 Kennedy's first defeat: Minimum-wage bill beaten in House by 1 vote.

26 First meeting of Prime Minister Macmillan and President Kennedy—in Key West, Fla., on Laos crisis.

28 Kennedy urges missile build-up, raising military budget to $43.8 billion, highest in peacetime.

29 Southeast Asia Treaty Organization pledges "appropriate action" if Communists continue aggression in Laos.

29 23rd Amendment to Constitution allows people of District of Columbia to vote for President for first time since 1800.

## APRIL 1961

3 White House declaration urges end to Cuba's Communist ties.

4 United Air Lines becomes biggest in U.S. as it buys Capital Airlines.

5 Prime Minister Macmillan in Washington for talks with Kennedy.

11 Adolf Eichmann goes on trial in Jerusalem, accused of managing Nazi slaughter of 6 million Jews.

12 Moscow announces putting first man into space in orbit around earth—Maj. Yuri A. Gagarin.

13 Adenauer and Kennedy complete talks in Washington.

17 Cuba invaded by an estimated 1,200 anti-Castro exiles.

18 Khrushchev promises "all necessary assistance" to Cuba against invasion.

20 Cuban government says exile invasion is crushed. Kennedy says U.S. won't allow communism to take over Cuba.

21 French military units seize Algiers in insurrection against de Gaulle government in Paris.

23 De Gaulle assumes emergency powers to quell Algerian insurrection by French troops.

24 Britain and U.S.S.R. issue joint appeal for cease-fire in Laos.

26 Insurrection in Algeria collapses; 3 French generals leading it vanish.

28 Congolese troops hold political leaders, pressuring them to agree on confederation.

## MAY 1961

1 Castro proclaims Cuba a "socialist" nation, meaning "communist."

3 Cease-fire ordered in Laos by government and Communist rebels.

3 Britain finds a Foreign Office diplomat, George Blake, has spied for Russia for nearly ten years.

4 2 Navy balloonists set height record— 21½ miles. One is killed during pickup operation.

5 First U.S. spaceman: Navy Cmdr. Alan B. Shepard, Jr., rockets 116.5 miles up in 302-mile trip.

9 U.S. offers to put 5 Polaris nuclear submarines in NATO pool of defenses.

13 Gary Cooper, 60, dies of cancer.

14 Buses bearing white and Negro integrationists stoned and burned in Alabama.

16 Military junta seizes control of South Korea; pledges anticommunism.

16 International conference about Laos opens in Geneva.

20 France opens peace talks with Algerian rebels at Evian-les-Bains.

21 Martial law proclaimed in Montgomery, Ala.; white mob threatens Negro rally in Baptist church.

22 Supreme Court rules Du Pont must rid itself of 63 million General Motors shares, worth nearly $3 billion.

24 Kennedy urges Americans to contribute to buying tractors to ransom 1,200 Cuban rebels captured by Castro regime.

25 Kennedy asks Congress for $1.8 billion to speed up space exploration, including man to moon.

26 U.S. Air Force jet bomber sets record flying Atlantic—New York to Paris in 3 hours, 20 minutes.

27 First Republican in Texas to win state-wide election: John G. Towers wins remainder of Vice President Johnson's term.

29 Department of Justice calls on Interstate Commerce Commission to wipe out racial segregation on interstate buses.

30 Generalissimo Rafael Trujillo, dictator of Dominican Republic for 31 years, slain by assassins.

31 2 French generals get 15-year prison terms for leading insurrection in Algeria in April.

## JUNE 1961

3–4 Kennedy talks with Khrushchev in Vienna.

5 Supreme Court orders Communist party to register. (June 8—Communists announce defiance.)

7 Geneva conference on Laos suspended because fighting continues despite cease-fire agreement.

12 Soviet Union kills Geneva conference on treaty to ban nuclear tests.

19 Supreme Court bans "belief in God" oath as requirement for public office in 8 states.

20 Adolf Eichmann takes stand in own defense in Jerusalem trial; says he was only a small cog in Nazi machinery.

21 Kennedy opens first big plant in Freeport, Tex., to make fresh water out of sea water.

23 Deal to trade U.S. tractors for Cuba's release of invader-prisoners fails.

25 20 Freedom Riders from 6 states arrive in Jackson, Miss., and go to jail.

26 Kuwait, sheikdom in Middle East, is threatened with annexation by Iraq.

27 Dr. Arthur Michael Ramsey is enthroned as Archbishop of Canterbury.

## JULY 1961

1 British armed forces land in Kuwait to counter Iraqi invasion threat.

2 Ernest Hemingway killed when shotgun he is cleaning goes off.

2 Britain and Iraq charge each other with endangering Middle East peace over Kuwait in testimony before U.N. Security Council.

5 80 killed, 266 wounded as Moslem rioters battle French troops and police in Algeria.

6 Russia and North Korea sign mutual military assistance pact.

8 Khrushchev cancels armed force cutbacks, raises arms budget because of world tension; asks Big Four summit meeting on German peace treaty.

9 Russia reveals dozen new types of warplanes at Moscow air show.

13 House Ways and Means Committee kills Kennedy proposal to increase taxes on stock dividends.

14 Pope John XXIII issues encyclical urging prosperous nations to help underdeveloped lands overcome poverty.

15 U.S. note to Moscow charges Russia with sabotaging Geneva nuclear testban talks.

17 U.S., Britain, and France reject Khrushchev proposals on Berlin and Germany.

19 French and Tunisian forces clash at Bizerte naval base.

20 French forces break Tunisian blockade of Bizerte; Tunis asks U.N. to halt French aggression.

21 Virgil Grissom becomes second American astronaut, making 118-mile-high, 303-mile-long rocket flight over Atlantic.

22 U.N. Security Council calls for immediate cease-fire in Tunisia and restoration of armed units to pre-crisis positions; France halts offensive.

23 France refuses U.N. peace offer on Bizerte until security of French base is assured.

24 Armed Cuban-born waiter commandeers Eastern Air Lines Electra; forces pilot and passengers to fly to Havana.

25 Cuba releases 32 passengers and crew of 5 aboard captured Electra, but retains plane.

26 President Kennedy asks Congress to boost armed forces, defense spending; seeks authority to call up 250,000 reservists; wins bipartisan backing.

28 U.N. Secretary Hammarskjöld declares French troops in Bizerte block truce plan.

30 Soviet Communist-party blueprint strengthens Khrushchev world leadership, stresses need for "peaceful coexistence."

## AUGUST 1961

3 Ex-convict and son foiled in attempt to hijack Continental Airlines jet plane at El Paso and fly to Havana.

6 Gherman Stepanovich Titov is launched in space ship *Vostok II;* makes 17½ orbits in 25 hours, covering 434,960 miles before landing safely.

9 Pan American jet plane hijacked by Algerian after leaving Mexico City for Panama; flown to Havana. Plane and passengers promptly released and returned to Miami.

12 East Germany closes all crossings between East and West Berlin, with full backing of Soviet Union, to halt flood of refugees.

16 Hijacked Eastern Air Lines Electra returned from Cuba to U.S. with crew in exchange for return of captured patrol boat to Cuba.

20 U.S. sends token reinforcement of 1,500 troops across East Germany to West Berlin garrison without Communist interference; Vice President Johnson makes quick trip to Berlin to boost morale there.

23 Communist East Germany imposes new curbs on East Berlin travel; Allies place tanks along East-West border.

24 U.S. warns Russia that interference with access to West Berlin would be "an aggressive act."

25 President Janio Quadros of Brazil resigns, blaming opponents at home and abroad. Ranieri Mazzilli, speaker of Chamber of Deputies, becomes president pro tem.

27 Military junta threatens to block succession to Brazilian presidency by João Goulart, leftist vice president.

28 Metropolitan Opera season assured as Labor Secretary Goldberg induces company and union to accept binding arbitration.

29 6 killed, 81 rescued as jet plane snaps cable of Mont Blanc scenic aerial tramway at Chamonix, France.

30 Soviet Union announces resumption of nuclear weapons testing.

## SEPTEMBER 1961

1 Trans World Airlines Constellation crashes at Hinsdale, Ill., killing all 78 persons aboard.

1 Soviets explode atomic bomb above ground in Central Asia.

2 Nehru says Soviet atomic tests increase war peril; asks resumption of East-West negotiations.

3 Kennedy and Macmillan propose to Khrushchev that all 3 powers ban above-ground nuclear tests to prevent radioactive fallout.

5 U.S. to resume underground and lab tests of nuclear weapons to avoid fallout danger.

7 João Goulart becomes figurehead President of Brazil after amended Constitution gives executive power to Premier Tancredo Neves.

9 Gen. de Gaulle unhurt as assassin's bomb misfires.

9–13 Hurricane Carla hits Gulf Coast, kills 40, causes estimated $200 million damage in Texas, Louisiana, and nearby states.

11 United Auto Workers settles main wage dispute with General Motors, but 255,-000 members strike over local working conditions.

12 Philosopher Bertrand Russell and wife jailed by British court for protest against nuclear arms.

13 U.N. army fights troops of Katanga Province in Congo.

14 Big Four Western foreign ministers discuss Berlin crisis in Washington.

15 U.N. forces locked in major battle with forces of President Moise Tshombe in Katanga Province.

17 Chancellor Konrad Adenauer loses absolute majority in Bonn Parliament following West German elections.

17 37 die in Chicago crash of Northwest Orient Airlines Electra II.

18 U.N. Secy.-Gen. Dag Hammarskjöld, 12 others die in air crash near Ndola, Northern Rhodesia; U.N. chief was on mission to end Katanga fighting.

19 Soviets stall on U.N. plan to name interim successor for Dag Hammarskjöld.

20 General Motors and United Auto Workers reach agreement to end strike.

20 U.N. and President Tshombe of Katanga concur on cease-fire.

22 Interstate Commerce Commission orders end of racial discrimination against bus travelers.

23 Kennedy urges U. S. Steel Corp. to hold price line despite pending union wage demands.

25 Kennedy addresses U.N., warning of atomic war danger; says West is firm but not rigid on Berlin; asks world peace drive; backs single U.N. head.

26 Gromyko tells U.N. that German peace treaty should be top issue before General Assembly; rejects U.S. atom peace plan.

27 Nixon to run for California Governor in 1962.

28 Rebellion of Syrian army threatens survival of United Arab Republic.

29 Syria quits U.A.R.

## OCTOBER 1961

1 N.Y. Yankee Roger Maris hits 61st homer on last day of 162-game season to set new record; Babe Ruth's 60 homers remains record for 154-game season.

4 Ex-Gov. Goodwin Knight says Nixon aide promised him top political job not to oppose Nixon for California Governor.

6 Gromyko meets Kennedy; no progress indicated.

7 U.S. weighs sending troops to Vietnam and Laos as Red pressure increases.

8 Neutralist Prince Souvanna Phouma to head coalition government of Laos.

9 New York Yankees beat Cincinnati Reds to take World Series in 5 games.

10 Macmillan warns Gromyko of "grave danger" in Soviet unilateral action on Berlin.

13 Soviets say they will accept U.N. Acting Secretary-General with full executive powers.

14 All U.S. and Canadian civilian planes grounded 12 hours in air-defense test.

15 Red China Premier Chou En-lai reaches Moscow for 22nd World Congress of Communist Party.

17 Khrushchev announces plan to test 50-megaton bomb on Oct. 30–31; U.S. asks Soviet to reconsider test.

## DIED—November 1960 to October 1961

| Day | Name | Age |
|---|---|---|
| | **NOVEMBER 1960** | |
| 16 | GABLE, Clark (actor) | 59 |
| 28 | WRIGHT, Richard (writer) | 52 |
| | **DECEMBER 1960** | |
| 13 | THOMAS, John Charles (singer) | 69 |
| 14 | RATOFF, Gregory (director) | 63 |
| | **JANUARY 1961** | |
| 4 | FITZGERALD, Barry (actor) | 72 |
| 10 | HAMMETT, Dashiell (writer) | 66 |
| 13 | RING, Blanche (actress) | 89 |
| 18 | DOOLEY, Dr. Thomas (medical missionary) | 34 |
| 23 | LORGE, Dr. Irving (psychologist) | 55 |
| 31 | THOMPSON, Dorothy (writer) | 66 |
| | **FEBRUARY 1961** | |
| 3 | WONG, Anna May (actress) | 54 |
| 9 | TYDINGS, Millard E. (Former Sen., D., Md.) | 70 |
| 15 | OWEN, Maribel Vinson (skater) | 49 |
| 15 | OWEN, Laurence (skater—daughter of M. V. Owen) | 16 |
| 15 | OWEN, Maribel (skater—daughter of M. V. Owen) | 20 |
| 16 | VANCE, Dazzy (baseball pitcher) | 69 |
| 20 | GRAINGER, Percy (pianist) | 78 |
| | **MARCH 1961** | |
| 8 | BEECHAM, Sir Thomas (conductor) | 81 |
| 28 | CROSLEY, Powel, Jr. (owner, Cincinnati Reds) | 74 |
| | **APRIL 1961** | |
| 5 | CANBY, Henry Seidel (critic) | 82 |
| 6 | BORDET, Jules (scientist) | 90 |
| 7 | JORDAN, Marian ("Molly McGee") (radio star) | 62 |
| 10 | RICKEY, Branch, Jr. (baseball executive) | 47 |
| | **MAY 1961** | |
| 13 | COOPER, Gary (film star) | 60 |
| 19 | HOWARD, Joe (song writer) | 93 |
| 23 | DAVIS, Joan (comedienne) | 48 |
| | **JUNE 1961** | |
| 2 | KAUFMAN, George S. (dramatist) | 71 |
| 6 | JUNG, Dr. Carl G. (psychologist) | 85 |
| 30 | DE FOREST, Lee (inventor) | 87 |
| | **JULY 1961** | |
| 2 | HEMINGWAY, Ernest (author) | 61 |
| 9 | CHAMBERS, Whittaker (accuser of Alger Hiss) | 60 |
| 17 | COBB, Ty (baseball player) | 74 |
| | **AUGUST 1961** | |
| 9 | SMITH, Gen. Walter Bedell (former chief of staff to Gen. Eisenhower, World War II) | 65 |
| 18 | HAND, Learned (jurist) | 89 |
| 30 | COBURN, Charles (actor) | 84 |
| | **SEPTEMBER 1961** | |
| 12 | STRAUS, Nathan (former chairman, USHA) | 72 |
| 18 | HAMMARSKJÖLD, Dag (U.N. Secy.-Gen.) | 56 |
| 22 | DAVIES, Marion (actress) | 64 |
| 24 | WELLES, Sumner (diplomat) | 69 |
| | **OCTOBER 1961** | |
| 1 | COOK, Donald (actor) | 60 |
| 5 | WARAM, Percy (actor) | 80 |
| 11 | MARX, Chico (comedian) | 70 |

# REVIEWS OF THE YEAR

## FILMS IN 1961

### By BOSLEY CROWTHER, Movie Critic, New York Times

In the realm of motion pictures, the most conspicuous development of the year was the penetration of the rich American market by an uncommon number of foreign films. Never before, not even in the heyday of the great French films before World War II, or the comparatively brief but fertile period of the Italian "neorealists" right after the war, have foreign-made pictures enjoyed such success in the United States. The phenomenon has caused a new regard for the shifting taste of the so-called mass audience.

While the top American pictures continued to run to the "blockbuster" type—such large and sumptuous eye-fillers, in color and wide screen, as *The Guns of Navarone, West Side Story, Exodus, Fanny, King of Kings, El Cid,* and *Come September*—the foreign films ran to less display of physical and pictorial riches (they were mostly in black and white) and more emphasis on sophistication of themes and cinematic techniques.

*La Dolce Vita,* the Italian film of Federico Fellini which was the sensational hit in Europe in 1960, followed its continental pattern when it opened in New York in April. Immediately it was deluged with critical and popular acclaim, and soon thereafter it was repeating this success in other cities across the land. Telling an episodic story of sophisticates and hedonists in modern Rome, a story which showed wide-spread corruption on several levels but had a fundamentally moral tone, it was perceived by many critics as one of the great motion pictures of all time. Some, on the other hand, viewed it with shock, anxiety, and disgust. This only tended to stimulate public curiosity. An educated guess was that it will eventually earn between $5,000,000 and $10,000,000 in the United States. This would be the most ever earned by a foreign picture, and would, indeed, be an excellent "take" for a top American film.

Right up with *La Dolce Vita* was *Never on Sunday,* an infectiously gay and ribald Greek comedy about a happy prostitute in Piraeus and an American tourist who tried unsuccessfully to reform her. The prostitute was played by Melina Mercouri, a leading actress in Greece, and the tourist was played by Jules Dassin, an American who also wrote, directed, and produced the film for a reported $150,000. This one is also expected to earn at least $5,000,000 in the United States, which should set some sort of record for the ratio of investment and return.

Less spectacular as moneymakers but surprising for their manifest appeal to American movie-goers, even in smaller cities that do not generally get foreign films, were the Italian *Rocco and His Brothers* and *Two Women,* the latter starring Sophia Loren in what was generally hailed as the best performance of her career; the French films *The Truth* (with Brigitte Bardot),

*The Lovers,* and *Hiroshima, Mon Amour;* the Soviet Russian film *Ballad of a Soldier;* and Ingmar Bergman's Swedish film *The Virgin Spring.*

An important factor was that most of these pictures were distributed with dubbed English dialogue to replace the foreign language. Further extension of this practice was expected to broaden the circulation and popularity of foreign films in coming years.

Representing the best of American movies, in dramatic content and popularity, were the above-named "blockbusters"—all of which, incidentally, with the exception of *West Side Story,* were shot on locations and in studios abroad, indicating the extent and seriousness of what has become known as "the flight of production" from Hollywood.

*West Side Story,* which opened in October, gave every indication of being the year's most distinguished and applauded picture. It was a brilliant re-creation on the screen of the successful Broadway musical about interracial gang warfare in New York City. But *The Guns of Navarone,* a big and fiery war adventure film, appeared to be the leading "box office picture" of the year.

Other American films of distinction were: a powerful dramatization of the Nazi war-guilt trials, *Judgment at Nuremberg;* Otto Preminger's caustic rendering of a Washington novel and play, *Advise and Consent;* an almost complete carry-over to the screen of a popular play on racial resentment, *A Raisin in the Sun;* a topical drama of pool-sharks, *The Hustler;* and a study of premarital sex problems, *Splendor in the Grass.*

Two fine and powerful films from Britain were also adornments of the year. They were *Tunes of Glory,* a drama of rivalry in high military ranks, starring John Mills and Alec Guinness; and *Saturday Night and Sunday Morning,* a scorching drama of a young factory worker in Lancashire.

Because of the notable increase of sordid themes and material in American movies, marked in such ambitious pictures as *Butterfield 8, Go Naked in the World, By Love Possessed,* and *Sanctuary,* to name but a few, there developed an amorphous agitation among parent groups and clergymen to "clean up the screen" by imposition of further censorship and restraints. The agitation became so strident in the public utterances of church leaders and in the press that Hollywood producers tacitly acceded to some "tightening up" in their own self-restraining Production Code and pointed proudly in defense of the whole medium to such conspicuously moral and inspirational pictures as *El Cid* and the story of Jesus Christ, *King of Kings.* (In the latter film, incidentally, the role of Christ was played by Jeffrey Hunter, a moderately popular young actor, whose future career was expected to be considerably affected thereby.)

Censorship on municipal levels also caused difficulties and annoyances. Censors in Chicago and Atlanta obstructed many films in their communities and precipitated court actions. As a consequence of the refusal of the Chicago censor to license a film called *Don Juan,* the distributor carried his appeal to the United States Supreme Court, which ruled that the licensing system was a legitimate municipal function. This did not confirm that the censors were to have free rein, however. In a subsequent case, the Illinois court disallowed the censor's right to obstruct a French film, *The Lovers*. Thus the status of censorship in Chicago remained unresolved.

Likewise, the censors continued to function in Atlanta, even though a municipal judge overruled their ban on *Never on Sunday*. Abilene, Texas, put into operation a stringent municipal censor board.

As usual, the American film producers attempted to advance new young stars to take the place of such irreplaceable veterans as Clark Gable and Gary Cooper, whose deaths were major sorrows and losses in Hollywood. Mr. Gable's death prior to the release of his last film, *The Misfits,* in which he starred with Marilyn Monroe, cast a certain inevitable shadow over this film, which was not brightened by its contents. It was one of the big disappointments of the year.

Other conspicuous disappointments, artistically and box office-wise, were *One-Eyed Jacks,* a diffuse western which Marlon Brando directed and in which he starred; *Cimarron,* an over-blown remake of an early sound-film success; and *Goodbye Again,* a dreary romance starring Ingrid Bergman and Yves Montand.

The recovery of Elizabeth Taylor from a critical illness early in the year was hailed by her fans, however, as a blessing of providence and the future was considered fairly glowing when she began acting in *Cleopatra* in Rome in the early fall.

## THE YEAR IN BOOKS
### By CHARLES POORE, Book Critic, New York Times

Three outstanding events marked the year in the world of books. They were: Robert Frost's splendid bardic eminence at the inauguration of President John Fitzgerald Kennedy, the surprising recession in the long Civil-War-book bull market, and the tragic death of Ernest Hemingway.

Other aspects had significant places in the tally. The gold-papered rush of amalgamations among book publishers calmed down. Or paused to shape up, according to your point of view. At any rate it seemed to be more important to keep going in publishing than to go public. Few writers bought yachts but many did well. The fact that the new President was himself a laureled young author heartened all who believe—peculiar electronic evidence to the contrary notwithstanding—that reading and writing are here to stay.

Those totem poles of the people's taste, the best-seller lists, blazoned literature's own continuity. As 1960 gave way to 1961 there was flowing interest in volumes as various as James Michener's *Hawaii* and Harper Lee's *To Kill a Mockingbird,* both novels but without any other notable similiarity. Also, William Shirer's *The Rise and Fall of the Third Reich* and Vance Packard's *The Waste Makers,* both impressive indictments, though on far differing scales of human values. Later in the year, other books, other issues, appeared.

Among them were dozens of gaudily jacketed new volumes that had no plausible claim to existence beyond the industrious hope of their creators, the genial faith of their editors and publishers, and the indulgent charity of the public. Since effective measures of book-birth-control were still to be devised, nothing much could be done about that. The day might come, though, pessimists darkly hinted, when it would be desirable to pay prolific authors of atrocious books not to write. Meantime, in general, books ranked high within our contemporary arts.

Robert Frost's appearance at the President's inauguration enhanced that standing. In all the history of man no poet ever before had such a tremendous audience as he did on that day of democratic pomp and circumstance. A wild snowy wind right out of his own New England blew his manuscript. He did not need it. What he had to say was in his mind and heart. Through television and radio it reached the millions around the earth. It would be pleasant to record that a renaissance of interest in poets and poetry followed. It did not. Yet the spirit of the republic of letters was strengthened by the occasion.

The values that spirit produces are never absolute. One generation's masterpiece is always in peril of being another generation's bore. A book may nevertheless do well if it serves a given time's needs and interests. In such cases the question of immortality is either ludicrous or irrelevant. In 1961, for example, such books as John Gunther's *Inside Europe Today* and Theodore White's *The Making of the President, 1960,* were notably useful in charting the fitful course of contemporary life on our rather feverish planet. They gave more practical light than the dozen volumes of Arnold Toynbee's *A Study of History*—including Toynbee's reconsiderations, which allowed him to reconsider his own judgments and his critics to expand their attacks.

What collapsed the Civil War book boom? It was decidedly not a lack of zeal among writers and publishers. Not by a very long cannon shot. They'd been getting ready to share the glory and the booty of the centennial years for a long time.

They had worked like troopers in blue and gray. As the hundredth anniversary dates of this battle or that campaign rolled around, books about the irrepressible conflict began to march across America in legions. Interest, however, so far as the great public was concerned, proved to be repressible.

Although *The American Heritage Picture History of the Civil War*—that's a grapeshot burst of a title, isn't it?—had been popular early in the year, interest thereafter was dim. One explanation might be that the Civil War revival had run its course without waiting for the centennial. Or, to put it bluntly, people were just plain tired of it all, at least for the time being. But perhaps the true answer was not so simple. Perhaps the true answer was that the books available, with such exceptions as Martin Duberman's biography of a prime mover and shaker of the era, *Charles Francis Adams: 1807-1886,* didn't anywhere near measure up to those varied classics of the Civil War—Stephen Crane's *The Red Badge of Courage,* Carl Sandburg's *Lincoln,* Stephen Vincent Benét's *John Brown's Body,* Douglas Southall Freeman's *Lee,* and the results of Bruce Catton's endless marches over the hallowed grounds.

If life on earth did not end during the year, it was not for lack of blueprints to cataclysmic atomic doom. Some novels and assorted jeremiads were merely sensational, offering bigger bangs for fewer bucks. Most, however, seemed to be animated by a genuine fear for man's fate. Yet the very varieties of fission, fusion and confusion these books dramatized tended to dissipate their effective force. The cry of wolf! wolf! went up so often that it became commonplace. More disquieting than most new books was the continuing revelation of what great powers were actually doing to widen the dimensions of death. Modern man might not yet be obsolete, but the modern novelist was having a hard time keeping up with international events that tended to make his wildest science-fiction nightmares obsolescent.

The specter of censorship loomed when Henry Miller's seedy saga of Americans and Paris, long a contraband favorite, was offered for public sale in America. Again a law of diminishing returns appeared to operate. There was far less interest in Miller's dated audacities than there had been during the uproars over, say, D. H. Lawrence's *Lady Chatterley's Lover,* or James Joyce's *Ulysses.*

Why? Partly, no doubt, because Miller was not so influential a writer as Lawrence, just as Lawrence, in that department, was inferior to Joyce. It seemed significant that the champions of the Miller grind were rather elderly celebrities of the Nineteen Twenties and Nineteen Thirties eras, rather than young rebels against those durable targets, censorship and conformity. Neither the home-grown hairy Beatniks nor the imported Angry Young Men appeared in rat packs at the Millerian barricades. They had long since gone deeper into howling glooms of their own devising.

It is curiously provincial, anyway, to regard book censorship as an isolated phenomenon. The demand for it is only part of the general arc of any given era's standards and tolerances. The expanded freedom of expression in other forms of art—notably the chaotic American theatre of our day—made *Tropic of Cancer* a minor target in a time when bigger ones, such as the prevalence of crime and violence in television shows, claimed major attention and concern.

The paperbacks flourished stupendously. An optimistic bookman suggested that they might be selling at a rate of perhaps a million copies a day. The haphazard race for distribution was dramatized by the fact that Carson McCullers' *Clock Without Hands* appeared on the best-seller lists before it was published, and J. D. Salinger's *Franny and Zooey* was advertised for sale before it was released for review.

A popular novel, an outstanding good-gracious-what-next polemic, a gaudy memoir, went through an increasingly complex series of contractions and expansions. Its serialization in a magazine might collide with its appearance in hard-cover book form, and then abridgments of it might appear just as it was being offered in a reduced-price promotion by a book club. You had your choice of what you would pay. Meantime, there were more and more billions of books in the world. There was a way to cope with that, too. The rapid-reading sorcerers were happy to teach you how to read at the rate of hundreds of pages per hour, or thereabouts. How much of that could be retained, though, was an awesome mystery.

The death of Hemingway ended an era. It was an era, writers of all nations who paid tribute to him agreed, that he had done much to shape. He left behind him an incomparable technique. He deepened modern man's sense of tragedy. But a part of his heritage, we should remember, was also a rare gift for laughter.

## THE THEATRE

### By HENRY HEWES, Drama Critic, Saturday Review

The 1960–61 Broadway theatre season was the grayest within recent memory. There were fewer productions, fewer hits, and even the handful of successes that did emerge were admired with a not inconsiderable amount of reservation.

Take, for instance, Tad Mosel's adaptation of the late James Agee's novel, *A Death in the Family.* Under the title of *All the Way Home,* the play appeared as not much more than a loosely collated series of true-to-life episodes leading up to and following the accidental death of a young father. Soberly appreciative notices failed to generate much activity at the box-office and its producers announced that they were closing the play after its fourth performance. However, Ed Sullivan made a special plea to his TV audience urging them to see *All the Way Home.* There was an immediate rush of ticket-buying and the producers declared that the play had been miraculously saved —for a week at least. Soon there was a second wave of curiosity resulting in a moderate but steady flow of people to see "The Miracle on Forty-Fourth Street," and in April it won both the Drama Critics' Circle Award and the Pulitzer Prize.

Oddly enough, a much better play, Tennessee Williams' *Period of Adjustment,* failed to attract enthusiastic audiences or even unenthusiastic prizes. Departing from the formula of blockbusting sex-operas, Mr. Williams took a comic, though nonetheless caustic, look at the present low estate of marriage in suburban America. In it two squabbling couples went through a "little old period of adjustment" to an existence that has been watered down to coarse materialism and neurotic love. The fact that it all ended in reconciliation was interpreted by some as a sentimental gesture on the part of Mr. Williams, but to others it made the play more true and more ironically bitter.

A play that truly represented the character of New York living was Hugh Wheeler's *Big Fish, Little Fish,* which was beautifully directed by Sir John Gielgud and featured a highly memorable performance by Martin Gabel as a flabby, and desperate, but at the same time arrogant and self-indulgent ex-publisher.

Other new American plays included Arthur Laurents's *Invitation to a March,* which took capricious and undisciplined swipes at American conformism; Jean Kerr's *Mary Mary,* in which her amusing dialogue and her accurate observations seemed just funny enough to triumph over her slight plot about a harrassed book publisher who finds out, first, that he cannot afford a divorce, and, then, that he doesn't really want one anyway; and Henry Denker's *A Far Country,* which was content merely to present Freud's famous psychoanalysis of the hysteric Elizabeth von R. The latter play, however, featured

Kim Stanley's painstakingly accurate and emotionally rich portrayal, which built up into a magnificent shocked scream when she discovered her repressed guilt. Furthermore, Sam Wanamaker's astute performance as Freud's brilliant colleague, who placed scientific truth second to maintaining his comfortable position in Austria's then anti-Semitic society, added poignance to the case history.

Adapted from books were John Hersey's *The Wall,* Morris L. West's *The Devil's Advocate,* Pierre Boulle's *Face of a Hero,* and Allen Drury's *Advise and Consent.* The latter, an often effective melodrama exposing the ruthless nature our politics may acquire under the pressures of an apparently permanent international emergency, invented distortions of recent history that, if taken as gospel, would indict the liberal's position.

Plays from abroad did much to keep the season from being a complete washout. Shelagh Delaney's *A Taste of Honey,* the bluntly told saga of an affection-starved daughter of a careless mother in a provincial English city, provided a fascinating slice of life and exceptional performances by Angela Lansbury as the mother, and by Andrew Ray as a young homosexual who befriends the daughter in time of need. But topping them all was Miss Plowright's energetic and rhythmic portrayal of the daughter.

Brendan Behan's *The Hostage* exploded as a delightfully free-swinging rebellion against respectability, form, and death. Eugene Ionesco's *The Rhinoceros,* a play which demonstrated that the little man was the only one left with enough common sense and human decency to withstand the onslaught of isms, not only surprised everyone by being able to run almost a year on Broadway, but also by getting customers without resorting to the traditional device of using critics' blurbs in its advertising.

Indeed the foreign contingent might singlehandedly have turned the season into a good one, had its two finest entries been produced here in the same way that they had been originally in Paris. The first, Jean Anouilh's *Becket,* which was intended as a subtle study of the relationship between two very different witty men, was mounted ornately as a religious spectacle. Sir Laurence Oliver was miscast in the title role, as was Anthony Quinn as King Henry II. Later in the season Sir Laurence switched roles, and while this did not restore Anouilh's original concept, it did make for a tremendously exciting tragedy of a King forced by history to do away with his best friend.

The second masterwork to suffer distortion was the French musical, *Irma la Douce,* which was given in its cute and prettified British version. Marguerite Monnot's marvelous score could still be heard underneath the mundane English lyrics, but whereas the French original had moved us by showing us deadly real people involved in an absurd plot, the Broadway version concocted characters as unreal as the events.

In the field of new musicals the biggest disappointment was Lerner and Loewe's *Camelot,* which came to be known as "The Big Deal on Forty-Fourth Street." Phil Silvers carried the mediocre *Do Re Mi* with his personal comic technique. Tammy Grimes blossomed into stardom and bruises with her virtuoso performance as *The Unsinkable Molly Brown,* a foundering musical about social climbing in turn-of-the-century Colorado. With such sub-par musical offerings, it was not surprising when *Carnival,* a beautifully designed and astutely directed show based on the film "Lili," won the Drama Critics' Circle Award as the season's best musical more or less by default.

Again a major part of the season's excitement was provided by the Off-Broadway Theatre. In Greenwich Village's espresso palaces untried talent held forth. This new classification, called "Coffee House Theatre," spawned "The Premise," where four young performers improvised on themes suggested by the audience, and "Take 3," where a trio of zanies improvised on themes of their own choosing in a delightfully mad excursion called *Stewed Prunes.* These were Off-Broadway's answer to Mike Nichols' and Elaine May's successful uptown invasion of Broadway.

In the regular Off-Broadway theatre itself there were three promising new playwrights unveiled, Michael Shurtleff (*Call Me by my Rightful Name*), Arnold Weinstein (*The Red Eye of Love*), and Robert D. Hock (*Borak*), but these were overshadowed by second plays by two playwrights who had had Off-Broadway debuts the season before. Edward Albee's *The American Dream* and *The Death of Bessie Smith* scored a big hit, and Jack Richardson's *Gallows Humor* revealed an Anouilh-like poetic view of life which, alas, was partly destroyed by the comic emphasis of the production. There were more musicals Off-Broadway than ever before, and while none of them equalled the success of the long running *The Fantasticks,* one, *Smiling the Boy Fell Dead,* deserved a better fate than it received.

Best of all, perhaps, was the production of Jean Genet's *The Blacks,* which delighted many of us by dealing with the Negro problem without the trite recourse to theses or the usual inhibition of taboos. And Claudel's *Noontide* and Brecht's *In the Jungle of Cities* both received American premieres that captured a surprising amount of their poetry.

Perhaps the most important contribution of Off-Broadway was the discovery, made first by the Living Theatre and then by Circle-in-the-Square, that plays could be kept running indefinitely by playing two or three different attractions in alternation each week. And Joseph Papp and his free New York Shakespeare Festival in Central Park was at last given partial financial subsidy by the city. The increasing unsatisfactoriness of the Broadway formula and the steady progress that Off-Broadway is making towards a more responsible and creative theatre suggest that a change may be underway.

## OPERA, CONCERT MUSIC, BALLET
### By IRVING KOLODIN, Music Critic, Saturday Review
### OPERA

The newest figure of consequence on the musical scene in 1961 was not a singer, a pianist, a violinist, or even a conductor. It was, rather, the Secretary of Labor, Arthur J. Goldberg, whose office became a court of final resort late in August when negotiations for a contract between the Metropolitan Opera Association and its orchestral musicians failed of resolution by ordinary means of mediation. Fourteen other unions with which the opera does business had come to agreement, some for periods covering as many as five seasons. But the demands of the orchestral players for half again as much as they received previously brought a cancellation edict from the management, a storm of protest from the press, and a directive from President John F. Kennedy that a solution be found.

Secretary Goldberg's invitation for the two sides to meet with him in Washington on August 28 was significant for several reasons. On the one hand, it conveyed the Administration's opinion that the Metropolitan was a "vital national resource" whose failure to operate would be a serious loss. On the other, it was a confession of national inadequacy that in such circumstances no agency concerned with culture or the arts existed to exert an influence, that Verdi and Wagner and those who loved them were parties to a labor-management dispute.

The expression of concern from the White House aroused interest, and hope, from others engaged in similar noncommercial ventures elsewhere, even before Secretary Goldberg's award was pronounced in mid-Autumn. For, the thesis ran, if the existence of an opera company or an orchestra or a ballet group could be set in the framework of a "national resource" the Administration implied some commitment to those whose finances were strained to meet ordinary demands and were now being urged to meet extraordinary ones. But some who saw further than the immediate issue of whether the present base pay of $170 a week (for a 32-week season) should be sharply increased doubted that the Administration was prepared to make a sufficiently substantial contribution to offset the decline, from private sources, that would follow on assistance from the city, state, or nation. Thus, on balance, it might leave the hard-pressed opera, orchestra, or whatever, worse off than before.

Paradoxically, the Metropolitan's threatened suspension—twice affirmed before it was rescinded as a first condition to Secretary Goldberg's participation, personally, as arbitrator—came at a time when demand for Metropolitan Opera tickets was at an all-time high, new subscriptions series (made possible by termination of the long-standing series of visits to Philadelphia because costs had far outrun income) were quickly sold out, and the late weeks of the 1960–1961 season had brought one of the most brilliant productions in the eleven years of Rudolf Bing's direction. Tickets for this *Turandot* were as scarce as those for a new hit musical—though without comparable profit, for the cost of raising the curtain exceeded the income from even a sold-out house.

Nevertheless the artistic results made possible by a gift from John S. Newberry of Detroit gave off the kind of well-balanced glow possible only to an opera company commanding the Metropolitan's resources. Among those brought together to match their talents against the last and most difficult of Puccini's operas to perform (the difficulties had kept it out of hearing in New York since 1931) were soprano Birgit Nilsson in the title role and a new Italian tenor of heroic vocal power, Franco Corelli, as the Prince Calaf.

The death in late 1960 of Dimitri Mitropoulos imposed a long search for a conductor of sufficient stature to dominate the large chorus and orchestra specified by the composer. It was finally resolved by the agreement of Leopold Stokowski to make his Metropolitan Opera debut, though there were some anxious moments when the 79-year-old conductor went to the hospital with a back ailment. Though he required assistance to get in and out of the orchestra pit, he made the musical experience a full partner to the inspired scenic production of Cecil Beaton.

*Turandot* did much to redeem a season in which inferior revivals of Flotow's *Martha* and Donizetti's *L'Elisir d'Amore* were unhappily preceded by substandard versions of more usual repertory for which such past stars as Jussi Bjoerling and Leonard Warren, who had died in mid-career, were no longer available. A bold venture, for the first time in Metropolitan history, with Verdi's *Nabucco* (the first success of Verdi's long career) pleased some, left others—especially the miscellaneous audience which viewed it on the season's opening night—unconvinced.

Fortunately there were some offsets to the dismal pattern of deprivation which cost the musical world such prominent artists as Bjoerling, Warren, and Mitropoulos in barely more than a year. New singers of high quality included the American sopranos Eileen Farrell and Leontyne Price. Miss Farrell, who was "new" only in the sense that she finally made a Metropolitan debut after twenty years of prominence on the radio and in concerts, paid the price for her preference during this time for home and a family in a lessening of her once peerless vocal power, a lack of the acting skill to make all the points of Gluck's *Orfeo* or Ponchielli's *La Gioconda*. However, she was still superior to most contemporary Europeans of the same vocal variety. Miss Price, who graduated from prominence in the Gershwins' *Porgy and Bess* to full-fledged stardom by way of Vienna and Milan, surpassed any prior Negro singer at the Metropolitan in the conviction as well as the artistry of her Leonora in *Il Trovatore,* her Aïda, and her warmly feminine Madame Butterfly. The Chisholms who started Miss Price on her way from Laurel, Mississippi, could be rightfully proud of a powerful contribution to inter-racial esteem.

With Renata Tebaldi limiting her appearances because of a painful spinal condition and Maria Callas performing infrequently, the way was wide open for a fresh vocal sensation. This was more than dimly discernible to be the Australian soprano Joan Sutherland when she made her New York debut in a concert performance of Bellini's long-forgotten opera *Beatrice di Tenda,* in which she had already sung at Milan's La Scala. Miss Sutherland was well known to a small circle of international opera devotees for her excellent if unspectacular singing as a Verdi-Mozart soprano at Covent Garden, at the Vancouver Festival of 1958, and in a modest range of recordings. Within a matter of months (or so it seemed) Miss Sutherland put herself to developing some latent talent for the kind of singing called coloratura, and gave Londoners their first opportunity in years to cheer a Commonwealth singer in *Lucia.* By fall 1961 she had become internationally identified with this specialty, with engagements in San Francisco, Chicago, and Dallas, preceding her first Metropolitan *Lucia*.

Miss Sutherland's pre-eminence was one subject of agreement among the established operatic enterprises coast to coast; another was the stimulus to native creation provided by the Ford Foundation. On the West Coast, such a grant provided a world premiere for Norman dello Joio's *Blood Moon* (with Mary Costa in the leading role), and in Chicago, Vittorio Giannini conducted his *The Harvest*. The Metropolitan took a more leisurely course, with quasi-commitments but no date scheduled for the works in which it expressed interest. Locally the slack was taken up by the New York City Opera, whose ambitious fall season included two works made possible by Ford Foundation money: Douglas Moore's setting of Henry James's *The Wings of the Dove* and Robert Ward's adaptation of Arthur Miller's *The Crucible*.

## CONCERT MUSIC
### By IRVING KOLODIN, Music Critic, Saturday Review

The concern with money demands and fringe benefits that brought national attention to the Metropolitan Opera in the late summer of 1961 had its counterpart among those with management responsibility for several of the nation's prominent symphony orchestras. None reached quite the same point of aggravated immobility—an orchestra's board of directors has only one unionized group to placate—but, with the opening concerts only weeks away, negotiations were still in progress between personnel of the Philadelphia Orchestra, the New York Philharmonic, and their respective employers. In St. Louis, the local symphony orchestra clung to a thin thread of survival with only the season immediately ahead assured.

In this area, however, there was a paragon to which the others could look hopefully and perhaps enviously. This was the Boston Symphony, whose high standards of execution had long been affiliated with an equally high sense of human relations. Historically, this was a heritage from the celebrated Col. Henry Lee Higginson, the Boston banker and music patron who personally provided the funds to make performance in a symphony orchestra the first obligation of the players he hired in the 1880's (in the few "permanent" orchestras elsewhere, symphony musicians played in restaurants or cafes, theaters or dance halls, between concerts). Higginson thought he left the orchestra financially secure at his death in 1920, but the ever-upward trend of living costs and wages put a continuing burden on those who succeeded him.

Through such developments as the Pop concerts directed by Arthur Fiedler, the "Esplanade" series on the Charles River (an outdoor post-Pop series financed by the city), and the Berkshire Festival at Lenox, Mass. (popularly known as "Tanglewood" from the estate it now owns), the Boston Symphony had evolved a satisfying year-round sequence by the early fifties. In the following decade, each had become so solidly established that, by extending its own season in Boston slightly and acceding to the ever-increasing demand for tickets at Tanglewood, the management could promise its players a symphonic millennium by 1962: year-round paychecks. Save for a two-week interval preceding the resumption of the winter season in Boston, the musicians would be playing, and paying, their own way 52 weeks a year. Earnings from a considerable recording schedule were further inducements for the players to consider themselves part of a financial as well as artistic elite.

Something comparable was in the making with the New York Philharmonic Orchestra, though with a different artistic emphasis. Thanks to the national prominence of Leonard Bernstein, his wide appeal as a television educator and symbol of a new era in music to a youthful public, the players in the Philharmonic were able to augment their base pay (approximately $8,000 a year minimum) with half again as much from the extras of recordings, television, tours, etc. Post- and pre-season visits to far places (the latest to Japan) had become an established part of the Philharmonic program, with the summer season at the Stadium for those who wanted it.

Desirable as the ends were, the variations in procedure produced some differences in artistic results also. In order to accommodate his other activities and preserve sufficient energy for the wide-ranging tours, Bernstein was available for less than half the season's activities in New York—two six-week stints at the beginning and end of the season which made him a new kind of symphonic figurehead: resident guest conductor. This was not only a deprivation to the public, which saw little of him during the four months in-between, but also a hardship to the players, who had to accommodate themselves to other, even more fleeting visitors during 16 of the 28-week season. The Stadium season had also deteriorated considerably in quality, with greater frequency than ever of Pop nights, operetta nights, and whatever "draws" the moment provided. Nevertheless the board appraised the situation as, on the whole, satisfactory by giving Bernstein a seven-year extension of his contract. It stipulated only that if he couldn't find more than twelve weeks a winter to devote to the Philharmonic after a year or two, it reserved the right to engage a conductor of comparable stature to share the season with him.

The kind of foresight that was responsible for the healthy look of the Boston Symphony's financial prospect also expressed itself in a decision that would assure unbroken responsibility when time came for the retirement of Charles Munch. Sometime in midwinter, Munch decided that 1961–1962 would be his last season in Boston and so advised his board of directors. As in 1949, when it selected Munch to succeed Serge Koussevitzky after the latter had served a full 25 years it did not temporize in deciding on the man it wanted. In a space of weeks, it settled the pros and cons of the available candidates by engaging Erich Leinsdorf, one of several guest conductors during the time in which Munch had made his decision.

A musician of scope and versatility, Leinsdorf had been associated with two symphony orchestras—in Cleveland and in Rochester—since he made his American debut as an uncommonly adept conductor of 26 at the Metropolitan in 1938. Curiously, he had returned to operatic conducting at the Metropolitan and abroad for several years prior to the time of decision in

Boston. Thus his name had acquired a new identity, his fame a new shine. Not since 1917, when Karl Muck had resigned under wartime pressures, had the Boston Symphony been under the direction of a conductor with Leinsdorf's German orientation. On either side of the Russian Koussevitzky there had been the Parisian Monteux and Munch.

Such a capacity for decision was decidedly unusual among managements of American orchestras—possibly because of a lack, in other cities, of the unified viewpoint that prevails in Boston. It was known that Detroit would soon part company with Paul Paray, but he agreed to return for the beginning of the 1962–1963 season while a successor was sought. Los Angeles lost Georg Solti even before he began his three-year engagement as a result, it was said, of his displeasure in not being consulted when Zubin Mehta, the young Indian musician, was given more authority than a subordinate commonly enjoys. But with his new status as artistic director of London's Covent Garden to occupy his major effort, and guest engagements as numerous as he chose to accept, Solti may well have decided that Los Angeles was no longer where he chose to spend a sizable part of each winter. Almost as soon as he became available, he accepted a tempting effort for a two-month stint in Dallas in the fall of 1961, where Paul Kletzki had given up on his project to make that Southwest group among the nation's best. In Houston, the veteran Leopold Stokowski gave way to Sir John Barbirolli, who still retained his traditional place at the head of the Hallé Orchestra, in Manchester, England. Finally, an uneasy situation prevailed in Chicago, where guest conductors in profusion were marshaled to fill time left vacant by the continuing absence of the ailing Fritz Reiner.

In the main, the concert stage continued to be dominated by familiar names, especially that of Artur Rubinstein, who presented an unprecedented series of ten Carnegie Hall concerts in forty days (October–November, 1961) to celebrate the twenty-fifth anniversary of his affiliation with manager S. Hurok. Rubinstein's share of the receipts went to ten charities (one per concert) ranging from musicians to mental health. It was a Gillels rather than a Richter year among Russian pianists, with the first of all the participants in "cultural exchange" returning for the third time. The now familiar name of Oistrakh nevertheless promised something new for this winter with the debut of the celebrated David's son Igor—also a violinist and also the well-tried veteran of several tours in Western Europe.

# BALLET
### By IRVING KOLODIN, Music Critic, Saturday Review

Despite the aggravated tensions of a year in which Laos, Berlin, and renewed atomic testing made peaceful coexistence something close to a contradiction in terms, it was a good year for "cultural exchange"—which is to say, for ballet. The Soviet Ministry of Culture approved a second American tour for the vastly popular Moiseyev Dance Company (which this time returned with a "Rock 'n Roll" take-off) and also authorized a first American visit for the Kirov Ballet of Leningrad, second only to the Bolshoi of Moscow in home esteem.

Earlier in the year, the Kirov company had visited Paris and London, with one consequence that attracted attention among many not normally interested in dancing. This was the defection, as the company was boarding planes from Paris to London, of its principal male dancer, Rudolf Nureyev. The young man's motive appeared to be personal rather than political; he had become attached to a Chilean girl he met in Paris. Apparently this aroused suspicion, and it was decided to return him "to his sick mother in Moscow." Nureyev, who had no mother in Moscow, sick or otherwise, broke away from those who were leading him from the London plane towards one for "home" and asked asylum. He was granted it—also star status with the Parisian ballet of the Marquis de Cuevas.

Whether this was in any respect responsible for some changes in company personnel when the Leningrad group came to New York could only be conjecture, but several of its female dancers who enjoyed particular success in London (Ospenko, in particular) were not among the visitors. However, those they did send for appearances at the Metropolitan Opera House in *Swan Lake, Sleeping Beauty,* and *Giselle* were uniformly of extremely high quality, rather more slenderly formed and better looking than their counterparts of the Bolshoi Ballet, though not possessed of as much audience appeal.

For those versed in ballet, the visit of the Kirov company was especially anticipated for the legendary connection of the physical plant in which it operates with such celebrities of the past as Pavlova, Nijinsky, and Karsavina. For it was from the Maryinsky Theatre of Petersburg (now the Kirov of Leningrad) that these dancers came to the West, also the great Michel Fokine and the many ballets which made up the nucleus of the "Russian ballet" brought by Serge Diaghilev to Paris before World War I.

So far as style and execution were concerned, the leading dancers of the Kirov company—especially the female—had many outstanding characteristics of their own, especially a development of the muscles that permitted deep back bends, high thrusts of the legs, and unusual use of the hands. It was readily recognized, too, that whereas the Bolshoi performers tended to bravura and strong dramatic emphasis, the Kirov company stressed softer, more lyric lines, a disposition to motion for its own sake. In this touring version of *Swan Lake,* for example, the story-telling resource of "mime" was almost wholly eliminated. Instead, one dance sequence followed another, with occasional disregard for the provisions in Tchaikovsky's music for an exchange of gestures, a passage of emotion not contained in the choreography per se.

Almost any first-class company of the West (England's Royal Ballet as well as the American Ballet Theatre or the New York City Ballet directed by George Balanchine) would envy the remarkably high standard of the corps de ballet as well as the numerous soloists, but neither the decor nor the theatrical totality the Russians presented. Its *Swan Lake* is far from the luminously lovely spectacle by Leslie Hurry which the Royal Ballet presented in its most recent visit of a year ago, and its costuming was far inferior, in taste and colorfulness, to that considered the norm of the American companies.

Despite a top price of $12 per seat (a concession to the mammoth costs of maintaining the large company during its visit, meeting the bill for a sizable complement of stagehands, and a suitably "symphonic" orchestra), desirable seats were scarce even before the company opened its engagement on September 11. And with headlines reflecting a grinding pressure of Soviet action on several fronts visible on nearby newsstands, only a solitary picket proclaiming "Russian visitors are unwelcome" came between first nighters who had paid up to $25 per seat and the crowded lobbies. A supplementary season of ten performances in Madison Square Garden (the larger capacity permitted a more modest charge of $8 for the best seats) was presented before the company departed for a lengthy tour that included Montreal and Toronto.

Some beneficial results to the home side of "cultural exchange" could be noted in the reappearance of the American Ballet Theatre in a fifteen-performance engagement at the Fifty-fourth Street Theatre prior to a tour of its own. The work that had gone into the preparations for its trip to the Soviet Union in 1960 resulted in a standard of performance on the whole higher than that seen when the company had last had a New York showing. Birgit Culberg of Denmark was responsible for two of the new ballets, *Eden* and *Moon Reindeer;* Harold Lander for *Etudes;* and William Dollar for *Divertimento Rossini*.

Meanwhile, without benefit of such stimulus, Balanchine's New York City Ballet continued to sustain the high standards associated with its appearances at the New York City Center. His far-flung fantasy found equally congenial material for animated response in musical sources old and new, with one recent work (*Modern Jazz: Variants*) welcoming the participation of the Modern Jazz Quartet, and another finding its impulse in sound produced by electronic means. In terms of balletic progress, New Yorkers specifically and Americans in general had no cause to regret that Balanchine had left St. Petersburg when he did, in the mid-twenties, while the Maryinsky was still the Maryinsky, rather than waiting to come here with it as the Kirov.

# TELEVISION

## By MERRILL PANITT, Editor, TV Guide

Having blotted the ink on his commission as Chairman of the Federal Communications Commission, New Frontiersman Newton N. Minow set himself an unprecedented—to some, unforgivable—labor. He actually spent a full, mind-boggling day watching television.

Fresh from his ordeal, he challenged the nation's broadcasters, in solemn conclave assembled, to do the same: "I invite you to sit down in front of your television set when your station goes on the air and stay there without a book, magazine, newspaper, profit and loss sheet or rating book to distract you—and keep your eyes glued to that set until the station signs off. I can assure you that you will observe a vast wasteland."

This devastating critique ("VAST WASTELAND" fit easily into three-line newspaper headlines under the words NEW FCC CHAIRMAN and TERMS TELEVISION) from television's watchdog followed a stern lecture from the broadcasters' own employee and spokesman, Florida's distinguished former governor, LeRoy Collins. Said Collins, busily chomping on the hands that feed him $50,000 a year: "You, the licensee, have been given the steward-ship of this medium. And you should say to those who seek to utilize that medium—for whatever purposes—that *you* are responsible for its standards."

But were the broadcasters indignant at Collins? Were they incensed by Minow's unveiled threat that unless they operated in what the Commission considered to be the public interest they'd lose their licenses? You bet they were. They muttered imprecations, mostly incoherent. They shouted "censor-ship!" very coherently. Minow brushed off the charge with a well-documented brief which proved—to his satisfaction at least—that the FCC is empowered by law to determine whether a station's programming is or is not in the public interest.

Minow obviously was ready to go farther than any of his predecessors to make all broadcasters feel as much responsibility to the public as they did to their stockholders. Collins wanted to head off government action. Thus he urged broadcasters to do their own reforming.

Newspapers and magazines generously donated space to relate in exquisite detail exactly what was wrong with their chief advertising competitor. To these opinions were added the public testimony—at FCC and Congressional committee hearings—of such deep thinkers as David Susskind, Georgie Jessel, and others including James V. Bennett, the Federal prison director, who once wired stations warning them not to air an episode of *The Un-touchables* because he didn't like the way his prison guards were portrayed.

Everyone (with the possible exception of the viewers—who kept tuning to shoot-em-up Westerns and police shows) was convinced that there was too much "unnecessary" violence on the air. Everyone (with the possible exception of the viewers—who, according to the ratings, couldn't have cared less) was convinced that television should devote more time to informational programs. Everyone (with the possible exception of the viewers—who switched their sets on an average of six hours a day) was convinced that the general level of programming was mediocre.

Minow's threat alone was enough to make the networks scrap the most violent episodes of shows being rerun during the summer, and order their West Coast film producers to go easy on the blood and thunder in new shows. There was a boom in situation comedies for the fall 1961 season and only one new Western was scheduled. That lone entry was titled *Frontier Circus*—possibly in honor of the Administration. There were also a number of news-documentary-informational-type programs set for fall, most of which went at bargain-basement rates to sponsors who could serve, and save, at the same time. The networks would lose money on them, but not as much as if they weren't sponsored at all.

What escaped most critics of the medium was that it was doing magnificently what it was best-equipped to do—report and interpret current events vividly and understandably. In a year of tremendous international tension, no Ameri-can who used his television set sensibly could miss exactly *what* was happening and *why* it was happening, in Berlin, in the slowly integrating South, in Laos, in Cape Canaveral, in Cuba, in South America.

The flights of Commander Alan B. Shepard Jr. and Capt. Virgil I. Grissom, America's first spacemen, were televised live, then repeated several times for those who missed the events. Before the flights, and after them, television cameras left no doubt as to their meaning and what they promised for the future. While the Russians had less interest in publicizing their space techniques before and during the earth orbiting flights of Cosmonauts Gagarin and Titov, whatever film they did release was carried on American television, as were the triumphal receptions given the Soviet heroes.

President Kennedy, elected—according to a number of surveys, and according to a *survey* of surveys—because of his television appeal during the Great Debates of the 1960 campaign, was inaugurated before an audience of 65 million, which saw—as an unscheduled added attraction—dignitaries beating out a small fire caused by a short circuit in the podium equipment.

At the outset of his administration, the President made frequent television appearances. There was, of course, detailed coverage of his trip to Paris, Vienna and London to confer with world leaders, but he also turned up in the nation's living rooms, congratulating a magazine on its 25th anniversary, urging support for his foreign aid legislation, paying tribute to poet Robert Frost, appealing for funds for the Red Cross, and as the subject of NBC's reports on JFK.

How to cover Presidential press conferences, usually held at about noon in Washington, was a subject of heated discussion among newspapermen, television men, and administration press representatives. After an experimental live telecast of one conference, it was tacitly agreed that perhaps the best technique was to video tape them for showing during the late afternoon hours, when more viewers could see them.

Reporters assigned to cover news of television could always depend upon attacks on the medium coming from FCC or Congressional hearings, but it was becoming harder to find bright new quotes condemning television. Besides, judging from the size of the headlines, readers were more interested in television's intramural fights.

Allen Funt, whose *Candid Camera* shennanigans were introduced on the air each week by Arthur Godfrey, blasted Godfrey for hogging the camera instead of letting the show's filmed stunts take the limelight. The feud between Funt and Godfrey continued for weeks behind the scenes, while on the air every Sunday night the two of them appeared side-by-side, smiling and complimenting one another. Upshot: Godfrey was replaced in the fall of 1961 by Durward Kirby—an announcer who undoubtedly had promised in advance to be a good boy.

Then there was the Ed Sullivan-Jack Paar middleweight bout, which concerned Sullivan's obligation to pay performers salaries in the thousands of dollars while the same performers appeared with Paar for the union minimum of $320. Sullivan ruled that if a performer accepted the Paar rate for the

Paar show, he'd have to take the same rate for the Sullivan show. Verbal blasts on and off the air culminated in Paar's gallant offer to debate the issue —on his show—with Sullivan. Sullivan was having no part of the Paar show, the Paar studio audience or the Paar home audience. There was no real decision in all this, the argument just sort of petered out.

Congressman Alfred E. Santangelo (D., N.Y.) launched a campaign, on behalf of the Federation of Italian-American Democratic Organizations, to boycott *The Untouchables* because all the heavies in the show—Chicago gangsters of the Capone era—were given Italian names. After meetings, statements, a sponsor withdrawal and picketing by a gentleman named Anthony (Tough Tony) Anastasia, producer Desi Arnaz promised to portray Italians in a better light on the show.

Jackie Gleason returned as moderator—for just one performance—of the worst panel-quiz show yet—*You're In The Picture.* The next week he came on without the panel to explain, in a half-hour public apology, how perfectly horrible the show was. Example: "It made the H-bomb look like a two-inch salute." Thereafter, for several weeks, Gleason filled the time slot by chatting idly with assorted friends and characters—including one memorable conversation with a chimpanzee.

Dave Garroway, mourning his wife's tragic suicide and his own inability, as head of the *Today* show, to devote enough time to his children and to "look, think and listen to people," decided to leave *Today*. He was replaced by NBC newsman John Chancellor and the daily morning program immediately started emphasizing news more than it had under Garroway's aegis.

Other news: a man named Therm Gibson bowled six strikes in a row on a program called *Jackpot Bowling,* an achievement of extraordinary impressiveness to all bowlers. Mr. Gibson's reward was a check for $75,000.

One of the joys of the 1960-61 season was *Winston Churchill,* a Sunday evening recounting of the statesman's career, done with newsreels and still pictures and narrated, chiefly with Churchill's own words, by Richard Burton and Gary Merrill. Other highlights were to be found in specials, among them a fine production of "Macbeth" with Dame Judith Anderson and Maurice Evans that surprisingly won not only the Television Academy's Emmy Award, but the TV Guide Award voted by the viewers.

Possibly the most surprising hit of the year was the adaptation of Mitch Miller's "Sing Along" records to a television series. The bearded oboist had a goodly part of the audience singing old songs along with his all-male chorus. Miller's success secret: "We concentrate on the sound." It was a radical departure for television.

# MEDICINE

### By GILBERT CANT, Medicine Editor, Time Magazine

With an increasingly educated public becoming more aware of the blessings of medical progress in the last half-century, the demand for health is greater in the United States today than ever before or anywhere in the world. This demand is expressed in urgent calls for the prompt discovery of causes and cures for such common and deadly ailments as cancer and heart disease. Fortunately the demand also finds a more constructive expression in readiness to pay for what is now recognized as a costly process. In 1961 medical research enjoyed the support of record expenditures, adding up to almost a billion dollars from all sources, and with the federal government alone paying more than half the total.

Notable progress was made in efforts to control infectious diseases (both viral and bacterial), in the use of artificial heartbeat machines and the artificial kidney, in sensitive methods of diagnosis, and toward explaining the mysterious mechanisms of cancer. But 1961 was also marked in a few places by actual retreats to more defensible positions.

The most conspicious example of such a withdrawal was in connection with live-virus vaccines, taken by mouth, against poliomyelitis. The year began with high optimism that these preparations would soon be available to replace the killed-virus (Salk) vaccine, which must be injected. U.S. authorities had approved the oral vaccine developed by Dr. Albert Sabin of Cincinnati, which almost 100 million people in the Soviet Union have already taken with good results and no reported ill effects. Of the three categories of poliovirus, Types I and II presented no greater technical problems than had been expected. In August, the U.S. Public Health Service licensed distribution of Type I vaccine made by an American manufacturer in British laboratories.

But Type III, which has lately been causing proportionately more paralytic polio than formerly, proved unexpectedly stubborn. To satisfy government standards of safety, the live-virus vaccine must be incapable of causing appreciable damage to nerve cells even when it is injected directly into the brains of monkeys. American manufacturers had difficulty in preparing the Sabin strain of Type III and getting it to pass this rigorous test. The result was to postpone the general release of across-the-board Sabin vaccine until the 1961 polio season was long past. Fortunately, and thanks mainly to Salk vaccine, it proved to be the mildest polio year since record-keeping began in 1912. And the first approved Sabin vaccine, kept in a government stockpile by presidential order, was available just in time for emergency use of 350,000 doses in a local epidemic around Syracuse, N.Y.

A promising experimental vaccine against measles ran into similar, though not quite the same, difficulties, and its release for general use was also postponed. Late in the year it was suggsted that the frequent undesirable effects of the vaccine—fever and a rash—might be avoided if children also received a shot of gamma globulin.

Infectious hepatitis rose to a record peak. Many cases in the New York–New Jersey area were traced, by good medical detective work, to the eating of raw clams taken from sewage-polluted beds in Raritan Bay. For the first time, there was the prospect of a vaccine against this debilitating disease. The evasive virus which causes it was grown in the laboratory for several "generations." Then Dr. Joseph D. Boggs of Chicago gave different virus preparations to volunteer inmates of Joliet Penitentiary, some of whom had to catch hepatitis to show that others were protected by a crude vaccine.

Perhaps the most significant of 1961 research, and certainly the most difficult to interpret, was that which involved the nucleic acids, bridging the gap between viral diseases and cancer. The fact that many animal cancers are caused by viruses has led to an intensive search—so far in vain—for viruses guilty of causing human cancer. Dr. Joseph Huppert of the Pasteur Institute in Paris suggested one explanation: it may be that only part of a human cell's nucleus is changed by a bit of nucleic acid from a virus, which could not be detected in this form. He has put "naked" nucleic acid from human cancers into animals and induced cancer. Dr. Helene Toolan of Sloan-Kettering Institute got indirect evidence of a similar process from human tumors grown in animals. There were renewed reports that virus particles from human cancers had been photographed with the electron microscope and might be used eventually to prepare an anti-cancer vaccine, but this optimism was cruelly premature.

In the long dispute over the role of the typically high-fat American diet in heart disease there was no new, conclusive evidence. But the American Heart Association made its most forthright statement to date: "The reduction or control of fat consumption under medical supervision, with reasonable substitution of polyunsaturated for saturated fats, is recommended as a possible means of preventing atherosclerosis and decreasing the risk of heart attacks and strokes." This would mean cutting down on the "hard" animal fats in meat and dairy products, and increasing the proportion of unhydrogenated vegetable oils and fish oils in the diet.

In October, a team of Harvard surgeons suggested that it may be possible to stave off the crippling damage of many heart attacks if the patients are hooked up promptly to a simple pump connected with an electrocardiograph. By delivering a "counterpulse" when the heart is relaxed between beats, the pump forces extra blood through the coronary arteries and encourages their smaller branches to expand quickly and carry more blood. Trials with human patients were beginning. And for patients whose hearts cannot maintain a healthy beat unaided, handy, portable electric pacemakers—hitherto little more than hospital curiosities—became available at moderate cost.

Lifesaving use of the artificial kidney has been limited to acute emergencies because the patient had to have tubes inserted in an artery and a vein of a leg or arm, and this operation could not be repeated more than half a dozen times. From the University of Washington, Dr. Belding Scribner reported that several patients who otherwise would have died of kidney disease were being treated regularly with the artificial kidney. The secret was the permanent implantation of tubes in the forearm. Though the method is not suitable for many cases and cannot be used outside a few medical centers, it opens a line of research to make similar techniques more widely useful and available.

Parkinsonism or "shaking palsy" has been increasing far more rapidly than either the population as a whole or the number of elderly people among whom it is now most frequent. Two Harvard researchers were able to find encouraging news buried in these depressing statistics. The average age of Parkinsonism victims, they find, has been rising consistently ever since a 1915–25 epidemic of a mysterious viral encephalitis. Most recent cases of Parkinsonism are believed to be late reactions to a seemingly mild, long-ago infection with this virus, which has now disappeared. Therefore, the Harvard men believe Parkinsonism will become a rarity within 20 years. They think it has already passed its peak.

For many patients whose illnesses make conventional gas anesthesia undesirable, a University of Mississippi team offered a disarmingly simple answer: an electric "shock" so modified that it causes no shock and virtually no sensation. A weak current at 22 to 30 volts, and at 700 cycles per second, is applied through electrodes at the temples. Patients report no discomfort from either the anesthesia or the surgery performed under it.

After an operation, many patients dread the return to the surgeon to have the stitches taken out. The best way around this, some considerate surgeons decided, was not to use stitches in the first place. Instead, they used a synthetic porous tape, which does not irritate the skin like ordinary adhesives. It lets the wound ooze, and is washable. And it doesn't hurt when it is taken off.

# SCIENCE IN 1961
## By JONATHAN NORTON LEONARD, Science Editor, Time Magazine

The year 1961 was not a specially glorious one in science. One likely reason was that space flight, which is engineering not science, absorbed a large part of the world's best brainpower while contributing very little to man's understanding of nature. Another important fraction of available brainpower was diverted to the weapons and communication systems of the cold war. In both Communist and non-Communist countries many brilliant, creative scientists worked on short-range, practical projects of nationalistic competition and had no time for the long-range, seemingly impractical research that makes for real progress in science.

Even though 1961 was not what it might have been, some sciences moved forward at an exciting clip. One of them was astronomy, which is the grandfather of the sciences and has always influenced man's philosophical imagination. During 1961, the world's astronomers were delightedly putting to use a set of new instruments for probing the universe. Most important of these are radio telescopes, which study radio waves coming from space instead of the light waves used by conventional telescopes. In ever-increasing profusion they brought new information about the heavens, including pictures of the invisible clouds and rivers of cold hydrogen that hang between the stars. The radio waves from space also told about galaxies (star clouds) so distant that their waves, traveling with the speed of light (186,272 miles per sec.), started in the earth's direction billions of years before either the earth or the sun was formed from cosmic dust and gas. This long-belated news from the depths of space has not been evaluated yet, but out of it may come the answer to the greatest question of all: How and when was the universe created, and is it still being created now?

So successful are radio telescopes that they are being built in many countries all over the world. Some of them are great "steerable dishes" more than 200 ft. in diameter; others are strange-looking arrays of wires, movable sheet-metal reflectors and giant corkscrews. These external parts are spectacular, but they would not be nearly as effective without new-type electronic devices to amplify the feeble radio waves from space. The most interesting of these is the maser, an incredibly sensitive amplifier whose heart is a crystal of synthetic ruby cooled almost to absolute zero ($-459.6$ F.) by liquid helium.

Masers are typical of a branch of science—solid-state physics—that soared to a dizzy peak in 1961. In electronics the phrase "solid state" means making use of electrons moving in the orderly lattices of solid crystals. Transistors were the first important solid-state devices, and they have been followed by a host of descendants and relatives. Some of them, often smaller than peppercorns, replace vacuum tubes in many kinds of electronic equipment. Others serve as the memories and "thinking" cells of giant computers. Still others turn light or heat into electricity, or turn electricity into sound or cold.

The maser, itself a solid-state device, has important descendants, too. One of them, the laser (light-maser) generates a peculiar kind of light whose waves are all exactly the same length and march exactly in step. A beam of this peculiar light, which scientists call "coherent," does not spread out and dissipate like an ordinary searchlight beam, but keeps its brightness for hundreds of miles. If a reasonably powerful source of coherent light were pointed toward a man standing on the moon, he would be able to see it plainly 240,000 miles away.

The laser, which has several forms, has not been perfected enough for practical use, but its inventors are sure that it will eventually revolutionize many kinds of science, as well as serve in both short- and long-distance communication. Coherent light can be amplified and modulated like a radio signal, and if ways are found to tune its single sharp wave length, it can be used to promote valuable chemical reactions. There is some chance that it can be made into a sort of death ray to attack airplanes or missiles.

The year 1961 also marked the peak of a new science with the cumbersome name of magnetohydrodynamics. It deals with plasma, which is gaseous matter whose atoms have been ionized by giving them electric charges. This can be done by heat, radiation, or electric charges, or in various other ways. Plasma is rare on earth, but stars are made almost entirely of it, so it is actually the commonest material in the universe.

Scientists call plasma the fourth state of matter because it does not behave like a solid, a liquid, or a normal gas. It pays little attention to gravitation, but swirls and streams and surges in response to fields of magnetic force. Sunspots are eddies of plasma driven by magnetism, and the great glowing filaments that spurt out of the sun are plasma, too.

Until very recently plasma was a laboratory curiosity, but by 1961 it had become vitally practical. The incandescent air flowing past the nose of a missile entering the atmosphere is a hot plasma and must be dealt with as such. It blocks radio signals and is visible to radars that could not possibly see the missile itself. The gaseous exhausts of climbing rockets are plasmas, too. An important problem in plasma physics is learning how to get controlled, nonexplosive energy out of the nuclear-fusion reaction of the H-bomb.

The year 1961 saw some progress toward this goal but no real solution. In another kind of plasma-power research came success. Scientists announced that a stream of hot plasma from burning fuel has been made to yield a powerful electric current without a boiler, turbine, or generator. Magneto-hydrodynamic power stations may be commonplace in the future.

The most spectacular scientific news of 1961 was the resumption of nuclear testing by Soviet Russia. The immediate purpose was to test and improve nuclear weapons, and the same had to be true of U.S. tests. But not all the results would be necessarily bad for humanity. Nuclear tests are experiments in physics that cannot be performed in any other way. Out of them may come scientific knowledge of use to men at peace, including the elusive secret of how to control hydrogen energy for peaceful purposes.

During 1961, oceanography came into its own. Scientists and governments realized that the oceans are the earth's last great frontier. Oceanographic ships working with newly devised instruments found important subsurface ocean currents that no one had dreamed of before. They discovered rich new fishing grounds, one of them in the Indian Ocean, handy to underfed Asia. In the bottoms of all the oceans they traced a network of strange cracks which indicate that the earth's crust has been growing slowly through geological ages.

A great U.S. project in geophysics got a start in 1961 when scientists experimented off California and Mexico with a drilling apparatus designed to bore a hole in the bottom of the ocean. Their ultimate purpose is to reach the Mohorovicic discontinuity, the sudden change of rock density that comes at the bottom of the earth's solid crust. Since the crust is much thinner under the oceans than under the land, American scientists have decided that the oceans are the best place to drill. The Russians, who are also planning to drill down to the "Moho," are planning to do it on land, or at least on some island in the ocean. The international competition to reach the "Moho" and learn about the almost unknown interior of the earth may develop into a rivalry like the race into space.

In the strange unreal world of theoretical physics, where waves are particles, and parts of an object can be bigger than the whole, a new level of mystery was added in 1961. Physicists had just about decided that they had found all except one of the elemental particles that form matter. They named the last particle *omega* in advance, but when they finally found it, they also found evidence that it might be only the first of a large family of particles. Apparently matter is even more complicated than the physicists thought.

In the life sciences, on which medicine and modern agriculture depend, there was steady advance in 1961 but few striking accomplishments. Perhaps the most important was the synthesis of ACTH, a hormone that controls many vital functions of the human body. The important thing about this synthesis is that ACTH is a protein, a class of chemical that has hitherto defied all efforts to make it in the laboratory. If ACTH can be synthesized, other synthetic proteins will surely follow, and there are literally millions of them that may play important parts in medicine and industry.

# SPACE AGE NEWS

## *By*
## WILLY LEY

In the 1961 edition of the *Information Please Almanac* I predicted that during 1961 the Russians "will be the first to have a man in orbit." As everybody now knows, they orbited two men during that year.

To counteract a large number of rumors and conjectures which have found their way into print, let me state that the United States Government is fully convinced that the Russian claims about these two orbits are absolutely correct. Of course, the government has not stated (and for very good reasons of its own does not wish to state) the facts on which this conviction is based; apparently there is additional evidence other than the normal satellite-tracking going on all the time which will catch any satellite larger than a coconut during its first orbit.

In both cases, the capsule carrying the cosmonaut (as the Russians call their astronauts) was named *Vostok*—*Vostok I* and *Vostok II*. The Russian word *vostok* means "east," but there may have been another reason for choosing this name. More than a century and a quarter ago, a Russian vessel, commanded by Admiral Fabian Gottlieb von Bellingshausen, was the first Russian ship to circumnavigate the globe at a very high southern latitude. The ship was named *Vostok*.

The Russians have promised that newspaper reporters and other news media, such as television, will be permitted to watch the third launching of a man into orbit. Until that happens there can be only conjectures as to the appearance of their spaceships. But from the reports, and from the performance of the large capsules carrying animals they orbited earlier, the following is a reasonable guess: the ship has an elongated shape with a fairly blunt rounded nose and short wings, possibly somewhat like the wings on our X-15 research aircraft. The ship, having orbited the earth, seems to re-enter as a whole supersonic glider and, after it has lost most of its speed, lands like a glider.

When the Russians orbited their animal-carrying capsules they probably decided that there was a possibility of a last-second crash. The ship might run into a boulder or a tree and thus ruin the whole experiment. For this reason the animal-carrying capsule was built to be detachable. When the ship had reached a reasonable altitude, say between 15,000 and 20,000 feet, the capsule was released by radio command, and descended by parachute.

This method seems to have been used for the manned flights, even though the cosmonaut, being a pilot, would no doubt be able to land his craft and avoid any last-second crash into a solid object. Why the feature of the separate capsule has been retained is not known, but there are two possibilities. The first is that this is what they had and they did not wish any delay by designing, and then building and testing, a new type of ship. They wanted to orbit a man before the *Mercury* capsule went into orbit. A delay of, say, six months might have seen the *Mercury* into orbit before the *Vostok*.

Secondly, there might be a sound engineering reason why the system of the detachable capsule was retained. Even if the re-entry of the *Vostok* is somewhat more gentle than that of the *Mercury,* the re-entering ship grows very hot. By means of various layers of insulation, the heating of the interior by the red-hot exterior can be slowed down. Here a separate capsule is a great help, and detaching the capsule and landing it by parachute relieves the pilot of the task of staying with his ship—the interior of which steadily grows hotter—to the last moment.

The first man to go into orbit was Major Yuri Alekseyevitch Gagarin, who took off at 9:07 A.M. (Moscow time) on April 12, 1961. The orbit plotted for him was strongly inclined to the equator. He almost passed over the Bering Strait on his way out; and if that half of the earth had not been in darkness then, he could have seen Tierra del Fuego on one side of his ship, and the tip of the Antarctic Peninsula (formerly Palmer Land) on the other side 40 minutes later.

His apogee point, 188 miles above sea level, was over the Pacific Ocean, just about half way between New Zealand and South America. The orbit proper lasted 89 minutes; the total elapsed time from take-off from a base near Lake Aral to the landing in an area north of the Caspian Sea was not quite two hours.

Radio Moscow waxed almost religious in their announcement, at 12:25 P.M., that: "At 10:55 Cosmonaut Gagarin safely returned to the sacred soil of our motherland."

Gagarin had made only one orbit around the earth. In fact, one may quibble, if so inclined, and say that it was not quite a complete orbit since the landing area is about 200 miles to the west of the take-off area.

The second man to go into orbit was Major Gherman Titov, whose flight was of much greater scientific importance than the flight of the *Vostok I.*

Major Titov took off—apparently from the same base—on Sunday, August 6, at 9 A.M. (Moscow time) and stayed in orbit for 25 hours, making a total of 17½ orbits around the earth. The weight of *Vostok II* was given as 10,408 lbs., which is, within a hundred pounds or so, the same as that of all the recent heavy Soviet satellites. The inclination of its orbit was nearly the same as that of *Vostok I.* While orbiting, Titov's ship approached the earth to within 110⅓ miles (perigee) and receded to as much as 159⅓ miles (apogee).

The important point of this flight was its long duration, which put Major Titov into a weightless state for nearly 25 hours. For years scientists have been wondering about the problem of eating in a weightless state. This had only been tested with weightless flights inside the atmosphere which never lasted longer than one minute, maximum. Another and far more difficult question was that of sleeping while in a weightless condition; that, of course, could not be tested at all in one minute. Titov ate a total of three meals while in orbit and said about one of them that he ate because this was on the time table, not because he felt hungry at the moment.

His lack of appetite may have had some connection with the fact, admitted by Russian scientists some six weeks later, that Titov felt "faintly seasick" all the time. This condition was not bad enough to interfere with his work and test program, and it improved after he slept for 7½ hours. It is quite possible that this was a purely individual reaction. We know from our own experiments that some people may be highly qualified as test pilots and be sensitive to weightlessness. It also works the other way around: people who have never flown before have shown not only resistance to but a liking for weightlessness. We already knew that eating in a weightless state was possible; spaceman Titov's three meals, therefore, were not surprising. What was important is that he also slept.

While the flight of the *Vostok I* has to be considered mainly as a cautious try, with the main emphasis on a safe landing and hence landing just as soon as possible under the circumstances, the flight of the *Vostok II* rates as a first-class space medical experiment. Naturally, many space scientists have stated all along that they considered eating and sleeping as possible while a person is weightless, but now it has been proved.

The only other major Russian space experiment was an unmanned probe to Venus on February 12, 1961. While the take-off went well and the Venus probe separated itself neatly from the orbiting satellite (*Sputnik VIII*), radio contact was lost, apparently much earlier than the Russians had expected. Even the big radio telescope in Jodrell Bank in England, which was loaned to the Russians for the purpose, was no help. Trajectory calculations indicate that the probe did not approach Venus any closer than 105,000 miles.

Before we go on to the American story, a bit of space age news has to be related concerning nearby space, but not with man-made activities. For nearly a century astronomers have been wondering whether our planet has only one moon. It became clear very soon that any additional moon, or moons, had to be very small, since even a hundred-foot moon in a thousand-mile orbit would be visible to the naked eye. A search carried on with specially designed equipment by Professor Clyde W. Tombaugh during 1953 to 1955 showed that no small earth satellites existed, although something the size of a small pebble might be in orbit somewhere. But this still left one possibility: the Earth could have additional satellites in the orbit of the Moon itself. If a small satellite moved in the Moon's orbit 60° ahead of the Moon (technically known as the $L_4$ position) or 60° behind the Moon (in the $L_5$ position), the orbits would be stable.

A Polish astronomer, Dr. K. Kordylewski, began a search several years ago for natural Earth satellites in these positions. But the search was fruitless, for Kordylewski looked for bodies large enough to show up as points of light in a telescope.

In 1956, his colleague and compatriot, Dr. Witkowski, suggested to him that such satellites might exist in the form of clouds of very fine cosmic dust. If so, they might be visible and more easily seen by the naked eye. Another condition was that the $L_4$ and $L_5$ spots had to be above the horizon, but the Moon had to be below the horizon because its bright light would mask such dust satellites. Dr. Kordylewski followed the advice and reported early in 1961 that he had observed very faint patches of light in both positions and had succeeded in photographing one in the trailing, or $L_5$, position. In early 1962, American astronomers will have a chance to check on this observation.

As for American space accomplishments, the United States in September put its fifty-second satellite successfully into orbit.

In addition to our man-in-space program we are working on three kinds of satellite systems, all of which probably will achieve what might be called a "preliminary working status" in 1962. They are: the *Tiros-Nimbus* meteorological observation satellite program, which will assist weather forecasts by pictures of the Earth's cloud cover broadcast from orbit. (One of these satellites produced the only complete picture of a hurricane in September 1961— hurricane Debbie.) The second is the *Transit* navigational satellite system, and the third is the communications satellite system. The *Transit* satellites that are in orbit provide hope that a working system will not be more than a year in the future. As for the communication satellites, it is probable that private persons will be able to make transatlantic phone calls "via satellite" by 1963.

The U.S. is also working on a fourth system—the *Midas* system for detecting the take-off of enemy ballistic missiles. Naturally nothing has been said about the early tests of this system.

It may be added that the Russians seem to have completely neglected to do any work on such systems. The reasons might be that our work is well ahead of theirs and, of course, the earth needs only *one* navigational system and only *one* meteorological system.

In America's man-in-space program there were four successful shots in 1961: three "inhabited" (as they are called) suborbital shots and the orbiting of a *Mercury* capsule with a "simulated person" inside.

The first of these suborbital shots took place on January 31, 1961. Carried by a *Redstone* rocket, the capsule attained a range of 414 miles with a peak of 156.5 miles. The inhabitant of the capsule was a 37-lb. chimpanzee officially labeled "Animal No. 65" but generally known as Ham because his normal behavior has been described as being "half ham, half human."

The first manned shot was that of Navy Commander Alan B. Shepard, Jr., on May 5, 1961, the second that of Air Force Captain Virgil I. Grissom on July 21. The flight, over a distance of 302 miles with a peak of 116.5 miles, was a complete success. The second flight was also a success; it went a distance of 303 miles with a peak of 118 miles, but was spoiled at the last moment when it landed in the water. A hatch cover blew prematurely, and Grissom had to abandon the capsule and swim; fortunately a spacesuit is quite buoyant. The weight of the capsule, plus the sea water sloshing into it, was too much for the rescue helicopter to carry. It had to be abandoned and sank to the bottom of the Atlantic Ocean.

But both shots were so satisfactory that further suborbital flights were discontinued. The next step was the orbiting of a *Mercury* capsule with a "dummy" inside—a device which would use up as much oxygen as a man and would "perspire" to the same degree as a man if the temperature climbed too high. This capsule was orbited by an *Atlas* rocket (the suborbital flights had used *Redstone* rockets) and made about the same flight as Gagarin. It went around the Earth once, lasted one hour and 49 minutes (one minute longer than Gagarin) with apogee at 158.6 miles. The date was September 13, 1961; take-off was from Cape Canaveral; landing was in the ocean 161 miles east of Bermuda. After the capsule had been successfully recovered it was found that there had been a minor leak somewhere in the oxygen system. But everybody was agreed that a man, wearing a spacesuit, would have survived the flight without any particular discomfort.

Though not directly connected with the man-in-space program the flights of the rocket-propelled research plane X-15 should be mentioned. After a number of preliminary flights in 1960, an altitude record of 169,600 feet was set on March 30, 1961, by test pilot (of NASA) Joe Walker. On October 4, 1961, Air Force Major Robert Rushworth flew the X-15 in a "crippled" condition. The bottom fin had been removed, and portions of the electronic systems were switched off in sequence, forcing the pilot to fly the ship manually. On October 11, 1961, Air Force Major Robert M. White set another record; he took the X-15 to 215,000 feet (with 99.9 per cent of the Earth's atmosphere below him) and reached a speed of 3,477 mph. During this flight, the pilot was weightless for two minutes, without experiencing any problems.

### U. S. Ballistic Missiles of Operational and Near-operational Status

| Name | Length (ft.) | Take-off Weight (lbs.) | Range (miles) | Fuel | Take-off thrust (lbs.) | Prime Contractor |
|---|---|---|---|---|---|---|
| GROUND–TO–GROUND: | | | | | | |
| Atlas | 82 | 265,000 | 6,000+ | Liquid | 360,000 | Convair |
| Titan | 90 | 222,000 | 7,000+ | Liquid | 340,000 | Martin |
| Thor | 62 | 110,000 | 1,500 | Liquid | 160,000 | Douglas |
| Jupiter | 59 | 110,000 | 1,500 | Liquid | 160,000 | Chrysler |
| Redstone | 63 | 61,000 | 200 | Liquid | 110,000 | Chrysler |
| Corporal | 46 | 12,000 | 50 | Liquid | 20,000 | Firestone |
| Sergeant | 30 | ...... | 50+ | Solid | ...... | JPL/Sperry |
| Honest John[1] | 27 | 6,000 | 15 | Solid | ...... | Emerson– |
| Little John | 15 | ...... | 15? | Solid | ...... | Douglas |
| Lacrosse | 19 | 2,300 | 20 | Solid | ...... | Martin |
| Polaris | 28 | 28,000 | 1,100 | Solid | ...... | Lockheed |
| SURFACE–TO–AIR: | | | | | | |
| Nike Ajax | 21 | ...... | 25 | Solid | ...... | Western El. |
| Nike Hercules | 27 | ...... | 75+ | Solid | ...... | Western El. |
| Terrier | 15 | 3,000 | 10 | Solid | ...... | Convair |
| AIR–TO–SURFACE: | | | | | | |
| Bullpup | 11 | 571 | 3 | Solid | ...... | Martin |
| Rascal | 32 | ...... | 100 | Liquid | ...... | Bell |
| ANTI–SUBMARINE: | | | | | | |
| Able | 8.5 | 500 | ...... | ...... | ...... | Avco |
| AIR–TO–AIR: | | | | | | |
| Falcon | 6.5 | 100 | ...... | Solid | ...... | Hughes |
| Genie[2] | 8 | ...... | 1.5 | Solid | ...... | Douglas |
| Sidewinder I-A | 9 | 155 | 2 | Solid | ...... | Philco |
| Sparrow I[3] | 12 | 300 | 5+ | Solid | ...... | Sperry |
| Sparrow III[3] | 12 | 350 | ...... | Solid | ...... | Raytheon |

[1] Honest John and Little John are unguided artillery Rockets. [2] Genie is an unguided rocket. [3] Sparrow I is being replaced by Sparrow III.

NOTE: A rather large number of other missiles are under development at the time the Almanac goes to print. Most of them are either direct improvements of missiles now in existence or new designs which will, when finished, replace other missiles slowly becoming obsolescent. The solid-fuel *Pershing* is meant to replace the liquid-fuel *Redstone*, just as the solid-fuel *Sergeant* has replaced the liquid-fuel *Corporal*. The *Skybolt* missile (to be fired from aircraft against ground targets) with its 1,000-mile range, will replace the *Rascal* with its 100-mile range. The three-stage solid-fuel *Minuteman* will, when finished, replace the *Atlas* and *Titan* as the ICBM (but *Atlas* and *Titan* will continue to be used as space boosters) and the upper two stages of the *Minuteman*, fired without its first-stage booster, might replace the *Jupiter* and the *Thor*. The *Nike-Zeus* is likely to become the anti-missile missile. The general trend is the replacement of existing missiles with others which have the same capabilities but are smaller and presumably cheaper.

## Russian Missiles

| Name | Length (ft.) | Take-off Weight (lbs.) | Range (miles) | Fuel | Take-off Thrust (lbs.) | Number of stages |
|------|------|------|------|------|------|------|
| GROUND–TO–GROUND: | | | | | | |
| T-1 | 50 | 38,000 | 600–700 | Liquid | 70,000 | one |
| T-2 | 85–91 | 110,000 | 1,500 | Liquid | 200,000 | two |
| T-3 | ca. 90 | 240,000 | 5,000 | Liquid | 500,000 | two |
| T-3A | ca. 110 | 260,000 | 6,000 | Liquid | 750,000 | two |
| T-3B | ca. 120 | 360,000 | 7,500 | Liquid | 1,000,000 | three |
| T-4[1] | 53 | ...... | 1,000 | Liquid | ...... | two |
| T-4A[2] | 121 | 230,000 | 10,000 | Liquid | 360,000 | three |
| T-5[3] | 36 | ...... | 50–100 | Solid | ...... | three |
| T-5B[4] | 31 | 6,000 | 15–25 | Solid | ...... | one |
| T-7A | 30 | 10,000 | 50–100 | Solid | ...... | one |
| SURFACE–TO–AIR: | | | | | | |
| T-6[5] | ...... | ...... | 20–25 | Solid | ...... | two |
| T-8[6] | 13 | ...... | ca. 20 | S/L | ...... | two |
| M-2 | 25 | ...... | ca. 20 | Solid | ...... | two |
| NAVY ROCKETS[7] | | | | | | |
| Golem I[8] | 54 | 23,000 | 400 | Liquid | 40,000 | one |
| Golem II | 60 | ...... | 1,200 | Liquid | ...... | one |
| Golem III | ca. 20 | ca. 3,000 | 20 | Solid | ...... | one |
| Golem IV | ...... | ca. 6,000 | 45 | Solid | ...... | one |
| Komet I[9] | ...... | ...... | 100 | Solid | ...... | one |
| Komet II | ...... | ...... | 600 | Solid | ...... | one |

NOTES:  [1] The T-4 missile seems to consist of the upper stages of the T-4A. Both T-4 and T-4A are experimental at the moment.  [2] T-4A is a winged missile (wing span 66 ft.) for winged re-entry which greatly extends the total range. It is catapulted from a rail sled for take-off.  [3] T-5 is designed to be launched in salvos.  [4] T-5B is about the same as our *Honest John*, unguided.  [5] Is fired from multiple launchers.  [6] Missile has liquid fuel, its booster uses solid fuel.  [7] The term "Navy Rockets" means Navy developments, some are also used by the Russian Army.  [8] Golem I and Golem II are designed to be fired from capsules towed by submarines, Golem III and Golem IV are operational from surface vessels though intended to be fired by submerged submarines.  [9] Komet I and Komet II are in use with the Army, program for adapting them to submarines is underway. The missile called Komet D is to be fired from aircraft against ground targets, it is turbojet propelled, 33.5 ft. long, range about 55 miles, still under development.

# The Detection of Ballistic Missiles

The firing of a ballistic missile over a range of several thousand miles can be discovered from space by special satellites (of which *Midas* is a prototype), and from the ground by long-range radars. The United States has completed the building of two of three long-range radar sites, which are known as BMEWS for Ballistic Missile Early Warning System. One is located in Thule, Greenland, and consists of four very large, fixed antennas. The second of these stations is in Clear, Alaska. The third, in Yorkshire, England, is expected to be completed in 1962. Each one of these stations will have a range of about 3,000 miles.

The trajectory of a ballistic missile, fired for a range of 6,000 miles or better, strongly resembles the trajectory of a missile placing an artificial satellite into orbit. But the trajectory of a missile which is to re-enter the atmosphere to strike a target on the ground has to be somewhat steeper than that of an orbiting missile. The peak of such a trajectory, located half-way between take-off pad and target, is likely to be more than a thousand miles from the surface, farther out than many satellite orbits.

This makes detection somewhat easier because the radar beam does not follow the curvature of the ground. If the radar is located about 700 miles from the launching pad, its beam, even if it is strictly horizontal, will pass some 60 miles over the launching pad and the missile will not be detected until it has reached that altitude. If the distance between radar and launching pad is 1,400 miles, the beam will pass 250 miles above the launching site. At a distance of 2,000 miles the beam will be nearly 600 miles above the pad, and at a distance of 3,000 miles it will be 1,100 miles above the launching site. These figures explain why it is necessary to locate the radar as close to the likely launching sites as possible.

Of course the BMEWS stations can only *detect* an enemy missile; the destruction of the missile would be up to anti-missile missiles, which still have to be developed.

# SPACE AGE NEWS CHRONOLOGY

## By

### WILLY LEY

---

## HIGH VERTICAL SHOTS AND LUNAR PROBES

| Date | Place of firing | Purpose and results |
| --- | --- | --- |
| Feb. 24, 1949 | White Sands Proving Ground, New Mexico | Two-stage rocket, V-2 plus WAC Corporal, first large two-stage rocket, to test separation in mid-flight. Fully successful, peak altitude of top stage 250 miles. |
| Winter, 1956–57 | Cape Canaveral | Runaway X-17 three-stage solid fuel nose cone test rocket. Lost by trackers, calculation indicates peak altitude near 1,000 miles. |
| Sept.–Oct., 1957 | Above Eniwetok, Pacific Ocean | Project Farside. Four-stage solid fuel rockets carried to over 80,000 ft. by plastic balloon. Six attempts, generally unsuccessful. Highest shot estimated at 3,000 miles (transmitter failed at 2,700 miles while rocket was still climbing). |
| Aug.–Sept. 1958 | Above South Atlantic | Project Argus, using modified X-17 rockets. Three shots, exploding small nuclear bombs 300 miles above sea level. |
| Aug. 27, 1958 | Kyzyl Kum Desert | Russian research rocket, carrying 3,726.45 lbs. to 279.6 miles. Two dogs in payload, recovered alive. |
| Oct. 11, 1958 | Cape Canaveral | Pioneer I, lunar probe. Reached maximum altitude of 71,300 miles. Re-entered atmosphere over South Pacific 43 hours and 17.5 min. after take-off. |
| Nov. 8, 1958 | Cape Canaveral | Pioneer II, lunar probe. Third stage failed to ignite, re-entered 42.4 minutes after take-off. Peak altitude not announced; must have been over 1,000 miles. |
| Dec. 6, 1958 | Cape Canaveral | Pioneer III, lunar probe. Reached maximum altitude of 66,654 miles. Discovered outer Van Allen layer. Burn-up over French Equatorial Africa 38 hours and 6 minutes after take-off. |

| Date | Place of firing | Purpose and results |
|---|---|---|
| Jan. 2, 1959 | Kyzyl Kum Desert | Russian lunar probe Metchtá ("Daydream") missed moon by 4,600 miles. Radio transmission stopped soon after passing moon, suggesting that rocket was fired for impact. Weight 3,245 lbs. Now in orbit around sun, 15-month period. |
| March 3, 1959 | Cape Canaveral | Pioneer IV, lunar probe. Passed moon on March 4 at a distance of 37,300 miles; now in orbit around sun similar to Metchtá's. Weight 13.4 lbs. |
| June (?), 1959 | Woomera, Australia | British Black Knight rocket carried nose cone to 300 miles. |
| July 2, 1959 | Kyzyl Kum Desert | Single-stage liquid fuel Russian rocket carried 4,400 lbs. of payload to above 200 miles. In payload two dogs and a young hare. Recovered alive and healthy. |
| July 7, 1959 | Wallops Island (Virginia) | Five-stage Javelin[1] rocket carried 45 lbs. of instruments to 600 miles; soon after, a Strongarm rocket carried 25 lbs. to 470 miles. |
| Sept. 12, 1959 | Kyzyl Kum Desert | Russian lunar probe, weighing 860 lbs. Impact on moon in the area of *Mare serenitatis* 35 hours after take-off. Not heavy enough to produce crater. |
| Nov. 10, 1959 | Wallops Island | Five-stage Strongarm rocket carried instrument payload to 1,050 miles. |
| Nov. 10, 1959 | Woomera, Australia | Black Knight reached 450 miles. |
| March 11, 1960 | Cape Canaveral | Pioneer V, space probe. Fired into orbit around sun between orbits of earth and of Venus. Orbital period 311 days, total weight 94.8 lbs. Radio transmission over record distance of more than 20 million miles. |
| July 1, 1960 | Wallops Island | First four-stage solid-fuel Scout with 193 lbs. payload. Fourth stage did not ignite; payload reached 860 miles peak altitude in spite of this failure. Impact 1,500 miles from Wallops Island in Atlantic. |
| Sept. 19, 1960 | Point Arguello, Calif. | Four-stage solid fuel NASA rocket fired into inner Van Allen belt. Peak altitude reached 1,200 miles. 83-lb. instrument capsule recovered 3 hours later by U.S.S. Rowan. |

[1] *Javelin, Strongarm* and other rockets, such as *Jason* (Argo E-5) and *Journeyman* (Argo D-8), are test vehicles which are made up, when needed, from existing missiles. *Strongarm's* first stage is an *Honest John*, the second and third stages are *Nike Ajax* boosters, the fourth stage a *Recruit* and the fifth a scaled down *Sergeant*. Another version has a T-55 Jato unit as the top stage. *Journeyman's* first stage consists of a *Sergeant* and two *Recruits* clustered together; the second and third stages are *Lance* rockets, and the fourth stage an *Altair* rocket.

| Date | Place of firing | Purpose and results |
|------|-----------------|---------------------|
| Sept. 21, 1960 | Cape Canaveral | Four-stage solid-fuel Blue Scout rocket, carrying 32.8 lbs. of instrumentation. Radio failed, estimated peak altitude 16,600 miles. Re-entered 7 hours after take-off. |
| Oct. 4, 1960 | Cape Canaveral | Scout rocket for radiation research. Peak altitude 3,500 miles. Impact in South Atlantic 5,800 miles down range. |
| Jan. 31, 1961 | Cape Canaveral | Mercury capsule carrying chimpanzee Ham fired by Redstone rocket. Peak altitude 155 miles, parachute landing 420 miles down range. Animal recovered in perfect condition. |
| Feb. 1, 1961 | Cape Canaveral | First firing of Minuteman, 4,000 miles down range. |
| Feb. 12, 1961 | Kyzyl Kum (?) | Russian Venus probe fired from orbiting Sputnik VIII. Must have passed Venus about May 20, 1961, but no signals received. Will orbit sun in orbit similar to that of Pioneer V. |
| March 3, 1961 | Cape Canaveral | Blue Scout II with 172 lbs. of instrumentation. Maximum altitude 1,580 miles, range 2,000 miles. |
| May 5, 1961 | Cape Canaveral | Mercury capsule Freedom VII with Commander Alan B. Shepard. Peak altitude 116.5 miles, range 302 miles. |
| July 21, 1961 | Cape Canaveral | Mercury capsule Liberty Bell VII with Captain Virgil I. Grissom. Peak altitude 118 miles, range 303 miles. |

# NUCLEAR TESTS, 1961 SERIES

**(August 30: Official Russian announcement that nuclear tests would be resumed.)**

| Number and date | Yield in megatons* | Location |
|-----------------|--------------------|----------| 
| | RUSSIAN TESTS† | |
| 1. Sept. 1 | 0.1–0.5 | Soviet Central Area (near Semipalatinsk) |
| 2. Sept. 4 | 0.1–0.5 | Same |
| 3. Sept. 5 | 0.1–0.5 | Same |
| 4. Sept. 6 | 0.1–0.5 | East of Stalingrad |
| 5. Sept. 10 | 0.5? | Novaya Zemlya |
| 6. Sept. 10 | 3–5 | Same |
| 7. Sept. 12 | 3–5 | Same |
| 8. Sept. 13 | 0.1–0.5 | Same |
| 9. Sept. 13 | 0.1–0.5 | Central Asia (Semipalatinsk) |
| 10. Sept. 14 | 3–5 | Novaya Zemlya |
| 11. Sept. 16 | 1 | Novaya Zemlya |
| 12. Sept. 17 | 0.5? | Central Asia (Semipalatinsk) |

| Number and date | Yield in megatons* | Location |
|-----------------|--------------------|----------|
| | RUSSIAN TESTS (cont'd)† | |
| 13. Sept. 18 | 1 | Novaya Zemlya |
| 14. Sept. 20 | 1 | Same |
| 15. Sept. 22 | 1 | Same |
| 16. Oct. 2 | 1 | Same |
| 17. Oct. 4 | 3–5 | Same |
| 18. Oct. 6 | 3–5 | Same |
| 19. Oct. 8 | 0.3 | Novaya Zemlya |
| 20. Oct. 12 | 0.2 | Central Asia (Semipalatinsk) |
| 21. Oct. 20 | ? | Novaya Zemlya |
| | U. S. TESTS | |
| 1. Sept. 14 | Low yield | Underground in Nevada |
| 2. Sept. 15 | Same | Same |
| 3. Oct. 10 | Same | Same |

\* The term *megaton* means "equivalent in explosive force to one million tons of TNT."
† All Russian tests were in the atmosphere.

# ARTIFICIAL SATELLITES

| Name | Firing Date | First perigee (miles) | First apogee (miles) | Orbital period (minutes) | Satellite weight (pounds) | Total weight in orbit (pounds) | Lifetime terminated |
|---|---|---|---|---|---|---|---|
| Sputnik I | Oct. 4, 1957 | 142 | 588 | 96.17 | 183.6 | ca. 8000 | Jan. 4, 1958 |
| Sputnik II | Nov. 3, 1957 | 140 | 1038 | 103.7 | 1120 | ca. 9000 | Apr. 14, 1958 |
| Explorer I | Jan. 31, 1958 | 224 | 1573 | 114.8 | 18.13 | 30.8 | Another 5 years |
| Vanguard I | Mar. 17, 1958 | 409 | 2453 | 134.3 | 3.25 | 53.25 | 1,000 years |
| Explorer III | Mar. 26, 1958 | 121 | 1746 | 115.9 | 18.56 | 31 | June 27, 1958 |
| Sputnik III | May 15, 1958 | 135 | 1167 | 106 | 2925 | 8000+ | April 6, 1960 |
| Explorer IV | July 26, 1958 | 163 | 1380 | 110.27 | 25.8 | 38.4 | Oct. 23, 1959 |
| Score (Atlas) | Dec. 18, 1958 | 110 | 920 | 101.46 | 160 | 8750 | Jan. 21, 1959 |
| Vanguard II | Feb. 17, 1959 | 347 | 2064 | 125.85 | 20.74 | 50.74 | Another 40 years |
| Discoverer I | Feb. 28, 1959 | 99 | 605 | 95.9 | 245 | 1300 | March 5, 1959 |
| Discoverer II | April 13, 1959 | 142 | 220 | 90.5 | 245 | 1610 | April 26, 1959 |
| Explorer VI | Aug. 7, 1959 | 157 | 26,400 | 12 h. 46 m. | 142 | .... | Est. late 1961 |
| Discoverer V | Aug. 13, 1959 | 150 | 450 | ca. 95 | 450 | 1700 | Sept. 28, 1959 |
| Discoverer VI | Aug. 19, 1959 | 138 | 537 | ca. 100 | 450 | 1700 | Oct. 20, 1959 |
| Vanguard III | Sept. 18, 1959 | 319 | 2329 | 135 | 50 | 100 | Another 40 years |
| Cosmic Rocket III | Oct. 4, 1959 | 24,840 | 291,870 | 15 d. | 613 | 3416 | May 19, 1960 |
| Explorer VII | Oct. 13, 1959 | 346 | 664 | 101.25 | 91.5 | .... | Another 20 years |
| Discoverer VII | Nov. 7, 1959 | 100 | 515 | 94.55 | 300 | 1700 | Nov. 26, 1959 |
| Discoverer VIII | Nov. 20, 1959 | 117 | 1040 | 103 | 300 | 1700 | Est. March, 1961 |
| Tiros I | April 1, 1960 | 429 | 468 | 99.1 | 270 | ca. 320 | About 100 years |
| Transit I B | April 13, 1960 | 239 | 472 | 95.9 | 265 | ca. 1500 | Est. Sept. 1961 |
| Discoverer XI | April 15, 1960 | 110 | 345 | 92.3 | 300 | 1700 | April 26, 1960 |
| Sputnik IV | May 15, 1960 | 189 | 222 | 91.1 | 9988 | ?? | July 17, 1960 |
| Midas II | May 24, 1960 | 300 | 318 | 94 | 3300 | ca. 5000 | Another 5 years |
| Transit II A | June 22, 1960 | 389 | 658 | 102 | 265 | 1500 | Another 50 years |
| Greb | June 22, 1960 | 382 | 658 | 102 | 42 | Same | Same |
| Echo I | Aug. 12, 1960 | 1018 | 1160 | 121.6 | 137.4 | .... | 1,000 years |
| Discoverer XIII | Aug. 10, 1960 | 266 | 436 | 96 | 300 | 1700 | Aug. 11, 1960 |
| Discovery XIV | Aug. 18, 1960 | 116 | 502 | 94.5 | 300 | 1700 | Aug. 19, 1960 |
| Sputnik V | Aug. 19, 1960 | 198.8 | 198.8 | 90.7 | 10,120 | .... | Aug. 20, 1960 |
| Discoverer XV | Sept. 13, 1960 | 130 | 472 | 94.24 | 1700 | 300 | Sept. 14, 1960 |
| Courier I | Oct. 4, 1960 | 500 | 745 | ca. 104 | 501 | .... | 1,000 years |
| Explorer VIII | Nov. 3, 1960 | 258 | 1422.6 | 112.7 | 90.4 | .... | About 20 years |
| Discoverer XVII | Nov. 12, 1960 | 118 | 615 | 96 | 300 | 2100 | Dec. 29, 1960 |
| Tiros II | Nov. 23, 1960 | 406 | 431 | 98 | 280 | .... | 200 years |
| Sputnik VI | Dec. 1, 1960 | 116.4 | 164.6 | 88.6 | 10,061 | .... | Dec. 3, 1960 |
| Discoverer XVIII | Dec. 7, 1960 | 154 | 459 | 93.8 | 300 | 2100 | Sometime in 1961 |
| Discoverer XIX | Dec. 20, 1960 | 128.3 | 390.5 | 93 | .... | 2100 | Sometime in 1961 |
| Samos II | Jan. 31, 1961 | 255 | 344 | 95 | .... | 2100 | About 10 years |
| Sputnik VII | Feb. 4, 1961 | 139 | 204 | 90 | 14,292 | .... | Feb. 26, 1961 |
| Sputnik VIII | Feb. 12, 1961 | 123 | 201.5 | 90 | 14,300 | .... | Feb. 25, 1961 |
| Explorer IX | Feb. 16, 1961 | 395 | 1605 | 118.3 | 80 | .... | 100 years |
| Discoverer XX | Feb. 17, 1961 | 177 | 486 | 95.4 | 300 | 2450 | Sometime in 1961 |
| Discoverer XXI | Feb. 18, 1961 | 149 | 659 | 93.8 | .... | 2450 | About 5 years |
| Transit IIIB and Lofti | Feb. 22, 1961 | 117 | 429 | 93.2 | 250 & 54 | .... | Sometime in 1961 |
| Sputnik IX | Mar. 9, 1961 | 110 | 155 | 88.2 | 10,360 | .... | March 9, 1961 |
| Sputnik X | Mar. 25, 1961 | 110 | 153 | 88 | 10,360 | .... | March 25, 1961 |
| Explorer X | Mar. 25, 1961 | 110 | 112,500 | 82.2 h. | 79 | .... | Probably Apr. 1961 |
| Discoverer XXIII | April 8, 1961 | .... | .... | .... | 300 | 2450 | Unknown |
| Vostok (Sputnik XI) | April 12, 1961 | 108.7 | 187.6 | 89.1 | 10,414 | .... | 108-minute lifetime |
| Explorer XI | April 27, 1961 | 302 | 1,113 | 107.9 | ca. 90 | .... | 3 years |
| Discoverer XXV | June 16, 1961 | 139.1 | 251.6 | 91 | 300 | 2450 | 1 month |
| Transit IV-A, Greb III, and Injun | June 29, 1961 | 547 | 620 | 103.8 | .... | .... | 1 year |
| Discoverer XXVI | July 7, 1961 | 142.0 | 410 | 93.5 | 300 | 2450 | About 1 year |
| Tiros III | July 12, 1961 | 457 | 510 | 100.3 | .... | .... | About 400 years |
| Midas III | July 12, 1961 | 2084 | 2191 | 161.5 | .... | .... | Indefinite |
| Vostok II | Aug. 6, 1961 | 110.3 | 115.3 | 88.6 | 10,400 | .... | 1 day |
| Ranger I | Aug. 23, 1961 | 105 | 312 | ca. 92 | 675 | .... | 3–4 months |
| Explorer XIII | Aug. 25, 1961 | 275 | 565 | 98 | 127 | .... | 50 years |
| Discoverer XXIX | Aug. 30, 1961 | 140 | 345 | 91 | 300 | 2100 | Sept. 2, 1961 |
| Discoverer XXX | Sept. 12, 1961 | 154 | 345 | 92 | 300 | 2450 | .... |
| Mercury–Atlas IV | Sept. 13, 1961 | 99.3 | 158.6 | 89 | 2700 | 11,000 | 1 orbit |
| Discoverer XXXI | Sept. 17, 1961 | 152 | 255 | 91 | 300 | 2450 | ............ |

(See the following page for additional information)

# Additional Information for the Table on Page 61

| | |
|---|---|
| Sputnik I. | Top stage of rocket re-entered and burned up during the first week of December 1957. |
| Sputnik II. | Carried dog Laika ("barker"), killed after nearly 100 hours in orbit. |
| Explorer I. | Oldest satellite still in orbit. |
| Vanguard I. | Enabled geophysicists to determine precise shape of earth. Its solar batteries are still working. First satellite known to have been slightly displaced by the sun's radiation pressure. |
| Explorer III. | Contributed to knowledge of radiation in space. |
| Sputnik III. | Surprisingly short lifetime for its heavy weight. |
| Explorer IV. | Most successful of the Explorer satellites, contributed to evaluation of Project Argus. |
| Score | Whole Atlas missile without booster in orbit. First broadcast from space. |
| Vanguard II. | Called the "cloud cover satellite," would have yielded better results if it had not tumbled. |
| Discoverer I. | First satellite in polar orbit. Tumbled, lasted only five days. |
| Discoverer II. | Ejected capsule to be recovered, but ejection took place over Spitsbergen instead of over Hawaii. |
| Explorer VI. | The so-called paddlewheel satellite. Radio ceased to broadcast (for unknown reasons) October 6, 1959. Its carrier rocket was never observed with certainty, probably still in orbit. |
| Discoverer V and VI. | Both ejected their capsules back into the atmosphere, but in both cases transmitters in capsules failed to work, so recovery was impossible. The carrier rocket of one is still in orbit. |
| Vanguard III. | The so-called icecream cone, last of the Vanguard shots. Radio out Feb. 14, 1960. |
| Cosmic Rocket III. | Orbital ellipse long enough to loop around the moon, first pictures of moon's "backside." Ran into earth on its 15th revolution. |
| Explorer VII. | Satellite still transmitting. Its carrier rocket is still in orbit too. |
| Discoverer VII, VIII and XI. | Recovery attempts failed in all cases. |
| Tiros I. | The spectacularly successful cloud cover satellite. Active life was 78 days during which a total of 22,952 pictures were transmitted to ground stations. Both the satelite and the carrier rocket are in orbit. |
| Transit IB. | First navigational satellite, 3 objects in orbit, satellite, rocket body and a metal ring. |
| Sputnik IV. | The figures in the table refer to the rocket carrier. The cabin section was supposed to be slowed down by retro rockets to re-enter the atmosphere. The radio command for this was sent on May 19, but the cabin had the wrong position so that the retro rockets accelerated it, resulting in a new orbit with the same perigee (189 miles) but a new apogee of 412 miles and an orbital period of 94.3 minutes. Satellite broke up, so there are now eight pieces in orbit, all likely to re-enter late in 1961. |
| Midas II. | The infrared detector satellite, details are classified. Carrier in orbit too. |
| Transit IIA. | Navigational test satellite. |
| Greb | Small radiation satellite, fired as "piggy-back" of Transit IIA. First instance of two satellites fired by one rocket. |
| Echo I. | The 100-foot inflated aluminized balloon used for "bouncing" telephone calls, wireless pictures and so forth. It and its carrier rocket will have an indefinite life time, though the useful lifetime of the balloon is estimated to be one year at most. |
| Discoverer XIII. | Capsule recovered, fished from Pacific Ocean. Recovery on day after firing. |
| Discoverer XIV. | Capsule recovered, caught in mid-air. Recovery on day after firing. |
| Sputnik V. | Soviet satellite carrying two dogs and a number of smaller animals, as well as microscopic animals and plants. Recovered safely on day after firing. First recovery of living beings from orbit, presumably by winged re-entry. |
| Discoverer XV. | Capsule re-entered and was seen floating in recovery area but sank before it could be reached. |
| Courier I. | Communications test satellite. |
| Explorer VIII. | "Radiation Laboratory"; good results. |
| Discoverer XVII. | Capsule caught in mid-air Nov. 14, 1960; second mid-air catch. |
| Tiros II. | Repeat of Tiros I. One camera failed, otherwise good. |
| Sputnik VI. | Carried 2 dogs and lower life forms. De-orbited on Dec. 2, 1960, but burned up on re-entry. |
| Discoverer XVIII. | Third mid-air catch of re-entered capsule. |
| Discoverer XIX. | No capsule in Discoverer XIX. Was test for Midas missile detection system. |
| Samos II. | First reconnaissance satellite; no details disclosed. |
| Sputnik VII. | Did not perform any detectable function. Believed to have been slated to carry out mission performed by Sputnik VIII. |
| Sputnik VIII. | Fired Venus probe from orbit; first successful experiment of this type. Probable orbit of Venus probe: perihelion, 66.7 million miles; aphelion, 94.6 million miles; orbital period, 300 days. |
| Explorer IX. | Two satellites, a 12-foot balloon and top rocket stage, both with transmitters. Orbited by all-solid-fuel Scout rocket. Balloon transmitter failed. |
| Discoverer XX. | Orbit achieved, capsule not ejected. Satellite broke into four pieces. |
| Discoverer XXI. | No capsule; test of engine re-sta.t in space. New orbital period after re-start, 97.8 minutes. |
| Transit IIIB. | The two satellites Transit IIIB and Lofti did not separate in orbit as planned, but are working. |
| Sputnik IX. | Also called Spaceship IV. Carried dog; successfully de-orbited after 17 revolutions and safely landed. |
| Sputnik X. | Also called Spaceship V. Carried dog, de-orbited and safely landed like Sputnik IX. |
| Explorer X. | Very long orbit. Instrumented for research on magnetic fields in space. Believed to have run into earth on third orbit. |
| Discoverer XXIII. | Almost no details disclosed. Capsule was ejected but in wrong direction, assuming larger orbit. |
| Vostok. | Spaceship Vostok ("East"), also called Spaceship VI or Sputnik XI. One orbit flown by Yuri Alexeyevitch Gagarin; total duration 108 minutes. Gagarin was weightless for 89 minutes. |
| Explorer XI. | Orbited telescope-like device. |
| Discoverer XXV. | Capsule recovered from sea after 33 orbits, June 18; rocket re-entered July 12. |
| Transit IV-A. | Three satellites orbited in one shot. Greb III and Injun separated from Transit but not from each other. Orbit of Greb III and Injun 548/619 miles; indefinite lifetime. |
| Discoverer XXVI. | Capsule caught in mid-air after 32 orbits. |
| Tiros III. | Cloud cover pictures. First picture of complete hurricane (Deborah, off African coast). |
| Midas III. | Missile detection system test. |
| Vostok II. | Manned ship, completed 17½ orbits; flown by Gherman Stepanovitch Titov. Landed successfully. Titov ate and slept in orbit but was "faintly seasick." |
| Ranger I. | Only partial success; orbit was supposed to have apogee at 685,000 miles and perigee at 37,500 miles. |
| Explorer XIII. | Orbited by solid-fuel Scout rocket; 50th U.S. satellite to achieve orbit. |
| Discoverer XXIX. | Capsule de-orbited after 33 revolutions; fished from ocean. |
| Discoverer XXX. | Capsule recovered in air on Sept. 14 after 33 orbits. |
| Mercury-Atlas IV. | Mercury capsule holding dummy that simulated breathing and perspiring. Landed in ocean 161 miles east of Bermuda 109 minutes after take-off; recovered by destroyer. |
| Discoverer XXXI. | Radiation detecting devices. |

# LIFE ON OTHER PLANETS

*By*

## WILLY LEY

What would have looked like wild fantasies to most people only fifteen years ago is now just "news," if unusual "news":

1. The President of the United States calls for a program to put a man on the moon within a decade.
2. Scientists with a giant radio telescope listen to radio noises from space; they hope to catch messages sent by alien intelligences. The attempt is abandoned when the scientists conclude that the equipment at their disposal is not yet good enough. (Note: they did not conclude that there was nothing to catch.)
3. Other scientists make studies on the feasibility of hollowing out whole asteroids to provide a home in space for selected groups of people who might set out on voyages lasting decades.

If any of this had been presented to well-read citizens (including many scientists) of the year 1935, they would have said two things: (1) that it couldn't be done, and (2) that it would be useless, even if it could be done.

But if the same plans or ideas had been presented to a similar group of citizens and scientists in 1905, their response would have been: If only it were possible to do so. And in saying that they would not only have been utterly sincere; they would even have behaved traditionally. For since about the year 1600, when it had become clear to anybody who managed to keep himself informed that Mercury and Venus, Mars and Jupiter were planets of our Sun just like our own Earth, the existence of "people" on other planets had simply been assumed.

Nobody doubted their existence, and even as critical a man as Immanuel Kant wrote in his *General Natural History and Theory of the Heavens* (1755): "Certainly most of the planets are inhabited and those that are not will be at one time." He ended his chapter *Of the Inhabitants of the Heavenly Bodies* with the sentence: "In fact these two planets, Earth and Mars, are the middle links of the planetary system and it is perhaps not improbable that their inhabitants stand in the middle, physically as well as morally, between the two extremes . . ."

With such backing from the pen of the most eminent philosopher, a general belief in inhabitants of other planets looked fully justified, and when, in 1877, Giovanni Virginio Schiaparelli discovered fine straight lines on the surface of the planet Mars, a fair number of astronomers—and almost all laymen—greeted this as a proof of the existence of intelligent inhabitants of that planet, considering the lines to be works of engineering. The general belief slowly faded, beginning in, say, 1912; and by 1930 the pendulum had swung to the other extreme. The lines on Mars, provided they existed at all, meant nothing. Mars was as thoroughly dead as the Moon; the planets beyond Mars were much too cold to harbor any life, and while the planet Venus could not categorically be ruled out, it was probably much too hot.

As for the planets of other stars, how did we know that they had any? A few American astrophysicists insisted that just one star, our Sun, had planets. It followed that Earth was the only inhabited planet in all the universe, and therefore mankind was the only intelligent race.

Fortunately science is a self-correcting process and after a few years quite a number of scientists began to examine once more the foundations of definite statements both old and new. It is almost needless to say that they came up with a good deal of new information and fresh thought. The current ideas about life in space differ radically from what was said thirty years ago. In fact they tend to approach the ideas of sixty years ago—of course, with many corrections and with much more factual material than was known then.

In the following pages I shall try to give a condensed report on present-day thinking about life on other planets, the ideas involved and their histories and background. But before I can go into this, it would be useful to say a few things about the planet Mars, which has been the center of controversy ever since Schiaparelli's maps of Mars were published.

To put it bluntly, many astronomers interested in these matters—very many practicing astronomers are not, which always comes as a great surprise to the layman—would say that there are two life-bearing planets in our solar system, Earth and Mars. But (and this is an important difference) they no longer think, as did some of their colleagues of fifty and sixty years ago, that Mars is "inhabited." That term means intelligent life forms. The Mars experts of today feel rather sure that the dark areas of Mars, which change their coloration with the Martian seasons, are areas of vegetation. It is a vegetation which is often described as "struggling for survival against the Martian desert." But if we accept the drawings made between 1877 and, say, 1900, as accurate, the struggle seems to be rather successful; the dark areas seem to be somewhat larger now than they were then. The presence of vegetation implies the presence of animal life, but there is no convincing evidence in favor of intelligent life.

Probably, then, Earth is the only "inhabited" planet in our solar system, though a second planet, Mars, also has some form of life. Whether Venus makes a third is not known yet; some temperature measurements indicate a temperature far above the boiling point of water. On the other hand, it is not absolutely certain that these temperatures are actually a surface phenomenon. They could originate in the equivalent of the stratosphere in the atmosphere of Venus.

But now let us proceed to the discussion of the principles involved. Evidently quite a number of different problems have to be considered: the nature of life itself, the nature of a planet which can harbor life, and the probable number of planets. Then there are side issues, such as the question of whether we have any evidence of extra-terrestrial life and whether we can assume that a planet suitable to harbor life actually does have life forms on it as a matter of course.

# WHAT IS LIFE?

Sitting behind the typewriter, smoking a cigar and looking around my study, I paused to think for a moment of the very large number of articles, pamphlets and books which have been written on the theme, "What is life?" It is a difficult question just because it seems to be so simple at first glance. The famous basic assumption of Descartes, *Cogito, ergo sum* ("I think, therefore I am") comes to mind; he could also have said, "I am alive, because I think." In short, the person who ponders that question has no doubt in his mind that *he* is alive.

I also don't doubt that a fly I hear at the window is alive, though it probably doesn't think. My cat, sleeping soundly on a chair, is alive too and the green plants also are alive. It is equally certain that my typewriter (though capricious on occasion) is not alive and that the radio (in spite of the noises it can produce) is not alive. While we, in the vast majority of all cases, have no doubt about the status of being alive, or not alive, as the case may be, of a certain object, it is difficult to express in a single sentence an answer to the question "what is life?" In fact, it seems to be impossible to do this because all the specialists who tried to find such an answer always ended up with a description of what a living thing *does*. Not what it *is,* but what it does.

It does a minimum of four things: it eats "foreign" substances which differ to a greater or lesser degree from its own body tissue. Then it "digests" these substances, and assimilates them into its body, which produces some waste material that is ejected. Furthermore, it "grows": it increases in size and bulk up to a certain point, which is different for different life forms. Finally it "propagates": it produces, or reproduces, its own kind.

Anything that can perform these four activities is considered to be alive. The reason why it is so useful to define life by what it does is that this method of definition draws a clear line between life and a few other things which are somewhat similar in performance. A crystal, for example, grows and produces "daughter crystals," but the crystal has to be in a solution of its own substance; it cannot produce chemical changes in other substances to produce its own. Acids, on the other hand, can and do "digest" foreign substances, but this does not add anything to their growth. The acid which attacks a foreign substance does not increase in amount; it is used up instead.

Some eighty years ago somebody wanted to prove that flames represent the earliest form of life, a form which preceded the current life on earth while the planet was still too hot. A flame, the man reasoned, attacks and digests other substances. While doing so it grows in bulk and, of course, one flame can beget many other flames. Very pretty-sounding reasoning; it just suffers from the fact that the flame is not an entity; it is the mere by-product of the rapid oxidation of substances which can be oxidized.

There is one more misleading similarity between a flame and an organism (in fact, it was this similarity which started the whole thought). A flame, when deprived of fuel, will go out, just as an organism deprived of food will die, even though most organisms have considerable stalling powers built into their systems. Generally speaking, it is true, however, that an organism needs a steady supply of energy in order to keep going. In larger life forms, the intake of this energy is normally intermittent, while the expenditure is more or less steady.

For almost all life forms the energy absorbed turns out to be, in the final analysis, solar energy. But the way solar energy is absorbed constitutes the fundamental differences between animals and plants. Plants are capable of "ingesting" solar energy directly; animals have to use a more roundabout way.

The process used by the plants is technically known as photosynthesis. A plant will absorb water (from the ground) and carbon dioxide (from the air). If there is also sunlight available, the water and the carbon dioxide will be turned into a more complicated chemical, with waste materials left over. Written in the form of a chemical equation, the making of the chemical glucose looks as follows:

$$6 H_2O + 6 CO_2 + \text{solar energy} \rightarrow C_6H_{12}O_6 + 6 O_2$$

In other words, 6 molecules of water and 6 molecules of carbon dioxide are converted into one molecule of glucose plus 6 molecules of oxygen which are discharged into the atmosphere.

Animals cannot build up molecules with the aid of solar energy; they need to derive that energy from the food they ingest. Two different processes are possible and both are in actual use. The first one is fermentation, used by many lower life forms. If a glucose molecule is used up by way of fermentation, the chemical equation reads:

$$C_6H_{12}O_6 \rightarrow 2 C_3H_6O_3 \text{ plus energy}$$

The symbols to the right of the arrow are the formula for lactic acid; the whole equation means that the organism derives energy from breaking down one glucose molecule into two molecules of lactic acid. This is the primitive method; the other one, far superior in energy yield, is the oxidation of the food.

Let us use the glucose molecule once more for an example. This is what happens:

$$C_6H_{12}O_6 + 6 O_2 \rightarrow 6 CO_2 + 6 H_2O + \text{energy}.$$

Here oxygen from the atmosphere is required (the waste matter discharged by the plants) and the glucose molecule is oxidized into 6 molecules of carbon dioxide which are discharged into the atmosphere because they are waste matter (the plants are waiting!) and 6 molecules of water. Some of the latter is retained, some is discharged.

The two main processes operating on earth, the photosynthesis of the plants, building up organic molecules with the discharge of oxygen, and the oxidation process of the animals, digesting organic molecules with the discharge of carbon dioxide, obviously complement each other, in that each depends on the waste material of the other. But on the whole, the animals are parasitic on the plants; the plants could get along without animals, since carbon dioxide is also produced by volcanoes, but the animals could not get along without the plants. (It has been estimated that the plants produce over a million million\* tons of fresh organic matter every year.) Hence the plants must have come first. And on any other planet animals are impossible without plants, if we define a "plant" as an organism using photosynthesis.

Another point which may have been noticed is that both processes require water. Since many life forms, even some highly evolved ones, can go into a period of withdrawl from active living, a planet which for half a year is so cold that all the water is frozen can conceivably still harbor life. But the over-all temperatures must be such that water will be liquid at least some of the time.

It is highly interesting that the presence of water as the main necessity of life forms was voiced at a time when chemistry was virtually nonexistent and biochemistry unheard of. It was the Dutch physicist and astronomer Christiaan Huyghens (1629–1695) who wrote, presumably near the end of his life, "water is most important because water is needed to partake of nutrition." The sentence can be found in his book *Cosmotheoros,* or *Conjectures Concerning the Inhabitants of the Planets*, which was published (in the Latin original) three years after his death. Huyghens would be most surprised (and pleased) to learn that scientists 250 years after his death insisted that even the origin of life required, first of all, liquid water.

In the past scientists often felt that the origin of life was such a complicated process that it was marvellous that it had taken place at all: at present most scientists feel that the origin of life is something that is virtually inevitable, provided some rather likely conditions exist. Since their reasoning was described in my article "Relearning Science" in the 1960 INFORMATION PLEASE ALMANAC and nothing fundamental has been added since, I'll quote the paragraph in question:

"Life originated in shallow waters either near the shore or in a lagoon where minerals had been dissolved out of the rocks . . . The atmosphere consisted essentially of argon and nitrogen but with a few additions like water vapor, carbon dioxide, carbon monoxide, ammonia, methane, and acetylene, the latter due to the reaction of natural carbides with sea water. If you prepare such a mixture and shoot electric sparks through it, a number of compounds are formed which a chemist would call 'organic,' including some of the amino acids which come close to, but are not yet, protein. The 'spark' which started all this—presumably millions of times over—was natural lightning. The result was something which, if it happened now, would be instantly eaten up by microorganisms. But there were no organisms of any type or size then. But if a very primitive organism came into existence, it would find a supply of food. This theory of the origin of life has been labeled 'the soup that ate itself.' It's a pretty phrase, but not quite correct—it was one part of the soup which ate the rest. This theory, incidentally, disposes of a question that used to be asked often in the past, namely, 'If living matter could originate from

\* The term "million million" has been used to avoid misunderstanding. Only in America is 1,000 million referred to as a billion; in England and in the non-English-speaking countries, a billion means a million million. In some of these countries, 1,000 million is called a milliard.

non-living matter, why doesn't it happen now?' It probably does happen now, but any 'protolife' that gets started now never has a chance to go any farther—it will be eaten up by the existing life forms. Life can originate only if it is not already present."

If this reasoning is correct, we can confidently expect life forms of some type on any planet which has water. If there is water, minerals will have been leached out of the rocks, the atmosphere can be expected to contain the necessary "impurities," and if the temperature is above the freezing point of water, lightning will occur.

It has been suggested on occasion that a planet may be "poisoned" by comparatively large amounts of chlorine (or of phosgene, a highly poisonous and rather simple chlorine compound of the formula $COCl_2$) or fluorine in the atmosphere. Naturally, as long as there are large amounts of chlorine or fluorine in the air, the life producing process just described cannot work. But both fluorine and chlorine are very active elements which combine most readily with other substances forming non-poisonous compounds (and phosgene breaks down in the presence of water into hydrochloric acid and carbon dioxide) so that their continued existence in the free state is an impossibility. Even oxygen, which is active, but much less so than fluorine and chlorine, would not exist in a free state if the plants did not keep making it all the time.

## FROM PLANET TO PLANET

Sixty years ago scientists were in an interesting dilemma. On the one hand they were convinced that every sun had planets and it seemed logical to assume that there was life on those planets which were neither too hot nor too cold. On the other hand it seemed that life could not originate easily, which made the lighthearted assumption of life on all planets capable of bearing it somewhat illogical.

But then two things happened which seemed to show a way out of this dilemma. The names of the two scientists who made these two things happen were Pyotr Nikolayevitch Lebyedev* (1866–1911) and Svante Arrhenius (1859–1927). The two scientific events were not directly connected, but they enhanced each other, and since the part played by Lebyedev can be told quickly I'll begin with him. As a physicist, Lebyedev knew well that the equations for electro-magnetic radiations, of which light is the best known example, had shown that light should exert pressure on the things it struck. Lebyedev worked out an experiment to show that it did. He took the spores of a puffball and heated them to nearly red hot (in a vacuum) to remove all the water from them. This reduced their weight, but not their size. Then he placed the very fine powder of the dehydrated spores and let them drift down inside a wide sealed glass tube. The experiment was run in very dim light, but a concentrated beam of very bright light shone crosswise through the glass tube. It could clearly be seen that the impact of the light rays exerted a push against the particles of the powder. We have much better and literally bigger examples now; both the small artificial satellite *Vanguard*

* Often spelled Petr Nikolaievich Lebedev.

*I* and the large *Echo I* balloon are visibly affected in their orbits by the pressure of sunlight. But in its day Lebyedev's experiment was the only proof for the actual existence of light pressure.

It was this light pressure upon which Svante Arrhenius built a theory. Arrhenius, a Swede, was professionally a chemist and physicist, later director of the Nobel Institute for Physical Chemistry and recipient of the 1903 Nobel Prize for Chemistry. Arrhenius drew a number of conclusions from work done by other scientists. Bacteriologists differ from their colleagues in the field of botany and zoology in that they don't want to keep the subjects of their studies alive but are forever thinking of ways to kill them. In these studies they had learned that bacteria formed so-called "spores," a dormant state. And if bacteria are hard to kill when they are active, it is three times as difficult when they are spores. The very lowest temperatures that could be produced—liquid hydrogen at the time—did not harm them. Ultra-violet radiation didn't seem to do much harm; electrical fields ditto.

Arrhenius noted that these spores were practically immune to anything that might happen to them in free space. He then reasoned that small bodies in space, instead of being gravitationally attracted by a sun, would be pushed away from it by light pressure which, in the case of small bodies of a certain size, is more powerful than gravitational attraction.

It had been calculated at the time—probably by Lebyedev—that a body had to be smaller than 1/100,000th of an inch if light pressure was to be more powerful than gravitational attraction. But it must not be too small; a single molecule, for example, would follow gravity and light pressure would not influence it at all. Svante Arrhenius calculated the size where light pressure would wield the greatest influence. This optimum size turned out to be around 100 million molecules, which would result in a tiny sphere 0.00016 millimeters (there are 25.4 millimeters in one inch) in diameter. Since the spores of bacteria are of about that size, Arrhenius felt justified to go on.

Let us say, he stated, that a spore has been pushed into the outermost atmosphere by electrical repulsion. It would then be caught up in the "light pressure wind" emitted by the Sun. Being pushed by the light waves, it would get to the orbit of Mars in 20 days, to the orbit of Jupiter in 80 days, to the orbit of Neptune in 14 months and to the vicinity of the nearest star in 9,000 years. Of course, at any point of the journey the spore might unite with other small bodies and finally become too large to be pushed by the light waves. Then it would fall back, re-crossing planetary orbits again.

Arrhenius offered one additional calculation.

At a considerable distance from the Sun the lack of heat would slow down the life processes. A terrestrial spore in the orbit of Neptune would not "run down" any more in 3 million years than during *one* day on the warm Earth. Taking everything together, Arrhenius could advance the belief that there are living, if dormant, spores almost anywhere in space, which will start the cycle of life on any planet which is ready to receive life. He called his theory "panspermy" from the Greek words for "all" and "seed."

Of course Arrhenius' theory must work both ways. Life could have come to the earth in this manner. On the other hand, if life did originate on Earth,

Earth would now fill space with spores which might start life elsewhere.

Arrhenius' theory is not discussed as much now as it was when it was new. Most chemists now feel that panspermy is not needed to explain life. But panspermy could be true just the same. We'll probably find out soon.

## METEORITES AS INDICATORS OF LIFE IN SPACE

A modern reader, after hearing of Arrhenius' theory of panspermy, is very likely to ask whether meteorites have ever provided us with an indication of life on other worlds.

The answer that can now be given to this question is "probably yes."

Naturally the probability of finding a fossil in a meteorite is small. If we assume, as is frequently done, that meteorites were originally part of a planet, we can get an idea about the probability of a fossil-bearing meteorite by calculating what would happen if our own planet exploded.

The volume of the Earth is 259,880 million cubic miles. Its surface area is 196,940,000 square miles. But we can assume fossil-bearing layers only for the land areas, which total 51,886,000 square miles. If we (somewhat generously, no doubt) consider the fossil-bearing strata to have a thickness of half a mile, this would give us a total of about 26 million cubic miles of earth's crust, or just about 1/100th of one per cent of earth's total volume in which fossils may occur. If our entire Earth were chopped up into a very large number of meteorites of equal volume, one in every ten thousand meteorites would come from a fossil-bearing layer. But since those layers are not often crammed with fossils and have many blank spots in between, it would be quite a stroke of good luck if one in a hundred thousand meteorites contained a trace of former life.

Though it was always realized that the probability of finding a fossil in a meteorite was small, a German investigator, one Dr. Otto Hahn, set out to find them. He obtained over thirty different specimens of a type of stony meteorite which is known to meteoriticists as "chondrite" and cut them into very thin sections for examination under the microscope. He was amazed and pleased to find that a large number of chondrites contained fossils—fossils of marine organisms. There were tiny sea urchins, corals of several types, sponges and so forth. The biggest specimen was nearly 1/10th of an inch across. The whole thing was an almost primitive mistake, perpetrated with high optimism. To anybody less enthusiastic it was clear at once that the so-called "organisms" were simply the crystalline structure of the meteorite itself.

The next sensational story about life in a meteorite came in 1930, just half a century after the publication of Hahn's book. Professor Charles B. Lipman announced that he had found not just fossils, but *live* bacteria in meteorites. Of course these meteorites had been in the ground for some time before they were picked up. But Lipman thought that he had eliminated any bacteria which might have been in the soil and adhered to the meteorite. Quoting from his own report: "This was attempted by first washing the surface of the specimen thoroughly with soap and hot water with the aid of a sterile brush. The specimen was then rinsed in distilled water, dried with a paper towel and placed in a solution of bactericide . . . After the exposure of the specimen to the bactericide [a 30% solution of hydrogen peroxide, W. L.] for the desired period, it was transferred to 95% alcohol for half a minute to a minute, grasped with sterile tongs and exposed to a large gas flame until the alcohol had all burned away and for a few seconds more. In the early experiments it was then quickly thrown into a sterile iron mortar and crushed and the powder distributed with a sterile spoon into several flasks of sterile media. In the later experiments the specimen was dropped directly . . . into a wide-mouthed flask."

After some time bacteria began to show up in the nutrient solution in the flasks, and Lipman stated that they were "similar to forms common on our Earth and probably identical with some."

Such a similarity was not impossible, of course, but it was suspicious. From 1933 to 1935 Sharat Kumar Roy of the Chicago Natural History Museum repeated Lipman's experiments, using meteorites from the same falls that Lipman had treated. Again, bacterial growth appeared in some of the test tubes, but this time the micro-organisms were identified as *Bacillus subtilis* and *Staphylococcus albus*. Both of these were long-known native species in the habit of showing up when unwanted.

Only last year this discussion would have ended with the statement that, so far, the evidence is wholly negative. This is no longer the case. During 1961 several reputable scientists have reported that they believe they have found evidence of life in meteorites. One group reported on something that might be called a "fossil" (stretching the term somewhat), while another group actually may have found some live extra-terrestrial bacteria.

The "fossil," amusingly enough, turned up in a chondrite.

It was a so-called "carboneceous chondrite," so named because it contained an unusually high percentage of carbon, several per cent in fact, while the normal content of carbon in a chondrite is about 0.15 per cent. The meteorite had fallen, in the presence of many witnesses, on May 14, 1864 near the town of Orgueil, France. It broke into about 50 fragments, the largest of them about the size of a human head, and it is now in Paris. A chemical analysis, establishing it as a carboneceous chondrite, was made soon after the fall.

The difference between the chemists of 1865 and the chemists of 1961 is that those of 1865 could establish the presence of carbon and the amount of carbon. The chemists of 1961 can count the number of carbon atoms in a molecule. This is what three American scientists, Drs. Douglas J. Hennessy, Warren J. Meinschein and Bartholomew Nagy have done. After counting the number of carbon atoms in the carbon-compound molecules of the Orgueil meteorite, they announced that they had found a trace of former life. The atom counts per molecule ran mostly to 19 and 21, far more often than 18, 20 or 22. Molecules containing 19 or 21 carbon atoms per molecule are typical of compounds formed by living matter, as for example butter, or the wax on an apple's skin, or the resinous substance on a palm frond. Hence Drs. Hennessy, Meinschein and Nagy declared that they were convinced that there was life on the planet from which this meteorite came. Of course, nobody can tell where that planet might have been located; even if the fall of the meteorite had been tracked with the most modern instruments, there is no way of calculating backwards beyond the portion of its orbit just before entering our atmosphere.

Other scientists are naturally cautious about accepting the results. The first and most obvious criticism, namely that the meteorite had been contaminated with organic matter while lying in the soil of France, could be refuted. Examination of the interior of the meteorite sample proved that it had been well sealed and had displayed no microscopic cracks up to the time it was crushed in the laboratory. The other cautious objection is that waxes of odd-numbered carbon atoms might be formed *without* the intervention of living things, even though no such waxes of non-organic origin are known on earth at present.

The report on the finding of such organic molecules reached the public in March 1961. Less than a month later, it was reported that another carbonaceous chondrite apparently harbored live bacteria from elsewhere in the universe. The exciting announcement came from examination of a fall that occurred at Murray, Kentucky, in 1950. The fact that this was a much more recent meteorite than Orgueil reduces the chances of bacterial contamination from earthly soil.

The report came from Dr. Frederick D. Sisler, microbiologist with the U.S. Geological Survey, and Dr. Walter Newton, chief of the germ-free laboratories at Bethseda, Maryland. They thoroughly sterilized the outside of the meteorite with ultra-violet light, hydrogen peroxide and chloride of mercury. Then they crushed it with a sterile pestle and mortar inside a germ-free cabinet. Finally they injected small amounts of the meteorite dust into germ-free laboratory rats and put other dust samples into a test tube of sterile nutrient solution. Contamination by earthly micro-organisms could be considered eliminated.

Injection of the dust into rats served as a cross check in several ways. *If* any terrestrial bacteria survived the sterilization of the outside of the meteorite, they would probably develop in the rats. The same went for viruses. But the rats just continued to live—they did not come down with diseases known or unknown; their bloodstreams remained germ free. But the nutrient solution turned cloudy after a few months. The biologists found what looked like bacteria, but of a species nobody had ever seen before. The meteorite microbes are twisted rods "shaped," to quote Dr. Sisler, "like sausages you might have twisted, thrown on the floor and jumped on." There can be little doubt that these "things" are alive and are organisms; whether they are "bacteria" in the ordinary meaning of that word is a different question. The discoverers themselves went on record that they did not consider the proof of "extra-terrestriality" of these organisms as definite. But they are certainly new to microbiology.

Additional information may come from another source.

Research with dust-catching Aerobee-Hi rockets is underway, and the very first shot produced a large yield of dust particles caught at the fringes of the earth's atmosphere. So far it is only known that dust was caught—wouldn't it be interesting if some of these dust motes turned out to be spores. Even if they were spores of well-known terrestrial bacteria, it would be a contribution to the thoughts of Arrhenius.

## THE CONCEPT OF THE ECOSPHERE

Since every planet receives its light and heat from its sun, the demand that water must be in liquid form at least some of the time automatically implies a certain distance from that sun. If the planet is so near its sun that all of the water it happens to have is in vapor form all the time, the normal life processes are impossible. Conversely, if the planet is so far from its sun that all its water remains permanently frozen, life cannot exist. (Of course, if at an earlier period life had time to grow intelligent and to develop a civilization with technology, this would be a different story; but we are talking about forms of life other than Man.)

There is, therefore, a figurative shell around a sun inside of which life can exist because the water on a planet inside this shell would be liquid some of the time. This shell has received a special name; it is called the "ecosphere." The word is derived from, or rather constructed in analogy to, the classical Greek term *oikoumene* which meant "the habitable world." A planet near the inner border of this ecosphere would be generally too hot for life, except in its polar areas. Likewise a planet at the outer border of the ecosphere would be generally too cold, except for its equatorial regions. Unfortunately, some theorists have dubbed such planets "polar planets" and "equatorial planets." At first hearing, the word "polar planet" seems to mean that the whole surface of this planet resembles our polar regions, and the term "equatorial planet" makes the same impression. But what is really meant by these terms is that a "polar planet" offers conditions suitable for life only near its poles, while an "equatorial planet" offers livable conditions only near its equator.

It is not very difficult to calculate the distance and extent of the ecosphere for any star, provided its size and its surface temperature are known. For a rather hot star, like Sirius, the inner border of the ecosphere will be a considerable distance from the surface of the star. For a rather cold star the inner border of the ecosphere will not be as far away.

If that calculation is made for our Sun, the approximate center of the ecosphere turns out to be just about 100 million miles from the Sun. The Earth, moving at a mean distance of 93 million miles, is therefore nicely inside the ecosphere. The planet Mars, moving around the Sun at a mean distance of 141.7 million miles, is still inside the ecosphere, but near its outer edge. It would qualify for the designation, "equatorial planet." The planet Venus, moving around the Sun at a mean distance of 67 million miles, is almost literally a borderline case, although we do not yet have enough information about Venus to be able to pronounce judgment. Venus might still be in the ecosphere, though rather close to its inner edge. Or it might be a bit too close to the Sun to be in the ecosphere. Mercury, moving around the Sun at a mean distance of only 36 million miles, is definitely too close.

Whether life could be expected on the planets of another sun would depend mainly on whether these planets are in that sun's ecosphere. It would be quite possible for a star to have a rather large number of planets but all of them too far away from it to assume the necessary degree of warmth. Similarly, a very hot sun may have all its planets inside the inner edge of its ecosphere.

# THE NUMBER OF POSSIBLE PLANETARY SYSTEMS

The next problem is to make a guess at the number of planetary systems in our galaxy; the reasoning would, of course, apply to other galaxies too. The usually accepted estimate for the total number of stars in our galaxy is 30,000 million, though it is possible that the actual number is higher by as much as twenty per cent. However, if we use the figure of 30,000 million as a basis, are we justified in assuming that every one of these suns has a planetary system?

The answer is "yes," or, if you wish to be careful, "in most cases."

Older readers may remember having read in popular books on astronomy that a planetary system came into existence as the result of so many special circumstances that planets should be exceedingly rare. Some popularizers even went as far as to state that our own solar system was probably unique. The astronomical theories leading to such statements are now all proven wrong and there is no need to discuss them anymore. The current theory, worked out originally during World War II by the German astronomer H. von Weizsäcker, with emendations by astronomers of several nations, assumes that a star forms when a rotating body of gas and cosmic dust begins to contract. The condensation in the center will finally grow hot enough to start atomic reactions in its interior and thereby become a star. But in addition to the central accumulation of the rotating nebula, there are a number of vortices at different distances from the center. These eventually become planets, which begin to form at about the same time as the sun in the center. According to this theory it can be taken for granted that a star is accompanied by planets. Some few exceptions may occur in reality, of course.

Now we can try to derive a few figures.

The stars are divided into a number of classes, according to their surface temperature. Class O are super-hot stars with a surface temperature of 30,000° centigrade; they are followed by class B, blue-white stars (Rigel is an example) with a surface temperature of about 22,000° centigrade. Next come the white stars (Sirius is an example) with a surface temperature of 11,000° centigrade; they are the class A stars. The class F stars (white-yellowish) have a surface temperature of 8000° centigrade—Procyon is an example. Then come the yellow stars, class G (like our own sun or Capella) with 6000° centigrade surface temperature. After that follows class K (orange; Arcturus is an example) with 4000° centigrade surface temperature, and class M, red stars (like Antares) with 3000° centigrade surface temperature. There are some even "cooler" classes which are of no interest right now, because we are mainly concerned with stars similar to our own Sun.

This means the three classes F, G and K. Taken together, these three classes are estimated to comprise slightly more than 60 per cent of all the stars in our galaxy. Since the total number is assumed to be 30,000 million, we find that there are, in our galaxy, 18,000 million F, G and K stars, which can be expected to have planetary systems. If we assume that the planets of these stars are outside their ecospheres in 99 out of 100 cases we still have 180 million planets capable of bearing life. There is, of course, no reason to make such an unfavorable assumption and the assumption is in all probability completely wrong. It is used here mainly for the purpose of keeping the numbers on the small side as much as possible. Going on in the same vein, we shall now assume that only one in a hundred of the planets so placed in their star's ecospheres as to be capable of bearing life, actually does bear life. Then we are down to a "mere" 1.8 million planets which do bear life. Now we'll assume that in only one per cent of these cases life progressed to intelligence comparable to human intelligence, and we find that 18,000 planets in our galaxy can be expected to be inhabited by intelligent beings. And this in spite of the most unfavorable assumptions possible.

But while such statistics can make it a virtual certainty that there is intelligent life elsewhere in our galaxy, they suffer from a drawback analogous to the statistics of life insurance companies. They can foretell with great accuracy how many people will die during a given year in a city of a given population. What they can't foretell is who is going to die. The statistics just attempted can tell that there must be life elsewhere. But they can't tell where.

## ANOTHER KIND OF LIFE?

All the reasoning presented thus far—and it is important to keep this in mind—was based on the fact that living tissue, protoplasm, of the type we know, needs water in its liquid form. Because of the need for liquid water, a certain temperature range had to be assumed, and from that the concept of the ecosphere emerged. Long before astronomers and biologists started talking about the ecosphere, a number of people, usually philosophers rather than scientists, had challenged the basic assumption, namely that life anywhere in the universe had to be of our kind, chemically speaking.

The living tissue we know is almost exclusively composed of atoms of rather low weight. The most numerous atoms in living tissue are those of hydrogen, carbon, nitrogen and oxygen. Present in small amounts are sodium, magnesium (especially in plants), silicon (in invertebrates), phosphorus, sulphur, chlorine, potassium, calcium, iron and copper (in crustaceans). The atomic weight of the heaviest of these elements (copper) is 63.54 and the only "heavyweight" which is of importance in living tissue is iodine (atomic weight 126.91). All this atomic array is focussed on the carbon atom; the carbon atom is always the "backbone" of all living molecules.

Couldn't there be life based on another set of elements?

A possible "competitor" to carbon which could be investigated to some extent is the element silicon. Chemists—whether they were interested in another kind of life or not—had been intrigued by the similarities between carbon and silicon for quite some time, say for the last seventy years, and had set out to make substances which are usually carbon compounds but which, in their make-up, had silicon atoms where there would be carbon atoms in the normal course of events.

There is, for example, a carbon compound with the formula $C_6H_{14}$, consisting of 6 carbon and 14 hydrogen atoms. The molecule is usually shown like this:

$$\begin{array}{ccccccccccc}
 & H & & H & & H & & H & & H & & H & \\
 & | & & | & & | & & | & & | & & | & \\
H- & C & - & C & - & C & - & C & - & C & - & C & -H \\
 & | & & | & & | & & | & & | & & | & \\
 & H & & H & & H & & H & & H & & H &
\end{array}$$

This is a nice stable compound.

A very similar compound, but with silicon instead of carbon, is this:

$$\begin{array}{ccccccccccc}
 & H & & H & & H & & H & & H & & H & \\
 & | & & | & & | & & | & & | & & | & \\
H- & Si & - & Si & - & Si & - & Si & - & Si & - & Si & -H \\
 & | & & | & & | & & | & & | & & | & \\
 & H & & H & & H & & H & & H & & H &
\end{array}$$

and it has actually been made. But unlike its carbon-based counterpart, it is *not* a stable compound. It is so unstable that just making it is a major feat. All silicon-hydrogen compounds burst into flames at room temperature just from being exposed to the atmosphere. There are stable silicon compounds, but they do not have an

$$Si-Si-Si-Si-Si$$

"backbone" in the center of the molecule. Instead they have an

$$Si-O-Si-O-Si-O-Si-O$$

chain; they are already oxidized!

All right, it was said, but this merely shows that the planets in the ecosphere are too hot for silicon life; maybe this silicon life takes over outside the ecosphere, where the temperatures are low enough to make such compounds stable. For an answer let us go back to our oxidation example, which was used to explain the difference between fermentation and oxidation. Instead of oxidizing $C_6H_{12}O_6$ we oxidize $Si_6H_{12}O_6$ and instead of 6 $CO_2$ plus 6 $H_2O$ we get 6 $SiO_2$ plus 6 $H_2O$. We can disregard the 6 $H_2O$ molecules; they are just water and the body of a silicon being could probably get rid of them whether the water were liquid or frozen. But instead of the six molecules of $CO_2$ (carbon dioxide), which can simply be exhaled, since they are a gas, there are six molecules of silicon dioxide, which is a very hard substance; its everyday name is quartz.

How could an organism get rid of such a substance?

The only way one could think of is that the quartz might form something like large scales which could be shed periodically. The over-all answer is that we simply do not know enough about chemistry at different temperature levels to declare categorically that life on a silicon basis is impossible. But from what we do know, it appears most unlikely. But even if it can exist, this would be just an addition to current ideas about the ecosphere of the stars; it would not invalidate the reasoning itself.

## THE MEN FROM PLANET X

One of my teachers, reminiscing about the time when he was a young astronomer, used to tell me that around the year 1900 lecture audiences usually fired a question at him which he dreaded. At that time most people interested in such questions were convinced that the planet Mars was inhabited by intelligent beings and the question dreaded by the young scientist was: "How do the Martians look?" Even two and a half decades later, when he talked about this, his voice took on a plaintive quality. "There is, of course," he would say "no answer to this question; it would be all guesswork."

Though he stated his conviction, he was not quite right. There is a fair amount that can logically be said about the intelligent inhabitants of another planet. The only assumptions to be made are: (a) carbon chemistry, (b) intelligence, and (c) evolution on a planet not too much larger or smaller than our earth. In fact, the first prescription for such an answer was written centuries ago by Christiaan Huyghens in his *Cosmotheoros*.

First he clarified what he meant by "inhabitants," as distinct from the animal life on another planet. "Men differ from Beasts in the Study of Nature" he declared, a simple statement about the function of intelligence which leads to science and technology. Then he went on and listed what else an "inhabitant" would have to have: (a) hands to make things, (b) feet to move around, (c) housing as a protection from the weather, (d) geometry and arithmetic and writing, and (e) upright posture to have their hands free. But in case somebody thought that the inhabitants of another planet would simply be human, Huyghens added "it follows not, therefore, that they have the same shape with us" because a rational soul could also inhabit a body of a different shape.

To see what the shape would be like, let us first eliminate a few wild thoughts. For example, an underwater civilization is quite impossible, because no implements which are either complicated (like a watch) or powerful (like a bulldozer) can be produced unless metals are available. Primitive man before he learned to smelt metals fashioned things of stones and bones. But what he did fashion was only the equivalent of sharper claws and bigger teeth. But the metals necessary for civilization can be smelted only in open air—hence the members of an alien civilization would have to be air breathers.

In physical construction they would have to resemble us in having an internal skeleton; a soft, if muscular tentacle, say like that of an octopus (or even an elephant's trunk) might be able to exert a considerable pull, but could not produce a strong push. And the exoskeletal construction of insects and crustaceans is possible only on a small scale, as we can clearly see from our own fauna. The largest beetle is about the size of a small mouse;

larger representatives of this type of construction, like sea spiders and lobsters, already need the support of the water.

The reason why creatures without an inner skeleton cannot grow large on land is the same that limits the growth even of land animals with an internal skeleton. It is a mathematical relationship which has received the name of cube/square law and it can be explained rather simply with a handful of cubes. Let's assume that the edge of each cube measures precisely one inch. For simplicity's sake we'll say that each cube weighs one ounce. One single cube, then, weighs one ounce and has a surface of six square inches. Now we put eight such cubes together to build a bigger cube. This one weighs eight ounces, but it does not have an outer surface of 8 times 6 square inches. Each surface measures 4 square inches, which makes the total for the six surfaces 24 square inches; compared to its surface it is already much heavier than the single cube. Now we use 27 cubes to build a still larger cube. It has a weight of 27 ounces and a surface of 6 times 9 square inches, or 54 square inches. The next larger cube would require 64 of the original cubes for its construction. Its weight would, of course, be 64 ounces, but its outside surface would be 6 times 16 square inches, or 96 square inches. The next bigger cube would need 125 of the original cubes to construct—would weigh 125 ounces but have a surface area of just 150 square inches.

It can clearly be seen that the weight increases more rapidly (namely, by the third power) than the surface (which increases by the second power only). If, as is the case with insects and crustaceans, the support for the body lies in the outer shell, the increasingly larger weight would either make the shell collapse, or else the shell would have to become so thick and so heavy that mobility would be seriously impaired. That's the reason why insects cannot be larger. With increase in size, even the internal skeleton has to grow more massive proportionally than the body, as can be seen by making the photographs of a mouse's skeleton and of an elephant's skeleton the same size and placing them side by side.

Hence our "alien" would have an internal skeleton and could not be too large—let's say up to twice the size of a gorilla. He also could not be too small; remember, we have assumed all along that he is intelligent. This means that his brain has to have a minimum number of cells to function. But the brain cells need body cells for their support. The minimum size for an intelligent alien is probably in the vicinity of about the size of a human midget.

As Huyghens said, "He must be upright to have his hands free." A logical statement, but couldn't he be built in such a way as to have his hands free without being "upright"? The shape of the classical centaur has been suggested as a compromise. Why shouldn't the vertebrates of another planet be six-limbed? Well, we don't know—but on earth we never had a six-limbed animal with an internal skeleton. It may just be an accident, but there may be biological reasons (unknown to us) why a six-limbed vertebrate body would not function.

So our alien comes out with a possible spread of body size between, say, 30 and 1200 pounds—upright, air-breathing, most likely with two "arms" and two legs and a head containing the main sense organs. The latter is necessary for the reason that nerve impulses from the sense organs must reach the brain as fast as possible—that's why they must be close together. And the "head" would have to be on top of the body because the brain, especially an intelligent brain, is a fairly delicate organ which must not be jarred. Hence the distance between brain and feet must be as long as body size permits so that the body tissues can exert a cushioning effect.

In spite of all these statements, "it follows not that they have the same shape with us"; accidents of evolution could produce a quite different overall appearance. An intelligent brain functions intelligently regardless of skin color; it would do the same regardless of fur or no fur, or outlandish skin texture. Likewise the presence or absence of a tail has nothing to do with intelligence. If you want to imagine the aliens as having horns or long canines sticking out of the mouth (decorated with inlays of gold or colored enamel if local fashion so decrees), nothing prevents you from doing so.

When it comes to detail there can be infinite variety but the overall shape is likely to be man-like, at least when seen from a distance in a dim light.

The actual meeting with intelligent aliens is likely to be the biggest turning point in human history. But there is no way of predicting whether it will ever take place, mainly because we don't know where they are. Our own solar system might be the cosmic equivalent, as far as location is concerned, of Easter or Pitcarin Islands, far away from the "population centers."

As far as we ourselves are concerned, interstellar flight is something we can dream about but for which we cannot do any "planning." The difference between the *Mercury* capsule or the Russian *Vostok* space capsule and an interstellar ship is about the same as that between a child's kite and a transoceanic passenger jet. So far we can just orbit the earth and shoot at the moon or past the moon. We can calculate that rockets we shall soon be able to build will make the trip to the planet Mars in 260 days. But Mars is "only" 35 million miles when at its nearest, while the distance to the nearest other sun, the alpha Centauri system, is nearly 25 million million miles.

Dreams about the farther future—interstellar trips, in this case—are both inevitable and useful, but in hard reality our first job is to reach our own moon. After that we can set out for the neighboring planets. And after that we'll see.

## THE MOON PROJECT

Man's first direct contact with the moon took place in 1947, when, for the first time, the moon's reflection of a radar beam was received in the United States. The next contact was much more material; it was the impact of Russia's *Cosmic Rocket II,* which struck 35 hours after its take-off on September 12, 1959. And just about a month later, *Cosmic Rocket III* took a set of pictures of the far side of the Moon from a temporary position beyond the Moon's orbit.

The Moon will obviously be the first goal of a trip beyond the atmosphere which aims at more than just orbiting the earth. The reason why the Moon will be the first goal is not that it is an especially inviting heavenly body. On the contrary! But it has the advantage of being the nearest heavenly body, only a quarter million miles away in round figures.

The diameter of the Moon is 2,160 miles, or just about a quarter of the diameter of the Earth. The gravitational pull at its surface is ⅙th of the normal gravitational pull at the surface of the Earth. There is no free water on the Moon and it does not have an atmosphere which would be breathable, even if condensed. It is now believed that the Moon has a very tenuous atmosphere consisting of the three rare gases argon, krypton and xenon (they are steadily produced as a by-product of natural radioactive decay of some elements), but it is probably so thin that even detecting it would be a considerable scientific accomplishment. And because the Moon turns so slowly on its axis, the "day" (meaning the period when the Sun is above the horizon) lasts two of our weeks and the night lasts equally long.

Because the Moon has no atmosphere worthy of that designation and because the view from a distance is often advantageous, that part of the Moon which is visible from the Earth has been well mapped. In fact, the Moon's surface is better mapped than some sections of the Earth's surface which are difficult of access. What our maps show are mountain ranges (named after mountain ranges on Earth) and thousands upon thousands of circular formations which have been called craters (named after famous men, especially astronomers) and which are taken to be caused by the impact of meteorites, large, very large and gigantic. Whether there are also real craters of volcanic origin is simply not certain at the moment. What can be seen from the Earth with the naked eye as dark spots are enormous plains, the *mare* plains. The word is derived from the Latin word *mare* for "sea" (the plural is *mária*) and was applied at a time when astronomers still thought that there were seas on the Moon. We now know that they are bone dry, but beyond that one negative fact, we do not know what they are.

The combination of the two facts, that the Moon could be well mapped but that we very often do not know just what it is that has been mapped, establishes the pattern of the exploration now being prepared. There will be two main phases of that exploration: a first phase with unmanned devices taking up, in round figures, the next five years, and a second phase with manned devices, which will follow after the unmanned devices have done all they can do.

## The Unmanned Phase

At first a number of experiments that have already been done will have to be repeated with more and more refinement. The Russian rocket which struck the Moon sent back telemetered information until the instant it crashed. The main scientific result was that the Moon's magnetic field is either non-existent or very weak. The tenuous atmosphere of rare gases, which is believed to exist, was not reported by this rocket; presumably it moved too fast. And, most unfortunate, the mass of that rocket was not large enough to cause a visible crater; if it had we could draw conclusions as to the nature of the ground where it struck from the size of the crater.

The first phase will begin with putting instruments (including a TV camera) into a tight orbit around the Moon. This feat will probably become the job of *Project Ranger*. If we can get TV pictures of the Moon's surface taken from only a hundred miles up, many things which are not quite clear on to-day's lunar maps, or which are subject to interpretation, will be settled. Of course this will be a mapping of the whole Moon, not just the part visible from Earth.

Then it will be useful to have one or two shots for impact. Since the 860 pounds of the Russian device were not enough to cause a visible crater, it might be practical to crash a load of ordinary high explosive. This would be especially useful if the impact could be observed from the earth. Astronomers believe that the whole surface of the Moon, except, of course, steep mountain flanks, is covered by a dust layer a few inches deep. The English astronomer Thomas Gold goes farther and assumes that the dark mare plains are enormous "dust bowls" where the dust may be thousands of feet deep in some places. An impact of a few hundred pounds of TNT, observed from earth, should solve this problem and if the mare plains are actually dust bowls of considerable depth it is obvious that manned ships will avoid landing there—the smoothness is otherwise an incentive to regard the mare as natural landing areas.

After close range TV mapping and a few impacts, there would come the first "soft landing" (*Project Surveyor*). To accomplish a "soft" landing on a body without an atmosphere is by no means easy. The fall of the payload toward the Moon has to be stopped by rocket firing in the direction of the movement. Ideally the falling motion should be braked to zero at the moment the altitude of the payload above the Moon's surface has become zero too. If a body were not braked by retro rockets, the impact on the lunar surface would be at least 2 miles per second; the impact velocity of the Russian rocket was somewhat higher than that.

We cannot expect, of course, that the braking will work as perfectly as desired in the beginning, therefore the instruments of these rocket payloads will be designed to survive a considerable shock. It has been said jokingly, but truthfully, that the "soft" landing for an instrument package would still break every bone in an astronaut's body. But the instrument package of *Project Surveyor* will broadcast a very large amount of scientific information to the Earth. First of all we shall receive direct temperature measurements. The presence of even the most tenuous atmosphere will be detected. Scientists are working on a compact instrument which will analyze soil samples and telemeter the results. A later version may include TV cameras, which would give us the first views of a lunar landscape as seen from a point on the surface.

The next step (*Project Prospector*) is to make the instrument package mobile, looking either like a small tank (this is the way the Russians intend doing it) or else like a tripod on wheels. Then the landed payload could be given radio commands to move in a certain direction, to stop in specific places and so forth. If *Project Surveyor,* the motionless instrument package, has failed to inform us about the conditions of the Moon's surface, *Prospector* will certainly do so.

## The Manned Phase

The switchover from the unmanned to the manned phase will not be sudden. Most likely the two phases will run parallel for a while and merge into each other. The manned phase will begin with the development of a space capsule which will carry more than one man (*Project Apollo*) and which will be able to stay in space for weeks. Of course anything like that is far too heavy to be carried by the *Atlas* or the *Titan* and will have to wait for the development of the *Saturn* booster. The *Saturn* will probably be declared reliable in about the latter part of 1964 or the early part of 1965; the development of the *Apollo* capsule should be more or less finished by then.

After preliminary orbiting flights, the three-man *Apollo* will be sent on a flight around the Moon. It is here that the two phases of the Moon Program may merge. An Apollo capsule orbiting the moon may direct one or several *Prospector* vehicles on the lunar surface in an effort to find a perfect landing site. A perfect landing site on the Moon would be quite some distance from the lunar equator, where the temperature around the middle of the two-week day rises above the boiling point of water. This would force special measures to be taken and would, at the very least, produce a period of relative inactivity for the duration of several earth days. A landing site far away from the lunar equator, under a latitude of about 60° North or South, would put the ship into an area where the temperature of the ground does not rise above 50–60° Fahrenheit. The lunar night would be very cold, of course (it would be very cold at the equator too) but it is always easier to heat something than it is to cool it.

For the first landing the explorers would eat and sleep in their ship. To venture outside the ship they would have to wear space suits, which are likely to be quite different from the suits now worn by the astronauts. The current space suit is a development of the pressure suit of the high altitude jet pilot. It is, of course, completely airtight as well as watertight and the oxygen which supports the astronaut is first made to circulate to keep him cool. The point is that a spacesuit, even in space, tends to become too hot very fast; the body of the astronaut generates an astonishing amount of heat, even if the man just sits still. But essentially to-day's space suit is one more protection for the astronaut in case the space capsule is punctured or starts leaking for some other reason. One might say that today's space suit is another form-fitting space capsule.

The space suit to be used on the surface of the Moon will have to be different. Because the gravitational pull on the Moon is so slight, the explorers may have difficulty walking, because they first have to learn how to control their muscles. They might fall, and if a sharp rock splinter punctures the suit, the man would most likely be lost. Fortunately, because of the low gravity, a man could carry a rather substantial armor, he would have no trouble walking in a suit which, on earth, would weigh 300 pounds. But this adds considerably to the payload the rocket would have to carry.

Because walking may be difficult, it has been proposed repeatedly to make space suits for use on the moon non-formfitting. They might look like large turtles, moving on large wheels with big low pressure tires. Instead of providing gloves of some kind, a large number of manipulating devices (similar to those used for manipulating radio-active substances) might be attached to the vehicle, each with a specialized instrument. One could be a scoop for dust or small gravel, emptying into a collection tube, another could be a rock drill for obtaining samples, and so forth. All such detail will be investigated and developed during the unmanned phase of the Moon program.

The first visit to the Moon is likely to be short, about two weeks. But at a later date a permanent base will be built. Again, the precise shape will depend on what is established during the unmanned phase and the first visit, but most experts feel that the base should be set up in a cave, if one can be found. It will not be too difficult to make the cave airtight and to fit it with an airlock. Inside, the 24-hour day and night cycle to which the explorers are used could be maintained, regardless of "lunar time" outside. The necessary oxygen would be produced by growing plants. Several lines of research for this purpose have already been carried out. One line worked with a single-celled algae of the genus *Chlorella*. It is not only an efficient oxygen producer, utilizing the carbon dioxide exhaled by the explorers; it also happens to be edible, either in the form of soup or, after drying, as an addition to flour for baking.

Researchers even found an eight-inch edible fish which grows very fast and is willing to live on *Chlorella* only. Experiments with higher and, of course, edible plants have also been made. It seems pretty certain that they could be grown under the protection of partly transparent plastic balloons in the natural sunlight of the moon's surface. The lunar base, then, could be made nearly self-supporting as regards food and fully self-supporting as regards oxygen.

The lunar base has to be considered both as an end in itself and as a stepping stone, comparable to a naval base on a distant island. Considered by itself, the lunar base will be a laboratory devoted to research in a number of fields. Astronomy (unhampered by the presence of an atmosphere) is only the most obvious one; the unique conditions on the moon will also be useful for research in electronics, mineralogy, crystallography, and some aspects of biology. It is quite possible that the lunar base will pay for itself because of the research done there. The second aspect is that which is usually associated with the word "base"—a base of operations for the further exploration of the solar system.

# Diplomatic Personnel To and From the U. S.

*Source:* U.S. Department of State.

| Country | U. S. Representative to* | Rank | Representative from* | Rank |
|---|---|---|---|---|
| Afghanistan | Henry A. Byroade | Amb. | Mohammed Hashim Maiwandwal | Amb. |
| Argentina | (Vacant) | Amb. | Dr. Emilio Donato del Carril | Amb. |
| Australia | William J. Sebald | Amb. | Sir Howard Beale | Amb. |
| Austria | H. Freeman Matthews | Amb. | Dr. Wilfried Platzer | Amb. |
| Belgium | Douglas MacArthur II | Amb. | Louis Scheyven | Amb. |
| Bolivia | Ben S. Stephansky | Amb. | Victor Andrade | Amb. |
| Brazil | Lincoln Gordon | Amb. | Carlos Alfredo Bernardes | Cd'A[1] |
| Bulgaria | Edward Page, Jr. | Min. | Dr. Peter G. Voutov | Min. |
| Burma | John S. Everton | Amb. | U On Sein | Amb. |
| Cambodia | William C. Trimble | Amb. | Nong Kimny | Amb. |
| Cameroun | Leland Barrows | Amb. | Aime-Raymond N'Thepe | Amb. |
| Canada | Livingston T. Merchant | Amb. | A. D. P. Heeney | Amb. |
| Central Afr. Rep. | W. Wendell Blancké[2] | Amb. | Michel Gallin-Douathe | Amb. |
| Ceylon | Frances E. Willis | Amb. | J. H. O. Paulusz | Cd'A[1] |
| Chad | John A. Calhoun | Amb. | Malick Adam Sow | Amb. |
| Chile | Charles W. Cole | Amb. | Walter Müller | Amb. |
| China[3] | Everett F. Drumright | Amb. | Dr. George K. C. Yeh | Amb. |
| Colombia | Fulton Freeman | Amb. | Dr. Carlos Sanz de Santamaría | Amb. |
| Congo (Brazzaville) | W. Wendell Blancké[2] | Amb. | Emmanuel Damongo Dadet | Amb. |
| Congo (Léopoldville) | Edmund A. Gullion | Amb. | (Vacant) | Amb. |
| Costa Rica | Raymond Telles | Amb. | Manuel G. Escalante | Amb. |
| Cuba[4] | | .... | | .... |
| Cyprus | Fraser Wilkins | Amb. | Zenon Rossides | Amb. |
| Czechoslovakia | Edward T. Wailes | Amb. | Dr. Miloslav Ružek | Amb. |
| Dahomey | Robinson McIlvaine | Amb. | Louis Ignacio Pinto | Amb. |
| Denmark | William M. Blair, Jr. | Amb. | Count Kield Gustav Knuth-Winterfeldt | Amb. |
| Dominican Rep.[5] | | .... | | .... |
| Ecuador | Maurice M. Bernbaum | Amb. | Dr. Alejandro T. Ponce L. | Amb. |
| Egypt | John S. Badeau | Amb. | Dr. Mostafa Kamel | Amb. |
| El Salvador | Murat W. Williams | Amb. | Dr. Francisco R. Lima | Amb. |
| Estonia | Legation closed | .... | Johannes Kaiv[6] | CG[7] |
| Ethiopia | Arthur L. Richards | Amb. | Berhanou Dinke | Amb. |
| Finland | Bernard A. Gufler | Amb. | Richard R. Seppälä | Amb. |
| France | James M. Gavin | Amb. | Hervé Alphand | Amb. |
| Gabon | Charles F. Darlington | Amb. | Joseph Ngoua | Amb. |
| Germany | Walter C. Dowling | Amb. | Wilhelm G. Grewe | Amb. |
| Ghana | Francis H. Russell | Amb. | W. M. Q. Halm | Amb. |
| Great Britain | David K. E. Bruce | Amb. | W. David Ormsby Gore | Amb. |
| Greece | Ellis O. Briggs | Amb. | Alexis S. Liatis | Amb. |
| Guatemala | John J. Muccio | Amb. | Carlos Alejos | Amb. |
| Guinea | William Attwood | Amb. | Dr. Seydou Conté | Amb. |
| Haiti | Robert Newbegin | Amb. | Ernest Bonhomme | Amb. |
| Honduras | Charles R. Burrows | Amb. | Dr. Céleo Dávila | Amb. |
| Hungary | (Vacant) | Min. | Tibor Zádor | Cd'A[1] |
| Iceland | James K. Penfield | Amb. | Thor Thors | Amb. |
| India | J. Kenneth Galbraith | Amb. | D. N. Chatterjee | Cd'A[1] |
| Indonesia | Howard P. Jones | Amb. | Dr. Zairin Zain | Amb. |
| Iran | Julius C. Holmes | Amb. | Ardeshir Zahedi | Amb. |
| Iraq | John D. Jernegan | Amb. | Ali Haider Sulaiman | Amb. |
| Ireland | Edward G. Stockdale | Amb. | Thomas J. Kiernan | Amb. |
| Israel | Walworth Barbour | Amb. | Avraham Harman | Amb. |
| Italy | G. Frederick Reinhardt | Amb. | Sergio Fenoaltea | Amb. |
| Ivory Coast | R. Borden Reams | Amb. | Konan Bédié | Amb. |
| Japan | Edwin O. Reischauer | Amb. | Koichiro Asakai | Amb. |
| Jordan | William B. Macomber, Jr. | Amb. | Yusuf Haikal | Amb. |
| Korea | Samuel D. Berger | Amb. | Gen. Il Kwon Chung | Amb. |
| Laos | Winthrop G. Brown | Amb. | Tianethone Chantharasy | Cd'A[1] |
| Latvia | Legation closed | .... | Dr. Arnolds Spekke | Min. |
| Lebanon | (Vacant) | Amb. | Nadim Dimechkie | Amb. |
| Liberia | Elbert G. Mathews | Amb. | S. Edward Peal | Amb. |
| Libya | J. Wesley Jones | Amb. | Dr. Mohieddine Fekini | Amb. |

| Country | U. S. Representative to* | Rank | Representative from* | Rank |
|---|---|---|---|---|
| Lithuania | Legation closed | .... | Joseph Kajeckas | Cd'A[1] |
| Luxembourg | James Wine | Amb. | George Heisbourg | Amb. |
| Malagasy Republic | Frederic P. Bartlett | Amb. | Louis Rakotomalala | Amb. |
| Malaya | Charles F. Baldwin | Amb. | Dato' Nik Ahmed Kamil | Amb. |
| Mali | Thomas K. Wright | Amb. | Abdoulaye Maiga | Amb. |
| Mauritania | Philip M. Kaiser[8] | Amb. | Souleymane Ould Cheikh Sidya | Amb. |
| Mexico | Thomas C. Mann | Amb. | Antonio Carrillo Flores | Amb. |
| Morocco | Philip W. Bonsal | Amb. | Dr. El-Mehdi Ben Aboud | Amb. |
| Nepal | Henry E. Stebbins | Amb. | Matrika Prasad Koirala | Amb. |
| Netherlands | John S. Rice | Amb. | Dr. J. H. van Roijen | Amb. |
| New Zealand | Anthony B. Akers | Amb. | G. R. Laking | Amb. |
| Nicaragua | Aaron S. Brown | Amb. | Dr. Guillermo Sevilla-Sacasa | Amb. |
| Niger | Mercer Cook | Amb. | Issoufou Saidou Djermakoye | Amb. |
| Nigeria | Joseph Palmer II | Amb. | J. M. Udochi | Amb. |
| Norway | Clifton R. Wharton | Amb. | Paul Koht | Amb. |
| Pakistan | William M. Rountree | Amb. | Aziz Ahmed | Amb. |
| Panamá | Joseph S. Farland | Amb. | Augusto Guillermo Arango | Amb. |
| Paraguay | William P. Snow | Amb. | Dr. Juan Plate | Amb. |
| Peru | James Loeb | Amb. | Fernando Berckemeyer | Amb. |
| Philippines | John D. Hickerson | Amb. | Gen. Carlos P. Romulo | Amb. |
| Poland | Jacob D. Beam | Amb. | Edward Drozniak | Amb. |
| Portugal | C. Burke Elbrick | Amb. | Frederico de Vasconcelos | Cd'A[1] |
| Rumania | (Vacant) | Min. | George Macovescu | Min. |
| Saudi Arabia | Parker T. Hart[9] | Amb. | Sheikh Abdullah Al-Khayyal | Amb. |
| Senegal | Philip M. Kaiser[8] | Amb. | Ousmane Soce Diop | Amb. |
| Sierra Leone | A. S. J. Carnahan | Amb. | Dr. R. E. Kelfa-Caulker | Amb. |
| Somalia | Andrew G. Lynch | Amb. | (Vacant) | Amb. |
| South Africa | Joseph C. Satterthwaite | Amb. | Dr. W. C. Naudé | Amb. |
| Spain | Anthony J. D. Biddle | Amb. | Mariano de Yturralde y Orbegoso | Amb. |
| Sudan | James S. Moose, Jr. | Amb. | Dr. Osman El Hadari | Amb. |
| Sweden | J. Graham Parsons | Amb. | Gunnar Jarring | Amb. |
| Switzerland | Robert M. McKinney | Amb. | August R. Lindt | Amb. |
| Syria | (Vacant) | Amb. | (Vacant) | Amb. |
| Thailand | Kenneth T. Young | Amb. | Visutr Arthayukti | Amb. |
| Togo | Leon B. Poullada | Amb. | Dr. André Akakpo | Amb. |
| Tunisia | Walter N. Walmsley | Amb. | Habib Bourguiba, Jr. | Amb. |
| Turkey | Raymond A. Hare | Amb. | Bülend Usakligil | Amb. |
| U.S.S.R. | Llewellyn E. Thompson | Amb. | Mikhail A. Menshikov | Amb. |
| Upper Volta | Thomas S. Estes | Amb. | Frédéric Fernand Guirma | Amb. |
| Uruguay | Edward J. Sparks | Amb. | Carlos A. Clulow | Amb. |
| Venezuela | Teodoro Moscoso | Amb. | Dr. José Antonio Mayobre | Amb. |
| Vietnam | Frederick E. Nolting, Jr. | Amb. | Tran Van Chuong | Amb. |
| Yemen | Parker T. Hart[9] | Min. | Assayed Ahmad Ali Zabarah | Cd'A |
| Yugoslavia | George F. Kennan | Amb. | Marko Nikezic | Amb. |

* As of Oct. 1961.
[1] Ad interim. [2] Accredited as Ambassador to Central African Republic and Congo (Brazzaville); resident in Brazzaville. [3] Formosa (Taiwan). [4] Diplomatic relations severed Jan. 3, 1961. [5] Diplomatic relations severed Aug. 26, 1960. [6] Legation in New York. [7] Acting. [8] Accredited as Ambassador to Mauritania and Senegal; resident in Dakar. [9] Accredited as Ambassador to Saudi Arabia and Minister to Yemen; resident in Jidda.

**(Amb.—Ambassador; Min.—Minister; CG—Consul General; Cd'A—Chargé d'Affaires)**

---

# The Liberty Bell

The Liberty Bell was cast in England in 1752 for the Pennsylvania Statehouse (now Independence Hall). Damaged in transit, it was recast in Philadelphia in 1753. It is inscribed with the words, "Proclaim liberty throughout all the land unto all the inhabitants thereof" (Lev. 25:10). The bell was rung on July 8, 1776, for the first public reading of the Declaration of Independence. Hidden in Allentown during the British occupation of Philadelphia, it was replaced in Independence Hall in 1778 where it remains today. The bell cracked on July 8, 1835, while tolling the death of Chief Justice John Marshall.

# SPEAKERS OF THE HOUSE OF REPRESENTATIVES

*Source: Congressional Directory.*

| Name and state | Congress | Dates served |
|---|---|---|
| Frederick A. C. Muhlenberg (Pa.) | 1 | 1789–1791 |
| Jonathan Trumbull (Conn.) | 2 | 1791–1793 |
| Frederick A. C. Muhlenberg (Pa.) | 3 | 1793–1795 |
| Jonathan Dayton (N. J.)[1] | 4–5 | 1795–1799 |
| Theodore Sedgwick (Mass.) | 6 | 1799–1801 |
| Nathaniel Macon (N. C.) | 7–9 | 1801–1807 |
| Joseph B. Varnum (Mass.) | 10–11 | 1807–1811 |
| Henry Clay (Ky.)[2] | 12–13 | 1811–1814 |
| Langdon Cheves (S. C.) | 13 | 1814–1815 |
| Henry Clay (Ky.)[3] | 14–16 | 1815–1820 |
| John W. Taylor (N. Y.) | 16 | 1820–1821 |
| Philip P. Barbour (Va.) | 17 | 1821–1823 |
| Henry Clay (Ky.) | 18 | 1823–1825 |
| John W. Taylor (N. Y.) | 19 | 1825–1827 |
| Andrew Stevenson (Va.)[4] | 20–23 | 1827–1834 |
| John Bell (Tenn.) | 23 | 1834–1835 |
| James K. Polk (Tenn.) | 24–25 | 1835–1839 |
| Robert M. T. Hunter (Va.) | 26 | 1839–1841 |
| John White (Ky.) | 27 | 1841–1843 |
| John W. Jones (Va.) | 28 | 1843–1845 |
| John W. Davis (Ind.) | 29 | 1845–1847 |
| Robert C. Winthrop (Mass.) | 30 | 1847–1849 |
| Howell Cobb (Ga.) | 31 | 1849–1851 |
| Linn Boyd (Ky.) | 32–33 | 1851–1855 |
| Nathaniel P. Banks (Mass.) | 34 | 1855–1857 |
| James L. Orr (S. C.) | 35 | 1857–1859 |
| Wm. Pennington (N. J.) | 36 | 1859–1861 |
| Galusha A. Grow (Pa.) | 37 | 1861–1863 |
| Schuyler Colfax (Ind.) | 38–40 | 1863–1869 |
| Theodore M. Pomeroy (N. Y.)[5] | 40 | 1869–1869 |
| James G. Blaine (Maine) | 41–43 | 1869–1875 |
| Michael C. Kerr (Ind.)[6] | 44 | 1875–1876 |
| Samuel J. Randall (Pa.) | 44–46 | 1876–1881 |
| J. Warren Keifer (Ohio) | 47 | 1881–1883 |
| John G. Carlisle (Ky.) | 48–50 | 1883–1889 |
| Thomas B. Reed (Maine) | 51 | 1889–1891 |
| Charles F. Crisp (Ga.) | 52–53 | 1891–1895 |
| Thomas B. Reed (Maine) | 54–55 | 1895–1899 |
| David B. Henderson (Iowa) | 56–57 | 1899–1903 |
| Joseph G. Cannon (Ill.) | 58–61 | 1903–1911 |
| Champ Clark (Mo.) | 62–65 | 1911–1919 |
| Frederick H. Gillett (Mass.) | 66–68 | 1919–1925 |
| Nicholas Longworth (Ohio) | 69–71 | 1925–1931 |
| John N. Garner (Tex.) | 72 | 1931–1933 |
| Henry T. Rainey (Ill.)[7] | 73 | 1933–1934 |
| Joseph W. Byrns (Tenn.)[8] | 74 | 1935–1936 |
| William B. Bankhead (Ala.)[9] | 74–76 | 1936–1940 |
| Sam Rayburn (Tex.) | 76–79 | 1940–1947 |
| Joseph W. Martin, Jr. (Mass.) | 80 | 1947–1949 |
| Sam Rayburn (Tex.) | 81–82 | 1949–1953 |
| Joseph W. Martin, Jr. (Mass.) | 83 | 1953–1955 |
| Sam Rayburn (Tex.) | 84– | 1955– |

[1] George Dent (Md.) was elected Speaker pro tempore for Apr. 20 and May 28, 1798. [2] Resigned during 2d session of 13th Congress. [3] Resigned between 1st and 2d sessions of 16th Congress. [4] Resigned during 1st session of 23d Congress. [5] Elected Speaker and served the day of adjournment. [6] Died between 1st and 2d sessions of 44th Congress. During 1st session, there were two Speakers pro tempore: Samuel S. Cox (N. Y.), appointed for Feb. 17, May 12 and June 19, 1876, and Milton Saylor (Ohio), appointed for June 4, 1876. [7] Died 1934 after adjournment of 2nd session of 73rd Congress. [8] Died during 2d session of 74th Congress. [9] Died during 3d session of 76th Congress.

---

# FLOOR LEADERS OF THE SENATE

*Source:* United States Senate, Secretary for the Majority.

### Democratic

Martin, Thomas S. (Va.) Maj. 1917–19
Hitchcock, Gilbert M. (Nebr.) Min. 1919–20
Underwood, Oscar W. (Ala.) Min. 1920–23
Robinson, Joseph T. (Ark.) Min. 1923–33 Maj. 1933–37
Barkley, Alben W. (Ky.) Maj. 1937–46 Min. 1947–48
Lucas, Scott W. (Ill.) Maj. 1949–50
McFarland, Ernest W. (Ariz.) Maj. 1951–52
Johnson, Lyndon B. (Tex.) Min. 1953–54 Maj. 1955–60
Mansfield, Mike (Mont.) Maj. 1961–

### Republican

Lodge, Henry Cabot (Mass.) Maj. 1919–24
Curtis, Charles (Kans.) Maj. 1925–29
Watson, James E. (Ind.) Maj. 1929–33
McNary, Chas. L. (Oreg.) Min. 1933–44
White, Wallace H., Jr. (Me.) Min. 1944–47 Maj. 1947–48
Wherry, Kenneth S. (Nebr.) Min. 1949–51
Bridges, Styles (N. H.) Min. 1951–52
Taft, Robert A. (Ohio) Maj. 1953
Knowland, Wm. F. (Cal.) Maj. 1953–54 Min. 1955–58
Dirksen, Everett McK. (Ill.) Min. 1959–

NOTE: Maj. stands for Majority Leader, Min., for Minority Leader.

# Principal Bills and Treaties Since 1900

## PARTY ABBREVIATIONS

| Dem.—Democratic | A.L.—American Labor | Ind.—Independent | Proh.—Prohibition |
|---|---|---|---|
| Rep.—Republican | F.L.—Farmer-Labor | Prog.—Progressive | Soc.—Socialist |

| Bill or treaty | Party | House vote Yea | House vote Nay | Senate vote Yea | Senate vote Nay | Date enacted |
|---|---|---|---|---|---|---|
| Hay-Pauncefote Treaty. England agreed the U. S. can build and control an Isthmian canal open to all nations on equal terms (ratified Dec. 16, 1901). | | No vote required | | 72 | 6 | Nov. 18, 1901 |
| Hay-Bunau-Varilla Treaty. Granted the U. S. a ten-mile strip in Panama in perpetuity for $10,000,000 in gold and an annuity of $250,000. | Dem. Rep. | No vote required | | 9 41 | 15 1 | Mar. 19, 1903 |
| Pure Food and Drug Act. Made shipments in interstate commerce of adulterated foods and drugs illegal. | | 240 | 17 | 63 | 4 | June 30, 1906 |
| Glass-Owen Bill. Established a Federal Reserve system. | | 298 | 60 | 43 | 25 | Dec. 23, 1913 |
| Federal Trade Commission. Established to enforce anti-trust laws. | | No roll-call vote | | 53 | 16 | Sept. 26, 1914 |
| Clayton Antitrust Act. Prohibited monopolistic price discrimination, restrictive sales or leases, intercorporate stock holding, interlocking directorates of competing companies capitalized at $1,000,000 or more. Exempted labor from antitrust laws and declared peaceful picketing legal. | | 244 | 54 | 35 | 24 | Oct. 15, 1914 |
| Federal Farm Loan Act. Created system of land banks to lend money to farmers on their land and permanent improvements. | | No roll-call vote | | 58 | 5 | July 17, 1916 |
| Keating-Owen Act. Forbade shipping in interstate commerce of goods produced by children. (Declared unconstitutional in 1918.) | | 337 | 46 | 52 | 12 | Sept. 1, 1916 |
| Adamson Act. Limited working hours of railroad employees to 8 per day on interstate railroads. | | 259 | 36 | 43 | 28 | Sept. 3–5, 1916* |
| Armed Neutrality Act. Allowed American vessels to be armed in war zones. | | ... | ... | Filibustered | | Defeated, Mar. 4, 1917 |
| Declaration of War. Against Germany (World War I). | | 373 | 50 | 82 | 6 | Apr. 6, 1917 |
| National Prohibition Act (Volstead Act). Prohibited manufacture, transportation and sale of beverages containing more than .5 per cent alcohol. | | 321 | 70 | Voice vote approval | | Vetoed, Oct. 27, 1919 |
| (Reconsideration vote) | | 176 | 55 | 65 | 20 | Oct. 28, 1919 |
| Treaty of Versailles. | Dem. Rep. | No vote required | | 4 35 | 42 13 | Defeated, Nov. 19, 1919 |
| Treaty of Versailles. | Dem. Rep | No vote required | | 21 28 | 23 12 | Defeated, Mar. 19, 1920 |
| Federal Intermediate Credit Act. Lent money to farmers to extent of 75 per cent of value of harvested crops and livestocks. | | 277 | 3 | No record vote | | Mar. 4, 1923 |
| Bonus Bill. Provided 20-year endowment policies for veterans. | Dem. Rep. F.L. Soc. Ind. | 177 175 1 1 1 | 20 34 ... ... ... | 32 33 2 .. .. | 9 8 .. .. .. | Vetoed, May 15, 1924 |
| (Reconsideration vote) | Dem. Rep. F.L. Soc. Ind. | 145 166 ... 1 1 | 21 57 ... ... ... | 27 30 2 .. .. | 9 17 .. .. .. | May 19, 1924 |

*As Sept. 3 was a Sunday, the bill was re-signed on the following Tuesday.

| Bill or treaty | Party | House vote | | Senate vote | | Date enacted |
|---|---|---|---|---|---|---|
| | | Yea | Nay | Yea | Nay | |
| World Court Membership. | Dem. | No vote required | | 36 | 2 | Jan. 27, 1926 |
| | Rep. | | | 40 | 14 | |
| | F.L. | | | .. | 1 | |
| Kellogg-Briand Pact. Outlawed wars and prescribed arbitration of international disputes. | | No vote required | | 85 | 1 | Jan. 15, 1929 |
| Agricultural Marketing Act. Created federal farm board with power to lend money to farm co-operatives and to create stabilization corporations to buy farm surplus and to store and sell abroad to maintain prices. | Dem. | 121 | 32 | 33 | 2 | June 15, 1929 |
| | Rep. | 245 | 2 | 21 | 32 | |
| | F.L. | 1 | ... | .. | .. | |
| Hawley-Smoot Tariff. Very high protective tariff, averaging 40.08 per cent but giving President power to initiate reduction or increase in rates. | Dem. | 14 | 132 | 5 | 30 | June 17, 1930 |
| | Rep. | 208 | 20 | 39 | 11 | |
| | F.L. | ... | 1 | .. | 1 | |
| War Debt Moratorium. Provided for moratorium on payment of interest and war debt installments by nations indebted to U. S. | Dem. | 120 | 95 | 33 | 6 | Dec. 23, 1931 |
| | Rep. | 196 | 5 | 36 | 6 | |
| | F.L. | 1 | ... | .. | .. | |
| Reconstruction Finance Corporation. Established with a working fund of $500,000,000 and power to borrow more to release frozen assets in banks and mortgage companies and to help bankrupt railroads. | Dem. | 153 | 43 | 29 | 5 | Jan. 22, 1932 |
| | Rep. | 182 | 12 | 34 | 3 | |
| Norris-LaGuardia Act. Limited granting of injunctions against labor; required open testimony in open court and outlawed yellow dog contracts. | | 363 | 13 | 75 | 5 | Mar. 23, 1932 |
| 3.2 Percent Liquor Law. Legalized manufacture and sale of 3.2 wines and beers. | Dem. | No record vote | | 33 | 19 | Mar. 22, 1933 |
| | Rep. | | | 10 | 17 | |
| Civilian Conservation Corps. Created to relieve unemployment and to work at reforestation, road building and flood control. | | No roll-call vote | | No roll-call vote | | Mar. 31, 1933 |
| Agricultural Adjustment Act. Created the AAA, which was authorized to limit acreage on specified crops at farmers' option and to pay benefits to farmers; money for this purpose to be raised by a process tax, which was declared unconstitutional Jan. 16, 1936. | | 315 | 98 | 52 | 31 | May 12, 1933 |
| Tennessee Valley Authority. Established to develop and sell electric power, to serve as yardstick for electricity rates, to develop rural electrification, to establish flood control, and to produce fertilizer. | Dem. | 284 | 2 | 48 | 3 | May 18, 1933 |
| | Rep. | 17 | 89 | 14 | 17 | |
| | F.L. | 5 | ... | 1 | .. | |
| Federal Securities Act. Required that all stock and bond issues be registered and approved. | | No roll-call vote | | No roll-call vote | | May 27, 1933 |
| Home Owners Refinancing Act. Established the HOLC, which took over mortgages in exchange for bonds in order to save home owners from losing homes. | | 383 | 4 | No record vote | | June 13, 1933 |
| Glass-Steagall Banking Act. Created Federal Deposit Insurance Corporation to insure deposits up to $5000 (later $10,000); required that private banks be either investment or deposit banks, but not both. | | No record vote | | No roll-call vote | | June 16, 1933 |
| National Industrial Recovery Act. Created NRA; authorized establishment of trade associations; suspended antitrust laws; authorized drawing-up of codes of Fair Competition to be accepted by President; guaranteed collective bargaining and required employers to accept approved maximum and minimum wage provisions. (Declared unconstitutional in 1935.) | Dem. | 266 | 25 | 46 | 4 | June 16, 1933 |
| | Rep. | 53 | 50 | 10 | 20 | |
| | F.L. | 4 | ... | 1 | .. | |
| Gold Reserve Act. Gave President power to devalue gold and to impound for treasury all gold in Federal System and to establish Exchange Stabilization Fund. | Dem. | 287 | 2 | 55 | 1 | Jan. 30, 1934 |
| | Rep. | 68 | 38 | 10 | 22 | |
| | F.L. | 5 | ... | 1 | .. | |
| Farm Mortgage Refinancing Act. Created Federal Farm Mortgage Corporation to assist farmers in payment of mortgages on easier interest terms. | | No record vote | | No record vote | | Jan. 31, 1934 |
| Tydings-McDuffie Act. Gave the Philippine Islands independence. | Dem. | No roll-call vote | | 51 | .. | Mar. 24, 1934 |
| | Rep. | | | 16 | 8 | |
| | F.L. | | | 1 | .. | |

| Bill or treaty | Party | House vote | | Senate vote | | Date enacted |
|---|---|---|---|---|---|---|
| | | Yea | Nay | Yea | Nay | |
| Securities and Exchange Act. Established Securities and Exchange Commission; required licensing of stock exchanges; made certain speculative practices illegal; gave Federal Reserve Board power to fix margins; required full financial statements from registered companies. | Dem. Rep. F.L. | 254 22 4 | 11 73 ... | 47 15 .. | 1 12 .. | June 6, 1934 |
| National Housing Act. Created Federal Housing Administration to administer funds for modernizing homes and for lending for new construction. | | 176 | 19 | No record vote | | June 28, 1934 |
| Federal Farm Bankruptcy Act (Frazier-Lemke Act). Declared moratorium on farm mortgage foreclosures. (Declared unconstitutional in May, 1935.) | | No record vote | | 60 | 16 | June 28, 1934 |
| World Court Ratification. (Defeated in Senate by lack of 2/3 majority vote.) | Dem. Rep. F.L. Prog. | No vote required | | 43 9 .. .. | 20 14 1 1 | Defeated, Jan. 29, 1935 |
| National Labor Relations Act (Wagner-Connery Act). Created the NLRB with power to determine appropriate collective bargaining unit subject to elections they supervised at request of the workers; to certify the duly chosen trade union and to take testimony about unfair employer practices and issue cease and desist orders. | Dem. Rep. F.L. Prog. | No record vote | | 49 12 1 1 | 4 8 .. .. | July 5, 1935 |
| Social Security Act. Created social security board to administer old age benefits based on earnings before the age of 65; unemployment administered under state laws and grants to states to aid the needy aged, blind, orphans, widows, etc. | | 372 | 33 | 76 | 6 | Aug. 14, 1935 |
| Farm Mortgage Moratorium Act. Allowed three-year moratorium on foreclosures with court permission upon payment of reasonable rental. | | No record vote | | No record vote | | Aug. 29, 1935 |
| Neutrality Act. Allowed President, for 6 months, to prohibit exports of arms, etc. (or their transportation by U. S. vessels) to belligerent countries. | | 211 | 83 | 79 | 2 | Aug. 31, 1935 |
| Soldiers' Bonus Bill. Made 9-year 3-per cent bonds redeemable on demand. | Dem. Rep. F.L. Prog. | 265 72 3 6 | 29 30 ... ... | 56 15 2 1 | 9 7 .. .. | Vetoed, Jan. 24, 1936 |
| | | (Reconsideration vote) | | | | |
| | Dem. Rep. F.L. Prog. | 248 66 3 7 | 32 29 ... ... | 57 16 2 1 | 12 7 .. .. | Jan. 27, 1936 |
| Soil Conservation and Domestic Allotment Act. Granted payments to farmers who let their land lie fallow or planted cover crops. | Dem. Rep. F.L. Prog. | 246 20 1 ... | 25 64 1 7 | 49 5 1 1 | 9 11 .. .. | Mar. 2, 1936 |
| Reciprocal Trade Agreement Act. Extended to June, 1940, period during which President is authorized to negotiate foreign trade under Trade Agreements Act of 1934. | | 284 | 0 | 58 | 24 | Mar. 1, 1937 |
| Neutrality Act. Forbade export of arms and ammunition to belligerents, the sale in this country of belligerents' securities, the use of American ships for carrying munitions; required belligerents to pay upon purchase and carry all purchases in their own ships (cash and carry clause). | | 377 | 12 | 41 | 15 | May 1, 1937 |
| Judiciary Act. Allowed voluntary retirement of Supreme Court justices and other federal court judges on full pension at age of 70. | | No roll-call vote | | Unanimous, no roll-call vote | | Aug. 25, 1937 |
| National Housing Act. Established U. S. Housing Authority to administer loans to communities and states for rural and urban construction. (Amended 1938.) | | 275 | 86 | 64 | 16 | Sept. 1, 1937 |

| Bill or treaty | Party | House vote Yea | Nay | Senate vote Yea | Nay | Date enacted |
|---|---|---|---|---|---|---|
| Agricultural Adjustment Act. Continued soil conservation program; provided parity payments and commodity loans to farmers; established crop insurance corporations and ever-normal granary plan. | Dem. Rep. F.L. Prog. Ind. | 243 14 5 1 ... | 54 74 ... 7 ... | 53 2 .. .. 1 | 17 11 2 1 .. | Feb. 16, 1938 |
| Wage and Hours Act. Provided minimum wage of 25 cents to rise to 40 cents after 6 years; limited hours from 44 per week the first year to 40 after the third year; goods produced by "oppressive child labor" could not be shipped in interstate commerce. | Dem. Rep. F.L. Prog. | 247 31 5 7 | 41 48 ... ... | No record vote | | June 25, 1938 |
| Alien Registration Act (Smith Act). Required fingerprinting of all aliens in U. S.; made it unlawful for anyone to advocate or teach overthrow of U. S. government or to belong to any group advocating such. | | 382 | 4 | No record vote | | June 28, 1940 |
| Selective Service Act. Established system for compulsory service in armed forces. (Extended in 1941.) | Dem. Rep. F.L. Prog. Ind. A.L. | 211 52 ... ... ... ... | 33 112 1 2 ... 1 | 50 8 .. .. .. .. | 17 10 2 1 1 .. | Sept. 16, 1940 |
| Lend-Lease. Provided system whereby U. S. lent goods and munitions to democratic nations in return for services and goods. | | 260 | 165 | 60 | 31 | Mar. 11, 1941 |
| Selective Service Act Extension. Extended period of service to not more than 30 months in time of peace and eliminated 900,000-man limit of Army. | Dem. Rep. Prog. A.L. | 182 21 ... ... | 65 133 3 1 | 38 7 .. .. | 16 13 1 .. | Aug. 18, 1941 |
| Declarations of World War II: Against Japan. | Dem. Rep. Prog. Ind. A.L. | 235 149 3 ... 1 | ... 1 ... ... ... | 56 24 1 1 .. | .. .. .. .. .. | Dec. 8, 1941 |
| Against Germany. | | 393 | 0 | 88 | 0 | Dec. 11, 1941 |
| U. N. Charter ratification. (For full text of Charter, see index.) | Dem. Rep. Prog. | No vote required | | 53 35 1 | .. 2 .. | July 28, 1945 |
| British Loan Act. Established $3,750,000,000 credit to Britain, including $650,000,000 in lend-lease. | Dem. Rep. Prog. A.L. | 157 61 ... 1 | 32 122 1 ... | 29 17 .. .. | 15 18 1 .. | July 15, 1946 |
| Atomic Energy Commission. Created five-man controlled commission without military representation but with military liaison; permitted Army and Navy to make atomic weapons; forbade distribution of fissionable materials or atomic energy information. | | No record vote | | No record vote | | Aug. 1, 1946 |
| Greek-Turkey Aid Bill. Authorized $400,000,000 to furnish aid to Greece and Turkey upon application, subject to withdrawal upon request of countries, of the U. N. Security Council or General Assembly, or of President if improperly used or unnecessary. | Dem. Rep. A.L. | 160 127 ... | 13 93 1 | 32 35 .. | 7 16 .. | May 22, 1947 |
| Treaty Ratifications: With Italy. | Dem. Rep. | No vote required | | 37 42 | 3 7 | June 14, 1947 |
| With Rumania. | | No vote required | | Voice vote approval | | June 14, 1947 |
| With Bulgaria. | | No vote required | | Voice vote approval | | June 14, 1947 |
| With Hungary. | | No vote required | | Voice vote approval | | June 14, 1947 |

| Bill or treaty | Party | House vote Yea | House vote Nay | Senate vote Yea | Senate vote Nay | Date enacted |
|---|---|---|---|---|---|---|
| Taft-Hartley Bill (Labor-Management Relations Act, 1947). Prohibited closed shops but allowed union shops by secret vote of majority of employes; made unions subject to damage suits for unfair labor practices, such as boycotts or jurisdictional strikes; required unions to file financial reports; required union leaders to file statements that they are not Communistic. | Dem. Rep. A.L. | 103 217 ... | 66 12 1 | 17 37 .. | 15 2 .. | Vetoed, June 20, 1947 |
| | | (Reconsideration vote) | | | | |
| | Dem. Rep. A.L. | 106 225 ... | 71 11 1 | 20 48 .. | 22 3 .. | June 23, 1947 |
| Presidential Succession Act. Made Speaker of House and President of Senate pro tempore next in line after Vice President. | | 365 | 11 | 50 | 35 | July 18, 1947 |
| National Security Act of 1947. Reorganized and co-ordinated armed forces under National Military Establishment headed by Secretary of Defense (of Cabinet rank) and including Secretaries of the Army, the Navy and the Air Force. | | Voice vote approval | | Voice vote approval | | July 26, 1947 |
| Foreign Assistance Act of 1948. Authorized $5.3 billion 1-year European Recovery Program, $275 million for military aid to Greece and Turkey, $463 million in economic and military aid for China, $60 million for U. N. Fund for Children. | Dem. Rep. A.L. | 150 167 0 | 11 62 2 | Voice vote approval | | Apr. 3, 1948 |
| Selective Service Act. Provided for registration of all men 18–25 and induction of enough men 19–25 to maintain Army of 837,000, Navy and Marine Corps of 666,882, and Air Force of 502,000. | | 259 | 136 | Voice vote approval | | June 24, 1948 |
| Displaced Persons Bill. Admitted 205,000 European displaced persons, including 3,000 orphans. | | Voice vote approval | | Voice vote approval | | June 25, 1948 |
| Foreign Aid Appropriations. Appropriated funds for 1 year: $5.055 billion for ERP, $400 million for China, $1.3 billion for occupied areas, $225 million for Greece and Turkey, $35 million for U. N. Fund for Children, $70,710,228 for IRO. | | 318 | 62 | Voice vote approval | | June 28, 1948 |
| Housing Bill. Authorized Federal loans for private construction of low-cost homes and apartments; liberalized loans to manufacturers of prefabricated houses. | | 351 | 9 | Voice vote approval | | Aug. 10, 1948 |
| Bill to raise salaries: President's, $75,000 to $100,000 with new $50,000 tax-free allowance; Vice President's and Speaker's, $20,000 to $30,000 with $10,000 tax-free allowance. | Dem. Rep. A.L. | Voice vote approval | | 42 26 .. | 0 9 .. | Jan. 19, 1949 |
| ERP authorization: $5,430,000,000 for European recovery, consisting of $1,150,000,000 for April–June and $4,280,000,000 for fiscal year starting July 1. | | Voice vote approval | | Voice vote approval | | Apr. 19, 1949 |
| North Atlantic Treaty. (For full text, consult index.) | Dem. Rep. | No vote required | | 50 32 | 2 11 | July 21, 1949 |
| National Security bill. Changed National Military Establishment to executive Department of Defense; made Departments of Army, Navy and Air Force "military departments." | | 356 | 7 | Voice vote approval | | Aug. 10, 1949 |
| Military Assistance Program. Authorized $1,314,010,000 in military aid: for Atlantic Pact countries, $1 billion; Greece and Turkey, $211,370,000; "general area" of China, $75,000,000; and South Korea, Iran and Philippines, $27,640,000. | Dem. Rep. A.L. | 172 51 0 | 24 84 1 | Voice vote approval | | Oct. 28, 1949 |
| Foreign-aid appropriations: $5,809,990,000, consisting of $4,852,380,000 for ERP, $912,500,000 for Army-occupied areas, $45,000,000 for Greek-Turkish aid, and $110,000 for joint Congressional Foreign-Aid Committee. | | Voice vote approval | | Voice vote approval | | Oct. 2, 1949 |
| Minimum-wage bill. Raised minimum wage from 40c to 75c an hour. | | 131 | 19 | Voice vote approval | | Oct. 26, 1949 |
| Farm bill. Supported prices for wheat, corn, cotton, rice, peanuts at 90% of parity through 1950, 80–90% through 1951, and 75–90% on sliding-scale basis thereafter. | | 175 | 34 | 46 | 7 | Oct. 31, 1949 |

| Bill or treaty | Party | House vote | | Senate vote | | Date enacted |
|---|---|---|---|---|---|---|
| | | Yea | Nay | Yea | Nay | |
| Housing bill. Authorized over $3.5 billion in government loans and mortgage insurance for expansion of housing program. Also turned over to state and local authorities about 150 wartime and veterans' housing projects. | | Voice vote approval | | Voice vote approval | | Apr. 20, 1950 |
| Bill to increase Air Force and Army. Expanded Air Force to 70 groups and from 410,000 to 502,000 men; expanded Army from 592,000 to 837,000 men. | | 315 | 4 | 76 | 0 | July 11, 1950 |
| Social Security bill. Will raise present employer's and employee's 1½% payroll tax to 2% in 1954, 2½% in 1960, 3% in 1965, and 3¼% in 1970; provided financial aid to permanently disabled persons in need. | | 374 | 1 | Voice vote approval | | Aug. 28, 1950 |
| Omnibus appropriations bill. Appropriated $35.554 billion, including $62.5 million loan to Spain, $14,680,084,443 for Defense Dept., $1.225 billion for rearming Western Europe, $2.526 billion for Marshall plan, $26.9 million for Point-4 program. | | Voice vote approval | | Voice vote approval | | Sept. 6, 1950 |
| Defense Production Act of 1950. Gave President power to curb prices, wages, and consumer credit, and to increase defense production. | | Voice vote approval | | Voice vote approval | | Sept. 8, 1950 |
| Bill to draft doctors, dentists, etc., up to 50 years of age, for 21-mo. service. | | Voice vote approval | | Voice vote approval | | Sept. 9, 1950 |
| Internal Security Act of 1950. Provided for registering of Communists and their internment in times of emergency. | Dem. | 186 | 18 | 24 | 6 | Vetoed Sept. 22, 1950 |
| | Rep. | 126 | 1 | 27 | 1 | |
| | A.L. | 0 | 1 | ... | ... | |
| | | (Reconsideration vote) | | | | |
| | Dem. | 161 | 45 | 26 | 10 | Sept. 23, 1950 |
| | Rep. | 125 | 2 | 31 | 0 | |
| | A.L. | 0 | 1 | ... | ... | |
| Emergency defense-appropriations bill. Appropriated $17,-099,902,285, including $3.734 billion for Navy, $3.166 billion for Army, $260 million for atomic-weapon research, etc. | | 286 | 30 | Voice vote approval | | Sept. 27, 1950 |
| Civil-defense bill. Provided $3.1 billion to be supplemented by state and local governments for bomb shelters and other civil defense. | | Voice vote approval | | Voice vote approval | | Jan. 12, 1951 |
| GI insurance law. Provided free $10,000 life insurance to all armed-forces personnel. | | Voice vote approval | | Voice vote approval | | Apr. 25, 1951 |
| Reciprocal Trade Agreements Act. Extended reciprocal trade agreement act to June 12, 1953, and directed President to end any concessions to Soviet bloc. | | Voice vote approval | | Voice vote approval | | June 16, 1951 |
| Draft act. Extended draft to July 1, 1955, and increased service to 24 months; provided preliminary study for universal military service. | | 339 | 41 | Voice vote approval | | June 19, 1951 |
| Pension bill. Raised to $120 a month the $60–$72 pensions to veterans disabled by nonservice disabilities. | | Voice vote approval | | Voice vote approval | | Vetoed Aug. 6, 1951 |
| | | (Reconsideration vote) | | | | |
| | | 318 | 45 | 69 | 9 | Sept. 18, 1951 |
| German peace resolution. Declared state of war with Germany ended. | | 376 | 0 | Voice vote approval | | Oct. 19, 1951 |
| Taft-Hartley Law amendment. Permitted union-shop contracts without first polling employees. | | 307 | 18 | Voice vote approval | | Oct. 22, 1951 |
| Atom-data bill. Authorized exchange of certain nonweapon atom data with friendly nations. | | Voice vote approval | | Voice vote approval | | Oct. 30, 1951 |
| Mutual Security Appropriation Bill. $7,328,903,976 voted for global military and economic aid, including $100 million for Spain. | | Voice vote approval | | Voice vote approval | | Oct. 31, 1951 |
| Japanese Peace Treaty. Formally ended state of war declared Dec. 8, 1941. | | No vote required | | 66 | 10 | Mar. 20, 1952 |
| Tidelands Oil Bill. Gave clear title to states for submerged oil and other mineral deposits off their shores. | | 247 | 89 | 50 | 35 | Vetoed, May 29, 1952 |
| | | (No reconsideration vote) | | | | |

| Bill or treaty | Party | House vote Yea | House vote Nay | Senate vote Yea | Senate vote Nay | Date enacted |
|---|---|---|---|---|---|---|
| McCarran-Walter Immigration and Nationality Act. Ended racial bars on immigration and retained quota system based on national origin. | | 205 | 53 | Voice vote approval | | Vetoed, June 25, 1952 |
| | | | (Reconsideration vote) | | | |
| | Dem. | 107 | 90 | 25 | 18 | June 27, 1952 |
| | Rep. | 170 | 23 | 32 | 8 | |
| | Ind. | 1 | 0 | . . . | . . . | |
| West German Peace Contracts. Established working basis for relations with Bonn Government. | | No vote required | | 77 | 5 | July 1, 1952 |
| New Puerto Rican Constitution. Made Puerto Rico a commonwealth and gave it greater home rule. | | Voice vote approval | | Voice vote approval | | July 3, 1952 |
| Fair Trade Acts of 1952. Allowed manufacturers and retailers to set prices on trade-marked articles where state laws concur. | | 196 | 10 | 64 | 16 | July 14, 1952 |
| Korea "G.I. Bill of Rights." Granted Korean veterans with 90 days service as of June 27, 1950, rights and benefits similar to those received by veterans of World War II. | | 322 | 1 | Voice vote approval | | July 16, 1952 |
| Social Security Amendment. Increased Social Security benefits to aged by 12½% and authorized pensioners to earn up to $75 a month. Minimum payments set at $5 a month. | | Voice vote approval | | Voice vote approval | | July 18, 1952 |
| Tidelands Oil Law. Gave coastal states right to all minerals in submerged lands within their historic boundaries; Federal government retained control of remainder of continental shelf. | Dem. Rep. Ind. | 97 188 0 | 59 18 1 | Voice vote approval | | May 22, 1953 |
| Refugee Immigration Act. Admitted 214,000 refugees in next 3 years over immigration quotas. | | 190 | 44 | Voice vote approval | | Aug. 7, 1953 |
| Statehood for Hawaii and Alaska. (Allowed to die in House.) | Rep. Dem. Ind. | . . . . . . . . . | . . . . . . . . . | 3 42 1 | 41 2 0 | Defeated, 1954 |
| Authorization of St. Lawrence Seaway. | Rep. Dem. Ind. | 144 96 1 | 64 94 0 | Voice vote approval | | May 13, 1954 |
| Public-housing bill. Allowed 35,000 units for year, but limited housing to cities where Federal slum clearance had displaced families. | | 358 | 30 | 59 | 21 | Aug. 2, 1954 |
| Tax revision to cost $1.363 million in revenue. | Rep. Dem. Ind. | 201 114 0 | 3 73 1 | 42 19 0 | 3 22 1 | Aug. 16, 1954 |
| Communist Control Act. Outlawed Communist party, though membership in party was not made crime. | | 265 | 2 | 79 | 0 | Aug. 24, 1954 |
| Farm bill. Provided flexible price support. | | 208 | 47 | 44 | 28 | Aug. 28, 1954 |
| Amendment to Atomic Energy Act of 1946. Allowed private interests to enter field of atomic power. | Rep. Dem. Ind. | Voice vote approval | | 6 38 1 | 35 6 0 | Aug. 30, 1954 |
| Social Security benefits increased and extended to additional 10,000,000 persons. | | Voice vote approval | | Voice vote approval | | Sept. 1, 1954 |
| Death penalty for peacetime espionage | | Voice vote approval | | Voice vote approval | | Sept. 3, 1954 |
| Revocation of citizenship of persons convicted by conspiracy to overthrow government by force. | | Voice vote approval | | Voice vote approval | | Sept. 3, 1954 |

| Bill or treaty | Party | House vote Yea | House vote Nay | Senate vote Yea | Senate vote Nay | Date enacted |
|---|---|---|---|---|---|---|
| Selective Service bill. Extended draft 4 years and doctors' draft 2 years. | | 388 | 5 | Voice vote approval | | June 30, 1955 |
| Funds for Dixon-Yates transmission line included in appropriations bill. | | Voice vote approval | | Voice vote approval[1] | | Canceled, July 11, 1955[2] |
| Military reserves bill. Raised present 800,000-man reserve to 2,900,000 by mid-1959. | Dem. Rep. | 169 146 | 38 40 | Voice vote approval | | Aug. 9, 1955 |
| Housing bill. Authorized construction of 45,000 public-housing units by mid-1956. | Dem. Rep. | 153 35 | 37 131 | Voice vote approval | | Aug. 11, 1955 |
| Federal minimum-wage bill. Increased minimum from 75¢ to $1 per hour. | Dem. Rep. | 192 170 | 29 25 | Voice vote approval | | Aug. 12, 1955 |
| Authorization of $1.2 billion "soil bank" program for paying farmers to withdraw acres from production. | Dem. Rep. | 172 132 | 12 47 | Voice vote approval | | May 28, 1956 |
| Highway bill. Called for expenditure of $33.482 billion for road building ($28.057 billion Federal expenditure and $5.425 billion outlay by states). | | Voice vote approval | | 89 | 1 | June 29, 1956 |
| School bill. Would have provided $1.6 billion in Federal aid for school construction. | Dem. Rep. | 119 75 | 105 119 | ... | ... | Defeated, July 5, 1956[3] |
| Foreign-aid authorization bill. Authorized $4 billion for foreign-aid program for another year. | | No record vote | | No record vote | | July 18, 1956 |
| Social Security bill. Made women eligible for benefits at 62, totally disabled workers at 50. | | Voice vote approval | | Voice vote approval | | Aug. 1, 1956 |
| Eisenhower Doctrine. Provided economic and military aid to Mideast nations. | | 350 | 60 | 73 | 19 | Mar. 9, 1957 |
| Housing bill. Permitted lower minimum down payments on government-insured housing: 3% on 1st $10,000 of appraised value, 15% on next $6,000, 30% on next $4,000. | | Voice vote approval | | Voice vote approval | | July 12, 1957 |
| U.S. ratification of treaty of International Atomic Energy Agency (IAEA). | Dem. Rep. | No vote required | | 35 32 | 9 10 | July 29, 1957 |
| Mutual security appropriations bill. Provided $2,768,760,000 in new funds and $667,050,000 in carry-over funds. | | 194 | 122 | 59 | 19 | Sept. 3, 1957 |
| Bill protecting FBI files from unrestricted use by defendant in criminal cases. | | 351 | 0 | 74 | 2 | Sept. 3, 1957 |
| Civil Rights Act of 1957. Created 6-member Civil Rights Commission; provided for additional Assistant Attorney General to head special Civil Rights section within Justice Department; barred interference with voting rights. | Dem. Rep. | 128 151 | 82 15 | 23 37 | 15 0 | Sept. 9, 1957 |
| Housing bill. Provided $1.85 billion to stimulate housing construction. | | Voice vote approval | | 86 | 0 | April 1, 1958 |
| Road bill. Added $1.8 billion to previous appropriations. | | Voice vote approval | | Voice vote approval | | April 16, 1958 |
| Postal rates and pay raise bill. Increased first-class mail from 3c to 4c per oz., etc. Provided 7½% pay raise to postal employees. | | 379 | 0 | 88 | 0 | May 27, 1958 |
| Jobless aid bill. Extended by 50% the duration of unemployment benefits for those who had exhausted their benefits. Provided on loan basis to the states, to be repaid by them. | Dem. Rep. | 60 163 | 148 17 | }88 | 0 | June 4, 1958 |
| Alaska statehood bill. (Alaska has also approved.) | Dem. Rep. | 117 91 | 81 85 | 31 33 | 13 7 | July 7, 1958 |
| Reciprocal trade bill. Extended program for 4 years; gave continued power to President to reduce tariffs on reciprocal by 20%. | Dem. Rep. | }161 | 56{ | 40 32 | 6 12 | Aug. 20, 1958 |
| Presidential pension bill. Gave $25,000 annually to ex-Presidents and $10,000 to their widows. | | 165 | 45 | Voice vote approval | | Aug. 25, 1958 |
| Foreign aid bill. Appropriated $3.3 billion for fiscal 1959, plus $644 million in carryover. | Dem. Rep. | Voice vote approval | | 25 26 | 9 8 | Aug. 29, 1958 |

[1] Passed with added provisions and sent back to House.   [2] Dixon-Yates contract ordered canceled by President and funds dropped by Congress from appropriations bill.   [3] Bill killed, since all money bills must originate in House

| Bill or treaty | Party | House vote Yea | House vote Nay | Senate vote Yea | Senate vote Nay | Date enacted |
|---|---|---|---|---|---|---|
| Debt limit rise. Raised limit to $283 billion permanently and to $288 billion temporarily. | | Voice vote approval | | 57 | 20 | Sept. 2, 1958 |
| Science education bill. Provided loans and fellowships to teachers and guidance counselors; encouraged foreign language study. ($800 million over 4 years.) | Dem. Rep. | Voice vote approval | | 37 29 | 7 8 | Sept. 2, 1958 |
| Bill admitting Hawaii as 50th state. | Dem. Rep. | 203 120 | 65 24 | 46 30 | 14 1 | Mar. 18, 1959 |
| Extension of draft for four years, until July 1, 1963. | Dem. Rep. | Voice vote approval | | 61 30 | 0 1 | Mar. 23, 1959 |
| Debt limit rise. Raised limit to $285 billion permanently and to $295 billion temporarily. | Dem. Rep. | 167 88 | 69 48 | Voice vote approval | | June 30, 1959 |
| Foreign aid bill. Authorized $3.6 billion for fiscal 1960. | Dem. Rep. | 182 89 | 83 59 | Voice vote approval | | July 24, 1959 |
| Veterans' pension revision. Increased and revised payments on basis of incomes. | | Voice vote approval | | Voice vote approval | | Aug. 29, 1959 |
| Public works appropriation bill. Appropriated $1,185,309,903 for fiscal 1960. | Dem. Rep. | 266 46 | 4 89 | 55 18 | 1 14 | Vetoed, Sept. 9, 1959 |
| (First Eisenhower veto to be overridden.) | | (Reconsideration vote) | | | | |
| | Dem. Rep. | 260 20 | 5 116 | 60 12 | 2 21 | Sept. 10, 1959 |
| Labor Reform Act of 1959. Guaranteed more democratic union procedure, etc. | Dem. Rep. | 214 138 | 51 1 | } 95 | 2 | Sept. 14, 1959 |
| Farm surplus bill. Extended for two years program of disposing of surplus farm products overseas; authorized "food stamp" plan through which $250 million worth of surplus food would be distributed annually for two-year period to needy Americans. | | Voice vote approval | | Voice vote approval | | Sept. 21, 1959 |
| Gasoline tax bill. Raised Federal tax on gasoline from 3¢ to 4¢ per gallon for 21 months starting Oct. 1, 1959. | | Voice vote approval | | 70 | 11 | Sept. 21, 1959 |
| Housing bill (third proposed). Authorized $1 billion, including $650 million for slum clearance in two-year period. | | Voice vote approval | | 86 | 7 | Sept. 23, 1959 |
| Civil rights bill. Made obstruction of integration in schools a crime and set up Federal referees in voter-registration disputes. | Dem. Rep. | 179 132 | 94 15 | 42 29 | 18 0 | May 6, 1960 |
| U.S.–Japanese Security Treaty. New mutual security treaty with Japan ratified despite Japanese student riots. | Dem. Rep. | No vote required | | } 90 | 2 | June 22, 1960 |
| Federal pay raise bill. Passed over President's veto (second Eisenhower veto overridden). Raised Federal employees pay 7½%. | Dem. Rep. | 256 89 | 13 56 | 55 19 | 9 15 | July 1, 1960 |
| Antarctic treaty. Twelve-country (including U.S.S.R.) agreement on use of Antarctic for continued scientific research. | Dem. Rep. | No vote required | | 38 28 | 17 4 | Aug. 10, 1960 |
| Foreign aid bill. Provided $3.98 billion for mutual security. | Dem. Rep. | 105 107 | 138 34 | 41 26 | 19 7 | Sept. 2, 1960 |
| Health care for aged bill. Provided $202 million in Federal aid to match $61 million from states. The medical aid funds will cover about 1.4 million needy persons over 65. | Dem. Rep. | 244 137 | 16 7 | 59 32 | 1 1 | Sept. 13, 1960 |

| Bill or treaty | Party | House vote Yea | House vote Nay | Senate vote Yea | Senate vote Nay | Date enacted |
|---|---|---|---|---|---|---|
| Five-star rank restored to Gen. Eisenhower. | | Voice vote approval | | Voice vote approval | | Mar. 14, 1961 |
| Columbia River Treaty. Provided for joint development by U.S. and Canada of water resources of Columbia River. | Dem. Rep. | No vote required | | 59 31 | 0 1 | Mar. 16, 1961 |
| Area redevelopment bill. Authorized loans and grants totaling $394 million to economically depressed areas. | Dem. Rep. | 208 43 | 42 125 | 48 15 | 11 16 | May 1, 1961 |
| Minimum wage bill. Raised hourly minimum wage for about 23.9 million covered workers from $1 to $1.15 an hour and expanded coverage. | Dem. Rep. | 208 133 | 43 35 | 51 14 | 11 17 | May 5, 1961 |
| Amendment to Social Security Act. Provided aid for dependent children of needy unemployed. | | Voice vote approval | | Voice vote approval | | May 8, 1961 |
| Inter-American aid bill. Authorized $600-million program for social and economic aid. | Dem. Rep. | 219 110 | 28 55 | Voice vote approval | | May 27, 1961 |
| Debt limit. Increased Federal debt limit from its permanent $285 billion ceiling to $292 billion during fiscal 1962. | Dem. Rep. | 191 40 | 35 113 | Voice vote approval | | June 29, 1961 |
| Amendment to Social Security Act. Increased benefits and allowed men as well as women to retire at 62. | Dem. Rep. | 251 149 | 0 14 | 57 33 | 0 0 | June 30, 1961 |
| Tax bill. Extended for year corporate income and excise tax rates. | Dem. Rep. | 203 92 | 27 61 | Voice vote approval | | June 30, 1961 |
| Housing bill. Authorized $6.1 billion for existing and new housing programs. | Dem. Rep. | 210 25 | 38 140 | 52 12 | 8 17 | June 30, 1961 |
| Foreign aid bill. Authorized $4-billion program of economic and military assistance. | Dem. Rep. | 195 92 | 63 77 | 46 20 | 13 11 | Sept. 4, 1961 |
| Bill making hijacking of airplanes a Federal offense. | Dem. Rep. | 226 148 | 5 0 | 60 32 | 0 0 | Sept. 5, 1961 |
| Education bill. Provided 2-year extension of Federal aid for "impacted" school areas, and extended National Defense Education Act. | Dem. Rep. | 221 157 | 23 9 | 52 28 | 7 0 | Sept. 18, 1961 |
| Bill making Peace Corps a permanent organization. | Dem. Rep. | 206 81 | 29 68 | Voice vote approval | | Sept. 21, 1961 |
| Bill establishing Disarmament Agency in State Department. | Dem. Rep. | 194 96 | 16 38 | 48 25 | 8 6 | Sept. 26, 1961 |

# How to Number the Presidents

Did Kennedy take office as the 34th President or as the 35th?

The difficulty started with Grover Cleveland. He became our 22nd President back in 1885. Then came Benjamin Harrison, who was obviously the 23rd President, serving from 1889–93. At this point, Cleveland returned to the White House for a second (but nonconsecutive) term.

Cleveland was still the same man who had been our 22nd President. But in his later term, it would look silly—some folks thought—to continue to call him our 22nd President. That would make the 22nd President follow the 23rd. Numbers should go in order—so ran the argument—and Cleveland should therefore be designated both as the 22nd President in his first term and as the 24th in his second term.

The people who argued the other way found an eloquent spokesman in John Kieran. He said: "Write down the names of all the Presidents, and you will only get 33. If you write Cleveland twice, you'll get 34—but in that case you've got

to write Franklin D. Roosevelt's name four times. Until they prove to me that Grover Cleveland was two men, Eisenhower can't be the 34th President."

The *Congressional Directory,* which must be considered the official final authority, grappled with the problem of numbering the Presidents. Until recent years, it has followed John Kieran's theory.

After the election of President Truman, and before the election of President Eisenhower, the *Congressional Directory* changed its official mind. In the 1956 *Congressional Directory,* Truman is the 33rd President, and Eisenhower is listed as the 34th. (Cleveland has two numbers—22nd and 24th.)

Since 1957, the *Directory* has listed the Presidents without numbering them—we don't know why. Although we are listing the Presidents on the basis of the *Congressional Directory* of 1956 we can't help thinking of John Kieran's remark: "Put the busts of all the Presidents in a row and count them and you will get 33, and only 33."

Wide World Photos

W FRONTIER TAKES OVER—President Eisenhower escorts John F.
nnedy to the latter's inauguration as the nation's 35th Chief Executive.
h look happy—which the happier?

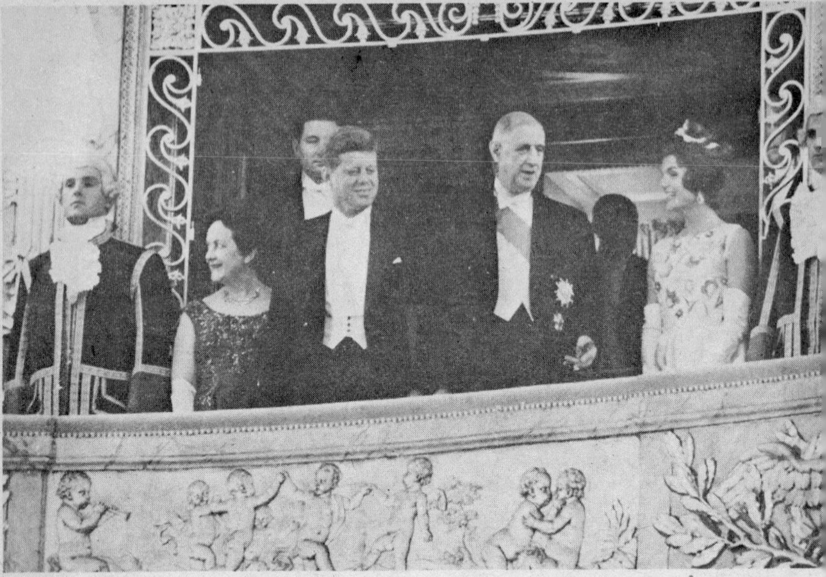

United Press Internat

VERSAILLES HOSPITALITY—Presidents Kennedy and de Gaulle their wives stand for the rendition of national anthems before a gala recept

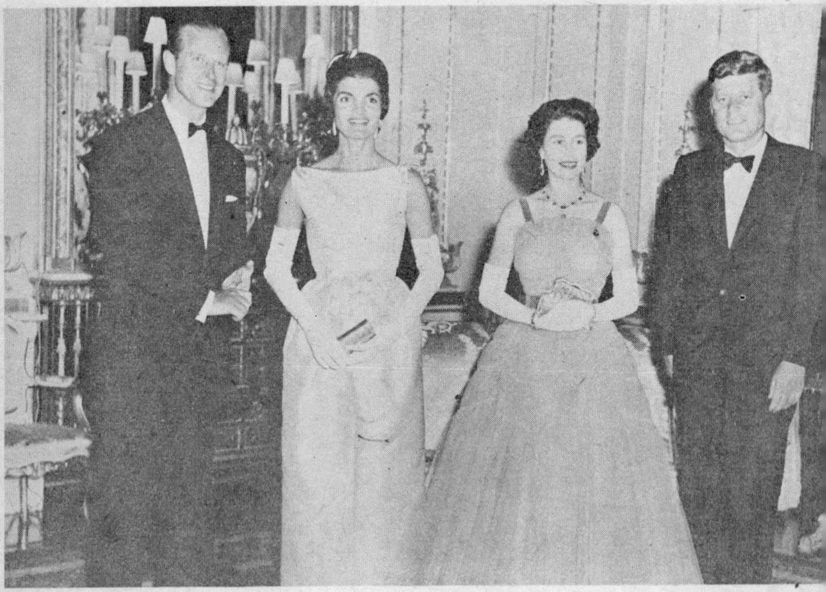

United Press Internat

ROYAL RECEPTION—President and Mrs. Kennedy pose with Qu Elizabeth and Prince Philip after a banquet at Buckingham Palace.

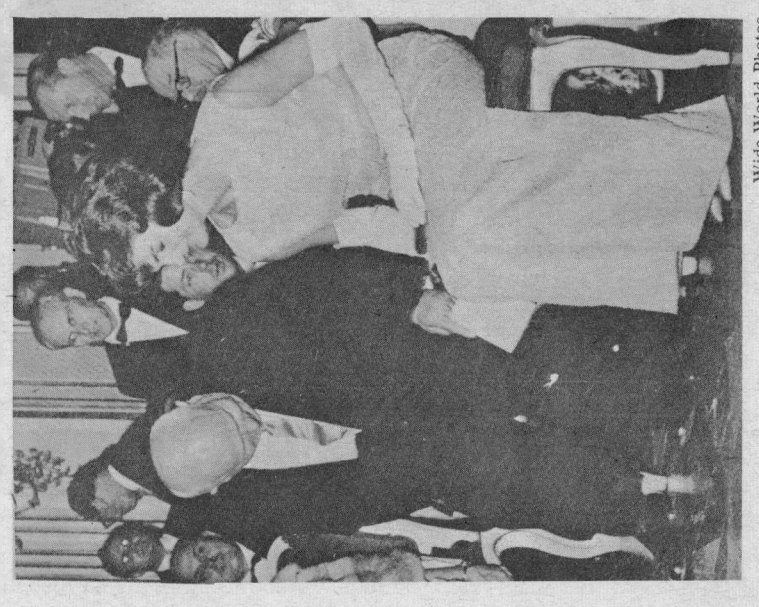

Wide World Photos

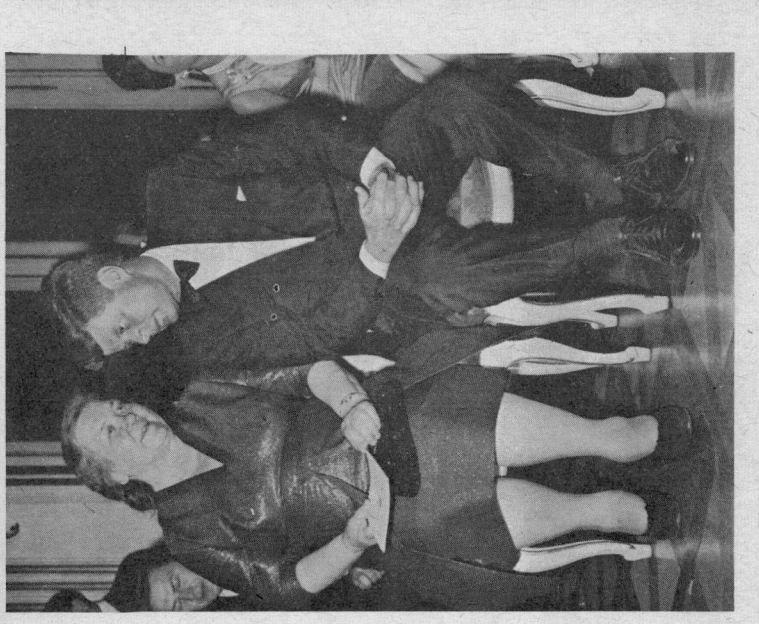

SOCIAL SUCCESS—Vienna Conference between President Kennedy and Premier Khrushchev failed to solve East-West problems, but the two leaders and their wives enjoyed a concert following a banquet in Schoenbrunn Palace.

Wide World Photos

**HOST KHRUSHCHEV**—Soviet Premier greets American President at Soviet Embassy in Vienna for their second day of talks, while Soviet Foreign Minister Andrei Gromyko (center) looks on.

London Daily Express

FLIGHT FROM COMMUNISM—Tired refugees from East Germany arrive in West Berlin.

Wide World Photos

LEAP FOR FREEDOM—A soldier of the East German Army jumps across a barbed-wire barricade to take refuge in democratic West Berlin.

Paris Match

DIVIDING LINE—Communist wall, which includes gravestones, separates a Roman Catholic church from many of its parishioners.

London Daily Express

DIVIDED WEDDING—Guests from East Berlin couldn't attend because of wall. What was left of the wedding party in West Berlin had to walk to reception because Communists blocked the roadway. Street was in East Berlin, sidewalk in West Berlin.

Paris Match

**ESPERATE LEAP**—West Berlin firemen await below with a net as refu-
ees prepare to leap from an East German building into the Free Berlin
reet below.

INTERNATIONAL CIVIL SERVANT—Dag Hammarskjöld, U.N. Secre
tary-General, received an ovation in 1960 when he told the General Assembly
"I shall remain at my post" in the face of Soviet opposition.

Paris Match

TRIBUTE—Members of the U.N. General Assembly stand in tribute to Dag Hammarskjöld after his death in a plane crash in Northern Rhodesia.

United Press International

CAREER'S END—Hammarskjöld family grave in Uppsala, Sweden, where the U.N. leader was buried.

The New York Times

KENNEDY AWAITING THE BIG MOMENT—The President about to address the U.N. General Assembly. A rare picture of Kennedy in a tense mood.

Sovfoto (Moscow, 1958)

**THE TROIKA**—The three-horse Russian sleigh that gave its name to the Soviet demand for three-man leadership of the U.N. Secretariat, allowing each man power of veto.

United Press International

**SOVIET AUDIENCE**—A glum delegation from the U.S.S.R. listens to President Kennedy's address before the General Assembly. Condemning Soviet troika scheme, the President said: "Even the three horses of the troika did not have three drivers, all going in different directions. They had only one—and so must the United Nations executive."

The New York Tim

U.S. representatives—Secretary of State Dean Rusk, Charles W. Yost, Am
bassador Stevenson, and Ambassador Charles E. Bohlen.

The New York Tim

Communist group—Russia's Valerian A. Zorin, Rumania's Eduard Mezin
cescu, S. G. Lapin, and Mme. Zoya Mironova of the U.S.S.R.

The New York Times

Ceylon's Felix Dias Bandaranaike and others.

The New York Times

Stevenson with Nigeria's Jaja Wachuku (right).

STORM'S FURY—High tides and winds accompanying hurricane Carla overturned cars and trucks on a shore road in Freeport, Texas.

Wide World Photos

HOUSE RAZED—A resident of Port O'Connor, Texas, sits in the midst of the debris that was once her home before it was wrecked by hurricane Carla.

Pictorial Parade, Inc.

FOOD FOR HOMELESS—Truck with emergency supply of bread inches along through flood waters left by hurricane Carla.

SEGREGATIONIST FIRE—A bus carrying "Freedom Riders" testing bus station segregation was set afire near Anniston, Ala., when halted by a flat tire.

Wide World Photos

PEACEFUL INTEGRATION—Negro first-graders enter previously all-white Alamo School in Galveston, Texas. There were no incidents.

Sovfoto

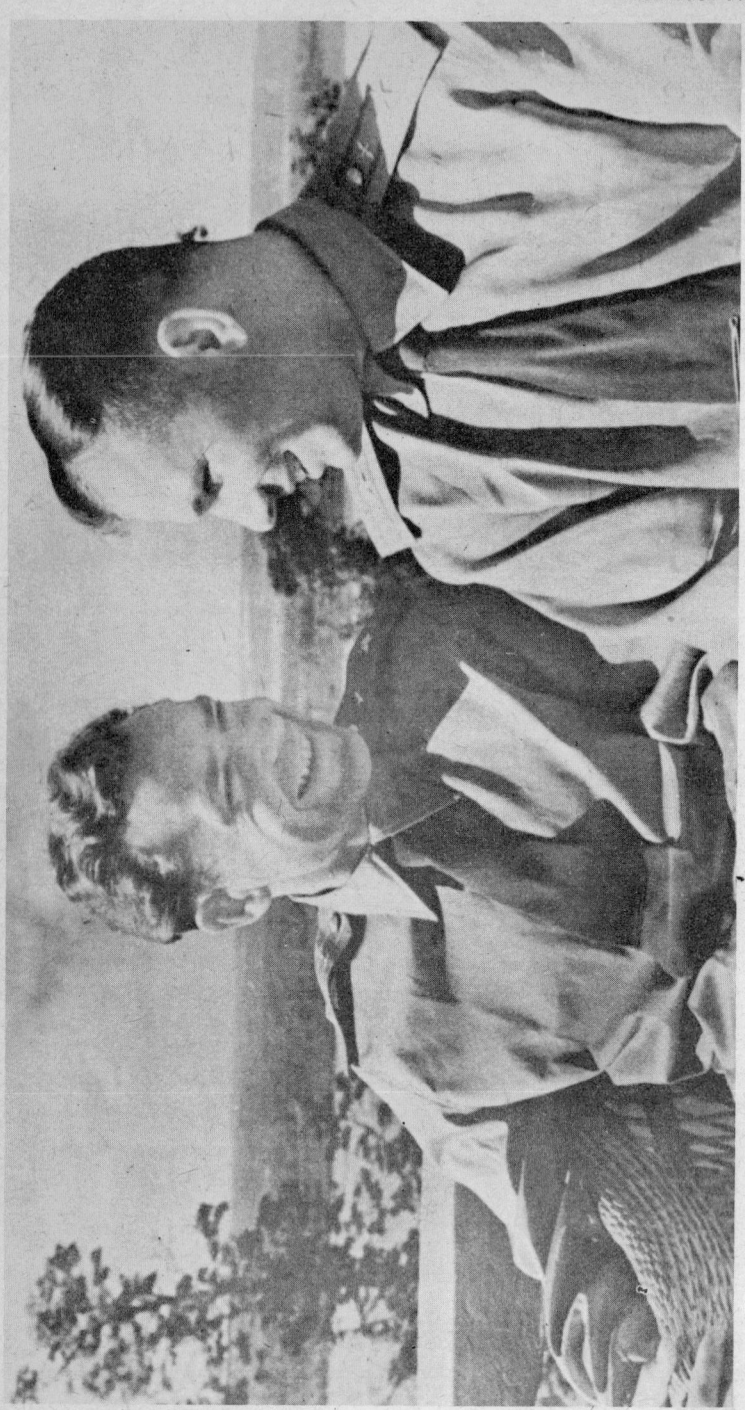

SOVIET COSMONAUTS—Gherman Titov and Yuri Gagarin relax together after Titov made world's second orbital flight. There were no pictures of the men entering or leaving space vehicles, only pictures before and afterward.

United Press International

AMERICAN ASTRONAUT—Cmdr. Alan Shepard, Jr., in space suit, leaves a medical center in Florida, followed by Capt. Virgil Grissom, who later made second flight.

JOURNEY'S START AND END—Mercury-Redstone rocket carrying Cmdr.
Alan Shepard, Jr., leaves the ground (left); the astronaut is being hoisted

United Press International

into a waiting helicopter after the successful completion of his suborbital
flight (right).

United Press International

CAPSULE LOST—Helicopter 32 tries in vain to raise Capt. Virgil Grissom's capsule, which sank. Circle indicates Grissom swimming, waiting for Helicopter to pick him up.

GRISSOM RESCUED—Helicopter 30 carries Capt. Virgil Grissom to safety.

A PLANE CRASHES IN BROOKLYN—Collision of two airliners over New York Harbor sent this craft plummeting into a heavily populated section of

Brooklyn, bringing death and destruction with it. The other airliner crashed in Staten Island.

BURNING CARRIER—Firemen battle to control blaze aboard 85% com-

Photo by Nat Fein, New York Herald Tribune

pleted U.S.S. *Constellation* under construction at Brooklyn Navy Yard.

Paris Match

ALPINE RESCUE—Tourist is lowered from a cable car near Chamonix, France, after jet plane cut one cable, killing six persons. Eighty-one were saved.

United Press International

**REBELLIOUS GENERALS**—Four of the leaders of the revolt against the de Gaulle government in Algiers: Zeller, Jouhaux, Salan, and Challe.

United Press International

**REVOLT'S AFTERMATH**—Generals Zeller (center) and Challe leave court in Paris after being sentenced to fifteen years' imprisonment.

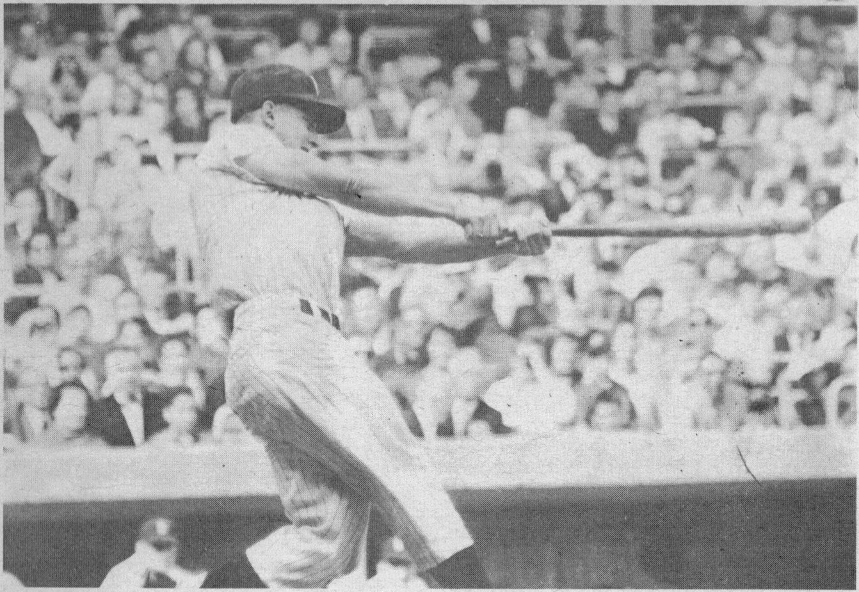

United Press International

IT'S GOING . . . GOING . . . GONE–Roger Maris, New York Yankee outfielder, became the first major leaguer ever to hit sixty-one home runs in one season.

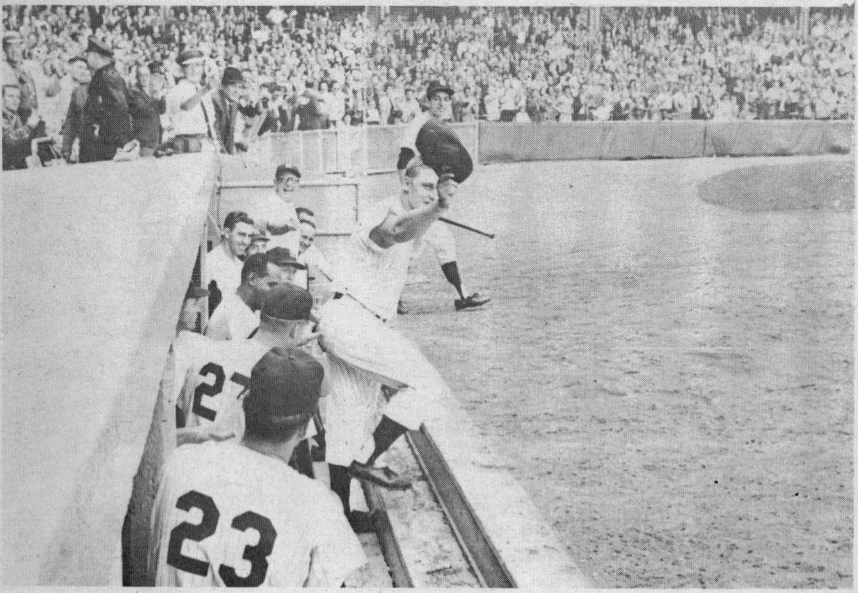

United Press International

DESERVED PLAUDITS—Roger Maris acknowledges the crowd's applause after hitting his sixty-first home run of the season in Yankee Stadium.

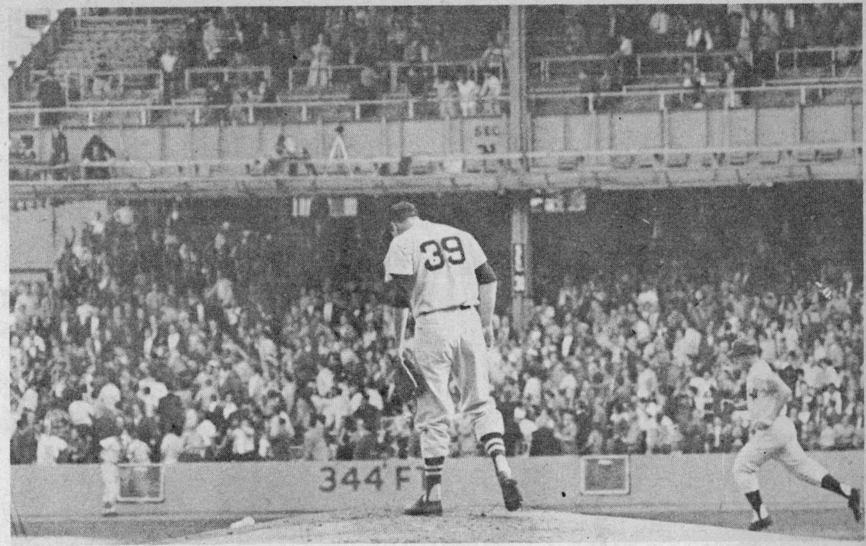


Wide World Photos

DEJECTED PITCHER—Red Sox pitcher Tracy Stallard kicks the mound after throwing the ball which allowed Maris to establish a home run record.

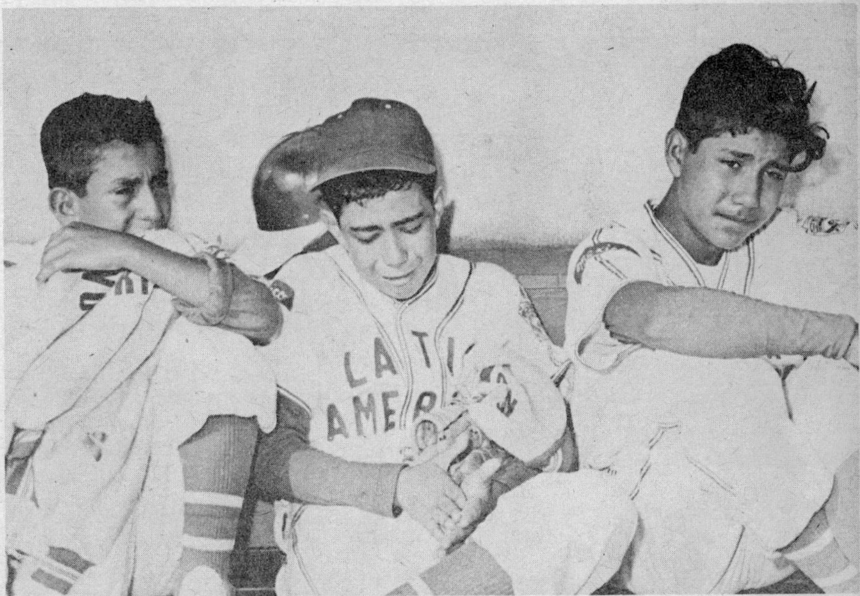

Wide World Photos

OTHER DEJECTED LOSERS—Members of Little League from Monterrey, Mexico, former champions, after losing in 1961 by only 1–0.

Wide World Photos

United Press International

A BABE RUTH RECORD BROKEN—Ford broke the pitching record for consecutive scoreless innings in World Series play established by Babe Ruth in 1918. Ford reached 32 scoreless innings in the 4th game with Cincinnati on Oct. 8, 1961.

THE MIGHTY BABE RUTH—The holder of two great records—60 home runs in one season in 1927 as a N. Y. Yankee player and a pitching record of 29⅔ scoreless innings in 1916 and 1918 while pitching for the Boston Red Sox.

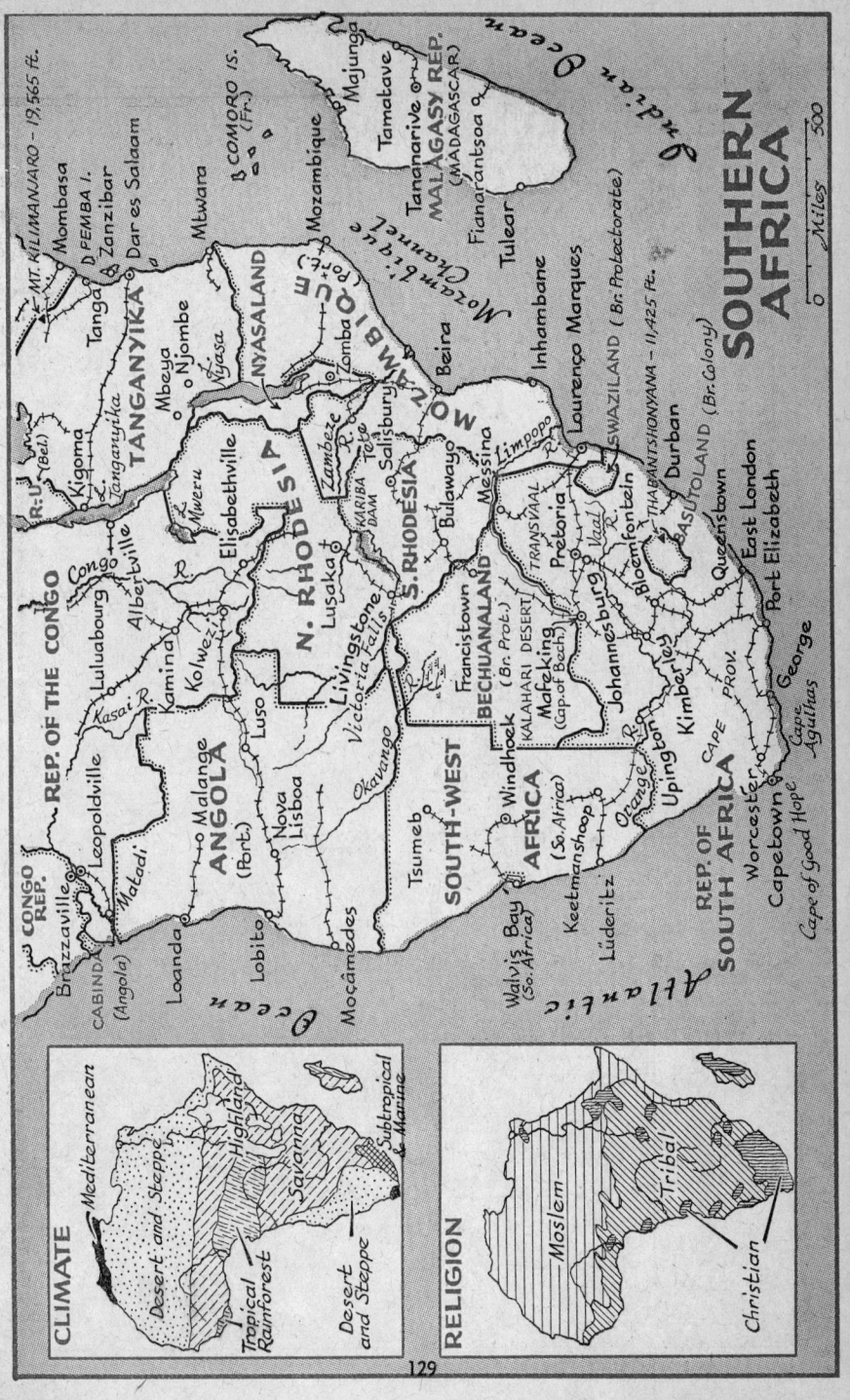

SOUTHERN AFRICA

0 — Miles — 500

Indian Ocean

MALAGASY REP.
(MADAGASCAR)

Majunga
Tananarive
Tamatave
Fianarantsoa
Tulear

MT. KILIMANJARO – 19,565 ft.
Mombasa
Tanga Zanzibar
PEMBA I.
Dar es Salaam
Mtwara
COMORO IS. (Fr.)
Mozambique

TANGANYIKA

Kigoma
R.-U. (Bel.)
Mbeya Njombe
Tanganyika L.
Mweru
Lake Nyasa

NYASALAND

Zomba (Port.)
MOZAMBIQUE

Mozambique Channel

Beira
Inhambane
Lourenço Marques
SWAZILAND (Br. Protectorate)
THABANTSHONYANA – 11,425 ft.
Durban

REP. OF THE CONGO

Luluabourg
Albertville
Elisabethville
Kamina
Kolwezi
Kasai R.

Congo

CONGO REP.
Brazzaville
Leopoldville
CABINDA (Angola)
Matadi

Loanda
Lobito
Moçâmedes

ANGOLA (Port.)
Malange
Nova Lisboa
Luso

N. RHODESIA

Mwinilunga R.
Lusaka
Livingstone
Victoria Falls
Okavango
Kabwe

S. RHODESIA

KARIBA DAM
Zambezi R.
Salisbury
Tete
Bulawayo
Messina
Limpopo

BECHUANALAND (Br. Prot.)

Francistown
KALAHARI DESERT
Mafeking (Cap. of Bech.)

SOUTH-WEST AFRICA (So. Africa)

Tsumeb
Windhoek
Walvis Bay (So. Africa)
Keetmanshoop
Lüderitz

Atlantic Ocean

REP. OF SOUTH AFRICA

TRANSVAAL
Pretoria
Johannesburg
Vaal R.
Bloemfontein
BASUTOLAND (Br. Colony)
Orange R.
Kimberley
Upington
Queenstown
East London
Port Elizabeth
George
Worcester
Capetown
Cape of Good Hope
Cape Agulhas
CAPE PROV.

## CLIMATE

Mediterranean
Desert and Steppe
Highland
Savanna
Tropical Rainforest
Desert and Steppe
Subtropical & Marine

## RELIGION

Moslem
Tribal
Christian

129

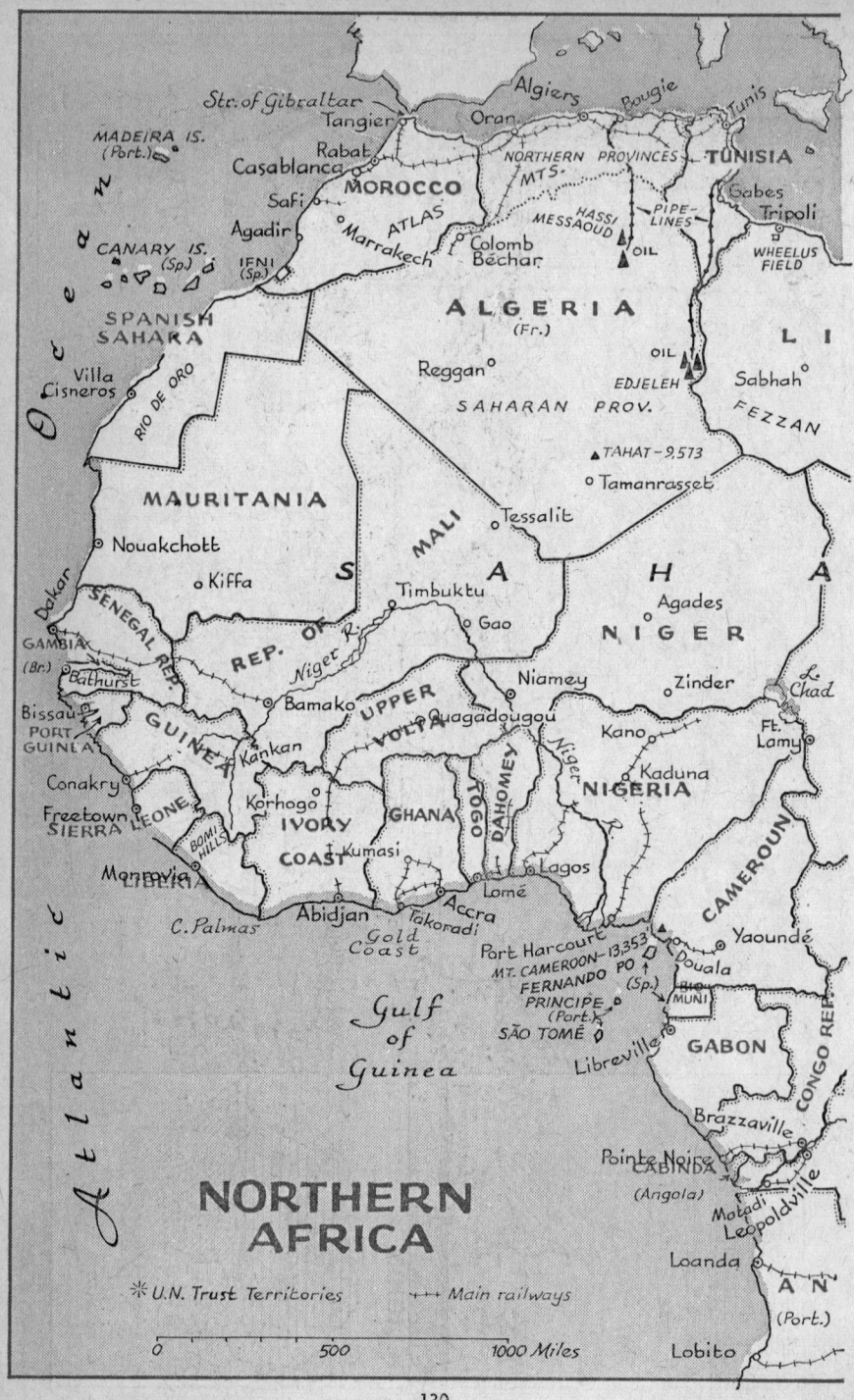

# NORTHERN AFRICA

* *U.N. Trust Territories*      +++ *Main railways*

0       500       1000 *Miles*

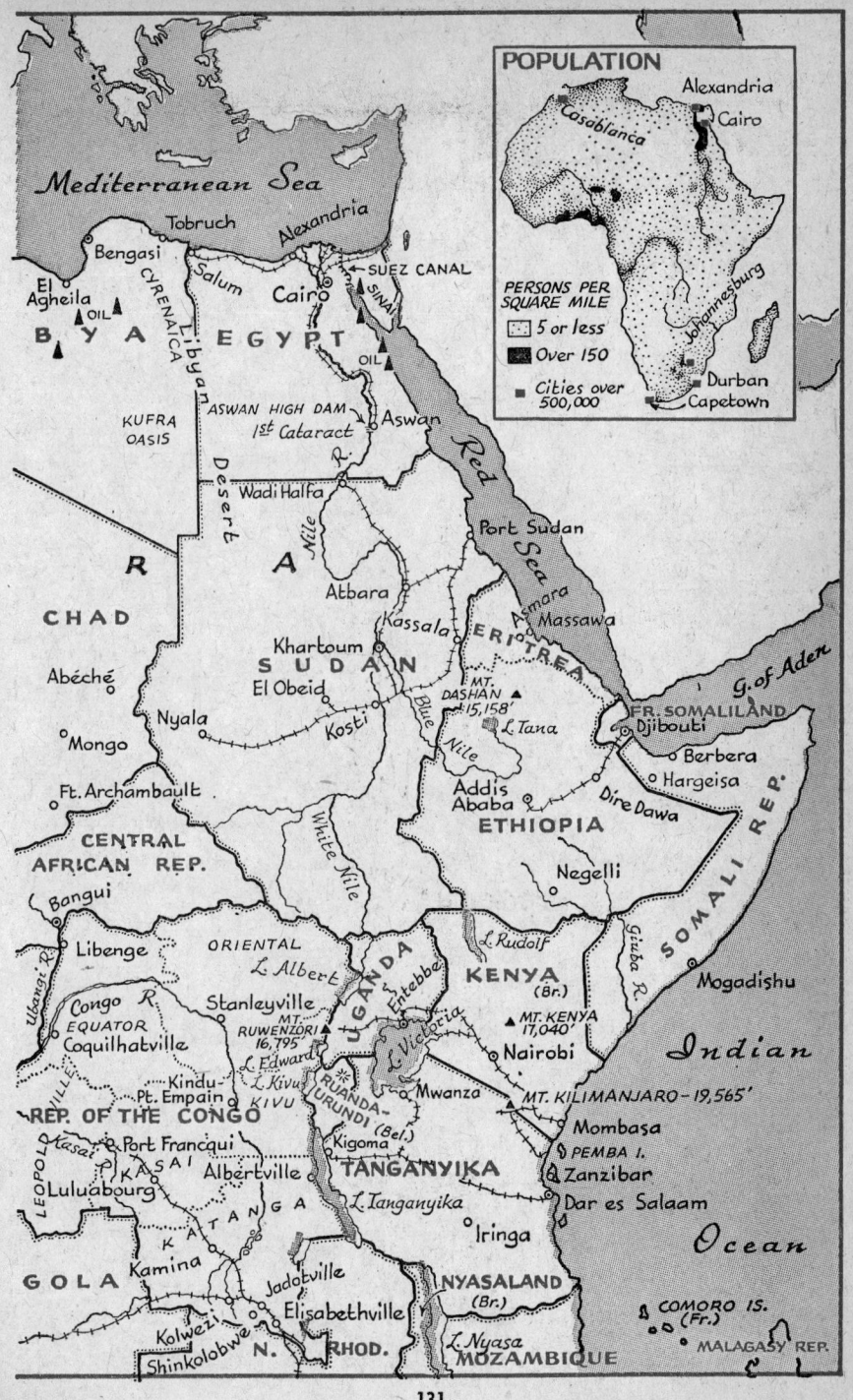

Mediterranean Sea

Tobruch
Bengasi
Salum
Alexandria
SUEZ CANAL
El Agheila
OIL
CYRENAICA
Cairo
SINAI
B Y A
Libyan
EGYPT
OIL

POPULATION
Casablanca
Alexandria
Cairo

PERSONS PER SQUARE MILE
5 or less
Over 150
Cities over 500,000

Johannesburg
Durban
Capetown

KUFRA OASIS
ASWAN HIGH DAM
1st Cataract
Aswan
R.

Desert

Wadi Halfa
Nile
Port Sudan
Red Sea

R
A
Atbara
Asmara
Massawa
CHAD
Kassala
ERITREA
G. of Aden
Abéché
Khartoum
MT. DASHAN 15,158'
L. Tana
FR. SOMALILAND
Djibouti
El Obeid
Blue Nile
Berbera
Mongo
Nyala
Kosti
Hargeisa
Ft. Archambault
Addis Ababa
Dire Dawa
White Nile
ETHIOPIA
SOMALI REP.
CENTRAL AFRICAN REP.
Negelli
Bangui
L. Rudolf
Libenge
ORIENTAL
L. Albert
UGANDA
Entebbe
KENYA (Br.)
Mogadishu
Ubangi R.
Congo R.
Stanleyville
MT. RUWENZORI 16,795'
L. Edward
MT. KENYA 17,040'
Indian
EQUATOR
Coquilhatville
L. Kivu
KIVU
L. Victoria
Nairobi
Kindu-
Pt. Empain
RUANDA-
Mwanza
MT. KILIMANJARO - 19,565'
REP. OF THE CONGO
URUNDI (Bel.)
Mombasa
Kasai
LEOPOL
Port Francqui
Kigoma
PEMBA I.
KASAI
Albertville
TANGANYIKA
Zanzibar
Luluabourg
Dar es Salaam
KATANGA
L. Tanganyika
Iringa
Ocean
GOLA
Kamina
Jadotville
NYASALAND (Br.)
COMORO IS. (Fr.)
Kolwezi
Elisabethville
Shinkolobwe
N. RHOD.
L. Nyasa
MALAGASY REP.
MOZAMBIQUE

131

# GERMANY
## AND DENMARK

═══ *Autobahn*

SWEDEN

Karlskrona
Halsingborg
Copenhagen
Malmo

Kattegat
Aarhus
Vejle
Esbjerg
Kolding
FÜNEN
Odense
ZEALAND
Korsor
Nyborg

North Sea

BORNHOLM (Den.)

Flensburg
Schleswig
HELGOLAND
Bremerhaven
Wilhelmshaven

Baltic Sea

RÜGEN
Swinemünde

Kiel
Lübeck
Altona
Hamburg
Harburg
Neubrandenburg

Rostock

Szczecin (Stettin)

EAST

NETHERLANDS

Oldenburg
Weser
Bremen
Osnabrück
Münster

Hanover

WEST

Wittenberge
Elbe

WESTERN SECTOR
BERLIN
SOVIET SECTOR

POLAND

Helmstedt
ACCESS ROUTES TO BERLIN
Magdeburg
Potsdam

Essen
RUHR
Dortmund
Düsseldorf
Rhine
Kassel
Cologne

GERMANY

Halle
Leipzig

Oder
Neisse R.
Dresden

Bad Hersfeld
Erfurt

AIR CORRIDORS TO BERLIN

Karl-Marxstadt (Chemnitz)

Aachen
BEL.
Bonn
Coblenz
Limburg
Fulda

Hof
Eger

Prague

Weisbaden
Frankfurt am Main
Mainz

CZECHOSLOVAKIA
Pilsen

LUXEM-BOURG
Trier
SAAR
Main R.
Bayreuth

Moselle R.
Kaiserslautern
Ludwigshafen
Mannheim
Heidleberg
Heilbronn

Nuremberg

Regensburg

GERMANY

Strasbourg
Kehl
Baden Baden
Stuttgart

Danube R.

FRANCE
Freiburg
Ulm
Augsburg
Munich

Chiem See
Salzburg

Constance
Oberammergau
Garmisch-Partenkirchen
Berchtesgaden
Königssee

Basel
BodenSee (L. Constance)
ZUGSPITZE 9721
LIECHTEN-STEIN
Inn R.
Innsbruck

AUSTRIA

SWITZERLAND

BRENNER PASS

ITALY

0 ___ Miles ___ 100

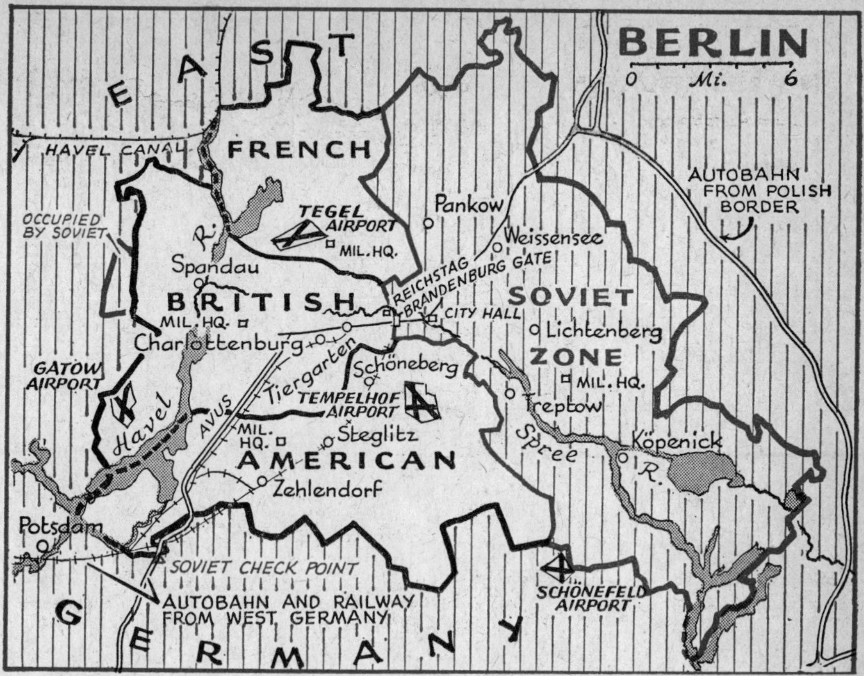

**BERLIN**

0  Mi.  6

E A S T

FRENCH

HAVEL CANAL

AUTOBAHN
FROM POLISH
BORDER

OCCUPIED
BY SOVIET

TEGEL
AIRPORT
MIL. HQ.

Pankow

Weissensee

Spandau

REICHSTAG
BRANDENBURG GATE

SOVIET

B R I T I S H

MIL. HQ.

CITY HALL

Lichtenberg

Charlottenburg

Tiergarten

Schöneberg

ZONE

MIL. HQ.

GATOW
AIRPORT

TEMPELHOF
AIRPORT

Treptow

AVUS

Havel

Spree

Köpenick

MIL.
HQ.

Steglitz

A M E R I C A N

Zehlendorf

Potsdam

SOVIET CHECK POINT

SCHÖNEFELD
AIRPORT

G E R M A N Y

AUTOBAHN AND RAILWAY
FROM WEST GERMANY

---

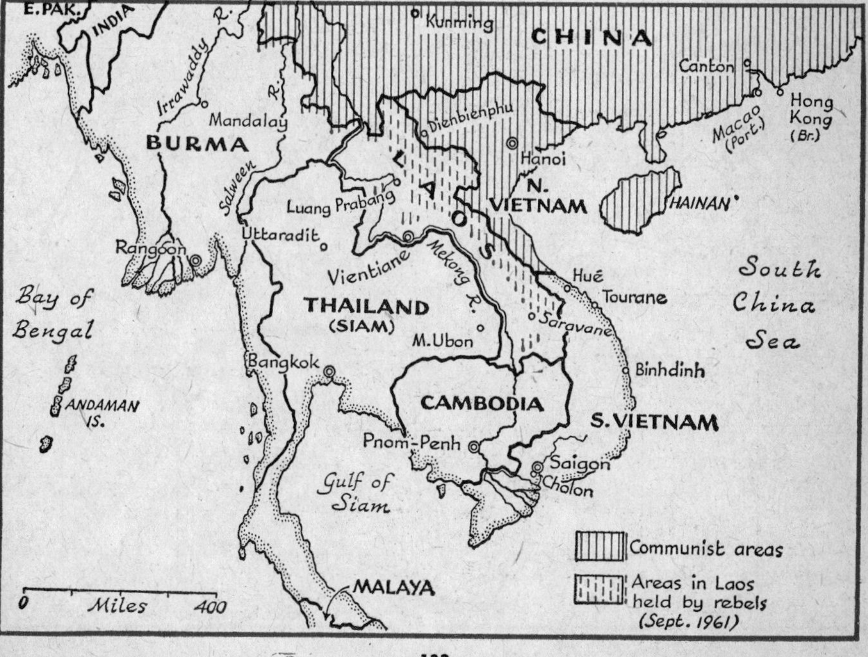

E. PAK.

INDIA

Kunming

C H I N A

Canton

Irrawaddy

Mandalay

Dienbienphu

Macao
(Port.)

Hong
Kong
(Br.)

BURMA

Salween

L A O S

Hanoi

N.
VIETNAM

HAINAN

Luang Prabang

Rangoon

Uttaradit

Mekong R.

Vientiane

Hué

South
China
Sea

Bay of
Bengal

THAILAND
(SIAM)

M. Ubon

Tourane

Saravane

Bangkok

CAMBODIA

Binhdinh

ANDAMAN
IS.

S. VIETNAM

Pnom-Penh

Saigon
Cholon

Gulf of
Siam

0    Miles    400

MALAYA

Communist areas

Areas in Laos
held by rebels
(Sept. 1961)

133

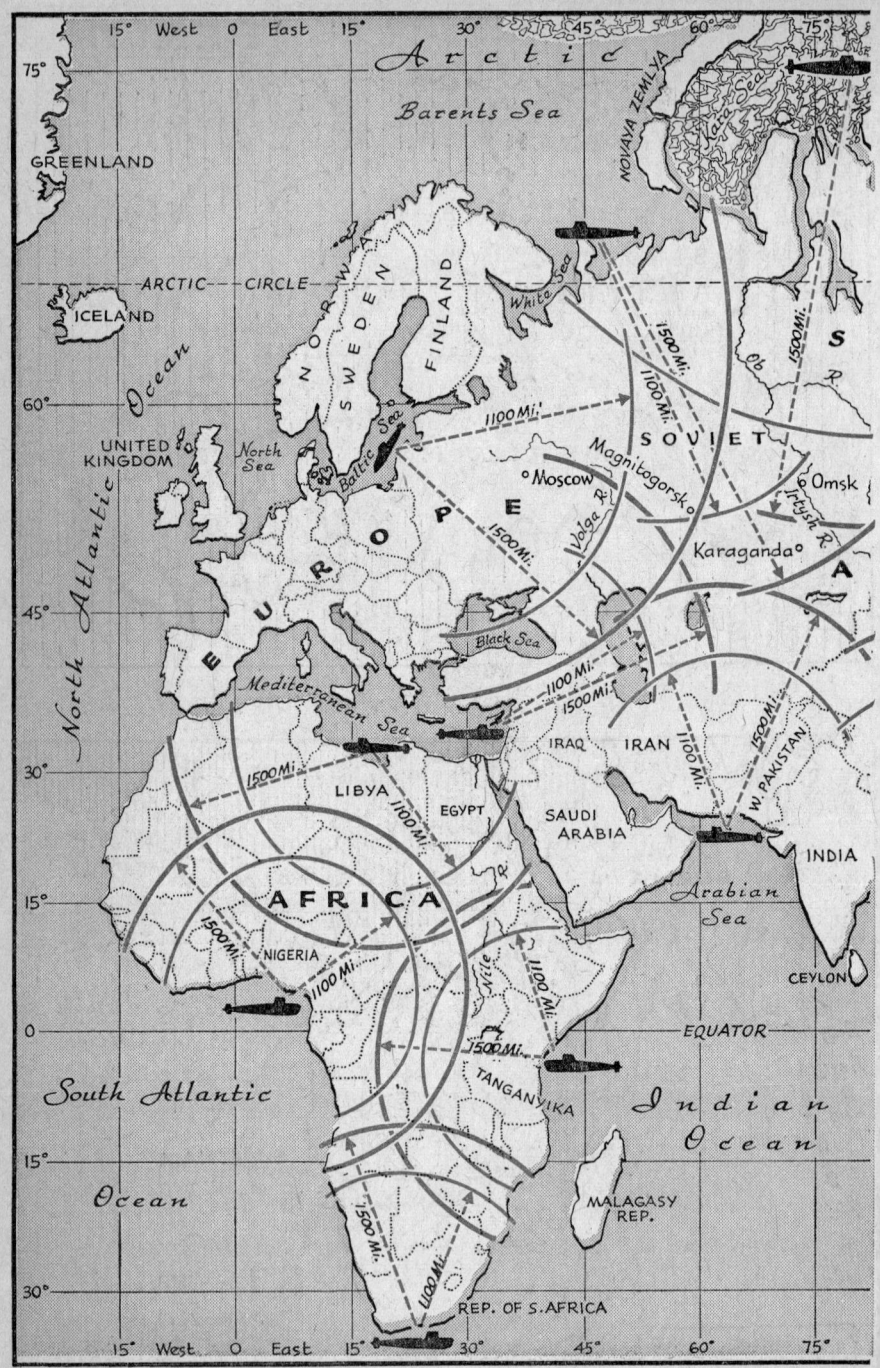

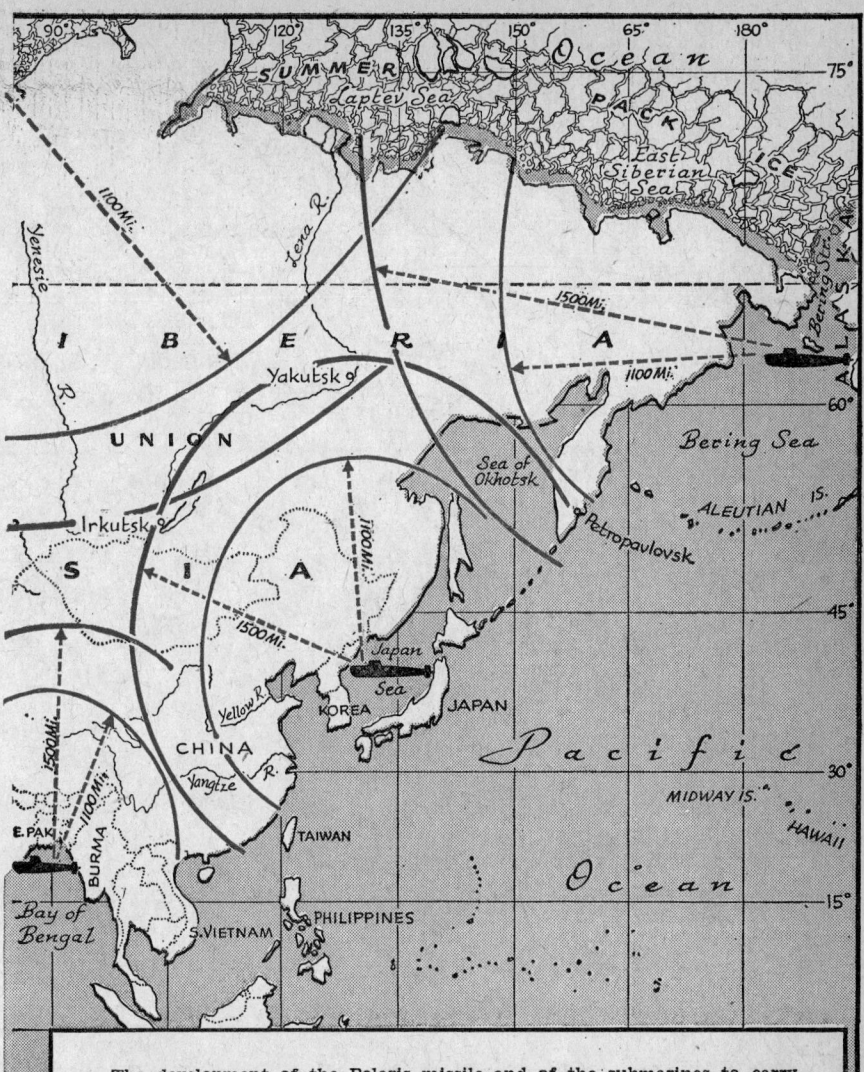

The development of the Polaris missile and of the submarines to carry them has given the United States a number of mobile missile bases which can change position at will and which will be very hard to detect. In fact a submarine hiding under the Arctic icepack may be considered virtually undetectable. The map shows positions which Polaris submarines might take. The two range circles are drawn for a range of 1,100 miles (that of the current Polaris missile) and for a range of 1,500 miles (the range of the improved Polaris missile now under development). It can be seen that a rather large area in Central Asia could not be reached with the 1,500-mile missile.

The different sizes of the range circles are caused by the distortion of the Mercator projection.

Each submarine carries 16 Polaris missiles which are ejected vertically by compressed air and ignite as soon as they break the surface of the water.

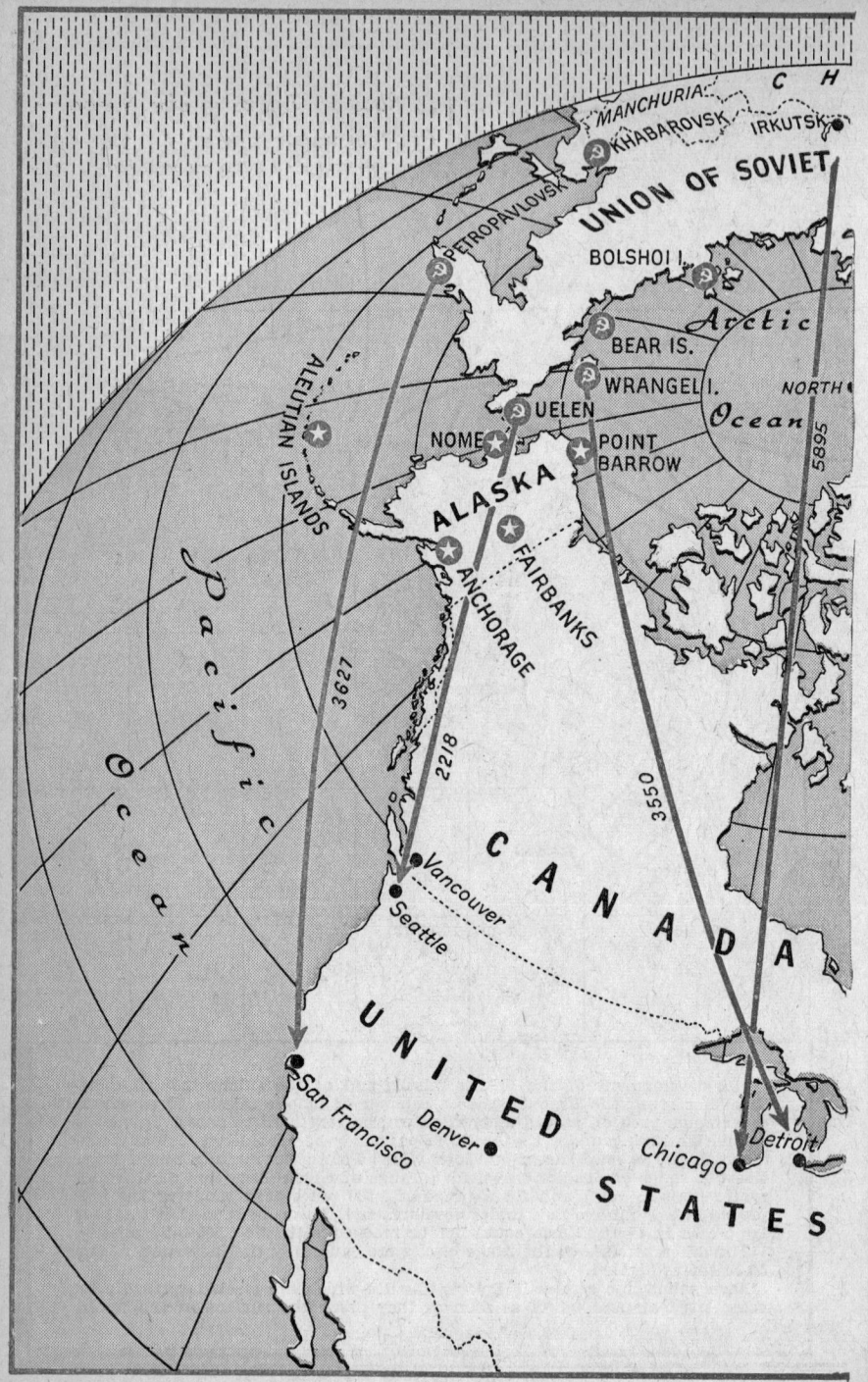

MANCHURIA
KHABAROVSK
IRKUTSK
C H

UNION OF SOVIET

PETROPAVLOVSK

BOLSHOI I.

*Arctic*

BEAR IS.

WRANGEL I.

NORTH

ALEUTIAN ISLANDS

UELEN

*Ocean*

NOME

POINT BARROW

ALASKA

5895

FAIRBANKS

ANCHORAGE

*Pacific*

3627

2218

3550

C A N A D A

*Ocean*

Vancouver

Seattle

U N I T E D

San Francisco

Denver

Chicago

Detroit

S T A T E S

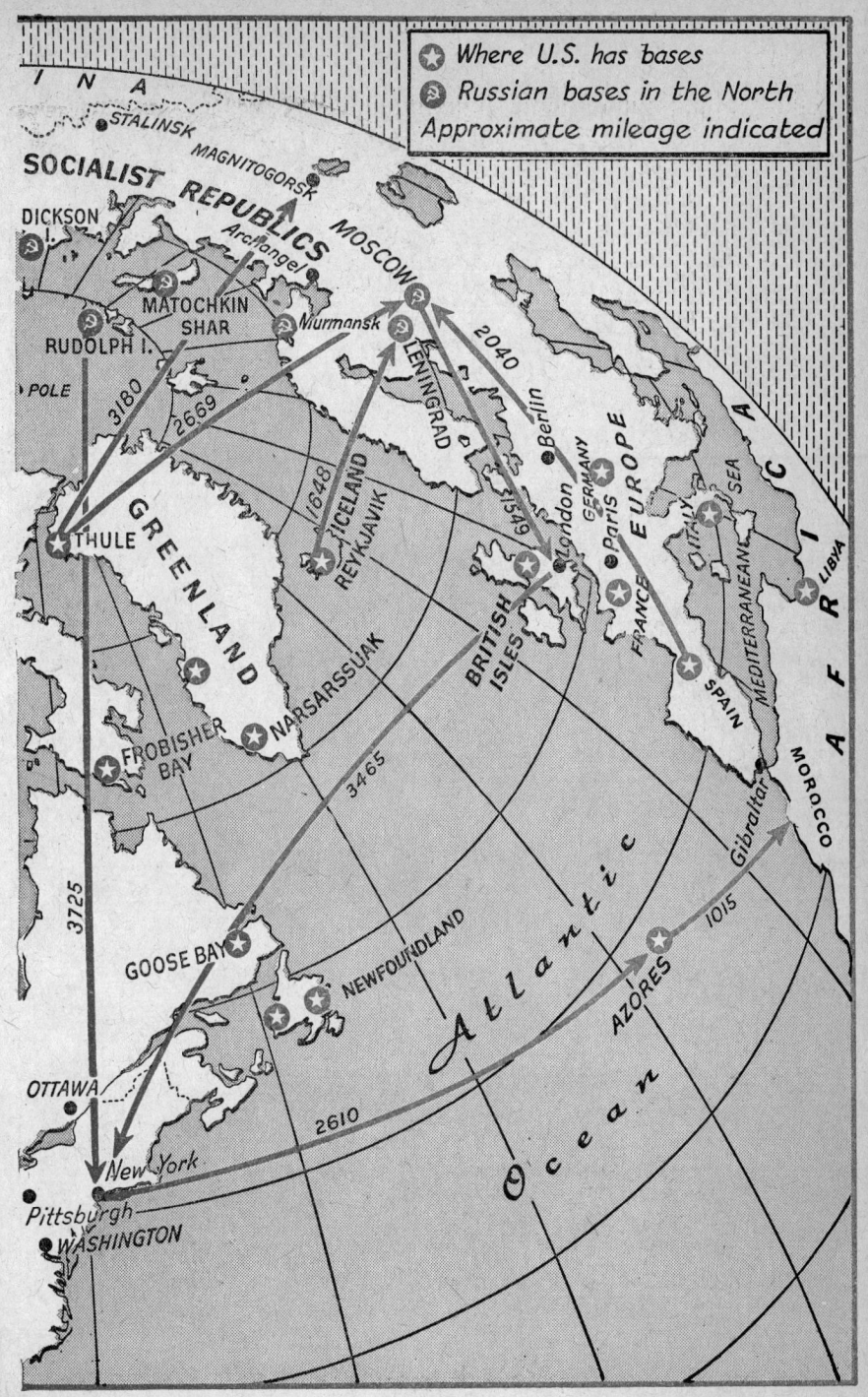

# SOUTH AMERICA

Miles 1000

PANAMA CANAL
CURAÇAO
WEST INDIES
Maracaibo
OIL
OIL
Caracas
TRINIDAD
VENEZUELA
BR. GUIANA
Georgetown
Paramaribo
Cayenne
DUTCH GUIANA
FR. GUIANA
AUXITE
COFFEE
Magdalena
OIL
Bogotá
Ciudad Bolívar
ANGEL FALLS
RON
Orinoco
COLOMBIA
MANGANESE
COCOA
Quito
ECUADOR
Negro
Branco
Belém
Fortaleza
Guayaquil
COCOA
Iquitos
Manaus
R.
Amazon
RUBBER
Natal
OIL
Marañón
Juruá
Ucayali
Madeira
RUBBER
B  R  A  Z  I  L
Parnaiba
Recife
COPPER
PERU
STEEL
Lima
Callao
COPPER
Tapajós
Xingu
MATO
GROSSO
Araguaia
São Francisco
DIAMONDS
COCOA
Salvador
TUNGSTEN
La Paz
Brasília
FEDERAL DISTRICT
CATTLE
Arequipa
TIN
BOLIVIA
Corumbá
STEEL
Belo Horizonte
MANGANESE
Sucre
TIN
CATTLE
Paraná
COFFEE
RON
Antofagasta
TIN
PARAGUAY
Campinas
São Paulo
Rio de Janeiro
NITRATES
Asunción
COFFEE
COPPER
Tucumán
CHILE
MANGANESE
RON
Salado
Paraguay
Uruguay
CATTLE
Pôrto Alegre
MT. ACONCAGUA 22,835 FT.
Córdoba
Rosario
Rio Grande
Valparaiso
Santiago
Buenos Aires
URUGUAY
Montevideo
Rio de la Plata
CATTLE
Colorado
COAL
Negro
Bahía Blanca
A  R  G  E  N  T  I  N  A
P  A  M  P  A  S
A  N  D  E  S
PATAGONIA
OIL
Punta Arenas
TIERRA DEL FUEGO
Strait of Magellan
Cape Horn

## CLIMATE

Tropical Rainforest
Savanna
Highland
Subtropical
Marine
Desert and Steppe

## POPULATION

■ Cities over 500,000

PERSONS PER SQUARE MILE
☐ 5 or less
▨ Over 150

## OCCUPATIONS

Virgin Forest
Lumbering
Agriculture
Livestock raising and grazing
Fishing

138

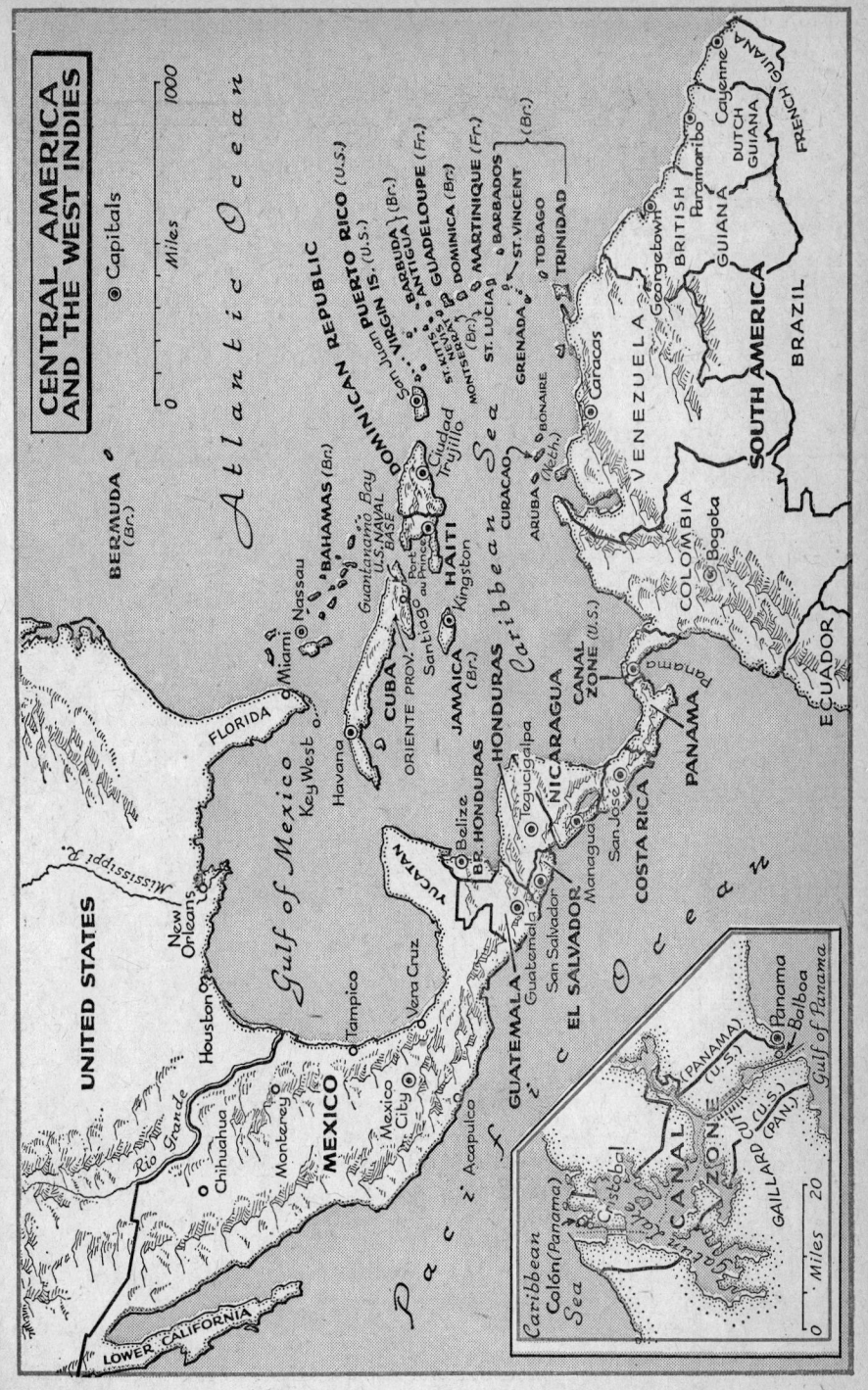

CENTRAL AMERICA AND THE WEST INDIES

● Capitals

Miles
0        1000

Atlantic Ocean

BERMUDA (Br.)

BAHAMAS (Br.)

Miami
Nassau
FLORIDA
Key West
Havana
CUBA
ORIENTE PROV.

Gulf of Mexico

New Orleans
Houston
Mississippi R.

UNITED STATES

MEXICO
Monterrey
Chihuahua
Rio Grande
Mexico City
Acapulco
Vera Cruz
Tampico
LOWER CALIFORNIA

YUCATAN
Belize
BR. HONDURAS
GUATEMALA
Guatemala
San Salvador
EL SALVADOR
HONDURAS
Tegucigalpa
NICARAGUA
Managua
COSTA RICA
San José
PANAMA
Panama
CANAL ZONE (U.S.)

Pacific Ocean

JAMAICA (Br.)
Kingston
Santiago
HAITI
Port au Prince
Guantanamo Bay
U.S. NAVAL BASE

DOMINICAN REPUBLIC
Ciudad Trujillo

Caribbean Sea

PUERTO RICO (U.S.)
San Juan
VIRGIN IS. (U.S.)
ST. KITTS
NEVIS (Br.)
MONTSERRAT (Br.)
BARBUDA (Br.)
ANTIGUA (Br.)
GUADELOUPE (Fr.)
DOMINICA (Br.)
MARTINIQUE (Fr.)
ST. LUCIA (Br.)
BARBADOS
ST. VINCENT
GRENADA
TOBAGO
TRINIDAD (Br.)

CURACAO
ARUBA (Neth.)
BONAIRE

Caracas
VENEZUELA
Bogota
COLOMBIA
ECUADOR

Georgetown
BRITISH GUIANA
Paramaribo
DUTCH GUIANA
Cayenne
FRENCH GUIANA

SOUTH AMERICA
BRAZIL

Caribbean Sea
Colón (Panama)
Cristóbal
CANAL ZONE
GAILLARD CUT (U.S.)
(U.S.)
(PANAMA)
COLOMBIA (PAN.)
Panama
Balboa
Gulf of Panama

Miles
0        20

139

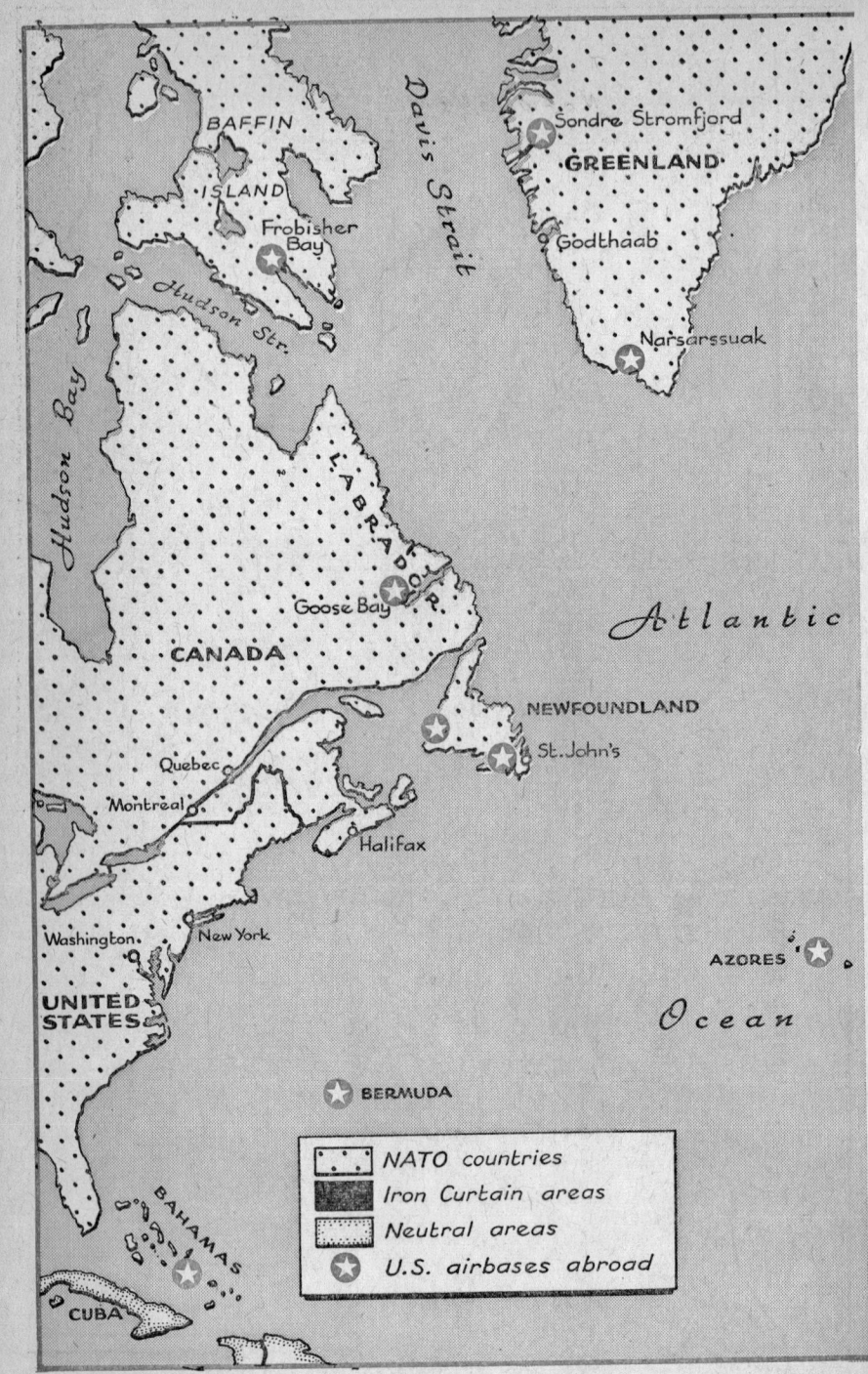

BAFFIN ISLAND

Davis Strait

Frobisher Bay

Hudson Str.

Hudson Bay

Sondre Stromfjord

GREENLAND

Godthaab

Narsarssuak

LABRADOR

Goose Bay

CANADA

Atlantic

NEWFOUNDLAND

Quebec

St. John's

Montreal

Halifax

Washington

New York

AZORES

Ocean

UNITED STATES

BERMUDA

BAHAMAS

CUBA

| | |
|---|---|
| ·.·. | NATO countries |
| ▓ | Iron Curtain areas |
| ▫ | Neutral areas |
| ⊛ | U.S. airbases abroad |

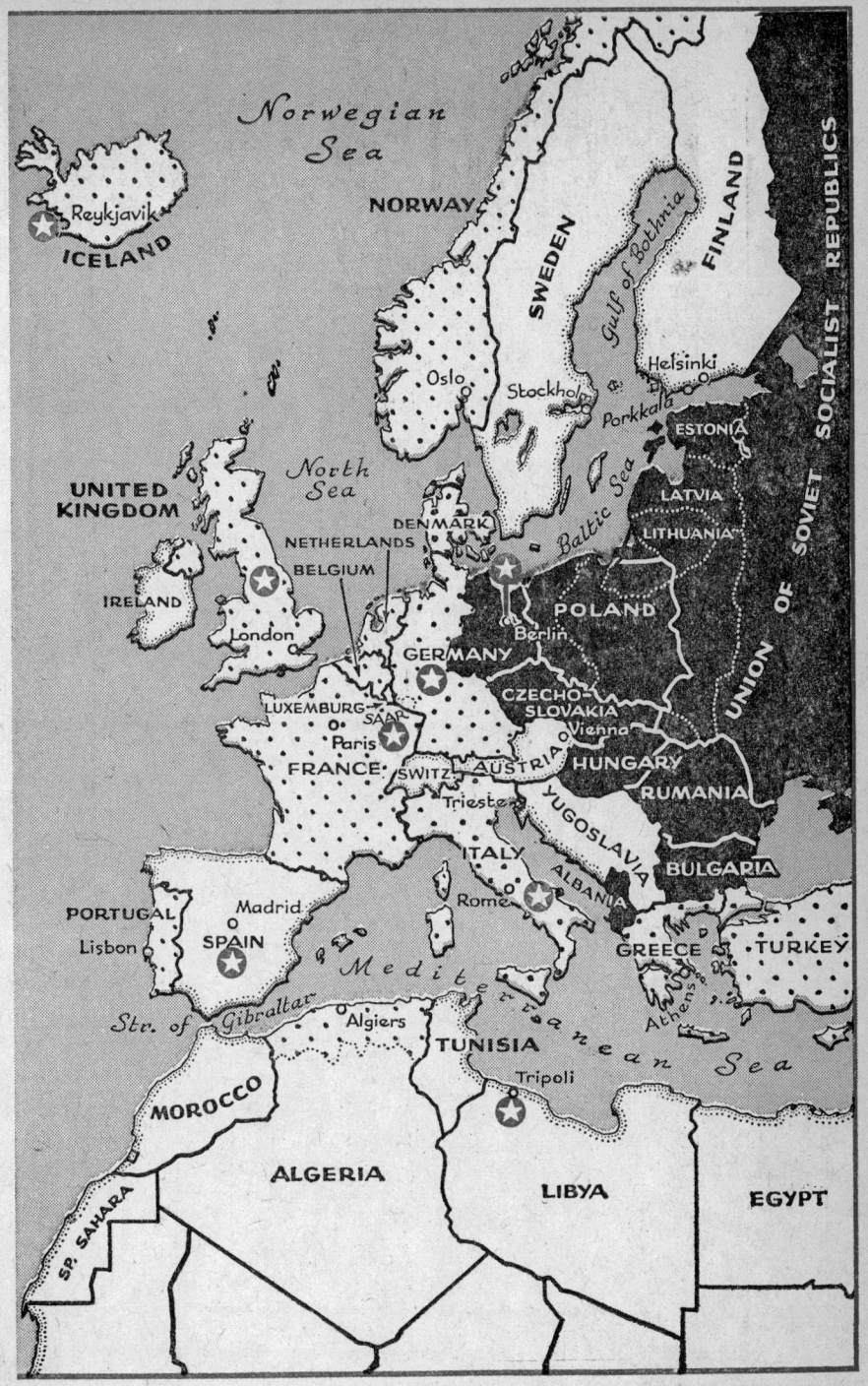

Norwegian
Sea

ICELAND
Reykjavik

NORWAY

SWEDEN

FINLAND

Gulf of Bothnia

Oslo

Stockholm

Helsinki

Porkkala

UNION OF SOVIET SOCIALIST REPUBLICS

North
Sea

UNITED
KINGDOM

IRELAND

London

NETHERLANDS
BELGIUM

DENMARK

Baltic Sea

Berlin

POLAND

ESTONIA

LATVIA

LITHUANIA

GERMANY

LUXEMBURG
SAAR
Paris

FRANCE

SWITZ. AUSTRIA

Vienna

CZECHO-
SLOVAKIA

HUNGARY

RUMANIA

Trieste

YUGOSLAVIA

ITALY

ALBANIA

BULGARIA

Rome

PORTUGAL

Madrid

SPAIN

Lisbon

Mediterranean Sea

GREECE

Athens

TURKEY

Str. of Gibraltar

Algiers

TUNISIA

Tripoli

MOROCCO

SP. SAHARA

ALGERIA

LIBYA

EGYPT

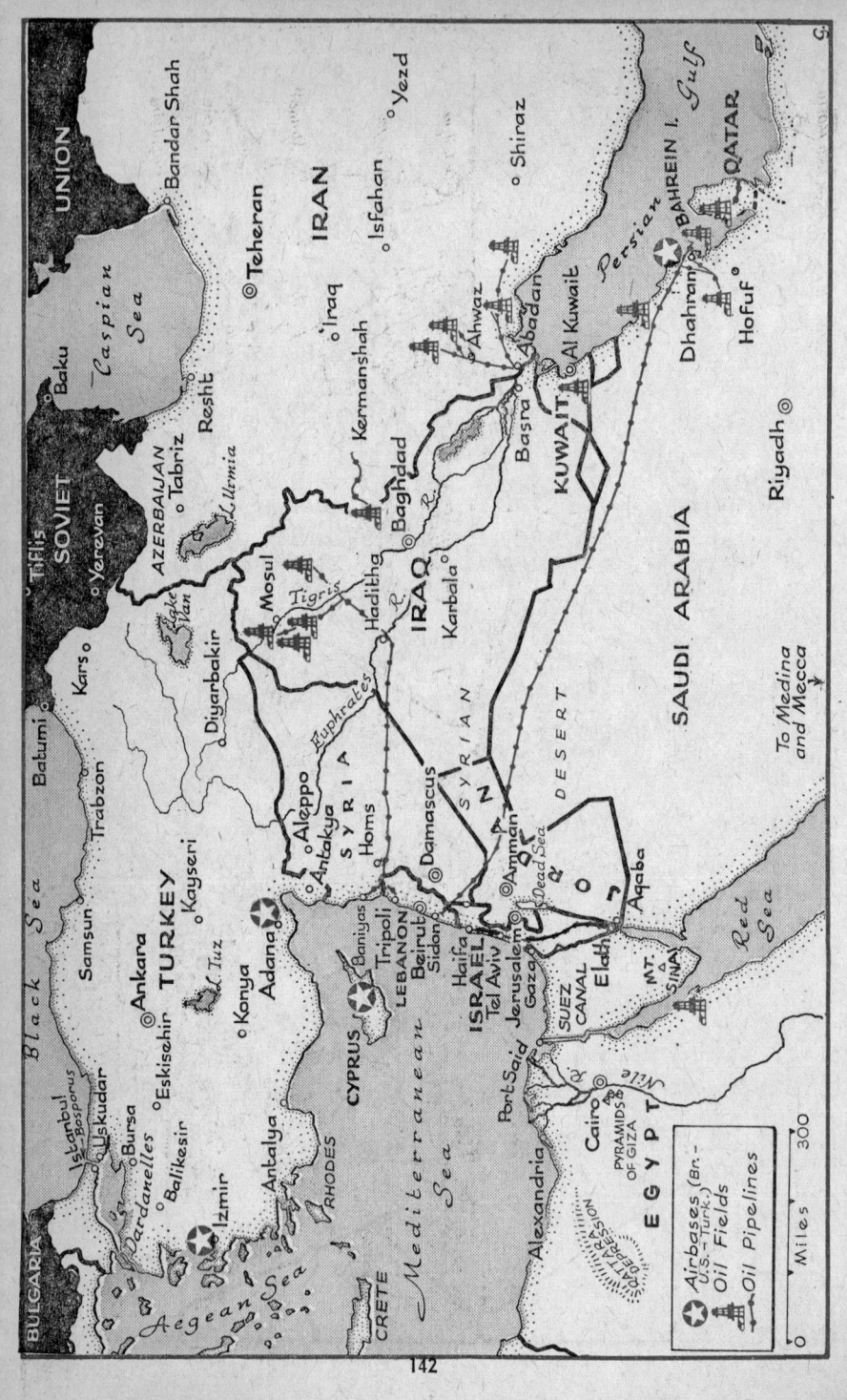

142

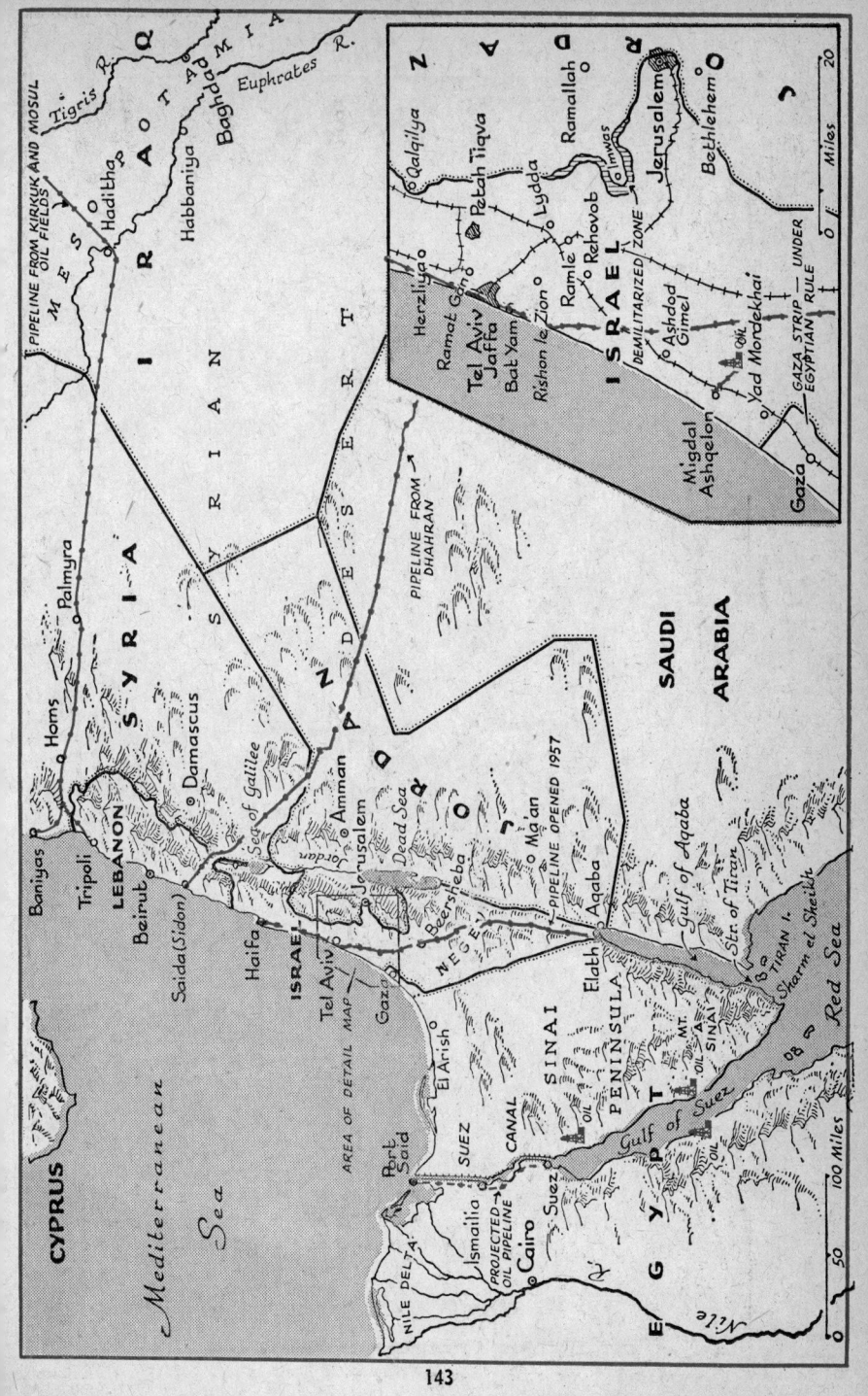

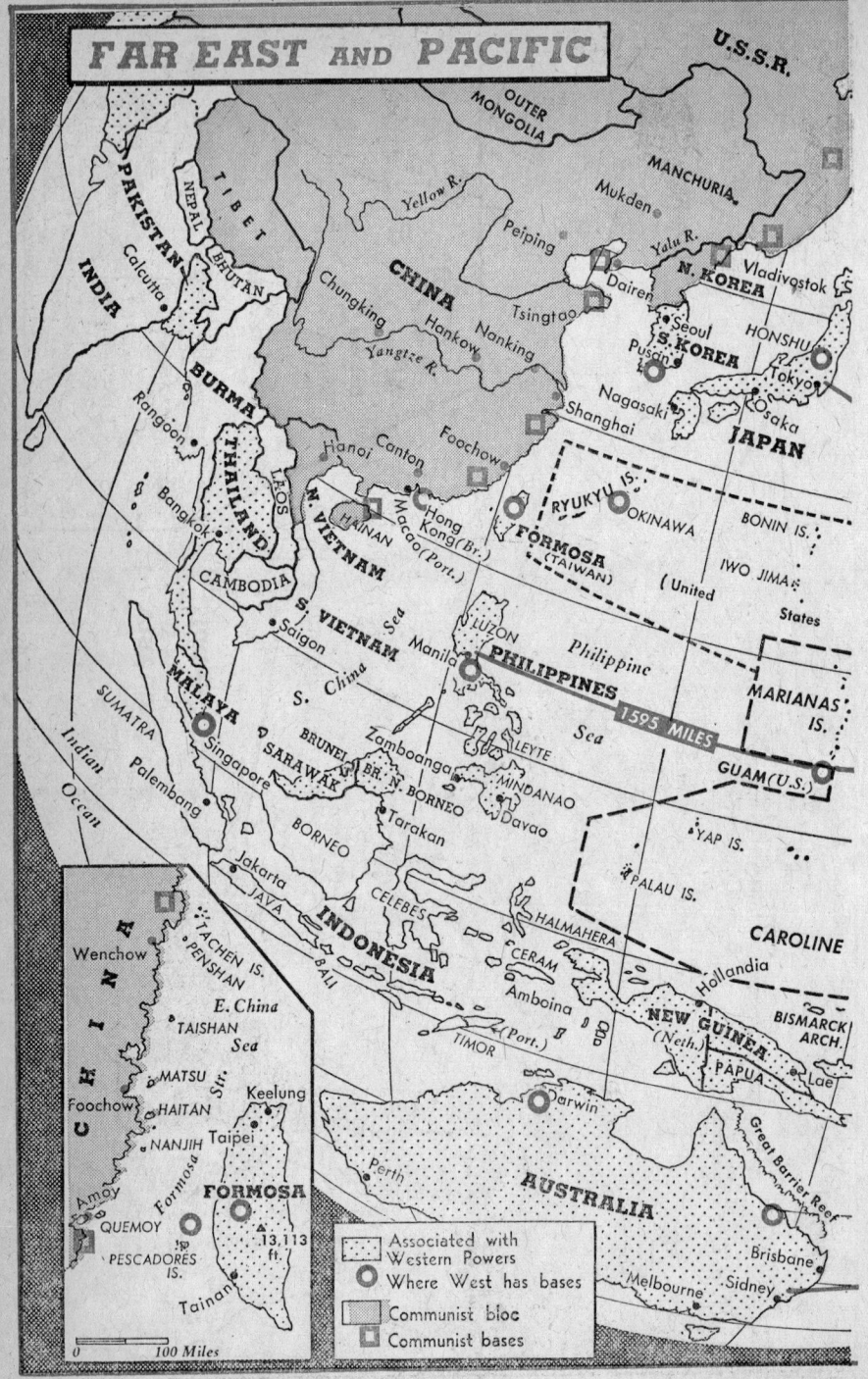

# FAR EAST AND PACIFIC

U.S.S.R.

OUTER MONGOLIA

MANCHURIA

Mukden

Peiping

Yellow R.

Vladivostok

N. KOREA

Yalu R.

HONSHU

PAKISTAN

NEPAL

BHUTAN

TIBET

CHINA

INDIA

Calcutta

BURMA

Chungking

Hankow

Nanking

Tsingtao

Dairen

Seoul

S. KOREA

Pusan

Tokyo

Osaka

JAPAN

Nagasaki

Rangoon

Yangtze R.

Foochow

Shanghai

THAILAND

LAOS

Hanoi

Canton

Hong Kong (Br.)

Macao (Port.)

RYUKYU IS.

OKINAWA

BONIN IS.

Bangkok

N. VIETNAM

HAINAN

FORMOSA (TAIWAN)

IWO JIMA

Saigon

CAMBODIA

S. VIETNAM

S. China Sea

Manila

LUZON

PHILIPPINES

Philippine Sea

(United States

MARIANAS IS.

MALAYA

SUMATRA

Singapore

BRUNEI

SARAWAK

BR. N. BORNEO

Zamboanga

LEYTE

1595 MILES

Palembang

Indian Ocean

Jakarta

JAVA

BALI

BORNEO

Tarakan

MINDANAO

Davao

GUAM (U.S.)

YAP IS.

PALAU IS.

CELEBES

HALMAHERA

CERAM

Amboina

(Port.)

CAROLINE

INDONESIA

TIMOR

NEW GUINEA (Neth.)

Hollandia

BISMARCK ARCH.

PAPUA

Lae

Darwin

AUSTRALIA

Perth

Brisbane

Sidney

Melbourne

## CHINA inset

CHINA

Wenchow

TACHEN IS.

PENSHAN

E. China Sea

TAISHAN

MATSU

HAITAN

Foochow

NANJIH

Taipei

Keelung

Formosa Str.

FORMOSA

13,113 ft.

Amoy

QUEMOY

PESCADORES IS.

Tainan

0        100 Miles

Associated with Western Powers

Where West has bases

Communist bloc

Communist bases

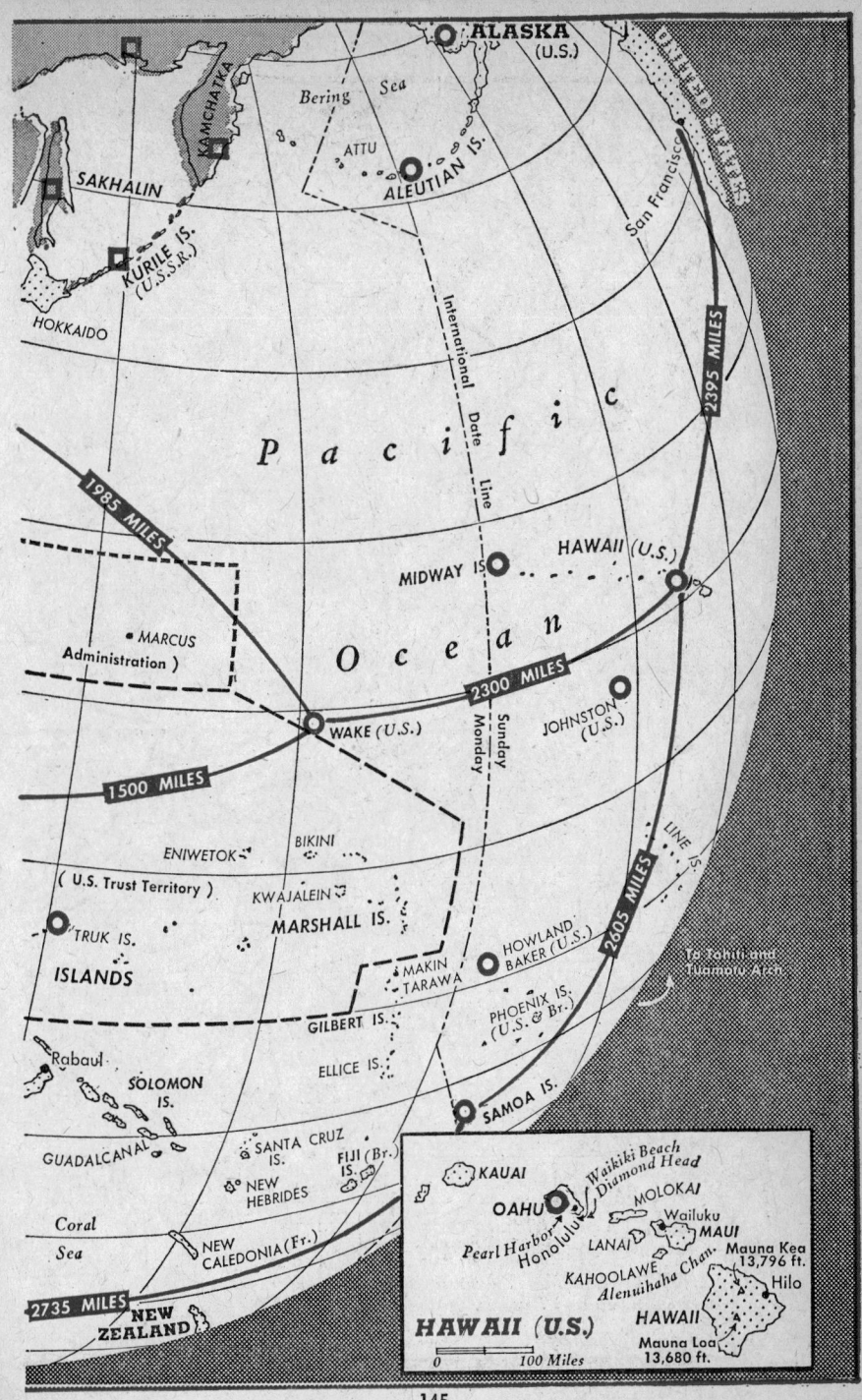

ALASKA (U.S.)

Bering Sea

KAMCHATKA

ATTU

ALEUTIAN IS.

SAKHALIN

KURILE IS.
(U.S.S.R.)

HOKKAIDO

San Francisco

2395 MILES

P a c i f i c

International Date Line

1985 MILES

O c e a n

MIDWAY IS.

HAWAII (U.S.)

• MARCUS
Administration )

2300 MILES

Sunday Monday

JOHNSTON
(U.S.)

WAKE (U.S.)

1500 MILES

ENIWETOK

BIKINI

( U.S. Trust Territory )

KWAJALEIN

LINE IS.

TRUK IS.

MARSHALL IS.

ISLANDS

MAKIN
TARAWA

HOWLAND
BAKER (U.S.)

2605 MILES

To Tahiti and
Tuamotu Arch.

Rabaul

GILBERT IS.

PHOENIX IS.
( U.S. & Br.)

SOLOMON
IS.

ELLICE IS.

GUADALCANAL

SANTA CRUZ
IS.

NEW
HEBRIDES

FIJI (Br.)
IS.

SAMOA IS.

Coral
Sea

NEW
CALEDONIA (Fr.)

2735 MILES

NEW
ZEALAND

KAUAI

Waikiki Beach
Diamond Head

OAHU

MOLOKAI

Wailuku

Pearl Harbor
Honolulu

LANAI

MAUI

KAHOOLAWE

Mauna Kea
13,796 ft.

Alenuihaha Chan.

Hilo

HAWAII (U.S.)

HAWAII

Mauna Loa
13,680 ft.

0      100 Miles

EURASIA

**C** CENTO (*Central Treaty Organization, formerly Baghdad Pact*) Plus U.S.A.

**S** SEATO (*Southeast Asia Treaty Organization*) Plus New Zealand & U.S.A.

⊙ Capital cities

146

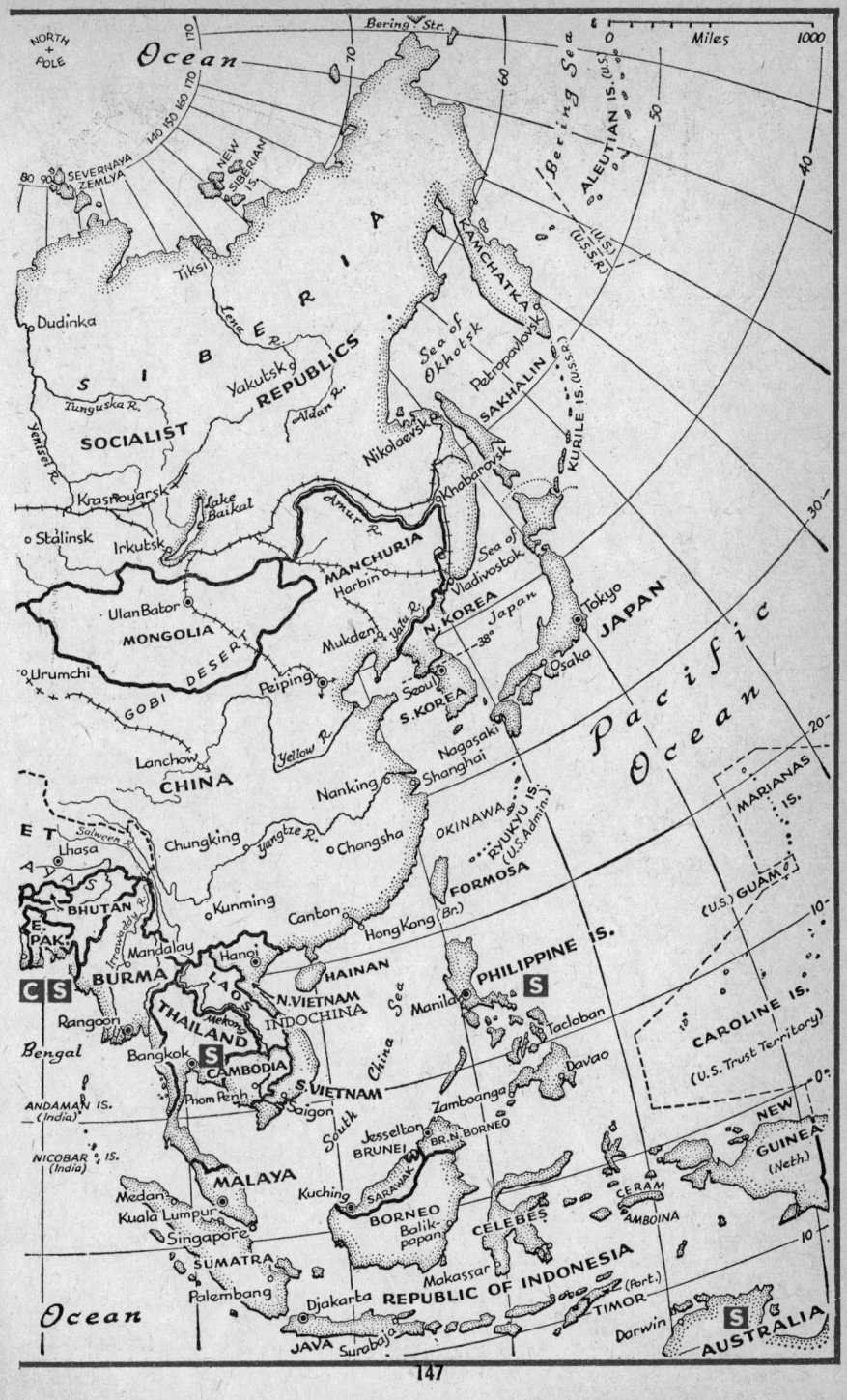

NORTH POLE

Ocean

Bering Str.

Bering Sea

Miles                    1000

ALEUTIAN IS. (U.S.)

(U.S.S.R.)

SEVERNAYA ZEMLYA

NEW SIBERIAN IS.

KAMCHATKA

S I B E R I A

Dudinka

Tiksi

Lena R.

Yakutsk

SOCIALIST

REPUBLICS

Aldan R.

Sea of Okhotsk

Petropavlovsk

SAKHALIN

KURILE IS. (U.S.S.R.)

Tunguska R.

Yenisei R.

Krasnoyarsk

Stalinsk

Irkutsk

Lake Baikal

Nikolaevsk

Khabarovsk

Amur R.

MANCHURIA

Harbin

Sea of Japan

Vladivostok

JAPAN

Urumchi

UlanBator

MONGOLIA

GOBI DESERT

Mukden

Yalu R.

N. KOREA

Tokyo

Osaka

Peiping

Seoul

S. KOREA

Pacific

Lanchow

Yellow R.

CHINA

Nanking

Nagasaki

Shanghai

Ocean

MARIANAS IS.

Lhasa

Salween R.

BHUTAN

E. PAK.

Chungking

Yangtze R.

Changsha

OKINAWA

RYUKYU IS. (U.S. Admin.)

FORMOSA

(U.S.) GUAM

Kunming

Canton

Hong Kong (Br.)

CAROLINE IS.

(U.S. Trust Territory)

BURMA

Mandalay

Irrawaddy R.

HAINAN

PHILIPPINE IS.

S

C S

Rangoon

LAOS

Hanoi

N. VIETNAM

INDOCHINA

China

Sea

Manila

S

THAILAND

Mekong R.

Bengal

Bangkok

S

CAMBODIA

S. VIETNAM

Tacloban

Davao

ANDAMAN IS. (India)

Phom Penh

Saigon

Zamboanga

NICOBAR IS. (India)

South

China

Sea

Jesselton

BRUNEI

BR. N. BORNEO

NEW GUINEA (Neth.)

MALAYA

SARAWAK

CERAM

Medan

Kuala Lumpur

Kuching

BORNEO

Balikpapan

CELEBES

AMBOINA

Singapore

SUMATRA

Makassar

REPUBLIC OF INDONESIA

TIMOR (Port.)

S

Palembang

Djakarta

Darwin

AUSTRALIA

Ocean

JAVA

Suroboja

147

EUROPE AND THE NEAR EAST

⭐ Countries in which West has bases
▓ Communist bloc    ⦿ Capitals

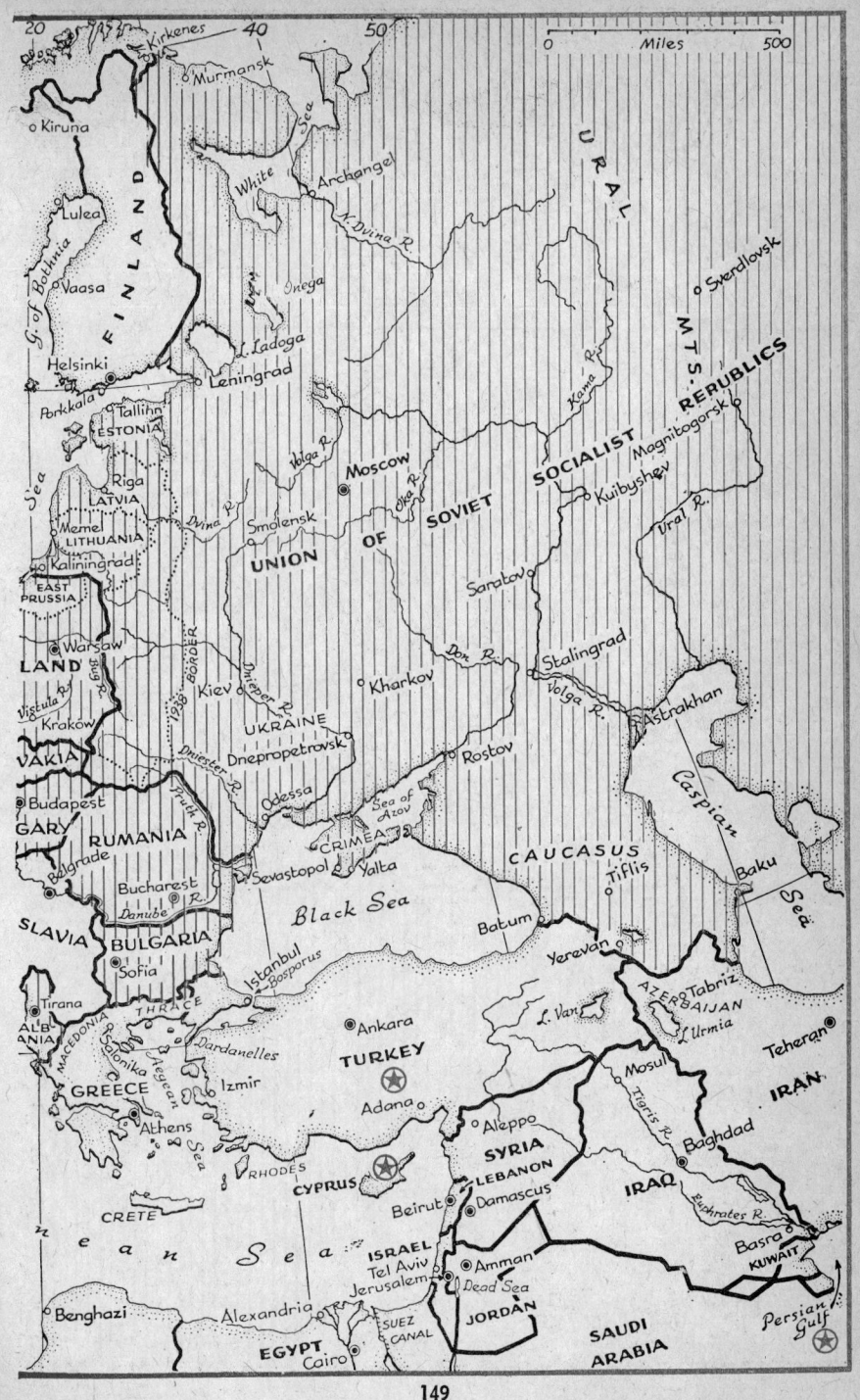

# UNITED STATES

( EXCLUDING ALASKA AND HAWAII )

150

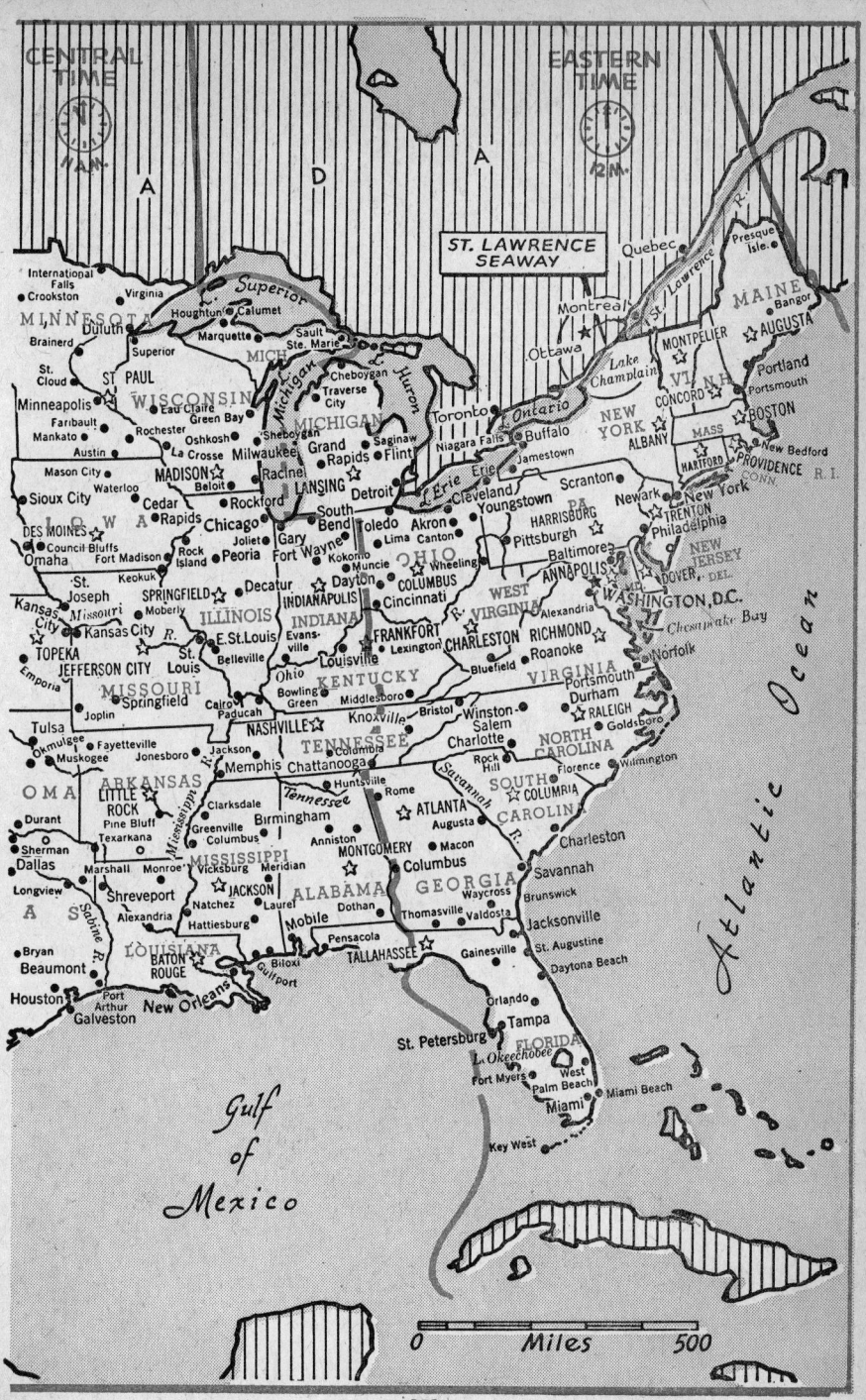

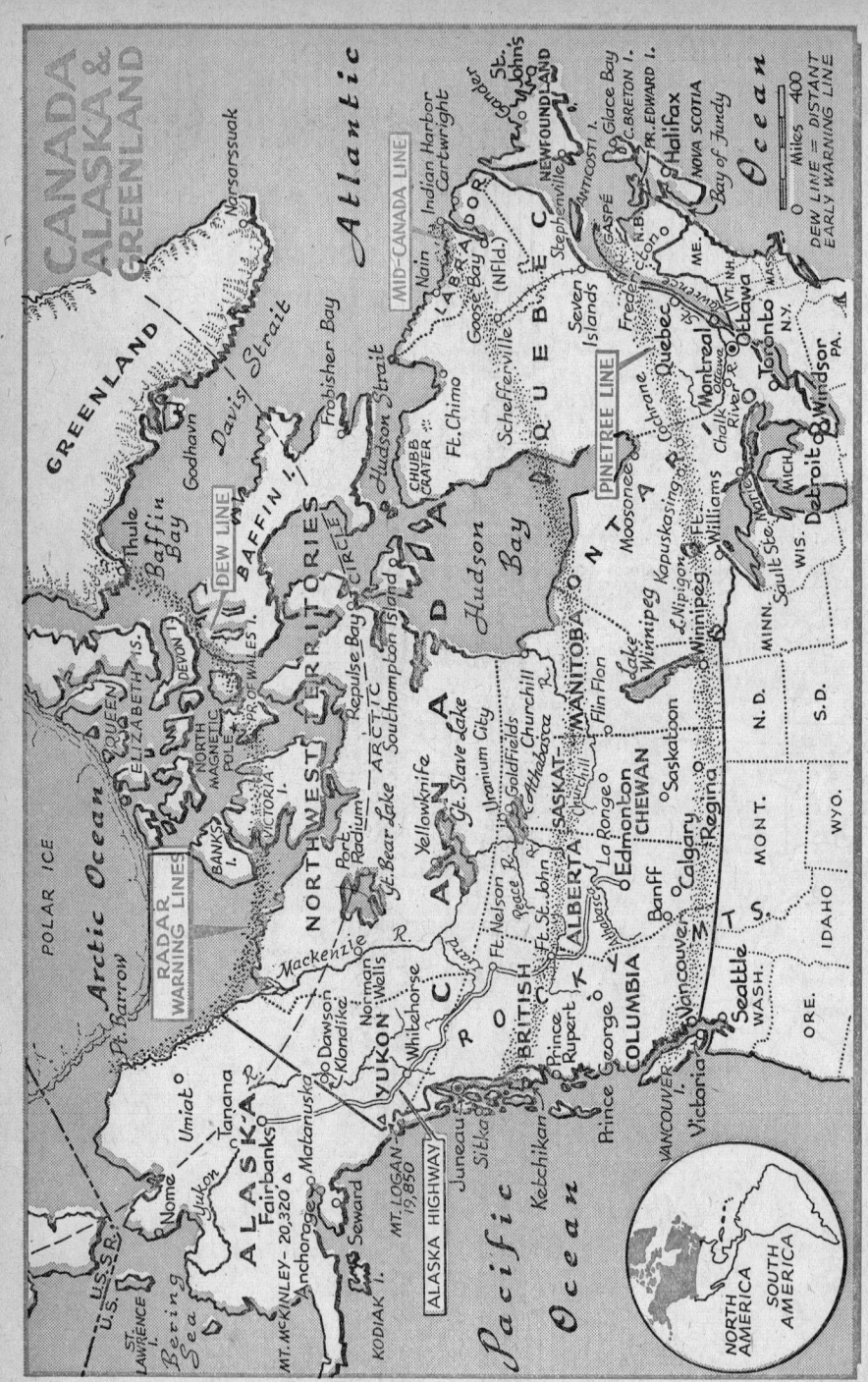

CANADA
ALASKA &
GREENLAND

GREENLAND

Atlantic

Ocean

0 Miles 400
O——O DEW LINE = DISTANT
EARLY WARNING LINE

MID-CANADA LINE

DEW LINE

PINETREE LINE

RADAR
WARNING LINES

Arctic Ocean

POLAR ICE

U.S.S.R.

Bering Sea

Pacific Ocean

ALASKA HIGHWAY

NORTH
AMERICA

SOUTH
AMERICA

152

BRITISH ISLES

Atlantic

Ocean

Stromness
C. Wrath
ORKNEY IS.
I. of LEWIS
HARRIS
Scapa Flow
Thurso
John o'Groats
Ullapool
Wick
I. of SKYE
Kyle
Moray Firth
GLEN MORE
Inverness
Loch Ness
HIGHLANDS
Peterhead
I. of MULL
Grampian Mts.
Aberdeen
HEBRIDES
SCOTLAND
ISLAY
Perth
Dundee
Greenock
Clydebank
BELL ROCK
St. Andrews
North Channel
Glasgow
Firth of Forth
Prestwick
Clyde
Edinburgh
Ayr
Tweed R.
Berwick
Londonderry
Southern
HOLY ISLAND
N. IRELAND
Uplands
L. Neagh
Dumfries
Carrick
ROMAN WALL
Belfast
Carlisle
Newcastle
Downpatrick
LAKE DIST.
South Shields
I. of MAN
Sunderland
Drogheda
Douglas
PENNINES
IRELAND
Irish Sea
Middlesbrough
Shannon
Dublin
Liverpool
Blackpool
Wicklow
Birkenhead
Manchester
York
Holyhead
Leeds
Waterford
ANGLESEY
Hull
Bangor
Chester
Wexford
Sheffield
St. George Channel
Cambrian Mts.
Stoke
WALES
Derby
Milford Haven
Birmingham
Nottingham
THE WASH
Coventry
THE FENS
Stratford on Avon
Trent R.
Norwich
Swansea
Severn R.
ENGLAND
Cardiff
Bristol
Cambridge
Barnstaple
Bath
Oxford
Ipswich
LAND'S END
Exeter
Salisbury
THE MOORS
LONDON
Harwich
Thames
Penzance
Plymouth
Southampton
Thames
Canterbury
Weymouth
Dover
Bournemouth
THE DOWNS
Portsmouth
Brighton
I. of WIGHT
Hastings
Strait of Dover
Calais
BEL.

English Channel

North Sea

Irish Sea

CHANNEL IS. (Br.)
Cherbourg
FRANCE

0    Miles    100

153

**GREAT BRITAIN**

LONDON

*English Channel*

*Atlantic Ocean*

GERMANY

*Rhine R.*

**BEL.** **LUX.**
Str. of Dover
Dunkerque
Calais Lille Valenciennes
SAAR
Amiens Cambrai Laon Sedan Nancy
Dieppe Compiègne Rheims Strasbourg
LeHavre Rouen Beauvais Châlons-sur-M. Baccarat
Cherbourg Caen Versailles Troyes
St.Lo **PARIS** Seine Sens Dijon **SWITZ.**
CHANNEL IS.(Br.) Fontainebleau
Mont St.Michel Chartres Orleans Geneva
Rennes LeMans R. JURA MTS. Chamonix
Brest **F R A N C E** Blois 5,771
**BRITTANY** Tours Bourges Saône R. Chambéry
Loire Châteauroux Vichy Lyon ALPS
Lorient Poitiers Clermont- St. Grenoble
St.Nazaire Nantes Ferrand Etienne
Limoges △6188' Monte Carlo
Rochefort Cognac CENTRAL Nice
*Gironde R.* Brive PLATEAU Orange RIVIERA
Avignon Aix
**Bordeaux** Garonne Nîmes Arles
*Bay of Biscay* Montpellier Toulon
LANDES R. Albi Marseille
Biarritz **Toulouse** Narbonne
Hendaye Lourdes Prades Perpignan
San Sebastián P Y R E N E E S ANDORRA
Santander Gerona
Gijón **Bilbao** Burgos Barcelona
Ferrol Oviedo Lérida
Coruña **GALICIA** Ebro R. Tarragona BALEARIC MINORCA
León Zaragoza Tortosa
Vigo Palencia A R A G O N MAJORCA
(Duero) R. Teruel Palma ISLANDS
Oporto Douro R. **Valladolid** Valencia
Salamanca IVIZA
**MADRID** **S P A I N** FORMENTERA
Coimbra Toledo Júcar R.
Tajo (Tagus) Alcázar Albacete
PORTUGAL Ciudad Alicante
Guadiana Real
**LISBON** Badajoz Linares Murcia
Evora Córdoba Cartagena Algiers
Setúbal Guadalquivir R. Oran
Sevilla **ANDALUSIA** Granada
Faro Malaga *Mediterranean Sea*
Cádiz LaLinea
*Strait of Gibraltar* GIBRALTAR(Br.)
Ceuta
Tangier

# FRANCE
# SPAIN
# & PORTUGAL

△ MOUNTAIN PEAK
Heights in feet

0 *Miles* 300

ITALY
AUSTRIA &
SWITZERLAND

MOUNTAIN PASS
MOUNTAIN PEAK

0    Miles    200

155

# Forms of Address

Reprinted by permission. From Webster's New International Dictionary, 2nd Edition, copyright 1959 by G. & C. Merriam Co., Publishers of the Merriam-Webster Dictionaries.

**Abbot.** *Address:* The Right Reverend _____ _____, Abbot of _____. *Begin:* Right Reverend and dear Father.

**Alderman.** *Address:* Honorable _____ _____. *Begin:* Dear Sir.

**Ambassador.** *Address:* His Excellency, _____ _____, Ambassador of _____ at _____. *Begin:* Sir; *or* Excellency.

**Ambassador and his wife.** *Address:* His Excellency, The _____ Ambassador and Mrs. _____ _____. *Begin:* Your Excellencies.

**Archbishop (Anglican).** *Address:* The Most Reverend His Grace the Lord Archbishop of _____. *Begin:* My Lord Archbishop; *or* Your Grace.

**Archbishop (Roman Catholic).** *Address:* The Most Reverend _____ _____, D.D., Archbishop of _____. *Begin:* Your Excellency.

**Archdeacon.** *Address:* The Venerable The Archdeacon of _____. *Begin:* Venerable Sir.

**Army Officers.** *Address:* The Commander in Chief, Army of the U. S.; *or* (use officer's rank) _____ _____, U.S.A. *Begin:* Sir; *or* My dear General _____.

**Assemblyman.** *Address:* The Honorable _____ _____, Member of Assembly; *or* Assemblyman _____. *Begin:* Sir; *or* My dear Mr. _____.

**Assistant Secretary (Assistant to a Cabinet Officer).** *Address:* Honorable _____ _____, Assistant Secretary of _____. *Begin:* Sir; *or* Dear Mr. _____.

**Associate Justice.** *Address:* The Honorable _____ _____, United States Supreme Court; *or* Mr. Justice _____, The Supreme Court. *Begin:* Mr. Justice; *or* Dear Justice.

**Baron.** *Address:* The Right Honourable Lord _____; *or* The Lord _____. *Begin:* My Lord.

**Baroness.** *Address:* The Right Honourable the Baroness _____; *or* The Lady _____. *Begin:* Madam.

**Baronet.** *Address:* Sir John _____, Bt. *or* Bart. *Begin:* Sir.

**Baronet's wife.** See *Lady,* below.

**Baron's wife.** See *Baroness,* above.

**Bishop (Anglican).** *Address:* The Right Reverend the Lord Bishop of _____; *or* The Lord Bishop of _____. *Begin:* My Lord Bishop; *or* My Lord.

**Bishop (Methodist).** *Address:* Reverend Bishop _____ _____. *Begin:* Dear Sir; *or* My dear Bishop _____.

**Bishop (Protestant Episcopal).** *Address:* To the Right Reverend _____ _____, Bishop of _____. *Begin:* Right Reverend and Dear Sir; *or* Dear Bishop _____.

**Bishop (Roman Catholic).** *Address:* The Most Reverend _____ _____, Bishop of _____. *Begin:* Your Excellency; *or* Most Reverend Sir.

**Cabinet Officers (U. S.).** *Address:* The Honorable the Secretary of State (or Labor, etc.); The Secretary of State, etc. *Begin:* Sir; *or* My dear Mr. Secretary.

**Canon.** *Address:* The Very Reverend Canon _____ _____; *or* The Very Reverend _____, Canon of _____. *Begin:* Very Reverend Canon; *or* Dear Canon _____.

**Cardinal.** *Address:* His Eminence John, Cardinal _____. *Begin:* Your Eminence.

**Cardinal (if also an Archbishop).** *Address:* His Eminence _____, Cardinal _____, Archbishop of _____. *Begin:* Your Eminence.

**Chargé d'Affaires.** *Address:* The Chargé d'Affaires of _____; *or* _____ _____, Esq., Chargé d'Affaires. *Begin:* Dear Sir; *or* My dear Mr. _____.

**Chief Justice of the U. S.** *Address:* The Chief Justice of the U. S.; *or* The Chief Justice, The Supreme Court, Washington, D. C. *Begin:* My dear Mr. Chief Justice; *or* Sir.

**Clergyman.** *Address:* The Reverend _____ _____; *or* (if doctor of divinity) The Rev. Dr. _____ _____. *Begin:* Dear Sir; *or* Reverend Sir.

**Clerk of Senate or House.** *Address:* The Honorable _____ _____, Clerk of _____. *Begin:* Sir; *or* Dear Sir.

**Commissioner of Bureau.** *Address:* The Honorable _____ _____, Commissioner of the Bureau of _____. *Begin:* Sir; *or* Dear Sir.

**Congressman.** *Address:* Honorable James H. Smith, House of Representatives. *Begin:* Sir; *or* Dear Sir.

**Consul.** *Address:* To the American Consul at _____; *or* _____ _____, Esq., American Consul at _____. *Begin:* Dear Sir.

**Countess.** *Address:* To the Right Honourable The Countess of _____. *Begin:* Madam.

**Dame.** *Address:* Dame _____ _____. *Begin:* Madam.

**Deacon. (Anglican and Protestant Episcopal).** *Address:* The Reverend Deacon _____. *Begin:* Reverend Sir.

**Dean (Ecclesiastic).** *Address:* The Very Reverend the Dean of _____. *Begin:* Very Reverend Sir; *or* Sir.

**Dean, Rural (Roman Catholic Church).** *Address:* The Very Reverend _____ _____, R.D., *or* V.F. *Begin:* Very Reverend Father.

**Dean of a College or Graduate School.** *Address:* Dean _____ _____. *Begin:* Dear Sir; *or* Dear Dean _____.

**Divorced woman.** *Address:* Ordinarily use the maiden name with *Mrs.* Some divorced women prefer to resume the *Miss.*

**Doctor of Divinity.** *Address:* _____ _____, D.D.; *or* Rev. Dr. _____. *Begin:* Dear Sir; *or* Dear Dr. _____.

**Doctor of Philosophy, Laws, Medicine, etc.** *Address:* _____ _____, Ph.D. (LL.D.)

(M.D.); *or* Dr. _____ _____. *Begin:* Dear Sir; *or* Dear Dr. _____.

**Dowager.** See *Widow,* below.

**Duchess.** *Address:* Her Grace the Duchess of _____; *or* The Most Noble the Duchess of _____. *Begin:* Madam; *or* Your Grace.

**Duchess of the Blood Royal.** *Address:* Her Royal Highness The Duchess of _____. *Begin:* Madam; *or* May it please your Royal Highness.

**Duke.** *Address:* His Grace the Duke of _____; *or* The Most Noble the Duke of _____. *Begin:* My Lord Duke; *or* Your Grace.

**Duke of the Blood Royal.** *Address:* His Royal Highness The Duke of _____. *Begin:* Sir; *or* May it please your Royal Highness.

**Earl.** *Address:* The Right Honourable The Earl of _____; *or* The Earl of _____. *Begin:* My Lord.

**Earl's wife.** See *Countess,* above.

**Envoy.** Same as Minister (Diplomatic).

**Esquire.** *Address:* _____ _____, Esq. *Begin:* Sir; *or* Dear Mr. _____. (Note.— *Esq.* is never used if the person is addressed by any other title, even *Mr.*)

**Governor.** *Address:* (In Mass. and by courtesy in some other states) His Excellency, The Governor of _____; *or* His Excellency _____ _____; *or* (in other states of the U. S.) The Honorable the Governor of _____; *or* Hon. _____ _____, Governor of _____. *Begin:* Sir; *or* Dear Sir.

**Governor-General of Canada.** *Address:* His Excellency The Right Honourable _____, (plus rank or title, if any). *Begin:* My Lord; *or* Sir.

**Governor-General's wife.** *Address:* Her Excellency _____ _____. *Begin:* Madam.

**Judge (U.S.A.).** *Address:* The Honorable _____ _____, U. S. District Judge. *Begin:* Dear Sir; *or* My dear Judge _____.

**King.** *Address:* The King's Most Excellent Majesty; *or* His Most Gracious Majesty, King _____. *Begin:* Sir; *or* May it please your Majesty.

**King's Counsel.** *Address:* To _____ _____, Esq., K.C. *Begin:* Sir.

**Knight.** *Address:* Sir John _____ (initials of his order, if any, as K.C.B.). *Begin:* Sir.

**Knight's wife.** See *Lady,* below.

**Lady.** *Address:* Lady _____, *or* (if daughter of a baron or viscount) Hon. Lady _____; *or* (if the daughter of an earl, marquis, or duke) Lady Florence _____. *Begin:* Madam; *or* Your Ladyship.

**Lawyer.** *Address:* _____ _____, Esq.; *or* Mr. _____ _____, Attorney at Law. *Begin:* Dear Sir; *or* My dear Mr. _____.

**Lieutenant Governor.** *Address:* The Honorable _____, Lt. Governor of _____. *Begin:* Sir; *or* Dear Sir.

**Maid of Honor.** *Address:* The Honourable Miss _____. *Begin:* Madam.

**Marchioness.** *Address:* The Most Honourable the Marchioness of _____. *Begin:* Madam.

**Marquis.** *Address:* The Most Honourable the Marquis of _____; *or* The Marquis of _____. *Begin:* My Lord Marquis.

**Mayor (in Canadian cities and towns, and English boroughs).** *Address:* The Right Worshipful the Mayor of _____ (English); His Worship, The Mayor of _____ (Canadian). *Begin:* Sir.

**Mayor (in the U. S.).** *Address:* The Honorable _____ _____, Mayor of _____; *or* The Mayor of the City of _____. *Begin:* Sir; *or* Dear Mr. Mayor.

**Member of Parliament (or of a Provincial Legislative Council or Legislature, etc.).** To the ordinary form of address add M.P. (*or* M.P.P.; *or* M.L.A., etc.). *Begin:* Sir.

**Minister (Diplomatic).** *Address:* The Honorable _____ _____, Minister of _____. *Begin:* Sir; *or* My dear Mr. Minister.

**Minister (Religious).** See *Clergyman,* above.

**Moderator (Presbyterian Church).** *Address:* The Right Reverend _____. *Begin:* Right Reverend Sir.

**Monsignor.** *Address:* The Right Reverend Monsignor _____ _____. *Begin:* Right Reverend and dear Monsignor.

**Mother Superior of a Sisterhood.** *Address:* The Reverend Mother Superior, Convent of _____; *or* Reverend Mother _____, O.S.D. (or other initials of the order). *Begin:* Reverend Mother; *or* Dear Madam.

**Naval Officers.** *Address:* The Admiral of the Navy of the U. S.; *or* Captain _____ _____, U.S.N. *Begin:* Sir; *or* Dear Commander _____; but for officers below the rank of commander, Dear Mr. _____.

**Nun.** See *Sister of a Religious Order,* listed below.

**Papal Nuncio or Internuncio or Apostolic Delegate.** *Address:* His Excellency, The Papal Nuncio (*or* Internuncio *or* Apostolic Delegate) to _____. *Begin:* Your Excellency.

**Patriarch (Eastern Church).** *Address:* His Beatitude the Patriarch of _____; *or* His Beatitude the Lord _____, Patriarch of _____. *Begin:* Most Reverend Lord; *or* Your Beatitude.

**Pope.** *Address:* To His Holiness Pope _____. *Begin:* Most Holy Father; *or* Your Holiness.

**President of a College or University.** *Address:* _____ _____ _____, LL.D. (*or* if he is not an LL.D., use the initials of his highest degree), President of _____ University; *or* President, _____ University. If he is a clergyman, address as Reverend _____ _____, LL.D., President of _____ University. *Begin:* Dear Sir; *or* Dear President _____.

**President of a Theological Seminary.** *Address:* The Rev. President _____ _____. *Begin:* Dear Sir; *or* Dear President _____.

**President of State Senate.** *Address:* The Honorable _____ _____, President of the Senate of _____. *Begin:* Sir.

**President of the Senate of the U. S.** *Address:* The Honorable, The President of the Senate of the U. S.; *or* The Honorable _____ _____, President of the Senate. *Begin:* Sir.

**President of the U. S.** *Address:* The President, The White House. *Begin:* Mr. President; *or* The President; *or* My dear Mr. President.

**Priest (Roman Catholic Church).** *Address:* Reverend _____ _____, O.S.M. (or other initials of his order). *Begin:* Dear Father _____ (religious name).

**Prime Minister of Canada.** *Address:* The Right Honourable _____, P.C., Prime Minister of Canada. *Begin:* Sir.

**Prince of the Blood Royal.** *Address:* His Royal Highness Prince _____. *Begin:* Sir.

**Prince of Wales.** *Address:* His Royal Highness The Prince of Wales. *Begin:* Sir; *or* May it please your Royal Highness.

**Princess of the Blood Royal.** *Address:* Her Royal Highness the Princess _____ (Christian name). *Begin:* Madam.

**Privy Councillor (British Imperial).** *Address:* To the Right Honourable _____ _____, P.C. *Begin:* Sir. Note.—If other titles are used, they should come after *The Right Honourable;* as, The Right Honourable Sir John _____.

**Privy Councillor (of Canada).** *Address:* The Honourable _____. *Begin:* Sir.

**Professor in a College or University.** *Address:* Professor _____; *or* _____ _____, Ph.D. (*or* LL.D., M.D., etc., using only the initials of his highest degree, if the degrees are in the same field), Professor of _____. *Begin:* Dear Sir; *or* My dear Professor.

**Professor in a Theological Seminary.** *Address:* The Reverend Professor _____ _____; *or* The Rev. _____ _____, D.D. *Begin:* Dear Sir; *or* Dear Professor _____.

**Queen.** *Address:* The Queen's Most Excellent Majesty; *or* Her Gracious Majesty, The Queen. *Begin:* Madam; *or* May it please your Majesty.

**Queen Mother.** *Address:* Her Gracious Majesty Queen _____. *Begin:* Madam; *or* May it please your Majesty.

**Rabbi.** *Address:* Rabbi _____ _____; *or* The Rev. _____ _____. *Begin:* Reverend Sir; *or* My dear Rabbi _____. (If he holds a doctor's degree, Dr. may be substituted for Rabbi.)

**Rector of a Religious House or of a Seminary.** *Address:* The Very Reverend _____ _____, O.S.B. (*or* other initials of order), Rector, Brothers of St. Francis. *Begin:* Very Reverend and dear Father (*or* Brother).

**Representative.** See *Congressman,* above.

**Senator (U. S.)** *Address:* The Honorable _____ _____, the U. S. Senate, Washington, D. C. *Begin:* Dear Sir; *or* My dear Senator.

**Sister of a Religious Order.** *Address:* Sister _____, (followed by the initials of the order). *Begin:* Dear Sister; *or* My dear Sister _____.

**Speaker of the House of Commons (Canada).** *Address:* The Honourable _____ _____, The Speaker of the House of Commons. *Begin:* Dear Mr. Speaker.

**Speaker of the House of Representatives of the U. S.** *Address:* The Honorable _____ _____, Speaker of the House of Representatives. *Begin:* Sir; *or* My dear Mr. Speaker.

**State Senator.** Like Senator (U. S.).

**Undersecretary of State (U.S.A.).** *Address:* The Undersecretary of State; *or* The Honorable _____ _____, Undersecretary of State. *Begin:* Sir; *or* Dear Mr. _____.

**Vice-President.** *Address:* The Vice-President; *or* The Honorable _____ _____, Vice-President of the U. S. *Begin:* Mr. Vice-President; *or* Sir.

**Viscount.** *Address:* The Right Honourable the Viscount _____; *or* The Viscount _____. *Begin:* My Lord.

**Viscountess.** *Address:* The Right Honourable the Viscountess _____; *or* The Viscountess _____. *Begin:* Madam.

**Widow.** *Address:* Ordinarily address by her former title; as, Mrs. John Smith, not Mrs. Mary Alice Smith, unless the latter form is preferred by the person herself.

---

# The Confederate States of America, 1861–65

**President—Jefferson Davis; born, Christian (now Todd) Co., Ky., June 3, 1808; died, Dec. 6, 1889. Vice President—Alexander H. Stephens.**

## CABINET*

| Secretary of State | Secretary of War | Secretary of Navy | Attorney General |
|---|---|---|---|
| Robert Toombs........ 1861 | | Stephen R. Mallory.... 1861 | |
| Robert M. T. Hunter... 1861 | Leroy P. Walker....... 1861 | | Judah P. Benjamin.... 1861 |
| Judah P. Benjamin.... 1862 | Judah P. Benjamin.... 1861 | | Thomas Bragg........ 1861 |
| | George W. Randolph... 1862 | Postmaster General | |
| Secretary of Treasury | James A. Seddon...... 1862 | Henry T. Ellett........ 1861 | Thomas N. Watts...... 1862 |
| Christopher Memminger 1861 | John C. Breckinridge... 1865 | John H. Reagan....... 1861 | George Davis.......... 1864 |
| George A. Trenholm... 1864 | | | |

* Dates are those of appointment.

# ★ CELEBRATED PERSONS ★

> Locations and dates are those of birth. A name in parentheses is the original name or form of the name of the individual.
>
> The listings in this section have been gathered from various sources, including the subjects thereof, but the *Information Please Almanac* cannot guarantee the the accuracy of each individual item. We have learned to accept the date and place of birth that any lady or gentleman claims for herself or himself and not argue about it. Where we have not been able to learn the date and place of birth, we have not attempted to invent the items.

**AARON,** Hank (Henry) (baseball player); Mobile, Ala., Feb. 5, 1934.

**ABBOTT,** Bud (William) (actor); Asbury Park, N. J., Oct. 2, 1898.

**ABBOTT,** George (director & dramatist); Forestville, N. Y., June 25, 1889.

**ABEL,** Walter (actor); St. Paul, Minn., June 6, 1898.

**ACHESON,** Dean (U. S. statesman); Middletown, Conn., Apr. 11, 1893.

**ADAMS,** Sherman (former Asst. to Pres., U. S.); East Dover, Vt., Jan. 8, 1899.

**ADDAMS,** Charles (cartoonist); Westfield, N. J., Jan. 7, 1912.

**ADENAUER,** Konrad (Chancellor, Ger. Fed. Rep.); Cologne, Ger., Jan. 5, 1876.

**ADLER,** Larry (harmonica player); Baltimore, Md., Feb. 10, 1914.

**AHERNE,** Brian (actor); King's Norton, Worcestershire, England, May 2, 1902.

**AIKEN,** Conrad (poet); Savannah, Ga., Aug. 5, 1889.

**ALBANESE,** Licia (soprano); Bari, It., July 22, 1913.

**ALBERT,** Eddie (Edward Albert Heimberger) (actor); Rock Island, Ill., Apr. 22, 1908.

**ALDA,** Robert (actor); New York City, Feb. 26, 1914.

**ALI,** Mohammed (Pakistani statesman & diplomat); Barisal, E. Bengal, Oct. 19, 1909.

**ALLEN,** Gracie (comedienne); San Francisco, Calif., July 26, 1906.

**ALLEN,** Mel (Melvin Allen Israel) (sports announcer); Birmingham, Ala., Feb. 14, 1919.

**ALLEN,** Steve (comedian); New York City; Dec. 26, 1921.

**ALLYSON,** June (Jan Allyson) (actress); New York City, Oct. 7, 1923.

**ALSOP,** Joseph W., Jr. (journalist); Avon, Conn., Oct. 11, 1910.

**ALSOP,** Stewart (journalist); New York City, May 17, 1914.

**ALSTON,** Walter (baseball manager); Butler Co., Ohio, Dec. 1, 1911.

**AMECHE,** Don (actor); Kenosha, Wis., May 31, 1908.

**AMORY,** Cleveland (author); Nahant, Mass., Sept. 2, 1917.

**AMOS** (Freeman F. Gosden) (actor); Richmond, Va., May 5, 1899.

**ANDERSON,** Eddie. *See* Rochester.

**ANDERSON,** Dame Judith (actress); Adelaide, Austr., Feb. 10, 1898.

**ANDERSON,** Marian (contralto); Philadelphia, Pa., Feb. 17, 1902.

**ANDERSON,** Robert Woodruff (playwright); New York City, Apr. 28, 1917.

**ANDREWS,** Dana (actor); Collins, Miss., Jan. 1, 1912.

**ANDREWS,** Julie (Julia Wells) (actress); Walton-on-Thames, Eng., Oct. 1, 1935.

**ANDY** (Charles J. Correll) (actor); Peoria, Ill., Feb. 2, 1890.

**ANGELES,** Victoria de los (Victoria Gamez Cima) (soprano); Barcelona, Sp., Nov. 1, 1923.

**ANGELI,** Pier (Anna Maria Pierangeli) (actress); Cagliari, It., June 19, 1932.

**ANTONELLI,** Johnny (baseball player); Rochester, N. Y., Apr. 12, 1930.

**ARCARO,** Eddie (jockey); Cincinnati, Ohio, Feb. 19, 1916.

**ARCHIPENKO,** Alexander (sculptor); Kiev, Rus., May 30, 1887.

**ARDEN,** Elizabeth (cosmetician); Ontario, Can., 1891.

**ARDEN,** Eve (Eunice Quedens) (actress); Mill Valley, Calif.

**ARLEN,** Harold (Hyman Arluck) (composer); Buffalo, N. Y., Feb. 15, 1905.

**ARMOUR,** Thomas Dickson (Tommy) (golfer); Edinburgh, Scot., Sept. 24, 1895.

**ARMSTRONG,** Henry (boxer); St. Louis, Mo., Dec. 12, 1912.

**ARMSTRONG,** Louis (trumpeter); New Orleans, La., July 4, 1900.

**ARMSTRONG-JONES,** Antony, Earl of Snowdon (husband of Princess Margaret of Great Britain); London, Eng., Mar. 7, 1930.

**ARNAZ,** Desi (Desiderio) (actor & band leader); Santiago, Cuba, Mar. 2, 1917.

**ARNESS,** James (actor); Minneapolis, Minn., May 26, 1923.

**ARNO,** Peter (Curtis Arnoux Peters) (cartoonist); New York City, Jan. 8, 1904.

**ARQUETTE,** Cliff ("Charley Weaver," TV comedian); Toledo, Ohio, Dec. 28, 1905.

**ARRAU,** Claudio (pianist); Chillán, Chile, Feb. 6, 1904.

**ASTAIRE,** Fred (Frederick Austerlitz) (dancer & actor); Omaha, Neb., May 10, 1899.

**ATKINSON,** Brooks (drama critic); Melrose, Mass., Nov. 28, 1894.

ATKINSON, Ted (jockey); Toronto, Ont., Can., June 17, 1916.

ATTLEE, Clement R. (British statesman); London, Eng., Jan. 3, 1883.

AUDEN, W. H. (Wystan Hugh Auden) (poet); York, Eng., Feb. 21, 1907.

AUTRY, Gene (actor); Tioga, Tex., Sept. 29, 1907.

BACALL, Lauren (actress); New York City, Sept. 16, 1924.

BACCALONI, Salvatore (basso); Rome, It., Apr. 14, 1900.

BACKHAUS, Wilhelm (pianist); Leipzig, Ger., Mar. 26, 1884.

BAILEY, Pearl (singer); Newport News, Va., Mar. 29, 1918.

BAINTER, Fay (actress); Los Angeles, Calif., 1893.

BAKER, Josephine (singer); St. Louis, Mo., 1907.

BALANCHINE, George (ballet director); St. Petersburg, Rus., Jan. 9, 1904.

BALDWIN, Faith (novelist); New Rochelle, N. Y., Oct. 1, 1893.

BALL, Lucille (actress); Jamestown, N. Y., Aug. 6, 1911.

BANCROFT, Anne (Annemarie Italiano) (actress); New York City, Sept. 17, 1931.

BANKHEAD, Tallulah (actress); Huntville, Ala., Jan. 31, 1903.

BANKS, Ernie (baseball player); Dallas, Tex., Jan. 31, 1931.

BANNISTER, Roger (mile runner); Harrow, Eng., Mar. 24, 1929.

BARBER, Red (Walter L.) (sports announcer); Columbus, Miss., Feb. 17, 1908.

BARBER, Samuel (composer); West Chester, Pa., Mar. 9, 1910.

BARBIROLLI, Sir John (orchestra conductor); London, Eng., Dec. 2, 1899.

BARDOT, Brigitte (actress); Paris, Fr., 1935.

BARTHELMESS, Richard (actor); New York City, May 9, 1897.

BARTHOLOMEW, Freddie (actor); London, Eng., Mar. 28, 1924.

BARTON, James (actor); Gloucester, N. J., Nov. 1, 1890.

BARUCH, Bernard (financier); Camden, S. C., Aug. 19, 1870.

BASIE, Count (William) (band leader); Red Bank, N. J., Aug. 21, 1906.

BATCHELOR, Clarence Daniel (cartoonist); Osage City, Kans.

BATISTA y ZALDÍVAR, Fulgencio (former President, Cuba); Banes, Cuba, Jan. 16, 1901.

BAUDOUIN (King, Belgium); Palace of Laeken, Belg., Sept. 7, 1930.

BAUER, Hank (Henry) (baseball player); E. St. Louis, Ill., July 31, 1922.

BAXTER, Anne (actress); Michigan City, Ind., May 7, 1923.

BEACH, Edward Latimer (author & submarine commander); New York City, Apr. 20, 1918.

BEEBE, William (zoologist); Brooklyn, N. Y., July 29, 1877

BEGLEY, Ed (Edward) (actor); Hartford, Conn., Mar. 25, 1901.

BEHAN, Bredan (dramatist); Dublin, Ire., Feb. 9, 1923.

BEHRMAN, S. N. (Samuel N.) (dramatist); Worcester, Mass., June 9, 1893.

BELAFONTE, Harry (singer); New York City, Mar. 1, 1927.

BELLAMY, Ralph (actor); Chicago, Ill., June 17, 1905.

BEMELMANS, Ludwig (essayist); Meran, Tirol, Apr. 27, 1898.

BENDIX, William (actor); New York City, Jan. 14, 1906.

BEN-GURION, David (David Green) (Premier, Israel); Plónsk, Pol., Oct. 16, 1886.

BENNETT, Joan (actress); Palisades, N. J., Feb. 27, 1910.

BENNETT, Robert Russell (composer); Kansas City, Mo., June 15, 1894.

BENNY, Jack (Benjamin Kubelsky) (comedian); Waukegan, Ill., Feb. 14, 1894.

BENTON, Thomas Hart (painter); Neosho, Mo., Apr. 15, 1889.

BERG, Patty (Patricia Jane) (golfer); Minneapolis, Minn., Feb. 13, 1918.

BERGEN, Edgar (ventriloquist); Chicago, Ill., Feb. 16, 1903.

BERGMAN, Ingmar (movie producer & director); Uppsala, Swed., July 14, 1918.

BERGMAN, Ingrid (actress); Stockholm, Swed., 1917.

BERLE, Milton (Milton Berlinger) (comedian); New York City, July 12, 1908.

BERLIN, Irving (Isidore Baline) (song writer); Temum, Russia, May 11, 1888.

BERLIN, Richard E. (publisher); Omaha, Nebr., Jan. 18, 1894.

BERMAN, Shelley (Sheldon) (comedian); Chicago, Ill., Feb. 3, 1926.

BERNSTEIN, Leonard (composer & conductor); Lawrence, Mass., Aug. 25, 1918.

BERRA, Yogi (Lawrence) (baseball player); St. Louis, Mo., May 12, 1925.

BERRYMAN, James T. (cartoonist); Washington, D. C., June 8, 1902.

BIKEL, Theodore (actor & singer); Vienna, Aus., May 2, 1924.

BING, Rudolf (opera executive); Vienna, Aus., Jan. 9, 1902.

BLACKMER, Sidney (actor); Salisbury, N. C., July 13, 1898.

BLAIK, Earl H. (football coach); Detroit, Mich., Feb. 15, 1897.

BLAINE, Vivian (Vivian Stapleton) (actress); Newark, N. J., Nov. 21, 1921.

BLITZSTEIN, Marc (composer); Philadelphia, Pa., Mar. 2, 1905.

BLOOM, Claire (actress); London, Eng., Feb. 15, 1931.

BLOOMGARDEN, Kermit (theatrical producer); Brooklyn, N. Y., Dec. 15, 1904.

BOGARDE, Dirk (actor); Hampstead, London, Eng., Mar. 28, 1921.

BOHLEN, Charles E. (author and diplomat); Clayton, N. Y., Aug. 30, 1904.

BOHR, Niels (physicist); Copenhagen, Den., Oct. 7, 1885.

BOLGER, Ray (actor); Dorcester, Mass, Jan. 10, 1906.

BOLT, Tommy (golfer); Hawarth, Okla., March 31, 1919.

BOONE, Pat (Charles) (singer); Jacksonville, Fla., June 1, 1934.

BOONE, Richard (actor); Los Angeles, California.

BOOTH, Shirley (Thelma Booth Ford) actress); New York City, Aug. 30, 1907.

BORGE, Victor (pianist & comedian); Copenhagen, Den., Jan. 3, 1909.

BORGNINE, Ernest (actor); Hamden, Conn., Jan. 24, 1917.

BORZAGE, Frank (movie director); Salt Lake City, Utah, Apr. 23, 1893.

BOSWELL, Connie (singer); New Orleans, La., Dec. 3.

BOWEN, Catherine Drinker (biographer); Haverford, Pa., Jan. 1, 1897.

BOWLES, Chester (author and former diplomat); Springfield, Mass., Apr. 5, 1901.

BOYD, William (actor); Cambridge, Ohio, June 5, 1898.

BOYER, Charles (actor); Figeac, Fr., Aug. 28, 1899.

BOYER, Ken (baseball player); Liberty, Mo., May 20, 1931.

BOYLE, Kay (novelist & poet); St. Paul, Minn., Feb. 19, 1903.

BRADLEY, Omar N. (U. S. general); Clark, Mo., Feb. 12, 1893.

BRAILOWSKY, Alexander (pianist); Kiev, Rus., Feb. 16, 1896.

BRANDO, Marlon (actor); Omaha, Nebr., Apr. 3, 1924.

BRANDT, Willy (Herbert Frahm) (Mayor, W. Berlin); Lübeck, Ger., Dec. 18, 1913.

BRAQUE, Georges (painter); Argenteuil, Fr., May 13, 1882.

BRAUN, Wernher von (rocket engineer); Wirsitz, Ger., Mar. 23, 1912.

BRAZZI, Rossano (actor); Bologna, It., Sept. 18, 1916.

BRENNAN, Walter (actor); Lynn, Mass., July 25, 1894.

BREWER, Teresa (singer); Toledo, Ohio, May 7, 1931.

BRINKLEY, David (news commentator); Wilmington, N. C., July 10, 1920.

BRISCOE, Robert (Irish statesman); Dublin, Ire., Sept. 25, 1894.

BRITTEN, Benjamin (composer); Lowestoft, Eng., Nov. 22, 1913.

BROOK, Peter (theatrical director); London, Eng., Mar. 21, 1925.

BROOKS, Van Wyck (literary critic); Plainfield, N. J., Feb. 16, 1886.

BROWN, Cecil (radio commentator); New Brighton, Pa., Sept. 14, 1907.

BROWN, Joe E. (actor); Holgate, Ohio, July 28, 1892.

BROWN, John Mason (drama critic); Louisville, Ky., July 3, 1900.

BROWN, Pamela (actress); London, Eng., July 8, 1918.

BROWN, Vanessa (Smylla Brind) (actress); Vienna, Aus., Mar. 24, 1928.

BROWNELL, Herbert, Jr. (U. S. statesman); Peru, Nebr., Feb. 20, 1904.

BRUBECK, Dave (jazz pianist); Concord, Calif., Dec. 6, 1920.

BRUNDAGE, Avery (sports executive); Detroit, Mich., Sept. 28, 1887.

BRYNNER, Yul (actor); Sakhalin (an island off Japan), July 11, 1917.

BUCHWALD, Art (Arthur) (columnist); Mount Vernon, N. Y., Oct. 20, 1925.

BUCK, Pearl S. (novelist); Hillsboro, W. Va., June 26, 1892.

BUHL, Bob (baseball player); Saginaw, Mich., Aug. 12, 1928.

BULGANIN, Nikolai A. (Soviet statesman); Nizhni-Novgorod, Rus., June 11, 1895.

BUNCHE, Ralph J. (U. N. official); Detroit, Mich., Aug. 7, 1904.

BURDETTE, Lou (baseball player); Nitro, W. Va., Nov. 22, 1926.

BURKE, Adm. Arleigh A. (U. S. naval officer); Boulder, Colo., Oct. 19, 1901.

BURKE, Billie (actress); Washington, D C., Aug. 7, 1886.

BURNS, George (Nathan Birnbaum) (comedian); New York City, Jan. 20, 1896.

BURROWS, Abe (playwright & producer); New York City, Dec. 18, 1910.

BURTON, Richard (Richard Jenkins) (actor); Pontrhydyfen, Wales, Nov. 10, 1925.

BUSH, Vannevar (engineer); Everett, Mass., Mar. 11, 1890.

BUTLER, Richard Austen (British statesman); Attock Serai, India, Dec. 9, 1902.

BUTTONS, Red (Aaron Chwatt) (comedian); New York City, Feb. 5, 1919.

BYINGTON, Spring (actress); Colorado Springs, Colo., Oct. 17, 1898.

CADMUS, Paul (painter & etcher); New York City. Dec. 17, 1904.

CAESAR, Sid (comedian); Yonkers, N. Y., Sept. 8, 1922.

CAGNEY, James (actor); New York City, July 17, 1904.

CAIN, James M. (novelist); Annapolis, Md., July 1, 1892.

CALDER, Alexander ("mobile" sculptor); Lawnton, Pa., July 22, 1898.

CALDWELL, Erskine (novelist); White Oak, Ga., Dec. 17, 1903.

CALDWELL, Taylor (novelist); Preswich, Eng., Sept 7, 1900.

CALLAS, Maria (soprano); New York City, Dec. 4, 1923.

CALLOWAY, Cab (band leader); Rochester, N. Y., Dec. 25, 1907.

CAMPANELLA, Roy (baseball player); Homestead, Pa., Nov. 19, 1921.

CANHAM, Edwin D. (editor); Auburn, Maine, Feb. 13, 1904.

CANIFF, Milton (cartoonist); Hillsboro, Ohio, Feb. 28, 1907.

CANTOR, Eddie (Edward Iskowitz) (comedian); New York City, Jan. 31, 1892.

CAPOTE, Truman (novelist); New Orleans, La., Sept. 30, 1924.

CAPP, Al (cartoonist); New Haven, Conn., Sept. 28, 1909.

CAPRA, Frank (movie director); Palermo, Sicily, May 18, 1897.

CAREY, MacDonald (actor); Sioux City, Iowa, Mar. 15, 1913.

CARLE, Frankie (pianist); Providence, R. I., Mar. 15, 1903.

CARLSON, Richard (actor); Albert Lea, Minn, Apr. 29, 1912.

CARMICHAEL, Hoagy (song writer); Bloomington, Ind., Nov. 22, 1899.

CARNEY, Art (actor); Mt. Vernon, N. Y., Nov. 4, 1918.

CARNOVSKY, Morris (actor); St. Louis, Mo., 1898.

CARON, Leslie (actress); Paris, July 1, 1931.

CARROLL, Leo G. (actor); Weedon, Eng.

CARROLL, Paul Vincent (dramatist); Dundalk, Ire., July 10, 1900.

CARSON, Jack (actor); Carman, Can., Oct. 27, 1910.

CARSON, Rachel (science writer); Springdale, Pa., May 27, 1907.

CASADESUS, Robert (pianist); Paris, Fr., Apr. 7, 1899.

CASALS, Pablo (cellist); Vendrell, Sp., Dec. 29, 1876.

CASTRO RUZ, Fidel (Premier, Cuba); Mayari, Oriente, Cuba, Aug. 13, 1927.

CAVALLARO, Carmen (pianist); New York City, May 6, 1913.

CHAGALL, Marc (painter); Vitebsk, Rus., July 7, 1887.

CHAMBERLAIN, Wilt (Wilton) (basketball player); Philadelphia, Pa., Aug. 21, 1936.

CHAMPION, Gower (dancer & actor); Geneva, Ill., June 22, 1921.

CHAMPION, Marge (dancer & actress); Los Angeles, Calif., Sept. 2, 1923.

CHANNING, Carol (comedienne); Seattle, Wash., Jan. 31, 1921.

CHAPLIN, Charles (comedian); London, Eng., Apr. 16, 1889.

CHARISSE, Cyd (Tula Finklea) (actress, dancer); Amarillo, Tex., Mar. 8, 1923.

CHASE, Ilka (actress); New York City, Apr. 8, 1905.

CHASE, Stuart (writer); Somersworth, N. H., Mar. 8, 1888.

CHÁVEZ, Carlos (composer); near Mexico City, Mex., June 13, 1899.

CHAYEFSKY, Paddy (Sidney) (dramatist); New York City, Jan. 29, 1923.

CHEVALIER, Maurice (actor); Paris, Fr., Sept. 12, 1888.

CHIANG Kai-shek (President, Nat. China); Feng-hwa, China, Oct. 31, 1887.

CHIRICO, Giorgio de (painter); Volos, Gr., July 10, 1888.

CHOU En-lai (Premier, Comm. China); Huai-yin, China, 1898.

CHRISTIE, Agatha (novelist); Torquay, Eng., 189?.

CHURCHILL, Sarah (actress); London, Eng., Oct. 7, 1914.

CHURCHILL, Sir Winston S. (British statesman); Oxfordshire, Eng., Nov. 30, 1874.

CLAIR, René (René Chomette) (movie director); Paris, Fr., Nov. 11, 1898.

CLAIRE, Ina (Ina Fagan) (actress); Washington, D. C., Oct. 15, 1892.

CLARK, Dane (actor); New York City, Feb. 18, 1915.

CLARK, Dick (Richard) (TV personality); Mt. Vernon, N. Y., Nov. 30, 1929.

CLIBURN, Van (Harvey Lavan Cliburn, Jr.) (pianist); Shreveport, La., July 12, 1934.

CLIFT, Montgomery (actor); Omaha, Nebr., Oct. 17, 1920.

CLOETE, Stuart (novelist); Paris, Fr., July 23, 1897.

CLOONEY, Rosemary (singer); Maysville, Ky., May 23, 1928.

CLURMAN, Harold (stage director); New York City, Sept. 18, 1901.

COBB, Lee J. (actor); New York City, Dec. 9, 1911.

COCA, Imogene (comedienne); Philadelphia, Pa.

COCTEAU, Jean (poet & dramatist); Maisons-Laffitte, Fr., July 5, 1891.

COLAVITO, Rocky (baseball player); New York City, Aug. 10, 1933.

COLBERT, Claudette (Lily Chauchoin) (actress); Paris, Fr., Sept. 13, 1905.

COLE, Nat King (Nathaniel Adams Coles) (singer); Montgomery, Ala., Mar. 17, 1919.

COLLINS, Dorothy (Marjorie Chandler) (singer); Windsor, Can., Nov. 18, 1926.

COMMAGER, Henry S. (historian); Pittsburgh, Pa., Oct. 25, 1902.

COMO, Perry (Pierino) (singer); Canonsburg, Pa., May 18, 1913.

COMPTON, Arthur H. (physicist); Wooster, Ohio, Sept. 10, 1892.

CONANT, James B. (scientist & educator); Dorchester, Mass., Mar. 26, 1893.

CONDON, Eddie (musician); Goodland, Ind., Nov. 16, 1905.

CONLEY, Donald (baseball player); Muskogee, Okla., Nov. 10, 1930.

CONNALLY, John Bowden, Jr. (Secy. of Navy); Floresville, Tex., Feb. 27, 1917.

CONNELLY, Marc (dramatist); McKeesport, Pa., Dec. 13, 1890.

CONROY, Frank (actor); Derby, Eng., Oct. 14, 1890.

CONTE, Richard (actor); New York City, Mar. 24, 1914.

COOGAN, Jackie (actor); Los Angeles, Calif., Oct. 26, 1914.

COOPER, Jackie (actor); Los Angeles, Calif., Sept. 15, 1922.

COPLAND, Aaron (composer); Brooklyn, N. Y., Nov. 14, 1900.

COREY, Wendell (actor); Dracut, Mass., Mar. 20, 1914.

CORNELL, Katharine (actress); Berlin, Ger., Feb. 16, 1898.

CORRELL, Charles J. See Andy

COSTAIN, Thomas Bertram (novelist); Brantford, Ont., Can., May 8, 1885.

COTTEN, Joseph (actor); Petersburg, Va., 1905.

COTTON, Thomas Henry (golfer); Cheshire, Eng., Jan. 26, 1907.

COWARD, Noel (dramatist & actor); Teddington, Eng., Dec. 16, 1899.

COWLES, Gardner (publisher); Algona, Iowa, Jan. 31, 1903.

COX, Wally (Wallace Maynard Cox) (comedian); Detroit, Mich., Dec. 6, 1924.

COZZENS, James Gould (novelist); Chicago, Ill., Aug. 19, 1903.

CRAIN, Jeanne (actress); Barstow, Calif., May 25, 1925.

CRAWFORD, Broderick (actor); Philadelphia, Pa., Dec. 9, 1911.

CRAWFORD, Cheryl (theatrical producer); Akron, Ohio, Sept. 24, 1902.

CRAWFORD, Joan (Lucille LeSueur) (actress); San Antonio, Tex., Mar. 23, 1908.

CRONIN, A. J. (Archibald J. Cronin) (novelist); Cardross, Scot., July 19, 1896.

CRONIN, Joe (baseball executive); San Francisco, Calif., Oct. 12, 1906.

CRONKITE, Walter (news commentator); St. Joseph, Mo., Nov. 4, 1916.

CRONYN, Hume (actor); London, Ont., Can., July 18, 1911.

CROSBY, Bing (Harry) (actor & singer); Tacoma, Wash., May 2, 1904.

CROSBY, Bob (band leader & actor); Spokane, Wash., Aug. 23, 1913.

CROSBY, John (TV critic); Milwaukee, Wis., May 18, 1912.

CROSS, Milton (radio announcer); New York City, Apr. 16, 1897.

CROUSE, Russel (dramatist); Findlay, Ohio, Feb. 20, 1893.

CUGAT, Xavier (orchestra leader); Barcelona, Sp., Jan. 1, 1900.

CUKOR, George (movie director); New York City, July 7, 1899.

CULLEN, William Lawrence (Bill) (radio-TV entertainer); Pittsburgh, Pa., February 18, 1920.

CULP, Robert (actor); Berkeley, Calif., Aug. 16, 1931.

CUMMINGS, E. E. (Edward Estlin Cummings) (poet); Cambridge, Mass., Oct. 14, 1894.

CUMMINGS, Robert (actor); Joplin, Mo., June 9, 1910.

CURTICE, Harlow H. (industrialist); Eaton Rapids, Mich., Aug. 15, 1893.

CURTIS, Tony (Bernard Schwartz) (actor); New York City, June 3, 1925.

CURTIZ, Michael (movie director); Budapest, Hung., Dec. 24, 1888.

CURZON, Clifford (pianist); London, Eng., May 18, 1907.

DACHÉ, Lilly (hat designer); Beigles, Fr.

DAHL, Arlene (actress); Minneapolis, Minn., Aug. 11.

DALI, Salvador (painter); Figueras, Sp., May 11, 1904.

DALY, John (news commentator); Johannesburg, S. Afr., Feb. 20, 1914.

DAMONE, Vic (Vito Farinola) (singer); Brooklyn, N. Y., June 12, 1928.

DANDRIDGE, Dorothy (actress); Cleveland, Ohio.

DANILOVA, Alexandra (dancer); Peterhof, Rus.

DARCEL, Denise (Denise Billecard) (actress); Paris, Fr., Sept. 8, 1925.

DARIN, Bobby (Walden Robert Cassotto) (singer); New York City, May 14, 1937.

DARNELL, Linda (actress); Dallas, Tex.

DARREN, James (James Ercolani) (actor); Philadelphia, Pa., June 8, 1936.

DARRIEUX, Danielle (actress); Bordeaux, Fr., May 1, 1917.

DAVIS, Bette (actress); Lowell, Mass., Apr. 5, 1908.

DAVIS, Miles (jazz trumpeter); Alton, Ill., May 25, 1926.

DAVIS, Sammy, Jr. (singer); New York City, Jan. 1926.

DAVIS, Stuart (painter); Philadelphia, Pa., Dec. 7, 1894.

DAY, Doris (Doris von Kappelhoff) (singer); Cincinnati, Ohio, Apr. 3, 1924.

DAY, J. Edward (Postmaster General); Jacksonville, Ill., Oct. 11, 1914.

DAY, Laraine (Loraine Johnson) (actress); Roosevelt, Utah, Oct. 13, 1920.

DEAN, Dizzy (Jay Hanna Dean) (baseball player and announcer); Lucas, Ark., Jan. 16, 1911.

DEAN, Jimmy (singer); Plainview, Tex., Aug. 10, 1928.

DE GAULLE, Charles (President, France); Lille, Fr., Nov. 22, 1890.

DE HAVILLAND, Olivia (actress); Tokyo, Jap., July 1, 1916.

DEMARET, Jim (golfer); Houston, Tex., May 10, 1910.

DE MILLE, Agnes (choreographer); New York City.

DEMPSEY, Jack (William H.) (boxer); Manassa, Colo., June 24, 1894.

DERAIN, André (painter); Chatou, Fr., June 10, 1880.

DE ROCHEMONT, Louis (movie producer); Chelsea, Mass., Jan. 13, 1899.

DE SICA, Vittorio (actor & movie director); Sora, It., July 7, 1901.

DE VALERA, Éamon (President, Ireland); New York City, Oct. 14, 1882.

DEVINE, Andy (actor); Flagstaff, Ariz., Oct. 7, 1905.

DEWEY, Thomas E. (U. S. statesman); Owosso, Mich., Mar. 24, 1902.

DE WILDE, Brandon (actor); New York City, Apr. 9, 1942.

DIEFENBAKER, John G. (Pr. Min., Canada); Grey County, Ont., Can., September 18, 1895.

DIETRICH, Marlene (Maria Magdalena von Losch) (actress); Berlin, Germany, Dec. 27, 1904.

DILLMAN, Bradford (actor); San Francisco, Calif., Apr. 14, 1930.

DILLON, Douglas (Secy. of Treasury); Geneva, Switz., Aug. 21, 1909.

DIMAGGIO, Joe (baseball player); Martinez, Calif., Nov. 25, 1914.

DISNEY, Walt (animated cartoonist); Chicago, Ill., Dec. 5, 1901.

DOLIN, Anton (dancer & choreographer); Slinfold, Sussex, Eng., July 27, 1904.

DONLEVY, Brian (actor); Portadown, Ire., Feb. 9, 1903.

DOOLITTLE, James H. (aviator); Alameda, Calif., Dec. 14, 1896.

DORATI, Antal (orchestra conductor); Budapest, Hung., Apr. 9, 1906.

DOS PASSOS, John (novelist); Chicago, Ill., Jan. 14, 1896.

DOUGLAS, Kirk (Issur Danielovitch) (actor); Amsterdam, N. Y., Dec. 9, 1916.

DOUGLAS, Melvyn (Melvyn Hesselberg) (actor); Macon, Ga., Apr. 5, 1901.

DOWLING, Eddie (Edward Goucher) (actor & director); Woonsocket, R. I., Dec. 9, 1894.

DRAKE, Alfred (singer & actor); New York City, Oct. 7, 1914

DRAPER, Paul (dancer); Florence, It., Oct. 25, 1911.

DRUMMOND, Roscoe (journalist); Theresa, N. Y.

DRYSDALE, Don (baseball player); Van Nuys, Calif., July 23, 1936.

**DUBINSKY,** David (David Dobnievski) (labor leader); Brest-Litovsk, Poland, Feb. 22, 1892.

**DUCLOS,** Jacques (French Communist leader); Louey, Fr., Oct. 2, 1896.

**DUKE,** Patty (Anna Marie Duke) (actress); New York City, Dec. 14, 1946.

**DULLES,** Allen W. (former CIA Director, U. S.); Watertown, N. Y., Apr. 7, 1893.

**DU MAURIER,** Daphne, (novelist); London, Eng., May 13, 1907.

**DUNNE,** Irene (actress); Louisville, Ky., Dec. 20, 1904.

**DUNNOCK,** Mildred (actress); Baltimore, Md., Jan. 25.

**DURANTE,** Jimmy (comedian); New York City, Feb. 10, 1893.

**DUROCHER,** Leo (former baseball manager); West Springfield, Mass., July 27, 1906.

**DYKES,** Jimmie (baseball coach); Philadelphia, Pa., Nov. 10, 1896.

**ECKSTINE,** Billy (singer); Pittsburgh, Pa., July 8, 1914.

**EDDY,** Nelson (baritone); Providence, R. I., June 29, 1901.

**EDEN,** Sir Anthony (British statesman); England, June 12, 1897.

**EGLEVSKY,** André (dancer); Moscow, Rus., Dec. 21, 1917.

**EISENHOWER,** Dwight D. (former President, U. S.); Denison, Tex., Oct. 14, 1890.

**EISENHOWER,** Milton S. (educator); Abilene, Kans., Sept. 15, 1899.

**EKBERG,** Anita (actress); Malmö, Swed.

**ELDRIDGE,** Florence (Florence McKechnie) (actress); Brooklyn, N. Y., Sept. 5, 1901.

**ELIOT,** T. S. (Thomas Stearns Eliot) (poet); St. Louis, Mo., Sept. 26, 1888.

**ELIZABETH II** (Queen, Gr. Brit., etc.); London, Eng., Apr. 21, 1926.

**ELLINGTON,** Duke (Edward) (band leader); Washington, D. C., Apr. 29, 1899.

**ELLIOTT,** Herb (mile runner); Perth, Australia, Feb. 25, 1938.

**ELMAN,** Mischa (violinist); Stalnoye, Rus., Jan. 20, 1891.

**EMERSON,** Faye (actress); Elizabeth, La., July 8, 1917.

**EVANS,** Dame Edith (actress); London, Eng., Feb. 8, 1888.

**EVANS,** Maurice (actor); Dorchester, Eng., June 3, 1901.

**EWELL,** Tom (Yewell Tompkins) (actor); Owensboro, Ky., Apr. 29, 1909.

**FABIAN** (Fabian Anthony Forte) (singer); Philadelphia, Pa., Feb. 6, 1943.

**FABRAY,** Nanette (Nanette Fabarés) (actress); San Diego, Calif., Oct. 27, 1922.

**FADIMAN,** Clifton (literary critic); Brooklyn, N. Y., May 15, 1904.

**FAIRBANKS,** Douglas, Jr., (actor); New York City, Dec. 9, 1909.

**FAIRLESS,** Benjamin F. (industrialist); Pigeon Run, Ohio, May 3, 1890.

**FALKENBURG,** Jinx (Eugenia) (actress); Barcelona, Sp., Jan. 21, 1919.

**FARRELL,** Eileen (soprano); Willimantic, Conn., Feb. 13, 1920.

**FARRELL,** James T. (novelist); Chicago, Ill., Feb. 27, 1904.

**FAULKNER,** William (novelist); New Albany, Miss., Sept. 25, 1897.

**FERBER,** Edna (novelist); Kalamazoo, Mich., Aug. 15, 1887.

**FERNANDEL** (Fernand Contandin) (actor); Marseille, France, May 8, 1903.

**FERRER,** Jose (actor); Santurce, P. R., Jan. 8, 1912.

**FERRER,** Mel (actor); Elberon, N. J., Aug. 25, 1917.

**FIELD,** Betty (actress); Boston, Mass., Feb. 8, 1918.

**FIELD,** Marshall, Jr. (publisher); New York City, June 15, 1916.

**FIELDS,** Gracie (actress); Rochdale, Eng., Jan. 9, 1898.

**FISHER,** Eddie (singer); Philadelphia, Pa., Aug. 10, 1928.

**FITZGERALD,** Ella (singer); Newport News, Va., Apr. 25, 1918.

**FITZSIMMONS,** Sunny Jim (horse trainer); Sheepshead Bay, N. Y., July 23, 1874.

**FLAGSTAD,** Kirsten (soprano); Hamar, Nor., July 12, 1895.

**FLEMING,** Rhonda (Marilyn Louis) (actress); Los Angeles, Calif., Aug. 10, 1923.

**FOCH,** Nina (actress); Leyden, Neth., Apr. 20, 1924.

**FONDA,** Henry (actor); Grand Island, Nebr., May 16, 1905.

**FONTAINE,** Joan (actress); Tokyo, Jap., Oct. 22, 1917.

**FONTANNE,** Lynn (actress); London, Eng., 1887.

**FONTEYN,** Dame Margot (Margaret Hookham) (ballerina); Reigate, Eng., May 18, 1919.

**FORD,** Glenn (Gwyllyn Ford) (actor); Quebec, Can., May 1, 1916.

**FORD,** Henry, II (industrialist); Detroit, Mich., Sept. 4, 1917.

**FORD,** John (movie director); Cape Elizabeth, Maine, Feb. 1, 1895.

**FORD,** Tennessee Ernie (entertainer); Fordtown, Tenn., Feb. 13, 1919.

**FORD,** Whitey (Edward) (baseball player); New York City, Oct. 21, 1928.

**FORESTER,** C. S. (Cecil Scott Forester) (novelist); Cairo, Egypt, Aug. 27, 1899.

**FOX,** Nellie (Jacob Nelson Fox) (baseball player); St. Thomas, Pennsylvania, Dec. 25, 1927.

**FRANCESCATTI,** Zino (violinist); Marseille, Fr., Aug. 9, 1905.

**FRANCIOSA,** Anthony (Anthony Papaleo) (actor); New York City, Oct. 25, 1928.

**FRANCIS,** Arlene (Arlene Francis Kazanjian) (actress); Boston, Mass., 1908.

**FRANCIS,** Connie (Connie Franconero) (singer); Newark, N.J., Dec. 12, 1938.

**FRANCO,** Francisco (Chief of State, Spain); El Ferrol, Sp., Dec. 4, 1892.

**FRAWLEY,** William (actor); Burlington, Iowa, Feb. 26, 1893.

**FREDERICK IX** (King, Denmark); nr. Copenhagen, Den., Mar. 11, 1899.

**FREEMAN,** Orville L. (Secy. of Agriculture); Minneapolis, Minn., May 9, 1918.

**FRICK,** Ford C. (baseball executive); Wawaka, Ind., Dec. 19, 1894.

**FRIEND,** Robert (baseball player); Lafayette, Ind., Mar. 24, 1930.

FRIML, Rudolf (composer); Prague, Czech., Dec. 7, 1884.

FRISCH, Frank F. (baseball player and announcer); New York City, Sept. 9, 1898.

FROST, Robert (poet); San Francisco, Calif., Mar. 26, 1875.

FRY, Christopher (dramatist); Bristol, Eng., Dec. 18, 1907.

FUNSTON, George Keith (financial executive); Waterloo, Iowa, Oct. 12, 1910.

GABIN, Jean (actor); Paris, Fr., May 17, 1904.

GABOR, Eva (actress); Budapest, Hung.

GABOR, Zsa Zsa (Sari) (actress); Budapest, Hung., Feb. 6, 1923.

GAITSKELL, Hugh (British statesman); London, Eng., Apr. 9, 1906.

GALBRAITH, John (economist); Iona Station, Ont., Canada, Oct. 15, 1908.

GALLICO, Paul (author); New York City, July 26, 1897.

GALLUP, George H. (public-opinion statistician); Jefferson, Iowa, Nov. 18, 1901.

GARBO, Greta (Greta Gustafsson) (actress); Stockholm, Swed., Sept. 18, 1905.

GARDEN, Mary (soprano); Aberdeen, Scot., Feb. 20. 1877.

GARDNER, Ava (actress); Smithfield, N. C., Dec. 24, 1922.

GARDNER, Erle Stanley (novelist); Malden, Mass., July 17, 1889.

GARGARIN, Yuri (Soviet cosmonaut); Gzhatsk, U.S.S.R., Mar. 9, 1934.

GARLAND, Judy (Frances Gumm) (actress); Grand Rapids, Minn., June 10, 1922.

GARNER, James (actor); Norman, Okla., Apr. 17, 1928.

GARROWAY, Dave (comedian); Schenectady, N. Y., July 13, 1913.

GARSON, Greer (actress); County Down, No. Ire.

GAXTON, William (Arturo Caxiola) (actor); San Francisco, Calif., Dec. 2, 1893.

GAYNOR, Mitzi (actress); Chicago, Ill., Sept. 4, 1931.

GEDDES, Barbara Bel (actress); New York City, Oct. 31, 1922.

GENEVIEVE (Ginette Marguerite Auger) (actress & singer); Paris, Fr., Apr. 17, 1930.

GENN, Leo (actor); London, Eng., Aug. 9, 1905.

GERSHWIN, Ira (lyricist); New York City, Dec. 6, 1896.

GIBSON, Althea (tennis player); Silver, S. C., Aug. 25, 1927.

GIELGUD, Sir John (actor); London, Eng., Apr. 14, 1904.

GILELS, Emil (pianist); Odessa, Ukr., 1916.

GILES, Warren (baseball executive); Tiskilwa, Ill., May 28, 1896.

GILLESPIE, Dizzy (John Birks Gillespie) (musician); Cheraw, S. C., Oct. 21, 1917.

GIMBEL, Bernard F. (merchant); Vincennes, Ind., Apr. 10, 1885.

GISH, Dorothy (actress); Massillon, Ohio, Mar. 11, 1898.

GISH, Lillian (actress); Springfield, Ohio, Oct. 14, 1896.

GLEASON, Jackie (actor); Brooklyn, N. Y., Feb. 26, 1916.

GOBEL, George (comedian); Chicago, Ill., May 20, 1920.

GODDARD, Paulette (actress); Great Neck, N. Y., June 3, 1911.

GODFREY, Arthur (entertainer); New York City, Aug. 31, 1903.

GOLDBERG, Arthur Joseph (Secy. of Labor); Chicago, Ill., Aug. 8, 1908.

GOLDBERG, Rube (Reuben) (cartoonist); San Francisco, Calif., July 4, 1883.

GOLDWYN, Samuel (Samuel Goldfish) (movie producer); Warsaw, Pol., 1882.

GONZALEZ, Pancho (tennis player); Los Angeles, Calif., May 9, 1928.

GOODMAN, Benny (clarinetist); Chicago, Ill., May 30, 1909.

GORDON, Max (play producer); New York City, 1892.

GORDON, Ruth (actress); Wollaston, Mass., Oct. 30, 1896.

GOREN, Charles H. (bridge export); Philadelphia, Pa., Mar. 4, 1901.

GORME, Eydie (singer); New York City, Aug. 16, 1931.

GOSDEN, Freeman F. *See* Amos.

GOULD, Chester (cartoonist); Pawnee, Okla., 1900.

GOULD, Glenn (pianist); Toronto, Canada, Sept. 25, 1932.

GOULD, Morton (composer); Richmond Hill, N. Y., Dec. 10, 1913.

GRABLE, Betty (actress); St. Louis, Mo., Dec. 18, 1916.

GRAHAM, Billy (William F.) (evangelist); Charlotte, N. C., Nov. 7, 1918.

GRAHAM, Martha (choreographer); Pittsburgh, Pa.

GRAHAME, Gloria (Gloria Grahame Hallward) (actress); Los Angeles, Calif., Nov. 28, 1924.

GRANGE, Red (Harold) (football player and announcer); Forksville, Pa., June 13, 1904.

GRANGER, Stewart (James Stewart) (actor); London, Eng., May 6, 1913.

GRANT, Cary (Archibald A. Leach) (actor); Bristol, Eng., Jan. 18, 1904.

GRAVES, Robert (poet & novelist); London, Eng., July 26, 1895.

GRAY, Harold (cartoonist); Kankakee, Ill., Jan. 20, 1894.

GRAYSON, Kathryn (Zelma Hednick) (actress); Winston-Salem, N. C., Feb. 9, 1923.

GRECO, José (dancer); Montorio nei Frentani, It., Dec. 23, 1918.

GREEN, Paul (dramatist); Lillington, N. C. Mar. 17, 1894.

GREENE, Graham (novelist); Berkhampstead, Eng., Oct. 2, 1904.

GRIFFITH, Andy (Andrew Samuel) (actor); Mount Airy, N. C., June 1, 1928.

GRIMM, Charley (baseball executive); St. Louis, Mo., Aug. 28, 1898.

GRISSOM, Virgil Ivan (astronaut); Mitchell, Ind., Apr. 3, 1926.

GRISWOLD, A. Whitney (educator); Morristown, N. J., Oct. 27, 1906.

GROFÉ, Ferde (composer); New York City, Mar. 27, 1892.

GROMYKO, Andrei A. (Soviet statesman); Starye Gromyki, Rus., July 5, 1909.

GRONCHI, Giovanni (President, Italy); Pontedera, It., Sept. 10, 1887.

GROPIUS, Walter (architect); Berlin, Ger., May 18, 1883.

GROVE, Lefty (Robert M.) (baseball player); Lonaconing, Md., Mar. 6, 1900

GRUENTHER, Gen. Alfred M. (Pres., Red Cross); Platte Center, Nebr., Mar. 3, 1899.

GUINNESS, Sir Alec (actor); Marylebone, London, Eng., Apr. 2, 1914.

GULDAHL, Ralph (golfer); Dallas, Tex., Nov. 22, 1912.

GUNTHER, John (journalist & author); Chicago, Ill., Aug. 30, 1901.

GUSTAVUS VI (King, Sweden); Stockholm, Swed., Nov. 11, 1882.

HACKETT, Francis (critic & novelist); Kilkenny, Ire., Jan. 21, 1883.

HAGEN, Walter (golfer); Rochester, N. Y., Dec. 21, 1892.

HAGERTY, James C. (former Pres. Press Secy., U. S.); Plattsburgh, N. Y., May 9, 1909.

HAILE SELASSIE I (Emperor, Ethiopia); Ethiopia, July 17, 1891.

HALAS, George (football coach); Chicago, Ill., Feb. 2, 1895.

HANSON, Howard (composer); Wahoo, Nebr., Oct. 28, 1896.

HARDWICKE, Sir Cedric (actor); Lye, Eng., Feb. 19, 1893.

HARRIDGE, Will (baseball executive); Chicago, Ill., Oct. 16, 1886.

HARRIS, Bucky (Stanley R.) (baseball manager); Port Jervis, N. Y., Nov. 8, 1896.

HARRIS, Jed (stage producer); Vienna, Aus., Feb. 25, 1900.

HARRIS, Julie (actress); Grosse Pointe Park, Mich., Dec. 2, 1925.

HARRIS, Phil (band leader); Linton, Ind., June 24, 1906.

HARRIS, Roy (composer); Lincoln Co., Okla., Feb. 12, 1898.

HARRISON, Rex (actor); Huyton, Eng., Mar. 5, 1908.

HARRISON, Wallace K. (architect); Worcester, Mass., Sept. 28, 1895.

HART, Moss (dramatist); New York City, Oct. 24, 1904.

HARVEY, Laurence (Larushka Skikne) (actor); Joniskis, Lithuania, Jan. 10, 1928.

HATLO, Jimmy (cartoonist); Providence, R. I., Sept. 1, 1898.

HAVOC, June (June Hovick) (actress); Seattle, Wash.

HAWKINS, Jack (actor); London, Eng., Sept. 14.

HAYES, Helen (Helen Hayes Brown) (actress); Washington, D. C., Oct. 10, 1900.

HAYWARD, Leland (theatrical producer); Nebraska City, Nebr., Sept. 13, 1902.

HAYWARD, Susan (Edythe Marrener) (actress); Brooklyn, N. Y., June 30, 1919.

HAYWORTH, Rita (Margarita Cansino) (actress); New York City, Oct. 17, 1918.

HEALD, Henry T. (educator); Lincoln, Nebr., Nov. 8, 1904.

HEARST, David W. (publisher); New York City, Dec. 2, 1915.

HEARST, Randolph A. (publisher); New York City, Dec. 2, 1915.

HEARST, William Randolph, Jr. (publisher); New York City, Jan. 27, 1908.

HECHT, Ben (novelist & dramatist); New York City, Feb. 28, 1894.

HEFLIN, Van (actor); Walters, Okla., Dec. 13, 1910.

HEIFETZ, Jascha (violinist); Vilna, Rus., Feb. 2, 1901.

HEISS, Carol (Elizabeth) (skater); New York City, Jan. 30, 1940.

HELLMAN, Lillian (dramatist); New Orleans, La., June 20, 1905.

HENDERSON, Skitch (pianist); Birmingham, Eng., Jan. 27, 1918.

HENIE, Sonja (skater); Oslo, Nor., Apr. 8, 1913.

HENREID, Paul (actor); Trieste, Jan. 10, 1908.

HEPBURN, Audrey (actress); Brussels, Belg., May 4, 1929.

HEPBURN, Katharine (actress); Hartford, Conn., Nov. 8, 1909.

HERBLOCK (Herbert L. Block) (cartoonist); Chicago, Ill., Oct. 13, 1909.

HERMAN, Woody (band leader); Milwaukee, Wis., May 16, 1913.

HERSEY, John R. (novelist); Tientsin, China, June 17, 1914.

HERTER, Christian A. (U. S. statesman); Paris, Fr., Mar. 28, 1895.

HESS, Dame Myra (pianist); London, Eng., Feb. 25, 1890.

HESTON, Charlton (actor); Evanston, Ill., Oct. 4, 1924.

HEYERDAHL, Thor (author & explorer); Larvik, Nor., Oct. 6, 1914.

HILDEGARDE (Hildegarde Loretta Sell) (entertainer); Adell, Wis., Feb. 1, 1906.

HILLARY, Sir Edmund (explorer); New Zealand, July 20, 1919.

HILLIARD, Harriet. See Nelson, Harriet.

HINDEMITH, Paul (composer); Hanau, Ger., Nov. 16, 1895.

HIROHITO (Emperor, Japan); Japan, Apr. 29, 1901.

HIRSCH, Max (horse trainer); Fredericksburg, Tex., July 12, 1880.

HITCHCOCK, Alfred J. (movie director); England, Aug. 13, 1899.

HO Chi-minh (President, Dem. Rep. of Vietnam); Annam, Indo-China, c. 1891.

HOAD, Lew (Lewis) (tennis player); Glebe, NSW, Australia, Nov. 23, 1934.

HOBSON, Laura Z. (Laura K Zametkin) (novelist); New York City.

HODGES, Gil (Gilbert) (baseball player); Princeton, Ind., Apr. 4, 1924.

HODGES, Luther H. (Secy. of Commerce); Pittsylvania Co., Va., Mar. 9, 1898.

HOGAN, Ben (golfer); Dublin, Tex., Aug. 13, 1912.

HOLBROOK, Hal (Harold) (actor); Cleveland, Ohio, Feb. 17, 1925.

HOLDEN, William (William Franklin Beedle, Jr.) (actor); O'Fallon, Ill., Apr. 17, 1918.

HOLLIDAY, Judy (Judith Tuvim) (actress); New York City, June 21, 1923.

HOLM, Celeste (actress & singer); New York City, Apr. 29, 1919.

HOOVER, Herbert C. (U. S. statesman); West Branch, Iowa, Aug. 10, 1874.

HOOVER, J. Edgar (FBI Director, U. S.); Washington, D. C., Jan. 1, 1895.

HOPE, Bob (Leslie Townes Hope) (comedian); London, Eng., May 29, 1903.

HOPPER, Hedda (Elda Furry) (columnist); Hollidaysburg, Pa., June 2, 1890.

HORNE, Lena (singer) Brooklyn, New York, 1918.

HORNSBY, Rogers (baseball player and coach); Winters, Tex., Apr. 27, 1896.

HOROWITZ, Vladimir (pianist); Kiev, Rus., Oct. 1, 1904.

HORTON, Edward Everett (actor); Brooklyn, N. Y., Mar. 18, 1886.

HORTON, Robert (actor); Los Angeles, Calif., July 29.

HOUSEMAN, John (John Haussmann) (stage & movie director); Bucharest, Rum., Sept. 22, 1902.

HOWARD, Roy W. (publisher); Gano, Ohio, Jan. 1, 1883.

HOWE, Quincy (historian & commentator; Boston, Mass., Aug. 17, 1900.

HOWELL, Jim Lee (football coach); Lonoke, Ark., Sept. 27, 1914.

HUBBELL, Carl (baseball executive); Carthage, Mo., June 22, 1903.

HUDSON, Rock (Roy Fitzgerald) (actor); Winnetka, Ill., Nov. 17, 1925.

HUGHES, Langston (poet); Joplin, Mo., Feb. 1, 1902.

HULL, Henry (actor); Louisville, Ky., Oct. 3, 1890.

HUNTER, Kim (Janet Cole) (actress); Detroit, Mich., Nov. 12, 1922.

HUNTER, Tab (actor); New York City, July 11, 1931.

HUNTLEY, Chet (commentator); Cardwell, Mont., Dec. 10, 1911.

HUROK, Sol (impresario); Pogar, Rus., Apr. 9, 1888.

HUSSEIN I (King, Jordan); Jordan, May 2, 1935.

HUSTON, John (movie director); Nevada, Mo., Aug. 5, 1906.

HUTCHINS, Robert M. (educator); Brooklyn, N. Y., Jan. 17, 1899.

HUTTON, Barbara (heiress); New York City, Nov. 14, 1912.

HUTTON, Betty (Betty Thornberg) (singer); Battle Creek, Mich., Feb. 26, 1921.

HUXLEY, Aldous (novelist); Godalming, Eng., July 26, 1894.

HUXLEY, Julian S. (biologist); England, June 22, 1887.

IBERT, Jacques (composer); Paris, Fr., Aug. 15, 1890.

INGE, William (dramatist); Independence, Kans., May 3, 1913.

IONESCO, Eugene (dramatist); Slatina, Rum., Nov. 26, 1912.

IRELAND, John (actor); Vancouver, B. C., Can., Jan. 30, 1915.

ISHERWOOD, Christopher (novelist); Disley, Cheshire, Eng., Aug. 26, 1904.

ITURBI, José (pianist); Valencia, Sp., Nov. 28, 1895.

IVES, Burl (folksinger & actor); Hunt, Ill., June 14, 1909.

JACOBS, Hirsch (horse trainer); New York City, Apr. 8, 1904.

JACKSON, Mahalia (singer); New Orleans, La., Oct. 26, 1912.

JAFFE, Sam (actor); New York City, Mar. 8, 1898.

JAMES, Harry (trumpeter); Albany, Ga., Mar. 15, 1916.

JAMESON, Margaret Storm (novelist); Whitby, Eng., 1897.

JEANMAIRE, Renée (dancer & actress); Paris, Fr., Apr. 29, 1924.

JEBB, Sir Gladwyn (British statesman); England, Apr. 25, 1900.

JEFFERS, Robinson (poet); Pittsburgh, Pa., Jan. 10, 1887.

JESSEL, George (comedian); New York City, Apr. 3, 1898.

JESSUP, Philip C. (U. S. statesman); New York City, Jan. 5, 1897.

JOHANSSON, Ingemar (boxer); Göteborg, Swed., Sept. 22, 1932.

JOHN XXIII (Angelo Giuseppe Roncalli) (Pope); Sotto il Monte, It., Nov. 25, 1881.

JOHN, Augustus (painter); Tenby, Wales, Jan. 4, 1879.

JOHNS, Glynis (actress); Durban, So. Af., Oct. 5, 1923.

JOHNSON, Lyndon B. (Vice President, U. S.); nr. Johnson City, Tex., Aug. 27, 1908.

JOHNSON, Rafer (athlete & actor); Hillsboro, Tex., Aug. 18, 1935.

JOHNSON, Van (actor); Newport, R. I., Aug. 20, 1916.

JOHNSTON, Eric A. (movie executive); Washington, D. C., Dec. 21, 1896.

JONES, Bobby (golfer); Atlanta, Ga., Mar. 17, 1902.

JONES, James (novelist); Robinson, Ill., Nov. 6, 1921.

JONES, Jennifer (Phyllis Isley) (actress); Tulsa, Okla., Mar. 2, 1919.

JONES, Sam (baseball player); Stewartsville, Ohio, Dec. 14, 1925.

JORDAN, James. See McGee.

JOURDAN, Louis (actor); Marseilles, Fr., June 18, 1921.

JULIANA (Queen, Netherlands); The Hague, Neth., Apr. 30, 1909.

KADAR, János (Hungarian statesman); Hungary, 1912.

KAISER, Henry J. (industrialist); Sprout Brook, N. Y., May 9, 1882.

KALINE, Al (Albert) (baseball player); Baltimore, Md., Dec. 19, 1934.

KALTENBORN, Hans V. (radio commentator); Milwaukee, Wis., July 9, 1878.

KANIN, Garson (dramatist & director); Rochester, N. Y., Nov. 24, 1912.

KANTOR, MacKinlay (novelist); Webster City, Iowa, Feb. 4, 1904.

KARLOFF, Boris (William Henry Pratt) (actor); Dulwich, Eng., Nov. 23, 1887.

KAYE, Danny (David Daniel Kominski) (comedian); Brooklyn, N. Y., Jan. 18, 1913.

KAYE, Nora (Nora Koreff) (ballerina); New York City, 1920.

KAYE, Sammy (band leader); Cleveland, Ohio, Mar. 13, 1910.

KAZAN, Elia (movie & stage director); Constantinople, Turk., Sept. 7, 1909.

KEATON, Buster (comedian); Piqua, Kans., Oct. 4, 1896.

KEEL, Howard (singer & actor); Gillespie, Ill., Apr. 13.

KELLAND, Clarence Budington (novelist); Portland, Mich., July 11, 1881.

**KELLER,** Helen (author & social worker); Tuscumbia, Ala., June 27, 1880.

**KELLY,** Emmett (circus clown); Sedan, Kans., 1898.

**KELLY,** Gene (actor); Pittsburgh, Pa., Aug. 23, 1912.

**KELLY,** Grace (actress & Princess of Monaco); Philadelphia, Pa., Nov. 12, 1929.

**KELLY,** Jack (actor); Astoria, N. Y., Sept. 16, 1927.

**KELLY,** Walt (cartoonist); Philadelphia, Pa., Aug. 25, 1913.

**KENNAN,** George F. (author and former diplomat); Milwaukee, Wisconsin, February 16, 1904.

**KENNEDY,** Arthur (actor); Worcester, Mass., Feb. 17, 1914.

**KENNEDY,** John F. (President, U. S.); Brookline, Mass., May 29, 1917.

**KENNEDY,** Robert F. (U.S. Attorney General); Brookline, Mass., Nov. 20, 1925.

**KENT,** Rockwell (painter); Tarrytown Heights, N. Y., June 21, 1882.

**KERENSKY,** Alexander (former Russian Premier); Simbirsk, Rus., 1881.

**KEROUAC,** Jack (novelist); Lowell, Mass., Mar. 12, 1922.

**KERR,** Deborah (actress); Helensburgh, Scot., Sept. 30, 1921.

**KEYES,** Frances Parkinson (novelist); Univ. of Va., July 21, 1885.

**KHACHATURIAN,** Aram (composer); Tiflis, Rus., June 6, 1903.

**KHRUSHCHEV,** Nikita S. (Premier, U.S.S.R.); Kalinovka, Rus., Apr. 17, 1894.

**KIDD,** Michael (choreographer); Brooklyn, N. Y., 1917.

**KIEPURA,** Jan (tenor); Sosnowiec, Pol., May 16, 1902.

**KIERAN,** John (author); New York City, Aug. 2, 1892.

**KILGALLEN,** Dorothy (columnist); Chicago, Ill., July 3, 1913.

**KILLEBREW,** Harmon (baseball player); Payette, Idaho, June 29, 1936.

**KING,** Alexander (writer-commentator-artist); Vienna, Austria, Nov. 13, 1900.

**KING,** Dennis (actor); Coventry, Eng., Nov. 2, 1897.

**KING,** Henry (movie director); Christianburg, Va., Jan. 24, 1896.

**KINGSLEY,** Sidney (Sidney Kirschner) (dramatist); New York City, Oct. 18, 1906.

**KIPNIS,** Alexander (basso); Ukraine, Feb. 1, 1896.

**KIRK,** Grayson (educator); Jeffersonville, Ohio, Oct. 12, 1903.

**KIRK,** Lisa (singer); Charleroi, Pa.

**KIRKPATRICK,** Ralph (harpsichordist); Leominster, Mass., June 10, 1911.

**KIRSTEN,** Dorothy (soprano); Montclair, N. J., July 6, 1919.

**KITT,** Eartha (singer & actress); North, S. C., Jan. 26, 1928.

**KNIGHT,** John S. (publisher); Bluefield, W. Va., Oct. 26, 1894.

**KNOPF,** Alfred A. (publisher); New York City, Sept. 12, 1892.

**KODÁLY,** Zoltán (composer); Kecskemét, Hung., Dec. 16, 1882.

**KOESTLER,** Arthur (novelist); Budapest, Hung., Sept. 5, 1905.

**KOKOSCHKA,** Oskar (painter); Pöchlarn, Aus., Mar. 1, 1886.

**KOSTELANETZ,** Andre (orchestra conductor); Petrograd, Rus., Dec. 22, 1901.

**KOVACS,** Ernie (comedian); Trenton, N. J., Jan. 23, 1919.

**KRAMER,** John A. (tennis player); Las Vegas, Nev., Aug. 1, 1921.

**KRAMER,** Stanley E. (movie producer); New York City, Sept. 29, 1913.

**KREISLER,** Fritz (violinist); Vienna, Aus., Feb. 2, 1875.

**KROCK,** Arthur (journalist); November 16, 1886.

**KRUPA,** Gene (drummer & band leader); Chicago, Ill., Jan. 15, 1909.

**KUBELIK,** Rafael (orchestra conductor); Bychory, Bohemia, June 29, 1914.

**KUENN,** Harvey (baseball player); Milwaukee, Wis., Dec. 4, 1930.

**KURTZ,** Efrem (orchestra conductor); St. Petersburg, Rus., Nov. 7, 1900.

**LADD,** Alan (actor); Hot Springs, Ark., Sept. 3, 1913.

**LA FARGE,** Oliver (author & anthropologist); New York City, Dec. 19, 1901.

**LAHR,** Bert (Irving Lahrheim) (comedian); New York City, Aug. 13, 1895.

**LAINE,** Frankie (Frank Paul LoVecchio) (singer); Chicago, Ill., Mar. 30, 1913.

**LAMARR,** Hedy (actress); Vienna, Aus.

**LAMAS,** Fernando (actor); Buenos Aires, Arg., Jan. 9.

**LAMOUR,** Dorothy (actress); New Orleans, La., Dec. 10, 1914.

**LANCASTER,** Burt (actor); New York City, Nov. 2, 1913.

**LANCHESTER,** Elsa (Elsa Sullivan) (actress); London, Eng., Oct. 28, 1902.

**LANDERS,** Ann (Mrs. Jules Lederer) (columnist); Sioux City, Iowa, July 14, 1918.

**LANDY,** John (mile runner); Australia, Apr. 4, 1930.

**LANG,** Fritz (movie director); Vienna, Aus., Dec. 5, 1890.

**LANG,** Paul Henry (musicologist); Budapest, Hung., Aug. 28, 1901.

**LA ROSA,** Julius (singer); Brooklyn, N. Y., Jan. 2, 1930.

**LAUGHTON,** Charles (actor); Scarborough, Eng., July 1, 1899.

**LAWFORD,** Peter (actor); London, Eng., Sept. 7, 1923.

**LAWRENCE,** David (journalist); Philadelphia, Pa., Dec. 25, 1888.

**LAWRENCE,** Marjorie (soprano); Deans Marsh, Austr., Feb. 17, 1909.

**LAWRENCE,** Steve (Sidney Leibowitz) (singer); New York City, July 8, 1935.

**LEAHY,** Frank (football coach); O'Neill, Nebr., Aug. 21, 1908.

**LEAN,** David (movie director); Croydon, Eng., Mar. 25, 1908.

**LE CORBUSIER** (Charles-Édouard Jeanneret) (architect); La Chaux De Fonds, Switz., Oct. 6, 1887.

**LEE,** Gypsy Rose (Rose Hovik) (entertainer); Seattle, Wash., Feb. 9, 1914.

LEE, Peggy (Norma Egstrom) (singer); Jamestown, N. Dak., May 26, 1920.

LE GALLIENNE, Eva (actress & director); London, Eng., Jan. 11, 1899.

LEHMAN, Herbert H. (former U. S. Senator); New York City, Mar. 28, 1878.

LEHMANN, Lotte (soprano); Perleberg, Ger., July 2, 1885.

LEIGH, Janet (Jeanette Morrison) (actress); Merced, Calif., July 6, 1927.

LEIGH, Vivien (Vivien Mary Hartley) (actress); Darjeeling, India, Nov. 5, 1913.

LEIGHTON, Margaret (actress); Birmingham, Eng., Feb. 26, 1922.

LEINSDORF, Erich (orchestra conductor); Vienna, Aus., Feb. 4, 1912.

LEMMON, Jack (actor); Boston, Mass., Feb. 8, 1925.

LERNER, Alan Jay (librettist); New York City, Aug. 31, 1918.

LERNER, Max (social writer); Minsk, Rus., Dec. 20, 1902.

LE ROY, Mervyn (movie producer & director); San Francisco, Calif., Oct. 15, 1900.

LEVANT, Oscar (pianist); Pittsburgh, Pa., Dec. 27, 1906.

LEVENE, Sam (actor); New York City, 1907.

LEVI, Carlo (novelist); Turin, It., Nov. 29, 1902.

LEVIN, Herman (theatrical producer); Philadelphia, Pa., Mar. 1, 1908.

LEWIS, Fulton, Jr. (columnist); Washington, D. C., Apr. 30, 1903.

LEWIS, Jerry (comedian); Newark, N. J., Mar. 16, 1926.

LEWIS, Joe E. (comedian); New York City.

LEWIS, John L. (labor leader); Lucas, Iowa, Feb. 12, 1880.

LEWIS, Ted (band leader); Circleville, Ohio.

LEY, Willy (science writer); Berlin, Ger., Oct. 2, 1906.

LIBERACE (Wladziu Liberace) (pianist); West Allis, Wis., May 16, 1919.

LILLIE, Beatrice (actress); Toronto, Can., May 29, 1898.

LIN Yutang (philosopher); Changchow, China, Oct. 10, 1895.

LINDBERGH, Anne Morrow (writer); Englewood, N. J., 1907.

LINDBERGH, Charles A. (aviator); Detroit, Mich., Feb. 4, 1902.

LINDSAY, Howard (dramatist); Waterford, N. Y., Mar. 29, 1889.

LINKLETTER, Art (actor); Moose Jaw, Sask., Can., July 17, 1912.

LIPCHITZ, Jacques (sculptor); Druskieniki, Lith., Aug. 22, 1891.

LIPPMANN, Walter (author & journalist); New York City, Sept. 23, 1889.

LITTLE, Lou (football coach); Leominster, Mass., Dec. 6, 1893.

LITTLE, W. Lawson, Jr. (golfer); Newport, R. I., Jan. 23, 1910.

LIVESY, Roger (actor); Barry, Wales, June 25, 1906.

LLEWELLYN, Richard (novelist); St. David's, Wales.

LLOYD, Harold (comedian); Burchard, Nebr., Apr. 20, 1894.

LLOYD, Selwyn (British diplomat); West Kirby, Eng., July 28, 1904.

LOCKE, Bobby (Arthur D'Arcy) (golfer); Transvaal, So. Africa, Nov. 20, 1917.

LOCKWOOD, Margaret (actress); Karachi, India, Sept. 15, 1916.

LODGE, Henry Cabot, Jr. (former U. N. Delegate, U. S.); Nahant, Mass., July 5, 1902.

LOESSER, Frank (song writer); New York City, June 29, 1910.

LOEWE, Frederick (song writer); Vienna, Aus., June 10, 1904.

LOGAN, Joshua (director & dramatist); Texarkana, Tex., Oct. 5, 1908.

LOLLOBRIGIDA, Gina (actress); Subiaco, It., 1928.

LOMBARDO, Guy (band leader); London, Can., June 19, 1902.

LONDON, Julie (Julie Peck) (singer); Santa Rosa, Calif., Sept. 26, 1926.

LOOS, Anita (novelist); Sisson, Calif., Apr. 26, 1893.

LOPEZ, Al (baseball manager); Tampa, Fla., Aug. 20, 1908.

LOPEZ, Vincent (band leader); Brooklyn, N. Y., Dec. 10, 1898.

LOREN, Sophia (Sofia Scicolone) (actress); Rome, It., Sept. 20, 1934.

LORRE, Peter (actor); Rosenberg, Hung., June 26, 1904.

LOUIS, Joe (Joe Louis Barrow) (boxer); Lexington, Ala., May 13, 1914.

LOVEJOY, Frank (actor); New York City, Mar. 28.

LOW, David (cartoonist); Dunedin, N. Z., Apr. 7, 1891.

LOWELL, Robert (poet); Boston, Mass., Mar. 1, 1917.

LOY, Myrna (Myrna Williams) (actress); near Helena, Mont., Aug. 2, 1905.

LUCE, Clare Boothe (playwright and former diplomat); New York City, Apr. 10, 1903.

LUCE, Henry R. (publisher); Shantung, China, Apr. 3, 1898.

LUKAS, Paul (actor); Budapest, Hung., May 26, 1895.

LUNT, Alfred (actor); Milwaukee, Wis., Aug. 19, 1893.

LUPINO, Ida (actress); London, Eng., Feb. 4, 1918.

MacARTHUR, Douglas (U. S. general); Little Rock Barracks, Ark., Jan. 26, 1880.

MacDONALD, Jeanette (soprano); Philadelphia, Pa., June 18, 1907.

MacKENZIE, Gisele (Marie Marguerite Louise Gisele LaFleche) (singer); Winnipeg, Canada, Jan. 10, 1927.

MacLEISH, Archibald (poet); Glencoe, Ill., May 7, 1892.

MACMILLAN, Harold (British Prime Minister); London, Eng., Feb. 10, 1894.

MacMURRAY, Fred (actor); Kankakee, Ill., Aug. 30, 1908.

MacRAE, Gordon (singer); East Orange, N. J., Mar. 12, 1921.

MADISON, Guy (Robert Moseley) (actor); Bakersfield, Calif., Jan. 19, 1922.

MAGNANI, Anna (actress); Rome, It., Mar. 7, 1908.

MAILER, Norman (novelist); Long Branch, N. J., Jan. 31, 1923.

MAIN, Marjorie (Mary Tomlinson Krebs) (actress); Acton, Ind., Feb. 24, 1890.

MAKARIOS III, Archbishop (Michael Christedoulos Mouskos) (Greek Orthodox prelate); Ano Panayia, Paphos, Cyprus, Aug. 13, 1913.

MALDEN, Karl (actor); Chicago, Ill., Mar. 22, 1913.

MALENKOV, Georgi M. (Soviet statesman); Orenburg, Rus., Jan. 8, 1902.

MALONE, Dorothy (actress) Chicago, Ill., Jan. 30, 1925.

MALRAUX, André (novelist); Paris, Fr., Nov. 3, 1901.

MANGANO, Silvana (actress); Rome, It.

MANGRUM, Lloyd (golfer); Dallas, Tex., Aug. 1, 1914.

MANKIEWICZ, Joseph L. (movie director); Wilkes-Barre, Pa., Feb. 11, 1909.

MANSFIELD, Jayne (Jane Palmer) (actress); Bryn Mawr, Pa., Apr. 19, 1933.

MANTLE, Mickey (baseball player); Spavinaw, Okla., Oct. 20, 1931.

MANTOVANI, Annunzio (orchestra conductor); Venice, 1905.

MAO Tse-tung (Chmn. of Politburo, Comm. China); Shao Shan, China, 1893.

MARCEAU, Marcel (mime); Strasbourg, Fr., Mar. 22, 1923.

MARCH, Fredric (Frederick Bickel) (actor); Racine, Wis., Aug. 31, 1897.

MARCH, Hal (Harold Mendelson) (actor); San Francisco, Calif., Apr. 22, 1920.

MARCIANO, Rocky (Rocco Marchegiano) (boxer); Brockton, Mass., Sept. 1, 1924.

MARGARET ROSE (Princess, Gr. Brit.); Glamis Castle, Angus, Scot., Aug. 21, 1930.

MARIS, Roger (baseball player); Hibbing, Minn., Sept. 10, 1934.

MARITAIN, Jacques (philosopher); Paris, Fr., Nov. 18, 1882.

MARKOVA, Alicia (ballerina); London, Eng., Dec. 1, 1910.

MARSHALL, Herbert (actor); London, Eng., May 23, 1890.

MARSHALL, Thurgood (lawyer); Baltimore, Md., July 2, 1908.

MARTIN, Dean (comedian & singer); Steubenville, Ohio, June 7, 1917.

MARTIN, Joseph W., Jr. (U. S. Representative, Mass.); No. Attleboro, Mass., Nov. 3, 1884.

MARTIN, Mary (actress); Weatherford, Tex., Dec. 1, 1914.

MARTIN, Tony (actor & singer); San Francisco, Calif., Dec. 25, 1914.

MARTIN, William McChesney, Jr. (financial executive); St. Louis, Mo., Dec. 17, 1906.

MARTINELLI, Giovanni (tenor); Montagnana, It., Oct. 22, 1885.

MARX, Chico (Leonard) (comedian); New York City, Mar. 22, 1891.

MARX, Groucho (Julius) (comedian); New York City, Oct. 2, 1895.

MARX, Harpo (Arthur) (comedian); New York City, Nov. 23, 1893.

MASEFIELD, John (poet); Ledbury, Eng., June 1, 1878.

MASON, James (actor); Huddersfield, Eng., May 15, 1909.

MASSEY, Raymond (actor); Toronto, Ont., Can., Aug. 30, 1896.

MASSEY, Vincent (Canadian statesman); Toronto, Ont., Can., Feb. 20, 1887.

MASSINE, Léonide (choreographer); Moscow, Rus., Aug. 9, 1896.

MATHIAS, Bob (athlete); Tulare, Calif., Nov. 17, 1930.

MATHIS, Johnny (singer); San Francisco, Calif., Sept. 30, 1935.

MATTHEWS, Ed (Edwin) (baseball player); Texarkana, Tex., Oct. 13, 1931.

MATURE, Victor (actor); Louisville, Ky., Jan. 19, 1916.

MAUGHAM, William Somerset (novelist); Paris, Fr., Jan. 25, 1874.

MAURIAC, François (novelist); Bordeaux, Fr., Oct. 11, 1885.

MAUROIS, André (Émile Herzog) (novelist); Elbeuf, Fr., July 26, 1885.

MAXWELL, Elsa (columnist); Keokuk, Iowa, May 24, 1883.

MAYER, Dick (golfer); Stamford, Conn., Aug. 29, 1922.

MAYNOR, Dorothy (soprano); Norfolk, Va., Sept. 3, 1910.

MAYS, Willie (baseball player); Fairfield, Ala., May 6, 1931.

McBRIDE, Mary Margaret (author); Paris, Mo., Nov. 16, 1899.

McCAREY, Leo (movie director); Los Angeles, Calif., Oct. 3, 1898.

McCARTHY, Joe (baseball manager); Philadelphia, Pa., Apr. 21, 1887.

McCLOY, John J. (banker); Philadelphia, Pa., Mar. 31, 1895.

McCORMACK, Patty (actress); New York City, Aug. 21, 1945.

McCREA, Joel (actor); Los Angeles, Calif., Nov. 5, 1906.

McDONALD, David J. (labor leader); Pittsburgh, Pa., Nov. 22, 1902.

McDONALD, Marie (Marie Frye) (actress); Burgin, Ky.

McDOWALL, Roddy (actor); London, Eng., Sept. 17, 1928.

McGEE, Fibber (James Jordan) (actor); Peoria, Ill., Nov. 16, 1896.

McGUIRE, Dorothy (actress); Omaha, Nebr., June 14, 1919.

McKENNA, Siobhan (actress); Belfast, Ire., May 24, 1923.

McNAMARA, Robert S. (Secy. of Defense); San Francisco, Calif., June 9, 1916.

MEAD, Margaret (anthropologist); Philadelphia, Pa., Dec. 16, 1901.

MEANY, George (labor leader); New York City, Aug. 16, 1894.

MEDINA, Harold R. (U. S. jurist); Brooklyn, N. Y., Feb. 16, 1888.

MEEKER Ralph (Ralph Rathgeber) (actor); Minneapolis, Minn., Nov. 21, 1920.

MEIR, Golda (Golda Myerson) (Israeli stateswoman); Kiev, Rus.

MEITNER, Lise (physicist); Vienna, Aus., Nov. 7, 1878.

MENDÈS-FRANCE, Pierre (French statesman); Paris, Fr., Jan. 11, 1905.

MENJOU, Adolphe (actor); Pittsburgh, Pa., Feb. 18, 1890.

MENOTTI, Gian-Carlo (composer); Cadegliano, It., July 7, 1911.

MENUHIN, Yehudi (violinist); New York City, Apr. 22, 1916.

MENZIES, Robert Gordon (Prime Minister, Australia); Jeparit, Australia, Dec. 20, 1894.

MERCER, Johnny (singer & song writer); Savannah, Ga., Nov. 18, 1909.

MEREDITH, Burgess (actor); Cleveland, Ohio, Nov. 16, 1908.

MERMAN, Ethel (Ethel Zimmerman) (actress & singer); Astoria, N. Y., Jan. 16, 1909.

MERRICK, David (David Margulois) (theatrical producer); St. Louis, Mo., Nov. 27, 1912.

MERRILL, Robert (baritone); Brooklyn, N. Y., June 4, 1919.

MERTON, Thomas (poet & religious writer); Prades, Fr., Jan. 31, 1915.

MESTA, Perle (hostess); Sturgis, Mich., 1891.

MESTROVIĆ, Ivan (sculptor); Vrpolje, Yugos., Aug. 15, 1883.

METALIOUS, Grace (author); Manchester, N. H., Sept. 8, 1924.

MICHENER, James A. (novelist); New York City, Feb. 3, 1907.

MIDDLECOFF, Cary (golfer); Halls, Tenn., Jan. 6, 1921.

MIELZINER, Jo (stage designer); Paris, Fr., Mar. 19, 1901.

MIKOYAN, Anastas I. (Soviet statesman); Sanain, Armenia, Nov. 25, 1895.

MILANOV, Zinka (soprano); Zagreb, Yugos., May 17, 1908.

MILHAUD, Darius (composer); Aix-en-Provence, Fr., Sept. 4, 1892.

MILLAND, Ray (actor); Neath, Wales, Jan. 3, 1907.

MILLER, Arthur (dramatist); New York City, 1915.

MILLER, Gilbert (theatrical producer); New York City, July 3, 1884.

MILLER, Henry (author); New York City, Dec. 26, 1891.

MILLER, Mitch (Mitchell) (musician); Rochester, N. Y., July 4, 1911.

MILSTEIN, Nathan (violinist); Odessa, Russ., Dec. 31, 1904.

MINEO, Sal (actor & singer); New York City, Jan. 10, 1939.

MINNELLI, Vincente (movie director); Chicago, Ill., Feb. 28.

MIRÓ, Joan (painter); Barcelona, Sp., Apr. 21. 1893.

MITCHELL, Guy (singer); Detroit, Mich., Feb. 27, 1927.

MITCHELL, Thomas (actor); Elizabeth, N. J., July 11, 1895.

MITCHUM, Robert (actor); Bridgeport, Conn., Aug. 6, 1917.

MOISEIWITSCH, Benno (pianist); Odessa, Rus., Feb. 22, 1890.

MOLLET, Guy (French statesman); Flers, Orne, Fr., Dec. 31, 1905.

MOLOTOV, Vyacheslav M. (V. M. Skryabin) (Soviet statesman); Kukarka, Rus., Mar. 9, 1890.

MONK, Thelonious (jazz musician); New York City, Oct. 10, 1920.

MONROE, Marilyn (Norma Jean Mortenson) (actress); Los Angeles, June 1, 1926.

MONROE, Vaughn (band leader); Akron, Ohio, Oct. 7, 1912.

MONSARRAT, Nicholas (novelist); Liverpool, Eng., Mar. 22, 1910.

MONTALBAN, Ricardo (actor); Mexico City, Mex., Nov. 25.

MONTEUX, Pierre (orchestra conductor); Paris, Fr., Apr. 4, 1875.

MONTGOMERY, Robert (Henry, Jr.) (actor); Beacon, N. Y., May 21, 1904.

MONTGOMERY OF ALAMEIN, 1st Viscount of Hindhead (Sir Bernard Law Montgomery) (British field marshal); Donegal, Ire., Nov. 17, 1887.

MOORE, Archie (boxer); Collinsville, Ill., Dec. 13, 1916.

MOORE, Garry (Thomas Garrison Morfit) (comedian); Baltimore, Md., Jan. 31, 1915.

MOORE, Henry (sculptor); Castleford, Eng., July 30, 1898.

MOORE, Marianne (poet); Kirkwood, Mo., Nov. 15, 1887.

MOORE, Terry (Helen Koford) (actress); Los Angeles, Calif., Jan. 7, 1929.

MOORE, Victor (actor); Hammonton, N. J., Feb. 24, 1876.

MOOREHEAD, Agnes (actress); Clinton, Mass., Dec. 6, 1906.

MORINI, Erica (violinist); Vienna, Aus., Jan. 5, 1910.

MORLEY, Robert (actor); Wiltshire, Eng., May 26, 1908.

MOSES, Grandma (Anna Mary Robertson) (painter); Greenwich, N. Y., September 7, 1860.

MOSES, Robert (NYC public official); New Haven, Conn., Dec. 18, 1888.

MOSTEL, Zero (actor & comedian); Brooklyn, N.Y., Feb. 28, 1915.

MUMFORD, Lewis (author); Flushing, N. Y., Oct. 19, 1895.

MUNCH, Charles (orchestra conductor); Strasbourg, Ger., Sept. 1891.

MUNI, Paul (Muni Weisenfreund) (actor); Lemberg, Aus., Sept. 22, 1895.

MUNSEL, Patrice (soprano); Spokane, Wash., May 14, 1925.

MURPHY, George (actor); New Haven, Conn., July 4, 1904.

MURRAY, Arthur (dancing teacher); New York City, Apr. 4, 1895.

MURRAY, Ken (Don Court) (actor); New York City, July 14, 1903.

MURROW, Edward R. (radio commentator); Greensboro, N. C.

MUSIAL, Stan (baseball player); Donora, Pa., Nov. 21, 1920.

NAISH, J. Carrol (actor); New York City, Jan. 21, 1900.

NASH, Ogden (poet); Rye, N. Y., Aug. 19, 1902.

NASSER, Gamal Abdel; Asyut province, Upper Egypt, Jan. 15, 1918.

NATWICK, Mildred (actress); Baltimore, Md., June 19, 1908.

NEHRU, Jawaharlal (Prime Minister, India); Allahabad, India, Nov. 14, 1889.

NELSON, David (actor); Oct. 24, 1936.

NELSON, John Byron, Jr. (golfer); Fort Worth, Tex., Feb. 4, 1912.

NELSON, Harriet Hilliard (Peggy Lou Snyder) (actress & singer); Des Moines, Iowa.

**NELSON,** Ozzie (Oswald) (actor & band leader); Jersey City, N. J., 1906.

**NELSON,** Ricky (Eric) (actor & singer); Teaneck, N. J., May 8, 1940.

**NENNI,** Pietro (Italian Socialist leader); Faenza, It., Feb. 9, 1891.

**NEVINS,** Allan (historian); Camp Point, Ill., May 20, 1890.

**NEWCOMBE,** Don (baseball player); Madison, N. J., July 14, 1926.

**NEWHOUSE,** Samuel I. (publisher); New York City, May 24, 1895.

**NEWMAN,** Paul (actor); Cleveland, Ohio, Jan. 26, 1925.

**NGO** Dinh Diem (President, Rep. of Vietnam); Quang Binh, Annam, 1901.

**NIEBUHR,** Reinhold (theologian); Wright City, Mo., June 21, 1892.

**NILSSON,** Birgit (soprano); West Karup, Sweden, May 17, 1923.

**NIVEN,** David (actor); Kirriemuir, Scot., Mar. 1, 1910.

**NIXON,** Richard M. (former Vice President, U. S.); Yorba Linda, Calif., Jan. 9, 1913.

**NKRUMAH,** Kwame (Prime Minister, Ghana); Nkroful, Br. W. Af., 1909.

**NOGUCHI,** Isamu (sculptor); Los Angeles, Calif., Nov. 7, 1904.

**NOLAN,** Lloyd (actor); San Francisco, Calif., Aug. 11, 1902.

**NORRIS,** Kathleen (novelist); San Francisco, Calif., July 16, 1880.

**NORSTAD,** Gen. Lauris (Supr. Comdr. NATO); Minneapolis, Minn., Mar. 24, 1907.

**NOVAËS,** Guiomar (pianist); São João de Boa Vista, Braz., Feb. 28, 1895.

**NOVAK,** Kim (Marilyn Novak) (actress); Chicago, Ill., Feb. 13, 1933.

**NOVOTNA,** Jarmila (soprano); Prague, Czechoslovakia, Sept. 23, 1911.

**NUGENT,** Elliott (author, actor & director); Dover, Ohio, Sept. 20, 1899.

**OBERON,** Merle (Merle O'Brien Thompson) (actress); Tasmania, Feb. 19, 1911.

**O'BRIAN,** Hugh (Hugh J. Krampe) (actor); Rochester, N. Y., Apr. 19, 1925.

**O'BRIEN,** Edmond (actor); New York City, Sept. 10, 1915.

**O'BRIEN,** Margaret (Angela Maxine O'Brien) (actress); San Diego, California, Jan. 15, 1937.

**O'BRIEN,** Pat (actor); Milwaukee, Wis., Nov. 11, 1899.

**O'CASEY,** Sean (dramatist); Dublin, Ire., 1881.

**O'CONNOR,** Donald (actor); Chicago, Ill., Aug. 28, 1925.

**ODETS,** Clifford (dramatist); Philadelphia, Pa., July 18, 1906.

**ODETTA** (Odetta Holmes) (folk singer); Birmingham, Ala., Dec. 31, 1930.

**O'HARA,** John (novelist); Pottsville, Pa., Jan. 31, 1905.

**O'HARA,** Maureen (Maureen FitzSimons) (actress); Dublin, Ire., Aug. 17, 1921.

**OISTRAKH,** David (violinist); Odessa, Russ., 1908.

**O'KEEFFE,** Georgia (painter); Sun Prairie, Wis., Nov. 15, 1887.

**O'KELLY,** Seán T. (Irish statesman); Dublin, Ire., Aug. 25, 1882.

**OLAF V** (King, Norway); Sandringham, Eng., July 2, 1903.

**OLIVIER,** Sir Laurence (actor); Dorking, Eng., May 22, 1907.

**OPPENHEIMER,** J. Robert (physicist); New York City, Apr. 22, 1904.

**ORMANDY,** Eugene (orchestra conductor); Budapest, Hung., Nov. 18, 1899.

**OSBORN,** Paul (dramatist); Evansville, Ind., Sept. 4, 1901.

**OSBORNE,** John (dramatist); London, Eng., Dec. 12, 1929.

**OWENS,** Jesse (sprinter); Decatur, Ala., Sept. 12, 1913.

**PAAR,** Jack (comedian); Canton, Ohio, May 1, 1918.

**PAGE,** Geraldine (actress); Kirksville, Mo., Nov. 22, 1924.

**PAGE,** Patti (Clara Ann Fowler) (singer); Claremore, Okla., 1927.

**PALANCE,** Jack (actor); Latimer, Pa., Feb. 18, 1920.

**PALEY,** William S. (broadcasting executive); Chicago, Ill., Sept. 28, 1901.

**PALMER,** Arnold (golfer); Youngstown, Pa., Sept. 10, 1929.

**PALMER,** Lilli (actress); Posen, Germany, May 27, 1917.

**PARKER,** Dorothy (poet & story writer); West End, N. J., Aug. 22, 1893.

**PARKER,** Eleanor (actress); Cedarville, Ohio, June 26, 1922.

**PARKINSON,** C. (Cyril) Northcote (author); Durham, Eng., July 30, 1909.

**PARSONS,** Louella O. (columnist); Freeport, Ill., Aug. 6, 1893.

**PASTERNAK,** Joseph (movie producer); Silagy-Somlyo, Rum., Sept. 19, 1901.

**PATTERSON,** Floyd (boxer); Waco, N. C., Jan. 4, 1935.

**PAUL I** (King, Greece); Athens, Gr., Dec. 14, 1901.

**PAULING,** Linus Carl (chemist); Portland, Oreg., Feb. 28, 1901.

**PEALE,** Norman Vincent (clergyman & author); Bowersville, Ohio, May 31, 1898.

**PEARSON,** Drew (columnist); Evanston, Ill., Dec. 13, 1897.

**PEARSON,** Hesketh (author); Hawford, Worcs., Eng., Feb. 20, 1887.

**PEARSON,** Lester B. (Canadian statesman); Toronto, Ont., Can., Apr. 23, 1897.

**PEATTIE,** Donald Culross (nature writer); Chicago, Ill., June 21, 1898.

**PECK,** Gregory (actor); La Jolla, Calif., Apr. 5, 1916.

**PEERCE,** Jan (tenor); New York City, 1904.

**PEGLER,** Westbrook (columnist); Minneapolis, Minn., Aug. 2, 1894.

**PERELMAN,** S. J. (Sidney J.); (humorist); Brooklyn, N. Y., Feb. 1, 1904.

**PERKINS,** Tony (Anthony) (actor); New York City, Apr. 14, 1932.

**PERÓN,** Juan D. (former President, Argentina); nr. Lobos, Arg., Oct. 8, 1895.

**PETERS,** Roberta (Roberta Peterman) (soprano); New York City, May 4, 1930.

**PETRI,** Egon (pianist); Hanover, Ger., Mar. 23, 1881.

PETRILLO, James C. (labor leader); Chicago, Ill., Mar. 16, 1892.

PHILIP (Philip Mountbatten) (Duke of Edinburgh); Corfu, June 10, 1921.

PIAF, Edith (singer); Paris, France, Dec. 19, 1915.

PIATIGORSKY, Gregor (cellist); Ekaterinoslav, Rus., Apr. 17, 1903.

PICASSO, Pablo (painter); Málaga, Sp., Oct. 25, 1881.

PICCARD, Auguste (physicist); Basel, Switz., Jan. 28, 1884.

PICCARD, Jean Félix (aeronautics engineer); Basel, Switz., Jan. 28, 1884.

PICKFORD, Mary (Gladys Mary Smith) (actress); Toronto, Can., Apr. 8, 1893.

PIDGEON, Walter (actor); East St. John, N. B., Can., Sept. 23, 1898.

PIERCE, Billy (baseball player); Detroit, Mich., Apr. 2, 1927.

PITTS, Zasu (actress); Parsons, Kans., Jan. 3, 1898.

PLAYER, Gary (golfer); Johannesburg, So. Af.

PODRES, Johnny (baseball player); Witherbee, N. Y., Sept. 30, 1932.

POITIER, Sidney (actor); Miami, Fla., Feb. 20, 1924.

PONS, Lily (soprano); Cannes, Fr., Apr. 13, 1904.

PORTER, Cole (song writer); Peru, Ind., June 9, 1893.

PORTER, Katherine Anne (story writer); Indian Creek, Tex., May 15, 1894.

POULENC, Francis (composer); Paris, Fr., Jan. 7, 1899.

POWELL, Dick (actor); Mt. View, Ark., Nov. 14, 1904.

POWELL, William (actor); Pittsburgh, Pa., July 29, 1892.

PREMINGER, Otto (movie producer & director); Vienna, Aus., Dec. 5, 1906.

PRESLEY, Elvis (singer); Tupelo, Miss., Jan. 8, 1935.

PRESTON, Robert (Robert Preston Meservey) (actor); Newton Highlands, Mass., 1918.

PRICE, George (cartoonist); Coytesville, N. J., June 9, 1901.

PRICE, Leontyne (soprano); Laurel, Miss., Feb. 10, 1929.

PRICE, Vincent (actor); St. Louis, Mo., May 27, 1911.

PRIESTLEY, J. B. (John B.) (novelist & dramatist); Bradford, Eng., Sept. 13, 1894.

PRIMROSE, William (violist); Glasgow, Scot., Aug. 23, 1904.

PUSEY, Nathan M. (educator); Council Bluffs, Iowa, Apr. 4, 1907.

QUASIMODO, Salvatore (poet); Modica, Italy, Aug. 20, 1901.

QUINN, Anthony (actor); Chihuahua, Mex., Apr. 21, 1916.

RABI, Isidor (physicist); Austria, July 29, 1898.

RAFT, George (actor); New York City, Sept. 27, 19??.

RAINIER III (Sovereign Prince of Monaco); Monaco, May 31, 1923.

RAINS, Claude (actor); London, Eng., Nov. 10, 1889.

RANK (1st Baron of Sutton-Scotney) (Joseph Arthur Rank) (movie producer); Hull, Eng., Dec. 23, 1888.

RATHBONE, Basil (actor); Johannesburg, So. Af., June 13, 1892.

RATTIGAN, Terence (dramatist); London, Eng., June 10, 1911.

RAWLS, Betsy (golfer); Spartanburg, S. C., May 4, 1928.

RAY, Johnnie (singer); Roseburg, Oreg., Jan. 10, 1927.

RAYBURN, Sam (Speaker of House, U. S..); Roane Co., Tenn., Jan. 6, 1882.

RAYE, Martha (Margie Yvonne Reed) (actress); Butte, Mont., Aug. 27, 1916.

REAGAN, Ronald (actor); Tampico, Ill., Feb. 6, 1911.

REDGRAVE, Sir Michael (actor); Bristol, Eng., Mar. 20, 1908.

REESE, Pee Wee (Harold) (baseball player & announcer); Ekron, Ky., July 23, 1919.

REID, Helen Rogers (publisher); Appleton, Wis., Nov. 23, 1882.

REINER, Carl (actor); New York City, Mar. 20, 1922.

REINER, Fritz (orchestra conductor); Budapest, Hung., Dec. 19, 1888.

REMARQUE, Erich Maria (novelist); Osnabrük, Ger., June 22, 1898.

REMICK, Lee (Ann) (actress); Quincy, Mass., Dec. 14, 1935.

RENNIE, Michael (actor); Bradford, Yorks., Eng., Aug. 25, 1909.

RESTON, James (journalist); Clydebank, Scot., Nov. 3, 1909.

REUTHER, Walter P. (labor leader); Wheeling, W. Va., Sept. 1, 1907.

REYNOLDS, Debbie (Mary Frances Reynolds) (actress); El Paso, Tex., Apr. 1, 1932.

RHEE, Syngman (former President, South Korea); Seoul, Kor., Mar. 26, 1875.

RIBICOFF, Abraham A. (Secy. of Health, Education, and Welfare); New Britain, Conn., Apr. 9, 1910.

RICE, Elmer (Elmer Reizenstein) (dramatist); New York City, Sept. 28, 1892.

RICHARD, Maurice (hockey player); Montreal, Que., Can., Aug. 4, 1921.

RICHARDS, Paul (baseball manager); Waxahachie, Tex., Nov. 21, 1908.

RICHARDSON, Sir Ralph (actor); Cheltenham, Glos., Eng., Dec. 19, 1902.

RICKENBACKER, Eddie (Edward V.) (airline executive); Columbus, Ohio, Oct. 8, 1890.

RICKEY, Branch (baseball executive); Stockdale, Ohio, Dec. 20, 1881.

RICKOVER, Vice Adm. Hyman G. (U. S. naval officer); Russia, Jan. 27, 1900.

RIDGWAY, Gen. Matthew B. (U. S. Army officer); Ft. Monroe, Va., Mar. 3, 1895.

RITCHARD, Cyril (actor); Sydney, Australia, Dec. 1, 1898.

RITTER, Thelma (actress); Brooklyn, N. Y., Feb. 14, 1905.

RIZZUTO, Phil (baseball player and announcer); New York City, Sept. 25, 1918.

ROARK, Helen Wills Moody (tennis player); Centerville, Calif., Oct. 6, 1905.

ROBBINS, Jerome (Jerome Rabinowitz) (choreographer); NYC, Oct. 11, 1918.

ROBERTS, Robin (baseball player); Springfield, Ill., Sept. 30, 1926.

ROBESON, Paul (baritone); Princeton, N. J., Apr. 9, 1898.

ROBINSON, Edward G. (Emanuel Goldenberg) (actor); Bucharest, Rum., Dec. 12, 1893.

ROBINSON, Frank (baseball player); Beaumont, Tex., Aug. 31, 1935.

ROBINSON, Jackie (baseball player); Cairo, Ga., Jan. 31, 1919.

ROBINSON, Ray (boxer); Detroit, Mich., May 3, 1920.

ROBSON, Dame Flora (actress); South Shields, Eng., Mar. 28, 1902.

ROCHESTER (Eddie Anderson) (comedian); Oakland, Calif., Sept. 18, 1905.

ROCKEFELLER, David (business executive); New York City, June 12, 1915.

ROCKEFELLER, John D., 3rd (business executive); New York City, Mar. 21, 1906.

ROCKEFELLER, Laurance S. (business executive); New York City, May 26, 1910.

ROCKEFELLER, Winthrop (business executive); New York City, May 1, 1912.

ROCKWELL, Norman (illustrator); New York City, Feb. 3, 1894.

RODGERS, Richard (song writer); New York City, June 28, 1902.

ROGERS, Buddy (Charles) (actor); Olathe, Kans., Aug. 13, 1904.

ROGERS, Ginger (Virginia McMath) (actress); Independence, Mo., July 16, 1911.

ROGERS, Roy (Leonard Slye) (actor); Cincinnati, Ohio, Nov. 5, 1912.

ROGERS, Will, Jr. (actor); New York City, Oct. 20, 1911.

ROMAINS, Jules (Louis Farigoule) (novelist); Saint-Julien Chapteuil, Fr., Aug. 26, 1885.

ROME, Harold (song writer); Hartford, Conn., May 27, 1908.

ROMERO, Cesar (actor); New York City, Feb. 15, 1907.

ROMULO, Carlos P. (Philippine statesman); Manila, Phil., Jan. 14, 1899.

ROONEY, Mickey (Joe Yule, Jr.) (actor); Brooklyn, N. Y., Sept. 23, 1922.

ROOSEVELT, Eleanor (U. S. stateswoman); New York City, Oct. 11, 1884.

ROSE, Billy (William S. Rosenberg) (stage producer); New York City, September 6, 1899.

ROSEWALL, Ken (tennis player); Sydney, NSW, Australia, Nov. 2, 1934.

ROSSELLINI, Roberto (movie director); Rome, It., May 8, 1906.

ROSTOW, Walt Whitman (educator & govt. official); New York City, Oct. 7, 1916.

RUBINSTEIN, Artur (pianist); Warsaw, Pol., Jan. 28, 1889.

RUDOLPH, Wilma Glodean (sprinter); St. Bethlehem, Tenn., June 23, 1940.

RUGGLES, Charles (actor); Los Angeles, Calif., Feb. 8, 1892.

RUSK, Dean (Secy. of State); Cherokee Co., Ga., Feb. 9, 1909.

RUSSELL, Bertrand (philosopher); Trelleck, Eng., May 18, 1872.

RUSSELL, Jane (actress); Bemidji, Minn., June 21, 1921.

RUSSELL, Rosalind (actress); Waterbury, Conn., June 4, 1912.

RYAN, Robert (actor); Chicago, Ill., Nov. 11, 1913.

SAHL, Mort (Morton Lyon Sahl) (comedian); Montreal, Canada, May 11, 1927.

SAINT, Eva Marie (actress); Newark, N. J., July 4, 1924.

ST. DENIS, Ruth (Ruth Denis) (dancer); Newark, N. J., Jan 20, 1880.

ST. LAURENT, Louis S. (Canadian statesman); Compton, Que., Can., Feb. 1, 1882.

SALAZAR, António de Oliveira (Premier, Portugal); Santa Comba, Port., 1889.

SALINGER, J. D. (Jerome David Salinger) (novelist); New York City, Jan. 1, 1919.

SALINGER, Pierre (Press Secy. to Pres.); San Francisco, Calif., June 14, 1925.

SALK, Jonas (physician); New York City, Oct. 28, 1914.

SANDBURG, Carl (poet & biographer); Galesburg, Ill., Jan. 6, 1878.

SANDE, Earl (horse trainer); Groton, S. Dak., Nov. 19, 1898.

SANDERS, George (actor); St. Petersburg, Rus., 1906.

SANDS, Tommy (singer); Chicago, Ill., Aug. 27, 1937.

SARAZEN, Gene (golfer); Harrison, N. Y., Feb. 27, 1902.

SARNOFF, David (radio executive); Uzlian, Rus., Feb. 27, 1891.

SAROYAN, William (story writer & dramatist); Fresno, Calif., Aug. 31, 1908.

SARTRE, Jean-Paul (philosopher); Paris, Fr., June 21, 1905.

SAYÃO, Bidú (soprano); Rio de Janeiro, Braz., May 11, 1906.

SCHAEFER, Jake (billiards player); Chicago, Ill., Oct. 18, 1894.

SCHARY, Dore (movie producer); Newark, N. J., Aug. 31, 1905.

SCHEFFING, Bob (Robert) (baseball manager); Overland, Mo., Aug. 11, 1915.

SCHELL, Maria (actress); Vienna, Aus., Jan. 15, 1926.

SCHIAPARELLI, Elsa (fashion designer); Rome, It.

SCHILDKRAUT, Joseph (actor); Vienna, Aus., Mar. 22, 1895.

SCHIPA, Tito (tenor); Lecce, It., Jan. 2, 1890.

SCHLESINGER, Arthur M., Jr. (historian); Columbus, Ohio, Oct. 15, 1917.

SCHLESINGER, Arthur M., Sr. (historian); Xenia, Ohio, Feb. 27, 1888.

SCHOENDIENST, Al (Albert) (baseball player); Germantown, Ill., Feb. 2, 1923.

SCHULBERG, Budd (novelist); New York City, Mar. 27, 1914.

SCHUMAN, William (composer); New York City, Aug. 4, 1910.

SCHWARZKOPF, Elisabeth (soprano); Jarotschin, Posen, Ger., Dec. 9, 1915.

SCHWEITZER, Albert (physician & philosopher); Kaysersburg, Alsace, Jan. 14, 1875.

SCORE, Herb (baseball player); Rosedale, N. Y., June 7, 1933.

SCOTT, Barbara Ann (skater); Ottawa, Can., May 9, 1928.

SCOTT, Hazel (pianist); Port of Spain, Trin., June 11, 1920.

SCOTT, Randolph (actor); Orange Co., Va., Jan. 23, 1903.

SCOTT, Zachary (actor); Austin, Tex., Feb. 24, 1914.

SEABORG, Glenn T. (nuclear chemist); Ishpeming, Mich., Apr. 19, 1912.

SEDGMAN, Frank (tennis player); Mont Albert, Victoria, Austr., Oct. 29, 1927.

SEGOVIA, Andrés (guitarist); Linares, Sp., Feb. 18, 1894.

SEGURA, Francisco (tennis player); Guayaquil, Ec., June 20, 1921.

SELLERS, Peter (actor); Southsea, England, Sept. 8, 1925.

SELZNICK, David O. (movie producer); Pittsburgh, Pa., May 10, 1902.

SERKIN, Rudolf (pianist); Eger, Boh., Mar. 28, 1903.

SERLING, Rod (playwright); Syracuse, N. Y., Dec. 25, 1924.

SESSIONS, Roger (composer); Brooklyn, N. Y. Dec. 28, 1896.

SEVAREID, Eric (news commentator); Velva, N. D., Nov. 26, 1912.

SHANTZ, Bobby (baseball player); Pottstown, Pa., Sept. 26, 1925.

SHAPLEY, Harlow (astronomer); Nashville, Mo., Nov. 2, 1885.

SHARETT, Moshé (Moshé Shertok) (Israeli statesman); Kherson, Rus., Oct. 3, 1894.

SHAUGHNESSY, Frank J. (baseball executive); Albion, Ill., Apr. 8, 1885.

SHAW, Artie (clarinetist); New York City, May 23, 1910.

SHAW, Irwin (dramatist & novelist); New York City, Feb. 27, 1913.

SHEARER, Moira (ballerina); Dunfermline, Fifes., Scot., Jan. 17, 1926.

SHEEAN, Vincent (novelist & essayist); Pana, Ill., Dec. 5, 1899.

SHEEN, Fulton J. (clergyman & author); El Paso, Ill., May 8, 1895.

SHEPARD, Alan B., Jr. (astronaut); East Derry, N.H., Nov. 18, 1923.

SHERIDAN, Ann (actress); Denton, Tex., Feb. 21, 1915.

SHERRIFF, Robert (dramatist); Kingston-on-Thames, Eng., June 6, 1896.

SHOEMAKER, Willie (jockey); Fabens, Tex., Aug. 19, 1931.

SHOLOKHOV, Mikhail (novelist); Veshenskaya, Rus., May 24, 1905.

SHORE, Dinah (singer); Winchester, Tenn., Mar. 1, 1917.

SHOSTAKOVICH, Dmitri (composer); St. Petersburg, Rus., Sept. 26, 1906.

SHULMAN, Max (humorist); St. Paul, Minn., Mar. 14, 1919.

SHUMLIN, Herman (theatrical producer); Atwood, Colo., Dec. 6, 1898.

SIGNORET, Simone (Simone Kaminker) (actress); Wiesbaden, Germany, Mar. 25, 1921.

SIKORSKY, Igor I. (aircraft designer); Kiev, Rus., May 25, 1889.

SILONE, Ignazio (Secondo Tranquilli) (novelist); Pescina dei Marsi, It., May 1, 1900.

SILVERS, Phil (Philip Silversmith) (comedian); Brooklyn, N. Y., May 11, 1912.

SIMENON, Georges (Georges Sim) (novelist); Liége, Belg., Feb. 13, 1903.

SIMMONS, Jean (actress); Crouch Hill, London, Eng., Jan. 31, 1929.

SIMONSON, Lee (stage designer); New York City, June 26, 1888.

SINATRA, Frank (singer & actor); Hoboken, N. J., Dec. 12, 1917.

SINCLAIR, Upton (novelist); Baltimore, Md., Sept. 20, 1878.

SIQUEIROS, David (painter); Chihuahua, Mex., Dec. 29, 1896.

SITWELL, Dame Edith (poet); Scarborough, Eng., 1887.

SITWELL, Sir Osbert (poet & satirist); London, Eng., Dec. 6, 1892.

SKELTON, Red (Richard) (comedian); Vincennes, Ind., July 18, 1913.

SKINNER, Cornelia Otis (actress); Chicago, Ill., May 30, 1901.

SLEZAK, Walter (actor); Vienna, Aus., May 3, 1902.

SLOAN, Alfred P., Jr. (business executive); New Haven, Conn., May 23, 1875.

SMITH, H. Allen (humorist); McLeansboro, Ill., Dec. 19, 1907.

SMITH, Howard K. (news commentator); Ferriday, La., May 12, 1914.

SMITH, Kate (Kathryn) (singer); Greenville, Mo., May 1, 1909.

SMITH, Lillian (novelist); Jasper, Florida, 1897.

SMITH, Red (Walter) (sports writer); Green Bay, Wis., Sept. 25, 1905.

SMYTHE, Conn (hockey executive); Toronto, Ont., Can., Feb. 1, 1895.

SNEAD, Sam (golfer); Hot Springs, Va., May 27, 1912.

SNIDER, Duke (Edwin) (baseball player); Los Angeles, Calif., Sept. 19, 1926.

SOTHERN, Ann (Harriette Lake) (actress); Valley City, N. Dak., Jan. 22, 1911.

SOUSTELLE, Jacques (French govt. official); Montpellier, Hérault, Fr., Feb. 3, 1912.

SPAAK, Paul Henri (Belgian statesman); Brussels, Belg., Jan. 25, 1899.

SPAHN, Warren (baseball player); Buffalo, N. Y., Apr. 23, 1921.

SPENDER, Stephen (poet); nr. London, Eng., Feb. 28, 1909.

SPEWACK, Bella (dramatist); Hungary, 1899.

SPEWACK, Sam (dramatist); Russia, 1899.

SPILLANE, Mickey (Frank Spillane) (novelist); Brooklyn, N. Y., Mar. 9, 1918.

SPOCK, Benjamin (pediatrician); New Haven, Conn., May 2, 1903.

SPROUL, Robert G. (educator); San Francisco, Calif., May 22, 1891.

STAGG, A. Alonzo (football coach); West Orange, N. J., Aug. 16, 1862.

STANLEY, Kim (Patricia Reid) (actress); Tularosa, N. Mex., Feb. 11, 1925.

STANWYCK, Barbara (Ruby Stevens) (actress); Brooklyn, N. Y., July 16, 1907.

STARR, Kay (Starks) (singer); Dougherty, Okla., July 21, 1922.

STASSEN, Harold E. (lawyer); West St. Paul, Minn., Apr. 13, 1907.

STEFANSSON, Vilhjalmur (explorer); Arnes, Can., Nov. 3, 1879.

STEICHEN, Edward (photographer); Luxemburg, Mar. 27, 1879.

STEIGER, Rod (actor); Westhampton, N. Y., Apr. 14, 1925.

STEINBECK, John (novelist); Salinas, Calif., Feb. 27, 1902.

STENGEL, Casey (Charles D.) (baseball manager); Kansas City, Mo., July 30, 1891.

STERN, Isaac (violinist); Kreminiecz, Rus., July 21, 1920.

STEVENS, George (movie producer); Oakland, Calif., 1905.

STEVENS, Mark (actor); Cleveland, Ohio, Dec. 13.

STEVENS, Risë (mezzo-soprano); New York City, June 11, 1913.

STEVENSON, Adlai E. (U. S. statesman); Los Angeles, Calif., Feb. 5, 1900.

STEWART, James (actor); Indiana, Pa., May 20, 1908.

STICKNEY, Dorothy (actress); Dickinson, N. Dak., June 21, 1900.

STOKOWSKI, Leopold (orchestra conductor); London, Eng., Apr. 18, 1882.

STONE, Edward D. (architect); Fayetteville, Ark., Mar. 9, 1902.

STRANAHAN, Frank R. (golfer); Toledo, Ohio, Aug. 5, 1922.

STRASBERG, Susan (actress); New York City, May 22, 1938.

STRAUSS, Lewis L. (former AEC Chmn., U. S.); Charleston, W. Va., Jan. 31, 1896.

STRAVINSKY, Igor (composer); Oranienbaum, Rus., June 17, 1882.

STREETER, Edward (novelist); New York City, Aug. 1, 1891.

SUGGS, Louise (golfer); Atlanta, Ga., Sept. 7, 1923.

SUKARNO (President & Premier, Indonesia); Surabaja, Java, 1901.

SULLIVAN, Barry (Patrick Barry) (actor); New York City, Aug. 29, 1912.

SULLIVAN, Ed (columnist & TV performer); New York City, Sept. 28, 1902.

SULLIVAN, Frank (humorist); Saratoga Springs, N. Y., Sept. 22, 1892.

SULZBERGER, Arthur H. (publisher); New York City, Sept. 12, 1891.

SUMAC, Yma (singer); Ichocan, Peru, Sept. 10, 1927.

SUZUKI, Pat (singer); Cressey, Calif.

SWANSON, Gloria (Josephine Swenson) (actress); Chicago, Ill., Mar. 27, 1898.

SWARTHOUT, Gladys (mezzo-soprano); Deepwater, Mo., Dec. 25, 1904.

SZELL, George (orchestra conductor); Budapest, Hung., June 7, 1897.

SZIGETI, Joseph (violinist); Budapest, Hung., Sept. 5, 1892.

TALBURT, Harold M. (cartoonist); Toledo, Ohio, Feb. 19, 1895.

TALLCHIEF, Maria (ballerina); Fairfax, Okla., Jan. 24, 1925.

TANDY, Jessica (actress); London, Eng., June 7, 1909.

TATE, Allen (poet); Winchester, Ky., Nov. 19, 1899.

TAYLOR, Deems (composer); New York City, Dec. 22, 1885.

TAYLOR, Elizabeth (actress); London, Eng., Feb. 27, 1932.

TAYLOR, Harold (educator); Toronto, Canada, Sept. 28, 1914.

TAYLOR, Gen. Maxwell D. (U. S. Army officer); Keytesville, Mo., Aug. 26, 1901.

TAYLOR, Robert (S. Arlington Brugh) (actor); Filley, Nebr., Aug. 5, 1911.

TEBALDI, Renata (soprano); Pesaro, It., Jan. 2, 1922.

TEBBETTS, Birdie (George R.) (baseball manager); Nashua, N. H., Nov. 10, 1914.

TELLER, Edward (physicist); Budapest, Hung., Jan. 15, 1908.

TEMPLE, Shirley (actress); Santa Monica, Calif., Apr. 23, 1928.

TEMPLETON, Alec (pianist); Cardiff, Wales, July 4, 1910.

TERRY-THOMAS (Thomas Terry Hoar Stevens) (actor); London, Eng., July 14, 1911.

THEBOM, Blanche (mezzo-soprano); Monessen, Pa., Sept. 19, 1919.

THOMAS, Danny (Amos Jacobs) (comedian); Deerfield, Mich., Jan. 6, 1914.

THOMAS, Lowell (lecturer & author); Woodington, Ohio, Apr. 6, 1892.

THOMAS, Norman (Socialist leader); Marion, Ohio, Nov. 20, 1884.

THOMSON, Virgil (composer); Kansas City, Mo., Nov. 25, 1896.

THOREZ, Maurice (Fr. Communist leader); Noyelles-Gaudault, Fr., Apr. 28, 1900.

THORNDIKE, Dame Sybil (actress); Gainsborough, Lincs., Eng., Oct. 24, 1882.

THURBER, James (humorist); Columbus, Ohio, Dec. 8, 1894.

TIERNEY, Gene (actress); Brooklyn, N. Y., Nov. 20, 1920.

TILLICH, Paul (theologian); Starzeddel, Kreis Guben, Prussia, Aug. 20, 1886.

TITO (Josip Brozovich or Broz) (President, Yugoslavia); Croatia, May 25, 1892.

TITOV, Maj. Gherman Stepanovitch (Soviet cosmonaut); Verkhneye Zhilino, Siberia, 1940.

TOGLIATTI, Palmiro (Italian Communist leader); Genoa, It., Mar. 26, 1893.

TONE, Franchot (actor); Niagara Falls, N. Y., Feb. 27, 1905.

TOUREL, Jennie (mezzo-soprano); Montreal, Can., June 22, 1910.

TOYNBEE, Arnold J. (historian); London, Eng., Apr. 14, 1889.

TRACY, Spencer (actor); Milwaukee, Wis., Apr. 5, 1900.

TRAUTMAN, George M. (baseball executive); Bucyrus, Ohio, Jan. 11, 1890.

TRILLING, Lionel (author & educator); New York City, July 4, 1905.

TRUEX, Ernest (actor); Kansas City, Mo., Sept. 19, 1890.

TRUMAN, Harry S. (U. S. statesman); Lamar, Mo., May 8, 1884.

TRUMAN, Margaret (soprano); Independence, Mo., Feb. 17, 1924.

TUCKER, Richard (tenor); New York City, Aug. 28, 1914.

TUCKER, Sophie (Sophie Abuza) (entertainer); Russia, 1884.

TUDOR, Anthony (choreographer); London, Eng., Apr. 4, 1909.

TUNNEY, Gene (James J.) (boxer); New York City, May 25, 1898.

TURLEY, Bob (baseball player); Troy, Ill., Sept. 19, 1930.

TURNER, Lana (Julia Jean Turner) (actress); Wallace, Idaho, Feb. 8, 1920.

TWINING, Gen. Nathan F. (ex-Chmn., Joint Chiefs of Staff, U. S.); Monroe, Wis., Oct. 11, 1897.

**TWITTY,** Conway (Harold Jenkins) (singer); Friars Point, Miss., Sept. 1, 1933.

**UDALL,** Stewart L. (Secy. of Interior); St. Johns, Ariz., Jan. 31, 1920.

**ULBRICHT,** Walter (Chmn., Council of State, Ger. Dem. Rep.); Leipzig, Ger., June 30, 1893.

**UNTERMEYER,** Louis (poet & anthologist); New York City, Oct. 1, 1885.

**UREY,** Harold C. (chemist); Walkerton, Ind., Apr. 29, 1893.

**USTINOV,** Peter (dramatist & actor); London, Eng., 1921.

**VALLEE,** Rudy (Hubert) (actor & band leader); Island Pond, Vt., July 28, 1901.

**VAN BUREN,** Abigail (Mrs. Morton Phillips) (columnist); Sioux City, Iowa, July 14, 1918.

**VANDERBILT,** Alfred G. (horse-racing executive); London, Eng., Sept. 22, 1912.

**VAN DOREN,** Mark (poet & critic); Hope, Ill., June 13, 1894.

**VANIER,** George P. (Gov. Gen., Canada); Montreal, Que., Can., Apr. 23, 1888.

**VAUGHAN,** Sarah (singer); Newark, N. J., Mar. 27, 1924.

**VERDON,** Gwen (actress); Culver City, Calif.

**VIDAL,** Gore (dramatist & novelist); West Point, N. Y., Oct. 3, 1925.

**VIDOR,** King (movie director & producer); Galveston, Tex., Feb. 8, 1895.

**VON BRAUN.** See Braun.

**WAGNER,** Robert (actor); Detroit, Mich., Feb. 10, 1930.

**WAGNER,** Robert F. (Mayor, NYC); New York City, Apr. 20, 1910.

**WALCOTT,** Jersey Joe (Arnold Cream) (boxer); Merchantville, N. J., Jan. 31, 1914.

**WALKER,** Mickey (boxer); Elizabeth, N. J., July 13, 1901.

**WALKER,** Nancy (Ann Myrtle Swoyer) (actress); Philadelphia, Pa.

**WALLACE,** DeWitt (publisher); St. Paul, Minn., Nov. 12, 1889.

**WALLACE,** Henry A. (U. S. statesman); Adair Co., Iowa, Oct. 7, 1888.

**WALLACE,** Mike (TV personality) (Myron Wallace); Brookline, Mass., May 9, 1918.

**WALTARI,** Mika (novelist); Helsinki, Fin., Sept. 19, 1908.

**WALTER,** Bruno (Bruno Walter Schlesinger) (conductor); Berlin, Ger., Sept. 17, 1876.

**WARD,** Barbara (writer & economist); York, Eng., May 23, 1914.

**WARING,** Fred (band leader); Tyrone, Pa., June 9, 1900.

**WARREN,** Robert Penn (novelist); Guthrie, Ky., Apr. 24, 1905.

**WATERS,** Ethel (actress & singer); Chester, Pa., Oct. 31, 1900.

**WAUGH,** Alec (Alexander Raban Waugh) (novelist); London, Eng., July 8, 1898.

**WAUGH,** Evelyn (novelist); London, 1903.

**WAYNE,** David (David McMeekan) (actor); Traverse City, Mich., Jan. 30, 1914.

**WAYNE,** John (Marion Michael Morrison) (actor); Winterset, Iowa, May 26, 1907.

**WEBB,** Clifton (Webb Parmelee Hollenbeck) (actor); Indianapolis, Ind., Nov. 19, 1893.

**WEBB,** Jack (actor); Santa Monica, Calif., Apr. 2, 1920.

**WEBSTER,** Margaret (actress & director); New York City, Mar. 15, 1905.

**WEEDE,** Robert (baritone) (Robert Wiedefeld); Baltimore, Md., Feb. 22, 1903.

**WELD,** Tuesday (Susan) (actress); New York City, Aug. 27, 1943.

**WELK,** Lawrence (band leader); Strasburg, N. Dak., Mar. 11, 1903.

**WELLES,** Orson (actor & director); Kenosha, Wis., May 6, 1915.

**WEST,** Mae (actress); Brooklyn, N. Y., Aug. 17, 1892.

**WEST,** Rebecca (Cicily Fairfield) (novelist); Edinburgh, Scot., Dec. 25, 1892.

**WHITE,** E. B. (Elwyn Brooks White) (writer); Mt. Vernon, N. Y., July 11, 1899.

**WHITE,** Paul Dudley (physician); Roxbury, Mass., June 6, 1886.

**WHITEMAN,** Paul (band leader); Denver, Colo., 1891.

**WHITNEY,** C. V. (horse racing executive); New York City, Feb. 20, 1899.

**WHITNEY,** John Hay (U. S. diplomat); Ellsworth, Me., Aug. 17, 1904.

**WHORF,** Richard (actor); Winthrop, Mass., June 4, 1906.

**WIDMARK,** Richard (actor); Sunrise, Minn., Dec. 26, 1914.

**WILDE,** Cornel (actor); New York City, Oct. 13, 1915.

**WILDER,** Billy (movie director); Vienna, Aus., June 22, 1906.

**WILDER,** Thornton (novelist); Madison, Wis., Apr. 17, 1897.

**WILDING,** Michael (actor); Westcliff, Essex, Eng., July 23, 1912.

**WILLARD,** Jess (boxer); Pottawatomie Co., Kans., Dec. 29, 1883.

**WILLIAMS,** Andy (singer); Wall Lake, Iowa, Dec. 3, 1928.

**WILLIAMS,** Emlyn (dramatist); Mostyn, Wales, Nov. 26, 1905.

**WILLIAMS,** Esther (swimmer & actress); Los Angeles, Calif., Aug. 8, 1923.

**WILLIAMS,** Gluyas (cartoonist); San Francisco, Calif., July 23, 1888.

**WILLIAMS,** Ted (baseball player); San Diego, Calif., Oct. 30, 1918.

**WILLIAMS,** Tennessee (Thomas L. Williams) (dramatist); Columbus, Miss., Mar. 26, 1914.

**WILLIAMS,** William Carlos (poet); Rutherford, N. J., Sept. 17, 1883.

**WILLSON,** Meredith (composer & actor); Mason City, Iowa, May 18, 1902.

**WILSON,** Edmund (literary critic); Red Bank, N. J., May 8, 1895.

**WILSON,** Sloan (novelist); Norwalk, Conn., May 8, 1920.

**WINCHELL,** Walter (columnist); New York City, Apr. 7, 1897.

**WINDSOR,** Duchess of (Bessie Wallis Warfield); Blue Ridge Summit, Pa., June 19, 1896.

**WINDSOR,** Duke of (formerly King Edward VIII, Gr. Brit.); Richmond Park, Eng., June 23, 1894.

**WINTERS,** Jonathan (comedian); Dayton, Ohio, Nov. 11, 1925.

WINTERS, Shelley (Shirley Schrift) (actress); East St. Louis, Ill., Aug. 18, 1922.

WOOD, Craig (golfer); Lake Placid, N. Y., Nov. 18, 1901.

WOODWARD, Joanne (actress); Thomasville, Ga., Feb. 27, 1931.

WOOLLEY, Monty (Edgar) (actor); New York City, Aug. 17, 1888.

WOUK, Herman (novelist); New York City, May 27, 1915.

WRIGHT, Teresa (actress); New York City, Oct. 27, 1918.

WYATT, Jane (actress); Campgaw, N. J., Aug. 12, 1912.

WYETH, Andrew (painter); Chadds Ford, Pa., July 12, 1917.

WYLER, William (movie director); Mulhouse, Fr., July 1, 1902.

WYLIE, Philip (novelist); Beverly, Mass., May 12, 1902.

WYMAN, Jane (Sarah Jane Fulks) (actress); St. Joseph, Mo., Jan. 4, 1914.

WYNN, Ed (Edwin Leopold) (comedian); Philadelphia, Pa., Nov. 9, 1886.

WYNN, Keenan (actor); New York City, July 27, 1916.

YOUNG, Loretta (Gretchen Young) (actress); Salt Lake City, Utah, Jan. 6, 1913.

YOUNG, Robert (actor); Chicago, Ill., Feb. 22, 1907.

ZANUCK, Darryl F. (movie director); Wahoo, Nebr., Sept. 5, 1902.

ZIMBALIST, Efrem (violinist); Rostov-on-Don, Rus., Apr. 9, 1889.

ZWEIG, Arnold (novelist); Grosz-Glogau, Silesia, Nov. 10, 1887.

# ★ CELEBRATED PERSONS OF THE PAST ★

For the Presidents of the United States, consult the entry Presidents in the index. For the Rulers of England, France, Germany and Russia, consult the entry Rulers. In many instances below, the original name or form of the name of the individual is shown in parentheses.

ABELARD, Peter (Pierre Abélard) (philosopher & theologian); b. near Nantes, Fr. (1079–1142).

ADAMS, Charles Francis (diplomat); b. Boston, Mass. (1807–1886).

ADAMS, Franklin Pierce (columnist, author); b. Chicago, Ill. (1881–1960).

ADAMS, Henry Brooks (historian); b. Boston, Mass. (1838–1918).

ADAMS, James Truslow (historian); b. Brooklyn, N. Y. (1878–1949).

ADAMS, Maude (Maude Kiskadden) (actress); b. Salt Lake City, Utah (1872–1953).

ADAMS, Samuel (American Revolutionary patriot); b. Boston, Mass. (1722–1803).

ADAMS, Samuel Hopkins (novelist); b. Dunkirk, N. Y. (1871–1958).

ADDAMS, Jane (social worker); b. Cedarville, Ill. (1860–1935).

ADE, George (humorist); b. Kentland, Ind. (1866–1944).

ADLER, Alfred (psychoanalyst); b. Vienna, Aus. (1870–1937).

AESCHYLUS (dramatist); b. Eleusis, Attica (525–456 B.C.).

AESOP (fabulist); birthplace unknown (lived c. 600 B.C.).

ALCOTT, Louisa May (novelist); b. Germantown, Pa. (1832–1888).

ALDEN, John (American Pilgrim); b. England (1599?–1687).

ALEXANDER the Great (monarch & conqueror); b. Pella, Macedonia (356–323 B.C.).

ALGER, Horatio (author); b. Revere, Mass. (1834–1899).

ALLEN, Ethan (American Revolutionary soldier); b. Litchfield, Conn. (1738–1789).

ALLEN, Fred (John Florence Sullivan) (comedian); b. Cambridge, Mass. (1894–1956).

ANDERSEN, Hans Christian (fairy-tale writer); b. Odense, Den. (1805–1875).

ANDERSON, Maxwell (dramatist); b. Atlantic, Pa. (1888–1959).

ANTHONY, Mark (Marcus Antonius) (statesman); b. Rome (83?–30 B.C.).

ANTHONY, Susan Brownell (woman suffragist); b. Adams, Mass. (1820–1906).

AQUINAS, St. Thomas (philosopher); b. near Aquino, It. (1225?–1274).

ARCHIMEDES (physicist & mathematician); b. Syracuse, Sicily (287?–212 B.C.).

ARISTOPHANES (dramatist); b. Athens (448?–380 B.C.).

ARISTOTLE (philosopher); b. Stagira (384–322 B.C.).

ARNOLD, Benedict (American traitor); b. Norwich, Conn. (1741–1801).

ARNOLD, Matthew (poet & critic); b. Laleham, Mid., Eng. (1822–1888).

ASCH, Sholem (novelist); b. Kutno, Pol. (1880–1957).

ASTOR, John Jacob (financier); b. Waldorf, Ger. (1763–1848).

ATTILA (King of Huns, called "Scourge of God") (406?–453).

AUDUBON, John James (naturalist & artist); b. Haiti (1785–1851).

AUER, Leopold (violinist & teacher); b. Veszprim, Hung. (1845–1930).

AUGUSTINE, Saint (Aurelius Augustinus) (philosopher); b. Numidia (354–430).

AUGUSTUS (Gaius Octavius) (Roman emperor); b. Rome (63 B.C.–A.D. 14).

AUSTEN, Jane (novelist); b. Steventon, Hamps., Eng. (1775–1817).

BACH, Johann Sebastian (composer); b. Eisenach, Ger. (1685–1750).

BACON, Francis (philosopher & essayist); b. London, England (1561–1626).

BACON, Roger (philosopher & scientist); b. Ilchester, Som., Eng. (1214?–1294).

BAEDEKER, Karl (travel-guidebook publisher); b. Essen, Ger. (1801–1859).

**BALBOA,** Vasco Núñez de (explorer); b. Jerez de los Caballeros, Sp. (1475–1517).

**BALZAC,** Honoré de (novelist); b. Tours, Fr. (1799–1850).

**BANTING,** Sir Frederick Grant (research physician); b. Canada (1891–1941).

**BARA,** Theda (Theodosia Goodman) (actress); b. Cincinnati, Ohio (1890–1955).

**BARKLEY,** Alben William (U. S. statesman); b. Graves Co., Ky. (1877–1956).

**BARNUM,** Phineas Taylor (showman); b. Bethel, Conn. (1810–1891).

**BARRIE,** Sir James Matthew (novelist & dramatist); b. Kirriemuir, Forfarshire, Scot. (1860–1937).

**BARRY,** Philip (dramatist); b. Rochester, N. Y. (1896–1949).

**BARRYMORE,** Ethel (actress); b. Philadelphia, Pa. (1879–1959).

**BARRYMORE,** John (actor); b. Philadelphia, Pa. (1882–1942).

**BARRYMORE,** Lionel (actor); b. Philadelphia, Pa. (1878–1954).

**BARTÓK,** Béla (composer); b. Nagyszentmiklos, Transylvania, Hung. (1881–1945).

**BARTON,** Clara (Clarissa Harlowe Barton) (social worker); b. Oxford, Mass. (1821–1912).

**BAUDELAIRE,** Charles Pierre (poet); b. Paris, Fr. (1821–1867).

**BECKET,** Thomas à (Archbishop of Canterbury); b. London, Eng. (1118?–1170).

**BEDE,** Saint ("The Venerable Bede") (scholar); b. Monkwearmouth, Eng. (673–735).

**BEECHAM,** Sir Thomas (Godfrey Thomas Beecham); b. St. Helens, Eng. (1879–1961).

**BEECHER,** Henry Ward (clergyman); b. Litchfield, Conn. (1813–1887).

**BEERBOHM,** Sir Max (author); b. London, Eng. (1872–1956).

**BEETHOVEN,** Ludwig van (composer); b. Bonn, Ger. (1770–1827).

**BELASCO,** David (dramatist & producer); b. San Francisco, Calif. (1854–1931).

**BELL,** Alexander Graham (inventor); b. Edinburgh, Scot. (1847–1922).

**BELLAMY,** Edward (author); b. Chicopee Falls, Mass. (1850–1898).

**BELLOWS,** George Wesley (painter & lithographer); b. Columbus, Ohio (1882–1925).

**BENCHLEY,** Robert Charles (humorist); b. Worcester, Mass. (1889–1945).

**BENEŠ,** Eduard (Czech statesman); b. Kožlany, Bohemia (1884–1948).

**BENÉT,** Stephen Vincent (poet & story writer); b. Bethlehem, Pa. (1898–1943).

**BENÉT,** William Rose (poet & novelist); b. Ft. Hamilton, N. Y. (1886–1950).

**BENJAMIN,** Judah Philip (Confederate statesman); b. St. Thomas, BWI (1811–1884).

**BENNETT,** Enoch Arnold (novelist & dramatist); b. Hanley, Staffs., Eng. (1867–1931).

**BENNETT,** James Gordon (editor); b. Keith, Banffshire, Scot. (1795–1872).

**BERKSON,** Seymour (publisher); b. Chicago, Ill. (1905–1959).

**BERLIOZ,** Louis Hector (composer); b. La Côte-St.-André, Fr. (1803–1869).

**BERNHARDT,** Sarah (Rosine Bernard) (actress); b. Paris, Fr. (1844–1923).

**BEVIN,** Ernest (British statesman); b. Somersetshire, Eng. (1881–1951).

**BIERCE,** Ambrose Gwinnett (journalist); b. Meigs Co., Ohio (1842–?1914).

**BISMARCK-SCHÖNHAUSEN,** Prince Otto Eduard Leopold von (German statesman); b. Schönhausen, Prus. (1815–1898).

**BIZET,** Georges (Alexandre César Léopold Bizet) (composer); b. Paris, Fr. (1838–1875).

**BLACKSTONE,** Sir William (jurist); b. London, Eng. (1723–1780).

**BLAKE,** William (poet & artist); b. London, Eng. (1757–1827).

**BLUM,** Léon (French statesman); b. Paris, Fr. (1872–1950).

**BOCCACCIO,** Giovanni (author); b. Paris, Fr. (1313–1375).

**BOGART,** Humphrey DeForest (actor); b. New York City (1900–1957).

**BOLÍVAR,** Simón (South American liberator); b. Caracas, Venez. (1783–1830).

**BOND,** Carrie (nee Jacobs) (composer of songs); b. Janesville, Wis. (1862–1946).

**BOONE,** Daniel (frontiersman); b. near Reading, Pa. (1734–1820).

**BOOTH,** Edwin Thomas (actor); b. Bel Air, Md. (1833–1893).

**BOOTH,** Evangeline Cory (religious leader); b. London, Eng. (1865–1950).

**BOOTH,** John Wilkes (actor; assassin of Lincoln); b. Hartford County, Md. (1838–1865).

**BOOTH,** William (called General Booth) (religious leader); b. Nottingham, Eng. (1829–1912).

**BORGIA,** Cesare (nobleman & soldier); b. Rome (1475?–1507).

**BORGIA,** Lucrezia (Duchess of Ferrara); b. Rome (1480–1519).

**BOSWELL,** James (diarist & biographer); b. Edinburgh, Scot. (1740–1795).

**BOTTICELLI,** Sandro (Alessandro di Mariano dei Filipepi) (painter); b. Florence (1444?–1510).

**BOWIE,** James (soldier); b. Burke Co., Ga. (1799–1836).

**BRAHMS,** Johannes (composer); b. Hamburg, Ger. (1833–1897).

**BRAILLE,** Louis (teacher of blind); b. Coupvray, Fr. (1809–1852).

**BRANDEIS,** Louis Dembitz (jurist); b. Louisville, Ky. (1856–1941).

**BRICE,** Fanny (Fannie Borach) (comedienne); b. New York City (1892–1951).

**BRISBANE,** Arthur (journalist) b. Buffalo, N. Y. (1864–1936).

**BROMFIELD,** Louis (novelist); b. Mansfield, Ohio (1896–1956).

**BRONTË,** Charlotte (novelist); b. Thornton, Yorks., Eng. (1816–1855).

**BRONTË,** Emily Jane (novelist); b. Thornton, Yorks., Eng. (1818–1848).

**BROOKE,** Rupert (poet); b. Rugby, War., Eng. (1887–1915).

**BROUN,** Matthew Heywood Campbell (journalist); b. Brooklyn, N. Y. (1888–1939).

**BROWN,** John (abolitionist); b. Torrington, Conn. (1800–1859).

**BROWNING,** Elizabeth Barrett (poet); b. Coxhoe Hall, Durham, England (1806–1861).

**BROWNING,** Robert (poet); b. London, Eng. (1812–1889).

**BRUEGHEL,** Pieter (painter); b. near Breda. Flanders (1520–1569).

**BRUTUS,** Marcus Junius (Roman politician) (85?–42 B.C.).

**BRYAN,** William Jennings (orator & politician); b. Salem, Ill. (1860–1925).

**BRYANT,** William Cullen (poet & editor); b. Cummington, Mass. (1794–1878).

**BUDDHA.** *See* Gautama Buddha.

**BUFFALO BILL** (William Frederick Cody) (scout); b. Scott Co., Iowa (1846–1917).

**BUNYAN,** John (preacher & author); b. Elstow, Eng. (1628–1688).

**BURBANK,** Luther (horticulturist); b. Lancaster, Mass. (1849–1926).

**BURKE,** Edmund (statesman); b. Dublin, Ire. (1729–1797).

**BURNS,** Robert (poet); b. Alloway, Scot. (1759–1796).

**BURR,** Aaron (U. S. political leader); b. Newark, N. J. (1756–1836).

**BUTLER,** Nicholas Murray (educator); b. Elizabeth, N. J. (1862–1947).

**BUTLER,** Samuel (author); b. Langar, Notts., Eng. (1835–1902).

**BYRD,** Richard Evelyn (explorer); b. Winchester, Va. (1888–1957).

**BYRON,** George Gordon (6th Baron Byron) (poet); b. London, Eng. (1788–1824).

**CABELL,** James Branch (novelist); b. Richmond, Va. (1879–1958).

**CABOT,** John (Giovanni Caboto) (navigator); b. Genoa (1450–1498).

**CABOT,** Sebastian (navigator); b. Venice (1476?–1557).

**CAESAR,** Gaius Julius (Roman statesman); b. Rome (100?–44 B.C.).

**CALHERN,** Louis (Carl Henry Vogt) (actor); b. New York City (1895–1956).

**CALHOUN,** John Caldwell (statesman); b. near Calhoun Mills, S. C. (1782–1850).

**CALVIN,** John (Jean Chauvin) (religious reformer); b. Noyon, Picardy (1509–1564).

**CANBY,** Henry Seidel (literary critic); b. Wilmington, Del. (1878–1961).

**CARDOZO,** Benjamin Nathan (jurist); b. New York City (1870–1938).

**CARLYLE,** Thomas (essayist & historian); b. Ecclefechan, Dumfriesshire, Scot. (1795–1881).

**CARNEGIE,** Andrew (industrialist); b. Dunfermline, Scot. (1835–1919).

**CARROLL,** Lewis (Charles Lutwidge Dodgson) (author & mathematician); b. Daresbury, Ches., Eng. (1832–1898).

**CARSON,** Kit (Christopher) (scout); b. Madison Co., Ky. (1809–1868).

**CARUSO,** Enrico (Errico) (tenor); b. Naples, It. (1873–1921).

**CARVER,** George Washington (botanist); b. Missouri (1864–1943).

**CARY,** Arthur Joyce Lunel (novelist); b. Londonderry, Ire. (1888–1957).

**CASANOVA DE SEINGALT,** Giovanni Jacopo (adventurer); b. Venice (1725–1798).

**CATHER,** Willa Sibert (novelist); b. Winchester, Va. (1876–1947).

**CATO,** Marcus Porcius (called Cato the Elder) (statesman); b. Tusculum (234–149 B.C.).

**CATT,** Carrie Chapman (nee Lane) (woman suffragist); b. Ripon, Wis. (1859–1947).

**CELLINI,** Benvenuto (goldsmith & sculptor); b. Florence (1500–1571).

**CERVANTES SAAVEDRA,** Miguel de (novelist); b. Alcalá de Henares, Sp. (1547–1616).

**CÉZANNE,** Paul (painter); b. Aix-en-Provence, Fr. (1839–1906).

**CHALIAPIN,** Feodor Ivanovitch (basso); b. Kazan, Rus. (1873–1938).

**CHAMPLAIN,** Samuel de (explorer); b. nr. Rochefort, Fr. (1567?–1635).

**CHANEY,** Lon (actor); b. Colorado Springs, Colo. (1883–1930).

**CHARLEMAGNE** (Holy Roman Emperor); birthplace unknown (742–814).

**CHAUCER,** Geoffrey (poet); b. London, Eng. (1340?–1400).

**CHEKHOV,** Anton Pavlovich (dramatist & story writer); b. Taganrog, Rus. (1860–1904).

**CHESTERTON,** Gilbert Keith (author); b. Kensington, Eng. (1874–1936).

**CHIPPENDALE,** Thomas (cabinetmaker); b. Otley, Eng. (1718?–1779).

**CHOPIN,** Frédéric François (composer); b. nr. Warsaw, Pol. (1810–1849).

**CICERO,** Marcus Tullius (orator & statesman); b. Arpinum, It. 106–43 B.C.).

**CLARK,** Bobby (Robert Edwin Clark) (comedian); b. Springfield, Ohio (1888–1960).

**CLARK,** William (explorer); b. Caroline Co., Va. (1770–1838).

**CLAY,** Henry (statesman); b. Hanover Co., Va. (1777–1852).

**CLEMENCEAU,** Georges (statesman); b. Mouilleron-en-Pareds, Vendée, Fr. (1841–1929).

**CLEMENS,** S. L. *See* Twain

**CLEOPATRA** (Queen of Egypt); b. Alexandria, Egy. (69–30 B.C.).

**COBB,** Irvin Shrewsbury (humorist); b. Paducah, Ky. (1876–1944).

**COBB,** Tyrus Raymond (Ty) (baseball player); b. Banks Co., Ga. (1886–1961).

**COBURN,** Charles Douville (actor); b. Savannah, Ga. (1877–1961).

**CODY,** W. F. *See* Buffalo Bill.

**COHAN,** George Michael (actor & dramatist); b. Providence, R. I. (1878–1942).

**COHEN,** Morris Raphael (philosopher & educator); b. Minsk, Rus. (1880–1947).

**COLERIDGE,** Samuel Taylor (poet); b. Ottery St. Mary, Dev., Eng. (1772–1834).

**COLLETTE** (Sidonie-Gabriele Colette) (novelist); b. St.-Sauveur, Fr. (c.1873–1954).

**COLMAN,** Ronald (actor); b. Richmond, Surrey, Eng. (1891–1958).

**COLUMBUS,** Christopher (Cristoforo Colombo) (discoverer of America); b. Genoa (1451–1506).

**COMPTON,** Karl Taylor (physicist); b. Wooster, Ohio (1887–1954).

**CONFUCIUS** (K'ung Fu-tzŭ) (philosopher); b. Shantung prov., China (c. 551–479 B.C.).

**CONGREVE,** William (dramatist); b. nr. Leeds, Eng. (1670–1729).

**CONRAD,** Joseph (Teodor Józef Konrad Korzeniowski) (novelist); b. Berdichev, Ukraine (1857–1924).

**COOPER,** Gary (Frank James Cooper) (actor); b. Helena, Mont. (1901–1961).

COOPER, James Fenimore (novelist); b. Burlington, N. J. (1789–1851).

COOPER, Peter (industrialist & philanthropist); b. New York City (1791–1883).

COPERNICUS, Nicolaus (Mikolaj Kopernik) (astronomer); b. Thorn, Pol. (1473–1543).

CORBETT, James John (boxer); b. San Francisco, Calif. (1866–1933).

CORNEILLE, Pierre (dramatist); b. Rouen, Fr. (1606–1684).

COROT, Jean Baptiste Camille (painter); b. Paris, Fr. (1796–1875).

CORREGGIO, Antonio Allegri da (painter); b. Correggio, It. (1494–1534).

CORTÉS (or CORTEZ), Hernando (explorer); b. Medellín, Sp. (1485–1547).

COWL, Jane (Jane Cowles) (actress); b. Boston, Mass. (1884–1950).

COWPER, William (poet); b. Great Berkhamstead, Herts., Eng. (1731–1800).

COX, James Middleton (publisher); b. Jacksonburg, Ohio (1870–1957).

CRANE, Stephen (novelist & poet); b. Newark, N. J. (1871–1900).

CROCE, Benedetto (philosopher); b. Pescasseroli, Aquila, It. (1866–1952).

CROCKETT, Davy (David) (frontiersman); b. Greene Co., Tenn. (1786–1836).

CURIE, Marie (Marja Sklodowska) (physical chemist); b. Warsaw, Pol. (1867–1934).

CURIE, Pierre (chemist); b. Paris, Fr. (1859–1906).

CUSTER, George Armstrong (army officer); b. New Rumley, Ohio (1839–1876).

DAMROSCH, Walter Johannes (orchestra conductor); b. Breslau, Ger. (1862–1950).

DANA, Charles Anderson (editor); b. Hinsdale, N. H. (1819–1897).

D'ANNUNZIO, Gabriele (soldier & author); b. Francaville al Mare, Pescara, It. (1863–1938).

DANTE (or DURANTE) ALIGHIERI (poet); b. Florence (1265–1321).

DANTON, Georges Jacques (French Revolutionary leader); b. Arcis-sur-Aube, Fr. (1759–1794).

DARROW, Clarence Seward (lawyer); b. Kinsman, Ohio (1857–1938).

DARWIN, Charles Robert (naturalist); b. Shrewsbury, Shrops., Eng. (1809–1882).

DAUMIER, Honoré (caricaturist); b. Marseille, Fr. (1808–1879).

DAVID (King of Israel & Judah) (died c.973 B.C.).

DAVIDSON, Jo (sculptor); b. New York City (1883–1952).

DAVIS, Elmer Holmes (radio commentator); b. Aurora, Ind. (1890–1958).

DAVIS, Jefferson (Pres. of Confederacy); b. Christian (now Todd) Co., Ky. (1808–1889).

DAVIS, Joan (Madonna Josephine Davis) (actress); b. St. Paul, Minn. (1912–1961).

DEAN, James (actor); b. Marion, Ind. (1931–1955).

DEBS, Eugene Victor (Socialist leader); b. Terre Haute, Ind. (1855–1926).

DEBUSSY, Claude Achille (composer); b. St. Germain-en-Laye, Fr. (1862–1918).

DEFOE, Daniel (novelist); b. London, Eng. (1659?–1731).

DEGAS, Hilaire Germain Edgar (painter); b. Paris, Fr. (1834–1917).

DE MILLE, Cecil Blount (movie director); b. Ashfield, Mass. (1881–1959).

DEMOSTHENES (orator); b. Athens (385?–322 B.C.).

DESCARTES, René (philosopher & mathematician); b. La Haye, Fr. (1596–1650).

DE SOTO, Hernando (explorer); b. Barcarrota, Sp. (1500?–1542).

DE VOTO, Bernard Augustine (author); b. Ogden, Utah (1897–1955).

DEWEY, George (naval officer); b. Montpelier, Vt. (1837–1917).

DEWEY, John (philosopher & educator); b. Burlington, Vt. (1859–1952).

DICKENS, Charles John Huffam (novelist); b. Portsea, Eng. (1812–1870).

DICKINSON, Emily Elizabeth (poet); b. Amherst, Mass. (1830–1886).

DIOGENES (philosopher); b. Sinope, Asia Minor (412?–323 B.C.).

DIOR, Christian (fashion designer); b. Granville, Normandy, Fr. (1905–1957).

DISRAELI, Benjamin (statesman); b. London, Eng. (1804–1881).

DODGSON, C. L. *See* Carroll, Lewis.

DONAT, Robert (actor); b. Withington, Eng. (1905–1958).

DONNE, John (poet); b. London, Eng. (1573–1631).

DOOLEY, Thomas Anthony (physician & author); b. St. Louis, Mo. (1927–1961).

DORSEY, Jimmy (James Francis Dorsey) (band leader); b. Shenandoah, Pa. (1904–1957).

DORSEY, Tommy (Thomas Francis Dorsey, Jr.) (band leader); b. Mahanoy Plane, Pa. (1905–1956).

DOSTOEVSKI, Fyodor Mikhailovich (novelist); b. Moscow, Rus. (1821–1881).

DOUGLAS, Stephen Arnold (politician); b. Brandon, Vt. (1813–1861).

DOYLE, Sir Arthur Conan (novelist & spiritualist); b. Edinburgh, Scot. (1859–1930).

DRAKE, Sir Francis (navigator); b. Tavistock, Devons., Eng. (1545?–1596).

DRAPER, Ruth (actress); b. New York City 1884–1956).

DREISER, Theodore (novelist); b. Terre Haute, Ind. (1871–1945).

DRESSLER, Marie (Leila Koerber) (actress); b. Cobourg, Ont., Can. (1869–1934).

DREYFUS, Alfred (French army officer); b. Alsace (1859–1935).

DRYDEN, John (poet); b. Northamptonshire, Eng. (1631–1700).

DULLES, John Foster (U. S. statesman); b. Washington, D. C. (1888–1959).

DUMAS, Alexandre (called Dumas père) (novelist); b. Villers-Cotterets, Fr. (1802–1870).

DUMAS, Alexandre (called Dumas fils) (novelist); b. Paris, Fr. (1824–1895).

DU MAURIER, George Louis Palmella Busson (novelist); b. Paris, Fr. (1834–1896).

DUNCAN, Isadora (dancer); b. San Francisco, Calif. (1878–1927).

DUSE, Eleonora (actress); b. Chioggia, It. (1859–1924).

DVOŘÁK, Antonin (composer); b. Mühl-hausen, Bohemia (1841–1904).

EARHART, Amelia (aviator); b. Atchison, Kans. (1898–1937).

EDDY, Mary Morse (nee Baker) (religious leader); b. Bow, N. H. (1821–1910).

EDISON, Thomas Alva (inventor); b. Milan, Ohio (1847–1931).

EDMAN, Irwin (philosopher); b. New York City (1896–1954).

EHRLICH, Paul (bacteriologist); Silesia prov., Prus. (1854–1915).

EINSTEIN, Albert (physicist); b. Ulm, Ger. (1879–1955).

ELGAR, Sir Edward (composer); b. Worces-ter, Eng. (1857–1934).

ELIOT, George (Mary Ann Evans) (novelist); b. Warickshire, Eng. (1819–1880).

EMERSON, Ralph Waldo (philosopher & poet); b. Boston, Mass. (1803–1882).

ENESCO, Georges (composer); b. Dorohoi, Rum. (1881–1955).

ENGELS, Friedrich (Socialist writer); b. Bar-men, Ger. (1820–1895).

EPICURUS (philosopher); b. Samos (341–270 B.C.).

EPSTEIN, Sir Jacob (sculptor); b. New York City (1880–1959).

ERASMUS, Desiderius (Gerhard Gerhards) (scholar); b. Rotterdam (1466?–1536).

ERICSON, Leif (navigator) (c.10th cent. A.D.).

EUCLID (mathematician) (c.300 B.C.).

EURIPIDES (dramatist); b. Salamis (c. 484–407 B.C.).

FAIRBANKS, Douglas (actor); b. Denver, Colo. (1883–1939).

FALLA, Manuel de (composer); b. Cadiz, Sp. (1876–1946).

FARADAY, Michael (physicist); b. Newing-ton, Sur., Eng. (1791–1867).

FERMI, Enrico (physicist); b. Rome, It. (1901–1954).

FIELD, Eugene (poet); b. St. Louis, Mo. (1850–1895).

FIELD, Marshall, III (publisher & philan-thropist); b. Chicago, Ill. (1893–1956).

FIELDING, Henry (novelist); b. nr. Glaston-bury, 'Som., Eng. (1707–1754).

FIELDS, W. C. (Claude William Dukenfield) (actor); b. Philadelphia, Pa. (1880–1946).

FISKE, Minnie Maddern (nee Davey) (ac-tress); b. New Orleans, La. (1865–1932).

FITZGERALD, Barry (William Joseph Shields) (actor); b. Dublin, Ire. (1888–1961).

FITZGERALD, Francis Scott Key (novelist); b. St. Paul, Minn. (1896–1940).

FITZSIMMONS, Robert Prometheus (boxer); b. Cornwall, Eng. (1862–1917).

FLAUBERT, Gustave (novelist); b. Rouen, Fr. (1821–1880).

FLEMING, Sir Alexander (bacteriologist); b. Lochfield, Scot. (1881–1955).

FORD, Henry (industrialist); b. Greenfield, Mich. (1863–1947).

FOSTER, Stephen Collins (composer); b. nr. Pittsburgh, Pa. (1826–1864).

FRANCE, Anatole (Jacques Anatole François Thibault) (author); b. Paris (1844–1924).

FRANKLIN, Benjamin (statesman & scien-tist); b. Boston, Mass. (1706–1790).

FRAZER, Sir James George (anthropologist); b. Glasgow, Scot. (1854–1941).

FREUD, Sigmund (psychoanalyst); b. Frei-berg, Moravia (1856–1939).

FULTON, Robert (inventor); b. Lancaster Co., Pa. (1765–1815).

GABLE, William Clark (actor); b. Cadiz, Ohio (1901–1960).

GAINSBOROUGH, Thomas (painter); b. Sud-bury, Suff., Eng. (1727–1788).

GALILEI, Galileo (astronomer & physicist); b. Pisa, It. (1564–1642).

GALSWORTHY, John (novelist & dramatist); b. Coombe, Sur., Eng. (1867–1933).

GANDHI, Mohandas Karamchand (called Ma-hatma Gandhi) (Hindu leader); b. Por-bandar, India (1869–1948).

GARIBALDI, Giuseppe (Italian nationalist leader); b. Nice, Fr. (1807–1882).

GARRICK, David (actor); b. Hereford, Heref., Eng. (1717–1779).

GARRISON, William Lloyd (abolitionist); b. Newburyport, Mass. (1805–1879).

GAUGUIN, Eugène Henri Paul (painter); b. Paris, Fr. (1848–1903).

GAUTAMA BUDDHA (Prince Siddhartha) (phi-losopher); b. Kapilavastu, India (563?–?483 B.C.).

GEDDES, Norman Bel (stage designer); b. Adrian, Mich. (1893–1958).

GEHRIG, Lou (Henry Louis Gehrig) (base-ball player); b. New York City (1903–1941).

GENGHIS KHAN (Temujin) (conqueror); b. nr. Lake Baikal in Asia (1162–1227).

GEORGE, Henry (economist); b. Philadelphia, Pa. (1839–1897).

GERONIMO (Goyathlay) (Apache chieftain); b. Arizona (1829–1909).

GERSHWIN, George (composer); b. Brooklyn, N. Y. (1898–1937).

GIBBON, Edward (historian); b. Putney, Eng. (1737–1794).

GIBSON, Charles Dana (illustrator); b. Rox-bury, Mass. (1867–1944).

GIDE, André (author); b. Paris, Fr. (1869–1951).

GILBERT, Sir William Schwenck (dramatist & librettist); b. London, England (1836–1911).

GIOTTO di Bondone (painter); b. Vespig-namo, It. (1276?–?1337).

GLADSTONE, William Ewart (statesman); b. Liverpool, Eng. (1809–1898).

GLEASON, James (actor); b. New York City (1886–1959).

GLUCK, Christoph Willibald (composer); b. Erasbach, Bavaria (1714–1787).

GOEBBELS, Joseph Paul (Nazi leader); b. Rheydt, Ger. (1897–1945).

GOERING, Hermann (Nazi leader); b. Rosen-heim, Bavaria (1893–1946).

GOETHALS, George Washington (engineer); b. Brooklyn, N. Y. (1858–1928).

GOETHE, Johann Wolfgang von (poet); b. Frankfurt am Main, Ger. (1749–1832).

GOGH, Vincent van (painter); b. Groot-Zundert, Brabant, Hol. (1853–1890).

GOGOL, Nikolai Vasilievich (novelist); b. nr. Mirgorod, Poltava, Ukr. (1809–1852).

GOLDSMITH, Oliver (dramatist & poet); b. County Longford, Ire. (1728–1774).

GOMPERS, Samuel (labor leader); b. London, Eng. (1850–1924).

GOODYEAR, Charles (inventor); b. New Haven, Conn. (1800–1860).

GORKI, Maxim (Alexei Maximovich Peshkov) (author); b. Nizhni Novgorod, Rus. (1868–1936).

GOULD, Jay (Jason) (financier); b. Roxbury, N. Y. (1836–1892).

GOUNOD, Charles François (composer); b. Paris, Fr. (1818–1893).

GOYA Y LUCIENTES, Francisco José de (painter); b. Fuendetodos, Sp. (1746–1828).

GRAY, Thomas (poet); b. London, Eng. (1716–1771).

GRECO, El (Domenicos Theotocopoulos) (painter); b. Candia, Crete (c.1542–1614).

GREELEY, Horace (journalist & politician); b. Amherst, N. H. (1811–1872).

GRIEG, Edvard Hagerup (composer); b. Bergen, Nor. (1843–1907).

GRIFFITH, David Lewelyn Wark (movie producer); b. La Grange, Ky. (1875–1948).

GRIMM, Jacob (mythologist); b. Hanau, Ger. (1785–1863).

GRIMM, Wilhelm (mythologist); b. Hanau, Ger. (1786–1859).

GUITRY, Sacha (Alexandre) (actor & movie director); b. St. Petersburg, Rus. (1885–1957).

GUTENBERG, Johann (printer); b. Mainz, Ger. (1400?–?1468).

HALE, Nathan (American Revolutionary officer); b. Coventry, Conn. (1755–1776).

HALS, Frans (painter); b. Antwerp, Hol. (1580?–1666).

HAMILTON, Alexander (statesman); b. Leeward Is. (1757?–1804).

HAMMARSKJÖLD, Dag (U. N. statesman); b. Jönköping, Swed. (1905–1961).

HAMMERSTEIN, Oscar, II (librettist, producer); b. New York City (1895–1960).

HAMMETT, Samuel Dashiell (novelist); b. St. Marys Co., Md. (1894–1961).

HANCOCK, John (statesman); b. Braintree, Mass. (1737–1793).

HAND, Learned (jurist); b. Albany, N.Y. (1872–1961).

HANDEL, George Frederick (Georg Friedrich Händel) (composer); b. Halle, Ger. (1685–1759).

HANDY, William Christopher (blues composer); b. Florence, Ala. (1873–1958).

HANNIBAL (Carthaginian general) (247–183 B.C.).

HARDY, Thomas (novelist); b. Dorsetshire, Eng. (1840–1928).

HARLOW, Jean (Harlean Carpenter) (actress); b. Kansas City, Mo. (1911–1937).

HARTE, Bret (Francis Brett Harte) (author); b. Albany, N. Y. (1836–1902).

HARVEY, William (physician); b. Folkestone, Kent, Eng. (1578–1657).

HAWTHORNE, Nathaniel (novelist); b. Salem, Mass. (1804–1864).

HAY, John Milton (statesman); b. Salem, Ind. (1838–1905).

HAYDN, Franz Joseph (composer); b. Rohrau, Aus. (1732–1809).

HEARST, William Randolph (publisher); b. San Francisco, Calif. (1863–1951).

HEGEL, Georg Wilhelm Friedrich (philosopher); b. Stuttgart, Ger. (1770–1831).

HEINE, Heinrich (Harry) (poet); b. Düsseldorf, Ger. (1797–1856).

HEMINGWAY, Ernest Miller (author); b. Oak Park, Ill. (1898–1961).

HENRY, O. (William Sydney Porter) (story writer); b. Greensboro, N. C. (1862–1910).

HENRY, Patrick (statesman); b. Hanover Co., Va. (1736–1799).

HEPPLEWHITE, George (furniture designer) b. England (?–1786).

HERBERT, Victor (composer); b. Dublin, Ire. (1859–1924).

HEROD (Herdoes) (called Herod the Great) (King of Judea) (73?–4 B.C.).

HERODOTUS (historian); b. Halicarnassus, Asia Minor (c.484–425 B.C.).

HERRIOT, Édouard (French statesman); b. Troyes, Fr. (1872–1957).

HERSHOLT, Jean (actor); b. Copenhagen, Den. (1886–1956).

HINDENBURG, Paul von (Paul Ludwig Hans Anton von Beneckendorff und von Hindenburg) (statesman); b. Posen, Prus. (1847–1934).

HINES, Duncan (author); b. Bowling Green, Ky. (1880–1959).

HIPPOCRATES (physician); b. Kos, Dodecanese (460?–?377 B.C.).

HITLER, Adolf (German dictator); b. Branau, Aus. (1889–1945).

HOFMANN, Josef Casimir (pianist); b. Kracow, Pol. (1876–1957).

HOGARTH, William (painter & engraver); b. London, Eng. (1697–1764).

HOLBEIN, Hans (the Elder) (painter); b. Augsburg, Bavaria (1465?–1524).

HOLBEIN, Hans (the Younger) (painter); b. Augsburg, Bavaria (1497?–1543).

HOLMES, Oliver Wendell (author); b. Cambridge, Mass. (1809–1894).

HOLMES, Oliver Wendell (jurist); b. Boston, Mass. (1841–1935).

HOMER (Greek poet) (c.850 B.C.?).

HOMER, Winslow (painter); b. Boston, Mass. (1836–1910).

HONEGGER, Arthur (composer); b. Le Havre, Fr. (1892–1955).

HOPPE, Willie (William Frederick Hoppe) (billiards player); b. Cornwall, N. Y. (1887–1959).

HORACE (Quintus Horatius Flaccus) (poet); b. Venosa, Lucania (65–8 B.C.).

HOUDINI, Harry (Ehrich Weiss) (magician); b. Appleton, Wis. (1874–1926).

HOUSMAN, Alfred Edward (poet); b. Fockburg, Worcs., Eng. (1859–1936).

HOUSTON, Samuel (political leader); b. Rockbridge Co., Va. (1793–1863).

HOWARD, Leslie (actor); b. London, Eng. (1893–1943).

HOWE, Elias (inventor); b. Spencer, Mass. (1819–1867).

HOWELLS, William Dean (author); b. Martin's Ferry, Ohio (1837–1920).

HUDSON, Henry (English navigator) (?–1611).

HUGHES, Charles Evans (jurist); b. Glens Falls, N. Y. (1862–1948).

HUGO, Victor Marie (author); b. Besançon, Fr. (1802–1885).

HULL, Josephine (nee Josephine Sherwood) (actress); b. Newtonville, Mass. (1886–1957).

HUME, David (philosopher); b. Edinburgh, Scot. (1711–1776).

HUSTON, Walter (Walter Houghston) (actor); b. Toronto, Ont., Can. (1884–1950).

HUXLEY, Thomas Henry (biologist); b. Ealing, Eng. (1825–1895).

IBSEN, Henrik (dramatist); b. Skien, Nor. (1828–1906).

INNESS, George (painter); b. nr. Newburgh, N. Y. (1825–1894).

IRVING, Washington (author); b. New York City (1783–1859).

JACKSON, Thomas Jonathan (general); b. Clarksburg, Va. (now W. Va.) (1824–1863).

JAMES, Henry (novelist); b. New York City (1843–1916).

JAMES, Jesse Woodson (outlaw); b. Clay Co., Mo. (1847–1882).

JAMES, William (psychologist); b. New York City (1842–1910).

JANIS, Elsie (Elsie Bierbower) (actress); b. Columbus, Ohio (1889–1956).

JAY, John (statesman & jurist); b. New York City (1745–1829).

JEFFRIES, James J. (boxer); b. Carroll, Ohio (1875–1953).

JENNER, Edward (physician); Berkeley, Glos., Eng. (1749–1823).

JOAN OF ARC (Jeanne d'Arc) (saint & patriot); b. Domremy-la-Pucelle, Fr. (1412–1431).

JOHNSON, Jack (John Arthur Johnson) (boxer); b. Galveston, Tex. (1876–1946).

JOHNSON, Samuel (lexicographer & author); b. Lichfield, Staffs., Eng. (1709–1784).

JOLIOT-CURIE, Frédéric (physicist); b. Paris, Fr. (1900–1958).

JOLIOT-CURIE, Irène (Irène Curie) (physicist); b. France (1897–1956).

JOLLIET (or JOLIET), Louis (explorer); b. Beaupré, Can. (1645–1700).

JOLSON, Al (Asa Yoelson) (actor & singer); b. St. Petersburg, Rus. (1886–1950).

JONES, John Paul (John Paul) (naval officer); b. Scotland (1747–1792).

JONSON, Ben (Benjamin) (poet & dramatist); b. Westminster, Eng. (1572–1637).

JOYCE, James (novelist); b. Dublin, Ire. (1882–1941).

JOYCE, Peggy Hopkins (nee Margaret Upton) (actress); b. Norfolk, Va. (1893?–1957).

JUÁREZ, Benito Pablo (statesman); b. Guelatao, Oaxaca, Mex. (1806–1872).

JUNG, Carl Gustav (psychoanalyst); b. Basel, Switz. (1875–1961).

KANT, Immanuel (philosopher); b. Königsberg, Prus. (1724–1804).

KAUFMAN, George S. (dramatist); b. Pittsburgh, Pa. (1389–1961).

KEATS, John (poet); b. London, Eng. (1795–1821).

KEMAL ATATÜRK (Mustafa Kemal) (statesman); b. Salonika, Turk. (1881–1938).

KEPLER, Johannes (astronomer); b. Weil, Württemberg, Ger. (1571–1630).

KERN, Jerome David (composer); b. New York City (1885–1945).

KETTERING, Charles Franklin (engineer); b. nr. Loudonville, Ohio (1876–1958).

KEY, Francis Scott (lawyer); b. Frederick (now Carroll) Co., Md. (1779–1843).

KEYNES (1st Baron of Tilton) (John Maynard Keynes) (economist); b. Cambridge, Eng. (1883–1946).

KIDD, William (called Capt. Kidd) (pirate); b. Greenock, Scot. (1645?–1701).

KILMER, Alfred Joyce (poet); b. New Brunswick, N. J. (1886–1918).

KIPLING, Rudyard (author); b. Bombay, India (1865–1936).

KNOX, John (religious reformer); b. Haddington, E. Lothian, Scot. (1505–1572).

KOSCIUSKO, Thaddeus (Tadeusz Andrzej Bonawentura Kościuszko) (military officer); b. Lithuania, Pol. (1746–1817).

KOUSSEVITZKY, Serge (Sergei) Alexandrovitch (orchestra conductor); b. Russia (1874–1951).

KUBLAI KHAN (Mongol conqueror) (1216–1294).

LAFAYETTE, Marquis de (Marie Joseph Paul Yves Roch Gilbert du Motier) (military officer); b. Auvergne, Fr. (1757–1834).

LA FOLLETTE, Robert Marin (politician); b. Primrose, Wis. (1855–1925).

LA GUARDIA, Fiorello Henry (politician); b. New York City (1882–1947).

LAMARCK, Chevalier de (Jean Baptiste Pierre Antoine de Monet) (naturalist); b. Bazantin, Picardy (1744–1829).

LAMB, Charles (essayist); b. London, Eng. (1775–1834).

LANDIS, Kenesaw Mountain (jurist); b. Millville, Ohio (1866–1944).

LANGTRY, Lily (nee Emily Le Breton) (actress); b. island of Jersey (1852–1929).

LAO-TZU (or LAO-TSE) (Li Erh) (philosopher); b. Honan prov., China (c.604–531 B.C.).

LARDNER, Ring (Ringgold Wilmer Lardner) (story writer); b. Niles, Mich. (1885–1933).

LA SALLE, Sieur de (Robert Cavelier) (explorer); b. Rouen, Fr. (1643–1687).

LAUDER, Sir Harry (Harry MacLennan) (singer); b. Portobello, Scot. (1870–1950).

LAVOISIER, Antoine Laurent (chemist); b. Paris, Fr. (1743–1794).

LAWRENCE, David Herbert (novelist); b. Nottingham, Eng. (1885–1930).

LAWRENCE, Gertrude (Gertrud Klasen) (actress); b. London, Eng. (1900–1952).

LAWRENCE OF ARABIA (Thomas Edward Lawrence; later changed name to Shaw); (author & soldier); b. Portmadoc, Wales (1888–1935).

LEAR, Edward (nonsense poet); b. London, Eng. (1812–1888).

LEE, Robert Edward (Confederate general); b. Stratford Estate, Va. (1807–1870).

LEHÁR, Franz (composer); b. Komárom, Hung. (1870–1948).

LENIN, Nikolai (Vladimir Ilich Ulyanov) (statesman); b. Simbirsk, Rus. (1870–1924).

LEONARD, Benny (Benjamin Leiner) (boxer); b. New York City (1896–1947).

LEWIS, Meriwether (explorer); b. Albemarle Co., Va. (1774–1809).

LEWIS, Sinclair (novelist); b. Sauk Centre, Minn. (1885–1951).

LIND, Jenny (Johanna Maria Lind) (soprano); b. Stockholm, Swed. (1820–1887).

LISTER (1st Baron of Lyme Regis) (Joseph Lister) (surgeon); b. Upton, Essex, Eng. (1827–1912).

LISZT, Franz (composer & pianist); b. Raiding, Hung. (1811–1886).

LIVINGSTONE, David (missionary & explorer); b. Lanarkshire, Scot. (1813–1873).

LLOYD GEORGE, David (statesman); b. Manchester, Eng. (1863–1945).

LOCKE, John (philosopher); b. Somersetshire, Eng. (1632–1704).

LODGE, Henry Cabot (legislator); b. Boston, Mass. (1850–1924).

LOMBARD, Carole (Carol Jane Peters) (actress); b. Ft. Wayne, Ind. (1908–1942).

LOMBROSO, Cesare (criminologist); b. Verona, It. (1836–1909).

LONDON, Jack (John Griffith London) (novelist); b. San Francisco (1876–1916).

LONG, Huey Pierce (politician); b. Winnfield, La. (1893–1935).

LONGFELLOW, Henry Wadsworth (poet); b. Portland, Maine (1807–1882).

LOWELL, Amy (poet); b. Brookline, Mass. (1874–1925).

LOWELL, James Russell (poet); b. Cambridge, Mass. (1819–1891).

LOYOLA, St. Ignatius of (Íñigo de Oñez y Loyola) (founder of Jesuits); b. Gúipuzcoa prov., Sp. (1491–1556).

LUBITSCH, Ernst (movie director); b. Berlin, Ger. (1892–1947).

LUDENDORFF, Erich Friedrich Wilhelm (general); b. Kruszevnia, Ger. (1865–1937).

LUTHER, Martin (religious reformer); b. Eisleben, Ger. (1483–1546).

MacARTHUR, Charles (dramatist); b. Scranton, Pa. (1895–1956).

MACAULAY, Thomas Babington (author); b. Leicestershire, Eng. (1800–1859).

MacDONALD, James Ramsay (statesman); b. Lossiemouth, Scot. (1866–1937).

MacDOWELL, Edward Alexander (composer); b. New York City (1861–1908).

MACFADDEN, Bernarr (physical culturist); b. nr. Mill Spring, Mo. (1868–1955).

MACHIAVELLI, Niccolò (political philosopher); b. Florence (1469–1527).

MACK, Connie (Cornelius Alexander McGillicuddy) (baseball executive); b. East Brookfield, Mass. (1862–1956).

MAETERLINCK, Count Maurice (author); b. Ghent, Belg. (1862–1949).

MAGELLAN, Ferdinand (Fernando de Magalhães) (navigator); b. Sabrosa, Port. (1480?–1521).

MAGSAYSAY, Ramón (statesman); b. Iba, Luzon, Philippines (1907–1957).

MAHAN, Alfred Thayer (naval historian); b. West Point, N. Y. (1840–1914).

MAHLER, Gustav (composer & conductor); b. Kalischt, Bohemia (1860–1911).

MANET, Édouard (painter); b. Paris, Fr. (1832–1883).

MANN, Horace (educator); b. Franklin, Mass. (1796–1859).

MANN, Thomas (novelist); b. Lübeck, Ger. (1875–1955).

MANSFIELD, Katherine (story writer); b. Wellington, N. Z. (1888–1923).

MARAT, Jean Paul (French revolutionist); b. Boudry, Neuchâtel, Switzerland (1743–1793).

MARCONI, Guglielmo (inventor); b. Bologna, It. (1874–1937).

MARCUS AURELIUS (Marcus Annius Verus) (Roman emperor); b. Rome (121–180).

MARIE ANTOINETTE (Josèphe Jeanne Marie Antoinette) (Queen of France); b. Vienna, Aus. (1755–1793).

MARKHAM, Charles Edwin (poet); b. Oregon City, Oreg. (1852–1940).

MARLOWE, Christopher (dramatist); b. Canterbury, Eng. (1564–1593).

MARLOWE, Julia (Sarah Frances Frost) (actress); b. Cumberlandshire, Eng. (1866–1950).

MARQUAND, John Phillips (novelist); b. Wilmington, Del. (1893–1960).

MARQUETTE, Jacques (missionary & explorer); b. Laon, Fr. (1637–1675).

MARSHALL, George Catlett (general); b. Uniontown, Pa. (1880–1959).

MARSHALL, John (jurist); b. nr. Germantown, Va. (1755–1835).

MARX, Karl (Socialist writer); b. Treves, Prus. (1818–1883).

MARY STUART (Queen of Scotland); b. Linlithgow, Scot. (1542–1587).

MASARYK, Thomas Garrigue (statesman); b. Hodonin, Moravia (1850–1937).

MASSENET, Jules Émile Frédéric (composer); b. Montaud, Fr. (1842–1912).

MASTERS, Edgar Lee (poet); b. Garnett, Kans. (1869–1950).

MATISSE, Henri (painter); b. Cateau, Fr. (1869–1954).

MAUPASSANT, Henri René Albert Guy de (story writer); b. Normandy, Fr. (1850–1893).

MAXIMILIAN (Ferdinand Maximilian Joseph) (Emperor of Mexico); b. Vienna, Aus. (1832–1867).

MAXWELL, James Clerk (physicist); b. Edinburgh, Scot. (1831–1879).

McCARTHY, Joseph Raymond (U. S. Senator); b. Grand Chute, Wis. (1908–1957).

McCORMACK, John (tenor); b. Athlone, Ire. (1884–1945).

McCORMICK, Cyrus Hall (inventor); b. Rockbridge Co., Va. (1809–1884).

McGRAW, John Joseph (baseball manager); b. Truxton, N. Y. (1873–1934).

MEDICI, Lorenzo de' (called Lorenzo the Magnificent) (Florentine ruler); b. Florence (1449–1492).

MELBA, Dame Nellie (Helen Porter Mitchell) (soprano); b. nr. Melbourne, Australia (1861–1931).

MELLON, Andrew William (financier); b. Pittsburgh, Pa. (1855–1937).

MELVILLE, Herman (novelist); b. New York City (1819–1891).

MENCKEN, Henry Louis (author); b. Baltimore, Md. (1880–1956).

MENDEL, Gregor Johann (botanist); b. Heinzendorf, Silesia (1822–1884).

MENDELEYEV, Dmitri Ivanovich (chemist); b. Tobolsk, Siberia (1834–1907).

MENDELSSOHN-BARTHOLDY, Jakob Ludwig Felix (composer); b. Hamburg, Ger. (1809–1847).

**MESMER,** Franz Anton (physician); b. Itzmang, nr. Constance, Baden (1733–1815).

**METTERNICH,** Prince Klemens Wenzel Nepomuk Lothar von (statesman); b. Coblenz, Aus. (1773–1859).

**MICHELANGELO BUONARROTI** (painter & sculptor); b. Caprese, Tuscany, It. (1475–1564).

**MILL,** John Stuart (philosopher); b. London, Eng. (1806–1873).

**MILLAY,** Edna St. Vincent (poet); b. Rockland, Maine (1892–1950).

**MILLER,** Glenn (band leader); b. Clarinda, Iowa (1909?–1944).

**MILNE,** Alan Alexander (author); b. London, Eng. (1882–1956).

**MILTON,** John (poet); b. London, Eng. (1608–1674).

**MINUIT,** Peter (Governor of New Amsterdam); b. Wesel, Rhenish Prussia (1580–1638).

**MITCHELL,** Margaret (novelist); b. Atlanta, Ga. (1900–1949).

**MITROPOULOS,** Dimitri (orchestra conductor); b. Athens, Gr. (1896–1960).

**MOHAMMED** (prophet); b. Mecca, Arabia (570–632).

**MOLIÈRE** (Jean Baptiste Poquelin) (dramatist); b. Paris, Fr. (1622–1673).

**MOLNÁR,** Ferenc (dramatist); b. Budapest, Hung. (1878–1952).

**MONET,** Claude (painter); b. Paris, Fr. (1840–1926).

**MONTAIGNE,** Michel Eyquem de (essayist); b. nr. Bordeaux, Fr. (1533–1592).

**MONTEZUMA II** (Aztec emperor); b. Mexico (1480?–1520).

**MOORE,** Thomas (poet); b. Dublin, Ire. (1779–1852).

**MORE,** Sir Thomas (statesman & author); b. London, Eng. (1478–1535).

**MORGAN,** Helen (singer); b. Danville, Ohio (1900?–1941).

**MORGAN,** John Pierpont (financier); b. Hartford, Conn. (1837–1913).

**MORLEY,** Christopher Darlington (novelist); b. Haverford, Pa. (1890–1957).

**MORSE,** Samuel Finley Breese (painter & inventor); b. Charlestown, Mass. (1791–1872).

**MOUSSORGSKY,** Modest Petrovich (composer); b. Karev, Rus. (1839–1881).

**MOZART,** Wolfgang Amadeus (Johannes Chrysostomus Wolfgangus Theophilus Mozart) (composer); b. Salzburg, Aus. (1756–1791).

**MURILLO,** Bartolomé Esteban (painter); b. Seville, Sp. (1617–1682).

**MUSSOLINI,** Benito (Italian dictator); b. Dovia, Forlì, It. (1883–1945).

**NAPOLEON BONAPARTE** (Emperor of the French); b. Ajaccio, Corsica (1769–1821).

**NAST,** Thomas (cartoonist); b. Landau, Ger. (1840–1902).

**NATHAN,** George Jean (theater critic); b. Ft. Wayne, Ind. (1882–1958).

**NATION,** Carry Amelia (temperance leader); b. Garrard Co., Ky. (1846–1911).

**NELSON,** Viscount Horatio (naval officer); b. Burnham Thorpe, Norf., Eng. (1758–1805).

**NERO** (Nero Claudius Caesar Drusus Germanicus) (Roman emperor); b. Antium, Latium, It. (A.D. 37–68).

**NEWTON,** Sir Isaac (mathematician & scientist); b. nr. Grantham, Lincs., Eng. (1642–1727).

**NIETZSCHE,** Friedrich Wilhelm (philosopher); b. nr. Lützen, Saxony (1844–1900).

**NIGHTINGALE,** Florence (nurse); b. Florence, It. (1820–1910).

**NIJINSKY,** Waslaw (dancer); b. Warsaw, Pol. (1890–1950).

**NOBEL,** Alfred Bernhard (industrialist); b. Stockholm, Swed. (1833–1896).

**NOSTRADAMUS** (Michel de Notredame) (astrologer); b. St. Remi, Fr. (1503–1566).

**OCHS,** Adolph Simon (publisher); b. Cincinnati, Ohio (1858–1935).

**OFFENBACH,** Jacques (composer); b. Cologne, Ger. (1819–1880).

**OMAR KHAYYÁM** (poet & astronomer); b. Nishapur, Khurasan, Persia (died c. 1123).

**O'NEILL,** Eugene Gladstone (dramatist); b. New York City (1888–1953).

**OROZCO,** José Clemente (painter); b. Zapotlán, Jalisco, Mex. (1883–1949).

**OSLER,** Sir William (physician); b. Bondhead, Ont., Can. (1849–1919).

**OTT,** Mel (Melvin Thomas Ott) (baseball player); b. Gretna, La. (1909–1958).

**OVID** (Publius Ovidius Naso) (poet); b. Sulmona, It. (43 B.C.–?A.D. 17).

**PADEREWSKI,** Ignace Jan (pianist & statesman); b. Podolia prov., Pol. (1860–1941).

**PAGANINI,** Nicolò (violinist); b. Genoa, It. (1782–1840).

**PAINE,** Thomas (political philosopher); b. Thetford, Eng. (1737–1809).

**PARNELL,** Charles Stewart (Irish nationalist leader); b. Avondale, Wicklow, Ire. (1846–1891).

**PASCAL,** Blaise (philosopher); b. Clermont, Fr. (1623–1662).

**PASTEUR,** Louis (chemist); b. Dole, Jura, Fr. (1822–1895).

**PAVLOV,** Ivan Petrovich (physiologist); b. Ryazan dist., Rus. (1849–1936).

**PAVLOVA,** Anna (ballerina); b. St. Petersburg, Rus. (1885–1931).

**PEARY,** Robert Edwin (explorer); b. Cresson, Pa. (1856–1920).

**PENN,** William (American colonist); b. London, Eng. (1644–1718).

**PEPYS,** Samuel (diarist); b. Bampton, Eng. (1633–1703).

**PERICLES** (statesman); b. Athens (died 429 B.C.).

**PERÓN,** María Eva Duarte de (political leader); b. Los Toldos, Arg. (1919–1952).

**PERSHING,** John Joseph (general); b. Linn Co., Mo. (1860–1948).

**PETRARCH** (Francesco Petrarca) (poet); b. Arezzo, It. (1304–1374).

**PINZA,** Ezio (basso); b. Rome, It. (1892–1957).

**PIRANDELLO,** Luigi (dramatist & novelist); b. nr. Girgenti, Sicily (1867–1936).

**PITT,** William ("Younger Pitt") (statesman); b. nr. Bromley, Eng. (1759–1806).

**PIUS XII** (Eugenio Pacelli) (Pope); b. Rome, It. (1876–1958).

**PIZARRO,** Francisco (explorer); b. Trujillo, Sp. (1470?–1541).

PLATO (Aristocles) (philosopher); b. Athens (?) (427?–347 B.C.).

PLUTARCH (biographer); b. Chaeronea, Boeotia (A.D. 46?–?120).

POCAHONTAS (Matoaka) (American Indian princess); b. Virginia (?) (1595?–1617).

POE, Edgar Allan (poet & story writer); b. Boston, Mass. (1809–1849).

POLO, Marco (traveler); b. Venice (1254?–?1324).

POMPEY (Gnaeua Pompeius Magnus) (general); b. Rome (?) (106–48 B.C.).

PONCE de LEÓN, Juan (explorer); b. Servas, Sp. (1460?–1521).

POPE, Alexander (poet); b. London, Eng. (1688–1744).

POST, Wiley (aviator); b. Texas (1900–1935).

POWER, Tyrone Edmund (actor); b. Cincinnati, Ohio (1914–1958).

PRIESTLEY, Joseph (chemist); b. nr. Leeds, Eng. (1733–1804).

PROKOFIEFF, Sergei Sergeevich (composer); b. St. Petersburg, Rus. (1891–1953).

PROUST, Marcel (novelist); b. Paris, Fr. (1871–1922).

PTOLEMY (Claudius Ptolemaeus) (astronomer & geographer); b. Ptolemais Hermii (2nd century A.D.).

PUCCINI, Giacomo (composer); b. Lucca, It. (1858–1924).

PULITZER, Joseph (publisher); b. Makó, Hung. (1847–1911).

PUSHKIN, Alexander Sergeevich (poet & dramatist); b. Moscow, Rus. (1799–1837).

PYLE, Ernest Taylor (journalist); b. Dana, Ind. (1900–1945).

PYTHAGORAS (mathematician & philosopher); b. Samos (6th century B.C.).

RABELAIS, François (satirist); b. nr. Chinon, Fr. (1494?–1553).

RACHMANINOFF, Sergei Wassilievtch (pianist & composer); b. Oneg Estate, Novgorod, Rus. (1873–1943).

RACINE, Jean Baptiste (dramatist); b. La Ferté-Milon, Fr. (1639–1699).

RALEIGH, Sir Walter (courtier & navigator); b. London, Eng. (1552?–1618).

RAPHAEL (Raffaello Santi) (painter); b. Urbino, It. (1483–1520).

RASPUTIN, Grigori Efimovich (monk); b. Tobolsk prov., Siberia (1871?–1916).

RATOFF, Gregory (movie director); b. St. Petersburg, Rus. (1897–1960).

RAVEL, Maurice Joseph (composer); b. Ciboure, Fr. (1875–1937).

REED, Walter (army surgeon); b. Belroi, Va. (1851–1902).

REINHARDT, Max (Max Goldmann) (theater producer); b. nr. Vienna, Aus. (1873–1943).

REMBRANDT (Harmensz van Rijn Rembrandt) (painter); b. Leyden, Hol. (1606–1669).

RENOIR, Pierre Auguste (painter); b. Limoges, Fr. (1841–1919).

RESPIGHI, Ottorino (composer); b. Bologna, It. (1879–1936).

REVERE, Paul (silversmith); b. Boston, Mass. (1735–1818).

REYNOLDS, Sir Joshua (painter); b. nr. Plymouth, Eng. (1723–1792).

RHODES, Cecil John (South African statesman); b. Bishop Stortford, Herts., Eng. (1853–1902).

RICE, Grantland (sports writer); b. Murfreesboro, Tenn. (1880–1954).

RICHELIEU, Duc de (Armand Jean du Plessis) (cardinal); b. Paris (1585–1642).

RILEY, James Whitcomb (poet); b. Greenfield, Ind. (1849–1916).

RIMSKY-KORSAKOV, Nikolai Andreevich (composer); b. Tikhvin, Rus. (1844–1908).

RINEHART, Mary (nee Roberts) (novelist); b. Pittsburgh, Pa. (?–1958).

RIVERA, Diego (painter); b. Guanajuato, Mex. (1886–1957).

ROBESPIERRE, Maximilien François Marie Isidore de (French Revolutionist); b. Arras, Fr. (1758–1794).

ROBINSON, Bill (Luther) (dancer); b. Richmond, Va. (1878–1949).

ROBINSON, Edwin Arlington (poet); b. Head Tide, Maine (1869–1935).

ROCKEFELLER, John Davison (capitalist); b. Richford, N. Y. (1839–1937).

ROCKEFELLER, John Davison, Jr. (industrialist); b. Cleveland, Ohio (1874–1960).

ROCKNE, Knute Kenneth (football coach); b. Voss, Nor. (1888–1931).

RODIN, François Auguste René (sculptor); b. Paris, Fr. (1840–1917).

ROENTGEN, Wilhelm Konrad (physicist); b. Lennep, Prus. (1845–1923).

ROGERS, Will (William Penn Adair Rogers) (humorist); b. Oologah, Okla. (1879–1935).

ROLLAND, Romain (author); b. Clamecy, Fr. (1866–1944).

ROMBERG, Sigmund (composer); b. Hungary (1887–1951).

ROSSETTI, Dante Gabriel (painter & poet); b. London, Eng. (1828–1882).

ROSSINI, Gioacchino Antonio (composer); b. Pesaro, It. (1792–1868).

ROSTAND, Edmond (dramatist); b. Marseilles, Fr. (1868–1918).

ROUSSEAU, Jean Jacques (philosopher); b. Geneva, Switz. (1712–1778).

RUBENS, Peter Paul (painter); b. Siegen, Westphalia (1577–1640).

RUNYON, Alfred Damon (journalist); b. Manhattan, Kans. (1884–1946).

RUSKIN, John (art critic); b. London, Eng. (1819–1900).

RUSSELL, Lillian (Helen Louise Leonard) (soprano); b. Clinton, Iowa (1861–1922).

RUTH, Babe (George Herman Ruth) (baseball player); b. Baltimore, Md. (1895–1948).

SAINT-GAUDENS, Augustus (sculptor); b. Dublin, Ire. (1848–1907).

SAINT-SAËNS, Charles Camille (composer); b. Paris, Fr. (1835–1921).

SAND, George (Amandine Lucille Aurore Dudevant, nee Dupin) (novelist); b. Paris, Fr. (1804–1876).

SANTAYANA, George (philosopher); b. Madrid, Sp. (1863–1952).

SAPPHO (poet); b. Lesbos (lived c.600 B.C.).

SARGENT, John Singer (painter); b. Florence, It., of American parents (1856–1925).

SARTO, Andrea del (Andrea Domenico d'Agnolo di Francesco) (painter); b. Florence (1486–1531).

SAUL (King of Israel) (11th century B.C.).

SCHILLER, Johann Christoph Friedrich von (dramatist & poet); b. Marbach, Wurttemberg, Ger. (1759–1805).

SCHÖNBERG, Arnold (composer); Vienna, Aus. (1874–1951).

SCHOPENHAUER, Arthur (philosopher); b. Danzig (1788–1860).

SCHUBERT, Franz Peter (composer); b. Vienna, Aus. (1797–1826).

SCHUMANN, Robert Alexander (composer); b. Zwickau, Saxony, Ger. (1810–1856).

SCHUMANN-HEINK, Ernestine (nee Roessler) (contralto); b. nr. Prague, Boh. (1861–1936).

SCHURZ, Carl (U. S. army officer & journalist); b. nr. Cologne, Ger. (1829–1906).

SCOTT, Robert Falcon (explorer); b. Devenport, Eng. (1868–1912).

SCOTT, Sir Walter (novelist); b. Edinburgh, Scot. (1771–1832).

SHAKESPEARE, William (dramatist); b. Stratford on Avon, Eng. (1564–1616).

SHAW, George Bernard (dramatist); b. Dublin, Ire. (1856–1950).

SHELLEY, Percy Bysshe (poet); b. nr. Horsham, Sus., Eng. (1792–1822).

SHERATON, Thomas (furniture designer); Stockton-on-Tees, Eng. (1751–1806).

SHERIDAN, Richard Brinsley (dramatist); b. Dublin, Ire. (1751–1816).

SHERMAN, William Tecumseh (army officer); b. Lancaster, Ohio (1820–1891).

SHERWOOD, Robert Emmet (dramatist); b. New Rochelle, N. Y. (1896–1955).

SIBELIUS, Jean (Johann Julius Christian Sibelius) (composer), b. Tavastehus, Fin. (1865–1957).

SKINNER, Otis (actor); b. Cambridge, Mass. (1858–1942).

SLOAN, John (painter); b. Lock Haven, Pa. (1871–1951).

SMITH, Adam (economist); b. Kirkaldy, Fifes., Scot. (1723–1790).

SMITH, Alfred Emanuel (politician); b. New York City (1873–1944).

SMITH, John (American colonist); b. Willoughby, Lincs., Eng. (1580–1631).

SMITH, Joseph (religious leader); b. Sharon, Vt. (1805–1844).

SOCRATES (philosopher); b. Athens (469–399 B.C.).

SOLOMON (King of Israel); b. Jerusalem (?) (died c.933 B.C.).

SOLON (lawgiver); b. Salamis, Gr. (638?–?559 B.C.).

SOPHOCLES (dramatist); b. nr. Athens (496?–406 B.C.).

SOTHERN, Edward Hugh (actor); b. New Orleans, La. (1859–1933).

SOUSA, John Philip (composer); b. Washington, D. C. (1854–1932).

SPEAKER, Tris (Tristram E. Speaker) (baseball player); b. Hubbard, Tex. (1888–1958).

SPENCER, Herbert (philosopher); b. Derby, Eng. (1820–1903).

SPENGLER, Oswald (philosopher); b. Blankenburg, Ger. (1880–1936).

SPENSER, Edmund (poet); b. London, Eng. (1552?–1599).

SPINOZA, Baruch (philosopher); b. Amsterdam, Hol. (1632–1677).

STALIN, Joseph Vissarionovich (Iosif V. Dzhugashvili) (statesman); b. nr. Tiflis, Georgia, Rus. (1879–1953).

STANISLAVSKI (Konstantin Sergeevich Alekseev) (stage producer); b. Moscow, Rus. (1863–1938).

STANLEY, Sir Henry Morton (John Rowlands) (explorer); b. Denbigh, Wales (1841–1904).

STEIN, Gertrude (author); b. Allegheny, Pa. (1874–1946).

STEINMETZ, Charles Proteus (engineer); b. Breslau, Ger. (1865–1923).

STENDHAL (Marie Henri Beyle) (novelist); b. Grenoble, Fr. (1783–1842).

STERNE, Laurence (novelist); b. Clonmel, Ire. (1713–1768).

STEVENSON, Robert Louis Balfour (novelist & poet); b. Edinburgh, Scot. (1850–1894).

STOKES, Thomas Lunsford, Jr. (journalist); b. Atlanta, Ga. (1898–1958).

STONE, Lucy (woman suffragist); b. nr. West Brookfield, Mass. (1818–1893).

STOWE, Harriet Elizabeth (nee Beecher) (novelist); b. Litchfield, Conn. (1811–1896).

STRADIVARI, Antonio (violinmaker); b. Cremona, It. (1644–1737).

STRAUS, Oskar (composer); b. Vienna, Aus. (1870–1954).

STRAUSS, Johann (composer); b. Vienna, Aus. (1825–1899).

STRAUSS, Richard (composer); b. Munich, Ger. (1864–1949).

STUART, Gilbert Charles (painter); b. Rhode Island (1755–1828).

STUYVESANT, Peter (Governor of New Amsterdam); b. W. Friesland, Neth. (1592–1672).

SULLAVAN, Margaret Brooke (actress); b. Norfolk, Va. (1911–1960).

SULLIVAN, Sir Arthur Seymour (composer); b. London, Eng. (1842–1900).

SULLIVAN, Francis Loftus (actor); b. London, Eng. (1903–1956).

SULLIVAN, John Lawrence (boxer); b. Boston, Mass. (1858–1918).

SUN Yat-Sen (statesman); b. nr. Macao, China (1866–1925).

SWIFT, Jonathan (satirist); b. Dublin, Ire. (1667–1745).

SWINBURNE, Algernon Charles (poet); b. London, Eng. (1837–1909).

SWOPE, Herbert Bayard (journalist); b. St. Louis, Mo. (1882–1958).

SYNGE, John Millington (dramatist); b. nr. Dublin, Ire. (1871–1909).

TAFT, Robert Alphonso (legislator); b. Cincinnati, Ohio (1889–1953).

TAGORE, Sir Rabindranath (poet); b. Calcutta, India (1861–1941).

TALLEYRAND-PÉRIGORD, Charles Maurice de (statesman); b. Paris, Fr. (1754–1838).

TAMERLANE (Timur) (Mongol conqueror); b. nr. Samarkand, Sib. (1336?–1405).

TARKINGTON, Newton Booth (novelist); b. Indianapolis, Ind. (1869–1946).

TCHAIKOVSKY (or TSCHAIKOWSKY), Peter (Pëtr) Ilich (composer); b. Ural region, Rus. (1840–1893).

TECUMSEH (Shawnee Indian chief); b. nr. Springfield, Ohio (1768?–1813).

**TENNYSON,** Alfred (1st Baron Tennyson) (poet); b. Somersby, Lincs., Eng. (1809–1892).

**TERRY,** Ellen Alicia (actress); b. Coventry, Eng. (1848–1928).

**TETRAZZINI,** Luisa (soprano); b. Florence, It. (1871–1940).

**THACKERAY,** William Makepeace (novelist); b. Calcutta, India (1811–1863).

**THOMAS,** Dylan Marlais (poet); b. Caermarthenshire, Wales (1914–1953).

**THOREAU,** Henry David (naturalist & author); b. Concord, Mass. (1817–1862).

**THORPE,** Jim (James Francis Thorpe) (athlete); b. nr. Prague, Oklahoma (1888–1953).

**TILDEN,** William Tatem, II (tennis player); b. Philadelphia, Pa. (1893–1953).

**TINTORETTO,** Il (Jacopo Robusti) (painter); b. Venice (1518–1594).

**TITIAN** (Tiziano Vecelli) (painter); b. Pieve di Cadore, Venezia, It. (1477–1576).

**TODD,** Mike (Avrom Goldbogen) (movie producer); b. Minneapolis (1909–1958).

**TOLSTOI,** Count Leo (Lev) Nikolaevich (novelist); b. Tula prov., Rus. (1828–1910).

**TOSCANINI,** Arturo (orchestra conductor); b. Parma, It. (1867–1957).

**TOULOUSE-LAUTREC** (Henri Marie Raymond de Toulouse-Lautrec Monfa) (painter); b. Albi, Fr. (1864–1901).

**TROTSKY,** Leon (Lev Davidovich Bronstein) (statesman); b. Elisavetgrad, Rus. (1879–1940).

**TRUJILLO Y MOLINA,** Rafael Leonidas (Dom. Rep. dictator); b. San Cristóbal, Dom. Rep. (1891–1961).

**TURGENEV,** Ivan Sergeevich (novelist); b. Orel, Rus. (1818–1883).

**TWAIN,** Mark (Samuel Langhorne Clemens) (author); b. Florida, Mo. (1835–1910).

**TWEED,** William Marcy (politician); b. New York City (1823–1878).

**VALENTINO,** Rudolph (Rodolpho d'Antonguolla) (actor); b. Castellaneta, It. (1895–1926).

**VANDENBERG,** Arthur Hendrick (legislator); b. Grand Rapids, Mich. (1884–1951).

**VANDERBILT,** Cornelius (financier); b. Port Richmond, N. Y. (1794–1877).

**VAN DRUTEN,** John William (dramatist); b. London, Eng. (1901–1957).

**VANDYKE** (or VAN DYCK), Sir Anthony (painter); b. Antwerp, Hol. (1599–1641).

**VAUGHAN WILLIAMS,** Ralph (composer); b. Down Ampney, Eng. (1872–1958).

**VELÁZQUEZ,** Diego Rodríguez de Silva y (painter); b. Seville, Sp. (1599–1660).

**VERDI,** Giuseppe (composer); b. Roncole, Parma, It. (1813–1901).

**VERMEER,** Jan (or Jan van der Meer van Delft) (painter); b. Delft, Hol. (1632–1675).

**VERNE,** Jules (author); b. Nantes, Fr. (1828–1905).

**VILLA,** Pancho (Doroteo Arango) (bandit); b. Rio Grande, Mex. (1877–1923).

**VILLON,** François (François de Montcorbier) (poet); b. Paris, Fr. (1431–c.1463).

**VINCI,** Leonardo da (painter & scientist); b. Vinci, Tuscany, It. (1452–1519).

**VIRGIL** (or VERGIL) (Publius Vergilius Maro) (poet); b. Mantua, Gaul (70–19 B.C.).

**VOLTAIRE** (François Marie Arouet) (author); b. Paris, Fr. (1694–1778).

**VON STROHEIM,** Erich Oswald Hans Carl Maria von Nordenwall (actor); b. Vienna, Aus. (1885–1957).

**WAGNER,** Honus (John Wagner) (baseball player); b. Mansfield, Pa. (1874–1955).

**WAGNER,** Wilhelm Richard (composer); b. Leipzig, Ger. (1813–1883).

**WALTON,** Izaak (author); b. Stafford, Eng. (1593–1683).

**WARD,** Fannie (actress); b. St. Louis, Mo. (1872–1952).

**WASHINGTON,** Booker Taliaferro (educator); b. Franklin Co., Va. (1856–1915).

**WATSON,** Thomas John (industrialist); b. Campbell, N. Y. (1874–1956).

**WATT,** James (inventor); b. Greenock, Scot. (1736–1819).

**WAYNE,** Anthony (military officer); b. Waynesboro, Pa. (1745–1796).

**WEBER,** Karl Maria Friedrich Ernst von (composer); b. nr. Lübeck, Ger. (1786–1826).

**WEBSTER,** Daniel (statesman); b. Salisbury, N. H. (1782–1852).

**WEBSTER,** Noah (lexicographer); b. West Hartford, Conn. (1758–1843).

**WEILL,** Kurt (composer); b. Dessau, Ger. (1900–1950).

**WEIZMANN,** Chaim (Israeli statesman); b. Grodno prov., Rus. (1874–1952).

**WELCH,** Joseph Nye (lawyer); b. Primghar, Iowa (1890–1960).

**WELLINGTON,** Duke of (Arthur Wellesley) (statesman); b. Ireland (1769–1852).

**WELLS,** Herbert George (author); b. Bromley, Kent, Eng. (1866–1946).

**WESLEY,** John (religious leader); b. Lincolnshire, Eng. (1703–1791).

**WESTINGHOUSE,** George (inventor); b. Central Bridge, N. Y. (1846–1914).

**WHARTON,** Edith Newbold (nee Jones) (novelist); b. New York City (1862–1937).

**WHISTLER,** James Abbott McNeill (painter); b. Lowell, Mass. (1834–1903).

**WHITE,** William Allen (journalist); b. Emporia, Kans. (1868–1944).

**WHITMAN,** Walt (Walter) (poet); b. West Hills, N. Y. (1819–1892).

**WHITNEY,** Eli (inventor); b. Westboro, Mass. (1765–1825).

**WHITTIER,** John Greenleaf (poet); b. Haverhill, Mass. (1807–1892).

**WILDE,** Oscar Fingal O'Flahertie Wills (author); b. Dublin, Ire. (1854–1900).

**WILKINS,** Sir George Hubert (explorer); b. Mt. Bryan East, Australia (1888–1958).

**WILLIAMS,** Roger (clergyman); b. London, Eng. (1603?–1683).

**WILLKIE,** Wendell Lewis (lawyer); b. Elwood, Ind. (1892–1944).

**WINTHROP,** John (1st Gov., Mass. Bay Colony); b. Suffolk, Eng. (1588–1649).

**WISE,** Stephen Samuel (rabbi); b. Budapest, Hung. (1874–1949).

**WOLFE,** Thomas Clayton (novelist); b. Asheville, N. C. (1900–1938).

**WOLSEY,** Thomas (prelate & statesman); b. Ipswich, Eng. (1475?–1530).

**WOOD,** Grant (painter); b. Anamosa, Iowa (1892–1942).

**WOOLF,** Adeline Virginia (nee Stephens) (novelist); b. London, Eng. (1882–1941).

**WOOLLCOTT,** Alexander (author); b. Phalanx, N. J. (1887–1943).

**WORDSWORTH,** William (poet); b. Cockermouth, Cumb., Eng. (1770–1850).

**WRIGHT,** Frank Lloyd (architect); b. Richland Center, Wis. (1869–1959).

**WRIGHT,** Orville (inventor); b. Dayton, Ohio (1871–1948).

**WRIGHT,** Richard (novelist); b. nr. Natchez, Miss. (1908–1960).

**WRIGHT,** Wilbur (inventor); b. Millville, Ind. (1867–1912).

**YEATS,** William Butler (poet); b. nr. Dublin, Ire. (1865–1939).

**YOUNG,** Brigham (religious leader); b. Whitingham, Vt. (1801–1877).

**YOUNG,** Cy (Denton True Young) (baseball player); b. Gilmore, Ohio (1867–1955).

**YOUNG,** Robert Ralph (railroad executive); b. Canadian, Tex. (1897–1958).

**ZAHARIAS,** Mildred ("Babe") (nee Didrikson) (athlete); b. Port Arthur, Tex. (1912–1956).

**ZIEGFELD,** Florenz (theatrical producer); b. Chicago, Ill. (1869–1932).

**ZOLA,** Émile (novelist); b. Paris, Fr. (1840–1902).

**ZOROASTER** (religious leader); b. Persia (lived about the 6th century B.C.).

---

# American Academy of Arts and Letters

## (633 W. 155th St., New York 32, N.Y.)

The American Academy of Arts and Letters was created as a section of the National Institute of Arts and Letters in 1904, and was incorporated by an Act of Congress signed by the President on Apr. 17, 1916. Its membership is limited to 50 persons chosen from those who at any time have been on the list of membership of the Institute.

The object of the Academy is to give greater definiteness to the work of the Institute in furthering the interests of literature and the fine arts in the U. S.

### Members of the Academy

Conrad Aiken
Wystan Hugh Auden
Samuel Barber
Peter Blume
Van Wyck Brooks
Pearl S. Buck
Charles E. Burchfield
Gilmore D. Clarke
Aaron Copland
E. E. Cummings
John Dos Passos
Barry Faulkner
William Faulkner

Robert Frost
Edith Hamilton
John Hersey
Charles Hopkinson
Edward Hopper
Anna Hyatt Huntington
Robinson Jeffers
Leon Kroll
Joseph Wood Krutch
Lee Lawrie
Walter Lippmann
Archibald MacLeish

Paul Manship
Ivan Mestrovic
Douglas Moore
Marianne Craig Moore
Lewis Mumford
Allan Nevins
Reinhold Niebuhr
Walter Piston
Edward W. Redfield
Carl Sandburg
Roger Sessions
Henry R. Shepley

Eugene Speicher
John E. Steinbeck
Igor Stravinsky
Deems Taylor
Virgil Thomson
Chauncey Brewster Tinker
Mark Van Doren
Robert Penn Warren
Thornton Wilder
William Carlos Williams
Andrew Wyeth

### Honorary Members of the Academy-Institute

Germán Arciniegas
Elizabeth Bowen
Sir Maurice Bowra
Georges Braque
Benjamin Britten
Marc Chagall
Carlos Chávez
Jean Cocteau
Isak Dinesen
André Dunoyer de Segonzac
T. S. Eliot
E. M. Forster
Romulo Gallegos

Graham Greene
Hu Shih
Aldous Huxley
Augustus E. John
Charles Edouard J. Le Corbusier
Alexis Leger
G. Francesco Malipiero
André Malraux
Jacques Maritain
John Masefield
W. Somerset Maugham

François Mauriac
Gian-Carlo Menotti
Darius Milhaud
Joan Miró
Henry Moore
Jawaharlal Nehru
Pier Luigi Nervi
Sir Harold Nicolson
Francis Poulenc
Jules Romains
Bertrand Russell
Henri Sauguet
Albert Schweitzer

Dmitri Shostakovich
Ignazio Silone
Dame Edith Sitwell
Sir Osbert Sitwell
Sir Charles Snow
Rufino Tamayo
Arnold J. Toynbee
George Macaulay Trevelyan
Jacques Villon
José Luis Zorilla de San Martín

---

# National Institute of Arts and Letters

## (633 W. 155th St., New York 32, N. Y.)

The National Institute of Arts and Letters was founded in 1898 by the American Social Science Association and was incorporated by an Act of Congress signed by the President on Feb. 4, 1913, for the furtherance of literature and the fine arts in the U. S. Its membership is limited to 250 native or naturalized citizens qualified by notable achievements in art, literature or music. It confers certain awards and honors for work of distinction; and, together with its affiliate, the American Academy of Arts and Letters, it elects as honorary members many distinguished artists from other countries.

An exhibition of the works of newly elected members and recipients of honors is held every spring, and other art, book and manuscript exhibitions are held from time to time. For recipients of grants in music, a recording of their works is provided.

## Members of the Institute

### Dept. of Literature

Léonie Adams
Conrad Aiken
Newton Arvin
Wystan Hugh Auden
Djuna Barnes
Jacques Barzun
Hamilton Basso
William Beebe
Samuel N. Behrman
Saul Bellow
Elizabeth Bishop
Richard P. Blackmur
Louise Bogan
Kay Boyle
Crane Brinton
Van Wyck Brooks
John Mason Brown
Pearl S. Buck
Kenneth Burke
Erskine Caldwell
Henry Seidel Canby
Rachel L. Carson
Bruce Catton
Stuart Chase
John Cheever
Marchette Chute
John Ciardi
Robert M. Coates
Padraic Colum
Henry S. Commager
Marc Connelly
Malcolm Cowley
James Gould Cozzens
E. E. Cummings
Babette Deutsch
John Dos Passos
W. E. Burghardt Du Bois
Will Durant
Richard Eberhart
James T. Farrell
William Faulkner
Edna Ferber
Dudley Fitts
Janet Flanner
Waldo Frank
Robert Frost
Paul Eliot Green
Francis Hackett
Hermann Hagedorn
Edith Hamilton
Lillian Hellman
John Hersey
Robert Silliman Hillyer
William Ernest Hocking
Paul Horgan
Langston Hughes
Rolfe Humphries
Christopher Isherwood
Randall Jarrell
Robinson Jeffers

Matthew Josephson
Helen Keller
Alfred Kreymborg
Louis Kronenberger
Joseph Wood Krutch
Oliver La Farge
Harry Levin
Walter Lippmann
Robert Lowell
Archibald MacLeish
Mary McCarthy
Carson McCullers
William McFee
Phyllis McGinley
Margaret Mead
Arthur Miller
Henry Miller
Marianne Craig Moore
Lewis Mumford
Ogden Nash
Robert Nathan
John G. Neihardt
Allan Nevins
Reinhold Niebuhr
John O'Hara
Dorothy Parker
Donald Culross Peattie
S. J. Perelman
Arthur Stanwood Pier
Katherine Anne Porter
Elmer Rice
Conrad Richter
Theodore Roethke
Carl Sandburg
William Saroyan
Arthur M. Schlesinger, Jr.
Karl Shapiro
Vincent Sheean
Upton Sinclair
John E. Steinbeck
Burton E. Stevenson
Allen Tate
Chauncey Brewster Tinker
Lionel Trilling
Louis Untermeyer
Mark Van Doren
Carl Van Vechten
Robert Penn Warren
Eudora Welty
Glenway Wescott
John Hall Wheelock
Richard Wilbur
Thornton Wilder
Tennessee Williams
William Carlos Williams
Stark Young

### Dept. of Art

Ivan Albright
Edmond Amateis
Peggy Bacon
Pietro Belluschi
Thomas H. Benton
Louis Betts
George Biddle
Isabel Bishop
Peter Blume
Louis Bouché
Alexander Brook
Gordon Bunshaft
Charles E. Burchfield
Alexander Calder
Gilmore D. Clarke
Gardner Cox
Peter Dalton
Stuart Davis
José de Creeft
Willem de Kooning
Donald De Lue
Jean de Marco
Edwin Dickinson
Sidney E. Dickinson
Marcel Duchamp
Aymar Embury II
Philip Evergood
Barry Faulkner
John F. Folinsbee
Laura Gardin Fraser
Leo Friedlander
Morris Graves
Eric Gugler
Walker Hancock
Wallace K. Harrison
Herbert Haseltine
Malvina Hoffman
Charles Hopkinson
Edward Hopper
Donal Hord
Anna Hyatt Huntington
C. Paul Jennewein
John C. Johansen
Karl Knaths
Henry Kreis
Leon Kroll
Armin Landeck
Gertrude Lathrop
Lee Lawrie
Rico Lebrun
Clare Leighton
Julian Levi
Jack Levine
Jacques Lipchitz
Loren MacIver
Jean MacLane
Oronzio Maldarelli
Paul Manship
Ivan Mestrovic
Ludwig Mies van der Rohe
Bruce Moore
Thomas W. Nason

Hobart Nichols
Georgia O'Keeffe
Abram Poole
Henry Varnum Poor
Brenda Putnam
Michael Rapuano
Abraham Rattner
Edward W. Redfield
Ernest David Roth
Eugene F. Savage
Henry Schnakenberg
Zoltan Sepeshy
Ben Shahn
Henry R. Shepley
Raphael Soyer
Eugene Speicher
Francis Speight
Edward Durell Stone
Walter Stuempfig
Mark Tobey
Ralph Walker
Franklin C. Watkins
Sidney B. Waugh
Max Weber
Katharine Lane Weems
Stow Wengenroth
Andrew Wyeth
William Zorach

### Dept. of Music

Samuel Barber
Leonard Bernstein
Marc Blitzstein
Elliott Carter
Aaron Copland
Henry Cowell
Norman Dello Joio
Louis Gruenberg
Howard Hanson
Roy Harris
Paul Hindemith
Philip James
Ernst Krenek
Otto Luening
Douglas Moore
Arne Oldberg
Walter Piston
Quincy Porter
John Powell
Richard Rodgers
Bernard Rogers
Carl Ruggles
William Schuman
Roger Sessions
Leo Sowerby
Igor Stravinsky
Deems Taylor
Randall Thompson
Virgil Thomson
Ernst Toch
Edgard Varèse

# U. S. Postal Regulations

*Source:* U. S. Post Office.

## FIRST CLASS:

Letters and written and sealed matter: 4¢ for each oz., except that drop letters are subject to 3¢ for each oz. when deposited for local delivery at offices not having letter-carrier service, provided they are not collected or delivered by rural or star-route carriers.

Government postal cards: single, 3¢; double, 6¢.

Private mailing or post cards: 3¢.

Limit of size: Min. size, 2¾" x 4"; max. 3-9/16" x 5-9/16".

Limit of weight when mailed from one first-class post office to another: 40 lb. in local, first and second zones, 20 lb. in third to eighth zones.

Limit of weight when mailed to or from second-, third- and fourth-class post offices: 70 lb.

## AIR PARCEL POST (OVER 8 OZ. TO 70 LB.):

The zone rates shall apply to mailable matter of any class carried by air. Such matter shall not exceed 100 in. in length and girth combined, including written and other matter of the first class, whether sealed or unsealed.

Parcels weighing less than 10 lb. and measuring more than 84 in., but not more than 100 in. in length and girth combined, shall be subject to the 10-lb. rate.

Parcels containing first-class matter for the weights and zones indicated below must bear postage at the rate of 4¢ for each oz. or fraction thereof:

### First-Class Only

| Zone | Weighing over | But not over | Pay |
|---|---|---|---|
| 1, 2, 3....... | 15 oz. | 1 lb. | $0.64 |
| | 1 lb. 11 oz. | 2 lb. | 4¢ ea. oz. |
| | 2 lb. 7 oz. | 3 lb. | 4¢ ea. oz. |
| | 3 lb. 3 oz. | 70 lb. | 4¢ ea. oz. |
| 4........... | 1 lb. 12 oz. | 2 lb. | 4¢ ea. oz. |
| | 2 lb. 9 oz. | 3 lb. | 4¢ ea. oz. |
| | 3 lb. 5 oz. | 4 lb. | 4¢ ea. oz. |
| | 4 lb. 2 oz. | 70 lb. | 4¢ ea. oz. |
| 5........... | 1 lb. 15 oz. | 2 lb. | $1.28 |
| | 2 lb. 13 oz. | 3 lb. | 4¢ ea. oz. |
| | 3 lb. 11 oz. | 4 lb. | 4¢ ea. oz. |
| | 4 lb. 9 oz. | 5 lb. | 4¢ ea. oz. |
| | 5 lb. 7 oz. | 6 lb. | 4¢ ea. oz. |
| | 6 lb. 5 oz. | 7 lb. | 4¢ ea. oz. |
| | 7 lb. 3 oz. | 8 lb. | 4¢ ea. oz. |
| | 8 lb. 1 oz. | 70 lb. | 4¢ ea. oz. |

Other parcels are subject to the following rates:

## Air Parcel-Post Zone Rates*

| Zone and (miles) | First lb. | Addl. lbs. |
|---|---|---|
| First, Second & Third (to 300) . | 60¢ | 48¢ |
| Fourth (300–600) ............ | 65¢ | 50¢ |
| Fifth (600–1,000) ........... | 70¢ | 56¢ |
| Sixth (1,000–1,400) .......... | 75¢ | 64¢ |
| Seventh (1,400–1,800) ........ | 75¢ | 72¢ |
| Eighth (over 1,800) .......... | 80¢ | 80¢ |

\* Fractions of a lb. are charged as a full lb.

The eighth-zone rate shall be charged on air parcel post between the U. S. or its Territories and possessions and overseas A.P.O.'s and Fleet post offices, as well as naval vessels and commands afloat addressed in care of Fleet post offices at New York or San Francisco.

For restrictions to certain A.P.O.'s and F.P.O.'s, consult local post office.

Limit of size to A.P.O. or F.P.O.: 100 in. length and girth; limit of weight: 70 lb.

Air parcels mailed at New York, N. Y., and addressed to Puerto Rico and the Virgin Is. are subject to the seventh-zone rate.

## AIRMAIL (LIMIT 8 OZ.):

7¢ for each oz. or fraction thereof within the continental U. S., within any Territory or possession of the U. S., or between any of the foregoing. This includes airmail to or from Alaska, Hawaii, Puerto Rico, Virgin Islands of the U. S., Canton Island, Canal Zone, Guam and any other place where the U. S. mail service is in operation.

Post cards: 5¢.

## SECOND CLASS (NO WEIGHT LIMIT):

Newspapers, magazines, and other periodicals containing notice of second-class entry.

For rates for publications mailed by the publishers or registered news agents, consult local postmaster.

Transient rate for matter mailed by others than the publishers or registered news agents: 2¢ for the first 2 oz., 1¢ for each additional oz. However, if the fourth-class rate is cheaper, it shall apply.

## THIRD CLASS (UNDER 16 OZ.):

Merchandise, books, printed matter, and all other mailable matter not in first or second class.

Regular rate: 3¢ for the first 2 oz., 1½¢ for each additional oz.

Bulk rate: fee $20 per year or fraction thereof, separately addressed identical pieces of third-class matter in quantities of not less than 20 lb. or of not less than 200 pieces are subject to the lb. rates of postage applicable to the entire bulk mailed at one time.

## Catalog Zone Rates

The zone rates below shall apply to individually addressed catalogs and similar printed advertising matter in bound form weighing 16 oz. or more but not exceeding 10 lb.

| Weight, 1 pound and not exceeding— | Zones and (miles) | | | | | | | |
|---|---|---|---|---|---|---|---|---|
| | Local | 1 & 2 (to 150)* | 3 (150–300) | 4 (300–600) | 5 (600–1,000) | 6 (1,000–1,400) | 7 (1,400–1,800) | 8 (Over 1,800) |
| | Cents | Cents | Cents | Cents | Cents | Cents | Cents | Cents |
| 1.5 pounds...... | 14 | 16 | 18 | 20 | 22 | 24 | 26 | 28 |
| 2.0 pounds...... | 16 | 20 | 22 | 24 | 26 | 29 | 32 | 35 |
| 2.5 pounds...... | 18 | 23 | 25 | 27 | 29 | 33 | 37 | 41 |
| 3.0 pounds...... | 18 | 24 | 26 | 28 | 31 | 36 | 40 | 45 |
| 3.5 pounds...... | 19 | 25 | 28 | 30 | 34 | 39 | 44 | 50 |
| 4.0 pounds...... | 20 | 27 | 29 | 32 | 36 | 42 | 48 | 54 |
| 4.5 pounds...... | 20 | 28 | 31 | 34 | 39 | 45 | 51 | 59 |
| 5.0 pounds...... | 21 | 29 | 32 | 36 | 41 | 48 | 55 | 63 |
| 5.5 pounds...... | 22 | 30 | 34 | 38 | 43 | 51 | 59 | 68 |
| 6.0 pounds...... | 22 | 31 | 35 | 40 | 46 | 54 | 62 | 72 |
| 6.5 pounds...... | 23 | 33 | 37 | 42 | 48 | 57 | 66 | 77 |
| 7.0 pounds...... | 24 | 34 | 38 | 44 | 51 | 60 | 70 | 81 |
| 7.5 pounds...... | 25 | 35 | 40 | 46 | 53 | 63 | 74 | 86 |
| 8.0 pounds...... | 25 | 36 | 41 | 47 | 55 | 66 | 77 | 90 |
| 8.5 pounds...... | 26 | 37 | 43 | 49 | 58 | 69 | 81 | 95 |
| 9.0 pounds...... | 27 | 39 | 44 | 51 | 60 | 72 | 85 | 99 |
| 9.5 pounds...... | 27 | 40 | 46 | 53 | 63 | 75 | 88 | 104 |
| 10.0 pounds..... | 28 | 41 | 47 | 55 | 65 | 78 | 92 | 108 |

* Exception: In the first or second zone, where the distance by the shortest regular practicable mail route is 300 miles or more, the rate shall be the same as for the third zone.

*Note.*—These rates apply to individually addressed catalogs and similar printed advertising matter in bound form, weighing 16 ounces or over, but not exceeding 10 pounds, and consisting of 24 or more pages.

The bulk rate for miscellaneous printed matter, etc., is 16¢ for each lb., with a minimum charge of 2½¢ per piece. For books and catalogs of 24 pages or more, seeds, etc., the rate is 10¢ for each lb., with a minimum charge of 2½¢ per piece.

Pieces of such size or form as to prevent ready facing and tying in bundles and requiring individual distributing throughout mailed singly or in bulk are subject to a minimum charge of 3½¢ each.

## FOURTH CLASS (PARCEL POST) 16 OZ. AND OVER):

Merchandise, books, printed matter, and all other mailable matter not in first, second, or third classes.

The zone rates opposite shall apply to fourth-class matter, except books, library books, publications or records for the blind, and certain controlled circulation publications.

Limit of size‡: 72 in. in length and girth combined.

Limit of weight: 16 oz. to 40 lb. in local, first, and second zones, 16 oz. to 20 lb. in third to eighth zones.

Note: The following five items have a size limit of 100 in. in length and girth combined, a weight limit of 16 oz. to 70 lb.: (1) parcels sent to or from rural or star routes; (2) parcels sent to or from second-, third-, and fourth-class post offices; (3) parcels containing baby fowl, live plants, trees, shrubs, or agricultural commodities (not including manufactured products thereof); (4) parcels containing books; (5) parcels mailed between the U. S. and any Army or Fleet post office or between the U. S. and any Territory or possession of the U. S.

## BOOKS (LIMIT 70 LB.):

Books (containing no advertising matter other than incidental announcements of books), 16-mm. film in final state for viewing, 16-mm. film catalogs, school test materials, printed music (in bound or sheet form), phonograph recordings, and manuscripts for books, periodical articles, and music, 9¢ first lb., 5¢ each additional lb. (Rate applies for films and catalogs except when mailed to commercial theaters.) Must be endorsed "Educational Material."

## LIBRARY BOOKS (LIMIT 70 LB.):

Books sent by authorized libraries to readers and when returned by such readers, 4¢ first lb., 1¢ each additional lb. Rate also applies to printed music (in bound or sheet form), bound volumes of academic theses, phonograph recordings and other library materials.

## MONEY ORDERS:

Money orders for amounts from 1¢ to $100 are issued upon written application made by the remitter or his agent showing the amount of the order and the names and addresses of payee and remitter.

| Amount or order | Fee | |
|---|---|---|
| | Domestic | International |
| $0.01 to $10.00............ | 20¢ | 40¢ |
| $10.01 to $50.00.......... | 30¢ | 60¢ |
| $50.01 to $100.00......... | 35¢ | 70¢ |

## Fourth-Class Zone Rates

| Weight, 1 pound and not exceeding | Local | 1 & 2 (to 150)* | 3 (150–300) | 4 (300–600) | 5 (600–1,000) | 6 (1,000–1,400) | 7 (1,400–1,800) | 8 (Over 1,800) |
|---|---|---|---|---|---|---|---|---|
| | | | | Zones and (miles) | | | | |
| 2 pounds....... | $0.24 | $0.33 | $0.35 | $0.39 | $0.45 | $0.51 | $ 0.58 | $ 0.64 |
| 3 pounds....... | .26 | .38 | .41 | .47 | .55 | .64 | .74 | .83 |
| 4 pounds....... | .28 | .43 | .47 | .55 | .65 | .77 | .90 | 1.02 |
| 5 pounds....... | .30 | .48 | .53 | .63 | .75 | .90 | 1.06 | 1.21 |
| 6 pounds....... | .32 | .53 | .59 | .70 | .85 | 1.03 | 1.22 | 1.40 |
| 7 pounds....... | .34 | .58 | .65 | .77 | .95 | 1.16 | 1.38 | 1.59 |
| 8 pounds....... | .36 | .63 | .71 | .84 | 1.05 | 1.29 | 1.54 | 1.78 |
| 9 pounds....... | .38 | .68 | .77 | .91 | 1.15 | 1.42 | 1.70 | 1.97 |
| 10 pounds....... | .40 | .73 | .83 | .98 | 1.25 | 1.55 | 1.86 | 2.16 |
| 11 pounds....... | .42 | .77 | .89 | 1.05 | 1.35 | 1.67 | 2.02 | 2.34 |
| 12 pounds....... | .44 | .81 | .95 | 1.12 | 1.45 | 1.79 | 2.18 | 2.52 |
| 13 pounds....... | .46 | .85 | 1.01 | 1.19 | 1.55 | 1.91 | 2.34 | 2.70 |
| 14 pounds....... | .48 | .89 | 1.07 | 1.26 | 1.65 | 2.03 | 2.50 | 2.88 |
| 15 pounds....... | .50 | .93 | 1.13 | 1.33 | 1.75 | 2.15 | 2.66 | 3.06 |
| 16 pounds....... | .52 | .97 | 1.18 | 1.40 | 1.85 | 2.27 | 2.81 | 3.24 |
| 17 pounds....... | .54 | 1.01 | 1.23 | 1.47 | 1.95 | 2.39 | 2.96 | 3.42 |
| 18 pounds....... | .56 | 1.05 | 1.28 | 1.54 | 2.05 | 2.51 | 3.11 | 3.60 |
| 19 pounds....... | .58 | 1.09 | 1.33 | 1.61 | 2.15 | 2.63 | 3.26 | 3.78 |
| 20 pounds....... | .60 | 1.13 | 1.38 | 1.68 | 2.25 | 2.75 | 3.41 | 3.96 |
| 21 pounds....... | .62 | 1.17 | 1.43 | 1.75 | 2.34 | 2.87 | 3.56 | 4.14 |
| 22 pounds....... | .64 | 1.21 | 1.48 | 1.82 | 2.43 | 2.99 | 3.71 | 4.32 |
| 23 pounds....... | .66 | 1.25 | 1.53 | 1.89 | 2.52 | 3.11 | 3.86 | 4.50 |
| 24 pounds....... | .68 | 1.29 | 1.58 | 1.96 | 2.61 | 3.23 | 4.01 | 4.68 |
| 25 pounds....... | .70 | 1.33 | 1.63 | 2.03 | 2.70 | 3.35 | 4.16 | 4.86 |
| 26 pounds....... | .72 | 1.37 | 1.68 | 2.10 | 2.79 | 3.47 | 4.31 | 5.04 |
| 27 pounds....... | .74 | 1.41 | 1.73 | 2.17 | 2.88 | 3.59 | 4.46 | 5.22 |
| 28 pounds....... | .76 | 1.45 | 1.78 | 2.24 | 2.97 | 3.71 | 4.61 | 5.40 |
| 29 pounds....... | .78 | 1.49 | 1.83 | 2.31 | 3.06 | 3.83 | 4.76 | 5.58 |
| 30 pounds....... | .80 | 1.53 | 1.88 | 2.38 | 3.15 | 3.95 | 4.91 | 5.76 |
| 31 pounds....... | .82 | 1.57 | 1.93 | 2.45 | 3.24 | 4.06 | 5.05 | 5.93 |
| 32 pounds....... | .84 | 1.61 | 1.98 | 2.52 | 3.33 | 4.17 | 5.19 | 6.10 |
| 33 pounds....... | .86 | 1.65 | 2.03 | 2.59 | 3.42 | 4.28 | 5.33 | 6.27 |
| 34 pounds....... | .88 | 1.69 | 2.08 | 2.66 | 3.51 | 4.39 | 5.47 | 6.44 |
| 35 pounds....... | .90 | 1.73 | 2.13 | 2.73 | 3.60 | 4.50 | 5.61 | 6.61 |
| 36 pounds....... | .92 | 1.77 | 2.18 | 2.80 | 3.69 | 4.61 | 5.75 | 6.78 |
| 37 pounds....... | .94 | 1.81 | 2.23 | 2.87 | 3.78 | 4.72 | 5.89 | 6.95 |
| 38 pounds....... | .96 | 1.85 | 2.28 | 2.94 | 3.87 | 4.83 | 6.03 | 7.12 |
| 39 pounds....... | .98 | 1.89 | 2.33 | 3.01 | 3.96 | 4.94 | 6.17 | 7.29 |
| 40 pounds....... | 1.00 | 1.93 | 2.38 | 3.08 | 4.05 | 5.05 | 6.31 | 7.46 |
| 41 pounds....... | 1.02 | 1.97 | 2.43 | 3.15 | 4.14 | 5.16 | 6.45 | 7.62 |
| 42 pounds....... | 1.04 | 2.01 | 2.48 | 3.22 | 4.23 | 5.27 | 6.59 | 7.78 |
| 43 pounds....... | 1.06 | 2.05 | 2.53 | 3.29 | 4.32 | 5.38 | 6.73 | 7.94 |
| 44 pounds....... | 1.08 | 2.09 | 2.58 | 3.36 | 4.41 | 5.49 | 6.87 | 8.10 |
| 45 pounds....... | 1.10 | 2.13 | 2.63 | 3.43 | 4.50 | 5.60 | 7.01 | 8.26 |
| 46 pounds....... | 1.12 | 2.17 | 2.68 | 3.50 | 4.59 | 5.71 | 7.15 | 8.42 |
| 47 pounds....... | 1.14 | 2.21 | 2.73 | 3.57 | 4.68 | 5.82 | 7.29 | 8.58 |
| 48 pounds....... | 1.16 | 2.25 | 2.78 | 3.64 | 4.77 | 5.93 | 7.43 | 8.74 |
| 49 pounds....... | 1.18 | 2.29 | 2.83 | 3.71 | 4.86 | 6.04 | 7.57 | 8.90 |
| 50 pounds....... | 1.20 | 2.33 | 2.88 | 3.78 | 4.95 | 6.15 | 7.71 | 9.06 |
| 51 pounds....... | 1.22 | 2.37 | 2.93 | 3.84 | 5.03 | 6.26 | 7.84 | 9.22 |
| 52 pounds....... | 1.24 | 2.41 | 2.98 | 3.90 | 5.11 | 6.37 | 7.97 | 9.38 |
| 53 pounds....... | 1.26 | 2.45 | 3.03 | 3.96 | 5.19 | 6.48 | 8.10 | 9.54 |
| 54 pounds....... | 1.28 | 2.49 | 3.08 | 4.02 | 5.27 | 6.59 | 8.23 | 9.70 |
| 55 pounds....... | 1.30 | 2.53 | 3.13 | 4.08 | 5.35 | 6.70 | 8.36 | 9.86 |
| 56 pounds....... | 1.32 | 2.57 | 3.18 | 4.14 | 5.43 | 6.81 | 8.49 | 10.02 |
| 57 pounds....... | 1.34 | 2.61 | 3.23 | 4.20 | 5.51 | 6.92 | 8.62 | 10.18 |
| 58 pounds....... | 1.36 | 2.65 | 3.28 | 4.26 | 5.59 | 7.03 | 8.75 | 10.34 |
| 59 pounds....... | 1.38 | 2.69 | 3.33 | 4.32 | 5.67 | 7.14 | 8.88 | 10.50 |
| 60 pounds....... | 1.40 +[1] | 2.73 +[2] | 3.38 +[3] | 4.38 +[4] | 5.75 +[5] | 7.25 +[6] | 9.01 +[7] | 10.66 +[8] |

[1] 2¢ for ea. lb. over 60 lbs.　[2] 4¢ for ea. lb. over 60 lbs.　[3] 5¢ for ea. lb. over 60 lbs.　[4] 6¢ for ea. lb. over 60 lbs.
[5] 8¢ for ea. lb. over 60 lbs.　[6] 11¢ for ea. lb. over 60 lbs.　[7] 13¢ for ea. lb. over 60 lbs.　[8] 16¢ for ea. lb. over 60 lbs.

## EXCEPTIONS

* In the first or second zone, where the distance by the shortest regular practicable mail route is 300 miles or more, the rate is the same as for the third zone.

Note.—Parcels less than 10 pounds, measuring over 84 inches but not exceeding 100 inches in length and girth combined, are chargeable with a minimum rate equal to that for a 10-pound parcel for the zone to which addressed.

## Special Delivery and Special Handling

| Weight | Special delivery First class* | Special delivery 2nd, 3rd, 4th class | Special handling (4th class only) |
|---|---|---|---|
| Up to 2 lb. ........ | 30¢ | 55¢ | 25¢ |
| Over 2 lb. to 10 lb. ... | 45¢ | 65¢ | 35¢ |
| Over 10 lb. ........ | 60¢ | 80¢ | 50¢ |

* Including air mail and air parcel post.

The prepayment of the special-delivery fee entitles mail to the most expeditious handling and special delivery.

Prepayment of the special-handling fee entitles fourth-class matter to the most expeditious handling, transportation, and delivery possible, but not special delivery.

## REGISTERED MAIL:

Fees for domestic registered mail (first-, second- and third-class matter, and sealed fourth-class matter on which postage at the first-class rate has been paid):

| Declared value (must be full value) | Fee if mailer has no commercial or other insurance | Fee if mailer has commercial or other insurance |
|---|---|---|
| $ 0.00 to $ 10.00 | $ .50[1] | $ .50[2] |
| 10.01 to 100.00 | .75[1] | .75[2] |
| 100.01 to 200.00 | 1.00[1] | 1.00[2] |
| 200.01 to 400.00 | 1.25[1] | 1.25[2] |
| 400.01 to 600.00 | 1.50[1] | 1.50[2] |
| 600.01 to 800.00 | 1.75[1] | 1.75[2] |
| 800.01 to 1,000.00 | 2.00[1] | 2.00[2] |
| 1,000.01 to 2,000.00 | 2.25[1] | 2.15[3] |
| 2,000.01 to 3,000.00 | 2.50[1] | 2.30[3] |
| 3,000.01 to 4,000.00 | 2.75[1] | 2.45[3] |
| 4,000.01 to 5,000.00 | 3.00[1] | 2.60[3] |
| 5,000.01 to 6,000.00 | 3.25[1] | 2.75[3] |
| 6,000.01 to 7,000.00 | 3.50[1] | 2.90[3] |
| 7,000.01 to 8,000.00 | 3.75[1] | 3.05[3] |
| 8,000.01 to 9,000.00 | 4.00[1] | 3.20[3] |
| 9,000.01 to 10,000.00 | 4.25[1] | 3.35[3] |
| 10,000.01 to 1,000,000.00 | 4.25+[4,5] | 3.35+[3,5] |
| 1,000,000.01 to 15,000,000.00 | 152.75+[4,6] | 151.85+[3,6] |
| Over 15,000,000.00 | [4,7] | [3,7] |

[1] Postal liability: declared value. [2] Postal liability: declared value or prorated. [3] Postal liability: $1,000 maximum or prorated. [4] Postal liability: $10,000. [5] Fee increased 15 cents per $1,000 or fraction above $10,000. [6] Fee increased 10 cents per $1,000 or fraction above $1,000,000. [7] Additional fee charges may be applied based on consideration of weight, space and value.

Restricted delivery, 50¢. Return receipts: showing to whom and when delivered, 10¢; to whom, when and address where delivered, 35¢; requested after mailing, showing to whom and when delivered, 25¢.

## CERTIFIED MAIL:

Certified mail service provides for a receipt to the sender and a record of delivery at the office of address. No record is kept at the office where mailed. It is handled in the ordinary mails and no insurance coverage is provided.

Any first-class mail having no intrinsic value will be accepted as certified mail.

This does not exclude articles of a non-negotiable character and other matter which would involve a cost of duplication if lost or destroyed. The mail may be sent by air on payment of the required postage. Return receipt service, requested at the time of mailing only, and special delivery service are available.

Fees are as follows: Fee in addition to postage, 20¢; return receipt showing to whom and when delivered, 10¢; return receipt showing to whom, when, and address where delivered, 35¢; restricted delivery, 50¢.

## INSURED MAIL:

Fees for domestic insured mail (third- and fourth-class matter):

| Insurance coverage | Fee |
|---|---|
| $ 0.00 to $ 10.00 | 10¢ |
| 10.01 to 50.00 | 20¢ |
| 50.01 to 100.00 | 30¢ |
| 100.01 to 200.00 | 40¢ |

## C.O.D. MAIL:

Fees for domestic unregistered C.O.D. mail (third- and fourth-class matter and sealed domestic mail matter of any class bearing postage at the first-class rate):

| Charges to be remitted* | Fee |
|---|---|
| $ .01 to $ 5.00 | $ .40 |
| 5.01 to 10.00 | .50 |
| 10.01 to 25.00 | .70 |
| 25.01 to 50.00 | .80 |
| 50.01 to 100.00 | .90 |
| 100.01 to 200.00 | 1.00 |

* Includes insurance. Additional insurance available.

Fees for domestic registered C.O.D. mail (sealed domestic mail of any class bearing postage at the first-class rate):

| Amount collectible and indemnity payable | Fee |
|---|---|
| $ .01 to $ 10.00 | $ .80 |
| 10.01 to 50.00 | 1.10 |
| 50.01 to 100.00 | 1.20 |
| 100.01 to 200.00* | 1.40 |

* Limit of collections.

When indemnity in excess of $200 is desired, the fees for domestic registered C.O.D. mail are:

| Indemnity limit | Fee |
|---|---|
| $200.01 to $ 300.00 | $1.50 |
| 300.01 to 400.00 | 1.60 |
| 400.01 to 500.00 | 1.70 |
| 500.01 to 600.00 | 1.80 |
| 600.01 to 700.00 | 1.90 |
| 700.01 to 800.00 | 2.00 |
| 800.01 to 1000.00 | 2.10 |

## MISCELLANEOUS:

In registered and insured mail, a receipt card will be returned to the sender upon request. When a card is requested showing to whom and when the delivery was made, the rate is 10¢ if the request is made at the time of mailing, 25¢ if made thereafter. When a card is requested showing to whom and when the delivery was made and the address, the rate is 35¢ and must be paid at the time of mailing.

Fees for effecting delivery of domestic registered, insured, and C.O.D. mail to addressee only or to addressee or order: 50¢.

Fee for notifying sender or his representative of inability to deliver a C.O.D. article: 5¢.

Certificates of mailing for ordinary mail of any class: 5¢ for each article described thereon. Additional certificates for ordinary, registered, insured and C.O.D. mail: 2¢ for each article described thereon.

C.O.D. mail cannot be sent to Navy personnel on board ships or at overseas shore stations.

**FOREIGN REGULAR MAIL:**

Letters and letter packages: To Canada and Mexico, 4¢ per oz. or fraction. To all other countries, 11¢ for 1st oz., 7¢ per additional oz. or fraction. Weight limit: 4 lb. 6 oz. (60 lb. to Canada).

Post cards: To Canada and Mexico, 3¢ each, 6¢ with reply paid. To all other countries, 7¢ each, 14¢ with reply paid.

**FOREIGN AIRMAIL:**

Air-letter sheets: Air letters, consisting of sheets which can be folded into the form of an envelope and sealed, are acceptable for dispatch by airmail to all foreign countries. The sheets are sold at all post offices at 11¢ each. No enclosures, adhesive tape or stickers are permitted.

Post cards: 5¢ each to Canada and Mexico; 11¢ each to all other countries.

## Airmail Rates from U. S. to Selected Countries

| Country | Airmail[1] | Air parcel post | | | Country | Airmail[1] | Air parcel post | | |
| | | Initial unit[2] | Addl. weight[3] | Limit, lbs. | | | Initial unit[2] | Addl. weight[3] | Limit, lbs.[1] |
|---|---|---|---|---|---|---|---|---|---|
| Albania | $.15 | $2.12 | $.49 | 22 | Indonesia | $.25 | $2.21 | $.96 | 11 |
| Algeria | .15 | ... | ... | .. | Iran | .25 | 1.70 | .61 | 44 |
| Argentina | .10 | 1.56 | .67 | 44 | Iraq | .25 | 1.89 | .60 | 44 |
| Australia | .25 | 1.66 | .76 | 22 | Ireland | .15 | 1.31 | .42 | 22 |
| Austria | .15 | 1.71 | .46 | 44 | Israel | .25 | 1.86 | .57 | 22 |
| Bahamas | .13 | 1.39 | .16 | 22 | Italy | .15 | 1.67 | .49 | 44 |
| Belgium | .15 | 1.53 | .42 | 44 | Jamaica | .13 | 1.50 | .20 | 22 |
| Bermuda | .13 | 1.12 | .22 | 33 | Japan | .25 | 1.39 | .50 | 22 |
| Bolivia | .15 | 1.57 | .43 | 44 | Jordan | .25 | 1.73 | .56 | 22 |
| Brazil | .15 | 1.87 | .49 | 44[4] | Korea, Rep. of | .25 | 1.43 | .54 | 22 |
| British Guiana | .15 | 1.54 | .31 | 22 | Lebanon | .25 | 1.73 | .56 | 44[10] |
| British Honduras | .13 | 1.30 | .30 | 22 | Liberia | .25 | 1.42 | .53 | 22 |
| Bulgaria | .15 | 1.36 | .47 | 22 | Mexico | .07[5] | 1.12 | .22 | 44 |
| Burma | .25 | 2.10 | .91 | 22 | Morocco | .15 | 1.67 | .49 | 44 |
| Canada[5,6] | .07 | ... | ... | .. | Netherlands | .15 | 1.50 | .42 | 44 |
| Ceylon | .25 | 2.12 | .81 | 22 | New Zealand | .25 | 1.89 | .67 | 22 |
| Chile | .15 | 1.85 | .55 | 22 | Nicaragua | .13 | 1.32 | .26 | 44 |
| China | .25 | 1.56[7] | .66 | 44 | Norway | .15 | 1.35 | .45 | 44 |
| Colombia | .15 | 1.82 | .31 | 44 | Pakistan | .25 | 2.20 | .77 | 22 |
| Costa Rica | .13 | 1.31 | .26 | 44 | Panamá | .13 | 1.58 | .28 | 70[7] |
| Cuba | .13 | 1.36 | .17 | 22 | Paraguay | .15 | 1.57 | .43 | 44 |
| Czechoslovakia | .15 | 1.38 | .48 | 44 | Peru | .15 | 1.83 | .37 | 44 |
| Denmark | .15 | 1.35 | .45 | 44 | Philippines | .25 | 1.93 | .74 | 44[7] |
| Dominican Republic | .13 | 1.42 | .23 | 44 | Poland | .15 | 1.65 | .47 | 44 |
| Ecuador | .15 | 1.76 | .30 | 44 | Portugal | .15 | 1.30 | .40 | 22 |
| Egypt (U.A.R.) | .15 | 1.47 | .58 | 44 | Rumania | .15 | ... | ... | .. |
| El Salvador | .13 | 1.40 | .27 | 44 | Saudi Arabia[11] | .25 | 1.97 | .63 | 22 |
| Ethiopia | .25 | 1.80 | .69 | 44 | South Africa, Rep. of | .25 | 1.69 | .80 | 11 |
| Finland | .15 | 1.38 | .49 | 44 | Spain | .15 | 1.77 | .44 | 22 |
| France | .15 | 1.89 | .47 | 44 | Surinam | .15 | 1.42 | .33 | 44 |
| French Guiana | .15 | 1.39 | .35 | 11 | Sweden | .15 | 1.35 | .45 | 44 |
| Germany | .15 | 1.34 | .44 | 44[8] | Switzerland | .15 | 1.52 | .43 | 44 |
| Greece | .15 | 1.66 | .53 | 22 | Syria (U.A.R.) | .25 | 1.57 | .58 | 44[12] |
| Guatemala | .13 | 1.59 | .29 | 44 | Thailand | .25 | 2.08 | .74 | 22 |
| Haiti | .13 | 1.43 | .22 | 44 | Turkey | .25 | 1.44 | .54 | 44 |
| Honduras | .13 | 1.35 | .29 | 44[9] | U.S.S.R. | .25 | 1.81 | .60 | 44 |
| Hong Kong | .25 | 1.68 | .79 | 22 | United Kingdom[13] | .15 | 1.32 | .42 | 22 |
| Hungary | .15 | 1.37 | .48 | 44 | Uruguay | .15 | 1.86 | .56 | 44 |
| Iceland | .15 | 1.69 | .35 | 44 | Venezuela | .10 | 1.72 | .26 | 44 |
| India | .25 | 1.70 | .80 | 22 | Yugoslavia | .15 | 1.38 | .49 | 44 |

(Footnotes are on opposite page.)

# The White House

*Source:* National Park Service.

The White House, the official residence of the President, is located on Pennsylvania Avenue in Washington, D. C. The site covering about 18 acres was selected by President Washington and Pierre Charles L'Enfant, and the architect was James Hoban. The design of the mansion is said to have been suggested by the Duke of Leinster's Palace in Ireland. The cornerstone was laid Oct. 13, 1792, and the first residents were President and Mrs. John Adams in Nov., 1800. The building was fired by the British in 1814.

The sandstone exterior was painted white during the course of construction.

The rooms for public functions are on the first floor; on the second and third are the President's apartments. The most celebrated public room is the East Room, where formal receptions take place. Other public rooms are the Red Room, the Green Room, and the Blue Room. The State Dining Room is used for formal dinners.

The Executive Office, a three-story structure at the west end of the West Terrace, was added to the original building in 1902 to accommodate the President's office staff, and several additions have since been made. In 1942, a three-story building was erected at the end of the East Terrace, and now serves as the White House main entrance. In 1946, a second-story balcony was added to the White House inside the Ionic pillars of the south portico.

From Nov., 1948, to Mar., 1952, the White House was closed for social engagements and sightseers because of a full-scale renovation of the building. The walls were retained and strengthened, and the interior was rebuilt. There are now 132 rooms instead of the former 62.

---

# The Great Seal of the United States

On July 4, 1776, the Continental Congress appointed a committee consisting of Benjamin Franklin, John Adams and Thomas Jefferson "to bring in a device for a seal of the United States of America." After many delays, a verbal description of a design by William Barton was finally approved by Congress on June 20, 1782. The seal shows an American bald eagle with a ribbon in its mouth bearing the device *E pluribus unum* (One out of many). In its talons are the arrows of war and an olive branch of peace.

## "In God We Trust"

"In God We Trust" first appeared on U.S. coins after April 22, 1864, when Congress passed an act authorizing the coinage of a 2-cent piece bearing this motto. Thereafter, Congress extended its use to other coins. On July 30, 1956, it became the national motto.

---

### Footnotes for Table on Opposite Page.

NOTE: For rates to countries not shown in this table, consult local postmaster. Leaders (......) indicate that there is no air-parcel-post service to the country.
[1] For letters and letter packages. Unless otherwise indicated, rate shown is per each ½ oz., and weight is limited to 4 lb., 6 oz. For rates for commercial papers, printed matter, samples of merchandise, small packages, 8-oz. merchandise packages, combination packages and articles grouped together, consult local postmaster. [2] Rate for 4 oz. or fraction thereof. [3] Rate for each additional 4 oz. or fraction thereof. [4] Parcels for Brazil exceeding 22 lb. accepted for following offices only: Belem (Para), Belo Horizonte, Florianopolis, Fortaleza, Manaus, Pelotas, Porto Alegre, Recife (Pernambuco), Rio de Janeiro, Rio Grande (Rio Grande do Sul), Salvador (Bahia), Santos and Sao Paulo. [5] Per oz.; post cards each 5¢. [6] Articles limited to 60 lb. in weight. [7] Parcels for many offices are limited to 11 lb., 22 lb. or 44 lb. Consult local postmaster for limitations. [8] Gift parcels to East Germany are limited to 22 lb.; other parcels may weigh up to 44 lb. [9] Parcels for Honduras exceeding 22 lb. accepted for following offices only: Amapala, Comayagua, La Ceiba, Olanchito, Progreso, Puerto Castilla, Puerto Cortez, San Pedro Sula, Tegucigalpa and Tela. [10] Parcels for Lebanon exceeding 11 lb. not accepted for following offices: Ain-Zhalta, Baino, Falougha, Hermel, Koubayat, Maser-el-Chouf, Ras-Baalbeck and Souk-el-Gharb. [11] Parcels for Saudi Arabia limited to the following places only: Al Gaba, Al Lith, Al Wejh, Daha, Dammam, Dhahran, Hassa, Jiddah, Jizam, Katif, Khobar, Mecca, Medina, Qunfidha, Rabigh, Rastanurra, Rivadh, Umm Lej and Yenbo. [12] Limit to Chahba and Salkhad is 11 lb.; limit to Tel-Abiad and Yabroud is 22 lb. [13] Great Britain and Northern Ireland.

# Executive Departments and Agencies

*Source: U. S. Government Organization Manual.*

**(Unless otherwise indicated, addresses shown are in Washington, D.C.)**

## Executive Office of the President

### THE WHITE HOUSE OFFICE

1600 Pennsylvania Ave., NW.

*Special Counsel to the President:* Theodore C. Sorensen.

*Deputy Special Counsel to the President:* Myer Feldman.

*Assistant Special Counsels to the President:* Richard N. Goodwin, Lee C. White.

*Press Secretary to the President:* Pierre E. G. Salinger.

*Associate Press Secretary to the President:* Andrew T. Hatcher.

*Special Assistants to the President:* McGeorge Bundy, Lawrence F. O'Brien, P. Kenneth O'Donnell, Jerome B. Wiesner, Ralph A. Dungan, Frederick G. Dutton, James M. Landis, Frank D. Reeves, Arthur Schlesinger, Jr., Harris L. Wofford, Jr.

*Deputy Special Assistant to the President:* Walt Whitman Rostow.

*Administrative Assistants to the President:* Timothy J. Reardon, Jr., Henry Hall Wilson, Jr., Mike N. Manatos.

*Special Assistant to the President—Director, Food for Peace:* George McGovern.

*Physician to the President:* Dr. Janet Travell.

*Military Aide to the President:* Brig. Gen. Chester V. Clifton, USA.

*Naval Aide to the President:* Comdr. Tazewell T. Shepard, Jr., USN.

*Air Force Aide to the President:* Col. Godfrey T. McHugh, USAF.

*Executive Clerk:* William J. Hopkins.

*Personal Secretary to the President:* Mrs. Evelyn N. Lincoln.

*Social Secretary:* Letitia Baldrige.

*Chief Usher:* J. Bernard West.

*Activities:* Serves President in performance of activities incident to his office.

### BUREAU OF THE BUDGET

Executive Office Bldg.

*Established:* June 10, 1921.

*Director:* David E. Bell.

*Activities:* Assists President in preparing budget and formulating fiscal program; supervises administration of budget; coordinates advice on proposed legislation; plans improvements in statistical services; keeps President informed of progress of activities by government agencies so that Congressional appropriations are spent most economically.

### COUNCIL OF ECONOMIC ADVISERS (CEA)

Executive Office Bldg.

*Members: 3. Established:* Feb. 20, 1946.

*Chairman:* Walter W. Heller.

*Other members:* Kermit Gordon, James Tobin.

*Activities:* Assists President in preparation of economic reports to Congress; studies economic trends; appraises government activities on nation's economy; recommends economic policies.

### NATIONAL SECURITY COUNCIL (NSC)

Executive Office Bldg.

*Members: 5. Established:* July 26, 1947.

*Chairman:* John F. Kennedy, President of the U. S.

*Other members:* Lyndon B. Johnson, Vice President; Dean Rusk, Secretary of State; Robert S. McNamara, Secretary of Defense; Frank B. Ellis, Director of Office of Emergency Planning.

*Activities:* Assesses and appraises objectives, commitments and risks of U. S. in relation to our actual and potential military power in interests of national security.

### CENTRAL INTELLIGENCE AGENCY (CIA)

2430 E Street N.W.

*Established:* 1947.

*Director:* John A. McCone.

*Deputy Director:* Gen. C. P. Cabell, USAF.

*Activities:* Coordinates intelligence activities of certain government departments and agencies by making recommendations to the National Security Council; correlates and evaluates intelligence and disseminates the results; performs certain additional services for existing intelligence agencies when the National Security Council determines that these can be more efficiently accomplished centrally; and performs such other functions as the National Security Council may direct.

### NATIONAL AERONAUTICS AND SPACE COUNCIL

Executive Office Bldg.

*Members: 9. Established:* 1958.

*Chairman:* Lyndon B. Johnson, Vice President of the U. S.

*Other members:* Dean Rusk, Secretary of State; Robert S. McNamara, Secretary of Defense; James E. Webb, Administrator of National Aeronautics and Space Administration; Glenn T. Seaborg, Chairman of Atomic Energy Commission.

*Activities:* Advises President regarding policies, plans, programs, and accomplishments of U. S. agencies engaged in aeronautical and space activities.

### OFFICE OF EMERGENCY PLANNING*

Executive Office Bldg.

*Established:* July 20, 1961. Formerly the Office of Civil and Defense Mobilization.

*Director:* Frank B. Ellis.

* Planning is done with the cooperation of the Departments of Defense; Health, Education, and Welfare; and Agriculture.

*Activities:* Advises President on coordination of military, industrial, and civilian mobilization in the event of nuclear warfare.

## Executive Departments

### DEPARTMENT OF STATE

2201 C St., NW.

*Established:* 1781 as Department of Foreign Affairs; reconstituted, 1789, following adoption of Constitution; name changed to Department of State Sept. 15, 1789.

*Secretary:* Dean Rusk.

*Under Secretary:* Chester Bowles.

*Activities:* Determines government policy in relation to international problems; formulates measures for promoting friendship with other countries; develops policies and programs for U. S. participation in U. N. and other international organizations; conducts correspondence with our representatives abroad and with accredited foreign representatives here.

### DEPARTMENT OF THE TREASURY

15th St. & Pennsylvania Ave., NW.

*Established:* Sept. 2, 1789.

*Secretary:* Douglas Dillon.

*Under Secretary:* Henry H. Fowler.

*Activities:* Manages national finances; grants warrants for money drawn from Treasury pursuant to legal appropriations; handles collection of revenue; keeps and renders public accounts; prepares plans for improvement of revenue and for support of public credit; reports annually to Congress on condition of public finances; controls coinage and printing of money; administers Coast Guard, Bureau of Narcotics, and Secret Service.

### DEPARTMENT OF DEFENSE

The Pentagon

*Established:* July 26, 1947, as National Military Establishment; name changed to Department of Defense on Aug. 10, 1949. Subordinate to Secretary of Defense are Secretaries of Army, Navy, Air Force.

*Secretary:* Robert S. McNamara.

*Deputy Secretary:* Roswell L. Gilpatric.

*Secretary of Army:* Elvis J. Stahr, Jr.

*Secretary of Navy:* John B. Connally.

*Commandant, Marine Corps:* Gen. David M. Shoup.

*Secretary of Air Force:* Eugene M. Zuckert.

*Joint Chiefs of Staff:*\* Gen. Lyman L. Lemnitzer, chairman; Gen. George H. Decker, Army; Adm. Arleigh, A. Burke, Navy; Gen. Curtis E. Lemay, Air Force; Gen. David M. Shoup, Marine Corps (on Marine Corps matters only).

*Activities:* Provides for security of U. S. by establishing integrated policies and procedures; co-ordinates and directs the activities of 3 separately administered military departments (Army, Navy, Air Force).

\* Consisting of chairman and chiefs of each service.

### DEPARTMENT OF JUSTICE

Constitution Ave. & 10th St., NW.

*Established:* Office of Attorney General was created Sept. 24, 1789. Although he was one of original Cabinet members, he was not executive department head until June 22, 1870, when Department of Justice was established.

*Attorney General:* Robert F. Kennedy.

*Deputy Atty. Gen.:* Byron R. White.

*Director of FBI:* J. Edgar Hoover.

*Activities:* Provides means for enforcing Federal laws; investigates and detects violations; represents U. S. in legal matters generally and gives advice and opinions when requested by President or heads of executive departments; directs FBI, Bureau of Prisons, Immigration and Naturalization Service.

### POST OFFICE DEPARTMENT

12th St. & Pennsylvania Ave., NW.

*Established:* Office of Postmaster General and temporary post office system created Sept. 22, 1789. Act of Feb. 20, 1792, made detailed provisions for Post Office Department. Postmaster General became Cabinet member in 1829. Department received executive status June 8, 1872.

*Postmaster General:* J. Edward Day.

*Deputy Postmaster General:* H. W. Brawley.

*Activities:* Maintains Postal Service of U. S. and executes all laws relative to it; negotiates, subject to approval of President, postal treaties with foreign governments.

### DEPARTMENT OF THE INTERIOR

C St. between 18th & 19th Sts., NW.

*Established:* Mar. 3, 1849.

*Secretary:* Stewart L. Udall.

*Under Secretary:* James K. Carr.

*Activities:* Develops and conserves natural resources of U. S. and territories; supervises public business relating to such offices as Bureau of Land Management, Bureau of Reclamation, Geological Survey, Bureau of Indian Affairs, National Park Service, Bureau of Mines, Fish and Wildlife Service, Office of Territories, etc.

### DEPARTMENT OF AGRICULTURE

14th St. & Independence Ave., SW.

*Established:* May 15, 1862. Administered by Commissioner of Agriculture until 1889, when it was made executive department and office of Secretary was created.

*Secretary:* Orville L. Freeman.

*Under Secretary:* Charles S. Murphy.

*Activities:* Conducts comprehensive research and educational program relating to agriculture; provides crop reports, commodity standards, meat inspection and other marketing services; administers national forests; aids in flood control; administers price-support and production-adjustment programs; makes loans to farmers.

## DEPARTMENT OF COMMERCE

14th St. between Constitution Ave. & E St., NW.

*Established:* Department of Commerce and Labor was created Feb. 14, 1903. On Mar. 4, 1913, all labor activities were transferred out of Department of Commerce and Labor and it was renamed Department of Commerce.

*Secretary:* Luther H. Hodges.

*Under Secretary:* Edward Gudeman.

*Activities:* Fosters and develops foreign and domestic commerce of U. S.; maintains Bureau of the Census, Office of Business Economics, Coast and Geodetic Survey, Maritime Administration, Patent Office, Bureau of Public Roads, National Bureau of Standards, Weather Bureau, etc.

## DEPARTMENT OF LABOR

14th St. & Constitution Ave., NW.

*Established:* Bureau of Labor was created in 1884 under Department of the Interior; later became independent department without executive rank. Returned to bureau satus in Department of Commerce and Labor, but on Mar. 4, 1913, became independent executive department under its present name.

*Secretary:* Arthur J. Goldberg.

*Under Secretary:* W. Willard Wirtz.

*Activities:* Promotes welfare of wage earners of U. S., improving working conditions and advancing opportunities for profitable employment; directs collection and collation of statistics concerning labor conditions; promulgates and enforces certain maximum-hour, minimum-wage, child-labor, safety and health standards.

## DEPARTMENT OF HEALTH, EDUCATION AND WELFARE

330 Independence Ave., SW.

*Established:* Apr. 11, 1953, replacing Federal Security Agency created in 1939.

*Secretary:* Abraham A. Ribicoff.

*Under Secretary:* Ivan A. Nestingen.

*Activities:* Supervises and co-ordinates various organizations within the department. Organizations are: Food and Drug Administration, Office of Education, Office of Vocational Rehabilitation, Public Health Service, St. Elizabeths Hospital, Social Security Administration; also following federally supported corporations: American Printing House for the Blind, Gallaudet College and Howard University.

## Independent Agencies

(Titles and addresses of independent agencies not described below follow on page 202.)

### Executive Department

## ATOMIC ENERGY COMMISSION (AEC)

Main office: Germantown, Md.; D.C. office: 1717 H St., NW.

*Members:* 5. *Established:* Aug. 1, 1946.

*Chairman:* Glenn T. Seaborg.

*Other members:* Robert E. Wilson, John S. Graham, Loren K. Olson, Leland J. Haworth.

*Activities:* Promotes federal and private research and development; controls dissemination of information and production, ownership and use of fissionable materials.

## CIVIL AERONAUTICS BOARD (CAB)

1825 Connecticut Ave.

*Members:* 5. *Established:* June 30, 1940.

*Chairman:* Alan S. Boyd.

*Activities:* Regulates economic aspects of U. S. air carrier operation; assists in development of international air transportation; promotes safety in civil aviation.

## FARM CREDIT ADMINISTRATION (FCA)

South Bldg., Dept. of Agriculture.

*Established:* July 17, 1916.

*Chairman:* George W. Lightburn.

*Activities:* Supervises and coordinates cooperative credit system for agriculture; provides long- and short-term credit to farmers and their cooperative marketing and business service organizations.

## FEDERAL COMMUNICATIONS COMMISSION (FCC)

Post Office Dept. Bldg.

*Members:* 7. *Established:* 1934.

*Chairman:* Newton N. Minow.

*Activities:* Regulates interstate and foreign communications by wire and radio, including amateur radio and TV; regulates operator's licenses; classifies radio stations and prescribes their services; enforces use of radio for safety purposes on U. S. ships.

## FEDERAL MEDIATION AND CONCILIATION SERVICE (FMCS)

Department of Labor Bldg.

*Established:* 1947.

*Director:* William E. Simkin.

*Activities:* Assists in labor-management disputes in industries affecting interstate commerce to reach settlements by mediation or conciliation; promotes better relations between labor and management.

## FEDERAL POWER COMMISSION (FPC)

General Accounting Office Bldg., 441 G St., NW.

*Members:* 5. *Established:* June 23, 1930.

*Chairman:* Joseph C. Swidler.

*Activities:* Licenses hydroelectric projects on U. S. Government lands or navigable waters; has jurisdiction over interstate commerce involving sale of electric energy and natural gas and companies engaged therein; handles transmission of electric energy and natural gas between U. S. and foreign countries.

## FEDERAL RESERVE SYSTEM (FRS), BOARD OF GOVERNORS OF

20th St. & Constitution Ave., NW.

*Members:* 7. *Established:* Dec. 23, 1913.

*Chairman:* William McC. Martin, Jr.
*Activities:* Supervises Federal Reserve banks; influences credit conditions; regulates open-market operations; issues Federal Reserve notes.

## FEDERAL TRADE COMMISSION (FTC)

Pennsylvania Ave. at 6th St., NW.
*Members:* 5. *Established:* Sept. 26, 1914.
*Chairman:* Paul Rand Dixon.
*Activities:* Prevents unfair competition, deceptive practices, false advertising, price discrimination, monopolies.

## HOUSING AND HOME FINANCE AGENCY (HHFA)

1626 K St., NW.
*Established:* July 27, 1947.
*Administrator:* Robert C. Weaver.
*Activities:* Provides single agency responsible for principal housing programs and functions of Federal government; supervises and co-ordinates activities of Federal National Mortgage Association (FNMA), Federal Housing Administration (FHA), Public Housing Administration (PHA), Voluntary Home Mortgage Credit Program, Urban Renewal Administration, and Community Facilities Administration.

## INTERSTATE COMMERCE COMMISSION (ICC)

12th St. & Constitution Ave., NW.
*Members:* 11. *Established:* Feb. 4, 1887.
*Chairman:* Everett Hutchinson.
*Activities:* Regulates railroads, motor carriers, water carriers and freight forwarders as to rates, through-routes, services and bills of lading; authorizes mergers or consolidations; authorizes issue of securities by carriers.

## NATIONAL LABOR RELATIONS BOARD (NLRB)

1717 Pennsylvania Ave., NW.
*Members:* 5. *Established:* July 5, 1935.
*Chairman:* Frank W. McCulloch.
*Activities:* Prevents unfair labor practices by employers or labor organizations; conducts secret ballots among employees to determine their choice of bargaining representatives.

## SECURITIES AND EXCHANGE COMMISSION (SEC)

425 2nd St., NW.
*Members:* 5. *Established:* June 6, 1934.
*Chairman:* William L. Cary.
*Activities:* Registers and issues regulations for securities and exchanges; registers securities offered for public sale; penalizes violators of regulations subject to appeal to U. S. Court of Appeals.

## SELECTIVE SERVICE SYSTEM (SSS)

451 Indiana Ave., NW.
*Established:* 1948.
*Director:* Lt. Gen. Lewis B. Hershey.

*Activities:* Handles registration, examination, classification and selection for induction into armed forces or other disposition of men required to register under Universal Military Training and Service Act.

## SMALL BUSINESS ADMINISTRATION (SBA)

811 Vermont Ave., NW.
*Established:* July 30, 1953.
*Administrator:* John E. Horne.
*Activities:* Aids and assists the interests of small business firms to insure a fair share of total government contracts; makes loans to small firms and victims of flood and disaster.

## TENNESSEE VALLEY AUTHORITY (TVA)

New Sprankle Bldg., Knoxville, Tenn. (Wash. office: Woodward Bldg., 15th & H Sts., NW.)
*Members:* 3. *Established:* May 18, 1933.
*Chairman:* Herbert D. Vogel.
*Other members:* A. R. Jones, Aubrey J. Wagner.
*Activities:* Provides navigable channel and flood control of Tennessee River and some of its larger tributaries; disposes of surplus electric power; improves, increases and cheapens fertilizer production.

## U. S. CIVIL SERVICE COMMISSION (CSC)

8th & F Sts., NW.
*Members:* 3. *Established:* Jan. 16, 1883.
*Chairman:* John W. Macy, Jr.
*Activities:* Provides examinations to test fitness of applicants for positions in competitive service; provides personnel in response to requests from appointing officers; investigates applicants for national security purposes; classifies positions; provides leadership to Federal agencies in personnel matters.

## U. S. INFORMATION AGENCY (USIA)

1776 Pennsylvania Ave., NW.
*Established:* Aug. 1, 1953.
*Director:* Edward R. Murrow.
*Activities:* Directs information to foreign peoples, such as explanation of policies of U. S. Government and delineation of U. S. life and culture.

## U. S. TARIFF COMMISSION

E St. between 7th & 8th Sts., NW.
*Members:* 6. *Established:* Sept. 8, 1916.
*Chairman:* Joseph E. Talbot.
*Activities:* Investigates customs laws, unfair competition and foreign and domestic manufacturing costs; advises the President on duty rates.

## VETERANS ADMINISTRATION (VA)

Vermont Ave. between H & I Sts., NW.
*Established:* July 21, 1930.
*Administrator:* J. S. Gleason, Jr.
*Activities:* Administers laws authorizing benefits for veterans and dependents or beneficiaries. Included are hospitals, pensions, insurance, loans, education, etc.

## Other Independent Agencies— Executive Department

American Battle Monuments Commission— Room 2018—Munitions Bldg.

Canal Zone Government—312 Pennsylvania Bldg., Washington 4, D.C.

Commission of Fine Arts—Dept. of the Interior Bldg., Eighteenth and C Sts., NW.

Development Loan Fund—1025 Fifteenth St., NW.

District of Columbia—District Bldg., Pennsylvania Ave. and Fourteenth St., NW.

District of Columbia Redevelopment Land Agency—919 Eighteenth St., NW.

Export-Import Bank of Washington—811 Vermont Ave., NW.

Federal Aviation Agency (FAA)—1711 New York Ave., NW.

Federal Coal Mine Safety Board of Review —811 Vermont Ave., NW.

Federal Deposit Insurance Corporation— National Press Bldg.

Federal Home Loan Bank Board—101 Indiana Ave., NW.

Foreign Claims Settlement Commission of the U.S.—Tariff Commission Bldg.

General Services Administration (GSA)— General Services Bldg., Eighteenth and F Sts., NW.

Indian Claims Commission—Room 4136, General Accounting Office Bldg., 441 G St., NW.

National Aeronautics and Space Administration (NASA)—1520 H St., NW.

National Capital Housing Authority—1729 New York Avenue, NW.

National Capital Planning Commission— 7013 Interior Bldg., Eighteenth and C Streets, NW.

National Capital Transportation Agency— 726 Jackson Place, NW.

National Mediation Board—1230 Sixteenth St., NW.

National Science Foundation (NSF)—1951 Constitution Ave., NW.

Panama Canal Company—312 Pennsylvania Bldg., Washington 4, D.C.

Railroad Retirement Board (RRB)—844 Rush St., Chicago 11, Ill.

Renegotiation Board—1910 K St., NW.

St. Lawrence Seaway Development Corp.— Seaway Circle, Massena, N.Y.

Smithsonian Institution—Smithsonian Institution Bldg., The Mall, Jefferson Dr. between 9th and 12th Sts., SW.

Subversive Activities Control Board—Lafayette Bldg., 811 Vermont Ave., NW.

Tax Court of the U.S.—Internal Revenue Bldg., Twelfth St. and Constitution Ave., NW.

Virgin Islands Corporation—General Office, St. Croix, V.I.

## Legislative Department

### GENERAL ACCOUNTING OFFICE (GAO)

441 G St., NW.

*Established:* June 10, 1921.

*Comptroller General of the U. S.:* Joseph Campbell.

*Activities:* Performs independent audits of government financial transactions to provide basis for settlement of accounts and to evaluate management of financial affairs by agencies; exercises power of disallowance based on Comptroller General's settlement of accounts and claims; issues reports to Congress on its findings.

### LIBRARY OF CONGRESS

First St., SE, between East Capitol St. and Independence Ave.

*Established:* Apr. 24, 1800.

*Librarian of Congress:* L. Quincy Mumford.

*Activities:* Intended primarily for service of Congress, it has come to include entire governmental establishment and the public. (For further description, consult index.)

# Assassinations and Attempts in U. S. Since 1865

CERMAK, Anton J. (Mayor of Chicago): Shot Feb. 15, 1933, in Miami by Giuseppe Zangara, who attempted to assassinate Franklin D. Roosevelt; Cermak died Mar. 6.

GARFIELD, James A. (President of U. S.): Shot July 2, 1881, in Washington, D. C., by Charles J. Guiteau; died Sept. 19.

LINCOLN, Abraham (President of U. S.): Shot Apr. 14, 1865, in Washington, D. C., by John Wilkes Booth; died Apr. 15.

LONG, Huey P. (U. S. Senator from Louisiana): Shot Sept. 8, 1935, in Baton Rouge by Dr. Carl A. Weiss; died Sept. 10.

McKINLEY, William (President of U. S.): Shot Sept. 6, 1901, in Buffalo by Leon Czolgosz; died Sept. 14.

ROOSEVELT, Franklin D. (President-elect of U. S.): Escaped assassination unhurt Feb. 15, 1933, in Miami. *See* Cermak.

ROOSEVELT, Theodore (ex-President of U. S.): Escaped assassination (though shot) Oct. 14, 1912, in Milwaukee while campaigning for President.

SEWARD, William H. (Secretary of State): Escaped assassination (though injured) Apr. 14, 1865, in Washington, D. C., by Lewis Powell (or Paine), accomplice of John Wilkes Booth.

TRUMAN, Harry S. (President of U. S.): Escaped assassination unhurt Nov. 1, 1950, in Washington, D. C., as 2 Puerto Rican nationalists attempted to shoot their way into Blair House.

# WEATHER AND CLIMATE
## Devastating North Atlantic Hurricanes of the 20th Century

The following is a selected list of North Atlantic hurricanes based on casualties, damage and general public interest. Facts about each storm are taken from Weather Bureau records, although in some cases only estimates of wind speed are available. Data given in this list pertain only to U. S. land areas except where indicated otherwise.

| Date | Areas hardest hit | Land stations with highest wind speed | Deaths (U. S. only) | Est. damage (millions) | Remarks |
|------|-------------------|---------------------------------------|---------------------|------------------------|---------|
| 1900, Sept. 8......... | Galveston, Tex. | Galveston, Tex. (120* mph) | 6,000 | $ 20 | Damage due to both winds and storm wave. Galveston Is. inundated. |
| 1909, Sept. 10–12..... | La.; Miss. | New Orleans, La. (68 mph) | 350 | 5 | Winds 50–75 mi. W of New Orleans, where deaths occurred, were stronger than 68 mph. |
| 1915, Aug. 5–24....... | East Tex.; La. | Galveston, Tex. (120 mph) | 275 | 50 | Water 5–6 ft. deep in Galveston business district. 90% of homes demolished. Warnings issued well ahead of time. |
| 1915, Sept. 22–Oct. 2.. | Mid-Gulf Coast | Burrwood, La. (140 mph) | 275 | 13 | Many casualties due to persons insisting on staying in low-lying areas despite warnings. |
| 1919, Sept. 2–14...... | Fla.; La.; Tex. | Sand Key, Fla. (84* mph) | 284 | 22 | 488 persons drowned at sea. |
| 1926, Sept. 6–22...... | Fla.; Ala. | Miami Beach, Fla. (132 mph) | 100 | 105 | Most deaths were in Miami area. Said to have been one of most destructive storms of century. |
| 1928, Sept. 6–20...... | Southern Fla. | Lake Okeechobee, Fla. (75* mph) | 1,836 | 25 | 1,870 injured. Nearly all deaths were in Lake Okeechobee area. Winds estimated as high as 160 mph caused Lake to overflow into populated areas. |
| 1935, Aug. 31–Sept. 8 . | Southern Fla. | Tampa, Fla. (75 mph) | 376 | 6 | Sustained winds over Florida Keys est. 150–200 mph. Remembered as "Labor Day Storm," one of most violent on record. |
| 1938, Sept. 16–22..... | Long Island, N. Y. Southern New Eng. | Blue Hills Obs., Mass. (186 mph) | 600 | 250 | Unusually destructive. Storm center moved as fast as 56 mph at times. 1,754 injured. Damage est. as high as $330 million. |
| 1940, Aug. 5–15....... | Ga.; S. C.; N. C. | Savannah, Ga. (73 mph) | 50 | 3 | 30 of deaths were due to disastrous flooding inland as far west as Tennessee. |
| 1944, Sept. 8–16...... | N. C. to New England | Cape Henry, Va. (134 mph) | 46 | 100 | 344 deaths at sea. Shipping lanes were crowded with war-time activity. |
| 1944, Oct. 13–21...... | Fla. to Carolinas | Dry Tortugas Is. (120 mph) | 18 | 100 | About 300 were killed in Cuba area before storm reached U. S. Evacuation of thousands from threatened areas in Fla. prevented higher toll. |
| 1945, Aug. 24–29...... | Texas | Seadrift, Tex. (135 mph) | 3 | 20 | Several other coastal localities recorded 135 mph. One of most intense hurricanes in Texas. |
| 1947, Sept. 10–19..... | Fla.; Mid-Gulf Coast | Hillsboro Light, Fla. (155 mph) | 51 | 110 | Damage especially heavy along Gulf Coast. Onshore winds resulted in high water. |
| 1949, Aug. 23–29...... | Fla. to Carolinas | Jupiter, Fla. (153 mph) | 2 | 52 | Center of storm crossed Lake Okeechobee. Levees held back water, which rose 12 ft. (Compare casualties with 1928.) |
| 1950, Oct. 15–19...... | Florida | Miami, Fla. (125 mph) | 4 | 28 | "KING"—small but violent storm. Struck Miami, then moved up Florida peninsula. |

| Date | Areas hardest hit | Land stations with highest wind speed | Deaths (U.S. only) | Est. damage (millions) | Remarks |
|---|---|---|---|---|---|
| 1954, Aug. 26–31...... | N. C. to Maine | Block Island, R. I. (135 mph) | 60 | 461 | "CAROL"—more damage than any other single storm to this date. Water and high waves flooded low-lying areas; 1,000 injuries in Long Island–New England area. |
| 1954, Sept. 6–11...... | N. J. to Maine | Massachusetts Bay (135 mph) | 21 | 7 | "EDNA"—New England again heavily hit. |
| 1954, Oct. 5–16....... | S. C. to N. Y. | New York, N. Y. (113 mph) (See Remarks) | 95 | 252 | "HAZEL"—several N. C. localities had winds of 130–150 mph with unusually heavy wave damage resulting. Est. 400–1,000 casualties in Haiti. In Canada there were 78 deaths, mostly due to flooding. |
| 1955, Aug. 11–13...... | N. C. to Pa. and N. Y. | Ft. Macon, N. C. (100 mph) | 25 | 46 | "CONNIE"—center passed over Morehead City and Beaufort flooding these cities. 12.35 in. of rain in New York City. |
| 1955, Aug. 17–19...... | N. C. to New England | Wilmington, N. C. (83 mph) | 184 | 832 | "DIANE"—worst floods in history in Southern New England. 16 in. of rain in Hartford area. |
| 1955, Sept. 19–20..... | North Carolina | Cherry Point, N. C. (107 mph) | 7 | 88 | "IONE"—center passed over Morehead City and Beaufort but lost force rapidly thereafter. Recurved to sea south of Norfolk. |
| 1956, Sept. 24–26..... | Northwest Florida | Burrwood, La. (110 mph) | 15 | 25 | "FLOSSY"—center passed in northeasterly direction over Burrwood, La., at 4 a.m. and over Pensacola, Fla., at 3 p.m. on Sept. 24. Lost force rapidly thereafter, but dumped heavy rains in southeastern states. |
| 1957, June 26–28...... | Southwest Texas and Southwest Louisiana | Lake Charles, La. (105 mph) | 390 | 150 | "AUDREY"—gave an early start to the hurricane season and wiped out Cameron, La. Two weeks later "BERTHA," a less destructive tropical storm, struck in exactly the same area. |
| 1960, Aug. 29–Sept. 15 | Florida to New England | Ft. Myers, Fla. (121 mph) Block Island, R. I. (130 mph) (See Remarks) | 50 | 500 | "DONNA"—hurricane winds from a single storm swept the entire Atlantic seaboard from Florida to New England for the first time in a 75-year record. Winds estimated near 140 mph with gusts 175–180 mph on Central Keys and lower southwest Florida coast. 115 deaths in Antilles, most from flash floods in Puerto Rico. |

\* Wind-measuring equipment disabled at speed indicated.
NOTE: Additional hurricanes are listed in *News Chronology of 1961.*

## Tropical Storms and Hurricanes, 1886-1960

|  | Jan.–Apr. | May | June | July | Aug. | Sept. | Oct. | Nov. | Dec. | Total |
|---|---|---|---|---|---|---|---|---|---|---|
| Number of tropical storms.................. | 2 | 10 | 40 | 43 | 136 | 198 | 140 | 26 | 4 | 599 |
| Number of tropical storms that reached hurricane intensity........................... | 1 | 2 | 17 | 24 | 101 | 127 | 65 | 11 | 2 | 350 |

# Groups of Tornadoes That Caused Outstanding Damage

*Source:* Data for 1884–1953, reprinted from *Tornadoes of the United States* by S. D. Flora.
Copyright, 1954, by University of Oklahoma Press. Used by permission. Also U. S. Weather Bureau.

| Date | Number of tornadoes | Deaths | Property losses | States in which storms occurred |
|---|---|---|---|---|
| 1884, Feb. 19......... | 60 | 800 | * | Mississippi, Alabama, North and South Carolina, Tennessee, Kentucky, Indiana |
| 1917, May 26–27...... | * | 249 | $ 5,555,000 | Illinois, Indiana, Arkansas, Kentucky, Tennessee, Alabama, Mississippi |
| 1920, Apr. 20......... | 6 | 220 | 3,525,000 | Mississippi, Alabama, Tennessee |
| 1924, Apr. 29–30...... | 22 | 115 | 4,372,300 | Oklahoma, Arkansas, Alabama, Georgia, Louisiana, North and South Carolina, Virginia |
| 1924, June 28........ | 4 | 96 | 13,050,000 | Ohio and Pennsylvania |
| 1925, Mar. 18........ | 8 | 792 | 17,872,000 | Missouri, Illinois, Indiana, Kentucky, Tennessee, Alabama |
| 1927, May 8–9........ | 36 | 227 | 7,877,000 | Texas, Louisiana, Missouri, Nebraska, Indiana, Michigan |
| 1932, Mar. 21........ | 27 | 321 | 5,514,000 | Alabama, Mississippi, Georgia, Tennessee |
| 1936, Apr. 5–6....... | 22 | 498 | 21,800,000 | Arkansas, Alabama, Tennessee, Georgia, South Carolina |
| 1944, June 23........ | 4 | 153 | 5,160,000 | Pennsylvania, West Virginia, Maryland |
| 1947, Apr. 9–10...... | 8 | 167 | 10,030,750 | Texas, Oklahoma, Kansas |
| 1952, Mar. 21–22..... | 31 | 343 | 15,327,100 | Arkansas, Tennessee, Missouri, Mississippi, Alabama, Kentucky |
| 1953, June 7–9....... | 12 | 234 | 93,230,840 | Michigan, Ohio, and New England states. |
| 1954, Mar. 13........ | 4 | 8 | 9,000,000 | Georgia. Heavy damage at Lawson Air Base and Ft. Benning. |
| 1955, May 25......... | 13 | 102 | 11,747,500 | Oklahoma and Kansas. Completely destroyed Udall, Kans., and part of Blackwell, Okla. |
| 1956, Apr. 2–3........ | 51 | 40 | 19,000,000 | Oklahoma, Kansas, Tennessee, Michigan, Wisconsin |
| 1957, May 20–21...... | 37 | 44 | 15,000,000 | Missouri, Oklahoma, Colorado, Kansas |
| 1959, Feb. 10........ | (†) | 21 | 12,000,000 | Missouri |

* Not definitely known; believed to be large.  † No information available.
NOTE: Additional storms are listed in *News Chronology of 1961*.

# CLIMATE OF SELECTED U. S. CITIES

*Source:* U. S. Weather Bureau.
Asterisk (*) indicates less than one-half; T—indicates trace; n.a.—indicates not available.

| Month | Temperature | | | | Precipitation | | | Percentage possible sunshine | Percentage relative humidity at noon |
|---|---|---|---|---|---|---|---|---|---|
| | Average maximum | Average minimum | Absolute maximum | Absolute minimum | Amount | Snowfall, inches | Days with precipitation | | |

**BAKERSFIELD, CALIFORNIA (KERN COUNTY AIRPORT) Lat 35° 25′ N, Long 119° 03′ W**

| Month | Average maximum | Average minimum | Absolute maximum | Absolute minimum | Amount | Snowfall, inches | Days with precipitation | Percentage possible sunshine | Percentage relative humidity at noon |
|---|---|---|---|---|---|---|---|---|---|
| January......... | 57 | 37 | 82 | 14 | 1.02 | T | 6 | n.a. | 71 |
| April............ | 76 | 50 | 100 | 30 | 0.75 | 0.0 | 5 | n.a. | 46 |
| July............. | 101 | 67 | 118 | 46 | 0.01 | 0.0 | * | n.a. | 30 |
| October......... | 81 | 52 | 104 | 31 | 0.37 | 0.0 | 2 | n.a. | 42 |
| Annual.......... | 79 | 51 | 118 | 13 | 6.40 | T | 38 | n.a. | 47 |

**CARIBOU, MAINE (MUNICIPAL AIRPORT) Lat 46° 52′ N, Long 68° 01′ W**

| Month | Average maximum | Average minimum | Absolute maximum | Absolute minimum | Amount | Snowfall, inches | Days with precipitation | Percentage possible sunshine | Percentage relative humidity at noon |
|---|---|---|---|---|---|---|---|---|---|
| January......... | 18 | −1 | 51 | −32 | 2.24 | 21.9 | 14 | n.a. | 69 |
| April............ | 43 | 26 | 80 | 2 | 2.63 | 6.3 | 13 | n.a. | 59 |
| July............. | 75 | 54 | 95 | 40 | 4.03 | 0.0 | 14 | n.a. | 58 |
| October......... | 51 | 33 | 79 | 14 | 3.47 | 2.0 | 12 | n.a. | 61 |
| Annual.......... | 47 | 28 | 96 | −41 | 35.94 | 105.0 | 161 | n.a. | 62 |

**CHICAGO, ILLINOIS (MIDWAY AIRPORT) Lat 41° 47′ N, Long 87° 45′ W**

| Month | Average maximum | Average minimum | Absolute maximum | Absolute minimum | Amount | Snowfall, inches | Days with precipitation | Percentage possible sunshine | Percentage relative humidity at noon |
|---|---|---|---|---|---|---|---|---|---|
| January......... | 33 | 17 | 67 | −20 | 1.84 | 7.5 | 10 | 43 | 71 |
| April............ | 58 | 39 | 91 | 17 | 2.82 | 0.4 | 13 | 53 | 53 |
| July............. | 85 | 64 | 105 | 49 | 2.73 | 0.0 | 9 | 69 | 51 |
| October......... | 64 | 44 | 91 | 14 | 2.56 | 0.3 | 7 | 64 | 52 |
| Annual.......... | 50 | 41 | 105 | −23 | 32.78 | 35.5 | 120 | 58 | 58 |

| Month | Temperature | | | | Precipitation | | | Percentage possible sunshine | Percentage relative humidity at noon |
| | Average maximum | Average minimum | Absolute maximum | Absolute minimum | Amount | Snowfall, inches | Days with precipitation | | |
|---|---|---|---|---|---|---|---|---|---|

### DALLAS, TEXAS (LOVE FIELD) Lat 32° 51' N, Long 96° 51' W

|  | | | | | | | | | |
|---|---|---|---|---|---|---|---|---|---|
| January | 55 | 36 | 88 | −3 | 2.47 | 1.0 | 7 | 47 | 62 |
| April | 77 | 56 | 96 | 30 | 3.87 | 0.0 | 9 | 58 | 56 |
| July | 95 | 76 | 111 | 56 | 1.97 | 0.0 | 5 | 78 | 50 |
| October | 80 | 58 | 100 | 26 | 2.67 | 0.0 | 6 | 66 | 51 |
| Annual | 77 | 56 | 111 | −3 | 34.51 | 1.7 | 81 | 66 | 54 |

### DENVER, COLORADO (STAPLETON AIRFIELD) Lat 39° 46' N, Long 104° 53' W

|  | | | | | | | | | |
|---|---|---|---|---|---|---|---|---|---|
| January | 42 | 16 | 76 | −29 | 0.50 | 8.9 | 6 | 70 | 44 |
| April | 61 | 34 | 86 | 4 | 2.05 | 10.2 | 9 | 62 | 39 |
| July | 87 | 58 | 104 | 42 | 1.36 | 0.0 | 9 | 70 | 32 |
| October | 66 | 37 | 90 | −2 | 1.01 | 3.1 | 6 | 72 | 34 |
| Annual | 64 | 36 | 105 | −30 | 14.22 | 59.3 | 86 | 69 | 38 |

### DULUTH, MINNESOTA (WILLIAMSON–JOHNSON AIRPORT) Lat 46° 50' N, Long 92° 11' W

|  | | | | | | | | | |
|---|---|---|---|---|---|---|---|---|---|
| January | 17 | −1 | 52 | −35 | 1.23 | 16.4 | 11 | 51 | 73 |
| April | 46 | 28 | 88 | −5 | 2.50 | 6.6 | 10 | 56 | 59 |
| July | 77 | 56 | 97 | 40 | 3.64 | 0.0 | 11 | 69 | 61 |
| October | 53 | 35 | 86 | 9 | 2.22 | 1.2 | 9 | 53 | 62 |
| Annual | 47 | 29 | 97 | −35 | 29.76 | 76.2 | 132 | 56 | 65 |

### GREAT FALLS, MONTANA (MUNICIPAL AIRPORT) Lat 47° 29' N, Long 111° 21' W

|  | | | | | | | | | |
|---|---|---|---|---|---|---|---|---|---|
| January | 32 | 14 | 62 | −33 | 0.55 | 8.3 | 8 | 54 | 62 |
| April | 56 | 33 | 87 | −6 | 0.95 | 4.4 | 8 | 64 | 45 |
| July | 84 | 55 | 102 | 42 | 1.35 | T | 7 | 80 | 36 |
| October | 59 | 37 | 91 | 7 | 0.72 | 2.7 | 6 | 61 | 47 |
| Annual | 56 | 34 | 105 | −35 | 14.06 | 54.7 | 98 | 65 | 50 |

### KANSAS CITY, MISSOURI (MUNICIPAL AIRPORT) Lat 39° 07' N, Long 94° 35' W

|  | | | | | | | | | |
|---|---|---|---|---|---|---|---|---|---|
| January | 39 | 21 | 75 | −20 | 1.43 | 5.3 | 7 | 50 | 65 |
| April | 66 | 46 | 95 | 16 | 3.61 | 0.6 | 11 | 58 | 51 |
| July | 91 | 71 | 112 | 53 | 2.83 | 0.0 | 8 | 76 | 49 |
| October | 70 | 49 | 98 | 17 | 2.93 | T | 7 | 68 | 49 |
| Annual | 66 | 46 | 113 | −22 | 35.36 | 19.6 | 100 | 64 | 55 |

### LOS ANGELES, CALIFORNIA (CITY OFFICE) Lat 34° 03' N, Long 118° 14' W

|  | | | | | | | | | |
|---|---|---|---|---|---|---|---|---|---|
| January | 65 | 45 | 90 | 28 | 2.38 | T | 6 | 71 | 46 |
| April | 71 | 52 | 100 | 36 | 1.17 | 0.0 | 4 | 67 | 50 |
| July | 83 | 62 | 109 | 49 | T | 0.0 | * | 81 | 49 |
| October | 77 | 56 | 104 | 40 | 0.50 | 0.0 | 2 | 74 | 47 |
| Annual | 74 | 54 | 110 | 28 | 14.64 | T | 37 | 74 | 47 |

### MIAMI, FLORIDA (INTERNATIONAL AIRPORT) Lat 25° 48' N, Long 80° 16' W

|  | | | | | | | | | |
|---|---|---|---|---|---|---|---|---|---|
| January | 78 | 59 | 87 | 28 | 2.06 | 0.0 | 6 | n.a. | 55 |
| April | 85 | 65 | 93 | 39 | 3.99 | 0.0 | 7 | n.a. | 56 |
| July | 91 | 74 | 100 | 68 | 6.73 | 0.0 | 17 | n.a. | 64 |
| October | 86 | 70 | 94 | 51 | 8.23 | 0.0 | 15 | n.a. | 64 |
| Annual | 85 | 67 | 100 | 28 | 56.48 | 0.0 | 128 | n.a. | 60 |

### MIAMI BEACH, FLORIDA Lat 25° 47' N, Long 80° 08' W

|  | | | | | | | | | |
|---|---|---|---|---|---|---|---|---|---|
| January | 76 | 64 | 84 | 35 | 2.04 | 0.0 | 7 | n.a. | n.a. |
| April | 81 | 70 | 90 | 48 | 2.61 | 0.0 | 7 | n.a. | n.a. |
| July | 88 | 77 | 98 | 69 | 3.83 | 0.0 | 15 | n.a. | n.a. |
| October | 84 | 74 | 92 | 55 | 7.07 | 0.0 | 15 | n.a. | n.a. |
| Annual | 82 | 71 | 98 | 35 | 42.90 | 0.0 | 127 | n.a. | n.a. |

| Month | Temperature | | | | Precipitation | | | | Percentage relative humidity at noon |
|---|---|---|---|---|---|---|---|---|---|
| | Average maximum | Average minimum | Absolute maximum | Absolute minimum | Amount | Snowfall, inches | Days with precipitation | Percentage possible sunshine | |
| **NASHVILLE, TENNESSEE (BERRY FIELD) Lat 36° 07′ N, Long 86° 41′ W** | | | | | | | | | |
| January......... | 49 | 31 | 78 | −15 | 4.93 | 3.6 | 12 | 36 | 68 |
| April............ | 71 | 49 | 90 | 25 | 3.69 | 0.1 | 11 | 60 | 50 |
| July............ | 91 | 69 | 107 | 51 | 3.96 | 0.0 | 10 | 63 | 55 |
| October........ | 74 | 50 | 94 | 26 | 2.52 | 0.0 | 7 | 62 | 52 |
| Annual......... | 71 | 50 | 107 | −15 | 45.19 | 10.4 | 119 | 56 | 56 |
| **NEW ORLEANS, LOUISIANA (CITY OFFICE) Lat 29° 57′ N, Long 90° 04′ W** | | | | | | | | | |
| January......... | 64 | 48 | 83 | 15 | 4.78 | T | 10 | 49 | 67 |
| April............ | 78 | 62 | 91 | 38 | 5.45 | 0.0 | 7 | 64 | 59 |
| July............ | 90 | 76 | 102 | 66 | 7.09 | 0.0 | 15 | 61 | 63 |
| October........ | 80 | 65 | 94 | 40 | 3.66 | 0.0 | 7 | 72 | 59 |
| Annual......... | 78 | 63 | 102 | 7 | 63.70 | 0.1 | 119 | 61 | 62 |
| **NEW YORK, NEW YORK (CENTRAL PARK) Lat 40° 47′ N, Long 73° 58′ W** | | | | | | | | | |
| January:........ | 39 | 26 | 72 | −6 | 3.57 | 7.6 | 11 | 49 | 61 |
| April............ | 59 | 42 | 92 | 12 | 3.35 | 1.1 | 11 | 59 | 54 |
| July............ | 85 | 67 | 106 | 52 | 4.22 | 0.0 | 11 | 66 | 57 |
| October........ | 66 | 50 | 94 | 28 | 3.03 | T | 8 | 61 | 56 |
| Annual......... | 62 | 46 | 106 | −15 | 43.36 | 30.0 | 121 | 59 | 58 |
| **PHOENIX, ARIZONA (SKY HARBOR AIRPORT) Lat 33° 26′ N, Long 112° 01′ W** | | | | | | | | | |
| January......... | 65 | 35 | 85 | 16 | 0.60 | T | 4 | 77 | 47 |
| April............ | 84 | 50 | 104 | 32 | 0.35 | T | 2 | 88 | 27 |
| July............ | 105 | 75 | 118 | 61 | 0.70 | 0.0 | 4 | 84 | 31 |
| October........ | 88 | 54 | 105 | 36 | 0.40 | 0.0 | 3 | 88 | 33 |
| Annual......... | 86 | 53 | 118 | 16 | 7.19 | T | 34 | 86 | 33 |
| **SALT LAKE CITY, UTAH (MUNICIPAL AIRPORT) Lat 40° 46′ N, Long 111° 58′ W** | | | | | | | | | |
| January......... | 36 | 17 | 60 | −22 | 1.20 | 13.6 | 10 | 47 | 70 |
| April............ | 63 | 37 | 85 | 14 | 1.76 | 3.2 | 9 | 68 | 42 |
| July............ | 92 | 61 | 107 | 41 | 0.61 | 0.0 | 4 | 82 | 27 |
| October........ | 67 | 39 | 88 | 18 | 1.34 | 0.5 | 6 | 73 | 42 |
| Annual......... | 64 | 39 | 107 | −30 | 14.79 | 51.7 | 86 | 69 | 46 |
| **SAN FRANCISCO, CALIFORNIA (CITY OFFICE) Lat 37° 47′ N, Long 122° 25′ W** | | | | | | | | | |
| January......... | 55 | 45 | 78 | 29 | 4.03 | T | 11 | 54 | 68 |
| April............ | 62 | 49 | 89 | 40 | 1.49 | 0.0 | 6 | 70 | 64 |
| July............ | 64 | 53 | 99 | 47 | 0.01 | 0.0 | 1 | 64 | 75 |
| October........ | 68 | 54 | 96 | 43 | 1.07 | 0.0 | 4 | 70 | 62 |
| Annual......... | 63 | 51 | 101 | 27 | 20.63 | T | 67 | 66 | 67 |
| **SEATTLE, WASHINGTON (CITY OFFICE) Lat 47° 36′ N, Long 122° 20′ W** | | | | | | | | | |
| January......... | 45 | 36 | 67 | 3 | 4.49 | 4.9 | 19 | 27 | 79 |
| April............ | 59 | 44 | 87 | 30 | 1.94 | T | 13 | 48 | 63 |
| July............ | 75 | 56 | 100 | 46 | 0.52 | 0.0 | 5 | 62 | 62 |
| October........ | 61 | 48 | 82 | 29 | 3.08 | T | 14 | 36 | 79 |
| Annual......... | 60 | 46 | 100 | 3 | 32.05 | 8.6 | 151 | 45 | 71 |
| **WASHINGTON, D. C. (NATIONAL AIRPORT) Lat 38° 51′ N, Long 77° 02′ W** | | | | | | | | | |
| January......... | 44 | 29 | 79 | 5 | 3.24 | 4.2 | 11 | 45 | 57 |
| April............ | 65 | 44 | 95 | 24 | 3.06 | T | 10 | 55 | 46 |
| July............ | 86 | 68 | 103 | 55 | 4.26 | 0.0 | 10 | 64 | 53 |
| October........ | 67 | 49 | 94 | 30 | 2.85 | T | 8 | 58 | 54 |
| Annual......... | 65 | 48 | 103 | 1 | 40.57 | 14.7 | 115 | 56 | 52 |

# ASTRONOMY AND CALENDAR

## By
### WILLY LEY

★

## Astronomical Facts

Ever since the first artificial satellite went into orbit, astronomical facts have become a topic of everyday conversation. Most people are conversant with a few of the basic facts, such as that the earth makes an orbit around the sun and the moon travels an orbit around the earth. It is also generally known that there are several other planets going around the sun and that some of them have moons of their own. But beyond these simple facts the conversation usually bogs down. This is, strange as it may seem, mostly due to the fact that people do not know which words and terms to use. I have been asked how many light-years it is to the moon, and when we can expect an expedition to "another universe." Both these questions are completely meaningless, mainly because the wrong terms were used. The first job, then, is to straighten out the terminology.

### Terminology

*Planet* is the term used for a body in orbit around the sun. Its origin is Greek; even in antiquity it was known that a number of "stars" did not stay in the same relative positions to the other stars, as did the majority of all stars. There were five such restless "stars" known—Mercury, Venus, Mars, Jupiter, and Saturn—and the Greeks referred to them as *planetes*, a word which means "wanderers." That the earth is one of the planets was realized later and, of course, additional planets were discovered after the invention of the telescope. A planet, then, is a body in orbit around the sun, regardless of its size.

*Satellite* (or "moon") is the term for a body in orbit around a planet. As long as our own moon was the only moon known, there was no need for a general term for the moons of planets. But when Galileo Galilei discovered the four main moons of the planet Jupiter, Johannes Kepler (in a letter to Galileo) suggested "satellite" (from the Latin *satelles*, which means attendant) as a general term for such bodies. It is used interchangeably with "moons"; astronomers speak and write about the moons of Neptune, Saturn, etc. The size

does not matter; a satellite is a body in orbit around a planet.

*Orbit* is the term for the path traveled by a body in space. It comes from the Latin *orbis*, which means circle, circuit, etc., and *orbita*, which means a rut or a wheel track. Theoretically, four mathematical figures are possible orbits; two are open (hyperbola and parabola) and two are closed (ellipse and circle), but in reality all closed orbits are ellipses. These ellipses can be nearly circular, as are the orbits of most planets, or very elongated, as are the orbits of most comets. In each case the sun is in one focal point of the ellipse, and the other focal point is empty. For satellite orbits, the planet stands in one focal point of the orbit. When discussing orbits generally, the term "primary" is often used; it means the body in the focal point. For planets, the point of the orbit closest to the sun is called the perihelion, and the point farthest from the sun is called the aphelion. For orbits around the earth, the corresponding terms are perigee and apogee; for orbits around other planets, corresponding terms are coined when necessary.

*Space vehicle orbits.* Here a few special terms became necessary. For space vehicles operating inside the orbit of our natural moon, the term "cislunar operations" has been coined by Krafft Ehricke. A space vehicle orbit connecting two planets would be called an "interplanetary orbit"; an orbit to another star would be called an "interstellar orbit."

*Star* is the term for a body like our sun, which is the nearest star. Stars are very large (our sun has a diameter of 860,000 miles and is a comparatively small star), and are intensely hot, deriving their energy from nuclear reactions going on in their interiors.

*Solar system.* Our solar system consists of one star (the sun), the planets from Mercury to Pluto and all their moons, several thousand minor planets (also called asteroids or, better, planetoids), and an equally large number of comets. Since a very large number of other stars, though probably not all, are also likely to have

# Astronomical Constants

| | |
|---|---|
| 1 light-year | 5,880,000,000,000 mi. |
| parsec (*parallax of one second*, for stellar distances) | 3.259 light yrs. |
| velocity of light | 186,272 mi./sec. |
| astronomical unit or distance earth-to-sun | 93,003,000 mi. |
| mean distance, earth to moon | 238,860 mi. |
| general precession | 50".26 |
| obliquity of the ecliptic | 23° 27' 8".26—0".4684($t$—1900) * |
| equatorial radius of the earth | 3963.34 statute mi. |
| polar radius of the earth | 3949.99 statute mi. |
| earth's mean radius | 3958.89 statute mi. |
| oblateness of the earth | $\frac{1}{297.0}$ |
| equatorial horizontal parallax of the moon | 57' 2".70 |
| earth's mean velocity in orbit | 18.5 mi./sec. |
| sidereal year | 365$^d$.2564 |
| tropical year | 365$^d$.2422 |
| sidereal month | 27$^d$.3217 |
| synodic month | 29$^d$.5306 |
| sidereal day | 23$^h$ 56$^m$ 4$^s$.091 of mean solar time |
| mean solar day | 24$^h$ 3$^m$ 56$^s$.555 of sidereal time |

* $t$ refers to the year in question, for example 1958.

---

comets, planets, and so forth, it is correct to speak of "other solar systems." Some astronomers, however, mindful of the fact that the "sol" part of the term refers specifically to our sun, prefer to speak of the "planetary system of (name of star)."

*Galaxy.* All the stars you can see in the sky (with a very few exceptions) are part of a galaxy—a system of, roughly, 30 billion stars. The few exceptions are other galaxies. Our own galaxy, the rim of which we see as the "Milky Way," is about 100,000 light-years in diameter and about 10,000 light-years in thickness. Its shape is generally that of a thick lens; more precisely it is a "spiral nebula," a term first used for other galaxies when they were discovered and before it was realized that these were separate and distant galaxies. The nearest other galaxy (visible to the naked eye) is the one in the constellation Andromeda; it is somewhat larger than our own galaxy. While the spiral nebulae are other galaxies, the "gaseous nebulae," like the one in Orion, are parts of our own galaxy, as are also a number of diffuse objects that bear the misleading name of "planetary nebulae." This name was used because, in the telescope, they show a visible diameter, as do planets, while all the stars, even in the strongest telescope, dimensionless points.

*Light-year,* etc. A light-year is the distance traveled by light in one year (see table of Astronomical Constants). For distances inside a solar system, this unit is too large to be used, as can be shown by two examples. The distance sun-to-earth would be just eight light-minutes, while the distance earth-to-moon would be about 1¼ light-seconds. The yardstick used inside the solar system is the "astronomical unit," abbreviated A.U., which is the mean distance from the sun to the earth, or 93 million miles. Interstellar distances are expressed in light-years or in parsecs (see table), while intergalactic distances are expressed in megaparsecs—millions of parsecs.

*Universe.* Some scientists and writers have used the term "island universe" when referring to a galaxy. But "universe" by itself simply comprises everything, the whole of space that we know.

## The Sun

With the exception of the moon and the five naked-eye planets all the lights you see in the sky are stars, of which our sun is neither the largest nor the most spectacular but merely the one which happens to be closest to us. Stars in the universe are grouped in galaxies (spiral nebulae) and our sun is a member of one of these galaxies, the edges of which we see as the Milky Way.

All these stars are gigantic balls of superheated gas, kept hot by atomic reactions in their centers. In our sun (and in the vast majority of the others) this atomic reaction is hydrogen fusion; four hydrogen atoms are combined to form one helium atom. The temperature at the core of our sun must be 20 million degrees centigrade, the surface temperature is around 6,000 degrees centigrade, or about 11,000 degrees Fahrenheit. The diameter of the sun is 865,390 miles so that its surface area is approximately 12,000 times that of the earth. Compared to other stars our sun is just a bit below average in size and temperature. Its fuel supply (hydrogen) is estimated to last for another 7 billion years.

Our sun is not motionless in space; in fact it has two proper motions. One is a straight-line motion (as far as is known) in the direction of the constellation Hercules at the rate of about 12 miles per second. But since the sun is a part of the Milky Way system and since the whole system rotates slowly around its own center, the sun also moves at the rate of 175 miles per second as part of the rotating Milky Way system.

In addition to this the sun rotates on its axis. Observing the motion of the sun spots (darkish areas which look like enormous whirling storms) and the exceptionally bright spots called "solar flares" which are usually associated with sun spots has shown that the rotational period of our sun is just short of 25 days. But this figure is valid for the sun's equator only; the sections near the sun's poles seem to have a rotational period of 34 days. Naturally, since the sun generates its own heat and light, there is no temperature difference between poles and equator.

What we call the sun's "surface" is technically known as the photosphere. Since the whole sun is a ball of very hot gas, there is really no such thing as a surface; it is a question of visual impression. Out-side the photosphere we have another layer called the "chromosphere," which extends several thousand miles beyond the photosphere. It is in steady motion and often enormous "prominences" can be seen to burst from it, extending as much as 100,-000 miles into space. Outside the chromosphere there is the so-called "corona." The corona consists of very tenuous gases (essentially hydrogen), but it makes a magnificent sight when the sun is eclipsed.

## The Moon

The earth is the planet nearest to the sun of all the planets which have moons. The two planets nearer the sun, Mercury and Venus, do not have any moons. The next planet farther out, Mars, has two very small moons. Jupiter has four major moons and presumably many minor ones, of which eight are now known. Saturn, the ringed planet, has nine known moons, of which one (Titan) is larger than the planet Mercury. Uranus has five known moons (four of them large), while Neptune has one large and one small moon. Pluto is moonless and considered by some a "runaway moon" of Neptune.

Our own moon, with a diameter of 2,160

## The Brightest Stars

| Star | Constellation | Position, 1950 R.A. | Dec. | Mag. | Dist. | On meridian 9 p.m. |
|------|---------------|------|------|------|-------|---------------------|
| | | h m | ° ′ | | l.-y. | |
| Sirius | Canis Major | 6 42.9 | −16 39 | −1.6 | 8 | Feb. 16 |
| Canopus | Carina | 6 22.8 | −52 40 | −0.9 | 650 | Feb. 11 |
| Alpha Centauri | Centaurus | 14 36.2 | −60 38 | +0.1 | 4 | June 16 |
| Vega | Lyra | 18 35.2 | +38 44 | 0.1 | 23 | Aug. 15 |
| Capella | Auriga | 5 13.0 | +45 57 | 0.2 | 42 | Jan. 24 |
| Arcturus | Boötes | 14 13.4 | +19 27 | 0.2 | 32 | June 10 |
| Rigel | Orion | 5 12.1 | − 8 15 | 0.3 | 545 | Jan. 24 |
| Procyon | Canis Minor | 7 36.7 | + 5 21 | 0.5 | 10 | Mar. 2 |
| Achernar | Eridanus | 1 35.9 | −57 29 | 0.6 | 70 | Nov. 30 |
| Beta Centauri | Centaurus | 14 0.3 | −60 8 | 0.9 | 130 | June 7 |
| Altair | Aquila | 19 48.3 | + 8 44 | 0.9 | 18 | Sept. 1 |
| Betelgeuse | Orion | 5 52.5 | + 7 24 | 0.9 | 300 | Feb. 3 |
| Aldebaran | Taurus | 4 33.0 | +16 25 | 1.1 | 54 | Jan. 14 |
| Spica | Virgo | 13 22.6 | −10 54 | 1.2 | 190 | May 28 |
| Pollux | Gemini | 7 42.3 | +28 9 | 1.2 | 31 | Mar. 3 |
| Antares | Scorpius | 16 26.3 | −26 19 | 1.2 | 170 | July 14 |
| Fomalhaut | Piscis Austrinus | 22 54.9 | −29 53 | 1.3 | 27 | Oct. 20 |
| Deneb | Cygnus | 20 39.7 | +45 6 | 1.3 | 465 | Sept. 16 |
| Regulus | Leo | 10 5.7 | +12 13 | 1.3 | 70 | Apr. 9 |
| Beta Crucis | Crux | 12 44.8 | −59 25 | 1.5 | 465 | May 18 |
| Eta Carinae | Carina | 10 43.1 | −59 25 | 1—7 | ... | Apr. 17 |
| Alpha-one Crucis | Crux | 12 23.8 | −62 49 | 1.6 | 150 | May 13 |
| Castor | Gemini | 7 31.4 | +32 0 | 1.6 | 44 | Feb. 28 |
| Gamma Crucis | Crux | 12 28.4 | −56 50 | 1.6 | ... | May 15 |
| Epsilon Canis Majoris | Canis Major | 6 56.7 | −28 54 | 1.6 | 325 | Feb. 19 |
| Epsilon Ursae Majoris | Ursa Major | 12 51.8 | +56 14 | 1.7 | 50 | May 20 |
| Bellatrix | Orion | 5 22.4 | + 6 18 | 1.7 | 215 | Jan. 27 |
| Lambda Scorpii | Scorpius | 17 30.2 | −37 4 | 1.7 | 205 | July 30 |
| Epsilon Carinae | Carina | 8 21.5 | −59 21 | 1.7 | 325 | Mar. 13 |
| Mira | Cetus | 2 16.8 | − 3 12 | 2—9 | 250 | Dec. 11 |

## Planet Table

| | Mean distance from sun in millions of miles | Period of revolution around the sun | Eccentricity of orbit | Inclination to ecliptic ° ' | Diameter miles | Period of rotation on axis | Inclination of equator to orbit plane ° | Surface gravity (earth =1) | Density H₂O=1 | Oblateness | Mean velocity in orbit mi./sec. | Max. stellar mag. |
|---|---|---|---|---|---|---|---|---|---|---|---|---|
| Sun..... | ...... | ........ | | | 865,400 | 24d.64† | 7.2 | 28 | 1.4 | 0 | ...... | −26.7 |
| Moon..... | ...... | (27d.322)* | 0.05 | 5  8 | 2,160 | 27d.322 | 6.7 | 0.16 | 3.3 | 0 | 0.63 | −12.6 |
| Mercury.. | 36.00 | 87d.969 | 0.21 | 7  0 | 3,100 | 88d | 7 | 0.28 | 3.8 | 0 | 30 | −1.2 |
| Venus.... | 67.27 | 224d.701 | 0.01 | 3  24 | 7,700 | ? ‡ | ? | 0.85 | 5.1 | 0 | 22 | −4.4 |
| Earth.... | 93.00 | 365d.256 | 0.02 | 0  0 | 7,927 | 23h 56m | 23.4 | 1.00 | 5.5 | 1/297 | 18.5 | .... |
| Mars..... | 141.71 | 1y.881 | 0.09 | 1  51 | 4,200 | 24h 37m | 25.2 | 0.38 | 4.0 | 1/192 | 15 | −2.8 |
| Jupiter... | 483.88 | 11y.862 | 0.05 | 1  18 | 88,700 | 9h 50m† | 3.1 | 2.6 | 1.3 | 1/15 | 8 | −2.5 |
| Saturn... | 887.14 | 29y.458 | 0.06 | 2  29 | 75,100 | 10h 14m† | 26.8 | 1.2 | 0.7 | 1/9.5 | 6 | −0.4 |
| Uranus... | 1783.98 | 84y.013 | 0.05 | 0  46 | 32,000 | 10 ¾ h | 98 | 1.1 | 1.3 | 1/14 | 4 | +5.7 |
| Neptune... | 2795.46 | 164y.794 | 0.01 | 1  46 | 27,700 | 15h.8 | 29 | 1.4 | 2.2 | 1/40 | 3 | +7.8 |
| Pluto.... | 3675.27 | 248y.430 | 0.25 | 17  9 | 3,600 | ?? | ?? | ?? | ? | ?? | <3 | +14 |

* Period of revolution around the earth.  † This is the rotation at the equator.  ‡ Rotation of Venus is uncertain but is probably a few weeks.  § The equatorial diameters of the earth, Jupiter, and Saturn are given; polar diameters are: earth, 7,900.0 mi., Jupiter 82,789 mi., Saturn 67,170 mi.

SATELLITES. The number of known moons in the solar system is now as follows: for the earth 1; Mars 2; Jupiter 12; Saturn 9; Uranus 5; Neptune 2.

OTHER DATA ON THE EARTH: Equatorial circumference, 24,902.4 mi.; total area, 196,949,970 sq. mi.; mass, 6.6 sextillion tons; mean diameter, 7,917.8 mi.

---

miles, is one of the large moons in our solar system and is especially large when compared to the planet around which it goes. In fact the common center of gravity of the earth-moon system is only about 1,000 miles below the earth's surface. The closest our moon can come to us (perigee) is 221,463 miles; the farthest it can go away (apogee) is 252,710 miles. Like all the other moons in our solar system the period of rotation of our moon is equal to its period of revolution around the earth. Hence from earth we can see only one hemisphere of the moon. Both periods are 27 days, 7 hours, 43 minutes and 11.47 seconds. But while the rotation of the moon is regular, its velocity in its orbit is not, since it moves more slowly in apogee than in perigee. Consequently some portions near the rim which are not normally visible will appear briefly. This phenomenon is called "libration," and by taking advantage of the librations astronomers have succeeded in mapping approximately 59 per cent of the lunar surface. The other 41 per cent can never be seen from the earth but should be well mapped by circumlunar camera-carrying rockets within a few years.

Though the moon goes around the earth in the time mentioned, the interval from new moon to new moon is 29 days, 12 hours, 44 minutes and 2.78 seconds. This delay of nearly two days is due to the fact that the earth is moving around the sun, so that the moon needs two extra days to reach a spot in its orbit where no part is illuminated by the sun, as seen from earth.

If the plane of the earth's orbit around the sun (the ecliptic) and the plane of the moon's orbit around the earth were the same, the moon would be eclipsed by the earth every time it is full, and the sun would be eclipsed by the moon every time the moon is "new" (it would be better to call it the "black moon" when it is in this position). But because the two orbits do not coincide, the moon's shadow normally misses the earth and the earth's shadow misses the moon. The inclination of the two orbital planes to each other is 5 degrees. The tides are, of course, caused by the moon, but in the open ocean they are surprisingly low, amounting to about one yard. The very high tides which can be observed near the shore in some places are due to funnelling effects of the shorelines. At new moon and at full moon the tides raised by the moon are re-enforced by the sun; these are the "spring tides." If the sun's tidal raising power does not re-enforce that of the moon we get the low "neap tides."

### The Planets

Of the nine known planets of our solar system, two, Mercury and Venus, move around the sun in orbits smaller than that of the earth. Because all planets "shine" by reflected sunlight, these two become invisible to us when they are nearest to us. We then see their unilluminated night-sides. As these planets move away from this position they first appear as sickles, and as the sickle widens their brilliance increases. When (as seen from earth) they are as far from the sun as they can be, they are said to be at "maximum elongation." Then they approach the sun (apparently, that is) and become invisible again because of their proximity to it.

Mercury, the innermost planet, is rather small in actual size, and though it is a naked-eye object, it is rather difficult to see because even at extreme elongation it is still in a sky illuminated by sunlight, though the sun itself will be below the horizon. Venus is the opposite of a difficult object; it hangs in the sky like a distant searchlight trained at us. As late as a hundred years ago a French warship tried to shoot it down because it was thought to be an enemy balloon, and in recent years Venus has often been reported as a "flying saucer."

Mars, the next planet outside the earth's orbit, will become especially bright when nearest to us because we then see its daylight side fully illuminated by the sun. This happens roughly every two years and two months. The last time was in December 1960, the next time will be in February 1963.

The planet beyond the orbit of Mars is not a planet, but an estimated 30,000 pieces of matter, known collectively as the asteroids, or planetoids. The first and, incidentally, the largest was discovered during the New Year's night of 1801 by the Italian astronomer Father Piazzi, and its orbit was calculated by the German mathematician Karl Friedrich Gauss. (Gauss invented a new method of calculating orbits on that occasion.) A German amateur astronomer, the physician Olbers, discovered the second asteroid. The number now known, catalogued, and named is around 1,600; the estimated total is about 20 times that figure. A few asteroids do not move in orbits beyond the orbit of Mars, but in orbits which cross the orbit of Mars. The first of them was named Eros because of this peculiar orbit. It had become the rule to bestow female names on the asteroids, but when it was found that Eros crossed the orbit of a major planet, it received a male name. Since then around two dozen orbit-crossers have been discovered, and they are often

referred to as the "male asteroids." A few of them—Albert, Adonis, Apollo, Amor, and Icarus—cross the orbit of the earth, and two of them may come closer than our moon; but the crossing is like a bridge crossing a highway, not like two highways intersecting. Hence there is no danger of collision from these bodies. They are all small, three to five miles in diameter, and therefore very difficult objects to identify, even when quite close.

Beyond the "asteroid belt" is the largest planet of our solar system, Jupiter. Even when nearest the earth, Jupiter is still almost 800 million miles away. But because of its size it may rival Venus in brilliance when near. The next planet beyond Jupiter is Saturn, famous for its rings. It is never an object of overwhelming brilliance but will look like a bright star. Uranus, the next planet, can occasionally become bright enough to be seen with the naked eye if you know just where to look; normally it is an object for good field-glasses or small portable telescopes. The same goes for Neptune. Pluto, the planet "beyond Neptune," as it is usually called, is now approaching the perihelion of its orbit and for the rest of this century will be closer to the sun than Neptune. Even then it can be seen only with a large telescope.

## Comets

The appearance of a large and brilliant comet in the skies cannot be predicted any earlier than 1986 when Halley's comet will approach perihelion (the point of its orbit closest to the sun) again. But a large and brilliant comet is possible at any time. More than 1,000 comets are on the lists now, with several new ones being discovered every year. But while you have a comet visible to the unaided eye almost every year, none of them since the last appearance of Halley's comet in 1910–11 has been conspicuous to a casual watcher.

Since comets appeared in the sky with-

### The First Ten Minor Planets

| Name | Year of discovery | Mean distance from sun (millions of miles) | Orbital period (years) | Diameter (miles) | Magnitude |
|---|---|---|---|---|---|
| 1. Ceres | 1801 | 257.0 | 4.60 | 485 | 7.4 |
| 2. Pallas | 1802 | 257.4 | 4.61 | 304 | 8.0 |
| 3. Juno | 1804 | 247.8 | 4.36 | 118 | 8.7 |
| 4. Vesta | 1807 | 219.3 | 3.63 | 243 | 6.5 |
| 5. Astraea | 1845 | 239.3 | 4.14 | 50 | 9.9 |
| 6. Hebe | 1847 | 225.2 | 3.78 | 121 | 8.5 |
| 7. Iris | 1847 | 221.4 | 3.68 | 121 | 8.4 |
| 8. Flora | 1847 | 204.4 | 3.27 | 56 | 8.9 |
| 9. Metis | 1848 | 221.7 | 3.69 | 78 | 8.9 |
| 10. Hygeia | 1849 | 292.6 | 5.59 | 40 ? | 9.5 |

## 20 Famous Comets

| Year and no. | Name of comet | Period, years |
|---|---|---|
| 1744 | De Chéseaux's Comet............ | ..... |
| 1806 | Biela's Comet................... | 6.7 |
| 1811 I | Great Comet of 1811............ | 3000 |
| 1812 | Di Vico's Comet................ | 70.7 |
| 1815 | Olbers' Comet.................. | 74.0 |
| 1819 I | Encke's Comet................. | 3.3 |
| 1819 | Pons-Winnecke Comet.......... | 6.0 |
| 1835 III | Halley's Comet................. | 76.3 |
| 1843 I | Great Comet of 1843........... | 512.4 |
| 1844 II | Great Comet of 1844........... | 102,050 |
| 1858 VI | Donati's Comet................. | 2,040 (?) |
| 1864 II | Great Comet of 1864........... | 2,800,000 |
| 1871 III | Tuttle's Comet................. | 13.8 |
| 1874 III | Coggia's Comet................ | 6,000 (?) |
| 1879 | Brorsen's Comet............... | 5.6 |
| 1881 II | Tebbutt's Comet............... | ..... |
| 1889 VI | Swift's 2nd Comet............. | 7.0 |
| 1892 III | Holmes' Comet................ | 6.9 |
| 1923 | d'Arrest's Comet.............. | 6.6 |
| 1925 II | Comet Schwassmann-Wachmann.. | 16.2 |

out any warning, people in classical times and especially during the Middle Ages believed that they had a special "meaning," which, of course, was bad. Since a natural catastrophe of some sort or a military conflict occurs every year, it was quite simple to blame the comet which happened to be visible. But even in the past there were some people who used logical reasoning. When, in Roman times, a comet was blamed for the loss of a battle and hence was called a "bad omen," a Roman writer observed that the victors in the battle probably did not think so.

Up until the middle of the sixteenth century comets were believed to be phenomena of the upper atmosphere; they were usually "explained" as "burning vapors" which had risen from "distant swamps." That nobody had ever actually seen burning vapors rise from a swamp did not matter.

But a large comet which appeared in 1577 was carefully observed by Tycho Brahe, a Danish astronomer who is often, and with the best of reasons, called "eccentric" but who insisted on precise measurements for everything. It was Tycho Brahe's accumulation of literally thousands of precise measurements which later enabled his younger collaborator, Johannes Kepler, to discover the laws of planetary motion. Measuring the motion of the comet of 1577, Tycho Brahe could show that it had been far beyond the atmosphere, even though he could not give figures for the distance. Tycho Brahe's work proved that comets were astronomical and not meteorological phenomena.

In 1682 the first Astronomer Royal of Great Britain, Dr. Edmund Halley, checked the orbit of a bright comet that was in the sky then and compared it with earlier comet orbits which were known in part. Halley found that the comet of 1682 was the third to move through what appeared to be the same orbit. And the three appearances were roughly 76 years apart. Halley concluded that this was the same comet, moving around the sun in a closed orbit, like the planets. He predicted that it would re-appear in 1758 or 1759. Halley himself died in 1742, but a large comet appeared sixteen years after his death as predicted and was immediately referred to as "Halley's comet."

Astronomers refer to comets as "periodic" or as "non-periodic" comets, but the latter term does not mean that these comets have no period; it merely means that their period is not known. The actual periods of comets run from 3.3 years (the shortest known) to several thousand years. Their orbits are elliptical, like those of the planets, but they are very eccentric, long and narrow ellipses. Only comet Schwassmann-Wachmann has an orbit which has such a low eccentricity (for a cometary orbit) that it could be the orbit of a minor planet.

When a comet, coming from deep space, approaches the sun, it is at first indistinguishable from a minor planet. Somewhere between the orbits of Mars and Jupiter its outline becomes fuzzy; it is said to develop a "coma" (the word used here is the Latin word *coma,* which means "hair," not the phonetically identical Greek word which means "deep sleep"). Then, near the orbit of Mars, the comet develops its tail, which at first trails behind. This grows steadily as the comet comes closer and closer to the sun. As it rounds the sun (as first pointed out by Johannes Kepler) the tail always points away from the sun so that the comet, when moving away from the sun, points its tail ahead like the landing lights of an airplane.

The reason for this behavior is that the tail is pushed in these directions by the radiation pressure of the sun. It sometimes happens that a comet loses its tail at perihelion; it then grows another one. Although the tail is clearly visible against the black of the sky, it is very tenuous. It has been said that if the tail of Halley's comet could be compressed to the density of iron, it would fit into a small suitcase.

The chemical make-up of comets has been explained by Fred L. Whipple. Comets are enormous "snowballs" of frozen gases (mostly carbon dioxide, methane or marsh gas, water vapor, etc.) containing very little solid material. The whole behaviour of a comet, therefore, is explainable as the behavior of a ball of frozen gas being heated by the sun.

## Important Meteor Showers

| Date | | Meteor stream | Radiant in constellation |
|---|---|---|---|
| Jan. | 1–4 | Quadrantids | Boötes |
| Feb. | 5–10 | Alpha Aurigids | Auriga |
| Mar. | 10–12 | Zeta Boötids | Boötes |
| Apr. | 19–23 | Lyrids | Hercules |
| May | 1–6 | May Aquarids | Aquarius |
| May | 30 | Eta Pegasids | Pegasus |
| June | 27–30 | Pons-Winnecke meteors | Draco |
| July | 14 | Alpha Cygnids | Cygnus |
| July | 26–31 | Delta Aquarids | Aquarius |
| Aug. | 10–14 | Perseids | Cassiopeia |
| Aug. | 10–20 | Kappa Cygnids | Cygnus |
| Aug. | 21–31 | Zeta Draconids | Draco |
| Sept. | 22 | Alpha Aurigids | Auriga |
| Oct. | 2 | Quadrantids | Boötes |
| Oct. | 9 | Giacobinids | Draco |
| Oct. | 18–23 | Orionids | Orion |
| Nov. | 14–18 | Leonids | Leo |
| Dec. | 10–13 | Geminids | Gemini |

## Meteors and Meteorites

The term "meteor" for what is usually called a "shooting star" bears an unfortunate resemblance to the term "meteorology," the science of weather and weather forecasting. This resemblance is due to an ancient misunderstanding which wrongly considered meteors an atmospheric phenomenon. Actually the streak of light in the sky which scientists call a meteor is essentially an astronomical phenomenon: the entry of a small piece of cosmic matter into our atmosphere.

The distinction between "meteors" and "fireballs" (formerly also called "bolides") is merely one of convenience; a fireball is an unusually bright meteor. Incidentally, it also means that a fireball is larger than a faint meteor. A bright fireball produces enough light to see by and may light up the night landscape like the full moon.

Bodies which enter our atmosphere become visible when they are about 60 miles above the ground. The fact that they grow hot enough to emit light is not due to the "friction" of the atmosphere, as one can often read. The phenomenon responsible for the heating is one of compression. Since unconfined air cannot move faster than the speed of sound but the entering meteorite moves with 30 to 60 times the speed of sound, the air simply cannot get out of the way. Therefore it is compressed like the air in the cylinder of a Diesel engine and is heated by compression. This heat—or part of it—is transferred to the moving body. The details of this process are now fairly well understood as a result of re-entry tests with ballistic-missile nose cones.

The average weight of a body producing a faint "shooting star" is only a small fraction of an ounce. Even a bright fireball may not weigh more than 2 or 3 pounds. Naturally the smaller bodies are worn to dust by the passage through the atmosphere; only rather large ones reach the ground. Those that are found are called meteorites. (The "meteor," to repeat, is the term for the light streak in the sky.)

The largest meteorite known is still imbedded in the ground near Grootfontein in SW Africa and is estimated to weigh 70 tons. The second largest known is the 34-ton Anighito (on exhibit in the Hayden Planetarium, New York), which was found by Admiral Peary at Cape York in Greenland. The largest meteorite found in the United States is the Willamette meteorite (found in Oregon, weight ca. 15 tons), but large portions of this meteorite weathered away before it was found and its weight as it struck the ground may have been 20 tons.

All these are iron meteorites (an iron meteorite normally contains about 7 per cent nickel), which form one class of meteorites. The other class are the stony meteorites and between them there are the so-called "stony irons." The so-called "Tektites" consist of glass similar to our volcanic glass obsidian, and because of the similarity there is doubt in a number of cases whether the glass is of terrestrial or of extra-terrestrial origin.

Though no meteorite larger than the Grootfontein is actually known, we do know that the earth has, on occasion, been struck by much larger bodies. Evidence for such hits are the meteorite craters, of which an especially good example is located near the Cañon Diablo in Arizona. Another meteor crater in the United States is a rather old crater near Odessa, Texas. A large number of others are known, but some of them have not actually been proved to be meteoritic in origin, as for example Lake Bosumtwi in West Africa.

The meteor showers are caused by multitudes of very small bodies travelling in swarms; these showers, though looking most spectacular on occasion, do not seem to contain large pieces.

## The Auroras

The "northern lights" (*Aurora borealis*) as well as the "southern lights" (*Aurora australis*) are upper-atmosphere phenomena but of astronomical origin. The auroras center around the magnetic (not the geographical) poles of the earth, which explains why, in the Western Hemisphere, they have been seen as far to the south as New Orleans or Florida while the equivalent latitude in the eastern hemisphere never sees an aurora. The northern magnetic pole happens to be in the Western Hemisphere.

The lower limit of an aurora is at about 50 miles. Upper limits have been estimated to be as high as 400 miles, but this figure is an estimate, not a measurement. Since about 1880 a connection between the auroras on earth and the sun spots has been suspected and has gradually come to be accepted. It was said that the sunspots probably eject "particles" (later the word electrons was substituted) which on striking the earth's atmosphere, cause the auroras. But this explanation suffered from certain difficulties. Sometimes a very large sunspot group on the sun, with individual spots bigger than the earth itself, would not cause an aurora. Moreover, even if a sunspot caused an aurora, the time that passed between the appearance of the one and the occurrence of the other was highly unpredictable.

In addition to these two theoretical difficulties there was a practical one. If an aurora was the result of earth being hit by a stream of electrons from the sun, the aurora should, of course, be "bipolar," meaning that it should appear near both the North and South Poles simultaneously. The practical difficulty here was that when the North Pole has winter and darkness, the South Pole has summer and bright daylight, so that an *aurora australis*, if there were one, would simply be invisible with the sun shining in the southern sky at the same time.

This practical problem has been solved by means of an instrument especially developed for the International Geophysical Year. The answer was affirmative; auroras *are* bipolar. The other problem of the time lag is, in all probability, answered by the discovery of the Van Allen layer by artificial satellite *Explorer I*. The Van Allen layer is a double layer of charged subatomic particles around the earth. The inner layer, with its center some 1,500 miles from the ground, reached from about 40° N. to about 40° S. and does not touch the atmosphere. The outer layer, much larger and with its center several thousand miles from the ground, does touch the atmosphere in the vicinity of the magnetic poles.

It seems probable that the "leakage" of electrons from the outer Van Allen layer causes the auroras. A new burst of electrons from the sun seems to be caught in the outer layer first. Under the assumption that all electrons are first caught in the outer layer, the time lag can be understood. There has to be an "overflow" from the outer layer to produce an aurora.

## The Atmosphere

Astronomically speaking, the presence of our atmosphere is deplorable. Though reasonably transparent to visible light, the atmosphere may absorb as much as 60 per

## Notable Telescopes of the World

### Refractor Telescopes

| Size in inches | Observatory | Location |
|---|---|---|
| 40 | Yerkes | Williams Bay, Wis. |
| 36 | Lick | Mt. Hamilton, Calif. |
| 32.7 | Paris (Univ. of) | Meudon, France |
| 31.5 | Astrophysical | Potsdam, Germany |
| 30 | Allegheny | Pittsburgh, Pa. |
| 30 | Bischoffsheim | Nice, France |
| 30 | Poulkova | Leningrad, U.S.S.R. |

### Reflector Telescopes

| | | |
|---|---|---|
| 200 | Palomar | Palomar Mt., Calif. |
| 120 | Lick | Mt. Hamilton, Calif. |
| 100 | Mt. Wilson | Pasadena, Calif. |
| 82 | McDonald | Mt. Locke, Texas |
| 74 | Dunlap | Richmond Hill, Ont. |
| 72 | Lord Ross (dismantled) | Parsonstown, Ireland |
| 72 | Dominion Astrophysical | Victoria, B. C. |
| 69 | Perkins | Delaware, Ohio |
| 61 | Harvard | Harvard, Mass. |
| 60 | Bloemfontein | Bloemfontein, U. of S. Af. |
| 60 | Mt. Wilson | Pasadena, Calif. |
| 60 | Córdoba | Bosque Alegre, Argentina |

## Radio Telescopes

| Diameter in feet | Location | Remarks |
|---|---|---|
| 250 | Jodrell Bank, England | ....... |
| 210 | St. Mary's, Sydney, Australia | building |
| 142 | Palo Alto, Calif. | building |
| 90 | Owens Valley, Calif. | (290 ft.) |
| 84 | Millstone Hill, Mass. | ....... |
| 82 | Dwingeloo, Netherlands | ....... |
| 82 | White Lake, B. C., Canada | building |
| 60 | Lebedev Institute, Crimea | ....... |
| 40 | Table Mesa, Calif. | ....... |

cent of the visible and near-visible light. It is opaque to most other wavelengths, except certain fairly short radio waves. In addition to absorbing much light, our atmosphere bends light rays entering slantwise (for a given observer) so that the true position of a star not too high above the horizon is not what is seems to be. One effect is that we see the sun above the horizon before it actually is. And the steady movement of the atmosphere causes the "twinkling" of the stars, which may be romantic but is a nuisance when it comes to observing. On "bad" nights the image of a star may jump out of the narrow field of vision of a telescope.

The composition of our atmosphere near the ground is 78 per cent nitrogen and 21 per cent oxygen, the remaining 1 per cent consisting of other gases, most of it argon. The composition stays the same to an altitude of at least 70 miles (except that higher up two impurities, carbon dioxide and water vapor, are missing) but the pressure drops very fast. At 18,000 feet half of the total mass of the atmosphere is below, and at 100,000 feet, 99 per cent of the mass of the atmosphere is below. The upper limit of the atmosphere is usually given as 120 miles; no definitive figure is possible, since there is no boundary line between the incredibly attenuated gases 120 miles up and space.

## Time and Calendar

The two natural cycles on which time measurements are based are the year and the day. The year is defined as the time required for the earth to complete one revolution around the sun, while the day is the time required for the earth to complete one turn upon its axis. Unfortunately the earth needs 365 days plus about six hours to go around the sun once, so that the year does not consist of so and so many days; the fractional day has to be taken care of by an extra day every fourth year.

But because the earth, while turning upon its axis, also moves around the sun there are two kinds of days. A day may be defined as the interval between the highest point of the sun in the sky on two successive days. This, averaged out over the year, produces the customary 24-hour day. But one might also define a day as the time interval between the moments when a certain point in the sky, say a conveniently located star, is directly overhead. This is called

*Siderial time.* Astronomers use a point which they call the "vernal equinox" for the actual determination. Such a sidereal day is somewhat shorter than the "solar day," namely by about 3 minutes and 56 seconds of so-called "mean solar time."

*Apparent solar time* is the time based directly on the sun's position in the sky. In ordinary life the day runs from midnight to midnight. It begins when the sun is invisible by being 12 hours from its zenith. Astronomers use the so-called "Julian Day," which runs from noon to noon; the concept was invented by the astronomer Joseph Scaliger, who named it after his father Julius. To avoid the problems caused by leap-year days and so forth, Scaliger picked a conveniently remote date in the past and suggested just counting days without regard to weeks, months and years. The Julian Day 2,437,665.5 is January 1, 1962. The reason for having the Julian Day run from noon to noon is the practical one that astronomical observations usually extend across the midnight hour, which would require a change in date (or in the Julian Day number) if the astronomical day, like the civil day, ran from midnight to midnight.

*Mean solar time,* rather than apparent solar time, is what is actually used most of the time. The mean solar time is based on the position of a fictitious "mean sun." The reason why this fictitious sun has to be introduced is the following: the earth turns on its axis regularly; it needs the same number of seconds regardless of the season. But the movement of the earth around the sun is not regular because the earth's orbit is an ellipse. This has the result (as explained in the section The Seasons) that the earth moves faster in January and slower in July. Though it is the earth which changes velocity it looks to us as if the sun did. In January, when the earth moves faster, the *apparent* movement of the sun looks faster. The "mean sun" of time measurements, then, is a sun which moves regularly all year round; the real sun will be either ahead or behind the "mean sun." The difference between the real sun and the fictitious mean sun is called the *equation of time.*

When the real sun is west of the mean sun we have the "sun fast" condition, with the real sun crossing the meridian ahead of the mean sun. The opposite is the "sun slow" situation when the real sun crosses the meridian after the mean sun. Of course what is observed is the real sun. The equation of time is needed to establish mean solar time, which is kept by the reference clocks.

But if all clocks were actually set by mean solar time we would be plagued by a welter of time differences which would be "correct" but a major nuisance. A clock on Long Island, correctly showing mean solar time for its location (this would be *local civil time*) would be slightly ahead of a clock in Newark, New Jersey. The Newark clock would be slightly ahead of a clock in Trenton, New Jersey which, in turn, would be ahead of a clock in Philadelphia. This condition actually prevailed in the past until 1883.

*Standard time* was introduced. Standard time is the correct mean solar time for a designated meridian, and this time is used for a certain area to the east and west of this meridian. In the United States four meridians have been designated to supply standard times; they are 75°, 90°, 105° and 120° west of Greenwich. The 75° meridian determines Eastern Standard Time. It happens to run through Camden, New Jersey, where standard time, therefore, is actual mean solar time and local civil time. The 90° meridian (which happens to pass through the western part of Memphis, Tenn.) determines Central Standard Time, the 105° meridian (passing through Denver) determines Mountain Standard Time and the 120° meridian (which runs through Lake Tahoe) determines Pacific Standard Time.

Canada, extending over more territory

# Perpetual Calendar 1800-2000 A.D.

| Day of the month | Jan. Oct. | Apr. Jul. *Jan.* | Sept. Dec. | Jun. | Feb. Mar. Nov. | Aug. *Feb.* | May | |
|---|---|---|---|---|---|---|---|---|
| 1  8 15 22 29 | A | B | C | D | E | F | G | Mon. |
| 2  9 16 23 30 | G | A | B | C | D | E | F | Tue. |
| 3 10 17 24 31 | F | G | A | B | C | D | E | Wed. |
| 4 11 18 25 | E | F | G | A | B | C | D | Thur. |
| 5 12 19 26 | D | E | F | G | A | B | C | Fri. |
| 6 13 20 27 | C | D | E | F | G | A | B | Sat. |
| 7 14 21 28 | B | C | D | E | F | G | A | Sun. |

### EXAMPLES

(1) Given Nov. 20, 1891, to find the day of the week. Under Nov., opposite 20, is G. In the 1891 column, opposite G is Fri., *ans.*

(2) Given Fri., Oct. —, 1868, to find the possible days of the month. In the 1868 column, opposite Fri. is G. Under Oct., G gives 2, 9, 16, 23, 30, *ans.* the Fridays of Oct., 1868.

(3) Given Mon., — 5, 1811, to find the possible months. In the 1811 column, opposite Mon. is B. Opposite 5, B gives Aug., the only common-year month available, *ans.*

(4) Given Sat., Feb. 29, —, to find the possible years. Under Feb., leap-year, opposite 29, is F. Opposite Sat. F gives leap-years 1812, 1840 1868, 1896, etc., *ans.*

NOTE: In leap-years (those shown in italics), use the Jan. and Feb. in italics, but do not use these for common years. The years 1800 and 1900 were not leap-years; 2000 will be a leap-year.

| Jan. Oct. | Apr. Jul. *Jan.* | Sept. Dec. | Jun. | Feb. Mar. Nov. | Aug. *Feb.* | May |
|---|---|---|---|---|---|---|
| .... | .... | 1800 | 1801 | 1802 | 1803 | .... |
| 1804 | 1805 | 1806 | 1807 | .... | 1808 | 1809 |
| 1810 | 1811 | .... | 1812 | 1813 | 1814 | 1815 |
| .... | 1816 | 1817 | 1818 | 1819 | .... | 1820 |
| 1821 | 1822 | 1823 | .... | 1824 | 1825 | 1826 |
| 1827 | .... | 1828 | 1829 | 1830 | 1831 | .... |
| 1832 | 1833 | 1834 | 1835 | .... | 1836 | 1837 |
| 1838 | 1839 | .... | 1840 | 1841 | 1842 | 1843 |
| .... | 1844 | 1845 | 1846 | 1847 | .... | 1848 |
| 1849 | 1850 | 1851 | .... | 1852 | 1853 | 1854 |
| 1855 | .... | 1856 | 1857 | 1858 | 1859 | .... |
| 1860 | 1861 | 1862 | 1863 | .... | 1864 | 1865 |
| 1866 | 1867 | .... | 1868 | 1869 | 1870 | 1871 |
| .... | 1872 | 1873 | 1874 | 1875 | .... | 1876 |
| 1877 | 1878 | 1879 | .... | 1880 | 1881 | 1882 |
| 1883 | .... | 1884 | 1885 | 1886 | 1887 | .... |
| 1888 | 1889 | 1890 | 1891 | .... | 1892 | 1893 |
| 1894 | 1895 | .... | 1896 | 1897 | 1898 | 1899 |
| 1900 | 1901 | 1902 | 1903 | .... | 1904 | 1905 |
| 1906 | 1907 | .... | 1908 | 1909 | 1910 | 1911 |
| .... | 1912 | 1913 | 1914 | 1915 | .... | 1916 |
| 1917 | 1918 | 1919 | .... | 1920 | 1921 | 1922 |
| 1923 | .... | 1924 | 1925 | 1926 | 1927 | .... |
| 1928 | 1929 | 1930 | 1931 | .... | 1932 | 1933 |
| 1934 | 1935 | .... | 1936 | 1937 | 1938 | 1939 |
| .... | 1940 | 1941 | 1942 | 1943 | .... | 1944 |
| 1945 | 1946 | 1947 | .... | 1948 | 1949 | 1950 |
| 1951 | .... | 1952 | 1953 | 1954 | 1955 | .... |
| 1956 | 1957 | 1958 | 1959 | .... | 1960 | 1961 |
| 1962 | 1963 | .... | 1964 | 1965 | 1966 | 1967 |
| .... | 1968 | 1969 | 1970 | 1971 | .... | 1972 |
| 1973 | 1974 | 1975 | .... | 1976 | 1977 | 1978 |
| 1979 | .... | 1980 | 1981 | 1982 | 1983 | .... |
| 1984 | 1985 | 1986 | 1987 | .... | 1988 | 1989 |
| 1990 | 1991 | .... | 1992 | 1993 | 1994 | 1995 |
| .... | 1996 | 1997 | 1998 | 1999 | .... | 2000 |

## Symbols

| | | |
|---|---|---|
| ☉ the sun | ♃ Jupiter | ⚹ occultation |
| ☽ the moon | ♄ Saturn | ☍ opposition |
| ☿ Mercury | ♅ Uranus | ● new moon |
| ♀ Venus | ♆ Neptune | ☽ first quarter |
| ⊕ the earth | ♇ Pluto | ○ full moon |
| ♂ Mars | ☌ conjunction | ☾ last quarter |

## The Zodiac and Average Date of Sun Entering

| Sign | | Constellation | Sign | | Constellation |
|---|---|---|---|---|---|
| Aries | Mar. 21 | Apr. 18 | Libra | Sept. 23 | Oct. 31 |
| Taurus | Apr. 20 | May 14 | Scorpius | Oct. 23 | Nov. 23 |
| Gemini | May 21 | June 21 | [Ophiuchus] | | Nov. 29 |
| Cancer | June 21 | July 20 | Sagittarius | Nov. 22 | Dec. 17 |
| Leo | July 23 | Aug. 10 | Capricornus | Dec. 22 | Jan. 19 |
| Virgo | Aug. 23 | Sept. 16 | Aquarius | Jan. 20 | Feb. 16 |
| | | | Pisces | Feb. 19 | Mar. 11 |

from west to east, adds one time zone on either side: Atlantic Standard Time (based on 60° west of Greenwich) for New Brunswick, Nova Scotia and Québec, and Yukon Standard Time (determined by the 135° meridian) for its extreme West. Alaska, extending still farther to the west, adds two more time zones, Alaska Standard Time (determined by the 150° meridian which passes through Anchorage) and Nome Standard Time, based on the 165° meridian just east of Nome.

In general the earth is divided into 24 such time zones, which run one hour apart. For practical purposes the time zones sometimes show indentations and there are a few "subzones" which differ from the neighboring zone by only half an hour, e.g., Newfoundland.

*The Date-line.* While the time zones are based on the natural event of the sun crossing the meridian, the date must be an arbitrary decision. The meridians are traditionally counted from the meridian of the observatory of Greenwich in England, which is called the zero meridian. The logical place for changing the date is 12 hours, or 180°, from Greenwich. Fortunately the 180th meridian runs mostly through the open Pacific. The date line makes a zig-zag in the north to incorporate the eastern tip of Siberia into the Siberian time system and then another one to incorporate a number of islands into the Alaska time system. In the south there is a similar zig-zag for the purpose of tying a number of British-owned islands to the New Zealand time system. Otherwise the date line is the same as 180° from Greenwich. At points to the east of the date-line the calendar is one day earlier than at points to the west of it. A traveller going eastward across the date-line from one island to another would not have to re-set his watch because he would stay inside the time zone (provided he does so where the date-line does *not* coincide with the 180° meridian), but it would be the same time of the previous day.

## The Seasons

The seasons are caused by the tilt of the earth's axis (23½°) and not by the fact that the earth's orbit around the sun is an ellipse. The average distance of the

earth from the sun is 93 million miles; the difference between aphelion (farthest away) and perihelion (closest to the sun) is 3 million miles, so that perihelion is about 91½ million miles from the sun. The earth goes through the perihelion point a few days after New Year, just when the northern hemisphere has winter. Aphelion is passed during the first days in July. This by itself shows that the distance from the sun is not important within these limits. What is important is that when the earth passes through perihelion, the northern end of the earth's axis happens to tilt away from the sun, so that the places beyond the Tropic of Cancer receive only slanting rays from a sun low in the sky.*

The tilt of the earth's axis is responsible for four lines you find on every globe. When, say, the North Pole is tilted away from the sun as much as possible, the farthest points in the North which can still be reached by the sun's rays is 23½° from the pole. This is the Arctic Circle. The Antarctic Circle is the corresponding limit 23½° from the South Pole; the sun's rays cannot reach beyond this point when we have mid-summer in the North.

When the sun is vertically above the equator, the day is of equal length all over the earth. This happens twice a year, and these are the "equinoxes" in March and in September. After having been over the equator in March, the sun will seem to move northward. The northernmost point where the sun can be straight overhead is 23½° north of the equator. This is the Tropic of Cancer; the sun can never be vertically overhead to the north of this line. Similarly the sun cannot be vertically overhead to the south of a line 23½° south of the equator—the Tropic of Capricorn.

This explains the climatic zones. In the belt (the Greek word *zone* means "belt") between the Tropic of Cancer and the Tropic of Capricorn, the sun can be straight overhead; this is the tropical zone. The two zones where the sun cannot be overhead but will be above the horizon every day of the year are the two temperate zones; the two areas where the sun will not rise at all for varying lengths of time are the two polar areas, Arctic and Antarctic.

\* The earth passes perihelion (point of its orbit closest to the sun) on January 2 and aphelion (point of the orbit farthest from the sun) on July 5.

# Astronomical Events

## Eclipses

There will be five eclipses in 1962—two of the sun and three of the moon. The dates for the eclipses of the sun are February 4–5 and July 31; the dates for the

eclipses of the moon are February 19, July 17, and August 15. The majority of these eclipses will not be visible from the United States.

*1. Total eclipse of the sun,* February 4–5.

The path of totality extends across the Pacific Ocean. The only major land across which it goes is New Guinea. The beginning will be visible from the sea coast portion of the states bordering the Pacific and from Hawaii, but not from Alaska.

2. *Partial eclipse of the moon,* February 19. The beginning will be visible in North America, the northwestern portion of South America, the Pacific Ocean, Australia, New Zealand, and eastern Asia. The end will be visible from Alaska, Asia, and eastern Europe.

Moon enters penumbra   6:04.4 A.M., E.S.T.
Middle of eclipse      8:03.2 A.M.
Moon leaves penumbra   10:02.0 A.M.

(The moon does not enter the umbra in any of the three 1962 eclipses.)

3. *Partial eclipse of the moon,* July 17. The beginning will be visible in North America (except the northeastern section), western South America, Antarctica, Australia, New Zealand, and the east coast of Asia. The end will be visible from the same areas, but as far as North America is concerned, only from the extreme tip of Alaska.

Moon enters penumbra   5:27.4 A.M., E.S.T.
Middle of eclipse      6:54.4 A.M.
Moon leaves penumbra   8:21.5 A.M.

4. *Annular eclipse of the sun* (sun appears as a luminous ring along the center of the eclipse path), July 31. The eclipse path extends across northern Madagascar, central Africa, and the central Atlantic Ocean to the northern part of South America. The only section of the United States where the eclipse will be visible (at sunrise) is Florida

and the southeastern portion of Georgia.

5. *Partial eclipse of the moon,* August 15. Not visible from the United States. The beginning will be visible in Australia, New Zealand, southern and southeastern Asia, eastern Europe, and eastern Africa. The end will be visible from western Australia, Asia except the northeastern part, Europe, Africa, and the southern Atlantic Ocean.

Moon enters penumbra   1:15.8 P.M., E.S.T.
Middle of eclipse      2:57.1 P.M.
Moon leaves penumbra   4:38.5 P.M.

## Mercury and Venus

The planet Mercury will assume the position of greatest elongation (maximum angular distance from the sun, as seen from the earth) six times during 1962. The dates are:

Jan. 20 at 7 P.M., E.S.T. Eastern elongation of 19°

Mar. 3 at midnight, E.S.T. Western elongation of 27°

May 13 at 5 P.M., E.S.T. Eastern elongation of 22°

July 1 at 7 A.M., E.S.T. Western elongation of 22°

Sept. 10 at 6 P.M., E.S.T. Eastern elongation of 27°

Oct. 21 at 11 P.M., E.S.T. Western elongation of 18°

The planet Venus reaches greatest elongation (east) of 46° on Sept. 3 at 2 P.M., E.S.T. Greatest brilliancy is reached twice —the first time on Oct. 8 at 5 P.M., E.S.T. (magnitude —4.3), and the second time on Dec. 18 at 7 P.M., E.S.T. (magnitude —4.4).

---

# Morning and Evening Stars, 1962

### MERCURY

Evening star, Jan 1 to Feb. 5
Morning star, Feb. 5 to Apr. 16
Evening star, Apr. 16 to June 7
Morning star, June 7 to July 29
Evening star, July 29 to Oct. 6
Morning star, Oct. 6 to Nov. 25
Evening star, Nov. 25 to Dec. 31

### VENUS

Morning star, Jan. 1 to Jan. 27
Evening star, Jan. 27 to Nov. 12
Morning star, Nov. 12 to Dec. 31

### MARS

Morning star, Jan. 1 to Dec. 31

### JUPITER

Evening star, Jan. 1 to Feb. 8
Morning star, Feb. 8 to Aug. 31
Evening star, Aug. 31 to Dec. 31

### SATURN

Evening star, Jan. 1 to Jan. 22
Morning star, Jan. 22 to July 31
Evening star, July 31 to Dec. 31

### URANUS

Morning star, Jan. 1 to Feb. 17
Evening star, Feb. 17 to Aug. 24
Morning star, Aug. 24 to Dec. 31

### NEPTUNE

Morning star, Jan. 1 to May 3
Evening star, May 3 to Nov. 6
Morning star, Nov. 6 to Dec. 31

### PLUTO

Morning star, Jan. 1 to Feb. 27
Evening star, Feb. 27 to Sept. 2
Morning star, Sept. 2 to Dec. 31

# Phases of the Moon for 1962

| | Date | E. S. T. | C. S. T. | M. S. T. | P. S. T. |
|---|---|---|---|---|---|
| New moon     JANUARY......... | 6 | 7:36 A | 6:36 A | 5:36 A | 4:36 A |
| First quarter.................... | 13 | 0:02 A | *11:02 P | *10:02 P | *9:02 P |
| Full moon...................... | 20 | 1:17 P | 12:17 P | 11:17 A | 10:17 A |
| Last quarter.................... | 28 | 6:37 P | 5:37 P | 4:37 P | 3:37 P |
| New moon     FEBRUARY........ | 4 | 7:10 P | 6:10 P | 5:10 P | 4:10 P |
| First quarter.................... | 11 | 10:50 A | 9:50 A | 8:50 A | 7:50 A |
| Full moon...................... | 19 | 8:18 A | 7:18 A | 6:18 A | 5:18 A |
| Last quarter.................... | 27 | 10:50 A | 9:50 A | 8:50 A | 7:50 A |
| New moon     MARCH.......... | 6 | 5:31 A | 4:31 A | 3:31 A | 2:31 A |
| First quarter.................... | 12 | 11:39 P | 10:39 P | 9:39 P | 8:39 P |
| Full moon...................... | 21 | 2:56 A | 1:56 A | 0:56 A | *11:56 P |
| Last quarter.................... | 28 | 11:11 P | 10:11 P | 9:11 P | 8:11 P |
| New moon     APRIL........... | 4 | 2:45 P | 1:45 P | 12:45 P | 11:45 A |
| First quarter.................... | 11 | 2:51 P | 1:51 P | 12:51 P | 11:51 A |
| Full moon...................... | 19 | 7:34 P | 6:34 P | 5:34 P | 4:34 P |
| Last quarter.................... | 27 | 8:00 A | 7:00 A | 6:00 A | 5:00 A |
| New moon     MAY............. | 3 | 11:25 P | 10:25 P | 9:25 P | 8:25 P |
| First quarter.................... | 11 | 7:45 A | 6:45 A | 5:45 A | 4:45 A |
| Full moon...................... | 19 | 9:32 A | 8:32 A | 7:32 A | 6:32 A |
| Last quarter.................... | 26 | 2:06 P | 1:06 P | 12:06 P | 11:06 A |
| New moon     JUNE............ | 2 | 8:27 A | 7:27 A | 6:27 A | 5:27 A |
| First quarter.................... | 01 | 1:22 A | 0:22 A | *11:22 P | *10:22 P |
| Full moon...................... | 17 | 9:03 P | 8:03 P | 7:03 P | 6:03 P |
| Last quarter.................... | 24 | 6:43 P | 5:43 P | 4:43 P | 3:43 P |
| New moon     JULY............ | 1 | 6:53 P | 5:53 P | 4:53 P | 3:53 P |
| First quarter.................... | 9 | 6:40 P | 5:40 P | 4:40 P | 3:40 P |
| Full moon...................... | 17 | 6:41 A | 5:41 A | 4:41 A | 3:41 A |
| Last quarter.................... | 23 | 11:19 P | 10:19 P | 9:19 P | 8:19 P |
| New moon...................... | 31 | 7:24 A | 6:24 A | 5:24 A | 4:24 A |
| First quarter     AUGUST........... | 8 | 10:55 A | 9:55 A | 8:55 A | 7:55 A |
| Full moon...................... | 15 | 3:10 A | 2:10 P | 1:10 P | 12:10 P |
| Last quarter.................... | 22 | 5:27 A | 4:27 A | 3:27 A | 2:27 A |
| New moon...................... | 29 | 10:09 P | 9:09 P | 8:09 P | 7:09 P |
| First quarter     SEPTEMBER....... | 7 | 1:06 A | 0:06 A | *11:06 P | *10:06 P |
| Full moon...................... | 13 | 11:12 P | 10:12 P | 9:12 P | 8:12 P |
| Last quarter.................... | 20 | 2:36 P | 1:36 P | 12:36 P | 11:36 A |
| New moon...................... | 28 | 2:40 P | 1:40 P | 12:40 P | 11:40 A |
| First quarter     OCTOBER......... | 6 | 2:55 P | 1:55 P | 12:55 P | 11:55 A |
| Full moon...................... | 13 | 7:33 A | 6:33 A | 5:33 A | 4:33 A |
| Last quarter.................... | 20 | 3:48 A | 2:48 A | 1:48 A | 0:48 A |
| New moon...................... | 28 | 8:05 A | 7:05 A | 6:05 A | 5:05 A |
| First quarter     NOVEMBER....... | 5 | 2:15 A | 1:15 A | 0:15 A | *11:15 P |
| Full moon...................... | 11 | 5:04 P | 4:04 P | 3:04 P | 2:04 P |
| Last quarter.................... | 18 | 9:10 P | 8:10 P | 7:10 P | 6:10 P |
| New moon...................... | 27 | 1:30 A | 0:30 A | *11:30 P | *10:30 P |
| First quarter     DECEMBER......... | 4 | 11:48 A | 10:48 A | 9:48 A | 8:48 A |
| Full moon...................... | 11 | 4:28 A | 3:28 A | 2:28 A | 1:28 A |
| Last quarter.................... | 18 | 5:43 P | 4:43 P | 3:43 P | 2:43 P |
| New moon...................... | 26 | 5:59 P | 4:59 P | 3:59 P | 2:59 P |

* On the previous day.

## 1961

### JANUARY
| S | M | T | W | T | F | S |
|---|---|---|---|---|---|---|
| 1 | 2 | 3 | 4 | 5 | 6 | 7 |
| 8 | 9 | 10 | 11 | 12 | 13 | 14 |
| 15 | 16 | 17 | 18 | 19 | 20 | 21 |
| 22 | 23 | 24 | 25 | 26 | 27 | 28 |
| 29 | 30 | 31 | – | – | – | – |

### FEBRUARY
| S | M | T | W | T | F | S |
|---|---|---|---|---|---|---|
| – | – | – | 1 | 2 | 3 | 4 |
| 5 | 6 | 7 | 8 | 9 | 10 | 11 |
| 12 | 13 | 14 | 15 | 16 | 17 | 18 |
| 19 | 20 | 21 | 22 | 23 | 24 | 25 |
| 26 | 27 | 28 | | | | |

### MARCH
| S | M | T | W | T | F | S |
|---|---|---|---|---|---|---|
| – | – | – | 1 | 2 | 3 | 4 |
| 5 | 6 | 7 | 8 | 9 | 10 | 11 |
| 12 | 13 | 14 | 15 | 16 | 17 | 18 |
| 19 | 20 | 21 | 22 | 23 | 24 | 25 |
| 26 | 27 | 28 | 29 | 30 | 31 | – |

### APRIL
| S | M | T | W | T | F | S |
|---|---|---|---|---|---|---|
| – | – | – | – | – | – | 1 |
| 2 | 3 | 4 | 5 | 6 | 7 | 8 |
| 9 | 10 | 11 | 12 | 13 | 14 | 15 |
| 16 | 17 | 18 | 19 | 20 | 21 | 22 |
| 23/30 | 24 | 25 | 26 | 27 | 28 | 29 |

### MAY
| S | M | T | W | T | F | S |
|---|---|---|---|---|---|---|
| – | 1 | 2 | 3 | 4 | 5 | 6 |
| 7 | 8 | 9 | 10 | 11 | 12 | 13 |
| 14 | 15 | 16 | 17 | 18 | 19 | 20 |
| 21 | 22 | 23 | 24 | 25 | 26 | 27 |
| 28 | 29 | 30 | 31 | – | – | – |

### JUNE
| S | M | T | W | T | F | S |
|---|---|---|---|---|---|---|
| – | – | – | – | 1 | 2 | 3 |
| 4 | 5 | 6 | 7 | 8 | 9 | 10 |
| 11 | 12 | 13 | 14 | 15 | 16 | 17 |
| 18 | 19 | 20 | 21 | 22 | 23 | 24 |
| 25 | 26 | 27 | 28 | 29 | 30 | – |

### JULY
| S | M | T | W | T | F | S |
|---|---|---|---|---|---|---|
| – | – | – | – | – | – | 1 |
| 2 | 3 | 4 | 5 | 6 | 7 | 8 |
| 9 | 10 | 11 | 12 | 13 | 14 | 15 |
| 16 | 17 | 18 | 19 | 20 | 21 | 22 |
| 23/30 | 24/31 | 25 | 26 | 27 | 28 | 29 |

### AUGUST
| S | M | T | W | T | F | S |
|---|---|---|---|---|---|---|
| – | – | 1 | 2 | 3 | 4 | 5 |
| 6 | 7 | 8 | 9 | 10 | 11 | 12 |
| 13 | 14 | 15 | 16 | 17 | 18 | 19 |
| 20 | 21 | 22 | 23 | 24 | 25 | 26 |
| 27 | 28 | 29 | 30 | 31 | – | – |

### SEPTEMBER
| S | M | T | W | T | F | S |
|---|---|---|---|---|---|---|
| – | – | – | – | – | 1 | 2 |
| 3 | 4 | 5 | 6 | 7 | 8 | 9 |
| 10 | 11 | 12 | 13 | 14 | 15 | 16 |
| 17 | 18 | 19 | 20 | 21 | 22 | 23 |
| 24 | 25 | 26 | 27 | 28 | 29 | 30 |

### OCTOBER
| S | M | T | W | T | F | S |
|---|---|---|---|---|---|---|
| 1 | 2 | 3 | 4 | 5 | 6 | 7 |
| 8 | 9 | 10 | 11 | 12 | 13 | 14 |
| 15 | 16 | 17 | 18 | 19 | 20 | 21 |
| 22 | 23 | 24 | 25 | 26 | 27 | 28 |
| 29 | 30 | 31 | – | – | – | – |

### NOVEMBER
| S | M | T | W | T | F | S |
|---|---|---|---|---|---|---|
| – | – | – | 1 | 2 | 3 | 4 |
| 5 | 6 | 7 | 8 | 9 | 10 | 11 |
| 12 | 13 | 14 | 15 | 16 | 17 | 18 |
| 19 | 20 | 21 | 22 | 23 | 24 | 25 |
| 26 | 27 | 28 | 29 | 30 | – | – |

### DECEMBER
| S | M | T | W | T | F | S |
|---|---|---|---|---|---|---|
| – | – | – | – | – | 1 | 2 |
| 3 | 4 | 5 | 6 | 7 | 8 | 9 |
| 10 | 11 | 12 | 13 | 14 | 15 | 16 |
| 17 | 18 | 19 | 20 | 21 | 22 | 23 |
| 24/31 | 25 | 26 | 27 | 28 | 29 | 30 |

## 1962

### JANUARY
| S | M | T | W | T | F | S |
|---|---|---|---|---|---|---|
| – | 1 | 2 | 3 | 4 | 5 | 6 |
| 7 | 8 | 9 | 10 | 11 | 12 | 13 |
| 14 | 15 | 16 | 17 | 18 | 19 | 20 |
| 21 | 22 | 23 | 24 | 25 | 26 | 27 |
| 28 | 29 | 30 | 31 | – | – | – |

### FEBRUARY
| S | M | T | W | T | F | S |
|---|---|---|---|---|---|---|
| – | – | – | – | 1 | 2 | 3 |
| 4 | 5 | 6 | 7 | 8 | 9 | 10 |
| 11 | 12 | 13 | 14 | 15 | 16 | 17 |
| 18 | 19 | 20 | 21 | 22 | 23 | 24 |
| 25 | 26 | 27 | 28 | | | |

### MARCH
| S | M | T | W | T | F | S |
|---|---|---|---|---|---|---|
| – | – | – | – | 1 | 2 | 3 |
| 4 | 5 | 6 | 7 | 8 | 9 | 10 |
| 11 | 12 | 13 | 14 | 15 | 16 | 17 |
| 18 | 19 | 20 | 21 | 22 | 23 | 24 |
| 25 | 26 | 27 | 28 | 29 | 30 | 31 |

### APRIL
| S | M | T | W | T | F | S |
|---|---|---|---|---|---|---|
| 1 | 2 | 3 | 4 | 5 | 6 | 7 |
| 8 | 9 | 10 | 11 | 12 | 13 | 14 |
| 15 | 16 | 17 | 18 | 19 | 20 | 21 |
| 22 | 23 | 24 | 25 | 26 | 27 | 28 |
| 29 | 30 | – | – | – | – | – |

### MAY
| S | M | T | W | T | F | S |
|---|---|---|---|---|---|---|
| – | – | 1 | 2 | 3 | 4 | 5 |
| 6 | 7 | 8 | 9 | 10 | 11 | 12 |
| 13 | 14 | 15 | 16 | 17 | 18 | 19 |
| 20 | 21 | 22 | 23 | 24 | 25 | 26 |
| 27 | 28 | 29 | 30 | 31 | – | – |

### JUNE
| S | M | T | W | T | F | S |
|---|---|---|---|---|---|---|
| – | – | – | – | – | 1 | 2 |
| 3 | 4 | 5 | 6 | 7 | 8 | 9 |
| 10 | 11 | 12 | 13 | 14 | 15 | 16 |
| 17 | 18 | 19 | 20 | 21 | 22 | 23 |
| 24 | 25 | 26 | 27 | 28 | 29 | 30 |

### JULY
| S | M | T | W | T | F | S |
|---|---|---|---|---|---|---|
| 1 | 2 | 3 | 4 | 5 | 6 | 7 |
| 8 | 9 | 10 | 11 | 12 | 13 | 14 |
| 15 | 16 | 17 | 18 | 19 | 20 | 21 |
| 22 | 23 | 24 | 25 | 26 | 27 | 28 |
| 29 | 30 | 31 | – | – | – | – |

### AUGUST
| S | M | T | W | T | F | S |
|---|---|---|---|---|---|---|
| – | – | – | 1 | 2 | 3 | 4 |
| 5 | 6 | 7 | 8 | 9 | 10 | 11 |
| 12 | 13 | 14 | 15 | 16 | 17 | 18 |
| 19 | 20 | 21 | 22 | 23 | 24 | 25 |
| 26 | 27 | 28 | 29 | 30 | 31 | – |

### SEPTEMBER
| S | M | T | W | T | F | S |
|---|---|---|---|---|---|---|
| – | – | – | – | – | – | 1 |
| 2 | 3 | 4 | 5 | 6 | 7 | 8 |
| 9 | 10 | 11 | 12 | 13 | 14 | 15 |
| 16 | 17 | 18 | 19 | 20 | 21 | 22 |
| 23/30 | 24 | 25 | 26 | 27 | 28 | 29 |

### OCTOBER
| S | M | T | W | T | F | S |
|---|---|---|---|---|---|---|
| – | 1 | 2 | 3 | 4 | 5 | 6 |
| 7 | 8 | 9 | 10 | 11 | 12 | 13 |
| 14 | 15 | 16 | 17 | 18 | 19 | 20 |
| 21 | 22 | 23 | 24 | 25 | 26 | 27 |
| 28 | 29 | 30 | 31 | – | – | – |

### NOVEMBER
| S | M | T | W | T | F | S |
|---|---|---|---|---|---|---|
| – | – | – | – | 1 | 2 | 3 |
| 4 | 5 | 6 | 7 | 8 | 9 | 10 |
| 11 | 12 | 13 | 14 | 15 | 16 | 17 |
| 18 | 19 | 20 | 21 | 22 | 23 | 24 |
| 25 | 26 | 27 | 28 | 29 | 30 | – |

### DECEMBER
| S | M | T | W | T | F | S |
|---|---|---|---|---|---|---|
| – | – | – | – | – | – | 1 |
| 2 | 3 | 4 | 5 | 6 | 7 | 8 |
| 9 | 10 | 11 | 12 | 13 | 14 | 15 |
| 16 | 17 | 18 | 19 | 20 | 21 | 22 |
| 23/30 | 24/31 | 25 | 26 | 27 | 28 | 29 |

## 1963

### JANUARY
| S | M | T | W | T | F | S |
|---|---|---|---|---|---|---|
| – | – | 1 | 2 | 3 | 4 | 5 |
| 6 | 7 | 8 | 9 | 10 | 11 | 12 |
| 13 | 14 | 15 | 16 | 17 | 18 | 19 |
| 20 | 21 | 22 | 23 | 24 | 25 | 26 |
| 27 | 28 | 29 | 30 | 31 | – | – |

### FEBRUARY
| S | M | T | W | T | F | S |
|---|---|---|---|---|---|---|
| – | – | – | – | – | 1 | 2 |
| 3 | 4 | 5 | 6 | 7 | 8 | 9 |
| 10 | 11 | 12 | 13 | 14 | 15 | 16 |
| 17 | 18 | 19 | 20 | 21 | 22 | 23 |
| 24 | 25 | 26 | 27 | 28 | – | – |

### MARCH
| S | M | T | W | T | F | S |
|---|---|---|---|---|---|---|
| – | – | – | – | – | 1 | 2 |
| 3 | 4 | 5 | 6 | 7 | 8 | 9 |
| 10 | 11 | 12 | 13 | 14 | 15 | 16 |
| 17 | 18 | 19 | 20 | 21 | 22 | 23 |
| 24/31 | 25 | 26 | 27 | 28 | 29 | 30 |

### APRIL
| S | M | T | W | T | F | S |
|---|---|---|---|---|---|---|
| – | 1 | 2 | 3 | 4 | 5 | 6 |
| 7 | 8 | 9 | 10 | 11 | 12 | 13 |
| 14 | 15 | 16 | 17 | 18 | 19 | 20 |
| 21 | 22 | 23 | 24 | 25 | 26 | 27 |
| 28 | 29 | 30 | – | – | – | – |

### MAY
| S | M | T | W | T | F | S |
|---|---|---|---|---|---|---|
| – | – | – | 1 | 2 | 3 | 4 |
| 5 | 6 | 7 | 8 | 9 | 10 | 11 |
| 12 | 13 | 14 | 15 | 16 | 17 | 18 |
| 19 | 20 | 21 | 22 | 23 | 24 | 25 |
| 26 | 27 | 28 | 29 | 30 | 31 | – |

### JUNE
| S | M | T | W | T | F | S |
|---|---|---|---|---|---|---|
| – | – | – | – | – | – | 1 |
| 2 | 3 | 4 | 5 | 6 | 7 | 8 |
| 9 | 10 | 11 | 12 | 13 | 14 | 15 |
| 16 | 17 | 18 | 19 | 20 | 21 | 22 |
| 23/30 | 24 | 25 | 26 | 27 | 28 | 29 |

### JULY
| S | M | T | W | T | F | S |
|---|---|---|---|---|---|---|
| – | 1 | 2 | 3 | 4 | 5 | 6 |
| 7 | 8 | 9 | 10 | 11 | 12 | 13 |
| 14 | 15 | 16 | 17 | 18 | 19 | 20 |
| 21 | 22 | 23 | 24 | 25 | 26 | 27 |
| 28 | 29 | 30 | 31 | – | – | – |

### AUGUST
| S | M | T | W | T | F | S |
|---|---|---|---|---|---|---|
| – | – | – | – | 1 | 2 | 3 |
| 4 | 5 | 6 | 7 | 8 | 9 | 10 |
| 11 | 12 | 13 | 14 | 15 | 16 | 17 |
| 18 | 19 | 20 | 21 | 22 | 23 | 24 |
| 25 | 26 | 27 | 28 | 29 | 30 | 31 |

### SEPTEMBER
| S | M | T | W | T | F | S |
|---|---|---|---|---|---|---|
| 1 | 2 | 3 | 4 | 5 | 6 | 7 |
| 8 | 9 | 10 | 11 | 12 | 13 | 14 |
| 15 | 16 | 17 | 18 | 19 | 20 | 21 |
| 22 | 23 | 24 | 25 | 26 | 27 | 28 |
| 29 | 30 | – | – | – | – | – |

### OCTOBER
| S | M | T | W | T | F | S |
|---|---|---|---|---|---|---|
| – | – | 1 | 2 | 3 | 4 | 5 |
| 6 | 7 | 8 | 9 | 10 | 11 | 12 |
| 13 | 14 | 15 | 16 | 17 | 18 | 19 |
| 20 | 21 | 22 | 23 | 24 | 25 | 26 |
| 27 | 28 | 29 | 30 | 31 | – | – |

### NOVEMBER
| S | M | T | W | T | F | S |
|---|---|---|---|---|---|---|
| – | – | – | – | – | 1 | 2 |
| 3 | 4 | 5 | 6 | 7 | 8 | 9 |
| 10 | 11 | 12 | 13 | 14 | 15 | 16 |
| 17 | 18 | 19 | 20 | 21 | 22 | 23 |
| 24 | 25 | 26 | 27 | 28 | 29 | 30 |

### DECEMBER
| S | M | T | W | T | F | S |
|---|---|---|---|---|---|---|
| 1 | 2 | 3 | 4 | 5 | 6 | 7 |
| 8 | 9 | 10 | 11 | 12 | 13 | 14 |
| 15 | 16 | 17 | 18 | 19 | 20 | 21 |
| 22 | 23 | 24 | 25 | 26 | 27 | 28 |
| 29 | 30 | 31 | – | – | – | – |

## Seasons for the Northern Hemisphere, 1962
### Eastern Standard Time

March 20, 9:30 P.M., sun enters sign of Aries, Spring begins.
June 21, 4:24 P.M., sun enters sign of Cancer, Summer begins.
September 23, 7:35 A.M., sun enters sign of Libra, Autumn begins.
December 22, 3:15 A.M., sun enters sign of Capricornus, Winter begins.

# Longitude, Latitude, Time and Magnetic Declination of U. S. and Canadian Cities

The last column shows the magnetic declination or angle which the magnetic meridian makes with the true (geographic) meridian. The value being marked w or e, the north end of the compass needle points west or east respectively of true north by that number of degrees.

| City | Long. w. | Lat. n. | Time* | Dec. |
|---|---|---|---|---|
| | ° ′ | ° ′ | | ° |
| Albany, N. Y. | 73 45 | 42 40 | 12:00 noon | 13 w |
| Amarillo, Tex. | 101 50 | 35 11 | 11:00 a.m. | 12 e |
| Anchorage, Alaska | 149 54 | 61 13 | 7:00 a.m. | 29 e |
| Atlanta, Ga. | 84 23 | 33 45 | 12:00 noon | 2 e |
| Atlantic City, N. J. | 74 25 | 39 22 | 12:00 noon | 10 w |
| Austin, Nev. | 117 4 | 39 29 | 9:00 a.m. | 18 e |
| Baker, Oreg. | 117 50 | 44 47 | 9:00 a.m. | 21 e |
| Baltimore, Md. | 76 38 | 39 18 | 12:00 noon | 8 w |
| Bangor, Maine | 68 47 | 44 48 | 12:00 noon | 19 w |
| Birmingham, Ala. | 86 50 | 33 30 | 11:00 a.m. | 3 e |
| Bismarck, N. Dak. | 100 47 | 46 48 | 11:00 a.m. | 14 e |
| Boise, Idaho | 116 13 | 43 36 | 10:00 a.m. | 19 e |
| Boston, Mass. | 71 5 | 42 21 | 12:00 noon | 15 w |
| Buffalo, N. Y. | 78 50 | 42 55 | 12:00 noon | 7 w |
| Calgary, Alta. | 114 1 | 51 1 | 10:00 a.m. | 23 e |
| Carlsbad, N. Mex. | 104 15 | 32 26 | 10:00 a.m. | 13 e |
| Charleston, S. C. | 79 56 | 32 47 | 12:00 noon | 2 w |
| Charleston, W. Va. | 81 38 | 38 21 | 12:00 noon | 2 w |
| Charlotte, N. C. | 80 50 | 35 14 | 12:00 noon | 2 w |
| Cheyenne, Wyo. | 104 52 | 41 9 | 10:00 a.m. | 15 e |
| Chicago, Ill. | 87 37 | 41 50 | 11:00 a.m. | 4 e |
| Cincinnati, Ohio | 84 30 | 39 8 | 12:00 noon | 1 e |
| Cleveland, Ohio | 81 37 | 41 28 | 12:00 noon | 5 w |
| Columbia, S. C. | 81 2 | 34 0 | 12:00 noon | 1 w |
| Columbus, Ohio | 83 1 | 40 0 | 12:00 noon | 2 w |
| Dallas, Tex. | 96 46 | 32 46 | 11:00 a.m. | 9 e |
| Denver, Colo. | 105 0 | 39 45 | 10:00 a.m. | 14 e |
| Des Moines, Iowa | 93 37 | 41 35 | 11:00 a.m. | 7 e |
| Detroit, Mich. | 83 3 | 42 20 | 12:00 noon | 3 w |
| Dubuque, Iowa | 90 40 | 42 31 | 11:00 a.m. | 5 e |
| Duluth, Minn. | 92 5 | 46 49 | 11:00 a.m. | 7 e |
| Eastport, Maine | 67 0 | 44 54 | 12:00 noon | 21 w |
| El Centro, Calif. | 115 33 | 32 38 | 9:00 a.m. | 15 e |
| El Paso, Tex. | 106 29 | 31 46 | 11:00 a.m. | 13 e |
| Eugene, Oreg. | 123 5 | 44 3 | 9:00 a.m. | 22 e |
| Fargo, N. Dak. | 96 48 | 46 52 | 11:00 a.m. | 10 e |
| Flagstaff, Ariz. | 111 41 | 35 13 | 10:00 a.m. | 15 e |
| Fresno, Calif. | 119 48 | 36 44 | 9:00 a.m. | 17 e |
| Garden City, Kans. | 100 53 | 37 58 | 10:00 a.m. | 13 e |
| Grand Junction, Colo. | 108 33 | 39 5 | 10:00 a.m. | 15 e |
| Grand Rapids, Mich. | 85 40 | 42 58 | 11:00 a.m. | 1 e |
| Havre, Mont. | 109 43 | 48 33 | 10:00 a.m. | 20 e |
| Helena, Mont. | 112 2 | 46 35 | 10:00 a.m. | 19 e |
| Honolulu, Hawaii | 157 50 | 21 18 | 7:00 a.m. | — |
| Hoquiam, Wash. | 123 54 | 46 59 | 9:00 a.m. | 23 e |
| Hot Springs, Ark. | 93 3 | 34 31 | 11:00 a.m. | 8 e |
| Idaho Falls, Idaho | 112 1 | 43 30 | 10:00 a.m. | 18 e |
| Indianapolis, Ind. | 86 10 | 39 46 | 11:00 a.m. | 1 e |
| Jackson, Miss. | 90 12 | 32 20 | 11:00 a.m. | 7 e |
| Jacksonville, Fla. | 81 40 | 30 22 | 12:00 noon | 1 e |
| Juneau, Alaska | 134 24 | 58 18 | 9:00 a.m. | — |
| Kansas City, Mo. | 94 35 | 39 6 | 11:00 a.m. | 9 e |
| Key West, Fla. | 81 48 | 24 33 | 12:00 noon | 3 e |
| Kingston, Ont. | 76 30 | 44 15 | 12:00 noon | 12 w |
| Klamath Falls, Oreg. | 121 44 | 42 10 | 9:00 a.m. | 19 e |
| Knoxville, Tenn. | 83 56 | 35 57 | 11:00 a.m. | 0 |
| Lander, Wyo. | 108 40 | 42 50 | 10:00 a.m. | 17 e |
| Las Vegas, Nev. | 115 12 | 36 10 | 9:00 a.m. | 16 e |
| Lewiston, Idaho | 117 2 | 46 24 | 9:00 a.m. | 21 e |
| Lincoln, Nebr. | 96 40 | 40 50 | 11:00 a.m. | 10 e |
| London, Ont. | 81 34 | 43 2 | 12:00 noon | 5 w |
| Los Angeles, Calif. | 118 15 | 34 3 | 9:00 a.m. | 16 e |
| Louisville, Ky. | 85 46 | 38 15 | 11:00 a.m. | 1 e |
| Manchester N. H. | 71 30 | 43 0 | 12:00 noon | 16 w |
| Memphis, Tenn. | 90 3 | 35 9 | 11:00 a.m. | 6 e |
| Miami, Fla. | 80 12 | 25 46 | 12:00 noon | 1 e |
| Milwaukee, Wis. | 87 55 | 43 2 | 11:00 a.m. | 2 e |
| Minneapolis, Minn. | 93 14 | 44 59 | 11:00 a.m. | 7 e |
| Mobile, Ala. | 88 3 | 30 42 | 11:00 a.m. | 5 e |
| Montgomery, Ala. | 86 18 | 32 21 | 11:00 a.m. | 3 e |
| Montpelier, Vt. | 72 32 | 44 15 | 12:00 noon | 16 w |
| Montreal, Que. | 73 35 | 45 30 | 12:00 noon | 16 w |
| Moose Jaw, Sask. | 105 31 | 50 37 | 10:00 a.m. | 18 e |
| Nashville, Tenn. | 86 47 | 36 10 | 11:00 a.m. | 3 e |
| Needles, Calif. | 114 36 | 34 50 | 9:00 a.m. | 15 e |
| Nelson, B. C. | 117 17 | 49 30 | 9:00 a.m. | 23 e |
| New Haven, Conn. | 72 55 | 41 19 | 12:00 noon | 12 w |
| New Orleans, La. | 90 4 | 29 57 | 11:00 a.m. | 6 e |
| New York, N. Y. | 73 58 | 40 47 | 12:00 noon | 12 w |
| Nogales, Ariz. | 110 56 | 31 21 | 10:00 a.m. | 14 e |
| Nome, Alaska | 165 30 | 64 25 | 6:00 a.m. | 19 e |
| North Platte, Nebr. | 100 46 | 41 8 | 11:00 a.m. | 12 e |
| Oklahoma City, Okla. | 97 28 | 35 26 | 11:00 a.m. | 10 e |
| Ottawa, Ont. | 75 43 | 45 24 | 12:00 noon | 14 w |
| Philadelphia, Pa. | 75 10 | 39 57 | 12:00 noon | 10 w |
| Phoenix, Ariz. | 112 4 | 33 29 | 10:00 a.m. | 15 e |
| Pierre, S. Dak. | 100 21 | 44 22 | 11:00 a.m. | 12 e |
| Pittsburgh, Pa. | 79 57 | 40 27 | 12:00 noon | 5 w |
| Port Arthur, Ont. | 89 17 | 48 30 | 11:00 a.m. | 1 e |
| Portland, Maine | 70 15 | 43 40 | 12:00 noon | 17 w |
| Portland, Oreg. | 122 41 | 45 31 | 9:00 a.m | 23 e |
| Providence, R. I. | 71 24 | 41 50 | 12:00 noon | 15 w |
| Quebec, Que. | 71 11 | 46 49 | 12:00 noon | 20 w |
| Raleigh, N. C. | 78 39 | 35 46 | 12:00 noon | 4 w |
| Reno, Nev. | 119 49 | 39 30 | 9:00 a.m. | 18 e |
| Richfield, Utah | 112 5 | 38 46 | 10:00 a.m. | 17 e |
| Richmond, Va. | 77 29 | 37 33 | 12:00 noon | 6 w |
| Roanoke, Va. | 79 57 | 37 17 | 12:00 noon | 3 w |
| Sacramento, Calif. | 121 30 | 38 35 | 9:00 a.m. | 17 e |
| St. John, N. B. | 66 10 | 45 18 | 1:00 p.m. | 22 w |
| St. Louis, Mo. | 90 12 | 38 35 | 11:00 a.m. | 5 e |
| Salmon, Idaho | 113 54 | 45 11 | 10:00 a.m. | 20 e |
| Salt Lake City, Utah | 111 54 | 40 46 | 10:00 a.m. | 17 e |
| San Antonio, Tex. | 98 33 | 29 23 | 11:00 a.m. | 10 e |
| San Diego, Calif. | 117 10 | 32 42 | 9:00 a.m. | 15 e |
| San Francisco, Calif. | 122 26 | 37 47 | 9:00 a.m. | 18 e |
| San Juan, P. R. | 66 10 | 18 30 | 1:00 p m. | — |
| Santa Fe, N. Mex. | 105 57 | 35 41 | 10:00 a.m. | 13 e |
| Sault Ste. Marie, Mich. | 84 21 | 46 30 | 11:00 a.m. | 4 w |
| Savannah, Ga. | 81 5 | 32 5 | 12:00 noon | 0 |
| Scranton, Pa. | 75 39 | 41 24 | 12:00 noon | 10 w |
| Seattle, Wash. | 122 20 | 47 37 | 9:00 a.m. | 23 e |
| Shreveport, La. | 93 42 | 32 28 | 11:00 a.m. | 8 e |
| Sioux Falls, S. Dak. | 96 44 | 43 33 | 11:00 a.m. | 11 e |
| Sitka, Alaska | 135 15 | 57 10 | 9:00 a.m. | 30 e |
| Spokane, Wash. | 117 26 | 47 40 | 9:00 a.m. | 23 e |
| Springfield, Ill. | 89 38 | 39 48 | 11:00 a.m. | 4 e |
| Springfield, Mass. | 72 34 | 42 6 | 12:00 noon | 14 w |
| Springfield, Mo. | 93 17 | 37 13 | 11:00 a.m. | 7 e |
| Syracuse, N. Y. | 76 8 | 43 2 | 12:00 noon | 11 w |
| Tampa, Fla. | 82 27 | 27 57 | 12:00 noon | 2 e |
| Toronto, Ont. | 79 24 | 43 40 | 12:00 noon | 8 w |
| Trinidad, Colo. | 104 30 | 37 10 | 10:00 a.m. | 14 e |
| Victoria, B. C. | 123 21 | 48 25 | 9:00 a.m. | 24 e |
| Watertown, N. Y. | 75 55 | 43 58 | 12:00 noon | 13 w |
| Wichita, Kans. | 97 17 | 37 43 | 11:00 a.m. | 10 e |
| Wilmington, N. C. | 77 57 | 34 14 | 12:00 noon | 3 w |
| Winnipeg, Man. | 97 7 | 49 54 | 11:00 a.m. | 11 e |

* Corresponding to 12:00 noon, E.S.T.

# Longitude and Latitude of Foreign Cities
## and Time Corresponding to 12:00 Noon, E.S.T.

| City | Long. | Lat. | Time |
|------|-------|------|------|
| Aberdeen, Scotland........ | 2 9 w | 57 9 n | 5:00 p.m. |
| Adelaide, Australia......... | 138 36 e | 34 55 s | 2:30 a.m.* |
| Algiers, Algeria............ | 3 0 e | 36 50 n | 5:00 p.m. |
| Amsterdam, Netherlands... | 4 53 e | 52 22 n | 6:00 p.m. |
| Ankara, Turkey............ | 32 55 e | 39 55 n | 7:00 p.m. |
| Asunción, Paraguay........ | 57 40 w | 25 15 s | 1:00 p.m. |
| Athens, Greece............ | 23 43 e | 37 58 n | 7:00 p.m. |
| Auckland, New Zealand.... | 174 45 e | 36 52 s | 5:00 a.m.* |
| Bangkok, Thailand......... | 100 30 e | 13 45 n | 0:00 a.m.* |
| Barcelona, Spain........... | 2 9 e | 41 23 n | 6:00 p.m. |
| Belém, Brazil.............. | 48 29 w | 1 28 s | 2:00 p.m. |
| Belfast, Northern Ireland... | 5 56 w | 54 37 n | 5:00 p.m. |
| Belgrade, Yugoslavia....... | 20 32 e | 44 52 n | 6:00 p.m. |
| Berlin, Germany........... | 13 25 e | 52 30 n | 6:00 p.m. |
| Birmingham, England...... | 1 55 w | 52 25 n | 5:00 p.m. |
| Bogotá, Colombia.......... | 74 15 w | 4 32 n | 12:00 noon |
| Bombay, India............. | 72 48 e | 19 0 n | 9:30 p.m. |
| Bordeaux, France.......... | 0 31 w | 44 50 n | 6:00 p.m. |
| Bremen, Germany......... | 8 49 e | 53 5 n | 6:00 p.m. |
| Brisbane, Australia........ | 153 8 e | 27 29 s | 3:00 a.m.* |
| Bristol, England........... | 2 35 w | 51 28 n | 5:00 p.m. |
| Brussels, Belgium.......... | 4 22 e | 50 52 n | 6:00 p.m. |
| Bucharest, Rumania....... | 26 7 e | 44 25 n | 7:00 p.m. |
| Budapest, Hungary........ | 19 5 e | 47 30 n | 6:00 p.m. |
| Buenos Aires, Argentina... | 58 22 w | 34 35 s | 2:00 p.m. |
| Cairo, Egypt.............. | 31 21 e | 30 2 n | 7:00 p.m. |
| Calcutta, India............ | 88 24 e | 22 34 n | 9:30 p.m. |
| Canton, China............ | 113 15 e | 23 7 n | 1:00 a.m.* |
| Capetown, South Africa.... | 18 22 e | 33 55 s | 7:00 p.m. |
| Caracas, Venezuela........ | 67 2 w | 10 28 n | 11:30 p.m. |
| Cayenne, French Guiana.. | 52 18 w | 4 49 n | 1:30 p.m. |
| Chihuahua, Mexico......... | 106 5 w | 28 37 n | 11:00 a.m. |
| Chungking, China.......... | 106 34 e | 29 46 n | 0:00 a.m.* |
| Copenhagen, Denmark..... | 12 34 e | 55 40 n | 6:00 p.m. |
| Córdoba, Argentina....... | 64 10 w | 31 28 s | 2:00 p.m. |
| Dakar, Senegal............ | 17 28 w | 14 40 n | 4:00 p.m. |
| Darwin, Australia.......... | 130 51 e | 12 28 s | 2:30 a.m.* |
| Dublin, Ireland............ | 6 15 w | 53 20 n | 5:00 p.m. |
| Durban, South Africa...... | 30 53 e | 29 53 s | 7:00 p.m. |
| Edinburgh, Scotland....... | 3 10 w | 55 55 n | 5:00 p.m. |
| Frankfurt, Germany....... | 8 41 e | 50 7 n | 6:00 p.m. |
| Georgetown, British Guiana. | 58 15 w | 6 45 n | 1:15 p.m. |
| Glasgow, Scotland......... | 4 15 w | 55 50 n | 5:00 p.m. |
| Guatemala City, Guatemala.. | 90 31 w | 14 37 n | 11:00 a.m. |
| Guayaquil, Ecuador........ | 79 56 w | 2 10 s | 12:00 noon |
| Hamburg, Germany........ | 10 2 e | 53 33 n | 6:00 p.m. |
| Hammerfest, Norway....... | 23 38 e | 70 38 n | 6:00 p.m. |
| Havana, Cuba............. | 82 23 w | 23 8 n | 12:00 noon |
| Helsinki, Finland.......... | 25 0 e | 60 10 n | 7:00 p.m. |
| Hobart, Tasmania.......... | 147 19 e | 42 52 s | 3:00 a.m.* |
| Iquique, Chile............. | 70 7 w | 20 10 s | 1:00 p.m. |
| Irkutsk, U.S.S.R........... | 104 20 e | 52 30 n | 1:00 a.m.* |
| Jakarta, Indonesia......... | 106 48 e | 6 16 s | 0:30 a.m.* |
| Jibuti, French Somaliland... | 43 3 e | 11 30 s | 8:00 p.m. |
| Johannesburg, South Africa... | 28 4 e | 26 12 s | 7:00 p.m. |
| Kingston, Jamaica......... | 76 49 w | 17 59 n | 12:00 noon |
| La Paz, Bolivia............ | 68 22 w | 16 27 s | 1:00 p.m. |
| Leeds, England............ | 1 30 w | 53 45 n | 5:00 p.m. |
| Leningrad, U.S.S.R........ | 30 18 e | 59 56 n | 8:00 p.m. |
| Léopoldville, Congo........ | 15 17 e | 4 18 s | 8:00 p.m. |

| City | Long. | Lat. | Time |
|------|-------|------|------|
| Lima, Peru............... | 77 2 w | 12 0 s | 12:00 noon |
| Lisbon, Portugal.......... | 9 9 w | 38 44 n | 5:00 p.m. |
| Liverpool, England........ | 3 0 w | 53 25 n | 5:00 p.m. |
| London, England.......... | 0 5 w | 51 32 n | 5:00 p.m. |
| Lyon, France............. | 4 50 e | 45 45 n | 6:00 p.m. |
| Madrid, Spain............ | 3 42 w | 40 26 n | 6:00 p.m. |
| Makassar, Indonesia...... | 119 30 e | 5 9 s | 1:00 a.m.* |
| Manchester, England...... | 2 15 w | 53 30 n | 5:00 p.m. |
| Manila, Philippines....... | 120 57 e | 14 35 n | 1:00 a.m.* |
| Marseille, France......... | 5 20 e | 43 20 n | 6:00 p.m. |
| Mazatlán, Mexico......... | 106 25 w | 23 12 n | 10:00 a.m. |
| Mecca, Saudi Arabia...... | 39 45 e | 21 29 n | 8:00 p.m. |
| Melbourne, Australia...... | 144 58 e | 37 47 s | 3:00 a.m.* |
| Mexico City, Mexico...... | 99 7 w | 19 26 n | 11:00 a.m. |
| Milan, Italy.............. | 9 10 e | 45 27 n | 6:00 p.m. |
| Montevideo, Uruguay...... | 56 10 w | 34 53 s | 2:00 p.m. |
| Moscow, U.S.S.R.......... | 37 36 e | 55 45 n | 8:00 p.m. |
| Munich, Germany......... | 11 35 e | 48 8 n | 6:00 p.m. |
| Nagasaki, Japan.......... | 129 57 e | 32 48 n | 2:00 a.m.* |
| Nagoya, Japan............ | 136 56 e | 35 7 n | 2:00 a.m.* |
| Nairobi, Kenya........... | 36 55 e | 1 25 s | 8:00 p.m. |
| Nanking, China........... | 118 53 e | 32 3 n | 1:00 a.m.* |
| Naples, Italy............. | 14 15 e | 40 50 n | 6:00 p.m. |
| Newcastle-on-Tyne, Eng... | 1 37 w | 54 58 n | 5:00 p.m. |
| Odessa, U.S.S.R.......... | 30 48 e | 46 27 n | 8:00 p.m. |
| Osaka, Japan............. | 135 30 e | 34 32 n | 2:00 a.m.* |
| Oslo, Norway............. | 10 42 e | 59 57 n | 6:00 p.m. |
| Panamá City, Panamá..... | 79 32 w | 8 58 n | 12:00 noon |
| Paramaribo, Surinam...... | 55 15 w | 5 45 n | 12:30 p.m. |
| Paris, France............. | 2 20 e | 48 48 n | 6:00 p.m. |
| Peiping, China............ | 116 25 e | 39 55 n | 1:00 a.m.* |
| Perth, Australia........... | 115 52 e | 31 57 s | 1:00 a.m.* |
| Plymouth, England........ | 4 5 w | 50 25 n | 5:00 p.m. |
| Port Moresby, Papau...... | 147 8 e | 9 25 s | 3:00 a.m.* |
| Prague, Czechoslovakia.... | 14 26 e | 50 5 n | 6:00 p.m. |
| Rangoon, Burma.......... | 96 0 e | 16 50 n | 11:30 p.m. |
| Reykjavik, Iceland........ | 21 58 w | 64 4 n | 4:00 p.m. |
| Rio de Janeiro, Brazil..... | 43 12 w | 22 57 s | 2:00 p.m. |
| Rome, Italy.............. | 12 27 e | 41 54 n | 6:00 p.m. |
| Santiago, Chile........... | 70 45 w | 33 28 s | 1:00 p.m. |
| São Paulo, Brazil.......... | 46 31 w | 23 31 s | 2:00 p.m. |
| São Salvador, Brazil....... | 38 27 w | 12 56 s | 2:00 p.m. |
| Shanghai, China.......... | 121 28 e | 31 10 n | 1:00 a.m.* |
| Singapore, Singapore...... | 103 55 e | 1 14 n | 0:30 a.m.* |
| Sofia, Bulgaria........... | 23 20 e | 42 40 n | 7:00 p.m. |
| Stockholm, Sweden....... | 18 3 e | 59 17 n | 6:00 p.m. |
| Sydney, Australia......... | 151 0 e | 34 0 s | 3:00 a.m.* |
| Tananarive, Malagasy Rep. | 47 33 e | 18 50 s | 8:00 p.m. |
| Teheran, Iran............ | 51 45 e | 35 45 n | 8:30 p.m. |
| Tokyo, Japan............. | 139 45 e | 35 40 n | 2:00 a.m.* |
| Tripoli, Libya............ | 13 12 e | 32 57 n | 6:00 p.m. |
| Venice, Italy............. | 12 20 e | 45 26 n | 6:00 p.m. |
| Veracruz, Mexico......... | 96 10 w | 19 10 n | 11:00 a.m. |
| Vienna, Austria........... | 16 20 e | 48 14 n | 6:00 p.m. |
| Vladivostok, U.S.S.R...... | 132 0 e | 43 10 n | 3:00 a.m.* |
| Warsaw, Poland.......... | 21 0 e | 52 14 n | 6:00 p.m. |
| Wellington, New Zealand.. | 174 47 e | 41 17 s | 5:00 a.m.* |
| Zürich, Switzerland....... | 8 31 e | 47 21 n | 6:00 p.m. |

* On the following day.

# AVIATION

★

## Famous Firsts in Aviation

1782—First balloon flight. Jacques and Joseph Montgolfier of Annonay, Fr., sent up a small smoke-filled balloon about mid-November.

1783—First hydrogen-filled balloon flight. Jacques A. C. Charles, Paris physicist, supervised construction by A. J. and M. N. Robert of a 13-ft. diameter balloon which was filled with hydrogen. It got up to about 3,000 ft. and traveled about 16 mi. in a 45-min. flight (Aug. 27).

1783—First human balloon flights. A Frenchman, Jean Pilâtre de Rozier, made the first captive-balloon ascension (Oct. 15). With the Marquis d'Arlandes, Pilâtre de Rozier made the first free flight, reaching a peak altitude of about 500 ft., and traveling about 5½ mi. in 20 min. (Nov. 21).

1784—First powered balloon. Gen. Jean Baptiste Marie Meusnier developed the first propeller-driven and elliptically-shaped balloon—the crew cranking three propellers on a common shaft to give the craft a speed of about 3 mi. per hr.

1784—First woman to fly. Mme. Thible, a French opera singer (June 4).

1793—First balloon flight in America. Jean Pierre Blanchard, a French pilot, made it from Philadelphia to near Woodbury, Gloucester Co., N. J., in a little over 45 min. (Jan. 9).

1794—First military use of the balloon. Jean Marie Coutelle, using a balloon built for the French Army, made two 4 hr. observation ascents. The military value of the ascents seems to have been in damage to the enemy's morale.

1797—First parachute jump. André-Jacques Garnerin dropped from about 6,500 ft. over Monceau Park in Paris in a 23-ft. diameter 'chute made of white canvas with a basket attached (Oct. 22).

1843—First air transport company. In London, William S. Henson and John Stringfellow filed articles of incorporation for the Aerial Transit Company (Mar. 24). It failed.

1852—First dirigible. Henri Giffard, a French engineer, flew in a controllable (more or less) steam-engine-powered balloon, 144 ft. long and 39 ft. in diameter, inflated with 88,000 cu. ft. of coal gas. It reached 6.7 mi. per hr. on a flight from Paris to Trappe (Sept. 24).

1860—First aerial photographers. Samuel Archer King and William Black made two photos of Boston, still in existence.

1872—First gas-engine powered dirigible. Paul Haenlein, a German engineer, flew in a semi-rigid-frame dirigible, powered by a 4-cylinder internal-combustion engine running on coal gas drawn from the supporting bag.

1873—First transatlantic attempt. *The New York Daily Graphic* sponsored the attempt with a 400,000 cu. ft. balloon carrying a lifeboat. A rip in the bag during inflation brought collapse of the balloon and the project.

1897—First successful metal dirigible. An all-metal dirigible, designed by David Schwarz, a Hungarian, took off from Berlin's Tempelhof Field and, powered by a 16-hp. Daimler engine, got several miles before leaking gas caused it to crash (Nov. 13).

1900—First Zeppelin flight. Germany's Count Ferdinand von Zeppelin flew the first of his long series of rigid-frame airships. It attained a speed of 18 mi. per hr. and got 3½ mi. before its steering gear failed (July 2).

1903—First successful heavier-than-air machine flight. Aviation was really born on the sand dunes at Kitty Hawk, N.C., when Orville Wright crawled to his prone position between the wings of the biplane he and his brother Wilbur had built, opened the throttle of their homemade 12-hp. engine and took to the air. He covered 120 ft. in 12 sec. Later that day, in one of four flights, Wilbur stayed up 59 sec. and covered 852 ft. (Dec. 17).

1904—First airplane maneuvers. Orville Wright made the first turn with an airplane (Sept. 15); 5 days later his brother Wilbur made the first complete circle.

1905—First airplane flight over half an hour. Orville Wright kept his craft up 33 min. 17 sec. (Oct. 4).

1906—First European airplane flight. Alberto Santos-Dumont, a Brazilian, flew a heavier-than-air machine at Bagatelle Field, Paris (Sept. 13).

1908—First airplane fatality. Lt. Thomas E. Selfridge, U.S. Army Signal Corps, was in a group of officers evaluating the Wright plane at Fort Myer, Va. He was up about 75 ft. with Orville Wright when the propeller hit a bracing wire and was broken, throwing the plane out of control, killing Selfridge and seriously injuring Wright (Sept. 17).

1910—First licensed woman pilot. Baroness Raymonde de la Roche of France, who learned to fly in 1909, received ticket No. 36 on March 8.

**1910—First flight from shipboard.** Lt. Eugene Ely, USN, took a Curtiss plane off from the deck of cruiser *Birmingham* at Hampton Roads, Va., and flew to Norfolk (Nov. 14). The following January he reversed the process, flying from Camp Selfridge to the deck of the armored cruiser *Pennsylvania* in San Francisco Bay (Jan. 18).

**1911—First U.S. woman pilot.** Harriet Quimby, a magazine writer, who got ticket No. 37.

**1913—First multi-engined aircraft.** Built and flown by Igor Ivan Sikorsky while still in his native Russia.

**1914—First aerial combat.** In August, Allied and German pilots and observers started shooting at each other with pistols and rifles—with negligible results.

**1915—First air raids on England.** German Zeppelins started dropping bombs on four English communities (Jan. 19).

**1918—First U.S. air squadron.** The U.S. Army Air Corps made its first independent raids over enemy lines, in DH-4 planes (British-designed) powered with 400-hp. American-designed Liberty engines (Apr. 8).

**1918—First regular airmail service.** Operated for the Post Office Department by the Army, the first regular service was inaugurated with one round trip a day (except Sunday) between Washington, D.C., and New York City (May 15).

**1919—First transatlantic flight.** The NC-4, one of four Curtiss flying boats commanded by Lt. Comdr. Albert C. Read, reached Lisbon, Port. (May 27) after hops from Trepassy Bay, Nfld. to Horta, Azores (May 16–17), to Ponta Delgada (May 20). The Liberty-powered craft was piloted by Walter Hinton.

**1919—First nonstop transatlantic flight.** Capt. John Alcock and Lt. Arthur Whitten Brown, British World War I flyers, made the 1,900 mi. from St. John's, Nfld. to Clifden, Ire., in 16 hr. 12 min. in a Vickers-Vimy bomber with two 350-hp. Rolls-Royce engines (June 15–16).

**1919—First lighter-than-air transatlantic flight.** The British dirigible R-34, commanded by Maj. George H. Scott, left Firth of Forth, Scot. (July 2) and touched down at Mineola, L. I., 108 hr. later. The eastbound trip was made in 75 hr. (completed July 13).

**1919—First scheduled passenger service (using airplanes).** Aircraft Travel and Transport inaugurated London-Paris service (Aug. 25). Later the company started the first trans-channel mail service on the same route (Nov. 10).

**1921—First naval vessel sunk by aircraft.** Two battleships being scrapped by treaty were sunk by bombs dropped from Army planes in demonstration put on by Brig. Gen. William S. Mitchell (July 21).

**1921—First helium balloon.** The C-7, nonrigid Navy dirigible was first to use noninflammable helium as lifting gas, making a flight from Hampton Roads, Va., to Washington, D.C. (Dec. 1).

**1922—First member of Caterpillar Club.** Lt. (later Maj. Gen.) Harold Harris bailed out of a crippled plane he was testing at McCook Field, Dayton, Ohio (Oct. 20), and became the first man to join the Caterpillar Club—those whose lives have been saved by parachute.

**1923—First nonstop transcontinental flight.** Lts. John A. Macready and Oakley Kelly flew a single-engine Fokker T-2 nonstop from New York to San Diego, a distance of just over 2,500 mi. in 26 hr. 50 min. (May 2–3).

**1923—First autogyro flights.** Juan de la Cierva, brilliant Spanish mathematician, made the first successful flight in a rotary wing aircraft in Madrid (June 9).

**1924—First round-the-world flight.** Four Douglas Cruiser biplanes of the U.S. Army Air Corps took off from Seattle under command of Maj. Frederick Martin (Apr. 6). 175 days later two of the planes (Lt. Lowell Smith's and Lt. Erik Nelson's) landed in Seattle after a circuitous route—one source saying 26,345 mi., another saying 27,553 mi.

**1926—First polar flight.** Then-Lt. Cmdr. Richard E. Byrd, acting as navigator, and Floyd Bennett as pilot, flew a trimotor Fokker from Kings Bay, Spitsbergen, over the North Pole and back in 15½-hr. flight (May 8–9).

**1927—First solo transatlantic flight.** Charles Augustus Lindbergh lifted his Wright-powered Ryan monoplane, *Spirit of St. Louis*, from Roosevelt Field, L. I., to stay aloft 33 hr. 39 min. and cover 3,600 mi. to Le Bourget Field outside Paris (May 20–21).

**1927—First transatlantic passenger.** Charles A. Levine was piloted by Clarence D. Chamberlin from Roosevelt Field, L.I., to Eisleben, Ger., in a Wright-powered Bellanca (June 4–5).

**1928—First east-west transatlantic crossing.** Baron Guenther von Huenefeld, piloted by German Capt. Hermann Koehl and Irish Capt. James Fitzmaurice, left Dublin for New York City (Apr. 12) in a single-engine all-metal Junkers monoplane. Some 37 hr. later they cracked up on Greely Island, Labrador. Rescued.

**1928—First U.S.-Australia flight.** Sir Charles Kingsford-Smith and Capt. Charles T. P. Ulm, Australians, and two American navigators, Harry W. Lyon and James Warner, crossed the Pacific from Oakland to Brisbane. They went via

Hawaii and the Fiji Islands in a tri-motor Fokker (May 31–June 8).

**1928—First trans-Arctic flight.** Sir Hubert Wilkins, Australian explorer, piloted by Carl Ben Eielson, flew from Point Barrow, Alaska, to Spitsbergen (mid-April).

**1929—First of the endurance records.** With Air Corps Maj. Carl Spaatz in command and Capt. Ira Eaker as chief pilot, an Army Fokker, aided by refueling in the air, remained aloft 150 hr. 40 min. at Los Angeles (Jan. 1–7).

**1929—First blind flight.** James H. Doolittle proved the feasibility of instrument flying when he took off and landed entirely on instruments (Sept. 24).

**1929—First rocket engine flight.** Fritz von Opel, German auto maker, stayed aloft in his small rocket-powered craft for 75 sec., covering nearly 2 mi. (Sept. 30).

**1929—First South Pole flight.** Comdr. Richard E. Byrd, with Bernt Balchen as pilot, Harold I. June, radio operator, and Capt. A. C. McKinley, photographer, flew a trimotor Fokker from the Bay of Whales, Little America, over the South Pole and back (Nov. 28–29).

**1930—First Paris–New York nonstop flight.** Dieudonné Coste and Maurice Bellonte, French pilots, flew a Hispano-powered Breguet biplane from Le Bourget Field to Valley Stream, L. I., in 37 hr. 18 min. (Sept. 2–3).

**1931—First flight into the stratosphere.** Prof. Auguste Piccard, Swiss physicist, and Charles Knipfer, ascended in a balloon from Augsburg, Ger., and reached a height of 51,793 ft. in a 17-hr. flight that terminated on a glacier near Innsbruck, Austria (May 27).

**1931—First nonstop transpacific flight.** Hugh Herndon and Clyde Pangborn took off from Sabishiro Beach, Japan, dropped their landing gear and flew 4,860 mi. to near Wenatchee, Wash., in 41 hr. 13 min. (Oct. 4–5).

**1932—First woman's transatlantic solo.** Amelia Earhart, flying a Pratt & Whitney Wasp-powered Lockheed Vega, flew alone from Harbor Grace, Nfld., to Ireland in approximately 15 hr. (May 20–21).

**1932—First westbound transatlantic solo.** James A. Mollison, British pilot, took a de Havilland Puss Moth from Portmarnock, Ire., to Pennfield, N. B. (Aug. 18).

**1932—First woman airline pilot.** Ruth Rowland Nichols, first woman to hold three international records at the same time—speed, distance, altitude—was employed by N.Y.-New England Airways.

**1933—First round-the-world solo.** Wiley Post took a Lockheed Vega, *Winnie Mae*, 15,596 mi. around the world in 7 days 18 hr. 49½ min. (July 15–22).

**1937—First successful helicopter.** Hanna Reitsch, German woman pilot, flew Dr. Heinrich Focke's FW-61 in free, fully-controlled flight at Bremen (July 4).

**1939—First turbojet flight.** Just before their invasion of Poland, the Germans flew a Heinkel He-178 plane powered by a Heinkel S3B turbojet (Aug. 27).

**1942—First American jet plane flight.** Robert Stanley, chief pilot for Bell Aircraft Corp., flew the Bell XP-59 *Airacomet* at Muroc Army Base, Calif. (Oct. 1).

**1947—First piloted supersonic flight in an airplane.** Capt. Charles E. Yeager, U.S. Air Force, flew the X-1, rocket-powered research plane built by Bell Aircraft Corp., faster than the speed of sound at Muroc Air Force Base, Calif. (Oct. 14).

**1949—First round-the-world nonstop flight.** Capt. James Gallagher and USAF crew of 13 flew a Boeing B-50A Superfortress around the world nonstop from Ft. Worth, Tex., returning to same point; 23,452 mi. in 94 hr. 1 min., with 4 aerial refuelings enroute (Feb. 27–Mar. 2).

**1950—First nonstop transatlantic jet flight.** Col. David C. Schilling (USAF) flew 3,300 mi. from England to Limestone, Maine, in 10 hr. 1 min. (Sept. 22).

**1950—First jet-plane battle.** Four U.N. jets attacked by 8 to 12 Communist jets near Sinuiju, Korea. One enemy jet reported shot down; no U.N. losses (Nov. 8).

**1951—First solo across North Pole.** Charles F. Blair, Jr., flew a converted P-51 (May 29).

**1952—First jetliner service.** De Havilland Comet flight inaugurated by BOAC between London and Rome (Apr. 21). Round trip: 4 hr. 46 min. flying time.

**1952—First transatlantic helicopter flight.** Capt. Vincent H. McGovern and 1st Lt. Harold W. Moore piloted 2 Sikorsky H-19s from Westover, Mass., to Prestwick, Scot. (3,410 mi.). Trip was made in 5 steps, with flying time of 42 hr. 25 min. (July 15–31).

**1952—First transatlantic round trip in same day.** British Canberra twin-jet bomber flew from Aldergrove, N. Ire., to Gander, Nfld., and back in 7 hr. 59 min. flying time (Aug. 26).

**1955—First transcontinental round trip in same day.** Lt. John M. Conroy piloted F-86 Sabrejet across U.S. (Los Angeles-New York) and back—5,085 mi.—in 11 hr. 33 min. 27 sec. (May 21).

**1957—First round-the-world, nonstop jet plane flight.** Maj. Gen. Archie J. Old, Jr., USAF, led a flight of 3 Boeing B-52 bombers, powered with 8 10,000-lb.-thrust Pratt & Whitney Aircraft J57 engines around the world in 45 hrs., 19 min.; distance 24,325 mi.; average speed 525 m.p.h. (Completed Jan. 18.)

**1958—First transatlantic jet passenger service.** BOAC, New York to London (Oct. 4). Pan American started daily service, N.Y. to Paris (Oct. 26).

**1958—First domestic jet passenger service.** National Airlines inaugurated service between New York and Miami (Dec. 10).

# World "Class" Airplane Records

*Source:* National Aeronautic Association.

## (Speed over measured straightaway course)

| Speed (mph) | Date | Type plane | Pilot | Place |
|---|---|---|---|---|
| 294.38 | Sept. 5, '32 | Gee Bee Racer | Maj. J. H. Doolittle (U.S.A.) | Cleveland |
| 304.98 | Sept. 4, '33 | Wedell-Williams | James R. Wedell (U.S.A.) | Glenview, Ill. |
| 314.32 | Dec. 25, '34 | Caudron | Raymond Delmotte (France) | Istres |
| 352.39 | Sept. 13, '35 | Hughes Special | Howard Hughes (U.S.A.) | Santa Anna |
| 379.63 | Nov. 11, '37 | BF-113R | Herman Wurster (Germany) | Augsburg |
| 469.22 | Apr. 26, '39 | ME-109R | Fritz Wendel (Germany) | Augsburg |
| 606.25 | Nov. 7, '45 | Gloster Meteor IV | Gp. Capt. H. Wilson (Gr. Britain) | Herne Bay |
| 615.78 | Sept. 7, '46 | Gloster Meteor | Gp. Capt. E. M. Donalson (Gr. Britain) | Little Hampton |
| 650.80 | Aug. 25, '47 | Douglas D-558 | Maj. Marion Carl, USMC (U.S.A.) | Muroc AFB, Calif. |
| 670.98 | Sept. 15, '48 | North American F-86A | Maj. R. L. Johnson (USAF) | Muroc AFB, Calif. |
| 698.51 | Nov. 19, '52 | North American F-86D | Capt. James S. Nash (USAF) | Salton Sea, Calif. |
| 755.15 | Oct. 29, '53 | North American YF | Lt. Col. F. K. Everest, Jr. (USAF) | Salton Sea, Calif. |
| 822.27 | Aug. 20, '55 | North American F-100C | Col. Horace A. Hanes (U.S.A.) | Palmdale, Calif. |
| 1,132.14 | Mar. 10, '56 | Fairey Delta 2 | L. Peter Twiss, D.S.C. (Gr. Britain) | Ford-Chichester, Eng. |
| 1,207.63 | Dec. 12, '57 | McDonnell F-101A | Maj. Adrian E. Drew (USAF) | Edwards, Calif. |
| 1,404.09 | May 16, '58 | Lockheed F104 | Capt. Walter W. Irwin (USAF) | Edwards, Calif. |
| 1,483.85 | Oct. 31, '59 | Sukhoi S-66 | G. Mossolov (U.S.S.R.) | U.S.S.R. |
| 1,525.96 | Dec. 15, '59 | F-106A Delta Wing Monoplane | Maj. Joseph W. Rogers (USAF) | Edwards, Calif. |

(Fastest U.S. transcontinental: Lt. Gustav B. Klatt (USAF)—McDonnell RF-101C Voodoo—from Ontario Airport, Ontario, Calif., to Floyd Bennett Field, Brooklyn, N. Y.—2,445.9 mi. in 3 hr., 7 min., 43.64 sec.; average speed 781.741 mph—Nov. 27, 1957.)

## Distance (Straight Line)

| Distance (mi.) | Date | Crew | From | To |
|---|---|---|---|---|
| 4,911.93 | Sept. 27–29, '29 | Costes & Bellonte (France) | Le Bourget | Moulant |
| 5,011.35 | July 28–30, '31 | Russel N. Boardman, John Polando (U.S.A.) | New York | Istanbul |
| 5,656.93 | Aug. 5–7, '33 | Maurice Rossi, Paul Codos (France) | New York | Ryack |
| 6,305.66 | July 12–14, '37 | Col. M. Gromov, Youmachev, Daniline (U.S.S.R.) | Moscow | San Jacinto, Calif. |
| 7,158.44 | Nov. 5–7, '38 | Sqd. Ldr. R. Kellett (Gr. Britain) | Ismalia (Suez) | Darwin |
| 7,916.00 | Nov. 19–20, '45 | Col. C. S. Irvine & Lt. Col. G. R. Stanley, (U.S.A.) | Guam | Washington, D. C. |
| 11,235.60 | Sept. 29–Oct. 1, '46 | Comdr. Thomas D. Davies, Comdrs. Eugene P. Rankin, Walter S. Reid, Lt. Comdr. Ray A. Tabeling (U.S.A.) | Perth, Australia | Columbus, Ohio |

(Longest light airplane distance; Maximillian A. Conrad—U. S. Piper Comanche 250, Lycoming 0-540-AIA5 (250 hp.), from Casablanca, Morocco, to Los Angeles, Calif., 7,668.48 mi.—June 2-4, 1959.

## Distance (Closed Course)

| Distance (mi.) | Date | Crew | Place |
|---|---|---|---|
| 5,088.267 | May 31–June 2, '30 | Maj. U. Maddalena & Lt. F. Cecconi (Italy) | Montecelio |
| 6,444.881 | June 7–10, '31 | J. LeBrix & M. Doret (France) | Istres |
| 6,587.441 | Mar. 23–26, '32 | Bossoutrot & Rossi (France) | Oran |
| 7,239.588 | May 13–15, '38 | Comm. Fujita & Sgt. Maj. Takahashi (Japan) | Kisarasu |
| 8,037.899 | July 30–Aug. 1 '39 | Angelo Tondi, Roberto Dagasso, Ferrucio Vignoli (Italy) | Rome |
| 8,854.308 | Aug. 1–2, '47 | Lt. Col. O. F. Lassiter (U.S.A.) Capt. W. J. Valentine (U.S.A.) | Tampa, Fla. |
| 10,078.84 | Dec. 13–14, '60 | Lt. Col. J. R. Grissom (USAF) | Edwards, Calif. |

## Altitude

| Height (feet) | Date | Crew | Place |
|---|---|---|---|
| 43,166 | June 4, '30 | Lt. Apollo Soucek (U.S.A.) | Washington |
| 43,976 | Sept. 16, '32 | Capt. Cyril F. Uwins (Gr. Britain) | Filton, Bristol |
| 44,819 | Sept. 28, '33 | G. Lemoine (France) | Villacoublay |
| 47,352 | April 11, '34 | Com. Renato Donati (Italy) | Rome |
| 49,944 | Sept. 28, '36 | Sqd. Ldr. F. R. D. Swain (Gr. Britain) | South Farnborough |
| 53,937 | June 30, '37 | Fl. Lt. M. J. Adam (Britain) | Farnborough |
| 56,046 | Oct. 22, '38 | Col. Mario Pezzi (Italy) | Montecelio |
| 59,445* | Mar. 23, '48 | John Cunningham (Gr. Britain) | Hatfield |
| 63,668* | May 4, '53 | Walter F. Gibb (Gr. Britain) | Bristol |
| 65,889* | Aug. 29, '55 | Walter F. Gibb (Gr. Britain) | Bristol |
| 70,308* | Aug. 28, '57 | Michael Randrup (Gr. Britain) | Luton, Eng. |
| 91,243* | May 7, '58 | Maj. H. C. Johnson (USAF) | Palmdale, Calif. |
| 103,389 | Nov. 14, '59 | Capt. Joe B. Jordan (USAF) | Edwards, Calif. |
| 113,891 | Apr. 28, '61 | G. Mossolov (U.S.S.R.) | U.S.S.R. |

* Jet-propelled aircraft.

## Helicopter Records
*Source:* National Aeronautic Association.

### DISTANCE, AIRLINE
International: 1,217.14 mi.

Elton J. Smith (U. S.) in Bell 47-D1 helicopter powered by 200-hp. Franklin; from Ft. Worth, Tex., to Niagara Falls, N. Y., Sept. 17, 1952.

### DISTANCE, CLOSED CIRCUIT
International: 1,199.078 mi.

Lt. Col. Harry L. Bush and Maj. William C. Dysinger (USA) in Vertol H21-C helicopter powered by 1275-hp. Wright R-1820-103; Robbinsville, N. J., Aug. 11, 1956.

### ALTITUDE
International: 36,037 ft.

Jean Boulet (France) in S.E. 3150/022 "Alouette" F-ZWVB helicopter powered by Turbomeca Artouste III 500-hp engine; Bretigny sur Orge, June 13, 1958.

### MAXIMUM SPEED
International: 162.743 mph.

Maj. Roy L. Anderson (USMC), pilot, Robert S. Decker, co-pilot (U. S.), in Sikorsky HR2S-1 helicopter powered by 2 Pratt & Whitney R-2800-54 engines; Windsor Locks, Conn., Nov. 11, 1956.

### SPEED FOR 100 K.M. (CLOSED CIRCUIT)
International: 167.09 mph.

Boris Zemskov & Nicholai Liechine (USSR) in MI-6 helicopter powered by 4700-hp. TB-2-BM; Golitsyno, USSR, Nov. 21, 1959.

### SPEED FOR 500 K.M. (CLOSED CIRCUIT)
International: 148.449 mph.

Col. J. L. Marinelli in Bell HU-1 helicopter powered by Lycoming T53-L-1A gas turbine engine; Hurst-Harrison (Tex.) course, July 19, 1960.

### SPEED FOR 1,000 K.M. (CLOSED CIRCUIT)
International: 132.633 mph.

Capts. Claude E. Hargett & Ellis D. Hill (USA) in Sikorsky H-34 helicopter powered by 1275-hp. Wright R-1820; Milford, Conn., July 12, 1956.

## Certificated U. S. Airplane Pilots
*Source:* Federal Aviation Agency.

| Year (As of Dec. 31) | Total | Airline transport | Commercial | Private |
|---|---|---|---|---|
| 1943....... | 173,206 | 2,315 | 63,940 | 106,950 |
| 1944....... | 183,383 | 3,046 | 68,449 | 111,888 |
| 1945....... | 296,895 | 5,815 | 162,873 | 128,207 |
| 1946....... | 400,061 | 7,654 | 203,251 | 189,156 |
| 1947....... | 433,241[1] | 7,059[1] | 181,912[1] | 244,270[1] |
| 1948....... | 491,306[2] | 7,762[2] | 176,845[2] | 306,699[2] |
| 1949....... | 525,174 | 9,025 | 187,769 | 328,380 |
| 1951....... | 580,574 | 10,813 | 197,000 | 371,861 |
| 1952....... | 581,218 | 11,357 | 193,575 | 376,286 |
| 1953....... | 585,974 | 12,757 | 195,363 | 377,854 |
| 1954....... | 613,695 | 13,341 | 201,441 | 398,913 |
| 1955....... | 643,201 | 13,700 | 211,142 | 418,359 |
| 1956....... | 669,079 | 15,295 | 221,096 | 432,688 |
| 1957....... | 702,519 | 16,900 | 237,149 | 448,470 |
| 1958....... | 731,078 | 18,303 | 245,541 | 467,234 |
| 1959....... | 758,339 | 19,364 | 255,377 | 483,598 |
| 1960....... | 783,232 | 20,985 | 262,437 | 499,810 |

[1] As of April 1, 1948.   [2] As of May 1, 1949.   NOTE: No figures available for 1950.

## U. S. Scheduled Airlines, 1960
*Source:* Civil Aeronautics Board.

| Airline | Certificated route mileage[1] | Revenue passenger-miles, 1960 |
|---|---|---|
| | **Domestic** | |
| Aaxico[2]............... | 3,166 | .......... |
| Alaska[3]............... | 1,665 | 31,296,000[4] |
| Allegheny............... | 3,451 | 131,293,000 |
| Aloha............... | 379 | 53,704,000 |
| American............... | 26,612 | 6,257,252,000 |
| Avalon[5]............... | 37 | .......... |
| Bonanza............... | 2,613 | 63,527,000 |
| Braniff ............... | 10,147 | 1,052,502,000 |
| Capital............... | 9,883 | 1,492,332,000 |
| Central............... | 4,359 | 32,358,000 |
| Continental ............... | 9,406 | 885,490,000 |
| Delta............... | 16,576 | 1,832,106,000 |
| Eastern............... | 25,128 | 4,045,679,000 |
| Flying Tiger[2] ............... | 20,520 | .......... |
| Frontier ............... | 8,503 | 88,021,000 |
| Hawaiian ............... | 389 | 73,796,000 |
| Helicopter (Chicago) ....... | 294 | 5,202,000 |
| Helicopter (Los Angeles).... | 389 | 1,355,000 |
| Helicopter (New York)...... | 222 | 2,918,000 |
| Lake Central............... | 4,739 | 35,834,000 |
| Mohawk............... | 3,184 | 116,084,000 |
| National............... | 3,607 | 1,016,138,000 |
| North Central............... | 8,539 | 168,880,000 |
| Northeast............... | 6,849 | 564,943,000 |
| Northwest............... | 13,833 | 1,336,636,000 |
| Ozark............... | 5,878 | 98,616,000 |
| Pacific............... | 2,187 | 103,374,000 |
| Pacific Northern[3]......... | 3,440 | 115,614,000[4] |
| Piedmont............... | 3,981 | 93,879,000 |
| Riddle[2]............... | 3,800 | .......... |
| Southern............... | 5,483 | 46,613,000 |
| Trans-Texas............... | 5,579 | 70,308,000 |
| Trans World............... | 22,113 | 4,450,933,000 |
| United............... | 17,860 | 5,354,955,000 |
| West Coast............... | 3,766 | 92,806,000 |
| Western............... | 7,607 | 944,233,000 |
| **TOTAL**............... | 266,184 | 30,658,677,000 |
| | **Foreign or Overseas** | |
| Aerovias Sud Americana[2].... | 9,860 | .......... |
| American............... | 3,375 | 114,159,000 |
| Braniff............... | 8,366 | 128,432,000 |
| Caribbean Atlantic......... | 566 | 27,007,000 |
| Delta............... | 3,630 | 38,281,000 |
| Eastern............... | 9,536 | 718,673,000 |
| Mackey............... | 2,414 | 21,523,000 |
| National............... | 114 | 24,364,000 |
| Northwest............... | 13,613 | 317,328,000 |
| Pan American............... | 190,747 | 4,832,647,000 |
| Panagra............... | 10,643 | 198,101,000 |
| Resort[6]............... | ...... | .......... |
| Riddle[2]............... | 3,800 | .......... |
| Samoan[7]............... | ...... | .......... |
| Seaboard & Western[2]...... | 15,163 | .......... |
| South Pacific[8]............... | 2,955 | 4,532,000 |
| Transportation Corporation .. | 2,095 | 207,694,000 |
| Trans World............... | 38,664 | 1,039,220,000 |
| United............... | 1,768 | 403,742,000 |
| Western............... | 1,640 | 83,020,000 |
| **TOTAL**............... | 318,949 | 8,158,723,000 |

[1] As of Dec. 31, 1960.  [2] All-cargo carrier.  [3] Alaska-Washington State mileage.  [4] Includes intra-Alaska operations not separately reported.  [5] Service inaugurated June 24, 1960.  [6] Scheduled service discontinued.  [7] Service inaugurated July 14, 1959, but reports are incomplete.  [8] Service inaugurated April 1, 1960.

# U. S. Airlines Transport Planes

*Source:* Aircraft Industries Assn. and National Aviation Education Council.

| Manufacturer | Type | Passengers | Maximum speed, mph | Maximum weight | Wingspan | Overall length |
|---|---|---|---|---|---|---|
| **TURBOJETS\*** | | | | | | |
| 4-engine | | | | | | |
| Douglas............... | DC-8 | 116–176 | 610[1] | 276,000 | 142' 4'' | 150' 6'' |
| Boeing................. | 707 | 108–189 | 600 | 248,000 | 134' 6'' | 130' 10'' |
| | 720 | 88–149 | 615 | 213,000 | 130' 10'' | 136' 2'' |
| Convair................ | 880 | 88–110 | 615 | 184,500 | 120' 0'' | 129' 4'' |
| 2-engine | | | | | | |
| Sud Aviation............ | Caravelle[2] | 80 | 510 | 99,210 | 112' 6'' | 104' 10'' |
| **PROPJETS\*** | | | | | | |
| 4-engine | | | | | | |
| Lockheed............... | Electra | 66–98 | 400[3] | 116,000 | 99' 0'' | 104' 6'' |
| Vickers................ | Viscount | 40–63 | 340 | 64,500 | 93' 8'' | 81' 10'' |
| 2-engine | | | | | | |
| Fairchild.............. | F-27 | 40 | 300 | 37,500 | 95' 2'' | 77' 2'' |
| **PISTON** | | | | | | |
| 4-engine | | | | | | |
| Douglas............... | DC-7 | 69–99 | 410 | 122,000 | 117' 6'' | 106' 6'' |
| | DC-6 | 54 | 370 | 100,000 | 117' 6'' | 106' 6'' |
| | DC-4 | 44–60 | 240 | 73,000 | 117' 6'' | 93' 5'' |
| Lockheed............... | Super-Constellation | | | | | |
| | (1049) | 94 | 346 | 140,000 | 123' 0'' | 113' 7'' |
| | 1649[4] | 47–99 | 377 | 156,000 | 150' 0'' | 116' 2'' |
| Boeing................. | 377 (Stratocruiser) | 50–80 | 375 | 148,000 | 141' 2'' | 110' 4'' |
| 2-engine | | | | | | |
| Convair............... | 440 | 44–52 | 280 | 49,100 | 105' 4'' | 79' 2'' |
| Martin................. | 404 | 40 | 300 | 44,900 | 93' 3'' | 72' 0'' |
| Douglas............... | DC-3 | 21 | 230 | 25,200 | 95' 0'' | 64' 5'' |

\* NOTE: A turbojet (often called "pure jet") is a gas turbine producing an exhaust rather similar to a rocket exhaust which propels the aircraft. A propjet is also a gas turbine, but the turbine is used to spin a propeller. In a propjet about 60 per cent of the propulsive force is due to the propeller, the other 40 per cent is due to the jet.

[1] The different series of the jetliners usually have different engines, hence the maximum speed is not quite the same for the different series. [2] Introduced in 1961. [3] Maximum speed currently restricted to 250 mph pending modifications designed to eliminate the possibility of accidents. [4] The Lockheed 1649 is variously called "Superstar," "Starliner" and "Jetstream" (by TWA).

Principal operators of the airliners listed above: *Boeing 377*—Northwest, Pan American; *Boeing 707* and *720*—American, Pan American, TWA; *Caravelle*—United; *Constellation,* etc.—Eastern, TWA, United; *Convair*—Braniff, Eastern, United; *Douglas DC-3*—Allegheny, Bonanza, Braniff, Continental, Delta, Frontier, Lake Central, Mohawk, North Central, Northeast, Ozark, Trans-Texas, and others. *Douglas DC-4*—Northwest, Pan American; *Douglas DC-6*—American, Braniff, Delta, Eastern. Northwest, Pan American, United; *Douglas DC-7*—American, Delta, Eastern, Northwest, Pan American, United; *Douglas DC-8*—Delta, United; *Fairchild F-27*—Piedmont, West Coast; *Martin 404*—Eastern, TWA; *Viscount*—Continental, Northeast, United.

---

# U. S. Warplane Production Record, 1940-45

*Source:* Civil Aeronautics Administration.

| Type | 1940 | 1941 | 1942 | 1943 | 1944 | 1945 | 1940–45 |
|---|---|---|---|---|---|---|---|
| Total................ | 6,019 | 19,433 | 47,836 | 85,898 | 96,318 | 47,714 | 303,218 |
| Bombers............. | 1,191 | 4,115 | 12,627 | 29,355 | 35,003 | 16,492 | 98,783 |
| Fighters............. | 1,685 | 4,416 | 10,769 | 23,988 | 38,873 | 21,696 | 101,427 |
| Photographic and reconnaissance...... | 121 | 727 | 1,468 | 734 | 259 | 531 | 3,840 |
| Transport............ | 290 | 532 | 1,984 | 7,012 | 9,834 | 4,629 | 24,281 |
| Trainer.............. | 2,731 | 9,373 | 17,631 | 19,939 | 7,577 | 1,309 | 58,560 |
| Other\*.............. | 1 | 270 | 3,357 | 4,870 | 4,772 | 3,057 | 16,327 |

\* Includes special-purpose, rotary-wing, and liaison aircraft.

# Important American Aircraft Types (U.S. Air Force)

*Source:* U. S. Air Force.

| Type | Manufacturer | Power plant[1] | Max. take-off ratings | Span, feet | Length, feet | Height, feet | Max. take-off weight | Speed, mph | Crew |
|------|--------------|----------------|-----------------------|------------|--------------|--------------|----------------------|------------|------|
| **BOMBERS** | | | | | | | | | |
| B-47 | Boeing | 6 J47 GE-25 | 6,000 lb. | 116.0 | 107.0 | 28.0 | 230,000 | 600 class | 3 |
| KB-50 | Boeing | 4 R4360 PW-35 | 3,500 hp. | 141.2 | 99.0 | 32.7 | 173,000 | Over 400 | 6 |
| B-52 | Boeing | 8 J57 P | 10,000 lb. | 185.0 | 156.0 | 48.0 | Over 400,000 | Over 600 | 6 |
| B-57 | Martin | 2 J-65 W | Over 7,200 lb. | 64.0 | 65.6 | 14.8 | 50,000 | Over 500 | 2 |
| B-58 | Convair | 4 J-79 | Over 10,000 lb.[4] | 56.10 | 96.9 | 31.5 | 160,000 | Over 1,300 | 3 |
| B-66 | Douglas | 2 J71 A-13 | 10,000 lb. | 72.6 | 75.2 | 23.7 | 78,000 | 600-700 | 3 |
| **FIGHTERS** | | | | | | | | | |
| F-84F | Republic | 1 J65 W-3 | 7,200 lb. | 33.6 | 43.4 | 14.4 | 25,000 | Over 650 | 1 |
| F-86F | North American | 1 J47 GE-27 | 5,970 lb. | 37.0 | 38.0 | 15.0 | 17,000 | 650 class | 1 |
| F-86L | North American | 1 J47 GE-33 | 7,650 lb. | 37.0 | 40.0 | 15.0 | 18,000 | Over 650 | 1 |
| F-89 | Northrop | 2 J35 A-35 | 7,500 lb[2] | 56.2 | 53.4 | 17.7 | 40,000 | 600 class | 2 |
| F-100 | North American | 1 J57 P-21 | 10,000 lb. | 38.0 | 47.0 | 16.0 | 28,000 | Over 800 | 1 |
| F-101 | McDonnell | 2 J57 | 15,000 lb. | 39.8 | 67.5 | 18.0 | Over 40,000 | Ovder 1,200 | 1 |
| RF-101 | McDonnell | 2 J-57 | 15,000 lb. | 39.8 | 69.0 | 18.0 | 40,000 | Over 1,000 | 1 |
| F-102 | Convair | 1 J57 P-23 | 10,000 lb. | 38.0 | 68.5 | 21.3 | Over 25,000 | Supersonic | 1 |
| F-104 | Lockheed | J79 | 15,000 lb. | 21.11 | 54.9 | 13.6 | 20,000 | Over 1,400 | 1 |
| F-105 | Republic | J-75-5 | 23,500 lb. | 34.11 | 63.1 | 19.8 | 45,000 | Supersonic | 1 |
| F-106 | Convair | J75-9P | 23,500 lb. | 38.0 | 70.9 | 28.0 | 35,000 | Over 1,400 | 1 |
| **TRANSPORTS** | | | | | | | | | |
| C-47 | Douglas | 2 R1830-90D P | 1,200 hp. | 95.0 | 64.4 | 16.10 | 28,500 | 200 top | 5 |
| C-54 | Douglas | 4 R2000-9 P | 1,450 hp. | 117.6 | 93.9 | 27.6 | 73,000 | 300 top | 3-5 |
| KC-97 | Boeing | 4 R4360-59 | 3,500 hp. | 141.3 | 110.4 | 38.3 | 175,000 | Over 350 | 5 |
| C-118 | Douglas | 4 R2800-CB-17 P | 2,500 hp. | 117.6 | 105.7 | 28.8 | 107,000 | Over 360 | 5 |
| C-119 | Fairchild | 2 R3350-85 W | 3,250 hp. | 109.4 | 86.6 | 26.2 | 74,000 | 250 | 3-5 |
| C-121 | Lockheed | 4 R3350 | 3,250 hp. | 123.0 | 116.0 | 23.0 | 125,000 | 370 | 5 |
| C-123 | Fairchild | 2 R2800-99W P | 2,500 hp. | 119.0 | 75.8 | 34.1 | 50,000 | 240 top | 2-4 |
| C-124 | Douglas | 4 R4360-63 A | 3,800 hp. | 174.2 | 130.0 | 48.3 | 194,500 | Over 300 | 5 |
| C-130 | Lockheed | 4 T56 A-1A | 3,750 hp. | 132.6 | 97.7 | 38.0 | 135,000 | Over 350 | 4-5 |
| C-131 | Convair | R2800-99W | 2,500 hp. | 91.8 | 74.8 | 27.4 | 47,000 | Over 300 | 3 |
| KC-135 | Boeing | 4 J-57-43W | 10,000 lb. | 130.10 | 136.3 | 38.5 | 297,000 | Over 600 | 4 |
| **HELICOPTERS** | | | | | | | | | |
| H-13 | Bell | 1 V-435 | 200 hp. | 35.2 | 31.0 | 9.6 | 2,500 | 100 | 1 |
| H-19 | Sikorsky | 1 R1340-57 P | 600 hp. | 53.0 | 41.2 | 15.6 | 7,500 | Over 100 | 1-3 |
| H-21 | Vertol | 1 R1820-13 | 1,425 hp. | 44.0 | 52.6 | 14.6 | 15,000 | Over 110[3] | 2-3 |
| H-43 | Kaman | 1 T-53-L-1A | 860 hp. | 51.5 | 25.2 | 12.7 | 6,948 | 120 top | 1-3 |
| **TRAINERS** | | | | | | | | | |
| T-29 | Convair | 2 p&W R-2800-99W | 2,500 hp. | 91.8 | 74.8 | 27.4 | 47,000 | 300 | 3 |
| T-33 | Lockheed | 1 J-33-A-35 | 5,200 lb. | 37.6 | 37.8 | 11.7 | 16,000 | 600 | 2 |
| T-37 | Cessna | 2 J-69-T-25 | 920 lb. | 33.10 | 29.4 | 9.5 | 6,403 | 350 | 2 |
| T-38 | Northrop | 2 J-85 | 2,450 lb. | 25.3 | 43.4 | 11.9 | 11,000 | 850 | 2 |
| T-39 | North American | 2 GE J-60-P | 2,450 lb. | 42.43 | 43.75 | 15.50 | 15,000 | 500 | 2 |
| **MISCELLANEOUS** | | | | | | | | | |
| L-20 | DeHavilland | R-985-AN-100-3 | 450 hp. | 48.0 | 30.4 | 10.5 | 4,820 | 180 | 1 |
| SA-16 | Grumman | 2 R-1820-76 | 1,425 hp. | 80.0 | 62.1 | 24.4 | 30,000 | 230 | 6 |
| U-3A | Cessna | 2 I0-470-D | 260 hp. | 35.9 | 29.7 | 10.2 | 4,990 | 200 | 2 |
| U-4 | Aero | 2 60-480 | 295 hp. | 44.1 | 35.5 | 14.6 | 6,000 | 190 | 2 |

[1] A—Allison; GE—General Electric; P—Pratt & Whitney; W—Wright. [2] With afterburner. [3] Knots. [4] Plus afterburner. [5] At 2,600 rpm.

# UNITED STATES STATISTICS

## POPULATION

### Population Growth of the United States

*Source:* U. S. Bureau of the Census.

| Colonial estimates | | National censuses | | | | Projections* | |
|---|---|---|---|---|---|---|---|
| Year | Population | Year | Population | Land area, sq. mi. | Pop. per sq. mi. | Year | Population† |
| | | | | | | | NOTE A |
| 1610...... | 210 | 1790...... | 3,929,214 | 867,980 | 4.5 | 1960...... | 181,154,000 |
| 1620...... | 2,499 | 1800...... | 5,308,483 | 867,980 | 6.1 | 1965...... | 198,950,000 |
| 1630...... | 5,700 | 1810...... | 7,239,881 | 1,685,865 | 4.3 | 1970...... | 219,474,000 |
| 1640...... | 27,947 | 1820...... | 9,638,453 | 1,753,588 | 5.5 | 1975...... | 243,880,000 |
| | | | | | | 1980...... | 272,557,000 |
| 1650...... | 51,700 | 1830...... | 12,866,020 | 1,753,588 | 7.3 | | |
| | | | | | | | NOTE B |
| 1660...... | 84,800 | 1840...... | 17,069,453 | 1,753,588 | 9.7 | 1960...... | 180,126,000 |
| 1670...... | 114,500 | 1850...... | 23,191,876 | 2,944,337 | 7.9 | 1965...... | 195,747,000 |
| 1680...... | 155,600 | 1860...... | 31,443,321 | 2,973,965 | 10.6 | 1970...... | 213,810,000 |
| 1690...... | 213,500 | 1870...... | 39,818,449 | 2,973,965 | 13.4 | 1975...... | 235,246,000 |
| | | | | | | 1980...... | 259,981,000 |
| 1700...... | 275,000 | 1880...... | 50,155,783 | 2,973,965 | 16.9 | | |
| | | | | | | | NOTE C |
| 1710...... | 357,500 | 1890...... | 62,947,714 | 2,973,965 | 21.2 | 1960...... | 179,773,000 |
| 1720...... | 474,388 | 1900...... | 75,994,575 | 2,974,159 | 25.6 | 1965...... | 193,643,000 |
| 1730...... | 654,950 | 1910...... | 91,972,266 | 2,973,890 | 30.9 | 1970...... | 208,199,000 |
| 1740...... | 889,000 | 1920...... | 105,710,620 | 2,973,776 | 35.5 | 1975...... | 225,552,000 |
| | | | | | | 1980...... | 245,409,000 |
| 1750...... | 1,207,000 | 1930...... | 122,775,046 | 2,977,128 | 41.2 | | |
| | | | | | | | NOTE D |
| 1760...... | 1,610,000 | 1940...... | 131,669,275 | 2,977,128 | 44.2 | 1960...... | 179,420,000 |
| 1770...... | 2,205,000 | 1950...... | 151,132,000‡ | 2,974,726 | 50.8 | 1965...... | 191,517,000 |
| 1780...... | 2,781,000 | 1960...... | 179,323,175§ | 3,548,913 | 50.5 | 1970...... | 202,541,000 |
| | | | | | | 1975...... | 215,790,000 |
| | | | | | | 1980...... | 230,834,000 |

* For the United States excluding Alaska and Hawaii.   † Figures relate to July 1 and include armed forces overseas.
‡ Including armed forces overseas.   § Figure includes Alaska and Hawaii; it excludes armed forces overseas, estimated at 680,000.
   NOTE A: Projection assumes that fertility will average 10% above the 1955–57 level for the whole projection period 1958–80.   NOTE B: Projection assumes that fertility will remain constant at the 1955–57 level for the whole projection period 1958–80.   NOTE C: Projection assumes that fertility will decline from the 1955–57 level to the 1949–51 level by 1965–70, then remain at this level to 1980.   NOTE D: Projection assumes that fertility will decline from the 1955–57 level to the 1942–44 level by 1965–70, then remain at this level to 1980.

## Estimates of World Population by Regions, 1650–1960

*Source:* W. F. Willcox, 1650–1900; United Nations, 1920–60.

| | Estimated population in millions | | | | | | |
|---|---|---|---|---|---|---|---|
| Date | Africa | North America[1] | Latin America[2] | Asia (exc. U.S.S.R.)[3] | Europe and Asiatic U.S.S.R.[3] | Oceania | World total |
| 1650........... | 100 | 1 | 7 | 257 | 103 | 2 | 470 |
| 1750........... | 100 | 1 | 10 | 437 | 144 | 2 | 694 |
| 1850........... | 100 | 26 | 33 | 656 | 274 | 2 | 1,091 |
| 1900........... | 141 | 81 | 63 | 857 | 423 | 6 | 1,571 |
| 1920........... | 140 | 117 | 91 | 966[4] | 487[5] | 8.8 | 1,810 |
| 1940........... | 172 | 146 | 131 | 1,212[4] | 573[5] | 11.3 | 2,246 |
| 1950........... | 200 | 167 | 163 | 1,376[4] | 576[5] | 13.0 | 2,495 |
| 1959........... | 237 | 196 | 235 | 1,624[4] | 634[5] | 16.1 | 2,907 |
| 1960........... | 244 | 199 | 206 | 1,665 | 641[5] | 16.4 | 2,971 |

[1] U.S. including Alaska and Hawaii; Bermuda; Canada; Greenland; and St. Pierre and Miquelon.   [2] Mexico, Central and South America, and Caribbean islands.   [3] Estimates for Asia and Europe by Willcox have been adjusted to include population of Asiatic U.S.S.R. with that of Europe rather than Asia.   [4] Includes Syria and Asiatic Turkey but excludes U.S.S.R.   [5] Includes European Turkey and U.S.S.R.

# Distribution of U. S. Population According to Size of Place, 1790 to 1960

Source: U. S. Bureau of the Census.

| Census year | Total population | Total urban | Urban places of | | | Total rural | Number of urban places of specified size | | |
|---|---|---|---|---|---|---|---|---|---|
| | | | 1,000,000 or more | 100,000 to 1,000,000 | Under 100,000 | | 1,000,000 or more | 100,000 to 1,000,000 | Under 100,000 |
| 1790....... | 3,929,214 | 5.1 | — | — | 5.1 | 94.9 | — | — | 24 |
| 1800....... | 5,308,483 | 6.1 | — | — | 6.1 | 93.9 | — | — | 33 |
| 1810....... | 7,239,881 | 7.3 | — | — | 7.3 | 92.7 | — | — | 46 |
| 1820....... | 9,638,453 | 7.2 | — | 1.3 | 5.9 | 92.8 | — | 1 | 60 |
| 1830....... | 12,866,020 | 8.8 | — | 1.6 | 7.2 | 91.2 | — | 1 | 89 |
| 1840....... | 17,069,453 | 10.8 | — | 3.0 | 7.8 | 89.2 | — | 3 | 128 |
| 1850....... | 23,191,876 | 15.3 | — | 5.1 | 10.2 | 84.7 | — | 6 | 230 |
| 1860....... | 31,443,321 | 19.8 | — | 8.4 | 11.4 | 80.2 | — | 9 | 383 |
| 1870....... | 38,558,371 | 25.7 | — | 10.7 | 15.0 | 74.3 | — | 14 | 649 |
| 1880....... | 50,155,783 | 28.2 | 2.4 | 10.0 | 15.8 | 71.8 | 1 | 19 | 919 |
| 1890....... | 62,947,714 | 35.1 | 5.8 | 9.6 | 19.7 | 64.9 | 3 | 25 | 1,320 |
| 1900....... | 75,994,575 | 39.7 | 8.5 | 10.2 | 21.0 | 60.3 | 3 | 35 | 1,699 |
| 1910....... | 91,972,266 | 45.7 | 9.2 | 12.9 | 23.6 | 54.3 | 3 | 47 | 2,212 |
| 1920....... | 105,710,620 | 51.2 | 9.6 | 16.3 | 25.3 | 48.8 | 3 | 65 | 2,654 |
| 1930....... | 122,775,046 | 56.2 | 12.3 | 17.3 | 26.6 | 43.8 | 5 | 88 | 3,072 |
| 1940....... | 131,669,275 | 56.5 | 12.1 | 16.8 | 27.6 | 43.5 | 5 | 87 | 3,372 |
| 1950*...... | 150,697,361 | 59.0 | 11.5 | 18.0 | 29.5 | 41.0 | 5 | 102 | 3,916 |
| 1950†...... | 150,697,361 | 64.0 | 11.5 | 17.9 | 34.6 | 36.0 | 5 | 101 | 4,635 |
| 1960†...... | 179,323,175 | 69.9 | 9.8 | 17.7 | 42.4 | 30.1 | 5 | 129 | 5,311 |

* Old urban definition.    † New urban definition.

# White and Negro Population by State, 1960 Census

Source: U. S. Bureau of the Census.

| State | White | Negro | Other | State | White | Negro | Other |
|---|---|---|---|---|---|---|---|
| Alabama............ | 2,283,609 | 980,271 | 2,860 | Montana........... | 650,738 | 1,467 | 22,562 |
| Alaska............. | 174,546 | 6,771 | 4,304 | Nebraska.......... | 1,374,764 | 29,262 | 7,304 |
| Arizona............ | 1,169,517 | 43,403 | 89,241 | Nevada............ | 263,443 | 13,484 | 8,351 |
| Arkansas ......... | 1,395,703 | 388,787 | 1,782 | New Hampshire .. | 604,334 | 1,903 | 684 |
| California.......... | 14,455,230 | 883,861 | 378,113 | New Jersey ....... | 5,539,003 | 514,875 | 12,904 |
| Colorado........... | 1,700,700 | 39,992 | 13,255 | New Mexico....... | 875,763 | 17,063 | 58,197 |
| Connecticut ....... | 2,423,816 | 107,449 | 3,969 | New York.......... | 15,287,071 | 1,417,511 | 77,722 |
| Delaware .......... | 384,327 | 60,688 | 1,277 | North Carolina ... | 3,399,285 | 1,116,021 | 40,849 |
| D. C.............. | 345,263 | 411,737 | 6,956 | North Dakota...... | 619,538 | 777 | 12,131 |
| Florida ........... | 4,063,881 | 880,186 | 7,493 | Ohio .......... | 8,909,698 | 786,097 | 10,602 |
| Georgia........... | 2,817,223 | 1,122,596 | 3,297 | Oklahoma.......... | 2,107,900 | 153,084 | 67,300 |
| Hawaii ........... | 202,230 | 4,943 | 425,599 | Oregon ........... | 1,732,037 | 18,133 | 18,517 |
| Idaho ........... | 657,383 | 1,502 | 8,306 | Pennsylvania....... | 10,454,004 | 852,750 | 12,612 |
| Illinois ........... | 9,010,252 | 1,037,470 | 33,436 | Rhode Island....... | 838,712 | 18,332 | 2,444 |
| Indiana........... | 4,388,554 | 269,275 | 4,669 | South Carolina .... | 1,551,022 | 829,291 | 2,281 |
| Iowa ............ | 2,728,709 | 25,354 | 3,474 | South Dakota ... | 653,098 | 1,114 | 26,302 |
| Kansas ........... | 2,078,666 | 91,445 | 8,500 | Tennessee ........ | 2,977,753 | 586,876 | 2,460 |
| Kentucky ......... | 2,820,083 | 215,949 | 2,124 | Texas ........... | 8,374,831 | 1,187,125 | 17,721 |
| Louisiana.......... | 2,211,715 | 1,039,207 | 6,100 | Utah ............ | 873,828 | 4,148 | 12,651 |
| Maine ........... | 963,291 | 3,318 | 2,656 | Vermont........... | 389,092 | 519 | 270 |
| Maryland ......... | 2,573,919 | 518,410 | 8,360 | Virginia........... | 3,142,443 | 816,258 | 8,248 |
| Massachusetts....... | 5,023,144 | 111,842 | 13,592 | Washington ....... | 2,751,675 | 48,738 | 52,801 |
| Michigan ......... | 7,085,865 | 717,581 | 19,748 | West Virginia....... | 1,770,133 | 89,378 | 910 |
| Minnesota......... | 3,371,603 | 22,263 | 19,998 | Wisconsin ........ | 3,858,903 | 74,546 | 18,328 |
| Mississippi......... | 1,257,546 | 915,743 | 4,852 | Wyoming ......... | 322,922 | 2,183 | 4,961 |
| Missouri............ | 3,922,967 | 390,853 | 5,993 | TOTAL, U. S. ...... | 158,831,732 | 18,871,831 | 1,619,612 |

# Distribution of U. S. Population by Race, 1850-1960

*Source:* U. S. Bureau of the Census.

| Year | White | Nonwhite | | | | | | Total Nonwhite |
|---|---|---|---|---|---|---|---|---|
| | | Negro | Indian | Japanese | Chinese | All other | | |
| 1850.............. | 19,553,068 | 3,638,808 | ....... | ....... | ...... | ...... | | 3,638,808 |
| 1860.............. | 26,922,537 | 4,441,830 | 44,021 | ....... | 34,933 | ...... | | 4,520,784 |
| 1870.............. | 33,589,377 | 4,880,009 | 25,731 | 55 | 63,199 | ...... | | 4,968,994 |
| 1880.............. | 43,402,970 | 6,580,793 | 66,407 | 148 | 105,465 | ...... | | 6,752,813 |
| 1890.............. | 55,101,258 | 7,488,676 | 248,253 | 2,039 | 107,488 | ...... | | 7,846,456 |
| 1900.............. | 66,809,196 | 8,833,994 | 237,196 | 24,326 | 89,863 | ...... | | 9,185,379 |
| 1910.............. | 81,731,957 | 9,827,763 | 265,683 | 72,157 | 71,531 | 3,175 | | 10,240,309 |
| 1920.............. | 94,820,915 | 10,463,131 | 244,437 | 111,010 | 61,639 | 9,488 | | 10,889,705 |
| 1930.............. | 110,286,740 | 11,891,143 | 332,397 | 138,834 | 74,954 | 50,978 | | 12,488,306 |
| 1940.............. | 118,214,870 | 12,865,518 | 333,969 | 126,947 | 77,504 | 50,467 | | 13,454,405 |
| 1950.............. | 134,942,028 | 15,042,286 | 343,410 | 141,768 | 117,629 | 110,240 | | 15,755,333 |
| Urban.......... | 86,756,435 | 9,392,608 | 56,108 | 100,735 | 109,434 | 52,366 | | 9,711,251 |
| Rural nonfarm.... | 28,470,339 | 2,491,377 | 178,678 | 14,260 | 5,844 | 20,827 | | 2,710,986 |
| Rural farm...... | 19,715,254 | 3,158,301 | 108,624 | 26,773 | 2,351 | 37,047 | | 3,333,096 |
| 1960 .......... | 158,831,732 | 18,871,831 | 523,591 | 464,332 | 237,292 | 394,397 | | 20,491,443 |

# United States Population Distribution by Age, Race, Nativity and Sex, 1850–1960

*Source:* Mortimer Spiegelman, *Introduction to Demography,* and Bureau of Census

| Year | Total | Age | | | | | | Race and Nativity | | | |
|---|---|---|---|---|---|---|---|---|---|---|---|
| | | Under 5 | 5–19 | 20–44 | 45–64 | 65 and over | | White | | | Nonwhite |
| | | | | | | | | Total | Native born | Foreign born | |
| | | | | | Per cent distribution | | | | | | |
| 1850*......... | 100.0 | 15.1 | 37.4 | 35.1 | 9.8 | 2.6 | | 84.3 | 74.6 | 9.7 | 15.7 |
| 1860†......... | 100.0 | 15.4 | 35.8 | 35.7 | 10.4 | 2.7 | | 85.6 | 72.6 | 13.0 | 14.4 |
| 1870†......... | 100.0 | 14.3 | 35.4 | 35.4 | 11.9 | 3.0 | | 87.1 | 72.9 | 14.2 | 12.9 |
| 1880†......... | 100.0 | 13.8 | 34.3 | 35.9 | 12.6 | 3.4 | | 86.5 | 73.4 | 13.1 | 13.5 |
| 1890‡......... | 100.0 | 12.2 | 33.9 | 36.9 | 13.1 | 3.9 | | 87.5 | 73.0 | 14.5 | 12.5 |
| 1900......... | 100.0 | 12.1 | 32.3 | 37.8 | 13.7 | 4.1 | | 87.9 | 74.5 | 13.4 | 12.1 |
| 1910......... | 100.0 | 11.6 | 30.4 | 39.1 | 14.6 | 4.3 | | 88.9 | 74.4 | 14.5 | 11.1 |
| 1920......... | 100.0 | 11.0 | 29.8 | 38.4 | 16.1 | 4.7 | | 89.7 | 76.7 | 13.0 | 10.3 |
| 1930......... | 100.0 | 9.3 | 29.5 | 38.3 | 17.5 | 5.4 | | 89.8 | 78.4 | 11.4 | 10.2 |
| 1940......... | 100.0 | 8.0 | 26.4 | 38.9 | 19.8 | 6.9 | | 89.8 | 81.1 | 8.7 | 10.2 |
| 1950§......... | 100.0 | 10.7 | 23.2 | 37.7 | 20.3 | 8.1 | | 89.5 | 82.8 | 6.7 | 10.5 |
| 1959§......... | 100.0 | 11.2 | 27.2 | 32.7 | 20.2 | 8.7 | | 88.8 | ¶ | ¶ | 11.2 |
| 1960 ......... | 100.0 | 11.3 | 27.2 | 32.2 | 20.1 | 9.2 | | 88.6 | ¶ | ¶ | 11.4 |
| | | | | | Males per 100 females | | | | | | |
| 1850*......... | 104.3 | 102.4 | 100.9 | 108.1 | 106.4 | 101.3 | | 105.2 | 103.1 | 123.8 | 99.1 |
| 1860†......... | 104.7 | 102.4 | 101.2 | 107.9 | 111.5 | 98.3 | | 105.3 | 103.7 | 115.1 | 101.2 |
| 1870†......... | 102.2 | 102.9 | 101.2 | 99.2 | 114.5 | 100.5 | | 102.8 | 100.6 | 115.3 | 98.4 |
| 1880†......... | 103.6 | 103.0 | 101.3 | 104.0 | 110.2 | 101.4 | | 104.0 | 102.1 | 115.9 | 100.7 |
| 1890‡......... | 105.0 | 103.6 | 101.4 | 107.3 | 108.3 | 104.2 | | 105.4 | 102.9 | 118.7 | 102.2 |
| 1900......... | 104.4 | 102.1 | 100.9 | 105.8 | 110.7 | 102.0 | | 104.9 | 102.8 | 117.4 | 101.0 |
| 1910......... | 106.0 | 102.5 | 101.3 | 108.1 | 114.4 | 101.1 | | 106.6 | 102.7 | 129.2 | 101.3 |
| 1920......... | 104.0 | 102.5 | 100.8 | 102.8 | 115.2 | 101.3 | | 104.4 | 101.7 | 121.7 | 100.9 |
| 1930......... | 102.5 | 103.0 | 101.4 | 100.5 | 109.1 | 100.5 | | 102.9 | 101.1 | 115.8 | 99.1 |
| 1940......... | 100.7 | 103.2 | 102.0 | 98.1 | 105.2 | 95.5 | | 101.2 | 100.1 | 111.1 | 96.7 |
| 1950§......... | 99.0 | 103.9 | 102.9 | 97.0 | 100.2 | 89.6 | | 99.4 | 99.0 | 103.9 | 96.2 |
| 1959§......... | 98.0 | 103.8 | 104.0 | 97.8 | 94.5 | 82.8 | | 98.3 | ¶ | ¶ | 95.6 |
| 1960 ......... | 97.1 | 103.4 | 102.7 | 95.6 | 95.7 | 82.8 | | 97.4 | ¶ | ¶ | 94.7 |

* Excludes nonwhite races other than Negro.   † Excludes Indians in Indian Territory and on Indian reservations. ‡ The age figures exclude all persons residing on Indian reservations, whether white or nonwhite; these persons are included in the race and nativity distributions.   § Includes armed forces overseas and other persons abroad.   ¶ Not available.   NOTE: For 1850 and 1860, the data in the census reports at ages 40–49 and 60–69 are published in 10-year age groupings; these were subdivided into 5-year age groupings by the author.

## U. S. Population by Age, Sex and Race, 1959-1960

*Source:* U. S. Bureau of the Census.

| Age | White, 1959 | | Nonwhite, 1959 | | All persons, 1960 | |
|---|---|---|---|---|---|---|
| | Male | Female | Male | Female | Male | Female |
| Under 5 years.......... | 8,639,000 | 8,285,000 | 1,443,000 | 1,429,000 | 10,329,729 | 9,991,172 |
| Under 1 year.......... | 1,650,000 | 1,586,000 | 279,000 | 278,000 | 2,089,909 | 2,022,040 |
| 1 and 2 years......... | 3,503,000 | 3,360,000 | 589,000 | 581,000 | 4,169,806 | 4,035,322 |
| 3 and 4 years......... | 3,485,000 | 3,339,000 | 574,000 | 569,000 | 4,070,014 | 3,933,810 |
| 5 to 9 years............. | 8,240,000 | 7,855,000 | 1,310,000 | 1,296,000 | 9,504,368 | 9,187,412 |
| 10 to 14 years.......... | 7,354,000 | 7,011,000 | 1,037,000 | 1,029,000 | 8,524,289 | 8,249,203 |
| 15 to 19 years.......... | 5,794,000 | 5,594,000 | 781,000 | 787,000 | 6,633,661 | 6,585,582 |
| 20 to 24 years.......... | 4,932,000 | 4,835,000 | 694,000 | 701,000 | 5,272,340 | 5,528,421 |
| 25 to 29 years.......... | 4,886,000 | 4,861,000 | 620,000 | 671,000 | 5,333,075 | 5,536,049 |
| 30 to 34 years.......... | 5,293,000 | 5,402,000 | 605,000 | 704,000 | 5,846,224 | 6,102,962 |
| 35 to 39 years.......... | 5,451,000 | 5,641,000 | 600,000 | 670,000 | 6,079,512 | 6,401,597 |
| 40 to 44 years.......... | 5,066,000 | 5,249,000 | 516,000 | 589,000 | 5,675,881 | 5,924,362 |
| 45 to 49 years.......... | 4,820,000 | 5,004,000 | 515,000 | 579,000 | 5,357,925 | 5,521,560 |
| 50 to 54 years.......... | 4,260,000 | 4,428,000 | 432,000 | 457,000 | 4,734,829 | 4,871,125 |
| 55 to 59 years.......... | 3,631,000 | 3,854,000 | 361,000 | 380,000 | 4,127,245 | 4,302,620 |
| 60 to 64 years.......... | 3,132,000 | 3,444,000 | 273,000 | 284,000 | 3,409,319 | 3,733,133 |
| 65 to 69 years.......... | 2,511,000 | 2,844,000 | 187,000 | 204,000 | 2,931,088 | 3,326,822 |
| 70 to 74 years.......... | 1,842,000 | 2,176,000 | 127,000 | 138,000 | 2,185,216 | 2,553,716 |
| 75 to 79 years.......... | 1,206,000 | 1,573,000 | 90,000 | 105,000 | 1,359,424 | 1,694,135 |
| 80 to 84 years.......... | 594,000 | 817,000 | 50,000 | 58,000 | 665,093 | 914,834 |
| 85 years and over....... | 319,000 | 449,000 | 41,000 | 50,000 | 362,276 | 566,976 |
| All ages............ | 77,969,000 | 79,321,000 | 9,682,000 | 10,131,000 | 88,331,494 | 90,991,681 |
| Under 18 years.......... | 27,937,000 | 26,719,000 | 4,275,000 | 4,242,000 | 32,615,929 | 31,586,081 |
| 65 years and over....... | 6,472,000 | 7,858,000 | 495,000 | 555,000 | 7,503,097 | 9,056,483 |
| Median age, years....... | 29.1 | 31.1 | 21.9 | 23.7 | 28.7 | 30.3 |

NOTE: Data relate to the total population of the continental United States, including the armed forces overseas.

## Immigrants and Emigrants; United States, 1911–1960

*Source:* U. S. Immigration and Naturalization Service and U. S. Bureau of the Census.

| Period* | Immigrants | Emigrants | Excess of immigrants over emigrants | Period* | Immigrants | Emigrants | Excess of immigrants over emigrants |
|---|---|---|---|---|---|---|---|
| 1911–15.......... | 4,459,831 | 1,444,530 | 3,015,301 | 1941–45......... | 170,952 | 42,696 | 128,256 |
| 1916–20.......... | 1,275,980 | 702,464 | 573,516 | 1946–50......... | 864,087 | 113,703 | 750,384 |
| 1921–25.......... | 2,638,913 | 697,397 | 1,941,516 | 1951–55......... | 1,087,638 | 134,220 | 953,418 |
| 1926–30.......... | 1,468,296 | 347,679 | 1,120,617 | 1956–60......... | 1,427,841 | (†) | ....... |
| 1931–35.......... | 220,209 | 323,863 | −103,654 | 1959............ | 260,686 | (†) | ....... |
| 1936–40.......... | 308,222 | 135,875 | 172,347 | 1960............ | 265,398 | (†) | ....... |

* Fiscal years ending June 30.    † Not available.

## Persons Naturalized Since 1907

*Source:* U. S. Immigration and Naturalization Service.

| Period* | Civilian | Military | Total | Period* | Civilian | Military | Total |
|---|---|---|---|---|---|---|---|
| 1907–10.......... | 111,738 | ...... | 111,738 | 1954............ | 104,086 | 13,745 | 117,831 |
| 1911–20.......... | 884,672 | 244,300 | 1,128,972 | 1956............ | 138,681 | 7,204 | 145,885 |
| 1921–30.......... | 1,716,979 | 56,206 | 1,773,185 | 1957............ | 137,198 | 845 | 138,043 |
| 1931–40.......... | 1,498,573 | 19,891 | 1,518,464 | 1958............ | 118,950 | 916 | 119,866 |
| 1941–50.......... | 1,837,229 | 149,799 | 1,987,028 | 1959............ | 102,623 | 1,308 | 103,931 |
| 1951–60.......... | 1,148,241 | 41,705 | 1,189,946 | 1960............ | 117,848 | 1,594 | 119,442 |
| 1952............ | 87,070 | 1,585 | 88,655 | 1907–60......... | 7,197,432 | 511,901 | 7,709,333 |

* Fiscal years ending June 30.

# Immigration by Country of Origin, 1820 to 1960

*Source:* Immigration and Naturalization Service.

(Figures are totals, not annual averages, and were tabulated as follows: 1820-67, alien passengers arrived; 1868-91 and 1895-97, immigrant aliens arrived; 1892-94 and 1898 to present, immigrant aliens admitted. Data before 1906 relate to country whence alien came; since 1906, to country of last permanent residence.)

| Countries | 1820-1910 | 1911-1920 | 1921-1930 | 1931-1940 | 1941-1950 | 1951-1960 | 1820-1960 |
|---|---|---|---|---|---|---|---|
| Europe: Albania[1] | ........ | ........ | 1,663 | 2,040 | 85 | 59 | 3,847 |
| Austria[2] | 3,172,461 | 453,649 | 32,868 | 3,563 | 24,860 | 67,106 | 3,754,507 |
| Belgium | 103,796 | 33,746 | 15,846 | 4,817 | 12,189 | 18,575 | 188,969 |
| Bulgaria[3] | 39,440 | 22,533 | 2,945 | 938 | 375 | 104 | 66,335 |
| Czechoslovakia[1] | ........ | 3,426 | 102,194 | 14,393 | 8,347 | 918 | 129,278 |
| Denmark | 258,053 | 41,983 | 32,430 | 2,559 | 5,393 | 10,984 | 351,402 |
| Estonia[1] | ........ | ........ | 1,576 | 506 | 212 | 185 | 2,479 |
| Finland[1] | ........ | 756 | 16,691 | 2,146 | 2,503 | 4,925 | 27,021 |
| France | 470,868 | 61,897 | 49,610 | 12,623 | 38,809 | 51,121 | 684,928 |
| Germany[2] | 5,351,746 | 143,945 | 412,202 | 114,058 | 226,578 | 477,765 | 6,726,294 |
| Great Britain: England | 2,212,071 | 249,944 | 157,420 | 21,756 | 112,252 | 156,171 | 2,909,614 |
| Scotland | 488,749 | 78,357 | 159,781 | 6,887 | 16,131 | 32,854 | 782,759 |
| Wales | 59,540 | 13,107 | 13,012 | 735 | 3,209 | 2,589 | 92,192 |
| Not specified[4] | 793,741 | ........ | ........ | ........ | ........ | 3,884 | 797,625 |
| Greece | 186,204 | 184,201 | 51,084 | 9,119 | 8,973 | 47,608 | 487,189 |
| Hungary[2] | ........ | 442,693 | 30,680 | 7,861 | 3,469 | 36,637 | 521,340 |
| Ireland | 4,212,169 | 146,181 | 220,591 | 13,167 | 26,967 | 57,332 | 4,676,407 |
| Italy | 3,086,356 | 1,109,524 | 455,315 | 68,028 | 57,661 | 185,491 | 4,962,375 |
| Latvia[1] | ........ | ........ | 3,399 | 1,192 | 361 | 352 | 5,304 |
| Lithuania[1] | ........ | ........ | 6,015 | 2,201 | 683 | 242 | 9,141 |
| Luxemburg[1] | ........ | ........ | 727 | 565 | 820 | 684 | 2,796 |
| Netherlands | 175,943 | 43,718 | 26,948 | 7,150 | 14,860 | 52,277 | 320,896 |
| Norway[5] | 665,189 | 66,395 | 68,531 | 4,740 | 10,100 | 22,935 | 837,890 |
| Poland[6] | 165,182 | 4,813 | 227,734 | 17,026 | 7,571 | 9,985 | 432,311 |
| Portugal | 132,989 | 89,732 | 29,994 | 3,329 | 7,423 | 19,588 | 283,055 |
| Rumania[7] | 72,117 | 13,311 | 67,646 | 3,871 | 1,076 | 1,039 | 159,060 |
| Spain | 69,296 | 68,611 | 28,958 | 3,258 | 2,898 | 7,894 | 180,915 |
| Sweden[5] | 1,021,165 | 95,074 | 97,249 | 3,960 | 10,665 | 21,697 | 1,249,810 |
| Switzerland | 237,401 | 23,091 | 29,676 | 5,512 | 10,547 | 17,675 | 323,902 |
| Turkey In Europe | 85,800 | 54,677 | 14,659 | 737 | 580 | 2,653 | 159,106 |
| U.S.S.R.[8] | 2,359,048 | 921,201 | 61,742 | 1,356 | 548 | 584 | 3,344,479 |
| Yugoslavia[3] | ........ | 1,888 | 49,064 | 5,835 | 1,576 | 8,225 | 66,588 |
| Other Europe | 2,605 | 8,111 | 9,603 | 2,361 | 3,983 | 8,155 | 34,818 |
| Total Europe | 25,421,929 | 4,376,564 | 2,477,853 | 348,289 | 621,704 | 1,328,293 | 34,574,632 |
| | | | | | | | |
| Asia: China | 326,060 | 21,278 | 29,907 | 4,928 | 16,709 | 9,657 | 408,539 |
| India | 5,409 | 2,082 | 1,886 | 496 | 1,761 | 1,973 | 13,607 |
| Japan[9] | 158,344 | 83,837 | 33,462 | 1,948 | 1,555 | 46,250 | 325,396 |
| Turkey in Asia[10] | 106,481 | 79,389 | 19,165 | 328 | 218 | 866 | 206,447 |
| Other Asia | 16,942 | 5,973 | 12,980 | 7,644 | 11,537 | 88,707 | 143,783 |
| Total Asia[15] | 613,236 | 192,559 | 97,400 | 15,344 | 31,780 | 147,453 | 1,097,772 |
| | | | | | | | |
| America: Canada & Newfoundland[11] | 1,230,501 | 742,185 | 924,515 | 108,527 | 171,718 | 377,952 | 3,555,398 |
| Central America | 10,365 | 17,159 | 15,769 | 5,861 | 21,665 | 44,751 | 115,570 |
| Mexico[12] | 77,645 | 219,004 | 459,287 | 22,319 | 60,589 | 299,811 | 1,138,655 |
| South America | 29,385 | 41,899 | 42,215 | 7,803 | 21,831 | 91,628 | 234,761 |
| West Indies | 233,146 | 123,424 | 74,899 | 15,502 | 49,725 | 123,091 | 619,787 |
| Other America[13] | ........ | ........ | 31 | 25 | 29,276 | 59,711 | 89,043 |
| Total America | 1,581,042 | 1,143,671 | 1,516,716 | 160,037 | 354,804 | 996,944 | 5,753,214 |
| | | | | | | | |
| Africa | 9,581 | 8,443 | 6,286 | 1,750 | 7,367 | 14,092 | 47,519 |
| Australia & New Zealand | 31,654 | 12,348 | 8,299 | 2,231 | 13,805 | 11,506 | 79,843 |
| Pacific Islands[15] | 8,859 | 1,079 | 427 | 780 | 5,437 | 4,698 | 21,280 |
| Countries not specified | 252,691[14] | 1,147 | 228 | ........ | 142 | 12,493 | 266,701 |
| | | | | | | | |
| Total all countries | 27,918,992 | 5,735,811 | 4,107,209 | 528,431 | 1,035,039 | 2,515,479 | 41,840,961 |

[1] Countries established since beginning of World War I are theretofore included with countries to which they belonged. [2] Data for Austria-Hungary not reported until 1861. Austria and Hungary recorded separately after 1905. Austria included with Germany 1938-45. [3] Bulgaria, Serbia, Montenegro first reported in 1899. Bulgaria reported separately since 1920. In 1920, separate enumeration for Kingdom of Serbs, Croats, Slovenes; since 1922, recorded as Yugoslavia. [4] United Kingdom not specified; for 1901-51, included in "Other Europe." [5] Norway included with Sweden 1820-68. [6] Included with Austria-Hungary, Germany and Russia 1899-1919. [7] No record of immigration until 1880. [8] Since 1931, U.S.S.R. has been broken down into European Russia and Siberia or Asiatic Russia. [9] No record of immigration until 1861. [10] No record of immigration until 1869. [11] Includes all British North American possessions 1820-98. [12] No record of immigration 1886-93. [13] Included with "Countries not specified" prior to 1925. [14] Includes 32,897 persons returning in 1906 to their homes in U. S. [15] From 1952, Asia included Philippines. From 1934-51, Philippines included in Pacific Islands; before 1934, recorded in separate tables as insular travel.

# The Working Population of the U. S., 1820–1960

*Source:* U. S. Bureau of the Census.

| Year | Working population | | Per cent of working population in | | Year | Working population | | Per cent of working population in | |
| | Number (thousands) | Per cent of total population ages 10 and over[1] | Farm occupation | Nonfarm occupation | | Number (thousands) | Per cent of total population ages 10 and over[1] | Farm occupation | Nonfarm occupation |
|---|---|---|---|---|---|---|---|---|---|
| 1820 | 2,881 | 44.4 | 71.8 | 28.2 | 1900 | 29,073 | 50.2 | 37.5 | 62.5 |
| 1830 | 3,932 | 45.5 | 70.5 | 29.5 | 1910 | 37,371 | 52.2 | 31.0 | 69.0 |
| 1840 | 5,420 | 46.6 | 68.6 | 31.4 | 1920 | 42,434 | 51.3 | 27.0 | 73.0 |
| 1850 | 7,697 | 46.8 | 63.7 | 36.3 | 1930 | 48,830 | 49.5 | 21.4 | 78.6 |
| 1860 | 10,533 | 47.0 | 58.9 | 41.1 | 1940 | 52,789 | 52.2 | 16.1 | 83.9 |
| 1870 | 12,925 | 44.4 | 53.0 | 47.0 | 1950 | 60,054 | 53.5 | 11.6 | 88.4 |
| 1880 | 17,392 | 47.3 | 49.4 | 50.6 | 1960 | 70,636 | 55.9 | 8.9 | 91.1 |
| 1890 | 23,318 | 49.2 | 42.6 | 57.4 | | | | | |

[1] For 1820 to 1930, the data relate to the population and gainful workers at ages 10 and over. For 1940 to 1960, the data relate to the population and labor force at ages 14 and over; the farm and nonfarm percentages relate only to the experienced labor force.

# Experienced Civilian Labor Force, 1950 in Thousands*

*Source:* U. S. Department of Commerce.

| | |
|---|---|
| Total, 14 years & over | 58,999 |
| Professional, technical & kindred workers | 4,988 |
| Accountants & auditors | 383 |
| Actors & actresses | 18 |
| Airplane pilots & navigators | 14 |
| Architects | 25 |
| Artists & art teachers | 81 |
| Authors, editors & reporters | 108 |
| Chemists | 76 |
| Chiropractors | 13 |
| Clergymen | 168 |
| College presidents, professors, instructors | 126 |
| Dancers & dancing teachers | 17 |
| Dentists | 75 |
| Draftsmen | 125 |
| Engineers, technical | 534 |
| Lawyers & judges | 181 |
| Librarians | 56 |
| Musicians & music teachers | 161 |
| Nurses, professional | 404 |
| Optometrists | 15 |
| Osteopaths | 5 |
| Pharmacists | 89 |
| Photographers | 55 |
| Physicians & surgeons | 192 |
| Radio operators | 16 |
| Religious workers | 42 |
| Social & welfare workers, except group | 76 |
| Surveyors | 28 |
| Veterinarians | 13 |
| Farmers & farm managers | 4,321 |
| Managers, officials & proprietors, excl. farm | 5,076 |
| Clerical & kindred workers | 7,070 |
| Bookkeepers | 736 |
| Cashiers | 234 |
| Stenographers, typists & secretaries | 1,622 |
| Sales workers | 4,044 |
| Insurance agents & brokers | 307 |
| Sales & sales clerks | 3,407 |
| Craftsmen, foremen & kindred workers | 8,153 |
| Carpenters | 985 |
| Electricians | 324 |
| Foremen, not elsewhere classified | 854 |
| Machinists | 534 |
| Mechanics & repairmen | 1,768 |
| Painters, construction & maintenance | 431 |
| Operators & kindred workers | 11,715 |
| Private household workers | 1,488 |
| Service workers, except private household | 4,512 |
| Barbers, beauticians & machinists | 389 |
| Bartenders | 208 |
| Boarding & lodging house keepers | 29 |
| Charwomen & cleaners | 124 |
| Cooks, except private household | 463 |
| Elevator operators | 94 |
| Practical nurses | 144 |
| Waiters & waitresses | 713 |
| Farm laborers & foremen | 2,515 |
| Laborers, except farm & mine | 3,751 |
| Occupation not reported | 1,366 |

# Indian Population Residing on Reservations Under Agency Control

**Top 16 agencies by population, 1950)***

*Source:* Bureau of Indian Affairs.

| | |
|---|---|
| Five Civilized Tribes Agency (Okla.) | 37,382 |
| Navajo Agency & Reservation (Ariz.) | 32,838 |
| Navajo Agency & Reservation (N. Mex.) | 20,714 |
| Southern Plains Agency (Okla.) | 14,841 |
| United Pueblo Agency (N. Mex.) | 12,935 |
| California Agency (Calif.) | 10,000 |
| Pine Ridge Agency & Reservation (S. Dak.) | 6,636 |
| Consolidated Chippewa Agency (Minn.) | 6,376 |
| Pima Agency (Ariz.) | 5,918 |
| Rosebud Agency (S. Dak.) | 5,698 |
| Turtle Mountain Agency (N. Dak.) | 4,546 |
| Papago Agency (Ariz.) | 4,468 |
| Hope Agency & Reservation (Ariz.) | 4,011 |
| Great Lakes Agency (Wis.) | 3,916 |
| Blackfeet Agency & Reservation (Mont.) | 3,546 |
| San Carlos Agency & Reservation (Ariz.) | 3,136 |

* Complete reports of 1960 census not available on time for this edition.

# Women in the Working Population of the U. S., 1870–1960

*Source:* U. S. Bureau of the Census.

| Year | Working women* | | |
| --- | --- | --- | --- |
| | Number (thousands) | Per cent of female population ages 10 and over* | Per cent of total working population ages 10 and over* |
| 1870............ | 1,917 | 13.3 | 14.8 |
| 1880............ | 2,647 | 14.7 | 15.2 |
| 1890............ | 4,006 | 17.4 | 17.2 |
| 1900............ | 5,319 | 18.8 | 18.3 |
| 1910............ | 7,445 | 21.5 | 19.9 |
| 1920............ | 8,637 | 21.4 | 20.4 |
| 1930............ | 10,752 | 22.0 | 22.0 |
| 1940............ | 12,845 | 25.4 | 24.3 |
| 1950............ | 16,501 | 28.9 | 27.5 |
| 1960†........... | 23,893 | 26.5 | 32.7 |

* For 1870 to 1930, the data relate to the population and gainful workers at ages 10 and over; for 1940 and 1950, the data relate to the population and labor force at ages 14 and over. † December.

# Percent Unemployed in the Civilian Labor Force, 1929–60

*Source:* U. S. Bureau of Labor Statistics.

| Year | Per cent unemployed | Year | Per cent unemployed[1] |
| --- | --- | --- | --- |
| 1929......... | 3.2 | 1945....... | 1.9 |
| 1930......... | 8.7 | 1946....... | 3.9 |
| 1931......... | 15.9 | 1947....... | 3.9 |
| 1932......... | 23.6 | 1948....... | 3.8 |
| 1933......... | 24.9 | 1949....... | 5.9 |
| 1934......... | 21.7 | 1950....... | 5.3 |
| 1935......... | 20.1 | 1951....... | 3.3 |
| 1936......... | 16.9 | 1952....... | 3.1 |
| 1937......... | 14.3 | 1953....... | 2.9 |
| 1938......... | 19.0 | 1954....... | 5.6 |
| 1939......... | 17.2 | 1955....... | 4.4 |
| 1940......... | 14.6 | 1956....... | 4.2 |
| 1941......... | 9.9 | 1957....... | 4.3 |
| 1942......... | 4.7 | 1958....... | 6.8 |
| 1943......... | 1.9 | 1959....... | 5.5 |
| 1944......... | 1.2 | 1960[2]..... | 5.6 |

[1] From 1957 on, new criteria were used. [2] Includes Alaska and Hawaii. NOTE: Estimates since 1940 are derived from sample surveys and are subject to sampling variations.

# MARRIAGE AND DIVORCE

(New statutory enactments and recent judicial decisions or interpretation may affect the following summary, therefore Government officials or an attorney should be consulted for advice.)

## Marriages and Divorces in the United States, 1890–1960

*Source:* Public Health Service, U. S. Dept. of Health, Education and Welfare.

| Year | Marriage | | Divorce[2] | | Year | Marriage | | Divorce[2] | |
| --- | --- | --- | --- | --- | --- | --- | --- | --- | --- |
| | Number | Rate[1] | Number | Rate[1] | | Number | Rate[1] | Number | Rate[1] |
| 1890.......... | 570,000 | 9.0 | 33,461 | .5 | 1932........ | 981,903 | 7.9 | 164,241 | 1.3 |
| 1895.......... | 620,000 | 8.9 | 40,387 | .6 | 1933........ | 1,098,000 | 8.7 | 165,000 | 1.3 |
| 1900.......... | 709,000 | 9.3 | 55,751 | .7 | 1934........ | 1,302,000 | 10.3 | 204,000 | 1.6 |
| 1905.......... | 842,000 | 10.0 | 67,976 | .8 | 1936........ | 1,369,000 | 10.7 | 236,000 | 1.8 |
| 1908.......... | 857,461 | 9.7 | 76,852 | .9 | 1937........ | 1,451,296 | 11.3 | 249,000 | 1.9 |
| 1909.......... | 897,354 | 9.9 | 79,671 | .9 | 1938........ | 1,330,780 | 10.3 | 244,000 | 1.9 |
| 1910.......... | 948,166 | 10.3 | 83,045 | .9 | 1939........ | 1,403,633 | 10.7 | 251,000 | 1.9 |
| 1911.......... | 955,287 | 10.2 | 89,219 | 1.0 | 1940........ | 1,595,879 | 12.1 | 264,000 | 2.0 |
| 1912.......... | 1,004,602 | 10.5 | 94,318 | 1.0 | 1941........ | 1,695,999 | 12.7 | 293,000 | 2.2 |
| 1913.......... | 1,021,398 | 10.5 | 91,307 | .9 | 1942........ | 1,772,132 | 13.2 | 321,000 | 2.4 |
| 1914.......... | 1,025,092 | 10.3 | 100,584 | 1.0 | 1943........ | 1,577,050 | 11.7 | 359,000 | 2.6 |
| 1915.......... | 1,007,595 | 10.0 | 104,298 | 1.0 | 1944........ | 1,452,394 | 10.9 | 400,000 | 2.9 |
| 1917.......... | 1,144,200 | 11.1 | 121,564 | 1.2 | 1946........ | 2,291,045 | 16.4 | 610,000 | 4.3 |
| 1918.......... | 1,000,109 | 9.7 | 116,254 | 1.1 | 1947........ | 1,991,878 | 13.9 | 483,000 | 3.4 |
| 1919.......... | 1,150,186 | 11.0 | 141,527 | 1.3 | 1948........ | 1,811,155 | 12.4 | 408,000 | 2.8 |
| 1920.......... | 1,274,476 | 12.0 | 170,505 | 1.6 | 1949........ | 1,579,798 | 10.6 | 397,000 | 2.7 |
| 1921.......... | 1,163,863 | 10.7 | 159,580 | 1.5 | 1950........ | 1,667,231 | 11.1 | 385,144 | 2.6 |
| 1922.......... | 1,134,151 | 10.3 | 148,815 | 1.4 | 1951........ | 1,594,694 | 10.4 | 381,000 | 2.5 |
| 1923.......... | 1,229,784 | 11.0 | 165,096 | 1.5 | 1952........ | 1,539,318 | 9.9 | 392,000 | 2.5 |
| 1924.......... | 1,184,574 | 10.4 | 170,952 | 1.5 | 1953........ | 1,546,000 | 9.8 | 390,000 | 2.5 |
| 1925.......... | 1,188,334 | 10.3 | 175,449 | 1.5 | 1954........ | 1,490,000 | 9.2 | 379,000 | 2.4 |
| 1927.......... | 1,201,053 | 10.1 | 196,292 | 1.6 | 1956........ | 1,585,000 | 9.5 | 382,000 | 2.3 |
| 1928.......... | 1,182,497 | 9.8 | 200,176 | 1.7 | 1957........ | 1,518,000 | 8.9 | 381,000 | 2.2 |
| 1929.......... | 1,232,559 | 10.1 | 205,876 | 1.7 | 1958........ | 1,451,000 | 8.4 | 368,000 | 2.1 |
| 1930.......... | 1,126,856 | 9.2 | 195,961 | 1.6 | 1959........ | 1,494,000 | 8.5 | 395,000 | 2.2 |
| 1931.......... | 1,060,914 | 8.6 | 188,003 | 1.5 | 1960[3]...... | 1,527,000 | 8.5 | (4) | (4) |

[1] Per 1,000 population. Divorce rates for 1917–19 and 1941–46 are based on population including armed forces overseas. Marriage rates are based on population excluding armed forces overseas. [2] Includes annulments. [3] Provisional. [4] Not available. NOTE: Figures for marriages for all years include partial or complete estimates for some states; figures for divorces are estimated, except for 1900, 1905 and 1922–32. Alaska is included beginning 1959, Hawaii beginning 1960.

# Marital Status of the Population, 1960
*Source:* U. S. Bureau of the Census.

| State and Census division | Males | | | | Females | | | |
|---|---|---|---|---|---|---|---|---|
| | Population 14 yrs. old & over | % distribution* | | | Population 14 yrs. old & over | % distribution* | | |
| | | Single | Married | Widowed or divorced | | Single | Married | Widowed or divorced |
| Alabama | 1,059,866 | 25.6 | 69.4 | 5.0 | 1,157,626 | 19.2 | 65.0 | 15.8 |
| Alaska | 89,132 | 34.5 | 59.4 | 16.1 | 59,626 | 16.6 | 76.8 | 6.6 |
| Arizona | 435,986 | 24.9 | 69.1 | 6.0 | 435,196 | 17.7 | 68.7 | 13.6 |
| Arkansas | 606,401 | 23.9 | 69.8 | 6.3 | 643,007 | 16.9 | 66.7 | 16.4 |
| California | 5,530,596 | 24.8 | 68.5 | 6.7 | 5,652,177 | 16.4 | 66.7 | 16.9 |
| Colorado | 594,482 | 24.4 | 69.6 | 6.0 | 616,527 | 17.7 | 67.4 | 14.9 |
| Connecticut | 881,494 | 25.1 | 69.7 | 5.2 | 942,847 | 20.7 | 65.4 | 13.9 |
| Delaware | 151,235 | 24.0 | 70.7 | 5.3 | 157,955 | 18.7 | 67.9 | 13.4 |
| D. C. | 265,503 | 31.0 | 61.8 | 7.2 | 313,161 | 26.9 | 53.8 | 19.3 |
| Florida | 1,730,220 | 21.6 | 71.8 | 6.6 | 1,827,398 | 14.9 | 68.4 | 16.7 |
| Georgia | 1,290,444 | 26.0 | 69.1 | 4.9 | 1,397,751 | 18.7 | 65.1 | 16.2 |
| Hawaii | 232,805 | 36.4 | 57.7 | 5.9 | 193,684 | 22.9 | 66.4 | 10.7 |
| Idaho | 226,097 | 24.4 | 69.8 | 5.8 | 221,295 | 16.4 | 71.4 | 12.2 |
| Illinois | 3,498,909 | 24.6 | 69.2 | 6.2 | 3,719,766 | 19.0 | 65.6 | 15.4 |
| Indiana | 1,580,100 | 22.6 | 71.3 | 6.1 | 1,670,751 | 17.3 | 67.8 | 14.9 |
| Iowa | 941,937 | 23.8 | 70.4 | 5.8 | 999,250 | 18.7 | 66.6 | 14.7 |
| Kansas | 754,886 | 23.1 | 71.1 | 5.8 | 783,472 | 16.6 | 68.6 | 14.8 |
| Kentucky | 1,036,635 | 26.3 | 67.9 | 5.8 | 1,074,053 | 18.9 | 65.9 | 15.2 |
| Louisiana | 1,037,798 | 25.8 | 69.0 | 5.2 | 1,126,618 | 19.6 | 65.2 | 15.2 |
| Maine | 334,141 | 25.8 | 67.3 | 6.9 | 349,182 | 19.6 | 64.5 | 15.9 |
| Maryland | 1,054,302 | 25.4 | 69.5 | 5.1 | 1,100,932 | 19.1 | 67.2 | 13.7 |
| Massachusetts | 1,767,940 | 27.6 | 66.6 | 5.8 | 1,971,652 | 24.3 | 60.4 | 15.3 |
| Michigan | 2,622,801 | 23.9 | 70.4 | 5.7 | 2,725,768 | 18.4 | 68.1 | 13.5 |
| Minnesota | 1,148,286 | 27.3 | 67.6 | 5.1 | 1,196,196 | 21.5 | 65.1 | 13.4 |
| Mississippi | 693,456 | 27.4 | 67.2 | 5.4 | 746,017 | 19.8 | 64.2 | 16.0 |
| Missouri | 1,496,446 | 23.1 | 70.4 | 6.5 | 1,620,617 | 17.6 | 65.4 | 17.0 |
| Montana | 234,200 | 26.9 | 66.3 | 6.8 | 224,198 | 17.0 | 69.0 | 14.0 |
| Nebraska | 488,723 | 24.7 | 69.8 | 5.5 | 507,502 | 18.2 | 67.4 | 14.4 |
| Nevada | 105,363 | 23.6 | 67.5 | 6.5 | 96,690 | 13.6 | 71.9 | 14.5 |
| New Hampshire | 209,518 | 25.2 | 68.3 | 6.5 | 223,616 | 20.1 | 64.4 | 15.5 |
| New Jersey | 2,125,478 | 23.4 | 70.5 | 6.1 | 2,278,413 | 19.4 | 66.3 | 14.3 |
| New Mexico | 305,452 | 25.9 | 69.0 | 5.1 | 301,432 | 18.7 | 69.6 | 11.7 |
| New York | 5,888,946 | 26.1 | 68.5 | 5.4 | 6,498,895 | 21.7 | 63.2 | 15.1 |
| North Carolina | 1,518,107 | 27.8 | 68.3 | 3.9 | 1,600,462 | 20.8 | 65.9 | 13.3 |
| North Dakota | 217,868 | 31.7 | 63.9 | 4.4 | 208,074 | 21.5 | 66.9 | 11.6 |
| Ohio | 3,267,146 | 22.7 | 71.1 | 6.2 | 3,499,338 | 18.3 | 66.7 | 15.0 |
| Oklahoma | 812,235 | 22.7 | 70.7 | 6.6 | 856,059 | 15.3 | 67.3 | 17.4 |
| Oregon | 616,766 | 22.6 | 70.5 | 6.9 | 634,518 | 16.2 | 68.7 | 15.1 |
| Pennsylvania | 3,915,461 | 25.2 | 69.0 | 5.8 | 4,270,170 | 21.2 | 64.2 | 14.6 |
| Rhode Island | 303,887 | 27.7 | 66.5 | 5.8 | 323,812 | 22.4 | 62.7 | 14.9 |
| South Carolina | 768,653 | 30.4 | 65.7 | 3.9 | 810,626 | 21.9 | 63.7 | 14.4 |
| South Dakota | 233,532 | 28.3 | 66.5 | 5.2 | 229,543 | 19.4 | 67.7 | 12.9 |
| Tennessee | 1,199,101 | 24.9 | 69.8 | 5.3 | 1,300,251 | 18.9 | 65.4 | 15.7 |
| Texas | 3,212,658 | 24.0 | 70.4 | 5.6 | 3,349,072 | 16.7 | 67.8 | 15.5 |
| Utah | 281,896 | 25.2 | 70.4 | 4.4 | 289,631 | 19.5 | 68.7 | 11.8 |
| Vermont | 132,187 | 27.7 | 66.2 | 6.1 | 141,327 | 21.7 | 62.5 | 15.8 |
| Virginia | 1,368,706 | 27.7 | 67.5 | 4.8 | 1,393,767 | 19.6 | 66.4 | 14.0 |
| Washington | 1,003,704 | 24.7 | 68.5 | 6.8 | 1,001,924 | 16.3 | 68.6 | 15.1 |
| West Virginia | 627,445 | 26.0 | 68.2 | 5.8 | 667,970 | 20.0 | 65.1 | 14.9 |
| Wisconsin | 1,347,890 | 26.2 | 68.2 | 5.6 | 1,395,184 | 20.5 | 66.1 | 13.4 |
| Wyoming | 114,875 | 24.2 | 69.5 | 6.3 | 108,991 | 15.4 | 72.2 | 12.4 |
| New England States | 3,629,167 | 26.6 | 67.6 | 5.8 | 3,952,436 | 22.6 | 62.3 | 15.1 |
| Middle Atlantic States | 11,929,885 | 25.5 | 69.0 | 5.5 | 13,047,478 | 21.1 | 64.4 | 14.5 |
| East North Central States | 12,316,847 | 23.9 | 70.1 | 6.0 | 13,010,807 | 18.6 | 66.8 | 14.6 |
| West North Central States | 4,478,688 | 25.9 | 68.7 | 5.4 | 4,670,054 | 19.3 | 66.4 | 14.3 |
| South Atlantic States | 8,774,615 | 26.0 | 68.8 | 5.2 | 9,270,022 | 18.9 | 66.1 | 15.0 |
| East South Central States | 3,935,058 | 26.2 | 68.3 | 5.5 | 4,277,947 | 19.3 | 65.0 | 15.7 |
| West South Central States | 5,669,092 | 24.1 | 70.1 | 5.8 | 5,974,756 | 17.1 | 68.9 | 14.0 |
| Mountain States | 2,098,622 | 27.4 | 66.1 | 6.5 | 2,089,218 | 19.3 | 65.8 | 14.9 |
| Pacific States | 7,473,003 | 25.0 | 68.3 | 6.7 | 7,541,929 | 16.6 | 67.2 | 16.2 |
| TOTAL, U. S. | 61,362,055 | 25.1 | 69.1 | 5.8 | 64,913,989 | 19.1 | 65.9 | 15.0 |

* Total for ages 14 and over = 100%.

# Marriage Information, by State

*Sources:* Legal information, *Information Please Almanac* questionnaires to states; Marriage statistics, Public Health Service, U. S. Dept. of Health, Education and Welfare.

| | Legal minimum marriage age | | | | | Waiting period[1] | | Marriages[2] | |
| State | With parental consent[3] | | Without parental consent | | Blood test required | Before license | After license | 1959 | 1960[4] |
| | M | F | M | F | | | | | |
|---|---|---|---|---|---|---|---|---|---|
| Alabama | 17 | 14 | 21 | 18 | yes | none | none | 30,722 | 31,884 |
| Alaska | 18 | 16 | 21 | 18 | yes | 3 da. | none. | 1,763 | 1,893 |
| Arizona | 18 | 16 | 21 | 18 | yes | none | none | 10,251 | 10,293 |
| Arkansas | 18 | 16 | 21 | 18 | yes | 3 da. | none | 18,394 | 18,703 |
| California | 18 | 16 | 21 | 18 | yes | none | none | 101,314 | 107,015 |
| Colorado | 16 | 16 | 21 | 18 | yes | none | none | 15,518[14] | 15,901 |
| Connecticut | 16 | 16 | 21 | 21 | yes | 4 da. | none | 17,509 | 17,735 |
| Delaware | 18 | 16 | 21 | 18 | yes | none | 24 hr.[5] | 2,383 | 2,392 |
| D. C. | 18 | 16 | 21 | 18 | no | 3 da.[6] | none | 8,377[14] | 8,524 |
| Florida | 18 | 16 | 21 | 21 | yes | 3 da. | none | 38,588 | 39,606 |
| Georgia | 17 | 14 | 21 | 18 | yes | 5 da.[7] | none | 48,928 | 44,341 |
| Hawaii | 18 | 16 | 20 | 20 | yes | 3 da. | none | 4,958 | 5,252 |
| Idaho | 15 | 15 | 18 | 18 | yes | none | none | 9,343 | 10,327 |
| Illinois | 18 | 16 | 21 | 18 | yes | none | none | 87,281 | 88,200 |
| Indiana | 18 | 16 | 21 | 18 | yes | 3 da. | none | 40,982 | 43,036 |
| Iowa | 16 | 14 | 21 | 18 | yes | none | none | 25,116 | 24,760 |
| Kansas | 18 | 16 | 21 | 18 | yes | 3 da. | none | 16,040 | 15,830 |
| Kentucky | 18 | 16 | 21 | 21 | yes | 3 da. | none | 18,323 | 26,733 |
| Louisiana | 18 | 16 | 21 | 21 | yes | none | 72 hr. | 21,453 | 24,210 |
| Maine | 16 | 16 | 21 | 18 | yes | 5 da. | none | 7,599 | 7,142 |
| Maryland | 18 | 16 | 21 | 18 | no | 48 hr. | none | 39,770 | 41,728 |
| Massachusetts | 18 | 16 | 21 | 18 | yes | 3 da. | none | 35,950[15] | 46,538 |
| Michigan | 18 | 16[8] | 18 | 18 | yes | 3 da. | none | 58,826 | 59,607 |
| Minnesota | 18 | 16 | 21 | 18 | no | 5 da. | none | 23,188 | 23,532 |
| Mississippi | 17 | 15 | 21 | 18 | yes | 3 da. | none | 20,447 | 21,238 |
| Missouri | 15 | 15 | 21 | 18 | yes | 3 da. | none | 35,380[13] | 36,442 |
| Montana | 18 | 16 | 21 | 18 | yes | none | none | 6,228 | 5,821 |
| Nebraska | 18 | 16 | 21 | 18 | yes | none | none | 10,724 | 10,652 |
| Nevada | 18 | 16 | 21 | 18 | no | none | none | 60,365[14] | 61,783 |
| New Hampshire | 20[19] | 18[19] | 20 | 18 | yes | 5 da. | none | 7,287 | 7,265 |
| New Jersey | 18 | 16 | 21 | 18 | yes | 72 hr. | none | 38,659 | 39,861 |
| New Mexico | 18 | 16 | 21 | 18 | yes | none | none | 11,113 | 7,352 |
| New York | 16 | 14[9] | 21 | 18 | yes | none | (10) | 120,517 | 125,481 |
| North Carolina | 16 | 16 | 18 | 18 | yes | none[11] | none | 29,986[14] | 31,691 |
| North Dakota | 18 | 15 | 21 | 18 | yes | none | none | 4,282 | 3,996 |
| Ohio | 18 | 16 | 21 | 21 | yes | 5 da. | none | 66,877 | 67,797 |
| Oklahoma | 18 | 15 | 21 | 18 | yes | none[17] | none | 30,170[15] | 28,488 |
| Oregon | 18 | 15 | 21 | 18 | yes | 3 da. | none | 10,166 | 10,726 |
| Pennsylvania | 16 | 16 | 21 | 21 | yes | 3 da. | none | 71,719 | 74,582 |
| Rhode Island | 18 | 16 | 21 | 21 | yes | none[12] | none | 5,770 | 5,786 |
| South Carolina | 18 | 14 | 18 | 18 | no | 24 hr. | none | 38,661 | 40,007 |
| South Dakota | 18 | 15 | 21 | 18 | yes | none | none | 5,861 | 5,804 |
| Tennessee | 16[16] | 16[16] | 21 | 18 | yes | 3 da. | none | 30,213 | 30,763 |
| Texas | 16[16] | 14[16] | 21 | 18 | yes | none[17] | 3 da. | 93,258[15] | 92,315 |
| Utah | 16 | 14 | 21 | 18 | yes | none | none | 6,734 | 7,195 |
| Vermont | 18 | 16 | 21 | 18 | yes | none | 5 da. | 3,235 | 3,044 |
| Virginia | 18 | 16 | 21 | 21 | yes | none | none | 37,768 | 37,470 |
| Washington | 14 | 12 | 21 | 18 | yes[18] | 3 da. | none | 28,556[14] | 28,303 |
| West Virginia | 18 | 16 | 21 | 18 | yes | 3 da | none | 13,294 | 13,877 |
| Wisconsin | 18 | 16 | 21 | 18 | yes | 5 da. | none | 25,637 | 24,629 |
| Wyoming | 18 | 16 | 21 | 21 | yes | none | none | 3,077 | 3,287 |

[1] In some states, waiting period may be waived or reduced by court order.  [2] By place of occurrence.  [3] In most states, persons younger than the age shown may be married by court permission.  [4] Provisional figures; data represent marriages reported for 33 states; marriage intentions filed for 1 state; and marriage licenses issued for remaining states.  [5] 96 hours if nonresidents.  [6] Day of application and day of pickup not included in 3-day waiting period.  [7] If parties cannot establish they are of legal age; 3 days if under legal age and parents sign for them.  [8] Consent of one parent or guardian necessary for female only.  [9] Females 14 to 16 years old must also have consent of judge of Children's Court.  [10] Marriage may not be solemnized within 3 days from date on which specimen was taken for serological test, and not until 24 hours after issuance of marriage license. Waiting period may be waived by court order.  [11] Except in Pamlico County, 48 hours.  [12] 5-day waiting period if woman is nonresident.  [13] Data incomplete.  [14] Marriage licenses.  [15] Data estimated.  [16] Parent must appear in person or provide doctor's affidavit of illness.  [17] 3 days if either party is under legal age.  [18] For males only.  [19] 14 and 13 provided Court's permission is obtained.

# Grounds for Divorce

Source: *Information Please Almanac* questionnaires to the states.

| State | Adultery | Cruelty | Desertion | Alcoholism | Impotence | Felony conviction | Neglect to provide | Insanity | Pregnancy at marriage[1] | Bigamy | Separation | Indignities | Drug addiction | Violence | Fraudulent contract | Others |
|---|---|---|---|---|---|---|---|---|---|---|---|---|---|---|---|---|
| Alabama | yes | yes | yes[2] | yes | yes | yes[50] | yes[3] | yes[4] | yes | ... | ... | ... | yes | yes | ... | (5) |
| Alaska | yes | yes | yes | yes | yes | yes | yes | yes | ... | ... | ... | yes | yes | ... | ... | (49) |
| Arizona | yes | yes | yes | yes | yes | yes[6] | yes | ... | yes | yes | yes[4] | yes | yes | yes | yes | (5,7-13) |
| Arkansas | yes | yes | yes[2] | yes | yes | yes | yes | ... | yes | yes | yes[14] | yes | yes | yes | yes | (12,15,16) |
| California | yes | yes[53] | yes | yes[53] | yes | yes | yes[53] | yes[14] | ... | yes | ... | yes | ... | yes | yes | (7) |
| Colorado | yes | yes | yes[2] | yes | yes | yes | yes[4] | ... | yes | yes[2] | ... | yes | yes | ... | ... | (7) |
| Connecticut | yes | yes | yes[14] | ... | ... | yes[18] | ... | yes[4] | ... | yes | ... | ... | ... | ... | ... | (10,17,19) |
| Delaware | yes | yes | yes[3] | yes[3] | ... | yes[20] | ... | yes[4] | ... | yes | ... | ... | ... | ... | ... | (21-23,36) |
| D. C. | yes | yes[57] | yes[3] | ... | ... | ... | yes | ... | ... | ... | yes[4] | ... | ... | ... | ... |  |
| Florida | yes | yes | yes[2] | yes | yes | ... | ... | yes | yes | yes | yes | ... | yes | ... | yes | (12,17,24,47) |
| Georgia | yes | yes | yes[2] | yes | yes | yes[20] | ... | yes | yes | yes | yes | ... | yes | ... | yes | (12,16) |
| Hawaii | yes | yes | yes[58] | yes[2] | ... | yes[59] | ... | yes[60] | yes[14] | ... | ... | ... | yes[2] | ... | ... | (61) |
| Idaho | yes | yes | yes | ... | ... | yes | yes | yes | yes[14] | ... | yes | ... | ... | ... | ... | (17,51) |
| Illinois | yes | yes | yes[2] | yes[3] | yes | yes | ... | ... | ... | yes | ... | ... | ... | ... | ... | (10,26,27) |
| Indiana | yes | yes | yes[3] | yes | yes | ... | yes[3] | yes[4] | ... | ... | ... | ... | ... | ... | ... | (10) |
| Iowa | yes | yes | yes | yes | yes | ... | yes | ... | ... | ... | ... | ... | ... | yes | ... |  |
| Kansas | yes | yes | yes[2] | yes | yes | yes | yes | ... | yes[4] | ... | ... | ... | ... | yes | ... | (12,16) |
| Kentucky | yes | yes | yes | yes | yes | yes | ... | yes[4] | ... | ... | yes[4] | ... | ... | yes | yes | (11,28,29) |
| Louisiana | yes | yes | yes | yes | ... | yes | yes | ... | ... | ... | yes[8] | ... | ... | ... | ... | (26,30) |
| Maine | yes | yes | yes | yes | yes | yes[18] | yes | ... | ... | ... | ... | ... | yes | ... | ... | (15) |
| Maryland | yes | yes | yes[31] | ... | yes[45] | yes[32] | ... | yes[14] | ... | yes[14] | ... | ... | yes | ... | ... | (32) |
| Massachusetts | yes | yes | yes[15] | yes | yes[34] | yes | ... | ... | ... | ... | yes | ... | ... | ... | ... |  |
| Michigan | yes | yes | yes[3] | yes | yes | yes[35] | yes | yes | ... | yes | ... | yes | yes | ... | ... |  |
| Minnesota | yes | yes | yes[2] | yes[2] | yes | yes | ... | yes[4] | ... | ... | yes[8] | ... | ... | ... | ... |  |
| Mississippi | yes | yes | yes | yes | yes | yes | ... | yes[56] | yes | yes | yes | ... | ... | ... | ... | (7,12,16) |
| Missouri | yes | yes | yes | yes | yes | yes | yes | ... | ... | yes | ... | yes | ... | ... | ... | (7-10) |
| Montana | yes | yes | yes | ... | ... | yes | yes | yes | ... | ... | ... | ... | ... | ... | ... | (17) |
| Nebraska | yes | yes | yes | yes | ... | yes | yes[35] | yes | ... | ... | ... | ... | ... | ... | ... |  |
| Nevada | yes | yes | yes[2] | yes | yes | yes | yes | yes[3] | ... | ... | ... | ... | ... | ... | ... | (10,36) |
| New Hampshire | yes | yes | yes[3] | yes[3] | yes | yes[6] | ... | yes[3] | ... | ... | ... | ... | ... | yes | ... | (28,41,48) |
| New Jersey | yes | yes | yes[3] | ... | ... | ... | ... | ... | ... | ... | ... | ... | ... | ... | ... |  |
| New Mexico | yes | yes | yes | yes | yes | yes | yes | yes | ... | ... | ... | ... | ... | ... | ... | (49) |
| New York | yes | ... | ... | ... | ... | ... | ... | ... | ... | ... | ... | ... | ... | ... | ... |  |
| North Carolina | yes | ... | ... | ... | yes | ... | ... | yes[37] | ... | ... | ... | ... | ... | ... | ... | (5) |
| North Dakota | yes | yes | yes[2] | yes[2] | ... | yes | yes[2] | yes[4] | ... | ... | ... | ... | ... | ... | ... |  |
| Ohio | yes | yes | yes[14] | yes | yes | ... | ... | ... | yes | ... | ... | ... | ... | ... | yes | (15,24,38) |
| Oklahoma | yes | yes | yes[2] | yes | yes | yes | yes | ... | yes[2] | ... | ... | ... | ... | ... | yes | (24,39,49) |
| Oregon | yes | yes | yes[2] | yes[33] | yes | yes | ... | yes[14] | ... | ... | ... | yes | ... | ... | ... |  |
| Pennsylvania | yes | yes | yes[3] | ... | yes[45] | yes[20] | ... | ... | ... | yes | ... | yes | ... | ... | yes | (12) |
| Rhode Island | yes | yes | yes[4] | yes | yes | yes[52] | yes[2] | yes[16] | ... | yes[37] | ... | yes | yes | ... | yes | (40,62) |
| South Carolina | yes | yes | yes[2] | yes | ... | ... | ... | ... | ... | ... | ... | yes | ... | ... | ... |  |
| South Dakota | yes | yes | yes[2] | yes[2] | ... | yes | yes[4] | yes[2] | ... | ... | ... | ... | ... | yes | ... | (7) |
| Tennessee | yes | yes | yes[3] | yes | yes | yes | yes[4] | yes[2] | ... | ... | ... | ... | ... | yes | ... | (10,26,41,46) |
| Texas | yes[54] | yes | yes[14] | ... | ... | yes[55] | yes[4] | ... | ... | ... | yes[52] | yes | ... | yes | ... |  |
| Utah | yes | yes | yes[14] | yes | yes | yes[35] | yes[4] | ... | ... | ... | yes[14] | ... | ... | ... | ... |  |
| Vermont | yes | yes | yes[14] | ... | ... | yes[35] | yes[4] | ... | ... | ... | yes[14] | ... | ... | ... | ... | (19) |
| Virginia | yes | ... | yes[2] | ... | yes | yes | ... | yes | ... | ... | ... | ... | ... | ... | ... | (5,13,42,43) |
| Washington | yes | yes | yes[2] | yes | yes | yes | yes | yes[3] | ... | yes[4] | yes | ... | ... | yes | ... |  |
| West Virginia | yes | yes | yes[3] | yes | ... | yes | ... | ... | ... | ... | ... | yes | ... | ... | ... |  |
| Wisconsin | yes | yes | yes[2] | yes | yes | yes[35] | ... | ... | ... | ... | yes[4] | ... | ... | ... | ... | (44) |
| Wyoming | yes | yes | yes[2] | yes | yes | yes | yes[2] | yes[3] | ... | ... | yes[3] | yes | ... | ... | ... | (8,9,45) |

[1] If unknown to husband. [2] 1 year. [3] 2 years. [4] 5 years. [5] Crime against nature. [6] With imprisonment of 1 year. [7] Absence of 1 year. [8] Felony before marriage. [9] Husband a vagrant. [10] Infamous crime. [11] Loathsome disease. [12] Relationship within prohibited degree. [13] Wife a prostitute. [14] 3 years. [15] Absence of 3 years. [16] Insanity at time of marriage. [17] Habitual intemperance. [18] With imprisonment for life. [19] Absence of 7 years. [20] With imprisonment of 2 years. [21] Wife under 16 at time of marriage. [22] Husband under 18 at time of marriage. [23] Feeble-mindedness or epilepsy for 5 years. [24] Defendant obtained divorce from plaintiff in any other state or country. [25] Absence. [26] Attempt by one party on life of other. [27] Infected other party with communicable venereal disease. [28] Joining a religious cult disbelieving in marriage. [29] Unchaste behavior of wife after marriage. [30] Public defamation. [31] 18 months. [32] With imprisonment of 3 years, 18 months of which have been served. [33] Excessively vicious conduct; any cause which, by laws of state, renders marriage null and void at its inception. [34] With imprisonment of 5 years. [35] With imprisonment of 3 years. [36] Noncohabitation for 3 years. [37] 10 years. [38] 1 year, if contracted after marriage. [39] Gross neglect of duty. [40] Any other gross misbehaviour or wickedness. [41] Absence of 2 years. [42] Infamous crime before marriage. [43] Fugitive from justice and absent for 2 years. [44] Absence of 5 years under

(Footnotes continued on next page.)

# Per Cent of Population Ever Married: U. S., 1890–1960

*Source:* U. S. Bureau of the Census.

| Age group, years | 1890 | 1900 | 1910 | 1920 | 1930 | 1940 | 1950 | 1960 |
|---|---|---|---|---|---|---|---|---|
| Males: 14–19...... | 0.4 | 0.9 | 1.0 | 1.8 | 1.5 | 1.5 | 2.6 | 2.9 |
| 20–24.......... | 19.2 | 22.1 | 24.6 | 29.0 | 28.9 | 27.8 | 43.9 | 45.3 |
| 25–29.......... | 53.8 | 54.0 | 56.9 | 60.3 | 63.1 | 64.0 | }81.5{ | 77.0 |
| 30–34.......... | 73.3 | 72.2 | 73.7 | 75.7 | 78.7 | 79.3 |  | 87.5 |
| 35–44.......... | 84.5 | 82.9 | 83.1 | 83.7 | 85.6 | 86.0 | 89.3 | 90.8 |
| 45–54.......... | 90.7 | 89.6 | 88.7 | 87.8 | 88.5 | 88.9 | 89.4 | 91.3 |
| Females: 14–19..... | 8.0 | 9.4 | 9.7 | 10.8 | 10.9 | 10.0 | 15.2 | 12.0 |
| 20–24.......... | 48.1 | 48.3 | 51.4 | 54.3 | 53.8 | 52.8 | 68.4 | 71.1 |
| 25–29.......... | 74.5 | 72.4 | 74.9 | 76.8 | 78.2 | 77.2 | }89.2{ | 90.5 |
| 30–34.......... | 84.8 | 83.3 | 83.8 | 85.0 | 86.7 | 85.3 |  | 93.1 |
| 35–44.......... | 90.1 | 88.8 | 88.5 | 88.6 | 89.9 | 89.6 | 91.6 | 94.1 |
| 45–54.......... | 92.9 | 92.1 | 91.4 | 90.3 | 90.8 | 91.3 | 92.2 | 92.8 |

# Marriage Prospects of Single Men and Women

*Source:* U. S. Bureau of the Census.

| Age | Per cent of population single[1] Male | Female | Per cent who ever marry[2] Male | Female | Age | Per cent of population single[1] Male | Female | Per cent who ever marry[2] Male | Female |
|---|---|---|---|---|---|---|---|---|---|
| 15.............. | 99.1 | 98.0 | 92.2 | 93.5 | 33.............. | 11.9 | 8.3 | 58.5 | 42.1 |
| 16.............. | 99.2 | 94.0 | 92.4 | 93.5 | 34.............. | 11.0 | 8.1 | 54.1 | 38.0 |
| 17.............. | 98.4 | 86.4 | 92.5 | 93.5 | 35.............. | 10.9 | 9.3 | 49.7 | 34.3 |
| 18.............. | 96.1 | 75.6 | 92.6 | 93.3 | 36.............. | 10.3 | 8.1 | 45.6 | 31.0 |
| 19.............. | 90.7 | 62.4 | 92.7 | 92.9 | 37.............. | 9.7 | 7.8 | 41.6 | 27.9 |
| 20.............. | 82.2 | 50.0 | 92.6 | 92.1 | 38.............. | 9.9 | 8.3 | 38.1 | 25.2 |
| 21.............. | 70.2 | 38.7 | 92.3 | 90.8 | 39.............. | 8.9 | 7.5 | 34.8 | 22.6 |
| 22.............. | 58.6 | 30.1 | 91.8 | 89.0 | 40.............. | 9.9 | 9.3 | 31.7 | 20.2 |
| 23.............. | 47.1 | 23.9 | 90.0 | 86.3 | 41.............. | 8.5 | 7.5 | 28.8 | 18.1 |
| 24.............. | 38.4 | 19.8 | 89.6 | 82.8 | 42.............. | 8.8 | 8.1 | 26.0 | 16.1 |
| 25.............. | 32.2 | 16.5 | 88.0 | 78.5 | 43.............. | 8.2 | 7.5 | 23.5 | 14.4 |
| 26.............. | 27.6 | 15.0 | 85.9 | 73.7 | 44.............. | 8.7 | 7.7 | 21.2 | 12.8 |
| 27.............. | 22.7 | 12.7 | 83.4 | 68.9 | 45.............. | 9.5 | 8.9 | 19.1 | 11.3 |
| 28.............. | 19.4 | 11.6 | 80.3 | 64.4 | 50.............. | 9.6 | 8.8 | 11.1 | 6.1 |
| 29.............. | 16.6 | 10.4 | 76.6 | 59.9 | 55.............. | 8.9 | 8.0 | 6.2 | 3.2 |
| 30.............. | 15.9 | 10.8 | 72.3 | 55.3 | 60.............. | 9.2 | 8.6 | 3.3 | 1.6 |
| 31.............. | 13.3 | 9.2 | 67.5 | 50.8 | 65 and over....... | 8.3 | 8.9 | 1.9 | 0.8 |
| 32.............. | 13.1 | 9.2 | 63.0 | 46.4 |  |  |  |  |  |

[1] Per cent single within specified year of age in 1950, in 3½% sample of population. [2] Per cent of persons single at beginning of year of age who marry during that year and all later years. NOTE: "Single" means those never married; that is, it excludes widowed and divorced. Hence, "marriage prospects" refers to likelihood of first marriage only.

# Median Age at First Marriage in the U. S., 1890–1960

*Source:* U. S. Bureau of the Census.

| Year | Males | Females | Year | Males | Females | Year | Males | Females | Year | Males | Females |
|---|---|---|---|---|---|---|---|---|---|---|---|
| 1890...... | 26.1 | 22.0 | 1920..... | 24.6 | 21.2 | 1950..... | 23.9 | 21.6 | 1959..... | 22.3 | 20.2 |
| 1900...... | 25.9 | 21.9 | 1930..... | 24.3 | 21.3 | 1957..... | 22.5 | 20.3 | 1960..... | 22.8 | 20.3 |
| 1910...... | 25.1 | 21.6 | 1940..... | 24.3 | 21.5 | 1958..... | 22.4 | 20.2 |  |  |  |

### Footnotes for Grounds for Divorce (contd.)

legal separation judgment. [45] If at time of marriage and incurable. [46] Indignities. [47] Ungovernable temper. [48] Noncohabitation for 2 years. [49] Incompatibility. [50] Imprisonment for 2 years, sentence being for 7 years or more. [51] Noncohabitation for 5 years. [52] 7 years. [53] 1 year. [54] Wife s adultery. Husband s adultery when combined with abandonment. [55] Suit for divorce cannot be sustained until 12 months after final judgment of conviction. Divorce cannot be obtained if plaintiff s testimony contributed toward conviction. [56] Absence of 3 years and/or insanity at time of marriage. [57] Limited divorce; may be grounds for absolute divorce 2 years later. [58] 6 months. [59] Imprisonment for life or for 7 years or more. [60] Not less than 60 days. [61] Either party has contracted Hansen's disease (leprosy). [62] Absence of one spouse; presumption of death.

# Divorce Information, by State

*Sources:* Legal information, questionnaires to states; Divorce statistics, Public Health Service,
U. S. Dept. of Health, Education and Welfare.

| State | Residence for divorce | Period before parties may remarry | | Divorces[1] | |
|---|---|---|---|---|---|
| | | Plaintiff | Defendant | 1959 | 1960[2] |
| Alabama | 1 yr. | 60 da. | 60 da. | 14,975 | 17,397 |
| Alaska | 1 yr. | none | none | 679 | 762 |
| Arizona | 1 yr. | 1 yr. | 1 yr. | 6,503[4] | ..... |
| Arkansas | 90 da. | none | none | 5,617[5] | 3,660 |
| California | 1 yr. | none | none | 47,572[5] | ..... |
| Colorado | 1 yr. | none | none | 5,900[4] | ..... |
| Connecticut | 3 yr. | none | none | 2,897 | 2,560 |
| Delaware | 2 yr. | none | none | 617 | 683 |
| D. C. | 1 yr.[6] | none | none | 1,230 | 1,142 |
| Florida | 6 mo. | none | none | 19,550 | 19,823 |
| Georgia | 6 mo. | none | none | 8,609 | 8,258 |
| Hawaii | 2 yr. | none | none | 1,378 | 1,271 |
| Idaho | 6 wk. | none | none | 2,652 | 2,517 |
| Illinois | 1 yr. | none | none | 22,700[5] | ..... |
| Indiana | 1 yr. | none | none | 8,228[5] | ..... |
| Iowa | 1 yr. | 1 yr.[7] | 1 yr.[7] | 4,594 | 4,589 |
| Kansas | 1 yr. | 6 mo. | 6 mo. | 4,963 | 4,884 |
| Kentucky | 1 yr. | none | none | 6,888[5] | ..... |
| Louisiana | 1 yr. | none[8] | none[8] | 3,666[5] | ..... |
| Maine | 6 mo. | none | none | 1,977 | 1,609 |
| Maryland | 1 yr. | none | none | 5,319 | 5,301 |
| Massachusetts | 5 yr.[23] | none | 2 yr. | 5,458 | ..... |
| Michigan | 1 yr. | (9) | (9) | 16,168 | ..... |
| Minnesota | 1 yr. | 6 mo. | 6 mo. | 3,820 | 4,239 |
| Mississippi | 1 yr. | (10) | (10) | 5,108 | 5,556 |
| Missouri | 1 yr.[11] | none | none | 11,824 | 11,268 |
| Montana | 1 yr. | none | none | 2,062 | 2,005 |
| Nebraska | 1 yr. | none | none | 2,201 | ..... |
| Nevada | 6 wk. | none | none | 9,509 | ..... |
| New Hampshire | 1 yr. | none | none | 1,049 | 1,001 |
| New Jersey | 2 yr. | none[12] | none[12] | 4,446 | 4,590 |
| New Mexico | 1 yr.[13] | none | none | 2,093[5] | 1,677 |
| New York | (14) | none | 3 yr.[15] | 7,691 | ..... |
| North Carolina | 2 yr. | none | none | 6,369 | 6,144 |
| North Dakota | 1 yr. | (9) | (9) | 590 | 593 |
| Ohio | 1 yr. | none | none | 22,655 | 23,274 |
| Oklahoma | 6 mo. | 6 mo. | 6 mo. | 13,133[5] | 12,919 |
| Oregon | 1 yr. | 6 mo. | 6 mo. | 6,009 | 5,719 |
| Pennsylvania | 1 yr. | none | none | 13,891 | 22,598 |
| Rhode Island | 2 yr. | none | none | 1,049 | ..... |
| South Carolina | 1 yr. | none | none | 3,034 | 2,896 |
| South Dakota | 1 yr. | none | none[16] | 763 | 815 |
| Tennessee | 1 yr. | none | none[17] | 9,205 | 8,649 |
| Texas | 1 yr. | 1 yr.[18] | 1 yr.[18] | 35,623 | ..... |
| Utah | 3 mo. | 3 mo.[12] | 3 mo.[12] | 1,336 | 2,166 |
| Vermont | (24) | none | 2 yr.[19] | 487 | 457 |
| Virginia | 1 yr. | 4 mo. | 4 mo.[25] | 7,111 | 7,299 |
| Washington | 1 yr. | none | none | 9,341 | ..... |
| West Virginia | 1 yr.[20] | 60 da.[21] | 60 da.[21] | 3,398[5] | ..... |
| Wisconsin | 2 yr. | 1 yr.[22] | 1 yr.[22] | 4,657 | ..... |
| Wyoming | 60 da. | none | none | 1,220 | 1,312 |

[1] By place of legal residence, including reported annulments. Leaders ( . . . .) indicate data unavailable.   [2] Provisional. [3] Divorced persons may remarry each other at any time.   [4] Estimated.   [5] Incomplete.   [6] 2 yrs. if cause for divorce occurred outside D. C.   [7] Unless otherwise set out by judge.   [8] For husband; 10 mo. for wife. In case of adultery, guilty party cannot marry accomplice.   [9] At discretion of court.   [10] Until court is adjourned that grants the divorce. Court may prohibit defendant in adultery cases from remarrying.   [11] Less than year under special circumstances. [12] 3 mo. between first and final judgment; in Utah, 90 days between first and final judgment, during which parties must consult counseling services.   [13] Servicemen acquire residence by being continuously stationed at military base in state for 1 year.   [14] Action for divorce may be maintained where: (1) both parties were residents of state when offense was committed; (2) parties were married within state; (3) plaintiff was resident of state when offense was committed and is resident when action is commenced; (4) offense was committed within state and injured party is resident of state when action is commenced.   [15] By modification of degree by court.   [16] In case of adultery, guilty party may not marry, except to innocent party, until death of innocent party.   [17] Party guilty of adultery may never marry the correspondent.   [18] For cruelty only, but technically not usually observed.   [19] Period may be shortened by court.   [20] 2 years if residence is acquired after cause of divorce action arose. No residence required in case of adultery if personal service can be had within state.   [21] Attorney can lengthen waiting period if desired.   [22] Divorce judgment may be vacated by court upon motion of either party within 1-year waiting period.   [23] For nonresidents at time of marriage; 3 yr. for residents at time of marriage.   [24] Six mo. before filing and 1 year before final decree.   [25] Six mo. in case of adultery.

# BIRTHS

## Registered Live Births and Birth Rates, 1958-60

*Source:* Public Health Service, U. S. Dept. of Health, Education and Welfare.

| State | 1958[1] Number | 1958[1] Rate | 1959[1] Number | 1959[1] Rate | 1960[2] Number | 1960[2] Rate |
|---|---|---|---|---|---|---|
| Alabama | 82,428 | 26.1 | 82,328 | 25.8 | 80,480 | 24.6 |
| Alaska | ..... | .... | 6,292 | 32.9 | 7,496 | 32.9 |
| Arizona | 33,000 | 28.1 | 34,640 | 28.1 | 36,172 | 27.4 |
| Arkansas | 40,892 | 23.4 | 40,718 | 23.3 | 41,455 | 23.2 |
| California | 349,598 | 24.5 | 359,088 | 24.5 | 360,770 | 22.8 |
| Colorado | 41,842 | 25.3 | 42,024 | 25.0 | 44,707 | 25.4 |
| Connecticut | 56,374 | 23.9 | 56,626 | 23.4 | 55,676 | 21.9 |
| Delaware | 11,574 | 26.1 | 11,758 | 25.9 | 11,607 | 25.9 |
| D. C. | 19,658 | 23.7 | 20,094 | 23.9 | 32,930 | 43.2 |
| Florida | 107,996 | 23.9 | 112,798 | 23.7 | 114,551 | 22.9 |
| Georgia | 99,928 | 26.4 | 99,620 | 26.0 | 95,552 | 24.2 |
| Hawaii | ..... | .... | ..... | .... | 17,332 | 27.0 |
| Idaho | 16,762 | 25.7 | 17,188 | 25.9 | 17,023 | 25.4 |
| Illinois | 234,980 | 23.5 | 240,208 | 23.5 | 235,994 | 23.3 |
| Indiana | 112,452 | 24.6 | 112,854 | 24.3 | 111,417 | 23.8 |
| Iowa | 62,372 | 22.4 | 64,616 | 23.0 | 64,767 | 23.5 |
| Kansas | 51,766 | 24.5 | 52,528 | 24.5 | 49,176 | 22.6 |
| Kentucky | 74,258 | 24.1 | 73,850 | 23.6 | 73,673 | 24.2 |
| Louisiana | 90,294 | 29.1 | 90,968 | 28.7 | 90,013 | 27.5 |
| Maine | 23,134 | 24.5 | 23,088 | 24.3 | 23,618 | 24.2 |
| Maryland | 75,960 | 25.7 | 77,060 | 25.4 | 68,999 | 22.1 |
| Massachusetts | 115,020 | 23.5 | 114,240 | 23.1 | (3) | (3) |
| Michigan | 202,900 | 25.9 | 198,576 | 24.9 | 193,886 | 24.7 |
| Minnesota | 84,992 | 25.4 | 88,390 | 26.0 | 87,179 | 25.4 |
| Mississippi | 59,242 | 27.5 | 60,720 | 27.8 | 59,465 | 27.3 |
| Missouri | 96,866 | 23.0 | 98,640 | 23.2 | 101,684 | 23.5 |
| Montana | 17,270 | 25.6 | 17,666 | 25.7 | 17,349 | 25.6 |
| Nebraska | 32,972 | 23.0 | 34,096 | 23.4 | 33,902 | 24.0 |
| Nevada | 6,792 | 25.0 | 7,046 | 25.2 | 7,344 | 25.5 |
| New Hampshire | 13,198 | 22.7 | 13,464 | 22.7 | 13,234 | 21.7 |
| New Jersey | 130,196 | 22.5 | 130,856 | 22.1 | 126,368 | 20.7 |
| New Mexico | 28,650 | 33.5 | 30,220 | 34.4 | 29,104 | 30.4 |
| New York | 360,662 | 22.1 | 360,820 | 21.9 | 360,152 | 21.4 |
| North Carolina | 110,698 | 24.8 | 110,884 | 24.5 | 110,063 | 24.1 |
| North Dakota | 16,528 | 25.9 | 16,986 | 26.5 | 16,561 | 26.1 |
| Ohio | 234,350 | 24.6 | 232,778 | 24.0 | 229,937 | 23.6 |
| Oklahoma | 50,286 | 22.3 | 51,354 | 22.6 | 50,146 | 21.5 |
| Oregon | 36,278 | 20.8 | 36,646 | 20.8 | 38,687 | 21.8 |
| Pennsylvania | 250,208 | 22.4 | 247,004 | 21.8 | 241,031 | 21.2 |
| Rhode Island | 18,350 | 21.2 | 18,716 | 21.4 | 19,290 | 22.5 |
| South Carolina | 60,702 | 25.4 | 60,276 | 24.9 | 59,713 | 25.0 |
| South Dakota | 17,316 | 25.3 | 18,000 | 26.2 | 17,697 | 25.9 |
| Tennessee | 82,770 | 23.9 | 83,152 | 23.8 | 82,850 | 23.2 |
| Texas | 246,498 | 26.4 | 249,240 | 26.2 | 251,120 | 26.1 |
| Utah | 25,508 | 29.7 | 25,708 | 29.2 | 26,130 | 29.2 |
| Vermont | 9,416 | 25.3 | 9,464 | 25.4 | 8,501 | 21.7 |
| Virginia | 96,664 | 24.8 | 96,632 | 24.2 | 89,692 | 22.5 |
| Washington | 65,664 | 23.7 | 65,750 | 23.3 | 64,747 | 22.6 |
| West Virginia | 44,212 | 22.5 | 42,282 | 21.5 | 40,550 | 21.8 |
| Wisconsin | 96,202 | 24.4 | 98,632 | 24.6 | 99,392 | 25.1 |
| Wyoming | 8,134 | 25.8 | 8,212 | 25.7 | 8,339 | 25.1 |
| United States | 4,203,812 | 24.3 | 4,244,796 | 24.1 | 4,231,797 | 23.6 |

[1] By place of residence. [2] By place of occurrence. [3] Not available. Figures for 1959 used in computing total.
NOTE: Rates are per 1,000 estimated midyear population in each specified area.

## Live Births in the United States, 1910–1960
*Source:* Public Health Service, U. S. Dept. of Health, Education and Welfare.

| Year | Births[1] | Rate[2] | Year | Births[1] | Rate[2] | Year | Births[1] | Rate[2] |
|---|---|---|---|---|---|---|---|---|
| 1910........ | 2,777,000 | 30.1 | 1927...... | 2,802,000 | 23.5 | 1944...... | 2,939,000 | 21.2 |
| 1911........ | 2,809,000 | 29.9 | 1928...... | 2,674,000 | 22.2 | 1945...... | 2,858,000 | 20.4 |
| 1912........ | 2,840,000 | 29.8 | 1929...... | 2,582,000 | 21.2 | 1946...... | 3,411,000 | 24.1 |
| 1913........ | 2,869,000 | 29.5 | 1930...... | 2,618,000 | 21.3 | 1947...... | 3,817,000 | 26.6 |
| 1914........ | 2,966,000 | 29.9 | 1931...... | 2,506,000 | 20.2 | 1948...... | 3,637,000 | 24.9 |
| 1915........ | 2,965,000 | 29.5 | 1932...... | 2,440,000 | 19.5 | 1949...... | 3,649,000 | 24.5 |
| 1916........ | 2,964,000 | 29.1 | 1933...... | 2,307,000 | 18.4 | 1950...... | 3,632,000 | 24.1 |
| 1917........ | 2,944,000 | 28.5 | 1934...... | 2,396,000 | 19.0 | 1951[3]...... | 3,823,000 | 24.9 |
| 1918........ | 2,948,000 | 28.2 | 1935...... | 2,377,000 | 18.7 | 1952[3]...... | 3,913,000 | 25.1 |
| 1919........ | 2,740,000 | 26.1 | 1936...... | 2,355,000 | 18.4 | 1953[3]...... | 3,965,000 | 25.0 |
| 1920........ | 2,950,000 | 27.7 | 1937...... | 2,413,000 | 18.7 | 1954[3]...... | 4,078,000 | 25.3 |
| 1921........ | 3,055,000 | 28.1 | 1938...... | 2,496,000 | 19.2 | 1955...... | 4,104,000 | 25.0 |
| 1922........ | 2,882,000 | 26.2 | 1939...... | 2,466,000 | 18.8 | 1956[3]...... | 4,218,000 | 25.2 |
| 1923........ | 2,910,000 | 26.0 | 1940...... | 2,559,000 | 19.4 | 1957[3]...... | 4,308,000 | 25.3 |
| 1924........ | 2,979,000 | 26.1 | 1941...... | 2,703,000 | 20.3 | 1958[3]...... | 4,255,000 | 24.6 |
| 1925........ | 2,909,000 | 25.1 | 1942...... | 2,989,000 | 22.2 | 1959[3]...... | 4,295,000 | 24.3 |
| 1926........ | 2,839,000 | 24.2 | 1943...... | 3,104,000 | 22.7 | 1960[4]...... | 4,247,000 | 23.6 |

[1] Figures through 1959 include adjustment for underregistration; 1960 figure represents number registered. For comparison, the 1959 registered count was 4,245,000.  [2] Rates are per 1,000 population estimated as of July 1 for each year except 1940 and 1950, which are as of April 1, the census date; for 1941–46 based on population including armed forces overseas.  [3] Based on 50% sample of births.  [4] Provisional.  NOTE: Alaska is included beginning 1959, Hawaii beginning 1960.

## Live Births by Order of Birth, 1940-59
*Source:* Public Health Service, U. S. Dept. of Health, Education and Welfare.

| Year & race | Total | Birth Order | | | | | | |
|---|---|---|---|---|---|---|---|---|
| | | 1st | 2nd | 3rd | 4th | 5th | 6th & 7th | 8th & over |
| 1940.......... | 2,558,647 | 940,116 | 639,236 | 349,941 | 205,443 | 131,099 | 154,138 | 138,674 |
| 1945.......... | 2,858,449 | 961,456 | 763,494 | 445,705 | 248,607 | 148,251 | 159,100 | 131,836 |
| 1947.......... | 3,816,770 | 1,574,001 | 1,018,873 | 523,722 | 266,976 | 151,703 | 156,269 | 125,226 |
| 1950.......... | 3,631,512 | 1,140,398 | 1,096,716 | 630,102 | 314,067 | 165,808 | 162,039 | 122,382 |
| 1951[1]........ | 3,822,961 | 1,195,333 | 1,116,358 | 685,721 | 351,234 | 180,341 | 170,285 | 123,689 |
| 1952[1]........ | 3,913,115 | 1,169,490 | 1,121,825 | 732,939 | 386,813 | 199,921 | 178,022 | 124,105 |
| 1953[1]........ | 3,964,750 | 1,149,993 | 1,119,751 | 752,655 | 412,076 | 216,238 | 189,545 | 124,492 |
| 1954[1]........ | 4,078,055 | 1,159,644 | 1,119,393 | 785,066 | 442,800 | 234,717 | 206,708 | 129,727 |
| 1955.......... | 4,104,112 | 1,138,375 | 1,103,633 | 799,598 | 461,561 | 249,060 | 219,752 | 132,133 |
| 1956[1]........ | 4,218,035 | 1,165,552 | 1,109,403 | 820,686 | 483,232 | 263,395 | 236,310 | 139,457 |
| 1957[1]........ | 4,308,251 | 1,180,072 | 1,110,646 | 838,289 | 504,372 | 278,500 | 250,292 | 146,080 |
| 1958[1]........ | 4,255,005 | 1,140,328 | 1,085,413 | 826,025 | 511,090 | 285,603 | 257,392 | 149,154 |
| 1959[1]........ | 4,294,829 | 1,133,011 | 1,076,384 | 830,962 | 526,308 | 297,710 | 272,655 | 157,799 |
| White[1]........ | 3,622,216 | 987,973 | 948,858 | 726,151 | 443,882 | 234,614 | 191,297 | 89,441 |
| Nonwhite[1]..... | 672,613 | 145,038 | 127,526 | 104,811 | 82,426 | 63,096 | 81,358 | 68,358 |

| | | Birth Rate | | | | | | |
|---|---|---|---|---|---|---|---|---|
| 1940.......... | 79.9 | 29.3 | 20.0 | 10.9 | 6.4 | 4.1 | 4.8 | 4.3 |
| 1945.......... | 85.9 | 28.9 | 22.9 | 13.4 | 7.5 | 4.5 | 4.8 | 4.0 |
| 1947.......... | 113.3 | 46.7 | 30.3 | 15.6 | 7.9 | 4.5 | 4.6 | 3.7 |
| 1950.......... | 106.2 | 33.3 | 32.1 | 18.4 | 9.2 | 4.8 | 4.7 | 3.6 |
| 1951[1]........ | 111.3 | 34.8 | 32.5 | 20.0 | 10.2 | 5.2 | 5.0 | 3.6 |
| 1952[1]........ | 113.5 | 33.9 | 32.5 | 21.3 | 11.2 | 5.8 | 5.2 | 3.6 |
| 1953[1]........ | 114.7 | 33.3 | 32.4 | 21.8 | 11.9 | 6.3 | 5.5 | 3.6 |
| 1954[1]........ | 117.6 | 33.5 | 32.3 | 22.6 | 12.8 | 6.8 | 6.0 | 3.7 |
| 1955.......... | 118.0 | 32.7 | 31.7 | 23.0 | 13.3 | 7.2 | 6.3 | 3.8 |
| 1956[1]........ | 120.8 | 33.4 | 31.8 | 23.5 | 13.8 | 7.5 | 6.8 | 4.0 |
| 1957[1]........ | 122.7 | 33.6 | 31.6 | 23.9 | 14.4 | 7.9 | 7.1 | 4.2 |
| 1958[1]........ | 120.1 | 32.2 | 30.6 | 23.3 | 14.4 | 8.1 | 7.3 | 4.2 |
| 1959[1]........ | 120.2 | 31.7 | 30.1 | 23.3 | 14.7 | 8.3 | 7.6 | 4.4 |
| White[1]........ | 114.6 | 31.3 | 30.0 | 23.0 | 14.0 | 7.4 | 6.1 | 2.8 |
| Nonwhite[1]..... | 163.0 | 35.2 | 30.9 | 25.4 | 20.0 | 15.3 | 19.7 | 16.6 |

NOTE: Birth order refers to number of children born alive to mother. Figures are shown to the last digit as computed for convenience in summation. They are not assumed to be accurate to the last digit. Figures for births of order not stated are distributed, including births that occurred in Massachusetts, which did not require the reporting of birth order. Rates are live births per 1,000 female population aged 15–44 years in each specified group. Population enumerated as of April 1 for 1940 and 1950, and estimated as of July 1 for all other years. Births are adjusted for underregistration. Beginning with 1959, Alaska is included.  [1] 1951–54 and 1956–59 are based on birth data from a 50% sample.

# Crude Birth Rate for Selected Countries, 1938, 1953, 1955, 1960

*Source:* Statistical Office of the United Nations.

| Country | Rate[1] | | | | Country | Rate[1] | | | |
|---|---|---|---|---|---|---|---|---|---|
| | 1938 | 1953 | 1955 | 1960 | | 1938 | 1953 | 1955 | 1960 |
| **North America** | | | | | **Europe (cont.)** | | | | |
| Canada........... | 20.7 | 28.1 | 28.2 | 26.8[2] | Hungary.......... | 19.9 | 21.5 | 21.4 | 14.6[2] |
| Costa Rica......... | 45.5 | 48.4 | 49.6 | 55.1[2] | Ireland........... | 19.4 | 21.2 | 21.1 | 21.4[2] |
| El Salvador........ | 43.7 | 47.9 | 47.9 | 44.8[2] | Italy............ | 23.8 | 17.7 | 18.1 | 18.4[2] |
| Mexico........... | 43.5 | 45.0 | 46.4 | 45.5[2] | Luxemburg........ | 14.9 | 16.2 | 16.3 | 16.8[2] |
| Nicaragua......... | 40.8 | 42.3 | 42.9 | 44.4[2] | Netherlands....... | 20.5 | 21.7 | 21.3 | 20.8[2] |
| Panama[4]......... | 45.5 | 37.9 | 39.4 | 40.6[2] | Norway.......... | 15.4 | 18.7 | 18.5 | 17.4[2] |
| Puerto Rico........ | 38.6 | 35.1 | 34.4 | 31.4[2] | Portugal.......... | 26.6 | 23.4 | 23.9 | 23.4[2] |
| United States...... | 17.6[3] | 24.7 | 24.7 | 23.6[2] | Rumania.......... | 29.5 | 23.8 | 25.6 | 18.9[5] |
| **South America** | | | | | Spain............ | 20.1 | 20.6 | 20.6 | 21.9[2] |
| Chile............. | 36.1 | 34.6 | 33.3 | .... | Sweden.......... | 14.9 | 15.4 | 14.8 | 13.6[2] |
| Peru[6]........... | .... | 36.0 | 37.7 | .... | Switzerland....... | 15.2 | 17.0 | 17.1 | 17.8[2] |
| Venezuela[6]........ | 33.7 | 46.1 | 47.2 | .... | United Kingdom... | 15.5 | 15.9 | 15.5 | 17.5[2] |
| **Europe** | | | | | **Asia** | | | | |
| Austria........... | 13.9 | 14.8 | 15.6 | 17.6[2] | Ceylon........... | 35.8 | 38.7 | 37.3 | .... |
| Belgium.......... | 16.0 | 16.6 | 16.8 | 16.8[2] | India[8].......... | 33.3 | 24.8 | 27.0 | 26.3[5] |
| Bulgaria.......... | 22.8 | 20.9 | 20.1 | .... | Israel............ | 26.3[9] | 32.1[10] | 29.2[10] | 26.9[2,10] |
| Czechoslovakia..... | 16.7 | 21.2 | 20.3 | 15.9[2] | Japan[11]......... | 27.1[12] | 21.5[12] | 19.4 | 17.1[2] |
| Denmark.......... | 18.1 | 17.9 | 17.3 | 16.6[2] | **Other** | | | | |
| Finland........... | 21.0[7] | 21.9 | 21.2 | 18.5 | Australia[13]....... | 17.4 | 22.9 | 22.6 | 22.4[2] |
| France............ | 15.0 | 18.9 | 18.6 | 17.9[2] | New Zealand[14].... | 18.0 | 24.1 | 24.9 | 28.4 |
| Germany, West.... | 19.7 | 15.8 | 16.0 | 17.7 | U. of So. Africa[15].. | 25.0 | 25.1 | 24.6 | 25.0[2] |

[1] Number of births per 1,000 population. [2] Provisional. [3] Excluding Alaska and Hawaii. [4] Excluding tribal Indians. Figures for 1953, 1955 and 1960 include Indians in Bocas del Toro and Darien provinces. [5] Official rate. [6] Excluding Indian jungle population. [7] Finnish nationals in Finland only. [8] Data are for a changing group of states and territories which, in 1955, included a population of about 217 million. [9] Jewish population only. [10] Excluding Bedouin population in the Negev. [11] Japanese nationals in Japan only. [12] Excluding Amami Islands. Also excluding Tokara Archipelago in 1938. [13] Excluding full-blooded aborigines. [14] Excluding Maoris. [15] White population only (about 20% of total). NOTE: Leaders (....) indicate information is not available.

# Registered Live Births and Birth Rates by Race in the U. S.

*Source:* Public Health Service, U. S. Dept. of Health, Education and Welfare.

**Rates per 1,000 population in each specified group, enumerated as of Apr. 1 for 1940 and 1950, and estimated as of July 1 for 1945 (including armed forces overseas).**

| Race | Births, 1959* | Rates | | | Race | Births, 1959* | Rates | | |
|---|---|---|---|---|---|---|---|---|---|
| | | 1950 | 1945 | 1940 | | | 1950 | 1945 | 1940 |
| White........... | 3,597,430 | 22.7 | 19.1 | 17.5 | Japanese....... | 8,780 | 24.1 | 22.9 | 14.8 |
| Negro........... | 605,962 | 31.0 | 23.3 | 21.7 | Other.......... | 7,170 | 18.3 | 20.7 | 21.0 |
| Indian.......... | 20,430 | 39.0 | 26.8 | 28.6 | All races....... | 4,244,796 | 23.6 | 19.5 | 17.9 |
| Chinese.......... | 5,024 | 42.9 | 17.1 | 14.2 | | | | | |

* Based on 50% sample of registered births. Includes Alaska.

# Multiple Births in the United States, 1951-57

*Source:* Statistical Bulletin of the Metropolitan Life Insurance Co.

| Age and color of mother | Number of confinements* | Cases of multiple births per million confinements | | | |
|---|---|---|---|---|---|
| | | Total | Twins | Triplets | Quadruplets |
| Total—All ages............... | 27,697,757 | 10,634 | 10,539 | 93 | 1.1 |
| Under 20.................. | 3,394,344 | 6,275 | 6,244 | 31 | † |
| 20–24.................... | 8,785,632 | 8.585 | 8,523 | 62 | 0.2 |
| 25–29.................... | 7,725,235 | 11,156 | 11,058 | 97 | 1.1 |
| 30–34.................... | 4,847,641 | 13,808 | 13,664 | 141 | 2.5 |
| 35–39.................... | 2,318,987 | 15,937 | 15,749 | 185 | 3.4 |
| 40–44.................... | 590,395 | 12,642 | 12,520 | 122 | † |
| 45 and over............... | 35,523 | 7,572 | 7,544 | 28 | † |
| Color—All ages | | | | | |
| White.................... | 23,751,611 | 10,145 | 10,059 | 85 | 1.0 |
| Nonwhite................. | 3,946,146 | 13,576 | 13,423 | 141 | 1.8 |

* Confinements from which at least one infant was born alive. † Cases too few to warrant computation. Source of basic data: Various reports by the National Office of Vital Statistics.

## Live Births by Age of Mother; U. S., 1940-1959

*Source:* Public Health Service, U. S. Dept. of Health, Education and Welfare.

| Year and race | Total[1] | Age of mother | | | | | | | |
|---|---|---|---|---|---|---|---|---|---|
| | | Under 15 yrs.[2] | 15–19 yrs. | 20–24 yrs. | 25–29 yrs. | 30–34 yrs. | 35–39 yrs. | 40–44 yrs. | 45 yrs. and over[3] |
| 1940..... | 2,558,647 | 3,865 | 332,667 | 799,537 | 693,268 | 431,468 | 222,015 | 68,269 | 7,558 |
| 1945..... | 2,858,449 | 4,028 | 298,868 | 832,746 | 785,299 | 554,906 | 296,852 | 78,853 | 6,897 |
| 1947..... | 3,816,770 | 4,911 | 445,047 | 1,254,902 | 1,069,820 | 635,647 | 318,516 | 81,605 | 6,322 |
| 1950..... | 3,631,512 | 5,413 | 432,911 | 1,155,167 | 1,041,360 | 610,816 | 302,780 | 77,743 | 5,322 |
| 1951[4]..... | 3,822,961 | 5,460 | 456,523 | 1,220,900 | 1,090,147 | 649,542 | 313,843 | 81,137 | 5,409 |
| 1952[4]..... | 3,913,115 | 5,358 | 449,163 | 1,232,057 | 1,120,702 | 690,940 | 326,299 | 83,018 | 5,578 |
| 1953[4]..... | 3,964,750 | 5,634 | 466,495 | 1,239,197 | 1,126,449 | 702,219 | 333,652 | 85,730 | 5,374 |
| 1954[4]..... | 4,078,055 | 6,396 | 488,313 | 1,275,313 | 1,137,123 | 731,850 | 344,490 | 89,122 | 5,448 |
| 1955..... | 4,014,112 | 6,181 | 493,770 | 1,290,939 | 1,133,155 | 732,540 | 352,320 | 89,777 | 5,430 |
| 1956[4]..... | 4,218,035 | 6,656 | 530,017 | 1,341,970 | 1,144,456 | 735,734 | 361,933 | 91,834 | 5,435 |
| 1957[4]..... | 4,308,251 | 7,269 | 559,703 | 1,377,463 | 1,153,327 | 740,199 | 371,902 | 92,819 | 5,569 |
| 1958[4]..... | 4,255,005 | 6,930 | 563,338 | 1,383,242 | 1,120,494 | 720,354 | 364,660 | 90,593 | 5,394 |
| 1959[4]..... | 4,294,829 | 7,054 | 580,079 | 1,421,300 | 1,110,918 | 709,234 | 369,261 | 91,463 | 5,520 |
| White[4]..... | 3,622,216 | 2,644 | 449,350 | 1,210,687 | 955,530 | 606,840 | 314,815 | 77,930 | 4,420 |
| Nonwhite[4] | 672,613 | 4,410 | 130,729 | 210,613 | 155,388 | 102,394 | 54,446 | 13,533 | 1,100 |

### Birth rate

| | | | | | | | | | |
|---|---|---|---|---|---|---|---|---|---|
| 1940..... | 79.9 | 0.7 | 54.1 | 135.6 | 122.8 | 83.4 | 46.3 | 15.6 | 1.9 |
| 1945..... | 85.9 | 0.8 | 51.1 | 138.9 | 132.2 | 100.2 | 56.9 | .16.6 | 1.6 |
| 1947..... | 113.3 | 0.9 | 79.3 | 209.7 | 176.0 | 111.9 | 58.9 | 16.6 | 1.4 |
| 1950..... | 106.2 | 1.0 | 81.6 | 196.6 | 166.1 | 103.7 | 52.9 | 15.1 | 1.2 |
| 1951[4]..... | 111.3 | 1.0 | 86.9 | 212.0 | 174.2 | 108.3 | 54.1 | 15.3 | 1.2 |
| 1952[4]..... | 113.5 | 0.9 | 85.4 | 218.1 | 180.4 | 113.1 | 56.1 | 15.3 | 1.2 |
| 1953[4]..... | 114.7 | 0.9 | 87.5 | 224.5 | 183.8 | 113.0 | 57.3 | 15.5 | 1.1 |
| 1954[4]..... | 117.6 | 1.0 | 89.8 | 235.6 | 188.5 | 116.4 | 58.8 | 15.8 | 1.1 |
| 1955..... | 118.0 | 0.9 | 89.7 | 240.4 | 190.8 | 115.8 | 59.5 | 15.7 | 1.1 |
| 1956[4]..... | 120.8 | 1.0 | 94.2 | 251.3 | 195.5 | 116.4 | 60.8 | 15.9 | 1.0 |
| 1957[4]..... | 122.7 | 1.0 | 96.1 | 257.6 | 200.5 | 118.0 | 60.8 | 16.0 | 1.0 |
| 1958[4]..... | 120.1 | 0.9 | 91.6 | 255.1 | 198.9 | 116.3 | 58.6 | 15.6 | 1.0 |
| 1959[4]..... | 120.2 | 0.9 | 90.9 | 256.4 | 200.6 | 116.1 | 58.5 | 15.7 | 1.0 |
| White[4]..... | 114.6 | 0.4 | 80.3 | 250.0 | 196.4 | 112.3 | 55.8 | 14.8 | 0.9 |
| Nonwhite[4] | 163.0 | 4.3 | 166.1 | 300.0 | 230.9 | 145.4 | 81.1 | 23.0 | 1.9 |

NOTE: Data refer only to births occurring within the U. S., including Alaska beginning with 1959. Births are adjusted for underregistration. Figures are shown to the last digit as computed for convenience in summation. They are not assumed to be accurate to the last digit. Figures for age of mother not stated are distributed. Rates are live births per 1,000 female population in each specified group, enumerated as of April 1 for 1940 and 1950, and estimated as of July 1 for all other years. [1] Rates computed by relating total births, regardless of age of mother, to female population aged 15–44 years. [2] Rates computed by relating births to mothers under 15 years, to female population aged 10–14. [3] Rates computed by relating births to mothers 45 years and over, to female population aged 45–49 years. [4] 1951–54 and 1956–59 are based on a 50% sample of births.

## Households, Families and Married Couples in the United States from 1890 to 1960

*Source:* U. S. Bureau of the Census.

| Date | Households | | Families | | Married couples |
|---|---|---|---|---|---|
| | Number | Average population per household | Number | Average population per family | Number |
| June    1890.............. | 12,690,000 | 4.93 | . . . | . . | . . . |
| April   1930.............. | 29,905,000 | 4.01 | . . . | . . | 25,174,000 |
| April   1940.............. | 34,949,000 | 3.67 | 32,166,000 | 3.76 | 28,517,000 |
| March 1950.............. | 43,554,000 | 3.37 | 39,303,000 | 3.54 | 36,091,000 |
| March 1958.............. | 50,402,000 | 3.35 | 43,714,000 | 3.65 | 39,182,000 |
| March 1959.............. | 51,302,000 | 3.35 | 44,202,000 | 3.66 | 39,529,000 |
| March 1960.............. | 52,610,000 | 3.35 | 45,062,000 | 3.68 | 40,205,000 |

# Number of Families and Households, 1940-1960

*Source:* Statistical Bureau of the Metropolitan Life Insurance Company and reports by the Bureau of the Census.

| State | Families | | Households | | Persons per household, 1960 |
|---|---|---|---|---|---|
| | 1940 | 1950 | 1950 | 1960 | |
| Alabama | 646,000 | 729,765 | 779,950 | 884,116 | 3.62 |
| Alaska | not avail. | not avail. | 31,047 | 57,250 | 3.49 |
| Arizona | 116,000 | 181,985 | 209,415 | 366,630 | 3.45 |
| Arkansas | 472,000 | 477,200 | 520,960 | 523,552 | 3.35 |
| California | 1,816,000 | 2,827,110 | 3,311,850 | 4,981,024 | 3.05 |
| Colorado | 278,000 | 338,205 | 386,065 | 529,424 | 3.21 |
| Connecticut | 412,000 | 512,280 | 552,545 | 752,736 | 3.27 |
| Delaware | 64,000 | 79,730 | 87,125 | 128,582 | 3.37 |
| D. C. | 165,000 | 198,180 | 226,545 | 252,066 | 2.87 |
| Florida | 473,000 | 721,460 | 810,860 | 1,550,044 | 3.11 |
| Georgia | 715,000 | 824,095 | 881,675 | 1,070,287 | 3.58 |
| Hawaii | not avail. | 96,460 | 111,849 | 153,064 | 3.87 |
| Idaho | 128,000 | 148,710 | 167,120 | 193,839 | 3.37 |
| Illinois | 2,008,000 | 2,287,955 | 2,536,905 | 3,084,738 | 3.18 |
| Indiana | 892,000 | 1,039,105 | 1,147,025 | 1,387,910 | 3.28 |
| Iowa | 644,000 | 686,785 | 768,080 | 841,357 | 3.19 |
| Kansas | 460,000 | 507,665 | 575,780 | 672,907 | 3.14 |
| Kentucky | 671,000 | 717,535 | 770,625 | 851,867 | 3.47 |
| Louisiana | 554,000 | 648,410 | 714,335 | 892,344 | 3.57 |
| Maine | 201,000 | 223,175 | 246,615 | 280,355 | 3.34 |
| Maryland | 431,000 | 581,840 | 628,615 | 863,003 | 3.48 |
| Massachusetts | 1,025,000 | 1,171,805 | 1,286,490 | 1,534,732 | 3.23 |
| Michigan | 1,308,000 | 1,624,875 | 1,752,955 | 2,238,650 | 3.42 |
| Minnesota | 665,000 | 747,680 | 834,205 | 991,981 | 3.35 |
| Mississippi | 504,000 | 508,960 | 551,465 | 568,070 | 3.74 |
| Missouri | 986,000 | 1,057,260 | 1,184,170 | 1,359,826 | 3.09 |
| Montana | 133,000 | 145,775 | 171,375 | 202,240 | 3.25 |
| Nebraska | 327,000 | 344,720 | 384,660 | 433,448 | 3.16 |
| Nevada | 27,000 | 40,945 | 49,235 | 91,520 | 3.02 |
| New Hampshire | 120,000 | 134,255 | 149,475 | 180,020 | 3.24 |
| New Jersey | 1,030,000 | 1,263,570 | 1,350,245 | 1,806,295 | 3.27 |
| New Mexico | 119,000 | 159,885 | 175,770 | 251,209 | 3.69 |
| New York | 3,379,000 | 3,862,050 | 4,276,635 | 5,248,261 | 3.11 |
| North Carolina | 772,000 | 939,215 | 984,255 | 1,204,715 | 3.66 |
| North Dakota | 139,000 | 144,855 | 159,215 | 173,362 | 3.55 |
| Ohio | 1,761,000 | 2,077,595 | 2,274,890 | 2,852,321 | 3.33 |
| Oklahoma | 587,000 | 590,840 | 658,285 | 734,593 | 3.08 |
| Oregon | 291,000 | 411,690 | 474,090 | 558,222 | 3.09 |
| Pennsylvania | 2,345,000 | 2,639,925 | 2,874,195 | 3,350,604 | 3.30 |
| Rhode Island | 167,000 | 198,630 | 216,795 | 257,335 | 3.18 |
| South Carolina | 410,000 | 477,780 | 511,020 | 603,551 | 3.81 |
| South Dakota | 149,000 | 160,625 | 177,630 | 194,821 | 3.39 |
| Tennessee | 686,000 | 808,145 | 859,660 | 1,003,301 | 3.48 |
| Texas | 1,580,000 | 1,978,950 | 2,175,045 | 2,777,646 | 3.36 |
| Utah | 130,000 | 169,925 | 186,410 | 241,532 | 3.62 |
| Vermont | 84,000 | 90,100 | 100,160 | 110,732 | 3.39 |
| Virginia | 593,000 | 785,060 | 837,275 | 1,074,442 | 3.53 |
| Washington | 451,000 | 625,185 | 730,760 | 894,168 | 3.09 |
| West Virginia | 434,000 | 479,265 | 512,560 | 521,142 | 3.51 |
| Wisconsin | 758,000 | 867,990 | 947,670 | 1,146,040 | 3.36 |
| Wyoming | 60,000 | 72,235 | 82,730 | 99,187 | 3.26 |
| United States | 32,166,000 | 38,407,440 | 42,394,311 | 53,021,061 | 3.29 |

# Projected Population by 1970 for Leading States

*Source:* U. S. Bureau of the Census. Figures exclude armed forces overseas.

| State | 1960 | Rank | 1965 | Rank | 1970 | Rank |
|---|---|---|---|---|---|---|
| New York | 16,782,304 | 1 | 18,628,000 | 1 | 20,023,000 | 2 |
| California | 15,717,204 | 2 | 17,661,000 | 2 | 20,296,000 | 1 |
| Pennsylvania | 11,319,366 | 3 | 11,917,000 | 3 | 12,508,000 | 3 |
| Illinois | 10,081,158 | 4 | 10,613,000 | 6 | 11,353,000 | 6 |
| Ohio | 9,706,397 | 5 | 11,109,000 | 4 | 12,258,000 | 4 |
| Texas | 9,579,677 | 6 | 10,697,000 | 5 | 11,752,000 | 5 |

# MORTALITY

## Death Rates in the United States, 1900–1960

*Source:* Public Health Service, U. S. Dept. of Health, Education and Welfare.

| Year | Rate | Year | Rate | Year | Deaths | Rate |
|------|------|------|------|------|--------|------|
| 1900 | 17.2 | 1921 | 11.5 | 1942 | 1,385,187 | 10.3 |
| 1901 | 16.4 | 1922 | 11.7 | 1943 | 1,459,544 | 10.9 |
| 1902 | 15.5 | 1923 | 12.1 | 1944 | 1,411,338 | 10.6 |
| 1903 | 15.6 | 1924 | 11.6 | 1945 | 1,401,719 | 10.6 |
| 1904 | 16.4 | 1925 | 11.7 | 1946 | 1,395,617 | 10.0 |
| 1905 | 15.9 | 1926 | 12.1 | 1947 | 1,445,370 | 10.1 |
| 1906 | 15.7 | 1927 | 11.3 | 1948 | 1,444,337 | 9.9 |
| 1907 | 15.9 | 1928 | 12.0 | 1949 | 1,443,607 | 9.7 |
| 1908 | 14.7 | 1929 | 11.9 | 1950 | 1,452,454 | 9.6 |
| 1909 | 14.2 | 1930 | 11.3 | 1951 | 1,482,099 | 9.7 |
| 1910 | 14.7 | 1931 | 11.1 | 1952 | 1,496,838 | 9.6 |
| 1911 | 13.9 | 1932 | 10.9 | 1953 | 1,517,541 | 9.6 |
| 1912 | 13.6 | 1933 | 10.7 | 1954 | 1,481,091 | 9.2 |
| 1913 | 13.8 | 1934 | 11.1 | 1955 | 1,528,717 | 9.3 |
| 1914 | 13.3 | 1935 | 10.9 | 1956 | 1,564,476 | 9.4 |
| 1915 | 13.2 | 1936 | 11.6 | 1957 | 1,633,128 | 9.6 |
| 1916 | 13.8 | 1937 | 11.3 | 1958 | 1,647,886 | 9.5 |
| 1917 | 14.0 | 1938 | 10.6 | 1959 | 1,656,814 | 9.4 |
| 1918 | 18.1 | 1939 | 10.6 | 1960 | 1,702,000 | 9.5 |
| 1919 | 12.9 | 1940 | 10.8 |      |        |     |
| 1920 | 13.0 | 1941 | 10.5 |      |        |     |

NOTE: Includes only deaths occurring within the registration area. Beginning with 1933, area includes entire U. S.; with 1959 includes Alaska, and with 1960 includes Hawaii. Excludes fetal deaths. Rates per 1,000 population residing in area, as of April 1 for 1940 and 1950, and estimated as of July 1 for all other years.  [1] Provisional.

## Death Rates by Age, Color and Sex; U. S., 1900–1960

*Source:* Public Health Service, U. S. Dept. of Health, Education and Welfare.

| Age group, years | 1900 | 1920 | 1940 | 1950 | 1960[1] | 1900 | 1920 | 1940 | 1950 | 1960[1] |
|------------------|------|------|------|------|---------|------|------|------|------|---------|
| | White Males | | | | | White Females | | | | |
| Under 1 | 175.9 | 98.1 | 56.7 | 34.0 | 28.8 | 142.6 | 76.1 | 43.6 | 25.7 | 21.4 |
| 1– 4 | 20.2 | 9.8 | 2.8 | 1.4 | 1.1 | 18.7 | 9.0 | 2.4 | 1.1 | .8 |
| 5–14 | 3.8 | 2.7 | 1.1 | .7 | .5 | 3.8 | 2.3 | .8 | .5 | .3 |
| 15–24 | 5.8 | 4.2 | 2.0 | 1.5 | 1.3 | 5.6 | 4.3 | 1.4 | .7 | .5 |
| 25–34 | 8.1 | 5.9 | 2.8 | 1.9 | 1.5 | 8.1 | 6.5 | 2.2 | 1.1 | .8 |
| 35–44 | 10.6 | 7.7 | 5.1 | 3.8 | 3.3 | 9.6 | 7.3 | 3.7 | 2.4 | 1.9 |
| 45–54 | 15.5 | 12.0 | 11.4 | 9.8 | 9.2 | 14.0 | 10.9 | 7.5 | 5.5 | 4.4 |
| 55–64 | 28.5 | 24.2 | 25.2 | 23.0 | 21.9 | 25.5 | 21.7 | 16.8 | 12.9 | 10.6 |
| 65–74 | 59.1 | 54.2 | 54.0 | 48.6 | 51.8 | 53.4 | 49.9 | 41.5 | 32.4 | 29.4 |
| 75–84 | 128.2 | 122.5 | 122.0 | 105.3 | 104.1 | 118.9 | 116.4 | 104.8 | 84.8 | 75.7 |
| 85 and over | 269.2 | 253.6 | 251.4 | 221.2 | 221.1 | 256.7 | 247.0 | 235.0 | 196.8 | 224.4 |
| | Nonwhite Males | | | | | Nonwhite Females | | | | |
| Under 1 | 369.3 | 167.7 | 101.2 | 59.9 | 55.4 | 299.5 | 131.1 | 77.4 | 47.5 | 44.2 |
| 1– 4 | 43.4 | 15.0 | 5.3 | 2.7 | 2.0 | 43.5 | 14.2 | 4.4 | 2.3 | 1.7 |
| 5–14 | 7.8 | 3.7 | 1.6 | 1.0 | .8 | 10.1 | 3.9 | 1.4 | .7 | .5 |
| 15–24 | 11.8 | 9.9 | 5.0 | 2.9 | 2.1 | 11.2 | 10.8 | 5.0 | 2.2 | 1.1 |
| 25–34 | 12.5 | 12.2 | 8.5 | 5.0 | 3.9 | 11.7 | 13.5 | 7.4 | 3.9 | 2.5 |
| 35–44 | 14.2 | 14.4 | 13.2 | 8.6 | 7.7 | 15.6 | 16.0 | 11.7 | 7.5 | 5.8 |
| 45–54 | 24.7 | 20.1 | 24.5 | 18.6 | 15.1 | 23.9 | 23.4 | 21.1 | 15.5 | 10.5 |
| 55–64 | 42.1 | 31.1 | 37.1 | 34.8 | 31.8 | 42.1 | 35.8 | 33.2 | 27.6 | 23.7 |
| 65–74 | 71.6 | 60.2 | 62.8 | 57.9 | 72.3 | 66.4 | 60.4 | 52.3 | 46.1 | 52.4 |
| 75–84 | 131.4 | 116.0 | 108.8 | 90.3 | 90.5 | 113.2 | 106.4 | 84.1 | 70.6 | 62.4 |
| 85 and over | 249.3 | 247.1 | 199.7 | 160.2 | 114.5 | 195.8 | 221.2 | 159.7 | 133.7 | 95.7 |

[1] Estimated from a 10% sample of death certificates. Alaska and Hawaii are included.

# Deaths and Infant Deaths in Each State Reporting, 1959-60

*Source:* Public Health Service, U. S. Dept. of Health, Education and Welfare.

| State | 1959[1] Total deaths Number | 1959[1] Total deaths Rate | 1959[1] Infant mortality Number | 1959[1] Infant mortality Rate | 1960[2] Total deaths Number | 1960[2] Total deaths Rate | 1960[2] Infant mortality Number | 1960[2] Infant mortality Rate |
|---|---|---|---|---|---|---|---|---|
| Alabama | 28,688 | 9.0 | 2,616 | 31.8 | 29,927 | 9.1 | 2,583 | 32.1 |
| Alaska | 1,145 | 6.0 | 270 | 42.9 | 1,236 | 5.4 | 303 | 40.4 |
| Arizona | 9,602 | 7.8 | 1,147 | 33.1 | 10,498 | 8.0 | 1,131 | 31.3 |
| Arkansas | 16,800 | 9.6 | 1,081 | 26.5 | 18,057 | 10.1 | 1,075 | 25.9 |
| California | 128,464 | 8.8 | 8,487 | 23.6 | 130,672 | 8.2 | 8,177 | 22.7 |
| Colorado | 14,842 | 8.8 | 1,212 | 28.8 | 15,767 | 9.0 | 1,203 | 26.9 |
| Connecticut | 23,409 | 9.7 | 1,267 | 22.4 | 23,505 | 9.2 | 1,166 | 20.9 |
| Delaware | 3,957 | 8.7 | 292 | 24.8 | 4,352 | 9.7 | 267 | 23.0 |
| District of Columbia | 8,819 | 10.5 | 739 | 36.8 | 10,127 | 13.3 | 1,022 | 31.1 |
| Florida | 44,387 | 9.3 | 3,574 | 31.7 | 49,548 | 9.9 | 3,412 | 29.8 |
| Georgia | 33,393 | 8.7 | 3,242 | 32.5 | 33,257 | 8.4 | 2,750 | 28.8 |
| Hawaii | ...... | .... | ...... | .... | 3,598 | 5.6 | 399 | 23.0 |
| Idaho | 5,443 | 8.2 | 382 | 22.2 | 5,253 | 7.8 | 388 | 22.8 |
| Illinois | 101,356 | 9.9 | 6,008 | 25.0 | 101,661 | 10.1 | 5,868 | 24.9 |
| Indiana | 44,146 | 9.5 | 2,641 | 23.4 | 44,601 | 9.5 | 2,679 | 24.0 |
| Iowa | 28,338 | 10.1 | 1,389 | 21.5 | 28,744 | 10.4 | 1,415 | 21.8 |
| Kansas | 20,576 | 9.6 | 1,189 | 22.6 | 20,882 | 9.6 | 1,123 | 22.8 |
| Kentucky | 28,742 | 9.2 | 2,018 | 27.3 | 29,386 | 9.6 | 2,020 | 27.4 |
| Louisiana | 28,255 | 8.9 | 2,996 | 32.9 | 29,882 | 9.1 | 2,860 | 31.8 |
| Maine | 10,843 | 11.4 | 603 | 26.1 | 10,687 | 11.0 | 511 | 21.6 |
| Maryland | 27,057 | 8.9 | 2,202 | 28.6 | 27,832 | 8.9 | 1,991 | 28.9 |
| Massachusetts | 54,556 | 11.0 | 2,546 | 22.3 | (3) | (3) | (3) | (3) |
| Michigan | 66,819 | 8.4 | 4,845 | 24.4 | 67,450 | 8.6 | 4,637 | 23.9 |
| Minnesota | 30,903 | 9.1 | 1,861 | 21.1 | 32,467 | 9.5 | 1,908 | 21.9 |
| Mississippi | 20,913 | 9.6 | 2,366 | 39.0 | 21,321 | 9.8 | 2,305 | 38.8 |
| Missouri | 46,631 | 11.0 | 2,416 | 24.5 | 48,967 | 11.3 | 2,501 | 24.6 |
| Montana | 6,584 | 9.6 | 432 | 24.5 | 6,459 | 9.5 | 429 | 24.7 |
| Nebraska | 13,896 | 9.5 | 800 | 23.5 | 13,993 | 9.9 | 589 | 17.4 |
| Nevada | 2,396 | 8.6 | 228 | 32.4 | 2,754 | 9.6 | 224 | 30.5 |
| New Hampshire | 6,727 | 11.4 | 297 | 22.1 | 6,524 | 10.7 | 299 | 22.6 |
| New Jersey | 58,263 | 9.8 | 3,218 | 24.6 | 57,617 | 9.4 | 3,048 | 24.1 |
| New Mexico | 6,190 | 7.0 | 993 | 32.9 | 6,569 | 6.9 | 988 | 33.9 |
| New York | 176,206 | 10.7 | 8,921 | 24.7 | 177,932 | 10.6 | 8,722 | 24.2 |
| North Carolina | 35,833 | 7.9 | 3,624 | 32.7 | 38,688 | 8.5 | 3,523 | 32.0 |
| North Dakota | 5,334 | 8.3 | 403 | 23.7 | 5,419 | 8.5 | 411 | 24.8 |
| Ohio | 91,354 | 9.4 | 5,815 | 25.0 | 93,073 | 9.6 | 5,377 | 23.4 |
| Oklahoma | 22,017 | 9.7 | 1,237 | 24.1 | 22,489 | 9.6 | 1,256 | 25.0 |
| Oregon | 16,699 | 9.5 | 921 | 25.1 | 16,798 | 9.5 | 908 | 23.5 |
| Pennsylvania | 119,387 | 10.5 | 6,147 | 24.9 | 120,706 | 10.6 | 5,949 | 24.7 |
| Rhode Island | 8,804 | 10.1 | 449 | 24.0 | 8,921 | 10.4 | 428 | 22.2 |
| South Carolina | 19,817 | 8.2 | 2,107 | 35.0 | 20,371 | 8.5 | 2,023 | 33.9 |
| South Dakota | 6,297 | 9.2 | 413 | 22.9 | 6,739 | 9.9 | 463 | 26.2 |
| Tennessee | 31,806 | 9.1 | 2,516 | 30.3 | 34,394 | 9.6 | 2,521 | 30.4 |
| Texas | 73,563 | 7.7 | 7,105 | 28.5 | 76,958 | 8.0 | 6,808 | 27.1 |
| Utah | 5,902 | 6.7 | 515 | 20.0 | 6,197 | 6.9 | 534 | 20.4 |
| Vermont | 4,377 | 11.8 | 224 | 23.7 | 4,442 | 11.4 | 196 | 23.1 |
| Virginia | 33,305 | 8.3 | 2,996 | 31.0 | 33,792 | 8.5 | 2,731 | 30.4 |
| Washington | 26,338 | 9.3 | 1,576 | 24.0 | 26,648 | 9.3 | 1,524 | 23.5 |
| West Virginia | 17,697 | 9.0 | 1,150 | 27.2 | 18,276 | 9.8 | 1,029 | 25.4 |
| Wisconsin | 37,310 | 9.3 | 2,311 | 23.4 | 38,245 | 9.6 | 2,221 | 22.3 |
| Wyoming | 2,628 | 8.2 | 221 | 26.9 | 2,806 | 8.5 | 236 | 28.3 |
| United States | 1,656,814 | 9.4 | 112,008 | 26.4 | 1,701,043 | 9.5 | 108,677 | 25.7 |

[1] By place of residence. [2] By place of occurrence. [3] Not available. Figures for 1959 used in computing total.
NOTE: Data exclude fetal deaths. Rates for total deaths are per 1,000 estimated midyear population in each area. Infant mortality rates are deaths under one year per 1,000 live births in each area.

# Average of Annual Death Rates for Selected Causes; U. S., 1900–1960

*Source:* Public Health Service, U. S. Dept. of Health, Education and Welfare.

| | Death rates per 100,000 in | | | | | | |
|---|---|---|---|---|---|---|---|
| | 5th Revision | | | | | 6th Revision | 7th Revision |
| Cause of death | 1900–04 | 1920–24 | 1940–44 | 1945–49 | 1950 | 1950 | 1960[1] |
| Typhoid fever | 26.7 | 7.3 | 0.6 | 0.2 | 0.1 | 0.1 | ([3]) |
| Communicable diseases of childhood | 65.2 | 33.8 | 4.6 | 2.3 | 1.4 | 1.3 | ([3]) |
| Measles | 10.0 | 7.3 | 1.1 | 0.6 | 0.3 | 0.3 | 0.2 |
| Scarlet fever | 11.8 | 4.0 | 0.4 | 0.1 | 0.0 | 0.2 | ([3]) |
| Whooping cough | 10.7 | 8.9 | 2.2 | 1.0 | 0.7 | 0.7 | 0.1 |
| Diphtheria | 32.7 | 13.7 | 1.0 | 0.7 | 0.3 | 0.3 | 0.0 |
| Diarrhea and enteritis | 115.3 | 42.8 | 9.8 | 6.5 | 5.0 | 5.1 | 4.2 |
| Pneumonia and influenza | 184.3 | 140.3 | 63.7 | 42.2 | 35.2 | 31.3 | 36.6 |
| Influenza | 22.8 | 34.8 | 13.0 | 5.0 | 3.5 | 4.4 | 4.5 |
| Pneumonia | 161.5 | 105.5 | 50.7 | 37.2 | 31.7 | 26.9 | 32.0 |
| Tuberculosis | 184.7 | 96.7 | 43.4 | 33.3 | 23.5 | 22.5 | 5.9 |
| Cancer | 67.7 | 86.9 | 123.1 | 133.7 | 137.8 | 139.8 | 147.4 |
| Diabetes mellitus | 12.2 | 17.1 | 26.2 | 26.8 | 28.5 | 16.2 | 17.1 |
| Cardiovascular-renal diseases | 359.5 | 369.9 | 490.4 | 489.2 | 489.0 | 510.8 | 518.9 |
| Diseases of the heart | 153.0 | 169.8 | 303.2 | 325.1 | 327.4 | 356.8 | 366.4 |
| Cerebral hemorrhage | 106.3 | 93.5 | 91.7 | 91.3 | 91.7 | 104.0 | 107.1 |
| Chronic nephritis | 84.3 | 81.5 | 72.1 | 55.0 | 46.3 | 16.4 | 6.9 |
| Syphilis | 12.9 | 17.6 | 12.7 | 8.8 | 6.7 | 5.0 | 1.7 |
| Appendicitis | 9.4 | 14.0 | 7.2 | 3.5 | 2.2 | 2.0 | 1.1 |
| Accidents, all forms | 79.2 | 70.8 | 73.0 | 68.2 | 63.5 | 60.6 | 51.9 |
| Motor vehicle accidents | ([3]) | 12.9 | 22.7 | 22.3 | 23.1 | 23.1 | 20.6 |
| Infant mortality[2] | ([3]) | 76.7 | 42.4 | 33.3 | 29.2 | 29.2 | 25.7 |
| Neonatal mortality[2] | ([3]) | 39.7 | 26.2 | 22.9 | 20.5 | 20.5 | 18.6 |
| Fetal mortality[2] | ([3]) | 39.2[4] | 28.5 | 24.3 | 22.9 | 22.9 | ([3]) |
| Maternal mortality[2] | ([3]) | 6.9 | 2.8 | 1.4 | 0.9 | 0.8 | 0.3 |
| All causes | 1,621.6 | 1,196.6 | 1,062.0 | 1,003.3 | 963.8 | 963.8 | 945.7 |

[1] Estimated from a 10 per cent sample of death certificates. [2] Rates per 1,000 live births. [3] Not available. [4] 1922–24. NOTE: Includes only deaths occurring within the registration area. Beginning with 1933, area includes the entire United States; beginning with 1960, it includes Alaska and Hawaii. Rates per 100,000 population residing in area, enumerated as of April 1 for 1940 and 1950 and estimated as of July 1 for all other years. Average rates computed from 5-year totals of deaths occurring in area and corresponding population. The death rates for 1950 are shown on the basis of both the Fifth and Sixth Revisions of the International Lists of Causes of Death. Due to major changes between the Fifth and Sixth Revisions, the death rates are not strictly comparable.

# Death Rates by Marital Status, Age, and Sex; U. S., Annual Average for 1949–51

*Source:* D. Shurtleff, "Mortality and Marital Status," Public Health Reports, March 1955.

| | Male | | | | | Female | | | | |
|---|---|---|---|---|---|---|---|---|---|---|
| Age (in years) | Single | Married | Widowed | Divorced | Total[1] | Single | Married | Widowed | Divorced | Total[1] |
| Under 20[3] | 3.4 | 1.6 | 2.0 | 2.3 | 3.4 | 2.6 | 1.0 | 4.8 | 1.6 | 2.5 |
| 20–24 | 2.2 | 1.5 | 5.7 | 3.4 | 1.9 | 1.2 | .9 | 3.4 | 1.7 | 1.0 |
| 25–34 | 3.6 | 1.7 | 8.6 | 5.8 | 2.2 | 2.2 | 1.2 | 4.1 | 2.6 | 1.4 |
| 35–44 | 8.5 | 3.6 | 12.1 | 11.8 | 4.3 | 3.9 | 2.6 | 6.2 | 4.5 | 2.9 |
| 45–54 | 17.8 | 9.3 | 21.6 | 23.2 | 10.7 | 7.0 | 5.7 | 10.3 | 8.1 | 6.5 |
| 55–59 | 30.0 | 17.8 | 30.4 | 36.5 | 20.0 | 11.5 | 10.2 | 14.8 | 13.8 | 11.4 |
| 60–64 | 41.0 | 25.8 | 39.5 | 48.6 | 29.0 | 16.6 | 15.7 | 20.7 | 21.1 | 17.5 |
| 65–69 | 55.0 | 36.5 | 50.0 | 66.1 | 41.1 | 24.8 | 23.5 | 28.1 | 33.1 | 26.0 |
| 70–74 | 78.8 | 54.3 | 69.1 | 91.9 | 60.4 | 42.3 | 39.0 | 44.8 | 58.2 | 43.2 |
| 75 and over | 137.3 | 100.3 | 139.0 | 173.3 | 119.4 | 103.6 | 76.0 | 106.2 | 129.2 | 101.6 |
| All ages[2] | 5.4 | 12.1 | 70.5 | 26.1 | 11.1 | 3.9 | 5.8 | 41.1 | 8.8 | 8.3 |

[1] Includes deaths for which marital status was not stated. [2] Includes deaths for which age was not stated. [3] Rates for "Total" and "Single" are based on deaths and population at ages 0–19 years. Rates for "Married," "Widowed," and "Divorced" are based on deaths and population at ages 15–19 years. NOTE: Rates are per 1,000 population in each specified group enumerated in the Census of April 1, 1950. Deaths among armed forces overseas are excluded.

# Average Annual Accidental Death Rates, 1957-58 and 1949-50

**(Rates per 100,000 population by place of residence)**

*Source:* Statistical Bulletin of the Metropolitan Life Insurance Co., June 1961.

| Area | Accidents total 1957-58 | Accidents total 1949-50 | Motor vehicle 1957-58 | Motor vehicle 1949-50 | Falls 1957-58 | Falls 1949-50 | Fire-and burns by other means 1957-58 | Fire-and burns by other means 1949-50 | Drowning* 1957-58 | Drowning* 1949-50 |
|---|---|---|---|---|---|---|---|---|---|---|
| UNITED STATES | 54.2 | 60.7 | 22.0 | 22.2 | 11.3 | 14.4 | 4.3 | 4.8 | 3.0 | 3.4 |
| New England | 47.5 | 51.6 | 12.9 | 12.8 | 17.2 | 20.3 | 3.8 | 3.6 | 2.5 | 3.2 |
| Maine | 55.8 | 62.1 | 19.3 | 17.3 | 9.8 | 16.5 | 5.8 | 6.6 | 4.4 | 4.6 |
| New Hampshire | 49.7 | 56.5 | 16.7 | 16.3 | 12.6 | 17.4 | 4.6 | 6.0 | 3.3 | 3.9 |
| Vermont | 63.2 | 64.5 | 24.4 | 19.5 | 13.2 | 16.3 | 6.3 | 4.6 | 2.2 | 5.7 |
| Massachusetts | 50.6 | 51.5 | 11.1 | 11.3 | 22.4 | 23.2 | 3.6 | 3.0 | 2.4 | 2.8 |
| Rhode Island | 35.2 | 48.4 | 9.7 | 10.6 | 14.5 | 23.0 | 2.6 | 2.0 | 1.8 | 3.6 |
| Connecticut | 39.0 | 44.8 | 12.7 | 12.9 | 12.2 | 15.4 | 3.4 | 3.2 | 2.2 | 3.0 |
| Middle Atlantic | 43.8 | 50.4 | 15.0 | 14.9 | 14.1 | 17.3 | 3.2 | 3.3 | 2.2 | 2.9 |
| New York | 42.2 | 50.2 | 14.2 | 14.1 | 14.0 | 18.6 | 3.2 | 3.2 | 2.3 | 3.1 |
| New Jersey | 40.3 | 42.6 | 13.9 | 13.3 | 12.4 | 13.4 | 3.3 | 2.9 | 2.4 | 2.9 |
| Pennsylvania | 47.9 | 54.2 | 16.8 | 16.6 | 15.0 | 17.3 | 3.3 | 3.8 | 2.0 | 2.5 |
| East North Central | 50.1 | 61.8 | 21.2 | 24.0 | 12.2 | 17.0 | 3.6 | 4.3 | 2.3 | 2.9 |
| Ohio | 52.1 | 61.7 | 21.3 | 23.1 | 14.7 | 18.5 | 3.6 | 4.1 | 2.1 | 2.5 |
| Indiana | 58.5 | 68.4 | 24.8 | 27.9 | 15.2 | 18.1 | 3.8 | 4.4 | 2.1 | 2.8 |
| Illinois | 48.4 | 59.8 | 20.2 | 22.3 | 10.8 | 16.5 | 4.1 | 4.5 | 2.3 | 2.9 |
| Michigan | 44.8 | 61.1 | 20.2 | 26.0 | 9.4 | 15.2 | 3.0 | 4.8 | 2.4 | 3.1 |
| Wisconsin | 50.3 | 60.5 | 21.8 | 22.8 | 11.8 | 16.8 | 3.0 | 3.5 | 2.5 | 3.1 |
| West North Central | 59.1 | 66.6 | 24.7 | 23.0 | 13.6 | 18.6 | 3.9 | 5.2 | 2.6 | 3.2 |
| Minnesota | 53.7 | 60.3 | 22.6 | 19.8 | 12.0 | 17.1 | 2.9 | 4.3 | 2.6 | 3.8 |
| Iowa | 56.8 | 66.0 | 24.5 | 23.4 | 13.6 | 20.7 | 3.3 | 5.1 | 1.9 | 2.7 |
| Missouri | 62.3 | 67.7 | 24.0 | 22.8 | 15.9 | 19.9 | 5.8 | 6.4 | 2.7 | 2.9 |
| North Dakota | 58.6 | 68.3 | 26.0 | 21.5 | 8.1 | 15.1 | 3.0 | 4.4 | 3.6 | 4.3 |
| South Dakota | 65.5 | 72.3 | 29.7 | 27.6 | 11.9 | 14.6 | 2.8 | 4.9 | 3.0 | 3.4 |
| Nebraska | 57.4 | 67.4 | 25.1 | 22.1 | 13.7 | 18.9 | 3.1 | 4.0 | 2.3 | 3.3 |
| Kansas | 63.1 | 71.7 | 27.5 | 27.2 | 13.3 | 17.4 | 4.0 | 5.5 | 3.0 | 3.3 |
| South Atlantic | 57.8 | 61.2 | 23.5 | 23.8 | 8.2 | 9.8 | 5.9 | 5.8 | 4.1 | 3.7 |
| Delaware | 51.9 | 61.9 | 21.2 | 24.5 | 8.0 | 14.0 | 5.5 | 7.1 | 3.9 | 4.1 |
| Maryland | 45.7 | 54.4 | 17.3 | 18.2 | 10.4 | 13.4 | 4.1 | 4.9 | 3.7 | 3.7 |
| District of Columbia | 49.6 | 56.2 | 14.0 | 15.9 | 15.1 | 17.4 | 4.5 | 4.9 | 2.2 | 3.4 |
| Virginia | 55.5 | 61.5 | 20.9 | 23.8 | 8.8 | 9.4 | 6.4 | 6.4 | 3.4 | 3.6 |
| West Virginia | 65.8 | 69.9 | 22.9 | 20.7 | 11.4 | 12.7 | 7.1 | 5.9 | 3.3 | 4.5 |
| North Carolina | 54.9 | 57.6 | 25.5 | 25.6 | 5.8 | 6.8 | 5.1 | 5.3 | 3.9 | 2.9 |
| South Carolina | 63.4 | 65.0 | 26.0 | 28.0 | 5.6 | 7.1 | 8.7 | 7.6 | 5.0 | 3.7 |
| Georgia | 61.6 | 59.8 | 26.6 | 24.0 | 6.5 | 8.9 | 6.9 | 6.4 | 3.7 | 2.9 |
| Florida | 63.1 | 66.1 | 26.1 | 27.5 | 8.8 | 9.8 | 4.9 | 4.4 | 6.0 | 5.9 |
| East South Central | 61.4 | 61.6 | 25.5 | 24.0 | 8.6 | 9.4 | 6.7 | 6.8 | 3.4 | 3.2 |
| Kentucky | 66.4 | 68.4 | 25.0 | 24.8 | 12.7 | 13.8 | 6.0 | 6.5 | 3.3 | 3.3 |
| Tennessee | 52.7 | 55.1 | 22.5 | 22.6 | 7.8 | 9.6 | 5.7 | 5.8 | 2.7 | 2.4 |
| Alabama | 63.8 | 62.4 | 29.1 | 25.9 | 6.9 | 7.2 | 7.3 | 6.6 | 3.1 | 2.9 |
| Mississippi | 64.6 | 61.5 | 25.4 | 22.4 | 6.3 | 6.3 | 8.8 | 9.2 | 5.1 | 4.8 |
| West South Central | 63.5 | 66.2 | 27.7 | 25.6 | 8.0 | 10.4 | 6.1 | 6.4 | 3.9 | 4.6 |
| Arkansas | 67.5 | 62.2 | 27.0 | 20.6 | 7.2 | 10.0 | 9.6 | 7.8 | 4.2 | 3.6 |
| Louisiana | 71.6 | 59.7 | 26.6 | 19.9 | 9.1 | 8.8 | 7.2 | 6.4 | 4.6 | 4.8 |
| Oklahoma | 69.5 | 66.5 | 31.0 | 24.4 | 11.2 | 13.7 | 5.9 | 6.4 | 3.5 | 3.2 |
| Texas | 58.5 | 69.4 | 27.4 | 29.1 | 7.1 | 10.2 | 5.2 | 6.2 | 3.7 | 5.2 |
| Mountain | 72.0 | 81.5 | 32.3 | 32.6 | 9.3 | 12.2 | 3.5 | 5.2 | 4.5 | 5.1 |
| Montana | 79.3 | 96.7 | 31.9 | 29.7 | 11.4 | 18.4 | 4.1 | 7.2 | 5.1 | 5.7 |
| Idaho | 77.3 | 83.9 | 35.3 | 33.7 | 8.7 | 11.0 | 2.2 | 4.6 | 6.0 | 6.5 |
| Wyoming | 78.2 | 103.4 | 35.9 | 42.5 | 7.9 | 11.2 | 4.8 | 5.5 | 4.1 | 5.9 |
| Colorado | 61.3 | 71.3 | 24.7 | 27.8 | 11.7 | 14.7 | 2.8 | 3.9 | 3.2 | 4.6 |
| New Mexico | 83.5 | 82.3 | 43.0 | 37.0 | 7.4 | 7.3 | 3.5 | 7.2 | 4.6 | 4.7 |
| Arizona | 74.5 | 80.9 | 37.3 | 36.1 | 6.0 | 8.3 | 4.5 | 5.5 | 5.1 | 5.7 |
| Utah | 59.2 | 70.8 | 24.0 | 27.8 | 9.5 | 13.1 | 2.6 | 3.6 | 4.3 | 4.1 |
| Nevada | 94.0 | 108.1 | 41.4 | 46.7 | 10.5 | 9.8 | 6.1 | 8.2 | 5.4 | 5.3 |
| Pacific | 56.1 | 65.2 | 26.3 | 28.5 | 9.4 | 10.7 | 3.1 | 4.1 | 3.4 | 3.8 |
| Washington | 60.5 | 70.8 | 22.9 | 21.7 | 11.7 | 14.2 | 3.5 | 4.8 | 4.9 | 5.5 |
| Oregon | 63.7 | 77.5 | 26.1 | 28.4 | 9.0 | 12.6 | 3.4 | 4.4 | 4.9 | 5.5 |
| California | 54.3 | 62.2 | 27.0 | 30.0 | 8.9 | 9.7 | 3.0 | 3.8 | 2.9 | 3.2 |

* Excludes water transportation.

Source of basic data: Various reports of the National Office of Vital Statistics.

# Crude Death Rate for Selected Countries, 1938, 1953, 1955, 1960

*Source:* Statistical Office of the United Nations.

| Country | Rate[1] 1938 | 1953 | 1955 | 1960 |
|---|---|---|---|---|
| **North America** | | | | |
| Canada | 9.7 | 8.6 | 8.2 | 7.8[2] |
| Costa Rica | 17.7 | 11.7 | 10.5 | 8.6[2] |
| El Salvador | 19.1 | 14.7 | 14.2 | 10.8[2] |
| Mexico | 22.9 | 15.9 | 13.7 | 11.5[2] |
| Nicaragua | 14.5 | 10.2 | 9.2 | 8.0[2] |
| Panama[4] | 14.2 | 9.2 | 9.2 | 8.4[2] |
| Puerto Rico | 18.7 | 8.1 | 7.2 | 6.7[2] |
| United States | 10.6[3] | 9.6 | 9.3 | 8.5[2] |
| **South America** | | | | |
| Chile | 23.1 | 12.4 | 13.0 | .... |
| Peru[6] | 16.2 | 12.2 | 11.8 | .... |
| Venezuela[6] | 18.3 | 9.9 | 10.3 | .... |
| **Europe** | | | | |
| Austria | 14.0 | 12.0 | 12.2 | 12.6[2] |
| Belgium | 13.2 | 12.1 | 12.3 | 12.9[2] |
| Bulgaria | 13.7 | 9.3 | 9.1 | .... |
| Czechoslovakia | 13.2 | 10.5 | 9.6 | 9.2[2] |
| Denmark | 10.3 | 9.0 | 8.7 | 9.6[2] |
| Finland | 12.8[7] | 9.6 | 9.3 | 8.9 |
| France | 15.8 | 13.1 | 12.2 | 11.4[2] |
| Germany, West | 11.4 | 11.2 | 11.0 | 11.4 |

| Country | Rate[1] 1938 | 1953 | 1955 | 1960 |
|---|---|---|---|---|
| **Europe (contd )** | | | | |
| Hungary | 14.3 | 11.7 | 9.9 | 10.1[2] |
| Ireland | 13.6 | 11.7 | 12.6 | 11.5[2] |
| Italy | 14.1 | 10.0 | 9.3 | 9.7[2] |
| Luxemburg | 12.7 | 12.6 | 11.5 | 12.1[2] |
| Netherlands | 8.5 | 7.7 | 7.6 | 7.6[2] |
| Norway | 9.9 | 8.5 | 8.5 | 9.0[2] |
| Portugal | 15.4 | 11.3 | 11.3 | 10.4[2] |
| Rumania | 19.2 | 11.6 | 9.7 | 8.2[5] |
| Spain | 19.3 | 9.7 | 9.4 | 8.9[2] |
| Sweden | 11.5 | 9.7 | 9.5 | 10.0[2] |
| Switzerland | 11.6 | 10.2 | 10.1 | 9.8[2] |
| United Kingdom | 11.8 | 11.4 | 11.7 | 11.5[2] |
| **Asia** | | | | |
| Ceylon | 21.0 | 10.7 | 10.8 | .... |
| India[8] | 23.7 | 14.5 | 11.7 | 11.1[5] |
| Israel | 8.1[9] | 6.7[10] | 6.1[10] | 5.7[2,10] |
| Japan[11] | 17.7[12] | 8.9[12] | 7.8 | 7.5[2] |
| **Other** | | | | |
| Australia[13] | 9.6 | 9.1 | 8.9 | 8.6[2] |
| New Zealamd[14] | 9.7 | 8.8 | 9.0 | 9.4 |
| U. of So. Africa[15] | 9.5 | 8.6 | 8.1 | 8.6[2] |

[1] Number of deaths per 1,000 population. [2] Provisional. [3] Excluding Alaska and Hawaii. [4] Excluding tribal Indians. Figures for 1953, 1955 and 1960 include Indians in Bocas del Toro and Darien Provinces. [5] Official rate. [6] Excluding Indian jungle population. [7] Finnish nationals in Finland only. [8] Data are for a changing group of States and Territories which, in 1955, had a population of about 217 million. [9] Jewish population only. [10] Excluding Bedouin population in the Negev. [11] Japanese nationals in Japan only. [12] Excluding Amami Islands. Also excluding Tokara Archipelago in 1938. [13] Excludes full-blooded aborigines. [14] Excluding Maoris. [15] White population only (about 20% of total). NOTE: Leaders (...) indicate information is not available.

---

# Transportation-Accident Death Rates, 1958-60

*Source:* National Safety Council.

| Kind of transportation | 1960 Passenger miles | Passenger deaths | Death rate[1] | 1958-60 average death rate[1] |
|---|---|---|---|---|
| Passenger automobiles and taxis | 1,120,000,000,000 | 24,600 | 2.2 | 2.3 |
| Passenger automobiles on turnpikes | 25,000,000,000 | 260 | 1.0 | 1.2 |
| Buses | 53,900,000,000 | 60 | 0.11 | 0.16 |
| Railroad passenger trains | 21,260,000,000 | 33 | 0.16 | 0.16 |
| Scheduled air transport planes (domestic) | 32,300,000,000 | 326 | 1.01 | 0.73 |

[1] Per 100,000,000 passenger miles. [2] Drivers of passenger automobiles are considered passengers.

---

# One Accidental Death Every 6 Minutes

*Source:* National Safety Council.

**The nation's 1960 accident totals can be figured at the following approximate rates:**

| Class of accident | | One every | | Class of accident | | One every | |
|---|---|---|---|---|---|---|---|
| All accidents | Deaths | 6 | minutes | Workers off-job | Deaths | 18 | minutes |
| | Injuries | 3 | seconds | | Injuries | 14 | seconds |
| Motor-vehicle | Deaths | 14 | minutes | Home | Deaths | 19 | minutes |
| | Injuries | 26 | seconds | | Injuries | 8 | seconds |
| Work | Deaths | 38 | minutes | Public non-motor-vehicle | Deaths | 32 | minutes |
| | Injuries | 16 | seconds | | Injuries | 15 | seconds |

# Motor-Vehicle Deaths by Type of Accident, 1935 to 1960

*Source:* National Safety Council.

| Year | Total deaths* | Deaths from collisions with— | | | | | | | Deaths from non-collision accidents |
|------|------|------|------|------|------|------|------|------|------|
| | | Pedestrians | Other motor vehicles | Railroad trains | Street cars | Bicycles | Animal-drawn vehicle or animal | Fixed objects | |
| 1935 | 36,369 | 14,350 | 8,750 | 1,587 | 253 | 450 | 250 | 1,010 | 9,720 |
| 1937 | 39,643 | 15,500 | 10,320 | 1,810 | 264 | 700 | 200 | 1,160 | 9,690 |
| 1939 | 32,386 | 12,400 | 8,700 | 1,330 | 150 | 710 | 200 | 1,000 | 7,900 |
| 1941 | 39,969 | 13,550 | 12,500 | 1,840 | 118 | 910 | 250 | 1,350 | 9,450 |
| 1942 | 28,309 | 10,650 | 7,300 | 1,754 | 124 | 650 | 240 | 850 | 6,740 |
| 1943 | 23,823 | 9,900 | 5,300 | 1,448 | 171 | 450 | 160 | 700 | 5,690 |
| 1944 | 24,282 | 9,900 | 5,700 | 1,663 | 175 | 400 | 140 | 700 | 5,600 |
| 1945 | 28,076 | 11,000 | 7,150 | 1,703 | 163 | 500 | 130 | 800 | 6,600 |
| 1946 | 33,411 | 11,600 | 9,400 | 1,703 | 174 | 540 | 130 | 950 | 8,900 |
| 1947 | 32,697 | 10,450 | 9,900 | 1,736 | 102 | 550 | 150 | 1,000 | 8,800 |
| 1948 | 32,259 | 9,950 | 10,200 | 1,474 | 83 | 500 | 100 | 1,000 | 8,950 |
| 1949 | 31,701 | 8,800 | 10,500 | 1,452 | 56 | 550 | 140 | 1,100 | 9,100 |
| 1950 | 34,763 | 9,000 | 11,650 | 1,541 | 89 | 440 | 120 | 1,300 | 10,600 |
| 1951 | 36,996 | 9,150 | 13,100 | 1,573 | 46 | 390 | 100 | 1,400 | 11,200 |
| 1952 | 37,794 | 8,900 | 13,500 | 1,429 | 32 | 430 | 130 | 1,450 | 11,900 |
| 1953 | 37,955 | 8,750 | 13,400 | 1,506 | 26 | 420 | 120 | 1,500 | 12,200 |
| 1954 | 35,586 | 8,000 | 12,800 | 1,269 | 28 | 380 | 90 | 1,500 | 11,500 |
| 1955 | 38,426 | 8,200 | 14,500 | 1,490 | 15 | 410 | 90 | 1,600 | 12,100 |
| 1956 | 39,628 | 7,900 | 15,200 | 1,377 | 11 | 440 | 100 | 1,600 | 13,000 |
| 1957 | 38,702 | 7,850 | 15,400 | 1,376 | 13 | 460 | 80 | 1,700 | 11,800 |
| 1958 | 36,981 | 7,650 | 14,200 | 1,316 | 9 | 450 | 80 | 1,650 | 11,600 |
| 1959 | 37,910 | 7,850 | 14,900 | 1,202 | 6 | 480 | 70 | 1,600 | 11,800 |
| 1960 | 38,200 | 7,750 | 14,800 | 1,311 | 5 | 460 | 80 | 1,700 | 12,100 |

* Yearly totals do not quite equal sums of the various types because totals for most types are estimated, and these have been made only to the nearest 10 deaths for some types and to the nearest 50 deaths for others.

# Motor-Vehicle Traffic Deaths by States, 1959-60

*Source:* National Safety Council.

| State | 1959 | Rate[1] | 1960 | Rate[1] | State | 1959 | Rate[1] | 1960 | Rate[1] |
|-------|------|------|------|------|-------|------|------|------|------|
| Alabama | 834 | 7.0 | 871 | 7.1 | Montana | 248 | 7.5 | 222 | 6.5 |
| Alaska | 34 | ... | 39 | ... | Nebraska | 342 | 5.1 | 292 | 4.3 |
| Arizona | 517 | 8.6 | 508 | 7.9 | Nevada | 180 | 9.6 | 165 | 8.3 |
| Arkansas | 458 | 6.6 | 448 | 6.2 | New Hampshire | 122 | 5.1 | 104 | 4.2 |
| California | 3,588 | 5.3 | 3,723 | 5.3 | New Jersey | 762 | 3.1 | 741 | 2.9 |
| Colorado | 404 | 5.2 | 433 | 5.4 | New Mexico | 456 | 8.7 | 405 | 7.8 |
| Connecticut | 249 | 2.6 | 273 | 2.8 | New York | 2,222 | 4.8 | 2,046 | 4.3 |
| Delaware | 83 | 4.0 | 87 | 4.1 | North Carolina | 1,193 | 6.7 | 1,220 | 6.7 |
| D. C. | 61 | 2.4 | 71 | 2.7 | North Dakota | 163 | 6.8 | 156 | 6.7 |
| Florida | 1,113 | 5.5 | 1,249 | 5.9 | Ohio | 1,853 | 4.8 | 1,907 | 5.0 |
| Georgia | 995 | 6.2 | 1,035 | 6.3 | Oklahoma | 642 | 5.9 | 657 | 5.8 |
| Hawaii | 95 | 6.0 | 117 | ... | Oregon | 492 | 6.1 | 462 | 5.6 |
| Idaho | 222 | 7.1 | 226 | 7.0 | Pennsylvania | 1,685 | 4.3 | 1,609 | 4.0 |
| Illinois | 1,795 | 4.9 | 1,725 | 4.4 | Rhode Island | 91 | 3.0 | 60 | 1.9 |
| Indiana | 1,125 | 5.4 | 1,124 | 5.2 | South Carolina | 684 | 7.7 | 702 | 7.8 |
| Iowa | 680 | 5.6 | 619 | 4.4 | South Dakota | 222 | 7.2 | 233 | 6.8 |
| Kansas | 567 | 5.7 | 512 | 5.1 | Tennessee | 773 | 5.7 | 787 | 5.6 |
| Kentucky | 750 | 7.0 | 765 | 7.0 | Texas | 2,453 | 5.3 | 2,254 | 4.9 |
| Louisiana | 803 | 7.2 | 840 | 7.5 | Utah | 205 | 5.4 | 256 | 6.4 |
| Maine | 136 | 3.4 | 178 | 4.3 | Vermont | 89 | 5.7 | 102 | 6.2 |
| Maryland | 524 | 4.8 | 511 | 4.5 | Virginia | 850 | 5.3 | 756 | 4.7 |
| Massachusetts | 557 | 3.2 | 578 | 3.3 | Washington | 548 | 4.8 | 559 | 4.8 |
| Michigan | 1,473 | 4.8 | 1,596 | 5.0 | West Virginia | 398 | 6.5 | 359 | 5.9 |
| Minnesota | 664 | 4.7 | 723 | 4.6 | Wisconsin | 821 | 5.5 | 927 | 5.9 |
| Mississippi | 549 | 6.9 | 622 | 7.7 | Wyoming | 170 | 7.8 | 167 | 7.3 |
| Missouri | 990 | 5.1 | 1,046 | 5.3 | | | | | |

[1] Number of deaths per 100,000,000 vehicle-miles. NOTE: Figures are per state traffic authorities and indicate place of accident rather than of death.

# CRIME

## City Arrests, Distribution by Sex, 1960

*Source:* Federal Bureau of Investigation.

**(Data in this table are from reports furnished the FBI by 2,460 cities over 2,500 in population. This represents a total population of 81,660,735.)**

| Offense charged | Males | Per cent | Females | Per cent | Total | Per cent |
|---|---|---|---|---|---|---|
| Criminal homicide: | | | | | | |
|   Murder and nonnegligent manslaughter ..... | 3,687 | .1 | 820 | .2 | 4,507 | .1 |
|   Manslaughter by negligence ............. | 1,575 | * | 191 | * | 1,766 | * |
| Robbery.................... | 27,986 | .9 | 1,340 | .3 | 29,326 | .8 |
| Aggravated assault ...................... | 44,284 | 1.4 | 7,993 | 2.0 | 52,277 | 1.4 |
| Other assaults | 121,035 | 3.7 | 13,503 | 3.3 | 134,538 | 3.7 |
| Burglary—breaking or entering ........... | 106,961 | 3.3 | 3,086 | .8 | 110,047 | 3.0 |
| Larceny—theft................. | 172,581 | 5.3 | 34,967 | 8.6 | 207,548 | 5.6 |
| Auto theft................... | 52,084 | 1.6 | 1,940 | .5 | 54,024 | 1.5 |
| Embezzlement and fraud ................ | 27,426 | .8 | 5,124 | 1.3 | 32,550 | .9 |
| Stolen property; buying, receiving, etc. ..... | 9,177 | .3 | 872 | .2 | 10,049 | .3 |
| Forgery and counterfeiting................. | 15,778 | .5 | 3,180 | .8 | 18,958 | .5 |
| Forcible rape .................... | 6,068 | .2 | ..... | ... | 6,068 | .2 |
| Prostitution and commercialized vice............. | 6,856 | .2 | 18,995 | 4.7 | 25,851 | .7 |
| Other sex offenses (includes statutory rape) .. | 36,024 | 1.1 | 8,508 | 2.1 | 44,532 | 1.2 |
| Narcotic drug laws................... | 20,014 | .6 | 3,416 | .8 | 23,430 | .6 |
| Weapons; carrying, possessing, etc.... | 32,613 | 1.0 | 1,907 | .5 | 34,520 | .9 |
| Offenses against family and children........... | 30,876 | .9 | 3,327 | .8 | 34,203 | .9 |
| Liquor laws.................... | 73,604 | 2.2 | 13,214 | 3.3 | 86,818 | 2.4 |
| Driving while intoxicated .............. | 137,700 | 4.2 | 8,681 | 2.1 | 146,381 | 4.0 |
| Disorderly conduct...................... | 387,258 | 11.8 | 62,186 | 15.3 | 449,444 | 12.2 |
| Drunkenness.................... | 1,223,276 | 37.4 | 103,131 | 25.4 | 1,326,407 | 36.1 |
| Vagrancy..................... | 134,956 | 4.1 | 11,149 | 2.7 | 146,105 | 4.0 |
| Gambling....................... | 108,509 | 3.3 | 10,734 | 2.6 | 119,243 | 3.2 |
| Suspicion....................... | 111,868 | 3.4 | 14,914 | 3.7 | 126,782 | 3.4 |
| All other offenses................... | 380,171 | 11.6 | 73,291 | 18.0 | 453,462 | 12.3 |
| TOTAL ARRESTS, 1960.................... | 3,272,367 | 100.0 | 406,469 | 100.0 | 3,678,836 | 100.0 |

## City Arrests, by Age Groups, 1960*

*Source:* Federal Bureau of Investigation.

| Age | Arrests | Age | Arrests | Age | Arrests | Age | Arrests | Age | Arrests |
|---|---|---|---|---|---|---|---|---|---|
| Under 15..... | 215,868 | 18 | ...... 106,795 | 22 | ...... 91,247 | 30–34 | ... 406,639 | 50 & over | 595,021 |
| 15........... | 86,642 | 19 | ...... 98,839 | 23 | ...... 84,267 | 35–39 | ... 422,045 | Not known .. | 2,504 |
| 16........... | 110,446 | 20 | ...... 90,321 | 24 | ...... 84,904 | 40–44 | ... 370,567 | TOTAL...... | 3,678,836 |
| 17........... | 113,949 | 21 | ...... 98,109 | 25–29 | ... 380,086 | 45–49 | ...... 320,587 | | |

\* Data from same sources as table above: 2,460 cities over 2,500.

## Crime Index Totals, 1957-60

*Source:* Federal Bureau of Investigation.

| Crime index classification | Estimated number of offenses | | Change, 1960 over 1957–59 average | |
|---|---|---|---|---|
| | 1957–59 average | 1960 | Number | Per cent |
| Murder....................... | 8,290 | 9,140 | +850 | +10 |
| Forcible rape................. | 14,240 | 15,560 | +1,320 | +9 |
| Robbery...................... | 72,540 | 88,970 | +16,430 | +23 |
| Aggravated assault............ | 116,020 | 130,230 | +14,210 | +12 |
| Burglary..................... | 663,500 | 821,100 | +157,600 | +24 |
| Larceny, $50 and over.......... | 388,800 | 474,900 | +86,100 | +22 |
| Auto theft.................... | 284,200 | 321,400 | +37,200 | +13 |
| TOTAL..................... | 1,547,590 | 1,861,300 | +313,710 | +20 |

# Sentenced Federal Prisoners Received from Courts, 1945-1960

Fiscal years ending June 30
*Source:* Federal Bureau of Prisons.

| Offense | 1945 | 1948 | 1950 | 1954 | 1956 | 1958 | 1959 | 1960 |
|---|---|---|---|---|---|---|---|---|
| Counterfeiting | 47 | 64 | 260 | 88 | 54 | 70 | 110 | 76 |
| Drug laws: Marihuana | 454 | 588 | 878 | 509 | 325 | 303 | 246 | 288 |
| Narcotics | 680 | 855 | 1,151 | 1,366 | 1,189 | 1,264 | 1,123 | 1,168 |
| Embezzlement and fraud | 340 | 531 | 609 | 445 | 453 | 540 | 590 | 665 |
| Forgery | 626 | 954 | 1,274 | 1,484 | 1,572 | 1,545 | 1,687 | 1,778 |
| Immigration laws | 3,996 | 3,200 | 3,463 | 7,277 | 1,771 | 1,654 | 1,637 | 1,548 |
| Income tax | 15 | 103 | 164 | 203 | 241 | 189 | 185 | 165 |
| Juvenile delinquency | 911 | 677 | 658 | 829 | 825 | 953 | 869 | 889 |
| Kidnaping | 20 | 36 | 41 | 41 | 19 | 26 | 36 | 21 |
| Liquor laws | 2,988 | 1,838 | 2,304 | 2,143 | 2,183 | 2,378 | 2,440 | 2,226 |
| Robbery | 45 | 68 | 92 | 193 | 212 | 242 | 293 | 275 |
| Theft from interstate commerce | 475 | 430 | 270 | 320 | 318 | 292 | 327 | 334 |
| Transportation, etc., of stolen motor vehicle | 1,072 | 2,612 | 2,486 | 2,838 | 2,835 | 3,295 | 3,400 | 3,271 |
| White-slave traffic | 209 | 221 | 185 | 242 | 206 | 134 | 139 | 120 |
| Govt. reservation, D. C., high seas and terr. cases | 986 | 1,069 | 1,145 | 1,487 | 1,365 | 1,667 | 1,748 | 1,492 |
| Other | 1,748 | 1,868 | 2,104 | 1,851 | 1,882 | 1,914 | 2,141 | 2,132 |
| National security offenses: | | | | | | | | |
| Selective Service Acts | 2,613 | 236 | 136 | 342 | 136 | 197 | 164 | 135 |
| Other national-defense and security laws | 2,150 | 319 | 130 | 167 | 132 | 104 | 128 | 54 |
| Military court-martial cases: Army | 1,793 | 851 | 606 | 639 | 952 | 82 | 5 | 130 |
| Navy | 32 | 267 | 107 | 33 | 30 | 8 | 13 | 16 |
| **TOTAL ALL OFFENSES** | 21,200 | 16,787 | 18,063 | 22,497 | 16,700 | 16,857 | 17,281 | 16,783 |

# Methods of Execution in the United States

*Source: Information Please Almanac questionnaires to the states.*

| State | Method | State | Method |
|---|---|---|---|
| Alabama | Electrocution | New Hampshire | Hanging |
| Alaska | No death penalty | New Jersey | Electrocution |
| Arizona | Lethal gas | New Mexico | Lethal gas |
| Arkansas | Electrocution | New York | Electrocution |
| California | Lethal gas | North Carolina | Lethal gas |
| Colorado | Lethal gas | North Dakota | No death penalty |
| Connecticut | Electrocution | Ohio | Electrocution |
| Delaware | No death penalty | Oklahoma | Lethal gas[1] |
| D. C. | Electrocution | Oregon | Lethal gas |
| Florida | Electrocution | Pennsylvania | Electrocution |
| Georgia | Electrocution | Rhode Island | No death penalty[2] |
| Hawaii | No death penalty | South Carolina | Electrocution |
| Idaho | Hanging | South Dakota | Electrocution |
| Illinois | Electrocution | Tennessee | Electrocution |
| Indiana | Electrocution | Texas | Electrocution |
| Iowa | Hanging | Utah | Hanging or shooting[3] |
| Kansas | Hanging | | |
| Kentucky | Electrocution | Vermont | Electrocution |
| Louisiana | Electrocution | Virginia | Electrocution |
| Maine | No death penalty | Washington | Hanging |
| Maryland | Lethal gas | West Virginia | Electrocution |
| Massachusetts | Electrocution | Wisconsin | No death penalty |
| Michigan | No death penalty | Wyoming | Lethal gas |
| Minnesota | No death penalty | U. S. (Fed. Gov't.) | [4] |
| Mississippi | Lethal gas | American Samoa | Hanging |
| Missouri | Lethal gas | Canal Zone | Hanging |
| Montana | Hanging | Guam | Hanging |
| Nebraska | Electrocution | Puerto Rico | No death penalty |
| Nevada | Lethal gas | Virgin Islands | No death penalty |

[1] Electrocution until gas chamber is provided. [2] However, a person who commits murder while under sentence of imprisonment for life shall be hanged. [3] Condemned man has choice. [4] Method shall be that used by state in which sentence is imposed. If state does not have death penalty, Federal judge shall prescribe method for carrying out death sentence. NOTE. Method shown with each state is maximum penalty for murder and certain other crimes. In most states having capital punishment, jury or judge can specify whether sentence shall be death or life imprisonment

# HOSPITALS

## Hospital Facilities in the U. S., 1960

*Source:* American Hospital Association.

| State | Total—all hospitals | | | State | Total—all hospitals | | |
|---|---|---|---|---|---|---|---|
| | No. of hospitals | No. of beds | Admissions during year* | | No. of hospitals | No. of beds | Admissions during year* |
| Alabama | 130 | 24,035 | 406,094 | Nebraska | 113 | 14,599 | 223,595 |
| Alaska | 23 | 1,674 | 36,161 | Nevada | 19 | 1,968 | 44,690 |
| Arizona | 70 | 8,191 | 190,244 | New Hampshire | 38 | 7,852 | 94,400 |
| Arkansas | 80 | 14,693 | 233,694 | New Jersey | 147 | 56,255 | 716,887 |
| California | 466 | 124,380 | 1,985,741 | New Mexico | 54 | 5,763 | 134,536 |
| Colorado | 93 | 17,708 | 306,596 | New York | 474 | 228,628 | 2,290,414 |
| Connecticut | 71 | 25,972 | 338,685 | North Carolina | 174 | 34,372 | 679,613 |
| Delaware | 16 | 5,508 | 60,295 | North Dakota | 64 | 7,422 | 123,491 |
| D. of C. | 23 | 15,623 | 202,217 | Ohio | 263 | 81,743 | 1,297,807 |
| Florida | 162 | 30,979 | 669,530 | Oklahoma | 132 | 19,352 | 319,181 |
| Georgia | 142 | 29,987 | 532,946 | Oregon | 79 | 13,480 | 249,376 |
| Hawaii | 32 | 6,724 | 97,890 | Pennsylvania | 329 | 116,530 | 1,512,347 |
| Idaho | 49 | 3,544 | 91,831 | Rhode Island | 24 | 9,831 | 112,056 |
| Illinois | 327 | 108,071 | 1,443,775 | South Carolina | 80 | 18,561 | 314,337 |
| Indiana | 135 | 33,932 | 574,197 | South Dakota | 65 | 7,743 | 120,276 |
| Iowa | 127 | 22,626 | 394,574 | Tennessee | 154 | 29,217 | 518,775 |
| Kansas | 151 | 18,580 | 326,886 | Texas | 550 | 65,903 | 1,425,383 |
| Kentucky | 132 | 23,019 | 421,557 | Utah | 36 | 4,679 | 110,922 |
| Louisiana | 139 | 24,645 | 521,682 | Vermont | 31 | 4,680 | 62,819 |
| Maine | 57 | 9,015 | 130,177 | Virginia | 119 | 33,972 | 503,858 |
| Maryland | 79 | 31,978 | 340,933 | Washington | 127 | 22,519 | 429,370 |
| Massachusetts | 211 | 69,035 | 776,280 | West Virginia | 93 | 16,040 | 307,896 |
| Michigan | 252 | 72,759 | 1,082,598 | Wisconsin | 198 | 33,663 | 640,633 |
| Minnesota | 203 | 37,095 | 571,456 | Wyoming | 33 | 3,682 | 60,780 |
| Mississippi | 106 | 14,772 | 275,435 | | | | |
| Missouri | 144 | 39,120 | 598,330 | Total | 6,876 | 1,657,970 | 25,027,152 |
| Montana | 60 | 5,851 | 123,906 | | | | |

* Data estimated for nonreporting hospitals. Excludes newborn.

# EXPECTATION OF LIFE

## Expectation of Life and Mortality Rates, 1959

*Source:* Metropolitan Life Insurance Co., from abridged life tables published by National Vital Statistics Division

| Age, years | Expectation of Life in Years | | | | | Mortality Rate per 1,000 | | | | |
|---|---|---|---|---|---|---|---|---|---|---|
| | Total Persons | White | | Nonwhite | | Total Persons | White | | Nonwhite | |
| | | Male | Female | Male | Female | | Male | Female | Male | Female |
| 0 | 69.7 | 67.3 | 73.9 | 60.9 | 66.2 | 26.4 | 26.3 | 20.0 | 48.4 | 40.1 |
| 1 | 70.5 | 68.2 | 74.4 | 63.0 | 68.0 | 1.7 | 1.5 | 1.3 | 3.6 | 3.0 |
| 2 | 69.7 | 67.3 | 73.5 | 62.3 | 67.2 | 1.0 | 1.0 | .8 | 2.0 | 1.6 |
| 3 | 68.7 | 66.3 | 72.6 | 61.4 | 66.3 | .8 | .8 | .6 | 1.3 | 1.1 |
| 4 | 67.8 | 65.4 | 71.6 | 60.5 | 65.4 | .7 | .7 | .6 | 1.0 | .9 |
| 5 | 66.8 | 64.4 | 70.7 | 59.5 | 64.4 | .6 | .6 | .5 | .9 | .8 |
| 6 | 65.9 | 63.5 | 69.7 | 58.6 | 63.5 | .5 | .6 | .4 | .8 | .7 |
| 7 | 64.9 | 62.5 | 68.7 | 57.6 | 62.5 | .5 | .5 | .4 | .7 | .6 |
| 8 | 63.9 | 61.5 | 67.8 | 56.7 | 61.5 | .4 | .5 | .3 | .6 | .5 |
| 9 | 63.0 | 60.6 | 66.8 | 55.7 | 60.6 | .4 | .5 | .3 | .6 | .4 |
| 10 | 62.0 | 59.6 | 65.8 | 54.7 | 59.6 | .4 | .4 | .3 | .6 | .4 |
| 11 | 61.0 | 58.6 | 64.8 | 53.8 | 58.6 | .4 | .4 | .3 | .6 | .4 |
| 12 | 60.0 | 57.6 | 63.8 | 52.8 | 57.6 | .4 | .5 | .3 | .7 | .4 |

## Expectation of Life and Mortality Rates (Contd.)

| Age, years | Expectation of Life in Years | | | | | Mortality Rate per 1,000 | | | | |
| | Total Persons | White | | Nonwhite | | Total Persons | White | | Nonwhite | |
| | | Male | Female | Male | Female | | Male | Female | Male | Female |
|---|---|---|---|---|---|---|---|---|---|---|
| 13............ | 59.1 | 56.7 | 62.9 | 51.8 | 56.7 | .5 | .6 | .3 | .9 | .5 |
| 14............ | 58.1 | 55.7 | 61.9 | 50.9 | 55.7 | .6 | .8 | .4 | 1.1 | .6 |
| 15............ | 57.1 | 54.7 | 60.9 | 49.9 | 54.7 | .7 | 1.0 | .4 | 1.3 | .7 |
| 16............ | 56.2 | 53.8 | 59.9 | 49.0 | 53.8 | .8 | 1.1 | .5 | 1.5 | .8 |
| 17............ | 55.2 | 52.9 | 59.0 | 48.1 | 52.8 | .9 | 1.3 | .5 | 1.7 | .9 |
| 18............ | 54.3 | 51.9 | 58.0 | 47.1 | 51.9 | 1.0 | 1.4 | .5 | 1.9 | 1.0 |
| 19............ | 53.3 | 51.0 | 57.0 | 46.2 | 50.9 | 1.1 | 1.5 | .5 | 2.0 | 1.1 |
| 20............ | 52.4 | 50.1 | 56.0 | 45.3 | 50.0 | 1.1 | 1.6 | .6 | 2.2 | 1.2 |
| 21............ | 51.4 | 49.1 | 55.1 | 44.4 | 49.0 | 1.2 | 1.7 | .6 | 2.3 | 1.3 |
| 22............ | 50.5 | 48.2 | 54.1 | 43.5 | 48.1 | 1.2 | 1.7 | .6 | 2.5 | 1.4 |
| 23............ | 49.6 | 47.3 | 53.1 | 42.6 | 47.2 | 1.3 | 1.7 | .6 | 2.7 | 1.5 |
| 24............ | 48.6 | 46.4 | 52.2 | 41.7 | 46.2 | 1.3 | 1.6 | .6 | 2.9 | 1.6 |
| 25............ | 47.7 | 45.5 | 51.2 | 40.9 | 45.3 | 1.2 | 1.5 | .7 | 3.1 | 1.7 |
| 26............ | 46.7 | 44.5 | 50.2 | 40.0 | 44.4 | 1.2 | 1.5 | .7 | 3.3 | 1.8 |
| 27............ | 45.8 | 43.6 | 49.3 | 39.1 | 43.5 | 1.3 | 1.4 | .7 | 3.5 | 2.0 |
| 28............ | 44.9 | 42.7 | 48.3 | 38.2 | 42.5 | 1.3 | 1.5 | .8 | 3.7 | 2.2 |
| 29............ | 43.9 | 41.7 | 47.3 | 37.4 | 41.6 | 1.4 | 1.5 | .8 | 3.9 | 2.4 |
| 30............ | 43.0 | 40.8 | 46.4 | 36.5 | 40.7 | 1.5 | 1.6 | .9 | 4.1 | 2.6 |
| 31............ | 42.0 | 39.8 | 45.4 | 35.7 | 39.8 | 1.6 | 1.7 | .9 | 4.3 | 2.9 |
| 32............ | 41.1 | 38.9 | 44.5 | 34.8 | 39.0 | 1.7 | 1.8 | 1.0 | 4.5 | 3.1 |
| 33............ | 40.2 | 38.0 | 43.5 | 34.0 | 38.1 | 1.8 | 1.9 | 1.1 | 4.8 | 3.4 |
| 34............ | 39.2 | 37.0 | 42.6 | 33.1 | 37.2 | 1.9 | 2.0 | 1.2 | 5.1 | 3.7 |
| 35............ | 38.3 | 36.1 | 41.6 | 32.3 | 36.3 | 2.0 | 2.1 | 1.2 | 5.4 | 4.0 |
| 36............ | 37.4 | 35.2 | 40.7 | 31.5 | 35.5 | 2.1 | 2.3 | 1.3 | 5.8 | 4.3 |
| 37............ | 36.5 | 34.3 | 39.7 | 30.7 | 34.6 | 2.3 | 2.5 | 1.4 | 6.2 | 4.6 |
| 38............ | 35.5 | 33.4 | 38.8 | 29.9 | 33.8 | 2.5 | 2.7 | 1.6 | 6.7 | 5.0 |
| 39............ | 34.6 | 32.4 | 37.8 | 29.1 | 33.0 | 2.7 | 3.0 | 1.7 | 7.2 | 5.3 |
| 40............ | 33.7 | 31.5 | 36.9 | 28.3 | 32.1 | 3.0 | 3.3 | 1.9 | 7.8 | 5.7 |
| 41............ | 32.8 | 30.7 | 36.0 | 27.5 | 31.3 | 3.3 | 3.7 | 2.1 | 8.4 | 6.2 |
| 42............ | 31.9 | 29.8 | 35.0 | 26.7 | 30.5 | 3.6 | 4.1 | 2.3 | 9.1 | 6.6 |
| 43............ | 31.1 | 28.9 | 34.1 | 26.0 | 29.7 | 4.0 | 4.6 | 2.5 | 9.7 | 6.9 |
| 44............ | 30.2 | 28.0 | 33.2 | 25.2 | 28.9 | 4.3 | 5.0 | 2.7 | 10.3 | 7.3 |
| 45............ | 29.3 | 27.2 | 32.3 | 24.5 | 28.1 | 4.7 | 5.6 | 3.0 | 10.9 | 7.7 |
| 46............ | 28.4 | 26.3 | 31.4 | 23.7 | 27.3 | 5.2 | 6.2 | 3.2 | 11.7 | 8.2 |
| 47............ | 27.6 | 25.5 | 30.5 | 23.0 | 26.6 | 5.7 | 6.8 | 3.5 | 12.5 | 8.7 |
| 48............ | 26.7 | 24.6 | 29.6 | 22.3 | 25.8 | 6.3 | 7.6 | 3.8 | 13.4 | 9.5 |
| 49............ | 25.9 | 23.8 | 28.7 | 21.6 | 25.0 | 6.9 | 8.5 | 4.2 | 14.4 | 10.4 |
| 50............ | 25.1 | 23.0 | 27.8 | 20.9 | 24.3 | 7.6 | 9.4 | 4.6 | 15.4 | 11.4 |
| 51............ | 24.3 | 22.2 | 26.9 | 20.2 | 23.6 | 8.3 | 10.4 | 5.0 | 16.6 | 12.4 |
| 52............ | 23.5 | 21.5 | 26.1 | 19.5 | 22.9 | 9.1 | 11.5 | 5.4 | 17.9 | 13.5 |
| 53............ | 22.7 | 20.7 | 25.2 | 18.9 | 22.2 | 9.9 | 12.5 | 5.9 | 19.5 | 14.8 |
| 54............ | 21.9 | 20.0 | 24.4 | 18.2 | 21.5 | 10.8 | 13.7 | 6.4 | 21.4 | 16.2 |
| 55............ | 21.1 | 19.2 | 23.5 | 17.6 | 20.8 | 11.8 | 15.0 | 7.0 | 23.5 | 17.8 |
| 56............ | 20.4 | 18.5 | 22.7 | 17.1 | 20.2 | 12.8 | 16.3 | 7.6 | 25.7 | 19.4 |
| 57............ | 19.6 | 17.8 | 21.8 | 16.5 | 19.6 | 13.9 | 17.7 | 8.3 | 27.7 | 20.9 |
| 58............ | 18.9 | 17.1 | 21.0 | 15.9 | 19.0 | 15.0 | 19.2 | 9.0 | 29.3 | 22.2 |
| 59............ | 18.2 | 16.5 | 20.2 | 15.4 | 18.4 | 16.1 | 20.7 | 9.8 | 30.8 | 23.2 |
| 60............ | 17.5 | 15.8 | 19.4 | 14.9 | 17.8 | 17.3 | 22.4 | 10.7 | 32.1 | 24.2 |
| 61............ | 16.8 | 15.2 | 18.6 | 14.4 | 17.3 | 18.6 | 24.1 | 11.6 | 33.6 | 25.3 |
| 62............ | 16.1 | 14.5 | 17.8 | 13.9 | 16.7 | 20.2 | 26.2 | 12.9 | 36.0 | 27.1 |
| 63............ | 15.4 | 13.9 | 17.0 | 13.4 | 16.2 | 22.3 | 28.8 | 14.4 | 39.9 | 29.7 |
| 64............ | 14.7 | 13.3 | 16.3 | 12.9 | 15.7 | 24.7 | 31.7 | 16.3 | 45.0 | 33.1 |
| 65............ | 14.1 | 12.7 | 15.6 | 12.5 | 15.2 | 27.4 | 34.8 | 18.3 | 50.9 | 36.8 |
| 66............ | 13.5 | 12.2 | 14.8 | 12.1 | 14.7 | 30.1 | 38.1 | 20.4 | 56.9 | 40.5 |
| 67............ | 12.9 | 11.6 | 14.1 | * | * | 33.0 | 41.6 | 22.7 | * | * |
| 68............ | 12.3 | 11.1 | 13.4 | * | * | 36.0 | 45.1 | 25.2 | * | * |
| 69............ | 11.7 | 10.6 | 12.8 | * | * | 39.1 | 48.6 | 28.0 | * | * |

* Not shown because of deficiencies in basic data.
Note: Interpolated in the Statistical Bureau of the Metropolitan Life Insurance Company from the abridged life tables published by the National Vital Statistics Division in *Vital Statistics of the United States, 1959.*

# Expectation of Life in the United States, 1850-1959

*Source:* Statistical Bulletin of the Metropolitan Life Insurance Company. Compiled from various publications of the National Vital Statistics Division, National Center for Health Statistics, and the Bureau of the Census.

| Calendar period | Age | | | | | | | | |
|---|---|---|---|---|---|---|---|---|---|
| | 0 | 10 | 20 | 30 | 40 | 50 | 60 | 70 | 80 |
| **White Males** | | | | | | | | | |
| 1850*........... | 38.3 | 48.0 | 40.1 | 34.0 | 27.9 | 21.6 | 15.6 | 10.2 | 5.9 |
| 1890*........... | 42.50 | 48.45 | 40.66 | 34.05 | 27.37 | 20.72 | 14.73 | 9.35 | 5.40 |
| 1900–1902†...... | 48.23 | 50.59 | 42.19 | 34.88 | 27.74 | 20.76 | 14.35 | 9.03 | 5.10 |
| 1901–1910†...... | 49.32 | 50.86 | 42.39 | 34.80 | 27.55 | 20.59 | 14.17 | 8.96 | 5.07 |
| 1909–1911†...... | 50.23 | 51.32 | 42.71 | 34.87 | 27.43 | 20.39 | 13.98 | 8.83 | 5.09 |
| 1919–1921‡...... | 56.34 | 54.15 | 45.60 | 37.65 | 29.86 | 22.22 | 15.25 | 9.51 | 5.47 |
| 1920–1929‡...... | 57.85 | 54.65 | 45.84 | 37.51 | 29.35 | 21.65 | 14.75 | 9.17 | 5.26 |
| 1929–1931........ | 59.12 | 54.96 | 46.02 | 37.54 | 29.22 | 21.51 | 14.72 | 9.20 | 5.26 |
| 1930–1939........ | 60.62 | 55.86 | 46.77 | 38.06 | 29.57 | 21.71 | 14.86 | 9.29 | 5.30 |
| 1939–1941........ | 62.81 | 57.03 | 47.76 | 38.80 | 30.03 | 21.96 | 15.05 | 9.42 | 5.38 |
| 1949–1951........ | 66.31 | 58.98 | 49.52 | 40.29 | 31.17 | 22.83 | 15.76 | 10.07 | 5.88 |
| 1959............ | 67.3 | 59.6 | 50.1 | 40.8 | 31.5 | 23.0 | 15.8 | 10.1 | 5.9 |
| **White Females** | | | | | | | | | |
| 1850*........... | 40.5 | 47.2 | 40.2 | 35.4 | 29.8 | 23.5 | 17.0 | 11.3 | 6.4 |
| 1890*........... | 44.46 | 49.62 | 42.03 | 35.36 | 28.76 | 22.09 | 15.70 | 10.15 | 5.75 |
| 1900–1902†...... | 51.08 | 52.15 | 43.77 | 36.42 | 29.17 | 21.89 | 15.23 | 9.59 | 5.50 |
| 1901–1910†...... | 52.54 | 52.89 | 44.39 | 36.75 | 29.28 | 21.86 | 15.09 | 9.52 | 5.43 |
| 1909–1911†...... | 53.62 | 53.57 | 44.88 | 36.96 | 29.26 | 21.74 | 14.92 | 9.38 | 5.35 |
| 1919–1921‡...... | 58.53 | 55.17 | 46.46 | 38.72 | 30.94 | 23.12 | 15.93 | 9.94 | 5.70 |
| 1920–1929‡...... | 60.62 | 56.41 | 47.46 | 39.20 | 30.97 | 22.97 | 15.70 | 9.71 | 5.46 |
| 1929–1931........ | 62.67 | 57.65 | 48.52 | 39.99 | 31.52 | 23.41 | 16.05 | 9.98 | 5.63 |
| 1930–1939........ | 64.52 | 58.98 | 49.71 | 40.90 | 32.24 | 23.96 | 16.44 | 10.19 | 5.76 |
| 1939–1941........ | 67.29 | 60.85 | 51.38 | 42.21 | 33.25 | 24.72 | 17.00 | 10.50 | 5.88 |
| 1949–1951........ | 72.03 | 64.26 | 54.56 | 45.00 | 35.64 | 26.76 | 18.64 | 11.68 | 6.59 |
| 1959............ | 73.9 | 65.8 | 56.0 | 46.4 | 36.9 | 27.8 | 19.4 | 12.1 | 6.5 |
| **Nonwhite Males§** | | | | | | | | | |
| 1900–1902†...... | 32.54 | 41.90 | 35.11 | 29.25 | 23.12 | 17.34 | 12.62 | 8.33 | 5.12 |
| 1901–1910†...... | 32.57 | 40.73 | 33.78 | 27.97 | 22.23 | 16.64 | 11.87 | 8.29 | 5.43 |
| 1909–1911†...... | 34.05 | 40.65 | 33.46 | 27.33 | 21.57 | 16.21 | 11.67 | 8.00 | 5.53 |
| 1919–1921‡...... | 47.14 | 45.99 | 38.36 | 32.51 | 26.53 | 20.47 | 14.74 | 9.58 | 5.83 |
| 1920–1929‡...... | 46.90 | 44.86 | 36.76 | 30.65 | 24.55 | 18.83 | 13.66 | 9.12 | 5.54 |
| 1929–1931........ | 47.55 | 44.27 | 35.95 | 29.45 | 23.36 | 17.92 | 13.15 | 8.78 | 5.42 |
| 1930–1939........ | 50.06 | 46.56 | 38.05 | 31.11 | 24.65 | 18.98 | 14.13 | 9.53 | 6.01 |
| 1939–1941........ | 52.26 | 48.34 | 39.52 | 32.05 | 25.06 | 19.06 | 14.37 | 10.11 | 6.58 |
| 1949–1951........ | 58.91 | 52.96 | 43.73 | 35.31 | 27.29 | 20.25 | 14.91 | 10.74 | 7.07 |
| 1959............ | 60.9 | 54.7 | 45.3 | 36.5 | 28.3 | 20.9 | 14.9 | 11.2 | 9.4 |
| **Nonwhite Females§** | | | | | | | | | |
| 1900–1902†...... | 35.04 | 43.02 | 36.89 | 30.70 | 24.37 | 18.67 | 13.60 | 9.62 | 6.48 |
| 1901–1910†...... | 35.65 | 42.52 | 36.17 | 30.09 | 23.81 | 18.08 | 13.17 | 9.52 | 6.50 |
| 1909–1911†...... | 37.67 | 42.84 | 36.14 | 29.61 | 23.34 | 17.65 | 12.78 | 9.22 | 6.05 |
| 1919–1921‡...... | 46.92 | 44.54 | 37.15 | 31.48 | 25.60 | 19.76 | 14.69 | 10.25 | 6.58 |
| 1920–1929‡...... | 47.95 | 44.86 | 36.98 | 30.93 | 24.67 | 18.85 | 14.01 | 10.01 | 6.49 |
| 1929–1931........ | 49.51 | 45.33 | 37.22 | 30.67 | 24.30 | 18.60 | 14.22 | 10.38 | 6.90 |
| 1930–1939........ | 52.62 | 48.29 | 39.90 | 32.88 | 26.11 | 20.09 | 15.28 | 10.88 | 7.18 |
| 1939–1941........ | 55.56 | 50.75 | 42.04 | 34.40 | 27.19 | 20.95 | 16.10 | 11.82 | 8.02 |
| 1949–1951........ | 62.70 | 56.17 | 46.77 | 38.02 | 29.82 | 22.67 | 16.95 | 12.29 | 8.15 |
| 1959............ | 66.2 | 59.6 | 50.0 | 40.7 | 32.1 | 24.3 | 17.8 | 13.3 | 10.2 |

* Massachusetts only; white and nonwhite combined, the latter being about one percent of the total. † Original Death Registration States. ‡ Death Registration States of 1920. § Data for periods 1900–1902 to 1929–1931 and 1939–1941 relate to Negroes only

# Expectation of Life by Age and Sex; Selected Countries

*Source:* Statistical Office of the United Nations.

| Country | Period | Males | | | | | | Females | | | | | |
|---|---|---|---|---|---|---|---|---|---|---|---|---|---|
| | | \multicolumn{12}{Average future lifetime in years at stated age} | | | | | | | | | | | |
| | | 0 | 1 | 10 | 20 | 40 | 60 | 0 | 1 | 10 | 20 | 40 | 60 |
| **North America** | | | | | | | | | | | | | |
| United States[8] | 1958 | 66.4 | 67.5 | 59.0 | 49.4 | 31.1 | 15.6 | 72.7 | 73.5 | 64.9 | 55.2 | 36.2 | 19.1 |
| Canada | 1955–57 | 67.6 | 69.0 | 60.7 | 51.2 | 32.7 | 16.5 | 72.9 | 74.0 | 65.5 | 55.8 | 36.7 | 19.3 |
| Mexico | 1940 | 37.9 | 44.4 | 45.4 | 37.6 | 24.8 | 13.4 | 39.8 | 46.2 | 47.9 | 40.0 | 26.6 | 13.5 |
| Puerto Rico[2] | 1939–41 | 45.1 | 50.4 | 48.6 | 40.1 | 30.1 | 17.0 | 46.9 | 51.5 | 50.0 | 41.8 | 32.4 | 19.3 |
| **South America** | | | | | | | | | | | | | |
| Chile | 1952 | 49.8 | 56.8 | 51.4 | 42.7 | 27.3 | 14.0 | 53.9 | 60.6 | 55.7 | 47.1 | 31.3 | 16.4 |
| Venezuela[3] | 1941–42 | 45.8 | 51.2 | 48.2 | 39.9 | 26.2 | 14.0 | 47.6 | 52.5 | 49.7 | 41.6 | 28.5 | 15.8 |
| **Europe** | | | | | | | | | | | | | |
| Austria | 1949–51 | 61.9 | 65.9 | 58.0 | 48.7 | 30.7 | 15.1 | 67.0 | 70.1 | 62.2 | 52.6 | 34.2 | 17.3 |
| Belgium | 1946–49 | 62.0 | 65.3 | 57.4 | 48.0 | 30.6 | 15.5 | 67.3 | 69.7 | 61.7 | 52.3 | 34.2 | 17.5 |
| Czechoslovakia | 1958 | 67.2 | 68.5 | 60.1 | 50.6 | 32.1 | 15.8 | 72.3 | 73.2 | 64.6 | 54.9 | 35.8 | 18.2 |
| Denmark | 1951–55 | 69.9 | 71.2 | 62.7 | 53.1 | 34.4 | 17.5 | 72.6 | 73.4 | 64.8 | 55.0 | 35.9 | 18.4 |
| England and Wales | 1959 | 68.1 | 68.8 | 60.2 | 50.6 | 31.6 | 15.1 | 73.8 | 74.3 | 65.6 | 55.8 | 36.6 | 19.0 |
| Finland | 1951–55 | 63.4 | 64.7 | 56.5 | 47.0 | 29.2 | 14.1 | 69.8 | 70.9 | 62.5 | 52.8 | 34.2 | 16.9 |
| France | 1952–56 | 65.0 | 66.8 | 58.5 | 48.9 | 30.7 | 15.2 | 71.2 | 72.4 | 64.1 | 54.4 | 35.6 | 18.5 |
| Germany (Fed. Rep.) | 1958–59 | 66.7 | 68.4 | 60.0 | 50.5 | 32.1 | 15.7 | 71.7 | 73.0 | 64.5 | 54.8 | 35.7 | 18.1 |
| Greece[4] | 1926–30 | 49.1 | 53.2 | 52.4 | 44.3 | 29.8 | 16.0 | 50.9 | 55.1 | 54.5 | 46.4 | 32.4 | 17.5 |
| Hungary | 1958 | 65.1 | 68.6 | 60.3 | 50.8 | 32.4 | 16.0 | 69.4 | 72.0 | 63.6 | 54.0 | 35.1 | 17.3 |
| Iceland | 1941–50 | 66.1 | 67.4 | 59.5 | 50.5 | 34.3 | 18.2 | 70.3 | 71.3 | 63.2 | 54.0 | 36.5 | 19.6 |
| Ireland | 1950–52 | 64.5 | 66.9 | 58.8 | 49.3 | 31.3 | 15.4 | 67.1 | 68.8 | 60.6 | 51.2 | 33.3 | 16.8 |
| Italy | 1954–57 | 65.8 | 68.5 | 60.5 | 51.0 | 32.5 | 16.2 | 70.0 | 72.4 | 64.4 | 54.7 | 35.8 | 18.2 |
| Netherlands | 1953–55 | 71.0 | 71.8 | 63.4 | 53.7 | 34.8 | 17.8 | 73.9 | 74.3 | 65.7 | 56.0 | 36.7 | 18.9 |
| Norway | 1951–55 | 71.1 | 72.0 | 63.7 | 54.1 | 35.5 | 18.5 | 74.7 | 75.2 | 66.7 | 57.0 | 37.8 | 19.9 |
| Poland | 1958 | 62.8 | 67.5 | 59.4 | 49.9 | 31.7 | 15.6 | 68.9 | 72.9 | 64.7 | 54.9 | 35.8 | 18.8 |
| Portugal | 1957–58 | 59.8 | 64.9 | 58.9 | 49.4 | 31.4 | 15.4 | 65.0 | 69.7 | 63.7 | 54.1 | 35.5 | 18.1 |
| Scotland | 1959 | 66.0 | 67.2 | 58.7 | 49.0 | 30.1 | 14.2 | 71.4 | 72.2 | 63.6 | 53.8 | 34.7 | 17.6 |
| Spain | 1950 | 58.8 | 63.1 | 56.5 | 47.5 | 36.7 | 15.2 | 63.5 | 67.6 | 61.2 | 52.0 | 34.6 | 17.7 |
| Sweden | 1957 | 70.8 | 71.2 | 62.7 | 53.1 | 34.4 | 17.3 | 74.3 | 74.5 | 65.8 | 56.0 | 36.7 | 18.9 |
| Switzerland | 1948–53 | 66.4 | 67.8 | 59.6 | 50.2 | 31.9 | 15.7 | 70.9 | 71.9 | 63.6 | 53.9 | 35.0 | 17.8 |
| U.S.S.R. | 1957–58 | 64 | * | * | * | * | * | 71 | * | * | * | * | * |
| **Asia** | | | | | | | | | | | | | |
| China (Taiwan) | 1936–41 | 41.1 | 47.6 | 45.6 | 37.2 | 22.7 | 11.3 | 45.7 | 51.5 | 50.8 | 42.4 | 27.7 | 14.2 |
| India[6] | 1941–50 | 32.5 | 39.0 | 39.0 | 33.0 | 20.5 | 10.1 | 31.7 | 37.3 | 39.5 | 32.9 | 21.1 | 11.3 |
| Israel (Jews) | 1959 | 70.2 | 71.4 | 62.9 | 53.2 | 34.2 | 17.1 | 72.3 | 73.3 | 64.7 | 54.9 | 35.8 | 18.4 |
| Japan[5] | 1959 | 65.2 | 66.7 | 58.8 | 49.3 | 31.3 | 15.2 | 69.9 | 71.1 | 63.1 | 53.5 | 35.1 | 18.1 |
| Korea | 1938 | 47.2 | 51.1 | 49.9 | 41.6 | 26.2 | 12.8 | 50.6 | 54.5 | 53.2 | 45.1 | 30.0 | 14.8 |
| Thailand | 1947–48 | 48.7 | 52.0 | 47.9 | 39.8 | 25.6 | 12.7 | 51.9 | 55.2 | 50.9 | 42.7 | 28.4 | 14.2 |
| **Africa** | | | | | | | | | | | | | |
| Egypt | 1936–38 | 35.7 | 42.1 | 46.9 | 39.8 | 26.1 | 13.3 | 41.5 | 48.1 | 54.5 | 46.1 | 30.8 | 16.3 |
| U. of So. Africa (white population) | 1945–47 | 63.8 | 65.5 | 57.7 | 48.4 | 30.4 | 15.3 | 68.3 | 69.6 | 61.7 | 52.3 | 34.1 | 18.0 |
| **Oceania** | | | | | | | | | | | | | |
| Australia[7] | 1953–55 | 67.1 | 67.9 | 59.5 | 50.1 | 31.7 | 15.5 | 72.8 | 73.2 | 64.8 | 55.1 | 36.0 | 18.8 |
| New Zealand (Europeans) | 1950–52 | 68.3 | 69.0 | 60.6 | 51.2 | 32.7 | 16.2 | 72.4 | 72.9 | 64.4 | 54.6 | 35.6 | 18.5 |

* Not available.　[1] Provisional.　[2] Figures in 40 and 60 columns are for ages 35 and 55 respectively.　[3] Unofficial estimates.　[4] Excluding Dodecanese.　[5] Japanese nationals in Japan only.　[6] Data are for states of Uttar Pradesh, Bihar, Orissa, Assam, Manipur, Madras, Mysore, Travancore-Cochin, Coorg, Bombay, Saurashtra, Kutch, Madhya Pradesh, Madhya Bharat, Hyderabad, Bhopal and Vinhya Pradesh, comprising a population of 294,749,000 in 1951.　[7] Excluding full-blooded aborigines, estimated at 46,638 in June 1947.　[8] Excludes Alaska and Hawaii.

# HISTORICAL AND NEWS EVENTS
## FROM ANCIENT TO MODERN TIMES
(See also our section entitled *Headline History of Our Times,* page 295)

**Actium, Battle of** (31 B.C.). Octavius defeats Mark Anthony.

**Alexander the Great** conquers Greece, Persia, Egypt and part of India (334-323 B.C.). Major battles: Granicus (334 B.C.), Issus (333), Arbela (331).

**American Revolution** (1775-83). Outstanding events: 1775—Battle of Lexington-Concord (Apr. 19). Battle of Bunker Hill (June 17). 1776—Battle of Long Island (Aug. 27). 1777—Burgoyne surrenders at Saratoga (Oct. 17). 1781—Battle of Cowpens (Jan. 17). Battle of Yorktown (Sept. 28-Oct. 19), and British surrender by Cornwallis. 1783—Treaty signed by U. S. and Britain (Sept. 3).

**"Babylonian Captivity"** of Papacy with seat at Avignon (1309-77).

**Bacon's Rebellion** (May 10-Oct. 18, 1676). Nathaniel Bacon leads unsuccessful insurrection in Virginia because of abuses in government administration and taxation.

**Balfour Declaration** (Nov. 2, 1917) promises Jewish homeland in Palestine.

**Balkan Wars** (1912-13). Bulgaria, Serbia, Greece and Montenegro defeat Turkey; later, Bulgaria attacks Serbia and Greece and is defeated.

**Bastille destroyed** (July 14, 1789).

**Benedictine Order** founded at Monte Cassino (c. A.D. 529).

**Bible** translated by Wycliffe into English (1382-84); Douay Version published (1582 & 1609-10); King James Version published (1611).

**Black Death** (beginning c. 1347) wipes out at least one-quarter of population of Europe.

**Black Friday** (Sept. 24, 1869). Financial panic results from gold corner in U. S.

**Boer War** (1899-1902). Boers defeated by British; sign peace treaty at Pretoria (May 31, 1902).

**Boston Massacre** (Mar. 5, 1770). British soldiers fire on Boston mob, killing 3.

**Boston Tea Party** (Dec. 16, 1773). Colonials dump tea in Boston Harbor because of tea tax.

**Boxer Rebellion** (1900). Uprising by secret society in northern China against foreigners.

**Brown, John,** and 18 followers raid Harpers Ferry (Oct. 16, 1859) and seize arsenal; taken prisoners by U. S. Marines (Oct. 18); Brown hanged (Dec. 2).

**Burr-Hamilton duel.** *See* Hamilton.

**Cape-to-Cairo Railroad** completed (1918).

**Carthage** founded by Phoenicians (c. 900 B.C.); destroyed by Romans (146 B.C.).

**Châlons, Battle of** (A.D. 451). Attila the Hun defeated by Romans.

**Charlemagne** crowned Emperor of the West (A.D. 800).

**Charles I** beheaded (Jan. 30, 1649). *See also* Great Rebellion.

**Children's Crusade** (1212). About 50,000 unarmed children set out to recover Holy Sepulchre; all lost or die on the way.

**Chinese-Japanese War** (1894-95). Japan wins Formosa, Pescadores and part of southern Manchuria; Korea becomes independent (annexed by Japan 1910).

**Christianity** made official religion of Roman Empire (A.D. 330).

**Civil War, American** (1861-65). Outstanding events: 1861—First Battle of Bull Run (July 21). 1862—*Monitor* defeats *Merrimack* (Mar. 9). Battle of Antietam (Sept. 15-17). 1863—Lincoln's Emancipation Proclamation (Jan. 1). Battle of Gettysburg (July 1-3). Grant captures Vicksburg (July 4). Battle of Lookout Mountain (Nov. 23-25). 1864—Battle of the Wilderness (May 5-6). Sherman's March through Georgia (Nov. 14-Dec. 22). 1865—Lee surrenders at Appomattox (Apr. 9).

**Code Napoléon,** unified codification of French law, adopted (1804).

**Code of Hammurabi** (c. 2300 B.C.). Oldest existing written code of laws.

**Communist Manifesto** issued by Karl Marx and Friedrich Engels (1848).

**Compromise of 1850** admits California as free state; organizes Utah and New Mexico as territories without mention of slavery; prohibits slave trade in D. C.; returns fugitive slaves to masters; pays Texas $10 million for her claim to New Mexico.

**Confederacy** proclaimed by seceding states (Feb. 9, 1861); Jefferson Davis named President.

**Congress of Vienna** (1814-15). European powers, under leadership of Metternich, meet to settle problems of territory and government resulting from Napoleonic Wars.

**Constantinople** founded (as Byzantium) by Greeks (c. 660 B.C.); made capital of Eastern Roman Empire by Constantine the Great (A.D. 330); captured by

Turks (1453); renamed Istanbul (1930).

**Council of Nicaea** (A.D. 325). Called by Constantine the Great; establishes official creed of Christianity (Nicene Creed).

**Council of Trent** (1545–64). Called by Pope Paul III, at suggestion of Emperor Charles V, to establish Catholic Counter Reformation.

**"Coxey's Army"** (March. 25–May 1, 1894). Jacob S. Coxey leads 20,000 unemployed on Washington, D. C.

**Crimean War** (1853–56). Russia loses claim to Greek Christians under Turkish flag.

**Crucifixion of Christ** (c. A.D. 29). According to New Testament, Christ rose from the dead 2 days later.

**Crusades** (1096–1291). European Christians, in 7 periods of conflict, attempt to recover Holy Land from Moslems. *See also* Children's Crusade.

**Custer massacre** (June 25, 1876). Gen. George A. Custer and his forces killed at Battle of Little Big Horn by Sioux.

**Divine Comedy** begun by Dante (1307); probably finished in last year of his life (1321).

**Dominican Order** founded (1215).

**Dorr Rebellion** (1841–42). Thomas W. Dorr leads unsuccessful attempt to extend franchise in Rhode Island; franchise extended 1843.

**Dred Scott case** (1846). Dred Scott, Negro slave, sues for freedom on claim he has lived for a time on free soil; U. S. Supreme Court rules (Mar. 6, 1857) that Scott is not a citizen and has no standing in court.

**Dreyfus case** (1894). Capt. Alfred Dreyfus found guilty of treason in France and sentenced to Devil's Island. Finally acquitted (1906).

**Easter Rebellion** (April. 24, 1916). Irish nationalists unsuccessfully attempt to throw off British rule.

**Edict of Nantes** (1598). Extends toleration to Huguenots (French Protestants); its revocation (1685) causes widespread persecution of Huguenots.

**Evolution trial.** *See* Scopes.

**Fawkes, Guy.** *See* Gunpowder Plot.

**Feudalism,** lord-vassal social system, established throughout Europe (9th century); begins to break up (14th–15th centuries).

**Franciscan Order** founded (1210).

**Franco-Prussian War** (1870–71). France defeated by German states; loses Alsace-Lorraine.

**Freedom of press** established in America as John Peter Zenger, New York editor, is acquitted in libel case against Gov. Cosby (1735).

**French and Indian War.** *See* Seven Years' War.

**French Revolution** (1789–99). Outstanding events: 1789—Bastille destroyed (July 14). Feudal rights abolished (Aug. 4). 1792—September Massacres (Sept. 2–6). France becomes republic (Sept. 21). 1793—Louis XVI beheaded (Jan. 21); Marie Antoinette beheaded (Oct. 16). Reign of Terror (spring 1793–summer 1794). 1795—Napoleon heads army. Directory established (Oct. 27). (Revolution merges into Napoleonic Wars.)

**Gold rush** develops as gold is discovered at Sutter's Mill, near Sacramento, Calif. (Jan. 2, 1848).

**Great Rebellion** (1642–49). Civil wars in England. Charles I beheaded (Jan. 30, 1649); Cromwell establishes Commonwealth (1649).

**Great Wall of China** begun (255 B.C.).

**Gregorian Calendar** replaces Julian Calendar in Catholic countries (1582), in Britain and her Colonies (1752), in Russia (1918).

**Gunpowder Plot** (1605). Guy Fawkes, agent of conspirators against King and Parliament, seized as he is about to blow up House of Lords (Nov. 5).

**Hamilton-Burr duel** (July 11, 1804) results in Hamilton's death next day.

**Hastings, Battle of** (1066). Normans led by William the Conqueror invade England.

**Hegira** (A.D. 622). Mohammed flees from Mecca to Medina. Year I of Moslem calendar.

**Holy Alliance** formed by Russia, Austria and Prussia (Sept. 26, 1815); intended to regulate government according to Christianity but actually used for repressing political liberty.

**Holy Roman Empire** founded by Otto the Great (962); dissolved by Napoleon (1805).

**Huguenots.** *See* Edict of Nantes; St. Bartholomew Massacre.

**Hundred Years' War** (1338–1453). England loses lands in France. Major battles: Crécy (1346), Poitiers (1356), Agincourt (1415).

**Industrial Revolution** begins in England (c. 1760). Machines gradually replace hand tools, bringing about vast industrial and social changes.

**Inquisition** established (c. 1233) to combat heresy; put under state control in Spain (1480); abolished in France (1772), in Spain (1834).

**International, First** (1864). Founded in London to further world socialism; dissolved in Philadelphia (1876).

**International, Second** (1889). Founded in Paris to celebrate 100th anniversary of French Revolution.

**International, Third** (1919). Founded in Moscow as protest against inactivity of Second International; dissolved (1943). Also called *Communist International* or *Comintern*.

**Jamestown, Va.,** settled by British under Capt. John Smith (1607).

**Jerusalem** destroyed by Nebuchadnezzar (586 B.C.); returned to Jews by Cyrus (538 B.C.); captured by Titus (A.D. 70); captured by Crusaders (1099); captured by Saladin (1187).

**Jesuits** (Society of Jesus) founded by Ignatius of Loyola (1534).

**Joan of Arc** burned at stake (1431).

**Justinian Code** (A.D. 533). Codification of Roman law by Byzantine Emperor Justinian.

**Kansas-Nebraska Act** (1854) abrogates Missouri Compromise; permits territories of Kansas and Nebraska local option on slavery question; results in rioting and bloodshed.

**Leopold-Loeb case** (1924). Nathan Leopold and Richard Loeb kidnap and kill Bobby Franks in Chicago (May 22); sentenced to life imprisonment (July 21); Loeb killed by fellow convict (Jan. 28, 1936); Leopold receives parole (Feb. 20, 1958).

**Lindbergh flight** (May 20–21, 1927). Charles A. Lindbergh makes first solo flight across Atlantic.

**Locarno Conferences** (Oct. 1925) seek to insure peace and preserve boundaries in Europe by mutual guarantees.

**Louis XVI** beheaded (Jan. 21, 1793). *See also* French Revolution.

**Magna Carta,** charter listing rights and privileges of English barons, proclaimed at Runnymede (June 15, 1215); King John forced by barons to accept it.

**Manhattan Island** purchased by Peter Minuit from Indians (1626) for trinkets worth 60 guilders (about $24).

**Mary, Queen of Scots,** convicted in England (1586) of being accomplice in plot to murder Queen Elizabeth; beheaded (Feb. 8, 1587).

**Maximilian,** Emperor of Mexico, executed by Benito Juárez (June 19, 1867) after Napoleon III of France withdraws support of Mexican empire.

**Merrimack.** *See* Monitor.

**Mexican War** (1846–1848) ends in American victory; Treaty of Guadalupe Hidalgo signed (1848).

**Ming Dynasty** (1368–1644). Noted for great development of culture and art in China.

**Missouri Compromise** (1820) admits Maine as free state, Missouri as slave state; slavery prohibited in Louisiana Territory north of 36° 30′. *See also* Kansas-Nebraska Act.

**Monitor,** Union ship, defeats *Merrimack,* Confederate ship (Mar. 9, 1862).

**Mooney, Tom,** sentenced to death for bomb explosion in San Francisco during Preparedness Day Parade (1916); sentence commuted to life (1918); freed (1939).

**Mormonism** (Church of Jesus Christ of Latter-day Saints) founded by Joseph Smith at Fayette, N. Y. (Apr. 6, 1830).

**Moses** leads Jews out of Egypt (c. 1300 B.C.).

**Napoleonic Wars** (1796–1815). Outstanding events: 1798—Campaign in Egypt. 1805 —Nelson defeats French at Battle of Trafalgar (Oct. 21). French defeat Russians and Austrians at Battle of Austerlitz (Dec. 2). 1813—French defeated in Battle of Leipzig (Oct. 16–19). 1814— Napoleon abdicates (Apr. 11); sent to Elba. 1815—Napoleon flees Elba (Feb. 26). Napoleon defeated in Battle of Waterloo (June 18). *See also* Congress of Vienna.

**Northwest Ordinance** (1787). Adopted for territory north of Ohio River. Establishes method for admitting new states; prohibits slavery in territory.

**Orthodox Eastern Church** excommunicated by Pope Leo IX (1054); schism final between Western and Eastern Churches.

**Parliament** established in England (1295).

**Peloponnesian War** (431–404 B.C.). Sparta under Lysander defeats Athens.

**Persian Wars** (499–478 B.C.). Greece defeats Persia. Major battles: Marathon (490 B.C.), Thermopylae (480), Salamis (480), Plataea (479), Mycale (479).

**Pilgrims** land at Plymouth Rock (Dec. 21, 1620).

**Plague in London** ("Great Plague") causes 68,596 deaths (1665).

**Plymouth Rock.** *See* Pilgrims.

**Poland** partitioned out of existence among Prussia, Russia and Austria (1772, 1793, 1795).

**Pony Express** (1860–61). Between St. Joseph, Mo., and Sacramento, Calif.

**Pullman strike** (June–July 1894). Strike smashed by Federal troops; Eugene V. Debs jailed for contempt.

**Punic Wars** (264–146 B.C.). Romans defeat Carthaginians and destroy Carthage (146 B.C.). Major battles: Cannae (216 B.C.), Zama (202).

**Rasputin** ("Black Monk"), confessor to Tsarina, murdered (Dec. 31, 1916).

**Reformation** (beginning 16th century). Outstanding events: Luther nails his 95 theses to church door at Wittenberg, Germany (1517). Zwingli begins Reformation in Switzerland (1519). Luther burns papal bull and canon law (1520). Calvin publishes *Institutes of the Christian Religion* (1536). Act of Supremacy makes King head of Church of England (1534). Calvin organizes Geneva as theocratic state (1541). Knox establishes Presbyterian Church in Scotland (1560).

**Renaissance** (14th–16th centuries). Revival of classical learning in Europe stimulates vigorous activity in arts, literature, humanities, etc.

**Roman Empire** established under Augustus (27 B.C.); divided into Western and Eastern Empires (A.D. 395); Western Empire falls (476); Eastern Empire falls with capture of Constantinople (1453).

**Rome** founded, according to legend, by Romulus (753 B.C.); burned, perhaps by Nero (A.D. 64); sacked by Visigoths under Alaric (410); sacked by Vandals under Genseric (455).

**Russo-Japanese War** (1904–05). Port Arthur surrenders to Japanese (Jan. 2, 1905); Treaty of Portsmouth, N. H. (Sept. 5).

**Russo-Turkish War** (1877–78). Power of Turkey in Europe broken; redivision of southeastern Europe at Congress of Berlin (June 13–July 13, 1878).

**St. Bartholomew, Massacre of** (Aug. 24–Oct. 3, 1572). Some 50,000 Huguenots (French Protestants) killed in Paris and provinces at instigation of Catherine de Médici.

**St. Valentine's Day Massacre** in Chicago (Feb. 14, 1929). 6 members of Moran gang lined up against wall by rival gang and shot.

**Savonarola,** Florentine priest and dictator, tried for sedition and heresy (1498); hanged and burned (May 23).

**Scopes Evolution Trial** held at Dayton, Tenn. (July 10–21, 1925). John T. Scopes prosecuted by William Jennings Bryan for teaching evolution in Tennessee school; defended by Clarence Darrow. Scopes convicted but decision later set aside.

**Seven Years' War** (1756–63). France, Austria, Sweden, Russia vs. England and Prussia. Clive defeats French at Battle of Plassey (1757), giving British supremacy in India; England wins Canada; Prussia retains Silesia. (American phases of war known as French and Indian War, 1754–63.)

**Shays' Rebellion** (1786). Capt. Daniel Shays leads unsuccessful insurrection against Massachusetts government because of economic crisis.

**Slavery** in British Empire abolished by Parliament (1833).

**Slavery** introduced into American Colonies at Jamestown, Va. (1619); abolished in U. S. by 13th Amendment (1865).

**Snyder-Gray case** (1927). Ruth Snyder and Judd Gray murder her husband, Albert Snyder (Mar. 20); both executed at Sing Sing (Jan. 12, 1928).

**Spanish-American War** (1898). Outstanding events: U. S. battleship *Maine* blown up in Havana harbor (Feb. 15). Dewey destroys Spanish fleet at Manila (May 1). Charge of San Juan Hill (July 1). Cervera's fleet destroyed off Santiago, Cuba, by U. S. ships (July 3). Treaty of Paris (Dec. 10).

**Spanish Armada** destroyed by British (1588).

**Spartacus,** Roman slave and gladiator, leads unsuccessful slave insurrection (73–71 B.C.).

**Stamp Act** (effective Nov. 1, 1765). First direct tax placed on America by Britain; protested by Stamp Act Congress in New York (Oct. 7–25); repealed by Britain (Mar. 18, 1766).

**Texan war of independence from Mexico** (1836). Major battles: Alamo (Mar. 6), San Jacinto (Apr. 21).

**Thaw-White case** (1906). Harry K. Thaw, millionaire, murders Stanford White, noted architect, in Madison Square Garden (June 25).

**Thirty Years' War** (1618–1648). England, Holland, France, Sweden and German Protestants against Spain, Italy and German Catholics; Peace of Westphalia ends conflict, Alsace going to France, Swiss independence recognized, and German secularized states given religious freedom.

**Tours, Battle of** (A.D. 732). Charles Martel defeats Moslems, checking their advance in western Europe. Also called Battle of Poitiers.

**Trojan War** (c. 1200 B.C.). Greeks defeat Trojans; destroy city of Troy.

**Tutankhamen's tomb** discovered near Luxor by Lord Carnarvon and Howard Carter (1922).

**Tweed Ring,** corrupt New York political group headed by Wm. Marcy Tweed, Tammany Boss, broken up (1872); Tweed convicted (Nov. 5).

**War of 1812** (1812–1815). Outstanding events: 1813—Battle of Lake Erie (Sept. 10). 1814—British burn White House at Washington (Aug. 24–25). Battle of Lake Champlain (Sept. 11). U. S. signs treaty with Britain at Ghent (Dec. 24). 1815—Battle of New Orleans (Jan. 8). (Slowness of communications was responsible for continuation of hostilities after treaty.)

**Wars of the Roses** (1455–85). House of York (white rose) against House of Lancaster (red rose). Richard III slain at Battle of Bosworth Field (1485); Tudor line started by Henry VII.

**Whisky Insurrection** (July–Nov. 1794). Farmers in western Pennsylvania revolt unsuccessfully against excise tax of 1791.

**Witch trials** in Salem, Mass., result in death sentences for 19 women by Judge Samuel Sewall (1692).

**Woman suffrage** first granted in U. S. by Wyoming Territory (1869).

**World War I** (1914–18). Central Powers (Austria-Hungary, Germany, Bulgaria, Turkey) vs. Allies (U. S., Britain, France, Russia, Belgium, Serbia, Greece, Rumania, Montenegro, Portugal, Italy, Japan). Outstanding events: 1914— Austria declares war on Serbia (July 28). Germany declares war on Russia (Aug. 1) and on France (Aug. 3). Germany invades Belgium (Aug. 4). Britain declares war on Germany (Aug. 4). Germans defeat Russians at Tannenberg, East Prussia (Aug. 31). First Battle of the Marne (Sept. 5–12). 1915 Dardanelles campaign against Turkey fails. 1916—Battle of Jutland (May 31). Battles of the Somme (July–Nov.). Germans turned back at Verdun (Sept. 3). Rumania overrun by Central Powers; fall of Bucharest (Dec. 6). 1917— Germany begins unrestricted submarine warfare. U. S. declares war (Apr. 6). Battle of Caporetto (Oct. 24–Dec. 26). 1918—Second Battle of the Somme (Aug. 21–Sept. 3). Third Battle of the Aisne (May 27–June 6). Second Battle of the Marne (July 15–Aug. 7). U. S. troops take St. Mihiel (Sept. 13). Battle of the Meuse-Argonne (Sept. 20– Nov. 11). Allies break Hindenburg line (Oct. 5). Armistice signed (Nov. 11).

**Zenger case.** *See* Freedom of press.

## The Flag at Half-Staff

The flag shall be flown at half-staff 30 days for the President of the U. S. or a former President; 10 days for the Vice President, the Chief Justice, a retired Chief Justice, or the Speaker of the House; until interment for an Associate Justice, a Cabinet member, a former Vice President, a Senator, a Representative, a state or territorial governor, etc. For other officials, the President or custom shall rule. Jurisdiction on naval vessels, government buildings, etc., is left to those in charge.

## Firsts in America

Occasionally other sources may differ with this list. Our selection is based on our editorial judgment.

**Admiral in U. S. Navy:** David Glasgow Farragut, 1866.

**Air-mail route, first transcontinental:** Between New York City and San Francisco, 1920.

**Assembly, representative:** House of Burgesses, founded in Virginia, 1619.

**Bank established:** Bank of North America, Philadelphia, 1781.

**Birth in America of English parents:** Virginia Dare, born Roanoke Island, N. C., 1587.

**Botanic garden:** Established by John Bartram in Philadelphia, 1728. (Oldest existing one was established in Cambridge, Mass., in 1807.)

**Cartoon, colored:** "The Yellow Kid," by Richard Outcault, in *New York World,* 1895.

**College in America:** Harvard, founded 1636.

**College to confer degrees on women:** Oberlin (Ohio) College, 1841.

**College to establish coeducation:** Oberlin (Ohio) College, 1833.

**Electrocution of a criminal:** William Kemmler in Auburn Prison, Auburn, N. Y., Aug. 6, 1890.

**Five and Ten Cents Store:** Founded by Frank Woolworth, Utica, N. Y., 1879 (moved to Lancaster, Pa., same year).

**Fraternity:** Phi Beta Kappa; founded Dec. 5, 1776, at College of William and Mary.

**Law to be declared unconstitutional by U. S. Supreme Court:** Judiciary Act of 1789. Case: Marbury vs. Madison, 1803.

**Library, circulating:** Philadelphia, 1731.

**Newspaper published for a continuous period:** *The Boston News-Letter,* April, 1704.

**Newspaper, illustrated daily:** *New York Daily Graphic,* 1873.

**Newspaper published daily:** *Pennsylvania Packet and General Advertiser,* Philadelphia, Sept., 1784.

**Newsreel:** Pathé Frères of Paris, in 1910, circulated a weekly issue of their *Pathé Journal.*

**Oil well, commercial:** Titusville, Pa., 1859.

**Panel quiz show on radio:** *Information Please,* May 17, 1938.

**Postage stamps issued:** 1847.

**President pro tempore of the U. S. Senate:** John Langdon, of New Hampshire, 1789.

Railroad, transcontinental: Central Pacific and Union Pacific railroads joined at Promontory, Utah, May 10, 1869.

Savings bank: The Provident Institute for Savings, Boston, 1816.

Science museum: Founded by Charleston (S. C.) Library Society, 1773.

Skyscraper: Home Insurance Co., Chicago, 1885 (10 floors, 2 added later).

Slaves brought into America: At Jamestown, Va., 1619, from a Dutch ship.

Sorority: Kappa Alpha Theta, at De Pauw University, 1870.

State to abolish capital punishment: Michigan, 1847.

State to enter Union after original 13: Vermont, 1791.

Steam-heated building: Eastern Hotel, Boston, 1845.

Steam railroad (carried passengers and freight): Baltimore & Ohio, 1830.

Strike on record by union: Journeymen Printers, New York, 1776.

Subway: Opened in Boston, 1897.

"Tabloid" picture newspaper: *The Illustrated Daily News* (now *The Daily News*), New York City, 1919.

Vaudeville theater: Gaiety Museum, Boston, 1883.

Woman cabinet member: Frances Perkins, Secretary of Labor, 1933.

Woman candidate for President: Victoria Claflin Woodhull, nominated by National Woman's Suffrage Assn. on ticket of Nation Radical Reformers, 1872.

Woman doctor of medicine: Elizabeth Blackwell; M.D. from Geneva Medical College of Western New York, 1849.

Woman elected governor of a state: Mrs. Nellie Tayloe Ross, Wyoming, 1925.

Woman elected to U. S. Senate: Mrs. Hattie Caraway, Arkansas; elected Nov. 1932.

Woman graduate of law school: Mrs. Ada H. Kepley, Union College of Law, Chicago, 1870.

Woman member of U. S. House of Representatives: Jeannette Rankin; elected Nov. 1916.

Woman member of U. S. Senate: Mrs. Rebecca Latimer Felton of Georgia; appointed Oct. 3, 1922.

Woman suffrage granted: Wyoming Territory, 1869.

Written constitution: *Fundamental Orders of Connecticut*, 1639.

# Societies and Foundations

*Source:* Questionnaires to Societies and Foundations.

AMERICAN BIBLE SOCIETY: Founded 1816 to translate, publish and encourage wider distribution of Holy Scriptures.

AMERICAN RED CROSS: Founded 1881. Programs include services to armed forces and veterans and their families, disaster relief, and other health, safety, and welfare activities.

BOY SCOUTS OF AMERICA: Founded 1910. Purpose is to promote character development, citizenship training and physical fitness for boys.

CAMP FIRE GIRLS, INC.: Founded 1910, to perpetuate spiritual ideals of the home and to stimulate and aid habits making for health and character.

CARNEGIE CORPORATION OF NEW YORK: Founded 1911 by Andrew Carnegie to advance knowledge and understanding in U. S. and certain British Commonwealth areas. Grants awarded to colleges and organizations engaged in basic research and studies of American education. Assets (1960): $214,000,000 (cost basis).

CARNEGIE ENDOWMENT FOR INTERNATIONAL PEACE: Founded 1910 by Andrew Carnegie. To work toward international peace. Assets (June 30, 1960): $21,210,490.

COMMONWEALTH FUND: Founded 1918 by Mrs. Stephen V. Harkness. Purpose is to promote health chiefly through grants for medical education and related activities. Endowment (1961): $77,000,000.

DUKE ENDOWMENT, THE: Founded 1924 by James B. Duke. Purpose is to assist North and South Carolina institutions, including universities, hospitals, orphanages and the Methodist Church. Income (Dec. 31, 1960): $168,318,421.28.

ELKS, BENEVOLENT AND PROTECTIVE ORDER OF: Founded 1868 to practice charity, justice, brotherly love and fidelity. Charitable expenditures (1960): $7,028,698.27 (by Lodges, 1880–1960, $153,389,768.64).

FIELD FOUNDATION, INC.: Founded 1940 by Marshall Field. Present purpose is to promote the welfare of children and improve intercultural and interracial relations. Assets (1961): Over $30,000,000.

FORD FOUNDATION: Founded 1936 by Henry and Edsel Ford to advance human welfare by identifying problems of national importance and granting funds for efforts toward their solution, primarily through educational means. Assets (Sept. 30, 1960): $2,195,509,083.

FREEMASONRY: Originated in England (1717); brought to America about 1733. It includes Symbolic Lodge (3 basic degrees), Royal Arch, Council of Royal and Select Masters, Knights Templar, and Scottish Rite. It is universal in its philosophy, nonsectarian in membership.

GIRL SCOUTS OF THE U.S.A.: Founded 1912. Purpose is to help girls develop as happy, resourceful individuals. Activities program emphasizes out-of-doors, creative arts, and community service.

GUGGENHEIM (JOHN SIMON) MEMORIAL FOUNDATION: Founded 1925. Purpose is to offer fellowships in all fields. Endowment (1961): $45,000,000.

W. K. KELLOGG FOUNDATION: Founded 1930 by W. K. Kellogg. Operates by making grants supporting experimental programs in health, agricultural and educational fields. Assets (Aug. 31, 1960): $72,668,186, book value; $254,634,186, market value.

KIWANIS INTERNATIONAL: Founded 1915 to render service to youth, community and nation.

KNIGHTS OF COLUMBUS: Founded 1882. Purpose is to render pecuniary aid to its sick, disabled and needy members; promotes social and intellectual intercourse among its members and conducts educational, charitable, social, relief and religious work.

KNIGHTS OF PYTHIAS: Founded 1864. Purpose is to promote social and fraternal well-being of its members. Auxiliary bodies: Dramatic Order of Knights Khorassan, Junior Order of Knights of Pythias, Order of Pythian Sisters.

LEAGUE OF WOMEN VOTERS OF THE UNITED STATES: Founded in 1920 upon ratification of 19th Amendment to inform the electorate and increase citizen participation in government. Annual expenditure: about $1,600,000.

LIONS CLUBS, INTERNATIONAL ASSOCIATION OF: Founded 1917. Purpose is to recognize community needs and develop means of meeting them. World's largest service club organization.

NATIONAL ASSOCIATION FOR THE ADVANCEMENT OF COLORED PEOPLE: Organized 1909. It seeks equal citizenship rights for Negroes through legal action, legislation and education.

NATIONAL FOUNDATION (formerly National Foundation for Infantile Paralysis, Inc.): Founded 1938 by F. D. Roosevelt. Funds are raised by the annual March of Dimes in January. Financed research resulting in development of Salk and Sabin vaccines. Program includes medical research, patient care, efforts to prevent birth defects, arthritis, virus diseases, future health problems, as well as polio.

NATIONAL GEOGRAPHIC SOCIETY: Founded 1888. Purpose is to increase and diffuse geographic knowledge. Publishes monthly *National Geographic Magazine*, weekly *Geographic School Bulletins*, maps, books, and *National Geographic News Bulletins*.

ODD FELLOWS, INDEPENDENT ORDER OF: Introduced into U. S. in 1819. Purpose is to promote social relations and to provide benefits for members.

ROCKEFELLER FOUNDATION: Founded 1913 to promote well-being of mankind throughout world; makes grants to agencies in fields of medical and natural sciences, agricultural sciences, social sciences and humanities. Principal Fund (Dec. 31, 1960): $469,576,720.

ROTARY INTERNATIONAL: Founded 1905. Purpose is to foster the ideal of service in business and community life and promote international understanding.

RUSSELL SAGE FOUNDATION: Founded 1907 by Mrs. Russell Sage to improve social and living conditions in U. S. Program emphasizes utilization of social sciences in professional practice. Assets (Sept. 1960): $28,650,000.

SLOAN FOUNDATION, ALFRED P.: Founded 1934 by Alfred P. Sloan, Jr. Purpose is to increase and spread economic knowledge and promote basic research in science and other subjects. Assets (Dec. 1960): $200,150,000.

TWENTIETH CENTURY FUND: Founded 1919 by Edward A. Filene to promote research and public education on economic and social problems. Assets (Dec. 31, 1960): $20,240,000.

YOUNG MEN'S CHRISTIAN ASSOCIATION: Founded 1844. Purpose is to improve spiritual, social, recreational and physical lives of young people. Total current income, $161,841,680.

YOUNG WOMEN'S CHRISTIAN ASSOCIATION OF THE U.S.A.: Founded 1858 to advance physical, social, intellectual and spiritual interests of young women and to build fellowship of women devoted to pursuit of Christian ideals.

## Longest Broadway Runs
Source: *Variety.*

1. Life with Father .............. 3,224
2. Tobacco Road ................ 3,182
3. Abie's Irish Rose ............ 2,327
4. My Fair Lady ................ 2,275†
5. Oklahoma! ................... 2,176
6. Harvey ...................... 1,775
7. South Pacific ................ 1,694
8. Born Yesterday .............. 1,642
9. The Voice of the Turtle ....... 1,557
10. Arsenic and Old Lace .......... 1,444
11. Helzapoppin .................. 1,404

## Top Grossing Films*
Source: *Variety.*

1. The Ten Commandments .. $34,200,000
2. Gone With the Wind ..... 33,500,000
3. Ben Hur ................ 33,000,000
4. Around World in 80 Days .. 22,000,000
5. The Robe ............... 17,500,000
6. South Pacific ........... 16,300,000
7. Bridge on the River Kwai .. 15,000,000
8. Greatest Show on Earth .. 12,800,000
9. From Here to Eternity .... 12,500,000
10. This Is Cinerama ........ 12,500,000
11. White Christmas ........ 12,000,000

* Figures are rentals collected by film distributors from exhibitors in U. S. and Canada.    † As of Sept. 6, 1961.

# FEDERAL INCOME TAX

If you are a citizen or a resident of the United States, and if your gross income for the year amounts to $600 or more, you are required to file a return. This requirement applies to minors, as well as adults, and must be met even if you do not pay a tax.

If you are more than 65 years old, you are required to file only if your gross income is $1,200 or more.

You must pay part of your tax in installments in the year in which you earned the income. This is the "pay-as-you-go" system. You are generally required to pay the rest of your tax when you file your return. It may turn out that you don't owe any additional tax when you file your return, or you may even be entitled to a refund, in which case the refund will be paid to you automatically after your return is filed.

The "pay-as-you-go" system works in two ways, through withholding and declaration of estimated tax. You may be subject to either or both of these requirements.

If you are married, you and your wife are allowed to report your combined income and your combined deductions on a single return. This is called a joint return. Your combined income is then taxed as though half were yours and half hers. This will usually result in a lower tax.

## Withholding Table for Employees Paid Weekly

| If the wages are— | | And the number of withholding exemptions claimed is— | | | | | | | | | | |
|---|---|---|---|---|---|---|---|---|---|---|---|---|
| | | 0 | 1 | 2 | 3 | 4 | 5 | 6 | 7 | 8 | 9 | 10 or more |
| At least | But less than | The amount of tax to be withheld shall be— | | | | | | | | | | |
| $0 | $13 | 18% of wages | $0 | $0 | $0 | $0 | $0 | $0 | $0 | $0 | $0 | $0 |
| $13 | $14 | $2.40 | .10 | 0 | 0 | 0 | 0 | 0 | 0 | 0 | 0 | 0 |
| $14 | $15 | 2.60 | .30 | 0 | 0 | 0 | 0 | 0 | 0 | 0 | 0 | 0 |
| $15 | $16 | 2.80 | .50 | 0 | 0 | 0 | 0 | 0 | 0 | 0 | 0 | 0 |
| $16 | $17 | 3.00 | .70 | 0 | 0 | 0 | 0 | 0 | 0 | 0 | 0 | 0 |
| $17 | $18 | 3.20 | .80 | 0 | 0 | 0 | 0 | 0 | 0 | 0 | 0 | 0 |
| $18 | $19 | 3.30 | 1.00 | 0 | 0 | 0 | 0 | 0 | 0 | 0 | 0 | 0 |
| $19 | $20 | 3.50 | 1.20 | 0 | 0 | 0 | 0 | 0 | 0 | 0 | 0 | 0 |
| $20 | $21 | 3.70 | 1.40 | 0 | 0 | 0 | 0 | 0 | 0 | 0 | 0 | 0 |
| $21 | $22 | 3.90 | 1.60 | 0 | 0 | 0 | 0 | 0 | 0 | 0 | 0 | 0 |
| $22 | $23 | 4.10 | 1.70 | 0 | 0 | 0 | 0 | 0 | 0 | 0 | 0 | 0 |
| $23 | $24 | 4.20 | 1.90 | 0 | 0 | 0 | 0 | 0 | 0 | 0 | 0 | 0 |
| $24 | $25 | 4.40 | 2.10 | 0 | 0 | 0 | 0 | 0 | 0 | 0 | 0 | 0 |
| $25 | $26 | 4.60 | 2.30 | 0 | 0 | 0 | 0 | 0 | 0 | 0 | 0 | 0 |
| $26 | $27 | 4.80 | 2.50 | .20 | 0 | 0 | 0 | 0 | 0 | 0 | 0 | 0 |
| $27 | $28 | 5.00 | 2.60 | .30 | 0 | 0 | 0 | 0 | 0 | 0 | 0 | 0 |
| $28 | $29 | 5.10 | 2.80 | .50 | 0 | 0 | 0 | 0 | 0 | 0 | 0 | 0 |
| $29 | $30 | 5.30 | 3.00 | .70 | 0 | 0 | 0 | 0 | 0 | 0 | 0 | 0 |
| $30 | $31 | 5.50 | 3.20 | .90 | 0 | 0 | 0 | 0 | 0 | 0 | 0 | 0 |
| $31 | $32 | 5.70 | 3.40 | 1.10 | 0 | 0 | 0 | 0 | 0 | 0 | 0 | 0 |
| $32 | $33 | 5.90 | 3.50 | 1.20 | 0 | 0 | 0 | 0 | 0 | 0 | 0 | 0 |
| $33 | $34 | 6.00 | 3.70 | 1.40 | 0 | 0 | 0 | 0 | 0 | 0 | 0 | 0 |
| $34 | $35 | 6.20 | 3.90 | 1.60 | 0 | 0 | 0 | 0 | 0 | 0 | 0 | 0 |
| $35 | $36 | 6.40 | 4.10 | 1.80 | 0 | 0 | 0 | 0 | 0 | 0 | 0 | 0 |

| If the wages are— | | And the number of withholding exemptions claimed is— | | | | | | | | | | |
|---|---|---|---|---|---|---|---|---|---|---|---|---|
| | | 0 | 1 | 2 | 3 | 4 | 5 | 6 | 7 | 8 | 9 | 10 or more |
| At least | But less than | The amount of tax to be withheld shall be— | | | | | | | | | | |
| $36 | $37 | $6.60 | $4.30 | $2.00 | $0 | $0 | $0 | $0 | $0 | $0 | $0 | $0 |
| $37 | $38 | 6.80 | 4.40 | 2.10 | 0 | 0 | 0 | 0 | 0 | 0 | 0 | 0 |
| $38 | $39 | 6.90 | 4.60 | 2.30 | 0 | 0 | 0 | 0 | 0 | 0 | 0 | 0 |
| $39 | $40 | 7.10 | 4.80 | 2.50 | .20 | 0 | 0 | 0 | 0 | 0 | 0 | 0 |
| $40 | $41 | 7.30 | 5.00 | 2.70 | .40 | 0 | 0 | 0 | 0 | 0 | 0 | 0 |
| $41 | $42 | 7.50 | 5.20 | 2.90 | .50 | 0 | 0 | 0 | 0 | 0 | 0 | 0 |
| $42 | $43 | 7.70 | 5.30 | 3.00 | .70 | 0 | 0 | 0 | 0 | 0 | 0 | 0 |
| $43 | $44 | 7.80 | 5.50 | 3.20 | .90 | 0 | 0 | 0 | 0 | 0 | 0 | 0 |
| $44 | $45 | 8.00 | 5.70 | 3.40 | 1.10 | 0 | 0 | 0 | 0 | 0 | 0 | 0 |
| $45 | $46 | 8.20 | 5.90 | 3.60 | 1.30 | 0 | 0 | 0 | 0 | 0 | 0 | 0 |
| $46 | $47 | 8.40 | 6.10 | 3.80 | 1.40 | 0 | 0 | 0 | 0 | 0 | 0 | 0 |
| $47 | $48 | 8.60 | 6.20 | 3.90 | 1.60 | 0 | 0 | 0 | 0 | 0 | 0 | 0 |
| $48 | $49 | 8.70 | 6.40 | 4.10 | 1.80 | 0 | 0 | 0 | 0 | 0 | 0 | 0 |
| $49 | $50 | 8.90 | 6.60 | 4.30 | 2.00 | 0 | 0 | 0 | 0 | 0 | 0 | 0 |
| $50 | $51 | 9.10 | 6.80 | 4.50 | 2.20 | 0 | 0 | 0 | 0 | 0 | 0 | 0 |
| $51 | $52 | 9.30 | 7.00 | 4.70 | 2.30 | 0 | 0 | 0 | 0 | 0 | 0 | 0 |
| $52 | $53 | 9.50 | 7.10 | 4.80 | 2.50 | .20 | 0 | 0 | 0 | 0 | 0 | 0 |
| $53 | $54 | 9.60 | 7.30 | 5.00 | 2.70 | .40 | 0 | 0 | 0 | 0 | 0 | 0 |
| $54 | $55 | 9.80 | 7.50 | 5.20 | 2.90 | .60 | 0 | 0 | 0 | 0 | 0 | 0 |
| $55 | $56 | 10.00 | 7.70 | 5.40 | 3.10 | .80 | 0 | 0 | 0 | 0 | 0 | 0 |
| $56 | $57 | 10.20 | 7.90 | 5.60 | 3.20 | .90 | 0 | 0 | 0 | 0 | 0 | 0 |
| $57 | $58 | 10.40 | 8.00 | 5.70 | 3.40 | 1.10 | 0 | 0 | 0 | 0 | 0 | 0 |
| $58 | $59 | 10.50 | 8.20 | 5.90 | 3.60 | 1.30 | 0 | 0 | 0 | 0 | 0 | 0 |
| $59 | $60 | 10.70 | 8.40 | 6.10 | 3.80 | 1.50 | 0 | 0 | 0 | 0 | 0 | 0 |
| $60 | $62 | 11.00 | 8.70 | 6.40 | 4.10 | 1.70 | 0 | 0 | 0 | 0 | 0 | 0 |
| $62 | $64 | 11.30 | 9.00 | 6.70 | 4.40 | 2.10 | 0 | 0 | 0 | 0 | 0 | 0 |
| $64 | $66 | 11.70 | 9.40 | 7.10 | 4.80 | 2.50 | .20 | 0 | 0 | 0 | 0 | 0 |
| $66 | $68 | 12.10 | 9.80 | 7.40 | 5.10 | 2.80 | .50 | 0 | 0 | 0 | 0 | 0 |
| $68 | $70 | 12.40 | 10.10 | 7.80 | 5.50 | 3.20 | .90 | 0 | 0 | 0 | 0 | 0 |
| $70 | $72 | 12.80 | 10.50 | 8.20 | 5.90 | 3.50 | 1.20 | 0 | 0 | 0 | 0 | 0 |
| $72 | $74 | 13.10 | 10.80 | 8.50 | 6.20 | 3.90 | 1.60 | 0 | 0 | 0 | 0 | 0 |
| $74 | $76 | 13.50 | 11.20 | 8.90 | 6.60 | 4.30 | 2.00 | 0 | 0 | 0 | 0 | 0 |
| $76 | $78 | 13.90 | 11.60 | 9.20 | 6.90 | 4.60 | 2.30 | 0 | 0 | 0 | 0 | 0 |
| $78 | $80 | 14.20 | 11.90 | 9.60 | 7.30 | 5.00 | 2.70 | .40 | 0 | 0 | 0 | 0 |
| $80 | $82 | 14.60 | 12.30 | 10.00 | 7.70 | 5.30 | 3.00 | .70 | 0 | 0 | 0 | 0 |
| $82 | $84 | 14.90 | 12.60 | 10.30 | 8.00 | 5.70 | 3.40 | 1.10 | 0 | 0 | 0 | 0 |
| $84 | $86 | 15.30 | 13.00 | 10.70 | 8.40 | 6.10 | 3.80 | 1.50 | 0 | 0 | 0 | 0 |
| $86 | $88 | 15.70 | 13.40 | 11.00 | 8.70 | 6.40 | 4.10 | 1.80 | 0 | 0 | 0 | 0 |
| $88 | $90 | 16.00 | 13.70 | 11.40 | 9.10 | 6.80 | 4.50 | 2.20 | 0 | 0 | 0 | 0 |
| $90 | $92 | 16.40 | 14.10 | 11.80 | 9.50 | 7.10 | 4.80 | 2.50 | .20 | 0 | 0 | 0 |
| $92 | $94 | 16.70 | 14.40 | 12.10 | 9.80 | 7.50 | 5.20 | 2.90 | .60 | 0 | 0 | 0 |
| $94 | $96 | 17.10 | 14.80 | 12.50 | 10.20 | 7.90 | 5.60 | 3.30 | .90 | 0 | 0 | 0 |
| $96 | $98 | 17.50 | 15.20 | 12.80 | 10.50 | 8.20 | 5.90 | 3.60 | 1.30 | 0 | 0 | 0 |
| $98 | $100 | 17.80 | 15.50 | 13.20 | 10.90 | 8.60 | 6.30 | 4.00 | 1.70 | 0 | 0 | 0 |
| $100 | $105 | 18.50 | 16.10 | 13.80 | 11.50 | 9.20 | 6.90 | 4.60 | 2.30 | 0 | 0 | 0 |
| $105 | $110 | 19.40 | 17.00 | 14.70 | 12.40 | 10.10 | 7.80 | 5.50 | 3.20 | .90 | 0 | 0 |
| $110 | $115 | 20.30 | 17.90 | 15.60 | 13.30 | 11.00 | 8.70 | 6.40 | 4.10 | 1.80 | 0 | 0 |
| $115 | $120 | 21.20 | 18.80 | 16.50 | 14.20 | 11.90 | 9.60 | 7.30 | 5.00 | 2.70 | .40 | 0 |
| $120 | $125 | 22.10 | 19.70 | 17.40 | 15.10 | 12.80 | 10.50 | 8.20 | 5.90 | 3.60 | 1.30 | 0 |
| $125 | $130 | 23.00 | 20.60 | 18.30 | 16.00 | 13.70 | 11.40 | 9.10 | 6.80 | 4.50 | 2.20 | 0 |
| $130 | $135 | 23.90 | 21.50 | 19.20 | 16.90 | 14.60 | 12.30 | 10.00 | 7.70 | 5.40 | 3.10 | .80 |
| $135 | $140 | 24.80 | 22.40 | 20.10 | 17.80 | 15.50 | 13.20 | 10.90 | 8.60 | 6.30 | 4.00 | 1.70 |
| $140 | $145 | 25.70 | 23.30 | 21.00 | 18.70 | 16.40 | 14.10 | 11.80 | 9.50 | 7.20 | 4.90 | 2.60 |
| $145 | $150 | 26.60 | 24.20 | 21.90 | 19.60 | 17.30 | 15.00 | 12.70 | 10.40 | 8.10 | 5.80 | 3.50 |
| $150 | $160 | 27.90 | 25.60 | 23.30 | 21.00 | 18.70 | 16.40 | 14.10 | 11.70 | 9.40 | 7.10 | 4.80 |
| $160 | $170 | 29.70 | 27.40 | 25.10 | 22.80 | 20.50 | 18.20 | 15.90 | 13.50 | 11.20 | 8.90 | 6.60 |

| If the wages are— | | And the number of withholding exemptions claimed is— | | | | | | | | | | |
|---|---|---|---|---|---|---|---|---|---|---|---|---|
| | | 0 | 1 | 2 | 3 | 4 | 5 | 6 | 7 | 8 | 9 | 10 or more |
| At least | But less than | The amount of tax to be withheld shall be— | | | | | | | | | | |
| $170 | $180 | $31.50 | $29.20 | $26.90 | $24.60 | $22.30 | $20.00 | $17.70 | $15.30 | $13.00 | $10.70 | $8.40 |
| $180 | $190 | 33.30 | 31.00 | 28.70 | 26.40 | 24.10 | 21.80 | 19.50 | 17.10 | 14.80 | 12.50 | 10.20 |
| $190 | $200 | 35.10 | 32.80 | 30.50 | 28.20 | 25.90 | 23.60 | 21.30 | 18.90 | 16.60 | 14.30 | 12.00 |
| | | 18 percent of the excess over $200 plus— | | | | | | | | | | |
| $200 and over | | 36.00 | 33.70 | 31.40 | 29.10 | 26.80 | 24.50 | 22.20 | 19.80 | 17.50 | 15.20 | 12.90 |

## Rate Table for Separate Returns

If your taxable income is:                          Your tax is:

Not over $2,000 .......................... 20% of the taxable income
Over $    2,000 but not over $    4,000....... $      400, plus 22% of excess over $    2,000
Over $    4,000 but not over $    6,000....... $      840, plus 26% of excess over $    4,000
Over $    6,000 but not over $    8,000....... $    1,360, plus 30% of excess over $    6,000
Over $    8,000 but not over $  10,000....... $    1,960, plus 34% of excess over $    8,000
Over $  10,000 but not over $  12,000....... $    2,640, plus 38% of excess over $  10,000
Over $  12,000 but not over $  14,000....... $    3,400, plus 43% of excess over $  12,000
Over $  14,000 but not over $  16,000....... $    4,260, plus 47% of excess over $  14,000
Over $  16,000 but not over $  18,000....... $    5,200, plus 50% of excess over $  16,000
Over $  18,000 but not over $  20,000....... $    6,200, plus 53% of excess over $  18,000
Over $  20,000 but not over $  22,000....... $    7,260, plus 56% of excess over $  20,000
Over $  22,000 but not over $  26,000....... $    8,380, plus 59% of excess over $  22,000
Over $  26,000 but not over $  32,000....... $  10,740, plus 62% of excess over $  26,000
Over $  32,000 but not over $  38,000....... $  14,460, plus 65% of excess over $  32,000
Over $  38,000 but not over $  44,000....... $  18,360, plus 69% of excess over $  38,000
Over $  44,000 but not over $  50,000....... $  22,500, plus 72% of excess over $  44,000
Over $  50,000 but not over $  60,000....... $  26,820, plus 75% of excess over $  50,000
Over $  60,000 but not over $  70,000....... $  34,320, plus 78% of excess over $  60,000
Over $  70,000 but not over $  80,000....... $  42,120, plus 81% of excess over $  70,000
Over $  80,000 but not over $  90,000....... $  50,220, plus 84% of excess over $  80,000
Over $  90,000 but not over $100,000....... $  58,620, plus 87% of excess over $  90,000
Over $100,000 but not over $150,000....... $  67,320, plus 89% of excess over $100,000*
Over $150,000 but not over $200,000....... $111,820, plus 90% of excess over $150,000*
Over $200,000 .......................... $156,820, plus 91% of excess over $200,000*

* The tax cannot in any event be more than 87% of taxable income.

## Rate Table for Head of Household Returns

If your taxable income is:                          Your tax is:

Not over $2,000 .......................... 20% of the taxable income
Over $    2,000 but not over $    4,000....... $      400, plus 21% of excess over $    2,000
Over $    4,000 but not over $    6,000....... $      820, plus 24% of excess over $    4,000
Over $    6,000 but not over $    8,000....... $    1,300, plus 26% of excess over $    6,000
Over $    8,000 but not over $  10,000....... $    1,820, plus 30% of excess over $    8,000
Over $  10,000 but not over $  12,000....... $    2,420, plus 32% of excess over $  10,000
Over $  12,000 but not over $  14,000....... $    3,060, plus 36% of excess over $  12,000
Over $  14,000 but not over $  16,000....... $    3,780, plus 39% of excess over $  14,000
Over $  16,000 but not over $  18,000....... $    4,560, plus 42% of excess over $  16,000
Over $  18,000 but not over $  20,000....... $    5,400, plus 43% of excess over $  18,000
Over $  20,000 but not over $  22,000....... $    6,260, plus 47% of excess over $  20,000
Over $  22,000 but not over $  24,000....... $    7,200, plus 49% of excess over $  22,000
Over $  24,000 but not over $  28,000....... $    8,180, plus 52% of excess over $  24,000
Over $  28,000 but not over $  32,000....... $  10,260, plus 54% of excess over $  28,000
Over $  32,000 but not over $  38,000....... $  12,420, plus 58% of excess over $  32,000
Over $  38,000 but not over $  44,000....... $  15,900, plus 62% of excess over $  38,000

## Rate Table for Head of Household Returns (contd.)

If your combined taxable income is:                     Your tax is:

| | | |
|---|---|---|
| Over $ 44,000 but not over $ 50,000 | $ 19,620, plus 66% of excess over $ 44,000 |
| Over $ 50,000 but not over $ 60,000 | $ 23,580, plus 68% of excess over $ 50,000 |
| Over $ 60,000 but not over $ 70,000 | $ 30,380, plus 71% of excess over $ 60,000 |
| Over $ 70,000 but not over $ 80,000 | $ 37,480, plus 74% of excess over $ 70,000 |
| Over $ 80,000 but not over $ 90,000 | $ 44,880, plus 76% of excess over $ 80,000 |
| Over $ 90,000 but not over $100,000 | $ 52,480, plus 80% of excess over $ 90,000 |
| Over $100,000 but not over $150,000 | $ 60,480, plus 83% of excess over $100,000 |
| Over $150,000 but not over $200,000 | $101,980, plus 87% of excess over $150,000 |
| Over $200,000 but not over $300,000 | $145,480, plus 90% of excess over $200,000* |
| Over $300,000 | $235,480, plus 91% of excess over $300,000* |

* The tax cannot in any event be more than 87% of taxable income.

## Rate Table for Joint Returns

If your combined taxable income is:                     Your tax is:

| | | |
|---|---|---|
| Not over $4,000 | 20% of taxable income |
| Over $ 4,000 but not over $ 8,000 | $ 800, plus 22% of excess over $ 4,000 |
| Over $ 8,000 but not over $ 12,000 | $ 1,680, plus 26% of excess over $ 8,000 |
| Over $ 12,000 but not over $ 16,000 | $ 2,720, plus 30% of excess over $ 12,000 |
| Over $ 16,000 but not over $ 20,000 | $ 3,920, plus 34% of excess over $ 16,000 |
| Over $ 20,000 but not over $ 24,000 | $ 5,280, plus 38% of excess over $ 20,000 |
| Over $ 24,000 but not over $ 28,000 | $ 6,800, plus 43% of excess over $ 24,000 |
| Over $ 28,000 but not over $ 32,000 | $ 8,520, plus 47% of excess over $ 28,000 |
| Over $ 32,000 but not over $ 36,000 | $ 10,400, plus 50% of excess over $ 32,000 |
| Over $ 36,000 but not over $ 40,000 | $ 12,400, plus 53% of excess over $ 36,000 |
| Over $ 40,000 but not over $ 44,000 | $ 14,520, plus 56% of excess over $ 40,000 |
| Over $ 44,000 but not over $ 52,000 | $ 16,760, plus 59% of excess over $ 44,000 |
| Over $ 52,000 but not over $ 64,000 | $ 21,480, plus 62% of excess over $ 52,000 |
| Over $ 64,000 but not over $ 76,000 | $ 28,920, plus 65% of excess over $ 64,000 |
| Over $ 76,000 but not over $ 88,000 | $ 36,720, plus 69% of excess over $ 76,000 |
| Over $ 88,000 but not over $100,000 | $ 45,000, plus 72% of excess over $ 88,000 |
| Over $100,000 but not over $120,000 | $ 53,640, plus 75% of excess over $100,000 |
| Over $120,000 but not over $140,000 | $ 68,640, plus 78% of excess over $120,000 |
| Over $140,000 but not over $160,000 | $ 84,240, plus 81% of excess over $140,000 |
| Over $160,000 but not over $180,000 | $100,440, plus 84% of excess over $160,000 |
| Over $180,000 but not over $200,000 | $117,240, plus 87% of excess over $180,000 |
| Over $200,000 but not over $300,000 | $134,640, plus 89% of excess over $200,000* |
| Over $300,000 but not over $400,000 | $223,640, plus 90% of excess over $300,000* |
| Over $400,000 | $313,640, plus 91% of excess over $400,000* |

* The tax cannot in any event be more than 87% of combined taxable income.

# SOCIAL SECURITY

The Social Security Act was passed in 1935 and subsequently amended in 1939, 1950, 1952, 1954, 1958, and 1961.

The act is administered by the Department of Health, Education and Welfare, of which the Social Security Administration is a part.

## Old-Age, Survivors, and Disability Insurance

### WHO IS COVERED?

Almost everyone who works fairly regularly. Self-employed doctors are the only large group not covered by this social security program.

To qualify for benefits or make payments possible for your survivors you must be in work covered by the law for a certain number of "quarters of coverage" after 1936 (for self-employment, after 1950). The number of quarters needed differs for different persons and depends on the date of your birth; in general, it is related to the length of time from 1950, or from your twenty-first birthday and the time you reach 62. No one needs more than 40 quarters, and no one can qualify with less than 6. Your local social security office can tell you how long you need to work in covered employment under the present law.

## WHO PAYS FOR THE INSURANCE?

Both workers and employers pay for the workers' insurance. Self-employed persons pay their own tax annually along with their income tax. Tax rates are scheduled to go up gradually until 1968:

| Years | Workers and Employers Each to Pay | Self-employed to Pay |
|---|---|---|
| 1961 | 3% | 4.5% |
| 1962 | 3⅛% | 4.7% |
| 1963–65 | 3⅜% | 5.4% |
| 1966–67 | 4⅛% | 6.2% |
| 1968 | 4⅝% | 6.9% |

## HOW TO APPLY FOR BENEFITS

You apply for benefits by filing a claim either in person or by mail at your nearest social security office. You can get the address either from the post office or from the phone book under the listing, United States Government—Department of Health, Education and Welfare—Social Security Administration. You will need certain kinds of proof, depending upon the type of benefit you are claiming. If it is an old-age benefit, you should have proof of age. A wife claiming old-age benefits based on her husband's earnings should have both proof of age and a copy of the marriage certificate. If formal proof is not available, the social security office will tell you what kinds of information will be acceptable.

## WHAT DOES SOCIAL SECURITY OFFER?

The social security tax you pay gives you three different kinds of protection: (1) retirement benefits, (2) survivors' benefits, and (3) disability benefits.

*Retirement benefits.* A worker becomes eligible for a full old-age benefit at age 65, if he has retired under the definition in the law. A worker may retire at 62 and get 80% of his full benefit for the rest of his life. The closer he is to age 65 when he starts collecting his benefit, the larger is the fraction of his full benefit that he will get.

The amount of the old-age benefit you are entitled to at 65 is the key to all other benefits under the program. The old-age benefit is based on average monthly earnings, generally those after 1950. (Amounts over $4,800 a year are not counted.) The table on the following page gives examples of benefits.

Using the table as a guide, you will see that average monthly earnings of $300 would give you a benefit of $105 a month when you retire at 65.

If your wife is also 65, then she will get a wife's benefit that is equal to half your benefit. So if your benefit is $105 your wife gets $52.50 (cents are rounded to the nearest dime).

If your wife is younger than you, but not under 62, she can draw a reduced benefit that depends on the number of months before she will be 65. If she draws her benefit when she is 62, she will get about ⅜ of your basic benefit, or $39.40. (She will get this amount for the rest of her life, unless you should die first; then she can start getting the full widow's benefit, described below.)

If your wife is entitled to a worker's old-age benefit on her own earnings she can draw whichever—the worker's or the wife's—is larger. No one can draw two benefits at the same time.

If you have children under 18 when you retire, they will get a benefit equal to half your benefit at age 65, and so will your wife, in that case, even if she is under 62. However, total benefits based on your earnings cannot be more than $254.10 a month or 80% of your average monthly wage. When your children reach age 18, their benefits will stop, except a benefit that is going to a child who is permanently and totally disabled. Such a child can continue to get his benefit as long as his disability meets the definition in the law.

If you are a woman worker entitled to an old-age benefit and you have a dependent husband aged 62 or over, he may draw a benefit similar to a wife's benefit at 62.

*Survivor benefits.* This feature of the social security program gives you valuable life insurance protection—in some cases over $30,000 worth. The amount of protection is again geared to what the worker would be entitled to at 65. If you can estimate from the table what your basic monthly benefit would be at 65, this is what your survivors would get:

1. A cash payment to cover your burial expenses. This comes to 3 times the basic monthly benefit but no more than $255.

2. A benefit for each child until he reaches 18. Each eligible child receives 75% of the basic benefit. (A disabled child can continue to collect benefits after age 18.)

3. A mother's benefit for your widow, if she has children under 18 in her care. Her benefit is 75% of the basic benefit. She can collect this until the youngest child reaches 18. Payments stop then (they will start again when she is 62 at a slightly higher amount). If she has a disabled child in her care who is getting a benefit after 18, then her benefit continues, too.

Total family benefits cannot go over

## What Benefits You Get Under Social Security

| Based on an average monthly wage of | Monthly retirement benefits | | | Monthly survivors' benefits | | |
|---|---|---|---|---|---|---|
| | Worker's benefit at 65[1] | Worker at 65 with 62-year-old wife[1] | Worker with 65-year-old wife[1] | Widow under 62 and 1 child | Widow under 62 and 2 children | Widow age 62[2] |
| $100 | $ 59.00 | $ 81.20 | $ 88.50 | $ 88.60 | $ 88.50 | $ 44.30 |
| $150 | 73.00 | 100.40 | 109.50 | 109.60 | 120.00 | 54.80 |
| $200 | 84.00 | 115.50 | 126.00 | 126.00 | 161.60 | 63.00 |
| $250 | 95.00 | 130.70 | 142.50 | 142.60 | 202.40 | 71.30 |
| $300 | 105.00 | 144.40 | 157.50 | 157.60 | 236.40 | 78.80 |
| $350 | 116.00 | 159.50 | 174.00 | 174.00 | 254.00 | 87.00 |
| $400 | 127.00 | 174.70 | 190.50 | 190.60 | 254.00 | 95.30 |

[1] Also indicates amount worker or worker and wife (aged 62 or 65) would get if disabled.   [2] Also indicates amount that would be paid to one child or parent.

$254.10 a month or 80% of your average monthly wage.

4. If there are no children under 18, your wife can get a widow's benefit starting at age 62. This would come to 82½% of the basic benefit.

5. Dependent parents can sometimes collect survivors' benefits. They are usually eligible if: (a) they were getting at least half their support from the deceased worker when he died, (b) they have reached 62, and (c) they are not eligible for an old-age benefit based on their own earnings. A single surviving parent can then get 82½% of the basic benefit. If two parents are eligible, each would get 75%.

A woman worker can provide survivors' benefits for any of these dependents, if she has been contributing at least half their support: (1) her children under age 18, (2) her disabled child after 18, if the child is unmarried and was disabled before 18, (3) her dependent widowed husband at age 62, if he hasn't remarried, or (4) her parents if they meet the tests in paragraph 5 above.

*Here is an example of survivors' benefits in one family situation:* John Jones dies, leaving a wife and two children aged one and three. His average monthly wage was $300. This would have given him an old-age benefit of $105, if he had lived to 65. This is what his family gets: (1) a cash burial payment of $255; (2) a total monthly benefit of $157.60 for the two children; and (3) a $78.80 monthly benefit for Mrs. Jones. Total benefits for the family come to $236.40 a month while the two children are under 18. When the older child reaches 18 his benefits stop, but the younger child continues to receive $78.80 a month. Mrs. Jones and the younger child then collect a total of $157.50 a month for two years until the child reaches 18. Then all payments stop. When Mrs. Jones becomes 62 (assuming she hasn't remarried), she will be paid $86.70 a month.

*Disability benefits.* These are a new feature of the social security insurance system. Disability benefits are paid to two groups of people:

1. An insured worker with a total disability can collect his full old-age benefit instead of waiting until 65. Eligible dependents of disabled workers will receive the usual benefits. To be eligible for disability benefits, a person must: (a) have worked in employment (or self-employment) covered by social security for about 5 out of the 10 years before he became disabled; (b) be suffering from a physical or mental disability of indefinite duration; and (c) be so disabled that he can't work, or at least "engage in any substantial gainful activity." If he meets those tests, his benefits will start after a 6-month waiting period.

The applicant is referred to the State vocational rehabilitation agency and, if rehabilitation services are proposed and the applicant refuses them without good cause, his disability benefit is suspended.

2. The permanently disabled child of a deceased or retired person who was covered by social security can collect benefits after age 18 (when children's benefits are ordinarily cut off). If the child is eligible, his mother can also get a benefit. The child must: (a) have been disabled before age 18 (but he need not have been drawing benefits before 18), (b) be unmarried, and (c) have been dependent on the deceased or retired worker. The child's benefit would be 75% of the father's basic benefit and his mother would get the same amount. A disabled child can get a benefit based on his mother's earnings, instead of his father's, if she has contributed to at least half his support and has died or is drawing an old-age benefit.

The disabled child's benefit can actually be paid to adults, if the above tests are met. For example, an unmarried person, aged 40, who was born blind and is dependent on his father for support can

## Examples of Monthly Payments Beginning 1961

| Average yearly earnings after 1950 | $800 or less | $1,200 | $1,800 | $2,400 | $3,000 | $3,600 | $4,200 | $4,800 |
|---|---|---|---|---|---|---|---|---|
| Retirement at 65.......... ⎫ Disability benefits........ ⎭ | $ 40.00 | $ 59.00 | $ 73.00 | $ 84.00 | $ 95.00 | $105.00 | $116.00 | $127.00 |
| Retirement at 64............ | 37.40 | 55.10 | 68.20 | 78.40 | 88.70 | 98.00 | 108.30 | 118.60 |
| Retirement at 63............ | 34.70 | 51.20 | 63.30 | 72.80 | 82.40 | 91.00 | 100.60 | 110.10 |
| Retirement at 62............ | 32.00 | 47.20 | 58.40 | 67.20 | 76.00 | 84.00 | 92.80 | 101.60 |
| Wife's benefit at 65 or with child in her care ...... | 20.00 | 29.50 | 36.50 | 42.00 | 47.50 | 52.50 | 58.00 | 63.50 |
| Wife's benefit at 64.......... | 18.40 | 27.10 | 33.50 | 38.50 | 43.60 | 48.20 | 53.20 | 58.30 |
| Wife's benefit at 63.......... | 16.70 | 24.60 | 30.50 | 35.00 | 39.60 | 43.80 | 48.40 | 53.00 |
| Wife's benefit at 62.......... | 15.00 | 22.20 | 27.40 | 31.50 | 35.70 | 39.40 | 43.50 | 47.70 |
| Widow 62 or over ........ | 40.00 | 48.70 | 60.30 | 69.30 | 78.40 | 86.70 | 95.70 | 104.80 |
| Widow under 62 and 1 child... | 60.00 | 88.50 | 109.60 | 126.00 | 142.60 | 157.60 | 174.00 | 190.60 |
| Widow under 62 and 2 children | 60.00 | 88.50 | 120.00 | 161.60 | 202.40 | 236.40 | 254.00 | 254.00 |
| One surviving child.......... | 40.00 | 44.30 | 54.80 | 63.00 | 71.30 | 78.80 | 87.00 | 95.30 |
| Two surviving children........ | 60.00 | 88.50 | 109.60 | 126.00 | 142.60 | 157.60 | 174.00 | 190.60 |
| Maximum family payment..... | 60.00 | 88.50 | 120.00 | 161.60 | 202.40 | 240.00 | 254.00 | 254.00 |
| Lump-sum death payment | 120.00 | 177.00 | 219.00 | 252.00 | 255.00 | 255.00 | 255.00 | 255.00 |

collect a disabled child's benefit as soon as his father starts drawing an old-age benefit or dies.

## YOU CAN EARN INCOME WITHOUT LOSING BENEFITS

If you are 72 or over, you can earn any amount. If you are under 72, you can earn $1,200 a year without losing any benefits. (Only earned income is counted, not pensions, dividends, etc.). If you earn more than $1,200 in a year, $1 of your benefits (or your family benefits) may be withheld for each $2 you earn from $1,200 to $1,700. For every $1 you earn over $1,700, $1 in benefits may be withheld. Family benefits include all benefits payable to you and to any dependents receiving payments based on your social security record. But you will not lose the benefit for any month in which you did not work as an employee for $100 or more and did not perform substantial services in self-employment. For example, if you earned $3,000 in 3 months and were idle the rest of the year, you would lose no more than 3 months' benefits.

If a widow with young children loses her benefits by working, the children will continue to get theirs.

If you earn over $1,200 a year while drawing benefits (and are under 72), you must report those earnings.

## HOW TO PROTECT MY SOCIAL SECURITY ACCOUNT

1. *Always show your social security card when you start a new job.* In that way you will be sure that your earnings will be credited to *your* social security account and not someone else's. If you lose your social security card, apply for a new one. When a woman marries, she should apply for a new card showing her married name.

2. *Make a periodic check of earnings credited to your social security account.* You can do this by mailing postcard Form OAR-7004 to the Social Security Administration, Baltimore 35, Md. (You can get this form at any social security office.) The reply will show total wages credited to your account since 1936 or when you started working. It's a good idea to check once every three years and prevent errors.

## PUBLIC ASSISTANCE

The federal government makes grants to the states to help them provide financial assistance, medical care, and other social services to the needy aged, blind, or disabled, or to children dependent because of the death, disability, absence, or unemployment of a parent; and medical care for those aged persons who can provide for their maintenance but are unable to pay for their medical care. In addition, in all states some help is provided from state and/or local funds only to some other needy persons.

Under the Social Security Act, federal sharing in state assistance costs is based on each state's average monthly payment (including medical costs) times the number of recipients in each program. The Act fixes maximums on the amount of payment to be shared, and sets the ratio of federal contributions. The state may make higher payments by using their own funds. Administrative costs in all the programs are shared equally by the federal and state governments.

In determining "need" for assistance, all income and resources of the individual are considered, except that in aid to the blind, some of the blind person's earned income is disregarded. In medical assistance for the aged, the amount of income and resources permitted is determined by each state.

Within these and other general patterns set by the requirements of the Social Security Act and their administrative interpretations, each state initiates and administers its own public assistance programs, including the determination of who is eligible to receive assistance, and how much can be granted and under what conditions. Assistance is in the form of cash payments made to recipients, except for payments for medical care. Other social services are provided, in some instances, to help assistance recipients increase their capacity for self-care and self-support or to strengthen family life.

In old-age assistance, aid to the blind, and aid to the permanently and totally disabled, federal funds provide four fifths of payments, up to $30 per recipient. In aid to dependent children, the federal share is fourteen seventeenths of payments up to $17 per recipient.

In the program of medical assistance for the aged, established in 1960, federal participation in payments made by the state to suppliers of medical care is not restricted by any specific maximum, and the federal share ranges from 50 to 80 percent, depending on the relationship between the per capita income in the state and the national per capita income.

Administrative costs in all the programs are shared equally by the federal and state governments.

---

## Unemployment Insurance

Unemployment insurance is managed jointly by the states and the national government. Most states began paying benefits in 1938 and 1939.

### UNDER WHAT CONDITIONS CAN THE WORKER COLLECT?

The laws vary from state to state. In general, a waiting period of one week after his first claim is required before collecting unemployment insurance; the worker must be able to work, must not have quit without good cause or have been discharged for misconduct; he must not be involved in a labor dispute; above all, he must be ready and willing to work. He may be disqualified if he refuses, without good cause, to accept a job which is suitable for him in terms of his qualifications and experience, unless the wages, hours, and working conditions offered are substantially less favorable than those prevailing for similar jobs in the community. Other restrictions on payments involve leaving for marriage, for further education, or because of pregnancy.

## State Unemployment Compensation Maximums
*Source:* U. S. Department of Labor, Bureau of Employment Security.

| Total | Maximum Weekly Benefit Amount[1] | Maximum Duration | Total | Maximum Weekly Benefit Amount[1] | Maximum Duration |
|---|---|---|---|---|---|
| Alabama | 28 | 20 | Montana | 34 | 26 |
| Alaska | 45–70 | 26 | Nebraska | 34 | 26 |
| Arizona | 35 | 26 | Nevada | 37.50–57.50 | 26 |
| Arkansas | 30 | 26 | New Hampshire | 38 | 26 |
| California | 55 | 26 | New Jersey | 50 | 26 |
| Colorado | 44 | 32½ | New Mexico | 36 | 30 |
| Connecticut | 45–67 | 26 | New York | 50 | 26 |
| Delaware | 40 | 26 | North Carolina | 35 | 26 |
| D. C. | 30 | 26 | North Dakota | 36 | 24 |
| Florida | 33 | 26 | Ohio | 42–53 | 26 |
| Georgia | 35 | 26 | Oklahoma | 32 | 39 |
| Hawaii | 55 | 26 | Oregon | 40 | 26 |
| Idaho | 43[2] | 26 | Pennsylvania | 40 | 30 |
| Illinois | 38–59 | 26 | Puerto Rico | 16 | 12 |
| Indiana | 36 | 26 | Rhode Island | 36–48 | 26 |
| Iowa | 30–44 | 26 | South Carolina | 33 | 22 |
| Kansas | 42 | 26 | South Dakota | 33 | 24 |
| Kentucky | 37 | 26 | Tennessee | 32 | 22 |
| Louisiana | 35 | 28 | Texas | 28 | 24 |
| Maine | 33 | 26 | Utah | 43 | 36 |
| Maryland | 35–43 | 26 | Vermont | 40 | 26 |
| Massachusetts | 40–(3) | 36 | Virginia | 32 | 20 |
| Michigan | 30–55 | 26 | Washington | 42 | 30 |
| Minnesota | 38 | 26 | West Virginia | 32 | 26 |
| Mississippi | 30 | 26 | Wisconsin | 50 | 34 |
| Missouri | 40 | 26 | Wyoming | 49–55 | 26 |

[1] Maximum amounts. When two amounts are shown, higher includes dependents' allowances. [2] Based in preliminary average weekly wages of $81.68 for 1960. [3] Amount limited only by average weekly wage.

The unemployed worker must go to the local state employment service office to file his claim for unemployment benefits and must register for work. If a suitable opening is available, he must accept it or lose his unemployment payments, unless he has good cause for the refusal. If a worker moves out of his own state, he can still collect at his new residence; the state where he is now located will act as agent for the other state, which pays his benefits.

Benefits are paid only to unemployed workers who have had at least a certain amount of recent past employment or earnings in a job covered by the state law. The amount of employment or earnings, and the period used to measure them, vary from state to state, but the intent of the various laws is to limit benefits to workers whose recent records indicate that they are members of the labor force. The amount of benefits an unemployed worker may receive for any week is also determined by application to his past wages of a formula specified in the law. The general objective is to provide a weekly benefit which is about half the worker's customary weekly wages, up to a maximum set by the law (see table). In a majority of states, the total benefits a worker may receive in a 12-month period is limited to a fraction (from one quarter to one half) of his total wages in a prior 12-month period, as well as to a stated number of weeks. Thus, not all workers in a state are entitled to benefits for the number of weeks shown in the table.

## WHO PAYS FOR THE INSURANCE?

The cost is borne by the employer in all but three states. Each state has a sliding scale of rates. The standard rate is set at 2.7% of taxable payroll in most states. But employers with records of steady employment (that is, with little unemployment benefits paid to their former workers) are rewarded with rates lower than the standard 2.7%. The estimated average rate for employers in 1960 was 1.9%. Tax is payable on only the first $3,000 of a worker's pay, except in California, Delaware, Hawaii, Massachusetts, Nevada, Oregon, Rhode Island, and West Virginia, where the limit is set at $3,600, and in Alaska, where the limit is $7,200. Employees as well as employers pay a tax in Alabama (0.1%), New Jersey (0.25%), and Alaska (0.5%).

Employers pay an additional unemployment tax to the Federal government—0.4% of the first $3,000 paid to each employee. This money is used for the federal and state costs of administering the employment security program, including both unemployment insurance and the employment service. Any amounts over these costs, up to $200 million, is put in a special fund on which the states may draw when their benefit payment funds are low; any remaining excess is distributed to the states in proportion to their taxable payrolls. These excess funds may be used for benefit payments, or may be used for administrative expenses if so appropriated by the state legislature.

Requirements vary from state to state, but all states cover firms having at least 4 employees for 20 weeks or more a year. In some states, firms with only one employee are covered. Certain classes of workers are specifically exempt under some or all state laws—employees of the state and its political subdivisions, farm workers, domestic workers, members of the employer's family, insurance agents on commission, workers in nonprofit organizations, student nurses, internes, and casual labor.

## Railroad Workers

These are covered by the Railroad Retirement Act, passed in 1935 and amended in 1937 and 1946. The social security provisions of this act are administered by the Railroad Retirement Board.

---

# Great Disasters

## Earthquakes and Volcanic Eruptions

**A.D. 79** Aug. 24, ITALY: eruption of Mt. Vesuvius buried cities of Pompeii and Herculaneum, killing thousands of persons.

**1755** Nov. 1, PORTUGAL: one of the most severe of recorded earthquakes leveled Lisbon and was felt as far away as southern France and North Africa; between 10,000 and 20,000 killed in Lisbon alone.

**1883** Aug. 26–28, NETHERLANDS INDIES: eruption of Krakatoa; violent explosions destroyed two-thirds of island. Sea waves occurred as far away as Cape Horn, and possibly England. Estimated 36,000 dead.

**1902** May 8, MARTINIQUE, WEST INDIES: Mt. Pelée erupted and wiped out city of St. Pierre; 40,000 dead.

**1906** April 18, SAN FRANCISCO: earthquake accompanied by fire razed more than 4 sq. mi.; more than 500 dead or missing; property damage about 250–300 millions.

**1908** Dec. 28, MESSINA, SICILY: about 85,000 killed and city totally destroyed by one of most disastrous of recorded earthquakes.

1923  Sept. 1, JAPAN: earthquake destroyed third of Tokyo and most of Yokohama; more than 90,000 killed.

1935  May 31, INDIA: earthquake at Quetta killed an estimated 50,000.

1939  Jan. 24, CHILE: earthquake razed some 50,000 sq. mi.; 30,000 killed.

1939  Dec. 27, NORTHERN TURKEY: severe quakes destroyed city of Erzingan; about 100,000 casualties.

1949  Aug. 5, ECUADOR: earthquake killed about 6,000 and razed 50 towns.

1950  Aug. 15, INDIA: second heaviest earthquake on record affected 30,-000 sq. mi. in Assam; 20,000–30,000 believed killed.

1951  Jan. 18–21, PAPUA TERRITORY, NEW GUINEA: eruption of Mt. Lamington killed more than 3,000.

1954  Sept. 9, ALGERIA: about 1,500 reported dead in Northern Algerian earthquake.

1956  June 17, AFGHANISTAN: about 2,000 killed during 10-day series of earthquakes in vicinity of Kabul.

1957  July 2, NORTHERN IRAN: 1,564 reported dead in earthquake.

1957  July 28, MEXICO: about 60 dead in quakes centering in Mexico City and vicinity of Acapulco.

1957  Dec. 13–15, WESTERN IRAN: 1,392 dead in earthquake.

1960  Apr. 24, LAR, IRAN: 700 dead in earthquakes.

1960  May 21–22, 27–29, CHILE: 5,700 persons dead, millions left homeless in earthquakes.

## Floods, Avalanches and Tidal Waves
### WORLD

1228  HOLLAND: 100,000 persons reputedly drowned by sea flood in Friesland.

1642  CHINA: Rebels destroyed Kaifeng seawall; 300,000 drowned.

1887  CHINA: hundreds of thousands of lives were lost in Honan province in overflow of Hwang Ho River.

1896  JAPAN: earthquake and tidal wave at Sanriku killed 27,000.

1939  CHINA: floods in north; casualties estimated at 10,000,000 homeless, starved or drowned.

1946  ALASKA-HAWAII: series of tidal waves in Pacific originating off Alaska killed about 150 in Hawaii.

1947  JAPAN: floods in wake of typhoon killed 2,000 persons on Honshu Is.

1948  TURKEY: hundreds of persons were drowned when two rivers in southern Turkey burst their dikes.

1948  CHINA: about 1,000 reported dead in floods near Foochow.

1950  CHINA: floods in eastern and southern China left 1,000,000 homeless and killed 500.

1951  ALPS: snow avalanches killed more than 200 in Alpine regions of Switzerland, Italy, France and Austria.

1951  MANCHURIA: floods killed 1,800; 3,000 missing.

1953  NORTHWEST EUROPE: storm followed by floods devastated North Sea coastal areas. Netherlands was hardest hit, with 1,794 dead.

1954  IRAN: flash flood reportedly killed 2,000 religious pilgrims.

1955  INDIA: floods in Punjab, Patiala and at Delhi killed 1,700.

1956  CHINA: floods in three provinces following typhoon killed over 2,000.

1960  AGADIR, MOROCCO: 10,000–12,000 dead as earthquake set off tidal wave and fire, destroying most of city.

1961  UKRAINE: mud slide killed 145.

### UNITED STATES

1889  PENNSYLVANIA: more than 2,000 died in Johnstown flood.

1913  OHIO AND INDIANA: floods of Ohio and Indiana rivers took 730 lives.

1927  MISSISSIPPI VALLEY: floods inundated 20,000 sq. mi.; 700,000 were left homeless.

1937  MISSISSIPPI, ALLEGHENY AND OHIO: Floods in valleys killed hundreds.

1954  TEXAS-MEXICO BORDER: flood of the Rio Grande river killed 50 or more.

1955  NORTHERN CALIF., OREG.: Rains caused $150,000,000 damage, 74 deaths.

## Tornadoes, Typhoons and Hurricanes
### (For tornadoes and hurricanes in the U. S., see Index)
### WORLD

1864  Oct. 5, INDIA: most of Calcutta denuded by cyclone; 70,000 killed.

1876  Oct. 31, INDIA: cyclone, tidal wave swept 3,000 sq. mi.; 215,000 killed.

1882  June 6, INDIA: cyclone and tidal wave killed 100,000 in Bombay.

1906  CHINA: typhoon at Hong Kong killed about 10,000.

1930  Sept. 3, SANTO DOMINGO (now Ciudad Trujillo): hurricane killed about 2,000 and injured 6,000.

1934  Sept. 21, JAPAN: hurricane killed more than 4,000 on Honshu.

1935 Oct. 25, HAITI: hurricane, flood killed 2,000 in Jérémie and Jacmel.

1942 Oct. 16, INDIA: cyclone devastated Bengal; about 40,000 lives lost.

1949 Oct. 31–Nov. 2, PHILIPPINES: 1,000 believed dead following typhoon.

1952 Oct. 20–22, INDO-CHINA, PHILIPPINES: typhoons killed more than 1,000.

1953 Sept. 25, VIÊT-NAM: typhoon left about 1,000 dead.

1954 Sept. 26, JAPAN: typhoon off Hakodate killed 1,200–1,600.

1955 Sept. 19, MEXICO: Hurricane Hilda killed over 200 in Tampico area.

1958 Sept. 27–28, JAPAN: Typhoon Ida killed over 600 persons.

## Fires and Explosions

### WORLD

1666 Sept. 2, ENGLAND: "Great Fire of London" destroyed St. Paul's Church, etc. Damage 10 million pounds.

1812 Sept. 14, RUSSIA: fire started by Russians in Moscow after French occupation destroyed 30,800 houses.

1917 Dec. 6, CANADA: explosion and fire at Halifax when ammunition ship collided with a vessel; 1,500 persons dead.

1922 ASIA MINOR: more than three-fifths of Smyrna destroyed by fire following Turkish occupation.

1948 July 28, GERMANY: Hundreds killed in Ludwigshaven works explosion.

1949 Sept. 2, CHINA: fire on Chungking waterfront killed 1,700.

1955 June 11, FRANCE: crash and explosion of racing car into crowd during Grand Prix race, Le Mans, killed 82.

1956 Aug. 7, COLOMBIA: about 1,200 reported killed when 7 army ammunition trucks exploded at Cali.

1956 Aug. 8, BELGIUM: 262 died in coal mine fire at Marcinelle.

1958 Feb. 19, BAHREIN: British freighter *Seistan* exploded; 53 killed.

1960 Jan. 21, SOUTH AFRICA: rock slide in mine trapped 417 miners.

1960 July 14, GUATEMALA CITY: hospital for insane destroyed by fire; 225 dead.

1960 Nov. 13, SYRIA: 152 children killed in movie-house fire.

### UNITED STATES

1835 Dec. 16, NEW YORK CITY: 530 buildings destroyed by fire.

1871 Oct. 8, CHICAGO: the "Chicago Fire" burned 17,450 buildings, killed 250 persons; 196 million damage.

1871 Oct. 8, PESHTIGO, WIS.: over 1,200 lives lost; 2 billion trees burned.

1872 Nov. 9, BOSTON: fire destroyed 800 buildings; 75 million damage.

1903 Dec. 30, CHICAGO: Iroquois Theatre fire killed 602.

1904 Feb. 7, BALTIMORE, MD.: Business section burned; 125 million damage.

1937 March 18, NEW LONDON, TEXAS: explosion destroyed schoolhouse; 413 children and 14 teachers killed.

1942 Nov. 28, BOSTON: Cocoanut Grove night club fire killed about 500.

1944 July 17, PORT CHICAGO: 300 killed as ammunition ships explode.

1946 Dec. 7, ATLANTA: fire in Winecoff Hotel killed 119.

1947 March 25, CENTRALIA, ILL.: explosion in coal mine killed 111 miners.

1947 April 16–18, TEXAS CITY, TEXAS: most of city destroyed, over 500 dead following explosion on ship.

1951 Dec. 21, near WEST FRANKFORT, ILL.: 119 coal miners died in explosion.

1953 Oct. 16, BOSTON, MASS.: explosion and fire aboard U.S.S. *Leyte* killed 37.

1956 Nov. 25, near SAN DIEGO, CALIF.: Forest fires destroyed about 40,000 ac.; 11 killed.

1957 Feb. 4, near BISHOP, VA.: 37 died in coal mine blast.

1957 Feb. 5, RENO, NEV.: gas explosions destroyed city block; 2 died.

1958 April 18, OKINAWA: underwater explosion of U. S. munitions ship, sunk in World War II, killed 40 persons.

1958 Dec. 1, CHICAGO, ILL.: fire at Our Lady of the Angels school killed 96.

1959 Mar. 5, near LITTLE ROCK, ARK.: fire destroyed dormitory of Negro Boys Industrial School; 21 dead.

1960 Dec. 19, BROOKLYN, N. Y.: blaze on aircraft carrier *Constellation* killed 49 workmen.

## Shipwrecks (not including military or naval action)

### WORLD

1833 May 11, LADY OF THE LAKE: bound from England to Quebec, struck iceberg; 215 perished.

1853 Sept. 29, ANNIE JANE: emigrant vessel off coast of Scotland; 348 died.

1912 March 5, PRINCIPE DE ASTURIAS: Spanish steamer struck rock off Sebastien Pt.; 500 drowned.

1912 April 15, TITANIC: sank after colliding with iceberg; 1,513 died.

1914 May 29, EMPRESS OF IRELAND: sank after collision in St. Lawrence River; 1,024 perished.

1928  Nov. 12, VESTRIS: British steamer sank in gale off Virginia; 110 died.

1931  June 14, French excursion steamer overturned in gale off St. Nazaire; approximately 450 died.

1939  June 1, Submarine THETIS: sank in Liverpool Bay, Eng.; 99 perished.

1942  Oct. 2, QUEEN MARY: rammed and sank a British cruiser; 338 aboard the cruiser died.

1948  Dec. 3, KIANGYA: Chinese refugee ship wrecked in explosion; about 1,000 believed dead.

1949  Jan. 27, TAIPING: Chinese liner collided with collier and both sank; at least 600 died.

1949  Sept. 17, NORONIC: Canadian Great Lakes cruise ship burned at Toronto dock; about 130 died.

1950  Jan. 12, TRUCULENT: British submarine sank in Thames estuary after collision with tanker; 64 dead.

1951  April 16, AFFRAY: British sub sank in English channel; 75 dead.

1953  Jan. 9, CHANG TYONG-HO: South Korean ferry foundered off Pusan; 249 reported dead.

1953  Jan. 31, PRINCESS VICTORIA: British ferry sank in Irish Sea; 133 lost.

1953  Aug. 1, MONIQUE: French motor ship with 120 aboard disappeared in South Pacific.

1956  July 25, ANDREA DORIA: Italian liner collided with Swedish liner *Stockholm* off Nantucket Island, Mass., sinking next day; 52, mostly passengers aboard Italian ship, dead or unaccounted for; more than 1,600 rescued.

1958  March 1, Passenger ferry sank in squall in Sea of Marmara, Turkey; over 200 killed.

1959  Jan. 30, HANS HEDTOFT: Danish passenger-cargo ship hit iceberg and sank off Greenland; 95 dead.

### U. S. AND U. S. LINES

1865  April 27, SULTANA: boiler explosion on Mississippi River steamboat near Memphis; 1,450 killed.

1898  Nov. 26, CITY OF PORTLAND: Loss of 157 off Cape Cod.

1904  June 15, GENERAL SLOCUM: excursion steamer burned in New York Harbor; 1,021 perished.

1915  July 24, EASTLAND: Great Lakes excursion steamer overturned in Chicago River; 812 died.

1934  Sept. 8, MORRO CASTLE: about 130 persons killed in fire off Asbury Pk., N. J.

1939  May 23, Submarine SQUALUS: sank with 59 men off Hampton Beach, N. H.; 33 crew members saved.

1945  April 9, U. S. ship, loaded with aerial bombs, exploded at Bari, Italy; at least 360 killed.

1952  Jan. 10, FLYING ENTERPRISE: freighter sank about 35 miles off southwest England after valiant 12-day effort by captain, Henrik K. Carlsen, to save ship.

1952  April 26, HOBSON: minesweeper collided with aircraft carrier *Wasp* and sank during night maneuvers in mid-Atlantic; 176 persons lost.

1954  Oct. 7, MORMACKITE: freighter capsized off Cape Henry, Va.; 37 lost.

1956  Sept. 15, PELAGIA: freighter sank in storm off Norway; 32 lost.

---

## Aircraft Accidents (not including military or naval action)
### WORLD

1921  Aug. 24, ENGLAND: *ZR-2,* British dirigible, broke in two on trial trip near Hull; 62 died.

1930  Oct. 5, FRANCE: British dirigible, *R-101,* crashed at Beauvais; 47 died.

1935  May 18, U.S.S.R.: stunt flier crashed into the *Maxim Gorkey;* 49 persons killed.

1938  July 24, COLOMBIA: military plane crashed into grandstand during air review at Bogotá, killing 53.

1947  Feb. 15, COLOMBIA: Avianca airliner crashed near Bogotá; 53 killed.

1950  March 12, near CARDIFF, WALES: crash of chartered airliner killed 80.

1950  Nov. 13, near GRENOBLE, FRANCE: Canadian plane carrying Holy Year pilgrims crashed; 58 dead.

1956  Feb. 18, near VALLETTA, MALTA: Scottish airliner crash killed 50.

1956  Feb. 20, near CAIRO, EGYPT: desert crash of French airliner; 52 died.

1956  June 20, off ASBURY PARK, N. J.: Venezuelan airliner exploded and fell into Atlantic, killing 74.

1956  Dec. 9, near CHILLIWACK, B. C., CANADA: Canadian airliner crashed; all 62 aboard killed.

1957  March 17, near CEBU CITY, PHILIPPINES: Pres. Ramón Magsaysay and 24 others killed in crash.

1957  July 16, BIAK ISLAND, NEW GUINEA: Dutch airliner crash killed 57.

1957  Aug. 11, near QUEBEC, CANADA: 79 died in crash of chartered airliner.

1958  Feb. 6, near MUNICH, GERMANY: British airliner crashed and burned;

21 persons, including 7 members of Manchester soccer team, were killed.

1958 Aug. 14, near IRELAND: Dutch KLM Super-Constellation crashed into North Atlantic; 99 killed.

1958 Oct. 17, near KANASH, U.S.S.R.: Soviet jet airliner crashed; 75 dead.

1959 Jan. 16, MAR DEL PLATA, ARGENTINA: Argentine airliner crashed; 51 dead.

1959 June 26, MILAN, ITALY: TWA Constellation broke apart and crashed; 68 killed.

1959 Sept. 24, BORDEAUX, FRANCE: French airliner crashed, killing 53.

1960 Jan. 19, near ANKARA, TURKEY: Scandinavian Airlines crash killed 41.

1960 Jan. 21, MONTEGO BAY, JAMAICA: Columbian airliner exploded; 37 died.

1960 Feb. 5, near COCHABAMBA, BOLIVIA: Bolivian airliner crashed, killing 59.

1960 Feb. 25, RIO DE JANEIRO, BRAZIL: U.S. Navy plane flying Navy musicians to perform at dinner given by visiting Pres. Eisenhower, collided with Brazilian airliner, killing 61.

1960 Feb. 25, SHANNON, IRELAND: Alitalia airliner crashed; 33 dead.

1960 June 24, GUANABARA BAY, BRAZIL: Real Airliner crashed in fog; 51 dead.

1960 Aug. 29, DAKAR, SENEGAL: French plane crashed into sea; 63 dead.

1961 Feb. 15, near BRUSSELS, BELGIUM: 72 on board and 1 farmer killed in crash of Sabena plane; U. S. figure skating team wiped out.

1961 May 10, SAHARA DESERT: Air France liner crashed, taking 79 lives.

## U. S. AND U. S. LINES

1925 Sept. 3, CALDWELL, OHIO: U. S. dirigible *Shenandoah* broke apart; 14 dead.

1933 April 4, NEW JERSEY COAST: U. S. dirigible *Akron* crashed; 73 died.

1937 May 6, LAKEHURST, N. J.: German zeppelin *Hindenburg* destroyed by fire at tower mooring; 36 killed.

1947 June 13, near LEESBURG, VA.: 50 killed in crash of airliner.

1947 Oct. 24, BRYCE CANYON, UTAH: airliner crashed into hillside after catching fire in midair; 52 killed.

1949 June 7, near SAN JUAN, P. R.: crash of converted army transport into ocean killed 53; 28 rescued.

1949 Nov. 1, WASH., D. C.: fighter plane rammed airliner, killing 55.

1950 Aug. 31, near CAIRO, EGYPT: crash of U. S. airliner killed 55, including 23 Americans.

1951 March 23, ATLANTIC OCEAN: U. S. Air Force transport with 53 aboard disappeared.

1951 April 25, near KEY WEST, FLA.: Cuban airliner and U. S. Navy plane collided; 43 killed.

1951 June 30, ROCKY MOUNTAIN NATIONAL PARK, COLO.: airliner crash killed 50.

1951 Dec. 16, ELIZABETH, N. J.: nonscheduled airliner crash killed 56.

1952 Jan. 22, ELIZABETH, N. J.: 29 killed, including former Sec. of War Robert P. Patterson, when airliner hit apartments; 7 were on ground.

1952 Feb. 11, ELIZABETH, N. J.: third major air disaster in Elizabeth within 2 months fatally injured 33.

1952 April 29, NORTH CENTRAL BRAZIL: airliner bound for New York crashed in jungle; 50 died.

1952 Dec. 20, MOSES LAKE, WASHINGTON: crash of Air Force "Globemaster" killed 87 servicemen, injured 28.

1953 Feb. 14, GULF OF MEXICO: airliner crash during storm killed 46.

1953 June 18, near TOKYO, JAPAN: crash of U. S. Air Force "Globemaster" killed 129 servicemen.

1953 July 11, PACIFIC OCEAN: airliner crashed about 325 mi. east of Wake Island; 58 persons were killed.

1954 Oct. 31, ATLANTIC OCEAN: U. S. navy plane with 42 aboard lost.

1955 March 22, near HONOLULU, HAWAII: crash of U. S. navy transport plane killed 66.

1955 Aug. 11, near EDELWEILER, GERMANY: two U. S. troop carriers collided; 66 air force personnel killed.

1955 Oct. 6, near LARAMIE, WYO.: airliner hit mountain; 66 died.

1955 Nov. 1, near LONGMONT, COLO.: criminally placed time-bomb destroyed airliner in flight, killing 44.

1956 June 30, GRAND CANYON, ARIZ.: 128 died in collision of two airliners; worst commercial air disaster to date.

1956 July 13, near FORT DIX, N. J.: 45 of 66 aboard killed in crash of U. S. Air Force transport.

1956 Oct. 11, ATLANTIC OCEAN: U. S. A. F. plane disappeared; 59 aboard.

1957 Feb. 1, NEW YORK, N. Y.: airliner crash on Rikers Island killed 20 of 101 aboard.

1957 March 21, PACIFIC OCEAN: U. S. Air Force plane disappeared; 67 lost.

1958 Feb. 1, LOS ANGELES, CALIF.: military air transport and Navy bomber collided in flight; 47 servicemen killed.

1958 March 27, BRIDGEPORT, TEX.: 2 Air Force transports collided; 18 killed.

1958 April 6, MIDLAND, MICH.: Capital Airlines plane crashed; 47 killed.

1958 April 21, near LAS VEGAS, NEV.: airliner and Air Force jet plane collided in flight; 49 killed.

1959 Feb. 3, NEW YORK, N. Y.: American Airlines Lockheed Electra turboprop plane crashed in East River; 65 dead.

1959 May 12, near BALTIMORE, MD.: Capital Airlines Viscount turboprop plane exploded and crashed; 31 dead.

1959 Sept. 29, near BUFFALO, TEXAS: Braniff turboprop Electra exploded in midair; 34 dead.

1959 Nov. 16, GULF OF MEXICO: National Airlines plane crashed, killing 42.

1960 Jan. 6, En route from N. Y. to Miami: National Airlines plane disintegrated; 34 died. Bomb suspected.

1960 Jan. 18, near HOLDCROFT, VA.: Capital Airlines plane crash killed 50.

1960 Mar. 17, over TELL CITY, INDIANA: Northwest Airlines turboprop Electra exploded in midair, killing 63.

1960 Sept. 19, near GUAM: crash shortly after take-off of World Airways plane took 78 lives.

1960 Oct. 4, BOSTON HARBOR: Eastern Airlines plane sank; 61 dead.

1960 Dec. 16, NEW YORK CITY: United and Trans World planes collided in fog, crashed in 2 boroughs, killing 134 in air and on ground.

1960 Dec. 17, MUNICH, GER.: USAF Convair hit church steeple; 53 dead.

## Railroad Accidents

### WORLD

1857 March 17, DES JARDINS (SOULANGES) CANAL, CANADA: train derailed on bridge; about 60 killed.

1864 June 29, near BELOEIL, CANADA: about 90 killed when train ran through open switch.

1879 Dec. 28, DUNDEE, SCOTLAND: train blown off Tay bridge; 73 drowned.

1881 June 24, near CUARTLA, MEX.: about 200 died when train fell into river.

1882 July 13, near TCHERNY, RUSSIA: more than 150 killed in derailment.

1889 June 12, near ARMAGH, IRELAND: about 80 killed in collision.

1891 June 14, near BASEL, SWITZERLAND: about 100 killed in collision.

1915 May 22, GRETNA, SCOTLAND: two passenger trains and troop train collided; 227 killed.

1917 Dec. 12, MODANE, FRANCE: almost 550 killed in derailment of troop train near mouth of Mt. Cenis tunnel.

1939 Dec. 22, near MAGDEBURG, GERMANY: more than 125 killed in collision; 99 killed in another wreck near Friedrichshafen.

1940 Jan. 29, OSAKA, JAPAN: 200 killed in collision.

1944 March 2, near SALERNO, ITALY: 521 suffocated when Italian train stalled in tunnel.

1949 Oct. 22, near NOWY DWOR, POLAND: more than 200 reported killed in derailment of Danzig-Warsaw express.

1950 April 6, near RIO DE JANEIRO, BRAZIL: train wrecked when bridge collapsed; 108 killed or missing.

1952 March 4, near RIO DE JANEIRO, BRAZIL: about 120 reported killed in collision of 2 trains.

1952 Oct. 8, HARROW-WEALDSTONE, ENGLAND: two express trains crashed into commuter train; 112 dead.

1953 Dec. 24, near WAIOURI, NEW ZEALAND: train plunged through bridge; 155 dead and others missing.

1953 Dec. 24, near SAKVICE, CZECHOSLOVAKIA: 2 trains crashed; over 100 dead.

1956 Sept. 2, near MAHBUBNAGAR, INDIA: at least 120 killed when bridge collapsed under train.

1957 Sept. 1, near KENDAL, JAMAICA: about 175 killed when train plunged into ravine.

1957 Sept. 29, near MONTGOMERY, WEST PAKISTAN: express train crashed into standing oil train; nearly 300 killed.

1957 Dec. 4, ST. JOHN'S, ENGLAND: 92 killed, 187 injured as one commuter train crashed into another in fog.

1960 Nov. 14, CZECHOSLOVAKIA: 2 trains collided; 110 dead, 106 injured.

### UNITED STATES

1943 Dec. 16, near RENNERT, N. C.: 72 killed in derailment and collision.

1944 Dec. 31, near OGDEN, UTAH: 48 killed in collision.

1946 April 25, NAPERVILLE, ILL.: at least 47 killed in collision.

1950 Feb. 17, ROCKVILLE CENTRE, N. Y.: head-on crash of two commuter trains killed 30.

1950 Nov. 22, RICHMOND HILL, N. Y.: 79 died when one commuter train crashed into rear of another.

1951 Feb. 6, WOODBRIDGE, N. J.: 85 died when commuter train plunged through temporary overpass.

1958 Sept. 15, near BAYONNE, N. J.: over 40 killed when train went through open drawbridge.

# SCIENCE

## MEASURES AND WEIGHTS
### UNITS OF LENGTH

**Metric System**

The meter was originally intended to be one ten-millionth of the earth's quadrant, a quadrant being one-quarter of a circumference. However, because of the difficulty of determining such a length with accuracy, this definition was abandoned. The meter is now considered to be the distance at 0°C between two microscopic marks on the International Prototype Meter, a platinum-iridium bar, kept by the International Bureau of Weights and Measures at Sèvres, France, a suburb of Paris.

In 1927, the International Conference on Weights and Measures adopted a secondary definition of the meter in terms of lightwaves. According to this definition, one meter is equivalent to 1,553,164.13 wave lengths of the red light from cadmium.

| Unit | Comparison | English equivalent |
|---|---|---|
| Millimeter (mm) | .001 meter | .0394 inch |
| Centimeter (cm) | .01 meter | .3937 inch |
| Decimeter (dm) | .1 meter | 3.937 inches |
| Meter (m) | | 3.2808 feet |
| Dekameter (dkm) | 10 meters | 32.8083 feet |
| Hectometer (hm) | 100 meters | 328.0833 feet |
| Kilometer (km) | 1000 meters | .62137 mile |

**English System**

According to legend, the yard was established by Henry I as the distance from the point of his nose to the end of his thumb when his arm was outstretched. The British Imperial Yard was defined in 1878 by the Weights and Measures Act as the distance at 62°F between two fine lines on gold studs sunk in a bronze bar known as the "No. 1 Standard Yard." This is equivalent to .914399 meter. In the United States, the yard is defined in terms of the meter, using as a standard the U. S. Prototype Meter. According to this definition, the yard is 3600/3937 (or .914402) meter, slightly longer than the British Imperial Yard.

| Unit | Comparison | Metric equivalent |
|---|---|---|
| Inch (in.) | | 25.4000 millimeters |
| Foot (ft) | 12 inches | .3048 meter |
| Yard (yd) | 36 inches 3 feet | .9144 meter |
| Rod (rd) | 16½ feet 5½ yards | 5.0292 meters |
| Furlong (fur.) | 660 feet 220 yards 40 rods | 201.1684 meters |
| Mile (mi)* | 5280 feet 1760 yards 320 rods 8 furlongs | 1.6093 kilometers |

\* Known as statute mile. See nautical mile under Miscellaneous Units.

## UNITS OF AREA

**Metric System**

| Unit | Comparison | English equivalent |
|---|---|---|
| Square millimeter (mm²) | .000001 m² | .0015 sq in. |
| Square centimeter (cm²) | .0001 m² | .155 sq in. |
| Square decimeter (dm²) | .01 m² | 15.5 sq in. |
| Square meter (m²)* | | 10.7639 sq ft |
| Square dekameter (dkm²)† | 100 m² | 3.9537 sq rd |
| Square hectometer (hm²)‡ | 10,000 m² | 2.471 acres |
| Square kilometer (km²) | 1,000,000 m² | .3861 sq mi |

\* Also known as a centare (ca).
† Also known as an are (a).
‡ Also known as a hectare (ha).

**English System**

| Unit | Comparison | Metric equivalent |
|---|---|---|
| Square inch (sq in.) | | 6.4516 cm² |
| Square foot (sq ft) | 144 sq in. | .0929 m² |
| Square yard (sq yd) | 1296 sq in. 9 sq ft | .8361 m² |
| Square rod (sq rd) | 272¼ sq ft 30¼ sq yds | 25.293 m² |
| Acre | 43,560 sq ft 4,840 sq yd 160 sq rd | .4047 ha |
| Square mile (sq mi) | 27,878,400 sq ft 3,097,600 sq yd 102,400 sq rd 640 acres | 2.5900 km² |

## UNITS OF VOLUME

**Metric System**

| Unit | Comparison | English equivalent |
|---|---|---|
| Cubic millimeter (mm³) | .000000001 m³ | .00006 cu in. |
| Cubic centimeter (cm³) | .000001 m³ | .061 cu in. |
| Cubic decimeter (dm³) | .001 m³ | 61.0234 cu in. |
| Cubic meter (m³)* | | 35.3145 cu ft |

\* Also known as a stere (s).

**English System**

| Unit | Comparison | Metric equivalent |
|---|---|---|
| Cubic inch (cu in.) | | 16.3872 cm³ |
| Cubic foot (cu ft) | 1728 cu in. | .0283 m³ |
| Cubic yard (cu yd) | 46,656 cu in. 27 cu ft | .7646 m³ |
| Cord (cd) | 128 cu ft | 3.6246 m³ |

# UNITS OF WEIGHT OR MASS

The term *mass* denotes the amount of matter contained in an object, while the term *weight* denotes the gravitational pull of the earth on the object. For practical purposes, the two terms are synonymous.

## Metric System

The gram was originally intended to be equal to the mass of one cubic centimeter of pure water at 4°C. However, because of the difficulty of making exact measurement, a small error was made; and it has since been found that a kilogram of pure water occupies 1.000028 cubic decimeters. The standard for the kilogram is a platinum-iridium cylinder, called the International Prototype Kilogram, which is kept at the International Bureau of Weights and Measures in France.

| Unit | Comparison | English equivalents | | |
|------|-----------|------|------|------|
| | | Avdp. | Troy | Apoth. |
| Milligram (mg) | .001 gram | .0154 grain | .0154 grain | .0154 grain |
| Centigram (cg) | .01 gram | .1543 grain | .1543 grain | .1543 grain |
| Decigram (dg) | .1 gram | 1.5432 grains | 1.5432 grains | 1.5432 grains |
| Gram (g) | | .0353 ounce | .0322 ounce | .0322 ounce |
| Dekagram (dkg) | 10 grams | .3527 ounce | .3215 ounce | .3215 ounce |
| Hectogram (hg) | 100 grams | 3.5274 ounces | 3.2151 ounces | 3.2151 ounces |
| Kilogram (kg) | 1000 grams | 2.2046 pounds | 2.6792 pounds | 2.6792 pounds |
| Metric ton (t) | 1000 kg | 1.1023 tons * | | |

\* Short tons. A metric ton is equivalent to .9842 long ton.

## English System

The English System is complicated by the existence of three different kinds of weight: *avoirdupois weight,* used for common purposes; *troy weight,* used for weighing gold, silver, etc.; and *apothecaries weight,* used for making up medical prescriptions.

The British Imperial Pound (avoirdupois) is defined as the mass of a pure platinum cylinder kept by the Standards Department of the Board of Trade. In the United States, the pound (avoirdupois) is defined in terms of the kilogram, using as a standard the U. S. Prototype Kilogram. According to this definition, the pound is equal to .4535924277 kilogram, making it infinitesimally smaller than the British Imperial Pound.

### Avoirdupois Weight

| Unit | Comparison | Metric equivalent |
|------|-----------|-------------------|
| Grain | | .0648 gram |
| Dram (dr avdp) | 27.3438 grains | 1.7718 grams |
| Ounce (oz avdp) | 16 drams | 28.3495 grams |
| | 437.5 grains | |
| Pound (lb avdp) | 7000 grains | 4536 kilogram |
| | 256 drams | |
| | 16 ounces | |
| Hundredweight (cwt)* | 100 pounds | 45.3592 kilograms |
| Ton (tn)† | 2000 pounds | .9072 metric ton |

\* Known as the short hundredweight, which is in use in the United States and Canada. Great Britain uses the long hundredweight (112 lb or 50.8024 kg).

† Known as the short ton, which is in use in the United States and Canada. Great Britain uses the long ton (2,240 lb or 1.01605 metric tons).

### Troy Weight

| Unit | Comparison | Metric equivalent |
|------|-----------|-------------------|
| Grain | | .0648 gram |
| Pennyweight (dwt) | 24 grains | 1.5552 grams |
| Ounce (oz t) | 480 grains | 31.1035 grams |
| | 20 pennyweights | |
| Pound (lb t)* | 5760 grains | .3732 kilogram |
| | 240 pennyweights | |
| | 12 ounces | |

\* Declared illegal in Great Britain.

### Apothecaries Weight

| Unit | Comparison | Metric equivalent |
|------|-----------|-------------------|
| Grain | | .0648 gram |
| Scruple (s ap or ℈) | 20 grains | 1.296 grams |
| Dram (dr ap or ʒ) | 60 grains | 3.8879 grams |
| | 3 scruples | |
| Ounce (oz ap or ℥) | 480 grains | 31.1035 grams |
| | 24 scruples | |
| | 8 drams | |
| Pound (lb ap) | 5760 grains | .3732 kilogram |
| | 288 scruples | |
| | 96 drams | |
| | 12 ounces | |

# UNITS OF CAPACITY

## Metric System

The liter is a secondary unit of capacity defined as the volume occupied by one kilogram of pure water at 4°C. It was intended that the liter should exactly equal one cubic decimeter, but as an error was made in measurement, has since been found to equal 1.000028 cubic decimeters.

| Unit | Comparison | English equivalents | |
|------|-----------|------|------|
| | | Liquid | Dry |
| Milliliter (ml) | .001 liter | .0338 fl oz | .0018 pt |
| Centiliter (cl) | .01 liter | .3381 fl oz | .0182 pt |
| Deciliter (dl) | .1 liter | 3.3815 fl oz | .1816 pt |
| Liter (l) | | 1.0567 qt | .9081 qt |
| Dekaliter (dkl) | 10 liters | 2.6418 gal | 1.1351 pk |
| Hectoliter (hl) | 100 liters | 26.4178 gal | 2.8378 bu |

### English System

In Great Britain, the standard unit of capacity for measuring both liquid and dry commodities is the British Imperial Gallon. It is defined as the volume of ten pounds of pure water at 62°F and contains 277.418 cubic inches. The bushel is defined as eight gallons (2218.192 cubic inches).

In the United States, there are two separate standards. The unit for measuring liquids is the gallon, which is defined as 231 cubic inches; the unit for measuring dry commodities is the bushel, which is defined as 2150.42 cubic inches.

### Liquid Measure (U. S.)

| Unit | Comparison | Cubic inches | Metric equivalent |
|---|---|---|---|
| Minim (min or m)* | | .0038 | .0616 ml |
| Fluid dram (fl dr) | 60 min | .2256 | 3.6966 ml |
| Fluid ounce (fl oz) | 8 fl dr | 1.8047 | 29.5729 ml |
| Gill (gi) | 32 fl dr<br>4 fl oz | 7.2188 | 118.292 ml |
| Pint (pt) | 16 fl oz<br>4 gi | 28.875 | .4732 liter |
| Quart (qt) | 32 fl oz<br>8 gi<br>2 pt | 57.75 | .9463 liter |
| Gallon (gal) | 32 gi<br>8 pt<br>4 qt | 231 | 3.7853 liters |

\* Approximately one drop.

## UNITS OF CIRCULAR MEASURE

| Unit | Comparison |
|---|---|
| Second (″) | |
| Minute (′) | 60 seconds |
| Degree (°) | 60 minutes |
| Right angle | 90 degrees |
| Straight angle | 180 degrees |
| Circle | 360 degrees |

### Dry Measure (U. S.)

| Unit | Comparison | Cubic inches | Metric equivalent |
|---|---|---|---|
| Pint (pt) | | 33.6003 | .5506 liter |
| Quart (qt) | 2 pints | 67.2006 | 1.1012 liters |
| Peck (pk) | 16 pints<br>8 quarts | 537.605 | 8.8096 liters |
| Bushel (bu) | 64 pints<br>32 quarts<br>4 pecks | 2150.42 | 35.2383 liters |

## COMMON FORMULAS

### Circumference

Circle: $C=\pi d$, in which $\pi$ is 3.1416 and $d$ the diameter.

### Area

Triangle: $A=\dfrac{ab}{2}$, in which $a$ is the base and $b$ the height.

Square: $A=a^2$, in which $a$ is one of the sides.

Rectangle: $A=ab$, in which $a$ is the base and $b$ the height.

Trapezoid: $A=\dfrac{h(a+b)}{2}$, in which $h$ is the height, $a$ the longer parallel side, and $b$ the shorter.

Regular pentagon: $A=1.720a^2$, in which $a$ is one of the sides.

Regular hexagon: $A=2.598a^2$, in which $a$ is one of the sides.

Regular octagon: $A=4.828a^2$, in which $a$ is one of the sides.

Circle: $A=\pi r^2$, in which $\pi$ is 3.1416 and $r$ the radius.

### Volume

Cube: $V=a^3$, in which $a$ is one of the edges.

Rectangular prism: $V=abc$, in which $a$ is the length, $b$ the width, and $c$ the depth.

Pyramid: $V=\dfrac{Ah}{3}$, in which $A$ is the area of the base and $h$ the height.

Cylinder: $V=\pi r^2 h$, in which $\pi$ is 3.1416, $r$ the radius of the base, and $h$ the height.

Cone: $V=\dfrac{\pi r^2 h}{3}$, in which $\pi$ is 3.1416, $r$ the radius of the base, and $h$ the height.

Sphere: $V=\dfrac{4\pi r^3}{3}$, in which $\pi$ is 3.1416 and $r$ the radius.

### Miscellaneous

Speed per second acquired by falling body: $v=32t$, in which $t$ is the time in seconds.

Distance in feet traveled by falling body: $d=16t^2$, in which $t$ is the time in seconds.

Speed of sound in feet per second through any given temperature of air:

$V=\dfrac{1087\sqrt{273+t}}{16.52}$, in which $t$ is the temperature Centigrade.

Cost per hour of operation of electrical device: $C=\dfrac{Wtc}{1000}$, in which $W$ is the number of watts, $t$ the time in hours, and $c$ the cost per kilowatt-hour.

Conversion of matter into energy (Einstein's Theorem): $E=mc^2$, in which $E$ is the energy in ergs, $m$ the mass of the matter in grams, and $c$ the speed of light in centimeters per second. ($c^2=9\cdot10^{20}$).

### Abbreviations

The National Bureau of Standards recommends that the period be omitted after all abbreviations of units unless the abbreviation forms an English word, and that the same abbreviation be used for both singular and plural.

## FAHRENHEIT AND CENTIGRADE SCALES

Zero on the Fahrenheit scale represents the temperature produced by the mixing of equal weights of snow and common salt.

Absolute zero is theoretically the lowest possible temperature, the point at which all molecular motion would cease.

---

|                        | F      | C       |
| ---------------------- | ------ | ------- |
| Boiling point of water | 212°   | 100°    |
| Freezing point of water| 32°    | 0°      |
| Absolute zero          | −459.6°| −273.1° |

To convert Fahrenheit to Centigrade, subtract 32 and multiply by 5/9.

To convert Centigrade to Fahrenheit, multiply by 9/5 and add 32.

## ROMAN NUMERALS

Roman numerals áre expressed by letters of the alphabet and are rarely used today except for formality or variety.

There are three basic principles for reading Roman numerals:

1. A letter repeated once or twice repeats its value that many times. (XXX= 30, CC=200, etc.).

2. One or more letters placed after another letter of greater value increases the greater value by the amount of the smaller. (VI=6, LXX=70, MCC=1200, etc.).

3. A letter placed before another letter of greater value decreases the greater value by the amount of the smaller. (IV=4, XC= 90, CM=900, etc.).

| Letter | Value | Letter | Value     |
| ------ | ----- | ------ | --------- |
| I      | 1     | LX     | 60        |
| II     | 2     | LXX    | 70        |
| III    | 3     | LXXX   | 80        |
| IV     | 4     | XC     | 90        |
| V      | 5     | C      | 100       |
| VI     | 6     | D      | 500       |
| VII    | 7     | M      | 1,000     |
| VIII   | 8     | V̄      | 5,000     |
| IX     | 9     | X̄      | 10,000    |
| X      | 10    | L̄      | 50,000    |
| XX     | 20    | C̄      | 100,000   |
| XXX    | 30    | D̄      | 500,000   |
| XL     | 40    | M̄      | 1,000,000 |
| L      | 50    |        |           |

## SIMPLE INTEREST FOR $100

To find the interest for any amount of money, move the decimal point of that amount two places to the left and multiply by the figure obtained from the table.

For figuring simple interest, the year is considered to have 360 days.

|        | 1 Day     | 7 Days    | 1 Month   | 3 Months  | 6 Months   | 1 Year      |
| ------ | --------- | --------- | --------- | --------- | ---------- | ----------- |
| 2%     | $.00556   | $.03889   | $.16667   | $.50000   | $1.00000   | $2.00000    |
| 2½%    | .00694    | .04861    | .20833    | .62500    | 1.25000    | 2.50000     |
| 3%     | .00833    | .05833    | .25000    | .75000    | 1.50000    | 3.00000     |
| 3½%    | .00972    | .06806    | .29167    | .87500    | 1.75000    | 3.50000     |
| 4%     | .01111    | .07778    | .33333    | 1.00000   | 2.00000    | 4.00000     |
| 4½%    | .01250    | .08750    | .37500    | 1.12500   | 2.25000    | 4.50000     |
| 5%     | .01389    | .09722    | .41667    | 1.25000   | 2.50000    | 5.00000     |
| 5½%    | .01528    | .10694    | .45833    | 1.37500   | 2.75000    | 5.50000     |
| 6%     | .01667    | .11667    | .50000    | 1.50000   | 3.00000    | 6.00000     |
| 6½%    | .01806    | .12639    | .54167    | 1.62500   | 3.25000    | 6.50000     |
| 7%     | .01944    | .13611    | .58333    | 1.75000   | 3.50000    | 7.00000     |
| 8%     | .02222    | .15556    | .66667    | 2.00000   | 4.00000    | 8.00000     |
| 9%     | .02500    | .17500    | .75000    | 2.25000   | 4.50000    | 9.00000     |
| 10%    | .02778    | .19444    | .83333    | 2.50000   | 5.00000    | 10.00000    |

## MISCELLANEOUS UNITS

AGATE: Originally a measurement of type size (5½ points). Now equal to 1/14 inch. Used in printing for measuring column length.

ANGSTROM (A or λ): .0001 micron or .0000001 mm. Used for measuring length of light waves.

ASTRONOMICAL UNIT (A.U.): 93,003,000 miles, the average distance of the earth from the sun. Used in astronomy.

BALE: A large bundle of goods. In the U. S., the approximate weight of a bale of cotton is 500 pounds. The weight varies in other countries.

**BARREL (bbl):** For liquids, 31½ gallons or 7326.5 cubic inches. For dry commodities, except cranberries: 105 dry quarts or 7056 cubic inches. For cranberries: 5826 cubic inches.

**BOARD FOOT (fbm):** 144 cubic inches (12 in. x 12 in. x 1 in.). Used for lumber.

**BOLT:** 40 yards. Used for measuring cloth.

**CABLE:** About 100 fathoms or 600 feet. Used for measuring lengths of cable.

**CARAT (c):** 200 milligrams or 3.086 grains troy. Originally the weight of a seed of the carob tree in the Mediterranean region. Used for weighing precious stones. Also a measure of the purity of gold alloy, indicating how many parts out of 24 are pure. Eighteen carat gold, for example, is ¾ pure.

**CHAIN (ch):** a chain 66 feet or one-tenth of a furlong in length, divided into 100 parts called links. One mile is equal to 80 chains. Used in surveying and sometimes called Gunter's chain.

**CUBIT:** 18 inches or 45.72 cm. Derived from distance between elbow and tip of middle finger.

**ELL, ENGLISH:** 1¼ yards or 1/32 bolt. Used for measuring cloth.

**FATHOM (fath):** 6 feet or 1.8288 m. Derived from the distance to which a man can stretch his arms. Used for measuring cables and depths of water.

**FREIGHT TON (also called MEASUREMENT TON):** 40 cubic feet of merchandise. Used for cargo freight.

**GREAT GROSS:** 12 gross or 1728.

**GROSS:** 12 dozen or 144.

**HAND:** 4 inches or 10.16 cm. Derived from the width of the hand. Used for measuring the height of horses at withers.

**HOGSHEAD (hhd):** 2 liquid barrels or 14,653 cubic inches.

**HORSEPOWER:** The power needed to lift 33,000 pounds a distance of one foot in one minute (about 1½ times the power an average horse can exert). Used for measuring the power of steam engines, etc.

**KNOT:** Not a distance, but the rate of speed of one nautical mile per hour. Used for measuring speed of ships.

**LEAGUE:** Rather indefinite and varying measure, but usually estimated at 3 miles in English-speaking countries.

**LIGHT-YEAR:** 5,880,000,000,000 miles, the distance light travels in a year at the rate of 186,272 miles per second. (If an astronomical unit were represented by one inch, a light-year would be represented by about one mile.) Used for measurements in interstellar space.

**LINK:** One-hundredth of a chain or 7.92 inches. Used in surveying.

**MAGNUM:** Two-quart bottle. Used for measuring wine, etc.

**MICRON (μ):** .001 millimeter. Used for scientific measurements.

**MIL:** .001 inch. Used for measuring size of wire. The area of a cross-section of wire is usually expressed in circular mils, a circular mil being the area of a circle one mil in diameter. A wire one inch in diameter has a cross-section area of one million circular mils.

**MILLIMICRON (mμ):** .001 micron or .000001 mm. Used for scientific measurements.

**NAUTICAL MILE (also called GEOGRAPHICAL or SEA MILE):** Equal to a minute or 1/21600 of a great circle of the earth. Length varies in different countries. In Great Britain, it is 6080 feet or 1853.2 meters, and in the United States, it is 6080.2 feet or 1853.248 meters. The International Hydrographic Bureau proposed in 1929 a length of 1852 meters or 6076.097 feet, which has been adopted by several countries.

**PARSEC:** Approximately 3.26 light-years or 19.2 trillion miles. Term is combination of first syllables of *parallax* and *second*, and distance is that of imaginary star when lines drawn from it to both earth and sun form a maximum angle or parallax of one second (1/3600 degree). Used for measuring interstellar distances.

**PI (π):** 3.14159265+. The ratio of the circumference of a circle to its diameter. For practical purpose, the value is used to four decimal places: 3.1416.

**PICA:** ⅙ inch or 12 points. Used in printing for measuring column width, etc.

**PIPE:** 2 hogsheads. Used for measuring wine and other liquids.

**POINT:** .013837 (approximately 1/72) inch or 1/12 pica. Used in printing for measuring type size.

**QUINTAL:** 100,000 grams or 220.46 pounds avoirdupois.

**QUIRE:** Used for measuring paper. Sometimes 24 sheets but more often 25. There are 20 quires in a ream.

**REAM:** Used for measuring paper. Sometimes 480 sheets, but more often 500 sheets.

**SCORE:** 20 units.

**SPAN:** 9 inches or 22.86 cm. Derived from the distance between the end of the thumb and the end of the little finger when both are outstretched.

**STONE:** Legally 14 pounds avoirdupois in Great Britain.

**TOWNSHIP:** U. S. land measurement of almost 36 square miles. The south border is 6 miles long. The east and west borders, also 6 miles long, follow the meridians, making the north border slightly less than six miles long. Used in surveying.

**TUN:** 252 gallons, but often larger. Used for measuring wine and other liquids.

# DECIMAL EQUIVALENTS OF COMMON FRACTIONS

| | | | | | | | |
|---|---|---|---|---|---|---|---|
| 1/2 | .5000 | 1/32 | .0313 | 3/11 | .2727 | 6/11 | .5455 |
| 1/3 | .3333 | 1/64 | .0156 | 4/5 | .8000 | 7/8 | .8750 |
| 1/4 | .2500 | 2/3 | .6667 | 4/7 | .5714 | 7/9 | .7778 |
| 1/5 | .2000 | 2/5 | .4000 | 4/9 | .4444 | 7/10 | .7000 |
| 1/6 | .1667 | 2/7 | .2857 | 4/11 | .3636 | 7/11 | .6364 |
| 1/7 | .1429 | 2/9 | .2222 | 5/6 | .8333 | 7/12 | .5833 |
| 1/8 | .1250 | 2/11 | .1818 | 5/7 | .7143 | 8/9 | .8889 |
| 1/9 | .1111 | 3/4 | .7500 | 5/8 | .6250 | 8/11 | .7273 |
| 1/10 | .1000 | 3/5 | .6000 | 5/9 | .5556 | 9/10 | .9000 |
| 1/11 | .0909 | 3/7 | .4286 | 5/11 | .4545 | 9/11 | .8182 |
| 1/12 | .0833 | 3/8 | .3750 | 5/12 | .4167 | 10/11 | .9091 |
| 1/16 | .0625 | 3/10 | .3000 | 6/7 | .8571 | 11/12 | .9167 |

## Handy Conversion Factors

| To change | To | Multiply by |
|---|---|---|
| acres | hectares | .4047 |
| bushels (U. S.) | hectoliters | .3524 |
| centimeters | inches | .3937 |
| cubic feet | cubic meters | .0283 |
| cubic meters | cubic feet | 35.3145 |
| cubic meters | cubic yards | 1.3079 |
| cubic yards | cubic meters | .7646 |
| feet | meters | .3048 |
| gallons (U. S.) | liters | 3.7853 |
| grains | grams | .0648 |
| grams | grains | 15.4324 |
| grams | ounces avdp. | .0353 |
| hectares | acres | 2.4710 |
| hectoliters | bushels (U. S.) | 2.8378 |
| inches | millimeters | 25.4000 |
| inches | centimeters | 2.5400 |
| kilograms | pounds ap or t | 2.6792 |
| kilograms | pounds avdp. | 2.2046 |
| kilometers | miles | .6214 |
| liters | gallons (U. S.) | .2642 |
| liters | pecks | .1135 |
| liters | pints (dry) | 1.8162 |
| liters | pints (liquid) | 2.1134 |
| liters | quarts (dry) | .9081 |
| liters | quarts (liquid) | 1.0567 |
| meters | feet | 3.2808 |
| meters | yards | 1.0936 |
| metric tons | tons (long) | .9842 |
| metric tons | tons (short) | 1.1023 |
| miles | kilometers | 1.6093 |
| millimeters | inches | .0394 |
| ounces avdp. | grams | 28.3495 |
| pecks | liters | 8.8096 |
| pints (dry) | liters | .5506 |
| pints (liquid) | liters | .4732 |
| pounds ap or t | kilograms | .3732 |
| pounds avdp. | kilograms | .4536 |
| quarts (dry) | liters | 1.1012 |
| quarts (liquid) | liters | .9463 |
| square feet | square meters | .0929 |
| square meters | square feet | 10.7639 |
| square meters | square yards | 1.1960 |
| square yards | square meters | .8361 |
| tons (long) | metric tons | 1.0160 |
| tons (short) | metric tons | .9072 |
| yards | meters | .9144 |

## Perfect Squares and Cubes, 1 to 2025

| Number | Square root | Cube root | Number | Square root | Cube root |
|---|---|---|---|---|---|
| 1 | 1 | 1 | 512 | .. | 8 |
| 4 | 2 | .. | 529 | 23 | .. |
| 8 | .. | 2 | 576 | 24 | .. |
| 9 | 3 | .. | 625 | 25 | .. |
| 16 | 4 | .. | 676 | 26 | .. |
| 25 | 5 | .. | 729 | 27 | 9 |
| 27 | .. | 3 | 784 | 28 | .. |
| 36 | 6 | .. | 841 | 29 | .. |
| 49 | 7 | .. | 900 | 30 | .. |
| 64 | 8 | 4 | 961 | 31 | .. |
| 81 | 9 | .. | 1000 | .. | 10 |
| 100 | 10 | .. | 1024 | 32 | .. |
| 121 | 11 | .. | 1089 | 33 | .. |
| 125 | .. | 5 | 1156 | 34 | .. |
| 144 | 12 | .. | 1225 | 35 | .. |
| 169 | 13 | .. | 1296 | 36 | .. |
| 196 | 14 | .. | 1331 | .. | 11 |
| 216 | .. | 6 | 1369 | 37 | .. |
| 225 | 15 | .. | 1444 | 38 | .. |
| 256 | 16 | .. | 1521 | 39 | .. |
| 289 | 17 | .. | 1600 | 40 | .. |
| 324 | 18 | .. | 1681 | 41 | .. |
| 343 | .. | 7 | 1728 | .. | 12 |
| 361 | 19 | .. | 1764 | 42 | .. |
| 400 | 20 | .. | 1849 | 43 | .. |
| 441 | 21 | .. | 1936 | 44 | .. |
| 484 | 22 | .. | 2025 | 45 | .. |

## Mean and Median

The mean, also called the average, of a series of quantities is obtained by finding the sum of the quantities and dividing it by the number of quantities. In the series 1,3,5,18,19,20,25, the mean or average is 13 —i.e., 91 divided by 7.

The median of a series is that point which so divides it that half the quantities are on one side, half on the other. In the above series, the median is 18.

The median often better expresses the common-run, since it is not, as is the mean, affected by an excessively high or low figure. In the series 1,3,4,7,55, the median of 4 is a truer expression of the common-run than is the mean of 14.

# Chemical Elements

| Atomic number | Element | Symbol | Atomic weight | Density gm/cc | Melting point °C. | Boiling point °C. | Valence | Number of isotopes† | Discoverer | Date discovered |
|---|---|---|---|---|---|---|---|---|---|---|
| 1 | Hydrogen | H | 1.0080 | 0.07‡ | −259.14 | −252.7 | 1 | 3 | Cavendish | 1766 |
| 2 | Helium | He | 4.003 | 0.15‡ | <−272.2 | −268.9 | 0 | 4 | Ramsay | 1895 |
| 3 | Lithium | Li | 6.940 | 0.534 | 186. | >1200. | 1 | 5 | Arfvedson | 1817 |
| 4 | Beryllium | Be | 9.013 | 1.84 | 1350. | 1500. | 2 | 4 | Vauquelin | 1798 |
| 5 | Boron | B | 10.82 | 2.535§ | 2300. | 2500. | 3 | 5 | Gay-Lussac and Thénard; Davy | 1808 |
| 6 | Carbon | C | 12.011 | 2.25** | >3500. | 4200. | 2, 3 or 4 | 6 | Prehistoric | .... |
| 7 | Nitrogen | N | 14.008 | 0.810‡ | −209.86 | −195.3 | 3 or 5 | 6 | Rutherford | 1772 |
| 8 | Oxygen | O | 16.0000 | 1.14‡ | −218.4 | −183.00 | 2 | 6 | Priestley | 1774 |
| 9 | Fluorine | F | 19.00 | 1.14‡ | −223. | −187. | 1 | 4 | Moissan | 1886 |
| 10 | Neon | Ne | 20.183 | 0.90035 (g/10°C. 760mm) | −248.67 | −245.9 | 0 | 5 | Ramsay and Travers | 1898 |
| 11 | Sodium | Na | 22.991 | 0.9287‡ | 97.5 | 880. | 1 | 6 | Davy | 1807 |
| 12 | Magnesium | Mg | 24.32 | 1.741 | 651. | 1110. | 2 | 6 | Davy | 1808 |
| 13 | Aluminum | Al | 26.98 | 2.699‡ | 660.0 | 1800. | 3 | 6 | Wöhler | 1827 |
| 14 | Silicon | Si | 28.09 | 2.42** | 1420. | 2600. | 4 | 6 | Berzelius | 1824 |
| 15 | Phosphorus | P | 30.975 | 1.83 (white) | 44.1 | 280. | 3 or 5 | 6 | Brand | 1669 |
| 16 | Sulfur | S | 32.066 | 2.0–1 | 112.8 | 444.6 | 2, 4 or 6 | 7 | Prehistoric | .... |
| 17 | Chlorine | Cl | 35.457 | 1.507‡ | −101.6 | −34.6 | 1, 3, 5 or 7 | 7 | Scheele | 1774 |
| 18 | Argon | A | 39.944 | 1.423‡ | −189.2 | −185.7 | 0 | 8 | Rayleigh and Ramsay | 1894 |
| 19 | Potassium | K | 39.100 | 0.87 | 62.3 | 760. | 1 | 8 | Davy | 1807 |
| 20 | Calcium | Ca | 40.08 | 1.54 | 810. | 1170. | 2 | 10 | Davy | 1808 |
| 21 | Scandium | Sc | 44.96 | 3.62 (10°C.) | 1200. | 2400. | 3 | 8 | Nilson | 1879 |
| 22 | Titanium | Ti | 47.90 | 4.5 | 1800. | >3000. | 3 or 4 | 8 | Gregor | 1791 |
| 23 | Vanadium | V | 50.95 | 5.69 | 1710. | 3000. | 2, 3, 4 or 5 | 8 | Sefström | 1830 |
| 24 | Chromium | Cr | 52.01 | 6.92 | 1615. | 2200. | 2, 3 or 6 | 8 | Vauquelin | 1798 |
| 25 | Manganese | Mn | 54.94 | 7.42 | 1260. | 1900. | 2, 3, 4 6 or 7 | 6 | Gahn | 1774 |
| 26 | Iron | Fe | 55.85 | 7.85–88 | 1535. | 3000. | 2, 3 or 6 | 8 | Prehistoric | .... |
| 27 | Cobalt | Co | 58.94 | 8.9 | 1480. | 2900. | 2 or 3 | 9 | Brandt | 1735 |
| 28 | Nickel | Ni | 58.71 | 8.60–90 | 1452. | 2900. | 2 or 3 | 11 | Cronstedt | 1751 |
| 29 | Copper | Cu | 63.54 | 8.30–95 | 1083. | 2300. | 1 or 2 | 10 | Prehistoric | .... |
| 30 | Zinc | Zn | 65.38 | 7.04–16 | 419.43 | 907. | 2 | 12 | Identified by Marggraf | 1746 |
| 31 | Gallium | Ga | 69.72 | 5.903 | 29.75 | >1600. | 2 or 3 | 11 | Boisbaudran | 1875 |
| 32 | Germanium | Ge | 72.60 | 5.46 | 958.5 | 2700. | 4 | 13 | Winkler | 1886 |
| 33 | Arsenic | As | 74.91 | 5.73 | 814. (36 atm.) | 615. | 3 or 5 | 11 | Albertus Magnus | 1250§§ |
| 34 | Selenium | Se | 78.96 | 4.3–8 | 220. | 688. | 2, 4 or 6 | 14 | Berzelius | 1818 |
| 35 | Bromine | Br | 79.916 | 3.12‡ | −7.2 | 58.78 | 1, 3, 5 or 7 | 15 | Balard | 1826 |
| 36 | Krypton | Kr | 83.80 | 2.16‡ | −169. | −151.8 | 0 | 19 | Ramsay and Travers | 1898 |
| 37 | Rubidium | Rb | 85.48 | 1.532 | 38.5 | 700. | 1 | 16 | Bunsen and Kirchhoff | 1861 |
| 38 | Strontium | Sr | 87.63 | 2.50–58 | 800. | 1150. | 2 | 16 | Davy | 1808 |
| 39 | Yttrium | Y | 88.92 | 3.80 | 1490. | 2500. | 3 | 15 | Gadolin | 1794 |
| 40 | Zirconium | Zr | 91.22 | 6.44 | 1700. | >2900. | 4 | 12 | Klaproth | 1789 |
| 41 | Niobium*** (Columbium) | Nb | 92.91 | 8.4 | 1950. | >3300. | 3 or 5 | 10 | Hatchett | 1801 |
| 42 | Molybdenum | Mo | 95.95 | 9.01 | 2620 ±10 | 3700. | 2, 3, 4, 5 or 6 | 13 | Hjelm | 1781 |
| 43 | Technetium | Tc | 99.* | 11.487 | 2300. | ..... | 2, 3, 4 or 6 | 12¶¶ | Perrier and Segrè | 1937 |
| 44 | Ruthenium | Ru | 101.1 | 12.06 | 2450. | >2700. | 3, 4, 6 or 8 | 13 | Klaus | 1844 |
| 45 | Rhodium | Rh | 102.91 | 12.44 | 1955. | >2500. | 3 | 10 | Wollaston | 1803 |
| 46 | Palladium | Pd | 106.4 | 12.16 (20°C.) | 1555. | 2200. | 2 or 4 | 13 | Wollaston | 1803 |
| 47 | Silver | Ag | 107.880 | 10.503†† | 960.5 | 1950. | 1 | 13 | Prehistoric | .... |
| 48 | Cadmium | Cd | 112.41 | 8.648 | 320.9 | 767. | 2 | 14 | Stromeyer | 1817 |
| 49 | Indium | In | 114.82 | 7.28 | 155. | 1450. | 1 or 3 | 13 | Reich and Richter | 1863 |
| 50 | Tin | Sn | 118.70 | 7.29 | 231.83 | 2260. | 2 or 4 | 18 | Prehistoric | .... |
| 51 | Antimony | Sb | 121.76 | 6.618 | 630.5 | 1380. | 3 or 5 | 16 | Early historic times | .... |
| 52 | Tellurium | Te | 127.61 | 6.25** | 452. | 1390. | 2, 4, or 6 | 17 | von Reichenstein | 1782 |
| 53 | Iodine | I | 126.91 | 4.94 | 113.5 | 184.35 | 1, 3, 5 or 7 | 18 | Courtois | 1811 |
| 54 | Xenon | Xe | 131.30 | 3.52‡ | −140. | −109.1 | 0 | 23 | Ramsay and Travers | 1898 |

| Atomic number | Element | Symbol | Atomic weight | Density gm/cc | Melting point °C. | Boiling point °C. | Valence | Number of isotopes† | Discoverer | Date discovered |
|---|---|---|---|---|---|---|---|---|---|---|
| 55 | Cesium | Cs | 132.91 | 1.873 | 26. | 670. | 1 | 18 | Bunsen and Kirchhoff | 1860 |
| 56 | Barium | Ba | 137.36 | 3.78 | 850. | 1140. | 2 | 17 | Davy | 1808 |
| 57 | Lanthanum | La | 138.92 | 6.5 | 826. | 1800. | 3 | 15 | Mosander | 1839 |
| 58 | Cerium | Ce | 140.13 | 6.9 | 770. | 1400. | 3 or 4 | 14 | Klaproth; Berzelius and Hisinger | 1803 |
| 59 | Praseodymium | Pr | 140.92 | 6.475 | 940. | 3450. | 3, 4 or 5 | 9 | Auer von Welsbach | 1885 |
| 60 | Neodymium | Nd | 144.27 | 6.96 | 840. | 3300. | 3 | 13 | Auer von Welsbach | 1885 |
| 61 | Promethium | Pm | 145.* | ..... | ..... | ..... | 3 | 12¶¶ | Marinsky and Glendenin | 1945 |
| 62 | Samarium | Sm | 150.35 | 7.7–8 | 1350. | 1900. | 2 or 3 | 14 | Boisbaudran | 1879 |
| 63 | Europium | Eu | 152.0 | 5.24 | 1100. | 1700. | 2 or 3 | 12 | Demarcay | 1901 |
| 64 | Gadolinium | Gd | 157.26 | 7.95 | 1350. | 3000. | 3 | 13 | Marignac | 1880 |
| 65 | Terbium | Tb | 158.93 | 8.33 | 1400. | 2800. | 3 or 4 | 10 | Mosander | 1843 |
| 66 | Dysprosium | Dy | 162.51 | 8.56 | 1475. | 2600. | 3 | 10 | Boisbaudran | 1886 |
| 67 | Holmium | Ho | 164.94 | 8.76 | 1475. | 2700. | 3 | 7 | Soret | 1878 |
| 68 | Erbium | Er | 167.27 | 9.06 | 1475. | 2600. | 3 | 9 | Mosander | 1843 |
| 69 | Thulium | Tm | 168.94 | 9.34 | 1500. | 2400. | 3 | 6 | Cleve | 1879 |
| 70 | Ytterbium | Yb | 173.04 | 9.01 | 824. | 1800. | 3 | 10 | Marignac | 1878 |
| 71 | Lutetium | Lu | 174.99 | 9.74 | 1650. | 3500. | 3 or 4 | 8 | Urbain | 1907 |
| 72 | Hafnium | Hf | 178.50 | 13.3 | 1700. | 3200. | 4 | 11 | Coster and von Hevesy | 1923 |
| 73 | Tantalum | Ta | 180.95 | 16.6 | 2850. | 4100. | 3 or 5 | 9 | Ekeberg | 1802 |
| 74 | Tungsten (Wolfram) | W | 183.86 | 18.6–19.1 | 3370. | 5900. | 2, 4, 5 or 6 | 12 | d'Elhuyar | 1783 |
| 75 | Rhenium | Re | 186.22 | 20.53 (20°C.) | 3000. | ..... | 4 | 7 | Noddack and Berg | 1925 |
| 76 | Osmium | Os | 190.2 | 22.5 | 2700. | 5300. | 2, 3, 4 or 8 | 13 | Tennant | 1804 |
| 77 | Iridium | Ir | 192.2 | 22.42 | 2350. | 4800. | 3 or 4 | 7 | Tennant | 1804 |
| 78 | Platinum | Pt | 195.09 | 21.37 | 1755. | 4300. | 2 or 4 | 9 | De Ulloa | 1748 |
| 79 | Gold | Au | 197.0 | 19.3†† | 1063.0 | 2600. | 1 or 3 | 12 | Prehistoric | .... |
| 80 | Mercury | Hg | 200.61 | 13.596‡ | −38.87 | 356.90 | 1 or 2 | 14 | Prehistoric | .... |
| 81 | Thallium | Tl | 204.39 | 11.86 | 303.5 | 1650. | 1 or 3 | 13 | Crookes | 1861 |
| 82 | Lead | Pb | 207.21 | 11.347†† | 327.5 | 1620. | 2 or 4 | 15 | Prehistoric | .... |
| 83 | Bismuth | Bi | 209.00 | 9.80 | 271. | 1450. | 3 or 5 | 17 | Identified by Geoffroy | 1753 |
| 84 | Polonium | Po | 210. | ..... | ..... | ..... |  | 19 | Curie | 1898 |
| 85 | Astatine | At | 210.* | ..... | 470. | ..... | 1, 3, 5 or 7 | 15 | Corson et al | 1940 |
| 86 | Radon | Rn | 222. | 9.739‡ | −71. | −61.8 | 0 | 12 | Dorn | 1900 |
| 87 | Francium | Fr | 223.* | ..... | 23. | ..... | 1 | 10 | Perey | 1939 |
| 88 | Radium | Ra | 226.05 | 6.0 | 960. | 1140. | 2 | 7 | Curie | 1898 |
| 89 | Actinium | Ac | 227. | ..... | ..... | ..... | 3 | 6 | Debierne | 1899 |
| 90 | Thorium | Th | 232.05 | 11.13 | 1845. | 3000. | 4 | 10 | Berzelius | 1828 |
| 91 | Protactinium | Pa | 231. | ..... | ..... | ..... | 5 | 9 | Hahn and Meitner | 1917 |
| 92 | Uranium | U | 238.07 | 18.7 | 1850. | 3927. | 3, 4 or 6 | 12 | Klaproth | 1789 |
| 93 | Neptunium | Np | 237.* | 17.7 | ..... | ..... | 3, 4, 5 or 6 | 10¶¶ | McMillan and Abelson | 1940 |
| 94 | Plutonium | Pu | 242.* | ..... | ..... | ..... | 3, 4, 5 or 6 | 9¶¶ | Seaborg et al | 1940 |
| 95 | Americium | Am | 243.* | 11.7 | >850. | ..... | 3 | 6¶¶ | Seaborg et al | 1944 |
| 96 | Curium | Cm | 242. | ..... | ..... | ..... | 3 | 6¶¶ | Seaborg et al | 1944 |
| 97 | Berkelium | Bk | 249.* | ..... | ..... | ..... | 3 or 4 | 3¶¶ | Seaborg et al | 1950 |
| 98 | Californium | Cf | 249.* | ..... | ..... | ..... | 3 | 2¶¶ | Seaborg et al | 1950 |
| 99 | Einsteinium | E | 253. | ..... | ..... | ..... | 3 | 5¶¶ | Ghiorso et al | 1954 |
| 100 | Fermium | Fm | 255. | ..... | ..... | ..... | 3 | 1¶¶ | Studier et al | 1954 |
| 101 | Mendelevium | Mv | 256.* | ..... | ..... | ..... | 3 | 1¶¶ | Ghiorso et al | 1955 |
| 102 | Nobelium | No | 253 | ..... | ..... | ..... | 3 | 1¶¶ | Sw., Br., & Am. | 1957 |

\* Mass number of the isotope of longest known half-life.

† Isotopes are different forms of the same element, having the same atomic number but different atomic weights. The number of isotopes given includes only those that are stable and natural occurring, excluding those marked ¶¶.

‡ Liquid.　§ Amorphous.　¶ Graphite.　\*\* Crystalline.　†† Compressed.　‡‡ Cast.　§§ Exact date doubtful —born 1193 and died 1280.　¶¶ Have been artificially produced.　\*\*\* New name adopted by International Union of Chemistry, replacing old name in parentheses.　< Is less than.　> Is greater than.

NOTE: Figures in parentheses are tentative or theoretical. Quantities made of elements from 96 to 102 have been too small to establish melting points and similar facts.

The number of isotopes of each element is increased by discovery or by manufacture.

# Scientific Inventions, Discoveries and Theories
*Source: Encyclopaedia Britannica.*

## Inventions

**Adding machine, recording:** William S. Burroughs, 1888.

**Airplane:** Wilbur and Orville Wright, 1903.

**Air brake, railroad:** George Westinghouse, 1868.

**Air pump:** Otto von Guericke, 1650.

**Automobile:** (Product of inventions of many men. Gottlieb Daimler is frequently given credit, c.1887.)

**Bakelite:** Leo H. Baekeland, 1908.

**Balloon, hot-air:** Joseph and Jacques Montgolfier, 1783.

**Barometer:** Evangelista Torricelli, 1643.

**Camera, Kodak:** George Eastman, 1888.

**Carburetor, spray:** Charles E. Duryea, 1892.

**Cellophane:** J. E. Brandenberger, 1911.

**Celluloid:** John W. and I. S. Hyatt, 1870.

**Clock, pendulum:** Christiaan Huygens, 1656.

**Converter, Bessemer:** William Kelly, 1851. (Patent bought by Sir Henry Bessemer, who made a similar invention in 1856.)

**Cotton gin:** Eli Whitney, 1793.

**Cyanide:** Nikodem Caro and Adolf Frank, 1905.

**Cyclotron:** Ernest O. Lawrence, 1931.

**Daguerreotype process:** Louis J. M. Daguerre, 1839.

**Diesel engine:** Rudolf Diesel, 1897.

**Dynamite:** Alfred B. Nobel, 1862.

**Dynamo:** Michael Faraday, 1831.

**Dynamo, industrial:** Zénobe Gramme, 1872.

**Electromagnet:** William Sturgeon, 1823.

**Electroplating:** Luigi Brugnatelli, 1805.

**Elevator, passenger:** Elisha G. Otis, 1857.

**Elevator safety device:** Elisha G. Otis, 1852.

**Engine, high-speed internal-combustion:** Gottlieb Daimler, 1885.

**Filament, tungsten:** Irving Langmuir, 1915.

**Flying shuttle:** John Kay, 1733.

**Food preservation, hermetically sealed (meat):** François (Nicolas) Appert, 1810, with little success.

**Fountain pen:** Lewis E. Waterman, 1884. (First successful one.)

**Frequency modulation (FM):** Edwin H. Armstrong, 1933.

**Guncotton:** Christian Schönbein, 1845.

**Gyrocompass:** Elmer A. Sperry, 1905.

**Gyroscope:** Léon Foucault, 1852.

**Helicopter:** Igor I. Sikorsky, 1909; Louis C. Bréguet equipped first passenger carrying helicopter, 1909; first successful modern helicopter, Heinrich K. J. Focke, 1937–41.

**Hydroplane:** Charles M. Ramus propounded idea around 1870; Glenn H. Curtiss, 1911.

**Jet propulsion (aircraft):** Sir Frank Whittle, 1930.

**Lamp, electric incandescent:** (Inventor uncertain; Thomas A. Edison, who made a lamp in 1879, is sometimes credited.)

**Lens, bifocal:** Benjamin Franklin, c.1760.

**Lightning rod:** Benjamin Franklin, 1752.

**Linotype machine:** Ottmar Mergenthaler, 1885 (patent); first used, 1886.

**Lithography:** Aloys Senefelder, 1796.

**Machine gun:** Richard J. Gatling, 1861.

**Match, friction:** John Walker, 1827.

**Mercury-vapor lamp:** Peter C. Hewitt, 1912.

**Microscope, compound:** Zacharias Janssen, 1590.

**Microscope, electron:** Vladimir Zworykin et al., 1939.

**Miner's safety lamp:** Sir Humphry Davy, 1815.

**Monotype machine:** Tolbert Lanston, 1887.

**Motion pictures:** Thomas A. Edison, 1893.

**Motion pictures, sound:** (Product of various inventions. First picture with synchronized musical score: *Don Juan,* Warner Bros., 1926. First picture with spoken dialogue: *The Jazz Singer,* Warner Bros., 1927.)

**Motor, A-C:** Nikola Tesla, 1892.

**Ophthalmoscope:** Hermann von Helmholtz, 1851.

**Phonograph:** Thomas A. Edison, 1877.

**Photography, color:** Gabriel Lippmann, 1891.

**Power loom:** Edmund Cartwright, 1785.

**Printing, movable-type:** Johann Gutenberg (?), c.1440.

**Printing press, rotary:** Richard Hoe, 1847.

**Radar:** Gregory Breit & Merle A. Tuve, 1925.

**Radio:** (Product of various inventions. First practical system of wireless telegraphy: Guglielmo Marconi, 1895.)

**Radio telephone:** Lee De Forest, 1906.

**Radio tube, diode:** Sir John Ambrose Fleming, 1904.

**Radio tube, triode:** Lee De Forest, 1906.

**Rayon:** George Andemars (first known patent), 1855; perfected by Sir Joseph W. Swan, 1883.

**Reaper:** Cyrus McCormick, 1834.

**Revolver:** Samuel Colt, 1835.

**Rifle, automatic:** John M. Browning, 1918.

**Rubber, vulcanized:** Ch. Goodyear, 1839.

**Screw propeller:** John Ericsson, 1837.

**Self-starter, automobile:** Charles F. Kettering, 1911.

**Sewing machine:** Elias Howe, 1846 (patented). Idea of lock-slick machine conceived independently by Walter Hunt, 1832–4.

**Spinning frame:** Sir Richard Arkwright, 1769.

**Spinning jenny:** James Hargreaves, 1764.

**Spinning mule:** Samuel Crompton, 1779.

**Steamboat:** Robert Fulton, 1807. (First commercially successful one in U. S.)

Steam engine: James Watt, 1765. (First practical one.)

Tank, military: Sir Ernest Swinton, 1914.

Telegraph, electromagnetic recording: Samuel F. B. Morse, 1837.

Telephone: Alexander Graham Bell, 1876.

Telescope: Hans Lippershey (?), c.1608.

Television: Successful demonstration by J. L. Baird in England and C. F. Jenkins in U. S., in early 1920's. (First commercial TV: July 1, 1941, over WNBT, New York.)

Thermometer: Galileo Galilei, 1593.

Tire, pneumatic: John B. Dunlop, 1888.

Tractor, caterpillar: Benjamin Holt, 1900.

Transformer, electric: Wm. Stanley, 1885.

Transistor: John Bardeen, William Shockley and Walter Brattain, 1948.

Typewriter: First practical one invented by Christopher Sholes, Carlos Glidden and Samuel W. Soule in 1867; patented by Sholes in 1868.

Zeppelin: Ferdinand von Zeppelin, 1900.

## Discoveries and Theories

Adrenaline, isolation of: Jokichi Takamine, 1901.

Aluminum manufacture by electrolytic action: Charles M. Hall, 1886.

Antitoxin, diphtheria: Emil von Behring, 1890.

Atom smashing with slow neutrons: Enrico Fermi, 1934. (Experiment repeated by Lise Meitner and Otto Hahn in 1938.)

Atomic numbers: Henry Moseley, 1913.

Atomic theory: John Dalton, 1803.

Aureomycin: Benjamin M. Duggar, 1948.

Bacteria: Anton van Leeuwenhoek, 1683.

Blood, circulation of: William Harvey, 1628.

Classification of plants and animals: Carolus Linnaeus, 1737–53.

Combustion, nature of: Antoine Lavoisier, 1777.

Conditioned reflex: Ivan Pavlov, c.1910.

Deuterium (heavy hydrogen): Harold C. Urey, 1931.

Displacement of water, principle of: Archimedes, 3rd century B.C.

Electromagnetic waves: Heinrich Hertz, 1886.

Electron: Sir Joseph J. Thomson, 1897.

Electron, wave nature of: Louis Victor de Broglie, 1924.

Ether, first used as anesthetic: Crawford W. Long, 1842.

Evolution by natural selection: Charles Darwin, 1859.

Falling bodies, law of: Galileo Galilei, 1590.

Gases, laws governing: Joseph Gay-Lussac, 1809.

Gravitation, law of: Sir Isaac Newton, 1687.

Helium on sun: Sir Joseph Lockyer, 1868.

Heredity, laws of: Gregor Mendel, 1865.

Induction, electric: Joseph Henry, 1828.

Insulin: Sir Frederick G. Banting and J. J. R. MacLeod, 1922.

Intelligence testing, modern: Alfred Binet and Theodore Simon, 1905.

Isotopes, mass spectra of: Francis W. Aston, 1919.

Isotopes, theory of: Frederick Soddy, 1912.

Light, electromagnetic theory of: James Clerk Maxwell, 1873.

Light, velocity of: Olaus Römer, 1675.

Molecular hypothesis: Amadeo Avogadro, 1811.

Neutron: James Chadwick, 1932.

Ohm's Law: Georg S. Ohm, 1827.

Ozone: Christian Schönbein, 1839.

Penicillin: Sir Alexander Fleming, 1929.

Periodic table: Dmitri Mendeleev, 1869.

Positron: Carl D. Anderson, 1932.

Proton: Ernest Rutherford, 1919.

Psychoanalysis: Sigmund Freud, c.1904.

Quantum mechanics: Werner Heisenberg, 1925.

Quantum theory: Max von Planck, 1901.

Rabies preventive: Louis Pasteur, 1885.

Radioactivity: Antoine Becquerel, 1896.

Radioactivity, artificial: Frédéric and Irène Joliot–Curie, 1934.

Relativity, theories of: Albert Einstein, 1905–53.

Sabin oral antipolio vaccine: Accepted as suitable for licensing, 1960.

Salk antipolio vaccine: Jonas E. Salk, announced successful 1955.

Schick test of susceptibility to diphtheria: Béla Schick, 1913.

Secretin, isolation of: Sir William Bayliss and Ernest Starling, 1902.

Soda manufacture from salt: Ernest Solvay, 1861.

Solar system, heliocentricity of: Nicolaus Copernicus, 1530. (Also Aristarchus of Samos, 3rd century B.C.)

Spectrum analysis: Robert Bunsen and Gustav Kirchhoff, 1859.

Sulfa drugs as bactericides: Gerhard Domagk, 1932.

Surgery, antiseptic: Sir Joseph Lister, 1867.

Tuberculosis bacillus: Robert Koch, 1882.

Vaccination: Edward Jenner, 1796.

Virus, crystallized: Wendell M. Stanley, 1935.

Vitamin A: Elmer V. McCollum and M. Davis, 1912–14.

Vitamin B: Elmer V. McCollum, 1915–16.

Vitamin C: A. Holst and T. Froehlich, 1912.

Vitamin D: Elmer V. McCollum, 1922.

Vitamin D, irradiated: Harry Steenbock, 1924.

Wassermann test for syphilis: August von Wassermann, 1906.

Wilson Cloud Chamber: Charles T. R. Wilson, 1911.

X-rays: Wilhelm Roentgen, 1895.

# Communicable Diseases

*Source: Control of Communicable Diseases in Man,* an official report of the American Public Health Assn.

| Disease | Incubation period* | Period of communicability |
|---|---|---|
| Chickenpox (varicella)......... | 2 to 3 weeks | From 1 day before appearance of vesicles to 6 days after. |
| Common cold................. | 12 to 72 hours; usually 24 hrs. | From 1 day before onset to 5 days after. |
| Conjunctivitis................. | 1 to 3 days | During course of active infection. |
| Diphtheria................... | 2 to 5 days | Usually 2 weeks or less; seldom more than 4 weeks. |
| Dysentery, amebic............ | 3 to 4 weeks (varies widely) | During infection; possibly for years if untreated. |
| Food poisoning: Botulism..... | Within 18 hours | Not applicable. |
| Salmonella infection......... | 6 to 48 hours in epidemics | 3 days to 3 weeks (extremely variable). |
| Staphylococcus intoxication .. | ½ to 4 hours | Not applicable. |
| German measles (rubella)..... | 14 to 21 days; usually 18 | At least 4 days after onset of catarrhal symptoms. |
| Gonorrhea.................... | 3 to 9 days; sometimes longer | Indefinitely unless treated. |
| Impetigo contagiosa.......... | 2 to 5 days; sometimes longer | Until lesions are healed. |
| Influenza.................... | Usually 1 to 3 days | Probably for brief time before and 1 week after onset. |
| Measles (rubeola)............ | 10 days (to onset) 14 days (to rash) | From 4 days before rash appears to 5 days after. |
| Meningitis, meningococcal..... | 2 to 10 days | Usually 1 day after appropriate medication. |
| Mumps....................... | 12 to 26 days; commonly 18 | From 7 days before distinctive symptoms up to 9 days after, or until swelling subsides. |
| Pneumonia: Bacterial......... | Usually 1 to 3 days | Unknown. |
| Virus..................... | Believed to be 7 to 21 days; commonly 12 | Unknown. |
| Poliomyelitis................. | 3 to 21 days; commonly 7 to 12 | From late incubation to first few days after onset; persists in feces for 3 to 6 weeks or more. |
| Rabies (hydrophobia)......... | 2 to 6 weeks or longer | From animals, 3 to 5 days before onset and during course of the disease. |
| Rheumatic fever............. | Not applicable† | Not known to be communicable. |
| Scarlet fever and streptococcal sore throat................. | 2 to 5 days | During incubation and clinical illness, about 10 days. May last for months in untreated patients. |
| Smallpox.................... | 7 to 16 days; commonly 12 | From first symptoms to disappearance of scabs and crusts, a period of 2 to 3 weeks. |
| Syphilis..................... | 10 days to 10 weeks; usually 3 weeks | Variable and not definitely known. |
| Tetanus..................... | 4 days to 3 weeks | Not communicable from man to man. |
| Trichinosis.................. | 2 to 28 days after eating infected meat; usually 9 days | Not directly transmitted from man to man. |
| Tuberculosis................. | 4 to 6 weeks (to primary phase) | As long as tubercle bacilli are discharged by patient. |
| Typhoid fever................ | 1 to 3 weeks | As long as typhoid bacilli appear in excreta; 2 to 5% of patients become permanent carriers. |
| Whooping cough (pertussis).... | Commonly 7 days, almost uniformly within 10 days, and not exceeding 21 days | From 7 days after exposure to 3 weeks after onset of typical paroxysms. |

\* Usual limits.   † Usually precipitated by a previous infection.

# Gestation, Incubation and Longevity of Certain Animals

*Source:* T. Donald Carter, American Museum of Natural History.

| Animal | Gestation and incubation, in days & (average) | Longevity, in years & (record exceptions) | Animal | Gestation and incubation, in days & (average) | Longevity, in years & (record exceptions) |
|---|---|---|---|---|---|
| Ass...................... | 340–385 | 18–20 (46) | Kangaroo............. | c. 39 | 10–12 (16) |
| Bear..................... | 180–240* | 15–20 (34) | Lion.................. | 105–111 | 10 (29) |
| Cat...................... | 52–65 | 10–12 (21) | Mare................. | 304–419 (336) | 20–25 (50+) |
| Chicken.................. | 21 | 7–8 (14) | Monkey............... | 149–179* (164) | 12–15* (29) |
| Cow..................... | c. 280 | 9–12 (25) | Mouse................ | 19–31* | 1–3 (4) |
| Deer.................... | 140–250 | 10–15 (26) | Parakeet (Budgerigar). | 17–20 (18) | 8 (12+) |
| Dog..................... | 55–70 (63) | 10–12 (24) | Pigeon............... | 18 | 10–12 (39) |
| Duck.................... | 21–35* (28) | 10 (15) | Rabbit............... | 27–36 (31) | 6–8 (15) |
| Elephant................ | 515–760* (628) | 30–40 (98) | Rat.................. | 21–30 (22) | 3 (5) |
| Ewe..................... | 121–180* | 12 (16) | Sow.................. | 101–130 (115) | 10 (22) |
| Goat.................... | 135–163 (150) | 12 (17) | Squirrel............. | 28–35 | 8–9 (15) |
| Groundhog.............. | 28–35 | 4–7 | Vixen (fox)........... | 51–60 | 8–10 (14) |
| Guinea pig............... | 63–71 | 3 (6) | Whale................ | 276–365* | ........ |
| Hamster, golden........ | 15–19 | 2 | Wolf................. | 63 | 10–12 (16) |
| Hippopotamus......... | 220–255 | 30 (49+) | Woman............... | 270+ or − | 72† |

\* Depending on kind.   † Latest life expectancy charts list this age.

# Calories and Vitamins of Selected Foods

*Source:* U. S. Department of Agriculture, Home and Garden Bulletin No. 72 (Sept. 1960).

| Food and (amount)[1] | Energy, calories | Vitamin A value, Int. Units | Vitamin B1 (thiamine), mg. | Vitamin B2 (riboflavin), mg. | Niacin, mg. | Vitamin C (ascorbic acid), mg. |
|---|---|---|---|---|---|---|
| Apples (1 medium R) | 70 | 50 | .04 | .02 | .1 | 3 |
| Bacon (2 sl. C[2]) | 95 | 0 | .08 | .05 | .8 | ... |
| Bananas (1 medium R) | 85 | 190 | .05 | .06 | .7 | 10 |
| Beans: snap, green (1 cup C[3]) | 25 | 830 | .09 | .12 | .6 | 18 |
| Beef: round, lean and fat (3 oz. C[4]) | 220 | 20 | .07 | .19 | 4.8 | ... |
| Beef: sirloin, lean and fat (3 oz. C[4]) | 330 | 50 | .05 | .16 | 4.0 | ... |
| Beets: diced (1 cup C) | 70 | 30 | .03 | .07 | .5 | 11 |
| Bread: rye (1 sl.) | 55 | 0 | .04 | .02 | .3 | 0 |
| Bread: white, enriched[5] (1 sl.) | 60 | trace | .06 | .04 | .5 | trace |
| Bread: wholewheat (1 sl.) | 55 | trace | .06 | .05 | .7 | trace |
| Butter (1 tbs.) | 100 | 460[6] | ... | ... | ... | 0 |
| Buttermilk: cultured[7] (1 cup) | 90 | 10 | .10 | .44 | .2 | 2 |
| Cabbage: finely shredded (1 cup R) | 25 | 80 | .06 | .05 | .3 | 50 |
| Carrots: diced (1 cup C) | 45 | 18,130 | .07 | .07 | .7 | 6 |
| Cheese: Swiss (1 oz.) | 105 | 320 | .01 | .06 | trace | 0 |
| Cheese: cottage, creamed[7] (1 cup) | 240 | 430 | .07 | .66 | .2 | 0 |
| Chicken: broiled[8] (3 oz. C) | 185 | 260 | .04 | .15 | 7.1 | ... |
| Chocolate: unsweetened (1 oz.) | 145 | 20 | .01 | .06 | .3 | 0 |
| Corn: sweet (1 ear C) | 65 | 300[9] | .09 | .08 | 1.1 | 6 |
| Crackers: graham (2 medium) | 55 | 0 | .04 | .02 | .2 | 0 |
| Cream: light, table or coffee (1 cup) | 525 | 2,140 | .07 | .35 | .1 | trace |
| Eggs (1 large R) | 80 | 590 | .05 | .15 | trace | 0 |
| Flour: wheat, enriched, sifted (1 cup) | 400 | 0 | .48 | .29 | 3.8 | 0 |
| Grapefruit: white (½ medium) | 50 | 10 | .05 | .02 | .2 | 50 |
| Ham: smoked, lean and fat (3 oz. C) | 290 | 0 | .39 | .15 | 3.1 | ... |
| Hamburger: broiled (3 oz. C) | 245 | 30 | .07 | .02 | 4.6 | ... |
| Honey: strained or extracted (1 tbs.) | 60 | 0 | trace | .01 | trace | 1 |
| Ice cream (⅛ qt. brick) | 145 | 370 | .03 | .13 | .1 | 1 |
| Lamb: leg roast, lean and fat (3 oz. C) | 235 | ... | .13 | .23 | 4.7 | ... |
| Lemons (1 medium) | 20 | 10 | .03 | .01 | .1 | 38 |
| Liver: beef, fried (2 oz. C) | 120 | 30,330 | .15 | 2.25 | 8.4 | 18 |
| Macaroni: enriched (1 cup C[10]) | 190 | 0 | .23 | .14 | 1.9 | 0 |
| Margarine[11] (1 tbs.) | 100 | 460 | ... | ... | ... | 0 |
| Milk: cow's, fluid, whole (1 cup) | 165 | 390 | .08 | .42 | .2 | 2 |
| Molasses: cane, light (1 tbs.) | 50 | ... | .01 | .01 | trace | ... |
| Oatmeal (1 cup C) | 150 | 0 | .22 | .05 | .4 | 0 |
| Oranges (1 medium) | 70 | 290 | .12 | .03 | .4 | 66 |
| Oysters: meat only (1 cup R) | 160 | 740 | .30 | .39 | 6.6 | ... |
| Peaches (1 medium R) | 35 | 1,320[12] | .02 | .05 | 1.0 | 7 |
| Peanut butter (1 tbs.) | 90 | 0 | .02 | .02 | 2.8 | 0 |
| Peanuts: roasted, chopped (1 tbs.) | 50 | 0 | .03 | .01 | 1.5 | 0 |
| Peas: green (1 cup C) | 110 | 1,150 | .40 | .22 | 3.7 | 24 |
| Plums (1 R) | 30 | 200 | .04 | .02 | .3 | 3 |
| Pork: roast, lean and fat (3 oz. C) | 310 | 0 | .78 | .22 | 4.7 | ... |
| Potatoes: baked[13] (1 medium C) | 90 | trace | .10 | .04 | 1.7 | 20 |
| Prunes: unsweetened (1 cup C) | 305 | 1,850 | .08 | .19 | 1.8 | 3 |
| Raisins (1 cup) | 460 | 30 | .18 | .13 | .9 | 2 |
| Rice: white (1 cup C) | 200 | 0 | .02 | .01 | .7 | 0 |
| Salmon: pink, canned (3 oz.) | 120 | 60 | .03 | .16 | 6.8 | ... |
| Sausage: pork, bulk, canned (4 oz.) | 340 | 0 | .23 | .27 | 3.4 | ... |
| Spaghetti: enriched (1 cup C) | 155 | 0 | .19 | .11 | 1.5 | 0 |
| Spinach (1 cup C) | 45 | 21,200 | .14 | .36 | 1.1 | 54 |
| Sugar: granulated (1 tbs.) | 50 | 0 | 0 | 0 | 0 | 0 |
| Sweet potatoes: baked[13] (1 medium C) | 155 | 8,970 | .10 | .07 | .7 | 24 |
| Tomatoes (1 medium R) | 30 | 1,640 | .08 | .06 | .8 | 35 |
| Turnips: diced (1 cup C) | 40 | trace | .06 | .09 | .6 | 28 |
| Veal: cutlet, broiled[8] (3 oz. C) | 185 | ... | .06 | .21 | 4.6 | ... |

[1] R—raw; C—cooked. [2] Broiled or fried crisp. [3] Cooked short time in small amount of water. [4] Broiled. [5] 1% to 2% nonfat dry milk. [6] Year-round average. [7] Made from skim milk. [8] Bone out. [9] Based on yellow corn; white corn contains only a trace. [10] 8 to 10 minutes. [11] Vitamin A added. [12] Yellow-fleshed varieties; value negligible in white-fleshed varieties. [13] Peeled after baking.

NOTE: Leaders (...) indicate that no basis could be found for imputing a value, although there was some reason to believe that a measurable amount of the constituent might be present.

# Atomic Energy

Just as the Space Age is said to have started with the orbiting of Sputnik I, the Atomic Age is said to have started with the explosion of a test bomb on July 16, 1945, near Alamogordo, N. Mex., at 5:30 A.M. local time. The bomb was placed on top of a steel tower, and observers were stationed in bunkers 10,000 yards away. The explosion vaporized the steel tower, produced a mushroom cloud rising to 40,000 ft., and melted the desert sand into glass for distances up to 800 yards from the tower.

The first operational use of an atom bomb took place only three weeks later, when a uranium bomb was exploded over Hiroshima, Japan, on Aug. 6, 1945. The bomb, cylindrical in shape, 10 ft. long with a diameter of 2 ft. 4 in., weighed about 9,000 lbs. Its explosive force was equal to 20,000 tons of TNT, hence the term "20 kiloton bomb." Three days later a plutonium bomb was exploded over Nagasaki.

Of course, the Atomic Age did not begin with the explosion of the test bomb at Alamogordo, just as the Space Age did not begin with the orbiting of the first artificial satellite. In both cases these visible feats were just experiments which proved the theory that had been built up patiently over decades.

At the turn of the century, scientists began to wonder whether the atoms of the chemical elements might not be composed of smaller particles. This was actually a contradiction in terms, because the Greek word *atomos*, from which the word *atom* was derived, meant "indivisible." But there were some indications of particles smaller than an atom—the electrons. In 1905, Albert Einstein suggested that matter might just be "condensed energy" and gave the conversion formula $E = mc^2$, in which $E$ represents the energy, $m$ the mass, and $c$ the velocity of light. If this formula was correct, a small piece of matter should represent enormous amounts of energy.

## FISSION AND FUSION

As is now generally known, atomic energy can be released in two ways. One is the *fission* of elements with very heavy atoms, such as uranium and plutonium, which will split when struck by a neutron, a subatomic particle. The splitting of the heavy atom releases more neutrons, which are then available to split other atoms—the so-called chain reaction. The other way of obtaining atomic energy is *fusion;* four light atoms (hydrogen) are fused together into the next heavier element (helium). The fusion reaction requires enormous heat and very high pressures. These pressures, coupled with very high temperatures, can most easily be produced by exploding a fission bomb, which is the reason why it is often said that a fission bomb is the trigger for a fusion (hydrogen) bomb.

Interestingly enough, the fusion reaction was discovered first, though only on paper. For the period from, say, 1910 to 1930, most physicists believed that the release of atomic energy, if it could be done, would be of no practical value. They asserted that causing the release would require more energy than could be obtained. Most astronomers, on the other hand, were convinced that atomic energy is released in the sun and the other stars because there was no other way to account for the energy the stars radiated into space. Trying to account for the energy radiated by the stars led to theoretical papers predicting what we now call the fusion reaction. At the time (1930), atomic fission was still unknown; it was discovered first by Fermi in 1934, and the process was repeated by Hahn and Strassmann in 1938. But nobody yet knew that the sudden bursts of energy observed in the experiments were due to the fission of the uranium-235 atom. This was established (by way of calculation) by Dr. Lise Meitner. Once it was known what happened, the way to a premeditated release of atomic energy was clear.

But nobody could be quite certain whether the release would take the form of an explosion or whether it would be slow enough to be used to generate power. American scientists proceeded under the assumption that the release would be sudden and violent (and the Alamogordo test proved them right), while Professor Heisenberg in Germany thought the slow release to be more likely, which is the reason why the Germans did not start a large-scale atomic energy project.

## INTERNATIONAL SCOREBOARD

The beneficial aspects of atomic energy lie in the field of research (physical, chemical, and medical); it provides both new materials and new techniques. Practical applications of the slow release of fission energy are the power reactors, including the power plants for seagoing vessels. The international scoreboard is this:

Fission bomb explosions: U.S., U.S.S.R., and France.

Fusion bomb explosions: U.S. and U.S.S.R.

Power reactors: U.S., U.S.S.R., U.K., France (Israel building, with French help).

Fusion reactors, experimental only: U.S., U.K., and probably U.S.S.R.

Atomic rocket propulsion, under development: U.S. and probably U.S.S.R.

(NOTE: The United Kingdom has the knowledge to build both fission and fusion bombs but has not actually done so.)

## Some Record Passages of Atlantic (Screw) Steamships since 1900
### WESTWARD PASSAGES

| Date | Ship and (flag*) | European port | Time D. | Time H. | Time M. | Speed knots | Nautical miles |
|---|---|---|---|---|---|---|---|
| 1900,01 | DEUTSCHLAND (G) | Southampton | 5 | 11 | 54 | 23.15 | 3,044 |
| 1910 | LUSITANIA† (B) | Queenstown | 4 | 11 | 40 | 25.88 | .... |
| 1929 | BREMEN† (G) | Cherbourg | 4 | 17 | 42 | 27.83 | .... |
| 1930 | EUROPA† (G) | Cherbourg | 4 | 17 | 6 | 27.91 | 3,157 |
| 1933 | REX† (I) | Gibraltar | 4 | 13 | 58 | 28.92 | 3,181 |
| 1935 | NORMANDIE† (F) | Bishop's Rock | 4 | 3 | 2 | 29.98 | 3,015 |
| 1938 | QUEEN MARY† (B) | Bishop's Rock | 3 | 21 | 48 | 30.99 | 2,907 |
| 1952 | UNITED STATES† (US) | Bishop's Rock | 3 | 12 | 12 | 34.51 | 2,906 |

### EASTWARD PASSAGES

| Date | Ship and (flag*) | European port | Time D. | Time H. | Time M. | Speed knots | Nautical miles |
|---|---|---|---|---|---|---|---|
| 1900,01 | DEUTSCHLAND† (G) | Eddystone Lt. | 5 | 7 | 38 | 23.51 | 2,082 |
| 1904 | KAISER WILHELM II† (G) | Plymouth | 5 | 8 | 16 | 23.58 | .... |
| 1910 | LUSITANIA† (B) | Queenstown | 4 | 15 | 50 | 25.57 | .... |
| 1929 | MAURETANIA† (B) | Plymouth | 4 | 17 | 50 | 27.22 | 3,098 |
| 1933 | BREMEN† (G) | Cherbourg | 4 | 16 | 15 | 28.51 | 3,199 |
| 1937 | NORMANDIE† (F) | Bishop's Rock | 4 | .. | 6 | 30.99 | 2,978 |
| 1938 | QUEEN MARY† (B) | Bishop's Rock | 3 | 20 | 42 | 31.69 | 2,938 |
| 1952 | UNITED STATES† (US) | Bishop's Rock | 3 | 10 | 40 | 35.59 | 3,144 |

\* (B)—British; (G)—German; (I)—Italian; (F)—French. † Vessels which have held the Blue Riband. *Source:* Maritime Adm.

## Largest Transatlantic Liners Calling at U. S. and Canadian Ports
*Source:* Trans-Atlantic Passenger Steamship Conference.

| Line | Name of ship | Flag | Length, ft. | Tonnage | Passengers |
|---|---|---|---|---|---|
| American Export............. | Constitution; Independence¹... | United States | 683 | 30,293 | 1,088 |
| Canadian Pacific............. | Empress of Canada............ | British | 650 | 27,300 | 1,048 |
| | Empress of Britain; Empress of England¹.................. | British | 640 | 25,500 | 1,050 |
| Cunard.................... | Queen Elizabeth.............. | British | 1,031 | 83,673 | 2,195 |
| | Queen Mary.................. | British | 1,019 | 81,237 | 1,902 |
| | Mauretania.................. | British | 772 | 35,674 | 1,131 |
| | Caronia..................... | British | 715 | 34,172 | 863 |
| | Sylvania.................... | British | 608 | 21,989 | 946 |
| | Carinthia................... | British | 608 | 21,947 | 936 |
| | Ivernia..................... | British | 608 | 21,717 | 951 |
| | Saxonia..................... | British | 608 | 21,637 | 939 |
| French..................... | France...................... | French | 1,035 | 68,000 | 2,000 |
| | Flandre..................... | French | 594 | 20,464 | 707 |
| Greek...................... | Olympia..................... | Liberian | 616 | 22,980 | 1,311 |
| | Arkadia..................... | Greek | 594 | 20,259 | 1,383 |
| Hamburg-Atlantic............ | Hanseatic................... | German | 672 | 30,029 | 1,276 |
| Holland-America............. | Rotterdam................... | Netherlands | 748 | 38,645 | 1,461 |
| | Nieuw Amsterdam............. | Netherlands | 759 | 36,667 | 1,249 |
| | Statendam................... | Netherlands | 642 | 24,294 | 951 |
| Home....................... | Homeric..................... | Panamanian | 639 | 25,487 | 1,228 |
| Italian.................... | Leonardo da Vinci............ | Italian | 763 | 33,500 | 1,326 |
| | Cristoforo Colombo........... | Italian | 695 | 29,191 | 1,191 |
| | Giulio Cesare; Augustus¹..... | Italian | 680 | 27,100 | 1,159 |
| | Vulcania.................... | Italian | 631 | 24,496 | 1,356 |
| | Saturnia.................... | Italian | 630 | 24,346 | 1,383 |
| National Hellenic American..... | Queen Frederica............. | Greek | 582 | 21,570 | 1,148 |
| North German Lloyd........... | Bremen..................... | German | 700 | 32,336 | 1,122 |
| Portuguese.................. | Santa Maria................. | Portuguese | 610 | 20,906 | 1,078 |
| Swedish American........... | Gripsholm................... | Swedish | 631 | 23,190 | 842 |
| | Kungsholm.................. | Swedish | 600 | 21,140 | 810 |
| United States............... | United States .............. | United States | 990 | 53,330 | 1,930 |
| | America..................... | United States | 723 | 33,961 | 1,046 |

¹ Sister ships.

# HEADLINE HISTORY OF OUR TIMES

## Based on Newspaper Accounts of Important Events

*The Headline History is based on the date when historical events came to the knowledge of the public through the newspapers. The events themselves may have occurred at a different date. For events previous to Headline History, see Page 260 for Historical and News Events from Ancient to Modern Times. This is compiled by the Encyclopaedia Britannica staff, and it begins with the Battle of Actium in 31 B.C. It includes a chronology of World War I.*

*See also Conferences and Treaties, pages 301–306.*

**1917**

*Mar. 8*—Russian Revolution begins.

*Apr. 6*—U. S. enters World War I.

**1918**

*Jan. 8*—Wilson's 14-point address to Congress calls for self-determination, removal of economic barriers, League of Nations.

*July 16*—Tsar Nicholas II and family shot.

*Nov. 11*—World War I ends.

**1919**

*June 28*—Versailles Treaty signed.

**1920**

*Jan. 10*—League of Nations officially inaugurated as Versailles Treaty goes into effect.

*Jan. 16*—Prohibition in U. S. goes into effect.

*Mar. 19*—Senate finally rejects Treaty of Versailles because of League of Nations proviso.

**1922**

*Oct. 27*—Mussolini marches on Rome.

**1923**

*Nov. 8-9*—Munich beer hall putsch led by Hitler put down; Hitler sentenced to 5 years, serves less than 1; writes *Mein Kampf* in jail.

**1925**

*July 10-21*—Scopes evolution trial held in Dayton, Tenn.

**1927**

*May 20-21*—Lindbergh flies solo across Atlantic.

*Aug. 23*—Sacco and Vanzetti executed.

*Nov.*—Trotsky expelled from Communist party.

**1929**

*Oct. 24*—Worst stock crash wipes out thousands of accounts.

**1931**

*Sept. 18-19*—Explosion on Manchurian railway serves as pretext for Japan to begin occupation of Manchuria.

**1932**

*Jan. 7*—Stimson Doctrine: U. S. will not recognize gains achieved by armed force; recognition of Manchukuo withheld.

*Jan. 28*—Japan begins invasion of international settlement of Shanghai.

*June 7*—Bonus March on Washington, D. C.

**1933**

*Jan. 30*—Hitler made Chancellor of Germany by Hindenburg.

*Mar. 5*—Reichstag elections give Nazis and Nationalist allies 52% of vote.

*Mar. 6*—Roosevelt proclaims bank holiday; embargoes gold.

*Mar. 12*—FDR's first "Fireside Chat."

*Mar. 23*—Reichstag gives Hitler blanket powers for 4 years; 94 Social Democrats opposed; many Social Democrats and all Communists under arrest or in hiding.

*Mar. 28*—Nazis begin systematic boycott of Jewish businessmen, doctors, lawyers.

*May 18*—Tennessee Valley Authority (TVA) established.

*June 16*—National Industrial Recovery Act (NIRA) signed. Declared unconstitutional May 27, 1935.

*Dec. 5*—Prohibition ends in U. S.

**1935**

*Mar. 16*—Hitler defies Versailles Treaty by re-establishing universal military training in Germany.

*Aug. 14*—Social Security Act signed; establishes old-age benefits and unemployment insurance. Upheld by Supreme Court May 24, 1937.

*Aug. 20*—Third International decides Russia will side with democracies against Fascist states.

*Sept. 15*—Nuremberg laws deprive Jews of citizenship and bar intermarriage.

*Oct. 3*—Italy invades Ethiopia.

*Oct. 7*—League of Nations condemns Italy.

## 1936

*Jan. 20*—George V dies; Prince of Wales becomes Edward VIII.

*Mar. 7*—Hitler sends German troops into Rhineland, defying Versailles Treaty; denounces Locarno Pact.

*July 17*—Spanish civil war begins; troops led by Gen. Francisco Franco revolt in Spanish Morocco; uprisings follow all over Spain.

*Aug. 19–23*—Zinoviev and Kamenev executed in Russia as collaborators with Trotsky and Nazi secret police.

*Oct. 1*—Franco named Chief of State by rebels; establishes capital at Burgos.

*Oct. 27*—Rome-Berlin Axis formed.

*Nov. 18*—Italy and Germany recognize Franco regime in Spain.

*Nov. 25*—Japan signs anti-Comintern treaty with Germany; Italy adheres Nov. 6, 1937.

*Dec. 1–23*—Buenos Aires conference: 21 American republics pledge to consult if peace is imperiled; no nation to interfere with another's domestic affairs.

*Dec. 11*—Edward VIII abdicates; his brother becomes George VI.

## 1937

*June 12*—Marshal Tukhachevsky and 7 generals executed in Russia for espionage and high treason.

## 1938

*Sept. 29–30*—Britain, France, Italy, Germany in parley at Munich agree to dismemberment of Czechoslovakia; Chamberlain returns to London with "peace in our time."

## 1939

*Mar. 15*—Hitler enters Prague.

*Apr. 28*—Hitler rebuffs FDR's peace plea in Polish quarrel.

*Aug. 24*—Germany and Russia sign 10-year nonaggression pact.

*Sept. 1*—Germany invades Poland and annexes Danzig; Britain and France give Hitler ultimatum.

*Sept. 3*—Britain and France declare war.

*Sept. 28*—Poland partitioned by Germany and Russia.

## 1940

*May 10*—Nazis invade Netherlands, Belgium, Luxemburg.
*May 10*—Chamberlain resigns as Prime Minister; Churchill takes over.

*May 12*—Germans cross French frontier.

*May 26–June 3*—Dunkerque evacuation:

about 335,000 out of 400,000 Allied soldiers rescued from Belgium by civilian and naval craft from Britain.

*June 10*—Italy declares war on France and Britain; invades France.

*June 14*—Germans enter Paris; city undefended.

*June 22*—France and Germany sign armistice at Compiègne.

*Nov. 14*—Nazis bomb Coventry.

## 1941

*Apr. 17*—Yugoslavia surrenders; Gen. Mikhailović continues guerrilla warfare; Tito leads left-wing guerrillas.

*Apr. 27*—Nazi tanks enter Athens; remnants of British army quit Greece.

*June 22*—Hitler attacks Russia.

*Aug. 14*—Atlantic Charter: FDR and Churchill agree on war aims.

*Dec. 7*—Japan attacks Pearl Harbor, Philippines, Guam, forcing U. S. into war Dec. 8; Pacific Fleet crippled.

*Dec. 8*—U. S. and Britain declare war on Japan.

*Dec. 11*—Germany and Italy declare war on U. S.; Congress declares war on those countries.

## 1942

*Feb. 15*—British surrender Singapore.

*Apr. 9*—U. S. forces on Bataan surrender.

*Nov. 8*—U. S. and Britain land great army in French North Africa.

## 1943

*Jan. 14–24*—Casablanca Conference: Churchill and FDR agree on unconditional-surrender goal.

*Feb. 1–2*—German 6th Army surrenders at Stalingrad; turning point of war in Russia.

*May 12*—Remnants of Nazis trapped on Cape Bon, ending war in Africa.

*June 10*—FDR signs withholding tax.

*July 25*—Mussolini deposed; Badoglio is Premier.

*Sept. 3*—Allied troops land on Italian mainland.

*Sept. 8*—Italy surrenders.

*Sept. 10*—Nazis seize Rome.

*Nov. 22–26*—Cairo Conference: FDR, Churchill, Chiang-Kai-shek pledge defeat of Japan, free Korea.

*Nov. 28–Dec. 1*—Teheran Conference: FDR, Churchill, Stalin agree on invasion plans.

## 1944

*June 6*—D-Day: Allies launch Normandy invasion.

*July 20*—Hitler wounded in bomb plot.

*Aug. 25*—Paris liberated.

*Oct. 20*—Americans invade Philippines.

*Dec. 16*—Germans launch counteroffensive in Belgium (Battle of Bulge).

## 1945

*Feb. 11*—Yalta Agreement signed by FDR, Churchill and Stalin.

*Apr. 12*—FDR dies; Truman is President.

*May 1*—Adm. Doenitz takes command in Germany; death of Hitler announced.

*May 2*—Berlin falls.

*May 7*—V-E Day: Germany signs unconditional surrender terms at Reims.

*July 17-Aug. 2*—Potsdam Conference: Truman, Churchill (Attlee after July 28), Stalin establish council of foreign ministers to prepare peace treaties; plan German postwar government and reparations.

*Aug. 6*—A-bomb blasts Hiroshima.

*Aug. 8*—Russia declares war on Japan.

*Aug. 9*—Nagasaki hit by A-bomb.

*Aug. 14*—Japan surrenders.

*Sept. 2*—Japanese sign surrender terms aboard battleship *Missouri* (V-J Day).

*Oct. 24*—U. N. officially established.

*Nov. 15*—Truman, Attlee and Mackenzie King decide in Washington Conference that A-bomb secrets will not be shared until U. N. adopts control plan.

*Dec. 27*—Moscow Conference, attended by Byrnes, Molotov and Bevin, makes preliminary plans for atomic-energy control, peace treaties and Korea.

## 1946

*Jan. 10*—1st meeting of U. N. General Assembly opens in London.

*Apr. 8-18*—Final Assembly session at Geneva dissolves League of Nations.

*Apr. 29*—U. S. proposes treaty with Britain, Russia and France to keep Germany disarmed 25 years; Russia cool to idea.

*May 31*—U. S. and Britain demand free elections in Rumania.

*Oct. 1*—Verdict in Nuremberg war trial: 12 Nazi leaders (including 1 tried in absentia) sentenced to hang; 7 imprisoned; 3 acquitted.

*Oct. 15*—Goering commits suicide a few hours before 10 other Nazis are executed Oct. 16.

## 1947

*Jan. 28*—U. S. rebukes Polish Communists for rigging election.

*Feb. 10*—Peace treaties for Italy, Rumania, Bulgaria, Hungary, Finland signed in Paris.

*Mar. 4*—Russia rejects U. S. plan for U. N. atomic-energy control.

*Mar. 12*—Truman asks Congress for $400 million to save Greece and Turkey from Communist expansion (Truman Doctrine).

*July 12-15*—16 nations meet in Paris to study Marshall Plan (Russia and 8 others stay away).

*Aug. 1*—Security Council calls on Dutch and Indonesians to cease hostilities.

*Aug. 15*—India freed by Britain.

*Oct. 5*—Moscow announces formation of new 9-nation Communist Information Bureau (Cominform).

*Nov. 14*—General Assembly votes commission to set up free government for all of Korea.

## 1948

*Jan. 17*—U. N. Good Offices Commission effects truce in Indonesia.

*Jan. 30*—Gandhi assassinated.

*Feb. 23-25*—Communists seize power in Czechoslovakia.

*Apr. 21*—Security Council votes plebiscite in Kashmir to decide whether province goes to India or Pakistan; both sides object.

*May 14*—Nation of Israel proclaimed; British end mandate at midnight; Arab armies attack.

*June 11*—U. N. appeal brings temporary truce in Palestine.

*June 18*—Russia stops traffic between Berlin and Western occupation zones in Germany.

*June 21*—Berlin airlift begins; ends May 12, 1949.

*June 22*—Russian veto prevents Security Council from approving atomic-control plan favored by majority.

*June 28*—Stalin and Tito break.

*Aug. 15*—Independent Republic of Korea is proclaimed, following election supervised by U. N.

*Nov. 4*—General Assembly approves U. S.-sponsored atomic control plan.

*Nov. 12*—Verdict in Japanese war trial: Tojo and 6 others sentenced to hang (hanged Dec. 23); 18 imprisoned.

## 1949

*Jan. 7*—Cease-fire in Palestine.

*Jan. 20*—Truman proposes Point 4 Program to help world's backward areas.

*Feb. 8*—Cardinal Mindszenty sentenced in Hungary to life imprisonment.

*Feb. 24*—Israel signs armistice with Egypt.

*Apr. 4*—Start of NATO; treaty signed by 12 nations.

*May 11*—U. N. admits Israel.

*Sept. 21*—German Federal Republic (West Germany) established.

*Sept. 24*—Truman discloses Russia has set off atomic explosion.

## 1950

*Jan. 13*—Russia boycotts Security Council (until Aug. 1) because Red China was refused admittance to U. N.

*Jan. 31*—Truman orders development of hydrogen bomb.

*June 25*—North Koreans cross 38th parallel to invade South Korea.

*June 27*—Truman orders U. S. air and sea aid to South Koreans.

*June 27*—Security Council (at that time boycotted by Russia) calls on U. N. members to help repel North Korean aggression.

*Oct. 7*—U. S. 1st Cavalry makes 1st U. S. crossing of 38th parallel.

*Nov. 20*—U. S. 7th Division unit reaches Manchurian border.

## 1951

*Feb. 1*—General Assembly condemns (44–7) Red China as an aggressor.

*Mar. 19*—6 nations initial Schuman Plan to pool European coal and steel market. (In effect Feb. 10, 1953.)

*Apr. 11*—Truman removes MacArthur from all commands.

*June 23*—Russia proposes truce.

*July 10*—Truce talks begin in Korea.

*Sept. 8*—Japanese peace treaty signed in San Francisco by 49 nations.

## 1952

*Feb. 6*—George VI dies; his daughter becomes Elizabeth II.

*Feb. 20–25*—NATO conference approves European Army; sets goal of 50 divisions and 4,000 planes by end of 1952.

*May 26*—Western Allies and West Germany sign peace contract at Bonn.

## 1953

*Mar. 5*—Stalin dies.

*Mar. 6*—Malenkov becomes Soviet Premier; Beria is Minister of Interior; Molotov is Foreign Minister.

*Apr. 10*—Dag Hammarskjöld begins term as U. N. Secretary General.

*June 8*—Agreement on POWs reached at Panmunjom; India to head 5-nation commission for custodianship of POWs refusing repatriation.

*June 17*—East Berliners rise against Communist rule; quelled by tanks.

*June 18–21*—Pres. Rhee frees 27,000 anti-Red POWs in defiance of U. N.-

Red prisoner agreement; truce talks halted June 20.

*July 10*—Truce talks are resumed.

*July 27*—Korean armistice signed.

*Aug. 20*—Moscow announces explosion of hydrogen bomb.

## 1954

*Jan. 21*—1st atomic-powered submarine, *Nautilus,* launched at Groton, Conn.

*Jan. 26*—U. S. Senate ratifies (81–6) mutual security treaty with Republic of Korea.

*May 7*—Dienbienphu falls to Indo-China Red rebels.

*July 21*—Indo-China truce signed at Geneva conference; Reds get half of Vietnam.

*Sept. 6*—Eisenhower launches world atomic pool without Russia.

*Sept. 8*—8-nation Southeast Asia defense treaty signed at Manila.

*Oct. 23*—West Germany is granted sovereignty and is admitted to NATO and Western European Union.

## 1955

*Jan. 17*—Submarine *Nautilus* goes to sea under atomic power.

*Apr. 5*—Churchill resigns; Eden succeeds him Apr. 6.

*Apr. 12*—Scientists OK Salk vaccine.

*May 31*—Supreme Court leaves school desegregation to regional Federal courts.

*July 16*—Hungary releases Cardinal Mindszenty. (See Feb. 8, 1949.)

*Sept. 19*—Argentina ousts Perón.

*Sept. 24*—Pres. Eisenhower suffers coronary thrombosis in Denver.

*Sept. 27*—Egypt to buy Soviet arms.

## 1956

*Feb. 22*—U. S. releases 40,000 kg. of Uranium 235 (worth $1 million) for peaceful atomic power at home and abroad.

*Mar. 9*—Archbishop Makarios of Cyprus is sent into exile by Britain.

*Mar. 20*—Khrushchev calls Stalin murderer. (Speech made Feb. 24.)

*Apr. 7*—Spain proclaims Spanish Morocco independent after 44 years.

*May 21*—First aerial H-bomb tested over Namu I., Bikini Atoll (10-million tons TNT equivalent).

*June 9*—Eisenhower undergoes operation to relieve blockage of small intestine due to ileitis; physicians say he will be physically fit to run for re-election.

*June 12*—Scientists report radiation is peril to future of race.

*June 28–30*—Workers' uprising against Communist rule in Poznan, Poland is crushed by tanks.

*July 19*—U. S. withdraws its offer to help Egypt build Aswan dam on Nile.

*July 26*—Egypt announces seizure of Suez Canal control.

*Sept. 29*—France and Germany agree that the Saar will return to Germany Jan. 1.

*Oct. 19*—Japan and Russia sign agreement ending technical state of war.

*Oct. 21*—Polish Communists restore Wladyslaw Gomulka to power, as party First Secretary.

*Oct. 24*—Soviet troops and tanks in Hungary fight anti-Communist rebellion, Imre Nagy is new premier.

*Oct. 26*—82 nations agree at U. N. on new International Atomic Energy Agency for peaceful use of atom. U. S. offers it 11,000 lb. of Uranium 235.

*Oct. 29*—Israel launches attack on Egypt's Sinai Peninsula and drives toward Suez Canal.

*Oct. 31*—British air attacks begin in Egypt.

*Nov. 4*—U. N. votes to organize its police force to restore peace to Egypt.

*Nov. 5*—British and French invade Egypt at Port Said.

*Nov. 6*—British, French cease fire at Port Said and halt Suez advance.

*Nov. 23*—Russians kidnap Hungary's Premier Imre Nagy and replace him with Janos Kadar.

*Dec. 12*—U. N. General Assembly condemns Russia for aggression in Hungary. Vote: 55 yes, 8 no, with 13 abstaining.

*Dec. 22*—Anglo-French forces withdraw from Egypt.

## 1957

*Jan. 5*—Eisenhower asks special joint session of Congress for power to use military and economic aid in Middle East—Eisenhower Doctrine.

*Jan. 9*—Prime Minister Anthony Eden resigns after only 21 months in office; succeeded by Harold Macmillan, Chancellor of Exchequer, on Jan. 10.

*Mar. 5*—Eisenhower Doctrine for Mideast passes Senate, 72–19; House completes Congressional approval, 350–60, on Mar. 7.

*Mar. 6*—New nation, Ghana, formerly British colony in Africa known as Gold Coast, attains full independence.

*June 24*—Scientists tell Eisenhower we now can produce nuclear weapons 95% free of radioactivity.

*Aug. 31*—Federation of Malaya comes into existence as newest free nation in world.

*Sept. 24*—Eisenhower sends Army troops to Little Rock, Ark., to quell mob and protect school integration.

*Nov. 3*—Soviet Russia launches earth satellite with dog in it.

*Nov. 26*—Eisenhower suffers slight stroke.

## 1958

*Jan. 31*—Army's Jupiter-C rocket fires first U. S. earth satellite, Explorer I, into orbit.

*Feb. 1*—Egypt and Syria merge into one nation—United Arab Republic.

*Mar. 27*—Khrushchev becomes Premier of Soviet Union as Bulganin resigns.

*Mar. 31*—Soviet government announces suspension of nuclear-weapons tests; demands U. S. and Britain also stop.

*June 30*—Congress votes Alaska into Union as 49th state.

*July 15*—Eisenhower orders U. S. Marines into Lebanon at request of Pres. Chamoun, who fears overthrow.

*Aug. 8*—U. S. atomic submarine *Nautilus* crosses top of world under North Pole.

*Aug. 22*—Eisenhower offers 1-year suspension of U. S. nuclear-arms tests.

*Sept. 12*—U. S. Supreme Court orders immediate racial integration in Little Rock high school; Gov. Faubus orders all 4 high schools closed.

*Sept. 22*—Sherman Adams resigns as Assistant to President, denying any wrong-doing.

*Oct. 9*—Pope Pius XII dies at 82.

*Oct. 28*—Cardinal Roncalli becomes Pope John XXIII.

## 1959

*Jan. 1*—President Batista resigns and flees Cuba. Castro's revolt wins.

*Jan. 8*—De Gaulle takes office as President of France for 7 years.

*Feb. 11*—Greece and Turkey agree on independence for Cyprus after long dispute.

*Feb. 27*—Dave Beck, former boss of Teamsters' Union, sentenced to 5 years in prison, fined $60,000 for income tax evasion.

*Mar. 12*—Congress votes admission of Hawaii as 50th state.

*Apr. 2*—Tibet's Dalai Lama escapes into India.

*Apr. 18*—Christian A. Herter named Secretary of State to succeed cancer-stricken John Foster Dulles, who resigned.

*Apr. 25*—St. Lawrence Seaway opens, allowing ocean ships to go into Midwest.

*June 23*—British set atom spy Klaus Fuchs free after 9 years in prison and put him on plane for East Germany.

*July 5*—France gives Saar completely back to Germany, ending economic controls.

*Aug. 12*—Little Rock public high schools reopen at court order, admitting 5 Negroes; police use clubs on protesting mob.

*Sept. 14*—Soviet rocket hits moon in 35-hour trip over 236,875 miles.

*Sept. 16*—Pres. de Gaulle tells Algeria it can vote on its destiny 4 years after rebellion ceases.

*Sept. 18*—Khrushchev, speaking to U.N. General Assembly, asks disarmament of all nations within 4 years.

*Nov. 2*—Charles Van Doren confesses fake on TV "21".

*Nov. 7*—Supreme Court upholds Taft-Hartley law injunction halting 116-day steel strike for 80 days.

*Dec. 3*—Eisenhower flies to Europe, Asia, Africa on 11-nation goodwill trip.

*Dec. 26*—Gov. Nelson A. Rockefeller withdraws from Republican Presidential race.

## 1960

*Jan. 19*—U. S. and Japan sign treaty of alliance and mutual security.

*Jan. 23*—Navy bathyscaph sets world record, diving with 2 men to 7 mi. under Pacific Ocean.

*Feb. 13*—France explodes its first atomic device, in Sahara.

*Feb. 19*—Son born to Queen Elizabeth II of Britain; her third child.

*Mar. 15*—East-West disarmament talks renewed in Geneva after 2½-year gap.

*Mar. 30*—South Africa under martial law as 30,000 Negroes demonstrate at Capetown.

*Apr. 14*—Polaris missile fired from under ocean for first time, in California.

*Apr. 26*—President Syngman Rhee of South Korea resigns after riots.

*May 2*—Caryl Chessman executed in California; fought off death sentence for 12 years.

*May 7*—U. S. admits our U-2 plane downed deep in U.S.S.R. was on spy mission.

*May 16*—Khrushchev kills Paris summit conference because of U-2 incident; tells Eisenhower not to visit Soviet Union.

*May 29*—Syngman Rhee, ousted President of South Korea, flies into exile in Hawaii.

*May 31*—Supreme Court awards states offshore oil rights, favoring Texas and Florida.

*July 7*—Eisenhower bars almost all remaining Cuban sugar imports.

*July 11*—Moscow admits having shot down U. S. reconnaissance plane RB-47 over Barents Sea on July 1.

*July 12*—U. S. says plane was 30 mi. away from U.S.S.R.

*July 14*—U.N. votes to send troops to Republic of Congo (formerly Belgian) to end chaos.

*July 20*—First 2 Polaris missiles launched from atomic submarine beneath sea, off Cape Canaveral, Fla.

*Aug. 7*—Cuba begins confiscation of $770 million of U. S. property.

*Aug. 19*—Russia sentences U-2 American spy flyer, Francis Gary Powers, to 10 years.

*Aug. 20*—Organization of American States votes diplomatic break with Dominican Republic under Trujillo dictatorship.

*Sept. 6*—2 U. S. defectors from National Security Agency—Bernon F. Mitchell, 31, and William H. Martin, 29—turn up in Moscow.

*Sept. 12*—Hurricane Donna hits Long Island and New England; leaves 152 dead. Called costliest ever; losses $29 million.

*Sept. 22*—U.N. admits 13 new members from Africa, plus Cyprus.

*Sept. 26*—Kennedy and Nixon clash in first presidential TV debate.

*Oct. 3*—Eisenhower becomes oldest U. S. President ever; 11 days short of 70th birthday.

*Oct. 13*—Khrushchev ends 25-day visit to U. S.

*Oct. 25*—Rev. Martin Luther King, Negro integration leader, sentenced to 4 months in jail for lacking driver license in Georgia.

*Oct. 29*—U.N. decides to send 15-man Asian-African conciliation team to Congo.

*Dec. 16*—Airliners collide over New York City; 132 die.

*Dec. 19*—50 die in fire on unfinished aircraft carrier *Constellation* in Brooklyn Navy Yard.

**(For 1961, see front of book.)**

# U. S. POSTWAR TREATIES

## Organization of American States (OAS) and the Rio Treaty

In Sept., 1947, eighteen Latin American countries (Nicaragua and Ecuador were excluded) and the United States signed at Rio de Janeiro the Rio Treaty under which all signatories agreed to protect against aggression every state in the Western Hemisphere. In Apr., 1948, all the American nations (twenty-one—Canada not included) joined in the Organization of American States (OAS) to implement the Rio Treaty and form a collective security system.

## North Atlantic Treaty Organization (NATO)

### (Formed: April 4, 1949)

Members: United States, Canada, Iceland, Norway, Great Britain, Netherlands, Denmark, Belgium, Luxemburg, Portugal, France, Italy, Greece, Turkey, West Germany

In 1948, the United States government began talks with the signers of the Brussels Pact and Canada concerning the formation of a regional defense treaty in the North Atlantic area. It represented the first important security pact with European nations since the French Alliance of 1778 and marked the first time in United States history that the United States pledged itself to go to war in support of allies before the actual outbreak of hostilities. The U. S. Senate ratified the treaty July 21, 1949.

The United States, acting under Article 3 of the Treaty, began a program of military assistance which at the end of the fiscal year 1959 amounted to over $10 billion. Roughly half of all United States military assistance has gone to members of NATO. However, approximately 85% of NATO's military preparation has come from the European countries themselves.

NATO now united most of the countries of the Atlantic community plus Greece, Turkey, and West Germany, which were added to the original membership. Its organization comprises the top foreign, economic, defense, and financial ministers of the member countries. The military responsibilities of NATO are divided into two major commands—SHAPE for Europe and SACLANT for the Atlantic Ocean area.

*Following are key quotations from the North Atlantic Treaty text. (Complete text in 1960 Information Please Almanac.)*

From Article 1: "The Parties undertake . . . to refrain in their international relations from the threat or use of force in any manner inconsistent with the purposes of the United Nations."

From Article 2: "The Parties . . . will seek to eliminate conflict in their international economic policies and will encourage economic collaboration between any or all of them."

From Article 5: "The Parties agree that an armed attack against one or more of them in Europe or North America shall be considered an attack against them all; and consequently they agree that, if such an armed attack occurs, each of them, in exercise of the right of individual or collective self-defense recognized by Article 51 of the Charter of the United Nations, will assist the Party or Parties so attacked by taking forthwith, individually and in concert with other Parties, such action as it deems necessary, including the use of armed force, to restore and maintain the security of the North Atlantic area."

From Article 9: "The Parties hereby establish a council, on which each of them shall be represented, to consider matters concerning the implementation of this Treaty."

## Tripartite Security Treaty

### (United States, Australia, New Zealand)

**Major provisions of the Tripartite agreement signed on Sept. 1, 1951, at San Francisco:**

1. The parties undertake to settle by peaceful means any international disputes in which they may be involved.

2. The parties will maintain and develop their individual and collective capacity to resist armed attack.

3. The parties will consult together whenever the territorial integrity, political independence or security of any of the parties is threatened in the Pacific.

4. Each party recognizes that an armed attack in the Pacific area on either of the other parties would be dangerous to its own peace and safety.

5. The parties hereby establish a council, consisting of their foreign ministers or their deputies, to consider matters concerning the implementation of this treaty.

6. This treaty shall remain in force indefinitely.

---

A Defense Treaty similar in its provisions to the Tripartite Security Treaty was signed by the U. S. and the Philippines in Washington, D. C., Aug. 30, 1951.

## Japanese Peace Treaty

The Japanese Peace Treaty was signed at San Francisco on September 8, 1951, by 49 nations; the U.S.S.R., Poland, and Czechoslovakia were present but refused to sign. Among the major provisions of the treaty are the following:

**Peace:** The state of war between Japan and the Allies is terminated.

**Sovereignty:** Japan's full sovereignty is recognized as is its right to apply for U. N. membership.

**Territory:** Japan recognizes the independence of Korea; renounces all rights, titles, or claims to Formosa, the Pescadores, the Kuriles, Sakhalin, the Pacific islands formerly under mandate to Japan, the Antarctic area, Spratly Island, and the Paracels.

Japan agrees to U. N. trusteeship over the Ryukyu and Daito Islands, the Bonins, Rosario Island, the Volcano Islands, Parece Vela, and Marcus Island. Disposition of Japanese property on these islands is to be negotiated by Japan and the administering authorities.

**Security:** Japan agrees to settle its international disputes peaceably, to refrain from the threat of or the use of force and to abide by the principles of the U. N.

All occupation forces are to be withdrawn as soon as possible but not later than 90 days after a majority of the signatory countries have given notice of ratification of this treaty. Nothing in this provision shall, however, prevent the stationing or retention of foreign armed forces in Japanese territory by agreement with one or more of the Allies.

**Political-Economic Clauses:** Japan may enter into fisheries treaties; may negotiate most-favored-nation trade and maritime treaties with the Allies; renounces all special rights and interests in China.

Japan accepts the judgments of the International Military Tribunal and Allied War Crimes Courts.

**Claims and Property:** Japan recognizes its responsibility to pay reparations but the Allies recognize its limited economic capacity; therefore, Japan shall pay through goods to be manufactured in Japan from raw materials provided by the victimized nations and by services. The Allies may retain certain properties seized from Japan but require the latter to return their properties within 6 months. Japan recognizes Allied industrial, literary, and artistic property rights. It agrees to indemnify prisoners of war who suffered unduly but renounces similar claims against the Allies.

**Settlement of Disputes:** Any disagreements arising out of the interpretation of this treaty and not otherwise settled shall be submitted to the International Court of Justice.

## Anzus Treaty
### (Effective 1952)

**Members:** Australia, New Zealand, United States

This security treaty involves a commitment less comprehensive than that of NATO and closer to the SEATO obligations. Article 3 stipulates that the parties will consult whenever in the opinion of any of them the territorial integrity, political independence, or security of any of the parties is threatened in the Pacific. Under Article 4, each party recognizes that an armed attack in the Pacific area on any of the parties would be considered dangerous to its own peace and safety, and agrees to act to meet the common danger in accordance with its constitutional processes.

## Southeast Asia Treaty Organization (SEATO)
### (Signed: Sept., 1954)

**Members:** United States, Great Britain, France, Australia, New Zealand, Pakistan, Thailand, Philippines

Weaker than NATO, SEATO does not include rigid provisions for collective defense but states that armed attack on any member would be regarded as a threat to safety of the others. SEATO represents the United States' desire to counterbalance the power of Communist China. Yet three major non-Communist countries—Indonesia, Burma, and India—are not members.

## Central Treaty Organization (CENTO) (Formerly Baghdad Pact)
### (Signed: Nov., 1955)

**Members:** Turkey, Iran, Great Britain, Pakistan, United States. (Another original member, Iraq, withdrew in Mar., 1959. The U. S. gradually became a member.)

Although it inspired the pact, the U. S. did not become a full member until July 28, 1958, shortly after the revolutionary coup in Iraq, which threatened the collapse of the Baghdad Pact. The pact's purpose continues to be that of providing a defense shield on the northern tier of the Middle East against Soviet penetration. The headquarters were transferred in Oct., 1958, from Baghdad to Ankara, and the name was changed from Baghdad Pact to Central Treaty Organization in Aug., 1959.

## U. S.–Japanese Treaty
(Signed: Jan. 19, 1960)

This treaty affirms the obligation of the parties to settle international differences in a manner consistent with the U.N. Charter, to strengthen economic and other ties between the two countries, and to resist armed attack individually and by mutual assistance.

### Summary of Major Provisions

Article I: The Parties undertake to settle by peaceful means any international disputes in which they may be involved. They will endeavor to strengthen the United Nations so that its mission of peace may be discharged more effectively.

Article II: They will seek to eliminate conflict and encourage collaboration in their economic policies.

Article III: They will maintain and develop, subject to their constitutional provisions, their capacities to resist attack.

Article IV: They will consult together whenever the security of Japan or the Far East is threatened.

Article V: Each Party recognizes that an armed attack against either in the territories under the administration of Japan would be dangerous to its own peace and declares that it would meet the common danger in accordance with its constitution.

Such measures shall be reported to the Security Council and be terminated when the Security Council has taken the measures necessary to restore international peace and security.

Article VI: For the security of Japan and the Far East, the United States is granted the use by its land, air, and naval forces of facilities and areas in Japan.

Article VII: This Treaty does not affect the rights and obligations of the Parties under the Charter of the United Nations or the responsibility of the United Nations for the maintenance of international peace and security.

Article X: After this Treaty has been in force for ten years, either Party may give notice to the other Party of its intention to terminate the Treaty, in which case it shall terminate one year later.

# MAJOR U. S. POSTWAR POLICY DECISIONS

## Truman Doctrine

President Truman took a decisive step in March, 1947, when he obtained from Congress authorization to spend $400 million to aid Greece and Turkey. His move followed directly on withdrawal of aid to those countries by Great Britain, whose resources were dwindling. Greece suffered from Communist guerrilla infiltration; Turkey lived under threat of Russia's constant pressures. Besides the appropriation, Congress authorized shipment of military equipment and dispatch of a military and technical mission. By 1950, the Red guerrillas had given up the struggle, and in Turkey results were much more immediately successful. The Truman Doctrine is regarded as the first significant experiment in the policy of "containment," although it preceded by four months the intellectual presentation of this policy by George Kennan.

## The Marshall Plan

After World War II, recovery programs among the nations of Europe, as well as contributions from the United States, were un-co-ordinated. In June, 1947, Gen. George C. Marshall, then Secretary of State, asserted the need for integrated recovery efforts against "hunger, poverty, desperation, and chaos." Congress, in April,

1948, appropriated $5.4 billion. The United States established the Economic Cooperation Administration while European nations set up the Organization for European Economic Administration. Under a system of counterpart funds, each participating government set aside, in its own currency, amounts matching the aid it received. As the European Recovery Program, Marshall Plan aid was economic in its early stages but with the worsening international situation—particularly after Korea—emphasis was shifted to rearmament. When ERP ended in Dec., 1951, a year ahead of schedule, it had cost $11 billion, but substantial amounts had been committed to collateral military ventures.

## Eisenhower Doctrine

In January, 1957, President Eisenhower, noting the unsettled state of the Middle East, asked authority from Congress to co-operate with any nation in that area for economic development, to undertake programs of military assistance for such nations which desired it and to use U. S. armed forces to protect Mid-East countries "requesting such aid" against "overt armed aggression from any nation controlled by international communism." In March, Congress authorized expenditures up to $200 million for 1957. Anti-Communist declarations were immediately forthcoming from Lebanon and Libya; and, more important, King Hussein of Jordan took a strong stand against the leftist drift in his country. Arms also were shipped to the area to counter the build-up of Soviet military equipment in Syria.

# ALLIED POLICY DECISIONS OF WORLD WAR II

## The Cairo Conference

**Important provisions of the Conference, which was held Nov. 22-26, 1943:**

The several military missions have agreed upon future military operations against Japan. The Three Great Allies expressed their resolve to bring unrelenting pressure against their brutal enemies by sea, land, and air. This pressure is already rising.

The Three Great Allies are fighting this war to restrain and punish the aggression of Japan. They covet no gain for themselves and have no thought of territorial expansion. It is their purpose that Japan shall be stripped of all the islands in the Pacific which she has seized or occupied since the beginning of the first World War in 1914, and that all the territories Japan has stolen from the Chinese, such as Manchuria, Formosa, and the Pescadores, shall be restored to the Republic of China. Japan will also be expelled from all other territories which she has taken by violence and greed. The aforesaid Three Great Powers, mindful of the enslavement of the people of Korea, are determined that in due course Korea shall become free and independent.

With these objectives in view the three Allies, in harmony with those of the United Nations at war with Japan, will continue to persevere in the serious and prolonged operations necessary to procure the unconditional surrender of Japan.

## The Teheran Conference

### (Nov. 28–Dec. 1, 1943)

The President of the United States of America, the Premier of the Union of Soviet Socialist Republics, and the Prime Minister of the United Kingdom have consulted with each other and, with the Prime Minister of Iran, desire to declare the mutual agreement of their three Governments regarding relations with Iran.

The Governments of the United States of America, the Union of Soviet Socialist Republics, and the United Kingdom recognize the assistance which Iran has given in the prosecution of the war against the common enemy, particularly by facilitating transportation of supplies from overseas to the Soviet Union. The three Governments realize that the war has caused special economic difficulties for Iran and they are agreed that they will continue to make available to the Government of Iran such economic assistance as may be possible, having regard to the heavy demands made upon them by their worldwide military operations and to the worldwide shortage of transport, raw materials, and supplies for civilian consumption.

With respect to the post-war period, the Governments of the United States of America, the Union of Soviet Socialist Republics, and the United Kingdom are in accord with the Government of Iran that any economic problem confronting Iran at the close of hostilities should receive full consideration along with those of the other members of the United Nations by conferences or international agencies held or created to deal with international economic matters.

The Governments of the United States of America, the Union of Soviet Socialist Republics, and the United Kingdom are at one with the Government of Iran in their desire for the maintenance of the independence, sovereignty, and territorial integrity of Iran. They count upon the participation of Iran together with all other peace-loving nations in the establishment of international peace, security, and prosperity after the war in accordance with the principles of the Atlantic Charter, to which all four governments have continued to subscribe.

## The Yalta Conference

**Important provisions of the Conference, which was held Feb. 4-11, 1945:**

### The Occupation and Control of Germany

We have agreed on common policies and plans for enforcing the unconditional surrender terms which we shall impose together on Nazi Germany after German armed resistance has been finally crushed. These terms will not be made known until the final defeat of Germany has been accomplished. Under the agreed plan, the forces of the three powers will each occupy a separate zone of Germany. Coordinated administration and control has been provided for under the plan through a central Control Commission, consisting of the supreme commanders of the three powers, with headquarters in Berlin. It has been agreed that France should be invited by the three powers, if she should so desire, to take over a zone of occupation, and to participate as a fourth member of the Control Commission. The limits of the

French zone will be agreed upon by the four Governments concerned through their representatives on the European Advisory Commission.

It is our inflexible purpose to destroy German militarism and nazism and to ensure that Germany will never again be able to disturb the peace of the world. We are determined to disarm and disband all German armed forces; break up for all time the German General Staff that has repeatedly contrived the resurgence of German militarism; remove or destroy all German military equipment; eliminate or control all German industry that could be used for military production; bring all war criminals to just and swift punishment and exact reparation in kind for the destruction wrought by the Germans; wipe out the Nazi Party, Nazi laws, organizations, and institutions, remove all Nazi and militarist influences from public office and from the cultural and economic life of the German people; and take in harmony such other measures in Germany as may be necessary to the future peace and safety of the world. It is not our purpose to destroy the people of Germany, but only when nazism and militarism have been extirpated will there be hope for a decent life for Germans, and a place for them in the comity of nations.

### Terms Under Which Russia Entered the War Against Japan

The leaders of the Three Great Powers—the Soviet Union, the United States of America, and Great Britain—have agreed that in two or three months after Germany has surrendered and the war in Europe has terminated the Soviet Union shall enter into the war against Japan on the side of the Allies on condition that:

1. The status quo in Outer Mongolia (The Mongolian People's Republic) shall be preserved;

2. The former rights of Russia violated by the treacherous attack of Japan in 1904 shall be restored, viz.:

(a) the southern part of Sakhalin as well as all the islands adjacent to it shall be returned to the Soviet Union,

(b) the commercial port of Dairen shall be internationalized, the preeminent interests of the Soviet Union in this port being safeguarded and the lease of Port Arthur as a naval base of the U.S.S.R. restored,

(c) the Chinese-Eastern Railroad and the South-Manchurian Railroad which provides an outlet to Dairen shall be jointly operated by the establishment of a joint Soviet-Chinese Company, it being understood that the preeminent interests of the Soviet Union shall be safeguarded and that China shall retain full sovereignty in Manchuria;

3. The Kurile Islands shall be handed over to the Soviet Union.

It is understood that the agreement concerning Outer Mongolia and the ports and railroads referred to above will require concurrence of Generalissimo Chiang Kai-shek. The President will take measures in order to obtain this concurrence on advice from Marshal Stalin.

The Heads of the Three Great Powers have agreed that these claims of the Soviet Union shall be unquestionably fulfilled after Japan has been defeated.

For its part the Soviet Union expresses its readiness to conclude with the National Government of China a pact of friendship and alliance between the U.S.S.R. and China in order to render assistance to China with its armed forces for the purpose of liberating China from the Japanese yoke.

## The Potsdam Declaration

Text of the declaration issued at Potsdam, Germany, July 26, 1945, outlining the terms under which Japan would be allowed to surrender:

1. We, the President of the United States, the President of the national government of the Republic of China, and the Prime Minister of Great Britain, representing the hundreds of millions of our countrymen, have conferred and agreed that Japan shall be given the opportunity to end this war.

2. The prodigious land, sea, and air forces of the United States, the British Empire, and China, many times reinforced by their armies and air fleets from the west, are poised to strike the final blow at Japan. This military power is sustained and inspired by the determination of all allied nations to prosecute the war against Japan until she ceases to resist.

3. The result of the futile and senseless German resistance to the might of the aroused free peoples of the world stands forth in awful clarity as an example to the people of Japan.

The might that now converges on Japan is immeasurably greater than that which, when applied to the resisting Nazis, necessarily laid waste to the land, the industry, and the method of life of the whole German people.

The full application of our military power, backed by our resolve, will mean the inevitable and complete destruction of the Japanese armed forces and just as inevitably the utter devastation of the Japanese homeland.

4. The time has come for Japan to decide whether she will continue to be con-

trolled by these self-willed militaristic advisers whose unintelligent calculations have brought the empire of Japan to the threshold of annihilation, or whether she will follow the path of reason.

5. The following are our terms: we will not deviate from them; there are no alternatives; we shall brook no delay.

6. There must be eliminated for all time the authority and influence of those who have deceived and misled the people of Japan into embarking on world conquest, for we insist that a new order of peace, security, and justice will be impossible until irresponsible militarism is driven from the world.

7. Until such a new order is established and until there is convincing proof that Japan's war-making power is destroyed, points in Japanese territory to be designated by the Allies shall be occupied to secure the achievement of the basic objectives we are here setting forth.

8. The terms of the Cairo declaration shall be carried out and Japanese sovereignty shall be limited to the Islands of Honshu, Hokkaido, Kyushu, Shikoku, and such minor islands as we determine.

9. Japanese military forces after being completely disarmed shall be permitted to return to their homes with the opportunity to lead peaceful and productive lives.

10. We do not intend that the Japanese shall be enslaved as a race or destroyed as a nation, but stern justice shall be meted out to all war criminals, including those who have visited cruelties upon our prisoners.

The Japanese government shall remove all obstacles to the revival and strengthening of democratic tendencies among the Japanese people. Freedom of speech and religion and of thought, as well as respect for the fundamental human rights, shall be established.

11. Japan shall be permitted to maintain such industries as will sustain her economy and permit the payment of just reparation in kind, but not those industries which will enable her to rearm for war.

To this end, access to, as distinguished from control of, raw materials shall be permitted. Eventual Japanese participation in world trade relations shall be permitted.

12. The occupying forces of the Allies shall be withdrawn from Japan as soon as these objectives have been accomplished and there has been established in accordance with the freely expressed will of the Japanese people a peacefully inclined and responsible government.

13. We call upon the government of Japan to proclaim now the unconditional surrender of all Japanese armed forces, and to provide proper and adequate assurances of their good faith in such action. The alternative for Japan is prompt and utter destruction.

## Western European Integration

The European Economc Community was established in Rome on March 25, 1957. Members: France, West Germany, Italy, Belgium, the Netherlands, and Luxembourg. This grouping has become known as the Common Market, or the "Inner Six." The purpose was to reduce tariffs and other trade barriers among the six countries with the hope of eventually creating a vast free-trade area comparable to the United States. The members also planned a common tariff policy toward imports from the rest of the world. On Aug. 10, 1961, Britain and Denmark applied for membership, the former subject to certain conditions intended to protect its commitments to other members of the Commonwealth.

A second group, the European Free Trade Association, unofficially called the "Outer Seven," was formed in Stockholm on Nov. 20, 1959, by seven countries: Austria, Great Britain, Denmark, Norway, Portugal, Sweden, and Switzerland. It aims to eliminate tariffs among members by Jan., 1970. The chief difference is that members are free to pursue individual trade policies in relation to the rest of the world.

All these countries have been associated for a decade in the more loosely constructed Organization for European Economic Co-operation.

In Jan., 1960, the United States entered into active participation at a Paris conference, and proposed a new trans-Atlantic trade organization which would include both European groups plus the United States and Canada. One purpose was to minimize rivalry between the two European groups.

## Warsaw Pact—Reds' "NATO"
### (Signed: May 14, 1955)

Members: Albania, Bulgaria, Czechoslovakia, East Germany, Hungary, Poland, Rumania, U.S.S.R.

The Warsaw Pact is the Communist equivalent of NATO. Article 4 contains the same provisions as Article 5 of NATO, stating that an attack on one shall be regarded as an attack on all. Article 5 provides for a unified military command.

# English Language Daily and Sunday U. S. Newspapers

## (as of Sept. 30, 1960)

*Source: Editor & Publisher.*

| State | Morning papers & circulation | | Evening papers & circulation | | Total M & E & circulation | | Sunday papers & circulation | |
|---|---|---|---|---|---|---|---|---|
| Alabama | 4 | 213,541 | 15 | 457,507 | 19 | 671,048 | 14 | 560,456 |
| Alaska | .. | ....... | 6 | 51,176 | 6 | 51,176 | 1 | 4,102 |
| Arizona | 3 | 165,853 | 10 | 150,824 | 13 | 316,677 | 5 | 249,292 |
| Arkansas | 6 | 145,172 | 29 | 237,454 | 35 | 382,626 | 11 | 313,317 |
| California | 18 | 2,008,225 | 111 | 3,088,171 | 129 | 5,096,396 | 28 | 3,953,270 |
| Colorado | 3 | 205,922 | 21 | 410,497 | 24 | 616,419 | 8 | 619,162 |
| Connecticut | 6 | 220,252 | 19 | 573,239 | 25 | 793,491 | 6 | 473,219 |
| Delaware | 1 | 32,171 | 2 | 84,496 | 3 | 116,667 | .. | ....... |
| District of Columbia | 1 | 403,010 | 2 | 458,947 | 3 | 861,957 | 2 | 770,180 |
| Florida | 15 | 965,789 | 30 | 649,756 | 45 | 1,615,545 | 30 | 1,468,947 |
| Georgia | 6 | 401,467 | 23 | 519,389 | 29 | 920,856 | 10 | 801,934 |
| Hawaii | 1 | 64,287 | 4 | 137,520 | 5 | 201,807 | 3 | 187,870 |
| Idaho[1] | 4 | 68,543 | 12 | 80,913 | 15 | 149,456 | 5 | 113,586 |
| Illinois | 9 | 1,841,989 | 74 | 2,011,205 | 83 | 3,853,194 | 18 | 3,014,660 |
| Indiana | 9 | 437,496 | 79 | 1,186,751 | 88 | 1,624,247 | 18 | 1,084,526 |
| Iowa[1] | 4 | 289,112 | 42 | 654,794 | 45 | 943,906 | 9 | 830,792 |
| Kansas[1] | 5 | 211,263 | 48 | 418,264 | 52 | 629,527 | 15 | 375,543 |
| Kentucky[1] | 7 | 320,310 | 22 | 408,124 | 28 | 728,434 | 13 | 534,651 |
| Louisiana | 4 | 350,931 | 14 | 381,564 | 18 | 732,495 | 8 | 592,457 |
| Maine | 5 | 194,386 | 4 | 54,557 | 9 | 248,943 | 1 | 97,705 |
| Maryland | 4 | 233,618 | 8 | 537,245 | 12 | 770,863 | 3 | 662,361 |
| Massachusetts[1] | 6 | 900,740 | 45 | 1,459,629 | 50 | 2,360,369 | 8 | 1,464,088 |
| Michigan | 1 | 501,115 | 53 | 1,520,475 | 54 | 2,021,590 | 11 | 1,665,346 |
| Minnesota | 5 | 387,833 | 26 | 695,385 | 31 | 1,083,218 | 5 | 934,494 |
| Mississippi | 4 | 77,786 | 16 | 210,482 | 20 | 288,268 | 8 | 175,860 |
| Missouri | 7 | 775,413 | 46 | 1,059,367 | 53 | 1,834,780 | 13 | 1,451,892 |
| Montana | 4 | 100,060 | 14 | 71,828 | 18 | 171,888 | 10 | 153,864 |
| Nebraska | 3 | 167,117 | 17 | 298,949 | 20 | 466,066 | 5 | 342,898 |
| Nevada | 2 | 34,895 | 6 | 55,271 | 8 | 90,166 | 3 | 73,807 |
| New Hampshire[1] | 1 | 24,412 | 9 | 99,419 | 9 | 123 831 | 1 | 42,266 |
| New Jersey | 5 | 412,287 | 22 | 1,052,502 | 27 | 1,464,789 | 10 | 979,330 |
| New Mexico | 1 | 46,764 | 18 | 139,013 | 19 | 185,777 | 13 | 156,278 |
| New York | 22 | 4,900,960 | 66 | 3,670,942 | 88 | 8,571,902 | 20 | 9,275,740 |
| North Carolina | 9 | 541,619 | 38 | 554,870 | 47 | 1,096,489 | 15 | 735,441 |
| North Dakota | 2 | 34,525 | 9 | 125,002 | 11 | 159,527 | 2 | 87,315 |
| Ohio | 8 | 835,955 | 86 | 2,539,064 | 94 | 3,375,019 | 20 | 2,074,012 |
| Oklahoma | 7 | 309,388 | 44 | 423,601 | 51 | 732,989 | 41 | 657,346 |
| Oregon | 4 | 235,011 | 17 | 323,838 | 21 | 558,849 | 7 | 527,630 |
| Pennsylvania[1] | 28 | 1,433,403 | 97 | 2,778,230 | 123 | 4,211,633 | 14 | 3,225,008 |
| Rhode Island | 1 | 61,175 | 6 | 235,769 | 7 | 296,944 | 2 | 197,727 |
| South Carolina | 8 | 344,285 | 9 | 148,252 | 17 | 492,537 | 7 | 373,651 |
| South Dakota | 2 | 5,686 | 11 | 160,806 | 13 | 166,492 | 14 | 113,685 |
| Tennessee | 7 | 486,305 | 23 | 566,467 | 30 | 1,052,772 | 12 | 785,722 |
| Texas | 24 | 1,238,880 | 92 | 1,692,366 | 116 | 2,931,246 | 79 | 2,563,259 |
| Utah | 1 | 100,788 | 4 | 137,247 | 5 | 238,035 | 4 | 236,720 |
| Vermont | 2 | 52,687 | 7 | 39,584 | 9 | 92,271 | 1 | 11,710 |
| Virginia | 9 | 403,292 | 22 | 485,594 | 31 | 888,886 | 12 | 590,001 |
| Washington | 6 | 336,905 | 21 | 632,197 | 27 | 969,102 | 10 | 833,268 |
| West Virginia | 9 | 233,652 | 21 | 253,395 | 30 | 487,047 | 8 | 365,963 |
| Wisconsin | 3 | 264,907 | 35 | 891,384 | 38 | 1,156,291 | 6 | 894,662 |
| Wyoming | 6 | 37,406 | 4 | 37,660 | 10 | 75,066 | 4 | 38,398 |
| Total U. S., Sept. 30, 1960 | 312 | 24,028,788 | 1,459 | 34,852,958 | 1,763 | 58,881,746 | 563 | 47,698,651 |
| Total U. S., Sept. 30, 1959 | 306 | 23,547,046 | 1,455 | 34,752,677 | 1,755 | 58,299,723 | 564 | 47,848,477 |
| Total U. S., Sept. 30, 1958 | 308 | 23,206,964 | 1,460 | 34,387,490 | 1,756 | 57,594,454 | 558 | 47,041,223 |
| Total U. S., Sept. 30, 1957[2] | 309 | 23,170,552 | 1,453 | 34,634,893 | 1,755 | 57,805,445 | 544 | 47,044,349 |
| Total U. S., Sept. 30, 1956[2] | 314 | 22,491,500 | 1,454 | 34,610,010 | 1,761 | 57,101,510 | 546 | 47,162,246 |
| Total U. S., Sept. 30, 1955[2] | 316 | 22,183,408 | 1,454 | 33,963,951 | 1,760 | 56,147,359 | 541 | 46,447,658 |
| Total U. S., Sept. 30, 1954[2] | 317 | 21,705,436 | 1,448 | 33,367,044 | 1,765 | 55,072,480 | 544 | 46,176,450 |

[1] "All-day" newspapers are listed in morning and evening columns, and their circulations are divided between morning and evening figures. Adjustments have been made in state and U. S. total figures.  [2] Excludes newspapers and circulations for Alaska and Hawaii.

# U. S. Daily Newspapers

*Source:* Audit Bureau of Circulations: Publishers' Statements for 6-mo. period ending Mar. 31, 1961.

**(NOTE: Where two or more newspapers are listed under a city, the order is according to size of total daily circulation.)**

| City and newspaper | Net Paid Circulation | | |
|---|---|---|---|
| | Morning[1] | Evening[1] | Sunday |
| Akron (Ohio): BEACON JOURNAL.................... | ....... | 168,252 | 179,588 |
| Albany (N. Y.): TIMES–UNION (M & S); KNICKERBOCKER NEWS (E)......... | 67,962 | 65,084 | 117,693 |
| Anderson (S. C.): INDEPENDENT (M & S); DAILY MAIL (E)................. | 53,389 | 7,367 | 53,559 |
| Atlanta: CONSTITUTION (M); JOURNAL (E); JOURNAL & CONSTITUTION (S) | 200,913 | 260,449 | 501,826 |
| Baltimore: SUN.................... | 191,506[2] | 218,803[2] | 321,598 |
|     NEWS–POST (E); AMERICAN (S)................. | ....... | 226,547[2] | 312,632 |
| Birmingham: POST–HERALD (M); NEWS (E & S)..... | 97,974 | 191,415 | 225,824 |
| Boston: RECORD (M); AMERICAN (E); ADVERTISER (S) | 352,842[2] | 163,139[2] | 457,587 |
|     GLOBE..................... | 191,392[2] | 150,616[2] | 447,775 |
|     HERALD (M & S); TRAVELER (E)............ | 171,201[2] | 170,018[2] | 298,569 |
|     CHRISTIAN SCIENCE MONITOR............ | ....... | 214,447 | ....... |
| Buffalo: NEWS........................ | ....... | 286,635[2] | ....... |
|     COURIER–EXPRESS................. | 156,327 | ....... | 303,950 |
| Charleston (W. Va.): GAZETTE (M); DAILY MAIL (E); GAZETTE–MAIL (S).... | 68,879 | 52,382 | 106,490 |
| Charlotte (N. C.): OBSERVER (M & S); NEWS (E)............. | 163,450 | 64,257 | 182,331 |
| Chattanooga (Tenn.): TIMES (M & S); NEWS–FREE PRESS (E)........... | 53,419 | 59,934 | 82,535 |
| Chicago: TRIBUNE..................... | 864,471 | ....... | 1,209,155 |
|     SUN–TIMES.................... | 546,957[2] | ....... | 666,044 |
|     NEWS..................... | ....... | 537,792[2] | ....... |
|     AMERICAN.................... | ....... | 450,340[2] | 571,997 |
|     WALL STREET JOURNAL (Midwest Edition)........ | 227,457[2] | ....... | ....... |
| Cincinnati: POST & TIMES–STAR.............. | ....... | 275,101 | ....... |
|     ENQUIRER..................... | 217,072 | ....... | 291,469 |
| Cleveland: PRESS & NEWS................ | ....... | 385,347 | ....... |
|     PLAIN DEALER.................... | 323,406 | ....... | 509,613 |
| Columbus (Ohio): DISPATCH................ | ....... | 213,868 | 286,127 |
|     CITIZEN–JOURNAL................... | 107,766 | ....... | ....... |
| Dallas: NEWS..................... | 220,529 | ....... | 238,993 |
|     TIMES HERALD.................... | ....... | 188,744[2] | 196,932 |
| Dayton (Ohio): NEWS................. | ....... | 151,589 | 187,184 |
| Denver: POST..................... | ....... | 265,980[2] | 348,937 |
|     ROCKY MOUNTAIN NEWS............. | 174,261 | ....... | 170,409 |
| Des Moines: REGISTER (M & S); TRIBUNE (E)........ | 230,093 | 127,266 | 521,194 |
| Detroit: NEWS..................... | ....... | 733,583 | 920,607 |
|     FREE PRESS..................... | 573,273 | ....... | 622,237 |
| Fort Worth: STAR–TELEGRAM.............. | 106,964 | 135,863 | 208,237 |
| Grand Rapids (Mich.): PRESS................ | ....... | 125,737 | 87,682 |
| Harrisburg (Pa.): PATRIOT (M); NEWS (E); PATRIOT–NEWS (S)........... | 41,433 | 77,263 | 154,757 |
| Hartford (Conn.): TIMES................ | ....... | 128,101 | ....... |
|     COURANT..................... | 111,167 | ....... | 156,684 |
| Honolulu: STAR–BULLETIN................ | ....... | 104,933[2] | 112,684 |
| Houston: POST..................... | 227,627[2] | ....... | 247,741 |
|     CHRONICLE..................... | ....... | 216 450[2] | 240,669 |
|     PRESS..................... | ....... | 101,583[2] | ....... |
| Indianapolis: STAR (M & S); NEWS (E)............ | 214,506 | 164,503 | 339,749 |
|     TIMES..................... | ....... | 91,695 | 104,014 |
| Jacksonville (Fla.): TIMES–UNION (M & S); JOURNAL (E)......... | 179,461 | 64,250 | 184,817 |
| Kansas City (Mo.): TIMES (M); STAR (E & S)....... | 332,802 | 337,482 | 363,708 |
| Knoxville: NEWS–SENTINEL................. | ....... | 106,076 | 142,553 |
| Little Rock: ARKANSAS GAZETTE............ | 89,150 | ....... | 101,513 |
|     DEMOCRAT..................... | ....... | 85,474 | 101,604 |
| Long Beach (Calif.): INDEPENDENT PRESS–TELEGRAM.............. | 39,023 | 110,911 | 140,479 |
| Los Angeles: TIMES..................... | 552,220 | ....... | 975,126 |
|     HERALD & EXPRESS................ | ....... | 378,613[2] | ....... |
|     EXAMINER..................... | 375,552 | ....... | 704,827 |
|     MIRROR..................... | ....... | 292,091[2] | ....... |
| Louisville: COURIER–JOURNAL (M & S); TIMES (E)............ | 219,072 | 173,571 | 319,300 |
| Memphis: COMMERCIAL APPEAL (M & S); PRESS SCIMITAR (E)............ | 222,531 | 147,486 | 260,477 |
| Miami: HERALD..................... | 336,211 | ....... | 389,076 |
|     NEWS..................... | ....... | 157,012[2] | 135,810 |
| Milwaukee: JOURNAL..................... | ....... | 377,582 | 516,220 |
|     SENTINEL..................... | 194,242 | ....... | 220,441 |

[1] Unless otherwise indicated, figure is an average of the Monday-through-Saturday circulation. [2] Figure is an average of the Monday-through-Friday circulation; i.e., Saturday circulation, if any, has not been used in making the average. [3] Post office address is Garden City, N. Y.

| City and newspaper | Net Paid Circulation | | |
|---|---|---|---|
| | Morning[1] | Evening[1] | Sunday |
| Minneapolis: TRIBUNE (M & S); STAR (E) | 229,421 | 302,738 | 666,395 |
| Nashville: TENNESSEAN (M & S); BANNER (E) | 130,968 | 103,936 | 205,487 |
| Nassau County (Long Island, N. Y.): NEWSDAY[3] | ....... | 328,801 | ....... |
| New Orleans: TIMES-PICAYUNE (M & S); STATES & ITEM (E) | 195,482 | 166,834[2] | 309,325 |
| New York City: NEWS | 1,980,338[2] | ....... | 3,244,667 |
| MIRROR | 840,644[2] | ....... | 1,198,750 |
| TIMES | 744,763[2] | ....... | 1,400,826 |
| JOURNAL-AMERICAN | ....... | 639,116[2] | 810,248 |
| WORLD-TELEGRAM & SUN | ....... | 477,595[2] | ....... |
| HERALD TRIBUNE | 367,991[2] | ....... | 486,160 |
| POST | ....... | 343,140[2] | 280,192 |
| LONG ISLAND PRESS (Jamaica, N. Y.) | ....... | 301,177 | 383,678 |
| WALL STREET JOURNAL (Eastern Edition) | 292,742[2] | ....... | ....... |
| STAR-JOURNAL (Long Island City) | ....... | 103,611 | ....... |
| Newark (N. J.): NEWS | ....... | 285,433[2] | 406,708 |
| STAR-LEDGER | 227,741[2] | ....... | 394,731 |
| Norfolk-Portsmouth-South Norfolk: VIRGINIAN PILOT (M); NORFOLK LEDGER-DISPATCH & PORTSMOUTH STAR (E); VIRGINIAN PILOT & PORTSMOUTH STAR (S) | 113,683 | 97,261 | 147,520 |
| Oakland (Calif.): TRIBUNE | ....... | 211,009 | 237,173 |
| Oklahoma City: OKLAHOMAN (M & S); TIMES (E) | 166,416 | 121,512 | 254,526 |
| Omaha: WORLD-HERALD | 126,847 | 125,385 | 264,902 |
| Orlando (Fla.): SENTINEL (M & S); STAR (E) | 87,137 | 29,887 | 114,134 |
| Philadelphia: BULLETIN | ....... | 720,794[2] | 712,956 |
| INQUIRER | 605,850[2] | ....... | 1,022,262 |
| NEWS | ....... | 275,294[2] | ....... |
| Phoenix: REPUBLIC (M & S); GAZETTE (E) | 140,146 | 88,190 | 207,715 |
| Pittsburgh: PRESS | ....... | 367,671 | 575,446 |
| POST-GAZETTE, SUN-TELEGRAPH | 294,442 | ....... | 338,182 |
| Portland (Maine): PRESS-HERALD (M); EXPRESS (E); TELEGRAM (S) | 52,713 | 29,025 | 99,347 |
| Portland (Oreg.): OREGONIAN | 207,837 | ....... | 273,688 |
| JOURNAL | ....... | 148,510[2] | 169,842 |
| Providence (R. I.): JOURNAL (M & S); BULLETIN (E) | 61,390 | 145,633 | 192,956 |
| Raleigh (N. C.): NEWS & OBSERVER (M & S); TIMES (E) | 126,437 | 22,982 | 138,509 |
| Richmond (Va.): TIMES-DISPATCH (M & S); NEWS-LEADER (E) | 140,486 | 117,634 | 188,227 |
| Rochester (N. Y.): DEMOCRAT & CHRONICLE (M & S); TIMES-UNION (E) | 127,519 | 131,041 | 187,830 |
| Sacramento: BEE | ....... | 166,549 | 174,314 |
| St. Louis: POST-DISPATCH | ....... | 406,947[2] | 577,436 |
| GLOBE-DEMOCRAT | 341,503[2] | ....... | 352,715 |
| St. Paul: PIONEER PRESS (M & S); DISPATCH (E) | 95,454 | 125,779 | 191,385 |
| St. Petersburg (Fla.): TIMES | 124,880 | ....... | 127,272 |
| Salt Lake City: TRIBUNE (M & S); DESERT NEWS-SALT LAKE TELEGRAM (E) | 99,914 | 85,552 | 182,763 |
| San Antonio: EXPRESS (M); NEWS (E); EXPRESS-NEWS (S) | 68,712[2] | 71,387[2] | 109,443 |
| LIGHT | ....... | 111,673[2] | 130,434 |
| San Diego: EVENING TRIBUNE | ....... | 122,432 | ....... |
| UNION | 104,005 | ....... | 208,342 |
| San Francisco: CHRONICLE | 291,555 | ....... | 325,016 |
| EXAMINER | 277,978 | ....... | 450,991 |
| NEWS-CALL-BULLETIN | ....... | 200,521[2] | ....... |
| WALL STREET JOURNAL (Pacific Coast Edition) | 123,431[2] | ....... | ....... |
| San Jose (Calif.): MERCURY (M); NEWS (E); MERCURY-NEWS (S) | 66,080 | 52,579 | 105,404 |
| Seattle: TIMES | ....... | 231,140[2] | 260,602 |
| POST-INTELLIGENCER | 219,531[2] | ....... | 250,904 |
| Shreveport (La.): TIMES (M & S); JOURNAL (E) | 85,347 | 47,630 | 109,600 |
| South Bend-Mishawaka (Ind.): TRIBUNE | ....... | 113,091 | 117,057 |
| Spokane (Wash.): SPOKESMAN-REVIEW | 88,081 | ....... | 135,887 |
| Syracuse (N. Y.): HERALD-JOURNAL (E); HERALD-AMERICAN (S) | ....... | 131,688 | 206,462 |
| POST-STANDARD | 97,616[2] | ....... | 102,288 |
| Tampa (Fla.): TRIBUNE (M & S); TIMES (E) | 151,577 | 45,434 | 166,247 |
| Toledo: BLADE | ....... | 183,927[2] | 181,856 |
| Tulsa (Okla.): WORLD (M & S); TRIBUNE (E) | 95,985 | 74,960 | 152,242 |
| Washington (D. C.): POST | 412,846[2] | ....... | 477,262 |
| EVENING STAR: SUNDAY STAR | ....... | 280,744[2] | 320,365 |
| NEWS | ....... | 184,986[2] | ....... |
| Wichita (Kans.): EAGLE (M); EAGLE & BEACON (E & S) | 125,649 | 84,399 | 161,068 |
| Wilmington (Del.): NEWS (M); JOURNAL (E) | 31,817 | 76,562 | ....... |
| Worcester (Mass.): TELEGRAM (M & S); GAZETTE (E) | 56,564 | 94,318 | 101,956 |
| Youngstown (Ohio): VINDICATOR | ....... | 104,029 | 152,286 |

## Leading Magazines: United States and Canada

*Souree:* Audit Bureau of Circulations: Publishers' Statements for 6-month period ending Dec. 31, 1960.

| Magazine | Circulation[1] | Magazine | Circulation[1] |
|---|---|---|---|
| American Girl (M) | 746,983 | National Geographic Magazine (M) | 2,517,846 |
| American Home (M) | 3,675,676 | Nation's Business (M) | 760,104 |
| Argosy (M) | 1,357,683 | Newsweek (W) | 1,442,836 |
| Better Homes & Gardens (M) | 5,037,498 | New Yorker (W) | 425,781 |
| Boys' Life (M) | 2,047,313 | Outdoor Life (M) | 1,106,581 |
| Cavalier (M) | 448,596 | Parents' Magazine & Better Home- | |
| Chatelaine (M)[2] | 767,250 | making (M) | 1,841,600 |
| Coronet (M) | 3,122,628 | Photoplay (M) | 1,350,763 |
| Cosmopolitan (M) | 857,669 | Playboy (M) | 1,144,077 |
| Ebony (M) | 631,849 | Popular Mechanics (M) | 1,364,603 |
| Esquire (M) | 875,053 | Popular Science Monthly (M) | 1,277,352 |
| Everywoman's Family Circle (M) | 5,616,029 | Reader's Digest (M) | 12,592,912 |
| Field & Stream (M) | 1,159,919 | Reader's Digest (Canadian English | |
| Flower & Garden Magazine (M) | 496,807 | Edition) (M)[2] | 882,884 |
| Flower Grower (M) | 400,443 | Redbook Magazine (M) | 3,220,354 |
| Glamour (M) | 1,140,144 | Saturday Evening Post (W) | 6,377,367 |
| Good Housekeeping (M) | 4,961,039 | Science & Mechanics (M) | 424,226 |
| Grit (W) | 787,697 | Secrets (M) | 471,098 |
| Harper's Bazaar (M) | 468,119 | Seventeen (M) | 1,155,550 |
| Holiday (M) | 921,061 | Sport (M) | 556,950 |
| Hot Rod Magazine (M) | 638,373 | Sports Afield (M) | 1,109,165 |
| House & Garden (M) | 833,155 | Sports Illustrated (W) | 939,828 |
| House Beautiful (M) | 902,083 | Stag (M) | 405,563 |
| Ladies' Home Journal (M) | 6,550,415 | Sunset (M) | 648,356 |
| Liberty (M)[2] | 579,574 | 'Teen (M) | 669,867 |
| Life (W) | 6,764,686 | Time (W) | 2,541,977 |
| Living for Young Homemakers (M) | 711,491 | True (M) | 2,408,348 |
| Look (BW) | 6,322,417 | True Confessions (M) | 1,227,950 |
| Maclean's Magazine (BW)[2] | 520,377 | True Romance (M) | 453,490 |
| Mademoiselle (M) | 535,095 | True Story (M) | 2,328,287 |
| McCall's (M) | 6,560,452 | TV Guide (all editions) (W) | 7,079,511 |
| Mechanix Illustrated (M) | 1,105,442 | TV Radio Mirror (M) | 646,760 |
| Modern Romances (M) | 1,057,164 | U. S. News & World Report (W) | 1,235,745 |
| Modern Screen (M) | 1,311,665 | Vogue (SM) | 482,650 |
| Motion Picture (M) | 1,166,259 | Woman's Day (M) | 5,051,066 |
| Motor Trend (M) | 432,287 | Workbasket (M) | 1,111,967 |

[1] Average total paid circulation for the 6-month period indicated above. This table lists weekly, biweekly, monthly and bimonthly magazines of more than 400,000 circulation, but excludes most official organs of associations and religious or scholastic magazines. [2] Canadian publication. NOTE: W—weekly; BW—biweekly; M—monthly; SM—semimonthly.

---

# Radio and Television Stations and Networks

*Source:* National Association of Broadcasters.

| Major networks | Standard broadcast stations (Apr. 1, 1961) | | TV Stations (Apr. 1, 1961) |
|---|---|---|---|
| | Owned and operated | Affiliated | Owned and operated |
| ABC—American Broadcasting Company | 6 | 358 | 5 |
| CBS—Columbia Broadcasting System | 7 | 210 | 5 |
| MBS—Mutual Broadcasting System | .. | 421 | .. |
| NBC—National Broadcasting Company | 6 | 201 | 5 |

| Number of stations* (Apr. 1, 1961) | Operating | Permits for construction | Total |
|---|---|---|---|
| Standard broadcast | 3,561 | 150 | 3,711 |
| FM (Frequency modulation) | 856 | 206 | 1,062 |
| Television | 542 | 99 | 641 |

* Including territories and possessions.

# RELIGION

## Estimated Membership of the Principal Religions of the World

*Source: Britannica Book of the Year, 1961.*

**Statistics of the world's religions are only very rough approximations. Aside from Christianity, few religions, if any, attempt to keep statistical records; and even Protestants and Catholics employ different methods of counting members. All persons of whatever age who have received baptism in the Catholic Church are counted as members, while in most Protestant Churches only those who "join" the church are numbered. The compiling of statistics is further complicated by the fact that in China one may be at the same time a Confucian, a Taoist and a Buddhist. In Japan, one may be both a Buddhist and a Shintoist.**

| Religion | North America | South America | Europe | Asia | Africa | Australasia[1] | Total |
|---|---|---|---|---|---|---|---|
| Total Christian........ | 184,176,306 | 131,131,141 | 480,079,626 | 47,276,172 | 34,836,280 | 11,303,501 | 888,803,026 |
| Roman Catholic...... | 106,874,000[2] | 128,488,000 | 241,030,000[3] | 35,419,000 | 22,855,000 | 2,867,000 | 537,533,000 |
| Eastern Orthodox.... | 2,979,883 | 41,156 | 126,601,957 | 2,569,216 | 4,870,113 | 74,660 | 137,136,985 |
| Protestant......... | 74,322,423 | 2,601,985 | 112,447,619 | 9,287,956 | 7,111,167 | 8,361,841 | 214,133,041 |
| Jewish[4]............... | 5,663,450 | 634,880 | 3,445,550 | 1,971,870 | 551,250 | 68,500 | 12,335,500 |
| Moslem.............. | 35,500 | 353,500 | 12,802,000 | 328,238,000 | 88,791,000 | 105,000 | 430,325,000 |
| Zoroastrian........... | ......... | ......... | ......... | 140,000 | ......... | ......... | 140,000 |
| Shinto.............. | ......... | ......... | ......... | 50,500,000 | ......... | ......... | 50,500,000 |
| Taoist............... | 15,000 | 17,000 | 12,000 | 50,000,000 | 1,200 | 8,000 | 50,053,200 |
| Confucian............ | 86,000 | 95,000 | 50,000 | 300,000,000 | 7,500 | 52,000 | 300,290,500 |
| Buddhist............ | 165,000 | 135,000 | 10,000 | 151,500,000 | ......... | ......... | 151,810,000 |
| Hindu.............. | 27,500 | 306,000 | ......... | 331,388,500 | 636,500 | 112,200 | 332,470,700 |
| Primitive............ | 50,000 | 1,000,000 | ......... | 45,000,000 | 75,000,000 | 100,000 | 121,150,000 |
| Others or none........ | 69,356,244 | 2,513,479 | 80,376,324 | 326,828,958 | 41,783,270 | 3,476,799 | 524,335,074 |
| Grand total........... | 259,575,000 | 136,186,000 | 576,775,500 | 1,632,843,500 | 241,607,000 | 15,226,000 | 2,862,213,000 |

[1] Includes Australia, New Zealand and Oceania. [2] Includes Catholics in Central America and the West Indies. [3] Includes Communist-controlled Eurasia. [4] Includes total Jewish population, whether or not related to the synagogue.

## History of Leading Religious Groups in the United States

### (50,000 members or over.)

*Source: Yearbook of American Churches*

### Baptist

**American Baptist Association.**—A group of Independent Missionary Baptist Churches organized into an association in 1905. Members (1960): 648,000.

**American Baptist Convention.**—The early historical local independency of Baptist churches in America tended to impede the formation of any general organization until in 1814 a General Missionary Convention was formed to permit Baptists to express themselves in terms of missionary activities. In 1845, the state conventions in the South withdrew to organize the Southern Baptist Convention. In 1907, the Northern Baptist Convention was organized, a delegated body under whose direction the many agencies of the Baptists in the North and West now operate. In May, 1950, the name was changed to the American Baptist Convention. Members (1959): 1,543,198.

**Baptist General Conference of America.**—Formerly known as the Swedish Baptist General Conference of America. It has operated as a general conference since 1879. Members (1960): 72,056.

**Conservative Baptist Association of America.**—Organized in 1947, it is a body with no authority over the local churches. Adherents consider the Bible infallible. Members (1960): 300,000.

**Free Will Baptists.**—A body of Arminian Baptists, organized in 1787 by Benjamin Randall in New Hampshire. Members (1960): 191,448.

**The General Association of Regular Baptist Churches.**—Founded in 1932 in Chicago by a group of churches which had withdrawn from the Northern Baptist Convention. Members (1960): 136,292.

**General Baptists.**—An Arminian group of Baptists, organized in 1607 and transplanted to the Colonies in 1714. It died down in the East but was revived in the Midwest in 1823 under Rev. Benoni Stinson. Members (1960): 58,530.

**National Baptist Convention, U. S. A., Inc.**—The older and parent convention of Negro Baptists. This body is to be distinguished from the National Baptist Convention of America, usually referred to as the "unincorporated" body. Members (1958): 5,000,000.

**National Baptist Convention of America.**—This is a body usually referred to as the "unincorporated" convention, not to be confused with the "incorporated" National

Baptist Convention, U. S. A., Inc., from which this body withdrew. Organized in 1895. Members (1956) : 2,668,799.

**National Baptist Evangelical Life and Soul Saving Assembly of U. S. A.**—Organized in 1921 by A. A. Banks, Sr., as a charitable, educational, and evangelical organization. Members (1951) : 57,674.

**National Primitive Baptist Convention of the U. S. A.**—A group of Negro Baptists opposed to all forms of church organization. Members (1957) : 80,983.

**North American Baptist Association.**—Organized 1950 in Little Rock, Ark., as the result of a division in the American Baptist Association. In theology these churches are militantly fundamentalist. Members (1959) : 330,265.

**Primitive Baptists.**—A large group of Baptists, largely through the South, who are opposed to all centralization, to modern missionary societies, and to Sunday schools. They are sometimes called "anti-missionary" Baptists. Members (1950) : 72,000.

**Southern Baptist Convention.**—In 1845, Southern Baptists withdrew from the General Missionary Convention over the question of slavery and other matters and formed the Southern Baptist Convention. Members (1960) : 9,731,591.

**United Baptists.**—This group dates from meetings of Regular Baptists and Separate Baptists held in Richmond, Va., in 1787, and a meeting under the name United Baptists in Clark County, Ky., in 1801. Members (1955) : 63,641.

**The United Free Will Baptist Church.**—A body which set up its organization in 1901. Though ecclesiastically distinct, they are in close relations with the Free Will Baptists. Members (1958) : 100,000.

## Catholic and Orthodox

**Armenian Church of North America.**—The American branch of the Ancient Church of Armenia. Established in the U. S. in 1889. Diocesan organization under the jurisdiction of the Holy See of Etchmiadzin, Armenia, U.S.S.R. Members (1960) : 125,000.

**The American Carpatho-Russian Orthodox Greek Catholic Church.**—This church is a self-governing diocese in communion with the Ecumenical Patriarchate of Constantinople. On Sept. 19, 1938, the late Patriarch Benjamin I canonized the diocese in the name of the Orthodox Church of Christ. Members (1960) : 100,000.

**Greek Archdiocese of North and South America:**—Greek-speaking Orthodox Christians have had parishes in the U. S. for the last seventy years. These were first under the jurisdiction of the Metropolitan of Athens and later under the Patriarchate of Constantinople. Political changes in Europe have been reflected in this country

and have brought difficulties in all branches of the Orthodox Church. In 1931, a general convention held in New York City under the presidency of Archbishop Athenagoras brought a large measure of unity and order. Members (1960) : 1,200,000.

**North American Catholic Church.**—This body is identical with the Roman Catholic Church in worship, faith, etc., but differs in discipline. It was received into union with the Eastern Orthodox Church by the Archbishop of Beirut in 1911 and by the Orthodox Patriarch of Alexandria in 1912. Members (1959) : 71,521.

**Polish National Catholic Church of America.**—After long dissatisfaction with Roman Catholic Administration in many Polish parishes, this group was organized in 1904. Members (1960) : 282,411.

**The Roman Catholic Church.**—The largest single group of Christians in the U. S., the Roman Catholic Church is under the spiritual leadership of Pope John XXIII. This group dates back to the priests who accompanied Columbus on his second voyage to the New World. A settlement, later discontinued, was made at St. Augustine, Fla. The continuous history of this Church in the colonies began at St. Mary's in 1634, in Maryland. Members (1960) : 42,104,900.

**Romanian Orthodox Episcopate of America.**—This body of Eastern Orthodox Christians of Rumanian descent is under the spiritual supervision and canonical jurisdiction of the Bishop of the Romanian Orthodox Church of North and South America. Members (1960) : 50,000.

**The Russian Orthodox Church Outside Russia.**—Organized in 1920 to unite the missions and parishes of the Russian Orthodox Church outside of Russia. Members (1955) : 55,000.

**The Russian Orthodox Greek Catholic Church of America.**—The Russian Orthodox Catholic Church entered Alaska in 1792. In 1872, its headquarters were moved from Sitka to San Francisco and, in 1905, to New York. It administers churches in the U. S. (including Alaska and the Aleutians), Canada, South America, and Japan. Members (1957) : 755,000.

## U. S. Church Membership, 1960

*Source: Yearbook of American Churches.*

| Religious group | Members |
|---|---|
| Buddhist | 20,000 |
| Old Catholic and Polish National Catholic | 589,819 |
| Eastern Orthodox | 2,698,663 |
| Jewish | 5,367,000 |
| Roman Catholic | 42,104,900 |
| Protestant | 63,668,835 |
| Total | 114,449,217 |

NOTE: Compiled from figures furnished by 259 religious bodies in the U. S.

**Serbian Eastern Orthodox Church.—** This body of the Eastern Orthodox Church has its own diocese and is under jurisdiction of the Serbian Patriarchate (Yugoslavia). Members (1960) : 125,000.

**Syrian Antiochian Orthodox Church.—** This body is a division of the Orthodox Church which is under the jurisdiction of the Patriarch of Antioch. It is a member of the Federation of Orthodox Greek Catholic Churches in America. Members (1959) : 115,000.

**Ukrainian Orthodox Church of U.S.A.—** This church was organized in the U. S. in 1919. Members (1960) : 85,000.

## Lutheran

**The American Lutheran Church.—** This Church is the result of the merger in 1961 of the American Lutheran Church, the Evangelical Lutheran Church, and the United Evangelical Lutheran Church. Members (1960) : 2,242,259.

**Augustana Evangelical Lutheran Church.** —This group, whose constituency originally was of Swedish extraction, is a member of the American Lutheran Conference and is also a participating body in the National Lutheran Council. Organized in 1860. Members (1960) : 608,289.

**Evangelical Lutheran Church.—** This body merged in 1961 with two other bodies to form the American Lutheran Church. See that church above.

**The Evangelical Lutheran Joint Synod of Wisconsin and Other States.—** This group, a constituent part of the Synodical Conference, was organized in Wisconsin in 1850. Members (1960) : 235,073.

**Lutheran Church-Missouri Synod.—** This group, the largest constituent part of the Synodical Conference, was organized in 1847, holds to an unwavering confessionalism, and is the leader in the conservative group among the Lutherans. Members (1960) : 2,391,195.

**Lutheran Free Church.—** This body was organized in 1897 as the result of differences of opinion in the United Norwegian Church over control of the Augsburg Seminary. It became a constituent part of the American Lutheran Conference in 1930. Members (1960) : 87,250.

**United Evangelical Lutheran Church.—** This body merged in 1961 with two other bodies to form the American Lutheran Church. See that church above.

**United Lutheran Church in America.—** This group dates back to the Ministerium of Pennsylvania which was organized in 1748, and beyond that to early colonial days. It represents the union of the General Synod, General Council, and United Synod of the South in 1918. Members (1960) : 2,385,224.

## Methodist

**African Methodist Episcopal Church.—** This group was formed in Philadelphia in 1816 and extended throughout the South after the Civil War. Members (1951): 1,166,301.

**African Methodist Episcopal Zion Church.—** This group was organized in 1796, coming out of the John Street Methodist Church, New York. Members (1959) : 780,000.

**Christian Methodist Episcopal Church—** In 1870, the General Conference of the M.E. Church, South, approved the request of its colored membership for the formation of their conferences into a separate body. Members (1951) : 392,167.

**Free Methodist Church of North America.** —This body, organized in 1860, grew out of a movement in the Genesee Conference of the Methodist Episcopal Church towards a more original Methodism. Members (1960) : 55,338.

**The Methodist Church.—** In April, 1939, the Uniting Conference forming The Methodist Church was held by representatives of the Methodist Episcopal Church, the Methodist Episcopal Church, South, and the Methodist Protestant Church. The Methodist Church in the United States originated with the efforts of John and Charles Wesley, leaders of the revival movement in England in the eighteenth century. Methodist emigrants from Ireland planted Methodism in America about 1760. In 1771 Francis Asbury, one of Wesley's preachers, later a Bishop, landed in Philadelphia. The Methodist Episcopal Church was organized in 1784–85. The Methodist Episcopal Church, South, dated from 1846, the separation from the Methodist Episcopal Church having taken place over the slavery issue. The Methodist Protestant Church dated from 1830 and was organized over the issue of lay representation. Members (1960) : 9,893,094.

## Presbyterian

**Cumberland Presbyterian Church.—** In 1806, a presbytery (Cumberland) of the Presbyterian Church was dissolved by the Synod of Kentucky on account of its attitude toward revivalism. Members of the presbytery organized as an independent body in 1810 and became the Cumberland Presbyterian Church. When this body attempted to reunite with the Presbyterian Church in 1906, a minority preferred to continue as an independent church. Members (1960) : 88,452.

**Presbyterian Church in the U. S.—** This group is the branch of the Presbyterian Church which separated from the main body at the time of the Civil War. It is often called the "Southern" Presbyterian Church. Members (1960) : 902,849.

The United Presbyterian Church in the U.S.A.—This group was formed in 1958 by a merger of the Presbyterian Church in the U.S.A. (dating from 1640) and the United Presbyterian Church of North America (established in 1858 by a merger of groups tracing their heritage to covenanter and seceder churches in Scotland). Members (1960): 3,259,011.

## Other Religious Bodies

Apostolic Overcoming Holy Church of God.—A Negro body incorporated in Alabama in 1919. Members (1956): 75,000.

Assemblies of God.—Independent, pentecostal, evangelical, missionary churches associated for co-operative effort in district and general councils. Organized in Arkansas in 1914. Members (1960): 508,602.

Buddhist Churches of America.—Organized in 1914 as the Buddhist Mission of North America, this group was incorporated in 1942 under the present name and represents Buddhism in this country, the faith based on "the anatman doctrine, supplemented by the idea of karma, and nirvana, the holy ease or a blissful mental state of absolute freedom from evil." Members (1960): 20,000.

The Christian and Missionary Alliance.—An evangelical, evangelistic, and missionary movement organized in 1887. It stresses "the deeper Christian life and consecration to the Lord's service." Members (1960): 59,657.

Christian Churches (Disciples of Christ).—In the revival period of the early nineteenth century, a movement under Thomas Campbell and his son, Alexander, resulted in the establishment of a fellowship called Christians or Disciples. They believe that sects are unscriptural. Members (1960): 1,801,821.

Christian Reformed Church.—A group of Dutch Calvinists which dissented from the Reformed Church in America in 1857 and which was strengthened by later accessions from the same source and by immigration. Members (1960): 242,593.

Church of Christ, Scientist.—Founded by Mary Baker Eddy in 1879. As defined by Mrs. Eddy, Christian Science is the scientific system of divine healing and the reinstatement of primitive Christianity.*

The Church of God.—Inaugurated by Bishop A. J. Tomlinson, who served as General Overseer 1903–43. Episcopal in administration. Members (1959): 74,209.

Church of God (Anderson, Ind.).—This group is one of the largest of the groups which have taken the name "Church of God." Its headquarters are at Anderson, Ind. It originated about 1880. Members (1960): 142,796.

*Membership figure not available. The manual of the church forbids "the numbering of people and the reporting of such statistics for publication."

Church of God (Cleveland, Tenn.).—This body, to be differentiated from the Church of God at Anderson, Ind., is a holiness group and pentecostal. It began in 1886 in Tennessee, under the name of Christian Union, reorganized in 1902 as the Holiness Church. In 1907 it adopted the name above. Members (1960): 170,261.

Church of God in Christ.—Organized in Arkansas in 1895, by C. P. Jones and C. H. Mason, who believed there was no salvation without holiness; incorporated 1897. Members (1960): 392,635.

Church of the Brethren (Conservative Dunkers).—German pietists from Krefeld, Germany, under the leadership of Peter Becker, entered the colonies in 1719, and settled at Germantown, Philadelphia, Pa. They were called Dunkers (baptizers) and were immersionists. The members are conservative as to attire, oaths or affirmations, resistance to force, temperance, etc. Members (1960): 199,947.

Church of the Nazarene.—One of the larger holiness bodies, organized in Pilot Point, Tex., Oct. 1908. It is in general accord with the early doctrines of Methodism and emphasizes entire sanctification. Members (1960): 307,629.

Churches of Christ.—This body is made up of a large group of churches, formerly reported with the Disciples of Christ but, since the religious census of 1906, reported separately. They are strictly congregational and have no organization larger than the local congregation. Members (1960): 2,163,493.

Congregational Christian Churches.—Congregational churches date back to the Pilgrim Fathers and the early colonists of New England in 1620. This body merged in July, 1961, with the Evangelical and Reformed Church to form the United Church of Christ. Members (1960): 1,427,863.

Evangelical and Reformed Church.—This body, now part of the United Church of Christ, was formed on June 26, 1934, at Cleveland, Ohio, by a union of the Evangelical Synod of North America and the Reformed Church in the United States. In July, 1961, the Evangelical and Reformed Church merged with the Congregational Christian Churches to form the United Church of Christ. Members (1960): 813,271.

Evangelical Covenant Church of America. A transplantation to the U. S., in 1885, of a free-church movement in the Swedish state church. Until recently the name has been the Swedish Evangelical Mission Covenant. Members (1960): 60,090.

The Evangelical United Brethren Church.—This group had its origin in Johnstown, Pa., November 16, 1946, in the consummation of organic union between the Evangelical Church and the Church of the United Brethren in Christ. Both these former communions had their beginning in Pennsylvania in the evangelistic movement of the early 19th century. Jacob Albright was the founder of the Evangelical Church, and Dr. Philip William Otterbein was the founder of the United Brethren Church in 1800. Members (1960): 748,216.

**Friends, The Five Years Meeting of.**— The Five Years Meeting of Friends was formed in 1902 by 13 Yearly Meetings entering into a loose confederation. Since then, two of the original Yearly Meetings have withdrawn (Kansas and Oregon) and three Yearly Meetings outside the U. S. have joined. Members (1960): 71,552.

**International Church of the Foursquare Gospel.**—An evangelistic missionary body organized by Aimee Semple McPherson in 1927. The parent church is Angelus Temple in Los Angeles. Members (1960): 82,624.

**Jehovah's Witnesses.**—A group calling themselves primitive Christians. They believe that the Kingdom under Christ will replace all earthly governments. Members (1959): 239,418.

**Jewish Congregations.**—Jews arrived in the colonies before 1650. The first congregation is recorded in 1656, in New York City, the Shearth Israel (Remnant of Israel). Members (1960): 5,367,000.

**Latter-day Saints, Church of Jesus Christ of.**—A group in which the Bible, the Book of Mormon, the Doctrine and Covenants, and the Pearl of Great Price are regarded as the word of God. The primitive church organization is sought. Members (1960): 1,486,887.

**Latter-day Saints, Reorganized Church of Jesus Christ of.**—A division among the Latter-day Saints (Mormons) occurred on the death of Joseph Smith in 1844. His son, Joseph Smith, became presiding officer of this group, which has headquarters at Independence, Mo. Members (1960): 155,291.

**Mennonite Church.**—The largest group of the Mennonites who began arriving in the U. S. in 1683, settling in Germantown, Pa. They derive their name from Menno Simons, born 1496. Members (1960): 73,125.

**Moravian Church (Unitas Fratrum).**—In 1735, Moravian missionaries of the pre-Reformation faith of John Huss came to Georgia and, in 1740, to Pennsylvania. They established the Moravian Church. Members (1960): 61,368.

**Pentecostal Assemblies of the World, Inc.**—A pentecostal holiness group originating in the early part of the century and found largely in the Midwest. Members (1960): 45,000.

**Pentecostal Church of God of America, Inc.**—Organized in 1919 at Chicago, Ill. Members (1958): 103,500.

**The Protestant Episcopal Church.**—This group entered the colonies with the earliest settlers as the Church of England. It became autonomous, adopted its present name in 1789. Members (1959): 3,444,265.

**Reformed Church in America.**—This group was established by the earliest Dutch settlers of New York as the Reformed Protestant Dutch Church in 1628. Members (1960): 225,927.

**The Salvation Army.**—An evangelistic organization, with a military government, first set up by General William Booth in England and introduced into the U. S. in 1880. Members (1960): 254,141.

**Seventh-day Adventists.**—This body developed out of the Adventist movement (1833–1844), which emphasized the imminent personal return of Jesus Christ. It emphasized the observance of the seventh-day Sabbath and in 1863 was numerous enough to organize a conference. Members (1960): 317,852.

**Spiritualists, International General Assembly of.**—Organized in Buffalo, N. Y., in 1936. Members (1956): 164,072.

**Unitarian Churches.**—The Unitarian movement in Congregationalism, beginning in the eighteenth century, produced the American Unitarian Association in 1825. In 1865 a national conference was organized Members (1960): 101,205.

**United Church of Christ.**—A merger in 1961 of the Evangelical and Reformed Church and the Congregational Christian Churches. See statistics under those churches, above.

**United Pentecostal Church, Inc.**—Pentecostal Church, Inc., and Pentecostal Assemblies of Jesus Christ merged in 1945 at St. Louis. Members (1960): 175,000.

**Universalist Church of America.**—The philosophy of Universalism originated in the first century A.D. and was carried to America in the eighteenth century. Members (1959): 70,542.

# Active Bishops of the Protestant Episcopal Church

*Source:* Alexander M. Rodger, Secretary, The House of Bishops, 207 Fairmount Rd., Ridgewood, N. J.

**(Note: M—Missionary Bishop; C—Coadjutor; S—Suffragan)**

**Presiding Bishop:** Arthur C. Lichtenberger, New York City. Vice President of National Council: John B. Bentley, 218 Park Ave. South, New York 10, N. Y.

Alabama: Chas. C. J. Carpenter, George M. Murray (C), Birmingham.

Alaska: Wm. J. Gordon, Jr. (M), Fairbanks.

Albany (N. Y.): Allen W. Brown.

Arizona: Arthur B. Kinsolving II, Phoenix.

Arkansas: Robert R. Brown, Little Rock.

Atlanta (Ga.): Randolph R. Claiborne.

Bethlehem (Pa.): Frederick J. Warnecke.

California: James A. Pike, George R. Millard (S), San Francisco.

Central America: David E. Richards (M), San José, Costa Rica.

Central Brazil: Edmund K. Sherrill (M), Rio de Janeiro.

Central New York: Walter M. Higley, Syracuse.

Chicago: Gerald F. Burrill, Charles L. Street (S).

Colorado: Joseph S. Minnis, Edwin B. Thayer (S), Denver.

Connecticut: Walter H. Gray, John H. Esquirol (S), Hartford.

Cuba: (Vacant).

Dallas (Tex.): C. Avery Mason, Joseph M. Harte (S).

Delaware: J. Brooke Mosley, Wilmington.

Dominican Republic: Paul A. Kellogg (M), Ciudad Trujillo.

East Carolina: Thomas H. Wright, Wilmington, N. C.

Eastern Oregon: Lane W. Barton (M), Bend.

Easton (Md.): Allen J. Miller.

Eau Claire (Wis.): William W. Horstick.

Erie (Pa.): William Crittenden.

European Churches: Stephen F. Bayne, Jr., London, Eng.

Florida: Hamilton West, Jacksonville.

Fond du Lac (Wis.): William H. Brady.

Georgia: Albert R. Stuart, Savannah.

Haiti: C. A. Voegeli (M), Port-au-Prince.

Harrisburg (Pa.): J. Thomas Heistand, Harrisburg; Earl M. Honaman (S), Williamsport.

Honolulu: Harry S. Kennedy (M).

Idaho: Norman L. Foote (M), Boise.

Indianapolis: John P. Craine.

Iowa: Gordon V. Smith, Des Moines.

Kansas: Edward C. Turner, Topeka.

Kentucky: C. Gresham Marmion, Jr., Louisville.

Lexington (Ky.): William R. Moody.

Liberia: Bravid W. Harris (M), Monrovia.

Long Island: James P. DeWolfe, Jonathan G. Sherman (S), Garden City, N. Y.

Los Angeles: Francis E. I. Bloy, Ivol I. Curtis (S).

Louisiana: Girault M. Jones, New Orleans; Iveson B. Noland (C), Alexandria.

Maine: Oliver L. Loring, Portland.

Maryland: Noble C. Powell, Harry L. Doll, (C), Baltimore.

Massachusetts: Anson Phelps Stokes, Jr., Boston, Frederic C. Lawrence (S).

Mexico: José G. Saucedo (M), Mexico City.

Michigan: Richard S. Emrich, Archie H. Crowley (S), Robert L. De Witt (S), Detroit.

Milwaukee: Donald H. V. Hallock.

Minnesota: Hamilton H. Kellogg, Philip F. McNairy (S), Minneapolis.

Mississippi: Duncan M. Gray, Jackson.

Missouri: George L. Cadigan, St. Louis.

Montana: Chandler W. Sterling, Helena.

National Council: Daniel Corrigan, Director of Home Department, New York City.

Nebraska: Howard R. Brinker, Russell T. Rauscher (C), Omaha.

Nevada: William G. Wright (M), Reno.

New Hampshire: Charles F. Hall, Concord.

New Jersey: Alfred L. Banyard, Trenton.

New Mexico and Southwest Texas: Charles J. Kinsolving III, Albuquerque, N. Mex.

New York: Horace W. B. Donegan, Charles F. Boynton (S), J. Stuart Wetmore (S), New York City.

Newark (N. J.): Leland Stark, Donald MacAdie (S).

North Carolina: Richard H. Baker, Thomas A. Fraser, Jr. (C), Raleigh.

North Dakota: Richard Emery (M), Fargo.

Northern California: Clarence R. Haden, Jr., Sacramento.

Northern Indiana: Reginald Mallett, South Bend.

Northern Michigan: Herman R. Page, Menominee.

Northwest Texas: George H. Quarterman, Amarillo.

Ohio: Nelson M. Burroughs, Cleveland.

Oklahoma: Chilton Powell, Oklahoma City.

Olympia (Wash.): William F. Lewis, Seattle.

Oregon: James W. F. Carman, Portland.

Panama Canal Zone: Reginald H. Gooden (M), Ancon.

Pennsylvania: Oliver J. Hart, J. Gillespie Armstrong (C), Philadelphia.

Philippines: Lyman C. Ogilby (M), Benito C. Cabanban (S), Manila.

Pittsburgh: Austin Pardue, William S. Thomas (S).

Puerto Rico: Albert E. Swift (M), Santurce.

Quincy (Ill.): William Lickfield.

Rhode Island: John S. Higgins, Providence, R. I.

Rochester (N. Y.): Dudley S. Stark.

San Joaquin (Calif.): Sumner F. D. Walters, Stockton.

South Carolina: Gray Temple, Charleston.

South Dakota: Conrad H. Gesner (M), Sioux Falls.

South Florida: Henry I. Louttit, Winter Park.

Southern Brazil: Egmont M. Krischke (M), Porto Alegre.

Southern Ohio: Roger W. Blanchard, Cincinnati.

Southern Virginia: George P. Gunn, Norfolk; David S. Rose (S), Petersburg.

Southwestern Brazil: Plinio L. Simões (M), Santa Maria.

Southwestern Virginia: William H. Marmion, Roanoke.

Spokane (Wash.): Russell S. Hubbard (M).

Springfield (Ill.): Charles A. Clough.

Tennessee: Theodore N. Barth, Memphis; John Vander Horst (C), Chattanooga.

Texas: John E. Hines, Houston; Percy Goddard (S), Tyler.

Upper South Carolina: C. Alfred Cole, Columbia, S. C.

Utah: Richard S. Watson (M), Salt Lake City.

Vermont: Harvey D. Butterfield, Burlington.

Virginia: Robert F. Gibson, Jr., Samuel B. Chilton (S), Richmond.

Washington (D. C.): Angus Dun, William F. Creighton (C).

West Missouri: Edward R. Welles, Grandview.

West Texas: Everett H. Jones, R. Earl Dicus (S), San Antonio.

West Virginia: Wilburn C. Campbell, Charleston.

Western Kansas: Arnold M. Lewis (M), Salina.

Western Massachusetts: Robert M. Hatch, Springfield.

Western Michigan: Charles E. Bennison, Grand Rapids.

Western New York: Lauriston L. Scaife, Buffalo.

Western North Carolina: M. George Henry, Asheville, N. C.

Wyoming: James W. Hunter (M), Laramie.

---

# Bishops of The Methodist Church

*Source:* Methodist Information, New York City.

President: Bishop Paul E. Martin, Houston, Tex. (to April 1962). President-designate: Bishop Marshall R. Reed, Detroit, Mich. Secretary: Bishop Roy H. Short, Box 871, Nashville 2, Tenn.

Dionisio D. Alejandro; Manila, Philippines.
Ralph T. Alton; Madison, Wis.
Hobart B. Amstutz; Singapore, Malaya.
Sante Uberto Barbieri; Buenos Aires.
Newell S. Booth; Elisabethville, Congo.
Charles W. Brashares; Chicago, Ill.
W. Y. Chen; China.
Matthew W. Clair, Jr.; St. Louis, Mo.
Kenneth W. Copeland; Lincoln, Nebr.
Fred P. Corson; Philadelphia, Pa.
Ralph E. Dodge; Salisbury, Southern Rhodesia.
F. Gerald Ensley; Des Moines, Iowa.
Eugene M. Frank; St. Louis, Mo.
Marvin A. Franklin; Jackson, Miss.
Paul V. Galloway; San Antonio, Tex.
Paul N. Garber; Richmond, Va.
Edwin R. Garrison; Aberdeen, S. Dak.
Charles F. Golden; Nashville, Tenn.
A. Raymond Grant; Portland, Oreg.
Walter C. Gum; Louisville, Ky.
Odd Hagen; Stockholm, Sweden.
Paul Hardin, Jr.; Columbia, S. C.
Nolan B. Harmon; Charlotte, N. C.
Marquis L. Harris; Atlanta, Ga.
James W. Henley; Jacksonville, Fla.
Fred G. Holloway; Charleston, W. Va.
Gerald Kennedy; Los Angeles, Calif.
John Wesley Lord; Washington, D. C.
Edgar A. Love; Baltimore, Md.

Paul E. Martin; Houston, Tex.
William C. Martin; Dallas, Tex.
James K. Mathews; Boston, Mass.
W. Vernon Middleton; Pittsburgh, Pa.
Shot K. Mondol; Delhi, India.
Noah W. Moore, Jr.; New Orleans, La.
T. Otto Nall; Minneapolis, Minn.
Everett W. Palmer; Seattle, Wash.
Glenn R. Phillips; Denver, Colo.
W. Kenneth Pope; Little Rock, Ark.
Richard C. Raines; Indianapolis, Ind.
Marshall R. Reed; Detroit, Mich.
Roy H. Short; Nashville, Tenn.
Ferdinand Sigg; Zürich, Switzerland.
Mangal Singh; Bombay, India.
Eugene Slater; Topeka, Kans.
John Owen Smith; Atlanta, Ga.
W. Angie Smith; Oklahoma City, Okla.
John A. Subhan; Hyderabad, India.
Gabriel Sundaram; Lucknow, India.
Prince Albert Taylor, Jr.; Monrovia, Liberia.
Donald H. Tippett; San Francisco, Calif.
José L. Valencia; Baguio, Philippines.
Edwin E. Voigt; Springfield, Ill.
Aubrey G. Walton; New Orleans, La.
W. Ralph Ward, Jr.; Syracuse, N. Y.
Hazen G. Werner; Columbus, Ohio.
Lloyd C. Wicke; New York, N. Y.
Friedrich Wunderlich; Frankfurt, Germany.

# Archbishops of Canterbury

| Sequence | Name | Created | Sequence | Name | Created |
|---|---|---|---|---|---|
| 1 | Augustine (consecrated Bishop 597) | 601 | 51 | Walter Reynolds | 1313 |
| 2 | Laurentius | 604 | 52 | Simon Mepeham | 1328 |
| 3 | Mellitus | 619 | 53 | John de Stratford | 1333 |
| 4 | Justus | 624 | 54 | Thomas Bradwardine | 1349 |
| 5 | Honorius | 627 | 55 | Simon Islip | 1349 |
| 6 | Deusdedit | 655 | 56 | Simon Langham | 1366 |
| 7 | Theodorus | 668 | 57 | William Whittlesey | 1368 |
| 8 | Beorhtweald | 692 | 58 | Simon of Sudbury | 1375 |
| 9 | Tatwine | 731 | 59 | William Courtenay | 1381 |
| 10 | Nothelm | 735 | 60 | Thomas Arundel | 1396 |
| 11 | Cuthbeorht | 740 | 61 | Roger Walden | 1398 |
| 12 | Breguwine | 761 | 62 | Thomas Arundel (restored) | 1399 |
| 13 | Jaenbeorht | 765 | 63 | Henry Chicheley | 1414 |
| 14 | Æthelheard | 793 | 64 | John Stafford | 1443 |
| 15 | Wulfred | 805 | 65 | John Kemp | 1452 |
| 16 | Feologild | 832 | 66 | Thomas Bourchier | 1454 |
| 17 | Ceolnoth | 833 | 67 | John Morton | 1486 |
| 18 | Æthelred | 870 | 68 | Henry Dean | 1501 |
| 19 | Plegmund | 890 | 69 | William Warham | 1503 |
| 20 | Æthelhelm | 914 | 70 | Thomas Cranmer | 1533 |
| 21 | Wulfhelm | 923 | 71 | Reginald Pole | 1556 |
| 22 | Oda | 942 | 72 | Matthew Parker | 1559 |
| 23 | Ælfsige | 959 | 73 | Edmund Grindal | 1576 |
| 24 | Beorhthelm | 959 | 74 | John Whitgift | 1583 |
| 25 | Dunstan | 959 | 75 | Richard Bancroft | 1604 |
| 26 | Æthelgar | 988 | 76 | George Abbot | 1611 |
| 27 | Sigeric Serio | 990 | 77 | William Laud | 1633 |
| 28 | Ælfric | 995 | 78 | William Juxon | 1660 |
| 29 | Ælfheah | 1005 | 79 | Gilbert Sheldon | 1663 |
| 30 | Lyfing | 1013 | 80 | William Sancroft | 1678 |
| 31 | Æthelnoth | 1020 | 81 | John Tillotson | 1691 |
| 32 | Eadsige | 1038 | 82 | Thomas Tenison | 1695 |
| 33 | Robert (Champart) of Jumièges | 1051 | 83 | William Wake | 1716 |
| 34 | Stigand | 1052 | 84 | John Potter | 1737 |
| 35 | Lanfranc | 1070 | 85 | Thomas Herring | 1747 |
| 36 | Anselm | 1093 | 86 | Matthew Hutton | 1757 |
| 37 | Ralph d'Escures | 1114 | 87 | Thomas Secker | 1758 |
| 38 | William de Corbeil | 1123 | 88 | Frederick Cornwallis | 1768 |
| 39 | Theobald | 1138 | 89 | John Moore | 1783 |
| 40 | Thomas à Becket | 1162 | 90 | Charles Manners-Sutton | 1805 |
| 41 | Richard (of Dover) | 1174 | 91 | William Howley | 1828 |
| 42 | Baldwin | 1185 | 92 | John Bird Sumner | 1848 |
| 43 | Hubert Walter | 1193 | 93 | Charles Thomas Longley | 1862 |
| 44 | Stephen Langton | 1207 | 94 | Archibald Campbell Tait | 1868 |
| 45 | Richard le Grant (of Wetharshed) | 1229 | 95 | Edward White Benson | 1883 |
| 46 | Edmund Rich | 1234 | 96 | Frederick Temple | 1896 |
| 47 | Boniface of Savoy | 1245 | 97 | Randall Thomas Davidson | 1903 |
| 48 | Robert Kilwardby | 1273 | 98 | Cosmo Gordon Lang | 1928 |
| 49 | John Pecham (Peckham) | 1279 | 99 | William Temple | 1942 |
| 50 | Robert Winchelsea | 1294 | 100 | Geoffrey Francis Fisher | 1945 |
|  |  |  | 101 | Arthur Michael Ramsey | 1961 |

(NOTE: Anglicans consider the line of Archbishops unbroken from Augustine to the present day. Roman Catholics consider the office vacant since 1558, the death of Pole.)

## History of the Christian Church in England

5th century  Arrival in England of Angles, Saxons and Jutes. Church isolated from Rome.

597  Augustine sent to convert Saxons.

1534  Act of Supremacy makes king head of Church of England.

1554  Church again united with Rome under reign of Mary.

1558  Church restored to Crown at accession of Elizabeth.

1611  King James version of Bible.

1646  Puritan rebellion. Presbyterianism becomes state religion.

1660  Restoration. Power of Church of England restored under Charles II.

1739  John Wesley founds Methodism.

1829  Catholic emancipation.

1833–45  Oxford Movement attempts to bring Church of England closer to ideals of ancient Church. This movement continues as important influence.

# Roman Catholic Pontiffs

*Source: The National Catholic Almanac.*

St. Peter, of Bethsaida in Galilee, Prince of the Apostles, was the first Pope. He resided first in Antioch and then for twenty-five years in Rome, where he suffered martyrdom in 64 or 67 of the modern era. He was followed by St. Linus.

| Name | Birthplace | Acces. | End of reign | Name | Birthplace | Acces. | End of reign |
|---|---|---|---|---|---|---|---|
| St. Linus | Tuscia | 67 | 76 | Sabinianus | Tuscia | 604 | 606 |
| St. Anacletus (Cletus) | Rome | 76 | 88 | Boniface III | Rome | 607 | 607 |
| | | | | St. Boniface IV | Marsi | 608 | 615 |
| St. Clement | Rome | 88 | 97 | St. Deusdedit (Adeodatus I) | Rome | 615 | 618 |
| St. Evaristus | Greece | 97 | 105 | | | | |
| St. Alexander I | Rome | 105 | 115 | Boniface V | Naples | 619 | 625 |
| St. Sixtus I | Rome | 115 | 125 | Honorius I | Campania | 625 | 638 |
| St. Telesphorus | Greece | 125 | 136 | Severinus | Rome | 640 | 640 |
| St. Hyginus | Greece | 136 | 140 | John IV | Dalmatia | 640 | 642 |
| St. Pius I | Aquileia | 140 | 155 | Theodore I | Greece | 642 | 649 |
| St. Anicetus | Syria | 155 | 166 | St. Martin I | Todi | 649 | 655 |
| St. Soter | Campania | 166 | 175 | St. Eugenius I | Rome | 654 | 657 |
| St. Eleutherius | Epirus | 175 | 189 | St. Vitalian | Segni | 657 | 672 |
| St. Victor I | Africa | 189 | 199 | Adeodatus II | Rome | 672 | 676 |
| St. Zephyrinus | Rome | 199 | 217 | Donus | Rome | 676 | 678 |
| St. Callistus I | Rome | 217 | 222 | St. Agatho | Sicily | 678 | 681 |
| St. Urban I | Rome | 222 | 230 | St. Leo II | Sicily | 682 | 683 |
| St. Pontian | Rome | 230 | 235 | St. Benedict II | Rome | 684 | 685 |
| St. Anterus | Greece | 235 | 236 | John V | Syria | 685 | 686 |
| St. Fabian | Rome | 236 | 250 | Conon | Unknown | 686 | 687 |
| St. Cornelius | Rome | 251 | 253 | St. Sergius I | Syria | 687 | 701 |
| St. Lucius I | Rome | 253 | 254 | John VI | Greece | 701 | 705 |
| St. Stephen I | Rome | 254 | 257 | John VII | Greece | 705 | 707 |
| St. Sixtus II | Greece | 257 | 258 | Sisinnius | Syria | 708 | 708 |
| St. Dionysius | Unknown | 259 | 268 | Constantine | Syria | 708 | 715 |
| St. Felix I | Rome | 269 | 274 | St. Gregory II | Rome | 715 | 731 |
| St. Eutychian | Luni | 275 | 283 | St. Gregory III | Syria | 731 | 741 |
| St. Caius | Dalmatia | 283 | 296 | St. Zachary | Greece | 741 | 752 |
| St. Marcellinus | Rome | 296 | 304 | Stephen II | Rome | 752 | 752 |
| St. Marcellus I | Rome | 308 | 309 | Stephen III | Rome | 752 | 757 |
| St. Eusebius | Greece | 309 | 309 | St. Paul I | Rome | 757 | 767 |
| St. Melchiades | Africa | 311 | 314 | Stephen IV | Sicily | 768 | 772 |
| St. Sylvester I | Rome | 314 | 335 | Adrian I | Rome | 772 | 795 |
| St. Marcus | Rome | 336 | 336 | St. Leo III | Rome | 795 | 816 |
| St. Julius I | Rome | 337 | 352 | Stephen V | Rome | 816 | 817 |
| St. Liberius | Rome | 352 | 366 | St. Paschal I | Rome | 817 | 824 |
| St. Damasus I | Spain | 366 | 384 | Eugenius II | Rome | 824 | 827 |
| St. Siricius | Rome | 384 | 399 | Valentine | Rome | 827 | 827 |
| St. Anastasius I | Rome | 399 | 401 | Gregory IV | Rome | 827 | 844 |
| St. Innocent I | Albano | 401 | 417 | Sergius II | Rome | 844 | 847 |
| St. Zozimus | Greece | 417 | 418 | St. Leo IV | Rome | 847 | 855 |
| St. Boniface I | Rome | 418 | 422 | Benedict III | Rome | 855 | 858 |
| St. Celestine I | Campania | 422 | 432 | St. Nicholas | Rome | 858 | 867 |
| St. Sixtus III | Rome | 432 | 440 | Adrian II | Rome | 867 | 872 |
| St. Leo I (the Great) | Tuscia | 440 | 461 | John VIII | Rome | 872 | 882 |
| | | | | Marinus I | Gallese | 882 | 884 |
| St. Hilary | Sardo | 461 | 468 | St. Adrian III | Rome | 884 | 885 |
| St. Simplicius | Tivoli | 468 | 483 | Stephen VI | Rome | 885 | 891 |
| St. Felix III (II) | Rome | 483 | 492 | Formosus | Portus | 891 | 896 |
| St. Gelasius I | Africa | 492 | 496 | Boniface VI | Rome | 896 | 896 |
| Anastasius II | Rome | 496 | 498 | Stephen VII | Rome | 896 | 897 |
| St. Symmachus | Sardo | 498 | 514 | Romanus | Gallese | 897 | 897 |
| St. Hormisdas | Frosinone | 514 | 523 | Theodore II | Rome | 897 | 897 |
| St. John I | Tuscia | 523 | 526 | John IX | Tivoli | 898 | 900 |
| St. Felix IV (III) | Sannio | 526 | 530 | Benedict IV | Rome | 900 | 903 |
| Boniface II | Rome | 530 | 532 | Leo V | Ardea | 903 | 903 |
| John II | Rome | 533 | 535 | Sergius III | Rome | 904 | 911 |
| St. Agapitus I | Rome | 535 | 536 | Anastasius III | Rome | 911 | 913 |
| St. Silverius | Campania | 536 | 537 | Landus | Sabina | 913 | 914 |
| Vigilius | Rome | 537 | 555 | John X | Tossignano | 914 | 928 |
| Pelagius I | Rome | 556 | 561 | Leo VI | Rome | 928 | 928 |
| John III | Rome | 561 | 574 | Stephen VIII | Rome | 928 | 931 |
| Benedict I | Rome | 575 | 579 | John XI | Rome | 931 | 935 |
| Pelagius II | Rome | 579 | 590 | Leo VII | Rome | 936 | 939 |
| St. Gregory I (the Great) | Rome | 590 | 604 | Stephen IX | Rome | 939 | 942 |
| | | | | Marinus II | Rome | 942 | 946 |

| Name | Birthplace | Acces. | End of reign | Name | Birthplace | Acces. | End of reign |
|---|---|---|---|---|---|---|---|
| Agapitus II | Rome | 946 | 955 | Bl. Benedict XI | Treviso | 1303 | 1304 |
| John XII | Tusculum | 955 | 964 | Clement V | France | 1305 | 1314 |
| Leo VIII | Rome | 963 | 965 | John XXII | Cahors | 1316 | 1334 |
| Benedict V | Rome | 964 | 966 | Benedict XII | France | 1334 | 1342 |
| John XIII | Rome | 965 | 972 | Clement VI | France | 1342 | 1352 |
| Benedict VI | Rome | 973 | 974 | Innocent VI | France | 1352 | 1362 |
| Benedict VII | Rome | 974 | 983 | Bl. Urban V | France | 1362 | 1370 |
| John XIV | Pavia | 983 | 984 | Gregory XI | France | 1370 | 1378 |
| John XV | Rome | 985 | 996 | Urban VI | Naples | 1378 | 1389 |
| Gregory V | Saxony | 996 | 999 | Boniface IX | Naples | 1389 | 1404 |
| Sylvester II | Alvernia | 999 | 1003 | Innocent VII | Sulmona | 1404 | 1406 |
| John XVII | Rome | 1003 | 1003 | Gregory XII | Venetia | 1406 | 1415 |
| John XVIII | Rome | 1004 | 1009 | Martin V | Rome | 1417 | 1431 |
| Sergius IV | Rome | 1009 | 1012 | Eugene IV | Venetia | 1431 | 1447 |
| Benedict VIII | Tusculum | 1012 | 1024 | Nicholas V | Sarzana | 1447 | 1455 |
| John XIX | Tusculum | 1024 | 1032 | Callistus III | Valencia | 1455 | 1458 |
| Benedict IX * | Tusculum | 1032 | 1044 | Pius II | Siena | 1458 | 1464 |
| Sylvester III | Rome | 1045 | 1045 | Paul II | Venetia | 1464 | 1471 |
| Benedict IX | .... | 1045 | 1045 | Sixtus IV | Savona | 1471 | 1484 |
|   (2nd time) | | | | Innocent VIII | Genoa | 1484 | 1492 |
| Gregory VI | Rome | 1045 | 1046 | Alexander VI | Valencia | 1492 | 1503 |
| Clement II | Saxony | 1046 | 1047 | Pius III | Siena | 1503 | 1503 |
| Benedict IX | .... | 1047 | 1048 | Julius II | Savona | 1503 | 1513 |
|   (3rd time) | | | | Leo X | Florence | 1513 | 1521 |
| Damasus II | Bavaria | 1048 | 1048 | Adrian VI | Utrecht | 1522 | 1523 |
| St. Leo IX | Egisheim-Dagsburg | 1049 | 1054 | Clement VII | Florence | 1523 | 1534 |
| Victor II | Dollnstein-Hirschberg | 1055 | 1057 | Paul III | Rome | 1534 | 1549 |
| Stephen X | Lorraine | 1057 | 1058 | Julius III | Rome | 1550 | 1555 |
| Nicholas II | Burgundy | 1059 | 1061 | Marcellus II | Montepulciano | 1555 | 1555 |
| Alexander II | Milan | 1061 | 1073 | Paul IV | Naples | 1555 | 1559 |
| St. Gregory VII | Tuscia | 1073 | 1085 | Pius IV | Milan | 1559 | 1565 |
| Bl. Victor III | Benevento | 1086 | 1087 | St. Pius V | Bosco | 1566 | 1572 |
| Bl. Urban II | France | 1088 | 1099 | Gregory XIII | Bologna | 1572 | 1585 |
| Paschal II | Ravenna | 1099 | 1118 | Sixtus V | Grottammare | 1585 | 1590 |
| Gelasius II | Gaeta | 1118 | 1119 | Urban VII | Rome | 1590 | 1590 |
| Callistus II | Burgundy | 1119 | 1124 | Gregory XIV | Cremona | 1590 | 1591 |
| Honorius II | Fiagnano | 1124 | 1130 | Innocent IX | Bologna | 1591 | 1591 |
| Innocent II | Rome | 1130 | 1143 | Clement VIII | Florence | 1592 | 1605 |
| Celestine II | Città di Castello | 1143 | 1144 | Leo XI | Florence | 1605 | 1605 |
| | | | | Paul V | Rome | 1605 | 1621 |
| Lucius II | Bologna | 1144 | 1145 | Gregory XV | Bologna | 1621 | 1623 |
| Bl. Eugene III | Pisa | 1145 | 1153 | Urban VIII | Florence | 1623 | 1644 |
| Anastasius IV | Rome | 1153 | 1154 | Innocent X | Rome | 1644 | 1655 |
| Adrian IV | England | 1154 | 1159 | Alexander VII | Siena | 1655 | 1667 |
| Alexander III | Siena | 1159 | 1181 | Clement IX | Pistoia | 1667 | 1669 |
| Lucius III | Lucca | 1181 | 1185 | Clement X | Rome | 1670 | 1676 |
| Urban III | Milan | 1185 | 1187 | Innocent XI | Como | 1676 | 1689 |
| Gregory VIII | Benevento | 1187 | 1187 | Alexander VIII | Venetia | 1689 | 1691 |
| Clement III | Rome | 1187 | 1191 | Innocent XII | Naples | 1691 | 1700 |
| Celestine III | Rome | 1191 | 1198 | Clement XI | Urbino | 1700 | 1721 |
| Innocent III | Anagni | 1198 | 1216 | Innocent XIII | Rome | 1721 | 1724 |
| Honorius III | Rome | 1216 | 1227 | Benedict XIII | Rome | 1724 | 1730 |
| Gregory IX | Anagni | 1227 | 1241 | Clement XII | Florence | 1730 | 1740 |
| Celestine IV | Milan | 1241 | 1241 | Benedict XIV | Bologna | 1740 | 1758 |
| Innocent IV | Genoa | 1243 | 1254 | Clement XIII | Venetia | 1758 | 1769 |
| Alexander IV | Anagni | 1254 | 1261 | Clement XIV | Rimini | 1769 | 1774 |
| Urban IV | Troyes | 1261 | 1264 | Pius VI | Cesena | 1775 | 1799 |
| Clement IV | France | 1265 | 1268 | Pius VII | Cesena | 1800 | 1823 |
| Bl. Gregory X | Piacenza | 1271 | 1276 | Leo XII | Fabriano | 1823 | 1829 |
| Bl. Innocent V | Savoy | 1276 | 1276 | Pius VIII | Cingoli | 1829 | 1830 |
| Adrian V | Genoa | 1276 | 1276 | Gregory XVI | Belluno | 1831 | 1846 |
| John XXI | Portugal | 1276 | 1277 | Pius IX | Senigallia | 1846 | 1878 |
| Nicholas III | Rome | 1277 | 1280 | Leo XIII | Carpineto | 1878 | 1903 |
| Martin IV | France | 1281 | 1285 | St. Pius X | Riese | 1903 | 1914 |
| Honorius IV | Rome | 1285 | 1287 | Benedict XV | Genoa | 1914 | 1922 |
| Nicholas IV | Ascoli | 1288 | 1292 | Pius XI | Desio | 1922 | 1939 |
| St. Celestine V | Isernia | 1294 | 1294 | Pius XII | Rome | 1939 | 1958 |
| Boniface VIII | Anagni | 1294 | 1303 | John XXIII | Sotto Il Monte | 1958 | |

* If the triple removal of Benedict IX was not valid, Sylvester III, Gregory VI and Clement II were antipopes.
NOTE: This list of Popes, adapted from the *Annuario Pontificio*, is in accordance with the recent revisions made by Monsignor Mercati, Prefect of the Vatican's archives. All Popes before Sylvester I are listed as martyrs; other martyrs were: St. John I, St. Silverius and St. Martin I. The accession year is that during which the Pope was elected.

# The College of Cardinals
## Cardinal Bishops

| Year of creation | Name | Office or dignity | Nationality |
|---|---|---|---|
| 1936 | Eugene Tisserant | Bishop of Ostia, Porto, and Santa Rufina; Dean of the Sacred College of Cardinals; Secretary of the Sacred Congregation for the Oriental Church; Prefect of the Sacred Congregation of Ceremonies; Librarian and Archivist of the Holy Roman Church; Chamberlain of the Sacred College. | French |
| 1946 | Clemente Micara | Bishop of Velletri; Vicar General of Rome | Italian |
| 1937 | Giuseppe Pizzardo | Bishop of Albano; Secretary of the Supreme Sacred Congregation of the Holy Office; Prefect of the Sacred Congregation of Seminaries and Universities | Italian |
| 1946 | Benedetto Aloisi Masella | Bishop of Palestrina; Prefect of the Sacred Congregation of the Sacraments; Archpriest of St. John Lateran's Basilica; Prefect of the Sacred Congregation of Sacramental Discipline; Chamberlain of the Holy Roman Church | Italian |
| 1953 | Gaetano Cicognani | Bishop of Frascati; Member of the Sacred Congregation of the Basilica of St. Peter, the Consistorial Congregation, the Sacred Congregations of the Council and the Sacraments | Italian |

## Cardinal Priests

| Year | Name | Office or dignity | Nationality |
|---|---|---|---|
| 1929 | Emanuel Goncalves Cerejeira | Patriarch of Lisbon | Portuguese |
| 1930 | Achilles Lienart | Bishop of Lille | French |
| 1933 | Maurilio Fossati | Archbishop of Turin | Italian |
| 1933 | Elia dalla Costa | Archbishop of Florence | Italian |
| 1935 | Ignazio Tappouni | Syrian Patriarch of Antioch | Iraqian |
| 1935 | Santiago Copello | Chancellor of the Holy Roman Church | Argentine |
| 1937 | Pierre Marie Gerlier | Archbishop of Lyon | French |
| 1946 | Gregory Peter XV Agagianian | Prefect of the Sacred Congregation for the Propagation of the Faith | Armenian |
| 1946 | James McGuigan | Archbishop of Toronto | Canadian |
| 1946 | Emile Roques | Archbishop of Rennes | French |
| 1946 | Carlo Carmelo de Vasconcelos Motta | Archbishop of São Paulo | Brazilian |
| 1946 | Norman Gilroy | Archbishop of Sydney | Australian |
| 1946 | Francis J. Spellman | Archbishop of New York | American |
| 1946 | Teodosio Clemente de Gouveia | Archbishop of Lourenço Marques, Mozambique | Portuguese |
| 1946 | Jaime de Barros Camara | Archbishop of Rio de Janeiro; Ordinary for Oriental Catholics in Brazil | Brazilian |
| 1946 | Enrique Pla y Deniel | Archbishop of Toledo and Primate of Spain | Spanish |
| 1946 | Manuel Arteaga y Betancourt | Archbishop of Havana | Cuban |
| 1946 | Joseph Frings | Archbishop of Cologne | German |
| 1946 | Jozsef Mindszenty | Archbishop of Esztergom and Primate of Hungary | Hungarian |

| Year of creation | Name | Office or dignity | Nationality |
|---|---|---|---|
| 1946 | Ernesto Ruffini | Archbishop of Palermo; Apostolic Administrator of the Byzantium Rite Eparchy of Piani Dei Greci | Italian |
| 1946 | Antonio Caggiano | Archbishop of Buenos Aires | Argentine |
| 1946 | Thomas Tien, S. V. D. | Archbishop of Peiping | Chinese |
| 1953 | Augusto Alvaro da Silva | Archbishop of San Salvador in Bahia | Brazilian |
| 1953 | Valerio Valeri | Prefect of Sacred Congregation of Affairs of Religious | Italian |
| 1953 | Pietro Ciriaci | Prefect of Sacred Congregation of the Council | Italian |
| 1953 | Maurice Feltin | Archbishop of Paris | French |
| 1953 | Carlos Maria de la Torre | Archbishop of Quito | Ecuadorian |
| 1953 | Giuseppe Siri | Archbishop of Genoa | Italian |
| 1953 | John F. D'Alton | Archbishop of Armagh, Primate of all Ireland | Irish |
| 1953 | James Francis McIntyre | Archbishop of Los Angeles | American |
| 1953 | Giacomo Lercaro | Archbishop of Bologna | Italian |
| 1953 | Stefan Wyszynski | Archbishop of Gniezno and Warsaw | Polish |
| 1953 | Benjamin de Arriba y Castro | Archbishop of Tarragona | Spanish |
| 1953 | Fernando Quiroga y Palacios | Archbishop of Santiago di Compostela | Spanish |
| 1953 | Paul Émile Leger, S.S. | Archbishop of Montreal | Canadian |
| 1953 | Valerian Gracias | Archbishop of Bombay | Indian |
| 1958 | Giovanni Battista Montini | Archbishop of Milan | Italian |
| 1958 | Giovanni Urbani | Patriarch of Venice | Italian |
| 1958 | Paolo Giobbe | Apostolic Datary | Italian |
| 1958 | Fernando Cento | Member of Roman Curia | Italian |
| 1958 | Carlo Chiarlo | Member of Roman Curia | Italian |
| 1958 | Amleto Giovanni Cicognani | Secretary of State of the Holy See | Italian |
| 1958 | José Garibi y Rivera | Archbishop of Guadalajara | Mexican |
| 1958 | Antonio Maria Barbieri | Archbishop of Montevideo | Uruguayan |
| 1958 | William Godfrey | Archbishop of Westminster, London | British |
| 1958 | Carlo Confalonieri | Secretary of the Sacred Congregation for Seminaries and Universities | Italian |
| 1958 | Richard James Cushing | Archbishop of Boston | American |
| 1958 | Alfonso Castaldo | Archbishop of Naples | Italian |
| 1958 | Paul Marie A. Richaud | Archbishop of Bordeaux | French |
| 1958 | José M. Bueno y Monreal | Archbishop of Seville | Spanish |
| 1958 | Franziskus König | Archbishop of Vienna | Austrian |
| 1958 | Julius Döpfner | Bishop of Berlin | German |
| 1959 | Paolo Marella | | Italian |
| 1959 | Gustavo Testa | Sacred Congregations for the Oriental Church, for Extraordinary Ecclesiastical Affairs, and of the Basilica of St. Peter | Italian |
| 1959 | Aloysius J. Muench | Sacred Congregations for Extraordinary Ecclesiastical Affairs, of Rites, and of Religious | American |
| 1959 | Albert G. Meyer | Sacred Congregations for the Propagation of the Faith, of Seminaries and Universities, and of the Basilica of St. Peter | American |
| 1960 | Luigi Traglia | Vicegerent of Rome | Italian |
| 1960 | Peter Tatsuo Doi | Archbishop of Tokyo | Japanese |
| 1960 | Joseph Lefebvre | Archbishop of Bourges | French |
| 1960 | Bernard Jan Alfrink | Archbishop of Utrecht | Dutch |
| 1960 | Rufino J. Santos | Archbishop of Manila | Philippino |
| 1960 | Laurian Rugambwa | Bishop of Rutabo, Tanganyika | African |

| Year of creation | Name | Office or dignity | Nationality |
|---|---|---|---|
| 1961 | Joseph Ferretto | Sacred Consistorial of the Council, Propagation of the Faith (Congregations) | Italian |
| 1961 | Joseph Ritter | Archbishop of St. Louis | American |
| 1961 | José Quintero | Archbishop of Caracas | Venezuelan |
| 1961 | Luis Concha | Archbishop of Bogotá | Colombian |

### Cardinal Deacons

| Year | Name | Office | Nationality |
|---|---|---|---|
| 1953 | Alfredo Ottaviani | Pro-Secretary of the Supreme Congregation of the Holy Office | Italian |
| 1958 | Alberto di Jorio | Member of Roman Curia | Italian |
| 1958 | Francesco Bracci | Secretary of the Sacred Congregation of the Sacraments | Italian |
| 1958 | Francesco Roberti | Secretary of the Sacred Congregation of the Council | Italian |
| 1958 | Andrea Jullien | Member of Roman Curia | French |
| 1959 | William T. Heard | Sacred Congregation of Sacramental Discipline, The Supreme, the Supreme Tribunal of the Apostolic Signature, and the Pontifical for the Codification of Oriental Canon Law | Scotch |
| 1959 | Augustine Bea, S.J. | Sacred Congregations of Rites and of Seminaries and Universities and the Pontifical Commission for Biblical Studies | German |
| 1959 | Arcadio Larraona, C.M.F. | Sacred Congregations of the Council and of Religious, and the Pontifical Commission for the Authentic Interpretation of the Code of Canon Law | Spanish |
| 1959 | Francesco Morano | Sacred Congregations of Sacramental Discipline and of Ceremonies, and the Supreme Tribunal of the Apostolic Signature | Italian |
| 1960 | Antonio Bacci | Secretary of Briefs to Princes | Italian |

## Roman Catholic Hierarchy of the U. S.

*Source:* National Catholic Welfare Conference, Washington, D. C.

(Note: A—Auxiliary; C—Coadjutor. Archbishops are shown in boldface type, Bishops in lightface. An Archbishop heading a diocese is called an "Archbishop ad Personam"; i.e., he bears the personal title of Archbishop. The Apostolic Delegate to the U. S. is Archbishop Egidio Vagnozzi.)

### Archdioceses

Baltimore, Md.: Francis P. Keough; Lawrence J. Shehan (C).

Boston, Mass.: Richard Cardinal Cushing; Eric F. MacKenzie (A); Jerehiah E. Minihan (A); Thomas J. Riley (A).

Chicago, Ill.: Albert G. Meyer; Bernard J. Sheil (A); Wm. D. O'Brien (A); Raymond P. Hillinger (A); Aloysius J. Wycislo (A); Cletus F. O'Donnell (A).

Cincinnati, Ohio: Karl J. Alter; Paul F. Leibold (A).

Denver, Colo.: Urban J. Vehr; David M. Maloney (A).

Detroit, Mich.: John F. Dearden; A. M. Zaleski (A); H. E. Donnelly (A); J. A. Donovan (A).

Dubuque, Iowa: Leo Binz; George J. Biskup (A).

Hartford, Conn.: Henry J. O'Brien; John F. Hackett (A).

Indianapolis Ind.: Paul C. Schulte.

Kansas City, Kans.: Edward J. Hunkeler.

Los Angeles, Calif.: James Francis Cardinal McIntyre; Timothy Manning (A); Alden J. Bell (A).

Louisville, Ky.: John A. Floersh; Charles G. Maloney (A).

Milwaukee, Wis.: William E. Cousins; Roman R. Atkielski (A).

Newark, N. J.: Thomas A. Boland; Martin W. Stanton (A); Walter Curtis (A).

New Orleans, La.: Joseph F. Rummel; L. Abel Caillouet (A); John P. Cody (C).

New York, N. Y.: Francis Cardinal Spellman; Stephen J. Donahue (A); Joseph F. Flannelly (A); Fulton J. Sheen (A); Edward V. Dargin (A); Joseph M. Pernicone (A); Raymond A. Lane; John W. Comber (A); Paul Yu Pin; James H. Griffiths (A); William R. Arnold (A); Philip J. Furlong (A); John M. Fearns (A); John J. McGuire (A); Edward E. Swanstrom (A).

Omaha, Nebr.: Gerald T. Bergan.

Philadelphia, Pa.: John J. Krol; Cletus J. Benjamin (A); Francis J. Furey (A); Joseph Mary Yuen Ching Ping.

Portland, Oreg.: Edward D. Howard.

St. Louis, Mo.: Joseph Cardinal Ritter; Glennon P. Flavin (A).

St. Paul, Minn.: William O. Brady; Leonard P. Cowley (A).

San Antonio, Tex.: Robert E. Lucey; Stephen A. Leven (A).

San Francisco, Calif.: John J. Mitty; Hugh A. Donohoe (A); Merlin J. Guilfoyle (A).

San Juan, P. R.: James P. Davis.

Santa Fe, N. Mex.: Edwin V. Byrne.

Seattle, Wash.: Thomas A. Connolly; Thomas E. Gill (A).

Washington, D. C.: Patrick A. O'Boyle; Philip M. Hannan (A).

## Dioceses

Alaska (vicariate): Francis D. Gleeson, S.J., Vicar Apostolic.

Albany, N. Y.: William A. Scully; Edward J. Maginn (A).

Alexandria, La.: Charles P. Greco.

Allentown, Pa.: Joseph McShea.

Altoona-Johnstown, Pa.: J. C. McCormick.

Amarillo, Tex.: John L. Morkovsky.

Arecibo, P. R.: Alfred F. Mendez, C.S.C.

Atlanta, Ga.: Francis E. Hyland.

Austin, Tex.: Louis J. Reicher.

Bahamas (Vicariate): Paul L. Hagarty, O.S.B., Vicar Apostolic.

Baker City, Oreg.: Francis P. Leipzig.

Baton Rouge, La.: Robert E. Tracy.

Belleville, Ill.: Albert R. Zuroweste.

Bismarck, N. Dak.: Hilary B. Hacker.

Boise, Idaho: James J. Byrne.

Bridgeport, Conn.: Lawrence J. Shehan.

Brooklyn, N. Y.: Bryan J. McEntegart; J. J. Boardman (A); Joseph P. Denning (A); Charles R. Mulrooney (A).

Buffalo, N. Y.: Joseph A. Burke; Leo R. Smith (A).

Burlington, Vt.: R. F. Joyce.

Camden, N. J.: Celestine J. Damiano.

Caroline-Marshall Islands (vicariate): Vincent I. Kennally.

Charleston, S. C.: Paul J. Hallinan.

Cheyenne, Wyo.: Hubert M. Newell.

Cleveland, Ohio: Edward F. Hoban; Floyd L. Begin (A).

Columbus, Ohio: Clarence G. Issenmann; Edward G. Hettinger (A).

Corpus Christi, Tex.: Mariano S. Garriga; Adolph Marx (A).

Covington, Ky.: Richard Ackerman.

Crookston, Minn.: Laurence A. Glenn.

Dallas-Ft. Worth, Tex.: Thomas K. Gorman; Augustine Danglmayr (A).

Davenport, Iowa: Ralph L. Hayes.

Des Moines, Iowa: Edward C. Daly, O.P.

Dodge City, Kans.: Marion F. Forst.

Duluth, Minn.: Francis J. Schenk.

El Paso, Tex.: Sidney M. Metzger.

Erie, Pa.: John M. Gannon; Edward P. McManaman (A).

Evansville, Ind.: Henry J. Grimmelsman.

Fall River, Mass.: James L. Connolly; James J. Gerrard (A).

Fargo, N. Dak.: Leo F. Dworschak.

Fort Wayne-South Bend, Ind.: Leo A. Pursley.

Gallup, N. Mex.: B. T. Espelage, O.F.M.

Galveston, Tex.: Wendelin J. Nold.

Gary, Ind.: A. G. Grutka.

Grand Island, Nebr.: John L. Paschang.

Grand Rapids, Mich.: Allen J. Babcock.

Great Falls, Mont.: William J. Condon.

Green Bay, Wis.: Stanislaus V. Bona; John B. Grellinger (A).

Greensburg, Pa.: William G. Connare.

Guam (vicariate): Apollinaris W. Baumgartner, O.F.M. Cap., Vicar Apostolic.

Harrisburg, Pa.: George L. Leech; Lawrence F. Schott (A).

Helena, Mont.: Joseph M. Gilmore.

Honolulu, Hawaii: J. J. Sweeney; J. J. Scanlan (A).

Jamaica (Vicariate): John J. McEleney, S.J., Vicar Apostolic.

Jefferson City, Mo.: Joseph H. Marling, C.PP.S.

Joliet, Ill.: Martin D. McNamara.

Juneau, Alaska: Dermot O'Flanagan.

Kansas City-St. Joseph, Mo.: (Vacant).

La Crosse, Wis.: John P. Treacy.

Lafayette, Ind.: John J. Carberry.

Lafayette, La.: Maurice Schexnayder.

Lansing, Mich.: Joseph H. Albers.

Lincoln, Nebr.: Jas. V. Casey.

Little Rock, Ark.: Albert L. Fletcher.

Madison, Wis.: William P. O'Connor.

Manchester, N. H.: Ernest J. Primeau.

Marquette, Mich.: Thomas L. Noa.

Miami, Fla.: Coleman F. Carroll.

Mobile-Birmingham, Ala.: T. J. Toolen; Joseph A. Durick (A).

Monterey-Fresno, Calif.: Aloysius J. Willinger, C.Ss.R.; Harry A. Clinch (A).

Nashville, Tenn.: William L. Adrian.

Natchez-Jackson, Miss.: Richard O. Gerow; Joseph Brunini (A).

New Ulm, Minn.: Alphonse Schadweiler.

Norwich, Conn.: Vincent J. Hines.

Ogdensburg, N. Y.: J. J. Navagh.

Oklahoma City-Tulsa, Okla.: Victor J. Reed.

Owensboro, Ky.: Henry J. Soenneker.

Paterson, N. J.: James A. McNulty.

Peoria, Ill.: John B. Franz.

Pittsburgh, Pa.: John J. Wright.

Ponce, P. R.: James E. McManus, C.Ss.R.

Portland, Maine: Daniel J. Feeney.

Providence, R. I.: Russell J. McVinney; Thomas F. Maloney (A).

Pueblo, Colo.: Charles A. Buswell.

Raleigh, N. C.: Vincent S. Waters.

Rapid City, S. Dak.: William T. McCarty, C.Ss.R.

Reno, Nev.: Robert J. Dwyer.

Richmond, Va.: John J. Russell; Joseph H. Hodges (A).

Rochester, N. Y.: James E. Kearney; Lawrence B. Casey (A).

Rockford, Ill.: Loras T. Lane.
Rockville Centre, N. Y.: W. P. Kellenberg.
Sacramento, Calif.: Joseph T. McGucken.
Saginaw, Mich.: Stephen S. Woznicki.
St. Augustine, Fla.: Joseph P. Hurley.
St. Cloud, Minn.: Peter W. Bartholome.
Salina, Kans.: Frederick W. Freking.
Salt Lake City, Utah: J. Lennox Federal.
San Diego, Calif.: Charles F. Buddy; Richard H. Ackerman (A).
Savannah, Ga.: Thomas J. McDonough.
Scranton, Pa.: Jerome D. Hannan; Henry T. Klonowski (A).
Sioux City, Iowa: Joseph M. Mueller.
Sioux Falls, S. Dak.: Lambert A. Hoch.
Spokane, Wash.: Bernard Topel.
Springfield, Ill.: William A. O'Connor.
Springfield, Mass.: Christopher J. Weldon.
Springfield-Cape Girardeau, Mo.: Charles M. Helmsing.
Steubenville, Ohio: John K. Mussio.
Superior, Wis.: George A. Hammes.
Syracuse, N. Y.: Walter A. Foery; David F. Cunningham (A).
Toledo, Ohio: George J. Rehring.

Trenton, N. J.: George W. Ahr; James J. Hogan (A).
Tucson, Ariz.: Daniel J. Gercke; Francis J. Green (A).
Wheeling, W. Va.: John J. Swint.
Wichita, Kans.: Mark K. Carroll; Leo C. Byrne (C).
Wilmington, Del.: Michael Hyle.
Winona, Minn.: Edward A. Fitzgerald.
Worcester, Mass.: Bernard J. Flanagan.
Yakima, Wash.: Joseph P. Dougherty.
Youngstown, Ohio: Emmet M. Walsh; James W. Malone (A).
Military Ordinariate: Francis Cardinal Spellman, Military Vicar; William Arnold, Military Delegate; Philip J. Furlong (A).
Philadelphia, Pa. (Byzantine Rite): Constantine Bohachevsky; Joseph Schmondiuk (A).
Pittsburgh, Pa. (Greek Rite): Nicholas T. Elko; Stephen Kocisko (A).
Stamford, Conn. (Ukrainian Greek Catholic Diocese): Ambrose Senyshyn.

# Antipopes

Antipopes were those who falsely claimed Papal Sovereignty. The dates and, in some cases, Roman numerals after the names account for occasional discrepancies in the succession of the Popes.

| Name | Birthplace | Acces. | End of reign | Name | Birthplace | Acces. | End of reign |
|------|-----------|--------|--------------|------|-----------|--------|--------------|
| St. Hippolytus | Rome | 217 | 235 | Clement III | Parma | 1080 | 1100 |
| Novatian | Rome | 251 | ... | Theodoric | ..... | .... | 1100 |
| Felix II | Rome | 355 | 365 | Albert | ..... | .... | 1102 |
| Ursinus | ..... | 366 | 367 | Sylvester IV | Rome | 1105 | 1111 |
| Eulalius | ..... | 418 | 419 | Gregory VIII | France | 1118 | 1121 |
| Lawrence | ..... | 498 | 501 | Celestine II | Rome | .... | 1124 |
| Dioscorus | Alexandria | 530 | 530 | Anacletus II | Rome | 1130 | 1138 |
| Theodore | ..... | ... | 687 | Victor IV | ..... | 1138 | 1138 |
| Paschal | ..... | ... | 687 | Victor IV* | Montecelio | 1159 | 1164 |
| Constantine | Nepi | 767 | 769 | Paschal III | ..... | 1164 | 1168 |
| Philip | ..... | 768 | 768 | Callistus III | Arezzo | 1168 | 1178 |
| John | ..... | ... | 844 | Innocent III | Sezze | 1179 | 1180 |
| Anastasius | ..... | 855 | 855 | Nicholas V | Corvaro | 1328 | 1330 |
| Christopher | Rome | 903 | 904 | Clement VII | ..... | 1378 | 1394 |
| Boniface VII | Rome | 974 | 974 | Benedict XIII | Aragon | 1394 | 1423 |
| Boniface VII (2nd time) | ..... | 984 | 985 | Alexander V | Crete | 1409 | 1410 |
| John XVI | Rossano | 997 | 998 | John XXIII | Naples | 1410 | 1415 |
| Gregory | ..... | ... | 1012 | Felix V | ..... | 1439 | 1449 |
| Benedict X | Rome | 1058 | 1059 | | | | |
| Honorius II | Verona | 1061 | 1072 | | | | |

\* Did not recognize his predecessor of 1138, who, only two months after claiming the Papacy, submitted to the rightful Pope, Innocent II.

# Jewish Congregational and Rabbinical Organizations

Central Conference of American Rabbis: 40 W. 68th St., New York 23, N. Y.

Rabbinical Alliance of America: 154 Nassau St., New York 38, N. Y.

Rabbinical Assembly of America: 3080 Broadway, New York 27, N. Y.

Rabbinical Council of America, Inc.: 84 Fifth Ave., New York 11, N. Y.

Synagogue Council of America: 110 W. 42nd St., New York 36, N. Y.

Union of American Hebrew Congregations: 838 Fifth Ave., New York 21, N. Y.

Union of Orthodox Jewish Congregations of America: 84 Fifth Ave., New York 11, N. Y.

Union of Orthodox Rabbis of the U. S. and Canada: 132 Nassau St., New York 38, N. Y.

United Synagogue of America: 3080 Broadway, New York 27, N. Y.

# Movable Holidays, 1962 to 1971

## CHRISTIAN AND SECULAR

| Year | Ash Wed. | Easter | Pentecost | Labor Day | Election Day | Thanksgiving | 1st Sun. Advent |
|------|----------|--------|-----------|-----------|--------------|--------------|-----------------|
| 1962 | Mar.  7 | Apr. 22 | June 10 | Sept. 3 | Nov. 6 | Nov. 22 | Dec.  2 |
| 1963 | Feb. 27 | Apr. 14 | June  2 | Sept. 2 | Nov. 5 | Nov. 28 | Dec.  1 |
| 1964 | Feb. 12 | Mar. 29 | May  17 | Sept. 7 | Nov. 3 | Nov. 26 | Nov. 29 |
| 1965 | Mar.  3 | Apr. 18 | June  6 | Sept. 6 | Nov. 2 | Nov. 25 | Nov. 28 |
| 1966 | Feb. 23 | Apr. 10 | May  29 | Sept. 5 | Nov. 8 | Nov. 24 | Nov. 27 |
| 1967 | Feb.  8 | Mar. 26 | May  14 | Sept. 4 | Nov. 7 | Nov. 23 | Dec.  3 |
| 1968 | Feb. 28 | Apr. 14 | June  2 | Sept. 2 | Nov. 5 | Nov. 28 | Dec.  1 |
| 1969 | Feb. 19 | Apr.  6 | May  25 | Sept. 1 | Nov. 4 | Nov. 27 | Nov. 30 |
| 1970 | Feb. 11 | Mar. 29 | May  17 | Sept. 7 | Nov. 3 | Nov. 26 | Nov. 29 |
| 1971 | Feb. 24 | Apr. 11 | May  30 | Sept. 6 | Nov. 2 | Nov. 25 | Nov. 28 |

Shrove Tuesday: 1 day before Ash Wednesday.
Palm Sunday: 7 days before Easter.
Maundy Thursday: 3 days before Easter.
Good Friday: 2 days before Easter.

Holy Saturday: 1 day before Easter.
Ascension Day: 10 days before Pentecost.
Trinity Sunday: 7 days after Pentecost.
Corpus Christi: 11 days after Pentecost.

## JEWISH

| Year | Purim | 1st day Passover | 1st day Shabuoth | 1st day Rosh Hashana | Yom Kippur | 1st day Sukkoth | Simhath Torah | 1st day Hanukkah |
|------|-------|------------------|------------------|----------------------|------------|-----------------|---------------|------------------|
| 1962 | Mar. 20 | Apr. 19 | June  8 | Sept. 29 | Oct.  8 | Oct. 13 | Oct. 21 | Dec. 22 |
| 1963 | Mar. 10 | Apr.  9 | May  29 | Sept. 19 | Sept. 28 | Oct.  3 | Oct. 11 | Dec. 11 |
| 1964 | Feb. 27 | Mar. 28 | May  17 | Sept.  7 | Sept. 16 | Sept. 21 | Sept. 29 | Nov. 30 |
| 1965 | Mar. 18 | Apr. 17 | June  6 | Sept. 27 | Oct.  6 | Oct. 11 | Oct. 19 | Dec. 19 |
| 1966 | Mar.  6 | Apr.  5 | May  25 | Sept. 15 | Sept. 24 | Sept. 29 | Oct.  7 | Dec.  8 |
| 1967 | Mar. 26 | Apr. 25 | June 14 | Oct.  5 | Oct. 14 | Oct. 19 | Oct. 27 | Dec. 27 |
| 1968 | Mar. 14 | Apr. 13 | June  2 | Sept. 23 | Oct.  2 | Oct.  7 | Oct. 15 | Dec. 16 |
| 1969 | Mar.  4 | Apr.  3 | May  23 | Sept. 13 | Sept. 22 | Sept. 27 | Oct.  5 | Dec.  5 |
| 1970 | Mar. 14 | Apr. 15 | June  6 | Oct.  1 | Oct. 10 | Oct. 15 | Oct. 30 | Oct. 25 |
| 1971 | Mar. 10 | Apr. 10 | May  30 | Sept. 20 | Sept. 29 | Oct.  4 | Oct. 12 | Dec. 13 |

Length of Jewish holidays (O = Orthodox, C = Conservative, R = Reform):

Passover: O & C, 8 days (holy days: first 2 and last 2); R 7 days (holy days: first and last).
Shabuoth: O & C, 2 days; R, 1 day.
Rosh Hashana: O & C, 2 days; R, 1 day.
Yom Kippur: All groups, 1 day.
Sukkoth: All groups, 7 days (holy days: O & C, first 2; R, first only). O & C observe two additional days: Shemini

Atsereth (Eighth Day of the Feast) and Simhath Torah (Rejoicing of the Law). R observes Shemini Atsereth but not Simhath Torah.
Hanukkah: All groups, 8 days.

NOTE: All holidays begin at sundown on the evening before the date given.

# Religious and Secular Holidays, 1962

### (Legal holidays falling on Sunday are observed on Monday)

NEW YEAR'S DAY—Monday, Jan. 1— A legal holiday in all states and the District of Columbia, New Year's Day has its origin in Roman times, when sacrifices were offered to Janus, the two-faced Roman deity who looked back on the past and forward to the future.

EPIPHANY—Saturday, Jan. 6—Falls the twelfth day after Christmas and commemorates the manifestation of Jesus as the Son of God, as represented by the adoration of the Magi, the baptism of Jesus,

and the miracle of the wine at the marriage feast at Cana. Epiphany originally marked the beginning of the carnival season preceding Lent, and the evening (sometimes the eve) is known as Twelfth Night.

LINCOLN'S BIRTHDAY—Monday, Feb. 12—A legal holiday in many states, this day was first formally observed in Washington, D. C., in 1866, when both houses of Congress gathered for a memorial address in honor of the late President.

ST. VALENTINE'S DAY—Wednesday, Feb. 14—This day is the festival of two 3rd-century martyrs, both named St. Valentine. It is not known why this day is associated with lovers. It may derive from an old pagan festival about this time of year, or it may have been inspired by the belief that birds mate on this day.

WASHINGTON'S BIRTHDAY—Thursday, Feb. 22—The birthday of George Washington is celebrated as a legal holiday in almost every state of the Union, the District of Columbia, and all territories. The observance began in 1796.

SHROVE TUESDAY—Mar. 6—Falls the day before Ash Wednesday and marks the end of the carnival season, which once began on Epiphany but is now usually celebrated the last three days before Lent. In France, the day is known as Mardi Gras (Fat Tuesday), and Mardi Gras celebrations are also held in several American cities, particularly in New Orleans. The day is sometimes called Pancake Tuesday by the English because fats, which were prohibited during Lent, had to be used up.

ASH WEDNESDAY—Mar. 7—The first day of the Lenten season, which lasts forty days. Having its origin sometime before A.D. 1000, it is a day of public penance and is marked in the Roman Catholic Church by the burning of the palms blessed on the previous Palm Sunday. With his thumb, the priest then marks a cross upon the forehead of each worshipper. The Anglican Church and a few Protestant groups in the United States also observe the day, but generally without the use of ashes.

ST. PATRICK'S DAY—Saturday, Mar. 17—St. Patrick, patron saint of Ireland, has been honored in America since the first days of the nation. There are many dinners and meetings but perhaps the most notable part of the observance is the annual St. Patrick's Day parade on Fifth Avenue in New York City.

PALM SUNDAY—Apr. 15—Is observed the Sunday before Easter to commemorate the entry of Jesus into Jerusalem. The procession and the ceremonies introducing the benediction of palms probably had their origin in Jerusalem.

FIRST DAY OF PASSOVER (Pesach)—Thursday, Apr. 19 (Nisan 15)—The Feast of the Passover, also called the Feast of Unleavened Bread, commemorates the escape of the first-born of the Jews from the Angel of Death. As the Jews fled Egypt, they ate unleavened bread, and from that time the Jews have allowed no leavening in the houses during Passover, bread being replaced by matzoth.

GOOD FRIDAY—Apr. 20—This day commemorates the Crucifixion, which is retold during services from the Gospel according to St. John. A feature in Roman Catholic churches is the Liturgy of the Passion; there is no Consecration, the Host having been consecrated the previous day. The eating of hot cross buns on this day is said to have started in England.

EASTER SUNDAY—April 22—Observed in all Christian churches, Easter commemorates the Resurrection of Jesus. It is celebrated on the first Sunday after the full moon which occurs on or next after March 21 and is therefore celebrated between March 22 and April 25 inclusive. This date was fixed by the Council of Nicaea in 325.

MEMORIAL DAY—Wednesday, May 30—Also known as Decoration Day, Memorial Day is a legal holiday in most of the states and in the territories, and is also observed by the armed forces. In 1868, General John A. Logan, Commander in Chief of the Grand Army of the Republic, issued an order designating the day as one in which the graves of soldiers would be decorated. The holiday was originally devoted to honoring the memory of those who fell in the Civil War, but is now also dedicated to the memory of the dead of all wars.

ASCENSION DAY—Thursday, May 31—Took place in the presence of His apostles 40 days after the Resurrection of Jesus. It is traditionally held to have occurred on Mount Olivet in Bethany.

FIRST DAY OF SHABUOTH (Hebrew Pentecost)—Friday, June 8 (Sivan 6)—This festival, sometimes called the Feast of Weeks, or of Harvest, or of the First Fruits, falls fifty days after Passover and originally celebrated the end of the seven-week grain harvesting season. In later tradition, it also celebrated the giving of the Law to Moses on Mt. Sinai, and both aspects have come down to the present.

PENTECOST (Whitsunday)—June 10—This day commemorates the descent of the Holy Ghost upon the Apostles fifty days after the Resurrection. The sermon by the Apostle Peter, which led to the baptism of 3,000 who professed belief, originated the ceremonies that have since been followed. "Whitsunday" is believed to have come from "white Sunday" when, among the English, white robes were worn by those baptized on the day.

FLAG DAY—Thursday, June 14—This day commemorates the adoption by the Continental Congress on June 14, 1777, of the Stars and Stripes as the U. S. flag. Although it is a legal holiday only in Pennsylvania, President Truman, on Aug. 3, 1949, signed a bill requesting the President to call for its observance each year by proclamation.

INDEPENDENCE DAY—Wednesday, July 4—The day of the adoption of the Declaration of Independence in 1776, celebrated in all states and territories. The observance began in the next year in the city of Philadelphia.

LABOR DAY—Monday, Sept. 3—Observed the first Monday in September in all states and territories, Labor Day was first celebrated in New York in 1882 under the sponsorship of the Central Labor Union, following the suggestion of Peter J. McGuire, of the Knights of Labor, that the day be set aside in honor of labor.

FIRST DAY OF ROSH HASHANA (Jewish New Year)—Saturday, Sept. 29 (Tishri 1)—This day marks the beginning of the Jewish year 5723 and opens the Ten Days of Penitence closing with Yom Kippur.

YOM KIPPUR (Day of Atonement)—Monday, Oct. 8 (Tishri 10)—This day marks the end of the Ten Days of Penitence that began with Rosh Hashana. It is described in *Leviticus* as a "Sabbath of rest," and synagogue services begin the preceding sundown, resume the following morning, and continue through the day to sundown.

COLUMBUS DAY—Friday, Oct. 12—A legal holiday in many states, commemorating the discovery of America by Columbus in 1492. Quite likely the first celebration of Columbus Day was that organized in 1792 by the Society of St. Tammany, or Columbian Order, more widely known as Tammany Hall.

FIRST DAY OF SUKKOTH (Feast of Tabernacles)—Saturday, Oct. 13 (Tishri 15)—This festival, also known as the Feast of the Ingathering, originally celebrated the fruit harvest, and the name comes from the booths or tabernacles in which the Jews lived during the harvest, although one tradition traces it to the shelters used by the Jews in their wandering through the wilderness. During the festival many Jews build small huts in their back yards or on the roofs of their houses.

HALLOWEEN—Wednesday, Oct. 31—The eve of All Saints' Day, formerly called All Hallows and Hallowmass. Halloween is traditionally associated in some countries with old customs such as bonfires, masquerading and the telling of ghost stories. These are old Celtic practices that marked the beginning of winter.

ALL SAINTS' DAY—Thursday, Nov. 1 This is a Roman Catholic and Anglican holiday celebrating all saints, known and unknown.

ELECTION DAY (in certain states)—Tuesday, Nov. 6—Since 1845, by Act of Congress, the first Tuesday after the first Monday in November is the date for choosing Presidential electors. State elections are also generally held on this day.

VETERANS DAY—Sunday, Nov. 11—Armistice Day was established in 1926 to commemorate the signing in 1918 of the Armistice ending World War I. On June 1, 1954, the name was changed to Veterans Day so as to honor all men and women who have served America in its armed forces.

THANKSGIVING—Thursday, Nov. 22—Observed nationally on the fourth Thursday in November by Act of Congress (1941), the first such national proclamation having been issued by President Lincoln in 1863, on the urging of Mrs. Sarah J. Hale, editor of *Godey's Lady's Book*. Most Americans believe that the holiday dates back to the day of thanks ordered by Governor Bradford of Plymouth Colony in New England in 1621 but scholars point out that days of thanks stem from ancient times.

FIRST SUNDAY OF ADVENT—Dec. 2—Advent is the season in which the faithful must prepare themselves for the advent of the Saviour on Christmas. The four Sundays before Christmas are marked by special church services.

FIRST DAY OF HANUKKAH (Festival of Lights)—Saturday, Dec. 22 (Kislev 25)—This festival was instituted by Judas Maccabaeus in 165 B.C. to celebrate the purification of the Temple of Jerusalem, which had been desecrated three years earlier by Antiochus Epiphanes, who set up a pagan altar and offered sacrifices to Zeus Olympius. In Jewish homes, a light is lighted the first night, and on each succeeding night of the eight-day festival, another is lighted.

CHRISTMAS (Feast of the Nativity)—Tuesday, Dec. 25—The most widely celebrated holiday of the Christian year, Christmas is observed as the anniversary of the birth of Jesus. Christmas customs are centuries old. The mistletoe, for example, comes from the Druids, who, in hanging the mistletoe, hoped for peace and good fortune. Use of such plants as holly comes from the ancient belief that such plants blossomed at Christmas. Comparatively recent is the Christmas tree, first set up in Germany in the 17th century, and the use of candles on trees developed from the belief that candles appeared by miracle on the trees at Christmas. Colonial Manhattan Islanders introduced the name Santa Claus, a corruption of the Dutch name for the 4th-century Asia-Minor St. Nicholas.

# Legal Holidays in the 50 States, D. C., and Puerto Rico

## Holidays Widely Observed

**January 1, New Year's Day:** All states, D. C., Puerto Rico.

**February 12, Lincoln's Birthday:** Alaska, Arizona, California, Colorado, Connecticut, Delaware, Illinois, Indiana, Iowa, Kansas, Kentucky, Maryland, Michigan, Minnesota, Missouri, Montana, Nebraska, New Jersey, New Mexico, New York, North Dakota, Ohio, Oregon, Pennsylvania, South Dakota, Tennessee, Utah, Vermont, Washington, West Virginia, Wisconsin, Wyoming.

**February 22, Washington's Birthday:** All states[1] (except Louisiana, Nevada, Oklahoma[3]); D. C., Puerto Rico.

**May 30, Memorial (or Decoration) Day:** All states (except Alabama, Georgia, Louisiana, South Carolina, Texas); D. C., Puerto Rico.

**July 4, Independence Day:** All states, D. C., Puerto Rico.

**September (1st Monday), Labor Day:** All states, D. C., Puerto Rico.

**October 12, Columbus Day:** All states (except Alaska, Arkansas, D. C., Hawaii, Idaho, Iowa, Kansas, Louisiana, Maine, Mississippi, Nevada, North Carolina, Oklahoma,[3] Oregon, South Carolina, South Dakota, Tennessee, Virginia, Wyoming); Puerto Rico.

**November (1st Tuesday after 1st Monday), Election Day:** Alaska, Arizona, Arkansas, California, Colorado, Delaware, Florida, Hawaii, Illinois, Indiana, Iowa, Louisiana, Maryland, Michigan, Missouri, Montana, New Hampshire, New Jersey, New York, North Carolina, North Dakota, Ohio, Oklahoma, Oregon, Pennsylvania, Rhode Island, South Carolina, South Dakota, Tennessee, Texas, Virginia, Washington, West Virginia, Wisconsin, Wyoming, Puerto Rico.

**November 11, Veterans Day (formerly Armistice Day):** All states (except Louisiana); D. C., Puerto Rico.

**November (4th Thursday), Thanksgiving Day:** All states, D. C., Puerto Rico.

**December 25, Christmas:** All states, D. C., Puerto Rico.

## Other Holidays

**January 6, Three Kings' Day:** Puerto Rico.

**January 11, De Hostos' Birthday:** Puerto Rico.

**January 19, Robert E. Lee's Birthday:** Alabama, Arkansas, Florida, Georgia, Kentucky, Mississippi, North Carolina, South Carolina, Tennessee, Texas, Virginia.[2]

**January 20, Inauguration Day (every 4 yrs.):** D. C.

**January 30, F. D. Roosevelt's Birthday:** Kentucky.

**February or March (1 day before Ash Wednesday), Mardi Gras (Shrove Tuesday):** Alabama, Florida (in some counties), Louisiana.

**February 14, Statehood Day:** Arizona.

**March (first Tuesday), Town Meeting Day:** Vermont.

**March 2, Texas Independence Day.**

**March 15, Andrew Jackson's Birthday:** Tennessee.

**March 17, Evacuation Day:** Massachusetts (in Suffolk Co. only).

**March or April (2 days before Easter), Good Friday:** California (12 M.–3 P.M.), Connecticut, Delaware, Florida, Hawaii, Illinois, Indiana, Louisiana, Maryland, Minnesota, New Jersey, North Dakota, Pennsylvania, Tennessee, Puerto Rico.

**March or April (1 day after Easter), Easter Monday:** North Carolina.

**March 22, Emancipation Day:** Puerto Rico.

**March 25, Maryland Day.**

**March 26, Kuhio Day:** Hawaii.

**March 30, Seward's Day:** Alaska.

**April (date set by governor), Arbor Day:** Wyo.

**April 12, Halifax Resolutions Anniversary:** N. C.

**April 13, Thomas Jefferson's Birthday:** Alabama, Missouri, Oklahoma,[3] Virginia.

**April 16, De Diego's Birthday:** Puerto Rico.

**April 19, Patriots' Day:** Maine, Massachusetts.

**April 21, San Jacinto Day:** Texas.

**April 22, Oklahoma Day.**[3]

**April 22, Arbor Day:** Nebraska.

**April (last Friday), Arbor Day:** Utah.

**April 26, Confederate Memorial Day:** Alabama, Florida, Georgia, Mississippi.

**April (4th Monday), Fast Day:** New Hampshire.

**May 1, Bird Day:** Oklahoma.

**May 4, Rhode Island Independence Day**

**May (2nd Sunday), Mother's Day:** Arizona, Oklahoma.

**May 10, Confederate Memorial Day:** North Carolina, South Carolina.

**May 20, Mecklenburg Independence Day:** N. C.

**June 3, Jefferson Davis' Birthday:** Alabama, Florida, Georgia, Kentucky, Mississippi, South Carolina, Tennessee, Texas.

**June 9, Senior Citizen's Day:** Oklahoma.[3]

**June 11, Kamehameha Day:** Hawaii.

**June 14, Flag Day:** Pennsylvania.

**June 17, Bunker Hill Day:** Massachusetts (in Suffolk Co. only).

**June 20, West Virginia Day.**

**July 13, Nathan Bedford Forrest's Birthday:** Tenn.

**July 17, Muñoz Rivera's Birthday:** Puerto Rico.

**July 24, Pioneer Day:** Utah.

**July 25, Constitution Day:** Puerto Rico.

**July 27, Barbosa's Birthday:** Puerto Rico.

**August 1, Colorado Day.**

**August 14, V-J Day:** Arkansas, Rhode Island.

**August 16, Bennington Battle Day:** Vermont.

**August 30, Huey P. Long Day:** Louisiana.

**September (1st Saturday after full moon), Indian Day:** Oklahoma.[3]

**September 9, Admission Day:** California.

**September 12, Defenders' Day:** Maryland.

**September 16, Cherokee Strip Day:** Oklahoma.[3]

**October (Thursday of State Fair Week):** South Carolina.

**October 10, Oklahoma Historical Day.**[3]

**October 18, Alaska Day.**

**October 31, Nevada Day**

**November 1, All Saints' Day:** Louisiana.

**November 4, Will Rogers Day:** Oklahoma.[3]

**November 19, Discovery Day:** Puerto Rico.

[1] Designated President's Day in Hawaii. [2] Called Lee-Jackson Day. [3] Not a holiday unless proclaimed by Governor

# EDUCATION
## Elementary and Secondary Public School Statistics, 1959–60

*Source: Information Please Almanac Questionnaire and U. S. Office of Education.*
**NOTE: The average yearly expenditure is based on average daily attendance.**

| State | No. schools elementary and secondary | Pupils Elementary | Pupils Secondary | Teachers Elementary | Teachers Secondary | Average yearly expenditure per pupil | All teachers Minimum salary | All teachers Maximum salary |
|---|---|---|---|---|---|---|---|---|
| **NORTH ATLANTIC** | | | | | | | | |
| Connecticut........ | 968 | 343,611 | 136,862 | 12,232 | 7,773 | $375.20 | $3,500 | $10,723 |
| Delaware.......... | 174 | 47,572 | 34,634 | 1,977 | 1,711 | 433.00 | 3,600 | 6,700 |
| Maine............. | 1,184 | 155,898[7] | 48,885[7] | 5,609 | 2,566 | 301.90 | 2,600 | 7,000 |
| Maryland[4]........ | 1,068 | 358,022 | 249,341 | 12,305 | 11,215 | 351.63 | 3,500 | 9,120 |
| Massachusetts..... | 2,053 | 560,365 | 277,278 | 20,983 | 14,570 | 333.34 | 4,000 | n.a. |
| New Hampshire..... | 489 | 72,468 | 33,501 | 2,768 | 1,736 | 330.92 | 2,900 | 8,100 |
| New Jersey........ | 1,975 | 739,862 | 314,543 | 30,225 | 16,041 | 435.76 | 3,600 | n.a. |
| New York.......... | 4,673 | 1,630,000[8] | 1,150,000[8] | 62,300 | 57,200 | 647.92 | 4,000 | 14,500 |
| Pennsylvania...... | 2,485 | 1,133,576 | 817,015 | 38,355 | 36,298 | 401.41 | 3,600 | 6,000 |
| Rhode Island...... | 350 | 79,963[8] | 54,550[8] | 2,694 | 2,561 | 386.00 | 3,400 | 8,090 |
| Vermont........... | 555 | 53,393 | 21,498 | 2,100 | 1,010 | 269.19[3] | 2,500[2] | 6,900[2] |
| District of Columbia | 174 | 80,805 | 40,643 | 2,593 | 1,782 | 417.53 | 4,800 | 7,848 |
| **GREAT LAKES & PLAINS** | | | | | | | | |
| Illinois.......... | 2,042 | 1,287,537 | 454,172 | 49,108 | 23,006 | 411.50[1] | 3,200 | 10,100 |
| Indiana........... | 2,558 | 709,496[5] | 274,035[5] | 25,248[5] | 9,752[5] | 347.11 | 2,600 | 5,600 |
| Iowa.............. | 3,114 | 381,276 | 196,459 | 14,903 | 11,361 | 351.00 | n.a. | n.a. |
| Kansas[6]......... | n.a. | 352,000 | 113,000 | 12,980 | 8,630 | 361.06[1] | 3,153[1,11] | 5,552[1,12] |
| Michigan.......... | 4,928 | 1,045,537 | 635,203 | 36,691 | 27,251 | 418.79 | 3,500 | 7,500 |
| Minnesota......... | 3,332 | 413,758 | 278,578 | 15,152 | 13,940 | 405.00 | 3,000 | 7,275 |
| Missouri.......... | 2,029 | 628,045[7] | 196,350[7] | 20,727 | 9,357 | 336.52 | 1,800 | 9,063 |
| Nebraska.......... | 3,399 | 193,319 | 89,678 | 8,811 | 5,038 | 308.16[1] | 2,500 | 7,500 |
| North Dakota...... | 1,816 | 100,897[7] | 37,266[7] | 5,202 | 2,326 | 353.01 | 2,700 | 6,000 |
| Ohio.............. | 4,157 | 1,306,759 | 644,093 | 45,524 | 28,205 | 330.68 | 3,500 | n.a. |
| South Dakota...... | 2,855 | 111,212[7] | 38,136[7] | 5,695 | 1,982 | 355.64 | 1,800[1] | 7,100[1] |
| Wisconsin[6]...... | 4,691 | 517,000 | 208,000 | 19,900 | 9,050 | 380.59 | 1,800 | 9,500 |
| **SOUTHEAST** | | | | | | | | |
| Alabama........... | 2,364 | 444,200[8] | 344,934[8] | 14,690 | 11,771 | 194.40 | 3,721[2] | 4,065[2] |
| Arkansas.......... | 1,705 | 240,021[8] | 182,139[8] | 7,820 | 7,202 | 242.48 | 2,700 | 5,200 |
| Florida........... | 2,060 | 575,533 | 403,632 | 20,807 | 16,458 | 299.78 | 3,200 | 9,410 |
| Georgia........... | 1,856 | 646,280[9] | 285,259[9] | 21,290 | 11,530 | 224.45 | 2,200 | 4,200 |
| Kentucky.......... | 3,720 | 443,452 | 174,752 | 15,730 | 7,769 | 246.72 | 1,300 | 5,265 |
| Louisiana......... | 1,866 | 559,000 | 155,000 | 15,956 | 10,642 | 372.31 | 3,400 | 6,700 |
| Mississippi....... | 1,944 | 387,000 | 188,000 | 10,915 | 7,776 | 191.48 | 2,900 | 3,454[2] |
| North Carolina.... | 2,919 | 839,916[7] | 262,110[7] | 26,911 | 10,547 | 229.00 | 2,946 | 4,557 |
| South Carolina.... | 1,419 | 375,152 | 205,768 | 12,330 | 8,526 | 213.00 | 2,394 | 3,717 |
| Tennessee......... | 3,021 | 604,017 | 190,743 | 21,934 | 7,707 | 217.03 | 3,819[2] | 3,819[2] |
| Virginia.......... | 2,386 | 582,872 | 264,356 | 19,737 | 12,926 | 256.07 | 2,800 | 7,572 |
| West Virginia..... | 3,943 | 266,915 | 170,741 | 9,658 | 6,698 | 244.24 | 2,689 | 6,839 |
| **WEST & SOUTHWEST** | | | | | | | | |
| Arizona........... | 611 | 236,491 | 70,375 | 8,369 | 2,815 | 413.54 | n.a. | n.a. |
| California........ | 5,709 | 2,282,000 | 1,071,600 | 74,500 | 44,750 | 409.32 | 4,500 | 10,400 |
| Colorado.......... | 1,400 | 243,295 | 148,922 | 9,323 | 7,360 | 380.77 | 3,380[1] | 8,000[1] |
| Idaho............. | 655 | 88,879[8] | 70,039[8] | 3,409 | 2,939 | 323.51 | 2,400 | 6,900 |
| Montana........... | 1,706 | 99,696[7] | 46,619[7] | 4,479 | 2,400 | 347.69 | 2,400 | 8,950 |
| Nevada............ | 229 | 42,424 | 21,954 | 1,848 | 881 | 432.97 | 4,000 | 8,250 |
| New Mexico........ | 679 | 133,138[8] | 89,815[8] | 5,116 | 4,075 | 376.71 | 4,000 | 6,500 |
| Oklahoma.......... | 2,498 | 328,500[10] | 210,500[10] | 11,600 | 8,690 | 298.26 | 3,200 | 5,100 |
| Oregon............ | 1,289 | 270,433[7] | 118,157[7] | 10,856 | 6,229 | 428.74 | 5,207[2] | 5,626[2] |
| Texas............. | 5,663 | 1,678,809 | 472,427 | 54,330 | 26,354 | 288.81 | 4,490[2] | 4,490[2] |
| Utah.............. | 570 | 142,986 | 94,799 | 4,629 | 3,897 | 309.88 | 3,586 | 6,564 |
| Washington........ | 1,618 | 476,338 | 162,095 | 14,241 | 10,353 | 373.30 | 5,277[2] | 5,604[2] |
| Wyoming........... | 546 | 48,615 | 30,317 | 2,219 | 1,742 | 435.00 | 3,200 | 6,000 |
| Alaska............ | 181 | 33,579 | 9,727 | 1,328 | 488 | 529.89 | 4,500 | 6,900 |
| Hawaii............ | 220 | 85,409 | 59,283 | 2,928 | 2,029 | 327.73 | 3,960 | 6,300 |
| **TOTAL.........** | 103,846[13] | 24,457,321 | 11,847,783 | 861,035 | 548,960 | ...... | ...... | ...... |

[1] 1958–59.   [2] Average, not absolute, minimum and maximum.   [3] Per elementary pupil; $428.45 per secondary pupil. [4] Includes librarians and guidance personnel.   [5] As of June 1960.   [6] Excludes vocational schools.   [7] Elementary comprises kindergarten through grade 8; secondary comprises grades 9–12.   [8] Elementary comprises kindergarten through grade 6; secondary comprises grades 7–12.   [9] Elementary comprises kindergarten through grade 7; secondary comprises grades 8–12.   [10] Estimated for 1960–61 school year.   [11] Average annual salary for elementary teachers.   [12] Average annual salary for secondary teachers.   [13] Does not include Kansas.

# State Compulsory School Attendance Laws

*Source:* U. S. Office of Education.

| State | Enactment[1] | Age limits | State | Enactment[1] | Age limits |
|---|---|---|---|---|---|
| Alabama | 1915 | 7–16 | Montana | 1883 | 7–16 |
| Alaska | 1929 | 7–16 | Nebraska | 1887 | 7–16 |
| Arizona | 1899 | 8–16 | Nevada | 1873 | 7–17 |
| Arkansas | 1909 | 7–16 | New Hampshire | 1871 | 6–16 |
| California | 1874 | 8–16 | New Jersey | 1875 | 7–16 |
| Colorado | 1889 | 8–16 | New Mexico | 1891 | 6–17 |
| Connecticut | 1872 | 7–16 | New York | 1874 | 7–16 |
| Delaware | 1907 | 7–16 | North Carolina | 1907 | 7–16 |
| D. C. | 1864 | 7–16 | North Dakota | 1883 | 7–16 |
| Florida | 1915 | 7–16 | Ohio | 1877 | 6–18 |
| Georgia | 1916 | 7–16 | Oklahoma | 1907 | 7–18 |
| Hawaii | 1896 | 6–16 | Oregon | 1889 | 7–18 |
| Idaho | 1887 | 7–16 | Pennsylvania | 1895 | 8–17 |
| Illinois | 1883 | 7–16 | Rhode Island | 1883 | 7–16 |
| Indiana | 1897 | 7–16 | South Carolina[3] | .... | .... |
| Iowa | 1902 | 7–16 | South Dakota | 1883 | 7–16 |
| Kansas | 1874 | 7–16 | Tennessee | 1905 | 7–17 |
| Kentucky | 1896 | 7–16 | Texas | 1915[4] | 7–16 |
| Louisiana | 1910 | 7–16 | Utah | 1890 | 6–18 |
| Maine | 1875 | 7–15 | Vermont | 1867 | 7–16 |
| Maryland | 1902 | 7–16 | Virginia[5] | .... | .... |
| Massachusetts | 1852 | 7–16 | Washington | 1871 | 8–16 |
| Michigan | 1871 | 6–16 | West Virginia | 1897 | 7–16 |
| Minnesota | 1885 | 7–16 | Wisconsin | 1879 | 7–16 |
| Mississippi[2] | .... | .... | Wyoming | 1876 | 7–17 |
| Missouri | 1905 | 7–16 | | | |

[1] Date of enactment of 1st compulsory school attendance law. [2] Mississippi repealed its compulsory attendance law in 1956. [3] South Carolina repealed its compulsory attendance law in 1955. [4] A compulsory school attendance law was contained in a law of 1873 establishing free public schools. However, the provision was omitted in superseding legislation passed in 1876. [5] Virginia repealed its compulsory attendance law in 1959.

# Enrollment in Full-time Day Schools, 1909-58

*Source:* U. S. Office of Education.

| Level of instruction, by type of school | 1909–1910 | 1919–1920 | 1929–1930 | 1939–1940 | 1949–1950 | 1957–1958 |
|---|---|---|---|---|---|---|
| Kindergarten: Public[1] | 293,970[2] | 481,266 | 723,443 | 594,647 | 1,034,203 | 1,771,753 |
| Nonpublic[1] | 52,219[2] | 29,683 | 54,456 | 57,341 | 133,000 | 353,000 |
| Residential schools for exceptional children | (3) | (3) | 5,164[4] | 5,777 | 4,459[5] | (3) |
| Other[6] | (3) | (3) | 3,400 | 3,144 | 3,650 | 11,164 |
| Total kindergarten | 346,189 | 510,949 | 786,463 | 660,909 | 1,175,312 | 2,135,917 |
| | | | | | | |
| Grades 1–8 inclusive: Public[1] | 16,604,821 | 18,897,661 | 20,555,150 | 18,237,451 | 18,352,603 | 23,897,067 |
| Nonpublic[1] | 1,506,218 | 1,455,878 | 2,255,430 | 2,095,938 | 2,574,777[7] | 3,943,806[7] |
| Residential schools for exceptional children | 71,307 | 99,234[8] | 124,153[4] | 55,954 | 48,894[5] | 63,300[9] |
| Other[6] | (3) | (3) | (3) | 76,769 | 55,655 | 86,900 |
| Total grades 1–8 | 18,182,346 | 20,452,773 | 22,953,377 | 20,466,112 | 21,031,929 | 27,991,073 |
| Total kindergarten through grade 8 | 18,528,535 | 20,963,722 | 23,739,840 | 21,127,021 | 22,207,241 | 30,126,990 |
| | | | | | | |
| Grades 9–12[10]: Public high schools[1] | 915,061 | 2,200,389 | 4,399,422 | 6,601,444 | 5,724,621 | 7,859,771 |
| Nonpublic high schools[1] | 117,400 | 213,920 | 341,158 | 457,768 | 672,362[7] | 930,608[7] |
| Residential schools for exceptional children | 4,005 | 4,500[8] | 4,388[4] | 9,727 | 9,784[5] | 23,201[12] |
| Other[6] | 78,932 | 81,367 | 66,832 | 61,040 | 46,242 | 55,007 |
| Total grades 9–12[10] | 1,115,398 | 2,500,176 | 4,811,800 | 7,129,979 | 6,453,009 | 8,868,586 |
| Total kindergarten through grade 12[10] | 19,643,933 | 23,463,898 | 28,551,640 | 28,257,000 | 28,660,250 | 38,995,576 |
| | | | | | | |
| Higher education: Publicly controlled | 166,560 | 315,382 | 532,647 | 796,531 | 1,354,902 | 1,876,898 |
| Privately controlled | 188,655 | 282,498 | 568,090 | 697,672 | 1,304,119 | 1,407,019 |
| Total higher education | 355,215 | 597,880 | 1,100,737 | 1,494,203 | 2,659,021 | 3,283,917 |
| Total all levels[11] | 19,999,148 | 24,061,778 | 29,652,377 | 29,751,203 | 31,319,271 | 42,279,493 |

[1] Does not include subcollegiate departments of institutions of higher education, residential schools for exceptional children, or Federal schools. [2] 1911–12. [3] Not available. [4] 1926–27. [5] 1945–46. [6] Subcollegiate departments of institutions of higher education, and Federal schools. [7] Estimated. [8] 1917–18. [9] Preliminary data; includes enrollment in kindergarten. [10] And postgraduate. [11] Does not include schools of nursing not affiliated with institutions of higher education. [12] Preliminary data.

# Statistics of State School Systems, 1949-59

Source: U. S. Office of Education.

| Years | Enrollment | | | | | | | | Current expenditure per pupil in average daily attendance | Expenditure for textbooks free to pupils |
|---|---|---|---|---|---|---|---|---|---|---|
| | Total | Kindergarten through grade 8 | | Grades 9 through 12 and postgraduate | | High-school graduates | | | | |
| | | Boys | Girls | Boys | Girls | Boys | Girls | | | |
| 1949–1950.... | 25,111,000 | 10,018,000 | 9,387,000 | 2,812,000 | 2,895,000 | 505,394 | 558,050 | | $208.83 | $48,076,000 |
| 1951–1952.... | 26,563,000 | 10,649,000 | 10,032,000 | 2,885,000 | 2,997,000 | 501,723 | 553,863 | | 244.24 | 53,677,000 |
| 1953–1954*... | 28,836,000 | 11,609,000 | 10,937,000 | 3,085,000 | 3,205,000 | 544,575 | 584,966 | | 264.76 | 72,660,000 |
| 1955–1956.... | 31,162,800 | 12,491,700 | 11,798,500 | 3,415,700 | 3,456,900 | 606,502 | 645,552 | | 294.22 | 75,626,000 |
| 1957–1958... | 33,529,000 | 13,239,000 | 12,430,000 | 3,864,000 | 3,995,000 | 648,046 | 684,985 | | 341.14 | 101,890,000 |
| 1958–1959... | 36,274,097 | 26,580,774** | | 8,257,867** | | 699,738 | 735,718 | | n.a. | n.a. |

\* Number of boys and girls in elementary and secondary schools in 1953–54 are estimated from total enrollment.
\*\* Breakdown by sex not available.

# Federal Government Funds for Education, 1959-60

Source: U. S. Office of Education.

| Program | Amount in thousands | Program | Amount in thousands |
|---|---|---|---|
| Elementary–Secondary Education............ | $1,131,412 | Fellowships and Grants................. | $ 53,265 |
| National Defense Education Act.......... | 80,129 | Research Grants and Contracts......... | 448,012 |
| Vocational Education................ | 30,235 | Loans: Student Loans of the National Defense Education Act and College Housing | |
| Federally Affected School Areas............ | 233,500 | Loans.......................... | 259,619 |
| School Lunch........................ | 305,511 | Veterans Education Programs............ | 248,492 |
| Revenue from Public Lands—Sales and Leases | 83,492 | Federal Personnel: Military Academies and | |
| Indian Education..................... | 47,133 | Outservice Training.................... | 54,701 |
| Education of Dependents of Military Personnel | 34,150 | Surplus Property.................... | 67,095 |
| Surplus Property..................... | 252,405 | Land-Grant Colleges................. | 5,052 |
| Science Education—National Science Foundation. | 4,463 | Other............................ | 8,453 |
| School Aid in Special Areas—District of Columbia, Canal Zone, Territories and Dependencies, Atomic Energy Commission Facilities. | 20,745 | Adult Education....................... | 234,748 |
| | | Programs Not Classified By Level........... | 118,484 |
| | | Administration—Office of Education........ | 10,327 |
| Teacher Training Programs................. | 39,480 | Rural Library Services.............. | 7,500 |
| Other............................ | 169 | Department of State Programs.......... | 58,449 |
| Higher Education..................... | 1,209,052 | Department of Defense Programs......... | 20,456 |
| Traineeships and Training Grants.......... | 64,363 | Other............................ | 21,752 |
| | | TOTAL............................ | $2,693,696 |

# Exceptional Children in Special Education Programs, 1956-58

(PUBLIC SCHOOLS ONLY) Source: U. S. Office of Education.

| Area of exceptionality | Total nursery and kindergarten | Elementary | Secondary | Not separately classified | Grand total |
|---|---|---|---|---|---|
| Blind........................ | 257 | 2,027 | 495 | 65 | 2,844 |
| Partially seeing.................. | 18 | 6,441 | 1,916 | 223 | 8,598 |
| Deaf............................. | 930 | 3,935 | 883 | 676 | 6,424 |
| Hard of hearing.................. | 7 | 10,393 | 2,470 | 243 | 13,113 |
| Speech impaired.................. | 1,514 | 442,138 | 38,974 | 4,318 | 486,944 |
| Crippled...................... | 1,188 | 22,692 | 4,358 | 1,073 | 29,311 |
| Special health problems............ | 12 | 16,241 | 6,655 | 169 | 23,077 |
| Socially and emotionally maladjusted...... | 2 | 18,415 | 7,580 | 2,263 | 28,260 |
| Gifted........................ | 155 | 19,808 | 32,159 | 147 | 52,269 |
| Mentally retarded[1] (upper range)[2]........ | .... | .... | .... | 201,406 | 201,406 |
| Mentally retarded[1] (middle range)[3]........ | .... | .... | .... | 16,779 | 16,779 |
| Other[4]....................... | 1,034 | 9,596 | 833 | 1,578 | 13,041 |
| TOTAL........................ | 5,117 | 551,686 | 96,323 | 228,940 | 882,066 |

[1] Enrollment data for mentally retarded pupils were not collected according to elementary and secondary classifications. [2] Includes children with approximately 50 to 75 I.Q. [3] Includes children with approximately 25 to 50 I.Q. [4] "Other" includes the following pupils reported in combined categories of exceptionality: Blind and partially seeing, 119; deaf and hard of hearing, 1,993; speech impaired and hard of hearing, 4,493; crippled and special health problems, 4,686; special health problem and socially maladjusted, 22; upper and middle range mentally retarded, 1,403; and multi-handicapped, 325.

# High-school and College Graduates, 1900-59

## (Public and private schools)

*Source:* U. S. Office of Education.

| Year of graduation | HIGH SCHOOL | | | COLLEGE* | | |
|---|---|---|---|---|---|---|
| | Men | Women | Total | Men | Women | Total |
| 1900.................... | 38,075 | 56,808 | 94,883 | 22,173 | 5,237 | 27,410 |
| 1910.................... | 63,676 | 92,753 | 156,429 | 28,762 | 8,437 | 37,199 |
| 1920.................... | 123,684 | 187,582 | 311,266 | 31,980 | 16,642 | 48,622 |
| 1929-30................. | 300,376 | 366,528 | 666,904 | 73,615 | 48,869 | 122,484 |
| 1939-40................. | 578,718 | 642,757 | 1,221,475 | 109,546 | 76,954 | 186,500 |
| 1947-48................. | 562,863 | 627,046 | 1,189,909 | 175,615 | 95,571 | 271,186 |
| 1949-50................. | 570,700 | 629,000 | 1,199,700 | 328,841 | 103,217 | 432,058 |
| 1950-51................. | 562,500 | 619,300 | 1,181,800 | 278,240 | 104,306 | 382,546 |
| 1951-52................. | 569,200 | 627,300 | 1,196,500 | 225,981 | 104,005 | 329,986 |
| 1952-53†................ | 572,800 | 625,500 | 1,198,300 | 199,793 | 103,256 | 303,049 |
| 1953-54................. | 612,500 | 663,600 | 1,276,100 | 186,528 | 104,297 | 290,825 |
| 1954-55†................ | 645,300 | 699,100 | 1,344,400 | 182,463 | 102,675 | 285,138 |
| 1955-56................. | 679,500 | 735,300 | 1,414,800 | 198,233 | 110,579 | 308,812 |
| 1956-57†................ | 692,200 | 746,900 | 1,439,100 | 221,231 | 116,432 | 337,663 |
| 1957-58................. | 725,500 | 780,400 | 1,505,900 | 240,990 | 121,564 | 362,554 |
| 1958-59†................ | 788,000 | 851,000 | 1,639,000 | 252,960 | 128,963 | 381,923 |

* 1st-level degree in given field of study.    † High-school graduates are estimated.

# Enrollment in Vocational Classes, 1960*

*Source:* U. S. Office of Education.

| Type of program | Evening classes | Part-time classes | Day classes | All classes |
|---|---|---|---|---|
| Agriculture............................ | 266,729 | 65,548 | 463,960 | 796,237 |
| Area programs........................ | 68,342† | ...... | 32,937‡ | 101,279 |
| Distributive occupations................ | 264,106 | 39,678 | ...... | 303,784 |
| Home economics....................... | 586,335 | 54,914 | 946,860 | 1,588,109 |
| Practical nursing...................... | 15,562† | ...... | 24,688‡ | 40,250 |
| Trades and industry.................... | 485,020 | 181,149 | 272,321 | 938,490 |
| Total................................ | 1,686,094 | 341,289 | 1,740,766 | 3,768,149 |

* Provisional figures, subject to final review of state reports.    † Extension.    ‡ Preparatory.

# Number Surviving Through College Entrance per 1,000 Pupils

*Source:* U. S. Office of Education.

| Grade or year | 1940-1941 | 1942-1943 | 1943-1944 | 1944-1945 | 1945-1946 | 1946-1947 | 1947-1948 | 1948-1949 | 1949-1950 | 1950-1951 | 1951-1952* | 1952-1953* |
|---|---|---|---|---|---|---|---|---|---|---|---|---|
| Elementary: Fifth............ | 1,000 | 1,000 | 1,000 | 1,000 | 1,000 | 1,000 | 1,000 | 1,000 | 1,000 | 1,000 | 1,000 | 1,000 |
| Sixth................. | 968 | 954 | 972 | 952 | 959 | 954 | 971 | 984 | 984 | 981 | 981 | 974 |
| Seventh............... | 910 | 909 | 914 | 929 | 944 | 945 | 948 | 956 | 967 | 968 | 965 | 965 |
| Eighth................ | 836 | 847 | 870 | 858 | 875 | 919 | 919 | 929 | 918 | 921 | 937 | 936 |
| High School: I.............. | 781 | 807 | 827 | 848 | 872 | 872 | 858 | 863 | 874 | 886 | 890 | 904 |
| II................... | 697 | 713 | 745 | 748 | 766 | 775 | 748 | 795 | 795 | 809 | 820 | 838 |
| III.................. | 566 | 604 | 630 | 650 | 662 | 641 | 670 | 706 | 698 | 709 | 719 | 733 |
| IV................... | 507 | 539 | 557 | 549 | 552 | 583 | 594 | 619 | 614 | 632 | 640 | 653 |
| Graduates.............. | 481 | 505 | 524 | 522 | 524 | 553 | 559 | 581 | 574 | 582 | 593 | 604 |
| Year of graduation........... | 1948 | 1950 | 1951 | 1952 | 1953 | 1954 | 1955 | 1956 | 1957 | 1958 | 1959 | 1960 |
| Enter college................ | † | 205 | 218 | 234 | 266 | 283 | 286 | 301 | 303 | 308 | 313 | 319 |

* Preliminary data.    † Because of veteran students, it is not possible to calculate retention rates.

# White and Negro School Statistics, 1953-54*

**(Public elementary and secondary schools in 17 Southern states and the District of Columbia)**

*Source:* U. S. Office of Education.

| State | Enrollment | | Instructional staff[1] | | Average annual salary of instructional staff | | Expenditure[2] per pupil in A.D.A.[3] | |
|---|---|---|---|---|---|---|---|---|
| | White | Negro | White | Negro | White | Negro | White | Negro |
| Alabama | 460,507 | 243,140 | 15,764 | 7,912 | $2,834 | $2,681 | $111.99 | $105.02 |
| Arkansas | 315,111 | 99,844 | 10,907 | 2,902 | 2,360 | 2,008 | 99.08 | 71.78 |
| Delaware | 47,237 | 9,968 | 2,109 | 411 | ..... | ..... | ..... | ..... |
| D. C. | 49,106 | 60,029 | 1,770 | 1,941 | 4,998 | 4,614 | 240.27 | 186.71 |
| Florida | 487,698 | 140,779 | 17,836 | 5,300 | 3,836 | 3,613 | 175.92 | 160.61 |
| Georgia | 533,508 | 274,123 | 19,848 | 8,576 | ..... | ..... | ..... | ..... |
| Kentucky | 553,051 | 38,517 | 18,843 | 1,422 | ..... | ..... | ..... | ..... |
| Louisiana | 343,914 | 208,577 | 13,228 | 6,342 | ..... | ..... | 165.08 | 122.07 |
| Maryland | 338,308 | 89,984 | 12,691 | 3,022 | ..... | ..... | ..... | ..... |
| Mississippi | 263,478 | 263,930 | 9,609 | 6,777 | 2,261 | 1,302 | 98.15 | 43.17 |
| Missouri | 637,705 | 65,962 | 23,564 | 2,034 | ..... | ..... | ..... | ..... |
| North Carolina | 683,284 | 284,782 | 23,971 | 8,944 | 3,335 | 3,406 | 132.46 | 124.85 |
| Oklahoma | 446,989 | 36,111 | 17,521 | 1,615 | 3,265 | 3,346 | 161.57 | 165.88 |
| South Carolina | 304,908 | 234,529 | 11,219 | 7,181 | ..... | ..... | ..... | ..... |
| Tennessee | 598,247 | 118,048 | 20,329 | 3,771 | ..... | ..... | ..... | ..... |
| Texas | 1,388,828 | 215,465 | 50,717 | 7,697 | ..... | ..... | ..... | ..... |
| Virginia | 523,165 | 172,112 | 19,252 | 5,868 | 3,076 | 3,104 | ..... | ..... |
| West Virginia | 426,345 | 25,646 | 15,437 | 983 | ..... | ..... | ..... | ..... |
| TOTAL | 8,401,389 | 2,581,546 | 304,615 | 82,698 | ..... | ..... | ..... | ..... |

[1] Includes supervisors, principals, teachers, etc. [2] For instruction. [3] Average daily attendance. * Latest data available.

# Degrees Granted by Institutions of Higher Education, 1959-60

**(Aggregate United States[1])**

*Source:* U. S. Office of Education.

| Field of study | Bachelor's and first professional | | Second level (master's, except first professional) | | Doctor's | |
|---|---|---|---|---|---|---|
| | Men | Women | Men | Women | Men | Women |
| Agriculture | 4,805 | 93 | 984 | 12 | 404 | 7 |
| Architecture | 1,744 | 57 | 305 | 14 | 17 | .... |
| Biological Sciences | 11,693 | 3,962 | 1,668 | 486 | 1,086 | 119 |
| Business and commerce | 47,629 | 3,893 | 4,476 | 167 | 133 | 2 |
| Education | 26,178 | 64,001 | 18,126 | 15,386 | 1,281 | 309 |
| Engineering | 37,663 | 145 | 7,133 | 26 | 783 | 3 |
| English and journalism | 9,001 | 13,455 | 1,670 | 1,522 | 321 | 84 |
| Fine and applied arts | 6,141 | 7,025 | 1,763 | 1,129 | 238 | 54 |
| Foreign languages and literature | 2,098 | 3,400 | 593 | 541 | 166 | 63 |
| Health professions | 15,170 | 9,387 | 1,075 | 797 | 99 | 8 |
| Dentistry | 3,221 | 26 | .... | .... | .... | .... |
| Medicine | 6,680 | 394 | .... | .... | .... | .... |
| Nursing | 81 | 6,580 | 14 | 585 | .... | .... |
| Pharmacy | 3,076 | 416 | 120 | 11 | 50 | 1 |
| Other | 2,112 | 1,971 | 941 | 201 | 49 | 7 |
| Home economics | 60 | 4,390 | 11 | 473 | 6 | 34 |
| Law | 9,073 | 241 | 496 | 24 | 24 | .... |
| Mathematical subjects | 8,312 | 3,125 | 1,428 | 337 | 285 | 18 |
| Physical sciences | 14,041 | 2,016 | 3,060 | 327 | 1,776 | 62 |
| Chemistry (excl. biochemistry) | 6,005 | 1,598 | 1,025 | 203 | 1,000 | 48 |
| Physics | 4,166 | 172 | 1,038 | 35 | 477 | 10 |
| Other | 3,870 | 246 | 997 | 89 | 299 | 4 |
| Psychology | 4,785 | 3,326 | 981 | 425 | 544 | 97 |
| Religion | 7,563 | 1,439 | 1,124 | 207 | 265 | 11 |
| Social sciences | 35,801 | 16,001 | 4,765 | 1,233 | 1,117 | 120 |
| Economics | 6,816 | 672 | 650 | 58 | 223 | 14 |
| History | 10,014 | 4,769 | 1,353 | 441 | 310 | 32 |
| Political science | 5,401 | 1,256 | 593 | 129 | 184 | 17 |
| Sociology | 3,171 | 4,011 | 327 | 113 | 135 | 26 |
| Other | 10,399 | 5,293 | 1,842 | 492 | 265 | 31 |
| TOTAL[2] | 255,504 | 139,385 | 50,937 | 23,560 | 8,801 | 1,028 |

[1] Includes the 48 contiguous states, D. C., Alaska, Hawaii and outlying parts. [2] Includes studies not listed in this table.

# School Enrollment, 5 to 34 Years Old, October 1957 to October 1960

*Source:* U. S. Bureau of the Census.

| Sex and age | October 1957 | | October 1959 | | October 1960 | |
|---|---|---|---|---|---|---|
| | Number enrolled | % enrolled | Number enrolled | % enrolled | Number enrolled | % enrolled |
| **MALE** | | | | | | |
| 5 and 6 years............ | 2,963,000 | 78.3 | 3,158,000 | 79.5 | 3,292,000 | 80.8 |
| 7 to 13 years............. | 11,584,000 | 99.5 | 12,556,000 | 99.3 | 13,074,000 | 99.5 |
| 14 to 17 years............ | 4,646,000 | 91.1 | 5,041,000 | 91.4 | 5,248,000 | 91.4 |
| 18 and 19 years......... | 780,000 | 43.3 | 918,000 | 45.6 | 1,063,000 | 47.8 |
| 20 to 24 years........... | 897,000 | 21.3 | 892,000 | 19.6 | 936,000 | 19.9 |
| 25 to 29 years........... | 493,000 | 9.5 | 446,000 | 8.9 | 415,000 | 8.4 |
| 30 to 34 years............ | 146,000 | 2.6 | 181,000 | 3.3 | 206,000 | 3.7 |
| TOTAL, 5 to 34 years... | 21,509,000 | 57.5 | 23,192,000 | 59.1 | 24,234,000 | 60.0 |
| **FEMALE** | | | | | | |
| 5 and 6 years............ | 2,866,000 | 79.0 | 3,064,000 | 80.5 | 3,146,000 | 80.6 |
| 7 to 13 years............. | 11,121,000 | 99.5 | 12,070,009 | 99.6 | 12,547,000 | 99.6 |
| 14 to 17 years............ | 4,421,000 | 87.8 | 4,798,000 | 89.0 | 4,994,000 | 89.2 |
| 18 and 19 years......... | 629,000 | 28.1 | 683,000 | 29.2 | 754,000 | 30.0 |
| 20 to 24 years........... | 439,000 | 8.2 | 391,000 | 7.1 | 414,000 | 7.4 |
| 25 to 29 years............ | 111,000 | 1.9 | 92,000 | 1.7 | 99,000 | 1.8 |
| 30 to 34 years............ | 70,000 | 1.1 | 80,000 | 1.3 | 72,000 | 1.2 |
| TOTAL, 5 to 34 years... | 19,657,000 | 50.0 | 21,178,000 | 52.0 | 22,025,000 | 52.8 |
| **TOTAL** | | | | | | |
| 5 and 6 years............ | 5,829,000 | 78.6 | 6,222,000 | 80.0 | 6,438,000 | 80.7 |
| 7 to 13 years............. | 22,705,000 | 99.5 | 24,626,000 | 99.4 | 25,621,000 | 99.5 |
| 14 to 17 years............ | 9,067,000 | 89.5 | 9,839,000 | 90.2 | 10,242,000 | 90.3 |
| 18 and 19 years......... | 1,409,000 | 34.9 | 1,601,000 | 36.8 | 1,817,000 | 38.4 |
| 20 to 24 years............ | 1,336,000 | 14.0 | 1,283,000 | 12.7 | 1,350,000 | 13.1 |
| 25 to 29 years............ | 604,000 | 5.5 | 538,000 | 5.1 | 514,000 | 4.9 |
| 30 to 34 years............ | 216,000 | 1.8 | 261,000 | 2.2 | 278,000 | 2.4 |
| TOTAL, 5 to 34 years... | 41,166,000 | 53.6 | 44,370,000 | 55.5 | 46,259,000 | 56.4 |

NOTE: Figures include children enrolled in kindergarten.

# Estimated Public and Private School Enrollment, By Type of School, 1959-61

(Estimates are for total enrollment during the school year. These figures are larger than the figures for fall enrollment.)

*Source:* U. S. Office of Education.

| Grade level and type of school | Enrollment | | Grade level and type of school | Enrollment | |
|---|---|---|---|---|---|
| | 1959–60 | 1960–61 | | 1959–60 | 1960–61 |
| **Kindergarten through Grade 8** | | | **Kindergarten through Grade 12** | | |
| Public school system[1].......... | 27,800,000 | 28,600,000 | Public school system[1].......... | 36,200,000 | 37,600,000 |
| Nonpublic schools[1]............. | 5,400,000 | 5,600,000 | Nonpublic schools[1]............. | 6,500,000 | 6,800,000 |
| Other schools[2]................. | 180,000 | 180,000 | Other schools[2]................. | 270,000 | 270,000 |
| Total, kindergarten through grade 8.................... | 33,380,000 | 34,380,000 | Total, kindergarten through grade 12................... | 42,970,000 | 44,670,000 |
| **Grades 9 through 12** | | | **Higher Education** | | |
| Public school system[1].......... | 8,400,000 | 9,000,000 | Universities, colleges, professional schools, junior colleges, normal schools, and teachers colleges (degree-credit enrollment)...................... | 3,750,000 | 3,980,000 |
| Nonpublic schools[1]............. | 1,100,000 | 1,200,000 | | | |
| Other schools[2]................. | 90,000 | 90,000 | | | |
| Total, grades 9 through 12....... | 9,590,000 | 10,290,000 | Grand total................... | 46,720,000 | 48,650,000 |

[1] Regular full-time. [2] Includes Federal schools for Indians, federally operated elementary-secondary schools on posts, model and practice schools in teacher-training institutions, subcollegiate departments of colleges, and residential schools for exceptional children.

# Selected Academic Degree Abbreviations

*Source:* Material condensed from *American Universities and Colleges*, 1960, pub. by American Council on Education.

**A.B.** Bachelor of Arts
**Ae.E.** Aeronautical Engineer
**A.M.** Master of Arts
**A.M.T.** Master of Arts in Teaching
**B.A.** Bachelor of Arts
**B.A.E.** Bachelor of Arts in Education, or Bachelor of Art Education, Aeronautical Engineering, Agricultural Engineering, or Architectural Engineering
**B.Ag.** Bachelor of Agriculture
**B.App.Arts** Bachelor of Applied Arts
**B.Arch.** Bachelor of Architecture
**B.B.A.** Bachelor of Business Administration
**B.C.E.** Bachelor of Civil Engineering
**B.Ch.E.** Bachelor of Chemical Engineering
**B.D.** Bachelor of Divinity
**B.E.** Bachelor of Education or Bachelor of Engineering
**B.E.E.** Bachelor of Electrical Engineering
**B.F.** Bachelor of Forestry
**B.F.A.** Bachelor of Fine Arts
**B.J.** Bachelor of Journalism
**B.L.S.** Bachelor of Library Science
**B.Litt.** Bachelor of Literature
**B.M.** Bachelor of Medicine or Bachelor of Music
**B.Mus.** Bachelor of Music
**B.N.** Bachelor of Nursing
**B.Pharm.** Bachelor of Pharmacy
**B.R.E.** Bachelor of Religious Education
**B.S.** Bachelor of Science
**B.Th.** Bachelor of Theology
**C.E.** Civil Engineer
**Chem.E.** Chemical Engineer
**D.D.** Doctor of Divinity
**D.D.S.** Doctor of Dental Surgery or Doctor of Dental Science
**D.L.S.** Doctor of Library Science
**D.M.D.** Doctor of Dental Medicine
**D.O.** Doctor of Osteopathy
**D.M.S.** Doctor of Medical Science
**D.P.A.** Doctor of Public Administration
**D.P.H.** Doctor of Public Health
**D.R.E.** Doctor of Religious Education
**D.S.W.** Doctor of Social Welfare
**D.Sc.** Doctor of Science
**D.V.M.** Doctor of Veterinary Medicine
**E.A.A.** Engineer in Aeronautics and Astronautics
**Ed.D.** Doctor of Education
**E.E.** Electrical Engineer
**E.M.** Engineer of Mines
**E.Met.** Engineer of Metallurgy

**G.N.** Graduate Nurse
**I.E.** Industrial Engineer
**J.D.** Doctor of Jurisprudence
**J.S.D.** Doctor of the Science of Law
**L.H.D.** Doctor of Humane Letters
**Litt.M.** Master of Letters
**LL.B.** Bachelor of Laws
**LL.D.** Doctor of Laws
**LL.M.** Master of Laws
**M.A.** Master of Arts
**M.Aero.E.** Master of Aeronautical Engineering
**M.B.A.** Master of Business Administration
**M.C.E.** Master of Civil Engineering
**M.C.S.** Master of Commercial Science
**M.D.** Doctor of Medicine
**M.E.** Mechanical Engineer or Master of Education
**M.Ed.** Master of Education
**M. Eng.** Mining Engineer or Master of Engineering
**M.F.** Master of Forestry
**M.F.A.** Master of Fine Arts
**M.L.S.** Master of Library Science
**M.M.** Master of Music
**M.M.E.** Master of Mechanical Engineering or Master of Music Education
**M.Mus.** Master of Music
**M. Nurs.** Master of Nursing
**M.P.A.** Master of Public Administration, Professional Accounting or Public Affairs
**M.P.H.** Master of Public Health
**M.R.E.** Master of Religious Education
**M.S.** Master of Science
**M.S.W.** Master of Social Work
**M.Th.** Master of Theology
**N.E.** Nuclear Engineer
**O.D.** Doctor of Optometry
**Pharm.D.** Doctor of Pharmacy
**Ph.B.** Bachelor of Philosophy
**Ph.C.** Pharmaceutical Chemist
**Ph.D.** Doctor of Philosophy
**Ph.M.** Master of Philosophy
**S.B.** Bachelor of Science
**Sc.D.** Doctor of Science
**S.J.D.** Doctor of Juridical Science
**S.Sc.D.** Doctor of Social Science
**S.T.B.** Bachelor of Sacred Theology
**S.T.D.** Doctor of Sacred Theology
**S.T.M.** Master of Sacred Theology
**Th.B.** Bachelor of Theology
**Th.D.** Doctor of Theology
**Th.M.** Master of Theology

# Academic Costume: Colors Associated with Fields

| | | | |
|---|---|---|---|
| Agriculture | Maize | Medicine | Green |
| Arts, Letters, Humanities | White | Music | Pink |
| Commerce, Accountancy, Business | Drab | Nursing | Apricot |
| | | Pharmacy | Olive green |
| Dentistry | Lilac | Philosophy | Dark blue |
| Economics | Copper | Physical Education | Sage green |
| Education | Light Blue | Public Admin. including Foreign Service | Peacock blue |
| Engineering | Orange | | |
| Fine Arts, Architecture | Brown | Public Health | Salmon pink |
| Forestry | Russet | Science | Golden yellow |
| Journalism | Crimson | Social Work | Citron |
| Law | Purple | Theology | Scarlet |
| Library Science | Lemon | Veterinary Science | Gray |

# Accredited U. S. Colleges and Universities
## Spring Semester, 1961

Only schools fully accredited by at least one of the six regional accrediting associations are listed. The number of students is for matriculated undergraduate and graduate students who are working for a degree.

| Institution, location and (date founded) | Chief executive | Students[1] | Control |
|---|---|---|---|
| Abilene Christian College; Abilene, Tex. (1906) | Don H. Morris | 2,262 C | Private |
| Adams State College; Alamosa, Colo. (1921) | Fred J. Plachy | 1,157 C | State |
| Adelphi College; Garden City & Sayville, N. Y. (1896) | Paul Dawson Eddy | 5,600 C | Private |
| Adrian College; Adrian, Mich. (1859) | John H. Dawson | 852 C | Methodist |
| Agnes Scott College; Decatur, Ga. (1889) | Wallace M. Alston | 640 F | Private |
| Air Force Institute of Technology; Wright-Patterson AFB, O. (1919) | Maj. Gen. C. E. Combs | 272 M | National |
| Akron, University of; Akron, Ohio (1870) | Norman P. Auburn | 5,372 C | City |
| Alabama, University of; Tuscaloosa, Ala. (1831)[2] | Frank A. Rose | 13,183 C | State |
| Alabama College; Montevallo, Ala. (1896) | Howard M. Phillips | 1,318 C | State |
| Alaska, University of; College, Alaska (1922)[2] | William R. Wood | 867 C | State |
| Albany State College; Albany & Columbus, Ga. (1903) | W. H. Dennis, Jr. | 794 C | State |
| Albertus Magnus College; New Haven, Conn. (1925) | Sister Marie Louise | 362 F | Catholic |
| Albion College; Albion, Mich. (1835) | Louis W. Norris | 1,355 C | Methodist |
| Albright College; Reading, Pa. (1856) | H. V. Masters | 827 C | Evan. Un. Breth. |
| Alderson-Broaddus College; Philippi, W. Va. (1871) | Richard E. Shearer | 516 C | Baptist |
| Alfred University; Alfred, N. Y. (1857) | M. Ellis Drake | 1,360 C | State |
| Allegheny College; Meadville, Pa. (1815) | Lawrence L. Pelletier | 1,187 C | Private |
| Alliance College; Cambridge Springs, Pa. (1912) | Arthur P. Coleman | 246 C | Private |
| Alma College; Alma, Mich. (1886) | Robert D. Swanson | 715 C | Presbyterian |
| Alverno College; Milwaukee, Wis. (1890) | Sister M. Augustine | 1,111 F | Catholic |
| American International College; Springfield, Mass. (1885)[2] | R. Adm. John F. Hines | 915 C | Private |
| American University; Washington, D. C. (1893) | Hurst R. Anderson | 7,530 C | Methodist |
| Amherst College; Amherst, Mass. (1821) | Calvin H. Plimpton | 979 M | Private |
| Anderson College & Theological Seminary; Anderson, Ind. (1917) | Robert H. Reardon | 1,071 C | Church of God |
| Andrews University; Berrien Springs, Mich. (1874)[3] | F. O. Rittenhouse | 1,300 C | 7th Day Adven. |
| Anna Maria College for Women; Paxton, Mass. (1946) | Sister Irene Marie | 336 F | Catholic |
| Annhurst College; South Woodstock, Conn. (1941) | Mother Claire Helen | 247 F | Catholic |
| Antioch College; Yellow Springs, Ohio (1852) | James P. Dixon | 1,444 C | Private |
| Appalachian State Teachers College; Boone, N. C. (1903) | W. H. Plemmons | 2,627 C | State |
| Aquinas College; Grand Rapids, Mich. (1886) | Arthur F. Bukowski | 823 C | Catholic |
| Arizona, University of; Tucson, Ariz. (1885) | Richard A. Harvill | 12,518 C | State |
| Arizona State College; Flagstaff, Ariz. (1899) | J. Lawrence Walkup | 1,916 C | State |
| Arizona State University; Tempe, Ariz. (1885) | G. Homer Durham | 10,324 C | State |
| Arkansas, University of; Fayetteville & Little Rock, Ark. (1871) | David W. Mullins | 5,952 C | State |
| Arkansas A & M College; College Heights, Ark. (1909) | J. W. Mears | 892 C | State |
| Arkansas A, M & Normal College; Pine Bluff, Ark. (1873) | Lawrence A. Davis | 1,596 C | State |
| Arkansas College; Batesville, Ark. (1872) | Paul M. McCain | 205 C | Presbyterian |
| Arkansas Polytechnic College; Russellville, Ark. (1909) | J. W. Hull | 1,262 C | State |
| Arkansas State College; Jonesboro & Beebe, Ark. (1909) | Carl R. Reng | 3,001 C | State |
| Arkansas State Teachers College; Conway, Ark. (1907) | Silas D. Snow | 1,823 C | State |
| Arlington State College; Arlington, Tex. (1917) | Jack R. Woolf | 6,457 C | State |
| Art Center School, The; Los Angeles, Calif. (1930) | E. A. Adams | 1,082 C | Private |
| Asbury College; Wilmore, Ky. (1890) | Z. T. Johnson | 896 C | Private |
| Ashland College; Ashland, Ohio (1878) | Glenn L. Clayton | 718 C | Brethren |
| Assumption College; Worcester, Mass. (1904) | V. Rev. A. Desautels | 462 M | Catholic |
| Athenaeum of Ohio; Cincinnati, Ohio (1831) | Rt. Rev. J. J. Schneider | 432 M | Catholic |
| Atlanta University System: | | | |
|   Atlanta University; Atlanta, Ga. (1865) | Rufus E. Clement | 864 C | Private |
|   Morehouse College; Atlanta, Ga. (1867) | Benjamin E. Mays | 790 M | Private |
|   Spelman College; Atlanta, Ga. (1881) | Albert E. Manley | 520 F | Baptist |
| Atlantic Christian College; Wilson, N. C. (1902) | Arthur D. Wenger | 1,069 C | Disc. of Christ |
| Atlantic Union College; South Lancaster, Mass. (1882) | Robert L. Reynolds | 538 C | 7th Day Adven. |
| Auburn University; Auburn, Ala. (1856) | Ralph B. Draughon | 7,863 C | State |
| Augsburg College & Theological Seminary; Minneapolis (1869) | Bernhard Christensen | 942 C | Lutheran |
| Augustana College; Rock Island, Ill. (1860) | Conrad Bergendoff | 1,350 C | Lutheran |
| Augustana College; Sioux Falls, S. Dak. (1860) | Lawrence M. Stavig | 1,351 C | Lutheran |
| Aurora College; Aurora, Ill. (1893) | Theodore P. Stephens | 1,326 C | Adven. Christ. |
| Austin College; Sherman, Tex. (1849) | J. D. Moseley | 857 C | Presbyterian |
| Austin Peay State College; Clarksville, Tenn. (1927) | Halbert Harvill | 1,319 C | State |
| Babson Institute; Babson Park, Mass. (1919) | Gordon M. Trim | 650 M | Private |
| Baker University; Baldwin, Kans. (1858) | W. J. Scarborough | 576 C | Methodist |
| Baldwin-Wallace College; Berea, Ohio (1845) | Alfred B. Bonds, Jr. | 2,013 C | Methodist |
| Ball State Teachers College; Muncie, Ind. (1918) | John R. Emens | 6,452 C | State |
| Bank Street College of Education; New York, N. Y. (1916) | John H. Niemeyer | 400 C | Private |
| Barat College of the Sacred Heart; Lake Forest, Ill. (1857) | Mother Margaret Burke | 376 F | Catholic |

| Institution, location and (date founded) | Chief executive | Students[1] | Control |
|---|---|---|---|
| Bard College; Annandale-on-Hudson, N. Y. (1860) | Reamer Kline | 297 C | Private |
| Barnard College; New York, N. Y. (1889)[4] | Millicent C. McIntosh | 1,425 F | Private |
| Barry College; Miami, Fla. (1940) | Rev. Mother M. Gerald | 574 F | Cathol c |
| Bates College; Lewiston, Maine (1864) | Charles F. Phillips | 834 C | Private |
| Baylor University; Waco, Dallas & Houston, Tex. (1845) | William R. White | 5,410 C | Baptist |
| Beaver College; Jenkintown & Glenside, Pa. (1853) | Edward D. Gates | 654 F | Presbyterian |
| Belhaven College; Jackson, Miss. (1883) | R. F. Cooper | 258 C | Presbyterian |
| Bellarmine College; Louisville, Ky. (1950) | Rt. Rev. A. F. Horrigan | 1,185 M | Catholic |
| Belmont Abbey College; Belmont, N. C. (1876) | V. Rev. John A. Oetgen | 419 Co | Catholic |
| Belmont College; Nashville, Tenn. (1951) | Herbert C. Gabhart | 395 C | Baptist |
| Beloit College; Beloit, Wis. (1846) | Miller Upton | 935 C | Private |
| Bemidji State College; Bemidji, Minn. (1919) | Charles R. Sattgast | 1,399 C | State |
| Bennett College; Greensboro, N. C. (1873) | Willa B. Player | 555 F | Methodist |
| Bennington College; Bennington, Vt. (1925) | William C. Fels | 336 F | Private |
| Berea College; Berea, Ky. (1855) | Francis S. Hutchins | 1,224 C | Private |
| Berry College; Mount Berry, Ga. (1902) | John R. Bertrand | 606 C | Private |
| Bethany College; Bethany, W. Va. (1840) | Perry E. Gresham | 721 C | Private |
| Bethany College; Lindsborg, Kans. (1881) | L. Dale Lund | 600 C | Lutheran |
| Bethany Nazarene College; Bethany, Okla. (1909) | Roy H. Cantrell | 822 C | Nazarene |
| Bethel College; McKenzie, Tenn. (1842) | Roy N. Baker | 550 C | Presbyterian |
| Bethel College; North Newton, Kans. (1887) | Vernon H. Neufeld | 524 C | Mennonite |
| Bethel College and Seminary; St. Paul, Minn. (1871) | Carl H. Lundquist | 819 C | Baptist |
| Bethune-Cookman College; Daytona Beach, Fla. (1904) | Richard V. Moore | 606 C | Private |
| Birmingham-Southern College; Birmingham, Ala. (1856) | Henry King Stanford | 977 C | Methodist |
| Black Hills Teachers College; Spearfish, S. Dak. (1883) | Russell E. Jonas | 650 C | State |
| Blackburn College; Carlinville, Ill. (1857) | Robert P. Ludlum | 390 C | Private |
| Bloomfield College; Bloomfield, N. J. (1868) | Theodore A. Rath | 401 C | Presbyterian |
| Bloomsburg State College; Bloomsburg, Pa. (1839) | Harvey A. Andruss | 1,684 C | State |
| Blue Mountain College; Blue Mountain, Miss. (1873) | Wilfred C. Tyler | 296 F | S. Baptist |
| Bluefield State College; Bluefield, W. Va. (1895) | L. B. Allen | 570 C | State |
| Bluffton College; Bluffton, Ohio (1899) | Lloyd L. Ramseyer | 390 C | Mennonite |
| Boston College; Chestnut Hill, Mass. (1863)[2] | V. Rev. Michael P. Walsh | 7,964 C | Catholic |
| Boston University; Boston, Mass. (1839) | Harold C. Case | 17,458 C | Private |
| Bowdoin College; Brunswick, Maine (1794) | James S. Coles | 790 M | Private |
| Bowling Green State University; Bowling Green, Ohio (1910)[2] | Ralph W. McDonald | 6,081 C | State |
| Bradley University; Peoria, Ill. (1897) | T. W. Van Arsdale, Jr. | 4,346 C | Private |
| Brandeis University; Waltham, Mass. (1948) | Abram L. Sachar | 1,560 C | Private |
| Brenau College; Gainesville, Ga. (1878) | Josiah Crudup | 412 F | Private |
| Brescia College; Owensboro, Ky. (1925) | Sister Joan M. Lechner | 628 C | Catholic |
| Briar Cliff College; Sioux City & Dubuque, Iowa (1930) | Sister Mary Matilda | 420 F | Catholic |
| Bridgeport, University of; Bridgeport, Conn. (1927) | James H. Halsey | 2,575 C | Private |
| Bridgewater College; Bridgewater, Va. (1880) | Warren D. Bowman | 586 C | Brethren |
| Brigham Young University; Provo, Utah (1875) | Ernest L. Wilkinson | 9,936 C | Latter-day Saints |
| Brooklyn, Polytechnic Institute of; Brooklyn, N. Y. (1854) | Ernst Weber | 4,073 C | Private |
| Brooklyn College. See New York, College of the City of | | | |
| Brown University; Providence, R. I. (1764)[5] | Barnaby C. Keeney | 3,990 Co | Private |
| Bryn Mawr College; Bryn Mawr, Pa. (1885) | Katharine E. McBride | 990 F | Private |
| Bucknell University; Lewisburg, Pa. (1846) | Merle M. Odgers | 2,260 C | Private |
| Buena Vista College; Storm Lake, Iowa (1891) | Wendell Q. Halverson | 493 C | Presbyterian |
| Buffalo, University of; Buffalo, N. Y. (1846) | C. C. Furnas | 11,178 C | Private |
| Butler University; Indianapolis, Ind. (1855) | M. O. Ross | 3,539 C | Disc. of Christ |
| Caldwell College for Women; Caldwell, N. J. (1939) | Sister M. Marguerite | 671 F | Catholic |
| California, University of; Berkeley, Calif. (1868) | Clark Kerr | 47,539 C | State |
|    Berkeley Campus | Edward W. Strong | 20,789 C | State |
|    Davis Campus | Emil M. Mrak | 2,868 C | State |
|    Los Angeles Campus (UCLA) | Franklin D. Murphy | 17,218 C | State |
|    Riverside Campus | Herman T. Spieth | 1,510 C | State |
|    San Diego (formerly La Jolla) Campus | Herbert F York | 100 C | State |
|    San Francisco Campus | John B. deC. M. Saunders | 1,771 C | State |
|    Santa Barbara Campus | Samuel B. Gould | 3 283 C | State |
| California College of Arts & Crafts; Oakland, Calif. (1907) | Harry X. Ford | 464 C | Private |
| California Institute of Technology; Pasadena, Calif. (1891) | Lee A. DuBridge | 1,225 M | Private |
| California School of Fine Arts. See San Francisco Art Institute | | | |
| California State College; California, Pa. (1852) | Michael Duda | 2,231 C | State |
| California State Polytechnic College; San Luis Obispo, Calif. (1901)[2] | Julian A. McPhee | 6,214 C | State |
| California Western University; San Diego, Calif. (1924) | William C. Rust | 1,521 C | Methodist |
| Calvin College; Grand Rapids, Mich. (1876) | William Spoelhof | 2,093 C | Christian Ref. |
| Canisius College; Buffalo, N. Y. (1870) | V. Rev. J. J. McGinley | 1,735 C | Catholic |
| Capital University; Columbus, Ohio (1850) | Harold L. Yochum | 1,277 C | Lutheran |
| Cardinal Glennon College; St. Louis, Mo. (1900) | V. Rev. Edward F. Riley | 220 M | Catholic |
| Cardinal Stritch College; Milwaukee, Wis. (1937) | Sister Mary Aquin | 375 F | Catholic |
| Carleton College; Northfield, Minn. (1866) | Laurence M. Gould | 1,154 C | Private |

| Institution, location and (date founded) | Chief executive | Students[1] | Control |
|---|---|---|---|
| Carnegie Institute of Technology; Pittsburgh, Pa. (1900) | John C. Warner | 3,362 C | Private |
| Carroll College; Helena, Mont. (1909) | Rt. Rev. R. G. Hunthausen | 685 C | Catholic |
| Carroll College; Waukesha, Wis. (1846) | Robert D. Steele | 870 C | Presbyterian |
| Carson-Newman College; Jefferson City, Tenn. (1851) | Harley Fite | 1,301 C | S. Baptist |
| Carthage College; Carthage, Ill. (1847) | Harold H. Lentz | 575 C | Lutheran |
| Cascade College; Portland, Oreg. (1918) | Thomas A. Leupp | 238 C | Private |
| Case Institute of Technology; Cleveland, Ohio (1880) | T. Keith Glennan | 2,145 M | Private |
| Catawba College; Salisbury, N. C. (1851) | A. R. Keppel | 809 C | Evan. & Ref. |
| Catholic University of America; Washington, D. C. (1889) | Rt. Rev. W. J. McDonald | 4,045 C[22] | Catholic |
| Catholic University of Puerto Rico; Ponce, P. R. (1948)[2] | Most Rev. J. E. McManus | 2,149 C | Catholic |
| Cedar Crest College; Allentown, Pa. (1867) | Dale H. Moore | 445 F | Evan. & Ref. |
| Centenary College of Louisiana; Shreveport, La. (1825) | Joe J. Mickle | 1,401 C | Methodist |
| Central College; Fayette, Mo. (1854) | Ralph L. Woodward | 726 C | Methodist |
| Central College; Pella, Iowa (1853) | Arend D. Lubbers | 496 C | Reformed Church |
| Central Connecticut State College; New Britain, Conn. (1849) | Herbert D. Welte | 2,303 C | State |
| Central Michigan University; Mt. Pleasant, Mich. (1892) | Judson W. Foust | 6,577 C | State |
| Central Missouri State College; Warrensburg, Mo. (1871) | Warren C. Lovinger | 3,602 C[6] | State |
| Central State College; Edmond, Okla. (1890) | Garland Godfrey | 3,737 C | State |
| Central State College; Wilberforce, Ohio (1887) | Charles H. Wesley | 1,679 C | State |
| Central Washington College of Education; Ellensburg, Wash. (1891) | Perry H. Mitchell | 1,939 C | State |
| Centre College of Kentucky; Danville, Ky. (1819) | Thomas A. Spragens | 448 C | Private |
| Chaminade College of Honolulu; Honolulu, Hawaii (1955) | Rev. Robert R. Mackey | 268 C | Catholic |
| Chapman College; Orange, Calif. (1861) | John L. Davis | 573 C | Disc. of Christ |
| Charleston, College of; Charleston, S. C. (1770) | George D. Grice | 301 C | Private |
| Chatham College; Pittsburgh, Pa. (1869) | Edward D. Eddy, Jr. | 501 F | Private |
| Chattanooga, University of; Chattanooga, Tenn. (1886) | LeRoy A. Martin | 2,088 C | Private |
| Chestnut Hill College; Philadelphia, Pa. (1871) | Sister Catharine Frances | 588 F | Catholic |
| Cheyney State College; Cheyney, Pa. (1837) | James H. Duckrey | 833 C | State |
| Chicago, School of the Art Institute of; Chicago, Ill. (1866) | Norman B. Boothby | 689 C | Private |
| Chicago, University of; Chicago, Ill. (1891) | George Welles Beadle | 6,567 C | Private |
| Chicago Teachers College; Chicago, Ill. (1869) | Raymond M. Cook | 5,776 C | City |
| Chico State College; Chico, Calif. (1887) | Glenn Kendall | 3,282 C | State |
| Chouinard Art Institute; Los Angeles, Calif. (1921) | Mitchell A. Wilder | 605 C | Private |
| Christian Brothers College; Memphis, Tenn. (1854) | Brother Lambert Thomas | 704 M | Catholic |
| Cincinnati, University of; Cincinnati, Ohio (1819) | Walter C. Langsam | 17,538 C | City |
| Citadel, The—The Military College of S. C.; Charleston (1842) | Gen. Mark W. Clark | 1,900 M | State |
| City College. See New York, College of the City of | | | |
| Claflin College; Orangeburg, S. C. (1869) | H. V. Manning | 396 C | Methodist |
| Claremont Graduate School; Claremont, Calif. (1925) | Robert J. Bernard | 639 C | Private |
| Claremont Men's College; Claremont, Calif. (1946) | George C. S. Benson | 415 M | Private |
| Clarion State College; Clarion, Pa. (1867) | James Gemmell | 1,348 C | State |
| Clark College; Atlanta, Ga. (1869) | James P. Brawley | 763 C | Methodist |
| Clark University; Worcester, Mass. (1887) | Howard B. Jefferson | 1,023 C | Private |
| Clarke College; Dubuque & Mt. Carmel, Iowa (1843) | Sister Mary Benedict | 911 F | Catholic |
| Clarkson College of Technology; Potsdam, N. Y. (1896) | William G. Van Note | 1,463 M | Private |
| Clemson Agricultural College; Clemson, S. C. (1889) | Robert Cook Edwards | 3,751 C | State |
| Coe College; Cedar Rapids, Iowa (1851) | Joseph E. McCabe | 643 C | Private |
| Coker College; Hartsville, S. C. (1908) | Fenton Keyes | 358 F | Private |
| Colby College; Waterville, Maine (1813) | Robert E. L. Strider | 1,167 C | Private |
| Colgate University; Hamilton, N. Y. (1819) | Everett N. Case | 1,388 M | Private |
| Colorado, University of; Boulder & Denver, Colo. (1876) | Quigg Newton | 10,992 C | State |
| Colorado College; Colorado Springs, Colo. (1874) | Louis T. Benezet | 1,140 C | Private |
| Colorado School of Mines; Golden, Colo. (1874) | John W. Vanderwilt | 1,016 C | State |
| Colorado State College; Greeley, Colo. (1890) | William R. Ross | 3,889 C | State |
| Colorado State University; Fort Collins, Colo. (1870) | William E. Morgan | 5,432 C | State |
| Columbia College; Columbia, S. C. (1854) | R. Wright Spears | 650 F | Methodist |
| Columbia Union College; Takoma Park, Md. (1904)[7] | Charles B. Hirsch | 906 C | 7th Day Adven. |
| Columbia University; New York, N. Y. (1754)[4] | Grayson Kirk | 20,374 C | Private |
| Concord College; Athens, W. Va. (1875) | Joseph F. Marsh, Jr. | 1,647 C | State |
| Concordia College; Moorhead, Minn. (1891) | Joseph L. Knutson | 1,601 C | Lutheran |
| Concordia Teachers College; River Forest, Ill. (1864) | Martin L. Koehneke | 954 C | Lutheran |
| Concordia Teachers College; Seward, Nebr. (1894) | Paul A. Zimmerman | 670 C | Lutheran |
| Connecticut, University of; Storrs, Conn. (1881)[2] | Albert N. Jorgensen | 11,244 C | State |
| Connecticut College; New London, Conn. (1911) | Rosemary Park | 1,005 F | Private |
| Converse College; Spartanburg, S. C. (1889) | Robert T. Coleman, Jr. | 584 F | Private |
| Cooper Union; New York, N. Y. (1859) | R. F. Humphreys | 1,123 C | Private |
| Cornell College; Mount Vernon, Iowa (1853) | A. F. Christ-Janer | 673 C | Private |
| Cornell University; Ithaca & New York, N. Y. (1865) | Deane W. Malott | 10,912 C | State & Private |
| Cranbrook Academy of Art; Bloomfield Hills, Mich. | Zoltan Sepeshy | 115 C[25] | Private |
| Creighton University; Omaha, Nebr. (1878) | V. Rev. Carl M. Reinert | 2,965 C | Catholic |
| Culver-Stockton College; Canton, Mo. (1853) | Fred Helsabeck | 548 C | Disc. of Christ |
| Dakota Wesleyan University; Mitchell, S. Dak. (1885) | Jack J. Early | 722 C | Methodist |

| Institution, location and (date founded) | Chief executive | Students[1] | Control |
|---|---|---|---|
| Dana College; Blair, Nebr. (1884) | C. C. Madsen | 837 C | U. Evan. Luth. |
| Danbury State College; Danbury, Conn. (1903) | Ruth A. Haas | 932 C | State |
| Dartmouth College; Hanover, N. H. (1769) | John Sloan Dickey | 3,075 M | Private |
| David Lipscomb College; Nashville, Tenn. (1891) | Athens Clay Pullias | 1,138 C | Ch. of Christ |
| Davidson College; Davidson, N. C. (1837) | D. Grier Martin | 950 M | Presbyterian |
| Davis & Elkins College; Elkins, W. Va. (1904) | David K. Allen | 492 C | Presbyterian |
| Dayton, University of; Dayton, Ohio (1850) | V. Rev. R. A. Roesch | 6,563 C | Catholic |
| Delaware, University of; Newark, Del. (1833) | J. A. Perkins | 3,518 C | State |
| Delaware State College; Dover, Del. (1891) | Luna I. Mishoe | 357 C | State |
| Delta State College; Cleveland, Miss. (1924) | James M. Ewing | 965 C | State |
| Denison University; Granville, Ohio (1831) | A. Blair Knapp | 1,453 C | Baptist |
| Denver, University of; Denver, Colo. (1864) | Chester M. Alter | 4,505 C | Methodist |
| DePaul University; Chicago, Ill. (1898) | V. Rev. C. J. O'Malley | 7,014 C | Catholic |
| DePauw University; Greencastle, Ind. (1837) | Russell J. Humbert | 2,181 C | Private |
| Detroit, University of; Detroit, Mich. (1877) | Rev. L. V. Britt | 10,028 C | Catholic |
| Dickinson College; Carlisle, Pa. (1773) | Gilbert Malcolm | 1,088 C | Private |
| Dillard University; New Orleans, La. (1930) | Albert W. Dent | 848 C | Private |
| District of Columbia Teachers College; Washington, D. C. (1851) | Paul O. Carr | 810 C | City |
| Doane College; Crete, Nebr. (1872) | Donald M. Typer | 300 C | Cong.-Prot. Epis. |
| Dominican College of San Rafael; San Rafael, Calif. (1890) | Sister M. Patrick | 697 F | Catholic |
| Douglass College; New Brunswick, N. J. (1918)[8] | Ruth M. Adams | 1,693 F | State |
| Drake University; Des Moines, Iowa (1881) | Henry G. Harmon | 4,508 C | Private |
| Drew University; Madison, N. J. (1868) | Robert F. Oxnam | 850 C | Methodist |
| Drexel Institute of Technology; Philadelphia, Pa. (1891) | James Creese | 8,841 C | Private |
| Dropsie College; Philadelphia, Pa., and New York, N. Y. (1907) | Abraham A. Neuman | 170 C | Jewish |
| Drury College; Springfield, Mo. (1873) | James F. Findlay | 809 C | Congregational |
| Dubuque, University of; Dubuque, Iowa (1852) | Gaylord M. Couchman | 570 C | Presbyterian |
| Duchesne College of the Sacred Heart; Omaha, Nebr. (1881) | Mother Dorothy Clark | 303 F | Private |
| Duke University; Durham, N. C. (1838) | Deryl Hart | 5,972 Co | Private |
| Dunbarton College of Holy Cross; Washington, D. C. (1935) | Sister M. M. Dolores | 427 F | Catholic |
| Duquesne University; Pittsburgh, Pa. (1878) | Rev. H. J. McAnulty | 5,256 C | Catholic |
| D'Youville College; Buffalo, N. Y. (1908) | Sister Catherine of Siena | 728 F | Catholic |
| Earlham College; Richmond, Ind. (1847) | Landrum R. Bolling | 861 C | Quaker |
| East Carolina College; Greenville, N. C. (1907) | Leo W. Jenkins | 4,271 C | State |
| East Central State College; Ada, Okla. (1909) | Charles F. Spencer | 1,623 C | State |
| East Stroudsburg State College; East Stroudsburg, Pa. (1893) | LeRoy J. Koehler | 1,409 C | State |
| East Tennessee State College; Johnson City, Tenn. (1911) | Burgin E. Dossett | 4,524 C | State |
| East Texas Baptist College; Marshall, Tex. (1914) | Howard C. Bennett | 432 C | Baptist |
| East Texas State College; Commerce, Texas (1889) | James G. Gee | 2,955 C | State |
| Eastern Baptist College; St. Davids, Pa. (1932) | Gilbert L. Guffin | 342 C | Baptist |
| Eastern Baptist Theological Seminary; Philadelphia, Pa. (1925) | Gilbert L. Guffin | 207 C | Baptist |
| Eastern Illinois University; Charleston, Ill. (1895) | Quincy Doudna | 2,642 C | State |
| Eastern Kentucky State College; Richmond, Ky. (1906) | Robert R. Martin | 3,272 C | State |
| Eastern Mennonite College; Harrisonburg, Va. (1917) | John R. Mumaw | 483 C | Mennonite |
| Eastern Michigan University; Ypsilanti, Mich. (1849) | Eugene B. Elliott | 5,019 C | State |
| Eastern Montana College of Education; Billings, Mont. (1927) | H. L. Steele | 1,169 C | State |
| Eastern Nazarene College; Quincy, Mass. (1918) | Edward S. Mann | 771 C | Nazarene |
| Eastern New Mexico University; Portales, N. Mex. (1935) | D. C. Moyer | 1,611 C | State |
| Eastern Oregon College; La Grande, Oreg. (1929) | Frank B. Bennett | 865 C[9] | State |
| Eastern Washington State College; Cheney, Wash. (1890) | Don S. Patterson | 2,206 C[9] | State |
| Edgewood College of the Sacred Heart; Madison, Wis. (1927) | Sister Mary Nona | 496 F | Catholic |
| Edinboro State College; Edinboro, Pa. (1857) | Thomas R. Miller | 1,413 C | State |
| Elizabethtown College; Elizabethtown, Pa. (1899) | Roy E. McAuley | 715 C | Brethren |
| Elmhurst College; Elmhurst, Ill. (1871) | Robert C. Stanger | 1,267 C | Evan. & Ref. |
| Elmira College; Elmira, N. Y. (1855) | J. Ralph Murray | 1,426 F[6] | Private |
| Elon College; Elon College, N. C. (1889) | James E. Danieley | 1,109 C | Cong. Christian |
| Emerson College; Boston, Mass. (1880) | S. J. McKinley | 576 C | Private |
| Emmanuel College; Boston, Mass. (1919) | Sister Ann Bartholomew | 950 F | Catholic |
| Emmanuel Missionary College. See Andrews University | | | |
| Emory & Henry College; Emory, Va. (1836) | Earl G. Hunt, Jr. | 704 C | Methodist |
| Emory University; Atlanta & Oxford, Ga. (1836) | S. Walter Martin | 3,963 C | Methodist |
| Emporia, College of; Emporia, Kans. (1882) | Richard Hanna | 394 C | Presbyterian |
| Erskine College; Due West, S. C. (1839) | J. M. Lesesne | 618 C | Assoc. Ref. Presb. |
| Evansville College; Evansville, Ind. (1854) | Melvin W. Hyde | 2,781 C | Private |
| Fairfield University; Fairfield, Conn. (1942) | Rev. James E. FitzGerald | 1,839 M | Catholic |
| Fairleigh Dickinson University; Rutherford, N. J. (1941)[2] | Peter Sammartino | 13,639 C | Private |
| Fairmont State College; Fairmont, W. Va. (1867) | E. K. Feaster | 1,389 C | State |
| Farmington State Teachers College; Farmington, Maine (1864) | Ermo Houston Scott | 484 C | State |
| Fayetteville State Teachers College; Fayetteville, N. C. (1877) | Rudolph Jones | 778 C | State |
| Fenn College; Cleveland, Ohio (1923) | G. Brooks Earnest | 2,992 C | Private |
| Ferris Institute; Big Rapids, Mich. (1884) | Victor F. Spathelf | 3,250 C | State |
| Finch College; New York, N. Y. (1900) | Roland R. De Marco | 300 F | Private |

| Institution, location and (date founded) | Chief executive | Students[1] | Control |
|---|---|---|---|
| Fisk University; Nashville, Tenn. (1866) | Stephen J. Wright | 846 C | Private |
| Flora Macdonald College; Red Springs, N. C. (1896)[10] | C. G. Vardell, Jr. | 399 C | S. Presbyterian |
| Florence State College; Florence, Ala. (1872) | E. B. Norton | 1,642 C | State |
| Florida, University of; Gainesville, Fla. (1853) | J. Wayne Reitz | 11,720 C | State |
| Florida A & M University; Tallahassee, Fla. (1887) | George W. Gore, Jr. | 2,690 C | State |
| Florida Southern College; Lakeland, Fla. (1885) | Charles T. Thrift, Jr. | 2,361 C | Methodist |
| Florida State University; Tallahassee, Fla. (1857) | Gordon W. Blackwell | 8,762 C | State |
| Fontbonne College; St. Louis, Mo. (1917) | Sister M. Alfred Noble | 525 F | Catholic |
| Fordham University; New York, N. Y. (1841)[2] | Rev. Laurence J. McGinley | 10,246 C | Catholic |
| Fort Hays Kansas State College; Hays, Kans. (1902) | M. C. Cunningham | 2,877 C[6] | State |
| Fort Valley State College; Fort Valley, Ga. (1895) | Cornelius V. Troup | 868 C | State |
| Franklin & Marshall College; Lancaster, Pa. (1787) | F. deW. Bolman, Jr. | 1,270 M | Private |
| Franklin College of Indiana; Franklin, Ind. (1834) | H. W. Richardson | 572 C | Baptist |
| Fresno State College; Fresno & Bakersfield, Calif. (1911) | Arnold E. Joyal | 6,061 C | State |
| Friends University; Wichita, Kans. (1898) | Lowell E. Roberts | 645 C | Quaker |
| Furman University; Greenville, S. C. (1825) | John L. Plyler | 1,414 C | S. Baptist |
| Gallaudet College; Washington, D. C. (1864) | Leonard M. Elstad | 391 C | Private |
| Gannon College; Erie, Pa. (1944) | Rt. Rev. W. J. Nash | 1,618 M | Catholic |
| Geneva College; Beaver Falls, Pa. (1848) | Edwin C. Clarke | 864 C | Reformed Presb. |
| George Fox College; Newberg, Oreg. (1891) | Milo C. Ross | 162 C | Quaker |
| George Peabody College for Teachers; Nashville, Tenn. (1875) | Henry H. Hill | 1,540 C | Private |
| George Pepperdine College. See Pepperdine College | | | |
| George Washington University; Washington, D. C. (1821) | Thomas H. Carroll | 8,260 C | Private |
| George Williams College; Chicago, Ill. (1890)[2] | John R. McCurdy | 293 C | Private |
| Georgetown College; Georgetown, Ky. (1798) | Robert L. Mills | 1,250 C | S. Baptist |
| Georgetown University; Washington, D. C. (1789) | V. Rev. Edward B. Bunn | 6,067 C | Catholic |
| Georgia, University of; Athens, Ga. (1785) | O. C. Aderhold | 6,846 C | State |
| Georgia, Woman's College of; Milledgeville, Ga. (1889) | Robert E. Lee | 765 F | State |
| Georgia Institute of Technology; Atlanta, Ga. (1888) | Edwin D. Harrison | 5,407 C | State |
| Georgia Southern College; Statesboro, Ga. (1908) | Z. S. Henderson | 1,289 C | State |
| Georgia State College of Business Admin.; Atlanta, Ga. (1914) | Noah Langdale, Jr. | 3,126 C | State |
| Georgian Court College; Lakewood, N. J. (1908)[2] | Mother Marie Anna | 384 F | Catholic |
| Gettysburg College; Gettysburg, Pa. (1832) | Willard Stewart Paul | 1,608 C | Lutheran |
| Glassboro State College; Glassboro, N. J. (1923) | Thomas E. Robinson | 1,517 C | State |
| Glenville State College; Glenville, W. Va. (1872) | Harry B. Heflin | 760 C | State |
| Goddard College; Plainfield, Vt. (1938) | Royce S. Pitkin | 153 C | Private |
| Golden Gate College; San Francisco, Calif. (1901) | Russell T. Sharpe | 1,502 C | Private |
| Gonzaga University; Spokane, Wash. (1887) | V. Rev. E. W. Morton | 1,707 C | Catholic |
| Good Counsel College; White Plains, N. Y. (1923) | Mother Mary Dolores | 421 F | Catholic |
| Goshen College; Goshen, Ind. (1894) | Paul M. Mininger | 762 C | Mennonite |
| Goucher College; Baltimore, Md. (1885) | Otto F. Kraushaar | 761 F | Private |
| Graceland College; Lamoni, Iowa (1895) | Harvey H. Grice | 774 C | Reorg. Lat.-day Sts. |
| Grambling College; Grambling, La. (1901) | R. W. E. Jones | 2,564 C | State |
| Great Falls, College of; Great Falls, Mont. (1932) | Sister Rita | 920 C | Catholic |
| Greensboro College; Greensboro, N. C. (1838) | Harold H. Hutson | 535 C | Methodist |
| Greenville College; Greenville, Ill. (1892) | H. J. Long | 637 C | Free Methodist |
| Grinnell College; Grinnell, Iowa (1846) | Howard R. Bowen | 1,101 C | Private |
| Grove City College; Grove City, Pa. (1884) | J. Stanley Harker | 1,428 C[22] | Private |
| Guilford College; Greensboro, N. C. (1837) | Clyde A. Milner | 1,385 C | Quaker |
| Gustavus Adolphus College; St. Peter, Minn. (1862) | Edgar M. Carlson | 1,116 C | Lutheran |
| Hamilton College; Clinton, N. Y. (1812) | Robert W. McEwen | 738 M | Private |
| Hamline University; St. Paul, Minn. (1854) | Paul H. Giddens | 991 C | Methodist |
| Hampden-Sydney College; Hampden-Sydney, Va. (1776) | Thomas E. Gilmer | 400 M | Presbyterian |
| Hampton Institute; Hampton, Va. (1868) | Jerome H. Holland | 1,350 C | Private |
| Hanover College; Hanover, Ind. (1827) | John E. Horner | 783 C | Presbyterian |
| Hardin-Simmons University; Abilene, Tex. (1891) | Evan Allard Reiff | 1,534 C | Baptist |
| Harding College; Searcy, Ark. (1924)[2] | George S. Benson | 1,012 C | Ch. of Christ |
| Harpur College. See New York, State University of | | | |
| Harris Teachers College; St. Louis, Mo. (1857) | Glynn E. Clark | 1,233 C | City |
| Hartt College of Music (U. of Hartford); Hartford, Conn. (1920)[2] | Moshe Paranov | 325 C | Private |
| Hartwick College; Oneonta, N. Y. (1928) | Frederick M. Binder | 712 C | Lutheran |
| Harvard University; Cambridge, Mass. (1636)[11] | Nathan M. Pusey | 13,260 C[6] | Private |
| Harvey Mudd College; Claremont, Calif. (1955) | Joseph B. Platt | 193 C | Private |
| Hastings College; Hastings, Nebr. (1882) | Theron B. Maxson | 785 C | Presbyterian |
| Haverford College; Haverford, Pa. (1833) | Hugh Borton | 455 M | Private |
| Hawaii, University of; Honolulu & Hilo, Hawaii (1907) | Laurence H. Snyder | 8,889 C | State |
| Hebrew Teachers College; Brookline, Mass. (1921) | Eisig Silberschlag | 134 C | Private |
| Hebrew Union College—Jewish Inst. of Religion; Cincinnati (1875)[2] | Nelson Glueck | 389 M | Jewish |
| Heidelberg College; Tiffin, Ohio (1850) | Terry Wickham | 836 C | Evan. & Ref. |
| Henderson State Teachers College; Arkadelphia, Ark. (1929) | D. D. McBrien | 1,400 C | State |
| Hendrix College; Conway, Ark. (1884) | Marshall T. Steel | 561 C | Methodist |
| High Point College; High Point, N. C. (1924) | Wendell M. Patton | 978 C | Methodist |

| Institution, location and (date founded) | Chief executive | Students[1] | Control |
|---|---|---|---|
| Hillsdale College; Hillsdale, Mich. (1844) | J. Donald Phillips | 662 C | Private |
| Hillyer College (U. of Hartford); West Hartford, Conn. (1879) | Alan S. Wilson | 784 C | Private |
| Hiram College; Hiram, Ohio (1850) | Paul F. Sharp | 672 C | Private |
| Hobart & William Smith Colleges; Geneva, N. Y. (24) | Rev. L. M. Hirshson | 942 Co[23] | Private |
| Hofstra College; Hempstead & Old Westbury, N. Y. (1935) | John C. Adams | 6,552 C | Private |
| Hollins College; Hollins College, Va. (1842) | John A. Logan, Jr. | 665 F | Private |
| Holy Cross, College of the; Worcester, Mass. (1843) | V. Rev. Raymond J. Swords | 1,723 M | Catholic |
| Holy Family College; Manitowoc, Wis. (1935) | Sister M. Brideen | 173 F | Private |
| Holy Names, College of the; Oakland & Los Gatos, Calif. (1868) | Sister Imelda Maria | 669 F | Catholic |
| Holy Names College; Spokane, Wash. (1939) | Sister Marian Raphael | 358 F | Catholic |
| Hood College; Frederick, Md. (1893) | Randle Elliott | 637 F | Private |
| Hope College; Holland, Mich. (1851) | Irwin J. Lubbers | 1,431 C | Reformed Church |
| Houghton College; Houghton, N. Y. (1883) | Stephen W. Paine | 785 C | Wesleyan Meth. |
| Houston, University of; Houston, Tex. (19 ⌣) | A. D. Bruce | 10,610 C | Private |
| Howard College; Birmingham, Ala. (1842) | Leslie S. Wright | 2,001 C[22] | S. Baptist |
| Howard Payne College; Brownwood, Tex. (1889) | Guy D. Newman | 1,181 C | Baptist |
| Howard University; Washington, D. C. (1867) | James M. Nabrit, Jr. | 5,056 C | Private & Natl. |
| Humboldt State College; Arcata, Calif. (1913) | Cornelius H. Siemens | 2,002 C | State |
| Hunter College. See New York, College of the City of | | | |
| Huntingdon College; Montgomery, Ala. (1854) | Hubert Searcy | 849 C | Methodist |
| Huron College; Huron, S. Dak. (1883) | Daniel E. Kerr | 396 C | Presbyterian |
| Huston-Tillotson College; Austin, Tex. (1877) | J. J. Seabrook | 403 C | Private |
| Idaho, College of; Caldwell, Idaho (1891) | Tom E. Shearer | 686 C | Presbyterian |
| Idaho, University of; Moscow & Lewiston, Idaho (1889) | D. R. Theophilus | 4,032 C | State |
| Idaho State College; Pocatello, Idaho (1901) | Donald E. Walker | 2,329 C | State |
| Illinois, University of; Urbana & Chicago, Ill. (1867) | David D. Henry | 26,010 C | State |
| Illinois College; Jacksonville, Ill. (1829) | L. Vernon Caine | 537 C | Presb.-Cong. |
| Illinois Institute of Technology; Chicago, Ill. (1892) | John T. Rettaliata | 6,667 C | Private |
| Illinois State Normal University; Normal, Ill. (1857) | Robert G. Bone | 4,205 C | State |
| Illinois Wesleyan University; Bloomington, Ill. (1850) | Lloyd M. Bertholf | 1,081 C | Methodist |
| Immaculata College; Immaculata, Pa. (1920) | Sister Mary of Lourdes | 670 F | Catholic |
| Immaculate Heart College; Los Angeles, Calif. (1906) | Sister Mary Humiliata | 1,476 F | Catholic |
| Incarnate Word College; San Antonio, Tex. (1881) | S. Thomas Greenburg | 1,180 F | Catholic |
| Indiana Central College; Indianapolis, Ind. (1902) | I. Lynd Esch | 1,435 C | Evan. Un. Breth. |
| Indiana State College; Indiana, Pa. (1875) | Willis E. Pratt | 3,569 C | State |
| Indiana State College; Terre Haute, Ind. (1870) | Raleigh W. Holmstedt | 4,290 C | State |
| Indiana University; Bloomington & Indianapolis, Ind. (1820)[2] | Herman B Wells | 24,963 C | State |
| Inter American University; San Germán, P. R. (1912)[2] | Ronald C. Bauer | 1,413 C | Private |
| Iona College; New Rochelle, N. Y. (1940) | Brother R. B. Power | 2,014 M | Catholic |
| Iowa, State College of; Cedar Falls, Iowa (1876) | J. W. Maucker | 3,443 C | State |
| Iowa, State University of; Iowa City, Iowa (1847) | Virgil M. Hancher | 10,388 C | State |
| Iowa State University of Science & Tech.; Ames, Iowa (1858) | James H. Hilton | 9,726 C[6] | State |
| Iowa Wesleyan College; Mt. Pleasant, Iowa (1842) | J. Raymond Chadwick | 541 C | Methodist |
| Ithaca College; Ithaca, N. Y. (1892) | Howard I. Dillingham | 1,473 C | Private |
| Jackson College. See Tufts University | | | |
| Jacksonville State College; Jacksonville, Ala. (1883) | Houston Cole | 2,389 C | State |
| Jamestown College; Jamestown, N. Dak. (1884) | John A. Fisher | 464 C | Presbyterian |
| Jersey City State College; Jersey City, N. J. (1929) | Michael B. Gilligan | 1,956 C | State |
| Jewish Theological Seminary of America; New York, N. Y. (1887)[2] | Louis Finkelstein | 526 C | Jewish |
| John Carroll University; Cleveland, Ohio (1886) | V. Rev. H. E. Dunn | 3,079 M | Catholic |
| Johns Hopkins University; Baltimore, Md. (1876)[2] | Milton S. Eisenhower | 4,714 M | Private |
| Johnson C. Smith University; Charlotte, N. C. (1867) | Rufus P. Perry | 807 C | Presbyterian |
| Judson College; Marion, Ala. (1838) | C. A. Anderson | 284 F | S. Baptist |
| Juilliard School of Music; New York, N. Y. (1905) | William Schuman | 650 C | Private |
| Juniata College; Huntingdon, Pa. (1876) | Calvert N. Ellis | 708 C | Brethren |
| Kalamazoo College; Kalamazoo, Mich. (1833) | Weimer K. Hicks | 675 C | Baptist |
| Kansas, University of; Lawrence & Kansas City, Kans. (1865) | W. Clarke Wescoe | 9,414 C | State |
| Kansas City, University of; Kansas City, Mo. (1933) | Richard M. Drake | 2,768 C | Private |
| Kansas State College of Pittsburg; Pittsburg, Kans. (1903) | Leonard H. Axe | 2,741 C | State |
| Kansas State Teachers College; Emporia, Kans. (1863) | John E. King | 3,647 C | State |
| Kansas State Univ. of Agr. & Appl. Sci.; Manhattan, Kans. (1863) | James A. McCain | 7,178 C | State |
| Kansas Wesleyan University; Salina, Kans. (1886) | D. Arthur Zook | 394 C | Methodist |
| Keene Teachers College; Keene, N. H. (1909) | Lloyd P. Young | 800 C | State |
| Kent State University; Kent, Ohio (1910) | George A. Bowman | 8,251 C | State |
| Kentucky, University of; Lexington, Ky. (1865)[2] | Frank G. Dickey | 6,900 C | State |
| Kentucky State College; Frankfort, Ky. (1886) | Rufus B. Atwood | 541 C | State |
| Kentucky Wesleyan College; Owensboro, Ky. (1858) | Harold P. Hamilton | 636 C | Methodist |
| Kenyon College; Gambier, Ohio (1824) | F. Edward Lund | 580 M | Private |
| Keuka College; Keuka Park, N. Y. (1890) | William S. Litterick | 432 F | Baptist |
| King College; Bristol, Tenn. (1867) | R. T. L. Liston | 289 C | Presbyterian |
| King's College; Wilkes-Barre, Pa. (1946) | Rev. George P. Benaglia | 1,012 M | Catholic |
| Knox College; Galesburg, Ill. (1837) | Sharvy G. Umbeck | 938 C | Private |

| Institution, location and (date founded) | Chief executive | Students[1] | Control |
|---|---|---|---|
| Knoxville College; Knoxville, Tenn. (1875) | James A. Colston | 604 C | U. Presbyterian |
| Kutztown State College; Kutztown, Pa. (1866) | Italo L. de Francesco | 1,610 C | State |
| Lafayette College; Easton, Pa. (1826) | K. Roald Bergethon | 1,463 M | Presbyterian |
| La Grange College; La Grange, Ga. (1831) | W. G. Henry, Jr. | 390 C | Methodist |
| Lake Erie College; Painesville, Ohio (1856) | Paul Weaver | 526 F | Private |
| Lake Forest College; Lake Forest, Ill. (1857) | William G. Cole | 703 C | Presbyterian |
| Lamar State College of Technology; Beaumont, Tex. (1923) | F. L. McDonald | 4,541 C | State |
| Lambuth College; Jackson, Tenn. (1843) | Luther L. Gobbel | 622 C | Methodist |
| Lander College; Greenwood, S. C. (1872) | B. M. Grier | 425 C | Private |
| Langston University; Langston, Okla. (1897) | William H. Hale | 613 C | State |
| La Salle College; Philadelphia, Pa. (1863) | Brother D. Bernian | 4,313 M | Catholic |
| La Sierra College; La Sierra, Calif. (1922) | W. M. Landeen | 983 C | 7th Day Adven. |
| La Verne College; La Verne, Calif. (1891) | Harold D. Fasnacht | 517 C | Brethren |
| Lawrence College; Appleton, Wis. (1847) | Douglas M. Knight | 929 C | Private |
| Lebanon Valley College; Annville, Pa. (1866) | Frederic K. Miller | 676 C | Evan. Un. Breth. |
| Lehigh University; Bethlehem, Pa. (1865) | Harvey A. Neville | 3,297 M | Private |
| Le Moyne College; Memphis, Tenn. (1871) | Hollis Freeman Price | 531 C | Am. Miss. Assn. |
| Le Moyne College; Syracuse, N. Y. (1946) | Rev. Robert F. Grewen | 1,205 C | Catholic |
| Lenoir Rhyne College; Hickory, N. C. (1891) | Voigt R. Cromer | 955 C | Lutheran |
| Lesley College; Cambridge, Mass. (1909) | Don A. Orton | 393 F | Private |
| Lewis and Clark College; Portland, Oreg. (1867) | John R. Howard | 1,048 C | Presbyterian |
| Limestone College; Gaffney, S. C. (1845) | A. J. Eastwood | 452 Co | Private |
| Lincoln Memorial University; Harrogate, Tenn. (1897) | Robert C. Provine | 409 C | Private |
| Lincoln University; Jefferson City, Mo. (1866) | Earl E. Dawson | 1,427 C | State |
| Lincoln University; Lincoln University, Pa. (1854) | Marvin Wachman | 367 C | Private |
| Lindenwood College; St. Charles, Mo. (1827) | F. L. McCluer | 536 F | Presbyterian |
| Linfield College; McMinnville, Oreg. (1849) | Harry L. Dillin | 946 C | Baptist |
| Little Rock University; Little Rock, Ark. (1927) | Carey V. Stabler | 1,433 C | Private |
| Livingston State College; Livingston, Ala. (1835) | D. P. Culp | 614 C | State |
| Lock Haven State College; Lock Haven, Pa. (1870) | Richard T. Parsons | 1,023 C | State |
| Loma Linda University; Loma Linda & Los Angeles, Calif. (1905)[12] | Godfrey T. Anderson | 962 C | 7th Day Adven. |
| Long Beach State College; Long Beach, Calif. (1949) | Carl W. McIntosh | 9,839 C | State |
| Long Island University; Brooklyn, N. Y. (1926)[2] | Adm. R. L. Conolly | 7,405 C | Private |
| Longwood College; Farmville, Va. (1884) | F. G. Lankford, Jr. | 1,031 F | State |
| Loras College; Dubuque, Iowa (1839) | Msgr. Dorrance V. Foley | 1,260 M | Catholic |
| Loretto Heights College; Loretto, Colo. (1918) | Sister Frances M. Walsh | 798 F | Catholic |
| Los Angeles County Art Institute. See Otis Art Institute. | | ......... | ......... |
| Los Angeles St. Coll. of App. Arts & Sci.; Los Angeles, Calif. (1947) | Howard S. McDonald | 14,642 C | State |
| Louisiana College; Pineville, La. (1906) | G. Earl Guinn | 995 C | Baptist |
| Louisiana Polytechnic Institute; Ruston, La. (1894) | Ralph L. Ropp | 3,410 C | State |
| Louisiana State University & A & M College; Baton Rouge (1860)[2] | Troy H. Middleton | 11,901 C | State |
| Louisville, University of; Louisville, Ky. (1798) | Philip Davidson | 5,210 C | City |
| Lowell Technological Institute; Lowell, Mass. (1895) | Martin J. Lydon | 1,171 C | State |
| Loyola College; Baltimore, Md. (1852) | V. Rev. V. F. Beatty | 1,170 M | Catholic |
| Loyola University; Chicago, Ill. (1870) | V. Rev. J. F. Maguire | 10,140 C | Catholic |
| Loyola University; New Orleans, La. (1911) | V. Rev. W. P. Donnelly | 2,488 C | Catholic |
| Loyola University of Los Angeles; Los Angeles, Calif. (1911) | V. Rev. C. S. Casassa | 1,583 M | Catholic |
| Luther College; Decorah, Iowa (1861) | J. W. Ylvisaker | 1,168 C | Lutheran |
| Lycoming College; Williamsport, Pa. (1812) | D. Frederick Wertz | 644 C | Methodist |
| Lynchburg College; Lynchburg, Va. (1903) | Orville W. Wake | 765 C | Disc. of Christ |
| Macalester College; St. Paul, Minn. (1853) | Harvey M. Rice | 1,586 C | Private |
| MacMurray College; Jacksonville, Ill. (1846) | Gordon E. Michalson | 912 Co | Methodist |
| Madison College; Harrisonburg, Va. (1908) | G. Tyler Miller | 1,443 F | State |
| Madonna College; Livonia, Mich. (1947) | Sister Mary Raynelda | 370 F | Catholic |
| Maine, University of; Orono & Portland, Maine (1865) | Lloyd H. Elliott | 3,830 C | State |
| Manchester College; North Manchester, Ind. (1889) | A. Blair Helman | 1,125 C | Brethren |
| Manhattan College; New York, N. Y. (1853) | Brother A. Philip | 2,934 M | Catholic |
| Manhattan School of Music; New York, N. Y. (1917) | John Brownlee | 571 C | Private |
| Manhattanville College of the Sacred Heart; Purchase, N. Y. (1841) | Mother E. M. O'Byrne | 807 F | Catholic |
| Mankato State College; Mankato, Minn. (1867) | C. L. Crawford | 5,600 C | State |
| Mansfield State College; Mansfield, Pa. (1857) | Lewis W. Rathgeber | 1,006 C | State |
| Marian College; Indianapolis & Oldenburg, Ind. (1937) | V. Rev. F. J. Reine | 670 C | Catholic |
| Marian College of Fond du Lac; Fond du Lac, Wis. (1936) | Sister M. Fidelis | 340 F | Catholic |
| Marietta College; Marietta, Ohio (1797) | W. Bay Irvine | 1,213 C | Private |
| Marquette University; Milwaukee, Wis. (1881) | V. Rev. E. J. O'Donnell | 10,659 C | Catholic |
| Marshall University; Huntington, W. Va. (1837) | Stewart H. Smith | 2,746 C | State |
| Mary Baldwin College; Staunton, Va. (1842) | Samuel R. Spencer, Jr. | 390 F | Presbyterian |
| Mary Hardin-Baylor College; Belton, Tex. (1845)[2] | Arthur K. Tyson | 614 F | Baptist |
| Mary Immaculate Seminary; Northampton, Pa. | James M. McGlinchey | 70 M[25] | Catholic |
| Mary Manse College; Toledo, Ohio (1922) | Sister John Baptist | 1,075 F | Catholic |
| Mary Washington College; Fredericksburg, Va. (1908)[18] | Grellet C. Simpson | 1,746 F | State |
| Marycrest College; Davenport, Iowa (1939) | Mother Mary Geraldine | 845 F | Catholic |

| Institution, location and (date founded) | Chief executive | Students[1] | Control |
|---|---|---|---|
| Marygrove College; Detroit, Mich. (1910) | Sister M. Honora | 946 F | Catholic |
| Maryknoll Seminary; Glen Ellyn, Ill. (1949) | V. Rev. G. M. Buckley | 339 M | Catholic |
| Maryknoll Teachers College; Maryknoll, N. Y. (1931) | Sister Jeanne M. Lyons | 126 F | Catholic |
| Maryland, University of; College Park, & Baltimore, Md. (1807) | Wilson H. Elkins | 12,199 C | State |
| Maryland State College; Princess Anne, Md. (1886) | John T. Williams | 506 C | State |
| Maryland State Teachers College; Frostburg, Md. (1898) | R. Bowen Hardesty | 962 C | State |
| Maryland State Teachers College; Salisbury, Md. (1925) | Wilbur Devilbiss | 365 C | State |
| Maryland State Teachers College; Towson, Md. (1866) | Earle T. Hawkins | 1,533 C | State |
| Marylhurst College; Marylhurst, Oreg. (1930)[2] | Sister Miriam Barbara | 557 F | Catholic |
| Marymount College; Salina, Kans. (1922) | Sister Etta L. Knaup | 432 F | Catholic |
| Marymount College; Tarrytown, N. Y. (1907) | Mother M. Brendan | 650 F | Catholic |
| Marymount Manhattan College; New York, N. Y. (1948) | Mother M. R. McKay | 511 F | Catholic |
| Maryville College; Maryville, Tenn. (1819) | Joseph J. Copeland | 706 C | Presbyterian |
| Maryville College of the Sacred Heart; St. Louis, Mo. (1872) | Mother M. Blish | 250 F | Catholic |
| Marywood College; Scranton, Pa. (1915) | Sister M. Eugenia | 1,276 F | Catholic |
| Massachusetts, University of; Amherst, Mass. (1863) | John W. Lederle | 6,153 C | State |
| Massachusetts College of Art; Boston, Mass. (1873) | Robert L. Bertolli | 500 C | State |
| Massachusetts Institute of Technology; Cambridge, Mass. (1861) | Julius A. Stratton | 6,289 C | Private |
| Massachusetts State College; Bridgewater, Mass. (1840) | Clement C. Maxwell | 1,214 C | State |
| Massachusetts State College; Fitchburg, Mass. (1894) | Ralph F. Weston | 752 C | State |
| Massachusetts State College; Framingham, Mass. (1839) | D. Justin McCarthy | 663 F | State |
| Massachusetts State College; Lowell, Mass. (1897) | Daniel H. O'Leary | 540 C | State |
| Massachusetts State College; North Adams, Mass. (1894) | Eugene L. Freel | 321 C | State |
| Massachusetts State College; Salem, Mass. (1854) | Frederick A. Meier | 1,143 C | State |
| Massachusetts State College; Westfield, Mass. (1839) | F. S. Conlin | 910 C | State |
| Massachusetts State College; Worcester, Mass. (1871) | Eugene A. Sullivan | 1,511 C | State |
| McMurry College; Abilene, Tex. (1920) | Gordon R. Bennett | 1,119 C | Methodist |
| McNeese State College; Lake Charles, La. (1939) | W. N. Cusic | 2,506 C | State |
| McPherson College; McPherson, Kans. (1887) | D. W. Bittinger | 506 C | Brethren |
| Medical Evangelists, College of. See Loma Linda University | | | |
| Memphis State University; Memphis, Tenn. (1912) | C. C. Humphreys | 4,989 C | State |
| Mercer University; Macon & Atlanta, Ga. (1833) | Rufus C. Harris | 1,326 C | S. Baptist |
| Mercy College; Detroit, Mich. (1941) | Sister Mary Lucille | 730 F | Catholic |
| Mercyhurst College; Erie, Pa. (1926) | Mother M. Loretta | 457 F | Catholic |
| Meredith College; Raleigh, N. C. (1891) | Carlyle Campbell | 645 F | S. Baptist |
| Merrimack College; North Andover, Mass. (1947) | Rev. Vincent A. McQuade | 1,026 C | Catholic |
| Miami, University of; Coral Gables, Fla. (1925)[2] | Jay F. W. Pearson | 13,453 C | Private |
| Miami University; Oxford, Ohio (1809)[2] | John D. Millett | 6,518 C | State |
| Michigan, University of; Ann Arbor, Mich. (1817)[2] | Harlan Hatcher | 24,229 C[6] | State |
| Michigan College of Mining & Technology; Houghton, Mich. (1885)[2] | J. R. Van Pelt | 2,963 C | State |
| Michigan State University; E. Lansing & Rochester, Mich. (1855) | John A. Hannah | 21,228 C[9] | State |
| Middle Tennessee State College; Murfreesboro, Tenn. (1911) | Quill E. Cope | 2,604 C | State |
| Middlebury College; Middlebury & Ripton, Vt. (1800) | Samuel S. Stratton | 1,255 C | Private |
| Midland College; Fremont, Nebr. (1887) | Paul W. Dieckman | 575 C | Lutheran |
| Midwestern University; Wichita Falls, Tex. (1922) | Travis A. White | 1,484 C | City |
| Millersville State College; Millersville, Pa. (1855) | D. L. Biemesderfer | 1,848 C | State |
| Millikin University; Decatur, Ill. (1901) | Paul L. McKay | 1,142 C | Presbyterian |
| Mills College; Oakland, Calif. (1852) | C. Easton Rothwell | 711 F | Private |
| Mills College of Education; New York, N. Y. (1909) | Amy Hostler | 195 F | Private |
| Millsaps College; Jackson, Miss. (1892) | H. E. Finger, Jr. | 832 C | Methodist |
| Milwaukee-Downer College; Milwaukee, Wis. (1851) | John B. Johnson, Jr. | 182 F | Private |
| Minneapolis School of Art; Minneapolis, Minn. (1886) | Wilhelmus B. Bryan | 248 C | Private |
| Minnesota, University of; Minneapolis, Minn. (1851)[2] | O. Meredith Wilson | 28,277 C[6] | State |
| Misericordia, College; Dallas, Pa. (1924) | Sister Mary C. McHale | 956 F | Private |
| Mississippi, University of; Oxford & Jackson, Miss. (1848) | John D. Williams | 4,810 C | State |
| Mississippi College; Clinton, Miss. (1826) | R. A. McLemore | 1,735 C | S. Baptist |
| Mississippi Southern College; Hattiesburg, Miss. (1910) | William D. McCain | 3,999 C | State |
| Mississippi State College for Women; Columbus, Miss. (1884) | Charles P. Hogarth | 1,442 F | State |
| Mississippi State University; Starkville, Miss. (1878) | D. W. Colvard | 4,398 C | State |
| Missouri, University of; Columbia & Rolla, Mo. (1839) | Elmer Ellis | 13,355 C | State |
| Missouri Valley College; Marshall, Mo. (1889) | M. Earle Collins | 503 C | Presbyterian |
| Monmouth College; Monmouth, Ill. (1853) | Robert W. Gibson | 783 C | U. Presbyterian |
| Monmouth College; West Long Branch, N. J. (1933) | Edward G. Schlaefer | 2,338 C | Private |
| Montana School of Mines; Butte, Mont. (1893) | Edwin G. Koch | 311 C | State |
| Montana State College; Bozeman, Mont. (1893)[2] | Roland R. Renne | 3,495 C | State |
| Montana State University; Missoula, Mont. (1893) | H. K. Newburn | 3,364 C | State |
| Montclair State College; Upper Montclair, N. J. (1908) | E. D. Partridge | 2,494 C | State |
| Moore Institute of Art, Sci. & Ind.; Philadelphia, Pa. (1844) | Harold R. Rice | 310 F | Private |
| Moorhead State College; Moorhead, Minn. (1887) | John J. Neumaier | 1,201 C | State |
| Moravian College; Bethlehem, Pa. (1742) | Raymond S. Haupert | 839 C | Moravian |
| Morehead State College; Morehead, Ky. (1922) | Adron Doran | 2,459 C[6] | State |
| Morehouse College. See Atlanta University System | | | |

| Institution, location and (date founded) | Chief executive | Students[1] | Control |
|---|---|---|---|
| Morgan State College; Baltimore, Md. (1867) | Martin D. Jenkins | 2,791 C | State |
| Morningside College; Sioux City, Iowa (1894) | J. Richard Palmer | 963 C | Methodist |
| Morris Brown College; Atlanta, Ga. (1881) | Frank Cunningham | 833 C | Af. Meth. Epis. |
| Morris Harvey College; Charleston, W. Va. (1888) | L. Riggleman | 2,463 C | Private |
| Mount Angel College; Mount Angel, Oreg. (1887) | Mother M. G. Piennett | 230 C | Catholic |
| Mount Angel Seminary; St. Benedict, Oreg. (1889) | Rt. Rev. Damian Jentges. | 132 M | Catholic |
| Mount Holyoke College; South Hadley, Mass. (1837) | Richard G. Gettell | 1,428 F | Private |
| Mount Mary College; Milwaukee, Wis. (1913)[2] | Sister Mary J. Francis | 1,069 F | Catholic |
| Mount Mercy College; Cedar Rapids, Iowa (1928) | Sister Mary Ildephonse. | 330 F | Catholic |
| Mount Mercy College; Pittsburgh, Pa. (1929) | Sister M. Muriel | 596 F | Private |
| Mount St. Agnes College; Baltimore, Md. (1890) | Sister Mary Cleophas | 384 F | Private |
| Mount St. Joseph, College of; Mt. St. Joseph, Ohio (1854) | Sister Maria Corona | 691 F | Catholic |
| Mount St. Joseph Teachers College; Buffalo, N. Y. (1937) | Mother M. Hubert | 360 F | Catholic |
| Mount St. Mary College; Hooksett, N. H. (1934) | Sister Mary Vianney | 217 F | Catholic |
| Mount St. Mary's College; Emmitsburg, Md. (1808) | Rt. Rev. J. L. Sheridan. | 703 M | Catholic |
| Mount St. Mary's College; Los Angeles, Calif. (1925) | Sister Rose Gertrude | 1,169 F | Catholic |
| Mount St. Scholastica College; Atchison, Kans. (1924) | Mother M. Alfred Schroll | 511 F | Catholic |
| Mount St. Vincent, College of; New York, N. Y. (1847) | Sister Catharine Marie | 640 F | Catholic |
| Mount Union College; Alliance, Ohio (1846) | Carl C. Bracy | 909 C | Methodist |
| Muhlenberg College; Allentown, Pa. (1848) | Erling N. Jensen | 1,035 C | Lutheran |
| Mundelein College; Chicago, Ill. (1930) | Sister Mary Ann Ida | 1,129 F | Catholic |
| Murray State College; Murray, Ky. (1922) | R. H. Woods | 2,920 C | State |
| Muskingum College; New Concord, Ohio (1837) | Robert N. Montgomery. | 1,162 C | U. Presbyterian |
| National College of Education; Evanston, Ill. (1886)[2] | K. Richard Johnson | 833 C | Private |
| Nazareth College; Kalamazoo, Mich. (1924) | Sister Marie Kathleen | 283 F[22] | Catholic |
| Nazareth College; Louisville & Nazareth, Ky. (1920) | Sister M. G. Murphy | 1,311 F | Catholic |
| Nazareth College of Rochester; Rochester, N. Y. (1924) | Sister Helen Daniel | 798 F | Catholic |
| Nebraska, University of; Lincoln & Omaha, Nebr. (1869) | Clifford M. Hardin | 8,372 C | State |
| Nebraska State Teachers College; Chadron, Nebr. (1911) | Barton L. Kline | 691 C | State |
| Nebraska State Teachers College; Kearney, Nebr. (1903) | Herbert L. Cushing | 2,285 C | State |
| Nebraska State Teachers College; Peru, Nebr. (1867) | Neal S. Gomon | 616 C | State |
| Nebraska State Teachers College; Wayne, Nebr. (1910) | W. A. Brandenburg | 1,285 C | State |
| Nebraska Wesleyan University; Lincoln, Nebr. (1887) | Vance D. Rogers | 1,009 C | Methodist |
| Nevada, University of; Reno & Las Vegas, Nev. (1874) | Charles J. Armstrong | 2,843 C | State |
| New Church, Academy of the; Bryn Athyn, Pa. (1877) | Rt. Rev. W. D. Pendleton | 82 C | Ch. of New Jerus. |
| New England Conservatory of Music; Boston, Mass. (1867)[2] | James Aliferis | 395 C | Private |
| New Hampshire, University of; Durham, N. H. (1866) | Eldon L. Johnson | 3,389 C | State |
| New Haven College; New Haven, Conn. (1920) | Marvin K. Peterson | 1,125 C | Private |
| New Mexico, University of; Albuquerque, N. Mex. (1889) | Tom L. Popejoy | 6,072 C | State |
| New Mexico Highlands University; Las Vegas, N. Mex. (1893) | Thomas C. Donnelly | 1,000 C | State |
| New Mexico Institute of Mining & Tech.; Socorro, N. Mex. (1889) | E. J. Workman | 255 C | State |
| New Mexico State University; University Park; N. Mex. (1888). | R. B. Corbett | 3,064 C | State |
| New Mexico Western College; Silver City, N. Mex. (1893) | J. Cloyd Miller | 718 C | State |
| New Rochelle, College of; New Rochelle, N. Y. (1904) | Mother Mary Peter Carthy | 987 F | Catholic |
| New School For Social Research; New York, N. Y. (1919) | Henry David | 6,072 C | Private |
| New York, College of the City of: | ...... | ...... | ......... |
| Brooklyn College; Brooklyn, N. Y. (1930) | Harry D. Gideonse | 12,218 C | City |
| City College; New York, N. Y. (1847) | Buell G. Gallagher | 16,680 C | City |
| Hunter College; New York, N. Y. (1870) | John J. Meng | 10,225 C | City |
| Queens College; Flushing, N. Y. (1937) | Harold W. Stoke | 7,346 C | City |
| New York, State University of; Albany, N. Y. (1948) | Thomas H. Hamilton | 31,151 C | State |
| Liberal Arts: Harpur College; Binghamton, N. Y. (1946) | Glenn C. Bartle | 1,229 C | State |
| Medical Colleges: Brooklyn, N. Y. (1857) | Robert A. Moore | 613 C | State |
| Syracuse, N. Y. (1834) | Carlyle Jacobsen | 451 C | State |
| Colleges of Education: Albany, N. Y. (1844) | Evan R. Collins | 3,208 C | State |
| Brockport, N. Y. (1841) | Donald M. Tower | 1,740 C | State |
| Buffalo, N. Y. (1869) | Paul G. Bulger | 3,907 C | State |
| Cortland, N. Y. (1863) | Donovan C. Moffett | 2,488 C | State |
| Fredonia, N. Y. (1867) | Harry W. Porter | 1,184 C | State |
| Geneseo, N. Y. (1867) | Francis J. Moench | 1,532 C | State |
| New Paltz, N. Y. (1886) | William J. Haggerty | 1,960 C | State |
| Oneonta, N. Y. (1887) | Royal F. Netzer | 1,891 C | State |
| Oswego, N. Y. (1861) | Foster S. Brown | 2,424 C | State |
| Plattsburgh, N. Y. (1889) | George W. Angell | 1,504 C | State |
| Potsdam, N. Y. (1889) | Frederick W. Crumb | 1,325 C | State |
| Other Professional Colleges: L. I. Center, Oyster Bay (1957) | John F. Lee | 439 C | State |
| College of Forestry at Syracuse U.; Syracuse, N. Y. (1911) | Hardy L. Shirley | 723 M | State |
| Maritime College at Ft. Schuyler; New York, N. Y. (1874) | Vice Adm. H. C. Moore. | 515 M | State |
| College of Ceramics at Alfred U.; Alfred, N. Y. (1900) | John F. McMahon | 421 C | State |
| College of Agriculture at Cornell U.; Ithaca, N. Y. (1904) | Charles E. Palm | 2,236 C | State |
| College of Home Econ. at Cornell U.; Ithaca, N. Y. (1900) | Helen G. Canoyer | 734 F | State |
| School of Ind. & Labor Rel., Cornell U.; Ithaca, N. Y. (1945). | John W. McConnell | 369 C | State |

| Institution, location and (date founded) | Chief executive | Students[1] | Control |
|---|---|---|---|
| Veterinary College at Cornell U.; Ithaca, N. Y. (1894) | George C. Poppensiek... | 258 C | State |
| New York University; New York, N. Y. (1831) | Carroll V. Newsom... | 37,199 C | Private |
| Newark College of Engineering; Newark, N. J. (1881) | Robert W. Van Houten .. | 3,432 C | State & City |
| Newark State College; Union, N. J. (1855) | Eugene G. Wilkins...... | 1,395 C | State |
| Newberry College; Newberry, S. C. (1856) | A. G. D. Wiles........ | 639 C | United Luth. |
| Newcomb College; New Orleans, La. (1886)[14] | John R. Hubbard....... | 887 F | Private |
| Newton College of the Sacred Heart; Newton, Mass. (1946) | Mother G. Husson..... | 615 F | Catholic |
| Niagara University; Niagara Falls, N. Y. (1856) | V. Rev. V. T. Swords..... | 1,600 C | Catholic |
| North Carolina, Agr. & Tech. College of; Greensboro, N. C. (1891) | Samuel D. Proctor...... | 2,225 C | State |
| North Carolina, University of: | ...... | ...... | .......... |
|   Consolidated Office; Chapel Hill, N. C. (1931) | William C. Friday...... | 17,091 C | State |
|     North Carolina State College; Raleigh, N. C. (1887) | John T. Caldwell....... | 5,949 C | State |
|     University of N. C. at Chapel Hill; Chapel Hill, N. C. (1789).. | William B. Aycock...... | 8,382 C | State |
|     Woman's College; Greensboro, N. C. (1892) | W. W. Pierson...... | 2,760 F | State |
| North Carolina College at Durham; Durham, N. C. (1910) | Alfonso Elder......... | 2,051 C | State |
| North Central College; Naperville, Ill. (1861) | Arlo L. Schilling........ | 890 C | Evan. Un. Breth. |
| North Dakota, University of; Grand Forks, N. Dak. (1883) | George W. Starcher..... | 4,130 C | State |
| North Dakota State Teachers College; Dickinson, N. Dak. (1917) | O. A. DeLong.......... | 651 C | State |
| North Dakota State Teachers College; Mayville, N. Dak. (1890) | T. S. Jenkins.......... | 588 C | State |
| North Dakota State Teachers College; Minot, N. Dak. (1913) | C. P. Lura............ | 1,289 C | State |
| North Dakota State Teachers College; Valley City, N. Dak. (1890) | R. L. Lokken........... | 711 C | State |
| North Dakota State Univ. of Agr. & App. Sci.; Fargo, N. Dak. (1890) | Fred S. Hultz.......... | 3,300 C | State |
| North Georgia College; Dahlonega, Ga. (1873) | Merritt E. Hoag....... | 678 C | State |
| North Texas State College; Denton, Tex. (1890) | J. C. Matthews......... | 6,932 C | State |
| Northeast Louisiana State College; Monroe, La. (1931) | George T. Walker...... | 2,374 C | State |
| Northeast Missouri State Teachers College; Kirksville, Mo. (1867) | Walter H. Ryle........ | 2,763 C | State |
| Northeastern State College; Tahlequah, Okla. (1909) | Harrell E. Garrison...... | 2,587 C | State |
| Northeastern University; Boston, Mass. (1898) | Asa S. Knowles........ | 18,000 C | Private |
| Northern Baptist Theological Seminary; Chicago, Ill. (1913) | Benjamin P. Browne.... | 239 C | Baptist |
| Northern Illinois University; De Kalb & Oregon, Ill. (1895) | Leslie A. Holmes....... | 6,655 C | State |
| Northern Michigan College; Marquette, Mich. (1899) | Edgar L. Harden....... | 1,994 C | State |
| Northern Montana College; Havre, Mont. (1929) | L. O. Brockmann...... | 586 C | State |
| Northern State Teachers College; Aberdeen, S. Dak. (1901) | J. Howard Kramer...... | 1,275 C | State |
| Northland College; Ashland, Wis. (1892) | Gus Turbeville........ | 370 C | Private |
| Northrop Institute of Technology; Inglewood, Calif. (1942) | James L. McKinley..... | 1,100 M | Private |
| Northwest Missouri State College; Maryville, Mo. (1905) | J. W. Jones.......... | 1,893 C | State |
| Northwest Nazarene College; Nampa, Idaho (1913) | John E. Riley.......... | 564 C | Nazarene |
| Northwestern State College; Alva, Okla. (1897) | Jesse W. Martin........ | 1,048 C | State |
| Northwestern State College of La.; Natchitoches, La. (1884) | John S. Kyser......... | 2,746 C | State |
| Northwestern University; Evanston & Chicago, Ill. (1851) | J. Roscoe Miller....... | 9,626 C | Private |
| Norwich University; Northfield, Vt. (1819) | Maj. Gen. E. N. Harmon. | 914 M | Private |
| Notre Dame, College of; Belmont & Saratoga, Calif. (1851) | Sister Catharine Julie... | 292 F | Catholic |
| Notre Dame, University of; Notre Dame, Ind. (1842) | Rev. T. M. Hesburgh.... | 6,239 M | Catholic |
| Notre Dame College; Cleveland, Ohio (1922) | Sister Mary Loyole..... | 390 F | Catholic |
| Notre Dame College; St. Louis, Mo. (1954) | Mother M. Theodosia... | 305 F | Catholic |
| Notre Dame College of Staten Island; Staten Island, N. Y. (1931) | Mother St. Egbert...... | 350 F | Catholic |
| Notre Dame of Maryland, College of; Baltimore, Md. (1873) | Sister Margaret Mary... | 963 F | Catholic |
| Notre Dame Seminary; New Orleans, La. (1923) | John McQuade........ | 109 M | Catholic |
| Oakwood College; Huntsville, Ala. (1896) | Garland Millet......... | 327 C | 7th Day Adven. |
| Oberlin College; Oberlin, Ohio (1833) | Robert Kenneth Carr.... | 2,252 C | Private |
| Occidental College; Los Angeles, Calif. (1887) | Arthur G. Coons....... | 1,436 C | Private |
| Oglethorpe University; Atlanta, Ga. (1835) | Donald C. Agnew....... | 320 C | Private |
| Ohio Northern University; Ada, Ohio (1871) | F. Bringle McIntosh..... | 1,443 C | Methodist |
| Ohio State University; Columbus, Ohio (1870)[2] | Novice G. Fawcett...... | 22,879 C | State |
| Ohio University; Athens, Ohio (1804)[2] | John C. Baker.......... | 7,507 C | State |
| Ohio Wesleyan University; Delaware, Ohio (1841) | David A. Lockmiller..... | 2,034 C | Methodist |
| Oklahoma, University of; Norman, Okla. (1892)[2] | George L. Cross....... | 9,603 C[26] | State |
| Oklahoma Baptist University; Shawnee, Okla. (1910) | John Wesley Raley..... | 1,384 C | S. Baptist |
| Oklahoma City University; Oklahoma City, Okla. (1904) | Jack S. Wilkes......... | 1,212 C | Methodist |
| Oklahoma College for Women; Chickasha, Okla. (1908) | Freeman H. Beets...... | 746 F | State |
| Oklahoma State University; Stillwater & Okmulgee, Okla. (1891) | Oliver S. Willham...... | 10,074 C | State |
| Olivet Nazarene College; Kankakee, Ill. (1907) | Harold W. Reed........ | 958 C | Nazarene |
| Omaha, Municipal University of; Omaha, Nebr. (1908) | Milo Bail............. | 6,045 C | City |
| Oregon, University of; Eugene & Portland, Oreg. (1872) | William C. Jones....... | 6,749 C | State |
| Oregon College of Education; Monmouth, Oreg. (1882) | Roy E. Lieuallen....... | 1,030 C[9] | State |
| Oregon State University; Corvallis, Oreg. (1868) | A. L. Strand.......... | 7,353 C | State |
| Otis Art Institute; Los Angeles, Calif. (1920)[15] | Jarvis Barlow.......... | 81 C | County |
| Ottawa University; Ottawa, Kans. (1865) | Andrew B. Martin...... | 547 C | Baptist |
| Otterbein College; Westerville, Ohio (1847) | Lynn W. Turner....... | 898 C | Evan. Un. Breth. |
| Ouachita Baptist College; Arkadelphia, Ark. (1885) | Ralph A. Phelps, Jr..... | 1,106 C | S. Baptist |
| Our Lady of Cincinnati College; Cincinnati, Ohio (1935) | Sister Mary Virginia.... | 915 F | Catholic |
| Our Lady of the Elms, College of; Chicopee, Mass. (1928) | Sister Rose William..... | 516 F | Catholic |

| Institution, location and (date founded) | Chief executive | Students[1] | Control |
|---|---|---|---|
| Our Lady of the Lake College; San Antonio, Tex. (1896) | John L. McMahon | 676 F | Catholic |
| Ozarks, College of the; Clarksville, Ark. (1834) | William S. Findley | 350 C | Presb., USA |
| Pace College; New York, N. Y. (1906) | Edward J. Mortola | 4,324 C | Private |
| Pacific, University of the; Stockton & Dillon Beach, Calif. (1851) | Robert E. Burns | 2,165 C | Methodist |
| Pacific Lutheran University; Tacoma, Wash. (1890) | S. C. Eastvold | 1,622 C | Lutheran |
| Pacific Oaks Friends School; Pasadena, Calif. (1945) | Evangeline Burgess | 18 C | Private |
| Pacific Union College; Angwin, Calif. (1882) | R. W. Fowler | 991 C | 7th Day Adven. |
| Pacific University; Forest Grove, Oreg. (1849) | M. A. F. Ritchie | 737 C | Private |
| Pan American College; Edinburg, Tex. (1927) | Ralph Schilling | 1,935 C | State & county |
| Panhandle A & M College; Goodwell, Okla. (1909) | Marvin McKee | 964 C | State |
| Park College; Parkville, Mo. (1875) | Paul H. Morrill | 427 C | Presbyterian |
| Parsons College; Fairfield, Iowa (1875) | Millard G. Roberts | 1,563 C | Presbyterian |
| Pasadena College; Pasadena, Calif. (1902) | O. J. Finch | 1,002 C | Nazarene |
| Paterson State College; Wayne, N. J. | Marion E. Shea | 2,649 C[25] | State |
| Peabody Conservatory of Music; Baltimore, Md. (1868) | Peter Mennin | 370 C | Private |
| Pembroke College; Providence, R. I. (1891)[5] | Nancy D. Lewis | 873 F[22] | Private |
| Pembroke State College; Pembroke, N. C. (1887) | Walter J. Gale | 500 C | State |
| Pennsylvania, University of; Philadelphia, Pa. (1740) | Gaylord P. Harnwell | 12,480C | Private |
| Pennsylvania Military College; Chester, Pa. (1821) | Clarence R. Moll | 1,643 M | Private |
| Pennsylvania State College of Optometry; Philadelphia, Pa. (1919) | Lawrence Fitch | 110 C | Private |
| Pennsylvania State Colleges. See individual colleges | | | |
| Pennsylvania State University; University Park, Pa. (1855)[2] | Eric A. Walker | 20,080 C | State |
| Pepperdine College; Los Angeles, Calif. (1937) | M. Norvel Young | 1,072 C | Private |
| Pfeiffer College; Misenheimer, N. C. (1885) | J. Lem Stokes, II | 767 C | Methodist |
| Philadelphia College of Textiles & Science; Philadelphia, Pa. (1884) | Bertrand W. Hayward | 421 C | Private |
| Philadelphia Museum College of Art; Philadelphia, Pa. (1876) | E. M. Benson | 1,060 C | Private |
| Philander Smith College; Little Rock, Ark. (1868) | Roosevelt D. Crockett | 705 C | Methodist |
| Phillips University; Enid, Okla. (1906) | Hallie G. Gantz | 1,126 C | Disc. of Christ |
| Pittsburgh, University of; Pittsburgh & Johnstown, Pa. (1787) | Edward H. Litchfield | 10,457 C[9] | Private |
| Plymouth Teachers College; Plymouth, N. H. (1870) | Harold E. Hyde | 674 C | State |
| Pomona College; Claremont, Calif. (1887) | E. Wilson Lyon | 1,063 C | Private |
| Portland, University of; Portland, Oreg. (1901) | Rev. Howard J. Kenna | 1,663 C | Catholic |
| Portland State College; Portland, Oreg. (1955) | Branford P. Millar | 3,926 C | State |
| Prairie View A & M College; Prairie View, Tex. (1876) | Edward B. Evans | 2,519 C | State |
| Pratt Institute; Brooklyn, N. Y. (1887) | Robert F. Oxnam | 4,044 C | Private |
| Presbyterian College; Clinton, S. C. (1880) | Marshall W. Brown | 495 C | Presbyterian |
| Presbyterian School of Christian Education; Richmond, Va. (1914) | Charles E. S. Kraemer | 116 C | Presbyterian |
| Princeton University; Princeton, N. J. (1746) | Robert F. Goheen | 3,828 M | Private |
| Principia College; Elsah, Ill. (1898) | David K. Andrews | 509 C | Private |
| Providence College; Providence, R. I. (1917) | V. Rev. R. J. Slavin | 2,139 M | Catholic |
| Puerto Rico, University of; Río Piedras, P. R. (1903)[2] | Jaime Benítez | 18,059 C | Terr. govt. |
| Puget Sound, University of; Tacoma, Wash. (1888) | R. Franklin Thompson | 1,018 C | Methodist |
| Purdue, University; Lafayette, Ind. (1869)[2] | Frederick L. Hovde | 14,206 C | State |
| Queens College; Charlotte, N. C. (1857) | Edwin R. Walker | 464 F | Presbyterian |
| Queens College (NYC). See New York, College of the City of | | | |
| Quincy College; Quincy, Ill. (1860) | Rev. Julian Woods | 800 C | Catholic |
| Quinnipiac College; Hamden, Conn. (1929) | Nils G. Sahlin | 1,164 C | Private |
| Radcliffe College; Cambridge, Mass. (1879)[11] | Mary I. Bunting | 1,798 F | Private |
| Radford College; Radford, Va. (1910)[16] | Charles K. Martin, Jr. | 1,500 F | State |
| Randolph-Macon College; Ashland, Va. (1830) | J. Earl Moreland | 665 M | Methodist |
| Randolph-Macon Woman's College; Lynchburg, Va. (1891) | William F. Quillian, Jr. | 664 F | Methodist |
| Redlands, University of; Redlands, Calif. (1907) | George H. Armacost | 1,555 C | Baptist |
| Reed College; Portland, Oreg. (1909) | Richard H. Sullivan | 753 C | Private |
| Regis College; Denver, Colo. (1887) | Richard F. Ryan | 986 M | Catholic |
| Regis College; Weston, Mass. (1927) | Sister Mary Alice | 700 F | Catholic |
| Rensselaer Polytechnic Institute; Troy, N. Y. (1824)[2] | Richard G. Folsom | 4,447 M[23] | Private |
| Rhode Island, University of; Kingston & Providence, R. I. (1892) | Francis H. Horn | 3,447 C | State |
| Rhode Island College; Providence, R. I. (1854) | William C. Gaige | 1,300 C | State |
| Rhode Island School of Design; Providence, R. I. (1877)[2] | John R. Frazier | 790 C | Private |
| Rice University; Houston, Tex. (1891) | Carey Croneis | 1,844 C | Private |
| Richmond, University of; Richmond, Va. (1830) | George M. Modlin | 1,933 Co | Baptist |
| Rider College; Trenton, N. J. (1865) | Franklin F. Moore | 2,318 C | Private |
| Ripon College; Ripon, Wis. (1851) | Fred O. Pinkham | 700 C | Private |
| Rivier College; Nashua, N. H. (1933) | Sister Clarice de St. Marie | 370 F | Private |
| Roanoke College; Salem, Va. (1842) | H. Sherman Oberly | 722 C | Lutheran |
| Rochester, University of; Rochester, N. Y. (1850) | Cornelis W. de Kiewiet | 6,350 C | Private |
| Rochester Institute of Technology; Rochester, N. Y. (1829) | Mark Ellingson | 2,116 C | Private |
| Rockford College; Rockford, Ill. (1847) | John A. Howard | 480 C | Private |
| Rockhurst College; Kansas City, Mo. (1910) | V. Rev. M. E. Van Ackeren | 1,637 M | Catholic |
| Rocky Mountain College; Billings, Mont. (1883) | Philip M. Widenhouse | 277 C | Cong.-Methodist |
| Rollins College; Winter Park, Fla. (1885) | Hugh F. McKean | 800 C | Private |
| Roosevelt University; Chicago, Ill. (1945) | Edward J. Sparling | 5,184 C | Private |

| Institution, location and (date founded) | Chief executive | Students[1] | Control |
|---|---|---|---|
| Rosary College; River Forest, Ill. (1848) | Sister M. Aurelia | 824 F | Catholic |
| Rosary Hill College; Buffalo, N. Y. (1947) | Sister M. Angela | 600 F | Catholic |
| Rose Polytechnic Institute; Terre Haute, Ind. (1874) | Ralph A. Morgen | 427 M | Private |
| Rosemont College; Rosemont, Pa. (1922) | Mother Mary Aidan | 571 F | Catholic |
| Russell Sage College; Troy & Albany, N. Y. (1916) | Lewis A. Froman | 2,270 F | Private |
| Rutgers, The State University; New Brunswick, N. J. (1766)[2,8] | Mason W. Gross | 17,100 C, Co | State |
| Sacramento State College; Sacramento, Calif. (1947) | Guy A. West | 6,084 C | State |
| Sacred Heart, College of the; Santurce, P. R. (1935) | Mother R. A. Arsuaga | 206 F | Catholic |
| Sacred Heart Dominican College; Houston, Tex. (1946) | Sister M. Antoinette | 417 F | Catholic |
| Sacred Heart Seminary; Detroit, Mich. (1919) | Msgr. A. A. Matyn | 235 M | Catholic |
| St. Ambrose College; Davenport, Iowa (1882) | Rt. Rev. W. J. Collins | 1,063 M | Catholic |
| St. Andrews Presbyterian College. See Flora Macdonald College. | | | |
| St. Anselm's College; Manchester, N. H. (1889) | Bernard G. Holmes | 1,196 M | Catholic |
| St. Augustine's College; Raleigh, N. C. (1867) | James A. Boyer | 472 C | Prot. Epis. |
| St. Benedict, College of; St. Joseph, Minn. (1913) | Sister R. Westkaemper | 422 F | Catholic |
| St. Benedict's College; Atchison, Kans. (1858) | Rev. Brendan Downey | 643 M | Catholic |
| St. Bernard College; St. Bernard, Ala. (1892) | Rev. Brian Egan | 539 Co | Catholic |
| St. Bernardine of Siena College; Loudonville, N. Y. (1937) | Rev. Edmund F. Christy | 1,620 M | Catholic |
| St. Bonaventure University; St. Bonaventure, N. Y. (1856) | V. Rev. Brian Lhota | 1,929 C | Catholic |
| St. Catherine, College of; St. Paul, Minn. (1905) | Sister Mary William | 1,085 F | Catholic |
| St. Cloud State College; St. Cloud, Minn. (1869) | George F. Budd | 3,016 C | State |
| St. Edward's Seminary. See Sulpician Seminary | | | |
| St. Edward's University; Austin, Tex. (1885) | Brother Raymond Fleck | 510 M | Catholic |
| St. Elizabeth, College of; Convent Station, N. J. (1899) | Sister Hildegarde Marie | 931 F | Catholic |
| St. Francis, College of; Joliet, Ill. (1920) | Sister Mary Elvira | 526 F | Catholic |
| St. Francis College; Brooklyn, N. Y. (1884) | Rev. Brother Urban | 1,500 M | Catholic |
| St. Francis College; Fort Wayne, Ind. (1890) | Sister M. Rosanna | 552 F | Catholic |
| St. Francis College; Loretto, Pa. (1847) | Rev. C. J. Devlin | 991 C | Catholic |
| St. John College; Cleveland, Ohio (1928) | Lawrence P. Cahill | 860 F | Catholic |
| St. John Fisher College; Rochester, N. Y. (1951) | V. Rev. C. J. Lavery | 520 M | Catholic |
| St. John's College; Annapolis, Md. (1696) | Richard D. Weigle | 249 C | Private |
| St. John's Seminary College; Camarillo, Calif. (1926) | V. Rev. W. J. Kenneally | 205 M | Catholic |
| St. John's University; Collegeville, Minn. (1857) | Abbot B. W. Dworschak | 1,297 M | Catholic |
| St. John's University; Jamaica & Brooklyn, N. Y. (1870) | V. Rev. John A. Flynn | 9,830 C | Catholic |
| St. Joseph College; Emmitsburg, Md. (1809) | Sister Hilda Gleason | 481 F | Catholic |
| St. Joseph College; West Hartford, Conn. (1932) | Sister M. Theodore | 650 F | Catholic |
| St. Joseph on the Rio Grande, Coll. of; Albuquerque, N. Mex. (1940) | Sister M. V. Schuller | 425 C | Catholic |
| St. Joseph's College; Philadelphia, Pa. (1851) | V. Rev. J. Joseph Bluett | 2,737 M | Catholic |
| St. Joseph's College; Rensselaer, Ind. (1889) | V. Rev. R. H. Gross | 1,016 M | Catholic |
| St. Joseph's College for Women; Brooklyn, N. Y. (1916) | Sister Vincent Therese | 554 F | Catholic |
| St. Joseph's Seminary; Washington, D. C. (1888) | V. Rev. James F. Didas | 38 M | Catholic |
| St. Lawrence University; Canton, N. Y. (1856) | Eugene G. Bewkes | 1,320 C | Private |
| St. Louis University; St. Louis, Mo. (1818)[2] | Paul C. Reinert | 9,300 C | Catholic |
| St. Martin's College; Olympia, Wash. (1895) | Rt. Rev. Raphael Heider | 310 M | Catholic |
| St. Mary, College of; Omaha, Nebr. (1923) | Sister Mary Alice | 410 F | Catholic |
| St. Mary College; Xavier, Kans. (1923) | Arthur M. Murphy | 420 F | Catholic |
| St. Mary of the Springs, College of; Columbus, Ohio (1911) | Sister M. Angelita | 346 F | Catholic |
| St. Mary-of-the-Woods Coll.; St. Mary-of-the-Woods, Ind. (1840). | Sister Marie Perpetua | 572 F | Catholic |
| St. Mary's College; Notre Dame, Ind. (1844) | Sister M. Madeleva | 1,076 F | Catholic |
| St. Mary's College; Winona, Minn. (1913) | Brother I. Basil | 902 M | Catholic |
| St. Mary's College of California; St. Mary's College, Calif. (1863) | Brother S. Albert | 815 M | Catholic |
| St. Mary's Dominican College; New Orleans, La. (1910) | Sister Mary Louise | 463 F | Catholic |
| St. Mary's Seminary & University; Baltimore, Md. (1791)[2] | Lloyd P. McDonald | 750 M | Catholic |
| St. Mary's University; San Antonio, Tex. (1852) | V. Rev. W. J. Buehler | 2,031 C | Catholic |
| St. Michael's College; Winooski, Vt. (1904) | V. Rev. Gerald E. Dupont | 850 M | Catholic |
| St. Norbert College; West De Pere, Wis. (1898) | V. Rev. D. M. Burke | 1,073 C | Catholic |
| St. Olaf College; Northfield, Minn. (1874) | Clemens M. Granskou | 1,753 C | Lutheran |
| St. Patrick's Seminary; Menlo Park & Mtn. View, Calif. (1898) | Rev. Edward J. Wagner | 161 M | Catholic |
| St. Paul Seminary; St. Paul, Minn. (1895) | Rev. Louis J. McCarthy | 332 M[22] | Catholic |
| St. Paul's College; Lawrenceville, Va. (1888) | Earl H. McClenney | 370 C | Prot. Epis. |
| St. Peter's College; Jersey City, N. J. (1872) | V. Rev. E. F. Clark | 1,928 M | Catholic |
| St. Procopius College; Lisle, Ill. (1887) | Rev. D. W. Kucera | 506 M | Catholic |
| St. Rose, College of; Albany, N. Y. (1920) | Sister Catherine Francis | 1,300 F | Catholic |
| St. Scholastica, College of; Duluth, Minn. (1912) | Sister Ann E. Scanlon | 450 F | Catholic |
| St. Teresa, College of; Kansas City, Mo. (1916) | Sister Mary D. Tammany | 490 F | Catholic |
| St. Teresa, College of; Winona, Minn. (1907)[2] | Sister M. C. Bowe | 803 F | Catholic |
| St. Thomas, College of; St. Paul, Minn. (1885) | Rt. Rev. J. P. Shannon | 1,900 M | Catholic |
| St. Thomas, University of; Houston, Tex. (1947) | Rev. John F. Murphy | 547 C | Catholic |
| St. Vincent College; Latrobe, Pa. (1846) | Rev. Quentin L. Schaut | 845 M | Catholic |
| St. Xavier College; Chicago, Ill. (1847) | Sister Mary Josetta | 960 F | Catholic |
| Salem College; Winston-Salem, N. C. (1772) | Dale H. Gramley | 416 F | Moravian |
| Salve Regina College; Newport, R. I. (1947) | Sister Mary Hilda | 435 F | Catholic |

| Institution, location and (date founded) | Chief executive | Students[1] | Control |
|---|---|---|---|
| Sam Houston State Teachers College; Huntsville, Tex. (1879) | Harmon Lowman | 4,190 C | State |
| San Diego, Univ. of, College for Men; San Diego, Calif. (1954) | V. Rev. Russell Wilson | 504 M | Catholic |
| San Diego College for Women; San Diego, Calif. (1949) | Mother Frances Danz | 517 F | Catholic |
| San Diego State Coll.; San Diego & Imperial Valley, Calif. (1897) | Malcolm A. Love | 11,074 C | State |
| San Fernando Valley State College; Northridge, Calif. (1958) | Ralph Prator | 6,200 C | State |
| San Francisco, University of; San Francisco, Calif. (1855) | V. Rev. J. F. X. Connolly | 4,009 C | Catholic |
| San Francisco Art Institute; San Francisco, Calif. (1874)[17] | Gurdon Woods | 203 C | Private |
| San Francisco College for Women; San Francisco, Calif. (1921)[2] | Mother Catherine Parks | 454 F | Catholic |
| San Francisco Conservatory of Music; San Francisco, Calif. (1917) | Robin Laufer | 37 C | Private |
| San Francisco State College; San Francisco, Calif. (1899) | Glenn S. Dumke | 11,874 C | State |
| San Jose State College; San Jose, Calif. (1857) | John T. Wahlquist | 14,288 C | State |
| San Luis Rey College; San Luis Rey, Calif. (1929) | Rev. Valentine Healy | 66 M | Catholic |
| Santa Clara, University of; Santa Clara & Los Gatos, Calif. (1851) | V. Rev. P. A. Donohoe | 1,816 C | Catholic |
| Sarah Lawrence College; Bronxville, N. Y. (1926) | Paul L. Ward | 468 F | Private |
| Scarritt College for Christian Workers; Nashville, Tenn. (1892) | D. Dillon Holt | 101 C | Methodist |
| Scranton, University of; Scranton, Pa. (1888) | V. Rev. John J. Long | 2,316 M | Catholic |
| Scripps College; Claremont, Calif. (1926) | Frederick Hard | 269 F | Private |
| Seattle Pacific College; Seattle, Wash. (1891)[2] | C. Dorr Demaray | 1,156 C | Methodist |
| Seattle University; Seattle, Wash. (1891) | V. Rev. A. A. Lemieux | 2,880 C | Catholic |
| Seton Hall University; South Orange, N. J. (1856)[2] | Rt. Rev. J. J. Dougherty | 9,449 C | Catholic |
| Seton Hill College; Greensburg, Pa. (1883) | Rev. William G. Ryan | 571 F | Private |
| Shepherd College; Shepherdstown, W. Va. (1871) | Oliver S. Ikenberry | 793 C | State |
| Shimer College; Mount Carroll, Ill. (1853) | F. Joseph Mullin | 246 C | Private |
| Shippensburg State College; Shippensburg, Pa. (1871) | Ralph E. Heiges | 1,320 C | State |
| Shorter College; Rome, Ga. (1873) | Randall H. Minor | 489 C | S. Baptist |
| Siena College; Memphis, Tenn. (1922) | Sister Albertus Magnus | 156 F | Private |
| Siena Heights College; Adrian, Mich. (1919) | Sister Benedicta Marie | 573 F | Catholic |
| Simmons College; Boston, Mass. (1899) | William E. Park | 1,428 F | Private |
| Simpson College; Indianola, Iowa (1860) | William E. Kerstetter | 684 C | Methodist |
| Sioux Falls College; Sioux Falls, S. Dak. (1883) | Reuben P. Jeschke | 492 C | Baptist |
| Skidmore College; Saratoga Springs, N. Y. (1911)[2] | Val H. Wilson | 1,259 F | Private |
| Slippery Rock State College; Slippery Rock, Pa. (1889) | Norman N. Weisenfluh | 1,386 C | State |
| Smith College; Northampton, Mass. (1871) | Thomas C. Mendenhall | 2,406 F | Private |
| Snow College; Ephraim, Utah (1888)[18] | Floyd S. Holm | 438 C | State |
| South, University of the; Sewanee, Tenn. (1857) | Edward McCrady | 690 M | Prot. Epis. |
| South Carolina, University of; Columbia, S. C. (1801)[2] | Robert L. Sumwalt | 5,543 C | State |
| South Carolina State College; Orangeburg, S. C. (1896) | B. C. Turner | 1,341 C | State |
| South Dakota, State University of; Vermillion, S. Dak. (1882) | Ila Delbert Weeks | 2,255 C | State |
| South Dakota School of Mines & Tech.; Rapid City, S. Dak. (1885) | F. L. Partlo | 800 C | State |
| South Dakota State Coll. of A & M Arts; Brookings, S. Dak. (1881) | Hilton M. Briggs | 2,503 C | State |
| Southeast Missouri State College; Cape Girardeau, Mo. (1873) | Mark F. Scully | 2,374 C | State |
| Southeastern Louisiana College; Hammond, La. (1925) | Luther H. Dyson | 1,934 C | State |
| Southeastern State College; Durant, Okla. (1909) | A. E. Shearer | 1,565 C | State |
| Southern California, University of; Los Angeles, Calif. (1880) | Norman Topping | 16,568 C[22] | Private |
| Southern Connecticut State College; New Haven, Conn. (1893) | Hilton C. Buley | 2,863 C | State |
| Southern Illinois University; Carbondale, Ill. (1869)[2] | Delyte W. Morris | 12,171 C | State |
| Southern Methodist University; Dallas, Tex. (1911) | Willis M. Tate | 4,996 C | Methodist |
| Southern Missionary College; Collegedale, Tenn. (1893)[2] | C. N. Rees | 553 C | 7th Day Adven. |
| Southern Oregon College; Ashland, Oreg. (1926) | Elmo N. Stevenson | 1,378 C | State |
| Southern State College; Magnolia, Ark. (1909) | Imon E. Bruce | 965 C | State |
| Southern State Teachers College; Springfield, S. Dak. (1897) | W. W. Ludeman | 550 C | State |
| Southern Univ. & A & M Coll.; Baton Rouge & New Orleans (1880) | Felton G. Clark | 5,128 C | State |
| Southern Utah, College of; Cedar City, Utah (1897)[18] | Royden C. Braithwaite | 752 C[9] | State |
| Southwest Missouri State College; Springfield, Mo. (1906) | Roy Ellis | 3,044 C | State |
| Southwest Texas State College; San Marcos, Tex. (1899) | J. G. Flowers | 2,508 C | State |
| Southwestern At Memphis; Memphis, Tenn. (1848) | Peyton Nalle Rhodes | 699 C | Presbyterian |
| Southwestern College; Winfield, Kans. (1885) | C. Orville Strohl | 582 C | Methodist |
| Southwestern Louisiana, University of; Lafayette, La. (1898) | Joel L. Fletcher | 4,488 C | State |
| Southwestern State College; Weatherford, Okla. (1903) | Al Harris | 1,838 C | State |
| Southwestern University; Georgetown, Tex. (1840) | Durwood Fleming | 653 C | Methodist |
| Spelman College. See Atlanta University System | | | |
| Spring Hill College; Mobile, Ala. (1830)[2] | V. Rev. A. Wm. Crandell | 1,256 C | Catholic |
| Springfield College; Springfield, Mass. (1885) | Glenn A. Olds | 1,210 C | Private |
| Stanford University; Stanford, Calif. (1885)[2] | J. E. Wallace Sterling | 8,877 C | Private |
| Stephen F. Austin State College; Nacogdoches, Tex. (1923) | R. W. Steen | 1,925 C | State |
| Sterling College; Sterling, Kans. (1887) | William M. McCreery | 449 C | U. Presbyterian |
| Stetson University; DeLand & St. Petersburg, Fla. (1883) | J. Ollie Edmunds | 1,331 C | S. Baptist |
| Steubenville, College of; Steubenville, Ohio (1946) | Rev. Kevin R. Keelan | 754 C | Private |
| Stevens Institute of Technology; Hoboken, N. J. (1870) | J. H. Davis | 1,890 M | Private |
| Stillman College; Tuscaloosa, Ala. (1876) | Samuel B. Hay | 450 C | Presbyterian |
| Stonehill College; North Easton, Mass. (1948) | Rev. R. H. Sullivan | 638 C | Catholic |
| Stout State College; Menomonie, Wis. (1893) | Verne C. Fryklund | 1,387 C | State |

| Institution, location and (date founded) | Chief executive | Students[1] | Control |
|---|---|---|---|
| Suffolk University; Boston, Mass. (1906) | Dennis C. Haley | 1,700 C | Private |
| Sul Ross State College; Alpine, Tex. (1917) | Bryan Wildenthal | 1,154 C | State |
| Sulpician Seminary of the Northwest; Kenmore, Wash. (1931)[19] | V. Rev. J. R. Sullivan | 300 M | Catholic |
| Susquehanna University; Selinsgrove, Pa. (1858) | Gustave W. Weber | 670 C | Lutheran |
| Swarthmore College; Swarthmore, Pa. (1864) | Courtney Smith | 937 C | Private |
| Sweet Briar College; Sweet Briar, Va. (1901) | Anne G. Pannell | 549 F | Private |
| Syracuse University; Syracuse & Utica, N. Y. (1870) | William P. Tolley | 16,481 C | Private |
| Talladega College; Talladega, Ala. (1867) | Arthur D. Gray | 411 C | Private |
| Tampa, University of; Tampa, Fla. (1931) | David M. Delo | 1,830 C | State |
| Tarkio College; Tarkio, Mo. (1883) | William H. Schechter | 307 C | U. Presbyterian |
| Taylor University; Upland, Ind. (1846) | B. Joseph Martin | 783 C | Private |
| Temple University; Philadelphia, Pa. (1884)[3] | Millard E. Gladfelter | 11,943 C | Private |
| Tennessee, University of; Knoxville, Tenn. (1794)[2] | Andrew David Holt | 10,918 C | State |
| Tennessee Agr. & Ind. State University; Nashville, Tenn. (1912) | Walter S. Davis | 3,833 C | State |
| Tennessee Polytechnic Institute; Cookeville, Tenn. (1915) | Everett Derryberry | 2,474 C | State |
| Tennessee Wesleyan College; Athens, Tenn. (1857) | Ralph W. Mohney | 614 C | Methodist |
| Texas, A & M College of; College Station, Tex. (1876) | Earl Rudder | 6,580 M | State |
| Texas, University of; Austin, Tex. | H. H. Ransom | 23,529 C | State |
|    Main University; Austin, Tex. (1883) | H. H. Ransom | 18,039 C | State |
|    Dental Branch; Houston, Tex. (1905) | John V. Olson | 427 C | State |
|    Medical Branch; Galveston, Tex. (1890) | John B. Truslow | 672 C | State |
|    Southwestern Medical School; Dallas, Tex. (1943) | A. J. Gill | 419 C | State |
|    Texas Western College; El Paso, Tex. (1913) | Joseph M. Ray | 3,972 C | State |
| Texas Christian University; Fort Worth, Tex. (1873) | McGruder E. Sadler | 5,681 C | Christian Chs. |
| Texas College of Arts & Ind.; Kingsville & Weslaco, Tex. (1917) | Ernest H. Poteet | 3,074 C | State |
| Texas Lutheran College; Seguin, Tex. (1891) | Marcus C. Rieke | 571 C | Lutheran |
| Texas Southern University; Houston, Tex. (1947) | Samuel M. Nabrit | 3,168 C | State |
| Texas Technological College; Lubbock, Tex. (1923) | R. C. Goodwin | 8,682 C | State |
| Texas Wesleyan College; Ft. Worth, Tex. (1891) | Law Sone | 1,193 C | Methodist |
| Texas Western College. See Texas, University of | ........ | ........ | ........ |
| Texas Woman's University; Denton, Tex. (1901) | John A. Guinn | 2,554 F | State |
| Thiel College; Greenville, Pa. (1866) | Chauncey G. Bly | 859 C | Lutheran |
| Tift College; Forsyth & Atlanta, Ga. (1849) | Carey T. Vinzant | 546 F | Baptist |
| Toledo, University of; Toledo, Ohio (1872) | William S. Carlson | 5,947 C | City |
| Tougaloo Southern Christian College; Tougaloo, Miss. (1869) | A. D. Beittel | 526 C | [20] |
| Transylvania College; Lexington, Ky. (1780) | Irvin E. Lunger | 527 C | Private |
| Trenton State College; Trenton, N. J. (1855) | Edwin L. Martin | 3,974 C | State |
| Trinity College; Burlington, Vt. (1925) | Sister Mary Claver | 320 F | Catholic |
| Trinity College; Hartford, Conn. (1823) | Albert C. Jacobs | 1,504 M | Private |
| Trinity College; Washington, D. C. (1897) | Sister Margaret | 699 F | Catholic |
| Trinity University; San Antonio, Tex. (1869) | James W. Laurie | 1,641 C | Presbyterian |
| Troy State College; Troy, Ala. (1887) | Charles B. Smith | 1,330 C | State |
| Tufts University; Medford & Boston, Mass. (1852)[21] | Nils Y. Wessell | 4,298 C | Private |
| Tulane University; New Orleans, La. (1834)[14] | H. E. Longenecker | 6,150 Co | Private |
| Tulsa, University of; Tulsa, Okla. (1894) | Ben G. Henneke | 4,384 C | Private |
| Tusculum College; Greeneville, Tenn. (1794) | Raymond C. Rankin | 386 C | Private |
| Tuskegee Institute; Tuskegee Institute, Ala. (1881) | L. H. Foster | 2,125 C | Private |
| Union College; Barbourville, Ky. (1879) | Mahlon A. Miller | 662 C | Methodist |
| Union College; Lincoln, Nebr., & Denver, Colo. (1891) | David J. Bieber | 668 C | 7th Day Adven. |
| Union College & University; Schenectady & Albany, N. Y. (1795) | Carter Davidson | 2,523 M | Private |
| Union University; Jackson, Tenn. (1825) | Warren F. Jones | 625 C | S. Baptist |
| U. S. Air Force Academy; Colorado Springs; Colo. (1955) | Maj. Gen. W. S. Stone | 1,769 M | National |
| U. S. Coast Guard Academy; New London, Conn. (1876) | R. Adm. S. H. Evans | 560 M | National |
| U. S. Merchant Marine Academy; Kings Point, N. Y. (1942) | R. Adm. G. McLintock | 900 M | National |
| U. S. Military Academy; West Point, N. Y. (1802) | Maj. Gen. W.Westmoreland | 2,512 M | National |
| U. S. Naval Academy; Annapolis, Md. (1845) | R. Adm. J. F. Davidson | 3,738 M | National |
| U. S. Naval Postgraduate School; Monterey, Calif. (1909) | R. Adm. M. E. Dornin | 1,261 C | National |
| Upland College; Upland, Calif. (1920) | John Z. Martin | 158 C | Breth. in Christ |
| Upper Iowa University; Fayette, Iowa (1857) | Eugene E. Garbee | 1,134 C | Private |
| Upsala College; East Orange, N. J. (1893) | Evald B. Lawson | 2,046 C | Lutheran |
| Ursinus College; Collegeville, Pa. (1869) | Donald L. Helfferich | 890 C | Private |
| Ursuline College; Louisville, Ky. (1938) | Mother M. Cosma | 350 F | Catholic |
| Ursuline College for Women; Cleveland, Ohio (1871) | Mother Marie Sands | 320 F | Catholic |
| Utah, University of; Salt Lake City, Utah (1850)[2] | A. Ray Olpin | 11,388 C[6] | State |
| Utah State Univ. of Agr. & App. Sciences; Logan, Utah (1888)[18] | Daryl Chase | 4,856 C | State |
| Valdosta State College; Valdosta, Ga. (1906) | J. Ralph Thaxton | 710 C | State |
| Valparaiso University; Valparaiso, Ind. (1859) | O. P. Kretzmann | 2,462 C | Lutheran |
| Vanderbilt University; Nashville, Tenn. (1872) | Harvie Branscomb | 3,585 C | Private |
| Vassar College; Poughkeepsie, N. Y. (1861) | Sarah Gibson Blanding | 1,445 F | Private |
| Vermont, University of; Burlington, Vt. (1791) | John T. Fey | 3,158 C | State |
| Villa Madonna College; Covington, Ky. (1921) | Rt. Rev. J. F. Murphy | 603 C | Catholic |
| Villa Maria College; Erie, Pa. (1925) | Mother M. A. A'Hearn | 733 F | Catholic |

| Institution, location and (date founded) | Chief executive | Students[1] | Control |
|---|---|---|---|
| Villanova University; Villanova, Pa. (1842) | Rev. John A. Klekotka | 4,882 M | Catholic |
| Virginia, Medical College of; Richmond, Va. (1838) | R. B. Smith, Jr. | 1,514 C | State |
| Virginia, University of; Charlottesville, Va. (1819)[2],[13] | Edgar F. Shannon, Jr. | 5,138 C | State |
| Virginia Military Institute; Lexington, Va. (1839) | Maj. Gen. G. R. E. Shell | 1,063 M | State |
| Virginia Polytechnic Institute; Blacksburg, Va. (1872)[16] | Walter S. Newman | 4,827 C[6] | State |
| Virginia State College; Petersburg & Norfolk, Va. (1882) | R. P. Daniel | 2,641 C | State |
| Virginia Union University; Richmond, Va. (1865) | Thomas H. Henderson | 1,017 C | Baptist |
| Viterbo College; La Crosse, Wis. (1931) | Sister M. Justille | 328 F | Catholic |
| Wabash College; Crawfordsville, Ind. (1832) | Byron K. Trippet | 621 M | Private |
| Wagner College; Staten Island, N. Y. (1883) | Richard H. Heindel | 1,528 C | Lutheran |
| Wake Forest College; Winston-Salem, N. C. (1834) | Harold W. Tribble | 2,248 C | Baptist |
| Walla Walla College; College Place, Wash. (1892)[2] | Percy W. Christian | 1,212 C | 7th Day Adven. |
| Wartburg College; Waverly, Iowa (1852) | C. H. Becker | 994 C | Lutheran |
| Washburn University of Topeka; Topeka, Kans. (1865) | W. J. McKeefery | 2,775 C | City |
| Washington, University of; Seattle, Wash. (1861) | Charles E. Odegaard | 18,143 C[6] | State |
| Washington & Jefferson College; Washington, Pa. (1781) | Boyd C. Patterson | 736 M | Private |
| Washington & Lee University; Lexington, Va. (1749) | Fred C. Cole | 1,100 M | Private |
| Washington College; Chestertown, Md. (1782) | Daniel Z. Gibson | 438 C | Private |
| Washington Missionary College. See Columbia Union College | | ...... | .......... |
| Washington State University; Pullman, Wash. (1890) | C. Clement French | 6,344 C | State |
| Washington University; St. Louis, Mo. (1853) | Ethan A. H. Shepley | 11,793 C | Private |
| Wayland Baptist College; Plainview, Tex. (1908) | Albert Hope Owen | 528 C | S. Baptist |
| Wayne State University; Detroit, Mich. (1868) | Clarence B. Hilberry | 20,980 C | State |
| Waynesburg College; Waynesburg & Uniontown, Pa. (1849) | Paul R. Stewart | 1,017 C | Presbyterian |
| Webb Institute of Naval Architecture; Glen Cove, N. Y. (1889) | William T. Alexander | 80 M | Private |
| Webster College; St. Louis, Mo. (1915) | Sister M. F. Barberis | 677 F | Catholic |
| Wellesley College; Wellesley, Mass. (1870) | Margaret Clapp | 1,723 F | Private |
| Wells College; Aurora, N. Y. (1868) | L. J. Long | 456 F | Private |
| Wesleyan College; Macon, Ga. (1836) | W. Earl Strickland | 485 F | Methodist |
| Wesleyan University; Middletown, Conn. (1831) | Victor L. Butterfield | 925 M | Private |
| West Chester State College; West Chester, Pa. (1871) | T. Noel Stern | 2,676 C | State |
| West Liberty State College; West Liberty, W. Va. (1837)[2] | Paul N. Elbin | 1,286 C | State |
| West Texas State College; Canyon, Tex. (1910) | James P. Cornette | 2,981 C | State |
| West Virginia Institute of Technology; Montgomery, W. Va. (1895) | William B. Axtell | 952 C | State |
| West Virginia State College; Institute, W. Va. (1891) | William J. L. Wallace | 1,763 C | State |
| West Virginia University; Morgantown, W. Va. (1867) | Clyde L. Colson | 6,299 C | State |
| West Virginia Wesleyan College; Buckhannon, W. Va. (1890) | Stanley H. Martin | 1,097 C | Methodist |
| Western Carolina College; Cullowhee, N. C. (1889) | Paul A. Reid | 1,438 C | State |
| Western College for Women; Oxford, Ohio (1853) | Herrick B. Young | 391 F | Private |
| Western Illinois University; Macomb, Ill. (1899) | A. L. Knoblauch | 2,987 C | State |
| Western Kentucky State College; Bowling Green, Ky. (1906) | Kelly Thompson | 3,532 C | State |
| Western Maryland College; Westminster, Md. (1867) | Lowell S. Ensor | 730 C | Methodist |
| Western Michigan University; Kalamazoo, Mich. (1903) | James W. Miller | 8,827 C | State |
| Western Montana College of Education; Dillon, Mont. (1897) | James E. Short | 485 C | State |
| Western Reserve University; Cleveland, Ohio (1826) | John Schoff Millis | 7,336 C | Private |
| Western State College of Colorado; Gunnison, Colo. (1901) | Grant Venn | 1,050 C | State |
| Western Washington State College; Bellingham, Wash. (1899) | James L. Jarrett | 2,891 C | State |
| Westmar College; Le Mars, Iowa (1890) | H. H. Kalas | 517 C | Evan. Un. Breth. |
| Westminster College; Fulton, Mo. (1851) | Robert L. D. Davidson | 575 M | Presbyterian |
| Westminster College; New Wilmington, Pa. (1852) | Will W. Orr | 1,326 C | U. Presbyterian |
| Westminster College; Salt Lake City, Utah (1875) | Frank E. Duddy, Jr. | 460 C | Interdenom. |
| Westminster Theological Seminary; Philadelphia, Pa. (1929) | Cornelius Van Til | 100 M | Private |
| Westmont College; Santa Barbara, Calif. (1940) | Roger J. Voskuyl | 456 C | Private |
| Wheaton College; Norton, Mass. (1834) | Elizabeth S. May | 779 F | Private |
| Wheaton College; Wheaton, Ill. (1860)[2] | V. Raymond Edman | 1,791 C | Private |
| Wheelock College; Boston, Mass. (1888)[2] | Frances Mayfarth | 428 F | Private |
| Whitman College; Walla Walla, Wash. (1859) | Louis B. Perry | 843 C | Private |
| Whittier College; Whittier, Calif. (1901)[2] | Paul S. Smith | 1,349 C | Private |
| Whitworth College; Spokane, Wash. (1890) | Frank F. Warren | 1,421 C | Private |
| Wichita, University of; Wichita, Kans. (1895) | Harry F. Corbin | 5,186 C | City |
| Wiley College; Marshall, Tex. (1873) | T. W. Cole, Sr. | 447 C | Methodist |
| Wilkes College; Wilkes-Barre, Pa. (1933) | Eugene S. Farley | 1,577 C | Private |
| Willamette University; Salem, Oreg. (1842) | G. Herbert Smith | 1,195 C | Methodist |
| William & Mary, College of; Williamsburg, Va. (1693)[2] | Davis Y. Paschall | 2,271 C | State |
| William Carey College; Hattiesburg, Miss. (1906) | J. Ralph Noonkester | 434 C | S. Baptist |
| William Jewell College; Liberty, Mo. (1849) | Walter Pope Binns | 931 C | Baptist |
| William Penn College; Oskaloosa, Iowa (1873) | S. A. Watson | 363 C | Quaker |
| William Smith College. See Hobart & William Smith Colleges | | ...... | .......... |
| Williams College; Williamstown, Mass. (1793) | John E. Sawyer | 1,130 M | Private |
| Willimantic State College; Willimantic, Conn. (1889) | J. Eugene Smith | 391 C | State |
| Wilmington College; Wilmington, Ohio (1870) | James M. Read | 633 C | Quaker |
| Wilson College; Chambersburg, Pa. (1869) | Paul Swain Havens | 538 F | Private |

| Institution, location and (date founded) | Chief executive | Students[1] | Control |
|---|---|---|---|
| Winona State College; Winona, Minn. (1858) | Nels Minné | 1,177 C | State |
| Winston-Salem Teachers College; Winston-Salem, N. C. | F. L. Atkins | 912 C[25] | State |
| Winthrop College; Rock Hill, S. C. (1886) | Charles Shepard Davis | 1,548 F | State |
| Wisconsin, University of; Madison & Milwaukee, Wis. (1848)[2] | Conrad A. Elvehjem | 27,386 C | State |
| Wisconsin State College; Eau Claire, Wis. (1916) | Leonard Haas | 2,110 C | State |
| Wisconsin State College; La Crosse, Wis. (1909) | Rexford S. Mitchell | 1,809 C | State |
| Wisconsin State College; Oshkosh, Wis. (1871) | Roger E. Guiles | 2,184 C | State |
| Wisconsin State College; River Falls, Wis. (1874) | E. H. Kleinpell | 1,365 C | State |
| Wisconsin State College; Stevens Point, Wis. (1894) | William C. Hansen | 2,420 C | State |
| Wisconsin State College; Superior, Wis. (1896) | Jim Dan Hill | 1,303 C[22] | State |
| Wisconsin State College; Whitewater, Wis. (1868) | Robert C. Williams | 1,886 C | State |
| Wisconsin State College & Inst. of Tech.; Platteville, Wis. (1866) | Bjarne R. Ullsvik | 1,623 C | State |
| Wittenberg University; Springfield, Ohio (1845) | Clarence C. Stoughton | 2,526 C | Un. Lutheran |
| Wofford College; Spartanburg, S. C. (1854) | Charles F. Marsh | 703 M | Methodist |
| Woodstock College; Woodstock, Md. (1869) | Rev. Edward J. Sponga | 257 M | Catholic |
| Wooster, College of; Wooster, Ohio (1866) | Howard F. Lowry | 1,264 C | Presbyterian |
| Worcester Polytechnic Institute; Worcester, Mass. (1865) | Arthur Bronwell | 1,133 M | Private |
| Wyoming, University of; Laramie, Wyo. (1887) | George Duke Humphrey | 3,663 C | State |
| Xavier University; Cincinnati, Ohio (1831) | V. Rev. Paul L. O'Connor | 3,662 M | Catholic |
| Xavier University of Louisiana; New Orleans, La. (1925) | Sister M. Josephina | 825 C | Catholic |
| Yale University; New Haven, Conn. (1701) | A. Whitney Griswold | 7,550 M | Private |
| Yankton College; Yankton, S. Dak. (1881) | Adrian Rondileau | 311 C | Private |
| Yeshiva University; New York, N. Y. (1886) | Samuel Belkin | 4,951 Co | Jewish |
| Youngstown University; Youngstown, Ohio (1908) | Howard W. Jones | 6,682 C | Private |

[1] M—all or predominantly male; F—all or predominantly female; C—coeducational; Co—co-ordinate, i.e., separate schools for men and women. In schools marked M and F, members of the opposite sex are in many cases admitted for special courses or graduate work.
[2] Other campus or campuses elsewhere.
[3] Formerly Emmanuel Missionary College.
[4] Barnard College is women's school of Columbia University.
[5] Pembroke College is women's school of Brown University.
[6] Enrollment for fall 1960. Formerly Washington Missionary College.

[8] Douglass College is women's school of Rutgers University.
[9] Enrollment for winter 1960–61.
[10] In Sept. 1961 will move to Laurinburg, N. C., with new name of St. Andrews Presbyterian College, under presidency of Ansley C. Moore.
[11] Radcliffe College is women's school of Harvard University.
[12] Formerly College of Medical Evangelists.
[13] Mary Washington College is women's school of University of Virginia.
[14] Newcomb College is women's school of Tulane University.
[15] Formerly Los Angeles County Art Institute.
[16] Radford College is women's school of Virginia Polytechnic Institute.

[17] Formerly California School of Fine Arts.
[18] Snow College and College of Southern Utah are branches of Utah State University.
[19] Formerly St. Edward's Seminary.
[20] American Missionary Assn. and United Christian Mission Society.
[21] Jackson College is women's school of Tufts University.
[22] Enrollment for spring 1960.
[23] Enrollment for spring 1959.
[24] Hobart College (1822) is for men; William Smith College (1908) is for women.
[25] Enrollment for fall 1959.
[26] Enrollment for campus at Norman.

# U. S. Junior Colleges

(*Source:* **Junior College Journal**, *Jan. 1961. Published by American Association of Junior Colleges*)

| Institution | Location |
|---|---|
| **ALABAMA** | |
| *Privately controlled* | |
| Alabama Christian College | Montgomery |
| Daniel Payne College | Birmingham |
| Marion Institute | Marion |
| Sacred Heart Junior College | Cullman |
| Snead Junior College | Boaz |
| The Southern Union College | Wadley |
| Walker College | Jasper |
| **ALASKA** | |
| *Publicly controlled* | |
| Anchorage Community College | Anchorage |
| Juneau–Douglas Comm. Coll. | Juneau |
| Ketchikan Comm. College | Ketchikan |
| Palmer Community College | Palmer |
| *Privately controlled* | |
| Sheldon Jackson Junior College | Sitka |

| Institution | Location |
|---|---|
| **ARIZONA** | |
| *Publicly controlled* | |
| Eastern Arizona Junior College | Thatcher |
| Phoenix College | Phoenix |
| **ARKANSAS** | |
| *Publicly controlled* | |
| Arkansas St. Coll. Beebe Br. | Beebe |
| *Privately controlled* | |
| Fort Smith Junior College | Fort Smith |
| Shorter College | Little Rock |
| Southern Baptist College | Walnut Ridge |
| **CALIFORNIA** | |
| *Publicly controlled* | |
| Allan Hancock College | Santa Maria |
| American River Jr. College | Sacramento |
| Antelope Valley College | Lancaster |

| Institution | Location |
|---|---|
| Bakersfield College.................... | Bakersfield |
| Cabrillo College...................... | Watsonville |
| Cerritos Junior College............... | Norwalk |
| Chaffey College...................... | Alta Loma |
| Citrus College....................... | Azusa |
| City College of San Francisco......... | San Francisco |
| Coalinga College..................... | Coalinga |
| College of Marin..................... | Kentfield |
| Compton College..................... | Compton |
| Contra Costa College................. | San Pablo |
| Diablo Valley College................ | Concord |
| East Los Angeles College............. | Los Angeles |
| El Camino College.................... | El Camino |
| Foothill College..................... | Mountain View |
| Fresno City College.................. | Fresno |
| Fullerton Junior College.............. | Fullerton |
| Glendale College..................... | Glendale |
| Hartnell College..................... | Salinas |
| Imperial Valley College.............. | Imperial |
| Lassen Junior College................ | Susanville |
| Long Beach City College.............. | Long Beach |
| Los Angeles City College............. | Los Angeles |
| Los Angeles Harbor College........... | Los Angeles |
| Los Angeles Metropolitan College of Business........................... | Los Angeles |
| Los Angeles Pierce College........... | Woodland Hills |
| Los Angeles Trade–Technical College... | Los Angeles |
| Los Angeles Valley College........... | Van Nuys |
| Modesto Junior College............... | Modesto |
| Monterey Peninsula College........... | Monterey |
| Mt. San Antonio Junior College........ | Walnut |
| Napa Junior College.................. | Napa |
| Oakland City College................. | Oakland |
| Oceanside–Carlsbad Junior College..... | Oceanside |
| Orange Coast College................. | Costa Mesa |
| Palo Verde College................... | Blythe |
| Palomar College...................... | San Marcos |
| Pasadena City College................ | Pasadena |
| Porterville College................... | Porterville |
| Reedley College...................... | Reedley |
| Riverside City College................ | Riverside |
| Sacramento City College.............. | Sacramento |
| Sacramento Evening City College....... | Sacramento |
| San Benito College................... | Hollister |
| San Bernardino Valley College......... | San Bernardino |
| San Diego Junior College............. | San Diego |
| San Jose City College................ | San Jose |
| San Mateo, College of................ | San Mateo |
| Santa Ana College................... | Santa Ana |
| Santa Barbara City College........... | Santa Barbara |
| Santa Monica City College............ | Santa Monica |
| Santa Rosa Junior College............ | Santa Rosa |
| Sequoias, College of the.............. | Visalia |
| Shasta College....................... | Redding |
| Sierra College....................... | Auburn |
| Siskiyous, College of the............. | Weed |
| Stockton College..................... | Stockton |
| Taft College......................... | Taft |
| Vallejo Junior College................ | Vallejo |
| Ventura College...................... | Ventura |
| Yuba College........................ | Marysville |

Privately controlled

| Institution | Location |
|---|---|
| California Concordia College........... | Oakland |
| Cogswell Polytechnic College.......... | San Francisco |
| Deep Springs College................. | Deep Springs |
| Humphreys College................... | Stockton |
| Los Angeles Pacific College........... | Los Angeles |
| Menlo College....................... | Menlo Park |

## COLORADO

Publicly controlled

| Institution | Location |
|---|---|
| Ft. Lewis Agric. & Mech. College....... | Durango |

| Institution | Location |
|---|---|
| Lamar Junior College................. | Lamar |
| Mesa County Junior College........... | Grand Junction |
| Northeastern Junior College........... | Sterling |
| Otero Junior College................. | La Junta |
| Pueblo Junior College................ | Pueblo |
| Trinidad State Junior College......... | Trinidad |

Privately controlled

| Institution | Location |
|---|---|
| Colorado Woman's College............ | Denver |

## CONNECTICUT

Privately controlled

| Institution | Location |
|---|---|
| Connecticut, Junior College of......... | Bridgeport |
| Hartford College..................... | Hartford |
| Mitchell College..................... | New London |
| New Haven College................... | New Haven |
| Quinnipiac College................... | Hamden |
| St. Thomas Seminary................. | Bloomfield |

## DELAWARE

Privately controlled

| Institution | Location |
|---|---|
| Wesley College...................... | Dover |

## DISTRICT OF COLUMBIA

Privately controlled

| Institution | Location |
|---|---|
| George Washington Univ. Jr. Coll....... | Washington |
| Georgetown Visitation Jr. Col.......... | Washington |
| Immaculata Junior College............ | Washington |
| Marjorie Webster Jr. Col.............. | Washington |
| Mt. Vernon Junior College............ | Washington |
| Strayer Jr. Col. of Finance............ | Washington |
| Wash. Hall Junior College............ | Washington |

## FLORIDA

Publicly controlled

| Institution | Location |
|---|---|
| Brevard Junior College............... | Cocoa |
| Central Florida Junior College......... | Ocala |
| Chipola Junior College................ | Marianna |
| Daytona Beach Junior College......... | Daytona Beach |
| Gibbs Junior College................. | St. Petersburg |
| Gulf Coast Junior College............. | Panama City |
| Hampton Junior College............... | Ocala |
| Manatee Junior College............... | Bradenton |
| North Florida Junior College.......... | Madison |
| Palm Beach Junior College............ | Lake Worth |
| Pensacola Junior College.............. | Pensacola |
| Roosevelt Junior College.............. | W. Palm Beach |
| Rosenwald Comm. Jr. College......... | Panama City |
| St. Johns River Junior College......... | Palatka |
| St. Petersburg Junior College......... | St. Petersburg |
| Volusia County Comm. College........ | Daytona Beach |
| Washington Junior College............ | Pensacola |

Privately controlled

| Institution | Location |
|---|---|
| Broward County, Junior College of...... | Ft. Lauderdale |
| Carver Junior College................. | Cocoa |
| Dade County Junior College........... | Miami |
| Edward Waters College................ | Jacksonville |
| Florida Christian College............. | Tampa |
| Indian River Junior College............ | Ft. Pierce |
| Jacksonville Univ. Jr. College.......... | Jacksonville |
| Lincoln Junior College................ | Ft. Pierce |
| Orlando Junior College............... | Orlando |
| St. Leo College...................... | St. Leo |
| Suwanee River Junior College......... | Madison |

## GEORGIA

Publicly controlled

| Institution | Location |
|---|---|
| Abraham Baldwin Agric. Col........... | Tifton |
| Armstrong Col. of Savannah........... | Savannah |
| Augusta College..................... | Augusta |
| Columbus College.................... | Columbus |

| Institution | Location |
|---|---|
| Georgia Military College | Milledgeville |
| Georgia Southwestern College | Americus |
| Middle Georgia College | Cochran |
| South Georgia College | Douglas |

Privately controlled

| Institution | Location |
|---|---|
| Andrew College | Cuthbert |
| Birdwood Junior College | Thomasville |
| Brewton Parker College | Mt. Vernon |
| Emmanuel College | Franklin Sprgs. |
| Emory-at-Oxford | Oxford |
| Gordon Military College | Barnesville |
| Norman College | Norman Park |
| Reinhardt College | Waleska |
| Truett-McConnell College | Cleveland |
| Young Harris College | Young Harris |

## HAWAII

Privately controlled

| | |
|---|---|
| The Church College of Hawaii | Laie, Oahu |
| Maunaolu College | Paia, Maui |

## IDAHO

Publicly controlled

| | |
|---|---|
| Boise Junior College | Boise |
| Lewis-Clark Normal Sch | Lewiston |
| North Idaho Junior College | Coeur d'Alene |

Privately controlled

| | |
|---|---|
| College of St. Gertrude | Cottonwood |
| Ricks College | Rexburg |

## ILLINOIS

Publicly controlled

| | |
|---|---|
| Belleville Junior College | Belleville |
| Bloom Township Community College | Chicago Heights |
| Centralia Township Jr. Col | Centralia |
| Chicago City Junior College | |
| Amundsen Branch | Chicago |
| Bogan Branch | Chicago |
| Crane Branch | Chicago |
| Fenger Branch | Chicago |
| Southeast Branch | Chicago |
| Wilson Branch | Chicago |
| Wright Branch | Chicago |
| Danville Junior College | Danville |
| Elgin Community College | Elgin |
| Joliet Junior College | Joliet |
| La Salle–Peru–Oglesby Jr. Col | La Salle |
| Lyons Township Jr. Col | La Grange |
| Moline Community College | Moline |
| Morton Junior College | Cicero |
| Mt. Vernon Com. Col | Mt. Vernon |
| Thornton Junior College | Harvey |

Privately controlled

| | |
|---|---|
| Canton Junior College | Canton |
| De Lourdes College (Junior) | Des Plaines |
| The Felician College | Chicago |
| Kendall College | Evanston |
| Lincoln College | Lincoln |
| Mallinckrodt College | Wilmette |
| Monticello College | Alton |
| Peoria College of Bradley Univ. | Peoria |
| St. Bede Junior College | Peru |
| St. Joseph's Seminary | Westmont |
| Springfield Junior College | Springfield |
| Trinity College | Worth |

## INDIANA

Publicly controlled

| | |
|---|---|
| Vincennes University | Vincennes |

| Institution | Location |
|---|---|
| Privately controlled | |
| Ancilla Domini College | Donaldson |

## IOWA

Publicly controlled

| | |
|---|---|
| Boone Junior College | Boone |
| Burlington College | Burlington |
| Centerville Comm. College | Centerville |
| Clarinda Community College | Clarinda |
| Clinton Junior College | Clinton |
| Creston Community College | Creston |
| Eagle Grove Junior College | Eagle Grove |
| Ellsworth Junior College | Iowa Falls |
| Emmetsburg Comm. College | Emmetsburg |
| Estherville Junior College | Estherville |
| Fort Dodge Community College | Fort Dodge |
| Keokuk Community College | Keokuk |
| Marshalltown Jr. College | Marshalltown |
| Mason City Junior College | Mason City |
| Muscatine Junor College | Muscatine |
| Webster City Junior College | Webster City |

Privately controlled

| | |
|---|---|
| Dordt College | Sioux Center |
| Grand View College | Des Moines |
| Mt. St. Clare College | Clinton |
| Northwestern College | Orange City |
| Ottumwa Heights College | Ottumwa |
| Waldorf College | Forest City |

## KANSAS

Publicly controlled

| | |
|---|---|
| Arkansas City Junior College | Arkansas City |
| Chanute Junior College | Chanute |
| Coffeyville College | Coffeyville |
| Dodge City College | Dodge City |
| El Dorado Junior College | El Dorado |
| Fort Scott Junior College | Fort Scott |
| Garden City Junior College | Garden City |
| Highland Junior College | Highland |
| Hutchinson Junior College | Hutchinson |
| Independence Comm. Col | Independence |
| Iola Junior College | Iola |
| Kansas City Junior College | Kansas City |
| Parsons Junior College | Parsons |
| Pratt Junior College | Pratt |

Privately controlled

| | |
|---|---|
| Central College | McPherson |
| Donnelly College | Kansas City |
| Friends Bible School | Haviland |
| Hesston College | Hesston |
| Miltonvale Wesleyan | Miltonvale |
| St. John's College | Winfield |

## KENTUCKY

Publicly controlled

| | |
|---|---|
| Paducah Junior College | Paducah |

Privately controlled

| | |
|---|---|
| Bethel College | Hopkinsville |
| Caney Junior College | Pippa Passes |
| Lees Junior College | Jackson |
| Lindsey Wilson College | Columbia |
| Loretto Junior College | Nerinx |
| Midway Junior College | Midway |
| St. Catharine Junior College | St. Catharine |
| Sue Bennett College | London |

| Institution | Location |
|---|---|

**LOUISIANA**

Privately controlled

St. Joseph Seminary.................. St. Benedict

**MAINE**

Publicly controlled

Univ. of Maine in Portland............. Portland

Privately controlled

Oblate College & Seminary............ Bar Harbor
Thomas Junior College............... Waterville
Westbrook Junior College............. Portland

**MARYLAND**

Publicly controlled

Baltimore Junior College.............. Baltimore
Catonsville Community College........ Catonsville
Charles County Junior College.......... La Plata
Essex Community College............. Essex
Frederick Community College........... Frederick
Hagerstown Junior College............ Hagerstown
Harford Junior College............... Bel Air
Montgomery Junior College............ Takoma Park
Prince George's Comm. Coll............ Suitland
St. Mary's Seminary Junior College..... St. Mary's City

Privately controlled

Baltimore College of Commerce........ Baltimore
Baltimore Jr. Coll., Univ. of............ Baltimore
Eastern College..................... Baltimore
St. Charles College.................. Catonsville
St. Peters College................... Baltimore
Villa Julie College................... Stevenson
Xaverian College.................... Silver Spring

**MASSACHUSETTS**

Publicly controlled

Holyoke Junior College............... Holyoke
Newton Junior College................ Newtonville
Quincy Junior College................ Quincy

Privately controlled

Bay Path Junior College.............. Longmeadow
Becker Junior College................ Worcester
Berkshire Community College.......... Pittsfield
Boston University of Basic Studies...... Boston
Bradford Junior College.............. Bradford
Burdett College..................... Boston
Cambridge Junior College............ Cambridge
Chamberlayne Junior College.......... Boston
Dean Junior College................. Franklin
Endicott Junior College............... Beverly
Fisher Junior College................ Boston
Franklin Tech. Institute.............. Boston
Garland Junior College............... Boston
Lasell Junior College................ Auburndale
Leicester Junior College.............. Leicester
Nichols College of Bus. Adm.......... Dudley
Pine Manor Junior College............ Wellesley
Wentworth Institute................. Boston
Worcester Junior College............. Worcester

**MICHIGAN**

Publicly controlled

Alpena Community College............ Alpena
Bay City Junior College.............. Bay City
Community Coll. & Tech. Inst......... Benton Harbor
Flint Comm. Jr. Coll................. Flint
Gogebic Community College........... Ironwood
Grand Rapids Junior College.......... Grand Rapids

| Institution | Location |
|---|---|

Henry Ford Community College....... Dearborn
Highland Park Junior College......... Highland Park
Jackson Junior College............... Jackson
Kellogg Community College............ Battle Creek
Lansing Community College........... Lansing
Muskegon Community College......... Muskegon
North Central Michigan Coll.......... Petoskey
Northwestern Michigan College....... Traverse City
Port Huron Junior College............ Port Huron
South Macomb Community College..... Warren

Privately controlled

Spring Arbor College................. Spring Arbor
Suomi College...................... Hancock

**MINNESOTA**

Publicly controlled

Austin Junior College................ Austin
Brainerd Junior College.............. Brainerd
Ely Junior College................... Ely
Eveleth Junior College............... Eveleth
Hibbing Junior College............... Hibbing
Itasca Junior College................ Coleraine
Rochester Junior College............. Rochester
Virginia Junior College............... Virginia
Worthington Junior College........... Worthington

Privately controlled

Bethany Lutheran College............ Mankato
Concordia College................... St. Paul
Crosier Seminary.................... Onamia

**MISSISSIPPI**

Publicly controlled

Coahoma Junior College.............. Clarksdale
Copiah–Lincoln Junior College......... Wesson
East Central Junior College........... Decatur
East Mississippi Jr. Coll.............. Scooba
Harris Junior College................ Meridian
Hinds Junior College................ Raymond
Holmes Junior College............... Goodman
Itawamba Junior College............. Fulton
Jones County Junior College.......... Ellisville
Meridian Municipal Jr. Coll........... Meridian
Northeast Mississippi Junior College... Booneville
Northwest Mississippi Junior College.... Senatobia
Pearl River Junior College........... Poplarville
Perkinston Junior College............ Perkinston
Southwest Mississippi Junior College ... Summit
Sunflower Junior College............. Moorhead
Utica Junior College................. Utica

Privately controlled

All Saints' Episcopal Junior College..... Vicksburg
J. P. Campbell College............... Jackson
Clarke Memorial College............. Newton
Gulf Park College................... Gulfport
Mary Holmes College................ West Point
Natchez Junior College.............. Natchez
Okolona College.................... Okolona
Piney Woods Junior College.......... Piney Woods
Prentiss Institute................... Prentiss
Wood Junior College................ Mathiston

**MISSOURI**

Publicly controlled

Flat River Junior College............. Flat River
Harris Teachers College.............. St. Louis
Joplin Junior College................ Joplin

| Institution | Location |
|---|---|
| Kansas City, Junior College of | Kansas City |
| Moberly Junior College | Moberly |
| St. Joseph Junior College | St. Joseph |
| Trenton Junior College | Trenton |

Privately controlled

| | |
|---|---|
| Christian College | Columbia |
| Cottey College | Nevada |
| Hannibal–LaGrange College | Hannibal |
| Kemper School, The | Boonville |
| Mercy Junior College | St. Louis |
| St. Mary's Junior College | O'Fallon |
| St. Paul's College | Concordia |
| School of the Ozarks, Jr. Coll. of | Point Lookout |
| Southwest Baptist College | Bolivar |
| Stephens College | Columbia |
| Wentworth Military Academy | Lexington |
| William Woods College | Fulton |

## MONTANA

Publicly controlled

| | |
|---|---|
| Custer County Junior College | Miles City |
| Dawson County Junior College | Glendive |

## NEBRASKA

Publicly controlled

| | |
|---|---|
| Fairbury Junior College | Fairbury |
| McCook College | McCook |
| Norfolk Junior College | Norfolk |
| Scottsbluff College | Scottsbluff |

Privately controlled

| | |
|---|---|
| Luther Junior College | Wahoo |

## NEW HAMPSHIRE

Privately controlled

| | |
|---|---|
| Colby Junior College | New London |

## NEW JERSEY

Publicly controlled

| | |
|---|---|
| Trenton Junior College | Trenton |

Privately controlled

| | |
|---|---|
| Assumption Junior College | Mendham |
| Centenary College for Women | Hackettstown |
| Immaculate Conception Junior College | Lodi |
| Monmouth College | West Long Branch |
| Mother of the Savior Seminary | Blackwood |
| St. Joseph's College | Princeton |
| Tombrock Junior College | Paterson |
| Union Junior College | Cranford |
| Villa Walsh College | Morristown |

## NEW MEXICO

Publicly controlled

| | |
|---|---|
| Carlsbad Community College | Carlsbad |
| New Mexico Military Inst. | Roswell |

## NEW YORK

Publicly controlled

| | |
|---|---|
| Auburn Community College | Auburn |
| Bronx Community College | Bronx |
| Broome Tech. Community College | Binghamton |
| Corning Community College | Corning |
| Dutchess Community College | Poughkeepsie |
| Erie County Tech. Inst. | Williamsville |
| Fashion Inst. of Tech. | New York |
| Hudson Valley Community College | Troy |
| Jamestown Community College | Jamestown |
| Mohawk Valley Tech. Inst. | Utica |

| Institution | Location |
|---|---|
| New York City Community College | Brooklyn |
| Orange County Community College | Middletown |
| State University of New York | |
|   Agricultural & Tech. Inst. | Alfred |
|   Agricultural & Tech. Inst. | Canton |
|   Agricultural & Tech. Inst. | Cobleskill |
|   Agricultural & Tech. Inst. | Delhi |
|   Agricultural & Tech. Inst. | Farmingdale |
|   Agricultural & Tech. Inst. | Morrisville |
| Staten Island Community College | Staten Island |
| Westchester Community College | Valhalla |

Privately controlled

| | |
|---|---|
| Bellarmine College | Plattsburgh |
| Bennett College | Millbrook |
| Briarcliff College | Briarcliff Manor |
| Catharine McAuley College | Rochester |
| Cazenovia Junior College | Cazenovia |
| Concordia Collegiate Inst. Jr. College | Bronxville |
| Divine Word Seminary | Conesus |
| Epiphany Apostolic College | Newburgh |
| Eymard Preparatory Sem. | Hyde Park |
| Finch College | New York |
| Holy Cross Preparatory | Dunkirk |
| Junior College of Albany | Albany |
| La Salette Seminary | Altamont |
| Mater Christi Seminary | Albany |
| Nassau Communtiy College | Mineola |
| New York Institute of Technology | New York |
| Our Lady of Hope Mission Sem. | Newburgh |
| Packer Collegiate Institute | Brooklyn |
| Paul Smith's College | Paul Smiths |
| Queen of the Apostles College | Harriman |
| Queensborough Community College | Bayside |
| Rockland Community College | Suffern |
| Saint Clare College | Williamsville |
| Saint Joseph Seraphic Sem. | Callicoon |
| Sancta Maria Junior College | Buffalo |
| Suffolk Community College | Lake Ronkonkoma |
| William H. Miner, The Agricultural Research Institute | Chazy |

## NORTH CAROLINA

Publicly controlled

| | |
|---|---|
| Asheville-Biltmore College | Asheville |
| Carver College | Charlotte |
| Charlotte College | Charlotte |
| Gaston Technical Institute | Gastonia |
| Wilmington College | Wilmington |

Privately controlled

| | |
|---|---|
| Brevard College | Brevard |
| Campbell College | Buie's Creek |
| Chowan College | Murfreesboro |
| Gardner-Webb Junior College | Boiling Springs |
| Immanuel Lutheran College | Greensboro |
| Lees-McRae College | Banner Elk |
| Louisburg College | Louisburg |
| Mars Hill College | Mars Hill |
| Mitchell College | Statesville |
| Mt. Olive Junior College | Mount Olive |
| Oak Ridge Military Institute | Oak Ridge |
| Peace College | Raleigh |
| Pineland College and Edwards Military Institute | Salemburg |
| Presbyterian Junior College | Maxton |
| Sacred Heart Junior College | Belmont |
| St. Mary's College | Raleigh |
| Warren Wilson Junior College | Swannanoa |
| Wingate College | Wingate |

| Institution | Location |
|---|---|

**NORTH DAKOTA**

Publicly controlled

| Institution | Location |
|---|---|
| Bismarck Junior College............. | Bismarck |
| Devils Lake Junior College........... | Devils Lake |
| North Dakota School of Forestry....... | Bottineau |
| North Dakota State School of Science... | Wahpeton |

**OHIO**

Privately controlled

| Institution | Location |
|---|---|
| Franklin University.................. | Columbus |
| Lourdes Junior College............... | Sylvania |
| Ohio College of Applied Science....... | Cincinnati |
| Salmon P. Chase College.............. | Cincinnati |
| Sinclair College..................... | Dayton |
| Tiffin University..................... | Tiffin |
| Urbana Junior College................ | Urbana |

**OKLAHOMA**

Publicly controlled

| Institution | Location |
|---|---|
| Altus Junior College................. | Altus |
| Cameron State Agricultural College.... | Lawton |
| Connors State Agricultural College.... | Warner |
| Eastern Oklahoma A & M College....... | Wilburton |
| El Reno Junior College............... | El Reno |
| Murray State Agricultural College..... | Tishomingo |
| Muskogee Junior College.............. | Muskogee |
| Northeastern Oklahoma A & M College.. | Miami |
| Northern Oklahoma Junior College..... | Tonkawa |
| Oklahoma Military Academy........... | Claremore |
| Poteau Community College............ | Poteau |
| Sayre Junior College................. | Sayre |
| Seminole Junior College.............. | Seminole |

Privately controlled

| Institution | Location |
|---|---|
| Bacone College...................... | Bacone |
| Oklahoma Christian College........... | Oklahoma City |
| St. Gregory's College................ | Shawnee |

**OREGON**

Publicly controlled

| Institution | Location |
|---|---|
| Central Oregon College............... | Bend |
| Oregon Technical Institute............ | Klamath Falls |

Privately controlled

| Institution | Location |
|---|---|
| Concordia College.................... | Portland |
| Multnomah College................... | Portland |

**PENNSYLVANIA**

Publicly controlled

| Institution | Location |
|---|---|
| Hershey Junior College............... | Hershey |
| Pennsylvania State University Centers | |
| .............................. | Allentown |
| .............................. | Altoona |
| .............................. | DuBois |
| .............................. | Erie |
| .............................. | Hazleton |
| .............................. | McKeesport |
| .............................. | New Castle |
| .............................. | New Kensington |
| .............................. | Abington |
| .............................. | Pottsville |
| .............................. | Scranton |
| .............................. | Wilkes-Barre |
| .............................. | Wyomissing |
| .............................. | York |

Privately controlled

| Institution | Location |
|---|---|
| Academy of the New Church.......... | Bryn Athyn |
| Ambler Junior College of Temple Univ... | Ambler |

| Institution | Location |
|---|---|
| Baptist Inst. for Christian Workers...... | Bryn Mawr |
| Community College of Temple Univ..... | Philadelphia |
| Eastern Pilgrim College.............. | Allentown |
| Gwynedd–Mercy Jr. College........... | Gwynedd Valley |
| Harcum Junior College................ | Bryn Mawr |
| Johnstown Coll., Univ. of Pittsburgh.... | Johnstown |
| Keystone Junior College............... | La Plume |
| Lackawanna Junior College........... | Scranton |
| Manor Junior College................. | Philadelphia |
| Mt. Aloysius Junior College........... | Cresson |
| Novitiate of St. Isaac Jogues........... | Wernersville |
| Penn Hall Junior College.............. | Chambersburg |
| Spring Garden Institute............... | Philadelphia |
| Tech. Inst. of Temple Univ............. | Philadelphia |
| Valley Forge Military Academy........ | Wayne |
| York Junior College.................. | York |

**RHODE ISLAND**

Privately controlled

| Institution | Location |
|---|---|
| Roger Williams Jr. College............ | Providence |

**SOUTH CAROLINA**

Privately controlled

| Institution | Location |
|---|---|
| Anderson College..................... | Anderson |
| Central Wesleyan College.............. | Central |
| Coastal Carolina Junior College........ | Conway |
| Friendship Junior College.............. | Rock Hill |
| North Greenville Junior College........ | Tigerville |
| Our Lady of Mercy Junior College...... | Charleston |
| Southern Methodist College............ | Aiken |
| Spartanburg Junior College............ | Spartanburg |
| Voorhees School and Junior College..... | Denmark |

**SOUTH DAKOTA**

Privately controlled

| Institution | Location |
|---|---|
| Freeman Junior College............... | Freeman |
| Presentation Junior College........... | Aberdeen |
| Wessington Springs College............ | Wessington Sps. |

**TENNESSEE**

Privately controlled

| Institution | Location |
|---|---|
| Freed–Hardeman College.............. | Henderson |
| Hiwassee College.................... | Madisonville |
| Lee College.......................... | Cleveland |
| Martin College....................... | Pulaski |
| Morristown College................... | Morristown |
| Owen College........................ | Memphis |

**TEXAS**

Publicly controlled

| Institution | Location |
|---|---|
| Alvin Junior College.................. | Alvin |
| Amarillo College..................... | Amarillo |
| Blinn College........................ | Brenham |
| Cisco Junior College................. | Cisco |
| Clarendon Junior College............. | Clarendon |
| Del Mar College..................... | Corpus Christi |
| Frank Phillips College................ | Borger |
| Gainesville College................... | Gainesville |
| Hardin Junior College................ | Wichita Falls |
| Henderson County Junior College...... | Athens |
| Houston, University of—Jr. Coll. Div... | Houston |
| Howard County Junior College........ | Big Spring |
| Kilgore College....................... | Kilgore |
| Laredo Junior College................ | Laredo |
| Lee College.......................... | Baytown |
| Navarro Junior College............... | Corsicana |
| Odessa College....................... | Odessa |
| Pan American College—Jr. Coll. Div..... | Edinburg |

| Institution | Location |
|---|---|
| Panola College | Carthage |
| Paris Junior College | Paris |
| Ranger College | Ranger |
| St. Phillip's College | San Antonio |
| San Angelo College | San Angelo |
| San Antonio College | San Antonio |
| South Plains College | Levelland |
| Southwest Texas Junior College | Uvalde |
| Tarleton State College | Stephenville |
| Temple Junior College | Temple |
| Texarkana College | Texarkana |
| Texas Southmost College | Brownsville |
| Tyler District College | Tyler |
| Tyler Junior College | Tyler |
| Victoria College, The | Victoria |
| Weatherford College | Weatherford |
| Wharton County Junior College | Wharton |

Privately controlled

| | |
|---|---|
| Allen Academy, The | Bryan |
| Decatur Baptist College | Decatur |
| Jacksonville College | Jacksonville |
| LeTourneau Tech. Inst. of Texas | Longview |
| Lon Morris College | Jacksonville |
| Lubbock Christian College | Lubbock |
| Lutheran Concordia College of Texas | Austin |
| Mary Allen College | Crockett |
| Schreiner Institute | Kerrville |
| South Texas Junior College | Houston |
| Southwestern Bible Inst. Jr. College | Waxahachie |
| Southwestern Junior College | Keene |

## UTAH

Publicly controlled

| | |
|---|---|
| Carbon College | Price |
| Dixie Junior College | St. George |
| Snow College | Ephraim |
| Weber College | Ogden |

## VERMONT

Privately controlled

| | |
|---|---|
| Green Mountain College | Poultney |
| Vermont College | Montpelier |

## VIRGINIA

Publicly controlled

| | |
|---|---|
| Clinch Valley College–Univ. of Virginia | Wise |
| Danville Branch–Virginia Polytechnic Institute | Danville |
| Norfolk Division of Virginia State College | Norfolk |

Privately controlled

| | |
|---|---|
| Averett College | Danville |
| Bluefield College | Bluefield |
| Ferrum Junior College | Ferrum |
| Frederick College | Portsmouth |
| Marion College | Marion |
| Marymount College | Arlington |
| Shenandoah College | Winchester |
| Southern Seminary and Junior College | Buena Vista |
| Stratford College | Danville |
| Sullins College | Bristol |
| Virginia Intermont College | Bristol |

## WASHINGTON

Publicly controlled

| | |
|---|---|
| Centralia College | Centralia |
| Clark College | Vancouver |
| Columbia Basin College | Pasco |

| Institution | Location |
|---|---|
| Everett Junior College | Everett |
| Grays Harbor College | Aberdeen |
| Lower Columbia Junior College | Longview |
| Olympic College | Bremerton |
| Skagit Valley College | Mt. Vernon |
| Wenatchee Valley College | Wenatchee |
| Yakima Valley Junior College | Yakima |

Privately controlled

| | |
|---|---|
| Tacoma Catholic Junior College | Tacoma |

## WEST VIRGINIA

Publicly controlled

| | |
|---|---|
| Potomac State College | Keyser |

Privately controlled

| | |
|---|---|
| Beckley College | Beckley |
| Greenbrier College | Lewisburg |

## WISCONSIN

Publicly controlled

| | |
|---|---|
| County Teachers Colleges: | |
| Ashland | Ashland |
| Barron | Rice Lake |
| Buffalo | Alma |
| Columbia | Columbus |
| Dodge | Mayville |
| Door–Kewaunee | Algoma |
| Green | Monroe |
| Juneau | New Lisbon |
| Langlade | Antigo |
| Lincoln | Merrill |
| Manitowoc | Manitowoc |
| Marinette | Marinette |
| Outagamie | Kaukauna |
| Polk | Frederic |
| Racine–Kenosha | Union Grove |
| Richland | Richland Center |
| Sauk | Reedsburg |
| Sheboygan | Sheboygan Falls |
| Taylor | Medford |
| Vernon | Viroqua |
| Waushara | Wautoma |
| Wood | Wisconsin Rapids |
| Milwaukee Institute of Technology | Milwaukee |
| Univ. of Wisconsin, Extension Centers: | |
| Fox Valley | Menasha |
| Green Bay | Green Bay |
| Kenosha | Kenosha |
| Manitowoc | Manitowoc |
| Marathon County | Wausau |
| Marinette | Marinette |
| Racine | Racine |
| Sheboygan | Sheboygan |

Privately controlled

| | |
|---|---|
| Concordia College | Milwaukee |
| Milwaukee Sch. of Engineering | Milwaukee |
| St. Lawrence Seminary | Mt. Calvary |
| Salvatorian Seminary | St. Nazianz |

## WYOMING

Publicly controlled

| | |
|---|---|
| Casper College | Casper |
| Goshen Cty. Comm. College | Torrington |
| Northwest Comm. College | Powell |
| Sheridan College | Sheridan |
| Western Wyoming Junior College | Rock Springs |

# GEOGRAPHY

## Miscellaneous Data for the United States

*Source:* U. S. Geological Survey.

Highest point: Mount McKinley, Alaska .................................. 20,320 ft.
Lowest point: Death Valley, Calif. ............. 282 ft. below sea level
Most northern point: Point Barrow, Alaska ...................... 71° 23′ N. lat.
Most southern point: KaLae, on island of Hawaii .................. 18° 56′ N. lat.
Most eastern point: West Quoddy Head, Maine ..................... 66° 57′ W. long.
Most western point: Kure Island, Hawaii† ........................ 178° 22′ W. long.
Places farthest apart: Cape Wrangell, Alaska, and Mangrove Point, Florida ... 6,940 mi.

Geographic center: In Butte County, South Dakota* ..................  { 44° 58′ N. lat.
{ 103° 46′ W. long.

Boundaries: Between Alaska and Canada .............................. 1,538 mi.
Between the 48 contiguous states and Canada (including Great Lakes) ..... 3,987 mi.
Between the United States and Mexico ................................ 2,013 mi.

\* West of Castle Rock.   † Attu Island, Alaska, is west of Kure, but its longitude is east of Greenwich, not west.

# Mountain Peaks in the U. S. 14,000 Feet or More Above Sea Level

*Source:* U. S. Geological Survey.

| Name of summit | State | Height, ft. |
|---|---|---|
| McKinley | Alaska | 20,320 |
| North Peak | Alaska | 19,370 |
| *St. Elias | Alaska | 18,008 |
| Foraker | Alaska | 17,395 |
| Blackburn | Alaska | 16,523 |
| Bona | Alaska | 16,421 |
| Sanford | Alaska | 16,208 |
| *Vancouver | Alaska | 15,700 |
| *Fairweather | Alaska | 15,300 |
| *Hubbard | Alaska | 14,950 |
| Bear | Alaska | 14,850 |
| Hunter | Alaska | 14,580 |
| Brown Tower | Alaska | 14,530 |
| *Alverstone | Alaska | 14,500 |
| Whitney | Calif. | 14,494 |
| Elbert | Colo. | 14,431 |
| Harvard | Colo. | 14,420 |
| Massive | Colo. | 14,418 |
| Rainier | Wash. | 14,410 |
| Williamson | Calif. | 14,494 |
| La Plata | Colo. | 14,340 |
| Blanca | Colo. | 14,317 |
| Uncompahgre | Colo. | 14,301 |
| Crestone | Colo. | 14,291 |
| Lincoln | Colo. | 14,284 |
| Grays | Colo. | 14,274 |
| Antero | Colo. | 14,269 |
| Torreys | Colo. | 14,264 |
| Evans | Colo. | 14,260 |
| Castle | Colo. | 14,259 |
| Longs | Colo. | 14,255 |
| Quandary | Colo. | 14,252 |
| Wilson | Colo. | 14,246 |
| White | Calif. | 14,246 |
| North Palisade | Calif. | 14,242 |
| Cameron | Colo. | 14,238 |
| Shavano | Colo. | 14,229 |
| Princeton | Colo. | 14,197 |
| Belford | Colo. | 14,196 |
| Yale | Colo. | 14,194 |
| Creston Needle | Colo. | 14,191 |
| Bross | Colo. | 14,169 |
| Sill | Calif. | 14,162 |
| Shasta | Calif. | 14,162 |
| El Diente | Colo. | 14,159 |
| Maroon | Colo. | 14,158 |
| Tabeguache | Colo. | 14,155 |
| Oxford | Colo. | 14,153 |
| Point Success | Wash. | 14,150 |
| Sneffels | Colo. | 14,150 |
| Democrat | Colo. | 14,142 |
| Capitol | Colo. | 14,137 |
| Liberty Cap | Wash. | 14,133 |
| Lindsey | Colo. | 14,125 |
| Pikes Peak | Colo. | 14,110 |
| Kit Carson | Colo. | 14,100 |
| Windom | Colo. | 14,091 |
| Eolus (Aeolus) | Colo. | 14,086 |
| Russell | Calif. | 14,086 |
| Snowmass | Colo. | 14,077 |
| Columbia | Colo. | 14,071 |
| *Augusta | Alaska | 14,070 |
| Culebra | Colo. | 14,069 |
| Missouri | Colo. | 14,067 |
| Sunlight | Colo. | 14,060 |
| Split | Calif. | 14,058 |
| Red Cloud | Colo. | 14,050 |
| Handies | Colo. | 14,049 |
| Bierstadt | Colo. | 14,046 |
| Humboldt | Colo. | 14,044 |
| Middle Palisade | Calif. | 14,040 |
| Little Bear | Colo. | 14,040 |
| Sherman | Colo. | 14,037 |
| Stewart | Colo. | 14,032 |
| Langley | Calif. | 14,027 |
| Tyndall | Calif. | 14,018 |
| Sunshine | Colo. | 14,018 |
| Wetterhorn | Colo. | 14,017 |
| Wilson | Colo. | 14,017 |
| Muir | Calif. | 14,015 |
| San Luis | Colo. | 14,014 |
| Wrangell | Alaska | 14,006 |
| Huron | Colo. | 14,003 |
| Pyramid | Colo. | 14,000 |
| Grizzly | Colo. | 14,000 |
| North Maroon | Colo. | 14,000 |

\* Mountains whose summits are on the international boundary between Canada and Alaska.

## The Continental Divide

The Continental Divide is a ridge of high ground which runs irregularly north and south through the Rocky Mountains and separates eastward-flowing from westward-flowing streams. The waters which flow eastward empty into the Atlantic Ocean, chiefly by way of the Gulf of Mexico; those which flow westward empty into the Pacific.

# Highest, Lowest, and Average Altitudes in the United States

*Source:* U. S. Geological Survey.

| State | Average elevation, ft. | Highest point | Elevation, ft. | Lowest point | Elevation, ft. |
|---|---|---|---|---|---|
| Alabama | 500 | Cheaha Mountain | 2,407 | Gulf of Mexico | Sea level |
| Alaska | 1,900 | Mount McKinley | 20,320 | Pacific Ocean† | Sea level |
| Arizona | 4,100 | Humphreys Peak | 12,670 | Colorado River | 100 |
| Arkansas | 650 | Magazine Mountain | 2,823 | Ouachita River | 55 |
| California | 2,900 | Mount Whitney | 14,494 | Death Valley | 282* |
| Colorado | 6,800 | Mount Elbert | 14,431 | Arkansas River | 3,350 |
| Connecticut | 500 | Mt. Frissell | 2,380 | Long Island Sound | Sea level |
| Delaware | 60 | Ebright Road | 442 | Atlantic Ocean | Sea level |
| D. C. | 150 | Tenleytown | 410 | Potomac River | Sea level |
| Florida | 100 | Sec. 30, T6N, R20W[1] | 345 | Atlantic Ocean | Sea level |
| Georgia | 600 | Brasstown Bald | 4,784 | Atlantic Ocean | Sea level |
| Hawaii | 1,990 | Mauna Kea | 13,796 | Pacific Ocean | Sea level |
| Idaho | 5,000 | Borah Peak | 12,662 | Snake River | 720 |
| Illinois | 600 | Charles Mound | 1,241 | Mississippi River | 279 |
| Indiana | 700 | Franklin Township | 1,253 | Ohio River | 320 |
| Iowa | 1,100 | T100N., R.44W[2] | 1,675 | Mississippi River | 480 |
| Kansas | 2,000 | In T11S R43W[3] | 4,025 | Verdigris River | 700 |
| Kentucky | 750 | Black Mountain | 4,145 | Mississippi River | 257 |
| Louisiana | 100 | Driskill Mountain | 535 | New Orleans | 5* |
| Maine | 600 | Mount Katahdin | 5,268 | Atlantic Ocean | Sea level |
| Maryland | 350 | Backbone Mountain | 3,360 | Atlantic Ocean | Sea level |
| Massachusetts | 500 | Mount Greylock | 3,491 | Atlantic Ocean | Sea level |
| Michigan | 900 | Sec. 2, T50N., R31W[4] | 1,980 | Lake Erie | 572 |
| Minnesota | 1,200 | Misquah Hills | 2,230 | Lake Superior | 602 |
| Mississippi | 300 | Woodall Mountain | 806 | Gulf of Mexico | Sea level |
| Missouri | 800 | Taum Sauk Mountain | 1,772 | St. Francis River | 230 |
| Montana | 3,400 | Granite Peak | 12,799 | Kootenai River | 1,800 |
| Nebraska | 2,600 | Johnson Township | 5,424 | Southeast corner of State | 840 |
| Nevada | 5,500 | Boundary Peak, White Mountains | 13,145 | Colorado River | 470 |
| New Hampshire | 1,000 | Mount Washington | 6,288 | Atlantic Ocean | Sea level |
| New Jersey | 250 | High Point | 1,803 | Atlantic Ocean | Sea level |
| New Mexico | 5,700 | Wheeler Peak | 13,160 | Red Bluff Reservoir | 2,817 |
| New York | 1,000 | Mount Marcy | 5,344 | Atlantic Ocean | Sea level |
| North Carolina | 700 | Mount Mitchell | 6,684 | Atlantic Ocean | Sea level |
| North Dakota | 1,900 | White Butte | 3,530 | Red River | 750 |
| Ohio | 850 | Campbell Hill | 1,550 | Ohio River | 433 |
| Oklahoma | 1,300 | Black Mesa | 4,978 | Red River | 300 |
| Oregon | 3,300 | Mount Hood | 11,245 | Pacific Ocean | Sea level |
| Pennsylvania | 500 | Mt. Davis, Negro Mountains | 3,213 | Delaware River | Sea level |
| Rhode Island | 200 | Jerimoth Hill | 812 | Atlantic Ocean | Sea level |
| South Carolina | 350 | Sassafras Mountain | 3,560 | Atlantic Ocean | Sea level |
| South Dakota | 2,200 | Harney Peak | 7,242 | Big Stone Lake | 962 |
| Tennessee | 900 | Clingmans Dome | 6,642 | Mississippi River | 182 |
| Texas | 1,700 | Guadalupe Peak | 8,751 | Gulf of Mexico | Sea level |
| Utah | 6,100 | Kings Peak | 13,498 | Beaverdam Creek | 2,000 |
| Vermont | 1,000 | Mount Mansfield | 4,393 | Lake Champlain | 95 |
| Virginia | 950 | Mount Rogers | 5,720 | Atlantic Ocean | Sea level |
| Washington | 1,700 | Mount Rainier | 14,410 | Pacific Ocean | Sea level |
| West Virginia | 1,500 | Spruce Knob | 4,860 | Potomac River | 240 |
| Wisconsin | 1,050 | Rib Mountain | 1,941 | Lake Michigan | 581 |
| Wyoming | 6,700 | Gannett Peak | 13,785 | Belle Fourche River | 3,100 |

\* Below sea level.    [1] Walton County.    [2] Osceola County.    [3] Wallace County.    [4] Baraga County.

## Forest Resources of the United States

*Source:* U. S. Forest Service.

Nearly 1/3 of the U. S. is forest land including over 1,000 different kinds of trees. Commercial areas include land capable of producing timber of commercial quantity and quality, and available now or prospectively for such use. Almost all the old-growth forest is in the West. Noncommercial areas include alpine, semidesert, and other forest types of low timber productivity, though much of it is important for watershed protection.

### U. S. Forest Land in Acres, 1953[1]

| | |
|---|---|
| Old growth | 50,009,000 |
| Young-growth sawtimber | 132,699,000 |
| Pole timber stands | 169,483,000 |
| Seedling and sapling stands | 94,784,000 |
| Nonstocked and other areas | 41,634,000 |
| Total, commercial forest land | 488,609,000 |
| Noncommercial forest | 175,585,000 |
| Total, all forest land | 664,194,000 |

[1] Generally considered to represent 1961 conditions. Includes 16,508,000 acres in coastal Alaska but does not include interior Alaska and Hawaii.

# Rivers of the U. S.

*Source:* U. S. Geological Survey.

**(300 or more miles long)**

ALABAMA (315 mi.): From junction of Tallapoosa R. and Coosa R. in Alabama to Mobile R.

ALLEGHENY (325 mi.): From Potter Co. in Pennsylvania to junction with Monongahela R. at Pittsburgh to form Ohio R.

ALTAMAHA-OCMULGEE (392 mi.): From junction of Yellow R. and South R., Newton Co. in Ga. to Atlantic Ocean.

APALACHICOLA-CHATTAHOOCHEE (500 mi.): From Towns Co. in Ga. to Gulf of Mexico in Fla.

ARKANSAS (1,450 mi.): From Lake Co. in Colorado to Mississippi R. in Arkansas.

BIG BLACK (330 mi.): From Webster Co. in Mississippi to Mississippi R.

BIG HORN (336 mi.): From junction of Popo Agie R. and Wind R. in Wyoming to Yellowstone R. in Montana.

BRAZOS (870 mi.): From junction of Salt Fork and Double Mountain Fork in Texas to Gulf of Mexico.

CANADIAN (906 mi.): From Colfax Co. in N. Mex. to Arkansas R. in Okla.

CEDAR (329 mi.): From south central Minnesota to Iowa R. in Iowa.

CIMARRON (600 mi.): From Colfax Co. in New Mexico to Arkansas R. in Okla.

CLARK FORK-PEND OREILLE (505 mi.): From Silver Bow Co. in Mont. to Columbia R. in British Columbia.

COLORADO (1,360 mi.): From Rocky Mountain National Park in Colorado to Arizona-Sonora boundary line.

COLORADO (840 mi.): From Dawson Co. in Texas to Matagorda Bay.

COLUMBIA (1,214 mi.): From Columbia Lake in British Columbia to Pacific Ocean (entering between Oreg. and Wash.)

COLVILLE (350 mi.): From Brooks Range in Alaska to Beaufort Sea.

CONNECTICUT (407 mi.): From Third Connecticut Lake in New Hampshire to Long Island Sound in Connecticut.

CUMBERLAND (687 mi.): From junction of forks in Harlan Co. in Kentucky to Ohio R.

DES MOINES (327 mi.): From Humboldt Co. in Iowa to Mississippi R.

GILA (630 mi.): From southwest New Mexico to Colorado R. in Arizona.

GREEN (360 mi.): From Lincoln Co. in Kentucky to Ohio R. in Kentucky.

GREEN (730 mi.): From Sublette Co. in Wyoming to Colorado R. in Utah.

HUDSON (306 mi.): From Essex Co. in New York to Upper New York Bay (entering between New York and New Jersey).

JAMES (sometimes called DAKOTA) (710 mi.): From Wells Co. in North Dakota to Missouri R. in South Dakota.

JAMES (340 mi.): From junction of Jackson R. and Cowpasture R. in Virginia to Hampton Roads.

KANAWHA-NEW (352 mi.): From junction of North and South Forks of New R. in North Carolina to Ohio R.

KOYUKUK (500 mi.): From Brooks Range in Alaska to Yukon R.

KUSKOKWIM (550 mi.): From Alaska Range in Alaska to Kuskokwim Bay.

LITTLE COLORADO (300 mi.): From Apache Co. in Arizona to Colorado R.

LITTLE MISSOURI (560 mi.): From northeast Wyoming to Missouri R. in North Dakota.

MILK (625 mi.): From junction of forks in Alberta Province to Missouri R.

MINNESOTA (332 mi.): From Big Stone Lake between Minnesota and South Dakota to Mississippi R. at St. Paul.

MISSISSIPPI (2,348 mi.): From Lake Itasca in Minn. to mouth of Southwest Pass.

MISSOURI (2,466 mi.): From junction of Jefferson R., Gallatin R., and Madison R. in Montana to Mississippi R. near St. Louis.

MOBILE-ALABAMA-COOSA (639 mi.): From junction of Etowah R. and Oostanaula R. in Georgia to Mobile Bay.

NEOSHO (460 mi.): From Morris Co. in Kansas to Arkansas R. in Oklahoma.

NIOBRARA (431 mi.): From Niobrara Co. in Wyoming to Missouri R. in Nebraska.

NOATAK (350 mi.): From Brooks Range in Alaska to Kotzebue Sound.

NORTH CANADIAN (760 mi.): From Union Co. in New Mexico to Canadian R. in Oklahoma.

NORTH PLATTE (618 mi.): From Jackson Co. in Colorado to junction with So. Platte R. in Nebraska to form Platte R.

NUECES (338 mi.): From near Edwards-Real Co. border in Texas to Nueces Bay.

OHIO (981 mi.): From junction of Allegheny R. and Monongahela R. at Pittsburgh to Mississippi R. between Illinois and Kentucky.

OSAGE (500 mi.): From junction of Elm Creek and Onion Creek in Kansas to Missouri R. in Missouri.

OUACHITA (605 mi.): From Polk Co. in Arkansas to Red R. in Louisiana.

PEARL (490 mi.): From Neshoba Co. in Mississippi to Gulf of Mexico between Mississippi and Louisiana.

PECOS (735 mi.): From Mora Co. in New Mexico to Rio Grande in Texas.

PEE DEE-YADKIN (435 mi.): From Watauga Co. in N. C. to Winyah Bay in S. C.

PLATTE (310 mi.): From junction of North Platte R. and South Platte R. in Nebraska to Missouri R. below Omaha.

PORCUPINE (450 mi.): From Yukon Territory, Canada, to Yukon R. in Alaska.

POWDER (375 mi.): From junction of forks in Johnson Co. in Wyoming to Yellowstone R. in Montana.

RED (1,018 mi.): From junction of forks in Tillman Co. in Oklahoma to Mississippi R. in Louisiana.

RED (officially called RED RIVER OF THE NORTH) (545 mi.): From junction of Otter Tail R. and Bois de Sioux R. in Minnesota to Lake Winnipeg in Manitoba.

REPUBLICAN (445 mi.): From junction of North Fork and Arikaree R. in Nebraska to junction with Smoky Hill R. in Kansas to form Kansas R.

RIO GRANDE (1,885 mi.): From San Juan Co. in Colorado to Gulf of Mexico.

ROANOKE (380 mi.): From junction of forks in Montgomery Co. in Virginia to Albemarle Sound in North Carolina.

ROCK (300 mi.): From Washington Co. in Wisconsin to Mississippi R. in Illinois.

SABINE (380 mi.): From junction of forks in Hunt Co. in Texas to Sabine Lake between Texas and Louisiana.

SACRAMENTO (382 mi.): From Siskiyou Co. in California to Suisun Bay.

SAINT FRANCIS (425 mi.): From Iron Co. in Missouri to Mississippi R. in Ark.

SALMON (420 mi.): From Custer Co. in Idaho to Snake R.

SAN JOAQUIN (350 mi.): From junction of forks in Madera Co. in California to Suisun Bay.

SAN JUAN (360 mi.): From Archuleta Co. in Colorado to Colorado R. in Utah.

SANTEE - WATEREE - CATAWBA (538 mi.): From McDowell Co. in North Carolina to Atlantic Ocean in South Carolina.

SAVANNAH (314 mi.): From junction of Tugaloo R. and Seneca R. in South Carolina to Atlantic Ocean between Georgia and South Carolina.

SMOKY HILL (540 mi.): From Cheyenne Co. in Colorado to junction with Republican R. in Kansas to form Kansas R.

SNAKE (1,038 mi.): From Ocean Plateau in Wyoming to Columbia R. in Wash.

SOUTH PLATTE (424 mi.): From Park Co. in Colorado to junction with North Platte R. in Nebraska to form Platte R.

SUSQUEHANNA (444 mi.): From Otsego Lake in New York to Chesapeake Bay in Maryland.

TALLAHATCHIE (301 mi.): From Tippah Co. in Mississippi to junction with Yalobusha R. to form Yazoo R.

TANANA (800 mi.): From Wrangell Mts. in Yukon Territory, Canada, to Yukon R. in Alaska.

TENNESSEE (652 mi.): From junction of Holston R. and French Broad R. in Tennessee to Ohio R. in Kentucky.

TOMBIGBEE (409 mi.): From junction of forks in Monroe Co. in Mississippi to Mobile R. in Alabama.

TRINITY (360): From junction of forks in Kaufman Co. in Texas to Galveston Bay.

WABASH (475 mi.): From Darke Co. in Ohio to Ohio R. between Ill. and Ind.

WASHITA (500 mi.): From Hemphill Co. in Texas to Red R. in Oklahoma.

WHITE (690 mi.): From Madison Co. in Arkansas to Mississippi R.

WISCONSIN (430 mi.): From Vilas Co. in Wisconsin to Mississippi R.

YELLOWSTONE (671 mi.): From Park Co. in Wyoming to Missouri R. in N. Dak.

YUKON (1,800 mi.): From junction of Lewes R. and Pelly R. in Yukon Territory, Canada, to Bering Sea in Alaska.

## Coastline of the United States

### Fourth (April 1, 1961) Edition

*Source:* U.S. Coast and Geodetic Survey.

| State | Lengths, statute miles | |
|---|---|---|
| | General coastline* | Tidal shoreline† |
| **Atlantic Coast:** | | |
| Maine | 228 | 3,478 |
| New Hampshire | 13 | 131 |
| Massachusetts | 192 | 1,519 |
| Rhode Island | 40 | 384 |
| Connecticut | ... | 618 |
| New York | 127 | 1,850 |
| New Jersey | 130 | 1,792 |
| Pennsylvania | ... | 89 |
| Delaware | 28 | 381 |
| Maryland | 31 | 3,190 |
| Virginia | 112 | 3,315 |
| North Carolina | 301 | 3,375 |
| South Carolina | 187 | 2,876 |
| Georgia | 100 | 2,344 |
| Florida (Atlantic) | 580 | 3,331 |
| Total Atlantic coast | 2,069 | 28,673 |
| **Gulf Coast:** | | |
| Florida (Gulf) | 770 | 5,095 |
| Alabama | 53 | 607 |
| Mississippi | 44 | 359 |
| Louisiana | 397 | 7,721 |
| Texas | 367 | 3,359 |
| Total Gulf coast | 1,631 | 17,141 |
| **Pacific Coast:** | | |
| California | 840 | 3,427 |
| Oregon | 296 | 1,410 |
| Washington | 157 | 3,026 |
| Hawaii | 750 | 1,052 |
| Alaska (Pacific) | 5,580 | 31,383 |
| Total Pacific coast | 7,623 | 40,298 |
| **Arctic Coast:** | | |
| Alaska (Arctic) | 1,060 | 2,521 |
| Total Arctic coast | 1,060 | 2,521 |
| STATES TOTAL | 12,383 | 88,633 |

* Figures are lengths of general outline of seacoast. Measurements made with unit measure of 30 minutes of latitude on charts as near scale of 1:1,200,000 as possible. Coastline of bays and sounds is included to point where they narrow to width of unit measure, and distance across at such point is included. † Figures obtained in 1939–40 with recording instrument on largest-scale maps and charts then available. Shoreline of outer coast, offshore islands, sounds, bays, rivers, and creeks is included to head of tidewater, or to point where tidal waters narrow to width of 100 feet.

# THE UNITED STATES

★

## STATES, TERRITORIES AND CITIES

(State flower, bird, etc., are official unless otherwise indicated; dates in parentheses are those of adoption. Largest cities include incorporated places only.)

### ALABAMA

Capital: Montgomery.
Governor: John Patterson, Dem. (to Jan. 1963).
Lieut. Governor: Albert B. Boutwell (to Jan. 1963).
Secy. of State: Bettye Frink (to Jan. 1963).
Controller: John Graves (indeterminate).
Atty. General: McDonald Gallion (to Jan. 1963).
Organized as territory: Mar. 3, 1817.
Entered Union & (rank): Dec. 14, 1819 (22).
Seceded from Union: Jan. 11, 1861.
Re-entered Union: July 13, 1868.
Present constitution adopted: 1901.
Motto: *Audemus jura nostra defendere* (We dare defend our rights).
State flower: Camellia (1959).
State bird: Yellowhammer (1927).
State song: "Alabama" (1931).
State tree: Southern pine (longleaf) (1949).
Nickname: Yellowhammer State.
Origin of name: May come from Choctaw meaning "thicket-clearers" or "vegetarian-gatherers".
1940 population & (rank): 2,832,961 (17).
1950 population & (rank): 3,061,743 (17).
1960 population & (rank): 3,266,740 (19).
Land area & (rank): 51,060 sq. mi. (28).
Geographic center: In Chilton Co., 12 mi. SW of Clanton.
Number of counties: 67.
Largest cities (1960 census): Birmingham (340,-887); Mobile (202,779); Montgomery (134,-393); Huntsville (72,365); Tuscaloosa (63,-370).
State forests: 8 (14,248.58 ac.).
State parks: 39 (41,959.35 ac.).
Total gross tax receipts (1956–57): $618,203,837.
Total gross tax disbursements (1956–57): $624,-466,789.

Alabama is the leading heavy-industry state in the South. Textiles, iron and steel, and sawmill products lead its manufacturing, which centers around the "Pittsburgh of the South"—Birmingham. Industry is growing rapidly in other areas, including the Tennessee River Valley, with its great Muscle Shoals power plant. Lumber, marble, dolomite and petroleum are other important products. Alabama ranks high in the production of cotton, cattle, corn, hay, nuts, broiler chickens and sweet potatoes.

At Tuskegee Institute, founded by Booker T. Washington, Dr. George Washington Carver carried out his famed agricultural research.

The Confederacy was founded at Montgomery in Feb. 1861, and for a time the city was the Confederate capital.

In 1540, Hernando de Soto and his treasure seekers were the first white men to see the state, although Cabeza de Vaca may have preceded him in 1528.

### ALASKA

Capital: Juneau.
Governor: William A. Egan, Dem. (to Jan. 1963).
Secy. of State: Hugh Wade (to Dec. 1962).
Director, Div. of Finance: William S. Brown (apptd. by Gov.).
Atty. General: Ralph E. Moody (to Dec. 1962).
Organized as territory: 1912.
Entered Union & (rank): Jan. 3, 1959 (49).
Constitution ratified: April 24, 1956.
Motto: None.
State flower: Forget-me-not.
State bird: Willow ptarmigan.
State song: "Alaska's Flag."
Nickname: Commonly called "The Last Frontier" or "Land of the Midnight Sun."
Origin of name: Corruption of native word meaning "great country."
1939 population: 72,524.
1950 population: 128,643.
1960 population & (rank): 226,167 (50).
Land area & (rank): 586,400 sq. mi. (1).
Geographic center: 10 mi. southeast of Lake Minchumina.
Number of counties: State to have boroughs; number not decided by first legislature.
Largest cities (1960 census): Anchorage (44,-237); Fairbanks (13,311); Juneau (6,797); Ketchikan (6,483); Sitka (3,237).
State forests: None.
State parks: None.
General revenue (1959–60): $44,389,271.
General expenditure (1959–60): $27,084,790.

Alaska, newest and largest of the states, was called "Seward's Folly" in 1867, when that Secretary of State arranged for its purchase from Russia for $7,200,000. Since then Alaska has returned approximately $3,500,-000,000 worth of products to the U. S.

Canned salmon is Alaska's principal product. It mines gold, supplies all domestically mined U. S. tin and also turns out platinum, coal, antimony, silver, mercury, tungsten and chromium.

The Pribilof Islands, in the Bering Sea, are famous as the breeding ground of the Alaska fur seal, which is under careful government control. Beaver, muskrat, otter, mink and other furs also abound. Alaska's first pulp mill at Ketchikan, constructed at a cost of $54 million, began operation in 1954. Its second, constructed at Sitka at a cost of $60,000,000, began operation in Nov. 1959.

Mt. McKinley, in the south central part, is 20,320 feet high, the tallest peak in North

America. With its wild interior, still partly unexplored, the state is a hunter's paradise. With one person for every four and a half square miles in 1950, Alaska is by far the most thinly settled of the states. Sitka was its capital until 1912.

Alaska has magnificent glaciers and active volcanoes. Winter temperatures in the interior have been known to register 78° below zero. However, summer temperatures in the same area have been recorded at 99° above zero; and large parts of the state, especially in the southeast, enjoy mild climate in both summer and winter.

The Aleutians include the following island groups (and major islands): Fox Islands (Unimak, Akutan, Unalaska, Umnak); Islands of the Four Mountains (Chuginadak, Kagamil, Carlisle, Herbert); Andreanof Islands (Atka, Tanaga, Adak, Kanaga); Rat Islands (Kiska, Amchitka, Semisopochnoi, Rat); Near Islands (Agattu, Attu, Shemya). In June 1942, the Japanese occupied Attu and Kiska. However, Attu was retaken by the U. S. in May 1943; Kiska was evacuated by the Japanese in Aug. 1943 after extensive shelling and bombing of the island.

Vitus Bering, a Dane working for the Russians, and Alexei Chirikov discovered Alaska and the Aleutians in 1741.

## ARIZONA

Capital: Phoenix.
Governor: Paul Fannin, Rep. (to Jan. 1963).
Secy. of State: Wesley Bolin (to Jan. 1963).
State Auditor: Jewell W. Jordan (to Jan. 1963).
Atty. General: Robert W. Pickrell (to Jan. 1963).
State Treasurer: J. W. Kelly (to Jan. 1963).
Organized as territory: Feb. 24, 1863.
Entered Union & (rank): Feb. 14, 1912 (48).
Present constitution adopted: 1911.
Motto: *Ditat Deus* (God enriches).
State flower: Flower of saguaro cactus (1931).
State bird: Cactus wren (1931).
State colors: Blue and old gold (1915).
State song: "Arizona," a march song (1919).
State tree: Paloverde (1957).
Nickname: Grand Canyon State.
Origin of name: From the Indian "Arizonac," meaning ' little spring."
1940 population & (rank): 499,261 (43).
1950 population & (rank): 749,587 (37).
1960 population & (rank): 1,302,161 (35).
Land area & (rank): 113,575 sq. mi. (6).
Geographic center: In Yavapai Co., 55 mi. SE of Prescott.
Number of counties: 14.
Largest cities (1960 census): Phoenix (439,170); Tucson (212,892); Mesa (33,772); Tempe (24,897); Yuma (23,974).
State forests: None.
State parks: 1 dedicated; 2 selected but not dedicated.
State revenue (1959-60): $196,515,689.
State expenditure (1959-60): $184,583,875.

Manufacturing now ranks first among Arizona's revenue-producing industries. Next in rank is the mining of copper, gold, vanadium, uranium and silver, the production of copper exceeding that of any other state.

Agriculture is the third-largest revenue-producing industry. By means of irrigation, its once arid acres produce alfalfa, cotton, wheat, sorghum, vegetables, citrus fruits and dates. Income from livestock ranks high from both range and feeder cattle.

Phoenix is a popular health and winter resort and a shipper of cotton and vegetables, Tucson is a winter resort, Douglas loads cattle and smelts copper, and Yuma is an agricultural center.

With the Hopi, Navajo (the largest in numbers) and Apache tribes, Arizona has the largest U. S. Indian population, spread over fourteen reservations. It also has some of the country's most famous scenery. In the north is the Grand Canyon; in the east are the Petrified Forest and Painted Desert.

Marcos de Niza, a Franciscan friar, entered the area in 1539 in search of the mythical Seven Cities of Cibola, and was followed a year later by Coronado.

## ARKANSAS

Capital: Little Rock.
Governor: Orval Faubus, Dem. (to Jan. 1963).
Lieut. Governor: Nathan Gordon (to Jan. 1963).
Secy. of State: Nancy J. Hall (to Jan. 1963.)
Controller: L. A. Mashburn (to Jan. 1963).
Atty. General: J. Frank Holt (to Jan. 1963).
Organized as territory: Mar. 2, 1819.
Entered Union & (rank): June 15, 1836 (25).
Seceded from Union: May 6, 1861.
Re-entered Union: June 22, 1868.
Present constitution adopted: 1874.
Motto: *Regnat populus* (The people rule).
State flower: Apple Blossom (1901).
State tree: Pine (1939).
State bird: Mockingbird (1929).
State song: "The Arkansas Traveler" (1949).
Nickname: Land of Opportunity.
Origin of name: From the Quapaw Indians.
1940 population & (rank): 1,949,387 (24).
1950 population & (rank): 1,909,511 (30).
1960 population & (rank): 1,786,272 (31).
Land area & (rank): 52,499 sq. mi. (27).
Geographic center: In Pulaski Co., 12 mi. N of W of Little Rock.
Number of counties: 75.
Largest cities (1960 census): Little Rock (107,-813); North Little Rock (58,032); Fort Smith (52,991); Pine Bluff (44,037); Hot Springs (28,337).
State forests: 1 (19,434 ac.).
State parks: 16 (19,113 ac.).
State tax receipts (1958-59): $152,754,747.
Taxes from all sources (1958-59): $242,347,647.*
State general expenditure (1958-59): $244,866,-578.

*\* Includes federal and non-revenue taxes.*

Arkansas produces 96% of the nation's high-grade domestic bauxite ore—the source of aluminum. It also has the only diamond mine in North America. Located near Murfreesboro in Pike County, the mine is used as a tourist attraction on a "finders-keepers" basis.

The state is almost equally divided between mountains and delta areas and has more year-round fishable lakes and streams than any other state. There are two large national forests in the Ouachita and Ozark mountain ranges. Hot Springs, the nation's first national reservation, entertains fifteen times its population in guests each year. Its forty-seven curative springs, which are under the supervision of the Federal Government, flow water at 147°F. the year round.

Arkansas is a leader in the production of cotton and soybeans, and also produces large quantities of rice, corn, wheat and other grains, fruit, vegetables, broilers, turkeys and livestock. Lumber provides 51% of the state's industrial employment, and several of the country's largest wood and wood products processing plants are located in Arkansas. The largest archery manufacturing plant in the nation is in Pine Bluff. The state also ranks high in the production of oil and natural gas.

## CALIFORNIA

**Capital:** Sacramento.
**Governor:** Edmund G. Brown, Dem. (to Jan. 1963).
**Lieut. Governor:** Glenn M. Anderson (to Jan. 1963).
**Secy. of State:** Frank M. Jordan (to Jan. 1963).
**Controller:** Alan Cranston (to Jan. 1963).
**Atty. General:** Stanley Mosk (to Jan. 1963).
**Entered Union & (rank):** Sept. 9, 1850 (31).
**Present constitution adopted:** 1879.
**Motto:** *Eureka* (I have found it).
**State flower:** Golden poppy (1903).
**State tree:** California redwoods (Sequoia sempervirens & Sequoia gigantea) (1937 & 1953).
**State bird:** California valley quail (1931).
**State animal:** California grizzly bear (1953).
**State fish:** California golden trout (1947).
**State insect:** California dog-face butterfly (unofficial).
**State colors:** Blue and gold (1951).
**State song:** "I Love You, California" (1951).
**Nickname:** Golden State.
**Origin of name:** From a book, *Amadís de Gaula,* by García Ordóñez de Montalvo, c. 1500.
**1940 population & (rank):** 6,907,387 (5).
**1950 population & (rank):** 10,586,223 (2).
**1960 population & (rank):** 15,717,204 (2).
**Land area & (rank):** 156,573 sq. mi. (3).
**Geographic center:** In Madera Co., 35 mi. NE of Madera.
**Number of counties:** 58.
**Largest cities (1960 census):** Los Angeles (2,479,015); San Francisco (740,316); San Diego (573,224); Oakland (367,548); Long Beach (344,168).
**State forests:** 8 (70,235 ac.).
**State parks and beaches:** 160 (700,000 ac.).
**State general revenue (1961-62 estimated):** $1,694,335,699.
**State general expenditure (1961-62 estimated):** $1,726,416,097.

California earns more money from raising food and catching fish than any other state, and it stands high in oil production, lumbering and manufacturing. It has more motor vehicles than any other state or any foreign country. Out-of-state tourist visitors and the travel and recreation expenditures of the state's residents continue to play an important part in the expansion of trade and employment opportunities. Irrigation makes possible the production of more than 200 commercial crops.

Nature is spectacular. Death Valley, in the southeast, is 282 feet below sea level, the lowest spot in the nation; Lassen Peak is the only active U. S. volcano outside of Alaska and Hawaii, although its last eruptions were recorded in the years from 1914 to 1917; the General Sherman Tree in Sequoia National Park is estimated to be about 3,500 years old; and a stand of bristlecone pine trees in the White Mountains is estimated to be over 4,000 years old. San Pedro is the world's largest man-made harbor, and the Bank of America National Trust and Savings Association, founded by the Giannini family, is the largest privately owned bank in the U. S. and ranks usually first or second in the world.

Gold, which was responsible for the state's settlement boom, is still found here, but the state's most important mineral products today are oil, natural gas and its liquids, cement, miscellaneous stones, borates, and mercury.

California is a leader in electrical energy, and its cities specialize in aircraft and parts, missiles, food processing, electrical and electronic equipment, machinery and fabricated metal products.

The San Francisco-Oakland and Golden Gate bridges are among the world's engineering marvels.

Juan Rodríguez Cabrillo, Portuguese navigator, was probably the first white man to see the state in 1542.

## COLORADO

**Capital:** Denver.
**Governor:** Stephen L. R. McNichols, Dem. (to Jan. 1963).
**Lieut. Governor:** Robert L. Knous (to Jan. 1963).
**Secy. of State:** George J. Baker (to Jan. 1963).
**Controller:** E. G. Spurlin (indefinite).
**Atty. General:** Duke W. Dunbar (to Jan. 1963).
**Organized as territory:** Feb. 28, 1861.
**Entered Union & (rank):** Aug. 1, 1876 (38).
**Present constitution adopted:** 1876.
**Motto:** *Nil sine Numine* (Nothing without Providence).
**State flower:** Rocky Mountain columbine (1899).
**State tree:** Colorado blue spruce (1939).
**State bird:** Lark bunting (1931).
**State animal:** Rocky Mountain bighorn sheep.
**State colors:** Blue and white (1911).
**State song:** "Where the Columbines Grow" (1915).
**Nickname:** Centennial State.
**Origin of name:** From the Spanish, meaning "red."
**1940 population & (rank):** 1,123,296 (33).
**1950 population & (rank):** 1,325,089 (34).
**1960 population & (rank):** 1,753,947 (33).
**Land area & (rank):** 103,884 sq. mi. (8).
**Geographic center:** In Park Co., 30 mi. NW of Pikes Peak.
**Number of counties:** 63.
**Largest cities (1960 census):** Denver (493,887); Pueblo (91,181); Colorado Springs (70,194); Aurora (48,548); Boulder (37,718).

State forests: 1 (70,980 ac.).
Total state revenue (1958): $365,920,645.
Total state expenditure (1958): $365,080,733.

Colorado has the highest mean elevation of any state, with 54 of its peaks over 14,000 feet in height and more than 1,000 going beyond the 10,000-foot mark. It began as a miner of gold but has been predominantly agricultural in recent times. Livestock, wheat, hay, beans, sugar beets, corn, potatoes, barley, and truck vegetables head the crop list. Like California and Arkansas, the state has a highly developed irrigation system to counteract its dry climate and promote farming.

Colorado is one of the nation's largest producers of uranium and vanadium; also mined are gold, silver, lead, zinc, copper, molybdenum, coal and several nonmetallics. The state is also a leading oil producer.

Pueblo, the "Pittsburgh of the West," makes iron, steel, brick, tile and foundry products. Colorado Springs is perhaps the most popular tourist center in the Rocky Mountain sector. Mount Evans Highway is the highest auto road in North America. The world's highest suspension bridge stretches 1,053 feet over the Royal Gorge of the Arkansas River. Summit Lake, 12,740 feet high, near the top of Mt. Evans, is the highest lake in the U. S. reached by an auto road.

Of archeological interest are the cliff dwellings located in the southwestern part of the state.

## CONNECTICUT

Capital: Hartford.
Governor: John N. Dempsey, Dem. (to Jan. 1963).
Lieut. Governor: Anthony J. Armentano (to Jan. 1963).
Secy. of State: Ella T. Grasso (to Jan. 1963).
Comptroller: Raymond S. Thatcher (to Jan. 1963).
Atty. General: Albert L. Coles (to Jan. 1963).
Entered Union & (rank): Jan. 9, 1788 (5).
Present constitution adopted: 1818; revised effective 1955.
Motto: *Qui transtulit sustinet* (He who transplanted still sustains).
State flower: Mountain laurel (1907).
State tree: White oak (1947).
State bird: American robin (1943).
State song: None.
Nickname: Constitution State.
Origin of name: From an Indian word (Quinnehtukqut) meaning "beside the long tidal river."
1940 population & (rank): 1,709,242 (31).
1950 population & (rank): 2,007,280 (28).
1960 population & (rank): 2,535,234 (25).
Land area & (rank): 4,899 sq. mi. (48).
Geographic center: In Hartford Co., at East Berlin.
Number of counties: 8.
Largest cities (1960 census): Hartford (162,-178); Bridgeport (156,748); New Haven (152,048); Waterbury (107,130); Stamford (92,713).
State forests: 27 (123,817 ac.).
State parks: 74 (21,958 ac.).
State general revenue (1960): $410,559,381.

State general expenditure (1960): $448,340,580.

Connecticut earned its sobriquet, the "Arsenal of the Nation," by its ability to turn out firearms and ammunition in early days, and from this developed an ability to turn out precision instruments of all classes.

Connecticut's cities produce a variety of products, some of which are: arms, sewing machines, airplanes, typewriters, motors, hardware, cutlery, tools, clocks, locks, pottery, machinery, brass products and hats. Hartford, which has the oldest U. S. newspaper still being published—the *Courant*, established 1764—is the insurance capital of the nation.

Connecticut devotes its farmland mainly to dairying, fruit growing and poultry raising. It stands high in tobacco growing and no crop in the nation receives as high a price per acre as her shade-grown tobacco.

The state is a popular resort area both for its beaches on Long Island Sound and for its inland lakes and forested hills. The southwest part of the state is a suburban area of New York City.

Connecticut was the first state to have a written constitution, the *Fundamental Orders*, adopted by three original towns of Colonial days in Jan. 1639.

## DELAWARE

Capital: Dover.
Governor: Elbert N. Carvel, Dem. (to Jan. 1965).
Lieut. Governor: Eugene P. Lamont (to Jan. 1965).
Secy. of State: Elisha Dukes (to Jan. 1965).
State Treasurer: Belle Everett (to Jan. 1963).
Atty. General: J. D. Bove, Jr. (to Jan. 1963).
Entered Union & (rank): Dec. 7, 1787 (1).
Present constitution adopted: 1897.
Motto: Liberty and independence.
State colors: Colonial blue and buff.
State flower: Peach blossom.
State tree: American holly.
State bird: Blue hen chicken.
State song: "Our Delaware."
Nicknames: Diamond State; First State.
Origin of name: In honor of Sir Thomas West, Lord De La Warr.
1940 population & (rank): 266,505 (46).
1950 population & (rank): 318,085 (46).
1960 population & (rank): 446,292 (46).
Land area & (rank): 1,978 sq. mi. (49).
Geographic center: In Kent Co., 11 mi. S of Dover.
Number of counties: 3.
Largest cities (1960 census): Wilmington (95,-827); Newark (11,404; Elsmere (7,319); Dover (7,250); Milford (5,795).
State forests: 6 (4,945 ac.).
State parks: 3.
State general revenue (fiscal 1960): $72,768,277.
State general expenditure (fiscal 1960): $73,475,-410.

Little Delaware, at the lowest mean elevation of any state, grows a great variety of small fruit and vegetables and is a U. S. pioneer in the industry of food canning. Peaches, strawberries, corn, wheat, lima beans, asparagus, tomatoes and soybeans are the leading crops. Fishing in the bay is an important industry. Delaware's chicken farms are one of the great supply sources for the big markets of the East.

Manufactures in Delaware include chemicals, vulcanized fiber, glazed kid and morocco leathers, textiles, paper, dental supplies, metal products, machinery, machine tools and transportation equipment of every major type. In 1844, the *Bangor,* the first iron seagoing propellor-type vessel constructed in the U. S., was launched at Wilmington.

Delaware was the first state to ratify the U. S. Constitution, on Dec. 7, 1787. During the Civil War, although a slave state, Delaware refused to secede from the Union; the southern part of the state, however, supplied many supporters to the Confederacy.

Henry Hudson discovered Delaware Bay in his exploration of 1609. First settlers in the state were Dutchmen, who arrived in 1631, but who were shortly afterwards massacred by the Indians.

## DISTRICT OF COLUMBIA

### (City of Washington)

**Land ceded to Congress:** 1788 by Maryland; 1789 by Virginia (retroceded to Virginia Sept. 7, 1846).
**Seat of government transferred to D. C.:** Dec. 1, 1800.
**Created municipal corporation:** Feb. 21, 1871.
**Present form of government established:** June 11, 1878.
**President of Board of Commissioners:** Walter N. Tobriner.
**Members of Board of Commissioners:** Robert E. McLaughlin and Brig. Gen. F. J. Clarke.
**Motto:** *Justitia omnibus* (Justice to all).
**Flower:** American beauty rose.
**Tree:** Scarlet oak.
**Origin of name:** In honor of Columbus.
**1940 population & (rank as city):** 663,091 (11).
**1950 population & (rank as city):** 802,178 (9).
**1960 population & (rank as city):** 763,956 (9).
**Land area:** 61 sq. mi.
**Geographic center:** Near corner of Fourth and L Sts., NW.
**Altitude:** Highest, 420 ft.; lowest, sea level.
**Location:** Between Virginia and Maryland, on Potomac River.
**Churches:** Protestant, 451; Roman Catholic, 41; Jewish, 16; others, 10.
**City parks:** 780 (6,945.5 ac.).
**Telephones (May 31, 1959):** 608,912.
**Radio sets:** 582,793.
**Television sets:** 402,046.
**Radio stations:** AM, 7; FM, 9.
**Television stations:** 4.
**Assessed valuation (June 1960):** $3,964,048,487.
**City tax rate (1960):** $2.30 per $100.
**Bonded debt:** None.
**Revenue (1960):** $218,678,638.
**Expenditures (1960):** $231,640,300.

The District of Columbia—identical with the City of Washington—is the capital of the U. S. and the first carefully planned capital in the world.

D. C. history began in 1790 when Congress directed selection of a new capital site, 10 miles square, along the Potomac. When the site was determined, it included thirty and three-quarters square miles on the Virginia side of the river. In 1846, however, Congress returned that area to Virginia.

The city was planned and partly laid out by Major Pierre Charles L'Enfant, a French engineer. This work was perfected and completed by Major Andrew Ellicott. In 1814, during the war of 1812, a British force fired the capital, and it was from the white paint applied to cover fire damage that the President's home came to be called the White House.

Washington's skyline is dominated by the Capitol and the Washington Monument, towering 555 feet. The Capitol, while not in the city center, is the key to the street address system. The city is laid out in rectangular blocks, created by streets intersecting at right angles. In addition, diagonal arteries fan out from various centers. Pennsylvania Avenue—the radial lines are generally named for the states—is the most famous of them, with the White House at number 1600.

The Capitol is 751 feet long and 350 feet wide. It has 431 rooms. The two wings, constructed of marble, house the Senate and the House; and the central part of the building contains the Rotunda, the Statuary Hall and the old Supreme Court chamber. Visitors may go through the building from 9 A.M. until 4:30 P.M. Congress normally convenes at noon, and the floor of the Senate and House must be cleared by 11:45 A.M. The galleries in the Senate and House chambers are open to visitors during sessions.

Washington has many other famous buildings and monuments—the Library of Congress, Jefferson Memorial, Lincoln Memorial, Grant Memorial, Tomb of the Unknown Soldier (Arlington Cemetery), Treasury Building, the Pentagon, Petersen House (where Lincoln died) and scores of others.

Washington is administered by three commissioners appointed by the President of the U. S. Two must have been civilian residents of the District for at least three years before their appointment. They are confirmed by the Senate and serve terms of three years each. The other commissioner is detailed from time to time from the Corps of Engineers of the U. S. Army. He must be a captain or of higher grade and must have served at least fifteen years in the Corps.

## FLORIDA

**Capital:** Tallahassee.
**Governor:** Farris Bryant, Dem. (to Jan. 1965).
**Secy. of State:** Tom Adams (to Jan. 1965).
**Comptroller:** Ray E. Green (to Jan. 1965).
**Atty. General:** Richard W. Ervin (to Jan. 1965).
**Organized as territory:** Mar. 30, 1822.
**Entered Union & (rank):** Mar. 3, 1845 (27).
**Seceded from Union:** Jan. 10, 1861.
**Re-entered Union:** June 25, 1868.
**Present constitution adopted:** 1885.
**Motto:** In God we trust.
**State flower:** Orange blossom (1909).
**State bird:** Mockingbird (1927).
**State song:** "Suwannee River" (1935).
**Nickname:** Sunshine State.

**Origin of name:** From the Spanish, meaning "feast of flowers" (Easter).
**1940 population & (rank):** 1,897,414 (27).
**1950 population & (rank):** 2,771,305 (20).
**1960 population & (rank):** 4,951,560 (10).
**Land area & (rank):** 54,252 sq. mi. (26).
**Geographic center:** In Citrus Co., 12 mi. W of N of Brooksville.
**Number of counties:** 67.
**Largest cities (1960 census):** Miami (291,688); Tampa (274,970); Jacksonville (201,030); St. Petersburg (181,298); Orlando (88,135).
**State forests:** 4 (204,035 ac.).
**State parks:** 23 (74,936 ac.).
**State government receipts (1959–60):** $995,439,161.
**State government expenditures (1959–60):** $928,844,257.

Industry and agriculture are Florida's biggest pursuits, but hotel statistics point to its chief fame—resorts and tourists. Along its coastline, dozens of communities more than double in population during the winter season when northerners flee snow and cold.

Oranges and grapefruit lead Florida's crop list, then come tomatoes, tobacco, beans, celery, potatoes and field corn. Truck gardening, commercial fishing and cattle are leading industries. Deep-sea fishing for sport is a leading tourist hobby. Industry is becoming increasingly important, with metal-working and chemicals now added to lumber, paper and citrus processing. Tampa is one of the largest cigar manufacturers and Jacksonville ships lumber and turpentine.

Florida's low elevation is dotted by some 30,000 small lakes and the Everglades National Park in the south. St. Augustine, founded in 1565, is the oldest town of European origin in the U. S. Key West, exclusive resort city, is connected to the mainland by a unique causeway.

In 1513, Ponce de León, seeking the mythical "Fountain of Youth," was the first white man to see the state.

# GEORGIA

**Capital:** Atlanta.
**Governor:** Ernest Vandiver, Dem. (to Jan. 1963).
**Lieut. Governor:** Garland Byrd (to Jan. 1963).
**Secy. of State:** Ben Fortson (to Jan. 1963).
**Comptroller General:** Zach Cravey (to Jan. 1963).
**Atty. General:** Eugene Cook (to Jan. 1963).
**Entered Union & (rank):** Jan. 2, 1788 (4).
**Seceded from Union:** Jan. 19, 1861.
**Re-entered Union:** July 15, 1870.
**Present constitution adopted:** 1945.
**Motto:** Wisdom, justice and moderation.
**State flower:** Cherokee rose (1916).
**State tree:** Live oak (1937).
**State bird:** Brown thrasher (1935).
**State song:** "Georgia" (1922).
**Nicknames:** Peach State; Empire State of the South.
**Origin of name:** In honor of George II of England.
**1940 population & (rank):** 3,123,723 (14).
**1950 population & (rank):** 3,444,578 (13).
**1960 population & (rank):** 3,943,116 (16).

**Land area & (rank):** 58,274 sq. mi. (21).
**Geographic center:** In Twiggs Co., 18 mi. SE of Macon.
**Number of counties:** 159.
**Largest cities (1960 census):** Atlanta (487,455); Savannah (149,245); Columbus (116,779); Augusta (70,626); Macon (69,764).
**State forests:** 24,056,600 ac. (63.8% of total state area).
**State parks:** 44 (60,794 ac.) (37 in operation).
**State general revenue (1960):** $565,472,856.
**State general allocations (1960):** $532,204,327

Georgia is typical of the changing South. The value of its factory products has passed the value of its farm products, and industrialization is ever increasing. Atlanta is achieving importance as an industrial center. Cotton and lumber products, fertilizer, processed food and a great variety of other items are among the factory output of Macon, Augusta, Savannah and Columbus.

Georgia ranks high in cotton, tobacco, peanuts and pecans. Georgia's peaches are nationally famous. From its vast stands of pine come more than half of the world's resin and turpentine, and 79% of the U. S. supply. The state is one of the leaders in the value of its clay products. Cattle grazing is extensive. Georgia marble is widely used.

Warm Springs has the celebrated foundation operated to aid infantile paralysis victims. It was there that President Franklin D. Roosevelt died on April 12, 1945.

Hernando de Soto, a Spaniard, in 1540, looked over the red clay of Georgia, and General James Oglethorpe founded its first British colony February 12, 1733, at Savannah.

# HAWAII

**Capital:** Honolulu (on Oahu).
**Governor:** William F. Quinn, Rep. (to Dec. 1962).
**Lieut. Governor:** James K. Kealoha (to Dec. 1962).
**Comptroller:** Michael M. Miyake (to Dec. 1962).
**Atty. General:** Shiro Kashiwa (to Dec. 1962).
**Organized as territory:** 1900.
**Entered Union & (rank):** Aug. 21, 1959 (50).
**Motto:** *Ua Mau Ke Ea O Ka Aina I Ka Pono* (The life of the land is perpetuated in righteousness).
**State flower:** Hibiscus.
**State song:** "Hawaii Ponoi" (unofficial).
**State bird:** Nene (Hawaiian goose).
**Nickname:** Aloha State.
**Origin of name:** Uncertain. The islands may have been named by Hawaii Loa, their traditional discoverer. Or they may have been named after Hawaii or Hawaiki, the traditional home of the Polynesians.
**1940 population:** 423,330.
**1950 population:** 499,794.
**1960 population & (rank):** 632,772 (43).
**Land area & (rank):** 6,415 sq. mi. (47).
**Counties:** 4.
**Largest cities (1960 census):** Honolulu (294,194); Hilo (25,966).*
**State parks:** 13.
**State revenue (fiscal 1960):** $251,515,166.
**State expenditure (fiscal 1960):** $226,365,159.

*Honolulu and Hilo have legally established limits and are therefore treated as incorporated places. All other places are unincorporated.

Hawaii, 2,100 miles west-southwest of San Francisco, is a 390-mile chain of islets and 8 main islands—Hawaii, Kahoolawe, Maui, Lanai, Molokai, Oahu, Kauai, and Niihau. Kure (Ocean) Island, an uninhabited islet in the Leeward Islands, is administratively part of Hawaii.

Hawaii's temperature is mild and the soil is fertile for tropical fruits and vegetables. Cane sugar and pineapple are its chief products, approximately 59% of the world's canned pineapple being produced in the islands. Hawaii also grows coffee, rice, -bananas, nuts and potatoes. Some livestock and poultry are raised. The tourist business is Hawaii's fourth largest source of income.

Hawaii's highest peak, Mauna Kea, rises to 13,769 feet. Mauna Loa, 13,680 feet in height, is the largest volcanic mountain in the world in cubic content.

Hawaii was discovered in 1778 by Captain James Cook, who named it the Sandwich Islands. It was ruled by native monarchs until 1893, thereafter as a republic until 1898, when it ceded itself to the U. S.

# IDAHO

Capital: Boise.
Governor: Robert E. Smylie, Rep. (to Jan. 1963).
Lieut. Governor: W. E. Drevlow (to Jan. 1963).
Secy. of State: Arnold Williams (to Jan. 1963).
State Auditor: Joe R. Williams (to Jan. 1963).
Atty. General: Frank L. Benson (to Jan. 1963).
Organized as territory: Mar. 3, 1863.
Entered Union & (rank): July 3, 1890 (43).
Present constitution adopted: 1890.
Motto: *Esto perpetua* (May you last forever).
State flower: Syringa (1931).
State tree: White pine (1935).
State bird: Mountain bluebird (1931).
State song: "Here We Have Idaho."
Nicknames: Gem State; Gem of the mountains.
Origin of name: From a Shoshoni Indian word meaning "sunup."
1940 population & (rank): 524,873 (42).
1950 population & (rank): 588,637 (43).
1960 population & (rank): 667,191 (42).
Land area & (rank): 82,708 sq. mi. (11).
Geographic center: In Custer Co., 24 mi. S by W of Challis.
Number of counties: 44, plus small part of Yellowstone Park.
Largest cities (1960 census): Boise (34,481); Idaho Falls (33,161); Pocatello (28,534); Twin Falls (20,126); Nampa (18,013).
State forests: 925,000 ac.
State parks: 4 (9,000 ac.).
State revenue (1959-61): total all funds, $211,310,000; total general fund, $75,600,000.
State expenditure (1959-61): total all funds, $211,309,876; total general fund, $75,553,428.

Most of Idaho slopes to the west from high, central wilderness mountains and the continental divide peaks in the east. One third of the state is covered by forests.

Mining, lumbering and irrigation farming have been important for years. The state's most impressive growth began when World War II military needs made processing agricultural products a big industry. Crops include potatoes, wheat, apples, corn, barley and hops. Light manufacturing is steadily increasing.

Tourist trade is important. Streams and lakes provide fishing, camping and boating sites. The nation's largest elk herds draw hunters from all over the world, and the famed Sun Valley resort attracts thousands of visitors each year to its swimming and skiing facilities.

# ILLINOIS

Capital: Springfield.
Governor: Otto Kerner, Dem. (to Jan. 1965).
Lieut. Governor: Samuel H. Shapiro (to Jan. 1965).
Secy. of State: Charles F. Carpentier (to Jan. 1965).
Auditor: Michael J. Howlett (to Jan. 1965).
Atty. General: William G. Clark (to Jan. 1965).
Organized as territory: Feb. 3, 1809.
Entered Union & (rank): Dec. 3, 1818 (21).
Present constitution adopted: 1870.
Motto: State sovereignty, national union.
State flower: Violet (1908).
State tree: Oak (1908).
State bird: Cardinal (1929).
State song: "Illinois" (1925).
State slogan: Land of Lincoln.
Nickname: Prairie State.
Origin of name: From an Indian word and French suffix meaning "tribe of superior men."
1940 population & (rank): 7,897,241 (3).
1950 population & (rank): 8,712,176 (4).
1960 population & (rank): 10,081,158 (4).
Land area & (rank): 55,930 sq. mi. (24).
Geographic center: In Logan Co., 28 mi. NE of Springfield.
Number of counties: 102.
Largest cities (1960 census): Chicago (3,550,404); Rockford (126,706); Peoria (103,162); Springfield (83,271); East St. Louis (81,712).
State forests: 3 (10,278 ac.).
State parks, memorials, conservation areas: 78 (90,000 ac.).
State revenue (1958-60): $2,939,363,628 (State Treasurer's report).
State expenditures (1958-60): $3,241,628,366 (State Treasurer's report).

Illinois anchors the Midwest like a rich giant, versatile in every big wealth-making industry. It stands high in manufacturing, coal mining, farm cash income, oil production. The sprawling Chicago district (including a slice of Indiana) is a great iron and steel producer, meat packer, grain exchange and railroad center. Chicago is also a busy long-flight airport city and Great Lakes port area. The Illinois sand and gravel business is exceeded only by that of California.

In agriculture, Illinois is first in soy beans and high in corn, oats, wheat, barley, rye, potatoes and truck vegetables. Hog raising and dairying are important industries of the state.

Illinois manufactures almost everything. Railroad cars, clothing, furniture, tractors, liquor, watches and farm implements are some of the items made in several of its cities. An important U. S. arsenal is located on a Mississippi island off Rock Island.

Central Illinois is noted for shrines and memorials associated with the life and works of Abraham Lincoln, greatest son of Illinois. In Springfield are the Lincoln Home and Lincoln Tomb. At New Salem State Park, 20 miles northwest of Springfield, the reconstructed village of New Salem stands as a notable Lincoln memorial.

## INDIANA

Capital: Indianapolis.
Governor: Matthew E. Welsh, Dem. (to Jan. 1965).
Lieut. Governor: Richard O. Ristine (to Jan. 1965).
Secy. of State: Charles O. Hendricks (to Jan. 1965).
Treasurer: Robert E. Hughes (to Feb. 1965).
Atty. General: Edwin K. Steers (to Jan. 1965).
Organized as territory: May 7, 1800.
Entered Union & (rank): Dec. 11, 1816 (19).
Present constitution adopted: 1851.
Motto: The Crossroads of America.
State flower: Peony (1957).
State tree: Tulip tree (1931).
State bird: Cardinal (1933).
State song: "On the Banks of the Wabash, Far Away" (1913).
Nickname: Hoosier State.
Origin of name: Meaning "land of Indians."
1940 population & (rank): 3,427,796 (12).
1950 population & (rank): 3,934,224 (12).
1960 population & (rank): 4,662,498 (11).
Land area & (rank): 36,185 sq. mi. (38).
Geographic center: In Boone Co., 14 mi. W of N of Indianapolis.
Number of counties: 92.
Largest cities (1960 census): Indianapolis (476,258); Gary (178,320); Ft. Wayne (161,-776); Evansville (141,543); South Bend (132,445).
State forests: 14 (120,000 ac.).
State parks: 20 (43,977.39 ac.) and 14 (703.66 ac.) state memorials.
State general revenue (1958–59): $560,360,000.
State general expenditure (1958–59): $549,302,000.

Indiana's fifty-one-mile Michigan waterfront is one of the great industrial centers of the world, turning out iron and steel and oil products to make this state a leader in manufacturing. Its cities have some of the world's largest industrial plants and their great output is further swelled by the inland factories. The list of products is endless—automobiles, farm implements, aviation and railroad equipment, sewing machines are made from iron ore mined in the Great Lakes region.

In farming the state stands high in soy beans, corn, tobacco, onions, wheat, oats, rye and tomatoes.

Indianapolis is the second largest U. S. city not on a navigable body of water. Wyandotte Cave, the second largest in the U. S., is located in Crawford County of Southern Indiana. West Baden and French Lick are well known for their mineral springs. Indiana was one of the early states to adopt the secret ballot based on the Australian system.

## IOWA

Capital: Des Moines.
Governor: Norman A. Erbe, Rep. (to Jan. 1963).
Lieut. Governor: W. L. Mooty (to Jan. 1963).
Secy. of State: Melvin D. Synhorst (to Jan. 1963).
Treasurer: M. L. Abrahamson (to Jan. 1963).
Atty. General: Evan Hultman (to Jan. 1963).
Organized as territory: June 12, 1838.
Entered Union & (rank): Dec. 28, 1846 (29).
Present constitution adopted: 1857.
Motto: Our liberties we prize and our rights we will maintain.
State flower: Wild rose (1897).
State bird: Eastern goldfinch (1933).
State colors: Red, white and blue (in state flag).
State song: "Song of Iowa."
Nickname: Hawkeye State.
Origin of name: Probably from an Indian word meaning "I-o-w-a, this is the place."
1940 population & (rank): 2,538,268 (20).
1950 population & (rank): 2,621,073 (22).
1960 population & (rank): 2,757,537 (24).
Land area & (rank): 56,032 sq. mi. (23).
Geographic center: In Story County, 5 mi. NE of Ames.
Number of counties: 99.
Largest cities (1960 census): Des Moines (208,-982); Cedar Rapids (92,035); Sioux City (89,159); Davenport (88,981); Waterloo (71,-755).
State forests: 7 (13,469 ac.).
State parks: 90 (28,437 ac.).
State general revenue (1959–60): $175,814,084.
State general expenditure (1959–60): $166,841,409.

Iowa stands in a class by itself as an agricultural state, supplying 10% of the nation's food supply. It ranks first in livestock income, value of cattle, sheep and hogs marketed, production averages of oats and corn; ranks second in production of chickens, eggs, and soybeans. Nearly 95% of the state's total acreage is in farms, and the fertility of its soil is unsurpassed. Of all the Grade A land in the country, 25% is in Iowa.

However, the value of Iowa's manufactured products is more than double that of her agricultural products. The top industrial activity is meat packing. Des Moines fittingly leads all cities in the publication of farm journals and is also a large insurance center.

West Branch is the birthplace of Herbert Hoover, who was the first President of the U. S. to be born west of the Mississippi.

## KANSAS

Capital: Topeka.
Governor: John Anderson, Jr., Rep. (to Jan. 1963).
Lieut. Governor: Harold H. Chase (to Jan. 1963).
Secy. of State: Paul R. Shanahan (to Jan. 1963).
Treasurer: Walter H. Peery (to Jan. 1963).

Atty. General: William M. Ferguson (to Jan. 1963).

Organized as territory: May 30, 1854.

Entered Union & (rank): Jan. 29, 1861 (34).

Present constitution adopted: 1859.

Motto: *Ad astra per aspera* (To the stars through difficulties).

State flower: Sunflower (1903).

State tree: Cottonwood (1937).

State bird: Western meadow lark (1937).

State animal: Buffalo (1955).

State song: "Home on the Range" (1947).

State march: "The Kansas March" (1935).

Nicknames: Sunflower State; Jayhawk State.

Origin of name: From a Siouan word meaning "people of the south wind."

1940 population & (rank): 1,801,028 (29).

1950 population & (rank): 1,905,299 (31).

1960 population & (rank): 2,178,611 (28).

Land area & (rank): 82,048 sq. mi. (13).

Geographic center: In Barton Co., 15 mi. NE of Great Bend.

Number of counties: 105.

Largest cities (1960 census): Wichita (254,698); Kansas City (121,901); Topeka (119,484); Salina (43,202); Hutchinson (37,574).

State forests: 1 (4,000 ac.).

State parks: 22 (14,394 ac.).

State operating revenue (1959–60): $358,613,713.

State operating expenditure (1959–60): $329,853,904.

Kansas finds its strength in wheat growing, flour milling and a variety of manufacturing enterprises. Slaughtering and meat packing are also extensively pursued. In the western part of the state, where a replica of Dodge City's Front Street recalls the old West and the city's heyday as a famous cowtown, rich prairie land sprawls over a large area and gives an abundance of winter wheat and fine grazing.

Corn, sorghums, oats, barley, soy beans and potatoes are other crops. Besides oil, Kansas mines zinc, coal, salt and lead.

The state is the geographical center of the 48 contiguous states, and the geodetic center of the North American continent.

Wichita, a growing industrial center, is a leader in the production of military and civilian aircraft. Kansas City is an important transportation, milling, and meat-packing center.

After being dry since the Murray Liquor Law of 1881, Kansas repealed prohibition in March 1949.

Points of unusual interest in Kansas include: President Eisenhower's boyhood home and the new Eisenhower Memorial Museum at Abilene (Presidential Library will open in 1961); John Brown's well-preserved cabin at Osawatomie; recreated Front Street at Dodge City; and two historic military reservations—Ft. Leavenworth and Ft. Riley.

## KENTUCKY

Capital: Frankfort.

Governor: Bert Combs, Dem. (to Dec. 1963).

Lieut. Governor: Wilson W. Wyatt (to Dec. 1963).

Secy. of State: Henry H. Carter (to Jan. 1964).

Director of Finance: Robert F. Matthews (to Dec. 1963).

Atty. General: John B. Breckinridge (to Jan. 1964).

Entered Union & (rank): June 1, 1792 (15).

Present constitution adopted: 1891.

Motto: United we stand, divided we fall.

State flower: Goldenrod.

State bird: Kentucky cardinal.

State song: "My Old Kentucky Home."

Nickname: Bluegrass State.

Origin of name: From an Iroquoian Indian word "Ken-tah-ten" meaning "land of tomorrow."

1940 population & (rank): 2,845,627 (16).

1950 population & (rank): 2,944,806 (19).

1960 population & (rank): 3,038,156 (22).

Land area & (rank): 39,863 sq. mi. (36).

Geographic center: In Marion Co., 3 mi. W of N of Lebanon.

Number of counties: 120.

Largest cities (1960 census): Louisville (390,639); Lexington (62,810); Covington (60,376); Owensboro (42,471); Paducah (34,479).

State forests: 6 (48,000 ac.).

State parks: 31 (35,565 ac.).

Total state revenue (1959–60): $373,041,036.

Total state expenditure (1959–60): $471,043,986.

Kentucky prides itself on producing some of the nation's best tobacco, horses and whisky. It stands high in the production of native asphalt, hemp, coal, corn, oil.

Among the manufactured items produced by its cities are furniture, aluminum ware, brooms, shoes, lumber products, machinery, textiles and iron and steel products. Besides coal and oil, important minerals are natural gas and quarry products.

Louisville, the largest city, famed for the Kentucky Derby at Churchill Downs, has a large municipal university, distills whisky and is a great cigarette maker. The Blue Grass country is the home of some of the world's finest race horses. Lexington, standing in the center of this country, is a leading tobacconist. Mammoth Cave, with its many miles of underground passages, is one tourist attraction. Another is Kentucky Lake, 184 miles wide, one of the largest man-made bodies of water in the world.

Kentucky was credited with a star in the Confederate flag because a secessionist group in the southwest part of the state set up a short-lived government and joined the Confederacy. The legitimate government, however, remained in the Union throughout the Civil War.

Marquette and Joliet in 1673 saw Kentucky when it was the "Dark and Bloody Ground," fiercely contested by Indian tribes. Daniel Boone explored the country in 1767.

## LOUISIANA

Capital: Baton Rouge.

Governor: James H. Davis, Dem. (to May 1964).

Lieut. Governor: C. C. Aycock (to May 1964).

Secy. of State: Wade O. Martin, Jr. (to May 1964).

Comptroller: Roy R. Theriot (to May 1964).

Atty. General: Jack P. Gremillion (to May 1964).

Organized as territory: Mar. 26, 1804.

**Entered Union & (rank):** Apr. 30, 1812 (18).
**Seceded from Union:** Jan. 26, 1861.
**Re-entered Union:** May 26, 1865.
**Present constitution adopted:** 1921.
**Motto:** Union, justice and confidence.
**State flower:** Magnolia (1900).
**State bird:** Pelican (unofficial).
**State song:** "Song of Louisiana."
**Nicknames:** Pelican State; Creole State; Sugar State.
**Origin of name:** In honor of Louis XIV of France.
**1940 population & (rank):** 2,363,880 (21).
**1950 population & (rank):** 2,683,516 (21).
**1960 population & (rank):** 3,257,022 (20).
**Land area & (rank):** 45,106 sq. mi. (32).
**Geographic center:** In Avoyelles Parish, 3 mi. SE of Marksville.
**Number of parishes (counties):** 64.
**Largest cities (1960 census):** New Orleans (627,525); Shreveport (164,372); Baton Rouge (152,419); Lake Charles (63,392); Monroe (52,219).
**State forests:** 1 (8,000 ac.).
**State parks:** 15 (13,323 ac.).
**State general revenue (1959–60):** $891,955,524.
**State general expenditure (1959–60):** $724,592,-242.

Louisiana, which still calls its counties parishes after the Spanish religious divisions, is one of the leading states in fur trapping, with a rich annual bag of mink, muskrat, opossum and raccoon pelts. Other important agricultural products are sugar cane, sweet potatoes, rice and cotton. The state is rapidly becoming industrialized, and is an important producer of petroleum and petrochemicals, pulp and paper, natural gas, sulfur, chemicals and salt.

New Orleans, home of the Mardi Gras, avoids flooding only by an expensive levee and spillway system. Its industry is making increased use of raw materials from South and Central America. The Vieux Carré, in this Old World city, called by many the "Little Paris" of the New World, has some of the celebrated restaurants of the nation.

Louisiana has a great variety and abundance of game birds. Its state-owned wildlife sanctuaries are among the world's largest.

Hernando de Soto, in the year 1540, is usually considered the first white man to see the state, but claims are made for Narvaez, who is reputed to have seen the state as early as 1528.

## MAINE

**Capital:** Augusta.
**Governor:** John H. Reed, Rep. (to Jan. 1963).
**Secy. of State:** Paul A. MacDonald (to Jan. 1963).
**Controller:** Henry L. Cranshaw (Indefinite).
**Atty. General:** Frank E. Hancock (to Jan. 1963).
**Entered Union & (rank):** Mar. 15, 1820 (23).
**Present constitution adopted:** 1820.
**Motto:** *Dirigo* (I guide).
**State flower:** White pine cone and tassel (1895).
**State tree:** Pine tree.
**State bird:** Chickadee (1927).
**State song:** "State of Maine Song" (1937).

**Nickname:** Pine Tree State.
**Origin of name:** From the French province of Mayne.
**1940 population & (rank):** 847,226 (35).
**1950 population & (rank):** 913,774 (35).
**1960 population & (rank):** 969,265 (36).
**Land area & (rank):** 31,012 sq. mi. (39).
**Geographic center:** In Piscataquis Co., 18 mi. N of Dover-Foxcroft.
**Number of counties:** 16.
**Largest cities (1960 census):** Portland (72,566); Lewiston (40,804); Bangor (38,912); Auburn (24,449); South Portland (22,788).
**State forests:** 1 (21,000 ac.).
**State parks:** 11 (203,533 ac.).
**State general revenue (1960):** $139,942,972.
**State general expenditure (1960):** $140,104,894.

Two major changes in Maine's constitution were voted in 1957: (1) the state's general election is now held in November instead of September, making the expression "As Maine goes so goes the nation" no longer valid, and (2) the governor now has a 4-year term and may succeed himself.

Maine produces one out of every seven potatoes raised in the U. S., and 95% of the nation's blueberries. The chicken broiler industry has climbed from $300,000 after the last war to over $46 million today.

Maine is one of the world's largest pulp-paper producers. It ranks fifth in boot and shoe manufacturing. It has the largest forest area in the East, and planned cutting promises an unending wood supply for pulp-paper mills, lumber mills and hardwood processing plants.

The state leads the world in the production of the familiar flat tins of sardines, producing 200 million of them normally. Lobstermen catch 90% of the nation's total of true lobsters.

In 1959, the Appalachian range within the state was named the "Longfellow Mountains of Maine," in honor of Henry Wadsworth Longfellow, who was born in the state. Mt. Katahdin (5,267 ft.) is the highest peak.

## MARYLAND

**Capital:** Annapolis.
**Governor:** J. Millard Tawes, Dem. (to Jan. 1963).
**Secy. of State:** Lloyd L. Simpkins (appointed by governor).
**Comptroller of the Treasury:** Louis L. Goldstein (to Jan. 1963).
**Atty. General:** Thomas B. Finan (to Dec. 1962).
**Entered Union & (rank):** Apr. 28, 1788 (7).
**Present constitution adopted:** 1867.
**Motto:** *Fatti maschii, parole femine* (Manly deeds, womanly words).
**State flower:** Black-eyed susan (1918).
**State tree:** White oak (1941).
**State bird:** Baltimore oriole (1882).
**State song:** "Maryland! My Maryland!" (1939).
**Nicknames:** Free State; Old Line State.
**Origin of name:** In honor of Henrietta Maria (Queen of Charles I of England).
**1940 population & (rank):** 1,821,244 (28).
**1950 population & (rank):** 2,343,001 (24).
**1960 population & (rank):** 3,100,689 (21).
**Land area & (rank):** 9,874 sq. mi. (42).

**Geographic center:** In Anne Arundel Co., 3 mi. E of Collington.
**Number of counties:** 23, plus 1 independent city.
**Largest cities (1960 census):** Baltimore (939,-024); Hagerstown (36,660); Cumberland (33,415); Rockville (26,090); Annapolis (23,-385).
**State forests:** 11 (119,186 ac.).
**State parks:** 17 (16,550 ac.).
**State general revenue (1960):** $476,245,728.
**State general expenditure (1960):** $454,461,795.

Maryland is cut almost in two by Chesapeake Bay, and the many estuaries and rivers create one of the longest water fronts of any state. The Bay produces more seafood—oysters, crabs, clams, fin fish—than any comparable body of water, and is a major crabbing center. Important agricultural products, in order of cash value, are dairy products, poultry and poultry products, tobacco, corn, vegetables, wheat, and soy beans. Maryland is a leader in vegetable canning and broiler raising. Sand and gravel, lime and cement, stone, coal, and clay are the chief mineral products.

Manufactures, which center in Baltimore, include missiles, airplanes, steel, clothing, and chemicals. The port of Baltimore ranks second in the country in foreign trade tonnage. Baltimore is the home of The Johns Hopkins University and Hospital. In Annapolis, home of the U. S. Naval Academy, is one of the earliest state houses (1772-1779) still in regular use by a State government.

The Charter of Maryland was granted in 1632 to Lord Baltimore, who died before it had passed the Great Seal; it was issued to his oldest son, Cecil. The first settlers landed at St. Mary's in 1634.

## MASSACHUSETTS

**Capital:** Boston.
**Governor:** John A. Volpe, Rep. (to Jan. 1963).
**Lieut. Governor:** Edward F. McLaughlin, Jr. (to Jan. 1963).
**Secy. of the Commonwealth:** Kevin H. White (to Jan. 1963).
**Atty. General:** Edward J. McCormack, Jr. (to Jan. 1963).
**Treasurer & Receiver General:** John T. Driscoll (to Jan. 1963).
**Auditor of the Commonwealth:** Thomas J. Buckley (to Jan. 1963).
**Entered Union & (rank):** Feb. 6, 1788 (6).
**Present constitution adopted:** 1780.
**Motto:** *Ense petit placidam sub libertate quietem* (By the sword we seek peace, but peace only under liberty).
**State flower:** Mayflower (1918).
**State tree:** American elm (1941).
**State bird:** Chickadee (1941).
**State colors:** Blue and gold.
**State song:** None.
**Nicknames:** Bay State; Old Colony State.
**Origin of name:** From two Indian words meaning "great mountain place."
**1940 population & (rank):** 4,316,721 (8).
**1950 population & (rank):** 4,690,514 (9).
**1960 population & (rank):** 5,148,578 (9).
**Land area & (rank):** 7,867 sq. mi. (45).
**Geographic center:** In Worcester Co., in N part of city of Worcester.

**Number of counties:** 14.
**Largest cities (1960 census):** Boston (697,197); Worcester (186,587); Springfield (174,463); Cambridge (107,716); New Bedford (102,477).
**State forests:** 28 (170,000 ac.).
**State parks:** 14 (9,236 ac.).*
**State general revenue (1959):** $692,459,640.
**State general expenditure (1959):** $657,406,126.

*\* The Metropolitan District Commission, an agency of the Commonwealth serving municipalities in the Boston area, has over 14,000 acres of parkways and reservations under its jurisdiction.*

Massachusetts is the leading shoe producer in the U. S., and has been one of the leaders in the making of textiles since the beginning of American history. Top-ranking industries are electrical and other machinery, leather and leather products, apparel, and other finished goods and textile mill products. Logan International Airport at East Boston, the nearest major airport in the U. S. to Europe, ranks among the worlds greatest aerodromes. It has one of the longest commercial runways (10,022 ft.) and the longest air passenger terminal building in the world (3,053 ft.).

Agricultural products, ranked in order of importance (1957), are poultry, dairy products, greenhouse and nursery products, vegetables, fruit, cranberries and tobacco. The state is the leader in producing carnations and cranberries.

The growth of factories brought to this state an influx of foreigners and today Boston has one of the largest Irish populations in the nation.

Faneuil Hall in Boston was known as the "Cradle of Liberty." From the belfry of Christ Church (Old North Church), on Copp's Hill, Paul Revere received the lantern message that began his famous ride. Boston was also the site of the Battle of Bunker Hill.

The Pilgrims landed at Plymouth Rock in 1620 as the first large group to settle here but legend has it that Eric the Red and his Norsemen saw the state in the year 1000.

## MICHIGAN

**Capital:** Lansing.
**Governor:** John B. Swainson, Dem. (to Jan. 1963).
**Lieut. Governor:** T. John Lesinski (to Jan. 1963).
**Secy. of State:** James M. Hare (to Jan. 1963).
**Auditor General:** Otis M. Smith (to Jan. 1963).
**Atty. General:** Paul L. Adams (to Jan. 1963).
**Organized as territory:** Jan. 11, 1805.
**Entered Union & (rank):** Jan. 26, 1837 (26).
**Present constitution adopted:** 1908.
**Motto:** *Si quaeris peninsulam amoenam circumspice* (If you seek a pleasant peninsula, look around you).
**State flower:** Apple blossom (1897).
**State bird:** Robin (unofficial).
**State animal:** Wolverine (unofficial).
**State song:** "Michigan, My Michigan" (unofficial).
**Nickname:** Wolverine State.
**Origin of name:** From two Indian words meaning "great lake."
**1940 population & (rank):** 5,256,106 (7).

1950 population & (rank): 6,371,766 (7).
1960 population & (rank): 7,823,194 (7).
Land area & (rank): 57,019 sq. mi. (22).
Geographic center: In Wexford Co., 5 mi. W of N of Cadillac.
Number of counties: 83.
Largest cities (1960 census): Detroit (1,670,144); Flint (196,940); Grand Rapids (177,313); Dearborn (112,007); Lansing (107,807).
State forests: 23 (3,762,464 ac.).
State parks: 79 (179,556 ac.).
State general revenue (1959–60): $1,107,927,015.
State general expenditure (1959–60): $1,097,229,-962.

On a map of Michigan, draw an eighty-five-mile circle around Detroit and it will contain the home plants of the companies that make 14 out of 16 American automobiles. This industry, which sprang up about fifty years ago from the carriage-building business, is not the only activity of this state. Airplane parts, furniture, diesel engines, hoists, pumps, boilers are among its leading items of production. Most of the nation's refrigerators are made in Michigan. On its farms are grown dry beans, grapes, peaches, potatoes, sugar beets, etc.

Michigan is split completely in two parts. The northern peninsula is mining and timber country. The southern part is agricultural and manufacturing country. Connecting Lakes Superior and Huron is the busiest canal in the world—the Sault Ste. Marie.

Michigan has the greatest inland fisheries in the world and markets at least 20 species from carp, trout, perch, pike to lake herring.

The state's 11,037 inland lakes and 2,242 miles of Great Lakes shoreline make it a good vacation land. The artificial ski jump on Iron Mountain is among the highest in the world.

## MINNESOTA

Capital: St. Paul.
Governor: Elmer L. Andersen, Rep. (to Jan. 1963).
Lieut. Governor: Karl F. Rolvaag (to Jan. 1963).
Secy. of State: Joseph L. Donovan (to Jan. 1963).
State Auditor: Stafford King (to Jan. 1963).
Atty. General: Walter F. Mondale (to Jan. 1963).
Organized as territory: Mar. 3, 1849.
Entered Union & (rank): May 11, 1858 (32).
Present constitution adopted: 1858.
Motto: *L'Etoile du Nord* (The North Star).
State flower: Moccasin flower (1902).
State tree: Norway pine.
State bird: Loon.
State song: "Hail Minnesota."
Nicknames: North Star State; Gopher State; Land of 10,000 Lakes.
Origin of name: From a Dakota Indian word meaning "sky-tinted water."
1940 population & (rank): 2,792,300 (18).
1950 population & (rank): 2,982,483 (18).
1960 population & (rank): 3,413,864 (18).
Land area & (rank): 80,009 sq. mi. (14).
Geographic center: In Crow Wing Co., 10 mi. SW of Brainerd.

Number of counties: 87.
Largest cities (1960 census): Minneapolis (482,872); St. Paul (313,411); Duluth (106,884); Bloomington (50,498); St. Louis Park (43,310).
State forests: 34 (3,039,236 ac.).
State parks: 69 (106,000 ac.).
Total gross receipts (1959–60): $821,481,333.
Total net expenditures (1959–60): $816,041,935.

A few square miles of Northern Minnesota, in the Mesabi, Cuyuna and Vermilion Ranges, produce most of the nation's iron ore, and provide the activity for the port of Duluth. Farm and factory are equally important in Minnesota. Its farms produce oats, butter, eggs, milk, corn, wheat, potatoes, etc. Its factory production follows the pattern of the Midwest. Machinery, furniture, foundry products, etc. are manufactured.

Minneapolis is the trade center of the Northwest. Its twin city, St. Paul, is the nation's biggest publisher of calendars and law books.

With over 11,000 lakes, the state is famous for its fishing, hunting and trapping, and it has many famous resort regions.

In 1655, Radisson and Groseilliers, French traders from Canada, were the first white men to see the state.

## MISSISSIPPI

Capital: Jackson.
Governor: Ross R. Barnett, Dem. (to Jan. 1964).
Lieut. Governor: Paul B. Johnson, Jr. (to Jan. 1964).
Secy. of State: Heber L. Ladner (to Jan. 1964).
Treasurer: Evelyn Gandy (to Jan. 1964).
Atty. General: Joe T. Patterson (to Jan. 1964).
Organized as territory: Apr. 7, 1798.
Entered Union & (rank): Dec. 10, 1817 (20).
Seceded from Union: Jan. 9, 1861.
Re-entered Union: Feb. 23, 1870.
Present constitution adopted: 1890.
Motto: *Virtute et armis* (By valor and arms).
State flower: Flower or bloom of the magnolia or evergreen magnolia (1952).
State tree: Magnolia (1938).
State bird: Mockingbird (1944).
State song: "Way Down South in Mississippi" (1948).
Nickname: Magnolia State.
Origin of name: From an Indian word meaning "Father of Waters."
1940 population & (rank): 2,183,796 (23).
1950 population & (rank): 2,178,914 (26).
1960 population & (rank): 2,178,141 (29).
Land area & (rank): 47,223 sq. mi. (31).
Geographic center: In Leake Co., 9 mi. N of W of Carthage.
Number of counties: 82.
Largest cities (1960 census): Jackson (144,422); Meridian (49,374); Biloxi (44,053); Greenville (41,502), Hattiesburg (34,989).
State forests: 1 (1,760 ac.).
State parks: 10 state-owned (10,972 ac.); 2 state-leased (1,910 ac.).
State general revenue (1959–60): $239,280,363.
State general expenditure (1959–60): $235,614,-808.

Mississippi, the stronghold of the Old

South, has until the past decade been one of the least industrialized states, with more than half its population making a living from the soil. A recent program of industrialization, however, has attracted numerous manufacturing concerns. Cotton, nevertheless, is still king. The world's largest cotton plantation of 35,000 acres is located at Scott. Other crops are corn, peanuts, oats, pecans, soybeans, rice, tung nuts, sugar cane and hay.

Mississippi's Central Hills have produced a serious soil-erosion problem due to the overemphasis placed on cotton growing through the years. Introduction of livestock and dairying and the pasture improvement programs attendant to it have helped in recent years to remedy this situation.

Mississippi was first to ratify the 18th Amendment, and it is the only state that still bans the sale of hard liquor. In 1950, it had the third largest Negro population in the U. S.

The state abounds in historical landmarks and is the home of the Vicksburg National Military Park commemorating Grant's victory.

## MISSOURI

**Capital:** Jefferson City.
**Governor:** John M. Dalton, Dem. (to Jan. 1965).
**Lieut. Governor:** Hilary A. Bush (to Jan. 1965).
**Secy. of State:** Warren E. Hearnes (to Jan. 1965).
**Treasurer:** Milton Carpenter (to Jan. 1965).
**Atty. General:** Thomas F. Eagleton (to Jan. 1965).
**Organized as territory:** June 4, 1812.
**Entered Union & (rank):** Aug. 10, 1821 (24).
**Present constitution adopted:** 1945.
**Motto:** *Salus populi suprema lex esto* (The welfare of the people shall be the supreme law).
**State flower:** Hawthorn (1923).
**State bird:** Bluebird (1927).
**State colors:** Red, white and blue (1913).
**State song:** "Missouri Waltz" (1949).
**State tree:** Dogwood (1955).
**Nickname:** Show-me State.
**Origin of name:** From an Indian word probably meaning "muddy water."
**1940 population & (rank):** 3,784,664 (10).
**1950 population & (rank):** 3,954,653 (11).
**1960 population & (rank):** 4,319,813 (13).
**Land area & (rank):** 69,138 sq. mi. (18).
**Geographic center:** In Miller Co., 20 mi. SW of Jefferson City.
**Number of counties:** 114, plus 1 independent city.
**Largest cities (1960 census):** St. Louis (750,-026); Kansas City (475,539); Springfield (95,865); St. Joseph (79,673); Independence (62,328).
**State forests:** 9 (175,519 ac.).
**State parks:** 32 (71,436 ac.). Also 5 Memorial Shrines.
**State cash receipts (1959–60):** $519,078,991.
**State general expenditure (1959–60):** $509,958,-232.

Missouri is composed of fertile farmlands in the north, flat lowlands in the southeast, rolling plains in the west, and the rugged Ozark Mountains which extend through the center of the state south into Arkansas. Once noted for its corncob pipes and Missouri mules, the state is now a popular vacationland. It has seven major lakes and numerous fishing streams, springs and caves. Bagnell Dam, across the Osage River in the Ozarks, completed in 1931, created one of the largest artificial lakes in the world, covering 64,000 acres of surface area and having a shoreline that extends for 1,372 miles.

Missouri is a leading producer of automobiles, machinery, shoes and beer. It also grows corn, soybeans, wheat, oats, barley, potatoes, tobacco and cotton. Eads Bridge, spanning the Mississippi River at St. Louis, probably handles more freight cars than any other bridge in the world.

Historically, Missouri played a leading role as a gateway to the west, St. Joseph, Mo., being the eastern starting point of the Pony Express. During the Civil War Missourians' loyalties were divided between North and South, but the state remained in the Union.

The birthplaces of Harry S. Truman and Mark Twain, as well as the Truman Library in Independence, are tourist attractions.

## MONTANA

**Capital:** Helena.
**Governor:** Donald G. Nutter, Rep. (to Jan. 1965).
**Lieut. Governor:** Tim M. Babcock (to Jan. 1965).
**Secy. of State:** Frank Murray (to Jan. 1965).
**Auditor:** John J. Holmes (to Jan. 1965).
**Atty. General:** Forrest Anderson (to Jan. 1965).
**Organized as territory:** May 26, 1864.
**Entered Union & (rank):** Nov. 8, 1889 (41).
**Present constitution adopted:** 1889.
**Motto:** *Oro y plata* (Gold and silver).
**State flower:** Bitterroot (1895).
**State tree:** Ponderosa pine (1949).
**State bird:** Western meadow lark (1931).
**State song:** "Montana" (1945).
**Nickname:** Treasure State.
**Origin of name:** Chosen from Mexican dictionary by J. M. Ashley. It is a Mexicanized Spanish word.
**1940 population & (rank):** 559,456 (39).
**1950 population & (rank):** 591,024 (42).
**1960 population & (rank):** 674,767 (41).
**Land area & (rank):** 145,736 sq. mi. (4).
**Geographic center:** In Fergus Co., 12 mi. W of Lewistown.
**Number of counties:** 56, plus small part of Yellowstone National Park.
**Largest cities (1960 census):** Great Falls (55,-357); Billings (52,851); Butte (27,877); Missoula (27,090); Helena (20,227).
**State forests:** 7 (488,078 ac.).
**State parks:** 23 (9,213 ac.).
**State general revenue (1959–60):** $159,888,088.
**State general expenditure (1959–60):** $158,608,-325.

Montana's story is the old Western story —few settlers until a gold strike in 1862 brought an influx. Mining is its present occupation, and copper, lead, zinc, silver, coal, and oil are taken from its earth.

Butte, sitting on the "richest hill in the world," is the center of the area that once supplied half of the U. S. copper (its most important mineral). Livestock, wool, lumber and dude ranching round out its interests. Agriculture is dependent on irrigation.

The state as a whole still possesses the frank character of the old days, reflected in the legend that the only reason Helena was selected as the name to replace Last Chance Gulch was because of the suggestion of profanity in the front part of that name. Glacier National Park is a popular tourist area with its rugged scenery, hunting areas and dude ranches. While little development has been made, Montana offers fine potentialities for winter sports.

## NEBRASKA

Capital: Lincoln.
Governor: Frank B. Morrison, Dem. (to Jan. 1963).
Lieut. Governor: Dwight W. Burney (to Jan. 1963).
Secy. of State: Frank Marsh (to Jan. 1963).
Atty. General: C. A. H. Meyer (to Jan. 1963).
Organized as territory: May 30, 1854.
Entered Union & (rank): Mar. 1, 1867 (37).
Present constitution adopted: 1875 (extensively amended 1919-20).
Motto: Equality before the law.
State flower: Goldenrod (1895).
State tree: American elm (1937).
State bird: Western meadow lark (1929).
State song: "My Nebraska" (unofficial).
Nickname: Cornhusker State.
Origin of name: From an Oto Indian word meaning "flat water."
1940 population & (rank): 1,315,834 (32).
1950 population & (rank): 1,325,510 (33).
1960 population & (rank): 1,411,330 (34).
Land area & (rank): 76,612 sq. mi. (15).
Geographic center: In Custer Co., 10 mi. NW of Broken Bow.
Number of counties: 93.
Largest cities (1960 census): Omaha (301,-598); Lincoln (128,521); Grand Island (25,-742); Hastings (21,412); Fremont (19,698).
State forests: 2.
State parks: 7 (1,036 ac.).
State general revenue (1960): $163,927,141.
State general expenditure (1959-60): $171,361,587.

Nebraska lives by its expansive sea of grain, reflected in its bumper crops of rye, corn and wheat. There are more varieties of grass growing in this state, valuable for forage, than in any other state in the nation. Its sizable cattle and hog industries help to make Omaha a great stockyard and meat-packing center. Flour, freight cars, farm machinery, precision instruments, brick and tile are products of Nebraska.

Oil was discovered in 1939, and natural gas in 1949. The state was 14th in oil production in the U. S. for 1956.

In 1937, Nebraska became the only state in the Union to have a unicameral (one-house) legislature. Members are elected to it without party designation.

## NEVADA

Capital: Carson City.
Governor: Grant Sawyer, Dem. (to Jan. 1963).
Lieut. Governor: Rex Bell (to 1963).
Secy. of State: John Koontz (to 1963).
State Treasurer: Dan W. Franks (to 1963).
Controller: Keith L. Lee (to 1963).
Atty. General: Roger D. Foley (to 1963).
Organized as territory: Mar. 2, 1861.
Entered Union & (rank): Oct. 31, 1864 (36).
Present constitution adopted: 1864.
Motto: All for our country.
State flower: Sagebrush (unofficial; official state emblem as of 1917).
State tree: Single-leaf piñon (1953).
State bird: Mountain bluebird (unofficial).
State colors: Cobalt blue and silver (unofficial).
State song: "Home Means Nevada" (1933).
Nicknames: Sagebrush State; Silver State; Battle Born State.
Origin of name: Spanish: meaning "snowclad."
1940 population & (rank): 110,247 (48).
1950 population & (rank): 160,083 (48).
1960 population & (rank): 285,278 (49).
Land area & (rank): 109,788 sq. mi. (7).
Geographic center: In Lander Co., 23 mi. SE of Austin.
Number of counties: 17.
Largest cities (1960 census): Las Vegas (64,405); Reno (51,470); North Las Vegas (18,422); Sparks (16,618); Henderson (12,525).
State forests: None.
State parks: 10 (10,179 ac.).
State revenue (1959-60): $62,818,619.
State expenditure (1959-60): $59,314,388.

Nevada was made famous by the discovery of the fabulous Comstock Lode in 1859, and its mines have produced large quantities of gold, silver, copper, lead, zinc, mercury, and tungsten. Oil was discovered in Feb., 1954. There are also uranium deposits.

In 1931, the state created a new industry by writing an easy divorce law and Reno has since become the "divorce capital of the nation." Gambling was legalized and the gaming tables now pay a tax to add to the state's income.

Near Las Vegas, on the Colorado River, stands the Hoover Dam which has twice changed its name (Hoover to Boulder to Hoover).

The state's agricultural crop consists mainly of hay, wheat, barley and potatoes.

Nevada was the first state to use gas for capital punishment.

## NEW HAMPSHIRE

Capital: Concord.
Governor: Wesley Powell, Rep. (to Jan. 1963).
Secy. of State: Robert L. Stark (to Jan. 1963).
Controller: Leonard S. Hill (to Dec. 1963).
Atty. General: Gardner C. Turner (to Jan. 1966).
Entered Union & (rank): June 21, 1788 (9).
Present constitution adopted: 1784.
Motto: Live free or die.
State flower: Purple lilac (1919).
State tree: White birch (1947).
State bird: Purple finch (1957).
State song: "Old New Hampshire" (1949).
Nickname: Granite State.
Origin of name: From the English county of Hampshire.

1940 population & (rank): 491,524 (45).
1950 population & (rank): 533,242 (44).
1960 population & (rank): 606,921 (45).
Land area & (rank): 9,014 sq. mi. (44).
Geographic center: In Belknap Co., 3 mi. E of Ashland.
Number of counties: 10.
Largest cities (1960 census): Manchester (88,-282); Nashua (39,096); Concord (28,991); Portsmouth (25,833); Dover (19,131).
State forests: 142 (63,805 ac.).
State parks: 40 (approx. 20,000 ac.).
State general revenue (1960): $111,016,356.
State general expenditure (1960): $92,160,100.

New Hampshire is the only state that ever played host at the formal conclusion of a foreign war when, in 1905, Portsmouth was the scene of the treaty ending the Russo-Japanese War. The sandy and stony loam of this state needs liberal fertilization for the growing of its principal crops—fruit, truck vegetables, corn, oats, hay and potatoes. Its chief manufacturing is the production of textiles, leather goods, pulp and paper products.

New Hampshire was the first state to declare its independence from Great Britain and to adopt a constitution. Mt. Washington has recorded some of the world's strongest wind velocities, the last recording of record proportions being registered at 231 miles per hour. The state also has the largest legislative body; it varies from 375 to 400.

With 1,300 lakes and good climate for both winter sports and summer vacations, the state is highly popular as a resort area.

# NEW JERSEY

Capital: Trenton.
Governor: Robert B. Meyner, Dem. (to Jan. 1962).
Secy. of State: Edward J. Patten (to Jan. 1962).
Treasurer: John A. Kervick (to Jan. 1962).
Atty. General: David D. Furman (to Jan. 1962).
Entered Union & (rank): Dec. 18, 1787 (3).
Present constitution adopted: 1947.
Motto: Liberty and prosperity.
State flower: Purple violet (1913).
State bird: Eastern goldfinch (1935).
State tree: Red oak (1950).
State colors: Buff and blue.
State song: None.
Nickname: Garden State.
Origin of name: From the Channel Isle of Jersey.
1940 population & (rank): 4,160,165 (9).
1950 population & (rank): 4,835,329 (8).
1960 population & (rank): 6,066,782 (8).
Land area & (rank): 7,521 sq. mi. (46).
Geographic center: In Mercer Co., 5 mi. SE of the State capital.
Number of counties: 21.
Largest cities (1960 census): Newark (405,220); Jersey City (276,101); Paterson (143,663); Camden (117,159); Trenton (114,167).
State forests: 11 (161,391 ac.).
State parks: 23 (27,025 ac.).
State general revenue (1960–61): $745,128,689.
State general expenditure (1960–61): $747,893,904.

New Jersey, situated in an area of wide industrial diversification between the major markets of Philadelphia and New York, is known as the crossroads of the East. Products from over 15,000 factories and shops can be delivered overnight to about 52 million people, representing 12 states and the District of Columbia. The greatest single industry is chemicals, and New Jersey is one of the foremost research centers of the world. Oil refining and shipbuilding are represented at Linden and Camden by some of the largest installations of their kind.

Of the total land area, 43% is forested and nearly 34.6% is devoted to agriculture. The state rates high in practically all garden vegetables. Among its fruit crops are the famous cultivated blueberries, which originated in New Jersey. The poultry industry is one of the principal phases of the state's agriculture, and dairying occupies a prominent place.

The oldest U. S. highway of any length was built in Sussex County. The New Jersey Turnpike links New York, Pennsylvania and Delaware. Its new span at Florence over the Delaware River connects with the Pennsylvania Turnpike, giving motorists an uninterrupted road from New York to Chicago. Garden State Parkway (toll) is now open from Cape May to the N. Y. Thruway (173 mi.).

Its fortunate topography and geographic location make New Jersey a popular resort state with over 100 resort areas.

# NEW MEXICO

Capital: Santa Fe.
Governor: Edwin L. Mechem, Rep. (to Jan. 1963).
Lieut. Governor: Tom Bolack (to Jan. 1963).
Secy. of State: Betty Florina (to Jan. 1963).
Atty. General: Earl E. Hartley (to Jan. 1963).
Organized as territory: Sept. 9, 1850.
Entered Union & (rank): Jan. 6, 1912 (47).
Present constitution adopted: 1912.
Motto: *Crescit eundo* (It grows as it goes).
State flower: Yucca (1927).
State tree: Piñon (1949).
State bird: Road runner (1949).
State fish: Cutthroat trout (1955).
State colors: Flaming red and golden orange (1915).
State song: "O, Fair New Mexico" (1916).
Nicknames: Land of Enchantment; Sunshine State.
Origin of name: From the country of Mexico.
1940 population & (rank): 531,818 (42).
1950 population & (rank): 681,187 (39).
1960 population & (rank): 951,023 (37).
Land area & (rank): 121,510 sq. mi. (5).
Geographic center: In Torrance Co., 12 mi. W of S of Willard.
Number of counties: 32.
Largest cities (1960 census): Albuquerque (201,-189); Roswell (39,593); Santa Fe (34,676); Las Cruces (29,367); Hobbs (26,275).
State forests: 300,000 ac. of forested lands.
State parks: 8 (92,818 ac.).
State general revenue (1959): $230,290,000.
State general expenditure (1959): $209,136,000.

New Mexico's chief industries are mining and the raising of cattle and crops. Irrigation is vital.

The state contains the largest Indian reservation in the U. S. with over 16,000,000 acres, inhabited by the Navajo tribe. The Apaches and Utes live in three other reservations in this state (the Jicarilla Apache, at Horse Lake; the Mescalero Apache, northeast of Alamogordo; the Navajo, in San Juan and McKinley counties; and the Southern Ute, in the northern part of San Juan County). Carlsbad Caverns, the largest in the world, attract many visitors annually. The Rio Grande State Park, established in March, 1959, will be over 80 miles long when it is fully developed.

The state's dry and healthful climate makes it a great recuperative mecca for tuberculars. Santa Fe, the oldest seat of government in the U. S., was founded by the Spaniards in 1609–10.

Los Alamos is the site of an atomic-energy laboratory. The first atomic explosion in history was at the Alamogordo air base. The state exceeds all others in the production and milling of uranium ore.

## NEW YORK

**Capital:** Albany.
**Governor:** Nelson A. Rockefeller, Rep. (to Jan. 1963).
**Lieut. Governor:** Malcolm Wilson, Rep. (to Jan. 1963).
**Secy. of State:** Caroline K. Simon (apptd. by Governor).
**Comptroller:** Arthur Levitt, Dem. (to Jan. 1963).
**Atty. General:** Louis J. Lefkowitz, Rep. (to Jan. 1963).
**Entered Union & (rank):** July 26, 1788 (11).
**Present constitution adopted:** 1777 (last revised 1938).
**Motto:** *Excelsior* (Ever upward).
**State flower:** Rose (1955).
**State tree:** Sugar maple (1956).
**State bird:** Bluebird (unofficial).
**State song:** None.
**Nickname:** Empire State.
**Origin of name:** In honor of the English Duke of York.
**1940 population & (rank):** 13,479,142 (1).
**1950 population & (rank):** 14,830,192 (1).
**1960 population & (rank):** 16,782,304 (1).
**Land area & (rank):** 47,939 sq. mi. (30).
**Geographic center:** In Madison Co., 6 mi. E of S of Oneida.
**Number of counties:** 62.
**Largest cities (1960 census):** New York (7,781,-984); Buffalo (532,759); Rochester (318,611); Syracuse (216,038); Yonkers (190,634).
**State Forest Preserves:** Adirondacks, 2,252,-269 ac.; Catskills, 235,076 ac.
**State parks:** 82 (approx. 200,000 ac., including parkways).
**State general fund income (1960):** $1,828,000,000.
**State general fund outgo (1960):** $1,827,400,000.

New York, with the great metropolis of New York City, is the spectacular nerve center of the nation. It leads in population, manufacturing, foreign trade, commercial and financial transactions, book and magazine publishing, theatrical production, etc.

New York City is not only a national but an international leader. It is the busiest seaport in the world; New York International Airport is one of the busiest in the world. First in manufacturing since 1824, the city today has a gigantic clothing and fur industry and also makes chemicals, paints, drugs, machinery, paper, wood, and textile products and houses the tallest buildings in the world.

Nearly all the rest of the state's manufacturing is done along the Hudson River north to Albany and through the Mohawk Valley, Central New York, and Southern Tier regions to Buffalo. The St. Lawrence seaway and power projects are opening the North Country to industrial expansion. The seaway has given the state a second seacoast, and the power project is the second largest power source on the continent. By 1961, when the Niagara power development begins operations, New York State will have the largest hydroelectric installation in the free world.

Planes, heavy and light electrical equipment, locomotives, radio and TV sets, auto bodies and parts, washing machines, typewriters, photographic and optical equipment, shirts, and flour are manufactured. Dairying, truck gardening, and the raising of potatoes, onions, and cabbage keep the New York farmer prosperous. Winemaking is a major industry in the state.

New York's extremely rapid commercial growth may be partly attributed to Governor De Witt Clinton, who pushed through the construction of the Erie Canal (Buffalo to Albany) which was opened in 1825. Today, the 559-mile New York Thruway connects New York City with Buffalo and with Connecticut, Massachusetts and Pennsylvania express highways. Two new toll-free superhighways, the Adirondack Northway (linking Albany with the Canadian border) and the North-South-Expressway (crossing central New York from the Pennsylvania border to the Thousand Islands) are under construction.

The convention and tourist business is one of the state's greatest sources of income.

For a short time, New York City was the U. S. Capital and George Washington was inaugurated there as the first President on April 30, 1789.

Plans for observance of the centennial of the Civil War (1961–65) and for a New York Worlds' Fair in 1964–65 were approved in legislation adopted in 1960.

## NORTH CAROLINA

**Capital:** Raleigh.
**Governor:** Terry Sanford, Dem. (to Jan. 1965).
**Lieut. Governor:** H. Cloyd Philpott (to Jan. 1965).
**Secy. of State:** Thad Eure (to Jan. 1965).
**Auditor:** Henry L. Bridges (to Jan. 1965).
**Atty. General:** T. W. Bruton (to Jan. 1965).
**Entered Union & (rank):** Nov. 21, 1789 (12).
**Seceded from Union:** May 20, 1861.
**Re-entered Union:** July 20, 1868.
**Present constitution adopted:** 1876.
**Motto:** *Esse quam videri* (To be rather than to seem) (1893).

State flower: Dogwood (1941).
State bird: Cardinal (1943).
State song: "The Old North State" (1927).
State colors: Red and blue (1945).
Nickname: Tar Heel State.
Origin of name: In honor of Charles I of England.
1940 population & (rank): 3,571,623 (11).
1950 population & (rank): 4,061,929 (10).
1960 population & (rank): 4,556,155 (12).
Land area & (rank): 49,067 sq. mi. (29).
Geographic center: In Chatham Co., 10 mi. NW of Sanford.
Number of counties: 100.
Largest cities (1960 census): Charlotte (201,-564); Greensboro (119,574); Winston-Salem (111,135); Raleigh (93,931); Durham (78,-302).
State forests: 1.
State parks: 11 (35,628 ac.).
State revenue (excluding Federal funds, 1959–60): $445,490,809.
State expenditure (excluding Federal Funds, 1959–60): $416,064,286.

North Carolina is the nation's largest tobacconist and textile producer. It holds first place in the Southeast in population and in the value of its industrial and agricultural production. This production is highly diversified, with furniture, chemicals and paper constituting enormous industries. Tobacco, corn, cotton, hay, peanuts and truck and vegetable crops are of major importance.

The state leads the South in social and economic reforms. Its educational pay scale is the same for white and Negro teachers.

There are 18 state and national parks and forests, including the Great Smoky Mountains National Park, the Blue Ridge Parkway and the new Cape Hatteras National Seashore. Mt. Mitchell, on the Parkway near Asheville, is the highest mountain in the Eastern U. S. (6,684 ft. above sea level).

The largest military reservation in the U. S. (Fort Bragg) and the largest Marine amphibious training base (Camp LeJeune) are in North Carolina.

The first English colony in America was established on Roanoke Island in 1585. Virginia Dare, who was born there in 1587, was the first child of English parentage born in America.

## NORTH DAKOTA

Capital: Bismarck.
Governor: William L. Guy, Dem. (to Jan. 1963).
Lieut. Governor: Orville W. Hagen, Rep. (to Jan. 1963).
Secy. of State: Ben Meier (to Jan. 1963).
Auditor: Curtis Olson (to Jan. 1963).
Atty. General: Leslie R. Burgum (to Jan. 1963).
Organized as territory: Mar. 2, 1861.
Entered Union & (rank): Nov. 2, 1889 (39).
Present constitution adopted: 1889.
Motto: Liberty and union, now and forever: one and inseparable.
State flower: Wild prairie rose (1907).
State tree: American elm (1947).
State bird: Western meadow lark (1947).

State song: "North Dakota Hymn" (1947).
Nickname: Sioux State; Flickertail State.
Origin of name: From the Dakotah tribe, meaning "allies."
1940 population & (rank): 641,935 (39).
1950 population & (rank): 619,636 (41).
1960 population & (rank): 632,446 (44).
Land area & (rank): 69,457 sq. mi. (17).
Geographic center: In Sheridan Co., 5 mi. SW of McClusky.
Number of counties: 53.
Largest cities (1960 census): Fargo (46,662); Grand Forks (34,451); Minot (30,604); Bismarck (27,670); Jamestown (15,163).
State forests: None.
State parks: 5 (2,981 ac.).
State collections (1959–60): $139,398,239.
State disbursements (1959–60): $139,769,631.

North Dakota, politically progressive, operates the only state-owned bank, flour mill and grain elevator in the nation. The state owes its main activity to agriculture with over 87 per cent of its acreage devoted to the growth of barley, wheat, rye, oats and livestock. Most of its manufacturing consists of dairy products.

The finest farming land is in the Red River Valley, celebrated in song. Cattle raising is centered in the Missouri Valley.

"Number One Northern Hard," a wheat first grown in this state, still brings premium prices for its excellence of quality.

The completion of Garrison Dam on the Missouri River will result in extensive irrigation and the production of 400,000 kw. of electricity for use in the Missouri Basin areas.

In 1951, oil was discovered near Tioga by the Amerada Petroleum Corp.

The geographic center of the North American continent is located in Pierce County, latitude 48°10'N, longitude 100°10'W.

## OHIO

Capital: Columbus.
Governor: Michael V. DiSalle, Dem. (to Jan. 1963).
Lieut. Governor: John W. Donahey (to Jan. 1963).
Secy. of State: Ted W. Brown (to Jan. 1963).
Auditor: James A. Rhodes (to Jan. 1965).
Treasurer: Joseph T. Ferguson (to Jan. 1963).
Atty. General: Mark McElroy (to Jan. 1963).
Entered Union & (rank): Mar. 1, 1803 (17).
Present constitution adopted: 1851.
Motto: With God, all things are possible.
State flower: Scarlet carnation (1904).
State tree: Buckeye.
State bird: Cardinal (1933).
State song: None.
Nickname: Buckeye State.
Origin of name: From an Iroquoian word meaning "great river."
1940 population & (rank): 6,907,612 (4).
1950 population & (rank): 7,946,627 (5).
1960 population & (rank): 9,706,397 (5).
Land area & (rank): 40,972 sq. mi. (35).
Geographic center: In Delaware Co., 25 mi. N of Columbus.
Number of counties: 88.
Largest cities (1960 census): Cleveland (876,-

050); Cincinnati (502,550); Columbus (471,-316); Toledo (318,003); Akron (290,351).
**State forests:** 21, incl. 3 nurseries (153,487 ac.).
**State parks:** 54 (66,661 ac.).
**State general revenue (1959–60):** $1,624,417,213.
**State general expenditure (1959–60):** $1,589,594,-110.

With vast coal and oil fields on the one hand, with Great Lakes iron ore close by on the other, Ohio automatically developed into one of the nation's greatest industrial states. The vast and varied factory output of its cities runs from wire, nails, nuts, bolts, paper, radios, cash registers, golf clubs, refrigerators to motors of all kinds and sizes. Cleveland is one of the world's largest handlers of iron ore. Toledo is the nation's largest shipper of coal. Akron makes most of the automobile tires used in the U. S.

Ohio's thousands of factories almost overshadow its importance in two other basic industries—mining and agriculture. Its fertile soil produces soy beans, corn, wheat, grapes and tobacco. Dairying and greenhouse products are important. Mining is centered in coal, oil, sand, gravel and clay.

## OKLAHOMA

**Capital:** Oklahoma City.
**Governor:** J. Howard Edmondson, Dem. (to Jan. 1963).
**Lieut. Governor:** George Nigh (to Jan. 1963).
**Secy. of State:** William N. Christian (to Jan. 1963).
**Treasurer:** William A. Burkhart (to Jan. 1963).
**Atty. General:** Mac Q. Williamson (to Jan. 1963).
**Organized as territory:** May 2, 1890.
**Entered Union & (rank):** Nov. 16, 1907 (46).
**Present constitution adopted:** 1907.
**Motto:** *Labor omnia vincit* (Labor conquers all things).
**State flower:** Mistletoe (1893).
**State tree:** Redbud (1937).
**State bird:** Scissor-tailed Flycatcher (1951).
**State colors:** Green and white (1915).
**State song:** "Oklahoma" (1953).
**Nickname:** Sooner State.
**Origin of name:** From two Choctaw Indian words meaning "red people."
**1940 population & (rank):** 2,336,434 (22).
**1950 population & (rank):** 2,233,351 (25).
**1960 population & (rank):** 2,328,284 (27).
**Land area & (rank):** 68,887 sq. mi. (19).
**Geographic center:** In Oklahoma Co., 8 mi. N of Oklahoma City.
**Number of counties:** 77.
**Largest cities (1960 census):** Oklahoma City (324,253); Tulsa (261,685); Lawton (61,697); Enid (38,859); Muskogee (38,059).
**State forests:** None.
**State parks:** 16 (52,891.16 ac.).
**Total state revenue (1959–60):** $437,411,430.
**Total state expenditure (1959–60):** $435,809,163.

Oil has made Oklahoma a rich state and Tulsa one of the world's wealthiest cities per capita. The smelting of zinc, oil refining, meat packing and flour milling are its chief factory industries. Wheat, corn, oats, cotton, sorghums and potatoes are its agricultural crops of chief importance.

In 1834, Oklahoma was set aside as Indian Territory. It remained so until Apr. 22, 1889, when the first opening to homestead settlement occurred. On that one day, 50,000 people swarmed in, and the term "sooners" was born to apply to those who had sneaked into the state sooner than the noon deadline. A series of land openings by "runs" and lotteries extended through 1901, and sales by sealed bid of remaining lands were held in 1906 and 1910.

In 1959, Oklahomans voted to end the state prohibition law, which had been in effect for 51 years.

## OREGON

**Capital:** Salem.
**Governor:** Mark O. Hatfield, Rep. (to Jan. 1963).
**Secy. of State:** Howell Appling, Jr. (to Jan. 1965).
**Treasurer:** Howard C. Belton (to Jan. 1965).
**Atty. General:** Robert Y. Thornton (to Jan. 1965).
**Organized as territory:** Aug. 14, 1848.
**Entered Union & (rank):** Feb. 14, 1859 (33).
**Present constitution adopted:** 1859.
**Motto:** The Union (1957).
**State flower:** Oregon grape (1899).
**State tree:** Douglas fir (1939).
**State bird:** Western meadow lark (1927).
**State colors:** Navy blue and gold (1959).
**State song:** "Oregon, My Oregon" (1927).
**Nickname:** Beaver State.
**Origin of name:** Unknown. However, it is generally accepted that the name, first used by Jonathan Carver in 1778, was taken from the writings of Maj. Robert Rogers, an English army officer.
**1940 population & (rank):** 1,089,684 (34).
**1950 population & (rank):** 1,521,341 (32).
**1960 population & (rank):** 1,768,687 (32).
**Land area & (rank):** 96,248 sq. mi. (10).
**Geographic center:** In Crook Co., 25 mi. E of S of Prineville.
**Number of counties:** 36.
**Largest cities (1960 census):** Portland (372,-676); Eugene (50,977); Salem (49,142); Medford (24,425); Corvallis (20,669).
**State forests:** 765,951 ac.
**State parks:** 174 (59,490 ac.).
**State general revenue (1960):** $383,244,000.
**State general expenditure (1960):** $368,000,000.

Oregon, with the greatest U. S. reserve of standing timber, has a billion-dollar forestry industry. Its salmon fishing industry, centered at Astoria at the mouth of the Columbia River, is one of the world's largest.

In agriculture, the state leads in growing peppermint, holly, lily bulbs, caneberries, filberts, Blue Lake beans and cover seed crops, and also raises strawberries, hops, wheat and other grains, sugar beets, potatoes, green peas, fiber flax, dairy products, livestock and poultry.

Crater Lake National Park, Mount Hood, and Bonneville Dam on the Columbia are major tourist attractions.

With the low-cost electric power provided by Bonneville Dam, McNary Dam and other dams in the Pacific Northwest, Oregon has developed steadily as a manufacturing state. Leading manufactures are lumber and lumber products, metalwork, machinery, aluminum, chemicals, paper and food processing.

# PENNSYLVANIA

Capital: Harrisburg.
Governor: David L. Lawrence, Dem. (to Jan. 1963).
Lieut. Governor: John M. Davis (to Jan. 1963).
Secy. of the Commonwealth: E. James Trimarchi, Jr. (term indefinite).
Auditor General: Thomas Z. Minehart (to May 1965).
Atty. General: Anne X. Alpern (term indefinite).
Entered Union & (rank): Dec. 12, 1787 (2).
Present constitution adopted: 1874.
Motto: Virtue, liberty and independence.
State flower: Mountain laurel (1933).
State tree: Hemlock (1931).
State bird: Ruffed grouse (1931).
State colors: Blue and gold.
State song: None.
Nickname: Keystone State.
Origin of name: In honor of Adm. Sir William Penn, father of William Penn. It means "Penn's Woodland."
1940 population & (rank): 9,900,180 (2).
1950 population & (rank): 10,498,012 (3).
1960 population & (rank): 11,319,366 (3).
Land area & (rank): 45,007 sq. mi. (33).
Geographic center: In Center Co., 2 1/2 mi. SW of Bellefonte.
Number of counties: 67.
Largest cities (1960 census): Philadelphia (2,-002,512); Pittsburgh (604,332); Erie (138,-440); Scranton (111,443); Allentown (108,-347).
State forests: 20 (1,881,403 ac.).
State parks: 72 (164,179 ac.).
Total revenue subject to appropriations (biennium ending May 31, 1961): $1,831,599,845.
Total expenditures (biennium ending May 31, 1961): $1,870,092,108.

From the steel mills of Pittsburgh through the mid-state coal mines and oil wells to the shipyards and factories of Philadelphia, Pennsylvania bristles with heavy industry. Approximately 26% of all American iron and steel is made in Pennsylvania. Other manufactures include locomotives, boilers, engines, blast furnaces, trucks, buses, wire, textiles, knit goods and nylon and rayon products. Virtually all of the U. S. anthracite (hard coal) deposits are located in Pennsylvania.

Agricultural products include apples, peaches, potatoes, corn, hay, barley, wheat, buckwheat and tobacco.

Pennsylvania is rich in historical lore. Philadelphia was the seat of the Federal government almost continuously from 1776 until 1800, and there the Declaration of Independence was signed and the Constitution drawn up. Valley Forge, of the Revolution, and Gettysburg, the turning-point of the Civil War, are both in Pennsylvania. The Liberty Bell stands in Independence Square in Philadelphia.

# RHODE ISLAND

Capital: Providence.
Governor: John A. Notte, Jr., Dem. (to Jan. 1963).
Lieut. Governor: Edward P. Gallogly (to Jan. 1963).
Secy. of State: August P. La France (to Jan. 1963).
Controller: Charles W. Hill (civil service).
Atty. General: J. J. Nugent (to Jan. 1963).
Entered Union & (rank): May 29, 1790 (13).
Present constitution adopted: 1843.
Motto: Hope.
State flower: Violet (unofficial).
State tree: Maple (unofficial).
State bird: Rhode Island Red (official).
State colors: Blue, white and gold (in state flag).
State song: "Rhode Island" (1946).
Nickname: Little Rhody.
Origin of name: From the Greek island of Rhodes.
1940 population & (rank): 713,346 (36).
1950 population & (rank): 791,896 (36).
1960 population & (rank): 859,488 (39).
Land area & (rank): 1,058 sq. mi. (50).
Geographic center: In Kent Co., 2.8 mi. S by W of Crompton.
Number of counties: 5.
Largest cities (1960 census): Providence (207,-498); Pawtucket (81,001); Warwick (68,-504); Cranston (66,766); Woonsocket (47,-080).
State forests: 9 (15,600 ac.).
State parks: 7 (8,196 ac.).
State general revenue (1959–60): $110,739,728.
State general expenditure (1959–60): $109,334,-643.

Rhode Island, with the greatest density of population barring the District of Columbia, boasts one of the highest proportion of industrial workers of all the states. Leading industry is textiles, largely concentrated in Providence County, particularly Pawtucket and Woonsocket. However, today the combined metal and machinery groups exceed textiles in importance.

Providence is one of the largest U. S. jewelry centers, and is important in the production of machinery and metal products.

With more than eight-tenths of the population living in urban areas, adjacent parts of the state are interested in dairying, poultry and truck farming. Nursery and greenhouse products and stock, potatoes, corn, apples, oats and hay lead the crop list. Of the state's land area, about one-tenth is farm cropland and open pasture; six-tenths is forested.

Newport is the site of the Naval War College and was long a show place for the luxurious summer homes built by some of New York's wealthiest people. The U. S. Naval Air Station is at Quonset in the town of North Kingstown.

Roger Williams founded Providence, and subsequently Rhode Island, in 1636.

# SOUTH CAROLINA

Capital: Columbia.
Governor: Ernest F. Hollings, Dem. (to Jan. 1963).

Lieut. Governor: Burnet R. Maybank (to Jan. 1963).

Secy. of State: O. Frank Thornton (to Jan. 1963).

Comptroller General: Eldridge C. Rhodes (to Jan. 1963).

Atty. General: Daniel R. McLeod (to Jan. 1963).

Entered Union & (rank): May 23, 1788 (8).

Seceded from Union: Dec. 20, 1860.

Re-entered Union: July 18, 1868.

Present constitution adopted: 1895.

Mottoes: *Animus opibusque parati* (Prepared in mind and resources) and *Dum spiro spero* (While I breathe, I hope).

State flower: Carolina yellow jessamine (1924).

State tree: Palmetto tree (1939).

State bird: Carolina wren (1948).

State song: "Carolina" (1911).

Nickname: Palmetto State.

Origin of name: In honor of Charles II of England.

1940 population & (rank): 1,899,804 (26).

1950 population & (rank): 2,117,027 (27).

1960 population & (rank): 2,382,594 (26).

Land area & (rank): 30,272 sq. mi. (40).

Geographic center: In Richland Co., 13 mi. SE of Columbia.

Number of counties: 46.

Largest cities (1960 census): Columbia (97,433); Greenville (66,188); Charleston (65,925); Spartanburg (44,352); Anderson (41,316).

State forests: 4 (123,000 ac.).

State parks: 22 (46,000 ac.).

State total revenue (1959–60): $214,096,728.

State general expenditure (1959–60): $214,096,728.

Once primarily agricultural, South Carolina has built so many big textile and other mills that today the state's factories are eight times the output of its farms in cash value. Agriculture has not, however, been completely replaced and today the chief products are livestock, cotton, tobacco, peaches, corn, hay, oats, sweet potatoes, and peanuts, which are enhanced by the recent development of modern soil-conservation methods. Charleston makes asbestos, wood, pulp, and steel products.

Civil War hostilities were started in this state at Charleston, when, on April 12, 1861, South Carolina men bombarded and captured Fort Sumter.

## SOUTH DAKOTA

Capital: Pierre.

Governor: Archie Gubbrud, Rep. (to Jan. 1963).

Lieut. Governor: Joe Bottum (to Jan. 1963).

Secy. of State: Essie Wiedenman (to Jan. 1963).

State Auditor: Betty Lou Larson (to Jan. 1963).

State Treasurer: Al Hamre (to Jan. 1963).

Atty. General: A. C. Miller (to Jan. 1963).

Organized as territory: Mar. 2, 1861.

Entered Union & (rank): Nov. 2, 1889 (40).

Present constitution adopted: 1889.

Motto: Under God the people rule.

State flower: American pasqueflower (1903).

State tree: Black Hills spruce (1947).

State bird: Ring-necked pheasant (1943).

State animal: Coyote (1949).

State colors: Blue and gold (in state flag).

State song: "Hail! South Dakota" (1943).

Nicknames: Sunshine State; Coyote State.

Origin of name: Same as for North Dakota.

1940 population & (rank): 642,961 (38).

1950 population & (rank): 652,740 (40).

1960 population & (rank): 680,514 (40).

Land area & (rank): 76,378 sq. mi. (16).

Geographic center: In Hughes Co., 8 mi. NE of Pierre.

Number of counties: 67 (64 county governments).

Largest cities (1960 census): Sioux Falls (65,466); Rapid City (42,399); Aberdeen (23,073); Huron (14,180); Watertown (14,077).

State forests: 4 (86,000 ac.).

State parks: 10 (90,000 ac.).*

State general revenue (1958–59): $123,741,457.

State general expenditure (1958–59): $121,139,429.

* The acreage shown includes 92 recreation areas and 50 roadside parks in addition to the 11 state parks.

Seventy-five per cent of the population of South Dakota is actively interested in agriculture. Its leading crops are rye, barley, oats, corn, wheat. Cattle raising and dairying are its stronger industries. The richest U. S. gold mine, the Homestake, is at Lead.

The Black Hills, a great tourist attraction, are the highest mountains east of the Rockies. Mt. Rushmore, in this group, is celebrated for the likenesses of Washington, Jefferson, Lincoln and Theodore Roosevelt, which were carved in stone by the late Gutzon Borglum. The Badlands offer very scenic masses of bare rock and clay unrelieved by any vegetation. It was in this state that the Sioux Indians, angered at the influx of the white men who were searching for gold, started the hostilities which ended in Custer's Massacre, on June 25, 1876, in Montana. A 600-ft. likeness of the Sioux chief is now being carved on Crazy Horse Mountain.

## TENNESSEE

Capital: Nashville.

Governor: Buford Ellington, Dem. (to Jan. 1963).

Lieut. Governor: William D. Baird (to Jan. 1963).

Secy. of State: Joe C. Carr (to Jan. 1965).

Comptroller: William R. Snodgrass (to Jan. 1963).

Atty. General: George F. McCanless to Sept. 1966).

Entered Union & (rank): June 1, 1796 (16).

Seceded from Union: June 24, 1861.

Re-entered Union: July 24, 1866.

Present constitution adopted: 1870, amended for first time 1953.

Motto: Agriculture, commerce.

State flower: Iris (1933).

State tree: Tulip poplar (1947).

State bird: Mockingbird (1933).

State songs: "My Homeland, Tennessee" (1925) and "When It's Iris Time in Tennessee" (1935).

Nickname: Volunteer State.

Origin of name: From the name of the ancient capital of the Cherokee tribe.

1940 population & (rank): 2,915,841 (15)

1950 population & (rank): 3,291,718 (16).
1960 population & (rank): 3,567,089 (17).
Land area & (rank): 41,762 sq. mi. (34).
Geographic center: In Rutherford Co., 5 mi. NE of Murfreesboro.
Number of counties: 95.
Largest cities (1960 census): Memphis (497,-524); Nashville (170,874); Chattanooga (130,009); Knoxville (111,827); Jackson (34,-376).
State forests: 14 (155,752 ac.).
State parks: 21 (130,000 ac.).
State general revenue (1958-59): $428,393,000.
State general expenditure (1958-59): $440,654,-000.

Tennessee won world prominence in 1945, for the atom bomb was made possible by the Clinton Engineer Works, which was located at Oak Ridge.

The state is now predominately industrial, with production including chemicals, food, textiles, virgin aluminum, shoes, lumber products, and metal work. Mineral products include phosphates, zinc, copper, lead, sinter iron, pyrites, high-grade pottery clay, coal and marble. Tennessee's agricultural production includes livestock, cotton, corn, tobacco, hay, dairy products, poultry and eggs.

Tennessee is the home of TVA, which operates 29 dams and distributes power from 3 dams on the Cumberland River maintained by the Army Corps of Engineers. Benefits of flood control, navigation and electrical power reach into 6 other states (Kentucky, Alabama, North Carolina, Georgia, Virginia, and Mississippi). The Tennessee River, already the most completely used major river in the world, is insufficient to supply energy needs, and the power system is being doubled by use of steam generating plants.

## TEXAS

Capital: Austin.
Governor: Price Daniel, Dem. (to Jan. 1963).
Lieut. Governor: Ben Ramsey (to Jan. 1963).
Secy. of State: P. Frank Lake (to Jan. 1963).
Comptroller: Robert S. Calvert (to Jan. 1963).
Atty. General: Will Wilson (to Jan. 1963).
Entered Union & (rank): Dec. 29, 1845 (28).
Seceded from Union: Mar. 2, 1861.
Re-entered Union: Mar. 30, 1870.
Present constitution adopted: 1876.
Motto: Friendship.
State flower: Bluebonnet (1901).
State tree: Pecan (1919).
State bird: Mockingbird (1927).
State song: "Texas, Our Texas" (1930).
Nickname: Lone Star State.
Origin of name: From an Indian word meaning "friends."
1940 population & (rank): 6,414,824 (6).
1950 population & (rank): 7,711,194 (6).
1960 population & (rank): 9,579,677 (6).
Land area & (rank): 262,840 sq. mi. (2).
Geographic center: In McCulloch Co., 20 mi. NE of Brady.
Number of counties: 254.
Largest cities (1960 census): Houston (938,219); Dallas (679,684); San Antonio (587,718); Ft. Worth (356,268); El Paso (276,687).

State forests: 4 (6,306 ac.).
State parks: 60 (46 developed).
State revenue receipts (1959-60): $1,250,001,415.
State Government cost (1959-60): $1,184,384,436.

Texas is the richest political subdivision in the world with the possible exception of the Russian Ukraine, and is the only state that may, by Congressional statute, divide into five parts if it so desires. There is very little possibility of this ever being done because Texas and Texans live by its bigness. Texas is a natural leader in oil, natural gas, cotton, cattle, helium, sheep, wool, onions, and turkeys.

The distance from El Paso to Beaumont is a greater distance than from New York to Chicago. Over the Neches River, at Port Arthur, is the most elevated highway bridge over tidal waters in the world.

Cabeza de Vaca explored the state in 1528. Since 1685, it has been under the jurisdiction of 6 separate governments: those of France, Spain, Mexico, the Republic of Texas, the Confederacy, and the United States.

## UTAH

Capital: Salt Lake City.
Governor: George D. Clyde, Rep. (to Jan. 1965).
Secy. of State: Lamont F. Toronto (to Jan. 1965).
Atty. General: Walter L. Budge (to Jan. 1965).
Organized as territory: Sept. 9, 1850.
Entered Union & (rank): Jan. 4, 1896 (45).
Present constitution adopted: 1896.
Motto: Industry.
State flower: Sego lily (1911).
State tree: Blue spruce (1933).
State bird: Seagull (1955).
State emblem: Beehive.
State song: "Utah, We Love Thee."
Nickname: Beehive State.
Origin of name: From the Ute tribe, meaning "people of the mountains."
1940 population & (rank): 550,310 (41).
1950 population & (rank): 688,862 (38).
1960 population & (rank): 890,627 (38).
Land area & (rank): 82,339 sq. mi. (12).
Geographic center: In Sanpete Co., 3 mi. N of Manti.
Number of counties: 29.
Largest cities (1960 census): Salt Lake City (189,454); Ogden (70,197); Provo (36,047); Logan (18,731); Orem (18,394).
State forests: None.
State parks: 13 (8,964.75 ac.).
Total state receipts (1959-60): $224,986,843.
Total state disbursements (1959-60): $205,542,-549.

Utah, rich in natural resources, has long been recognized for its copper, gold, silver, lead and zinc. Also, it produces all the elements necessary for the manufacture of steel: iron, lime, dolomite, fluorspar, manganese and coal for coking. The state is also developing an oil industry and in 1959 rose to 11th in rank among states in total production.

Utah's crops requiring extensive irrigation include sugar beets, potatoes, hay, onions and wheat. Various garden crops, such as beans, peas and tomatoes, and fruits, such as pears, peaches, apples and apricots, make up an ever-growing industry. Eggs and commercial poultry are also among the products of Utah.

Brigham Young led the Mormons into the area in 1847.

Great Salt Lake, lying in the north central area, has long been a world wonder. It has no known outlet, and its salt content is about six times that of the ocean. Because of its natural beauty and pioneer culture, Utah is an ideal place for tourists to visit.

## VERMONT

**Capital:** Montpelier.
**Governor:** F. Ray Keyser, Jr., Rep. (to Jan. 1963).
**Lieut. Governor:** Ralph A. Foote (to Jan. 1963).
**Secy. of State:** Howard E. Armstrong (to Jan. 1963).
**Treasurer:** George H. Amidan (to Jan. 1963).
**Auditor of Accounts:** David V. Anderson (to Jan. 1963).
**Atty. General:** Thomas M. Debevoise (to Jan. 1963).
**Entered Union & (rank):** Mar. 4, 1791 (14).
**Present constitution adopted:** 1793.
**Motto:** Vermont—freedom and unity.
**State flower:** Red clover (1894).
**State tree:** Sugar maple (1949).
**State bird:** Hermit thrush (1941).
**State song:** "Hail to Vermont" (1937).
**Nickname:** Green Mountain State.
**Origin of name:** From the French, meaning "green mountain."
**1940 population & (rank):** 359,231 (46).
**1950 population & (rank):** 377,747 (45).
**1960 population & (rank):** 389,881 (47).
**Land area & (rank):** 9,276 sq. mi. (43).
**Geographic center:** In Washington Co., 4.5 mi. SSE of Roxbury Village.
**Number of counties:** 14.
**Largest cities (1960 census):** Burlington (35,-531); Rutland (18,325); Barre (10,387); St. Albans (8,806); Montpelier (8,782).
**State forests:** 28 (82,690 ac.).
**State parks:** 26 (7,314.5 ac.).
**State revenue (1960):** $89,309,027.
**State expenditure (1960):** $96,897,649.

Vermont, the only New England state without a seacoast (and the last to be settled because of this), leads the nation in marble, granite, asbestos and maple syrup production. In ratio to population it keeps more dairy cows than any other state. Vermont's soil is devoted to dairying, truck farming and fruit growing, its rugged area precluding extensive farming. This same quality, however, along with a bracing dry climate, makes the state popular as a summer resort and as a center of winter sports.

From 1777 to 1791, Vermont was an independent state of indefinite status with some national perquisites and then was the first state after the original thirteen to join the Union. It was also the first state to forbid slavery and the first to adopt universal manhood suffrage (1777). Vermont has been Republican since 1854; only Georgia on the Democratic side ties that record.

## VIRGINIA

**Capital:** Richmond.
**Governor:** James Lindsay Almond, Jr., Dem. (to Jan. 1962).
**Lieut. Governor:** A. E. Stephens (to Jan. 1962).
**Secy. of the Commonwealth:** Martha Bell Conway (apptd. by Governor).
**Comptroller:** Sidney C. Day, Jr. (apptd. by Governor).
**Atty. General:** Albertis S. Harrison, Jr. (apptd. by Governor).
**Entered Union & (rank):** June 25, 1788 (10).
**Seceded from Union:** Apr. 17, 1861.
**Re-entered Union:** Jan. 27, 1870.
**Present constitution adopted:** 1902.
**Motto:** *Sic semper tyrannis* (Thus always to tyrants).
**State flower:** American dogwood (1918).
**State bird:** Cardinal.
**State song:** "Carry Me Back to Old Virginny" (1940).
**Nicknames:** The Old Dominion; Cavalier State.
**Origin of name:** In honor of Elizabeth, "Virgin Queen" of England.
**1940 population & (rank):** 2,677,773 (19).
**1950 population & (rank):** 3,318,680 (15).
**1960 population & (rank):** 3,966,949 (14).
**Land area & (rank):** 39,838 sq. mi. (37).
**Geographic center:** In Appomattox Co., 11 mi. S of E of Amherst.
**Number of counties:** 98, plus 32 independent cities.
**Largest cities (1960 census):** Norfolk (304,869); Richmond (219,958); Portsmouth (114,773); Newport News (113,662); Roanoke (97,110).
**State forests:** 7 (47,338 ac.).
**State parks:** 8 (21,523 ac.).
**State revenue (1960):** $637,807,186.
**State expenditure (1960):** $656,400,427.

The history of America is closely tied to that of Virginia, particularly in the colonial period. Jamestown, founded in 1607, was the first permanent English settlement in North America, and slavery was introduced there in 1619. The surrenders ending both the American Revolution and the Civil War occurred in Virginia. The state is called the "Mother of Presidents" because 8 chief executives of the U. S. were born there.

Points of historic interest include Mount Vernon and other places associated with Washington; Monticello, home of Jefferson; Stratford, home of the Lees; Richmond, capital of the Confederacy and of Virginia; and Williamsburg, the restored Colonial capital.

Among Virginia's natural wonders are the famous Natural Bridge and the limestone caverns of the Shenandoah Valley. The most important natural resources are beds of bituminous coal, forest lands, oyster beds and commercial fisheries.

Manufacturing includes chemicals, textiles, lumber and wood products, foods, transportation equipment (including shipbuilding), apparel and furniture. Agricultural products include livestock, poultry, dairy goods, tobacco, apples, grains and hay crops.

# WASHINGTON

Capital: Olympia.
Governor: Albert D. Rosellini, Dem. (to Jan. 1965).
Lieut. Governor: John A. Cherberg (to Jan. 1965).
Secy. of State: Victor A. Meyers (to Jan. 1965).
State Treasurer: Tom Martin (to Jan. 1965).
Atty. General: John J. O'Connell (to Jan. 1965).
Organized as territory: Mar. 2, 1853.
Entered Union & (rank): Nov. 11, 1889 (42).
Present constitution adopted: 1889.
Motto: *Al-Ki* (Indian word meaning Bye and Bye).
State flower: Rhododendron (1949).
State tree: Hemlock (1947).
State bird: Goldfinch (1951).
State colors: Green and gold (1925).
State song: "Washington, My Home" (1959).
Nicknames: Evergreen State; Chinook State.
Origin of name: In honor of Geo. Washington.
1940 population & (rank): 1,736,191 (30).
1950 population & (rank): 2,378,963 (23).
1960 population & (rank): 2,853,214 (23).
Land area & (rank): 66,709 sq. mi. (20).
Geographic center: In Chelan Co., 10 mi. SW of Wenatchee.
Number of counties: 39.
Largest cities (1960 census): Seattle (557,087); Spokane (181,608); Tacoma (147,979); Yakima (43,284); Everett (40,304).
State forest lands: 2,137,000 ac.
State parks: 67 active (73,832 ac.) (119 total).
State revenue (all funds, 1960): $700,708,353.
State expenditures (all funds, 1960): $622,437,-264.

Washington is one of the leaders in lumber production. Its rugged surface is rich in stands of Douglas fir, hemlock, yellow and white pine, spruce, larch and cedar. The state's other first is apples. Food and lumber products, aircraft and missiles, and a wide variety of other goods flow from Washington factories.

The Columbia River contains one third of the potential water power of America. Largest dam is Grand Coulee, greatest power producer in the world. Other mighty dams on the Columbia include Chief Joseph, Rock Island, Bonneville, McNary and The Dalles, which are shared with Oregon. There are 90 dams in Washington, built for various purposes including power, irrigation, flood control, water storage, etc.

The Hanford Engineer Works, north of Pasco, has been set up as the world's first full-scale plant for atomic weapons material.

# WEST VIRGINIA

Capital: Charleston.
Governor: W. W. Barron, Dem. (to Jan. 1965).
Secy. of State: Joe F. Burdett (to Jan. 1965).
State Auditor: Denzil Gainer (to Jan. 1965).
Atty. General: Donald Robertson (to Jan. 1965).
Entered Union & (rank): June 20, 1863 (35).
Present constitution adopted: 1872.

Motto: *Montani semper liberi* (Mountaineers always free).
State flower: Rhododendron (1903).
State tree: Sugar maple (1949).
State bird: Cardinal (1949).
State animal: Black bear.
State colors: Blue and gold (unofficial).
State songs: "West Virginia, My Home Sweet Home" (approved 1947 as one of songs of state); "West Virginia Hills" (by custom).
Nickname: Mountain State.
Origin of name: Same as for Virginia.
1940 population & (rank): 1,901,974 (25).
1950 population & (rank): 2,005,552 (29).
1960 population & (rank): 1,860,421 (30).
Land area & (rank): 24,079 sq. mi. (41).
Geographic center: In Braxton Co., 4 mi. E of Sutton.
Number of counties: 55.
Largest cities (1960 census): Charleston (85,-796); Huntington (83,627); Wheeling (53,-400); Parkersburg (44,797); Weirton (28,-201).
State forests: 9 (78,351 ac.).
State parks: 20 (40,974 ac.).
State general revenue (1959-60): $116,069,245.
State general expenditure (1959-60): $113,840,-509.

Mountainous West Virginia is the coal mining leader of the nation. The state also ranks high in steel, glass, aluminum and chemical manufacture, natural gas, oil, quarry products and hardwood lumber. Cattle is the main agricultural product. Leading crops include wheat, corn, oats, hay, tobacco and fruit.

West Virginia was created when its residents refused to secede from the Union and severed the state from Virginia during the Civil War era.

Like many mountain states, West Virginia has an equable climate without extremes. White Sulphur Springs, in Greenbrier County, is a famous health resort.

# WISCONSIN

Capital: Madison.
Governor: Gaylord A. Nelson, Dem. (to Jan. 1963).
Lieut. Governor: Warren P. Knowles (to Jan. 1963).
Secy. of State: Robert C. Zimmerman (to Jan. 1963).
Dir. of Bureau of Finance: E. C. Giessel (term indefinite).
Atty. General: John W. Reynolds (to Jan. 1963).
Organized as territory: Apr. 20, 1836.
Entered Union & (rank): May 29, 1848 (30).
Present constitution adopted: 1848.
Motto: Forward.
State flower: Violet.
State tree: Sugar maple.
State bird: Robin.
State animal: Badger; "wild life" animal: white-tailed deer.
State fish: Musky (Muskellunge).
State song: "On Wisconsin."
Nickname: Badger State.
Origin of name: French corruption of an Indian word meaning "gathering of waters."
1940 population & (rank): 3,137,587 (13).

1950 population & (rank): 3,434,575 (14).
1960 population & (rank): 3,951,777 (15).
Land area & (rank): 54,705 sq. mi. (25).
Geographic center: In Wood Co., 9 mi. SE of Marshfield.
Number of counties: 72.
Largest cities (1960 census): Milwaukee (741,-324); Madison (126,706); Racine (89,144); West Allis (68,157); Kenosha (67,899).
State forests: 9 (364,839 ac.).
State parks: 32 (19,174 ac.).
State total net revenue, all funds (1959–60): $736,442,147.
State total net expenditure, all funds (1959–60): $686,862,395.

Wisconsin leads the U. S. in milk and cheese production. In 1959, the state ranked first in the number of milk cows (2,501,000), and produced 14.4% of the nation's total output of milk. Other important farm products are: potatoes, cabbage, maple sugar, cranberries and cherries. The state ranks first in producing peas, corn and beets for canning.

About 40 years ago Wisconsin's forests became depleted, but in recent years phenomenal strides in reforestation have been made. The chief industrial products of the state are automobiles, machinery, furniture, paper, beer and processed foods.

Wisconsin pioneered in social legislation, providing pensions for the blind (1907), aid to dependent children (1913) and old-age assistance (1925). In 1932, it was the first state to enact an unemployment compensation law. In labor legislation, the state has also pioneered in important laws, among them the first workmen's compensation law actually to take effect. Wisconsin had the first state-wide primary-election law and the first successful income-tax law. Probably the greatest legislative innovation in 1959 was the creation of a streamlined form of county government for the Menommec Indian Reservation, which will become a separate county no longer under Federal supervision.

## WYOMING

Capital: Cheyenne.
Acting Governor: Jack R. Gage.
Secy. of State: Jack R. Gage (to Jan. 1963).

Auditor: Minnie Mitchell (to Jan. 1963).
Treasurer: C. J. Rogers (to Jan. 1963).
Atty. General: Norman B. Gray (apptd. by Governor).
Organized as territory: July 25, 1868.
Entered Union & (rank): July 10, 1890 (44).
Present constitution adopted: 1890.
Motto: Equal rights (1955).
State flower: Indian paintbrush (1917).
State tree: Cottonwood (1947).
State bird: Meadow lark (1927).
State insignia: Bucking horse (unofficial).
State song: "Wyoming" (1955).
Special legal holiday: Arbor Day (by Governor's designation).
Nickname: Equality State.
Origin of name: From the Indian, meaning "mountains and valleys alternating"; named after the Wyoming Valley in Pa.
1940 population & (rank): 250,742 (47).
1950 population & (rank): 290,529 (47).
1960 population & (rank): 330,066 (48).
Land area & (rank): 97,411 sq. mi. (9).
Geographic center: In Fremont Co., 58 mi. N of E of Lander.
Number of counties: 23, plus Yellowstone National Park.
Largest cities (1960 census): Cheyenne (43,505); Casper (38,930); Laramie (17,520); Sheridan (11,651); Rock Springs (10,371).
State forests: None.
State parks: 2 (1,060 ac.).
Estimated income available (General Fund, 1961–63): $40,842,391.
Estimated expenditure (General Fund, 1961–63): $37,296,562.

Wealthy in wool, cattle, oil, uranium, and coal, Wyoming was first in U. S. history to insure woman's place in politics. In 1869, it gave women the vote and Mrs. Nellie Tayloe Ross, who held office in 1925–27, was the first U. S. woman governor.

Second in mean elevation to Colorado, Wyoming has many lures for the tourist trade, notably Yellowstone National Park. Cheyenne is famous for its annual "Frontier Days" celebration, which brings in visitors from everywhere. One of the world's largest subbituminous coal fields lies near Gillette. Big game hunting is good in many parts of the state.

## COMMONWEALTH OF PUERTO RICO

Capital: San Juan.
Governor: Luis Muñoz Marín, Pop. Dem. (to Jan. 1965).
Song: "La Borinqueña."
1940 population: 1,869,255.
1950 population: 2,210,703.
1960 population: 2,349,544.
Area: 3,435 sq. mi.
Largest cities (1960 census): San Juan (432,-377); Ponce (114,286); Mayagüez (50,147); Caguas (32,015); Arecibo (28,828).

Puerto Rico is an island about 100 mi. long and 35 mi. wide at the northeastern end of the Caribbean Sea. It is a self-governing Commonwealth freely and vol-

untarily associated with the U. S. Under its Constitution, a Governor and a Legislative Assembly are elected by direct vote for a 4-year period. The judiciary is vested in a Supreme Court and lower courts established by law. The people elect a Resident Commissioner to the U. S. House of Representatives, where he has a voice but no vote. The island was formerly an unincorporated territory of the U. S. after being ceded by Spain as a result of the Spanish-American War.

The Commonwealth, established in 1952, is one of the most densely populated areas of the world, with about 683 inhabitants per square mile. However, it has one of the highest standards of living in Latin America. Featuring Puerto Rican economic development is Operation Bootstrap. This program has established more than 600 new factories and has greatly increased agricultural production, transportation and communications facilities, electric power, housing, and other industries.

Columbus discovered the island on his second voyage to America in 1493.

# NON-SELF-GOVERNING U. S. TERRITORIES

## AMERICAN SAMOA

Capital: Pago Pago (on Tutuila Island).
Governor: Peter Tali Coleman.
1940 population: 12,908.
1950 population: 18,937.
1960 population: 20,051.
Area: 76 sq. mi.

American Samoa, a group of 5 volcanic islands and 2 coral atolls located some 2,400 miles south of Hawaii in the South Pacific Ocean, is an insular possession of the U. S. administered by the Department of the Interior.

By the Treaty of Berlin signed Dec. 2, 1899, and ratified Feb. 16, 1900, the U. S. was internationally acknowledged to have rights extending over all the islands of the Samoa group east of longitude 171° west of Greenwich. On Apr. 17, 1900, the chiefs of Tutuila and Aunu'u ceded those islands to the U. S. In 1904, the King and chiefs of Manu'a ceded the islands of Ofu, Olosega and Tau (composing the Manu'a group) to the U. S. Swains Island, some 200 miles north of Samoa, was included as part of the territory by Act of Congress Mar. 4, 1925; and on Feb. 20, 1929, Congress formally accepted sovereignty over the entire group and placed the responsibility for administration in the hands of the President. From 1900–51, by Presidential direction, the Department of the Navy governed the territory. On July 1, 1951, administration was transferred to the Department of the Interior. The first constitution for the territory was signed on Apr. 27, 1960.

The principal products are copra, mats, handicrafts and canned fish.

## BAKER, HOWLAND AND JARVIS

These Pacific islands were not to play a role in the extraterritorial plans of the U. S. until May 13, 1936, when the U. S. perfected its claim. President F. D. Roosevelt, at that time, placed them under the control of and jurisdiction by the Secretary of the Interior for administration purposes.

Baker Island is a saucer-shaped atoll with an area of approximately one square mile and an elevation of 20 feet. It is about 1,650 miles from Hawaii.

Howland Island, 36 miles to the northeast, is approximately one and a half miles long and half a mile wide and rises to an elevation of 18 feet.

Jarvis Island is several hundred miles to the east and is approximately two miles long by one and an eighth miles wide.

Baker, Howland, and Jarvis have been uninhabited since 1942.

## CANAL ZONE

Headquarters: Balboa Heights, C. Z.; 21 West St., New York City; 425 Thirteenth St., N. W., Washington, D. C.
Governor-President: Maj. Gen. W. A. Carter.
1940 population: 51,827.
1950 population: 52,822.
1960 population: 42,122.
Area: 553 sq. mi.

The Canal Zone is a 50-mile strip between the Atlantic and Pacific Oceans which was granted to the U. S. in perpetuity by the Republic of Panamá by treaty in 1903 (ratified Feb. 26, 1904) for the purpose of building, maintaining, protecting, and operating a canal. The zone extends roughly 5 miles on either side of the center line of the Panama Canal.

The 1903 treaty empowered the U. S. to act as sovereign within the zone to the exclusion of the exercise of any such sovereign rights by the Republic.

In return for the perpetual sovereign grant, the U. S. guaranteed the independence of the Republic and agreed to pay $10,000,000 to Panama upon ratification of the treaty and $250,000 in gold annually, beginning 9 years after ratification. The annual payments were increased to $430,000 after the U. S. went off the gold standard. The annuity was increased to $1,930,000 by the 1955 treaty.

The history of the Canal goes back to 1534, when King Charles V of Spain ordered a survey made. In 1876 a concession to construct a Panama Canal was granted by Columbia to an American citizen, Anthony de Gogorza. A revised concession was granted in 1878 to St. Lucien N. B. Nise, who represented a French company. Construction of the waterway was formally inaugurated in Jan. 1880 by the French Canal Co. Twenty years later, the French gave up their efforts to build a canal and sold their canal rights and properties to the U. S. for $40,000,000, the transfer being made May 4, 1904, in Panama City. The construction of the canal was completed 10 years later.

The Canal is 40.27 miles from shore line to shore line and 50.72 miles from deep water in the Caribbean to deep water in the Pacific. The Panama Railroad, completed in 1855 by private U. S. enterprise, is owned by the Panama Canal Co. It roughly parallels the Canal channel, running 47.64 miles from Colon to Panama City and is the oldest transcontinental railroad in the Americas.

The Panama Canal Locks lift or lower ships 85 feet between sea level and Gatún Lake level in 3 steps on each side of the Isthmus. On the Atlantic side the three steps are at Gatún Locks. On the Pacific side there are two steps at Miraflores Locks and one step at the Pedro Miguel Locks. Each of the twin chambers in every flight of locks has a usable length of 1,000 feet, a width of 110 feet, and a minimum depth of water of 40 feet.

The Canal Zone is, in effect, a U. S. government reservation, and in general no private enterprise is permitted except that relating directly to the operation of the waterway. The Governor, who is appointed by the U. S. President, administers the Canal Zone Government, which is charged with the civil government, including health, sanitation and protection of the Zone. The Governor is also ex officio President of the Panama Canal Company, which is a corporate agency of the U. S. charged with the operation of the Canal and related business activities.

## CANTON AND ENDERBURY

Canton and Enderbury islands, the largest of the Phoenix group, are jointly administered by the United States and Great Britain after and agreement signed on Apr. 6, 1939. Canton is triangular in shape and the largest of the eight islands of this group. It lies approximately 1,600 miles southwest of Hawaii in the Pacific and was discovered at the turn of the eighteenth century by U. S. whalers. It was surveyed by Commander R. W. Meade who named it after a whaler ship. It had, in 1960, a population of 320, including Europeans. Enderbury is rectangular in shape and is 3.5 miles long by 1.5 miles wide. It is unpopulated and lies about 32 miles southeast of Canton.

## GUAM

**Capital:** Agaña.
**Governor:** Joseph Flores.
**1940 population:** 22,290.
**1950 population:** 59,498.
**1960 population:** 67,044.
**1959 area:** 209 sq. mi.

Guam, the largest of the Mariana Islands, is independent of the trusteeship assigned to the U. S. in 1947. It was acquired by the U. S. from Spain in 1898 (occupied 1899) and was placed under the Navy Department.

In World War II, Guam was seized by the Japanese on Dec. 11, 1941; but on July 27, 1944, it was once more in U. S. hands.

On Aug. 1, 1950, President Truman signed a bill which granted U. S. citizenship to the people of Guam and established self-government. However, the people do not have an elected representative in Washington, D.C., and they do not vote in national elections. The Executive Branch of the Guam government is under the general supervision of the U.S. Secretary of Agriculture.

Military installations are an important factor in Guam's economy, followed by agriculture.

## JOHNSTON ISLAND

This island was originally discovered by Captain Charles James Johnston of *H.M.S. Cornwallis* on Dec. 14, 1807. On July 27, 1858, it was claimed by Hawaii and later became a possession of the U. S. The island is about 600 miles southwest of Hawaii and about 1½ miles long by half a mile wide.

## KINGMAN REEF

This reef was discovered by Captain W. E. Kingman in Nov. 1853 and is the smallest land of U. S. sovereignty. It is 150 feet long by 120 feet wide at high tide. At low tide, two other islets of this atoll appear. Kingman Reef is located approximately 1,000 miles south of Hawaii.

## MIDWAY

Midway, lying about 1,200 miles west-northwest of Hawaii, was discovered by Captain N. C. Brooks of the Hawaiian bark *Gambia* on July 5, 1859, in the name of the U. S. It was formally declared a U. S. possession in 1867, and in 1903 Theodore Roosevelt made it a naval reservation.

Sand and Eastern Islands, with 850 acres and 328 acres respectively, are its largest individual islands.

The total group comprises an area of 2 square miles and has no native population. The Navy Department maintains an installation and has jurisdiction over the island.

## VIRGIN ISLANDS OF THE U. S.

**Capital:** Charlotte Amalie (on St. Thomas).
**Governor:** Ralph Paiewonsky.
**1940 population:** 24,889.
**1950 population:** 26,665.
**1960 population:** 32,099 (St. Thomas, 16,201; St. Croix, 14,973; St. John, 925).
**Area:** 132 sq. mi. (St. Croix, 82; St. Thomas, 32; St. John, 18).

The Virgin Islands, consisting of 9 main islands and some 75 islets, were discovered by Columbus in 1493. Since 1666, England has held 6 of the main islands; the other 3 (St. Croix, St. Thomas and St. John), as well as about 50 of the islets, were eventually acquired by Denmark, which named them the Danish West Indies. In 1917, these islands were purchased by the U. S. from Denmark for $25 million.

Congress granted U. S. citizenship to Virgin Islanders in 1927; and, in 1931, administration was transferred from the Navy to the Department of the Interior. Universal suffrage was given in 1936 to all persons who could read and write the English language. The Governor is appointed by the President of the U. S.

About 85% of the population is Negro, and there is limited farming, fishing and cattle raising. Vegetables, citrus fruits and coconuts are raised, and the chief items of export are sugar, rum and bay rum. Tourism is the principal industry.

## WAKE ISLAND

Wake Island, about halfway between Midway and Guam, is actually the three islets of Wilkes, Peale and Wake. They were discovered by the British in 1796 and annexed by the U. S. in 1898. The entire area comprises 3 square miles. In 1938, Pan American Airways established a seaplane base and it has been used as a commercial base since then. On Dec. 8, 1941, it was attacked by the Japanese, who finally took possession on Dec. 23. It was surrendered by the Japanese on Sept. 4, 1945.

The Federal Aviation Agency maintains a station on the island and has jurisdiction, with the Navy, over the island. There is no native population.

## Pacific Islands Under U. S. Administration

In accordance with Article 3 of the Treaty of Peace with Japan, which entered into force on April 28, 1952, Japan agreed to concur in any proposal of the United States to the United Nations to place under its trusteeship system, with the United States as the sole administering authority, the Ryukyus, the Bonins, and certain other islands southwest of Japan. Japan also agreed that, pending the making of such a proposal and affirmative action thereon, the United States would have the right to exercise full jurisdiction over these islands. As of this date, no action has been taken by the United States toward bringing about this trusteeship.

All of these islands are administered, on behalf of the President, by the Secretary of Defense, who has delegated this responsibility to the Department of the Army for the Ryukyus and to the Department of the Navy for the Bonins and the other islands.

The Ryukyus, totaling some 64 islands, extend from southern Japan to Formosa (Taiwan). They have a total area of 848 square miles and a population of 882,000. The largest island is Okinawa, which has an area of 454 square miles and a population of 758,100 (as of December 1960). The principal exports from the Ryukyus are sugar, pineapple, fresh vegetables, and marine products. The local Ryukyuan government has a popularly elected legislature, an appointive chief executive, and an independent judiciary. The high commissioner is presently Lieutenant General Paul W. Caraway, of the U.S. Army, and the chief executive of the government of the Ryukyu Islands is Seisaku Ota.

The other islands under U.S. administration include Rosario Island, the Volcanos, Parece Vela, Marcus Island, and the Bonins. Typically Oriental by race, the inhabitants of the Bonin group are descendants in part of American and European settlers who came from the Sandwich Islands (Hawaii), New England, and Bermuda in 1830. Japan annexed these islands in 1878 and later sought to wipe out Western influence in the Bonins through intermarriage and immigration. However, Western names, such as Savory, Washington, Gilley, and Gonzales, have continued to this day.

## U. S. Trusteeships

In 1885, Germany assumed a protectorate over the Marshall Islands; and, in 1899, she purchased the Northern Mariana and Caroline Islands from Spain. These islands were occupied by the Japanese in 1914 and were mandated to Japan by the League of Nations in 1919. On Apr. 2, 1947, the U. N. Security Council approved a trusteeship agreement proposed by the U. S. under which the Northern Mariana, Caroline and Marshall Islands became a Strategic Trust Territory under the administration of the U. S. The measure was approved by the President, with the agreement of Congress, on July 18, 1947. Administration was transferred from the Navy to the Department of the Interior on July 1, 1951. However, administration of Saipan and Tinian was transferred back to the Navy on Jan. 1, 1953. On July 17 of the same year, administration of the remaining islands of the Northern Marianas, with the exception of Rota, was also transferred back to the Navy.

The entire group comprises more than 2,000 islands, but the total land area is only 687 sq. mi., many of the islands being only tiny coral reefs. The Micronesians are the main cultural group, the inhabitants of the Northern Marianas being most advanced.

### MARIANA ISLANDS

The Mariana Islands, east of the Philippines and south of Japan, include the islands of Guam, Rota, Saipan, Tinian, Pagan, Guguan, Agrihan and Aguijan. Guam, the largest, is independent of the trusteeship, having been acquired by the U. S. from Spain in 1898. (For information on Guam, *see* preceding page.)

Chief crops are copra and fresh fruits and vegetables.

### CAROLINE ISLANDS

The Caroline Islands, east of the Philippines and south of the Marianas, include the ap, Truk and the Palau groups and the islands of Ponape and Kusaie, as well as many coral atolls.

The islands are composed chiefly of volcanic rock, and their peaks rise 2,000 to 3,000 feet above sea level. Chief exports of the islands are copra, trochus and handicrafts.

### MARSHALL ISLANDS

The Marshall Islands, east of the Carolines, are divided into two chains: the western or Ralik group, including the atolls Jaluit, Kwajalein, Wotho, Bikini and Eniwetok; and the eastern or Ratak group, including the atolls Mili, Majuro, Maloelap, Wotje and Likiep.

The islands are of the coral-reef type and rise only a few feet above sea level. The chief crop is coconuts; exports include copra, tortoise shell, mother-of-pearl, etc.

Bikini and Eniwetok have been the scene of several atom-bomb tests.

# THE FIFTY LARGEST CITIES OF THE UNITED STATES

Since we planned the INFORMATION PLEASE ALMANAC as a book of national scope and interest, we avoided emphasis on and identification with a single city or state, as has been characteristic of all almanacs heretofore. To obtain accurate and authoritative information we have gone to the city officials. We appreciate their co-operation. The tabular material listed here is the latest provided by the sources.

## AKRON, OHIO

Incorporated as city: 1865.
Mayor-Manager: Leo Berg (to Dec. 1961).
1950 population & (rank): 274,605 (39).
1960 population & (rank): 290,351 (45).
1950–60 population change: +5.7%.
1960 land area: 55 sq. mi.
Altitude: 1,081 ft.
Location: In NE part of state, on Little Cuyahoga River.
County: Seat of Summit Co.
Churches: 316 of all denominations in county.
City-owned parks: 73 (4,400 ac.).
Telephones (1960): 159,027.*
Television sets (1960): 147,840.
Radio stations: AM, 4; FM, 1.
Television stations: 1.
Assessed valuation (1960): $793,000,000.†
City tax rate (1960): $37.90 per $1,000.†
Bonded debt (1960): $41,729,400.
Revenue (1960): $26,787,194.
Expenditure (1960): $23,687,077.

*Excluding switchboards and extentions.   †Collection year, 1961.

## ATLANTA, GA.

Incorporated as city: 1847.
Mayor: William B. Hartsfield (to Jan 1962).
1950 population & (rank): 331,314 (33).
1960 population & (rank): 487,454 (24).
1950–60 population change: +47.1%.
1960 area: 128.0 sq. mi.
Altitude: Highest, 1,050 ft.; lowest, 940.
Location: In NW central part of state, near Chattahoochee River.
Counties: In Fulton and De Kalb Cos.; seat of Fulton Co.
Churches: For whites, more than 352; for Negroes, more than 270.
City-owned parks and parkways: 150 (3,000 ac.).
Telephones (1960): 441,302.
Families with radios (1960): 250,000.
Television sets (1960): 267,000.
Radio stations: AM, 15; FM, 5.
Television stations: 3.
Assessed valuation (1961): $1,075,572,621.
City tax rate (1961): $29.25 per $1,000.
Bonded debt (Jan. 1, 1961): $76,811,180.
Revenue (1960): $55,787,130.
Expenditure (1960): $53,939,979.

## BALTIMORE, MD.

Incorporated as city: 1797.
Mayor: J. Harold Grady (to May 1963).
1950 population & (rank): 949,708 (6).
1960 population & (rank): 939,024 (6).
1950–60 population change: −1.1%.
1960 land area: 73.7 sq. mi.
Altitude: Highest, 490 ft.; lowest, sea level.
Location: On Patapsco River, about 12 mi. from Chesapeake Bay.
County: Independent city.
Churches: Roman Catholic, 68; Jewish, 50; Protestant and others, 356.

City-owned parks: 148 park areas and tracts (5,768 ac.).
Telephone subscribers (Jan. 1, 1961): 248,148.
Radio stations: AM, 11.; FM, 9.
Television stations: 3.
Assessed valuation (1961): $3,466,866,348.
City tax rate (1961): $3.60 per $100.
Net bonded debt (Jan. 1, 1960): $287,947,891.
Current revenue (1960 budget): $177,951,370.
Current expenditure (1960 budget): $175,024,786.

## BIRMINGHAM, ALA.

Incorporated as city: 1871.
Mayor: James W. Morgan (to Nov. 1961).
1950 population & (rank): 326,037 (34).
1960 population & (rank): 340,887 (36).
1950–60 population change: +4.6%.
1959 land area: 68.76 sq. mi.
Altitude: Highest, 1,052 ft.; lowest, 565.
Location: In N central part of state.
County: Seat of Jefferson Co.
Churches: Protestant, 570; Roman Catholic, 26; Jewish, 3.
City-owned parks: 68 (1,400 ac.).
Telephones (1960): 243,202.
Television sets (1959): 142,800.
Radio stations: AM, 13; FM, 4.
Television stations: 5.
Assessed valuation (1960): $500,000,000.
City tax rate (1961): $36 per $1,000.
Net bonded debt (1960): $31,595,520.
Tax Revenue (1960): $31,634,212.
Expenditure (1960): $31,719,192.

## BOSTON, MASS.

Incorporated as city: 1822.
Mayor: John F. Collins (to Jan. 1964).
1950 population & (rank): 801,444 (10).
1960 population & (rank): 697,197 (13).
1950–60 population change: −13.0%.
1960 area: 67.6 sq. mi.
Altitude: Highest, 330 ft.; lowest, sea level.
Location: On Massachusetts Bay, at mouths of Charles and Mystic Rivers.
County: Seat of Suffolk Co.
Churches: Protestant, 263; Roman Catholic, 79; Jewish, 24; others, 74.
City-owned parks & parkways: 2,710.82 ac.
Telephones: 409,000.
Radio sets (Greater Boston Area): 2,348,292.
Television sets (Greater Boston Area): 906,800.
Radio stations: AM, 9; FM, 8.
Television stations: 4.
Assessed valuation (1960): $1,465,525,100.
City tax rate (1960): $100.70 per $1,000.
Net bonded debt (1960): $101,016,708.
Revenue (1960): $310,312,877.
Expenditure (1960): $321,775,275.*

*Includes payment for investment of general cash in amount of $12,942,747 in U.S. Treasury Bills.

## BUFFALO, N. Y.

Incorporated as city: 1832.
Mayor: Frank A. Sedita (to Dec. 31, 1961).
1950 population & (rank): 580,132 (15).

1960 population & (rank): 532,759 (20).
1950–60 population change: —8.2%.
1940 area: Land, 42.67 sq. mi.; inland water, 10.8.
Altitude: Highest, 680 ft.; lowest, 571.
Location: At east end of Lake Erie, on Niagara River.
County: Seat of Erie Co.
Churches: Protestant, 290; Roman Catholic, 74; Jewish, 12; others, 30.
City-owned parks: 10 public parks (3,000 ac.).
Telephones (Jan. 1960): 358,006.
Radio sets: 350,000.
Television sets: 160,000.
Radio stations: AM, 8; FM, 6.
Television stations: 3.
Assessed valuation (1961–62): $1,078,600,000.
City tax rate (1961–62): $44.45 per $1,000.
Net bonded debt (1960): $77,008,783.
Revenue (1960–61): $84,280,000.
Expenditure (1960–61): $84,369,900.

## CHICAGO, ILL.

Incorporated as city: 1837.
Mayor: Richard J. Daley (to Apr. 1963).
1950 population & (rank): 3,620,962 (2).
1960 population & (rank): 3,550,404 (2).
1950–60 population change: —1.9%.
1960 area: Land, 225.12 sq. mi.; inland water, 5.37.
Altitude: Highest, 672 ft.; lowest, 581.
Location: On lower west shore of Lake Michigan.
County: Seat of Cook Co.
Churches*: Protestant, 1,421; Roman Catholic, 292; Jewish, 54.
City-owned parks: 423 (staffed, 212).
Telephones (Apr. 1, 1961): 1,929,732.
Radio sets (Jan. 1960): 1,549,000.†
Television sets (Jan. 1960): 1,488,570.‡
Radio stations: AM, 23; FM, 21.
Television stations: 5.
Assessed valuation (1960): $10,429,524,480.
City tax rate (1960): north of 87th St., $4.668; south of 87th St., $4.688. Both per $100.
Gross bonded debt (Jan. 1961): $659,329,000.
Revenue (1960): $538,027,000.
Expenditure (1960): $464,675,000.

\* Store front churches excluded.  † Metropolitan area.
‡ Cook County.

## CINCINNATI, OHIO

Incorporated as city: 1819.
Mayor: Walton H. Bachrach (to Dec. 1961).
City Manager: C. A. Harrell (Apptd. 1954).
1950 population & (rank): 503,998 (18).
1960 population & (rank): 502,550 (21).
1950–60 population change: —0.3%.
1959 land area: 77.3181 sq. mi.
Altitude: Highest, 960 ft.; lowest, 441.
Location: In SW corner of state on Ohio River.
County: Seat of Hamilton Co.
Churches: 373.
City-owned parks: 84 (3,870 ac.).
Telephones (1961): 334,167.
Homes with radios (1960): 266,040.*
Homes with television (1960): 259,280.*
Radio stations: AM, 8; FM, 3 (Greater Cincinnati).
Television stations: 4.
Assessed valuation (1960): $1,574,553,770.

\* Data for Hamilton County.

City tax rate (1961): $11.44 per $1,000.
Bonded debt (1960): $171,944,911.
Receipts (1960): $70,499,069.
Expenses (1960): $59,643,555.

## CLEVELAND, OHIO

Incorporated as city: 1836.
Mayor: Anthony J. Celebrezze (to Nov. 1961).
1950 population & (rank): 914,808 (7).
1960 population & (rank): 876,050 (8).
1950–60 population change: —4.2%.
1960 area: 75.66 sq. mi.
Altitude: Highest, 865 ft.; lowest, 573.
Location: On Lake Erie at mouth of Cuyahoga River.
County: Seat of Cuyahoga Co.
Churches: Protestant, 377; Roman Catholic, 118; Jewish, 36; others, 6.
City-owned parks: 39 (2,600 ac.).
Telephones (1960): 855,621.*
Radio sets (1960): 1,291,750.
Televison sets (1960): 1,310,000.
Radio stations: AM, 8; FM, 8.
Television stations: 3.
Assessed valuation (1961): $2,862,976,353.
City tax rate (1961): $39.50 per $1,000.
Bonded debt (Dec. 31, 1960): $221,853,000.
Revenue (1960): $146,472,719.
Expenditure (1960): $113,736,504.

\* Metropolitan area.

## COLUMBUS, OHIO

Incorporated as city: 1834.
Mayor: W. Ralston Westlake (to Jan. 1964).
1950 population & (rank): 375,901 (28).
1960 population & (rank): 471,316 (28).
1950–60 population change: +25.4%.
Altitude: Highest, 902 ft.; lowest, 702.
Location: In central part of state, on Scioto River.
County: Seat of Franklin Co.
Churches: Protestant, 400; Roman Catholic, 40; Jewish, 5.
City-owned parks: 57 (2,772.81 ac.).
Telephones (Dec. 1959): 335,108.
Homes with radios (1958): 196,000.
Television sets (1958): 165,600.*
Radio stations: AM, 6; FM, 4.
Television stations: 3.
Assessed valuation (1960): $1,173,230,220.
City tax rate (1960): $27.40 per $1,000.
Net bonded debt (1961): $76,590,649.
Revenue (1960): $33,828,924.
Expenditure (1960): $33,901,805.

\* Metropolitan area.

## DALLAS, TEX.

Incorporated as city: 1856.
Mayor: Earle Cabell (to May 1963).
City Manager: Elgin E. Crull (apptd. 1952).
1950 population & (rank): 434,462 (22).
1960 population & (rank): 679,684 (14).
1950–60 population change: +56.4%.
1959 area: 277 sq. mi.
Altitude: Highest, 685 ft.; lowest, 375.
Location: In NE part of state, on Trinity River.
County: Seat of Dallas Co.
Churches: 800.
City-owned parks: 118 (7,988 ac.).
Telephones (Jan. 1, 1961): 451,824.

Radio sets (1960): 427,600.
Television homes (1960): 203,670.
Radio stations: AM, 12, FM, 5.
Television stations: 3.
Assessed valuation (1960): $2,334,338,720.
City tax rate (1960–61): $1.56 per $100.
Net bonded debt (Oct. 1, 1960): $108,627,631.
Revenue (1960–61): $73,852,078.
Expenditure (1960–61): $73,852,078.

## DAYTON, OHIO

Incorporated as city: 1805.
Mayor: R. William Patterson (to Jan. 1962).
City Manager: Herbert W. Starick (apptd. July 1953).
1950 population & (rank): 243,872 (44).
1960 population & (rank): 262,332 (49).
1950–60 population change: +7.6%.
1959 land area: 34.7 sq. mi.
Altitude: Highest 981 ft.; lowest, 727.
Location: In SW part of state, on Miami River.
County: Seat of Montgomery Co.
Churches: Protestant, 300; Roman Catholic, 30; Jewish, 3.
City-owned parks: 66 (1,799 ac.).
Telephones (1960): 252,139.
Radio sets (1960): 259,184.*
Television sets (1960): 246,592.
Radio stations: AM, 4; FM, 3.
Television stations: 2.
Assessed valuation (1960): $833,977,590.
Real estate city tax rate (1960): $10 per $1,000.†
Bonded debt (1960): $42,827,000.
Revenue (1960 General Fund): $13,122,099.
Expenditure (1960 General Fund): $12,968,231.

* Dwellings only; Metropolitan area. † Dayton also has a ¾% City Income Tax on salaries and net profits of business.

## DENVER, COLO.

Incorporated as city: 1861.
Mayor: Richard Y. Batterton (to July 1963).
1950 population & (rank): 415,786 (24).
1960 population & (rank): 493,887 (23).
1950–60 population change: +18.8%.
1959 area: Land, 73.8 sq. mi.; inland water, 85.
Altitude: Highest, 5,470 ft.; lowest, 5,130.
Location: In NE central part of state, on South Platte River.
County: Coextensive with Denver Co.
Churches: Protestant, 360; Roman Catholic, 53; Jewish, 14.
City-owned parks: 100 (2,200 developed acres).
City-owned mountain parks: 40 (13,447.6 ac.).
Families with telephones (1960): 223,579.
Radio stations: AM, 11; FM, 3.
Television stations: 5.
Assessed valuation (1960): $1,120,765,400.
City tax rate (1960): $20.70 per $1,000.
Bonded debt (1960): $16,508,000.
Revenue (1960): $102,636,145.
Expenditure (1960): $79,275,122.

## DETROIT, MICH.

Incorporated as city: 1806.
Mayor: Louis C. Miriani (to Jan. 1962).
1950 population & (rank): 1,849,568 (5).
1960 population & (rank): 1,670,144 (5).
1950–60 population change: −9.7%.
1957 area: Land, 139.6 sq. mi.; inland water, 4.1.

Altitude: Highest, 685 ft.; lowest, 574.
Location: In Southeast part of state, on Detroit River.
County: Seat of Wayne Co.
Churches*: Protestant, 1,494; Catholic, 333; Jewish, 32.
City-owned parks: 361 sites (5,831 ac.).
Telephones: 1,566,136.*
Radio sets: 1,061,980.
Television sets: 1,043,610.
Radio stations: AM, 15; FM, 20.*
Television stations: 5.*
Assessed valuation (1960): $5,672,174,774.
City tax rate (1960–61): $25.258 per $1,000.†
Net bonded debt (June 30, 1960): $407,565,620.
Revenue (1959–60): $242,227,319.
Expenditure (1959–60): $241,431,747.

* Metropolitan area. † Excludes school system.

## EL PASO, TEX.

Incorporated as city: 1873.
Mayor: Ralph Seitsinger (to Apr. 1963).
1950 population & (rank): 130,485 (75).
1960 population & (rank): 276,687 (46).
1950–60 population change: +112.0%.
1950 land area: 25.6 sq. mi.
Altitude: 4,000 ft.
Location: In far west part of state, on Rio Grande.
County: Seat of El Paso Co.
Churches: Protestant, 136; Roman Catholic, 25; Jewish, 2; others, 10.
City-owned parks: 96 (655 ac.).
Telephones (1960): 97,953.
Radio sets (1961): 95,200.*
Television sets (1961): 84,900.*
Radio stations: AM, 7; FM, 1.
Television stations: 3.
Assessed valuation (1960): $475,000,000.
City tax rate (1961): $1.65 per $100 (based on 50% of valuation).
Bonded debt (Feb. 1961): $23,005,140.†
Revenue (1960–61): $17,315,758.†
Expenditure (1960–61): $16,223,272.†

* Metropolitan area. † Excludes revenue bond financing of water-sewer system.

## FORT WORTH, TEX.

Incorporated as city: 1873.
Mayor: John Justin, Jr. (to Apr. 1963).
City Manager: L. P. Cookingham (apptd. 1959).
1950 population & (rank): 278,778 (38).
1960 population & (rank): 356,268 (34).
1950–60 population change: +27.8%.
1960 area: 153.11 sq. mi.
Altitude: Highest, 780 ft.; lowest, 520.
Location: In N Central part of state, on Trinity River.
County: Seat of Tarrant Co.
Churches: Protestant, 586; Roman Catholic, 18; Jewish, 2.
City-owned parks: 65 (4,957 ac.).
Telephones (1960): 239,108.
Radio sets (1960): 493,230.
Television sets (1960): 211,643.
Radio stations: AM, 6; FM, 2.
Television stations: 2.
Assessed valuation (1960): $822,463,900.
City tax rate (1960): $1.71 per $100.
Bonded debt (1960): $81,145,980.
Revenue (1960): $20,249,245.
Expenditure (1960): $20,259,803.

# HONOLULU, HAWAII

Incorporated as city & county: 1909.
Mayor: Neal S. Blaisdell (to Jan. 2, 1965).
1950 population of city: 248,034.
1950 population of city & county: 353,020.
1960 population of city & (rank): 294,179 (43).
1950–60 population change: +18.6%.
1959 area of city & county: 604 sq. mi.
Altitude: Highest, 4,025 ft.; lowest, sea level.
Location: County comprises entire island of Oahu; city is on southeast part of island.
Churches: Roman Catholic, 27; Buddhist, 19; Jewish, 1; Protestant & other, 146.
City-owned parks: 2,721.28 ac.
Telephones (1960): 200,000.
Television sets (1960): 107,069.
Radio stations: AM, 11; FM, 1.
Television stations: 3.
Assessed valuation (1960): $1,527,489,601.
City tax rate (1960): $11.70 per $1,000.
Bonded debt (1960): $65,033,000.
Net revenue (1960): $41,929,403 (1959 surplus: $3,250,223).
Net expenditure (1960): $40,043,251.

# HOUSTON, TEX.

Incorporated as city: 1837.
Mayor: Lewis Cutrer (to Jan. 1962).
1950 population & (rank): 596,163, (14).
1960 population & (rank): 938,219 (7).
1950–60 population change: +57.4%.
1961 land area: 349.4 sq. mi.
Altitude: Highest, 54 ft; lowest, sea level.
Location: In SE part of state, near Gulf of Mexico.
County: Seat of Harris Co.
Churches: Approximately 1,275.*
City-owned parks: 138 (4,454 ac.).
Telephones: (1961): 543,019.*
Households with radio sets: 384,000.*
Households with television sets: 337,400.*
Radio stations: AM, 11; FM, 8.
Television stations: 4.
Assessed valuation (1960): $2,329,076,000.
City tax rate (1961): $2 per $100.
Bonded debt (Jan. 1, 1961): $244,643,500.
Revenue (1960 General Fund): $58,905,015.
Expenditure (1960 General Fund): $59,427,884.
  * Metropolitan area (Harris County).

# INDIANAPOLIS, IND.

Incorporated as city: 1874.
Mayor: Charles H. Boswell (to Dec. 1963).
1950 population & (rank): 427,173 (23).
1960 population & (rank): 476,258 (26).
1950–60 population change: +11.5%.
1960 land area: 77 sq. mi.
Altitude: Highest, 816 ft.; lowest, 667.
Location: In central part of state, on West Fork of White River.
County: Seat of Marion County.
Churches: 515.
City-owned parks: 32 (3,519 ac.).
Telephones (Dec. 1960): 352,806.
Radio sets: 194,000 (radio families).
Television sets: 199,500 (TV families).
Radio stations: AM, 6; FM, 2.
Television stations: 4.
Assessed valuation (1960): $813,497,655.
City tax rate (1960): $7.742 per $100.

Gross debt (Dec. 31, 1960): $77,580,000.
Revenue (1959): $29,087,285.*
Expenditure (1959): $27,592,661.*
  * Excludes schools and county and township government.

# JERSEY CITY, N. J.

Incorporated as city: 1855.
Mayor: Thomas Gangemi (to June 1965).
1950 population & (rank): 299,017 (37).
1960 population & (rank): 276,101 (47).
1950–60 population change: —7.7%.
1960 area: 19.2 sq. mi.
Altitude: Highest, 150 ft.; lowest, 14 ft. above mean sea level.
Location: In NE part of state, on Hudson River and Upper New York Bay.
County: Seat of Hudson Co.
Churches: Protestant, 90; Roman Catholic, 26; Jewish, 7; others, 26.
Telephones (1960): 111,000.
Assessed valuation (1960): $494,017,628.
City tax rate (1960): $98.23 per $1,000.
Bonded debt (Dec. 31, 1959): $34,460,090.*
Revenue (1960): $57,852,986.
Expenditures (1960): $58,684,461.
  * Includes bonds and notes authorized and not issued of $7,390,090.

# KANSAS CITY, MO.

Incorporated as city: 1850.
Mayor: H. Roe Bartle (to Apr. 1963).
City Manager: R. P. Weatherford, Jr.
1950 population & (rank): 456,622 (20).
1960 population & (rank): 475,539 (27).
1950–60 population change: +4.1%.
1960 land area: 167.83 sq. mi.
Altitude: Highest, 1,014 ft.; lowest, 722 ft.
Location: In western part of state, at conjunction of Missouri and Kansas Rivers.
County: Located in Jackson & Clay Counties.
Churches: Protestant, 500; Roman Catholic, 45; Jewish, 4.
City-owned parks: 59 (4,093 ac.).
Telephones in Kansas City District Exchange (Mar. 31, 1961): 532,285.
Television households (est. Jan. 1961): 160,500.
Radio stations: AM, 9; FM, 8.
Television stations: 3.
Assessed valuation (1961): $1,006,762,282.
City tax rate (1961–62): $15 per $1,000.
Bonded debt (Apr. 30, 1961): $59,172,000.
Revenue (1960–61): $34,297,485.
Expenditure (1960–61): $35,231,336.

# LONG BEACH, CALIF.

Founded: 1881.
Mayor: Edwin W. Wade (to July 1963).
City Manager: John R. Mansell (apptd. 1961).
1950 population & (rank): 250,767 (41).
1960 population & (rank): 344,168 (35).
1950–60 population change: +37.2%.
1960 land area: 46.46 sq. mi.
Altitude: Highest, 170 ft.; lowest, sea level.
Location: On San Pedro Bay, south of Los Angeles.
County: In Los Angeles Co.
Churches: 184.
City-owned parks: 37 (1,725.86 ac.).
Telephones (1961): 194,757.
Radio stations: AM, 2; FM, 3.
Television stations: None.
Assessed valuation (1960–61): $716,550,940.

City tax rate (1960–61): $1.37 per $100.
Bonded debt (June 30, 1961): $36,881,500.
Revenue (1960–61): $63,905,488.
Expenditure (1960–61): $85,039,257.

## LOS ANGELES, CALIF.

Incorporated as city: 1850.
Mayor: Sam Yorty (to June 1965).
1950 population & (rank): 1,970,358 (4).
1960 population & (rank): 2,479,015 (3).
1950–60 population change: +25.8%.
1960 area: 457.93 sq. mi.
Altitude: Highest, 5,081 ft.; lowest, sea level.
Location: In SW part of state, on Pacific Ocean.
County: Seat of Los Angeles Co.
Churches: 1,603 Catholic, Protestant and Jewish, plus unknown number of others.
City-owned parks: 112 (10,490 ac.).
Telephones (1961): 1,586,000.
Radio sets (1961): 1,788,328 in homes, 695,248 in automobiles.
Television sets in homes (1961): 793,800.
Radio stations: AM, 30; FM, 15 (includes 9 combinations).*
Television stations: 7.
Assessed valuation (1960–61): $4,690,616,620.
City tax rate (1960–61): $1.9422 per $100.
Gross debt (June 30, 1960): General obligation bonds, $251,408,000; revenue bonds, $415,-210,000.
Revenue (cash receipts, 1959–60): $524,043,510 (includes bonds sold).
Expenditure (1959–60): $536,746,222 (includes capital expenditures).
*Metropolitan area.

## LOUISVILLE, KY.

Incorporated as city: 1828.
Mayor: Bruce Hoblitzell (to Dec. 1961).
1950 population & (rank): 369,129 (30).
1960 population & (rank): 390,639 (31).
1950–60 population change: +5.8%.
1960 land area: 57.07 sq. mi.
Altitude: Highest, 761 ft.; lowest, 382 ft.
Location: In north central part of state, on Ohio River.
County: Seat of Jefferson Co.
Churches*: 648.
City-owned parks: 8 parks; 57 playgrounds (total: 3,600 ac.).
Telephones (1960)*: 239,420.
Radio sets (1960)†: 126,660.
Television sets (1960)*: 195,150.
Radio stations: AM, 7; FM, 0.
Television stations: 2.
Assessed valuation (Jan. 1, 1959): $753,587,885.
City tax rate (1959): $1.50 per $100 (city purposes only; exclusive of schools).
Net bonded debt (Dec. 31, 1960): $49,230,637.
Revenue (1960): $18,430,018 (general corporate purposes only).
Expenditure (1960): $18,208,227 (general corporate purposes only).
*Jefferson County.	†Metropolitan area.

## MEMPHIS, TENN.

Incorporated as city: 1826.
Mayor: Henry Loeb (to Jan. 1964).
1950 population & (rank): 396,000 (26).
1960 population & (rank): 497,524 (22).
1950–60 population change: +25.6%.

1960 land area: 140.68 sq. mi.
Altitude: Highest, 300 ft.
Location: In SW corner of state, on Mississippi River.
County: Seat of Shelby Co.
Churches: Roman Catholic, 19; Jewish, 5; Protestant & other, 539.
City-owned parks: 120 (3,510 ac.); playgrounds, 30.
Telephones (Mar. 31, 1961): 238,150.
Radio sets (Jan. 1961): 161,890.
Television sets (May 1961): 155,700.
Radio stations: AM, 9; FM, 3.
Television stations: 4.
Assessed valuation (1960): $1,108,365,743.
City tax rate (1960): $1.80 per $100.
Bonded debt (Dec. 31, 1960): $94,653,000.
Revenue (1960): $28,607,905.
Expenditure (1960): $28,985,781.

## MIAMI, FLA.

Incorporated as city: 1896.
Mayor: Robert King High (to Nov. 1961).
City manager: Melvin L. Reese (apptd. Mar. 1960).
1950 population & (rank): 249,276 (42).
1960 population & (rank): 291,688 (44).
1950–60 population change: +17.0%.
1959 area: Land, 34.32 sq. mi.; inland water, 19.50.
Altitude: Average, 12 ft.
Location: In SE part of state, on Biscayne Bay.
County: Seat of Dade Co.
Churches: Metropolitan Miami (Dade County), 581.
City-owned parks: 52.
Telephones (1960): 516,715.
Radio sets (1960): 680,000.
Television sets (1960): 462,100.
Radio stations: AM, 12; FM, 6 (4 AM-FM).
Television stations: 3 commercial, 1 educational.
Gross assessed valuation (1960): $1,096,926,330.
City tax rate (1960–61): $20.59 per $1,000 valuation above $5,000 homestead exemption.
Net bonded debt (June 30, 1960): $39,599,602.
Revenue (1959–60): $31,755,214.
Expenditure (1959–60): $31,160,367.

## MILWAUKEE, WIS.

Incorporated as city: 1846.
Mayor: Henry W. Maier (to Apr. 1964).
1950 population & (rank): 637,392 (13).
1960 population & (rank): 741,324 (11).
1950–60 population change: +16.3%.
1960 land area: 91.10 sq. mi.
Altitude: 581.22 ft.
Location: In SE part of state, on Lake Michigan.
County: Seat of Milwaukee Co.
Churches: 570 in county.
County-owned parks: 102 (10,355 ac.).
Telephones (1961): 515,663.*
Families with radio sets (1961): 354,870.*
Families with television sets (1960): 303,700.*
Radio stations: AM, 7; FM, 7.*
Television stations: 5.
Assessed valuation (1961): $1,974,345,250.
City-school tax rate (1960): $43.37 per $1,000.
Gross debt (Dec. 31, 1959): $119,732,423.
Revenue (1959): $137,252,897.
Expenditure (1961 budget): $156,674,100.
* Milwaukee County.

## MINNEAPOLIS, MINN.

Incorporated as city: 1867.
Mayor: Arthur Naftalin (to July 1963).
1950 population & (rank): 521,718 (17).
1960 population & (rank): 482,872 (25).
1950–60 population change: —7.4%.
1954 area: Land, 58.79 sq. mi.; inland water, 5.0.
Altitude: Highest, 945 ft.; lowest, 695.
Location: In SE central part of state, on Mississippi River.
County: Seat of Hennepin Co.
Churches: 419.
City-owned parks: 152.
Telephones (1960): 336,919.
Radio sets (1960): 432,000.
Television sets (1960): 172,000.
Radio stations: AM, 11; FM, 4.
Television stations: 5.
Assessed valuation (1960): $405,503,575.
City tax rate (1960): $1.9132 per $100.
Net debt (Feb. 28, 1961): $26,342,579.
Revenue (1958): $89,238,589.
Expenditure (1958): $89,238,589.

## NEW ORLEANS, LA.

Incorporated as city: 1805.
Mayor: de Lesseps S. Morrison (to May 1962).
1950 population & (rank): 570,445 (16).
1960 population & (rank): 627,525 (15).
1950–60 population change: +10.0%.
1954 area: Land, 199.4 sq. mi.; inland water, 164.1.
Altitude: Highest, 15 ft.; lowest, 4 below sea level.
Location: In SE part of state, between Mississippi River and Lake Pontchartrain.
Parish: Seat of Orleans Parish.
Churches: 625.
City-owned parks: 69 (1,700 ac.).
Telephones (1960): 343,000.
Radio sets (1960): 231,200.
Television sets (1960): 209,000.
Radio stations: AM, 10; FM, 4.
Television stations: 4.
Assessed valuation (1961): $997,000,000.
City tax rate (1961): $3.1275 per $100.
Bonded debt (Jan. 1, 1961): $95,073,000.
Revenue (1961 operating budget): $34,128,520.
Expenditure (1961 operating budget): $34,128,520.

## NEW YORK, N. Y.

Chartered as "Greater New York": 1898.
Mayor: Robert F. Wagner (to Dec. 1961).
Borough Presidents: Bronx, James J. Lyons; Brooklyn, John Hayes; Manhattan, Edward R. Dudley; Queens, John P. Clancy; Richmond, Albert V. Maniscalco.
1950 population & (rank): 7,891,957 (1).
1960 population & (rank): 7,781,984 (1).
1950–60 population change: —1.4%.
1955 area: 319.1 sq. mi.
Altitude: Highest, 409 ft.; lowest, sea level.
Counties: Consists of 5 counties: Bronx, Kings (Brooklyn), New York (Manhattan), Queens, Richmond (Staten Island).
Location: SE part of state, at mouth of Hudson River.
Churches: Protestant, 1,626; Jewish, 1,249; Roman Catholic, 428.

City-owned parks: 1,293 (35,464 ac.).
Telephones: 4,410,000.
Families with radios: 2,400,000.
Families with television sets: 2,260,000.
Radio stations: AM & FM, 10; AM only, 8; FM only, 7.
Television stations: 6.
Assessed valuation (1960–61): $24,944,418,337.
City tax rate (1960–61): $4.12 per $100.
Bonded debt (June 30, 1960): $3,362,921,088.
Revenue (1959–60): $2,225,655,074.
Expenditure (1960–61): $2,345,483,576.

## NEWARK, N. J.

Incorporated as city: 1836.
Mayor: Leo P. Carlin (to July 1962).
1950 population & (rank): 438,776 (21).
1960 population & (rank): 405,220 (30).
1950–60 population change: —7.6%.
1955 area: Land, 23.57 sq. mi.; inland water, 3.2.
Altitude: Highest, 273.4 ft.; lowest, sea level.
Location: In NE part of state, on Passaic River and Newark Bay.
County: Seat of Essex Co.
Churches: Roman Catholic, 35; Jewish, 31; Protestant and others, 265.
City-owned parks: 41 (38.84 ac.).
County-governed parks in city: 7 (752.9 ac.).
Telephones (1960): 257,300 (includes fringe areas).
Radio stations: AM, 4; FM, 2.
Television stations: 1.
Assessed valuation (1961): $743,314,446.
City tax rate (1961): $10.11 per $100.
Net bonded debt (1960): $46,181,000.
Revenue (1960): $93,987,957.
Expenditure (1960): $93,987,957.

## NORFOLK, VA.

Incorporated as city: 1845.
Mayor: W. F. Duckworth (to Aug. 31, 1962).
City Manager: Thomas F. Maxwell (apptd. Feb. 1956).
1950 population & (rank): 213,513 (48).
1960 population & (rank): 305,872 (41).
1950–60 population change: +43.3%.
1959 land area: 61.84 sq. mi.
Location: In SE part of state, on Elizabeth River and Hampton Roads.
County: Independent city.
Churches: 375.
Telephones (1959): 122,677.
Radio stations: AM, 6; FM, 3.
Television stations: 3.
Assessed valuation (1961): $503,491,920.
City tax rate (1958): Real and personal, $3 per $100; machinery, $1 per $100.
Bonded debt (1960): $58,587,640.
Revenue (1961 anticipated): $42,336,534.*
Expenditure (1961 budget): $41,804,923.

*Does not include cash surplus.

## OAKLAND, CALIF.

Incorporated as city: 1854.
Mayor: John C. Houlihan (to June 1965).
City Manager: Wayne E. Thompson (appt. Aug. 1954).
1950 population & (rank): 384,575 (27).
1960 population & (rank): 367,548 (33).
1950–60 population change: —4.4%.
1961 land area: 53.3 sq. mi.

Altitude: Highest, 1,700 ft.; lowest, sea level.
Location: In west central part of state, on east side of San Francisco Bay.
County: Seat of Alameda Co.
Churches: Protestant, 147; Roman Catholic, 23; Jewish, 3; others, 84.
City-owned parks: 943.6 ac.
Telephones (1961): 384,131.*
Radio sets (1961): 885,000.†
Television sets (1961): 283,600.†
Radio stations: AM, 4; FM, 4.
Television stations: 5 (Bay area).
Assessed valuation (1960–61): $629,631,963.
City tax rate (1960–61): $2.91 per $100.
Bonded debt (June 30, 1960): $22,994,000.
Revenue (1959–60, all funds): $48,286,415.‡
Expenditure (1959–60, all funds): $41,119,499.‡

* Oakland directory area.   † Metropolitan area.
‡Includes bond capital fund activity.

## OKLAHOMA CITY, OKLA.

Incorporated as city: 1890.
Mayor: James Norick (to Apr. 1963).
City Manager: Sheldon L. Stirling.
1950 population & (rank): 243,504 (45).
1960 population & (rank): 324,253 (37).
1950–60 population change: +33.2%.
1961 land area: 432.8 sq. mi.
Altitude: Highest, 1,276 ft.; lowest, 1,070.
Location: In central part of state, on North Canadian River.
County: Seat of Oklahoma Co.
Churches: Protestant & others, 340; Catholic, 15; Jewish, 2.
City-owned parks: 82 (9,924 ac.).
Telephones (1961): 216,762.
Television sets: Not available.
Radio stations: AM, 8; FM, 2.
Television stations: 4.
Assessed valuation (1960): Gross, $357,830,459; net, $298,130,029.
City tax rate (1961): $19.84 per $1,000.
Bonded debt (1960): $63,300,500.
Revenue (1960): $12,812,207.
Expenditure (1960): $13,203,587.

## OMAHA, NEBR.

Incorporated as city: 1857.
Mayor: James J. Dworak (to May 1965).
1950 population & (rank): 251,117 (40).
1960 population & (rank): 301,598 (42).
1950–60 population change: +20.1%.
1961 land area: 53.6 sq. mi.
Altitude: Highest, 1,270 ft.
Location: In eastern part of state, on Missouri River.
County: Seat of Douglas Co.
Churches: Protestant, 200; Roman Catholic, 37; Jewish, 3.
City-owned parks: 3,400 ac.
Telephones (1961): 195,532.
Radio sets: 343,600.
Television sets: 97,000.
Radio stations: AM, 7; FM, 3.
Television stations: 3.
Assessed valuation (1961): $518,706,683.
City tax rate (1961): $17.90 per $1,000.
Bonded debt (Jan. 1, 1961): $14,989,187.
Revenue (1960): $22,981,156.*
Expenditure (1960): $21,275,459.

* Balance of revenue on hand on Dec. 31, 1960: $10,509,868.

## PHILADELPHIA, PA.

First charter as city: 1701.
Mayor: Richardson Dilworth (to Jan. 1964).
1950 population & (rank): 2,071,605 (3).
1960 population & (rank): 2,002,512 (4).
1950–60 population change: —3.3%.
1960 land area: 129.71 sq. mi.
Altitude: Highest, 440 ft.; lowest, sea level.
Location: In SE part of state, at junction of Schuylkill and Delaware Rivers.
County: Seat of Philadelphia Co. (co-terminous).
Churches: Roman Catholic, 147; Jewish, 155; Protestant and other, 1,130.
City-owned parks: 113 (8,184 ac.).
Telephones (1961): 1,846,359.
Television sets (1961): 606,700.
Radio stations: AM, 12; FM, 12.
Television stations: 5.
Assessed valuation (1961): $4,028,506,410.
City tax rate (1961): $3.80 per $100.
Net bonded debt (Jan. 1, 1961): $657,222,000 (tax supported).
Revenue (1960): $216,409,000.
Expenditure (1960): $216,608,000.

## PHOENIX, ARIZ.

Incorporated as city: 1881.
Mayor: Samuel Mardian, Jr. (to Jan. 1962).
City Manager: Samuel E. Vickers (apptd. Mar. 1961).
1950 population & (rank): 106,818 (98).
1960 population & (rank): 439,170 (29).
1950–60 population change: +311.1%.
1950 land area: 17.1 sq. mi.
Altitude: Highest, 2,690 ft.; lowest, 1,017.
Location: In center of state, on Salt River.
County: Seat of Maricopa Co.
Churches: Protestant, 344; Roman Catholic, 16; Jewish, 4; others, 2.
City-owned parks: 52 (21,610.16 ac.).
Telephones (1961): 250,453.
Radio sets (1960): 187,000.
Television sets (1960): 153,248.
Radio stations: AM, 17; FM, 5.
Television stations: 5.
Assessed valuation (1960–61): $450,624,500.
City tax rate (1960–61): $1.75 per $100.
Bonded debt (June 30, 1960): $82,521,000.
Revenue (1959–60): $27,969,688.
Expenditure (1959–60): $28,728,751.

## PITTSBURGH, PA.

Incorporated as city: 1816.
Mayor: Joseph M. Barr (to Dec. 1961).
1950 population & (rank): 676,806 (12).
1960 population & (rank): 604,332 (16).
1950–60 population change: —10.7%.
1960 land area: 55.23 sq. mi.
Altitude: Highest, 1,240 ft.; lowest, 715.
Location: In SW part of state, at beginning of Ohio River.
County: Seat of Allegheny Co.
Churches: Protestant, 348; Roman Catholic, 86; Jewish, 28; Orthodox, 26.
City-owned parks: 25; 13 parklets (2,010 ac.).
Telephones (1960): 541,262.
Radio sets (1958): 454,900.
Television sets (1959): 443,670.*
Radio stations: AM, 10; FM, 6.
Television stations: 4.

* Allegheny County.

Assessed valuation (1961): Land, $424,170,339; buildings, $791,880,193.
City tax rate (1961): Land, $37 per $1,000; buildings, $18.50 per $1,000.
Bonded debt (Jan. 1, 1961): $56,426,800.
Revenue (1961 budget): $59,135,658.
Expenditure (1961 budget): $59,111,642.

## PORTLAND, OREG.

Incorporated as city: 1851.
Mayor: Terry D. Shrunk (to Jan. 1965).
1950 population & (rank): 373,628 (29).
1960 population & (rank): 372,676 (32).
1950–60 population change: —.3%.
1960 land area: 78 sq. mi.
Altitude: Highest, 1,073 ft.; lowest, sea level.
Location: In NW part of state, on Willamette River.
County: Seat of Multnomah Co.
Churches: Protestant, 475; Roman Catholic, 35; Jewish, 10; Buddhist, 2.
City-owned parks: 120 (6,203 ac.).
Telephones (1960): 271,541.
Radio stations: AM, 10; FM, 6.
Television stations: 3.
Assessed valuation (1960–61): $842,422,720 (at 40% of true cash value).
City tax rate (1959–60): $6.50 per $100 (at 40% of true cash value).
Bonded debt (June 30, 1960): $39,774,129.
Revenue (1960–61): $59,390,070.
Expenditure (1960–61): $59,390,070.

## ROCHESTER, N. Y.

Incorporated as city: 1834.
Mayor: Peter Barry (to Dec. 1961).
City Manager: F. Dow Hamblin (apptd. 1959).
1950 population & (rank): 332,488 (32).
1960 population & (rank): 318,611 (38).
1950–60 population change: —4.2%.
1960 land area: 36.4 sq. mi.
Altitude: Highest, 655 ft.; lowest, 246 ft.
Location: In W. part of state, on Genesee R.
County: Seat of Monroe Co.
Churches: Protestant, 128; Roman Catholic, 38; Jewish, 19; others, 22.
City-owned parks: 23 (2,000 ac.).
Telephones (1959): 219,052.
Radio sets (1958): 174,200.
Television sets (1958): 162,070.
Radio stations: AM, 6; FM, 2.
Television stations: 3.
Assessed valuation (1960–61): $668,680,886.
City tax rate (1960–61): $47.51 per $1,000.
Bonded debt (Apr. 12, 1960): $48,080,250.
Revenue (1959–60): $61,756,820.
Expenditure (1959–60): $57,704,316.

## ST. LOUIS, MO.

Incorporated as city: 1822.
Mayor: Raymond R. Tucker (to Apr. 1965).
1950 population & (rank): 856,796 (8).
1960 population & (rank): 750,026 (10).
1950–60 population change: —12.5%.
1953 land area: 61.0 sq. mi.
Altitude: Highest, 605 ft.; lowest, 410 ft.
Location: On Mississippi River.
County: Independent city, not in county.
Churches: 1,117.

City-owned parks: 71 (3,198.60 ac.).
Telephones (1961): 743,000.
Homes with radios: 616,300 (est.).
Television sets (1961): 640,000 (est.).
Radio stations: AM, 13; FM, 3.
Television stations: 5.
Assessed valuation (1960): $1,506,790,067.
City tax rate (1960): $3.79 per $100.
Bonded debt (1960): $79,064,200.
Revenue (1960): $64,903,614.
Expenditure (1960): $63,298,422.

## ST. PAUL, MINN.

Chartered as city: 1853.
Mayor: George J. Vavoulis (to June 1962).
1950 population & (rank): 311,349 (35).
1960 population & (rank): 313,411 (40).
1950–60 population change: +0.7%.
1955 land area: 55.44 sq. mi.
Altitude: Highest, 1,045 ft.; lowest, 683.
Location: In SE central part of state, on Mississippi River.
County: Seat of Ramsey Co.
Churches: Protestant, 250; Catholic, 54; Jewish, 4.
City-owned parks: 5 (2,300 ac.).
Telephones (1961): 245,628 (metropolitan area).
Radio stations: 4.
Television stations: 4.
Assessed valuation (1960): $244,185,114.
Tax rate (1961): City, $132.25 per $1,000; total rate, $186.09 per $1,000.
Bonded debt (Feb. 28, 1961): Gross, $68,966,000; net, $41,231,000.
Revenue (1960): $72,349,143.
Expenditure (1960): $71,799,186.

## SAN ANTONIO, TEX.

Incorporated as city: 1837.
Mayor: Walter W. McAllister (to May 1963).
City Manager: Lynn H. Andrews (apptd. Feb. 1958).
1950 population & (rank): 408,442 (25).
1960 population & (rank): 587,718 (17).
1950–60 population change: +43.9%.
1959 land area: 160.27 sq. mi.
Altitude: 717 ft.
Location: In south central part of state, on San Antonio River.
County: Seat of Bexar Co.
City-owned parks: Approx. 3,000 ac.
Radio stations: AM, 9; FM, 3.
Television stations: 4.
Assessed valuation (1961): $864,613,850.
City tax rate (1961): $1.82 per $100.
Bonded debt (1960): $41,515,108.
Revenue (1960): $23,690,876.
Expenditure (1960): $23,153,493.

## SAN DIEGO, CALIF.

Incorporated as city: 1850; again in 1872.
Mayor: Charles C. Dail (to May 1963).
City Manager: George E. Bean (apptd. Dec. 1957).
1950 population & (rank): 334,387 (31).
1960 population & (rank): 573,224 (18).
1950–60 population change: +71.4%.
1960 land area: 196.5 sq. mi.
Altitude: Highest, 822 ft.; lowest, sea level.
Location: In south part of state, on San Diego Bay.
County: Seat of San Diego.

Churches: Roman Catholic, 30; Jewish, 5; Protestant & other, 278.
City-owned parks: 78 (6,775 ac.).
Telephones: 222,364.
Radio stations: AM, 9; FM, 3.
Television stations: 2.
Assessed valuation (1960–61): $875,698,460.
City tax rate (1960–61): $1.85 per $100.
Bonded debt (1960–61): $34,454,500.
Revenue (1960–61): $68,236,682.
Expenditure (1960–61): $68,236,682.

## SAN FRANCISCO, CALIF.

Incorporated as city: 1850.
Mayor: George Christopher (to Jan. 1964).
1950 population & (rank): 775,357 (11).
1960 population & (rank): 740,316 (12).
1950–60 population change: −4.3%.
1960 area: Land, 44.6 sq. mi.; inland water, 48.5.
Altitude: Highest, 900 ft.; lowest, sea level.
Location: Between Pacific Ocean and San Francisco Bay.
County: Coextensive with San Francisco Co.
Churches: 493 of all denominations.
City-owned parks & squares: 52.
Telephones (Jan. 1961): Residential, 241,443; commercial, 91,768.
Homes with radios: 298,295.
Television sets: 278,307.
Radio stations: AM, 12; FM, 15.
Television stations in operation: 4.
Assessed valuation (1961–62): $2,142,546,429.
City tax rate (1960–61): $8.48 per $100.
Bonded debt (July 1, 1960): $220,960,000.
General city revenue bonds (1959–60): $202,412,-389.
General city expenditures (1959–60): $198,600,-879.

## SEATTLE, WASH.

Incorporated as city: 1869.
Mayor: Gordon S. Clinton (to April, 1964).
1950 population & (rank): 467,591 (19).
1960 population & (rank): 557,087 (19).
1950–60 population change: +19.1%.
1960 area: Land, 91.57 sq. mi.; inland water, 3.07 sq. mi.
Altitude: Highest, 540 ft.; lowest, sea level.
Location: In west central part of state, on Puget Sound.
County: Seat of King Co.
Churches: Protestant, 267; Roman Catholic, 30; Jewish, 6.
City-owned parks: 183 (3,154 ac.).
Telephones (1960): 253,490.
Homes with radios (1960): 360,890.
Homes with television sets (1960): 331,660.
Radio stations: AM, 13; FM, 4.
Television stations: 6.
Assessed valuation (1960): $730,716,061.
City tax rate (1960): $55.40 per $1,000.
Bonded debt (Dec. 31, 1960): $33,247,000.
General govt. revenue (1960): $52,053,647.
General govt. expenditure (1960): $51,196,569.

## TAMPA, FLA.

Incorporated as city: 1855.
Mayor: Julian B. Lane (to Sept. 1963).
1950 population & (rank): 124,681 (84).
1960 population & (rank): 274,970 (48).

1950–60 population change: +120.5%.
1950 land area: 19.0 sq. mi.
Altitude: Highest, 62 ft.; lowest, 4.
Location: In west central part of state, on Tampa Bay.
County: Seat of Hillsborough Co.
City-owned parks: 21 major parks.
Telephones (1961): 128,307.
Households with radios (1961): 119,010.
Radio stations: AM, 10; FM, 2.
Television stations: 4.
Assessed valuation (1961): $554,968,352.
City tax rate (1961): $23.30 per $1,000.
Bonded debt (Sept. 1960): $59,531,000.
Total budgeted receipts, including taxes (1959–60): $27,727,185.
Total budgeted expenditures (1959–60): $26,619,-091.

## TOLEDO, OHIO

Incorporated as city: 1837.
Mayor: Michael J. Damas (to Dec. 1961).
City Manager: John R. Alspach (apptd. Apr. 1960).
1950 population & (rank): 303,616 (36).
1960 population & (rank): 318,003 (39).
1950–60 population change: +4.7%.
1960 land area: 46.94 sq. mi.
Altitude: 630 ft.
Location: In NW part of state, on Maumee River at Lake Erie.
County: Seat of Lucas Co.
Churches: Protestant, 254; Roman Catholic, 36; Jewish, 5; other, 86.
City-owned parks & playgrounds: 53 (2,129 ac.).
Telephones (1960): 216,867.
Radio sets (1960): 285,000.
Television sets (1960): 124,000.
Radio stations: AM, 4; FM, 4.
Television stations: 2.
Assessed valuation (1960): $881,664,730.
City tax rate (1960): $30.50 per $1,000.
Bonded debt: All offset by trust fund.
Revenue (1960): $44,205,706.
Expenditure (1960): $44,562,199.

## TULSA, OKLA.

Incorporated as city: 1898.
Mayor: James L. Maxwell (to May 1962).
1950 population & (rank): 182,740 (51).
1960 population & (rank): 261,685 (50).
1950–60 population change: +43.2%.
1950 land area: 26.7 sq. mi.
Altitude: 674 ft.
Location: In NE part of state, on Arkansas River.
County: Seat of Tulsa Co.
Churches: Protestant, 448; Roman Catholic, 21; Jewish, 2; others, 12.
City-owned parks: 6 (3,459 ac.).
Telephones (1961): 174,332.
Radio stations: AM, 7; FM, 4.
Television stations: 3.
Assessed valuation (1960): $331,198,724.
City tax rate (1960): $63.90 per $1,000.
Bonded debt (June 30, 1960): $67,090,000.
Revenue (1959–60): $18,537,507.
Expenditure (1959–60): $18,231,949.

## WASHINGTON, D. C. See index.

# Tabulated Data on State Governments

*Source:* Questionnaires to the states.

| State | GOVERNOR Term | GOVERNOR Annual salary | LEGISLATURE[1] Membership U[3] | L[4] | Term U[3] | L[4] | Salaries of members[5] | HIGHEST COURT[2] Members | Term | Annual salary |
|---|---|---|---|---|---|---|---|---|---|---|
| Alabama | 4[6] | $25,000 | 35 | 106 | 4 | 4 | $ 30 per diem[7] | 7 | 6 | $14,000 |
| Alaska | 4 | 25,000 | 20 | 40 | 4 | 2 | 3,000 per annum[7] | 3 | 10 | 22,500[8] |
| Arizona | 2 | 18,500 | 28 | 80 | 2 | 2 | 1,800 per annum[9] | 5 | 6 | 15,000 |
| Arkansas | 2 | 10,000 | 35 | 100 | 4 | 2 | 1,800 per annum | 7 | 8 | 15,000 |
| California | 4 | 40,000 | 40 | 80 | 4 | 2 | 6,000 per annum | 7 | 12 | 26,000[30] |
| Colorado | 4 | 20,000 | 35 | 65 | 4 | 2 | 4,800 per biennium | 7 | 10 | 15,000 |
| Connecticut | 4 | 15,000 | 36 | 279 | 2 | 2 | 2,500 per term | 5 | 8 | 21,500[9] |
| Delaware | 4 | 17,500 | 17 | 35 | 4 | 2 | 3,000 per annum | 3 | 12 | 17,000[10] |
| Florida | 4[6] | 22,500 | 38 | 95 | 4 | 2 | 1,200 per annum[11] | 7 | 6 | 17,500 |
| Georgia | 4[6] | 12,000 | 54 | 205 | 2 | 2 | 50 per diem | 7 | 6 | 18,000 |
| Hawaii | 4 | 25,000 | 25 | 51 | 4 | 2 | 2,500 per session[29] | 5 | 7 | 22,000[10] |
| Idaho | 4 | 15,000 | 44 | 59 | 2 | 2 | 10 per diem[11] | 5 | 6 | 13,500 |
| Illinois | 4 | 30,000 | 58 | 177 | 4 | 2 | 12,000 per biennium | 7 | 9 | 20,000 |
| Indiana | 4[6] | 15,000 | 50 | 100 | 4 | 2 | 1,800 per annum | 5 | 6 | 15,000 |
| Iowa | 2 | 17,500 | 50 | 108 | 4 | 2 | 30 per diem | 9 | 6 | 16,000 |
| Kansas | 2 | 16,500 | 40 | 125 | 4 | 2 | 5 per diem | 7 | 6 | 14,000[8] |
| Kentucky | 4[6] | 18,000 | 38 | 100 | 4 | 2 | 25 per diem[5] | 7 | 8 | 12,000 |
| Louisiana | 4[6] | 20,000 | 39 | 101 | 4 | 4 | 50 per diem[12] | 7 | 14 | 18,500[10] |
| Maine | 4 | 15,000 | 33 | 151 | 2 | 2 | 1,600 per session | 6 | 7 | 14,000[8] |
| Maryland | 4[13] | 15,000 | 29 | 123 | 4 | 4 | 1,800 per annum | 7 | 15 | 21,000[8] |
| Massachusetts | 2 | 20,000 | 40 | 240 | 2 | 2 | 6,700 per annum | 7 | Life | 22,000[8] |
| Michigan | 2 | 25,000 | 34 | 110 | 2 | 2 | 5,000 per annum | 8 | 8 | 25,500 |
| Minnesota | 2 | 19,000 | 67 | 131 | 4 | 2 | 4,800 per session[14] | 7 | 6 | 19,000[8] |
| Mississippi | 4[6] | 25,000 | 49 | 140 | 4 | 4 | 3,000 per session | 9 | 8 | 13,500[15] |
| Missouri | 4[6] | 25,000 | 34 | 157 | 4 | 2 | 4,800 per annum | 7 | 12 | 18,500 |
| Montana | 4 | 12,500 | 56 | 94 | 4 | 2 | 20 per diem | 5 | 6 | 11,000 |
| Nebraska | 2 | 14,000 | 43[16] | | 2[16] | | 2,400 per annum | 7 | 6 | 13,000 |
| Nevada | 4 | 20,000[32] | 17 | 37 | 4 | 2 | 25 per diem[17] | 3 | 6 | 20,000 |
| New Hampshire | 2 | 15,500 | 24 | (18) | 2 | 2 | 200 per biennium | 5 | (19) | 15,000 |
| New Jersey | 4[13] | 30,000 | 21 | 60 | 4 | 2 | 5,000 per annum | 7 | (20) | 26,000[8] |
| New Mexico | 2[13] | 17,500 | 32 | 66 | 4 | 2 | 20 per diem | 5 | 8 | 17,500 |
| New York | 4 | 50,000 | 58 | 150 | 2 | 2 | 7,500 per annum | 7 | 14 | 36,500[21] |
| North Carolina | 4[6] | 25,000 | 50 | 120 | 2 | 2 | 15 per diem[22] | 7 | 8 | 16,000 |
| North Dakota | 2 | 10,000 | 49 | 113 | 4 | 2 | 5 per diem | 5 | 10 | 14,000 |
| Ohio | 4 | 25,000 | 38 | 139 | 4 | 2 | 5,000 per annum | 7 | 6 | 20,000[30] |
| Oklahoma | 4[6] | 25,000[32] | 44 | (23) | 4 | 2 | 15 per diem | 9 | 6 | 16,500 |
| Oregon | 4[13] | 25,000 | 30 | 60 | 4 | 2 | 600 per annum | 7 | 6 | 19,000 |
| Pennsylvania | 4[6] | 35,000 | 50 | 210 | 4 | 2 | 6,000 per session | 7 | 21 | 30,000[10] |
| Rhode Island | 2 | 15,000 | 44 | 100 | 2 | 2 | 5 per diem[17] | 5 | (24) | 17,000[8] |
| South Carolina | 4[6] | 15,000 | 46 | 124 | 4 | 2 | 1,800 per session[31] | 5 | 10 | 12,500[8] |
| South Dakota | 2[13] | 13,000 | 35 | 75 | 2 | 2 | 1,800 per biennium | 5 | 6 | 11,000 |
| Tennessee | 4[6] | 18,500[32] | 33 | 99 | 2 | 2 | 10 per diem[25] | 5 | 8 | 15,000[26] |
| Texas | 2 | 25,000 | 31 | 150 | 4 | 2 | 4,800 per annum[22] | (27) | 6 | 20,000 |
| Utah | 4 | 13,200 | 25 | 64 | 4 | 2 | 500 per annum[28] | 5 | 10 | 13,200 |
| Vermont | 2 | 12,500 | 30 | 246 | 2 | 2 | 70 per week | 5 | 2 | 10,500[10] |
| Virginia | 4[6] | 20,000 | 40 | 100 | 4 | 2 | 1,080 per session | 7 | 12 | 17,500[8] |
| Washington | 4 | 22,500 | 49 | 99 | 4 | 2 | 1,200 per annum | 9 | 6 | 20,000 |
| West Virginia | 4[6] | 17,500 | 32 | 100 | 4 | 2 | 1,500 per annum | 5 | 12 | 17,500 |
| Wisconsin | 2 | 20,000 | 33 | 100 | 4 | 2 | 300 per month | 7 | 10 | 17,500[10] |
| Wyoming | 4 | 15,000 | 27 | 56 | 4 | 2 | 12 per diem | 4 | 8 | 13,000 |

[1] General Assembly in Arkansas, Colorado, Connecticut, Delaware, Georgia, Illinois, Indiana, Iowa, Kentucky, Maryland, Missouri, Ohio, Pennsylvania, Rhode Island, South Carolina, Tennessee, Vermont, Virginia; Legislative Assembly in Montana, North Dakota, Oregon; General Court in Massachusetts, New Hampshire; Legislature in other states. Meets annually in Alaska, Arizona, California, Colorado, Delaware, Georgia, Hawaii, Kansas, Maryland, Massachusetts, Michigan, New Jersey, New Mexico, New York, Pennsylvania, Rhode Island, South Carolina, West Virginia, Wisconsin; biennially in other states. [2] Known as Court of Appeals in Kentucky, Maryland, New York; Supreme Court of Appeals in Virginia, West Virginia; Supreme Judicial Court in Maine, Massachusetts; Supreme Court of Errors in Connecticut; Supreme Court in other states. [3] Upper house; known as Senate in all states. [4] Lower house; known as Assembly in California, Nevada, New York, Wisconsin; House of Delegates in Maryland, Virginia, West Virginia; House of General Assembly in New Jersey; House of Representatives in other states. [5] Does not include additional payment for expenses, mileage, etc. [6] Cannot succeed himself. [7] Plus $35 per diem while in session. [8] Chief Justice's salary is $1,000 higher. [9] Plus $20 per diem for special sessions, etc. [10] Chief Justice's salary is $500 higher. [11] Plus $15 per diem while in session. [12] Plus $150 per month allowance while not in session. [13] May not serve a third consecutive term. [14] House salary; Senate salary is $9,600. [15] Chief Justice's salary is $750 higher. [16] Unicameral legislature. [17] For 60 days only. [18] Varies from 350 to 400. [19] Until 70 years old. [20] During good behavior; retired at 70. [21] Chief Justice's salary is $2,500 higher. [22] Plus $12 per diem for first 120 days of regular session. [23] Varies from 120 to 123. [24] Term of good behavior. [25] For 75 days only. [26] Chief Justice's salary is $1,500 higher. [27] 9 members in Supreme Court (highest in civil cases); 3 members in Court of Criminal Appeals. [28] Plus $5 per diem while in session. [29] Per regular session; $1,500 for each budget session. [30] Chief Justice's salary is $2,000 higher. [31] Plus $10 per diem. [32] Effective 1963.

# Tabulated Data on City Governments

*Source:* Questionnaires to the cities.

| City | MAYOR Term, years | MAYOR Salary[1] | City manager's salary[1,2] | COUNCIL OR COMMISSION Name | Members | Term, years | Salary[1] |
|---|---|---|---|---|---|---|---|
| Akron, Ohio | 2 | $16,000 | ...... | Council | 13 | 2 | $3,900 |
| Atlanta, Ga. | 4 | 20,000 | ...... | Bd. of Aldermen | 17 | 4 | 300[17] |
| Baltimore, Md. | 4 | 15,000 | ...... | Council | 21 | 4 | 4,200[13] |
| Birmingham, Ala. | 4 | 13,000 | ...... | Commission | 3 | 4 | 13,000 |
| Boston, Mass. | 4 | 20,000 | ...... | Council | 9 | 2 | 5,000 |
| Buffalo, N. Y. | 4 | 20,000 | ...... | Council | 15 | 2[4] | 6,000[20] |
| Chicago, Ill. | 4 | 35,000 | ...... | Council | 50 | 4 | 8,000 |
| Cincinnati, Ohio | 2 | 10,608 | $30,000 | Council | 9 | 2 | 8,000 |
| Cleveland, Ohio | 2 | 25,000 | ...... | Council | 33 | 2 | 5,000 |
| Columbus, Ohio | 4 | 15,000 | ...... | Council | 7 | 4 | 4,800 |
| Dallas, Tex. | 2 | 20[8] | 26,046 | Council | 9 | 2 | 20[8] |
| Dayton, Ohio | 4 | 1,800 | 25,000 | Commission | 5 | 4 | 1,200 |
| Denver, Colo. | 4 | 14,000 | ...... | Council | 9 | 4 | 3,000[10] |
| Detroit, Mich. | 4 | 25,000 | ...... | Council | 9 | 4 | 12,000 |
| El Paso, Tex. | 2 | 9,600 | ...... | Council | 5[12] | 2 | 4,800 |
| Ft. Worth, Tex. | 2 | 10[22] | 30,000 | Council | 9 | 2 | 10[22] |
| Honolulu, Hawaii | 4 | 20,000 | ...... | Council | 9 | 4 | 6,000 |
| Houston, Tex. | 2 | 20,000 | ...... | Council | 8 | 2 | 300[7] |
| Indianapolis, Ind. | 4 | 13,200 | ...... | Council | 9 | 4 | 1,800[16] |
| Jersey City, N. J. | 4 | 12,500 | ...... | Council | 9 | 4 | 12,000 |
| Kansas City, Mo. | 4 | 15,000 | 26,500 | Council | 9[12] | 4 | 4,800 |
| Long Beach, Calif. | 3 | 200[3] | 23,400 | Council | 9 | 3 | 200[3] |
| Los Angeles, Calif. | 4 | 25,000 | ...... | Council | 15 | 4 | 12,000 |
| Louisville, Ky. | 4 | 12,000 | ...... | Bd. of Aldermen | 12 | 2 | 2,400 |
| Memphis, Tenn. | 4 | 17,500 | ...... | Commission | 5 | 4 | 12,000 |
| Miami, Fla. | 2 | 5,000 | 22,500 | Commission | 5[12] | 4 | 5,000 |
| Milwaukee, Wis. | 4 | 24,000 | ...... | Council | 20 | 4 | 9,000 |
| Minneapolis, Minn. | 2 | 12,000 | ...... | Council | 13 | 2 | 7,000 |
| New Orleans, La. | 4 | 25,000 | ...... | Council | 7 | 4 | 7,500 |
| New York, N. Y. | 4 | 40,000 | 30,000[21] | Council | 25 | 4 | 7,000 |
| Newark, N. J. | 4 | 25,000 | ...... | Council | 9 | 4 | 6,000[13] |
| Norfolk, Va. | 2 | 3,600 | 30,000 | Council | 7 | 4 | 2,400 |
| Oakland, Calif. | 4 | 7,500 | 26,250 | Council | 9[12] | 4 | 120[5] |
| Oklahoma City, Okla. | 4 | 1,000 | 19,500 | Council | 8 | 4 | 10[5] |
| Omaha, Nebr. | 4 | 17,500 | ...... | Council | 7 | 4 | 3,000 |
| Philadelphia, Pa. | 4 | 30,000 | 26,500[11] | Council | 17 | 4 | 15,000[9] |
| Phoenix, Ariz. | 2 | 6,000 | 25,500 | Council | 7[12] | 2 | 3,000 |
| Pittsburgh, Pa. | 4 | 20,000 | ...... | Council | 9 | 4 | 10,000 |
| Portland, Oreg. | 4 | 15,017 | ...... | Commission | 4 | 4 | 12,500 |
| Rochester, N. Y. | 2 | 2,500 | 20,160 | Council | 9 | 4 | 5,000 |
| St. Louis, Mo. | 4 | 25,000 | ...... | Bd. of Aldermen | 29 | 4 | 3,000 |
| St. Paul, Minn. | 2 | 10,800 | ...... | Council | 7[12] | 2 | 9,720 |
| San Antonio, Tex. | 2 | 3,000[15] | 25,000 | Council | 9 | 2 | 20[8] |
| San Diego, Calif. | 4 | 12,000 | 28,000 | Council | 6 | 4 | 5,000 |
| San Francisco, Calif. | 4 | 31,980 | 28,128[14] | Bd. of Supervisors | 11 | 4 | 4,800 |
| Seattle, Wash. | 4 | 20,000 | ...... | Council | 9 | 4 | 10,000 |
| Tampa, Fla. | 4 | 15,000 | ...... | Council | 8 | 4 | 4,800 |
| Toledo, Ohio | 2 | 9,400 | 20,000 | Council | 9[23] | 2 | 3,600 |
| Tulsa, Okla. | 2 | 12,000 | ...... | Commission | 4 | 2 | 9,000 |

[1] Annual, unless otherwise indicated. [2] City Manager's term is indefinite and at will of Council. [3] Per month. [4] For 8 District Councilmen; 4 years for 5 Councilmen-at-large. [5] Per Council meeting. [6] For 3 members; 2 years for 9 members. [7] Per month part-time. [8] Per council meeting; not over $1,040 per year. [9] President receives $20,000. [10] President receives $4,000. [11] Appointed by Mayor, with title of Managing Director. [12] Including Mayor. [13] Also $2,500 in lieu of secretarial expenses; President receives $6,500, plus $3,000 for secretarial expenses. [14] Chief Administrative Officer; appointed by Mayor, for life. [15] Plus Council pay. [16] President and Chairman of Finance Comm. receive $2,400. [17] Per month; President receives $350. [18] President receives $6,500; Vice President, $4,725. [19] President receives $4,000. [20] President receives $12,000. [21] Appointed at pleasure of Mayor, with title of City Administrator. [22] Per week and per Council meeting. [23] Including Mayor and Vice-Mayor; latter receives $5,600.

# United States Population by State, 1790 to 1960

*Source:* U. S. Bureau of the Census.

| State | 1790 | 1900 | 1950 | 1960 | % change 1950–60 | Land area, sq. mi. | Pop. per sq. mi. | Population rank |
|---|---|---|---|---|---|---|---|---|
| Alabama | ....... | 1,828,697 | 3,061,743 | 3,266,740 | 6.7 | 51,060 | 64.0 | 19 |
| Alaska | ....... | 63,592 | 128,643 | 226,167 | 78.1 | 586,400 | 0.4 | 50 |
| Arizona | ....... | 122,931 | 749,587 | 1,302,161 | 73.7 | 113,575 | 11.5 | 35 |
| Arkansas | ....... | 1,311,564 | 1,909,511 | 1,786,272 | −6.5 | 52,499 | 34.0 | 31 |
| California | ....... | 1,485,053 | 10,586,223 | 15,717,204 | 48.5 | 156,573 | 100.4 | 2 |
| Colorado | ....... | 539,700 | 1,325,089 | 1,753,947 | 32.4 | 103,884 | 16.9 | 33 |
| Connecticut | 237,946 | 908,420 | 2,007,280 | 2,535,234 | 26.3 | 4,899 | 517.5 | 25 |
| Delaware | 59,096 | 184,735 | 318,085 | 446,292 | 40.3 | 1,978 | 225.6 | 46 |
| D. C. | ....... | 278,718 | 802,178 | 763,956 | −4.8 | 61 | 12,523.9 | ... |
| Florida | ....... | 528,542 | 2,771,305 | 4,951,560 | 78.7 | 54,252 | 91.3 | 10 |
| Georgia | 82,548 | 2,216,331 | 3,444,578 | 3,943,116 | 14.5 | 58,274 | 67.7 | 16 |
| Hawaii | ....... | 154,001 | 499,794 | 632,772 | 26.6 | 6,415 | 98.6 | 43 |
| Idaho | ....... | 161,772 | 588,637 | 667,191 | 13.4 | 82,708 | 8.1 | 42 |
| Illinois | ....... | 4,821,550 | 8,712,176 | 10,081,158 | 15.7 | 55,930 | 180.2 | 4 |
| Indiana | ....... | 2,516,462 | 3,934,224 | 4,662,498 | 18.5 | 36,185 | 128.9 | 11 |
| Iowa | ....... | 2,231,853 | 2,621,073 | 2,757,537 | 5.2 | 56,032 | 49.2 | 24 |
| Kansas | ....... | 1,470,495 | 1,905,299 | 2,178,611 | 14.3 | 82,048 | 26.6 | 28 |
| Kentucky | 73,677 | 2,147,174 | 2,944,806 | 3,038,156 | 3.2 | 39,863 | 76.2 | 22 |
| Louisiana | ....... | 1,381,625 | 2,683,516 | 3,257,022 | 21.4 | 45,106 | 72.2 | 20 |
| Maine | 96,540 | 694,466 | 913,774 | 969,265 | 6.1 | 31,012 | 31.3 | 36 |
| Maryland | 319,728 | 1,188,044 | 2,343,001 | 3,100,689 | 32.3 | 9,874 | 314.0 | 21 |
| Massachusetts | 378,787 | 2,805,346 | 4,690,514 | 5,148,578 | 9.8 | 7,867 | 654.5 | 9 |
| Michigan | ....... | 2,420,982 | 6,371,766 | 7,823,194 | 22.8 | 57,019 | 137.2 | 7 |
| Minnesota | ....... | 1,751,394 | 2,982,483 | 3,413,864 | 14.5 | 80,009 | 42.7 | 18 |
| Mississippi | ....... | 1,551,270 | 2,178,914 | 2,178,141 | † | 47,223 | 46.1 | 29 |
| Missouri | ....... | 3,106,665 | 3,954,653 | 4,319,813 | 9.2 | 69,138 | 62.3 | 13 |
| Montana | ....... | 243,329 | 591,024 | 674,767 | 14.2 | 145,736 | 4.6 | 41 |
| Nebraska | ....... | 1,066,300 | 1,325,510 | 1,411,330 | 6.5 | 76,612 | 18.4 | 34 |
| Nevada | ....... | 42,335 | 160,083 | 285,278 | 78.2 | 109,788 | 2.6 | 49 |
| New Hampshire | 141,885 | 411,588 | 533,242 | 606,921 | 13.8 | 9,014 | 67.3 | 45 |
| New Jersey | 184,139 | 1,883,669 | 4,835,329 | 6,066,782 | 25.5 | 7,521 | 806.6 | 8 |
| New Mexico | ....... | 195,310 | 681,187 | 951,023 | 39.6 | 121,510 | 7.8 | 37 |
| New York | 340,120 | 7,268,894 | 14,830,192 | 16,782,304 | 13.2 | 47,939 | 350.1 | 1 |
| North Carolina | 393,751 | 1,893,810 | 4,061,929 | 4,556,155 | 12.1 | 49,067 | 92.9 | 12 |
| North Dakota | ....... | 319,146 | 619,636 | 632,446 | 2.1 | 69,457 | 9.1 | 44 |
| Ohio | ....... | 4,157,545 | 7,946,627 | 9,706,397 | 22.1 | 40,972 | 236.9 | 5 |
| Oklahoma | ....... | 790,391* | 2,233,351 | 2,328,284 | 4.3 | 68,887 | 33.8 | 27 |
| Oregon | ....... | 413,536 | 1,521,341 | 1,768,687 | 16.3 | 96,248 | 18.4 | 32 |
| Pennsylvania | 434,373 | 6,302,115 | 10,498,012 | 11,319,366 | 7.8 | 45,007 | 251.5 | 3 |
| Rhode Island | 68,825 | 428,556 | 791,896 | 859,488 | 8.5 | 1,058 | 812.4 | 39 |
| South Carolina | 249,073 | 1,340,316 | 2,117,027 | 2,382,594 | 12.5 | 30,272 | 78.7 | 26 |
| South Dakota | ....... | 401,570 | 652,740 | 680,514 | 4.3 | 76,378 | 8.9 | 40 |
| Tennessee | 35,691 | 2,020,616 | 3,291,718 | 3,567,089 | 8.4 | 41,762 | 85.4 | 17 |
| Texas | ....... | 3,048,710 | 7,711,194 | 9,579,677 | 24.2 | 262,840 | 36.4 | 6 |
| Utah | ....... | 276,749 | 688,862 | 890,627 | 29.3 | 82,339 | 10.8 | 38 |
| Vermont | 85,425 | 343,641 | 377,747 | 389,881 | 3.2 | 9,276 | 42.0 | 47 |
| Virginia | 747,610 | 1,854,184 | 3,318,680 | 3,966,949 | 19.5 | 39,838 | 99.6 | 14 |
| Washington | ....... | 518,103 | 2,378,963 | 2,853,214 | 19.9 | 66,709 | 42.8 | 23 |
| West Virginia | ....... | 958,800 | 2,005,552 | 1,860,421 | −7.2 | 24,079 | 77.3 | 30 |
| Wisconsin | ....... | 2,069,042 | 3,434,575 | 3,951,777 | 15.1 | 54,705 | 72.2 | 15 |
| Wyoming | ....... | 92,531 | 290,529 | 330,066 | 13.6 | 97,411 | 3.4 | 48 |
| Total | 3,929,214 | 76,212,168 | 151,325,798 | 179,323,175 | 18.5 | 3,548,913 | 50.5 | .. |

* Includes population of Indian Territory; 1900, 392,960.   † Less than 0.1 percent loss.

# Population of U. S. Cities, 1920-1960

(Over 50,000 population in 1960)

*Source:* U. S. Bureau of the Census.

| City | 1920 population | 1940 population | 1950 population | 1960 population | 1960 rank | % change 1950-60 |
|------|----------------:|----------------:|----------------:|----------------:|----------:|-----------------:|
| Abilene, Tex. | 10,274 | 26,612 | 45,570 | 90,368 | 149 | 98.3 |
| Akron, Ohio | 208,435 | 244,791 | 274,605 | 290,351 | 45 | 5.7 |
| Alameda, Calif. | 28,806 | 36,256 | 64,430 | 63,855 | 232 | −0.9 |
| Albany, Ga. | 11,555 | 19,055 | 31,155 | 55,890 | 274 | 79.5 |
| Albany, N. Y. | 113,344 | 130,577 | 134,995 | 129,726 | 93 | −3.9 |
| Albuquerque, N. Mex. | 15,157 | 35,449 | 96,815 | 201,189 | 60 | 107.8 |
| Alexandria, Va. | 18,060 | 33,523 | 61,787 | 91,023 | 148 | 47.3 |
| Alhambra, Calif. | 9,096 | 38,935 | 51,359 | 54,807 | 279 | 6.7 |
| Allentown, Pa. | 73,502 | 96,904 | 106,756 | 108,347 | 116 | 1.5 |
| Altoona, Pa | 60,331 | 80,214 | 77,177 | 69,407 | 207 | −10.1 |
| Amarillo, Tex. | 15,494 | 51,686 | 74,246 | 137,969 | 88 | 85.8 |
| Anaheim, Calif. | 5,526 | 11,031 | 14,556 | 104,184 | 123 | 615.7 |
| Ann Arbor, Mich. | 19,516 | 29,815 | 48,251 | 67,340 | 216 | 39.6 |
| Asheville, N. C. | 28,504 | 51,310 | 53,000 | 60,192 | 254 | 13.6 |
| Atlanta, Ga. | 200,616 | 302,288 | 331,314 | 487,455 | 24 | 47.1 |
| Atlantic City, N. J. | 50,707 | 64,094 | 61,657 | 59,544 | 256 | −3.4 |
| Augusta, Ga. | 52,548 | 65,919 | 71,508 | 70,626 | 202 | −1.2 |
| Aurora, Ill. | 36,397 | 47,170 | 50,576 | 63,715 | 233 | 25.9 |
| Austin, Tex. | 34,876 | 87,930 | 132,459 | 186,545 | 67 | 40.8 |
| Bakersfield, Calif. | 18,638 | 29,252 | 34,784 | 56,848 | 269 | 63.4 |
| Baltimore, Md. | 733,826 | 859,100 | 949,708 | 939,024 | 6 | −1.1 |
| Baton Rouge, La. | 21,782 | 34,719 | 125,629 | 152,419 | 80 | 21.3 |
| Bay City, Mich. | 47,554 | 47,956 | 52,523 | 53,604 | 288 | 2.1 |
| Bayonne, N. J. | 76,754 | 79,198 | 77,203 | 74,215 | 191 | −3.9 |
| Beaumont, Tex. | 40,422 | 59,061 | 94,014 | 119,175 | 102 | 26.8 |
| Berkeley, Calif. | 56,036 | 85,547 | 113,805 | 111,268 | 114 | −2.2 |
| Berwyn, Ill. | 14,150 | 48,451 | 51,280 | 54,224 | 283 | 5.7 |
| Bethlehem, Pa. | 50,358 | 58,490 | 66,340 | 75,408 | 190 | 13.7 |
| Billings, Mont. | 15,100 | 23,261 | 31,834 | 52,851 | 292 | 66.0 |
| Binghamton, N. Y. | 66,800 | 78,309 | 80,674 | 75,941 | 189 | −5.9 |
| Birmingham, Ala. | 178,806 | 267,583 | 326,037 | 340,887 | 36 | 4.6 |
| Bloomfield, N. J. | 22,019 | 41,623 | 49,307 | 51,867 | 297 | 5.2 |
| Bloomington, Minn. | .... | .... | .... | 50,498 | 308 | .... |
| Boston, Mass. | 748,060 | 770,816 | 801,444 | 697,197 | 13 | −13.0 |
| Bridgeport, Conn. | 143,555 | 147,121 | 158,709 | 156,748 | 79 | −1.2 |
| Brockton, Mass. | 66,254 | 62,343 | 62,860 | 72,813 | 192 | 15.8 |
| Buffalo, N. Y. | 506,775 | 575,901 | 580,132 | 532,759 | 20 | −8.2 |
| Burbank, Calif. | 2,913 | 34,337 | 78,577 | 90,155 | 150 | 14.7 |
| Cambridge, Mass. | 109,694 | 110,879 | 120,740 | 107,716 | 119 | −10.8 |
| Camden, N. J. | 116,309 | 117,536 | 124,555 | 117,159 | 103 | −5.9 |
| Canton, Ohio | 87,091 | 108,401 | 116,912 | 113,631 | 109 | −2.8 |
| Cedar Rapids, Iowa | 45,566 | 62,120 | 72,296 | 92,035 | 145 | 27.3 |
| Charleston, S. C. | 67,957 | 71,275 | 70,174 | 65,925 | 228 | −6.1 |
| Charleston, W. Va. | 39,608 | 67,914 | 73,501 | 85,796 | 161 | 16.7 |
| Charlotte, N. C. | 46,338 | 100,899 | 134,042 | 201,564 | 59 | 50.4 |
| Chattanooga, Tenn. | 57,895 | 128,163 | 131,041 | 130,009 | 92 | −.7 |
| Chester, Pa. | 58,030 | 59,285 | 66,039 | 63,658 | 234 | −3.6 |
| Chicago, Ill. | 2,701,705 | 3,396,808 | 3,620,962 | 3,550,404 | 2 | −1.9 |
| Chicopee, Mass. | 36,214 | 41,664 | 49,211 | 61,553 | 248 | 25.1 |
| Cicero, Ill. | 44,995 | 64,712 | 67,544 | 69,130 | 208 | 2.3 |
| Cincinnati, Ohio | 401,247 | 455,610 | 503,998 | 502,550 | 21 | −.3 |
| Cleveland, Ohio | 796,841 | 878,336 | 914,808 | 876,050 | 8 | −4.2 |
| Cleveland Heights, Ohio | 15,236 | 54,992 | 59,141 | 61,813 | 246 | 4.5 |
| Clifton, N. J. | 26,470 | 48,827 | 64,511 | 82,084 | 174 | 27.2 |
| Colorado Springs, Colo. | 30,105 | 36,789 | 45,472 | 70,194 | 204 | 54.4 |
| Columbia, S. C. | 37,524 | 62,396 | 86,914 | 97,433 | 135 | 12.1 |
| Columbus, Ga. | 31,125 | 53,280 | 79,611 | 116,779 | 104 | 46.7 |
| Columbus, Ohio | 237,031 | 306,087 | 375,901 | 471,316 | 28 | 25.4 |
| Compton, Calif. | 1,478 | 16,198 | 47,991 | 71,812 | 199 | 49.6 |
| Corpus Christi, Tex. | 10,522 | 57,301 | 108,287 | 167,690 | 74 | 54.9 |
| Council Bluffs, Iowa | 36,162 | 41,439 | 45,429 | 55,641 | 276 | 22.5 |
| Covington, Ky. | 57,121 | 62,018 | 64,452 | 60,376 | 253 | −6.3 |
| Cranston, R. I. | 29,407 | 47,085 | 55,060 | 66,766 | 222 | 21.3 |
| Dallas, Tex. | 158,976 | 294,734 | 434,462 | 679,684 | 14 | 56.4 |
| Davenport, Iowa | 56,727 | 66,039 | 74,549 | 88,981 | 155 | 19.4 |

| City | 1920 population | 1940 population | 1950 population | 1960 population | 1960 rank | % change 1950-60 |
|---|---|---|---|---|---|---|
| Dayton, Ohio............... | 152,559 | 210,718 | 243,872 | 262,332 | 49 | 7.6 |
| Dearborn, Mich............. | 2,470 | 63,584 | 94,994 | 112,007 | 110 | 17.9 |
| Decatur, Ill................. | 43,818 | 59,305 | 66,269 | 78,004 | 184 | 17.7 |
| Denver, Colo................ | 256,491 | 322,412 | 415,786 | 493,887 | 23 | 18.8 |
| Des Moines, Iowa............ | 126,468 | 159,819 | 177,965 | 208,982 | 55 | 17.4 |
| Detroit, Mich............... | 993,678 | 1,623,452 | 1,849,568 | 1,670,144 | 5 | −9.7 |
| Downey, Calif............... | .... | .... | .... | 82,505 | 170 | .... |
| Dubuque, Iowa.............. | 39,141 | 43,892 | 49,671 | 56,606 | 271 | 14.0 |
| Duluth, Minn............... | 98,917 | 101,065 | 104,511 | 106,884 | 122 | 2.3 |
| Durham, N. C............... | 21,719 | 60,195 | 71,311 | 78,302 | 183 | 9.8 |
| East Chicago, Ind........... | 35,967 | 54,637 | 54,263 | 57,669 | 267 | 6.3 |
| East Orange, N. J .......... | 50,710 | 68,945 | 79,340 | 77,259 | 185 | −2.6 |
| East St. Louis, Ill........... | 66,767 | 75,609 | 82,295 | 81,712 | 175 | −.7 |
| El Paso, Tex................. | 77,560 | 96,810 | 130,485 | 276,687 | 46 | 112.0 |
| Elizabeth, N. J.............. | 95,783 | 109,912 | 112,817 | 107,698 | 120 | −4.5 |
| Erie, Pa.................... | 93,372 | 116,955 | 130,803 | 138,440 | 87 | 5.8 |
| Euclid, Ohio................ | 3,363 | 17,866 | 41,396 | 62,998 | 240 | 52.2 |
| Eugene, Oreg............... | 10,593 | 20,838 | 35,879 | 50,977 | 305 | 42.1 |
| Evanston, Ill................ | 37,234 | 65,389 | 73,641 | 79,283 | 182 | 7.7 |
| Evansville, Ind.............. | 85,264 | 97,062 | 128,636 | 141,543 | 86 | 10.0 |
| Fall River, Mass............. | 120,485 | 115,428 | 111,963 | 99,942 | 131 | 10.7 |
| Flint, Mich................. | 91,599 | 151,543 | 163,143 | 196,940 | 62 | 20.7 |
| Fort Lauderdale, Fla......... | 2,065 | 17,996 | 36,328 | 83,648 | 164 | 130.2 |
| Fort Smith, Ark............. | 28,870 | 36,584 | 47,942 | 52,991 | 290 | 10.5 |
| Fort Wayne, Ird............ | 86,549 | 118,410 | 133,607 | 161,776 | 78 | 21.1 |
| Fort Worth, Tex............. | 106,482 | 177,662 | 278,778 | 356,268 | 34 | 27.8 |
| Fresno, Calif................ | 45,086 | 60,685 | 91,669 | 133,929 | 90 | 46.1 |
| Fullerton, Calif............. | 4,415 | 10,442 | 13,958 | 56,180 | 273 | 302.5 |
| Gadsden, Ala................ | 14,737 | 36,975 | 55,725 | 58,088 | 263 | 4.2 |
| Galveston, Tex.............. | 44,.55 | 60,862 | 66,568 | 67,175 | 217 | .9 |
| Garden Grove, Calif.......... | .... | .... | 3,762 | 84,238 | 163 | 2,139.2 |
| Gary, Ind................... | 55,378 | 111,719 | 133,911 | 178,320 | 70 | 33.2 |
| Glendale, Calif.............. | 13,536 | 82,582 | 95,702 | 119,442 | 101 | 24.8 |
| Grand Rapids, Mich.......... | 137,634 | 164,292 | 176,515 | 177,313 | 71 | .5 |
| Great Falls, Mont............ | 24,121 | 29,928 | 39,214 | 55,357 | 278 | 41.2 |
| Green Bay, Wis.............. | 31,017 | 46,235 | 52,735 | 62,888 | 241 | 19.3 |
| Greensboro, N. C............ | 19,861 | 59,319 | 74,389 | 119,574 | 99 | 60.7 |
| Greenville, S. C ............ | 23,127 | 34,734 | 58,161 | 66,188 | 225 | 13.8 |
| Hamilton, Ohio.............. | 39,675 | 50,592 | 57,951 | 72,354 | 197 | 24.9 |
| Hammond, Ind............... | 36,004 | 70,184 | 87,594 | 111,698 | 112 | 27.5 |
| Hampton, Va................ | 6,138 | 5,898 | 5,966 | 89,258 | 151 | 1,396.1 |
| Harrisburg, Pa.............. | 75,917 | 83,893 | 89,544 | 79,697 | 180 | −11.0 |
| Hartford, Conn.............. | 138,036 | 166,267 | 177,397 | 162,178 | 77 | −8.6 |
| Hayward, Calif.............. | 3,487 | 6,736 | 14,272 | 72,700 | 193 | 409.4 |
| Hialeah, Fla................ | .... | 3,958 | 19,676 | 66,972 | 220 | 240.4 |
| High Point, N. C............ | 14,302 | 38,495 | 39,973 | 62,063 | 245 | 55.3 |
| Holyoke, Mass............... | 60,203 | 53,750 | 54,661 | 52,689 | 293 | −3.6 |
| Honolulu, Hawaii............ | 83,327 | 179,326 | 248,034 | 294,194 | 43 | 18.5 |
| Houston, Tex................ | 138,276 | 384,514 | 596,163 | 938,219 | 7 | 57.4 |
| Huntington, W. Va........... | 50,177 | 78,836 | 86,353 | 83,627 | 165 | −3.2 |
| Huntsville, Ala.............. | 8,018 | 13,050 | 16,437 | 72,365 | 196 | 340.3 |
| Independence, Mo............ | 11,686 | 16,066 | 36,963 | 62,328 | 244 | 68.6 |
| Indianapolis, Ind............ | 314,194 | 386,972 | 427,173 | 476,258 | 26 | 11.5 |
| Inglewood, Calif............. | 3,286 | 30,114 | 46,185 | 63,390 | 237 | 37.3 |
| Irvington, N. J.............. | 25,480 | 55,328 | 59,201 | 59,379 | 257 | .3 |
| Jackson, Mich............... | 48,374 | 49,656 | 51,088 | 50,720 | 306 | −.7 |
| Jackson, Miss............... | 22,817 | 62,107 | 98,271 | 144,422 | 84 | 47.0 |
| Jacksonville, Fla............. | 91,558 | 173,065 | 204,517 | 201,030 | 61 | −1.7 |
| Jersey City, N. J............ | 298,103 | 301,173 | 299,017 | 276,101 | 47 | −7.7 |
| Johnstown, Pa............... | 67,327 | 66,668 | 63,232 | 53,949 | 285 | −14.7 |
| Joliet, Ill................... | 38,442 | 42,365 | 51,601 | 66,780 | 221 | 29.4 |
| Kalamazoo, Mich............ | 48,487 | 54,097 | 57,704 | 82,089 | 173 | 42.3 |
| Kansas City, Kans........... | 101,177 | 121,458 | 129,553 | 121,901 | 98 | −5.9 |
| Kansas City, Mo............. | 324,410 | 399,178 | 456,622 | 475,539 | 27 | 4.1 |
| Kenosha, Wis............... | 40,472 | 48,765 | 54,368 | 67,899 | 213 | 24.9 |
| Kettering, Ohio.............. | .... | .... | .... | 54,462 | 282 | .... |
| Knoxville, Tenn.............. | 77,818 | 111,580 | 124,769 | 111,827 | 111 | −10.4 |
| Lake Charles, La............. | 13,088 | 21,207 | 41,272 | 63,392 | 236 | 53.6 |
| Lakewood, Calif.............. | .... | .... | .... | 67,126 | 219 | .... |
| Lakewood, Ohio.............. | 41,732 | 69,160 | 68,071 | 66,154 | 226 | −2.8 |

| City | 1920 population | 1940 population | 1950 population | 1960 population | 1960 rank | % change 1950–60 |
|---|---|---|---|---|---|---|
| Lancaster, Pa.............. | 53,150 | 61,345 | 63,774 | 61,055 | 250 | −4.3 |
| Lansing, Mich............... | 57,327 | 78,753 | 92,129 | 107,807 | 118 | 17.0 |
| Laredo, Tex................. | 22,710 | 39,274 | 51,910 | 60,678 | 252 | 16.9 |
| Las Vegas, Nev............. | 2,304 | 8,422 | 24,624 | 64,405 | 231 | 161.6 |
| Lawrence, Mass............. | 94,270 | 84,323 | 80,536 | 70,933 | 201 | −11.9 |
| Lawton, Okla............... | 8,930 | 18,055 | 34,757 | 61,697 | 247 | 77.6 |
| Lexington, Ky.............. | 41,534 | 49,304 | 55,534 | 62,810 | 242 | 13.1 |
| Lima, Ohio.............. | 41,326 | 44,711 | 50,246 | 51,037 | 304 | 1.5 |
| Lincoln, Nebr.............. | 54,948 | 81,984 | 98,884 | 128,521 | 95 | 30.0 |
| Lincoln Park, Mich......... | .... | 15,236 | 29,310 | 53,933 | 286 | 45.7 |
| Little Rock, Ark........... | 65,142 | 88,039 | 102,213 | 107,813 | 117 | 5.5 |
| Livonia, Mich.............. | .... | 8,728 | 17,534 | 66,702 | 223 | 280.4 |
| Long Beach, Calif.......... | 55,593 | 164,271 | 250,767 | 344,168 | 35 | 37.2 |
| Lorain, Ohio............... | 37,295 | 44,125 | 51,202 | 68,932 | 209 | 34.6 |
| Los Angeles, Calif......... | 576,673 | 1,504,277 | 1,970,358 | 2,479,015 | 3 | 25.8 |
| Louisville, Ky............. | 234,891 | 319,077 | 369,129 | 390,639 | 31 | 5.8 |
| Lowell, Mass............... | 112,759 | 101,389 | 97,249 | 92,107 | 144 | −5.3 |
| Lubbock, Tex............... | 4,051 | 31,853 | 71,747 | 128,691 | 94 | 79.3 |
| Lynchburg, Va.............. | 30,070 | 44,541 | 47,727 | 54,790 | 280 | 15.0 |
| Lynn, Mass................. | 99,148 | 98,123 | 99,738 | 94,478 | 140 | −5.3 |
| Macon, Ga.................. | 52,995 | 57,865 | 70,252 | 69,764 | 206 | −.7 |
| Madison, Wis............... | 38,378 | 67,447 | 96,056 | 126,706 | * | 31.9 |
| Malden, Mass............... | 49,103 | 58,010 | 59,804 | 57,676 | 266 | −3.6 |
| Manchester, N. H........... | 78,384 | 77,685 | 82,732 | 88,282 | 157 | 6.7 |
| Medford, Mass.............. | 39,038 | 63,083 | 66,113 | 64,971 | 230 | −1.7 |
| Memphis, Tenn.............. | 162,351 | 292,942 | 396,000 | 497,524 | 22 | 25.6 |
| Meriden, Conn.............. | 29,867 | 39,494 | 44,088 | 51,850 | 299 | 17.6 |
| Miami, Fla................. | 29,571 | 172,172 | 249,276 | 291,688 | 44 | 17.0 |
| Miami Beach, Fla........... | 644 | 28,012 | 46,282 | 63,145 | 239 | 36.4 |
| Midland, Tex............... | 1,795 | 9,352 | 21,713 | 62,625 | 243 | 188.4 |
| Milwaukee, Wis............. | 457,147 | 587,472 | 637,392 | 741,324 | 11 | 16.3 |
| Minneapolis, Minn.......... | 380,582 | 492,370 | 521,718 | 482,872 | 25 | −7.4 |
| Mobile, Ala................ | 60,777 | 78,720 | 129,000 | 202,779 | 58 | 57.1 |
| Monroe, La................. | 12,675 | 28,309 | 38,572 | 52,219 | 295 | 35.3 |
| Montgomery, Ala............ | 43,464 | 78,084 | 106,525 | 134,393 | 89 | 26.2 |
| Mount Vernon, N. Y......... | 42,726 | 67,362 | 71,899 | 76,010 | 188 | 5.7 |
| Muncie, Ind................ | 36,524 | 49,720 | 58,479 | 68,603 | 210 | 17.3 |
| Nashville, Tenn............ | 118,342 | 167,402 | 174,307 | 170,874 | 73 | −2.0 |
| New Bedford, Mass.......... | 121,217 | 110,341 | 109,189 | 102,477 | 125 | −6.1 |
| New Britain, Conn.......... | 59,316 | 68,685 | 73,726 | 82,201 | 172 | 11.5 |
| New Haven, Conn............ | 162,537 | 160,605 | 164,443 | 152,048 | 81 | −7.5 |
| New Orleans, La........... | 387,219 | 494,537 | 570,445 | 627,525 | 15 | 10.0 |
| New Rochelle, N. Y......... | 36,213 | 58,408 | 59,725 | 76,812 | 186 | 28.6 |
| New York, N. Y............. | 5,620,048 | 7,454,995 | 7,891,957 | 7,781,984 | 1 | −1.4 |
|   Bronx borough........... | 732,016 | 1,394,711 | 1,451,277 | 1,424,815 | ... | −1.8 |
|   Brooklyn borough.......... | 2,018,356 | 2,698,285 | 2,738,175 | 2,627,319 | ... | −4.0 |
|   Manhattan borough........ | 2,284,103 | 1,889,924 | 1,960,101 | 1,698,281 | ... | −13.4 |
|   Queens borough........... | 469,042 | 1,297,634 | 1,550,849 | 1,809,578 | ... | 16.7 |
|   Richmond borough........ | 116,531 | 174,441 | 191,555 | 221,991 | ... | 15.9 |
| Newark, N. J............... | 414,524 | 429,760 | 438,776 | 405,220 | 30 | −7.6 |
| Newport News, Va........... | 35,596 | 37,067 | 42,358 | 113,662 | 108 | 168.3 |
| Newton, Mass............... | 46,054 | 69,873 | 81,994 | 92,384 | 143 | 12.7 |
| Niagara Falls, N. Y........ | 50,760 | 78,029 | 90,872 | 102,394 | 126 | 12.7 |
| Norfolk, Va................ | 115,777 | 144,332 | 213,513 | 304,869 | 41 | 43.3 |
| North Little Rock, Ark...... | 14,048 | 21,137 | 44,097 | 58,032 | 264 | 42.8 |
| Norwalk, Calif............. | .... | .... | .... | 88,739 | 156 | .... |
| Norwalk, Conn.............. | 27,743 | 39,849 | 49,460 | 67,775 | 214 | 37.0 |
| Oak Park, Ill.............. | 39,858 | 66,015 | 63,529 | 61,093 | 249 | −3.8 |
| Oakland, Calif............. | 216,261 | 302,163 | 384,575 | 367,548 | 33 | −4.4 |
| Odessa, Tex. .............. | .... | 9,573 | 29,495 | 80,338 | 179* | 172.4 |
| Ogden, Utah................ | 32,804 | 43,688 | 57,112 | 70,197 | 203 | 22.9 |
| Oklahoma City, Okla........ | 91,295 | 204,424 | 243,504 | 324,253 | 37 | 33.2 |
| Omaha, Nebr................ | 191,601 | 223,844 | 251,117 | 301,598 | 42 | 20.1 |
| Orlando, Fla............... | 9,282 | 36,736 | 52,367 | 88,135 | 158 | 68.3 |
| Palo Alto, Calif........... | 5,900 | 16,774 | 25,475 | 52,287 | 294 | 105.2 |
| Parma, Ohio................ | .... | 16,365 | 28,897 | 82,845 | 168 | 186.7 |
| Pasadena, Calif............ | 45,354 | 81,864 | 104,577 | 116,407 | 105 | 11.3 |
| Pasadena, Tex.............. | .... | 3,436 | 22,483 | 58,737 | 262 | 161.3 |
| Passaic, N. J.............. | 63,841 | 61,394 | 57,702 | 53,963 | 284 | −6.5 |
| Paterson, N. J............. | 135,875 | 139,656 | 139,336 | 143,663 | 85 | 3.1 |

| City | 1920 population | 1940 population | 1950 population | 1960 population | 1960 rank | % change 1950–60 |
|---|---|---|---|---|---|---|
| Pawtucket, R. I. | 64,248 | 75,797 | 81,436 | 81,001 | 177 | .5 |
| Pensacola, Fla. | 31,035 | 37,449 | 43,479 | 56,752 | 270 | 30.5 |
| Peoria, Ill. | 76,121 | 105,087 | 111,856 | 103,162 | 124 | −7.8 |
| Philadelphia, Pa. | 1,823,779 | 1,931,334 | 2,071,605 | 2,002,512 | 4 | −3.3 |
| Phoenix, Ariz. | 29,053 | 65,414 | 106,818 | 439,170 | 29 | 311.1 |
| Pittsburgh, Pa. | 588,343 | 671,659 | 676,806 | 604,332 | 16 | −10.7 |
| Pittsfield, Mass. | 41,763 | 49,684 | 53,348 | 57,879 | 265 | 8.5 |
| Pomona, Calif. | 13,505 | 23,539 | 35,405 | 67,157 | 218 | 89.7 |
| Pontiac, Mich. | 34,273 | 66,626 | 73,681 | 82,233 | 171 | 11.6 |
| Port Arthur, Tex. | 22,251 | 46,140 | 57,530 | 66,676 | 224 | 15.9 |
| Portland, Maine | 69,272 | 73,643 | 77,634 | 72,566 | 194 | −6.5 |
| Portland, Oreg. | 258,288 | 305,394 | 373,628 | 372,676 | 32 | −.3 |
| Portsmouth, Va. | 54,387 | 50,745 | 80,039 | 114,773 | 106 | 43.4 |
| Providence, R. I. | 237,595 | 253,504 | 248,674 | 207,498 | 56 | −16.6 |
| Pueblo, Colo. | 43,050 | 52,162 | 63,685 | 91,181 | 147 | 43.2 |
| Quincy, Mass. | 47,876 | 75,810 | 83,835 | 87,409 | 159 | 4.3 |
| Racine, Wis. | 58,593 | 67,195 | 71,193 | 89,144 | 154 | 25.2 |
| Raleigh, N. C. | 24,418 | 46,897 | 65,679 | 93,931 | 141 | 43.0 |
| Reading, Pa. | 107,784 | 110,568 | 109,320 | 98,177 | 133 | −10.2 |
| Reno, Nev. | 12,016 | 21,317 | 32,497 | 51,470 | 301 | 58.4 |
| Richmond, Calif. | 16,843 | 23,642 | 99,545 | 71,854 | 198 | −27.8 |
| Richmond, Va. | 171,667 | 193,042 | 230,310 | 219,958 | 52 | −4.5 |
| Riverside, Calif. | 19,341 | 34,696 | 46,764 | 84,332 | 162 | 80.3 |
| Roanoke, Va. | 50,842 | 69,287 | 91,921 | 97,110 | 136 | 5.6 |
| Rochester, N. Y. | 295,750 | 324,975 | 332,488 | 318,611 | 38 | −4.2 |
| Rock Island, Ill. | 35,177 | 42,775 | 48,710 | 51,863 | 298 | 6.5 |
| Rockford, Ill. | 65,651 | 84,637 | 92,927 | 126,706 | * | 36.4 |
| Rome, N. Y. | 26,341 | 34,214 | 41,682 | 51,646 | 300 | 23.9 |
| Roseville, Mich. | .... | 9,023 | 15,816 | 50,195 | 310 | 217.4 |
| Royal Oak, Mich. | 6,007 | 25,087 | 46,898 | 80,612 | 178 | 71.9 |
| Sacramento, Calif. | 65,908 | 105,958 | 137,572 | 191,667 | 63 | 39.3 |
| Saginaw, Mich. | 61,903 | 82,794 | 92,918 | 98,265 | 132 | 5.8 |
| St. Clair Shores, Mich. | .... | 10,405 | 19,823 | 76,657 | 187 | 286.7 |
| St. Joseph, Mo. | 77,939 | 75,711 | 78,588 | 79,673 | 181 | 1.4 |
| St. Louis, Mo. | 772,897 | 816,048 | 856,796 | 750,026 | 10 | −12.5 |
| St. Paul, Minn. | 234,698 | 287,736 | 311,349 | 313,411 | 40 | .7 |
| St. Petersburg, Fla. | 14,237 | 60,812 | 96,738 | 181,298 | 69 | 87.4 |
| Salt Lake City, Utah | 118,110 | 149,934 | 182,121 | 189,454 | 65 | 4.0 |
| San Angelo, Tex. | 10,050 | 25,802 | 52,093 | 58,815 | 260 | 12.9 |
| San Antonio, Tex. | 161,379 | 253,854 | 408,442 | 587,718 | 17 | 43.9 |
| San Bernardino, Calif. | 18,721 | 43,646 | 63,058 | 91,922 | 146 | 45.8 |
| San Diego, Calif. | 74,361 | 203,341 | 334,387 | 573,224 | 18 | 71.4 |
| San Francisco, Calif. | 506,676 | 634,536 | 775,357 | 740,316 | 12 | −4.3 |
| San Jose, Calif. | 39,642 | 68,457 | 95,280 | 204,196 | 57 | 114.3 |
| San Leandro, Calif. | 5,703 | 14,601 | 27,542 | 65,962 | 227 | 139.5 |
| San Mateo, Calif. | 5,979 | 19,403 | 41,782 | 69,870 | 205 | 67.2 |
| Santa Ana, Calif. | 15,485 | 31,921 | 45,533 | 100,350 | 130 | 120.4 |
| Santa Barbara, Calif. | 19,441 | 34,958 | 44,913 | 58,768 | 261 | 30.8 |
| Santa Clara, Calif. | 5,220 | 6,650 | 11,702 | 58,880 | 259 | 403.2 |
| Santa Monica, Calif. | 15,252 | 53,500 | 71,595 | 83,249 | 167 | 16.3 |
| Savannah, Ga. | 83,252 | 95,996 | 119,638 | 149,245 | 82 | 24.7 |
| Schenectady, N. Y. | 88,723 | 87,549 | 91,785 | 81,682 | 176 | −11.0 |
| Scranton, Pa. | 137,783 | 140,404 | 125,536 | 111,443 | 113 | −11.2 |
| Seattle, Wash. | 315,312 | 368,302 | 467,591 | 557,087 | 19 | 19.1 |
| Shrevepor,. La. | 43,874 | 98,167 | 127,206 | 164,372 | 76 | 29.2 |
| Sioux City, Iowa | 71,227 | 82,364 | 83,991 | 89,159 | 153 | 6.2 |
| Sioux Falls, S. Dak. | 25,202 | 40,832 | 52,696 | 65,466 | 229 | 24.2 |
| Skokie, Ill. | 763 | 7,172 | 14,832 | 59,364 | 258 | 300.2 |
| Somerville, Mass. | 93,091 | 102,177 | 102,351 | 94,697 | 139 | −7.5 |
| South Bend, Ind. | 70,983 | 101,268 | 115,911 | 132,445 | 91 | 14.3 |
| South Gate, Calif. | .... | 26,945 | 51,116 | 53,831 | 287 | 5.3 |
| Spokane, Wash. | 104,437 | 122,001 | 161,721 | 181,608 | 68 | 12.3 |
| Springfield, Ill. | 59,183 | 75,503 | 81,628 | 83,271 | 166 | 2.0 |
| Springfield, Mass. | 129,614 | 149,554 | 162,399 | 174,463 | 72 | 7.4 |
| Springfield, Mo. | 39,631 | 61,238 | 66,731 | 95,865 | 137 | 43.7 |
| Springfield, Ohio | 60,840 | 70,662 | 78,508 | 82,723 | 169 | 5.4 |
| Stamford, Conn. | 35,096 | 47,938 | 74,293 | 92,713 | 142 | 24.8 |
| Stockton, Calif. | 40,296 | 54,714 | 70,853 | 86,321 | 160 | 21.8 |
| Sunnyvale, Calif. | 1,675 | 4,373 | 9,829 | 52,898 | 291 | 438.2 |
| Syracuse, N. Y. | 171,717 | 205,967 | 220,583 | 216,038 | 53 | −2.1 |

| City | 1920 population | 1940 population | 1950 population | 1960 population | 1960 rank | % change 1950–60 |
|---|---|---|---|---|---|---|
| Tacoma, Wash. | 96,965 | 109,408 | 143,673 | 147,979 | 83 | 3.0 |
| Tampa, Fla. | 51,608 | 108,391 | 124,681 | 274,970 | 48 | 120.5 |
| Terre Haute, Ind. | 66,083 | 62,693 | 64,214 | 72,500 | 195 | 12.9 |
| Toledo, Ohio | 243,164 | 282,349 | 303,616 | 318,003 | 39 | 4.7 |
| Topeka, Kans. | 50,022 | 67,833 | 78,791 | 119,484 | 100 | 51.6 |
| Torrance, Calif. | .... | 9,950 | 22,241 | 100,991 | 128 | 354.1 |
| Trenton, N. J. | 119,289 | 124,697 | 128,009 | 114,167 | 107 | −10.8 |
| Troy, N. Y. | 71,996 | 70,304 | 72,311 | 67,492 | 215 | −6.7 |
| Tucson, Ariz. | 20,292 | 35,752 | 45,454 | 212,892 | 54 | 368.4 |
| Tulsa, Okla. | 72,075 | 142,157 | 182,740 | 261,685 | 50 | 43.2 |
| Tuscaloosa, Ala. | 11,996 | 27,493 | 46,396 | 63,370 | 238 | 36.6 |
| Tyler, Tex. | 12,085 | 28,279 | 38,968 | 51,230 | 303 | 31.5 |
| Union City, N. J. | 20,651 | 56,173 | 55,537 | 52,180 | 296 | −6.0 |
| University City, Mo. | 6,792 | 33,023 | 39,892 | 51,249 | 302 | 28.5 |
| Utica, N. Y. | 94,156 | 100,518 | 101,531 | 100,410 | 129 | −1.1 |
| Vallejo, Calif. | 21,107 | 20,072 | 26,038 | 60,877 | 251 | 133.8 |
| Waco, Tex. | 38,500 | 55,982 | 84,706 | 97,808 | 134 | 15.5 |
| Waltham, Mass. | 30,915 | 40,020 | 47,187 | 55,413 | 277 | 17.4 |
| Warren, Mich. | .... | 582 | 727 | 89,246 | 152 | 12,142.2 |
| Warren, Ohio | 27,050 | 42,837 | 49,856 | 59,648 | 255 | 19.6 |
| Warwick, R. I. | 13,481 | 28,757 | 43,028 | 68,504 | 211 | 59.2 |
| Washington, D. C. | 437,571 | 663,091 | 802,178 | 763,956 | 9 | −4.8 |
| Waterbury, Conn. | 91,715 | 99,314 | 104,477 | 107,130 | 121 | 2.5 |
| Waterloo, Iowa | 36,230 | 51,743 | 65,198 | 71,755 | 200 | 10.1 |
| Waukegan, Ill. | 19,226 | 34,241 | 38,946 | 55,719 | 275 | 43.1 |
| Wauwatosa, Wis. | 5,818 | 27,769 | 33,324 | 56,923 | 268 | 70.8 |
| West Allis, Wis. | 13,745 | 36,364 | 42,959 | 68,157 | 212 | 58.7 |
| West Covina, Calif. | .... | 1,072 | 4,499 | 50,645 | 307 | 1,025.7 |
| West Palm Beach, Fla. | 8,659 | 33,693 | 43,162 | 56,208 | 272 | 30.2 |
| Wheeling, W. Va. | 56,208 | 61,099 | 58,891 | 53,400 | 289 | −9.3 |
| White Plains, N. Y. | 21,031 | 40,327 | 43,466 | 50,485 | 309 | 16.1 |
| Wichita, Kans. | 72,217 | 114,966 | 168,279 | 254,698 | 51 | 51.4 |
| Wichita Falls, Tex. | 40,079 | 45,112 | 68,042 | 101,724 | 127 | 49.5 |
| Wilkes-Barre, Pa. | 73,833 | 86,236 | 76,826 | 63,551 | 235 | −17.3 |
| Wilmington, Del. | 110,168 | 112,504 | 110,356 | 95,827 | 138 | −13.2 |
| Winston-Salem, N. C. | 48,395 | 79,815 | 87,811 | 111,135 | 115 | 26.6 |
| Worcester, Mass. | 179,754 | 193,694 | 203,486 | 186,587 | 66 | −8.3 |
| Yonkers, N. Y. | 100,176 | 142,598 | 152,798 | 190,634 | 64 | 24.8 |
| York, Pa. | 47,512 | 56,712 | 59,953 | 54,504 | 281 | −9.1 |
| Youngstown, Ohio | 132,358 | 167,720 | 168,330 | 166,689 | 75 | −1.0 |

\* Rockford, Ill., and Madison, Wis., share 96th place in rank.

## Territorial Expansion of U. S.

*Source:* U. S. Bureau of the Census.

### CONTINENTAL UNITED STATES

| Accession | Date | Area, sq. mi.[1] |
|---|---|---|
| Territory in 1790 | .... | 888,811 |
| Louisiana Purchase | 1803 | 827,192 |
| Florida | 1819 | 58,560 |
| By treaty with Spain | 1819 | 13,443 |
| Texas | 1845 | 390,144 |
| Oregon | 1846 | 285,580 |
| Mexican Cession | 1848 | 529,017 |
| Gadsden Purchase | 1853 | 29,640 |
| Total | .... | 3,022,387 |

### OUTLYING TERRITORY

| Accession | Date | Area, sq. mi.[1] |
|---|---|---|
| Alaska[3] | 1867 | 586,400 |
| Hawaii[3] | 1898 | 6,423 |
| Puerto Rico | 1899 | 3,435 |
| Guam | 1899 | 206 |
| American Samoa | 1900 | 76 |
| Panama Canal Zone | 1904 | 553 |
| Corn Islands[2] | 1914 | 4 |
| Virgin Islands of U. S. | 1917 | 133 |
| Trust territory | 1947 | 8,475 |
| All other | .... | 38 |
| Total | .... | 605,743 |
| Aggregate, 1960 | .... | 3,628,130 |

[1] Total land and water area.  [2] Leased from Nicaragua for 99 years.  [3] Became state in 1959.

## Total Population U. S. and Possessions

*Source:* U. S. Bureau of the Census.

| Area | 1940 | 1950 | 1960 |
|---|---|---|---|
| United States | 131,669,275 | 150,697,361 | 179,323,175[1] |
| Alaska[2] | 72,524 | 128,643 | (3) |
| American Samoa | 12,908 | 18,937 | 20,040 |
| Canal Zone | 51,827 | 52,822 | 41,684 |
| Guam | 22,290 | 59,498 | 66,910 |
| Hawaii[2] | 423,330 | 499,794 | (3) |
| Philippines | 16,356,000 | ...... | ...... |
| Puerto Rico | 1,869,255 | 2,210,703 | 2,353,297 |
| Virgin Is. of U. S. | 24,889 | 26,665 | 31,904 |
| Total | 150,502,298 | 153,694,423 | 181,837,010 |

[1] Excludes members of Armed Forces overseas, estimated at 680,000.  [2] Became state in 1959.  [3] Included in U. S. total.

# Patents

*Source:* Patent Office.

A patent, in the most general sense, is a document issued by a government, conferring some special right or privilege. The term is now restricted mainly to patents for inventions; occasionally, land patents.

The grant of a patent for an invention gives the inventor the privilege, for a limited period of time, of excluding others from practicing a certain art or from making, using, or selling a certain article. However, it does not give him the right to make, use, or sell his own invention if it is an improvement on some unexpired patent whose claims are infringed thereby.

In the U. S., the law provides that a patent may be granted, for a term of 17 years, to any person who has invented or discovered any new and useful art, machine, manufacture, or composition of matter, as well as any new and useful improvements thereof. A patent may also be granted to a person who has invented or discovered and asexually reproduced a new and distinct variety of plant (other than a tuber-propagated one) or has invented a new, original and ornamental design for an article of manufacture.

A patent is granted only upon a regularly filed application, complete in all respects; upon payment of the fees; and upon determination that the disclosure is complete and that the invention is new and useful. The disclosure must be of such nature as to enable others to reproduce the invention.

A complete application, which must be addressed to the Commissioner of Patents, Washington, D. C., consists of a petition, specification and claims, oath, drawing (whenever the nature of the case admits of it) and a filing fee of $30 for cases having 20 claims or less. An additional fee of $1 per claim is required for cases having more than 20 claims. The filing fee is not returned to the applicant if the patent is refused. If the patent is allowed, another fee of $30 (and $1 each for claims allowed in excess of 20) is required before the patent is issued. The fees for design patents vary.

Applications are considered in the order in which they are received. Patents are not granted for printed matter, for methods of doing business, or for devices for which claims contrary to natural laws are made. Applications for a perpetual-motion machine have been made from time to time, but until a working model is presented that actually fulfills the claim, no patent will be issued.

# Trademarks

*Source:* Patent Office.

A trademark may be defined as a word, letter, device, or symbol, as well as some combination of these, which is used in connection with merchandise and which points distinctly to the origin or ownership of it.

Certificates of registration of trademarks are issued under the seal of the Patent Office and may be registered by the owner if he is engaged in interstate or foreign commerce, since any Federal jurisdiction over trademarks arises under the commerce clause of the Constitution. Trademarks may be registered by foreign owners who comply with our law, as well as by citizens of foreign countries with which the U. S. has treaties relating to trademarks. American citizens may register trademarks in foreign countries by complying with the laws of those countries. The right to registration and protection of trademarks in many foreign countries is guaranteed by treaties.

General jurisdiction in trademark cases is given to the Federal courts. Decisions of examiners on applications or oppositions are subject to appeal to the Trademark Trial and Appeal Board and from it to the U. S. Court of Customs and Patent Appeals. Before adopting a trademark, a person should make a search of prior marks in order to avoid infringing unwittingly upon them.

The duration of a trademark registration is 20 years, but it may be renewed indefinitely for 20-year periods, provided the trademark is still in use at the time of expiration.

# Television Statistics

*Source:* ELECTRONIC TECHNICIAN Magazine.

| Year | TV sets mfd. | Retail value | Picture tubes mfd. | Retail value | TV stations | Homes with TV* | TV sets in use in U. S. |
|---|---|---|---|---|---|---|---|
| 1946 | 10,000 | $ 5,000,000 | 20,000 | $ 1,000,000 | 5 | 8,000 | 8,000 |
| 1947 | 250,000 | 100,000,000 | 300,000 | 15,000,000 | 20 | 250,000 | 250,000 |
| 1948 | 1,000,000 | 350,000,000 | 1,500,000 | 75,000,000 | 48 | 1,000,000 | 1,000,000 |
| 1949 | 3,000,000 | 950,000,000 | 3,500,000 | 210,000,000 | 100 | 4,000,000 | 4,000,000 |
| 1950 | 7,500,000 | 2,200,000,000 | 8,000,000 | 400,000,000 | 107 | 10,400,000 | 10,500,000 |
| 1951 | 5,600,000 | 1,800,000,000 | 6,000,000 | 300,000,000 | 108 | 15,500,000 | 15,750,000 |
| 1953 | 7,300,000 | 1,675,000,000 | 9,900,000 | 360,000,000 | 350 | 26,000,000 | 28,000,000 |
| 1957 | 6,400,000 | 1,050,000,000 | 13,100,000 | 410,000,000 | 521 | 39,500,000 | 47,200,000 |
| 1959 | 6,400,000 | 1,100,000,000 | 13,000,000 | 400,000,000 | 570 | 44,000,000 | 52,000,000 |
| 1960 | 6,000,000 | 855,000,000 | 13,000,000 | 410,000,000 | 590 | 45,000,000 | 54,000,000 |

* Includes dwellings such as apartment hotels.

# Copyrights

*Source:* Copyright Office.

A copyright is a statutory right obtained by authors, musicians, and artists or their assigns, upon compliance with the provisions of the copyright law, to prevent the reproduction of their works without their consent. The U. S. Constitution (Article I, Section 8) empowers Congress "to promote the progress of science and useful arts, by securing for limited times to authors and inventors the exclusive right to their respective writings and discoveries." The copyright owner possesses the exclusive right to print, reprint, publish, copy, and vend the copyrighted work. Among some of the other rights possessed by the copyright owner are the exclusive rights to translate and dramatize literary works, to control public performance of dramas, and, in the case of nondramatic literary works and musical compositions, to control public performance for profit. Special provisions in regard to mechanical reproductions of musical compositions are included. Copyright protection extends to books; pamphlets; periodicals and contributions to periodicals; lectures, sermons, and monologues; dramas and dramatico-musical compositions; musical compositions; maps; works of art or models and designs for works of art; reproductions of a work of art; drawings or plastic works of scientific or technical character; photographs; prints and pictorial illustrations; commercial prints and labels; and motion pictures.

Copyright term endures 28 years from date of registration in the Copyright Office for unpublished material and from the date of publication for published works. The copyright may be renewed for an additional period of 28 years, provided application for such renewal is made within one year prior to the date of expiration of the original term. The copyright of a book or similar publication is secured by publication of such work after printing on the title page, or the page immediately following, the required copyright notice. This notice consists of the word *Copyright*, the abbreviation *Copr.* or the symbol ©, the name of the copyright owner, and the year date of publication. It is important to bear in mind that copyright comes into being at the time of first publication if this required notice appears on the work. If publication occurs without this notice, the work falls into the public domain, and the Copyright Office cannot register the claim. In short, the Copyright Office does not grant copyrights; the obtaining of such protection depends on whether or not the claimant follows the statutory formalities at the time of publication. In view of the fact that those formalities vary with the different classes of works subject to copyright, persons interested in securing copyright should obtain circular No. 35 from the Register of Copyrights, Library of Congress, Washington 25, D. C.

The law requires that, promptly after the work has been published, two copies thereof (foreign works, one copy) must be promptly deposited in the Copyright Office. These copies should be accompanied by the proper application form and the statutory fee of $4. If the work is a commercial print or label published in connection with the sale or advertisement of an article of merchandise, the fee is $6.

The Act of Aug. 31, 1954, modified a number of existing formalities, primarily with regard to certain foreign works, and was designed to implement the Universal Copyright Convention, which took effect on Sept. 16, 1955. One principal modification is that U. S. authors and publishers may use the symbol © instead of the word *Copyright* or the abbreviation *Copr.* The symbol must be accompanied by the name of the copyright owner and the year date of publication. The use of this form may obtain automatic copyright protection in countries adhering to the Universal Copyright Convention.

Application forms, etc., may be obtained free from the Copyright Office. Bulletin 14, the U. S. copyright law, can be purchased from the Register of Copyrights, or from the Superintendent of Documents, U. S. Government Printing Office, for 25¢.

---

# Radio and Audio Statistics
# for the United States

*Source:* ELECTRONIC TECHNICIAN Magazine.

| Radio† | | Audio | |
|---|---:|---|---:|
| Radios: Homes with* | 54,500,000 | Phonographs sold, 1960 | 4,700,000 |
|   Secondary sets in home | 56,500,000 | Phonographs in U. S. | 41,500,000† |
|   Sets in business | 14,500,000 | Tape recorders sold, 1960 | 500,000 |
|   Automobile radios | 41,500,000 | Tape recorders in U. S. | 3,500,000† |
| Total radios | 167,000,000 | Home hi-fi servicing | $150,000,000 |
| Amateur stations licensed | 240,000 | Hi-fi audio $ volume, 1960 | $210,000,000 |

\* Includes dwellings such as apartment hotels.    † As of Jan. 1, 1961.

# Motor Vehicle Laws as of 1961

*Source:* American Automobile Association.

| State | Date new license plates can be used | Driver's license required | Minimum age of drivers | State gasoline tax | % state tax[1] | Certificate of title required |
|---|---|---|---|---|---|---|
| Alabama | Oct. 1 | yes | 16 | $.07 | 1½ | no |
| Alaska | Jan. 1 | yes | 16 | .07 | .. | yes |
| Arizona | Dec. 1 | yes | 18 | .05 | 3 | yes |
| Arkansas | Jan. 1 | yes | 14 | .065 | 3 | yes |
| California | Jan. 1 | yes | 16 | .06 | 3 | yes |
| Colorado | Dec. 1 | yes | 17 | .06 | 2 | yes |
| Connecticut | Mar. 1 | yes | 16 | .06 | 3[2] | yes |
| Delaware | ([3]) | yes | 16 | .05 | .. | yes |
| District of Columbia | Mar. 1 | yes | 16 | .06 | 2 | yes |
| Florida | Jan. 1 | yes | 16 | .07 | 1 | yes |
| Georgia | Jan. 1 | yes | 16 | .065 | 3 | no |
| Hawaii | Jan. 3 | yes | 15 | ([4]) | .. | yes |
| Idaho | Dec. 1 | yes | 16 | .06 | .. | yes |
| Illinois | Dec. 1 | yes | 16 | .05 | 3 | yes |
| Indiana | Jan. 3 | yes | 16[5] | .06 | .. | yes |
| Iowa | Dec. 1 | yes | 16 | .06 | 2 | yes |
| Kansas | Jan. 1 | yes | 16 | .05 | 2½ | yes |
| Kentucky | Dec. 29 | yes | 16 | .07 | 3 | ([6]) |
| Louisiana | Dec. 1 | yes | 15 | .07 | 2 | yes |
| Maine | Dec. 25 | yes | 17 | .07 | 3 | no |
| Maryland | Mar. 1 | yes | 16 | .06 | 2 | yes |
| Massachusetts | Jan. 1 | yes | 16 | .055 | ([7]) | no |
| Michigan | ([8]) | yes | 16 | .06 | 4 | yes |
| Minnesota | Nov. 15 | yes | 15 | .05 | .. | no[9] |
| Mississippi | Nov. 1 | yes | 17 | .07 | 2 | no |
| Missouri | On issue | yes | 16 | .03 | 2 | yes |
| Montana | On issue | yes | 15 | .06 | ... | yes |
| Nebraska | Jan. 1 | yes | 16 | .07 | .. | yes |
| Nevada | June 1 | yes | 16 | .06 | 2 | yes |
| New Hampshire | Mar. 1 | yes | 16 | .07 | ... | no |
| New Jersey | On issue | yes | 17 | .05 | ... | yes |
| New Mexico | Dec. 15 | yes | 18 | .06 | 1 | yes |
| New York | Jan. 1 | yes | 18 | .06 | .. | no |
| North Carolina | Jan. 1 | yes | 16 | .07 | 1[10] | yes |
| North Dakota | Nov. 1 | yes | 16 | .06 | 2 | yes |
| Ohio | Mar. 1 | yes | 16 | .07 | 3 | yes |
| Oklahoma | Dec. 11 | yes | 16 | .065 | 2 | yes |
| Oregon | On issue | yes | 16 | .06 | .. | yes |
| Pennsylvania | Mar. 15 | yes | 18 | .07 | 4 | yes |
| Rhode Island | Mar. 1 | yes | 16 | .07 | 3 | no |
| South Carolina | Sept. 6 | yes | 16 | .07 | 3 | yes |
| South Dakota | Jan. 1 | yes | 16 | .06 | 2[11] | yes |
| Tennessee | Mar. 1 | yes | 16 | .07 | 3 | yes |
| Texas | Feb. 1 | yes | 16 | .05 | 1½ | yes |
| Utah | Dec. 15 | yes | 16 | .06 | 2 | yes |
| Vermont | Feb. 1 | yes | 18 | .065 | 2 | no |
| Virginia | Mar. 15 | yes | 18 | .07 | .. | yes |
| Washington | Jan. 2 | yes | 16 | .075 | 4 | yes |
| West Virginia | June 1 | yes | 16 | .07 | 2 | yes |
| Wisconsin | On issue | yes | 16 | .06 | .. | yes |
| Wyoming | Dec. 1 | yes | 15 | .05 | 2 | yes |

[1] Applicable to car sales. [2] Sales or use tax on first registration of new or used cars. [3] Three months before current registration expires. [4] $.085 to $.11; varies by county. [5] Plus one month. [6] Bill of sale must be filed. [7] Excise tax based on car value. [8] At discretion of Secretary of State. [9] Required for initial registration of vehicles previously registered in other states. [10] $80 maximum. [11] Registry tax on first registration in state. NOTE: Speed limits are not given in the above table because they vary widely within each state, depending on the kind of road, the condition of the road, the weather, the light, local ordinances, etc. In many states no maximum speed is specified, the requirement being what is "reasonable and proper."

# Road Mileages Between U. S. Cities

*Source:* American Automobile Association.

| Cities | Birming-ham | Boston | Buffalo | Chicago | Cleveland | Dallas | Denver |
|---|---|---|---|---|---|---|---|
| Birmingham, Ala. | .... | 1,223 | 1,130 | 663 | 651 | 659 | 1,379 |
| Boston, Mass. | 1,223 | .... | 463 | 980 | 651 | 1,728 | 2,025 |
| Buffalo, N. Y. | 1,130 | 463 | .... | 524 | 188 | 1,427 | 1,562 |
| Chicago, Ill. | 663 | 980 | 524 | .... | 349 | 1,006 | 1,038 |
| Cleveland, Ohio | 651 | 651 | 188 | 349 | .... | 1,139 | 1,351 |
| Dallas, Tex. | 659 | 1,728 | 1,427 | 1,006 | 1,139 | .... | 800 |
| Denver, Colo. | 1,379 | 2,025 | 1,562 | 1,038 | 1,351 | 800 | .... |
| Detroit, Mich. | 759 | 735 | 247 | 272 | 167 | 1,278 | 1,323 |
| El Paso, Tex. | 1,286 | 2,527 | 1,938 | 1,654 | 1,750 | 627 | 725 |
| Houston, Tex. | 742 | 1,965 | 1,549 | 1,173 | 1,361 | 243 | 1,043 |
| Indianapolis, Ind. | 508 | 935 | 488 | 188 | 302 | 928 | 1,051 |
| Kansas City, Mo. | 714 | 1,429 | 982 | 503 | 794 | 527 | 644 |
| Los Angeles, Calif. | 2,121 | 3,162 | 2,699 | 2,175 | 2,457 | 1,486 | 1,202 |
| Louisville, Ky. | 394 | 971 | 550 | 300 | 362 | 892 | 1,168 |
| Memphis, Tenn. | 248 | 1,360 | 958 | 541 | 765 | 474 | 1,131 |
| Miami, Fla. | 803 | 1,540 | 1,434 | 1,384 | 1,346 | 1,346 | 2,182 |
| Minneapolis, Minn. | 1,088 | 1,405 | 962 | 425 | 774 | 991 | 916 |
| New Orleans, La. | 357 | 1,580 | 1,392 | 943 | 1,108 | 490 | 1,280 |
| New York, N. Y. | 851 | 208 | 384 | 850 | 501 | 1,646 | 1,833 |
| Omaha, Nebr. | 926 | 1,472 | 1,010 | 486 | 835 | 699 | 552 |
| Philadelphia, Pa. | 759 | 301 | 393 | 756 | 426 | 1,576 | 1,763 |
| Phoenix, Ariz. | 1,699 | 2,834 | 2,245 | 1,816 | 2,057 | 1,040 | 826 |
| Pittsburgh, Pa. | 812 | 576 | 223 | 463 | 131 | 1,278 | 1,465 |
| St. Louis, Mo. | 548 | 1,196 | 729 | 300 | 541 | 676 | 901 |
| Salt Lake City, Utah | 1,890 | 2,427 | 1,964 | 1,440 | 1,789 | 1,270 | 530 |
| San Francisco, Calif. | 2,443 | 3,186 | 2,723 | 2,199 | 2,548 | 1,807 | 1,270 |
| Seattle, Wash. | 2,779 | 3,098 | 2,600 | 2,076 | 2,608 | 2,153 | 1,403 |
| Washington, D. C. | 624 | 435 | 407 | 698 | 368 | 1,399 | 1,614 |

| Cities | Detroit | El Paso | Houston | Indian-apolis | Kansas City | Los Angeles | Louisville |
|---|---|---|---|---|---|---|---|
| Birmingham, Ala. | 759 | 1,286 | 742 | 508 | 714 | 2,121 | 394 |
| Boston, Mass. | 735 | 2,527 | 1,965 | 935 | 1,429 | 3,162 | 971 |
| Buffalo, N. Y. | 247 | 1,938 | 1,549 | 488 | 982 | 2,699 | 550 |
| Chicago, Ill. | 272 | 1,654 | 1,173 | 188 | 503 | 2,175 | 300 |
| Cleveland, Ohio | 167 | 1,750 | 1,361 | 302 | 794 | 2,457 | 362 |
| Dallas, Tex. | 1,278 | 627 | 243 | 928 | 527 | 1,486 | 892 |
| Denver, Colo. | 1,323 | 725 | 1,043 | 1,051 | 644 | 1,202 | 1,168 |
| Detroit, Mich. | .... | 1,722 | 1,307 | 272 | 766 | 2,447 | 370 |
| El Paso, Tex. | 1,722 | .... | 736 | 1,450 | 1,039 | 816 | 1,416 |
| Houston, Tex. | 1,307 | 736 | .... | 1,035 | 770 | 1,566 | 999 |
| Indianapolis, Ind. | 272 | 1,450 | 1,035 | .... | 498 | 2,196 | 114 |
| Kansas City, Mo. | 766 | 1,039 | 770 | 498 | .... | 1,728 | 524 |
| Los Angeles, Calif. | 2,447 | 816 | 1,566 | 2,196 | 1,728 | .... | 2,183 |
| Louisville, Ky. | 370 | 1,416 | 999 | 114 | 524 | 2,183 | .... |
| Memphis, Tenn. | 716 | 1,091 | 591 | 444 | 466 | 1,874 | 381 |
| Miami, Fla. | 1,407 | 1,998 | 1,288 | 1,274 | 1,526 | 2,832 | 1,126 |
| Minneapolis, Minn. | 697 | 1,480 | 1,234 | 611 | 464 | 2,018 | 725 |
| New Orleans, La. | 1,116 | 1,135 | 385 | 844 | 868 | 1,976 | 751 |
| New York, N. Y. | 636 | 2,161 | 1,593 | 727 | 1,221 | 3,025 | 773 |
| Omaha, Nebr. | 758 | 1,045 | 942 | 591 | 212 | 1,689 | 736 |
| Philadelphia, Pa. | 580 | 2,091 | 1,501 | 657 | 1,151 | 2,919 | 693 |
| Phoenix, Ariz. | 2,029 | 400 | 1,163 | 1,757 | 1,346 | 399 | 1,783 |
| Pittsburgh, Pa. | 287 | 1,793 | 1,394 | 359 | 853 | 2,621 | 395 |
| St. Louis, Mo. | 515 | 1,209 | 821 | 241 | 257 | 1,916 | 267 |
| Salt Lake City, Utah | 1,712 | 1,137 | 1,537 | 1,547 | 1,155 | 735 | 1,679 |
| San Francisco, Calif. | 2,471 | 1,221 | 2,019 | 2,306 | 1,914 | 415 | 2,438 |
| Seattle, Wash. | 2,531 | 2,078 | 2,449 | 2,262 | 2,047 | 1,177 | 2,547 |
| Washington, D. C. | 522 | 2,026 | 1,511 | 563 | 1,051 | 2,799 | 599 |

# Road Mileages Between U. S. Cities

Source: American Automobile Association.

| Cities | Memphis | Miami | Minne-apolis | New Orleans | New York | Omaha | Phila-delphia |
|---|---|---|---|---|---|---|---|
| Birmingham, Ala. | 248 | 803 | 1,088 | 357 | 851 | 926 | 759 |
| Boston, Mass. | 1,360 | 1,540 | 1,405 | 1,580 | 208 | 1,472 | 301 |
| Buffalo, N. Y. | 958 | 1,434 | 962 | 1,392 | 384 | 1,010 | 393 |
| Chicago, Ill. | 541 | 1,384 | 425 | 943 | 850 | 486 | 756 |
| Cleveland, Ohio | 765 | 1,346 | 774 | 1,108 | 501 | 835 | 426 |
| Dallas, Tex. | 474 | 1,346 | 991 | 490 | 1,646 | 699 | 1,576 |
| Denver, Colo. | 1,131 | 2,182 | 916 | 1,280 | 1,833 | 552 | 1,763 |
| Detroit, Mich. | 716 | 1,407 | 697 | 1,116 | 636 | 758 | 580 |
| El Paso, Tex. | 1,091 | 1,998 | 1,480 | 1,135 | 2,161 | 1,045 | 2,091 |
| Houston, Tex. | 591 | 1,288 | 1,234 | 385 | 1,593 | 942 | 1,501 |
| Indianapolis, Ind. | 444 | 1,274 | 611 | 844 | 727 | 591 | 657 |
| Kansas City, Mo. | 466 | 1,526 | 464 | 868 | 1,221 | 212 | 1,151 |
| Los Angeles, Calif. | 1,874 | 2,832 | 2,018 | 1,976 | 3,025 | 1,689 | 2,919 |
| Louisville, Ky. | 381 | 1,126 | 725 | 751 | 773 | 736 | 693 |
| Memphis, Tenn. | .... | 1,022 | 863 | 386 | 1,152 | 678 | 1,060 |
| Miami, Fla. | 1,022 | .... | 1,818 | 899 | 1,332 | 1,738 | 1,224 |
| Minneapolis, Minn. | 863 | 1,818 | .... | 1,275 | 1,284 | 364 | 1,190 |
| New Orleans, La. | 386 | 899 | 1,275 | .... | 1,208 | 1,080 | 1,116 |
| New York, N. Y. | 1,152 | 1,332 | 1,284 | 1,208 | .... | 1,300 | 93 |
| Omaha, Nebr. | 678 | 1,738 | 364 | 1,080 | 1,300 | .... | 1,230 |
| Philadelphia, Pa. | 1,060 | 1,224 | 1,190 | 1,116 | 93 | 1,230 | .... |
| Phoenix, Ariz. | 1,474 | 2,411 | 1,742 | 1,548 | 2,474 | 1,378 | 2,534 |
| Pittsburgh, Pa. | 804 | 1,276 | 897 | 1,169 | 368 | 932 | 298 |
| St. Louis, Mo. | 301 | 1,269 | 562 | 701 | 968 | 469 | 898 |
| Salt Lake City, Utah | 1,619 | 2,607 | 1,283 | 1,801 | 2,290 | 954 | 2,184 |
| San Francisco, Calif. | 2,195 | 3,270 | 2,141 | 2,297 | 3,049 | 1,713 | 2,943 |
| Seattle, Wash. | 2,532 | 3,582 | 1,642 | 2,683 | 2,926 | 1,773 | 2,832 |
| Washington, D. C. | 925 | 1,111 | 1,132 | 1,227 | 227 | 1,167 | 135 |

| Cities | Phoenix | Pitts-burgh | St. Louis | Salt Lake City | San Francisco | Seattle | Wash-ington |
|---|---|---|---|---|---|---|---|
| Birmingham, Ala. | 1,699 | 812 | 548 | 1,890 | 2,443 | 2,779 | 624 |
| Boston, Mass. | 2,834 | 576 | 1,196 | 2,427 | 3,186 | 3,098 | 435 |
| Buffalo, N. Y. | 2,245 | 223 | 729 | 1,964 | 2,723 | 2,600 | 407 |
| Chicago, Ill. | 1,816 | 463 | 300 | 1,440 | 2,199 | 2,076 | 698 |
| Cleveland, Ohio | 2,057 | 131 | 541 | 1,789 | 2,548 | 2,608 | 368 |
| Dallas, Tex. | 1,040 | 1,278 | 676 | 1,270 | 1,807 | 2,153 | 1,399 |
| Denver, Colo. | 826 | 1,465 | 901 | 530 | 1,270 | 1,403 | 1,614 |
| Detroit, Mich. | 2,029 | 287 | 515 | 1,712 | 2,471 | 2,531 | 522 |
| El Paso, Tex. | 400 | 1,793 | 1,209 | 1,137 | 1,221 | 2,078 | 2,026 |
| Houston, Tex. | 1,163 | 1,394 | 821 | 1,537 | 2,019 | 2,449 | 1,511 |
| Indianapolis, Ind. | 1,757 | 359 | 241 | 1,547 | 2,306 | 2,262 | 563 |
| Kansas City, Mo. | 1,346 | 853 | 257 | 1,155 | 1,914 | 2,047 | 1,051 |
| Los Angeles, Calif. | 399 | 2,621 | 1,916 | 735 | 415 | 1,177 | 2,799 |
| Louisville, Ky. | 1,783 | 395 | 267 | 1,679 | 2,438 | 2,547 | 599 |
| Memphis, Tenn. | 1,474 | 804 | 301 | 1,619 | 2,195 | 2,532 | 925 |
| Miami, Fla. | 2,411 | 1,276 | 1,269 | 2,607 | 3,270 | 3,582 | 1,111 |
| Minneapolis, Minn. | 1,742 | 897 | 562 | 1,283 | 2,141 | 1,642 | 1,132 |
| New Orleans, La. | 1,548 | 1,269 | 701 | 1,801 | 2,297 | 2,683 | 1,227 |
| New York, N. Y. | 2,474 | 368 | 968 | 2,290 | 3,049 | 2,926 | 227 |
| Omaha, Nebr. | 1,378 | 932 | 469 | 954 | 1,713 | 1,773 | 1,167 |
| Philadelphia, Pa. | 2,534 | 298 | 898 | 2,184 | 2,943 | 2,832 | 135 |
| Phoenix, Ariz. | .... | 2,116 | 1,516 | 763 | 827 | 1,531 | 2,399 |
| Pittsburgh, Pa. | 2,116 | .... | 600 | 1,886 | 2,645 | 2,438 | 235 |
| St. Louis, Mo. | 1,516 | 600 | .... | 1,412 | 2,171 | 2,259 | 804 |
| Salt Lake City, Utah | 763 | 1,886 | 1,412 | .... | 759 | 889 | 1,778 |
| San Francisco, Calif. | 827 | 2,645 | 2,171 | 759 | .... | 874 | 2,885 |
| Seattle, Wash. | 1,531 | 2,438 | 2,259 | 889 | 874 | .... | 2,673 |
| Washington, D. C. | 2,399 | 235 | 804 | 1,778 | 2,885 | 2,673 | .... |

## Air Distances Between U. S. Cities

*Source:* U. S. Coast and Geodetic Survey.

| Cities | Birming-ham | Boston | Buffalo | Chicago | Cleveland | Dallas | Denver |
|---|---|---|---|---|---|---|---|
| Birmingham, Ala. | .... | 1,052 | 776 | 578 | 618 | 581 | 1,095 |
| Boston, Mass. | 1,052 | .... | 400 | 851 | 551 | 1,551 | 1,769 |
| Buffalo, N. Y. | 776 | 400 | .... | 454 | 173 | 1,198 | 1,370 |
| Chicago, Ill. | 578 | 851 | 454 | .... | 308 | 803 | 920 |
| Cleveland, Ohio | 618 | 551 | 173 | 308 | .... | 1,025 | 1,227 |
| Dallas, Tex. | 581 | 1,551 | 1,198 | 803 | 1,025 | .... | 663 |
| Denver, Colo. | 1,095 | 1,769 | 1,370 | 920 | 1,227 | 663 | .... |
| Detroit, Mich. | 641 | 613 | 216 | 238 | 90 | 999 | 1,156 |
| El Paso, Tex. | 1,152 | 2,072 | 1,692 | 1,252 | 1,525 | 572 | 557 |
| Houston, Tex. | 567 | 1,605 | 1,286 | 940 | 1,114 | 225 | 879 |
| Indianapolis, Ind. | 433 | 807 | 435 | 165 | 263 | 763 | 1,000 |
| Kansas City, Mo. | 579 | 1,251 | 861 | 414 | 700 | 451 | 558 |
| Los Angeles, Calif. | 1,802 | 2,596 | 2,198 | 1,745 | 2,049 | 1,240 | 831 |
| Louisville, Ky. | 331 | 826 | 483 | 269 | 311 | 726 | 1,038 |
| Memphis, Tenn. | 217 | 1,137 | 803 | 482 | 630 | 420 | 879 |
| Miami, Fla. | 665 | 1,255 | 1,181 | 1,188 | 1,087 | 1,111 | 1,726 |
| Minneapolis, Minn. | 862 | 1,123 | 731 | 355 | 630 | 862 | 700 |
| New Orleans, La. | 312 | 1,359 | 1,086 | 833 | 924 | 443 | 1,082 |
| New York, N. Y. | 864 | 188 | 292 | 713 | 405 | 1,374 | 1,631 |
| Omaha, Nebr. | 732 | 1,282 | 883 | 432 | 739 | 586 | 488 |
| Philadelphia, Pa. | 783 | 271 | 279 | 666 | 360 | 1,299 | 1,579 |
| Phoenix, Ariz. | 1,456 | 2,300 | 1,906 | 1,453 | 1,749 | 887 | 586 |
| Pittsburgh, Pa. | 608 | 483 | 178 | 410 | 115 | 1,070 | 1,320 |
| St. Louis, Mo. | 400 | 1,038 | 662 | 262 | 492 | 547 | 796 |
| Salt Lake City, Utah | 1,466 | 2,099 | 1,699 | 1,260 | 1,568 | 999 | 371 |
| San Francisco, Calif. | 2,013 | 2,699 | 2,300 | 1,858 | 2,166 | 1,483 | 949 |
| Seattle, Wash. | 2,082 | 2,493 | 2,117 | 1,737 | 2,026 | 1,681 | 1,021 |
| Washington, D. C. | 661 | 393 | 292 | 597 | 306 | 1,185 | 1,494 |

| Cities | Detroit | El Paso | Houston | Indian-apolis | Kansas City | Los Angeles | Louisville |
|---|---|---|---|---|---|---|---|
| Birmingham, Ala. | 641 | 1,152 | 567 | 433 | 579 | 1,802 | 331 |
| Boston, Mass. | 613 | 2,072 | 1,605 | 807 | 1,251 | 2,596 | 826 |
| Buffalo, N. Y. | 216 | 1,692 | 1,286 | 435 | 861 | 2,198 | 483 |
| Chicago, Ill. | 238 | 1,252 | 940 | 165 | 414 | 1,745 | 269 |
| Cleveland, Ohio | 90 | 1,525 | 1,114 | 263 | 700 | 2,049 | 311 |
| Dallas, Tex. | 999 | 572 | 225 | 763 | 451 | 1,240 | 726 |
| Denver, Colo. | 1,156 | 557 | 879 | 1,000 | 558 | 831 | 1,038 |
| Detroit, Mich. | .... | 1,479 | 1,105 | 240 | 645 | 1,983 | 316 |
| El Paso, Tex. | 1,479 | .... | 676 | 1,264 | 839 | 701 | 1,254 |
| Houston, Tex. | 1,105 | 676 | .... | 865 | 644 | 1,374 | 803 |
| Indianapolis, Ind. | 240 | 1,264 | 865 | .... | 453 | 1,809 | 107 |
| Kansas City, Mo. | 645 | 839 | 644 | 453 | .... | 1,356 | 480 |
| Los Angeles, Calif. | 1,983 | 701 | 1,374 | 1,809 | 1,356 | .... | 1,829 |
| Louisville, Ky. | 316 | 1,254 | 803 | 107 | 480 | 1,829 | .... |
| Memphis, Tenn. | 623 | 976 | 484 | 384 | 369 | 1,603 | 320 |
| Miami, Fla. | 1,152 | 1,643 | 968 | 1,024 | 1,241 | 2,339 | 919 |
| Minneapolis, Minn. | 543 | 1,157 | 1,056 | 511 | 413 | 1,524 | 605 |
| New Orleans, La. | 939 | 983 | 318 | 712 | 680 | 1,673 | 623 |
| New York, N. Y. | 482 | 1,905 | 1,420 | 646 | 1,097 | 2,451 | 652 |
| Omaha, Nebr. | 669 | 878 | 794 | 525 | 166 | 1,315 | 580 |
| Philadelphia, Pa. | 443 | 1,836 | 1,341 | 585 | 1,038 | 2,394 | 582 |
| Phoenix, Ariz. | 1,690 | 346 | 1,017 | 1,499 | 1,049 | 357 | 1,508 |
| Pittsburgh, Pa. | 205 | 1,590 | 1,137 | 330 | 781 | 2,136 | 344 |
| St. Louis, Mo. | 455 | 1,034 | 679 | 231 | 238 | 1,589 | 242 |
| Salt Lake City, Utah | 1,492 | 689 | 1,200 | 1,356 | 925 | 579 | 1,402 |
| San Francisco, Calif. | 2,091 | 995 | 1,645 | 1,949 | 1,506 | 347 | 1,986 |
| Seattle, Wash. | 1,938 | 1,376 | 1,891 | 1,872 | 1,506 | 959 | 1,943 |
| Washington, D. C. | 396 | 1,728 | 1,220 | 494 | 945 | 2,300 | 476 |

# Air Distances Between U. S. Cities

*Source:* U. S. Coast and Geodetic Survey.

| Cities | Memphis | Miami | Minneapolis | New Orleans | New York | Omaha | Philadelphia |
|---|---|---|---|---|---|---|---|
| Birmingham, Ala. . . . . . . . | 217 | 665 | 862 | 312 | 864 | 732 | 783 |
| Boston, Mass. . . . . . . . . . | 1,137 | 1,255 | 1,123 | 1,359 | 188 | 1,282 | 271 |
| Buffalo, N. Y. . . . . . . . . . | 803 | 1,181 | 731 | 1,086 | 292 | 883 | 279 |
| Chicago, Ill. . . . . . . . . . . | 482 | 1,188 | 355 | 833 | 713 | 432 | 666 |
| Cleveland, Ohio . . . . . . . . | 630 | 1,087 | 630 | 924 | 405 | 739 | 360 |
| Dallas, Tex. . . . . . . . . . . | 420 | 1,111 | 862 | 443 | 1,374 | 586 | 1,299 |
| Denver, Colo. . . . . . . . . . | 879 | 1,726 | 700 | 1,082 | 1,631 | 488 | 1,579 |
| Detroit, Mich. . . . . . . . . . | 623 | 1,152 | 543 | 939 | 482 | 669 | 443 |
| El Paso, Tex. . . . . . . . . . | 976 | 1,643 | 1,157 | 983 | 1,905 | 878 | 1,836 |
| Houston, Tex. . . . . . . . . . | 484 | 968 | 1,056 | 318 | 1,420 | 794 | 1,341 |
| Indianapolis, Ind. . . . . . . | 384 | 1,024 | 511 | 712 | 646 | 525 | 585 |
| Kansas City, Mo. . . . . . . . | 369 | 1,241 | 413 | 680 | 1,097 | 166 | 1,038 |
| Los Angeles, Calif. . . . . . . | 1,603 | 2,339 | 1,524 | 1,673 | 2,451 | 1,315 | 2,394 |
| Louisville, Ky. . . . . . . . . | 320 | 919 | 605 | 623 | 652 | 580 | 582 |
| Memphis, Tenn. . . . . . . . . | . . . . | 872 | 699 | 358 | 957 | 529 | 881 |
| Miami, Fla. . . . . . . . . . . . | 872 | . . . . | 1,511 | 669 | 1,092 | 1,397 | 1,019 |
| Minneapolis, Minn. . . . . . | 699 | 1,511 | . . . . | 1,051 | 1,018 | 290 | 985 |
| New Orleans, La. . . . . . . | 358 | 669 | 1,051 | . . . . | 1,171 | 847 | 1,089 |
| New York, N. Y. . . . . . . . | 957 | 1,092 | 1,018 | 1,171 | . . . . | 1,144 | 83 |
| Omaha, Nebr. . . . . . . . . . | 529 | 1,397 | 290 | 847 | 1,144 | . . . . | 1,094 |
| Philadelphia, Pa. . . . . . . . | 881 | 1,019 | 985 | 1,089 | 83 | 1,094 | . . . . |
| Phoenix, Ariz. . . . . . . . . . | 1,263 | 1,982 | 1,280 | 1,316 | 2,145 | 1,036 | 2,083 |
| Pittsburgh, Pa. . . . . . . . . | 660 | 1,010 | 743 | 919 | 317 | 836 | 259 |
| St. Louis, Mo. . . . . . . . . . | 240 | 1,061 | 466 | 598 | 875 | 354 | 811 |
| Salt Lake City, Utah . . . . . | 1,250 | 2,089 | 987 | 1,434 | 1,972 | 833 | 1,925 |
| San Francisco, Calif. . . . . | 1,802 | 2,594 | 1,584 | 1,926 | 2,571 | 1,429 | 2,523 |
| Seattle, Wash. . . . . . . . . . | 1,867 | 2,734 | 1,395 | 2,101 | 2,408 | 1,369 | 2,380 |
| Washington, D. C. . . . . . . | 765 | 923 | 934 | 966 | 205 | 1,014 | 123 |

| Cities | Phoenix | Pittsburgh | St. Louis | Salt Lake City | San Francisco | Seattle | Washington |
|---|---|---|---|---|---|---|---|
| Birmingham, Ala. . . . . . . . | 1,456 | 608 | 400 | 1,466 | 2,013 | 2,082 | 661 |
| Boston, Mass. . . . . . . . . . | 2,300 | 483 | 1,038 | 2,099 | 2,699 | 2,493 | 393 |
| Buffalo, N. Y. . . . . . . . . . | 1,906 | 178 | 662 | 1,699 | 2,300 | 2,117 | 292 |
| Chicago, Ill. . . . . . . . . . . | 1,453 | 410 | 262 | 1,260 | 1,858 | 1,737 | 597 |
| Cleveland, Ohio . . . . . . . . | 1,749 | 115 | 492 | 1,568 | 2,166 | 2,026 | 306 |
| Dallas, Tex. . . . . . . . . . . | 887 | 1,070 | 547 | 999 | 1,483 | 1,681 | 1,185 |
| Denver, Colo. . . . . . . . . . | 586 | 1,320 | 796 | 371 | 949 | 1,021 | 1,494 |
| Detroit, Mich. . . . . . . . . . | 1,690 | 205 | 455 | 1,492 | 2,091 | 1,938 | 396 |
| El Paso, Tex. . . . . . . . . . | 346 | 1,590 | 1,034 | 689 | 995 | 1,376 | 1,728 |
| Houston, Tex. . . . . . . . . . | 1,017 | 1,137 | 679 | 1,200 | 1,645 | 1,891 | 1,220 |
| Indianapolis, Ind. . . . . . . | 1,499 | 330 | 231 | 1,356 | 1,949 | 1,872 | 494 |
| Kansas City, Mo. . . . . . . . | 1,049 | 781 | 238 | 925 | 1,506 | 1,506 | 945 |
| Los Angeles, Calif. . . . . . . | 357 | 2,136 | 1,589 | 579 | 347 | 959 | 2,300 |
| Louisville, Ky. . . . . . . . . | 1,508 | 344 | 242 | 1,402 | 1,986 | 1,943 | 476 |
| Memphis, Tenn. . . . . . . . . | 1,263 | 660 | 240 | 1,250 | 1,802 | 1,867 | 765 |
| Miami, Fla. . . . . . . . . . . . | 1,982 | 1,010 | 1,061 | 2,089 | 2,594 | 2,734 | 923 |
| Minneapolis, Minn. . . . . . | 1,280 | 743 | 466 | 987 | 1,584 | 1,395 | 934 |
| New Orleans, La. . . . . . . | 1,316 | 919 | 598 | 1,434 | 1,926 | 2,101 | 966 |
| New York, N. Y. . . . . . . . | 2,145 | 317 | 875 | 1,972 | 2,571 | 2,408 | 205 |
| Omaha, Nebr. . . . . . . . . . | 1,036 | 836 | 354 | 833 | 1,429 | 1,369 | 1,014 |
| Philadelphia, Pa. . . . . . . . | 2,083 | 259 | 811 | 1,925 | 2,523 | 2,380 | 123 |
| Phoenix, Ariz. . . . . . . . . . | . . . . | 1,828 | 1,272 | 504 | 653 | 1,114 | 1,983 |
| Pittsburgh, Pa. . . . . . . . . | 1,828 | . . . . | 559 | 1,668 | 2,264 | 2,138 | 192 |
| St. Louis, Mo. . . . . . . . . . | 1,272 | 559 | . . . . | 1,162 | 1,744 | 1,724 | 712 |
| Salt Lake City, Utah . . . . | 504 | 1,668 | 1,162 | . . . . | 600 | 701 | 1,848 |
| San Francisco, Calif. . . . . | 653 | 2,264 | 1,744 | 600 | . . . . | 678 | 2,442 |
| Seattle, Wash. . . . . . . . . . | 1,114 | 2,138 | 1,724 | 701 | 678 | . . . . | 2,329 |
| Washington, D. C. . . . . . . | 1,983 | 192 | 712 | 1,848 | 2,442 | 2,329 | . . . . |

# Air Distances Between World Cities

*Source: Encyclopaedia Britannica.*

| Cities | Berlin | Buenos Aires | Cairo | Calcutta | Capetown | Caracas | Chicago |
|---|---|---|---|---|---|---|---|
| Berlin, Germany | .... | 7,402 | 1,795 | 4,368 | 5,981 | 5,247 | 4,405 |
| Buenos Aires, Argentina | 7,402 | .... | 7,345 | 10,265 | 4,269 | 3,168 | 5,598 |
| Cairo, Egypt | 1,795 | 7,345 | .... | 3,539 | 4,500 | 6,338 | 6,129 |
| Calcutta, India | 4,368 | 10,265 | 3,539 | .... | 6,024 | 9,605 | 7,980 |
| Capetown, South Africa | 5,981 | 4,269 | 4,500 | 6,024 | .... | 6,365 | 8,494 |
| Caracas, Venezuela | 5,247 | 3,168 | 6,338 | 9,605 | 6,365 | .... | 2,501 |
| Chicago, Ill., U. S. | 4,405 | 5,598 | 6,129 | 7,980 | 8,494 | 2,501 | .... |
| Hong Kong (Victoria) | 5,440 | 11,472 | 5,061 | 1,648 | 7,375 | 10,167 | 7,793 |
| Honolulu, Hawaii, U. S. | 7,309 | 7,561 | 8,838 | 7,047 | 11,534 | 6,013 | 4,250 |
| Istanbul, Turkey | 1,078 | 7,611 | 768 | 3,638 | 5,154 | 6,048 | 5,477 |
| Lisbon, Portugal | 1,436 | 5,956 | 2,363 | 5,638 | 5,325 | 4,041 | 3,990 |
| London, England | 579 | 6,916 | 2,181 | 4,947 | 6,012 | 4,660 | 3,950 |
| Los Angeles, Calif., U. S. | 5,724 | 6,170 | 7,520 | 8,090 | 9,992 | 3,632 | 1,745 |
| Manila, Philippines | 6,132 | 11,051 | 5,704 | 2,203 | 7,486 | 10,620 | 8,143 |
| Mexico City, Mexico | 6,047 | 4,592 | 7,688 | 9,492 | 8,517 | 2,232 | 1,691 |
| Montreal, Canada | 3,729 | 5,615 | 5,414 | 7,607 | 7,931 | 2,449 | 744 |
| Moscow, U.S.S.R. | 1,004 | 8,376 | 1,803 | 3,321 | 6,300 | 6,173 | 4,974 |
| New York, N. Y., U. S. | 3,965 | 5,297 | 5,602 | 7,918 | 7,764 | 2,132 | 713 |
| Paris, France | 545 | 6,870 | 1,995 | 4,883 | 5,807 | 4,736 | 4,134 |
| Rio de Janeiro, Brazil | 6,220 | 1,200 | 6,146 | 9,377 | 3,773 | 2,810 | 5,296 |
| Rome, Italy | 734 | 6,929 | 1,320 | 4,482 | 5,249 | 5,196 | 4,808 |
| San Francisco, Calif., U. S. | 5,661 | 6,467 | 7,364 | 7,814 | 10,247 | 3,904 | 1,858 |
| Shanghai, China | 5,218 | 12,201 | 5,183 | 2,117 | 8,061 | 9,501 | 7,061 |
| Stockholm, Sweden | 504 | 7,808 | 2,111 | 4,195 | 6,444 | 5,420 | 4,278 |
| Sydney, Australia | 10,006 | 7,330 | 8,952 | 5,685 | 6,843 | 9,513 | 9,272 |
| Tokyo, Japan | 5,540 | 11,408 | 5,935 | 3,194 | 9,156 | 8,799 | 6,299 |
| Warsaw, Poland | 320 | 7,662 | 1,630 | 4,048 | 5,958 | 5,517 | 4,667 |
| Washington, D. C., U. S. | 4,169 | 5,218 | 5,800 | 8,084 | 7,901 | 2,059 | 597 |

| Cities | Hong Kong | Honolulu | Istanbul | Lisbon | London | Los Angeles | Manila |
|---|---|---|---|---|---|---|---|
| Berlin, Germany | 5,440 | 7,309 | 1,078 | 1,436 | 579 | 5,724 | 6,132 |
| Buenos Aires, Argentina | 11,472 | 7,561 | 7,611 | 5,956 | 6,916 | 6,170 | 11,051 |
| Cairo, Egypt | 5,061 | 8,838 | 768 | 2,363 | 2,181 | 7,520 | 5,704 |
| Calcutta, India | 1,648 | 7,047 | 3,638 | 5,638 | 4,947 | 8,090 | 2,203 |
| Capetown, South Africa | 7,375 | 11,534 | 5,154 | 5,325 | 6,012 | 9,992 | 7,486 |
| Caracas, Venezuela | 10,167 | 6,013 | 6,048 | 4,041 | 4,660 | 3,632 | 10,620 |
| Chicago, Ill., U. S. | 7,793 | 4,250 | 5,477 | 3,990 | 3,950 | 1,745 | 8,143 |
| Hong Kong (Victoria) | .... | 5,549 | 4,984 | 6,853 | 5,982 | 7,195 | 693 |
| Honolulu, Hawaii, U. S. | 5,549 | .... | 8,109 | 7,820 | 7,228 | 2,574 | 5,299 |
| Istanbul, Turkey | 4,984 | 8,109 | .... | 2,012 | 1,552 | 6,783 | 5,664 |
| Lisbon, Portugal | 6,853 | 7,820 | 2,012 | .... | 985 | 5,621 | 7,546 |
| London, England | 5,982 | 7,228 | 1,552 | 985 | .... | 5,382 | 6,672 |
| Los Angeles, Calif., U. S. | 7,195 | 2,574 | 6,783 | 5,621 | 5,382 | .... | 7,261 |
| Manila, Philippines | 693 | 5,299 | 5,664 | 7,546 | 6,672 | 7,261 | .... |
| Mexico City, Mexico | 8,782 | 3,779 | 7,110 | 5,390 | 5,550 | 1,546 | 8,835 |
| Montreal, Canada | 7,729 | 4,910 | 4,789 | 3,246 | 3,282 | 2,427 | 8,186 |
| Moscow, U.S.S.R. | 4,439 | 7,037 | 1,091 | 2,427 | 1,555 | 6,003 | 5,131 |
| New York, N. Y., U. S. | 8,054 | 4,964 | 4,975 | 3,364 | 3,458 | 2,451 | 8,498 |
| Paris, France | 5,985 | 7,438 | 1,400 | 904 | 213 | 5,588 | 6,677 |
| Rio de Janeiro, Brazil | 11,021 | 8,285 | 6,389 | 4,796 | 5,766 | 6,331 | 11,259 |
| Rome, Italy | 5,768 | 8,022 | 843 | 1,161 | 887 | 6,732 | 6,457 |
| San Francisco, Calif., U. S. | 6,897 | 2,393 | 6,703 | 5,666 | 5,357 | 347 | 6,967 |
| Shanghai, China | 764 | 4,941 | 4,962 | 6,654 | 5,715 | 6,438 | 1,150 |
| Stockholm, Sweden | 5,113 | 6,862 | 1,348 | 1,856 | 890 | 5,454 | 5,797 |
| Sydney, Australia | 4,584 | 5,073 | 9,294 | 11,302 | 10,564 | 7,530 | 3,944 |
| Tokyo, Japan | 1,794 | 3,853 | 5,560 | 6,915 | 5,940 | 5,433 | 1,866 |
| Warsaw, Poland | 5,144 | 7,355 | 863 | 1,715 | 899 | 5,922 | 5,837 |
| Washington, D. C., U. S. | 8,147 | 4,519 | 5,215 | 3,562 | 3,663 | 2,300 | 8,562 |

# Air Distances Between World Cities
Source: *Encyclopaedia Britannica.*

| Cities | Mexico City | Montreal | Moscow | New York | Paris | Rio de Janeiro | Rome |
|---|---|---|---|---|---|---|---|
| Berlin, Germany | 6,047 | 3,729 | 1,004 | 3,965 | 545 | 6,220 | 734 |
| Buenos Aires, Argentina | 4,592 | 5,615 | 8,376 | 5,297 | 6,870 | 1,200 | 6,929 |
| Cairo, Egypt | 7,688 | 5,414 | 1,803 | 5,602 | 1,995 | 6,146 | 1,320 |
| Calcutta, India | 9,492 | 7,607 | 3,321 | 7,918 | 4,883 | 9,377 | 4,482 |
| Capetown, South Africa | 8,517 | 7,931 | 6,300 | 7,764 | 5,807 | 3,773 | 5,249 |
| Caracas, Venezuela | 2,232 | 2,449 | 6,173 | 2,132 | 4,736 | 2,810 | 5,196 |
| Chicago, Ill., U. S. | 1,691 | 744 | 4,974 | 713 | 4,134 | 5,296 | 4,808 |
| Hong Kong (Victoria) | 8,782 | 7,729 | 4,439 | 8,054 | 5,985 | 11,021 | 5,768 |
| Honolulu, Hawaii, U. S. | 3,779 | 4,910 | 7,037 | 4,964 | 7,438 | 8,285 | 8,022 |
| Istanbul, Turkey | 7,110 | 4,789 | 1,091 | 4,975 | 1,400 | 6,389 | 843 |
| Lisbon, Portugal | 5,390 | 3,246 | 2,427 | 3,364 | 904 | 4,796 | 1,161 |
| London, England | 5,550 | 3,282 | 1,555 | 3,458 | 213 | 5,766 | 887 |
| Los Angeles, Calif., U. S. | 1,546 | 2,427 | 6,003 | 2,451 | 5,588 | 6,331 | 6,732 |
| Manila, Philippines | 8,835 | 8,186 | 5,131 | 8,498 | 6,677 | 11,259 | 6,457 |
| Mexico City, Mexico | .... | 2,318 | 6,663 | 2,094 | 5,716 | 4,771 | 6,366 |
| Montreal, Canada | 2,318 | .... | 4,386 | 320 | 3,422 | 5,097 | 4,080 |
| Moscow, U.S.S.R. | 6,663 | 4,386 | .... | 4,665 | 1,544 | 7,175 | 1,474 |
| New York, N. Y., U. S. | 2,094 | 320 | 4,665 | .... | 3,624 | 4,817 | 4,281 |
| Paris, France | 5,716 | 3,422 | 1,544 | 3,624 | .... | 5,699 | 697 |
| Rio de Janeiro, Brazil | 4,771 | 5,097 | 7,175 | 4,817 | 5,699 | .... | 5,684 |
| Rome, Italy | 6,366 | 4,080 | 1,474 | 4,281 | 697 | 5,684 | .... |
| San Francisco, Calif., U. S. | 1,887 | 2,539 | 5,871 | 2,571 | 5,558 | 6,621 | 6,240 |
| Shanghai, China | 8,022 | 7,053 | 4,235 | 7,371 | 5,754 | 11,336 | 5,677 |
| Stockholm, Sweden | 5,959 | 3,667 | 762 | 3,924 | 958 | 6,651 | 1,234 |
| Sydney, Australia | 8,052 | 9,954 | 9,012 | 9,933 | 10,544 | 8,306 | 10,136 |
| Tokyo, Japan | 7,021 | 6,383 | 4,647 | 6,740 | 6,034 | 11,533 | 6,135 |
| Warsaw, Poland | 6,365 | 4,009 | 715 | 4,344 | 849 | 6,467 | 817 |
| Washington, D. C., U. S. | 1,887 | 488 | 4,858 | 205 | 3,829 | 4,796 | 4,434 |

| Cities | San Francisco | Shanghai | Stockholm | Sydney | Tokyo | Warsaw | Washington |
|---|---|---|---|---|---|---|---|
| Berlin, Germany | 5,661 | 5,218 | 504 | 10,006 | 5,540 | 320 | 4,169 |
| Buenos Aires, Argentina | 6,467 | 12,201 | 7,808 | 7,330 | 11,408 | 7,662 | 5,218 |
| Cairo, Egypt | 7,364 | 5,183 | 2,111 | 8,952 | 5,935 | 1,630 | 5,800 |
| Calcutta, India | 7,814 | 2,117 | 4,195 | 5,685 | 3,194 | 4,048 | 8,084 |
| Capetown, South Africa | 10,247 | 8,061 | 6,444 | 6,843 | 9,156 | 5,958 | 7,901 |
| Caracas, Venezuela | 3,904 | 9,501 | 5,420 | 9,513 | 8,799 | 5,517 | 2,059 |
| Chicago, Ill., U. S. | 1,858 | 7,061 | 4,278 | 9,272 | 6,299 | 4,667 | 597 |
| Hong Kong (Victoria) | 6,897 | 764 | 5,113 | 4,584 | 1,794 | 5,144 | 8,147 |
| Honolulu, Hawaii, U. S. | 2,393 | 4,941 | 6,862 | 5,073 | 3,853 | 7,355 | 4,519 |
| Istanbul, Turkey | 6,703 | 4,962 | 1,348 | 9,294 | 5,560 | 863 | 5,215 |
| Lisbon, Portugal | 5,666 | 6,654 | 1,856 | 11,302 | 6,915 | 1,715 | 3,562 |
| London, England | 5,357 | 5,715 | 890 | 10,564 | 5,940 | 899 | 3,663 |
| Los Angeles, Calif., U. S. | 347 | 6,438 | 5,454 | 7,530 | 5,433 | 5,922 | 2,300 |
| Manila, Philippines | 6,967 | 1,150 | 5,797 | 3,944 | 1,866 | 5,837 | 8,562 |
| Mexico City, Mexico | 1,887 | 8,022 | 5,959 | 8,052 | 7,021 | 6,365 | 1,887 |
| Montreal, Canada | 2,539 | 7,053 | 3,667 | 9,954 | 6,383 | 4,009 | 488 |
| Moscow, U.S.S.R. | 5,871 | 4,235 | 762 | 9,012 | 4,647 | 715 | 4,858 |
| New York, N. Y., U. S. | 2,571 | 7,371 | 3,924 | 9,933 | 6,740 | 4,344 | 205 |
| Paris, France | 5,558 | 5,754 | 958 | 10,544 | 6,034 | 849 | 3,829 |
| Rio de Janeiro, Brazil | 6,621 | 11,336 | 6,651 | 8,306 | 11,533 | 6,467 | 4,796 |
| Rome, Italy | 6,240 | 5,677 | 1,234 | 10,136 | 6,135 | 817 | 4,434 |
| San Francisco, Calif., U. S. | .... | 6,140 | 5,361 | 7,416 | 5,135 | 5,841 | 2,442 |
| Shanghai, China | 6,140 | .... | 4,825 | 4,899 | 1,097 | 4,951 | 7,448 |
| Stockholm, Sweden | 5,361 | 4,825 | .... | 9,696 | 5,051 | 501 | 4,123 |
| Sydney, Australia | 7,416 | 4,899 | 9,696 | .... | 4,866 | 9,696 | 9,758 |
| Tokyo, Japan | 5,135 | 1,097 | 5,051 | 4,866 | .... | 5,249 | 6,772 |
| Warsaw, Poland | 5,841 | 4,951 | 501 | 9,696 | 5,249 | .... | 4,457 |
| Washington, D. C., U. S. | 2,442 | 7,448 | 4,123 | 9,758 | 6,772 | 4,457 | .... |

# PARLIAMENTARY PROCEDURE

*by*

Dan Golenpaul

Parliamentary procedures are rules for the conduct of a meeting in an orderly and democratic manner. Their purpose is to ensure the rule by a majority and to protect the rights of all members of an organization or assembly in meetings and in connection with all activities of the organization. The application of parliamentary rules is solely for this purpose.

Very often, though, individuals employ the rules for a contest of wits. This practice can be interesting and the life of the meeting, but it can also be a nuisance and a field day for parliamentary pests. The degree to which this activity may be tolerated should be dictated by circumstances. A certain amount of indulgence may be necessary because it is part of the game and is inevitably an expression of many egos that meet in a group.

Under no circumstances, however, should a chairman or members permit anyone to use the rules of procedure to trick and confuse members or to impede the function of a meeting. To prevent these occurrences, a knowledge of parliamentary rules is important. We will do our best in the limited space permitted to impart a little learning. (But remember, a little learning is a dangerous thing.) What we are setting forth here should be adequate to take care of most situations in organizations made up of friendly people who want to conduct their business in an orderly, friendly manner.

If it is necessary for you to be a member of a group that is involved in bitter conflicts, then we advise that you go to more technical and authoritative works on parliamentary procedure such as *Robert's Rules of Order, Cushing's Manual, Sturgis' Standard Code of Parliamentary Procedure* and others. We also suggest that you go to the meetings with a good lawyer and a baseball bat.

## HOW TO FORM AN ORGANIZATION

People form or join organizations because they have a common interest or purpose that can best be advanced and attained through group activity. Whether the character of the organization be social, political, educational, communal, fraternal or athletic, its purpose and government are usually expressed in by-laws. They are not required to be elaborate, technical or legal.

## BY-LAWS

By-laws should simply state the objects of the organization, the rights and duties of members, the qualifications of members, the number required to constitute a quorum, the dues, the necessary governing officers and how they should be elected, their terms of office, when meetings should be held and where, the order of business and, in the case of large and impersonal organizations, an authority for settling parliamentary disputes. (An organization usually adopts as its guide such works as mentioned heretofore.)

## FIRST MEETING

At the first meeting of a group, temporary officers are chosen: a chairman, a secretary and a committee to prepare a draft of by-laws. The meeting is called to order by the member of the group who has assumed the leadership in the formation of the organization. He or she opens the meeting by the simple statement: "I now call the meeting to order," and asks the members to make nominations for chairman. When this announcement is made, members may ask for the floor by raising their hands, and, when recognized, offer a name in nomination. The person presiding can be nominated as can any other member present. Nominations require no seconding. A majority vote is necessary for the election of the chairman. The same procedure is required for the secretary and committee on by-laws.

The officers selected at the first meeting may serve until the next meeting or for a limited period, to be decided by a majority vote of the members present.

## SECOND MEETING

At the second meeting, the report of the committee on by-laws is presented to the membership. The entire report may be accepted by a motion to adopt the report. A two-thirds vote is required. If the entire report is not acceptable to the membership, each provision may be considered separately; consideration consists of debating, amending, accepting or rejecting. The vote required on each provision is two-thirds of the membership present instead of the usual majority. Because by-laws are the fundamental basis of the organization, they should be acceptable to as many members as possible.

By-laws can be amended at any time during the life of the organization. Any proposals for changes in the by-laws require prior notice in writing to the entire membership before acting upon the proposed amendments at any meeting.

## ELECTION OF OFFICERS

With the adoption of the by-laws providing for the type of officers for the organization, and the length of their terms, the organization proceeds to elect such officers. The usual officers for most groups are a president, vice-president, recording secretary, corresponding secretary, treasurer, sergeant at arms, and committees. Some have an executive secretary, a paid job, but an organization would have to be large to warrant a paid official.

All members are eligible for office when an organization is first formed. But later the by-laws may require a certain minimum period of membership as a qualification to hold office. Nominations are made by the simple statement: "I nominate so-and-so." The nominations do not require a second and a majority vote is necessary for election.

## DUTIES OF OFFICERS

**President:** The president, as in government, is top man in an organization. Some organizations call this official "chairman." President sounds better, and is more appropriate when he performs not only the functions of presiding at meetings, but other duties in directing the organization. Chairman is the proper designation for one elected only to preside at a meeting.

Their duties as presiding officers are identical, regardless of title; they call the meeting to order, then present the order of business which the meeting is to act upon. They recognize members who desire the floor for a proposal or a discussion. They are supposed to see that everyone who wishes to speak has the opportunity, and to do as little talking themselves as possible. The presiding officer has the right to take part in a discussion. When he does, the vice-chairman should take the chair until the presiding officer has concluded his talk.

A chairman is really a moderator who directs, controls and regulates proceedings. He is neither a boss nor an antagonist and is not to be regarded as such by the members. It is the chairman's primary job to keep the meetings moving smoothly. He should prevent members from abusing their privileges without interference, but should not curb their rights. The chair must entertain all motions that are seconded and must restate them for the members. He must call for a vote on motions and declare the motion adopted or defeated on the basis of the vote. He should allow for a re-count or a roll call whenever requested to do so. When referring to himself, the presiding officer usually says: "The chair recognizes Mr. Blank" instead of "I recognize Mr. Blank."

The president or permanent chairman is usually an ex-officio member of all committees. Although he is not obligated to attend all meetings, he may if he so desires.

**Secretary:** The duties of a secretary are to keep the records of the organization, to record the minutes of the meetings, to handle the correspondence (unless the organization is large enough to require a corresponding secretary), such as notifying members of regular meetings or of a special meeting, reading the minutes at the meeting, etc.

The minutes of a secretary should indicate when the meeting was held, where it took place, who presided, what business was transacted, when the meeting adjourned, etc.

**Treasurer:** The treasurer's duties are to handle the funds of the organization, to collect the dues, to pay the bills when authorized, to keep the books for the organization with records of income and expenditures, and to render reports on finances at the regular meetings.

Sergeant-at-Arms: The duties of the sergeant-at-arms are to assist the chairman in preserving order among the people present at a meeting, members and visitors, to act as a sort of usher by checking people at the door to see that only those entitled to be present at the meeting are admitted, and to escort anyone out if requested to do so by the chairman.

## COMMITTEES

The purpose of committees is to expedite the transaction of business on matters that require more time than the meeting permits, or on matters that require time for investigation and special study. Committees are essential in a large organization, but are really not necessary for a small group that can handle its limited business at the regular membership meetings.

The types of committee may vary according to the needs of an organization. A "standing" committee has a fixed term of office and gives continuous service. A "special" committee serves temporarily to investigate and report on some special project or condition.

The top committee in most organizations is the executive committee, sometimes made up of the chairmen of the various committees, sometimes selected from the general membership. Other committees are: membership committees, athletic committees, education committees, social or house committees, committees on finance, temporary committees to deal with a temporary specific problem, etc.

Committees may be appointed by the presiding officer, or be elected by the group, depending upon the by-laws. We think it best for committees to be elected by the membership. The chairman of the committee is either designated by the presiding officer, elected by the committee, or is the person obtaining the most votes in the election. Committees should consist of an odd number of members to assure a majority vote and a minimum of stalemates. As far as possible, the by-laws governing the conduct of a meeting or organization govern the committees as well.

Most committees are usually made up of small groups and, therefore, their meetings are less formal than regular organization meetings. Motions do not require seconding, speeches are not as restricted and limited, and the chairman attending the committee, or the president of the organization, if attending the committee meeting, participates in the discussions on a par with the other members.

Providing for numerous officers is a good thing because it distributes responsibility among more members. This is important to keep in mind in connection with committees; while good people should be placed on many committees, it is best and advisable to have as many members on committees as possible.

The committee chairman reports for the committee to the general membership meeting. Reports of the committee may consist only of information requiring no action or may contain recommendations for certain action which is often the equivalent of a proposed motion.

When there is a difference of opinion among committee members, the majority report offered is considered the committee report. The dissenting members have the right, however, to submit a minority report proposing a different course of action. Both reports must be heard or read at the same meeting. No action on the majority report is in order until the minority report is disposed of. It can be disposed of in either of two ways. (a) Any member may object to consideration of the minority report and such objection must be voted on immediately without debate. If carried, the minority report is dropped. (b) If the objection to consideration is not upheld, then a motion to substitute the minority report for the majority report is in order. If this motion is carried, the majority report is eliminated and the minority report becomes the committee report and is the only report before the body. If the motion to substitute is not carried, then the meeting proceeds to deal with the majority report.

It is well to bear in mind that any report or motion belongs to the membership.

If they are not satisfied with either report, they can dissolve the committee and act directly from the floor or appoint a new committee.

The chairman of the committee calls the meetings of the committee. If he fails or refuses to do so, or if he is absent, any two members of the committee may call a meeting. The chairman of a committee usually acts as its secretary.

If a committee fails to render a report on a matter referred to it within a reasonable time, the membership may force it to do so by drawing up a petition bearing the number of signatures required in the by-laws. This is called discharging a committee.

## ORDER OF BUSINESS

The chairman calls the meeting to order. He must determine whether a quorum is present. The number of members required to constitute a quorum is stipulated in the by-laws, usually one more than half of the membership, or as low as one-tenth of the membership. Without a quorum, business cannot be legally conducted. The secretary reads the minutes of the previous meeting and they are adopted, perhaps with corrections, or as read. Officers and committees make any reports they have. Old business left over from the previous meeting is transacted. New business is brought up, discussed and acted upon. At the close, the chairman says that he will entertain a motion for adjournment.

## RULES OF DEBATE

The presiding officers should first recognize the mover of a proposal, or the member of a committee presenting a report, and should try to alternate recognition between those favoring and those opposing a proposition. Any member is entitled to speak on the main question and on each amendment as presented. He must confine himself to the question under consideration, must avoid personalities, and must not accuse others of ill motives. In some groups the by-laws limit each speaker to a fixed number of minutes. The meeting may vote to extend the time of a speaker if it so desires. Debate can only be halted by a motion for the previous question and a two-thirds vote is required.

## VOTING RULES

There are several methods of taking a vote. The simplest is by voice—"ayes" and "noes." This may be challenged by any member who thinks that the chairman did not hear correctly, in which case the vote is taken by a show of hands, or by standing. Roll call votes, recorded by the secretary, are required in some instances. The closed ballot (written votes) also is commonly used, especially in the election of officers. Only attending members may vote, unless the by-laws specifically permit proxy voting. A tie vote defeats a motion. The chairman is allowed to break a tie, though, if he has not previously voted. Some organizations permit a chairman to vote only in case of a tie, while others allow him to vote as a regular member.

A majority vote is generally required to pass ordinary motions or to adopt ordinary actions. There are certain motions which require a two-thirds vote of those present. These generally include the following: amendments to the by-laws, to take up a question out of its proper order, to suspend the rules, to support an objection to the consideration of a question, to take up the previous question, to limit debate, to expel a member or officer, to discharge a committee, or to refer back to a committee. No vote can be made unanimous if even one member present objects.

## WHAT HAPPENS TO A MOTION

A motion is a proposal for action by an organization. It is made by any member who asks the chair for the floor and is properly recognized. Most motions require a second before being placed before the group. Not more than one main motion may be considered at a time. The procedure is simple. One merely says, "I move the following." The chairman then asks if anyone seconds the motion. If it is properly seconded, the chairman announces that a motion has been made and seconded, calls for a discussion and repeats the motion on request. A motion may be voted on without discussion, but discussion is required if requested by any member.

A motion causes many things to happen. It provokes debate, suggests modifications, clarifies the thinking and expresses the will of the group on a question. Once a motion is presented to the membership, it belongs to them to treat and dispose of in any one of several ways and can only be withdrawn with the consent of the membership.

**A motion may be amended.** This means that the motion may be modified or qualified by adding, substituting, or eliminating words or whole paragraphs. **These changes must be relevant to the main motion.**

For example, a motion is made for the organization to publish a magazine and stipulates (a) the publication to be a monthly, (b) to have two editors, (c) to cost the members $1.00 a year, etc. This motion may be amended as follows: (a) to substitute "weekly" for "monthly," (b) to provide salaries for the two editors, (c) to eliminate the dollar charge for the magazine. All these amendments are in order because while the original motion has been amplified or qualified by the amendments, the proposal for publishing a magazine still prevails.

Amendments that are irrelevant are not permissible, such as an amendment requiring the editors to watch television. This is improper (perhaps for other reasons) because it is extraneous to the main question of proposing the publication of a magazine.

Amendments that negate the purpose of the motion, such as a proposal that the organization should not publish a magazine, are out of order because if the membership is entirely opposed to the idea, it can vote against the main motion or dismiss it in other parliamentary ways.

Other important rules governing amendments are:

1. There is no limit to the number of amendments that may be offered, but each amendment must be disposed of before a new one may be proposed.

2. After all amendments have been acted on, the meeting votes on the main motion, and all of the adopted amendments are incorporated in the main motion.

3. All amendments require a majority vote for passage.

4. A rejected amendment may not be resubmitted in identical form and no amendment may be offered reversing an amendment previously adopted.

This is not all that can happen to a motion. In addition to amendments to the motion, you are also permitted to make amendments to the amendments. For example, the original motion stipulates that the magazine should have two editors. An amendment provides that the editors be paid salaries. This amendment can be amended to provide what the salary should be.

Now, if you are thinking of whether you can amend the amendment to the amendment, the answer is "No." Although this has really gone far enough, there is something else you are allowed to do, for better or worse, and that is to introduce a substitute for the motion itself or for any of the amendments or for everything that has been proposed on the question. The substitute for an amendment does not modify the amendment, but replaces it and is subject to the same rules that apply to amendments.

When amendments pile up to the point of confusing the membership, resorting to a substitute for the entire proposition may be helpful. The best way to do this, under the circumstances, is for someone to move to have a special committee designated to prepare a substitute motion for the whole.

If the motion is adopted, the committee-elect should withdraw from the meeting to try to reconcile any contradictions contained in the motion or the amendments. It should bring forth a clear substitute that expresses the intentions of most of the proposals.

Let us not lose sight of the fact that the purpose of a motion is not to create an endless chain of acts, but to get something done. In this connection, it is well to bear in mind that the motion and amendments do not necessarily conflict and that the proposer of a motion may accept the amendments without discussion or vote.

**Motions that cannot be amended:** These include such motions as questions of order or appeal, objections to consideration of the question, or motions to adjourn, to call for the order of the day, to vote, to withdraw a motion, to take up a question out of proper order, to suspend the rules, to table, to take from the table, to reconsider, to consider the previous question, to postpone indefinitely, to amend an amendment, or to nominate. Motions to postpone indefinitely, to limit debate, or to recess can be amended as to time only.

## DELAYING OR CANCELING CONSIDERATION OF A MOTION

It is not binding on a meeting to deal with a motion at the time it is proposed. On the contrary, the membership has the choice of postponing or renewing consideration of a motion. Here are some of the ways to attain such objectives.

**Objection to consideration:** Consideration of any issue may be stopped before discussion begins on the question, even though it involves interrupting the speaker, by objecting to its consideration. This objection may be made by any member and does not require a second. Objection to consideration calls for an immediate vote without debate or amendment and requires a two-thirds vote. If carried, the motion is dropped for all time. The purpose of the act is to prevent the meeting from dealing with a question that may be offensive. This reason should be primary. Other reasons may be that it might waste the time of the meeting or it may be inappropriate to deal with the question at the time. This action is very drastic and should not be employed to gag any member except the village idiot at his worst.

**Motion to postpone indefinitely:** This is a polite way of killing a motion, at least for the moment. It differs from "Objection to consideration" insofar as the motion to postpone indefinitely and the motion itself are debatable and cannot be made while a member has the floor. This motion requires a second and calls for a majority vote. It cannot be amended and cannot be brought up again.

**Motion to "lay on the table":** If the meeting does not want to consider the motion at all, the procedure is to make a motion to "lay the question on the table." This suspends consideration of the main motion and amendments until such time as the group chooses to take it up again, which can be later at the same meeting after other business has been transacted or at any subsequent meeting. This motion must be seconded, requires a majority vote, may not be debated or amended or postponed. The only way to bring the motion back is to move to "take it off the table."

**Motion to postpone to a definite date:** This is an expression of the will of the meeting to put off consideration of the proposal until later in the same session or until a subsequent meeting. The object of such an act is to delay consideration of the question until more members are present, or to enable members to acquire further information before making their decisions. This motion is debatable only as to the advisability of postponement. The subject matter of the motion is not debatable. It is open for amendment as to time only and requires a majority vote.

**Motion to refer to a committee:** This is usually done if a meeting feels that a question requires more time and information before it acts upon it. A motion to refer to a committee names an existing committee or creates a special committee for its consideration and may be accompanied by instructions. Seconding and a majority vote are required for passage of this motion. It can be debated only as to the desirability and advisability of referring it to the committee. It can be amended only as to the nature of the committee and as to the instructions.

## HOW TO REOPEN A QUESTION

To avoid finality of decisions that may be harmful to the best interests of the members, certain actions previously taken by the members are subject to review by them. Such review may apply to matters acted upon, matters postponed, or matters delegated to committees.

**Motion to reconsider:** This deals with something acted upon by a meeting which the members would like to reconsider at another time during the same meeting. It is a motion that should be made by one who has voted with the majority, whether in the affirmative or the negative, and is made because the voter has changed his mind on the matter in the light of new information. Very often a member deliberately votes for or against motions so that he can move for reconsideration of the subject later in the meeting when there may be a better chance for passing or defeating the motion because more members are present, or because he will have an opportunity to persuade other members to change their votes. This is both good parliamentary procedure and democratic.

A motion to reconsider requires a second, a majority vote, is debatable and cannot be renewed. If a motion to reconsider is carried, the question is before the assembly with its original parliamentary status. Motions that cannot be reconsidered include: motions to take from the table, to lay on the table, or a motion for indefinite postponement that has been defeated.

**To take from the table:** This motion allows a group to take up a subject that was set aside by a motion to table it at a previous meeting. This resumption of consideration on a question rates priority over any new motions and can be introduced when there is no other business before the body. Motion to take a question from the table requires a second and a majority vote, is not debatable and cannot be amended.

**A motion to rescind:** This motion enables the membership to re-evaluate some action taken in the past because it may have been adopted without full understanding of the consequences at that time. The point of rescinding a previous act of an organization does not apply to any legally binding act committing the organization, nor to the election of members or officers. This motion calls for a second and majority vote unless the original motion involved required a two-thirds vote. It is debatable and cannot be amended.

Several important techniques for keeping informed about proceedings, preventing violations and protecting the rights of members, correcting errors, and expediting the business at hand, are:

**Moving the Previous Question:** This asks that the discussion be stopped at once on any motion before the body. A move for the previous question cannot interrupt the speaker. It requires a second, is not de-

batable, cannot be amended, and requires a two-thirds vote. Its purpose is to say "Let's stop talking and vote."

**Point of Information:** This is a method of obtaining information about what is occurring through the medium of the chairman or the speaker. This interruption request is permissible even when one is speaking. It is unusual for the speaker or the chair to ignore such a request. Since it is intended only to secure information, it is not proper to use this as a device to make a statement or delay proceedings.

**Point of Order:** This questions the correctness of any action at the time it occurs. The only time that a point of order can be employed *after* an action has taken place is if it involves a violation of by-laws, constitution, or the law. It is raised on the basis of a mistake or omission in procedure, of a violation of the rules of the organization, of decorum in debate, or of irrelevancy of debate and procedure. A point of order needs no seconding, cannot be amended and requires no vote.

A point of order may be raised by any member at any time. It is in the nature of a demand addressed to the chair, which is required to act immediately on the point of order raised. The procedure is as follows: A member announces, "I rise to a point of order." This automatically halts any discussion or action until the chairman rules on the point of order. If the chairman concurs, he announces that the point of order was well taken, and proceeds to correct whatever is in question.

**Appeal:** If any other member takes exception to this ruling, he may appeal from the decision of the chair. Another basis for an appeal may result when the chair declares the point of order not well taken. This appeal is usually made by the person raising the point of order. All appeals require a second, are debatable and are subject to a majority vote of the membership. If they vote for the appeal, the chairman's decision is reversed. If they vote against the appeal, the chairman's decision is upheld. In the event of a tie vote, the chairman is sustained. If the chairman is a member of the organization, he has the right to vote and may make the tie.

Discussions on some appeals are not customary, such as questions of indecorum, violation of rules of speaking, or order of business.

Sometimes the chairman is in doubt on a point of order. When he is, he may defer to someone present for advice, or ask the members to discuss and vote on the point of order. This is the only time that a point of order is debatable. Their vote determines the chairman's decision.

**Motion to adjourn:** This motion is in order at any time, but should be employed with discretion. Obviously, it should not interfere with the organization's efforts to get business done. This motion requires a second, is not debatable, cannot be amended, and must be voted on immediately. A majority vote is necessary. Any motion for adjournment that refers to a specific time or place for the next meeting is subject to debate and amendment.

We have tried to project the reader into actual participation in the forming of an organization and the conduct of a meeting, and we have given more attention to the processes than to the discussion of technical rules. In following this course, we may have omitted some matters that do not occur at every meeting, but that do happen occasionally and should be understood.

**Removal of officers:** This is sometimes an unhappy necessity. Misconduct of an officer may involve neglect of duties, abuse of privileges, or incompetence. The removal of an officer is accomplished by preferring charges which should be of a serious nature and supported by proof. The charges may be considered at a general meeting or referred to a committee to investigate and to recommend a course of action. A two-thirds vote of the members present is required to remove an officer. A motion to remove an officer is debatable.

**Expulsion of members:** If a member violates his obligations and duties or is involved in an act that may bring disrepute to the organization, he is subject to charges and a hearing before a committee or the membership and can be expelled by a two-thirds vote. This action is debatable. Obviously, such actions should not be undertaken unless the charges are serious and supported by substantial proof. It would be deplorable if the exercise of such a drastic action were based on a frivolous issue or personal bias. Sometimes the behavior of a member at a meeting requires disciplinary action in the form of a motion for immediate expulsion. This is not debatable and requires a two-thirds vote.

**Question of privilege:** A member may interrupt a meeting at any time to raise a question involving the comfort or convenience of the membership. It may concern such matters as the physical condition of the meeting hall, the seating of the members, the conduct of persons present, or the ability to hear speakers. This request requires no second, is not debatable, cannot be amended and is decided by the chair.

**Suspension of the rules:** The object of a proposal to suspend the rules is to permit a meeting to do something that is ordinarily prohibited by the rules of parliamentary procedure or by the adopted order of business. The suspension of rules is generally employed to deal with an emergency or special condition, such as permitting a guest speaker to start earlier than scheduled or allowing for the interruption of the regular order of business by a visiting committee. There are other circumstances under which the suspension of rules is permitted, but these cases are too complicated to be treated here. This motion cannot interrupt a speaker, requires a second, cannot be debated or amended, and requires a two-thirds vote.

We have endeavored to outline some of the basic rules for the benefit of the many people who want some simple knowledge of how to form an organization, how to conduct a meeting, or how to participate in one; also to help spectators at a convention understand what is going on. Beyond this, we refer you to the authorities on parliamentary procedure.

However important rules are for guidance in most human activities, there is no doubt that much is accomplished through informal discussion and action, and we do not hesitate to urge small friendly groups to do their business with as little formality and as few restrictions as possible. If this does not always work, we hope our book is there to serve you.

# CROSSWORD PUZZLE GUIDE

★

Since most persons who can read and write occasionally or frequently indulge in the indoor pastime of working crossword puzzles, this section is offered as a handy help to solvers who may be stumped for a two-letter word meaning "three-toed sloth" or a three-letter word meaning "native of Mindanao."

We have those two words here, and plenty more. We have the Greek, Roman, Norse and Egyptian deities of myth and legend. And we have those "Greek letters" and "months of the Jewish year" so often needed to fill out little gaps.

The reader is warned that in mythology there are many confusing and even conflicting accounts of the identities and adventures of the various gods, goddesses and lesser figures. There is also considerable variation in the spelling of names, places and things. For instance, you may spell it ICON, IKON or EIKON, and similar options are plentiful all along the crossword line. If the reader will keep further possible variations in mind, it may help at a critical point.

Various other sections of our book will be found of use to the crossword puzzler—especially the section of world geography and statistics. See Geography in the index.

## First Aid to Crossword Puzzlers

(We cannot, of course, begin to list all the odd words you will meet with in your daily and Sunday crossword puzzles, for such words run into many thousands. But we have tried to include those which turn up most frequently, as well as many others which should be of help to you when you are unable to go any further.

Also, we do not guarantee that the definitions in your puzzle will be exactly the same as ours, although we have checked every word with a standard dictionary and have followed its definition.

In nearly every case, we have used as the key word the principal noun of the definition, rather than any adjective, adjective phrase, or noun used as an adjective. And, to simplify your searching, we have grouped the words according to the number of spaces you have to fill.)

### Words of Two Letters

Ambary, DA
And (French, Latin), ET
Article (Arabic), AL
  (French), LA, LE, UN
  (Spanish), EL, LA, UN
At the (French), AU
  (Spanish), AL
Behold, LO
Bird: Hawaiian, OO
Birthplace: Abraham's, UR
Bone, OS
Buddha, FO
Butterfly: Peacock, IO
Champagne, AY
Chaos, NU
Chief: Burmese, BO
Coin: Roman, AS
  Siamese, AT
Concerning, RE
Dialect: Chinese, WU
Double (Egy. relig.), KA
Drama: Japanese, NO
Egg (comb. form), OO
Esker, OS
Eye (Scotch), EE
Factor: Amplification, MU
Fifty (Greek), NU
Fish: Carplike, ID
Force, OD
Forty (Greek), MU
From (French, Latin, Spanish), DE
  (Latin prefix), AB

From the (French), DU
God: Babylonian, EA, ZU
  Egyptian sun, RA
  Hindu unknown, KA
  Semitic, EL
Goddess: Babylonian, AI
  Greek earth, GE
Gold (heraldry), OR
Gulf: Arctic, OB
Heart (Egy. relig.) AB
Indian: South American, GE
King: Of Bashan, OG
Language: Artificial, RO
  Assamese, AO
Lava: Hawaiian, AA
Letter: Greek, MU, NU, PI, XI
  Hebrew, HE, PE
Lily: Palm, TI
Measure: Annamese, LY
  Chinese, HO, HU, KO, LI, MU, PU, TO, TU
  Japanese, GO, JO, MO, RI, SE, TO
  Metric land, AR
  Netherlands, EL
  Portuguese, PE
  Siamese, WA
  Swedish, AM
  Type, EM, EN
Monk: Buddhist, BO

Month: Jewish, AB
Mouth, OS
Mulberry: Indian, AL
Native: Burmese, WA
Note: Of Scale, DO, FA, MI, LA, RE, TI
Of (French, Latin, Spanish), DE
Of the (French), DU
One (Scotch), AE
Pagoda: Chinese, TA
Plant: East Indian fiber, DA
Ridge: Sandy, AS, OS
River: Russian, OB
Sloth: Three-toed, AI
Soul (Egy. relig.), BA
Sound: Hindu mystic, OM
Suffix: Comparative, ER
The. See Article
To the: French, AU
  Spanish, AL
Tree: Buddhist sacred, BO
Tribe: Assamese, AO
Type: Jumbled, PI
Weight: Annamese, TA
  Chinese, LI
  Danish, ES
  Japanese, MO
  Roman, AS
Whirlwind: Faeroe Is., OE
Yes (German), JA
  (Italian, Spanish), SI
  (Russian), DA

## Words of Three Letters

Adherent, IST
Again, BIS
Age, ERA
Antelope: African, GNU, KOB
Apricot: Japanese, UME
Article (German), DAS, DEM, DEN, DER, DES, DIE, EIN
(French), LES, UNE
(Spanish), LAS, LOS, UNA
Banana: Polynesian, FEI
Barge, HOY
Bass: African, IYO
Beak, NEB, NIB
Beard: Grain, AWN
Beetle: June, DOR
Being, ENS
Berry: Hawthorn, HAW
Beverage: Hawaiian, AVA
Bird: Australian, EMU
Crowlike, JAY
Extinct, MOA
Fabulous, ROC
Frigate, IWA
Parson, POE, TUE, TUI
Sea, AUK
Blackbird, ANI, ANO
Born, NEE
Bronze: Roman, AES
Bugle: Yellow, IVA
By way of, VIA
Canton: Swiss, URI
Cap: Turkish, FEZ
Catnip, NEP
Character: In "Faerie Queene," UNA
Coin: Afghan, PUL
Albanian, LEK
British Guiana, BIT
Bulgarian, LEV, LEW
French, ECU, SOU
Indian, PIE
Japanese, SEN, YEN
Korean, WON
Lithuanian, LIT
Macao, Timor, AVO
Palestinian, MIL
Persian, PUL
Peruvian, SOL
Rumanian, BAN, LEU, LEY
Scandinavian, ORE
Siamese, ATT
*See also* Money of account
Collection: Facts, ANA
Commune: Belgian, ANS, ATH
Netherlands, EDE, EPE
Community: Russian, MIR
Constellation: Southern, ARA
Contraction: Poetic, EEN, EER, OER
Covering: Apex of roof, EPI

Crab: Fiddler, UCA
Crag: Rocky, TOR
Cry: Crow, rook, raven, CAW
Cup: Wine, AMA
Cymbal: Oriental, TAL, ZEL
Disease: Silkworm, UJI
Division: Danish territorial, AMT
Geologic, EON
Doctrine, ISM
Dowry, DOT
Dry (French), SEC
Dynasty: Chinese, CHI, HAN, SUI, WEI, YIN
Eagle: Sea, ERN
Earth (comb. form), GEO
Egg: Louse, NIT
Eggs: Fish, ROE
Emmet, ANT
Enzyme, ASE
Equal (comb. form), ISO
Extension: building, ELL
Far (comb. form), TEL
Farewell, AVE
Fiber: Palm, TAL
Finial, EPI
Fish: Carplike, IDE
Pikelike, GAR
Flatfish, DAB
Fleur-de-lis, LIS, LYS
Food: Hawaiian, POI
Formerly, NEE
Friend (French), AMI
Game: Card, LOO
Garment: Camel-hair, ABA
Gateway, DAR
Gazelle: Tibetan, GOA
Genus: Ducks, AIX
Grasses, POA
Grasses (maize), ZEA
Herbs or shrubs, IVA
Lizards, UTA
Rodents (incl. house mice), MUS
Ruminants (incl. cattle), BOS
Swine, SUS
Gibbon: Malay, LAR
God: Assyrian, SIN
Babylonian, ABU, ANU, BEL, HEA, SIN, UTU
Irish sea, LER
Phrygian, MEN
Polynesian, ORO
Goddess: Babylonian, AYA
Etruscan, UNI
Hindu, SRI, UMA, VAC
Teutonic, RAN
Governor: Algerian, DLY
Turkish, BEY
Grampus, ORC
Grape, UVA
Grass: Meadow, POA
Gypsy, ROM
Hail, AVE
Hare: Female, DOE

Hawthorn, HAW
Hay: Spread for drying, TED
Herb: Japanese, UDO
Perennial, PIA
Used for blue dye, WAD
Herd: Whales, GAM, POD
Hero: Spanish, CID
High (music), ALT
Honey (pharm.), MEL
Humorist: American, ADE
I (Latin), EGO
I love (Latin), AMO
Indian: Algonquian, FOX, SAC, WEA
Chimakuan, HOH
Keresan, SIA
Mayan, MAM
Shoshonean, UTE
Siouan, KAW, OTO
South American, ITE, ONA, URO, URU, YAO
Tierra del Fuego, ONA
Wakashan, AHT
Ingot, PIG
Inlet: Narrow, RIA
Island: Cyclades, IOS
Dodecanese, COS, KOS
(French), ILE
River, AIT
Jackdaw, DAW
John (Gaelic), IAN
Keelbill, ANI, ANO
Kiln, OST
King: British legendary, LUD
Kobold, NIS
Lace: To make, TAT
Lamprey, EEL
Language: Artificial, IDO
Bantu, ILA
Siamese, LAO, TAI
Leaf: Palm, OLA, OLE
Leaving, ORT
Left: Cause to turn, HAW
Letter: Greek, CHI, ETA, PHI, PSI, RHO, TAU
Hebrew, MEM, NUN, SIN, TAV, VAU
Lettuce, COS
Life (comb. form), BIO
Lily: Palm, TOI
Lizard, EFT
Louse: Young NIT
Love (Anglo-Irish), GRA
Lute: Oriental, TAR
Macaw: Brazilian, ARA
Marble, TAW
Match: Shooting (French), TIR
Meadow, LEA
Measure: Abyssinian, TAT
Algerian, PIK
Annamese, GON, MAU, NGU, QUO, SAO, TAO, TAT
Arabian, DEN, SAA

Belgian, VAT
Bulgarian, OKA, OKE
Chinese, FEN, TOU, YIN
Cloth, ELL
Cyprus, OKA, OKE, PIK
Czech, LAN, SAH
Danish, FOD, MIL, POT
Dominican Republic, ONA
Dutch, old, AAM
East Indian, KIT
Egyptian, APT, HEN, PIK, ROB
Electric, MHO, OHM
Energy, ERG
English, PIN
Estonian, TUN
French, POT
German, AAM
Greek, PIK
Hebrew, CAB, HIN, KOR, LOG
Hungarian, AKO
Icelandic, FET
Indian, GAZ, GUZ, JOW, KOS
Japanese, BOO, CHO, KEN, RIN, SHO, SUN, TAN
Malabar, ADY
Metric land, ARE
Netherlands, KAN, KOP, MUD, VAT, ZAK
Norwegian, FOT, POT
Persian, GAZ, GUZ, MOU, ZAR, ZER
Polish, CAL
Rangoon, DHA, LAN
Roman, PES, URN
Russian, FUT, LOF
Scotch, COP
Siamese, KEN, NIU, RAI, SAT, SEN, SOK, WAH, YOT
Somaliland, TOP
Spanish, PIE
Straits Settlements, PAU, TUN
Swedish, ALN, FOT, MIL, REF, TUM
Swiss, POT
Tunisian, SAA
Turkish, OKA, OKE, PIK
Wire, MIL
Würtemberg, IMI
Yarn, LEA
Yugoslavian, OKA, RIF
Milk, LAC
Milkfish, AWA
Moccasin, PAC
Money: Yap stone, FEI
Money of Account: Anglo-Saxon, ORA, ORE
French, SOU
Indian, LAC
Japanese, RIN
Oman, GAJ
Virgin Islands, BIT
*See also* Coin

Monkey: Capuchin, SAI
Morsel, ORT
Mother: Peer Gynt's, ASE
Mountain: Asia Minor, IDA
Mulberry:   Indian,   AAL, ACH, AWL
Muttonbird: New Zealand, OII
Nahoor, SNA
Native: Mindanao, ATA
Neckpiece, BOA
Newt, EFT
No (Scotch), NAE
Note: Guido's highest, ELA
Of scale, SOL
Nursemaid: Oriental, AMA, IYA
Ocher: Yellow, SIL
One (Scotch), YIN
Ornament: Pagoda, TEE
Oven: Polynesian, UMU
Ox: Tibetan, YAK
Pagoda: Chinese, TAA
Parrot: Hawk, HIA
New Zealand, KEA
Part: Footlike, PES
Particle: Electrified, ION
Pasha, DEY
Pass: Mountain, COL
Paste: Rice, AME
Pea: Indian split, DAL
Peasant: Philippine, TAO
Penpoint, NEB, NIB
Piece out, EKE
Pigeon, NUN
Pine: Textile screw, ARA
Pistol (slang), GAT
Pit: Baking, IMU
Plant: Pepper, AVA
Play: By Capek, RUR
Poem: Old French, DIT
Porgy: Japanese, TAI
Priest: Biblical high, ELI
Prince: Ethiopian, RAS
Pseudonym: Dickens', BOZ
Queen: Fairy, MAB
Quince: Bengal, BEL
Record: Ship's, LOG
Refuse: Flax (Scotch), PAB, POB
Resin, LAC
Resort, SPA
Revolver (slang), GAT
Right: Cause to turn, GEE
River: Scotch or English, DEE (Spanish), RIO
Swiss, AAR
Room: Harem, ODA
Rootstock: Fern, ROI
Rose (Persian), GUL
Ruff: Female, REE
Rule: Indian, RAJ
Sailor, GOB, TAR
Saint: Female (abbr.), STE
Mohammedan, PIR
Salt, SAL
Sash: Japanese, OBI
Scrap, ORT

Seed: Poppy, MAW
Small, PIP
Self, EGO
Serpent: Vedic sky, AHI
Sesame, TIL
Sheep: Female, EWE
Indian, SHA
Male, RAM
Sheepfold (Scotch), REE
Shelter, LEE
Shield, ECU
Shooting  match  (French), TIR
Shrew: European, ERD
Shrub: Evergreen, YEW
Silkworm, ERI
Snake, ASP, BOA
Soak, RET
Son-in-law: Mohammed's, ALI
Sorrel: Wood, OCA
Spade: Long, narrow, LOY
Spirit: Malignant, KER
Spot: Playing-card, PIP
Spread for drying, TED
Spring: Mineral, SPA
Sprite: Water, NIX
Statesman: Japanese, ITO
Stern: Toward, AFT
Stomach: Bird's, MAW
Street (French), RUE
Summer (French), ETE
Sun, SOL
Swamp, BOG, FEN
Swan: Male, COB
Tea: Chinese, CHA
Temple: Shinto, SHA
The. *See* Article
Thing (law), RES
Title: Etruscan, LAR
Monk's, FRA
Portuguese, DOM
Spanish, DON
Turkish, AGA, BEY
Tool: Cutting, ADZ, AXE
Mining, GAD
Piercing, AWL
Tree: Candlenut, AMA
Central American, EBO
East Indian, SAJ, SAL
Evergreen, YEW
Hawaiian, KOA, KOU
Indian, BEL, DAR
Linden, LIN
New Zealand, AKE
Philippine,   DAO,   TUA, TUI
Rubber, ULE
South American, APA
Tribe: New Zealand, ATI
Turmeric, REA
Twice, BIS
Twin: Siamese, ENG
Uncle (dialect), EAM, EME
Veil: Chalice, AER, AIR
Vessel: Wine, AMA
Vestment: Ecclesiastical, ALB

Vetch: Bitter, ERS
Victorfish, AKU
Vine: New Zealand, AKA
    Philippine, IYO
Wallaba, APA
Wapiti, ELK
Water (French), EAU
Waterfall, LIN
Watering place: Prussian,
    EMS
Weave: Designating plain,
    UNI
Weight: Annamese, CAN
    Bulgarian, OKA, OKE
    Burmese, MOO, VIS
    Chinese, FEN, HAO, KIN,
    SSU, TAN, YIN

Cyprus, OKA, OKE
Danish, LOD, ORT, VOG
East Indian, TJI
Egyptian, KAT, OKA, OKE
English, for wool, TOD
German, LOT
Greek, MNA, OKA, OKE
Indian, SER
Japanese, FUN, KIN, RIN,
    SHI
Korean, KON
Malacca, KIP
Mongolian, LAN
Netherlands, ONS
Norwegian, LOD
Polish, LUT
Rangoon, PAI
Roman, BES

Russian, LOT
Siamese, BAT, HAP, PAI
Swedish, ASS, ORT
Turkish, OKA, OKE
Yugoslavian, OKA, OKE
Whales: Herd, GAM, POD
Wildebeest, GNU
Wing, ALA
Witticism, MOT
Wolframite, CAL
Worm: African, LOA
Wreath: Hawaiian, LEI
Yale, ELI
Yam: Hawaiian, HOI
Yes (French), OUI
Young: Bring forth, EAN
Z (letter), ZED

## Words of Four Letters

Aborigine: Borneo, DYAK
Agave, ALOE
Animal: Footless, APOD
Ant: White, ANAI, ANAY
Antelope: African, ASSE,
    BISA, GUIB, KOBA,
    KUDU, ORYX, POKU,
    PUKU, TOPI, TORA
Apoplexy: Plant, ESCA
Apple, POME
Apricot, ANSU
Ardor, ELAN
Armadillo, APAR, PEBA,
    PEVA, TATU
Ascetic: Mohammedan,
    SUFI
Association: Chinese, TONG
Astronomer: Persian, OMAR
Avatar: Of Vishnu, RAMA
Axillary, ALAR
Band: Horizontal (heral-
    dry), FESS
Barracuda, SPET
Bark: Mulberry, TAPA
Base: Column, DADO
Bearing (heraldry), ORLE
Beer: Russian, KVAS
Beige, ECRU
Being, ESSE
Beverage: Japanese rice,
    SAKE
Bird: Asian, MINA, MYNA
    Egyptian sacred, IBIS
    Extinct, DODO, MAMO
    Flightless, KIWI
    Gull-like, TERN
    Hawaiian, IIWI, MAMO
    Parson, KOKO
    Unfledged, EYAS
Birds: As class, AVES
Black, EBON
    (French), NOIR
Blackbird: European, MERL
Boat: Flat-bottomed, DORY
Bone: Forearm, ULNA
Bones, OSSA
Box: Japanese, INRO
Bravo (rare), EUGE

Buffalo: Indian wild, ARNA
Bull (Spanish), TORO
Burden, ONUS
Cabbage: Sliced, SLAW
Caliph: Mohammedan,
    OMAR
Canoe: Malay, PRAU, PROA
Cap: Military, KEPI
Cape, NESS
Capital: Ancient Irish,
    TARA
Case: Article, ETUI
Cat: Wild, BALU, EYRA
Chalcedony, SARD
Chamber: Indian ceremo-
    nial, KIVA
Channel: Brain, ITER
Cheese: Dutch, EDAM
Chest: Sepulchral stone,
    CIST
Chieftain: Arab, EMIR
Church: Part of, APSE,
    NAVE
    (Scotch), KIRK
Claim (law), LIEN
Cluster: Flower, CYME
Coin: Chinese, TAEL, YUAN
    German, MARK
    Indian, ANNA
    Iranian, RIAL
    Italian, LIRA
    Moroccan, OKIA
    Siamese, BAHT
    South American, PESO
    Spanish, DURO, PESO
    Turkish, PARA
Commune: Belgian, AATH
Composition: Musical,
    OPUS
Compound: Chemical, DIOL
Constellation: Southern,
    PAVO
Council: Russian, DUMA
Counsel, REDE
Covering: Seed, ARIL
Cross: Egyptian, ANKH
Cry: Bacchanalian, EVOE
Cup (Scotch), TASS

Cupbearer, SAKI
Dagger, DIRK
    Malay, KRIS
Dam: River, WEIR
Dash, ELAN
Date: Roman, IDES
Dawn: Pertaining to, EOAN
Dean: English, INGE
Decay: In fruit, BLET
Deer: Sambar, MAHA
Disease: Skin, ACNE
Disk: Solar, ATEN
Dog: Hunting, ALAN
Drink: Hindu intoxicating,
    SOMA
Duck, SMEE, SMEW, TEAL
Dynasty: Chinese, CHEN,
    CHIN, CHOU, CHOW,
    HSIA, MING, SUNG,
    TANG, TSIN
    Mongol, YUAN
Eagle: Biblical, GIER
    Sea, ERNE
Egyptian: Christian, COPT
Ear: Pertaining to, OTIC
Entrance: Mine, ADIT
Esau, EDOM
Escutcheon: Voided, ORLE
Eskers, OSAR
Evergreen: New Zealand,
    TAWA
Fairy: Persian, PERI
Family: Italian, ESTE
Far (comb. form), TELE
Farewell, VALE
Father (French), PERE
Fennel: Philippine, ANIS
Fever: Malarial, AGUE
Fiber: East Indian, JUTE
Firn, NEVE
Fish: Carplike, DACE
    Hawaiian, ULUA
    Herringlike, SHAD
    Mackerellike, CERO
    Marine, HAKE
    Sea, LING, MERO, OPAH
    Spiny-finned, GOBY
Food: Tropical, TARO

Foot: Metric, IAMB
Formerly, ERST
Founder: Of Carthage, DIDO
France: Southern, MIDI
Furze, ULEX
Gaelic, ERSE
Gaiter, SPAT
Game: Card, FARO, SKAT
Garlic: European wild, MOLY
Garment: Hindu, SARI
    Roman, TOGA
Gazelle, CORA
Gem, JADE, ONYX, OPAL, RUBY
Genus: Amphibians (incl. frogs), RANA
    Amphibians (incl. tree toads), HYLA
    Antelopes, ORYX
    Auks, ALCA, URIA
    Bees, APIS
    Birds (American ostriches), RHEA
    Birds (cranes), GRUS
    Birds (magpies), PICA
    Birds (peacocks), PAVO
    Cetaceans, INIA
    Ducks (incl. mallards), ANAS
    Fishes (burbots), LOTA
    Fishes (incl. bowfins), AMIA
Genus: Geese (snow geese), CHEN
    Gulls, XEMA
    Herbs, ARUM, GEUM
    Insects (water scorpions), NEPA
    Lilies, ALOE
    Mammals (mankind), HOMO
    Orchids, DISA
    Owls, ASIO, BUBO, OTUS
    Palms, NIPA
    Sea birds, SULA
    Sheep, OVIS
    Shrubs, Eurasian, ULEX
    Shrubs (hollies), ILEX
    Shrubs (incl. Virginia Willow), ITEA
    Shrubs, tropical, EVEA
    Snakes (sand snakes), ERYX
    Swans, OLOR
    Trees, chocolate, COLA
    Trees (ebony family), MABA
    Trees (incl. maples), ACER
    Trees (Olives), OLEA
    Trees, tropical, EVEA
    Turtles, EMYS
Goat: Wild, IBEX, KRAS, TAHR, TAIR, THAR
God: Assyrian, ASUR

Babylonian, ADAD, ADDU, ENKI, ENZU, IRRA, NABU, NEBO, UTUG
    Celtic, LLEU, LLEW
    Hindu, AGNI, CIVA, DEVA, DEWA, KAMA, RAMA, SIVA, VAYU
    Phrygian, ATYS
    Semitic, BAAL
    Teutonic, HLER
Goddess: Babylonian, ERUA, GULA
    Hawaiian, PELE
    Hindu, DEVI, KALI, SHRI, VACH
Gooseberry: Hawaiian, POHA
Gourd, PEPO
Grafted (heraldry), ENTE
Grandfather (obsolete), AIEL
Grandparents: Pertaining to, AVAL
Grass: Hawaiian, HILO
Gray (French), GRIS
Green (heraldry), VERT
Groom: Indian, SYCE
Half (prefix), DEMI, HEMI, SEMI
Hamlet, DORP
Hammer-head: Part of, PEEN
Handle, ANSA
Harp: Japanese, KOTO
Hartebeest, ASSE, TORA
Hautboy, OBOE
Hawk: Taken from nest (falconry), EYAS
Hearing (law), OYER
Heater: For liquids, ETNA
Herb: Aromatic, ANET, DILL
    Fabulous, MOLY
    Perennial, GEUM, SEGO
    Pot, WORT
    Used for blue dye, WADE, WOAD
Hill: Flat-topped, MESA
    Sand, DENE, DUNE
Hoarfrost, RIME
Hog: Immature female, GILT
Holly, ILEX
House: Cow, BYRE
    (Spanish), CASA
Ice: Floating, FLOE
Image, ICON, IKON
Incarnation: Of Vishnu, RAMA
Indian: Algonquian, CREE, SAUK
    Central American, MAYA
    Iroquoian, ERIE
    Mexican, CORA
    Peruvian, CANA, INCA, MORO
    Shoshonean, HOPI
    Siouan, OTOE

    Southwestern, HOPI, PIMA, YUMA, ZUNI
Insect: Immature, PUPA
Instrument: Stringed, LUTE, LYRE
Ireland, EIRE, ERIN
Jacket: English, ETON
Jail (British), GAOL
Jar, OLLA
Judge: Mohammedan, CADI
Juniper: European, CADE
Kiln, OAST, OVEN
King: British legendary, LUDD, NUDD
Kiss, BUSS
Knife: Philippine, BOLO
Koran: Section of, SURA
Laborer: Spanish American, PEON
Lake: Mountain, TARN
    (Scotch), LOCH
Lamp: Miner's, DAVY
Landing place: Indian, GHAT
Language: Buddhist, PALI
    Japanese, AINU
Latvian, LETT
Layer: Of iris, UVEA
Leaf: Palm, OLAY, OLLA
Legislature: Ukrainian, RADA
Lemur, LORI
Leopard, PARD
Let it stand, STET
Letter: Greek, BETA, IOTA, ZETA
    Hebrew, AYIN, BETH, CAPH, KOPH, RESH, SHIN, TETH, YODH
    Papal, BULL
Lily, ALOE
Literature: Hindu sacred, VEDA
Lizard, GILA
    Monitor, URAN
Loquat, BIWA
Magistrate: Genoese or Venetian, DOGE
Man (Latin), HOMO
Mark: Omission, DELE
Marmoset: South American, MICO
Meadow: Fertile, VEGA
Measure: Electric, VOLT, WATT
    Force, DYNE
    Hebrew, OMER
    Printing, PICA
    Spanish or Portuguese, VARA
    Swiss land, IMMI
Medley, OLIO
Merganser, SMEW
Milk (French), LAIT
Molding, GULA
    Curved, OGEE
Mongoose: Crab-eating, URVA

Monk: Tibetan, LAMA
Monkey: African, MONA, WAAG
  Ceylonese, MAHA
  Cochin-China, DOUC
  South American, SAKI, TITI
Monkshood, ATIS
Month: Jewish, ADAR, ELUL, IYAR
Mother (French), MERE
Mountain: Thessaly, OSSA
Mouse: Meadow, VOLE
Mythology: Norse, EDDA
Nail (French), CLOU
Native: Philippine, MORO
Nest: Of pheasants, NIDE
Network, RETE
No (German), NEIN
Noble: Mohammedan, AMIR
Notice: Death, OBIT
Novel: By Zola, NANA
Nursemaid: Oriental AMAH, AYAH, EYAH
Nut: Philippine, PILI
Oak: Holm, ILEX
Oil (comb. form), OLEO
Ostrich: American, RHEA
Oven, KILN, OAST
Owl: Barn, LULU
Ox: Celebes wild, ANOE
  Extinct wild, URUS
Palm, ATAP, NIPA, SAGO
Parliament, DIET
Parrot: New Zealand, KAKA
Pass: Indian mountain, GHAT
Passage: Closing (music), CODA
Peach: Clingstone, PAVY
Peasant: Indian, RYOT
  Old English, CARL
Pepper: Australasian, KAVA
Perfume, ATAR
Persia, IRAN
Person: Extraordinary, ONER
Pickerel or pike, ESOX
Pitcher, EWER
Plant: Aromatic, NARD
  Century, ALOE
  Indigo, ANIL
  Pepper, KAVA
Platform: Raised, DAIS
Plum: Wild, SLOE
Pods: Vegetable, OKRA, OKRO
Poem: Epic, EPOS
Poet: Persian, OMAR
  Roman, OVID
Poison, BANE
  Arrow, INEE
Porkfish, SISI
Portico: Greek, STOA
Premium, AGIO
Priest: Mohammedan, IMAM
Prima donna, DIVA

Prong: Fork, TINE
Pseudonym: Lamb's, ELIA
Queen: Carthaginian, DIDO
  Hindu, RANI
Rabbit, CONY
Race: Of Japan, AINU
Rail: Ducklike, COOT
  North American, SORA
Redshank, CLEE
Refuse: After pressing, MARC
Regiment: Turkish, ALAI
Reliquary, ARCA
Resort: Italian, LIDO
Ridges: Sandy, ASAR, OSAR
River: German, ELBE, ODER
  Italian, ADDA
  Siberian, LENA
Road: Roman, ITER
Rockfish: California, RENA
Rodent: Mouselike, VOLE
  South American, PACA
Rootstock, TARO
Salamander, NEWT
Salmon: Silver, COHO
  Young, PARR
Same (Greek), HOMO
  (Latin), IDEM
Sauce: Fish, ALEC
School: English, ETON
Seaweed, AGAR, ALGA, KELP
Secular, LAIC
Sediment, SILT
Seed: Dill, ANET
  Of vetch, TARE
Serf, ILOT
Sesame, TEEL
Settlement: Eskimo, ETAH
Shark: Atlantic, GATA
  European, TOPE
Sheep: Wild, UDAD
Sheltered, ALEE
Shield, EGIS
Ship: Jason's, ARGO
  Left side of, PORT
  Two-masted, BRIG
Shrine: Buddhist, TOPE
Shrub: New Zealand, TUTU
Sign: Magic, RUNE
Silkworm, ERIA
Skin: Beaver, PLEW
Skink: Egyptian, ADDA
Slave, ESNE
Sloth: Two-toed, UNAU
Smooth, LENE
Snow: Glacial, NEVE
Soapstone, TALC
Society: African secret, EGBO, PORO
Son: Of Seth, ENOS
Song (German), LIED
  Unaccompanied, GLEE
Sound: Lung, RALE
Sour, ACID
Sow: Young, GILT
Spike: Brad-shaped, BROB

Spirit: Buddhist evil, MARA
Stake: Poker, ANTE
Star: Temporary, NOVA
Starch: East Indian, SAGO
Stone: Precious, OPAL
Strap: Bridle, REIN
Strewn (heraldry), SEME
Sweetsop, ATES, ATTA
Sword: Fencing, EPEE, FOIL
Tambourine: African, TAAR
Tapir: Brazilian, ANTA
Tax, CESS
Tea: South American, MATE
Therefore (Latin), ERGO
Thing: Extraordinary, ONER
Three (dice, cards, etc.), TREY
Thrush: Hawaiian, OMAO
Tide, NEAP
Tipster: Racing, TOUT
Tissue, TELA
Title: Etruscan, LARS
  Hindu, BABU
  Indian, RAJA
  Mohammedan, EMIR, IMAM
  Persian, BABA
  Spanish, DONA
  Turkish, AGHA, BABA
Toad: Largest known, AGUA
  Tree, HYLA
Tool: Cutting, ADZE
Track: Deer, SLOT
Tract: Sandy, DENE
Tree: Apple, SORB
  Central American, EBOE
  East Indian, TEAK
  Eucalyptus, YATE
  Guiana and Trinidad, MORA
  Javanese, UPAS
  Linden, LIME, LINN, TEIL, TILL
  Sandarac, ARAR
  Sassafras, AGUE
  Tamarisk salt, ATLE
Tribe: Moro, SULU
Trout, CHAR
Urchin: Street, ARAB
Vessel: Arab, DHOW
Vestment: Ecclesiastical, COPE
Vetch, TARE
Vine: East Indian, SOMA
Violinist: Famous, AUER
Vortex, EDDY
Wampum, PEAG
Wapiti, STAG
Waste: Allowance for, TRET
Watchman: Indian, MINA
Water (Spanish), AGUA
Waterfall, LINN
Wavy (heraldry), ONDE, UNDE
Wax, CERE
  Chinese, PELA

Weed: Biblical, TARE
Weight: Ancient, MINA
   Danish (pl.), ESER
   East Asian, TAEL
   Greek,' MINA
   Siamese, BAHT
Well done (rare), EUGE
Whale, CETE

Killer, ORCA
White, HUSE, HUSO
Whirlpool, EDDY
Wife: Of Geraint, ENID
Willow: Virginia, ITEA
Wine, PORT
Winged, ALAR
   (Heraldry), AILE

Wings, ALAE
Withered, SERE
Without (French), SANS
Wool: To comb, CARD
Work, OPUS
Wrong: Civil, TORT
Young: Bring forth, YEAN

## Words of Five Letters

Abode of dead: Babylonian, ARALU
Aborigine: Borneo, DAYAK
Aftersong, EPODE
Aloe, AGAVE
Animal: Footless, APODE
Ant, EMMET
Antelope:   African,   ADDAX,   BEISA,
   CAAMA,   ELAND,   GUIBA,   ORIBI,
   TIANG
   Goat, GORAL, SEROW
   Indian, SASIN
   Siberian, SAIGA
Arch: Pointed, OGIVE
Armadillo, APARA, POYOU, TATOU
Arrowroot, ARARU
Artery: Trunk, AORTA
Association: Russian, ARTEL
   Secret, CABAL
Author: English, READE
Automaton, GOLEM, ROBOT
Award: Motion-picture, OSCAR
Basket: Fishing, CREEL
Beer: Russian, KVASS
Bible: Mohammedan, KORAN
Bird: Asian, MINAH, MYNAH
   Indian, SHAMA
   Larklike, PIPIT
   Loonlike, GREBE
   Oscine, VIREO
   South American, AGAMI
   Swimming, GREBE
Black: (French), NOIRE
   (Heraldry), SABLE
Blackbird: European, MERLE, OUSEL,
   OUZEL
Block: Glacial, SERAC
Blue (heraldry), AZURE
Boat: Eskimo, BIDAR, UMIAK
Bobwhite, COLIN, QUAIL
Bone (comb. form), OSTEO
   Leg, TIBIA
   Thigh, FEMUR
Broom: Twig, BESOM
Brother (French), FRERE
   Moses', AARON
Canoe: Eskimo, BIDAR, KAYAK
Cape: Papal, FANON, ORALE
Caravansary, SERAI
Card: Old playing, TAROT
Caterpillar: New Zealand, AWETO
Catkin, AMENT
Cavity: Stone, GEODE
Cephalopod, SQUID
Cetacean, WHALE
Chariot, ESSED
Cheek: Pertaining to, MALAR
Chieftain: Arab, EMEER
Child (Scotch), BAIRN

Cigar, CLARO
Coating: Seed, TESTA
Cockatoo: Palm, ARARA
Coin: Costa Rican, COLON
   Danish, KRONE
   Ecuadorian, SUCRE
   English, GROAT, PENCE
   French, FRANC
   German, KRONE, TALER
   Hungarian, PENGO
   Icelandic, KRONA
   Indian, RUPEE
   Iraqi, DINAR
   Norwegian, KRONE
   Polish, ZLOTY
   Russian, COPEC, KOPEK, RUBLE
   Swedish, KRONA
   Turkish, ASPER
   Yugoslav, DINAR
Collar: Papal, FANON, ORALE
   Roman, RABAT
Commune: Italian, TREIA
Composition: Choral, MOTET
Compound: Chemical, ESTER
Conceal (law), ELOIN
Council: Ecclesiastical, SYNOD
Court: Anglo-Saxon, GEMOT
   Inner, PATIO
Crest: Mountain, ARETE
Crown: Papal, TIARA
Cuttlefish, SEPIA
Date: Roman, NONES
Decree: Mohammedan, IRADE
   Russian, UKASE
Deposit: Loam, LOESS
Desert: Gobi, SHAMO
Devilfish, MANTA
Disease: Cereals, ERGOT
Disk, PATEN
Dog: Wild, DHOLE, DINGO
Dormouse, LEROT
Drum, TABOR
Duck: Sea, EIDER
Dynasty: Chinese, CHING, LIANG, SHANG
Earthquake, SEISM
Eel, ELVER, MORAY
Ermine: European, STOAT
Ether: Crystalline, APIOL
Fabric: Velvetlike, PANNE
Fabulist, AESOP
Family: Italian, CENCI
Fiber: West Indian, SISAL
Fig: Smyrna, ELEME, ELEMI
Figure: Of speech, TROPE
Finch: European, SERIN
Fish: American small, KILLY
Flower: Garden, ASTER
Friend (Spanish), AMIGO

Fruit: Tropical, MANGO
Fungus: Rye, ERGOT
Furze, GORSE
Gateway, TORAN, TORII
Gem, AGATE, BERYL, PEARL, TOPAZ
Genus: Barnacles, LEPAS
  Bears, URSUS
  Birds (loons), GAVIA
  Birds (nuthatches), SITTA
  Cats, FELIS
  Dogs, CANIS
  Fishes (chiros), ELOPS
  Fishes (perch), PERCA
  Geese, ANSER
  Grasses, STIPA
  Grasses (incl. oats), AVENA
  Gulls, LARUS
  Hares, rabbits, LEPUS
  Hawks, BUTEO
  Herbs, old world, INULA
  Herbs, trailing or climbing, APIOS
  Herbs, tropical, TACCA, URENA
  Horses, EQUUS
  Insects (olive flies), DACUS
  Lice, plant, APHIS
  Lichens, USNEA
  Lizards, AGAMA
  Moles, TALPA
  Mollusks, OLIVA
  Monkeys, CEBUS
  Palms, ARECA
  Pigeons, GOURA
  Plants (amaryllis family), AGAVE
  Ruminants (goats), CAPRA
  Shrubs, Asiatic, SABIA
  Shrubs (heath), ERICA
  Shrubs (incl. raspberry), RUBUS
  Shrubs, tropical, IXORA, TREMA,
    URENA
  Ticks, ARGAS
  Trees (of elm family), TREMA, ULMUS
  Trees, tropical, IXORA, TREMA
Goat: Bezoar, PASAN
God: Assyrian, ASHIR, ASHUR, ASSUR
  Babylonian, DAGAN, SIRIS
  Gaelic, DAGDA
  Hindu, BHAGA, INDRA, SHIVA
  Japanese, EBISU
  Philistine, DAGON
  Phrygian, ATTIS
  Teutonic, AEGIR, GYMIR
  Welsh, DYLAN
Goddess: Babylonian, ISTAR, NANAI
  Hindu, DURGA, GAURI, SHREE
Group: Of six, HEXAD
Grove: Sacred to Diana, NEMUS
Growing out, ENATE
Guitar: Hindu, SITAR
Gull: PEWEE, PEWIT
Hartebeest, CAAMA
Headdress: Jewish or Persian, TIARA
  Liturgical, MITER, MITRE
Heath, ERICA
Herb: Grasslike marsh, SEDGE
Heron, EGRET
Hog: Young, SHOAT, SHOTE
Image, EIKON
Indian: Cariban, ARARA

Iroquoian, HURON
Mexican, AZTEC, OPATA, OTOMI
Muskhogean, CREEK
Siouan, OSAGE, TETON
Spanish American, ARARA, CARIB
Inflorescence: Racemose, AMENT
Insect: Immature, LARVA
Intrigue, CABAL
Iris: Yellow, SEDGE
Juniper, GORSE, RETEM
Kidneys: Pertaining to, RENAL
King: British legendary, LLUDD
Kite: European, GLEDE
Kobold, NISSE
Land: Cultivated, ARADA, ARADO
Landholder (Scotch), LAIRD, THANE
Language: Dravidian, TAMIL
Lariat, LASSO, REATA
Laughing, RIANT
Lawgiver: Athenian, DRACO, SOLON
Leaf: Calyx, SEPAL
  Fern, FROND
Lemur, LORIS
Letter: English, AITCH
  Greek, ALPHA, DELTA, GAMMA,
    KAPPA, OMEGA, SIGMA, THETA
  Hebrew, ALEPH, CHETH, GIMEL,
    SADHE, ZAYIN
Lichen, USNEA
Lighthouse, PHARE
Lizard: Old World, AGAMA
Loincloth, DHOTI
Louse: Plant, APHID
Macaw: Brazilian, ARARA
Mahogany: Philippine, ALMON
Mammal: Badgerlike, RATEL
  Civetlike, GENET
  Giraffelike, OKAPI
  Raccoonlike, COATI
Man (French), HOMME
Marble, AGATE
Mark: Insertion, CARET
Market place: Greek, AGORA
Marsupial: Australian, KOALA
Measure: Electric, FARAD, HENRY
  Energy, JOULE
  Metric, LITER, STERE
  Printing, AGATE
  Russian, VERST
Mixture: Smelting, MATTE
Mohicans: Last of, UNCAS
Molding: Convex, OVOLO, TORUS
Mole, TALPA
Monkey: African, PATAS
  Capuchin, SAJOU
  Howling, ARABA
Monkshood, ATEES
Month: Jewish, NISAN, SIVAN, TEBET
Museum (French), MUSEE
Musketeer, ATHOS
Native: Aleutian, ALEUT
  New Zealand, MAORI
Neckpiece: Ecclesiastical, AMICE
Nerve (comb. form), NEURO
Nest: Eagle's or hawk's, AERIE
  Insect's, NIDUS
Net: Fishing, SEINE
Newsstand, KIOSK

Nitrogen, AZOTE
Noble: Mohammedan, AMEER
Nodule: Stone, GEODE
Nostrils, NARES
Notched irregularly, EROSE
Nymph: Mohammedan, HOURI
Official: Roman, EDILE
Oleoresin, ELEMI
Opening: Mouthlike, STOMA
Oration: Funeral, ELOGE
Ostiole, STOMA
Page: Left-hand, VERSO
  Right-hand, RECTO
Palm, ARECA, BETEL
Park: Colorado, ESTES
Perfume, ATTAR
Philosopher: Greek, PLATO
Pillar: Stone, STELA, STELE
Pinnacle: Glacial, SERAC
Plain, LLANO
Plant: Century, AGAVE
  Climbing, LIANA
  Dwarf, CUMIN
  East Asian perennial, RAMIE
  Medicinal, SENNA
  Mustard family, CRESS
Plate: Communion, PATEN
Poem: Lyric, EPODE
Point: Lowest, NADIR
Poplar, ABELE, ALAMO, ASPEN
Porridge: Spanish American, ATOLE
Post: Stair, NEWEL
Priest: Mohammedan, IMAUM
Protozoan, AMEBA
Queen: (French), REINE
  Hindu, RANEE
Rabbit, CONEY
Rail, CRAKE
Red (heraldry), GULES
Religion: Moslem, ISLAM
Resin, ELEMI
Revoke (law), ADEEM
Rich man, MIDAS, NABOB
Ridge: Sandy, ESKAR, ESKER
River: French, LOIRE, SEINE
Rockfish: California, REINA
Rootstock: Fragrant, ORRIS
Ruff: Female, REEVE
Sack: Pack, KYACK
Salt: Ethereal, ESTER
Saltpeter, NITER, NITRE
Salutation: Eastern, SALAM
Sandpiper: Old World, TEREK
Scented, OLENT
School: Fish, SHOAL
  French public, LYCEE
Scriptures: Mohammedan, KORAN
Seaweeds, ALGAE
Seed: Aromatic, ANISE
Seraglio, HAREM, SERAI
Serf, HELOT
Sheep: Wild, AUDAD
Sheeplike, OVINE
Shield, AEGIS
Shoe: Wooden, SABOT
Shoots: Pickled bamboo, ACHAR
Shot: Billiard, CAROM, MASSE
Shrine: Buddhist, STUPA

Shrub: Burning bush, WAHOO
  Ornamental evergreen, TOYON
  Used in tanning, SUMAC
Silk: Watered, MOIRE
Sister (French), SOEUR
  (Latin), SOROR
Six: Group of, HEXAD
Skeleton: Marine, CORAL
Slave, HELOT
Snake, ABOMA, ADDER, COBRA, RACER
Soldier: French, POILU
  Indian, SEPOY
Sour, ACERB
Spirit: Air, ARIEL
Staff: Shepherd's, CROOK
Starwort, ASTER
Steel (German), STAHL
Stockade: Russian, ETAPE
Stop (nautical), AVAST
Storehouse, ETAPE
Subway: Parisian, METRO
Tapestry, ARRAS
Tea: Paraguayan, YERBA
Temple: Hawaiian, HEIAU
Terminal: Positive, ANODE
Theater: Greek, ODEON, ODEUM
Then (French), ALORS
Thread: Surgical, SETON
Thrush: Wilson's, VEERY
Title: Hindu, BABOO
  Indian, RAJAH, SAHEB, SAHIB
  Mohammedan, EMEER, IMAUM
Tree: Buddhist sacred, PIPAL
  East Indian cotton, SIMAL
  Hickory, PECAN
  Light-wooded, BALSA
  Malayan, TERAP
  Mediterranean, CAROB
  Mexican, ABETO
  Mexican pine, OCOTE
  New Zealand, MAIRE
  Philippine, ALMON
  Rain, SAMAN
  South American, UMBRA
  Tamarack, LARCH
  Tamarisk salt, ATLEE
  West Indian, ACANA
Trout, CHARR
Troy, ILION, ILIUM
Twin: Siamese, CHANG
Vestment: Ecclesiastical, STOLE
Violin: Famous, AMATI, STRAD
Volcano: Mud, SALSE
Wampum, PEAGE
War cry: Greek, ALALA
Wavy (heraldry), UNDEE
Weight: Jewish, GERAH
Wen, TALPA
Wheat, SPELT
Wheel: Persian water, NORIA
Whitefish, CISCO
Willow, OSIER
Window: Bay, ORIEL
Wine, MEDOC, RHINE, TINTA, TOKAY
Winged, ALATE
Woman (French), FEMME
Year: Excess of solar over lunar, EPACT
Zoroastrian, PARSI

## Words of Six or More Letters

Agave, MAGUEY
Alkaloid: Crystalline, ESERIN, ESERINE
Alligator, CAYMAN
Amphibole, EDENITE, URALITE
Ant: White, TERMITE
Antelope: African, DIKDIK, DUIKER, GEMSBOK, IMPALA, KOODOO
   European, CHAMOIS
   Indian, NILGAI, NILGAU, NILGHAI, NILGHAU
Ape: Asian or East Indian, GIBBON
Appendage: Leaf, STIPEL, STIPULE
Armadillo, PELUDO, TATOUAY
Arrowroot, ARARAO
Ascetic: Jewish, ESSENE
Ass: Asian wild, ONAGER
Avatar: Of Vishnu, KRISHNA
Babylonian, ELAMITE
Badge: Shoulder, EPAULET
Baldness, ALOPECIA
Barracuda, SENNET
Bark: Aromatic, SINTOC
Bearlike, URSINE
Beetle, ELATER
Bible: Zoroastrian, AVESTA
Bird: Sea, PETREL
   South American, SERIEMA
   Wading, AVOCET, AVOSET
Bone: Leg, FIBULA
Branched, RAMATE
Brother (Latin), FRATER
Bunting: European, ORTOLAN
Call: Trumpet, SENNET
Canoe: Eskimo, BAIDAR, OOMIAK
Caravansary, IMARET
Cat: Asian or African, CHEETAH
   Leopardlike, OCELOT
Cenobite: Jewish, ESSENE
Centerpiece: Table, EPERGNE
Cetacean, DOLPHIN, PORPOISE
Chariot, ESSEDA, ESSEDE
Chief: Seminole, OSCEOLA
Claim: Release as (law), REMISE
Clock: Water, CLEPSYDRA
Cloud, CUMULUS, NIMBUS
Coach: French hackney, FIACRE
Coin: Czech, KORUNA
   Ethiopian, TALARI
   Finnish, MARKKA
   German, THALER
   Greek, DRACHMA
   Haitian, GOURDE
   Honduran, LEMPIRA
   Hungarian, FORINT
   Indo-Chinese, PIASTER
   Netherlands, GUILDER
   Panamanian, BALBOA
   Paraguayan, GUARANI
   Portuguese, ESCUDO
   Russian, COPECK, KOPECK, ROUBLE
   Spanish, PESETA
   Venezuelan, BOLIVAR
Communion: Last holy, VIATICUM
Conceal (law), ELOIGN
Confection, PRALINE
Construction: Sentence, SYNTAX
Convexity: Shaft of column, ENTASIS

Court: Anglo-Saxon, GEMOTE
Cow: Sea, DUGONG, MANATEE
Cylindrical, TERETE
Dagger, STILETTO
   Malay, CREESE, KREESE
Date: Roman, CALENDS, KALENDS
Deer, CARIBOU, WAPITI
Disease: Plant, ERINOSE
Doorkeeper, OSTIARY
Dragonflies: Order of, ODANATA
Drink: Of gods, NECTAR
Drum: TABOUR
   Moorish, ATABAL, ATTABAL
Duck: Fish-eating, MERGANSER
   Sea, SCOTER
Dynasty: Chinese, MANCHU
Eel, CONGER
Edit, REDACT
Envelope: Flower, PERIANTH
Eskimo, AMERIND
Ether: Crystalline, APIOLE
Excuse (law), ESSOIN
Eyespots, OCELLI
Fabric, ESTAMENE, ESTAMIN, ETAMINE
Falcon: European, KESTREL
Figure: Used as column, CARYATID, TELAMON
Fine: For punishment, AMERCE
Fish: Asian fresh-water, GOURAMI
   Pikelike, BARRACUDA
Five: Group of, PENTAD
Fly: African, TSETSE
Foot: Metric, ANAPEST, IAMBUS
Foxlike, VULPINE
Frying pan, SPIDER
Fur, KARAKUL
Galley: Greek or Roman, BIREME, TRIREME
Game: Card, ECARTE
Garment: Greek, CHLAMYS
Gateway, GOPURA, TORANA
Genus: Birds (ravens, crows), CORVUS
   Eels, CONGER
   Fishes, ANABAS
   Foxes, VULPES
   Herbs, ANEMONE
   Insects, CICADA
   Lemurs, GALAGO
   Mints (incl. catnip), NEPETA
   Mollusks, ANOMIA, ASTARTE, TEREDO
   Mollusks (incl. oysters), OSTREA
   Monkeys (spider monkeys), ATELES
   Thrushes (incl. robins), TURDUS
   Trees (of elm family), CELTIS
   Trees (incl. dogwood), CORNUS
   Trees, tropical American, SAPOTA
   Wrens, NANNUS
Gibbon, SIAMANG, WOUWOU
Gland: Salivary, RACEMOSE
Goat: Bezoar, PASANG
Goatlike, CAPRINE
God: Assyrian, ASSHUR, ASSHUR
   Babylonian, BABBAR, MARDUK, MERODACH, NANNAR, NERGAL, SHAMASH
   Hindu, BRAHMA, KRISHNA, VISHNU
   Tahitian, TAAROA
Goddess: Babylonian, ISHTAR

Hindu, CHANDI, HAIMAVATI, LAKSHMI, PARVATI, SARASVATI, SARASWATI
Government, POLITY
Governor: Persian, SATRAP
Grandson (Scotch), NEPOTE
Group: Of five, PENTAD
    Of nine, ENNEAD
    Of seven, HEPTAD
Hare: In first year, LEVERET
Harpsichord, SPINET
Herb: Alpine, EDELWEISS
    Chinese, GINSENG
    South African, FREESIA
Hermit, EREMITE
Hero: Legendary, PALADIN
Heron, BITTERN
Horselike, EQUINE
Hound: Short-legged, BEAGLE
House (French), MAISON
Idiot, CRETIN
Implement: Stone, NEOLITH
Incarnation: Hindu, AVATAR
Indian, APACHE, COMANCHE, PAIUTE, SENECA
Inn: Turkish, IMARET
Insects: Order of, DIPTERA
Instrument: Japanese banjolike, SAMISEN
    Musical, CLAVIER, SPINET
Interstice, AREOLA
Ironwood, COLIMA
Juniper: Old Testament, RAETAM
Kettledrum, ATABAL
King: Fairy, OBERON
Kneecap, PATELLA
Knife, MACHETE
Langur: Sumatran, SIMPAI
Legislature: Spanish, CORTES
Lemur: African, GALAGO
    Madagascar, AYEAYE
Letter: Greek, EPSILON, LAMBDA, OMICRON, UPSILON
    Hebrew: DALETH, LAMEDH, SAMEKH
Lighthouse, PHAROS
Lizard, IGUANA
Llama, ALPACA
Lockjaw, TETANUS
Locust, CICADA, CICALA
Macaw: Brazilian, MARACAN
Maid: Of Astolat, ELAINE
Mammal: Madagascar, TENDRAC, TENREC
Man (Spanish), HOMBRE
Marmoset: South American, TAMARIN
Marsupial, BANDICOOT, WOMBAT
Massacre, POGROM
Mayor: Spanish, ALCALDE
Measure: Electric, AMPERE, COULOMB, KILOWATT
Medicine: Quack, NOSTRUM
Member: Religious order, CENOBITE
Molasses, TREACLE
Monkey: African, GRIVET, NISNAS
    Asian, LANGUR
    Philippine, MACHIN
    South American, PINCHE, SAIMIRI, SAMIRI, SAPAJOU
Monster, CHIMERA, GORGON

(Comb. form), TERATO
    Cretan, MINOTAUR
Month: Jewish, HESHVAN, KISLEV, SHEBAT, TAMMUZ, TISHRI, VEADAR
Mountain: Asia Minor, ARARAT
Mulct, AMERCE
Musketeer, ARAMIS, PORTHOS
Nearsighted, MYOPIC
Net, TRAMMEL
New York City, GOTHAM
Nine: Group of, ENNEAD
Nobleman: Spanish, GRANDEE
Official: Roman, AEDILE
Onyx: Mexican, TECALI
Order: Dragonflies, ODANATA
    Insects, DIPTERA
Organ: Plant, PISTIL
Ornament: Shoulder, EPAULET
Overcoat: Military, CAPOTE
Ox: Wild, BANTENG
Oxidation: Bronze or copper, PATINA
Paralysis: Incomplete, PARESIS
Pear: Alligator, AVOCADO
Persimmon: Mexican, CHAPOTE
Pipe: Peace, CALUMET
Plaid (Scotch), TARTAN
Plain, PAMPAS, STEPPE, TUNDRA
Plant: Buttercup family, ANEMONE
    Century, MAGUEY
    On rocks, LICHEN
Plowing: Fit for, ARABLE
Poem: Heroic, EPOPEE
    Six-lined, SESTET
Point: Highest, ZENITH
Potion: Love, PHILTER, PHILTRE
Protozoan, AMOEBA
Punish, AMERCE
Purple (heraldry), PURPURE
Queen: Fairy, TITANIA
Race: Skiing, SLALOM
Rat, BANDICOOT, LEMMING
Retort, RIPOST, RIPOSTE
Ring: Harness, TERRET
    Little, ANNULET
Rodent: Jumping, JERBOA
    Spanish American, AGOUTI, AGOUTY
Sailor: East Indian, LASCAR
Salmon: Young, GRILSE
Salutation: Eastern, SALAAM
Sandpiper, PLOVER
Sandy, ARENOSE
Sapodilla, SAPOTA, SAPOTE
Saw: Surgical, TREPAN
Seven: Group of, HEPTAD
Sexes: Common to both, EPICENE
Shawl: Mexican, SERAPE
Sheathing: Flower, SPATHE
Sheep: Wild, AOUDAD, ARGALI
Shipworm, TEREDO
Shoes: Mercury's winged, TALARIA
Shortening: Syllable, SYSTOLE
Shrub, SPIRAEA
Sickle-shaped, FALCATE
Silver (heraldry), ARGENT
Snake, ANACONDA
Speech: Loss of, APHASIA
Spiral, HELICAL
Staff: Bishop's, CROSIER, CROZIER

Stalk: Plant, PETIOLE
State: Swiss, CANTON
Studio, ATELIER
Swan: Young, CYGNET
Swimming, NATANT
Sword-shaped, ENSATE
Terminal: Negative, CATHODE
Third (music), TIERCE
Thrust: Fencing, RIPOST, RIPOSTE
Tile: Pertaining to, TEGULAR
Tomb: Empty, CENOTAPH
Tooth (comb. form), ODONTO
Tower: Mohammedan, MINARET
Tree: African timber, BAOBAB
  Black gum, TUPELO
  East Indian, MARGOSA
  Locust, ACACIA
  Malayan, SINTOC
  Marmalade, SAPOTE
Urn: Tea, SAMOVAR
Vehicle, LANDAU, TROIKA

Verbose, PROLIX
Viceroy: Egyptian, KHEDIVE
Vulture: American, CONDOR

Warehouse (French), ENTREPOT
Whale: White, BELUGA
Whirlpool, VORTEX
Will: Addition to, CODICIL
  Having left, TESTATE
Wind, CHINOOK, MONSOON, SIMOOM,
  SIMOON, SIROCCO
Window: In roof, DORMER
Wine, BARBERA, BURGUNDY, CABER-
  NET, CHABLIS, CHIANTI, CLARET,
  MUSCATEL, RIESLING, SAUTERNE,
  SHERRY, ZINFANDEL
Wolfish, LUPINE
Woman: Boisterous, TERMAGANT
Woolly, LANATE
Workshop, ATELIER

Zoroastrian, PARSEE

# Old-Testament Names

(We do not pretend that this list is all-inclusive. We include only those names which in our opinion one meets most often in crossword puzzles.)

AARON: First high priest of Jews; son of Amram; brother of Miriam and Moses; father of Abihu, Eleazer, Ithamar, and Nadab.

ABEL: Son of Adam; slain by Cain.

ABIGAIL: Wife of Nabal; later, wife of David.

ABIHU: Son of Aaron.

ABIMELECH: King of Gerar.

ABNER: Commander of army of Saul and Ishbosheth; slain by Joab.

ABRAHAM (or ABRAM): Patriarch; forefather of the Jews; son of Terah; husband of Sarah; father of Isaac and Ishmael.

ABSALOM: Son of David and Maacah; revolted against David; slain by Joab.

ACHISH: King of Gath; gave refuge to David.

ACHSA (or ACHSAH): Daughter of Caleb; wife of Othniel.

ADAH: Wife of Lamech.

ADAM: First man; husband of Eve; father of Cain, Abel, and Seth.

ADONIJAH: Son of David and Haggith.

AGAG: King of Amalek; spared by Saul; slain by Samuel.

AHASUERUS: King of Persia; husband of Vashti and, later, Esther; sometimes identified with Xerxes the Great.

AHIJAH: Prophet; foretold accession of Jeroboam.

AHINOAM: Wife of David.

AMASA: Commander of army of David; slain by Joab.

AMNON: Son of David and Ahinoam; ravished Tamar; slain by Absalom.

AMRAM: Husband of Jochebed; father of Aaron, Miriam and Moses.

ASENATH: Wife of Joseph.

ASHER: Son of Jacob and Zilpah.

BALAAM: Prophet; rebuked by his donkey for cursing God.

BARAK: Jewish captain; associated with Deborah.

BARUCH: Secretary to Jeremiah.

BATHSHEBA: Wife of Uriah; later, wife of David.

BELSHAZZAR: Crown prince of Babylon.

BENAIAH· Warrior of David; proclaimed Solomon King.

BEN-HADAD: Name of several kings of Damascus.

BENJAMIN: Son of Jacob and Rachel.

BEZALEEL: Chief architect of tabernacle.

BILBAH: Servant of Rachel; mistress of Jacob.

BILDAD: Comforter of Job.

BOAZ: Husband of Ruth; father of Obed.

CAIN: Son of Adam and Eve; slayer of Abel; father of Enoch.

CAINAN: Son of Enos.

CALEB: Spy sent out by Moses to visit Canaan; father of Achsa.

CANAAN: Son of Ham.

CHILION: Son of Elimelech; husband of Orpah.

CUSH: Son of Ham; father of Nimrod.

DAN: Son of Jacob and Bilhah.

DANIEL: Prophet; saved from lions by God.

DEBORAH: Hebrew prophetess; helped Israelites conquer Canaanites.

DELILAH: Mistress and betrayer of Samson.

ELAM: Son of Shem.

ELEAZAR: Son of Aaron; succeeded him as high priest.

ELI: High priest and judge; teacher of Samuel; father of Hophni and Phinehas.

ELIAKIM: Chief minister of Hezekiah.

ELIEZER: Servant of Abraham.

ELIHU: Comforter of Job.

ELIJAH (or ELIAS): Prophet; went to heaven in chariot of fire.

ELIMELECH: Husband of Naomi; father of Chilion and Mahlon.

ELIPHAZ: Comforter of Job.

ELISHA (or ELISEUS): Prophet; successor of Elijah.

ELKANAH: Husband of Hannah; father of Samuel.

ENOCH: Son of Cain.

ENOCH: Father of Methuselah.

ENOS: Son of Seth; father of Cainan.

EPHRAIM: Son of Joseph.

ESAU: Son of Isaac and Rebecca; sold his birthright to his brother Jacob.

ESTHER: Jewish wife of Ahasuerus; saved Jews from Haman's plotting.

EVE: First woman; created from rib of Adam.

EZRA (or ESDRAS): Hebrew scribe and priest.

GAD: Son of Jacob and Zilpah.

GEHAZI: Servant of Elisha.

GIDEON: Israelite hero; defeated Midianites.

GOLIATH: Philistine giant; slain by David.

HAGAR: Handmaid of Sarah; concubine of Abraham; mother of Ishmael.

HAGGITH: Mother of Adonijah.

HAM: Son of Noah; father of Cush, Mizraim, Phut, and Canaan.

HAMAN: Chief minister of Ahasuerus; hanged on gallows prepared for Mordecai.

HANNAH: Wife of Elkanah; mother of Samuel.

HANUN: King of Ammonites.

HARAN: Brother of Abraham; father of Lot.

HAZAEL: King of Damascus.

HEPHZI-BAH: Wife of Hezekiah; mother of Mannaseh.

HIRAM: King of Tyre.

HOLOFERNES: General of Nebuchadnezzar; slain by Judith.

HOPHNI: Son of Eli.

ISAAC: Hebrew patriarch; son of Abraham and Sarah; half brother of Ishmael; husband of Rebecca; father of Esau and Jacob.

ISHMAEL: Son of Abraham and Hagar; half brother of Isaac.

ISSACHAR: Son of Jacob and Leah.

ITHAMAR: Son of Aaron.

JABAL: Son of Lamech and Adah.

JABIN: King of Hazor.

JACOB: Hebrew patriarch, founder of Israel; son of Isaac and Rebecca; husband of Leah and Rachel; father of Asher, Benjamin, Dan, Gad, Issachar, Joseph, Judah, Levi, Naphtali, Reuben, Simeon, and Zebulun.

JAEL: Slayer of Sisera.

JAPHETH: Son of Noah.

JEHOIADA: High priest; husband of Jehoshabeath; revolted against Athaliah and made Joash King of Judah.

JEHOSHABEATH (or JEHOSHEBA): Daughter of Jehoram of Judah; wife of Jehoiada.

JEPHTHAH: Judge in Israel; sacrificed his only daughter because of vow.

JESSE: Son of Obed; father of David.

JETHRO: Midianite priest; father of Zipporah.

JEZEBEL: Phoenician princess; wife of Ahab; mother of Ahaziah, Athaliah, and Jehoram.

JOAB: Commander in chief under David; slayer of Abner, Absalom, and Amasa.

JOB: Patriarch; underwent many afflictions; comforted by Bildad, Elihu, Eliphaz and Zophar.

JOCHEBED: Wife of Amram.

JONAH: Prophet; cast into sea and swallowed by great fish.

JONATHAN: Son of Saul; friend of David.

JOSEPH: Son of Jacob and Rachel; sold into slavery by his brothers; husband of Asenath; father of Ephraim and Manassah.

JOSHUA: Successor of Moses; son of Nun.

JUBAL: Son of Lamech and Adah.

JUDAH: Son of Jacob and Leah.

JUDITH: Slayer of Holofernes.

KISH: Father of Saul.

LABAN: Father of Leah and Rachel.

LAMECH: Son of Methuselah; father of Noah.

LAMECH: Husband of Adah and Zillah; father of Jabal, Jubal, and Tubal-Cain.

LEAH: Daughter of Laban; wife of Jacob.

LEVI: Son of Jacob and Leah.

LOT: Son of Haran; escaped destruction of Sodom.

MAACAH: Mother of Absalom and Tamar.

MAHLON: Son of Elimelech; first husband of Ruth.

MANASSEH: Son of Joseph.

MELCHIZEDEK: King of Salem.

METHUSELAH: Patriarch; son of Enoch; father of Lamech.

MICHAL: Daughter of Saul; wife of David.

MIRIAM: Prophetess; daughter of Amram; sister of Aaron and Moses.

MIZRAIM: Son of Ham.

MORDECAI: Uncle of Esther; with her aid, saved Jews from Haman's plotting.

MOSES: Prophet and lawgiver; son of Amram; brother of Aaron and Miriam; husband of Zipporah.

NAAMAN: Syrian captain; cured of leprosy by Elisha.

NABAL: Husband of Abigail.

NABOTH: Owner of vineyard; stoned to death because he would not sell it to Ahab.

NADAB: Son of Aaron.

NAHOR: Father of Terah.

NAOMI: Wife of Elimelech; mother-in-law of Ruth.

NAPHTALI: Son of Jacob and Bilhah.

NATHAN: Prophet; reproved David for causing Uriah's death.

NEBUCHADNEZZAR (or NEBUCHAD-REZZAR): King of Babylon; destroyer of Jerusalem.

NEHEMIAH: Jewish leader; empowered by Artaxerxes to rebuild Jerusalem.

NIMROD: Mighty hunter; son of Cush.

NOAH: Patriarch; Son of Lamech; escaped Deluge by building Ark; father of Ham, Japheth and Shem.

NUN (or NON): Father of Joshua.

OBED: Son of Boaz; father of Jesse.

OG: King of Bashan.

ORPAH: Wife of Chilion.

OTHNIEL: Kenezite; judge of Israel; husband of Achsa.

PHINEHAS: Son of Eleazer.

PHINEHAS: Son of Eli.

PHUT (or PUT): Son of Ham.

POTIPHAR: Egyptian official; bought Joseph.

RACHEL: Wife of Jacob.

REBECCA (or REBEKAH): Wife of Isaac.

REUBEN: Son of Jacob and Leah.

RUTH: Wife of Mahlon, later of Boaz; daughter-in-law of Naomi.

SAMSON: Judge of Israel; famed for strength; betrayed by Delilah.

SAMUEL: Hebrew judge and prophet; son of Elkanah.

SARAH (or SARA, SARAI): Wife of Abraham.

SENNACHERIB: King of Assyria.

SETH: Son of Adam; father of Enos.

SHEM: Son of Noah; father of Elam.

SIMEON: Son of Jacob and Leah.

SISERA: Canaanite captain; slain by Jael.

TAMAR: Daughter of David and Maachah; ravished by Amnon.

TERAH: Son of Nahor; father of Abraham.

TUBAL-CAIN: Son of Lamech and Zillah.

URIAH: Husband of Bathsheba; sent to death in battle by David.

VASHTI: Wife of Ahasuerus; set aside by him.

ZADOK: High priest during David's reign.

ZEBULUN (or ZABULON): Son of Jacob and Leah.

ZILLAH: Wife of Lamech.

ZILPAH: Servant of Leah; mistress of Jacob.

ZIPPORAH: Daughter of Jethro; wife of Moses.

ZOPHAR: Comforter of Job.

# Kings of Judah and Israel

## Kings Before Division of Kingdom

SAUL: First King of Israel; son of Kish; father of Ish-Bosheth, Jonathan and Michal.

ISH-BOSHETH (or ESHBAAL): King of Israel; son of Saul.

DAVID: King of Judah; later of Israel; son of Jesse; husband of Abigail, Ahinoam, Bathsheba, Michal, etc.; father of Absalom, Adonijah, Amnon, Solomon, Tamar, etc.

SOLOMON: King of Israel and Judah; son of David; father of Rehoboam.

REHOBOAM: Son of Solomon; during his reign the kingdom was divided into Judah and Israel.

## Kings of Judah (Southern Kingdom)

REHOBOAM: First King.

ABIJAH (or ABIJAM or ABIA): Son of Rehoboam.

ASA: Probably son of Abijah.

JEHOSHAPHAT: Son of Asa.

JEHORAM (or JORAM): Son of Jehoshaphat; husband of Athaliah.

AHAZIAH: Son of Jehoram and Athaliah.

ATHALIAH: Daughter of King Ahab of Israel and Jezebel; wife of Jehoram.

JOASH (or JEHOASH): Son of Ahaziah.

AMAZIAH: Son of Joash.

UZZIAH (or AZARIAH): Son of Amaziah.

JOTHAM: Regent, later King; son of Uzziah.

AHAZ: Son of Jotham.

HEZEKIAH: Son of Ahaz; husband of Hephzi-Bah.

MANASSEH: Son of Hezekiah and Hephzi-Bah.

AMON: Son of Manasseh.

JOSIAH (or JOSIAS): Son of Amon.

JEHOAHAZ (or JOAHAZ): Son of Josiah.

JEHOIACHIN: Son of Jehoiakim.

JEHOIAKIM: Son of Josiah.

ZEDEKIAH: Son of Josiah; kingdom overthrown by Babylonians under Nebuchadnezzar.

## Kings of Israel (Northern Kingdom)

JEROBOAM I: Led secession of Israel.

NADAB: Son of Jeroboam I.

BAASHA: Overthrew Nadab.

ELAH: Son of Baasha.

ZIMRI: Overthrew Elah.

OMRI: Overthrew Zimri.

AHAB: Son of Omri; husband of Jezebel.

AHAZIAH: Son of Ahab.

JEHORAM (or JORAM): Son of Ahab.

JEHU: Overthrew Jehoram.

JEHOAHAZ (or JOAHAZ): Son of Jehu.

JEHOASH (or JOASH): Son of Jehoahaz.

JEROBOAM II: Son of Jehoash.
ZECHARIAH: Son of Jeroboam II.
SHALLUM: Overthrew Zechariah.
MENAHEM: Overthrew Shallum.

PEKAHIAH: Son of Menahem.
PEKAH: Overthrew Pekahiah.
HOSHEA: Overthrew Pekah; kingdom overthrown by Assyrians under Sargon II.

## Prophets

### Major

| | | | |
|---|---|---|---|
| ISAIAH | JEREMIAH | EZEKIEL | DANIEL |

### Minor

| | | | |
|---|---|---|---|
| HOSEA | OBADIAH | NAHUM | HAGGAI |
| JOEL | JONAH | HABAKKUK | ZECHARIAH |
| AMOS | MICAH | ZEPHANIAH | MALACHI |

## Foreign Phrases

**(NOTE: The English meanings given are not necessarily literal translations.)**

AB OVO: From the beginning.
ABSIT OMEN: Hope this is no bad luck.
AEQUO ANIMO: Undisturbed in mind.
AD VALOREM: According to its value.
ALEA JACTA EST: The die is cast.
ALMA MATER: One's college or school.
ALTER EGO: Other self.
AMICUS CURIAE: Friend of the court.
ANNO DOMINI: Year of our Lord.
BEL CANTO: A style of singing marked by virtuosity and beauty.
BETE NOIRE: Particular nemesis.
BONA FIDE: In good faith; genuine.
CARPE DIEM: Enjoy today.
CASUS BELLI: Cause of war.
CAVEAT EMPTOR: Buy at your own risk.
CORPUS DELICTI: Fundamental fact or facts necessary to commission of a crime.
CUI BONO: To whose advantage?
CUM GRANO SALIS: With a grain of salt.
DE FACTO: As a matter of fact; because of this fact.
DEO GRATIAS: Thanks be to God.
DEUS EX MACHINA: Artificially produced to bring a solution of some extreme difficulty.
ECCE HOMO: This is the man.
ERRARE HUMANUM (EST): To err is human.
FESTINA LENTE: Make haste slowly.
FIAT LUX: Let there be light.
FIDUS ACHATES: Faithful friend.
FLAGRANTE DELICTO: Caught in the act.
HABEAS CORPUS: Common-law writ to bring a person before a court or judge.
HIC JACET: Here lies. . . .
HOI POLLOI: The common people.
HONORIS CAUSA: For the sake of honor.

HORS D'OEUVRES: Appetizers.
IN VINO VERITAS: In wine there is truth.
IPSE DIXIT: An assertion made but not proved.
IPSO FACTO: By the very fact.
JEUNESSE DOREE: Gilded youth.
LABOR OMNIA VINCIT: Work overcomes all things.
LAISSEZ FAIRE: Noninterference.
MIRABILE DICTU: Wonderful to relate.
MULTUM IN PARVO: Much in little.
NIL ADMIRARI: To be astonished at nothing.
NOLENS, VOLENS: Willy-nilly.
O TEMPORA! O MORES!: What sad times and customs!
PERSONA GRATA: A favored person.
POST MORTEM: After death.
PRO BONO PUBLICO: For the public welfare.
PRO TEMPORE: For the time being.
RARA AVIS: Extraordinary person or thing.
REQUIESCAT IN PACE: Rest in peace.
SAVOIR FAIRE: Know-how; manners for all occasions.
SINE DIE: With no day set for the next meeting.
SINE QUA NON: Indispensable.
SPIRITUS FRUMENTI: Alcohol.
STATUS (IN) QUO: State in which anything is.
SUI GENERIS: In a class by itself.
SURSUM CORDA: Lift up your hearts.
TEMPUS FUGIT: Time flies.
ULTIMA THULE: The limit in an ideal way.
VAE VICTIS: Woe to the conquered.
VENI, VIDI, VICI: I came, I saw, I conquered.

# Greek and Roman Mythology

(Most of the Greek deities were adopted by the Romans, although in many cases there was a change of name. In the list below, information is given under the Greek name; the name in parentheses is the Latin equivalent. However, all Latin names are listed with cross references to the Greek ones. In addition, there are several deities which were exclusively Roman.)

**ACHERON:** *See* Rivers.

**ACHILLES:** Greek warrior; slew Hector at Troy; slain by Paris, who wounded him in his vulnerable heel.

**ACTAEON:** Hunter; surprised Artemis bathing; changed by her to stag and killed by his dogs.

**ADMETUS:** King of Thessaly; his wife, Alcestis, offered to die in his place.

**ADONIS:** Beautiful youth loved by Aphrodite.

**AEACUS:** One of three judges of dead in Hades; son of Zeus.

**AEËTES:** King of Colchis; father of Medea; keeper of Golden Fleece.

**AEGEUS:** Father of Theseus; believing Theseus killed in Crete, he drowned himself, Aegean Sea named for him.

**AEGISTHUS:** Son of Thyestes; slew Atreus; with Clytemnestra, his paramour, slew Agamemnon; slain by Orestes.

**AEGYPTUS:** Brother of Danaüs; his sons, except Lynceus, slain by Danaïdes.

**AENEAS:** Trojan; son of Anchises and Aphrodite; after fall of Troy, led his followers eventually to Italy; loved and deserted Dido.

**AEOLUS:** *See* Winds.

**AESCULAPIUS:** *See* Asclepius.

**AESON:** King of Ioclus; father of Jason; overthrown by his brother Pelias; restored to youth by Medea.

**AETHER:** Personification of sky.

**AETHRA:** Mother of Theseus.

**AGAMEMNON:** King of Mycenae; son of Atreus; brother of Menelaus; leader of Greeks against Troy; slain on his return home by Clytemnestra and Aegisthus.

**AGLAIA:** *See* Graces.

**AJAX:** Greek warrior; killed himself at Troy because Achilles' armor was awarded to Odysseus.

**ALCESTIS:** Wife of Admetus; offered to die in his place but saved from death by Hercules.

**ALCMENE:** Wife of Amphitryon; mother by Zeus of Hercules.

**ALCYONE:** *See* Pleiades.

**ALECTO:** *See* Furies.

**ALECTRYON:** Youth changed by Ares into cock.

**ALTHAEA:** Wife of Oeneus; mother of Meleager.

**AMAZONS:** Female warriors in Asia Minor; supported Troy against Greeks.

**AMOR:** *See* Eros.

**AMPHION:** Musician; husband of Niobe; charmed stones to build fortifications for Thebes.

**AMPHITRITE:** Sea goddess; wife of Poseidon.

**AMPHITRYON:** Husband of Alcmene.

**ANCHISES:** Father of Aeneas.

**ANCILE:** Sacred shield that fell from heavens; palladium of Rome.

**ANDRAEMON:** Husband of Dryope.

**ANDROMACHE:** Wife of Hector.

**ANDROMEDA:** Daughter of Cepheus; chained to cliff for monster to devour; rescued by Perseus.

**ANTEIA:** Wife of Proetus; tried to induce Bellerophon to elope with her.

**ANTEROS:** God who avenged unrequited love.

**ANTIGONE:** Daughter of Oedipus; accompanied him to Colonus; performed burial rite for Polynices and was buried alive.

**ANTINOÜS:** Leader of suitors of Penelope; slain by Odysseus.

**APHRODITE (VENUS):** Goddess of love and beauty; daughter of Zeus; mother of Eros.

**APOLLO:** God of beauty, poetry, music; later identified with Helios as Phoebus Apollo; son of Zeus and Leto.

**AQUILO:** *See* Winds.

**ARACHNE:** Maiden who challenged Athena to weaving contest; changed to spider.

**ARES (MARS):** God of war; son of Zeus and Hera.

**ARGO:** Ship in which Jason and followers sailed to Colchis for Golden Fleece.

**ARGUS:** Monster with hundred eyes; slain by Hermes; his eyes placed by Hera into peacock's tail.

**ARIADNE:** Daughter of Minos; aided Theseus in slaying Minotaur; deserted by him on island of Naxos and married to Dionysus.

**ARION:** Musician; thrown overboard by pirates but saved by dolphin.

**ARTEMIS (DIANA):** Goddess of moon; huntress; twin sister of Apollo.

**ASCLEPIUS (AESCULAPIUS):** Mortal son of Apollo; slain by Zeus for raising dead; later deified as god of medicine. Also known as Asklepios.

**ASTARTE:** Phoenician goddess of love; variously identified with Aphrodite, Selene, and Artemis.

ASTRAEA: Goddess of Justice; daughter of Zeus and Themis.

ATALANTA: Princess who challenged her suitors to a foot race; Hippomenes won race and married her.

ATHENA (MINERVA): Goddess of wisdom; known poetically as Pallas Athene; sprang fully armed from head of Zeus.

ATLAS: Titan; held world on his shoulders as punishment for warring against Zeus; son of Iapetus.

ATREUS: King of Mycenae; father of Menelaus and Agamemnon; brother of Thyestes, three of whose sons he slew and served to him at banquet; slain by Aegisthus.

ATROPOS: *See* Fates.

AURORA: *See* Eos.

AUSTER: *See* Winds.

AVERNUS: Infernal regions; name derived from small vaporous lake near Vesuvius which was fabled to kill birds and vegetation.

BACCHUS: *See* Dionysus.

BELLEROPHON: Corinthian hero; killed Chimera with aid of Pegasus; tried to reach Olympus on Pegasus and was thrown to his death.

BELLONA: Roman goddess of war.

BOREAS: *See* Winds.

BRIAREUS: Monster of hundred hands; son of Uranus and Gaea.

BRISEIS: Captive maiden given to Achilles; taken by Agamemnon in exchange for loss of Chryseis, which caused Achilles to cease fighting, until death of Patroclus.

CADMUS: Brother of Europa; planter of dragon seeds from which first Thebans sprang.

CALLIOPE: *See* Muses.

CALYPSO: Sea nymph; kept Odysseus on her island Ogygia for seven years.

CASSANDRA: Daughter of Priam; prophetess who was never believed; slain with Agamemnon.

CASTOR: *See* Dioscuri.

CELAENO: *See* Pleiades.

CENTAURS: Beings half man and half horse; lived in mountains of Thessaly.

CEPHALUS: Hunter; accidentally killed his wife Procris with his spear.

CEPHEUS: King of Ethiopia; father of Andromeda.

CERBERUS: Three-headed dog guarding entrance to Hades.

CERES: *See* Demeter.

CHAOS: Formless void; personified as first of gods.

CHARON: Boatman on Styx who carried souls of dead to Hades; son of Erebus.

CHARYBDIS: Female monster; personification of whirlpool.

CHIMERA: Female monster with head of lion, body of goat, tail of serpent; killed by Bellerophon.

CHIRON: Most famous of centaurs.

CHRONOS: Personification of time.

CHRYSEIS: Captive maiden given to Agamemnon; his refusal to accept ransom from her father Chryses caused Apollo to send plague on Greeks besieging Troy.

CIRCE: Sorceress; daughter of Helios; changed Odysseus' men into swine.

CLIO: *See* Muses.

CLOTHO: *See* Fates.

CLYTEMNESTRA: Wife of Agamemnon, whom she slew with aid of her paramour, Aegisthus; slain by her son Orestes.

COCYTUS: *See* Rivers.

CREON: Father of Jocasta; forbade burial of Polynices; ordered burial alive of Antigone.

CREUSA: Princess of Corinth, for whom Jason deserted Medea; slain by Medea, who sent her poisoned robe; also known as Glauke.

CREUSA: Wife of Aeneas; died fleeing Troy.

CRONUS (SATURN): Titan; god of harvests; son of Uranus and Gaea; dethroned by his son Zeus.

CUPID: *See* Eros.

CYBELE: Anatolian nature goddess; adopted by Greeks and identified with Rhea.

CYCLOPES: Race of one-eyed giants (singular: Cyclops).

DAEDALUS: Athenian artificer; father of Icarus; builder of Labyrinth in Crete; devised wings attached with wax for him and Icarus to escape Crete.

DANAE: Princess of Argos; mother of Perseus by Zeus, who appeared to her in form of golden shower.

DANAIDES: Daughters of Danaüs; at his command, all except Hypermnestra slew their husbands, the sons of Aegyptus.

DANAÜS: Brother of Aegyptus; father of Danaïdes; slain by Lynceus.

DAPHNE: Nymph; pursued by Apollo; changed to laurel tree.

DECUMA: *See* Fates.

DEINO: *See* Graeae.

DEMETER (CERES): Goddess of agriculture; mother of Persephone.

DIANA: *See* Artemis.

DIDO: Founder and queen of Carthage; stabbed herself when deserted by Aeneas.

DIOMEDES: Greek hero; with Odysseus, entered Troy and carried off Palladium, sacred statue of Athena.

DIOMEDES: Owner of man-eating horses, which Hercules, as ninth labor, carried off.

**DIONE:** Titan goddess; mother by Zeus of Aphrodite.

**DIONYSUS (BACCHUS):** God of wine; son of Zeus and Semele.

**DIOSCURI:** Twins Castor and Pollux; sons of Leda by Zeus.

**DIS:** *See* Hades.

**DRYADS:** Wood nymphs.

**DRYOPE:** Maiden changed to Hamadryad.

**ECHO:** Nymph who fell hopelessly in love with Narcissus; faded away except for her voice.

**ELECTRA:** Daughter of Agamemnon and Clytemnestra; sister of Orestes; urged Orestes to slay Clytemnestra and Aegisthus.

**ELECTRA:** *See* Pleiades.

**ELYSIUM:** Abode of blessed dead.

**ENDYMION:** Mortal loved by Selene.

**ENYO:** *See* Graeae.

**EOS (AURORA):** Goddess of dawn.

**EPIMETHEUS:** Brother of Prometheus; husband of Pandora.

**ERATO:** *See* Muses.

**EREBUS:** Spirit of darkness; son of Chaos.

**ERINYES:** *See* Furies.

**ERIS:** Goddess of discord.

**EROS (AMOR or CUPID):** God of love; son of Aphrodite.

**ETEOCLES:** Son of Oedipus, whom he succeeded to rule alternately with Polynices; refused to give up throne at end of year; he and Polynices slew each other.

**EUMENIDES:** *See* Furies.

**EUPHROSYNE:** *See* Graces.

**EUROPA:** Mortal loved by Zeus, who, in form of white bull, carried her off to Crete.

**EURUS:** *See* Winds.

**EURYALE:** *See* Gorgons.

**EURYDICE:** Nymph; wife of Orpheus.

**EURYSTHEUS:** King of Argos; imposed twelve labors on Hercules.

**EUTERPE:** *See* Muses.

**FATES:** Goddesses of destiny: Clotho (Spinner of thread of life), Lachesis (Determiner of length), and Atropos (Cutter of thread); also called Moirae. Identified by Romans with their goddesses of fate; Nona, Decuma, and Morta; called Parcae.

**FAUNS:** Roman deities of woods and groves.

**FAUNUS:** *See* Pan.

**FAVONIUS:** *See* Winds.

**FLORA:** Roman goddess of flowers.

**FORTUNA:** Roman goddess of fortune.

**FURIES:** Avenging spirits: Alecto, Megaera, and Tisiphone; known also as Erinyes or Eumenides.

**GAEA:** Goddess of earth; daughter of Chaos; mother of Titans; known also as Ge, Gea, Gaia, etc.

**GALATEA:** Statue of maiden carved from ivory by Pygmalion; given life by Aphrodite.

**GALATEA:** Sea nymph; loved by Polyphemus.

**GANYMEDE:** Beautiful boy; successor to Hebe as cupbearer of gods.

**GLAUCUS:** Mortal who became sea divinity by eating magic grass.

**GLAUKE:** *See* Creüsa.

**GOLDEN FLEECE:** Fleece from ram that flew Phrixos to Colchis; Aeëtes placed it under guard of dragon; carried off by Jason.

**GORGONS:** Female monsters: Euryale, Medusa, and Stheno; had snakes for hair; their glances turned mortals to stone. *See* Medusa.

**GRACES:** Beautiful goddesses: Aglaia (Brilliance), Euphrosyne (Joy), and Thalia (Bloom); daughters of Zeus.

**GRAEAE:** Sentinels for Gorgons: Deino, Enyo, and Pephredo; had one eye among them, which passed from one to another.

**HADES (DIS):** Name sometimes given Pluto; also, abode of dead, ruled by Pluto.

**HAEMON:** Son of Creon; promised husband of Antigone; killed himself in her tomb.

**HAMADRYADS:** Tree nymphs; lived and died with trees they inhabited.

**HARPIES:** Monsters with heads of women and bodies of birds.

**HEBE (JUVENTAS):** Goddess of youth; cupbearer of gods before Ganymede; daughter of Zeus and Hera.

**HECATE:** Goddess of sorcery and witchcraft.

**HECTOR:** Son of Priam; slayer of Patroclus; slain by Achilles.

**HECUBA:** Wife of Priam.

**HELEN:** Fairest woman in world; daughter of Zeus and Leda; wife of Menelaus; carried to Troy by Paris, causing Trojan War.

**HELIADES:** Daughters of Helios; mourned for Phaëthon and were changed to poplar trees.

**HELIOS (SOL):** God of sun; later identified with Phoebus Apollo.

**HELLE:** Sister of Phrixos; fell from ram of Golden Fleece; water where she fell named Hellespont.

**HEPHAESTUS (VULCAN):** God of fire; celestial blacksmith; son of Zeus and Hera; husband of Aphrodite.

**HERA (JUNO):** Queen of heaven; wife of Zeus.

**HERCULES:** Hero and strong man; son of Zeus and Alcmene; performed twelve labors or deeds to be free from bondage under Eurystheus; after death, his mortal share was destroyed, and he became immortal. Also known as Herakles or Heracles. Labors: (1) killing Nemean lion; (2) killing Lernaean Hydra; (3) capturing Erymanthian boar; (4) capturing Cerynean hind; (5) killing man-eating Stymphalian birds; (6) procuring girdle of Hippolyte; (7) cleaning Augean stables; (8) capturing Cretan bull; (9) capturing man-eating horses of Diomedes; (10) capturing cattle of Geryon; (11) procuring golden apples of Hesperides; (12) bringing Cerberus up from Hades.

**HERMES (MERCURY):** God of physicians and thieves; messenger of gods; son of Zeus and Maia.

**HERO:** Priestess of Aphrodite; Leander swam Hellespont nightly to see her; drowned herself at his death.

**HESPERUS:** Evening star.

**HESTIA (VESTA):** Goddess of hearth; sister of Zeus.

**HIPPOLYTE:** Queen of Amazons; wife of Theseus.

**HIPPOLYTUS:** Son of Theseus and Hippolyte; falsely accused by Phaedra of trying to kidnap her; slain by Poseidon at request of Theseus.

**HIPPOMENES:** Husband of Atalanta, whom he beat in foot race by dropping golden apples, which she stopped to pick up.

**HYACINTHUS:** Beautiful youth accidentally killed by Apollo, who caused flower to spring up from his blood.

**HYDRA:** Nine-headed monster in marsh of Lerna; slain by Hercules.

**HYGEIA:** Personification of health.

**HYMEN:** God of marriage.

**HYPERION:** Titan; early sun god; father of Helios.

**HYPERMNESTRA:** Daughter of Danaüs; refused to kill her husband Lynceus.

**HYPNOS (SOMNUS):** God of sleep.

**IAPETUS:** Titan; father of Atlas, Epimetheus, and Prometheus.

**ICARUS:** Son of Daedalus; flew too near sun with wax-attached wings and fell into sea and was drowned.

**IO:** Mortal maiden loved by Zeus; changed by Hera into heifer.

**IOBATES:** King of Lycia; sent Bellerophon to slay Chimera.

**IPHIGENIA:** Daughter of Agamemnon; offered as sacrifice to Artemis at Aulis; carried by Artemis to Tauris where she became priestess; escaped from there with Orestes.

**IRIS:** Goddess of rainbow; messenger of Zeus and Hera.

**ISMENE:** Daughter of Oedipus; sister of Antigone.

**IULUS:** Son of Aeneas.

**IXION:** King of Lapithae; for making love to Hera he was bound to endlessly revolving wheel in Tartarus.

**JANUS:** Roman god of gates and doors; represented with two opposite faces.

**JASON:** Son of Aeson; to gain throne of Ioclus from Pelias, went to Colchis and brought back Golden Fleece; married Medea; deserted her for Creüsa.

**JOCASTA:** Wife of Laius; mother of Oedipus; unwittingly became wife of Oedipus; hanged herself when relationship was discovered.

**JUNO:** *See* Hera.

**JUPITER:** *See* Zeus.

**JUVENTAS:** *See* Hebe.

**LACHESIS:** *See* Fates.

**LAIUS:** Father of Oedipus, by whom he was slain.

**LAOCOÖN:** Priest of Apollo at Troy; warned against bringing wooden horse into Troy; destroyed with his two sons by serpents sent by Athena.

**LARES:** Roman ancestral spirits protecting descendants and homes.

**LAVINIA:** wife of Aeneas after defeat of Turnus.

**LEANDER:** Swam Hellespont nightly to see Hero; drowned in storm.

**LEDA:** Mortal loved by Zeus in form of Swan; mother of Helen, Clytemnestra, Dioscuri.

**LETHE:** *See* Rivers.

**LETO (LATONA):** Mother by Zeus of Artemis and Apollo.

**LUCINA:** Roman goddess of childbirth; identified with Juno.

**LYNCEUS:** Son of Aegyptus; husband of Hypermnestra; slew Danaüs.

**MAIA:** Daughter of Atlas; mother of Hermes.

**MAIA:** *See* Pleiades.

**MANES:** Souls of dead Romans, particularly of ancestors.

**MARS:** *See* Ares.

**MARSYAS:** Shepherd; challenged Apollo to music contest and lost; flayed alive by Apollo.

**MEDEA:** Sorceress; daughter of Aeëtes; helped Jason obtain Golden Fleece; when deserted by him for Creüsa, killed her children and Creüsa.

**MEDUSA:** Gorgon; slain by Perseus, who cut off her head.

**MEGAERA:** *See* Furies.

**MELEAGER:** Son of Althaea; his life would last as long as brand burning at his birth; Althaea quenched and saved it but destroyed it when Meleager slew his uncles.

**MELPOMENE:** *See* Muses.

**MEMNON:** Ethiopian king; made immortal by Zeus; son of Tithonus and Eos.

MENELAUS: King of Sparta; son of Atreus; brother of Agamemnon; husband of Helen.

MERCURY: *See* Hermes.

MEROPE: *See* Pleiades.

MEZENTIUS: Cruel Etruscan king; ally of Turnus against Aeneas; slain by Aeneas.

MIDAS: King of Phrygia; given gift of turning to gold all he touched.

MINERVA: *See* Athena.

MINOS: King of Crete; after death, one of three judges of dead in Hades; son of Zeus and Europa.

MINOTAUR: Monster, half man and half beast, kept in Labyrinth in Crete; slain by Theseus.

MNEMOSYNE: Goddess of memory; mother by Zeus of Muses.

MOIRAE: *See* Fates.

MOMUS: God of ridicule.

MORPHEUS: God of dreams.

MORS: *See* Thanatos.

MORTA: *See* Fates.

MUSES: Goddesses presiding over arts and sciences: Calliope (epic poetry), Clio (history), Erato (lyric and love poetry), Euterpe (music), Melpomene (tragedy), Polymnia or Polyhymnia (sacred poetry), Terpsichore (choral dance and song), Thalia (comedy and bucolic poetry), Urania (astronomy); daughters of Zeus and Mnemosyne.

NAIADS: Nymphs of waters, streams, and fountains.

NAPAEAE: Wood nymphs.

NARCISSUS: Beautiful youth loved by Echo; in punishment for not returning her love, he was made to fall in love with his image reflected in pool; pined away and became flower.

NEMESIS: Goddess of retribution.

NEOPTOLEMUS: Son of Achilles; slew Priam; also known as Pyrrhus.

NEPTUNE: *See* Poseidon.

NEREIDS: Sea nymphs; attendants on Poseidon.

NESTOR: King of Pylos; noted for wise counsel in expedition against Troy.

NIKE: Goddess of victory.

NIOBE: Daughter of Tantalus; wife of Amphion; her children slain by Apollo and Artemis; changed to stone but continued to weep her loss.

NONA: *See* Fates.

NOTUS: *See* Winds.

NOX: *See* Nyx.

NYMPHS: Beautiful maidens; inferior deities of nature.

NYX (NOX): Goddess of night.

OCEANIDS: Ocean nymphs; daughters of Oceanus.

OCEANUS: Eldest of Titans; god of waters.

ODYSSEUS (ULYSSES): King of Ithaca; husband of Penelope; wandered ten years after fall of Troy before arriving home.

OEDIPUS: King of Thebes; son of Laius and Jocasta; unwittingly murdered Laius and married Jocasta; tore his eyes out when relationship was discovered.

OENONE: Nymph of Mount Ida; wife of Paris, who abandoned her; refused to cure him when he was poisoned by arrow of Philoctetes at Troy.

OPS: *See* Rhea.

OREADS: Mountain nymphs.

ORESTES: Son of Agamemnon and Clytemnestra; brother of Electra; slew Clytemnestra and Aegisthus; pursued by Furies until his purification by Apollo.

ORION: Hunter; slain by Artemis and made heavenly constellation.

ORPHEUS: Famed musician; son of Apollo and Muse Calliope; husband of Eurydice.

PALES: Roman goddess of shepherds and herdsmen.

PALINURUS: Aeneas' pilot; fell overboard in his sleep and was drowned.

PAN (FAUNUS): God of woods and fields; part goat; son of Hermes.

PANDORA: Opener of box containing human ills; mortal wife of Epimetheus.

PARCAE: *See* Fates.

PARIS: Son of Priam; gave apple of discord to Aphrodite, for which she enabled him to carry off Helen; slew Achilles at Troy; slain by Philoctetes.

PATROCLUS: Great friend of Achilles; wore Achilles' armor and was slain by Hector.

PEGASUS: Winged horse that sprang from Medusa's body at her death; ridden by Bellerophon when he slew Chimera.

PELIAS: King of Ioclus; seized throne from his brother Aeson; sent Jason for Golden Fleece; slain unwittingly by his daughters at instigation of Medea.

PELOPS: Son of Tantalus; his father cooked and served him to gods; restored to life; Peloponnesus named for him.

PENATES: Roman household gods.

PENELOPE: Wife of Odysseus; waited faithfully for him for ten years while putting off numerous suitors.

PEPHREDO: *See* Graeae.

PERIPHETES: Giant; son of Hephaestus; slain by Theseus.

PERSEPHONE (PROSERPINE): Queen of infernal regions; daughter of Zeus and Demeter; wife of Pluto.

PERSEUS: Son of Zeus and Danaë; slew Medusa; rescued Andromeda from monster and married her.

PHAEDRA: Daughter of Minos; wife of Theseus; falsely accused Hippolytus of trying to kidnap her.

**PHAËTHON:** Son of Helios; drove his father's sun chariot and was struck down by Zeus before he set world on fire.

**PHILOCTETES:** Greek warrior who possessed Hercules' bow and arrows; slew Paris at Troy with poisoned arrow.

**PHINEUS:** Betrothed of Andromeda; tried to slay Perseus but turned to stone by Medusa's head.

**PHLEGETHON:** *See* Rivers.

**PHOSPHOR:** Morning star.

**PHRIXOS:** Brother of Helle; carried by ram of Golden Fleece to Colchis.

**PIRITHOÜS:** Son of Ixion; friend of Theseus; tried to carry off Persephone from Hades; bound to enchanted rock by Pluto.

**PLEIADES:** Alcyone, Celaeno, Electra, Maia, Merope, Sterope or Asterope, Taygeta; seven daughters of Atlas; transformed into heavenly constellation, of which six stars are visible (Merope is said to have hidden in shame for loving a mortal).

**PLUTO (DIS):** God of Hades; brother of Zeus.

**PLUTUS:** God of wealth.

**POLLUX:** *See* Dioscuri.

**POLYMNIA:** *See* Muses.

**POLYNICES:** Son of Oedipus; he and his brother Eteocles killed each other; burial rite, forbidden by Creon, performed by his sister Antigone.

**POLYPHEMUS:** Cyclops; devoured six of Odysseus' men; blinded by Odysseus.

**POLYXENA:** Daughter of Priam; betrothed to Achilles, whom Paris slew at their betrothal; sacrificed to shade of Achilles.

**POMONA:** Roman goddess of fruits.

**PONTUS:** Sea god; son of Gaea.

**POSEIDON (NEPTUNE):** God of sea; brother of Zeus.

**PRIAM:** King of Troy; husband of Hecuba; ransomed Hector's body from Achilles; slain by Neoptolemus.

**PRIAPUS:** God of regeneration.

**PROCRIS:** Wife of Cephalus, who accidentally slew her.

**PROCRUSTES:** Giant; stretched or cut off legs of victims to make them fit iron bed; slain by Theseus.

**PROETUS:** Husband of Anteia; sent Bellerophon to Iobates to be put to death.

**PROMETHEUS:** Titan; stole fire from heaven for man. Zeus punished him by chaining him to rock in Caucasus where vultures devoured his liver daily.

**PROTEUS:** Sea god; assumed various shapes when called on to prophesy.

**PSYCHE:** Beloved of Eros; punished by jealous Aphrodite; made immortal and united with Eros.

**PYGMALION:** King of Cyprus; carved ivory statue of maiden which Aphrodite gave life as Galatea.

**PYRAMUS:** Babylonian youth; made love to Thisbe through hole in wall; thinking Thisbe slain by lion, killed himself.

**PYRRHUS:** *See* Neoptolemus.

**PYTHON:** Serpent born from slime left by Deluge; slain by Apollo.

**QUIRINUS:** Roman war god.

**REMUS:** Brother of Romulus; slain by him.

**RHADAMANTHUS:** One of three judges of dead in Hades; son of Zeus and Europa.

**RHEA (OPS):** Daughter of Uranus and Gaea; wife of Cronus; mother of Zeus; identified with Cybele.

**RIVERS OF UNDERWORLD:** Acheron (woe), Cocytus (wailing), Lethe (forgetfulness), Phlegethon (fire), Styx (across which souls of dead were ferried by Charon).

**ROMULUS:** Founder of Rome; he and Remus suckled in infancy by she-wolf; slew Remus; deified by Romans.

**SARPEDON:** King of Lycia; son of Zeus and Europa; slain by Patroclus at Troy.

**SATURN:** *See* Cronus.

**SATYRS:** Hoofed demigods of woods and fields; companions of Dionysus.

**SCIRON:** Robber; forced strangers to wash his feet, then hurled them into sea where tortoise devoured them; slain by Theseus.

**SCYLLA:** Female monster inhabiting rock opposite Charybdis; menaced passing sailors.

**SELENE:** Goddess of moon.

**SEMELE:** Daughter of Cadmus; mother by Zeus of Dionysus; demanded Zeus appear before her in all his splendor and was destroyed by his lightnings.

**SIBYLS:** Various prophetesses; most famous, Cumaean sibyl, accompanied Aeneas into Hades.

**SILENI:** Minor woodland deities similar to satyrs (singular: silenus). Sometimes Silenus refers to eldest of satyrs, son of Hermes or of Pan.

**SILVANUS:** Roman god of woods and fields.

**SINIS:** Giant; bent pines, by which he hurled victims against side of mountain; slain by Theseus.

**SIRENS:** Minor deities who lured sailors to destruction with their singing.

**SISYPHUS:** King of Corinth; condemned in Tartarus to roll huge stone to top of hill; it always rolled back down again.

**SOL:** *See* Helios.

**SOMNUS:** *See* Hypnos.

**SPHINX:** Monster of Thebes; killed those who could not answer her riddle; slain by Oedipus. Name also refers to other monsters having body of lion, wings, and head and bust of woman.

**STEROPE:** *See* Pleiades.

**STHENO:** *See* Gorgons.

**STYX:** *See* Rivers.

SYMPLEGADES: Clashing rocks at entrance to Black Sea; Argo passed through, causing them to become forever fixed.

SYRINX: Nymph pursued by Pan; changed to reeds, from which he made his pipes.

TANTALUS: Cruel king; father of Pelops and Niobe; condemned in Tartarus to stand chin-deep in lake surrounded by fruit branches; as he tried to eat or drink, water or fruit always receded.

TARTARUS: Underworld below Hades; often refers to Hades.

TAYGETA: *See* Pleiades.

TELEMACHUS: Son of Odysseus; made unsuccessful journey to find his father.

TELLUS: Roman goddess of earth.

TERMINUS: Roman god of boundaries and landmarks.

TERPSICHORE: *See* Muses.

TERRA: Roman earth goddess.

THALIA: *See* Graces; Muses.

THANATOS (MORS): God of death.

THEMIS: Titan goddess of laws of physical phenomena; daughter of Uranus; mother of Prometheus.

THESEUS: Son of Aegeus; slew Minotaur; married and deserted Ariadne; later married Phaedra.

THISBE: Beloved of Pyramus; killed herself at his death.

THYESTES: Brother of Atreus; Atreus killed three of his sons and served them to him at banquet.

TIRESIAS: Blind soothsayer of Thebes.

TISIPHONE: *See* Furies.

TITANS: Early gods from which Olympian gods were derived; children of Uranus and Gaea.

TITHONUS: Mortal loved by Eos; changed into grasshopper.

TRITON: Demigod of sea; son of Poseidon.

TURNUS: King of Rutuli in Italy; betrothed to Lavinia; slain by Aeneas.

ULYSSES: *See* Odysseus.

URANIA: *See* Muses.

URANUS: Personification of Heaven; husband of Gaea; father of Titans; dethroned by his son Cronus.

VENUS: *See* Aphrodite.

VERTUMNUS: Roman god of fruits and vegetables; husband of Pomona.

VESTA: *See* Hestia.

VULCAN: *See* Hephaestus.

WINDS: Aeolus (keeper of winds), Boreas (Aquilo) (north wind), Eurus (east wind), Notus (Auster) (south wind), Zephyrus (Favonius) (west wind).

ZEPHYRUS: *See* Winds.

ZEUS (JUPITER): Chief of Olympian gods; son of Cronus and Rhea; husband of Hera.

## Norse Mythology

AESIR: Chief gods of Asgard.

ANDVARI: Dwarf; robbed of gold and magic ring by Loki.

ANGERBOTHA (Angrbotha): Giantess; mother by Loki of Fenrir, Hel, and Midgard serpent.

ASGARD (Asgarth): Abode of gods.

ASK (Aske, Askr): First man; created by Odin, Hoenir, and Lothur.

ASYNJUR: Goddesses of Asgard.

ATLI: Second husband of Gudrun; invited Gunnar and Hogni to his court, where they were slain; slain by Gudrun.

AUDHUMLA (Audhumbla): Cow that nourished Ymir; created Buri by licking ice cliff.

BALDER (Baldr, Baldur): God of light, spring, peace, joy; son of Odin; slain by Hoth at instigation of Loki.

BIFROST: Rainbow bridge connecting Midgard and Asgard.

BRAGI (Brage): God of poetry; husband of Ithunn.

BRANSTOCK: Great oak in hall of Volsungs; into it, Odin thrust Gram, which only Sigmund could draw forth.

BRYNHILD: Valkyrie; wakened from magic sleep by Sigurd; married Gunnar; instigated death of Sigurd; killed herself and was burned on pyre beside Sigurd.

BUR (Bor): Son of Buri; father of Odin, Hoenir, and Lothur.

BURI (Bori): Progenitor of gods; father of Bur; created by Audhumla.

EMBLA: First woman; created by Odin, Hoenir, and Lothur.

FAFNIR: Son of Rodmar, whom he slew for gold in Otter's skin; in form of dragon, guarded gold; slain by Sigurd.

FENRIR: Wolf; offspring of Loki; swallows Odin at Ragnarok and is slain by Vitharr.

FORSETI: Son of Balder.

FREY (Freyr): God of fertility and crops; son of Njorth; originally one of Vanir.

FREYA (Freyja): Goddess of love and beauty; sister of Frey; originally one of Vanir.

FRIGG (Frigga): Goddess of sky; wife of Odin.

GARM: Watchdog of Hel; slays, and is slain by, Tyr at Ragnarok.

GIMLE: Home of blessed after Ragnarok.

GIUKI: King of Nibelungs; father of Gunnar, Hogni, Guttorm, and Gudrun.

**GLATHSHEIM** (Gladsheim): Hall of gods in Asgard.

**GRAM** (meaning "Angry"): Sigmund's sword; rewelded by Regin; used by Sigurd to slay Fafnir.

**GREYFELL**: Sigmund's horse; descended from Sleipnir.

**GRIMHILD**: Mother of Gudrun; administered magic potion to Sigurd which made him forget Brynhild.

**GUDRUN**: Daughter of Giuki; wife of Sigurd; later wife of Atli and Jonakr.

**GUNNAR**: Son of Giuki; in his semblance Sigurd won Brynhild for him; slain at hall of Atli.

**GUTTORM**: Son of Giuki; slew Sigurd at Brynhild's request.

**HEIMDALL** (Heimdallr): Guardian of Asgard.

**HEL**: Goddess of dead and queen of underworld; daughter of Loki.

**HIORDIS**: Wife of Sigmund; mother of Sigurd.

**HOENIR**: One of creators of Ask and Embla; son of Bur.

**HOGNI**: Son of Giuki; slain at hall of Atli.

**HOTH** (Hoder, Hodur): Blind god of night and darkness; slayer of Balder at instigation of Loki.

**ITHUNN** (Ithun, Iduna): Keeper of golden apples of youth; wife of Bragi.

**JONAKR**: Third husband of Gudrun.

**JORMUNREK**: Slayer of Swanhild; slain by sons of Gudrun.

**JOTUNNHEIM** (Jotunheim): Abode of giants.

**LIF** and **LIFTHRASIR**: First man and woman after Ragnarok.

**LOKI**: God of evil and mischief; instigator of Balder's death.

**LOTHUR** (Lodur): One of creators of Ask and Embla.

**MIDGARD** (Midgarth): Abode of mankind; the earth.

**MIDGARD SERPENT**: Sea monster; offspring of Loki; slays, and is slain by, Thor at Ragnarok.

**MIMIR**: Giant; guardian of well in Jotunnheim at root of Yggdrasill; knower of past and future.

**MJOLLNIR**: Magic hammer of Thor.

**NAGLFAR**: Ship to be used by giants in attacking Asgard at Ragnarok; built from nails of dead men.

**NANNA**: Wife of Balder.

**NIBELUNGS**: Dwellers in northern kingdom ruled by Giuki.

**NIFLHEIM** (Nifelheim): Outer region of cold and darkness; abode of Hel.

**NJORTH**: Father of Frey and Freya; originally one of Vanir.

**NORNS**: Demigoddesses of fate: Urth (Urdur) (Past), Verthandi (Verdandi) (Present), Skuld (Future).

**ODIN** (Othin): Head of Aesir; creator of world with Vili and Ve; equivalent to Woden (Wodan, Wotan) in Teutonic mythology.

**OTTER**: Son of Rodmar; slain by Loki; his skin filled with gold hoard of Andvari to appease Rodmar.

**RAGNAROK**: Final destruction of present world in battle between gods and giants; some minor gods will survive, and Lif and Lifthrasir will repeople world.

**REGIN**: Blacksmith; son of Rodmar; foster-father of Sigurd.

**RERIR**: King of Huns; son of Sigi.

**RODMAR**: Father of Regin, Otter, and Fafnir; demanded Otter's skin be filled with gold; slain by Fafnir, who stole gold.

**SIF**: Wife of Thor.

**SIGGEIR**: King of Goths; husband of Signy; he and his sons slew Volsung and his sons, except Sigmund; slain by Sigmund and Sinfiotli.

**SIGI**: King of Huns; son of Odin.

**SIGMUND**: Son of Volsung; brother of Signy, who bore him Sinfiotli; husband of Hiordis, who bore him Sigurd.

**SIGNY**: Daughter of Volsung; sister of Sigmund; wife of Siggeir; mother by Sigmund of Sinfiotli.

**SIGURD**: Son of Sigmund and Hiordis; wakened Brynhild from magic sleep; married Gudrun; slain by Guttorm at instigation of Brynhild.

**SIGYN**: Wife of Loki.

**SINFIOTLI**: Son of Sigmund and Signy.

**SKULD**: *See* Norns.

**SLEIPNIR** (Sleipner): Eight-legged horse of Odin.

**SURT** (Surtr): Fire demon; slays Frey at Ragnarok.

**SVARTALFAHEIM**: Abode of dwarfs.

**SWANHILD**: Daughter of Sigurd and Gudrun; slain by Jormunrek.

**THOR**: God of thunder; oldest son of Odin; equivalent to Germanic deity Donar.

**TYR**: God of war; son of Odin; equivalent to Tiu in Teutonic mythology.

**ULL** (Ullr): Son of Sif; stepson of Thor.

**URTH**: *See* Norns.

**VALHALLA** (Valhall): Great hall in Asgard where Odin received souls of heroes killed in battle.

**VALI**: Odin's son; Ragnarok survivor.

**VALKYRIES**: Virgins, messengers of Odin, who selected heroes to die in battle and took them to Valhalla; generally considered as nine in number.

**VANIR**: Early race of gods; three survivors, Njorth, Frey, and Freya, are associated with Aesir.

VE: Brother of Odin; one of creators of world.

VERTHANDI: *See* Norns.

VILI: Brother of Odin; one of creators of world.

VINGOLF: Abode of goddesses in Asgard.

VITHARR (Vithar): Son of Odin; survivor of Ragnarok.

VOLSUNG: Descendant of Odin, and father of Signy, Sigmund; his descendants were called Volsungs.

YGGDRASILL: Giant ash tree springing from body of Ymir and supporting universe; its roots extended to Asgard, Jotunnheim, and Niflheim.

YMIR (Ymer): Primeval frost giant killed by Odin, Vili, and Ve; world created from his body; also, from his body sprang Yggdrasill.

## Egyptian Mythology

AARU: Abode of the blessed dead.

AMEN (Amon, Ammon): One of chief Theban deities; united with sun god under form of Amen-Ra.

AMENTI: Region of dead where souls were judged by Osiris.

ANUBIS: Guide of souls to Amenti; son of Osiris; jackal-headed.

APIS: Sacred bull, an embodiment of Ptah; identified with Osiris as Osiris-Apis or Serapis.

GEB (Keb, Seb): Earth god; father of Osiris; represented with goose on head.

HATHOR (Athor): Goddess of love and mirth; cow-headed.

HORUS: God of day; son of Osiris and Isis; hawk-headed.

ISIS: Goddess of motherhood and fertility; sister and wife of Osiris.

KHEPERA: God of morning sun.

KHNEMU (Khnum, Chnuphis, Chnemu, Chnum): Ram-headed god.

KHONSU (Khensu, Khuns): Son of Amen and Mut.

MENTU (Ment): Solar deity, sometimes considered god of war; falcon-headed.

MIN (Khem, Chem): Principle of physical life.

MUT (Maut): Wife of Amen.

NEPHTHYS: Goddess of the dead; sister and wife of Set.

NU: Chaos from which world was created, personified as a god.

NUT: Goddess of heavens; consort of Geb.

OSIRIS: God of underworld and judge of dead; son of Geb and Nut.

PTAH (Phtha): Chief deity of Memphis.

RA: God of the Sun, the supreme god; son of Nut; Pharaohs claimed descent from him; represented as lion, cat, or falcon.

SERAPIS: God uniting attributes of Osiris and Apis.

SET (Seth): God of darkness or evil; brother and enemy of Osiris.

SHU: Solar deity; son of Ra and Hathor.

TEM (Atmu, Atum, Tum): Solar deity.

THOTH (Dhouti): God of wisdom and magic; scribe of gods; ibis-headed.

## Rulers of England and Great Britain

### Saxons[1]

| Name | Born | Ruled[2] |
|---|---|---|
| Egbert[3] | c. 775 | 828– 839 |
| Ethelwulf | ? | 839– 858 |
| Ethelbald | ? | 858– 860 |
| Ethelbert | ? | 860– 866 |
| Ethelred I | ? | 866– 871 |
| Alfred the Great | 849 | 871– 899 |
| Edward the Elder | c. 870 | 899– 924 |
| Athelstan | 895 | 924– 939 |
| Edmund I the Deed-doer | 921 | 939– 946 |
| Edred | c. 925 | 946– 955 |
| Edwy the Fair | c. 943 | 955– 959 |
| Edgar the Peaceful | 943 | 959– 975 |
| Edward the Martyr | c. 962 | 975– 979 |
| Ethelred II the Unready | 968 | 979–1016 |
| Edmund II Ironside | c. 993 | 1016–1016 |

### Danes

| Name | Born | Ruled[2] |
|---|---|---|
| Canute | 995 | 1016–1035 |
| Harold I Harefoot | c.1016 | 1035–1040 |
| Hardecanute | c.1018 | 1040–1042 |

### Saxons

| Name | Born | Ruled[2] |
|---|---|---|
| Edward the Confessor | c.1004 | 1042–1066 |
| Harold II | c.1020 | 1066–1066 |

### House of Normandy

| Name | Born | Ruled[2] |
|---|---|---|
| William I the Conqueror | 1027 | 1066–1087 |
| William II Rufus | c.1056 | 1087–1100 |
| Henry I Beauclerc | 1068 | 1100–1135 |
| Stephen of Blois | c.1100 | 1135–1154 |

### House of Plantagenet

| Name | Born | Ruled[2] |
|---|---|---|
| Henry II | 1133 | 1154–1189 |
| Richard I Coeur de Lion | 1157 | 1189–1199 |
| John Lackland | 1167 | 1199–1216 |
| Henry III | 1207 | 1216–1272 |
| Edward I Longshanks | 1239 | 1272–1307 |
| Edward II | 1284 | 1307–1327 |
| Edward III | 1312 | 1327–1377 |
| Richard II | 1367 | 1377–1399[4] |

### House of Lancaster

| Name | Born | Ruled[2] |
|---|---|---|
| Henry IV Bolingbroke | 1367 | 1399–1413 |
| Henry V | 1387 | 1413–1422 |
| Henry VI | 1421 | 1422–1461[13] |

### House of York

| Name | Born | Ruled[2] |
|---|---|---|
| Edward IV | 1442 | 1461–1483[13] |
| Edward V | 1470 | 1483–1483 |
| Richard III | 1452 | 1483–1485 |

### House of Tudor

| Name | Born | Ruled[2] |
|---|---|---|
| Henry VII | 1457 | 1485–1509 |
| Henry VIII | 1491 | 1509–1547 |
| Edward VI | 1537 | 1547–1553 |
| Jane (Lady Jane Grey)[5] | 1537 | 1553–1553 |
| Mary I ("Bloody Mary") | 1516 | 1553–1558 |
| Elizabeth I | 1533 | 1558–1603 |

### House of Stuart

| Name | Born | Ruled[2] |
|---|---|---|
| James I[6] | 1566 | 1603–1625 |
| Charles I | 1600 | 1625–1649 |

### Commonwealth

| Name | Born | Ruled[2] |
|---|---|---|
| Council of State | .... | 1649–1653 |
| Oliver Cromwell[7] | 1599 | 1653–1658 |
| Richard Cromwell[7] | 1626 | 1658–1659[8] |

### Restoration of House of Stuart

| Name | Born | Ruled[2] |
|---|---|---|
| Charles II | 1630 | 1660–1685 |
| James II | 1633 | 1685–1688[9] |

### Restoration of House of Stuart (cont'd)

| Name | Born | Ruled[2] |
|---|---|---|
| William III[10] | 1650 | 1689–1702 |
| Mary II[10] | 1662 | 1689–1694 |
| Anne | 1665 | 1702–1714 |

### House of Hanover

| Name | Born | Ruled[2] |
|---|---|---|
| George I | 1660 | 1714–1727 |
| George II | 1683 | 1727–1760 |
| George III | 1738 | 1760–1820 |
| George IV | 1762 | 1820–1830 |
| William IV | 1765 | 1830–1837 |
| Victoria | 1819 | 1837–1901 |

### House of Saxe-Coburg[11]

| Name | Born | Ruled[2] |
|---|---|---|
| Edward VII | 1841 | 1901–1910 |

### House of Windsor[11]

| Name | Born | Ruled[2] |
|---|---|---|
| George V | 1865 | 1910–1936 |
| Edward VIII | 1894 | 1936–1936[12] |
| George VI | 1895 | 1936–1952 |
| Elizabeth II | 1926 | 1952– |

[1] Dates for Saxon Kings are still subjects of controversy. [2] Year of end of rule is also that of death, unless otherwise indicated. [3] Became King of West Saxons in 802; considered (from 828) first King of all England. [4] Died 1400. [5] Nominal Queen for 9 days; not counted as Queen by some authorities. She was beheaded in 1554. [6] Ruled in Scotland as James VI (1567–1625). [7] Lord Protector. [8] Died 1712. [9] Died 1701. [10] Joint rulers 1689–1694. [11] Name changed from Saxe-Coburg to Windsor in 1917. [12] Has been known since his abdication as the Duke of Windsor. [13] Henry VI reigned again briefly 1470–71.

## British Prime Ministers Since 1770

| Name | Term |
|---|---|
| Lord North (Tory) | 1770–1782 |
| Marquis of Rockingham (Whig) | 1782–1782 |
| Earl of Shelburne (Whig) | 1782–1783 |
| Duke of Portland (Coalition) | 1783–1783 |
| William Pitt, the Younger (Tory) | 1783–1801 |
| Henry Addington (Tory) | 1801–1804 |
| William Pitt, the Younger (Tory) | 1804–1806 |
| Baron Grenville (Whig) | 1806–1807 |
| Duke of Portland (Tory) | 1807–1809 |
| Spencer Perceval (Tory) | 1809–1812 |
| Earl of Liverpool (Tory) | 1812–1827 |
| George Canning (Tory) | 1827–1827 |
| Viscount Goderich (Tory) | 1827–1828 |
| Duke of Wellington (Tory) | 1828–1830 |
| Earl Grey (Whig) | 1830–1834 |
| Viscount Melbourne (Whig) | 1834–1834 |
| Sir Robert Peel (Tory) | 1834–1835 |
| Viscount Melbourne (Whig) | 1835–1841 |
| Sir Robert Peel (Tory) | 1841–1846 |
| Earl Russell (Whig) | 1846–1852 |
| Earl of Derby (Tory) | 1852–1852 |
| Earl of Aberdeen (Coalition) | 1852–1855 |
| Viscount Palmerston (Liberal) | 1855–1858 |
| Earl of Derby (Conservative) | 1858–1859 |
| Viscount Palmerston (Liberal) | 1859–1865 |
| Earl Russell (Liberal) | 1865–1866 |
| Earl of Derby (Conservative) | 1866–1868 |
| Benjamin Disraeli (Conservative) | 1868–1868 |
| William E. Gladstone (Liberal) | 1868–1874 |
| Benjamin Disraeli (Conservative) | 1874–1880 |
| William E. Gladstone (Liberal) | 1880–1885 |
| Marquis of Salisbury (Conservative) | 1885–1886 |
| William E. Gladstone (Liberal) | 1886–1886 |
| Marquis of Salisbury (Conservative) | 1886–1892 |
| William E. Gladstone (Liberal) | 1892–1894 |
| Earl of Rosebery (Liberal) | 1894–1895 |
| Marquis of Salisbury (Conservative) | 1895–1902 |
| Earl Balfour (Conservative) | 1902–1905 |
| Sir H. Campbell-Bannerman (Liberal) | 1905–1908 |
| Herbert H. Asquith (Liberal) | 1908–1915 |
| Herbert H. Asquith (Coalition) | 1915–1916 |
| David Lloyd George (Coalition) | 1916–1922 |
| Andrew Bonar Law (Conservative) | 1922–1923 |
| Stanley Baldwin (Conservative) | 1923–1924 |
| James Ramsay MacDonald (Labour) | 1924–1924 |
| Stanley Baldwin (Conservative) | 1924–1929 |
| James Ramsay MacDonald (Labour) | 1929–1931 |
| James Ramsay MacDonald (Coalition) | 1931–1935 |
| Stanley Baldwin (Coalition) | 1935–1937 |
| Neville Chamberlain (Coalition) | 1937–1940 |
| Winston Churchill (Coalition) | 1940–1945 |
| Clement R. Attlee (Labour) | 1945–1951 |
| Sir Winston Churchill (Conservative) | 1951–1955 |
| Sir Anthony Eden (Conservative) | 1955–1957 |
| Harold Macmillan (Conservative) | 1957– |

## Birthstones

*Source: Jewelry Industry Council.*

|  |  |
|---|---|
| January | Garnet |
| February | Amethyst |
| March | Aquamarine or Bloodstone |
| April | Diamond |
| May | Emerald |
| June | Pearl, Alexandrite or Moonstone |
| July | Ruby |
| August | Peridot or Sardonyx |
| September | Sapphire |
| October | Opal or Tourmaline |
| November | Topaz |
| December | Turquoise or Zircon |

# Rulers of France

## Carolingian Dynasty

| Name | Born | Ruled[1] |
|---|---|---|
| Pepin the Short | c. 714 | 751–768 |
| Charlemagne[2] | 742 | 768–814 |
| Louis I the Debonair[3] | 778 | 814–840 |
| Charles I the Bald[4] | 823 | 840–877 |
| Louis II the Stammerer | 846 | 877–879 |
| Louis III[5] | c. 863 | 879–882 |
| Carloman[5] | ? | 879–884 |
| Charles II the Fat[6] | 839 | 884–887[7] |
| Eudes (Odo), Count of Paris | ? | 888–898 |
| Charles III the Simple[8] | 879 | 893–923[9] |
| Robert I[10] | c. 865 | 922–923 |
| Rudolf (Raoul), Duke of Burgundy | ? | 926–936 |
| Louis IV d'Outremer | c. 921 | 936–954 |
| Lothair | c. 941 | 954–986 |
| Louis V the Sluggard | c. 967 | 986–987 |

## Capetian Dynasty

| Name | Born | Ruled |
|---|---|---|
| Hugh Capet | c. 940 | 987–996 |
| Robert II the Pious[11] | c. 970 | 996–1031 |
| Henry I | 1008 | 1031–1060 |
| Philip I | 1052 | 1060–1108 |
| Louis VI the Fat | 1081 | 1108–1137 |
| Louis VII the Young | c.1121 | 1137–1180 |
| Philip II (Philip Augustus) | 1165 | 1180–1223 |
| Louis VIII the Lion | 1187 | 1223–1226 |
| Louis IX (St. Louis) | 1214 | 1226–1270 |
| Philip III the Bold | 1245 | 1270–1285 |
| Philip IV the Fair | 1268 | 1285–1314 |
| Louis X the Quarreler | 1289 | 1314–1316 |
| John I | 1316 | 1316–1316 |
| Philip V the Tall | 1294 | 1316–1322 |
| Charles IV the Fair | 1294 | 1322–1328 |

## House of Valois

| Name | Born | Ruled |
|---|---|---|
| Philip VI | 1293 | 1328–1350 |
| John II the Good | 1319 | 1350–1364 |
| Charles V the Wise | 1337 | 1364–1380 |
| Charles VI the Well-Beloved | 1368 | 1380–1422 |
| Charles VII | 1403 | 1422–1461 |
| Louis XI | 1423 | 1461–1483 |
| Charles VIII | 1470 | 1483–1498 |
| Louis XII the Father of the People | 1462 | 1498–1515 |
| Francis I | 1494 | 1515–1547 |
| Henry II | 1519 | 1547–1559 |
| Francis II | 1544 | 1559–1560 |
| Charles IX | 1550 | 1560–1574 |
| Henry III | 1551 | 1574–1589 |

## House of Bourbon

| Name | Born | Ruled |
|---|---|---|
| Henry IV of Navarre | 1553 | 1589–1610 |
| Louis XIII | 1601 | 1610–1643 |
| Louis XIV the Great | 1638 | 1643–1715 |
| Louis XV the Well-Beloved | 1710 | 1715–1774 |

## House of Bourbon (cont'd)

| Name | Born | Ruled[1] |
|---|---|---|
| Louis XVI | 1754 | 1774–1792[12] |
| Louis XVII (Louis Charles de France)[13] | 1785 | 1793–1795 |

## First Republic

| Name | | Ruled |
|---|---|---|
| National Convention | | 1792–1795 |
| Directory (Directoire) | | 1795–1799 |

## Consulate

| Name | Born | Ruled |
|---|---|---|
| Napoleon Bonaparte[14] | 1769 | 1799–1804 |

## First Empire

| Name | Born | Ruled |
|---|---|---|
| Napoleon I | 1769 | 1804–1815[15] |

## Restoration of House of Bourbon

| Name | Born | Ruled |
|---|---|---|
| Louis XVIII le Désiré | 1755 | 1814–1824 |
| Charles X | 1757 | 1824–1830[16] |

## Bourbon-Orleans line

| Name | Born | Ruled |
|---|---|---|
| Louis Philippe ("Citizen King") | 1773 | 1830–1848[17] |

## Second Republic

| Name | Born | Ruled |
|---|---|---|
| Louis Napoleon[18] | 1808 | 1848–1852 |

## Second Empire

| Name | Born | Ruled |
|---|---|---|
| Napoleon III (Louis Napoleon) | 1808 | 1852–1871[19] |

## Third Republic

| Name | Born | Ruled |
|---|---|---|
| Louis Adolphe Thiers[20] | 1797 | 1871–1873[21] |
| Marie E. P. M. de MacMahon[20] | 1808 | 1873–1879[22] |
| François P. J. Grévy[20] | 1807 | 1879–1887[23] |
| Sadi Carnot[20] | 1837 | 1887–1894 |
| Jean Casimir-Périer[20] | 1847 | 1894–1895[24] |
| François Félix Faure[20] | 1841 | 1895–1899 |
| Émile Loubet[20] | 1838 | 1899–1906[25] |
| Clement Armand Fallières[20] | 1841 | 1906–1913[26] |
| Raymond Poincaré[20] | 1860 | 1913–1920[27] |
| Paul E. L. Deschanel[20] | 1856 | 1920–1920[28] |
| Alexandre Millerand[20] | 1859 | 1920–1924[29] |
| Gaston Doumergue[20] | 1863 | 1924–1931[30] |
| Paul Doumer[20] | 1857 | 1931–1932 |
| Albert Lebrun[20] | 1871 | 1932–1940[31] |

## Vichy Government

| Name | Born | Ruled |
|---|---|---|
| Henri Philippe Pétain[32] | 1856 | 1940–1944[33] |

## Provisional Government

| Name | Born | Ruled |
|---|---|---|
| Charles de Gaulle[34] | 1890 | 1944–1946[35] |
| Félix Gouin[34] | 1884 | 1946–1946[35] |
| Georges Bidault[34] | 1899 | 1946–1947[35] |

## Fourth Republic

| Name | Born | Ruled |
|---|---|---|
| Vincent Auriol[20] | 1884 | 1947–1954[35] |
| René Coty[20] | 1882 | 1954–1959[35] |

## Fifth Republic

| Name | Born | Ruled |
|---|---|---|
| Charles de Gaulle[20] | 1890 | 1959– |

[1] Year of end of rule is also that of death, unless otherwise indicated. [2] Crowned Emperor of the West in 800. [3] Holy Roman Emperor 814–840. [4] Holy Roman Emperor 875–877 as Charles II. [5] Ruled jointly 879–882. [6] Holy Roman Emperor 881–887 as Charles III. [7] Died 888. [8] King 893–898 in opposition to Eudes. [9] Died 929. [10] Not counted in regular line of Kings of France by some authorities. Elected by nobles but killed in Battle of Soissons. [11] Sometimes called Robert I. [12] Executed 1793. [13] Titular King only. He died in prison according to official reports, but many pretenders appeared during the Bourbon restoration. [14] As First Consul. Napoleon held the power of government. In 1804, he became Emperor. [15] Abdicated first time June 1814. Re-entered Paris Mar. 1815, after escape from Elba; Louis XVIII fled to Ghent. Abdicated second time June 1815. He named as his successor his son, Napoleon II, who was not acceptable to the Allies. He died 1821. [16] Died 1836. [17] Died 1850. [18] President; became Emperor in 1852. [19] Died 1873. [20] President. [21] Died 1877. [22] Died 1893. [23] Died 1891. [24] Died 1907. [25] Died 1929. [26] Died 1931. [27] Died 1934. [28] Died 1922. [29] Died 1943. [30] Died 1937. [31] Died 1950. [32] Chief of State. [33] Died 1951. [34] Interim President. [35] Still alive.

# Rulers of Germany and Prussia

## Kings of Prussia

| Name | Born | Ruled[1] |
|------|------|----------|
| Frederick I[2] ............... | 1657 | 1701–1713 |
| Frederick William I ....... | 1688 | 1713–1740 |
| Frederick II the Great .... | 1712 | 1740–1786 |
| Frederick William II ..... | 1744 | 1786–1797 |
| Frederick William III ..... | 1770 | 1797–1840 |
| Frederick William IV ..... | 1795 | 1840–1861 |
| William I ................. | 1797 | 1861–1871[3] |

## Emperors of Germany

| Name | Born | Ruled[1] |
|------|------|----------|
| William I ................. | 1797 | 1871–1888 |
| Frederick III .............. | 1831 | 1888–1888 |
| William II ................ | 1859 | 1888–1918[4] |

## Heads of the Reich

| Name | Born | Ruled[1] |
|------|------|----------|
| Friedrich Ebert[5] .......... | 1871 | 1919–1925 |
| Paul von Hindenburg[5] .... | 1847 | 1925–1934 |
| Adolf Hitler[6,7] ............. | 1889 | 1934–1945 |
| Karl Doenitz[6] ............. | 1891 | 1945–1945[8] |

## German Federal Republic (Western)

| Name | Born | Ruled[1] |
|------|------|----------|
| Theodor Heuss[5] .......... | 1884 | 1949–1959[8] |
| Heinrich Luebke[5] ........ | 1895 | 1959– |

## German Democratic Republic (Eastern)

| Name | Born | Ruled[1] |
|------|------|----------|
| Wilhelm Pieck[5] .......... | 1876 | 1949–1960 |
| Walter Ulbricht[9] ......... | 1893 | 1960– |

[1] Year of end of rule is also that of death, unless otherwise indicated. [2] Was Elector of Brandenburg (1688–1701) as Frederick III. [3] Became Emperor of Germany in 1871. [4] Died 1941. [5] President. [6] Führer. [7] Named Chancellor by President Hindenburg in 1933. [8] Still alive. [9] Chairman of Council of State.

# Rulers of Russia Since 1533

| Name | Born | Ruled[1] |
|------|------|----------|
| Ivan IV the Terrible ...... | 1530 | 1533–1584 |
| Theodore I ................ | 1557 | 1584–1598 |
| Boris Godunov ...........c.1551 | | 1598–1605 |
| Theodore II ............... | 1589 | 1605–1605 |
| Demetrius I[2] ............. | ? | 1605–1606 |
| Basil IV Shuiski .......... | ? | 1606–1610[3] |
| "Time of Troubles" ....... | .... | 1610–1613 |
| Michael Romanov ......... | 1596 | 1613–1645 |
| Alexis I .................. | 1629 | 1645–1676 |
| Theodore III .............. | 1656 | 1676–1682 |
| Ivan V[4] ................ | 1666 | 1682–1689[5] |
| Peter I the Great[4] ........ | 1672 | 1682–1725 |
| Catherine I ............c.1684 | | 1725–1727 |
| Peter II .................. | 1715 | 1727–1730 |
| Anna ..................... | 1693 | 1730–1740 |
| Ivan VI ................... | 1740 | 1740–1741[6] |
| Elizabeth ................ | 1709 | 1741–1762 |
| Peter III ................. | 1728 | 1762–1762 |

| Name | Born | Ruled[1] |
|------|------|----------|
| Catherine II the Great .... | 1729 | 1762–1796 |
| Paul I ..................... | 1754 | 1796–1801 |
| Alexander I ............... | 1777 | 1801–1825 |
| Nicholas I ................ | 1796 | 1825–1855 |
| Alexander II .............. | 1818 | 1855–1881 |
| Alexander III ............. | 1845 | 1881–1894 |
| Nicholas II ............... | 1868 | 1894–1917[7] |

## Provisional Government

| Name | Born | Ruled[1] |
|------|------|----------|
| Prince Georgi Lvov[8] ...... | 1861 | 1917–1917[9] |
| Alexander Kerensky[8] ...... | 1881 | 1917–1917[10] |

## U.S.S.R.

| Name | Born | Ruled[1] |
|------|------|----------|
| Nikolai Lenin[8] ............ | 1870 | 1917–1924 |
| Joseph Stalin[11] ............ | 1879 | 1924–1953 |
| Georgi M. Malenkov[8] ...... | 1902 | 1953–1955[10] |
| Nikolai A. Bulganin[8] .... | 1895 | 1955–1958[10] |
| Nikita S. Khrushchev[8] .... | 1894 | 1958– |

[1] Year of end of rule is also that of death, unless otherwise indicated. [2] Also known as Pseudo-Demetrius. [3] Died 1612. [4] Ruled jointly until 1689, when Ivan was deposed. [5] Died 1696. [6] Died 1764. [7] Killed 1918. [8] Premier. [9] Died 1925. [10] Still alive. [11] General Secretary of Communist party; Premier 1941–53.

# Animal Names: Male, Female and Young
*Source:* Grace Davall, N.Y. Zoological Society.

| Animal | Male | Female | Young | Animal | Male | Female | Young |
|--------|------|--------|-------|--------|------|--------|-------|
| Ass | Jack | Jenny | Foal | Goose | Gander | Goose | Gosling |
| Bear | He-bear | She-bear | Cub | Horse | Stallion | Mare | Foal |
| Cat | Tom | Tabby | Kitten | Lion | Lion | Lioness | Cub |
| Cattle | Bull | Cow | Calf | Rabbit | Buck | Doe | ...... |
| Chicken | Rooster | Hen | Chick | Sheep | Ram | Ewe | Lamb |
| Deer | Buck | Doe | Fawn | Swan | Cob | Pen | Cygnet |
| Dog | Dog | Bitch | Pup | Swine | Boar | Sow | Shoat |
| Duck | Drake | Duck | Duckling | Tiger | Tiger | Tigress | Cub |
| Elephant | Bull | Cow | Calf | Whale | Bull | Cow | Calf |
| Fox | Dog | Vixen | Cub | Wolf | Dog | Bitch | Cub |

# Mason and Dixon's Line

Mason and Dixon's Line (often called the Mason-Dixon Line) is the boundary between Pennsylvania and Maryland, running at a north latitude of 39°43'19.11". The greater part of it was surveyed from 1763–67 by Charles Mason and Jeremiah Dixon, English astronomers who had been appointed to settle a dispute between the colonies. As the line was partly the boundary between the free and the slave states, it has come to signify the division between the North and the South.

# AWARDS

★

## NOBEL PRIZES

The Nobel prizes are awarded under the will of Alfred Bernhard Nobel, Swedish chemist and engineer, who died in 1896. The interest of the fund is divided annually among the persons who have made the most outstanding contributions in the field of physics, chemistry, and physiology or medicine, who have produced the most distinguished literary work of an idealist tendency, and who have contributed most toward world peace.

The prizes for physics and chemistry are awarded by the Swedish Academy of Science in Stockholm, the one for physiology or medicine by the Caroline Medical Institute in Stockholm, that for literature by the academy in Stockholm, and that for peace by a committee of five elected by the Norwegian Storting. The distribution of prizes was begun on December 10, 1901, the anniversary of Nobel's death. The amount of each prize varies with the income from the fund and since 1936 has stood at approximately £8,000.

No Nobel prizes were awarded for 1940, 1941 and 1942; prizes for Literature and Peace were not awarded for 1943.

| Year | Literature | Peace |
|------|-----------|-------|
| 1901 | René F. A. Sully Prudhomme (France) | Henri Dunant (Switzerland) and Frederick Passy (France) |
| 1902 | Theodor Mommsen (Germany) | Elie Ducommun and Albert Gobat (Switzerland) |
| 1903 | Björnstjerne Björnson (Norway) | Sir William R. Cremer (England) |
| 1904 | Frédéric Mistral (France) and José Echegaray (Spain) | Institut de Droit International (Belgium) |
| 1905 | Henryk Sienkiewicz (Poland) | Bertha von Suttner (Austria) |
| 1906 | Giosuè Carducci (Italy) | Theodore Roosevelt (U. S.) |
| 1907 | Rudyard Kipling (England) | Ernesto T. Moneta (Italy) and Louis Renault (France) |
| 1908 | Rudolf Eucken (Germany) | Klas P. Arnoldson (Sweden) and Frederik Bajer (Denmark) |
| 1909 | Selma Lagerlöf (Sweden) | Auguste M. F. Beernaert (Belgium) and Baron Paul H. B. B. d'Estournelles de Constant de Rebecque (France) |
| 1910 | Paul von Heyse (Germany) | Bureau International Permanent de la Paix (Switzerland) |
| 1911 | Maurice Maeterlinck (Belgium) | Tobias M. C. Asser (Holland) and Alfred H. Fried (Austria) |
| 1912 | Gerhart Hauptmann (Germany) | Elihu Root (U. S.) |
| 1913 | Rabindranath Tagore (India) | Henri La Fontaine (Belgium) |
| 1915 | Romain Rolland (France) | No award |
| 1916 | Verner von Heidenstam (Sweden) | No award |
| 1917 | Karl Gjellerup (Denmark) and Henrik Pontoppidan (Denmark) | International Red Cross |
| 1919 | Carl Spitteler (Switzerland) | Woodrow Wilson (U. S.) |
| 1920 | Knut Hamsun (Norway) | Léon Bourgeois (France) |
| 1921 | Anatole France (France) | Karl H. Branting (Sweden) and Christian L. Lange (Norway) |
| 1922 | Jacinto Benavente (Spain) | Fridtjof Nansen (Norway) |
| 1923 | William B. Yeats (Ireland) | No award |
| 1924 | Wladyslaw Reymont (Poland) | No award |
| 1925 | George Bernard Shaw (England) | Sir Austen Chamberlain (England) and Charles G. Dawes (U. S.) |
| 1926 | Grazia Deledda (Italy) | Aristide Briand (France) and Gustav Stresemann (Germany) |
| 1927 | Henri Bergson (France) | Ferdinand Buisson (France) and Ludwig Quidde (Germany) |
| 1928 | Sigrid Undset (Norway) | No award |
| 1929 | Thomas Mann (Germany) | Frank B. Kellogg (U. S.) |
| 1930 | Sinclair Lewis (U. S.) | Lars O. J. Söderblom (Sweden) |
| 1931 | Erik A. Karlfeldt (Sweden) | Jane Addams and Nicholas M. Butler (U. S.) |
| 1932 | John Galsworthy (England) | No award |
| 1933 | Ivan G. Bunin (Russia) | Sir Norman Angell (England) |
| 1934 | Luigi Pirandello (Italy) | Arthur Henderson (England) |
| 1935 | No award | Karl von Ossietzky (Germany) |
| 1936 | Eugene O'Neill (U. S.) | Carlos de S. Lamas (Argentina) |
| 1937 | Roger Martin du Gard (France) | Lord Cecil of Chelwood (England) |
| 1938 | Pearl S. Buck (U. S.) | Office International Nansen pour les Réfugiés (Switzerland) |
| 1939 | Frans Eemil Sillanpää (Finland) | No award |
| 1944 | Johannes V. Jensen (Denmark) | International Red Cross |
| 1945 | Gabriela Mistral (Chile) | Cordell Hull (U. S.) |
| 1946 | Hermann Hesse (Switzerland) | Emily G. Balch and John R. Mott (U. S.) |

| Year | Literature | Peace |
|------|------------|-------|
| 1947 | André Gide (France) | Am. Friends Service Com. (U. S.), Brit. Soc. of Friends' Service Council (Eng.) |
| 1948 | Thomas Stearns Eliot (England) | No award |
| 1949 | William Faulkner (U. S.) | Lord John Boyd Orr (Scotland) |
| 1950 | Bertrand Russell (England) | Ralph J. Bunche (U. S.) |
| 1951 | Pär Lagerkvist (Sweden) | Léon Jouhaux (France) |
| 1952 | François Mauriac (France) | Albert Schweitzer (Fr. Eq. Af.) |
| 1953 | Sir Winston Churchill (England) | George C. Marshall (U. S.) |
| 1954 | Ernest Hemingway (U. S.) | Office of U.N. High Commissioner for Refugees |
| 1955 | Halldór Kiljan Laxness (Iceland) | No award |
| 1956 | Juan Ramón Jiminez (Spain) | No award |
| 1957 | Albert Camus (France) | Lester B. Pearson (Canada) |
| 1958 | Boris Pasternak (U.S.S.R.) (declined prize) | Rev. Dominique Georges Henri Pire (Belgium) |
| 1959 | Salvatore Quasimodo (Italy) | Philip John Noel-Baker (England) |
| 1960 | St.-John Perse (Alexis St.-Léger Léger) (France) | No award |

| Year | Physics | Chemistry | Medicine |
|------|---------|-----------|----------|
| 1901 | Wilhelm K. Roentgen, for discovery of Roentgen rays. | Jacobus H. van't Hoff, for laws of chemical dynamics and osmotic pressure in solutions. | Emil A. von Behring, for work on serum therapy against diphtheria. |
| 1902 | Hendrik A. Lorentz and Pieter Zeeman, for work on influence of magnetism upon radiation. | Emil Fischer, for experiments in sugar and purin groups of substances. | Sir Ronald Ross, for work on malaria. |
| 1903 | A. Henri Becquerel, for work on discovery of spontaneous radioactivity. Pierre and Marie Curie; study of radiation. | Svante A. Arrhenius, for his electrolytic theory of dissociation. | Niels R. Finsen, for his treatment of lupus vulgaris, with concentrated light rays. |
| 1904 | John Strutt (Lord Rayleigh) for discovery of argon in investigating gas density. | Sir William Ramsay; discovery and determination of place of inert gaseous elements in air. | Ivan P. Pavlov, for work on the physiology of digestion. |
| 1905 | Philipp Lenard, for work with cathode rays. | Adolf von Baeyer, for work on organic dyes and hydroaromatic combinations. | Robert Koch, for work on tuberculosis. |
| 1906 | Joseph J. Thomson, for investigations on passage of electricity through gases. | Henri Moissan, for isolation of fluorine, and introduction of electric furnace. | Camillo Golgi and Santiago Ramón y Cajal, for work on structure of the nervous system. |
| 1907 | Albert A. Michelson, for spectroscopic and metrologic investigations. | Eduard Buchner; discovery of cell-less fermentation and investigations in biological chemistry. | Charles L. A. Laveran, for work with protozoa in the generation of disease. |
| 1908 | Gabriel Lippmann, for method of reproducing colors by photography. | Ernest Rutherford, for investigations into disintegration of elements. | Paul Ehrlich and Élie Metchnikoff, for work on immunity. |
| 1909 | Guglielmo Marconi and Ferdinand Braun, for development of wireless. | Wilhelm Ostwald, for work on catalysis and investigations into chemical equilibrium and reaction rates. | Theodor Kocher, for work on the thyroid gland. |
| 1910 | Johannes D. van der Waals, for work with the equation of state for gases and liquids. | Otto Wallach, for work in the field of alicyclic compounds. | Albrecht Kossel, for achievements in the chemistry of the cell. |
| 1911 | Wilhelm Wien, for his laws governing the radiation of heat. | Marie Curie, for discovery of elements radium and polonium. | Allvar Gullstrand, for work on the dioptrics of the eye. |
| 1912 | Gustaf Dalén, for discovery of automatic regulators used in lighting lighthouses and light buoys. | Victor Grignard, for reagent discovered by and named after him. Paul Sabatier, for the methods of hydrogenating organic compounds. | Alexis Carrel, for work on vascular ligature and grafting of blood vessels and organs. |

| Year | Physics | Chemistry | Medicine |
|------|---------|-----------|----------|
| 1913 | H. Kamerlingh-Onnes, for work leading to production of liquid helium. | Alfred Werner, for linking up atoms within the molecule. | Charles Richet, for work on anaphylaxy. |
| 1914 | Max von Laue, for discovery of diffraction of Roentgen rays passing through crystals. | Theodore W. Richards, for determining atomic weight of many chemical elements. | Robert Bárány, for work on physiology and pathology of the vestibular system. |
| 1915 | W. H. Bragg and W. L. Bragg, for analysis of crystal structure by means of X rays. | Richard Willstätter, for research into coloring matter of plants, especially chlorophyll. | No award. |
| 1917 | Charles G. Barkla, discovery of Roentgen radiation of the elements. | No award. | No award. |
| 1918 | Max Planck, for discoveries in connection with quantum theory. | Fritz Haber, for synthetic production of ammonia. | No award. |
| 1919 | Johannes Stark, discovery of Doppler effect in Canal rays and decomposition of spectrum lines by electric fields. | No award. | Jules Bordet, for discoveries in connection with immunity. |
| 1920 | Charles E. Guillaume, for discoveries of anomalies in nickel steel alloys. | Walther Nernst, for work in thermochemistry. | August Krogh, discovery of regulation of capillaries' motor mechanism. |
| 1921 | Albert Einstein, for discovery of the law of the photoelectric effect. | Frederick Soddy, for investigations into origin and nature of isotopes. | No award. |
| 1922 | Niels Bohr, for investigations of structure of atoms and radiations emanating from them. | Francis W. Aston, for discovery of isotopes in nonradioactive elements and for discovery of the whole number rule. | In 1923 the 1922 prize was divided between Archibald V. Hill for discovery relating to heat-production in muscles; and Otto Meyerhof, for correlation between consumption of oxygen and production of lactic acid in muscles. |
| 1923 | Robert A. Millikan, work on elementary charge of electricity and photoelectric phenomena. | Fritz Pregl, for method of microanalysis of organic substances discovered by him. | Frederick G. Banting and John J. R. Macleod, for discovery of insulin. |
| 1924 | Karl M. G. Siegbahn, for investigations in X-ray spectroscopy. | No award. | Willem Einthoven, for discovering the mechanism of the electrocardiogram. |
| 1925 | James Franck and Gustav Hertz, for discovery of laws governing impact of electrons upon atoms. | In 1926 the 1925 prize was awarded to Richard Zsigmondy, for work on the heterogeneous nature of colloid solutions. | No award. |
| 1926 | Jean B. Perrin, for works on discontinuous structure of matter and discovery of the equilibrium of sedimentation. | Theodor Svedberg, for work on disperse systems. | Johannes Fibiger, for discovery of the Spiroptera carcinoma. |
| 1927 | Arthur H. Compton, discovery of Compton phenomenon; and Charles T. R. Wilson, for method of perceiving paths taken by electrically charged particles. | In 1928 the 1927 prize was awarded to Heinrich Wieland, for investigations of bile acids and kindred substances. | Julius Wagner-Jauregg, for use of malaria inoculation in treatment of dementia paralytica. |

| Year | Physics | Chemistry | Medicine |
|------|---------|-----------|----------|
| 1928 | In 1929 the 1928 prize was awarded to Owen W. Richardson, for work on the phenomenon of thermionics and discovery of the Richardson Law. | Adolf Windaus, for investigations on constitution of the sterols and their connection with vitamins. | Charles Nicolle, for work on typhus exanthematicus. |
| 1929 | Prince Louis Victor de Broglie, for discovery of the wave character of electrons. | Arthur Harden and Hans K. A. S. von Euler-Chelpin, for research of fermentation of sugars. | Christiaan Eijkman, for discovery of the antineuritic vitamins; and Sir Frederick G. Hopkins, for discovery of growth-promoting vitamins. |
| 1930 | Sir Chandrasekhara V. Raman, for work on diffusion of light and discovery of the Raman effect. | Hans Fischer, for work on coloring matter of blood and leaves and for his synthesis of hemin. | Karl Landsteiner, for discovery of human blood groups. |
| 1931 | No award. | Karl Bosch and Friedrich Bergius, for invention and development of chemical high-pressure methods. | Otto H. Warburg, for discovery of the character and mode of action of the respiratory ferment. |
| 1932 | In 1933 the prize for 1932 was awarded to Werner Heisenberg, for creation of the quantum mechanics. | Irving Langmuir, for work in realm of surface chemistry. | Sir Charles S. Sherrington and Edgar D. Adrian, for discoveries of the function of the neuron. |
| 1933 | Erwin Schrödinger and Paul A. M. Dirac, for discovery of new fertile forms of the atomic theory. | No award. | Thomas H. Morgan, for discoveries on hereditary function of the chromosomes. |
| 1934 | No award. | Harold C. Urey, for discovery of heavy hydrogen. | George H. Whipple, George R. Minot, and William P. Murphy, for discovery of liver therapy against anemias. |
| 1935 | James Chadwick, for discovery of the neutron. | Frédéric and Irène Joliot-Curie, for synthesis of new radioactive elements. | Hans Spemann, for discovery of the organizer-effect in embryonic development. |
| 1936 | Victor F. Hess, for discovery of cosmic radiation; and Carl D. Anderson, for discovery of the positron. | Peter J. W. Debye, for investigations on dipole moments and diffraction of X rays and electrons in gases. | Sir Henry H. Dale and Otto Loewi, for discoveries on chemical transmission of nerve impulses. |
| 1937 | Clinton J. Davisson and George P. Thomson, for discovery of diffraction of electrons by crystals. | Walter N. Haworth, for research on carbohydrates and vitamin C; and Paul Karrer, for work on carotenoids, flavins and vitamins A and B. | Albert Szent-Györgyi von Nagyrapolt, for discoveries on biological combustion. |
| 1938 | Enrico Fermi, for identification of new radioactivity elements and discovery of nuclear reactions effected by slow neutrons. | Richard Kuhn, for carotinoid study and vitamin research (declined the prize). | Corneille Heymans, for importance of sinus and aorta mechanisms in the regulation of respiration. |
| 1939 | Ernest Orlando Lawrence, for the development of the cyclotron. | Adolf Friedrich Johann Butenandt, for work on sexual hormones (declined the prize); and Leopold Růžička, work with polymethylenes. | Gerhard Domagk, antibacterial effect of prontocilate. |

| Year | Physics | Chemistry | Medicine |
|------|---------|-----------|----------|
| 1943 | Otto Stern, for detection of magnetic momentum of protons. | George Hevesy De Heves, for work on use of isotopes as indicators. | Henrik Dam, Edward A. Doisy for the analysis of Vitamin K. |
| 1944 | Isidor Isaac Rabi, for work on magnetic movements of atomic particles. | Otto Hahn, for work on atomic fission. | Joseph Erlanger and Herbert Spencer Gasser, for work on functions of the nerve threads. |
| 1945 | Wolfgang Pauli, for work on atomic fissions. | Artturi Ilmari Virtanen, for research in the field of conservation of fodder. | Sir Alexander Fleming, Ernst Boris Chain, and Sir Howard Florey, for discovery of penicillin. |
| 1946 | Percy Williams Bridgman, studies and inventions in high-pressure physics. | James B. Sumner, crystallizing of enzymes. John H. Northrop and Wendell M. Stanley, preparing enzymes and virus proteins in pure form. | Herman J. Muller, hereditary effects of X ray on genes. |
| 1947 | Sir Edward Appleton, for discovery of layer which reflects radio short waves in the ionosphere. | Sir Robert Robinson, for research in plant substances. | Carl F. and Gerty T. Cori, for work on animal starch metabolism; Bernardo A. Houssay, for study of pituitary. |
| 1948 | Patrick M. S. Blackett, for improvement on Wilson chamber, discoveries in cosmic radiation. | Arne Tiselius, for biochemical discoveries and isolation of mouse paralysis virus. | Paul Mueller, for discovery of insect-killing properties of DDT. |
| 1949 | Hideki Yukawa, for mathematical prediction, 14 years ago, of the meson. | William Francis Giauque, for research in thermodynamics, especially effects of low temperature. | Walter Rudolf Hess, for research on brain control of body; and Antonio Caetano de Abreu Freire Egas Moniz, for development of brain operation. |
| 1950 | Cecil Frank Powell, for method of photographic study of atom nucleus, and for discoveries about mesons. | Otto Diels and Kurt Alder for discovery of diene synthesis enabling scientists to study structure of organic matter. | Philip S. Hench, Edward C. Kendall, and Tadeus Reichstein, for discoveries about hormones of adrenal cortex. |
| 1951 | Sir John Douglas Cockcroft and Ernest T. S. Walton, for work in 1932 on transmutation of atomic nuclei. | Glenn T. Seaborg and Edwin M. McMillan, for discovery of plutonium. | Max Theiler, for development of anti-yellow-fever vaccine. |
| 1952 | Edward Mills Purcell and Felix Bloch, for work in measurement of magnetic fields in atomic nuclei. | Archer John Porter Martin and Richard Laurence Millington Synge, for development of partition chromatography. | Selman A. Waksman, for co-discovery of streptomycin. |
| 1953 | Fritz Zernike, for development of "phase contrast" microscope. | Hermann Staudinger, for research in giant molecules. | Fritz A. Lipmann and Hans Adolph Krebs, for studies of living cells. |
| 1954 | Max Born, for work in quantum mechanics; and Walther Bothe, for work in cosmic radiation. | Linus Pauling, for study of forces holding together protein and other molecules. | John F. Enders, Thomas H. Weller and Frederick C. Robbins, for work with cultivation of polio virus. |
| 1955 | Polykarp Kusch and Willis E. Lamb, for work in atomic measurement. | Vincent du Vigneaud, for work on pituitary hormones. | Hugo Theorell, for work on oxidation enzymes. |
| 1956 | William Shockley, Walter H. Brattain and John Bardeen for developing electronic transistor. | Cyril Hinshelwood and Nikolai N. Semenov for parallel research on chemical reaction kinetics. | Dickinson W. Richards, Jr., André F. Cournand and Werner Forssmann for new techniques in heart disease. |

| Year | Physics | Chemistry | Medicine |
|---|---|---|---|
| 1957 | Tsung Dao Lee and Chen Ning Yang, for disproving principle of conservation of parity. | Sir Alexander Todd, for research with chemical compounds that are factors in heredity. | Daniel Bovet, for development of drugs to relieve allergies and relax muscles during surgery. |
| 1958 | Pavel A. Cherenkov, Ilya M. Frank, and Igor E. Tamm, for work resulting in development of cosmic-ray counter. | Frederick Sanger, for determining molecular structure of insulin. | Joshua Lederberg, for work with genetic mechanisms; George W. Beadle and Edward L. Tatum, for discovering how genes transmit hereditary characteristics. |
| 1959 | Emilio Segre and Owen Chamberlain, for demonstrating the existence of the anti-proton. | Jaroslav Heyrovsky, for development of polarography, an electrochemical method of analysis. | Severo Ochoa and Arthur Kornberg, for discoveries related to compounds within chromosomes, which play a vital role in heredity. |
| 1960 | Donald A. Glaser, for invention of "bubble chamber" to study subatomic particles. | Willard F. Libby, for "atomic time clock" to measure age of objects by measuring their radioactivity. | Sir Macfarlane Burnet and Peter Brian Medawar, for discovery of acquired immunological tolerance. |

---

# Pulitzer Prize Awards

Source: Columbia University, New York. (For years not listed, no award was made.)

## Pulitzer Prizes in Journalism

### Meritorious Public Service

1918 New York Times
1919 Milwaukee Journal
1921 Boston Post
1922 New York World
1923 Memphis Commercial Appeal
1924 New York World
1926 Columbus (Ga.) Enquirer Sun
1927 Canton (Ohio) Daily News
1928 Indianapolis Times
1929 New York Evening World
1931 Atlanta Constitution
1932 Indianapolis News
1933 New York World-Telegram
1934 Medford (Oreg.) Mail Tribune
1935 Sacramento Bee
1936 Cedar Rapids (Iowa) Gazette
1937 St. Louis Post-Dispatch
1938 Bismarck (N. Dak.) Tribune
1939 Miami Daily News
1940 Waterbury (Conn.) Republican & American
1941 St. Louis Post-Dispatch
1942 Los Angeles Times
1943 Omaha World-Herald
1944 New York Times
1945 Detroit Free Press
1946 Scranton (Pa.) Times
1947 Baltimore Sun
1948 St. Louis Post-Dispatch
1949 (Lincoln) Nebraska State Journal
1950 Chicago Daily News; St. Louis Post-Dispatch

1951 Miami Herald; Brooklyn Eagle
1952 St. Louis Post-Dispatch
1953 Whiteville (N. C.) News Reporter; Tabor City (N. C.) Tribune
1954 (Garden City, L. I.) Newsday
1955 Columbus (Ga.) Ledger & Sunday Ledger-Enquirer
1956 Watsonville (Calif.) Register-Pajaronian
1957 Chicago Daily News
1958 (Little Rock) Arkansas Gazette
1959 Utica (N. Y.) Observer Dispatch and the Utica Daily Press
1960 Los Angeles Times
1961 Amarillo (Tex.) Globe-Times

### Editorial

1917 New York Tribune
1918 Louisville Courier-Journal
1920 HARVEY E. NEWBRANCH (Omaha Evening World-Herald)
1922 FRANK M. O'BRIEN (New York Herald)
1923 WILLIAM ALLEN WHITE (Emporia [Kans.] Gazette)
1924 Boston Herald; Special prize: FRANK I. COBB (New York World)
1925 Charleston (S. C.) News and Courier

1926 New York Times (EDWARD M. KINGSBURY)
1927 Boston Herald (F. LAURISTON BULLARD)
1928 GROVER CLEVELAND HALL (Montgomery [Ala.] Advertiser)
1929 LOUIS ISAAC JAFFE (Norfolk Virginian-Pilot)
1931 CHARLES S. RYCKMAN (Fremont [Nebr.] Tribune)
1933 Kansas City (Mo.) Star
1934 E. P. CHASE (Atlantic [Iowa] News Telegraph)
1936 FELIX MORLEY (Washington [D.C.] Post); GEORGE B. PARKER (Scripps-Howard Newspapers)
1937 JOHN W. OWENS (Baltimore Sun)
1938 W. W. WAYMACK (Des Moines Register & Tribune)
1939 RONALD G. CALLVERT (Portland Oregonian)
1940 BART HOWARD (St. Louis Post-Dispatch)
1941 REUBEN MAURY (New York Daily News)
1942 GEOFFREY PARSONS (New York Herald Tribune)
1943 FORREST W. SEYMOUR (Des Moines Register & Tribune)
1944 Kansas City (Mo.) Star (HENRY J. HASKELL)
1945 GEORGE W. POTTER (Provi-

dence [R. I.] *Journal-Bulletin*)

1946 HODDING CARTER ([Greenville, Miss.] *Delta Democrat-Times*)

1947 WILLIAM H. GRIMES (*Wall Street Journal*)

1948 VIRGINIUS DABNEY (*Richmond Times-Dispatch*)

1949 JOHN H. CRIDER (*Boston Herald*); HERBERT ELLISTON (*Washington Post*)

1950 CARL M. SAUNDERS (*Jackson* [Mich.] *Citizen Patriot*)

1951 WILLIAM H. FITZPATRICK (*New Orleans States*)

1952 LOUIS LACOSS (*St. Louis Globe-Democrat*)

1953 VERMONT C. ROYSTER (*Wall Street Journal*)

1954 *Boston Herald* (DON MURRAY)

1955 *Detroit Free Press* (ROYCE HOWES)

1956 LAUREN K. SOTH (*Des Moines Register & Tribune*)

1957 BUFORD BOONE (*Tuscaloosa* [Ala.] *News*)

1958 HARRY S. ASHMORE (*Arkansas Gazette*)

1959 RALPH McGILL (*Atlanta Constitution*)

1960 LENOIR CHAMBERS (*Virginian-Pilot*)

1961 WILLIAM J. DORVILLIER (*San Juan* [P.R.] *Star*)

### Correspondence

1929 PAUL SCOTT MOWRER (*Chicago Daily News*)

1930 LELAND STOWE (*New York Herald Tribune*)

1931 H. R. KNICKERBOCKER (*Philadelphia Public Ledger* and *New York Evening Post*)

1932 WALTER DURANTY (*New York Times*); CHARLES G. ROSS (*St. Louis Post-Dispatch*)

1933 EDGAR ANSEL MOWRER (*Chicago Daily News*)

1934 FREDERICK T. BIRCHALL (*New York Times*)

1935 ARTHUR KROCK (*New York Times*)

1936 WILFRED C. BARBER (*Chicago Tribune*)

1937 ANNE O'HARE McCORMICK (*New York Times*)

1938 ARTHUR KROCK (*New York Times*)

1939 LOUIS P. LOCHNER (Associated Press)

1940 OTTO D. TOLISCHUS (*New York Times*)

1941 Group award*

*For the public services and the individual achievements of American news reporters in the war zones.

1942 CARLOS P. ROMULO (*Philippines Herald*)

1943 HANSON W. BALDWIN (*New York Times*)

1944 ERNIE PYLE (Scripps-Howard Newspaper Alliance)

1945 HAROLD V. (HAL) BOYLE (Associated Press)

1946 ARNALDO CORTESI (*New York Times*)

1947 BROOKS ATKINSON (*New York Times*)

1948 Discontinued

### Cartoon

1922 ROLLIN KIRBY (*New York World*)

1924 JAY NORWOOD DARLING (*New York Tribune*)

1925 ROLLIN KIRBY (*New York World*)

1926 D. R. FITZPATRICK (*St. Louis Post-Dispatch*)

1927 NELSON HARDING (*Brooklyn Eagle*)

1928 NELSON HARDING (*Brooklyn Eagle*)

1929 ROLLIN KIRBY (*New York World*)

1930 CHARLES R. MACAULEY (*Brooklyn Eagle*)

1931 EDMUND DUFFY (*Baltimore Sun*)

1932 JOHN T. McCUTCHEON (*Chicago Tribune*)

1933 H. M. TALBURT (*Washington Daily News*)

1934 EDMUND DUFFY (*Baltimore Sun*)

1935 ROSS A. LEWIS (*Milwaukee Journal*)

1937 C. D. BATCHELOR (*New York Daily News*)

1938 VAUGHN SHOEMAKER (*Chicago Daily News*)

1939 CHARLES G. WERNER (*Daily Oklahoman* [Oklahoma City])

1940 EDMUND DUFFY (*Baltimore Sun*)

1941 JACOB BURCK (*Chicago Times*)

1942 HERBERT L. BLOCK (NEA Service)

1943 JAY NORWOOD DARLING (*New York Herald Tribune*)

1944 CLIFFORD K. BERRYMAN (*Washington* [D. C.] *Evening Star*)

1945 BILL MAULDIN (United Features Syndicate)

1946 BRUCE ALEXANDER RUSSELL (*Los Angeles Times*)

1947 VAUGHN SHOEMAKER (*Chicago Daily News*)

1948 REUBEN L. GOLDBERG (*New York Sun*)

1949 LUTE PEASE (*Newark Evening News*)

1950 JAMES T. BERRYMAN (*Washington* [D. C.] *Evening Star*)

1951 REG (REGINALD W.) MANNING (*Arizona Republic* [Phoenix])

1952 FRED L. PACKER (*New York Mirror*)

1953 EDWARD D. KUEKES (*Cleveland Plain Dealer*)

1954 HERBERT L. BLOCK (*Washington* [D. C.] *Post & Times-Herald*)

1955 DANIEL R. FITZPATRICK (*St. Louis Post-Dispatch*)

1956 ROBERT YORK (*Louisville Times*)

1957 TOM LITTLE (*Nashville Tennessean*)

1958 BRUCE M. SHANKS (*Buffalo Evening News*)

1959 BILL MAULDIN (*St. Louis Post-Dispatch*)

1961 CAREY ORR (*Chicago Tribune*)

### News Photography

1942 MILTON BROOKS (*Detroit News*)

1943 FRANK NOEL (Associated Press)

1944 FRANK FILAN (Associated Press); EARLE L. BUNKER (*Omaha World-Herald*)

1945 JOE ROSENTHAL (Associated Press)

1947 ARNOLD HARDY

1948 FRANK CUSHING (*Boston Traveler*)

1949 NAT FEIN (*New York Herald Tribune*)

1950 BILL CROUCH (*Oakland Tribune*)

1951 MAX DESFOR (Associated Press)

1952 JOHN ROBINSON & DON ULTANG (*Des Moines Register & Tribune*)

1953 WILLIAM M. GALLAGHER (*Flint* [Mich.] *Journal*)

1954 MRS. WALTER M. SCHAU

1955 JOHN L. GAUNT, JR. (*Los Angeles Times*)

1956 *New York Daily News*

1957 HARRY A. TRASK (*Boston Traveler*)

1958 WILLIAM C. BEALL (*Washington Daily News*)

1959 WILLIAM SEAMAN (*Minneapolis Star*)

1960 ANDREW LOPEZ (United Press International)

1961 YASUSHI NAGAO (Mainichi Newspapers, Tokyo)

### National Telegraphic Reporting

1942 LOUIS STARK (*New York Times*)

1944 DEWEY L. FLEMING (*Baltimore Sun*)

1945 JAMES B. RESTON (*New York Times*)

1946 EDWARD A. HARRIS (*St. Louis Post-Dispatch*)

1947 EDWARD T. FOLLIARD (*Washington* [D. C.] *Post*)

### National Reporting

1948 BERT ANDREWS (*New York Herald Tribune*); NAT S. FINNEY (*Minneapolis Tribune*)

1949 C. P. TRUSSELL (*New York Times*)

1950 EDWIN O. GUTHMAN (*Seattle Times*)

1952 ANTHONY LEVIERO (*New York Times*)

1953 DON WHITEHEAD (Associated Press)

1954 RICHARD WILSON (Cowles Newspapers)

1955 ANTHONY LEWIS (*Washington Daily News*)

1956 CHARLES L. BARTLETT (*Chattanooga Times*)

1957 JAMES RESTON (*New York Times*)

1958 RELMAN MORIN (Associated Press) and CLARK MOLLENHOFF (*Des Moines Register & Tribune*)

1959 HOWARD VAN SMITH (*Miami News*)

1960 VANCE TRIMBLE (Scripps-Howard Newspaper Alliance)

1961 EDWARD R. CONY (*Wall Street Journal*)

### International Telegraphic Reporting

1942 LAURENCE EDMUND ALLEN (Associated Press)

1943 IRA WOLFERT (North American Newspaper Alliance, Inc.)

1944 DANIEL DE LUCE (Associated Press)

1945 MARK S. WATSON (*Baltimore Sun*)

1946 HOMER W. BIGART (*New York Herald Tribune*)

1947 EDDY GILMORE (Associated Press)

### International Reporting

1948 PAUL W. WARD (*Baltimore Sun*)

1949 PRICE DAY (*Baltimore Sun*)

1950 EDMUND STEVENS (*Christian Science Monitor*)

1951 KEYES BEECH & FRED SPARKS (*Chicago Daily News*); HOMER BIGART & MARGUERITE HIGGINS (*New York Herald Tribune*); RELMAN MORIN & DON WHITEHEAD (Associated Press)

1952 JOHN M. HIGHTOWER (Associated Press)

1953 AUSTIN C. WEHRWEIN (*Milwaukee Journal*)

1954 JIM G. LUCAS (Scripps-Howard Newspapers)

1955 HARRISON E. SALISBURY (*New York Times*)

1956 WILLIAM RANDOLPH HEARST, JR., & FRANK CONNIFF (Hearst newspapers) & KINGSBURY SMITH (INS)

1957 RUSSELL JONES (United Press)

1958 *New York Times*

1959 JOSEPH MARTIN & PHILIP SANTORA (*New York Daily News*)

1960 A. M. ROSENTHAL (*New York Times*)

1961 LYNN HEINZERLING (*Associated Press*)

### Reporting

1917 HERBERT B. SWOPE (*New York World*)

1918 HAROLD A. LITTLEDALE (*New York Evening Post*)

1920 JOHN J. LEARY, JR. (*New York World*)

1921 LOUIS SEIBOLD (*New York World*)

1922 KIRKE L. SIMPSON (Associated Press)

1923 ALVA JOHNSTON (*New York Times*)

1924 MAGNER WHITE (*San Diego Sun*)

1925 JAMES W. MULROY & ALVIN H. GOLDSTEIN (*Chicago Daily News*)

1926 WILLIAM BURKE MILLER (*Louisville Courier-Journal*)

1927 JOHN T. ROGERS (*St. Louis Post-Dispatch*)

1929 PAUL Y. ANDERSON (*St. Louis Post-Dispatch*)

1930 RUSSELL D. OWEN (*New York Times*); Special award: W. O. DAPPING (*Auburn* [N. Y.] *Citizen*)

1931 A. B. MACDONALD (*Kansas City* [Mo.] *Star*)

1932 W. C. RICHARDS, D. D. MARTIN, J. S. POOLER, F. D. WEBB, J. N. W. SLOAN (all of *Detroit Free Press*)

1933 FRANCIS A. JAMIESON (Associated Press)

1934 ROYCE BRIER (*San Francisco Chronicle*)

1935 WILLIAM H. TAYLOR (*New York Herald Tribune*)

1936 LAUREN D. LYMAN (*New York Times*)

1937 JOHN J. O'NEILL (*New York Herald Tribune*),

WILLIAM LEONARD LAURENCE (*New York Times*), HOWARD W. BLAKESLEE (Associated Press), GOBIND BEHARI LAL (Universal Service), DAVID DIETZ (Scripps-Howard Newspapers)

1938 RAYMOND SPRIGLE (*Pittsburgh Post-Gazette*)

1939 THOMAS L. STOKES (*New York World-Telegram*)

1940 S. BURTON HEATH (*New York World-Telegram*)

1941 WESTBROOK PEGLER (*New York World-Telegram*)

1942 STANTON DELAPLANE (*San Francisco Chronicle*)

1943 GEORGE WELLER (*Chicago Daily News*)

1944 PAUL SCHOENSTEIN & associates (*New York Journal-American*)

1945 JACK S. McDOWELL (*San Francisco Call-Bulletin*)

1946 WILLIAM LEONARD LAURENCE (*New York Times*)

1947 FREDERICK WOLTMAN (*New York World-Telegram*)

1948 GEORGE E. GOODWIN (*Atlanta Journal*)

1949 MALCOLM JOHNSON (*New York Sun*)

1950 MEYER BERGER (*New York Times*)

1951 EDWARD S. MONTGOMERY (*San Francisco Examiner*)

1952 GEORGE DE CARVALHO (*San Francisco Chronicle*)

1953 Editorial staff (*Providence Journal & Evening Bulletin*);* EDWARD J. MOWERY (*New York World-Telegram & Sun*)†

1954 *Vicksburg* (Miss.) *Sunday Post-Herald;** ALVIN SCOTT McCOY (*Kansas City* [Mo.] *Star*)†

1955 MRS. CARO BROWN (*Alice* [Tex.] *Daily Echo*);* ROLAND KENNETH TOWERY (*Cuero* [Tex.] *Record*)†

1956 LEE HILLS (*Detroit Free Press*);* ARTHUR DALEY (*New York Times*)†

1957 *Salt Lake Tribune;** WALLACE TURNER and WILLIAM LAMBERT (*Portland Oregonian*)†

1958 *Fargo* [N. Dak.] *Forum;** GEORGE BEVERIDGE (*Washington Evening Star*)†

1959 MARY LOU WERNER (*Washington Evening Star*);* JOHN HAROLD BRISLIN

Scranton [Pa.] *Tribune & Scrantonian*) †

1960 JACK NELSON (*Atlanta Constitution*); * MIRIAM OTTENBERG (*Washington Evening Star*) †

1961 SANCHE DE GRAMONT (*New York Herald Tribune*); * EDGAR MAY (*Buffalo Evening News*) †

* Reporting under pressure of edition deadlines.   † Reporting not under pressure of edition deadlines.

### Special Citations

1938 *Edmonton* [Alberta] *Journal*, special bronze plaque for editorial leadership in defense of freedom of press in Province of Alberta.

1941 *New York Times* for the public educational value of its foreign news report.

1944 BYRON PRICE, Director of the Office of Censorship, for the creation and administration of the newspaper and radio codes. MRS. WILLIAM ALLEN WHITE, for her husband's interest and services during the past seven years as a member of the Advisory Board of the Graduate School of Journalism, Columbia University.

1945 The cartographers of the American press for their war maps.

1947 (Pulitzer centennial year.) Columbia University and the Graduate School of Journalism, for their efforts to maintain and advance the high standards governing the Pulitzer Prize awards. The *St. Louis Post-Dispatch*, for its unswerving adherence to the public and professional ideals of its founder and its leadership in the field of American journalism.

1948 DR. FRANK D. FACKENTHAL, for his interest and service.

1951 CYRUS L. SULZBERGER (*New York Times*) for his exclusive interview with Archbishop Stepinac in a Yugoslav prison.

1952 *Kansas City Star* for coverage of 1951 floods; MAX KASE (*New York Journal-American*) for exposures of bribery in college basketball.

1953 *New York Times* for its 17-year publication of "News of the Week in Review."

1958 WALTER LIPPMANN (*New York Herald Tribune*) for his "wisdom, perception and high sense of responsibility" in his commentary on national and international affairs.

1960 GARRETT MATTINGLY, for *The Armada*.

1961 *American Heritage Picture History of the Civil War*, as a distinguished example of American book publishing.

### History of Services Rendered Public by American Press in Preceding Year

1918 MINNA LEWINSON, HENRY B. HOUGH

## Pulitzer Prizes in Letters

### Novel*

1918 *His Family*. By ERNEST POOLE

1919 *The Magnificent Ambersons*. By BOOTH TARKINGTON

1921 *The Age of Innocence*. By EDITH WHARTON

1922 *Alice Adams*. By BOOTH TARKINGTON

1923 *One of Ours*. By WILLA CATHER

1924 *The Able McLaughlins*. By MARGARET WILSON

1925 *So Big*. By EDNA FERBER

1926 *Arrowsmith*. By SINCLAIR LEWIS

1927 *Early Autumn*. By LOUIS BROMFIELD

1928 *The Bridge of San Luis Rey*. By THORNTON WILDER

1929 *Scarlet Sister Mary*. By JULIA PETERKIN

1930 *Laughing Boy*. By OLIVER LA FARGE

1931 *Years of Grace*. By MARGARET AYER BARNES

1932 *The Good Earth*. By PEARL S. BUCK

* Category changed to fiction for 1948 and thereafter.

1933 *The Store*. By T. S. STRIBLING

1934 *Lamb in His Bosom*. By CAROLINE MILLER

1935 *Now in November*. By JOSEPHINE WINSLOW JOHNSON

1936 *Honey in the Horn*. By HAROLD L. DAVIS

1937 *Gone With the Wind*. By MARGARET MITCHELL

1938 *The Late George Apley*. By JOHN PHILLIPS MARQUAND

1939 *The Yearling*. By MARJORIE KINNAN RAWLINGS

1940 *The Grapes of Wrath*. By JOHN STEINBECK

1942 *In This Our Life*. By ELLEN GLASGOW

1943 *Dragon's Teeth*. By UPTON SINCLAIR

1944 *Journey in the Dark*. By MARTIN FLAVIN

1945 *A Bell for Adano*. By JOHN HERSEY

1947 *All the King's Men*. By ROBERT PENN WARREN

1948 *Tales of the South Pacific*. By JAMES A. MICHENER

1949 *Guard of Honor*. By JAMES GOULD COZZENS

1950 *The Way West*. By A. B. GUTHRIE, JR.

1951 *The Town*. By CONRAD RICHTER

1952 *The Caine Mutiny*. By HERMAN WOUK

1953 *The Old Man and the Sea*. By ERNEST HEMINGWAY

1955 *A Fable*. By WILLIAM FAULKNER

1956 *Andersonville*. By MACKINLAY KANTOR

1958 *A Death in the Family*. By JAMES AGEE

1959 *The Travels of Jaimie McPheeters*. By ROBERT LEWIS TAYLOR

1960 *Advise and Consent*. By ALLEN DRURY

1961 *To Kill a Mockingbird*. By HARPER LEE

### Drama

1918 *Why Marry?* By JESSE LYNCH WILLIAMS

1920 *Beyond the Horizon*. By EUGENE O'NEILL

1921 *Miss Lulu Bett*. By ZONA GALE

1922 *Anna Christie*. By EUGENE O'NEILL

1923 *Icebound.* By OWEN DAVIS

1924 *Hell-Bent Fer Heaven.* By HATCHER HUGHES

1925 *They Knew What They Wanted.* By SIDNEY HOWARD

1926 *Craig's Wife.* By GEORGE KELLY

1927 *In Abraham's Bosom.* By PAUL GREEN

1928 *Strange Interlude.* By EUGENE O'NEILL

1929 *Street Scene.* By ELMER L. RICE

1930 *The Green Pastures.* By MARC CONNELLY

1931 *Alison's House.* By SUSAN GLASPELL

1932 *Of Thee I Sing.* By GEORGE S. KAUFMAN, MORRIE RYSKIND & IRA GERSHWIN

1933 *Both Your Houses.* By MAXWELL ANDERSON

1934 *Men in White.* By SIDNEY KINGSLEY

1935 *The Old Maid.* By ZOË AKINS

1936 *Idiot's Delight.* By ROBERT E. SHERWOOD

1937 *You Can't Take It With You.* By MOSS HART and GEORGE S. KAUFMAN

1938 *Our Town.* By THORNTON WILDER

1939 *Abe Lincoln in Illinois.* By ROBERT E. SHERWOOD

1940 *The Time of Your Life.* By WILLIAM SAROYAN

1941 *There Shall Be No Night.* By ROBERT E. SHERWOOD

1943 *The Skin of Our Teeth.* By THORNTON WILDER

1945 *Harvey.* By MARY CHASE

1946 *State of the Union.* By RUSSEL CROUSE and HOWARD LINDSAY

1948 *A Streetcar Named Desire.* By TENNESSEE WILLIAMS

1949 *Death of a Salesman.* By ARTHUR MILLER

1950 *South Pacific.* By RICHARD RODGERS, OSCAR HAMMERSTEIN 2ND, AND JOSHUA LOGAN

1952 *The Shrike.* By JOSEPH KRAMM

1953 *Picnic.* By WILLIAM INGE

1954 *The Teahouse of the August Moon.* By JOHN PATRICK

1955 *Cat on a Hot Tin Roof.* By TENNESSEE WILLIAMS

1956 *The Diary of Anne Frank.* By FRANCES GOODRICH & ALBERT HACKETT

1957 *Long Day's Journey Into Night.* By EUGENE O'NEILL

1958 *Look Homeward, Angel.* By KETTI FRINGS

1959 *J.B.* By ARCHIBALD MAC-LEISH

1960 *Fiorello.* By GEORGE ABBOTT, JEROME WEIDMAN, JERRY BOCK, and SHELDON HARNICK

1961 *All the Way Home.* By TAD MOSEL

## History

1917 *With Americans of Past and Present Days.* By J. J. JUSSERAND, Amb. of France to U. S.

1918 *A History of the Civil War, 1861–1865.* By JAMES FORD RHODES

1920 *The War with Mexico.* By JUSTIN H. SMITH

1921 *The Victory at Sea.* By WILLIAM SOWDEN SIMS in collaboration with BURTON J. HENDRICK

1922 *The Founding of New England.* By JAMES TRUSLOW ADAMS

1923 *The Supreme Court in United States History.* By CHARLES WARREN

1924 *The American Revolution—A Constitutional Interpretation.* By CHARLES HOWARD McILWAIN

1925 *A History of the American Frontier.* By FREDERIC L. PAXSON

1926 *The History of the United States.* By EDWARD CHANNING

1927 *Pinckney's Treaty.* By SAMUEL FLAGG BEMIS

1928 *Main Currents in American Thought.* By VERNON LOUIS PARRINGTON

1929 *The Organization and Administration of the Union Army, 1861–1865.* By FRED ALBERT SHANNON

1930 *The War of Independence.* By CLAUDE H. VAN TYNE

1931 *The Coming of the War: 1914.* By BERNADOTTE E. SCHMITT

1932 *My Experiences in the World War.* By JOHN J. PERSHING

1933 *The Significance of Sections in American History.* By FREDERICK J. TURNER

1934 *The People's Choice.* By HERBERT AGAR

1935 *The Colonial Period of American History.* By CHARLES McLEAN ANDREWS

1936 *The Constitutional History of the United States.* By ANDREW C. McLAUGHLIN

1937 *The Flowering of New England.* By VAN WYCK BROOKS

1938 *The Road to Reunion, 1865–1900.* By PAUL HERMAN BUCK

1939 *A History of American Magazines.* By FRANK LUTHER MOTT

1940 *Abraham Lincoln: The War Years.* By CARL SANDBURG

1941 *The Atlantic Migration, 1607–1860.* By MARCUS LEE HANSEN

1942 *Reveille in Washington.* By MARGARET LEECH

1943 *Paul Revere and the World He Lived In.* By ESTHER FORBES

1944 *The Growth of American Thought.* By MERLE CURTI

1945 *Unfinished Business.* By STEPHEN BONSAL

1946 *The Age of Jackson.* By ARTHUR M. SCHLESINGER, JR.

1947 *Scientists Against Time.* By JAMES PHINNEY BAXTER, 3RD

1948 *Across the Wide Missouri.* By BERNARD DEVOTO

1949 *The Disruption of American Democracy.* By ROY FRANKLIN NICHOLS

1950 *Art and Life in America.* By OLIVER W. LARKIN

1951 *The Old Northwest, Pioneer Period 1815–1840.* By R. CARLYLE BULEY

1952 *The Uprooted.* By OSCAR HANDLIN

1953 *The Era of Good Feelings.* By GEORGE DANGERFIELD

1954 *A Stillness at Appomattox.* By BRUCE CATTON

1955 *Great River: The Rio Grande in North American History.* By PAUL HORGAN

1956 *The Age of Reform.* By RICHARD HOFSTADTER

1957 *Russia Leaves the War: Soviet-American Relations, 1917–1920.* By GEORGE F. KENNAN

1958 *Banks and Politics in America: From the Revolution to the Civil War.* By BRAY HAMMOND

1959 *The Republican Era:*

1869–1901. By LEONARD D. WHITE, assisted by JEAN SCHNEIDER.

1960 *In the Days of McKinley.* By MARGARET LEECH

1961 *Between War and Peace: The Potsdam Conference.* By HERBERT FEIS

## Biography or Autobiography

1917 *Julia Ward Howe.* By LAURA E. RICHARDS and MAUDE HOWE ELLIOTT assisted by FLORENCE HOWE HALL

1918 *Benjamin Franklin, Self-Revealed.* By WILLIAM CABELL BRUCE

1919 *The Education of Henry Adams.* By HENRY ADAMS

1920 *The Life of John Marshall.* By ALBERT J. BEVERIDGE

1921 *The Americanization of Edward Bok.* By EDWARD BOK

1922 *A Daughter of the Middle Border.* By HAMLIN GARLAND

1923 *The Life and Letters of Walter H. Page.* By BURTON J. HENDRICK

1924 *From Immigrant to Inventor.* By MICHAEL IDVORSKY PUPIN

1925 *Barrett Wendell and His Letters.* By M. A. DEWOLFE HOWE

1926 *The Life of Sir William Osler.* By HARVEY CUSHING

1927 *Whitman.* By EMORY HOLLOWAY

1928 *The American Orchestra and Theodore Thomas.* By CHARLES EDWARD RUSSELL

1929 *The Training of an American. The Earlier Life and Letters of Walter H. Page.* By BURTON J. HENDRICK

1930 *The Raven.* By MARQUIS JAMES

1931 *Charles W. Eliot.* By HENRY JAMES

1932 *Theodore Roosevelt.* By HENRY F. PRINGLE

1933 *Grover Cleveland.* By ALLAN NEVINS

1934 *John Hay.* By TYLER DENNETT

1935 *R. E. Lee.* By DOUGLAS S. FREEMAN

1936 *The Thought and Character of William James.* By RALPH BARTON PERRY

1937 *Hamilton Fish.* By ALLAN NEVINS

1938 *Pedlar's Progress.* By ODELL SHEPARD. *Andrew Jackson.* By MARQUIS JAMES

1939 *Benjamin Franklin.* By CARL VAN DOREN

1940 *Woodrow Wilson. Life and Letters,* Vols. VII and VIII. By RAY STANNARD BAKER

1941 *Jonathan Edwards.* By OLA E. WINSLOW

1942 *Crusader in Crinoline.* By FORREST WILSON

1943 *Admiral of the Ocean Sea.* By SAMUEL ELIOT MORISON

1944 *The American Leonardo: The Life of Samuel F. B. Morse.* By CARLETON MABEE

1945 *George Bancroft: Brahmin Rebel.* By RUSSEL BLAINE NYE

1946 *Son of the Wilderness.* By LINNIE MARSH WOLFE

1947 *The Autobiography of William Allen White*

1948 *Forgotten First Citizen: John Bigelow.* By MARGARET CLAPP

1949 *Roosevelt and Hopkins.* By ROBERT E. SHERWOOD

1950 *John Quincy Adams and the Foundations of American Foreign Policy.* By SAMUEL FLAGG BEMIS

1951 *John C. Calhoun: American Portrait.* By MARGARET LOUISE COIT

1952 *Charles Evans Hughes.* By MERLO J. PUSEY

1953 *Edmund Pendleton 1721–1803.* By DAVID J. MAYS

1954 *The Spirit of St. Louis.* By CHARLES A. LINDBERGH

1955 *The Taft Story.* By WILLIAM S. WHITE

1956 *Benjamin Henry Latrobe.* By TALBOT F. HAMLIN

1957 *Profiles in Courage.* By JOHN F. KENNEDY

1958 *George Washington.* By DOUGLAS SOUTHALL FREEMAN (Vols. 1–6) and JOHN ALEXANDER CARROLL and MARY WELLS ASHWORTH (Vol. 7)

1959 *Woodrow Wilson, American Prophet.* By ARTHUR WALWORTH

1960 *John Paul Jones.* By SAMUEL ELIOT MORISON

1961 *Charles Sumner and the Coming of the Civil War.* By DAVID DONALD

## Poetry

1918 *Love Songs.* By SARA TEASDALE

1919 *Old Road to Paradise.* By MARGARET WIDDEMER; *Corn Huskers.* By CARL SANDBURG

1922 *Collected Poems.* By EDWIN ARLINGTON ROBINSON

1923 *The Ballad of the Harp-Weaver; A Few Figs from Thistles;* eight sonnets in *American Poetry, 1922, A Miscellany.* By EDNA ST. VINCENT MILLAY

1924 *New Hampshire: A Poem with Notes and Grace Notes.* By ROBERT FROST

1925 *The Man Who Died Twice.* By EDWIN ARLINGTON ROBINSON

1926 *What's O'Clock.* By AMY LOWELL

1927 *Fiddler's Farewell.* By LEONORA SPEYER

1928 *Tristram.* By EDWIN ARLINGTON ROBINSON

1929 *John Brown's Body.* By STEPHEN VINCENT BENÉT

1930 *Selected Poems.* By CONRAD AIKEN

1931 *Collected Poems.* By ROBERT FROST

1932 *The Flowering Stone.* By GEORGE DILLON

1933 *Conquistador.* By ARCHIBALD MACLEISH

1934 *Collected Verse.* By ROBERT HILLYER

1935 *Bright Ambush.* By AUDREY WURDEMANN

1936 *Strange Holiness.* By ROBERT P. T. COFFIN

1937 *A Further Range.* By ROBERT FROST

1938 *Cold Morning Sky.* By MARYA ZATURENSKA

1939 *Selected Poems.* By JOHN GOULD FLETCHER

1940 *Collected Poems.* By MARK VAN DOREN

1941 *Sunderland Capture.* By LEONARD BACON

1942 *The Dust Which Is God.* By WILLIAM ROSE BENÉT

1943 *A Witness Tree.* By ROBERT FROST

1944 *Western Star.* By STEPHEN VINCENT BENÉT

1945 *V-Letter and Other Poems.* By KARL SHAPIRO

1947 *Lord Weary's Castle.* By ROBERT LOWELL

1948 *The Age of Anxiety.* By W. H. AUDEN

1949 *Terror and Decorum.* By PETER VIERECK

1950 *Annie Allen.* By GWENDOLYN BROOKS

1951 *Complete Poems.* By CARL SANDBURG

1952 *Collected Poems.* By MA-RIANNE MOORE
1953 *Collected Poems 1917–1952.* By ARCHIBALD MAC-LEISH
1954 *The Waking.* By THEODORE ROETHKE
1955 *Collected Poems.* By WALLACE STEVENS
1956 *Poems—North & South.* By ELIZABETH BISHOP

1957 *Things of This World.* By RICHARD WILBUR
1958 *Promises: Poems 1954–1956.* By ROBERT PENN WARREN
1959 *Selected Poems, 1928–1958.* By STANLEY KUNITZ
1960 *Heart's Needle.* By WILLIAM SNODGRASS
1961 *Times Three: Selected Verse from Three Dec-* ades. By PHYLLIS MCGINLEY

### Special Citations

1944 *Oklahoma!* By RICHARD RODGERS and OSCAR HAMMERSTEIN 2ND
1957 KENNETH ROBERTS, for his historical novels.

## Pulitzer Prizes in Music

1943 *Secular Cantata No. 2, A Free Song.* By WILLIAM SCHUMAN
1944 *Symphony No. 4 (Op. 34).* By HOWARD HANSON
1945 *Appalachian Spring.* By AARON COPLAND
1946 *The Canticle of the Sun.* By LEO SOWERBY
1947 *Symphony No. 3.* By CHARLES IVES
1948 *Symphony No. 3.* By WALTER PISTON
1949 *Louisiana Story* music. By VIRGIL THOMSON

1950 *The Consul.* By GIAN-CARLO MENOTTI
1951 Music for opera *Giants in the Earth.* By DOUGLAS STUART MOORE
1952 *Symphony Concertante.* By GAIL KUBIK
1954 *Concerto for Two Pianos and Orchestra.* By QUINCY PORTER
1955 *The Saint of Bleecker Street.* By GIAN-CARLO MENOTTI

1956 *Symphony No. 3.* By ERNST TOCH
1957 *Meditations on Ecclesiastes.* By NORMAN DELLO JOIO
1958 *Vanessa.* By SAMUEL BARBER
1959 *Concerto for Piano & Orchestra.* By JOHN LA MONTAINE
1960 *Second String Quartet.* By ELLIOTT CARTER
1961 *Symphony No. 7.* By WALTER PISTON

## Overseas Press Club of America Awards, 1961

**Class 1**—Best daily newspaper or wire service reporting from abroad: Lynn Heinzerling, Associated Press.

**Class 2**—Best radio-television reporting from abroad: Radio: Edwin Newman, NBC; TV: CBS Eyewitness to History: "The Road Ahead."

**Class 3**—Best photographic reporting (still) from abroad: Yasushi Nagao, UPI.

**Class 4**—Best photographic reporting (motion picture) from abroad: Yung Su Kwon, NBC.

**Class 5**—Best magazine reporting of foreign affairs: *The Reporter.*

**Class 6**—Best interpretation of foreign affairs, daily newspaper or wire service: Robert Hewett, *Minneapolis Star & Tribune.*

**Class 7**—Best interpretation of foreign affairs, radio-television: NBC White Paper: "The U-2 Affair."

**Class 8**—Best book on foreign affairs: William L. Shirer for *The Rise and Fall of the Third Reich.*

**Class 9**—Ed Stout Award for best article or report on Latin America (any medium): CBS Reports: "Trujillo: Portrait of a Dictator."

**Class 10**—E. W. Fairchild Award for best business news reporting from abroad (any medium): Edwin L. Dale, Jr., *The New York Times.*

**Class 11**—Robert Capa Award for superlative photography, still or motion picture, requiring exceptional courage and enterprise abroad: Yung Su Kwon, NBC.

**Class 12**—George Polk Memorial Award for best reporting, any medium, requiring exceptional courage and enterprise abroad: Henry N. Taylor, Scripps-Howard Newspapers, and Lionel Durand, Newsweek.

## List of Motion Picture Academy Awards

### PRODUCTION

1928 *Wings,* Paramount

1929 *The Broadway Melody,* M-G-M
1930 *All Quiet on the Western Front,* Universal
1931 *Cimarron,* RKO Radio
1932 *Grand Hotel,* M-G-M
1933 *Cavalcade,* Fox
1934 *It Happened One Night,* Columbia
1935 *Mutiny on the Bounty,* M-G-M
1936 *The Great Ziegfeld,* M-G-M
1937 *The Life of Emile Zola,* Warner Bros.
1938 *You Can't Take It With You,* Columbia

### DIRECTOR AND MOVIE

Frank Borzage, *Seventh Heaven;* Lewis Milestone, *Two Arabian Nights*
Frank Lloyd, *The Divine Lady*
Lewis Milestone, *All Quiet on the Western Front*
Norman Taurog, *Skippy*
Frank Borzage, *Bad Girl*
Frank Lloyd, *Cavalcade*
Frank Capra, *It Happened One Night*
John Ford, *The Informer*
Frank Capra, *Mr. Deeds Goes to Town*
Leo McCarey, *The Awful Truth*
Frank Capra, *You Can't Take It With You*

| | | |
|---|---|---|
| 1939 | *Gone With the Wind,* Selznick-M-G-M | Victor Fleming, *Gone With the Wind* |
| 1940 | *Rebecca,* Selznick-UA | John Ford, *The Grapes of Wrath* |
| 1941 | *How Green Was My Valley,* 20th Century-Fox | John Ford, *How Green Was My Valley* |
| 1942 | *Mrs. Miniver,* M-G-M | William Wyler, *Mrs. Miniver* |
| 1943 | *Casablanca,* Warner Bros. | Michael Curtiz, *Casablanca* |
| 1944 | *Going My Way,* Paramount | Leo McCarey, *Going My Way* |
| 1945 | *The Lost Weekend,* Paramount | Billy Wilder, *The Lost Weekend* |
| 1946 | *The Best Years of Our Lives,* Goldwyn-RKO Radio | William Wyler, *The Best Years of Our Lives* |
| 1947 | *Gentleman's Agreement,* 20th Century-Fox | Elia Kazan, *Gentleman's Agreement* |
| 1948 | *Hamlet,* Rank-Two Cities-U-I | John Huston, *Treasure of Sierra Madre* |
| 1949 | *All the King's Men,* Rossen-Columbia | Joseph L. Mankiewicz, *A Letter to Three Wives* |
| 1950 | *All About Eve,* 20th Century-Fox | Joseph L. Mankiewicz, *All About Eve* |
| 1951 | *An American in Paris,* M-G-M | George Stevens, *A Place in the Sun* |
| 1952 | *The Greatest Show on Earth,* DeMille-Paramount | John Ford, *The Quiet Man* |
| 1953 | *From Here to Eternity,* Columbia | Fred Zinnemann, *From Here to Eternity* |
| 1954 | *On the Waterfront,* Horizon-American Corp., Columbia | Elia Kazan, *On the Waterfront* |
| 1955 | *Marty,* Hecht and Lancaster's Steven-United Artists | Delbert Mann, *Marty* |
| 1956 | *Around the World in 80 Days,* the Michael Todd Co., Inc.-UA | George Stevens, *Giant* |
| 1957 | *The Bridge on the River Kwai,* Horizon Picture, Columbia | David Lean, *The Bridge on the River Kwai* |
| 1958 | *Gigi,* Arthur Freed Productions, Inc., M-G-M | Vincente Minnelli, *Gigi* |
| 1959 | *Ben-Hur,* M-G-M | William Wyler, *Ben-Hur* |
| 1960 | *The Apartment,* Mirisch Co., Inc., United Artists | Billy Wilder, *The Apartment* |

| ACTRESS AND MOVIE | ACTOR AND MOVIE |
|---|---|

| | | |
|---|---|---|
| 1928 | Janet Gaynor, *Seventh Heaven, Street Angel, Sunrise* | Emil Jannings, *The Way of All Flesh, The Last Command* |
| 1929 | Mary Pickford, *Coquette* | Warner Baxter, *In Old Arizona* |
| 1930 | Norma Shearer, *The Divorcee* | George Arliss, *Disraeli* |
| 1931 | Marie Dressler, *Min and Bill* | Lionel Barrymore, *A Free Soul* |
| 1932 | Helen Hayes, *The Sin of Madelon Claudet* | Fredric March, *Dr. Jekyll and Mr. Hyde,* and Wallace Beery, *The Champ* |
| 1933 | Katharine Hepburn, *Morning Glory* | Charles Laughton, *The Private Life of Henry VIII* |
| 1934 | Claudette Colbert, *It Happened One Night* | Clark Gable, *It Happened One Night* |
| 1935 | Bette Davis, *Dangerous* | Victor McLaglen, *The Informer* |
| 1936 | Luise Rainer, *The Great Ziegfeld* | Paul Muni, *The Story of Louis Pasteur* |
| 1937 | Luise Rainer, *The Good Earth* | Spencer Tracy, *Captains Courageous* |
| 1938 | Bette Davis, *Jezebel* | Spencer Tracy, *Boys Town* |
| 1939 | Vivien Leigh, *Gone With the Wind* | Robert Donat, *Goodbye, Mr. Chips* |
| 1940 | Ginger Rogers, *Kitty Foyle* | James Stewart, *The Philadelphia Story* |
| 1941 | Joan Fontaine, *Suspicion* | Gary Cooper, *Sergeant York* |
| 1942 | Greer Garson, *Mrs. Miniver* | James Cagney, *Yankee Doodle Dandy* |
| 1943 | Jennifer Jones, *The Song of Bernadette* | Paul Lukas, *Watch on the Rhine* |
| 1944 | Ingrid Bergman, *Gaslight* | Bing Crosby, *Going My Way* |
| 1945 | Joan Crawford, *Mildred Pierce* | Ray Milland, *The Lost Weekend* |
| 1946 | Olivia de Havilland, *To Each His Own* | Fredric March, *The Best Years of Our Lives* |
| 1947 | Loretta Young, *The Farmer's Daughter* | Ronald Colman, *A Double Life* |
| 1948 | Jane Wyman, *Johnny Belinda* | Laurence Olivier, *Hamlet* |
| 1949 | Olivia de Havilland, *The Heiress* | Broderick Crawford, *All the King's Men* |
| 1950 | Judy Holliday, *Born Yesterday* | Jose Ferrer, *Cyrano de Bergerac* |
| 1951 | Vivien Leigh, *A Streetcar Named Desire* | Humphrey Bogart, *The African Queen* |
| 1952 | Shirley Booth, *Come Back, Little Sheba* | Gary Cooper, *High Noon* |
| 1953 | Audrey Hepburn, *Roman Holiday* | William Holden, *Stalag 17* |
| 1954 | Grace Kelly, *The Country Girl* | Marlon Brando, *On the Waterfront* |
| 1955 | Anna Magnani, *The Rose Tattoo* | Ernest Borgnine, *Marty* |
| 1956 | Ingrid Bergman, *Anastasia* | Yul Brynner, *The King and I* |
| 1957 | Joanne Woodward, *The Three Faces of Eve* | Alec Guinness, *The Bridge on the River Kwai* |

| 1958 | Susan Hayward, *I Want to Live!* | David Niven, *Separate Tables* |
| 1959 | Simone Signoret, *Room at the Top* | Charlton Heston, *Ben-Hur* |
| 1960 | Elizabeth Taylor, *Butterfield 8* | Burt Lancaster, *Elmer Gantry* |

| **ACTRESS (SUPPORTING ROLE)** | **ACTOR (SUPPORTING ROLE)** |
| --- | --- |

| 1936 | Gale Sondergaard, *Anthony Adverse* | Walter Brennan, *Come and Get It* |
| 1937 | Alice Brady, *In Old Chicago* | Joseph Schildkraut, *The Life of Emile Zola* |
| 1938 | Fay Bainter, *Jezebel* | Walter Brennan, *Kentucky* |
| 1939 | Hattie McDaniel, *Gone With the Wind* | Thomas Mitchell, *Stagecoach* |
| 1940 | Jane Darwell, *The Grapes of Wrath* | Walter Brennan, *The Westerner* |
| 1941 | Mary Astor, *The Great Lie* | Donald Crisp, *How Green Was My Valley* |
| 1942 | Teresa Wright, *Mrs. Miniver* | Van Heflin, *Johnny Eager* |
| 1943 | Katina Paxinou, *For Whom the Bell Tolls* | Charles Coburn, *The More the Merrier* |
| 1944 | Ethel Barrymore, *None But the Lonely Heart* | Barry Fitzgerald, *Going My Way* |
| 1945 | Anne Revere, *National Velvet* | James Dunn, *A Tree Grows in Brooklyn* |
| 1946 | Anne Baxter, *The Razor's Edge* | Harold Russell, *The Best Years of Our Lives* |
| 1947 | Celeste Holm, *Gentleman's Agreement* | Edmund Gwenn, *Miracle on 34th Street* |
| 1948 | Claire Trevor, *Key Largo* | Walter Huston, *Treasure of Sierra Madre* |
| 1949 | Mercedes McCambridge, *All the King's Men* | Dean Jagger, *Twelve O'Clock High* |
| 1950 | Josephine Hull, *Harvey* | George Sanders, *All About Eve* |
| 1951 | Kim Hunter, *A Streetcar Named Desire* | Karl Malden, *A Streetcar Named Desire* |
| 1952 | Gloria Grahame, *The Bad and the Beautiful* | Anthony Quinn, *Viva Zapata!* |
| 1953 | Donna Reed, *From Here to Eternity* | Frank Sinatra, *From Here to Eternity* |
| 1954 | Eva Marie Saint, *On the Waterfront* | Edmond O'Brien, *The Barefoot Contessa* |
| 1955 | Jo Van Fleet, *East of Eden* | Jack Lemmon, *Mister Roberts* |
| 1956 | Dorothy Malone, *Written on the Wind* | Anthony Quinn, *Lust for Life* |
| 1957 | Miyoshi Umeki, *Sayonara* | Red Buttons, *Sayonara* |
| 1958 | Wendy Hiller, *Separate Tables* | Burl Ives, *The Big Country* |
| 1959 | Shelley Winters, *The Diary of Anne Frank* | Hugh Griffith, *Ben-Hur* |
| 1960 | Shirley Jones, *Elmer Gantry* | Peter Ustinov, *Spartacus* |

## Some Other Academy Awards for 1960

**Art direction (black-and-white):** *The Apartment.* Art direction: Alexander Trauner. Set decoration: Edward G. Boyle.

**Art direction (color):** *Spartacus.* Art direction: Alexander Golitzen and Eric Orbom. Set decoration: Russell A. Gausman and Julia Heron.

**Cinematography (black-and-white):** Freddie Francis, *Sons and Lovers.*

**Cinematography (color):** Russell Metty, *Spartacus.*

**Costume design (black-and-white):** Edith Head and Edward Stevenson, *The Facts of Life.*

**Costume design (color):** Valles and Bill Thomas, *Spartacus.*

**Documentary (feature):** *The Horse With the Flying Tail,* Walt Disney Productions.

**Documentary (short subject):** *Giuseppina,* James Hill Production.

**Film editing:** Daniel Mandell, *The Apartment.*

**Foreign-language film:** The Virgin Spring (Swedish).

**Honorary awards:** Gary Cooper, Stan Laurel, and Hayley Mills.

**Jean Hersholt Humanitarian Award:** Sol Lesser.

**Music (scoring musical picture):** Morris Stoloff and Harry Sukman, *Song Without End* (*The Story of Franz Liszt*).

**Music (score of dramatic or comedy picture):** Ernest Gold, *Exodus.*

**Music (song):** "Never on Sunday" from *Never on Sunday.* Music and lyrics by Manos Hadjidakis.

**Short Subjects (cartoon):** *Munro,* Rembrandt Films.

**Short subjects (live action):** *Day of the Painter,* Little Movies.

**Sound:** *The Alamo,* Samuel Goldwyn Studio Sound Dept.

**Special effects:** *The Time Machine,* Galaxy Films Production, M-G-M. Gene Warren and Tim Baar (visual effects).

**Writing (screenplay—based on material from another medium):** Richard Brooks, *Elmer Gantry.*

**Writing (story and screenplay—written directly for the screen):** Billy Wilder and I. A. L. Diamond, *The Apartment.*

---

### Wedding Anniversary Gifts
*Source: Encyclopaedia Britannica.*

| 5th year—wood | 15th year—crystal | 25th year—silver |
| 10th year—tin | 20th year—china | 50th year—gold |

60th year in Great Britain, 75th year in America—diamond

# New York Film Critics' Awards

**(1—best motion picture; 2—best male performance; 3—best feminine performance; 4—best direction; 5—best foreign film; 6—special award; 7—screenplay writing..)**

**1940** 1. *The Grapes of Wrath,* 20th Century-Fox
2. Charles Chaplin, *The Great Dictator* (refused award)
3. Katharine Hepburn, *The Philadelphia Story*
4. John Ford, *The Grapes of Wrath; The Long Voyage Home*
5. *The Baker's Wife* (French)
6. Walt Disney, *Fantasia*

**1941** 1. *Citizen Kane,* RKO-Mercury
2. Gary Cooper, *Sergeant York*
3. Joan Fontaine, *Suspicion*
4. John Ford, *How Green Was My Valley*

**1942** 1. *In Which We Serve,* UA-Noel Coward
2. James Cagney, *Yankee Doodle Dandy*
3. Agnes Moorehead, *The Magnificent Ambersons*
4. John Farrow, *Wake Island*

**1943** 1. *Watch on the Rhine,* Warner Bros.
2. Paul Lukas, *Watch on the Rhine*
3. Ida Lupino, *The Hard Way*
4. George Stevens, *The More the Merrier*

**1944** 1. *Going My Way,* Paramount
2. Barry Fitzgerald, *Going My Way*
3. Tallulah Bankhead, *Lifeboat*
4. Leo McCarey, *Going My Way*

**1945** 1. *The Lost Weekend,* Paramount
2. Ray Milland, *The Lost Weekend*
3. Ingrid Bergman, *Spellbound* and *The Bells of St. Mary's*
4. Billy Wilder, *The Lost Weekend*
5. (None)
6. *The True Glory* and *The Fighting Lady*

**1946** 1. *The Best Years of Our Lives,* Goldwyn-RKO Radio
2. Laurence Olivier, *Henry V*
3. Celia Johnson, *Brief Encounter*
4. William Wyler, *The Best Years of Our Lives*
5. *Open City* (Italian)

**1947** 1. *Gentleman's Agreement,* 20th Century-Fox
2. William Powell, *Life With Father*
3. Deborah Kerr, *The Adventuress* and *Black Narcissus*
4. Elia Kazan, *Gentleman's Agreement* and *Boomerang*
5. *To Live in Peace* (Italian)

**1948** 1. *Treasure of Sierra Madre,* Warner Bros.
2. Sir Laurence Olivier, *Hamlet*
3. Olivia de Havilland, *The Snake Pit*
4. John Huston, *Treasure of Sierra Madre*
5. *Paisan* (Italian)

**1949** 1. *All the King's Men,* Rossen-Columbia
2. Broderick Crawford, *All the King's Men*
3. Olivia de Havilland, *The Heiress*
4. Carol Reed, *The Fallen Idol*
5. *The Bicycle Thief* (Italian)

**1950** 1. *All About Eve,* 20th Century-Fox
2. Gregory Peck, *Twelve O'Clock High*
3. Bette Davis, *All About Eve*
4. Joseph L. Mankiewicz, *All About Eve*
5. *Ways of Love* (Franco-Italian)

**1951** 1. *A Streetcar Named Desire,* Warner Bros.
2. Arthur Kennedy, *Bright Victory*
3. Vivien Leigh, *A Streetcar Named Desire*
4. Elia Kazan, *A Streetcar Named Desire*
5. *Miracle in Milan* (Italian)

**1952** 1. *High Noon,* United Artists
2. Ralph Richardson, *Breaking the Sound Barrier*
3. Shirley Booth, *Come Back, Little Sheba*
4. Fred Zinnemann, *High Noon*
5. *Forbidden Games* (French)

**1953** 1. *From Here to Eternity,* Columbia
2. Burt Lancaster, *From Here to Eternity*
3. Audrey Hepburn, *Roman Holiday*
4. Fred Zinnemann, *From Here to Eternity*
5. *Justice Is Done* (French)
6. *A Queen Is Crowned* (JARO) and *The Conquest of Everest* (JARO)

**1954** 1. *On the Waterfront,* Columbia
2. Marlon Brando, *On the Waterfront*
3. Grace Kelly, *The Country Girl, Rear Window, Dial M for Murder*
4. Elia Kazan, *On the Waterfront*
5. *Gate of Hell* (Japanese)

**1955** 1. *Marty,* United Artists
2. Ernest Borgnine, *Marty*
3. Anna Magnani, *The Rose Tattoo*
4. David Lean, *Summertime*
5. *Diabolique* (French) and *Umberto D.* (Italian)

**1956** 1. *Around the World in 80 Days.* The Michael Todd Co., Inc., UA
2. Kirk Douglas, *Lust For Life*
3. Ingrid Bergman, *Anastasia*
4. John Huston, *Moby Dick*
5. *La Strada* (Italian)

**1957** 1. *The Bridge on the River Kwai,* Columbia
2. Alec Guinness, *The Bridge on the River Kwai*
3. Deborah Kerr, *Heaven Knows, Mr. Allison*

4. David Lean, *The Bridge on the River Kwai*
5. *Gervaise* (French)

1958 1. *The Defiant Ones*, United Artists
2. David Niven, *Separate Tables*
3. Susan Hayward, *I Want to Live!*
4. Stanley Kramer, *The Defiant Ones*
5. *Mon Oncle* (French)
6. (None)
7. Nathan E. Douglas & Harold J. Smith, *The Defiant Ones*

1959 1. *Ben-Hur*, M-G-M
2. James Stewart, *Anatomy of a Murder*
3. Audrey Hepburn, *The Nun's Story*
4. Fred Zinnemann, *The Nun's Story*
5. *The 400 Blows* (French)
6. (None)
7. Wendell Mayes, *Anatomy.*

1960 1. *The Apartment,* United Artists; *Sons and Lovers,* 20th Century-Fox
2. Burt Lancaster, *Elmer Gantry*
3. Deborah Kerr, *The Sundowners*
4. Billy Wilder, *The Apartment;* Jack Cardiff, *Sons and Lovers*
5. *Hiroshima, Mon Amour* (French)
6. (None)
7. Billy Wilder & I. A. L. Diamond, *The Apartment.*

# New York Drama Critics' Circle Awards

1935-36 *Winterset,* by Maxwell Anderson
1936-37 *High Tor,* by Maxwell Anderson
1937-38 *Of Mice and Men,* by John Steinbeck
    *Shadow and Substance,* by Paul Vincent Carroll [1]
1938-39 (No award)
    *The White Steed,* by Paul Vincent Carroll [1]
1939-40 *The Time of Your Life,* by William Saroyan
1940-41 *Watch on the Rhine,* by Lillian Hellman
    *The Corn Is Green,* by Emlyn Williams[1]
1941-42 (No award)
    *Blithe Spirit,* by Noel Coward [1]
1942-43 *The Patriots,* by Sidney Kingsley
1943-44 (No award)
    *Jacobowsky and the Colonel,* by Franz Werfel-S. N. Behrman[1]
1944-45 *The Glass Menagerie,* by Tennessee Williams
1945-46 (No award)
    *Carousel,* by Richard Rodgers & Oscar Hammerstein II[2]
1946-47 *All My Sons,* by Arthur Miller
    *No Exit,* by Jean-Paul Sartre[1]
    *Brigadoon,* by Lerner and Loewe[2]
1947-48 *A Streetcar Named Desire,* by Tennessee Williams
    *The Winslow Boy,* by Terence Rattigan[1]

1948-49 *Death of a Salesman,* by Arthur Miller
    *The Madwoman of Chaillot,* by Jean Giraudoux - Maurice Valency[1]
    *South Pacific,* by Richard Rodgers, Oscar Hammerstein II & Joshua Logan[2]
1949-50 *The Member of the Wedding,* by Carson McCullers
    *The Cocktail Party,* by T. S. Eliot[1]
    *The Consul,* by Gian-Carlo Menotti[2]
1950-51 *Darkness at Noon,* by Sidney Kingsley[3]
    *The Lady's Not for Burning,* by Christopher Fry[1]
    *Guys and Dolls,* by Abe Burrows, Jo Swerling & Frank Loesser[2]
1951-52 *I Am a Camera,* by John Van Druten[4]
    *Venus Observed,* by Christopher Fry[1]
    *Pal Joey,* by Richard Rodgers, Lorenz Hart & John O'Hara[2]
    *Don Juan in Hell,* by George B. Shaw[5]
1952-53 *Picnic,* by William Inge
    *The Love of Four Colonels,* by Peter Ustinov[1]
    *Wonderful Town,* by Joseph Fields, Jerome Chodorov, Betty Comden, Adolph Green & Leonard Bernstein[2]

1953-54 *The Teahouse of the August Moon,* by John Patrick
    *Ondine,* by Jean Giraudoux[1]
    *The Golden Apple,* by John Latouche & Jerome Moross[2]
1954-55 *Cat on a Hot Tin Roof,* by Tennessee Williams
    ·*Witness for the Prosecution,* by Agatha Christie[1]
    *The Saint of Bleecker Street,* by Gian-Carlo Menotti[2]
1955-56 *The Diary of Anne Frank,* by Frances Goodrich & Albert Hackett
    *Tiger at the Gates,* by Jean Giraudoux-Christopher Fry[1]
    *My Fair Lady,* by Frederick Loewe & Alan Jay Lerner[2]
1956-57 *Long Day's Journey Into Night,* by Eugene O'Neill
    *Waltz of the Toreadors,* by Jean Anouilh[1]
    *The Most Happy Fella,* by Frank Loesser[2, 6]
1957-58 *Look Homeward, Angel,* by Ketti Frings[7]
    *Look Back in Anger,* by John Osborne[1]
    *The Music Man,* by Meredith Willson[2]
1958-59 *A Raisin in the Sun,* by Lorraine Hansberry

*The Visit,* by Fried-rich Duerrenmatt-Maurice Valency[1]

*La Plume de ma Tante,* by Robert Dhery & Gerard Calvi[2]

1959-60 *Toys in the Attic,* by Lillian Hellman
*Five Finger Exercise,* by Peter Shaffer[1]
*Fiorello,* by Jerome Weidman, George Abbott, Jerry Bock,

Sheldon Harnick[2]

1960-61 *All the Way Home,* by Tad Mosel[8]
*A Taste of Honey,* by Shelagh Delaney[1]
*Carnival,* by Michael Stewart[2]

[1] Citation for best foreign play. [2] Citation for best musical. [3] Based on a novel by Arthur Koestler. [4] Based on Christopher Isherwood's *Berlin Stories.* [5] For "distinguished and original contribution to the theater." [6] Based on Sidney Howard's *They Knew What They Wanted.* [7] Based on a novel by Thomas Wolfe. [8] Based on James Agee's *A Death in the Family.*

# The Hall of Fame for Great Americans

The Hall of Fame for Great Americans, established in 1900 on the campus of New York University, is an open-air colonnade with busts and tablets for 88 of the 89 persons so far honored for national achievements. New names are voted on every five years by a College of Electors of about 100 eminent men and women from all the states. To be elected to the Hall of Fame, an individual must have been dead more than 25 years (before 1922, the stipulation was 10 years), must have been a citizen of the U. S., and must receive a majority vote. Nominations may be made by any citizen.

| Names | Elected |
| --- | --- |
| John Adams (statesman) | 1900 |
| John Quincy Adams (statesman) | 1905 |
| Louis Agassiz (naturalist) | 1915 |
| Susan B. Anthony (reformer) | 1950 |
| John James Audubon (naturalist) | 1900 |
| George Bancroft (historian) | 1910 |
| Henry Ward Beecher (clergyman) | 1900 |
| Alexander Graham Bell (inventor) | 1950 |
| Daniel Boone (explorer) | 1915 |
| Edwin Booth (actor) | 1925 |
| Phillips Brooks (clergyman) | 1910 |
| William Cullen Bryant (poet) | 1910 |
| William Ellery Channing (clergyman) | 1900 |
| Rufus Choate (lawyer) | 1915 |
| Henry Clay (statesman) | 1900 |
| Samuel L. Clemens (author) | 1920 |
| Grover Cleveland (statesman) | 1935 |
| James Fenimore Cooper (author) | 1910 |
| Peter Cooper (philanthropist) | 1900 |
| Charlotte S. Cushman (actress) | 1915 |
| James Buchanan Eads (engineer) | 1920 |
| Thomas A. Edison (inventor) | 1960 |
| Jonathan Edwards (clergyman) | 1900 |
| Ralph Waldo Emerson (author) | 1900 |
| David G. Farragut (naval officer) | 1900 |
| Stephen C. Foster (song composer) | 1940 |
| Benjamin Franklin (statesman) | 1900 |
| Robert Fulton (inventor) | 1900 |
| Josiah Willard Gibbs (physicist) | 1950 |
| William Crawford Gorgas (physician) | 1950 |
| Ulysses S. Grant (statesman) | 1900 |
| Asa Gray (botanist) | 1900 |
| Alexander Hamilton (statesman) | 1915 |
| Nathaniel Hawthorne (author) | 1900 |
| Joseph Henry (physicist) | 1915 |
| Patrick Henry (statesman) | 1920 |
| Oliver Wendell Holmes (author) | 1910 |
| Mark Hopkins (educator) | 1915 |
| Elias Howe (inventor) | 1915 |
| Washington Irving (author) | 1900 |
| Andrew Jackson (statesman) | 1910 |
| Thomas ("Stonewall") Jackson (military officer) | 1955 |
| Thomas Jefferson (statesman) | 1900 |
| John Paul Jones (naval officer) | 1925 |
| James Kent (jurist) | 1900 |

| Names | Elected |
| --- | --- |
| Sidney Lanier (poet) | 1945 |
| Robert E. Lee (military officer) | 1900 |
| Abraham Lincoln (statesman) | 1900 |
| Henry W. Longfellow (poet) | 1900 |
| James Russell Lowell (poet) | 1905 |
| Mary Lyon (educator) | 1905 |
| Edward Alexander MacDowell * (composer) | 1960 |
| James Madison (statesman) | 1905 |
| Horace Mann (educator) | 1900 |
| John Marshall (jurist) | 1900 |
| Matthew F. Maury (oceanographer) | 1930 |
| Maria Mitchell (astronomer) | 1905 |
| James Monroe (statesman) | 1930 |
| Samuel F. B. Morse (inventor) | 1900 |
| William T. G. Morton (dentist) | 1920 |
| John Lothrop Motley (historian) | 1910 |
| Simon Newcomb (astronomer) | 1935 |
| Thomas Paine (author) | 1945 |
| Alice Freeman Palmer (educator) | 1920 |
| Francis Parkman (historian) | 1915 |
| George Peabody (philanthropist) | 1900 |
| William Penn (colonizer) | 1935 |
| Edgar Allan Poe (author) | 1910 |
| Walter Reed (surgeon) | 1945 |
| Theodore Roosevelt (statesman) | 1950 |
| Augustus Saint-Gaudens (sculptor) | 1920 |
| William T. Sherman (army officer) | 1905 |
| Joseph Story (jurist) | 1900 |
| Harriet Beecher Stowe (author) | 1910 |
| Gilbert Charles Stuart (painter) | 1900 |
| Henry David Thoreau (author) * | 1960 |
| Booker T. Washington (educator) | 1945 |
| George Washington (statesman) | 1900 |
| Daniel Webster (statesman) | 1900 |
| George Westinghouse (inventor) | 1955 |
| J. A. McNeill Whistler (painter) | 1930 |
| Walt Whitman (poet) | 1930 |
| Eli Whitney (inventor) | 1900 |
| John Greenleaf Whittier (poet) | 1905 |
| Emma Willard (educator) | 1905 |
| Frances Elizabeth Willard (reformer) | 1910 |
| Roger Williams (clergyman) | 1920 |
| Woodrow Wilson (statesman) | 1950 |
| Wilbur Wright* (inventor) | 1955 |

\* Not yet represented by a bust and tablet.

# WORLD GEOGRAPHY AND MISCELLANEOUS

## Explorations and Discoveries

### Africa

| Country or place | Event | Explorer or discoverer | Date |
|---|---|---|---|
| Sierra Leone | Visited | Hanno, Carthaginian seaman | c. 520 B.C. |
| Congo River | Mouth discovered | Cão, Portuguese navigator | c. A.D. 1484 |
| Cape of Good Hope | Doubled | Bartholomeu Diaz, Portuguese navigator | 1488 |
| Gambia River | Explored | Mungo Park, Scottish explorer | 1795 |
| Sahara Desert | Crossed | Denham and Clapperton, English explorers | 1822–23 |
| Zambezi River | Discovered | Livingstone, Scottish explorer | 1851 |
| Sudan | Explored | Barth, German explorer | 1852–55 |
| Victoria Falls | Discovered | Livingstone | 1855 |
| Lake Tanganyika | Discovered | Burton and Speke, British explorers | 1858 |
| Congo River | Traced | Stanley, British explorer | 1877 |

### Asia

| Country or place | Event | Explorer or discoverer | Date |
|---|---|---|---|
| Punjab (India) | Visited | Alexander the Great | 327 B.C. |
| China | Visited | Marco Polo, Italian traveler | c. A.D. 1272 |
| Tibet | Visited | Odoric, Italian monk | c. 1325 |
| Southern China | Explored | Conti, Italian adventurer | c. 1440 |
| India | Visited by Cape route | Vasco da Gama, Portuguese navigator | 1498 |
| Japan | Visited | St. Francis Xavier of Spain | 1549 |
| Arabia | Explored | Niebuhr, German explorer | 1762 |
| China | Explored | Richthofen, German scientist | 1868 |
| Mongolia | Explored | Przhevalsky, Russian explorer | 1870–73 |
| Central Asia | Explored | Hedin, Swedish scientist | 1890–1908 |

### Europe

| Country or place | Event | Explorer or discoverer | Date |
|---|---|---|---|
| Shetland Islands | Visited | Pytheas of Massilia (Marseille) | c. 325 B.C. |
| North Cape | Rounded | Ottar, Norwegian explorer | c. A.D. 870 |
| Iceland | Colonized | Norwegian noblemen | c. 890–900 |

### North America

| Country or place | Event | Explorer or discoverer | Date |
|---|---|---|---|
| Greenland | Colonized | Eric the Red, Norwegian navigator | c. A.D. 985 |
| Labrador; Nova Scotia (?) | Discovered | Leif Ericsson, Norse explorer | 1000 |
| West Indies | Discovered | Christopher Columbus, Italian navigator | 1492 |
| North America | Coast discovered | John Cabot, for British | 1497 |
| Pacific Ocean | Discovered | Balboa, Spanish explorer | 1513 |
| Florida | Explored | Ponce de León, Spanish explorer | 1513 |
| Mexico | Conquered | Cortez, Spanish adventurer | 1519 |
| St. Lawrence River | Discovered | Cartier, French navigator | 1534 |
| Southwest U. S. | Explored | Coronado, Spanish explorer | 1540–42 |
| Colorado River | Discovered | Alarcón, Spanish explorer | 1540 |
| Mississippi River | Discovered | Hernando de Soto, Spanish explorer | 1541 |
| Frobisher Bay | Discovered | Frobisher, English seaman | 1576 |
| Maine Coast | Explored | Champlain, French explorer | 1604 |
| Jamestown, Va. | Settled | Smith, English colonist | 1607 |
| Hudson River | Explored | Hudson, English navigator | 1609 |
| Hudson Bay (Canada) | Discovered | Hudson | 1610 |
| Baffin Bay | Discovered | Baffin, English navigator | 1616 |
| Lake Michigan | Navigated | Nicolet, French explorer | 1634 |
| Arkansas River | Discovered | Marquette and Joliet, French explorers | 1673 |
| Mississippi River | Explored | LaSalle, French explorer | 1682 |
| Bering Strait | Discovered | Bering, Danish explorer | 1728 |
| Alaska | Discovered | Bering | 1741 |
| Mackenzie River (Canada) | Discovered | Mackenzie, Scottish-Canadian explorer | 1789 |
| Northwest U. S. | Explored | Lewis and Clark | 1804–06 |

| Country or place | Event | Explorer or discoverer | Date |
|---|---|---|---|
| Northeast Passage (Arctic Ocean) | Navigated | Nordenskjold, Swedish explorer | 1879 |
| Greenland | Explored | Peary, American explorer | 1892 |
| Northwest Passage | Navigated | Amundsen, Norwegian explorer | 1906 |

### South America

| | | | |
|---|---|---|---|
| Continent | Visited | Columbus, Italian navigator | 1498 |
| Brazil | Discovered | Cabral, Portuguese explorer | 1500 |
| Peru | Conquered | Pizarro, Spanish explorer | 1532–33 |
| Amazon River | Explored | Orellana, Spanish explorer | 1541 |
| Cape Horn | Discovered | Schouten, Dutch navigator | 1615 |

### Oceania

| | | | |
|---|---|---|---|
| New Guinea | Visited | Menezes, Portuguese explorer | 1526 |
| Australia | Visited | Jansz, Dutch explorer | 1606 |
| Tasmania | Visited | Tasman, Dutch navigator | 1642 |
| Australia | Explored | Sturt, English explorer | 1828 |
| Australia | Explored | Burke and Wills, Australian explorers | 1861 |

### Arctic, Antarctic and Miscellaneous

| | | | |
|---|---|---|---|
| Ocean exploration | Expedition | Magellan's ships circled globe | 1519–22 |
| Spitsbergen | Visited | Barents, Dutch navigator | 1596 |
| Antarctic Circle | Crossed | Cook, English navigator | 1773 |
| Antarctica | Discovered | Palmer, U S. explorer (archipelago) and Bellingshausen, Russian navigator (mainland) | 1820–21 |
| Antarctica | Explored | Wilkes, American explorer | 1840 |
| North Pole | Discovered | Peary, American explorer | 1909 |
| South Pole | Discovered | Amundsen, Norwegian explorer | 1911 |

# The Seven Wonders of the World

### THE PYRAMIDS OF EGYPT

A group of three pyramids, *Khufu, Khafra,* and *Menkaura* at Giza, outside modern Cairo, is often called the first wonder of the world; it is also the oldest and only surviving "wonder." The largest pyramid, built by Khufu (Cheops), had an original estimated height of 482 ft. (now approximately 450 ft.). The exact date of its construction is unknown and has been estimated as early as 4700 B.C. but is probably closer to 2900 B.C.

### HANGING GARDENS OF BABYLON

Often listed as the second wonder, these gardens were supposedly built by Nebuchadnezzar about 600 B.C. to please his queen, Amuhia. They are also associated with the mythical Assyrian Queen, Semiramis. Archeologists surmise that the gardens were laid out atop a vaulted building, with provisions for raising water. The terraces were said to rise from 75 to 300 ft.

The Walls of Babylon, also built by Nebuchadnezzar, are sometimes referred to as the second (or the seventh) wonder instead of the Hanging Gardens.

### STATUE OF ZEUS (JUPITER) AT OLYMPIA

The work of Phidias (5th century B.C.), this colossal figure in gold and ivory was reputedly 40 ft. high. All trace of it is lost, except for reproductions on coins.

### TEMPLE OF ARTEMIS (DIANA) AT EPHESUS

A beautiful structure, begun about 350 B.C. in honor of a non-Hellenic goddess who later became identified with the Greek goddess of the same name. The temple, with Ionic columns 60 feet high, was destroyed by invading Goths A.D. 262.

### MAUSOLEUM AT HALICARNASSUS

This famous monument was erected by Queen Artemisia in memory of her husband, King Mausolus of Caria in Asia Minor, who died in 353 B.C. Some remains of the structure are in the British Museum. This shrine is the source of the modern word "mausoleum."

### COLOSSUS AT RHODES

This bronze statue of Helios (Apollo), about 105 ft. high, was the work of the sculptor Chares, who reputedly labored for 12 years before completing it in 280 B.C. It was destroyed during an earthquake in 224 B.C.

### PHAROS OF ALEXANDRIA

The seventh wonder was the Pharos (lighthouse) of Alexandria, built by Sostratus of Cnidus during the 3rd century B.C. on the island of Pharos off the coast of Egypt. It was destroyed by an earthquake in the 13th century.

# Representative Mountain Peaks of the World

| Mountain peak | Range | Location | Height, ft. |
|---|---|---|---|
| Everest | Himalayas | Tibet-Nepal | 29,028 |
| Godwin Austen (K2) | Karakoram | India | 28,250 |
| Kanchenjunga | Himalayas | Nepal | 28,140 |
| Makalu | Himalayas | Tibet-Nepal | 27,790 |
| Dhaulagari | Himalayas | Nepal | 26,795 |
| Gurla Mandhata | Himalayas | Tibet | 25,355 |
| Tirich Mir | Hindu Kush | Pakistan | 25,230 |
| Muztagh Ata (K5) | Pamirs | Sinkiang | 24,388 |
| Muztagh | Kunlun | Sinkiang | 23,890 |
| Aconcagua | Andes | Argentina | 22,835 |
| Dos Conos | Andes | Argentina | 22,507 |
| Ojos del Salado | Andes | Argentina-Chile | 22,408 |
| Huascarán | Andes | Peru | 22,205 |
| Llullaillaco | Andes | Argentina-Chile | 22,148 |
| Kailas | Himalayas | Tibet | 22,028 |
| Mercedario | Andes | Argentina | 21,883 |
| Tupungato | Andes | Argentina-Chile | 21,489 |
| Sajama | Andes | Bolivia | 21,391 |
| Chimborazo | Andes | Ecuador | 20,557 |
| McKinley | Alaska | Alaska | 20,320 |
| Logan | St. Elias | Canada (Yukon Territory) | 19,850 |
| Kilimanjaro | ........ | Tanganyika | 19,565 |
| Cotopaxi | Andes | Ecuador | 19,344 |
| Cayambe | Andes | Ecuador | 19,170 |
| Misti | Andes | Peru | 19,167 |
| Orizaba (Citlaltepetl) | Sierra Madre Oriental | Mexico | 18,696 |
| Elbrus | Caucasus | U.S.S.R. | 18,468 |
| St. Elias | St. Elias | Alaska-Canada | 18,008 |
| Vilcanota | Andes | Peru | 17,998 |
| Popocatepetl | Cordillera de Anáhuac | Mexico | 17,883 |
| Cerro de Cuz | Andes | Bolivia | 17,828 |
| Ixtaccihuatl | Cordillera de Anáhuac | Mexico | 17,338 |
| Tolima | Andes | Colombia | 17,109 |
| Dikh-Tau | Caucasus | U.S.S.R. | 17,054 |
| Kenya | ........ | Kenya | 17,040 |
| Ruwenzori | Ruwenzori | Congo-Uganda | 16,795 |
| Kazbek | Caucasus | U.S.S.R. | 16,545 |
| Bona | Wrangell | Alaska | 16,421 |
| Klyuchevskaya | Kamchatka | U.S.S.R. | 15,912 |
| Savalan | Elburz | Iran | 15,784 |
| Blanc | Alps | France | 15,781 |
| Lister | ........ | Antarctica | 15,384 |
| Fairweather | St. Elias | Alaska | 15,300 |
| Dashan | Simen | Ethiopia | 15,158 |
| Markham | ........ | Antarctica | 15,102 |
| Matterhorn | Alps | Switzerland-Italy | 14,780 |
| Whitney | Sierra Nevada | California | 14,495 |
| Elbert | Rockies | Colorado | 14,431 |
| Massive | Rockies | Colorado | 14,418 |
| Rainier | Cascades | Washington | 14,410 |
| Longs | Rockies | Colorado | 14,255 |
| Colima | Sierra Madre Occidental | Mexico | 14,239 |
| Shasta | Sierra Nevada | California | 14,162 |
| Pikes Peak | Rockies | Colorado | 14,110 |
| Finsteraarhorn | Alps | Switzerland | 14,026 |
| Mauna Kea | ........ | Hawaii | 13,796 |
| Gannett Peak | Rockies | Wyoming | 13,785 |
| Mauna Loa | ........ | Hawaii | 13,680 |
| Jungfrau | Bernese Alps | Switzerland | 13,667 |
| Cameroon | ........ | British Cameroons | 13,353 |
| Erebus | ........ | Antarctica | 13,202 |
| Robson | Rockies | British Columbia | 12,972 |
| Fujiyama (Fujisan) | ........ | Japan | 12,385 |
| Cook | Southern Alps | South Island, New Zealand | 12,349 |
| Hood | Cascades | Oregon | 11,245 |

## Large Islands of the World

| Island and status | Location | Area, sq. mi. |
|---|---|---|
| GREENLAND (Danish territory) | North Atlantic | 839,782 |
| NEW GUINEA (Under Dutch crown, west part; U. N. trust territory under Australian administration, northeast part; Australian territory, southeast part) | Southwest Pacific | 312,329 |
| BORNEO (Indonesia, south part; British protectorate and colonies, north part) | South China Sea | 290,012 |
| MADAGASCAR (Malagasy Republic) | Off southeast coast of Africa | 227,737 |
| BAFFIN (Canada, Northwest Territories) | Arctic | 183,810 |
| SUMATRA (Indonesia) | Northeast Indian Ocean | 163,145 |
| HONSHU (Japanese home island) | Sea of Japan—Pacific | 91,278 |
| GREAT BRITAIN (Eng., Scotland, Wales) | Off coast of northwest Europe | 88,140 |
| VICTORIA (Canada, Northwest Territories) | Arctic | 80,450 |
| ELLESMERE (Canada, Northwest Territories) | Arctic Ocean | 75,024 |
| CELEBES (Indonesia) | Southwest Pacific | 69,255 |
| SOUTH ISLAND, NEW ZEALAND | South Pacific | 58,093 |
| JAVA (Indonesia) | Northeast Indian Ocean | 48,504 |
| NORTH ISLAND, NEW ZEALAND | South Pacific | 44,281 |
| NEWFOUNDLAND (Canadian province) | North Atlantic | 42,734 |
| CUBA (Republic) | Caribbean Sea | 42,350 |
| LUZON | Philippine Islands | 40,814 |
| ICELAND (Republic) | North Atlantic | 39,688 |
| MINDANAO | Philippine Islands | 36,537 |
| HOKKAIDO (Japanese home island) | Sea of Japan—Pacific | 34,084 |
| IRELAND (Ireland, republic, south part; Northern Ireland, part of United Kingdom) | West of Great Britain | 31,840 |
| HISPANIOLA (Dominican Republic, east part; Haitian republic, west part) | Caribbean Sea | 30,075 |
| TASMANIA (Australian state) | South of Australia | 26,215 |
| BANKS (Canada, Northwest Territories) | Arctic | 25,992 |
| CEYLON (Member of Commonwealth of Nations) | Indian Ocean | 25,332 |
| SAKHALIN (U.S.S.R.) | North of Japan | 24,560 |
| DEVON (Canada, Northwest Territories) | Arctic | 20,484 |
| TIERRA DEL FUEGO (East part to Argentina; west part to Chile) | Southern tip of South America | 18,530 |
| MELVILLE (Canada, Northwest Territories) | Arctic | 16,164 |
| SOUTHAMPTON (Canada, N. W. Territories) | Hudson Bay | 16,114 |

## Oceans and Seas

| Name | Area, sq. mi. | Average depth, feet | Greatest known depth, ft. | Place of greatest known depth |
|---|---|---|---|---|
| Pacific Ocean | 63,801,700 | 14,048 | 35,400 | Off Mindanao |
| Atlantic Ocean | 31,830,800 | 12,880 | 30,246 | Off Puerto Rico |
| Indian Ocean | 28,356,300 | 13,002 | 22,968 | Off Sumatra-Java |
| Arctic Ocean | 5,440,200 | 3,953 | 17,850 | 77° 45′ N.; 175° W. |
| Mediterranean Sea* | 1,145,100 | 4,688 | 15,564 | Off Cape Matapan, Greece |
| Caribbean Sea | 1,049,500 | 8,685 | 22,788 | Off Cayman Islands |
| South China Sea | 895,400 | 5,419 | 18,090 | West of Luzon |
| Bering Sea | 875,800 | 4,714 | 13,422 | Off Buldir Island |
| Gulf of Mexico | 618,200 | 4,874 | 12,744 | Sigsbee Deep |
| Sea of Okhotsk | 589,800 | 2,749 | 11,400 | 146° 10′ E.; 46° 50′ N. |
| East China Sea | 482,300 | 617 | 9,126 | 25° 16′ N.; 125° E. |
| Hudson Bay | 475,800 | 420 | 600 | Near entrance |
| Sea of Japan | 389,100 | 4,429 | 12,276 | Central Basin |
| Andaman Sea | 308,000 | 2,854 | 12,392 | Off Car Nicobar Island |
| North Sea | 222,100 | 308 | 2,165 | Skagerrak |
| Red Sea | 169,100 | 1,611 | 7,254 | Off Port Sudan |
| Baltic Sea | 163,000 | 180 | 1,380 | Off Gotland |

* Including Black Sea and Sea of Azov. NOTE: For Caspian Sea, see Large Lakes of World elsewhere in this section.

## Famous Waterfalls of the World

| Waterfall | Location | River | Height, feet |
|---|---|---|---|
| Angel | Venezuela | Tributary of Caroní | 3,300 |
| Cuquenán, or Kukenaam | Venezuela-British Guiana | Cuquenán | 2,000 |
| Sutherland | South Island, N. Z. | Arthur | 1,904 |
| Tugela | Natal, South Africa | Tugela | 1,800 |
| Ribbon (Yosemite) | California | Creek, flowing into Yosemite | 1,612 |
| Upper Yosemite | California | Yosemite Creek, tributary of Merced | 1,430 |
| Gavarnie | Southwestern France | Gave de Pau | 1,385 |
| Takkakaw | British Columbia | Tributary of Yoho | 1,200 |
| Widow's Tears (Yosemite) | California | Tributary of Merced | 1,170 |
| Staubbach | Switzerland | Staubbach (Lauterbrunnen valley) | 980 |
| Trummelbach | Switzerland | Trummelbach (Lauterbrunnen) | 950 |
| Middle Cascade (Yosemite) | California | Yosemite Creek, tributary of Merced | 910 |
| Multnomah | Oregon | Multnomah Creek, tributary of Columbia | 850 |
| Vettisfos | Norway | Morkedöla | 850 |
| King Edward VII | British Guiana | Courantyne | 840 |
| Gersoppa | India | Sharavati | 830 |
| Kaieteur | British Guiana | Pataro | 741 |
| Kalambo | Tanganyika-N. Rhodesia | ........ | 705 |
| Fairy (Mt. Rainier Park) | Washington | Stevens Creek | 700 |
| Maradalsfos | Norway | Stream flowing into Ejkisdalsvand (lake) | 650 |
| Skykkjefos | Norway | In Skykkjedal (valley) of Inner Hardanger Fiord | 650 |
| Terni | Italy | Velino, tributary of Nera | 650 |
| Maletsunyane (Le Bihan) | Basutoland, Africa | Maletsunyane | 630 |
| Bridal Veil (Yosemite) | California | Bridal Veil Creek, tributary of Merced | 620 |
| Nevada (Yosemite) | California | Merced | 594 |
| Voringfos | Norway | Bjoreia | 535 |
| Skjaeggedalsfos | Norway | Tyssaå | 525 |
| Marina | British Guiana | Tributary of Kuribrong, a tributary of the Pataro | 500 |
| Tequendama | Colombia | Bogotá | 450 |
| King George's | Cape Province, South Africa | Orange | 450 |
| Herval Cascades | Brazil | ........ | 400 |
| Guayra | Paraguay-Brazil | Paraná | 374 |
| Ililouette (Yosemite) | California | Ililouette Creek, tributary of Merced | 370 |
| Granite (Mt. Rainier Park) | Washington | Granite Creek | 350 |
| Splendor of Sun | Nikko, Japan | ........ | 350 |
| Victoria | Southern Rhodesia | Zambezi | 343 |
| Comet (Mt. Rainier Park) | Washington | Van Trump Creek | 320 |
| Lower Yosemite | California | Yosemite Creek | 320 |
| Vernal (Yosemite) | California | Merced | 317 |
| Virginia | Northwest Territories, Canada | South Nahanni, tributary of Mackenzie | 315 |
| Lower Yellowstone | Wyoming | Yellowstone | 308 |
| Grand | Labrador, Canada | Hamilton | 302 |
| Sluiskin (Mt. Rainier Park) | Washington | Paradise | 300 |
| Snoqualmie | Washington | Snoqualmie | 270 |
| Seven Falls | Colorado | ........ | 266 |
| Tallulah | Georgia | Tallulah | 251 |
| Shoshone | Idaho | Snake | 195 |
| Narada (Mt. Rainier Park) | Washington | Paradise | 168 |
| Niagara | New York-Ontario | Niagara | 167 |
| Tower (Yellowstone) | Wyoming | Tower Creek, tributary of Yellowstone | 132 |

# Principal Rivers of the World

| River | Source | Outflow | Approx. length, miles |
|---|---|---|---|
| Nile | Lake Victoria | Mediterranean Sea | 4,160 |
| Amazon | Glacier-fed lakes, Peru | Atlantic Ocean | 3,900 |
| Mississippi-Missouri-Red Rock | Source of Red Rock River, Montana | Gulf of Mexico (mouth of Southwest Pass) | 3,890 |
| Ob | Altai Mts., U.S.S.R. | Gulf of Ob | 3,200 |
| Yangtze Kiang | Tibetan plateau | China Sea | 3,100 |
| Amur | Confluence of Shilka (U.S.S.R.) and Argun (Manchuria) Rivers | Tartary Strait | 2,900 |
| Congo | Between Lakes Nyasa and Tanganyika | Atlantic Ocean | 2,900 |
| Lena | Baikal Mts., U.S.S.R. | Arctic Ocean | 2,800 |
| Yenisei | Tannu Ola Mountains, western Mongolia | Arctic Ocean | 2,800 |
| Missouri-Red Rock | Source of Red Rock River, Montana | Mississippi River | 2,714 |
| Hwang Ho (Yellow) | East part of Kunlun Mts., west China | Gulf of Chihli | 2,700 |
| Niger | Border of Sierra Leone | Gulf of Guinea | 2,600 |
| Mackenzie | Head of Finlay River, British Columbia | Beaufort Sea (Arctic Ocean) | 2,514 |
| Mékong | Tibetan highlands | South China Sea | 2,500 |
| Missouri | Confluence of Jefferson and Madison rivers, Montana | Mississippi River | 2,466 |
| Paraná | Confluence of Paranaiba and Grande Rivers, southeast Brazil | Río de la Plata (Atlantic Ocean) | 2,450 |
| Mississippi | Lake Itasca, Minnesota | Gulf of Mexico (mouth of Southwest Pass) | 2,348 |
| Murray | Australian Alps, New South Wales | Indian (Southern) Ocean | 2,310 |
| Irtish | Altai Mts., U.S.S.R. | Ob River | 2,300 |
| Volga | Valdai plateau, U.S.S.R. | Caspian Sea | 2,300 |
| Madeira | Confluence of Gauporé and Maumoré Rivers, Bolivia-Brazil border | Amazon River | 2,000 |
| St. Lawrence | St. Louis River, Minn. | Gulf of St. Lawrence | 1,900 |
| Purús | Southwest Amazonas, Brazil | Amazon River | 1,850 |
| Rio Grande | San Juan Mts., Colorado | Gulf of Mexico | 1,800 |
| São Francisco | Southwest Minas Geraes, Brazil | Atlantic Ocean | 1,800 |
| Yukon | Junction of Lewes and Pelly, Yukon Territory | Bering Sea | 1,800 |
| Salween | Tibet, south of Kunlun Mountains | Gulf of Martaban | 1,750 |
| Danube | Black Forest, Germany | Black Sea | 1,725 |
| Euphrates | Dumlu Dagh (mountains), Turkey | Persian Gulf | 1,700 |
| Indus | Himalayas | Arabian Sea | 1,700 |
| Orinoco | Sierra Parima on Venezuela-Brazil boundary | Atlantic Ocean | 1,700 |
| Tocantins | Near Pyrenopolis, southeast Brazil | Pará River (Atlantic Ocean) | 1,700 |
| Brahmaputra | Himalayas | Ganges River (Bay of Bengal) | 1,680 |
| Si Kiang | Plateau of Yunnan, southwest China | China Sea | 1,650 |
| Nelson | Head of Bow River, west Alberta, Canada | Hudson Bay | 1,600 |
| Zambezi | 11°21′S.; 24°22′E., Northern Rhodesia, Africa | Indian Ocean | 1,600 |
| Ganges | Himalayas | Bay of Bengal | **1,540** |

| River | Source | Outflow | Approx. length, miles |
|---|---|---|---|
| Amu Darya (Oxus) | Nicholas Range, Pamir Mountains, U.S.S.R. | Lake Aral | 1,500 |
| Paraguay | Mato Grosso, Brazil | Paraná River | 1,500 |
| Yapurá | Andes, Colombia | Amazon River | 1,500 |
| Arkansas | Central Colorado | Mississippi River | 1,450 |
| Colorado | Grand County, Colorado | Gulf of California | 1,450 |
| Dnieper | Valdai Hills, U.S.S.R. | Black Sea | 1,400 |
| Negro | Watershed between Orinoco and Amazon | Amazon River | 1,400 |
| Ural | Southern Ural Mountains, U.S.S.R. | Caspian Sea | 1,400 |
| Ohio-Allegheny | Potter County, Pa. | Mississippi River | 1,306 |
| Orange | Basutoland, Africa | Atlantic Ocean | 1,300 |
| Irrawaddy | Confluence of N'mai and Mali Rivers, northeast Burma | Bay of Bengal | 1,250 |
| Columbia | Columbia Lake, British Columbia | Pacific Ocean | 1,214 |
| Saskatchewan | Western Alberta, Canada | Lake Winnipeg | 1,205 |
| Darling | Central part of Eastern Highlands, Australia | Murray River | 1,160 |
| Tigris | Taurus Mts., Turkey | Euphrates River (Persian Gulf) | 1,150 |
| Sungari | Sungari Reservoir, Manchuria, China | Amur River | 1,130 |
| Don | Lake Ivan, U.S.S.R. | Sea of Azov | 1,100 |

## Large Lakes of the World

| Name and location | Area, sq. mi. | Length, miles | Maximum depth, feet | Elevation above sea level, feet |
|---|---|---|---|---|
| Caspian, U.S.S.R.–Iran† | 169,300 | 795 | 3,612 | −86 |
| Superior, U. S. A.–Canada | 31,820 | 383 | 1,302 | 622 |
| Victoria, East Central Africa | 26,828 | 250 | 270 | 3,717 |
| Aral, U.S.S.R. | 26,233 | 280 | 222 | 155 |
| Huron, U. S. A.–Canada | 23,010 | 206 | 750 | 581 |
| Michigan, U. S. A. | 22,400 | 321 | 923 | 581 |
| Baikal, U.S.S.R. | 13,300 | 385 | 5,413 | 1,515 |
| Tanganyika, East Central Africa | 12,700 | 420 | 4,708 | 2,534 |
| Great Bear, Canada | 12,000 | 195 | 270* | 391 |
| Great Slave, Canada | 11,170 | 325 | —— | 495 |
| Nyasa, Southern Africa | 11,000 | 350 | 2,580 | 1,650 |
| Erie, U. S. A.–Canada | 9,940 | 241 | 210 | 572 |
| Winnipeg, Canada | 9,398 | 260 | 70 | 712 |
| Ontario, U. S. A.–Canada | 7,540 | 193 | 778 | 246 |
| Balkhash, U.S.S.R. | 7,115 | 430 | 36 | 900 |
| Ladoga, U.S.S.R. | 7,000 | 125 | 730 | 55 |
| Onega, U.S.S.R. | 3,764 | 145 | 408 | 125 |
| Rudolf, Eastern Africa | 3,475 | 185 | —— | 1,250 |
| Titicaca, Bolivia–Peru | 3,200 | 125 | 892 | 12,507 |
| Nicaragua, Nicaragua | 3,089 | 110 | 200 | 135 |
| Athabaska, Canada | 3,058 | 195 | —— | 699 |
| Reindeer, Canada | 2,444 | 155 | —— | 1,150 |
| Issyk-Kul, U.S.S.R. | 2,230 | 115 | 2,300 | 5,400 |
| Koko Nor, China | 2,200 | 66 | —— | 10,000 |
| Vänern, Sweden | 2,143 | 87 | 292 | 144 |
| Winnipegosis, Canada | 2,086 | 122 | 38 | 831 |
| Bangweulu, East Central Africa | 1,900 | 60 | 15 | 3,700 |
| Nipigon, Canada | 1,870 | 70 | —— | 852 |
| Manitoba, Canada | 1,817 | 120 | 12* | 813 |
| Urmia, Iran | 1,750* | 80–90 | 50 | 4,184 |
| Albert, Uganda, Africa | 1,640 | 100 | 50 | 2,037 |
| Dubawnt, Canada | 1,600 | 65 | —— | 500 |
| Great Salt, U. S. A. | 1,500 | 75 | 15–25* | 4,218 |
| Van, Turkey | 1,453 | 80 | —— | 5,643 |

* Average. † The name Caspian *Sea* is a misnomer; it is a land-locked lake, so classified by oceanographers.

# Volcanoes of the Earth

There are approximately 430 volcanoes (275 in the Northern Hemisphere and 155 in the Southern) with recorded eruptions in historical times. Of the 2,500 recorded eruptions, more than 2,000 have taken place in the Pacific area. Of known active volcanoes, about 80 are of the submarine type.

## ATLANTIC-INDIAN AREA

### Mediterranean Region

*Italy:* Mt. Vesuvius, southeast of Naples (3,858 ft.). Only active volcano on mainland of Europe. Pompeii buried by an eruption, A.D. 79. Latest eruption in 1944.

*Sicily:* Mt. Etna, eastern Sicily (10,741 ft.). Two new craters formed in eruptions of Feb.–Mar., 1947. Worst eruption in 50 years occurred Nov., 1950–Jan., 1951.

*Lipari Islands* (north of Sicily): Stromboli (about 3,000 ft.). Called "Lighthouse of the Mediterranean." Erupted 1956.

### Atlantic Area

*Canary Islands:* Pico de Teide (Teneriffe), on island of Teneriffe (12,192 ft.).

*Cape Verde Islands:* Fogo (over 8,000 ft.). Severe eruption in 1857; last until 1951.

*Iceland:* At least 25 volcanoes active in historic times. These volcanoes very similar to those in Hawaii. Askja (4,600 ft.) is the largest.

*Lesser Antilles (West Indian Islands):* Mt. Pelée, in northwestern Martinique (about 4,400 ft.). Eruption in 1902 destroyed town of St. Pierre and killed approximately 40,000.

### Indian Ocean Region

*Comoro Islands* (east of northern Mozambique): One volcano, Kartala (over 8,500 ft.), is visible for over 100 miles. Last erupted in 1904.

*Réunion Island* (east of Madagascar): Piton de la Fournaise (Le Volcan) (8,610 ft.). Large lava flows.

## THE PACIFIC AREA

### Northwest Portion

*Kamchatka:* 14–18 active volcanoes. Klyuchevskaya (Kluchev) (15,912 ft.) erupted in 1954.

*Kurile Islands:* At least 13 active volcanoes and several submarine outbreaks.

*Japan:* at least 33 active vents.

Fujiyama (Fujisan), southwest of Tokyo (12,385 ft.). Symmetrical in outline, snow-covered. Regarded as a sacred mountain.

Adzumayama (7,733 ft.).

Asamayama (8,182 ft.). Continuously active; violent eruption in 1783; latest in 1955.

*Bonin (Ogasawara) Islands:* Mt. Suribachi, on Iwo Jima (546 ft.). A sulfurous steaming volcano. Raising of U. S. flag over Mt. Suribachi was one of the dramatic episodes of World War II.

*Samoan archipelago:* Savaii. An eruption in 1905 did considerable damage. Niuafoou (Tin Can) between Samoa and Fiji Islands has a crater 6,000 feet below and 600 feet above water.

*Philippine Islands:* about 100 eruptive centers; Hibok Hibok on Camiguin island erupted in Sept. 1950, and again in Dec. 1951, when about 750 were reported killed or missing; eruptions continued during 1952–53.

*Hawaiian Group:* Mauna Loa (13,680 ft.). Also called "Long Mountain." Discharges more lava than any other volcano. Largest volcanic mountain in the world in cubic content, with crater of 3.7 sq. mi. Violent eruption in June, 1950, with lava pouring 25 mi. into the ocean.

Mauna Kea (13,796 ft.). Highest mountain in group.

Kilauea (4,090 ft.). A vent in side of Mauna Loa but apparently erupts independently of it. One of the most spectacular and active craters. Crater has an area of 4.14 sq. mi. Erupted 1952 and again in 1955, with considerable damage.

### Southwest Portion

*Sumatra:* Ninety volcanoes have been discovered; 12 are now active. The most famous, Krakatoa, is a small volcanic island in the Sunda Strait. Numerous volcanic discharges occurred in 1883. One explosion caused the disappearance of the highest peak and the northern part of the island. Fine dust was carried around the world in the upper atmosphere. Over 36,000 persons lost their lives in resultant tidal waves, which were felt as far away as Cape Horn. Active in 1928, 1950 and 1953.

*New Zealand:* Tarawera, on North Island. Severe eruption in 1886 destroyed the famous pink and white sinter terraces of Rotomahana, a hot lake.

Ngauruhoe (7,515 ft.). Emits steam and vapor incessantly. Major eruptions occurred 1952–54.

### Northeast Portion

*Aleutian area:* There are 32 active vents known, and numerous inactive cones.

*Alaska:* Wrangell (14,005 ft.) and Katmai (about 7,500 ft.).

On June 6, 1912, a violent eruption of

the volcano Nova Rupta occurred, during which the "Valley of Ten Thousand Smokes" was formed.

*California, Oregon, Washington:* Lassen Peak (10,453 ft.) in California is the only observed active volcano in the U. S. outside Alaska and Hawaii. The last period of activity was 1914–17. Other mountains of volcanic origin include Mt. Shasta (Calif.), Mt. Hood and the mountain containing Crater Lake (Oreg.), and Mt. Rainier (Wash.).

*Mexico:* Popocatepetl (17,883 ft.). Crater 673 ft. deep and 2½ mi. in circumference. Not entirely extinct; steam still escapes.

Colima (14,239 ft.), in group that has had frequent eruptions.

Orizaba (Citlaltepetl) (18,696 ft.).

Paricutín. First appeared in Feb., 1943. In less than a week a cone over 140 ft. high developed with a crater one quarter mile in circumference. Cone grew over 1,500 ft. in 1943. Erupted 1952.

Boquerón ("Big Mouth"). Newest volcano in Western Hemisphere, discovered Sept., 1952 on San Benedicto island, about 250 mi. south of Lower California.

*Guatemala:* Santa Maria Quezaltenango (12,361 ft.). Frequent activity between 1902–08 and 1922–28 after centuries of quiescence. Most dangerously active vent

of Central America. Other volcanoes include Tajumulco (13,814 ft.) and Atitlán (11,633 ft.).

*El Salvador:* Izalco, "beacon of Central America," which first appeared in 1770 and is still growing (erupted in 1950, 1956); San Salvador, which had a violent eruption in 1923, and Conchagua, which erupted with considerable damage early in 1947.

*Nicaragua:* Volcanoes include Telica, Coseguina and Momotombo. Between Momotombo on the west shore of Lake Managua and Coseguina overlooking the Gulf of Fonseca, there is a string of more than 20 cones, many still active. One of these, Cerro Negro, erupted in July, 1947, with considerable damage and loss of life, and again in 1948–50.

### Southeast Portion

*Colombia:* Huila (18,700 ft.), a vapor-emitting volcano, and Tolima (17,109 ft.).

Eruption of Puracé (15,420 ft.), 1949, killed 17.

*Ecuador:* Cotopaxi (19,344 ft.). Perhaps highest active volcano in the world. Possesses a beautifully formed cone.

Cayambe (19,170 ft.). Almost on equator.

*Chile and Argentina:* About 25 active or potentially active; destructive eruptions in 1948, 1955, and 1960.

## Principal Deserts of the World

| Desert | Location | Approximate size | Appx. elevation, ft. |
|---|---|---|---|
| Atacama............ | North Chile...................... | 400 mi. long.................... | 7,000–13,500 |
| Black Rock.......... | Northwest Nevada................ | About 1,000 sq. mi............ | 2,000–5,000 |
| Colorado............ | Southeast California from San Gorgonio Pass to Gulf of California | 200 mi. long and a maximum width of 50 mi.............. | Few feet above to 250 below sea level |
| Dasht-i-Kavir........ | Southeast of Caspian Sea in Iran... | ............................. | 2,000 |
| Dasht-i-Lut.......... | Northeast of Kerman in Iran....... | ............................. | 1,000 |
| Gobi (Shamo ) | Covers most of Mongolia.......... | 300,000 sq. mi................ | 3,000–5,000 |
| Great Arabian........ | Most of Arabia.................. | 1,500 mi. long................. | ................... |
| Syrian (El Hamad) | North of 30° N. Latitude........... | | 1,850 |
| Nefud (Red Desert) | South of Jauf.................... | 400 mi. by average of 200 mi. | 3,000 |
| Dahna............. | Southeast of Nefud............. | 400 by 30 mi................. | ................... |
| Rub' al Khali....... | South portion of Nejd............. | | |
| Great Australian...... | Western portion of Australia....... | About one-half the continent... | 600–1,000 |
| Great Salt Lake...... | West of Great Salt Lake to Nevada-Utah line. | 80 by 50 mi.................. | 4,500 |
| Kalahari............. | South Africa between the Orange and Zambezi Rivers | 400 by 600 mi., or about 120,000 sq. mi................. | Over 3,000 |
| Kara Kum (Desert of Khiva) | Southwest Turkestan south of Lake Aral | 110,000 sq. mi................ | ................... |
| Kizil Kum........... | Central Turkestan southeast of Lake Aral | 370 by 220 mi., or about 70,000 sq. mi................... | 160 near Lake Aral to 2,000 in southeast |
| Libyan.............. | Eastern Sahara west of Nile | More than 500,000 sq. mi...... | ................... |
| Mohave............. | North of Colorado Desert and south of Death Valley in SE Calif. | 15,000 sq. mi................. | 2,000 |
| Nubian.............. | From Red Sea to great west bend of the Nile | ............................. | 2,500 |
| Painted Desert....... | Northeast Arizona................ | 75 mi. wide.................. | High plateau 5,000 |
| Sahara.............. | Northern states of Africa to about 15° N. Lat. and from Red Sea to the Atlantic Ocean | 3,200 mi. greatest length along 20° N. Lat.; Area over 3,500,000 sq. mi............. | 440 below sea level to 11,000 above, ave. elevation, 1,400–1,600 |
| Takla Makan........ | S. Central Sinkiang in Tarim Basin | 700 mi. long.................. | ................... |
| Thar (Indian)........ | Chiefly Rajputana, India............ | About 300 mi. by 380 mi....... | About 500 |

## Population, Land Areas of the World and World Elevations

| Area | Estimated population, in thousands, 1959 | Approximate area, in thousands of sq. mi. | Per cent of total land area | Population density per sq. mi. | Elevation, feet — Highest | Elevation, feet — Lowest | Dimensions, miles — East-West | Dimensions, miles — North-South |
|---|---|---|---|---|---|---|---|---|
| **WORLD** | 2,905,000 | 58,333 | 100.0 | 49.8 | Mt. Everest, Asia, 29,028 | Dead Sea, Asia, 1,290 below sea level | 24,902 | 24,860 |
| **ASIA**, excluding Asiatic U.S.S.R.; including Philippines, Turkey, and Indonesia | 1,624,000 | 10,599 | 18.1 | 153.2 | Mt. Everest, Tibet-Nepal, 29,028 | Dead Sea, Palestine-Jordan, 1,290 below sea level | 5,400* | 5,300* |
| **AFRICA** | 261,000 | 11,684 | 20.0 | 20.2 | Mt. Kilimanjaro, Tanganyika, 19,565 | Qattara Depression, Egypt, 440 below sea level | 4,600 | 5,000 |
| **NORTH AMERICA**, including Central America | 261,000 | 9,355 | 16.0 | 27.9 | Mt. McKinley, Alaska, 20,320 | Death Valley, Calif., 282 below sea level | 3,200 | 4,000 |
| **SOUTH AMERICA** | 137,000 | 6,889 | 11.8 | 19.9 | Mt. Aconcagua, Argentina, 22,835 | Sea level | 3,200 | 4,600 |
| **ANTARCTICA** | Uninhabited | 6,000 | 10.3 | .... | Mt. Vinson, above 19,000 | Sea level | | |
| **EUROPE**, including Iceland; excluding European U.S.S.R. | 421,000 | 1,903 | 3.3 | 221.2 | Mt. Blanc, France, 15,781 | Sea level | 3,300† | 2,400† |
| **AUSTRALIA** | 10,281 | 2,974 | 5.1 | 3.5 | Mt. Kosciusko, 7,352 | Lake Eyre, 38 below sea level | 2,400 | 1,900 |
| **OCEANIA**, incl. New Zealand and British, U. S., French and Australian territories, possessions, etc. | 5,819 | 330 | .6 | 17.6 | Mauna Kea, Hawaii, 13,784 | Sea level | | |
| **U.S.S.R.** | 210,000 | 8,650 | 14.8 | 24.3 | Mt. Pobedy, 24,409 | Caspian Sea, 86 below sea level | 5,000 | 2,500 |

\* Including Asiatic U.S.S.R.    † Including European U.S.S.R.

## HIGH POPULATION DENSITIES (per square mile)

| | | | | | | | |
|---|---|---|---|---|---|---|---|
| Monaco | 34,653.5 | Japan | 655.8 | Italy | 421.7 | Korea | 357.6 |
| Netherlands | 916.3 | San Marino | 635.6 | Germany (East) | 390.8 | Switzerland | 332.4 |
| Belgium | 772.9 | Germany (West) | 557.6 | Lebanon | 386.1 | Haiti | 327.1 |
| Maldive Islands | 713.0 | United Kingdom | 556.0 | Ceylon | 379.4 | Luxembourg | 324.3 |

# Interesting Caves and Caverns of the World

**Aggtelek.** In village of same name, northern Hungary. Large stalactitic cavern about 5 miles long.

**Altamira Cave.** Near Santander, Spain. Contains animal paintings (Old Stone Age art) on roof and walls.

**Antiparos.** On island of same name in the Grecian Archipelago. Some stalactites are 20 ft. long. Brilliant colors and fantastic shapes.

**Blue Grotto.** On island of Capri, Italy. Cavern hollowed out in limestone by constant wave action. Now half filled with water because of sinking coast. Name derived from unusual blue light permeating the cave. Source of light is a submerged opening, light passing through the water.

**Carlsbad Caverns.** Southeast New Mexico. Largest underground labyrinth yet discovered. Three levels: 754, 900, and 1,320 feet below the surface.

**Fingal's Cave.** On island of Staffa off coast of western Scotland. Penetrates about 200 ft. inland. Contains basaltic columns almost 40 ft. high.

**Ice Cave.** Near Dobsina, Czechoslovakia. Noted for its beautiful crystal effects.

**Jenolan Caves.** In Blue Mountain plateau, New South Wales, Australia. Beautiful stalactitic formations.

**Kent's Cavern.** Near Torquay, England. Source of much information on Paleolithic man.

**Luray Cavern.** Near Luray, Virginia. Has large stalactitic and stalagmitic columns of many colors.

**Mammoth Cave.** Limestone cavern in central Kentucky. Cave area is about 10 miles in diameter but has at least 150 miles of irregular subterranean passageways at various levels. Temperature remains fairly constant at 54°F.

**Peak Cavern or Devil's Hole.** Derbyshire, England. About 2,250 ft. into a mountain. Lowest part is about 600 ft. below the surface.

**Postojnoc (Postumia) Grotto.** Near Postumia in Julian Alps, about 25 miles N.E. of Trieste. Stalactitic cavern, largest in Europe. Piuca (Pivka) River flows through part of it. Caves have numerous beautiful stalactites.

**Singing Cave.** Iceland. A lava cave; name derived from echoes of people singing in it.

**Wind Cave.** In Black Hills of South Dakota. Limestone caverns with stalactites and stalagmites almost entirely missing. Variety of crystal formations called "boxwork."

**Wyandotte Cave.** In Crawford County, southern Indiana. A limestone cavern with five levels of passages; one of the largest in North America. "Monumental Mountain," approximately 135 ft. high, is believed to be one of the world's largest underground "mountains."

## Geysers

Geysers exist in many volcanic regions of the world such as Japan and South America, but their greatest development is in Iceland, New Zealand and Yellowstone National Park.

**Iceland.** The principal geyser area is about 30 miles northwest of Mt. Hekla, where there are more than 100 geysers and hot springs in about two square miles. The main ones are the following:

*Great Geyser (Geysir).* Sends up a column 160 to 180 ft. high intermittently from an opening more than 9 ft. across and about 70 ft. deep.

*Strokkr (Churn).* Constant bubbling and occasional eruptions.

**New Zealand.** There is a great profusion of boiling springs, steam jets and mud volcanoes northeast of Lake Taupo on North Island. Main geysers are *Waikite*, with a 30–35 ft. column, *Pohutu* and *Waimauku*.

**United States.** There are 120 named geysers in Yellowstone National Park, Wyoming, and perhaps half that number unnamed. Most of the geysers and the 4,000 or more hot springs are located in the western portion of the park. The most important are the following:

Norris Geyser Basin has 24 or more active geysers; the number varies. There are scores of steam vents and hot springs. *Valentine* is highest, erupting 50–75 ft. at intervals varying from 18 hr. to 3 days or more. *Minuté*, 15–20 ft. high, several hours apart. Others include *Steamboat, Fearless, Veteran, Vixen, Corporal, Whirligig, Little Whirligig* and *Pinwheel*.

Lower Geyser Basin has at least 18 active geysers. *Fountain* throws water 50–75 ft. in all directions at unpredictable intervals. *Clepsydra* erupts violently from four vents up to 30 ft. *Great Fountain* plays every 8 to 15 hr. in spurts from 30 to 90 ft. high.

Midway Geyser Basin has vast steaming terraces of red, orange, pink and other colors; there are pools and springs, including the beautiful *Grand Prismatic Spring*. *Excelsior* crater discharges boiling water into Firehole River at the rate of 6 cu. ft. per second.

*Giant* erupts up to 200 ft. at intervals of 2½ days to 3 mo.; eruptions last about 1½ hr. *Daisy* sends water up to 75 ft. but is irregular and frequently inactive.

*Old Faithful* sends up a column varying from 116 to 175 ft. at intervals of .65 min., varying from 33 to 90 min. Eruptions last about 4 min., during which time about 12,000 gal. are discharged.

*Giantess* seldom erupts, but during its active periods sends up streams 150–200 ft.

Lion Group: *Lion* plays up to 60 ft.

every 2–4 days when active; *Little Cub* up to 10 ft. every 1–2 hr. *Big Cub* and *Lioness* seldom erupt.

*Castle* usually erupts twice daily to a height of 75 ft.

Mammoth Hot Springs: There are no geysers in this area. The formation is travertine. Sides of a hill are steps and terraces over which flow the steaming waters of hot springs laden with minerals. Each step is tinted by algae to many shades of orange, pink, yellow, brown, green and blue. Terraces are white where no water flows.

## Famous Ship Canals of the World

| Name | Location | Year opened | Length (mi.)† | Width (ft.) | Depth (ft.) | Locks |
|------|----------|-------------|---------------|-------------|-------------|-------|
| Albert | Belgium | 1939 | 80.0 | 53.0 | 16.5 | 6 |
| Amsterdam–Rhine | Netherlands | 1952 | 45.0 | 164.0 | 41.0 | 3 |
| Beaumont–Port Arthur | United States | 1916 | 40.0 | 200.0 | 34.0 | .. |
| Chesapeake and Delaware | United States | 1927 | 19.0 | 250.0 | 27.0 | .. |
| Houston | United States | 1914 | 43.0 | 300.0 | 34.0 | .. |
| Kiel | Germany | 1895 | 61.3 | 144.0 | 36.0 | 4 |
| Panama | Canal Zone | 1914 | 50.0 | 110.0 | 41.0 | 12 |
| St. Lawrence Seaway | U. S. & Canada | 1959 | 2,400.0‡ | § | 27.0 | 7 |
| Sault Ste. Marie | Canada | 1895 | 1.2 | 60.0 | 16.8 | 1 |
| Sault Ste. Marie | United States | 1915 | 1.6 | 80.0 | 25.0 | 4 |
| Suez | Egypt | 1869 | 100.6* | 197.0 | 34.0 | .. |
| Welland | Canada | 1931 | 27.6 | 80.0 | 25.0 | 8 |

\* From Port Said lighthouse to entrance channel in Suez roads. † In statute miles. ‡ Montreal to Duluth. § 442 ft.-550 ft.; there are 11 1/2 miles of locks, 80 ft. wide and 30 ft. deep.

## World Extremes of Climate

**Highest recorded shade temperature:**
  World: 136° F. at Azizia, Libya, North Africa, September 13, 1922.
  United States: 134° F. at Death Valley, California, July 10, 1913.
**Lowest recorded temperature:**
  World: −125.3° F. at Vostok, near south geomagnetic pole, Antarctica, August 25, 1958.
  In Siberia, −89.9° F. at Oimekon, February 6, 1933, and −89.7° F. at Verkhoyansk, February 5 and 7, 1892.
  United States: −70° F. at Rogers Pass, Montana, January 20, 1954.

**Highest mean annual temperature:**
  World: 88° F. at Lugh, Somaliland, Africa, 13-year average.

  United States: 77.6° F. at Key West, Florida, 30 year normal.

**Lowest mean annual temperature:**
  World: −71.0° F. at Sovietskaya (78° 24′ S. lat., 87° 35′ E. long.) (March 1958–Feb. 1959).
  United States: 10.1° at Barrow, Alaska, 30-year record.

**Maximum rainfall for 24-hour period:**
  World: 46 inches at Baguio, Luzon, Phillipines, July 14–15, 1911.
  Contiguous United States: 38.7 inches at Yankeetown, Florida, September 5–6, 1950. From a recording gauge: 26.12 inches at Hoegees Camp, California, January 22–23, 1942.
**Maximum rainfall in one month:**
  World: 366.14 inches at Cherrapunji, India, July, 1861 (over 150 inches fell in 5 consecutive days in August, 1841).
  United States: 71.54 inches at Helen Mine, California, January, 1909.
**Maximum average annual precipitation (calendar year):**
  World: 460 inches at Mt. Waialeale, Island of Kauai, Hawaiian Islands, 1912–1958; 450 inches at Cherrapunji, India, 74 year average.
  United States: 150.73 inches at Wynoochee, Washington, 13 year average.
**Minimum average annual precipitation (calendar year):**
  World: 0.02 inch at Arica, Chile, 43 year average.
  United States: 1.66 inches at Greenland Ranch, California, 44 year average. (Bagdad, California holds the U. S. record for the longest period with no measurable rain, 767 days, Oct. 3, 1912 to Nov. 8, 1914.)

**Other U. S. precipitation extremes:**
Wettest state: Louisiana, 65 year annual average of 57.34 inches.
Driest state: Nevada, 66 year annual average of 8.60 inches. (Average annual precipitation for the United States is about 29 inches.)
**Heavy U. S. snowfall records:**
Greatest average annual: 575.1 inches at Paradise Ranger Station, Rainier Park, Washington.
Greatest amount in one season: 1000.3 inches at Paradise Ranger Station, Rainier Park, Washington, 1955/56.
Greatest amount in a calendar month: 390 inches at Tamarack, California, Jan., 1911.
Greatest in 24 hours: 76 inches at Silver Lake, Colorado, April 14–15, 1921. (This storm, April 12–15, produced highest known rates in U. S. for durations up to 3 days —95 inches in 48 hours; 98 inches in 72 hours; 100 inches in 85 hours.)
In the New York City blizzard of December 26, 1947, 25.8 inches of snow fell in about 20 hours, almost 5 inches more than fell in the blizzard of March, 1888.
**Largest hailstone definitely recorded in U. S.:** 1½ pounds by weight, at Potter, Nebraska, July 6, 1928.

# Ancient Empires

The *Egyptian* and *Babylonian* empires, Near Eastern civilizations whose cultures mark the beginning of written history, had their origins in the nebulous period of ancient history prior to the year 4000 B.C. They developed rapidly in the fertile river valleys of the Nile in Egypt and the Tigris-Euphrates in Mesopotamia after the discovery of metals and the invention of writing. Their governments were all-powerful, with the people subjugated and without political rights. The Egyptians regarded their king as a god. In Babylon, the ruler was a priest-king, earthly representative of the gods. Nevertheless, these Near East cultures made great contributions to the eternal march of man; they advanced the ways of making and doing things, produced the earliest literature, developed the principles of law (the code of Hammurabi, Babylonian king of the 18th [or possibly 17th] century B.C., the oldest code of law) and science.

The influence of Babylon and Egypt was felt in the rise of the Semitic tribes of Syria, the Hittites in Asia Minor, and the people of the Aegean region. Between the years 1200 and 800 B.C., the small Syrian states grew to great power and then were overwhelmed by the great empire of the *Assyrians,* the warlike peasants of the Tigris valley, who took the lessons learned from the Babylonians and spread that culture over their domains. The Assyrians, like the Egyptians and the Babylonians, in turn fell under the power of the *Persian* kings in the century between 600 and 500 B.C. By 525 B.C., the Persian Empire extended from India to Egypt.

The lessons learned by these early Near Eastern civilizations were transmitted to *Greece,* which developed its illustrious empire in the Aegean region, after the inhabitants of the island of Crete had absorbed the Egyptian culture. The mainland Greeks overthrew the Cretans and in turn were succeeded by the Doric Greeks, who spread their culture across the Aegean, the Asia Minor coast, and into the Mediterranean and Black Sea regions. The characteristic Greek political institution was the city-state, first ruled by kings and often temporary monarchical tyrannies, and finally by the participation of free citizens. Literature and the arts flourished, and by the 5th century B.C., when Athens became the great city of the Greeks, drama had risen to full maturity with the great tragedies of Sophocles and Euripides and the comedies of Aristophanes. Architecture and art advanced apace. The Greeks, learning much from their Egyptian teachers, produced such superb buildings as the Parthenon and created amazingly beautiful statues through the use of living models. Religion, which was closely linked with art, also flourished, as did the development of philosophy, under Socrates, Plato and Aristotle. Wars weakened the city-states, and they fell to Alexander the Great in the 4th century B.C.

Last among the great ancient empires was the *Roman,* which developed in Italy and gained control over the Mediterranean region after absorbing the culture of Greece and combining with it new principles of law and art and teaching this new learning to the West. The development of the Roman civilization began in 510 or 509 B.C., when the peoples on the peninsula of Italy freed themselves from the rule of the Etruscans. The Romans, with a republican form of government, speedily conquered Italy and the Mediterranean region, and the Roman governors became men of great wealth, corrupting the city-state system and making it a graft-ridden machine of exploitation. The failure of the government to check this self-seeking influence brought on a revolt which resulted eventually in the rise of Julius Caesar to dictatorship in 46–44 B.C. Caesar's murder in the Senate at Rome was followed in 27 B.C. by the establishment of the one-man rule of Augustus over the Roman Empire. Legal practices were developed and became the foundations of modern law. This great ancient civilization began to crumble in the 3d century A.D.

# Languages of the World
## (spoken natively by 5,000,000 or more people)

| Language | Number speaking | Language | Number speaking |
|---|---|---|---|
| American Indian: including Mayan, Quéchua and 750–1,000 other languages and dialects | 15,000,000 | Madurese, Malay, Malagasy, Sundanese, Tagalog | 105,000,000 |
| Amharic (Ethiopia) | 5,600,000 | Iranian: including Baluchi, Kurdish, Persian, Pushtu | 26,500,000 |
| Annamese (Indo-China) | 20,000,000 | Italian | 50,000,000 |
| Arabic | 65,000,000 | Japanese | 90,000,000 |
| Bantu: including Swahili, Zulu (S. Africa) | 45,000,000 | Javanese | 41,000,000 |
| Bengali (India; Pakistan) | 70,000,000 | Kanarese (India) | 14,000,000 |
| Berber dialects (N. Africa) | 6,000,000 | Korean | 30,000,000 |
| Bihari (India) | 37,000,000 | Lahnda (India; Pakistan) | 13,000,000 |
| Bisayan (Philippines) | 9,000,000 | Madurese (Indonesia) | 6,500,000 |
| Bulgarian | 7,000,000 | Malay (Indonesia) | 14,000,000 |
| Burmese | 13,000,000 | Malayalam (India) | 14,000,000 |
| Catalan (Spain) | 6,000,000 | Marathi (India) | 27,000,000 |
| Chinese: including Mandarin, Cantonese and others | 510,000,000 | Munda (India) | 5,000,000 |
| Cushitic: including Somali (Ethiopia) | 7,000,000 | Oriya (India) | 13,000,000 |
| Czech | 8,500,000 | Persian | 12,000,000 |
| Dravidian: including Kanarese, Malayalam, Tamil, Telugu (India) | 95,000,000 | Polish | 30,000,000 |
| | | Portuguese | 76,000,000 |
| | | Punjabi (India; Pakistan) | 22,000,000 |
| Dutch | 15,000,000 | Pushtu (Afghanistan; Pakistan) | 8,000,000 |
| English | 290,000,000 | Rajasthani (India; Pakistan) | 17,000,000 |
| Ethiopian: including Amharic | 6,400,000 | Rumanian | 16,000,000 |
| Finno-Ugric: including Estonian, Finnish, Hungarian, Karelian, Lappish | 21,500,000 | Russian | 170,000,000 |
| | | Serbo-Croatian (Yugoslavia) | 15,000,000 |
| | | Siamese | 16,000,000 |
| Flemish (Belgium) | 5,000,000 | Sinhalese (Ceylon) | 5,500,000 |
| French | 65,000,000 | Spanish | 150,000,000 |
| German | 90,000,000 | Sudanic: including Hausa (Central Africa) | 75,000,000 |
| Greek | 8,000,000 | Sundanese (Indonesia) | 13,000,000 |
| Gujarati (India; Pakistan) | 16,000,000 | Swahili (E. Africa) | 8,000,000 |
| Hausa (Central Africa) | 9,000,000 | Swedish | 7,000,000 |
| Hindi (India; Pakistan) | 150,000,000 | Tagalog (Philippines) | 5,000,000 |
| Hungarian | 13,000,000 | Tamil (India) | 27,000,000 |
| Indic: including Assamese, Bengali, Bihari, Gujarati, Hindi, Lahnda, Marathi, Oriya, Punjabi, Rajasthani, Sindhi, Sinhalese | 415,000,000 | Telugu (India) | 33,000,000 |
| | | Tibeto-Burman: including Tibetan and Burmese | 20,000,000 |
| | | Turkic: including Kazakh, Tartar, Turkish, Uzbek | 45,000,000 |
| Indonesian: including Balinese, Visayan, Ilocano, Javanese, | | Turkish | 20,000,000 |
| | | Ukrainian | 33,000,000 |
| | | Uzbek (U.S.S.R.) | 6,000,000 |
| | | Yiddish | 5,000,000 |

## Universities—Medieval and Modern

Universities, in the modern sense of the term, sprang up in the 12th and 13th centuries in response to the resurgence of learning that preceded the Renaissance in Europe. Procedure at the early universities was informal, with students gathering at some place in a city to listen to a preeminent teacher. There were no campuses, buildings or endowments. Actually, the term "university" once meant a guild or corporation; there were, in the medieval period, "universities" of bootmakers, weavers, etc. Thus the university of learning was similar in organization to the guilds. The students filled the role of apprentices and the teachers were the masters.

The first European university was that of *Salerno* in the 9th century, when it was known as a school of medicine. By the 11th century, it had become one of the most famous medical schools of Europe.

*University of Bologna.* Originated about 1200 as student guilds for protection against the merchants and citizens of Bologna who had raised prices of food and lodging. It was famous for its legal scholars. The students were organized into two guilds and exercised a great deal of authority over the administration.

Other Italian universities famed in the Middle Ages included those at *Arezzo, Fer-*

*rara, Florence, Modena, Naples, Padua, Pavia, Perugia, Siena* and *Vicenza*.

*University of Paris.* Originated between 1150 and 1170 in a cathedral school on the Ile de la Cité, it was later moved to the left (south) bank of the Seine, although it remained under the authority of the chancellor of Notre Dame. It developed into the most famous continental center of learning of its day. Its four principal schools were theology, medicine, law and arts. By the 14th century, the university had some 40 colleges, of which the *Sorbonne* became the most celebrated.

The universities of Paris and Bologna had a marked influence in the subsequent creation of other university centers. About 1167–68 there was a migration of students from Paris to *Oxford* (founded in the 12th century) and about 1210, from Oxford to *Cambridge* (also founded in the 12th century).

Other famous universities of the Middle Ages include the *University of Toulouse* (1233), *Salamanca* (1243), *Seville* (1254), *Orléans* (1305), *Valladolid* (1346), *Prague* (1347), *Kraków* (1364), *Vienna* (1364), *Erfurt* (1379), *Heidelberg* (1385), *Cologne* (1388), *Leipzig* (1409), *Rostock* (1419) and *Louvain* (1426).

## The Renaissance

The Renaissance gave fresh impetus to the universities of Europe. In France three of importance arose in the 15th century —the *University of Aix* (1409, Provence), the *University of Poitiers* (1431) and the *University of Caen* (1437).

Other French institutions of note that arose in this era were at *Bordeaux* (1441), *Valence* (1452), *Nantes* (1463) and *Bourges* (1465). New European universities were also founded at *Trier* (1450), *Freiburg* (1455), *Ingolstadt* (1459), *Basel* (1460), *Budapest* (1475), *Mainz* (1476), *Uppsala* (1477), *Tübingen* (1477), *Copenhagen* (1479), *Wittenberg* (1502), *Frankfurt on Oder* (1506) and *Coimbra* (1537).

*St. Andrews,* founded in 1411, was the first university in Scotland. Others were the *University of Glasgow* (1453) and the *University of Aberdeen* (1494). The *College of Edinburgh* was established in the post-Reformation period (1582). In Ireland, *Trinity College* was founded in Dublin in 1591.

## Reformation and Post-Reformation

Until the Reformation, most of the institutions of higher learning in Europe were under the tutelage of the Catholic Church. After 1520, however, many established universities declared their independence of the Church. Cromwell's rule brought about new scholastic methods at both Oxford and Cambridge and the establishment of new colleges thoroughly imbued with Protestantism.

But the first Protestant university was that of *Marburg,* Germany, founded in 1527. Other Protestant universities were: *Königsberg* (1544); *Jena* (1558); *Helmstedt* (1575); *Altdorf* (1575); *Giessen* (1607); *Strasbourg* (1621); *Halle* (1693).

## 18th, 19th and 20th Centuries

Among the more famous institutions in this era was *Göttingen* (1736), whose school of history became celebrated throughout Europe. Others were: *Erlangen* (1743); *Berlin* (1809); *Lemberg* (Lwów) (1816); *Bonn* (1818); *Helsingfors* (1828); the *National University* at Athens (1837); *Bucharest* (1864); *Tokyo* (1877); *Sofia* (1888) and *Kyoto* (1897).

Among the more famous British universities established in the 19th and 20th centuries were the *University of London* (1828); *Manchester* (1851); the *Mason University College* in Birmingham, later *Birmingham University* (1900); *Liverpool* (1903); *Leeds* (1904); and the *University of Sheffield* (1905). The *University of Wales* (1893) is composed of the colleges of Aberystwyth, Bangor and Cardiff.

There are many large and important universities in the British Commonwealth. In Canada, the famous *McGill University* in Montreal was founded in 1821. Others are the *University of Toronto* (1827); *Queens University* at Kingston, Ont. (1841); *Laval University,* Quebec (1852); *Dalhousie,* Halifax (1818), and *Montreal University* (1878).

The early universities in India were patterned after London University rather than on the Oxford-Cambridge style, and were purely examining institutions. *Calcutta, Bombay* and *Madras* universities were founded in 1857 as examining bodies.

In Australia, the state plays an important role in the development of universities. The *University of Melbourne* (1853) has the largest enrollment. Among the others are *Adelaide* (1874); *Tasmania* (1890); *Queensland* (1909); *Sydney* (1850), and *Western Australia* (1911).

There are also many well-endowed universities in New Zealand, South Africa, and other parts of the Commonwealth.

By 1800, Russia had only three universities—*Vilna* (1578), *Dorpat* (1632) and *Moscow* (1755). Other institutions developed later were the *University of Kharkov* (1804); *Kazan* (1804); *Warsaw,* now Polish (originally established 1816, but closed 1832–69); *St. Petersburg* (1819); *St. Vladimir* in Kiev (1835); *Odessa* (1865) and *Tomsk,* in Siberia (1888). The building of universities after the Revolution of 1917 was spurred by the Soviet government.

In China, the growth of universities was hampered by the chaotic state of the government in the 1900's, the recurring civil wars and the conflict with Japan.

## The United States

Universities in the United States marched in step with the progress of the nation. The early settlers brought a heritage of European culture which they planted in New England soil. The first university in the country was started as *Harvard College* in 1636, with an endowment totaling 800 pounds. Harvard was to become probably the most famous of the American universities.

The *College of William and Mary* (1693) was the second institution of higher learning established in the colonies. Others started during the colonial period (current names only) are: *Yale* (1701); *University of Pennsylvania* (1740); *Princeton* (1746); *Washington and Lee* (1749); *Columbia* (1754); *Brown* (1764); *Rutgers* (1766) and *Dartmouth* (1770).

After the Revolution of 1776, the state tax-supported university was established. The *University of Virginia* (1819) was a notable early example of this type.

Colleges for women grew up in the second quarter of the 19th century. Among these are: *Mt. Holyoke* (1837); *Elmira* (1855); *Vassar* (1861); *Wells* (1868); *Hunter* (1870); *Wellesley* (1870); *Smith* (1871) and *Bryn Mawr* (1880).

In the latter part of the 19th century, universities established by private endowments arose. Typical of these are: *Cornell* (1865), which is also a land-grant institution; *Johns Hopkins* (1876); *Stanford* (1885) and the *University of Chicago* (1890).

# Libraries of the World

### Europe and Asia

Among the great libraries of the world, the *British Museum* remains in the first rank with more than 6,000,000 printed volumes and 60,000 manuscripts. It contains such outstanding treasures as the *Codex Alexandrinus* and the *Codex Sinaiticus* of the Bible, the best collection of Greek papyri from Egypt, and vast collections of original historical manuscripts of incalculable value. Some 150,000 volumes were destroyed in air raids during World War II, but many were replaced later.

One of the finest libraries in the world is the *Bibliothèque Nationale* in Paris, which has approximately 6,000,000 volumes, 155,000 manuscripts, 450,000 medals and coins, 5,000,000 prints and engravings and 400,000 maps.

The *State Library* in Berlin, founded in 1659–61, was amalgamated in 1947 with the library of the University of Berlin. Prior to World War II, the State Library had 2,850,000 volumes; the new combined library had only 1,500,000. The *State Library* at Munich also suffered extensive war losses, with some 500,000 volumes destroyed; it now contains about 2,000,000. Estimates have placed the war losses of all German libraries at between 20 and 25 million volumes.

The *Nationalbibliothek* in Vienna has about 1,500,000 volumes, a large collection of papyri, and a notable theater and motion picture collection.

While not as large as some of the European state libraries, the *Biblioteca Apostolica Vaticana* in Rome has many priceless old manuscripts bequeathed to the Vatican over the centuries, including the *Codex Vaticanus* of the 4th century.

Three of the more important Italian libraries are the *Biblioteca Nazionale* in Naples, with about 1,400,000 volumes; the *Biblioteca Nazionale Centrale* in Florence, with 4,000,000 volumes; and the *Biblioteca Nazionale Centrale* in Rome, with approximately 1,970,000 volumes.

Other large European libraries are the *Bibliothèque Royale* in Brussels (2,000,-000 volumes), the *Biblioteca Nacional* in Madrid (1,500,000); the *University Library* at Amsterdam (more than 1,500,000) and the *Royal Library* in Stockholm (900,000). The *Lenin State Library* in Moscow is said to contain 15,000,000 volumes (a figure that probably includes periodicals), besides many collections of valuable historical documents. In Leningrad, the *Public Library* claims 10,000,000 volumes, and the *Library of the Academy of Sciences* some 8,000,000. There are said to be 350,000 libraries in all parts of the U.S.S.R.

In the Far East, the most extensive libraries are found in Japan, although war damage in 1944–45 was severe. In Tokyo, the *National Diet Library* (formerly the *Imperial Library*) was organized in 1948 as a deposit center. With its various branches, it contains an estimated 4,100,-000 volumes. The *University Library* at Kyoto has about 1,820,000.

The oldest national libraries in South America are those of Argentina and Brazil, each founded in 1810; the former has about 600,000 volumes, the latter 1,000,000.

### The United States and Canada

The earliest libraries in the colonial era were privately owned, although in 1731 Benjamin Franklin projected the first subscription library in Philadelphia. Endowments helped to set up many of the large libraries, although many of these institutions are now receiving state or municipal support.

The largest library in the United States is the *Library of Congress,* established in 1800 by Congress. In 1957, it contained more than 11,050,000 books and pamphlets, and total collections of over 36,100,000. It extends services to members of Congress and other government departments, and also offers excellent facilities for persons engaged in scholarly research.

The *New York Public Library,* with some 6,400,000 volumes in 1957, is the largest public library in the U. S.

The *American Library Directory* for 1954 listed 12,478 libraries in the U. S., including 6,925 public (with 3,106 branches), 1,374 college and university, 1,923 special and 2,256 other types.

The growth of libraries attached to colleges and universities in the United States has been phenomenal, and some of the university libraries are among the largest in the country. Those with more than 1,000,000 volumes each in 1956 were as follows: Harvard, 6,075,000; Yale, 4,280,000; California, including branches, 3,632,000; Illinois, 3,090,000; Michigan, 2,325,000; Columbia, 2,117,000; Chicago, 1,911,000; Minnesota, 1,791,000; Cornell, 1,746,000; Princeton, 1,500,000; Pennsylvania, 1,475,-000; Stanford, 1,309,000; Texas, 1,273,000; Duke, 1,198,000; Northwestern, 1,185,000; Ohio State, 1,150,000; Johns Hopkins, 1,068,000; New York University, 1,041,000; Indiana, 1,000,000.

In Canada, the most important public library is that of Toronto, which has more than 875,000 volumes. Large Canadian university libraries include those at Queens (280,000), Toronto (609,000), McGill (720,-000), and Laval (339,000). The *American Library Directory* for 1954 listed a total of 719 libraries in Canada, including 683 public.

# Museums of the World
## (For Museums of the U. S., see index.)

The modern museum originated during the Renaissance, when the revival of interest in the arts and classical antiquity led princes, nobles and humanists to amass specimens of historical value and to house their collections in special buildings or galleries.

### Art Museums

*The British Museum,* London, contains some of the most famous historical objects of the world, including the Elgin Marbles and the Rosetta Stone.

*Victoria and Albert Museum,* London, whose primary object is to furnish examples to illustrate the history of art, emphasizes architecture and sculpture, ceramics, engraving, book production, paintings, textiles, etc. The library is devoted principally to fine and applied arts of all countries.

*National Gallery,* London, contains a great number of old Masters, including paintings by Da Vinci, Michelangelo, Tintoretto, Mantegna, Titian, Bellini, Jan van Eyck, Rubens, Rembrandt, Holbein, Constable and Turner.

*Tate Gallery,* London, established as part of the National Gallery, was badly damaged during air raids of World War II, but was completely restored by 1949.

*Wallace Collection,* London, has many *objets d'art* and curios of French origin, and first-rank canvases and etchings of Italian, Spanish, Flemish, Dutch and English artists.

In France, the most famous gallery is the *Louvre* in Paris, noted for the magnificence of its architecture as well as for its art collection, which is the largest in the world. Other Parisian museums of importance are *Cluny, Rodin, Guimet,* and *Carnavalet.*

Among the magnificent Italian museums, the *National Museum* at Naples contains one of the best arranged and classified collections. The *Uffizi Gallery* in Florence, founded by the Medicis, has one of the world's largest and best collections of Italian art. Other galleries in Florence are the *Gallery of Modern Art* (*Pitti Palace*) and the *National Museum* (*Bargello*). Rome has numerous museums, including several in the Vatican.

In Berlin, the *National Gallery* was damaged during World War II.

The *Royal Museum of Fine Arts* in Brussels has a fine collection of French, Flemish and Dutch masters and houses many canvases by Rubens, Van Dyck, Jordaens, Rembrandt, Frans Hals and Jan Steen.

The *State Museum* in Amsterdam contains superb works by Rembrandt, Vermeer and others.

Among the notable art museums in other countries are the world-famous *Museo del Prado* in Madrid; the *Tretyakov Gallery* and the *Pushkin State Museum of Fine Arts* in Moscow; the *Hermitage State Museum* in Leningrad; and the *National Museum* in Tokyo, famed for its many Oriental paintings and objects of art.

### Science Museums

The *Ashmolean Museum,* oldest in Great Britain, was founded in 1683 by Oxford

University and houses a collection of archeological and classical rarities.

*Science Museum* of London has exhibits of scientific instruments and appliances which review the progress of science and the history of invention. Other London museums of science are the *Natural History (British Museum)*, the *Imperial War Museum* (exhibits of both World Wars) and the *Geological Museum.*

The *Liverpool Museums* contain valuable collections of natural history and antiquities and are divided into departments of zoology, botany, geology, archeology and ethnology. The buildings were almost completely destroyed during World War II, although most of the exhibits were saved.

The *Manchester Museum* serves as both a municipal and a university museum. The *Bristol Museum* contains departments of geology, zoology, botany, archeology and Bristol antiquities. The *National Museum of Wales* at Cardiff has departments of art, archeology, botany, geology and zoology.

In Edinburgh, Scotland, are the famed *Royal Scottish Museum,* which has collections in art, ethnography, natural history, technology and archeology; and the *National Museum of Antiquities of Scotland,* noted for its coin and manuscript collections.

The *National Museum* in Dublin and the *Municipal Museum* in Belfast have important science collections.

Notable institutions of continental Europe include the *Natural History Museum* in Paris, the *Museum of Oceanog. aphy* in Monaco, the *Natural History Museum* in Lisbon, the *State Museum of Geology and Mineralogy* in Leyden (Netherlands), the *Museum of Natural History* in Stockholm, the *Natural History Museum* in Vienna, the *Hungarian National Museum* in Budapest, the *National Museum* in Prague, and the various science museums in Berne, Geneva, Zurich and Neuchâtel, Switzerland. Most larger cities of the U.S.S.R. have science museums of varying sizes, some specializing in local exhibits of natural history.

Famous science museums in Germany prior to World War II included the various sections of the *Staatliche Museen* in Berlin (re-established after the war) and the museum of ethnography in Hamburg.

In Calcutta is the *Indian Museum,* outstanding for its marine fauna and vertebrate fossils, and in Bombay the *Victoria and Albert Museum.*

In Australia are the *Queensland Museum* and the *Botanic Museum* in Brisbane, the *South Australian Museum* in Adelaide, and the *Australian Museum* in Sydney.

New Zealand contains the *Canterbury Museum,* Christchurch, rich in local fauna, flora and geological items, and a Maori and Polynesian ethnological collection.

In Africa, the *South African Museum,* Capetown, holds general and local history collections and others illustrating anthropology, ethnology and archeology. The *Durban Museum* contains much anthropological material. In Cairo are the notable collections of the *Egyptian Museum.*

Other museums of note include the *Archeological Museums* at Istanbul, the *Tokyo Science Museum,* the *National Museum of Natural History* in Santiago (Chile), the *National Museum* at Rio de Janeiro, and the *Argentine National Museum of Natural Sciences* at Buenos Aires.

# Zoological Gardens

North America has more than 30 major zoos, in the United States, Canada and Mexico. The *Quebec Zoological Society*'s collection is made up of Canadian species; Toronto has many exotic species.

The first zoological garden in the United States was established in Philadelphia in 1874. Since that time nearly every large city in the country has acquired a zoo. Among the largest are the celebrated *Bronx Zoo* and the *Central Park Zoo* in New York, the *Lincoln Park Zoo* and the *Brookfield Zoo* in Chicago, and those in St. Louis, Cincinnati, Detroit, Kansas City and San Diego. The *National Zoological Park* in Washington, D. C., in a beautiful setting of hills, woods and streams, was established in 1890 by an act of Congress. Some of the U. S. zoos exhibit their collections in open-air, barless pits; the Brookfield Zoo is an example.

In Europe, zoological gardens have long been popular public institutions. The *Jardin d'Acclimatation,* in the Bois de Boulogne, Paris, was established in 1858, and a model zoo at Vincennes was added in 1937 for the Paris Exposition.

Germany had about 20 zoological gardens, many of which were developed in the peacetime years between World Wars I and II. Large zoos were located in Berlin and Frankfurt am Main. In Munich, the animals were grouped according to the continent of their origin. Others were established at Dresden, Leipzig and Cologne. At Stellingen, the *Hagenbeck Garden* became an outstanding show place and distributing center for animals. Smaller collections were established at Düsseldorf, Elberfeld and Hanover. Several German zoos, notably that at Berlin, were destroyed during World War II.

The *Schönbrunn* at Vienna is one of the oldest zoos in Europe. The Budapest zoological gardens house a fine collection of European birds. At Antwerp, the *Royal Zoological Society* founded a large menagerie in 1843. It was seriously damaged by German bombs during World War II.

In the British Isles, the outstanding collection is in the garden of the *London Zoological Society* in Regent's Park. Although this zoo received a number of direct bomb hits in 1940–41 and again in 1944, it remained open throughout World War II; visitors during this period numbered 6,500,000. Manchester and Clifton have smaller gardens, and the one at Edinburgh is famous for its collection of penguins. The *Dublin Zoo* is noted for its lions, many of which were born there.

The Amsterdam zoo, with its East Indian collection and its aquarium, and the Rotterdam gardens are the two best known in the Netherlands. Built on a high elevation, the *Skansen Zoo* in Stockholm exhibits north European specimens. The most important gardens in the U.S.S.R. are found in Moscow, where northern as well as exotic species are collected. The zoo at Rome has part of its collection confined in barless pits. At Lisbon there is a small zoological garden, and in Madrid a part of the original royal menagerie. A new zoo notable for its landscaping was opened at Naples, Italy, in 1952.

# Famous Structures

(For Seven Wonders of the World, see index.)

### Ancient

*The Great Sphinx of Egypt,* one of the wonders of ancient Egyptian architecture, adjoins the pyramids of Giza and has a length of 189 ft. It was built in the 4th dynasty and was used as a temple.

Other Egyptian buildings of note include the *Temples of Karnak* and *Edfu* and the *Tombs at Beni Hassan.*

*The Parthenon of Greece,* built on the Acropolis in Athens, was the chief temple to the goddess Athena. It was believed to have been completed by 438 B.C. The present temple remained intact until the 5th century A.D. Today, though the Parthenon is in ruins, its majestic proportions are still discernible.

Other great structures of ancient Greece were the *Temples at Paestum* (about 540 and 420 B.C.); the *Temple of Poseidon* (about 460 B.C.); the *Temple of Apollo* at Corinth (about 540 B.C.); the *Temple of Apollo* at Bassae (about 450–420 B.C.); the famous *Erechtheum* atop the Acropolis (about 421–405 B.C.); the *Temple of Athena Niké* at Athens (about 426 B.C.); the *Olympieum* at Athens (174 B.C.–A.D. 131); the *Athenian Treasury* at Delphi (about 515 B.C.); the *Propylaea* of the Acropolis at Athens (437–432 B.C.); the *Theater of Dionysus* at Athens (about 350–325 B.C.); the *"House of Cleopatra"* at Delos (138 B.C.) and the *Theater* at Epidaurus (about 325 B.C.).

*The Colosseum (Flavian Amphitheater) of Rome,* the largest and most famous of the Roman amphitheaters, was opened for use A.D. 80. Elliptical in shape, it consisted of three stories and an upper gallery, rebuilt in stone in its present form in the third century A.D. Its seats rise in tiers, which in turn are buttressed by concrete vaults and stone piers. It could seat between 40,000 and 50,000 spectators. The Colosseum was principally used for gladiatorial combat.

*The Pantheon* at Rome, begun by Agrippa in 27 B.C. as a temple, was rebuilt in its present circular form by Hadrian (A.D. 110–25). Literally the Pantheon was intended as a temple for "all the gods." It is remarkable for its perfect preservation today, and it has served continuously for 20 centuries as a place of worship.

Famous Roman arches includes the *Arch of Constantine* (about A.D. 315) and the *Arch of Titus* (about A.D. 80).

### Later European

*St. Mark's Cathedral* in Venice (1063–67), one of the great examples of Byzantine architecture, was begun in the 9th century. Partly destroyed by fire in 976, it was later rebuilt as a Byzantine edifice.

Other famous Byzantine examples of architecture are *St. Sophia* in Constantinople (A.D. 532–37); *San Vitale* in Ravenna (542); *St. Paul's Outside the Walls,* Rome (5th century); the *Kremlin* baptism and marriage church, Moscow (begun in 1397); and *St. Lorenzo Outside the Walls,* Rome, begun in 588.

*The Cathedral Group* at Pisa (1067–1173), one of the most celebrated groups of structures built in Romanesque style, consists of the cathedral, the cathedral's baptistery, and the *Leaning Tower.* This trio forms a group by itself in the northwest corner of the city. The cathedral and baptistery are built in varicolored marble. The campanile (Leaning Tower) is 179 ft. high and leans more than 16 feet out of the perpendicular. There is little reason to believe that the architects intended to have the tower lean.

Other examples of Romanesque architecture include the *Vézelay Abbey* in France (1130); the *Church of Notre-Dame-*

*du-Port* at Clermont-Ferrand in France (1100); the *Church of San Zeno* (begun in 1138) at Verona, and *Durham Cathedral* in England.

The *Alhambra* (1248–1354), located in Granada, Spain, is universally esteemed as one of the greatest masterpieces of Moslem architecture. Designed as a palace and fortress for the Moorish monarchs of Granada, it is surrounded by a heavily fortified wall more than a mile in perimeter. The location of the Alhambra in the Sierra Nevada provides a magnificent setting for this jewel of Moorish Spain.

The *Tower of London* is a group of buildings and towers covering 13 acres along the north bank of the Thames. The central *White Tower,* begun in 1078 during the reign of William the Conqueror, was originally a fortress and royal residence, but was later used as a prison. The *Bloody Tower* is associated with Anne Boleyn and other notables.

*Westminster Abbey,* in London, was begun in 1045 and completed in 1065. It was rebuilt and enlarged in 1245–50.

*Notre-Dame de Paris* (begun in 1163), one of the great examples of Gothic architecture, is a twin-towered church with a steeple over the crossing and immense flying buttresses supporting the masonry at the rear of the church.

Other famous Gothic structures are *Chartres Cathedral* (12th century); *Sainte Chapelle,* Paris (1246–48); *Laon Cathedral,* France (1160–1205); *Rheims Cathedral* (about 1210–50; rebuilt after its almost complete destruction in World War I); *Rouen Cathedral* (13th–16th centuries); *Amiens Cathedral* (1218–69); *Beauvais Cathedral* (begun 1247); *Salisbury Cathedral* (1220–60); *York Minster* or the *Cathedral of St. Peter* (begun in the 7th century); *Milan Cathedral* (begun 1386); and *Cologne Cathedral* (13th–19th centuries; badly damaged in World War II).

The *Duomo* (cathedral) in Florence was founded in 1298, completed by Brunelleschi and consecrated in 1436. The oval-shaped dome dominates the entire structure.

The *Vatican* is a group of buildings in Rome comprising the official residence of the Pope. The *Basilica of St. Peter,* the largest church in the Christian world, was begun in 1450. The *Sistine Chapel,* begun in 1473, is noted for the art masterpieces of Michelangelo, Botticelli and others. The *Basilica of the Savior* (known as *St. John Lateran*) is the first-ranking Catholic Church in the world, for it is the cathedral of the Pope.

Other examples of Renaissance architecture are the *Palazzo Riccardi,* the *Palazzo Pitti* and the *Palazzo Strozzi* in Florence; the *Farnese Palace* in Rome; *Palazzo Grimani* (completed about 1550) in Venice;

the *Escorial* (1563–93) near Madrid; the *Town Hall* of Seville (1527–32); the *Louvre,* Paris; the *Château* at Blois, France; *St. Paul's Cathedral,* London (1675–1710; badly damaged in World War II); the *Ecole Militaire,* Paris (1752); the *Pazzi Chapel,* Florence, designed by Brunelleschi (1429); the Palace of *Fontainebleau* and the *Château de Chambord* in France.

The *Palace of Versailles,* containing the famous Hall of Mirrors, was built during the reign of Louis XIV and served as the royal palace until 1793.

Outstanding European buildings of the 18th and 19th centuries are the *Superga* at Turin, the *Hôtel-Dieu* in Lyon, the *Belvedere Palace* at Vienna, the *Royal Palace* of Stockholm, the *Opera House* of Paris (1863–75); the *Bank of England,* the *British Museum,* the *University of London* and the *Houses of Parliament,* all in London; the *Panthéon,* the *Church of the Madeleine,* the *Bourse* and the *Palais de Justice* in Paris.

The *Eiffel Tower,* in Paris, was built for the Exposition of 1889 by Alexandre Eiffel. It is 984 ft. high.

### Asiatic and African

The *Taj Mahal* (1632–50), at Agra, India, built by Shah Jahan as a tomb for his wife, is considered by some as the most perfect example of the Mogul style and by others as the most beautiful building in the world. Four slim white minarets flank the building, which is topped by a white dome; the entire structure is of marble.

Other examples of Indian architecture are the temples at Benares and Tanjore.

Among famed Moslem edifices are the *Dome of the Rock* or *Mosque of Omar,* Jerusalem (A.D. 691); the *Citadel* (1166), and the *Tombs of the Mamelukes* (15th century), in Cairo;; the *Tomb of Humayun* in Delhi; the *Blue Mosque* (1468) at Tabriz and the *Tamerlane Mausoleum* at Samarkand.

*Angkor Vat,* outside the city of Angkor Thom, Cambodia, is one of the most beautiful examples of Cambodian or Khmer architecture. The sanctuary was built during the 12th century.

*Great Wall of China* (228 B.C.?), designed specifically as a defense against nomadic tribes, has numerous large watch towers which could be called buildings. It was erected by Emperor Ch'in Shih Huang Ti and is 1,400 miles long. Built mainly of earth and stone, it varies in height between 18 and 30 feet.

Typical of Chinese architecture are the pagodas or temple towers. Among some of the better known pagodas are the *Great Pagoda of the Wild Geese* at Sian (founded in 652); *Nan t'a* (11th century) at Fang Shan; the *Pagoda of Sung Yueh Ssu* (A.D. 523) at Sung Shan, Honan.

Other well-known Chinese buildings are the *Drum Tower* (1273), the *Three Great Halls* in the Purple Forbidden City (1627), *Buddha's Perfume Tower* (19th century), the *Porcelain Pagoda* and the *Summer Palace*, all at Peiping.

## United States

*Rockefeller Center*, in New York City, extends from 5th to 6th Aves. between 48th and 52nd Sts. (and halfway to 7th Ave. between 50th and 51st Sts.). It occupies 14 ac. and has 16 buildings.

*Grant's Tomb*, at Riverside Dr. near 122nd St. in New York City, contains the bodies of Ulysses S. Grant and his wife. It was completed in 1897.

*The Cathedral of St. John the Divine*, at Cathedral Pkwy. and Amsterdam Ave. in New York City, was begun in 1892 but is not yet completed. When completed, it will be the largest Gothic cathedral in the world: 601 ft. long, 146 ft. wide at the nave, 320 ft. wide at the transept.

*St. Patrick's Cathedral*, at 5th Ave. and 50th St. in New York City, has a seating capacity of 4,500. The nave was opened in 1877; the cathedral was dedicated in 1879.

*Lincoln Memorial*, in Washington, D. C., was dedicated in 1922. It has 36 columns (the number of states in 1865), each 44 ft. high. The main chamber contains a statue of Lincoln.

*Independence Hall*, in Philadelphia, was the scene of the signing of the Declaration of Independence and the drawing up of the U. S. Constitution. It was built between 1732–41 as the State House. The Liberty Bell is on the first floor.

## Great Dams of the World

| Reservoir capacity, thousands of acre feet | Name | Location | Maximum height, feet | Date completed |
|---|---|---|---|---|
| 31,142 | Hoover | Colorado River, Ariz.-Nev. | 726 | 1936 |
| 28,040 | Glen Canyon | Colorado River, Arizona | 700 | * |
| n.a. | Kariba | Zambesi River, Rhodesia | 420 | * |
| 24,500 | Garrison | Missouri River, N. Dak. | 210 | 1954 |
| 19,600 | Oahe | Missouri River, S. Dak. | 230 | 1960 |
| 19,412 | Fort Peck | Missouri River, Mont. | 250 | 1940 |
| 9,402 | Grand Coulee | Columbia River, Wash. | 550 | 1942 |
| 6,200 | Fort Randall | Missouri River, S. Dak. | 150 | 1954 |
| 6,100 | Kentucky | Tennessee River, Ky. | 160 | 1944 |
| 6,089 | Wolf Creek | Cumberland River, Ky. | 242 | 1951 |
| 5,825 | Denison | Red River, Okla.-Tex. | 165 | 1944 |
| 5,407 | Bull Shoals | White River, Ark. | 278 | 1953 |
| 5,000 | Presidente Alemán | Rio Tonto, Mex. | 200 | 1955 |
| 4,500 | Shasta | Sacramento River, Calif. | 602 | 1945 |
| 4,085 | Falcon | Rio Grande, Tex.-Mex. | 128 | 1953 |
| 4,060 | Aswan | Nile River, Egypt | 174 | 1934 |
| 3,468 | Hungry Horse | Flathead, S. Fk., Mont. | 564 | 1953 |
| 3,263 | Lázaro Cárdenas (El Palmito) | Nazas River, Mex. | 295 | 1948 |
| 3,000 | Salt Springs | North Fork, Mokelumne River, Calif. | 345 | 1931 |
| 2,567 | Norris | Clinch River, Tenn. | 265 | 1936 |
| 2,500 | Trinity | Trinity River, California | 537 | 1960 |
| 2,432 | Alvaro Obregón (Oviachic) | Yaqui River, Sonora, Mex. | 187 | 1953 |
| 2,300 | Saluda | Saluda River, S. C. | 208 | 1930 |
| 2,207 | Elephant Butte | Rio Grande, N. Mex. | 301 | 1916 |
| 2,092 | Center Hill | Caney Fork River, Tenn. | 240 | 1950 |
| 2,051 | Canyon Ferry | Missouri River, Mont. | 225 | 1954 |
| 1,983 | Norfork | North Fork River, Ark. | 230 | 1944 |
| 1,980 | Chelsea | Gatineau River, Canada | 100 | 1927 |
| 1,951 | Marshall Ford (Mansfield) | Colorado River, Tex. | 278 | 1942 |
| 520 | Friant | San Joaquin River, California | 319 | 1942 |
| 493 | Anderson Ranch | Boise River, Idaho | 456 | 1950 |
| 456 | Shoshone | Shoshone Canyon, Wyoming | 329 | 1910 |
| 286 | Arrowrock | Boise River, Idaho | 350 | 1915 |
| n.a. | Vaiont | Italy | 840 | * |
| n.a. | Mauvoisin | Dranse River, Switzerland | 780 | 1957 |
| n.a. | Grand Dixence | Dixence River, Switzerland | 584† | * |
| n.a. | Bhakra | India | 680 | * |
| n.a. | Brownlee | Snake River, Idaho-Oregon | 400 | 1958 |

* Still under construction.   † Initial stage of 3 stages.   NOTE: n.a. indicates data not available.

# Notable Modern Bridges

| Length of channel span, feet | Name | Location | Type* | Year completed |
|---|---|---|---|---|
| 4,200 | GOLDEN GATE | San Francisco | S | 1937 |
| 3,800 | MACKINAC STRAITS | Michigan | S | 1957 |
| 3,500 | GEORGE WASHINGTON | New York City | S | 1931 |
| 2,800 | TACOMA NARROWS | Tacoma, Wash. | S | 1950 |
| 2,310 | TRANSBAY | San Francisco | S | 1936 |
| 2,300 | BRONX-WHITESTONE | New York City | S | 1939 |
| 2,150 | DELAWARE MEMORIAL | Near Wilmington, Del. | S | 1951 |
| 2,000 | WALT WHITMAN | South Philadelphia, Pa. | S | 1957 |
| 1,850 | AMBASSADOR | Detroit, Mich. | S | 1929 |
| 1,800 | QUEBEC | Near Quebec, Canada | C | 1917 |
| 1,750 | DELAWARE RIVER | Philadelphia, Pa. | S | 1926 |
| 1,700 | FORTH | Firth of Forth, Scotland | C | 1889 |
| 1,652 | KILL VAN KULL | Bayonne, N. J. | SA | 1931 |
| 1,650 | SYDNEY HARBOR | Sydney, Australia | SA | 1932 |
| 1,632 | BEAR MOUNTAIN | Peekskill, N. Y. | S | 1924 |
| 1,600 | CHESAPEAKE BAY | Near Annapolis, Md. | S | 1952 |
| 1,600 | WILLIAMSBURG | New York City | S | 1903 |
| 1,595.5 | BROOKLYN | New York City | S | 1883 |
| 1,550 | LIONS GATE | Vancouver, Canada | S | 1939 |
| 1,500 | MID-HUDSON | Poughkeepsie, N. Y. | S | 1930 |
| 1,500 | HOWRAH | Calcutta, India | C | 1943 |
| 1,470 | MANHATTAN | New York City | S | 1909 |
| 1,447 | ANGUS L. MACDONALD | Halifax, N. S., Canada | S | 1954 |
| 1,400 | TRANSBAY | Oakland, Calif. | C | 1936 |
| 1,380 | TRIBOROUGH | New York City | S | 1936 |
| 1,240 | COLOGNE-RODENKIRCHEN | Germany | S | 1954 |
| 1,212 | TAPPAN ZEE | Nyack, N. Y. | C | 1956 |
| 1,207 | ST. JOHNS | Portland, Oreg. | S | 1931 |
| 1,200 | LONGVIEW | Longview, Wash. | C | 1930 |
| 1,200 | MT. HOPE | Near Bristol, R. I. | S | 1929 |
| 1,182 | QUEENSBORO | New York City | C | 1909 |
| 1,114 | FLORIANÓPOLIS | Florianópolis, Brazil | S | 1926 |
| 1,100 | CARQUINEZ STRAIT | Near San Francisco | C | 1927 |
| 1,097 | MONTREAL HARBOR | Montreal, Canada | C | 1930 |
| 1,080 | DEER ISLE | Deer Isle, Me. | S | 1939 |
| 1,070 | RICHMOND-SAN RAFAEL | San Francisco Bay | C | 1956 |
| 1,057 | CINCINNATI | Cincinnati, Ohio | S | 1867 |
| 1,050 | COOPER RIVER | Charleston, S. C. | C | 1929 |
| 1,042 | NAGASAKI | Japan | SA | 1955 |
| 1,034 | COLOGNE-MÜLHEIM | Germany | S | 1951 |
| 1,010 | WHEELING | Wheeling, W. Va. | S | 1849 |
| 977.5 | HELL GATE | New York City | SA | 1917 |
| 963 | EAST ST. LOUIS | East St. Louis, Ill. | C | 1950 |
| 950 | RAINBOW | Niagara Falls, N. Y. | SA | 1941 |
| 949 | GRAND MERE | Quebec, Canada | S | 1928 |
| 936 | DUISBURG | Germany | S | 1954 |
| 924 | STORY | Queensland, Australia | C | 1940 |
| 875 | NATCHEZ | Natchez, Miss. | C | 1940 |
| 871 | BLUE WATER | Port Huron, Mich. | C | 1938 |
| 866 | SANDO | Sando, Sweden | CA | 1943 |
| 864 | SUNSHINE SKYWAY | St. Petersburg, Fla. | C | 1954 |
| 856 | SAVA RIVER | Belgrade, Yugoslavia | CG | 1956 |
| 845 | DUBUQUE | Dubuque, Iowa | CT | 1943 |
| 800 | KINGSTON-RHINECLIFF | Hudson River, N. Y. | CT | 1956 |
| 800 | THOUSAND ISLANDS | Alexandria Bay, N. Y. | S | 1938 |
| 800 | RIP VAN WINKLE | Catskill, N. Y. | C | 1935 |
| 800 | HENRY HUDSON | New York City | SA | 1936 |

* C—Cantilever. S—Suspension. SA—Steel Arch. CA—Concrete Arch. CT—Continuous Truss. CG—Continuous Girder.

# THE DECLARATION OF INDEPENDENCE

## In CONGRESS, July 4, 1776

### The unanimous Declaration of the thirteen united States of America.

WHEN in the Course of human events it becomes necessary for one people to dissolve the political bands which have connected them with another, and to assume among the powers of the earth, the separate and equal station to which the Laws of Nature and of Nature's God entitle them, a decent respect to the opinions of mankind requires that they should declare the causes which impel them to the separation.

We hold these truths to be self-evident, that all men are created equal, that they are endowed by their Creator with certain unalienable Rights, that among these are Life, Liberty and the pursuit of Happiness.—That to secure these rights, Governments are instituted among Men, deriving their just powers from the consent of the governed,—That whenever any Form of Government becomes destructive of these ends, it is the Right of the People to alter or to abolish it, and to institute new Government, laying its foundation on such principles and organizing its powers in such form, as to them shall seem most likely to effect their Safety and Happiness. Prudence, indeed, will dictate that Governments long established should not be changed for light and transient causes; and accordingly all experience hath shewn that mankind are more disposed to suffer, while evils are sufferable, than to right themselves by abolishing the forms to which they are accustomed. But when a long train of abuses and usurpations, pursuing invariably the same Object evinces a design to reduce them under absolute Despotism, it is their right, it is their duty, to throw off such Government, and to provide new Guards for their future security.—Such has been the patient sufferance of these Colonies; and such is now the necessity which constrains them to alter their former Systems of Government. The history of the present King of Great Britain is a history of repeated injuries and usurpations, all having in direct object the establishment of an absolute Tyranny over these States. To prove this, let Facts be submitted to a candid world.

He has refused his Assent to Laws, the most wholesome and necessary for the public good.

He has forbidden his Governors to pass Laws of immediate and pressing importance, unless suspended in their operation till his Assent should be obtained; and when so suspended, he has utterly neglected to attend to them.

He has refused to pass other Laws for the accommodation of large districts of people, unless those people would relinquish the right of Representation in the Legislature, a right inestimable to them and formidable to tyrants only.

He has called together legislative bodies at places unusual, uncomfortable, and distant from the depository of their Public Records, for the sole purpose of fatiguing them into compliance with his measures.

He has dissolved Representative Houses repeatedly, for opposing with manly firmness his invasions on the rights of the people.

He has refused for a long time, after such dissolutions, to cause others to be elected; whereby the Legislative Powers, incapable of Annihilation, have returned to the People at large for their exercise; the State remaining in the mean time exposed to all the dangers of invasion from without, and convulsions within.

---

NOTE: On April 12, 1776, the legislature of North Carolina authorized its delegates to the Continental Congress to join with others in a declaration of separation from Great Britain; the first colony to instruct its delegates to take the actual initiative was Virginia on May 15. On June 7, 1776, Richard Henry Lee of Virginia offered a resolution to the Congress to the effect "that these United Colonies are, and of right ought to be, free and independent States. . . ." A committee, consisting of Thomas Jefferson, John Adams, Benjamin Franklin, Robert R. Livingston, and Roger Sherman was organized to "prepare a declaration to the effect of the said first resolution." The Declaration of Independence was adopted on July 4, 1776.

Most delegates signed the Declaration August 2, but George Wythe (Va.) signed August 27; Richard Henry Lee (Va.), Elbridge Gerry (Mass.), and Oliver Wolcott (Conn.) in September; Matthew Thornton (N. H.), not a delegate until September, in November; and Thomas McKean (Del.), although present on July 4, not until 1781 by special permission, having served in the army in the interim.

He has endeavoured to prevent the population of these States; for that purpose obstructing the Laws for Naturalization of Foreigners; refusing to pass others to encourage their migrations hither, and raising the conditions of new Appropriations of Lands.

He has obstructed the Administration of Justice, by refusing his Assent to Laws for establishing Judiciary Powers.

He has made Judges dependent on his Will alone, for the tenure of their offices, and the amount and payment of their salaries.

He has erected a multitude of New Offices, and sent hither swarms of Officers to harass our people, and eat out their substance.

He has kept among us, in times of peace, Standing Armies without the Consent of our legislatures.

He has affected to render the Military independent of and superior to the Civil Power.

He has combined with others to subject us to a jurisdiction foreign to our constitution, and unacknowledged by our laws; giving his Assent to their Acts of pretended Legislation:

For quartering large bodies of armed troops among us:

For protecting them, by a mock Trial, from punishment for any Murders which they should commit on the Inhabitants of these States:

For cutting off our Trade with all parts of the world:

For imposing Taxes on us without our Consent:

For depriving us in many cases, of the benefits of Trial by Jury:

For transporting us beyond Seas to be tried for pretended offences:

For abolishing the free System of English Laws in a neighbouring Province, establishing therein an Arbitrary government, and enlarging its Boundaries so as to render it at once an example and fit instrument for introducing the same absolute rule into these Colonies:

For taking away our Charters, abolishing our most valuable Laws and altering fundamentally the Forms of our Governments:

For suspending our own Legislatures, and declaring themselves invested with power to legislate for us in all cases whatsoever.

He has abdicated Government here, by declaring us out of his Protection and waging War against us.

He has plundered our seas, ravaged our Coasts, burnt our towns, and destroyed the lives of our people.

He is at this time transporting large Armies of foreign Mercenaries to compleat the works of death, desolation and tyranny, already begun with circumstances of Cruelty & Perfidy scarcely paralleled in the most barbarous ages, and totally unworthy the Head of a civilized nation.

He has constrained our fellow Citizens taken Captive on the high Seas to bear Arms against their Country, to become the executioners of their friends and Brethren, or to fall themselves by their Hands.

He has excited domestic insurrections amongst us, and has endeavoured to bring on the inhabitants of our frontiers, the merciless Indian Savages, whose known rule of warfare, is an undistinguished destruction of all ages, sexes and conditions.

In every stage of these Oppressions We have Petitioned for Redress in the most humble terms: Our repeated Petitions have been answered only by repeated injury. A Prince, whose character is thus marked by every act which may define a Tyrant, is unfit to be the ruler of a free people.

Nor have We been wanting in attentions to our Brittish brethren. We have warned them from time to time of attempts by their legislature to extend an unwarrantable jurisdiction over us. We have reminded them of the circumstances of our emigration and settlement here. We have appealed to their native justice and magnanimity, and we have conjured them by the ties of our common kindred to disavow these usurpations, which would inevitably interrupt our connections and correspondence. They too have been deaf to the voice of justice and of consanguinity. We must, therefore, acquiesce in the necessity, which denounces our Separation, and hold them, as we hold the rest of mankind, Enemies in War, in Peace Friends.

WE, THEREFORE, the Representatives of the UNITED STATES OF AMERICA, in General Congress, Assembled, appealing to the Supreme Judge of the world for the rectitude of our intentions, do, in the Name, and by Authority of the good People of these Colonies, solemnly publish and declare, That these United Colonies are, and of Right ought to be

FREE AND INDEPENDENT STATES; that they are Absolved from all Allegiance to the British Crown, and that all political connection between them and the State of Great Britain, is and ought to be totally dissolved; and that as Free and Independent States, they have full Power to levy War, conclude Peace, contract Alliances, establish Commerce, and to do all other Acts and Things which Independent States may of right do.—And for the support of this Declaration, with a firm reliance on the protection of Divine Providence, we mutually pledge to each other our Lives, our Fortunes and our sacred Honor.

JOHN HANCOCK.

#### New Hampshire.
Josiah Bartlett,
Wm. Whipple,
Matthew Thornton.

#### Rhode Island.
Step. Hopkins,
William Ellery.

#### Connecticut.
Roger Sherman,
Sam'el Huntington,
Wm. Williams,
Oliver Wolcott.

#### New York.
Wm. Floyd,
Phil. Livingston,
Frans. Lewis,
Lewis Morris.

#### New Jersey.
Richd. Stockton,
Jno. Witherspoon,
Fras. Hopkinson,
John Hart,
Abra. Clark.

#### Pennsylvania.
Robt. Morris,
Benjamin Rush,
Benj. Franklin,
John Morton,
Geo. Clymer,
Jas. Smith,
Geo. Taylor,
James Wilson,
Geo. Ross.

#### Massachusetts-Bay.
Saml. Adams,
John Adams,
Robt. Treat Paine,
Elbridge Gerry.

#### Delaware.
Caesar Rodney,
Geo. Read,
Tho. M'Kean.

#### Maryland.
Samuel Chase,
Wm. Paca,
Thos. Stone,
Charles Carroll of Carrollton.

#### Virginia.
George Wythe,
Richard Henry Lee,
Th. Jefferson,
Benj. Harrison,
Ths. Nelson, Jr.,
Francis Lightfoot Lee,
Carter Braxton.

#### North Carolina.
Wm. Hooper,
Joseph Hewes,
John Penn.

#### South Carolina.
Edward Rutledge,
Thos. Heyward, Junr.,
Thomas Lynch, Junr.,
Arthur Middleton.

#### Georgia.
Button Gwinnett,
Lyman Hall,
Geo. Walton.

IN CONGRESS
JANUARY, 18, 1777.

*Ordered:*
That an authenticated copy of the Declaration of Independency, with the names of the Members of Congress subscribing the same, be sent to each of the United States, and that they be desired to have the same put on record.
By order of Congress.
Attest, CHAS. THOMSON, *Secy.* A true copy. JOHN HANCOCK, *Presidt.*

## The Statue of Liberty

The Statue of Liberty ("Liberty Enlightening the World") is a 225-ton, steel-reinforced copper female figure, 152 ft. in height, facing the ocean from Liberty* Island in New York Harbor. The right hand holds aloft a torch, and the left hand carries a tablet upon which is inscribed: "July 4, 1776."

The statue was designed by Frédéric Auguste Bartholdi, at the request of the Franco-American Union, as a present to the U. S. to commemorate the centennial of American independence. It cost $250,000.

The pedestal, almost 150 ft. in height, was erected by the U. S., and its cost of more than $270,000 was met by popular sub-

* Called Bedloe's Island prior to 1956.

scription in this country. The cornerstone was laid Aug. 5, 1884, and the unveiling of the statue took place Oct. 28, 1886.

On a tablet inside the pedestal is engraved the following sonnet, written by Emma Lazarus:

#### The New Colossus
Not like the brazen giant of Greek fame,
With conquering limbs astride from land to land;
Here at our sea-washed, sunset gates shall stand
A mighty woman with a torch, whose flame
Is the imprisoned lightning, and her name
Mother of Exiles. From her beacon hand
Glows world-wide welcome; her mild eyes command
The air-bridged harbor that twin cities frame.
"Keep, ancient lands, your storied pomp!" cries she
With silent lips. "Give me your tired, your poor,
Your huddled masses yearning to breathe free,
The wretched refuse of your teeming shore.
Send these, the homeless, tempest-tost to me,
I lift my lamp beside the golden door."

# CONSTITUTION
## of the UNITED STATES OF AMERICA

THE *oldest federal constitution in existence was framed by a convention of delegates from twelve of the thirteen original states in Philadelphia in May, 1787, Rhode Island failing to send a delegate. George Washington presided over the session, which lasted until September 17, 1787. The draft (originally a preamble and seven Articles) was submitted to all thirteen states and was to become effective when ratified by nine states. It went into effect on the first Wednesday in March, 1789, having been ratified by New Hampshire, the ninth state to approve, on June 21, 1788. The states ratified the Constitution in the following order:*

| | | | |
|---|---|---|---|
| Delaware | December 7, 1787 | South Carolina | May 23, 1788 |
| Pennsylvania | December 12, 1787 | New Hampshire | June 21, 1788 |
| New Jersey | December 18, 1787 | Virginia | June 25, 1788 |
| Georgia | January 2, 1788 | New York | July 26, 1788 |
| Connecticut | January 9, 1788 | North Carolina | November 21, 1789 |
| Massachusetts | February 6, 1788 | Rhode Island | May 29, 1790 |
| Maryland | April 28, 1788 | | |

## Outline of the Constitution

### ARTICLE I

SEC. 1. Legislative powers; in whom vested.

SEC. 2. House of Representatives, how and by whom chosen—Qualifications of a Representative—Representatives and direct taxes, how apportioned—Enumeration—Vacancies to be filled—Power of choosing officers, and of impeachment.

SEC. 3. Senators, how and by whom chosen—How classified—State Executive, when to make temporary appointments, in case, etc.—Qualifications of a Senator—President of the Senate, his right to vote—President pro tem., and other officers of the Senate, how chosen—Power to try impeachments—When President is tried, Chief Justice to preside—Sentence.

SEC. 4. Times, etc., of holding elections, how prescribed—At least one Session in each year.

SEC. 5. Membership—Quorum—Adjournments—Rules—Power to punish or expel—Journal—Time of adjournments, how limited, etc.

SEC. 6. Compensation—Privileges—Disqualification in certain cases.

SEC. 7. House to originate all revenue bills—Veto—Bill may be passed by two-thirds of each house, notwithstanding, etc.—Bill, not returned in ten days, to become a law—Provisions as to orders, concurrent resolutions, etc.

SEC. 8. Powers of Congress.

SEC. 9. Provision as to migration or importation of certain persons—Habeas Corpus—Bills of attainder, etc.—Taxes, how apportioned—No export duty—No commercial preference—Money, how drawn from treasury, etc.—No titular nobility—Officers not to receive presents, etc.

SEC. 10. States prohibited from the exercise of certain powers.

### ARTICLE II

SEC. 1. President; his term of office—Electors of President; number and how appointed—Electors to vote on same day—Qualification of President—On whom his duties devolve in case of his removal, death, etc.—President's compensation—His oath of office.

SEC. 2. President to be commander in chief—He may require opinions of Cabinet Officers, etc., may pardon—Treaty-making power—Nomination of certain officers—When President may fill vacancies.

SEC. 3. President shall communicate to Congress—He may convene and adjourn Congress, in case of disagreement, etc.—Shall receive ambassadors, execute laws, and commission officers.

SEC. 4. All civil offices forfeited for certain crimes.

### ARTICLE III

SEC. 1. Judicial powers—Tenure—Compensation.

SEC. 2. Judicial power; to what cases it extends—Original jurisdiction of Supreme Court — Appellate — Trial by jury, etc. — Trial, where.

SEC. 3. Treason defined—Proof of—Punishment of.

### ARTICLE IV

SEC. 1. Each State to give credit to the public acts, etc., of every other State.

SEC. 2. Privileges of citizens of each State—Fugitives from justice to be delivered up—Persons held to service having escaped, to be delivered up.

SEC. 3. Admission of new States—Power of Congress over territory and other property.

SEC. 4. Republican form of government guaranteed—Each State to be protected.

## ARTICLE V

Constitution; how amended—Proviso.

## ARTICLE VI

Certain debts, etc., declared valid—Supremacy of Constitution, treaties, and laws of the United States—Oath to support Constitution, by whom taken—No religious test.

## ARTICLE VII

What ratification shall establish Constitution.

## AMENDMENTS

I. Religious establishment prohibited—Freedom of speech, of the press, and right to petition.

II. Right to keep and bear arms.

III. No soldier to be quartered in any house, unless, etc.

IV. Right of search and seizure regulated.

V. Provisions concerning prosecution, trial, and punishment—Private property not to be taken for public use, without compensation.

VI. Further provision respecting criminal prosecutions.

VII. Right of trial by jury secured.

VIII. Excessive bail or fines and cruel punishments prohibited.

IX. Rule of construction of Constitution.

X. Same subject; rights of States.

XI. Same subject; judicial powers construed.

XII. Manner of choosing President and Vice President.

XIII. Slavery abolished.

XIV. Citizenship; representation—Public debt.

XV. Right of suffrage.

XVI. Taxes on incomes.

XVII. Election of Senators—Filling of vacancies.

XVIII. Prohibition.

XIX. Suffrage; not to be denied because of sex.

XX. Commencement of terms of President, Vice President, and members of Congress; time of assembling of Congress.

XXI. Repeal of Prohibition.

XXII. No person to serve as President for more than two terms.

XXIII. Electors for District of Columbia.

# The Constitution of the United States of America

PREAMBLE.—WE THE PEOPLE of the United States, in Order to form a more perfect Union, establish Justice, insure domestic Tranquility, provide for the common defence, promote the general Welfare, and secure the Blessings of Liberty to ourselves and our Posterity, do ordain and establish this Constitution for the United States of America.

## ARTICLE I

### Section 1

Legislative powers vested in Congress.—All legislative Powers herein granted shall be vested in a Congress of the United States, which shall consist of a Senate and House of Representatives.

### Section 2

Composition of the House of Representatives.—1. The House of Representatives shall be composed of Members chosen every second Year by the People of the several States, and the Electors in each State shall have the Qualifications requisite for Electors of the most numerous Branch of the State Legislature.

Qualifications of Representatives.—2. No Person shall be a Representative who shall not have attained to the Age of twenty-five Years, and been seven Years a Citizen of the United States, and who shall not, when elected, be an Inhabitant of that State in which he shall be chosen.

Apportionment of Representatives and direct taxes—census.*—3. [Representatives and direct Taxes shall be apportioned among the several States which may be included within this Union, according to their respective Numbers, which shall be determined by adding to the whole Number of free Persons, including those bound to Service for a Term of Years, and excluding Indians not taxed, three fifths of all other Persons.] The actual Enumeration shall be made within three Years after the first Meeting of the Congress of the United States, and within every subsequent Term of ten Years, in such Manner as they shall by Law direct. The Number of Representatives shall not exceed one for every thirty Thousand, but each State shall have at Least one Representative; and until such enumeration shall be made, the State of New Hampshire shall be entitled to chuse three, Massachusetts eight, Rhode-Island and Providence Plantations one, Connecticut five, New York six, New Jersey four, Pennsylvania eight, Delaware one, Maryland six, Virginia ten, North Carolina five, South Carolina five, and Georgia three.

Filling of vacancies in representation.—4. When vacancies happen in the Representation from any State, the Executive

---

* The clause included in brackets is amended by the 14th Amendment, Section 2.

Authority thereof shall issue Writs of Election to fill such Vacancies.

**Selection of officers; power of impeachment.—5.** The House of Representatives shall chuse their Speaker and other Officers; and shall have the sole Power of Impeachment.

## Section 3*

**The Senate.—**[1. The Senate of the United States shall be composed of two Senators from each State, chosen by the Legislature thereof, for six Years; and each Senator shall have one Vote.]

**Classification of Senators; filling of vacancies.—2.** Immediately after they shall be assembled in Consequence of the first Election, they shall be divided as equally as may be into three Classes. The Seats of the Senators of the first Class shall be vacated at the Expiration of the second Year, of the second Class at the Expiration of the fourth Year, and of the third Class at the Expiration of the sixth Year, so that one-third may be chosen every second Year; and if Vacancies happen by Resignation, or otherwise, during the Recess of the Legislature of any State, the Executive thereof may make temporary Appointments [until the next Meeting of the Legislature, which shall then fill such Vacancies].

**Qualification of Senators.—3.** No Person shall be a Senator who shall not have attained to the Age of thirty Years, and been nine Years a Citizen of the United States, and who shall not, when elected, be an Inhabitant of that State for which he shall be chosen.

**Vice President to be President of Senate. —4.** The Vice President of the United States shall be President of the Senate, but shall have no Vote, unless they be equally divided.

**Selection of Senate officers; President pro tempore.—5.** The Senate shall chuse their other Officers, and also a President pro tempore, in the Absence of the Vice President, or when he shall exercise the Office of President of the United States.

**Senate to try impeachments.—6.** The Senate shall have the sole Power to try all Impeachments. When sitting for that Purpose, they shall be on Oath or Affirmation. When the President of the United States is tried, the Chief Justice shall preside: And no Person shall be convicted without the Concurrence of two thirds of the Members present.

**Judgment in cases of impeachment.—7.** Judgment in Cases of Impeachment shall not extend further than to removal from Office, and disqualification to hold and enjoy any Office of honor, Trust, or Profit under the United States: but the Party convicted shall nevertheless be liable and subject to Indictment, Trial, Judgment and Punishment, according to Law.

## Section 4

**Control of congressional elections.—1.** The Times, Places and Manner of holding Elections for Senators and Representatives, shall be prescribed in each State by the Legislature thereof; but the Congress may at any time by Law make or alter such Regulations, except as to the Places of chusing Senators.

**Time for assembling of Congress.†—2.** The Congress shall assemble at least once in every Year, and such Meeting shall be on the first Monday in December, unless they shall by Law appoint a different Day.

## Section 5

**Each house to be the judge of the election and qualifications of its members; regulations as to quorum.—1.** Each House shall be the Judge of the Elections, Returns and Qualifications of its own Members, and a Majority of each shall constitute a Quorum to do Business; but a smaller Number may adjourn from day to day, and may be authorized to compel the Attendance of absent Members, in such Manner, and under such Penalties as each House may provide.

**Each house to determine its own rules.— 2.** Each House may determine the Rules of its Proceedings, punish its Members for disorderly Behaviour, and, with the Concurrence of two thirds, expel a Member.

**Journals and yeas and nays.—3.** Each House shall keep a Journal of its Proceedings, and from time to time publish the same, excepting such Parts as may in their Judgment require Secrecy; and the Yeas and Nays of the Members of either House on any question shall, at the Desire of one fifth of those Present, be entered on the Journal.

**Adjournment.—4.** Neither House, during the Session of Congress shall, without the Consent of the other, adjourn for more than three days, nor to any other Place than that in which the two Houses shall be sitting.

## Section 6

**Compensation and privileges of Members of Congress.—1.** The Senators and Representatives shall receive a Compensation for their Services, to be ascertained by Law, and paid out of the Treasury of the United States. They shall in all Cases, except Treason, Felony and Breach of the

---

* The 1st paragraph of this section and as much of the 2nd paragraph as relates to filling vacancies are amended by the 17th Amendment.
† Amended by the 20th Amendment, Section 2.

Peace, be privileged from Arrest during their Attendance at the Session of their respective Houses, and in going to and returning from the same; and for any Speech or Debate in either House, they shall not be questioned in any other Place.

**Incompatible offices; exclusions.—2.** No Senator or Representative shall, during the Time for which he was elected, be appointed to any civil Office under the Authority of the United States, which shall have been created, or the Emoluments whereof shall have been encreased during such time; and no Person holding any Office under the United States, shall be a Member of either House during his Continuance in Office.

## Section 7

**Revenue bills to originate in House.—1.** All Bills for raising Revenue shall originate in the House of Representatives; but the Senate may propose or concur with Amendments as on other Bills.

**Manner of passing bills; veto power of President.—2.** Every Bill which shall have passed the House of Representatives and the Senate, shall, before it becomes a Law, be presented to the President of the United States; If he approve he shall sign it, but if not he shall return it, with his Objections to that House in which it shall have originated, who shall enter the Objections at large on their Journal, and proceed to reconsider it. If after such Reconsideration two thirds of that House shall agree to pass the Bill, it shall be sent, together with the Objections, to the other House, by which it shall likewise be reconsidered, and if approved by two thirds of that House, it shall become a Law. But in all such Cases the Votes of both Houses shall be determined by Yeas and Nays, and the Names of the Persons voting for and against the Bill shall be entered on the Journal of each House respectively. If any Bill shall not be returned by the President within ten Days (Sundays excepted) after it shall have been presented to him, the Same shall be a Law, in like Manner as if he had signed it, unless the Congress by their Adjournment prevent its Return, in which Case it shall not be a Law.

**Concurrent orders or resolutions, to be passed by President.—3.** Every Order, Resolution, or Vote to which the Concurrence of the Senate and House of Representatives may be necessary (except on a question of adjournment) shall be presented to the President of the United States; and before the Same shall take Effect, shall be approved by him, or being disapproved by him, shall be repassed by two thirds of the Senate and House of Representatives, according to the Rules and Limitations prescribed in the Case of a Bill.

## Section 8

**General powers of Congress.** *

The Congress shall have Power.—1. To lay and collect Taxes, Duties, Imposts and Excises, to pay the Debts and provide for the common Defence and general Welfare of the United States; but all Duties, Imposts and Excises shall be uniform throughout the United States;

**Borrowing of money.—2.** To borrow Money on the credit of the United States;

**Regulation of commerce.—3.** To regulate Commerce with foreign Nations, and among the several States, and with the Indian Tribes;

**Naturalization and bankruptcy.—4.** To establish an uniform Rule of Naturalization, and uniform Laws on the subject of Bankruptcies throughout the United States;

**Money, weights and measures.—5.** To coin Money, regulate the Value thereof, and of foreign Coin, and fix the Standard of Weights and Measures;

**Counterfeiting.—6.** To provide for the Punishment of counterfeiting the Securities and current Coin of the United States;

**Post offices.—7.** To establish Post Offices and post Roads;

**Patents and copyrights.—8.** To promote the Progress of Science and useful Arts, by securing for limited Times to Authors and Inventors the exclusive Right to their respective Writings and Discoveries;

**Inferior courts.—9.** To constitute Tribunals inferior to the supreme Court;

**Piracies and felonies.—10.** To define and punish Piracies and Felonies committed on the high Seas, and Offences against the Law of Nations;

**War; marque and reprisal.—11.** To declare War, grant Letters of Marque and Reprisal, and make Rules concerning Captures on Land and Water;

**Armies.—12.** To raise and support Armies, but no Appropriation of Money to that Use shall be for a longer Term than two Years;

**Navy.—13.** To provide and maintain a Navy;

**Land and naval forces.—14.** To make Rules for the Government and Regulation of the land and naval Forces;

**Calling out militia.—15.** To provide for calling forth the Militia to execute the Laws of the Union, suppress Insurrections and repel Invasions;

**Organizing, arming and disciplining militia.—16.** To provide for organizing, arming, and disciplining, the Militia, and for governing such Part of them as may be

---

* By the 16th Amendment, Congress is given the power to lay and collect taxes on incomes.

employed in the Service of the United States, reserving to the States respectively, the Appointment of the Officers, and the Authority of training the Militia according to the discipline prescribed by Congress;

**Exclusive legislation over District of Columbia.**—17. To exercise exclusive Legislation in all Cases whatsoever, over such District (not exceeding ten Miles square) as may, by Cession of particular States, and the Acceptance of Congress, become the Seat of the Government of the United States, and to exercise like Authority over all Places purchased by the Consent of the Legislature of the State in which the Same shall be, for the Erection of Forts, Magazines, Arsenals, dock-Yards, and other needful Buildings;—And

**To enact laws necessary to enforce Constitution.**—18. To make all Laws which shall be necessary and proper for carrying into Execution the foregoing Powers, and all other Powers vested by this Constitution in the Government of the United States, or in any Department or Officer thereof.

### Section 9

**Migration or importation of certain persons not to be prohibited before 1808.**—1. The Migration or Importation of such Persons as any of the States now existing shall think proper to admit, shall not be prohibited by the Congress prior to the Year one thousand eight hundred and eight, but a Tax or duty may be imposed on such Importation, not exceeding ten dollars for each Person.

**Writ of habeas corpus not to be suspended; exception.**—2. The Privilege of the Writ of Habeas Corpus shall not be suspended, unless when in Cases of Rebellion or Invasion the public Safety may require it.

**Bills of attainder and ex post facto laws prohibited.**—3. No Bill of Attainder or ex post facto Law shall be passed.

**Capitation and other direct taxes.**—4. No Capitation, or other direct, Tax shall be laid, unless in Proportion to the Census or Enumeration herein before directed to be taken.*

**Exports not to be taxed.**—5. No Tax or Duty shall be laid on Articles exported from any State.

**No preference to be given to ports of any State; interstate shipping.**—6. No Preference shall be given by any Regulation of Commerce or Revenue to the Ports of one State over those of another: nor shall Vessels bound to, or from, one State, be obliged to enter, clear, or pay Duties in another.

**Money, how drawn from treasury; finan-**cial statements to be published.—7. No Money shall be drawn from the Treasury, but in Consequence of Appropriations made by Law; and a regular Statement and Account of the Receipts and Expenditures of all public Money shall be published from time to time.

**Titles of nobility not to be granted; acceptance by government officers of favors from foreign powers.**—8. No Title of Nobility shall be granted by the United States: And no Person holding any Office of Profit or Trust under them, shall, without the Consent of the Congress, accept of any present, Emolument, Office, or Title, of any kind whatever, from any King, Prince, or foreign State.

### Section 10

**Limitations of the powers of the several States.**—1. No State shall enter into any Treaty, Alliance, or Confederation; grant Letters of Marque and Reprisal; coin Money; emit Bills of Credit; make any Thing but gold and silver Coin a Tender in Payment of Debts; pass any Bill of Attainder, ex post facto Law, or Law impairing the Obligation of Contracts, or grant any Title of Nobility.

**State imposts and duties.**—2. No State shall, without the Consent of the Congress, lay any Imposts or Duties on Imports or Exports, except what may be absolutely necessary for executing its inspection Laws: and the net Produce of all Duties and Imposts, laid by any State on Imports or Exports, shall be for the Use of the Treasury of the United States; and all such Laws shall be subject to the Revision and Control of the Congress.

**Further restrictions on powers of States.**—3. No State shall, without the Consent of Congress, lay any Duty of Tonnage, keep Troops, or Ships of War in time of Peace, enter into any Agreement or Compact with another State, or with a foreign Power, or engage in War, unless actually invaded, or in such imminent Danger as will not admit of delay.

## ARTICLE II

### Section 1

**The President; the executive power.**—1. The executive Power shall be vested in a President of the United States of America. He shall hold his Office during the Term of four Years, and, together with the Vice President, chosen for the same Term, be elected, as follows

**Appointment and qualifications of presidential electors.**—2. Each State shall appoint, in such Manner as the Legislature thereof may direct, a Number of Electors, equal to the whole Number of Senators and

---

* See the 16th Amendment.

Representatives to which the State may be entitled in the Congress: but no Senator or Representative, or Person holding an Office of Trust or Profit under the United States, shall be appointed an Elector.

**Original method of electing the President and Vice-President.*—**[The Electors shall meet in their respective States, and vote by Ballot for two Persons, of whom one at least shall not be an Inhabitant of the same State with themselves. And they shall make a List of all the Persons voted for, and of the Number of Votes for each; which List they shall sign and certify, and transmit sealed to the Seat of the Government of the United States, directed to the President of the Senate. The President of the Senate shall, in the Presence of the Senate and House of Representatives, open all the Certificates, and the Votes shall then be counted. The Person having the greatest Number of Votes shall be the President, if such Number be a Majority of the whole Number of Electors appointed; and if there be more than one who have such Majority, and have an equal Number of Votes, then the House of Representatives shall immediately chuse by Ballot one of them for President; and if no person have a Majority, then from the five highest on the List the said House shall in like Manner chuse the President. But in chusing the President, the Votes shall be taken by States, the Representation from each State having one Vote; A quorum for this Purpose shall consist of a Member or Members from two thirds of the States, and a Majority of all the States shall be necessary to a Choice. In every Case, after the Choice of the President, the Person having the greatest Number of Votes of the Electors shall be the Vice President. But if there should remain two or more who have equal Votes, the Senate should chuse from them by Ballot the Vice President.]

**Congress may determine time of choosing electors and day for casting their votes.—**3. The Congress may determine the Time of chusing the Electors, and the Day on which they shall give their Votes; which Day shall be the same throughout the United States.

**Qualifications for the office of President.†**—4. No Person except a natural born Citizen, or a Citizen of the United States, at the time of the Adoption of this Constitution, shall be eligible to the Office of President; neither shall any Person be eligible to that Office who shall not have attained to the Age of thirty five Years, and been fourteen Years a Resident within the United States.

**Filling vacancy in the office of Presi-**dent.‡—5. In Case of the Removal of the President from Office, or of his Death, Resignation, or Inability to discharge the Powers and Duties of the said Office, the same shall devolve on the Vice President, and the Congress may by Law provide for the Case of Removal, Death, Resignation or Inability, both of the President and Vice President, declaring what Officer shall then act as President, and such Officer shall act accordingly, until the Disability be removed, or a President shall be elected.

**Compensation of the President.—**6. The President shall, at stated Times, receive for his Services, a Compensation, which shall neither be encreased nor diminished during the Period for which he shall have been elected, and he shall not receive within that Period any other Emolument from the United States, or any of them.

**Oath to be taken by the President.—**7. Before he enter on the Execution of his Office, he shall take the following Oath or Affirmation:—"I do solemnly swear (or affirm) that I will faithfully execute the Office of President of the United States, and will to the best of my Ability, preserve, protect and defend the Constitution of the United States."

### Section 2

**The President to be commander in chief of army and navy and head of executive departments; may grant reprieves and pardons.—**1. The President shall be Commander in Chief of the Army and Navy of the United States, and of the Militia of the several States, when called into the actual Service of the United States; he may require the Opinion, in writing, of the principal Officer in each of the executive Departments, upon any subject relating to the Duties of their respective Offices, and he shall have Power to grant Reprieves and Pardons for Offences against the United States, except in Cases of Impeachment.

**President may, with concurrence of Senate, make treaties, appoint ambassadors, etc.; appointment of inferior officers, authority of Congress over.—**2. He shall have Power, by and with the Advice and Consent of the Senate, to make Treaties, provided two thirds of the Senators present concur; and he shall nominate, and by and with the Advice and Consent of the Senate, shall appoint Ambassadors, other public Ministers and Consuls, Judges of the supreme Court, and all other Officers of the United States, whose Appointments are not herein otherwise provided for, and which shall be established by Law: but the Congress may by Law vest the Appointment of such inferior Officers, as they think proper, in the President alone, in

---

* This clause has been superseded by the 12th Amendment.
† For qualifications of the Vice President, see 12th Amendment.
‡ Amended by the 20th Amendment, Sections 3 and 4.

the Courts of Law, or in the Heads of Departments.

**President may fill vacancies in office during recess of Senate.**—3. The President shall have Power to fill up all Vacancies that may happen during the Recess of the Senate, by granting Commissions which shall expire at the End of their next Session.

### Section 3

**President to give advice to Congress; may convene or adjourn it on certain occasions; to receive ambassadors, etc.; have laws executed and commission all officers.**—He shall from time to time give to the Congress Information of the State of the Union, and recommend to their Consideration such Measures as he shall judge necessary and expedient; he may, on extraordinary Occasions, convene both Houses, or either of them, and in Case of Disagreement between them, with Respect to the Time of Adjournment, he may adjourn them to such Time as he shall think proper; he shall receive Ambassadors and other public Ministers; he shall take Care that the Laws be faithfully executed, and shall Commission all the Officers of the United States.

### Section 4

**All civil officers removable by impeachment.**—1. The President, Vice President and all civil Officers of the United States, shall be removed from Office on Impeachment for, and Conviction of, Treason, Bribery, or other high Crimes and Misdemeanors.

## ARTICLE III

### Section 1

**Judicial powers; how vested; term of office and compensation of judges.**—The judicial Power of the United States, shall be vested in one supreme Court, and in such inferior Courts as the Congress may from time to time ordain and establish. The Judges, both of the supreme and inferior Courts, shall hold their Offices during good Behaviour, and shall, at stated Times, receive for their Services, a Compensation, which shall not be diminished during their Continuance in Office.

### Section 2

**Jurisdiction of Federal courts.\***—1. The judicial Power shall extend to all Cases, in Law and Equity, arising under this Constitution, the Laws of the United States, and Treaties made, or which shall be made, under their Authority;—to all Cases affecting Ambassadors, other public Ministers and Consuls;—to all Cases of Admiralty and maritime Jurisdiction;—to Controversies to which the United States shall be a Party;—to Controversies between two or more States;—between a State and

Citizens of another State;—between Citizens of different States,—between Citizens of the same State claiming Lands under Grants of different States, and between a State, or the Citizens thereof, and foreign States, Citizens or Subjects.

**Original and appellate jurisdiction of Supreme Court.**—2. In all Cases affecting Ambassadors, other public Ministers and Consuls, and those in which a State shall be Party, the supreme Court shall have original Jurisdiction. In all the other Cases before mentioned, the supreme Court shall have appellate Jurisdiction, both as to Law and Fact, with such Exceptions, and under such Regulations as the Congress shall make.

**Trial of all crimes, except impeachment, to be by jury.**—3. The Trial of all Crimes, except in Cases of Impeachment, shall be by Jury; and such Trial shall be held in the State where the said Crimes shall have been committed; but when not committed within any State, the Trial shall be at such Place or Places as the Congress may by Law have directed.

### Section 3

**Treason defined; conviction of.**—1. Treason against the United States, shall consist only in levying War against them, or, in adhering to their Enemies, giving them Aid and Comfort. No Person shall be convicted of Treason unless on the Testimony of two Witnesses to the same overt Act, or on Confession in open Court.

**Congress to declare punishment for treason; proviso.**—2. The Congress shall have power to declare the Punishment of Treason, but no Attainder of Treason shall work Corruption of Blood, or Forfeiture except during the Life of the Person attainted.

## ARTICLE IV

### Section 1

**Each State to give full faith and credit to the public acts and records of other States.**—Full Faith and Credit shall be given in each State to the public Acts, Records, and judicial Proceedings of every other State. And the Congress may by general Laws prescribe the Manner in which such Acts, Records and Proceedings shall be proved, and the Effect thereof.

### Section 2

**Privileges of citizens.**—1. The Citizens of each State shall be entitled to all Privileges and Immunities of Citizens in the several States.

**Extradition between the several States.**—2. A Person charged in any State with Treason, Felony, or other Crime, who shall flee from Justice, and be found in another State, shall on Demand of the executive

---

\* This section is abridged by the 11th Amendment.

Authority of the State from which he fled, be delivered up, to be removed to the State having Jurisdiction of the Crime.

**Persons held to labor or service in one State, fleeing to another, to be returned.\*** —3. No Person held to Service or Labour in one State, under the Laws thereof, escaping into another, shall, in Consequence of any Law or Regulation therein, be discharged from such Service or Labour, but shall be delivered up on Claim of the Party to whom such Service or Labour may be due.

### Section 3

**New States.—**1. New States may be admitted by the Congress into this Union; but no new State shall be formed or erected within the Jurisdiction of any other State; nor any State be formed by the Junction of two or more States, or Parts of States, without the Consent of the Legislatures of the States concerned as well as of the Congress.

**Regulations concerning territory.—**2. The Congress shall have Power to dispose of and make all needful Rules and Regulations respecting the Territory or other Property belonging to the United States; and nothing in this Constitution shall be so construed as to Prejudice any Claims of the United States, or of any particular State.

### Section 4

**Republican form of government and protection guaranteed the several States.—** The United States shall guarantee to every State in this Union a Republican Form of Government, and shall protect each of them against Invasion; and on Application of the Legislature, or of the Executive (when the Legislature cannot be convened) against domestic Violence.

## ARTICLE V

**Ways in which the Constitution can be amended.—**The Congress, whenever two thirds of both Houses shall deem it necessary, shall propose Amendments to this Constitution, or, on the Application of the Legislatures of two thirds of the several States, shall call a Convention for proposing Amendments, which, in either Case, shall be valid to all Intents and Purposes, as Part of this Constitution, when ratified by the Legislatures of three fourths of the several States, or by Conventions in three fourths thereof, as the one or the other Mode of Ratification may be proposed by the Congress; Provided that no Amendment which may be made prior to the Year One thousand eight hundred and eight shall in any Manner affect the first and fourth Clauses in the Ninth Section of the first Article; and that no State, without its Consent, shall be deprived of its equal Suffrage in the Senate.

\* See the 13th Amendment.

## ARTICLE VI

**Debts contracted under the confederation secured.—**1. All Debts contracted and Engagements entered into, before the Adoption of this Constitution, shall be as valid against the United States under this Constitution, as under the Confederation.

**Constitution, laws and treaties of the United States to be supreme.—**2. This Constitution, and the Laws of the United States which shall be made in Pursuance thereof; and all Treaties made, or which shall be made, under the Authority of the United States, shall be the supreme Law of the Land; and the Judges in every State shall be bound thereby, any Thing in the Constitution or Laws of any State to the Contrary notwithstanding.

**Who shall take constitutional oath; no religious test as to official qualification.—** 3. The Senators and Representatives before mentioned, and the Members of the several State Legislatures, and all executive and judicial Officers, both of the United States and of the several States, shall be bound by Oath or Affirmation, to support this Constitution; but no religious Test shall ever be required as a Qualification to any Office or public Trust under the United States.

## ARTICLE VII

**Constitution to be considered adopted when ratified by nine States.—**The Ratification of the Conventions of nine States shall be sufficient for the Establishment of this Constitution between the States so ratifying the Same.

Done in Convention by the Unanimous Consent of the States present the Seventeenth Day of September in the Year of our Lord one thousand seven hundred and Eighty seven and of the Independence of the United States of America the Twelfth. In witness whereof We have hereunto subscribed our Names.

GO. WASHINGTON
*Presidt and Deputy from Virginia*

**NEW HAMPSHIRE**

John Langdon       Nicholas Gilman

**MASSACHUSETTS**

Nathaniel Gorham       Rufus King

**CONNECTICUT**

Wm Saml Johnson       Roger Sherman

**NEW YORK**

Alexander Hamilton

**NEW JERSEY**

Wil: Livingston       Wm Paterson
David Brearley       Jona: Dayton

**PENNSYLVANIA**

B Franklin       Thomas Mifflin
Robt Morris       Geo. Clymer
Thos FitzSimons       Jared Ingersoll
James Wilson       Gouv Morris

**DELAWARE**

Geo: Read       Gunning Bedford Jun
John Dickinson       Richard Bassett
Jaco: Broom

**MARYLAND**

James McHenry       Dan of St Thos Jenifer
Danl Carroll

VIRGINIA
John Blair —        James Madison Jr.

NORTH CAROLINA
Wm Blount        Richd Dobbs Spaight
Hu Williamson

SOUTH CAROLINA
J. Rutledge        Charles Cotesworth Pinckney.
Charles Pinckney        Pierce Butler

GEORGIA
William Few        Abr Baldwin
Attest: William Jackson, Secretary.

# AMENDMENTS TO THE CONSTITUTION OF THE UNITED STATES

(Amendments I to X inclusive, popularly known as the Bill of Rights, were proposed and sent to the states by the first session of the First Congress. They became effective Dec. 15, 1791.)

## ARTICLE I

**Freedom of religion, speech, of the press, and right of petition.**—Congress shall make no law respecting an establishment of religion, or prohibiting the free exercise thereof; or abridging the freedom of speech, or of the press; or the right of the people peaceably to assemble, and to petition the Government for a redress of grievances.

## ARTICLE II

**Right of people to bear arms not to be infringed.**—A well regulated Militia, being necessary to the security of a free State, the right of the people to keep and bear Arms, shall not be infringed.

## ARTICLE III

**Quartering of troops.**—No Soldier shall, in time of peace be quartered in any house, without the consent of the Owner, nor in time of war, but in a manner to be prescribed by law.

## ARTICLE IV

**Persons and houses to be secure from unreasonable searches and seizures.**—The right of the people to be secure in their persons, houses, papers, and effects, against unreasonable searches and seizures, shall not be violated, and no Warrants shall issue, but upon probable cause, supported by Oath or affirmation, and particularly describing the place to be searched, and the persons or things to be seized.

## ARTICLE V

**Trials for crimes; just compensation for private property taken for public use.**—No person shall be held to answer for a capital, or otherwise infamous crime, unless on a presentment or indictment of a Grand Jury, except in cases arising in the land or naval forces, or in the Militia, when in actual service in time of War or public danger; nor shall any person be subject for the same offence to be twice put in jeopardy of life or limb; nor shall be compelled in any criminal case to be a witness against himself, nor be deprived of life, liberty, or property, without due process of law; nor shall private property be taken for public use, without just compensation.

## ARTICLE VI

**Civil rights in trials for crimes enumerated.**—In all criminal prosecutions, the accused shall enjoy the right to a speedy and public trial, by an impartial jury of the State and district wherein the crime shall have been committed, which district shall have been previously ascertained by law, and to be informed of the nature and cause of the accusation; to be confronted with the witnesses against him; to have compulsory process for obtaining witnesses in his favor, and to have the Assistance of Counsel for his defence.

## ARTICLE VII

**Civil rights in civil suits.**—In Suits at common law, where the value in controversy shall exceed twenty dollars, the right of trial by jury shall be preserved, and no fact tried by a jury, shall be otherwise reexamined in any Court of the United States, than according to the rules of the common law.

## ARTICLE VIII

**Excessive bail, fines and punishments prohibited.**—Excessive bail shall not be required, nor excessive fines imposed, nor cruel and unusual punishments inflicted.

## ARTICLE IX

**Reserved rights of people.**—The enumeration in the Constitution, of certain rights, shall not be construed to deny or disparage others retained by the people.

## ARTICLE X

**Powers not delegated, reserved to states and people respectively.**—The powers not delegated to the United States by the Constitution, nor prohibited by it to the States, are reserved to the States respectively, or to the people.

## ARTICLE XI

(The proposed amendment was sent to the states Mar. 5, 1794, by the Third Congress. It became effective Jan. 8, 1798.)

**Judicial power of United States not to extend to suits against a State.**—The Judicial power of the United States shall not be construed to extend to any suit in law or equity, commenced or prosecuted against one of the United States by Citizens of another State, or by Citizens or Subjects of any Foreign State.

## ARTICLE XII

(The proposed amendment was sent to the states Dec. 12, 1803, by the Eighth Congress. It became effective Sept. 25, 1804.)

**Present mode of electing President and Vice-President by electors.\***—The Electors shall meet in their respective states, and vote by ballot for President and Vice-President, one of whom, at least, shall not be an inhabitant of the same state with themselves; they shall name in their ballots the person voted for as President, and in distinct ballots the person voted for as Vice-President, and they shall make distinct lists of all persons voted for as President, and of all persons voted for as Vice-President, and of the number of votes for each, which lists they shall sign and certify, and transmit sealed to the seat of the government of the United States, directed to the President of the Senate;—The President of the Senate shall, in the presence of the Senate and House of Representatives, open all the certificates and the votes shall then be counted;—The person having the greatest number of votes for President, shall be the President, if such number be a majority of the whole number of Electors appointed; and if no person have such majority, then from the persons having the highest numbers not exceeding three on the list of those voted for as President, the House of Representatives shall choose immediately, by ballot, the President. But in choosing the President, the votes shall be taken by states, the representation from each State having one vote; a quorum for this purpose shall consist of a member or members from two-thirds of the states, and a majority of all the states shall be necessary to a choice. And if the House of Representatives shall not choose a President whenever the right of choice shall devolve upon them, before the fourth day of March next following, then the Vice-President shall act as President, as in the case of the death or other constitutional disability of the President.—The person having the greatest number of votes as Vice-President, shall be the Vice-President, if such number be a majority of the whole number of Electors appointed, and if no person have a majority, then from the two highest numbers on the list, the Senate shall choose the Vice-President; a quorum for the purpose shall consist of two-thirds of the whole number of Senators, and a majority of the whole number shall be necessary to a choice. But no person constitutionally ineligible to the office of President shall be eligible to that of Vice-President of the United States.

## ARTICLE XIII

(The proposed amendment was sent to the states Feb. 1, 1865, by the Thirty-eighth Congress. It became effective Dec. 18, 1865.)

### Section 1

**Slavery prohibited.**—Neither slavery nor involuntary servitude, except as a punishment for crime whereof the party shall have been duly convicted, shall exist within the United States, or any place subject to their jurisdiction.

### Section 2

**Congress given power to enforce this article.**—Congress shall have power to enforce this article by appropriate legislation.

## ARTICLE XIV

(The proposed amendment was sent to the states June 16, 1866, by the Thirty-ninth Congress. It became effective July 28, 1868.)

### Section 1

**Citizenship defined; privileges of citizens.**—All persons born or naturalized in the United States, and subject to the jurisdiction thereof, are citizens of the United States and of the State wherein they reside. No State shall make or enforce any law which shall abridge the privileges or immunities of citizens of the United States; nor shall any State deprive any person of life, liberty, or property, without due process of law; nor deny to any person within its jurisdiction the equal protection of the laws.

### Section 2

**Apportionment of Representatives.**—Representatives shall be apportioned among the several States according to their respective numbers, counting the whole number of persons in each State, excluding Indians not taxed. But when the right to vote at any election for the choice of electors for President and Vice-President of the United States, Representatives in Congress, the Executive and Judicial officers of a State, or the members of the Legislature thereof, is denied to any of the male inhabitants of such State, being twenty-one years of age, and citizens of the United States, or in any way abridged, except for participation in rebellion, or other crime, the basis of representation therein shall be reduced in the proportion which the number of such male citizens shall bear to the whole number of male citizens twenty-one years of age in such State.

### Section 3

**Disqualification for office; removal of disability.**—No person shall be a Senator or Representative in Congress, or elector of President and Vice President, or hold any office, civil or military, under the United States, or under any State, who, having previously taken an oath, as a member of Congress, or as an officer of the United States, or as a member of any State legislature, or as an executive or judicial officer of any State, to support the Constitution of the United States, shall

---

\* Amended by the 20th Amendment, Sections 3 and 4.

have engaged in insurrection or rebellion against the same, or given aid or comfort to the enemies thereof. But Congress may by a vote of two-thirds of each House, remove such disability.

## Section 4

**Public debt not to be questioned; payment of debts and claims incurred in aid of rebellion forbidden.**—The validity of the public debt of the United States, authorized by law, including debts incurred for payment of pensions and bounties for services in suppressing insurrection or rebellion, shall not be questioned. But neither the United States nor any State shall assume or pay any debt or obligation incurred in aid of insurrection or rebellion against the United States, or any claim for the loss or emancipation of any slave; but all such debts, obligations and claims shall be held illegal and void.

## Section 5

**Congress given power to enforce this article.**—The Congress shall have power to enforce, by appropriate legislation, the provisions of this article.

## ARTICLE XV

(The proposed amendment was sent to the states Feb. 27, 1869, by the Fortieth Congress. It became effective Mar. 30, 1870.)

## Section 1

**Right of certain citizens to vote established.**—The right of citizens of the United States to vote shall not be denied or abridged by the United States or by any State on account of race, color, or previous condition of servitude.

## Section 2

**Congress given power to enforce this article.**—The Congress shall have power to enforce this article by appropriate legislation.

## ARTICLE XVI

(The proposed amendment was sent to the states July 12, 1909, by the Sixty-first Congress. It became effective Feb. 25, 1913.)

**Taxes on income; Congress given power to lay and collect.**—The Congress shall have power to lay and collect taxes on incomes, from whatever source derived, without apportionment among the several States, and without regard to any census or enumeration.

## ARTICLE XVII

(The proposed amendment was sent to the states May 16, 1912, by the Sixty-second Congress. It became effective May 31, 1913.)

**Election of United States Senators; filling of vacancies; qualifications of electors.**

1. The Senate of the United States shall be composed of two Senators from each State, elected by the people thereof, for six years; and each Senator shall have one vote. The electors in each State shall have the qualifications requisite for electors of the most numerous branch of the State legislatures.

2. When vacancies happen in the representation of any State in the Senate, the executive authority of such State shall issue writs of election to fill such vacancies: *Provided,* That the legislature of any State may empower the executive thereof to make temporary appointment until the people fill the vacancies by election as the legislature may direct.

3. This amendment shall not be so construed as to affect the election or term of any Senator chosen before it becomes valid as part of the Constitution.

## ARTICLE XVIII *

(The proposed amendment was sent to the states Dec. 18, 1917, by the Sixty-fifth Congress. It was approved by three-quarters of the states by Jan. 16, 1919, and became effective Jan. 16, 1920.)

**Manufacture, sale or transportation of intoxicating liquors, for beverage purposes, prohibited.**—1. After one year from the ratification of this article the manufacture, sale, or transportation of intoxicating liquors within, the importation thereof into, or the exportation thereof from the United States and all territory subject to the jurisdiction thereof for beverage purposes is hereby prohibited.

**Congress and the several States given concurrent power to pass appropriate legislation to enforce this article.**—2. The Congress and the several States shall have concurrent power to enforce this article by appropriate legislation.

**Provisions of article to become operative, when adopted by three-fourths of the States.**—3. This article shall be inoperative unless it shall have been ratified as an amendment to the Constitution by the legislatures of the several States, as provided in the Constitution, within seven years from the date of the submission hereof to the States by Congress.

## ARTICLE XIX

(The proposed amendment was sent to the states June 4, 1919, by the Sixty-sixth Congress. It became effective Aug. 26, 1920.)

**The right of citizens to vote shall not be denied because of sex.**—The right of citizens of the United States to vote shall not be denied or abridged by the United States or by any State on account of sex.

Congress shall have power to enforce this article by appropriate legislation.

## ARTICLE XX

(The proposed amendment, sometimes called the "Lame Duck Amendment," was sent to the states Mar. 3, 1932, by the Seventy-second Congress. It became effective Feb. 6, 1933; but, in accordance with Section 5, Sections 1 and 2 did not go into effect until Oct. 15, 1933.)

* Repealed by the 21st Amendment.

## Section 1

**Terms of President, Vice-President, Senators and Representatives.**—The terms of the President and Vice-President shall end at noon on the twentieth day of January, and the terms of Senators and Representatives at noon on the third day of January, of the years in which such terms would have ended if this article had not been ratified; and the terms of their successors shall then begin.

## Section 2

**Time of assembling Congress.**—The Congress shall assemble at least once in every year, and such meeting shall begin at noon on the third day of January, unless they shall by law appoint a different day.

## Section 3

**Filling vacancy in office of President.**— If, at the time fixed for the beginning of the term of the President, the President-elect shall have died, the Vice-President-elect shall become President. If a President shall not have been chosen before the time fixed for the beginning of his term, or if the President-elect shall have failed to qualify, then the Vice-President-elect shall act as President until a President shall have qualified; and the Congress may by law provide for the case wherein neither a President-elect nor a Vice-President-elect shall have qualified, declaring who shall then act as President, or the manner in which one who is to act shall be selected, and such person shall act accordingly until a President or Vice-President shall have qualified.

## Section 4

**Power of Congress in Presidential succession.**—The Congress may by law provide for the case of the death of any of the persons from whom the House of Representatives may choose a President whenever the right of choice shall have devolved upon them, and for the case of the death of any of the persons from whom the Senate may choose a Vice-President whenever the right of choice shall have devolved upon them.

## Section 5

**Time of taking effect.**—Sections 1 and 2 shall take effect on the 15th day of October following the ratification of this article.

## Section 6

**Ratification.**—This article shall be inoperative unless it shall have been ratified as an amendment to the Constitution by the legislatures of three-fourths of the several States within seven years from the date of its submission.

## ARTICLE XXI

(The proposed amendment was sent to the states Feb. 20, 1933, by the Seventy-second Congress. It became effective Dec. 5, 1933.)

## Section 1

**Repeal of Prohibition Amendment.**—The eighteenth article of amendment to the Constitution of the United States is hereby repealed.

## Section 2

**Transportation of intoxicating liquors.**— The transportation or importation into any State, Territory, or possession of the United States for delivery or use therein of intoxicating liquors, in violation of the laws thereof, is hereby prohibited.

## Section 3

**Ratification.**—This article shall be inoperative unless it shall have been ratified as an amendment to the Constitution by convention in the several States, as provided in the Constitution, within seven years from the date of the submission thereof to the States by the Congress.

## ARTICLE XXII

(The proposed amendment was sent to the states Mar. 21, 1947, by the Eightieth Congress. It became effective Feb. 26, 1951.)

## Section 1

**Limit to number of terms a President may serve.**—No person shall be elected to the office of the President more than twice, and no person who has held the office of President, or acted as President, for more than two years of a term to which some other person was elected President shall be elected to the office of the President more than once. But this Article shall not apply to any person holding the office of President when this Article was proposed by the Congress, and shall not prevent any person who may be holding the office of President, or acting as President, during the term within which this Article becomes operative from holding the office of President or acting as President during the remainder of such term.

## Section 2

**Ratification.**—This article shall be inoperative unless it shall have been ratified as an amendment to the Constitution by the legislatures of three-fourths of the several States within seven years from the date of its submission to the States by the Congress.

## ARTICLE XXIII

(The proposed amendment was sent to the states June 16, 1960, by the Eighty-sixth Congress. It became effective Mar. 29, 1961.)

### Section 1

**Electors for the District of Columbia.**— The District constituting the seat of Government of the United States shall appoint in such manner as the Congress may direct:

A number of electors of President and Vice President equal to the whole number of Senators and Representatives in Congress to which the District would be entitled if it were a State, but in no event more than the least populous State; they shall be in addiion to those appointed by the States, but they shall be considered, for the purposes of the election of President and Vice President, to be electors appointed by a State; and they shall meet in the District and perform such duties as provided by the twelfth article of amendment.

### Section 2

**Enforcement.**—The Congress shall have the power to enforce this article by appropriate legislation.

## HOW A PRESIDENT IS NOMINATED AND ELECTED

### Selection of Delegates

THE NATIONAL CONVENTIONS of both major parties are held sometime during the summer of a presidential-election year. Earlier, each party selects delegates by primaries, conventions, committees, etc.

For their 1960 National Convention, Democrats allowed each state 2½ votes for each Senator and Representative in Congress. Additional votes were allowed as follows: (a) ½ vote additional when the basic allocation resulted in a fractional vote; (b) additional votes for any state when required to make its total number of votes equal to the number the state had in the 1956 convention; and (c) ½ vote for each of the state's two members of the Democratic National Committee. Finally, the District of Columbia was given 8 votes, Puerto Rico 6, and the Virgin Islands and the Canal Zone 3 each, plus a vote for their National Committee members. The total number of votes thus provided was 1,521. Each state and territory was authorized to select either one delegate with a full vote or two delegates with ½ vote for each convention vote to which it was entitled (in addition to its National Committee members).

For their 1960 National Convention, Republicans allowed the following delegates: 4 delegates at-large from each state; 2 at-large for each Representative at-large in Congress from each state; 6 at-large from each state carried by the Republican candidate for President in the last presidential election, or electing, at that election or later, a Republican U. S. Senator or a governor; 1 delegate for each Congressional District casting 2,000 votes or more for the Republican candidate for President in the last presidential election or for the Republican nominee for the House of Representatives in the last congressional election; 1 delegate for each Congressional District casting 10,000 votes or more for the Republican candidate for President in the last presidential election or for the Republican nominee for the House of Representatives in the last congressional election. At the 1960 convention, the District of Columbia had 8 delegates at-large, Puerto Rico 3, and the Virgin Islands 1. The rules for the 1964 convention have not been changed for delegate membership, except that the District of Columbia will have 9 delegates, Puerto Rico 5, and the Virgin Islands 3.

Both parties provide for the selection of alternates. Republicans allow one alternate for each delegate. Democrats allow one alternate for each full convention vote.

### The Conventions

At each convention a temporary chairman is chosen. After a credentials committee seats the various delegates, a permanent chairman is elected. The convention then votes on a platform, drawn up by the platform committee.

By the third or fourth day, presidential nominations begin. The chairman calls the roll of states alphabetically. A state may place a candidate in nomination or yield to another state.

Voting, again alphabetically by voice vote, begins after all nominations have been made and seconded. A simple majority is required in each party, although this may require many ballots.

Finally, the vice-presidential candidate is selected. Although there is no law saying that the candidates *must* come from different states, it is practically necessary for this to be the case. Otherwise, according to the Constitution (*see* Amendment XII), electors from that state could vote for only one of the candidates and would have to cast their other vote for some person of another state. This could result in the awkward situation of a presidential candidate's receiving a majority electoral vote and his running mate's failing to.

### The Electoral College

The next step in the process is the nomination of electors in each state, according to its laws. These electors must not be Federal office holders. In the November election, the voters cast their votes for electors, not for President. In some states, the ballots include only the names of the presidential and vice-presidential candidates; in others, they include only names of the electors. Nowadays, it is rare for electors to be split between parties. The last such occurrence was in Tennessee in 1948* the last before that, in West Virginia in 1916. On three occasions (1824, 1876 and 1888), the presidential candidate with the largest popular vote failed to obtain an electoral-vote majority.

Each state has as many electors as it has Senators and Representatives. For the 1960 election, the total of electors was 537 (based on 100 Senators and 437 Representatives), of which 269 were needed to win.

On the first Monday after the second Wednesday in December, the electors cast their votes in their respective state capitols. Constitutionally they may vote for someone other than the party candidate but usually they do not since they are pledged to one party and its candidate on the ballot. Should the presidential or vice-presidential candidate die between the November election and the December meetings, the electors pledged to vote for him could vote for whomever they pleased. However, it seems certain that the national committee would attempt to get an agreement among the state party leaders for a replacement candidate.

The votes of the electors, certified by the states, are sent to Congress, where the president of the Senate opens the certificates and has them counted in the presence of both Houses on January 6. The new President is inaugurated at noon on January 20.

Should no candidate receive a majority of the electoral vote for President, the House of Representatives chooses a President from among the three highest candidates, voting, not as individuals, but as states, with a majority (now 26 needed to elect. Should no vice-presidential candidate obtain the majority, the Senate, voting as individuals, chooses from the highest two.

* In 1956, 1 of Alabama's 11 electoral votes was cast for Walter B. Jones. In 1960, 6 of Alabama's 11 electoral votes and 1 of Oklahoma's 8 electoral votes were cast for Harry Flood Byrd.

## Order of Presidential Succession

1. Vice President of the U. S.
2. Speaker of the House.
3. President pro tempore of the Senate.
4. Secretary of State.
5. Secretary of the Treasury.
6. Secretary of Defense.

7. Attorney General.
8. Postmaster General.
9. Secretary of the Interior.
10. Secretary of Agriculture.
11. Secretary of Commerce.
12. Secretary of Labor.

## How a Bill Becomes a Law

When a Senator or a Representative introduces a bill, he sends it to the clerk of his house, who gives it a number and title. This is the *first reading,* and the bill is referred to the proper committee.

The committee may decide the bill is unwise or unnecessary and *table* it, thus killing it at once. Or it may decide the bill is worthwhile and hold hearings to listen to facts and opinions presented by experts and other interested persons. After members of the committee have debated the bill and perhaps offered amendments, a vote is taken; and if the vote is favorable, the bill is sent back to the floor of the house.

The clerk reads the bill sentence by sentence to the house, and this is known as the *second reading.* Members may then debate the bill and offer amendments. In the House of Representatives, the time for debate is limited by a *cloture rule,* but there is no such restriction in the Senate except by a two-thirds vote for cloture. This makes possible a *filibuster,* in which one or more opponents hold the floor to defeat the bill.

The *third reading* is by title only, and the bill is put to a vote, which may be by voice or roll call, depending on the circumstances and parliamentary rules. Members who must be absent at the time but who wish to record their vote may be paired if each negative vote has a balancing affirmative one.

The bill then goes to the other house of Congress, where it may be defeated, or passed with or without amendments. If the bill is defeated, it dies. If it is passed with amendments, a joint Congressional committee must be appointed by both houses to iron out the differences.

After its final passage by both houses, the bill is sent to the President. If he approves, he signs it, and the bill becomes a law. However, if he disapproves, he *vetoes* the bill by refusing to sign it and sending it back to the house of origin with his reasons for the veto. The objections are read and debated, and a roll-call vote is taken. If the bill receives less than a two-thirds vote, it is defeated and goes no farther. But if it receives a two-thirds vote or greater, it is sent to the other house for a vote. If that house also passes it by a two-thirds vote, the President's veto is *overridden,* and the bill becomes a law.

Should the President desire neither to sign nor to veto the bill, he may retain it for ten days, Sundays excepted, after which time it automatically becomes a law without signature. However, if Congress has adjourned within those ten days, the bill is automatically killed, that process of indirect rejection being known as a *pocket veto.*

# U. S. National Conventions Since 1856

| Opening date | Party | Where held | Presidential nominee | Vote |
|---|---|---|---|---|
| June 17, 1856 | R | Philadelphia | John C. Frémont | 520 |
| June 2, 1856 | D | Cincinnati | James Buchanan | 296 |
| May 16, 1860 | R | Chicago | Abraham Lincoln | 364 |
| April 23, 1860 | D | Charleston & Baltimore | S. A. Douglas | 181 |
| June 7, 1864 | R[1] | Baltimore | Abraham Lincoln | Unanimous |
| Aug. 29, 1864 | D | Chicago | Geo. B. McClellan | 202½ |
| May 20, 1868 | R | Chicago | U. S. Grant | Unanimous |
| July 4, 1868 | D | New York City | Horatio Seymour | Unanimous |
| June 5, 1872 | R | Philadelphia | U. S. Grant | Unanimous |
| June 9, 1872 | D | Baltimore | Horace Greeley | 688 |
| June 14, 1876 | R | Cincinnati | R. B. Hayes | 384 |
| June 28, 1876 | D | St. Louis | S. J. Tilden | 508 |
| June 2, 1880 | R | Chicago | J. A. Garfield | 399 |
| June 23, 1880 | D | Cincinnati | W. S. Hancock | 705 |
| June 3, 1884 | R | Chicago | J. G. Blaine | 541 |
| July 11, 1884 | D | Chicago | Grover Cleveland | 683 |
| June 19, 1888 | R | Chicago | Benjamin Harrison | 544 |
| June 6, 1888 | D | St. Louis | Grover Cleveland | By acclamation |
| June 7, 1892 | R | Minneapolis | Benjamin Harrison | 535⅙ |
| June 21, 1892 | D | Chicago | Grover Cleveland | 617½ |
| June 16, 1896 | R | St. Louis | William McKinley | 661½ |
| July 7, 1896 | D | Chicago | William J. Bryan | 500 |
| June 19, 1900 | R | Philadelphia | William McKinley | Unanimous |
| July 4, 1900 | D | Kansas City | William J. Bryan | By acclamation |
| June 21, 1904 | R | Chicago | Theodore Roosevelt | Unanimous |
| July 6, 1904 | D | St. Louis | Alton B. Parker | 678 |
| June 16, 1908 | R | Chicago | William H. Taft | 702 |
| July 7, 1908 | D | Denver | William J. Bryan | 892½ |
| June 18, 1912 | R | Chicago | William H. Taft | 561 |
| June 25, 1912 | D | Baltimore | Woodrow Wilson | 990 |
| June 7, 1916 | R | Chicago | Charles E. Hughes | 949½ |
| June 14, 1916 | D | St. Louis | Woodrow Wilson | By acclamation |
| June 8, 1920 | R | Chicago | Warren G. Harding | 692⅕ |
| June 28, 1920 | D | San Francisco | James M. Cox | 732½ |
| June 10, 1924 | R | Cleveland | Calvin Coolidge | 1,065 |
| June 24, 1924[2] | D | New York City | John W. Davis | 839[3] |
| June 12, 1928 | R | Kansas City | Herbert Hoover | 837 |
| June 26, 1928 | D | Houston | Alfred E. Smith | 849½ |
| June 14, 1932 | R | Chicago | Herbert Hoover | 1,126½ |
| June 27, 1932 | D | Chicago | F. D. Roosevelt | 945 |
| June 9, 1936 | R | Cleveland | Alfred M. Landon | 984 |
| June 23, 1936 | D | Philadelphia | F. D. Roosevelt | By acclamation |
| June 24, 1940 | R | Philadelphia | Wendell L. Willkie | Unanimous |
| July 15, 1940 | D | Chicago | F. D. Roosevelt | Unanimous |
| June 26, 1944 | R | Chicago | Thomas E. Dewey | 1,056 |
| July 19, 1944 | D | Chicago | F. D. Roosevelt | 1,086–90 |
| June 21, 1948 | R | Philadelphia | Thomas E. Dewey | 1,094–0 |
| July 12, 1948 | D | Philadelphia | Harry S. Truman | 947½–263½ |
| July 17, 1948 | ([4]) | Birmingham | J. Strom Thurmond | By acclamation |
| July 22, 1948 | ([5]) | Philadelphia | Henry A. Wallace | By acclamation |
| July 7, 1952 | R | Chicago | Dwight D. Eisenhower | 845–361 |
| July 21, 1952 | D | Chicago | Adlai E. Stevenson | By acclamation |
| Aug. 20, 1956 | R | San Francisco | Dwight D. Eisenhower | Unanimous |
| Aug. 13, 1956 | D | Chicago | Adlai E. Stevenson | By acclamation |
| July 25, 1960 | R | Chicago | Richard M. Nixon | Unanimous |
| July 11, 1960 | D | Los Angeles | John F. Kennedy | Unanimous |

[1] The Convention adopted name Union party to attract War Democrats and others favoring prosecution of war. [2] In session until July 10, 1924. [3] 103d ballot. [4] States' Rights delegates from 13 Southern states. [5] Progressive party. NOTE: For allocation of convention votes to states, 1956 and 1960, see Conventions, National in Index.

# National Committee Chairmen Since 1921

*Source:* Republican and Democratic National Committees.

| Chairman and (state) | Term | Chairman and (state) | Term |
|---|---|---|---|
| **Republican** | | Meade Alcorn (Conn.) | 1957–59 |
| John T. Adams (Iowa) | 1921–24 | Thruston B. Morton (Ky.) | 1959–61 |
| William M. Butler (Mass.) | 1924–28 | William E. Miller (N. Y.) | 1961– |
| Hubert Work (Colo.) | 1928–29 | **Democratic** | |
| Claudius H. Huston (Tenn.) | 1929–30 | Cordell Hull (Tenn.) | 1921–24 |
| Simeon D. Fess (Ohio) | 1930–32 | Clem Shaver (W. Va.) | 1924–28 |
| Everett Sanders (Ind.) | 1932–34 | John J. Raskob (N. Y.) | 1928–32 |
| Henry P. Fletcher (Pa.) | 1934–36 | James A. Farley (N. Y.) | 1932–40 |
| John Hamilton (Kans.) | 1936–40 | Edward J. Flynn (N. Y.) | 1940–43 |
| Joseph W. Martin, Jr. (Mass.) | 1940–42 | Frank C. Walker (Mont.) | 1943–44 |
| Harrison E. Spangler (Iowa) | 1942–44 | Robert E. Hannegan (Mo.) | 1944–47 |
| Herbert Brownell, Jr. (N. Y.) | 1944–46 | J. Howard McGrath (R. I.) | 1947–49 |
| Carroll Reece (Tenn.) | 1946–48 | William M. Boyle, Jr. (Mo.) | 1949–51 |
| Hugh D. Scott, Jr. (Pa.) | 1948–49 | Frank E. McKinney (Ind.) | 1951–52 |
| Guy G. Gabrielson (N. J.) | 1949–52 | Stephen A. Mitchell (Ill.) | 1952–54 |
| Arthur E. Summerfield (Mich.) | 1952–53 | Paul M. Butler (Ind.) | 1955–60 |
| C. Wesley Roberts (Kans.) | 1953–53 | Henry M. Jackson (Wash.) | 1960–61 |
| Leonard W. Hall (N. Y.) | 1953–57 | John M. Bailey (Conn.) | 1961– |

**Republican National Committee:** 1625 Eye St. NW., Washington 6, D. C.
**Democratic National Committee:** 1730 K St. NW., Washington 6, D. C.

# The Confederate States of America

| State | Seceded from Union | Readmitted to Union | State | Seceded from Union | Readmitted to Union |
|---|---|---|---|---|---|
| 1. South Carolina | Dec. 20, 1860 | July 18, 1868 | 7. Texas | Mar. 2, 1861 | Mar. 30, 1870 |
| 2. Mississippi | Jan. 9, 1861 | Feb. 23, 1870 | 8. Virginia | Apr. 17, 1861 | Jan. 27, 1870 |
| 3. Florida | Jan. 10, 1861 | June 25, 1868 | 9. Arkansas | May 6, 1861 | June 22, 1868 |
| 4. Alabama | Jan. 11, 1861 | July 13, 1868 | 10. North Carolina | May 20, 1861 | July 20, 1868 |
| 5. Georgia | Jan. 19, 1861 | July 15, 1870 | 11. Tennessee | June 24, 1861 | July 24, 1866 |
| 6. Louisiana | Jan. 26, 1861 | May 26, 1865 | | | |

NOTE: 4 other slave states—Delaware, Kentucky, Maryland and Missouri—remained in the Union.

## Facts About Elections

Candidate with highest popular vote: Eisenhower (1956), 35,581,003.

Candidate with highest electoral vote: F. D. Roosevelt (1936), 523.

Candidate carrying most states: F. D. Roosevelt (1936), 46.

Candidate running most times: Norman Thomas, 6 (1928, 1932, 1936, 1940, 1944, 1948).

Candidate elected, defeated, then re-elected: Cleveland (1884, 1888, 1892).

## Election of 1876

In the election of 1876 Samuel J. Tilden, the Democratic candidate, received a popular majority but lacked one undisputed electoral vote to carry a clear majority of the electoral college. The crux of the problem was in the 22 electoral votes which were in dispute because Florida, Louisiana, South Carolina and Oregon each sent in 2 sets of election returns. In the 3 southern states Republican election boards threw out enough Democratic votes to certify the Republican candidate, Hayes. In Oregon, the Democratic governor disqualified a Republican elector, replacing him with a Democrat. Since the Senate was Republican and the House of Representatives Democrat, it seemed useless to refer the disputed returns to the two houses for solution. Instead Congress appointed an Electoral Commission with 5 representatives each from the Senate, the House and the Supreme Court. All but one Justice was named, giving the Commission 7 Republican and 7 Democratic members. The naming of the fifth Justice was left to the other four. He was a Republican who first favored Tilden but, under pressure from his party, switched to Hayes, ensuring his election by the Commission voting 8 to 7 on party lines.

## Election of 1872

The presidential and vice-presidential candidates of the Liberal Republicans and the northern Democrats in 1872 were Horace Greeley and B. Gatz Brown. Since Greeley died on November 29, before the electoral college could vote, his 66 electoral votes were cast for other opponents of Grant.

# Presidential Elections, 1789 to 1960

| Year | Presidential candidates | Party | Electoral vote | Year | Presidential candidates | Party | Electoral vote |
|------|-------------------------|-------|----------------|------|-------------------------|-------|----------------|
| 1789[1,2] | George Washington | (no party) | 69 | 1796[1] | John Adams | Federalist | 71 |
|  | John Adams | (no party) | 34 |  | Thomas Jefferson | Dem.-Rep. | 68 |
|  | Scattering | (no party) | 35 |  | Thomas Pinckney | Federalist | 59 |
|  | Votes not cast |  | 8 |  | Aaron Burr | Dem.-Rep. | 30 |
| 1792[1] | George Washington | Federalist | 132 |  | Scattering |  | 48 |
|  | John Adams | Federalist | 77 | 1800[1,3] | Thomas Jefferson | Dem.-Rep. | 73 |
|  | George Clinton | Anti-Federalist | 50 |  | Aaron Burr | Dem.-Rep. | 73 |
|  | Thomas Jefferson | Anti-Federalist | 4 |  | John Adams | Federalist | 65 |
|  | Aaron Burr | Anti-Federalist | 1 |  | Charles C. Pinckney | Federalist | 64 |
|  | Votes not cast |  | 6 |  | John Jay | Federalist | 1 |

[1] For the original method of electing the President and the Vice President, *see* Article II, Section 1, of the Constitution. [2] Only 10 states participated in the election. The New York legislature chose no electors, and North Carolina and Rhode Island had not yet ratified the Constitution. [3] As Jefferson and Burr were tied, the House of Representatives chose the President. In a vote by states, 10 votes were cast for Jefferson, 4 for Burr; 2 votes were not cast.

| Year | Presidential candidates | Party | Electoral vote | Vice-presidential candidates | Party | Electoral vote |
|------|-------------------------|-------|----------------|------------------------------|-------|----------------|
| 1804[1] | Thomas Jefferson | Dem.-Rep. | 162 | George Clinton | Dem.-Rep. | 162 |
|  | Charles C. Pinckney | Federalist | 14 | Rufus King | Federalist | 14 |
| 1808 | James Madison | Dem.-Rep. | 122 | George Clinton | Dem.-Rep. | 113 |
|  | Charles C. Pinckney | Federalist | 47 | Rufus King | Federalist | 47 |
|  | George Clinton | Dem.-Rep. | 6 | John Langdon | Ind. (no party) | 9 |
|  | Votes not cast |  | 1 | James Madison | Dem.-Rep. | 3 |
|  |  |  |  | James Monroe | Dem.-Rep. | 3 |
|  |  |  |  | Votes not cast |  | 1 |
| 1812 | James Madison | Dem.-Rep. | 128 | Elbridge Gerry | Dem.-Rep. | 131 |
|  | De Witt Clinton | Federalist | 89 | Jared Ingersoll | Federalist | 86 |
|  | Votes not cast |  | 1 | Votes not cast |  | 1 |
| 1816 | James Monroe | Dem.-Rep. | 183 | Daniel D. Tompkins | Dem.-Rep. | 183 |
|  | Rufus King | Federalist | 34 | John E. Howard | Federalist | 22 |
|  | Votes not cast |  | 4 | James Ross | Ind. (no party) | 5 |
|  |  |  |  | John Marshall | Federalist | 4 |
|  |  |  |  | Robert G. Harper | Ind. (no party) | 3 |
|  |  |  |  | Votes not cast |  | 4 |
| 1820 | James Monroe | Dem.-Rep. | 231 | Daniel D. Tompkins | Dem.-Rep. | 218 |
|  | John Quincy Adams | Ind. (no party) | 1 | Richard Stockton | Ind. (no party) | 8 |
|  | Votes not cast |  | 3 | Daniel Rodney | Ind. (no party) | 4 |
|  |  |  |  | Richard Rush | Ind. (no party) | 1 |
|  |  |  |  | Robert G. Harper | Ind. (no party) | 1 |
|  |  |  |  | Votes not cast |  | 3 |
| 1824[2] | John Quincy Adams | (no party) | 84 | John C. Calhoun | (no party) | 182 |
|  | Andrew Jackson | (no party) | 99 | Nathan Sanford | (no party) | 30 |
|  | William H. Crawford | (no party) | 41 | Nathaniel Macon | (no party) | 24 |
|  | Henry Clay | (no party) | 37 | Andrew Jackson | (no party) | 13 |
|  |  |  |  | Martin Van Buren | (no party) | 9 |
|  |  |  |  | Henry Clay | (no party) | 2 |
|  |  |  |  | Votes not cast |  | 1 |
| 1828 | Andrew Jackson | Democratic | 178 | John C. Calhoun | Democratic | 171 |
|  | John Quincy Adams | Natl. Rep. | 83 | Richard Rush | Natl. Rep. | 83 |
|  |  |  |  | William Smith | Democratic | 7 |
| 1832 | Andrew Jackson | Democratic | 219 | Martin Van Buren | Democratic | 189 |
|  | Henry Clay | Natl. Rep. | 49 | John Sergeant | Natl. Rep. | 49 |
|  | John Floyd | Ind. (no party) | 11 | Henry Lee | Ind. (no party) | 11 |
|  | William Wirt[3] | Antimasonic | 7 | Amos Ellmaker | Antimasonic | 7 |
|  | Votes not cast |  | 2 | William Wilkins | Ind. (no party) | 30 |
|  |  |  |  | Votes not cast |  | 2 |
| 1836 | Martin Van Buren | Democratic | 170 | Richard M. Johnson[4] | Democratic | 147 |
|  | William H. Harrison | Whig | 73 | Francis Granger | Whig | 77 |
|  | Hugh L. White | Whig | 26 | John Tyler | Democratic | 47 |
|  | Daniel Webster | Whig | 14 | William Smith | Ind. (no party) | 23 |
|  | W. P. Mangum | Ind. (no party) | 11 |  |  |  |
| 1840 | William H. Harrison[5] | Whig | 234 | John Tyler | Whig | 234 |
|  | Martin Van Buren | Democratic | 60 | Richard M. Johnson | Democratic | 48 |
|  |  |  |  | L. W. Tazewell | Ind. (no party) | 11 |
|  |  |  |  | James K. Polk | Democratic | 1 |

## Presidential Elections (continued)

| Year | Presidential candidates | Party | Electoral vote | Vice-presidential candidates | Party | Electoral vote |
|---|---|---|---|---|---|---|
| 1844 | James K. Polk | Democratic | 170 | George M. Dallas | Democratic | 170 |
|  | Henry Clay | Whig | 105 | Theo. Frelinghuysen | Whig | 105 |
| 1848 | Zachary Taylor[6] | Whig | 163 | Millard Fillmore | Whig | 163 |
|  | Lewis Cass | Democratic | 127 | William O. Butler | Democratic | 127 |
| 1852 | Franklin Pierce | Democratic | 254 | William R. King | Democratic | 254 |
|  | Winfield Scott | Whig | 42 | William A. Graham | Whig | 42 |
| 1856 | James Buchanan | Democratic | 174 | John C. Breckinridge | Democratic | 174 |
|  | John C. Frémont | Republican | 114 | William L. Dayton | Republican | 114 |
|  | Millard Fillmore | American[7] | 8 | A. J. Donelson | American[7] | 8 |
| 1860 | Abraham Lincoln | Republican | 180 | Hannibal Hamlin | Republican | 180 |
|  | John C. Breckinridge | Democratic | 72 | Joseph Lane | Democratic | 72 |
|  | John Bell | Const. Union | 39 | Edward Everett | Const. Union | 39 |
|  | Stephen A. Douglas | Democratic | 12 | H. V. Johnson | Democratic | 12 |
| 1864 | Abraham Lincoln[8] | Union[10] | 212 | Andrew Johnson | Union[10] | 212 |
|  | George B. McClellan | Democratic | 21 | G. H. Pendleton | Democratic | 21 |
| 1868 | Ulysses S. Grant | Republican | 214 | Schuyler Colfax | Republican | 214 |
|  | Horatio Seymour | Democratic | 80 | Francis P. Blair, Jr. | Democratic | 80 |
|  | Votes not counted[9] |  | 23 | Votes not counted[9] |  | 23 |

[1] The first election in wh.ch the electors voted for President and Vice President on separate ballots. (*See* Amendment XII to the Constitution.)   [2] As no candidate had an electoral-vote majority, the House of Representatives chose the President from the first three. In a vote by states, 13 votes were cast for Adams, 7 for Jackson, and 4 for Crawford. [3] The Antimasonic party on Sept. 26, 1831, was the first party to hold a nominating convention to choose candidates for President and Vice President.   [4] As Johnson did not have an electoral-vote majority, the Senate chose him 33–14 over Granger, the others being legally out of the race.   [5] Harrison died Apr. 4, 1841, and Tyler succeeded him Apr. 6. [6] Taylor died July 9, 1850, and Fillmore succeeded him July 10.   [7] Also known as the Know-Nothing party.   [8] Lincoln died Apr. 15, 1865, and Johnson succeeded him the same day.   [9] 23 Southern electoral votes were excluded.   [10] Name adopted by the Republican National Convention of 1864. Johnson was a War Democrat.

| Year | Presidential candidates | Party | Electoral vote | Popular vote | Vice-presidential candidates and party |
|---|---|---|---|---|---|
| 1872 | Ulysses S. Grant | Republican | 286 | 3,597,132 | Henry Wilson—R |
|  | Horace Greeley | Dem., Liberal Rep. | ([1]) | 2,834,125 | B. Gratz Brown—D, LR—(47) |
|  | Thomas A. Hendricks | Democratic | 42 |  | Scattering—(19) |
|  | B. Gratz Brown | Dem., Liberal Rep. | 18 |  | Votes not counted—(14) |
|  | Charles J. Jenkins | Democratic | 2 |  |  |
|  | David Davis | Democratic | 1 |  |  |
|  | Votes not counted |  | 17 |  |  |
| 1876[2] | Rutherford B. Hayes | Republican | 185 | 4,033,768 | William A. Wheeler—R |
|  | Samuel J. Tilden | Democratic | 184 | 4,285,992 | Thomas A. Hendricks—D |
|  | Peter Cooper | Greenback | 0 | 81,737 | Samuel F. Cary—G |
| 1880 | James A. Garfield[3] | Republican | 214 | 4,449,053 | Chester A. Arthur—R |
|  | Winfield S. Hancock | Democratic | 155 | 4,442,035 | William H. English—D |
|  | James B. Weaver | Greenback | 0 | 308,578 | B. J. Chambers—G |
| 1884 | Grover Cleveland | Democratic | 219 | 4,911,017 | Thomas A. Hendricks—D |
|  | James G. Blaine | Republican | 182 | 4,848,334 | John A. Logan—R |
|  | Benjamin F. Butler | Greenback | 0 | 175,370 | A. M. West—G |
|  | John P. St. John | Prohibition | 0 | 150,369 | William Daniel—P |
| 1888 | Benjamin Harrison | Republican | 233 | 5,440,216 | Levi P. Morton—R |
|  | Grover Cleveland | Democratic | 168 | 5,538,233 | A. G. Thurman—D |
|  | Clinton B. Fisk | Prohibition | 0 | 249,506 | John A. Brooks—P |
|  | Alson J. Streeter | Union Labor | 0 | 146,935 | Charles E. Cunningham—UL |
| 1892 | Grover Cleveland | Democratic | 277 | 5,556,918 | Adlai E. Stevenson—D |
|  | Benjamin Harrison | Republican | 145 | 5,176,108 | Whitelaw Reid—R |
|  | James B. Weaver | People's[4] | 22 | 1,041,028 | James G. Field—Peo |
|  | John Bidwell | Prohibition | 0 | 264,133 | James B. Cranfill—P |
| 1896 | William McKinley | Republican | 271 | 7,035,638 | Garret A. Hobart—R |
|  | William J. Bryan | Dem., People's[4] | 176 | 6,467,946 | Arthur Sewall—D—(149) |
|  |  |  |  |  | Thomas E. Watson—Peo—(27) |
|  | John M. Palmer | Natl. Dem. | 0 | 133,148 | Simon B. Buckner—ND |
|  | Joshua Levering | Prohibition | 0 | 132,007 | Hale Johnson—P |

| Year | Presidential candidates | Party | Electoral vote | Popular vote [1] | Vice-presidential candidates and party |
|---|---|---|---|---|---|
| **1900** | William McKinley[5] | Republican | 292 | 7,219,530 | Theodore Roosevelt—R |
| | William J. Bryan | Dem., People's[4] | 155 | 6,358,071 | Adlai E. Stevenson—D, Peo |
| | John G. Woolley | Prohibition | 0 | 208,914 | Henry B. Metcalf—P |
| | Eugene V. Debs | Social Democratic | 0 | 94,768 | Job Harriman—SD |
| **1904** | Theodore Roosevelt | Republican | 336 | 7,628,834 | Charles W. Fairbanks—R |
| | Alton B. Parker | Democratic | 140 | 5,084,491 | Henry G. Davis—D |
| | Eugene V. Debs | Socialist | 0 | 402,400 | Benjamin Hanford—S |
| | Silas C. Swallow | Prohibition | 0 | 258,536 | George W. Carroll—P |
| | Thomas E. Watson | People's | 0 | 117,183 | Thomas H. Tibbles—Peo |
| **1908** | William H. Taft | Republican | 321 | 7,679,006 | James S. Sherman—R |
| | William J. Bryan | Democratic | 162 | 6,409,106 | John W. Kern—D |
| | Eugene V. Debs | Socialist | 0 | 420,820 | Benjamin Hanford—S |
| | Eugene W. Chafin | Prohibition | 0 | 253,840 | Aaron S. Watkins—P |
| | Thomas L. Hisgen | Independence | 0 | 82,872 | John T. Graves—I |
| **1912** | Woodrow Wilson | Democratic | 435 | 6,286,214 | Thomas R. Marshall—D |
| | Theodore Roosevelt | Progressive | 88 | 4,126,020 | Hiram Johnson—Prog |
| | William H. Taft | Republican | 8 | 3,483,922 | Nicholas M. Butler—R[6] |
| | Eugene V. Debs | Socialist | 0 | 897,011 | Emil Seidel—S |
| | Eugene W. Chafin | Prohibition | 0 | 206,275 | Aaron S. Watkins—P |
| **1916** | Woodrow Wilson | Democratic | 277 | 9,129,606 | Thomas R. Marshall—D |
| | Charles E Hughes | Republican | 254 | 8,538,221 | Charles W. Fairbanks—R |
| | A. L. Benson | Socialist | 0 | 585,113 | G. R. Kirkpatrick—S |
| | J. Frank Hanly | Prohibition | 0 | 220,506 | Ira Landrith—P |
| **1920** | Warren G. Harding[7] | Republican | 404 | 16,152,200 | Calvin Coolidge—R |
| | James M. Cox | Democratic | 127 | 9,147,353 | Franklin D. Roosevelt—D |
| | Eugene V. Debs | Socialist | 0 | 917,799 | Seymour Stedman—S |
| | P. P. Christensen | Farmer-Labor | 0 | 265,411 | Max S. Hayes—FL |
| | Aaron S. Watkins | Prohibition | 0 | 189,408 | D. Leigh Colvin—P |
| **1924** | Calvin Coolidge | Republican | 382 | 15,725,016 | Charles G. Dawes—R |
| | John W. Davis | Democratic | 136 | 8,385,586 | Charles W. Bryan—D |
| | Robert M. LaFollette | Progressive, Socialist | 13 | 4,822,856 | Burton K. Wheeler—Prog S |
| **1928** | Herbert Hoover | Republican | 444 | 21,392,190 | Charles Curtis—R |
| | Alfred E. Smith | Democratic | 87 | 15,016,443 | Joseph T. Robinson—D |
| **1932** | Franklin D. Roosevelt | Democratic | 472 | 22,821,857 | John N. Garner—D |
| | Herbert Hoover | Republican | 59 | 15,761,841 | Charles Curtis—R |
| **1936** | Franklin D. Roosevelt | Democratic | 523 | 27 751,597 | John N. Garner—D |
| | Alfred M. Landon | Republican | 8 | 16,679,583 | Frank Knox—R |
| **1940** | Franklin D. Roosevelt | Democratic | 449 | 27,244,160 | Henry A. Wallace—D |
| | Wendell L. Willkie | Republican | 82 | 22,305,198 | Charles L. McNary—R |
| **1944** | Franklin D. Roosevelt[8] | Democratic | 432 | 25,602,504 | Harry S. Truman—D |
| | Thomas E. Dewey | Republican | 99 | 22,006,285 | John W. Bricker—R |
| **1948** | Harry S. Truman | Democratic | 303 | 24,105,695 | Alben W. Barkley—D |
| | Thomas E. Dewey | Republican | 189 | 21,969,170 | Earl Warren—R |
| | J. Strom Thurmond | States' Rights Dem. | 39 | 1,169,021 | Fielding L. Wright—SR |
| | Henry A. Wallace | Progressive | 0 | 1,156,103 | Glen Taylor—Prog |
| **1952** | Dwight D. Eisenhower | Republican | 442 | 33,824,351 | Richard M. Nixon—R |
| | Adlai E. Stevenson | Democratic | 89 | 27,314,987 | John J. Sparkman—D |
| **1956**[9] | Dwight D. Eisenhower | Republican | 457 | 35,581,003 | Richard M. Nixon—R |
| | Adlai E. Stevenson | Democratic | 73 | 26,031,322 | Estes Kefauver—D |
| **1960**[10] | John F. Kennedy | Democratic | 303 | 34,221,485 | Lyndon B. Johnson—D |
| | Richard M. Nixon | Republican | 219 | 34,108,684 | Henry Cabot Lodge—R |

[1] See Election of 1872 in Index.  [2] See Election of 1876 in Index.  [3] Garfield died Sept. 19, 1881, and Arthur succeeded him Sept. 20.  [4] The members of the People's party were known as Populists.  [5] McKinley died Sept. 14, 1901, and Roosevelt succeeded him the same day.  [6] James S. Sherman, Republican candidate for Vice President, died Oct. 30, 1912, and the Republican electoral votes were cast for Butler.  [7] Harding died Aug. 2, 1923, and Coolidge succeeded him Aug. 3.  [8] Roosevelt died Apr. 12, 1945, and Truman succeeded him the same day.  [9] One electoral vote from Alabama was cast for Walter B. Jones.  [10] Sen. Harry F. Byrd received 15 electoral votes.

# Electoral Vote
## for President, 1888-1924

| States | 1888 | | 1892 | | | 1896 | | 1900 | | 1904 | | 1908 | | 1912 | | | 1916 | | 1920 | | 1924 | | |
|---|---|---|---|---|---|---|---|---|---|---|---|---|---|---|---|---|---|---|---|---|---|---|---|
| | Harrison, Rep. | Cleveland, Dem. | Cleveland, Dem. | Harrison, Rep. | Weaver, Peo. | McKinley, Rep. | Bryan, Dem. | McKinley, Rep. | Bryan, Dem. | Roosevelt, Rep. | Parker, Dem. | Taft, Rep. | Bryan, Dem. | Wilson, Dem. | Taft, Rep. | Roosevelt, Prog. | Wilson, Dem. | Hughes, Rep. | Harding, Rep. | Cox, Dem. | Coolidge, Rep. | Davis, Dem. | LaFollette, Prog. |
| Alabama | | 10 | 11 | | | | 11 | | 11 | | 11 | | 11 | 12 | | | 12 | | | 12 | | 12 | |
| Arizona | | | | | | | | | | | | | | 3 | | | 3 | | | 3 | | 3 | |
| Arkansas | | 7 | 8 | | | | 8 | | 8 | | 9 | | 9 | 9 | | | 9 | | | 9 | | 9 | |
| California | 8 | | 8 | 1 | | 8 | 1 | 9 | | 10 | | 10 | | 2 | | 11 | 13 | | 13 | | 13 | | |
| Colorado | 3 | | | | 4 | | 4 | | 4 | 5 | | | 5 | 6 | | | 6 | | 6 | | 6 | | |
| Connecticut | | 6 | 6 | | | 6 | | 6 | | 7 | | 7 | | 7 | | | | 7 | 7 | | 7 | | |
| Delaware | | 3 | 3 | | | 3 | | 3 | | 3 | | 3 | | 3 | | | | 3 | 3 | | 3 | | |
| Florida | | 4 | 4 | | | | 4 | | 4 | | 5 | | 5 | 6 | | | 6 | | | 6 | | 6 | |
| Georgia | | 12 | 13 | | | | 13 | | 13 | | 13 | | 13 | 14 | | | 14 | | | 14 | | 14 | |
| Idaho | | | | | 3 | | 3 | | 3 | 3 | | 3 | | 4 | | | 4 | | 4 | | 4 | | |
| Illinois | 22 | | 24 | | | 24 | | 24 | | 27 | | 27 | | 29 | | | | 29 | 29 | | 29 | | |
| Indiana | 15 | | 15 | | | 15 | | 15 | | 15 | | 15 | | 15 | | | | 15 | 15 | | 15 | | |
| Iowa | 13 | | | 13 | | 13 | | 13 | | 13 | | 13 | | 13 | | | | 13 | 13 | | 13 | | |
| Kansas | 9 | | | | 10 | | 10 | 10 | | 10 | | 10 | | 10 | | | 10 | | 10 | | 10 | | |
| Kentucky | | 13 | 13 | | | 12 | 1 | | 13 | | 13 | | 13 | 13 | | | 13 | | | 13 | 13 | | |
| Louisiana | | 8 | 8 | | | | 8 | | 8 | | 9 | | 9 | 10 | | | 10 | | | 10 | | 10 | |
| Maine | 6 | | | 6 | | 6 | | 6 | | 6 | | 6 | | 6 | | | | 6 | 6 | | 6 | | |
| Maryland | | 8 | 8 | | | 8 | | 8 | | 1 | 7 | 2 | 6 | 8 | | | 8 | | 8 | | 8 | | |
| Massachusetts | 14 | | | 15 | | 15 | | 15 | | 16 | | 16 | | 18 | | | | 18 | 18 | | 18 | | |
| Michigan | 13 | | 5 | 9 | | 14 | | 14 | | 14 | | 14 | | | | 15 | | 15 | 15 | | 15 | | |
| Minnesota | 7 | | | 9 | | 9 | | 9 | | 11 | | 11 | | | | 12 | | 12 | 12 | | 12 | | |
| Mississippi | | 9 | 9 | | | | 9 | | 9 | | 10 | | 10 | 10 | | | 10 | | | 10 | | 10 | |
| Missouri | | 16 | 17 | | | | 17 | | 17 | 18 | | 18 | | 18 | | | 18 | | 18 | | 18 | | |
| Montana | | | | 3 | | | 3 | | 3 | 3 | | 3 | | 4 | | | 4 | | 4 | | 4 | | |
| Nebraska | 5 | | | 8 | | | 8 | | 8 | 8 | | | 8 | 8 | | | 8 | | 8 | | 8 | | |
| Nevada | 3 | | | | 3 | | 3 | | 3 | 3 | | | 3 | 3 | | | 3 | | 3 | | 3 | | |
| New Hampshire | 4 | | | 4 | | 4 | | 4 | | 4 | | 4 | | 4 | | | 4 | | 4 | | 4 | | |
| New Jersey | | 9 | 10 | | | 10 | | 10 | | 12 | | 12 | | 14 | | | | 14 | 14 | | 14 | | |
| New Mexico | | | | | | | | | | | | | | 3 | | | 3 | | 3 | | 3 | | |
| New York | 36 | | 36 | | | 36 | | 36 | | 39 | | 39 | | 45 | | | | 45 | 45 | | 45 | | |
| North Carolina | | 11 | 11 | | | | 11 | | 11 | | 12 | | 12 | 12 | | | 12 | | | 12 | | 12 | |
| North Dakota | | | 1 | 1 | 1 | 3 | | 3 | | 4 | | 4 | | 5 | | | 5 | | 5 | | 5 | | |
| Ohio | 23 | | 1 | 22 | | 23 | | 23 | | 23 | | 23 | | 24 | | | 24 | | 24 | | 24 | | |
| Oklahoma | | | | | | | | | | | | | 7 | 10 | | | 10 | | 10 | | | 10 | |
| Oregon | 3 | | | 3 | 1 | 4 | | 4 | | 4 | | 4 | | 5 | | | | 5 | 5 | | 5 | | |
| Pennsylvania | 30 | | | 32 | | 32 | | 32 | | 34 | | 34 | | | | 38 | | 38 | 38 | | 38 | | |
| Rhode Island | 4 | | | 4 | | 4 | | 4 | | 4 | | 4 | | 5 | | | | 5 | 5 | | 5 | | |
| South Carolina | | 9 | 9 | | | | 9 | | 9 | | 9 | | 9 | 9 | | | 9 | | | 9 | | 9 | |
| South Dakota | | | | 4 | | | 4 | 4 | | 4 | | 4 | | | | 5 | | 5 | 5 | | 5 | | |
| Tennessee | | 12 | 12 | | | | 12 | | 12 | | 12 | | 12 | 12 | | | 12 | | 12 | | | 12 | |
| Texas | | 13 | 15 | | | | 15 | | 15 | | 18 | | 18 | 20 | | | 20 | | | 20 | | 20 | |
| Utah | | | | | | | 3 | 3 | | 3 | | 3 | | | 4 | | 4 | | 4 | | 4 | | |
| Vermont | 4 | | | 4 | | 4 | | 4 | | 4 | | 4 | | | 4 | | | 4 | 4 | | 4 | | |
| Virginia | | 12 | 12 | | | | 12 | | 12 | | 12 | | 12 | 12 | | | 12 | | | 12 | | 12 | |
| Washington | | | | 4 | | | 4 | 4 | | 5 | | 5 | | | | 7 | 7 | | 7 | | 7 | | |
| West Virginia | | 6 | 6 | | | 6 | | 6 | | 7 | | 7 | | 8 | | | 1 | 7 | 8 | | 8 | | |
| Wisconsin | 11 | | 12 | | | 12 | | 12 | | 13 | | 13 | | 13 | | | | 13 | 13 | | | | 13 |
| Wyoming | | | | 3 | | | 3 | 3 | | 3 | | 3 | | 3 | | | 3 | | 3 | | 3 | | |
| Total | 233 | 168 | 277 | 145 | 22 | 271 | 176 | 292 | 155 | 336 | 140 | 321 | 162 | 435 | 8 | 88 | 277 | 254 | 404 | 127 | 382 | 136 | 13 |

NOTE: For electoral votes by state from 1948 to 1960, see succeeding pages.

# Presidential Election of 1948

## CANDIDATES FOR PRESIDENT AND VICE PRESIDENT

**Democratic**—Harry S. Truman, Missouri; Alben Barkley, Kentucky.

**Republican**—Thomas E. Dewey, New York; Earl Warren, California.

**States' Rights Democratic**—J. Strom Thurmond, South Carolina; Fielding L. Wright, Mississippi.

**Progressive[1]**—Henry A. Wallace, Iowa; Glen H. Taylor, Idaho.

**Socialist**—Norman Thomas, New York; Tucker P. Smith, Michigan.

**Prohibition**—Claude A. Watson, California; Dale Learn, Pennsylvania.

**Socialist Labor[2]**—Edward A. Teichert, Pennsylvania; Stephen Emery, New York.

| State | Total | Dem. | Rep. | SR Dem. | Plur. | Electoral D | R | S | Prog.[1] | Others[2] |
|---|---|---|---|---|---|---|---|---|---|---|
| Alabama | 214,980 | (4) | 40,930 | 171,443 | 130,513 S | .. | .. | 11 | 1,522 | 1,085 |
| Arizona | 177,065 | 95,251 | 77,597 | ....... | 17,654 D | 4 | .. | .. | 3,310 | 907 |
| Arkansas | 242,475 | 149,659 | 50,959 | 40,068 | 98,700 D | 9 | .. | .. | 751 | 1,038 |
| California | 4,021,538 | 1,913,134 | 1,895,269 | 1,228[5] | 17,865 D | 25 | .. | .. | 190,381 | 21,526 |
| Colorado | 515,237 | 267,288 | 239,714 | ....... | 27,574 D | 6 | .. | .. | 6,115 | 2,120 |
| Connecticut | 883,518 | 423,297 | 437,754 | ....... | 14,457 R | .. | 8 | .. | 13,713 | 8,754 |
| Delaware | 139,073 | 67,813 | 69,588 | ....... | 1,775 R | .. | 3 | .. | 1,050 | 622 |
| Florida | 577,643 | 281,988 | 194,280 | 89,755 | 87,708 D | 8 | .. | .. | 11,620 | ....... |
| Georgia | 418,760 | 254,646 | 76,691 | 85,055 | 169,591 D | 12 | .. | .. | 1,636 | 732 |
| Idaho | 214,816 | 107,370 | 101,514 | ....... | 5,856 D | 4 | .. | .. | 4,972 | 960 |
| Illinois | 3,984,046 | 1,994,715 | 1,961,103 | ....... | 33,612 D | 28 | .. | .. | ....... | 28,228 |
| Indiana | 1,656,214 | 807,833 | 821,079 | ....... | 13,246 R | .. | 13 | .. | 9,649 | 17,653 |
| Iowa | 1,038,264 | 522,380 | 494,018 | ....... | 28,362 D | 10 | .. | .. | 12,125 | 9,741 |
| Kansas | 788,819 | 351,902 | 423,039 | ....... | 71,137 R | .. | 8 | .. | 4,603 | 9,275 |
| Kentucky | 822,658 | 466,756 | 341,210 | 10,411 | 125,546 D | 11 | .. | .. | 1,567 | 2,714 |
| Louisiana | 416,326 | 136,344 | 72,657 | 204,290 | 67,946 S | .. | .. | 10 | 3,035 | ....... |
| Maine | 264,787 | 111,916 | 150,234 | ....... | 38,318 R | .. | 5 | .. | 1,884 | 753 |
| Maryland | 596,735 | 286,521 | 294,814 | 2,476[5] | 8,293 R | .. | 8 | .. | 9,983 | 2,941 |
| Massachusetts | 2,155,347 | 1,151,788 | 909,370 | ....... | 242,418 D | 16 | .. | .. | 38,157 | 56,032 |
| Michigan | 2,109,609 | 1,003,448 | 1,038,595 | ....... | 35,147 R | .. | 19 | .. | 46,515 | 21,051 |
| Minnesota | 1,212,226 | 692,966[6] | 483,617 | ....... | 209,349 D | 11 | .. | .. | 27,866 | 7,777 |
| Mississippi | 192,190 | 19,384[7] | 5,043[8] | 167,538[9] | 148,154 S | .. | .. | 9 | 225 | ....... |
| Missouri | 1,578,628 | 917,315 | 655,039 | ....... | 262,276 D | 15 | .. | .. | 3,998 | 2,276 |
| Montana | 224,278 | 119,071 | 96,770 | ....... | 22,301 D | 4 | .. | .. | 7,313 | 1,124 |
| Nebraska | 488,939 | 224,165 | 264,774 | ....... | 40,609 R | .. | 6 | .. | ....... | ....... |
| Nevada | 62,117 | 31,291 | 29,357 | ....... | 1,934 D | 3 | .. | .. | 1,469 | ....... |
| New Hampshire | 231,440 | 107,995 | 121,299 | 7 | 13,304 R | .. | 4 | .. | 1,970 | 169 |
| New Jersey | 1,949,555 | 895,455 | 981,124 | ....... | 85,669 R | .. | 16 | .. | 42,683 | 30,293 |
| New Mexico | 185,767 | 105,464 | 80,303 | ....... | 25,161 D | 4 | .. | .. | ....... | ....... |
| New York | 6,274,527 | 2,780,204[10] | 2,841,163 | ....... | 60,959 R | .. | 47 | .. | 509,559 | 143,601 |
| North Carolina | 791,209 | 459,070 | 258,572 | 69,652 | 200,498 D | 14 | .. | .. | 3,915 | ....... |
| North Dakota | 220,716 | 95,812 | 115,139 | 374 | 19,327 R | .. | 4 | .. | 8,391 | 1,000 |
| Ohio | 2,936,071 | 1,452,791 | 1,445,684 | ....... | 7,107 D | 25 | .. | .. | 37,596 | ....... |
| Oklahoma | 721,599 | 452,782 | 268,817 | ....... | 183,965 D | 10 | .. | .. | ....... | ....... |
| Oregon | 524,080 | 243,147 | 260,904 | ....... | 17,757 R | .. | 6 | .. | 14,978 | 5,051 |
| Pennsylvania | 3,735,149 | 1,752,426 | 1,902,197 | ....... | 149,771 R | .. | 35 | .. | 55,161 | 25,365 |
| Rhode Island | 326,098 | 188,619 | 134,892 | ....... | 53,727 D | 4 | .. | .. | 2,587 | ....... |
| South Carolina | 142,571 | 34,423 | 5,386 | 102,607 | 68,184 S | .. | .. | 8 | 154 | 1 |
| South Dakota | 250,105 | 117,653 | 129,651 | ....... | 11,998 R | .. | 4 | .. | 2,801 | ....... |
| Tennessee | 550,283 | 270,402 | 202,914 | 73,815 | 67,488 D | 11 | .. | 1 | 1,864 | 1 288 |
| Texas | 1,147,245 | 750,700 | 282,240 | 106,909 | 468,460 D | 23 | .. | .. | 3,764 | 3,632 |
| Utah | 276,305 | 149,151 | 124,402 | ....... | 24,749 D | 4 | .. | .. | 2,679 | 73 |
| Vermont | 123,382 | 45,557 | 75,926 | ....... | 30,369 R | .. | 3 | .. | 1,279 | 620 |
| Virginia | 419,256 | 200,786 | 172,070 | 43,393 | 28,716 D | 11 | .. | .. | 2,047 | 960 |
| Washington | 905,059 | 476,165 | 386,315 | ....... | 89,850 D | 8 | .. | .. | 31,692 | 10,887 |
| West Virginia | 748,750 | 429,188 | 316,251 | ....... | 112,937 D | 8 | .. | .. | 3,311 | ....... |
| Wisconsin | 1,276,800 | 647,310 | 590,959 | ....... | 56 351 D | 12 | .. | .. | 25,282 | 13,249 |
| Wyoming | 101,425 | 52,354 | 47,947 | ....... | 4,407 D | 3 | .. | .. | 931 | 193 |
| Total | 48,833,680 | 24,105,695 | 21,969,170 | 1,169,021 | 2,136,525 D | 303 | 189 | 39 | 1,156,103 | 433,691 |

[1] Independent Progressive in California; Peoples in Connecticut; Independent in Kansas, Mississippi, Ohio, South Dakota; American Labor in New York; People's Progressive in Wisconsin. [2] Industrial Government in Minnesota, New York, Pennsylvania; Independent Socialist Labor in Wisconsin. [3] Breakdown of other votes: Socialist 139,009; Prohibition 103,216; Socialist Labor 29,061; Socialist Workers 13,613; Christian Nationalist 42; Greenback 6; Vegetarian 4; blank 145,320; write-in 1,683; scattering 1,666; void 71. [4] Not on ballot. [5] Write-in votes. [6] Including Farmer-Labor votes. [7] National Democratic. [8] Contains 2,595 Republican and 2,448 Independent Republican votes. [9] Mississippi Democratic. [10] Includes 222,562 Liberal votes.

# Presidential Election of 1952

## CANDIDATES FOR PRESIDENT AND VICE PRESIDENT

Republican—Dwight D. Eisenhower, New York; Richard M. Nixon, California.

Democratic—Adlai E. Stevenson, Illinois; John J. Sparkman, Alabama.

Progressive[1]—Vincent Hallinan, California; Mrs. Charlotta A. Bass, New York.

Prohibition—Stuart Hamblen, California; Enoch A. Holtwick, Illinois.

Socialist Labor[2]—Eric Hass, New York; Stephen Emery, New York.

Socialist—Darlington Hoopes, Pennsylvania; Samuel H. Friedman, New York.

| State | Total | Rep. | Dem. | Plur. | Electoral R | Electoral D | Prog.[1] | Prohib. | Soc. Lab.[2] | Others[3] |
|---|---|---|---|---|---|---|---|---|---|---|
| Alabama | 426,120 | 149,231 | 275,075 | 125,844 D | .. | 11 | .... | 1,814 | .... | .... |
| Arizona | 260,570 | 152,042 | 108,528 | 43,514 R | 4 | .. | .... | .... | .... | .... |
| Arkansas | 404,800 | 177,155 | 226,300 | 49,145 D | .. | 8 | .... | 886 | 1 | 458 |
| California | 5,141,849 | 2,897,310 | 2,197,548 | 699,762 R | 32 | .. | 24,106 | 15,653 | .... | 7,232 |
| Colorado | 630,103 | 379,782 | 245,504 | 134,278 R | 6 | .. | 1,919 | .... | 352 | 2,546 |
| Connecticut | 1,096,911 | 611,012 | 481,649 | 129,363 R | 8 | .. | .... | .... | 535 | 3,715 |
| Delaware | 174,025 | 90,059 | 83,315 | 6,744 R | 3 | .. | 155 | 234 | 242 | 20 |
| Florida | 989,337 | 544,036 | 444,950 | 99,086 R | 10 | .. | .... | .... | .... | 351 |
| Georgia | 655,803 | 198,979 | 456,823 | 257,844 D | .. | 12 | .... | .... | .... | 1 |
| Idaho | 276,231 | 180,707 | 95,081 | 85,626 R | 4 | .. | 443 | .... | .... | .... |
| Illinois | 4,481,058 | 2,457,327 | 2,013,920 | 443,407 R | 27 | .. | .... | .... | 9,363 | 448 |
| Indiana | 1,955,325 | 1,136,259 | 801,530 | 334,729 R | 13 | .. | 1,222 | 15,335 | 979 | .... |
| Iowa | 1,268,773 | 808,906 | 451,513 | 357,393 R | 10 | .. | 5,085 | 2,882 | 139 | 248 |
| Kansas | 896,166 | 616,302 | 273,296 | 343,006 R | 8 | .. | .... | 6,038 | .... | 530 |
| Kentucky | 993,148 | 495,029 | 495,729 | 700 D | .. | 10 | 336 | 1,161 | 893 | .... |
| Louisiana | 651,952 | 306,925 | 345,027 | 38,102 D | .. | 10 | .... | .... | .... | .... |
| Maine | 351,786 | 232,353 | 118,806 | 113,547 R | 5 | .. | 332 | .... | 156 | 139 |
| Maryland | 902,074 | 499,424 | 395,337 | 104,087 R | 9 | .. | 7,313 | .... | .... | .... |
| Massachusetts | 2,383,398 | 1,292,325 | 1,083,525 | 208,800 R | 16 | .. | 4,636 | 886 | 1,957 | 69 |
| Michigan | 2,798,592 | 1,551,529 | 1,230,657 | 320,872 R | 20 | .. | 3,922 | 10,331 | 1,495 | 658 |
| Minnesota | 1,379,483 | 763,211 | 608,458[4] | 154,753 R | 11 | .. | 2,666 | 2,147 | 2,383 | 618 |
| Mississippi | 285,532 | (⁵) | 172,566 | 59,600 D | .. | 8 | .... | .... | .... | 112,966 |
| Missouri | 1,892,062 | 959,429 | 929,830 | 29,599 R | 13 | .. | 987 | 885 | 169 | 762 |
| Montana | 265,037 | 157,394 | 106,213 | 51,181 R | 4 | .. | 723 | 548 | .... | 159 |
| Nebraska | 609,660 | 421,603 | 188,057 | 233,546 R | 6 | .. | .... | .... | .... | .... |
| Nevada | 82,190 | 50,502 | 31,688 | 18,814 R | 3 | .. | .... | .... | .... | .... |
| New Hampshire | 272,950 | 166,287 | 106,663 | 59,624 R | 4 | .. | .... | .... | .... | .... |
| New Jersey | 2,419,554 | 1,374,613 | 1,015,902 | 358,711 R | 16 | .. | 5,589 | 989 | 5,815 | 16,646 |
| New Mexico | 238,608 | 132,170 | 105,661 | 26,509 R | 4 | .. | .... | 297 | 35 | 445 |
| New York | 7,128,241 | 3,952,815 | 3,104,601[6] | 848,214 R | 45 | .. | 64,211 | .... | 1,560 | 5,054 |
| North Carolina | 1,210,910 | 558,107 | 652,803 | 94,696 D | .. | 14 | .... | .... | .... | .... |
| North Dakota | 270,127 | 191,712 | 76,694 | 115,018 R | 4 | .. | 344 | 302 | .... | 1,075 |
| Ohio | 3,700,758 | 2,100,456 | 1,600,302 | 500,154 R | 25 | .. | .... | .... | .... | .... |
| Oklahoma | 948,984 | 518,045 | 430,939 | 87,106 R | 8 | .. | .... | .... | .... | .... |
| Oregon | 695,059 | 420,815 | 270,579 | 150,236 R | 6 | .. | .... | .... | .... | 3,665 |
| Pennsylvania | 4,580,717 | 2,415,789 | 2,146,269 | 269,520 R | 32 | .. | 4,200 | 8,771 | 1,347 | 4,341 |
| Rhode Island | 414,498 | 210,935 | 203,293 | 7,642 R | 4 | .. | 187 | .... | 83 | .... |
| South Carolina | 341,086 | 168,082[7] | 173,004 | 4,922 D | .. | 8 | .... | .... | .... | .... |
| South Dakota | 294,283 | 203,857 | 90,426 | 113,431 R | 4 | .. | .... | .... | .... | .... |
| Tennessee | 892,553 | 446,147 | 443,710 | 2,437 R | 11 | .. | 885 | 1,432 | .... | 379 |
| Texas | 2,076,006 | 1,102,878 | 969,288 | 133,590 R | 24 | .. | 294 | 1,983 | .... | 1,563 |
| Utah | 329,554 | 194,190 | 135,364 | 58,826 R | 4 | .. | .... | .... | .... | .... |
| Vermont | 153,539 | 109,717 | 43,355 | 66,362 R | 3 | .. | 282 | .... | .... | 185 |
| Virginia | 619,689 | 349,037 | 268,677 | 80,360 R | 12 | .. | 311 | .... | 1,160 | 504 |
| Washington | 1,102,708 | 599,107 | 492,845 | 106,262 R | 9 | .. | 2,460 | .... | 633 | 7,663 |
| West Virginia | 873,548 | 419,970 | 453,578 | 33,608 D | .. | 8 | .... | .... | .... | .... |
| Wisconsin | 1,607,370 | 979,744 | 622,175 | 357,569 R | 12 | .. | .... | .... | .... | 5,451 |
| Wyoming | 91,251 | 81,047 | 47,934 | 33,113 R | 3 | .. | .... | 194 | 36 | 40 |
| Total | 61,551,978 | 33,824,351 | 27,314,987[6] | 6,509,364 R | 442 | 89 | 132,608 | 72,768 | 29,333 | 177,931 |

[1] Independent Progressive in California; Peace Progressive in Massachusetts; American Labor in New York.   [2] Industrial Government in Minnesota, New York and Pennsylvania.   [3] Breakdown of Other votes: Independent (pledged to Republican candidate in Miss.), 112,966; Socialist, 18,322; Christian Nationalist, 10,557; Socialist Workers, 8,956; write-in, 4,431; Poor Man's, 4,203; scattering, 4,040; Independent, 3,665; Constitution, 2,911; Vincent Hallinan (Independent in Wis.), 2,174; People's party of Connecticut, 1,466; Farrell Dobbs (Independent in Wis.), 1,350; Darlington Hoopes (Independent in Wis.), 1,157; Eric Hass (Independent in Wis.), 770; Social Democrat, 504; America First, 233; Independent Progressive, 225; Liberty, 1.   [4] Democratic-Farmer Labor votes.   [5] 112,966 Independent votes were pledged to the Republican candidate; these are shown as Other votes.   [6] Includes 416,711 Liberal votes. [7] Includes 158,289 votes for separate set of electors for Republican candidates by petition.

# Presidential Election of 1956

### CANDIDATES FOR PRESIDENT AND VICE PRESIDENT

Republican—Dwight D. Eisenhower, New York; Richard M. Nixon, California.

Democratic—Adlai E. Stevenson, Illinois; Estes Kefauver, Tennessee.

Prohibition—Enoch A. Holtwick, Illinois; Edward M. Cooper, California.

Socialist—Darlington Hoopes, Pennsylvania; Samuel H. Friedman, New York.

Socialist Labor—Eric Hass, New York; Georgia Cozzini, Wisconsin.

Socialist Workers—Farrell Dobbs, New York; Myra Tanner Weiss, New York.

| State | Total | Rep. | Dem. | Plur. | Electoral vote R | D | Distribution of votes at National Conventions R | D |
|-------|-------|------|------|-------|---|---|---|---|
| Alabama | 496,861 | 195,694 | 280,844 | 85,150 D | .. | 10[1] | 21 | 26 |
| Arizona | 290,173 | 176,990 | 112,880 | 64,110 R | 4 | .. | 14 | 16 |
| Arkansas | 406,572 | 186,287 | 213,277 | 26,990 D | .. | 8 | 16 | 26 |
| California | 5,466,355 | 3,027,668 | 2,420,135 | 607,533 R | 32 | .. | 70 | 68 |
| Colorado | 663,074 | 394,479 | 263,997 | 130,482 R | 6 | .. | 18 | 20 |
| Connecticut | 1,117,121 | 711,837 | 405,079 | 306,758 R | 8 | .. | 22 | 20 |
| Delaware | 177,988 | 98,057 | 79,421 | 18,636 R | 3 | .. | 12 | 10 |
| Florida | 1,124,220 | 643,849 | 480,371 | 163,478 R | 10 | .. | 26 | 28 |
| Georgia | 668,920 | 222,778 | 444,388 | 221,610 D | .. | 12 | 23 | 32 |
| Idaho | 272,989 | 166,979 | 105,868 | 61,111 R | 4 | .. | 14 | 12 |
| Illinois | 4,407,407 | 2,623,327 | 1,775,682 | 847,645 R | 27 | .. | 60 | 64 |
| Indiana | 1,974,607 | 1,182,811 | 783,908 | 398,903 R | 13 | .. | 32 | 26 |
| Iowa | 1,234,564 | 729,187 | 501,858 | 227,329 R | 10 | .. | 26 | 24 |
| Kansas | 866,243 | 566,878 | 296,317 | 270,561 R | 8 | .. | 22 | 16 |
| Kentucky | 1,053,805 | 572,192 | 476,453 | 95,739 R | 10 | .. | 26 | 30 |
| Louisiana | 617,544 | 329,047 | 243,977 | 85,070 R | 10 | .. | 20 | 24 |
| Maine | 351,706 | 249,238 | 102,468 | 146,770 R | 5 | .. | 16 | 14 |
| Maryland | 932,351 | 559,738 | 372,613 | 187,125 R | 9 | .. | 24 | 18 |
| Massachusetts | 2,348,506 | 1,393,197 | 948,190 | 445,007 R | 16 | .. | 38 | 40 |
| Michigan | 3,080,468 | 1,713,647 | 1,359,998 | 353,749 R | 20 | .. | 46 | 44 |
| Minnesota | 1,340,005 | 719,302 | 617,525 | 101,777 R | 11 | .. | 28 | 30 |
| Mississippi | 248,149 | 56,372 | 144,498 | 88,126 D | .. | 8 | 15 | 22 |
| Missouri | 1,832,572 | 914,299 | 918,273 | 3,974 D | .. | 13 | 32 | 38 |
| Montana | 271,171 | 154,933 | 116,238 | 38,695 R | 4 | .. | 14 | 16 |
| Nebraska | 577,137 | 378,108 | 199,029 | 179,079 R | 6 | .. | 18 | 12 |
| Nevada | 96,689 | 56,049 | 40,640 | 15,409 R | 3 | .. | 12 | 14 |
| New Hampshire | 266,994 | 176,519 | 90,364 | 86,155 R | 4 | .. | 14 | 8 |
| New Jersey | 2,484,312 | 1,606,942 | 850,337 | 756,605 R | 16 | .. | 38 | 36 |
| New Mexico | 253,926 | 146,788 | 106,098 | 40,690 R | 4 | .. | 14 | 16 |
| New York | 7,093,336 | 4,340,340 | 2,750,769[2] | 1,589,571 R | 45 | .. | 96 | 98 |
| North Carolina | 1,165,592 | 575,062 | 590,530 | 15,468 D | .. | 14 | 28 | 36 |
| North Dakota | 253,991 | 156,766 | 96,742 | 60,024 R | 4 | .. | 14 | 8 |
| Ohio | 3,702,265 | 2,262,610 | 1,439,655 | 822,955 R | 25 | .. | 56 | 58 |
| Oklahoma | 859,350 | 473,769 | 385,581 | 88,188 R | 8 | .. | 22 | 28 |
| Oregon | 735,597 | 406,393 | 329,204 | 77,189 R | 6 | .. | 18 | 16 |
| Pennsylvania | 4,576,503 | 2,585,252 | 1,981,769 | 603,483 R | 32 | .. | 70 | 74 |
| Rhode Island | 387,609 | 225,819 | 161,790 | 64,029 R | 4 | .. | 14 | 16 |
| South Carolina | 300,583[3] | 75,700 | 136,372 | 60,672 D | .. | 8 | 16 | 20 |
| South Dakota | 293,857 | 171,569 | 122,288 | 49,281 R | 4 | .. | 14 | 8 |
| Tennessee | 939,404 | 462,288 | 456,507 | 5,781 R | 11 | .. | 28 | 32 |
| Texas | 1,955,168 | 1,080,619 | 859,958 | 220,661 R | 24 | .. | 54 | 56 |
| Utah | 333,995 | 215,631 | 118,364 | 97,267 R | 4 | .. | 14 | 12 |
| Vermont | 152,978 | 110,390 | 42,549 | 67,841 R | 3 | .. | 12 | 6 |
| Virginia | 697,978 | 386,459 | 267,760 | 118,699 R | 12 | .. | 30 | 32 |
| Washington | 1,150,889 | 620,430 | 523,002 | 97,428 R | 9 | .. | 24 | 26 |
| West Virginia | 830,831 | 449,297 | 381,534 | 67,763 R | 8 | .. | 16 | 24 |
| Wisconsin | 1,550,558 | 954,844 | 586,768 | 368,076 R | 12 | .. | 30 | 28 |
| Wyoming | 124,127 | 74,573 | 49,554 | 25,019 R | 3 | .. | 12 | 14 |
| Total | 62,027,040 | 35,581,003 | 26,031,322 | 9,549,681 R | 457 | 73[1] | 1,323* | 1,372* |

[1] Alabama's 11th electoral vote was cast for Walter B. Jones of Alabama. [2] Includes 292,557 Liberal-party votes.
[3] Includes 88,509 votes for electors nominated by petition.
* Note: This total includes National Convention votes allocated to the District of Columbia and United States territories as follows:
Republican: Alaska, 4; District of Columbia, 6; Hawaii, 10; Puerto Rico, 3; Virgin Islands, 1.
Democratic: Alaska, 6; District of Columbia, 6; Hawaii, 6; Puerto Rico, 6; Canal Zone, 3; Virgin Islands, 3.

# Presidential Election of 1960

## CANDIDATES FOR PRESIDENT AND VICE PRESIDENT

Democratic—John F. Kennedy, Massachusetts; Lyndon B. Johnson, Texas.
Republican—Richard M. Nixon, California; Henry Cabot Lodge, Massachusetts.

| State | Total | Dem. | Rep. | Plur. | Electoral vote D | Electoral vote R | Electoral vote Byrd[1] | Distribution of votes at National Conventions Dem. | Distribution of votes at National Conventions Rep. |
|---|---|---|---|---|---|---|---|---|---|
| Alabama | 570,225 | 324,050 | 237,981 | 86,069 D | 5 | .. | 6[2] | 29 | 22 |
| Alaska | 60,762 | 29,809 | 30,953 | 1,144 R | .. | 3 | .. | 9 | 6 |
| Arizona | 398,491 | 176,781 | 221,241 | 44,460 R | .. | 4 | .. | 17 | 14 |
| Arkansas | 428,509 | 215,049 | 184,508 | 30,541 D | 8 | .. | .. | 27 | 16 |
| California | 6,506,578 | 3,224,099 | 3,259,722 | 35,623 R | .. | 32 | .. | 81 | 70 |
| Colorado | 736,246 | 330,629 | 402,242 | 71,613 R | .. | 6 | .. | 21 | 18 |
| Connecticut | 1,222,868 | 657,055 | 565,813 | 91,242 D | 8 | .. | .. | 21 | 22 |
| Delaware | 195,963 | 99,590 | 96,373 | 3,217 D | 3 | .. | .. | 11 | 12 |
| Florida | 1,544,180 | 748,700 | 795,476 | 46,776 R | .. | 10 | .. | 29 | 26 |
| Georgia | 733,349 | 458,638 | 274,472 | 184,166 D | 12 | .. | .. | 33 | 24 |
| Hawaii | 184,705 | 92,410 | 92,295 | 115 D | 3 | .. | .. | 9 | 12 |
| Idaho | 300,450 | 138,853 | 161,597 | 22,744 R | .. | 4 | .. | 13 | 14 |
| Illinois | 4,757,409 | 2,377,846 | 2,368,988 | 8,858 D | 27 | .. | .. | 69 | 60 |
| Indiana | 2,135,360 | 952,358 | 1,175,120 | 222,762 R | .. | 13 | .. | 34 | 32 |
| Iowa | 1,273,810 | 550,565 | 722,381 | 171,816 R | .. | 10 | .. | 26 | 26 |
| Kansas | 928,825 | 363,213 | 561,474 | 198,261 R | .. | 8 | .. | 21 | 22 |
| Kentucky | 1,124,462 | 521,855 | 602,607 | 80,752 R | .. | 10 | .. | 31 | 26 |
| Louisiana | 807,891 | 407,339 | 230,980 | 176,359 D | 10 | .. | .. | 26 | 26 |
| Maine | 421,767 | 181,159 | 240,608 | 59,449 R | .. | 5 | .. | 15 | 16 |
| Maryland | 1,055,346 | 565,808 | 489,538 | 76,270 D | 9 | .. | .. | 24 | 24 |
| Massachusetts | 2,469,480 | 1,487,174 | 976,750 | 510,424 D | 16 | .. | .. | 41 | 38 |
| Michigan | 3,318,097 | 1,687,269 | 1,620,428 | 66,841 D | 20 | .. | .. | 51 | 46 |
| Minnesota | 1,541,887 | 779,933 | 757,915 | 22,018 D | 11 | .. | .. | 31 | 28 |
| Mississippi | 298,171 | 108,362 | 73,561 | 34,801 D | .. | .. | 8[2] | 23 | 12 |
| Missouri | 1,934,422 | 972,201 | 962,221 | 9,980 D | 13 | .. | .. | 39 | 26 |
| Montana | 277,579 | 134,891 | 141,841 | 6,950 R | .. | 4 | .. | 17 | 14 |
| Nebraska | 613,095 | 232,542 | 380,553 | 148,011 R | .. | 6 | .. | 16 | 18 |
| Nevada | 107,267 | 54,880 | 52,387 | 2,493 D | 3 | .. | .. | 15 | 12 |
| New Hampshire | 295,761 | 137,772 | 157,989 | 20,217 R | .. | 4 | .. | 11 | 14 |
| New Jersey | 2,773,111 | 1,385,415 | 1,363,324 | 22,091 D | 16 | .. | .. | 41 | 38 |
| New Mexico | 311,107 | 156,027 | 153,733 | 2,294 D | 4 | .. | .. | 17 | 14 |
| New York | 7,380,075 | 3,830,085[3] | 3,446,419 | 383,666 D | 45 | .. | .. | 114 | 96 |
| North Carolina | 1,368,556 | 713,136 | 655,420 | 57,716 D | 14 | .. | .. | 37 | 28 |
| North Dakota | 278,431 | 123,963 | 154,310 | 30,347 R | .. | 4 | .. | 11 | 14 |
| Ohio | 4,161,859 | 1,944,248 | 2,217,611 | 273,363 R | .. | 25 | .. | 64 | 56 |
| Oklahoma | 903,150 | 370,111 | 533,039 | 162,928 R | .. | 7 | 1 | 29 | 22 |
| Oregon | 775,462 | 367,402 | 408,060 | 40,658 R | .. | 6 | .. | 17 | 18 |
| Pennsylvania | 5,006,541 | 2,556,282 | 2,439,956 | 116,326 D | 32 | .. | .. | 81 | 70 |
| Rhode Island | 405,534 | 258,032 | 147,502 | 110,530 D | 4 | .. | .. | 17 | 14 |
| South Carolina | 386,688 | 198,129 | 188,558 | 9,571 D | 8 | .. | .. | 21 | 13 |
| South Dakota | 306,487 | 128,070 | 178,417 | 50,347 R | .. | 4 | .. | 11 | 14 |
| Tennessee | 1,051,792 | 481,453 | 556,577 | 75,124 R | .. | 11 | .. | 33 | 28 |
| Texas | 2,311,845 | 1,167,932 | 1,121,699 | 46,233 D | 24 | .. | .. | 61 | 54 |
| Utah | 374,709 | 169,248 | 205,361 | 36,113 R | .. | 4 | .. | 13 | 14 |
| Vermont | 167,317 | 69,186 | 98,131 | 28,945 R | .. | 3 | .. | 9 | 12 |
| Virginia | 771,449 | 362,327 | 404,521 | 42,194 R | .. | 12 | .. | 33 | 30 |
| Washington | 1,241,572 | 599,298 | 629,273 | 29,975 R | .. | 9 | .. | 27 | 24 |
| West Virginia | 837,781 | 441,786 | 395,995 | 45,791 D | 8 | .. | .. | 25 | 22 |
| Wisconsin | 1,729,082 | 830,805 | 895,175 | 64,370 R | .. | 12 | .. | 31 | 30 |
| Wyoming | 139,882 | 63,331 | 76,551 | 13,220 R | .. | 3 | .. | 15 | 12 |
| Total | 68,836,385 | 34,227,096 | 34,107,646 | 119,450 D | 303 | 219 | 15 | 1,521[4] | 1,331[5] |

[1] For Sen. Harry F. Byrd, of Virginia.   [2] Unpledged electors.   [3] Includes 406,176 Liberal votes.   [4] 24 National Convention votes allocated to District of Columbia and U. S. territories.   [5] 12 National Convention votes allocated to D. C. and U. S. territories.

## PARTY STRENGTH IN 83RD TO 87TH CONGRESSES

| | The Senate | | | | | The House | | | | |
|---|---|---|---|---|---|---|---|---|---|---|
| | 83rd 1953 | 84th 1955 | 85th 1957 | 86th 1959 | 87th 1961 | 83rd 1953 | 84th 1955 | 85th 1957 | 86th 1959 | 87th 1961 |
| Democratic | 47 | 48 | 49 | 65 | 64 | 213 | 232 | 234 | 283 | 260 |
| Republican | 48 | 47 | 47 | 35 | 36 | 221 | 203 | 201 | 154 | 176 |
| Other | 1 | 1 | 0 | 0 | 0 | 1 | 0 | 0 | 0 | 0 |

# Qualifications for Voting in the 50 States

(Minimum voting age is 18 in Georgia and Kentucky, 19 in Alaska, and 20 in Hawaii.
In all other states, the minimum age is 21.)
*Source:* Questionnaires to the states.

| State | Minimum length of U. S. citizenship | Residence[1] State | County | District | Literacy test | Poll tax[2] |
|---|---|---|---|---|---|---|
| Alabama | ...... | 1 yr. | 6 mo. | 3 mo.[3] | Yes | $1.50[14] |
| Alaska | ...... | 1 yr. | ...... | 30 da. | .... | .... |
| Arizona | 1 yr. | 1 yr. | 30 da. | 30 da. | Yes | .... |
| Arkansas | 1 yr. | 1 yr. | 6 mo. | 30 da.[4] | .... | 1.00 |
| California | 90 da. | 1 yr.[23] | 90 da. | 54 da.[4] | Yes | .... |
| Colorado | ...... | 1 yr. | 3 mo. | 30 da.[5] | .... | .... |
| Connecticut | ...... | 1 yr. | .... | 6 mo.[6] | Yes | .... |
| Delaware | ...... | 1 yr. | 3 mo. | 30 da. | Yes | .... |
| Florida | ...... | 1 yr. | 6 mo. | ...... | .... | .... |
| Georgia | ...... | 1 yr. | 6 mo. | 6 mo. | Yes | .... |
| Hawaii | ...... | 1 yr. | ...... | 3 mo. | .... | .... |
| Idaho | ...... | 6 mo. | 30 da. | ...... | .... | .... |
| Illinois | ...... | 1 yr. | 3 mo. | 30 da. | .... | .... |
| Indiana | ...... | 6 mo. | 2 mo.[9] | 30 da.[4] | .... | .... |
| Iowa | ...... | 6 mo. | 60 da. | 10 da.[4] | .... | .... |
| Kansas | ...... | 6 mo. | ...... | 30 da.[10] | .... | .... |
| Kentucky | ...... | 1 yr. | 6 mo. | 60 da.[4] | .... | .... |
| Louisiana | ...... | 1 yr. | 1 yr.[11] | 3 mo.[19] | Yes | .... |
| Maine | ...... | 6 mo. | ...... | 3 mo.[6] | Yes | .... |
| Maryland | ...... | 1 yr. | 6 mo. | 6 mo. | .... | .... |
| Massachusetts | ...... | 1 yr. | ...... | 6 mo.[6] | Yes | .... |
| Michigan | ...... | 6 mo. | ...... | 30 da.[6,24] | .... | .... |
| Minnesota | 3 mo. | 6 mo. | ...... | 30 da. | .... | .... |
| Mississippi | ...... | 2 yr. | 1 yr. | 1 yr. | (12) | 2.00 |
| Missouri | ...... | 1 yr. | 60 da. | 30 da.[8] | .... | .... |
| Montana | ...... | 1 yr. | 30 da. | 30 da.[8] | .... | .... |
| Nebraska | ...... | 6 mo. | 40 da. | 10 da. | .... | .... |
| Nevada | ...... | 6 mo | 30 da. | 10 da.[4] | .... | .... |
| New Hampshire | ...... | 6 mo. | ...... | 6 mo.[5] | Yes | .... |
| New Jersey | ...... | 6 mo. | 60 da. | ...... | .... | .... |
| New Mexico | ...... | 1 yr. | 3 mo. | 30 da.[4] | .... | .... |
| New York | 90 da. | 1 yr. | 4 mo. | 30 da. | Yes | .... |
| North Carolina | ...... | 1 yr. | 4 mo. | 4 mo. | Yes | .... |
| North Dakota | ...... | 1 yr. | 3 mo. | 30 da.[4] | .... | .... |
| Ohio | ...... | 1 yr. | 40 da. | 40 da.[4] | .... | .... |
| Oklahoma | ...... | 1 yr. | 6 mo. | 30 da.[4] | .... | .... |
| Oregon | ...... | 6 mo. | 30 da.[22] | 30 da.[4,22] | Yes | .... |
| Pennsylvania | 1 mo. | 1 yr.[13] | ...... | 60 da. | .... | .... |
| Rhode Island | 1 yr. | 1 yr. | ...... | 6 mo.[6] | .... | .... |
| South Carolina | 2 yr. | 2 yr. | 1 yr. | 4 mo. | .... | (18) |
| South Dakota | 5 yr. | 1 yr. | 3 mo.[7] | 30 da.[4,7] | .... | .... |
| Tennessee | ...... | 1 yr. | 3 mo. | 30 da.[3,24] | .... | .... |
| Texas | ...... | 1 yr. | 6 mo. | ...... | .... | 1.75[21] |
| Utah | 90 da. | 1 yr. | 4 mo. | 60 da.[4] | .... | .... |
| Vermont[20] | ...... | 1 yr. | ...... | 3 mo.[6,15] | .... | .... |
| Virginia | ...... | 1 yr. | 6 mo.[16] | 30 da.[4] | Yes | 1.50 |
| Washington | ...... | 1 yr. | 60 da. | 30 da.[17] | Yes | .... |
| West Virginia | ...... | 1 yr. | 2 mo. | ...... | .... | .... |
| Wisconsin | ...... | 1 yr.[23] | ...... | 10 da. | .... | .... |
| Wyoming | ...... | 1 yr. | 60 da. | 10 da. | (12) | .... |

[1] Registration of all or part of the voters is required in most states. [2] Annual levy. Although poll (or head) taxes are levied in several other states, those listed make payment of the tax a condition for voting. [3] Precinct or ward. [4] Precinct. [5] City or town, and 15 days in precinct. [6] City or town. [7] A person living in a new precinct or county for less than the period required may vote at either his old or new residence, provided he was qualified to vote at his old residence. [8] Precinct; 6 mo. in city or town. [9] Township. [10] Township or ward. [11] Parish. [12] Must be able to read, understand and/or write any section of state constitution. [13] 6 months if previously qualified elector or natural-born citizen of state. [14] 1953 act makes poll tax noncumulative except for 2 years preceding election in which elector offers to vote. [15] To qualify to vote for representatives to general assembly or justices. [16] County, city, or town. [17] City, town, ward, or precinct. [18] Repealed in 1945. [19] Precinct, municipality 4 mo. [20] A person must take freeman's oath as qualification for voting. [21] $1.50 levied by state; 25 cents levied by most counties, but not all. [22] To vote for county officials requires 30 days residence in the county; for municipal officials, 30 days in the municipality. State residents may vote in national and state-wide elections without 30 days local residence. [23] Residents of less than one year may vote in presidential elections if eligible to vote elsewhere prior to moving. [24] If person moves during 30-day period, he has to vote in old location.

## Lincoln's Gettysburg Address

The Battle of Gettysburg, one of the most noted battles of the Civil War, was fought on July 1, 2, and 3, 1863. On November 19, 1863, the field was dedicated as a national cemetery by President Lincoln in a two-minute speech that was to become immortal. At the time of its delivery the speech was relegated to the inside pages of the papers, while a two-hour address by Edward Everett, the leading orator of the time, caught the headlines.

The following is the text of the address revised by President Lincoln from his own notes:

FOURSCORE and seven years ago our fathers brought forth on this continent a new nation conceived in liberty and dedicated to the proposition that all men are created equal. Now we are engaged in a great civil war testing whether that nation, or any nation so conceived and so dedicated, can long endure. We are met on a great battlefield of that war. We have come to dedicate a portion of that field as a final resting-place for those who here gave their lives that that nation might live. It is altogether fitting and proper that we should do this. But, in a larger sense, we cannot dedicate, we cannot consecrate, we cannot hallow this ground. The brave men, living and dead, who struggled here have consecrated it far above our poor power to add or detract. The world will little note nor long remember what we say here, but it can never forget what they did here. It is for us the living rather to be dedicated here to the unfinished work which they who fought here have thus far so nobly advanced. It is rather for us to be here dedicated to the great task remaining before us—that from these honored dead we take increased devotion to that cause for which they gave the last full measure of devotion—that we here highly resolve that these dead shall not have died in vain, that this nation under God shall have a new birth of freedom, and that government of the people, by the people, for the people shall not perish from the earth.

## The Monroe Doctrine

The Monroe Doctrine was announced in President James Monroe's message to Congress, during his second term on December 2, 1823 in part as follows:

"In the discussions to which this interest has given rise, and in the arrangements by which they may terminate, the occasion has been deemed proper for asserting as a principle in which rights and interests of the United States are involved, that the American continents, by the free and independent condition which they have assumed and maintain, are henceforth not to be considered as subjects for future colonization by any European power. . . . We owe it, therefore, to candor and to the amicable relations existing between the United States and those powers to declare that we should consider any attempt on their part to extend their system to any portion of this hemisphere as dangerous to our peace and safety. With the existing colonies or dependencies of any European power we have not interfered and shall not interfere. But with the governments who have declared their independence and maintain it, and whose independence we have, on great consideration and on just principles, acknowledged, we could not view any interposition for the purpose of oppressing them or controlling in any other manner their destiny by any European power in any other light than as the manifestation of an unfriendly disposition toward the United States."

## Minority Presidents

Fourteen candidates have become President of the U. S. with a popular vote less than 50 per cent of the total vote cast. It should be noted, however, that in elections before 1872, presidential electors were not chosen by popular vote in all states. Adams' election in 1824 was by the House of Representatives, which chose him over Jackson, who had a plurality of both electoral and popular votes, but not a majority in the electoral college.

Besides Jackson in 1824, only two other candidates receiving the largest popular vote have failed to gain a majority in the electoral college—Samuel J. Tilden (D) in 1876 and Grover Cleveland (D) in 1888. The "minority" Presidents follow:

| Year | President | Electoral Pct. | Popular vote Pct. |
|------|-----------|------:|------:|
| 1824 | John Q. Adams.............. | 31.8 | 29.8 |
| 1844 | James K. Polk (D)........... | 61.8 | 49.3 |
| 1848 | Zachary Taylor (W)........... | 56.2 | 47.3 |
| 1856 | James Buchanan (D)........ | 58.7 | 45.3 |
| 1860 | Abraham Lincoln (R)........ | 59.4 | 39.9 |
| 1876 | Rutherford B. Hayes (R)....... | 50.1 | 47.9 |
| 1880 | James A. Garfield (R)........ | 57.9 | 48.3 |
| 1884 | Grover Cleveland (D)........ | 54.6 | 48.8 |
| 1888 | Benjamin Harrison (R)........ | 58.1 | 47.8 |
| 1892 | Grover Cleveland (D)........ | 62.4 | 46.0 |
| 1912 | Woodrow Wilson (D)......... | 81.9 | 41.8 |
| 1916 | Woodrow Wilson (D)......... | 52.1 | 49.3 |
| 1948 | Harry S. Truman (D)......... | 57.1 | 49.5 |
| 1960 | John F. Kennedy (D)......... | 56.4 | 49.7 |

# The Mayflower Compact

On September 6, 1620, the *Mayflower,* a sailing vessel of about 180 tons, started her memorable voyage from Plymouth, England with about 100* pilgrims aboard, bound for Virginia to establish a private permanent colony in North America. Arriving at Provincetown, Mass., on November 11 (November 21, new style calendar), forty-one of the passengers signed the famous "Mayflower Compact" as the boat lay at anchor in that Cape Cod harbor. A small detail of the pilgrims, led by William Bradford, assigned to select a place for permanent settlement landed at what is now Plymouth, Mass., on December 21, N.S.

The text of the compact follows:

IN THE NAME OF GOD, Amen. We, whose names are underwritten, the Loyal Subjects of our dread Sovereign Lord, King *James,* by the Grace of God, of *Great Britain, France* and *Ireland,* King, *Defender of the Faith,* &,

Having undertaken for the Glory of God, and Advancement of the Christian Faith, and the Honour of our King and Country, a voyage to plant the first colony in the northern Parts of Virginia; do by these Presents, solemnly and mutually in the Presence of God and one of another, covenant and combine ourselves together into a civil Body Politick, for our better Ordering and Preservation, and Furtherance of the Ends aforesaid; And by Virtue hereof to enact, constitute, and frame, such just and equal Laws, Ordinances, Acts, Constitutions and Offices, from time to time, as shall be thought most meet and convenient for the General good of the Colony; unto which we promise all due Submission and Obedience.

In WITNESS whereof we have hereunto subscribed our names at *Cape Cod* the eleventh of *November,* in the Reign of our Sovereign Lord, King *James* of *England, France* and *Ireland,* the eighteenth, and of *Scotland* the fifty-fourth. *Anno Domini,* 1620

| | | | |
|---|---|---|---|
| John Carver | William Mullins | Thomas Tinker | Edward Tilly |
| Digery Priest | Thomas English | Samuel Fuller | John Craxton |
| William Brewster | John Howland | Richard Clark | Thomas Rogers |
| Edmund Margesson | Stephen Hopkins | John Allerton | John Goodman |
| John Alden | Edward Winslow | Richard Warren | Edward Fuller |
| George Soule | Gilbert Winslow | Edward Liester | Richard Gardiner |
| James Chilton | Miles Standish | William Bradford | William White |
| Francis Cooke | Richard Bitteridge | Thomas Williams | Edward Doten |
| Joses Fletcher | Francis Eaton | Isaac Allerton | |
| John Ridgate | John Tilly | Peter Brown | |
| Christopher Martin | John Billington | John Turner | |

* Historians differ as to whether 100, 101, or 102 passengers were aboard.

---

# The Early Congresses

At the urging of Massachusetts and Virginia, the First Continental Congress met in Philadelphia on September 5, 1774, and was attended by representatives of all the colonies except Georgia. Patrick Henry of Virginia declared: "The distinctions between Pennsylvanians, New Yorkers and New Englanders are no more. I am not a Virginian but an American." This Congress, which adjourned October 26, 1774, passed intercolonial resolutions calling for extensive boycott by the colonies against British trade.

The following year, most of the delegates from the colonies were chosen by popular election to attend the Second Continental Congress, which assembled in Philadelphia on May 10. As war had already begun between the colonies and England, the chief problems before the Congress were the procuring of military supplies, the establishment of an army and proper defenses, the issuing of continental bills of credit, etc. On June 15, 1775, George Washington was elected to command the Continental army. Congress adjourned Dec. 12, 1776.

Other Continental Congresses were held in Baltimore (1776–77), Philadelphia (1777), Lancaster, Pa. (1777), York, Pa. 1777–78), and Philadelphia (1778–81).

In 1781, the Articles of Confederation, although establishing a league of the thirteen states rather than a strong central government, provided for the continuance of Congress. Known thereafter as the Congress of the Confederation, it held sessions in Philadelphia (1781–83), Princeton, N. J. (1783), Annapolis, Md. (1783–84), and Trenton, N. J. (1784). Five sessions were held in New York City between the years 1785 and 1789.

The Congress of the United States, established by the ratification of the Constitution, held its first meeting on Mar. 4, 1789, in New York City. Several sessions of Congress were held in Philadelphia, and the first meeting in Washington, D. C., was on Nov. 17, 1800.

## Presidents of the Continental Congresses

| Name | Elected | Born | Died |
|---|---|---|---|
| Peyton Randolph, Va. | Sept. 5, 1774 | c.1721 | 1775 |
| Henry Middleton, S. C. | Oct. 22, 1774 | 1717 | 1784 |
| Peyton Randolph, Va. | May 10, 1775 | c.1721 | 1775 |
| John Hancock, Mass. | May 24, 1775 | 1737 | 1793 |
| Henry Laurens, S. C. | Nov. 1, 1777 | 1724 | 1792 |
| John Jay, N. Y. | Dec. 10, 1778 | 1745 | 1829 |
| Samuel Huntington, Conn. | Sept. 28, 1779 | 1731 | 1796 |
| Thomas McKean, Del. | July 10, 1781 | 1734 | 1817 |
| John Hanson, Md. | Nov. 5, 1781 | 1715 | 1783 |
| Elias Boudinot, N. J. | Nov. 4, 1782 | 1740 | 1821 |
| Thomas Mifflin, Pa. | Nov. 3, 1783 | 1744 | 1800 |
| Richard Henry Lee, Va. | Nov. 30, 1784 | 1732 | 1794 |
| John Hancock, Mass.* | Nov. 23, 1785 | 1737 | 1793 |
| Nathaniel Gorham, Mass. | June 6, 1786 | 1738 | 1796 |
| Arthur St. Clair, Pa. | Feb. 2, 1787 | 1734 | 1818 |
| Cyrus Griffin, Va. | Jan. 22, 1788 | 1748 | 1810 |

* Resigned May 29, 1786, never having served, because of continued illness.

## The Star-Spangled Banner
### Francis Scott Key, 1814

O say, can you see, by the dawn's early light,
What so proudly we hail'd at the twilight's last gleaming?
Whose broad stripes and bright stars, thro' the perilous fight,
O'er the ramparts we watch'd, were so gallantly streaming?
And the rockets' red glare, the bombs bursting in air,
Gave proof thro' the night that our flag was still there.
O say, does that star-spangled banner yet wave
O'er the land of the free and the home of the brave?

On the shore dimly seen thro' the mists of the deep,
Where the foe's haughty host in dread silence reposes,
What is that which the breeze, o'er the towering steep,
As it fitfully blows, half conceals, half discloses?
Now it catches the gleam of the morning's first beam,
In full glory reflected, now shines on the stream:
'T is the star-spangled banner: O, long may it wave
O'er the land of the free and the home of the brave!

And where is that band who so vauntingly swore
That the havoc of war and the battle's confusion,
A home and a country should leave us no more?
Their blood has wash'd out their foul footsteps' pollution.
No refuge could save the hireling and slave
From the terror of flight or the gloom of the grave:
And the star-spangled banner in triumph doth wave
O'er the land of the free and the home of the brave.

O thus be it ever when free-men shall stand
Between their lov'd home and the war's desolation;
Blest with vict'ry and peace, may the heav'n-rescued land
Praise the Pow'r that hath made and preserv'd us a nation!
Then conquer we must, when our cause it is just,
And this be our motto: "In God is our trust!"
And the star-spangled banner in triumph shall wave
O'er the land of the free and the home of the brave!

ON SEPTEMBER 13, 1814, Francis Scott Key visited the British fleet in Chesapeake Bay to secure the release of Dr. William Beanes, who had been captured after the burning of Washington, D. C. The release was secured, but Key was detained on ship overnight during the shelling of Fort McHenry, one of the forts defending Baltimore. In the morning, he was so delighted to see the American flag still flying over the fort that he began a poem to commemorate the occasion. Entitled "The Star-Spangled Banner," the poem soon attained wide popularity as sung to the tune "Anacreon in Heaven." The origin of this tune is obscure, but it may have been written by John Stafford Smith, a British composer born in 1750. "The Star-Spangled Banner" was officially made the National Anthem by Congress in 1931, although already adopted as such by the Army and Navy.

# History of the Flag

*Source: Encyclopaedia Britannica.*

THE FIRST OFFICIAL AMERICAN flag, the Continental or Grand Union flag, was displayed on Prospect Hill, Jan. 1, 1776, in the American lines besieging Boston. It had thirteen alternate red and white stripes, with the British Union Jack in the upper left corner.

On June 14, 1777, the Continental Congress adopted the design for a new flag, which actually was the Continental flag with the red cross of St. George and the white cross of St. Andrew replaced on the blue field by thirteen stars, one for each state. No rule was made as to the arrangement of the stars, and while they were usually shown in a circle, there were various other designs. It is uncertain when the new flag was first flown, but its first official announcement is believed to have been on Sept. 3, 1777.

The first public assertion that Betsy Ross made the first Stars and Stripes appeared in a paper read before the Historical Society of Pennsylvania on March 14, 1870, by William J. Canby, a grandson. However, Mr. Canby on later investigation found no official documents of any action by Congress on the flag before June 14, 1777. Betsy Ross's own story, according to her daughter, was that Washington, Robert Morris, and George Ross, as representatives of Congress, visited her in Philadelphia in June 1776, showing her a rough draft of the flag and asking her if she could make one. However, the only actual record of the manufacture of flags by Betsy Ross is a voucher in Harrisburg, Pa., for 14 pounds and some shillings for flags for the Pennsylvania navy.

On Jan. 13, 1794, Congress voted to add two stars and two stripes to the flag in recognition of the admission of Vermont and Kentucky to the Union. By 1818, there were twenty states in the Union, and as it was obvious that the flag would soon become unwieldy, Congress voted April 18 to return to the original thirteen stripes and to indicate the admission of a new state simply by the addition of a star the following July 4. The forty-ninth star, for Alaska, was added on July 4, 1959; and the fiftieth star, for Hawaii, was added on July 4, 1960.

The first Confederate flag, adopted in 1861 by the Confederate convention in Montgomery, Ala., was called the Stars and Bars; but because of its similarity in colors to the American flag, there was much confusion in the Battle of Bull Run. To remedy this situation, Gen. G. T. Beauregard suggested a battle flag, which was used by the Southern armies throughout the war. The flag consisted of a red field on which was placed a blue cross of St. Andrew separated from the field by a white fillet and adorned with thirteen* white stars for the Confederate states. In May 1863, at Richmond, an official flag was adopted by the Confederate Congress. This flag was white and twice as long as wide; the union, two-thirds the width of the flag, contained the battle flag designed for Gen. Beauregard. A broad transverse stripe of red was added Feb. 4, 1865, so that the flag might not be mistaken for a signal of truce.

* 11 states formally seceded, and unofficial groups in Kentucky and Missouri adopted ordinances of secession. On this basis, these two states were admitted to the Confederacy, although the official state governments remained in the Union.

# Flag Etiquette

## (Public Law 829—77th Congress)

### JOINT RESOLUTION

To amend Public Law Numbered 623, approved June 22, 1942, entitled "Joint resolution to codify and emphasize existing rules and customs pertaining to the display and use of the flag of the United States of America."

*Resolved by the Senate and House of Representatives of the United States of America in Congress Assembled,* That Public Law Numbered 623, approved June 22, 1942, entitled "Joint resolution to codify and emphasize existing rules and customs pertaining to the display and use of the flag of the United States of America," be, and the same is hereby amended to read as follows:

That the following codification of existing rules and customs pertaining to the display and use of the flag of the United States of America be, and it is hereby established for the use of such civilians or civilian groups or organizations as may not be required to conform with regulations promulgated by one or more executive departments of the Government of the United States.

Sec. 2. (a) It is the universal custom to display the flag only from sunrise to sunset on buildings and on stationary flagstaffs in the open. However, the flag may be displayed at night upon special occasions when it is desired to produce a patriotic effect.

(b) The flag should be hoisted briskly and lowered ceremoniously.

(c) The flag should not be displayed on days when the weather is inclement.

(d) The flag should be displayed on all days when the weather permits, especially on New Year's Day, January 1; Inauguration Day, January 20; Lincoln's Birthday, February 12; Washington's Birthday, February 22; Army Day*, April 6; Easter Sunday (variable); Mother's Day, second Sunday in May; Memorial Day (half-staff until noon), May 30; Flag Day, June 14; Independence Day, July 4; Labor Day, first Monday in September; Constitution Day, September 17; Columbus Day, October 12; Navy Day*, October 27; Armistice Day, November 11 †; Thanksgiving Day, fourth Thursday in November; Christmas Day, December 25; such other days as may be proclaimed by the President of the United States; the birthdays of States (dates of admission); and on State holidays.

(e) The flag should be displayed daily, weather permitting, on or near the main administration building of every public institution.

(f) The flag should be displayed in or near every polling place on election days.

(g) The flag should be displayed during school days in or near every schoolhouse.

SEC. 3. That the flag, when carried in a procession with another flag or flags, should be either on the marching right; that is, the flag's own right, or, if there is a line of other flags, in front of the center of that line.

(a) The flag should not be displayed on a float in a parade except from a staff, or as provided in subsection (i).

(b) The flag should not be draped over the hood, top, sides, or back of a vehicle or of a railroad train or a boat. When the flag is displayed on a motorcar, the staff shall be fixed firmly to the chassis or clamped to the radiator cap.

(c) No other flag or pennant should be placed above or, if on the same level, to the right of the flag of the United States of America, except during church services conducted by naval chaplains at sea, when the church pennant may be flown above the flag during church services for the personnel of the Navy. No person shall display the flag of the United Nations or any other national or international flag equal, above, or in a position of superior prominence or honor to, or in place of, the flag of the United States at any place within the United States or any Territory or possession thereof: *Provided,* That nothing in this section shall make unlawful the continuance of the practice heretofore followed of displaying the flag of the United Nations in a position of superior prominence or honor, and other national flags in positions of equal prominence or honor, with that of the flag of the United States at the headquarters of the United Nations.††

(d) The flag of the United States of America, when it is displayed with another flag against a wall from crossed staffs, should be on the right, the flag's own right, and its staff should be in front of the staff of the other flag.

(e) The flag of the United States of America should be at the center and at the highest point of the group when a number of flags of States or localities or pennants of societies are grouped and displayed from staffs.

(f) When flags of States, cities, or localities, or pennants of societies are flown on the same halyard with the flag of the United States, the latter should always be at the peak. When the flags are flown from adjacent staffs, the flag of the United States should be hoisted first and lowered last. No such flag or pennant may be placed above the flag of the United States or to the right of the flag of the United States.

(g) When flags of two or more nations are displayed, they are to be flown from separate staffs of the same height. The flags should be of approximately equal size. International usage forbids the display of the flag of one nation above that of another nation in time of peace.

(h) When the flag of the United States is displayed from a staff projecting horizontally or at an angle from the window sill, balcony, or front of a building, the union of the flag should be placed at the peak of the staff unless the flag is at half-staff. When the flag is suspended over a sidewalk from a rope extending from a house to a pole at the edge of the sidewalk, the flag should be hoisted out, union first, from the building.

(i) When the flag is displayed otherwise than by being flown from a staff, it should be displayed flat, whether indoors or out, or so suspended that its folds fall as free as though the flag were staffed.

(j) When the flag is displayed over the middle of the street, it should be suspended vertically with the union to the north in an east and west street or to the east in a north and south street.

(k) When used on a speaker's platform, the flag, if displayed flat, should be displayed above and behind the speaker. When displayed from a staff in a church or public auditorium, if it is displayed in the chancel of a church, or on the speaker's platform in a public auditorium, the flag should occupy the position of honor and be placed at the clergyman's or speaker's right as he faces the congregation or audience. Any other flag so displayed in the chancel or on the platform should be placed at the clergyman's or speaker's left as he faces the congregation or audience. But when the flag is displayed from a staff in a church or public auditorium elsewhere than in the chancel or on the platform it shall be placed in the position of honor at the right of the congregation or audience as they face the chancel or platform. Any other flag so displayed should be placed on

---

* In 1949, Army Day and Navy Day were abandoned; Armed Forces Day is celebrated the 3rd Saturday of May.  † In 1954, changed to Veterans Day.  †† Section 3 (c) was amended by Public Law 107, approved July 9, 1953, to designate the position of the United Nations flag.

the left of the congregation or audience as they face the chancel or platform.

(*l*) The flag should form a distinctive feature of the ceremony of unveiling a statue or monument, but it should never be used as the covering for the statue or monument.

(*m*) The flag, when flown at half-staff, should be first hoisted to the peak for an instant and then lowered to the half-staff position. The flag should be again raised to the peak before it is lowered for the day. By "half-staff" is meant lowering the flag to one-half the distance between the top and bottom of the staff. Crepe streamers may be affixed to spearheads or flag-staffs in a parade only by order of the President of the United States.

(*n*) When the flag is used to cover a casket, it should be so placed that the union is at the head and over the left shoulder. The flag should not be lowered into the grave or allowed to touch the ground.

Sec. 4. That no disrespect should be shown to the flag of the United States of America, the flag should not be dipped to any person or thing. Regimental colors, State flags, and organization or institutional flags are to be dipped as a mark of honor.

(*a*) The flag should never be displayed with the union down save as a signal of dire distress.

(*b*) The flag should never touch anything beneath it, such as the ground, the floor, water, or merchandise.

(*c*) The flag should never be carried flat or horizontally, but always aloft and free.

(*d*) The flag should never be used as drapery of any sort whatsoever, never festooned, drawn back, nor up, in folds, but always allowed to fall free. Bunting of blue, white, and red, always arranged with the blue above, the white in the middle, and the red below, should be used for covering a speaker's desk, draping the front of a platform, and for decoration in general.

(*e*) The flag should never be fastened, displayed, used, or stored in such a manner as will permit it to be easily torn, soiled, or damaged in any way.

(*f*) The flag should never be used as a covering for a ceiling.

(*g*) The flag should never have placed upon it, nor on any part of it, nor attached to it any mark, insignia, letter, word, figure, design, picture, or drawing of any nature.

(*h*) The flag should never be used as a receptacle for receiving, holding, carrying, or delivering anything.

(*i*) The flag should never be used for advertising purposes in any manner whatsoever. It should not be embroidered on such articles as cushions or handkerchiefs and the like, printed or otherwise impressed on paper napkins or boxes or anything that is designed for temporary use and discard; or used as any portion of a costume or athletic uniform. Advertising signs should not be fastened to a staff or halyard from which the flag is flown.

(*j*) The flag, when it is in such condition that it is no longer a fitting emblem for display, should be destroyed in a dignified way, preferably by burning.

Sec. 5. That during the ceremony of hoisting or lowering the flag or when the flag is passing in a parade or in a review, all persons present should face the flag, stand at attention, and salute. Those present in uniform should render the military salute. When not in uniform, men should remove the headdress with the right hand holding it at the left shoulder, the hand being over the heart. Men without hats should salute in the same manner. Aliens should stand at attention. Women should salute by placing the right hand over the heart. The salute to the flag in the moving column should be rendered at the moment the flag passes.

Sec. 6. That when the national anthem is played and the flag is not displayed, all present should stand and face toward the music. Those in uniform should salute at the first note of the anthem, retaining this position until the last note. All others should stand at attention, men removing the headdress. When the flag is displayed, all present should face the flag and salute.

Sec. 7. That the pledge of allegiance* to the flag, "I pledge allegiance to the flag of the United States of America and to the Republic for which it stands, one Nation under God,† indivisible, with liberty and justice for all," be rendered by standing with the right hand over the heart. However, civilians will always show full respect to the flag when the pledge is given by merely standing at attention, men removing the headdress. Persons in uniform shall render the military salute.

Sec. 8. Any rule or custom pertaining to the display of the flag of the United States of America, set forth herein, may be altered, modified, or repealed, or additional rules with respect thereto may be prescribed, by the Commander-in-Chief of the Army and Navy of the United States, whenever he deems it to be appropriate or desirable; and any such alteration or additional rule shall be set forth in a proclamation.

Approved, December 22, 1942.

---

\* The idea originated in 1892 with James B. Upham, an editor of *Youth's Companion*. The claim that Upham was also the author is disputed by some who credit Francis Bellamy. † The phrase "under God" was added to the pledge on June 14, 1954.

# Members of the Supreme Court of the United States

*Source:* The Marshal, Supreme Court of the United States.

| Name | Birth Place | Birth Date | Religious Affiliation (Source: Library of Congress) | Appointment From | President | Oath Taken Date | Oath Taken Age | Service Terminated Date | Service Terminated Cause | Years Served | Service Terminated Age | Death Date | Death Age |
|---|---|---|---|---|---|---|---|---|---|---|---|---|---|
| **CHIEF JUSTICES** | | | | | | | | | | | | | |
| John Jay | N. Y. | 1745 | Episcopal | N. Y. | Washington | 1790 | 44 | 1795 | resigned | 5 | 49 | 1829 | 83 |
| John Rutledge | S. C. | 1739 | Church of England | S. C. | Washington | 1795 | 55 | 1795 | rejected | 0 | 56 | 1800 | 60 |
| Oliver Ellsworth | Conn. | 1745 | Congregational | Conn. | Washington | 1796 | 50 | 1800 | resigned | 4 | 55 | 1807 | 62 |
| John Marshall | Va. | 1755 | Episcopal | Va. | J. Adams | 1801 | 45 | 1835 | death | 34 | 79 | 1835 | 79 |
| Roger B. Taney | Md. | 1777 | Roman Catholic | Md. | Jackson | 1836 | 59 | 1864 | death | 28 | 87 | 1864 | 87 |
| Salmon P. Chase | N. H. | 1808 | Episcopal | Ohio | Lincoln | 1864 | 56 | 1873 | death | 8 | 65 | 1873 | 65 |
| Morrison R. Waite | Conn. | 1816 | Episcopal | Ohio | Grant | 1874 | 57 | 1888 | death | 14 | 71 | 1888 | 71 |
| Melville W. Fuller | Maine | 1833 | Protestant | Ill. | Cleveland | 1888 | 55 | 1910 | death | 21 | 77 | 1910 | 77 |
| Edward D. White | La. | 1845 | Roman Catholic | La. | Taft | 1910 | 65 | 1921 | death | 10 | 75 | 1921 | 75 |
| William H. Taft | Ohio | 1857 | Unitarian | Conn. | Harding | 1921 | 63 | 1930 | retired | 8 | 72 | 1930 | 72 |
| Charles E. Hughes | N. Y. | 1862 | Baptist | N. Y. | Hoover | 1930 | 67 | 1941 | retired | 11 | 79 | 1948 | 86 |
| Harlan F. Stone | N. H. | 1872 | Episcopal | N. Y. | F. Roosevelt | 1941 | 68 | 1946 | death | 4 | 73 | 1946 | 73 |
| Frederick M. Vinson | Ky. | 1890 | Methodist | Ky. | Truman | 1946 | 56 | 1953 | death | 7 | 63 | 1953 | 63 |
| Earl Warren | Calif. | 1891 | Baptist | Calif. | Eisenhower | 1953 | 62 | .... | .... | .... | .... | .... | .... |
| **ASSOCIATE JUSTICES** | | | | | | | | | | | | | |
| James Wilson | Scotland | 1742 | Episcopal | Pa. | Washington | 1789 | 47 | 1798 | death | 8 | 55 | 1798 | 55 |
| John Rutledge | S. C. | 1739 | Church of England | S. C. | Washington | 1790 | 50 | 1791 | resigned | 1 | 51 | 1800 | 60 |
| William Cushing | Mass. | 1732 | Unitarian | Mass. | Washington | 1790 | 57 | 1810 | death | 20 | 78 | 1810 | 78 |
| John Blair | Va. | 1732 | Presbyterian | Va. | Washington | 1790 | 58 | 1796 | resigned | 5 | 64 | 1800 | 68 |
| James Iredell | England | 1751 | Episcopal | N. C. | Washington | 1790 | 38 | 1799 | death | 9 | 48 | 1799 | 48 |
| Thomas Johnson | Md. | 1732 | Episcopal | Md. | Washington | 1792 | 59 | 1793 | resigned | 0 | 60 | 1819 | 86 |
| William Paterson | Ireland | 1745 | Presbyterian | N. J. | Washington | 1793 | 47 | 1806 | death | 13 | 60 | 1806 | 60 |
| Samuel Chase | Md. | 1741 | Episcopal | Md. | Washington | 1796 | 54 | 1811 | death | 15 | 70 | 1811 | 70 |
| Bushrod Washington | Va. | 1762 | Church of England | Va. | J. Adams | 1799 | 36 | 1829 | death | 30 | 67 | 1829 | 67 |
| Alfred Moore | N. C. | 1755 | Protestant | N. C. | J. Adams | 1800 | 45 | 1804 | resigned | 3 | 48 | 1810 | 55 |
| William Johnson | S. C. | 1771 | Presbyterian | S. C. | Jefferson | 1804 | 32 | 1834 | death | 30 | 62 | 1834 | 62 |
| Brockholst Livingston | N. Y. | 1757 | Presbyterian | N. Y. | Jefferson | 1807 | 49 | 1823 | death | 16 | 65 | 1823 | 65 |
| Thomas Todd | Va. | 1765 | Presbyterian | Ky. | Jefferson | 1807 | 42 | 1826 | death | 18 | 61 | 1826 | 61 |
| Gabriel Duval | Md. | 1752 | French Protestant | Md. | Madison | 1811 | 58 | 1835 | resigned | 23 | 82 | 1844 | 91 |
| Joseph Story | Mass. | 1779 | Calvinist | Mass. | Madison | 1812 | 32 | 1845 | death | 33 | 65 | 1845 | 65 |
| Smith Thompson | N. Y. | 1768 | Presbyterian | N. Y. | Monroe | 1823 | 55 | 1843 | death | 20 | 75 | 1843 | 75 |
| Robert Trimble | Va. | 1777 | Protestant | Ky. | J. Q. Adams | 1826 | 49 | 1828 | death | 2 | 51 | 1828 | 51 |
| John McLean | N. J. | 1785 | (?) | Ohio | Jackson | 1830 | 44 | 1861 | death | 31 | 76 | 1861 | 76 |
| Henry Baldwin | Conn. | 1780 | Not known | Pa. | Jackson | 1830 | 50 | 1844 | death | 14 | 64 | 1844 | 64 |
| James M. Wayne | Ga. | 1790 | Protestant | Ga. | Jackson | 1835 | 45 | 1867 | death | 32 | 77 | 1867 | 77 |

| Name | Birthplace | Religion | Born | Appointed by | From | Appointed | Age | Term ended | How ended | Yrs served | Age at end | Died | Age at death |
|---|---|---|---|---|---|---|---|---|---|---|---|---|---|
| Philip P. Barbour | Va. | Episcopal | 1783 | Jackson | Va. | 1836 | 52 | 1841 | death | 4 | 57 | 1841 | 57 |
| John Catron | Pa. | Presbyterian | 1786 | Van Buren | Tenn. | 1837 | 51 | 1865 | death | 28 | 79 | 1865 | 79 |
| John McKinley | Va. | Protestant | 1780 | Van Buren | Ala. | 1838 | 57 | 1852 | death | 14 | 72 | 1852 | 72 |
| Peter V. Daniel | Va. | Protestant | 1784 | Van Buren | Va. | 1842 | 57 | 1860 | death | 18 | 76 | 1860 | 76 |
| Samuel Nelson | N.Y. | Protestant | 1792 | Tyler | N.Y. | 1845 | 52 | 1872 | retired | 27 | 80 | 1873 | 81 |
| Levi Woodbury | N.H. | Protestant | 1789 | Polk | N.H. | 1845 | 55 | 1851 | death | 5 | 61 | 1851 | 61 |
| Robert C. Grier | Pa. | Presbyterian | 1794 | Polk | Pa. | 1846 | 52 | 1870 | retired | 23 | 75 | 1870 | 76 |
| Benjamin R. Curtis | Mass. | (?) | 1809 | Fillmore | Mass. | 1851 | 41 | 1857 | resigned | 5 | 47 | 1874 | 64 |
| John A. Campbell | Ga. | Protestant | 1811 | Pierce | Ala. | 1853 | 41 | 1861 | resigned | 8 | 49 | 1889 | 77 |
| Nathan Clifford | N.H. | Protestant | 1803 | Buchanan | Maine | 1858 | 54 | 1881 | death | 23 | 77 | 1881 | 78 |
| Noah H. Swayne | Va. | Quaker | 1804 | Lincoln | Ohio | 1862 | 57 | 1881 | retired | 18 | 76 | 1884 | 79 |
| Samuel F. Miller | Ky. | Protestant | 1816 | Lincoln | Iowa | 1862 | 46 | 1890 | death | 28 | 74 | 1890 | 74 |
| David Davis | Md. | Episcopal | 1815 | Lincoln | Ill. | 1862 | 46 | 1877 | resigned | 14 | 61 | 1886 | 71 |
| Stephen J. Field | Conn. | Congregational | 1816 | Lincoln | Calif. | 1863 | 46 | 1897 | retired | 34 | 81 | 1899 | 82 |
| William Strong | Conn. | Presbyterian | 1808 | Grant | Pa. | 1870 | 61 | 1880 | retired | 10 | 72 | 1895 | 87 |
| Joseph P. Bradley | N.Y. | Protestant | 1813 | Grant | N.J. | 1870 | 57 | 1892 | death | 21 | 78 | 1892 | 78 |
| Ward Hunt | N.Y. | Episcopal | 1810 | Grant | N.Y. | 1873 | 62 | 1882 | disabled | 9 | 71 | 1886 | 75 |
| John M. Harlan | Ky. | Presbyterian | 1833 | Hayes | Ky. | 1877 | 44 | 1911 | death | 33 | 78 | 1911 | 78 |
| William B. Woods | Ohio | Presbyterian | 1824 | Hayes | Ga. | 1881 | 56 | 1887 | death | 6 | 62 | 1887 | 62 |
| Stanley Matthews | Ohio | Protestant | 1824 | Garfield | Ohio | 1881 | 56 | 1889 | death | 7 | 64 | 1889 | 64 |
| Horace Gray | Mass. | (*) | 1828 | Arthur | Mass. | 1882 | 53 | 1902 | death | 20 | 74 | 1902 | 74 |
| Samuel Blatchford | N.Y. | Presbyterian | 1820 | Arthur | N.Y. | 1882 | 62 | 1893 | death | 11 | 73 | 1893 | 73 |
| Lucius Q. C. Lamar | Ga. | Methodist | 1825 | Cleveland | Miss. | 1888 | 62 | 1893 | death | 5 | 67 | 1893 | 67 |
| David J. Brewer | Asia Minor | Protestant | 1837 | Harrison | Kans. | 1890 | 52 | 1910 | death | 20 | 72 | 1910 | 72 |
| Henry B. Brown | Mass. | Protestant | 1836 | Harrison | Mich. | 1891 | 54 | 1906 | retired | 15 | 70 | 1913 | 77 |
| George Shiras, Jr. | Pa. | Presbyterian | 1832 | Harrison | Pa. | 1892 | 60 | 1903 | retired | 10 | 71 | 1924 | 92 |
| Howell E. Jackson | Tenn. | Baptist | 1832 | Harrison | Tenn. | 1893 | 60 | 1895 | death | 2 | 63 | 1895 | 63 |
| Edward D. White | La. | Roman Catholic | 1845 | Cleveland | La. | 1894 | 48 | 1910 | promoted | 16 | 65 | 1921 | 76 |
| Rufus W. Peckham | N.Y. | Episcopal | 1838 | Cleveland | N.Y. | 1896 | 57 | 1909 | death | 13 | 70 | 1909 | 71 |
| Joseph McKenna | Pa. | Roman Catholic | 1843 | McKinley | Calif. | 1898 | 54 | 1925 | retired | 26 | 81 | 1926 | 83 |
| Oliver W. Holmes | Mass. | Congregational | 1841 | T. Roosevelt | Mass. | 1902 | 61 | 1932 | retired | 29 | 90 | 1935 | 94 |
| William R. Day | Ohio | Protestant | 1849 | T. Roosevelt | Ohio | 1903 | 53 | 1922 | retired | 19 | 73 | 1923 | 74 |
| William H. Moody | Mass. | Protestant | 1853 | T. Roosevelt | Mass. | 1906 | 52 | 1910 | disabled | 3 | 56 | 1917 | 64 |
| Horace H. Lurton | Ky. | Episcopal | 1844 | Taft | Tenn. | 1910 | 65 | 1914 | death | 4 | 70 | 1914 | 70 |
| Charles E. Hughes | N.Y. | Baptist | 1862 | Taft | N.Y. | 1910 | 48 | 1916 | resigned | 5 | 54 | 1948 | 86 |
| Willis Van Devanter | Ind. | Episcopal | 1859 | Taft | Wyo. | 1911 | 51 | 1937 | retired | 26 | 78 | 1941 | 82 |
| Joseph R. Lamar | Ga. | Ch. of Disciples | 1857 | Taft | Ga. | 1911 | 53 | 1916 | death | 4 | 58 | 1916 | 59 |
| Mahlon Pitney | N.J. | Presbyterian | 1858 | Taft | N.J. | 1912 | 54 | 1922 | retired | 10 | 64 | 1924 | 66 |
| James C. McReynolds | Ky. | Disciples of Christ | 1862 | Wilson | Tenn. | 1914 | 52 | 1939 | retired | 26 | 78 | 1946 | 84 |
| Louis D. Brandeis | Ohio | Hebrew | 1856 | Wilson | Mass. | 1916 | 59 | 1939 | retired | 22 | 82 | 1941 | 85 |
| John H. Clarke | Ohio | Protestant | 1857 | Wilson | Ohio | 1916 | 59 | 1922 | resigned | 5 | 65 | 1945 | 88 |
| George Sutherland | England | Protestant | 1862 | Harding | Utah | 1922 | 60 | 1938 | retired | 15 | 75 | 1942 | 80 |
| Pierce Butler | Minn. | Roman Catholic | 1866 | Harding | Minn. | 1923 | 56 | 1939 | death | 16 | 73 | 1939 | 73 |
| Edward T. Sanford | Tenn. | Episcopal | 1865 | Harding | Tenn. | 1923 | 57 | 1930 | death | 7 | 64 | 1930 | 65 |
| Harlan F. Stone | N.H. | Episcopal | 1872 | Coolidge | N.Y. | 1925 | 52 | 1941 | promoted | 16 | 68 | 1946 | 74 |
| Owen J. Roberts | Pa. | Episcopal | 1875 | Hoover | Pa. | 1930 | 55 | 1945 | resigned | 15 | 70 | 1955 | 80 |

## Members of the Supreme Court of the United States (Contd.)

| Name | Birth | | Religious Affiliation (Source: Library of Congress) | Appointment | | Oath Taken | | Service Terminated | | | | Death | |
|---|---|---|---|---|---|---|---|---|---|---|---|---|---|
| | Place | Date | | From | President | Date | Age | Date | Cause | Years Served | Age | Date | Age |
| Benjamin N. Cardozo | N. Y. | 1870 | Hebrew | N. Y. | Hoover | 1932 | 61 | 1938 | death | 6 | 68 | 1938 | 68 |
| Hugo L. Black | Ala. | 1886 | Baptist | Ala. | F. Roosevelt | 1937 | 51 | .... | .... | .... | .... | .... | .... |
| Stanley F. Reed | Ky. | 1884 | Protestant | Ky. | F. Roosevelt | 1938 | 53 | 1957 | retired | 19 | 73 | .... | .... |
| Felix Frankfurter | Austria | 1882 | Hebrew | Mass. | F. Roosevelt | 1939 | 56 | .... | .... | .... | .... | .... | .... |
| William O. Douglas | Minn. | 1898 | Presbyterian | Conn. | F. Roosevelt | 1939 | 40 | .... | .... | .... | .... | .... | .... |
| Frank Murphy | Mich. | 1890 | Roman Catholic | Mich. | F. Roosevelt | 1940 | 49 | 1949 | death | 9 | 59 | 1949 | 59 |
| James F. Byrnes | S. C. | 1879 | Episcopal | S. C. | F. Roosevelt | 1941 | 62 | 1942 | resigned | 1 | 63 | .... | .... |
| Robert H. Jackson | N. Y. | 1892 | Episcopal | N. Y. | F. Roosevelt | 1941 | 49 | 1954 | death | 13 | 62 | 1954 | 62 |
| Wiley B. Rutledge | Ky. | 1894 | Unitarian | Iowa | F. Roosevelt | 1943 | 49 | 1949 | death | 6 | 55 | 1949 | 55 |
| Harold H. Burton | Mass. | 1888 | Unitarian | Ohio | Truman | 1945 | 57 | 1958 | retired | 13 | 70 | .... | .... |
| Tom C. Clark | Tex. | 1899 | Presbyterian | Tex. | Truman | 1949 | 49 | .... | .... | .... | .... | .... | .... |
| Sherman Minton | Ind. | 1890 | Protestant | Ind. | Truman | 1949 | 58 | 1956 | retired | 7 | 67 | .... | .... |
| John M. Harlan | Ill. | 1899 | Presbyterian | N. Y. | Eisenhower | 1955 | 55 | .... | .... | .... | .... | .... | .... |
| William J. Brennan, Jr. | N. J. | 1906 | Roman Catholic | N. J. | Eisenhower | 1956 | 50 | .... | .... | .... | .... | .... | .... |
| Charles E. Whittaker | Kans. | 1901 | Methodist | Mo. | Eisenhower | 1957 | 56 | .... | .... | .... | .... | .... | .... |
| Potter Stewart | Mich. | 1915 | Episcopal | Ohio | Eisenhower | 1959 | 44 | .... | .... | .... | .... | .... | .... |

[1] Professing Christian. [2] Unitarian, then Episcopal. [3] Unitarian or Congregaitonal.

## Impeachments

*U. S. Constitution, Article I, Section 3.*

The Senate shall have the sole Power to try all Impeachments. When sitting for that Purpose, they shall be on Oath or Affirmation. When the President of the United States is tried, the Chief Justice shall preside. And no Person shall be convicted without the Concurrence of two thirds of the Members present.

Judgment in Cases of Impeachment shall not extend further than to removal from Office, and disqualification to hold and enjoy any Office of honor, Trust, or Profit under the United States: but the Party convicted shall nevertheless be liable and subject to Indictment, Trial, Judgment and Punishment, according to Law.

## Federal Impeachments

*Source: Congressional Directory.*

The Senate has sat as a court of impeachment in the following cases:

WILLIAM BLOUNT, Senator from Tennessee; charges dismissed for want of jurisdiction, January 14, 1799.

JOHN PICKERING, Judge of the U. S. District Court for New Hampshire; removed from office March 12, 1804.

SAMUEL CHASE, Associate Justice of the Supreme Court; acquitted March 1, 1805.

JAMES H. PECK, Judge of the U. S. District Court for Missouri; acquitted Jan. 31, 1831.

WEST H. HUMPHREYS, Judge of the United States District Court for the middle, eastern, and western districts of Tennessee; removed from office June 26, 1862.

ANDREW JOHNSON, President of the United States; acquitted May 26, 1868.

WILLIAM W. BELKNAP, Secretary of War; acquitted Aug. 1, 1876.

CHARLES SWAYNE, Judge of the United States District Court for the northern district of Florida; acquitted Feb. 27, 1905.

ROBERT W. ARCHBALD, Associate Judge, United States Commerce Court; removed from office January 13, 1913.

GEORGE W. ENGLISH, Judge of the U. S. District Court for the eastern district of Illinois; resigned office November 4, 1926; impeachment proceedings dismissed.

HAROLD LOUDERBACK, Judge of the U. S. District Court for the northern district of California; acquitted May 24, 1933.

HALSTED L. RITTER, Judge of the U. S. District Court for the southern district of Florida; removed April 17, 1936.

# THE UNITED STATES ARMED SERVICES

## U. S. MILITARY ACADEMY
*Source:* U. S. Military Academy.

Established in 1802 by an Act of Congress, the U. S. Military Academy is located on the west bank of the Hudson River some 50 miles north of New York City. Admission may be gained only by appointment to one of the 2,536 cadetships authorized by law:

Noncompetitive:

| | |
|---|---:|
| Representatives (4 each) ........ | 1,748 |
| Senators (4 each) .............. | 400 |
| Other: | |
|   Vice Presidential .......... 3 | |
|   District of Columbia ...... 6 | |
|   Canal Zone Government ... 2 | |
|   Puerto Rico .............. 4 | 15 |

Competitive:

| | |
|---|---:|
| Army and Air Force: | |
|   Regular components .......... | 90 |
|   Reserve components .......... | 90 |
| Presidential .................... | 89 |
| Sons of deceased veterans ....... | 40 |
| Honor military & honor naval schools | 40 |
| **Foreign cadets*** .................. | 24 |
| Total ................ | 2,536 |

Graduation of the senior class normally leaves about 750 of these cadetships vacant and hence available to new candidates each year. Candidates may be nominated for these vacancies during the year preceding the admission date—the first Tuesday in July.

Candidates must be citizens of the U. S., be of good moral character, have never been married, be between the ages of 17 and 22, have a secondary-school education or its equivalent, and be able to meet the academic, medical, and physical aptitude requirements. Academic qualification is determined by an analysis of entire scholastic record, and performance on prescribed tests of the College Entrance Examination Board. The College Board tests which have been adopted by the Military Academy are—The Scholastic Aptitude Test and Achievement Tests in English Composition and Mathematics. The particular College Board tests which a candidate must take to qualify for entrance to the Military Academy depend upon the type of nomination the candidate receives and his previous academic performance. Entrance requirements and procedures for appointment are described in the U. S. Military Academy Catalogue, available without charge from The Registrar, U. S. Military Academy, West Point, New York.

Cadets receive their entire education at Government expense and are paid $111.15

* Philippines, 4; Canada and other American countries, 20.

per month. From this sum, they pay for their uniforms, textbooks, etc. Upon successful completion of the 4-year course, the graduate receives the degree of Bachelor of Science and is commissioned a second lieutenant in the Regular Army of the United States.

## U. S. NAVAL ACADEMY
*Source:* U. S. Naval Academy.

On October 10, 1845, the Naval School was established at Fort Severn, Annapolis, Maryland. Five years later it was renamed the United States Naval Academy, and the following year a regular four-year course was adopted. In June, 1959, the academic departments were grouped under three directors as follows: Director of Naval Science (Command—Weapons—Naval Hygiene); Director of Science and Engineering (Mathematics—Science—Engineering); and Director of Social Sciences and Humanities (English, History, and Government—Foreign Languages). The Executive Department and Physical Education came under the direction of the Commandant of Midshipmen.

Candidates are selected as follows:

5 from the District of Columbia.

40 sons of men and women killed in action or who have died, or may hereafter die of wounds or injuries, or disease contracted, in active service in World Wars I and II and other periods.

75 annually from among sons of officers and enlisted men in the regular Army, Navy, Marine Corps, Air Force and Coast Guard.

160 enlisted Navy and Marine personnel selected annually by competitive examination.

160 annually chosen by the Secretary of the Navy from the Naval and Marine Corps Reserves.

5 Puerto Ricans chosen by the Resident Commissioner of Puerto Rico.

1 on the recommendation of the Governor of Puerto Rico.

4 Filipinos designated by the President of the United States.

1 from the Canal Zone.

20 annually from schools designated by the Army and Navy as honor schools and from NROTC schools.

20 from the American republics and the Dominion of Canada.

Unlimited: Sons of persons who have been or shall hereafter be awarded the Medal of Honor.

Each Senator and Representative in Congress, and the Vice President may have not more than 5 Midshipmen at the Naval Academy. The Board of Commissioners selects the 5 from the District of Columbia. The President selects the 40 sons of deceased veterans of World Wars and the 75 sons of officers and enlisted men in the regular Army, Navy, Marine Corps, Air Force and Coast Guard. The President also appoints the sons of holders of the Medal of Honor.

Subject to the existence of vacancies and the availability of accommodations, the Secretary of the Navy may nominate for appointment a limited number of additional candidates. These must be recommended by the Academic Board from among the fully qualified, regularly nominated alternate and competitive candidates of the same year who were unable to enter because of the appointment of men preceding them in nomination.

Candidates for admission must be between 17 and 22 years of age on July 1 of their entering year. They may qualify by submitting acceptable scores on College Entrance Examination Board aptitude and achievement tests, or by presenting acceptable high school and college certificates. Details of the entrance requirements, scholastic and physical, may be obtained from the Naval Academy or from the Navy Department, Washington, 25, D.C. Candidates must also meet physical requirements and be unmarried.

Midshipmen are paid $111.15 per month. Graduates of the Academy are granted Bachelor of Science degrees and are commissioned as ensigns in the Navy or second lieutenants in the Marine Corps.

## U. S. COAST GUARD ACADEMY
*Source:* U. S. Coast Guard Academy.

The cadet system of the Coast Guard was established by law on July 31, 1876, when the "School of Instruction" for the Revenue Cutter Service, predecessor to the Coast Guard, was authorized.

The *J. C. Dobbin,* a converted schooner, served as the first schoolship, and was succeeded in 1878 by the bark *Chase,* a ship built for cadet training. First winter quarters were in a sail loft at New Bedford, Mass. The school was moved in 1900 to a two-story frame school at Curtis Bay, Md., to provide a more technical education; and in 1910 to Fort Trumbull, New London, Conn. In 1932 the Academy moved to its present site in the latter city.

The 4-year college-level curriculum leads to a Bachelor of Science degree and to a commission of ensign in the Coast Guard.

Cadets receive appointment to the Academy through a nation-wide competitive examination, held annually in February. Applications must be submitted by Jan. 10. Candidates must be between 17 and 22 years of age, physically sound, unmarried and at least 5′ 4″ tall. They must agree to remain unmarried until graduation and to serve at least 4 years on active duty. Cadets receive $1,333.80 per year to cover their uniform and incidental expenses, and are furnished their rations and quarters. Applications for appointment may be made to the Commandant (PTP), U. S. Coast Guard, Washington 25, D. C.

## U. S. MERCHANT MARINE ACADEMY
*Source:* U.S. Merchant Marine Academy.

The U. S. Merchant Marine Cadet Corps was established Mar. 15, 1938, and its Academy is located on the south shore of Long Island Sound at Kings Point, N. Y.

The Academy has a complement of 1,000 cadets representing every U. S. state, D. C., the Canal Zone, Puerto Rico, Guam, American Samoa and the Virgin Islands. In addition, it is authorized to admit for the full period of training not more than 12 candidates from Central and South American republics.

Competitive examinations are held annually among candidates nominated by Senators and members of the House of Representatives. Appointments to the Academy are governed by a state and territory quota system based on population. A candidate must be an unmarried citizen not less than 17 and not yet 22 years of age by July 1 of the year in which admission is sought. He must have 15 high school credits, including 3 units in mathematics (from algebra, geometry and/or trigonometry), 1 unit in science (physics or chemistry) and 3 in English.

The course is 4 years, consisting of 1 year as Fourth Classman at the Academy, 1 year as Third Classman aboard a merchant ship, and 2 years as Second and First Classman at the Academy. Study includes marine engineering, navigation, electricity, ship construction, naval science and tactics, economics, business, languages, history, and other subjects.

On completion of their courses, cadets are examined for their original Merchant Marine license as deck or engineer officers in any ship in the U. S. Merchant Marine. They also receive Bachelor of Science degrees and may be commissioned as officers in the U. S. Naval Reserve.

## U. S. AIR FORCE ACADEMY
*Source:* U. S. Air Force Academy.

The bill establishing the Air Force Academy was signed by President Eisenhower on Apr. 1, 1954. The first class of 306 cadets was sworn in on July 11, 1955, at Lowry Air Force Base, Denver, Colo., the Academy's temporary location. The Cadet Wing moved into the Academy's permanent home north of Colorado Springs in Aug. 1958.

Eventually the Academy will have a complement of over 2,500. Qualified sons of Medal of Honor winners will be admitted without regard to total vacancies, provided they pass minimum requirements.

Candidates must be citizens of the U. S., be at least 17 but less than 22 on July 1 of the year for which they seek admission, never have been married, be at least 5' 4" and not more than 6' 8" tall, and be able to meet the mental and physical requirements. A candidate is required to take the following examinations and tests: (1) the Air Force Academy Medical Examination; (2) the College Entrance Examination Board Tests; and (3) a physical aptitude examination.

Cadets receive their entire education at Government expense and, in addition, are paid $111.15 per month. From this sum, they pay for some of their uniforms, textbooks, etc. Upon completion of the 4-year course, leading to a bachelor's degree, a cadet who meets the physical qualifications is appointed a second lieutenant in the regular U. S. Air Force. Many go on to full-scale pilot training.

---

# History of the Armed Services
Source: U. S. Department of Defense.

## U. S. ARMY

When Gen. Washington, on July 3, 1775, took command of the colonial militia (about 8,000 men) besieging Boston, the event marked the union of the forces of the 13 separate colonies under one head, and the U. S. Army was born. In Jan. 1776, the Continental Congress decided that these troops should be separate in organization from those of local communities and established them as the U. S. Regular Army. When these forces were disbanded after the war, only some 80 officers and men were retained to guard U. S. Army stores. From this humble beginning, in the ensuing years, the strength of the U. S. Army rose or fell according to national and international conditions.

## U. S. NAVY

In Sept. and Oct. 1775, Gen. Washington maintained 5 schooners and a sloop with officers and men from his army for the purpose of preying on inbound English supply vessels and thereby caused the birth of the U. S. Navy. In Dec. 1775, the Continental Congress expanded this by providing for construction of naval craft and the appointment of a marine committee (one member from each colony) which continued until 1794 when further ships and manpower were provided for by act of Congress. Upon completion of these ships in 1798, a Navy Department was established as the controlling agency, and the secretary given Cabinet rank.

## U. S. AIR FORCE

Until creation of the National Military Establishment in September 1947, which united the services under one department, military aviation was a part of the U. S. Army. In the Army, aeronautical operations came under the Signal Corps from 1907 to 1918, when the U. S. Air Service was established. In 1926, the U. S. Air Corps came into being and remained until 1942, when the Army Air Forces succeeded it as the Army's air arm.

In the Navy, ship-based fighters and bombers are attached to the several fleets and are under the orders of the fleet commanders. Marine Corps aviation comes under control of the Navy.

In 1947, the U. S. Air Force was established as an independent military service under the National Military Establishment. At that time, the name U. S. Air Corps and the names of the services within the Army Air Forces were abolished.

## U. S. COAST GUARD

Our country's oldest continuous seagoing service, the U. S. Coast Guard traces its history back to 1790 when the First Congress authorized the construction of ten vessels for the collection of revenue. Known first as the Revenue Marine, and later as the Revenue Cutter Service, the Coast Guard received its present name in 1915 under an act of Congress combining the Revenue Cutter Service with the Life-Saving Service. In 1939, the Lighthouse Service of the Department of Commerce was also consolidated with this unit. The Bureau of Marine Inspection and Navigation was transferred temporarily to the Coast Guard in 1942, permanently in 1946. Through its antecedents, the Coast Guard is one of the oldest organizations under the Federal government and, until the Navy Department was established in 1798, served as the only U. S. armed force afloat. In time of peace it operates under the Treasury Department, serving as the Nation's primary agency for promoting marine safety and enforcing Federal maritime laws. In time of war, or on direction of the President, it is attached to the Navy Department.

## U. S. MARINE CORPS

Founded in 1775 and observing its official birthday on Nov. 10, the U. S. Marine Corps was developed to be able to serve to advantage on land or sea.

It has been used successfully in every U. S. war beginning with the Revolution, when it consisted of 2 battalions. It reached its high in achievement in World War II and in the Korean conflict when over 75% of its officers and men saw combat.

## Selective Service Classifications

**I-A:** Available for military service.

**I-A-O:** Conscientious objector available for noncombatant military service only.

**I-C:** Member of Armed Forces, Coast and Geodetic Survey or Public Health Service.

**I-D:** Member of reserve component or student taking military training.

**I-O:** Conscientious objector available for civilian work contributing to maintenance of national health, safety or interest.

**I-S:** Student deferred by statute.

**I-W:** Conscientious objector performing civilian work contributing to maintenance of national health, safety or interest.

**II-A:** Registrant deferred because of civilian occupation (except agriculture and activity in study).

**II-C:** Registrant deferred because of agricultural occupation.

**II-S:** Registrant deferred because of activity in study.

**III-A:** Registrant with child or children; and registrant deferred by reason of extreme hardship to dependents.

**IV-A:** Registrant who has completed service; sole surviving son.

**IV-B:** Official deferred by law.

**IV-C:** Alien.

**IV-D:** Minister of religion or divinity student.

**IV-F:** Physically, mentally or morally unfit.

**V-A:** Registrant over age of liability for military service.

## Highest Ranking Officers in the Armed Forces

### ARMY

**Generals of the Army:** Douglas MacArthur; Omar N. Bradley; Dwight D. Eisenhower.

**Generals:** Lyman L. Lemnitzer; Williston B. Palmer; George H. Decker; Bruce C. Clarke; Clyde D. Eddleman; Clark L. Ruffner; Charles D. Palmer; Carter B. Magruder; James E. Moore; James F. Collins; Herbert B. Powell.

### AIR FORCE

**Generals:** Thomas D. White; Lauris Norstad; Curtis E. LeMay; Laurence S. Kuter; Leon W. Johnson; Thomas S. Power; Frank F. Everest; Samuel E. Anderson; Charles P. Cabell; Emmett O'Donnell, Jr.; Frederic H. Smith, Jr.

### NAVY

**Fleet Admiral:** Chester W. Nimitz.

**Admirals:** Arleigh A. Burke; Harry D. Felt; James S. Russell; Charles R. Brown; Robert L. Dennison; Harold P. Smith; John H. Sides.

### MARINE CORPS

**General:** David M. Shoup.

**Lieutenant Generals:** Joseph C. Burger; Edward W. Snedeker; John C. Munn; Wallace M. Greene, Jr.; Alan Shapley.

### COAST GUARD

**Admiral:** Alfred C. Richmond, Commandant.

**Vice Admiral:** James A. Hirshfield, Assistant Commandant.

# U. S. Military Actions Other Than Declared Wars

**HAWAII (1893):** U. S. Marines, ordered to land by U. S. Minister Stevens, aided the revolutionary Committee of Safety in overthrowing the native government. Stevens then proclaimed Hawaii a U. S. protectorate. Annexation, resisted by the Democratic regime in Washington, was not formally accomplished until 1898.

**CHINA (1900):** Boxers (a group of Chinese revolutionists) occupied Peking and laid siege to foreign legations. U. S. troops joined an international expedition which relieved the city.

**PANAMÁ (1903):** After Colombia had rejected a proposed agreement for relinquishing sovereignty over the Panama Canal Zone, revolution broke out, aided by promoters of the Panama Canal Co. Two U. S. warships were standing by to protect American privileges. The U. S. recognized the Republic of Panamá on Nov. 6.

**DOMINICAN REPUBLIC (1904):** When the Dominican Republic failed to meet debts owed to the U. S. and foreign creditors, Theodore Roosevelt declared the U. S. intention of exercising "international police power" in the Western Hemisphere whenever necessary. The U. S. accordingly administered customs and managed debt payments of the Dominican Republic from 1905–07.

**NICARAGUA (1911):** The possibility of foreign control over Nicaragua's canal route led to U. S. intervention and agreement. The U. S. landed Marines in Nicaragua (Aug. 14, 1912) to protect American interests there. A small detachment remained until 1933.

**MEXICO (1914):** Mexican Dictator Huerta, opposed by President Wilson, had the support of European governments. An incident involving unarmed U. S. sailors in Tampico led to the landing of U. S. forces on Mexican soil. Vera Cruz was bombarded by the Navy to prevent the landing of munitions from a German vessel. At the point of war, both powers agreed to mediation by Argentina, Brazil and Chile. Huerta abdicated, and Carranza succeeded to the presidency.

**HAITI (1915):** U. S. Marines imposed a military occupation. Haiti signed a treaty making it a virtual protectorate of the U. S until troops were withdrawn in 1934.

MEXICO (1916): Raids by Pancho Villa cost American lives on both sides of the border. President Carranza consented to a punitive expedition lead by Gen. Pershing, but antagonism grew in Mexico. Wilson withdrew the U. S. force when war with Germany became imminent.

DOMINICAN REPUBLIC (1916): Renewed intervention in the Dominican Republic with internal administration by U. S. naval officers lasted until 1924.

## Insignia and Ranks of the Armed Forces

| Army, Air Force and Marines | | Navy and Coast Guard | | |
|---|---|---|---|---|
| Insignia | Rank | Insignia | Rank | Stripes[1] |
| Five silver stars | General of the Army, AF | Five silver stars | Fleet Admiral | 1—4—0 |
| Four silver stars | General | Four silver stars | Admiral | 1—3—0 |
| Three silver stars | Lieutenant General | Three silver stars | Vice Admiral | 1—2—0 |
| Two silver stars | Major General | Two silver stars | Rear Admiral | 1—1—0 |
| One silver star | Brigadier General | One silver star | Commodore | 1—0—0[2] |
| Silver eagle | Colonel | Silver eagle | Captain | 0—4—0 |
| Silver oak leaf | Lieutenant Colonel | Silver oak leaf | Commander | 0—3—0 |
| Gold oak leaf | Major | Gold oak leaf | Lt. Commander | 0—2—1 |
| Two silver bars | Captain | Two silver bars | Lieutenant | 0—2—0 |
| One silver bar | First Lieutenant | One silver bar | Lieutenant (jg) | 0—1—1 |
| One gold bar | Second Lieutenant | One gold bar | Ensign | 0—1—0 |
| Silver bar with 3 enamel bands[3] | Chief Warrant Officer (W-4) | Silver bar with 3 enamel bands[3] | Chief Warrant Officer (W-4) | 0—1—0[4] |
| Silver bar with 2 enamel bands[3] | Chief Warrant Officer (W-3) | Silver bar with 2 enamel bands[3] | Chief Warrant Officer (W-3) | 0—1—0[5] |
| Gold bar with 3 enamel bands[3] | Chief Warrant Officer (W-2) | Gold bar with 3 enamel bands[3] | Chief Warrant Officer (W-2) | 0—1—0[6] |
| Gold bar with 2 enamel bands[3] | Warrant Officer (W-1) | Gold bar with 2 enamel bands[3] | Warrant Officer (W-1) | 0—0—1[6] |

[1] Of gold embroidery; first figure is number of 2-in. stripes, second is number of 1/2-in. stripes, third is number of 1/4-in. stripes. [2] Wartime only. [3] Bar is 3/8 in. by 1 1/8 in. for Army, Air Force and Navy, 1/4 in. by 3/4 in. for Marine Corps. Enamel bands are brown for Army, sky blue for Air Force, scarlet for Marines and blue for Navy. [4] One break. [5] Two breaks. [6] Three breaks.

## Pay Grades of Enlisted Personnel

*Source:* Department of Defense, Public Information Office.

| Army ranks[1] | Air Force ranks | Marine ranks | Navy ranks | Pay grades |
|---|---|---|---|---|
| Sergeant Major | Chief Master Sergeant | Sergeant Major and Master Gunnery Sergeant | Mast. Ch. Petty Officer | E-9 |
| 1st Sgt. and Master Sgt. | Sr. Master Sergeant | 1st Sgt. and Master Sgt. | Sr. Ch. Petty Officer | E-8 |
| Sergeant 1st Class | Master Sergeant | Gunnery Sergeant | Chief Petty Officer | E-7 |
| Staff Sergeant | Technical Sergeant | Staff Sergeant | Petty Officer 1st Class | E-6 |
| Sergeant | Staff Sergeant | Sergeant | Petty Officer 2nd Class | E-5 |
| Corporal | Airman 1st Class | Corporal | Petty Officer 3rd Class | E-4 |
| Private 1st Class | Airman 2nd Class | Lance Corporal | Seaman | E-3 |
| Private | Airman 3rd Class | Private 1st Class Marine | Seaman Apprentice | E-2 |
| Private | Airman | Private | Seaman Recruit | E-1 |

[1] Army specialist pay grades correspond to numbers: Specialist Nine (E-9) etc.

## Monthly Salaries of Enlisted Personnel by Years of Service

E-9*—10–12 yrs service: $380; 12–14 yrs: $390; 14–16 yrs: $400; 16–18 yrs: $410; 18–20 yrs: $420; 20–22 yrs: $430; over 22 yrs: $440.

E-8*—8–10 yrs service: $310; 10–12 yrs: $320; 12–14 yrs: $330; 14–16 yrs: $340; 16–18 yrs: $350; 18–20 yrs: $360; 20–22 yrs: $370; over 22 yrs: $380.

E-7—Under 2 yrs service: $206.39; 2–4 yrs: $236; 4–6 yrs: $250; 6–8 yrs: $260; 8–10 yrs: $270; 10–12 yrs: $285; 12–14 yrs: $300; 14–16 yrs: $310; 16–18 yrs: $325; 18–20 yrs: $340; over 20 yrs: $350.

E-6—Under 2 yrs service: $175.81; 2–4 yrs: $200; 4–6 yrs: $225; 6–8 yrs: $235; 8–10 yrs: $245; 10–12 yrs: $255; 12–14 yrs: $265; 14–16 yrs: $275; 16–18 yrs: $280; over 18 yrs: $290.

E-5—Under 2 yrs service: $145.24; 2–4 yrs: $180; 4–6 yrs: $205; 6–8 yrs: $210; 8–10 yrs: $220; over 10 yrs $240.

E-4—Under 2 yrs service: $122.30; 2–3 yrs: $150; 3–4 yrs: $160; 4–6 yrs: $170; 6–8 yrs: $180; over 8 yrs: $190.

E-3—Under 2 yrs service: $99.37; 2–4 yrs: $124; over 4 yrs: $141.

E-2—Under 2 yrs service: $85.80; over 2 yrs: $108.

E-1—Under 4 mos service: $78; 4 mos–2 yrs: $83.20; over 2 yrs: $105.

* An enlisted member may not be placed in pay grade E-8 or E-9 until he has completed at least 8 years or 10 years, respectively, of cumulative service creditable in the computation of his basic pay.

MONTHLY ALLOWANCE FOR QUARTERS: No dependents, $51.30 for all pay grades; 1 dependent, $51.30 for pay grades E-1 through E-3, $77.10 for pay grades E-4 through E-9; 2 dependents, $77.10 for all pay grades; over 2 dependents, $96.90 for all pay grades.

# Pay Grades of Commissioned Officers and Warrant Officers

*Source:* Department of Defense, Public Information Office.

| Rank | | | | Monthly allowances for quarters | |
|---|---|---|---|---|---|
| Army, Air Force and Marine Corps | Navy, Coast Guard and Coast and Geodetic Survey | Public Health Service | Pay grade | With dependents | With no dependents |
| General | Admiral | ......................... | O-10 | $171.00 | $136.80 |
| Lieutenant General | Vice Admiral | | O-9 | 171.00 | 136.80 |
| Major General | Rear Admiral (upper half) | Surgeon General; Deputy Surgeon General; Assistant Surgeon General having rank of Major General | O-8 | 171.00 | 136.80 |
| Brigadier General | Rear Admiral (lower half) and Commodore | Assistant Surgeon General having rank of Brigadier General | O-7 | 171.00 | 136.80 |
| Colonel | Captain | Director Grade | O-6 | 136.80 | 119.70 |
| Lieutenant Colonel | Commander | Senior Grade | O-5 | 136.80 | 102.60 |
| Major | Lieutenant Commander | Full Grade | O-4 | 119.70 | 94.20 |
| Captain | Lieutenant | Senior Assistant Grade | O-3 | 102.60 | 85.50 |
| First Lieutenant | Lieutenant (junior grade) | Assistant Grade | O-2 | 94.20 | 77.10 |
| Second Lieutenant | Ensign | Junior Assistant Grade | O-1 | 85.50 | 68.40 |
| Chief Warrant Officer | Chief Warrant Officer | ......................... | W-4 | 119.70 | 94.20 |
| Chief Warrant Officer | Chief Warrant Officer | ......................... | W-3 | 102.60 | 85.50 |
| Chief Warrant Officer | Chief Warrant Officer | ......................... | W-2 | 94.20 | 77.10 |
| Warrant Officer | Warrant Officer | ......................... | W-1 | 85.50 | 68.40 |

## Monthly Salaries of Officers by Years of Service

**O-10\***—Under 2 yrs service: $1,200; 2–8 yrs: $1,250; 8–12 yrs: $1,300; 12–16 yrs: $1,400; 16–20 yrs: $1,500; 20–26 yrs: $1,600; over 26 yrs: $1,700.

**O-9**—Under 2 yrs service: $1,063.30; 2–3 yrs: $1,100; 3–8 yrs: $1,122; 8–12 yrs: $1,150; 12–16 yrs: $1,200; 16–26 yrs: $1,300; 20–26 yrs: $1,400; over 26 yrs: $1,500.

**O-8**—Under 2 yrs service: $963.30; 2–3 yrs: $1,000; 3–8 yrs: $1,022; 8–12 yrs: $1,100; 12–16 yrs: $1,150; 16–18 yrs: $1,200; 18–20 yrs: $1,250; 20–22 yrs: $1,300; over 22 yrs: $1,350.

**O-7**—Under 2 yrs service: $800.28; 2–6 yrs: $860; 6–10 yrs: $900; 10–14 yrs: $950; 14–16 yrs: $1,000; 16–18 yrs: $1,100; over 18 yrs: $1,175.

**O-6**—Under 2 yrs service: $592.80; 2–3 yrs: $628; 3–14 yrs: $670; 14–16 yrs: $690; 16–18 yrs: $800; 18–20 yrs: $840; 20–22 yrs: $860; 22–26 yrs: $910; over 26 yrs: $985.

**O-5**—Under 2 yrs service: $474.24; 2–3 yrs: $503; 3–10 yrs: $540; 10–12 yrs: $560; 12–14 yrs: $590; 14–16 yrs: $630; 16–18 yrs: $680; 18–20 yrs: $720; 20–22 yrs: $745; over 22 yrs: $775.

**O-4**—Under 2 yrs service: $400.14; 2–3 yrs: $424; 3–6 yrs: $455; 6–8 yrs: $465; 8–10 yrs: $485; 10–12 yrs: $520; 12–14 yrs: $550; 14–16 yrs: $570; 16–18 yrs: $610; over 18 yrs: $630.

**O-3†**—Under 2 yrs service: $326.04; 2–3 yrs: $346; 3–4 yrs: $372; 4–6 yrs: $415; 6–8 yrs: $440; 8–10 yrs: $460; 10–12 yrs: $480; 12–14 yrs: $510; over 14 yrs: $525.

**O-3‡**—4–6 yrs service: $415; 6–8 yrs: $440, 8–10 yrs: $460; 10–12 yrs: $480; 12–14 yrs: $510; over 14 yrs: $535.

**O-2†**—Under 2 yrs service: $259.36; 2–3 yrs: $291; 3–4 yrs: $360; 4–6 yrs: $370; over 6 yrs: $380.

**O-2‡**—4–6 yrs service: $370; 6–8 yrs: $380; 8–10 yrs: $395; 10–12 yrs: $415; 12–14 yrs: $435; over 14 yrs: $450.

**O-1†**—Under 2 yrs service: $222.30; 2–3 yrs: $251; over 3 yrs: $314.

**O-1‡**—4–6 yrs service: $314; 6–8 yrs: $335; 8–10 yrs: $350; 10–12 yrs: $365; 12–14 yrs: $380; over 14 yrs: $400.

**W-4**—Under 2 yrs service: $332.90; 2–4 yrs: $376; 4–6 yrs: $383; 6–8 yrs: $399; 8–10 yrs: $416; 10–12 yrs: $435; 12–14 yrs: $465; 14–16 yrs: $486; 16–18 yrs: $504; 18–20 yrs: $516; 20–22 yrs: $528; 22–26 yrs: $543; 26–30 yrs: $575; over 30 yrs: $595.

**W-3**—Under 2 yrs: $302.64; 2–4 yrs: $343; 4–6 yrs: $348; 6–8 yrs: $353; 8–10 yrs: $380; 10–12 yrs: $398; 12–14 yrs: $412; 14–16 yrs: $427; 16–18 yrs: $441; 18–20 yrs: $458; 20–22 yrs: $470; 22–26 yrs: $487; over 26 yrs: $506.

**W-2**—Under 2 yrs: $264.82; 2–4 yrs: $298; 4–6 yrs: $307; 6–8 yrs: $328; 8–10 yrs: $342; 10–12 yrs: $355; 12–14 yrs: $369; 14–16 yrs: $381; 16–18 yrs: $393; 18–20 yrs: $406; 20–22 yrs: $417; over 22 yrs: $440.

**W1**—Under 2 yrs: $219.42; 2–4 yrs: $266; 4–6 yrs: $285; 6–8 yrs: $299; 8–10 yrs: $313; 10–12 yrs: $334; 12–14 yrs: $345; 14–16 yrs: $354; 16–18 yrs: $364; 18–20 yrs: $375; over 20 yrs: $390.

\* While serving as Chairman of Joint Chiefs of Staff, Chief of Staff of the Army, Chief of Staff of the Air Force, Commandant of the Marine Corps, or Commandant of the U.S. Coast Guard, basic pay for this grade is $1,875 regardless of cumulative years of service. † For commissioned officers who have not been credited with over 4 years' active service as an enlisted member. ‡ For commissioned officers who have been credited with over 4 years' active service as an enlisted member.

## Special Incentive Pay Rates

Members of the uniformed services are entitled to receive special pay for special kinds of duty. In addition to the incentive rates for aircraft and submarine crews listed elsewhere in this section, the following types of hazardous duty receive flat rates of $110 per month for officers and $55 per month for enlisted personnel.

1. Frequent and regular participation in aerial flights *not* as a crew member.
2. Parachute jumping as an essential part of military duty.
3. Duty involving contact with lepers.
4. Demolition of explosives as primary duty (training included).
5. Submarine escape training tank duty.
6. Deep sea diving duty (including helium-oxygen diving).
7. Human acceleration or deceleration duty.
8. Low pressure chamber duty (inside observer).
9. Duty as human test subject in thermal stress experiments.

### Medical and Dental Officers

Monthly incentive pay for medical and dental officers is based on cumulative service:

0-2 years, $100; 2-6 years, $150; 6-10 years, $200; over 10 years, $250.

### Diving as in Salvage and Repair

The monthly rate is not less than $13 or more than $33, plus $5.50 for each diving hour spent in salvage or repair operations. Pay applies to pay grades E-1 through E-9 only.

### Sea and Foreign Duty

| Pay grade | Monthly rate | Pay grade | Monthly rate |
|---|---|---|---|
| E-7, E-8, E-9 | $22.50 | E-4 | $13.00 |
| E-6 | 20.00 | E-3 | 9.00 |
| E-5 | 16.00 | E-2, E-1 | 8.00 |

## Proficiency Pay

An enlisted member designated as possessing special proficiency in a military skill may—

(1) Be advanced to any enlisted pay grade that is higher than his pay grade at the time of designation; or

(2) Be paid proficiency pay at a monthly rate not to exceed the following maximum rates for the proficiency rating to which he is assigned: Rating P-1, $50; P-2, $100; P-3, $150.

An enlisted member with less than 8 or 10, as the case may be, cumulative years of enlisted service for basic pay purposes, who is advanced to pay grade E-8 or E-9, respectively, is entitled to the minimum amount of pay prescribed for that pay grade until his cumulative years of service entitle him to a higher rate.

## Special Pay for Certain Designated Officers

Officers in pay grades O-3 through O-6 who hold positions of unusual responsibility which are of a critical nature to the service concerned, may receive special pay, in addition to any other pay prescribed by law, at a monthly rate as follows: Pay grades O-3 and O-4, $50; O-5, $100; O-6, $150.

## Arlington National Cemetery

Arlington National Cemetery occupies 420 acres in Virginia on the Potomac River directly opposite Washington. This land was part of the estate of John Parke Custis, Martha Washington's son, who built the mansion which later became the home of Robert E. Lee. In 1864 Arlington became a national military cemetery. Many thousands of soldiers as well as hundreds of distinguished Americans are buried there. In 1921, an Unknown Soldier from World War I was buried in a temporary crypt in the cemetery; the completed tomb was dedicated in 1932. Two more Unknowns, one from World War II and one from the Korean War, were buried May 30, 1958. In April 1959, the 100,000th body was interred in Arlington National Cemetery.

## The American's Creed
*By William Tyler Page*

"I believe in the United States of America as a government of the people, by the people, for the people; whose just powers are derived from the consent of the governed; a democracy in a republic; a sovereign Nation of many sovereign States; a perfect union, one and inseparable; established upon those principles of freedom, equality, justice, and humanity for which American patriots sacrificed their lives and fortunes.

"I therefore believe it is my duty to my country to love it; to support its Constitution; to obey its laws; to respect its flag, and to defend it against all enemies."

NOTE: William Tyler Page, Clerk of the U.S. House of Representatives, wrote "The American's Creed" in 1917. It was accepted by the House on behalf of the American people on April 3, 1918.

# Incentive Pay for Hazardous Duty
## (As an Aircraft or Submarine Crew Member)

| Pay grade | Under 2 yrs. | Over 2 yrs. | Over 3 yrs. | Over 4 yrs. | Over 6 yrs. | Over 8 yrs. | Over 10 yrs. |
|---|---|---|---|---|---|---|---|
| O-9, O-10 | $165.00 | $165.00 | $165.00 | $165.00 | $165.00 | $165.00 | $165.00 |
| O-8 | 155.00 | 155.00 | 165.00 | 165.00 | 165.00 | 165.00 | 165.00 |
| O-7 | 150.00 | 150.00 | 160.00 | 160.00 | 160.00 | 160.00 | 160.00 |
| O-6 | 200.00 | 200.00 | 215.00 | 215.00 | 215.00 | 215.00 | 215.00 |
| O-5 | 190.00 | 190.00 | 205.00 | 205.00 | 205.00 | 205.00 | 205.00 |
| O-4 | 170.00 | 170.00 | 185.00 | 185.00 | 185.00 | 195.00 | 210.00 |
| O-3 | 145.00 | 145.00 | 155.00 | 165.00 | 180.00 | 185.00 | 190.00 |
| O-2 | 115.00 | 125.00 | 150.00 | 150.00 | 160.00 | 165.00 | 170.00 |
| O-1 | 100.00 | 105.00 | 135.00 | 135.00 | 140.00 | 145.00 | 155.00 |
| W-4 | 115.00 | 115.00 | 115.00 | 115.00 | 120.00 | 125.00 | 135.00 |
| W-3 | 110.00 | 115.00 | 115.00 | 115.00 | 120.00 | 120.00 | 125.00 |
| W-2 | 105.00 | 110.00 | 110.00 | 110.00 | 115.00 | 120.00 | 125.00 |
| W-1 | 100.00 | 105.00 | 105.00 | 105.00 | 110.00 | 120.00 | 125.00 |
| E-8, E-9 | 105.00 | 105.00 | 105.00 | 105.00 | 105.00 | 105.00 | 105.00 |
| E-7 | 80.00 | 85.00 | 85.00 | 85.00 | 90.00 | 95.00 | 100.00 |
| E-6 | 70.00 | 75.00 | 75.00 | 80.00 | 85.00 | 90.00 | 95.00 |
| E-5 | 60.00 | 70.00 | 70.00 | 80.00 | 80.00 | 85.00 | 90.00 |
| E-4 | 55.00 | 65.00 | 65.00 | 70.00 | 75.00 | 80.00 | 80.00 |
| E-3 | 55.00 | 60.00 | 60.00 | 60.00 | 60.00 | 60.00 | 60.00 |
| E-2 | 50.00 | 60.00 | 60.00 | 60.00 | 60.00 | 60.00 | 60.00 |
| E-1 | 50.00 | 55.00 | 55.00 | 55.00 | 55.00 | 55.00 | 55.00 |

| Pay grade | Over 12 yrs. | Over 14 yrs. | Over 16 yrs. | Over 18 yrs. | Over 22 yrs. | Over 26 yrs. | Over 30 yrs. |
|---|---|---|---|---|---|---|---|
| O-9, O-10 | $165.00 | $165.00 | $165.00 | $165.00 | $165.00 | $165.00 | $165.00 |
| O-8 | 165.00 | 165.00 | 165.00 | 165.00 | 165.00 | 165.00 | 165.00 |
| O-7 | 160.00 | 160.00 | 160.00 | 160.00 | 160.00 | 160.00 | 160.00 |
| O-6 | 215.00 | 215.00 | 220.00 | 245.00 | 245.00 | 245.00 | 245.00 |
| O-5 | 210.00 | 225.00 | 230.00 | 245.00 | 245.00 | 245.00 | 245.00 |
| O-4 | 215.00 | 220.00 | 230.00 | 240.00 | 240.00 | 240.00 | 240.00 |
| O-3 | 200.00 | 205.00 | 205.00 | 205.00 | 205.00 | 205.00 | 205.00 |
| O-2 | 180.00 | 185.00 | 185.00 | 185.00 | 185.00 | 185.00 | 185.00 |
| O-1 | 160.00 | 170.00 | 170.00 | 170.00 | 170.00 | 170.00 | 170.00 |
| W-4 | 145.00 | 155.00 | 160.00 | 165.00 | 165.00 | 165.00 | 165.00 |
| W-3 | 135.00 | 140.00 | 140.00 | 140.00 | 140.00 | 140.00 | 140.00 |
| W-2 | 130.00 | 135.00 | 135.00 | 135.00 | 135.00 | 135.00 | 135.00 |
| W-1 | 130.00 | 130.00 | 130.00 | 130.00 | 130.00 | 130.00 | 130.00 |
| E-8, E-9 | 105.00 | 105.00 | 105.00 | 105.00 | 105.00 | 105.00 | 105.00 |
| E-7 | 105.00 | 105.00 | 105.00 | 105.00 | 105.00 | 105.00 | 105.00 |
| E-6 | 95.00 | 100.00 | 100.00 | 100.00 | 100.00 | 100.00 | 100.00 |
| E-5 | 95.00 | 95.00 | 95.00 | 95.00 | 95.00 | 95.00 | 95.00 |
| E-4 | 80.00 | 80.00 | 80.00 | 80.00 | 80.00 | 80.00 | 80.00 |
| E-3 | 60.00 | 60.00 | 60.00 | 60.00 | 60.00 | 60.00 | 60.00 |
| E-2 | 60.00 | 60.00 | 60.00 | 60.00 | 60.00 | 60.00 | 60.00 |
| E-1 | 55.00 | 55.00 | 55.00 | 55.00 | 55.00 | 55.00 | 55.00 |

# Extra Pay for Wartime Service

Act of March 3, 1847, during the Mexican War, provided for $2 a month extra pay for "distinguished service." This continued in force beyond the war and applied in the Civil War.

In the Spanish American War, there was a 20 per cent increase of enlisted men's pay for war service.

In World War I, additional pay was offered for all types of services, usually as incentive for special qualifications as gun pointer, expert rifleman, etc. Among these items is pay for certificate of merit of $2 a month. By the new law passed in 1920, the number of reasons for additional pay had expanded. Recipients of the Medal of Honor, Distinguished Service Cross and Distinguished Service Medal received $2 a month extra, while each bar in lieu of these medals also added another $2 a month. Added to this was a foreign service bonus of 20 per cent.

Act of June 30, 1944 authorized compensation of $5 a month to enlisted men qualified as expert infantrymen and $10 to those qualified as combat infantrymen. These amounts were payable for the duration of war and six months thereafter.

By the Act of July 6, 1945 for the duration of war and for six months thereafter enlisted men entitled to wear Medical Badges received additional pay of $10.

Act of July 10, 1952 authorized $45 a month for each month beginning after May 31, 1950, for which the member was entitled to receive basic pay and during which he was a member of a combat unit in Korea. This applies to officers and enlisted men.

# U. S. Armed Forces Personnel

*Source:* U. S. Department of Defense, U. S. Coast Guard.

| Year[1] | Army | Air Force[2] | Navy | Marines | Men[3] | Women | Coast Guard[4] |
|---|---|---|---|---|---|---|---|
| 1935............. | 139,486 | ....... | 95,053 | 17,260 | 250,864 | 935 | 10,303 |
| 1939............. | 189,839 | ....... | 125,202 | 19,432 | 333,363 | 1,110 | 10,064 |
| 1940............. | 269,023 | ....... | 160,997 | 28,345 | 456,984 | 1,381 | 13,621 |
| 1941............. | 1,462,315 | ....... | 284,427 | 54,359 | 1,794,997 | 6,104 | 19,036 |
| 1942............. | 3,075,608 | ....... | 640,570 | 142,613 | 3,831,571 | 27,220 | 58,998 |
| 1943............. | 6,994,472 | ....... | 1,741,750 | 308,523 | 8,915,248 | 129,497 | 154,976 |
| 1944............. | 7,994,750 | ....... | 2,981,365 | 475,604 | 11,229,682 | 222,037 | 169,264 |
| 1945............. | 8,267,958 | ....... | 3,380,817 | 474,680 | 11,923,250 | 200,205 | 171,518 |
| 1946............. | 1,891,011 | ....... | 983,398 | 155,679 | 2,984,096 | 45,992 | 29,736 |
| 1947............. | 991,285 | ....... | 498,661 | 93,053 | 1,564,717 | 18,282 | 18,972 |
| 1949............. | 660,473 | 419,347 | 449,575 | 85,965 | 1,597,280 | 18,080 | 23,326 |
| 1950............. | 593,167 | 411,277 | 381,538 | 74,279 | 1,438,192 | 22,069 | 23,190 |
| 1951............. | 1,531,774 | 788,381 | 736,680 | 192,620 | 3,209,830 | 39,625 | 29,000 |
| 1953............. | 1,533,815 | 977,593 | 794,440 | 249,219 | 3,509,582 | 45,485 | 34,148 |
| 1955............. | 1,109,296 | 959,946 | 660,695 | 205,170 | 2,899,916 | 35,191 | 28,500 |
| 1957............. | 997,994 | 919,835 | 677,108 | 200,861 | 2,763,625 | 32,173 | 28,322 |
| 1958............. | 898,925 | 871,156 | 641,005 | 189,495 | 2,569,520[5] | 31,176 | 29,711 |
| 1959............. | 861,964 | 840,435 | 626,340 | 175,571 | ........ | 31,854 | 29,984 |
| 1960............. | 873,078 | 814,752 | 617,984 | 170,621 | ........ | 31,738 | 30,211 |

[1] As of June 30. [2] Before July 26, 1947, when the National Military Establishment was established, the Air Force was a part of the Army. [3] Not including men in the Coast Guard. [4] In peacetime, the Coast Guard operates under the Department of the Treasury; in time of war, it is attached to the Navy Department. [5] As of June 1.

# Veterans' Benefits

Although benefits of various kinds date back to Colonial days, veterans of World War I were the first to receive disability compensation for injuries, allotments for the support of dependents, life insurance, complete medical care and vocational rehabilitation. Beginning with 1940, these benefits were slowly broadened.

The following benefits available to veterans of World War II and the Korean War have specific time limitations and, in most cases, are applicable only to those whose discharge was not dishonorable.

Education and Training: *Veterans of the Korean War:* For a maximum period of 1½ times the duration of active service, not exceeding 36 months, the VA pays sums varying from $110 to $160 per month toward subsistence, tuition, supplies, etc.

Unemployment allowances: A Korea veteran may be eligible for unemployment pay under the Korean GI Bill or, if he left service after Oct. 27, 1958, under a 1958 law. Both benefits are administered through local state employment security agencies.

Loans: GI loans are made for a variety of purposes, such as: to buy or build a home; to conduct a business or farming enterprise; to buy livestock, machinery, tools and other equipment; and to use for working capital. The VA will guarantee the lender against loss up to 60% of a home loan with a maximum of $7,500. On other loans, the guarantee is up to 50% with a maximum of $4,000 involving real estate and $2,000 on non-real estate loans. The interest rate in all cases must not exceed 5¼% per year.

Compensation and rehabilitation benefits are available to those having some service-connected illness or disability:

Disability Compensation: The VA pays from $19 to $225 per month, and for specific conditions up to $450 per month, plus allowances for dependents, where the disability is rated 50% or more.

Vocational rehabilitation: Necessary training expenses, special equipment, etc., toward a definite job objective are paid for, plus a monthly allowance varying from $65 to $120 in addition to compensation.

Medical and dental care: This includes complete care in VA or certain other Federal hospitals. It also covers treatment (not requiring hospitalization) at a VA field station or by an approved private physician or dentist. Medicine, appliances, equipment, etc., are supplied. Full domiciliary care is also provided where necessary.

War Orphans Education: $110 a month for up to 36 months of schooling may be paid to sons and daughters of veterans who died of service-connected causes. Students must usually be between 18 and 23.

Pensions: The Veterans Pension Act of 1959, effective July 1, 1960, provides a sliding scale formula for pension benefits. These benefits are based on need to a greater extent than before. However, pensioners who were on the rolls prior to July 1 have a choice of remaining under the earlier system or of electing coverage under the new law. Widows and orphans of World War II and Korea veterans have been given the same eligibility status as World War I widows and orphans.

NOTE: See your local Veterans Administration (VA) for detailed information.

## ALLOWANCES FOR SUBSISTENCE

Officers receive $47.88 per month. Enlisted personnel receive allowances for subsistence under the following provisions: (1) when rations in kind are not available, $2.57 per day; (2) when permission to mess separately is granted, $1.10 per day; (3)* when assigned to duty under emergency conditions where no government messing facilities are available, up to and not to exceed $3.42 per day.

\* Applicable only within the U. S.

### U. S. Navy Combatant Vessels

| Type | Number |
|---|---|
| Attack Carriers | 14 |
| Anti-Submarine Carriers | 9 |
| Cruiser types | 15 |
| Destroyers | 225 |
| Submarines | 117* |
| Minecraft | 78 |
| Patrol Craft | 45 |
| Amphibious | 110 |
| Auxiliaries | 204 |
| Total | 817† |

\* Includes 17 nuclear submarines, 5 of which are Polaris type.   † Numbers are approximate; exact figures are classified information.

# U. S. Casualties in Major Wars

*Source:* Department of Defense.

| War | Branch of service | Numbers engaged | Battle deaths | Other deaths | Total deaths | Wounds not mortal | Total casualties[1] |
|---|---|---|---|---|---|---|---|
| **Revolutionary War** 1775 to 1783 | Army | ...... | 4,044 | ...... | ...... | 6,004 | ...... |
| | Navy | ...... | 342 | ...... | ...... | 114 | ...... |
| | Marines | ...... | 49 | ...... | ...... | 70 | ...... |
| | Total | ...... | 4,435 | ...... | ...... | 6,188 | ...... |
| **War of 1812** 1812 to 1815 | Army | ...... | 1,950 | ...... | ...... | 4,000 | ...... |
| | Navy | ...... | 265 | ...... | ...... | 439 | ...... |
| | Marines | ...... | 45 | ...... | ...... | 66 | ...... |
| | Total | 286,730 | 2,260 | ...... | ...... | 4,505 | ...... |
| **Mexican War** 1846 to 1848 | Army | ...... | 1,721 | 11,550 | 13,271 | 4,102 | 17,373 |
| | Navy | ...... | 1 | ...... | ...... | 3 | ...... |
| | Marines | ...... | 11 | ...... | ...... | 47 | ...... |
| | Total | 78,718 | 1,733 | ...... | ...... | 4,152 | ...... |
| **Civil War[2]** 1861 to 1865 | Army | 2,128,948 | 138,154 | 221,374 | 359,528 | 280,040 | 639,568 |
| | Navy | } 84,415 | 2,112 | 2,411 | 4,523 | 1,710 | 6,233 |
| | Marines | | 148 | 312 | 460 | 131 | 591 |
| | Total | 2,213,363 | 140,414 | 224,097 | 364,511 | 281,881 | 646,392 |
| **Spanish-American War** 1898 | Army | 280,564 | 369 | 2,061 | 2,430 | 1,594 | 4,024 |
| | Navy | 22,875 | 10 | 0 | 10 | 47 | 57 |
| | Marines | 3,321 | 6 | 0 | 6 | 21 | 27 |
| | Total | 306,760 | 385 | 2,061 | 2,446 | 1,662 | 4,108 |
| **World War I** 1917 to 1918 | Army | 4,057,101 | 50,510 | 55,868 | 106,378 | 193,663 | 300,041 |
| | Navy | 599,051 | 431 | 6,856 | 7,287 | 819 | 8,106 |
| | Marines | 78,839 | 2,461 | 390 | 2,851 | 9,520 | 12,371 |
| | Total | 4,734,991 | 53,402 | 63,114 | 116,516 | 204,002 | 320,518 |
| **World War II** 1941 to 1945 | Army[3] | 11,260,000 | 234,874 | 83,400 | 318,274 | 565,861 | 884,135 |
| | Navy | 4,183,466 | 36,950 | 25,664 | 62,614 | 37,778 | 100,392 |
| | Marines | 669,100 | 19,733 | 4,778 | 24,511 | 67,207 | 91,718 |
| | Total | 16,112,566 | 291,557 | 113,842 | 405,399 | 670,846 | 1,076,245 |
| **Korean War** 1950 to 1953 | Army | 2,834,000 | 27,704 | 9,429 | 37,133 | 77,596 | 114,729 |
| | Navy | 1,177,000 | 458 | 4,043 | 4,501 | 1,576 | 6,077 |
| | Marines | 424,000 | 4,267 | 1,261 | 5,528 | 23,744 | 29,272 |
| | Air Force | 1,285,000 | 1,200 | 5,884 | 7,084 | 368 | 7,452 |
| | Total | 5,720,000 | 33,629 | 20,617 | 54,246 | 103,284 | 157,530 |

[1] Excludes captured or interned and missing in action who were subsequently returned to military control.   [2] Union forces only.   Totals should probably be somewhat larger as data on disposition of prisoners are far from complete.   [3] Army data include Air Force.   NOTE: All data are subject to revision.   For wars before World War I, information represents best data from available records.   However, due to incomplete records and possible differences in usage of terminology, reporting systems, etc., figures should be considered estimates.   Leaders (......) indicate that information is not available.

# Casualties in World War II

### (Additional U. S. figures are to be found on p. 536)

| Country | Men in war | Battle deaths | Wounded |
|---|---|---|---|
| Australia | 1,000,000 | 26,976 | 180,864 |
| Austria | 800,000 | 280,000 | 350,117 |
| Belgium | 625,000 | 8,460 | 55,513[1] |
| Brazil[2] | 40,334 | 943 | 4,222 |
| Bulgaria | 339,760 | 6,671 | 21,878 |
| Canada | 1,041,080 | 32,412 | 53,145 |
| China[3] | 17,250,521 | 1,324,516 | 1,762,006 |
| Czechoslovakia | ....... | 6,683[4] | 8,017 |
| Denmark | ....... | 4,339 | ....... |
| Finland | 500,000 | 79,047 | 50,000 |
| France | ....... | 201,568 | 400,000 |
| Germany | 20,000,000 | 3,250,000[4] | 7,250,000 |
| Greece | ....... | 17,024 | 47,290 |
| Hungary | ....... | 147,435 | 89,313 |
| India | 2,393,891 | 32,121 | 64,354 |
| Italy | 3,100,000 | 149,496[4] | 66,716 |
| Japan | 9,700,000 | 1,270,000 | 140,000 |
| Netherlands | 280,000 | 6,500 | 2,860 |
| New Zealand | 194,000 | 11,625[4] | 17,000 |
| Norway | 75,000 | 2,000 | ....... |
| Poland | ....... | 664,000 | 530,000 |
| Rumania | 650,000[5] | 350,000[6] | ....... |
| South Africa, Union of | 410,056 | 2,473 | ....... |
| U.S.S.R. | ....... | 6,115,000[4] | 14,012,000 |
| United Kingdom | 5,896,000 | 357,116[4] | 369,267 |
| Yugoslavia | 3,741,000 | 305,000 | 425,000 |
| United States | 16,112,566 | 291,557 | 670,846 |

[1] Civilians only.  [2] Army and navy figures.  [3] Figures cover period July 7, 1937–Sept. 2, 1945, and concern only Chinese regular troops. They do not include casualties suffered by guerillas and local military corps.  [4] Deaths from all causes.  [5] Against Soviet Russia; 385,847 against Nazi Germany.  [6] Against Soviet Russia; 169,822 against Nazi Germany.  NOTE: The figures in this table are unofficial estimates obtained from various sources.

# Casualties in World War I

### (Additional U. S. figures are to be found on p. 536)

| | Total mobilized forces | Killed or died[1] | Wounded | Prisoners or missing | Total casualties |
|---|---|---|---|---|---|
| Austria-Hungary | 7,800,000 | 1,200,000 | 3,620,000 | 2,200,000 | 7,020,000 |
| Belgium | 267,000 | 13,716 | 44,686 | 34,659 | 93,061 |
| British Empire[2] | 8,904,467 | 908,371 | 2,090,212 | 191,652 | 3,190,235 |
| Bulgaria | 1,200,000 | 87,500 | 152,390 | 27,029 | 266,919 |
| France[2] | 8,410,000 | 1,357,800 | 4,266,000 | 537,000 | 6,160,800 |
| Germany | 11,000,000 | 1,773,700 | 4,216,058 | 1,152,800 | 7,142,558 |
| Greece | 230,000 | 5,000 | 21,000 | 1,000 | 27,000 |
| Italy | 5,615,000 | 650,000 | 947,000 | 600,000 | 2,197,000 |
| Japan | 800,000 | 300 | 907 | 3 | 1,210 |
| Montenegro | 50,000 | 3,000 | 10,000 | 7,000 | 20,000 |
| Portugal | 100,000 | 7,222 | 13,751 | 12,318 | 33,291 |
| Rumania | 750,000 | 335,706 | 120,000 | 80,000 | 535,706 |
| Russia | 12,000,000 | 1,700,000 | 4,950,000 | 2,500,000 | 9,150,000 |
| Serbia | 707,343 | 45,000 | 133,148 | 152,958 | 331,106 |
| Turkey | 2,850,000 | 325,000 | 400,000 | 250,000 | 975,000 |
| United States | 4,734,991 | 116,516 | 204,002 | ....... | 320,518 |

[1] Includes deaths from all causes.  [2] Official figures.

# U. S. Cabinet Members with Dates of Appointment

Although the Constitution made no provision for a President's advisory group, the heads of the three executive departments (State, Treasury and War) and the Attorney General were organized by Washington into such a group; and by about 1793, the name "Cabinet" was applied to it. With the exception of the Attorney General up to 1870 and the Postmaster General from 1829–72, Cabinet members have been heads of executive departments, although other government officials may be called to sit in whenever necessary.

A Cabinet member is appointed by the President, subject to the confirmation of the Senate; and as his term is not fixed, he may be replaced at any time by the President. At a change in Administration, it is customary for him to tender his resignation, but he remains in office until a successor is appointed.

The table of Cabinet members lists only those members who actually served after being duly commissioned. It does not include ad-interim appointments or cases where the appointee declined the office after appointment.

The dates shown are those of appointment. "Contd" indicates that the term continued from the previous Administration for a substantial amount of time. Those cases where the term continued for only a few days, until a new appointment could be made, are not indicated.

---

## WASHINGTON

**Secretary of State**

Thomas Jefferson...... 1789
Edmund Randolph..... 1794
Timothy Pickering..... 1795

**Secretary of the Treasury**

Alexander Hamilton.... 1789
Oliver Wolcott, Jr.... 1795

**Secretary of War**

Henry Knox .......... 1789
Timothy Pickering..... 1795
James McHenry....... 1796

**Attorney General**

Edmund Randolph..... 1789
William Bradford...... 1794
Charles Lee.......... 1795

## J. ADAMS

**Secretary of State**

Timothy Pickering.... Contd
John Marshall......... 1800

**Secretary of the Treasury**

Oliver Wolcott, Jr..... Contd
Samuel Dexter........ 1801

**Secretary of War**

James McHenry...... Contd
Samuel Dexter........ 1800

**Attorney General**

Charles Lee.......... Contd

**Secretary of the Navy**

Benjamin Stoddert.... 1798

## JEFFERSON

**Secretary of State**

James Madison....... 1801

**Secretary of the Treasury**

Samuel Dexter....... Contd
Albert Gallatin........ 1801

**Secretary of War**

Henry Dearborn....... 1801

**Attorney General**

Levi Lincoln.......... 1801
Robert Smith......... 1805
John Breckinridge..... 1805
Caesar A. Rodney..... 1807

**Secretary of the Navy**

Benjamin Stoddert... Contd
Robert Smith......... 1801

## MADISON

**Secretary of State**

Robert Smith......... 1809
James Monroe........ 1811

**Secretary of the Treasury**

Albert Gallatin....... Contd
George W. Campbell... 1814
Alexander J. Dallas.... 1814
William H. Crawford... 1816

**Secretary of War**

William Eustis......... 1809
John Armstrong....... 1813
James Monroe........ 1814
William H. Crawford... 1815

**Attorney General**

Caesar A. Rodney.... Contd
William Pinckney...... 1811
Richard Rush......... 1814

**Secretary of the Navy**

Paul Hamilton......... 1809
William Jones......... 1813
B. W. Crowninshield... 1814

## MONROE

**Secretary of State**

John Quincy Adams.... 1817

**Secretary of the Treasury**

William H. Crawford.. Contd

**Secretary of War**

John C. Calhoun....... 1817

**Attorney General**

Richard Rush........ Contd
William Wirt.......... 1817

**Secretary of the Navy**

B. W. Crowninshield.. Contd
Smith Thompson...... 1818
Samuel L. Southard... 1823

## J. Q. ADAMS

**Secretary of State**

Henry Clay........... 1825

**Secretary of the Treasury**

Richard Rush......... 1825

**Secretary of War**

James Barbour........ 1825
Peter B. Porter........ 1828

**Attorney General**

William Wirt......... Contd

**Secretary of the Navy**

Samuel L. Southard.. Contd

## JACKSON

**Secretary of State**

Martin Van Buren..... 1829
Edward Livingston..... 1831
Louis McLane......... 1833
John Forsyth.......... 1834

**Secretary of the Treasury**

Samuel D. Ingham..... 1829
Louis McLane......... 1831
William J. Duane...... 1833
Roger B. Taney....... 1833
Levi Woodbury........ 1834

**Secretary of War**

John H. Eaton......... 1829
Lewis Cass........... 1831

**Attorney General**

John M. Berrien....... 1829
Roger B. Taney....... 1831
Benjamin F. Butler.... 1833

**Postmaster General[1]**

William T. Barry...... 1829
Amos Kendall........ 1835

**Secretary of the Navy**

John Branch.......... 1829
Levi Woodbury........ 1831
Mahlon Dickerson..... 1834

## VAN BUREN

**Secretary of State**

John Forsyth......... Contd

**Secretary of the Treasury**

Levi Woodbury....... Contd

**Secretary of War**

Joel R. Poinsett....... 1837

**Attorney General**

Benjamin F. Butler... Contd
Felix Grundy.......... 1838
Henry D. Gilpin...... 1840

**Postmaster General**

Amos Kendall........ Contd
John M. Niles......... 1840

**Secretary of the Navy**

Mahlon Dickerson.... Contd
James K. Paulding..... 1838

## W. HARRISON

**Secretary of State**

Daniel Webster........ 1841

**Secretary of the Treasury**

Thomas Ewing........ 1841

**Secretary of War**

John Bell............. 1841

**Attorney General**

John J. Crittenden..... 1841

**Postmaster General**

Francis Granger....... 1841

**Secretary of the Navy**

George E. Badger...... 1841

## TYLER

### Secretary of State
Daniel Webster...... Contd
Abel P. Upshur........ 1843
John C. Calhoun....... 1844

### Secretary of the Treasury
Thomas Ewing....... Contd
Walter Forward....... 1841
John C. Spencer....... 1843
George M. Bibb....... 1844

### Secretary of War
John Bell............ Contd
John C. Spencer....... 1841
James M. Porter....... 1843
William Wilkins....... 1844

### Attorney General
John J. Crittenden.... Contd
Hugh S. Legaré....... 1841
John Nelson.......... 1843

### Postmaster General
Francis Granger...... Contd
Charles A. Wickliffe... 1841

### Secretary of the Navy
George E. Badger.... Contd
Abel P. Upshur....... 1841
David Henshaw....... 1843
Thomas W. Gilmer.... 1844
John Y. Mason........ 1844

## POLK

### Secretary of State
James Buchanan...... 1845

### Secretary of the Treasury
Robert J. Walker...... 1845

### Secretary of War
William L. Marcy...... 1845

### Attorney General
John Y. Mason........ 1845
Nathan Clifford....... 1846
Isaac Toucey......... 1848

### Postmaster General
Cave Johnson......... 1845

### Secretary of the Navy
George Bancroft....... 1845
John Y. Mason........ 1846

## TAYLOR

### Secretary of State
John M. Clayton....... 1849

### Secretary of the Treasury
William M. Meredith... 1849

### Secretary of War
George W. Crawford... 1849

### Attorney General
Reverdy Johnson...... 1849

### Postmaster General
Jacob Collamer........ 1849

### Secretary of the Navy
William B. Preston..... 1849

### Secretary of the Interior
Thomas Ewing........ 1849

## FILLMORE

### Secretary of State
Daniel Webster........ 1850
Edward Everett........ 1852

### Secretary of the Treasury
Thomas Corwin........ 1850

### Secretary of War
Charles M. Conrad..... 1850

### Attorney General
John J. Crittenden..... 1850

### Postmaster General
Nathan K. Hall........ 1850
Samuel D. Hubbard.... 1852

### Secretary of the Navy
William A. Graham..... 1850
John P. Kennedy....... 1852

### Secretary of the Interior
Thos. M. T. McKennan. 1850
Alex. H. H. Stuart..... 1850

## PIERCE

### Secretary of State
William L. Marcy...... 1853

### Secretary of the Treasury
James Guthrie........ 1853

### Secretary of War
Jefferson Davis........ 1853

### Attorney General
Caleb Cushing........ 1853

### Postmaster General
James Campbell....... 1853

### Secretary of the Navy
James C. Dobbin...... 1853

### Secretary of the Interior
Robert McClelland..... 1853

## BUCHANAN

### Secretary of State
Lewis Cass........... 1857
Jeremiah S. Black..... 1860

### Secretary of the Treasury
Howell Cobb.......... 1857
Philip F. Thomas...... 1860
John A. Dix........... 1861

### Secretary of War
John B. Floyd......... 1857
Joseph Hoit........... 1861

### Attorney General
Jeremiah S. Black..... 1857
Edwin M. Stanton..... 1860

### Postmaster General
Aaron V. Brown....... 1857
Joseph Holt........... 1859
Horatio King.......... 1861

### Secretary of the Navy
Isaac Toucey......... 1857

### Secretary of the Interior
Jacob Thompson...... 1857

## LINCOLN

### Secretary of State
William H. Seward..... 1861

### Secretary of the Treasury
Salmon P. Chase...... 1861
William P. Fessenden.. 1864
Hugh McCulloch....... 1865

### Secretary of War
Simon Cameron....... 1861
Edwin M. Stanton..... 1862

### Attorney General
Edward Bates......... 1861
James Speed.......... 1864

### Postmaster General
Montgomery Blair..... 1861
William Dennison...... 1864

### Secretary of the Navy
Gideon Welles......... 1861

### Secretary of the Interior
Caleb B. Smith........ 1861
John P. Usher......... 1863

## JOHNSON

### Secretary of State
William H. Seward.... Contd

### Secretary of the Treasury
Hugh McCulloch...... Contd

### Secretary of War
Edwin M. Stanton.... Contd
John M. Schofield.... 1868

### Attorney General
James Speed........ Contd
Henry Stanbery....... 1866
William M. Evarts..... 1868

### Postmaster General
William Dennison..... Contd
Alexander W. Randall.. 1866

### Secretary of the Navy
Gideon Welles........ Contd

### Secretary of the Interior
John P. Usher........ Contd
James Harlan......... 1865
Orville H. Browning.... 1866

## GRANT

### Secretary of State
Elihu B. Washburne.... 1869
Hamilton Fish......... 1869

### Secretary of the Treasury
George S. Boutwell.... 1869
William A. Richardson.. 1873
Benjamin H. Bristow... 1874
Lot M. Morrill........ 1876

### Secretary of War
John A. Rawlins....... 1866
William T. Sherman.... 1869
William W. Belknap.... 1869
Alphonso Taft......... 1879
James D. Cameron..... 1876

### Attorney General
Ebenezer R. Hoar...... 1869
Amos T. Akerman..... 1870
George H. Williams.... 1871
Edwards Pierrepont.... 1875
Alphonso Taft......... 1876

### Postmaster General
John A. J. Creswell.... 1869
James W. Marshall.... 1874
Marshall Jewell....... 1874
James N. Tyner....... 1876

### Secretary of the Navy
Adolph E. Borie....... 1869
George M. Robeson.... 1869

### Secretary of the Interior
Jacob D. Cox.......... 1869
Columbus Delano...... 1870
Zachariah Chandler.... 1875

## HAYES

### Secretary of State
William M. Evarts..... 1877

### Secretary of the Treasury
John Sherman........ 1877

### Secretary of War
George W. McCrary.... 1877
Alexander Ramsey..... 1879

### Attorney General
Charles Devens....... 1877

### Postmaster General
David M. Key......... 1877
Horace Maynard....... 1880

### Secretary of the Navy
Richard W. Thompson.. 1877
Nathan Goff, Jr....... 1881

### Secretary of the Interior
Carl Schurz........... 1877

## GARFIELD

### Secretary of State
James G. Blaine....... 1881

### Secretary of the Treasury
William Windom....... 1881

### Secretary of War
Robert T. Lincoln...... 1881

### Attorney General
Wayne MacVeagh...... 1881

### Postmaster General
Thomas L. James...... 1881

### Secretary of the Navy
William H. Hunt....... 1881

### Secretary of the Interior
Samuel J. Kirkwood... 1881

## ARTHUR

### Secretary of State
James G. Blaine...... Contd
F. T. Frelinghuysen.... 1881

### Secretary of the Treasury
William Windom...... Contd
Charles J. Folger...... 1881
Walter Q. Gresham.... 1884
Hugh McCulloch....... 1884

### Secretary of War
Robert T. Lincoln......Contd

### Attorney General
Wayne MacVeagh......Contd
Benjamin H. Brewster. 1881

### Postmaster General
Thomas L. James..... Contd
Timothy O. Howe...... 1881
Walter Q. Gresham.... 1883
Frank Hatton......... 1884

### Secretary of the Navy
William H. Hunt...... Contd
William E. Chandler.... 1882

### Secretary of the Interior
Samuel J Kirkwood.. Contd
Henry M. Teller....... 1882

## CLEVELAND

### Secretary of State
Thomas F. Bayard..... 1885

### Secretary of the Treasury
Daniel Manning....... 1885
Charles S. Fairchild.... 1887

### Secretary of War
William C. Endicott.... 1885

### Attorney General
Augustus H. Garland... 1885

### Postmaster General
William F. Vilas...... 1885
Don M. Dickinson..... 1888

### Secretary of the Navy
William C. Whitney.... 1885

### Secretary of the Interior
Lucius Q. C. Lamar.... 1885
William F. Vilas....... 1888

### Secretary of Agriculture
Norman J. Colman..... 1889

## HARRISON

### Secretary of State
James G. Blaine....... 1889
John W. Foster....... 1892

### Secretary of the Treasury
William Windom....... 1889
Charles Foster........ 1891

### Secretary of War
Redfield Proctor...... 1889
Stephen B. Elkins..... 1891

### Attorney General
William H. H. Miller.... 1889

### Postmaster General
John Wanamaker...... 1889

### Secretary of the Navy
Benjamin F. Tracy..... 1889

### Secretary of the Interior
John W. Noble........ 1889

### Secretary of Agriculture
Jeremiah M. Rusk..... 1889

## CLEVELAND

### Secretary of State
Walter Q. Gresham.... 1893
Richard Olney......... 1895

### Secretary of the Treasury
John G. Carlisle....... 1893

### Secretary of War
Daniel S. Lamont...... 1893

### Attorney General
Richard Olney......... 1893
Judson Harmon....... 1895

### Postmaster General
Wilson S. Bissell...... 1893
William L. Wilson...... 1895

### Secretary of the Navy
Hilary A. Herbert...... 1893

### Secretary of the Interior
Hoke Smith........... 1893
David R. Francis....... 1896

### Secretary of Agriculture
Julius Sterling Morton. 1893

## McKINLEY

### Secretary of State
John Sherman........ 1897
William R. Day........ 1898
John Hay............. 1898

### Secretary of the Treasury
Lyman J. Gage........ 1897

### Secretary of War
Russell A. Alger....... 1897
Elihu Root............ 1899

### Attorney General
Joseph McKenna...... 1897
John W. Griggs....... 1898
Philander C. Knox..... 1901

### Postmaster General
James A. Gary........ 1897
Charles E. Smith...... 1898

### Secretary of the Navy
John D. Long......... 1897

### Secretary of the Interior
Cornelius N. Bliss..... 1897
Ethan A. Hitchcock.... 1898

### Secretary of Agriculture
James Wilson......... 1897

## T. ROOSEVELT

### Secretary of State
John Hay............. Contd
Elihu Root............ 1905
Robert Bacon......... 1909

### Secretary of the Treasury
Lyman J. Gage....... Contd
Leslie M. Shaw....... 1902
George B. Cortelyou... 1907

### Secretary of War
Elihu Root........... Contd
William H. Taft....... 1904
Luke E. Wright....... 1908

### Attorney General
Philander C. Knox.... Contd
William H. Moody..... 1904
Charles J. Bonaparte... 1906

### Postmaster General
Charles E. Smith..... Contd
Henry C. Payne....... 1902
Robert J. Wynne ...... 1904
George B. Cortelyou... 1905
George von L. Meyer... 1907

### Secretary of the Navy
John D. Long......... Contd
William H. Moody..... 1902
Paul Morton.......... 1904
Charles J. Bonaparte... 1905
Victor H. Metcalf..... 1906
Truman H. Newberry.. 1908

### Secretary of the Interior
Ethan A. Hitchcock... Contd
James R. Garfield..... 1907

### Secretary of Agriculture
James Wilson........ Contd

### Secretary of Commerce and Labor
George B. Cortelyou... 1903
Victor H. Metcalf..... 1904
Oscar S. Straus....... 1906

## TAFT

### Secretary of State
Philander C. Knox..... 1909

### Secretary of the Treasury
Franklin MacVeagh.... 1909

### Secretary of War
Jacob M. Dickinson.... 1909
Henry L. Stimson...... 1911

### Attorney General
George W. Wickersham. 1909

### Postmaster General
Frank H. Hitchcock.... 1909

### Secretary of the Navy
George von L. Meyer... 1909

### Secretary of the Interior
Richard A. Ballinger... 1909
Walter L. Fisher....... 1911

### Secretary of Agriculture
James Wilson........ Contd

### Secretary of Commerce and Labor
Charles Nagel........ 1909

## WILSON

### Secretary of State
William J. Bryan...... 1913
Robert Lansing........ 1915
Bainbridge Colby...... 1920

### Secretary of the Treasury
William G. McAdoo.... 1913
Carter Glass......... 1918
David F. Houston...... 1920

### Secretary of War
Lindley M. Garrison.... 1913
Newton D. Baker...... 1916

### Attorney General
James C. McReynolds.. 1913
Thomas W. Gregory.... 1914
A. Mitchell Palmer..... 1919

### Postmaster General
Albert S. Burleson.... 1913

### Secretary of the Navy
Josephus Daniels...... 1913

### Secretary of the Interior
Franklin K. Lane...... 1913
John B. Payne........ 1920

### Secretary of Agriculture
David F. Houston...... 1913
Edwin T. Meredith..... 1920

### Secretary of Commerce
William C. Redfield.... 1913
Joshua W. Alexander... 1919

### Secretary of Labor
William B. Wilson...... 1913

## HARDING

### Secretary of State
Charles E. Hughes..... 1921

### Secretary of the Treasury
Andrew W. Mellon..... 1921

### Secretary of War
John W. Weeks........ 1921

### Attorney General
Harry M. Daugherty.... 1921

### Postmaster General
Will H. Hays.......... 1921
Hubert Work.......... 1922
Harry S. New......... 1923

### Secretary of the Navy
Edwin Denby.......... 1921

### Secretary of the Interior
Albert B. Fall......... 1921
Hubert Work.......... 1923

### Secretary of Agriculture
Henry C. Wallace..... 1921

### Secretary of Commerce
Herbert Hoover....... 1921

### Secretary of Labor
James J. Davis........ 1921

## COOLIDGE

### Secretary of State
Charles E. Hughes.... Contd
Frank B. Kellogg...... 1925

### Secretary of the Treasury
Andrew W. Mellon.... Contd

### Secretary of War
John W. Weeks....... Contd
Dwight F. Davis....... 1925

### Attorney General
Harry M. Daugherty... Contd
Harlan F. Stone........ 1924
John G. Sargent....... 1925

### Postmaster General
Harry S. New........ Contd

### Secretary of the Navy
Edwin Denby........ Contd
Curtis D. Wilbur....... 1924

### Secretary of the Interior
Hubert Work......... Contd
Roy O. West.......... 1928

### Secretary of Agriculture
Henry C. Wallace...... Contd
Howard M. Gore....... 1924
William M. Jardine.... 1925

### Secretary of Commerce
Herbert Hoover....... Contd
William F. Whiting..... 1928

### Secretary of Labor
James J. Davis....... Contd

## HOOVER

### Secretary of State
Frank B. Kellogg..... Contd
Henry L. Stimson...... 1929

### Secretary of the Treasury
Andrew W. Mellon.... Contd
Ogden L. Mills........ 1932

### Secretary of War
James W. Good........ 1929
Patrick J. Hurley...... 1929

### Attorney General
William D. Mitchell.... 1929

### Postmaster General
Walter F. Brown....... 1929

### Secretary of the Navy
Charles F. Adams..... 1929

### Secretary of the Interior
Ray Lyman Wilbur..... 1929

### Secretary of Agriculture
Arthur M. Hyde....... 1929

### Secretary of Commerce
Robert P. Lamont...... 1929
Roy D. Chapin........ 1932

### Secretary of Labor
James J. Davis....... Contd
William N. Doak....... 1930

## F. D. ROOSEVELT

### Secretary of State
Cordell Hull........... 1933
E. R. Stettinius, Jr..... 1944

### Secretary of the Treasury
William H. Woodin..... 1933
Henry Morgenthau, Jr... 1934

### Secretary of War
George H. Dern........ 1933
Harry H. Woodring..... 1936
Henry L. Stimson...... 1940

### Attorney General
Homer S. Cummings... 1933
Frank Murphy......... 1939
Robert H. Jackson..... 1940
Francis Biddle........ 1941

### Postmaster General
James A. Farley....... 1933
Frank C. Walker....... 1940

### Secretary of the Navy
Claude A. Swanson.... 1933
Charles Edison........ 1940
Frank Knox........... 1940
James Forrestal....... 1944

### Secretary of the Interior
Harold L. Ickes.......: 1933

### Secretary of Agriculture
Henry A. Wallace...... 1933
Claude R. Wickard..... 1940

### Secretary of Commerce
Daniel C. Roper....... 1933
Harry L. Hopkins...... 1938
Jesse H. Jones........ 1940
Henry A. Wallace..... 1945

### Secretary of Labor
Frances Perkins....... 1933

## TRUMAN

### Secretary of State
E. R. Stettinius, Jr.... Contd
James F. Byrnes...... 1945
George C. Marshall.... 1947
Dean Acheson........ 1949

### Secretary of the Treasury
Henry Morgenthau, Jr. Contd
Fred M. Vinson....... 1945
John W. Snyder....... 1946

### Secretary of Defense
James Forrestal....... 1947
Louis A. Johnson...... 1949
George C. Marshall.... 1950
Robert A. Lovett....... 1951

### Attorney General
Francis Biddle........ Contd
Tom C. Clark......... 1945
J. Howard McGrath.... 1949
James P. McGranery... 1952

### Postmaster General
Frank C. Walker...... Contd
Robert E. Hannegan... 1945
Jesse M. Donaldson.... 1947

### Secretary of the Interior
Harold L. Ickes....... Contd
Julius A. Krug........ 1946
Oscar L. Chapman..... 1949

### Secretary of Agriculture
Claude R. Wickard.... Contd
Clinton P. Anderson... 1945
Charles F. Brannan... 1948

### Secretary of Commerce
Henry A. Wallace..... Contd
W. Averell Harriman... 1946
Charles Sawyer....... 1948

### Secretary of Labor
Frances Perkins...... Contd
Lewis B. Schwellenbach 1945
Maurice J. Tobin...... 1948

### Secretary of War[2]
Henry L. Stimson...... Contd
Robert P. Patterson.... 1945
Kenneth C. Royall..... 1947

### Secretary of the Navy[2]
James Forrestal....... Contd

## EISENHOWER

### Secretary of State
John Foster Dulles..... 1953
Christian A. Herter.... 1959

### Secretary of the Treasury
George M. Humphrey.. 1953
Robert B. Anderson.... 1957

### Secretary of Defense
Charles E. Wilson..... 1953
Neil H. McElroy...... 1957
Thomas S. Gates, Jr.... 1959

### Attorney General
Herbert Brownell, Jr... 1953
William P. Rogers..... 1958

### Postmaster General
Arthur Summerfield... 1953

### Secretary of the Interior
Douglas McKay........ 1953
Frederick A. Seaton... 1956

### Secretary of Agriculture
Ezra Taft Benson...... 1953

### Secretary of Commerce
Sinclair Weeks........ 1953
Lewis L. Strauss[3].... 1958
Frederick H. Mueller.. 1959

### Secretary of Labor
Martin P. Durkin...... 1953
James P. Mitchell..... 1953

### Secretary of Health, Education and Welfare
Oveta Culp Hobby..... 1953
Marion B. Folsom..... 1955
Arthur S. Flemming... 1958

## KENNEDY

### Secretary of State
Dean Rusk............ 1961

### Secretary of the Treasury
C. Douglas Dillon...... 1961

### Secretary of Defense
Robert S. McNamara... 1961

### Attorney General
Robert F. Kennedy.... 1961

### Postmaster General
J. Edward Day........ 1961

### Secretary of the Interior
Stewart L. Udall....... 1961

### Secretary of Agriculture
Orville L. Freeman..... 1961

### Secretary of Commerce
Luther H. Hodges...... 1961

### Secretary of Labor
Arthur J. Goldberg..... 1961

### Secretary of Health, Education and Welfare
Abraham A. Ribicoff... 1961

[1] The Postmaster General did not become a Cabinet member until 1829. Earlier Postmasters General were: Samuel Osgood (1789), Timothy Pickering (1791), Joseph Habersham (1795), Gideon Granger (1801), Return J. Meigs, Jr. (1814) and John McLean (1823). [2] On July 26, 1947, the Departments of War and of the Navy were incorporated into the Department of Defense. [3] Not confirmed by the Senate.

## Plurality and Majority

In order to win a plurality, a candidate must receive a greater number of votes than anyone running against him. If he receives 50 votes, for example, and two other candidates receive 49 and 2, he will have a plurality of one vote over his closest opponent.

However, a candidate does not have a majority unless he receives more than 50% of the total votes cast. In the example above, the candidate does not have a majority, because his 50 votes are less than 50% of the 101 votes cast.

## Presidents and Vice Presidents of the U. S.

| Presidents & (parties)[1] | Born | State of birth | Religion | Died | Term | Age at inaug. | Age at death | Vice Presidents[2] | State of birth |
|---|---|---|---|---|---|---|---|---|---|
| 1. Washington (F)[3] | Feb. 22, 1732 | Va. | Episcopalian | Dec. 14, 1799 | 1789–1797 | 57 | 67 | 1. John Adams | Mass. |
| 2. J. Adams (F) | Oct. 30, 1735 | Mass. | Unitarian | July 4, 1826 | 1797–1801 | 61 | 90 | 2. Thomas Jefferson[4] | Va. |
| 3. Jefferson (DR) | Apr. 13, 1743 | Va. | Deist | July 4, 1826 | 1801–1809 | 57 | 83 | 3. Aaron Burr | N. J. |
| | | | | | | | | 4. George Clinton | N. Y. |
| 4. Madison (DR) | Mar. 16, 1751 | Va. | Episcopalian | June 28, 1836 | 1809–1817 | 57 | 85 | 5. George Clinton[5] | Mass. |
| | | | | | | | | 5. Elbridge Gerry[6] | N. Y. |
| 5. Monroe (DR) | Apr. 28, 1758 | Va. | Episcopalian | July 4, 1831 | 1817–1825 | 58 | 73 | 6. Daniel D. Tompkins | N. Y. |
| 6. J. Q. Adams (DR) | July 11, 1767 | Mass. | Unitarian | Feb. 23, 1848 | 1825–1829 | 57 | 80 | 7. John C. Calhoun | S. C. |
| 7. Jackson (D) | Mar. 15, 1767 | S. C. | Presbyterian | June 8, 1845 | 1829–1837 | 61 | 78 | John C. Calhoun[7] | |
| | | | | | | | | 8. Martin Van Buren | N. Y. |
| 8. Van Buren (D) | Dec. 5, 1782 | N. Y. | Reformed Dutch | July 24, 1862 | 1837–1841 | 54 | 79 | 9. Richard M. Johnson | Ky. |
| 9. W. H. Harrison (W)[8] | Feb. 9, 1773 | Va. | Episcopalian | Apr. 4, 1841 | 1841–1841 | 68 | 68 | 10. John Tyler | Va. |
| 10. Tyler (W) | Mar. 29, 1790 | Va. | Episcopalian | Jan. 18, 1862 | 1841–1845 | 51 | 71 | | |
| 11. Polk (D) | Nov. 2, 1795 | N. C. | Methodist | June 15, 1849 | 1845–1849 | 49 | 53 | 11. George M. Dallas | Pa. |
| 12. Taylor (W)[8] | Nov. 24, 1784 | Va. | Episcopalian | July 9, 1850 | 1849–1850 | 64 | 65 | 12. Millard Fillmore | N. Y. |
| 13. Fillmore (W) | Jan. 7, 1800 | N. Y. | Unitarian | Mar. 8, 1874 | 1850–1853 | 50 | 74 | | |
| 14. Pierce (D) | Nov. 23, 1804 | N. H. | Episcopalian | Oct. 8, 1869 | 1853–1857 | 48 | 64 | 13. William R. King[9] | N. C. |
| 15. Buchanan (D) | Apr. 23, 1791 | Pa. | Presbyterian | June 1, 1868 | 1857–1861 | 65 | 77 | 14. John C. Breckinridge | Ky. |
| 16. Lincoln (R)[10] | Feb. 12, 1809 | Ky. | Liberal | Apr. 15, 1865 | 1861–1865 | 52 | 56 | 15. Hannibal Hamlin | Maine |
| | | | | | | | | 16. Andrew Johnson[17] | N. C. |
| 17. Johnson (U)[17] | Dec. 29, 1808 | N. C. | [16] | July 31, 1875 | 1865–1869 | 56 | 66 | 17. Schuyler Colfax | N. Y. |
| 18. Grant (R) | Apr. 27, 1822 | Ohio | Methodist | July 23, 1885 | 1869–1877 | 46 | 63 | 18. Henry Wilson[11] | N. H. |
| 19. Hayes (R) | Oct. 4, 1822 | Ohio | Methodist | Jan. 17, 1893 | 1877–1881 | 54 | 70 | 19. William A. Wheeler | N. Y. |
| 20. Garfield (R)[12] | Nov. 19, 1831 | Ohio | Disciples of Christ | Sept. 19, 1881 | 1881–1881 | 49 | 49 | 20. Chester A. Arthur | Vt. |
| 21. Arthur (R) | Oct. 5, 1830 | Vt. | Episcopalian | Nov. 18, 1886 | 1881–1885 | 50 | 56 | | |
| 22. Cleveland (D) | Mar. 18, 1837 | N. J. | Presbyterian | June 24, 1908 | 1885–1889 | 47 | 71 | 21. Thomas A. Hendricks[13] | Ohio |
| 23. B. Harrison (R) | Aug. 20, 1833 | Ohio | Presbyterian | Mar. 13, 1901 | 1889–1893 | 55 | 67 | 22. Levi P. Morton | Vt. |
| 24. Cleveland (R)[14] | | | | | 1893–1897 | | | 23. Adlai E. Stevenson | Ky. |
| | | | | | | | | 24. Garret A. Hobart[15] | N. J. |
| 25. McKinley (R) | Jan. 29, 1843 | Ohio | Methodist | Sept. 14, 1901 | 1897–1901 | 54 | 58 | 25. Theodore Roosevelt | N. Y. |
| 26. T. Roosevelt (R) | Oct. 27, 1858 | N. Y. | Reformed Dutch | Jan. 6, 1919 | 1901–1909 | 42 | 60 | 26. Charles W. Fairbanks | Ohio |
| 27. Taft (R) | Sept. 15, 1857 | Ohio | Unitarian | Mar. 8, 1930 | 1909–1913 | 51 | 72 | 27. James S. Sherman[16] | N. Y. |
| 28. Wilson (D) | Dec. 28, 1856 | Va. | Presbyterian | Feb. 3, 1924 | 1913–1921 | 56 | 67 | 28. Thomas R. Marshall | Ind. |
| 29. Harding (R)[8] | Nov. 2, 1865 | Ohio | Baptist | Aug. 2, 1923 | 1921–1923 | 55 | 57 | 29. Calvin Coolidge | Vt. |
| 30. Coolidge (R) | July 4, 1872 | Vt. | Congregationalist | Jan. 5, 1933 | 1923–1929 | 51 | 60 | 30. Charles G. Dawes | Ohio |
| 31. Hoover (R) | Aug. 10, 1874 | Iowa | Quaker | | 1929–1933 | 54 | | 31. Charles Curtis | Kans. |
| 32. F. D. Roosevelt (D)[8] | Jan. 30, 1882 | N. Y. | Episcopalian | Apr. 12, 1945 | 1933–1945 | 51 | 63 | 32. John N. Garner | Tex. |
| | | | | | | | | 33. Henry A. Wallace | Iowa |
| | | | | | | | | 34. Harry S. Truman | Mo. |
| 33. Truman (D) | May 8, 1884 | Mo. | Baptist | | 1945–1953 | 60 | | 35. Alben W. Barkley | Ky. |
| 34. Eisenhower (R) | Oct. 14, 1890 | Tex. | Presbyterian | | 1953–1961 | 62 | | 36. Richard M. Nixon | Calif. |
| 35. Kennedy (D) | May 29, 1917 | Mass. | Roman Catholic | | 1961– | 43 | | 37. Lyndon B. Johnson | Tex. |

### Footnotes for Table on Preceding Page

[1] F—Federalist; DR—Democratic–Republican; D—Democratic; W—Whig; R—Republican; U—Union. [2] Same party as President, except as indicated. [3] No party for first election. The party system in the U. S. made its appearance during Washington's first term. [4] Democratic–Republican. [5] Died in office Apr. 20, 1812. [6] Died in office, Nov. 23, 1814. [7] Resigned Dec. 28, 1832, to become U. S. Senator. [8] Died in office. [9] Died in office Apr. 18, 1853. [10] Died in office (shot Apr. 14 by John Wilkes Booth). [11] Died in office Nov. 22, 1875. [12] Died in office (shot July 2 by Charles J. Guiteau). [13] Died in office Nov. 25, 1885. [14] Died in office (shot Sept. 6 by Leon F. Czolgosz). [15] Died in office Nov. 21, 1899. [16] Died in office Oct. 30, 1912. [17] The Republican National Convention of 1864 adopted the name Union party. It renominated Lincoln for President; for Vice President it nominated Johnson, a War Democrat. Although frequently listed as a Republican Vice President and President, Johnson undoubtedly considered himself strictly a member of the Union party. When that party broke apart after 1868, he returned to the Democratic party. [18] Johnson was not a professed church member; however, he admired the Baptist principles of church government.

# Wives and Children of the Presidents of the United States

| President | Wife's name | Year and place of wife's birth | Married | Wife Died | Children of President* Sons | Daughters |
|---|---|---|---|---|---|---|
| Washington | Mrs. Martha Dandridge Custis | 1732, Va. | 1759 | 1802 | .. | .. |
| John Adams | Abigail Smith | 1744, Mass. | 1764 | 1818 | 3 | 2 |
| Jefferson | Mrs. Martha Wayles Skelton | 1748, Va. | 1772 | 1782 | 1 | 5 |
| Madison | Mrs. Dorothy "Dolly" Payne Todd | 1768, N. C. | 1794 | 1849 | .. | .. |
| Monroe | Eliza Kortright | 1768, N. Y. | 1786 | 1830 | .. | 2 |
| J. Q. Adams | Louisa Catherine Johnson | 1775, England | 1797 | 1852 | 3 | 1 |
| Jackson | Mrs. Rachel Donelson Robards | 1767, Va. | 1791 | 1828 | .. | .. |
| Van Buren | Hannah Hoes | 1783, N. Y. | 1807 | 1819 | 4 | .. |
| W. H. Harrison | Anna Symmes | 1775, N. J. | 1795 | 1864 | 6 | 4 |
| Tyler | Letitia Christian | 1790, Va. | 1813 | 1842 | 3 | 4 |
| | Julia Gardiner | 1820, N. Y. | 1844 | 1889 | 5 | 2 |
| Polk | Sarah Childress | 1803, Tenn. | 1824 | 1891 | .. | .. |
| Taylor | Margaret Smith | 1788, Md. | 1810 | 1852 | 1 | 5 |
| Fillmore | Abigail Powers | 1798, N. Y. | 1826 | 1853 | 1 | 1 |
| | Mrs. Caroline Carmichael McIntosh | 1813, N. J. | 1858 | 1881 | .. | .. |
| Pierce | Jane Means Appleton | 1806, N. H. | 1834 | 1863 | 3 | .. |
| Buchanan | (Unmarried) | .... | .... | .... | .. | .. |
| Lincoln | Mary Todd | 1818, Ky. | 1842 | 1882 | 4 | .. |
| Johnson | Eliza McCardle | 1810, Tenn. | 1827 | 1876 | 3 | 2 |
| Grant | Julia Dent | 1826, Mo. | 1848 | 1902 | 3 | 1 |
| Hayes | Lucy Ware Webb | 1831, Ohio | 1852 | 1889 | 7 | 1 |
| Garfield | Lucretia Rudolph | 1832, Ohio | 1858 | 1918 | 5 | 2 |
| Arthur | Ellen Lewis Herndon | 1837, Va. | 1859 | 1880 | 2 | 1 |
| Cleveland | Frances Folsom | 1864, N. Y. | 1886 | 1947 | 2 | 3 |
| B. Harrison | Caroline Lavinia Scott | 1832, Ohio | 1853 | 1892 | 1 | 1 |
| | Mrs. Mary Scott Lord Dimmick | 1858, Pa. | 1896 | 1948 | .. | 1 |
| McKinley | Ida Saxton | 1847, Ohio | 1871 | 1907 | .. | 2 |
| T. Roosevelt | Alice Hathaway Lee | 1861, Mass. | 1880 | 1884 | .. | 1 |
| | Edith Kermit Carow | 1861, Conn. | 1886 | 1948 | 4 | 1 |
| Taft | Helen Herron | 1861, Ohio | 1886 | 1943 | 2 | 1 |
| Wilson | Ellen Louise Axson | 1860, Ga. | 1885 | 1914 | .. | 3 |
| | Mrs. Edith Bolling Galt | 1872, Va. | 1915 | .... | .. | .. |
| Harding | Mrs. Florence Kling DeWolfe | 1860, Ohio | 1891 | 1924 | .. | .. |
| Coolidge | Grace Anna Goodhue | 1879, Vt. | 1905 | 1957 | 2 | .. |
| Hoover | Lou Henry | 1875, Iowa | 1899 | 1944 | 2 | .. |
| F. D. Roosevelt | Anna Eleanor Roosevelt | 1884, N. Y. | 1905 | .... | 5 | 1 |
| Truman | Bess Wallace | 1885, Mo. | 1919 | .... | .. | 1 |
| Eisenhower | Mamie Geneva Doud | 1896, Iowa | 1916 | .... | 2 | .. |
| Kennedy | Jacqueline Lee Bouvier | 1929, N. Y. | 1953 | .... | 1 | 1 |

\* Includes children who died in infancy.

# Annual Salaries of Federal Officials

*Source:* U. S. Department of the Treasury

| | | | |
|---|---|---|---|
| President of the U. S. | $100,000[1] | Secretaries of the Army, Navy, Air Force | 22,000 |
| Vice President of the U. S. | 35,000[2] | Senators and Representatives | 22,500 |
| Cabinet members | 25,000 | Speaker of the House | 35,000[2] |
| Undersecretaries of executive departments | 21,000[3] | Chief Justice of the Supreme Court | 35,500 |
| Deputy Secretary of Defense | 22,500 | Associate Justices of the Supreme Court | 35,000 |

[1] Plus taxable $50,000 for expenses and a nontaxable sum (not to exceed $40,000 a year) for traveling and official entertainment expenses. [2] Plus taxable $10,000 for expenses. [3] Except Undersecretary of State, who receives $22,500. NOTE: All salaries shown above are taxable.

# BIOGRAPHIES OF THE PRESIDENTS

## GEORGE WASHINGTON

was born February 22, 1732 (February 11, 1731/2, old style) in Westmoreland County, Virginia. He early trained as a surveyor; but in 1752 he was appointed adjutant in the Virginia militia, and for the next three years he took an active part in the wars against the French and Indians, serving as General Braddock's aide in the disastrous campaign against Fort Duquesne. In 1759 he resigned from the militia, married Martha Dandridge Custis, a widow, and settled down as a gentleman farmer at Mount Vernon.

As a militiaman, he had been exposed to the arrogance of the British officers, and his experience as a planter with British commercial restrictions increased his anti-British sentiment. He opposed the Stamp Act of 1765 and after 1770 became increasingly prominent in organizing resistance. A delegate to the Continental Congress, Washington was selected as commander in chief of the Continental Army and took command at Cambridge, Massachusetts, on July 3, 1775.

Inadequately supported and sometimes covertly sabotaged by the Congress, in charge of troops who were inexperienced, badly equipped, and impatient of discipline, Washington conducted the war on the policy of avoiding major engagements with the British and wearing them down by harassing tactics. His able generalship, along with the French alliance and the growing weariness within Britain, brought the war to a conclusion with the surrender of Cornwallis at Yorktown on October 19, 1781.

The chaotic years under the Articles of Confederation led Washington to return to public life in the hope of promoting the formation of a strong central government. He presided over the Constitutional Convention and yielded to the universal demand that he serve as first President. In office, he sought to unite the nation in the service of establishing the authority of the new government at home and abroad. Greatly distressed by the emergence of the Hamilton-Jefferson rivalry, he worked to maintain neutrality but actually sympathized more with Hamilton. Following his unanimous re-election in 1792, his second term was dominated by the Federalists. His Farewell Address rebuked party spirit and warned against foreign entanglements.

He died at Mt. Vernon on December 14, 1799. Tall, dignified and impressive, Washington gave a public impression of austerity, though he was capable of gaiety in private. His life was characterized by a strict sense of duty to his people. The standard biographies are by Fitzpatrick, Ford, Hughes, and Stephenson.

## JOHN ADAMS

was born on October 30 (October 19, old style), 1735, at Braintree (now Quincy), Massachusetts. A Harvard graduate, he considered teaching and the ministry but finally turned to law and was admitted to the bar in 1758. He opposed the Stamp Act, served as lawyer for patriots indicted by the British and, by the time of the Continental Congresses, was in the vanguard of the movement for independence. In 1778 he went to France as commissioner. Subsequently he helped negotiate the peace treaty with Britain, and in 1785 became the U. S. envoy to London. Resigning in 1788, he was elected Vice President under Washington, and was re-elected in 1792.

Though a Federalist, Adams did not get along with Hamilton, who sought to prevent his election to the presidency in 1796, and thereafter intrigued against his administration. Adams was chosen with 71 electoral votes to 68 for his closest competitor, Thomas Jefferson, who became Vice President. In 1798 Adams' independent policy averted a war with France but completed the break with Hamilton and the right-wing Federalists while, at the same time, the enactment of the Alien and Sedition Acts, directed against foreigners and against critics of the government, exasperated the Jeffersonian opposition. The split between Adams and Hamilton elected Jefferson in 1800. Adams retired to his home in Quincy, Massachusetts. He later corresponded with Jefferson and they died on the same day, July 4, 1826.

Stout, somewhat vain and irascible, Adams was honest, fearless and essentially fair-minded. His *Defence of the Constitutions of Government of the United States* (1787) contains original and striking if conservative political ideas. He married Abigail Smith in 1764, and their life together was long and happy. The standard biographies are by Morse and Chinard.

## THOMAS JEFFERSON

was born on April 13 (April 2, old style), 1743, at Shadwell in Goochland (now Albemarle) County, Virginia. A William and Mary graduate, he studied law but from the start showed an interest in science and philosophy. His literary skill and political clarity brought him to the forefront of the revolutionary movement in Virginia. As delegate to the Continental Congress, he drafted the Declaration of Independence. In 1776 he entered the Virginia House of Delegates and initiated a comprehensive reform program for the abolition of feudal survivals in land tenure and the separation of church and state.

In 1779 he became governor, but constitutional limitations on his power combined with his own lack of executive energy caused an unsatisfactory administration, culminating in Jefferson's virtual abdication when the British invaded Virginia in 1781. He now retired to his beautiful home at Monticello, to his wife, Martha Wayles Skelton, whom he had married in 1772 and who died in 1782, and to his children.

Jefferson's *Notes on Virginia* (1784–85) illustrate his many-faceted interests, his limitless intellectual curiosity, his deep faith in agrarian democracy. Sent to Congress in 1783, he helped lay down the decimal system and drafted basic reports on the organization of the western lands. In 1785 he was appointed minister to France, where his Anglo-Saxon liberalism he had drawn from Locke was stimulated by contact with the thought which would soon ferment in the French Revolution. In 1789 Washington appointed him Secretary of State. While favoring the Constitution and a strengthened central government, Jefferson came to believe that Hamilton contemplated the establishment of a monarchy. Growing differences resulted in Jefferson's resignation on Dec. 31, 1793.

Elected Vice President in 1796, Jefferson continued to serve as spiritual leader of the opposition to Federalism, particularly to the repressive Alien and Sedition Acts. He was elected President in 1801 by the House of Representatives as a result of Hamilton's decision to throw the Federalist votes to him rather than to Aaron Burr, who had tied him in electoral votes. The purchase of Louisiana from France in 1803, though in violation of his earlier constitutional scruples, was the most notable act of his administration. Re-elected in 1804 with 162 electoral votes to 14 for the Federalist Charles C. Pinckney, Jefferson tried desperately during his second term to keep the United States out of the Napoleonic Wars in Europe, employing to this end the unpopular embargo policy.

After his retirement to Monticello in 1809, he developed his interest in education, founding the University of Virginia and watching its development with never-flagging interest. He died at Monticello on July 4, 1826. Tall, loose-jointed, a poor speaker, Jefferson had an enormous variety of interests and skills, ranging from education and science to architecture and music. Economically his conception of democracy presupposed an essentially rural community of small freeholds; but his deep and abiding faith in the common man provides inspiration for future generations. The standard biographies are by Chinard, Bowers, Kimball, Randall, and Malone.

## JAMES MADISON

was born in Port Conway, Virginia, on March 16, 1751 (March 5, 1750/1, old style). A Princeton graduate, he joined the struggle for independence on his return to Virginia in 1771. In the seventies and eighties he was active both in state politics, where he championed the Jefferson reform program, and in the Continental Congress. He was influential in the Constitutional Convention as leader of the group favoring a strong central government and as recorder of the debates; and he subsequently wrote, in collaboration with Alexander Hamilton and John Jay, the *Federalist* papers to aid the campaign for the adoption of the Constitution.

In the new Congress, Madison soon emerged as the leader in the House of the men who opposed Hamilton's financial program and his pro-British leanings in foreign policy. Retiring from Congress in 1797, he continued active in Virginia and drafted the Virginia Resolution protesting the Alien and Sedition Acts. His intimacy with Jefferson made him the natural choice for Secretary of State in 1801.

In 1809 Madison succeeded Jefferson as President, with 122 electoral votes to 47 for the Federalist, C. C. Pinckney, and 6 scattering. His attractive wife, Dolly Payne Todd, whom he married in 1794, brought a new social sparkle to the executive mansion. In the meantime, increasing tension with Britain culminated in the War of 1812—a war for which the United States was unprepared, and for which Madison lacked the executive talent to clear out incompetence and mobilize the nation's energies. Madison was re-elected in 1812, with 128 electoral votes to 89 for the Federalist, De Witt Clinton. In 1814 the British actually captured Washington and forced Madison to flee to Virginia.

In his domestic program, Madison capitulated to the Hamiltonian policies that he had resisted twenty years before, signing bills to establish a United States Bank and a higher tariff. Following his presidency, he remained in retirement in Virginia until his death on June 28, 1836. Small, wrinkled, unimpressive, Madison had an acute political intelligence but lacked executive force. The standard biographies are by Hunt, Brant, and Rives.

## JAMES MONROE

was born on April 28, 1758, in Westmoreland County, Virginia. A William and Mary graduate, he served in the army during the first years of the Revolution and was wounded at Trenton. He then entered Virginia politics and later national politics under the sponsorship of Jefferson. In 1786 he married Eliza Kortright.

Fearing centralization, Monroe opposed the adoption of the Constitution and, as senator from Virginia, was highly critical of the Hamiltonian program. In 1794 he was appointed minister to France where his ardent sympathies with the Revolution exceeded the wishes of the State Department. A troubled diplomatic career ended with his recall in 1796. From 1799 to 1802 he was governor of Virginia. In 1803 Jefferson sent him to France to help negotiate the Louisiana Purchase and for the next few years he was active in various continental negotiations.

In 1808 Monroe flirted with the radical wing of the Republican party, which opposed Madison's candidacy; but the presidential boom came to naught and, after a brief term as governor of Virginia in 1811, Monroe accepted Madison's offer of the State Department. During the war he vainly sought a field command and served as Secretary of War from Sept., 1814, to Mar., 1815.

Elected President in 1816 with 183 electoral votes to 34 for the Federalist Rufus King, and re-elected without opposition in 1820, Monroe, the last of the Virginia dynasty, pursued the course of systematic tranquilization which won for his terms the name "the era of good feeling." He continued Madison's surrender to the Hamiltonian domestic program, signed the Missouri Compromise, acquired Florida and, with the able assistance of his Secretary of State, John Quincy Adams, promulgated the Monroe Doctrine in 1823, declaring against foreign colonization or intervention in the Americas. He died in New York City on July 4, 1831.

A sound man of medium abilities, Monroe possessed qualities of judgment rather than of leadership. The standard biographies are by Morgan, Gilman, and Styron.

## JOHN QUINCY ADAMS

was born on July 11, 1767, at Braintree (now Quincy), Massachusetts, the son of John Adams. He spent his early years in Europe with his father, graduated from Harvard, and entered law practice. His anti-Jeffersonian newspaper articles won him political attention. In 1794 he became minister to the Netherlands, the first of several diplomatic posts which occupied him until his return to Boston in 1801. In 1797 he married Louisa Catherine Johnson.

In 1803 he was elected to the Senate, nominally as a Federalist, but his repeated displays of independence on such issues as the Louisiana Purchase and the embargo caused his party to compel his resignation

and ostracize him socially. In 1809 Madison rewarded him for his support of Jefferson by appointing him minister to St. Petersburg. He helped negotiate the Treaty of Ghent in 1814 and in 1815 became minister to London. In 1817 Monroe appointed him Secretary of State where he served with great distinction, gaining Florida from Spain without hostilities and playing an equal part with Monroe in formulating the Monroe Doctrine.

When no presidential candidate received a majority of electoral votes in 1824, Adams, with the support of Henry Clay, was elected by the House in 1825 over Andrew Jackson, who had the original plurality. Adams had ambitious plans of government activity to foster internal improvements and promote the arts and sciences; but congressional obstructionism combined with his own unwillingness or inability to play the role of a politician meant that little was accomplished. Retiring to Quincy after his defeat in 1828, he was elected to the House of Representatives in 1831 where, though nominally a Whig, he pursued as ever an independent course. He led the fight to force Congress to receive antislavery petitions and fathered the Smithsonian Institution.

Stricken on the floor of the House, he died on February 23, 1848. Tactless, brusque, conscientious, a rough and savage debater, Adams spared neither himself nor his enemies. His long and detailed *Diary* gives a unique picture of the personalities and politics of the times. The standard biographies are by Morse and Clark.

## ANDREW JACKSON

was born on March 15, 1767, in what is now generally agreed to be Waxhaw, South Carolina. After a turbulent boyhood as an orphan and a British prisoner, he moved west to Tennessee where he soon qualified for law practice but found time for such frontier pleasures as horse racing, cockfighting, and dueling. His marriage to Rachel Donelson Robards in 1791 was complicated by subsequent legal uncertainties about the status of her divorce. During the seventeen-nineties Jackson served in the Tennessee constitutional convention, the federal House of Representatives, the federal Senate, and the Tennessee supreme court.

After some years as a country gentleman, living at the Hermitage near Nashville, Jackson in 1812 was given command of Tennessee troops sent against the Creeks. He defeated the Indians at Horseshoe Bend in 1814; subsequently he became a major general and won the Battle of New Orleans over veteran British troops though after the treaty of peace had been signed at Ghent. In 1818 General Jackson invaded Florida, captured Pensacola and hanged two Englishmen named Arbuthnot and

Ambrister, creating an international incident. A presidential boom began for him in 1821 and in its service he returned to the Senate (1823–25). Though he won a plurality of electoral votes in 1824, he lost in the House when Clay threw his strength to Adams; he won easily in 1828 by an electoral vote of 178 to 83.

As President, Jackson greatly expanded the power and prestige of the presidential office and carried through an unexampled program of domestic reform, vetoing the bill to extend the United States Bank, moving toward a hard-money currency policy, and checking the program of federal internal improvements. He also vindicated federal authority against South Carolina with its doctrine of nullification and against France on the question of debts. The support given his policies by the workingmen of the East as well as by the farmers of the East, West, and South resulted in his triumphant re-election in 1832 over Clay by an electoral vote of 219 to 49, with 18 scattering and 2 not cast.

After watching the inauguration of his hand-picked successor, Martin Van Buren, Jackson retired to the Hermitage, where he maintained a lively interest in national affairs until his death on June 8, 1845. A tall, dignified man with a drawn and wrinkled face, Jackson has been endowed by partisan historians with a violence and irascibility he appears not to have possessed. His great contribution was to adjust the presidential office and the democratic doctrines of Jefferson to the new situation created by the Industrial Revolution. The standard biographies are by James, Bassett, and Parton.

## MARTIN VAN BUREN

was born on December 5, 1782, at Kinderhook, New York. After graduating from the village school, he became a law clerk, entered practice in 1803, and soon became active in state politics as state senator and attorney general. In 1821 he was elected to the United States Senate. He threw the support of his efficient political organization, known as the Albany Regency, to William H. Crawford in 1824 and to Jackson in 1828. After leading the opposition to Adams' administration in the Senate, he served briefly as governor of New York and resigned to become Jackson's Secretary of State. He soon became on close personal terms with Jackson and played an important part in turning the Jacksonian program from the lines intended by his original Western backers.

In 1832 Van Buren became Vice President; in 1836, President, with an electoral vote of 170 against 124 scattered among four opponents. The Panic of 1837 overshadowed his term. He attributed it to the overexpansion of the credit and favored the establishment of an independent treasury as repository for the federal funds. In 1840 he established a ten-hour day on public works. Defeated by Harrison in 1840, he was the leading contender for the Democratic nomination in 1844 until he publicly opposed immediate annexation of Texas and was subsequently beaten by the Southern delegations at the Baltimore convention. This incident increased his growing misgivings about the slave power.

After working behind the scenes among the antislavery Democrats, Van Buren joined in the movement which led to the Free-Soil party and became its candidate for President in 1848. He subsequently returned to the Democratic party while continuing to object to its pro-Southern policy. He died in Kinderhook on July 24, 1862. His *Autobiography* throws valuable sidelights on the political history of the times.

Small, erect, dapper, Van Buren had a reputation for slick politicking which won him such sobriquets as the Little Magician and the Red Fox of Kinderhook; but, as his later career showed, he was capable of taking firm and unpopular stands on public issues. His wife Hannah Hoes, whom he married in 1807, died in 1819.

The standard biographies are by Shepard and Lynch.

## WILLIAM HENRY HARRISON

was born in Charles City County, Virginia, on February 9, 1773. Joining the army in 1791, he was active in Indian fighting in the Northwest, became secretary of the Northwest Territory in 1798 and governor of Indiana in 1800. He married Anna Symmes in 1795. Growing discontent over white encroachments on Indian lands led to the formation of an Indian alliance under Tecumseh to resist further aggressions. In 1811 Harrison won a nominal victory over the Indians at Tippecanoe and in 1813 a more decisive one at the Battle of the Thames, where Tecumseh was killed.

After resigning from the army in 1814, Harrison had an obscure career in politics and diplomacy, ending up in twenty years as a county recorder in Ohio. Nominated for President in 1835 as a military hero whom the conservative politicians hoped to be able to control, he ran surprisingly well against Van Buren in 1836. Four years later he defeated Van Buren by an electoral vote of 234 to 60 but caught pneumonia and died in Washington a month after his inauguration, April 4, 1841. Harrison's qualities were those of a soldier rather than of a statesman or political leader. The standard biographies are by Cleaves and Goebel.

## JOHN TYLER

was born in Charles City County, Virginia, on March 29, 1790. A William and Mary graduate, he entered law practice and politics, serving in the House of Representatives (1816–21) and later as governor of Virginia (1825–27), and as senator. A thorough-going strict constructionist, he supported Crawford in 1824 and Jackson in 1828 but broke with Jackson over his Bank policy and became a member of the Southern state-rights group which co-operated with the Whigs. In 1836 he resigned from the Senate rather than follow instructions from the Virginia legislature to vote for a resolution expunging censure of Jackson from the Senate record.

Elected Vice President on the Whig ticket in 1840, Tyler succeeded to the presidency on Harrison's death. His strict-constructionist views soon caused a split with the Henry Clay wing of the Whig party and a stalemate on domestic questions. Tyler's more considerable achievements were his support of the Webster-Ashburton Treaty with Britain and his success in bringing about the annexation of Texas through joint congressional resolution.

After his presidency he lived in retirement in Virginia until the outbreak of the Civil War, when he emerged briefly as chairman of a peace convention and then as delegate to the provisional Congress of the Confederacy. He died on January 18, 1862. He was married first to Letitia Christian March in 1813 and, two years after her death in 1842, to Julia Gardiner. Witty, amiable, courteous, Tyler was a Virginia gentleman whose presidency was hamstrung by the basic contradiction between his own ideas and those of the party which put him on the ticket as Vice President. The standard biographies are by Chitwood and Tyler.

## JAMES KNOX POLK

was born in Mecklenburg County, North Carolina, on November 2, 1795. A graduate of the University of North Carolina, he moved west to Tennessee, was admitted to the bar and soon became prominent in state politics. In 1825 he was elected to the House of Representatives where he opposed Adams and, after 1829, became Jackson's floor leader in the fight against the Bank. In 1835 he became Speaker of the House. In 1839 he was elected governor of Tennessee but was beaten in tries for re-election in 1841 and 1843.

The supporters of Van Buren for the Democratic nomination in 1844 counted on Polk as his running mate; but, when Van Buren's stand on Texas alienated Southern support, the convention swung to Polk on the ninth ballot. He was elected over Henry Clay, the Whig candidate, by an electoral vote of 170 to 105. Rapidly disillusioning those who thought that he would not run his own administration, Polk proceeded steadily and precisely to achieve four major objectives—the acquisition of California, the settlement of the Oregon question, the reduction of the tariff, and the establishment of the independent treasury. He also enlarged the Monroe Doctrine to exclude all non-American intervention in American affairs, whether forcible or not, and he forced Mexico into a war which he waged to a successful conclusion. His wife Sarah Childress, whom he married in 1824, was a woman of charm and ability. Polk died in Nashville, Tennessee, on June 15, 1849.

Serious, hardworking, lacking in color, Polk has long been underrated by historians who mistakenly regarded him as a slaveholders' puppet; in fact, few presidents have so thoroughly controlled their own administration or have so ably accomplished the purposes they set for themselves. Polk's *Diary* reflects the mood and problems of his presidency. The standard biography is by McCormac.

## ZACHARY TAYLOR

was born at Montebello, Orange County, Virginia, on November 24, 1784. Embarking on a military career in 1808, Taylor fought in the War of 1812, the Black Hawk War, and the Seminole War, holding in between garrison jobs on the frontier or desk jobs in Washington. A brigadier general as a result of his victory over the Seminoles at Lake Okeechobee (1837), Taylor held a succession of Southwestern commands and in 1846 established a base on the Rio Grande, where his forces engaged in hostilities which precipitated the war with Mexico. He captured Monterrey in Sept., 1846, and, disregarding Polk's orders to stay on the defensive, defeated Santa Anna at Buena Vista in February, 1847, ending the war in the northern provinces.

Though Taylor had never cast a vote for President, his party affiliations were Whiggish, and his availability was increased by his difficulties with Polk. He was elected President over the Democrat Lewis Cass by an electoral vote of 163 to 127. During the revival of the slavery controversy, which was to result in the Compromise of 1850, Taylor began to take an increasingly firm stand against appeasing the South; but he died in Washington on July 9, 1850, in the midst of the fight over the Compromise. He married Margaret Mackall Smith in 1810. His bluff and simple soldierly qualities won him the name of Old Rough and Ready. During his brief term as President he displayed a growing insight into political questions. The standard biographies are by Hamilton and by Bent and McKinley.

## MILLARD FILLMORE

was born at Locke, Cayuga County, New York, on January 7, 1800. A lawyer, he entered politics as an Antimason under the sponsorship of Thurlow Weed, editor and party boss, and subsequently followed Weed into the Whig party. He served in the House of Representatives (1833–35 and 1837–43) and played a leading role in writing the tariff of 1842. Defeated for governor of New York in 1844, he became comptroller in 1848, was put on the Whig ticket with Taylor as a concession to the Clay wing of the party and became President upon Taylor's death in 1850.

As President, Fillmore broke with Weed and William H. Seward and associated himself with the pro-Southern Whigs, supporting the Compromise of 1850. Defeated for the Whig nomination in 1852, he ran for President in 1856 as candidate of the American or Know-Nothing party, which sought to unite the country against foreigners in the alleged hope of diverting it from the explosive slavery issue. Fillmore opposed Lincoln during the Civil War. He died in Buffalo on March 8, 1874. He was married in 1826 to Abigail Powers, who died in 1853, and in 1858 to Caroline Carmichael McIntosh. Urbane, gracious, colorless, and weak, Fillmore was an undistinguished President. The standard biography is by Griffis.

## FRANKLIN PIERCE

was born at Hillsboro, New Hampshire, on November 23, 1804. A Bowdoin graduate and lawyer, he won rapid political advancement in the Democratic party, in part because of the prestige of his father, Governor Benjamin Pierce. By 1831 he was Speaker of the New Hampshire House of Representatives; from 1833 to 1837 he served in the federal House and from 1837 to 1842 in the Senate. His wife, Jane Means Appleton, whom he had married in 1834, disliked Washington and the somewhat dissipated life led by Pierce; and in 1842 Pierce, resigning from the Senate, took up a successful law practice in Concord, New Hampshire.

During the Mexican War Pierce was a brigadier general. Thereafter he continued to oppose antislavery tendencies within the Democratic party. As a result, he was the Southern choice to break the deadlock at the Democratic convention of 1852 and was nominated on the 49th ballot. Pierce rolled up 254 electoral votes to 42 for Winfield Scott, the Whig candidate.

As President, Pierce followed a course of appeasing the South at home and of playing with schemes of territorial expansion abroad. The failure of both his foreign and domestic policies prevented his renomination; and he died in Concord, New Hampshire, on October 8, 1869, in relative obscurity. A kindly and courteous person, Pierce was weak, unstable, and lacking in presidential qualities. The standard biography is by Nichols.

## JAMES BUCHANAN

was born near Mercersburg, Pennsylvania, on April 23, 1791. A Dickinson graduate and a lawyer, he entered Pennsylvania politics as a Federalist. With the disappearance of the Federalist party, he became a Jacksonian Democrat. He served with ability in the House (1821–31), as minister to St. Petersburg (1832–33) and in the Senate (1834–45), and in 1845 became Polk's Secretary of State. Disappointed in the presidential nomination in 1852, Buchanan became minister to Britain in 1853 where he participated with other American diplomats in Europe in drafting the expansionist Ostend Manifesto.

In 1856 Buchanan received the Democratic nomination and won the election, gaining 174 electoral votes to 114 for John C. Frémont, the Republican candidate, and 8 for Millard Fillmore, American party. The growing crisis over slavery presented Buchanan with problems he lacked the will to tackle. His appeasement of the South alienated the Stephen Douglas wing of the Democratic party without reducing Southern militancy on slavery issues. While denying the right of secession, Buchanan also denied that the federal government could do anything about it. He supported the administration during the Civil War and died in Lancaster, Pennsylvania, on June 1, 1868.

The only President to remain a bachelor throughout his term, Buchanan used his charming niece Harriet Lane as White House hostess. Legalistic, indecisive, and timorous as President, Buchanan filled his other public offices capably. The standard biography is by Curtis.

## ABRAHAM LINCOLN

was born in Hardin (now Larue) County, Kentucky, on February 12, 1809. His family moved to Indiana and then to Illinois, and Lincoln gained what education he could along the way. While reading law, he worked in a store, managed a mill, surveyed, and split rails. In 1834 he went to the state legislature as a Whig and became the party's floor leader. For the next twenty years he remained in law practice in Springfield, except for a single term (1847–49) in Congress, where he denounced the Mexican War. In 1855 he was a candidate for senator and in 1856 he joined the new Republican party.

A leading but unsuccessful candidate for the vice-presidential nomination with Frémont, Lincoln gained national attention in 1858 when, as Republican candidate for senator from Illinois, he engaged in a series of debates with Stephen A. Douglas, the Democratic candidate. He lost the senatorial election, but continued to prepare the way for the 1860 Republican convention and was rewarded with the presidential nomination on the third ballot. He polled 180 electoral votes, as against the 123 of his three opponents, but had only a plurality of the popular vote.

From the start, Lincoln made clear that, unlike Buchanan, he believed the national government had the power to crush the rebellion. Not an abolitionist, he held the slavery issue subordinate to that of preserving the Union but soon perceived that the war could not be brought to a successful conclusion without freeing the slaves. His administration was hampered by the incompetence of many Union generals, the inexperience of the troops, and the harassing political tactics both of the Republican Radicals, who favored a hard policy toward the South, and the Democratic Copperheads, who desired a negotiated peace. The Gettysburg Address of November 19, 1863, marks the high point in the record of American eloquence. His patient search for a winning combination finally brought Generals Ulysses S. Grant and William T. Sherman to the top; and their series of victories in 1864 dispelled the mutterings from both Radicals and Peace Democrats which at one time seemed to threaten Lincoln's re-election. He received 212 electoral votes to 21 for George B. McClellan, the Democratic candidate. His inaugural address urged leniency toward the South: "With malice toward none, with charity for all . . . let us strive on to finish the work we are in; to bind up the nation's wounds . . ." This policy aroused growing opposition on the part of the Republican Radicals, but Lincoln was shot by John Wilkes Booth at Ford's Theater, Washington, on April 14, 1865, before the matter could be put to test. He died the following day.

Lincoln's marriage to Mary Todd in 1842 was often unhappy and turbulent, in part because of his wife's pronounced instability. By his remarkable literary artistry, his essential patience and devotion, his profound sense of the importance of government by, for and of the people, by the manner of his life and of his death, Lincoln has won a unique place in the hearts of Americans. The standard biographies are by Sandburg, Herndon, Nicolay, and Hay.

## ANDREW JOHNSON

was born at Raleigh, North Carolina, on December 29, 1808. Self-educated, he became a tailor in Greeneville, Tennessee, but soon went into politics, where he rose steadily. From 1843 to 1853 he served in the House of Representatives, 1853–57 as governor of Tennessee, and in 1857 was elected Senator. Politically he was a Jacksonian Democrat, and his specialty was the fight for a more equitable land policy. Alone among the Southern Senators, he stood by the Union during the Civil War. In 1862 he became war governor of Tennessee and carried out a thankless and difficult job with great courage. Johnson became Lincoln's running mate in 1864 as result of an attempt to give the ticket a nonpartisan and nonsectional character. Succeeding to the presidency on Lincoln's death, Johnson sought to carry out his policy but without his political skill. The result was a hopeless conflict with the Radical Republicans who dominated Congress, passed measures over Johnson's vetoes, and attempted to limit the power of the executive concerning appointments and removals. The conflict culminated with Johnson's impeachment for attempting to remove his disloyal Secretary of War in defiance of the Tenure of Office Act which required senatorial concurrence for such dismissals. The opposition failed by one vote to get the two-thirds necessary for conviction.

After his presidency, Johnson maintained an interest in politics and in 1875 was elected to the Senate. He died near Carter Station, Tennessee, on July 31, 1875. He married Eliza McCardle in 1827. An honest, courageous, and intelligent man, Johnson lacked the tact, patience, and self-control to be an effective President.

The standard biographies are by Winston, Stryker, and Milton.

## ULYSSES SIMPSON GRANT

was born (as Hiram Ulysses Grant) at Point Pleasant, Ohio, on April 27, 1822. He finished West Point in 1843 and served without particular distinction in the Mexican War. In 1848 he married Julia Dent. He resigned from the army in 1854, following warnings from his commanding officer about his drinking habits, and for the next six years held a wide variety of jobs in the Middle West. With the outbreak of the Civil War, he sought a command and soon, to his surprise, was made a brigadier general. His continuing successes in the western theaters, culminating in the capture of Vicksburg in 1863, brought him national fame and soon the command of all the Union armies. His dogged, implacable policy of concentrating on dividing and destroying the Confederate armies brought the war to an end in 1865. In 1866 he was made full general.

Grant's relations with Johnson grew steadily worse; and in 1868, as the Republican candidate for President, Grant was elected with 214 electoral votes to 80 for the Democrat Horatio Seymour. From the start Grant showed his unfitness for the office. His cabinet was weak, his domestic policy was confused, many of his intimate associates were corrupt. The notable achievement in foreign affairs was the settlement of controversies with Great Britain in the Treaty of London (1871), negotiated by his able Secretary of State, Hamilton Fish.

Nominated for a second term, he defeated Horace Greeley, the Democratic and Liberal Republican candidate, 286 votes to 63. The Panic of 1873 created difficulties for his second term.

After retiring from office, Grant toured Europe for two years and returned in time to accede to a third-term boom, but was beaten in the convention of 1880. Illness and bad business judgment darkened his last years, but he worked steadily at the *Personal Memoirs* which were to be so successful when published after his death at Mount McGregor, near Saratoga, New York, on July 23, 1885. Inarticulate, taciturn, loyal to his friends, he was an able general who should never have accepted the presidency. The standard biographies are by Hesseltine and Woodward.

## RUTHERFORD BIRCHARD HAYES

was born at Delaware, Ohio, on October 4, 1822. A graduate of Kenyon College and the Harvard Law School, he practiced law in Sandusky and then in Cincinnati, Ohio. In 1852 he married Lucy Webb. A Whig, he joined the Republican party in 1855. During the Civil War he rose to the rank of major general. He served in Congress from 1865 to 1867 and then confirmed a reputation for honesty and efficiency in two terms as governor of Ohio. His re-election as governor in 1875 made him the logical candidate for those Republicans who wished to stop James G. Blaine in 1876, and he was successfully nominated.

The result of the election was for some time in doubt and hinged upon disputed returns from South Carolina, Louisiana, Florida, and Oregon. Samuel J. Tilden, the Democratic candidate, had the larger popular vote but was adjudged by the strictly partisan decisions of the Electoral Commission to have one less electoral vote, 185 to 184. The national acceptance of this result was due in part to the general understanding that Hayes would pursue a conciliatory policy toward the South. He withdrew the troops from the South, took a conservative position on financial and labor issues, and urged civil service reform.

Hayes served only one term by his own wish and spent the rest of his life in various humanitarian endeavors. He died in Fremont, Ohio, on January 17, 1893. A hard-working, conscientious, sensible man, Hayes represented the best type of Republican of his day. The standard biographies are by Eckenrode and Williams.

## JAMES ABRAM GARFIELD,

the last President to be born in a log cabin, was born at Cuyahoga County, Ohio, on November 19, 1831. A Williams graduate, he taught school for a time and entered Republican politics in Ohio. In 1858 he married Lucretia Rudolph. During the Civil War he had a promising career, rising to the rank of major general of volunteers; but in 1863 he was elected to the House of Representatives where he served until 1880. His oratorical and parliamentary abilities soon made him the leading Republican in the House, though his record was marred by his unorthodox acceptance of a fee in the DeGolyer paving contract case and by suspicions of his complicity in the Crédit Mobilier scandal.

In 1880 Garfield was elected to the Senate, but instead became the presidential candidate on the 36th ballot as a result of a deadlock in the Republican convention. He gained 214 electoral votes to 155 for General Winfield Scott Hancock, the Democratic candidate. Garfield's administration was barely under way when he was shot by Charles J. Guiteau, a disappointed office seeker, in July. He died in Elberon, New Jersey, on September 19, 1881. An attractive and eloquent man, he was much beloved in his day.

The standard biographies are by Smith and Caldwell.

## CHESTER ALAN ARTHUR

was born at Fairfield, Vermont, on October 5, 1830. A graduate of Union College, he became a successful New York lawyer. In 1859 he married Ellen Herndon. During the Civil War he held administrative jobs in the Republican state administration and in 1871 was appointed collector of the Port of New York by Grant. This post gave him control over considerable patronage; and, though not personally corrupt, Arthur managed his power in the interests of the New York machine so openly that President Hayes in 1877 called for an investigation, and in 1878 Arthur was suspended from his responsibilities.

In 1880 Arthur was nominated for Vice President in the hope of conciliating the followers of Grant and the powerful New York machine. As President on Garfield's assassination, Arthur, stepping out of his familiar role as spoilsman, backed civil service reform, reorganized the cabinet and prosecuted political associates accused of post office graft. Losing machine support and failing to gain the reformers, he was not renominated. He died in New York City on November 18, 1886. A tall, handsome, dignified man with real administrative abilities, he was a better President than his previous record promised. The standard biography is by Howe.

## STEPHEN GROVER CLEVELAND

was born at Caldwell, New Jersey, on March 18, 1837. He was admitted to the bar in Buffalo, New York, in 1859 and lived there as a lawyer, with occasional incursions into Democratic politics, for more than twenty years. He did not participate in the Civil War. As mayor of Buffalo in 1881, he carried through a reform program so ably that the Democrats ran him successfully for governor in 1882. In 1884 he won the Democratic nomination for President. The campaign contrasted Cleveland's spotless public career with the uncertain record of James G. Blaine, the Republican candidate, and Cleveland received enough Mugwump (independent Republican) support to win by 219 to 182 electoral votes.

As President, Cleveland pushed civil service reform, opposed the pension grab and attacked the high tariff rates. While in the White House he married Frances Folsom (1886). Renominated in 1888, Cleveland was defeated by Benjamin Harrison, polling more popular but fewer electoral votes. In 1892 he was re-elected over Harrison, 277 to 145, with 22 votes for James B. Weaver, the Populist candidate. When the Panic of 1893 burst upon the country, Cleveland's attempts to solve it by sound-money measures alienated the free-silver wing of the party, while his tariff policy alienated the protectionists. In 1894 he sent troops to break the Pullman strike. In foreign affairs his firmness caused Great Britain to back down in the Venezuela border dispute.

In his last years Cleveland was an active and much respected public figure. He died in Princeton, New Jersey, on June 24, 1908. An honest, stubborn, high-principled man, Cleveland was an old-fashioned liberal in the nineteenth-century sense who was baffled by the new problems of industrial society. The standard biographies are by Nevins and McElroy.

## BENJAMIN HARRISON

was born in North Bend, Ohio, on August 20, 1833, the grandson of William Henry Harrison. A graduate of Miami University, he took up the law in Indiana and became active in Republican politics. In 1853 he married Caroline Lavinia Scott. During the Civil War he rose to the rank of brigadier general. A sound-money Republican, he was elected senator from Indiana in 1880 and in 1888 received the Republican nomination for President on the 8th ballot. Though behind on the popular vote, he won over Grover Cleveland in the electoral college by 233 to 168.

As President, Benjamin Harrison failed to please either the bosses or the reform element in the party. In foreign affairs he backed Secretary of State Blaine, whose policy foreshadowed later American imperialism. In 1892 Harrison was renominated, but Cleveland beat him in the election. His wife died in the White House in 1892, and Harrison married her niece, Mary Scott (Lord) Dimmick, in 1896. After his presidency, he resumed law practice. He died in Indianapolis, Indiana, on March 13, 1901. Harrison was an honest man of very medium abilities.

## WILLIAM McKINLEY

was born in Niles, Ohio, on January 29, 1843. He taught school, then served in the Civil War, rising from the ranks to become a major. Subsequently he opened a law office in Canton, Ohio, and in 1871 married Ida Saxton. Elected to Congress in 1876, he served there steadily till 1891, except for 1883–85. His faithful advocacy of business interests culminated in the passage of the highly protective McKinley Tariff of 1890. With the support of Mark Hanna, a shrewd Cleveland businessman interested in safeguarding tariff protection, McKinley became governor of Ohio in 1892 and Republican presidential candidate in 1896. The business community, alarmed by the progressivism of William Jennings Bryan, the Democratic candidate, spent considerable money to assure McKinley's victory, which was by the margin of 271 to 176 in the electoral college.

The chief event of McKinley's administration was the war with Spain, which resulted in our acquisition of the Philippines and other islands. With imperialism as an issue, McKinley defeated Bryan again in the election of 1900 by 292 to 155. On September 6, 1901, he was shot at Buffalo by Leon F. Czolgosz, an anarchist, and he died there on September 14.

The standard biography is by Olcott.

## THEODORE ROOSEVELT

was born in New York City on October 27, 1858. A Harvard graduate, he was early interested in ranching, in politics, and in writing picturesque historical narratives. He was a Republican member of the New York Assembly in 1882–84, an unsuccessful candidate for mayor of New York in 1886, a U. S. Civil Service Commissioner under Harrison, Police Commissioner of New York City in 1895, and Assistant Secretary of the Navy under McKinley in 1897. After exuding a belligerence which helped bring on the war with Spain, he resigned in 1898 to help organize a volunteer regiment named the Rough Riders and take a more direct part in the war. Always publicity-shrewd, he won the New York gubernatorial nomination in 1898 in spite of pronounced lack of enthusiasm on the part of the bosses.

After two years of T.R. in Albany, the New York bosses succeeded in getting him the vice-presidential nomination in 1900.

Roosevelt accepted it with reluctance, feeling that his career had been ruined. As President on McKinley's assassination, he perceived the new popular mood of progressivism and initiated a policy of trust busting, designed to control giant corporations. He also strengthened government powers over interstate commerce and launched a conservation program to save natural resources. In foreign affairs he pursued a truculent policy, permitting the instigation of a revolt in Panamá to dispose of Colombian objections to the Panama Canal and helping to maintain the balance of power in the East by bringing the Russo-Japanese war to an end. In 1904 he decisively defeated Alton B. Parker, his conservative Democratic opponent, by an electoral margin of 336 to 140.

Following his second term he went big-game hunting in Africa and toured Europe. On his return to the United States, his increasing coldness toward Taft led him to overlook his earlier disclaimer of third-term ambitions and to re-enter politics. Defeated by the machine in the Republican convention of 1912, he organized the Progressive party and polled more votes than Taft, though the split brought about the election of Wilson. From 1915 on, Roosevelt strongly favored intervention in the European war. He became deeply embittered at Wilson's refusal to allow him to raise a volunteer division. He died in Oyster Bay, New York, on January 6, 1919. He was married twice: in 1880 to Alice Hathaway Lee, who died in 1884; and in 1886 to Edith Kermit Carow.

The athletic advocate of the strenuous life, with his high voice, prominent teeth, and thick glasses, Roosevelt captured the imagination of the American people. He was one of the great personalities of American history. The standard biography is by Pringle.

## WILLIAM HOWARD TAFT

was born in Cincinnati, Ohio, on September 15, 1857. A Yale graduate, he entered Ohio Republican politics in the eighteen eighties. In 1886 he married Helen Herron. From 1887 to 1890, he served on the Ohio superior court; 1890–92, as solicitor general of the United States; 1892–1900, on the federal circuit court. In 1900 McKinley appointed him president of the Philippine Commission and in 1901 governor general. Taft had great success in pacifying the Filipinos, solving the problem of the church lands, improving economic conditions and establishing limited self-government. His period as Secretary of War 1904–08 further demonstrated his capacity as administrator and conciliator; and he was Roosevelt's hand-picked successor in 1908.

In the election he polled 321 electoral votes to 162 for William Jennings Bryan.

As President, though he carried on many of Roosevelt's policies, Taft got into increasing trouble with the progressive wing of the party and displayed mounting irritability and indecision. After his defeat in 1912, he became professor of constitutional law at Yale. In 1921 he was appointed Chief Justice of the United States. He died in Washington on March 8, 1930. Enormously large, deliberate, and good-humored, Taft excelled as an administrator and judge, not as a political leader.

The standard biography is by Pringle.

## THOMAS WOODROW WILSON

was born in Staunton, Virginia, on December 28, 1856. A Princeton graduate, he turned from law practice to post-graduate work in political science at Johns Hopkins University, receiving his Ph.D. in 1886. He taught at Bryn Mawr, Wesleyan, and Princeton, and in 1902 was made president of Princeton. After an unsuccessful attempt to democratize the social life of Princeton, he welcomed an invitation in 1910 to be the Democratic gubernatorial candidate in New Jersey. His success in fighting the machine and putting through a reform program attracted national attention.

In 1912, after a protracted contest at Baltimore, Wilson won the Democratic nomination on the 46th ballot. In the election he received 435 electoral votes to 88 for Roosevelt and 8 for Taft. During his first term Wilson proceeded under the standard of the New Freedom to enact a program of domestic reform, including the Federal Reserve Act, the Clayton Antitrust Act, the establishment of the Federal Trade Commission, and other measures designed to restore competition in the face of the great monopolies. In foreign affairs, while privately sympathetic with the Allies, he strove to maintain strict neutrality in the European war and warned both sides against encroachments on American interests.

Re-elected in 1916 as a peace candidate, he tried to mediate between the warring nations; but, when the Germans resumed unrestricted submarine warfare in 1917, Wilson brought the United States into what he now believed was a war to make the world safe for democracy. He supplied the classic formulations of Allied war aims; and the armistice of November, 1918, was negotiated on the basis of Wilson's Fourteen Points. In 1919 he strove at Versailles to lay the foundations for enduring peace. He accepted the imperfections of the Versailles Treaty in the expectation that they could be remedied by action within the

League of Nations. He probably could have secured ratification of the treaty if he had adopted a more conciliatory attitude toward the mild reservationists; but his insistence on all or nothing eventually caused the diehard isolationists and diehard Wilsonites to unite in rejecting a compromise.

In September, 1919, Wilson suffered a paralytic stroke which limited his future activity. After the presidency he lived on in retirement in Washington, dying February 3, 1924. He was married twice—in 1885 to Ellen Louise Axson, who died in 1914, and in 1915 to Edith Bolling Galt. A man of high principle, inspiring eloquence, and great intellectual ability, Wilson was the first leader to fire the imagination of the masses of the world with the vision of world peace. The standard biography is by Baker.

### WARREN GAMALIEL HARDING

was born in Morrow County, Ohio, on November 2, 1865. After attending Ohio Central College, Harding became interested in journalism and in 1884 bought the *Marion* (Ohio) *Star*. In 1891 he married a wealthy widow, Florence Kling De Wolfe. As his paper prospered, he entered Republican politics, serving as state senator (1899–1903), and as lieutenant governor (1904–06). In 1910 he was defeated for governor but in 1914 was elected to the Senate. His reputation as orator made him keynoter in the 1916 convention.

When the 1920 Republican convention was deadlocked between Leonard Wood and Frank O. Lowden, Harding was made the dark-horse nominee on his solemn affirmation that there was no reason in his past that he should not be. Straddling the League question, Harding was elected easily, with 404 electoral votes to 127 for James M. Cox, his Democratic opponent. His cabinet contained some able men, but also some manifestly unfit for public office. Harding's own intimates were mediocre when they were not corrupt. The impending disclosure of scandals in the Interior and Justice departments and in the Veterans' Bureau, as well as political setbacks, profoundly worried him. On his return from Alaska in 1923, he died suddenly at San Francisco on August 2. A handsome and genial man, undiscriminating in his associates, lacking in political ideas or fortitude, Harding was totally unfitted for the presidency.

### JOHN CALVIN COOLIDGE

was born in Plymouth, Vermont, on July 4, 1872. An Amherst graduate, he went into law practice at Northampton, Massachusetts, in 1897. He married Grace Anna Goodhue in 1905. He entered Republican state politics, becoming successively mayor of Northampton, state senator, lieutenant governor and, in 1919, governor. His conduct in regard to the Boston police strike in 1919 won him a somewhat undeserved reputation for decisive action and brought him the Republican vice-presidential nomination in 1920. After Harding's death Coolidge handled the Washington scandals with care and finally managed to save the Republican party from public blame for the widespread corruption.

In 1924 Coolidge won re-election without difficulty, getting 382 electoral votes to 136 for the Democrat, John W. Davis, and 13 for Robert M. La Follette running on the Progressive ticket. His second term, like his first, was characterized by a general satisfaction with the existing economic order. He stated that he did not choose to run in 1928.

After his presidency, Coolidge lived quietly in Northampton, writing an unilluminating *Autobiography* and conducting a syndicated column. He died in Northampton, Massachusetts, on January 5, 1933. His dry, Yankee humor, his frugality and glumness made him a paradoxically popular President in the boom period. The standard biographies are by White and Fuess.

### HERBERT CLARK HOOVER

was born at West Branch, Iowa, an August 10, 1874. A Stanford graduate, he worked from 1895 to 1913 as a mining engineer and consultant in North America, Europe, Asia, Africa, and Australia. In 1899 he married Lou Henry. During the First World War he served with distinction as chairman of the American Relief Committee in London, as chairman of the Commission for Relief in Belgium and as United States Food Administrator. His political affiliations were still sufficiently indeterminate for him to be mentioned as a possibility for both Republican and Democratic nominations in 1920; but after the election he served both Harding and Coolidge as Secretary of Commerce.

In the election of 1928 Hoover received 444 electoral votes to 87 for Alfred E. Smith, the Democratic candidate. He soon faced the worst depression in the nation's history; but his attacks upon it were hampered by his devotion to the theory that the forces which brought the crisis would soon bring the revival, and then by his belief that in too many areas the federal government had no power to act. In a succession of vetoes he struck down measures proposing a national employment system or national relief; he reduced income tax rates; and only at the end of his term did he yield to popular pressure and set up agencies such as the Reconstruction Finance Corporation to make emergency loans to assist business.

After his 1932 defeat, Hoover returned to private business. In 1946, President Truman charged him with various world food missions; and from 1947 to 1949 and again from 1953 to 1955, he was head of the Commission on Organization of the Executive Branch of the Government.

## FRANKLIN DELANO ROOSEVELT

was born in Hyde Park, New York, on January 30, 1882. A Harvard graduate, he attended Columbia Law School and was admitted to the New York bar. In 1910 he was elected to the New York state senate as a Democrat. Re-elected in 1912, he was appointed Assistant Secretary of the Navy by Woodrow Wilson in 1913. In 1920 his radiant personality and his war services resulted in his nomination for Vice President as James M. Cox's running mate. After his defeat, he returned to law practice in New York. In August, 1921, Roosevelt was stricken with infantile paralysis while at Campobello, New Brunswick. After a long and gallant fight against the disease he recovered partial use of his legs. In 1924 and 1928 he led the fight at the Democratic national conventions for the nomination of Governor Alfred E. Smith of New York; and in 1928 Roosevelt was himself induced to run for governor of New York. He was elected and was re-elected in 1930.

In 1932 Roosevelt received the Democratic nomination for President and immediately launched a campaign which brought new spirit to a weary and discouraged nation. He won the election over Herbert Hoover by a margin of 472 to 59 in the electoral college. His first term was characterized by an unfolding of the New Deal program, with greater benefits for labor, the farmers, and the unemployed, and the progressive estrangement of most of the business community.

At an early stage Roosevelt became aware of the menace to world peace involved in the existence of totalitarian fascism, and from 1937 on he tried to focus public attention on the trend of events in Europe and Asia. As a result he was widely denounced as a warmonger. He was re-elected in 1936 over Alfred M. Landon by the overwhelming electoral margin of 523 to 8; and the gathering international crisis caused him to decide to run again in 1940. He defeated Wendell L. Willkie by a vote of 449 to 82.

Roosevelt's program to bring maximum aid to Britain and, after June, 1941, to Russia was opposed, until the Japanese attack on Pearl Harbor restored national unity. During the war Roosevelt shelved the New Deal in the interests of conciliating the business community, both in order to get full production during the war and to prepare the way for a united acceptance of the peace settlements after the war. A series of conferences with Winston Churchill and Joseph Stalin laid down the bases for the postwar world. In 1944 he was elected to a fourth term, running against Governor Thomas E. Dewey of New York.

On April 12, 1945, Roosevelt died at Warm Springs, Georgia, shortly after his return from the Yalta Conference. His wife, Anna Eleanor Roosevelt, whom he married in 1905, is a woman of great ability who made significant contributions to her husband's policies. No President has been faced with so many staggering responsibilities, both at home and abroad.

## HARRY S. TRUMAN

was born on a farm near Lamar, Missouri, on May 8, 1884. During the First World War he served in France with the 129th Field Artillery. He married Bess Wallace in 1919. After engaging briefly and unsuccessfully in the haberdashery business in Kansas City, Truman entered local politics. Under the sponsorship of Thomas Pendergast, Democratic boss of Missouri, he held a number of local offices, preserving his personal honesty in the midst of a notoriously corrupt political machine. In 1934 he was elected to the Senate and was re-elected in 1940. During his first term he was a loyal but quiet supporter of the New Deal; but in the course of his second term, an appointment as head of a Senate committee to investigate war production brought out his special qualities of honesty, common sense, and hard work, and he won widespread respect.

Elected Vice President in 1944, Truman became President upon Roosevelt's death in 1945 and immediately had to face complex postwar problems, both domestic and foreign. His first attempts did not meet with marked success, and the Republicans won control of Congress in 1946. The next two years were distinguished by the Truman Doctrine, the Marshall Plan, and civil-rights proposals; and his general record, highlighted by a vigorous Fair Deal campaign, brought about his unexpected and impressive re-election in 1948.

Truman's second term was primarily concerned with the Cold War with the Soviet Union, the implementing of the North Atlantic Pact, the United Nations police action in Korea, and the vast rearmament program with its accompanying problems of economic stabilization.

On Mar. 29, 1952, Truman announced that he would not run again for the Presidency. He campaigned actively for Adlai E. Stevenson. After Eisenhower's inauguration, Truman returned to his Independence, Missouri, home to write his memoirs. He further busied himself with the organization of the Harry S. Truman Library in Independence, Missouri.

## DWIGHT DAVID EISENHOWER

was born in Denison, Texas, on October 14, 1890. His ancestors lived in Germany, and emigrated to America, settling in Pennsylvania, early in the 18th century. His father, David, had a general store in Hope, Kansas, which failed. After a brief time in Texas, the family moved to Abilene, Kansas.

After graduating from Abilene High School in 1909, Dwight Eisenhower did odd jobs for almost two years. He won an appointment to the Naval Academy at Annapolis, but it turned out that he was too old for admittance. Then he received an appointment in 1910 to West Point. He was graduated a 2nd lieutenant in 1915.

He did not see service in World War I, having been assigned to the 19th Infantry at Fort Sam Houston, Texas. There he met Mamie Geneva Doud, whom he married in Denver on July 1, 1916. Their first son died in infancy. Their second son is Major John Sheldon Doud Eisenhower.

A paper he wrote about 1930 attracted the attention of General Douglas MacArthur, then Chief of Staff, who asked that Eisenhower be assigned to his office. When MacArthur went to the Philippines as military adviser in 1935, Eisenhower accompanied him and remained with him until 1939.

General George C. Marshall brought him into the War Department General Staff and, in 1942, put him in command of the Allied invasion of North Africa. In 1944, Eisenhower was made Supreme Allied Commander of the invasion of Europe.

After the war, Eisenhower served as Army Chief of Staff from November, 1945, until February, 1948, when he was appointed president of Columbia University.

In December, 1950, President Truman recalled Eisenhower to active duty to command the North Atlantic Treaty Organization forces in Europe. He held this post until the end of May, 1952.

In the Republican Convention of July, 1952, in Chicago, Eisenhower won the Presidential nomination on the first ballot in a close race with Senator Robert A. Taft of Ohio. In November, he won the election, defeating Adlai E. Stevenson by an electoral vote of 442 to 89.

Through two terms, Eisenhower hewed to moderate domestic policies. He quested for peace through Free World strength in an era of new nationalisms, nuclear rockets, and space exploration. He fostered alliances pledging the U.S. to resist Red aggression in Europe, Asia, and Latin America. The Eisenhower doctrine of 1957 extended commitments to the Middle East. Arms budgets focused on nuclear "massive retaliation." Stepped-up space programs followed the Soviet Sputnik I (1957). Meetings with Soviet Premier Khrushchev in 1955 and 1959 saw some relaxation of tensions. But the 1960 Summit meeting died when Eisenhower rejected Khrushchev's demand for a U.S. apology for the U-2 "spy" flights over the U.S.S.R. Eisenhower proposed an international "atoms for peace" plan to the U.N. in 1954. His travels to advance Free World unity carried him as far as India.

At home, the popular President lacked G.O.P. Congressional majorities after 1954, but he was re-elected in 1956 by 457 electoral votes to 73 for Adlai E. Stevenson. Under early attack from Sen. Joseph R. McCarthy, R., Wis., he later saw McCarthy censured. He retained most Fair Deal programs, but stressed "fiscal responsibility" and sought more state participation. He was a moderate on civil rights, but used troops to balk anti-integration riots in Little Rock, Ark. Eisenhower ran in 1956 on a "Peace, Prosperity, Progress" platform, despite a heart attack suffered in September, 1955. An ileitis operation in June, 1956, curtailed his campaign. He kept Vice President Nixon as his 1956 running mate and put increased reliance on Nixon following the resignation under fire in 1958 of his top aide, Sherman Adams.

## JOHN FITZGERALD KENNEDY

was born in Brookline, Massachusetts, on May 29, 1917, into a wealthy Catholic family. His father, Joseph P. Kennedy, was American Ambassador to the Court of St. James from 1937 to 1940. There were nine children. John F. Kennedy and his wife, the former Jacqueline Lee Bouvier, have a daughter, Caroline, born November 27, 1957, and a son, John Fitzgerald, Jr., born November 25, 1960.

At Harvard, Kennedy was on the swimming team—a fact that later probably saved his life. Joining the Navy in 1941, he became skipper of a PT boat in the Pacific, which was sunk by a Japanese destroyer. Kennedy was given up for lost, but he swam to a safe island, towing an injured enlisted man.

After recovering from a war-aggravated spinal injury, Kennedy entered politics in 1946 and was elected to Congress. In 1952 he ran against the then Senator from Massachusetts, Henry Cabot Lodge, Jr., and won.

In 1957 Kennedy won the Pulitzer Prize for a book he had written earlier, *Profiles in Courage*, which gave biographical sketches of American political leaders of earlier days who had displayed courage in standing up for their convictions against odds.

(For news events of the Kennedy Administration, see front of book or Index.)

# THE EIGHTY-SEVENTH CONGRESS

*Source: Congressional Directory.*

## THE SENATE

The year in which present service began and the year in which it is due to expire are indicated in parentheses after each name. Only the last two numbers of the year are given; e.g., 63 for 1963. All terms expire in January.

### ALABAMA
Lister Hill, D (38–63)
John J. Sparkman, D (46–67)

### ALASKA
E. L. (Bob) Bartlett, D (59–67)
Ernest Gruening, D (59–63)

### ARIZONA
Carl Hayden, D (27–63)
Barry Goldwater, R (53–65)

### ARKANSAS
John L. McClellan, D (43–67)
J. W. Fulbright, D (45–63)

### CALIFORNIA
Thomas H. Kuchel, R (53–63)
Clair Engle, D (59–65)

### COLORADO
Gordon Allott, R (55–67)
John A. Carroll, D (57–63)

### CONNECTICUT
Prescott Bush, R (52–63)
Thomas J. Dodd, D (59–65)

### DELAWARE
John J. Williams, R (47–65)
J. Caleb Boggs, R (61–67)

### FLORIDA
Spessard L. Holland, D (46–65)
George A. Smathers, D (51–63)

### GEORGIA
Richard B. Russell, D (33–67)
Herman E. Talmadge, D (57–63)

### HAWAII
Hiram L. Fong, R (59–65)
Oren E. Long, D (59–63)

### IDAHO
Henry C. Dworshak, R (49–67)[1]
Frank Church, D (57–63)

### ILLINOIS
Paul H. Douglas, D (49–67)
Everett M. Dirksen, R (51–63)

### INDIANA
Homer E. Capehart, R (45–63)
Vance Hartke, D (59–67)

### IOWA
B. B. Hickenlooper, R (45–63)
Jack Miller, R (61–67)

### KANSAS
Andrew F. Schoeppel, R (49–67)
Frank Carlson, R (50–63)

### KENTUCKY
John S. Cooper, R (56–67)[2]
Thruston B. Morton, R (57–63)

### LOUISIANA
Allen J. Ellender, D (37–67)
Russell B. Long, D (48–63)

### MAINE
Margaret C. Smith, R (49–67)
Edmund S. Muskie, D (59–65)

### MARYLAND
John M. Butler, R (51–63)
J. Glenn Beall, R (53–65)

### MASSACHUSETTS
Leverett Saltonstall, R (45–67)
Benjamin Atwood Smith II, D (60–65)

### MICHIGAN
Pat McNamara, D (55–67)
Philip A. Hart, D (59–65)

### MINNESOTA
Hubert H. Humphrey, D (49–67)
Eugene J. McCarthy, D (59–65)

### MISSISSIPPI
James O. Eastland, D (43–67)[3]
John Stennis, D (47–65)

### MISSOURI
Stuart Symington, D (53–65)
Edward V. Long, D (60–63)

### MONTANA
Mike Mansfield, D (53–65)
Lee Metcalf, D (61–67)

### NEBRASKA
Roman L. Hruska, R (54–65)
Carl T. Curtis, R (55–67)

### NEVADA
Alan Bible, D (54–63)
Howard W. Cannon, D (59–65)

### NEW HAMPSHIRE
Styles Bridges, R (37–67)
Norris Cotton, R (54–63)

### NEW JERSEY
Clifford P. Case, R (55–67)
H. A. Williams, Jr., D (59–65)

### NEW MEXICO
Dennis Chavez, D (35–65)
Clinton P. Anderson, D (49–67)

### NEW YORK
Jacob K. Javits, R (57–63)
Kenneth B. Keating, R (59–65)

### NORTH CAROLINA
Sam J. Ervin, Jr., D (54–63)
B. Everett Jordan, D (58–67)

### NORTH DAKOTA
Milton R. Young, R (45–63)
Quentin N. Burdick, D (60–65)

### OHIO
Frank J. Lausche, D (57–63)
Stephen M. Young, D (59–65)

### OKLAHOMA
Robert S. Kerr, D (49–67)
Mike Monroney, D (51–63)

### OREGON
Wayne Morse, D (45–63)
Mrs. Maurine B. Neuberger, D (60–67)

### PENNSYLVANIA
Joseph S. Clark, D (57–63)
Hugh Scott, R (59–65)

### RHODE ISLAND
John O. Pastore, D (50–65)
Claiborne Pell, D (61–67)

### SOUTH CAROLINA
Olin D. Johnston, D (45–63)
Strom Thurmond, D (56–67)[4]

### SOUTH DAKOTA
Karl E. Mundt, R (48–67)
Francis Case, R (51–63)

### TENNESSEE
Estes Kefauver, D (49–67)
Albert Gore, D (53–65)

### TEXAS
R. W. Yarborough, D (57–65)
John G. Tower, R (61–67)

### UTAH
Wallace F. Bennett, R (51–63)
Frank E. Moss, D (59–65)

### VERMONT
George D. Aiken, R (41–63)
Winston L. Prouty, R (59–65)

### VIRGINIA
Harry Flood Byrd, D (33–65)
A. Willis Robertson, D (46–67)

### WASHINGTON
Warren G. Magnuson, D (44–63)
Henry M. Jackson, D (53–65)

### WEST VIRGINIA
Jennings Randolph, D (58–67)
Robert C. Byrd, D (59–65)

### WISCONSIN
Alexander Wiley, R (39–63)
William Proxmire, D (57–65)

### WYOMING
Gale W. McGee, D (59–65)
J. J. Hickey, D (61–67)

[1] Also served Nov. 6, 1946, to Jan. 3, 1949.  [2] Also served Nov. 6, 1946, to Jan. 3, 1949, and Nov. 5, 1952, to Jan. 3, 1955.  [3] Also served June 30 to Sept. 28, 1941.  [4] Also served Dec. 24, 1954, to Apr. 4, 1956.

# THE HOUSE OF REPRESENTATIVES

The apportionment based on the Seventeenth Census (1950) distributed the seats in the House among the states according to the method of equal proportions. By this method the per cent difference between the average number of Representatives per million people in any 2 states is made as small as possible. Also, the per cent difference between the average districts, i.e., the average number of persons per Representative, in any 2 states is made as small as possible. By equalizing the representation of all pairs of states, the method gives as nearly equal representation as possible to all states in proportion to their population.

The numerals indicate the Congressional Districts of the states, and the designation At-L means At-Large. An asterisk (*) indicates that the Congressman was returned to office in the 1960 elections. The terms of all Representatives end January, 1963.

## ALABAMA

**(9 Representatives)**

1. *Frank W. Boykin, D
2. *George Grant, D
3. *George W. Andrews, D
4. *Kenneth A. Roberts, D
5. *Albert Rains, D
6. *Armistead I. Selden, Jr., D
7. *Carl Elliott, D
8. *Robert E. Jones, Jr., D
9. *George Huddleston, Jr., D

## ALASKA

**(1 Representative)**

At-L. *Ralph J. Rivers, D

## ARIZONA

**(2 Representatives)**

1. *John J. Rhodes, R
2. Morris K. Udall, D

## ARKANSAS

**(6 Representatives)**

1. *E. C. Gathings, D
2. *Wilbur D. Mills, D
3. *James W. Trimble, D
4. *Oren Harris, D
5. *Dale Alford, D
6. Catherine D. Norrell, D

## CALIFORNIA

**(30 Representatives)**

1. *Clem Miller, D
2. *Harold T. Johnson, D
3. *John E. Moss, D
4. *William S. Mailliard, R
5. *John F. Shelley, D
6. *John F. Baldwin, Jr., R
7. *Jeffery Cohelan, D
8. *George P. Miller, D
9. *J. Arthur Younger, R
10. *Charles S. Gubser, R
11. *John J. McFall, D
12. *B. F. Sisk, D
13. *Charles M. Teague, R
14. *Harlan Hagen, D
15. *Gordon L. McDonough, R
16. Alphonzo Bell, R
17. *Cecil R. King, D
18. *Craig Hosmer, R
19. *Chet Holifield, D
20. *H. Allen Smith, R
21. *Edgar W. Hiestand, R
22. James C. Corman, D
23. *Clyde Doyle, D
24. *Glenard P. Lipscomb, R
25. John H. Rousselot, R
26. *James Roosevelt, D

27. *Harry R. Sheppard, D
28. *James B. Utt, R
29. *D. S. (Judge) Saund, D
30. *Bob Wilson, R

## COLORADO

**(4 Representatives)**

1. *Byron G. Rogers, D
2. Peter H. Dominick, R
3. *J. Edgar Chenoweth, R
4. *Wayne N. Aspinall, D

## CONNECTICUT

**(6 Representatives)**

1. *Emilio Q. Daddario, D
2. Horace Seely-Brown, Jr., R
3. *Robert N. Giaimo, D
4. Abner W. Sibal, R
5. *John S. Monagan, D
At-L. *Frank Kowalski, D

## DELAWARE

**(1 Representative)**

At-L. *Harris B. McDowell, Jr., D

## FLORIDA

**(8 Representatives)**

1. *William C. Cramer, R
2. *Charles E. Bennett, D
3. *Robert L. F. Sikes, D
4. *Dante B. Fascell, D
5. *A. S. (Syd) Herlong, Jr., D
6. *Paul G. Rogers, D
7. *James A. Haley, D
8. *D. R. (Billy) Matthews, D

## GEORGIA

**(10 Representatives)**

1. G. Elliott Hagan, D
2. *J. L. Pilcher, D
3. *E. L. (Tic) Forrester, D
4. *John J. Flynt, Jr., D
5. *James C. Davis, D
6. *Carl Vinson, D
7. John W. Davis, D
8. *Mrs. Iris F. Blitch, D
9. *Phil M. Landrum, D
10. Robert G. Stephens, Jr., D

## HAWAII

**(1 Representative)**

At-L. *Daniel K. Inouye, D

## IDAHO

**(2 Representatives)**

1. *Mrs. Gracie Pfost, D
2. Ralph R. Harding, D

## ILLINOIS

**(25 Representatives)**

1. *William L. Dawson, D
2. *Barratt O'Hara, D
3. *William T. Murphy, D
4. *Edward J. Derwinski, R
5. *John C. Kluczynski, D
6. *Thomas J. O'Brien, D
7. *Roland V. Libonati, D
8. *Dan Rostenkowski, D
9. *Sidney R. Yates, D
10. *Harold R. Collier, R
11. *Roman C. Pucinski, D
12. Edward R. Finnegan, D
13. *Marguerite S. Church, R
14. *Elmer J. Hoffman, R
15. *Noah M. Mason, R
16. John B. Anderson, R
17. *Leslie C. Arends, R
18. *Robert H. Michel, R
19. *Robert B. Chiperfield, R
20. Paul Findley, R
21. *Peter F. Mack, Jr., D
22. *William L. Springer, R
23. *George E. Shipley, D
24. *Melvin Price, D
25. *Kenneth J. Gray, D

## INDIANA

**(11 Representatives)**

1. *Ray J. Madden, D
2. *Charles A. Halleck, R
3. *John Brademas, D
4. *E. Ross Adair, R
5. *Edward Roush, D
6. Richard L. Roudebush, R
7. *William G. Bray, R
8. *Winfield K. Denton, D
9. Earl Wilson, R
10. Ralph Harvey, R
11. Donald C. Bruce, R

## IOWA

**(8 Representatives)**

1. *Fred Schwengel, R
2. James E. Bromwell, R
3. *H. R. Gross, R
4. John Kyl, R
5. *Neal Smith, D
6. *Merwin Coad, D
7. *Ben F. Jensen, R
8. *Charles B. Hoeven, R

## KANSAS

**(6 Representatives)**

1. *William H. Avery, R
2. Robert F. Ellsworth, R
3. Walter L. McVey, R

4. Garner E. Shriver, R
5. *J. Floyd Breeding, D
6. Robert Dole, R

## KENTUCKY
### (8 Representatives)
1. *Frank A. Stubblefield, D
2. *William H. Natcher, D
3. *Frank W. Burke, D
4. *Frank Chelf, D
5. *Brent Spence, D
6. *John C. Watts, D
7. *Carl D. Perkins, D
8. *Eugene Siler, R

## LOUISIANA
### (8 Representatives)
1. *F. Edward Hébert, D
2. *Hale Boggs, D
3. *Edwin E. Willis, D
4. *Overton Brooks, D
5. *Otto E. Passman, D
6. *James H. Morrison, D
7. *T. A. Thompson, D
8. *Harold B. McSween, D

## MAINE
### (3 Representatives)
1. Peter A. Garland, R
2. Stanley R. Tupper, R
3. *Clifford G. McIntire, R

## MARYLAND
### (7 Representatives)
1. *Thomas F. Johnson, D
2. *Daniel B. Brewster, D
3. *Edward A. Garmatz, D
4. *George H. Fallon, D
5. *Richard E. Lankford, D
6. Charles McC. Mathias, Jr., R
7. *Samuel N. Friedel, D

## MASSACHUSETTS
### (14 Representatives)
1. *Silvio O. Conte, R
2. *Edward P. Boland, D
3. *Philip J. Philbin, D
4. *Harold D. Donohue, D
5. F. Bradford Morse, R
6. *William H. Bates, R
7. *Thomas J. Lane, D
8. *Torbert H. Macdonald, D
9. *Hastings Keith, R
10. *Laurence Curtis, R
11. *Thomas P. O'Neill, Jr., D
12. *John W. McCormack, D
13. *James A. Burke, D
14. *Joseph W. Martin, Jr., R

## MICHIGAN
### (18 Representatives)
1. *T. M. Machrowicz, D
2. *George Meader, R
3. *August E. Johansen, R
4. *Clare E. Hoffman, R
5. *Gerald R. Ford, Jr., R
6. *Charles E. Chamberlain, R
7. *James G. O'Hara, D
8. James Harvey, R
9. *Robert P. Griffin, R
10. *Elford A. Cederberg, R

11. *Victor A. Knox, R
12. *John B. Bennett, R
13. *Charles C. Diggs, Jr., D
14. *Louis C. Rabaut, D
15. *John D. Dingell, D
16. *John Lesinski, D
17. *Martha W. Griffiths, D
18. *William S. Broomfield, R

## MINNESOTA
### (9 Representatives)
1. *Albert H. Quie, R
2. *Ancher Nelsen, R
3. Clark MacGregor, R
4. *Joseph E. Karth, D
5. *Walter H. Judd, R
6. *Fred Marshall, D
7. *H. Carl Andersen, R
8. *John A. Blatnik, D
9. *Odin Langen, R

## MISSISSIPPI
### (6 Representatives)
1. *Thomas G. Abernethy, D
2. *Jamie L. Whitten, D
3. *Frank E. Smith, D
4. *John Bell Williams, D
5. *Arthur Winstead, D
6. *William M. Colmer, D

## MISSOURI
### (11 Representatives)
1. *Frank M. Karsten, D
2. *Thomas B. Curtis, R
3. *Mrs. Leonor K. Sullivan, D
4. *William J. Randall, D
5. *Richard Bolling, D
6. *W. R. Hull, Jr., D
7. *Durward G. Hall, R
8. Richard H. Ichord, D
9. *Clarence Cannon, D
10. *Paul C. Jones, D
11. *Morgan M. Moulder, D

## MONTANA
### (2 Representatives)
1. Arnold Olsen, D
2. James F. Battin, R

## NEBRASKA
### (4 Representatives)
1. *Phil Weaver, R
2. *Glenn Cunningham, R
3. Ralph F. Beermann, R
4. Dave Martin, R

## NEVADA
### (1 Representative)
At-L. *Walter S. Baring, D

## NEW HAMPSHIRE
### (2 Representatives)
1. *Chester E. Merrow, R
2. *Perkins Bass, R

## NEW JERSEY
### (14 Representatives)
1. *William T. Cahill, R
2. *Milton W. Glenn, R
3. *James C. Auchincloss, R

4. *Frank Thompson, Jr., D
5. *Peter Frelinghuysen, Jr., R
6. *Mrs. Florence P. Dwyer, R
7. *William B. Widnall, R
8. Charles S. Joelson, D
9. *Frank C. Osmers, Jr., R
10. *Peter W. Rodino, Jr., D
11. *Hugh J. Addonizio, D
12. *George M. Wallhauser, R
13. *Cornelius E. Gallagher, D
14. *Dominick V. Daniels, D

## NEW MEXICO
### (2 Representatives)
At-L. *Joseph M. Montoya, D
At-L. *Thomas G. Morris, D

## NEW YORK
### (43 Representatives)
1. Otis G. Pike, D
2. *Steven B. Derounian, R
3. *Frank J. Becker, R
4. *Seymour Halpern, R
5. Joseph P. Addabbo, D
6. *Lester Holtzman, D
7. *James J. Delaney, D
8. *Victor L. Anfuso, D
9. *Eugene J. Keogh, D
10. *Mrs. Edna F. Kelly, D
11. *Emanuel Celler, D
12. Hugh L. Carey, D
13. *Abraham J. Multer, D
14. *John J. Rooney, D
15. *John H. Ray, R
16. *Adam C. Powell, D
17. *John V. Lindsay, R
18. *Alfred E. Santangelo, D
19. *Leonard Farbstein, D
20. William Fitts Ryan, D
21. *Herbert Zelenko, D
22. *James C. Healey, D
23. *Jacob H. Gilbert, D
24. *Charles A. Buckley, D
25. *Paul A. Fino, R
26. *Edwin B. Dooley, R
27. *Robert R. Barry, R
28. *Mrs. Katharine St. George, R
29. *J. Ernest Wharton, R
30. *Leo W. O'Brien, D
31. Carleton J. King, R
32. *Samuel S. Stratton, D
33. *Clarence E. Kilburn, R
34. *Alexander Pirnie, R
35. *R. Walter Riehlman, R
36. *John Taber, R
37. *Howard W. Robison, R
38. *Mrs. Jessica McC. Weis, R
39. *Harold C. Ostertag, R
40. *William E. Miller, R
41. *Thaddeus J. Dulski, D
42. *John R. Pillion, R
43. *Charles E. Goodell, R

## NORTH CAROLINA
### (12 Representatives)
1. *Herbert C. Bonner, D
2. *L. H. Fountain, D
3. David N. Henderson, D
4. *Harold D. Cooley, D

5. *Ralph J. Scott, D
6. Horace R. Kornegay, D
7. *Alton Lennon, D
8. *A. Paul Kitchin, D
9. *Hugh Q. Alexander, D
10. *Charles Raper Jonas, R
11. *Basil L. Whitener, D
12. *Roy A. Taylor, D

### NORTH DAKOTA
(2 Representatives)
At-L. *Don L. Short, R
At-L. Hjalmar C. Nygaard, R

### OHIO
(23 Representatives)
1. *Gordon H. Scherer, R
2. Donald D. Clancy, R
3. *Paul F. Schenck, R
4. *William M. McCulloch, R
5. *Delbert L. Latta, R
6. William H. Harsha, Jr., R
7. *Clarence J. Brown, R
8. *Jackson E. Betts, R
9. *Thomas L. Ashley, D
10. *Walter H. Moeller, D
11. *Robert E. Cook, D
12. *Samuel L. Devine, R
13. Charles A. Mosher, R
14. *William H. Ayres, R
15. Tom V. Moorehead, R
16. *Frank T. Bow, R
17. John M. Ashbrook, R
18. *Wayne L. Hays, D
19. *Michael J. Kirwan, D
20. *Michael A. Feighan, D
21. *Charles A. Vanik, D
22. *Mrs. Frances P. Bolton, R
23. *William E. Minshall, R

### OKLAHOMA
(6 Representatives)
1. *Page Belcher, R
2. *Ed Edmondson, D
3. *Carl Albert, D
4. *Tom Steed, D
5. *John Jarman, D
6. Victor Wickersham, D

### OREGON
(4 Representatives)
1. *Walter Norblad, R
2. *Al Ullman, D
3. *Mrs. Edith Green, D
4. Edwin R. Durno, R

### PENNSYLVANIA
(30 Representatives)
1. *William A. Barrett, D
2. *Mrs. Kathryn E. Granahan, D
3. *James A. Byrne, D
4. *Robert N. C. Nix, D
5. *William J. Green, Jr., D
6. *Herman Toll, D
7. *William H. Milliken, Jr., R
8. *Willard S. Curtin, R
9. *Paul B. Dague, R
10. William W. Scranton, R
11. *Daniel J. Flood, D

12. *Ivor D. Fenton, R
13. Richard S. Schweiker, R
14. *George M. Rhodes, D
15. *Francis E. Walter, D
16. John C. Kunkel, R
17. *Herman T. Schneebeli, R
18. J. Irving Whalley, R
19. George A. Goodling, R
20. *James E. Van Zandt, R
21. *John H. Dent, D
22. *John P. Saylor, R
23. *Leon H. Gavin, R
24. *Carroll D. Kearns, R
25. *Frank M. Clark, D
26. *Thomas E. Morgan, D
27. *James G. Fulton, R
28. *William S. Moorhead, D
29. *Robert J. Corbett, R
30. *Elmer J. Holland, D

### RHODE ISLAND
(2 Representatives)
1. Fernand J. St. Germain, D
2. *John E. Fogarty, D

### SOUTH CAROLINA
(6 Representatives)
1. *L. Mendel Rivers, D
2. *John J. Riley, D
3. *W. J. Bryan Dorn, D
4. *Robert T. Ashmore, D
5. *Robert W. Hemphill, D
6. *John L. McMillan, D

### SOUTH DAKOTA
(2 Representatives)
1. Ben Reifel, R
2. *E. Y. Berry, R

### TENNESSEE
(9 Representatives)
1. Louise G. Reece, R
2. *Howard H. Baker, R
3. *James B. Frazier, Jr., D
4. *Joe L. Evins, D
5. *J. Carlton Loser, D
6. *Ross Bass, D
7. *Tom Murray, D
8. *Robert A. Everett, D
9. *Clifford Davis, D

### TEXAS
(22 Representatives)
1. *Wright Patman, D
2. *Jack Brooks, D
3. *Lindley Beckworth, D
4. *Sam Rayburn, D
5. *Bruce Alger, R
6. *Olin E. Teague, D
7. *John Dowdy, D
8. *Albert Thomas, D
9. *Clark W. Thompson, D
10. *Homer Thornberry, D
11. *W. R. Poage, D
12. *Jim Wright, D
13. *Frank Ikard, D
14. *John Young, D
15. *Joe M. Kilgore, D
16. *J. T. Rutherford, D

17. *Omar Burleson, D
18. *Walter Rogers, D
19. *George Mahon, D
20. *Paul J. Kilday, D
21. *O. C. Fisher, D
22. *Bob Casey, D

### UTAH
(2 Representatives)
1. M. Blaine Peterson, D
2. *David S. King, D

### VERMONT
(1 Representative)
At-L. Robert T. Stafford, R

### VIRGINIA
(10 Representatives)
1. *Thomas N. Downing, D
2. *Porter Hardy, Jr., D
3. *J. Vaughan Gary, D
4. *Watkins M. Abbitt, D
5. *William M. Tuck, D
6. *Richard H. Poff, R
7. *Burr P. Harrison, D
8. *Howard W. Smith, D
9. *W. Pat Jennings, D
10. *Joel T. Broyhill, R

### WASHINGTON
(7 Representatives)
1. *Thomas M. Pelly, R
2. *Jack Westland, R
3. Mrs. Julia Butler Hansen, D
4. *Mrs. Catherine May, R
5. *Walt Horan, R
6. *Thor C. Tollefson, R
7. *Don Magnuson, D

### WEST VIRGINIA
(6 Representatives)
1. *Arch A. Moore, Jr., R
2. *Harley O. Staggers, D
3. *Cleveland M. Bailey, D
4. *Ken Hechler, D
5. *Mrs. Elizabeth Kee, D
6. *John M. Slack, Jr., D

### WISCONSIN
(10 Representatives)
1. Henry C. Schadeberg, R
2. *Robert W. Kastenmeier, D
3. Vernon W. Thomson, R
4. *Clement J. Zablocki, D
5. *Henry S. Reuss, D
6. *William K. Van Pelt, R
7. *Melvin R. Laird, R
8. *John W. Byrnes, R
9. *Lester R. Johnson, D
10. *Alvin E. O'Konski, R

### WYOMING
(1 Representative)
At-L. William Henry Harrison, R

### PUERTO RICO
(1 Resident Commissioner)[1]
*Antonio Fernós-Isern, Pop. Dem.

[1] Does not have a vote.

# CONGRESSIONAL COMMITTEES

## Committees of the Senate

**Aeronautical and Space Sciences (15 members)**
*Chairman:* Robert S. Kerr (Okla.)
*Ranking Rep.:* Styles Bridges (N. H.)

**Agriculture and Forestry (17 members)**
*Chairman:* Allen J. Ellender (La.)
*Ranking Rep.:* George D. Aiken (Vt.)

**Appropriations (27 members)**
*Chairman:* Carl Hayden (Ariz.)
*Ranking Rep.:* Styles Bridges (N. H.)

**Armed Services (17 members)**
*Chairman:* Richard B. Russell (Ga.)
*Ranking Rep.:* Leverett Saltonstall (Mass.)

**Banking and Currency (15 members)**
*Chairman:* A. Willis Robertson (Va.)
*Ranking Rep.:* Homer E. Capehart (Ind.)

**District of Columbia (7 members)**
*Chairman:* Alan Bible (Nev.)
*Ranking Rep.:* J. Glenn Beall (Md.)

**Finance (17 members)**
*Chairman:* Harry Flood Byrd (Va.)
*Ranking Rep.:* John J. Williams (Del.)

**Foreign Relations (17 members)**
*Chairman:* J. W. Fulbright (Ark.)
*Ranking Rep.:* Alexander Wiley (Wis.)

**Government Operations (9 members)**
*Chairman:* John L. McClellan (Ark.)
*Ranking Rep.:* Karl E. Mundt (S. D.)

**Interior and Insular Affairs (17 members)**
*Chairman:* Clinton P. Anderson (N. M.)
*Ranking Rep.:* Henry C. Dworshak (Idaho)

**Interstate and Foreign Commerce (17 members)**
*Chairman:* Warren G. Magnuson (Wash.)
*Ranking Rep.:* Andrew F. Schoeppel (Kan.)

**Judiciary (15 members)**
*Chairman:* James O. Eastland (Miss.)
*Ranking Rep.:* Alexander Wiley (Wis.)

**Labor and Public Welfare (15 members)**
*Chairman:* Lister Hill (Ala.)
*Ranking Rep.:* Barry Goldwater (Ariz.)

**Post Office and Civil Service (9 members)**
*Chairman:* Olin D. Johnston (S. C.)
*Ranking Rep.:* Frank Carlson (Kan.)

**Public Works (17 members)**
*Chairman:* Dennis Chavez (N. M.)
*Ranking Rep.:* Francis Case (S. D.)

**Rules and Administration (9 members)**
*Chairman:* Mike Mansfield (Mont.)
*Ranking Rep.:* Carl T. Curtis (Neb.)

## Committees of the House

**Agriculture (36 members)**
*Chairman:* Harold D. Cooley (N. C.)
*Ranking Rep.:* Charles B. Hoeven (Iowa)

**Appropriations (50 members)**
*Chairman:* Clarence Cannon (Mo.)
*Ranking Rep.:* John Taber (N. Y.)

**Armed Services (38 members)**
*Chairman:* Carl Vinson (Ga.)
*Ranking Rep.:* Leslie C. Arends (Ill.)

**Banking and Currency (30 members)**
*Chairman:* Brent Spence (Ky.)
*Ranking Rep.:* Clarence E. Kilburn (N. Y.)

**District of Columbia (25 members)**
*Chairman:* John L. McMillan (S. C.)
*Ranking Rep.:* James C. Auchincloss (N. J.)

**Education and Labor (31 members)**
*Chairman:* Adam C. Powell (N. Y.)
*Ranking Rep.:* Carroll D. Kearns (Pa.)

**Foreign Affairs (33 members)**
*Chairman:* Thomas E. Morgan (Pa.)
*Ranking Rep.:* Robert B. Chiperfield (Ill.)

**Government Operations (30 members)**
*Chairman:* William L. Dawson (Ill.)
*Ranking Rep.:* Clare E. Hoffman (Mich.)

**House Administration (25 members)**
*Chairman:* Omar Burleson (Tex.)
*Ranking Rep.:* Paul F. Schenck (Ohio)

**Interior and Insular Affairs (32 members)**
*Chairman:* Wayne N. Aspinall (Colo.)
*Ranking Rep.:* John P. Saylor (Pa.)

**Interstate and Foreign Commerce (33 members)**
*Chairman:* Oren Harris (Ark.)
*Ranking Rep.:* John B. Bennett (Mich.)

**Judiciary (35 members)**
*Chairman:* Emanuel Celler (N. Y.)
*Ranking Rep.:* William M. McCulloch (Ohio)

**Merchant Marine and Fisheries (31 members)**
*Chairman:* Herbert C. Bonner (N. C.)
*Ranking Rep.:* Thor C. Tollefson (Wash.)

**Post Office and Civil Service (25 members)**
*Chairman:* Tom Murray (Tenn.)
*Ranking Rep.:* Robert J. Corbett (Pa.)

**Public Works (34 members)**
*Chairman:* Charles A. Buckley (N. Y.)
*Ranking Rep.:* James C. Auchincloss (N. J.)

**Rules (15 members)**
*Chairman:* Howard W. Smith (Va.)
*Ranking Rep.:* Clarence J. Brown (Ohio)

**Science and Astronautics (25 members)**
*Chairman:* Overton Brooks (La.)
*Ranking Rep.:* Joseph W. Martin, Jr. (Mass.)

**Un-American Activities (9 members)**
*Chairman:* Francis E. Walter (Pa.)
*Ranking Rep.:* Gordon H. Scherer (Ohio)

**Veterans' Affairs (25 members)**
*Chairman:* Olin E. Teague (Tex.)
*Ranking Rep.:* William H. Ayres (Ohio)

**Ways and Means (25 members)**
*Chairman:* Wilbur D. Mills (Ark.)
*Ranking Rep.:* Noah M. Mason (Ill.)

# The Governors and Senators of the Fifty States

The years shown in parentheses are those of birth. Unless otherwise indicated, the Governor or Senator was born in the state in which he was elected to office.

| State | Governor | Senior Senator | Junior Senator |
|---|---|---|---|
| Alabama | John Patterson, D (1921) | Lister Hill, D (1894) | John J. Sparkman, D (1899) |
| Alaska | William A. Egan, D (1914) | E. L. (Bob) Bartlett, D (1904)[1] | Ernest Gruening, D (1887)[2] |
| Arizona | Paul Fannin, R (1907)[8] | Carl Hayden, D (1877) | Barry Goldwater, R (1909) |
| Arkansas | Orval Faubus, D (1910) | John L. McClellan, D (1896) | J. W. Fulbright, D (1905)[4] |
| California | Edmund G. Brown, D (1905) | Thomas H. Kuchel, R (1910) | Clair Engle, D (1911) |
| Colorado | Stephen L. R. McNichols, D (1914) | Gordon Allott, R (1907) | John A. Carroll, D (1901) |
| Connecticut | John N. Dempsey, D (1915)[27] | Prescott Bush, R (1895)[5] | Thomas J. Dodd, D (1907) |
| Delaware | Elbert N. Carvel, D (1910)[2] | John J. Williams, R (1904) | J. Caleb Boggs, R (1909) |
| Florida | Farris Bryant, D (1914) | Spessard L. Holland, D (1892) | George A. Smathers, D (1913)[6] |
| Georgia | Ernest Vandiver, D (1918) | Richard B. Russell, D (1897) | Herman E. Talmadge, D (1913) |
| Hawaii | William F. Quinn, R (1919)[2] | Hiram L. Fong, R (1907) | Oren E. Long, D (1889)[7] |
| Idaho | Robert E. Smylie, R (1914)[8] | Henry C. Dworshak, R (1894)[9] | Frank Church, D (1924) |
| Illinois | Otto Kerner, D (1908) | Paul H. Douglas, D (1892)[10] | Everett M. Dirksen, R (1896) |
| Indiana | Matthew E. Welsh, D (1912)[24] | Homer E. Capehart, R (1897) | Vance Hartke, D (1919) |
| Iowa | Norman A. Erbe, R (1919) | Bourke B. Hickenlooper, R (1896) | Jack Miller, R (1916)[22] |
| Kansas | John Anderson, Jr., R (1917) | Andrew F. Schoeppel, R (1894) | Frank Carlson, R (1893) |
| Kentucky | Bert T. Combs, D (1911) | John S. Cooper, R (1901) | Thruston B. Morton, R (1907) |
| Louisiana | James H. Davis, D | Allen J. Ellender, D (1890) | Russell B. Long, D (1918) |
| Maine | John H. Reed, R (1921) | Margaret C. Smith, R (1897) | Edmund S. Muskie, D (1914) |
| Maryland | J. Millard Tawes, D (1894) | John M. Butler, R (1897) | J. Glenn Beall, R (1894) |
| Massachusetts | John A. Volpe, R (1908) | Leverett Saltonstall, R (1892) | Benjamin A. Smith II, D (1916) |
| Michigan | John B. Swainson, D (1925)[25] | Pat McNamara, D (1894)[10] | Philip A. Hart, D (1912)[11] |
| Minnesota | Elmer L. Andersen, R (1909)[22] | Hubert H. Humphrey, D (1911)[12] | Eugene J. McCarthy, D (1916) |
| Mississippi | Ross R. Barnett, D (1898) | James O. Eastland, D (1904) | John Stennis, D (1901) |
| Missouri | John M. Dalton, D (1900) | Stuart Symington, D (1901)[10] | Edward V. Long, D (1908) |
| Montana | Donald G. Nutter, R (1916) | Mike Mansfield, D (1903)[2] | Lee Metcalf, D (1911) |
| Nebraska | Frank B. Morrison, D (1905)[13] | Roman L. Hruska, R (1904) | Carl T. Curtis, R (1905) |
| Nevada | Grant Sawyer, D (1918)[14] | Alan Bible, D (1909) | Howard W. Cannon, D (1912)[15] |
| New Hampshire | Wesley Powell, R (1915) | Styles Bridges, R (1898)[16] | Norris Cotton, R (1900) |
| New Jersey | Robert B. Meyner, D (1908)[11] | Clifford P. Case, R (1904) | H. A. Williams, Jr., D (1919) |
| New Mexico | Edwin L. Mechem, R (1912) | Dennis Chavez, D (1888) | Clinton P. Anderson, D (1895)[12] |
| New York | Nelson A. Rockefeller, R (1908)[16] | Jacob K. Javits, R (1904) | Kenneth B. Keating, R (1900) |
| North Carolina | Terry Sanford, D (1917) | Sam J. Ervin, Jr., D (1896) | B. Everett Jordan, D (1896) |
| North Dakota | William L. Guy, D (1919) | Milton R. Young, R (1897) | Quentin N. Burdick, D (1908) |
| Ohio | Michael V. DiSalle, D (1908)[2] | Frank J. Lausche, D (1895) | Stephen M. Young, D (1890) |
| Oklahoma | J. Howard Edmonson, D (1925) | Robert S. Kerr, D (1896) | A. S. (Mike) Monroney, D (1902) |
| Oregon | Mark O. Hatfield, R (1922) | Wayne Morse, D (1900)[18] | Maurine B. Neuberger, D (1907) |
| Pennsylvania | David L. Lawrence, D (1889) | Joseph S. Clark, D (1901) | Hugh Scott, R (1900)[17] |
| Rhode Island | John A. Notte, Jr., D (1909) | John O. Pastore, D (1907) | Claiborne Pell, D (1918)[2] |
| South Carolina | Ernest F. Hollings, D (1922) | Olin D. Johnston, D (1896) | Strom Thurmond, D (1902) |
| South Dakota | Archie M. Gubbrud, R (1910) | Karl E. Mundt, R (1900) | Francis Case, R (1896)[8] |
| Tennessee | Buford Ellington, D (1907)[19] | Estes Kefauver, D (1903) | Albert Gore, D (1907) |
| Texas | Price Daniel, D (1910) | R. W. Yarborough, D (1903) | John G. Tower, R |
| Utah | George D. Clyde, R (1898) | Wallace F. Bennett, R (1898) | Frank E. Moss, D (1911) |
| Vermont | F. Ray Keyser, Jr., R (1927) | George D. Aiken, R (1892) | Winston L. Prouty, R (1906) |
| Virginia | J. Lindsay Almond, Jr., D (1898) | Harry Flood Byrd, D (1887)[20] | A. Willis Robertson, D (1887)[20] |
| Washington | Albert D. Rosellini, D (1910) | Warren G. Magnuson, D (1905)[9] | Henry M. Jackson, D (1912) |
| West Virginia | William W. Barron, D (1911) | Jennings Randolph, D (1902) | Robert C. Byrd, D (1918)[21] |
| Wisconsin | Gaylord A. Nelson, D (1916) | Alexander Wiley, R (1884) | William Proxmire, D (1915)[22] |
| Wyoming | Jack R. Gage (1899)[23] | Gale W. McGee, D (1915)[23] | J. J. Hickey, D (1911) |

[1] Born in Washington. [2] Born in New York. [3] Born in Kentucky. [4] Born in Missouri. [5] Born in Ohio. [6] Born in New Jersey. [7] Born in Kansas. [8] Born in Iowa. [9] Born in Minnesota. [10] Born in Massachusetts. [11] Born in Pennsylvania. [12] Born in South Dakota. [13] Born in Colorado. [14] Born in Idaho. [15] Born in Utah. [16] Born in Maine. [17] Born in Virginia. [18] Born in Wisconsin. [19] Born in Mississippi. [20] Born in West Virginia. [21] Born in North Carolina. [22] Born in Illinois. [23] Born in Nebraska. [24] Born in Michigan. [25] Born in Canada. [26] Born in Montana. [27] Born in Ireland.

# The National Park System of the United States

*Source:* National Park Service.

The National Park System of the United States, administered by the National Park Service, a bureau of the Department of the Interior, embraces a total of 183 areas, containing approximately 22,491,0 acres in Federal ownership. Started with the establishment of Yellowstone National Park in 1872, the system includes not only the most extraordinary and spectacular scenic exhibits in the United States but also a large number of sites distinguished for their historic or prehistoric importance or scientific interest. The number and extent of the various types of areas which comprise the system, as of January 1, 1961, are as follows:

| Type of area | Number | Federal land (acres) | Lands within exterior boundaries not federally owned (acres) | Total lands within exterior boundaries (acres) |
|---|---|---|---|---|
| National Parks.................... | 29 | 13,208,144.10 | 251,061.60 | 13,459,205.70 |
| National Historical Parks.............. | 8 | 31,838.15 | 6,112.38 | 37,950.53 |
| National Memorial Park.............. | 1 | 69,023.64 | 1,350.66 | 70,374.30 |
| National Battlefield Parks........... | 3 | 5,549.36 | 1,938.74 | 7,488.10 |
| National Monuments................. | 83 | 8,981,309.73 | 143,679.85 | 9,124,989.58 |
| National Military Parks............. | 12 | 30,447.52 | 2,714.44 | 33,161.96 |
| National Battlefield............... | 1 | 323.86 | 7.00 | 330.86 |
| National Battlefield Sites.............. | 5 | 188.63 | 600.00 | 788.63 |
| National Historic Sites................ | 12 | 1,678.61 | 374.12 | 2,052.73 |
| National Memorials.............. | 14 | 4,517.58 | 207.38 | 4,724.96 |
| National Cemeteries................. | 10 | 215.10 | 5.00 | 220.10 |
| National Parkways............... | 3 | 93,657.60 | 21,086.45 | 114,744.05 |
| National Seashore Recreational Area..... | 1 | 24,705.23 | 3,794.77 | 28,500.00 |
| National Capital Parks[1]............... | 1 | 39,130.51 | 1,444.00 | 40,574.51 |
| Total, National Park System........... | 183 | 22,490,729.62 | 434,376.39 | 22,925,106.01 |

[1] Includes Catoctin Mountain Park, Chesapeake and Ohio Canal, Prince William Forest Park, Baltimore-Washington Parkway, Suitland Parkway among the 783 units administered by National Capital Parks.

## National Parks

| Name, location and year established as National Park | Area in U. S. ownership, acres | Outstanding characteristics |
|---|---|---|
| Acadia (Maine), 1919................ | 31,287.19 | Rugged seashore on Mt. Desert Island and adjacent mainland |
| Big Bend (Texas), 1944............. | 700,220.70 | Mountains and desert bordering the Rio Grande |
| Bryce Canyon (Utah), 1928.......... | 36,010.38 | Area of grotesque eroded rocks brilliantly colored |
| Carlsbad Caverns (N. Mex.), 1930..... | 45,846.59 | One of the world's largest known caves; spectacular flight of bats |
| Crater Lake (Oregon), 1902.......... | 160,290.33 | Deep blue lake in crater of inactive volcano |
| Everglades (Florida), 1947........... | 1,301,349.00 | Subtropical area with abundant bird and animal life |
| Glacier (Montana), 1910.............. | 1,009,109.90 | Rocky Mountain scenery with many glaciers and lakes |
| Grand Canyon (Arizona), 1919........ | 673,203.35 | Mile deep gorge, 4 to 18 miles wide, 217 miles long (105 in park) |
| Grand Teton (Wyoming). 1929........ | 302,255.68 | Picturesque range of high mountain peaks |
| Great Smoky Mts. (N. C.-Tenn.), 1930.. | 509,147.52 | Highest mountain range east of Black Hills; luxuriant plant life |
| Hawaii (Hawaii), 1916.............. | 196,040.61 | Spectacular volcanic area; luxuriant vegetation at lower levels |
| Hot Springs (Arkansas), 1921....... | 988.97 | 47 mineral hot springs said to have therapeutic value |
| Isle Royale (Michigan), 1940.......... | 539,338.51 | Largest wilderness island in Lake Superior; great moose herd |
| Kings Canyon (California), 1940....... | 453,768.38 | Huge canyons; high mountains; giant sequoias |
| Lassen Volcanic (California), 1916..... | 105,110.26 | Exhibits of impressive volcanic phenomena |
| Mammoth Cave (Kentucky), 1936..... | 50,695.73 | Vast limestone labyrinth with underground river |
| Mesa Verde (Colorado), 1906....... | 51,017.87 | Best preserved prehistoric cliff dwellings in United States |
| Mount McKinley (Alaska), 1917....... | 1,939,354.04 | Highest mountain in North America; spectacular wildlife |
| Mount Rainier (Washington), 1899..... | 241,571.09 | Single-peak glacial system; dense forests, flowered meadows |
| Olympic (Washington), 1938.......... | 888,557.79 | Finest mountain wilderness of Pacific Northwest |
| Platt (Oklahoma), 1906............. | 911.97 | Cold mineral springs with distinctive properties |
| Rocky Mountain (Colorado), 1915..... | 256,468.73 | Section of the Rocky Mountains; 65 named peaks over 10,000 feet |
| Sequoia (California), 1890............ | 385,418.92 | Giant sequoias; magnificent High Sierra scenery, including Mt. Whitney |
| Shenandoah (Virginia), 1935.......... | 193,177.75 | Tree-covered mountains; scenic Skyline Drive |
| Virgin Islands (U. S. Virgin Is.), 1956.. | 5,179.58 | Beaches; lush hills; prehistoric Carib Indian relics |
| Wind Cave (South Dakota), 1903...... | 28,052.66 | Limestone caverns in Black Hills, buffalo herd |
| Yellowstone (Wyoming-Montana-Idaho), 1872.................. | 2,213,206.55 | World's greatest geyser area; spectacular falls and canyon; one of world's great wildlife sanctuaries |
| Yosemite (California), 1890........... | 758,092.71 | Mountains; inspiring gorges and waterfalls; giant sequoias |
| Zion (Utah), 1919.................. | 132,470.32 | Multicolored gorge in heart of southern Utah desert |

## National Historical Parks

| Name and location | Acreage in U. S. ownership |
| --- | --- |
| Appomattox Court House (Va.) | 937.34 |
| Chalmette (Lousiana) | 69.61 |
| Colonial (Virginia) | 7,260.35 |
| Cumberland Gap (Ky.-Tenn.-Va.) | 20,184.20 |
| Independence (Pennsylvania) | 15.46 |
| Minute Man (Massachusetts) | 8.08 |
| Morristown (New Jersey) | 957.96 |
| Saratoga (New York) | 2,405.15 |

## National Monuments

| Name and location | Acreage |
| --- | --- |
| Ackia Battleground (Miss.) | 49.15 |
| Andrew Johnson (Tennessee) | 16.33 |
| Arches (Utah) | 34,249.94 |
| Aztec Ruins (New Mexico) | 27.14 |
| Badlands (South Dakota) | 99,985.92 |
| Bandelier (New Mexico) | 27,048.89 |
| Big Hole Battlefield (Montana) | 200.00 |
| Black Canyon of the Gunnison (Colorado) | 13,033.98 |
| Booker T. Washington (Va.) | 199.73 |
| Cabrillo (California) | 80.50 |
| Canyon de Chelly (Arizona) | 83,840.00 |
| Capitol Reef (Utah) | 36,115.65 |
| Capulin Mountain (N. Mex.) | 680.42 |
| Casa Grande (Arizona) | 472.50 |
| Castillo de San Marcos (Fla.) | 19.12 |
| Castle Clinton (New York) | 1.00 |
| Cedar Breaks (Utah) | 6,172.20 |
| Chaco Canyon (New Mexico) | 20,989.35 |
| Channel Islands (California) | 18,166.68 |
| Chiricahua (Arizona) | 10,480.90 |
| Colorado (Colorado) | 17,606.76 |
| Craters of the Moon (Idaho) | 48,003.86 |
| Custer Battlefield (Montana) | 765.34 |
| Death Valley (Calif.-Nev.) | 1,879,088.28 |
| Devils Postpile (California) | 798.46 |
| Devils Tower (Wyoming) | 1,266.91 |
| Dinosaur (Utah-Colorado) | 184,913.60 |
| Edison Laboratory (New Jersey) | 1.51 |
| Effigy Mounds (Iowa) | 1,204.36 |
| El Morro (New Mexico) | 880.80 |
| Fort Frederica (Georgia) | 209.97 |
| Fort Jefferson (Florida) | 47,125.00 |
| Fort Matanzas (Florida) | 227.76 |
| Fort McHenry (Maryland) | 43.26 |
| Fort Pulaski (Georgia) | 5,364.12 |
| Fort Sumter (South Carolina) | 2.40 |
| Fort Union (New Mexico) | 720.60 |
| Fort Vancouver (Wash.) | 74.71 |
| George Washington Birthplace (Virginia) | 393.68 |
| George Washington Carver (Missouri) | 210.00 |
| Gila Cliff Dwellings (N. Mex.) | 160.00 |
| Glacier Bay (Alaska) | 2,274,248.44 |
| Gran Quivira (New Mexico) | 610.94 |
| Grand Canyon (Arizona) | 193,040.00 |
| Grand Portage (Minnesota) | 315.00 |
| Great Sand Dunes (Colorado) | 34,979.88 |
| Harpers Ferry (W. Va.-Md.) | 469.23 |
| Homestead (Nebraska) | 162.73 |
| Hovenweep (Utah-Colorado) | 505.43 |
| Jewel Cave (South Dakota) | 1,274.56 |

| Name and location | Acreage in U. S. ownership |
| --- | --- |
| Joshua Tree (California) | 504,719.70 |
| Katmai (Alaska) | 2,697,590.00 |
| Lava Beds (California) | 46,238.69 |
| Lehman Caves (Nevada) | 640.00 |
| Meriwether Lewis (Tennessee) | 300.00 |
| Montezuma Castle (Arizona) | 783.09 |
| Mound City Group (Ohio) | 67.50 |
| Muir Woods (California) | 485.18 |
| Natural Bridges (Utah) | 2,649.70 |
| Navajo (Arizona) | 360.00 |
| Ocmulgee (Georgia) | 683.48 |
| Oregon Caves (Oregon) | 480.00 |
| Organ Pipe Cactus (Arizona) | 328,691.01 |
| Perry's Victory (Ohio) | 14.25 |
| Petrified Forest (Arizona) | 92,751.57 |
| Pinnacles (California) | 13,617.77 |
| Pipe Spring (Arizona) | 40.00 |
| Pipestone (Minnesota) | 275.93 |
| Rainbow Bridge (Utah) | 160.00 |
| Saguaro (Arizona) | 60,987.60 |
| Scotts Bluff (Nebraska) | 2,198.78 |
| Sitka (Alaska) | 54.16 |
| Statue of Liberty (New York) | 10.38 |
| Sunset Crater (Arizona) | 3,040.00 |
| Timpanogos Cave (Utah) | 250.00 |
| Tonto (Arizona) | 1,120.00 |
| Tumacacori (Arizona) | 10.15 |
| Tuzigoot (Arizona) | 42.67 |
| Walnut Canyon (Arizona) | 1,641.62 |
| White Sands (New Mexico) | 140,247.04 |
| Whitman (Washington) | 45.84 |
| Wupatki (Arizona) | 34,607.03 |
| Yucca House (Colorado) | 9.60 |

## National Military Parks

| Name and location | Acreage |
| --- | --- |
| Chickamauga and Chattanooga (Georgia-Tennessee) | 8,189.64 |
| Fort Donelson (Tennessee) | 118.84 |
| Fredericksburg and Spotsylvania (Virginia) | 2,513.76 |
| Gettysburg (Pennsylvania) | 2,793.92 |
| Guilford Courthouse (N. C.) | 150.53 |
| Horseshoe Bend (Alabama) | 2,040.00 |
| Kings Mountain (S. C.) | 3,950.00 |
| Moores Creek (North Carolina) | 42.23 |
| Pea Ridge (Arkansas) | 4,211.40 |
| Petersburg (Virginia) | 1,505.55 |
| Shiloh (Tennessee) | 3,556.77 |
| Vicksburg (Mississippi) | 1,374.88 |

## National Memorial Park

| | |
| --- | --- |
| Theodore Roosevelt (N. Dak.) | 69,023.64 |

## National Battlefield

| | |
| --- | --- |
| Stones River (Tennessee) | 323.86 |

## National Battlefield Parks

| | |
| --- | --- |
| Kennesaw Mountain (Georgia) | 2,882.62 |
| Manassas (Virginia) | 1,970.13 |
| Richmond (Virginia) | 691.61 |

## National Battlefield Sites

| | |
| --- | --- |
| Antietam (Maryland) | 183.63 |
| Brices Cross Roads (Mississippi) | 1.00 |
| Cowpens (South Carolina) | 1.00 |
| Fort Necessity (Pennsylvania) | 2.00 |
| Tupelo (Mississippi) | 1.00 |

## National Historic Sites

| Name and location | Acreage in U. S. ownership |
|---|---|
| Abraham Lincoln Birthplace (Kentucky) | 116.50 |
| Adams (Massachusetts) | 4.77 |
| Edison Home (New Jersey) | 13.54 |
| Fort Laramie (Wyoming) | 192.41 |
| Fort Raleigh (North Carolina) | 18.50 |
| Hampton (Maryland) | 45.42 |
| Home of Franklin D. Roosevelt (New York) | 93.69 |
| Hopewell Village (Pa.) | 848.06 |
| Jefferson National Expansion Memorial (Missouri) | 85.46 |
| Salem Maritime (Massachusetts) | 8.61 |
| San Juan (Puerto Rico) | 40.00 |
| Vanderbilt Mansion (New York) | 211.65 |

## National Memorials

| Name and location | Acreage |
|---|---|
| Coronado (Arizona) | 2,745.33 |
| Custis-Lee Mansion (Virginia) | 3.47 |
| De Soto (Florida) | 24.18 |
| Federal Hall (N. Y.) | .45 |
| Fort Caroline (Florida) | 119.51 |
| Fort Clatsop (Oregon) | 69.62 |
| General Grant (New York) | .76 |
| House Where Lincoln Died (D. C.) | .05 |
| Lincoln Memorial (D. C.) | .61 |
| Lincoln Museum (D. C.) | .18 |
| Mount Rushmore (S. Dak.) | 1,227.82 |
| Thomas Jefferson (D. C.) | 1.20 |

| Name and location | Acreage in U. S. ownership |
|---|---|
| Washington Monument (D. C.) | .37 |
| Wright Brothers (N. C.) | 324.03 |

## National Cemeteries[1]

| Name and location | Acreage |
|---|---|
| Antietam (Maryland) | 11.36 |
| Battleground (D. C.) | 1.03 |
| Fort Donelson (Tennessee) | 15.34 |
| Fredericksburg (Virginia) | 12.00 |
| Gettysburg (Pennsylvania) | 15.55 |
| Poplar Grove (Virginia) | 8.72 |
| Shiloh (Tennessee) | 10.25 |
| Stones River (Tennessee) | 20.09 |
| Vicksburg (Mississippi) | 117.85 |
| Yorktown (Virginia) | 2.91 |

## National Seashore Recreational Area

| Name and location | Acreage |
|---|---|
| Cape Hatteras (North Carolina) | 24,705.23 |

## National Parkways

| Name and location | Acreage |
|---|---|
| Blue Ridge (N. C.-Va.) | 62,874.31 |
| George Washington Memorial (Va.-Md.) | 4,336.13 |
| Natchez Trace (Tenn.-Ala.-Miss.) | 26,447.16 |

## National Capital Parks

| Name and location | Acreage |
|---|---|
| National Capital Parks (D. C.-Va.-Md.-W. Va.) | 39,130.51 |

[1] For Arlington National Cemetery, see index. It is not included here because it is under the jurisdiction of the Department of the Army rather than the National Park Service.

# Museums of the United States

*Source:* Questionnaires to Museums.

### NEW YORK CITY

**American Academy of Arts and Letters:** 633 W. 155th St., New York 32. Open: wkdys. & Sun. during exhib. 2–5 (closed Mon.). Otherwise by appt. Free.

Painting, sculpture by members of Academy and Natl. Inst. of Arts & Letters (by appt.): Fall exhibition of paintings eligible for purchase on Hassam Fund. Winter exhibition on special theme. Spring exhibition by new members and recipients of grants and honors.

**American Museum of Natural History:** Central Park W. at 79th St., New York 24. Open: wkdys. 10–5, Sun. & hldys. 1–5. Free.

All branches of natural sciences with exhibits including astronomy at American Museum-Hayden Planetarium.

**Brooklyn Museum:** Eastern Pkwy., Brooklyn 38, N. Y. Open: Wed.–Sat. 10–5, Sun. & hldys. 1–5 (closed Xmas). Closed Mon. & Tues. except main floor. Free.

American painting, Colonial to modern. 19th-20th-century European painting. Modern sculpture. Egyptian and primitive art. Ancient art and art of Near and Far East. Period rooms. Gallery shop with handicrafts of many countries.

**Cloisters:** Ft. Tryon Pk., New York 40. Open: wkdys. 10–5 (closed Mon.), Sun., hldys. 1–5 (May–Sept., Sun., 1–6). Free.

Cloisters, chapel, chapter house reconstructed from parts of medieval structures. Frescoes, polychromed statues, stained glass, Gothic tapestries. Medieval branch of Metropolitan Museum of Art.

**Frick Collection:** 1 E. 70th St., New York 21. Open: wkdys. 10–5 (closed Mon. & mo. of Aug.), Sun. & hldys. 1–5. Free.

Paintings, prints, drawings of 14th to 19th centuries. Italian Renaissance and French sculpture and furniture. Chinese and French porcelain. Concerts, lectures.

**Guggenheim (Solomon R.) Museum, Guggenheim Foundation:** 5th Ave. at 88th St., New York 28. Open: Tues.–Sat. 10–6, Wed. 10–9 (closed Mon.), Sun. 12–6. Adm. 50¢.

Works of leading 20th century foreign and American painters and sculptors.

**Hispanic Society of America (Museum & Library):** Broadway between W. 155th & 156th Sts., New York 32. Museum open: wkdys. 10–4:30, Sun. 2–5 (closed Mon., July 4, Thnks. Day, Xmas, New Year's Day). Library open: wkdys. 1–4:30 (closed Sun., Mon., hldys., mo. of Aug.). Free.

Paintings, sculpture, decorative arts, manuscripts and incunabula, representative of Hispanic culture. Works on Hispanic art, history, and published literature of which much is devoted to objects in the collection.

**Jewish Museum:** 5th Ave. at 92nd St., New York 28. Open: Mon.-Thurs. 1–5 (closed Fri., Sat.), Sun. 11–6. Free.

Jewish ceremonial and historical objects. Works of art, past and contemporary. Junior gallery, child's map of Israel.

**Metropolitan Museum of Art:** 5th Ave. at 82nd St., New York 28. Open: wkdys. 10–5 (closed Mon.), Sun., hldys. 1–5. Free.

Comprehensive collection of European and American paintings, sculpture, decorative arts, prints. Egyptian, Greek, Roman, Near Eastern, Asiatic art. Musical instruments, arms and armor. European and American period rooms. Costumes and textiles. *See also* Cloisters.

**Museum of Modern Art:** 11 W. 53rd St., New York 19. Open: wkdys. 11–6, Sun. 1–7. Adm. 95c (children 25c).

Founded 1929 to aid study of modern art and its application to manufacturing and practical life. Constantly changing exhibitions of contemporary painting, sculpture, prints, photography, architecture, industrial design, films.

**Museum of the American Indian, Heye Foundation:** Broadway at 155th St., New York 32. Open; Tues.-Sun. 1–5 (closed Mon., hldys., mos. of July & Aug.). Free.

Archaeology and ethnology of Americas from Arctic Circle to Tierra del Fuego.

**Museum of the City of New York:** 5th Ave. at 104th St., New York 29. Open: wkdys. 10–5 (closed Mon.), Sun., hldys. 1–5, closed Xmas. Free.

History and life of New York City. Period costumes, furniture, miniature scenes, portraits, paintings, prints, manuscripts, theater and music collection, silver, dolls and doll houses, etc.

**National Academy of Design:** 1083 5th Ave. (at 90th St.) New York 28. Open: wkdys. & Sun. 1–5 (during exhibitions).

Special annual exhibitions by selected organizations Oct. thru May.

**New York Historical Society:** Central Park W. at 77th St., New York 24. Museum open: wkdys. & Sun. 1–5, (Sat. 10–5, closed Mon.). Library open: Mon.-Sat., 10–5. (Closed NY Day, July 4, Thnks. Day, Xmas, month of Aug.). Free.

New York city and state historical exhibits. Early American paintings and portraits. Period rooms. Audubon watercolors. John Rogers statuettes. Large American history library.

**Roosevelt (Theodore) Museum:** 28 E. 20th St., New York 3. Open: wkdys. 10–5 (closed Mon.), Sun. & hldys. 1–5 (closed NY Day, Good Fri., Easter, Thnks. Day, Xmas). Adm. 40¢.

Restored birthplace of Roosevelt. Mounted lion shot by him in Africa. Photographs, letters, trophies, personal items.

**Whitney Museum of American Art:** 22 W. 54th St., New York 19. Open: wkdys. & Sun. 1–5 (closed major holidays). Free.

Sculpture, paintings, watercolors, drawings by 20th-century American artists. Exhibitions of contemporary and historical American art.

## CHICAGO

**Art Institute of Chicago:** Michigan Ave. at Adams St., Chicago 3, Ill. Open: wkdys. 9–5, Thurs. until 9:30, Sun. 12–5. Free.

Paintings, sculpture, prints, drawings. Oriental arts; European, American decorative arts; primitive art. Thorne Miniature Rooms.

**Chicago Academy of Sciences, Museum of Natural History:** Lincoln Park—2001 N. Clark St., Chicago 14, Ill. Open: daily 10–5. Free.

Exhibits of animal and plant life, minerals and fossils of Chicago region. Astronomical exhibits. Junior Academy of Science. Lectures. Movies for teachers, students and interested adults.

**Chicago Historical Society:** N. Clark St. at North Ave., Chicago 14, Ill. Open: wkdys. 9:30–4:30, Sun. 12:30–5:30. Free (Sun., Mem. Day, July 4, Lab. Day 25¢ for adults).

Exhibits and period rooms from discovery of America to present. Special emphasis on history of Chicago. Washington and Lincoln exhibits.

**Chicago Natural History Museum (formerly Field Museum):** Roosevelt Rd. at Lake Shore Dr., Chicago 5, Ill. Open: wkdys. & Sun.—Nov.–Feb. 9–4; May–Aug. 9–6; Mar., Apr., Sept., Oct. 9–5 (closed Xmas and NY Day). Adm. 25¢. (free Thurs., Sat., Sun.).

Exhibits in anthropology, botany, geology, zoology. Prehistoric skeletons. Dioramas of Stone-Age Europe. Vast Egyptian collection. Model of moon.

**Museum of Science and Industry:** 57th St. at Lake Michigan, Chicago 37, Ill. Open: fall & winter—wkdys. 9:30–4, Sun. & hldys. 10–6; spring & summer—everyday 9:30–5:30. Free (small fee to certain exhibits).

"Do it yourself" museum where learning is fun. Operating coal mine, real submarine, giant heart, Paul Bunyan house. Original "Atoms for Peace" Exhibit. U. S. science exhibits from Brussels World Fair.

**Oriental Institute Museum of the University of Chicago:** 1155 E. 58th St., Chicago 37, Ill. Open: Tues. & Weds. 10–12, 1–5, Thurs.-Sun. 10–5 (closed Mon.). Free.

Ancient Near Eastern objects, including 40-ton human-headed winged bull from Khorsabad in Assyria, 16-ft. statue of Tutankhamen from Egypt, colossal bull's head from Persepolis, statuary, glyptic, gold and ivory ornaments.

**Vanderpoel (John H.) Memorial Art Gallery:** Longwood Dr. at 96th St., Chicago 43, Ill. Open: wkdys. & Sun. 9–5 (closed hldys.). Free.

Paintings, watercolors, etchings, sculpture contributed by the artists in tribute to Mr. Vanderpoel.

## WASHINGTON, D. C.

**Corcoran Gallery of Art:** 17th St. at New York Ave., N. W., Washington 6, D. C. Open: wkdys. 10–4:30 (closed Mon.; Sat. 9–4:30), Sun. & hldys. 2–5 (closed Xmas, NY Day & July 4). Free.

Specializes in American art, but has notable collection of 17th century Dutch and 19th century French paintings. Persian rugs, Italian majolica, Greek and Roman antiquities. Barye bronzes. American sculpture. Annual and special exhibitions of U. S. art.

**Freer Gallery of Art, Smithsonian Institution:** Jefferson Dr. at 12th St., S.W., Washington 25, D. C. Open: daily 9–4:30 (closed Xmas). Free.

Oriental paintings, sculpture, bronzes, pottery, metalwork, manuscripts. Largest extant Whistler collection.

**National Air Museum, Smithsonian Institution:** The Mall, Independence Ave. nr. 10th St., S.W., Washington 25, D. C. Open: daily 9–4:30 (closed Xmas). Free.

Full-sized aircraft exhibited, including Wright brothers' *Kitty Hawk Flyer*, Lindbergh's *Spirit of St. Louis*, Wiley Post's *Winnie Mae*, *Bell Supersonic X-1*. Rocketry and Space Age exhibits.

**National Collection of Fine Arts, Smithsonian Institution:** Constitution Ave. at 10th St., Washington 25, D. C. Open: daily 9–4:30 (closed Xmas). Free.

Art collections given by Harriet Lane Johnston, Ralph Cross Johnson, William T. Evans, John Gellatly and others. Room devoted to Albert Pinkham Ryder.

**National Gallery of Art, Smithsonian Institution:** Constitution Ave. at 6th St., Washington 25, D. C. Open: wkdys. 10–5, Sun. 2–10 (closed Xmas & N Y Day). Free.

Paintings, sculpture, drawings, prints, decorative arts given by Mellon, Kress, Widener, Rosenwald, Dale, the Garbisches and others. Index of American Design.

**Smithsonian Institution:** on the Mall, Washington 25, D. C. Open: daily 9–4:30 (closed Xmas). Free.

Maintains the following museums and art galleries: Freer Gallery of Art, National Air Museum, National Collection of Fine Arts, National Gallery of Art, U. S. National Museum. *See* those entries.

**United States National Museum, Smithsonian Institution:** on the Mall, Washington 25, D. C. Open: daily 9–4:30 (closed Xmas). Free.

Exhibits in anthropology, zoology, botany, geology, paleontology, engineering, industry, technology, crafts, numismatics, philately, history, etc.

## PHILADELPHIA

**Academy of Natural Sciences of Philadelphia:** 19th and the Parkway, Philadelphia 3, Pa. Open: wkdys. 10–5 (summer 10–4), Sun. 1–5. Adm. 50¢ (children 25¢).

Large habitat groups of animals of North America, Africa, Asia. Hall of Earth History, Audubon Bird Hall. Minerals, gems. Aquarium. Live animal demonstrations.

**Franklin Institute of the State of Pennsylvania for the Promotion of the Mechanic Arts:** 20th St. at Benj. Franklin Pkwy., Philadelphia 3, Pa. Open: wkdys. 10–5 (closed Mon.), Sun. 12–5. Adm. 75¢.

Activities grouped into 7 major categories: Benj. Franklin Memorial; monthly Journal; lectures; library; medal awards; museum of science and industry, including planetarium; research laboratories.

**Pennsylvania Academy of the Fine Arts:** Broad and Cherry Sts., Philadelphia 2. Open: wkdys. 10–5 (closed Mon., Good Fri., Mem. Day, July 4, Thnks. Day, Xmas, NY Day), Sun. & some hldys. 1–5. Free.

Permanent collections include American art. Special exhibitions, lectures, gallery talks, concerts.

**Philadelphia Museum of Art:** Parkway at 26th St., Philadelphia 31, Pa. Open: wkdys. & Sun. 9–5 (closed all legal hldys.). Free.

Paintings: old masters, contemporary French, American, Mexican. Prints, decorative arts, period rooms. Oriental arts. Operates Colonial Chain of Houses in Fairmount Park, Rodin Museum, Samuel S. Fleischer Art Memorial.

## MUSEUMS IN OTHER CITIES
*(Free unless otherwise noted)*

**Alabama Museum of Natural History:** University of Alabama, Tuscaloosa. Open: wkdys. & Sun. 8–5.

All phases of natural history with emphasis on geology.

**Atomic Energy, American Museum of:** Oak Ridge, Tenn. Open: wkdys. 9:30–5; Sun. 12:30–6:30. Free.

Demonstrations, exhibits, motion pictures, models, etc. relating to atomic energy. Traveling exhibits available free to qualified exhibitors in U. S.*

**Baseball Hall of Fame and Museum, Natl.:** Main St., Cooperstown, N. Y.

Relics, pictures, documents of baseball history. Bronze plaques of game's immortals. *See also* Hall of Fame in index.

**Berkshire Museum:** Pittsfield, Mass. Open: wkdys. 10–5 (closed Mon.), Sun. 2–5. Free.

Painting, sculpture, decorative arts, loan exhibitions—ancient to modern; galleries of birds, animals, biology. Peary arctic sledge. Original "One Hoss Shay." First Wm. Stanley transformer. Little Cinema theater. Shows first-run movies.

**(Boston) Museum of Fine Arts:** 465–479 Huntington Ave., Boston 15, Mass. Open: wkdys. 10–5 (Tues., Oct.–May, 10–10; closed Mon. & hldys.), Sun. 1:30–5:30.

European and American paintings. Early American silver, furniture, interiors. Print collection largest in U. S. Noted Asiatic, Egyptian, Classical collections.

---

* Send inquiries to Museum Division, Oak Ridge Institute of Nuclear Studies, P. O. Box 117, Oak Ridge, Tenn.

**Buffalo Fine Arts Academy—Albright Art Gallery:** 1285 Elmwood Ave., Buffalo 22, N. Y. Open: Sun. & Mon. 2–6, rest of wk. 10–5 (closed Thnks. Day, Xmas, NY Day). Presently closed for construction until Jan. 30, 1962.

Comprehensive collection of contemporary painting. English 18th- and French 19th-century works. Sculpture 3000 B.C. to present.

**Buffalo Museum of Science:** Humboldt Park, Buffalo, N. Y. Open: Mon.–Sat. 10–5, Sun. & hldys. 1:30–5:30.

Extensive natural history collections. African and South Sea exhibits. Chinese pottery. Babylonian seals. Living museum.

**California Academy of Sciences:** Golden Gate Park, San Francisco 18. Open: wkdys. & Sun. 10–5.

North American and African habitat groups. Astronomical exhibits, clocks, watches, lamps, minerals, plants. Steinhart Aquarium. Morrison Planetarium. Continuous research program.

**California Palace of the Legion of Honor:** Lincoln Park, San Francisco. Open: daily 10–5 (hldys. 1–5). Free.

European and American paintings. Rodin sculpture and drawings. Furniture, tapestries, bronzes, porcelain. Egyptian art. Print and lithograph collection.

**Carnegie Institute:** 4400 Forbes Ave., Pittsburgh 13, Pa. Open: wkdys. 10–5 (Tues. during winter mos. 10–10), Sun. 2–5.

Department of Fine Arts: European and American paintings, ancient sculpture. Museum: exhibits in history and natural history. Music Hall. Carnegie Library.

**Cincinnati Art Museum:** Eden Park, Cincinnati 6, Ohio. Open: wkdys. 10–5, Sun. & hldys. 2–5 (closed Thnks. Day & Xmas).

Paintings, prints, decorative arts, period rooms, Near & Far Eastern potteries and bronzes. Egyptian, Greco-Roman, Medieval, Oriental sculptures. Ancient musical instruments.

**Cleveland Museum of Art:** 11150 East Boulevard, Cleveland 6, Ohio. Open: Tues. & Thurs. 10–6, Wed. 10 A.M.–10 P.M., Fri. during lecture season 10–10 (closed Mon., July 4, Thnks. Day, Xmas), Sat. 9–5, Sun. 1–6.

Classical and modern art of all nations and ages. Paintings, sculpture, graphic arts, furniture, silver, prints, arms and armor, textiles, Byzantine, Medieval, Early American collections.

**Cleveland Museum of Natural History:** 10600 East Blvd., Cleveland 6, Ohio. Open: wkdys. 9–5 (closed Mon.), Sun. 1–5:30.

Natural history exhibits from formation of our solar system to present—animals, plant life, geology. Mueller Planetarium, Hall of Nature.

**Colonial Williamsburg:** Williamsburg, Va. Open: daily. Adm. $3 for block ticket; students and servicemen $1.50. Children under 7 free; 7–11, 50¢.

Restoration of 18th-century capital of Virginia colony: 500 reconstructed or restored buildings, 84 ac. of gardens; 18th-century restaurants, buildings and craft shops.

**Colorado Springs Fine Arts Center:** 30 W. Dale St., Colorado Springs, Colo. Open: wkdys. 9–5 (closed Mon. from Sept. thru May), Sun. 1:30–5.

Contemporary paintings. Collection of Spanish-American New Mexican Santos. Southwest Indian arts and crafts.

**Corning Glass Center:** Corning, N. Y. Open: wkdys. & Sun. 9:30–5 (closed Mon. ex. June, July, Aug.).

Museum has most comprehensive collection of glass in world; Hall of Science and Industry shows many uses of glass; factory has comfortable gallery where visitors may watch glass being made.

**Currier Gallery of Art:** 192 Orange St., Manchester, N. H. Open: wkdys. 10–5, Sun. 2–5.

European and American paintings, 15th–20th century. American decorative arts of 18th century, including fine New England furniture, silver and early glass. Temporary exhibitions. Concerts and lectures.

**Davenport Public Museum:** Brady St. at 7th, Davenport, Iowa. Open: Mon.–Sat. 9–5 (closed Sun.).

Science, history, applied art exhibits, including anthropology, ethnology, Oriental and Mediterranean culture.

**Denver Art Museum:** 5 separate branches. Administration offices: Schleier Gallery, 1343 Acoma St., Denver 4, Colo. Open wkdys. 9–5 (Mon. 1–5), Sun. 2–5.

Ancient Mediterranean, European, American paintings and decorative arts. Oriental, South Sea, African, Latin American, American Indian arts and crafts.

**Denver Museum of Natural History:** City Park, Denver 6. Open: wkdys. 9–4:30, Sun. & hldys. 12–5. Winter: wkdys. 10–4:30, Sun. & hldys. 12–4:30.

Natural history of North and South America, Australia and South Pacific. Ecological exhibits of mammals and birds. Minerals, fossil mammal and reptile skeletons, New World archaeology.

**Detroit Historical Museum:** 5401 Woodward, Detroit 2. Open: Tues.–Sun. 9–6 (closed Mon.), Sun. 1–10.

Industrial, social history, marine and military exhibits. Streets of Detroit 1840–50, 1870–80. Large model railroad.

**Detroit Institute of Arts:** 5200 Woodward Ave., Detroit, Mich. Open: Sept.–June—wkdys. 1–6, 7–10 (Sat. 9–6, closed Mon.), Sun. 9–6; July & Aug.—wkdys. & Sun. 9–6 (closed Mon.); closed all hldys.

Survey of history as expressed in arts. Paintings, sculpture, furniture, glass, gold work, ivory, graphic arts, textiles, armor. Murals by Diego Rivera. Movies.

**Farmers' Museum:** Lake Rd., Route 80,

Cooperstown, N. Y. Open: May 1–Nov. 1, 9–6 daily. Re-created Village Crossroads, Nov. 1–Apr. 30, 9–5 daily exc. Mon. & Sun. A.M. Adm. $1.25 May 1–Nov. 1 (children 25¢).

Early farm and handicraft tools. School house, country store, smithy, print shop, doctor's and lawyer's offices, pharmacy, tavern, farm unit. Cardiff Giant. Operated by N. Y. State Historical Assn.

**Fenimore House:** Lake Rd., Route 80, Cooperstown, N. Y. Open: May 1–June 30 —daily 9–6; July 4–Labor Day—daily 9–9; Sept. 1–Oct. 31—daily 9–6; Nov. 1–Apr. 30 —daily 9–5. Adm. 75¢ (children 25¢).

American portraits, genre paintings. Browere life masks of Founding Fathers. Hamilton-Burr Room. James Fenimore Cooper memorabilia. Folk art. Library. Operated by N. Y. State Historical Assn.

**Florida State Museum:** Gainesville, Fla. Open: wkdys. 9:30–5, Sun. & hldys. 1–5.

Archaeology, ethnology, ornithology and other phases of natural history. Also history and industry.

**Gardner (Isabella Stewart) Museum:** 280 The Fenway, Boston 15, Mass. Open: Tues., Thurs., Sat. 10–4, Sun. 2–5, first Thurs. of each mo., 10 A.M.–10 P.M. (closed other days, natl. hldys., and during Aug.). Guided tours on closed days, including Mon. through Fri. in Aug., 11 A.M. and 2 P.M.

Renaissance art in building of Venetian palace style. Painting, sculpture, tapestries, furniture.

**Heard Museum:** 22 E. Monte Vista Rd., Phoenix, Ariz. Open (Oct. 1–June 1): wkdys. 10–5 (closed Mon.), Sun. 1–5.

Prehistoric and historic pottery, blankets, beadwork, carvings, weapons, etc., from various parts of world.

**Herron (John) Art Museum:** 110 E. 16th St., Indianapolis, Ind. Open: wkdys. 9–5 (closed Mon. & hldys.), Sun. 1–6.

European paintings from Renaissance to present. American paintings of 19th and 20th centuries. Egyptian, Greek, Asiatic sculpture and ceramics, Chinese bronzes, ceramics, jades.

**Huntington (Henry E.) Library and Art Gallery:** San Marino 9, Calif. Open: wkdys. & Sun. 1–4:30 (closed Mon. and during Oct.).

18th-century British paintings, including Gainsborough's "Blue Boy" & Lawrence's "Pinkie." English & American library exhibits. Gutenberg Bible. Franklin's autobiography in his handwriting. Botanical garden. Research facilities.

**Illinois State Museum:** Springfield, Ill. Open: wkdys. 8:30–5, Sun. 2–5.

Natural science and art. Anthropological, archaeological, botanical, geological, zoological collections. Traveling Museumobile & loan services for schools.

**International Folk Art, Museum of (Unit** of the Museum of N. Mex.): Off Old Pecos Rd., Santa Fe, N. Mex. Open: Mon.–Sat. 9–12, 1–5, Sun. 2–4 (1–5 summer).

Collection of folk art from 50 countries. **The Layton Collection:** Memorial Center, Milwaukee, Wis. Open: wkdys. 10–5, Sun. 1–5.

Exhibitions of selections from permanent collections.

**Los Angeles County Museum:** Exposition Park, Los Angeles 7, Calif. Open: Tues.–Sun. 10–5 (closed Mon., Thnks. Day, Xmas).

American, European, Eastern art. American Indian exhibits. Habitat groups of African and North American animals. California History Hall. La Brea fossils.

**Mint Museum of Art:** 501 Hempstead Pl., Charlotte, N. C. Open: wkdys. 10–5 (closed Mon.), Sun. 3–5.

American and European paintings and prints. Theater and art studios.

**Mound State Monument Archaeological Museum:** Moundville, Ala. Open: wkdys & Sun. 8–5 (closed Xmas). Adm. 50¢ adults, 25¢ children.

Uncovered Indian burials, etc., of Moundville Indians. Operated by Alabama Museum of Natural History.

**Mystic Seaport (Marine Historical Association, Inc.):** Mystic, Conn. Open: wkdys. & Sun. 9–5 (closed Thnks. Day, Xmas.). Adm. $2.00 (children 50¢).

Reconstructed seaport of Age of Sail. Typical waterfront street. *Charles W. Morgan,* last of wooden whaleships. Planetarium.

**Navajo Ceremonial Art, Museum of:** Camino Lejo, near old Pecos Rd., Santa Fe, N. Mex. Open: wkdys. 9–12, 1–4:30 (closed Mon.), Sun. 2–5. Adm. 50¢ adults; 25¢ children 6–12; Indians, free.

Sand paintings, ceremonial objects, baskets, blankets, silver. Music records of chants. Comparative material from Asia and elsewhere. Library.

**Nelson (William Rockhill) Gallery of Art and Atkins Museum of Fine Arts:** 4525 Oak, Kansas City 11, Mo. Open: Tues.–Sat. 10–5, Sun. 2–6 (closed Mon., NY Day, July 4, Thnks. Day, Xmas). Adm. 25¢ (children 10¢) (free Sat. & Sun.).

European paintings from 13th century to present. Paintings and sculpture from Kress Collection. Extensive Chinese collection. Egyptian, Greek, Roman collections. English pottery. Concerts, movies.

**New York State Historical Association:** Lake Rd., Route 80, Cooperstown, N. Y.

Administers Farmers' Museum and Fenimore House. *See* those entries.

**Newark Museum:** 43–49 Washington St., Newark 1, N. J. Open: Oct.–June—wkdys. 12–5:30 (Wed. & Thur. 12–5:30, 7–9:30), Sun. & hldys. 2–6; July–Sept.—wkdys. 12–5, Sun. & hldys. 2–6.

Collections: American painting, sculpture; Tibetan, Chinese, Japanese arts; decorative arts, ancient glass & ceramics; natural science, ethnology, mechanical models. Planetarium. Junior museum.

**Ringling (John & Mable) museums:** Sarasota, Fla. Museum of Art, Asolo Theater, John Ringling Residence, Museum of the Circus open wkdys. 9–4:30, Sun. 12:30–4:30. Closed Xmas and Thnks. Day. Adm.: Art Museum, $1; Residence, $1; Circus Museum, 50¢; general admission, $2.

Collection of old masters, especially Rubens. Only 18th-century Italian theater in America. Elaborate furnishings in Residence. Illustrative and historical material in Circus Museum.

**Rosicrucian Egyptian, Oriental Museum and Art Gallery:** San Jose, Calif. Open: wkdys. 9–12 & 1–5 (Sat. 1–5), Sun. 12–5.

Egyptian and Oriental antiquities. Mummies, statuary, jewelry, utensils, clothing. Reproductions of Egyptian rock tomb and temple. Art gallery.

**(St. Louis) City Art Museum:** Forest Park, St. Louis 5, Mo. Open: wkdys. & Sun. 10–5 (Tues. 2:30–9:30, closed Mon.).

Collection covers all fields of fine art: painting, sculpture, graphic art, decorative art, period rooms. Public restaurant.

**San Diego, Fine Arts Gallery of:** Plaza de Panama, Balboa Park, San Diego, Calif. Open: wkdys. 10–5, Sun. 1–5:30 (closed Mon. & mo. of Sept.).

European, American paintings, 14th century to present, with emphasis on Spanish, Italian, Flemish and Dutch art. Asiatic arts and prints.

**San Diego Museum of Man:** California Quadrangle, Balboa Park, San Diego, Calif. Open: wkdys. 10–4:45, Sun. 12–4:45.

Exhibits on Egypt; primitive weapons; Choco, North American, San Diego County Indians; Mayan archaeology; Mexican ethnology.

**San Diego Society of Natural History—Natural History Museum:** San Diego, Calif. Open: wkdys. & Sun. 10–4:30 (closed Xmas, NY Day).

Mammals, birds, fossils, shells, plants, insects, minerals. Emphasis on Southwestern U. S., Sonora and Lower California.

**San Francisco Museum of Art:** War Memorial Bldg., San Francisco, Calif. Open: Tues.–Fri. 12–10, Sat., Sun., Mon. 1–6.

Contemporary European, American paintings, sculpture, drawings, prints, architecture, photographs, decorative arts, including work by San Francisco artists. 40–50 exhibitions annually.

**Southwest Museum, Inc.:** Marmion Way at Museum Dr., Highland Pk., Los Angeles 65, Calif. Open: wkdys. & Sun. 1–5 (closed Mon., & certain hldys.).

American Indian exhibits, ancient and modern. Library. Casa de Adobe, reproduction of adobe hacienda, located at 4605 N. Figueroa St.; open Wed., Sat. & Sun. 2–5 P.M.

**Toledo Museum of Art:** Monroe at Scottwood, Toledo 1, Ohio. Open: wkdys. 9–5 (Mon. 1–5), Sun. hldys. 1–5 (closed Xmas, NY Day).

Dutch, French, English, American paintings. Old Masters. Prints, manuscripts, sculpture. Ancient, modern glass. Oriental, Egyptian art. Library, concerts. Founded by Edward Drummond Libbey.

**Virginia Museum of Fine Arts:** Boulevard at Grove Ave., Richmond 20. Open: wkdys. 2–6, 8–10 (closed Mon.), Sun. 2–6. Free Sat., Sun. (other days 30¢).

European, American, ancient Oriental art; French and American paintings. European tapestries; imperial Russian jewels. Theater with annual season of 6 plays.

**Wadsworth Atheneum:** 25 Atheneum Sq., N., Hartford 3, Conn. Open: wkdys. 10–5 (Sat. 9–5, closed Mon., Gd. Fri., July 4, Labor Day, Thnks. Day, Xmas, NY Day), Sun. 1:30–5:30.

European and American paintings and drawings from 1400 to present. Bronzes, porcelain, silver. American period rooms and furniture. Library, concerts, movies.

**Walters Art Gallery:** Charles and Centre Sts., Baltimore 1, Md. Open: Mon. 1:30–5, Tues.–Sat. 11–5 (July–Aug. wkdys. 11–4), Sun. & hldys. 2–5 (closed NY Day, July 4, Thnks. Day, Xmas Eve, Xmas).

Art from ancient empires to 19th-century Europe. Important collections of decorative arts and medieval illuminated books.

**Worcester Art Museum:** 55 Salisbury St., Worcester 8, Mass. Open: wkdys. 10–5 (Tues. in Nov.–Apr. 10–10), Sun. 2–5, hldys. 2–5 (closed July 4, Thnks. Day, Xmas).

Art from Egyptian to modern times, including Far East. Emphasis on painting and sculpture. Classes, lectures, concerts, films. Professional art school.

## Portraits and Designs of U. S. Paper Currency

| Currency | Portrait | Design on back | Currency | Portrait | Design on back |
|---|---|---|---|---|---|
| $1 | Washington | ONE between obverse and reverse of Great Seal of U. S. | $100 | Franklin | Independence Hall. |
| $2 | Jefferson | Monticello. | $500 | McKinley | Ornate FIVE HUNDRED across. |
| $5 | Lincoln | Lincoln Memorial. | $1,000 | Cleveland | Ornate ONE THOUSAND across. |
| $10 | Hamilton | U. S. Treasury Building. | $5,000 | Madison | Ornate FIVE THOUSAND across. |
| $20 | Jackson | White House. | $10,000 | Chase | Ornate TEN THOUSAND across. |
| $50 | Grant | U. S. Capitol. | $100,000* | Wilson | 100,000 superimposed over dollar sign. |

* For use only in transactions between Federal Reserve System and Treasury Department

# AMERICAN ECONOMY

ALTHOUGH we account for only 6.2% of the world's population, we own almost 50% of its wealth. We make, grow, build, sell, buy, and use more goods and services than any other country in the world. Of our population of over 179 million persons, about 65 million are employed, and over 46 million are enrolled in our schools and colleges (1960). Each year we spend more than $300 billion on personal goods and services, of which $88 billion go for food, tobacco, and alcohol alone. According to the American Automobile Association we spend $25 billion on vacations every year. Our personal savings amount to over $23 billion annually, in addition to which 4 out of every 5 families are covered by life insurance. Of our 50 million dwelling units, 55% are occupied by their owners. The millions of acres of fertile farmland produce more food than we can eat. Our productive capacity is the largest in the world: we own 29% of the world's railroad mileage, 68% of its automobiles, 51% of its trucks, 52% of its radios, 44% of its electric power output, 37% of its steel. Our natural resources are tremendous: each year we produce 41% of the world's output of petroleum and about 29% of its coal. Our merchant fleets have outstripped Britain's, and we have the greatest volume of foreign trade.

## Gross National Product or Expenditure
### (in millions of dollars)
*Source:* U. S. Department of Commerce.

| Item | 1929 | 1933 | 1938 | 1945 | 1948 | 1951 | 1960 | 1961* |
|---|---|---|---|---|---|---|---|---|
| Gross national product.............. | 104,436 | 55,964 | 85,227 | 213,558 | 259,426 | 328,975 | 503,200 | 500,800 |
| GNP in constant (1954) dollars....... | 181,944 | 126,606 | 174,965 | 314,044 | 297,205 | 341,965 | 439,200* | 433,400 |
| Personal consumption expenditures... | 78,952 | 46,392 | 64,641 | 121,699 | 178,313 | 209,805 | 327,800 | 330,700 |
| Durable goods.................... | 9,212 | 3,469 | 5,686 | 8,105 | 22,723 | 29,471 | 43,600 | 39,000 |
| Nondurable goods.............. | 37,677 | 22,251 | 33,985 | 73,222 | 98,737 | 110,135 | 152,400 | 153,700 |
| Services...................... | 32,063 | 20,672 | 24,970 | 40,372 | 56,853 | 70,199 | 131,700 | 137,500 |
| Gross private domestic investment.... | 16,231 | 1,391 | 6,661 | 10,430 | 43,087 | 56,334 | 72,800 | 59,800 |
| New construction.............. | 8,707 | 1,431 | 3,960 | 3,833 | 19,454 | 24,811 | 40,400 | 39,600 |
| Producers' durable equipment...... | 5,850 | 1,589 | 3,644 | 7,654 | 18,925 | 21,290 | 28,800 | 24,200 |
| Change in business inventories..... | 1,674 | −1,629 | −943 | −1,057 | 4,708 | 10,233 | 3,600 | −4,000 |
| Net foreign investment............. | 771 | 150 | 1,109 | −1,438 | 1,929 | 229 | 3,000 | 5,300 |
| Government purchases............. | 8,482 | 8,031 | 12,816 | 82,867 | 36,097 | 62,607 | 99,700 | 105,000 |
| Federal....................... | 1,311 | 2,018 | 5,280 | 75,923 | 20,867 | 40,915 | 52,400 | 54,700† |
| National security.............. | } 1,344 | 2,022 | 5,286 |  | 15,832 | 37,180 | 45,100 | 47,200 |
| Other........................ |  |  |  | ..... | 5,570 | 4,154 | 7,900 | 8,100 |
| Less: Government sales........ | 33 | 4 | 6 | 2,158 | 535 | 419 | 600 | 600 |
| State and local................... | 7,171 | 6,013 | 7,536 | 8,071 | 15,230 | 21,692 | 47,000 | 50,300 |

\* First quarter.  † Less Government sales.

## National Income by Distributive Shares
### (in millions of dollars)
*Source:* U. S. Department of Commerce.

| Type of share | 1929 | 1933 | 1939 | 1945 | 1948 | 1951 | 1953 | 1960 | 1960 % of total |
|---|---|---|---|---|---|---|---|---|---|
| National income...................... | 87,814 | 40,159 | 72,753 | 181,248 | 223,487 | 279,313 | 305,573 | 417,500 | 100.0 |
| Compensation of employees............ | 51,085 | 29,539 | 48,108 | 123,181 | 140,969 | 180,327 | 208,812 | 294,400 | 70.5 |
| Wages and salaries.................. | 50,423 | 28,997 | 45,941 | 117,577 | 135,214 | 170,788 | 198,030 | 272,475 | 65.3 |
| Supplements to wages and salaries... | 662 | 542 | 2,167 | 5,604 | 5,755 | 9,539 | 10,782 | 21,925 | 5.2 |
| Income of unincorporated enterprises and inventory valuation adjustment | 14,759 | 5,599 | 11,610 | 30,835 | 40,194 | 42,329 | 40,723 | 47,800 | 11.4 |
| Business and professional........... | 8,791 | 3,166 | 7,293 | 19,011 | 22,405 | 25,995 | 27,445 | 35,850 | 8.6 |
| Farm............................. | 5,968 | 2,433 | 4,317 | 11,824 | 17,789 | 16,334 | 13,278 | 11,925 | 2.8 |
| Rental income of persons.............. | 5,425 | 1,971 | 2,742 | 5,634 | 7,297 | 9,431 | 10,528 | 12,500 | 3.0 |
| Corporate profits and inventory valuation adjustment................. | 10,100 | −1,992 | 5,689 | 18,413 | 30,848 | 40,954 | 37,314 | 44,125 | 10.6 |
| Net interest....................... | 6,445 | 5,042 | 4,604 | 3,185 | 4,179 | 6,272 | 8,196 | 18,700 | 4.5 |

## How Consumers Spend Their Dollar
*Source:* U. S. Department of Commerce.

| Group | 1929 | 1932 | 1939 | 1945 | 1947 | 1949 | 1958 | 1959 | 1960 | 1960 % of total |
|---|---|---|---|---|---|---|---|---|---|---|
| | | | | (in millions of dollars) | | | | | | |
| Food and tobacco.............. | 21,374 | 12,719 | 21,072 | 45,924 | 58,274 | 58,384 | 82,999 | 85,027 | 87,548 | 26.6 |
| Clothing, accessories, and jewelry...... | 11,018 | 5,973 | 8,299 | 20,247 | 22,952 | 23,451 | 31,046 | 33,053 | 33,904 | 10.3 |
| Personal care...................... | 1,116 | 817 | 1,004 | 2,077 | 2,253 | 2,324 | 4,425 | 4,877 | 5,248 | 1.6 |
| Housing......................... | 11,421 | 8,964 | 8,940 | 12,205 | 15,567 | 19,295 | 37,656 | 39,924 | 42,209 | 12.8 |
| Household operation................ | 10,509 | 6,675 | 9,461 | 14,865 | 23,949 | 25,651 | 41,278 | 44,060 | 45,862 | 14.0 |
| Medical care and death expenses...... | 3,620 | 2,575 | 3,386 | 5,902 | 7,685 | 9,003 | 18,082 | 19,697 | 21,326 | 6.5 |
| Personal business.................. | 5,221 | 3,111 | 3,725 | 4,787 | 5,707 | 7,015 | 17,046 | 18,872 | 20,602 | 6.3 |
| Transportation..................... | 7,496 | 3,924 | 6,250 | 6,694 | 15,390 | 20,864 | 33,565 | 38,998 | 40,715 | 12.4 |
| Recreation........................ | 4,327 | 2,439 | 3,446 | 6,314 | 9,352 | 10,122 | 16,842 | 18,356 | 19,408 | 5.9 |
| Private education and research........ | 664 | 571 | 628 | 871 | 1,411 | 1,683 | 3,641 | 4,053 | 4,467 | 1.3 |
| Religious and welfare activities....... | 1,196 | 973 | 938 | 1,572 | 2,032 | 2,235 | 3,997 | 4,281 | 4,687 | 1.4 |
| Foreign travel and remittances—net.... | 799 | 467 | 317 | 1,621 | 837 | 1,131 | 2,621 | 2,798 | 2,950 | .9 |
| Total personal consumption expenditures.................. | 78,761 | 49,208 | 67,466 | 123,079 | 165,409 | 181,158 | 293,198 | 313,996 | 328,926 | 100.0 |

## Consumers' Price Index (1947–49 = 100)
*Source:* U. S. Bureau of Labor Statistics.

| Items | 1947 | 1948 | 1951 | 1953 | 1959 | 1960 | 1961* |
|---|---|---|---|---|---|---|---|
| All items...................... | 95.5 | 102.8 | 111.0 | 114.4 | 124.6 | 126.5 | 127.5 |
| Total food.................... | 95.9 | 104.1 | 112.6 | 112.8 | 118.3 | 119.7 | 121.2 |
| Apparel...................... | 97.1 | 103.5 | 106.9 | 104.8 | 107.9 | 109.4 | 109.8 |
| Housing total................. | 95.0 | 101.7 | 112.4 | 117.7 | 129.2 | 131.5 | 132.5 |
| Rent...................... | 94.4 | 100.7 | 113.1 | 124.1 | 139.7 | 141.8 | 143.1 |
| Gas and electricity........... | 97.6 | 100.0 | 103.1 | 106.6 | 119.9 | 124.8 | 125.9 |
| Solid fuels and fuel oil....... | 88.8 | 104.4 | 116.4 | 123.9 | 136.6 | 135.6 | 141.3 |
| Housefurnishings............. | 97.2 | 103.2 | 111.2 | 107.9 | 103.9 | 104.2 | 103.9 |
| Household operation.......... | 97.2 | 102.6 | 109.0 | 115.3 | 134.3 | 137.4 | 138.5 |
| Transportation................ | 90.6 | 100.9 | 118.4 | 129.7 | 146.3 | 146.2 | 145.7 |
| Medical care................. | 94.9 | 100.9 | 111.1 | 121.3 | 150.8 | 156.2 | 159.6 |
| Personal care................ | 97.6 | 101.3 | 110.5 | 112.8 | 131.2 | 133.3 | 133.6 |
| Reading and recreation......... | 95.5 | 100.4 | 106.5 | 108.0 | 118.6 | 121.5 | 123.4 |
| Other goods and services........ | 96.1 | 100.5 | 109.7 | 118.2 | 129.7 | 132.2 | 132.6 |

\* March.

## U. S. Consumption of Principal Foods*
(in pounds per capita)
*Source:* U. S. Department of Agriculture.

| Foods | 1935–39 avg. | 1947–49 avg. | 1961³ |
|---|---|---|---|
| Red meats.................. | 127.0 | 148.5 | 160.0 |
| Poultry.................... | 15.6 | 22.0 | 36.8 |
| Eggs¹..................... | 300.0 | 385.0 | 328.0 |
| Fluid milk and cream...... | 330.0 | 359.0 | 335.0 |
| Cheese.................... | 5.6 | 7.0 | 8.6 |
| Butter.................... | 17.0 | 10.6 | 7.8 |
| Margarine................. | 2.9 | 5.6 | 9.6 |
| Fats and oils².............. | 29.3 | 29.3 | 28.5 |
| Fresh fruits............... | 139.0 | 132.2 | n.a. |
| Processed fruits⁴........... | 25.5 | 41.9 | n.a. |
| Fresh vegetables.......... | 140.2 | 147.8 | n.a. |
| Processed vegetables⁴...... | 30.5 | 42.1 | n.a. |
| Potatoes, sweetpotatoes.... | 151.6 | 126.6 | n.a. |
| Sugar..................... | 97.4 | 95.1 | 98.0 |
| Corn products............. | 37.8 | 33.1 | 27.8 |
| Wheat flour............... | 160.0 | 137.0 | 116.0 |
| Coffee.................... | 14.0 | 18.2 | 16.1 |
| Cocoa.................... | 4.4 | 4.4 | 4.4 |

¹ Number, not pounds. ² Excludes butter and margarine. ³ Preliminary estimates. ⁴ Pack year. ⁵ Civilian consumption only.

## Consumer Credit
(in millions of dollars)
*Source:* Federal Reserve Board.

| End of year | Total | Installment credit | Non-installment credit* | Charge accounts |
|---|---|---|---|---|
| 1929...... | 6,444 | 3,151 | 1,691 | 1,602 |
| 1932...... | 3,567 | 1,521 | 1,026 | 1,020 |
| 1935...... | 4,911 | 2,694 | 1,034 | 1,183 |
| 1939...... | 7,222 | 4,503 | 1,305 | 1,414 |
| 1940...... | 8,338 | 5,514 | 1,353 | 1,471 |
| 1943...... | 4,901 | 2,136 | 1,325 | 1,440 |
| 1946...... | 8,384 | 4,172 | 2,136 | 2,076 |
| 1949...... | 17,305 | 11,590 | 2,920 | 2,795 |
| 1950...... | 21,395 | 14,703 | 3,401 | 3,291 |
| 1953...... | 31,393 | 23,005 | 4,114 | 4,274 |
| 1955...... | 38,882 | 28,958 | 5,129 | 4,795 |
| 1956...... | 42,511 | 31,897 | 5,619 | 4,995 |
| 1958...... | 45,544 | 34,057 | 6,427 | 5,060 |
| 1959 †..... | 52,119 | 39,852 | 7,163 | 5,104 |
| 1960 †..... | 56,049 | 43,281 | 7,581 | 5,187 |

\* Single payment loans and service credit. † Includes data for Alaska and Hawaii, beginning with Jan. and Aug. 1959.

## Minutes of Working Time Required for Purchase of Selected Consumer Items in 1957

*Source:* National Conference Industrial Board.

| Food | U. S. | Austria | Belgium | Sweden | France | West Germany | Italy | U. K. | Canada | Mexico | Japan | Australia | U.S.S.R. |
|---|---|---|---|---|---|---|---|---|---|---|---|---|---|
| Flour, wheat (1 kg.) | 7 | 27 | 36 | 13 | 34 | 21 | 39 | 15 | 7 | 30 | 41 | 10 | 59 |
| Rice (1 kg.) | 11 | 36 | 40 | 24 | 53 | 28 | 52 | 31 | ... | 51 | 64 | 17 | 200 |
| Bread, white (1 kg.) | 12 | 43 | 18 | 22 | 20 | 28 | 38 | 13 | 12 | 47 | 58 | 11 | 19 |
| Beef, sirloin[1] (1 kg.) | 61 | 265 | 296 | 149 | 326 | 142 | 387 | 116 | 70 | 168 | 356 | 65 | 200 |
| Pork, loin chops (1 kg.) | 56 | 204 | 220 | 93 | 190 | 160 | .... | 113 | 61 | 229 | 346 | 87 | 369[2] |
| Fish, fresh (1 kg.) | 27 | 130 | 143 | 46 | 71 | 67 | 328 | 59 | 31 | 181 | 81 | 110 | 297[2] |
| Butter (1 kg.) | 45[5] | 211 | 230 | 93 | 283 | 197 | 342 | 88 | 56 | 323 | 576 | 80 | 405[5] |
| Milk, pasteurized (1 liter) | 8[5] | 14 | 18 | 8 | 16 | 12 | 25 | 14 | 8 | 25 | 59 | 12 | 33[5] |
| Eggs, fresh (one) | 2[5] | 8 | 7 | 4 | 10 | 7 | 11 | 4 | 2 | 11 | 10 | 3 | 12[5] |
| Apples, eating (1 kg.) | 8 | 59 | 29 | 30 | 86 | 46 | 54 | 32 | 11 | 90 | ... | ... | 196 |
| Cabbage (1 kg.) | 5 | 14 | 10 | 6 | 15 | 9 | ... | 9 | 6 | 30 | 18 | ... | 81[2] |
| Potatoes (1 kg.) | 4 | 6 | 6 | 6 | 8 | 6 | 14 | 7 | 3 | 20 | 17 | 7 | 13 |
| Coffee (1 kg.) | 61 | 519 | 309 | 174 | 351 | 557 | 658 | 217 | 78 | 256 | ... | 195 | 985[2] |
| Tea (1 kg.) | 94[2] | 710 | 679 | 339 | 973 | 868 | 842 | 178 | 99 | 2,088 | 272 | 108 | 1,216 |
| Oleomargarine (1 kg.) | 19 | 84 | 59 | 44 | 97 | 57 | ... | 46 | 28 | 168 | 246 | 49 | 334[2] |
| Sugar (1 kg.) | 7[5] | 38 | 34 | 16 | 34 | 33 | 71 | 15 | 10 | 25 | 115 | 15 | 141[5] |
| Cigarettes (20) | 7[5] | 28 | 20 | 33[4] | 33 | 46 | 46[4] | 46 | 13 | 10 | 45 | 23 | 27[5] |
| Electricity (1 kwh.) | 2 | 3 | 9 | 2 | 9 | 6 | 12 | 2 | 1 | 7 | 9 | 1 | ... |
| Coal (100 kg.) | 90 | 723 | 509 | ... | 660 | 213 | 1,332 | 174 | 107 | 76 | 850 | ... | ... |

[1] Boneless.   [2] Estimated.   [3] Weighted average of 5 cities.   [4] Home produced.   [5] August 1959.

## New Construction Activity, by Type
### (in millions of dollars)
*Source:* U. S. Department of Commerce and U. S. Department of Labor

| Activity | 1929 | 1933 | 1940 | 1945 | 1949 | 1957 | 1960 |
|---|---|---|---|---|---|---|---|
| Total new construction activity | 10,793 | 2,879 | 8,682 | 5,633 | 22,789 | 48,115 | 55,148 |
| New private construction activity | 8,307 | 1,231 | 5,504 | 3,235 | 16,384 | 33,988 | 38,925 |
| Residential (nonfarm) | 3,625 | 470 | 2,985 | 1,100 | 8,267 | 17,019 | 22,022 |
| New dwelling units | 3,040 | 290 | 2,560 | 720 | 7,257 | 12,615 | 16,432 |
| Additions and alterations | 340 | 145 | 335 | 340 | 825 | 3,903 | 4,679 |
| Nonhousekeeping | 245 | 35 | 90 | 40 | 185 | 501 | ... |
| Nonresidential building, except farm and public utility | 2,694 | 406 | 1,025 | 1,020 | 3,228 | 9,556 | 8,632 |
| Industrial | 949 | 176 | 442 | 642 | 972 | 3,557 | 2,861 |
| Commercial[1] | 1,135 | 130 | 348 | 203 | 1,027 | 3,564 | 4,072 |
| Other | 610 | 100 | 235 | 175 | 1,229 | 2,435 | 4,658 |
| Public utility | 1,578 | 261 | 771 | 827 | 3,323 | 5,624 | 5,312 |
| Railroad | 510 | 94 | 167 | 264 | 352 | 406 | ... |
| Telephone and telegraph | 354 | 45 | 122 | 117 | 533 | 1,068 | ... |
| Other public utility | 714 | 115 | 482 | 446 | 2,438 | 4,150 | ... |
| Farm construction | 307 | 49 | 240 | 267 | 1,488 | 1,590 | 1,276 |
| All other private | 103 | 45 | 33 | 21 | 78 | 199 | ... |
| New public construction activity | 2,486 | 1,648 | 3,628 | 2,398 | 6,405 | 14,127 | 16,223 |
| Residential | ... | ... | 200 | 80 | 359 | 506 | ... |
| Nonresidential building | 659 | 230 | 615 | 937 | 2,068 | 4,503 | 4,753 |
| Industrial | ... | 2 | 164 | 755 | 177 | 473 | ... |
| Educational | 389 | 52 | 156 | 59 | 934 | 2,825 | ... |
| Hospital and institutional | 101 | 49 | 54 | 85 | 477 | 350 | ... |
| Other | 169 | 127 | 241 | 38 | 480 | 855 | ... |
| Military and Naval | 19 | 36 | 385 | 690 | 137 | 1,322 | 1,370 |
| Highway | 1,266 | 847 | 1,302 | 398 | 2,131 | 4,971 | 5,797 |
| Sewer and water | 253 | 95 | 338 | 97 | 619 | 1,344 | 1,487 |
| Conservation and development | 115 | 359 | 528 | 130 | 793 | 971 | ... |
| All other[2] | 23 | 16 | 260 | 66 | 298 | 117 | ... |

[1] Warehouses, office and loft buildings; stores, restaurants and garages.   [2] Miscellaneous public service enterprises and all Federal not included elsewhere.

## Number of Nonfarm Houses Built*

*Source:* U. S. Bureau of Labor Statistics, National
Bureau of Economic Research.

| Year | Houses | Year | Houses |
|------|--------|------|--------|
| 1900 | 204,000 | 1944 | 169,000 |
| 1910 | 475,000 | 1949 | 1,025,100 |
| 1920 | 247,000 | 1950 | 1,396,000 |
| 1929 | 509,000 | 1952 | 1,127,000 |
| 1933 | 93,000 | 1953 | 1,103,800 |
| 1937 | 336,000 | 1957 | 1,041,900 |
| 1939 | 515,000 | 1959 | 1,378,500 |
| 1943 | 350,000 | 1960 | 1,257,400 |

* Data represent new dwelling units started.

## Monthly Average Railroad Carloadings
### (in thousands of cars)
*Source:* Association of American Railroads.

| Year | Total | Year | Total |
|------|-------|------|-------|
| 1920 | 3,760 | 1948 | 3,643 |
| 1925 | 4,269 | 1949 | 2,992 |
| 1929 | 4,402 | 1950 | 3,242 |
| 1932 | 2,348 | 1951 | 3,437 |
| 1939 | 2,826 | 1952 | 3,165 |
| 1940 | 3,030 | 1953 | 3,192 |
| 1943 | 3,535 | 1957 | 2,963 |
| 1944 | 3,617 | 1958 | 2,517 |
| 1945 | 3,492 | 1959 | 2,581 |
| 1947 | 3,708 | 1960 | 2,536 |

## Industrial Production Indexes, by Groups
### (1947–49 average = 100)
*Source:* Board of Governors of the Federal Reserve System.

| Industry | 1950 | 1958 | 1959 | 1960 |
|----------|------|------|------|------|
| Durable manufactures | 116 | 141 | 165 | 169 |
| Ferrous metals | 114 | 94 | 108 | 110 |
| Nonferrous metals | 116 | ... | ... | ... |
| Fabricated metal products | 115 | 125 | 142 | 145 |
| Machinery | 114 | 140 | 169 | 174 |
| Transportation equipment | 120 | 197 | 228 | 238 |
| Instruments and related products | 114 | 175 | 209 | 221 |
| Stone, clay and glass products | 118 | 171 | 188 | 158 |
| Lumber and products | 113 | 110 | 124 | 118 |
| Furniture and misc. | 117 | 126 | 147 | 153 |
| Nondurable manufactures | 111 | 141 | 155 | 160 |
| Textile mill products | 111 | 109 | 126 | 121 |
| Apparel and allied products | 108 | 129 | 152 | 159 |
| Rubber products | 119 | 166 | 199 | 200 |

| Industry | 1950 | 1958 | 1959 | 1960 |
|----------|------|------|------|------|
| Leather and products | 101 | 109 | 119 | 113 |
| Paper and allied products | 118 | 155 | 170 | 172 |
| Printing and publishing | 111 | 133 | 143 | 152 |
| Chemicals and allied products | 121 | 210 | 240 | 255 |
| Petroleum and coal products | 110 | 148 | 158 | 161 |
| Food and beverage products | 103 | 123 | 128 | 132 |
| Tobacco manufactures | 101 | 121 | 127 | 130 |
| Total manufactures | 113 | 139 | 158 | 163 |
| Minerals | 105 | 120 | 125 | 127 |
| Fuels | 103 | 117 | 122 | 122 |
| Stone & earth minerals | 111 | 171 | 188 | 194 |
| Total industrial production | 112 | 141 | 159 | 164 |

## Electric Energy Output of Utilities*
### (in millions of kilowatt hours)
*Source:* Federal Power Commission.

| Year | Total | Privately owned | Publicly owned | Municipal | Federal | Co-operatives, power districts, state projects | % Public to total | Fuels | Fuels as % of total |
|------|-------|-----------------|----------------|-----------|---------|------------------------------------------------|-------------------|-------|---------------------|
| 1920 | 39,405 | 37,716 | 1,689 | 1,373 | 58 | 94 | 4.3 | 23,644 | 60.0 |
| 1929 | 92,180 | 87,514 | 4,667 | 3,498 | 300 | 451 | 5.1 | 59,533 | 64.6 |
| 1933 | 81,740 | 76,668 | 5,072 | 3,583 | 458 | 654 | 6.2 | 48,283 | 59.1 |
| 1939 | 127,642 | 115,078 | 12,564 | 5,688 | 5,476 | 944 | 9.8 | 84,078 | 65.9 |
| 1943 | 217,759 | 180,247 | 37,511 | 9,223 | 24,485 | 3,156 | 17.2 | 144,127 | 66.2 |
| 1951 | 370,673 | 301,845 | 68,828 | 17,617 | 44,120 | 6,204 | 18.6 | 270,922 | 73.1 |
| 1953 | 442,665 | 354,273 | 88,393 | 21,625 | 58,064 | 8,704 | 20.0 | 337,431 | 76.2 |
| 1956 | 600,668 | 459,015 | 141,653 | 28,006 | 100,711 | 12,937 | 23.6 | 478,639 | 79.7 |
| 1958 | 645,098 | 490,402 | 154,696 | 28,329 | 110,437 | 15,930 | 24.0 | 504,836 | 78.3 |
| 1959 | 710,006 | 544,234 | 165,772 | 34,618 | 109,052 | 22,102 | 23.3 | 572,224 | 80.6 |
| 1960† | 752,861 | 578,360 | 174,501 | 36,858 | 112,305 | 25,338 | 23.2 | 607,349 | 80.7 |

* Output by industrial establishments was as follows (in millions of kilowatt hours): 1939—33,667; 1943—49,781; 1951—62,685; 1953—71,505; 1956—84,136; 1958—79,654; 1959—85,245;   † 1960 preliminary—87,596.

## Fuel Production

*Source:* U. S. Dept. of Interior, U. S. Dept. of Commerce, and American Gas Association.

| Year | Coke, in thousands of short tons | Anthracite coal in thousands of short tons | Bituminous coal, in thousands of short tons | Natural gas, in millions of therms (produced and marketed)[1] | Manufactured gas, in millions of therms[2] | Crude petroleum, in thousands of 42-gal. barrels |
|---|---|---|---|---|---|---|
| 1929....... | 59,884 | 73,828 | 534,989 | 20,490[3] | 2,070[3] | 1,007,323 |
| 1933....... | 27,589 | 49,541 | 333,631 | 16,640[3] | 1,820 | 905,656 |
| 1939....... | 44,327 | 51,487 | 394,855 | 26,220 | 1,830 | 1,264,962 |
| 1941....... | 65,187 | 56,368 | 514,149 | 29,780 | 1,990 | 1,402,228 |
| 1945....... | 67,308 | 54,934 | 577,617 | 41,960 | 2,600 | 1,713,655 |
| 1949....... | 63,637 | 42,702 | 437,868 | 55,770 | 2,680 | 1,841,940 |
| 1951....... | 79,331 | 42,670 | 533,645 | 76,660 | 2,435 | 2,244,529 |
| 1956....... | 81,498 | 28,578 | 500,505 | 108,381 | 1,434 | 2,617,432 |
| 1957....... | 82,464 | 25,476 | 489,996 | 114,810 | 1,167 | 2,616,780 |
| 1959....... | 63,112 | 19,548 | 406,870 | 129,496 | 952 | 2,572,000 |
| 1960....... | 69,994 | 18,080 | 410,685 | 142,448 | 736 | 2,574,933 |

[1] Includes all natural gas in sales of natural gas mixed with manufactured gas. [2] Includes all manufactured gas products produced and purchased by gas utilities. [3] Estimated.

## Metals Production (in short tons)

*Source:* American Iron & Steel Institute, *Iron Age,* American Zinc Institute, American Bureau of Metal Statistics and U. S. Bureau of Mines.

| Year | Pig iron and ferroalloys | Steel ingots and castings | Rolled iron and steel products (tons) Total | Rolled iron and steel products (tons) Plates and sheets | Aluminum (primary) | Copper (smelter output from domestic ore) | Zinc (slab smelter output, all grades)* | Mine production of recoverable lead in the U. S. |
|---|---|---|---|---|---|---|---|---|
| 1929.......... | 47,727,661 | 63,205,490 | 45,997,746 | 13,928,670 | 113,986 | 1,001,432 | 631,601 | 672,498 |
| 1932.......... | 9,835,227 | 15,322,901 | 11,705,219 | 3,956,505 | 52,444 | 272,005 | 213,531 | 255,337 |
| 1939.......... | 35,677,097 | 52,798,714 | 39,067,553 | 13,931,919 | 163,545 | 712,675 | 538,198 | 420,967 |
| 1941.......... | 56,686,604 | 82,839,259 | 62,324,187 | 20,293,071 | 309,067 | 966,072 | 863,955 | 470,517 |
| 1943.......... | 62,769,947 | 88,836,512 | 63,292,673 | 22,543,040 | 920,179 | 1,092,939 | 971,873 | 406,544 |
| 1945.......... | 54,919,029 | 79,701,648 | 59,811,669 | 19,314,316 | 495,060 | 722,894 | 799,520 | 356,535 |
| 1948.......... | 61,911,559 | 88,640,470 | 69,191,952 | 25,694,480 | .623,456 | 834,813 | 850,105 | 339,413 |
| 1949.......... | 54,916,785 | 77,978,176 | 60,882,387 | 23,470,886 | 603,462 | 752,750 | 870,113 | 404,449 |
| 1951.......... | 72,448,543 | 105,199,848 | 81,911,320 | 31,869,683 | 836,881 | 928,330 | 931,833 | 342,644 |
| 1953.......... | 77,250,168 | 111,609,719 | 85,943,724 | 35,699,732 | 1,252,013 | 926,448 | 971,191 | 328,012 |
| 1954.......... | 59,806,242 | 88,311,652 | 68,464,640 | 28,406,447 | 1,460,565 | 835,472 | 868,242 | 322,271 |
| 1957.......... | 79,339,671 | 112,714,996 | 85,886,891 | 35,575,848 | 1,647,698 | 1,076,928 | 1,057,452 | 338,216 |
| 1958.......... | 57,764,100 | 85,254,885 | 65,105,455 | 29,683,253 | 1,564,341 | 1,001,615 | 781,664 | 265,520 |
| 1959.......... | 60,774,738 | 93,446,132 | 71,855,811 | 33,858,651 | 1,771,200 | 996,700 | 801,720 | 345,600 |
| 1960.......... | 67,958,144 | 99,281,601 | 76,446,483 | 37,046,117 | 2,014,600 | 1,121,200 | 820,200 | 243,800 |

* From 1940 includes both foreign and domestic ores.

## Business Population
### (in thousands of concerns)

*Source:* U. S. Department of Commerce, Dun & Bradstreet.

| Item | 1929 | 1933 | 1941 | 1943 | 1946 | 1949 | 1953 | 1958 | 1960 | 1961[6] |
|---|---|---|---|---|---|---|---|---|---|---|
| Total operating businesses[1] | 3,029 | 2,782 | 3,276 | 3,030 | 3,242 | 3,984 | 4,188 | 4,533 | 4,660 | 4,717 |
| Manufacturing........... | 257 | 167 | 230 | 243 | 264 | 323 | 331 | 329 | 324 | 324 |
| Wholesale trade........ | 148 | 142 | 190 | 182 | 210 | 260 | 283 | 309 | 317 | 323 |
| Retail trade.............. | 1,327 | 1,291 | 1,561 | 1,401 | 1,458 | 1,783 | 1,846 | 1,955 | 1,998 | 2,011 |
| Service industries........ | 591 | 575 | 615 | 579 | 614 | 739 | 750 | 828 | 872 | 893 |
| Contract construction..... | 234 | 185 | 194 | 164 | 199 | 339 | 405 | 466 | 475 | 479 |
| All others[5]............. | 472 | 422 | 486 | 460 | 498 | 539 | 573 | 647 | 674 | 687 |
| New Entrants[2]............. | (3) | (3) | 290 | 146 | 617 | 331 | 352 | 397 | 443 | ..... |
| Discontinued businesses[2]... | (3) | (3) | 271 | 337 | 209 | 307 | 299 | 347 | 386 | ..... |
| Commercial and industrial failures[4]................ | 22.9 | 19.9 | 11.8 | 3.2 | 1.1 | 9.2 | 8.9 | 15.0 | 15.4 | .... |

[1] 1929–33, annual average; 1941–60, as of Jan. 1. [2] Annual total. [3] Not available. [4] Closures resulting in a known loss to creditors. [5] Includes transportation, communications, public utilities, finance, insurance, real estate, and mining and quarrying. [6] Preliminary.

## Consumer Durable Goods Output

*Source: Electrical Merchandising Week;* Electronic Industries Association; Automobile Manufacturers Association, Inc.

| Year | Electric clothes washers Number sold, in thousands | Average retail price | Standard electric ranges Number sold, in thousands | Average retail price | Electric vacuum cleaners Number sold, in thousands | Average retail price | Electric refrigerators Number sold, in thousands | Average retail price | Radio sets Output in thousands | Average retail price[3] | Television sets Output in thousands | Average retail price[3] | Passenger cars Factory sales, in thousands | Average factory price |
|---|---|---|---|---|---|---|---|---|---|---|---|---|---|---|
| 1900.... | .... | ... | .... | ... | .... | ... | .... | ... | .... | ... | .... | ... | 4 | $1,229 |
| 1910.... | 3[1] | $ 75[1] | .... | ... | .... | ... | .... | ... | .... | ... | .... | ... | 181 | 1,190 |
| 1920.... | 600 | 120 | 40 | ... | 1,024 | $50 | 5[2] | $550[2] | .... | ... | .... | ... | 1,906 | 949 |
| 1925.... | 736 | 141 | 85 | $176 | 1,056 | 62 | 75 | 425 | .... | ... | .... | ... | 3,735 | 658 |
| 1929.... | 956 | 113 | 173 | 165 | 1,253 | 50 | 778 | 292 | .... | ... | .... | ... | 4,455 | 621 |
| 1932.... | 570 | 59 | 60 | 150 | 447 | 40 | 798 | 195 | 2,446 | $47 | .... | ... | 1,104 | 545 |
| 1937.... | 1,465 | 72 | 405 | 134 | 1,210 | 56 | 2,310 | 171 | 8,083 | 56 | .... | ... | 3,929 | 573 |
| 1941.... | 1,892 | 79 | 728 | 142 | 1,670 | 56 | 3,500 | 155 | 13,642 | 35 | .... | ... | 3,780 | 679 |
| 1946.... | 2,047 | 121 | 577 | 186 | 2,290 | 68 | 2,100 | 207 | 15,955 | 50 | .... | ... | 2,149 | 921 |
| 1948.... | 4,196 | 173 | 1,600 | 235 | 3,361 | 77 | 4,766 | 260 | 16,500 | 52 | 975 | $393 | 3,909 | 1,220 |
| 1950.... | 4,273 | 184 | 1,830 | 233 | 3,529 | 79 | 6,200 | 258 | 13,468 | 44 | 7,464 | 300 | 6,666 | .... |
| 1952.... | 3,267 | 217 | 1,400 | 245 | 2,842 | 92 | 4,075 | 275 | 10,431 | 34 | 6,096 | 308 | 4,321 | .... |
| 1955.... | 4,391 | 235 | 1,600 | 263 | 3,330 | 88 | 4,025 | 315 | 14,133 | 32 | 7,575 | 231 | 7,920 | .... |
| 1958.... | 3,770 | 248 | 810 | 255 | 3,295 | 89 | 3,117 | 320 | 11,747 | 32 | 4,920 | 205 | 4,258 | .... |
| 1959.... | 3,950 | 249 | 934 | 260 | 3,421 | 92 | 3,785 | 336 | 15,622 | 31 | 6,349 | 213 | 5,591 | .... |
| 1960.... | 3,381 | 243 | 860 | 260 | 3,350 | 92 | 3,475 | 325 | 17,127 | 32 | 5,708 | 219 | 6,675 | .... |

[1] 1909.   [2] 1921.   [3] Average retail prices not supplied by Electronic Industries Association.

## Wood Pulp, Paper and Lumber

*Source:* U. S. Bureau of the Census and National Lumber Manufacturers Assn.

| Year | Wood pulp (in thousands of short tons) | Paper and paperboard (in thousands of short tons) | Lumber (in millions of board feet) |
|---|---|---|---|
| 1919........ | 3,518 | 6,098 | 34,552 |
| 1929........ | 4,863 | 11,140 | 36,886 |
| 1939........ | 6,993 | 13,510 | 25,148 |
| 1941*....... | 10,011 | 17,934 | 33,613 |
| 1943........ | 9,060 | 17,036 | 34,289 |
| 1945........ | 10,167 | 17,371 | 28,122 |
| 1947........ | 11,946 | 21,114 | 35,404 |
| 1948........ | 12,872 | 21,897 | 36,762 |
| 1949........ | 12,207 | 20,315 | 32,901 |
| 1950........ | 14,849 | 24,375 | 38,902 |
| 1952........ | 16,473 | 24,418 | 37,462 |
| 1955........ | 20,829 | 29,892 | 39,108† |
| 1958........ | 21,614 | 30,229 | 33,275 |
| 1959........ | 24,155 | 34,020 | 36,530 |
| 1960........ | 25,056 | 34,090 | 34,577 |

\* Coverage for paper and paperboard increased in 1941.
† Subject to revision.

## Expenditures for New Plant and Equipment*

(in millions of dollars)

*Source:* Securities and Exchange Commission and U. S. Department of Commerce.

| Year | Manufacturing and mining | Transportation | All other† | Total |
|---|---|---|---|---|
| 1939....... | 2,269 | 645 | 2,598 | 5,512 |
| 1945....... | 4,366 | 1,122 | 3,204 | 8,692 |
| 1946....... | 7,217 | 1,506 | 6,125 | 14,848 |
| 1947....... | 9,394 | 2,187 | 9,031 | 20,612 |
| 1948....... | 10,016 | 2,604 | 9,439 | 22,059 |
| 1949....... | 7,941 | 2,239 | 9,105 | 19,285 |
| 1950....... | 8,198 | 2,323 | 10,084 | 20,605 |
| 1952....... | 12,617 | 2,896 | 10,980 | 26,493 |
| 1957....... | 17,200 | 3,680 | 16,620 | 36,900 |
| 1958....... | 12,375 | 2,254 | 15,897 | 30,526 |
| 1959....... | 13,044 | 2,978 | 16,619 | 32,641 |
| 1960....... | 15,460 | 2,980 | 17,240 | 35,680 |

\* Data exclude agriculture. † Includes electric and gas utilities, trade, service, communications, construction and finance. ‡ First 6 months, estimated.

## Industrial Production Indexes for Western Europe

*Source:* United Nations.
(1953 = 100)

| Country | 1948 | 1950 | 1955 | 1960 | Country | 1948 | 1950 | 1955 | 1960 |
|---|---|---|---|---|---|---|---|---|---|
| Austria.............. | 54 | 86 | 133 | 169 | Italy................ | 62 | 79 | 118 | 182 |
| Belgium............. | 88 | 90 | 116 | 126 | Luxembourg........ | 91 | 92 | 116 | 139 |
| Denmark............ | 82 | 98 | 112 | 142 | Netherlands........ | 71 | 88 | 118 | 157 |
| France.............. | 81 | 88 | 121 | 173 | Norway............. | 70 | 87 | 117 | 143 |
| Germany (Fed. Rep.).. | 40 | 72 | 129 | 180 | Sweden............. | 90 | 97 | 111 | 134 |
| Greece.............. | 52 | 78 | 130 | 172 | United Kingdom.... | 83 | 94 | 113 | 128 |
| Ireland............. | 70 | 91 | 107 | 122 | U.S.S.R............ | 45 | ... | 128 | 212 |

## Employment and Unemployment (in millions of persons)

*Sources:* U. S. Bureau of Labor Statistics, U. S. Bureau of the Census, and U. S. Bureau of Agricultural Economics.

| Activity | 1929 | 1932 | 1941 | 1943 | 1945 | 1950 | 1957 | 1959 | 1961[1] |
|---|---|---|---|---|---|---|---|---|---|
| Total employment............................ | 46.7 | 37.9 | 50.4 | 54.5 | 52.8 | 60.0 | 65.0 | 65.6 | 64.7 |
| Non-agricultural employment................. | 36.8 | 26.3 | 41.3 | 45.4 | 44.2 | 52.5 | 58.8 | 59.7 | 59.9 |
| Manufacturing......................... | 10.5 | 6.8 | 13.0 | 17.4 | 15.2 | 14.9 | 16.8 | 16.2 | 15.5 |
| Durable goods..................... | ... | ... | ... | 6.5 | 6.3 | 8.0 | 9.8 | 9.3 | 8.8 |
| Nondurable goods.................. | ... | ... | ... | 10.9 | 8.9 | 6.9 | 7.0 | 6.9 | 6.7 |
| Mining.............................. | 1.1 | 0.7 | .9 | .9 | .8 | .9 | 0.8 | 0.7 | 0.6 |
| Construction........................... | 1.5 | 1.0 | 1.8 | 1.6 | 1.1 | 2.3 | 3.0 | 2.7 | 2.2 |
| Transportation and public utilities.......... | 3.9 | 2.8 | 3.2 | 3.6 | 3.9 | 4.0 | 4.2 | 3.9 | 3.8 |
| Trade................................. | 6.4 | 4.9 | 7.6 | 7.3 | 7.7 | 9.5 | 11.5 | 11.4 | 11.3 |
| Retail............................. | ... | ... | ... | 5.7 | 5.9 | 7.0 | 8.4 | 8.3 | 8.2 |
| Wholesale......................... | ... | ... | ... | 1.6 | 1.8 | 2.5 | 3.1 | 3.1 | 3.1 |
| Finance............................ | 1.4 | 1.3 | 1.5 | 1.4 | 1.4 | 1.8 | 2.3 | 2.4 | 2.5 |
| Service............................ | 3.1 | 2.7 | 3.6 | 3.8 | 3.9 | 4.8 | 6.5 | 6.5 | 6.5 |
| Government........................ | 3.1 | 3.2 | 4.6 | 6.0 | 6.0 | 5.9 | 7.4 | 8.1 | 8.7 |
| Other, self-employed, domestic............. | 6.9 | 5.1 | 5.1 | 3.4 | 4.2 | 8.4 | (³) | (³) | (³) |
| Agricultural employment.................... | 9.9 | 9.6 | 9.1 | 9.1 | 8.6 | 7.5 | 6.2 | 5.9 | 4.7 |
| Unemployment........................... | 2.0 | 12.7 | 5.5 | 1.1 | 1.1 | 3.1 | 2.9 | 3.8 | 5.7 |
| Total civilian labor force.................... | 48.7 | 50.6 | 55.9 | 55.5 | 53.9 | 63.1 | 67.9 | 69.4 | 70.4 |
| Armed forces............................ | .3 | .3 | 1.5 | 8.9 | 11.3 | 1.5 | 2.8 | 2.5 | 2.5 |
| Total labor force......................... | 49.0 | 50.9 | 57.4² | 64.4 | 65.2 | 64.6 | 70.7 | 71.9 | 72.9 |

[1] Feb. ² Includes 1.9 million employed in public works. ³ Included in services, transportation and public utilities, and retail trade.

## Average Earnings and Hours Worked Per Week in Manufacturing Industries

*Source:* U. S. Department of Labor.

| Industry | 1947 Earnings | 1947 Hours worked | 1949 Earnings | 1949 Hours worked | 1951 Earnings | 1951 Hours worked | 1953 Earnings | 1953 Hours worked | 1958 Earnings | 1958 Hours worked | 1961² Earnings | 1961² Hours worked |
|---|---|---|---|---|---|---|---|---|---|---|---|---|
| All manufacturing[1].............. | $54.14 | 40.1 | $54.92 | 39.2 | $64.71 | 40.7 | $71.69 | 40.5 | $83.56 | 39.2 | $90.02 | 38.8 |
| Durable goods................. | 57.11 | 40.5 | 58.03 | 39.5 | 69.47 | 41.6 | 77.23 | 41.3 | 90.23 | 39.6 | 96.82 | 39.2 |
| Primary metal industries...... | 61.03 | 40.1 | 60.78 | 38.3 | 75.12 | 41.5 | 84.25 | 40.9 | 101.16 | 38.1 | 107.16 | 37.6 |
| Iron and steel foundries... | 58.45 | 40.7 | 55.09 | 37.2 | 71.66 | 42.4 | 76.33 | 40.6 | 86.00 | 37.3 | 92.62 | 36.9 |
| Nonferrous foundries....... | 59.96 | 40.0 | 60.92 | 39.0 | 73.74 | 41.9 | 80.97 | 41.1 | 92.81 | 39.6 | 109.75 | 40.8 |
| Fabricated metal products..... | 56.68 | 40.6 | 57.82 | 39.6 | 68.81 | 41.7 | 77.15 | 41.7 | 90.83 | 39.9 | 96.68 | 39.3 |
| Hand tools................ | 56.07 | 40.9 | 54.54 | 38.6 | 69.70 | 42.5 | 74.70 | 41.5 | 84.91 | 39.4 | 92.28 | 39.1 |
| Hardware................. | 54.26 | 40.4 | 56.28 | 39.3 | 66.49 | 41.3 | 75.89 | 41.7 | 89.37 | 40.1 | 92.28 | 39.1 |
| Structural metal products... | 58.17 | 41.2 | 59.90 | 40.5 | 71.49 | 42.3 | 80.75 | 42.5 | 93.42 | 40.1 | 99.85 | 39.8 |
| Electrical machinery........... | 55.66 | 40.1 | 56.96 | 39.5 | 64.84 | 41.3 | 71.81 | 40.8 | 85.22 | 39.6 | 93.53 | 39.8 |
| Machinery, except electrical... | 60.52 | 41.2 | 60.44 | 39.5 | 76.38 | 43.4 | 82.91 | 42.3 | 94.36 | 39.6 | 104.92 | 40.2 |
| Transportation equipment .... | 61.58 | 39.0 | 64.95 | 39.2 | 75.67 | 40.9 | 85.28 | 41.2 | 100.50 | 39.8 | 108.14 | 38.9 |
| Automobiles............... | 61.86 | 38.4 | 65.97 | 38.9 | 75.45 | 39.5 | 87.95 | 41.1 | 101.29 | 39.1 | 104.16 | 37.2 |
| Lumber and wood products..... | 51.38 | 41.5 | 51.72 | 40.6 | 59.98 | 40.8 | 65.93 | 40.7 | 75.01 | 39.8 | 77.80 | 38.9 |
| Furniture & fixtures.......... | 48.99 | 41.1 | 49.48 | 40.1 | 57.27 | 41.2 | 63.14 | 41.0 | 70.21 | 39.5 | 71.43 | 38.2 |
| Stone, clay and glass......... | 53.46 | 40.9 | 54.45 | 39.8 | 63.91 | 41.5 | 70.35 | 40.9 | 84.60 | 40.0 | 91.77 | 39.9 |
| Nondurable goods.............. | 50.61 | 39.6 | 51.41 | 38.8 | 58.46 | 39.5 | 63.60 | 39.5 | 75.76 | 38.8 | 81.41 | 38.4 |
| Textile—mill products........ | 45.59 | 39.2 | 44.83 | 37.7 | 51.60 | 38.8 | 53.57 | 39.1 | 56.56 | 38.6 | 61.56 | 38.0 |
| Cotton, silk, synthetic fibers. | 44.36 | 39.4 | 42.89 | 37.2 | 50.70 | 39.3 | 51.09 | 39.3 | 55.16 | 38.5 | .... | ... |
| Woolen and worsted goods.. | 52.45 | 40.1 | 51.19 | 38.9 | 57.87 | 39.1 | 61.93 | 39.7 | 65.34 | 40.7 | .... | ... |
| Apparel and other finished textiles.................. | 42.79 | 36.2 | 41.89 | 35.8 | 46.31 | 35.9 | 48.41 | 36.4 | 53.51 | 35.4 | 54.54 | 34.3 |
| Leather...................... | 41.66 | 37.2 | 41.61 | 36.6 | 46.86 | 36.9 | 51.65 | 37.7 | 57.61 | 36.7 | 62.75 | 37.8 |
| Food....................... | 51.87 | 42.0 | 53.58 | 41.5 | 59.92 | 41.9 | 66.33 | 41.2 | 81.55 | 40.6 | 90.45 | 40.1 |
| Tobacco.................... | 36.50 | 38.1 | 37.25 | 37.1 | 43.51 | 38.5 | 47.37 | 38.2 | 62.51 | 39.1 | 66.35 | 37.7 |
| Paper...................... | 55.25 | 42.8 | 55.96 | 41.7 | 65.51 | 43.1 | 72.67 | 43.0 | 88.49 | 41.9 | 96.28 | 41.5 |
| Printing and publishing....... | 66.73 | 39.3 | 70.28 | 38.7 | 77.21 | 38.8 | 85.58 | 38.9 | 97.97 | 37.8 | 106.22 | 37.8 |
| Chemicals.................. | 56.23 | 41.5 | 58.63 | 41.0 | 67.81 | 41.6 | 75.58 | 41.3 | 94.59 | 40.7 | 104.55 | 41.0 |
| Petroleum and natural gas.... | 69.23 | 40.7 | 72.36 | 40.4 | 80.98 | 40.9 | 90.17 | 40.8 | 110.85 | 40.5 | 131.04 | 41.6 |
| Rubber..................... | 56.78 | 39.0 | 57.79 | 38.3 | 68.61 | 40.6 | 77.78 | 40.3 | 92.38 | 39.3 | 99.57 | 39.2 |

[1] Average weekly earnings in 1919 = $23.29, 1929 = $26.40, 1932 = $17.86, 1939 = $24.23. Average hours worked per week in 1914 = 51.0, 1919 = 47.8, 1929 = 45.7, 1932 = 38.2, 1939 = 37.7. ² January.

## Average Earnings and Hours Worked Per Week in Nonmanufacturing Industries
*Source:* U. S. Department of Labor.

| Industry | 1947 Earnings | 1947 Hours worked | 1949 Earnings | 1949 Hours worked | 1951 Earnings | 1951 Hours worked | 1955 Earnings | 1955 Hours worked | 1961* Earnings | 1961* Hours worked |
|---|---|---|---|---|---|---|---|---|---|---|
| Anthracite mining | $62.77 | 37.7 | $56.78 | 30.2 | $66.66 | 30.3 | $84.50 | 33.4 | $ 90.74 | 36.3 |
| Bituminous coal mining | 66.59 | 40.7 | 63.28 | 32.6 | 77.79 | 35.2 | 96.26 | 37.6 | 112.85 | 34.3 |
| Metalliferous mining | 54.63 | 41.8 | 61.55 | 40.9 | 74.56 | 43.6 | 92.42 | 42.2 | 111.38 | 41.1 |
| Quarrying and nonmetallic mining.... | 50.54 | 45.0 | 56.38 | 43.3 | 67.05 | 45.0 | 80.99 | 44.5 | 98.18 | 42.5 |
| Telephone | 44.77 | 37.4 | 51.78 | 38.5 | 58.26 | 39.1 | 72.07 | 39.6 | 89.86 | 38.9 |
| Telegraph | 53.56 | 44.6 | 62.85 | 44.7 | 68.24 | 44.6 | 78.54 | 42.0 | 103.00 | 41.7 |
| Gas and electric utilities | 56.69 | 41.9 | 63.99 | 41.5 | 72.49 | 41.9 | 86.52 | 41.2 | 111.93 | 40.7 |
| Street railways and busses | 57.14 | 46.8 | 64.61 | 44.9 | 72.23 | 46.3 | 80.60 | 43.1 | 99.41 | 42.3 |
| Wholesale trade | 51.99 | 41.0 | 57.55 | 40.7 | 64.31 | 40.7 | 77.55 | 40.6 | 94.24 | 40.1 |
| Retail trade | 40.66 | 40.3 | 45.93 | 40.4 | 50.65 | 40.2 | 58.50 | 39.0 | 69.18 | 37.6 |
| Hotels (year-round) | 29.36 | 45.2 | 32.84 | 44.2 | 35.42 | 43.2 | 41.09 | 41.5 | 48.95 | 39.8 |
| Laundries | 32.71 | 42.6 | 34.98 | 41.5 | 37.81 | 41.1 | 40.70 | 40.3 | 47.72 | 38.8 |
| Dyeing and cleaning | 38.30 | 41.9 | 40.71 | 41.2 | 43.99 | 41.5 | 47.40 | 39.5 | 55.44 | 38.5 |
| Private building construction | 63.13 | 37.6 | 70.95 | 36.7 | 81.47 | 37.2 | 96.30 | 36.1 | 115.16 | 36.1 |

*Jan.

## State and Local Government Employment and Monthly Payroll: October 1960
*Source:* U. S. Department of Commerce.

| Function | Employees (in thousands) | Payroll (in millions) | Function | Employees (in thousands) | Payroll (in millions) |
|---|---|---|---|---|---|
| Total all functions | 6,387 | $2,215.0 | Hospitals | 597 | $169.3 |
| Education, total | 2,918 | 1,095.0 | Police | 341 | 129.0 |
| Public schools | 2,401 | 927.3 | Local fire protection | 220 | 65.1 |
| Institutions of higher learning | 487 | 156.7 | Natural resources | 143 | 46.8 |
| Other | 29 | 11.0 | Sanitation | 148 | 49.5 |
| Highways | 532 | 177.7 | Local utilities, total | 142 | 97.4 |
| Public welfare | 119 | 38.8 | General control | 476 | 129.3 |
| Health | 82 | 28.2 | All other | 569 | 188.8 |

## Why Strikes?

| Major issues | Percentage of total strikes 1949 | 1958 | 1959 | 1960 |
|---|---|---|---|---|
| Wage and hours | 46.6 | 50.8 | 50.5 | 47.8 |
| Union organization, wages and hours | 6.0 | 6.0 | 9.7 | 9.0 |
| Union organization | 15.7 | 9.8 | 8.2 | 7.2 |
| Recognition | 10.8 | 6.8 | 5.5 | 4.5 |
| Strengthening bargaining position | .5 | .6 | .5 | .4 |
| Union security | 2.2 | 1.9 | 1.5 | 1.8 |
| Discrimination | 1.8 | .2 | .1 | .1 |
| Other | .4 | .2 | .5 | .3 |
| Other working conditions | 25.0 | 23.7 | 20.5 | 24.0 |
| Job security | 12.6 | 11.7 | 10.5 | 10.8 |
| Shop conditions and policies | 9.7 | 9.7 | 8.7 | 11.4 |
| Work load | 2.1 | 2.2 | 1.0 | 1.4 |
| Other | .6 | .1 | .3 | .3 |
| Interunion or intraunion matters | 5.8 | 8.7 | 9.4 | 9.3 |
| Sympathy | 1.4 | 1.6 | 1.4 | 1.0 |
| Union rivalry or factionalism | 1.5 | .6 | 1.0 | .6 |
| Jurisdiction | 2.6 | 6.3 | 6.9 | 7.6 |
| Other | .3 | .2 | .1 | .1 |
| Not reported | .9 | 1.1 | 1.6 | 2.8 |
| All issues | 100.0 | 100.0 | 100.0 | 100.0 |

## Strikes and Lockouts
*Source:* U. S. Bureau of Labor Statistics.

| Year | Strikes and lockouts Number | Workers involved Number (thousands) | Man-days idle Number (thousands) |
|---|---|---|---|
| 1885 | 695 | 258 | n.a. |
| 1890 | 1,897 | 373 | n.a. |
| 1895 | 1,255 | 407 | n.a. |
| 1900 | 1,839 | 568 | n.a. |
| 1905 | 2,186 | 302 | n.a. |
| 1915 | 1,593 | n.a. | n.a. |
| 1917 | 4,450 | 1,227 | n.a. |
| 1920 | 3,411 | 1,463 | n.a. |
| 1925 | 1,301 | 428 | n.a. |
| 1929 | 921 | 289 | 5,352 |
| 1930 | 637 | 183 | 3,317 |
| 1932 | 841 | 324 | 10,502 |
| 1933 | 1,695 | 1,168 | 16,872 |
| 1935 | 2,014 | 1,117 | 15,456 |
| 1939 | 2,613 | 1,171 | 17,812 |
| 1943 | 3,752 | 1,981 | 13,501 |
| 1945 | 4,750 | 3,470 | 38,025 |
| 1949 | 3,606 | 3,030 | 50,500 |
| 1952 | 5,117 | 3,540 | 59,100 |
| 1957 | 3,673 | 1,390 | 16,500 |
| 1958 | 3,025 | 2,065 | 23,550 |
| 1959 | 3,708 | 1,880 | 69,000 |
| 1960 | 3,333 | 1,320 | 19,100 |

n.a. = not available.

## Membership of Representative American Labor Unions, 1960
*Source:* Bureau of Labor Statistics.

| Name of Union | Affiliation | No. of Members |
|---|---|---|
| Amalgamated Association of Street, Electric Railway and Motor Coach Employes......... | AFL–CIO | 124,637 |
| Amalgamated Clothing Workers...... | AFL–CIO | 376,000 |
| Amalgamated Meat Cutters and Butcher Workmen...... | AFL–CIO | 325,304 |
| American Federation of Musicians...... | AFL–CIO | 262,882 |
| Bricklayers, Masons and Plasterers...... | AFL–CIO | 159,126 |
| Brotherhood of Locomotive Firemen and Enginemen...... | AFL–CIO | 78,412 |
| Brotherhood of Maintenance of Way Employes...... | AFL–CIO | 183,000 |
| Brotherhood of Painters, Decorators and Paperhangers...... | AFL–CIO | 184,502 |
| Brotherhood of Railroad Trainmen..... | AFL–CIO | 200,111 |
| Brotherhood of Railway and Steamship Clerks...... | AFL–CIO | 360,899 |
| Building Service Employees International Union...... | AFL–CIO | 260,000 |
| Communications Workers of America...... | AFL–CIO | 255,365 |
| Hotel & Restaurant Employees' International Alliance...... | AFL–CIO | 436,315 |
| International Association of Bridge, Structural and Ornamental Iron Workers...... | AFL–CIO | 152,389 |
| International Association of Machinists...... | AFL–CIO | 992,689 |
| International Brotherhood of Boilermakers...... | AFL–CIO | 132,356 |
| International Brotherhood of Electrical Workers...... | AFL–CIO | 750,000 |
| International Brotherhood of Teamsters...... | Ind. | 1,418,246 |
| International Hod Carriers', Building and Common Laborers' Union...... | AFL–CIO | 476,598 |
| International Ladies' Garment Workers' Union...... | AFL–CIO | 442,901 |
| International Typographical Union...... | AFL–CIO | 110,449 |
| International Union of Mine, Mill and Smelter Workers...... | Ind. | 100,000 |
| International Union of Electrical, Radio and Machine Workers...... | AFL–CIO | 278,281 |
| National Association of Letter Carriers...... | AFL–CIO | 110,000 |
| National Federation of Post Office Clerks...... | AFL–CIO | 100,000 |
| Oil, Chemical and Atomic Workers...... | AFL–CIO | 180,175 |
| Retail Clerks International Association...... | AFL–CIO | 305,000 |
| Retail, Wholesale and Department Store Union...... | AFL–CIO | 160,000 |
| State, County and Municipal Employees...... | AFL–CIO | 200,000 |
| Textile Workers Union...... | AFL–CIO | 197,200 |
| Transport Workers Union...... | AFL–CIO | 135,000 |
| United Association of Plumbers and Steam Fitters...... | AFL–CIO | 255,800 |
| United Automobile, Aircraft and Agricultural Implement Workers...... | AFL–CIO | 1,027,000 |
| United Brotherhood of Carpenters and Joiners...... | AFL–CIO | 835,000 |
| United Electrical, Radio and Machine Workers...... | Ind. | 160,000 |
| United Mine Workers...... | Ind. | 600,000 |
| United Packinghouse Workers...... | AFL–CIO | 157,690 |
| United Papermakers and Paperworkers...... | AFL–CIO | 135,000 |
| United Rubber, Cork, Linoleum and Plastic Workers...... | AFL–CIO | 158,570 |
| United Steelworkers...... | AFL–CIO | 960,000 |

## Wholesale and Retail Trade: No. of Establishments, 1954 and 1958
*Source:* Bureau of Census, Department of Commerce.

| Kind of business group | 1954 | 1958 | Kind of business group | 1954 | 1958 |
|---|---|---|---|---|---|
| Retail trade, total.................. | 1,721,650 | 1,788,325 | Tobacco and tobacco products (except leaf)................. | 2,858 | 2,759 |
| Food group...................... | 384,616 | 355,508 | Dry goods, apparel............. | 9,389 | 9,199 |
| Eating and drinking places....... | 319,657 | 344,740 | Furniture, home furnishings..... | 4,815 | 5,359 |
| General merchandise group........ | 76,198 | 86,644 | Paper and its products.......... | 4,864 | 5,182 |
| Apparel group.................... | 119,743 | 118,759 | Farm products—raw materials... | 3,853 | 4,195 |
| Furniture, furnishings, appliance group............. | 97,607 | 103,417 | Automotive.................... | 15,540 | 20,823 |
| Automotive group................ | 85,953 | 93,655 | Electrical goods............... | 7,123 | 9,488 |
| Gasoline service stations......... | 181,747 | 206,302 | Hardware, plumbing, heating.... | 8,043 | 9,492 |
| Lumber, building, hardware group.. | 100,519 | 108,248 | Lumber, construction materials .. | 10,314* | 9,463 |
| Drug and proprietary stores....... | 56,009 | 56,232 | Machinery, equipment & supplies | 25,290 | 30,627 |
| Liquor........................ | 31,240 | 37,068 | Metals, metalwork (except scrap) | 3,935 | 4,792 |
| Other retail stores.............. | 221,093 | 240,140 | Waste materials............... | 8,189 | 9,491 |
| Wholesale trade, total............. | 252,318 | 285,996 | Other merchant wholesalers..... | 17,999 | 24,414 |
| Merchant wholesalers, total...... | 165,153 | 189,728 | Manufacturers' sales branches, offices...................... | 22,590 | 25,181 |
| Groceries, confectionery, meats .. | 29,795 | 30,022 | Petroleum bulk stations, terminals.. | 29,189 | 30,424 |
| Farm products................ | 3,853 | 4,195 | Agents, brokers................ | 22,131 | 26,567 |
| Beer, wines, distilled spirits..... | 7,309 | 7,325 | Assemblers of farm products....... | 13,255 | 14,096 |
| Drugs, chemicals, allied products | 5,837 | 7,097 | | | |

* This figure includes 1,996 ready-mix concrete distributors.

## Retail Sales by Kind of Business Group
### (in millions of dollars)
*Source:* U. S. Bureau of the Census.

| Kind of business | 1952 Amount | 1952 % | 1959 Amount | 1959 % | 1960 Amount | 1960 % |
|---|---|---|---|---|---|---|
| Durable-goods stores[1] | $ 55,270 | 33.7 | $ 71,662 | 33.2 | $ 71,018 | 32.3 |
| Automotive group | 28,337 | 17.3 | 39,333 | 18.4 | 39,533 | 17.0 |
| Motor-vehicle, other automotive dealers | 26,383 | 16.1 | 36,583 | 17.0 | 36,999 | 15.8 |
| Tire, battery, accessory dealers | 1,944 | 1.2 | 2,750 | 1.4 | 2,534 | 1.2 |
| Furniture and appliance group | 8,926 | 5.4 | 11,042 | 5.1 | 10,658 | 4.8 |
| Furniture, home furnishings stores | 5,255 | 3.2 | 6,989 | 3.2 | 6,795 | 3.1 |
| Household appliance, radio stores | 3,671 | 2.2 | 4,053 | 1.9 | 3,863 | 1.7 |
| Lumber, building, hardware group | 10,200 | 6.2 | 11,857 | 5.5 | 11,485 | 5.2 |
| Lumber, building-materials dealers | 7,572 | 4.6 | 9,106 | 4.2 | 8,639 | 3.9 |
| Hardware stores | 2,628 | 1.6 | 2,751 | 1.3 | 2,846 | 1.3 |
| Non-durable-goods stores[1] | 108,815 | 66.3 | 143,751 | 66.8 | 148,609 | 67.7 |
| Apparel group | 10,633 | 6.5 | 13,266 | 6.2 | 13,543 | 6.2 |
| Men's and boys' wear stores | 2,497 | 1.5 | 2,534 | 1.2 | 2,559 | 1.2 |
| Women's apparel, accessory stores | 4,233 | 2.6 | 5,254 | 2.4 | 5,321 | 2.4 |
| Family and other apparel stores | 2,210 | 1.3 | 3,114 | 1.4 | 3,213 | 1.5 |
| Shoe stores | 1,693 | 1.1 | 2,364 | 1.2 | 2,450 | 1.1 |
| Drug and proprietary stores | 4,717 | 2.9 | 7,150 | 3.3 | 7,517 | 3.4 |
| Eating and drinking places | 12,688 | 7.7 | 15,601 | 7.2 | 16,057 | 7.3 |
| Food group[1] | 39,771 | 24.2 | 51,681 | 24.0 | 54,035 | 24.5 |
| Grocery stores | 32,238 | 19.6 | 46,043 | 21.4 | 48,322 | 22.0 |
| Gasoline service | 9,976 | 6.1 | 16,793 | 7.8 | 17,594 | 8.0 |
| General-merchandise group | 18,694 | 11.4 | 23,391 | 10.9 | 25,857 | 11.8 |
| Department stores, excluding mail order | 10,277 | 6.3 | 13,609 | 6.3 | 13,854 | 6.2 |
| Mail order (catalog sales) | 1,339 | .8 | 1,778 | 0.8 | 1,842 | 0.8 |
| Variety stores | 2,996 | 1.8 | 3,950 | 1.8 | 3,943 | 1.8 |
| Other general merchandise stores | 4,082 | 2.5 | 4,054 | 2.0 | 6,218 | 3.0 |
| Liquor stores | 3,165 | 1.9 | 4,729 | 2.2 | 4,892 | 2.2 |
| All retail sales | 164,085 | 100.0 | 215,413 | 100.0 | 219,627 | 100.0 |

[1] Sales of other durable-goods stores, other food stores and other non-durable-goods stores not reported separately but included in totals.

## Wholesale Price Indexes by Major Commodity Groups
### (1947–49 = 100)
*Source:* U. S. Bureau of Labor Statistics.

| Commodity | 1948 | 1949 | 1951 | 1955 | 1960 | 1961* |
|---|---|---|---|---|---|---|
| All commodities | 104.4 | 99.2 | 114.8 | 110.7 | 119.6 | 120.0 |
| Farm products | 107.3 | 92.8 | 113.4 | 89.6 | 88.8 | 90.3 |
| Processed foods | 106.1 | 95.7 | 111.4 | 101.7 | 107.7 | 110.5 |
| Textile products & apparel | 104.4 | 95.5 | 110.6 | 95.3 | 94.2 | 94.8 |
| Hides, skins & leather products | 102.1 | 96.9 | 120.3 | 93.8 | 110.3 | 108.2 |
| Fuel, power & lighting materials | 107.1 | 101.9 | 106.7 | 107.9 | 113.8 | 117.8 |
| Chemicals & allied products | 103.8 | 94.8 | 110.0 | 106.6 | 110.2 | 110.8 |
| Rubber & products | 102.1 | 98.9 | 148.0 | 143.8 | 144.7 | 139.9 |
| Lumber & wood products | 107.2 | 99.2 | 123.9 | 123.6 | 121.3 | 114.9 |
| Pulp, paper & allied products | 102.9 | 98.5 | 119.6 | 119.3 | 133.2 | 132.8 |
| Metals & metal products | 103.9 | 104.8 | 122.8 | 136.6 | 153.8 | 152.5 |
| Machinery & motive products | 100.9 | 106.6 | 119.0 | 128.4 | 153.4 | 153.1 |
| Furniture & other household durables | 101.4 | 103.1 | 114.1 | 115.9 | 123.1 | 122.2 |
| Nonmetallic minerals—structural | 101.7 | 104.4 | 113.6 | 124.2 | 138.0 | 138.5 |
| Tobacco mfs. & bottled beverages | 100.4 | 101.6 | 108.1 | 121.6 | 131.8 | 132.1 |
| Miscellaneous | 103.1 | 96.1 | 104.9 | 92.0 | 92.1 | 94.7 |

* As of February.

## Sales of Leading Retail Outlets
*Sources: Fortune Magazine, Business Week, Moody's Manual of Industrials.*

### DEPARTMENT STORES

1960 Sales (in thousands)

| | |
|---|---|
| J. C. Penney Co. | $1,468,918 |
| Federated Department Stores | 785,358 |
| May Department Stores Co. | 684,839 |
| Allied Stores Corp | 680,492 |
| Macy's | 508,695 |
| Gimbel Bros., Inc. | 407,045 |
| Marshall Field & Co. | 234,201 |

### VARIETY STORES

| | |
|---|---|
| F. W. Woolworth Co. | $1,035,293 |
| W. T. Grant Co. | 512,687 |
| S. S. Kresge Co. | 418,200 |
| G. C. Murphy Co. | 245,562 |
| J. J. Newberry Co. | 265,818 |
| McCrory-McLellan Stores Corp | 200,269 |
| S. H. Kress & Co. | 144,572 |

### GROCERY STORES

| | |
|---|---|
| Great Atlantic & Pacific Tea Co. | $5,246,578 |
| Safeway Stores, Inc. | 2,468,973 |
| Kroger Co. | 1,870,290 |
| American Stores Co. | 1,011,489 |
| National Tea (Chicago) | 855,841 |
| Food Fair | 771,172 |
| Winn-Dixie | 721,532 |
| Grand Union | 604,274 |

### DRUG STORES

1960 Sales (in thousands)

| | |
|---|---|
| Walgreen Co. | $312,365 |
| Rexall Drug | 242,557 |
| Sterling Drug Co. | 218,526 |

### SHOE STORES

| | |
|---|---|
| International Shoe Co. | $296,470 |
| Brown Shoe | 295,802 |
| Melville Shoe Co. | 161,594 |
| Endicott Johnson Corp. | 141,468 |
| Edison Bros. Stores, Inc. | 133,239 |
| A. S. Beck Shoe Corp. | 76,867 |

### MAIL-ORDER HOUSES

| | |
|---|---|
| Sears, Roebuck & Co. | $4,134,320 |
| Montgomery Ward & Co. | 1,248,994 |
| Spiegel, Inc. | 268,834 |

### FURNITURE STORES

| | |
|---|---|
| Larchfield Corp. | $96,754 |
| Reliable Stores Corp. | 27,534 |
| Haverty Furniture Co., Inc. | 22,281 |

## Largest U. S. and Foreign Corporations
(millions of dollars)
*Source: Fortune Magazine.*

### Ten Largest Industrial Corporations

| | Sales | Assets[1] |
|---|---|---|
| General Motors | $12,736 | $8,553 |
| Standard Oil (N.J.) | 8,035 | 10,090 |
| Ford Motor | 5,238 | 4,032 |
| General Electric | 4,198 | 2,551 |
| U.S. Steel | 3,698 | 4,781 |
| Socony Mobil Oil | 3,178 | 3,455 |
| Chrysler | 3,007 | 1,369 |
| Texaco | 2,980 | 3,647 |
| Gulf Oil | 2,721 | 3,843 |
| Western Electric | 2,640 | 1,665 |

### Five Largest Commercial Banks

| | Assets[1] |
|---|---|
| Bank of America | $11,942 |
| Chase Manhattan Bank | 9,260 |
| First National City Bank | 8,832 |
| Chemical Bank New York Trust | 4,539 |
| Morgan Guaranty Trust | 4,424 |

### Five Largest Life Insurance Companies

| | Assets[1] |
|---|---|
| Metropolitan | $17,941 |
| Prudential | 16,551 |
| Equitable Life Assurance | 10,039 |
| New York Life | 7,158 |
| John Hancock Mutual | 6,127 |

[1] As of Dec. 31, 1960.

### Five Largest Foreign Industrial Corporations

| | Sales | Assets[1] |
|---|---|---|
| Royal Dutch-Shell (Britain-Holland) | $5,481 | $8,900 |
| Unilever (Britain-Holland) | 3,884 | 2,259 |
| British Petroleum Industries (Britain) | 1,811 | 2,019 |
| Imperial Chemical | 1,564 | 2,312 |
| Nestlé (Switzerland) | 1,519 | 239 |

### Five Largest Transportation Companies

| | Operating revenues (1960) | Assets[1] |
|---|---|---|
| Pennsylvania Railroad | $844 | $2,873 |
| Southern Pacific Transportation System | 760 | 2,517 |
| New York Central Railroad | 760 | 2,512 |
| Atchison, Topeka & Santa Fe Railway | 614 | 1,598 |
| Union Pacific Railroad | 494 | 1,553 |

### Five Largest Utilities

| | Assets[1] |
|---|---|
| American Tel & Tel | $22,558 |
| Pacific Gas & Electric | 2,479 |
| Consolidated Edison of N. Y. | 2,449 |
| Commonwealth Edison (Chicago) | 1,736 |
| Tennessee Gas | 1,734 |

## Number of Service Establishments and Places of Amusement, 1954 and 1958

*Source:* U. S. Department of Commerce.

| Kind of business | 1954 | 1958 | Kind of business | 1954 | 1958 |
|---|---|---|---|---|---|
| **PERSONAL SERVICES:** | | | Automobile rentals............... | 6,061* | 10,518* |
| | | | Automobile storage, parking....... | 8,572 | 10,998 |
| Barber shops..................... | 91,122 | 105,056 | Electrical repair shops............. | 32,164 | 51,269 |
| Barber and beauty shops.......... | 78,562 | 110,395 | Jewelry, watch, clock repair....... | 11,246 | 11,651 |
| Baths and masseurs............... | 2,265 | 2,866 | Locksmiths and gunsmiths......... | 1,801 | 2,468 |
| Cleaning and dyeing plants........ | 29,200 | 34,311 | Musical instrument repair......... | 2,972 | 3,504 |
| Costume and dress suit rentals..... | 515 | 687 | Radio repair..................... | 22,824† | 37,884 |
| Diaper service................... | 381 | 385 | Refrigerator repair............... | 5,037 | 5,748 |
| Funeral service, crematories....... | 18,387 | 20,767 | Saw, knife and tool sharpening and | | |
| Fur repair and storage........... | 1,439 | 1,091 | repair......................... | 2,746 | 4,230 |
| Hat cleaning.................... | 947 | 707 | Upholstery, furniture............. | 13,305 | 15,823 |
| Laundries, all types............. | 59,469 | 67,920 | Welding shops................... | 9,244 | 11,118 |
| Linen supply service............. | 1,371 | 1,588 | | | |
| Photographic studios............. | 17,293 | 20,028 | **AMUSEMENT PLACES:** | | |
| Rug cleaning and repairing........ | 1,777 | 2,506 | | | |
| Shoe repair shops................ | 26,843 | 25,642 | Amusement parks, devices and | | |
| Shoe shine parlors................ | 1,595 | 1,426 | shooting galleries............... | 2,488 | 3,682 |
| | | | Bands, orchestras, entertainers..... | 7,097 | 14,655 |
| **BUSINESS SERVICES:** | | | Bathing beaches (not municipal)... | 360 | 500 |
| Advertising agencies.............. | 88,661 | 113,923 | Billiard and pool parlors........... | 7,639 | 7,045 |
| Auctioneers..................... | 1,639 | 2,069 | Boat and canoe rental............. | 1,811 | 1,736 |
| Blueprinting and photostat........ | 1,019 | 1,360 | Bowling alleys................... | 5,062 | 6,871 |
| Coin-operated machines........... | 482 | 864 | Clubs, baseball.................. | 271 | 200 |
| Consumer credit reporting........ | 5,220 | 6,883 | Clubs, football.................. | 25 | 30 |
| Detective agencies................ | 1,123 | 2,831 | Dance halls, studios, schools....... | 2,265 | 6,869 |
| Disinfecting, exterminating........ | 3,270 | 4,231 | Race tracks, automobile........... | 454 | 578 |
| Employment agencies............. | 3,153 | 3,892 | Race tracks, dog................. | 145 | 249 |
| Interior decorating............... | 2,944 | 4,191 | Race tracks, horse................ | 1,246 | 4,449 |
| News syndicates................. | 467 | 868 | Riding academies................ | 689 | 861 |
| Outdoor advertising.............. | 1,307 | 1,713 | Skating rinks.................... | 1,799 | 2,254 |
| Photo finishing laboratories....... | 1,719 | 1,907 | Sports promoters, commercial oper- | | |
| Sign painting shops.............. | 5,703 | 7,110 | ators........................ | 7,799 | 6,028 |
| Telephone answering service....... | 1,171 | 1,656 | Swimming pools (not municipal)... | 652 | 1,031 |
| Window cleaning service.......... | 4,231 | 4,476 | Theatres, motion pictures......... | 18,491 | 16,354 |
| Window display service........... | 1,101 | 1,213 | Theatres and theatrical producers.. | 2,179 | 3,212 |
| **REPAIR SERVICES:** | | | | | |
| Automotive repair service and | | | | | |
| garages...................... | 79,709 | 103,724 | | | |

\* Includes truck rental      † Includes TV repair

## Advertising Expenditures by Medium

*Source: Printers' Ink.*

| Medium | 1948 Amount (million dollars) | 1948 % of total | 1950 Amount (million dollars) | 1950 % of total | 1958 Amount (million dollars) | 1958 % of total | 1959 Amount (million dollars) | 1959 % of total | 1960 Amount (million dollars) | 1960 % of total |
|---|---|---|---|---|---|---|---|---|---|---|
| Newspapers.............. | 1,749.6 | 36.0 | 2,063.2 | 36.3 | 3,120 | 30.6 | 3,517 | 31.7 | 3,546 | 31.5 |
| Radio.................. | 617.1 | 12.7 | 667.1 | 11.7 | 616 | 6.0 | 638 | 5.8 | 657 | 5.8 |
| Magazines.............. | 512.7 | 10.5 | 514.9 | 9.0 | 770 | 7.6 | 866 | 7.8 | 866 | 8.1 |
| Direct mail.............. | 689.1 | 14.2 | 803.2 | 14.1 | 1,560 | 15.3 | 1,573 | 14.2 | 1,573 | 14.0 |
| Business papers.......... | 250.9 | 5.2 | 251.1 | 4.4 | 540 | 5.3 | 566 | 5.1 | 569 | 5.2 |
| Outdoor................ | 132.1 | 2.7 | 142.5 | 2.5 | 199 | 2.0 | 193 | 1.8 | 193 | 1.8 |
| Farm papers*............ | 20.4 | .4 | 21.2 | .4 | 34 | 0.3 | 36 | 0.3 | 36 | 0.3 |
| Television............... | .... | ... | 185.0 | 3.3 | 1,360 | 13.3 | 1,526 | 13.7 | 1,495 | 13.8 |
| Miscellaneous............ | 891.7 | 18.3 | 1,043.1 | 18.3 | 1,997 | 19.6 | 2,175 | 19.6 | 2,181 | 19.5 |
| Total................. | 4,863.6 | 100.0 | 5,691.3 | 100.0 | 10,196 | 100.0 | 11,090 | 100.0 | 11,117 | 100.0 |

\* Regional farm papers.

## Financial Condition of U. S. Life Insurance Companies
### (in millions of dollars)
*Source:* Institute of Life Insurance.

| Year | Assets (admitted) Dec. 31 | Total income | Premium income | Payment to policyholders* |
|---|---|---|---|---|
| 1910..... | 3,876 | 781 | 593 | 387 |
| 1920..... | 7,320 | 1,764 | 1,381 | 745 |
| 1929..... | 17,482 | 4,337 | 3,343 | 1,962 |
| 1932..... | 20,754 | 4,653 | 3,495 | 3,087 |
| 1939..... | 29,243 | 5,453 | 3,776 | 2,642 |
| 1945..... | 44,797 | 7,674 | 5,159 | 2,667 |
| 1948..... | 55,512 | 9,751 | 7,157 | 3,237 |
| 1950..... | 64,020 | 11,337 | 8,189 | 3,731 |
| 1955..... | 90,432 | 16,544 | 12,546 | 5,383 |
| 1957..... | 101,309 | 19,333 | 14,775 | 6,661 |
| 1959..... | 113,650 | 21,790 | 16,622 | 7,531 |
| 1960..... | 119,576 | 23,007 | 17,365 | 8,118 |

* Beginning 1943, data include payments to U. S. residents by domestic and foreign companies.

## Life Insurance in Force in U. S.
### (in millions of dollars)
*Source: Spectator Yearbook* and Institute of Life Insurance.

| Dec. 31 | Ordinary | Group | Industrial | Total* |
|---|---|---|---|---|
| 1910....... | 11,783 | ..... | 3,125 | 14,908 |
| 1915....... | 16,650 | 100 | 4,279 | 21,029 |
| 1925....... | 52,892 | 4,247 | 12,318 | 69,475 |
| 1929....... | 75,686 | 8,994 | 17,349 | 102,086 |
| 1930....... | 78,576 | 9,801 | 17,963 | 106,413 |
| 1933....... | 70,872 | 8,681 | 16,630 | 96,246 |
| 1935....... | 70,684 | 10,208 | 17,471 | 98,464 |
| 1940....... | 79,346 | 14,938 | 20,866 | 115,530 |
| 1945....... | 101,550 | 22,172 | 27,675 | 151,762 |
| 1948....... | 131,158 | 37,068 | 31,253 | 201,208 |
| 1950....... | 149,071 | 47,793 | 33,415 | 234,168 |
| 1951....... | 159,054 | 54,398 | 34,870 | 253,140 |
| 1955....... | 216,600 | 101,300 | 39,682 | 372,332 |
| 1957....... | 264,678 | 133,794 | 40,139 | 458,359 |
| 1959....... | 315,953 | 159,807 | 39,688 | 542,128 |
| 1960....... | 340,268 | 175,424 | 39,563 | 586,448 |

* Includes credit insurance.

## Domestic Passenger Traffic by Major Carriers
### (in millions of passenger-miles)
*Source:* Interstate Commerce Commission; Corps of Engineers, U. S. A.; Civil Aeronautics Board; Assn. of American Railroads.

| Year | Steam railroads | | Buses | | Air carriers | | Electric Interurban railways | | Inland waterways[1] | |
|---|---|---|---|---|---|---|---|---|---|---|
| | Passenger-miles | % of total | Passenger-miles | % of total | Passenger-miles | % of total | Passenger-miles | % of total | Passenger-miles | % of total |
| 1939.......... | 22,713 | 65.0 | 9,100 | 26.0 | 683 | 2.0 | 956 | 2.7 | 1,486 | 4.3 |
| 1941.......... | 29,406 | 62.7 | 13,100 | 27.9 | 1,385 | 3.0 | 1,177 | 2.5 | 1,821 | 3.9 |
| 1944.......... | 95,663 | 74.2 | 26,920 | 20.8 | 2,178 | 1.7 | 2,042 | 1.6 | 2,187 | 1.7 |
| 1947.......... | 45,972 | 58.5 | 23,948 | 30.4 | 6,110 | 7.8 | 771 | 1.0 | 1,845 | 2.3 |
| 1949.......... | 35,133 | 52.8 | 22,411 | 33.7 | 6,753 | 10.1 | 842 | 1.3 | 1,402 | 2.1 |
| 1953.......... | 31,679 | 46.4 | 19,730 | 28.9 | 14,760 | 21.6 | 582 | 0.9 | 1,487 | 2.2 |
| 1957.......... | 25,914 | 31.8 | 24,998 | 30.7 | 28,302 | 34.7 | 337 | 0.4 | 1,930 | 2.4 |
| 1958.......... | 23,295 | 31.1 | 20,756 | 27.7 | 28,522 | 38.0 | 310 | 0.4 | 2,073 | 2.8 |
| 1959.......... | 22,075 | 28.6 | 20,364 | 26.4 | 32,366 | 42.0 | 298 | 0.4 | 2,026 | 2.6 |
| 1960[2].......... | 21,200 | 27.2 | 20,400 | 26.1 | 34,300 | 43.9 | 300 | 0.4 | 1,900 | 2.4 |

[1] Rivers, canals and Great Lakes.   [2] Estimated.

## Domestic Freight Traffic by Major Carriers
### (in millions of ton-miles)
*Source:* Interstate Commerce Commission; Corps of Engineers, U. S. A.; Civil Aeronautics Board; Assn. of American Railroads.

| Year | Steam railways[1] | | Inland waterways[2] | | Motor trucks | | Oil pipelines | | Air carriers[1] | |
|---|---|---|---|---|---|---|---|---|---|---|
| | Ton-miles | % of total | Ton-miles | % of total | Ton-miles | % of total | Ton-miles | % of total | Ton-miles | % of total |
| 1939.......... | 338,125 | 64.22 | 88,897 | 16.88 | 43,931 | 8.34 | 55,602 | 10.56 | 12 | (4) |
| 1941.......... | 480,730 | 64.68 | 130,916 | 17.61 | 63,258 | 8.51 | 68,428 | 9.20 | 19 | (4) |
| 1944.......... | 745,573 | 70.14 | 137,005 | 12.89 | 47,395 | 4.46 | 132,864 | 12.50 | 71 | (4) |
| 1947.......... | 663,442 | 67.51 | 135,964 | 13.84 | 77,918 | 7.93 | 105,161 | 10.70 | 158 | (4) |
| 1949.......... | 533,862 | 61.17 | 130,192 | 14.91 | 93,653 | 10.73 | 114,916 | 13.16 | 235 | (4) |
| 1951.......... | 654,340 | 59.05 | 168,143 | 15.17 | 133,160 | 12.02 | 152,115 | 13.73 | 378 | (4) |
| 1953.......... | 613,171 | 52.55 | 180,622 | 15.49 | 206,808 | 17.72 | 165,728 | 14.30 | 427 | (4) |
| 1957.......... | 626,222 | 46.3 | 231,792 | 17.2 | 260,856 | 19.3 | 232,660 | 17.2 | 601 | (4) |
| 1958.......... | 558,738 | 46.3 | 189,016 | 15.7 | 246,984 | 20.5 | 211,289 | 17.5 | 579 | (4) |
| 1959.......... | 582,497 | 45.0 | 195,559 | 15.2 | 288,519 | 22.3 | 226,991 | 17.5 | 646 | (4) |
| 1960[3].......... | 578,000 | 43.8 | 214,000 | 16.2 | 293,500 | 22.2 | 234,000 | 17.7 | 700 | (4) |

[1] Includes express and mail.   [2] Rivers, canals and domestic traffic on Great Lakes.   [3] Estimated.   [4] Negligible.

## Farm Income—Estimated Receipts from Major Farm Marketings
### (in millions of dollars)
*Source:* U. S. Department of Agriculture.

| Year | Cotton and cotton- seed | Tobacco | Food grains | Oil- bearing crops | Feed grains and hay | Vege- tables | Fruits and nuts | Meat animals | Dairy products | Poultry & eggs |
|---|---|---|---|---|---|---|---|---|---|---|
| 1919........... | 2,282 | 500 | 1,749 | 96 | 1,173 | 631 | 597 | 4,045 | 1,522 | 1,106 |
| 1929........... | 1,511 | 279 | 788 | 85 | 697 | 751 | 582 | 3,017 | 1,838 | 1,187 |
| 1932........... | 461 | 115 | 220 | 29 | 247 | 359 | 299 | 1,159 | 986 | 562 |
| 1939........... | 627 | 271 | 464 | 110 | 485 | 545 | 411 | 2,271 | 1,346 | 775 |
| 1944........... | 1,548 | 688 | 1,369 | 581 | 1,203 | 1,510 | 1,446 | 5,706 | 2,938 | 2,473 |
| 1947........... | 2,245 | 1,033 | 2,768 | 908 | 2,328 | 1,710 | 1,160 | 9,340 | 4,046 | 2,926 |
| 1949........... | 2,632 | 904 | 2,339 | 846 | 2,299 | 1,641 | 1,013 | 8,383 | 3,778 | 3,088 |
| 1951........... | 2,849 | 1,187 | 1,896 | 1,058 | 1,966 | 1,670 | 1,214 | 11,308 | 4,290 | 3,667 |
| 1955........... | 2,703 | 1,161 | 2,312 | 912 | 2,323 | 1,624 | 1,272 | 8,868 | 4,114 | 3,013 |
| 1957........... | 1,784 | 967 | 1,878 | 1,154 | 2,328 | 1,539 | 1,415 | 9,389 | 4,651 | 3,001 |
| 1958........... | 2,134 | 1,008 | 2,510 | 1,424 | 2,781 | 1,589 | 1,503 | 11,178 | 4,562 | 3,286 |
| 1959........... | 2,576 | 1,057 | 2,229 | 1,183 | 2,693 | 1,613 | 1,571 | 11,036 | 4,617 | 2,906 |
| 1960........... | 2,435 | 1,148 | 2,363 | 1,287 | 2,841 | 1,778 | 1,583 | 10,681 | 4,736 | 3,196 |

## Farm Income (in millions of dollars)
*Source:* U. S. Department of Agriculture.

| Year | Est. cash income | | | |
|---|---|---|---|---|
| | Crops | Livestock and livestock products | Government payments | Total cash income |
| 1919...... | 7,645 | 6,925 | ... | 14,570 |
| 1929...... | 5,120 | 6,179 | ... | 11,299 |
| 1931...... | 2,532 | 3,837 | ... | 6,369 |
| 1935...... | 2,957 | 4,117 | 573 | 7,647 |
| 1941...... | 4,605 | 6,470 | 544 | 11,619 |
| 1945...... | 9,419 | 12,001 | 742 | 22,162 |
| 1946...... | 10,835 | 13,719 | 772 | 25,326 |
| 1947...... | 13,231 | 16,523 | 314 | 30,068 |
| 1949...... | 12,586 | 15,426 | 185 | 28,197 |
| 1950...... | 12,575 | 16,198 | 283 | 29,056 |
| 1952...... | 14,627 | 18,498 | 292 | 33,417 |
| 1953...... | 13,797 | 17,178 | 213 | 31,188 |
| 1956...... | 13,792 | 16,207 | 554 | 30,553 |
| 1957...... | 12,381 | 17,376 | 1,016 | 30,773 |
| 1958...... | 14,259 | 19,301 | 1,089 | 34,649 |
| 1959...... | 14,291 | 18,855 | 681 | 33,146 |
| 1960...... | 14,840 | 18,906 | 693 | 33,746 |

## Farms—Population and Property
*Source:* U. S. Bureau of the Census.

| Item | 1930 | 1954 | 1959 |
|---|---|---|---|
| Farm population (thousands) .. | 29,447 | 22,099 | 21,172 |
| Number of farms (thousands).. | 6,289 | 4,782 | 3,704 |
| Tenancy as % of total........ | 42.2 | 24.4 | 20.5 |
| All land in farms (million acres) | 986 | 1,158 | 1,120 |
| Average acreage per farm..... | 156.9 | 242.2 | 302.4 |
| Value of farm property (mil- lions of dollars)*.......... | 56,973 | 97,577 | 123,128 |

* Includes land, buildings, livestock, implements and machinery.

## U. S. Farm Index (1910-14 = 100)
*Source:* U. S. Department of Agriculture.

| Year | Prices paid by farmers* | Prices rec'd by farmers† | Parity ratio |
|---|---|---|---|
| 1935-39 average . | 125 | 107 | 86 |
| 1945........... | 189 | 206 | 109 |
| 1948........... | 259 | 285 | 110 |
| 1950........... | 255 | 256 | 100 |
| 1952........... | 286 | 288 | 101 |
| 1955........... | 281 | 236 | 84 |
| 1959........... | 298 | 240 | 80 |
| 1960........... | 299 | 238 | 80 |
| 1961‡........... | 302 | 244 | 81 |

* Commodities, interest and taxes, and wage rates.
† All crops and livestock.   ‡ February.

## Farm to Retail Price Spreads for Farm Food Products*
*Source:* U. S. Department of Agriculture.

| Year | Retail cost (dollars) | Net farm value (dollars) | Farmer's share of consumer's dollars (%) |
|---|---|---|---|
| Average: | | | |
| 1913-19....... | 361 | 170 | 47 |
| 1920-24....... | 444 | 181 | 41 |
| 1925-29....... | 439 | 183 | 42 |
| 1933........... | 277 | 90 | 32 |
| 1937........... | 363 | 151 | 42 |
| 1939........... | 318 | 122 | 38 |
| 1945........... | 459 | 246 | 54 |
| 1949........... | 939 | 435 | 46 |
| 1950........... | 924 | 432 | 47 |
| 1953........... | 1,002 | 452 | 45 |
| 1957........... | 1,007 | 401 | 40 |
| 1958........... | 1,065 | 427 | 40 |
| 1959........... | 1,040 | 395 | 38 |
| 1960........... | 1,052 | 408 | 39 |

* Retail cost of 1935-39 average annual purchases of farm food products by a family of three average consumers; farm value of equivalent quantities sold by producers adjusted for value of by-products.

## Agricultural Output by States, 1960 Crops
*Source:* U. S. Department of Agriculture.

| State | Wheat (1,000 bu.) | Corn (1,000 bu.) | Cotton lint[1] | Potatoes (1,000 cwt.) | Tobacco (1,000 lbs.) | Cattle[2] (1,000 head) | Hogs[2] (1,000 head) |
|---|---|---|---|---|---|---|---|
| Alabama | 1,300 | 60,088 | 760 | 2,620 | 704 | 1,656 | 972 |
| Arizona | 858 | 1,056 | 835 | 2,352 | ..... | 1,014 | 29 |
| Arkansas | 4,420 | 11,799 | 1,350 | 402 | ..... | 1,388 | 416 |
| California | 7,744 | 15,750 | 1,950 | 28,672 | ..... | 4,203 | 340 |
| Colorado | 66,121 | 23,850 | ..... | 11,922 | ..... | 2,240 | 193 |
| Connecticut | ..... | 2,132 | ..... | 1,470 | 13,171 | 153 | 19 |
| Delaware | 775 | 9,734 | ..... | 2,200 | ..... | 53 | 35 |
| Florida | ..... | 16,762 | 16.5 | 4,548 | 29,061 | 1,596 | 393 |
| Georgia | 2,070 | 84,608 | 505 | 181 | 131,126 | 1,438 | 1,566 |
| Idaho | 35,031 | 5,440 | ..... | 42,400 | ..... | 1,401 | 147 |
| Illinois | 46,226 | 697,068 | 2 | 153 | ..... | 3,901 | 7,096 |
| Indiana | 41,844 | 356,796 | ..... | 1,762 | 11,200 | 2,103 | 4,801 |
| Iowa | 2,985 | 769,978 | ..... | 451 | ..... | 6,460 | 12,433 |
| Kansas | 290,640 | 90,270 | ..... | 207 | ..... | 4,473 | 1,142 |
| Kentucky | 5,191 | 83,153 | 8 | 884 | 357,508 | 2,115 | 1,400 |
| Louisiana | 1,218 | 13,558 | 505 | 392 | 320 | 1,818 | 279 |
| Maine | ..... | 440 | ..... | 34,040 | ..... | 200 | 21 |
| Maryland | 4,588 | 30,420 | ..... | 620 | 32,812 | 508 | 182 |
| Massachusetts | ..... | 1,674 | ..... | 1,346 | 5,492 | 153 | 117 |
| Michigan | 33,926 | 119,568 | ..... | 7,572 | ..... | 1,701 | 725 |
| Minnesota | 26,543 | 349,650 | ..... | 13,282 | ..... | 4,054 | 3,378 |
| Mississippi | 1,110 | 32,512 | 1,550 | 338 | ..... | 2,107 | 636 |
| Missouri | 37,648 | 224,031 | 470 | 560 | 4,650 | 4,099 | 3,893 |
| Montana | 79,517 | 3,556 | ..... | 1,302 | ..... | 2,133 | 151 |
| Nebraska | 85,712 | 340,471 | ..... | 2,840 | ..... | 5,175 | 2,427 |
| Nevada | 457 | 300 | 6 | 220 | ..... | 516 | 10 |
| New Hampshire | ..... | 561 | ..... | 342 | ..... | 99 | 13 |
| New Jersey | 1,617 | 12,350 | ..... | 3,995 | ..... | 198 | 160 |
| New Mexico | 4,546 | 1,848 | ..... | 426 | ..... | 1,174 | 54 |
| New York | 7,380 | 33,696 | ..... | 18,450 | ..... | 2,152 | 110 |
| North Carolina | 7,966 | 96,900 | 235 | 4,070 | 854,280 | 898 | 1,292 |
| North Dakota | 127,500 | 31,872 | ..... | 14,560 | ..... | 1,916 | 248 |
| Ohio | 52,500 | 260,984 | ..... | 3,666 | 21,895 | 2,272 | 2,653 |
| Oklahoma | 121,278 | 8,547 | 460 | 270 | ..... | 3,513 | 380 |
| Oregon | 26,542 | 4,485 | ..... | 7,700 | ..... | 1,435 | 184 |
| Pennsylvania | 15,782 | 79,360 | ..... | 8,700 | 52,700 | 1,951 | 525 |
| Rhode Island | ..... | 258 | ..... | 1,112 | ..... | 20 | 10 |
| South Carolina | 3,358 | 28,207 | 415 | 665 | 147,015 | 542 | 463 |
| South Dakota | 46,156 | 132,958 | ..... | 638 | ..... | 3,327 | 1,262 |
| Tennessee | 3,408 | 62,920 | 590 | 804 | 120,545 | 1,914 | 1,337 |
| Texas | 84,645 | 29,876 | 4,350 | 2,503 | ..... | 9,379 | 1,037 |
| Utah | 5,106 | 3,000 | ..... | 1,462 | ..... | 726 | 66 |
| Vermont | ..... | 2,958 | ..... | 323 | ..... | 431 | 11 |
| Virginia | 6,656 | 39,004 | 11 | 4,641 | 149,092 | 1,408 | 668 |
| Washington | 65,102 | 6,794 | ..... | 9,060 | ..... | 1,174 | 140 |
| West Virginia | 756 | 7,332 | ..... | 880 | 4,062 | 540 | 95 |
| Wisconsin | 1,680 | 162,035 | ..... | 8,970 | 24,740 | 4,296 | 1,767 |
| Wyoming | 5,541 | 2,059 | ..... | 704 | ..... | 1,116 | 29 |
| Total | 1,363,443 | 4,352,668 | 14,309 | 256,677 | 1,960,373 | 97,139 | 55,305 |

[1] Thousands of 500 lb. bales.   [2] Number on farms as of Jan. 1, 1961.

## Domestic Animals on Farms, Number and Value
*Source:* U. S. Department of Agriculture.

| January 1: | Number (thousands) | | | | | | Value of domestic animals (millions of dollars) |
|---|---|---|---|---|---|---|---|
| | Cattle | Dairy cows | Sheep | Swine | Chickens | Turkeys | |
| 1945 | 85,573 | 27,770 | 46,520 | 59,373 | 516,497 | 7,082 | 11,707 |
| 1951 | 82,083 | 23,722 | 30,635 | 62,852 | 442,657 | 5,091 | 22,165 |
| 1953 | 94,241 | 24,094 | 31,861 | 54,294 | 429,731 | 5,305 | 19,477 |
| 1957 | 94,502 | 22,916 | 30,840 | 51,703 | 390,137 | 5,799 | 11,132 |
| 1959 | 93,322 | 20,132 | 32,606 | 58,045 | 387,002 | 6,105 | 17,329 |
| 1960 | 96,236 | 19,527 | 33,170 | 59,026 | 369,484 | 5,633 | 15,206 |
| 1961 | 97,139 | 19,291 | 32,932 | 55,305 | 357,910 | 6,840 | 15,498 |

## Regional Economic Differences

*Source:* U. S. Depts. of Commerce and Labor and *Sales Management*, American Telephone and Telegraph Co. and Edison Electric Institute.

| State | 1950 % of employed in | | Income received per capita, 1960 | State income as % of total U. S. income 1960 | Est. retail sales* ($ millions, 1960) | % distribution of electric customers, Dec. 1960 | % households with telephone service, April 1960 |
|---|---|---|---|---|---|---|---|
| | Agriculture | Manufacturing | | | | | |
| New England.............. | .... | .... | $2,489 | 6.53 | $13,506 | 6.15 | 85 |
| Maine.................. | 9.3 | 34.2 | 1,894 | 0.46 | 1,123 | 0.61 | 72 |
| New Hampshire......... | 6.5 | 40.4 | 2,108 | 0.32 | 780 | 0.41 | 77 |
| Vermont............... | 18.2 | 24.6 | 1,893 | 0.18 | 474 | 0.24 | 74 |
| Massachusetts......... | 1.8 | 37.4 | 2,548 | 3.28 | 6,763 | 2.94 | 87 |
| Rhode Island........... | 1.5 | 44.0 | 2,217 | 0.47 | 1,005 | 0.50 | 80 |
| Connecticut........... | 2.9 | 42.6 | 2,871 | 1.82 | 3,361 | 1.45 | 92 |
| Middle Atlantic........ | .... | .... | ..... | 22.48 | 43,883 | 19.06 | 86 |
| New York.............. | 2.9 | 29.8 | 2,853 | 11.95 | 22,672 | 9.36 | 86 |
| New Jersey............. | 2.5 | 37.7 | 2,687 | 4.08 | 7,947 | 3.50 | 87 |
| Pennsylvania.......... | 4.1 | 35.5 | 2,282 | 6.45 | 13,264 | 6.20 | 85 |
| East North Central........ | .... | .... | 2,401 | 21.72 | 46,467 | 20.15 | 83 |
| Ohio.................. | 6.9 | 36.6 | 2,367 | 5.74 | 12,162 | 5.30 | 84 |
| Indiana............... | 11.6 | 34.8 | 2,198 | 2.56 | 5,629 | 2.66 | 79 |
| Illinois............... | 7.1 | 32.0 | 2,651 | 6.67 | 13,836 | 5.54 | 83 |
| Michigan.............. | 6.7 | 40.9 | 2,355 | 6.67 | 9,985 | 4.36 | 86 |
| Wisconsin............. | 18.6 | 30.6 | 2,177 | 2.15 | 4,855 | 2.29 | 83 |
| West North Central....... | .... | .... | 2,082 | 8.00 | 19,521 | 8.92 | 83 |
| Minnesota............. | 22.1 | 16.3 | 2,074 | 1.77 | 4,276 | 1.93 | 87 |
| Iowa.................. | 28.5 | 15.2 | 1,982 | 1.36 | 3,626 | 1.63 | 88 |
| Missouri.............. | 17.5 | 21.8 | 2,214 | 2.39 | 5,571 | 2.45 | 77 |
| North Dakota.......... | 44.2 | 2.9 | 1,826 | 0.29 | 791 | 0.34 | 74 |
| South Dakota......... | 40.5 | 4.9 | 1,919 | 0.33 | 832 | 0.39 | 75 |
| Nebraska............. | 29.6 | 9.2 | 2,113 | 0.74 | 1,832 | 0.90 | 85 |
| Kansas............... | 23.0 | 12.6 | 2,066 | 1.12 | 2,593 | 1.28 | 85 |
| South Atlantic......... | .... | .... | ..... | 12.09 | 28,387 | 13.58 | 66 |
| Delaware............. | 8.8 | 32.4 | 3,094 | 0.35 | 652 | 0.24 | 83 |
| Maryland............. | 6.1 | 24.9 | 2,415 | 1.87 | 3,626 ⎫ | 1.88 | ⎰ 80 |
| D. C. ................ | 0.2 | 7.3 | 3,000 | 0.57 | 1,433 ⎭ | | ⎱ 88 |
| Virginia.............. | 14.6 | 20.5 | 1,868 | 1.85 | 4,058 | 1.96 | 67 |
| West Virginia.......... | 9.8 | 18.9 | 1,692 | 0.78 | 1,644 | 0.98 | 64 |
| North Carolina........ | 24.6 | 27.9 | 1,584 | 1.80 | 4,360 | 2.34 | 58 |
| South Carolina......... | 26.1 | 27.9 | 1,403 | 0.84 | 1,908 | 1.17 | 53 |
| Georgia............... | 21.2 | 23.0 | 1,622 | 1.60 | 3,924 | 2.04 | 62 |
| Florida............... | 12.2 | 10.7 | 1,949 | 2.43 | 6,782 | 2.97 | 67 |
| East South Central........ | .... | .... | ..... | 4.42 | 10,829 | 6.28 | 59 |
| Kentucky.............. | 25.7 | 15.8 | 1,555 | 1.18 | 2,766 | 1.59 | 59 |
| Tennessee............. | 21.8 | 21.1 | 1,565 | 1.39 | 3,483 | 1.92 | 66 |
| Alabama.............. | 24.3 | 21.8 | 1,478 | 1.20 | 2,923 | 1.71 | 58 |
| Mississippi............ | 42.1 | 12.6 | 1,190 | 0.65 | 1,657 | 1.06 | 45 |
| West South Central....... | .... | .... | ..... | 7.67 | 18,889 | 9.38 | 67 |
| Arkansas.............. | 35.0 | 13.8 | 1,369 | 0.61 | 1,683 | 1.00 | 49 |
| Louisiana............. | 17.3 | 15.1 | 1,630 | 1.33 | 3,178 | 1.67 | 70 |
| Oklahoma............. | 20.5 | 9.8 | 1,859 | 1.08 | 2,520 | 1.40 | 73 |
| Texas................ | 16.0 | 13.5 | 1,943 | 4.65 | 11,508 | 5.31 | 69 |
| Mountain.............. | .... | .... | ..... | 3.55 | 8,847 | 3.70 | 72 |
| Montana.............. | 24.8 | 8.5 | 1,996 | 0.34 | 895 | 0.40 | 74 |
| Idaho................ | 26.8 | 9.2 | 1,824 | 0.30 | 881 | 0.39 | 73 |
| Wyoming.............. | 20.5 | 6.0 | 2,262 | 0.19 | 457 | 0.19 | 73 |
| Colorado.............. | 15.1 | 12.2 | 2,301 | 1.01 | 2,345 | 1.02 | 81 |
| New Mexico........... | 18.4 | 5.9 | 1,789 | 0.43 | 1,071 | 0.45 | 60 |
| Arizona............... | 14.7 | 8.8 | 1,983 | 0.65 | 1,693 | 0.65 | 60 |
| Utah................. | 12.4 | 12.2 | 1,936 | 0.43 | 1,039 | 0.44 | 84 |
| Nevada............... | 10.5 | 5.1 | 2,854 | 0.20 | 466 | 0.16 | 63 |
| Pacific................ | .... | .... | ..... | 13.54 | 29,502 | 12.17 | 81 |
| Washington............ | 9.3 | 21.2 | 2,334 | 1.66 | 3,752 | 1.69 | 81 |
| Oregon............... | 12.1 | 22.7 | 2,276 | 1.01 | 2,355 | 1.06 | 78 |
| California............. | 7.3 | 19.6 | 2,753 | 10.87 | 22,534 | 9.42 | 81 |
| Alaska............... | n.a. | n.a. | 2,724 | 0.15 | 217 ⎫ | 0.61 | ⎰ n.a. |
| Hawaii. ............. | n.a. | n.a. | 2,192 | 0.35 | 644 ⎭ | | ⎱ n.a. |
| Total.................. | 12.2 | 25.9 | 2,242 | 100.00 | 219,830 | 100.00 | 78 |

## Receipts and Expenditures of the National Government (in millions of dollars)

*Source:* U. S Treasury Department.

| Yearly average or year ended June 30 | Customs (including tonnage tax)[1] | Income and profits tax | Other (internal revenue) | Other receipts | Total receipts | Net receipts[2] | Department of the Army[3] | Department of the Navy | Interest on public debt | All other | Total expenditures[4] | Surplus (+) or deficit (−) |
|---|---|---|---|---|---|---|---|---|---|---|---|---|
| 1789–1800 | 6 | … | … | … | 7 | 7 | 2 | … | 3 | 1 | 6 | … |
| 1801–1810 | 12 | … | … | … | 13 | 13 | 2 | 1 | 4 | 2 | 9 | +4 |
| 1811–1820 | 16 | … | 2 | 3 | 21 | 21 | 11 | 5 | 5 | 3 | 24 | −3 |
| 1821–1830 | 20 | … | … | 2 | 22 | 22 | 4 | 3 | 4 | 5 | 16 | +6 |
| 1831–1840 | 20 | … | … | 10 | 30 | 30 | 8 | 5 | … | 11 | 24 | +6 |
| 1841–1850 | 24 | … | … | 3 | 27 | 27 | 13 | 7 | 1 | 11 | 32 | −5 |
| 1851–1860 | 54 | … | … | 6 | 60 | 60 | 16 | 12 | 3 | 29 | 60 | … |
| 1861–1865 | 69 | 17 | 55 | 20 | 161 | 161 | 548 | 65 | 35 | 36 | 684 | −523 |
| 1866–1870 | 179 | 51 | 171 | 46 | 447 | 447 | 128 | 28 | 135 | 86 | 377 | +70 |
| 1871–1875 | 186 | 8 | 113 | 30 | 337 | 337 | 40 | 23 | 112 | 112 | 287 | +50 |
| 1876–1880 | 146 | … | 117 | 25 | 288 | 288 | 37 | 16 | 100 | 102 | 255 | +33 |
| 1881–1885 | 202 | … | 132 | 33 | 367 | 367 | 43 | 16 | 64 | 135 | 258 | +109 |
| 1886–1890 | 216 | … | 127 | 32 | 375 | 375 | 40 | 18 | 44 | 177 | 279 | +96 |
| 1891–1895 | 177 | 4 | 150 | 26 | 353 | 353 | 50 | 29 | 30 | 255 | 364 | −11 |
| 1896–1900 | 185 | … | 207 | 43 | 435 | 435 | 111 | 48 | 38 | 260 | 457 | −22 |
| 1901–1905 | 260 | … | 255 | 44 | 559 | 559 | 133 | 86 | 28 | 288 | 535 | +24 |
| 1906–1910 | 311 | … | 257 | 56 | 628 | 628 | 169 | 113 | 23 | 334 | 639 | −11 |
| 1915 | 210 | 80 | 336 | 72 | 698 | 698 | 202 | 142 | 23 | 394 | 761 | −63 |
| 1918 | 180 | 2,314 | 872 | 299 | 3,665 | 3,665 | 4,870 | 1,279 | 190 | 6,358 | 12,697 | −9,032 |
| 1929 | 602 | 2,331 | 607 | 493 | 4,033 | 4,033 | 426 | 365 | 678 | 1,830 | 3,299 | +734 |
| 1933 | 251 | 746 | 858 | 225 | 2,080 | 2,021 | 435 | 349 | 689 | 3,150 | 4,623 | −2,602 |
| 1937 | 486 | 2,163 | 2,434 | 211 | 5,294 | 4,979 | 628 | 557 | 866 | 5,705 | 7,756 | −2,777 |
| 1939 | 319 | 2,189 | 2,972 | 188 | 5,668 | 5,104 | 695 | 673 | 941 | 6,657 | 8,966 | −3,862 |
| 1943 | 324 | 16,094 | 6,050 | 934 | 23,402 | 22,202 | 42,526 | 20,888 | 1,808 | 14,400 | 79,622 | −57,420 |
| 1945 | 355 | 35,173 | 8,729 | 3,493 | 47,750 | 44,762 | 50,490 | 30,047 | 3,617 | 14,549 | 98,703 | −53,941 |
| 1947 | 494 | 29,305 | 10,074 | 4,635 | 44,508 | 40,043 | 9,172 | 5,597 | 4,958 | 19,562 | 39,289 | +754 |
| 1949 | 384 | 29,482 | 10,825 | 2,082 | 42,773 | 38,246 | 7,862 | 4,435 | 5,339 | 20,730 | 40,057 | −1,811 |
| 1950 | 423 | 28,263 | 11,186 | 1,439 | 41,311 | 37,045 | 5,789 | 4,130 | 5,750 | 20,977 | 40,167 | −3,122 |
| 1951 | 624 | 37,753 | 13,354 | 1,639 | 53,369 | 48,143 | 8,636 | 5,863 | 5,613 | 18,163 | 44,633 | +3,510 |
| 1953 | 613 | 54,073 | 15,808 | 1,864 | 72,649 | 64,825 | 17,054 | 11,875 | 6,503 | 23,756 | 74,274 | −9,449 |
| 1956 | 705 | 56,632 | 18,476 | 3,006 | 78,820 | 68,165 | 9,274 | 9,744 | 6,787 | 23,986 | 66,540 | +1,626 |
| 1957 | 754 | 60,560 | 19,612 | 2,749 | 83,675 | 71,029 | 9,705 | 10,397 | 7,244 | 23,726 | 69,433 | +1,596 |
| 1958 | 800 | 59,102 | 20,877 | 3,196 | 83,974 | 69,117 | 9,776 | 10,913 | 7,607 | 25,203 | 71,936 | −2,819 |
| 1959 | 948 | 58,826 | 20,972 | 3,158 | 83,904 | 68,270 | 10,284 | 11,720 | 7,593 | 32,017 | 80,697 | −12,427 |
| 1960 | 1,123 | 67,125 | 24,650 | 4,064 | 96,962 | 77,763 | 10,294 | 11,642 | 9,180 | 27,052 | 77,233 | +1,224 |

[1] Beginning 1932, tonnage tax incl. in "Other receipts." [2] Net receipts equal total receipts less (a) appropriations to Federal old-age and survivors' insurance trust fund beginning fiscal year 1937 and (b) refunds of receipts beginning fiscal year 1931. [3] Formerly War Department. [4] Includes Air Force — 1949—$1,690,460,724; 1950—$3,520,632,580; 1951—$6,358,603,528; 1953—$15,085,227,952; 1956—$16,749,647,622; 1957—$18,361,000,000; 1958—$18,437,000,000; 1959—$19,083,300,000; 1960—$19,065,244,298.

## Money and Interest Rates
### (Per cent per annum)
*Source:* Federal Reserve Board.

| | Open market rate in New York City | | | Commercial loan rates | | |
|---|---|---|---|---|---|---|
| Year | Prime commercial paper, 4 to 6 months | Prime bankers' acceptances, 90 days | Call loans, renewal rate* | New York City | 7 other northern & eastern cities | 11 southern & western cities |
| 1929 | 5.85 | 5.03 | 7.61 | 5.76 | 5.82 | 5.93 |
| 1932 | 2.73 | 1.28 | 2.05 | 4.20 | 4.81 | 5.21 |
| 1933 | 1.73 | .63 | 1.16 | 3.43 | 4.46 | 5.04 |
| 1935 | .76 | .13 | .56 | 1.76 | 3.39 | 3.76 |
| 1938 | .81 | .44 | 1.00 | 1.69 | 2.75 | 3.26 |
| 1941 | .54 | .44 | 1.00 | 1.97 | 2.55 | 3.19 |
| 1945 | .75 | .44 | 1.00 | 1.99 | 2.51 | 2.73 |
| 1947 | 1.03 | .87 | 1.38 | 1.81 | 2.33 | 2.76 |
| 1949 | 1.48 | 1.12 | 1.63 | 2.37 | 2.71 | 3.10 |
| 1951 | 2.17 | 1.60 | 2.17 | 2.83 | 3.09 | 3.52 |
| 1953 | 2.52 | 1.88 | 3.06 | 3.47 | 3.68 | 4.04 |
| 1957 | 3.81 | 3.45 | 4.38 | 4.47 | 4.63 | 4.83 |
| 1958 | 2.46 | 2.04 | 3.38 | 4.12 | 4.34 | 4.67 |
| 1959 | 3.97 | 3.49 | 4.12 | 4.83 | 5.02 | 5.23 |
| 1960 | 3.85 | 3.54 | 4.75 | 4.67 | 5.15 | 5.45 |

* Average of daily quotations on the New York Stock Exchange.

## U. S. Money in Circulation by Denomination[1]
### (in millions of dollars)
*Source:* U. S. Treasury Department.

| Denomination | 1939 | 1940 | 1943 | 1945 | 1950 | 1951 | 1953 | 1957 | 1959 | 1960 |
|---|---|---|---|---|---|---|---|---|---|---|
| Coin | 590 | 648 | 1,019 | 1,274 | 1,554 | 1,654 | 1,812 | 1,789 | 2,304 | 2,427 |
| $1[2] | 559 | 610 | 909 | 1,039 | 1,113 | 1,182 | 1,249 | 1,302 | 1,511 | 1,533 |
| $2 | 36 | 39 | 70 | 73 | 64 | 67 | 72 | 77 | 85 | 88 |
| $5 | 1,019 | 1,129 | 1,973 | 2,313 | 2,049 | 2,120 | 2,119 | 2,102 | 2,216 | 2,246 |
| $10 | 1,772 | 2,021 | 5,194 | 6,782 | 5,998 | 6,329 | 6,565 | 6,615 | 6,672 | 6,691 |
| $20 | 1,576 | 1,800 | 5,705 | 9,201 | 8,529 | 9,177 | 9,819 | 9,985 | 10,476 | 10,536 |
| $50 | 460 | 538 | 1,481 | 2,327 | 2,422 | 2,544 | 2,732 | 2,696 | 2,803 | 2,815 |
| $100 | 919 | 1,112 | 2,912 | 4,220 | 5,043 | 5,207 | 5,581 | 5,575 | 5,913 | 5,954 |
| $500 | 191 | 227 | 407 | 454 | 368 | 355 | 333 | 283 | 261 | 249 |
| $1,000 | 425 | 523 | 749 | 801 | 588 | 556 | 486 | 391 | 341 | 316 |
| $5,000 | 20 | 30 | 9 | 7 | 4 | 4 | 4 | 3 | 3 | 3 |
| $10,000 | 32 | 60 | 22 | 24 | 12 | 12 | 11 | 9 | 5 | 10 |
| Total[3] | 7,598 | 8,732 | 20,449 | 28,515 | 27,741 | 29,206 | 30,781 | 31,082 | 32,591 | 32,869 |

[1] End of year.   [2] Paper currency only: $1 silver coins reported under coin.   [3] Includes unassorted currency.

## Public Debt of the United States
*Source:* U. S. Treasury Department.

| | Gross debt | | | Gross debt | |
|---|---|---|---|---|---|
| June 30— | Amount (in millions of dollars) | Per capita (dollars) | June 30— | Amount (in millions of dollars) | Per capita (dollars) |
| 1800* | $ 83 | $ 15.87 | 1945 | $ 258,682 | $ 1,848.60 |
| 1860 | 65 | 2.06 | 1947 | 258,286 | 1,792.05 |
| 1865 | 2,678 | 75.01 | 1950 | 257,357 | 1,696.75 |
| 1900 | 1,263 | 16.60 | 1951 | 255,222 | 1,653.42 |
| 1915 | 1,191 | 11.85 | 1953 | 266,071 | 1,666.81 |
| 1920 | 24,299 | 228.23 | 1954 | 271,260 | 1,670.23 |
| 1929 | 16,931 | 139.04 | 1955 | 274,374 | 1,660.38 |
| 1932 | 19,487 | 156.10 | 1956 | 276,200 | 1,624.71 |
| 1935 | 28,701 | 225.55 | 1957 | 270,527 | 1,582.00 |
| 1937 | 36,425 | 282.75 | 1958 | 276,343 | 1,587.60 |
| 1939 | 40,440 | 308.98 | 1959 | 284,706 | 1,607.35 |
| 1943 | 136,696 | 999.83 | 1960 | 286,331 | 1,586.07 |

* Figures for 1800 are as of Jan. 1.

## U. S. Aid to Foreign Countries

U. S. foreign aid totaled $74.4 billion from 1945 to 1960. Of this, $61 billions were grants; $35 billions for economic and $26 billions for military aid. The current rate of $4 billion per year is almost equally divided between economic and military aid.

The post-war period witnessed the highest outpouring of aid by one country (U. S.) in the history of the world. UNRRA provided needy people in war-stricken areas with emergency food, clothing and shelter. It was followed by the Marshall Plan (1948–52), which left European countries in better economic condition than they had been in 1938. This cost the U. S. $11 billions—$9 billions in grants and $2 billions in loans.

After the Marshall Plan the government began its military aid plan to Turkey, France, Japan, etc., as part of its over-all containment policy against Communism. In 1949 President Truman announced the establishment of the "Point IV" technical aid program. The least costly of U. S. aid programs, "Point IV" provides teams of technicians in underdeveloped countries to teach them efficient production methods and American know-how. The International Finance Corporation, inaugurated in 1956, helps finance industrial companies on the basis of one-half private and one-half IFC funds. The U. S. share of the corporation's $93 million capital is $35 million. Fifty-four other countries also contribute.

Loans for "sure-thing" development projects are made by the World Bank ($4.5 billions loaned since 1944) and the U. S. Export-Import Bank. These conservative agencies act only after careful study. Their repayment record is excellent.

In addition to government aid, private investors have supplied about 15 billions to set up factories, power plants and experimental ranches abroad.

Foreign aid given by the U. S. in 1960 totaled $4.0 billions, practically all of it in grants. The portions allocated for military and nonmilitary purposes included $1.4 billion to the Far East and Pacific; $1.4 billion to the Near East and South Asia; and $.4 billion to American Republics. In 1959 the U. S. set up the Inter-American Development Fund, which is scheduled to provide funds to aid development in Latin America. In 1961 an additional $500 million was voted for Latin-American improvement of health and living conditions.

The new Peace Corps is not expected to cost more than $5 million per year.

### Loans of the International Bank[1] (in millions of dollars)

*Source:* International Bank for Reconstruction and Development.

| Country | No. of loans | Original amount | Net amount[2] | Country | No. of loans | Original amount | Net amount[2] |
|---|---|---|---|---|---|---|---|
| Africa: Algeria and Sahara.. | 2 | $ 60.0 | $ 60.0 | Europe (contd.): Belgium.. | 4 | $ 76.0 | $ 76.0 |
| Congo.................. | 5 | 120.0 | 120.0 | Denmark.............. | 2 | 60.0 | 60.0 |
| East Africa.............. | 1 | 24.0 | 24.0 | Finland................ | 7 | 102.3 | 102.0 |
| Ethiopia................ | 4 | 23.5 | 23.5 | France................ | 1 | 250.0 | 250.0 |
| French West Africa....... | 1 | 7.5 | 7.1 | Iceland................ | 5 | 5.9 | 5.9 |
| Gabon.................. | 1 | 35.0 | 35.0 | Italy.................. | 7 | 299.6 | 298.0 |
| Kenya.................. | 1 | 5.6 | 5.6 | Luxemburg............ | 1 | 12.0 | 11.8 |
| Mauritania.............. | 1 | 66.0 | 66.0 | Netherlands........... | 10 | 244.0 | 236.5 |
| Nigeria................. | 1 | 28.0 | 28.0 | Norway............... | 5 | 120.0 | 120.0 |
| Rhodesia & Nyasaland.... | 5 | 146.5 | 146.5 | Turkey................ | 6 | 63.4 | 60.7 |
| Ruandi–Urundi......... | 1 | 4.8 | 4.8 | Yugoslavia............ | 4 | 90.7 | 90.7 |
| Sudan.................. | 1 | 54.5 | 54.5 | Western Hemisphere: | | | |
| Uganda................ | 1 | 8.4 | 8.4 | Brazil................. | 13 | 292.1 | 267.1 |
| Union of South Africa.... | 8 | 196.8 | 196.8 | Chile.................. | 8 | 106.6 | 106.2 |
| Asia: Burma............. | 3 | 33.4 | 33.4 | Colombia.............. | 17 | 178.7 | 178.6 |
| Ceylon................. | 2 | 26.5 | 23.9 | Costa Rica............ | 4 | 17.3 | 17.3 |
| India.................. | 25 | 700.6 | 678.3 | Ecuador.............. | 6 | 46.6 | 45.0 |
| Iran................... | 4 | 194.2 | 194.2 | El Salvador........... | 5 | 35.5 | 35.5 |
| Iraq................... | 1 | 12.8 | 6.3 | Guatemala............ | 1 | 18.2 | 18.2 |
| Israel.................. | 1 | 27.5 | 27.5 | Haiti................. | 1 | 2.6 | 2.6 |
| Japan.................. | 22 | 367.9 | 362.4 | Honduras............. | 4 | 19.9 | 19.9 |
| Lebanon................ | 1 | 27.0 | 27.0 | Mexico............... | 10 | 245.8 | 226.3 |
| Malaya................. | 1 | 35.6 | 30.6 | Nicaragua............. | 11 | 35.5 | 35.5 |
| Pakistan................ | 13 | 241.4 | 241.3 | Panama............... | 4 | 14.6 | 14.0 |
| Philippines............. | 1 | 21.0 | 18.5 | Paraguay............. | 1 | 5.0 | 4.5 |
| Thailand................ | 6 | 106.8 | 106.7 | Peru................. | 13 | 97.1 | 82.0 |
| United Arab Republic.... | 1 | 56.5 | 56.5 | Uruguay.............. | 4 | 71.0 | 71.0 |
| Australasia: Australia...... | 6 | 317.7 | 317.7 | | | | |
| Europe: Austria........... | 8 | 103.3 | 99.9 | Total.............. | 283 | $5,561.3 | $5,439.7 |

[1] As of March 31, 1961.   [2] Of the total $112.3 millions have been cancelled, refunded or terminated.

## U. S. Foreign Aid, 1945-59
### (in billions of dollars)
*Source:* U. S. Dept. of Commerce.

|                                  | 1945–50 | 1951–56 | 1957–59 | Total postwar period |
|----------------------------------|---------|---------|---------|----------------------|
| Net nonmilitary grants           | 17.1    | 11.0    | 4.8     | 32.9                 |
| Western Europe                   | 10.9    | 5.4     | 0.6     | 16.9                 |
| Asia, Africa and Near East       | 4.6     | 5.0     | 3.5     | 13.1                 |
| Rest of world                    | 1.6     | 0.6     | 0.7     | 2.9                  |
| Net government loans             | 9.4     | 1.5     | 0.9     | 11.8                 |
| Western Europe                   | 8.1     | 0.2     | —0.5    | 7.8                  |
| Asia, Africa and Near East       | 0.7     | 0.8     | 0.6     | 2.1                  |
| Rest of world                    | 0.6     | 0.5     | 0.8     | 1.9                  |
| Net military grants              | 1.8     | 16.6    | 7.2     | 25.6                 |
| Western Europe                   | 0.3     | 11.0    | 2.8     | 14.1                 |
| Asia, Africa and Near East       | 1.4     | 5.1     | 4.1     | 10.6                 |
| Rest of world                    | 0.1     | 0.5     | 0.3     | 0.9                  |
| Net total, grants and loans      | 28.3    | 29.2    | 12.9    | 70.4                 |

## Par Values of Member Currencies[1]
*Source:* International Monetary Fund.

| Member | Currency | U. S. cents per currency unit | Currency units per U. S. dollar | Member | Currency | U. S. cents per currency unit | Currency units per U. S. dollar |
|--------|----------|------------------------------|---------------------------------|--------|----------|------------------------------|---------------------------------|
| Australia | Pound | 224.000 | 0.446 429 | Indonesia | Rupiah | (3) | (3) |
| Austria | Schilling | 3.846 15 | 26.000 0 | Iran | Rial | 1.320 13 | 75.750 0 |
| Belgium | Franc | 2.000 00 | 50.000 0 | Iraq | Dinar | 280.000 | 0.357 143 |
| Bolivia | Boliviano | (3) | (3) | Israel | Pound | 55.555 6 | 1.800 00 |
| Brazil | Cruzeiro | (2) | (2) | Italy | Lira | 0.160 000 | 625.000 00 |
| Burma | Kyat | 21.000 0 | 4.761 90 | Japan | Yen | 0.277 778 | 360.000 |
| Canada[2] | Dollar | .... | .... | Jordan | Dinar | 280.000 | 0.357 143 |
| Ceylon | Rupee | 21.000 0 | 4.761 90 | Korea | Hwan | (3) | (3) |
| Chile | Escudo | .... | .... | Lebanon | Pound | 45.631 3 | 2.191 48 |
| China | Yuan | (3) | (3) | Luxemburg | Franc | 2.000 00 | 50.000 0 |
| Colombia | Peso | 51.282 5 | 1.949 98 | Mexico | Peso | 8.000 00 | 12.500 0 |
| Costa Rica | Colón | 17.809 4 | 5.615 00 | Netherlands | Guilder | 27.624 3 | 3.620 00 |
| Cuba | Peso | 100.000 | 1.000 00 | Nicaragua | Córdoba | 14.2857 | 7.000 00 |
| Denmark | Krone | 14.477 8 | 6.907 14 | Norway | Krone | 14.000 0 | 7.142 86 |
| Dominican Republic | Peso | 100.000 | 1.000 00 | Pakistan | Rupee | 21.000 0 | 4.761 90 |
| Ecuador | Sucre | 5.555 56 | 18.000 0 | Panamá | Balboa | 100.000 | 1.000 00 |
| Egypt | Pound | 287.156 | 0.348 242 | Paraguay | Guaraní | (4) | (4) |
| El Salvador | Colón | 40.000 0 | 2.500 00 | Peru | Sol | (5) | (5) |
| Ethiopia | Dollar | 40.250 0 | 2.484 47 | Philippines | Peso | 50.000 0 | 2.000 00 |
| Finland | Markka | 0.312 500 | 320.000 | Sweden | Krona | 19.330 4 | 5.173 21 |
| France | Franc | 20.255 | 4.937 06 | Syria | Pound | 45.631 3 | 2.191 48 |
| Germany, Federal Republic of | Deutsche Mark | 25.000 00 | 4.000 00 | Thailand | Baht | (3) | (3) |
| Greece | Drachma | (3) | (3) | Turkey | Lira | 11.111 1 | 9.000 00 |
| Guatemala | Quetzal | 100.000 | 1.000 00 | Union of South Africa | Rand | 140.000 | 0.714 286 |
| Haiti | Gourde | 20.000 0 | 5.000 00 | United Kingdom | Pound | 280.000 | 0.357 143 |
| Honduras | Lempira | 50.000 0 | 2.000 00 | United States | Dollar | 100.000 | 1.000 00 |
| Iceland | Króna | 2.631 58 | 38.000 0 | Uruguay | Peso | 13.513 5 | 7.400 00 |
| India | Rupee | 21.000 0 | 4.761 90 | Venezuela | Bolivar | 29.850 7 | 3.350 00 |
|        |          |         |          | Yugoslavia | Dinar | 0.333 333 | 300.000 |

[1] As of March 15, 1961.  [2] No fixed value.  [3] Par value not yet established.  [4] No transactions in the exchange market take place at rates governed by the par value last agreed with the Fund.  [5] In Nov. 1949, Peru introduced a new exchange system, but no agreement on a new par value has been reached.

## U. S. Exports of Leading Commodities

**(Value in millions of dollars)**

*Source:* U. S. Department of Commerce.

| Commodity | 1959 | 1960 |
|---|---|---|
| Crude materials:............................ | $ 1,913 | $ 2,586 |
| Coal.............................. | 378 | 354 |
| Cotton, unmanufactured.............. | 445 | 980 |
| Tobacco, unmanufactured............. | 346 | 378 |
| Soybeans.......................... | 282 | 335 |
| Crude petroleum.................... | 7 | 8 |
| Other.............................. | 455 | 531 |
| | | |
| Foodstuffs:............................ | 2,526 | 2,756 |
| Grains and preparations.............. | 1,420 | 1,650 |
| Wheat, including flour........... | 718 | 967 |
| Corn............................ | 286 | 281 |
| Fruits and vegetables............... | 385 | 389 |
| Meats and edible animal fats......... | 169 | 188 |
| Dairy products..................... | 96 | 87 |
| | | |
| Manufactures, including semimanufac- | | |
| tures:.......................... | 13,000 | 14,958 |
| Excluding type I and II "special | | |
| category'' items................ | 11,218 | 13,247 |
| Machinery....................... | 3,706 | 4,088 |
| Electrical machinery and apparatus... | 806 | 793 |
| Industrial machinery, total........ | 2,212 | 2,505 |
| Construction and mining machinery | 692 | 756 |
| Engines, turbines, and parts....... | 248 | 228 |
| Metalworking and machine tools ... | 312 | 368 |
| Tractors, parts and accessories....... | 355 | 387 |
| Automobiles, parts and accessories..... | 1,145 | 1,216 |
| Motor trucks and buses, commercial, | | |
| new............................ | 326 | 362 |
| Passenger automobiles, commercial, | | |
| new............................ | 224 | 235 |
| Chemicals and related products........ | 1,432 | 1,591 |
| Chemical specialties............... | 580 | 646 |
| Medicinal and pharmaceutical | | |
| preparations.................... | 284 | 275 |
| Industrial chemicals............... | 258 | 311 |
| Iron and steel products, including scrap | 540 | 852 |
| Petroleum products.................. | 395 | 421 |
| Textile manufactures................ | 634 | 694 |
| Cotton cloth, including duck[1]........ | 128 | 129 |
| Broad-woven fabrics of synthetic | | |
| fibers[1]........................ | 76 | 72 |
| Metal manufactures................. | 445 | 423 |
| Nonferrous metals and ferroalloys..... | 261 | 658 |
| Rubber manufactures................ | 326 | 372 |
| Paper and manufactures............. | 235 | 256 |
| | | |
| Including type II, but excluding | | |
| type I "special category'' items.... | 12,439 | 14,601 |
| Machinery....................... | 3,887 | 4,293 |
| Electrical machinery and apparatus... | 987 | 999 |
| Automobiles, parts and accessories..... | 1,258 | 1,293 |
| Chemicals and related products........ | 1,447 | 1,610 |
| Aircraft, parts and accessories ........ | 768 | 1,329 |
| Petroleum products.................. | 473 | 470 |
| Motor fuel, gasoline, and jet fuel..... | 98 | 72 |
| Lubricating oils.................... | 181 | 206 |
| Rubber manufactures[2]................ | 329 | 376 |
| Small arms and ammunition.......... | 229 | 229 |

[1] Excludes tire, pile, upholstery and drapery fabrics, and remnants. [2] Includes synthetic rubber.

## U. S. Imports of Leading Commodities

**(Value in millions of dollars)**

*Source:* U. S. Department of Commerce.

| Commodity | 1959 | 1960 |
|---|---|---|
| Crude materials:........................ | $ 3,097 | $ 3,014 |
| Crude petroleum.................... | 873 | 895 |
| Nonferrous ores and concentrates[1]...... | 323 | 363 |
| Manganese ore...................... | 75 | 82 |
| Copper ore and concentrates......... | 23 | 49 |
| Zinc-bearing ores.................. | 39 | 44 |
| Lead ore and flue dust.............. | 27 | 28 |
| Crude natural rubber................ | 383 | 322 |
| Iron ore.......................... | 312 | 322 |
| Wool, unmanufactured............... | 224 | 197 |
| Diamonds, rough, uncut, industrial... | 157 | 140 |
| Tobacco, unmanufactured............. | 111 | 115 |
| Undressed furs..................... | 96 | 96 |
| Other............................. | 620 | 564 |
| | | |
| Foodstuffs:............................ | 3,423 | 3,288 |
| Coffee............................ | 1,097 | 1,044 |
| Cane sugar........................ | 496 | 507 |
| Fruits, edible nuts and vegetables...... | 289 | 310 |
| Fish, including shellfish............. | 309 | 304 |
| Whiskey and other distilled spirits...... | 201 | 219 |
| Cocoa or cacao beans............... | 165 | 143 |
| Meat products..................... | 393 | 323 |
| Grains and preparations............. | 55 | 55 |
| Other............................. | 416 | 423 |
| | | |
| Semimanufactures:..................... | 3,306 | 3,092 |
| Nonferrous metals[2]................... | 848 | 805 |
| Copper........................ | 224 | 301 |
| Tin........................... | 103 | 88 |
| Aluminum...................... | 149 | 103 |
| Nickel metal and oxide............ | 148 | 144 |
| Lead.......................... | 75 | 63 |
| Zinc.......................... | 34 | 30 |
| Gas oil and fuel oil................. | 505 | 483 |
| Sawmill products................... | 337 | 310 |
| Woodpulp......................... | 315 | 305 |
| Diamonds, cut but not set........... | 86 | 78 |
| Iron and steel semimanufactures[3]...... | 279 | 208 |
| Industrial chemicals................ | 94 | 98 |
| Fertilizer materials................. | 62 | 59 |
| Other............................. | 779 | 746 |
| | | |
| Finished manufactures:................. | 5,168 | 5,258 |
| Paper and manufactures.............. | 743 | 763 |
| Newsprint...................... | 666 | 689 |
| Textile manufactures................ | 721 | 832 |
| Burlaps........................ | 91 | 95 |
| Cotton manufactures.............. | 202 | 252 |
| Wool manufactures............... | 171 | 208 |
| Fabrics of wool and mohair........ | 64 | 79 |
| Machinery, total................... | 656 | 711 |
| Agricultural implements and tractors.. | 169 | 135 |
| Vehicles and parts................. | 966 | 753 |
| Automobiles, new[4].............. | 735 | 514 |
| Aircraft........................ | 68 | 62 |
| Steel-mill manufactures............. | 345 | 298 |
| Clocks, watches, and parts........... | 74 | 71 |
| Iron and steel advanced manufactures.. | 112 | 125 |
| Other............................. | 1,546 | 1,705 |

[1] Includes ores of ferroalloying metals. [2] Includes ferroalloys. [3] Including pig iron and scrap. [4] Trucks and buses are excluded.

## U. S. Exports and General Imports by Countries and Areas

### (Value in millions of dollars)

*Source:* U. S. Department of Commerce.

| Area and country | Exports, including re-exports | | | General imports | | |
|---|---|---|---|---|---|---|
| | 1949 | 1959 | 1960 | 1949 | 1959 | 1960 |
| Total.......................................... | 11,936.0 | 17,621.4 | 20,500.0 | 6,592.0 | 15,207.2 | 14,653.9 |
| Canada........................................ | 1,925.5 | 3,824.5 | 3,808.1 | 1,550.8 | 3,042.0 | 2,901.7 |
| 20 American Republics........................ | 2,632.9 | 3,612.6 | 3,558.0 | 2,301.0 | 3,601.5 | 3,528.6 |
| Western Europe............................... | 3,973.0 | 5,450.1 | 7,155.6 | 909.0 | 4,522.7 | 4,183.9 |
| Other Areas.................................. | 3,404.6 | 4,734.2 | 5,978.3 | 1,831.2 | 4,041.0 | 4,039.7 |
| **NORTH AND SOUTH AMERICA** | (Excluding special categories)[1] | | | | | |
| Canada........................................ | 1,925.5 | 3,727.7 | 3,698.5 | 1,550.8 | 3,042.0 | 2,901.7 |
| 20 American Republics........................ | 2,632.9 | 3,514.7 | 3,454.8 | 2,301.0 | 3,601.5 | 3,528.6 |
| Mexico...................................... | 454.4 | 740.3 | 806.8 | 243.5 | 435.4 | 443.0 |
| Central American Republics.................. | 257.1 | 292.6 | 301.9 | 139.0 | 200.2 | 204.4 |
| Costa Rica................................ | 26.2 | 40.9 | 44.0 | 22.4 | 32.8 | 34.8 |
| El Salvador............................... | 24.8 | 36.9 | 42.4 | 40.2 | 37.4 | 32.2 |
| Guatemala................................. | 43.7 | 64.4 | 62.8 | 43.3 | 65.1 | 58.8 |
| Honduras.................................. | 32.7 | 32.4 | 34.4 | 15.2 | 24.6 | 33.6 |
| Nicaragua................................. | 14.8 | 27.7 | 29.6 | 6.7 | 15.4 | 20.8 |
| Panama, Republic of....................... | 114.9 | 90.3 | 88.8 | 11.2 | 24.9 | 24.1 |
| Cuba....................................... | 374.9 | 437.9 | 222.5 | 387.5 | 474.7 | 357.2 |
| Dominican Republic......................... | 36.9 | 59.8 | 41.3 | 24.4 | 75.2 | 110.9 |
| Haiti...................................... | 23.3 | 23.8 | 25.1 | 19.8 | 16.2 | 18.2 |
| Argentina.................................. | 123.5 | 231.0 | 349.0 | 97.5 | 125.8 | 98.7 |
| Bolivia.................................... | 34.6 | 23.5 | 24.5 | 48.5 | 7.6 | 8.7 |
| Brazil..................................... | 365.0 | 412.5 | 426.2 | 551.8 | 628.5 | 570.2 |
| Chile...................................... | 138.5 | 137.2 | 194.9 | 152.5 | 201.9 | 192.7 |
| Colombia................................... | 167.9 | 205.8 | 245.6 | 241.5 | 340.0 | 299.6 |
| Ecuador.................................... | 31.0 | 48.6 | 54.9 | 17.1 | 60.5 | 65.5 |
| Paraguay................................... | 7.5 | 8.0 | 8.8 | 5.7 | 8.5 | 8.5 |
| Peru....................................... | 81.9 | 121.9 | 141.1 | 40.2 | 118.9 | 182.2 |
| Uruguay.................................... | 33.4 | 33.3 | 61.8 | 54.0 | 18.4 | 20.7 |
| Venezuela.................................. | 503.0 | 738.7 | 550.2 | 278.1 | 889.9 | 948.3 |
| Netherlands Antilles....................... | 75.2 | 56.9 | 63.4 | 111.4 | 280.4 | 264.7 |
| **EUROPE** | | | | | | |
| Western Europe.............................. | 3,973.0 | 4,495.2 | 6,279.4 | 909.0 | 4,522.7 | 4,183.9 |
| Austria.................................... | 149.7 | 67.4 | 80.3 | 9.6 | 55.9 | 49.3 |
| Belgium and Luxembourg..................... | 300.9 | 350.3 | 435.4 | 94.2 | 416.0 | 364.2 |
| Denmark.................................... | 91.1 | 106.6 | 109.8 | 6.6 | 104.4 | 98.3 |
| France..................................... | 465.6 | 339.5 | 576.3 | 61.5 | 462.1 | 396.1 |
| Germany, Western[2]........................ | 817.3 | 747.5 | 1,067.0 | 45.5 | 920.0 | 896.8 |
| Greece..................................... | 152.2 | 51.5 | 60.3 | 15.7 | 34.0 | 33.4 |
| Iceland.................................... | 7.4 | 13.4 | 11.5 | 2.2 | 11.8 | 10.5 |
| Ireland.................................... | 60.7 | 30.3 | 38.6 | 1.7 | 26.2 | 28.3 |
| Italy...................................... | 451.3 | 407.8 | 642.4 | 70.9 | 387.6 | 393.1 |
| Trieste.................................... | 11.8 | 3.8 | 4.2 | .... | ([3]) | ([3]) |
| Netherlands................................ | 268.1 | 551.1 | 711.1 | 59.3 | 216.0 | 213.0 |
| Norway..................................... | 87.9 | 77.0 | 89.2 | 30.7 | 99.0 | 65.6 |
| Portugal................................... | 50.6 | 26.7 | 38.4 | 13.6 | 26.4 | 34.9 |
| Sweden..................................... | 81.0 | 207.3 | 299.9 | 54.4 | 184.6 | 170.2 |
| Switzerland................................ | 137.7 | 187.7 | 252.6 | 93.1 | 195.8 | 196.7 |
| Turkey..................................... | 82.9 | 123.7 | 123.9 | 55.7 | 82.2 | 60.2 |
| United Kingdom............................. | 662.0 | 884.9 | 1,406.9 | 227.6 | 1,137.2 | 992.6 |
| Finland.................................... | 26.0 | 43.6 | 56.3 | 27.4 | 48.8 | 52.2 |
| Spain...................................... | 49.2 | 152.7 | 188.5 | 24.3 | 77.5 | 87.7 |
| Yugoslavia................................. | 19.6 | 122.1 | 85.9 | 14.9 | 37.1 | 40.6 |
| Soviet Bloc................................ | 61.8 | 89.3 | 193.4 | 67.4 | 80.9 | 80.9 |
| **ASIA AND OCEANIA** | | | | | | |
| Western Asia................................ | 335.5 | 438.0 | 479.3 | 94.7 | 345.1 | 312.0 |
| Iran....................................... | 77.1 | 113.6 | 117.4 | 16.4 | 50.9 | 51.3 |
| Iraq....................................... | 12.2 | 27.5 | 37.0 | 5.7 | 34.5 | 27.2 |
| Israel[4].................................. | 76.8 | 116.5 | 125.0 | 6.0 | 27.5 | 27.3 |
| Kuwait..................................... | 22.3 | 46.6 | 40.6 | 38.8 | 158.8 | 123.4 |
| Lebanon.................................... | 39.7 | 39.7 | 42.9 | 2.1 | 3.3 | 3.5 |

| Area and country | Exports, including re-exports[1] | | | General imports | | |
|---|---|---|---|---|---|---|
| | 1949 | 1959 | 1960 | 1949 | 1959 | 1960 |
| Saudi Arabia | 81.6 | 49.6 | 43.3 | 19.9 | 56.4 | 65.2 |
| Far East | 1,823.7 | 2,630.1 | 3,614.2 | 1,214.5 | 2,595.1 | 2,674.7 |
| Southern, Southeastern and Eastern Asia | 1,650.1 | 2,307.5 | 3,140.4 | 1,089.1 | 2,257.5 | 2,408.7 |
| Malaya, Federation of | 36.2 | 8.7 | 18.0 | 195.5 | 159.4 | 156.3 |
| Ceylon | 17.1 | 23.1 | 14.3 | 34.8 | 34.7 | 38.7 |
| Hong Kong | 113.6 | 96.0 | 122.5 | 4.3 | 99.8 | 138.9 |
| India | 240.4 | 336.6 | 639.7 | 238.8 | 207.3 | 227.9 |
| Indonesia, Republic of | 119.4 | 65.4 | 83.2 | 120.4 | 190.4 | 216.1 |
| Japan | 466.1 | 965.1 | 1,328.4 | 82.0 | 1,028.7 | 1,148.6 |
| Korea, Republic of | 49.9 | 135.8 | 153.5 | 1.4 | 4.0 | 5.2 |
| Pakistan | 41.0 | 103.9 | 168.6 | 27.7 | 35.4 | 36.0 |
| Philippines, Republic of | 424.9 | 275.4 | 294.8 | 204.7 | 312.2 | 306.4 |
| Thailand (Siam) | 28.9 | 62.7 | 61.6 | 48.0 | 90.6 | 55.5 |
| Taiwan | 22.7 | 107.3 | 110.2 | 1.7 | 14.1 | 20.5 |
| Vietnam[5] | 16.2 | 56.4 | 53.1 | 1.1 | 10.7 | 4.4 |
| Australia | 124.4 | 266.0 | 386.5 | 97.6 | 196.9 | 142.0 |
| New Zealand | 40.1 | 48.3 | 74.5 | 24.4 | 135.6 | 119.0 |
| **AFRICA** | | | | | | |
| Africa, total | 590.8 | 686.5 | 760.8 | 337.5 | 588.9 | 535.0 |
| Algeria | 22.1 | 26.5 | 21.1 | 4.1 | 1.1 | 1.4 |
| Angola | 8.4 | 10.6 | n.a. | 7.2 | 37.2 | n.a. |
| Congo (former Belgian) | 46.5 | 30.8 | 26.3 | 36.3 | 107.1 | 68.3 |
| British East Africa, total[6] | 16.8 | 9.7 | n.a. | 22.4 | 47.8 | n.a. |
| Egypt | 50.0 | 105.9 | 150.4 | 9.4 | 16.8 | 31.6 |
| Ethiopia | 3.4 | 9.8 | 7.3 | 8.3 | 15.5 | 27.0 |
| Morocco | 27.8 | 39.0 | 33.6 | 5.8 | 10.4 | 10.4 |
| French West Africa, total | 33.2 | 26.0 | n.a. | 2.4 | 38.9 | n.a. |
| Liberia | 51.5 | 100.9 | 36.0 | 10.8 | 42.1 | 39.4 |
| Union of South Africa[6] | 257.4 | 220.7 | 277.2 | 116.4 | 117.1 | 107.9 |

[1] "Special category" exports not available by country of destination, except Canada, after 1949.   [2] Germany prior to 1952.   [3] Less than $50,000.   [4] Israel included Palestine prior to 1954.   [5] Vietnam, Cambodia, and Laos prior to 1958.   [6] South-West Africa and British High Commission territories of Bechuanaland, Basutoland, and Swaziland are included.

## Balance of Payments of the U. S., 1949-1960 (in millions of dollars)
*Source:* Department of Commerce, Office of Business Economics.

| Item | 1949 | 1950 | 1951 | 1957 | 1958 | 1959 | 1960 |
|---|---|---|---|---|---|---|---|
| Exports of goods and services, total | 16,061 | 14,427 | 20,333 | 29,168 | 25,606 | 25,683 | 29.065 |
| Military transfers under aid programs | 210 | 526 | 1,470 | 2,435 | 2,281 | 1,974 | 1,765 |
| Other goods and services, total | 15,851 | 13,901 | 18,863 | 26,733 | 23,325 | 23,709 | 27,300 |
| Merchandise, adjusted (excl. military expenditures) | 12,149 | 10,117 | 14,123 | 19,390 | 16,263 | 16,282 | 19,409 |
| Transportation | 1,238 | 1,033 | 1,556 | 1,999 | 1,672 | 1,646 | 1,816 |
| Travel | 392 | 419 | 473 | 785 | 825 | 902 | 968 |
| Income on investments | 1,395 | 1,593 | 1,882 | 2,881 | 2,922 | 3,043 | 3,205 |
| Other services | 677 | 739 | 829 | 1,306 | 1,643 | 1,836 | 1,902 |
| Imports of goods and services | 9,702 | 12,098 | 15,142 | 20,923 | 21,053 | 23,537 | 23,327 |
| Merchandise, adjusted (excl. military expenditures) | 6,879 | 9,108 | 11,202 | 13,291 | 12,951 | 15,294 | 14,722 |
| Transportation | 700 | 818 | 974 | 1,569 | 1,636 | 1,759 | 1,942 |
| Travel | 700 | 754 | 757 | 1,372 | 1,460 | 1,610 | 1,744 |
| Military expenditures | 621 | 576 | 1,270 | 3,165 | 3,412 | 3,109 | 3,048 |
| Other services | 802 | 842 | 939 | 1,526 | 1,594 | 1,765 | 1,871 |
| Balance on goods and services | 6,359 | 2,329 | 5,191 | 8,245 | 4,553 | 2,146 | 5,738 |
| Net unilateral transfers to foreign countries (−) | −5,837 | −4,533 | −4,962 | −4,753 | −4,619 | −4,398 | −4,254 |
| Military supplies and services | −210 | −526 | −1,470 | −2,435 | −2,281 | −1,974 | −1,765 |
| Grants and other government transfers | −5,106 | −3,563 | −3,106 | −1,775 | −1,798 | −1,849 | −1,856 |
| Private remittances | −521 | −444 | −386 | −543 | −540 | −575 | −633 |
| Direct investment [outflow of funds (−)] | −660 | −621 | −528 | −2,072 | −1,094 | −1,372 | −1,694 |
| Other U. S. capital | −545 | −800 | −696 | −2,102 | −2,721 | −1,356 | −3,271 |
| Foreign long-term capital [outflow (−)] | {−92{ | 53 | 182 | 634 | 24 | 555 | 297 |
| Increase or decrease (−) in foreign gold and liquid dollar assets | | 3,602 | 343 | −798 | 3,477 | 3,897 | 3,832 |
| Errors and omissions | 775 | −30 | 470 | 876 | 380 | 528 | −648 |

# LEADING NATIONS IN RICHES AND RESOURCES

*Sources:* Statistical Yearbook of the United Nations, 1960; Monthly Bulletin of Statistics, United Nations, 1961.

ℱ **The designation "n.d." means no data are available. In such cases, the relative rank of the nation is estimated.**

## Mineral and Metal Production

**ANTIMONY ORE (thousands of metric tons, metal content, 1959)**

1. China (mainland) . 15.0[1]
2. Un. of So. Africa . . 12.3
3. Bolivia . . . . . . . . . . 5.5
4. Mexico . . . . . . . . . . 3.3
5. Yugoslavia . . . . . . . 2.9
6. Czechoslovakia . . . 1.6
7. Australia . . . . . . . . 1.3
8. Algeria . . . . . . . . . . 1.2
9. Austria . . . . . . . . . . 0.8
10. Peru . . . . . . . . . . . . 0.7

[1] Estimate.

**BAUXITE (thousands of metric tons, 1959)**

1. Jamaica . . . . . . . . . 5,207
2. Surinam . . . . . . . . 3,430
3. France . . . . . . . . . . 1,745
4. British Guiana . . . 1,701
5. United States . . . . 1,700
6. U.S.S.R. . . . . . . . . . 1,100[1]
7. Hungary . . . . . . . . 938
8. Greece . . . . . . . . . . 900
9. Yugoslavia . . . . . . 815
10. Dominican Republic . . . . . . . . . . . . . . 771

[1] Estimate.

**CEMENT (thousands of metric tons, 1959)**

1. United States . . . 59,763
2. U.S.S.R. . . . . . . . . 38,781
3. West Germany . . 22,852
4. Japan . . . . . . . . . . 17,269
5. France . . . . . . . . . . 14,184
6. Italy . . . . . . . . . . 14,074
7. United Kingdom . 12,793
8. China (mainland) 12,270
9. India . . . . . . . . . . 6,936
10. Canada . . . . . . . . . 5,691

**CHROME (thousands of metric tons, 1959)**

1. Un. of So. Africa . . 301
2. U.S.S.R. . . . . . . . . . 300[1]
3. Philippines . . . . . . 294
4. Fed. of Rhodesia & Nyasaland . . . . . . . . 236
5. Turkey . . . . . . . . . . 206
6. India . . . . . . . . . . . . 38
7. Yugoslavia . . . . . . . 34
8. Argentina . . . . . . . 30[1]
9. Greece . . . . . . . . . . . 29
10. Cuba . . . . . . . . . . . . 23

[1] Estimate.

**COAL (millions of metric tons, 1960)**

1. U.S.S.R. . . . . . . . . . 513.6[1]
2. United States . . . . 372.2[1]

3. United Kingdom . 196.8[2]
4. West Germany . . 142.3[3]
5. China (mainland) 123.9[4]
6. Poland . . . . . . . . . . 104.4
7. France . . . . . . . . . . 56.0
8. India . . . . . . . . . . . . 52.7
9. Japan . . . . . . . . . . 51.1
10. Un. of So. Africa . . 38.0

[1] Including lignite. [2] Excluding No. Ireland. [3] Including Saar. [4] 1957.

**COPPER (thousands of metric tons, smelter, 1960)**

1. United States . . 1,147.8[1]
2. N. Rhodesia . . . . 566.4
3. Chile . . . . . . . . . . 506.4
4. Canada . . . . . . . . 378.0
5. U.S.S.R. . . . . . . . . 375.0[2]
6. West Germany . . 309.1[1]
7. Congo (Léopoldville) . . . . . . . . . . . 288.0[2]
8. Japan . . . . . . . . . . 249.6[1]
9. United Kingdom 217.2[1]
10. Belgium . . . . . . . . 211.2[1]

[1] Including secondary copper. [2] Estimate.

**GOLD (thousands of kilograms, 1959)**

1. Un. of So. Africa . 624.1
2. U.S.S.R. . . . . . . . . . 350.0[1]
3. Canada . . . . . . . . . 139.5
4. United States . . . . 50.9
5. Australia . . . . . . . . 33.8
6. Ghana . . . . . . . . . . 28.4
7. So. Rhodesia . . . . 17.6
8. Philippines . . . . . . 12.5
9. Colombia . . . . . . . 12.4
10. Congo (Léopoldville) . . . . . . . . . . 10.9

[1] Estimate.

**IRON ORE (millions of metric tons, 1960)[1]**

1. U.S.S.R. . . . . . . . . . 106.8
2. United States . . . . 89.0
3. France . . . . . . . . . . 66.9
4. Canada . . . . . . . . . 26.3[2]
5. Sweden . . . . . . . . . 21.3
6. Venezuela . . . . . . . 19.5
7. United Kingdom . 17.3
8. West Germany . . . 13.5
9. China (mainland) 11.0[3]
10. Luxembourg . . . . . 7.0

[1] Approximate metal content: U.S., 50%; U.S.S.R., 60%; France, 35%; Canada, 55%; United Kingdom, 30%; Venezuela, 65%; West Germany, 30%; China, unknown; Luxembourg, 30%. [2] Shipments only. [3] 1956 estimate.

**LEAD (thousands of metric tons, refined, 1960)**

1. United States . . . 378.0

2. U.S.S.R. . . . . . . . . 291.0[1]
3. Australia . . . . . . . 246.0
4. Mexico . . . . . . . . . 177.6
5. West Germany . . 147.7
6. Canada . . . . . . . . 144.0
7. France . . . . . . . . . 99.7[2]
8. Belgium . . . . . . . . 92.6[2]
9. United Kingdom . 92.5[2]
10. Yugoslavia . . . . . . 90.2

[1] Estimate. [2] Includes secondary lead.

**MANGANESE ORE (thousands of metric tons, metal content, 1959)**

1. U.S.S.R. . . . . . . . . 2,500
2. India . . . . . . . . . . 516
3. Brazil . . . . . . . . . . 421
4. Un. of So. Africa . . 360
5. Ghana . . . . . . . . . 257
6. Congo (Léopoldville) . . . . . . . . . . . 193
7. Morocco . . . . . . . . 185
8. Japan . . . . . . . . . . 118
9. United States . . . . 90
10. Mexico . . . . . . . . . 77

**PETROLEUM, CRUDE (millions of metric tons, 1960)**

1. United States . . . 347.7
2. Venezuela . . . . . . . 153.3
3. U.S.S.R. . . . . . . . . 147.6
4. Kuwait . . . . . . . . . 81.7
5. Saudi Arabia . . . . 61.7
6. Iran . . . . . . . . . . . 51.3
7. Iraq . . . . . . . . . . . 47.3
8. Canada . . . . . . . . . 25.9
9. Indonesia . . . . . . . 19.2[1]
10. Mexico . . . . . . . . . 14.4

[1] Estimate.

**PIG IRON AND FERRO-ALLOYS (millions of metric tons, 1960)**

1. United States . . . . 61.1[1]
2. U.S.S.R. . . . . . . . . 46.8
3. Germany . . . . . . . 25.9[2]
4. United Kingdom . 16.0
5. France . . . . . . . . . 14.3
6. Japan . . . . . . . . . . 12.3
7. Belgium . . . . . . . . 6.6
8. China (mainland) 5.1[3]
9. Czechoslovakia . . . 4.7
10. Poland . . . . . . . . . 4.6

[1] Excluding electric furnace production. [2] Including Saar. [3] 1956.

**SILVER (metric tons, 1959)**

1. Mexico . . . . . . . . 1,370.9
2. Canada . . . . . . . . 993.0
3. Peru . . . . . . . . . . 851.4
4. United States . . . 715.4[1]

| | | |
|---|---|---|
| 5. U.S.S.R. | ........ | 700.0[2] |
| 6. Australia | ...... | 468.9 |
| 7. West Germany | . | 352.3 |
| 8. Japan | ...... | 294.4 |
| 9. Congo (Léopold- | | |
| ville) | .......... | 148.0 |
| 10. Bolivia | ........ | 139.0 |

[1] Including Alaska.  [2] Estimate.

## TIN (thousands of metric tons, 1960)

| | | |
|---|---|---|
| 1. Malaya | ........ | 52.8 |
| 2. Indonesia | ........ | 22.9 |
| 3. Bolivia | ........ | 19.7 |
| 4. Thailand | ........ | 12.2 |
| 5. Congo (Léopold- | | |
| ville) | ............ | 10.2 |
| 6. China (mainland) | | 10.0[1] |
| 7. Nigeria | ........ | 7.8 |
| 8. Australia | ........ | 1.9 |
| 9. Burma | ........ | 1.4 |
| 10. {Un. of So. Africa .. | | 1.2 |
| {United Kingdom .. | | 1.2 |

[1] Estimate.

## URANIUM

World production data are generally unavailable, but U. S. output of uranium oxide was estimated at 10,-000 tons in 1957 as compared with 6,000 tons in 1956. A member of the AEC estimated the known world reserves of uranium concentrates at 25,000,000 tons in Dec., 1957. (In the U. S., an average of 5 lb. of uranium oxide is extrated from each ton of ore.) U. S. reserves of high-grade uranium were estimated at 200,000 tons in 1957; of lower grade, about 6,000,000 tons. The world's most important deposits of uranium are believed to be in the Congo (Léopoldville); in the Northwest Territories and elsewhere in Canada; in the Colorado plateau area of Colorado, New Mexico, Arizona, and Utah; and in Alaska. Deposits have also been found or reported in Australia, Bolivia, Brazil, Bulgaria, Burma, Ceylon, Chile, China (in Manchuria), Czechoslovakia, England, Ethiopia, Finland, France, Germany, Greece, Greenland, Hungary, India, Indonesia, Iran, Japan, Madagascar, Mexico, Mozambique, Nigeria, Norway, Panamá, Philippines, Portugal, Rumania, Sardinia, South Africa, Spain, Sweden, Switzerland, U.S.S.R., and Yugoslavia.

## ZINC (thousands of metric tons, 1960)

| | | |
|---|---|---|
| 1. United States | .... | 809.9[1] |
| 2. U.S.S.R. | ......... | 351.0[2] |
| 3. Belgium | .......... | 247.2[1] |
| 4. Canada | .......... | 236.4 |
| 5. West Germany | ... | 201.6 |
| 6. France | .......... | 180.7[1] |
| 7. Japan | .......... | 180.0[1] |
| 8. Poland | .......... | 175.2[1] |
| 9. Australia | ......... | 122.2 |
| 10. Italy | ............ | 79.4 |

[1] Including secondary zinc.  [2] 1956

# Agriculture

## BARLEY (thousands of metric-tons, 1959)

| | | |
|---|---|---|
| 1. China (main- | | |
| land) | .......... | 19,720[1] |
| 2. U.S.S.R. | ......... | n.d. |
| 3. United States | .. | 9,148 |
| 4. France | ........ | 4,931 |
| 5. Canada | ........ | 4,911 |
| 6. United Kingdom | | 4,080 |
| 7. Turkey | ........ | 3,300 |
| 8. West Germany | . | 2,834 |
| 9. India | ......... | 2,715 |
| 10. Denmark | ....... | 2,338 |

[1] Estimate.

## BUTTER (thousands of metric tons, 1960)

| | | |
|---|---|---|
| 1. United States | .. | 630.0 |
| 2. U.S.S.R. | ......... | 621.0[1] |
| 3. West Germany | .. | 405.6 |
| 4. France | ........ | 330.0[1] |
| 5. New Zealand | .... | 211.2 |
| 6. Australia | ....... | 198.0 |
| 7. East Germany | .. | 175.2 |
| 8. Denmark | ....... | 166.8 |
| 9. Canada | ........ | 144.0 |
| 10. Netherlands | .... | 99.7 |

[1] 1957.

## CATTLE (number in millions, 1958–59)

| | | |
|---|---|---|
| 1. India | ......... | 158.7[1] |
| 2. United States | ... | 96.6 |
| 3. Brazil | .......... | 71.4 |
| 4. U.S.S.R. | ........ | 70.8 |
| 5. China (mainland) | | 45.9 |
| 6. Argentina | ....... | 40.0 |

| | | |
|---|---|---|
| 7. Pakistan | ........ | 23.8 |
| 8. Mexico | ........ | 21.6 |
| 9. France | ......... | 18.5 |
| 10. Australia | ....... | 16.3 |

[1] 1955–56.

## CHEESE (thousands of metric tons, 1960 factory production)

| | | |
|---|---|---|
| 1. United States | .... | 668.4 |
| 2. France | ......... | 390.0[1] |
| 3. Italy | .......... | 329.0[1] |
| 4. Netherlands | ...... | 192.0 |
| 5. West Germany | ... | 163.2 |
| 6. U.S.S.R. | ........ | 136.2[2] |
| 7. Argentina | ....... | 116.3[3] |
| 8. Denmark | ........ | 114.0 |
| 9. United Kingdom | . | 111.6 |
| 10. New Zealand | .... | 93.2 |

[1] 1957.  [2] 1956.  [3] 1959.

## COTTON GINNED (thousands of metric tons, 1959)

| | | |
|---|---|---|
| 1. United States | .... | 3,170 |
| 2. China (mainland) | | 2,410 |
| 3. U.S.S.R. | ......... | 1,598 |
| 4. India | ........... | 682 |
| 5. Egypt | ........... | 457 |
| 6. Brazil | .......... | 449 |
| 7. Mexico | .......... | 360 |
| 8. Pakistan | ........ | 295 |
| 9. Turkey | .......... | 195 |
| 10. Sudan | .......... | 122 |

## FORESTS (millions of acres, latest data available, 1960)[1]

| | | |
|---|---|---|
| 1. U.S.S.R. | ......... | 2,275 |

| | | |
|---|---|---|
| 2. Brazil | .......... | 975 |
| 3. Canada | .......... | 835 |
| 4. United States | ... | 825 |
| 5. Fr. West Africa | . | 420[2] |
| 6. Fr. Eq. Africa | ... | 340[3] |
| 7. Indonesia | ....... | 300 |
| 8. Congo (Léopold- | | |
| ville) | ............ | 250 |
| 9. Sudan | .......... | 225 |
| 10. China | .......... | 210 |

[1] Of present or potential value.
[2] Area now comprising this former territory.  [3] Including Savannah.

## HOGS (number in millions, 1958–59)

| | | |
|---|---|---|
| 1. China (mainland) | | 160.0 |
| 2. United States | .... | 56.9 |
| 3. U.S.S.R. | ......... | 48.7 |
| 4. Brazil | .......... | 45.3 |
| 5. West Germany | ... | 14.7 |
| 6. Poland | .......... | 11.2 |
| 7. Mexico | .......... | 9.4 |
| 8. France | .......... | 8.4 |
| 9. East Germany | ... | 7.5 |
| 10. Canada | .......... | 6.9 |

## LAND, ARABLE (millions of acres, latest data available, 1960)

| | | |
|---|---|---|
| 1. U.S.S.R. | ......... | 585 |
| 2. United States | .... | 478 |
| 3. India | ............ | 325 |
| 4. China (mainland) | . | 250 |
| 5. Congo (Léopoldville) | | 120 |
| 6. Canada | .......... | 97 |
| 7. Argentina | ........ | 75 |

8. Fr. Eq. Africa[1] ..... 74
9. Pakistan ......... 60
10. France .......... 52

[1] Area now comprising this former territory.

## MEAT (thousands of metric tons, 1960)

1. United States ... 12,228
2. U.S.S.R. ........ 4,440
3. West Germany .. 2,316
4. France ......... 1,858[1]
5. Brazil ......... 1,843[2]
6. United Kingdom 1,716
7. Australia ...... 1,448
8. Argentina ...... 1,098[1]
9. Poland ......... 979
10. Denmark ....... 893

[1] 1959.  [2] 1957.

## MILK, COW'S (thousands of metric tons, 1960)

1. United States .. 55,752
2. U.S.S.R. ....... 46,000[1]
3. France ........ 20,600[2]
4. West Germany .. 19,236
5. United Kingdom 9,704
6. Canada ........ 8,364
7. India ......... 7,756
8. Australia ...... 6,600
9. Italy ......... 6,592[2]
10. Netherlands ... 6,072
11. East Germany .. 5,736
12. Denmark ...... 5,400
13. New Zealand ... 5,352
14. Argentina ..... 4,801[2]
15. Czechoslovakia . 3,444

[1] Estimate.  [2] 1957.

## OATS (thousands of metric tons, 1959)

1. United States .. 15,589
2. U.S.S.R. ....... n.d.
3. Canada ........ 6,445
4. France ........ 2,815
5. Poland ........ 2,483
6. United Kingdom 2,222
7. West Germany .. 2,020
8. Argentina ...... 983
9. Czechoslovakia .. 929
10. Sweden ........ 787

## POTATOES (thousands of metric tons, 1959)

1. U.S.S.R. ....... 90,000[1]
2. Poland ........ 35,700
3. West Germany .. 22,722

4. France ......... 12,903
5. United States ... 11,036
6. East Germany .. 11,011[1]
7. United Kingdom 6,929
8. Czechoslovakia . 6,334
9. Spain ......... 4,600
10. Italy ......... 3,954
11. Japan ......... 3,252
12. Netherlands ... 3,141

[1] Estimate.

## RICE (thousands of metric tons, 1959)

1. China (mainland) ......... 113,700[1]
2. India ......... 44,713
3. Japan ........ 15,626
4. Pakistan ...... 14,419
5. Indonesia ..... 12,402
6. Thailand ...... 7,275
7. Burma ........ 6,843
8. Vietnam ...... 5,311
9. Brazil ........ 4,082
10. Philippines ... 3,668

[1] 1958.

## RUBBER (thousands of metric tons, 1960)

1. United States ... 1,459[1]
2. Malaya ........ 722
3. Indonesia ...... 605
4. U.S.S.R. ...... n.d.
5. Thailand ...... 170
6. Canada ........ 162
7. Ceylon ........ 98
8. United Kingdom . 91
9. East Germany ... 86
10. West Germany .. 81

[1] Synthetic only.

## SHEEP (number in millions, 1958–59)

1. Australia ...... 152.7
2. U.S.S.R. ....... 129.9
3. China (mainland) 61.0
4. Argentina ...... 47.7
5. New Zealand ... 46.9
6. India ......... 39.2[1]
7. Un. of So. Africa 38.3[2]
8. United States ... 32.9
9. Turkey ........ 30.8
10. United Kingdom 27.6
11. Uruguay ....... 23.3[1]
12. Ethiopia ...... 21.8[2]
13. Brazil ........ 19.9

[1] 1955–56.  [2] 1956–57.

## SUGAR (thousands of metric tons, 1959)

1. U.S.S.R. ....... 6,513
2. Cuba .......... 5,964
3. Brazil ........ 3,108
4. India ......... 2,296
5. United States ... 2,025
6. West Germany ... 1,534
7. Philippines ..... 1,471
8. Mexico ........ 1,448
9. Italy ......... 1,389
10. Australia ..... 1,290
11. China (mainland) 1,130
12. France ....... 1,054
13. Un. of So. Africa 1,046
14. Puerto Rico .... 979
15. Poland ....... 973

## WHEAT (thousands of metric tons, 1959)

1. U.S.S.R. ....... 69,100
2. United States .. 30,704
3. China (mainland) ......... 28,950[1]
4. France ....... 11,544
5. Canada ....... 11,254
6. India ......... 9,929
7. Italy ......... 8,466
8. Turkey ....... 7,987
9. Argentina ..... 5,837
10. Australia ..... 5,307
11. Spain ........ 4,644
12. West Germany . 4,522
13. Yugoslavia .... 4,134

[1] 1958.

## WOOL (thousands of metric tons, greasy basis, 1959–60)

1. Australia ....... 766
2. U.S.S.R. ...... 347
3. New Zealand .... 256
4. Argentina ...... 197
5. Un. of So. Africa .. 145
6. United States ..... 143
7. China (mainland) 101[1]
8. Uruguay ....... 72
9. United Kingdom . 58
10. Turkey ....... 46
11. Spain ........ 38
12. India ........ 35
13. Brazil ........ 26
14. France ........ 25
15. Chile ......... 22

[1] Estimate.

# Industry, Trade, Communications

## AIRLINES (millions of passenger-kilometers, monthly average, 1960)

1. United States .. 5,212
2. United Kingdom . 530
3. France ........ 375[1]
4. U.S.S.R. ........ n.d.

5. Canada ........ 312[1]
6. { Australia ...... 217[1]
   { Brazil ....... 217[1]
8. Netherlands ..... 186[1]
9. Italy ......... 112
10. West Germany ... 107

[1] 1959.

## ALUMINUM (thousands of metric tons, 1960)

1. United States .. 2,139.6[1]
2. Canada ........ 543.6[2]
3. U.S.S.R. ...... 535.0[3]
4. West Germany . 302.6[1]
5. France ........ 279.2[1]

| | | |
|---|---|---|
| 6. Japan | | 181.2[1] |
| 7. Norway | | 165.4 |
| 8. United Kingdom | | 141.0 |
| 9. Italy | | 83.6 |
| 10. Austria | | 67.9 |

[1] Including secondary aluminum.
[2] 1959. [3] 1956.

## ELECTRICITY (millions of kwh., monthly average, 1960)

| | | |
|---|---|---|
| 1. United States | | 70,038 |
| 2. U.S.S.R. | | 24,300 |
| 3. West Germany | | 9,908 |
| 4. United Kingdom | | 9,904 |
| 5. Canada | | 9,501 |
| 6. Japan | | 8,259[1] |
| 7. France | | 5,376[1] |
| 8. Italy | | 4,524 |
| 9. East Germany | | 3,583 |
| 10. Sweden | | 2,900 |
| 11. Norway | | 2,580 |
| 12. Poland | | 2,441 |

[1] 1959.

## EMPLOYMENT INDEX (non-agricultural, 1960; 1953 = 100)[1]

| | | |
|---|---|---|
| 1. Yugoslavia | | 161 |
| 2. Japan | | 149 |
| 3. West Germany | | 132 |
| 4. Austria | | 124 |
| 5. Philippines | | 123 |
| 6. Canada | | 120 |
| 7. Poland | | 118 |
| 8. New Zealand | | 117 |
| 9. Australia | | 116 |
| Luxembourg | | 116 |

[1] Data on U.S.S.R. and satellites not available.

## EXPORT INDEX (1960; 1953 = 100)

| | | |
|---|---|---|
| 1. Israel | | 370 |
| 2. Japan | | 318 |
| 3. Yugoslavia | | 305 |
| 4. Norway | | 292 |
| 5. West Germany | | 261 |
| 6. France | | 256 |
| 7. Italy | | 244 |
| 8. Austria | | 221 |
| 9. Netherlands | | 187 |
| 10. Greece | | 180 |

[1] Volume of exports after eliminating price change effects; not including U.S.S.R. and satellites.

## INDUSTRIAL PRODUCTION INDEX (1960; 1953 = 100)

| | | |
|---|---|---|
| 1. Japan | | 261 |
| 2. Bulgaria | | 252 |
| 3. Yugoslavia | | 246 |
| 4. Pakistan | | 245 |
| 5. U.S.S.R. | | 212 |
| 6. China (Taiwan) | | 192 |
| Czechoslovakia | | 192 |
| 8. Italy | | 182 |
| 9. West Germany | | 180 |
| 10. France | | 173 |

## MERCHANT FLEETS (millions of gross tons, 1960)

| | | |
|---|---|---|
| 1. United States | | 24.8[1] |
| 2. United Kingdom | | 21.1 |
| 3. Liberia | | 11.3[2] |
| 4. Norway | | 11.2 |
| 5. Japan | | 6.9 |
| 6. Italy | | 5.1 |
| 7. Netherlands | | 4.9 |
| 8. France | | 4.8 |
| 9. East and West Germany | | 4.7 |
| 10. Greece | | 4.5 |
| 11. Panamá | | 4.2[2] |
| 12. Sweden | | 3.6 |

[1] Including Great Lakes shipping.
[2] Mostly vessels of other nations, flying under "flag of convenience," practically tax free.

## MOTOR VEHICLES (production in thousands, 1959)

| | | |
|---|---|---|
| 1. United States | | 6,729 |
| 2. West Germany | | 1,718 |
| 3. United Kingdom | | 1,560 |
| 4. France | | 1,283 |
| 5. U.S.S.R. | | 505 |
| 6. Italy | | 501 |
| 7. Japan | | 263 |
| 8. Canada | | 243 |
| 9. Australia | | 141[1] |
| 10. Sweden | | 112 |

[1] 1958.

## RAILWAYS (millions of metric tons carried, monthly average, 1960)

| | | |
|---|---|---|
| 1. United States | | 175.0[1] |
| 2. U.S.S.R. | | 114.3[2] |
| 3. West Germany | | 24.9 |

| | | |
|---|---|---|
| 4. Poland | | 23.9 |
| 5. United Kingdom | | 20.8 |
| 6. East Germany | | 19.8 |
| 7. France | | 18.9 |
| 8. Czechoslovakia | | 16.2 |
| 9. Japan | | 15.5 |
| 10. Canada | | 13.3[1] |

[1] Estimate. [2] 1956.

## RETAIL TRADE INDEX (1960; 1953 = 100)[1]

| | | |
|---|---|---|
| 1. Argentina | | 538 |
| 2. Yugoslavia | | 292 |
| 3. Japan | | 264 |
| 4. France | | 236 |
| 5. Rumania | | 200[2] |
| 6. Mexico | | 198[2] |
| 7. Hungary | | 187 |
| 8. Poland | | 183 |
| 9. Austria | | 175 |
| 10. Australia | | 166 |

[1] Internal commerce, principal nations only; data on U.S.S.R. unavailable. [2] Estimate.

## STEEL, CRUDE (millions of metric tons, 1960)

| | | |
|---|---|---|
| 1. United States | | 90.1 |
| 2. U.S.S.R. | | 65.3 |
| 3. West Germany | | 34.1[1] |
| 4. United Kingdom | | 24.7 |
| 5. Japan | | 22.1 |
| 6. France | | 17.3 |
| 7. Italy | | 8.2 |
| 8. Belgium | | 7.2 |
| 9. Czechoslovakia | | 6.8 |
| 10. Poland | | 6.7 |
| 11. Canada | | 5.3 |
| 12. China (mainland) | | 4.5[2] |
| 13. Luxembourg | | 4.1 |

[1] Including Saar. [2] 1956.

## TELEPHONES (number per 100 population, 1959)

| | | |
|---|---|---|
| 1. United States | | 36.2 |
| 2. Sweden | | 33.9 |
| 3. Switzerland | | 29.5 |
| 4. New Zealand | | 28.9 |
| 5. Canada | | 28.8 |
| 6. Denmark | | 22.4 |
| 7. Iceland | | 21.7 |
| 8. Australia | | 20.0 |
| 9. Norway | | 19.5 |
| 10. United Kingdom | | 14.9 |

## America's Tallest Buildings

| City | Building | Stories | Height, ft. | City | Building | Stories | Height, ft. |
|---|---|---|---|---|---|---|---|
| New York | Empire State | 102 | 1,250 | New York | 500 Fifth Avenue | 60 | 700 |
| New York | Chrysler | 77 | 1,046 | New York | Metropolitan Life | 50 | 700 |
| New York | 60 Wall Tower | 66 | 950 | New York | Chanin | 56 | 680 |
| New York | Bk. of Manhattan | 71 | 927 | New York | Lincoln | 53 | 673 |
| New York | R. C. A. | 70 | 850 | New York | Irving Trust | 50 | 654 |
| New York | Chase-Manhattan | 64 | 813 | New York | General Electric | 50 | 641 |
| New York | Woolworth | 60 | 792 | New York | Waldorf-Astoria | 47 | 625 |
| New York | City Bank-Farmers Trust | 57 | 741 | New York | 10 E. 40th St. | 48 | 621 |
| New York | Union Carbide | 52 | 720 | New York | New York Life | 40 | 617 |
| Cleveland | Terminal Tower | 52 | 708 | New York | Singer | 47 | 612 |

# Value of Exports and Imports

### (in millions of U. S. dollars)

*Sources: Statistical Yearbook*, United Nations, and *Monthly Bulletin of Statistics*, United Nations.

| Country | Exports[1] | Imports[1] | Country | Exports[1] | Imports[1] |
|---|---|---|---|---|---|
| Afghanistan | 49[2] | 58[2] | Ireland | 426 | 632 |
| Albania | 29[3] | 78[3] | Israel | 221 | 496 |
| Argentina | 1,079 | 1,189 | Italy | 3,669 | 4,730 |
| Australia | 1,967 | 2,367 | Japan | 4,055 | 4,492 |
| Austria | 1,120 | 1,416 | Jordan | 10 | 113 |
| Belgium–Luxembourg | 3,775 | 3,957 | Korea, South | 19 | 283 |
| Bolivia | 51 | 67[4] | Laos | 2[4] | 13[4] |
| Brazil | 1,269 | 1,462 | Lebanon | 40[4] | 261[4] |
| Bulgaria | 470[4] | 581[4] | Liberia | 65[4] | 43[4] |
| Burma | 224[4] | 265 | Malaya | 955 | 703 |
| Cambodia | 60 | 70[4] | Mexico | 760 | 1,187 |
| Canada | 5,563 | 5,667 | Morocco | 354 | 413 |
| Ceylon | 385 | 412 | Netherlands | 4,028 | 4,531 |
| Chile | 497[4] | 413[2] | New Zealand | 846 | 781 |
| China—mainland | 1,005[5] | 1,010[5] | Nicaragua | 65[4] | 67[4] |
| China—Taiwan (Formosa) | 157[4] | 231[4] | Norway | 880 | 1,461 |
| Colombia | 465 | 516 | Pakistan | 393 | 652 |
| Costa Rica | 88 | 110 | Panamá | 31 | 109 |
| Cuba | 675[4] | 808[3] | Paraguay | 31[4] | 26[4] |
| Czechoslovakia | 1,727[4] | 1,602[4] | Peru | 312[4] | 294[4] |
| Denmark | 1,485 | 1,802 | Philippines | 551 | 591 |
| Dominican Republic | 130[4] | 118[4] | Poland | 1,145[4] | 1,420[4] |
| Ecuador | 150 | 103 | Portugal | 326 | 544 |
| Egypt | 550 | 632 | Rumania | 430[3] | 415[3] |
| Eritrea and Ethiopia | 68[4] | 84[4] | Salvador, El | 117 | 123 |
| Finland | 989 | 1,062 | Spain | 501[4] | 795[4] |
| France | 6,864 | 6,281 | Sweden | 2,567 | 2,876 |
| Germany (East) | 2,122[4] | 1,918[4] | Switzerland | 1,880 | 2,243 |
| Germany (West) | 11,412 | 1,092 | Syria | 98[4] | 176[4] |
| Ghana | 286[4] | 317[4] | Thailand | 410 | 448 |
| Greece | 203 | 702 | Tunisia | 120 | 191 |
| Guatemala | 116 | 138 | Turkey | 321 | 468 |
| Haiti | 28[4] | 30[4] | Union of South Africa | 1,225 | 1,555 |
| Honduras | 69[4] | 62[4] | United Kingdom | 9,955 | 12,433 |
| Hungary | 766 | 790 | United States | 20,325 | 14,709 |
| Iceland | 67 | 89 | Uruguay | 129 | 244 |
| India | 1,366 | 1,903 | U.S.S.R. | 5,441[4] | 5,073[4] |
| Indonesia | 872[4] | 459[4] | Venezuela | 2,369[4] | 1,408[4] |
| Iran | 111[6] | 572[6] | Vietnam | 75[4] | 225[4] |
| Iraq | 606[4] | 326[4] | Yugoslavia | 567 | 827 |

[1] Figures are for 1960 unless otherwise indicated.   [2] 1948.   [3] 1958.   [4] 1959.   [5] Estimate.   [6] 1954.

---

# United Nations Headquarters

The first regular session of the General Assembly held at Central Hall, Westminster, London, voted that Interim Headquarters of the Organization should be located in New York. From London the U. N. moved to Hunter College in the Bronx. In August 1946, an Interim Headquarters was set up at Lake Success on Long Island, in a part of the Sperry Gyroscope Co.'s plant. The New York City building at Flushing Meadows, site of the 1939 World's Fair, was converted for the use of the General Assembly. The search for a permanent home ended in December 1946, when the General Assembly accepted an offer from John D. Rockefeller, Jr., of $8,500,000 for the purchase of the present Headquarters site—an 18-acre tract alongside Manhattan's East River. The U. S. Government loaned the U. N. $65,000,000 interest free, which is being repaid in annual installments.

Architectural plans drawn up by an international Board of Design were approved by the Assembly, and construction began in September 1948. By mid-1950, the 39-story Secretariat Building was ready for occupancy, and in the spring of 1951 "United Nations, New York" became the Organization's permanent address.

# World Education Statistics

*Source: Statistical Yearbook, United Nations, 1960.*

NOTE: where figures are not available, the abbreviation n.a. is used; where the illiteracy rate is very **slight** the abbreviation negl. is used.

| Country | Illiteracy rate, %[1] | Number of schools | Colleges and universities | Total students[2] | Country | Illiteracy rate, % | Number of schools | Colleges and universities | Total students[2] |
|---|---|---|---|---|---|---|---|---|---|
| Afghanistan.... | n.a. | 698[3] | 4[3] | 121,822[4] | Japan......... | negl. | 53,012[11] | 534 | 22,898,664[11] |
| Albania........ | high | 3,337[11] | 2[11] | 247,972[11] | Jordan......... | 50.0[16] | 1,341[12] | 5 | 266,634[12] |
| Argentina...... | 8 | 22,032[11] | 8[3] | 3,601,911[11] | Korea, South.. | n.a. | 7,048[11] | 26 | 4,632,367[11] |
| Australia...... | negl.[5] | 11,007[12] | 9[3] | 2,163,339[11] | Kuwait........ | n.a. | 98[11] | 2 | 32,791[11] |
| Austria........ | negl. | 7,389[11] | 14[11] | 1,113,606[11] | Laos.......... | 63.2[16] | 1,474[11] | 1 | 103,501[11] |
| Belgium........ | 3.1[6] | 18,352[12] | 19[12] | 1,840,252[12] | Lebanon....... | n.a. | 2,166 | 7 | 260,044 |
| Bolivia........ | 69.2 | 884[12] | 5[7] | 343,081[12] | Liberia........ | 95.0[4] | 580[12] | 3 | 53,979[12] |
| Brazil.......... | 51.0 | 91,450[11] | 11[11] | 7,052,465[11] | Luxemburg..... | negl. | 67 | 1 | 42,527[11] |
| Bulgaria....... | 24.2[7] | 13,328[11] | 32[12] | 1,555,701[11] | Malaya........ | 61.7[6] | 5,228[11] | 4[11] | 1,198,392 |
| Burma......... | 42.9 | 12,546[11] | 7[11] | 1,946,316[11] | Mexico........ | 38.0[14] | 32,437[12] | 135 | 4,468,354[12] |
| Cambodia...... | n.a. | 3,626 | 3 | 551,340[12] | Morocco...... | n.a. | n.a. | 6 | 670,175[12] |
| Canada........ | negl. | 35,961[12] | 120 | 3,733,304[12] | Nepal......... | n.a. | 1,322[8] | 14 | 73,400[8] |
| Ceylon........ | 42.0[8] | 7,422[11] | 3[11] | 1,973,519[11] | Netherlands... | negl. | 15,500[11] | 11 | 2,589,561[11] |
| Chile......... | 24.0[7] | 7,824[12] | 5 | 1,287,703[12] | New Zealand.. | 60 | 2,771[11] | 6 | 536,911[11] |
| China, mainland | n.a. | 512,761[4] | 194 | 58,266,136[4] | Nicaragua..... | negl. | 3,593[4] | 1 | 140,348[11] |
| China, Taiwan (Formosa).... | n.a. | 2,512[11] | 22 | 2,024,047[11] | Norway....... | negl.[8] | 7,405[12] | 8 | 595,841[12] |
| Colombia....... | 37.0[7] | 20,220[11] | 18 | 1,770,075[11] | Pakistan...... | 86.8[3] | 49,475 | 163 | 5,701,500[12] |
| Costa Rica..... | 21.0[14] | 1,975[10] | 2 | 222,170[10] | Panama....... | 28.0[14,17] | 1,233[12] | 1 | 170,826[12] |
| Cuba.......... | 25.0 | 10,207[13] | 7 | 892,678[13] | Paraguay...... | 60.0 | 4,038[10] | 1 | 330,269[10] |
| Czechoslovakia . | 1.7[9] | 19,567[11] | 27 | 2,544,007[11] | Peru.......... | 50.0 | 14,484[11] | 7 | 1,517,409[11] |
| Denmark....... | negl. | 3,688[11] | 12 | 792,852[11] | Philippines.... | 37.8 | 31,497[12] | n.a. | 4,625,826[12] |
| Dominican Rep.. | 57.0[9] | 4,903[10] | 1 | 517,511[10] | Poland....... | n.a. | 168,488[11] | 57 | 5,783,101[11] |
| Ecuador....... | 44.0 | 5,132[12] | 7 | 584,778[12] | Portugal...... | 41.7[14] | 17,793[12] | 13 | 1,037,285[12] |
| Egypt......... | 74.5[6] | 8,788[11] | 26[11] | 2,938,716[11] | Puerto Rico.... | 25.6[14] | 2,363[12] | 4 | 731,699[12] |
| Ethiopia–Eritrea | 70.0[11] | 607[11] | 2 | 166,909[11] | Rumania...... | 23.1[8] | 23,639[11] | 91 | 2,636,692[11] |
| Finland........ | negl. | 7,453[4] | 11 | 880,946[11] | El Salvador.... | 58.0[14] | 2,732[11] | 1 | 307,327[11] |
| France......... | 3.3 | 89,762[8] | 151 | 8,559,061[11] | Saudi Arabia.. | n.a. | 582[12] | 1 | 83,280[11] |
| Germany....... | negl. | 58,049[11] | 106 | 11,508,822[11] | Spain......... | 14.2[6] | 10,540[8] | 25 | 4,250,386[11] |
| Ghana........ | n.a. | 5,038[11] | 2 | 634,011[11] | Sweden....... | negl. | 8,916[9] | 15 | 1,292,645[11] |
| Greece........ | 23.5[4] | 11,684[12] | 8 | 1,244,112[12] | Switzerland... | negl. | (18) | 9 | 730,502[5,6] |
| Guatemala..... | 72.0[14] | 4,038[18] | 1 | 329,269[10] | Syria......... | n.a. | 3,315[12] | 1 | 449,239[12] |
| Haiti......... | 90.0 | 1,494[12] | 13 | 217,444[12] | Thailand...... | 46.3[6] | 24,789[12] | 5 | 3,756,571[12] |
| Honduras...... | 65.0[14] | 2,501[12] | 1 | 161,285[12] | Tunisia....... | n.a. | 1,886[12] | 6 | 349,986[12] |
| Hungary....... | 5.9[15] | 9,410[12] | 31 | 1,648,166[11] | Turkey....... | 65.4[14] | 20,572[12] | 13 | 2,670,293[12] |
| Iceland........ | negl. | 249 | 1 | 29,025[4] | Union of South Africa....... | 70.9[14] | 10,281[12] | 10 | 2,036,027[12] |
| India......... | 82.1[4] | 326,181[11] | 1,129 | 32,057,398[11] | United Kg'dm.. | negl. | 39,544[12] | 26 | 8,776,954[12] |
| Indonesia...... | 47.0[8] | 37,782[11] | 87 | 8,014,438[11] | United States.. | negl. | 124,685 | 681 | 46,259,000[19] |
| Iran.......... | high | 9,476[11] | 1 | 1,397,051[11] | Uruguay...... | 35.0 | 2,442[12] | 1 | 390,754[12] |
| Iraq.......... | n.a. | 2,831[11] | 12 | 652,887[11] | U.S.S.R...... | 10.0[16] | 238,946[11] | 765 | 35,979,800[11] |
| Ireland........ | negl. | 5,651[12] | 3 | 617,861[12] | Venezuela..... | 60.0 | 7,346 | 5 | 852,382[12] |
| Israel......... | 6.9[14] | 3,590[11] | 12 | 517,315[11] | Vietnam...... | n.a. | 6,387 | 18 | 1,222,604[11] |
| Italy......... | 10.0[8] | 68,377[12] | 34 | 7,990,308[12] | Yemen........ | n.a. | 2,159[5,6] | 1 | 94,697[5,6] |
| | | | | | Yugoslavia.... | 25.0[4] | 15,787[12] | 63 | 2,731,029[12] |

[1] For 10 years and older. [2] Includes colleges and universities. [3] 1954. [4] 1955. [5] For European population. [6] 1947. [7] 1953. [8] 1946. [9] 1956. [10] 1959. [11] 1958. [12] 1957. [13] For 6 years and older. [14] 1950. [15] 1948. [16] Estimate. [17] Excluding tribal Indians. [18] Incomplete. [19] 1960.

# Area and Population by Country

| Country | Area, sq. mi. | Population | Year[1] | Country | Area, sq. mi. | Population | Year[1] |
|---|---|---|---|---|---|---|---|
| Afghanistan............. | 250,966 | 13,000,000 | 1957E | Lebanon.............. | 4,015 | 1,550,000 | 1958E |
| Albania................ | 11,100 | 1,556,000 | 1959E | Liberia............... | 43,000 | 1,250,000 | 1956E |
| Argentina.............. | 1,072,477 | 20,956,000 | 1959E | Libya................. | 679,360 | 1,153,000 | 1958C |
| Australia.............. | 2,974,583 | 10,281,000 | 1960E | Liechtenstein.......... | 61 | 16,274 | 1959E |
| Austria................ | 32,374 | 7,049,000 | 1959E | Lithuania[3]............ | 25,174 | 2,713,000 | 1959E |
| Belgium............... | 11,779 | 9,104,000 | 1959E | Luxembourg........... | 998 | 324,000 | 1959E |
| Bhutan................ | 19,305 | 700,000 | 1959E | Malagasy Rep.......... | 227,800 | 5,071,000 | 1957E |
| Bolivia................ | 424,163 | 3,462,000 | 1960E | Malaya, Federation of... | 50,700 | 6,698,000 | 1959E |
| Brazil................. | 3,287,204 | 65,743,000 | 1960E | Maldive Islands........ | 115 | 82,000 | 1958E |
| Bulgaria............... | 42,729 | 7,798,000 | 1959C | Mali, Rep. of.......... | 464,874 | 3,700,000 | 1958E |
| Burma................. | 261,757 | 20,662,000 | 1960E | Mauritania, Islamic | | | |
| Cambodia.............. | 67,607 | 4,740,000 | 1958E | Rep. of............. | 419,230 | 623,800 | 1959E |
| Cameroun.............. | 166,796 | 3,200,000 | 1959E | Mexico............... | 759,178 | 34,625,903 | 1960PC |
| Canada................ | 3,851,116 | 17,814,000 | 1960E | Monaco............... | 0.61 | 21,000 | 1957E |
| Central African Rep..... | 238,224 | 1,130,000 | 1960E | Mongolian People's Rep.. | 591,121 | 909,600 | 1959E |
| Ceylon................ | 25,332 | 9,612,000 | 1959E | Morocco.............. | 171,305 | 11,598,070 | 1960PC |
| Chad, Rep. of.......... | 495,794 | 2,730,000 | 1959E | Nepal................ | 54,362 | 9,044,000 | 1959E |
| Chile.................. | 286,397 | 7,627,000 | 1960E | Netherlands........... | 12,529 | 11,480,000 | 1960E |
| China[2]................ | 3,768,736 | 679,232,000 | 1959E | New Zealand.......... | 110,686 | 2,372,000 | 1960E |
| Colombia.............. | 439,520 | 14,132,000 | 1960E | Nicaragua............ | 57,143 | 1,450,349 | 1959E |
| Congo, Rep. of | | | | Niger, Rep. of........ | 458,995 | 2,400,000 | 1958E |
| (Brazzaville)......... | 132,047 | 760,000 | 1958E | Nigeria, Federation of... | 339,169 | 33,854,000 | 1958E |
| Congo, Rep. of | | | | Norway.............. | 125,065 | 3,583,000 | 1960E |
| (Leopoldville)........ | 905,381 | 13,821,000 | 1959E | Pakistan.............. | 364,797 | 86,823,000 | 1959E |
| Costa Rica............ | 19,653 | 1,173,000 | 1960E | Panamá............... | 28,753 | 1,053,000 | 1960E |
| Cuba.................. | 44,218 | 6,743,000 | 1960E | Paraguay............. | 157,047 | 1,760,000 | 1960E |
| Cyprus................ | 3,572 | 563,000 | 1960E | Peru................. | 496,223 | 10,827,000 | 1960E |
| Czechoslovakia........ | 49,366 | 13,649,000 | 1960E | Philippines........... | 115,707 | 27,473,000 | 1960E |
| Dahomey, Rep. of....... | 44,696 | 1,719,000 | 1959E | Poland............... | 120,359 | 29,480,000 | 1960E |
| Denmark.............. | 16,619 | 4,547,000 | 1959E | Portugal.............. | 35,599 | 9,124,000 | 1960E |
| Dominican Rep......... | 18,816 | 2,994,000 | 1960E | Rumania............. | 91,639 | 18,256,000 | 1959E |
| Ecuador............... | 104,506 | 4,298,000 | 1960E | Saar................. | 991 | 996,000 | 1955E |
| Egypt................. | 386,100 | 25,365,000 | 1959E | Salvador, El.......... | 7,722 | 2,613,000 | 1960E |
| Estonia[3].............. | 17,375 | 1,196,000 | 1959E | San Marino........... | 23.6 | 15,000 | 1959E |
| Ethiopia[4]............. | 457,267 | 21,600,000 | 1958E | Saudi Arabia.......... | 617,762 | 6,036,000 | 1956E |
| Finland............... | 130,120 | 4,457,000 | 1960E | Senegal, Rep. of....... | 76,124 | 2,260,000 | 1958E |
| France................ | 212,822 | 45,097,000 | 1959E | Sierra Leone.......... | 27,925 | 2,260,000 | 1958C |
| Gabon Rep............ | 103,088 | 403,000 | 1958E | Somalia.............. | 246,202 | 1,900,000 | 1960E |
| Germany (east)[5]....... | 41,479 | 16,213,000 | 1959E | South Africa, Rep. of[12].. | 472,359 | 14,929,000 | 1960E |
| Germany (west)[6]...... | 95,738 | 53,373,000 | 1960E | Spain................ | 194,396 | 30,128,000 | 1960E |
| Ghana................ | 91,843 | 4,911,000 | 1959E | Sudan................ | 967,501 | 11,615,000 | 1960C |
| Greece[7].............. | 51,182 | 8,258,000 | 1959E | Sweden.............. | 173,623 | 7,471,345 | 1960E |
| Guatemala............. | 42,042 | 3,759,000 | 1960E | Switzerland........... | 15,941 | 5,298,000 | 1960E |
| Guinea................ | 94,926 | 2,665,000 | 1959E | Syria................. | 71,228 | 4,539,000 | 1959E |
| Haiti................. | 10,714 | 3,505,000 | 1960E | Thailand.............. | 198,456 | 22,718,000 | 1960E |
| Honduras.............. | 43,277 | 1,950,000 | 1960E | Tibet................ | 469,143 | 1,273,969 | 1953C |
| Hungary............... | 35,919 | 10,002,000 | 1960E | Togo................. | 22,008 | 1,162,000 | 1959E |
| Iceland............... | 39,768 | 172,000 | 1959E | Tunisia............... | 48,332 | 3,965,000 | 1960E |
| India[8]................ | 1,259,992 | 408,050,000 | 1960E | Turkey............... | 301,381 | 26,881,000 | 1959E |
| Indonesia[9]............ | 575,894 | 92,600,000 | 1960E | U.S.S.R.............. | 8,649,821 | 214,400,000 | 1960E |
| Iran.................. | 636,294 | 20,633,000 | 1960E | United Kingdom........ | 94,215 | 52,383,000 | 1960E |
| Iraq.................. | 171,600[10] | 6,952,000 | 1959E | United States......... | 3,614,210[13] | 179,660,000 | 1960C |
| Ireland............... | 27,136 | 2,834,000 | 1960E | Upper Volta, Rep. of.... | 105,839 | 3,472,000 | 1959E |
| Israel................ | 7,992 | 2,114,000 | 1960E | Uruguay.............. | 72,172 | 2,800,000 | 1958E |
| Italy................. | 116,304 | 49,052,000 | 1959E | Vatican City State....... | 0.17[14] | 1,000 | 1957E |
| Ivory Coast, Rep. of..... | 124,503 | 2,482,000 | 1959E | Venezuela............. | 352,143 | 6,709,000 | 1960E |
| Japan................ | 142,726 | 93,600,000 | 1960E | Vietnam (north)....... | 59,934 | 15,280,000 | 1959E |
| Jordan[11].............. | 37,301 | 1,636,000 | 1959E | Vietnam (south)........ | 75,290 | 13,960,000 | 1959E |
| Korea................ | 85,286 | 32,948,000 | 1959E | Yemen............... | 75,290 | 4,500,000 | 1959E |
| Laos.................. | 91,429 | 1,760,000 | 1959E | Yugoslavia............ | 98,766 | 18,655,000 | 1960E |
| Latvia[3].............. | 24,595 | 2,094,000 | 1959E | | | | |

[1] E—Estimated; C—Census; PC—Provisional Census.　[2] Including Formosa (Taiwan), Manchuria and Tibet. [3] Part of U.S.S.R. but still recognized by U. S. as independent country.　[4] Including Eritrea.　[5] Excluding East Berlin. [6] Excluding West Berlin.　[7] Including Dodecanese.　[8] Including Kashmir.　[9] Excluding Netherlands New Guinea. [10] Including desert area of 80,583 sq. mi.　[11] Including Arab Palestine.　[12] Excluding South-West Africa.　[13] Includes Alaska and Hawaii.　[14] 108.7 acres.

# Largest Cities of the World

(Exact rating of the cities of the world according to size is impossible because of the diversity of the years for which census or estimated population figures have been issued. Therefore, the rating shown in this table must be considered only approximate.)

| City and country | Population | Year* | City and country | Population | Year* |
|---|---|---|---|---|---|
| 1. Tokyo, Japan | 9,021,313 | 1959E | 11. São Paulo, Brazil | 3,315,553 | 1960E |
| 2. London (Greater), England | 8,346,137 | 1951C | 12. Tientsin, China | 3,100,000 | 1957E |
| 3. New York, N. Y., U.S.A. | 7,781,984 | 1960C | 13. Cairo, Egypt | 3,035,000 | 1959E |
| 4. Shanghai, China | 6,204,417 | 1953C | 14. Rio de Janeiro, Brazil | 3,030,619 | 1960E |
| 5. Moscow, U.S.S.R. | 5,032,000 | 1959C | 15. Leningrad, U.S.S.R. | 2,888,000 | 1959C |
| 6. Mexico City, Mexico | 4,700,000 | 1959E | 16. Paris, France | 2,820,534 | 1954C |
| 7. Peking, China | 4,140,000 | 1957E | 17. Osaka, Japan | 2,547,316 | 1955C |
| 8. Buenos Aires, Argentina | 3,845,279 | 1959E | 18. Calcutta, India | 2,520,921 | 1951C |
| 9. Chicago, Ill., U.S.A. | 3,550,404 | 1960C | 19. Los Angeles, Calif., U.S.A. | 2,479,015 | 1960C |
| 10. Berlin, Germany | 3,390,349 | 1960E | 20. Bombay, India | 2,329,020 | 1951C |

## Other Large Foreign Cities (over 640,000)

| City and country | Population | Year* | City and country | Population | Year* |
|---|---|---|---|---|---|
| Ahmedabad, India | 788,333 | 1951C | Lódz, Poland | 696,000 | 1959E |
| Alexandria, Egypt | 1,416,000 | 1959E | Madrid, Spain | 1,926,211 | 1959E |
| Algiers, Algeria | 750,000 | 1959E | Madras, India | 1,416,056 | 1951C |
| Amsterdam, Netherlands | 869,602 | 1960E | Manchester, England | 703,175 | 1951C |
| Ankara, Turkey | 646,151 | 1960C | Manila, Philippines | 1,205,340 | 1959E |
| Antwerp, Belgium | 841,686 | 1957E | Marseilles, France | 605,577 | 1954C |
| Bandung, Indonesia | 951,900 | 1958E | Melbourne, Australia | 1,777,700 | 1959E |
| Bangalore, India | 778,977 | 1951C | Milan, Italy | 1,384,666 | 1958E |
| Bangkok, Thailand | 1,204,894 | 1957E | Montevideo, Uruguay | 965,000 | 1959E |
| Barcelona, Spain | 1,477,811 | 1959E | Montreal, Canada | 1,109,439 | 1956C |
| Birmingham, England | 1,112,340 | 1951C | Mukden, Manchuria | 1,790,000 | 1952E |
| Bogotá, Colombia | 1,188,180 | 1960E | Munich, Germany | 1,065,104 | 1960E |
| Brussels, Belgium | 1,385,831 | 1957E | Nagoya, Japan | 1,336,780 | 1955C |
| Bucharest, Rumania | 1,291,351 | 1959E | Nanking, China | 1,020,000 | 1952E |
| Budapest, Hungary | 1,807,299 | 1960E | Naples, Italy | 1,115,798 | 1958E |
| Canton, China | 1,210,000 | 1952E | Novosibirsk, U.S.S.R. | 887,000 | 1959C |
| Capetown, South Africa | 729,200 | 1959E | Odessa, U.S.S.R. | 667,000 | 1959C |
| Caracas, Venezuela | 711,673 | 1959E | Port Arthur, Kwantung | 1,010,000 | 1952E |
| Casablanca, Morocco | 960,812 | 1960C | Prague, Czechoslovakia | 987,865 | 1959E |
| Chelyabinsk, U.S.S.R. | 688,000 | 1959C | Pusan, Korea | 1,049,363 | 1955C |
| Chungking, China | 2,000,000 | 1952E | Rangoon, Burma | 723,000 | 1960E |
| Cologne, Germany | 780,124 | 1960E | Recife, Brazil | 733,870 | 1960E |
| Copenhagen, Denmark | 942,058 | 1958E | Rome, Italy | 1,874,469 | 1958E |
| Delhi, India | 914,790 | 1951C | Rotterdam, Netherlands | 729,852 | 1960E |
| Düsseldorf, Germany | 691,740 | 1960E | Saigon-Cholon, Vietnam | 1,219,500 | 1958E |
| Essen, Germany | 727,929 | 1960E | Santiago, Chile | 830,897 | 1958E |
| Frankfurt am Main, Germany | 657,735 | 1960E | Seoul, Korea | 1,756,406 | 1960E |
| Genoa, Italy | 736,135 | 1958E | Singapore City, Singapore | 953,000 | 1958E |
| Glasgow, Scotland | 1,089,555 | 1951C | Sofia, Bulgaria | 800,000 | 1960E |
| Gorki, U.S.S.R. | 942,000 | 1959C | Stalino, U.S.S.R. | 701,000 | 1959C |
| Hamburg, Germany | 1,823,574 | 1960E | Stockholm, Sweden | 807,909 | 1960E |
| Harbin, Manchuria | 1,000,000 | 1952E | Surabaja, Indonesia | 1,135,300 | 1958E |
| Havana, Cuba | 785,455 | 1953C | Sverdlovsk, U.S.S.R. | 777,000 | 1959C |
| Hyderabad, India | 1,085,722 | 1951C | Sydney, Australia | 2,054,800 | 1959E |
| Istanbul, Turkey | 1,719,922 | 1960C | Taipei, Formosa | 809,169 | 1958E |
| Jakarta, Indonesia | 2,081,200 | 1958E | Tashkent, U.S.S.R. | 911,000 | 1959C |
| Johannesburg, South Africa | 1,052,600 | 1959E | Tblisi, U.S.S.R. | 694,000 | 1959C |
| Kanpur, India | 705,443 | 1951C | Teheran, Iran | 1,512,082 | 1956C |
| Karachi, Pakistan | 2,000,000 | 1959E | Toronto, Canada | 667,706 | 1956C |
| Kharkov, U.S.S.R. | 930,000 | 1959C | Tsingtao, China | 850,308 | 1948E |
| Kiev, U.S.S.R. | 1,102,000 | 1959C | Tunis, Tunisia | 695,000 | 1960E |
| Kobe, Japan | 979,305 | 1950C | Turin, Italy | 889,249 | 1958E |
| Kuibyshev, U.S.S.R. | 806,000 | 1959C | Victoria, Hong Kong | 1,000,000 | 1957E |
| Kyoto, Japan | 1,204,084 | 1955C | Vienna, Austria | 1,652,427 | 1959E |
| Lahore, Pakistan | 849,476 | 1951C | Warsaw, Poland | 1,088,000 | 1959E |
| Lima, Peru | 1,186,212 | 1958E | Wuhan, China | 1,090,000 | 1952E |
| Lisbon, Portugal | 790,434 | 1950C | Yokohama, Japan | 1,143,687 | 1955C |
| Liverpool, England | 789,532 | 1951C | | | |

*E—Estimated; C—Census.

# THE UNITED NATIONS

## Its Major Cases and Actions

(For new U. N. developments see News Chronology listed in Table of Contents.)

### IRAN

Iran presented the first case before the Security Council on Jan. 19, 1946, demanding an end to Russian "interference" in Azerbaijan province, which Russia had brought under its control through a puppet government. Iran also demanded that Russia keep her promise to withdraw all occupation troops by Mar. 2. The Council kept the matter on the agenda. Russia withdrew her troops May 6.

### GREECE

On Dec. 3, 1946, Greece complained to the Security Council that Communist-led rebels in northern Greece were being aided by Albania, Bulgaria and Yugoslavia. The Council named an investigating committee, which reported May 23, 1947, that those 3 nations were guilty. A Russian veto of July 29 prevented the Council's acceptance of the report. In Sept. 1948, the U. N. Balkan Commission, which continued to watch developments, again condemned the 3 nations for continuing aid to the Greek rebels. However, 3 months previously, on June 28, 1948, Marshal Tito's Yugoslavia had broken with Moscow. Thereafter, the Greek Communist-led rebellion faded out.

### ATOMIC ENERGY CONTROL

On Dec. 31, 1946, a U. N. commission of 11 nations recommended the "Baruch plan" sponsored by the U. S. for international control and inspection. Only Russia dissented. In June 1947, she submitted a vastly different control plan, limiting international inspection so greatly that the secret making of atomic bombs could not be discovered. On May 17, 1948, the U. N. commission voted (9–2) to suspend work on international atomic control, blaming Russia for the deadlock. A Russian veto of June 22 prevented the Security Council from approving the majority-approved control plan. The topic then went to the General Assembly, which, on Nov. 4, 1948, adopted (40–6) the U. S.-sponsored plan; but nothing could be done to put it into effect because of Soviet-bloc opposition.

### PALESTINE

A General Assembly special session met Apr. 28, 1947, at the request of Great Britain to consider Palestine. An 11-nation investigating commitee recommended Aug. 31 that Britain give up control and that an Arab and a Jewish state be established. This partition plan was approved by the Assembly in Nov. 1947, but proved impossible to enforce.

Britain ceased to govern Palestine on May 14, 1948. Israel proclaimed her independence and was attacked by 5 neighboring Arab nations. The U. N. made 6 appeals to both sides to stop the war; the last brought about a truce from June 11 to July 9. Intermittent fighting took place thereafter. Count Folke Bernadotte, the U. N. mediator, was murdered Sept. 17 near Jerusalem. He was succeeded by Dr. Ralph J. Bunche.

Israel signed an armistice with Egypt on Feb. 24, 1949, and with Jordan on Apr. 3. On May 11, the U. N. voted (37–12) to admit Israel as the 59th member.

### INDONESIA

On July 30, 1947, Australia called the Security Council's attention to the fighting between the Netherlands and the Indonesian Republic. The Council, on Aug. 1, ordered both sides to cease hostilities. A Good Offices Commission was sent to Indonesia, and it effected a truce Jan. 17, 1948. In Dec. 1948, the Dutch attacked Jokjakarta, then the Indonesian capital, and the Council again issued a cease-fire order. Dutch troops were withdrawn from around Jokjakarta in July 1949. Indonesia thereafter peacefully achieved independence from the Netherlands.

### INDIA-PAKISTAN

On Jan. 2, 1948, India appealed to the U. N. to stop alleged aggression by Pakistan. Fighting had broken out over which nation should control the province of Kashmir. The Security Council sent a commission, which proposed that Kashmir's future be determined by a plebiscite. The Council agreed on Apr. 21, but both sides raised objections. Early in 1949, the U. N. commission succeeded in obtaining a truce; and, on Mar. 14, 1950, the Council substituted a mediator, who was to seek demilitarization of the areas of Kashmir held by India and Pakistan and to try for a plebiscite. Two mediators failed.

### RUSSIAN BOYCOTT

Soviet Delegate Malik walked out of the Security Council on Jan. 13, 1950, because it had refused (6–3) Russia's demand that Nationalist China be replaced in the U. N. by Communist China. The boycott ended on Aug. 1. Again the Council voted (8–3) to refuse membership to Communist China.

## KOREA

Russia occupied the northern half of Korea after World War II, and the U. S. occupied the southern half below the 38th parallel. The understanding was that the occupying powers would set up an independent republic to govern the entire country. Russia refused to co-operate. The U. S. then referred the problem to the U. N., and the General Assembly voted Nov. 5, 1947, to send a commission to Korea to set up a free government. Russia, however, boycotted the commission and refused to allow it to enter North Korea. The commission therefore supervised free elections in South Korea and assisted in setting up the Republic of Korea with its capital at Seoul.

## HUNGARY

Sparked by student demonstrations, street riots in Hungary in Oct. 1956, took on the proportions of rebellion. The Communist government called for Soviet help, and Russian tanks rolled into Budapest on Oct. 24. The Communists sought to appease the rebellious people by putting in as Premier a man, Imre Nagy, who had been ousted from the party as a "Titoist."

Nagy promised to throw off Russian shackles, and by Nov. 1, Russian tanks and troops had withdrawn from Budapest. On Nov. 4, however, the Russian tanks returned in force, shooting freely and killing civilians. The Russians set up a new puppet government headed by János Kadar.

The General Assembly on Nov. 4, in a special session, called on Russia to get its troops out of Hungary "without delay."

In the ensuing 6 weeks, the General Assembly passed 4 more resolutions about the Soviet crushing of Hungary.

One of the resolutions (Dec. 12, 1956) was an outright condemnation of Russia for "violation of the Charter by the U.S.S.R. in depriving Hungary of its liberty and independence." The vote was 55 to 8, which constituted a world-wide indictment.

The General Assembly decided in January 1957 to name a five-man committee to investigate from outside Hungary. On it were representatives of Denmark, Tunisia, Uruguay, Ceylon and Australia.

The committee heard testimony from 111 Hungarians, mainly refugees, in Europe and America. It reported unanimously on June 20, 1957, that the Hungarian uprising had been a spontaneous revolt of the people and that the crushing of the revolt by Soviet Russian troops had cost between 2,500 and 3,000 lives.

Meanwhile, people had begun fleeing from Communist Hungary on a mass scale almost unprecedented. By the end of April 1957, some 175,000 Hungarians had sought asylum in Austria.

## SUEZ

On Oct. 29, 1956, Israeli armed forces launched a major attack into the Gaza Strip and into Egypt's Sinai Desert territory.

An emergency special session of the U. N. General Assembly adopted on the night of Nov. 1-2, by a vote of 64 in favor, 5 against, 6 abstentions, a United States resolution calling upon all parties involved in hostilities in the area to agree to an immediate cease-fire. By that time, Britain and France were involved in the fighting.

Heeding the General Assembly call, Britain and France announced on Nov. 3 that they would stop military action.

By direction of the General Assembly, a United Nations Emergency Force was established to keep the peace. The first units landed at Ismailia, midway point on the Suez Canal, on Nov. 11, 1956.

On Feb. 21, Israel agreed to pull out its last troops if the U. N. Emergency Force stationed peace-keeping troops on the Aqaba Gulf and in the Gaza Strip. The U. N. Emergency Force troops were so stationed, and they became the first uniformed peace-preserving unit in the history of the U. N.

The nations which contributed troops were Brazil, Canada, Colombia, Denmark, Finland, India, Norway, Sweden and Yugoslavia.

## LEBANON

In July, 1958, the United States responded to a plea for help from the little country of Lebanon at the eastern end of the Mediterranean, which had been in the throes of insurrection allegedly aided from its neighbor Syria, lately affiliated with Egypt in the new United Arab Republic. At Lebanon's request, U. S. Marines were landed there. Almost simultaneously, nearby Jordan requested and received British troops to safeguard the pro-West regime.

The U. N. already had a team of about 130 observers in Lebanon. In the Security Council, the Soviet Union now cast its 84th and 85th vetoes to kill resolutions (supported by the West) designed to strengthen U. N. forces in the Mideast.

The General Assembly was summoned into a rare emergency session which opened Aug. 8. A unanimous resolution directed Secretary-General Dag Hammarskjold to go to the Middle East and see what arrangements could be made to restore stability and facilitate withdrawal of U. S. and British troops.

## THE CONGO

The Belgian Congo became independent on June 30, 1960, after 75 years as a Belgian colony. Chaos ensued. Provinces seceded and announced their independence. Tribes fought tribes. Whites fled, fearing massacre.

Appeal from the Congo caused the U.N. to act swiftly. It sent a police force, with troops from 18 nations, mostly African but also some from Ireland, Canada, and Sweden.

There was trouble, with Congo firebrands occasionally attacking the U.N. forces. But on the whole, the operation seemed to bring a semblance of order out of the chaos.

The "Cold War" came into the picture. Soviet Russia demanded that the former Congo Premier, pro-Communist Patrice Lumumba, be restored to power. He was caught and killed in Katanga Province in February, 1961, and the Russians blamed the Belgians, who still had "advisers" in Katanga.

This led to a Soviet demand for reorganization of the U.N. Secretariat. Secretary General Dag Hammarskjöld must go, said Moscow. In his place there must be a "troika" control. (Troika is a Russian word for a carriage pulled by three horses.) This would consist of one man from the Communist bloc, one man from the West, and one man from an uncommitted neutralist nation. Any action they took would have to be unanimous. That meant that the Communist member would have veto power and could kill any action by the U.N. Secretariat.

The United States announced that it would use its veto power to kill any such reorganization of the U.N.

# Elected Member States Serving Terms on U. N. Councils

## Security Council

Jan. 1946–Dec. 1946: Egypt; Mexico; Netherlands.
Jan. 1946–Dec. 1947: Australia; Brazil; Poland.
Jan. 1947–Dec. 1948: Belgium; Colombia; Syria.
Jan. 1948–Dec. 1949: Argentina; Canada; Ukrainian S.S.R.
Jan. 1949–Dec. 1950: Cuba; Egypt; Norway.
Jan. 1950–Dec. 1951: Ecuador; India; Yugoslavia.
Jan. 1951–Dec. 1952: Brazil; Netherlands; Turkey.
Jan. 1952–Dec. 1953: Chile; Greece; Pakistan.
Jan. 1953–Dec. 1954: Colombia; Denmark; Lebanon.
Jan. 1954–Dec. 1955: Brazil; New Zealand; Turkey.
Jan. 1955–Dec. 1956: Belgium, Iran, Peru.
Jan. 1956–Dec. 1957: Australia; Cuba; Yugoslavia. Yugoslavia resigned at the end of 1956 and was replaced by the Philippines.
Jan. 1957–Dec. 1958: Colombia; Iraq; Sweden.
Jan. 1958–Dec. 1959: Canada; Japan; Panamá.
Jan. 1959–Dec. 1960: Argentina; Italy; Tunisia.
Jan. 1960–Dec. 1961: Ceylon; Ecuador; Poland. Poland resigned at the end of 1960 and was replaced by Turkey.
Jan. 1961–Dec. 1962: Chile; Liberia; United Arab Republic. Ireland will replace Liberia in 1962.

## Economic and Social Council

Jan. 1946–Dec. 1946: Colombia; Greece; Lebanon; Ukrainian S.S.R.; U. S.; Yugoslavia.
Jan. 1946–Dec. 1947: Cuba; Czechoslovakia; India; Norway; United Kingdom; U.S.S.R.
Jan. 1946–Dec. 1948: Belgium (resigned 1947 and replaced by Netherlands); Canada; Chile; China; France; Peru.
Jan. 1947–Dec. 1949: Byelorussian S.S.R.; Lebanon; New Zealand; Turkey; U. S.; Venezuela.
Jan. 1948–Dec. 1950: Australia; Brazil; Denmark; Poland; United Kingdom; U.S.S.R.
Jan. 1949–Dec. 1951: Belgium; Chile; China; France; India; Peru.

Jan. 1950–Dec. 1952: Canada; Czechoslovakia; Iran; Mexico; Pakistan; U. S.
Jan. 1951–Dec. 1953: Philippines; Poland; Sweden; United Kingdom; Uruguay; U.S.S.R.
Jan. 1952–Dec. 1954: Argentina; Belgium; China; Cuba; Egypt; France.
Jan. 1953–Dec. 1955: Australia; India; Turkey; U. S.; Venezuela; Yugoslavia.
Jan. 1954–Dec. 1956: Czechoslovakia; Ecuador; Norway; Pakistan; United Kingdom; U.S.S.R.
Jan. 1955–Dec. 1957: Argentina; China; Dom. Rep.; Egypt; France; Netherlands.
Jan. 1956–Dec. 1958: Brazil; Canada; Greece; Indonesia; U. S.; Yugoslavia.
Jan. 1957–Dec. 1959: Finland; Mexico; Pakistan; Poland; U.S.S.R.; United Kingdom.
Jan. 1958–Dec. 1960: Chile; China; Costa Rica; France; Netherlands; Sudan.
Jan. 1959–Dec. 1961: Afghanistan; Bulgaria; New Zealand; Spain; U. S.; Venezuela.
Jan. 1960–Dec. 1962: Brazil; Denmark; Japan; Poland; U.S.S.R.; United Kingdom.
Jan. 1961–Dec. 1963: El Salvador; Ethiopia; France; Jordan; Uruguay.
Apr. 1961–Dec. 1963: Italy.

## Trusteeship Council

### Nonadministering Members

Jan. 1947–Dec. 1949: Iraq; Mexico.
Jan. 1948–Dec. 1950: Costa Rica (resigned Sept. 1949 and replaced by Dominican Republic); Philippines.
Jan. 1950–Dec. 1952: Argentina (resigned with effect of Jan. 1, 1952 and replaced by El Salvador); Iraq.
Jan. 1951–Dec. 1953: Dominican Republic; Thailand.
Jan. 1953–Dec. 1955: El Salvador; Syria.
Jan. 1954–Dec. 1956: Haiti; India.
Jan. 1956–Dec. 1958: Burma; Guatemala; Syria.
Jan. 1957–Dec. 1959: Haiti; India.
Jan. 1959–Dec. 1961: Burma; Paraguay; United Arab Republic.
Jan. 1960–Dec. 1962: Bolivia; India.

# Principal Organs of the United Nations

## SECRETARIAT

### Secretaries-General

Trygve Lie, of Norway, Feb. 1, 1946, to Apr. 10, 1953.

Dag Hammarskjöld, of Sweden, Apr. 10, 1953, to Sept. 18, 1961 (killed in airplane accident; see News Chronology of 1961 in front of book).

## GENERAL ASSEMBLY

The General Assembly is composed of all member states. It does most of its work in committees, of which there are 4 types: main, procedural, standing and ad hoc.

### Main Committees

First Committee (Political and Security, including the regulation of armaments).
Special Political Committee.
Second Committee (Economic and Financial).
Third Committee (Social, Humanitarian and Cultural).
Fourth Committee (Trusteeship, including Non-Self-Governing Territories).
Fifth Committee (Administrative and Budgetary).
Sixth Committee (Legal).

### Presidents of the General Assembly

Paul-Henri Spaak, of Belgium, 1946, First Session.
Oswaldo Aranha, of Brazil, 1947, First Special Session and Second Regular Session.
Dr. José Arce, of Argentina, 1948, Second Special Session.
Herbert V. Evatt, of Australia, 1948, Third Session.
Carlos P. Romulo, of the Philippines, 1949, Fourth Session.
Nasrollah Entezam, of Iran, 1950, Fifth Session.
Luis Padilla Nervo, of Mexico, 1951, Sixth Session.
Lester B. Pearson, of Canada, 1952, Seventh Session.
Mrs. Vijaya Lakshmi Pandit, of India, 1953, Eighth Session.
Eelco N. van Kleffens, of the Netherlands, 1954, Ninth Session.
José Maza, of Chile, 1955, Tenth Session.
Rudecindo Ortega, of Chile, Nov., 1956, First and Second Emergency Special Sessions.
Prince Wan Waithayakon, of Thailand, 1956–57, Eleventh Session.
Sir Leslie Munro, of New Zealand, 1957–58, Twelfth Session and Third Emergency Special Session.
Charles Malik, of Lebanon, 1958–1959, Thirteenth Session.

Víctor Andrés Belaúnde, of Peru, 1959–60, Fourteenth Session and Fourth Emergency Special Session.

Frederick Henry Boland, of Ireland, 1960–61, Fifteenth Session and Third Special Session.

## SECURITY COUNCIL

The Security Council is composed of 5 permanent members—China, France, the U.S.S.R., the United Kingdom and the U. S. There are 6 nonpermanent members serving 2-year terms.

The Military Staff Committee is composed of the Chiefs of Staff of the 5 permanent members or their representatives; the Disarmament Commission, established in 1952 by the General Assembly under the Security Council, has, since 1959, been composed of all members of the U.N.

## ECONOMIC AND SOCIAL COUNCIL

The Economic and Social Council is composed of 18 members serving 3-year terms.

### Functional Commissions

Statistical Commission.
Population Commission.
Social Commission.
Commission on Human Rights.
Commission on the Status of Women.
Commission on Narcotic Drugs.
Commission on International Commodity Trade.

### Regional Economic Commissions

Economic Commission for Europe.
Economic Commission for Asia and the Far East.
Economic Commission for Latin America.
Economic Commission for Africa.

## TRUSTEESHIP COUNCIL

The Trusteeship Council is composed of 13 members; five members—Australia, Belgium, New Zealand, the United Kingdom, and the U.S.—which administer trust territories; three members—China, France, and the U.S.S.R.—which are permanent members of the Security Council but do not administer trust territories; and five other nonadministering members elected by the General Assembly for three-year terms. Upon the independence in 1960 of territories administered by Italy and France, Italy ceased to be a member of the Council, while France, as a permanent member of the Security Council, became a nonadministering member. Although membership is therefore no longer equally divided between administering and nonadministering countries, the General Assembly has decided to retain the present arrangement until the end of 1961.

As of April 1961, Trusteeship Agreements concerned the following territories (the

Administering Authority in each case is in italics):

Nauru—*Australia (on behalf of Australia, New Zealand and the United Kingdom).*
New Guinea—*Australia.*
Ruanda-Urundi—*Belgium.*
Western Samoa—*New Zealand.*
Cameroons, Tanganyika—*United Kingdom.*

The Trust Territory of the Pacific Islands—composed of the former Japanese-mandated islands of the Marshalls, Marianas (with the exception of Guam), and Carolines—is a strategic trust territory administered by the U.S.

Three trust territories became independent in 1960: the French Cameroons, Jan. 1; French Togoland, Apr. 27; and Italian Somaliland, July 1. Tanganyika will attain independence on Dec. 9, 1961, while Dec. 31, 1961, is the date tentatively set for Western Samoan independence. British Togoland, a former trust territory, became independent Mar. 7, 1957, joining the Gold Coast, a former British colony, to become the new state of Ghana. As a result of U.N.-supervised plebiscites held in the British Cameroons in February 1961, the Northern Cameroons joined Nigeria in June 1961, and the Southern Cameroons joined the Republic of Cameroun in October 1961.

## INTL. COURT OF JUSTICE

(The Court is composed of 15 judges, who serve for a 9-year term and may be re-elected. Expiration dates of terms are shown in parentheses. All terms expire February 5 of the year designated. The seat of the Court is The Hague, Netherlands.)

**President: Bohdan Winiarski, Poland** (1967)
**Vice President: Ricardo J. Alfaro, Panama** (1964)

Abdel Hamid Badawi, U.A.R. (1967)
Jules Basdevant, France (1964)
José Luis Bustamente y Rivero, Peru (1970)
Roberto Córdova, Mexico (1964)
Sir Gerald Fitzmaurice, U. K. (1964)
Philip C. Jessup, U. S. (1970)
Vladimir M. Koretsky, U.S.S.R. (1970)
Gaetano Morelli, Italy (1970)
L. M. Moreno Quintana, Argentina (1964)
Sir Percy Spender, Australia (1967)
Jean Spiropoulos, Greece (1967)
Kotaro Tanaka, Japan (1970)
V. K. Wellington Koo, China (1967)

# Agencies of the United Nations

**International Atomic Energy Agency (IAEA)**
*Established:* Statute for IAEA, approved on October 26, 1956 at a conference held at U. N. Headquarters, New York, came

into force on July 29, 1957. The Agency, while not a specialized agency, is under the aegis of the U. N.
*Purposes:* To promote the peaceful uses of atomic energy, and to ensure that assistance provided by it or at its request or under its supervision or control is not used in such a way as to further any military purpose.
*Headquarters:* Vienna, Austria.

## Specialized Agencies

**International Labour Organisation (ILO)**
*Established:* Apr. 11, 1919, when constitution was adopted as Part XIII of Treaty of Versailles.
*Purposes:* To contribute to establishment of lasting peace by promoting social justice; to improve, through international action, labor conditions and living standards; to promote economic and social stability.
*Headquarters:* Geneva, Switzerland.

**Food and Agriculture Organization of the United Nations (FAO)**
*Established:* Oct. 16, 1945, when constitution became effective.
*Purposes:* To raise nutrition levels and living standards; to secure improvements in production and distribution of food and agricultural products.
*Headquarters:* Viale delle Terme di Caracalla, Rome, Italy.

**United Nations Educational, Scientific and Cultural Organization (UNESCO)**
*Established:* Nov. 4, 1946, when 20th signatory to constitution deposited instrument of acceptance with government of United Kingdom.
*Purposes:* To promote collaboration among nations through education, science and culture in order to further justice, rule of law and human rights and freedoms without distinction of race, sex, language or religion.
*Headquarters:* UNESCO House, Place de Fontenoy, Paris 7e, France.

**World Health Organization (WHO)**
*Established:* Apr. 7, 1948, when 26 members of the U. N. had accepted its constitution adopted July 22, 1946, by International Health Conference in New York City.
*Purposes:* To aid attainment by all peoples of the world of highest possible level of health.
*Headquarters:* Palais des Nations, Geneva, Switzerland.

**International Bank for Reconstruction and Development (Bank)**
*Established:* Dec. 27, 1945, when Articles of Agreement drawn up at Bretton Woods Conference in July, 1944, came into force. Began operations June 25, 1946.
*Purposes:* To assist in reconstruction and development of economies of members by making loans directly and promoting private foreign investment; to promote the

balanced growth of international trade

*Headquarters:* 1818 H St., NW, Washington 25, D. C.

## International Development Association (IDA)

*Established:* Sept. 24, 1960. An affiliate of the International Bank, IDA has the same officers and staff as the Bank.

*Purposes:* To further economic development of its members by providing finance on terms which bear less heavily on balance of payments of members than those of conventional loans.

*Headquarters:* 1818 H St., NW, Washington 25, D. C.

## International Finance Corporation (IFC)

*Established:* Charter of IFC came into force on July 20, 1956. Although IFC is affiliated with the International Bank, it is a separate legal entity and its funds are entirely separate from those of the Bank. However, membership in the Corporation is open only to Bank members.

*Purposes:* Its objective is to further economic development by encouraging the growth of productive private enterprise in its member countries, particularly in the less developed areas. It is empowered to invest in productive private enterprises in association with private investors, and without government guarantee of repayment in cases where sufficient private capital is not available on reasonable terms; and to serve as a clearing house to bring together investment opportunities, private capital, both foreign and domestic, and experienced management.

*Headquarters:* 1818 H St., NW, Washington, D. C.

## International Monetary Fund (Fund)

*Established:* Dec. 27, 1945, when Articles of Agreement drawn up at Bretton Woods Conference in July 1944 came into force. Fund began operations on March 1, 1947.

*Purposes:* To promote international monetary co-operation and expansion of international trade; to promote exchange stability; to assist in establishment of multilateral system of payments in respect of current transactions between members.

*Headquarters:* 1818 H St., NW, Washington 25, D. C.

## International Civil Aviation Organization (ICAO)

*Established:* April 4, 1947, after working as a provisional organization since August 1945.

*Purposes:* To help governments along international air routes contribute toward safe, regular flights in the jet age by listing needed improvements and cooperating with national aviation officials in putting them into effect. They have, for example, helped in designing new airports and demonstrating new safety equipment. They are also concerned with international financing of services too expensive for some of the member nations to maintain alone, as well as helping less developed countries use small planes to overcome some of their economic handicaps. This agency also prepares for future developments and helps establish uniform practices and standards in international aviation.

*Headquarters:* Montreal.

## Universal Postal Union (UPU)

*Established:* July 1, 1875.

*Purposes:* Reciprocal exchange of correspondence by uniform procedures by all UPU members. It also helps governments modernize and speed up mailing procedures.

*Headquarters:* Berne, Switzerland.

## International Telecommunication Union (ITU)

*Established:* 1865.

*Purposes:* To extend technical assistance to help members keep up with present day telecommunication needs, to standardize communications equipment and procedures, and to lower costs. It also works for orderly sharing of radio frequencies, and makes studies and recommendations to benefit its members.

*Headquarters:* Geneva, Switzerland.

## World Meteorological Organization (WMO)

*Established:* April 4, 1951, succeeding the International Meteorological Organization, a non-governmental organization founded in 1878.

*Purposes:* The international exchange of weather reports and maximum standardization of observations. It also helps underdeveloped countries set up weather services for their own economic needs; seeks to fill gaps in observing stations; promotes meteorological investigations affecting jet aircraft, satellites, energy resources, etc.

*Headquarters:* Geneva, Switzerland.

## Inter-Governmental Maritime Consultative Organization (IMCO)

*Established:* January 13, 1959.

*Purposes:* To give advisory and consultative help to promote international cooperation in maritime navigation, and to encourage the highest standards of safety and navigation. It has started efforts to bring about a uniform system of measuring ship tonnage; systems now vary widely in different parts of the world. Other activities include cooperation with other U. N. agencies in relation to matters affecting the maritime field.

*Headquarters:* London.

### General Agreement on Tariffs and Trade (GATT)

*Established:* January 1, 1948.

*Purposes:* An International Trade Organization (ITO) was planned when the U. N. Agencies were first set up. Although this agency has not materialized, some of its objectives have been embodied in an international commercial treaty, the General Agreement on Tariffs and Trade (GATT). This provides a code of conduct for international trade and seeks to help raise living standards and promote economic growth.

*Headquarters:* Geneva, Switzerland.

## United Nations Costs

U. N. regular budget appropriations for 1961 were approved at $72,969,300. Member states contribute on a scale determined by the General Assembly. For 1961, the United States was assessed 32.51% of the net contributions, amounting to $63,437,463; the U.S.S.R. was assessed 13.62%; and the United Kingdom was assessed 7.78%.

## Members of the United Nations

| Country | Joined U.N. Organization[1] | Country | Joined U.N. Organization[1] | Country | Joined U.N. Organization[1] |
|---|---|---|---|---|---|
| Afghanistan | 1946 | France | 1945 | Nicaragua | 1945 |
| Albania | 1955 | Gabon | 1960 | Niger | 1960 |
| Argentina | 1945 | Ghana | 1957 | Nigeria | 1960 |
| Australia | 1945 | Greece | 1945 | Norway | 1945 |
| Austria | 1955 | Guatemala | 1945 | Pakistan | 1947 |
| Belgium | 1945 | Guinea | 1958 | Panamá | 1945 |
| Bolivia | 1945 | Haiti | 1945 | Paraguay | 1945 |
| Brazil | 1945 | Honduras | 1945 | Peru | 1945 |
| Bulgaria | 1955 | Hungary | 1955 | Philippines | 1945 |
| Burma | 1948 | Iceland | 1946 | Poland | 1945 |
| Byelorussian S.S.R. | 1945 | India | 1945 | Portugal | 1955 |
| Cambodia | 1955 | Indonesia | 1950 | Rumania | 1955 |
| Cameroun | 1960 | Iran | 1945 | Saudi Arabia | 1945 |
| Canada | 1945 | Iraq | 1945 | Senegal | 1960 |
| Central African Rep. | 1960 | Ireland | 1955 | Somalia | 1960 |
| Ceylon | 1955 | Israel | 1949 | South Africa | 1945 |
| Chad | 1960 | Italy | 1955 | Spain | 1955 |
| Chile | 1945 | Ivory Coast | 1960 | Sudan | 1956 |
| China | 1945 | Japan | 1956 | Sweden | 1946 |
| Colombia | 1945 | Jordan | 1955 | Thailand | 1946 |
| Congo (Brazzaville) | 1960 | Laos | 1955 | Togo | 1960 |
| Congo (Leopoldville) | 1960 | Lebanon | 1945 | Tunisia | 1956 |
| Costa Rica | 1945 | Liberia | 1945 | Turkey | 1945 |
| Cuba | 1945 | Libya | 1955 | Ukrainian S.S.R. | 1945 |
| Cyprus | 1960 | Luxembourg | 1945 | U.S.S.R. | 1945 |
| Czechoslovakia | 1945 | Malagasy Rep. | 1960 | United Arab Rep.[2] | 1945 |
| Dahomey | 1960 | Malaya, Fed. of | 1957 | United Kingdom | 1945 |
| Denmark | 1945 | Mali | 1960 | United States | 1945 |
| Dominican Rep. | 1945 | Mexico | 1945 | Upper Volta | 1960 |
| Ecuador | 1945 | Morocco | 1956 | Uruguay | 1945 |
| El Salvador | 1945 | Nepal | 1955 | Venezuela | 1945 |
| Ethiopia | 1945 | Netherlands | 1945 | Yemen | 1947 |
| Finland | 1955 | New Zealand | 1945 | Yugoslavia | 1945 |

[1] The U.N. officially came into existence on Oct. 24, 1945.  [2] Formed by the union in 1958 of Egypt and Syria. Both had joined the U.N. in 1945.

# Principal Officers of the Secretariat as of September 1, 1961

C. V. Narasimhan (India), *Chef de Cabinet* and Under-Secretary for Special Political Affairs.

Andrew W. Cordier (U. S.), Under-Secretary in Charge of General Assembly and Related Affairs.

Constantin A. Stavropoulos (Greece), Legal Counsel.

Bruce R. Turner (New Zealand), Controller.

W. A. B. Hamilton (U. K.), Director of Personnel.

Ralph J. Bunche (U. S.), Under-Secretary for Special Political Affairs.

Georgy P. Arkadev (U.S.S.R.), Under-Secretary for Political and Security Council Affairs.

Philippe de Seynes (France), Under-Secretary for Economic and Social Affairs.

Roberto M. Heurtematte (Panamá), Commissioner for Technical Assistance.

Paul Hoffman (U. S.), Managing Director of the U. N. Special Fund.

Vladimir Velebit (Yugoslavia), Executive Secretary, Economic Commission for Europe.

U Nyun (Burma), Executive Secretary, Economic Commission for Asia and the Far East.

Raúl Prebisch (Argentina), Executive Secretary, Economic Commission for Latin America.

Mekki Abbas (Sudan), Executive Secretary, Economic Commission for Africa.

Dragoslav Protitch (Yugoslavia), Under-Secretary for Trusteeship and Information from Non-Self-Governing Territories.

Hernane Tavares de Sa (Brazil), Under-Secretary for Public Information.

Victor Hoo (China), Under-Secretary for Conference Services.

David B. Vaughan (U. S.), Director of General Services.

Maurice Pate (U. S.), Executive Director of the U. N. Children's Fund (UNICEF).

David Owen (U. K.), Executive Chairman of the Technical Assistance Board.

P. P. Spinelli (Italy), Director of the U. N. European Office in Geneva.

Felix Schnyder (Switzerland), U. N. High Commissioner for Refugees (UNHCR).

John H. Davis (U. S.), Director, U. N. Relief and Works Agency for Palestine Refugees in the Near East (UNRWA).

---

## Security Council
### Representatives (as of Aug. 1961)

Ceylon: (Vacant).
Chile: Daniel Schweitzer.
China: Dr. Tingfu F. Tsiang.
Ecuador: Leopoldo Benites.
France: Armand Bérard.
Liberia: George Padmore.
Turkey: Turgut Menemencioglu.
U.S.S.R.: Valerian Zorin.
United Arab Republic: Omar Loutfi.
United Kingdom: Sir Patrick Dean.
United States: Adlai E. Stevenson.

## Economic and Social Council
### Representatives (32nd session, July–Aug. 1961)

Afghanistan: Abdul Rahman Pazhwak.
Brazil: Afrânio de Mello-Franco.
Bulgaria: Yordan Tchobanov.
Denmark: Aage Hessellund-Jensen; Mogens Wandel-Petersen.
El Salvador: Dr. Ruy Cesar Miranda Lupone.
Ethiopia: Kifle Wodajo.
France: Joannès Dupraz.
Italy: Giuseppe Cerulli-Irelli.
Japan: Shiroshichi Kimura.
Jordan: Dr. Nijmeddin Dajani.
New Zealand: Foss Shanahan; R. H. Wade.

Poland: Jerzy Michalowski; Adam Meller-Conrad.
Spain: Don José Manuel Aniel-Quiroga.
U.S.S.R.: M. A. Lesechko; A. S. Chistyakov.
United Kingdom: J. B. Godber; Miss B. Salt.
United States: Adlai E. Stevenson (to July 14), Philip M. Klutznick (from July 14); Walter M. Kotschnig.
Uruguay: Don Daniel Rodríguez Larreta.
Venezuela: Eddie Morales Crespo.

## Trusteeship Council
### Representatives (27th session, June–July 1961)

Australia: J. D. L. Hood.
Belgium: Alfred Claeys Bouuaert.
Bolivia: Carlos Salamanca.
Burma: U Thant.
China: Chiping H. C. Kiang.
France: Jacques Kosciusko-Morizet.
India: C. S. Jha.
New Zealand: Foss Shanahan.
Paraguay: Pacifico Montero de Vargas.
U.S.S.R.: Valentin I. Oberemko.
United Arab Republic: Mostapha Rateb Abdel Wahab.
United Kingdom: Sir Hugh Foot.
United States: J. B. Bingham.

---

## Security Council Vetoes

As of April 1961, 101 proposals brought before the United Nations Security Council had been defeated because of vetoes by permanent members. The U.S.S.R. cast 94 of these vetoes, the United Kingdom two, China one and France four (two in conjunction with the United Kingdom, one with the U.S.S.R. and one alone). The United States had cast no vetoes in the Security Council.

# Delegation Heads to the United Nations
## Members Represented at Headquarters*

Afghanistan: Abdul Rahman Pazhwak.
Albania: Halim Budo.
Argentina: Dr. Mario Amadeo.
Australia: James Plimsoll.
Austria: Dr. Franz Matsch.
Belgium: Walter Loridan.
Bolivia: Jaime Caballero Tamayo.
Brazil: Cyro de Freitas-Valle.
Bulgaria: Yordan Tchobanov.
Burma: U Thant.
Byelorussian S.S.R.: Feodosy N. Gryaznov.
Cambodia: Nong Kimny.
Cameroun: Aimé Raymond N'Thepe.
Canada: C. S. A. Ritchie.
Central African Republic: Michel Gallin-Douathe.
Ceylon: (Vacant).
Chad: Adam Malick Sow.
Chile: Daniel Schweitzer.
China: Dr. Tingfu F. Tsiang.
Colombia: Dr. German Zea.
Congo (Brazzaville): Emmanuel Dadet.
Congo (Léopoldville): (Vacant).
Costa Rica: Dr. Gonzalo Ortiz.
Cuba: Mario Carcia-Inchaustegui.
Cyprus: Zenon Rossides.
Czechoslovakia: Karel Kurka.
Dahomey: Louis Ignacio-Pinto.
Denmark: Aage Hessellund-Jensen.
Dominican Republic: (Vacant).
Ecuador: Dr. Leopoldo Benites.
El Salvador: Dr. Miguel Rafael Urquia.
Ethiopia: Dr. Tesfaye Gebre-Egzy.
Federation of Malaya: Dato Nik Ahmed Kamil.
Finland: Ralph Enckell.
France: Armand Bérard.
Gabon: Joseph N'Goua.
Ghana: Alex Quaison-Sackey.
Greece: Dimitri S. Bitsios.
Guatemala: Col. Guillermo Flores Avendaño.
Guinea: Diallo Telli.
Haiti: Carlet R. Auguste.
Honduras: Francisco Milla Bermudez.
Hungary: Peter Mod.
Iceland: Thor Thors.
India: C. S. Jha.
Indonesia: Sukardjo Wirjopranoto.
Iran: Dr. Mehdi Vakil.
Iraq: Dr. Adnan M. Pachachi.
Ireland: Frederick H. Boland.

Israel: Michael S. Comay.
Italy: Vittorio Zoppi.
Ivory Coast: Arsène Assouan Usher.
Japan: Katsuo Okazaki.
Jordan: Dr. Faouzi Al-Mulki.
Laos: Sisouk Na Champassak.
Lebanon: Georges Hakim.
Liberia: Nathan Barnes.
Libya: Dr. Mohieddine Fekini.
Luxembourg: Maurice Steinmetz.
Malagasy Republic: Louis Rakotomalala.
Mali: Abdoulaye Maiga.
Mexico: Dr. Luis Padilla Nervo.
Morocco: (Vacant).
Nepal: Matrika Prasad Koirala.
Netherlands: C. W. A. Schurmann.
New Zealand: Foss Shanahan.
Nicaragua: Dr. Guillermo Sevilla-Sacasa.
Niger: Issoufou Saidou Djermakoye.
Nigeria: Alhaji Muhammad Ngileruma.
Norway: Sivert A. Nielsen.
Pakistan: Said Hasan.
Panamá: Dr. Enrique Jimenez.
Paraguay: Dr. Pacífico Montero de Vargas.
Peru: Carlos Mackehenie.
Philippines: Dr. Francisco A. Delgado.
Poland: Bohdan Lewandowski.
Portugal: Dr. Vasco Vieira Garin.
Rumania: Silviu Brucan.
Saudi Arabia: Ahmad Shukairy.
Senegal: Ousmane Socé Diop.
Somalia: Hassan Nur Elmi.
South Africa: Bernardus G. Fourie.
Spain: Don José Felix de Lequerica.
Sudan: Omar Abdel Hamid Adeel.
Sweden: Mrs. Agda Rössel.
Thailand: (Vacant).
Togo: Dr. André Akakpo.
Tunisia: Habib Bourguiba, Jr.
Turkey: Turgut Menemencioglu.
Ukrainian S.S.R.: Petr P. Udovichenko.
U.S.S.R.: Valerian A. Zorin.
United Arab Republic: Omar Loutfi.
United Kingdom: Sir Patrick Dean.
United States: Adlai E. Stevenson.
Upper Volta: Frederic Guirma.
Uruguay: Prof. Enrique Rodríguez Fabregat.
Venezuela: Dr. Carlos Sosa-Rodríguez.
Yemen: Mohamed Kamil Abdul Rahim.
Yugoslavia: Miso Pavicevic.

* Permanent representatives to U. N. as of August 1961. Not all nations maintain permanent missions.

---

## U. S. Permanent Mission to U. N.

Adlai E. Stevenson; Ambassador Extraordinary and Plenipotentiary, Permanent Representative to U. N.

Francis Taylor Pearson Plimpton; Ambassador Extraordinary and Plenipotentiary, Deputy Permanent Representative to U. N.

Charles Woodruff Yost; Ambassador, Deputy Permanent Representative to U. N.

Philip Morris Klutznick; Minister, Representative on Economic and Social Council.

Jonathan Brewster Bingham; Minister, Representative on Trusteeship Council.

## U. S. Delegation to the 16th Session of the General Assembly
### (Beginning Sept. 19, 1961)
### Representatives

Adlai E. Stevenson, Chairman; Omar Burleson; Marguerite Stitt Church; Francis T. P. Plimpton; Arthur H. Dean.

### Alternate Representatives

Charles W. Yost; Clifton R. Wharton; Philip M. Klutznick; Jonathan B. Bingham; Gladys A. Tillett.

The U. S. Secretary of State serves as Chairman of the Delegation, *ex officio*, during his presence at the session.

# CHARTER OF THE UNITED NATIONS

WE the peoples of the United Nations determined to save succeeding generations from the scourge of war, which twice in our lifetime has brought untold sorrow to mankind, and

To reaffirm faith in fundamental human rights, in the dignity and worth of the human person, in the equal rights of men and women and of nations large and small, and

To establish conditions under which justice and respect for the obligations arising from treaties and other sources of international law can be maintained, and

To promote social progress and better standards of life in larger freedom, and for these ends

To practice tolerance and live together in peace with one another as good neighbors, and

To unite our strength to maintain international peace and security, and

To insure, by the acceptance of principles and the institution of methods, that armed force shall not be used, save in the common interest, and

To employ international machinery for the promotion of the economic and social advancement of all peoples, have resolved to combine our efforts to accomplish these aims.

Accordingly, our respective Governments, through representatives assembled in the city of San Francisco, who have exhibited their full powers found to be in good and due form, have agreed to the present Charter of the United Nations and do hereby establish an international organization to be known as the United Nations.

## CHAPTER I

## Purposes and Principles

### Article 1

The purposes of the United Nations are:

1. To maintain international peace and security, and to that end: to take effective collective measures for the prevention and removal of threats to the peace, and for the suppression of acts of aggression or other breaches of the peace, and to bring about by peaceful means, and in conformity with the principles of justice and international law, adjustment or settlement of international disputes or situations which might lead to a breach of the peace;

2. To develop friendly relations among nations based on respect for the principle of equal rights and self-determination of peoples, and to take other appropriate measures to strengthen universal peace;

3. To achieve international cooperation in solving international problems of an economic, social, cultural, or humanitarian character, and in promoting and encouraging respect for human rights and for fundamental freedoms for all without distinction as to race, sex, language, or religion; and

4. To be a center for harmonizing the actions of nations in the attainment of these common ends.

### Article 2

The Organization and its Members, in pursuit of the Purposes stated in Article 1, shall act in accordance with the following Principles:

1. The Organization is based on the principle of the sovereign equality of all its Members.

2. All Members, in order to ensure to all of them the rights and benefits resulting from membership, shall fulfill in good faith the obligations assumed by them in accordance with the present Charter.

3. All Members shall settle their international disputes by peaceful means in such a manner that international peace and security, and justice, are not endangered.

4. All Members shall refrain in their international relations from the threat or use of force against the territorial integrity or political independence of any state, or in any other manner inconsistent with the Purposes of the United Nations.

5. All Members shall give the United Nations every assistance in any action it takes in accordance with the present Charter, and shall refrain from giving assistance to any state against which the United Nations is taking preventive or enforcement action.

6. The Organization shall ensure that states which are not Members of the United Nations act in accordance with these Principles so far as may be necessary for the maintenance of international peace and security.

7. Nothing contained in the present Charter shall authorize the United Nations to intervene in matters which are essentially within the domestic jurisdiction of any state or shall require the Members to submit such matters to settlement under the present Charter; but this principle shall not prejudice the application of enforcement measures under Chapter VII.

## CHAPTER II

## Membership

### Article 3

The original Members of the United Nations shall be the states which, having participated in the United Nations Conference on International Organization at San Francisco, or having previously signed the Declaration by United Nations of January 1, 1942, sign the present Charter and ratify it in accordance with Article 110.

### Article 4

1. Membership in the United Nations is open to all other peace-loving states which accept the obligations contained in the present Charter and, in the judgment of the Organization, are able and willing to carry out these obligations.

2. The admission of any such state to membership in the United Nations will be effected by a decision of the General Assembly upon the recommendation of the Security Council.

### Article 5

A Member of the United Nations against which preventive or enforcement action has been taken by the Security Council may be suspended from the exercise of the rights and privileges of membership by the General Assembly upon the recommendation of the Security Council. The exercise of these rights and privileges may be restored by the Security Council.

### Article 6

A Member of the United Nations which has persistently violated the Principles contained in the present Charter may be expelled from the Organization by the General Assembly upon the recommendation of the Security Council.

### CHAPTER III

### Organs

### Article 7

1. There are established as the principal organs of the United Nations; a General Assembly, a Security Council, an Economic and Social Council, a Trusteeship Council, an International Court of Justice, and a Secretariat.

2. Such subsidiary organs as may be found necessary may be established in accordance with the present Charter.

### Article 8

The United Nations shall place no restrictions on the eligibility of men and women to participate in any capacity and under conditions of equality in its principal and subsidiary organs.

### CHAPTER IV

### The General Assembly
### Composition

### Article 9

1. The General Assembly shall consist of all the members of the United Nations.

2. Each Member shall have not more than five representatives in the General Assembly.

### Functions and Powers
### Article 10

The General Assembly may discuss any questions or any matters within the scope of the present Charter or relating to the powers and functions of any organs provided for in the present Charter, and, except as provided in Article 12, may make recommendations to the Members of the United Nations or to the Security Council or to both on any such questions or matters.

### Article 11

1. The General Assembly may consider the general principles of cooperation in the maintenance of international peace and security, including the principles governing disarmament and the regulation of armaments, and may make recommendations with regard to such principles to the Members or to the Security Council or to both.

2. The General Assembly may discuss any questions relating to the maintenance of international peace and security brought before it by any Member of the United Nations, or by the Security Council, or by a state which is not a Member of the United Nations, in accordance with Article 35, paragraph 2, and, except as provided in Article 12, may make recommendations with regard to any such question to the state or states concerned or to the Security Council or to both. Any such question on which action is necessary shall be referred to the Security Council by the General Assembly either before or after discussion.

3. The General Assembly may call the attention of the Security Council to situations which are likely to endanger international peace and security.

4. The powers of the General Assembly set forth in this Article shall not limit the general scope of Article 10.

### Article 12

1. While the Security Council is exercising in respect of any dispute or situation the functions assigned to it in the present Charter, the General Assembly shall not make any recommendations with regard to that dispute or situation unless the Security Council so requests.

2. The Secretary-General, with the consent of the Security Council, shall notify the General Assembly at each session of any matters relative to the maintenance of international peace and security which are being dealt with by the Security Council and shall similarly notify the General Assembly, or the Members of the United Na-

tions if the General Assembly is not in session, immediately the Security Council ceases to deal with such matters.

### Article 13

1. The General Assembly shall initiate studies and make recommendations for the purpose of:

(a) promoting international cooperation in the political field and encouraging the progressive development of international law and its codification;

(b) promoting international cooperation in the economic, social, cultural, educational, and health fields, and assisting in the realization of human rights and fundamental freedoms for all without distinction as to race, sex, language, or religion.

2. The further responsibilities, functions and powers of the General Assembly with respect to matters mentioned in paragraph 1 (b) above are set forth in Chapters IX and X.

### Article 14

Subject to the provisions of Article 12, the General Assembly may recommend measures for the peaceful adjustment of any situation, regardless of origin, which it deems likely to impair the general welfare or friendly relations among nations, including situations resulting from a violation of the provisions of the present Charter setting forth the Purposes and Principles of the United Nations.

### Article 15

1. The General Assembly shall receive and consider annual and special reports from the Security Council; these reports shall include an account of the measures that the Security Council has decided upon or taken to maintain international peace and security.

2. The General Assembly shall receive and consider reports from the other organs of the United Nations.

### Article 16

The General Assembly shall perform such functions with respect to the international trusteeship system as are assigned to it under Chapters XII and XIII, including the approval of the trusteeship agreements for areas not designated as strategic.

### Article 17

1. The General Assembly shall consider and approve the budget of the Organization.

2. The expenses of the Organization shall be borne by the Members as apportioned by the General Assembly.

3. The General Assembly shall consider and approve any financial and budgetary arrangements with specialized agencies referred to in Article 57 and shall examine the administrative budgets of such specialized agencies with a view to making recommendations to the agencies concerned.

## Voting

### Article 18

1. Each member of the General Assembly shall have one vote.

2. Decisions of the General Assembly on important questions shall be made by a two-thirds majority of the members present and voting. These questions shall include: recommendations with respect to the maintenance of international peace and security, the election of the nonpermanent members of the Security Council, the election of the members of the Economic and Social Council, the election of members of the Trusteeship Council in accordance with paragraph 1 (c) of Article 86, the admission of new Members to the United Nations, the suspension of the rights and privileges of membership, the expulsion of Members, questions relating to the operation of the trusteeship system, and budgetary questions.

3. Decisions on other questions, including the determination of additional categories of questions to be decided by a two-thirds majority, shall be made by a majority of the members present and voting.

### Article 19

A Member of the United Nations which is in arrears in the payment of its financial contributions to the Organization shall have no vote in the General Assembly if the amount of its arrears equals or exceeds the amount of the contributions due from it for the preceding two full years. The General Assembly may, nevertheless, permit such a Member to vote if it is satisfied that the failure to pay is due to conditions beyond the control of the Member.

## Procedure

### Article 20

The General Assembly shall meet in regular annual sessions and in such special sessions as occasion may require. Special sessions shall be convoked by the Secretary-General at the request of the Security Council or of a majority of the Members of the United Nations.

### Article 21

The General Assembly shall adopt its own rules of procedure. It shall elect its President for each session.

### Article 22

The General Assembly may establish such subsidiary organs as it deems necessary for the performance of its functions.

CHAPTER V

# The Security Council
## Composition
### Article 23

1. The Security Council shall consist of eleven Members of the United Nations. The Republic of China, France, the Union of Soviet Socialist Republics, the United Kingdom of Great Britain and Northern Ireland, and the United States of America shall be permanent members of the Security Council. The General Assembly shall elect six other Members of the United Nations to be non-permanent members of the Security Council, due regard being specially paid, in the first instance to the contribution of members of the United Nations to the maintenance of international peace and security and to the other purposes of the Organization, and also to equitable geographical distribution.

2. The non-permanent members of the Security Council shall be elected for a term of two years. In the first election of the non-permanent members, however, three shall be chosen for a term of one year. A retiring member shall not be eligible for immediate re-election.

3. Each member of the Security Council shall have one representative.

## Functions and Powers
### Article 24

1. In order to insure prompt and effective action by the United Nations, its Members confer on the Security Council primary responsibility for the maintenance of international peace and security, and agree that in carrying out its duties under this responsibility the Security Council acts on their behalf.

2. In discharging these duties the Security Council shall act in accordance with the Purposes and Principles of the United Nations. The specific powers granted to the Security Council for the discharge of these duties are laid down in Chapters VI, VII, VIII, and XII.

3. The Security Council shall submit annual and, when necessary, special reports to the General Assembly for its consideration.

### Article 25

The Members of the United Nations agree to accept and carry out the decisions of the Security Council in accordance with the present Charter.

### Article 26

In order to promote the establishment and maintenance of international peace and security with the least diversion for armaments of the world's human and economic resources, the Security Council shall be responsible for formulating, with the assistance of the Military Staff Committee referred to in Article 47, plans to be submitted to the Members of the United Nations for the establishment of a system for the regulation of armaments.

## Voting
### Article 27

1. Each member of the Security Council shall have one vote.

2. Decisions of the Security Council on procedural matters shall be made by an affirmative vote of seven members.

3. Decisions of the Security Council on all other matters shall be made by an affirmative vote of seven members including the concurring votes of the permanent members; provided that, in decisions under Chapter VI, and under paragraph 3 of Article 52, a party to a dispute shall abstain from voting.

## Procedure
### Article 28

1. The Security Council shall be so organized as to be able to function continuously. Each member of the Security Council shall for this purpose be represented at all times at the seat of the Organization.

2. The Security Council shall hold periodic meetings at which each of its members may, if it so desires, be represented by a member of the government or by some other specially designated representative.

3. The Security Council may hold meetings at such places other than the seat of the Organization as in its judgment will best facilitate its work.

### Article 29

The Security Council may establish such subsidiary organs as it deems necessary for the performance of its functions.

### Article 30

The Security Council shall adopt its own rules of procedure, including the method of selecting its President.

### Article 31

Any Member of the United Nations which is not a member of the Security Council may participate, without vote, in the discussion of any question brought before the Security Council whenever the latter considers that the interests of that Member are specially affected.

### Article 32

Any Member of the United Nations which is not a member of the Security

Council or any state which is not a Member of the United Nations, if it is a party to a dispute under consideration by the Security Council, shall be invited to participate, without vote, in the discussion relating to the dispute. The Security Council shall lay down such conditions as it deems just for the participation of a state which is not a Member of the United Nations.

## CHAPTER VI

## Pacific Settlement of Disputes

### Article 33

1. The parties to any dispute, the continuance of which is likely to endanger the maintenance of international peace and security, shall, first of all, seek a solution by negotiation, enquiry, mediation, conciliation, arbitration, judicial settlement, resort to regional agencies or arrangements, or other peaceful means of their own choice.

2. The Security Council shall, when it deems necessary, call upon the parties to settle their dispute by such means.

### Article 34

The Security Council may investigate any dispute, or any situation which might lead to international friction or give rise to a dispute, in order to determine whether the continuance of the dispute or situation is likely to endanger the maintenance of international peace and security.

### Article 35

1. Any Member of the United Nations may bring any dispute, or any situation of the nature referred to in Article 34 to the attention of the Security Council or of the General Assembly.

2. A state which is not a Member of the United Nations may bring to the attention of the Security Council or of the General Assembly any dispute to which it is a party if it accepts in advance, for the purposes of the dispute, the obligations of pacific settlement provided in the present Charter.

3. The proceedings of the General Assembly in respect of matters brought to its attention under this Article will be subject to the provisions of Articles 11 and 12.

### Article 36

1. The Security Council may, at any stage of a dispute of the nature referred to in Article 33 or of a situation of like nature, recommend appropriate procedures or methods of adjustment.

2. The Security Council should take into consideration any procedures for the settlement of the dispute which have already been adopted by the parties.

3. In making recommendations under this Article the Security Council should also take into consideration that legal disputes should as a general rule be referred by the parties to the International Court of Justice in accordance with the provisions of the Statute of the Court.

### Article 37

1. Should the parties to a dispute of the nature referred to in Article 33 fail to settle it by the means indicated in that Article, they shall refer it to the Security Council.

2. If the Security Council deems that the continuance of the dispute is in fact likely to endanger the maintenance of international peace and security, it shall decide whether to take action under Article 36 or to recommend such terms of settlement as it may consider appropriate.

### Article 38

Without prejudice to the provisions of Articles 33 to 37, the Security Council may, if all the parties to any dispute so request, make recommendations to the parties with a view to a pacific settlement of the dispute.

## CHAPTER VII

## Action with Respect to Threats to the Peace, Breaches of the Peace, and Acts of Aggression

### Article 39

The Security Council shall determine the existence of any threat to the peace, breach of the peace, or act of aggression and shall make recommendations, or decide what measures shall be taken in accordance with Articles 41 and 42, to maintain or restore international peace and security.

### Article 40

In order to prevent an aggravation of the situation, the Security Council may, before making the recommendations or deciding upon the measures provided for in Article 39, call upon the parties concerned to comply with such provisional measures as it deems necessary or desirable. Such provisional measures shall be without prejudice to the rights, claims, or position of the parties concerned. The Security Council shall duly take account of failure to comply with such provisional measures.

### Article 41

The Security Council may decide what measures not involving the use of armed force are to be employed to give effect.

to its decisions, and it may call upon the Members of the United Nations to apply such measures. These may include complete or partial interruption of economic relations and of rail, sea, air, postal, telegraphic, radio, and other means of communication, and the severance of diplomatic relations.

## Article 42

Should the Security Council consider that measures provided for in Article 41 would be inadequate or have proved to be inadequate, it may take such action by air, sea, or land forces as may be necessary to maintain or restore international peace and security. Such action may include demonstrations, blockade, and other operations by air, sea, or land forces of Members of the United Nations.

## Article 43

1. All Members of the United Nations, in order to contribute to the maintenance of international peace and security, undertake to make available to the Security Council, on its call and in accordance with a special agreement or agreements, armed forces, assistance, and facilities, including rights of passage, necessary for the purpose of maintaining international peace and security.

2. Such agreement or agreements shall govern the numbers and types of forces, their degree of readiness and general location, and the nature of the facilities and assistance to be provided.

3. The agreement or agreements shall be negotiated as soon as possible on the initiative of the Security Council. They shall be concluded between the Security Council and Members or between the Security Council and groups of Members and shall be subject to ratification by the signatory states in accordance with their respective constitutional processes.

## Article 44

When the Security Council has decided to use force it shall, before calling upon a Member not represented on it to provide armed forces in fulfillment of the obligations assumed under Article 43, invite that Member, if the Member so desires, to participate in the decisions of the Security Council concerning the employment of contingents of that Member's armed forces.

## Article 45

In order to enable the United Nations to take urgent military measures, Members shall hold immediately available national air-force contingents for combined international enforcement action. The strength and degree of readiness of these contingents and plans for their combined action shall be determined, within the limits laid down in the special agreement or agreements referred to in Article 43, by the Security Council with the assistance of the Military Staff Committee.

## Article 46

Plans for the application of armed force shall be made by the Security Council with the assistance of the Military Staff Committee.

## Article 47

1. There shall be established a Military Staff Committee to advise and assist the Security Council on all questions relating to the Security Council's military requirements for the maintenance of international peace and security, the employment and command of forces placed at its disposal, the regulation of armaments, and possible disarmament.

2. The Military Staff Committee shall consist of the Chiefs of Staff of the permanent members of the Security Council or their representatives. Any Member of the United Nations not permanently represented on the Committee shall be invited by the Committee to be associated with it when the efficient discharge of the Committee's responsibilities requires the participation of that Member in its work.

3. The Military Staff Committee shall be responsible under the Security Council for the strategic direction of any armed forces placed at the disposal of the Security Council. Questions relating to the command of such forces shall be worked out subsequently.

4. The Military Staff Committee, with the authorization of the Security Council and after consultation with appropriate regional agencies, may establish regional subcommittees.

## Article 48

1. The action required to carry out the decisions of the Security Council for the maintenance of international peace and security shall be taken by all the Members of the United Nations or by some of them, as the Security Council may determine.

2. Such decisions shall be carried out by the Members of the United Nations directly and through their action in the appropriate international agencies of which they are members.

## Article 49

The Members of the United Nations shall join in affording mutual assistance in carrying out the measures decided upon by the Security Council.

## Article 50

If preventive or enforcement measures against any state are taken by the Security Council, any other state, whether a

Member of the United Nations or not, which finds itself confronted with special economic problems arising from the carrying out of those measures shall have the right to consult the Security Council with regard to a solution of those problems.

## Article 51

Nothing in the present Charter shall impair the inherent right of individual or collective self-defense if an armed attack occurs against a Member of the United Nations, until the Security Council has taken measures necessary to maintain international peace and security. Measures taken by Members in the exercise of this right of self-defense shall be immediately reported to the Security Council and shall not in any way affect the authority and responsibility of the Security Council under the present Charter to take at any time such action as it deems necessary in order to maintain or restore international peace and security.

## CHAPTER VIII

### Regional Arrangements

#### Article 52

1. Nothing in the present Charter precludes the existence of regional arrangements or agencies for dealing with such matters relating to the maintenance of international peace and security as are appropriate for regional action, provided that such arrangements or agencies and their activities are consistent with the Purposes and Principles of the United Nations.

2. The Members of the United Nations entering into such arrangements or constituting such agencies shall make every effort to achieve pacific settlement of local disputes through such regional arrangements or by such regional agencies before referring them to the Security Council.

3. The Security Council shall encourage the development of pacific settlement of local disputes through such regional arrangements or by such regional agencies either on the initiative of the states concerned or by reference from the Security Council.

4. This Article in no way impairs the application of Articles 34 and 35.

#### Article 53

1. The Security Council shall, where appropriate, utilize such regional arrangements or agencies for enforcement action under its authority. But no enforcement action shall be taken under regional arrangements or by regional agencies without the authorization of the Security Council, with the exception of measures against any enemy state, as defined in par-

agraph 2 of this Article, provided for pursuant to Article 107 or in regional arrangements directed against renewal of aggressive policy on the part of any such state, until such time as the Organization may, on request of the Governments concerned, be charged with the responsibility for preventing further aggression by such a state.

2. The term enemy state as used in paragraph 1 of this Article applies to any state which during the Second World War has been an enemy of any signatory of the present Charter.

## Article 54

The Security Council shall at all times be kept fully informed of activities undertaken or in contemplation under regional arrangements or by regional agencies for the maintenance of international peace and security.

## CHAPTER IX

## International Economic and Social Cooperation

### Article 55

With a view to the creation of conditions of stability and well-being which are necessary for peaceful and friendly relations among nations based on respect for the principle of equal rights and self-determination of peoples, the United Nations shall promote:

(a) higher standards of living, full employment, and conditions of economic and social progress and development;

(b) solutions of international economic, social, health, and related problems; and international cultural and educational cooperation; and

(c) universal respect for, and observance of, human rights and fundamental freedoms for all without distinction as to race, sex, language, or religion.

### Article 56

All Members pledge themselves to take joint and separate action in cooperation with the Organization for the achievement of the purposes set forth in Article 55.

### Article 57

1. The various specialized agencies, established by intergovernmental agreement and having wide international responsibilities, as defined in their basic instruments, in economic, social, cultural, educational, health, and related fields, shall be brought into relationship with the United Nations in accordance with the provisions of Article 63.

2. Such agencies thus brought into relationship with the United Nations are

hereinafter referred to as specialized agencies.

## Article 58

The Organization shall make recommendations for the coordination of the policies and activities of the specialized agencies.

## Article 59

The Organization shall, where appropriate, initiate negotiations among the states concerned for the creation of any new specialized agencies required for the accomplishment of the purposes set forth in Article 55.

## Article 60

Responsibility for the discharge of the functions of the Organization set forth in this Chapter shall be vested in the General Assembly and, under the authority of the General Assembly, in the Economic and Social Council, which shall have for this purpose the powers set forth in Chapter X.

### CHAPTER X

## Economic and Social Council
## Composition

### Article 61

1. The Economic and Social Council shall consist of eighteen Members of the United Nations elected by the General Assembly.

2. Subject to the provisions of paragraph 3, six members of the Economic and Social Council shall be elected each year for a term of three years. A retiring member shall be eligible for immediate re-election.

3. At the first election, eighteen members of the Economic and Social Council shall be chosen. The term of office of six members so chosen shall expire at the end of one year, and of six other members at the end of two years, in accordance with arrangements made by the General Assembly.

4. Each member of the Economic and Social Council shall have one representative.

### Functions and Powers

### Article 62

1. The Economic and Social Council may make or initiate studies and reports with respect to international economic, social, cultural, educational, health, and related matters and may make recommendations with respect to any such matters to the General Assembly, to the Members of the United Nations, and to the specialized agencies concerned.

2. It may make recommendations for the purpose of promoting respect for, and observance of, human rights and fundamental freedoms for all.

3. It may prepare draft conventions for submission to the General Assembly, with respect to matters falling within its competence.

4. It may call, in accordance with the rules prescribed by the United Nations, international conferences on matters falling within its competence.

### Article 63

1. The Economic and Social Council may enter into agreements with any of the agencies referred to in Article 57, defining the terms on which the agency concerned shall be brought into relationship with the United Nations. Such agreements shall be subject to approval by the General Assembly.

2. It may coordinate the activities of the specialized agencies through consultation with and recommendations to such agencies and through recommendations to the General Assembly and to the Members of the United Nations.

### Article 64

1. The Economic and Social Council may take appropriate steps to obtain regular reports from the specialized agencies. It may make arrangements with the Members of the United Nations and with the specialized agencies to obtain reports on the steps taken to give effect to its own recommendations and to recommendations on matters falling within its competence made by the General Assembly.

2. It may communicate its observations on these reports to the General Assembly.

### Article 65

The Economic and Social Council may furnish information to the Security Council and shall assist the Security Council upon its request.

### Article 66

1. The Economic and Social Council shall perform such functions as fall within its competence in connection with the carrying out of the recommendations of the General Assembly.

2. It may, with the approval of the General Assembly, perform services at the request of Members of the United Nations and at the request of specialized agencies.

3. It shall perform such other functions as are specified elsewhere in the present Charter or as may be assigned to it by the General Assembly.

### Voting

### Article 67

1. Each member of the Economic and Social Council shall have one vote.

2. Decisions of the Economic and Social Council shall be made by a majority of the members present and voting.

## Procedure
### Article 68

The Economic and Social Council shall set up commissions in economic and social fields and for the promotion of human rights, and such other commissions as may be required for the performance of its functions.

### Article 69

The Economic and Social Council shall invite any Member of the United Nations to participate, without vote, in its deliberations on any matter of particular concern to that Member.

### Article 70

The Economic and Social Council may make arrangements for representatives of the specialized agencies to participate, without vote, in its deliberations and in those of the commissions established by it, and for its representatives to participate in the deliberations of the specialized agencies.

### Article 71

The Economic and Social Council may make suitable arrangements for consultation with non-governmental organizations which are concerned with matters within its competence. Such arrangements may be made with international organizations and, where appropriate, with national organizations after consultation with the Member of the United Nations concerned.

### Article 72

1. The Economic and Social Council shall adopt its own rules of procedure, including the method of selecting its President.

2. The Economic and Social Council shall meet as required in accordance with its rules, which shall include provision for the convening of meetings on the request of a majority of its members.

## CHAPTER XI

## Declaration Regarding Non-Self-Governing Territories
### Article 73

Members of the United Nations which have or assume responsibilities for the administration of territories whose peoples have not yet attained a full measure of self-government recognize the principle that the interests of the inhabitants of these territories are paramount, and ac-

cept as a sacred trust the obligation to promote to the utmost, within the system of international peace and security established by the present Charter, the well-being of the inhabitants of these territories, and, to this end:

(a) to ensure, with due respect for the culture of the peoples concerned, their political, economic, social, and educational advancement, their just treatment, and their protection against abuses;

(b) to develop self-government, to take due account of the political aspirations of the peoples, and to assist them in the progressive development of their free political institutions, according to the particular circumstances of each territory and its peoples and their varying stages of advancement;

(c) to further international peace and security;

(d) to promote constructive measures of development, to encourage research, and to cooperate with one another and, when and where appropriate, with specialized international bodies with a view to the practical achievement of the social, economic, and scientific purposes set forth in this Article; and

(e) to transmit regularly to the Secretary-General for information purposes, subject to such limitation as security and constitutional considerations may require, statistical and other information of a technical nature relating to economic, social, and educational conditions in the territories for which they are respectively responsible other than those territories to which Chapters XII and XIII apply.

### Article 74

Members of the United Nations also agree that their policy in respect of the territories to which this Chapter applies, no less than in respect of their metropolitan areas, must be based on the general principle of good-neighborliness, due account being taken of the interests and well-being of the rest of the world, in social, economic, and commercial matters.

## CHAPTER XII

## International Trusteeship System
### Article 75

The United Nations shall establish under its authority an international trusteeship system for the administration and supervision of such territories as may be placed thereunder by subsequent individual agreements. These territories are hereinafter referred to as trust territories.

### Article 76

The basic objectives of the trusteeship system, in accordance with the Purposes of the United Nations laid down in Article 1 of the present Charter, shall be:

(a) to further international peace and security;

(b) to promote the political, economic, social, and educational advancement of the inhabitants of the trust territories, and their progressive development towards self-government or independence as may be appropriate to the particular circumstances of each territory and its peoples and the freely expressed wishes of the peoples concerned, and as may be provided by the terms of each trusteeship agreement;

(c) to encourage respect for human rights and for fundamental freedoms for all without distinction as to race, sex, language, or religion, and to encourage recognition of the interdependence of the peoples of the world; and

(d) to ensure equal treatment in social, economic, and commercial matters for all Members of the United Nations and their nationals, and also equal treatment for the latter in the administration of justice, without prejudice to the attainment of the foregoing objectives and subject to the provisions of Article 80.

## Article 77

1. The trusteeship system shall apply to such territories in the following categories as may be placed thereunder by means of trusteeship agreements:

(a) territories now held under mandate;

(b) territories which may be detached from enemy states as a result of the Second World War; and

(c) territories voluntarily placed under the system by states responsible for their administration.

2. It will be a matter for subsequent agreement as to which territories in the foregoing categories will be brought under the trusteeship system and upon what terms.

## Article 78

The trusteeship system shall not apply to territories which have become Members of the United Nations, relationship among which shall be based on respect for the principle of sovereign equality.

## Article 79

The terms of trusteeship for each territory to be placed under the trusteeship system, including any alteration or amendment, shall be agreed upon by the states directly concerned, including the mandatory power in the case of territories held under mandate by a Member of the United Nations, and shall be approved as provided for in Articles 83 and 85.

## Article 80

1. Except as may be agreed upon in individual trusteeship agreements, made under Articles 77, 79, and 81, placing each territory under the trusteeship system, and until such agreements have been concluded, nothing in this Chapter shall be construed in or of itself to alter in any manner the rights whatsoever of any states or any peoples or the terms of existing international instruments to which Members of the United Nations may respectively be parties.

2. Paragraph 1 of this Article shall not be interpreted as giving grounds for delay or postponement of the negotiation and conclusion of agreements for placing mandated and other territories under the trusteeship system as provided for in Article 77.

## Article 81

The trusteeship agreement shall in each case include the terms under which the trust territory will be administered and designate the authority which will exercise the administration of the trust territory. Such authority, hereinafter called the administering authority, may be one or more states or the Organization itself.

## Article 82

There may be designated, in any trusteeship agreement, a strategic area or areas which may include part or all of the trust territory to which the agreement applies, without prejudice to any special agreement or agreements made under Article 43.

## Article 83

1. All functions of the United Nations relating to strategic areas, including the approval of the terms of the trusteeship agreements and of their alteration or amendment, shall be exercised by the Security Council.

2. The basic objectives set forth in Article 76 shall be applicable to the people of each strategic area.

3. The Security Council shall, subject to the provisions of the trusteeship agreements and without prejudice to security considerations, avail itself of the assistance of the Trusteeship Council to perform those functions of the United Nations under the trusteeship system relating to political, economic, social, and educational matters in the strategic areas.

## Article 84

It shall be the duty of the administering authority to ensure that the trust territory shall play its part in the maintenance of international peace and security. To this end the administering authority may make use of volunteer forces, facilities, and assistance from the trust territory in carrying out the obligations towards the Security Council undertaken in this regard by the administering authority, as well as for local defense and the maintenance of law and order within the trust territory.

### Article 85

1. The functions of the United Nations with regard to trusteeship agreements for all areas not designated as strategic, including the approval of the terms of the trusteeship agreements and of their alteration or amendment, shall be exercised by the General Assembly.

2. The Trusteeship Council, operating under the authority of the General Assembly, shall assist the General Assembly in carrying out these functions.

### CHAPTER XIII

## The Trusteeship Council
## Composition

### Article 86

1. The Trusteeship Council shall consist of the following Members of the United Nations:

(a) those Members administering trust territories;

(b) such of those Members mentioned by name in Article 23 as are not administering trust territories; and

(c) as many other Members elected for three-year terms by the General Assembly as may be necessary to ensure that the total number of members of the Trusteeship Council is equally divided between those Members of the United Nations which administer trust territories and those which do not.

2. Each member of the Trusteeship Council shall designate one specially qualified person to represent it therein.

## Functions and Powers

### Article 87

The General Assembly and, under its authority, the Trusteeship Council, in carrying out their functions, may:

(a) consider reports submitted by the administering authority;

(b) accept petitions and examine them in consultation with the administering authority;

(c) provide for periodic visits to the respective trust territories at times agreed upon with the administering authority; and

(d) take these and other actions in conformity with the terms of the trusteeship agreements.

### Article 88

The Trusteeship Council shall formulate a questionnaire on the political, economic, social, and educational advancement of the inhabitants of each trust territory, and the administering authority for each trust territory within the competence of the General Assembly shall make an annual report to the General Assembly upon the basis of such questionnaire.

## Voting

### Article 89

1. Each member of the Trusteeship Council shall have one vote.

2. Decisions of the Trusteeship Council shall be made by a majority of the members present and voting.

## Procedure

### Article 90

1. The Trusteeship Council shall adopt its own rules of procedure, including the method of selecting its President.

2. The Trusteeship Council shall meet as required in accordance with its rules, which shall include provision for the convening of meetings on the request of a majority of its members.

### Article 91

The Trusteeship Council shall, when appropriate, avail itself of the assistance of the Economic and Social Council and of the specialized agencies in regard to matters with which they are respectively concerned.

### CHAPTER XIV

## The International Court of Justice

### Article 92

The International Court of Justice shall be the principal judicial organ of the United Nations. It shall function in accordance with the annexed Statute, which is based upon the Statute of the Permanent Court of International Justice and forms an integral part of the present Charter.

### Article 93

1. All Members of the United Nations are *ipso facto* parties to the Statute of the International Court of Justice.

2. A state which is not a Member of the United Nations may become a party to the Statute of the International Court of Justice on condition to be determined in each case by the General Assembly upon the recommendation of the Security Council.

### Article 94

1. Each Member of the United Nations undertakes to comply with the decision of

the International Court of Justice in any case to which it is a party.

2. If any party to a case fails to perform the obligations incumbent upon it under a judgment rendered by the Court, the other party may have recourse to the Security Council, which may, if it deems necessary, make recommendations or decide upon measures to be taken to give effect to the judgment.

### Article 95

Nothing in the present Charter shall prevent Members of the United Nations from entrusting the solution of their differences to other tribunals by virtue of agreements already in existence or which may be concluded in the future.

### Article 96

1. The General Assembly or the Security Council may request the International Court of Justice to give an advisory opinion on any legal question.

2. Other organs of the United Nations and specialized agencies, which may at any time be so authorized by the General Assembly, may also request advisory opinions of the Court on legal questions arising within the scope of their activities.

### CHAPTER XV

## The Secretariat

### Article 97

The Secretariat shall comprise a Secretary-General and such staff as the Organization may require. The Secretary-General shall be appointed by the General Assembly upon the recommendation of the Security Council. He shall be the chief administrative officer of the Organization.

### Article 98

The Secretary-General shall act in that capacity in all meetings of the General Assembly, of the Security Council, of the Economic and Social Council, and of the Trusteeship Council, and shall perform such other functions as are entrusted to him by these organs. The Secretary-General shall make an annual report to the General Assembly on the work of the Organization.

### Article 99

The Secretary-General may bring to the attention of the Security Council any matter which in his opinion may threaten the maintenance of international peace and security.

### Article 100

1. In the performance of their duties the Secretary-General and the staff shall not seek or receive instructions from any government or from any other authority external to the Organization. They shall refrain from any action which might reflect on their position as international officials responsible only to the Organization.

2. Each Member of the United Nations undertakes to respect the exclusively international character of the responsibilities of the Secretary-General and the staff and not to seek to influence them in the discharge of their responsibilities.

### Article 101

1. The staff shall be appointed by the Secretary-General under regulations established by the General Assembly.

2. Appropriate staffs shall be permanently assigned to the Economic and Social Council, the Trusteeship Council, and, as required, to other organs of the United Nations. These staffs shall form a part of the Secretariat.

3. The paramount consideration in the employment of the staff and in the determination of the conditions of service shall be the necessity of securing the highest standards of efficiency, competence, and integrity. Due regard shall be paid to the importance of recruiting the staff on as wide a geographical basis as possible.

### CHAPTER XVI

## Miscellaneous Provisions

### Article 102

1. Every treaty and every international agreement entered into by any Member of the United Nations after the present Charter comes into force shall as soon as possible be registered with the Secretariat and published by it.

2. No party to any such treaty or international agreement which has not been registered in accordance with the provisions of paragraph 1 of this Article may invoke that treaty or agreement before any organ of the United Nations.

### Article 103

In the event of a conflict between the obligations of the Members of the United Nations under the present Charter and their obligations under any other international agreement, their obligations under the present Charter shall prevail.

### Article 104

The Organization shall enjoy in the territory of each of its Members such legal capacity as may be necessary for the exercise of its functions and the fulfillment of its purposes.

### Article 105

1. The Organization shall enjoy in the territory of each of its Members such privileges and immunities as are necessary for the fulfillment of its purposes.

2. Representatives of the Members of the United Nations and officials of the Organization shall similarly enjoy such privileges and immunities as are necessary for the independent exercise of their functions in connection with the Organization.

3. The General Assembly may make recommendations with a view to determining the details of the application of paragraphs 1 and 2 of this Article or may propose conventions to the Members of the United Nations for this purpose.

## CHAPTER XVII

## Transitional Security Arrangements

### Article 106

Pending the coming into force of such special agreements referred to in Article 43 as in the opinion of the Security Council enable it to begin the exercise of its responsibilities under Article 42, the parties to the Four-Nation Declaration, signed at Moscow, October 30, 1943, and France, shall, in accordance with the provisions of paragraph 5 of that Declaration, consult with one another and, as occasion requires with other Members of the United Nations with a view to such joint action on behalf of the Organization as may be necessary for the purpose of maintaining international peace and security.

### Article 107

Nothing in the present Charter shall invalidate or preclude action, in relation to any state which during the Second World War has been an enemy of any signatory to the present Charter, taken or authorized as a result of that war by the Governments having responsibility for such action.

## CHAPTER XVIII

## Amendments

### Article 108

Amendments to the present Charter shall come into force for all Members of the United Nations when they have been adopted by a vote of two-thirds of the members of the General Assembly and ratified in accordance with their respective constitutional processes by two-thirds of the Members of the United Nations, including all the permanent members of the Security Council.

### Article 109

1. A General Conference of the Members of the United Nations for the purpose of reviewing the present Charter may be held at a date and place to be fixed by a two-thirds vote of the members of the General Assembly and by a vote of any seven members of the Security Council. Each Member of the United Nations shall have one vote in the conference.

2. Any alteration of the present Charter recommended by a two-thirds vote of the conference shall take effect when ratified in accordance with their respective constitutional processes by two-thirds of the Members of the United Nations including all the permanent members of the Security Council.

3. If such a conference has not been held before the tenth annual session of the General Assembly following the coming into force of the present Charter, the proposal to call such a conference shall be placed on the agenda of that session of the General Assembly, and the conference shall be held if so decided by a majority vote of the members of the General Assembly and by a vote of any seven members of the Security Council.

## CHAPTER XIX

## Ratification and Signature

### Article 110

1. The present Charter shall be ratified by the signatory states in accordance with their respective constitutional processes.

2. The ratifications shall be deposited with the Government of the United States of America, which shall notify all the signatory states of each deposit as well as the Secretary-General of the Organization when he has been appointed.

3. The present Charter shall come into force upon the deposit of ratifications by the Republic of China, France, the Union of Soviet Socialist Republics, the United Kingdom of Great Britain and Northern Ireland, and the United States of America, and by a majority of the other signatory states. A protocol of the ratifications deposited shall thereupon be drawn up by the Government of the United States of America which shall communicate copies thereof to all the signatory states.

4. The states signatory to the present Charter which ratify it after it has come into force will become original Members of the United Nations on the date of the deposit of their respective ratifications.

### Article 111

The present Charter, of which the Chinese, French, Russian, English, and Spanish texts are equally authentic, shall remain deposited in the archives of the Government of the United States of America. Duly certified copies thereof shall be transmitted by that Government to the Governments of the other signatory states.

IN FAITH WHEREOF the representatives of the Governments of the United Nations have signed the present Charter.

DONE at the city of San Francisco the twenty-sixth day of June, one thousand nine hundred and forty-five.

# WORLD HISTORY

★

## A GUIDE TO MAIN HISTORICAL, POLITICAL, ECONOMIC, GEOGRAPHIC AND SOCIAL FACTS

*Prepared by the Editorial Staff of the*

### INFORMATION PLEASE ALMANAC

---

Although the general Index at the back of the book lists each country covered in this section, we have added this special index for quicker reference, plus a table of Newly Independent Countries.

NOTE: Dependencies not listed below will be found following the mother country. For page, see Index at back of book.

---

# NEWLY INDEPENDENT COUNTRIES
## (since 1950)

### AFRICA

| Country | Date of Independence | Previous Status |
|---|---|---|
| Cameroun | 1960 | Fr. Trust Territory |
| Central African Republic† | 1960 | Autonomous Rep., Member of French Community |
| Republic of Chad† | 1960† | Autonomous Rep., Member of French Community |
| Republic of the Congo (Brazzaville)† | 1960 | Autonomous Rep., Member of French Community |
| Republic of the Congo (Léopoldville) | 1960 | Belgian Colony |
| Cyprus* | 1959 | British Crown Colony |
| Republic of Dahomey†† | 1960 | Autonomous Republic, Member of French Community |
| Gabon Republic† | 1960 | Autonomous Republic, Member of French Community |
| Ghana* | 1957 | Protectorate and British Trust Territory |
| Guinea | 1958 | French Overseas Territory |
| Republic of the Ivory Coast†† | 1960 | Autonomous Republic, Member of French Community |
| Kuwait | 1961 | British Sheikdom-Protectorate |
| Libya | 1951 | Under British and French Military Occupation |
| Malagasy Republic† | 1960 | Autonomous Republic, Member of French Community |
| Republic of Mali†† | 1960 | Autonomous Republic, Member of French Community |
| Islamic Republic of Mauritania† | 1960 | Autonomous Republic, Member of French Community |
| Morocco | 1956 | French and Spanish Protectorates |
| Republic of the Niger†† | 1960 | Autonomous Republic, Member of French Community |
| Federation of Nigeria* | 1960 | British Colony, Protectorate and Trust Territory |
| Republic of Senegal† | 1960 | Autonomous Republic, Member of French Community |
| Sierra Leone* | 1961 | British Colony and Protectorate |
| Somalia* | 1960 | British Protectorate |
| Sudan | 1956 | Anglo-Egyptian Condominium |
| Tanganyika** | 1961 | British Trust Territory |
| Togo | 1960 | French Trust Territory |
| Tunisia | 1956 | French Protectorate |
| Republic of the Upper Volta†† | 1960 | Autonomous Republic, Member of French Community |

## ✓ IA AND OCEANIA

| | | |
|---|---|---|
| Cambodia...................... | 1954 | Associated State of French Union |
| Laos........................... | 1954 | Associated State of French Union |
| Federation of Malaya*........... | 1957 | British Protected States |
| Islamic Republic of Pakistan*.... | 1956 | British Dominion |
| Democratic Republic of Vietnam (North)....................... | 1954 | Associated State of French Union |
| Republic of Vietnam (South)...... | 1954 | Associated State of French Union |
| Western Samoa§................. | 1962 | New Zealand Trust Territory |

† Member of the French Community. * Member of the British Commonwealth. †† Associated with French Community. ** Independence scheduled for Dec. 9, 1961. § Independence tentatively scheduled for Jan. 1, 1962.

# WORLD HISTORY
## Countries, Territories, Dependencies

## Afghanistan (Kingdom)

**Area:** 250,966 square miles.
**Population** (est. 1957): 13,000,000 (Pushtu, 60.5%; Tajik, 30.7%; Uzbek, 5%; Mongolian and others, 3.8%).
**Density per square mile:** 52.3.
**Ruler:** Mohammed Zahir Shah.
**Prime Minister:** Ali Mohammed Daud.
**Principal cities** (est. 1954): Kabul, 310,-000 (capital); Kandahar, 195,000 (trading center); Herat, 150,000 (farming center).
**Monetary unit:** Afghani.
**Languages:** Pashto (official), Persian.
**Religion:** Mohammedan (Sunni, 90%; Shiah, 10%).

### STATUS IN THE WORLD TODAY

Afghanistan has adopted a policy of neutrality, or neutralism, in the current East-West struggle largely as a result of the following factors: its history as an object for many years of Anglo-Russian imperialist rivalry; its landlocked position; its 1,250-mile frontier with the U.S.S.R.; and its border troubles with Pakistan, the country's best and least expensive trade route with the rest of the world. Like other underdeveloped Asian nations, it has been using both American and Soviet assistance in its economic development program aimed at building up some of the power, transport, irrigation, and industrial sources it so badly needs. Latest estimates indicate that Afghanistan has received the equivalent of $161 million in loans and credits from the U.S.S.R., including $25 million for military aid, as against $59 million in grants and loans from the U.S.

One of the nation's principal problems is transportation over extremely difficult terrain. There are few roads and usable waterways. The exit route through Iran is the least useful and most expensive; that through the Soviet Union depends upon political accommodation. Twice in recent years—in 1950 and 1955—Pakistan has blocked its neighbor's transit to the sea because of a conflict over the border region of "Pushtunistan," the home of the Pathans. But in 1958 the two countries signed a Transit Agreement, and a U.S. loan to Pakistan will enable that nation to complete railroad lines to the Afghan border and the latter to connect with them. The U.S.S.R. took advantage of the 1950 dispute to sign a far-reaching trade agreement with Afghanistan and since then has intensified its efforts at penetration of the country, which has received $70 millions in military aid, including 60 jet fighters and 12 bombers from Russia.

HISTORY AND GOVERNMENT. Wedged among Pakistan, Iran, and the U.S.S.R. in southwestern Asia without outlet to the sea, Afghanistan did not become an independent state until 1747. Previously, it had been either a cluster of small states under nominal Arab rule, part of Mongol or Mogul empires, or dismembered among India, Persia, and the Uzbeks.

In 1880, Great Britain recognized Abdur Rahman Khan as Emir and gave him an annual subsidy of more than $500,000 to delegate management of his foreign relations to Britain.

On Aug. 8, 1919, a treaty was signed making Afghanistan free and independent of all British control. The country maintained strict neutrality in World War II, and was admitted to the U.N. in 1946.

Under the Constitution, promulgated in 1932, authority is vested in the sovereign and Parliament, which has a Senate of fifty members, who are named for life by the sovereign, and a National Assembly of 171 elected members. Executive power is exercised by the sovereign and Cabinet, headed by the Prime Minister.

ECONOMIC CONDITIONS. Only a fifth of the soil is under cultivation, the greater part of the country being mountainous and rocky. Farming is confined to the fertile valleys and plains, sometimes with the aid of irrigation. Two crops a year are usually grown. Important ones include fruits and nuts, castor beans, cereals, madder, tobacco, cotton and vegetables. Wheat is the staple food. The fat-tailed indigenous sheep is a principal source of meat and wearing apparel.

Industry is still in a primary stage of development. Manufactures include cotton and woolen textiles and clothing, soap, leather, matches, beet sugar and furniture.

Among the leading exports are karakul skins (mostly to the U.S.), cotton, wool, rugs, carpets, spices and dried fruits. Most of the trade normally is carried on through Pakistan; wool and cotton are exported to the U.S.S.R. in return for consumers' goods. Fifty per cent of foreign trade is with the U.S.S.R. In addition exports go to India, U.S., Great Britain and Poland.

Afghanistan has no railways or navigable streams. Camels and pack horses are still used by the natives.

Both mineral and forest resources are largely unexploited. There are deposits of beryllium, chromite, coal, copper, gold, iron ore, lapis lazuli, oil, silver and sulfur.

NATURAL FEATURES. Afghanistan, approximately the size of Texas, is split east to west by the Hindu Kush range of the Himalayas, rising in the east to heights of 24,000 feet. Except in the southwest, most of the country is covered by high snow-capped mountains and deep valleys.

---

## Albania (People's Republic)

(Republika Popullóre e Shqipërisë)
Area: 11,100 square miles.
Population (1959): 1,556,000 (Albanian 99.8%; others, .2%).
Density per square mile: 140.2.
Chairman of Presidium: Hadji Leshi.
Premier: Mehmet Shehu
Principal cities (est. 1958): Tirana, 119,000 (capital); Scutari, 40,900 (northern trading center); Koritsa, 34,400 (farming center).
Monetary unit: Lek.
Language: Albanian.
Religions (est. 1953): Moslem, 65%; Greek Orthodox, 23%; Roman Catholic, 11%; others, 1%.

---

### STATUS IN THE WORLD TODAY

Albania, a backward and mountainous country, is the Kremlin's sole and isolated outpost on the Mediterranean, accessible only by a circuitous sea route since the defection of Yugoslavia from the Cominform. While it is reported to shelter submarine pens for the Soviet navy, its few port facilities are generally inadequate for modern shipping, and its principal role is that of a gadfly pestering Marshal Tito's dissident, yet Communist, country. Soviet agents can slip across the common frontier in either direction, and propaganda attacks can be mounted against Yugoslavia in the name of the largely illiterate Albanian mountain folk. Albania played a similar role in the late 1940's, when Greek Communist rebels were engaged in civil war against the Athens government. Until the 1948 break between Tito and Moscow, the Albanian Labor (Communist) party was directly subordinate to the Yugoslav Communist party. Recently Albanian Communists have shown a tendency to sympathize more with Red China's theories than with Moscow's.

---

HISTORY AND GOVERNMENT. After the fall of the Roman Empire, Albania became part of the Byzantine Empire and was successively invaded by Goths, Serbs, and Bulgarians. From 1014 to 1204 it was again under Byzantine rule. An alliance of Albanian chieftains (1444–66) under Skanderbeg failed to halt the advance of the Turks, and the country remained under at least nominal Turkish rule for more than four centuries, until it proclaimed its independence on Nov. 28, 1912.

During World War I Albania was variously occupied by Italian, Greek, French, Serb and Austro-Bulgarian forces. On Aug. 2, 1920, Italy recognized Albanian independence and evacuated the country. In 1927, after concluding pacts which placed Albania in Italy's sphere of influence, Zogu, President of the new Albanian republic since 1925, proclaimed himself King Zog 1.

During the Greco-Italian war of 1940–41, the Greek armies pushed the Italians back from the Albanian border and occupied a large part of southern Albania. When Germany attacked Greece and Yugoslavia in April, 1941, however, the Greeks withdrew quickly, and the Axis occupation of Albania was complete.

Albania was free of the Axis yoke by the end of 1944, and a leftist provisional government under Colonel General Enver Hoxha was established.

Under its 1945 Constitution, Albania has a typical Soviet government. Supreme power is vested in the popularly elected National Assembly, to which the Cabinet, headed by the Premier, is responsible.

ECONOMIC CONDITIONS. Albania is still a primitive country where each family tries to provide most of its own needs. Nearly the whole population is engaged in combined farming and stock raising. Only a small portion of the central part is fit for tilling. Corn is the chief crop. Others are wheat, tobacco, oats, barley, rye, spelt, olives, and citrus fruit. Factories produce food products, cement and textiles; a large dam and power station was completed near Tirana in 1950.

Albania's postwar trade has been limited for the most part to the Soviet bloc. Important exports include crude oil, copper and chrome ore. In 1959 Russia extended a credit of 300 million rubles and agreed to furnish technical aid to Albanian industry.

Mineral wealth, thought to be considerable, is relatively unexploited. The principal mineral is petroleum. Others include asphalt, bitumen, bauxite, chromite, copper, lignite, and pyrites.

NATURAL FEATURES. Albania is a mountainous state, largely over 3,000 ft. above sea level, with a narrow, marshy coastal plain crossed by several rivers. The interior mountain plateaus and basins contain the centers of population.

## Andorra

This 191-square-mile autonomous and semi-independent state on the Franco-Spanish border has been under the joint suzerainty of the French state and the Spanish bishops of Urgel since 1278. It is a cluster of mountain valleys inhabited by about 6,000 hardy and traditionally independent people, whose principal pursuit is the tending of flocks. Catalán is the language spoken. A Council General of 24 members, elected for four years by the heads of families, choose the First Syndic, the supreme executive authority.

## Arabia

### POLITICAL DIVISIONS OF ARABIA

| Name | Area (sq. mi.) | Population |
|---|---|---|
| Aden (Colony, British) | 75 | 152,000[1] |
| Aden (Protectorate[2]) | 112,278 | 650,000[1] |
| Bahrein Islands (Sultanate) | 231 | 143,213[3] |
| Kuwait (Sheikdom) | 6,000 | 240,000 |
| Oman and Masqat (Sultanate) | 82,000 | 550,000[4] |
| Qatar (Sheikdom) | 8,500 | 45,000 |
| Saudi Arabia (Kingdom) | 872,722 | 6,036,000[1] |
| Trucial Coast (Sheikdoms) | 32,278 | 86,000[1] |
| Yemen (Kingdom) | 75,290 | 4,500,000[5] |

[1] 1956 estimated. [2] British protectorate. [3] 1959 census. [4] 1957 estimated. [5] 1953 estimated.

The Arabian peninsula is at the southwest extremity of Asia. Its rich oil deposits and proximity to Palestine gave it special importance after World War II. Once a political unit, today it consists of the kingdoms of Saudi Arabia and Yemen, the British colony of Aden and six political entities in special treaty relationship with Great Britain.

The peninsula, with an area more than three times that of Texas, and an extreme length of 1,400 miles, is generally a plateau sloping gently eastward from a mountain range that averages 5,000 feet in elevation and runs along its entire west side within ten or fifteen miles of the Red Sea. The range reaches a maximum of 12,336 feet in Yemen to the southwest. Arabia has no rivers and no forests and is principally a desert dotted with many oases.

Mohammed united all Arabs in the seventh century A.D., and his followers, led by the caliphs, founded a great empire with its capital at Medina. Later, the caliphate capital was transferred to Damascus and then Baghdad, but Arabia retained its importance because of the holy cities of Mecca and Medina. In the sixteenth and seventeenth centuries, the Turks established at least nominal rule over much of Arabia, and in the middle of the eighteenth century it was divided into separate principalities.

### Aden. See Index.

### Bahrein Islands (Sheikdom)

These islands form an archipelago off Arabia's east coast and are an independent state ruled by Sheik Sir Salman bin Hamad al Khalifah. The islands are the center of the Persian Gulf pearl fisheries and the site of an airport on the London-Australia route. The concession for exploitation of petroleum deposits, discovered in 1932, is held in equal proportion by the Standard Oil Co. of California and the Texas Co. Output in 1959 was 2,256,000 metric tons. Agriculture is of some importance. Most of the trade of the Saudi Arabian provinces of Nejd and Hasa pass through Bahrein. The capital is Manama (population 1959: 61,837).

### Kuwait (Independent Sheikdom)

**Area: 6,000 square miles.**
**Population: 240,000.**
**Density per sqare mile: 40.**
**Ruler: Sheik Abdullah as-Salim as-Subah.**
**Principal city: Kuwait (capital), 104,551.**
**Monetary unit: Persian Gulf Indian Rupee.**
**Language: Arabic.**
**Religion: Moslem.**

### STATUS IN THE WORLD TODAY

Kuwait, which declared its independence in June, 1961, still has to depend on Great

Britain to maintain this independence. No sooner had the sheikdom achieved its new status than it was threatened with annexation by Iraq, and British troops were hastily summoned from Africa and Asia to defend Kuwait. The reason other Arab states have cast covetous eyes on the sheikdom is that, despite its size, it is the world's largest oil producer, and last year its revenues from this source, $400,000,000, were, for instance, twice as great as Iraq's.

HISTORY. The reigning dynasty in Kuwait was established in 1756. Before it became a British Protectorate, the protection of Turkey several times prevented Kuwait from being absorbed by Saudi Arabia. The Sheik is absolute ruler.

ECONOMIC CONDITIONS. Kuwait is largely desert. Oil production, which began in 1945, totaled 69,540,000 metric tons in 1959. Petroleum reserves, estimated at 60 billion barrels, are under concession to the Kuwait Oil Co., Ltd. (owned jointly by Gulf Oil Corp. and British Petroleum Co., Ltd.). Most of the revenue is devoted to the well-being of the inhabitants.

Kuwait is also a trading center for the exchange of Arab goods from the interior for textiles, rice, sugar, and other necessities.

## Oman and Masqat (Sultanate)

Occupying the mountainous southeastern part of the peninsula, Oman is nominally an independent state under the rule of Sultan Said bin Taimur. It has been under British protection since the nineteenth century. The state is best known for its date cultivation, and its riding camels are considered the best in the world. Trade is mainly to and from India. The capital is Masqat (population 1954: 5,500).

## Qatar (Sheikdom)

Qatar occupies the whole of the Qatar peninsula in the Persian Gulf. It is ruled, under British protection, by Sheik Ahmed bin Ali bin Abdullah al Thani. The whole area is claimed by Saudi Arabia. Oil deposits are being exploited by a subsidiary of the Iraq Petroleum Co.; output in 1959 was about 7,992,000 metric tons.

## Saudi Arabia. See Index.

## Trucial Coast (Sheikdoms)

This area, extending along part of the Gulf of Oman and the southern coast of the Persian Gulf, is ruled by seven semi-independent sheiks. Treaties signed with Britain in 1853 and 1892 provided that the sheiks should not cede or sell any part of their land to any other power.

## Yemen. See Index.

# Argentina (Republic)
## (República Argentina)

Area: 1,072,477 square miles.
Population (est. 1960): 20,956,000 (approximately 97% of European descent, chiefly Spanish and Italian; 3% Indian and other).
Density per square mile: 19.3.
President: Arturo Frondizi.
Principal cities (est. 1959): Buenos Aires, 3,845,279 (capital and chief port); (est. 1956) Rosario, 572,893 (flour milling); Córdoba, 478,428 (northwest farming center); Avellaneda, 363,150 (industrial suburb of Buenos Aires); Lanús, 300,045 (suburb of Buenos Aires); Mar del Plata, 144,942 (seaport, meat packing).
Monetary unit: Peso.
Languages: Spanish (official), Italian.
Religions (census 1947): Roman Catholic, 92.7%; Protestant, 1.9%; Jewish, 1.6%; others and unknown, 3.8%.

## STATUS IN THE WORLD TODAY

Argentina's problems since the overthrow of Juan Perón and the inauguration of a constitutional President in May, 1958, have been primarily economic and are due largely to the mistaken economic policies of the recent dictator. They are threefold: labor, decapitalization, and a strongly unfavorable balance of payments.

Since Perón, for political reasons, had made the labor movement his movement and given it many concessions at the expense of other economic units in the nation, its attitude toward the new government of Dr. Arturo Frondizi at first was in doubt. One of his first moves was to decree a general wage increase for all wage and salary earners. Even so, there have been a number of conflicts since then between labor and the government, and resultant strikes. There is still considerable Peronista strength in the country.

The capital equipment of much of Argentina's economy, particularly in the field of transportation, is out of date. Agriculture, upon which Argentina depends for most of its foreign-exchange earnings, is under-equipped with implements and machinery. Much of the equipment of the manufacturing industry is inadequate.

Increasing exports and decreasing noncapital imports are two ways of reducing the country's unfavorable balance of trade, which recently has been about $300 million a year. But increased domestic consumption and a decline in the nation's output have reduced the agricultural products available for export. The Frondizi government hopes to remedy this by expanding agricultural production for export through increased local production of agricultural machinery, distribution of modern technical information, and a shift from highly competitive products such as wheat to corn and meat. The regime also hopes to reduce imports of petroleum, the largest single import item. Here it is somewhat handicapped by a nationalistic opposition to exploitation of Argentina's admittedly rich oil reserves by foreign companies.

## MAJOR POLITICAL PARTIES

Unión Cívica Radical Intransigente (left-wing Radicals) (111 seats in Chamber of Deputies), led by Alfredo Garcia; Unión Cívica Radical del Pueblo (moderate Radicals) (76 seats), led by Ricardo Balbin.

HISTORY. Discovered in 1516 by Juan Díaz de Solís, Argentina developed slowly under Spanish colonial rule. Buenos Aires was settled in 1580; the cattle industry was thriving as early as 1600.

Invading British forces were expelled in 1806–07, and when Napoleon conquered Spain, the Argentinians set up their own government in the name of the Spanish King in 1810. On July 9, 1816, independence was formally declared.

The Rosas dictatorship (1835–52) only temporarily ended the strife between Buenos Aires and the rest of the country and between adherents of a strong central government and states rights. Despite these internal differences, however, the country prospered. Gradually the non-aristocratic groups began to demand more political rights and representative government, and electoral reforms were finally enacted in 1912.

Argentina proclaimed neutrality at the outbreak of World War II, but in general co-operated in hemispheric defense programs. In the closing months of the war, the nation declared war on the Axis (March 27, 1945) and signed the Act of Chapultepec the following April 4. Diplomatic recognition and admission to the U. N. followed. Juan D. Perón, then an army colonel, emerged as strongman and won the 1946 presidential elections. Perón was re-elected in 1951.

Long-smouldering opposition, fanned by worsening relations with the Catholic Church, finally resulted in Perón's overthrow in Sept., 1955 in a coup led by the armed forces. Perón fled to exile and his party as well as Congress was dissolved. GOVERNMENT. Argentina is a federal union of 22 provinces and the federal district. Under the Constitution of 1853 (restored by decree on May 1, 1956), the President and Vice-President are elected every 6 years by electors who are chosen by direct vote. The President appoints his Cabinet. The Vice-President presides over the Senate but has no other powers. Neither is eligible for immediate re-election. The Congress has two houses—a 46-member Senate, elected by the provincial legislatures for 6-year terms, and a Chamber of Deputies, popularly elected for 6-year terms. One-third of each house is renewed every two years.

Each province has its own constitution, elected governor, legislature and judiciary, but the President may in a crisis take over the local government.

ECONOMIC CONDITIONS.

*Agriculture.* A farming and stock-raising nation, Argentina devotes some 40% of its area to pasture and 10% to cultivation. Cotton, sugar cane and fruits are important, and Argentina is the world's largest producer of yerba maté (Paraguay tea), the national beverage. The 1956 wine production (preliminary) was 354,300,000 gallons (1951–55 average: 412,000,000 gallons).

Cattle-raising predominates on the pampas, especially in Buenos Aires province. Sheep raising is more important in Patagonia. In 1957 there were 44,203,425 cattle, 45,737,860 sheep, 3,487,122 pigs, 5,482,453 horses. Wool exports in 1959 were 224,670 tons, greasy basis.

*Manufacturing.* Industrial expansion was accelerated during World War II by the shortage of imports, but industry is still closely allied to agriculture. The principal industry is meat packing, followed by flour milling, textiles, sugar refining, dairy products, quebracho extraction and wine. Jeep production was started in 1956 and a steel plant is under construction at San Nicolas.

*Trade.* Leading exports in 1959 were meat (30%), cereals and linseed (29%), wheat (12%), wool (12%), and hides (7%); leading imports, machinery and vehicles (26%), fuel and lubricants (21%), and iron and steel and manufactures (20%). Leading customers were the United Kingdom (23%), the U.S. (12%), Germany (9%), the Netherlands (12%), and Italy (10%); leading suppliers, the U.S. (23%), Brazil (6%), Venezuela (11%), the United Kingdom (9%), and West Germany (11%).

NATURAL FEATURES AND RESOURCES. Second in South America to Brazil in size and population, Argentina is a plain, rising from the Atlantic to the Chilean border and the towering Andes peaks, including Aconcagua, 22,835 feet, the highest peak in the world outside Asia. The northern area is the swampy and partly wooded Gran Chaco. South of that are the rolling, fertile pampas, rich for agriculture and grazing and supporting most of Argentina's population. Next southward is Patagonia, a region of cool, arid steppes with some wooded and fertile sections. The eastern part of Tierra del Fuego, the island southern tip of South America, belongs to Argentina.

The three great rivers which make up the Plata system—the Paraná, Paraguay and Uruguay—are important commercial arteries in northern Argentina. Rosario and Santa Fé, 260 and 360 miles respectively above Buenos Aires on the Paraná, are accessible to ocean vessels.

*Minerals.* Argentina must import most of nearly every mineral it uses. Oil is proced in Patagonia (1959: 6,384,000 metric tons). The government announced discovery of uranium deposits in Feb., 1947. Imports of fuels and lubricants totaled 9,993,900 metric tons in 1956.

*Forests.* The Gran Chaco area is the world's chief source of quebracho extract. Total exports of this tanning agent obtained from quebracho logs in 1954 were 153,000 metric tons, part of which was re-exported from Paraguay.

---

# Austria (Republic)
## (Republik Österreich)

**Area:** 32,374 square miles.
**Population** (est. 1959): 7,049,000 (practically all Austrian).
**Density per square mile:** 217.7.
**President:** Dr. Adolf Schärf.
**Chancellor:** Alfons Gorbach.
**Principal cities** (est. 1959): Vienna, 1,652,427 (capital, industrial center); Graz, 226,453 (industrial center); Linz, 184,685 (industrial center); Salzburg, 102,927 (tourist center); Innsbruck, 95,055 (tourist center).
**Monetary unit:** Schilling.
**Language:** German.
**Religions** (census 1951): Roman Catholic, 89%; Protestant, 6%; others, 5%.

---

### STATUS IN THE WORLD TODAY

Although theoretically neutral in the cold war, Austria, with its democratic institutions, is oriented toward Free Europe. Its foreign policy aims to avoid accusations of favoritism for either East or West. But public opinion appears to be pro-Free Europe and pro-American, and there is much resentment against the severe economic concessions exacted by the U.S.S.R. as the price of its withdrawal in 1955.

Stripped of her industrial areas after World War I, with no outlet to the sea, with a soft currency, and a population less than that of metropolitan New York, Austria has long been dependent upon outside aid. Her economic recovery in recent years has been one of the most dramatic success stories of the post-World War II era. Much of this may be attributed to Marshall Plan aid.

### MAJOR POLITICAL PARTIES

People's party (79 seats in Parliament), led by Chancellor Alfons Gorbach; Socialist party (78 seats), led by Vice-Chancellor Bruno Pittermann.

---

HISTORY AND GOVERNMENT. The history of Austria before World War I was closely identified with that of the Austro-Hungarian Monarchy and its ruling house, the Hapsburgs. The monarchy originated in a margravate founded by Charlemagne in the late eighth century. In 1252 Ottokar, King of Bohemia, gained possession of the Austrian territories, only to lose them to Rudolf of Hapsburg in 1276. In the next three centuries the Hapsburg power steadily grew until Charles V (1519–1556) ruled a vast area of Europe. In 1806, during the Napoleonic Wars, Emperor Francis I relinquished the crown of the Holy Roman Empire.

Austria emerged from the Congress of Vienna in 1815 as the dominant power on the Continent. The *Ausgleich* of 1867 provided for a dual sovereignty embracing the empire of Austria and the kingdom of Hungary under Francis Joseph I, who ruled until 1916.

In 1919 the Austro-Hungarian Monarchy was dissolved by the treaties of St. Germain and Trianon. Austria was left in political chaos and economic ruin. In 1934 Chancellor Englebert Dollfuss established a dictatorship, only to be assassinated by Nazi conspirators on July 25, 1934. He was succeeded by Kurt von Schuschnigg, whose futile effort to maintain Austria's independence ended with a bloodless Nazi occupation on March 12, 1938. The next day, *Anschluss* (union) with Germany was proclaimed. After World War II the United States and Great Britain removed Austria from the ranks of enemy states by declaring the Austrians a "liberated" people. She finally regained her independence on May 14, 1955, by a state treaty ending seventeen years of occupation, but only after long and difficult negotiations with the Russians.

The federal republic of Austria is composed of nine provinces, including Vienna. The President is elected by the people directly for a term of six years. The bicameral legislature consists of the *Bundesrat*, with fifty members chosen by the provincial assemblies, and the *Nationalrat*, with 165 members popularly elected for 4 years. The Chancellor and his Cabinet are responsible for governmental administration.

ECONOMIC CONDITIONS. Agriculture employs approximately one-third of the population but the country is heavily dependent on imported foodstuffs. Mixed farming predominates. Rye and wheat are the leading cereals. Stock raising and dairy farming, both in the Alpine pastures and the lowlands of the east, are of importance.

Austria is primarily an industrial country, with 41% of the population engaged in industry. Most important are the metallurgical, engineering, textile and food-processing industries. Medium- and small-sized firms with specialized lines predominate, although a few large enterprises exist. Nationalized plants employ about one-fifth of the industrial labor force. The major steel and aluminum plants are in Upper Austria.

Leading exports are iron and steel and other metals, timber and machinery, electrical equipment and vehicles; leading imports, machinery, electrical equipment and vehicles, food and mineral fuels. Leading customers in 1959 were West Germany (26%), Italy (17%), other EPU countries (17%), and the sterling area (6%); leading suppliers, West Germany (40%), the U.S. and Canada (8%), Italy (8%), other EPU countries (17%), and the United Kingdom (5%). Austria joined "Outer Seven" in 1959 to encourage free trade in this area.

NATURAL FEATURES AND RESOURCES. Austria covers an area about equal to that of Scotland and includes much of the mountainous territory of the eastern Alps (about 92.3 per cent of the country). The country contains many snowfields, glaciers, and snow-capped peaks. The principal river is the Danube. Forests and woodlands cover about 40%.

Austria possesses valuable mineral resources. In Styria lies one of the largest European deposits of iron ore. Copper is mined in Salzburg, Tyrol, and Lower Austria, and lead and zinc in Carinthia. Large supplies of coal and coke must be imported, but extensive water power resources are available for exploitation. Petroleum fields are in the Zistersdorf and Mühlberg areas, both in eastern Austria.

# Belgium (Kingdom)

## (Royaume de Belgique—
## Koninkrijk België)

**Area: 11,779 square miles.\***
**Population** (est. 1959): 9,104,000 (Walloon, Flemish).
**Density per square mile: 772.9.**
**Sovereign: Baudouin I.**
**Premier: Theo Lefevre.**
**Principal cities** (est. 1957, including certain suburbs): Brussels, 1,385,831 (capital); Antwerp, 841,686 (port and commercial center); Liège, 604,861 (iron and steel); Charleroi, 469,383 (industrial center); Ghent, 453,234 (textiles).

**Monetary unit:** Belgian franc.
**Languages** (est. 1954): Flemish, 50%; French, 34%; Flemish and French, 15%; German, 1%.

**Religion: Predominantly Roman Catholic.**

\* Including areas taken over from Germany in 1949.

## STATUS IN THE WORLD TODAY

Little Belgium, a staunch supporter of the Free World, probably makes a proportional contribution to the North Atlantic community second to none. As a small nation, it has always been one of the most enthusiastic participants in international attempts to bring order into the world, first in the League of Nations and then in the United Nations. It has also supported attempts to create supranational economic divisions, starting with the Benelux Customs Union which it established with the Netherlands and Luxembourg. Its economy is relatively stable, although it can supply only two-thirds of its food needs, has no natural resource except coal —which has become increasingly difficult to sell—and must export 40 per cent of its production. In competing with other nations for foreign trade, it is beginning to feel the effect of obsolescent equipment in some textile and chemical plants.

Riots early in 1959 against Europeans by Abako Congolese seeking independence focused attention on the Belgian Congo, where the Belgians have sought to rule with enlightenment. Voting rights were granted to all in 1959 (until then, even white settlers could not vote), and on June 30, 1960, the colony received its independence.

## MAJOR POLITICAL PARTIES

Christian Social party (96 seats in Chamber of Representatives), led by Premier Theo Lefevre; Socialist party (84 seats), led by Paul Henri Spaak.

HISTORY AND GOVERNMENT. Perhaps the earliest mention of the Belgians in history was in 57–50 B.C., when they were conquered by Julius Caesar. In the Middle Ages the Belgian towns became wealthy and virtually autonomous as great textile centers. Belgium became part of Burgundy in 1385 and, later, part of the Spanish domains of Charles V. By the Treaty of Utrecht, in 1713 Belgium went to Austria, though retaining its autonomy. During the wars that followed the French Revolution, Belgium was occupied and later annexed by France.

After the fall of Napoleon the Congress of Vienna (1815) joined the French Catholic Walloons of Belgium with the Germanic Protestant Flemings of Holland (United Provinces) to form the Kingdom of the Netherlands. The Belgians rose in revolt in 1830 and declared their independence. The Treaty of London (1831) guaranteed Belgian independence.

The invasion of Belgium by Germany in 1914 triggered the explosion of World War I. The Treaty of Versailles (1919) gave the strategic areas of Eupen, Malmédy, and

Moresnet to Belgium. On February 17, 1934, King Albert was killed while mountain climbing and was succeeded by his son, Leopold III. Leopold III formally abdicated on July 16, 1951, and his son became King Baudouin.

Belgium is one of the most highly industrialized nations in Europe, due in part to its coal reserves. Its economic advance has been notable. In spring, 1958, the $260 million Brussels World's Fair commenced a six-months run to portray the artifacts of today's technological revolution.

Belgium is a constitutional monarchy consisting of nine provinces. Its bicameral legislature has a Senate, with members elected for four years, partly directly and partly indirectly, and a 212-member Chamber of Deputies directly elected for four years by proportional representation. There is universal suffrage, and those who do not vote are fined. Belgium joined the North Atlantic Alliance in April, 1949.

ECONOMIC CONDITIONS. *Agriculture.* About 60 per cent of the total area of Belgium is under cultivation, and one-half the farmed area is devoted to forage crops.

Other crops are fodder beets, flax and fruit. The pastoral industry, especially dairy farming, flourishes. On Jan. 1, 1957, Belgium had 2,254,924 cattle, 1,276,437 hogs, 175,003 horses, and 37,540 sheep.

*Manufacturing.* Industry chiefly processes imported raw materials for re-export in semifinished or finished form. Of primary importance are iron and steel, nonferrous metals, fabricated metal products and textiles. Associated with iron and steel is a considerable engineering industry, shipbuilding in Antwerp, and machinery and railway stock in Brussels. The centuries-old textile industry produces linen (Courtrai); cotton (the southeast); and synthetic fibers. Antwerp, using the output of mines in the Congo and Angola, rivals Amsterdam in diamond cutting.

Chief customers in 1959 for Belgium-Luxembourg were the Netherlands (21%), France (9%), West Germany (13%), the U.S. and Canada (15%), other EPU countries (14%), and Britain (6%). Leading sources of imports were West Germany (16%), the Netherlands (16%), the U.S. and Canada (11%), France (13%), other EPU countries (9%), and Britain (9%). Chief exports (1958) were iron and steel and products (28%), thread and fabric (7%), coal, coke, and petroleum and products (6%), copper and products (5%), and precious stones and metals (5%).

NATURAL FEATURES AND RESOURCES. The northern third of Belgium is a plain extending eastward from the coast of the North Sea. North of the Sambre-Meuse Rivers is a low plateau, varying from 250 to more than 600 feet in height, and to the south lies the Ardennes plateau, rising to a maximum of about 2,300 feet. The shallowness of the North Sea off Belgium precludes the development of good harbors; some of the port advantages of Antwerp, on the Schelde River, are offset by the fact that the approaches to it are through Dutch territory.

The principal mineral is coal. The Ardennes coalfield, now nearly exhausted, extends southward into France. The Campine field lies in the northeast.

**RUANDA-URUNDI—Status: U. N. trust** territory.
**Area: 20,916 square miles.**
**Population (est. 1958): 4,700,000.**
**Capital: Usumbura.**
**Resident-General: Jean Paul Harroy.**
**Principal products: tin, coffee, gold, cotton, hides.**

Ruanda-Urundi, in east Africa, was assigned to Belgium as a mandate by the League of Nations at the end of World War I, before which it was a portion of German East Africa. The area, placed under U.N. trusteeship in Dec., 1946, is largely mountainous, with livestock grazing the principal native activity.

# Bhutan (Kingdom)

**Area: 19,305 square miles.**
**Population (est. 1959): 700,000 (mostly Bhotiya).**
**Density per square mile: 36.3.**
**Ruler: Maharaja Jigme Dorji Wangchuk.**
**Capital: Punakha.**
**Monetary unit: Indian rupee.**
**Language: Tibetan dialect.**
**Religion: Buddhism.**

HISTORY. Bhutan is a semi-independent state lying on the southeast slope of the Himalayas, bordered on the north and east by Tibet and on the south and west by the Republic of India. The area is said to have been invaded and settled by Tibetan troops in the 9th century A.D. After almost a century of conflict between the Bhutanese and the British in India, British troops invaded the country in 1865 and negotiated an agreement under which Britain undertook to pay an annual allowance to Bhutan on condition of good behavior. A treaty signed with India in Aug. 1949 increased this subsidy and placed Bhutan's foreign affairs under Indian control.

Until 1907, Bhutan's government was under the dual control of the clergy and laity, but the country is now ruled by a hereditary Maharaja.

The dominant people are the Bhotiyas, who are of Tibetan origin, speak a Tibetan dialect, and profess the same form of Buddhism as is prevalent in Tibet.

ECONOMIC CONDITIONS. The chief crops are rice, corn and millet; the fields, laid out on hillside terraces, are watered by an ingenious system of irrigation. Bhutan is famous for its small though sturdy mountain ponies. The chief industries are metal work, cloth weaving and fine basket and mat work. Trade is insignificant, and much of it is conducted by barter.

NATURAL FEATURES. The whole of Bhutan presents a succession of lofty and rugged mountains running generally from north to south and separated by deep valleys. Mountains in the north reach a height of 24,000 feet.

# Bolivia (Republic)
## (República Boliviana)

Area: 424,163 square miles.
Population (est. 1960): 3,462,000 (1950: Indian 52.9%, mestizo 32%, white 14.8%, others .3%).
Density per square mile: 8.2.
President: Víctor Paz Estenssoro.
Principal cities (est. 1959): La Paz, 409,-500 (de facto capital); Cochabamba, 99,099 (commercial center); Oruro, 77,874 (tin mines); Potosí, 52,278 (mining); Sucre, 44,-913 (legal capital).
Monetary unit: Boliviano.
Language: Spanish.
Religion: Roman Catholic.

### STATUS IN THE WORLD TODAY

The wave of democracy which has swept over South America in recent years has enabled the National Revolutionary Movement to stay in power since 1952 despite strikes, attempts at revolution, and an almost desperate economic situation. It has maintained its position because of the social revolution it inaugurated by nationalizing the tin mines—minerals are the source of more than 90 per cent of its foreign exchange; giving the Indians the right to vote; and distributing land among the landless farm workers who previously had had to work for the large landowners in return for small plots just big enough for their own sustenance. Virtually all Indians now have some land and are prospective recipients of more. And with extensive help from the U.S. Point Four program, the NRM government is giving them information on new and better methods of production and extending them credit.

While diversification of agriculture will help offset the payments Bolivia must make to import much of its basic foodstuffs, the primary problem is still the country's dependence upon tin exports, which in turn depend upon the world price of that metal. A world surplus of tin, the re-establishment of a quota system for world tin production and the "dumping"

of tin on the world market by the Soviet bloc at low prices have hurt Bolivia. And since miners have been frozen in their jobs, uneconomic mines have not been closed and workers have been given subsidies in the form of fixed prices at commissaries during inflation, the nationalized mines have been run at a deficit and the government has been forced to seek aid from the United States and the International Monetary Fund. One bright spot in an otherwise bleak economic picture has been the successful exploitation of petroleum deposits which has converted the country from a heavy importer of petroleum products to an exporter.

HISTORY. Famous since Spanish colonial days for its mineral wealth, modern Bolivia was once a part of the ancient Incan Empire. After the Spaniards had defeated the Incas during the first part of the 16th century, Bolivia was subjected to the Spanish Viceroyalty of Peru, and its predominantly Indian population was reduced to slavery. The country finally won its independence in 1825; the new republic was named after Simón Bolívar, South America's famed liberator.

Bolivia's political history since independence has been extremely stormy. Since 1825 it has had more than 60 revolutions, 70 Presidents and 11 Constitutions. No elected President has served out his term.

Harassed by internal strife, Bolivia lost great slices of territory to three neighbor nations. Several thousand square miles and its outlet to the Pacific were taken by Chile after a disastrous war in 1879–83. In 1903 a piece of Bolivia's Acre province, rich in rubber, was ceded to Brazil. And in 1938, after a war with Paraguay, Bolivia gave up claim to nearly 100,000 square miles of the Gran Chaco.

GOVERNMENT. Bolivia is a republic, electing by popular vote a President every four years, a 27-member Senate every six years, and a 110-member Chamber of Deputies every four years. The President appoints the members of his Cabinet. The Indian majority was virtually disfranchised until July, 1952, when the franchise was conferred on all those who had reached the age of 20, whether literate or illiterate.

ECONOMIC CONDITIONS. Production of such basic foodstuffs as wheat and rice is insufficient for domestic needs, and considerable quantities must be imported. Cattle are raised in the more temperate regions of the east and south, sheep in the departments of La Paz and Cochabamba, and llamas, alpacas, and vicuñas, important sources of hides, wool and, meat, are raised on the plateaus by Indians. The furbearing chinchilla, a native of the colder plateau regions, is also raised in Bolivia.

Tin and other minerals comprise almost the whole of Bolivia's exports. Since the country is landlocked, foreign trade must pass through free ports in Chile and river ports on the Amazon.

Chief exports in 1959 were tin (68%), lead (6%), tungsten (7%), zinc (5%), silver (5%), and petroleum and products (4%). Leading customers in 1957 were the United Kingdom (45%) and the U.S. (35%); leading suppliers, the U.S. (44%), Germany (11%), Argentina (12%), and Peru (7%). The U.S. has supplied $137 millions of economic aid.

NATURAL FEATURES AND RESOURCES. Landlocked Bolivia is a low alluvial plain throughout 60 per cent of its area toward the east, drained by the Amazon and Plata river systems. The western part, enclosed by two chains of the Andes, is a great plateau—the Altiplano, with an average altitude of 12,000 feet. More than 80 per cent of the population lives on the plateau, which also contains La Paz, the highest capital city in the world. Lake Titicaca, half the size of Lake Ontario, is one of the highest large lakes in the world, at an altitude of 12,507 feet. Islands in the lake hold ruins of the ancient Incan civilization.

Mining is the backbone of the economy. Tin, accounting normally for about 70 per cent of Bolivian exports, is by far the most important mineral, most of it coming from Potosí and Oruro. During World War II, Bolivia was the world's largest tin producer.

# Brazil (Republic)

## (Estados Unidos do Brasil)

Area: 3,287,204 square miles.
Population (est. 1960): 65,743,000 (1950: white, 61.7%; mestizo, 26.5%; Negro, 11.0%; other, 0.8%).
Density per square mile: 20.0.
President: João Goulart.
Prime Minister: Tancredo Neves.
Principal cities (est. 1960): São Paulo 3,315,553 (coffee and industrial center); Rio de Janeiro, 3,030,619 (chief port); Recife (Pernambuco), 733,870 (seaport); Salvador (Baía), 551,525 (seaport); Pôrto Alegre, 532,624 (seaport); Belo Horizonte, 527,270 (mining); Fortaleza (Ceará), 300,-000 (seaport); Brasilia, 120,000 (capital).
Monetary unit: Cruzeiro.
Language: Portuguese.
Religion: Roman Catholic, 95%.

## STATUS IN THE WORLD TODAY

Brazil's principal problem currently is economic, even though it is potentially one of the richest nations in the Western Hemisphere. After four centuries as an almost exclusively agricultural country, with only one export crop—coffee—it is now trying hard to industrialize itself. It is plagued by a constantly rising cost of living which has caused mounting discontent. One of its weaknesses is oil—it produces only one-fifth of its requirements through a state monopoly which does not permit participation of foreign or internal private capital. Consequently, the government seeks public funds abroad rather than private capital to develop this industry and for that reason has not met with any great success in obtaining foreign investments. It has also been loath to institute reforms which would curb inflation as a prerequisite to obtaining a loan from the International Monetary Fund to close the gap in the balance of payments. As a temporary measure, the United States has agreed to let Brazil postpone payments which are due on its debts. In the meantime, ultra-nationalists are blaming the United States for the high cost of living and are demanding nationalization of some American industries. These circles also make much of the argument that the United States gives far too little financial assistance to countries in this hemisphere in comparison with the amounts allotted to countries in Europe, Asia, and Africa. Brazil has a number of military agreements with the United States, including one for the use of an island as a tracking station for guided missiles.

## MAJOR POLITICAL PARTIES

Partido Social Democratico (113 seats in Chamber of Deputies), led by Abelardo Jurema; União Democratica Nacional (72 seats), led by João Agripino; Partido Trabalhista Brasileiro (60 seats), led by Dr. João Belchior Marques Goulart.

HISTORY. Brazil, the only Latin American nation deriving its culture and language from Portugal, is the largest country in South America, covering nearly half the continent. In the world, it ranks after the U.S.S.R., China, Canada and the U.S.

Brazil was discovered in 1500 by the Portuguese admiral, Pedro Alvares Cabral. Portugal began colonization in 1532 and Brazil became a royal colony in 1549.

During the Napoleonic wars, the Prince Regent of Portugal (later King John VI) fled his country in advance of the French armies, and set up his royal court at Rio de Janeiro in 1808. When John was drawn home by a revolution in 1820, the Brazilians rebelled at resuming colonial status and declared their independence in 1822 under Pedro, son of John VI. Pedro I abdicated in 1831 in favor of his five-year-old son, who became Emperor in 1840 as Pedro II.

Although a popular monarch, Pedro II was forced to abdicate in 1889 following a military revolt, after which a republic was set up.

GOVERNMENT. Under the Constitution of 1946, Brazil is a union of twenty states, five territories and one federal district. The President is popularly elected for a five-year term and may not succeed himself. The national Congress is composed of two houses—the Senate, whose members serve for eight-year terms, and the Chamber of Deputies, elected for four-year terms. Members of Congress are elected by equal, direct, compulsory and secret suffrage under proportional representation.

In Sept., 1961, when the resignation of President Janio Quadros meant the succession to the presidency of a left-winger, João Goulart, the Constitution was hastily revised to give all power to a Prime Minister elected by Congress.

ECONOMIC CONDITIONS. *Agriculture.* Agriculture is a mainstay of Brazil's economy, but only 4 per cent of its area is under cultivation, the rest being grazing, forest, or non-productive land. Brazil leads the world in production of coffee and castor beans, and ranks second in cacao. Production and export of both coffee and cacao are government-controlled. Coffee production in the 1958–59 season totaled 44,000,000 bags of 132 lbs. each.

Livestock is raised nearly everywhere, with the great centers in the central and northern states. On Dec. 31, 1958, there were 45,262,000 hogs, 19,921,000 sheep, and 71,420,000 cattle.

*Trade.* Leading exports in 1959 were coffee (57%), pine wood (4%), cacao (5%), iron ore (3%), and cotton (3%). Leading customers were the U.S. (46%), Argentina (3%), Germany (7%), U.K. (4%), and the Netherlands (4%); leading suppliers, the U.S. (34%), Germany (10%), Venezuela (8%), Argentina (8%), and the Netherlands Antilles (4%).

Major imports include machinery, Argentine wheat, vehicles, and petroleum products.

NATURAL FEATURES AND RESOURCES. Brazil covers about three-sevenths of South America, extends 2,965 miles north-south, 2,691 miles east-west, and borders every South American state except Chile and Ecuador.

More than a third of Brazil is drained by the Amazon and its more than 200 tributaries. The Amazon is navigable for ocean steamers to Iquitos, Peru, 2,300 miles upstream. Southern Brazil is drained by the Plata system—the Paraguay, Uruguay and Paraná Rivers. The most important stream entirely within Brazil is the São Francisco, navigable for a thousand miles but broken near its mouth by the 260-foot Paulo Affonso Falls, with estimated potential of 1,000,000 horsepower.

*Mineral Resources.* Brazil's vast mineral resources are among her least developed assets. The most important are coal (estimated reserves of 5,000,000,000 tons; estimated 1959 production, 2,200,000 metric tons) and iron ore (metal content 65%), found mainly in Minas Gerais (1957 output, 5,184,000 metric tons). Other important minerals in Brazil are gold (1959), 109,000 troy oz.; manganese ore (1959), 882,000 tons; petroleum (1959), 23,590,000 barrels; diamonds; silver; quartz crystals; and uranium.

*Forests and Fisheries.* The largest single forest commodities are timber, chiefly pine from the southern states, and the wax of the carnauba palm, used for insulation and phonograph records and produced commercially only in Brazil (exports 1959: 9,805 metric tons).

# BRITISH COMMONWEALTH OF NATIONS

## EUROPE

### United Kingdom of Great Britain and Northern Ireland

Area: 94,215 square miles (excluding Channel Islands and Isle of Man).
Population (est. 1960): 52,383,000 (English, Scotch, Welsh, Irish).
Density per square mile: 556.0.
Ruler: Queen Elizabeth II.
Prime Minister: Harold Macmillan.
Principal cities (census 1951): London (Greater), 8,346,137 (capital); Birmingham, 1,112,340 (iron and steel); Glasgow, 1,089,555 (seaport, shipbuilding); Liverpool, 789,532 (seaport); Manchester, 703,175 (textiles); Sheffield, 512,834 (steel, cutlery); Leeds, 504,954 (clothing); Edinburgh, 466,770 (capital, Scotland).
Monetary unit: Pound sterling (£).
Languages: English, Welsh, Gaelic.
Religion: Church of England (established church); Church of Wales (disestablished); Church of Scotland (established church—Presbyterian); Church of Ireland (disestablished); Roman Catholic; Methodist; Congregational; Baptist; Jewish.

## STATUS IN THE WORLD TODAY

Although Britain's interests are still worldwide and do not everywhere coincide with those of the United States—recognition of Red China and the attack on Suez, to name two instances—the American alliance is a cornerstone of British policy, as axiomatic with Labor as it is with the Conservatives. The alliance is dedicated to the winning of the cold war—and any "hot" war, if necessary—and to bringing freedom to the nations oppressed by Communist or other dictatorships. It is in the means of accomplishing these objectives that the two partners occasionally differ.

Being a great power is an expensive business, and Britain at times finds it difficult to maintain its status financially. There are many who argue that Britain should let its American partner carry the burden of expensive nuclear armaments rather than duplicating the effort, since Britain would be unlikely ever to be engaged in a nuclear war except at America's side. This would allow the United Kingdom to concentrate on mobile conventional forces, which are what she really will need for the small, regular, and far-flung operations likely to fall to her lot.

So Britain's defense, though seen as geared to America's under NATO, is also still conceived independently. Bases like Cyprus, Malta, Aden, Kenya, Singapore, and Hong Kong all make their claims on slender resources. It is a system wide open to the drain of constant small troubles which, once they arise, are fanned by the scouts of world communism. It is the requirements of small police operations and old-fashioned petty wars across the globe that many British feel must first be met.

In the field of diplomacy, too, there have been differences. It was Britain which maintained that a Foreign Ministers' conference in Geneva might be worthwhile when American opinion seemed disposed to regard such a meeting as fruitless unless a definite agenda could be agreed upon in advance. Yet when it came to negotiating with their adversaries, the British and Americans—and the French, too—presented a united front in offering counterproposals to Russia's demands that Berlin be abandoned by the West.

Economically, as Mr. Macmillan put it in 1957, most British people "have never had it so good." The working people in Britain enjoy almost full employment and most of them have larger pay envelopes than ever before. The gadgets of comfort—refrigerators, washing machines, automobiles, television sets—are almost as common in working-class as they are in middle-class families. On top of what wages will buy, there lie all the benefits of the Welfare State, which guarantees a livable minimum from the cradle to the grave.

But the Welfare State and the great-power status cost money, and to earn money Britain must export. She was able to get her export business going again after the war by large loans from the United States and by 1956 had doubled her prewar volume of exports and raised the proportion of engineering goods to over half the total. She is concentrating on the development of new products and new industries—electronics, petrochemicals, plastics and synthetic fibers. It is the export of machines that pays best—the more scientifically advanced, the better. Let the successful export of manufactured goods fail, and everything fails. "Export or die" has been the slogan since the war.

---

## MAJOR POLITICAL PARTIES

Conservative party (365 seats in House of Commons), led by Prime Minister Harold Macmillan; Labour party (258 seats), led by Hugh Gaitskell.

---

HISTORY. Roman invasions of the first century B.C. brought Britain into contact with the continent. When the Roman legions withdrew in the fifth century A.D., Britain fell easy prey to the invading hordes of Angles, Saxons, and Jutes from Scandinavia and the Low Countries. Seven large kingdoms were established, and the original Britons were forced into Wales and Scotland. It was not until the eleventh century that the country finally became united under the Danish King Canute. Following the death of Edward the Confessor (1066), a dispute about the succession arose, and William Duke of Normandy invaded England, defeating the Saxon noble, Harold II, at the Battle of Hastings (1066). The Norman conquest was accompanied by the introduction of Norman law and feudalism, changing the customs of England.

The reign of Henry II (1154–89), first of the Plantagenets, saw an increasing centralization of royal power at the expense of the nobles, but in 1215 John (1199–1216) was forced to sign the Magna Carta, which awarded the people, especially the nobles, certain basic rights. Edward I (1272–1307) continued the conquest of Ireland, reduced Wales to subjection, and

---

### AREA AND POPULATION OF MAJOR SUBDIVISIONS*

| Subdivision | Area sq. mi. | Population, est. June 1958 |
|---|---|---|
| England | 50,871 ⎫ | 45,244,000 |
| Wales | 7,474 ⎬ | |
| Scotland | 30,411 | 5,223,000 |
| Northern Ireland | 5,700 | 1,403,000 |

* Not including Channel Islands and Isle of Man

# The Commonwealth of Nations

The Commonwealth is an association of 12 sovereign, independent states—the United Kingdom, Canada, Australia, New Zealand, Cyprus, India, Pakistan, Ceylon, Ghana, the Federation of Malaya, Nigeria and Sierra Leone together with certain dependencies of various status: Colonies, Protectorates, Protected States and Trust Territories. All of these areas are listed here in alphabetical order by continents. General information on each area is given, pages 636 to 666, in the order in which it appears in this table.

## Europe

| Political subdivision | Area (sq. mi.) | Population |
|---|---|---|
| United Kingdom | 93,599 | 52,383,000[10] |
| Channel Islands | 75 | 100,000[8] |
| Isle of Man | 227 | 55,000[8] |
| Gibraltar | 2 | 25,721[9] |
| Malta | 122 | 323,667[8] |
| Cyprus | 3,572 | 563,000[10] |

## Africa

| Political subdivision | Area (sq. mi.) | Population |
|---|---|---|
| Basutoland | 11,716 | 685,000[10] |
| Bechuanaland | 275,000 | 337,000[9] |
| Gambia | 4,010 | 289,000[9] |
| Ghana | 92,100 | 4,911,000[10] |
| Kenya | 224,960 | 6,551,000[9] |
| Mauritius and dependencies | 720 | 621,000[9] |
| Nigeria | 339,169 | 34,296,000[10] |
| Rhodesia and Nyasaland, Federation of: | | |
| Northern Rhodesia | 288,130 | 2,430,000[10] |
| Nyasaland | 45,366 | 2,830,000[10] |
| Southern Rhodesia | 150,333 | 3,070,000[10] |
| St. Helena and dependencies | 162 | 5,412[8] |
| Seychelles | 156 | 43,149[9] |
| Sierra Leone | 27,925 | 2,260,000[8] |
| Swaziland | 6,704 | 275,000[9] |
| Tanganyika Territory | 361,800 | 9,238,000[10] |
| Uganda | 93,981 | 6,682,000[10] |
| Zanzibar and Pemba | 1,020 | 307,000[10] |

## America

| Political subdivision | Area (sq. mi.) | Population |
|---|---|---|
| Bahamas | 4,400 | 136,229[8] |
| Barbados[1] | 166 | 237,000[9] |
| Bermudas | 20 | 43,480[8] |
| British Guiana | 83,000 | 560,620[10] |
| British Honduras | 8,866 | 90,343[10] |
| Canada | 3,851,116 | 17,814,000[10] |
| Falkland Islands (excluding dependencies) | 4,618 | 2,191[9] |
| Jamaica and dependencies | 4,709 | 1,606,546[10] |

## America—(cont.)

| Political subdivision | Area (sq. mi.) | Population |
|---|---|---|
| Leeward Islands[1,2,3] | 423 | 138,421[8] |
| Trinidad and Tobago[1] | 1,980 | 817,000[9] |
| Windward Islands[1,3] | 825 | 332,216[8] |

## Asia

| Political subdivision | Area (sq. mi.) | Population |
|---|---|---|
| Aden colony | 108 | 140,000[7] |
| Aden protectorate | 112,000 | 660,000[8] |
| Borneo: | | |
| Colony of North Borneo | 29,387 | 416,435[8] |
| Brunei | 2,226 | 83,869[10] |
| Sarawak | 47,500 | 744,391[10] |
| Ceylon | 25,332 | 9,612,000[9] |
| Hong Kong | 398 | 2,918,000[10] |
| India, Republic of | 1,259,992 | 408,050,000[10] |
| Federation of Malaya | 50,700 | 6,698,000[9] |
| Maldive Islands | 115 | 82,000[8] |
| Singapore and dependencies | 224 | 1,634,000[10] |
| Pakistan | 364,797 | 86,823,000[9] |

## Oceania

| Political subdivision | Area (sq. mi.) | Population |
|---|---|---|
| Australia, Commonwealth of | 2,974,583 | 10,281,000[10] |
| Fiji | 7,055 | 381,000[9] |
| Gilbert and Ellice Islands | 349 | 45,000[9] |
| Nauru | 8 | 4,308[8] |
| New Hebrides | 5,700 | 51,242[8] |
| New Zealand and island territories | 110,686 | 2,372,000[10] |
| Norfolk Island | 14 | 1,033[8] |
| Papua—New Guinea | 183,490 | 1,831,530[9] |
| Solomon Islands | 11,500 | 117,500[9] |
| Tonga (Friendly Islands) | 269 | 62,000[9] |
| Western Samoa | 1,130 | 107,000[10] |

(Note: Each population figure is followed by superior number denoting the year of estimate or census: [10] for 1960, [9] for 1959, [8] for 1958, [7] for 1957, etc.

[1] Member of the British West Indies Federation, formed in January 1958. [2] The Virgin Islands have not joined the Federation. [3] There is no longer a common governor for the Leeward Is. nor for the Windward Is.

made some gains in Scotland. In 1314, however, English forces led by Edward II were ousted from Scotland after the battle of Bannockburn. The late thirteenth and early fourteenth centuries saw the development of a separate House of Commons with tax-raising powers.

Edward III's claim to the throne of France led to the Hundred Years' War (1338–1453), which ended with the loss of almost all the large English territory in France. In England the great poverty and discontent caused by the war was intensified by the Black Death, a plague which reduced the population by about one-third. The Wars of the Roses (1455–85), a struggle for the throne between the House of York and the House of Lancaster, were ended by the victory of Henry Tudor (Henry VII) at Bosworth Field (1485).

During the reign of Henry VIII (1509-47), the Church in England asserted its independence from the Roman Catholic Church. Under Edward VI and Mary, the two extremes of religious fanaticism were reached and it remained for Henry's daughter, Elizabeth I (1558-1603), to set up the Church of England on a moderate basis. In 1588 the Spanish Armada, a fleet sent out by Catholic King Philip II of Spain, was defeated by the English and destroyed during a storm. During Elizabeth's reign, England became a world power.

Elizabeth's heir was of the house of Stuart—James VI of Scotland—who joined the two crowns as James I (1603-25). The Stuart Kings incurred large debts and were forced either to depend on Parliament for taxes or to raise money by illegal means. In 1642 war broke out between Charles I and a large portion of the Parliament; Charles was defeated and executed in 1649, and the monarchy was then abolished. The Puritan Commonwealth endured for ten years, but after the death (1658) of Oliver Cromwell, the Lord Protector, the government fell to pieces and Charles II was restored to the throne in 1660. The struggle between the King and Parliament continued, but Charles II knew when to compromise. His brother James II (1685-88) possessed none of his ability and was ousted by the Revolution of 1688, which confirmed the predominant position of Parliament. James' daughter, Mary, and her husband, William of Orange, now ruled.

The reign of Queen Anne (1702-14) was marked by the Duke of Marlborough's victories over France at Blenheim, Oudenarde, and Malplaquet in the War of the Spanish Succession. England and Scotland meanwhile were joined together by the Act of Union (1707). Upon the death of Anne, the distant claims of the elector of Hanover were recognized, and he became King of England as George I.

The eighteenth century was a period of gradual growth and change. At home the unwillingness of the Hanoverian Kings to rule resulted in the formation by the King's ministers of a Cabinet, headed by a Prime Minister, which directed all public business. Abroad the constant wars with France resulted in expansion of the British Empire all over the globe, particularly in North America and India. This imperial growth was checked by the revolt of the American colonies (1775-81).

The age-long struggle with France broke out again in 1793, and during the lengthy Napoleonic Wars, which ended at Waterloo (1815), England was pitted at one time against almost all of Europe.

The Victorian era, named after Queen Victoria (1837-1901), saw the growth of a democratic system of government which had begun with the Reform Bill of 1832. The two important wars in Victoria's reign were the Crimean War against Russia (1853-56) and the Boer War (1899-1902). The latter was accompanied by enormous extension of England's sway in Africa.

The reign of Edward VII (1901-10) was marked by increasing uneasiness at home and abroad. Within four years after the accession of George V (1910), England entered World War I when Germany invaded Belgium. The nation was led by coalition Cabinets headed first by Herbert Asquith and then (Dec., 1916) by the Welsh statesman, David Lloyd George. The years after the war were marked by labor unrest which culminated in the general strike of 1926. A Labour ministry formed early in 1924 by Ramsay MacDonald fell in October of that year. In 1929 a second Labour government was formed, but the world economic depression forced a change in 1931, and a national government was formed, composed chiefly of Conservative members, although MacDonald remained Prime Minister until 1935. King Edward VIII succeeded to the throne in 1936 on his father's death but abdicated eleven months later (in order to marry an American, Wallis Warfield Simpson, whose second divorce was then pending) in favor of his brother, who became King George VI.

The efforts of Prime Minister Neville Chamberlain to meet by peaceful means the rising threat of Nazism in Germany failed with the German invasion of Poland (Sept. 1, 1939), which was followed by England's entry into World War II (Sept. 3, 1939). Serious Allied reverses in the spring of 1940 led to Chamberlain's resignation and the formation of another coalition war Cabinet by Conservative leader Winston Churchill, who led England through most of World War II. Churchill resigned as the coalition leader shortly after V-E Day, but then formed a "caretaker" government which remained in office until after the parliamentary elections of July 5, 1945, in which the Labour party won an overwhelming victory. The government formed by Clement R. Attlee on July 26 began a moderate socialistic program.

Internationally, the Attlee government continued Britain's close co-operation with the United States through the North Atlantic Treaty and in the Korean war, at the same time solidifying its position in western Europe in opposition to the U.S.S.R. The Labour regime, returned to office by a slight majority in the parliamentary elections of Feb., 1950, lost by a narrow margin in the Oct., 1951 elections. On Oct. 26 Winston Churchill again became Prime Minister at the head of a Conservative government. George VI died Feb. 6, 1952, and was succeeded by his daughter, Elizabeth II.

Churchill voluntarily stepped down on April 5, 1955, in favor of Sir Anthony Eden, who led the Conservatives to another victory in elections May 26, 1955. The Suez crisis and the abortive Anglo-French invasion of Egypt (Oct. 31, 1956) were followed by Eden's resignation on grounds of ill health (Jan. 9, 1957). Harold Macmillan succeeded him.

RULER. Queen Elizabeth II, born April 21, 1926, elder daughter of King George VI and Queen Elizabeth, succeeded to the throne on the death of her father, Feb. 6, 1952; married Nov. 20, 1947, to Prince Philip, Duke of Edinburgh, born June 10, 1921; their children are Prince Charles (heir presumptive), born Nov. 14, 1948, and Princess Anne, born Aug. 15, 1950. The Queen's sister is Princess Margaret Rose, born Aug. 21, 1930; her uncles are Prince Edward Albert, Duke of Windsor (formerly King Edward VIII), born June 23, 1894, and Prince Henry William, Duke of Gloucester, born March 31, 1900.

GOVERNMENT. The United Kingdom is a constitutional monarchy, with a Queen and a Parliament which has two houses: the House of Lords with about 830 hereditary peers, 26 spiritual peers, 16 Scottish representative peers, a number of Irish representative peers (vacancies are no longer filled), and a few life peers who hold or have held high judicial office; and the House of Commons, numbering since 1955 630 members elected by practically universal suffrage. Supreme legislative power is vested in Parliament, which holds office for five years unless sooner dissolved. The executive power of the Crown is exercised by the Cabinet, headed by the Prime Minister. The latter, normally the head of the party commanding a majority in the House of Commons, is appointed by the sovereign, with whose consent he in turn appoints the rest of the Cabinet. All ministers must be members of one or the other house of Parliament; they are individually and collectively responsible to the Crown, the Prime Minister and Parliament. The Cabinet proposes bills and arranges the business of Parliament, but it depends entirely on the votes of confidence in Commons. The lords cannot hold up "money" bills, but they can delay other bills for a period of at least one year.

By the Act of Union (1707) the Scottish Parliament was assimilated with that of England, and Scotland is now represented in Commons by seventy-one members. The Secretary of State for Scotland, a member of the Cabinet, is responsible for the administration of Scottish affairs.

ECONOMIC CONDITIONS. *Agriculture.* Agriculture remains one of Britain's chief industries, employing about 800,000 persons.

Livestock (Dec., 1959) included 11,479,000 cattle, 19,391,000 sheep, 6,008,000 hogs, and 87,831,000 poultry. Cattle occupy a predominant position in British agriculture, accounting for about 40 per cent of the total farm output.

*Industry.* The most important British manufacture is heavy goods such as machinery, tools, bridges, and locomotives; industry is concentrated in the north and Midlands of England. Sheffield is the center of the steel industry, while the china industry is concentrated in the Midlands The cotton industry is centered in Lancashire; Liverpool, Manchester, Oldham, Preston, and Bolton are the main manufacturing towns. The wool industry, England's oldest large trade, is located just east of the cotton towns, at Leeds, Bradford, and Hull in Yorkshire. An important industrial region is the central Lowlands of Scotland, where woolens and other fabrics, lace, glass, paper, steel, and pig iron are produced. Important shipyards are located along the coast.

The total working population in May, 1960 was 24,296,000.

*Trade.* The United Kingdom's economic prosperity is dependent on its foreign trade, and the nation made great efforts after World War II to build up its volume of exports.

Leading exports are machinery (non-electrical), road vehicles and aircraft, chemicals, electrical machinery, iron and steel.

Leading imports are meat, fruits and vegetables, cereals and cereal preparations, nonferrous base metals and wool.

Chief customers are United States, Australia, Canada, India, South Africa, and New Zealand.

Chief sources of imports for 1959 were sterling area (38%), continental European Payments Union countries (24%), the U.S. and Canada (17%), and Latin America (5%).

*Communications.* The merchant marine on June 30, 1959, represented about 19.1% of the world total and was second only to the U.S. merchant fleet.

Nationalization of the railway and canal systems in Great Britain became effective Jan. 1, 1948, and are now operated by the government's Transport Commission.

British air services throughout the world are nationalized under the Minister of Civil Aviation. Service is supplied by two public corporations—British Overseas Airways (BOAC) and British European Airways.

NATURAL FEATURES AND RESOURCES. The United Kingdom, consisting of England, Wales, Scotland, and Northern Ireland, is a third the size of Texas. England, in the southeast part of the British Isles, is separated from Scotland on the north by the granite Cheviot Hills; from them the Pennine chain of uplands extends south through the center of England, reaching its highest point in the Lake district in the northwest. To the west along the border of Wales—a land of steep hills and valleys —are the Cambrian Mountains, while the Cotswolds, a range of hills in Gloucestershire, extend into the surrounding shires. The remainder of England is plain land, though not necessarily flat, with the rocky sand-topped moors in the southwest, the rolling downs in the south and southeast and the reclaimed marshes of the low-lying Fens in the east central districts. Scotland is divided into three physical regions—the Highlands, the Central Lowlands, containing two-thirds of the population, and the Southern Uplands. The western Highland coast is intersected throughout by long, narrow sea-lochs, or fiords. Scotland also includes the Outer and Inner Hebrides and other islands off the west coast and the Orkney and Shetland Islands off the north coast.

Wales is generally hilly; the Snowdon range in the northern part culminates in Mt. Snowdon (3,557 ft.), highest in both England and Wales.

Important rivers flowing into the North Sea are the Thames, Humber, Tees, and Tyne. In the west are the Severn and the Wye, which empty into the Bristol Channel and are navigable, as are the Mersey and Ribble.

*Minerals.* Great Britain's most important mineral resource is coal, which was responsible to a large extent for British industrial supremacy during the late eighteenth and the nineteenth centuries. The coal mines were nationalized in 1946. Reserves have been variously estimated at from 150,000 million to 200,000 million tons. Prior to World War II, coal was exported in declining amounts to the continent, mainly to France, Sweden, Denmark and Italy. Since the war, however, Britain has been hard put to meet her own minimum domestic requirements.

Most of the British iron ore is produced in England, especially in Cumberland, Lancashire, and Staffordshire. Tin ore and copper are obtained almost exclusively from Cornwall, while lead comes mainly from Flint, Durham, and Derbyshire. Zinc occurs mainly in North Wales, the north of England, the Isle of Man, and the county of Dumfries in Scotland. The whole British supply of china clay (kaolin)—of

great importance in the ceramic, paper-making, bleaching, and chemical industries—comes from Cornwall. Petroleum production is negligible, but oil shale exists in large quantities.

*Water Power.* The most important potential sources of water power are in the highlands of Scotland, North Wales, and Cumberland. Nationalization of the electric and gas industries became effective in 1948.

*Forests and Fisheries.* Great Britain was once heavily forested, but centuries of timber cutting and clearing have denuded the country of the original forests. Consequently the nation is heavily dependent on imported timber.

Great Britain's sea fishing industry is among the most important in the world. The principal kinds of fish caught are herring, cod, haddock, plaice, and hake, classed as wet fish, and, among shellfish, oysters, crabs, and lobsters. The most important factor in the export trade is salted herring, which ordinarily represents about 70 per cent of the total. Principal grounds frequented by British fishermen are the North Sea; off Iceland; the Faeroes; south of Ireland; west of Scotland; west of Ireland; the Irish Sea; and the English Channel.

## NORTHERN IRELAND
### (Part of United Kingdom)

Area: 5,700 square miles.
Population (est. June 1958): 1,403,000.
Density per square mile: 246.0.
Governor: Lord Wakehurst.
Prime Minister: Viscount Brookeborough.
Principal cities (census 1951): Belfast, 443,671 (capital); Londonderry, 50,092.
Monetary unit: Pound sterling.
Language: English, Gaelic.
Religions (census 1951): Roman Catholic (34.4%), Presbyterian (29.9%), Church of Ireland (25.8%), Methodist (4.9%), others (5%).

Northern Ireland comprises the six predominantly Protestant counties of Antrim, Armagh, Down, Fermanagh, Londonderry, and Tyrone (collectively known as Ulster), which form the northern part of the island of Ireland. The area is an integral part of the United Kingdom, but under the terms of the Government of Ireland Act (1920) it has a semiautonomous government.

The government has only limited powers for local purposes, and many matters are reserved to the central government at Westminster. Executive authority is vested in the Crown-appointed Governor, who is advised by a Cabinet of eight ministers headed by the Prime Minister. The Parliament consists of the House of Commons of fifty-two members elected for 5-year terms, and the Senate of twenty-six members elected by the House of Commons. The area is also represented by twelve members in the British House of Commons.

Agriculture is the largest single industry; about two-thirds of the country is devoted to crops and pasture under a system of mixed farming. The leading crops include potatoes, oats, and flax. In 1955 there were 905,890 cattle, 878,480 sheep, and 696,410 hogs.

The two principal manufacturing industries are linen and shipbuilding, both centered in Belfast. The linen industry was established by Huguenot weavers who fled France after the revocation of the Edict of Nantes in 1685.

## ISLE OF MAN

Lieutenant Governor: Sir Herbert Garvey.

Located in the Irish Sea, equidistant from Scotland, Ireland, and England, the Isle of Man is administered according to its own laws by a government composed of the Lieutenant Governor, a Legislative Council, and a House of Keys, one of the most ancient legislative assemblies in the world.

## CHANNEL ISLANDS

Lieutenant Governor of Jersey: Gen. Sir G. W. E. J. Erskine.
Lieutenant Governor of Guernsey: Vice Adm. S. Geoffrey Robson.

This group of islands, lying in the English Channel off the northwest coast of France, is the only portion of the Duchy of Normandy belonging to the English Crown, to which it has been attached since the conquest of 1066. It was the only British possession occupied by Germany during World War II.

For purposes of government the islands are divided into Jersey (45 sq. mi.) and the bailiwick of Guernsey (24 sq. mi.), including Alderney (3 sq. mi.), Sark (2 sq. mi.), Herm, and Jethou. The islands are administered according to their own laws and customs by local governments headed by Crown-appointed Lieutenant Governors. Acts of Parliament in London are not binding on the islands unless they are specifically mentioned.

French is still the official language, although English is the main language of commerce.

GIBRALTAR—Status: Colony.
Governor: Gen. Sir Chas. Keightley.

Gibraltar, at the south end of the Iberian Peninsula, is a rocky promontory commanding the western entrance to the Mediterranean. Aside from its strategic importance, it is also a free port, naval base, and coaling station. It was captured by the Arabs crossing from Africa into Spain in A.D. 711. In the fifteenth century it passed to the Moorish ruler of Granada and later became Spanish. It was captured by an Anglo-Dutch force in 1704 during the War of the Spanish Succession and passed to Britain by the Treaty of Utrecht in 1713. Most of the inhabitants are of Spanish, Italian and Maltese descent.

MALTA—Status: Self-governing colony.
Capital: Valletta (population 18,801).
Governor: Sir Guy Grantham.
Prime Minister: (Post now vacant).
Agricultural products: potatoes, onions, cereals, fruits.

The Maltese islands lie between Europe and Africa, in the central channel linking the eastern and western Mediterranean. The inhabited islands are Malta (95 sq. mi.), Gozo (26 sq. mi.) and Comino (1 sq. mi.). The Knights of St. John (Malta), who obtained the islands from Charles V in 1530, reached their highest fame when they withstood an attack by superior Turkish forces in 1565. Napoleon seized Malta in 1798, but the French forces were ousted by British troops in 1799, and British rule was confirmed by the Treaty of Paris (1814). The principal importance of Malta is its strategic location as a naval base; it was heavily attacked by German and Italian aircraft during World War II but was never invaded by the Axis. Most of the population are Maltese, speaking the Phoenician Maltese language, a tongue akin to Syriac and Arabic. The islands are densely populated (2,554 per square mile in 1956).

Under its 1947 Constitution, Malta enjoyed a measure of self-government. In April, 1959, the British Colonial Office suspended the 1947 Constitution and issued an interim Constitution granting the Government power to enact ordinances and to accept or reject the advice of an Executive Council concerned with questions of domestic administration of the island. Defense and foreign affairs are reserved to the British government under Section 14 of the new Constitution.

# Cyprus (Republic)
## (Member of Commonwealth of Nations)

Area: 3,572 square miles.
Population (est. 1960): 563,000 (Greek Cypriots, 78.8%; Turkish Cypriots, 17.5%; Armenians, Maronites, Latins and others, 3.7%).
Density per square mile: 157.6.
President: Archbishop Makarios.
Vice-President: Dr. Fazil Kutchuk.
Principal cities: Nicosia, 81,700 (capital); Limassol, 38,000; Famagusta, 27,900.
Monetary unit: Cyprus pound.
Languages: Greek, Turkish, English.
Religions: Greek Orthodox, Moslem.

## STATUS IN THE WORLD TODAY

Cyprus, which achieved its independence Aug. 16, 1960, after more than 2,000 years of foreign domination, remained part of the NATO defense network in the Middle East. Britain retained two bases on the island.

---

HISTORY AND GOVERNMENT. Cyprus, third largest island in the Mediterranean, is roughly equidistant from Asia Minor to the north and Syria to the east. The site of early Phoenician and Greek colonies, it passed in 1571 from the rule of Venice to that of the Ottoman Empire, under which it remained until 1878, when it was ceded to Great Britain for administrative purposes. On the outbreak of hostilities with Turkey in World War I (Nov. 9, 1914), the island was formally annexed to Great Britain. Demands for self-determination and union with Greece (enosis), which had been accompanied by terrorism for several years, finally ended in February, 1959, when Britain, Turkey, Greece and representatives of the Turkish and Greek communities in Cyprus signed an agreement providing for the establishment of an independent Cypriot Republic.

Under the republic's constitution, for the protection of the Turkish minority the Vice-President as well as three of the ten cabinet ministers must be from the Turkish community, while the House of Representatives shall be elected by each community separately, 70 per cent Greek Cypriot and 30 per cent Turkish Cypriot representatives. Another unusual feature is that the two virtually self-governing communities have considerable legislative powers over their own communal affairs. The Greek Communal Chamber has 23 members, including one Armenian and one Maronite, while the Turkish Chamber has 30. Each community has the right to fix the number of members in its own chamber.

ECONOMIC CONDITIONS. Agriculture is the principal industry of the island. Sponge fishing as well as copper mining are also important. In 1956 34% of its exports went to West Germany, while 45% of its imports came from Britain. Principal exports are cupreous concentrates (32%) and pyrites (27%). The chief agricultural products are barley, wheat, potatoes, wine and fruit.

---

## ⋎ AFRICA

### BRITISH SOUTH AFRICAN TERRITORIES

**High Commissioner: Sir John Maud.**

The three British territories in southern Africa—Basutoland, Bechuanaland and Swaziland—are not part of the Union of South Africa but are administered by a High Commissioner responsible to the Secretary of State for Commonwealth Relations in the British Cabinet. He is also High Commissioner for the United Kingdom in the Union of South Africa.

**BASUTOLAND—Status: Colony.**
**Capital: Maseru (population 4,000).**
**Resident Commissioner: A. G. T. Chaplin.**
**Agricultural products: corn, wheat, sorghum.**

Basutoland is a mountainous enclave surrounded by the Union of South Africa and bounded by the Orange Free State, Cape Province and Natal. It was constituted a native state under British protection by a treaty signed with the native chief Moshesh in 1843. It was annexed to Cape Colony in 1871, but on Mar. 13, 1884, was restored to direct control by the Crown. The Resident Commissioner is advised by a council of 100, of whom 95 are nominated by the native chiefs who administer the affairs of their tribes.

The population is restricted almost entirely to the lowland strip in the west; the white population (1,926 in 1956) consists solely of officials, missionaries, traders, and a few labor agents for employers in the Union of South Africa. About 100,000 natives are regularly employed in the Union. Sheep raising is highly developed. Land is the common property of the nation and is held in trust by the chiefs.

**BECHUANALAND—Status: Protectorate.**
**Administrative center: Mafeking, in Cape Province (population 4,666).**
**Resident Commissioner: Robert P. Fawcus.**
**Agricultural products: hides and skins, cattle, butter, millet, maize.**
**Minerals: gold and silver.**

Bechuanaland lies in south central Africa, bounded on the south and southeast by the Union of South Africa, on the west by South-West Africa, on the north by Angola and Northern Rhodesia and on the northeast by Southern Rhodesia. Its average elevation is 3,300 feet and the greater part is gently undulating. The area was placed under British protection on Sept. 30, 1885, to prevent further Boer encroachment and has since remained a British protectorate. The form of government is similar to that of Basutoland.

Most of the inhabitants are Bantu, but there were 3,177 Europeans in 1956, a few of them farmers. The country is essentially pastoral, with cattle raising and dairy farming the chief industries. Gold is mined in the Tati district near Francistown. There is also some mining of silver and copper. Timber is produced for use as fuel and pit props.

SWAZILAND—Status: Protectorate.
Capital: Mbabane (population 1,600).
Resident Commissioner: B. A. Marwick.
Agricultural products: cattle, hides and skins, butter, tobacco, corn, millet.
Minerals: asbestos, tin, gold.

Swaziland lies at the southeastern corner of the Transvaal. It is largely hilly, with an average elevation of 4,000 feet in the west. It came under the protection of the Transvaal Republic in 1894 but was made a British protectorate in 1906 under the High Commissioner for South Africa.

The natives are mostly Swazi; there were 5,932 Europeans in 1956, mostly farmers. Grazing is the principal native occupation; there is excellent pasture in the high land to the west. Tropical and subtropical crops are raised in the lower areas. Tin is mined near Mbabane.

# EAST AFRICA HIGH COMMISSION

The East Africa High Commission, comprising the Governors of Kenya, Tanganyika and Uganda, administers the public utilities and other central services of those territories, and has power to legislate with respect thereto with the advice and consent of a Central Legislative Assembly. The governments of the three areas are otherwise independent of one another.

KENYA—Status: Colony and protectorate.
Capital: Nairobi (pop. est. 1959: 238,500).
Governor: Sir Patrick Muir Renison.
Foreign trade (1956): domestic exports, 25% to Britain; imports, 51% from Britain. Chief exports: coffee (47%), tea (9%), sisal (7%).
Agricultural products (exports 1956): coffee, tea, sisal.
Minerals: gold, sodium carbonate, silver, salt.
Forest products: wattle bark extract, timber.

Kenya extends along the Indian Ocean between Ethiopia and Tanganyika Territory and westward to Lake Victoria and Uganda. Formerly known as the East Africa Protectorate, it was held under a concession from the Sultan of Zanzibar by the Imperial British East Africa Company from 1888 to 1905. It became a Crown colony in 1920, the coastal strip leased from the Sultan becoming a protectorate.

The colony is predominantly agricultural, and a large area is cultivated by Europeans. Altitude ranges from sea level to more than 9,000 ft.; hence, the cultivation of tropical, subtropical and temperate crops is possible.

Kenya has been plagued since 1952 by serious outbreaks of native terrorism inspired by the anti-white Mau Mau secret society, which have taxed strengthened security forces, including British regular army units.

TANGANYIKA TERRITORY—Status: U. N. trust territory.
Capital: Dar es Salaam (pop. 1957: 128,-742).
Governor: Sir Richard G. Turnbull.
Foreign trade (1956): domestic exports, 31% to Britain; imports, 41% from Britain. Chief exports: sisal (24%), coffee (21%), cotton (17%), diamonds.
Agricultural products: sisal, coffee, cotton, peanuts, sugar cane, tea.
Minerals: gold, diamonds.
Forest products: gum arabic and copal, beeswax, timber.

Tanganyika Territory, with the Belgian Ruanda and Urundi, constituted German East Africa from 1884 until 1919. It was administered under League of Nations mandate by Britain until 1946, when it was placed under United Nations trusteeship. It was scheduled to become independent on Dec. 20, 1961.

Tanganyika's narrow coastal plain is bordered on the west by the precipitous eastern side of the Central African plateau. Mount Kilimanjaro (19,565 ft.) is the highest point on the African continent. The territory also includes adjacent islands in the Indian Ocean.

The territory is sparsely populated; two-thirds of it is uninhabited. It is the world's largest producer of sisal hemp.

UGANDA—Status: Protectorate.
Capital: Entebbe (pop. 1957: 8,500).
Governor: Sir Frederick Crawford.
Foreign trade (1956): exports, 28% to India; imports, 30% from Britain. Chief exports: cotton, coffee.
Agricultural products: cotton, coffee, sugar cane, rubber, tea, sisal.
Minerals: gold, tin.

Uganda lies immediately south of Anglo-Egyptian Sudan and west of Kenya, along the northwest shore of Lake Victoria. The surface is extremely diversified, with lofty plateaus, snow-capped peaks, swamps, forests and arid areas. A British protectorate over the area was proclaimed in 1894. A large measure of home rule is given the native states, notably Buganda, whose *kabaka* (king) is assisted by a ministry and native parliament.

Agriculture, including livestock, is the basis of the economy. Cotton is raised, principally by natives, and coffee, tea and rubber are grown on large plantations. Most natives possess large herds of cattle and sheep.

GAMBIA—Status: Colony and protectorate.
Capital: Bathurst (population, est. 1959, 21,000).
Governor: Sir Edward Windley.
Foreign trade. Chief export: peanuts (90%).
Agricultural products: peanuts, hides and skins, millet, rice, palm kernels.

Gambia, smallest of the British West African dependencies, is a stretch of land 200 miles long on both sides of the lower Gambia River, surrounded on all land sides by French West Africa and fronting on the Atlantic Ocean. During the 17th century it was settled by various companies of English merchants; slavery was the chief source of revenue until it was abolished in 1807. Gambia became a Crown colony in 1843. Except for the island of St. Mary, on which the capital stands, the area is administered as a protectorate.

The inhabitants, mostly Negroes or Negroids, are predominantly Mohammedan. The principal economic activity is the cultivation of peanuts. Internal transportation is by steamer and launch.

# Ghana (Republic)

**(Member of Commonwealth of Nations)**

Area: 92,100 square miles.

Population (est. 1959): 4,911,000 (almost entirely African).

Density per square mile: 53.3.

President: Kwame Nkrumah.

Principal cities (Preliminary census 1960): Accra, 388,231 (capital); Kumasi, 220,922 (rail center); Sekondi-Takoradi, 120,793 (rail terminus and port).

Monetary unit: Gold Coast pound.

Languages: Native tongues (Twi, Fanti, Ga), English.

Religions: Pagan, Mohammedan, Christian.

## STATUS IN THE WORLD TODAY

The official international policy of Ghana is one of "non-alignment" in the cold war, but the nation is leaning in a westerly direction and looks to the United States for financial aid in developing its economic resources. In relations with the rest of Africa, Prime Minister Nkrumah, who was educated in the United States, aspires to leadership of a pan-African movement, and, with Guinea, the only French colony to choose independence instead of a limited autonomy within the French Union, has formed the Union of Independent African States, little more than a very loose federation.

Politically, there has been criticism of Ghana for the sometimes undemocratic methods resorted to under Nkrumah's one-party control of the country: revising the constitution to meet the ruling party's fancy; dissolving the regional assemblies and curbing the powers of tribal chieftains; arresting and detaining opponents of the government, including members of Parliament, without trial. But supporters of the regime maintain that a strong hand is necessary for stability while the new nation suffers its growing pains.

Ghana has a prosperous economy based on cocoa, of which it is the world's largest producer, although it is at times vulnerable to price fluctuations on the world market. The cocoa crop 1958–9 amounted to over 250,000 tons. It also has large bauxite deposits and plans are well advanced to carry out a Volta River dam project which will furnish power for an aluminum industry in the interior as well as the development of other new industries.

## MAJOR POLITICAL PARTIES

Convention People's party (89 seats in National Assembly), led by President Kwame Nkrumah; United party (14 seats), led by S. D. Dombo.

HISTORY AND GOVERNMENT. Created an independent country on March 6, 1957, Ghana is the former British colony of the Gold Coast. The area was first seen by Portuguese traders in 1470. They were followed by the English (1553), the Dutch (1595), and the Swedes (1640). British rule over the Gold Coast began in 1820, but it was not until after quelling the severe resistance of the Ashanti in 1901 that it was firmly established. British Togoland, formerly a colony of Germany, was incorporated into Ghana by referendum in 1956. As the result of a plebiscite, Ghana became a republic on July 1, 1960.

ECONOMIC CONDITIONS. The mainstay of the economy is the cultivation of cacao, in the production of which Ghana leads the rest of the world. Secondary export crops include palm kernels, copra, kola nuts, coffee, and rubber.

Chief exports in 1958 were cacao (59%), wood and lumber (11%), diamonds (9%), gold (9%) and manganese ore (8%). Chief customers in 1955 were Britain (35%), the U. S. (14%) and the Netherlands (11%); leading suppliers, Britain (35%), Japan (10%), and the Netherlands (8%).

Mineral resources are abundant. Most important is gold, mined at Tarkwa, Bibiani, and Obuasi. Others include diamonds, manganese ore, and bauxite. Forest resources are extensive and large amounts of hardwoods, notably mahogany, are exported from the forests in the interior.

The coastal belt of the new nation, extending about 270 miles along the Gulf of Guinea, is sandy, marshy and generally exposed. Behind it is a gradually widening grass strip. The forested plateau region to the north is broken by ridges and hills.

MAURITIUS—Status: Colony.

Capital: Port Louis (pop. 1958: 85,200).

Governor: Sir Colville Deverell.

Foreign trade. Chief export: sugar (96%).

Agricultural products: sugar, tea, tobacco, copra.

Mauritius is a mountainous island of volcanic origin in the Indian Ocean, about 500 miles east of Madagascar. It was seized in 1810 from the French, who had settled it in 1715, and was formally ceded to Great Britain by the Treaty of Paris in 1814.

With over 700 persons per square mile, the island is one of the most densely populated regions in the world. There is a large white element, chiefly French and British, but British Indians are predominant. There are many half-castes.

# Nigeria (Republic)

(Member of Commonwealth of Nations)
Area: 339,169 square miles.
Population (est. 1960): 34,296,000.
Density per square mile: 101.1.
High Commissioner: Antony Head.
Federal Premier: A. A. T. Balewa.
Principal cities: (est. 1959): Ibadan, 500,000 (native metropolis); Lagos, 364,000 (capital); Ogbomosho, 139,535 (native city); Kano, 130,173 (textiles, leather goods, cattle).
Monetary unit: Nigerian pound.
Languages: Native tongues, Arabic, English.
Religions: Mohammedan, Pagan, Christian.

## STATUS IN THE WORLD TODAY

Nigeria became independent on Oct. 1, 1960, following the pattern set in 1957 by Ghana. In common with the other territories of West Africa, Nigeria has advanced rapidly on the road to self-government since 1945. Although British control over the colony was established in 1900, little effort was made before World War II to introduce popular representation. An efficient system of colonial administration was set up, at the head of which was a Legislative Council with a few African elected members, but not until 1946 were popularly elected Regional Houses of Assembly created.

Nigeria is perhaps the richest of the West African territories in variety of natural resources. About 75 per cent of the world's supply of columbite, a rare metal used in alloys for jet engines, comes from Nigeria. There are good prospects for commercial oil production in Eastern Nigeria. Nigerian industry is still in its early stages of development, but with the rapid spread of education it is expected that within a few years many of the products now imported will be manufactured at home with skilled Nigerian labor.

Nigeria, with an area twice that of California, is situated on the Gulf of Guinea in West Africa. Between 1879 and 1914 private colonial developments by the British, with reorganizations of the Crown's interest in the region, resulted in the formation of Nigeria as it exists today. During World War I, native troops of the West African frontier force joined with French forces to defeat the German garrison in the Cameroons. The Cameroons, a narrow strip along Nigeria's eastern border, became a League mandate after World War I, divided between France and Britain. In the British mandate area, Southern Cameroons subsequently elected to join the Cameroun Republic, while Northern Cameroons voted to join Nigeria. In early 1958, the British Secretary of State for Colonies announced the approval of a grant of $1,750,000 to assist in the expansion of educational facilities in Lagos. An additional $33.6 million loan for development of the country's economy was made when Nigeria became independent.

ECONOMIC CONDITIONS. Among the leading export crops are cacao, peanuts, palm kernels, palm oil, and rubber. Hides and skins are also important export items. Aside from small native industry, there is no manufacturing.

Chief exports in 1958 were peanuts (21%), cacao (18%), palm kernels (15%), and palm oil (9%). Leading customers were Britain (55%), the Netherlands (10%), and the U. S. (9%); leading suppliers, Britain (43%), Japan (13%), and Western Germany (8%).

Nigeria is a leading tin producer from mines on the Bauchi plateau. Other minerals are coal, gold, lead, silver, and tungsten. Over half the area is forested. Mahogany is the main timber export.

# FEDERATION OF RHODESIA AND NYASALAND

Governor General: Earl of Dalhousie.
Prime Minister: Sir Roy Welensky.
Foreign trade (1956): exports, 58% to Britain, 10% to Union of South Africa; imports, 41% from Britain, 34% from Union of South Africa. Chief exports: copper (38%), tobacco (15%), asbestos (4%).

## STATUS IN THE WORLD TODAY

The Central African Federation consists of the two British protectorates of Northern Rhodesia and Nyasaland and the self-governing British colony of South Rhodesia, and stretches for more than 1,000 miles south from the borders of Tanganyika to the northern rim of the Union of South Africa.

The Governor General of the Federation is appointed by the British Crown, and the Federal Assembly of 59 members is partly appointed and partly elected. The distribution of Assembly seats by territory grants 31 to Southern Rhodesia, 18 to Northern Rhodesia, and 10 to Nyasaland.

The rate of African advancement and the distribution of political power between the races are the major internal issues within the Federation. Southern Rhodesia is leading the Federation in pressing for dominion status. American private investments have been substantial in this area and the minerals of the Rhodesias, especially copper, have added further to the strategic importance of these territories.

NORTHERN RHODESIA—Status: Protectorate.
Capital: Lusaka (pop. 1956: 60,000).
Governor: Sir Evelyn Hone.
Agricultural products: tobacco, maize, wheat.
Minerals: copper, cobalt, vanadium, lead, zinc.

NYASALAND—Status: Protectorate.
Capital: Zomba (pop. 1956: 6,600).
Governor: Sir Robert Armitage.
Agricultural products: tobacco, tea, cotton.

SOUTHERN RHODESIA—Status: Self-governing colony.
Capital: Salisbury (pop. 1956: 125,000).
Governor: Humphrey Gibbs.
Prime Minister: Sir Edgar Whitehead.
Agricultural products: tobacco, corn, peanuts, meat, hides, and skins.
Minerals: asbestos, gold, coal, chrome ore.

ST. HELENA—Status: Colony.
Capital: Jamestown. (pop. est. 1959: 1,600).
Governor: Sir Robert Alford.
Foreign trade (1956): exports, 71% to Britain; imports, 44% from Britain. Chief export: hempen products (82%).
Agricultural products: flax, potatoes.

St. Helena is a volcanic island (47 sq. mi.) in the South Atlantic about 1,200 miles from the west coast of Africa. It is famous as the place of exile of Napoleon (1815–21). It was taken for Britain in 1651 by the British East India Company and became a Crown colony in 1833. Attached to it are Ascension Island (34 sq. mi.), 800 miles northwest, and the Tristan da Cunha group (45 sq. mi.), about 1,500 miles southwest. Most of the inhabitants are of mixed European, East Indian and African descent.

SEYCHELLES—Status: Colony.
Capital: Victoria (population 10,000).
Governor: Post vacant.
Foreign trade (1956): exports, 69% to India; imports, 38% from Britain. Chief export: copra (69%).
Agricultural products: cinnamon, patchouli oil, coconuts, maize, sugar cane.

This archipelago of about 92 islands in the Indian Ocean was seized from France by British troops in 1794 and ceded to Britain by the Treaty of Paris in 1814. The principal island is Mahé (55 sq. mi.), about 600 mi. northeast of Madagascar.

# Sierra Leone
(Member of Commonwealth of Nations)
Area: 27,925 square miles.
Population (1958): 2,260,000.
Density per square mile: 80.9.
Ruler: Queen Elizabeth II.
Governor General: Sir Maurice Dorman.
Prime Minister: Sir Milton Margai.
Principal cities (1958): Freetown (capital), 100,000; Makeni, 10,000; Moyamba, 3,700.
Monetary unit: West African pound.
Languages: Bantu, English.
Religions: Animist, Christian, Moslem.

## STATUS IN THE WORLD TODAY

This former Crown Colony, which achieved its independence April 27, 1961, has indicated it will maintain its close ties with Great Britain.

HISTORY AND GOVERNMENT. The coastal area was ceded to English settlers in 1788 as a home for Negroes discharged from the British armed forces and also for runaway slaves who had found asylum in London. The British protectorate over the hinterland was proclaimed in 1896.

ECONOMIC CONDITIONS. The country's principal exports, in order of value, are diamonds, iron ore (60% metal content) from deposits at Marampa, and oil palm products. Other exports, such as coffee and cocoa, contributed to a total valued at £21,900,000 in 1959. Imports in that year, valued at £23,500,000 included petroleum products, cotton products, cement, machinery, rice, flour, and tobacco.

SWAZILAND (See BRITISH SOUTH AFRICAN TERRITORIES).

TANGANYIKA & UGANDA (See EAST AFRICA HIGH COMMISSION)
ZANZIBAR—Status: Protectorate.
Capital: Zanzibar (pop. 1958: 57,923).
Sultan: Seyyid Sir Abdulla.
British Resident: Sir George Mooring.
Foreign trade (1958): exports, 60% to Indonesia and British Commonwealth; imports, 28% from Britain. Chief export: cloves (80%).
Agricultural products: cloves, clove oil, coconut oil, copra.

The protectorate consists principally of the islands of Zanzibar (640 sq. mi.) and Pemba (380 sq. mi.), just off the East African coast. Before 1890, the sultanate's territory also included a large area on the mainland, now comprising Italian Somaliland, Kenya and Tanganyika Territory. It was proclaimed a British protectorate Nov. 4, 1890. The British Resident administers the government, but the Sultan still retains considerable authority.

Principal industry is the production of cloves—about 80% of the world supply.

# WESTERN HEMISPHERE

**BAHAMAS—Status: Colony.**
Capital: Nassau (population 50,405).
Governor: Sir Robert Stapledon.
Foreign trade (1956): exports (57% to the U. S.); imports (53% from the U. S.). Chief exports: lumber (26%), crawfish. 1959 imports: £24,845,191; exports: £1,555,-761.
Agricultural products: tomatoes, citrus fruit, sisal.
Sea products: sponges, lobsters, crawfish.

The Bahamas are an archipelago of about 3,000 islands, islets (cays) and rocks, east of Florida and north of Cuba, extending from N.W. to S.E. for about 800 miles. Only about 20 of the islands are inhabited; the most important is New Providence (20 sq. mi.) on which Nassau is located. The islands were reached by Columbus in Oct., 1492, and were a favorite pirate resort in the early 18th century. They have been a Crown colony since 1717. The Constitution provides for a nominated Legislative Council and a popularly elected Assembly. The Governor is advised by an Executive Council.

About 82% of the population is Negro. The tourist trade is of paramount importance, especially at Nassau.

**BARBADOS—Status: Colony.**
Capital: Bridgetown (pop. 1958: 11,300).
Governor: Sir John Montagu Stow.
Chief Minister: Dr. H. G. H. Cummins.
Foreign trade (1956): exports (53% to Britain); imports (35% from Britain). Chief exports: sugar (67%), molasses (12%) rum. 1959 imports, W.I. $74,400,000; exports, W.I. $46,656,000.
Agricultural products: sugar (1959: 184,-000 tons), cotton, maize, cassava.
Manufactures: rum, molasses.
Monetary unit: West Indies dollar with a par value of 58¢ U.S.

Barbados, an island east of the Windward group in the West Indies, has been a British possession since 1627; it is believed to have been first visited by the Portuguese. The colony has a nominated Legislative Council and a popularly elected Assembly of 24 members. Under a ministerial system of government inaugurated Feb. 1, 1954, the Prime Minister and 4 other members of the Executive Committee (all 5 being members of the Assembly) exercise executive responsibility for most of the departments of government, except defense and foreign affairs.

The island is very densely populated (about 1,400 per sq. mi.). About 93 per cent of the inhabitants are Negro, 5 per cent white and the remainder of mixed blood. Approximately 70 per cent of the total area is cultivated and half of this is devoted to sugar, which is the staple product; there are sugar and molasses plants and several rum distilleries.

**BERMUDAS—Status: Colony.**
Capital: Hamilton (population 3,000).
Governor: Maj. Gen. Sir Julian Gascoigne.
Foreign trade (1956): exports, £511,581; re-exports, £4,154,343; imports, £13,159,853 (53% from the U. S.). Chief domestic exports: pharmaceuticals (42%), concentrated essences. 1959 imports, £10,447,709; exports, £9,627,932 (£829,402 domestic exports).
Agricultural products: lily bulbs, potatoes, vegetables, arrowroot.
Monetary unit: Bermuda pound at par with sterling.

The Bermudas comprise an archipelago of about 360 small islands, 580 miles east of North Carolina. The largest is (Great) Bermuda, or Main Island. Discovered by Juan Bermudez, a shipwrecked Spaniard, early in the 16th century, the islands were settled in 1612 by an offshoot of the Virginia Company and became a Crown colony in 1684. The Governor is assisted by nominated Executive and Legislative Councils and a popularly elected Assembly of 36 members. In 1940, sites on the islands were leased for 99 years to the U.S. for air and navy bases. Bermuda is also the headquarters of the West Indies and Atlantic squadron of the Royal Navy. The most important factor in the colony's economy is the tourist trade. The arable land is devoted to horticulture.

**BRITISH GUIANA—Status: Colony.**
Capital: Georgetown (population 1960: 72,991).
Governor: Sir Ralph Grey.
Foreign trade (1956): exports (40% to Canada, 32% to Britain); imports (45% from Britain). Chief exports: sugar (44%), bauxite (31%), rice (10%). 1959 imports, $110,620,386; exports, $101,985,268.
Agricultural products: sugar, rice, copra, coffee, fruit.
Minerals: bauxite, gold, diamonds.
Forest products: balata, timber.
Monetary unit: West Indian pound.

The only British possession in South America proper, British Guiana is on the northeastern coast between Venezuela and Surinam (Dutch Guiana). Settled by the Dutch in the 17th century, it was occupied by the British in 1796 and ceded to them at the end of the Napoleonic wars. Behind the low plain which contains the farm area is a higher area containing forest and mineral resources.

The colony was granted home rule in 1961, with Great Britain retaining control of defense and foreign affairs; and a government headed by Dr. Cheddi Jagan took office. Charges that Dr. Jagan planned to establish a Communist regime in 1953 led to suspension of the Constitution and British intervention to oust his government. Dr. Jagan, who denies charges of communism, says his party, which appeals primarily to Guiana voters of East Indian extraction, plans to convert the colony into a socialist state.

Forest resources, mostly unexploited, have been estimated at about 40,000,000,000 cubic feet of merchantable timber.

**BRITISH HONDURAS—Status: Colony.**
Capital: Belize (pop. 1960: 32,824).
Governor: Sir Colin Thornley.
Chief exports (1956): mahogany (24%), pine. 1958 imports: BH $18,516,000; exports: BH $9,088,000.
Agricultural products: bananas, sugar cane, citrus fruits.
Forest products: cedar lumber and logs, mahogany lumber, logs, pine lumber, chicle.
Monetary unit: British Honduras dollar (BH $1.43 = U.S. $1.00).

British Honduras is bounded on the north by Mexico and on the west and south by Guatemala. It was settled in 1662 by woodcutters from Jamaica. An irregular form of local government continued until 1871, when it became a Crown colony; it was separated from Jamaica in 1884. The Governor is assisted by an Executive Council and by a partially elected Legislative Assembly. A new constitution will permit the people to elect a Prime Minister.

The colony's economy is dependent upon timber and other forest exports. Agriculture has never been adequately developed.

# Canada

(Member of Commonwealth of Nations)
Area (land only): 3,851,116 square miles.*
Population (1960): 17,814,000 (1951: British 48%; French 31%; German 4%; Ukrainian 3%; others 14%).
Density per square mile: 4.6.
Ruler: Queen Elizabeth II.
Governor General: George P. Vanier.
Prime Minister: John Diefenbaker
Principal cities (census 1956): Montreal, 1,109,439 (seaport); Toronto, 667,706 (manufacturing center); Vancouver, 365,844 (Pacific seaport); Winnipeg, 255,093 (grain); Hamilton, 239,625 (iron and steel); Edmonton, 226,002 (petroleum); Ottawa, 222,129 (capital); Calgary, 181,780 (farming); Quebec, 170,703 (seaport); Windsor, 121,980 (automobiles).
Monetary unit: Canadian dollar.
Religions (census 1951): Roman Catholic 43%; United Church 20%; Anglican 15%; Presbyterian 6%; Baptist 4%; others 12%.
* Total area, including water: 3,845,774 square miles.

**STATUS IN THE WORLD TODAY**
Canada, like the United States, has emerged from its prewar isolation and, no longer a small power, has become an extremely active member of the group of Free World nations. Since 1945 the cornerstone of its foreign policy has been support of the U.N. In world politics it moves in three areas: the Commonwealth, NATO, and the Americas.

From the Canadian point of view, the Commonwealth maintains a bridge to Asia and Africa from the Western world and also lessens Canadian dependence upon the United States. NATO affords a perfect framework in which to use Canada's relatively small population and relatively great resources in conjunction with those of both the United Kingdom and the United States. It also, by means of its European members, gives Canada associates whose members do something to offset the power of the two great members. And in the Americas, with the possibility of attack on North America across the Arctic, Canada and the United States have set up a Permanent Joint Defense Committee. This has brought about the construction of the Distant Early Warning (DEW) line of radar installations and the creation of the North American Air Defense command (NORAD).

Canadian membership in the U.N. and in its Security Council, has been marked by a quickness to attempt to bring disputes into the hands of the U.N. Its action in calling for intervention by the U.N. in the dispute between Nationalist and Red China over Quemoy and Matsu islands is an example of Canada's preference for action by the U.N. instead of action by one or more of the great powers. At the time of the attack on Suez, Canada's reaction was to attempt to restore peace and to preserve the Commonwealth, whose Asian members were overwhelmingly on the side of Egypt. Its actions procured first the dispatch of Mr. Hammarskjöld to Egypt and then the provision of the United Nations Emergency Force to restore the frontiers on which the fighting began and to set a screen between the belligerents.

In the 1957 Canadian elections, there were distinct anti-American overtones. The amount of American capital investment, the control of American branch factories by American head offices and the excess of American imports over Canadian exports to the United States are a matter of concern to many Canadians who are not necessarily anti-American in sentiment. They merely wish to insure Canadian control of the country's economic development by a judicious diversification of foreign interests in Canada and of Canadian external trade. A desire to solve some of these differences prompted the visit of President Eisenhower to Ottawa in July, 1958, and the setting up of joint committees of the

## PROVINCES AND TERRITORIES

| Province | Land area, sq. mi. | Population (Census 1959) |
|---|---|---|
| Alberta | 248,800 | 1,243,000 |
| British Columbia | 359,279 | 1,570,000 |
| Manitoba | 219,723 | 885,000 |
| New Brunswick | 27,473 | 590,000 |
| Newfoundland | 152,734 | 449,000 |
| Nova Scotia | 20,547 | 716,000 |
| Ontario | 363,282 | 5,952,000 |
| Prince Edward Island | 2,184 | 102,000 |
| Quebec | 523,860 | 4,999,000 |
| Saskatchewan | 237,975 | 902,000 |
| **Territories** | | |
| Northwest Territories | 1,258,217 | 21,000 |
| Yukon | 205,346 | 13,000 |

| Provinces | Capital | Premier, 1959 |
|---|---|---|
| Alberta | Edmonton | Ernest C. Manning[1] |
| British Columbia | Victoria | William Bennett[1] |
| Manitoba | Winnipeg | Duff Roblin[2] |
| New Brunswick | Fredericton | Louis J. Robichaud[3] |
| Newfoundland | St. John's | Joseph Smallwood[3] |
| Nova Scotia | Halifax | Robert L. Stanfield[2] |
| Ontario | Toronto | Leslie Frost[2] |
| Prince Edward Island | Charlottetown | Walter R. Shaw[2] |
| Quebec | Quebec | Jean Lesage[3] |
| Saskatchewan | Regina | T. C. Douglas[4] |
| **Territories** | | |
| Northwest Territories | Ottawa | R. G. Robertson* |
| Yukon | Whitehorse | F. H. Collins* |

[1] Social Credit; [2] Progressive-Conservative; [3] Liberal; [4] Cooperative Commonwealth Federation.
* Commissioner.

American and Canadian cabinets and of Congress and Parliament. If these bodies can function, they may contribute not merely to a better understanding between the governments and legislatures of the two countries, but also their more effective co-operation in continental defense and in world politics.

### MAJOR POLITICAL PARTIES

Conservative party (208 seats in House of Commons), led by Prime Minister John Diefenbaker; Liberal party (49 seats), led by Lester Pearson.

HISTORY. The Norse explorer Leif Ericsson probably reached the shores of Canada (Labrador or Nova Scotia) in A.D. 1000, but the history of the white man in the country actually began in 1497, when John Cabot, an Italian in the service of Henry VII of England, reached the shore of Newfoundland or Nova Scotia. Canada was taken for France in 1534 by Jacques Cartier. The actual settlement of New France, as it was then called, began in 1604 at Port Royal in what is now Nova Scotia; in 1608 Quebec was founded. France's colonization efforts were not very successful, but French explorers by the end of the seventeenth century had penetrated beyond the Great Lakes to the western prairies and south along the Mississippi to the Gulf of Mexico. Meanwhile, the English Hudson's Bay Company had been established in 1670. Because of the valuable fisheries and fur trade, a conflict developed between the French and English; in 1713, Newfoundland, Hudson Bay, and Nova Scotia (Acadia) were lost to England.

During the Seven Years' War (1756–63), England extended its conquest, and the British general, Wolfe, won his famous victory over Montcalm outside Quebec (Sept. 13, 1759). The Treaty of Paris (1763) put Canada under English control.

At that time the population of Canada was almost entirely French, but in the next few decades thousands of British colonists emigrated to Canada from the British Isles and from the American colonies. In 1849 the right of Canada to self-government was recognized. By the British North America Act of 1867, the Dominion of Canada was created through the confederation of Upper and Lower Canada, Nova Scotia, and New Brunswick. Prince Edward Island joined the Dominion in 1873. In 1869 Canada had purchased from the Hudson's Bay Company the vast middle west (Rupert's Land) from which the provinces of Manitoba (1870), Alberta, and Saskatchewan (1905) were later formed. In 1871 British Columbia joined the Dominion. The country was linked from coast to coast in 1885 by the Canadian Pacific Railway.

During the formative years between 1867 and 1896, the Conservative party, led by Sir John A. Macdonald, governed the country, except during the years 1873–78. In 1896 the Liberal party took over and under Sir Wilfrid Laurier, an eminent French Canadian, ruled until 1911. In World War I, more than 500,000 Canadian soldiers fought for the Allied cause. After the Treaty of Versailles, Canada, a full-fledged nation, was admitted to the League of Nations and appointed its own representatives in foreign countries. By the Statute of Westminster (1931) the British Dominions, including Canada, were formally declared to be partner nations with Britain, "equal in status, in no way subordinate to each other," and bound together only by allegiance to a common Crown.

Newfoundland became Canada's tenth province on March 31, 1949, following a plebiscite held July 22, 1948, in which the people voted by a narrow margin to unite with Canada.

GOVERNMENT. Canada, a self-governing member of the Commonwealth of Nations, is a federal union of ten provinces whose powers are laid down in the British North America Act of 1867. The executive powers nominally rest in the hands of the Governor General, who represents the Queen and is appointed by her upon the recommendation of the Canadian government.

Actually the Governor General acts only with the advice of the Canadian Prime Minister and the members of the Cabinet, who at the same time sit in the federal Parliament. The Parliament has two houses: a Senate numbering 102 members appointed for life, and a House of Commons numbering 265 members apportioned according to provincial population. Elections are held at least every five years or whenever the party in power is voted down in the House of Commons or considers it expedient to appeal to the people. The Prime Minister is the leader of the majority party in the House of Commons. Laws must be passed by both houses of Parliament and signed by the Governor General in the Queen's name.

The ten provincial governments are nominally headed by Lieutenant Governors appointed by the federal government, but the executive power in each actually is vested in a Cabinet headed by a Prime Minister, who is leader of the majority party. In nine of the ten provinces the legislature is composed of a one-house assembly elected by the people for four years. In Quebec there is a second chamber, the Legislative Council, composed of nominees of the Provincial Government.

*Judicial System.* The judicial system consists of a Supreme Court in Ottawa (established in 1875), with appellate jurisdiction, and a Supreme Court in each province, as well as country courts with limited jurisdiction in most of the provinces. The Governor General in Council appoints the judges of these courts.

ECONOMIC CONDITIONS. *Agriculture.* Agriculture, including horticulture, fruit growing, and the raising of stock and poultry, is the largest single industry. Canada is one of the world's greatest wheat-exporting countries; production is concentrated in Manitoba, Saskatchewan, and Alberta.

Stock raising and dairy farming have grown greatly since 1920. Ontario and Quebec are the most important dairying provinces. On June 1, 1960, Canada had 11,501,-000 cattle, 5,483,000 hogs, 1,773,000 sheep, and 571,500 horses.

*Industry.* Canadian manufactures rely mainly on domestic raw materials; growing industries which depend largely on materials imported in a raw or semi-finished state include the manufacture of automobiles, sugar, and rubber goods, as well as the iron and steel industry in Nova Scotia, Quebec, and Ontario. The latter two provinces account for more than 80% of all manufactures. The abundance of cheap water power is one of the chief factors in the growth of Canadian industry. In 1958 there were 36,741 plants employing 1,289,-602 persons. The most important industries in terms of output were pulp and paper, nonferrous-metals smelting and refining, petroleum products, meatpacking, motor vehicles, and sawmill products.

*Trade.* Canada is one of the great trading

## Canadian Governors General and Prime Ministers Since 1867

| Term of office | Governor General | Term | Prime Minister | Party |
|---|---|---|---|---|
| 1867–1869 | Viscount Monck | 1867–1873 | Sir John A. Macdonald | Conservative |
| 1869–1872 | Baron Lisgar | 1873–1878 | Alexander Mackenzie | Liberal |
| 1872–1878 | Earl of Dufferin | 1878–1891 | Sir John A. Macdonald | Conservative |
| 1878–1883 | Marquess of Lorne | 1891–1892 | Sir John J. Abbot | Conservative |
| 1883–1888 | Marquess of Lansdowne | 1892–1894 | Sir John S. D. Thompson | Conservative |
| 1888–1893 | Baron Stanley | 1894–1896 | Sir Mackenzie Bowell | Conservative |
| 1893–1898 | Earl of Aberdeen | 1896 (2 mos) | Sir Charles Tupper | Conservative |
| 1898–1904 | Earl of Minto | 1896–1911 | Sir Wilfrid Laurier | Liberal |
| 1904–1911 | Earl Grey | 1911–1917 | Sir Robert L. Borden | Conservative |
| 1911–1916 | Duke of Connaught | 1917–1920 | Sir Robert L. Borden | Unionist |
| 1916–1921 | Duke of Devonshire | 1920–1921 | Arthur Meighen | Unionist-National, Conservative |
| 1921–1926 | Viscount Byng | | | |
| 1926–1931 | Viscount Willingdon | 1921–1926 | W. L. Mackenzie King | Liberal |
| 1931–1935 | Earl of Bessborough | 1926 (3 mos) | Arthur Meighen | Conservative |
| 1935–1940 | Baron Tweedsmuir | 1926–1930 | W. L. Mackenzie King | Liberal |
| 1940–1946 | Earl of Athlone | 1930–1935 | Richard B. Bennett | Conservative |
| 1946–1952 | Viscount Alexander | 1935–1948 | W. L. Mackenzie King | Liberal |
| 1952–1959 | Vincent Massey | 1948–1957 | Louis S. St. Laurent | Liberal |
| 1959– | George P. Vanier | 1957– | John Diefenbaker | Conservative |

nations of the world. The bulk of its foreign commerce is in raw or semi-finished products.

In 1959, Canada's principal customers were the United States (61%), Britain (15%), West Germany (2.5%), Japan (2.7%), and Norway (1.2%). Leading suppliers were the United States (68%), Britain (10%), Venezuela (3.6%), West Germany (2.2%), and Japan (1.8%). Leading exports were newsprint (14%), wheat (8.7%), wood pulp (6.0%), planks and boards (6.4%), uranium ores and concentrates (6.2%), and nickel (5.1%). Leading imports in 1959 were machinery (nonfarm) (10.4%), automobile parts (4.9%), crude petroleum (4.9%), rolling-mill products (steel) (2.8%), farm implements and machinery (4.9%), and petroleum products (3%).

*Communications.* Because Canada's exports are to a large extent bulky raw materials, cheap water transportation is essential. The country's system of canals, especially those connecting the Great Lakes, forms an integral part of the inland communications system.

NATURAL FEATURES AND RESOURCES. Covering most of the northern part of the North American continent and with an area larger than that of the United States, Canada's topography is extremely diversified. The northeastern region, including most of Quebec, northern Ontario and Manitoba, and the Northwest Territories, with Hudson Bay in the center, is an important source of minerals, wood pulp, and water power. In the east the mountainous maritime provinces have an irregular coast line on the Gulf of St. Lawrence and the Atlantic. The St. Lawrence plain, covering most of southern Quebec and Ontario, and the interior continental plain, covering southern Manitoba and Saskatchewan and most of Alberta, are the principal cultivable areas. They are separated by a forested plateau rising from Lakes Superior and Huron. Westward toward the Pacific, most of British Columbia, Yukon, and part of western Alberta are covered by parallel mountain ranges including the Rockies. The Pacific border of the coast range is ragged with fiords and channels. The highest point in Canada is Mt. Logan, 19,850 ft., located in the Yukon.

Canada has an abundance of large and small lakes. In addition to the Great Lakes on the United States border, there are nine others which are more than 100 miles long and 35 which are more than 50 miles long.

The two principal river systems are the Mackenzie and the St. Lawrence. The St. Lawrence, with its tributaries, is navigable for over 1,900 miles and is the commercial artery of eastern Canada.

As most of the Canadian rivers have waterfalls on their courses they are of considerable importance as sources of power.

*Minerals.* Canada's mineral resources are both rich and varied. Mining production in 1956 was valued at $2,067,699,096. Metals come mainly from two widely separated regions, the mountain ranges of the Pacific coast and the province of Ontario. Copper ore also exists in Quebec, Manitoba, and Newfoundland. Production of petroleum centers in Alberta. There are deposits of uranium in the Northwest Territories.

*Forests and Fisheries.* The total area of land covered by forests is estimated at 1,300,000 square miles, of which only 435,000 are productive and accessible. The manufacture of pulp and paper is one of the leading industries.

Fishing, Canada's oldest industry, is carried on along the Atlantic and Pacific coasts and on the inland lakes.

**FALKLAND ISLANDS AND DEPENDENCIES—Status: Crown Colony.**
**Governor: Sir Edwin P. Arrowsmith.**
**Capital: Stanley (population 1,135).**

This sparsely inhabited Crown colony consists of a group of islands in the south Atlantic about 250 miles east of the South American mainland. Dependencies include all islands and Antarctic territory between 20° and 50° w. long., south of 50° s. lat., and between 50° and 80° w. long., south of 58° s. lat. The chief industry is sheep raising, and apart from the production of wool, hides and skins, and tallow, there are no known resources. The whaling industry is carried on from South Georgia Island.

The islands were discovered by John Davis in 1592.

**JAMAICA AND DEPENDENCIES—Status: Colony.**
Capital: Kingston (population 125,526).
Governor: Sir Kenneth Blackburne.
Chief Minister: Norman W. Manley.
Foreign trade (1956)*: exports (49% to Britain); imports (37% from Britain). Chief exports: sugar and preparations (34%), bananas (14%), bauxite (12%). 1959 bauxite exports: 4,197,000 tons; sugar exports, 378,000 tons.
Agricultural products: sugar, rum, bananas, citrus fruits, ginger, coffee, pimento.
Mineral: bauxite.

* Excluding dependencies.

Jamaica, the largest island in the British West Indies (4,470 sq. mi.), is eighty miles south of the eastern end of Cuba. Its island dependencies include the Turks and Caicos Islands (about 600 mi. N.E.), Cayman Islands (about 300 mi. N.W.) and two uninhabited cays. It was discovered by Columbus in 1494 and remained in Spanish possession until 1655, when it was taken by the British. According to the Constitution of Nov. 20, 1944, as amended in 1953, the Governor is assisted by a House of Representatives, a Legislative Council (upper house), and an Executive Council, of whom the Chief Minister is appointed by the Governor subject to approval of the House of Representatives.

Sites were leased for 99 years to the U.S. in 1940 for naval and air bases.

The colony's economy depends on agriculture, and about 200,000 acres are under cultivation. Sugar took the place of bananas as the chief crop during World War II. Jamaica is virtually the sole source of pimento.

**LEEWARD ISLANDS—Status: Group of colonies.**
Chief export: sugar.
Agricultural products: sugar, cotton, coconuts, citrus fruits, tobacco.

The Leeward Islands, lying southeast of Puerto Rico, are a group of four colonies— Antigua (108 sq. mi.) and dependencies (63 sq. mi.); Virgin Islands (67 sq. mi.); St. Kitts, Nevis and dependency (152 sq. mi.); and Montserrat (33 sq. mi.). They are governed separately, each under an administrator.

In 1940, the United States acquired a 99-year lease on sites for a naval and air base on Antigua. The islands are agricultural.

**TRINIDAD AND TOBAGO—Status: Colony.**
Capital: Port of Spain (population 121,-150).
Governor: Sir Solomon Hochoy.
Chief Minister: Dr. Eric Williams.
Foreign trade (1956): exports (35% to Britain); imports (35% from Britain). Chief exports: crude petroleum and products (66%), sugar (8%), cacao (3%). 1959 imports: W.I. $447,360,000; exports: W.I. $445,440,000.
Agricultural products: raw sugar, cacao, coconuts, citrus fruit.
Manufactures: petroleum products
Minerals: crude petroleum, asphalt.
Monetary unit: West Indian dollar.

The islands of Trinidad and Tobago are sixteen and twenty-one miles, respectively, off Venezuela just north of the Orinoco delta. Both were discovered by Columbus in 1498 and remained Spanish possessions until 1797, when the British took them. They are administered by a Governor, assisted by an Executive Council and a Legislative Council, popularly elected. In 1941 the U.S. was granted 99-year leases on the islands for naval and air bases.

The soil is rich for the growing of tropical products; sugar and cacao are the principal crops. Trinidad is one of the leading oil producers of the Commonwealth, and the world's most notable source of asphalt, found in Pitch Lake, thirty-eight miles southeast of Port of Spain.

**WEST INDIES FEDERATION:** established Jan. 3, 1958, it includes Antigua, Barbados, Dominica, Grenada, Montserrat, Trinidad and Tobago, St. Lucia, St. Vincent, and St. Kitts-Nevis. It expected to attain Commonwealth status in 1962, but Jamaica's withdrawal in Sept. 1961 made this doubtful.

*Major political parties:* Federal Labour party (24 seats in House of Representatives), led by Norman Manley; Democratic Labour party (20 seats), led by Sir Alexander Bustamente.

**WINDWARD ISLANDS—Status: Group of colonies.**
Agricultural products: arrrowroot (St. Vincent), nutmeg (Grenada), mace (Grenada), cacao.

These islands, four in number, form the southern portion of the Lesser Antilles in the Caribbean; they extend approximately 250 miles from the French colony of Guadeloupe on the north to the British colony of Trinidad on the south. Their total area of about 820 square miles divides as follows: Dominica, 304; St. Lucia, 233; St. Vincent, 150; Grenada, 133. The four colonies are governed by different administrators.

Agriculture is the only industry. St. Vincent has a virtual monopoly on the world supply of arrowroot.

# ASIA

**ADEN—Status: Colony and Protectorate.**
Governor: Sir Charles Johnston.
Foreign trade: exports (16% to Britain); imports (30% from Kuwait).
Manufactures: crude petroleum refined (1959: 3,945,000 tons).

The British colony and protectorate of Aden is situated on the volcanic southern tip of the Arabian peninsula, along the Gulf of Aden. The colony (port) of Aden was annexed to Britain in 1839 and was part of the Bombay Presidency until 1932, when it became a separate province with the Chief Commissioner responsible to the Indian government. In 1937 it was transferred from Indian to Imperial control as a Crown colony. It is administered by a Governor and Commander-in-Chief, aided by an Executive Council and a Legislative Council. The 20-odd Sultans who rule their respective territories in the protectorate are responsible to him.

Aden colony is essentially a transshipment point and bunkering station and is also the commercial center for the Yemen and the African coast opposite. Aden airport is a station on the Khartoum-Karachi air route. Agriculture is unimportant except for some coffee and tobacco, and except for the large petroleum refinery of the British Petroleum Co., Ltd. (formerly Anglo-Iranian Oil Co.), which went into operation in 1954, manufacturing activity is limited to salt, cigarettes, and dhows.

## COLOMBO PLAN

The Colombo Plan, started among Commonwealth countries of Southeast Asia in 1950, focuses attention on recipient rather than donor. Its objective is to improve living standards of economically underdeveloped countries by coordinating their approach to foreign economic aid. Substantial contributions have been made by the U.S., the U.K., Australia, New Zealand and the International Bank for Reconstruction and Development.

## BORNEO

**COLONY OF NORTH BORNEO—Status:** Colony.
  Capital: Jesselton (population 15,500).
  Governor: Sir Wm. Goode.
  Foreign trade (1956)*: exports (23% to Britain); imports (24% from Britain). Chief exports: rubber (33%), timber (22%), copra (19%). 1959 exports: rubber, 22,900 tons; copra, 59,400 tons.
  Agricultural products: rubber, rice, copra.
  Forest products: timber, cutch, rattans.

\* Excluding transit trade.

The Colony of North Borneo, constituting the extreme northern portion of the island of Borneo, consists largely of highlands and occasional open valleys and plateaus. The territory was a British protectorate administered under a royal charter by the British North Borneo Company from 1881 until July 15, 1946, when it assumed the status of a Crown colony. It was occupied by Japanese troops from 1942 until 1945. Labuan (pop. 9,000; area, 35 sq. mi.), a small island off the North Borneo coast, was transferred from the jurisdiction of the Straits Settlements to that of North Borneo in 1946.

The population is comprised largely of aborigines living on a primitive cultural level. In 1951, 72.7 per cent of the population was native, 22.3 per cent Chinese; there were 1,213 Europeans. Mineral resources are believed to be considerable, but the colony's income is based on agricultural and jungle produce.

**BRUNEI—Status:** Protectorate.
  Capital: Brunei (population 17,000).
  Sultan: Sir Omar Ali Saifuddin.
  High Commissioner: D. C. White.
  Foreign trade: Chief export: petroleum (99%). 1959 crude oil: 5,295,552 tons.
  Agricultural products: rice, rubber.
  Mineral: petroleum.

Brunei lies on the northwestern coast of Borneo, entirely surrounded by Sarawak. It was placed under British protection in 1888, and in 1906 a treaty was concluded whereby the native Sultan yielded administration of the state to a British Resident.

The Governor of Sarawak was appointed High Commissioner for Brunei in 1948.

Most of the inhabitants are Malays and Borneans; in 1955, 19% were Chinese and only 1.5% European. The bulk of the population lives in and around the capital, situated on the Brunei River 9 miles from its mouth. The interior is largely forested and contains rich timber. All petroleum is exported to Sarawak for refining.

**SARAWAK—Status:** Colony.
  Capital: Kuching (population 50,585).
  Governor: Sir Alexander Waddell.
  Foreign trade. Chief exports: petroleum and products (73%), rubber (14%), pepper (5%).
  Agricultural products: rubber, pepper, copra, rice.
  Minerals: petroleum, gold, silver, coal.

Sarawak extends along the northwestern coast of Borneo for about 500 miles. In 1841 part of the present territory was granted by the Sultan of Brunei to Sir James Brooke. The state, enlarged by additional concessions made between 1861 and 1905, continued to be ruled by members of the Brooke family until the Japanese occupation in Dec. 1941. A British protectorate since 1888, Sarawak became a Crown colony July 15, 1946, through agreement between the British government and the then-ruling Rajah, Sir Charles Vyner Brooke.

The colony is mountainous and well watered; inland communication is largely by water. Most of the inhabitants are Malays, Dyaks, and Chinese. The most important mineral is petroleum, which was discovered at Miri in 1909 and subsequently worked by Sarawak Oilfields, Ltd. In 1959, 5,357,626 tons of crude and refined oil were produced. There are also forest resources.

# Ceylon

(Member of Commonwealth of Nations)
  Area: 25,332 square miles.
  Population (est. 1959): 9,612,000 (1953: Sinhalese, 69%; Tamil, 21%; Moors, 6%; Burghers and Eurasians, .5%; Europeans [6,909] and others, 3.5%).
  Density per square mile: 379.4.
  Ruler: Queen Elizabeth II.
  Governor General: Sir Oliver Goonetilleke.
  Prime Minister: Mrs. Sirimavo Bandaranaike.
  Principal cities (census 1953): Colombo, 426,127 (capital); Dehiwala—Mt. Lavinia, 78,213 (suburb of Colombo).
  Monetary unit: Ceylonese rupee.
  Languages: English, Sinhalese, Tamil.
  Religious (est.): Buddhist, 61%; Hindu, 22%; Moslem, 7%; Christian (mainly Roman Catholic), 9%; others, 1%.

## STATUS IN THE WORLD TODAY

A self-governing dominion in the British Commonwealth of nations, Ceylon at first was one of the most genuinely pro-Western nations among the newly independent nations of Asia. But when it could not sell rubber and other exports in Western markets at prices which would pay for the necessary imports of foodstuffs, it began to shift toward a neutralist policy which led to the first (in 1952) of a series of trade agreements with the Soviet-Sino bloc providing for the exchange of rubber for rice.

Ceylon depends upon three products—tea, rubber, and coconuts—to finance its food imports, since domestic production provides less than half the minimum needs. But rubber and coconut prices on the world market fluctuate more widely than those of almost any other products, while tea, more stable, has recently had price variations up to 11 per cent. Thus, Ceylon cannot control its livelihood. To diversify and develop its economy, the nation adopted in 1947 the first of two Six-Year Plans to develop new crops and expand secondary industry. When results failed to measure up to the goals set, Ceylon sought the help of an International Bank mission in 1951 to formulate a more comprehensive Six-Year Investment Program for 1954–1960, calling for a total expenditure of $531 million.

Faced with a dense population to add to its economic difficulties, Ceylon also has a serious ethnic problem. Over 70 per cent of the population are Sinhalese, principally Buddhists. Another 21 per cent are Tamil-speaking Hindus of South Indian extraction. More than half of these are so-called Ceylon Tamils, descendents of 11th century invaders, who enjoy full legal equality with the Sinhalese. The rest, Indian Tamils, were brought over as laborers by the British or are more recent arrivals. They are not especially wanted by the Sinhalese and only half of them are eligible for citizenship. The Sinhalese-Tamil linguistic-religious conflict erupted into communal rioting in May and June of 1958 in which hundreds of lives were lost. As a result of the unrest, the government banned two extreme communalist parties, one Tamil and one Sinhalese.

## MAJOR POLITICAL PARTIES

Sri Lanka Freedom party (65 seats in House of Representatives), led by Prime Minister Mrs. Sirimavo Bandaranaike; United National party (29 seats), led by Dudley Senanayke; Federal party (18 seats), led by S. J. V. Chesvanayakam.

HISTORY AND GOVERNMENT. Known to the Greeks and Romans as Taprobane and to Mohammedan seamen as Serendib, Ceylon is reputed to have been invaded from India in 504 B.C. by Vijaya, the first Sinhalese King. Buddhism was introduced in the third century B.C. In subsequent centuries the island was invaded and occupied several times by Indian princes.

Ceylon became a full-fledged, self-governing dominion on Feb. 4, 1948, with Stephen Senanayake as Prime Minister. On his death, Mar. 22, 1952, his son Dudley took office. The latter resigned on Oct. 12, 1953, and was succeeded by Sir John Kotelawala. The leftist People's United Front won the April, 1956, elections and its leader, S.W.R.D. Bandaranaike, formed a new government on Apr. 12. Bandaranaike was assassinated Sept. 26, 1959, and Wijayananda Dahanayake became Prime Minister.

Under the 1946 Constitution, Ceylon's government is headed by the Crown-appointed Governor General, who is advised by a Council of Ministers headed by the Prime Minister. The bicameral Parliament consists of a House of Representatives of 101 members, and a Senate of 30 members. Half of the senate is nominated by the Cabinet and the other half elected by the House of Representatives.

ECONOMIC CONDITIONS. Ceylon is heavily dependent on food imports, particularly rice, the staple food. A large part of the cultivated land (25 per cent of the total area) is devoted to the chief export crops—tea, rubber, and coconut products, all of which are grown for the most part on plantations. Other crops include rice, fruits, cinnamon, and citronella.

Leading exports are tea, rubber, and coconut oil. Leading customers are Britain (28%), sterling area (20%), the United States and Canada (15%), and EPU countries (12%); leading suppliers, Britain (25%), India (12%), other sterling area (17%), continental EPU countries (9%), and U.S. and Canada (8%).

NATURAL FEATURES AND RESOURCES. Most of the island is flat, but mountains in the south rise to 8,000 feet. The island extends to a maximum of 270 miles north and south, and 140 miles east and west.

Mineral resources include graphite (plumbago), gem stones, mica, magnesite, and vanadium.

HONG KONG—Status: Colony.
Capital: Victoria (population 1,000,000).
Governor: Sir Robert Black.
Foreign trade: Chief export: textiles.
Agricultural products: rice, sugar cane.
Major industries: shipbuilding, rope making, cement, sugar refining, textiles.

The colony of Hong Kong comprises the island of Hong Kong (32 sq. mi.), Stonecutters' Island, and the Kowloon peninsula and the New Territories on the adjoining mainland. The island of Hong Kong, located at the mouth of the Canton River about ninety miles southeast of Canton, was ceded to Britain in 1841.

Stonecutters' Island and Kowloon were annexed in 1860, and the New Territories, which are mainly agricultural lands, were leased from China in 1898 for ninety-nine years. Hong Kong was attacked by Japanese troops Dec. 7, 1941, and surrendered the following Christmas Day. It remained under the occupation of the Japanese until September, 1945.

Possessing an excellent natural harbor seventeen miles in extent, the only safe deep-sea anchorage between Shanghai and Indo-China, Hong Kong is the entrepôt for trade throughout southern China and the western Pacific.

The cities of Victoria and Kowloon contain the greater part of the population, which is overwhelmingly Chinese. Besides those Chinese engaged in agriculture or industry, many live in sampans or junks either in Victoria Harbour or neighboring bays, supporting themselves by fishing or by performing labor on the wharves.

# India (Republic)

(Member of Commonwealth of Nations)

Area: 1,259,992 square miles.*
Population (est. 1960): 408,050,000.* (Hindu, 85%; Moslem, 9.9%; Christian, 2.3%; Sikh, 1.7%; others [Jain, Buddhist, Zoroastrian, Jewish, etc.], 1.1%).
Density per square mile: 300.8.
President: Rajendra Prasad.
Prime Minister: Pandit Jawaharlal Nehru.
Principal cities (census 1951): Bombay, 2,329,020 (seaport; cotton and textiles); Calcutta, 2,520,921 (chief port); Madras, 1,416,056 (seaport); Hyderabad, 1,085,722 (trade center); Delhi, 914,790 (manufacturing); Ahmedabad, 788,333 (manufacturing); Bangalore, 778,977 (manufacturing); Kanpur (Cawnpore), 705,443 (textiles); New Delhi, 276,314 (capital).
Monetary unit: Rupee.
Principal languages: Hindi (official), English†, Bengali, Assamese, Gujarati, Kannada, Kashmiri, Malayalam, Marathi, Oriya, Punjabi, Sanskrit, Tamil, Telugu, Urdu.
* Including Jammu and Kashmir; status in dispute with Pakistan. † To be used for all official purposes until 1965.

## STATUS IN THE WORLD TODAY

India, a sovereign democratic republic which still retains membership in the British Commonwealth of Nations, is the leader of the neutralist bloc of nations in the current cold war. One reason is the determination of Prime Minister Jawaharlal Nehru that India should have the position and play the role of a great power in world affairs. A second is that through mediation and compromise it hopes to become a third force, or bridge, between the East and the West power blocs. A third

factor is invariable opposition, inherited from colonial days, to imperialism, but usually only of the Western variety, and a consequent innate suspicion of the West.

Thus India was among the leaders who demanded that France and Great Britain obey the United Nations mandate to withdraw from the Suez Canal during the 1956 attack, although the Indian government itself has refused to obey U.N. decisions in its dispute with Pakistan over Kashmir. Only belatedly, and in part forced by domestic public opinion as much as by loss of face in the non-Soviet world, did official India also speak out against the brutal Soviet oppression of the Hungarian revolt in the same year. Although it had agreed in June, 1954, with Communist China on the "five principles of peaceful coexistence," its reaction when Red China violated these principles in overthrowing the autonomous government of Tibet in 1959 was one of comparative mildness, even though Peiping charged that a Tibetan revolt had been planned in India. It did, however, give asylum to the deposed Dalai Lama. It faces the prospect of frontier troubles with its huge northern neighbor. Parts of India are already shown as belonging to Red China on maps which have been published in Peiping, and in 1960 it was disclosed that Red China had completed a base and a strategic road inside territory considered Indian before India ever heard of the project. Premier Chou En-lai came to India in April, 1960, for a week of talks about the frontier disputes, but the visit ended in failure

But because of the abject poverty which exists in India, the average illiterate Indian is too much concerned with eking out a mere existence even to think about his country's foreign policies. And to this problem of mass poverty, as India's Planning Commission described it, the government has turned most of its attention. Although like all other undeveloped countries India was fascinated by steel mills and power plants as symbols of industrial development, the core of its first Five-Year Program, started April 1, 1951, was agriculture, irrigation, land reclamation, and community development. It was in many ways a material success, and was accomplished with Western aid totaling $625 million. Not until a year before the end of the program did the U.S.S.R. enter the picture with an offer to build and equip a steel mill on terms more favorable than those hitherto secured from the West.

For its second Five-Year Plan, which ended in 1961, allocations to all parts of the economy were vastly increased and the emphasis upon direct industrialization sharply stepped up. India expected to finance this program mainly from internal resources, but still required $1,680

## POLITICAL SUBDIVISIONS OF REPUBLIC OF INDIA

| States | Area, sq. mi. | Population, census 1951* |
|---|---|---|
| Andhra Pradesh.. | 105,677 | 31,260,133 |
| Assam ../........ | 85,062 | 9,043,707 |
| Bihar .......... | 67,071 | 38,783,778 |
| Bombay ......... | 190,668 | 48,265,221 |
| Jammu and Kashmir† ..... | 85,861 | 4,410,000 |
| Kerala .......... | 15,006 | 13,549,118 |
| Madhya Pradesh.. | 171,250 | 26,071,637 |
| Madras .......... | 50,128 | 29,974,936 |
| Mysore .......... | 74,861 | 19,401,193 |
| Orissa .......... | 60,250 | 14,645,946 |
| Punjab ......... | 47,062 | 16,134,890 |
| Rahasthan ...... | 132,148 | 15,970,774 |
| Uttar Pradesh ... | 113,422 | 63,215,742 |
| West Bengal ..... | 33,927 | 26,302,386 |

| Centrally Administered Territories | Area, sq. mi. (approx.) | Population, census 1951* |
|---|---|---|
| Andaman and Nicobar Islands .. | 3,215 | 30,971 |
| Delhi ........... | 573 | 1,744,072 |
| Himachal Pradesh | 10,922 | 1,109,466 |
| Laccadive, Minicoy and Amindive Islands | 10 | 21,035 |
| Manipur ........ | 8,629 | 577,635 |
| Tripura ......... | 4,022 | 639,029 |

* Estimated on basis of census where territorial changes in unit have occurred since 1951. † Status in dispute with Pakistan

millions in external assistance. Emphasis in the third Five-Year Plan is again on agriculture because of the problem of a rapidly expanding population, estimated at 492 million in 1966.

### MAJOR POLITICAL PARTIES

Congress party (365 seats in House of the People—Lok Sabha), led by N. Sanjiva Reddi; Communist party (29 seats), led by S. A. Dange.

HISTORY. The Aryans or Hindus who invaded India between 2400 and 1500 B.C. from the northwest found a land already well civilized. Buddhism was founded in the sixth century B.C. and spread through northern India. The first exact date in Indian history is 327 B.C., when Alexander the Great invaded India. Meanwhile India continued to be divided into rival states.

In 1526, Mohammedan invaders founded the great Mogul empire, centered on Delhi, which lasted at least in name until 1857. Akbar the Great (1542–1605) strengthened this empire and became the ruler of a greater portion of India than had ever before acknowledged the suzerainty of one man. The long reign of his great-grandson, Aurangzeb (1658–1707) represents both the culmination of Mogul power and the beginning of its decay.

Vasco da Gama, the Portuguese explorer, visited India first in 1498, and for the next hundred years the Portuguese had a virtual monopoly on trade with the subcontinent. Meanwhile, the English founded the East India Company, which set up its first factory at Surat in 1612 and began expanding its influence, fighting against the Indian rulers and the French, Dutch, and Portuguese traders simultaneously.

Bombay, taken from the Portuguese, became the seat of English rule in 1687. The defeat of French and Moslem armies by Lord Clive in the decade ending in 1760

laid the foundation of the British Empire in India. From then until 1858, when the administration of India was formally transferred to the British Crown following the great mutiny of native troops in 1857, the East India Company was constantly occupied with the suppression of native uprisings and the extension of British rule.

After World War I, in which the Indian states sent more than 1,000,000 troops to fight beside the Allies, Indian nationalist unrest rose to new heights under the leadership of a little Hindu lawyer, Mohandas K. Gandhi, called Mahatma Gandhi. His tactics, of a politico-religious nature, called for non-violent revolts against British authority. He soon became the leading spirit of the All-India Congress Party, which was the spearhead of Indian revolt against British rule. In 1919 the British gave added responsibility to Indian officials, and by an act passed in 1935 India was given a federal form of government and a measure of self-rule.

During the 1940's the policy of both the wartime coalition government of Britain and later the Labour government envisaged an unpartitioned India as a self-governing federal dominion including both British India and the native states. In 1942, with the Japanese pressing hard on the eastern borders of India, the British war Cabinet decided to send Sir Stafford Cripps to India to try to reach a political settlement with nationalist leaders. The mission failed. Shortly thereafter the Congress Party took the position that the British must quit India. In August 1942, fearing mass civil disobedience, the government of India carried out widespread arrests of Congress leaders, including Gandhi.

Gandhi was released in May, 1944, and other leaders later. Negotiations for a settlement were resumed and they proved fruitless until the British Labour government sent a mission in 1946 which obtained the agreement of the Congress party and Mohammed Ali Jinnah's Moslem League to a long-term plan for a Constitution based on three separate groups of provinces with a minimal center. However, agreement was not reached on an interim government and the Moslem League later reverted to its position of unconditional partition. Finally, in February, 1947, the Labour government announced its determination to transfer power to "responsible Indian hands" by June, 1948, even if a Constitution had not been worked out.

With the appointment at the same time of Lord Mountbatten as Governor-General, events moved swiftly. By early June, 1947, agreement was reached on the partitioning of India along religious lines (a plan previously opposed by the predominant Hindus and by Britain) and on the splitting of the provinces of Bengal and the Punjab, which the Moslems had claimed in their entirety.

The Indian Independence Act, passed quickly by both houses of the British Parliament, received royal assent on July 18, 1947, and on Aug. 15 the Indian Empire, united under British rule for almost a century, passed into history.

GOVERNMENT. India is now a sovereign republic within the Commonwealth of Nations—a status approved by the other Commonwealth nations at London in April, 1949, on the condition that India recognize the King as head of the Commonwealth. Under the Constitution adopted by the Constituent Assembly on Nov. 26, 1949, India has a parliamentary type of government. The constitutional head of state is the president, who is elected every five years. Dr. Rajendra Prasad has held this office continuously since January 26, 1950. He is advised by a prime minister and cabinet based on a majority of the bicameral parliament, which consists of a Council of States, representing the constituent units of the Republic, and a House of the People, elected every five years by universal adult (21 years) suffrage.

*Native States.* Most of the 560-odd native states and subdivisions of pre-1947 India acceded to the new nation, and the central government pursued a vigorous policy of integration. This took three forms: (1) merger into adjacent provinces, (2) conversion into centrally administered areas, and (3) grouping into unions of states. Finally, under a controversial reorganization plan effective Nov. 1, 1956, the unions of states were abolished and merged into adjacent states, and India became a union of fourteen states and six centrally administered areas.

The status of the large princely state of Jammu and Kashmir on the northwest frontier is in dispute with Pakistan. It is 85 per cent Moslem, but its Hindu ruling prince acceded to India, which took over administration following invasion by Moslem troops in late 1947. The U.N. Security Council voted on April 21, 1948, to hold a plebiscite in the area, but it was never held. The part occupied by India was incorporated into India in Jan. 1957.

ECONOMIC CONDITIONS.

Leading customers in 1959 were Britain (28%), other sterling area (20%), the United States and Canada (18%), and Japan (5%); leading suppliers, Britain (19%), other sterling area (12%), the United States and Canada (25%), and continental EPU countries (24%). Leading exports were tea (20%), jute and bagging (16%), and cotton manufactures. Main imports included petroleum and products, machinery, raw cotton, and rice. By 1959 the U.S. had supplied $1,792,700,000 of economic aid to India.

In May 1960, the U.S. agreed to sell India 16,000,000 metric tons of wheat and 1,000,000 metric tons of rice over a four-year period.

A third five-year plan (1961–66) includes a total investment of £5,250,000,000 in the public sector and £3,000,000,000 in the private sector. Also the aim was to increase national income by 28% and per capita income by 14%.

The U.S.S.R. has agreed to supply £45,-000,000 for oil development, while the United Kingdom is supplying £50,000,000 for steel and capital goods development.

NATURAL FEATURES AND RESOURCES. The Indian republic contains a large part of the great Indo-Gangetic plain which extends from the Bay of Bengal on the east to the Afghan frontier and the Arabian Sea on the west. This plain is the richest and most densely settled part of the subcontinent. Another distinct natural region is the Deccan, a plateau of 2,000 to 3,000 feet elevation, occupying the southern portion of the subcontinent.

Forming a part of the republic are several groups of islands—the Laccadives (fourteen islands) in the Arabian Sea; the Andamans (204 islands) and the Nicobars (nineteen islands) in the Bay of Bengal.

India's three great river systems, all rising in the Himalayas, have extensive deltas. The Ganges flows south and then east for 1,540 miles across the northern plain to the Bay of Bengal; part of its delta, which begins 220 miles from the sea, is within the republic. The Indus, starting in Tibet, flows northwest for several hundred miles in Kashmir before turning southwest toward the Arabian Sea; it is important for irrigation in Pakistan. The Brahmaputra, also rising in Tibet, flows eastward first through India and then south into Pakistan and the Bay of Bengal.

*Minerals.* The republic has rich mineral resources. The most valuable is coal, deposited throughout most of the nation.

Assam and the Punjab produce oil. Other minerals include iron ore, monazite, diamonds, magnesite, uranium, zircon, silver, graphite, gypsum, tungsten ore, and sapphires.

# Malaya, Federation of

**(Member of Commonwealth of Nations)**
Area: 50,700 square miles.
Population (est. 1959): 6,698,000 (1947: Malayan, 49.5%; Chinese, 38.4%; Indian and Pakistani, 10.8%; others, 1.3%).
Density per square mile: 132.1.
Head of State: Sir Syed Putra.
Prime Minister: Tengku Abdul Rahman.
Principal cities (census 1958): Kuala Lumpur, 316,230 (capital); George Town, 234,903 (seaport); Ipoh, 125,770 (tin); Kluang, 75,649; Malacca, 69,848 (seaport, rubber, copra).
Monetary unit: Malayan dollar.
Languages: English, Malay, Chinese, Tamil.
Religions:    Moslems    (predominant), Christian, Buddhist.

### STATUS IN THE WORLD TODAY

Despite a clear pro-Western bias and continuing close ties with the British, Malaya has generally pursued a neutralist course and has declined to join the Southeast Asia Treaty Organization. It has followed this policy even though it has been torn by a Communist insurrection since 1948 which, although impossible to suppress completely, has now been reduced to little more than nuisance proportions but still demands large-scale military effort and expense.

Malaya faces a unique racial problem. As a result of indiscriminate immigration in the past, the Malays have become a minority in their own land. Today nearly 40 per cent of the population are Chinese, 12 per cent are Indians and others. Little progress has yet been made toward integrating the several races into a united Malayan nation. The Malays, easygoing and wedded to their traditional, agrarian way of life, fear and resent the Chinese, who have long since won a dominant position in the commercial life of the country. The ambitious, hardworking Chinese, in turn, are disgruntled over the favored political position which the Malays enjoy under the existing governmental set-up.

While the Federation is relatively well off in comparison with most of its Asian neighbors, the economic situation also holds many incalculable factors. Malaya produces only a third of its food requirements, and its prosperity is dependent upon the fluctuating world market for the country's two major exports, rubber and tin. Thus far relatively little progress has been made toward diversification and industrialization of the economy.

HISTORY AND GOVERNMENT. The Federation of Malaya consists of the states of Johore, Kedah, Kelantan, Negri Sembilan, Pahang, Perak, Perlis, Selangor, and Trengganu, and the former British settlements (crown colonies) of Malacca and Penang. The native states were brought under British administration by a process of commercial and political exploitation in the late nineteenth and early twentieth centuries.

As the result of agreements reached with the British government in 1956 and 1957, the Federation attained full independence within the Commonwealth on August 31, 1957. Sir Abdul Rahman was elected the first head of state, and Tengku Abdul Rahman (no relation) became prime minister.

Under the 1957 constitution Malaya is a sovereign constitutional monarchy within the Commonwealth of Nations, recognizing the Queen as head of the Commonwealth. The head of state is elected by the hereditary rulers of the states from among themselves for a 5-year term. He is advised by the prime minister and his cabinet. Malaya has a bicameral legislature. The Federal Senate is partly appointed by the Head of State to represent minority interests and partly elected by the legislative assembly of the states. The House of Representatives, or Lower House, is made up of 104 elected members.

About 65% of the cultivated area is devoted to rubber, of which Malaya is one of the world's largest producers (709,500 tons in 1959). Other export crops include coconuts and coconut oil, tea, and pineapples. Production of rice, the principal subsistence crop, falls far short of meeting local requirements.

Leading customers are Britain, the United States, and Japan; leading suppliers, Indonesia, Britain, and Thailand. Leading exports are rubber and tin.

Malaya is rich in minerals. Tin, the most important, occurs throughout the country but production is concentrated in Perak and Selangor. Tin production in 1959 was 38,160 metric tons. Other minerals include iron ore, coal, bauxite, tungsten, and manganese ore.

MALDIVE ISLANDS—Status: Protected state.
Capital: Malé (est. pop., 8,000).
Sultan: Amir Mohammed Farid Didi.
Prime Minister: Ibrahim Nasir.

HISTORY AND GOVERNMENT. The Maldive Islands, about 400 miles to the southwest of Ceylon in the Indian Ocean, were first visited by the Portuguese in the sixteenth century. They came under British protection in 1887 and were a dependency of the colony of Ceylon until 1948, when relations with Britain were formalized in a treaty which left domestic affairs in the hands of the islanders. Reactivation of a British airfield was announced Jan. 3, 1957.

For centuries a sultanate, the islands adopted a republican form of government in 1952, but the sultanate was restored in Feb., 1954, and is elective, not hereditary. The Sultan is elected by the parliament. The latter consists of a Senate of 80 members and a Lower House of 46 members elected by popular vote. All men and women over 18 have the franchise.

The people are great traders and fishermen. Besides fishing, coir making is the chief local industry. Exports include coir, coconuts, copra, millet, and fruit.

The islands consist of 12 coral atolls with about 2,000 small islands, of which about 300 are inhabited.

# Pakistan (Republic)

(Member of Commonwealth of Nations)*
Area: 364,797 square miles.
Population (estimated 1959): 86,823,000 (Moslem, 86%; Hindu, 13%; others, 1%).
Density per square mile: 238.0.
President: Mohammed Ayub Khan.
Prime Minister: (Post abolished in October, 1958.)
Principal cities (est. 1959): Karachi, 2,000,000; (census 1951): Lahore, 849,476 (capital, West Pakistan); Dacca, 411,279 (capital, East Pakistan); Hyderabad, 241,-801 (trade and rail center); Rawalpindi, 237,219 (capital).
Monetary unit: Pakistani rupee.
Principal languages: Bengali (official), Urdu (official), English,* Hindi, Punjabi.

* To be used for official purposes until 1976.

## STATUS IN THE WORLD TODAY

Pakistan, an Islamic republic which is still a member of the British Commonwealth of Nations, is, unlike India, an open supporter of the West. It has joined the Baghdad Pact, is a member of SEATO (Southeast Asia Treaty Organization), and participates regularly in various activities arising from membership in the Commonwealth. It has also associated itself with the Afro-Asian bloc in the U.N. and was a sponsor of the twenty-nine-nation Bandung Conference in April, 1955. Its difficulties with Afghanistan over the border area of "Pushtunistan" have been, in part,

smoothed over, as has its argument with India over division of the waters of the Indus River and its tributaries. But it is still embroiled in a bitter conflict with India over Kashmir, which it claims and which India has annexed, even though the dispute is technically before the U.N.

The nation is divided into two unequal parts separated by the 1,000-mile expanse of India: overcrowded East Pakistan, with more than half the population and only 15 per cent of the total land area, and West Pakistan, which has dominated the political life of the country since independence in 1947. Unlike most other ex-colonial nations, Pakistan had no prior existence except as fairly well-defined, predominantly Moslem areas within the great Indian subcontinent. Relations with India were also disturbed by savage communal riots between Moslems and Hindus which followed partition, and the vast transfers of population resulting from them.

Pakistan's economic difficulties as a new state have been heightened by internal political instability and the country's feeling that comparatively large defense expenditures (with U.S. military aid) were necessary because of its difficulties with India and Afghanistan. The first Five-Year Plan, started in 1955, brought little improvement in living standards but made some progress, particularly in the industrial field. The second plan envisages an outlay of $4.8 billion, with $1.7 billion of it from foreign aid. Manufacturing has accounted for a steadily rising share of the national income, and in certain consumer articles the country has achieved self-sufficiency and even an export potential. The plan's four objectives are: to raise national income and employment through industry, agriculture, and community development; to improve the balance of payments through raising exports and managing imports; to extend social services; and to pay special attention to some of Pakistan's more depressed areas, especially East Pakistan.

HISTORY AND GOVERNMENT. Pakistan, a self-governing member of the Commonwealth of Nations and one of the two successor states to British India, is the world's largest and most important Moslem state.

The history of Pakistan prior to 1947 is principally that of India (*see* India). Upon the transfer of power on Aug. 15, 1947, Mohammed Ali Jinnah became the first Governor General; he died on Sept. 11, 1948, and was succeeded by Khwaja Nazimuddin. The latter became Prime Minister upon the assassination of Liaquat Ali Khan, Oct. 16, 1951; he was replaced on Apr. 17, 1953, by Mohammed Ali. Chaudry Mohammed Ali succeeded him on Aug. 11, 1955. Pakistan was proclaimed a republic March 23, 1956, and Gov. Gen. Iskander Mirza was elected Provisional President. H. S. Suhrawardy, the first non-Moslem League Prime Minister, took office Sept. 12, 1956.

Under the Constitution of Feb. 29, 1956, Pakistan is a republic but continues its membership in the Commonwealth of Nations. The President is elected for five years by members of the central and provincial legislatures. The Prime Minister and his Cabinet were named by the President and were collectively responsible to the National Assembly. The Assembly has 300 members, divided equally between East and West Pakistan and directly elected for five years. On October 7, 1958, President Iskander Mirza proclaimed martial law, suspended the Constitution, dismissed the central and provincial governments, and banned all political parties. But on October 27, 1958, Mirza surrendered his power to General Ayub Khan, who abolished the post of Prime Minister and has been ruling as virtual dictator ever since. He purged corrupt and inefficient office holders, broke up the feudal land system, eliminated much of the black market, tax evasion and hoarding, and revolutionized education. A vote of confidence in February, 1960, extended his rule for five years and gave him power to write a new constitution. He expressed the hope that martial law could end and democracy return in 1961.

*Provinces.* Pakistan consists of two provinces—West and East Pakistan—approximately 1,000 miles apart, separated by the republic of India. The province of West Pakistan consists of Sind, Baluchistan, the former North-West Frontier Province, western Punjab, the princely state of Bahawalpur and a few other small native states. The province of East Pakistan consists of eastern Bengal and the Sylhet district of Assam. Pakistan contains large communal minorities of Hindus and Sikhs.

ECONOMIC CONDITIONS. Pakistan, poor in industry and natural resources, is mainly an agricultural nation. Upwards of 45,000,000 acres are under cultivation, almost half of which are irrigated, largely in Sind and west Punjab in western Pakistan. The Punjab contains important wheat-growing areas, and eastern Pakistan is rich in jute, rice, and tea. In 1959 there were 6,293,000 sheep, 6,752,000 buffalo, 23,624,000 cattle, 585,000 horses, and (1952) 477,000 camels.

The second five-year plan promises to be complete by 1963 instead of 1965. This plan aims at a 20% rise in output.

Pakistan is an exporter of agricultural products and an importer of manufactured commodities.

Chief exports in 1959 were jute (59%), raw cotton (17%), tea, wool, and jute manufactures. Leading customers in 1959 were Britain (18%), other sterling area (24%), Japan (8%), the United States and Canada (11%), and India (3%); leading suppliers, Britain (18%), Japan (6%), the United States and Canada (29%). Leading imports were machinery, petroleum and products, iron and steel and products, vehicles, and cotton piece goods.

Development of a unified nation is retarded by the fact that communication between East and West Pakistan is possible only through a thousand miles of Indian territory or by a long sea voyage.

Since partition, Pakistan has made much progress toward industrialization. The most important manufacturing area is in the vicinity of Lahore in the Punjab. Industries include cotton ginning, spinning and weaving, jute manufacturing, sugar refining, cement making, flour milling, railway and engineering workshops, and petroleum refining.

NATURAL FEATURES AND RESOURCES. Almost all of Sind and the west Punjab are a continuation of north-central plains leading up to rugged mountains in the north and west which traverse Baluchistan and the North-West Frontier Province. Eastern Pakistan is a low-lying, flat country with elevation averaging not more than 600 feet above sea level.

Mineral resources are limited to petroleum, coal, lignite, chromite, and gypsum. Vast quantities of natural gas were discovered at Sui, Baluchistan, in 1952.

**SINGAPORE—Status: independent state within Commonwealth of Nations.**
**Capital: Singapore (pop. 1958: 953,000).**
**Commissioner General in Southeast Asia: Earl of Selkirk.**
**High Commissioner for United Kingdom in Singapore: Lee Kuan Yew.**
**Prime Minister: Lee Kuan Yew.**
**Foreign trade: see Federation of Malaya.**

HISTORY AND GOVERNMENT. Singapore, founded in 1819 by Sir Stamford Raffles, comprises the island of Singapore and adjacent islets. It became a separate Crown colony of Great Britain on Apr. 1, 1946, when the former colony of the Straits Settlements was dissolved. Penang and Malacca were transferred to the Malayan Union, and the small island of Labuan to North Borneo. The Cocos or Keeling Islands were transferred to Australia in 1951 and Christmas Island in 1957.

Under its new 1959 Constitution, Singapore elected in May, 1959, for a term of 5 years and by universal suffrage, a legislative Assembly of 51 members. Voting is compulsory and half of the electorate is illiterate. But Britain still retains control of Singapore's defense and external affairs and may suspend the Constitution or dissolve the legislative Assembly. Executive power is in the hands of an Internal Security Council consisting of 7 members: the British Commissioner as Chairman, the Prime Minister and two other Ministers, two other British representatives, and one Malayan member.

The basis of Singapore's prosperity is its entrepôt trade. It handles a large part of the export trade of Malaya and also conducts a large volume of trade with Indonesia. Singapore has an excellent natural harbor and is the principal British naval base in the Far East. About 76 per cent of the population is Chinese and 12 per cent Malayan.

# OCEANIA

## Australia, Commonwealth of

### (Member of Commonwealth of Nations)

Area: 2,974,583 square miles.
Population (est. 1960): 10,281,000 (excluding full-blooded aborigines, estimated at 50,000).
Density per square mile: 3.5.
Ruler: Queen Elizabeth II.
Governor General: Field Marshal Sir William Slim.
Prime Minister: Robert Gordon Menzies.
Principal cities (est. 1959): Sydney, 2,-054,800 (seaport, wool market); Melbourne, 1,777,700 (seaport, wool, wheat); Brisbane, 567,000 (seaport, industrial center); Adelaide, 562,500 (seaport); Perth, 389,000 (western seaport); Canberra, 43,973 (capital).
Monetary unit: Australian pound (£A).
Language: English.
Religions (census 1947): Anglican, 39.0%; Roman Catholic, 20.7%; Presbyterian, 9.8%; Methodist, 11.5%; other Christians, 7.1%; others, 11.9%.

### STATUS IN THE WORLD TODAY

Situated on a continent located under the overhang of Asia, Australians are a paradox of history. Culturally they are wholly Western, but they exist in what is geographically "the East." They are "in" the Asiatic area and obviously remote from their Western fellows. What goes on in Indonesia, immediately over their heads like an umbrella, is obviously a more intimate worry to them than to the faraway Americans. They are Western and show few signs of any wish to be assimilated to "the East," either politically or culturally. In World War II their sparsely populated continent was one target of the expansionists in overpopulated Japan; hence the current Australian anxiety to sustain their position by rapidly building up the population and economic strength with immigrants from Europe. For what will the United States do if Australian security is actually (not theoretically) menaced by developments in Asia? Will the Americans again come to the rescue?

In formulating a foreign policy, the fundamental problem is how correctly to balance its relations with the United Kingdom on the one hand and the United States on the other. Ordinarily it has not been too difficult to keep these relations in balance. Australia has moved quite close to the United States in the Pacific and Asia without offending Britain and has followed a national line in Asia without tangling with the U.S. It does not recognize Red China. It participates in ANZUS and SEATO (Australia, New Zealand, United States defense pact and Southeast Asia Treaty Organization). It sided with the United Kingdom over Suez. With the right foreign policy, Australians hope to sustain their peculiar position in the critical decades ahead.

Economically, the emphasis since World War II has been on industrial expansion, and today far more people work in factories and offices than on the land. As a trading nation, Australia is closely tied to the United Kingdom and is deeply involved in the Imperial trading system and the Sterling Area. While it has drawn close to the U.S. since World War II, it still normally runs a dollar deficit as an international trader and must get dollar allocations from the sterling area authorities. The marked increase in the flow of American investment capital to Australia has not yet fully corrected the condition.

Politically, Australia has been ruled on the federal level since 1949 by a Liberal-party-Country-party coalition, led by Robert Gordon Menzies as Prime Minister. For eight years before Menzies came to power, the Labor party had ruled. It has been the driving force behind the growth of the welfare state in Australia, and much that it has done while in office is determinative of the climate in which its conservative opposition must function. Although out of power on the federal level, Labor often holds power in the states.

### MAJOR POLITICAL PARTIES

Liberal-Country party (77 seats in House of Representatives), led by Prime Minister Robert G. Menzies; Labour party (47 seats), led by Arthur C. Calwell.

HISTORY AND GOVERNMENT. Australia was the last continent to be discovered. The first Europeans to land were the Dutch, who sailed into the Gulf of Carpentaria in March, 1606. Later in the same year, Luis Vas de Torres, a Spaniard, sailed through the strait subsequently named for him, and may have touched at several points on the north coast. In 1642 Abel Tasman (for whom Tasmania was named) sailed from west to east along the southern shore and proved that Australia was not a part of the Antarctic Continent. The continent was called New Holland until about 1850.

In 1770 Captain James Cook, after visiting New Zealand, sailed to the east coast of New Holland and landed south of the present city of Sydney. His account of the country led to its being claimed and settled by Great Britain.

The first settlement, made in 1788 at Botany Bay, was founded as a penal station for criminals from England. Transportation of criminals was virtually suspended in 1839, and Australia had comparatively few white settlers until gold was discovered in Victoria in 1851, after which immigrants poured in. By 1860 all the states (then separate colonies) except Western Australia had been granted responsible government.

On January 1, 1901, the six Australian states united to form the Commonwealth of Australia. The Federal Parliament consists of a bicameral legislature. The House of Representatives has 124 members elected for 3 years by adult (male and female) suffrage. The Senate has 60 members elected by popular vote for 6 years. One-half of the Senate is elected every 3 years.

Federal judicial power is vested in a Federal Supreme Court of 7 justices, appointed by the Governor General in Council. Each state has its own judicial system.

ECONOMIC CONDITIONS. About 55 per cent of Australia's total area is suitable (mining excepted) only for pastoral pursuits. On March 31, 1958, there were 152,688,000 sheep, 16,296,000 cattle, 1,288,000 hogs, and 671,000 horses.

Sugar and cotton are grown in Queensland and New South Wales, tobacco in northeast Victoria, and vines chiefly in South Australia and Victoria.

New South Wales is the leading industrial state. Power for industry is derived almost entirely from coal.

In 1959 the leading customers were Britain (27%), other sterling area (18%), Japan (14%), France (6%), and the United States and Canada (11%); leading suppliers, Britain (36%), other sterling area (18%), the United States and Canada (17%), continental EPU and EF countries (15%), and Japan (4%). Chief exports were wool (39%), meat (8%), wheat (7%), and fruit (4%). Leading imports included petroleum and products, motor vehicles, iron and steel, and cotton piece goods.

The principal ports are Sydney, Melbourne, and Adelaide.

NATURAL FEATURES AND RESOURCES. Australia is approximately equal in area to the United States* and is more than three-fourths the size of Europe.

Along the east coast, ranges of mountains run from north to south, reaching their highest point in Mt. Kosciusko (7,352 ft.). The western half of the continent is occupied by a desert plateau which rises into barren, rolling hills near the west coast. It includes the Great Victoria Desert, to the south, and the Great Sandy Desert to the north. The island of Tasmania (26,215 sq. mi.) lies off the southeastern coast.

Australia possesses considerable mineral resources. Most important is gold, followed by coal, mined near Sydney, Brisbane, and in eastern Tasmania. The Broken Hill mines in New South Wales are one of the most valuable silver-lead-zinc areas in the world. Other important minerals in 1955 included tin, copper, iron ore, and uranium. Petroleum was discovered in Western Australia in 1953.

Forest products include timber (rough sawn), eucalyptus oil, sandalwood oil, tan bark and yacca gum. Sea products include bêche-de-mer, oysters, pearls, pearl shell, tortoise shell, and agar-agar.

DEPENDENCIES. Norfolk Island (13 sq. mi.), under Commonwealth administration since 1914, lies about 800 miles east of New South Wales. It enjoys a delightful subtropical climate. Citrus fruits, bananas and coffee are grown.

Nauru (about 8 sq. mi.), an important source of phosphate (exports about 1,000,000 tons annually), was annexed by Germany in 1888 and was placed under joint Australian, New Zealand and British mandate after World War I. In 1947 it was placed under U. N. trusteeship, with the same three administering powers. It lies 2,215 miles northeast of Sydney.

The Ashmore and Cartier Islands (.8 sq. mi.), about 200 mi. off the northeast coast, were placed under Australian authority in 1931, while the Heard and McDonald Islands (158 sq. mi.), about 2,500 mi. southwest of Fremantle, were transferred to Australian control in 1947.

The Australian Antarctic Territory (2,472,000 sq. mi.), comprising all the islands and territories other than Adélie Land situated south of 60° S. lat. and lying between 160° E. long. and 45° E. long., was placed under Australian authority by an order in council effective in 1936.

The Cocos (Keeling) Islands (5 sq. mi.; population 1,000) are a group of 27 small coral islands in the Indian Ocean about 1,160 mi. southwest of Singapore. Used as a link on the Australia-South Africa air route, they were placed under Australian administration in 1951. Christmas Island

* Not including Hawaii and Alaska.

(62 sq. mi.; population 2,000), about 850 mi. southeast of Singapore, was transferred to Australian control in 1957. It has important phosphate deposits.

### PAPUA AND NEW GUINEA, TERRITORY OF—Status: Australian territory and U.N. trust territory.

Capital: Port Moresby (population, 1949: 14,846).

Chief exports: copra, rubber, gold.

Agricultural products: coconuts, rubber, copra, cacao.

Minerals: gold, silver, platinum.

Effective July 1, 1949, the Australian territory of Papua and the U.N. trust territory of New Guinea were joined in an administrative union by act of the Australian Parliament. Provision is made for an executive and a legislative council.

Papua, comprising the southeastern part of the island of New Guinea, and the islands of the D'Entrecasteaux, Louisiade and nearby groups, was annexed by Queensland in 1883 and by the British Crown in 1888. It came under the control of the Australian Commonwealth in 1901 and became the Territory of Papua in 1906. Japan invaded Papua in early 1942, but in Dec. 1942, Australian control was restored.

The U.N. trust territory of New Guinea, comprising the northern section of eastern New Guinea (93,000 sq. mi.), was mandated in 1920 by the League of Nations to the government of the Commonwealth of Australia, together with the Bismarck Archipelago (New Britain, New Ireland and adjacent islands), the Admiralty Islands with several outlying groups, and the northern Solomon Islands (Bougainville and Buka). It was placed under United Nations trusteeship Dec. 13, 1946, with Australia as the administering power. Japanese troops occupied much of the territory in 1942–45. On June 30, 1959, there were 15,270 nonnatives in the territory.

### FIJI—Status: Colony.

Governor: Sir Kenneth Maddocks.

Capital: Suva (population 37,371).

Foreign trade (1955): exports, 38% to Britain; imports, 37% from Britain. Chief exports: sugar (49%), coconut oil (18%), gold (8%).

Agricultural products: sugar, coconut oil, copra, bananas, pineapples.

Minerals: gold.

Fiji colony consists of an archipelago of from 200 to 250 islands in the South Pacific Ocean about 1,740 miles northeast of Sydney, Australia. The larger islands, including Viti Levu (4,011 sq. mi.) and Vanua Levu (2,137 sq. mi.) are mountainous and of volcanic origin. The archipelago was ceded to Great Britain by the native ruler in 1874.

The population of the archipelago in Dec., 1955, included 6,402 Europeans, 146,-842 Fijians and 166,262 Indians. Importation of the latter to work the sugar plantations has led to important social and economic changes. There has been almost no intermarriage between Fijians and Indians, and considerable ill feeling has developed between them.

During World War II, the archipelago was an important air and naval station on the route from the United States west coast and Hawaii to Australia and New Zealand.

### TONGA (FRIENDLY ISLANDS)—Status: Protected state.

Ruler: Queen Salote Tupou.

Chief export: copra (86%).

This native Polynesian kingdom in the Pacific came under British protection through the Anglo-German agreement of November 14, 1899. The native Queen is advised by a British Agent; the 21-member native Legislative Council is partly elected and partly nominated. The only important products are copra and bananas.

### PITCAIRN ISLAND—Status: Colony.

Located in the South Pacific, about midway between Australia and South America, Pitcairn has an area of 2 square miles. It was settled in 1790 by British mutineers from the ship *Bounty*, commanded by Capt. Bligh. Overpopulation forced removal of the settlement to Norfolk Island in 1856, but about 40 soon returned. The island is administered by the Governor of Fiji through an elected council headed by a Chief Magistrate. The population is about 150.

# New Zealand

(Member of Commonwealth of Nations)

Area: 110,686 square miles (including outlying islands).

Population (estimated 1960): 2,372,000. (1951: European, 93.3%; Maori and half-caste, 5.9%; others, .8%).

Density per square mile: 21.4.

Ruler: Queen Elizabeth II.

Governor General: Viscount Cobham.

Prime Minister: Keith J. Holyoake.

Principal cities (est. 1960): Auckland (greater), 422,900 (seaport and naval base); Christchurch, 214,800 (cereals, stock raising); Wellington, 144,000 (capital); Dunedin City, 103,300 (textiles).

Monetary unit: New Zealand pound (£NZ).

Language: English.

Religions (census 1956): Church of England, 35.9%; Presbyterian, 22.3%; Roman Catholic, 14.3%; Methodist, 7.4%; Baptist, 1.6%; others, 18.5%.

## STATUS IN THE WORLD TODAY

New Zealand has not felt it wise or necessary to go as far as neighboring Australia in developing its own foreign policy and a machinery of diplomacy to implement it. It has, however, joined the ANZUS (Australia, New Zealand, United States) defense pact and SEATO (Southeast Asia Treaty Organization) and participated in the Colombo Plan, indications of a realization of its relationship to Asia on a regional basis. It has normally been satisfied to rest in the shadow of the United Kingdom where foreign affairs are concerned, but has now moved somewhat closer to Australia. Economically, it is closely linked to the United Kingdom, which takes about two-thirds of all its exports and furnishes about half its imports. During the Suez crisis of 1956, it stood with Britain, although its position might have been different had there been a Labor instead of a Nationalist administration.

## MAJOR POLITICAL PARTIES

National party (46 seats in House of Representatives), led by Prime Minister Keith J. Holyoake; Labour party (34 seats), led by Walter Nash.

**HISTORY AND GOVERNMENT.** New Zealand, about 1,250 miles east of Australia, consists of two main islands and a number of smaller outlying islands so scattered that they range from the tropical to the antarctic. The islands, which have approximately the area of Italy, were discovered and named New Zealand in 1642 by Abel Tasman, a Dutch navigator. Captain James Cook explored them in 1769. On Jan. 22, 1840, Britain formally annexed them.

New Zealand was granted self-government in 1852, a full parliamentary system and ministries in 1856 and dominion status on Sept. 26, 1907. Meanwhile, from 1861 to 1871 there was fierce intermittent fighting with the native Maoris. The Queen is represented by a Governor General, and the Cabinet is responsible to a unicameral Parliament of 76 white and 4 Maori members elected by popular vote for 3 years.
**ECONOMIC CONDITIONS.** Primarily a grazing country, New Zealand is one of the world's largest exporters of mutton, lamb, wool, butter, and cheese. In 1957, livestock included 42,500,000 sheep, 5,924,000 cattle, and 689,000 hogs. Outside of grass, the chief crop is wheat. Other crops are oats, barley, potatoes, onions, tobacco, fruits, and vegetables.

Leading customers in 1959 were Britain (56%), the United States and Canada (16%), EPU and EF countries (15%); leading suppliers, Britain (47%), Australia (18%), other sterling area (9%), the United States and Canada (11%), and West Germany (3%). Leading exports were wool (31%), lamb and mutton (15%), and butter (19%).

**NATURAL FEATURES AND RESOURCES.** New Zealand's two main components are North Island and South Island, separated by Cook Strait, which varies from 16 to 190 miles in width. North Island (44,281 sq. mi.) is 515 miles long and volcanic in its south-central part. It contains many hot springs and beautiful geysers.

South Island (58,093 sq. mi.) has the Southern Alps along its west coast, with Mt. Cook (12,349 feet) the highest point in New Zealand.

Principal minerals are coal and gold. Other minerals of importance include tungsten, pumice, silica sand, asbestos, scheelite, iron ore, and phosphate. About 30 per cent of the total area is forested.

Numerous rushing streams give New Zealand a great volume of hydroelectric power.
**DEPENDENCIES.** The Auckland Islands (234 sq. mi.) and Campbell Island (44 sq. mi.) are the principal outlying islands, which have a total area of 324 square miles. They are included within the geographical boundaries of New Zealand, as proclaimed in 1847. The Aucklands and Campbell are uninhabited. Six hundred miles north of the Aucklands are the volcanic Kermadec Islands (13 sq. mi.), annexed in 1887. The Union (or Tokelau) Islands (4 sq. mi.), transferred in 1925 from the Gilbert and Ellice Islands colony, were declared part of New Zealand effective Jan. 1, 1949.

In Polynesia a number of uninhabited islands were brought under New Zealand's control in 1901. Rarotonga and Mangaia in the Cook group total 84 square miles. Niue (or Savage Island) (115 sq. mi.) is the largest island outside the Cook group. New Zealand also administers the Ross Dependency (175,000 sq. mi.), an antarctic region claimed by Great Britain in 1923.

**WESTERN SAMOA—Status: New Zealand Trust Territory.**
  **Capital: Apia (population 16,000).**
  **Chief exports: cacao, copra, bananas.**
  **Principal products: copra, cacao, bananas, tropical fruits.**

The former German Samoan Islands were occupied by New Zealand troops in the opening weeks of World War I and were mandated to New Zealand by the League of Nations in 1920 as the Territory of Western Samoa. They came under U.N. trusteeship in 1947, with New Zealand continuing as the administering authority. In January, 1960, sovereignty over Western Samoa reverted completely to New Zealand.

The territory was tentatively scheduled for independence on Jan. 1, 1962.

The High Commissioner is assisted by an

Executive Council, a Legislative Assembly which has a Samoan majority and a consultative Native Council. There are nine islands, of which the largest and most populous are Savaii (703 sq. mi.) and Upolu (430 sq. mi.). They are largely mountainous but fertile. The inhabitants are predominantly Polynesian Christians.

## PACIFIC ISLANDS (British)

**High Commissioner in Western Pacific:** D. C. C. Trench.

Island groups in the Pacific administered by the British High Commissioner in the Western Pacific include (1) Gilbert and Ellice Islands, (2) British Solomon Islands, and (3) New Hebrides Condominium (see French Overseas Territories). The High Commissioner has headquarters at Honiara, Solomon Islands.

**GILBERT AND ELLICE ISLANDS—Status: Colony.**

The islands in these groups (including the Gilbert group; the Ellice group; Ocean Island [the seat of administration], Fanning, Washington and Christmas Islands; and the Phoenix group) were proclaimed a British protectorate in 1892 and annexed

as a colony in 1915. The most important product is high-grade phosphate.

Ownership of Canton and Enderbury islands in the Phoenix group was long in dispute between Great Britain and the United States until 1939, when an agreement for "use in common" was reached by the two governments. Several of the Gilbert islands were occupied by Japanese forces in World War II, and Tarawa was the scene of one of the fiercest battles in U.S. Marine Corps history in Nov. 1943.

**SOLOMON ISLANDS—Status: Protectorate.**

This British protectorate, lying east of New Guinea, includes the islands of Guadalcanal, Malaita, San Cristobal, New Georgia, Santa Isabel, Choiseul and numerous smaller islands. Bougainville, one of the group, is under Australian mandate. The islands, which came under British protection late in the 19th century, were the scene of several important U.S. naval and military victories during World War II. There are no native states, and administration is carried on by the High Commissioner, assisted by a nominated Advisory Council. The most important products are copra and kauri wood. The population is predominantly Melanesian.

# Bulgaria (People's Republic)

## (Narodna Republika Blgariya)

**Area:** 42,729 square miles.
**Population** (census 1959): 7,798,000 (1952: Bulgarian, 91%; Turkish, 6%; Gypsy, 2%; others, 1%).
**Density per square mile:** 182.5.
**Chairman of Presidium:** Dimiter Ganev.
**Premier:** Anton Yugov.
**Principal cities** (census 1956): Sofia, 644,727 (capital, railroad center); Plovdiv, 161,836 (commercial center); Varna, 124,951 (Black Sea port); Ruse, 83,453 (chief Danube port); Burgas, 72,526 (Black Sea port).
**Monetary unit:** Lev.
**Languages:** Bulgarian, Turkish.
**Religions:** Greek Orthodox, 84.4%; Mohammedan, 13.5%; Jewish, .8%; Roman Catholic, .8%; others, .5%.

### STATUS IN THE WORLD TODAY

Bulgaria, probably because its religion, language, and national origin are the same as those of Russia, has become what might be called a model satellite. Despite the tyrannical rule of the Communist party, the people do not seem to have the hatred for their rulers which the Hungarians demonstrated in their revolt. Predominantly agricultural, Bulgaria has more than two-thirds of its arable land held by

collective farms, the highest percentage among Russia's East European satellites. Unlike Yugoslavia or Poland, it has followed the Kremlin line without balking outwardly, operating under a personal dictatorship of the Stalin type as long as Stalin lived, then changing leadership and splitting the posts of party secretary and prime minister between two individuals when Stalin and the "cult of personality" were denounced. Although it once discussed the possibility of federation with Yugoslavia, it has, since 1948, loyally denounced Titoism whenever called upon to do so. One explanation is that even in Czarist days, Russia was considered a friendly, Slavic power rather than an inimical, exploiting imperialist state. Although its rulers showed marked pro-German feelings in both World Wars, the people regarded Russia with friendship. For in the nineteenth century, Russia was one of the champions of Bulgarian independence.

The relations between Bulgaria's Communist regime and the United States reached an all-time low in 1950, when Sofia accused the American Minister, Donald Heath, and other members of his staff of espionage. The United States responded by breaking off diplomatic relations and withdrawing its representatives. After three vain attempts to restore official relations, the Bulgarians finally apologized early in 1959 for having made the unfounded accusations against the American diplomats, and on that basis diplomatic relations were resumed.

---

**HISTORY AND GOVERNMENT.** The first Bulgarians, a tribe of wild horsemen akin to the Huns, crossed the Danube from the north in A.D. 679 and subjugated the Slavonic population of Moesia. They adopted a Slav dialect and Slavic customs and twice conquered most of the Balkan peninsula between 893 and 1280. After the Serbs subjected their kingdom in 1330, the Bulgars gradually fell prey to the Turks, and from 1396 to 1878 Bulgaria was a Turkish province. In 1878, Russia forced Turkey to give the country its independence; but the European powers, fearing that Bulgaria might become a Russian dependency, intervened. By the Treaty of Berlin (July, 1878), Bulgaria became autonomous under Turkish sovereignty.

In 1887, Prince Ferdinand of Saxe-Coburg-Gotha was elected ruler; on Oct. 5, 1908, he declared Bulgaria an independent kingdom.

Bulgaria joined Germany in World War I and lost. On Oct. 3, 1918, Tsar Ferdinand abdicated in favor of his son, who became Tsar Boris III. The Treaty of Neuilly the next year disarmed Bulgaria, reduced it to its 1878 size, and levied a heavy indemnity.

Boris assumed dictatorial powers in 1934–35. When Hitler awarded Bulgaria Southern Dobruja, taken from Rumania in 1940, the weak but land-hungry Boris joined the Nazis in war the next year and occupied parts of Yugoslavia and Greece. Later, with the fortunes of war swinging inexorably against them, the Germans tried to force Boris to send his troops against the Russians. Boris resisted and died under mysterious circumstances on Aug. 28, 1943.

Simeon II, infant son of Boris, became nominal ruler under a regency. Three days after Russia declared war on Bulgaria on Sept. 5, 1944, Bulgaria declared war on Germany. Russian troops streamed in the next day, and under an informal armistice a coalition "Fatherland Front" cabinet was set up under Kimon Georgiev.

Most of the population is Greek Orthodox. Clergy of all faiths are paid by the state. The national language, Bulgarian, is closely related to Russian; both employ the Cyrillic alphabet.

**ECONOMIC CONDITIONS.** Bulgaria is still predominantly agrarian, with most of the population engaged in agriculture. Because of the mountainous character of the country, however, less than half of the land is tilled or used for pasture. Collectivization is well advanced. More than half the cultivated area is devoted to cereals, including wheat, corn, barley, oats, and rye. Other crops are tobacco, alfalfa, cotton, flax, potatoes, and sugar. There are extensive vineyards in the southern valleys.

Industries are of minor importance and with few exceptions—tobacco leaf, wines and liquors, fertilizers, and flour—are confined to domestic markets. Industrialization is one of the chief aims of the Communist regime, however, and all industries of any importance have been nationalized. Both the first (1948–53) and the second (1953–57) five-year plans emphasized the development of heavy industry. Results of the plans were somewhat mixed. Low quality was a general complaint. Shortages occurred in mining and processing of nonferrous metals.

Foreign trade necessarily consists of the exchange of agricultural products for cheap manufactures.

Leading customers in 1959 were East Germany, the U.S.S.R., and Czechoslovakia, Hungary, Rumania, and Poland. Leading suppliers were the U.S.S.R. and the four above-named satellites. Tobacco is the principal export.

**NATURAL FEATURES AND RESOURCES.** Two mountain ranges and two great valleys mark Bulgaria's topography. The Balkan belt crosses the center of the country, almost due east-west, rising to a height of 7,800 feet. The Rhodope range breaks off from the Balkans in the west, curves and then straightens out to run nearly parallel along the southern border. Between the two ranges is the valley of the Maritsa, Bulgaria's principal river. Between the Balkan range and the Danube, which forms most of the northern boundary with Rumania, is the Danubian tableland, traversed by several short rivers. Southern Dobruja, a fertile region of 2,900 square miles below the Danube delta, is an area of low hills, fens and sandy steppes.

Soft coal is Bulgaria's principal mineral. Other minerals include chromite, gypsum, iron ore, manganese ore, rock salt, and silver.

---

# Burma (Republic)

**Area:** 261,757 square miles.
**Population** (est. 1960): 20,662,000 (1941: Burmans, 60%; Shans, 7%; Chins, 2%; Kachins, 1%; Indians, 6%; Chinese, 1%; Indo-Burmans, 1%; others, 22%).
**Density per square mile:** 78.9.
**President:** U Win Maung.
**Premier:** U Nu.
**Principal cities** (est. 1960): Rangoon, 723,000 (capital, chief port); Mandalay, 203,000 (river port, upper Burma); Moulmein, 107,250 (seaport).
**Monetary unit:** Kyat.
**Languages:** Burmese (70%), English.

**Religions:** Buddhist, 90%; Mohammedan, 3%; Hindu, 3%; Christian, 2%;
others, 2%.

## STATUS IN THE WORLD TODAY

Burma, which achieved its independence
on Jan. 4, 1948, has tried to follow a foreign policy of neutralism, or "third-force-
ism" to avoid involvement in the cold war.
Yet, despite the threat posed by its giant
northern neighbor, Communist China, it
has taken such pro-Western steps as supporting the U.N. on the Korean issue and
voting against the Soviet bloc on the
Hungarian issue.

Despite its neutralism, Burma's relations with Communist nations have not
been too happy. As the world's largest
rice-exporting nation, Burma found it difficult to dispose of its surpluses in 1954
and 1955 and turned to the Sino-Soviet
bloc for a far-reaching barter agreement
which would dispose of 25 per cent of annual rice stocks. Then, in trying to dispose
of the rest of its rice for cash elsewhere,
it found itself competing with its own
product, which the Communists had
dumped on the market at a low price.
Domestically, it was faced with an armed
Communist rebellion only two months
after achieving independence. And its relations with China were complicated by
the presence of Chinese Nationalist troops
in border areas, which gave the Communists a pretext to occupy frontier sections
of Burma. A partial settlement of the
frontier disputes was reached in a border
agreement signed in February, 1960. Both
sides yielded some land, but the agreement
did not settle all outstanding questions.

In its relations with the United States,
Burma received about $20 million in grant
aid between 1950 and 1953, but then terminated all grant-aid agreements because
of disappointment with the United States
over the removal of the Chinese Nationalist troops in the north. But after several years of economic dealings with the
Communist bloc, Burma resumed in 1957
arrangements for loans and the purchase
of surplus agricultural products along
with a $20 million loan from the Interna-
tional Bank for Reconstruction and Development.

Politically, Burma was ruled for the first
ten years of its independence by the Anti-
Fascist People's Freedom League (AFPFL),
a coalition originally organized as a wartime resistance movement. After expelling the Communist elements, the AFPFL
government gained steadily in strength
and demonstrated its ability to bring
about meaningful economic progress. But
gradually differences developed among the
AFPFL leaders, and when the leadership
split publicly, the Burmese Army took
power in September, 1958, in a bloodless
coup to prevent Communist elements from
seizing control. Army officers said that as
soon as they had put an end to the Communist insurrection and wiped out the
bands of guerrillas, elections would be
held and the administration turned over
to civilians. This was done in April, 1960.
Among the accomplishments of the Army
regime was the virtual suppression of in-
surgent groups, a cut in living costs, virtual elimination of corruption and improvement of morale in permanent government service.

## MAJOR POLITICAL PARTIES

"Clean" Anti-Fascist People's Freedom
League (AFPFL) (156 seats in Chamber of
Deputies), led by Prime Minister U Nu;
"Stable" AFPFL (34 seats), led by U Ba
Swe.

HISTORY AND GOVERNMENT. Lying on
the eastern side of the Bay of Bengal between India, China, and Thailand, the
Union of Burma came into existence as an
independent state on Jan. 4, 1948. In 1612
the British East India Company sent
agents to Burma, and in the seventeenth
and eighteenth centuries the Burmese
stoutly resisted the efforts of British,
Dutch, and Portuguese traders to establish
posts on the Bay of Bengal. Actual British
rule dated from 1826, and in 1886 British
troops forced the annexation of all Burma
to India. On April 1, 1937, the British
separated Burma from India and set it up
as a Crown colony with its own legislature
and a British Governor.

For hundreds of years a battlefield of
petty princes, Burma became a key battleground in World War II largely because the
800-mile Burma Road was the Allies' vital
supply line to China. The Japanese invaded the country in Dec., 1941, and by
May 1942, had occupied most of it, cutting
the road. In Aug., 1942, the Japanese set
up a puppet government.

After one of the most difficult campaigns
of the war, Allied forces liberated most of
Burma prior to the Japanese surrender on
Aug. 14, 1945.

The Constitution of Sept. 24, 1947,
provides for a government headed by the
President, who is elected by the two houses
of Parliament—the Chamber of Deputies,
consisting of 250 members elected for 4
years, and the Chamber of Nationalities,
consisting of 125 members elected for 4
years. The President appoints the Premier
on nomination of the Chamber of Deputies.
Four frontier areas—the Shan, Kachin, and
Karenni states, and the Chin special division—are constituent parts of the Union
but enjoy some autonomy. The Constitution contemplates a form of state social-

ism, with the operation of all public utilities and the exploitation of all natural resources to come eventually under state control.

SOCIAL AND ECONOMIC CONDITIONS. The natives in general are Mongolian; the Burmese are the most advanced. Indians, settled in the Irrawaddy delta region, supply most of the coolie labor, while the Chinese constitute the artisan and merchant class. Buddhism, the national religion, profoundly affects the national character; every village in the country has its temple.

Burma is essentially agricultural, with crop growing concentrated in the delta and river valleys. It is a leading producer of rice, the staple food, which occupies two-thirds of the cultivated area. Crops grown in the dry zone in upper Burma include millet, cotton, peanuts, and sesame. Other crops include tobacco, fruit, vegetables, and cereals. The number of rubber plantations has increased. The principal domestic animals are water buffalo, used as a beast of burden in the delta, and small humped oxen, which predominate in other areas. In July, 1959, Burma accepted $30 million from the U.S. to be received over a period of four years, and to cover the foreign-exchange costs of the construction of a highway connecting Rangoon with central Burma, and for physical construction at the University of Rangoon.

Leading industries include silk weaving and dyeing, rice husking, oil refining, and wood carving. The Baluchaung hydroelectric plant, one of the largest in Southeast Asia, was completed in March 1960.

Chief exports in 1958 were rice and products (70%) and teak and cotton. Leading customers were India (16%), Indonesia (17%), Japan (5%), Ceylon (11%), Britain (9%) and other sterling area (26%); leading suppliers were Britain (19%), Japan (23%), and India (13%).

NATURAL FEATURES AND RESOURCES. Slightly smaller than Texas, Burma is divided into three natural regions: the Arakan Yoma, a long, narrow mountain range forming the barrier between Burma and India; the Shan Plateau in the east, extending southward into Tenasserim; and the Central Basin, running down to the flat, fertile delta of the Irrawaddy in the south. This delta contains a network of intercommunicating canals and nine principal mouths.

Mineral resources are considerable but, in many cases, undeveloped.

Other minerals include lead, silver, zinc, nickel, cobalt, copper, gold, iron ore, molybdenum, coal, uranium (reported), rubies, sapphires, and jade.

More than half of Burma is forested. Teak, valuable for naval construction, is the main timber product. Its cutting is strictly controlled.

# Cambodia (Kingdom)

**Area: 66,607 square miles.**
**Population (est. 1959): 4,845,000.**
**Density per square mile: 72.7.**
**Chief of State: Prince Norodom Sihanouk.**
**Principal cities (est. 1959): Pnom-Penh, 355,180 (capital); (1941) Battambang, 23,-567 (rice).**
**Monetary unit: Riel.**
**Languages: Cambodian, French, Annamese.**
**Religion: Buddhism.**

### STATUS IN THE WORLD TODAY

Cambodia, which was relatively free of Communist subversive activity during the prolonged conflict between France and the Communist-led Viet Minh, has pursued a neutralist course in world politics, trying to steer a middle course between the world power blocs. The only part of former French Indo-China not partitioned by the Geneva agreements (July, 1954) which ended the nine-year Indo-China war, it remained for the most part outside the main theaters of military operations. While heavily dependent on aid from the United States (about $40 million annually) and to a lesser extent France, Cambodia has also received large-scale help from the Communist bloc, especially Red China. Allegations of American interference in Cambodia's internal affairs have been more than offset by the exposure of Communist subversive activities financed and directed from abroad. Despite the latter, Cambodia recognized Red China in 1958, and its prime minister then made a highly publicized visit to Peking.

The nation's long-range economic development plans are proceeding slowly. Although most American aid has gone to support Cambodia's armed forces, the United States has also contributed to other projects. The most spectacular is a highway connecting Pnom-Penh, the capital, with Kompong Som, on the Gulf of Siam, where the French are building a deep-water port to free Cambodian commerce from dependence on the Mékong river.

Political life in Cambodia has been dominated by the volatile, enigmatic personality of ex-King Norodom Sihanouk, who ascended the throne in 1941. Four years later he abdicated to play a more active role in politics. He organized the Popular Socialist Community, which has controlled the government ever since 1955. But since Norodom Sihanouk has consented to serve only intermittently as Prime Minister, political life has been characterized by marked cabinet instability.

---

HISTORY AND GOVERNMENT. Cambodia is bounded on the south and east by south Vietnam, on the north by Laos and Thailand, on the west by Thailand, and on the southwest by the Gulf of Siam. Its recorded history dates back to the beginning of the Christian era, when it was known as Fou-Nan. It was absorbed in about A.D. 600 by the Khmers, under whose rule magnificent temples were built at Angkor. The arrival of the French, who were granted a protectorate in 1863, prevented the annihilation of the Khmer empire by the Vietnamese and Siamese. It was occupied by Japan during World War II. Cambodia's legislature consists of a unicameral National Assembly of 61 members elected for 4 years by direct universal suffrage.

ECONOMIC CONDITIONS. About 76 per cent of the population is Cambodian, five per cent Anamese, and four per cent Chinese. The forested regions of the northeast are inhibited by various primitive peoples.

Agriculture is the basis of the economy. The chief crop is rice, grown principally in the Battambang area. Second in importance is rubber. Other crops include tobacco, kapok, cotton, pepper, and maize. Cattle breeding is of major importance. Native industries include silk and cotton weaving, rice milling, and the salting of fish obtained from Lake Tonle Sap during the low-water season.

Leading exports include rice, rubber, animal products, wool and hides, and skins. A large part of the trade is with France, the United States and Vietnam.

NATURAL FEATURES AND RESOURCES. Cambodia consists chiefly of a large alluvial plain ringed in by mountains and on the east by the Mékong river. The plain is centered on Lake Tonle Sap, which is a natural storage basin of the Mékong.

Forests cover about 75 per cent of the land but most are unexploited. Deposits of iron ore, limestone and phosphate exist but also are undeveloped.

---

# Cameroun (Republic)

Area: 166,796 square miles.
Population (est. 1959): 3,200,000 (16,500 Europeans).
Density per square mile: 19.2.
President: Ahmadou Ahidjo.
Premier: Charles Assale.
Principal cities: Douala, 120,000 (chief port); Yaounde, 55,000 (capital).
Monetary unit: Franc C.F.A. (Communauté Française de l'Atlantique).*

* One franc C.F.A. = 0.02 new French franc.

Languages: French, Foulbé, Bamiléké and many other dialects.
Religions: Animist, Christian, Moslem.

## HISTORY AND PRESENT STATUS

The Cameroun became independent on January 1, 1960, after 75 years of German and French rule. The Cameroon estuary and coast were discovered toward the end of the 15th century by the Portuguese navigator Fernando Po. Not until the end of the 17th century were the first European trading posts established. In 1884 the area became a German colony (Kamerun). After World War I the region was divided as a League of Nations mandate between Britain and France, four-fifths of it going to France. The mandate subsequently became a United Nations trusteeship, and in 1957 a self-government statute was enacted preliminary to independence. In 1961 the United Nations trust territories of Southern Cameroons and Northern Cameroons, administered by Great Britain, voted to join other nations: the former chose Cameroun, the latter Nigeria. The present government is patterned after the presidential regime of France, with a premier, cabinet and 100-man parliament. The president is elected for a five-year term.

ECONOMIC CONDITIONS. The principal exports are cacao, coffee, bananas, timber and cotton. Exports (1958) came to 22,290,000,000 fr. C.F.A., imports to 21,452,000,000 fr. C.F.A. Mineral resources include titanium, tin and gold. The biggest industrial plant is at Edea.

---

# Chile (Republic)
## (República de Chile)

Area: 286,397 square miles.
Population (est. 1960): 7,627,000.
Density per square mile: 26.6.
President: Jorge Alessandri.
Principal cities (est. 1958): Santiago, 830,897 (capital); Valparaíso, 271,431 (port); Concepción, 163,798 (farming center); Viña del Mar, 105,779 (resort center); Antofagasta, 77,240 (nitrates).
Monetary unit: Peso.
Language: Spanish.
Religion: Roman Catholic.

---

## STATUS IN THE WORLD TODAY

Like many other countries which have to depend on one or two products to earn foreign exchange, Chile's principal problem is economic. Nitrates and copper exports bring in nearly all its vitally needed earnings, and these vary as the world prices of the two minerals fluctuate. In addition, although Chile once exported wheat and other agricultural products, in the past twenty years it has become an increasingly large importer of these commodities and has consequently needed more foreign exchange. Industrialization, begun in World War I and stimulated by the depression, has helped to provide locally many manufactured goods formerly imported. To reduce its dependence on imported petroleum products, the government has started drilling for oil wells in southernmost Tierra del Fuego. It has also established a major steel industry in Talcahuano. But swiftly rising prices have brought about an inflation which has caused riots and strikes over such comparatively small increases in living costs as a rise in bus fares in Santiago.

## MAJOR POLITICAL PARTIES

Radical party (40 seats in Chamber of Deputies), led by Luis Bossay and Gabriel González; Liberal party (27 seats), led by Gregorio Amunategui; United Conservative party (18 seats), led by Jorge Pristo and Francisco Bulnes.

HISTORY. Europeans first arrived in 1536, when Diego de Almagro, an associate of Pizarro, led an unsuccessful invasion from Peru. Five years later another Spaniard, Pedro de Valdivia, founded Santiago. On Sept. 18, 1810, Chile rebelled against Spanish rule, but independence was not won completely until 1818, when Bernardo O'Higgins and José de San Martín finally crushed the Spanish armies.

Chile, which has never lost a war, fought with Bolivia and Peru in 1879–83 and won the province of Antofagasta, Bolivia's only outlet to the Pacific, as well as extensive areas from Peru. In World War I, Chile was neutral.

During the decade after the war the demand for social and political reform resulted in the enactment of reform bills, and a strong executive replaced the rather ineffective parliamentary system. A series of brief governments came about as a result of the 1929 depression, but stable regimes returned in 1932.

GOVERNMENT. The nation elects a President every six years, a Senate of 45 members every eight years (one-half renewable every four years), and a Chamber of Deputies of 147 members every four years. The President is assisted by a Cabinet responsible to him but subject to impeachment by Congress, which also may override a presidential veto by two-thirds vote. All literate citizens over 21 may vote.

ECONOMIC CONDITIONS. Chilean agriculture is mostly confined to the temperate central valley, similar to that of California. Productive land is extremely limited, and most of it must be irrigated. Wheat (1959–60: 1,190,000 metric tons) is the leading crop. Grapes, next to wheat in acreage, produced an estimated 118,800,000 gallons of wine in 1956. Feudal-type estates, averaging 2,500 acres, predominate. Cattle in 1958 totaled 2,590,000 and sheep 6,540,000. Wool production (1959) was about 49,800,000 pounds, greasy basis.

*Trade.* In 1959 the leading customers were the U.S. (31%), Britain (15%), West Germany (16%), the Netherlands (8%), and Argentina (5%); leading suppliers, the U.S. (33%), West Germany (10%), and Argentina (7%). Chief exports were copper (64%), nitrate of soda (7%), and iron ore (6%). Leading imports were machinery (20%), transportation equipment (5%), and petroleum (14%).

Except for mineral processing, most manufacturing is of low-priced consumer's goods, particularly textiles.

NATURAL FEATURES AND RESOURCES. A narrow, mountainous land, Chile has one-third of its area covered by the towering ranges of the Andes. In the north is the mineral-rich Atacama Desert, between the coast mountains and the Andes. In the center is a 700-mile-long valley, thickly populated, between the Andes and the coastal plateau. In the south, the Andes border on the ocean.

At the southern tip of Chile's mainland is Punta Arenas, the southernmost city in the world, and beyond that lies the Strait of Magellan and Tierra del Fuego, an island divided between Chile and Argentina. The Juan Fernández Islands, in the South Pacific about 400 miles west of the mainland, and Easter Island, about 2,000 miles west, are Chilean possessions.

The basis of the country's economy is its mineral resources in the northern desert provinces of Atacama, Antofagasta and Tarapacá, where the only natural nitrate in the world is found. Some 60 per cent of the world's iodine is obtained as a by-product of nitrate processing. Chile's world monopoly in nitrate, however, declined in importance with development of the synthetic product.

The world's largest copper reserve, estimated at 134 billion pounds, is in Chile, and also more than 900 million tons of high-grade iron ore. The reserve of Chilean coal, noted for quantity rather than quality, exceeds two billion tons.

# China (Republic)
## (Chung-Hua Min-Kuo)

**Area: 3,768,738 square miles.***
**Population (census 1959): 672,232,000.***
**Density per square mile: 178.5.**

\* Including Province of Formosa (Taiwan), Manchuria and Tibet. Census not taken in Formosa (population estimated at 7,591,298); population total excludes an estimated 11,743,320 Chinese resident abroad. The total population figure is regarded with considerable reserve.

President, Nationalist China: Generalissimo Chiang Kai-shek.
Premier: Chen Cheng.
President, Communist China: Liu Shaochi.
Premier: Chou En-lai.

Principal cities (census 1953): Shanghai, 6,204,417 (chief port, industrial and financial center); Peking (Peiping), 2,768,149 (capital, Communist China); (est. 1957) Tientsin, 3,100,000 (commercial center); (est. 1952) Chungking, 2,000,000 (river port, trade center); Mukden, 1,790,000 (Manchurian industrial center); Canton, 1,210,000 (southern commercial center); Wuhan, 1,090,000 (river port); Nanking, 1,020,000 (former Nationalist capital).
Monetary unit: Chinese dollar (yuan).
Language: Chinese.
Religions: Principally Confucian, Buddhist and Taoist.

## STATUS IN THE WORLD TODAY

Communist China, as the Asian partner of the U.S.S.R., carries out in Asia the policy which the Russians are particularly active in pushing in Africa and the Middle East—supporting nationalistic movements, opposing any American or Western moves as "imperialistic" and "colonial," giving economic assistance, although to an extremely limited degree, to newly established governments, and undermining, wherever possible, democratic institutions and administrations. Its most notable example of intervention was in the Korean conflict. But it is equally active in the nations which came into being in Southeast Asia and continuously dangles the bait of increased trade before Japan in return for diplomatic recognition. While it has been recognized by a fairly large number of countries, including the United Kingdom, it has yet to attain membership in the United Nations, despite repeated attempts by the U.S.S.R., or to oust Nationalist China from its seat on the Security Council.

China's model for the Communist state is found in Stalin's totalitarian institutions. Although Communist party leader Mao Tse-tung, in a 1957 speech entitled "Let One Hundred Flowers Bloom, Let One Hundred Schools of Thought Contend," seemed to indicate that there could be some criticism of the administration, those who took him at his word soon found themselves being "re-educated" in work camps or other institutions, and the flow of critical thought was quickly stopped. While there is no accurate way to measure the true feeling of the Chinese people toward the Communist regime, reports from the mainland indicate there is scattered resistance from a number of groups, with the government determined to stamp out all opposition ruthlessly.

There has been particular widespread discontent among the peasants, the demands upon agriculture having been severe during recent years. The Communists have been trying to modernize China by following the Soviet model of emphasis on heavy industry. The chief stress has been on capital-goods production which the current Five-Year Plan, begun in 1958, proposes to raise 18.8 per cent to 9.7 per cent for consumer goods. Industrial gains have been made. But since the state has used most of the "surplus" extracted from the countryside to develop industry, there has been little capital available to invest in agriculture. The Communists have tried to increase production, but the result has not been impressive. Figures on recent crops show that collectivization of the land has not solved China's problem of increasing agricultural production and in 1961 food was imported to ease famine conditions in some areas. State grain collection already has been slightly eased as the result of peasant withholding of grain, and travel restrictions have been tightened because of the exodus to the city.

The seriousness which Communist leaders attach to the food problem is underlined by the fact that in order to provide more farm labor, they have even broken up the traditional basic Chinese social unit—the family. Fathers and mothers are taken from their homes and housed in separate barracks to constitute male and female working gangs, while their children are placed in state-operated nurseries. At intervals, such as every two weeks, the families are permitted a brief reunion.

While the strains imposed on China's rural millions have been severe, it must be recognized that the over-all national income of Red China appears to have gone up each year by about 9 per cent. This has meant a per capita annual rise in income of 6–7 per cent. When compared with the economic gains of postwar Japan, China's achievements are not so impressive; but, when compared with the years of relative stagnation in China's past, they are impressive indeed.

HISTORY AND GOVERNMENT. By 2000 B.C., the Chinese were living in the Hwang Ho basin, and they had achieved an advanced stage of civilization by 1200 B.C. The great philosophers, Lao-tse, Confucius, Mo Ti, and Mencius lived during the Chou dynasty (about 1122 to 249 B.C.). The warring feudal states were first united under Emperor Ch'in Shih Huang Ti, during whose reign (246-210 B.C.) work was begun on the Great Wall. Under the Han dynasty

(206 B.C. to A.D. 220) China prospered and traded with the West.

The T'ang dynasty (618–907) has often been called the golden age of Chinese history. Painting, sculpture, and poetry flourished under royal patronage, and printing made its earliest known appearance.

The Mings, last of the native rulers (1368–1644), overthrew the Mongol, or Yuan, dynasty (1280–1368) established by Kublai Khan, whose dominions extended into eastern Europe. The weakening Mings in turn were overthrown in 1644 by invaders from the north, the Manchus.

The Chinese closely restricted foreign activities, and by the end of the 18th century only Canton (and the Portuguese port of Macao) were open to European merchants. Following the Anglo-Chinese War of 1839–42, however, several treaty ports were opened and Hong Kong was ceded to Britain. Treaties signed after further hostilities (1856–60) weakened Chinese sovereignty and removed foreigners from Chinese jurisdiction. The disastrous Chinese-Japanese War of 1894–95 was followed by a scramble for Chinese leases and concessions by European powers, which resulted in the Boxer Rebellion (1900), suppressed by an international force.

The death of the Empress Dowager Tzu Hsi in 1908 and the accession of the infant Emperor Hsüan T'ung (Pu-Yi) were followed by a nation-wide rebellion led by Dr. Sun Yat-sen, who became first President of the Provisional Chinese Republic in 1911. The Manchus abdicated on Feb. 12, 1912. Dr. Sun resigned in favor of Yuan Shih-k'ai, who suppressed the republicans but was forced by a serious rising in 1915–16 to abandon his intention of declaring himself Emperor. Yuan's death in June, 1916, was followed by years of civil war between rival militarists and Dr. Sun's republicans. The death in 1925 of Dr. Sun, who had controlled only the Canton area in opposition to the recognized regime, was followed by a revival of the Kuomintang party, which practically deified him. Nationalist forces, led by Gen. Chiang Kai-shek and advised originally by Communist experts, soon occupied most of China, setting up a Kuomintang regime in 1928. Internal strife continued, however, and Chiang broke with the Communists.

An alleged explosion on the South Manchurian Railway on Sept. 18, 1931, brought invasion of Manchuria by Japanese forces, who installed the last Manchu Emperor, Henry Pu-Yi, as nominal ruler of the puppet state of "Manchukuo." Japanese efforts to take China's northern provinces in July, 1937, were resisted by Chiang Kai-shek, who meanwhile had succeeded in uniting most of China behind him. Within two years, however, Japan seized most of the ports and railways. The Kuomintang government retreated first to Hankow and then to Chungking, while the Japanese set up a puppet government at Nanking headed by Wang Ching-wei.

When the Japanese surrendered in 1945, China signed a treaty with the Soviet Union providing for Soviet withdrawal from Manchuria, joint Chinese-Soviet control of Manchurian railways for 30 years, a joint Chinese-Soviet naval base at Port Arthur, and a free port at Dairen.

The surrender of Japan also touched off a civil war between Nationalist and Communist forces for control of China. By the end of 1949, all of the republic except the island of Formosa was under Communist control. Barricaded on Formosa, the Nationalist regime had little means at its disposal to make any effective counterattack upon the mainland. The U.S., however, after the outbreak of the Korean war in 1950, promised naval and air aid to repel any invasion of Formosa.

The Communists meanwhile set up, in September, 1949, a soviet-type government. After prolonged negotiations, the People's government and the Soviet Union signed a 30-year treaty of friendship and mutual aid on Feb. 14, 1950; its published terms provided for return of the Changchun railroad to China and the eventual return of Port Arthur and Dairen.

The Communist regime subsequently was recognized as the legal government of China by many nations but was unable to secure a place in the U.N. It threw several hundred thousand men into the Korean war of 1950–53 in a futile effort to drive U.N. forces from Korea.

ECONOMIC CONDITIONS.

*Agriculture.* In China, nearly 80 per cent of the population depends on the land for livelihood. Subsistence crops are necessarily emphasized, but China is still not self-sufficient in food. Cultivation is intensive, and irrigation is widely practiced. The Communists have organized communal farms which have not been very productive. The 1959–60 crops were insufficient and famines resulted. Droughts and floods caused the greatest difficulties. The three most important food crops are rice, wheat, and maize.

In northern China, wheat, barley, corn, sorghum, millet and other cereals, and beans and peas predominate, whereas in the south, rice, sugar, and indigo are most important. The Yangtze basin, one of the most favored agricultural regions in the world, is China's premier granary. Tea, the chief beverage, is grown mainly in the central uplands, coastal ranges and Szechwan.

Silkworm culture is practiced widely, especially in the lower Yangtze valley. Soybeans and cotton are of ever-increasing im-

portance. Other crops include fibers, tobacco, vegetable oils, cane sugar, and many
medicinal plants and spices.

The urgent need for subsistence crops
has confined grazing grounds for sheep
and cattle to the dry northwest and to
mountain pastures. However, such animals
as goats, poultry, and especially pigs are
raised everywhere. According to unofficial
estimates, Communist China had in 1953
28,812,000 cattle, 17,190,000 sheep, 77,-
376,000 hogs, 34,110,000 goats, and 11,885,-
000 buffalo.

*Industry.* Industrially, China is still in
its infancy. Development has been mainly
in the erection of textile mills, silk and
flour mills, match factories, tanneries, and
a few steel and cement mills. The production of consumer's goods far exceeds that
of producer's goods, which must still be
imported.

The communist regime is reported to be
concentrating upon Manchuria as China's
industrial center and to be shifting some
industries to the northwest.

*Trade.* According to official reports, the
U.S.S.R. and its satellites accounted for
80 per cent of Communist China's trade in
1957. Major exports include textiles and
products, tung oil, and pig bristles.

NATURAL FEATURES AND RESOURCES.
China has about 1¼ times the area of
the continental United States. Its coast
line is roughly a semi-circle, about 2,150
miles long. The greater part of the country is mountainous, and only in the lower
reaches of the Hwang Ho (Yellow) and
Yangtze Kiang rivers are there extensive
low plains.

The principal mountain ranges are
the Tien Shan, to the northwest; the Kunlun chain, which attains a maximum
height of 23,890 feet, running south of the
Takla Makan and Gobi deserts; and the
Trans-Himalaya, connecting the Kunlun
with the borders of China and Tibet. Manchuria is largely an undulating plain connected with the north China plain by a
narrow lowland corridor. Inner Mongolia
contains the relatively fertile southern and
eastern portions of the Gobi. The large
island of Hainan (13,500 sq. mi.) lies off
the southern coast.

Hydrographically, China proper consists
of three great river systems. The northern
part of the country is drained by the
Hwang Ho river, 2,700 miles long and
mostly unnavigable. The central part is
drained by the Yangtze Kiang, the fifth
longest river in the world (3,100 mi.). The
Si Kiang in the south is about 1,650 miles
long and navigable for a considerable distance. In addition, the Amur forms part of
the northeastern boundary.

*Minerals.* Mineral resources are considerable. Iron ore, far less plentiful than
coal, is mined principally in the lower
Yangtze valley and in north China. Tin,
mined in Yunnan and southwest Szechwan, has been a major mineral export. Of
some rarer minerals, notably antimony and
tungsten, China is sometimes the world's
leading producer. Lead, zinc, silver, mercury, and gold are also mined. The discovery of uranium has been reported in recent years.

*Forests and Fisheries.* China urgently needs
reforestation. Most remaining forests are
on inaccessible mountain slopes. Bamboo
is cultivated in groves throughout the
country south of the Tsinling mountains.

**FORMOSA (TAIWAN)—Status: Province
(Part of Republic of Nationalist China).**
Area: 13,885 square miles.
Population (estimated 1960, excluding
troops and militia): 10,611,000.
Principal cities (est. 1958): .Taipei,
809,169 (capital); Kaohsiung, 371,225 (seaport, industrial center); Tainan, 287,797
(agricultural products).
Foreign trade (1959): exports, U.S.
$164,000,000; (1959) imports, U.S. $150,400,-
00.* Chief exports (1958): sugar (59%),
rice (10%), canned pineapple (5%).
Agricultural products (est. 1959, in metric tons): sugar, 867,847; rice (paddy),
1,854,782.
Manufactures (1957): cement, 603,933
metric tons; cotton cloth, 130,000,000 sq.
yd.; paper, 59,634 tons; aluminum, 8,700
tons; steel bars, 67,900 tons.
Minerals: coal (1958: 3,181,000 metric
tons), gold, petroleum, silver, sulfur.

* Excludes U.S. aid imports ($95,374,000) and those
with self-provided exchange ($16,580,000).

---

## STATUS IN THE WORLD TODAY

Despite attempts by the Soviet Union
to obtain both *de jure* and *de facto* recognition of the Communist regime as the
government of China, the Nationalist government now located on Taiwan is still
recognized by the United Nations, the
United States, and a number of other nations as the legitimate government of the
mainland territory. President Chiang Kai-
shek still hopes to reconquer the China
over which he once ruled, and the Taiwan
regime consequently maintains an armed
force of more than 600,000 men. Similarly,
the Communist regime in Peiping has
pledged itself to "liberate" Taiwan and
make it part of Red China. Currently a
United States promise to defend Taiwan
against aggression has discouraged any
Communist invasion threats, and its assistance in protecting shipments of supplies to the offshore islands of Matsu and
Quemoy, held by Nationalist forces, has
cut down actual hostilities to desultory
exchanges of artillery shells. In March,
1960, President Chiang was re-elected for

a third six-year term by the National Assembly.

Economically, the Taiwan regime is dependent upon American aid, although it has made great strides in increasing both agricultural and industrial output. Although trade with both the United States and Japan has been considerably expanded, there is still an unfavorable balance of payments. Capital needs for economic development are still too great to be met locally, and military costs far exceed revenues available to the government.

---

**HISTORY AND GOVERNMENT.** Formosa is a large island in the western Pacific, separated from China to the west by the Taiwan straits (narrowest point, 90 mi.). The Pescadores (Bokoto) and other outlying islands (about 78 sq. mi.) became administratively a part of Formosa under Japanese rule. Formosa, ceded to Japan in 1895 after the Chinese-Japanese War, remained Japanese until it was restored to China in 1945, in accordance with the Cairo conference of 1943. It was the only territory under the control of the Nationalist regime after 1949. Under a 1955 mutual-defense treaty the United States is committed to defend Formosa and the Pescadores.

Formosa's internal affairs are administered by the provincial government headed by the Governor appointed by the Nationalist government. The provincial assembly is elected by direct popular vote.

Most of the inhabitants are of Chinese stock. There are also about 180,000 aboriginal tribesmen in the interior.

Formosa is essentially an agricultural country with the greater part of the population dependent on farming. It is self-sufficient in most basic foodstuffs and produces surpluses of a number of others, notably rice and sugar. Farms are generally small (average, 3 ac.). Cattle and water buffalo are the chief livestock.

Food processing is the island's major industry; it engaged over 6,000 plants in 1955. The textile industry is expanding, and industrial potential was increased by the first four-year program (1953–56).

The island is one of the world's chief sources of camphor, and government monopolies of camphor, salt, opium, and tobacco have been established. Forest resources are enormous.

Formosa is divided by a central mountain range running from north to south, which rises sharply on the east coast and declines gradually to the broad western plain, where cultivation is concentrated.

**TIBET—Status: Nominally independent; under Chinese Communist control.**

Area: 471,660 square miles.
Population (census 1953): 1,273,969.
Capital: Lhasa (about 20,000).
Ruler: the Panchen Lama.
Monetary unit: Sang.
Exports: wool, live animals, salt, hides, borax, tea, musk.
Agricultural products: barley, fruits, pulse, vegetables.
Minerals: borax, salt, coal, gold.

---

## STATUS IN THE WORLD TODAY

The complete suppression of autonomous government in Tibet in March, 1959, by Red Chinese troops has been cited as an example of Asian imperialism and has caused doubts in some Asian countries as to the validity of Communist China's pledge at the Bandung Asian conference to practice "peaceful co-existence" and "non-interference in the internal affairs of other countries." Although Peiping promised to respect Tibet's autonomy in a treaty signed in 1951, it immediately violated the treaty through systematic oppression and tyranny which finally brought about a revolt in 1959. The ruling Dalai Lama was forced to flee to India and a Panchen Lama, chosen by Peiping, was installed as puppet ruler. Since then, according to Tibetan exiles, the Chinese have embarked upon a policy of forced labor and compulsory exactions, confiscation of property, execution of leading Tibetans, and the destruction of national, ethnic, and religious groups of Tibet which amount to genocide.

---

**HISTORY AND GOVERNMENT.** Tibet, north and northeast of the Himalayas, is the highest country in the world, averaging 16,000 feet in elevation and having many peaks ranging up to more than 25,000 feet. Chinese suzerainty over Tibet was established in the eighteenth century. The area was invaded by a British expeditionary force in 1904, but the Anglo-Russian Convention of 1907 recognized China's influence and stipulated that neither Russia nor Britain should interfere in Tibet's affairs.

Chinese Communist troops invaded the area in October, 1950. An agreement signed with Communist China in May, 1951, recognized the Dalai Lama as spiritual and temporal ruler but made Tibet virtually a Chinese province.

The religion and predominant factor in Tibet's social system is Lamaism, a late form of Buddhism modified by animism and primitive magic. Education is in the control of the many monasteries, some of which have more than 1,000 monks. A large number of the population are lamas, mostly celibates. Both polyandry and polygyny are practiced.

# Colombia (Republic)
## (República de Colombia)

**Area:** 439,520 square miles.
**Population** (est. 1960): 14,132,000 (mestizo, 68%; white, 20%; Indian, 7%; Negro, 5%).
**Density per square mile:** 32.2.
**President:** Alberto Lleras Camargo.
**Principal cities** (est. 1960): Bogotá, 1,188,180 (capital); Medellín, 614,030 (industrial); Cali, 590,770 (coffee, mining); Barranquilla, 431,250 (seaport); Bucaramanga, 196,290 (industrial center); Cartagena, 173,520 (seaport).
**Monetary unit:** Peso.
**Language:** Spanish.
**Religion:** Roman Catholic.

## STATUS IN THE WORLD TODAY

Colombia did not believe that a dictatorship was justified merely because the country was economically prosperous. The cruel regime of General Rojas Pinilla, who took power with the backing of the army in 1953 and had himself elected President the following year by a constitutional assembly he himself had named, was finally overthrown in May, 1957. A military junta took over until elections could be held. The Liberals and Conservatives agreed that for twelve years, in the interests of political peace and preventing further military coups, the presidency would alternate between the two parties and congress would be equally divided between them. The congressional elections of March, 1958, gave the Liberals a three to two advantage over the Conservatives, and two months later Alberto Lleras Camargo, a Liberal, was inaugurated as President.

Colombia was primarily a coffee producer until World War II, but with the beginning of industrialization, the nation became self-sufficient in cotton and woolen textiles. Then came the establishment of steel, chemical, cement, and metallurgical industries, while agriculture became more diversified. The growth of the economy continued while the political situation deteriorated until the popular revolution of 1957.

HISTORY. Colombia, nearly nine times the size of New York state, is the only country in South America with frontage on both the Pacific and the Caribbean. Its northern coast was one of the first parts of the Americas to be visited by Spanish explorers. Darien, the first permanent European settlement on the American mainland, was founded in 1510.

New Granada, as Colombia was called until 1861, was comparatively neglected during the Spanish colonial era. After winning independence from Spain during a fourteen-year struggle ending in 1824, the country established a republic in 1831, including the area that now is Panamá. Intermittent civil war plagued Colombia until 1903, when Panamá, with United States backing, seceded from the republic.

The century-old boundary dispute with Peru over Leticia almost led to war in 1931, but a settlement was arranged through the League of Nations in 1934–35.

GOVERNMENT. Colombia's President, who appoints his own Cabinet, is elected every four years and is not eligible for immediate reelection. The Senate—upper house of Congress—has 80 members elected for four years by direct vote. The House of Representatives of 148 members is directly elected for two years. Congress was superseded temporarily by a national constituent assembly in 1954. All citizens over 21 may vote. On December 1, 1957, a popular plebiscite amended the Constitution establishing parity for 12 years between the Liberal and Conservative parties in both Houses of Congress and in the regional legislatures and municipal councils, in the Supreme Court, the central government, and the regional cabinets. In December, 1958, some seven months after President Camargo was elected, former President Pinilla was found guilty by the Senate of having violated the Colombian Constitution and of "abuse of power by improper conduct in the exercise of the office of President."

ECONOMIC CONDITIONS. Most of the people live by farming and cattle herding, but only a small part of the land is cultivated, and that by primitive means. Colombia's coffee, the nation's principal crop, is a mild variety that does not compete with Brazilian types. Cattle numbered 15,100,000 in Dec., 1959, according to U.S. government estimates.

The leading manufacturing industries are foodstuff processing, textiles and beverages. A new steel plant went into operation late in 1954; production in 1959 was 108,321 metric tons of steel ingots and 112,000 metric tons of rolled-steel products.

Leading exports in 1959 were coffee (77%), petroleum (16%), and bananas (2%). Leading customers were the U.S. (73%), West Germany (9%), Netherlands Antilles (4%), and Sweden (3%); leading suppliers, the U.S. (50%), Germany (10%), Britain (5%), and Canada (4%).

NATURAL FEATURES AND RESOURCES. Through the western half of the country, three Andean ranges run north and south, merging into one at the Ecuadorean border. The eastern half is a low, jungle-covered plain, drained by spurs of the Amazon and Orinoco, inhabited mostly by uncivilized Indians. The fertile plateau and valley of the eastern range is the most densely populated part of the country.

Rich in minerals, Colombia has the third largest oil industry in Latin America (70 per cent controlled by U.S. interests). The country is also rich in platinum and has world-famous emerald mines at Muzo in the eastern Andes.

Forest products include vanilla, quinine, ipecac, sarsaparilla, gums and balsams, tanning agents, and dyewoods.

# Congo, The Republic of the
## (Léopoldville)*

Area: 905,381 square miles.
Population (est. 1959): 13,821,000 (115,-804 non-Africans).
Density per square mile: 15.3.
President: Joseph Kasavubu.
Premier: Cyrille Adoula.
Principal cities (est. 1958): Léopoldville, 389,547 (capital); Elizabethville, 182,-638; Stanleyville, 79,951.
Monetary unit: Congolese franc.
Languages: Kiswahili, Tshiluba, Lingala, Kikogno.
Religions: Fetishism, Roman Catholic (4,200,439), Protestant (812,608), Moslem (150,000).
Ethnic groups: Bantu, Sudanese, Nilotics, Pygmies, Hamites.

* As distinguished from Republic of the Congo Brazzaville), formerly French.

### STATUS IN THE WORLD TODAY

When the former Belgian Congo colony declared its independence on June 30, 1960, its army mutinied, the government was unable to restore order, and a lack of trained public administrators hampered the entire country. The United Nations, summoned to help reestablish normal conditions, flew in troops from neutral countries under U.N. command, but the political situation was complicated by the demand for independence in Katanga, the wealthiest province, and in Kasai as well; and by the inter-party bickering which reflects the cold war. A parliamentary government was finally established in August, 1961, its forty ministers encompassing almost all shades of political factionalism.

HISTORY AND GOVERNMENT. The first thorough exploration of the (Belgian) Congo was sponsored by King Leopold II of Belgium. In 1885 he was recognized by the great powers as personal sovereign and proprietor of the Congo Free State, as it was then called. Four years later he turned his rights over to Belgium. After World War II, as independence movements spread through Africa, unrest in this area brought attempts at reform by Belgium. However, riots in Leopoldville beginning in January, 1959, led to a timetable for granting self-government which came to an abrupt end when violent outbreaks caused Belgium to withdraw.

ECONOMIC CONDITIONS. The mineral-rich Congo (not to be confused with the former French Congo colony, which also calls itself the Republic of the Congo) is one of the world's most important sources of uranium. It also is a source of copper (40 per cent of its exports), tin, diamonds (mainly industrial), gold, cobalt and zinc. In 1958, exports amounted to 19.1 billion francs, imports to 15.1 billion.

# Costa Rica (Republic)
## (República de Costa Rica)

Area: 19,653 square miles.
Population (est. 1960): 1,173,000 (1950: white and mestizo, 97.6%; Negro, 1.9%; Indian, .4%; Asiatic, .1%).
Density per square mile: 59.7.
President: Mario Echandi Jiménez.
Principal city (est. 1959): San José, 106,324 (capital and only large city).
Monetary unit: Colón.
Language: Spanish.
Religion: Roman Catholic (state).

### STATUS IN THE WORLD TODAY

Costa Rica, which has always claimed that it was the only Central American nation which spent more on education than it did on its army, has had a long tradition of democracy. It has generally chosen its chief executives by elections instead of coups d'etat and has usually been ruled by constitutional governments instead of military juntas or dictators. It is a country of predominantly small farmers producing excellent coffee for export and food crops largely for local consumption.

### MAJOR POLITICAL PARTIES

National Liberation party (20 seats in Legislative Assembly), led by Francisco Orlich; National Union party (11 seats), led by President Mario Echandi Jiménez; National Republican party (10 seats), led by Dr. Rafael Angel Calderón Guardia.

HISTORY AND GOVERNMENT. Costa Rica, discovered and probably named by Columbus in 1502, proclaimed its independence in 1821. It was part of a federation of Central American states until 1848, when the Republic of Costa Rica was established. A military dictatorship by Tomas Guardia was in effect most of the time from 1870 to 1882, but then constitutional government prevailed except for a brief period, 1917–1919.

Aside from boundary disputes with Nicaragua and Panama, Costa Rica's modern history was comparatively tranquil until 1948. A disputed presidential election caused internal disturbances which ended with the 1949 elections and a new constitution.

Under the 1949 Constitution the President and one-house Congress of 45 members are elected for terms of 4 years.

The army was abolished in 1950. There is a police force of 1,000 and 700 coast guardsmen.

ECONOMIC CONDITIONS. Coffee (1959–60: 905,000 bags), bananas, abacá, fiber, and cacao are the basic agricultural products.

Leading customers in 1959 were the U.S. (41%), West Germany (24%), and the Netherlands (4%); leading suppliers, the U.S. (40%), West Germany (10%), Japan (6%), and Britain (6%). Leading exports were coffee (51%), bananas (28%), and cacao (9%); imports included textiles, machinery, vehicles. and petroleum products.

NATURAL FEATURES AND RESOURCES. Most of Costa Rica is tableland, from 3,000 to 6,000 feet above sea level. Cocos Island (10 sq. mi.), about 300 miles off the Pacific Coast, is under Costa Rican sovereignty; although it is mostly tropical jungle, it is of potential strategic importance in the defenses of the Panama Canal.

The mountain slopes yield such forest products as balsa, cedar, dyewood, mahogany and rosewood.

## Cuba (Republic)
### (República de Cuba)

**Area:** 44,218 square miles.
**Population** (est. 1960): 6,743,000 (white, 72.8%; mulatto, 14.5%; Negro, 12.4%; Asiatic, .3%).
**Density per square mile:** 152.5.
**President:** Osvaldo Dorticos Torrado.
**Premier:** Fidel Castro.
**Principal cities** (census 1953): Havana, 785,455 (capital, industrial center); Mariano, 219,278 (Havana suburb); Santiago de Cuba, 163,237 (seaport, mining); Camagüey, 110,388 (cattle, sugar); Santa Clara, 77,398 (tobacco).
**Monetary unit:** Peso.
**Language:** Spanish.
**Religion:** Roman Catholic.

### STATUS IN THE WORLD TODAY

Cuba, under the leadership of Fidel Castro, has become the first and only open adherent to the Soviet orbit in the Western Hemisphere. The military dictatorship of President Batista, which the Castro forces overthrew on Jan. 1, 1959, under the guise of bringing democracy to the island republic, has been replaced by another dictatorship. Congress has been dissolved. There have been no elections, and Castro rules by decree. Politically and economically, Cuba has aligned itself completely with the Red bloc, with the customary attacks on United States "capitalist imperialism."

The first step which brought Castro into conflict with the United States was the confiscation of American sugar and cattle lands in a land-reform program. The owners were not compensated, although they had been promised payment in the form of twenty-year government bonds, which they did not consider just compensation. The land which was then given to peasants in "co-operatives" appeared to have been distributed as government-owned, collective farms.

Unable to continue its purchases of crude oil because its economic policies had caused depletion of its dollar exchange, Cuba signed an agreement with the U.S.S.R. to buy Russian oil. Foreign refineries which refused to handle the Russian crude were then also confiscated. The United States was finally forced to retaliate by cutting the sugar quota, under which Cuban sugar was purchased at a price well above the world market. Castro then began seizing virtually every American property of any importance in Cuba. Russia agreed to purchase the excess sugar—but probably only at world market prices. The United States finally broke off diplomatic relations on Jan. 3, 1961.

The pro-Communist policy of the new régime disenchanted a great many Castro supporters who had thought they were fighting for democracy. His first hand-picked President, Dr. Manuel Urrutia, resigned after assailing communism. Many other officials and private citizens fled the country. Nor did Castro's actions endear him with other Latin American nations, where he had counted on sympathetic support. His attempts to obtain official hemispheric denunciation of "economic aggression" by the U.S. failed completely.

On April 17, 1961, some 1,200 Cuban exiles attempted an invasion of Cuba. They had been trained by the United States and their action had been approved by it. But they were given no aerial cover; Castro's quick action blocked an anticipated uprising in Cuba proper planned to coincide with the invasion, and the attack was a fiasco.

A tragic aftermath of the invasion was Castro's offer to exchange the prisoners he had captured for agricultural tractors. The exchange came to naught when he increased his demands, which were denounced as "blackmail" and "inhuman," and were compared with Nazi methods.

HISTORY. The history of Cuba, largest of the many Caribbean islands, began for white men with discovery by Columbus on his first voyage in 1492. It was a Spanish colony until 1898, except for brief British occupancy in 1762–63. Open war raged between Cuban rebels and Spanish troops from 1867 to 1878. Fighting broke out again in 1895, and when the United States threatened to intervene, Spain felt its national dignity had been wounded. Strained relations between Spain and the U.S. led to war when the U.S. battleship *Maine* was blown up in Havana harbor in February, 1898. At the end of the brief Spanish-American War, Spain gave up Cuba.

Until creation of the Cuban republic in 1902, the island was ruled by United States military authorities. For the first thirty-two years of the republic's life, the United States held the right to intervene in any crisis—a right which was invoked during insurrections which occurred in 1906, 1912 and 1917.

ECONOMIC CONDITIONS. Half of the employed are engaged in agriculture, which normally accounts for more than 90 per cent of the exports. About two-thirds of the cultivated area is devoted to sugar cane. Other important crops are tobacco, coffee, cacao, fruits, vegetables, henequen, corn, pineapples, and rice.

Manufactured products include sugar, (1959–60: 5,688,859 tons), molasses, syrup, brandy, rum, alcohol, cigars, cigarettes, cigar boxes, sponges, cement, cordage, salt, dressed hides, dairy products, and canned goods. The leading industry is the processing of sugar cane and its products.

Leading exports in 1959 were sugar (76%), tobacco and products (8%), and molasses (3%). Leading customers were the U.S. (74%), Japan (6%), and Britain (5%); leading suppliers, the U.S. (72%), Japan (6%), Britain (3%), Canada (2%), Spain (2%), and India (2%).

NATURAL FEATURES AND RESOURCES. Long, narrow Cuba has mountainous areas in the southeast, central area, and west, but the rest of the country is flat or rolling.

Rich mineral beds, mostly in the eastern province of Oriente, include iron, copper, manganese, chromium and nickel. Iron ore reserves are 90 per cent held by U.S. steel interests. Virtually all mineral exports go to the United States; they include nickel, copper ore, and manganese ore.

# Czechoslovakia (Republic)
## (Ceskoslovenská Republika)

Area: 49,366 square miles.
Population (est. 1960): 13,649,000 (1949: Czech, 67.0%; Slovak, 23.7% German, 3.2%; Magyar, 3.2%; Polish, Jewish and others, 2.9%).
Density per square mile: 276.5.
President: Antonin Novotny.

Premier: Viliam Siroky.
Principal cities (est. 1959): Prague (Praha), 987,865 (capital, industrial center): Brünn (Brno), 312,330 (textiles); Bratislava, 256,700 (Danube port); Ostrava (Moravska Ostrava), 231,698 (iron and steel products); Pilsen (Plzen), 136,854 (Skoda steel works).
Monetary unit: Koruna.
Languages: Czech (67%), Slovak (25%), German (4%), Hungarian, Ukrainian, Polish.
Religions (est. 1947): Roman Catholic, 77%; Czechoslovak Church, 8%; Protestant, 7%; Greek Orthodox, .5%; Jewish, .5%; others and no confession, 7%.

## STATUS IN THE WORLD TODAY

Economically, Czechoslovakia is the most important satellite the Soviet Union has, since, with the possible exception of East Germany, it was the most highly industrialized nation taken over by the Communists in the wake of World War II. Agriculturally, it is also important in the Soviet scheme of things because, next to Bulgaria, it has the highest percentage of arable land and farm families organized in collectives. Even so, in the process of postwar industrialization it became an importer of foodstuffs and depends upon the Soviet Union for raw materials to keep its industries going. In return it is a chief supplier to the U.S.S.R. of steel, iron, and engineering products, shoes, textiles, and, of course, armaments.

Outwardly, Czechoslovakia is under the firm control of the Communist party. Its members toe the Moscow line faithfully. Many Czechs, whether Communist or not, still hold a measure of resentment against the West for having let them down in 1938 at Munich and are uneasy over the unlikely possibility that some or all of the 2,500,000 Sudeten Germans expelled after World War II might return. But underneath the serene surface, leaders of the Communist party have noted the following trends: a lack of interest among the youth and the workers in identifying themselves with communism; "unhealthy manifestations" among the workers, such as a tendency to drift into administrative positions as against jobs at the bench and success in extracting economic concessions from the authorities in terms of wages and fringe benefits. One factor is the promotion of workers to take the place of remnants of the middle class who survived in some managerial positions and are systematically moved to production jobs.

One problem inherited from prewar times which the Communists have tried, unsuccessfully, to solve is that of relations between the Czechs and Slovaks. They have invested heavily in Slovakia, which is primarily agricultural, to reduce the inequalities between its industrial development and that of the Czech lands. Although they have established a special provincial executive and a provincial assembly, the supremacy of the central Prague government is manifest and there is abundant evidence of Slovak "separatist" aspirations. Divergent attitudes toward religion also cause conflict.

---

HISTORY AND GOVERNMENT. It was probably about the fifth century A.D. that the ancestors of the Czechs and Slovaks settled in the region of modern Czechoslovakia. Slovakia passed under Magyar domination, but the Czechs founded the kingdom of Bohemia, which was among the most powerful in Europe for centuries. German encroachment began in the twelfth century and was furthered by the election in 1526 of a Hapsburg as Bohemian King. After the Czechs rebelled in 1618 and were defeated at the Battle of White Mountain in 1620, they were ruled for the next 300 years by the Hapsburgs as part of the Empire of Austria. In World War I, Czech and Slovak patriots, notably Thomas G. Masaryk and Milan Stefanik, went abroad to promote support for Czech-Slovak independence, while Czechoslovak legions fought against the Central Powers. On Oct. 28, 1918, Czechoslovakia proclaimed itself a republic; shortly thereafter Masaryk was unanimously elected first President.

Between World Wars I and II, Czechoslovakia supported the League of Nations, formed the Little Entente with Yugoslavia and Rumania, and co-operated closely with France. President Masaryk was succeeded by Dr. Eduard Beneš in 1935.

Meanwhile, Czechoslovakia's German minority, led by Konrad Henlein, began demanding autonomy.

At the Munich conference on Sept. 30, 1938, France and Britain agreed that the Nazis could take the Czech Sudetenland on the German border. Dr. Beneš resigned on October 5, and Czechoslovakia became a federal union in the German orbit. The Poles, meantime, seized Czechoslovakia's Teschen area, and Hungary had taken areas in Slovakia and Ruthenia. In March, 1939, the Nazis set up Slovakia as a puppet state, declared Bohemia and Moravia to be Nazi protectorates, and gave Hungary the remainder of Ruthenia. Both Slovakia and Bohemia-Moravia were occupied by German troops. Beneš organized a government-in-exile in London in 1940.

Soon after the government returned to Czechoslovakia in April 1945, Ruthenia, the easternmost province, was ceded to Russia. On July 3, 1946, Communist Klement Gottwald formed a six-party coalition Cabinet. Amid increasing pressure

from Moscow, Gottwald's Cabinet remained in office until a bloodless coup d'état of Feb. 23-25, 1948, when the Communists seized complete control. President Beneš resigned June 7 following parliamentary elections in which the Communists and their allies were unopposed. Parliament then elected Gottwald to the presidency.

Czechoslovakia's Soviet-type Constitution makes the 300-member unicameral Parliament the supreme organ of the state. The government is headed by the President, elected by Parliament for a seven-year term. The Prime Minister and his Cabinet are appointed by the President but responsible to Parliament.

ECONOMIC CONDITIONS. Nationalization of all enterprises with more than fifty employees as well as concerns of any size operating in key industries was completed between 1945 and 1948. Distribution of large estates had already been accomplished by the 1919 Land Reform Law. Total collectivization of agriculture was the professed aim of the Communist regime.

Sugar beets, wheat, corn, and high-grade barley and hops for beer brewing are cultivated in the low-lying areas. In more elevated regions, the cultivation of potatoes, rye, and oats predominates. Higher lands are also used for growing fodder crops or for grazing. In 1958 there were 4,091,000 cattle, 889,000 sheep, and 5,435,-000 hogs.

Abundance of coal and presence of iron ore give the country a big metallurgical industry. The Skoda steel works at Pilsen are among the largest in Europe.

Other industries are glass, porcelain, and pottery making, while large forest areas provide raw material for the timber, paper, and cellulose industries. Also highly developed are the textile industries, including cotton, wool, flax, and jute production, and the shoe industry. The famous Bat'a shoe factories are at Zlin.

Foreign trade is a state monopoly managed by government corporations.

NATURAL FEATURES AND RESOURCES. Czechoslovakia lies athwart the great central-European watershed between the Baltic, Black, and North Seas. Mountains form several of its boundaries. Many of the valleys are made fertile by the Danube, Elbe, and Vltava (Moldau) rivers and their tributaries.

Most important of Czechoslovakia's varied minerals are pit coal and lignite (53,-706,000 tons in 1959), with the principal coal fields in the Ostrava-Karvinná area, connected with the Polish fields of Upper Silesia.

Production of iron ore in 1959 was about

2,968,000 tons; much ore is imported to meet the demands of Czechoslovakia's flourishing iron and steel industry. Excellent porcelain raw materials, particularly kaolin, are obtained in western Bohemia and southern Moravia. Other minerals are antimony, gold, magnesite, oil, uranium, silver, and zinc.

# Denmark (Kingdom)
## (Kongeriget Danmark)

**Area:** 16,619 square miles.
**Population (est. 1959):** 4,547,000 (almost entirely Danish).
**Density per square mile:** 273.6.
**Sovereign:** King Frederick IX.
**Prime Minister:** Viggo Kampmann.
**Principal cities (est. 1958):** Copenhagen, including suburbs, 942,058 (capital); Arhus, 118,205 (shipbuilding); Odense, 109,136 (meat, dairy products); Alborg, 85,318 (seaport).
**Monetary unit:** Krone.
**Language:** Danish.
**Religion:** Evangelical Lutheran (state).

## STATUS IN THE WORLD TODAY

Smallest of the Scandinavian countries, Denmark adheres enthusiastically and without reservation to the free world in the current cold war. It has approved the construction of seven airfields on Danish soil under the NATO program and despite its small size maintains an army of some 100,000 men, plus 25,000 in the Home Guard. A basic tenet of its foreign policy is friendship with the United States. Its economy depends primarily on the export of dairy and meat products and the earnings of its merchant marine, which is one of the largest in the world on a per capita basis.

## MAJOR POLITICAL PARTIES

Social Democratic party (76 seats in Parliament-Folketing), led by Prime Minister Viggo Kampmann; Moderate Liberal party (38 seats), led by Erik Eriksen; Conservative party (32 seats), led by Einar P. Foss.

HISTORY AND GOVERNMENT. The smallest of the three Scandinavian countries, Denmark emerged with the establishment of the Norwegian dynasty of the Ynglinger in Jutland at the end of the eighth century. It was subjugated and Christianized by the German King Henry I in 934. Canute the Great (1014–1035) conquered England in 1015. In the late twelfth and early thirteenth centuries Denmark became for a time the dominant power in Northern Europe.

Denmark supported Napoleon, for which she was punished at the Congress of Vienna in 1815 by the loss of Norway to

Sweden. In 1864 Bismarck, together with the Austrians, made war on the little country as an initial step in the unification of Germany. Denmark was neutral in World War I. In 1939 Denmark signed a ten-year pact with Hitler, but less than a year later she was invaded by the Nazi Fuehrer. King Christian X cautioned his fellow countrymen to accept the occupation, but there was widespread resistance against the Nazi occupation. In 1944 Iceland declared its independence from Denmark, thus putting an end to a union that had existed since 1380.

Denmark has been a constitutional monarchy since 1849. Legislative power is held jointly by king and parliament. The Constitution of 1953 provides for a unicameral parliament called the *Folketing*, consisting of 179 popularly elected members serving for four years. The cabinet is presided over by the king, who appoints the prime minister. Women are eligible to succeed to the throne.

RULER. Frederick IX, of the house of Schleswig - Holstein - Sonderburg - Glücksburg, born March 11, 1899, became King April 20, 1947. In 1935 he married Princess Ingrid of Sweden, by whom he has three daughters: Margrethe (heiress apparent, born April 16, 1940), Benedikte (born 1944), Anne-Marie (born 1946).

ECONOMIC CONDITIONS. Livestock in July, 1959, included 3,376,000 cattle, 6,088,000 hogs, and (1948) 24,475,000 poultry.

The largest industries are food processing and iron and metal. Others include chemicals and pharmaceuticals wood and paper, clothing, textiles, machinery, beverages, and leather.

Leading suppliers in 1959 were Great Britain (21%), West Germany (21%), other EPU and EF countries (33%), and the U.S. and Canada (10%). Chief customers were Great Britain (26%), West Germany (20%), and the U.S. and Canada (11%). Leading exports were bacon (12%) and butter (8%). Leading imports were coal, coke, petroleum and petroleum products, machinery, vehicles, and textiles.

NATURAL FEATURES AND RESOURCES. Denmark, only three miles from Sweden at the closest point, consists of the Jutland peninsula and the islands in the Baltic. The largest islands are Zealand, the site of Copenhagen; Fünen; and far to the east, Bornholm. The narrow waters to the north are called Skagerrak; and to the east, Kattegat.

The terrain of the whole kingdom is low but not flat. Its highest point is about 500 feet, and there are many lakes, ponds and short rivers. Sand dunes line the western Jutland coast almost without a break.

Mineral resources are negligible. Large

quantities of coal and coke must be imported.

The fishing industry, centered at Copenhagen but carried on also in the shallow fiords and in the deeper waters of the Baltic, North Sea and Skagerrak, is a basic part of the Danish economy.

## Outlying Territories

**FAEROE ISLANDS—Status: Autonomous part of Denmark.**
Area: 540 square miles.
Population (est. 1959): 34,000.
Capital: Thorshavn (pop. 1955: 6,067).
Governor General: Niels Elkaer-Hansen.
Principal products: cod, whale oil, cod liver oil, wool, fertilizers, skins and leather.

This group of 21 islands, lying in the North Atlantic about 200 miles northwest of the Shetland Islands, joined Denmark in 1386 and has since been part of the Danish kingdom. The islands were occupied by British troops during World War II, after the German occupation of Denmark. The principal pursuits are fishing and sheep grazing. The Faeroes have home rule under a bill enacted in 1948; they also have two representatives in the Danish Folketing.

**GREENLAND—Status: Integral part of Kingdom of Denmark.**
Area: 839,782 square miles (almost 85 per cent glacier).
Population (census 1958): 28,000 (native except for 1,269 Europeans).
Capital: Godthaab (second governor's seat, Godhavn).
Governor General: Finn Nielsen.
Foreign trade (1958): exports, 50,016,000 kr. (47.4% to Denmark); imports, 102,275,-000 kr. (88.3% from Denmark). Chief exports: cryolite (40,970 metric tons), fish and products, hides and skins.

Greenland, the world's largest island, was colonized in 985–86 by Eric the Red. Danish sovereignty, which covered only the west coast, was extended over the whole island in 1917. In 1941 the United States signed an agreement with the Danish minister in Washington, placing it under U.S. protection during World War II but maintaining Danish sovereignty. A definitive agreement for the joint defense of Greenland within the framework of NATO was signed on April 27, 1951. A large U.S. air base at Thule in the far north was completed in 1953.

Under 1953 amendments to the Danish Constitution, Greenland is part of Denmark and has two representatives in the Danish Folketing. There is a popularly elected council.

Greenland is the world's only source of natural cryolite, important in the manufacture of aluminum.

## Dominican Republic
### (República Dominicana)

Area: 18,816 square miles.
Population (est. 1960): 2,994,000 (1950: mestizo and mulatto, 60%; white, 28%; Negro, 12%).
Density per square mile: 159.1.
President: Joaquin Balaguer.
Principal cities (estimated 1960): Ciudad Trujillo, 350,847 (capital; sugar); Santiago de los Caballeros, 74,137 (tobacco); San Francisco de Macorís, 24,705 (sugar); San Pedro de Macorís, 22,787 (sugar port).
Monetary unit: Dominican peso.
Language: Spanish.
Religion: Roman Catholic.

### STATUS IN THE WORLD TODAY

The assassination on May 30, 1961, of the Dominican dictator, Generalissimo Rafael Leonidas Trujillo, does not appear to have brought that Caribbean republic any closer to democracy. His hand-picked President remains in office. His son, Rafael, Jr., has taken over command of all the armed forces. The government has pursued an ostensibly liberal policy to show that it intends to promote political and personal liberty. But an investigating committee of the Organization of American States apparently was not impressed by this show of liberalism and decided it was still too early to judge the character and purpose of the existing regime. It did not recommend lifting the diplomatic sanctions imposed by the OAS late in 1960 because of charges that the Dominican Republic had plotted to assassinate the President of Venezuela.

The country had been under the thumb of Generalissimo Trujillo since 1930. He permitted no freedom of press or speech; opposition political parties were banned. He was believed to be a silent partner in many business enterprises since none could function without his approval.

Despite the lack of freedom in his own country, Trujillo supported the Free World in the field of foreign affairs and offered land for settlement by refugees from European persecution. After the overthrow of the Batista regime in Cuba—Ciudad Trujillo sheltered both Batista and ex-President Perón, of Argentina—he apparently worried about an insurrection against his administration launched from nearby democracies.

One positive aspect of the Trujillo regime was its economic policy. It built modern housing for the workers, more schools for the children, diversified the economy, which had been formerly dependent entirely on sugar production, and stimulated moderate industrialization. Santo Domingo, the capital, was completely rebuilt after a shattering earthquake and then re-named by Trujillo for himself. New hotels have been constructed in an attempt to attract tourists.

HISTORY. The Dominican Republic (formerly San Domingo) occupies the eastern two-thirds of the island which Columbus named La Española (now Hispaniola) when he discovered it on his first voyage in 1492. The other third is occupied by the republic of Haiti. The capital, Ciudad Trujillo, founded in 1496, is the oldest white settlement in the Western Hemisphere.

The Dominican Republic was variously under Spanish, French and Haitian domination until it established its independence in 1865 and then plunged into an unstable political history. U.S. Marines occupied it from 1916 to 1924, when a new Constitution was adopted. In 1930, Rafael Leónidas Trujillo y Molina, an army general, was elected President. The Dominican Republic has a bicameral Congress with both Senators and Deputies elected by direct vote for 5 years. The President is also elected by direct vote for 5 years but he may be re-elected indefinitely and rule by decree without Congressional approval.

ECONOMIC CONDITIONS. Primarily agricultural, the country produces sugar, coffee, cacao, tobacco, bananas, rice, corn, cassava, beans, and sweet potatoes. Cattle raising is of growing importance.

Sugar refining is the only important industry, although several new industries have been established in recent years.

Leading exports in 1959 were sugar (30%), coffee (14%), and cacao (12%). Chief customers were the U.S. (58%) and Britain (24%); leading suppliers, the U.S. (51%) and West Germany (6%). The main imports are cotton goods, iron and steel products, chemicals, and machinery.

NATURAL FEATURES. Crossed from northwest to southeast by a mountain range with maximum elevations exceeding 10,000 feet, the country has fertile, well-watered land on the northeast side, where nearly two-thirds of the population lives. The southwest part is arid and with poor soil except around Ciudad Trujillo. The country has many good harbors.

# Ecuador (Republic)
## (República del Ecuador)

Area: 104,506 square miles.
Population (est. 1960): 4,298,000 (1942: mestizo, 41%; Indian, 39%; white, 10%; Negro, 5%; others, 5%).
Density per square mile: 41.1.
President: Jose M. Velasco Ibarra.
Principal cities (est. 1959): Guayaquil, 410,000 (chief port); Quito, 267,700 (capital); Cuenca, 66,800 (trading center); Ambato, 44,300 (commercial center).
Monetary unit: Sucre.
Languages: Spanish, Quéchua.
Religion: Roman Catholic.

## STATUS IN THE WORLD TODAY

Although Ecuador has rich natural resources, its economic development on a large scale has been hampered by poor communications and the geographic fact that it is cut up into five regions by ranges of the Andes mountains. World War II gave it a start toward a better economic future when the demand for war materials boosted its exports of quinine, balsa wood, rubber, oil, and kapok, but the opening up of undeveloped territory is still a big job. Its principal exports are bananas, cocoa and coffee. Construction of a steel mill may lead to exploitation of such items as copper, manganese, and oil. The country, however, has been relatively free of problems which have beset other nations—political and economic instability—and in recent years its currency has been relatively stable, while the rise in the cost of living has not been so great as in other South American countries. Loans will be necessary for any long-range economic program, since its own resources are insufficient.

HISTORY. Mostly forested and mountainous and a little larger than Colorado, Ecuador has a long history replete with the forceful rule of dictators. The Spanish under Francisco Pizarro conquered the land in 1532 by defeating the Inca Atahualpa. The first revolt against Spain occurred in 1809, but the victory was not complete until the Battle of Pichincha on May 24, 1822. Ecuador then joined Venezuela and Colombia in a confederacy founded by Simón Bolívar and known as Colombia, but withdrew amicably and became independent in 1830. The country's subsequent history has been largely one of dictatorships.

For more than a hundred years, Ecuador disputed its boundary with Peru, frequently resorting to arms. After hostilities started again in 1941, both nations submitted to mediation, and in 1944 Ecuador lost most of the disputed area. But in 1960 Ecuador repudiated the Rio de Janeiro Treaty under which a settlement had been reached, and the dispute again became a disturbing factor in hemisphere relations.

GOVERNMENT. Under the 1946 (16th) Constitution, Ecuador elects a President for four years by direct vote, and he is ineligible for further service until at least one term intervenes. The Congress is bicameral, with a Senate and Chamber of Deputies.

ECONOMIC CONDITIONS. Although agriculture is the basis of Ecuador's economy, less than 12,000,000 acres are devoted to it. Cacao, the chief crop, is grown in coastal regions and lower river valleys. The plateaus and mountain valleys are used for grazing and dairying, and raising cereals and potatoes. After textiles, one of Ecuador's main industries is the manufacture of Panama hats, made of Toquilla straw.

Leading exports in 1958 were bananas (64%), coffee (12%), and cacao (15%). Leading customers were the U.S. (60%), West Germany (11%), and Colombia (5%); leading suppliers, the U.S. (50%), West Germany (11%), and Belgium (6%).

NATURAL FEATURES AND RESOURCES. Two high and parallel ranges of the Andes, traversing Ecuador from north to south, are topped by tall volcanic peaks.

Ecuador produces gold, silver, copper, lead, and petroleum. It is the world's chief source of light, strong balsa wood.

---

# Egypt (Province of U.A.R.)

## (Misr)

> Egypt and Syria united in February, 1958, to form the United Arab Republic.

Area: 386,100 square miles.
Population (est. 1959): 25,365,000 (1944: Egyptian, 95.4%; Arabian, 1.7%; Greek, .6%; others, 2.3%).
Density per square mile: 65.7.
President: Gamal Abdel Nasser.
Principal cities (est. 1959): Cairo, 3,035,-000 (capital); Alexandria, 1,416,000 (chief port); Port Said, 226,000 (Suez Canal terminus); Tanta, 175,400 (railroad center, Nile delta).
Monetary unit: Egyptian pound (£E).
Language: Arabic.
Religions: Moslem, 91%; Christian (mostly Copt and Greek Orthodox), 8%; others, 1%.

### STATUS IN THE WORLD TODAY

The primary objective of President Nasser since he took over the regime in Egypt, and later included Syria in the United Arab Republic, has been to become the leader of all Arab states in opposition to the Western nations, which he considers colonial and imperialist. His fortunes have risen and fallen in this respect in direct proportion to his diplomatic successes and failures. When he nationalized the Suez Canal, he became a hero in the Arab world because he had presented Great Britain and France with a *fait accompli* about which they could do nothing without being branded aggressors. Yet when they did intervene in 1956, at the time of Israel's attack against Egypt, the speed with which the Israeli armed forces overwhelmed Egypt's army in the Sinai peninsula dealt a severe blow to Nasser's military prestige. His interference in the internal affairs of other Arab states in trying to make himself the head of a Pan-Arab movement brought him in conflict with other Arab leaders. Jordan and Lebanon reacted violently against Radio Cairo's propaganda. Saudi Arabia was less than happy as its oil royalties dropped because Egyptian sabotage of the Suez Canal blocked oil shipments to Europe. Tunisia broke off diplomatic relations because of Egypt's interference. The Sudan stressed its independence after more than half a century of being governed jointly by Egypt and Great Britain.

Relations with these other Arab states began to improve, however, with the increase of Communist influence in the Middle East. Nasser had assigned 80 per cent of Egypt's cotton crop to the Soviet bloc in return for armaments and help in constructing the Aswan High Dam. But the U.S.S.R. was dumping Egyptian cotton on the world market at prices below those charged by Egypt, and Egyptian importers were becoming irritated at the poor quality of goods they were receiving from behind the Iron Curtain. Egypt was willing to accept Soviet aid, but it was definitely annoyed at any Communist attempts to share in any Arab government, a fact which led Nasser to denounce Arab Communists and to accuse the Soviet Union of working against true Arab nationalism in Iraq. Cairo is now soft-pedaling its propaganda broadcasts, which formerly were aimed at inciting pro-Nasser agitation against established regimes, and is working at mending its political fences in the Arab world. It is still willing to accept economic aid from the Soviet Union, especially in connection with construction of the Aswan Dam, but is increasingly aware of the danger of Communist political activity. It still has one thing in common with the other Arab states—its hatred of Israel—on which to build its Pan-Arab hegemony.

In September, 1959, the Soviet Union finally signed a contract for technical assistance and equipment for the first stage of the dam.

---

HISTORY AND GOVERNMENT. Egyptian history dates back to about 4000 B.C., when the kingdoms of upper and lower Egypt, already highly civilized, were united. Egypt's "Golden Age" coincided with the eighteenth and nineteenth dynasties (sixteenth to thirteenth centuries B.C.), during which the empire was established. Persia conquered Egypt in 525 B.C.; Alexander the Great subdued it in 332 B.C., and then the dynasty of the Ptolemies ruled the land until 30 B.C., when Cleopatra, last of the line, committed suicide and Egypt became a Roman province. From 641 to 1517 the Arab Caliphs ruled Egypt, and then the Turks took it and made it part of their Ottoman Empire. Napoleon's armies occupied the country from 1798 to 1801. In 1805, Mohammed Ali, leader of a band of Albanian soldiers, became Pasha of Egypt. After completion of the Suez Canal in 1869, both the French and British took increasing interest in Egypt.

British troops occupied Egypt in 1882, and British resident agents became its actual administrators, though it remained under nominal Turkish sovereignty. On December 18, 1914, this fiction was ended and Egypt became a protectorate of Great Britain.

Pressure by Egyptian nationalists forced Britain to declare Egypt an independent, sovereign state on Feb. 28, 1922, although the British reserved rights for the protection of the Suez Canal and the defense of Egypt. On Aug. 26, 1936, by an Anglo-Egyptian treaty of alliance, all British troops and officials were to be withdrawn, except from the Suez Canal zone. When World War II started, Egypt remained neutral. British imperial troops finally ended the Nazi threat to Suez in 1942 in the battle of El Alamein, which took place west of Alexandria.

In Oct., 1951, Egypt abrogated the 1936 treaty and the 1899 Anglo-Egyptian condominium of the Sudan. (See Sudan.) Rioting and attacks on British troops in the Suez Canal zone followed, reaching a climax in Jan., 1952. The army, led by Gen. Mohammed Naguib, seized power on July 23, 1952. On July 26, King Farouk abdicated in favor of his infant son. Naguib took over the premiership on Sept. 7, 1952, and promised far-reaching reforms. The monarchy was abolished and a republic proclaimed on June 18, 1953, with Naguib holding the posts of both provisional President and Premier. He relinquished the latter post on April 18, 1954, to Gamal Abdel Nasser, leader of the ruling military junta. Naguib was deposed by the Cabinet and junta on Nov. 14, 1954.

Nasser was confirmed as President in a popular referendum on June 23, 1956. According to the provisional Constitution of the United Arab Republic announced by Nasser in February, 1958, legislative power is vested in a "Council of the Nation" composed of members chosen by decree of the President of the United Arab Republic. Executive power is vested in the President of the United Arab Republic, who is assisted by Ministers appointed by him and responsible to him. Political parties have been abolished by Nasser for an indefinite period. In addition to the organs set up for joint jurisdiction over Egypt and Syria, certain executive organs were created to deal separately with these two provinces of the U.A.R. As of October 7, 1958, Egypt has a 15-member Executive Council appointed by and responsible to the President of the U.A.R.

SOCIAL AND ECONOMIC CONDITIONS. The majority of the people are Sunni Moslems. The Christians are mainly Copts, with an admixture of Armenian, Syrian, and Maronite sects. The population divides generally into fellahin (peasantry) and townspeople of the same blood, the Bedouin, or nomad, Arabs of the desert, and the Berbers, who occupy the Nile valley between Aswan and Dongola. The foreigners are chiefly Greeks (whose main center is Alexandria), French, British and Italians. The density of population in the small inhabited area in the Nile valley and delta (about 13,600 sq. mi.) is far greater than that of either the Netherlands or Belgium.

Agriculture is the chief industry, engaging more than half the population. Only about 3.5 per cent of the total area is arable, and only about 6,000,000 acres are actually under cultivation, almost entirely in the Nile valley and delta. More than half the cultivated area comprises farms of less than 20 acres. Irrigation is indispensable to agriculture; the Aswan reservoir above the first cataract of the Nile holds up to 5,500,000,000 cubic meters of water and the reservoir of Gebel Aulia, in the Sudan, 2,000,000,000 cubic meters. In the delta and in middle Egypt, where perennial or canal irrigation is possible, two or three crops a year can be grown. The chief cash crop is cotton, of which Egypt is one of the world's leading producers (1959: 455,000 metric tons).

Industry includes sugar refining, cotton ginning, cement manufacture, milling and pottery, soap and perfume making. The Sugar Company of Egypt holds a monopoly on the sugar refining industry.

In 1959, Egypt's chief customers were the Soviet area (44%), EPU and EF countries (21%), and the sterling area (9%); leading suppliers, the Soviet area (26%), the U.S. and Canada (13%), the sterling area (12%), EPU and EF countries (11%), West Germany (13%), and Italy (6%). Leading exports were raw cotton (71%) and rice (10%).

Imports included wheat, petroleum, fertilizers, iron and steel products, textiles, and machinery and vehicles.

Navigable throughout its course in Egypt, the Nile is used largely as a means of cheap transport for heavy goods. The principal port is Alexandria.

NATURAL FEATURES AND RESOURCES. Egypt, at the northeast corner of Africa, is a very rough square, with the historic

Nile flowing northward through its eastern third. On either side of the Nile valley are desert plateaus, spotted with oases. In the north, toward the Mediterranean, plateaus are low, while south of Cairo they rise to a maximum of 1,015 feet above sea level. At the head of the Red Sea, at the northeast corner of Egypt, is the triangular Sinai peninsula, between the Suez Canal and Israel.

The Nile delta starts 100 miles south of the Mediterranean and fans out to a sea front of 155 miles between Alexandria and Port Said. From Cairo north, the Nile branches into many streams, the principal of which are the Damietta and the Rosetta, joined by a network of canals.

The most important minerals are manganese ore, phosphate, and petroleum. Gold, iron ochres, nickel, sodium carbonate, sulfate talc, and tungsten also are mined.

Except for a narrow belt on the Mediterranean, Egypt lies in an almost rainless area, in which high daytime temperatures fall quickly at night.

SUEZ CANAL. The Suez Canal, in Egyptian territory between the Arabian Desert and the Sinai peninsula, is an artificial waterway about 100 miles long between Port Said on the Mediterranean and Suez on the Red Sea. Construction work, directed by the French engineer Ferdinand de Lesseps, was begun April 25, 1859, and the canal was opened Nov. 17, 1869. The cost was 432,807,882 francs. The concession is held by an Egyptian joint stock company, *Compagnie Universelle du Canal Maritime de Suez*, in which the British government holds 353,504 out of a total of 800,000 shares. The concession was to expire Nov. 17, 1968, but the company was nationalized July 26, 1956, by unilateral action of the Egyptian government. As a result of hostilities the canal was blocked between Nov., 1956, and March, 1957. In July, 1958, an agreement was finally signed in Geneva between the United Arab Republic and the shareholders of the former Suez Canal Company. Compensation was arranged for the period of twelve years which was still to have elapsed between 1956 and the end of the Company's 99-year concession in 1968. In the last few years, Nasser has been seizing or delaying cargoes coming from or going to Israel on the grounds that the U.A.R. still considers itself in a state of war with Israel.

## Estonia

**Area:** 17,375 square miles.
**Population** (est. 1959): 1,196,000 (1940: Estonians, 88%; Russians, 9%; Germans [Balts], 1%; others, 2%).
**Density per square mile:** 63.2.
**Principal cities** (est. 1959): Tallinn, 280,-000 (capital); Tartu, 74,000 (university town).
**Language:** Estonian (Finno-Ugrian).
**Religions:** Lutheran, 78%; Greek Orthodox, 19%; others, 3%.

HISTORY AND GOVERNMENT. Born out of World War I, this small Baltic state enjoyed two short decades of independence before it was absorbed again by its powerful neighbor, Russia. In the thirteenth century, the Estonians had been conquered by the Teutonic Knights of Germany, who reduced them to serfdom. In 1521, the Swedes took over, and the power of the German (Balt) landowning class was curbed somewhat. But after 1721, when Russia succeeded Sweden as the ruling power, the Estonians were subjected to a double bondage—the Balts and the tsarist officials. The oppression lasted until the closing months of World War I, when Estonia finally achieved independence.

Shortly after the start of World War II, the nation was occupied by Russian troops and was incorporated as the sixteenth republic of the U.S.S.R. in 1940. Germany occupied the nation from 1941 to 1944, when it was retaken by the Russians. Most of the nations of the world, including the United States and Great Britain, have not recognized the Soviet incorporation of Estonia.

## Ethiopia (Kingdom)
### (Abyssinia)

**Area:** 457,267 square miles.
**Population** (est. 1959): 21,800,000 (Abyssinian [Amhara], 20%; Galla, 50%; others, 30%).
**Density per square mile:** 47.6.
**Ruler:** Emperor Haile Selassie I.
**Prime Minister:** (Post vacant.)
**Principal cities** (est. 1956): Addis Ababa, 400,000 (capital); Asmara, 123,083 (capital, Eritrea); Dessié, 50,000 (grain center); Harar, 40,000 (coffee); Diré Dawa, 30,000 (railway workshops).
**Monetary unit:** Ethiopian paper dollar.
**Languages:** Amharic, Arabic.
**Religions:** Copt (Christian), Moslem.

### STATUS IN THE WORLD TODAY

Isolated for many centuries from the rest of the world by a belt of mountains, Ethiopia is struggling to modernize itself and to catch up with the twentieth century economically. Pro-Western in its foreign policy, it is receiving technical and monetary assistance from many sources: the World Bank, the United Nations, the United States Point Four program, and Belgian, Swiss, French, and even Russian advisers. Despite active propaganda by a relatively large Soviet diplomatic delegation in Addis Ababa, American military communications installations have been erected in the country.

Before World War II, Ethiopia's principal link with the outside world was the railroad to Djibouti in French Somaliland. Since 1952, the former Italian colony of Eritrea has been federated with Ethiopia, giving it another outlet to the sea through the port of Massaua. Trade has increased and exploration for mineral resources has been speeded up.

---

**HISTORY AND GOVERNMENT.** The ancient empire of Ethiopia attained its independence long before the creation of any of the modern states of Africa. Present-day Ethiopia became a sovereign state as an outgrowth of the consolidation of a number of former kingdoms which owed allegiance to the Ethiopian emperor, the King of Kings. Most of these old kingdoms (Shoa, Tigri, Gojjam, and others) are to-day provinces of Ethiopia.

The Ethiopian kingdom is one of the few African countries which have a recorded history. Men have migrated here from Asia Minor for well over two thousand years. The chief race today is the Amhara, numbering 2,000,000. They were converted to Christianity by the Egyptian Coptic Christians. Along with the Amharic people, there have come to Ethiopia over the centuries Greeks, Jews, Arabs, and Indians, so that today the kingdom is a mixture of peoples speaking over seventy different languages.

The fact that the ruling Amharic group have had to retain control over the country in the face of frequent tribal resistance accounts in part for some of the authoritarian aspects of Ethiopian government today. The kingdom remains essentially feudal in nature. At the top is the Emperor, Haile Selassie I (born 1891, crowned Emperor 1930), who traces his ancestry to the Queen of Sheba and to Menelek, King Solomon's first son. He retains virtually full governmental powers in his own hands, appointing the ministers who assist him and the governors who rule the outlying provinces.

In October, 1935, anxious to expand his small colonial empire, Mussolini invaded Ethiopia. Addis Ababa fell on May 5, 1936. With Italian Somaliland and Eritrea, Ethiopia became part of Italian East Africa until British and Ethiopian troops reconquered the country in 1941.

**ECONOMIC CONDITIONS.** Ethiopia is generally fertile, predominantly agricultural and pastoral, with many regions yielding two crops a year. The chief crops are maize, wheat, barley, rye, cotton, sugar cane, millet, hemp, vegetables, coffee, and teff (the common bread grain). The country's inadequate transport system, however, makes crop growing largely a local industry.

The country grazes several million cattle and many goats and sheep. Horses and mules are bred extensively as pack animals and mounts. There is little manufacturing except for small native industry, although the Italians built some industrial plants during their five-year occupation.

Chief exports in 1958 were coffee (55%), hides and skins (10%), and oil seeds (8%). Leading customers were the United States (25%), Aden (21%), and Italy (19%); leading suppliers, Italy (15%), India (14%), and the United States (13%). Major imports were cotton piece goods, machinery, sugar, and salt.

**NATURAL FEATURES AND RESOURCES.** Over its main plateau land, Ethiopia has several high mountains. The Blue Nile, or Abbai, rises in the northwest and flows in a great semicircle east, south, and northwest before entering Sudan. Its chief reservoir, Lake Tana, lies in the northwestern part of the plateau.

Gold, produced from placer mines worked by natives in the south and west, is Ethiopia's main mineral. Platinum also is mined in fair commercial quantities. Other minerals are rock salt, cinnabar, copper, iron, mercury, mica, potash, and sulfur. Oil deposits are believed to exist, and all drilling rights have been sold to the Sinclair Refining Company of the United States.

**ERITREA—Status: Federated with Ethiopia.**
Area: 45,946 sq. mi.
Population (est. 1957): 1,040,404.
Capital: Asmara (population: 123,083).
Sovereign: Haile Selassie I.
Chief Executive: Fitaurari Asfaha Woldemikael.
Agricultural products: coffee, barley, tobacco, sesame, hides, skins.
Minerals: gold, salt, potassium salts.
Sea product: pearls.

The first Italian inroad into Eritrea came in 1870, when the port of Assab and adjacent territory were bought from a native sultan; with British approval, Italian troops occupied Massaua in 1885. By a decree of Jan. 1, 1890, Italian possessions along the Red Sea were united into the colony of Eritrea.

As an autonomous, self-governing area, Eritrea has its own elected assembly which selects the chief executive. It is also represented in the Ethiopian Parliament. Matters reserved to the Ethiopian government include defense, foreign affairs, foreign trade, finance, communications.

The principal native elements are the Ethiopians and Tigrés, who have close ethnic, linguistic, and religious ties with peoples in neighboring Ethiopia. Irrigation is essential in the coastal plains, and agriculture is practiced largely on the interior plateau (average elevation: 6,500 ft.).

# Finland (Republic)
## (Suomen Tasavalta)

Area: 130,120 square miles.
Population (est. 1960): 4,457,000 (Finnish, 90%; Swedish, 10%).
Density per square mile: 34.3.
President: Urho Kekkonen.
Premier: Martti Miettunen.
Principal cities (est. Jan. 1, 1958): Helsinki, 445,190 (capital); Tampere, 121,422 (textiles, paper); Turku (Abo), 120,095 (seaport, shipbuilding); Lahti, 62,500 (glass, lumber); Oulu, 49,300 (seaport, shipbuilding).
Monetary unit: Markka (FM).
Languages: Finnish, Swedish.
Religions (1949): Evangelical Lutheran, 95.4%, Greek Orthodox, 2%; others, 2.6%.

## STATUS IN THE WORLD TODAY

Finland's foreign policy since the end of World War II has had to take into account two fundamentally conflicting factors: the fact that public opinion in this democracy is oriented toward the free world and especially toward friendship with the United States; and the harsh geographic reality that it is a neighbor of the U.S.S.R. and must trade with the Soviets as a matter of economic necessity. Yet, despite tricky propaganda campaigns and economic pressure, the Communists have not succeeded in electing enough representatives in the government to give the Kremlin any sort of voice in domestic affairs. It has, however, been successful in obtaining trade pacts and a treaty of friendship and mutual assistance.

Despite the loss of its principal industrial area to Soviet Russia, Finland has managed to expand industry, to balance its budget, and to keep its currency stable. It occupies a special place of esteem in the United States because it was the only nation after World War I which continued to make semi-annual payments on its debts when larger countries were defaulting on their war obligations.

## MAJOR POLITICAL PARTIES

Social Democrats (50 seats in Parliament), led by V. Tanner; Democratic Union (Communists and Socialist Union party) (50 seats), led by H. Kuusinen; Agrarian Union (48 seats), led by Vieno J. Sukselainen.

HISTORY AND GOVERNMENT. At the end of the seventh century the Finns, probably of Mongolian origin, came to Finland from their Volga settlements. Their repeated raids on the Scandinavian coast impelled Eric IX, the Swedish king, to conquer the country in 1157 and bring it into contact with Western Christendom. By 1809 the whole of Finland was conquered by Alexander I of Russia, who set up Finland as a Grand Duchy.

The first period of Russification (1899–1905) resulted in a lessening of the powers of the Finnish Diet. The Russian language was made official, and the Finnish military system was superseded by the Russian. The pace of Russification was intensified from 1908 to 1914. When Russian control was weakened as a consequence of the March Revolution of 1917, the Finnish Diet on July 20, 1917, proclaimed Finland's independence, which became complete on December 6, 1917.

When its territorial demands on Finland were rejected, the Soviet Union attacked Finland on November 30, 1939. The Finns made an amazing stand of three months. Finland finally capitulated, ceding 16,000 square miles to the U.S.S.R. Under German pressure the Finns joined the Nazis against Russia in 1941, but were defeated again, and ceded the Petsamo area to Soviet Russia.

The President of the Republic of Finland, chosen for six years by the Electoral College of 300 members, appoints the Cabinet. The single-chambered Diet, the *Eduskunta*, consists of 200 members popularly elected for three-year terms by proportional representation.

ECONOMIC CONDITIONS. The chief crops are oats, barley, rye, and potatoes. Grazing lands are extensive. In 1959, there were 1,965,000 cattle, 378,000 sheep, 457,000 hogs, and 170,293 reindeer.

The leading Finnish manufactures (1958) were wood and paper (about one-third the total value) food, luxury items, machinery and textiles. With the cession of the Karelian isthmus and the city of Viipuri to the U.S.S.R., Finland lost valuable manufacturing areas. Helsinki is the principal industrial center.

Chief exports in 1959 were wood and wood products (29%), paper (27%), and wood pulp (18%). Leading customers were Britain (23%), U.S.S.R. (17%), West Germany (11%), and the U.S. and Canada (6%); leading suppliers, U.S.S.R. (18%), Britain (13%), West Germany (17%), EPU and EF countries (29%), and the U.S. and Canada (6%).

NATURAL FEATURES AND RESOURCES. Finland stretches 700 miles from the Gulf of Finland on the south to Soviet Petsamo, north of the Arctic Circle. Off the southwest coast are the Åland Islands (approximately 300), controlling the entrance to the Gulf of Bothnia. Finland has more than 60,000 lakes. Of the few rivers, only the Oulu (Uleå) is navigable to any important extent.

Finland has no coal or oil, and many of its ore deposits are remote from transportation. Finland's sulfide ore is 4 per cent copper, 26 per cent sulfur and 27 per cent iron, with some zinc, cobalt, gold, and silver. Limestone, soapstone and red granite deposits are extensive, and uranium deposits are believed to exist. Wood and peat are the only natural fuels.

More than a third of Finland is covered with high-quality timber, the nation's richest natural resource.

The Swedish-populated Åland Islands (581 sq. mi.) have an autonomous status under a law passed in 1951.

# THE FRENCH COMMUNITY

## France (Republic)
### (République Française)

**Area:** 212,822 square miles.
**Population** (est. 1960): 45,355,000 (1954: French, 96.6%; others, 3.4%).
**Density per square mile:** 213.1.
**President:** Charles de Gaulle.
**Premier:** Michel Debré.
**Principal cities** (census 1954): Paris, 2,820,534 (capital); Marseilles, 605,577 (chief port); Lyons, 462,657 (silk, metal manufacture); Bordeaux, 250,306 (wine; seaport); Toulouse, 217,667 (tobacco; commercial center); Nice, 208,543 (resort center); Nantes, 197,915 (manufacturing).
**Monetary unit:** Franc.
**Religion** (est.): Roman Catholic, 97.5%; Protestant and others, 2.5%.

### STATUS IN THE WORLD TODAY

Under the energetic leadership of Gen. Charles de Gaulle, the newly established Fifth Republic of France appears to be making progress in restoring financial and political stability to that nation and making her a more effective partner in the association of free nations. After having lost the cream of their youth in two World Wars, the French, to whom the free world owes much of its way of life, are in no mood to accept the status of a second-class power. Under the leadership of de Gaulle they hope to recover that prestige that marked them as one of the great powers of the world.

The deepening French problem until May, 1958—political chaos, financial instability, and labor strife—caused great concern among the nations of the free world. France is indispensable to the Allies' position in Western Europe. Many constructive enterprises set into motion by the West were blocked by the continuing French crises. No single group could ever attain enough power to implement a consistent long-term policy. The inauguration of the Fifth Republic changed all that. From a parliamentary democracy France became a presidential one with a strong executive and balanced powers. The Premier is now, in effect, the President's chief executive and is largely responsible to the President instead of an unwieldy coalition of deputies in Parliament.

Creation of a strong executive has not, in itself, solved all of France's problems. A number of fiscal reforms have been initiated, but the problem of the drain on the French economy by the war in Algeria remains. There is still some labor unrest because of the high prices resulting from inflation. But the aircraft and metallurgical industries have given exports a boost, and the franc has been stabilized and revalued—one "new" franc equaling 100 former francs. France is also a key member of the European Common Market, the Coal and Steel Community and the European Atomic Energy Community.

The French desire to be considered a first-rate power has not been without its effects on military matters within NATO. Since the United States retains control over the atomic warheads of weapons sent abroad, it has had to move some of its planes to Britain and West Germany because the de Gaulle regime felt it was not compatible with French sovereignty not to have a voice in atomic matters. Then, too, partly in view of the war in Algeria, the units of the French fleet in the Mediterranean have been withdrawn from overall NATO command. Gen. de Gaulle, before assuming power, criticized both American leadership of NATO and what he asserted was the French government's slavish acceptance of it. But despite the present differences, which are relatively minor, the Allies feel that finally a stronger France will also mean a stronger NATO.

In September, 1959, Gen. de Gaulle announced that four years after the end of hostilities in Algeria, an election would be held to determine the area's future.

### MAJOR POLITICAL PARTIES

Union pour la Nouvelle République (UNR) (188 seats in National Assembly), led by Premier Michel Debré; Right Wing Independents and Peasants (IPAS) (132

# The French Community

The Constitution of the Fifth Republic of France, which was adopted by a referendum of the people on September 28, 1958, set up a Community which consisted of the French Republic and certain other States—formerly Overseas Territories of France—that voted to adopt the present Constitution and later chose the status of self-governing Republics. At the present time there are twelve such Republics. In the list below, the new Republics marked with an asterisk are associated with the French Community. The rest are members.

seats), led by Henri Bergasse and Raymond Pinchard.

---

**HISTORY AND GOVERNMENT.** France, the Gaul of ancient times, began its history as France, a separate nation, with the Treaty of Verdun (843), by which the territories roughly comprising what are today France, Germany, and Italy were divided among Charlemagne's three grandsons. Caesar conquered part of Gaul in 57–52 B.C. and the Franks overran it in the fifth century A.D. The first of the Capetians, Hugh Capet (987–996) ruled over the principality of the Île-de-France, from which the Capetian domain was gradually expanded by conquest, purchase, marriage, inheritance, and forfeiture. The task of breaking English power in France was begun by Philip II Augustus (1180–1223) and continued in a long series of conflicts called the Hundred Years' War, 1338–1453. Beginning as a feudal conflict between French kings and the English Angevin house, this strife ended as a national war, with France emerging as a modern centralized national state. The English had won at Crécy in 1346 and at Agincourt in 1415 but were defeated at Orléans in 1429 by the French under Joan of Arc.

Relics of half-overthrown medievalism still survived in eighteenth-century France. Louis XVI (1774–1792) was unable to solve the accumulated crises. The Old Regime, with its autocratic monarch and its privileged nobility, was an outworn society ready to collapse under the impact of revolution. The French Revolution, beginning in 1789, resulted from lack of intelligent government, lack of political liberty, an arbitrary system of taxation, survival of medieval abuses, economic evils, and the ideas of the intellectual reformers of the Age of Reason. It was a dramatic, bloody affair which kept France in turmoil for years.

Napoleon Bonaparte gave France a short period of glory and then the humiliation of a stunning defeat. Napoleon hardened the changes that had been brought about by the French Revolution and made some of them permanent before the forces of reaction set in; he spread revolutionary reforms to conquered German and Italian territories, nourished the growth of nationalism, and consolidated the Industrial Revolution in France.

The Congress of Vienna (1815), called to remake the map of Europe on the basis of "legitimacy" and "compensations" after the downfall of Napoleon, restored the Bourbons to the throne. Louis Philippe abdicated and fled to England at the start of the Revolution of 1848, and the Second French Republic was established.

Taking advantage of a factional split, Prince Louis Napoleon assumed control of France in the coup d'état of 1851. A year later, on December 2, 1852, he proclaimed himself Napoleon III, Emperor of the French. He founded his Second French Empire on nationalism, militarism, and imperialism. His opposition to the national unification of Germany collided head-on with Bismarck's plans. The result was the Franco-Prussian War (1870–71). Napoleon III was captured at Sedan, and the Second Empire collapsed in ruins.

Reconstruction after the Franco-Prussian War was rapid, with reorganization of the army and economic and social reforms, and a new France emerged from World War I as the dominant power on the Continent. But four years of hostile occupation and the fires of war had reduced the once-thriving area of Northeast France to ruins. The Third French Republic was plagued by political instability and economic chaos.

From 1919 on, the aim of French foreign policy was to maintain German weakness by a system of military alliances isolating Germany. The rise of Hitler and the establishment of the Nazi dictatorship meant the failure of France's foreign policy. On June 5, 1940, the mechanized Nazi troops attacked the French. As the German armies drew close to Paris, Italy declared war on France and England. The Germans marched into undefended Paris, and three days later Marshal Pétain, head of the French government then at Bordeaux, asked for an armistice. It was granted on June 22, 1940, and the French armies surrendered. Flooded with Nazi agents, France was betrayed as well as defeated. France was split into occupied and unoccupied zones. The unoccupied portion, Vichy

France, became a totalitarian state with Marshal Pétain as Chief of State.

France was liberated by the Allied armies in September, 1944. The French Committee of National Liberation, formed in Algiers in 1943, established a provisional government with General de Gaulle as President of Council. With the adoption of a new constitution on December 24, 1946, the Fourth French Republic came into existence.

The Fifth Republic was inaugurated on October 5, 1958, after approval by a popular referendum on September 28, 1958. The President of the Republic is elected for 7 years by an enlarged electoral college made up of members of Parliament, departmental and municipal counselors, representatives of the assemblies of Overseas Territories, and additional electors chosen by the mayors and municipal counselors. The President appoints the Premier and the Cabinet is responsible to Parliament. The President has the right to dissolve the National Assembly or to ask Parliament for reconsideration of a law. The Parliament consists of two Houses: the National Assembly and the Senate. The 546 members of the National Assembly of the Fifth Republic were elected in November, 1958, by direct suffrage. The Senate was elected by indirect suffrage in April and May, 1959, and includes representation from Metropolitan France and from Overseas Departments and Territories.

*Religion.* The predominant faith is Roman Catholicism, but church and state were separated in 1905. Diplomatic relations with the Vatican were resumed in 1921, and lesser church property was returned to diocesan associations in 1924.

*Population.* The people are not homogeneous, varying from section to section. During the inter-bellum period, the population remained almost static, with an increase of only 72,133 from 1931 to 1936 and a decrease of 3.3 per cent from 1936 to 1946. The period between 1946 and 1954 showed an increase of 5.6 per cent. France normally is almost self-sufficient in basic foodstuffs and leads the world in wine production.

ECONOMIC CONDITIONS. Silk culture once thrived in the lower Rhône valley, but production fell sharply between wars. Milk, butter, and cheese are important as exports. Livestock in Oct., 1959, included 18,466,000 cattle, 8,749,000 sheep, and 8,469,000 hogs.

*Industry.* Principal industrial areas are Paris, Artois, Lower Seine and Lyon; the textile industry is concentrated in the north. Leading manufactures are iron, steel, chemicals, textiles, automobiles, machinery, and beet sugar.

Principal suppliers in 1959 were the U.S.

and Canada (9%), EPU countries (33%), EPU overseas territories (25%), and Britain (4%), other sterling area (15%); leading customers, EPU countries (37%), continental EPU/EF overseas territories (32%), U.S. and Canada (9%), Britain (4%). Leading exports were metals, manufactures, textiles, and agricultural and food products.

NATURAL FEATURES AND RESOURCES. France is second in size to Russia among Europe's nations. In the Alps near the Italian and Swiss borders is France's highest point—Mont Blanc, 15,781 feet. The forest-covered Vosges Mountains are in the northeast and the Pyrenees are along the Spanish border. Except for extreme northern France, which is part of the Flanders plain, the country may be described as four river basins and a plateau. Three of the streams flow west—the Seine into the English Channel, the Loire into the Atlantic, and the Garonne into the Bay of Biscay. The Rhône flows south into the Mediterranean. For about a hundred miles, the Rhine is France's eastern border. West of the Rhône and northeast of the Garonne lies the Central Plateau, covering about 15 per cent of France's area, and rising to a maximum elevation of 6,188 feet. In the Mediterranean, about 115 miles east-south-east of Nice, is Corsica, the island of Napoleon's birth, with an area of 3,367 square miles.

*Minerals.* French coalfields, most extensive in the northeast, ordinarily supply about 70 per cent of domestic needs. Lorraine, Anjou and Normandy have valuable iron ore deposits. Provence has bauxite. Alsace has potash and oil. Limousin has kaolin, zinc, lead and tar.

*Forests and Fisheries.* France produces forest products, including resin, turpentine, timber, and nuts. The annual fish catch is among the largest in Europe.

# AFRICA

## Algeria (Part of Metropolitan France)

### (L'Algérie)

**Delegate General: Paul Delouvrier.**
**Population (est. 1959): 10,930,000.**
**Principal cities (1954 census): Algiers,\* 750,000 (capital); Oran, 274,772 (seaport); Constantine, 111,315 (trading center); Bône, 88,920 (seaport, phosphates).**
**Monetary unit: French franc.**
**Languages: Arabic, French.**
**Religions: Moslem (natives), Roman Catholic, Jewish.**
\* Estimated 1959.

### STATUS IN THE WORLD TODAY

The fight by Algerian nationalists for independence has had widespread political, diplomatic, military, and financial repercussions in France. Politically, it brought General de Gaulle to power when the Army and extremist French colonists virtually seceded, set up a "Committee of Public Safety," and demanded that de Gaulle be given power. Diplomatically, it has had serious effects on French relations with the other Moslem nations along the northern coast of the Mediterranean, with the French trying to stop the flow of arms from Arab sympathizers in these states. Militarily, it has forced France to detach troops from their NATO forces and send them to Algeria and tied down nearly half a million troops. Financially, the campaign has cost a great deal.

Although Algeria is considered part of metropolitan France, the natives, comprising 86 per cent of the population, never had all the same rights as Frenchmen, and when Morocco and Tunisia became independent, nationalists demanded the same status. When it was refused, fighting started, mostly of the guerrilla type. A number of moves to give the natives more political representation failed to satisfy the extremists. In 1947 Moslems were given the right to send deputies to the National Assembly in Paris. This was followed in 1958 by a bill establishing regional autonomy along geographic and ethnic lines with voting equality between Moslems and non-Moslems. The fighting continues, with nationalists demanding complete independence and the French colonists equally violently opposed to too many concessions to the Moslems.

Peace talks based on Gen. de Gaulle's policy of self-determination were started twice in 1961 and then suspended, largely because of a dispute over future ownership of the oil-rich Sahara region.

HISTORY AND GOVERNMENT. As ancient Numidia, Algeria became a Roman colony at the close of the Punic Wars (145 B.C.). Conquered by the Vandals about A.D. 440, it descended from a high state of prosperity and civilization to virtual barbarism, from which it partially recovered after invasion by the Moslems about A.D. 650. In 1492 the Moors and Jews, who had been expelled from Spain, settled in Algeria. Falling under Turkish control in 1518, Algiers became for three centuries the headquarters of the Barbary pirates who preyed on Mediterranean commerce. The French took Algiers in 1830. While Algeria is organically linked with France, its constitutional status is in a process of revision. In the meantime, the French Delegate General has full civil and military powers and is directly responsible to the French Premier.

ECONOMIC CONDITIONS. Approximately 86 per cent of the population is native,

12 per cent French, and 2 per cent other European. The native population is Berber, with Arab admixture physically assimilated.

The area under cultivation is about 15,-000,000 acres, more than 30 per cent of which is owned by European farmers, chiefly in the fertile coastlands. The principal crops are wheat, barley and oats. Algeria is a leading wine producer, with almost 7 per cent of the cultivated area devoted to vines. Tobacco, corn, vegetables, flax, silk, figs, and dates are also produced. Much of the area is adapted to grazing. In 1959 there were 5,478,000 sheep, 617,000 cattle, 2,014,000 goats, and 194,000 camels.

European industries include those dependent on crops, such as distilling and oil and flour milling, as well as the making of leather, tobacco and matches. There are also small native industries, particularly the traditional carpet weaving.

The chief exports were wine, iron ore, and citrus fruits; chief imports, petroleum and products, machinery and apparatus, and motor vehicles. France took 76 per cent of the exports and supplied 80 per cent of the imports.

NATURAL FEATURES AND RESOURCES. Low plains cover small areas near the coast, but 68 per cent of Algeria is a plateau between 2,625 and 5,250 feet above sea level. The region between the Sahara and the Mediterranean reaches a high point of 7,641 feet.

Algeria is a leading producer of phosphates. Iron ore (55 per cent metal) is found near the Tunisian frontier and on the Oran coast. Zinc, lead, and salt are also important minerals.

## The Central African Republic
### (Member of French Community)

Area: 238,224 square miles.
Population (1959 est.): 1,193,020.
Density per square mile: 5.0.
Chief of State: David Dacko.
Principal cities: Bangui, 79,634 (1959 est.) (capital); Berberati; Bambari.
Monetary unit: franc C.F.A.*
Ethnic groups: Bayas, Mandjas, Badas, Saras.
Languages: French and African languages.
Religions: Animism; some Christian.

### HISTORY AND PRESENT STATUS

The Central African Republic, formerly known as Ubangi-Shari, was organized by France as a territory in 1894. It achieved its independence on August 13, 1960. Legislative powers are exercised by a 50-member Assembly elected for a five-year term. The President is elected by the Assembly.

ECONOMIC CONDITIONS. Coffee, cotton, sesame, diamonds and lumber are the leading products. Foreign trade (1958) came to $20.6 million in imports and $14.8 million in exports, with cotton, coffee, diamonds and lumber in the lead.

## Chad, The Republic of
### (Member of French Community)

Area: 495,794 square miles.
Population: 2,730,000.
Density per square mile: 5.6.
Chief of State: François Tombalbaye.
Principal cities: Fort-Lamy, 54,000 (1960 est.) (capital); Fort-Archambault, Moundou, Abeche.
Monetary unit: franc C.F.A.*
Ethnic groups: Arabs, Saras, Peuls.
Languages: French, Arabic, and African languages.
Religions: Moslem, Animist, Christian.

### HISTORY AND PRESENT STATUS

Primarily a desert, except in the south, Chad was visited by French expeditions toward the end of the 19th century and became part of the Ubangi-Shari-Chad colony in 1910. Ten years later it was constituted a separate colony, became an autonomous republic within the French Union after World War II and attained its independence on August 11, 1960. An 85-member Legislative Assembly, elected for five years, designates the Premier by a simple majority and invests the cabinet by a two-thirds majority vote.

ECONOMIC CONDITIONS. Cotton, peanuts and livestock are the chief products, with cotton accounting for $8.4 million out of $26 million in exports (1958). Imports amounted to $34 million.

COMORO ISLANDS—Status: Overseas Territory.
Population: 181,288.
Capital: Dzaudzi.
Administrator: Georges Arnaud.

The Comoro Is. (832 sq. mi.) became an autonomous overseas territory effective Jan. 1, 1947. They are located in the Indian Ocean about 300 miles north of Madagascar. The population is largely Moslem. Exports include essential oils, sisal, vanilla, copra, cacao, and cloves.

## Congo, The Republic of the (Brazzaville)†
### (Member of French Community)

Area: 132,047 square miles.
Population: 770,600.

† As distinguished from The Republic of the Congo (Léopoldville), former Belgian colony.

---

* One franc C.F.A. (Communauté Française de l'Atlantique) equals 0.02 new French francs.

Density per square mile: 5.8.
Chief of State: Abbé Fulbert Youlou.
Principal cities: Brazzaville, 100,000 (capital); Pointe-Noire.
Monetary unit: franc C.F.A.†
Ethnic groups: Bavilis, Balalis, Batékés, M'Bochis.
Languages: French and African languages.
Religions: Animism, some Christian areas.

## HISTORY AND PRESENT STATUS

Formerly known as the Middle Congo, this area was placed under the protection of France during 1879–1882 by Pierre Savergnan de Brazza, founder of Brazzaville. During World War II the colony declared its independence of Vichy, and Brazzaville served as the center of Gen. de Gaulle's Free French forces in Africa. It subsequently became an autonomous republic under the French Community and on August 15, 1960 achieved its independence. Executive powers are exercised by the Premier designated by a 61-member Assembly, which is elected for a 5-year term.

ECONOMIC CONDITIONS. The chief agricultural products are cocoa, coffee, tobacco; okoume and limba woods are important forest products; and oil, lead and cassiterite (tin) are the principal minerals. Foreign trade (1958) came to $44 million in imports and $15.6 million in exports, chiefly lumber, palm oil, peanuts, lead ore and tobacco.

## Dahomey, The Republic of

### (Associated with French Community)

Area: 44,696 square miles.
Population (1960 est.): 1,800,000.
Density per square mile: 40.3.
Chief of State: Hubert Maga.
Principal cities: Porto Novo, 32,000 (capital); Cotonou.
Monetary unit: franc C.F.A.†
Ethnic groups: Fons and Adjas, Boribas, Yorubas, Mahis.
Languages: French and African.
Religions: Animist, Christian, Moslem.

## HISTORY AND PRESENT STATUS

Dahomey was a kingdom when, in 1851, King Gezo signed a commercial treaty with the French. Slavery expeditions led in 1892 to a war with the French, who had protectorates in the area. The following year the country's independence ended when it was organized as a territory by France. After World War II it became an autonomous republic within the French Union and on Aug. 1, 1960 was granted its independence within the Community. Legislative powers are exercised by a 70-member assembly elected for a five-year term. The Premier is chosen by the Assembly.

ECONOMIC CONDITIONS. The chief products are palm oil, coffee, karite (vegetable oil), cotton, kapok and phosphates. In 1958 imports amounted to $17.2 million, exports to $13.6 million, the most important of them being palm kernels, palm oil and coffee.

FRENCH SOMALILAND—Status: Overseas territory.
Population: 67,000.
Capital: Djibouti (population 31,900).
Governor: Ahmed Dimi.
Foreign trade (1958): domestic exports, 373,200,000 Djibouti fr.; imports 10,020,000,000 Djibouti fr. Chief exports: salt, hides.
Mineral: salt.

French Somaliland, at the southern entrance to the Red Sea, was acquired by France between 1883 and 1887 by treaties with the Somali sultans, although posts on the coast had been acquired in 1856. This small, largely arid and sparsely populated region is important chiefly because of the port of Djibouti, the main artery of Ethiopia's trade via the Djibouti-Addis Ababa railway. The area is administered by a Governor, responsible to the French government and assisted by a representative council. In October, 1958, French Somaliland voted in favor of the new Constitution establishing the French Fifth Republic, and in December, 1958, the 32-member Territorial Assembly of French Somaliland voted to remain an Overseas Territory within the French community. In 1955 there were an estimated 3,132 Europeans, 28,000 Somalis, 25,000 Danakils, and 6,000 Arabs.

## The Gabon Republic

### (Member of French Community)

Area: 103,088 square miles.
Population (1959 est.): 404,570.
Density per square mile: 3.9.
Chief of State: Léon M'Ba.
Principal cities: Libreville, 20,000 (capital); Port-Gentil.
Monetary unit: franc C.F.A.*
Ethnic groups: Pahouins, Pongwés, Adounas, Chiras, Punu and Lumbu.
Languages: French and African languages.

† One franc C.F.A. (Communauté Française de l'Atlantique) equals 0 02 new French francs.

Religions: Animist, Christian along the coast.

## HISTORY AND PRESENT STATUS

Gabon was first visited by the Portuguese navigator Diego Cam in the 15th century. In 1839 the French founded their first settlement on the left bank of the Gabon River and gradually occupied the hinterland during the second half of the 19th century. It was organized as a French territory in 1888, and became an autonomous republic within the French Union after World War II and an independent republic on Aug. 17, 1960. Legislative powers are exercised by a 40-member Assembly elected for a five-year term which names the Premier.

ECONOMIC CONDITIONS. Cocoa and akoume and acajou woods are the principal products besides the minerals, oil, gold, manganese and uranium. Foreign trade (1958) came to $31 million in imports and $33.6 million in exports, of which okoume accounted for $10.4 million and petroleum for $2.2 million.

# Ivory Coast, The Republic of the

## (Associated with French Community)

Area: 124,503 square miles.
Population (1960 est.): 3,267,000.
Density per square mile: 26.2.
Chief of State: Félix Houphouët-Boigny.
Principal cities: Abidjan, 160,000 (1960 est.) (capital); Bouake.
Monetary unit: franc C.F.A.*
Ethnic groups: Agnis, Baoulés, Senoufos, Kroumen, Mandes, Dan-fouros, and other groups.
Languages: French and African languages.
Religions: Animist, Moslem, Christian.

## HISTORY AND PRESENT STATUS

The Ivory Coast attracted both French and Portuguese merchants in the 15th century. French traders set up establishments early in the 19th century, and in 1842 the French obtained territorial concessions from local tribes, gradually extending their influence along the coast and inland. The area was organized as a territory in 1893, became an autonomous republic in the French Union after World War II and achieved independence on August 7, 1960. The government is headed by a Premier, named by a majority of the 100-member Assembly, which is elected for five years.

ECONOMIC CONDITIONS. The principal agricultural products are coffee, cocoa, bananas, and palm oil; acajou, tiama, iroko and makere are the chief forest products. Diamonds and gold are also produced. Foreign trade (1958) came to $91.2 million in imports and $125.8 million in exports, the latter consisting chiefly of coffee, cocoa and lumber.

# The Malagasy Republic (Madagascar)

## (Member of French Community)

Area: 227,800 square miles.
Population (1960 est.): 5,290,769.
Density per square mile: 23.2.
Chief of State: Philibert Tsiranana.
Principal cities (1960 est.): Tananarive, 210,000 (capital); Tamatave; Diego-Suarez; Majunga; Fianarantsoa; Tulear.
Monetary unit: franc C.F.A.*
Ethnic groups: Merina (or Hova), Betsimisaraka, Retsileo, Tsimihety, Antaisoka, Sakalava, Antandroy.
Languages: French, Malagasy and others.
Religions: Catholic, Protestant and others.

## HISTORY AND PRESENT STATUS

The fourth largest island in the world, Madagascar remained independent under native rulers until 1885 when it came under French protection. French troops conquered the island in 1895, and it became a French colony the following year. The last native ruler, Queen Rànavàlona III, was exiled. Serious native nationalist outbreaks occurred in 1947.

In September, 1958 Madagascar voted in favor of the new Constitution of the Fifth French Republic, and in October, 1958 the French High Commissioner in Madagascar proclaimed as lapsed the law under which Madagascar had been made a French Colony.

An autonomous republic within the French Community since October, 1958, the Malagasy Republic became an independent member of that Community on June 25, 1960.

ECONOMIC CONDITIONS. Agricultural products include coffee, rice, cloves, tobacco, sugar, vanilla, manioc, bananas, maize and coconuts. Gum, medicinal plants, rubber, tannins and dyewoods are produced in the forests; graphite, mica, phosphates and gold are among its mineral resources. Foreign trade (1958) came to $106.2 million in imports and $81 million in exports, some of the leading items being rice, coffee, sugar, peanuts, sisal, raffia, cloves and vanilla.

---

* One franc C.F.A. (Communauté Française de l'Atlantique) equals 0.02 new French francs.

## Mali, The Republic of

### (Associated with French Community)

**Area:** 464,874 square miles.
**Population (est. 1960):** 4,300,000.
**Density per square mile:** 9.2.
**Chief of State:** Modibo Keita.
**Principal cities (est. 1957):** Bamako, 69,-000 (capital); Gao.
**Monetary unit:** franc C.F.A.*
**Ethnic groups:** Bambara, Peuls, Markas, Songhais, Malinkes, Touareg and others.
**Languages:** French and African languages.
**Religions:** Moslem, Animist, Christian.

#### HISTORY AND PRESENT STATUS

Subjugated by France by the end of the 19th century, this area became a territory in 1904 and in 1946 became part of the French Union. On June 20, 1960 it became independent and, under the name of Sudanese Republic, was federated with the Republic of Senegal in the Mali Federation. However, Senegal seceded from the Federation and the Sudanese Republic changed its name to The Republic of Mali. Peanuts, corn, sesame and cotton are its principal products.

## Mauritania, The Islamic Republic of

### (Member of French Community)

**Area:** 419,230 square miles.
**Population (est. 1959):** 655,637.
**Density per square mile:** 1.6.
**Chief of State:** Mocktar Ould Daddah.
**Principal cities:** Nouakchott (capital, presently under construction).
**Monetary unit:** franc C.F.A.*
**Ethnic groups:** White Moors; a Negro minority, chiefly Tukulers and Sorakolles.
**Languages:** French, Arabic and Negro languages.
**Religion:** Moslem.

#### HISTORY AND PRESENT STATUS

Mauritania was first explored by the Portuguese in the 15th century, then by the Spanish in the 16th century, followed by the Dutch, who developed the gum trade. The French came in the early 19th century and organized the area as a territory in 1904. It achieved independence on Nov. 28, 1960. A 40-member Assembly elected for a five-year term designates the Premier.

**ECONOMIC CONDITIONS.** Mauritania produces dates, palm oil and grains. Gum arabic is a product of the forests and iron and copper are mined. Foreign trade statistics prior to independence were grouped with those of Senegal and Sudan.

## Niger, The Republic of the

### (Associated with French Community)

**Area:** 458,995 square miles.
**Population (1959 census):** 2,556,211.
**Density per square mile:** 5.6.
**President:** Hamani Diori.
**Principal cities (1959 census):** Niamey, 30,030 (capital); Zinder.
**Monetary unit:** franc C.F.A.*
**Ethnic groups:** Hausas, Djermas, Touareg, Peuls, and Songhais.
**Languages:** French and African languages.
**Religion:** Moslem and others.

#### HISTORY AND PRESENT STATUS

The Niger was organized as a territory by France in 1920 and attained independence within the French Community on Aug. 3, 1960. The President of the Council (Premier) is elected by the Assembly, a 60-member legislative body elected for a five-year term.

**ECONOMIC CONDITIONS.** The chief products are peanuts, livestock, gum arabic, tin and wolfram. Foreign trade (1958) amounted to $8.8 million in imports and $15.2 million in exports, chiefly peanuts, livestock and hides.

**RÉUNION (Bourbon)—Status:** Overseas Department.
**Population (est. 1959):** 324,000.
**Capital (1954 census):** St. Denis, 41,863.
**Prefect:** Jean Perreau-Pradier.
**Foreign trade (1958):** exports, 6,500,000,-000 fr. C.F.A.* (90% to France); imports, 10,000,000,000 fr. C.F.A. (65% from France).
**Chief exports:** sugar, essential oils.
**Agricultural products:** sugar, vanilla, coffee, maize.

Discovered by Portuguese navigators in the 16th century, the island, then uninhabited, was taken as a French possession in 1638. It is located about 450 miles east of Madagascar, in the Indian Ocean. In September, 1958, Réunion approved the Constitution of the Fifth French Republic and became an Overseas Department within the new French Community.

There is no indigenous population. About three-quarters of the inhabitants are of European origin; the remainder are Creoles, mulattoes, Negroes, Indians and other Asiatics.

## The Republic of Senegal

### (Member of French Community)

**Area:** 76,124 square miles.
**Population (est. 1960):** 2,550,000.
**Density per square mile:** 33.5.
**President:** Leopold S. Senghor.
**Premier:** Mamadow Dia.

* One franc C.F.A. (Communauté Française de l'Atlantique) equals 0.02 new French francs.

Principal cities (est. 1960): Dakar, 300,-000 (capital); Saint-Louis, Thies.
Monetary unit: franc C.F.A.*
Ethnic groups: Wolofs, Sereres, Peuls, Tukulers, and others.
Languages: French and African languages.
Religions: Moslem, Animist, Christian.

### HISTORY AND PRESENT STATUS

The Portuguese had some stations on the banks of the Senegal River in the 15th century, and the first French settlement was made at Saint-Louis about 1650. The British took parts of Senegal at various times, but the French gained possession in 1840 and organized Sudan as a territory in 1904. In 1946, together with other parts of French West Africa, Senegal became part of the French Union. On June 20, 1960, it became an independent Republic federated with the Sudanese Republic in the Mali Federation, from which it withdrew soon after. Peanuts, cotton, gum arabic and phosphates are its chief exports.

## Upper Volta, The Republic of the

### (Associated with French Community)

Area: 105,839 square miles.
Population (est. 1959): 4,000,000.
Density per square mile: 37.8.
Chief of State: Maurice Yameogo.
Principal cities: Ouagadougou, 65,000 (capital); Bobo-Dioulasso.
Monetary unit: franc C.F.A.*
Ethnic groups: Mossis, Bobos.
Languages: French and African languages.
Religions: Animist, Christian, Moslem.

### HISTORY AND PRESENT STATUS

The Upper Volta consists chiefly of the lands of the Mossi Empire, where France established a protectorate over the Kingdom of Ouagadougou in 1897. Upper Volta became a separate colony in 1919, was partitioned among the Niger, Sudan and Ivory Coast in 1933, and was reconstituted in 1947. An autonomous republic within the French Community, it became independent on Aug. 5, 1960. It has a 75-member Assembly elected for five years, which selects the President of the Council.

ECONOMIC CONDITIONS. The principal products are cotton, sisal and peanuts. Imports (1958) came to $7.2 million and exports to $4.4 million, of which livestock and karite (vegetable oil) were the leading items.

## WESTERN HEMISPHERE

FRENCH GUIANA (including ININI)—Status: Overseas Department.
Population (est. 1960): 32,000.
Capital (est. 1960): Cayenne, 15,000.
Prefect: René Erignac.
Foreign trade (1959): exports, 441,000,000 fr. (74.8% to France); imports, 3,291,000,-000 fr. (69.6% from France). Chief exports: rum, timber, gold.
Agricultural products: bananas, cacao, corn, manioc, rice, sugar cane.
Mineral: gold (699 kg. produced in 1958).

French Guiana, lying north of Brazil and east of Surinam (Dutch Guiana) on the northeast coast of South America, was first settled in 1626. Penal settlements, embracing the area around the mouth of the Maroni River and the Iles du Salut (including Devil's Island), were founded in 1852; they were replaced by refugee camps in the 1940's.

During World War II, French Guiana at first adhered to the Vichy government, but the Free French took over in March, 1943. French Guiana accepted in September, 1958, the new Constitution of the French Fifth Republic and became an Overseas Department within the new French Community.

GUADELOUPE—Status: Overseas Department.
Population (est. 1959): 264,000.
Capital: Basse-Terre (population 11,837).
Prefect: Albert Bonhomme.
Foreign trade (1958): exports, 14,236,-000,000 fr. (77% to France); imports, 20,-092,000,000 fr. (75% from France). Chief exports: sugar (61%), bananas, rum.
Agricultural products: sugar, bananas, coffee, cacao, manioc, vanilla.
Manufactures: rum, sugar.

Guadeloupe, lying in the West Indies about 300 miles southeast of Puerto Rico, was discovered by Columbus in 1493. French colonization began in 1635. The largest city and chief port is Pointe-à-Pitre (population 30,465). About half the cultivated area is devoted to sugar cane. The manufacturing of rum and spirits is the principal industry. In September, 1958, Guadeloupe voted in favor of the new Constitution of the French Fifth Republic and became an Overseas Department within the new French Community.

MARTINIQUE—Status: Overseas Department.
Population (est. 1959): 271,000.
Capital: Fort-de-France, 62,000.
Prefect: Michel Grollemund.
Foreign trade (1958): exports, 13,000,000-000 fr. (96% to France); imports, 17,000,-

---

* One franc C.F.A. (Communauté Française de l'Atlantique) equals 0.02 new French francs.

000,000 fr. (77% from France). Chief exports: sugar (42%), bananas, rum.

Agricultural products: sugar, bananas, pineapples, cacao, coffee.

Manufactures: rum, sugar.

Martinique, lying in the Lesser Antilles about 300 miles northeast of Venezuela, was probably discovered by Columbus in 1502 and was taken for France in 1635. Following the Franco-German armistice of 1940 it had a semi-autonomous status under the High Commissioner, Admiral Georges Robert, until 1943, when he relinquished his authority to the Free French. The area, administered by a Prefect assisted by an elected council, is represented in the French legislature. In September, 1958, Martinique voted in favor of the new Constitution of the French Fifth Republic and became an Overseas Department within the new French Community. The population is mainly Negro and mulatto. Most of the arable land is devoted to sugar cultivation. Fort-de-France, the capital and chief commercial center, has an excellent harbor.

**ST. PIERRE AND MIQUELON—Status:** Overseas territory.

Population: 5,000.

Capital: St. Pierre (population 4,295).

Administrator: Michel Maillard.

Foreign trade (1959): exports, 447,000,-000 fr. C.F.A.; imports, 1,005,900,000 fr. C.F.A. Chief export: fish and products.

The sole remnant of the French colonial empire in North America, these islands were first occupied by the French in 1660. Their only importance arises from proximity to the Grand Banks, located 10 miles south of Newfoundland, making them the center of the French Atlantic cod fisheries. In September, 1958, St. Pierre and Miquelon voted in favor of the new Constitution of the French Fifth Republic and became an Overseas Territory within the new French Community.

# OCEANIA

**FRENCH POLYNESIA—Status:** Overseas territory.

Governor: Aimé Grimald.

Capital: Papeete, on Tahiti (population 1957: 17,247).

Foreign trade (1958): exports, 796,000,-000 fr. C.F.P.* (52% to France); imports, 676,000,000 fr. C.F.P. (44% from France).

Chief exports: phosphate (33%), copra, vanilla.

Agricultural products: copra (exports 1956: 20,000 metric tons), sugar, vanilla, tobacco.

Mineral: phosphates, copra, vanilla.

The term French Polynesia is applied to the scattered French possessions in the eastern Pacific—Mangareva (Gambier), Makatea, Marquesas Islands, Rapa, Rurutu, Rimatara, Society Islands, Tuamotu Archipelago, Tubuai, and Raivavae—which were organized into a single colony in 1903. The appointed Governor is assisted by a Privy Council and a popularly elected Representative Assembly. The principal and most populous island—Tahiti, in the Society group (pop. 1951: 30,500)—was claimed as French in 1768. In September, 1958, French Polynesia voted in favor of the new Constitution of the French Fifth Republic and became an Overseas Territory within the new French Community. The natives are mostly Polynesians.

**NEW CALEDONIA AND DEPENDENCIES** —Status: Overseas territory.

Population: 69,255.

Capital: Nouméa (population 22,272).

Governor: Michel Kauma.

Foreign trade (1958): exports, 2,030,000,-000 fr. C.F.P.* (62% to France); imports, 3,438,000,000 fr. C.F.P. (56% from France). Chief exports: nickel (87%), chromite, coffee.

Agricultural products: coffee, copra, corn, cotton, manioc, rice, tobacco.

Minerals: nickel, chromite, iron ore.

Sea product: mother-of-pearl.

New Caledonia (6,533 sq. mi.), lying about 1,070 miles northeast of Sydney, Australia, was discovered by Captain James Cook in 1774 and annexed by France in 1853. The government, in the hands of an appointed Governor and an elective Council, also administers the Isle of Pines, the Wallis Archipelago, the Loyalty Islands, the Chesterfield Islands, Walpole, the Huon Islands, Futuna and Alofi, with a total area of 1,121 square miles. The area—taken over in the summer of 1940 by the Free French after a bloodless revolution—is one of the richest of the Pacific islands in mineral resources, particularly nickel and chrome ore. New Caledonia chose in 1958 to remain an Overseas Territory within the new French Community. The natives are Melanesians; about one-third of the population is white and one-fifth Indo-Chinese and Javanese. A French penal colony was established in the 19th century.

**NEW HEBRIDES—Status:** Anglo-French condominium.

Population: 55,713.

Capital: Vila (population 2,000).

Foreign trade (1958): exports, £2,218,552; imports, £1,463,580. Chief exports: copra (33,548 metric tons), cacao (921 metric tons), and coffee (167 metric tons).

Agricultural products: coconuts, cacao, coffee.

Sea products: trochus and burghaus shell.

The New Hebrides, under joint Anglo-French administration since February, 1906, lie northeast of New Caledonia. The islands, about 40 in number, joined the Free

---

* One franc C.F.P. (Colonies Françaises du Pacifique) equals .055 new French francs.

French movement after a plebiscite in July, 1940. Most of the natives are Melanesians of mixed blood; there were 659 British and 3,812 French in 1958. The largest island is Espiritu Santo (875 sq. mi.). The French and British high commissioners in the Pacific are represented by resident commissioners.

# GERMANY

HISTORY. In Caesar's time, the territory that is now Germany was inhabited by barbarous tribes that came originally perhaps from Central Asia. One of these Germanic tribes, the Franks, attained supremacy in western Europe under Charlemagne, who was crowned Holy Roman Emperor in A.D. 800. By the Treaty of Verdun (843), Charlemagne's lands east of the Rhine were ceded to the German Prince Louis. Additional territory acquired by the Treaty of Mersen (870) gave Germany approximately the area she maintained throughout the Middle Ages. For several centuries after Otto the Great was crowned King in 936, the German rulers were also usually heads of the Holy Roman Empire.

Relations between state and church were changed by the Reformation, which began with Martin Luther's 95 theses, and came to a head in 1547, when Charles V scattered the forces of the Protestant League at Mühlberg. Freedom of worship was obtained by the Peace of Augsburg (1555), but a Counter Reformation took place later, and a dispute over the succession to the Bohemian throne brought on the Thirty Years' War (1618–48) which devastated Germany and left the empire divided into hundreds of small principalities virtually independent of the Emperor. Meanwhile, Prussia was developing into a province of considerable strength. Frederick the Great (1740–86) reorganized the Prussian army and defeated Maria Theresa of Austria in a struggle over Silesia. The conflict with revolutionary France hastened the disintegration of the empire, and in 1806 Francis II of Austria laid down the Imperial German crown. After the defeat of Napoleon at Waterloo (1815), the struggle between Austria and Prussia for supremacy in Germany continued, reaching its climax in the defeat of Austria in the Seven Weeks' War (1866) and the formation of the Prussian-dominated North German Confederation (1867).

The architect of German unity was Otto von Bismarck (1815–1898), a conservative, monarchist, and militaristic Prussian Junker who had no use for "empty phrase-making and constitutions." From 1862 until his retirement in 1890 he dominated not only the German but also the entire European scene. He unified all Germany in a series of three wars against Denmark (1864), Austria (1866), and France (1870–1871). Historians differ on the responsibility for these wars, but many believe they were instigated and promoted by Bismarck in his zeal to obtain national unity through "blood-and-iron."

On January 18, 1871, King William I of Prussia was proclaimed William I, German Emperor, at the Hall of Mirrors, Versailles. The North German Confederation, created in 1867, was abolished, and the new Second German Reich, consisting of both North and South German states, was born. As King of Prussia, the German Emperor exercised what amounted to dictatorial control over all Germany. With a powerful army, an efficient bureaucracy, and a loyal bourgeoisie, Chancellor Bismarck consolidated a powerful centralized state under Prussian domination.

William II (1888–1918) dismissed Bismarck in 1890 and embarked upon a "New Course" stressing an intensified colonialism and a powerful navy. His chaotic foreign policy gradually culminated in the diplomatic isolation of Germany and the nearly fatal outcome of World War I.

The Second German Empire collapsed following the defeat of the German armies in 1918, the naval mutiny at Kiel, and the flight of William II to Holland. The Social Democrats, led by Ebert and Scheidemann, crushed the Communists and established a moderate republic. The Weimar Constitution of 1919 provided for a President to be elected for seven years by direct universal suffrage; a bicameral legislature, consisting of the *Reichsrat,* representing the states, and the *Reichstag,* representing the people. It contained a model Bill of Rights. Unfortunately, the value of this Constitution was weakened by including a provision (Article 48) enabling the President to rule by decree.

The Weimar Republic was neither loved, wanted, nor understood by the mass of Germans. They regarded it as a child of defeat, imposed upon a Germany whose legitimate aspirations to world leadership had been thwarted by a world conspiracy. Schooled in autocracy, obedience, and leadership, the people apparently were not ready for an advanced democratic form of government. Added to this were a crippling currency debacle, a tremendous burden of reparations, and acute economic distress.

Capital of Germany's misery was made by Adolf Hitler (1889–1945), a former Austrian war veteran, a fanatical hypomaniac, a remarkable orator, and a passionate nationalist. He aroused all the elements of discontent by promising a Greater Germany, the abrogation of the Treaty of Versailles, the restoration of Germany's lost colonies, and the destruction of the Jews. When the Social Democrats and the Communists refused to combine against the Nazi threat, they sealed the doom of the Weimar Republic. President von Hindenburg appointed Hitler as Chancellor on January 30, 1933.

*Adolf Hitler.* With the death of President von Hindenburg in 1934, Hitler became complete master of Germany. He repudiated the Treaty of Versailles and began full-scale rearmament. In 1935 he withdrew from the League of Nations, and in 1936 he reoccupied the Rhineland and signed the anti-Comintern pact with Japan, at the same time strengthening relations with Italy. Austria was annexed in March, 1938. By the Munich agreement (Sept., 1938) he gained the Czech Sudetenland, and in violation of this agreement he completed the dismemberment of Czechoslovakia in March, 1939. But his invasion of Poland on Sept. 1, 1939, precipitated British and French declarations of war.

On May 8, 1945, Germany surrendered unconditionally to Allied and Soviet military commanders, and on June 5 the four-nation Allied Control Council became the *de facto* government of Germany.

At the Berlin (or Potsdam) Conference (July 17–Aug. 2, 1945) President Truman, Stalin and Prime Minister Attlee set forth the principles by which the Allied Control Council was to be guided. They were: Germany's complete disarmament and demilitarization; destruction of its war potential; rigid control of industry; decentralization of the political and economic structure. Pending final determination of territorial questions at a peace conference, the three victors agreed in principle to the ultimate transfer of the city of Königsberg (now Kaliningrad) and its adjacent area to the Soviet Union and to the administration by Poland of former German territories lying generally east of the Oder-Neisse line.

For purposes of control, Germany, was divided in 1945 into four national occupation zones, each headed by a Military Governor, assisted by appropriate supervisory and operating staffs.

Efforts to unify Germany were totally unsuccessful, and the western powers were unable to agree with the U.S.S.R. on any fundamental issue. Work of the Allied Control Council was hamstrung by repeated Soviet vetoes; and finally, on March 20, 1948, the U.S.S.R. walked out of the Council. Meanwhile, the U.S. and Britain had taken steps to merge their zones

economically (Bizone); and on May 31, 1948, the U.S., Britain, France and the Benelux countries agreed to set up a German state comprising the three western zones. At the same time the western powers introduced a new German currency.

The Soviet Union replied to these measures by clamping a blockade on all ground communications between the western zones and Berlin. The western Allies, refusing to be driven out of the capital, immediately organized a gigantic airlift to fly supplies into the beleaguered city. Before the Russians were finally forced to lift the blockade on May 12, 1949, 60,000 men were engaged in the airlift.

In return for lifting the blockade, the U.S.S.R. asked only that the Big Four Foreign Ministers meet again to discuss German unification. The conference, meeting in Paris from May 23 to June 20, 1949, ended as usual in a deadlock.

The Big Four Foreign Ministers met once more at Berlin from Jan. 25 to Feb. 18, 1954, again without success. No progress toward German reunification was made thereafter, despite a number of frequent high-level meetings, the last series being held in Geneva in the summer of 1959.

# German Federal Republic
## (West Germany)

**Area: 95,738 square miles.***
**Population (est. 1960): 53,373,000 (predominantly German).**
**Density per square mile: 557.6.**
**President: Heinrich Luebke.**
**Chancellor: Konrad Adenauer.**
**Principal cities (est. 1960): Hamburg,** 1,823,574 (chief port); Munich, 1,065,104 (Bavarian capital); Cologne, 780,124 (transportation center); Essen, 727,929 (steel center); Düsseldorf, 691,740 (river port); Frankfurt am Main, 657,735 (manufacturing); Bonn, 146,216 (capital).
**Language: German.**
**Religions (census 1950): Protestant,** 52.2%; Roman Catholic, 43.8%; others, 4.0%.

* Excluding West Berlin.

### STATUS IN THE WORLD TODAY

West Germany has allied itself with the western free world in the cold war with communism, and both its leadership and its people are strongly oriented toward the United States and its foreign policy. On May 26, 1952, it was integrated into the North Atlantic Treaty Organization. Four years later the Bundestag legalized national armament, although clearly specifying that there would be civilian control over the military. Its maximum of twelve divisions will be under the command of the Supreme Allied Commander, Europe, at NATO headquarters. The Germans fear the colossus to the East. They know well how their brothers in East Germany suffer under the Communist yoke and they want none of it. And it is Soviet Russia which unilaterally established the Oder-Neisse line as the definitive eastern boundary of postwar Germany, a decision which West Germany does not recognize.

Some opposition to the extent of the nation's pro-Western policy does exist, by reason of the natural desire of all Germans for reunification of their country. The Social Democrats insist that if West Germany were not allied militarily with the free world, there might be a chance to negotiate reunification with the Kremlin. This argument, however, seemed to have lost considerable force in July, 1959, when Prime Minister Khrushchev announced that the line between East Germany and West Germany was the dividing line between Communism and capitalism which Russia would defend to the bitter end. In addition, there are some industrialists who feel they could expand their exports to Iron Curtain countries were it not for the restrictions placed on trade in strategic materials by the United States. All parties are agreed, however, on the necessity of maintaining a free Berlin instead of turning it over to the Communists.

West Germany's recovery after its defeat in World War II was little short of phenomenal. To some extent it was due to American aid of some $3.4 billion, as well as hard work. The recovery is a classic case of the free-market economy operating successfully with a limited number of strategically placed controls. It stands in contrast to the economy of East Germany, which has sunk to a much lower level.

German industry has forged ahead by leaps and bounds. By 1953 she had achieved an industrial output 59 per cent higher than 1936. From 1951 to 1956 West German exports tripled in value. West Germany pushed ahead of Britain for the number one trading position in South America. Her chemical exports passed those of Britain for the first time.

---

### MAJOR POLITICAL PARTIES

Christian Democratic party (243 seats in Bundestag), led by Chancellor Adenauer; Social Democratic party (190 seats), led by Willy Brandt.

---

HISTORY AND GOVERNMENT. The Federal Republic of West Germany, comprising those portions of Germany and Greater Berlin which had been assigned to the American, British, and French zones of control, was proclaimed on May 23, 1949, with its capital at Bonn.

The Constitution of the German Federal Republic embodies the best features of the French Declaration of the Rights of Man, the first ten amendments to the American Constitution, the British Bill of Rights, and the Weimar Constitution. It was adopted by the Parliamentary Council on May 8, 1949, and approved by the High Commissioners on May 12, 1949. It provides for a Federal President, chosen for a term of five years by a Federal Convention. The Parliament consists of two legislative houses. The upper house, the *Bundesrat*, represents and is appointed by the governments of the *Länder*, or states. The lower house, the *Bundestag*, is elected for a period of four years by universal suffrage. The Chancellor, or Prime Minister, is appointed by the President, though the *Bundestag* reserves the right to elect a Chancellor of its own preference. Each of the ten constituent *Länder* is required to have a republican form of government with an assembly chosen by the people.

ECONOMIC CONDITIONS. *Agriculture.* Agriculture is characterized by mixed farming, the climate and the soil permitting cultivation of a variety of crops and most types of livestock. Rye and potatoes are staple crops in the north; grains and sugar beets in the central regions. The northwestern and southern areas are noted for dairying, while the west is the chief fruit- and wine-producing region. The soil is generally poor, and high crop yields are dependent upon large-scale use of fertilizers.

In Dec., 1959, West Germany (excluding the Saar) had 12,127,000 cattle, 913,-000 horses, 14,654,000 hogs, and 1,113,000 sheep.

West Germany is not self-sustaining in food. Difficulties stem to a considerable extent from the fact that Poland now controls the area east of the Oder-Neisse, which contained 28 per cent of prewar Germany's arable land and produced about 25 per cent of its food.

*Industry.* West Germany's industry is well-developed and highly diversified. It accounted for about two-thirds of Germany's prewar industrial production and for a large part of iron and steel production.

Shipbuilding has regained its former prominence. Industrial production in 1956 was 140 per cent of the 1953 level.

West Germany is a member of the European Coal and Steel Community, which commenced activities on Aug. 10, 1952. It has jurisdiction over the production and allocation of coal and steel by its member nations.

*Trade.* Leading customers in 1959 were EPU countries (53%), the U.S. and Canada (11%), and Latin America (7%); leading suppliers, EPU countries (48%), the U.S. and Canada (13%), and Latin America (10%). Leading exports included machines, vehicles, electrical machinery and apparatus, iron and steel products, and coal; leading imports, copper (4%), iron ore (4%), cotton (4%), and wheat (3%).

Shipping on the Rhine is controlled by the Central Commission of the Rhine—an international body composed provisionally of U.S., British, French, Swiss, Dutch and Belgian representatives—which was reconvened in October, 1945.

NATURAL FEATURES AND RESOURCES. The northern plain, the central hill country and the southern mountain district constitute the main physical divisions of West Germany. The Bavarian plateau in the southwest averages 1,600 feet above sea level, but it reaches 9,721 feet in the Zugspitze, the highest point in Germany.

There are several important navigable rivers. In the south the Danube, rising in the Black Forest, flows east across Bavaria into Austria. The other important rivers flow north. The Rhine, which rises in Switzerland and flows across the Netherlands in two channels to the North Sea, is navigable by smaller vessels as far as Cologne. The Rhine and the Elbe, which also empties into the North Sea, are navigable within Germany for ships of 400 tons. The Weser, flowing into the North Sea, and the Main and Mosel (Moselle), both tributaries of the Rhine, are also important.

*Minerals and Forests.* Aside from rich deposits of coal and potash, West Germany's mineral wealth is not considerable. The Ruhr, Krefeld and Aachen districts constitute one of the world's greatest coal-mining regions.

About 23 per cent of the total area of West Germany is covered by commercial forests, which yield timber as well as material for paper, wood fiber, cellulose and other products.

# German Democratic Republic
## (East Germany)

**Area:** 41,479 square miles.*
**Population** (est. 1959): 16,213,000 (predominantly German).
**Density per square mile:** 390.8.
**Soviet High Commissioner:** G. M. Pushkin.
**Chairman, Council of State:** Walter Ulbricht.
**Premier:** Otto Grotewohl.
**Principal cities** (est. 1960): Leipzig, 592,-
* Excluding East Berlin.

821 (trading, publishing center); Dresden, 493,515 (railway center, Elbe port); Karl-Marxstadt (Chemnitz), 286,226 (textiles); Halle am der Saale, 278,700 (railway center); Magdeburg, 260,618 (iron and steel products).
**Monetary unit: Ostmark.**
**Religions** (census 1946): Protestant, 81.3%; Roman Catholic, 12.1%; others, 6.6%.

---

### STATUS IN THE WORLD TODAY

East Germany is probably the Kremlin's most important satellite because it has placed Soviet military and political influence deep inside western Europe. As such it is a springboard for further Communist expansion and a first line of defense. The Western powers have refused to acknowledge its legal existence as a state or separate sovereign entity, regarding it as a disguised Soviet dependency which is directly administered by the occupying authority. Its boundaries coincide with the zone of occupation conferred upon the Soviet Union at the end of World War II. The Russians, on the other hand, declared it a "country" in October, 1949, and bestowed upon it "full sovereignty" in September, 1957. This has given the U.S.S.R. an excuse for refusing to negotiate the reunification of Germany, claiming that it is a matter between the "state" of East Germany and the West German Republic. It seeks constantly to bolster the prestige of the East German regime and tried, unsuccessfully, to obtain equal status for it as a participant with other powers at the Foreign Ministers' conferences in Geneva in 1959. The presence of Soviet occupation troops is regulated by a status-of-forces agreement as in Hungary and Rumania, and their stationing in East Germany is formally regarded as temporary. But their function in keeping the Communist regime in power was dramatically demonstrated in June, 1953, when they were used to quell a workers' riot in East Berlin.

Economically, East Germany is tied to the Soviet bloc and has made nowhere near the progress achieved by West Germany. Not until the spring of 1958 was food-rationing abolished, but prices remain high and there is a scarcity of consumer items. A seven-year plan to coordinate the Soviet and East German economies calls for sizable expansion of the East German chemical industry and delivery of more chemical and machine industry products to Russia. In return, East Germany will receive greater supplies of raw materials, such as oil, pig iron, aluminum, copper, and steel. An economic program adopted in January, 1958, called for a 25% rise in industrial production in the next three years. Some progress has been made, and according to official figures, East Germany is the second industrial power in the Communist orbit, excluding Russia.

---

HISTORY AND GOVERNMENT. The so-called German Democratic Republic comprises the Soviet zone of occupation of eastern Germany. It was proclaimed on Oct. 7, 1949, with its seat at Berlin, on the basis of a Constitution adopted May 30, 1949, by a People's Congress chosen under a plebiscite arrangement in elections held in the Soviet zone and East Berlin on May 15 and 16, 1949. The Congress elected a People's Council (*Volksrat*) which was transformed on Oct. 7 into a provisional People's Chamber (*Volkskammer*). A Chamber of the States (*Länderkammer*) was nominated on Oct. 10, and on Oct. 11 both chambers elected Communist leader Wilhelm Pieck as President of the republic and Otto Grotewohl as Minister-President or Premier. The Constitution is Soviet in nature and the government is under complete Communist domination. Soviet government supervision is exercised by the Soviet High Commissioner.

The republic lies largely between the Elbe and Oder rivers, including most of Brandenburg, Mecklenburg and the industrial Saxon and Thuringian lands.

ECONOMIC CONDITIONS. About 22 per cent of the population is engaged in agricultural pursuits and the area is almost self-sufficient in foodstuffs. Postwar yields have, however, suffered from droughts and shortages of fertilizers.

Most of the industrial establishments, particularly in heavy industry, have been nationalized. The area accounted for 26 per cent of prewar Germany's industrial production, ranking first in textiles, paper and pulp and ceramics and glass (especially optical glass produced by the famous Jena works). A Two-Year Plan inaugurated in 1949 had the object of raising the volume of production to 81 per cent of the 1936 level by the end of 1950, while a Five-Year Plan initiated in 1951 aimed at doubling the 1936 level by 1955. Official production data for 1959 are as follows: pig iron (1,898,400 metric tons), raw steel (3,207,400 tons), cement (4,205,000 tons).

Foreign trade is carried on through government-owned trading companies. Trade is confined largely to U.S.S.R., Czechoslovakia and Poland. Important imports include foodstuffs, minerals and textiles; exports include machinery, engineering equipment and chemicals.

NATURAL RESOURCES. The area is not rich in minerals. It has only minor deposits of coal. It does have important deposits of lignite and crude potash.

## Berlin

Area: 341.2 square miles.
Population (est. 1960): 3,390,349.

Berlin, the capital of prewar Germany, is surrounded by the German Democratic Republic. It is occupied by the forces of the U.S., the U.K., France and the U.S.S.R., each having its own sector of occupation. The three western sectors contain 55 per cent of the area and two-thirds of the population.

The supreme authority in West Berlin is a tripartite Kommandatura, which has responsibility for the exercise of the powers reserved to the occupation forces under the Berlin Charter, a document analogous to the former West German Occupation Statute. With the termination of the Allied occupation of West Germany, Allied controls were substantially relaxed.

Other powers of government are exercised by a City Assembly elected by popular vote and a *Magistrat* (city council) chosen by the Assembly.

Supreme authority in the eastern sector of Berlin is exercised by the Soviet High Commissioner. Powers not exercised by him or by the German Democratic Republic are vested in a "rump" city government, which proclaimed itself in power Nov. 30, 1948. Major anti-Communist riots broke out in East Berlin in June, 1953.

---

## Greece (Kingdom)
### (Hellas)

Area: 51,182 square miles.
Population (est. 1959): 8,258,000 (1940, excluding the Dodecanese Greek, 92.8%; Turkish, 3.8%; Macedonian, 1.3%; Spanish, 1%; others, 1.1%).
Density per square mile: 161.3.
Sovereign: King Paul I.
Premier: Constantine Karamanlis.
Principal cities (census 1951, municipal areas only): Athens, 565,084 (capital); Salonika, 217,049 (seaport); Piraeus, 186,014 (port of Athens); Patras, 79,014 (seaport); Volos, 51,144 (seaport).

Monetary unit: Drachma.
Languages: Greek, Turkish.
Religions: Greek Orthodox, 96%; Mohammedan, 2%; Jewish, 1.1%; others, .9%.

---

### STATUS IN THE WORLD TODAY

Greece, which had to fight and overcome Communist guerrilla forces before it could even begin to recover from the effects of World War II, is a member of the North Atlantic Treaty Organization, which it joined in 1951. It has long had friendly ties with the United States, to which many of its nationals have emigrated, and with Great Britain. From 1955 until 1959, however, relations with these two countries as well as with Turkey were strained because of the question of Cyprus, a British colony. Greek Cypriots demanded union with Greece and undertook a campaign of terrorism and guerrilla warfare. The Turks on the island were vehemently opposed to any such union, and there was some feeling against the United States for not openly backing the Greek side. An agreement making Cyprus a republic, with constitutional safeguards for the Turkish minority, was reached in February of 1959, and peace was restored.

Traditionally one of the poorest countries in Europe, Greece has made a remarkable postwar recovery, thanks in part to funds supplied by the United States under the Truman Doctrine for the rehabilitation of both Greece and Turkey. Industrial production has soared, railroads and highways have been improved, and the national budget has been balanced. Destruction caused by the war, which was severe, has resulted in rebuilding of more than 1,500 villages and towns and of virtually all roads.

## MAJOR POLITICAL PARTIES

National Radical Union (172 seats in Chamber of Deputies as of Sept. 1961), led by Prime Minister Constantine Karamanlis; Union of Democratic Left (79 seats), led by Ioannis Passalidis; Liberal party (36 seats), led by Sophocles Venizelos.

HISTORY AND GOVERNMENT. Greece, with a recorded history going back to 766 B.C., reached the peak of its glory in the fifth century B.C., and by the middle of the second century B.C., it had declined to the status of a Roman province. It remained within the Eastern Roman Empire until Constantinople fell to the Crusaders in 1204. In 1453, the Turks took Constantinople, and by 1460 Greece was a Turkish province. The insurrection made famous by the poet Lord Byron broke out in 1821, and in 1827 Greece was set up an independent nation, with sovereignty guaranteed by Britain, France and Russia. Prince Otto of Bavaria was recognized as King five years later, but he was ousted by a revolution in 1862. Prince William of Denmark, as George I, succeeded him.

King George encouraged the adoption of a constitution which made possible the development of a democratic parliamentary system. Greek territory was considerably extended as a result of the Balkan Wars, but an expedition into Turkish Asia Minor after World War I was unsuccessful, and claims to Greek-inhabited areas were finally settled by an exchange of populations.

A republic was proclaimed in 1924, following the departure of King George II and a plebiscite which showed a republican majority. The monarchy was restored in 1935, however, following a coup d'etat. Greece resisted an Italian invasion so successfully in 1940 that Nazi Germany had to come to the aid of her Axis partner the following year. British and Greek troops liberated Greece in October, 1944. For some time after that guerrilla warfare was conducted by Communist sympathizers.

Greece is a constitutional hereditary monarchy. Its unicameral Parliament is elected by popular vote. Nominal executive power is vested in the King.

ECONOMIC CONDITIONS About three-quarters of the population engages in agricultural pursuits, although only one-fifth of the land is arable. Most of the cultivated area is devoted to cereals: wheat, barley, and maize. There are also olive trees, vines, tobacco, and currants. The principal fruits are oranges, lemons, figs, mandarins, apples, and pears. In Dec., 1959, there were 1,028,000 cattle, 9,555,000 sheep, and 660,000 hogs.

Development of large-scale Greek manufacturing is blocked by lack of coal resources and of capital. The most valuable products are textiles, chemicals and food items. Among other processed or manufactured products are olive oil, wine, spirits, flour, carpets, leather, cigarettes and building materials.

Leading customers in 1959 were West Germany (20%), other EPU countries (18%), and the U.S. and Canada (14%); leading suppliers, the U.S. and Canada (12%), West Germany (19%), and Britain (10%). Leading exports were tobacco (23%) and currants and raisins (17%).

The merchant marine plays a vital part in the national economy.

Reconstruction of the Greek transport system, financed by U.S. aid, was completed in 1949; it included extensive work on highways, port and dry-dock facilities, railways and bridges.

NATURAL FEATURES AND RESOURCES. North central Greece, Epirus and western Macedonia all are mountainous. The main chain of the Pindus Mountains rises to 9,000 feet in places, separating Epirus from the plains of Thessaly. Greek Thrace is mostly a lowland region separated from European Turkey by the lower Maritsa River.

Among the many islands are the Ionian group off the west coast; the Cyclades group to the southeast; other islands in the eastern Aegean, including Lesbos, Samos and Khios; and Crete, the fourth largest Mediterranean island.

The Dodecanese, a group of thirteen islands in the Aegean Sea near the coast of Asia Minor, were ceded to Greece by the 1947 Italian peace treaty and were formally transferred on March 7, 1948.

Greek minerals are varied but are exploited only moderately. Principal ones are lignite, iron ore, iron pyrites, magnesite, chromite, lead, bauxite, molybdenum, emery, marine salt and marble.

A fifth of the country is forested, largely with pine, fir and oak. Resin and turpentine are main forest products. The principal sea product is sponges.

# Guatemala (Republic)
## (República de Guatemala)

**Area:** 42,042 square miles.
**Population** (est. 1960): 3,759,000 (1950: Indian, 53.5%; mixed and other, 46.5%).
**Density per square mile:** 89.4.
**President:** Miguel Ydigoras Fuentes.
**Principal cities** (est. 1958): Guatemala, 355,254 (capital); Quezaltenango, 33,726 (coffee, sugar); Puerto Barrios, 19,268 (port); Mazatenango 13,728 (coffee).
**Monetary unit:** Quetzal.
**Language:** Spanish.
**Religion:** Roman Catholic.

### STATUS IN THE WORLD TODAY

Guatemala, the first nation to overthrow a Communist regime, in so doing deprived the Kremlin of a base of operations in the Western Hemisphere and forced its agents there to flee or go into hiding. Since that time—1954—the government has concentrated on improving the country's economic status, and with the help of the United States—$80 million of aid in four years—appeared to be on the way to prosperity until a drop in coffee prices slowed down the economy. Coffee constitutes more than 75 per cent of the country's exports. Strikes of railroad workers and port employees also contributed to unsettled conditions, although the government's policy of agrarian reform—giving fifty-acre plots of land to the landless—continued. Early in 1959 an austerity program was put into effect which included a surcharge of 100 per cent on tariffs on goods imported from twenty-eight countries with which Guatemala had an unfavorable balance of trade. In foreign affairs it was involved in a dispute with Mexico over fishing rights in what Guatemala claimed were its territorial waters. As a result of the strafing of Mexican fishing boats, Mexico broke off diplomatic relations, which were resumed in Sept., 1959.

### MAJOR POLITICAL PARTIES

P.R.D.M. (33 seats in Legislative Assembly), led by President Ydigoras Fuentes; M.D.N. (14 seats), led by Col. Cruz-Salazar.

**HISTORY AND GOVERNMENT.** Once the site of the ancient Mayan civilization, Guatemala, conquered by Spain in 1524, set itself up as a republic in 1839. From 1898 to 1920, the dictator Manuel Estrada Cabrera ran the country, and from 1931 to 1944 General Jorge Ubico Castañeda was the "strong man." In July, 1944, the National Assembly elected General Federico Ponce President, but he was overthrown in October, and in December Dr. Juan José Arévalo was elected as the head of a leftist regime which continued to press its reform program in the face of conservative resistance. He took office on March 15, 1945. Jacobo Arbenz Guzmán, administration candidate with pro-Communist leanings, won the Nov., 1950, elections, took office March 15, 1951, and was ousted in 1954.

A new Constitution has been adopted to take the place of that of 1945, which provided that a President be elected every six years by direct vote and could not succeed himself immediately. Legislative power was vested in a unicameral National Assembly of 66 members popularly elected for four-year terms, half the members being elected every two years.

**ECONOMIC CONDITIONS.** Agriculture engages 90 per cent of Guatemalans. Coffee accounts for a fifth of the cultivated land.

In 1958 the U.S. took 55% of the exports and supplied 49% of the imports. The chief exports were coffee (75%) and bananas (10%). Imports included flour, petroleum products, drugs, and textiles.

**NATURAL FEATURES AND RESOURCES.** Most of Guatemala is mountainous, with many volcanic peaks. The northern part is the great plain of Petén, largely uncultivated and sparsely populated. The narrow Pacific slope, well watered and fertile, is the most densely populated.

The country's vast forests, mostly in the Petén region, yield chicle for chewing gum, cinchona bark, a small amount of rubber, and dyewoods and cabinet woods.

# Guinea (Republic)

**Area:** 94,926 square miles.
**Population** (est. 1959): 2,726,888 (mostly Peulhs and Malinkés).
**Density per square mile:** 28.7.
**President:** Sékou Touré.
**Premier:** Sékou Touré.
**Principal cities** (est. 1960): Conakry, 75,000 (capital); Kankan, 30,000.
**Monetary unit:** Franc C.F.A. (Colonies Françaises d'Afrique, equal to 2 metropolitan francs).

Languages: French, native tongues (Twi, Fanti, Ga).

Religions: Animist, Moslem, Christian.

## STATUS IN THE WORLD TODAY

Guinea, formerly part of French West Africa, achieved its independence as the only colony to vote against the new French Constitution in September, 1958, declaring its new status on Oct. 2. Since then its avowed position in foreign affairs has been one of pan-African neutralism, and it has created, with Ghana, the Union of Independent African States, presently a loose federation aimed at closer ties in the future.

Western nations, during the first year of Guinea's independence, felt the nation was headed toward the left because of the Marxist trend of the government, headed by President Sékou Touré, and because of its early commercial ties with Iron Curtain countries. East European nations were the first to conclude trade agreement with Guinea, to send technical and commercial delegations, and "gift" shipments of arms, and have tied up an estimated 60 per cent of the country's exports. The Guinea government replied that Western nations, for fear of alienating France, were slow to recognize the new nation and that it wanted economic help wherever it could obtain it.

Economically, Guinea has long been subsidized by France, and the withdrawal of financial help and of administrative personnel upon achieving independence made the transition period difficult. Primarily an agricultural country, its principal exports are bananas and coffee, although it has undeveloped riches in gold, diamonds, iron ore, and bauxite. Private capital from five foreign countries is underwriting the first aluminum plant, but much more aid will be necessary to bring the Koukoure Dam project into being.

HISTORY AND GOVERNMENT. Previously part of French West Africa, Guinea achieved independence by rejecting in September, 1958, the new Constitution of the French Fifth Republic. On October 2, 1958, the Territorial Assembly of French Guinea proclaimed the independent Republic of Guinea and transformed itself into a Constituent Assembly. In December, 1958, Guinea was admitted to full membership in the United Nations.

ECONOMIC CONDITIONS. Guinea is well equipped economically to be independent. It is the second richest country in French Africa. It is rich in bauxite (1958: 800,000 metric tons) and has great reserves of hydraulic power.

Main exports are coffee, bananas, iron ore, bauxite, and palm kernels.

# Haiti (Republic)
## (République d'Haïti)

Area: 10,714 square miles.
Population (est. 1960): 3,505,000 (Negro, 95%; mulatto, 5%).
Density per square mile: 327.1.
President: François Duvalier.
Principal cities (census 1950)*: Port-au-Prince, 134,117 (capital, chief port); Cap Haïtien, 24,243 (seaport); Gonaïves, 13,634 (farming district); Les Cayes, 11,608 (seaport; coffee).
Monetary unit: Gourde.
Language: French.
Religion: Roman Catholic.

* Cities proper, excluding surrounding communes.

## STATUS IN THE WORLD TODAY

Intermittent political turbulence, although it has little real influence on the daily lives of the people of Haiti, continues to be the order of the day in this island republic, and as a result stability and systematic growth have yet to come to the country's politics and economy. The election of the present chief executive, President François Duvalier, put an end to one of the shorter periods of chaos which alternate with periods of dictatorship. Although his regime has attempted to restore some semblance of order to the nation's finances, it depends upon the armed forces for its tenure in office. Haiti is also unwillingly involved through purely geographical reasons in the conflict between the revolutionary forces in Cuba and the dictatorship in the neighboring Dominican Republic. The late Generalissimo Trujillo threatened to "protect" Haiti with his troops if the revolutionaries opposing him tried to land forces there.

Haiti is the one virtually all-Negro nation of the hemisphere. It is a country of small farmers, most of whom own and cultivate mere patches of land. It has the highest illiteracy rate, the deepest poverty, and one of the most meager endowments of natural resources of all the countries of the hemisphere. Despite political instability, the farmers continue to grow their infinitesimal amounts of coffee and corn which the womenfolk bring to the market on their heads. Close to the spirit of their African ancestors, they speak their own peculiar language— a mixture of African dialects, French, Spanish and English—and worship their pagan gods, only slightly influenced by the teachings of the Roman Catholic church.

HISTORY AND GOVERNMENT. Haiti started its struggle for independence under Toussaint L'Ouverture at the time of the French Revolution in the 1790's. Although this first attempt was suppressed by Napoleon Bonaparte, a successful uprising led by Jean Jacques Dessalines in 1804 finally established Haiti as an independent nation.

In December, 1945, a revolution put President Dumarsais Estimé in power. His regime was one of the few democratic episodes the country has experienced. There was freedom of press and speech, several political parties were organized, a labor movement was established, and a serious attempt was made to plan for the country's economic development. Rudimentary labor legislation was enacted and the foundations of a social security system were laid.

However, President Estimé's attempt to perpetuate himself in power after his term had expired in December, 1949, brought another revolution, the victor of which was General Paul Magloire, who ruled until December, 1956. His regime, a dictatorship, continued many of the social and economic policies of its predecessor. President Magloire, in turn, attempted to stay in office after his term had ended and was overthrown. From December, 1956, until September, 1957, when President Duvalier was installed, there was a period of chaos.

Normally the President is elected for six years by two-thirds vote of the National Assembly. That body consists of a 37-member Chamber of Deputies, elected for four years by popular vote, and a 21-member Senate elected for six years.

ECONOMIC CONDITIONS. Haiti is predominantly agricultural. Coffee, which made up 55% of Haitian exports, is the principal crop, followed by sisal, sugar cane, cotton, bananas, and cacao. Manufacturing is almost entirely for local consumption.

Leading exports in 1957 were coffee (62%), sisal (18%), and sugar (8%). Leading customers were the U.S. (33%), Belgium (21%), and Italy (13%); leading suppliers, the U.S. (62%), Canada (6%), Netherlands Antilles (5%), and Germany (4%).

NATURAL FEATURES AND RESOURCES. Haiti, about the size of Maryland, is two-thirds mountainous, with the rest marked by great valleys, extensive plateaus and small plains. The most densely populated and productive region is the Cul de Sac plain, near Port-au-Prince.

# Honduras (Republic)
## (República de Honduras)

**Area:** 43,277 square miles.
**Population** (est. 1960): 1,950,000 (1945: mestizo, 89.9%; Indian, 6.7%; Negro, 2.1%; white, 1.3%).
**Density per square mile:** 45.1.

**President: Ramon Villeda Morales.**
**Principal cities (census 1950):** Tegucigalpa (including twin city of Comayagüela), 72,385 (capital); San Pedro Sula, 21,139 (bananas); La Ceiba, 16,645 (seaport, bananas); Tela, 12,614 (seaport).
**Monetary unit: Lempira.**
**Language: Spanish.**
**Religion: Roman Catholic.**

## STATUS IN THE WORLD TODAY

Honduras, which has had a long history of military dictatorships and political instability, installed a democratically elected administration in January, 1958. There have been several attempted uprisings since then, although the army has pledged itself to uphold constitutional government, and there have been unofficial reports that the would-be rebels were backed by dictators in the Dominican Republic and neighboring Nicaragua. The signing on Feb. 26, 1959, of an agreement between Honduras and Nicaragua to prevent their territories from being used to mount rebellions against each other gave rise to hopes that Honduras might be able to concentrate on its economic problems. It has received several loans to diversify its current coffee-banana economy through the construction of a hydroelectric project and the establishment of a paper and pulp industry.

## MAJOR POLITICAL PARTIES

Liberal party (37 seats in Congress), led by President Ramon Villeda Morales; Nationalist party (18 seats), led by Gonzalo Carias.

HISTORY AND GOVERNMENT. Columbus discovered Honduras on his last voyage in 1502. Honduras declared its independence from Spain in 1838, and has been troubled by revolution and war ever since. American Marines intervened in 1903 and 1923. In 1931, 1932, and 1937 major revolutions were crushed by force. The Nicaragua-Honduras boundary dispute of 1937 almost caused war, and in April, 1945, the country was invaded from Guatemala by a group of Honduran exiles, who were suppressed. The Constitution of Honduras provides for a President elected by popular vote for only one term of 6 years and for a unicameral Congress elected by popular vote for 6 years.

ECONOMIC CONDITIONS. In 1959 the U.S. took 54% of the exports and supplied 53% of the imports. Leading exports were bananas (46%), coffee (24%), timber and lumber (9%), and silver (3%).

NATURAL FEATURES AND RESOURCES. Honduras, in the north central part of Central America, has a 400-mile Caribbean coast-line and a 40-mile Pacific frontage.

Generally mountainous, it has fertile plateaus and river valleys and narrow coastal plains.

Gold and silver are the most important mineral products of Honduras.

# Hungary (Republic)

**Area:** 35,919 square miles.
**Population (estimated 1960):** 10,002,000 (Magyar, German, Slovak).
**Density per square mile:** 278.6.
**Chairman of Presidium:** István Dobi.
**Prime Minister:** Janos Kadar.
**Principal cities (est. 1960):** Budapest, 1,807,299 (capital, Danube port); Miskolc, 143,364 (industrial center); Debrecen, 129,-671 (livestock); Szeged, 99,061 (textiles, wheat); Pécs, 114,713 (farming).
**Monetary unit:** Forint.
**Languages (census 1949):** Hungarian, 98.7%; Slovak, .3%; German, .2%; Rumanian, .2%; others, .6%.
**Religions (est. 1956):** Roman Catholic, 67%; Calvinist, 22.8%; Lutheran, 3.3%; Jewish, 1.5%; Greek Orthodox, 2.5%; others, 1%.

## STATUS IN THE WORLD TODAY

Hungary, where communism came at Soviet gunpoint and could be restored only by Red Army tanks when, in 1956, the Red puppets were swept out of office by a popular, nation-wide revolt, is outwardly tranquil now only because of the continued presence of Soviet troops. Recognizing the fact that even the workers were opposed to the regime, the government has liquidated the workers' councils as well as many of their leaders. Many intellectuals have been arrested and imprisoned. The shaky administration is determined to settle scores with all those who collaborated in overthrowing the "people's democratic order." Thousands were executed, placed in internment camps, imprisoned, or deported to Siberia. More than 200,000 managed to flee the country, however, and as a result the Communist party faces a manpower shortage in many fields, especially the professions. Economically, Hungary is at least a temporary liability to the Soviet bloc.

The revolution, although unsuccessful because of Soviet intervention, did, however, cause incalculable harm to the Communist cause. The bloody suppression precipitated a revulsion of feeling against the Reds and led to the disillusionment of many a Communist or Communist sympathizer. It also smashed the myth of invincibility of the totalitarian system from within and demonstrated the elemental strength of an aroused people. But the Iron Curtain has been rigidly drawn around Hungary to prevent the free world from learning additional facts about the revolt, and United Nations observers and committees have been refused admittance to the country.

---

HISTORY AND GOVERNMENT. About 2,000 years ago, Hungary was part of the Roman provinces of Pannonia and Dacia on the empire's borders. In A.D. 896 it was invaded by the Magyars, who founded a kingdom. Christianity was accepted during the reign of Stephen I (St. Stephen) from 997 to 1038. The peak of Hungary's great period of medieval power came in 1342–82 under King Louis the Great (Louis I) of Anjou, whose dominions touched the Baltic, Black, and Mediterranean seas. War with the Turks broke out in 1389, and when the Turks smashed a Hungarian army in 1526, western and northern Hungary accepted Hapsburg rule to escape Turkish occupation. Transylvania became independent under Hungarian princes. Intermittent war with the Turks was waged until a peace treaty was signed in 1699.

After the suppression of the 1848 revolt against Hapsburg rule led by Louis Kossuth, the dual monarchy of Austria-Hungary was set up in 1867.

The dual monarchy was defeated with the other Central Powers in World War I, and the new Hungary underwent hard times. First there was a short-lived republic in 1918. The chaotic Communist rule of 1919 under Béla Kun ended with the Rumanians occupying Budapest on Aug. 4, 1919. When the Rumanians left, Admiral Nicholas Horthy entered the capital with a national army. The Treaty of Trianon of June 4, 1920, cost Hungary 75 per cent of its land and more than 50 per cent of its population. Meanwhile, the National Assembly had restored the legal continuity of the old monarchy; and on March 1, 1920, Horthy was elected Regent.

Following the German invasion of Russia on June 22, 1941, Hungary joined the attack against the U.S.S.R., but the war was not popular and Hungarian troops were almost entirely withdrawn from the eastern front by May, 1943. German occupation troops set up a puppet government after Admiral Horthy's appeal for an armistice with advancing Soviet troops on October 15, 1944, had resulted in his overthrow. The German regime soon fled the capital, however, and on Dec. 23 a provisional government was formed in Soviet-occupied eastern Hungary. On Jan. 20, 1945, it signed an armistice in Moscow. On Feb. 1, 1946, the National Assembly approved a constitutional law abolishing the 1,000-year-old monarchy and establishing a republic.

ECONOMIC CONDITIONS. Agriculture is

the basis of Hungarian economic life, engaging more than half the population. The Land Reform Act issued in March, 1945, provided for the confiscation of all estates over 284 acres; about 8,000,000 acres were divided among some 500,000 families. Cereals grown in the fertile Danubian plains are the chief crops. Leading crops in 1960 were wheat, potatoes, barley, rye, oats, maize, and sugar beets.

In addition, cultivation of vines, fruit and garden produce is important; the famous Tokay wine is produced on the southern slopes of the Hegyalja in the northeast.

Horse-breeding is a traditionally important branch of agriculture. Hungarians have a great love for horses, and their excellent breeds were exported in large numbers before World War II. Livestock in 1959 included 2,155,000 sheep, 6,225,000 hogs, 2,002,000 cattle, and 717,000 horses.

The dominant industries are all based on agriculture, with flour milling in first place, followed by sugar refining, brewing and canning. The second group of industries make hardware and machinery. Most of the machine industry is concentrated in Budapest and Györ. Cotton leads the textile industry, especially in Budapest, which is also a center of woolen manufactures. Hemp and flax weaving are important. An estimated 1,150,000 persons were employed in industry in 1959. Almost all industrial facilities were nationalized under laws passed in 1946, 1948 and 1949. In addition, the Soviet Union took over all German-owned plants as reparations, and in 1946 Soviet-Hungarian companies were formed to exploit bauxite, petroleum, and air and river navigation; the Soviet shares in these companies were sold to Hungary in 1954.

Leading exports include passenger rail coaches, buses, textiles, live animals and products, and machinery.

NATURAL FEATURES AND RESOURCES. Most of Hungary is a fertile, rolling plain lying east of the Danube, and drained by the Danube and the Tisza Rivers. In the extreme northwest is the Little Hungarian Plain. South of that area is Lake Balaton, 250 square miles, the largest lake of western and central Europe.

While Hungary generally is mineral-poor, it has about 20 per cent of the world's known reserves of bauxite. The coal is of low quality and is insufficient to meet domestic needs. Other minerals include iron ore, manganese, and gold.

---

# Iceland (Republic)

## (Ísland)

**Area: 39,768 square miles.\***
Population (est. 1959): 172,000 (almost entirely Icelandic).

\* Including several off-shore islands.

Density per square mile: 4.3.
President: Asgeir Asgeirsson.
Prime Minister: Olafur Thors.
Principal city (est. 1957): Reykjavik, 67,589 (capital and only large city).
Monetary unit: Króna.
Languages: Icelandic,
Religion: Evangelical Lutheran.

---

### MAJOR POLITICAL PARTIES

Independence party (24 seats in Parliament-Althing), led by Prime Minister Olafur Thors; Progressive party (17 seats), led by Eysteinn Jonsson; People's union party (10 seats), led by Einar Olgeirsson.

---

HISTORY AND GOVERNMENT. Iceland was first settled shortly before 900, mainly by Norse. A Constitution drawn up about 930 created a form of democracy and provided for an Althing, or General Assembly, now the oldest legislative body in the world. In 1262–64, Iceland came under Norwegian rule and passed to ultimate Danish control through the formation of the Union of Kalmar in 1483. In 1874 Icelanders obtained their own Constitution. In 1918 Denmark recognized Iceland as a separate state with unlimited sovereignty, but still nominally under the Danish King. On June 17, 1944, after a popular referendum, the Althing proclaimed Iceland a completely independent republic.

The British occupied Iceland in 1940, immediately after the German invasion of Denmark. In 1942, the United States took over the burden of protection. Iceland refused to abandon its neutrality in World War II, and thus forfeited charter membership in the United Nations, but it was cooperative with the Allies throughout. Iceland joined the North Atlantic Treaty Organization in 1949, and in May 1951, U.S. troops again landed at Iceland's request to aid in its defense preparations. Withdrawal of an Icelandic request for evacuation of U.S. troops was announced Dec. 6, 1956.

Constitutionally, the President of Iceland is elected for four years by popular vote. Executive power of the state resides in the Prime Minister and his Cabinet. The Althing (Parliament) is composed of 52 members in two houses. At an election the 52 members elect 17 of themselves to constitute the Upper House, the remaining 35 members representing henceforth the Lower House. In May, 1959, the Althing approved a bill providing for a new system of proportional representation and increasing the number of elected representatives from 52 to 60. The Althing can dismiss the Cabinet and the latter can dissolve the former. The President of the Republic cannot veto bills and can be removed from office by the Althing provided this action is subsequently approved by majority vote in a national plebiscite.

ECONOMIC CONDITIONS. Approximately six-sevenths of Iceland is unproductive, and only one-half of one per cent is under cultivation. With about 20 per cent of the population engaged in farming, sheep raising is the most important branch of this industry. Hay, potatoes, and turnips are the principal crops.

Fish and fish products accounted for 93% of the exports in 1959. Leading customers were the U.S.S.R. (18%), the United States and Canada (17%), Britain (8%), and EPU countries (28%); leading suppliers, the United States and Canada (16%), the U.S.S.R. (16%), and EPU countries (34%).

NATURAL FEATURES AND RESOURCES. Iceland, a bleak, volcanic island about the size of Kentucky, has maximum dimensions of 298 by 194 miles; it is mostly tableland, high, rugged, and barren. It is one of the world's most volcanic regions.

Small fresh-water lakes are found throughout the island, and there are many natural oddities, including hot springs, geysers, sulfur beds, canyons, waterfalls, and swift rivers. More than 13 per cent of the area is covered by snowfields and glaciers, and most of the people live in the 7 per cent of the island comprising fertile coastlands. Vegetation is of the Arctic type, mostly stunted. Except for peat and fisheries, Iceland has no natural resources.

About one-tenth of the people are engaged in fishing, and fish and fish products make up the bulk of Iceland's exports. The annual catch averages approximately 580,-000 metric tons. Many European fishing craft visit Iceland's fisheries, which lead the world in cod and are important for herring, plaice and halibut.

# Indonesia (Republic)
## (Republik Indonesia)

**Area:** 575,894 square miles.
**Population (est. 1960):** 92,600,000. (Indonesian, except for an estimated 1,500,-000 Chinese and 100,000 Europeans in 1951).
**Density per square mile:** 160.8.
**President:** Sukarno.
**Premier:** Sukarno.
**Principal cities (est. 1958):** Jakarta, 2,-081,200 (capital); Surabaja, 1,135,300 (industrial center); Bandung, 951,900 (commercial center, west Java); Semarang, 444,800 (seaport, central Java); Surakarta, 393,547*, (industrial center); Makassar, 346,080*, (coffee, teak); Medan, 342,200 (rail center, Sumatra).
**Monetary unit:** Rupiah.
**Languages:** Bahasa Indonesia (Malay) (official), Dutch, Javanese, Sundanese, Madurese.

* 1957 estimated.

**Religions:** Moslem (predominant), Christian (about 2,500,000), Brahmin, Buddhist.

---

### STATUS IN THE WORLD TODAY

Indonesia, like many another former colony, is neutralist in its foreign policy, although the local Communist groups have tried to take advantage of the new country's political and economic difficulties to bring about a more pro-Soviet orientation. Under President Sukarno's conception of a "guided democracy," consisting in part of a cabinet representing all parties, they have had some part in the central government, although of late their influence has been curbed by anti-Communists in the army.

Domestic politics have been characterized by a multiplicity of parties and grave cabinet instability. The centralization of powers, particularly economic, in the hands of the government in Java eventually gave rise in 1958 to widespread antagonism in the other islands, which felt they were being drained economically for the benefit of the overcrowded Javanese, and led to armed rebellion. The central government quickly and efficiently put down the revolt, although scattered guerrilla resistance still exists in outlying districts. But the resentment and the regional grievances, including a steady leftward drift at Jakarta, had a moderating effect on the government, which has promised a fairer economic deal for the outer regions in the future.

Indonesia's economic difficulties were further aggravated by the seizure of Dutch properties as a result of the dispute over West New Guinea, which the Dutch refused to turn over to Indonesia at the time of independence and which the latter claimed as an integral part of the republic. There was a sudden dearth of shipping to carry Indonesian exports because of a lack of trained personnel to operate ships and to operate other seized industries. The West New Guinea dispute also led to a coolness toward the United States because of our refusal to support Indonesia in this matter.

In July, 1959, President Sukarno assumed dictatorial powers by dissolving the constituent assembly and reinstating the 1945 Constitution. Fiscal measures in August resulted in a financial crisis.

---

HISTORY. The sovereign state of Indonesia, a group of islands with a total area more than twice that of Texas, constitutes one of the world's richest natural areas. These islands—Sumatra, Java, Madura, central and southern Borneo, Celebes, and the Moluccas—would reach from San Francisco to Honolulu if their extent was transposed to the eastern Pacific. They have great wealth in tin, rubber, spices, oil, quinine, and copra.

During the first few centuries of the Christian era, most of the islands came under the influence of Hindu priests and traders, who spread their culture and religion. Moslem invasions began in the thirteenth century, and most of the area was Moslem by the fifteenth century. Portuguese traders arrived early in the sixteenth century but were ousted by the Dutch about 1595. After Napoleon subjugated the Netherlands homeland in 1811, the British seized the islands but returned them to the Dutch in 1816. In 1922 the islands were made an integral part of the Netherlands kingdom.

In World War II, the Japanese military occupation with nominal native self-government continued until Aug., 1945, except in outlying parts of New Guinea and Borneo. About the time of the Japanese surrender, a self-styled Indonesian Republic headed by Achmed Sukarno sprang up and took over effective control of parts of Sumatra and Java. Allied forces, mostly British Indian troops, moved in, and fighting between them and the nationalists continued until Nov. 15, 1946, when Dutch-Indonesian parleys resulted in a draft agreement that contemplated the formation by Jan. 1, 1949, of a Netherlands-Indonesian Union, consisting on the one hand of the Netherlands, the Netherlands Antilles and Surinam and on the other of the United States of Indonesia, which was to be a sovereign nation composed of three equal states—the Republic of Indonesia, East Indonesia, and Borneo. Differences of interpretation ensued, and the Dutch resorted to force on July 20, 1947. Both sides issued cease-fire orders on Aug. 4, 1947, in response to a call from the U.N. Security Council.

After the Dutch and the Republic signed another truce on Jan. 17, 1948, a provisional federal government for the whole area was installed on Mar. 9, 1948, but difficulties between the Dutch and the Republic continued. On Dec. 18, 1948, Dutch forces instituted "police" action against Republican areas and seized the Republican leaders. Hostilities ceased Jan. 1, 1949, following U.N. intervention. On May 7, the Dutch agreed to return the exiled Republican regime to central Java.

On Nov. 2, 1949, Dutch and Indonesian leaders agreed upon the terms of union between the Netherlands and Indonesia. Dr. Sukarno was elected President of the federation on Dec. 16 by representatives of the Indonesian states, and the first all-Indonesian Cabinet was formed with Mohammed Hatta as Premier. The transfer of sovereignty took place at Amsterdam on Dec. 27, 1949. In July, 1959, Sukarno decreed a full return to the 1945 Constitution.

ECONOMIC CONDITIONS. The islands of Java and Madura, with only 9 per cent of the area, have more than two-thirds of the population and are among the most densely settled areas in the world (more than 1,000 per sq. mi.). The people, including about 137 races and tribes, are mainly of Malayan stock, with the Javanese the most advanced.

Agriculture engages about 70 per cent of the adult males. Rich in a variety of crops, the islands prior to World War II produced about 31 per cent of the world's copra, 37 per cent of its rubber, 83 per cent of its pepper, and nearly all of its quinine. The big-estate agriculture on Java and Sumatra is devoted mainly to export. The rest is subsistence agriculture. Rice is the staple food and chief crop. Major plantation crops are rubber, tea, coffee, cinchona bark, palm kernels, and sugar. Others are copra, cacao, spices, agava fiber, and kapok. In addition to rice, the chief food crops are maize, cassava, sweet potatoes, peanuts, and soybeans.

In 1959 there were an estimated 5,081,-000 cattle, 2,634,000 sheep, 1,469,000 hogs (1956), 654,000 horses, and 2,866,000 buffalo.

Industry, especially in Java, developed rapidly after 1930. In addition to industries connected with the processing of the rich natural products, there were established chemical works, textile and paper mills, soap factories, breweries, shipyards, a Goodyear tire and rubber plant, and a General Motors assembly plant.

Indonesia is primarily an importer of consumer and capital goods and an exporter of mineral and plantation products.

Chief exports in 1959 were rubber (35%), petroleum and products (37%), tin (5%), and cocoanut products (3%). Leading customers were Singapore and Malaya (29%), the Netherlands (4%), the United States (17%), and Britain (13%); leading suppliers, the United States and Canada (16%), Japan (14%), the Netherlands (6%), and Britain (5%).

NATURAL FEATURES AND RESOURCES. A backbone of mountain ranges extends throughout the main islands of the archipelago. Earthquakes are frequent, and there are many active volcanoes, ninety of them in Sumatra. Borneo is heavily forested.

Petroleum is the principal mineral product of modern Indonesia. The tin industry attained prewar levels more rapidly than others after World War II. Other important minerals include bauxite, coal, salt, nickel, and manganese.

Most valuable timber is teak, found mostly in east Java. Ebony, sandalwood, and ironwood also are cut.

# Iran (Kingdom)

Area: 636,294 square miles.

Population (est. 1960)*: 20,633,000 (Iranian, Kurdish, Azerbaijani).

Density per square mile: 32.4.

Ruler: Mohammed Riza Pahlavi.

Premier: Ali Amini.

Principal cities (1956 census): Teheran, 1,512,082 (capital); Tabriz, 289,996 (manufacturing center); Isfahan, 254,708 (cotton, tobacco); Meshed, 241,989.

Monetary unit: Rial.

Languages: Iranian (Persian), Kurdish, Azerbaijani.

Religions: Moslem (Shiah), about 90%; Moslem (Sunni), about 5%; Armenian; Jewish; Nestorian; Parsi.

* U.N. estimate; no census ever taken.

---

## STATUS IN THE WORLD TODAY

Iran, as one of the Middle Eastern Islamic nations which is not of Arab stock, has not been subject to as much anti-Western pressure from nationalist pan-Arab sources as have other countries in the area. But as a nation bordering upon the Soviet Union, it has been subjected to extreme anti-Western pressure from Moscow because of the fact that it is a signatory to the Central Treaty Organization, a defense group comprising the "Upper Tier" of states between the U.S.S.R. and the Middle East.

As a major oil-producing nation and as a potential gateway to the rest of the Middle East, Iran has long been a target of Kremlin imperialism. Early in 1959, when Iran was negotiating a bilateral defense agreement with the United States, the Soviet Union offered to negotiate a nonaggression and economic pact if Iran would refuse to sign any agreement with the United States. Iran, however, elected to accept defense assistance from the United States, and again became the target of violent Communist abuse and of Moscow's threats to invoke sections of a 1921 treaty which permits the U.S.S.R. to move troops into Iran if forces of a hostile third nation enter the latter country. Iran countered by denouncing the treaty articles in question.

Although Iran is a major oil producer, it has had to obtain nearly $500 million in American aid since 1951. The Shah himself has taken steps to break down the feudal land-ownership system, which provided fuel for Communist propaganda, by distributing his own farm properties to peasants of more than 300 villages.

---

HISTORY. Oil-rich Iran, was called Persia before 1935. Its key location blocks the lower land gate to Asia and also stands in the way of traditional Russian ambitions for access to the Indian Ocean. After periods of Assyrian, Median, and Achaemenidian rule, Persia became a powerful empire under Cyrus the Great, reaching from the Indus to the Nile at its zenith in 525 B.C. It fell to Alexander in 331–30 B.C., to the Selucidae in 312–02 B.C., and to the Parthians about 130 B.C. A native Persian regime arose about A.D. 224, was weakened fighting the Turks, and fell to the Arabs in 637. In the twelfth century the Mongols took their turn ruling Persia, and in the early eighteenth century the Turks and Russians occupied it.

An Anglo-Russian convention of 1907 divided Iran into two spheres of influence. British attempts to impose a protectorate over all of Iran were defeated in 1919. On Feb. 26, 1921, General Riza Pahlavi seized the government and was elected hereditary Shah in 1925. Subsequently he did much to modernize the country and abolished all foreign extraterritorial rights.

Increased pro-Axis activity led to Anglo-Russian occupation of Iran in August, 1941, and deposition of the Shah in favor of his son, Mohammed Riza Pahlavi.

In November, 1945, a Soviet-inspired autonomist movement won control of Azerbaijan, Iran's northwest province. To protect their advantage, the Russians kept troops in that area past the treaty evacuation date of March 2, 1946. The Iranians promptly protested this breach of agreement to the United Nations. The Russians evacuated their troops on May 6.

Ali Razmara became Premier June 26, 1950, and pledged to restore efficient and honest government, but he was assassinated Mar. 7, 1951. Mohammed Mossadegh took over April 29. Parliament completed action on a bill nationalizing the oil industry over strong British protests.

Mossadegh was ousted Aug. 19, 1953, in a coup d'état led by Fazollah Zahedi, whom the Shah had named Premier. The oil dispute was settled in August, 1954. The present government is concentrating on land reform to appease the demands of peasant groups.

GOVERNMENT. Iran is a constitutional monarchy, and the Shah has the usual powers of the head of a parliamentary state. Executive power is exercised by a Cabinet headed by the Prime Minister, who is appointed by the Shah and is responsible to Parliament, the lower house of which (Majlis) has 136 popularly elected members and the upper house of which (Senate) has 60 members, half of whom are appointed by the Shah.

ECONOMIC CONDITIONS. Iran is predominantly agricultural. Large estates are numerous, and irrigation is common, especially on the central plateau. The principal crops are wheat and barley.

Other crops include rice, grapes, dates,

apricots, tobacco, tea, cotton, sugar beets, and corn. There are extensive grazing lands. In 1958 there were an estimated 27,200,000 sheep.

Iran must still import many manufactured necessities, but several new factories were established by the government after 1925, including sugar plants, rice and oil mills, textile factories, a cement factory, copper smelter, glycerine factory, and small arms factory. Both sugar and tobacco are government monopolies. The manufacture of carpets, for which Iran is famous, is a valuable industry.

In 1958–59 the leading customers were the United States and Canada (11%), the United Kingdom (14%), West Germany (8%), and other continental EPU countries (32%); leading suppliers, West Germany (21%), other continental EPU countries (15%), and the United States and Canada (18%). The principal exports are cotton, petroleum, and rugs.

NATURAL FEATURES AND RESOURCES. Iran is, in general, a plateau averaging 4,000 feet elevation. In addition, there are maritime lowlands along the Persian Gulf and the Caspian Sea. The Elburz Mountains in the north rise to 18,603 feet at Mt. Demavend. From northwest to southeast, the country is crossed by a desert 800 miles long.

Considerable mineral wealth exists, but only oil is exploited commercially. The principal field, near Shushar in the southwest, was worked until 1951 by the Anglo-Iranian Oil Company. The latter's concession began in 1901 and was to run until 1993, but its properties were nationalized by the Iranian government in April, 1951. Production under Iranian control was negligible. Under an agreement signed Sept. 19, 1954, Iran's oil is being produced, refined and marketed by a consortium of eight western oil companies, with 50 per cent of the profits going to Iran. The consortium began production Oct. 29, 1954.

---

# Iraq (Republic)

**Area:** 171,600 square miles.*
**Population** (1959 est.): 6,952,000 (Arab, 75%; Kurdish, 15%; Iranian, 3.75%; others, 6.25%).
**Density per square mile:** 40.5.
**President:** Najib al-Rubai.
**Premier:** Brig. Abdul Karim Kassem.
**Principal cities** (census 1957, cities proper): Baghdad, 355,958 (capital); Mosul, 179,646 (oil); Basra, 164,623 (chief port).
**Monetary unit:** Dinar.
**Languages:** Arabic, Kurdish.
**Religions** (census 1947): Moslem, 93.6%; Christian, 3.1%; Jewish, 2.5%; others, .8%.

\* Includes desert area of 80,583 square miles.

## STATUS IN THE WORLD TODAY

The military regime which has ruled Iraq since the coup d'etat of July, 1958, has thus far shown itself to be extremely anti-Western and ultra-nationalistic. It has gradually been expelling, or releasing, all military, economic, agricultural, educational, and other experts who had been brought in by the previous governments to help in the development of the country. Although it has enjoyed the support of the Communists since the beginning, it has discouraged all political parties, and a prominent Communist has yet to be named to high office. In fact, the Communists assailed Brigadier Kassem's choice of a Foreign Minister appointed on the first anniversary of the revolution. It remains to be seen how long the Communist-Kassem honeymoon lasts. As long as the Kassem regime carries out one of the basic Soviet aims—the elimination of all Western influence—there is no need for the popular front which is usually organized to help the Communists to power.

Although the Iraq revolutionary movement is nationalistic, and no doubt was influenced by the success of Nasser's nationalistic administration in Egypt, it is not pan-Arabic to the extent that the United Arab Republic expected. During the first year, relations between the two governments were anything but friendly, with the Cairo radio assailing the Communists and the U.A.R. allegedly having financed and organized a revolt against the Kassem regime by a group of young officers in the Mosul area early in 1959. A second "disturbance" in the same general area took place on the occasion of the anniversary, when pro-Communist Kurds were joined by a few officers in fighting against loyal troops in Kirkuk. In recent decades, leaders of nationalistic Kurds, who inhabit parts of Iraq, Iran, and Turkey, and who would like to see the creation of an independent Kurdistan, have fled to the U.S.S.R. and been trained there by the Kremlin. Approximately 1,000 of these returned to Iraq after the revolution and can be presumed to be busy spreading Soviet propaganda in all three countries. To many of the Iraqi Kurds, however, the Communist domination has become so oppressive that they have fled to neighboring Turkey.

With Iraq out of the Baghdad Pact, the name of the anti-Communist group was changed to the Central Treaty Organization, to be known as CENTO.

---

HISTORY. Iraq, a triangle of mountains, desert, and fertile river valley is bounded east by Iran, north by Turkey, west by Syria and Jordan, and south by Saudi Arabia. From earliest times it has been known as Mesopotamia—the land between the rivers—for it embraces a large part of the alluvial plains of the Tigris and Euphrates.

An advanced civilization existed in Mesopotamia by 4000 B.C. Sometime after 2000 B.C. it became the center of the ancient Babylonian and Assyrian empires. It was conquered by Cyrus the Great of Persia in 538 B.C., and by Alexander in 331 B.C. After an Arab conquest in A.D. 637–40, Baghdad became capital of the ruling caliphate. The country was cruelly pillaged by the Mongols in 1258, and during the sixteenth, seventeenth, and eighteenth centuries was the object of repeated Turkish-Persian competition.

Nominal Turkish suzerainty imposed in 1638 was replaced by direct Turkish rule in 1831. In World War I an Anglo-Indian force occupied most of the country, and Britain was given a mandate over the area in 1920. The British recognized Iraq as a kingdom in 1922 and terminated the mandate in 1932, when Iraq was admitted to the League of Nations. In World War II, Iraq generally adhered to its 1930 treaty of alliance with Britain, but in 1941 British troops were compelled to put down a pro-Axis revolt led by Prime Minister Rashid Ali. Iraq became a charter member of the Arab League in March, 1945, and Iraqi troops took part in the Arab invasion of Palestine in 1948. The 1930 treaty of alliance with Britain was terminated in April, 1955, and replaced by a defense co-operation agreement.

King Faisal II, born on May 2, 1935, succeeded his father, Ghazi I, who was killed in an automobile accident on April 4, 1939. King Faisal and his uncle, Crown Prince Abdul-Ilah, were assassinated in August, 1958, in a swift revolutionary coup which brought to power a military junta headed by Abdul Karim Kassem. The short-lived "Arab Union," formed by the federation of Iraq and Jordan in February, 1958, came abruptly to an end with recognition by the U.A.R. of the rebel government of Iraq.

ECONOMIC CONDITIONS. The chief economic activity is agriculture, dependent upon irrigation and confined to the valleys of the Tigris and Euphrates. Iraq supplies about 80 per cent of the world's dates. Chief among the cereal products of Iraq are barley, wheat, rice, sorghum, maize, and millet. Many fruits and some tobacco and cotton are grown. Grazing is the principal occupation of the many nomadic and seminomadic tribes.

Industry is still embryonic. Of some 100 firms, the most important are those making brick, tile, woolen textiles, vegetable oils, soap, glass, and cigarettes.

Chief exports in 1959 were petroleum (83%), dates (10%), and barley (2%). Leading suppliers in 1958 were Britain (31%), and the United States and Canada (11%); leading customers, France (21%), Italy (19%), and Britain (18%).

The only port for seagoing vessels is that of Basra, located on the Shatt-al-Arab River near the head of the Persian Gulf. NATURAL FEATURES AND RESOURCES. Iraq has arid desertland west of the Euphrates, a broad central valley between the Euphrates and Tigris, and mountains in the northeast. The fertile lower valley is formed by the delta of the two rivers, which join about 120 miles from the head of the Persian Gulf. The gulf coast line is 26 miles.

Oil production is concentrated at the Baba Gurgur fields near Kirkuk, which are operated on behalf of an international group by the British-managed Iraq Petroleum Company. Associated companies operate fields at Zubair and Rumaila near Basra and at Ain Zalah and Butmah. The Khanaqin Oil Company, a British Petroleum subsidiary, operates another field which produces only for local consumption.

Oil is piped to Tripoli in Lebanon, Baniyas in Syria, Fao on the Persian Gulf, and Haifa in Israel (suspended in 1948). The Iraqi government received an estimated $250 million in oil revenues in 1959.

---

# Ireland (Republic)

**Area:** 27,136 square miles (not including larger water bodies).*
**Population** (est. 1960): 2,834,000 (almost entirely Irish).
**Density per square mile:** 104.4.
**President:** Eamon de Valera.
**Prime Minister:** Sean Lemass.
**Principal cities** (census 1956): Dublin (Baile Atha Cliath), 539,476 (capital); Cork, 80,011 (seaport); Limerick (Luimneach), 50,886 (seaport).
**Monetary unit:** Irish pound.
**Languages:** Gaelic, English.
**Religions** (census 1946): Roman Catholic, 94.3%; Protestant Episcopal, 4.2%; Presbyterian, .8%; others, .7%.
* Total area: 27,136 square miles.

---

## STATUS IN THE WORLD TODAY

Although there is little doubt that the Irish believe in the basic principles of Free Europe and strongly oppose the Soviet way of life, the Republic of Ireland has remained firmly aloof from political commitments in Western European integration of Free World alliances. This attitude, as well as Eire's official neutrality in World War II, can be traced to the problem of the division of the island into the Republic, comprising the twenty-six southern counties, and the six northeastern counties of Ulster, with a separate government closely bound to England. Protestant in faith and largely industrial, whereas the Republic is predominantly Roman Catholic and agricultural, Northern Ireland remains detached from the rest, despite the demand for Irish unity which still persists in Eire, a feeling often expressed in border raids and bombings. The official policy of the government of Eire, however, is that the solution must come about in a peaceful manner. The foreign policy toward the United States is extremely friendly.

### MAJOR POLITICAL PARTIES

Republican party (Fianna Fail) (78 seats in House of Representatives—Dáil), led by Prime Minister Sean Lemass; United Ireland party (Fine Gael) (40 seats), led by James M. Dillon.

HISTORY. About the beginning of the Christian Era, Ireland was divided into five kingdoms, each with its own ruler, but each subject to the overlord of all Ireland who dwelt at Tara. St. Patrick introduced Christianity in A.D. 432.

Norse depredations along the coasts, starting in 795, ended in 1014 with Norse defeat at the Battle of Clontarf by forces under Brian. In the middle of the 12th century, the Pope gave all Ireland to the English Crown as a papal fief. In 1171 Henry II of England was acknowledged "Lord of Ireland," but local sectional rule continued for centuries, and English control over the whole island was not reasonably absolute until the 17th century. By the Act of Union (1800), England and Ireland became the "United Kingdom of Great Britain and Ireland."

A steady decline in the Irish economy followed in the next decades. The population had reached 8¼ million when the great potato famine of 1846–48 took many lives and drove millions to emigrate to America. By 1921 it was down to 4.3 million. In the meantime, anti-British agitation continued along with demands for Irish home rule. The advent of World War I delayed the institution of home rule and resulted in the 1916 Easter rebellion in Dublin. Guerrilla warfare against British forces followed proclamation of a republic by the rebels in 1919. The Irish Free State was established as a dominion in 1922, with the six northern counties as part of the United Kingdom. Ireland was neutral in World War II. Its last link with the British was broken in 1949, when the Republic of Ireland was proclaimed.

GOVERNMENT. Ireland is a sovereign, independent republic. The President, directly elected for seven years, names the Prime Minister on the nomination of the Chamber of Deputies. Parliament (Oireachtas) has two houses. The Chamber of Deputies (Dáil Eireann) has 147 members elected by proportional representation for a five-year term. The Senate (Seanad Eireann) has 60 members, of whom 11 are named by the Prime Minister, 6 by the universities, and 43 from vocational panels. Its powers, however, are limited.

The majority of the people are English speaking, although the government has attempted to promote the traditional Gaelic language, which is an essential part of the curriculum for all state schools.

ECONOMIC CONDITIONS. Principal crops are wheat, oats, potatoes, sugar beets. Other staple crops are rye, flax, turnips, cabbage, and hay. Livestock in June, 1959, included 4,657,000 cattle, 4,409,000 sheep, and 838,000 hogs.

Leading manufactures are ordinarily beverages, tobacco, wood, paper, clothing, textiles and metals. The hydroelectric plant erected on the Shannon River in County Limerick provides cheap electricity for homes and factories.

The United Kingdom (including Northern Ireland) was the leading customer in 1958 (74%). The United Kingdom was also the chief supplier (52%), followed by the U.S. and Canada (9%) and West Germany (4%). Major exports were live animals (42%), beef and veal (6%), beer (5%), and chocolate crumb (5%). Major imports were oils, fats, resins and gums, textiles, machinery, and vehicles.

NATURAL FEATURES AND RESOURCES. Occupying the entire island except for the six northern countries of Ulster, Ireland resembles a basin—a central plain rimmed with mountains, except in the Dublin region. The mountains are low, with the highest peak, Carrantuohill, located in Kerry County, rising to a height of 3,415 feet.

The principal river is the Shannon, which begins in the north central area, flows south and southwest for about 240 miles and empties into the Atlantic. About 20 per cent of the country is covered by bogs. Among the many lakes are the famous Lakes of Killarney in the southwest county of Kerry.

Ireland mines coal and gypsum.

## Israel (Republic)

Area: 7,992 square miles.
Population (est. 1960): 2,114,000 (1953: Jewish, 88.9%; Moslem, 7.6%; Christian, 2.5%; others, 1.0%).
Density per square mile: 264.5.
President: Itzhak Ben-Zvi.
Premier: David Ben-Gurion.

Principal cities (est. Dec. 31, 1958): Tel Aviv-Jaffa, 380,000 (industrial center); Haifa, 170,000 (chief port); Jerusalem (Israeli sector), 156,000 (capital).

Monetary unit: Israeli pound (£I).

## STATUS IN THE WORLD TODAY

Israel, friend of the West in the cold war, has been under military threat from its Arab neighbors ever since it achieved its independence in 1948. At first it was supported by the Soviet Union, but the Kremlin quickly decided that it was more worthwhile to win some measure of popular sympathy in the oil-producing Arab nations. In recent years it has consistently backed the Arab countries against Israel and, in response to Arab protests, has at times curtailed the flow of Jewish immigrants from behind the Iron Curtain to Israel.

Despite the constant threat of attack, which has meant devoting a considerable portion of the budget to defense, Israel has made tremendous strides economically, while at the same time absorbing large numbers of Jewish refugees from all parts of the world. Completion of a pipe line from the Red Sea to the Mediterranean will ease its dependence on use of the Suez Canal, which is barred to it frequently by the hostile Egyptians despite efforts of the United Nations to keep the waterway open to commerce of all nations. The swift Israeli conquest of the Sinai Peninsula in 1956 enhanced its military position vis-a-vis Egypt and detracted somewhat from the prestige of the Nasser regime. A U.N. force still guards the frontier between Israel and Egypt along the Gaza strip.

## MAJOR POLITICAL PARTIES

Israel Labor party (42 seats in Parliament-Knesset), led by Prime Minister David Ben Gurion; Herut party (17 seats), led by Menahem Begin; Liberal party (17 seats), led by Dr. Peretz Bernstein and Dr. Pinhas Rosen.

**HISTORY.** The history of Palestine, cradle of two of the great religions of the world, and homeland of the modern state of Israel, is mostly a chronicle of invasion, conquest, and confusing divisions. To the ancient Hebrews it was known as the "Land of Canaan"; the name Palestine is derived from that part of the country inhabited by the Philistines of Biblical times. About 1000 B.C. the Hebrews succeeded in establishing a single monarchy, which later split up into two kingdoms—Judah and Israel. The country was subsequently invaded and overcome by many peoples, including the Assyrians, Babylonians, Egyptians, Persians, Macedonians, Romans, and

Byzantines. In A.D. 634–36, Palestine was wrested from the Byzantine Empire by the Arabs. Frankish Crusaders captured Jerusalem in 1099 and set up a feudal kingdom which endured until the defeat of the Franks by Saladin (1187) and the restoration of Moslem rule. In 1516 suzerainty over the area was transferred from the Mamelukes of Egypt to the Turks. It remained part of the Ottoman Empire until World War I, when British forces under General Allenby defeated the Turks and captured Jerusalem (Dec. 9, 1917). The League of Nations mandate awarded to Great Britain was put in force on Sept. 29, 1923.

Meanwhile, a movement had been founded in 1897 by Theodor Herzl to create a Jewish homeland in Palestine, and a considerable number of Jewish immigrants had entered the country prior to World War I. On Nov. 2, 1917, British recognition was given both to the growing Arab nationalist movement and to Zionist aspirations by the Balfour Declaration.

A British royal commission report, July 7, 1937, recommended partition of Palestine into an Arab and a Jewish state separated by a mandated area in the vicinity of Jerusalem and at Nazareth. The Arabs opposed the proposal, advocating instead the establishment of an independent Palestine with full minority rights for the Jews. In May, 1939, the British government issued a White Paper declaring the establishment of a Jewish state contrary to British obligations to the Arabs and promising, after a transitory period of ten years, the establishment of an independent Palestine in which Arabs and Jews would share authority in government. During the next five years, 75,000 Jews were to be allowed to enter Palestine. These proposals did not satisfy either party, but the outbreak of World War II overshadowed all other issues.

End of European hostilities in 1945 brought a renewal of friction and the formation of the Arab League. Attempts to bring Jewish immigrants into Palestine illegally were intensified thereafter, and terrorism grew apace.

Termination of the British mandate May 14, 1948, and withdrawal of British forces brought new violence. An independent state of Israel was immediately proclaimed by the Jewish National Council, and Arab forces converged on Palestine from the south, north, and east, spearheaded by the crack British-trained Arab Legion of King Abdullah of Jordan. Within a few hours Arab-Jewish hostilities were in full swing. On June 11, however, there went into effect a four-week truce supervised by Count Folke Bernadotte, Swedish U.N. mediator in Palestine. Fighting resumed on July 9, with Israeli forces gaining on all fronts except in Jerusalem, part of which had been taken by Jordani troops prior to the truce. On July 17 a second truce was effected on order of the U.N. Security Council. Bernadotte was assassinated on Sept. 17 by unidentified Jewish terrorists, and his duties were taken over by Dr. Ralph Bunche of the United States. A final cease-fire took effect on Jan. 7, 1949, and an armistice agreement was concluded with Egypt on Feb. 24 and with Jordan on April 3.

During the hostilities Israel lost none of the territory allotted to it under the partition plan and increased that territory by about 50 per cent by gaining western Galilee, a broad corridor to Jerusalem through central Palestine and part of modern Jerusalem. In April, 1950, Jordan incorporated eastern and central Palestine, including the Old City of Jerusalem.

Israel's governmental structure took shape rapidly. The provisional leaders, Chaim Weizmann and David Ben-Gurion, were confirmed as President and Premier, respectively. Recognized by most non-Arab countries, the new nation was admitted to the U.N. on May 11, 1949.

Despite many Cabinet crises, Ben-Gurion's government met with increasing success the problems arising out of an unfavorable trade balance, large numbers of immigrants and need for foreign capital investment and additional industries.

Dr. Weizmann died Nov. 9, 1952, and Itzhak Ben-Zvi was elected to succeed him as President on Dec. 8.

Israeli troops invaded Egypt on Oct. 29, 1956, and quickly took the Gaza strip and almost all the Sinai peninsula up to the Suez canal. Following U.N. intervention, they were gradually withdrawn.

GOVERNMENT. The Israeli Constitution, adopted by the Constituent Assembly in 1949, provides a republican form of government headed by a President elected for a 5-year term by the Knesset (Chamber of Deputies). Legislative power is vested in the Knesset, whose 120 members are elected by the vote of all citizens who have reached the age of 21. The government is administered by the Cabinet, which is headed by the Premier and is responsible to the Chamber of Deputies.

The Knesset decided in June, 1950, that Israel would not have a formal written constitution but would acquire one gradually through the years. Israel is basically committed to the admission of every Jew who desires to settle within its borders, subject to control of the Knesset.

ECONOMIC CONDITIONS. Agriculture is the chief economic activity. The maritime plain, the plain of Esdraelon and the northern Jordan valley are the principal agricultural areas. Citrus growing, confined largely to the maritime plain, normally furnishes the major export crop. Others include olives, rice, fruits and vegetables, figs, tobacco, wheat, barley, corn, sesame, and potatoes. There are many collective rural settlements.

Industry is developing rapidly, especially the food-processing, textile, metalworking, and chemical groups. Diamond cutting, although dependent on rough diamond imports, is of major importance; and there are oil refineries and storage tanks at Haifa, a terminus of the pipeline from the Iraqi oil fields, which have been suspended since 1948.

Chief exports in 1958 were citrus fruits (29%) and polished diamonds (26%). Leading customers were Britain (19%) and the United States and Canada (17%); leading suppliers, the United States and Canada (30%), EPU countries (37%), and Britain (11%). Leading imports were wheat (7%), rough diamonds (6%), and iron and steel bars (3%).

NATURAL FEATURES AND RESOURCES. Northern Israel is largely a plateau traversed from north to south by mountains and broken by great depressions, also running from north to south.

The maritime plain of Israel is remarkably fertile, but the southern Negeb region, which comprises almost half the total area, is largely a wide desert steppe area. The Jordan, the only important river, rises in Syria and flows along the Jordan border through the Hule marshes and lake and the Sea of Tiberias (Galilee) into Jordani Palestine and thence into the Dead Sea, which is 1,290 feet below sea level.

Mineral resources are limited. They include gypsum, sulfur, limestone, and rock salt, together with potash and bromine from the Dead Sea.

# Italy (Republic)
## (Repubblica Italiana)

Area: 116,304 square miles.
Population (est. 1959): 49,052,000 (predominantly Italian).
Density per square mile: 421.7.
President: Giovanni Gronchi.
Premier: Amintore Fanfani.
Principal cities (est. 1958): Rome, 1,874,-469 (capital); Milan, 1,384,666 (leading financial, industrial center); Naples, 1,115,-798 (seaport); Turin, 889,249 (auto works); Genoa, 736,135 (seaport); Palermo, 570,568 (Sicilian seaport).
Monetary unit: Lira.
Religions: Roman Catholic, 99.6%; others (Protestant, Orthodox, Jewish), .4%.

## STATUS IN THE WORLD TODAY

The postwar Republic of Italy has been firmly pro-Western in the cold war and is a member of NATO. It has followed this policy despite a strong and persistent Communist opposition, although the majority of Italian Communists, with the exception of the leaders, reject the dominance of Moscow and regard their vote as a reaction against fascism and a short cut to economic betterment. In foreign affairs Italy has also tried to mediate between the Western and Arab powers, since it is no longer a colonial power, and has made considerable progress in obtaining oil concessions in the Middle East.

Western nations have helped Italy recover from the gravest sort of economic problems resulting from heavy damage in World War II. Under the Marshall Plan and ECA, Italy received $1.8 billion, while the United States paid most of the $450 million allocated by UNRRA for food relief and gave Italy twenty-nine ships. As a result of this pump priming, Italian agricultural and industrial production increased. But despite the remarkable progress in vitalizing economic life, only a beginning has been made. Agricultural production is still unable to meet the demands of the Italian people. Land reform, especially turning over large estates to the peasants, has been painfully slow. Energetic efforts are being made to close the gap between exports and imports, and there are still some 2,000,000 unemployed in a working population of 21,000,000.

## MAJOR POLITICAL PARTIES

Christian Democratic party (273 seats in Chamber of Deputies), led by Adone Zoli; Communist party (140 seats), led by Palmiro Togliatti; Socialist party (84 seats), led by Pietro Nenni.

HISTORY AND GOVERNMENT: Until A.D. 476, when the German Odoacer became head of the Roman Empire in the west, the history of Italy was largely the history of Rome. From A.D. 800 on, the Holy Roman Emperors, the Popes, Normans and Saracens all vied for control over various segments of the Italian peninsula. Numerous city states, such as Venice and Genoa, and many small principalities flourished in the late Middle Ages.

In 1713, after the War of the Spanish Succession, Milan, Naples, and Sardinia were handed over to Austria, which lost some of its Italian territories in 1735. After 1800 Italy was unified by Napoleon, who crowned himself King of Italy on May 26, 1805; but after the Congress of Vienna in 1815, Austria once again became the dominant power in Italy.

Recent Italian experience seems to be an extension of a troubled history. In 1815 the Congress of Vienna restored the Italies to their former position of confused disunity, like the Germanies a "geographical expression." The tyranny of the Restoration met with opposition by the *Carbonari* (charcoal burners), a secret society which demanded constitutional government and national unification. But Austrian armies crushed Italian uprisings in 1820, 1821, and 1831. In the 1830's Joseph Mazzini (1805–1872), brilliant liberal nationalist, organized the *Risorgimento* (Resurrection), which laid the foundation for Italian unity.

Disappointed Italian patriots looked to Sardinia for leadership. Count Camille di Cavour (1810–1861), Prime Minister of Sardinia in 1852 and the architect of United Italy, joined England and France in the Crimean War (1853–1856), and in 1859 helped France in a war against Austria, thereby obtaining Lombardy. By plebiscite in 1860, Modena, Parma, Tuscany, and the Romagna voted to join Sardinia. In 1860, Giuseppe Garibaldi (1807–1882) conquered Sicily and Naples and turned them over to Sardinia. Victor Emmanuel II, King of Sardinia, was proclaimed King of Italy on March 17, 1861.

Allied with Germany and Austria-Hungary in the Triple Alliance of 1882, Italy declared her neutrality upon the outbreak of World War I on the ground that Germany had embarked upon an offensive war. In 1915 Italy entered the war on the side of the Allies.

Benito Mussolini (1883–1945), a former Socialist, organized discontented Italians in 1919 into the Fascisti Party "to rescue Italy from Bolshevism." After winning the battle of the streets against the Communists, the Black Shirts marched on Rome on October 27, 1922. Mussolini was made Premier. The price of Fascist victory was the breakdown of parliamentary government. Mussolini destroyed Parliament, suspended civil rights, wiped out political opposition, and transformed Italy into a dictatorship. He gave his people everything but freedom. His basic slogan—"Believe, Obey, Fight."

Mussolini's foreign policy was expansionist, designed to make the Mediterranean an Italian lake (*Mare Nostrum*). His designs on Corsica, Savoy, Nice, and Tunis enraged the French. In 1935 his troops invaded Ethiopia (Abyssinia) and annexed it despite stubborn resistance. In 1936 he aligned himself with Hitler in the Rome-Berlin Axis. Italian troops fought for Franco in the Spanish Civil War of 1936–1939. After the defeat of France in 1940, Mussolini joined Nazi Germany in World War II. The myth of Italian military strength was broken on the sands of Libya by British tanks and in Albania by Greek bayonets. The Italian dictator was caught and executed by partisans at Dongo on Lake Como on April 28, 1945.

Following the overthrow of Mussolini's dictatorship and the armistice with the Allies (September 3, 1943), Italy joined the war against Germany as a co-belligerent. In May, 1946, King Victor Emmanuel III left the country after installing his son as King Humbert II. But a provisional coalition government held a popular plebiscite in June, 1946. The Italians voted for a republic. King Humbert abdicated and followed his father into exile.

The President is elected for a term of seven years by Parliament in joint session with regional representatives. The President nominates the Cabinet, which is headed by the Premier, or Prime Minister. Parliament is composed of two houses: a Senate with 246 elective Senators and Deputies, of 590 members elected by the people for a five-year term. All Italian citizens, including women over 21, are dutybound to vote.

PEACE TREATY OF 1947. The peace treaty which took effect Sept. 15, 1947, required Italian renunciation of all claims in Ethiopia and Greece, and the cession of the Dodecanese to Greece and of five small Alpine areas to France. In addition, the major part of the Istrain peninsula, including Fiume and Pola, went to Yugoslavia. The Free Territory of Trieste was carved out of the area to the west of the new Yugoslav frontier.

Italy was to pay reparations of $100,000,000 in kind over a seven-year period to the Soviet Union, $125,000,000 to Yugoslavia, $105,000,000 to Greece, $25,000,000 to Ethiopia and $5,000,000 to Albania; also to make two-thirds restitution for wartime damage to Allied property in Italy.

Zone A of Trieste (90 sq. mi.), including the city of Trieste, was transferred to Italy in Oct., 1954, and the remainder to Yugoslavia.

RELIGION. Although the country is predominantly Roman Catholic, religious freedom is permitted. Catholic religious teaching is given in all elementary and intermediate schools. Relations with the Church are regulated by the treaty with the Holy See of Feb. 11, 1929, which established the temporal power of the Pope over Vatican City.

ECONOMIC CONDITIONS.
*Agriculture.* Agriculture engages more than a third of the population. It is extremely diversified; differences of altitude, soil and climate allow the production of all European crops from rye to rice, from apples to oranges, and from hemp to cotton. Italy ranks next to France in wine production, and next to Spain in olive-oil production.

Livestock and dairy farming are important in Italy. Of the 50-odd varieties of Italian cheese, the best known are the hard parmesan and pecorino (the latter made from ewe's milk) and the soft bel paese and gorgonzola. In 1959 Italy had 8,978,000 cattle, 8,600,000 sheep, and 3,900,000 hogs.

*Industry.* Industrial production is centered in the north. The nature of the fascist corporate state had a tendency to foster industrial concentration prior to World War II. The textile industry is the largest and most important and supplies the home market as well as furnishing a large proportion of Italy's exports. The metal industries are handicapped by lack of coal, which must be imported in large quantities, and by insufficient iron-ore reserves. The chemical, clothing and food industries are also important. Italy is a member of the European Coal and Steel Community.

Production includes cotton yarn, woven cotton fabrics, rayon yarn, pig iron and ferroalloys, raw steel, cement, automobiles, and trucks.

*Trade.* Italy's leading customers by value in 1959 were EPU countries (45%) and the U.S. and Canada (13%). Main suppliers were EPU countries (41%), the U.S. and Canada (12%), Latin America (7%), Britain (6%), and Iraq (5%). Leading exports were machinery and vehicles, fruits and vegetables, synthetic fibers and manufactures and cotton and manufactures. Leading imports included cotton, coal and coke, wool, grain, and petroleum and products.

NATURAL FEATURES AND RESOURCES. Approximately 600 of boot-shaped Italy's 708 miles of length are in the long peninsula that projects into the Mediterranean from the fertile basin of the Po River. The Apennines, branching off from the Alps between Nice and Genoa, form the peninsula's backbone, and rise to a maximum height of 9,560 feet at the Gran Sasso d'Italia (Corno). The Alps are Italy's northern boundary.

Several islands form part of Italy. Sicily, 9,926 square miles, lies off the toe of the boot, across the Strait of Messina, with a steep and rock-bound northern coast and gentler slopes to the sea in the west and south. Mt. Etna, an active volcano, rises to 10,741 feet, and most of Sicily is more than 500 feet in elevation. Sixty-two miles southwest of Sicily lies Pantelleria, 45 square miles, and south of that are Lampedusa and Linosa. Sardinia, 9,301 square miles, just south of Corsica and about 125 miles west of the mainland, is mountainous, stony, and unproductive.

Italy has many northern lakes, lying below the snow-covered peaks of the Alps.

The largest are Garda (143 sq. mi.), Maggiore (83 sq. mi.), and Como (55 sq. mi.). The Po, the principal river, flows from the Alps on Italy's western border and crosses the Lombard plain to the Adriatic.

*Natural Resources.* Italy is ordinarily the world's largest producer of mercury; it is also an important producer of sulfur. The nation lacks, however, the staple minerals of coal, oil and iron, and is forced to import them.

In the south Tirol and in the central Apennines, abundant hydroelectric power resources and deposits of natural gas are being increasingly exploited.

# Japan (Empire)
## (Nippon)

**Area:** 142,726 square miles.
**Population** (est. 1960): 93,600,000.
**Density per square mile:** 655.8.
**Ruler:** Emperor Hirohito.
**Premier:** Hayato Ikeda.
**Principal cities** (census 1955): Tokyo, 6,969,104 * (capital; financial, manufacturing center); Osaka, 2,547,316 (chief industrial center); Nagoya, 1,336,780 (machinery, textiles); Kyoto, 1,204,084 (manufacturing); Yokohama, 1,143,687 (seaport); Kobe, 979,305 (seaport, shipbuilding).
**Monetary unit:** Yen.
**Language:** Japanese.
**Religions** (1938): Buddhism, 60%; Shintoism, 21%; Protestant (215,166); Roman Catholic (118,856).

  * Estimated Aug. 1, 1959: 9,021,313.

### STATUS IN THE WORLD TODAY

Japan, which has been transformed into a pacific democracy under civilian leadership, has aligned itself with the free world, and more particularly, with the United States. In 1951 the two countries concluded a mutual-defense assistance agreement, which was replaced by a new one in 1960. This made Japan an equal partner. It commits both countries to help each other in case either is attacked on Japanese territory; it also provides for prior consultation with Japan before forces from U.S. bases there can be used in any engagement other than the defense of Japan. Despite the U.S. concessions, leftists rioted but failed to prevent ratification.

Outside the military sphere, the United States has done its best to expand its trade and cultural ties with Japan, to encourage its allies to accept Japan as a partner, and to persuade the world community to recognize Japan again as a responsible and important member. The policy of the present government is one of economic expansion under close government supervision, reassessment of Occupation reforms and eventual revision of the constitution, gradual rearmament, and interdependence with the United States.

Serious international problems still plague Japan. The peace declaration of 1956 with the Soviet Union did not settle all issues with the U.S.S.R. The question of what kind of relations to develop with the other states of the Soviet bloc, particularly mainland China, is pressing. Korean claims and sensibilities still have to be pacified. Military relations with the United States require constant attention, as do trade relations with all countries. But Japan has been making satisfying progress in its international relations, and without the expense of supporting a large military establishment.

Increased imports are essential to Japan's economic growth, for the islands are small and poorly endowed. The key problem is how to secure the foreign exchange needed to pay for them. Japan is making every effort to expand its markets in the West but on several occasions has taken the extraordinary step of itself limiting its exports to avoid a raising of the barriers in the United States. Two other major markets beckon—south and southeast Asia and mainland China. In the former case, there are three obstacles: distrust of Japanese motives engendered before and during World War II, shortage of capital, and competition from West Germany, Britain, and others. In the latter case, the Japanese government has enforced a partial boycott in accord with the policy enunciated by America during the Korean War, while the Red Chinese government has adopted restrictive policies in attempting to use the promise of this trade to force the Tokyo regime to recognize it diplomatically. Limited trade continues on an individual-barter basis. Increased attention is being given in Japanese financial circles to the need for Japan itself to provide more capital for the development of the south and southeast Asia region.

### MAJOR POLITICAL PARTIES

Liberal-Democratic party (298 seats in House of Representatives), led by Premier Hayato Ikeda; Socialist party (127 seats), led by Mosaburo Suzuki.

HISTORY AND GOVERNMENT. A series of legends attributes creation of Japan to the sun goddess, from whom the later emperors were allegedly descended. The first of them was Jimmu Tennō, supposed to have ascended the throne on Feb. 11, 660 B.C.

Recorded Japanese history begins with the first contact with China in the 5th century A.D. Japan was then divided into strong feudal states, all nominally under the Emperor, but with real power often held by a court minister or clan. In 1185 Yoritomo, chief of the Minamoto clan, was designated Shogun (Generalissimo) with the actual administration of the islands under his control. A dual government system—Shogun and Emperor—persisted till 1867.

First contact with the West came about 1542, when a Portuguese ship off course arrived in Japanese waters. Portuguese traders, Jesuit missionaries, and Spanish, Dutch, and English traders followed. Suspicious of Christianity and of Portuguese support of a local Japanese revolt, the shoguns restricted all foreigners in 1636–38 except the Dutch, who were confined to Nagasaki. Western attempts to renew trading relations failed until 1853, when Commodore Matthew Perry sailed an American fleet into Tokyo Bay.

Japan now quickly made the transition from a medieval to a modern power. Feudalism was abolished and industrialization was speeded. An imperial army was established with conscription. The shogun system was abolished in 1867 by Emperor Meiji, and parliamentary government was established in 1889. After a brief war with China in 1894–95, Japan acquired Formosa (Taiwan), the Pescadores islands, and part of southern Manchuria. China also recognized the independence of Korea (Chosen), which Japan later annexed (1910).

In 1904–05 Japan defeated Russia in the Russo-Japanese War, gaining the territory of southern Sakhalin (Karafuto) and Russia's port and rail rights in Manchuria. In World War I, Japan, which took a negligible part in military operations, seized Germany's Pacific islands and leased areas in China. The Treaty of Versailles then awarded her a mandate over the islands.

At the Washington Conference of 1921–22, Japan agreed to respect Chinese national integrity. The series of Japanese aggressions which was to lead to the nation's downfall began in 1931 with the invasion of Manchuria. The following year, Japan set up this area as a puppet state, "Manchukuo," under Emperor Henry Pu-Yi, last of China's Manchu dynasty. On Nov. 25, 1936, Japan joined the Axis by signing the anti-Comintern pact. The invasion of China came the next year, and the Pearl Harbor attack on Dec. 7, 1941.

For many months after Pearl Harbor, the Japanese army and navy enjoyed spectacular success, but by the end of 1942 the tide had begun to turn. Three years later the dropping of the world's first atomic bomb in combat on Hiroshima, followed by a second one on Nagasaki, knocked Japan swiftly into surrender.

Japan surrendered formally Sept. 2, 1945, aboard the battleship *Missouri* in Tokyo Bay. Southern Sakhalin and the Kurile Islands reverted to Russia, and Formosa (Taiwan) and Manchuria to China. The Pacific islands remained under U.S. occupation.

General of the Army Douglas MacArthur was appointed Supreme Commander for the Allied Powers (SCAP) Aug. 14, 1945. An 11-power (later 13-power) Far Eastern Commission was created to lay down occupation policies, while the 4-power Allied council advised and consulted with SCAP in carrying them out.

Japan's Constitution, promulgated in November, 1946, replaced the Meiji Constitution of 1889. The new Constitution, sponsored by the U.S. during its occupation of Japan, brought fundamental changes to the Japanese political system, including the abandonment of the Emperor's divine rights. The Diet (Parliament) consists of a House of Representatives of 467 members elected for 4 years and a House of Councillors of 250 members, half of whom are elected every 3 years for 6-year terms. Executive power is vested in the cabinet headed by a Prime Minister, who is elected by the Diet from its members.

*Ruler.* Emperor Hirohito, born April 29, 1901, succeeded his father, Yoshihito, on Dec. 25, 1926. He was married on Jan. 26, 1924, to Princess Nagako, born in 1903. To them were born two sons, Crown Prince Akihito (Dec. 23, 1933) and Prince Masahito (Nov. 28, 1935), and 5 daughters. Succession to the Japanese throne is in the male line only.

ECONOMIC CONDITIONS.

*Agriculture.* Japan is traditionally a land of small farms and, except in Hokkaido, the northernmost island, there is almost no large-scale farming and animal husbandry. The average holding is less than three acres. Double cropping makes self-sufficiency possible, but on a low level of subsistence.

In 1957 there were 3,402,000 cattle, 1,600,000 hogs, and 1,000,000 sheep.

*Industry.* Prewar Japan was one of the world's leading industrial nations and the only country in the Far East with highly developed textile, steel, machinery, chemical, and electrical industries. The textile industry was dominant, but after 1931 considerable expansion took place in the heavy industries—metal, machinery-building, and chemical—which were adaptable to war purposes.

Postwar industrial rehabilitation proceeded slowly at first, but by the end of 1956 average industrial output was more than twice the 1934–36 level. Japan led the world in shipbuilding in 1959, completing vessels aggregating 6,276,689 gross tons, many of them super tankers.

The huge interlocking monopolies (*Zaibatsu*), controlling prewar business and finance, were dissolved in 1945, and reconcentration was prohibited by postwar legislation.

*Trade.* Before World War II, Japan ranked fifth in world trade. Private trade was resumed in 1947; by the mid-1950s, Japan had regained its place in world trade.

Leading customers in 1958 were the United States (23%), Hong Kong (5%), India (4%), and Malaya (3%); leading suppliers, the United States (34.8%), Australia (8%), Canada (4%), and Malaya (4%). Leading exports were textiles (35%), machinery (19%), iron and steel and manufactures (9%), and chemicals (4%). Imports included raw cotton (15%), petroleum and products (10%), wool (7%), wheat (5%), and iron ore (5%).

*Communications.* Before World War II the merchant marine carried almost 80 per cent of the foreign trade and was surpassed only by those of the United States and Britain. Wartime losses were enormous, but recovery was fairly steady. By 1959 there was a gross tonnage of 6,276,689, according to *Lloyd's Register*.

NATURAL FEATURES AND RESOURCES. Japan's four main islands are Honshu, Hokkaido, Kyushu, and Shikoku. The Ryukyu chain to the southwest is U.S.-occupied and the Kuriles to the northeast are Russian-occupied. The surface of the main islands consists largely of mountains separated by narrow valleys. There are about fifty more or less active volcanoes, including famous Fujiyama near Tokyo (12,385 ft.), continuously active Asamayama (8,182 ft.), and Adzumayama (7,733 ft.).

*Minerals.* Japan is relatively poor in minerals, and large imports of coal, petroleum, and iron ore are necessary. Other minerals include lead, silver, gold, and copper.

# Jordan, The Hashemite Kingdom of

**Area:** 37,301 square miles.*
**Population** (est. 1959): 1,636,000.*
**Density per square mile:** 43.9.*
**Ruler:** King Hussein I.
**Prime Minister:** Bahjat al-Talhouni.
**Principal cities** (est. 1959): Amman, 245,000 (capital); Jerusalem (Jordanian sector), 75,000 (religious center).
**Monetary unit:** Jordanian dinar.
**Language:** Arabic.
**Religions:** Moslem (Sunni), 92%; Christian, 8%.

\* Including Arab Palestine (area: 2,125 sq. mi.; population 1953, 745,786).

## STATUS IN THE WORLD TODAY

Jordan, although a cobelligerent with Egypt against Israel, has lately remained aloof from the movement for pan-Arabism because of attempts to undermine its independence and to overthrow King Hussein. These plots were blamed in Amman on Egyptian and Syrian elements in the United Arab Republic, and the Cairo radio retaliated for a considerable period of time with propaganda broadcasts urging the overthrow of King Hussein. At the time of the 1958 rebellion in Iraq, British paratroopers arrived to help safeguard Jordan's independence at the same time that United States Marines landed in Lebanon to help prevent the spread of violence in the Middle East. Since that time, the U.A.R. has appeared to be more preoccupied with the Communist threat posed by the new Baghdad regime.

Jordan has a considerable agricultural potential if it could come to an agreement with Israel on the use of the waters of the Jordan River. But it is still technically at war with Israel, and has incorporated part of Jerusalem into its territory. Egypt also still has to live up to its agreement to share in furnishing the economic aid to Jordan which it lost when the British withdrew.

HISTORY AND GOVERNMENT. An ancient land, Jordan was known in the time of Moses as Edom and Moab. It passed to the Amorites of Damascus and in A.D. 106 became part of the Roman province of Arabia. In 633–36 it was conquered by the Arabs.

Conquered from the Turks by the British in World War I, Jordan was separated from the Palestine mandate in 1920, and placed in 1921 under the rule of Abdullah ibn Hussein.

In 1923 Britain recognized Jordan's independence, subject to the mandate. In 1946, Britain abolished the mandate and recognized the independence of Jordan. That part of Palestine occupied by Jordani troops was formally incorporated by action of the Jordani Parliament on Apr. 24, 1950. Jordan's rejection of the Baghdad pact in Dec., 1955, set off a period of instability and tension.

Abdullah was assassinated June 20, 1951. His son Talal was deposed as mentally ill Aug. 11, 1952. Talal's son Hussein, born May 2, 1935, succeeded him. Jordan is a constitutional monarchy with a bicameral parliament. Its Chamber of Deputies of 40 members is elected for 4 years by male suffrage, and the 20 members of the Senate are appointed by the King.

Defense of the country is entrusted to the British-trained Arab Legion of about 20,000 men, the most effective force among all Arab armies. The Anglo-Jordanian treaty of Mar. 20, 1948, was terminated Mar. 13, 1957. Jordan had ousted the Legion's British commander on March 2, 1956, and Britain recalled most of its remaining military officers. In Jan., 1957, Egypt, Saudi Arabia, and Syria agreed to provide the equivalent of the former British defense subsidy. In February, 1958, Jordan and Iraq united to form the "Arab Federation," subsequently called the "Arab Union," but this federation came abruptly to an end with the revolutionary coup in Iraq in August, 1958.

ECONOMIC CONDITIONS. Life in Jordan is primitive; there are estimated to be 50,-000 nomads and 120,000 seminomads. At least 95 per cent of the total area is desert.

Most of the country is suitable only for pasturing sheep, goats, and camels. Cultivated land is limited to a relatively small area west of the Hejaz Railway. In the drier cultivated areas of the plateau, the inhabitants retain tribal organization and still live in tents. Foreign trade consists largely of the exchange of wheat, fresh fruit, wool, and live animals for sugar, tea, and other necessities. Main exports are phosphates (30%) and olive oil (0.6%).

# Korea (Chosen; Chosŏn)

Area: 85,286 square miles.
Population (est. 1959): 32,948,000, almost entirely Korean).
Density per square mile: 386.3.
President, South Korea: Yun Po Sun.
Premier, South Korea: Lt. Gen. Song Yo-Chan.
Premier, North Korea: Kim Il-sung.
Principal cities: Seoul (est. 1960) 1,756,-406 (capital, South Korea); Pusan (1955 census) 1,049,363 (chief port); Pyong-yang (est. 1952) 500,000 (capital, North Korea); Taegu (1955 census) 488,960 (silk center).
Monetary unit: Hwan.
Languages: Korean, Chinese, Japanese.
Religions: Buddhist, Confucianist, Taoist, Christian (500,300 Christians in 1938).

### STATUS IN THE WORLD TODAY

North Korea became a Communist satellite as the result of a military agreement which permitted Soviet Russia to accept the Japanese surrender north of the 38th parallel in Korea. Soviet forces occupied the northern zone, established a puppet government, and although an agreement was reached in Moscow in 1945 to establish a joint commission to unify the two zones under a provisional Korean government, supervised by a four-power trusteeship, there was no agreement on how this could be done. Since the Korean War, the country has been to all intents and purposes an appendage of Red China, and the ruling officials apparently have been build-

ing up the Communist military strength despite the provisions of the 1953 armistice agreement. In the spring of 1958 the Red Chinese announced that they had begun to move their "volunteers" out of North Korea and that they would complete their withdrawal by the end of the year. It may be that the North Korean forces have been so strengthened that they are considered now capable of defending or extending the regime themselves. This may have been the reason for Chou Enlai's call for all foreign troops to be evacuated from the peninsula as preliminary to an all-Korean election to establish a new, unified government. Intelligible military and economic data are lacking, but the Communist regime is reported to have received aid from eight of the Communist-bloc nations, the largest grants coming from the U.S.S.R. and Red China.

The Republic of Korea was strongly pro-democratic and anti-Communistic even before the Communist invasion from North Korea and has been a staunch supporter of the free world since its organization in 1948. Its struggle to build a free and independent country has met with staggering economic problems as a result of the civil war. Relief and reconstruction have gone forward, with nearly $2 billion in relief and aid having been given since 1950 by the United States and the United Nations. Even this has been insufficient, however; production has increased little beyond the 1949–50 level and has hardly kept pace with the growth in population. Trade has been encouraged, but the traditional exchange with Japan has not been restored and relations between the two countries are further complicated by a fisheries dispute. Because of the military build-up believed to have taken place in North Korea, the ROK has felt it imperative to maintain comparatively large military forces. These have been strengthened since June, 1957, when the U.N. command announced that breaches of the armistice agreement by the opposing side freed it to equip its own men with more modern weapons.

Although Dr. Syngman Rhee spent 50 years fighting for Korean independence, his rule as president became increasingly autocratic. He declared martial law and arrested assemblymen who opposed his legislative and constitutional proposals. When an amendment exempting him from a two-term limit as president failed to pass, his Liberal party declared it adopted anyway. Widespread charges of ballot-box stuffing, trickery, fraud and strong-arm tactics in the March, 1960, elections which returned him to a fourth term as president resulted in wide-spread riots. Under pressure at home and abroad to end police repression and restore democratic rule,

President Rhee finally resigned. A little more than a year later, in May, 1961, a military group overthrew the civilian regime in a coup d'état, charging that the civilians had not been zealous enough in eradicating corruption and Communist infiltration.

HISTORY. According to myth, Korea, a peninsula about 600 miles long, was founded in 2,333 B.C. by Tangun. His dynasty is said to have ruled until 1122 B.C. when a Chinese sage, Kija, established a dynasty supposed to have ruled until 193 B.C. Later, three kingdoms were established, one of which (Silla) absorbed the other two in A.D. 666–668. In 1627, the Manchus seized Korea and placed it again under Chinese sovereignty.

In the Chinese-Japanese War of 1894–95, Japan won predominant influence in Korea, and in 1910 Japan formally annexed it. A Korean bid for independence was crushed ruthlessly in 1919.

In Aug., 1945, at the end of World War II, Korea was occupied by Soviet and U.S. troops. The United States and the U.S.S.R. were unable to agree on the formation of an all-Korean provisional government, and in Nov., 1947 the U.N. General Assembly set up a commission, boycotted by the U.S.S.R., to arrange for elections. Elections were held in the U.S. zone on May 10, 1948, for a national assembly, which on July 12 adopted a republican Constitution and on July 20 elected Syngman Rhee President. The new republic was proclaimed on Aug. 15 and was recognized as the legal government of Korea by the U.N. General Assembly on Dec. 12, 1948. Meanwhile, a North Korean "People's Republic" had been formed in the Soviet zone north of the 38th parallel on May 1, 1948. It claimed jurisdiction over all of Korea.

On June 25, 1950, South Korea was attacked by North Korean Communist forces. U.S. armed intervention was ordered on June 27 by Pres. Truman and on the same day the U.N. invoked military sanctions against North Korea. Gen. Douglas MacArthur was named commander of U.N. forces on July 7. U.S. and South Korean troops fought a heroic holding action, but by the first week of August, they had been forced back to a 4,000 sq. mi. beachhead in southeast Korea. There they stood off superior North Korean forces until Sept. 15, when a major U.N. amphibious attack was launched far behind the Communist lines at Inchon, port of Seoul. By Sept. 30, U.N. forces were in complete control of South Korea; they then invaded North Korea and were nearing the Manchurian and Siberian borders when several hundred thousand Chinese Communist troops entered the conflict in late October. U.N.

forces then retreated successfully below the 38th parallel, where they repulsed several major attacks.

On May 24, 1951, UN forces recrossed the parallel and had made important new inroads into North Korea when truce negotiations began on July 10. An armistice was finally signed at Panmunjom on July 27, 1953, leaving a devastated Korea in need of large-scale rehabilitation. The armistice contemplated an international political conference on the status of Korea, but negotiations for arranging it broke down. The question was discussed without result at the Geneva conference on Far Eastern problems (April 26–June 19, 1954).

The U.S. and South Korea signed a mutual-defense treaty on Oct. 1, 1953, and in Aug., 1953 the U.S. Congress authorized up to $200,000,000 for rehabilitation and economic support of South Korea.

ECONOMIC CONDITIONS. The Korean population is more or less homogeneous and successfully withstood Japanese efforts to assimilate it. South Korea has 43 per cent of the peninsula's area and over two-thirds of its population. Korea is predominantly agricultural.

Industrial development was speeded in the last years of Japanese rule. The leading industries by value of output ordinarily are chemical, textile, food, beverage, and tobacco. Korea north of the 38th parallel has by far the larger portion of the country's industry and abundant hydroelectric resources.

Korea's prewar foreign trade was closely linked with that of Japan. South Korea's postwar trade has been financed to a large extent by U.S. funds. Most of the trade is with the United States, Japan, and Hong Kong. Chief imports were foods and manufactured goods; chief exports, raw materials, including tungsten, graphite, and raw silk. North Korea's trade is chiefly with Communist China and the U.S.S.R.

South Korea is insolvent and dependent on U.S. and other contributions.

NATURAL FEATURES AND RESOURCES. Korea's coast, with a rugged mountain range along the east, is fringed with more than 1,000 islands. Several rivers are navigable for more than 100 miles, including the Naktong in the south, the Han in the central region, and the Yalu in the northwest.

Leading products are coal, gold, silver, copper, tungsten ore, iron ore, graphite, lead, alum stone, and pyrite ore.

# Laos (Kingdom)

Area: 91,429 square miles.
Population (est. 1959): 1,760,000.
Density per square mile: 19.2.

Ruler: King Savang Vathana.
Premier: Prince Boun Oum.
Principal cities (est. 1957): Vientiane, 60,000 (administrative capital); Luang- prabang, 18,000 (royal capital).
Monetary unit: Kip.
Language: Laotian.
Religion: Buddhist.

## STATUS IN THE WORLD TODAY

Laos, a former province of French Indo-China which the Communists expected to take over without any trouble, has managed to maintain its independence with the help of American military and financial aid.

The Communists in the northern provinces have been supported from northern Vietnam and there have been a number of frontier incidents along the 800-mile frontier which Laos shares with that Communist satellite and Red China. The difficulty of patrolling this long border has also resulted in making Laos a haven for the thousands of refugees who have fled from Red China.

Economically the least developed former unit of Indo-China, Laos is sparsely populated and has just begun to modernize its backward economy. It has no railroads and few passable roads. It has been receiving between $30 and $40 million annually in American aid. Whatever the truth of charges of inept and unimaginative American administration and widespread corruption on the part of Laotian officials, the program does appear to have averted Communist threats to take over the country, although it may not, to date, have greatly speeded up the process of economic growth in Laos.

Renewed attacks by Communists in August, 1959, allegedly supported by forces from North Vietnam, brought a plea in the U.N. from Laos for intervention against invasion. In September, the Security Council voted to send a fact-finding commission. It found no evidence of organized aggression by outside forces, but it did find that some aid might have been sent to Communist rebels from North Vietnam.

During 1961, however, despite the U.N. findings, the Communists began transporting men, munitions, and supplies into Laos by air, and their forces had made considerable progress against the Laotian Army before a cease-fire was arranged. A 14-nation conference met in Geneva, Switzerland, to try to bring peace to the small kingdom, but hopes for an East-West agreement appeared dim after 10 weeks of talks.

HISTORY AND GOVERNMENT. Sparsely settled Laos occupies the northwestern portion of Indo-China. In the fourteenth century, a unified Lao kingdom of Lanxang was constituted on both sides of the Mékong river. It was divided in the seventeenth century into the two kingdoms of Vientiane, which was annexed by Siam in 1827, and Luangprabang, which recognized Siamese suzerainty shortly thereafter. In 1893 both kingdoms passed to France.

Laos was reunited in 1947 as a constitutional monarchy under the Luangprabang dynasty. In 1950 it became an associated state in the French Union. The transfer of sovereignty was completed by the Paris agreements of Dec. 29, 1954. The constitution of May, 1947, provides for a National Legislative Assembly elected by popular vote. In 1958 women were granted the franchise and voting qualifications were liberalized, thereby increasing the total number of Assembly seats from 38 to 59.

SOCIAL AND ECONOMIC CONDITIONS. About half the people are Laotians who live mainly in the Mékong valley, and half are mountain tribes of Chinese and Indonesian extraction. There are sizable Chinese and Vietnamese minorities.

About 95 per cent of the people are farmers. The chief food crop is rice; others are maize, vegetables, cotton, cardamons, and tobacco. The leading exports are benzoin, coffee, opium, and lac; cattle and teak are also exported. Laos is the least developed of the former Indo-Chinese states and has little modern industry. Tin is the only mineral of importance. The northern forests are rich in valuable timber, notably teak; the logs are floated down the Mékong. The latter, in spite of rapids, is the chief transportation route. There are no railroads and few all-weather roads.

# Latvia

Area: 24,595 square miles.
Population (est. 1959): /2,094,000 (1940: Lettish, 75.5% [1950: 58%]; Russian, 12%; German, 3.2%; Polish, 2.5%; others, 6.8%).
Density per square mile: 81.3.
Principal cities (est. 1959): Riga, 604,-500 (capital); Liepaja, 71,400 (seaport).
Language: Latvian.
Religions (census 1930): Lutheran, 56.6%; Roman Catholic, 23.7%; Greek Orthodox, 8.9%; others, 10.8%.

HISTORY AND GOVERNMENT. Descended from Aryan stock, the Latvians were early tribesmen who settled along the Baltic Sea and, lacking a central government, fell an easy prey to more powerful peoples. The German Teutonic Knights first conquered them in 1158 and ruled the area as two states—Livonia and Courland. Poland conquered the territory in 1562 and ruled until 1795 in Courland; control of Livonia was disputed between Sweden and Poland from 1562 to 1629. Sweden controlled Livonia from 1629 to 1721. Russia took over

Livonia in the latter year and Courland after the third partition of Poland in 1795. From that time until 1918, the Latvians remained Russian subjects, although they preserved their language, customs, and folklore. The Russian Revolution of 1917 gave them their opportunity for freedom, and the Latvian republic was proclaimed on Nov. 18, 1918.

The republic lasted little more than twenty years. It was occupied by Russian troops in 1939 and incorporated into the U.S.S.R. in 1940. German armies occupied the nation from 1941 to 1943–44, when they were driven out by the Russians. Most countries, including the United States, have refused to recognize the Soviet annexation of Latvia.

# Lebanon (Republic)

**Area:** 4,015 square miles.
**Population** (est. 1958): 1,550,000 (Arabian, Armenian, Circassian, Turk).
**Density per square mile:** 386.1.
**President:** Fouad Chehab.
**Premier:** Saeb Salaam.
**Principal cities** (est. 1958): Beirut, 400,-000 (capital, chief port); Tripoli, 115,000 (oil pipeline terminus).
**Monetary unit:** Lebanese pound (£L).
**Languages:** Arabic, French.
**Religions** (est. 1954): Christian, 54%; Moslem, 44%; others, 2%.

### STATUS IN THE WORLD TODAY

Since the 1958 insurrection, when Egypt was charged with intervention in Lebanon's internal affairs, and the landing of United States Marines—at Lebanon's request—during the uncertainty which followed the overthrow of the Hashemite monarchy in Iraq, this half-Christian, half-Moslem nation has moved closer to positive neutralism. It has, however, begun to deport Arab Communists, disarm the civilian population, and maintain strict neutrality between Nasser and Egypt, on the one hand, and Kassem and Iraq on the other. Its swift economic recovery following the civil strife was aided by $12.5 million from the United States, and the Lebanese, who had made their nation the most prosperous in the Middle East, are rapidly resuming their former position. Relations with the U.A.R. have been normalized, with a pledge by Nasser in March, 1959 to respect Lebanon's independence and the signing of an economic pact three months later.

HISTORY AND GOVERNMENT. In ancient times Lebanon was the mountainous hinterland of the Phoenician coast towns. From the seventh to the eleventh centuries there infiltrated into southern Lebanon the heretics of Islam, who finally coalesced into the Druse community.

In the nineteenth century the Turkish Sultanate encouraged the Druses to wage civil war against the Christian Maronites. After a massacre of 2,500 Christians in 1860. Lebanon was occupied by the French for a year. From 1864 to 1914, a Christian military government ruled the area under nominal Turkish sovereignty. After World War I, France received a League of Nations mandate over Syria and Lebanon. The French drew a Lebanese border in 1920 to offset predominantly Moslem Syria and proclaimed the area a republic under French control on May 23, 1926. Complete independence came on Nov. 26, 1941. Lebanon joined the Arab League and took part in the invasion of Palestine on May 15, 1948.

GOVERNMENT. The modern Lebanese republic is governed by a President elected by Parliament, for a six-year term, and a Cabinet of Ministers appointed by the President, but responsible to Parliament, which has 66 members elected for a four-year term by universal suffrage. Voting is compulsory.

ECONOMIC CONDITIONS. Lebanon produces tobacco, olives, grapes and other fruits, wheat, and silk. Manufacturing is confined mainly to local consumers' goods. The silk industry is important in Beirut and Tripoli. Tobacco manufacturing is a government monopoly. An oil refinery was opened at Tripoli in 1950 and its facilities are being currently expanded.

Leading customers in 1959 were Saudi Arabia (13%), Syria (15%), and France (2%); leading suppliers, Syria (9%), Britain (24%), and the United States and Canada (12%). The leading exports were wool, fruits, vegetables, barley, and cotton.

One of the oil pipelines from the Kirkuk field in Iraq terminates at Tripoli; the trans-Arabian pipeline from Saudi Arabia ends at Sidon.

# Liberia (Republic)

**Area:** c. 43,000 square miles.
**Population** (est. 1956): 1,250,000 (native Negro, 99%; American Negro, .8%; white, .1%; others, .1%).
**Density per square mile:** c. 29.1.
**President:** William V. S. Tubman.
**Principal city** (census 1958): Monrovia, 45,000 (capital and chief port).
**Monetary unit:** Liberian dollar.
**Languages:** English (official), native tongues.
**Religion:** Protestant Christian (official); Moslem, Catholic, tribal religion.

## STATUS IN THE WORLD TODAY

Liberia has never been a colonial possession. Created as a result of the efforts of the American Colonization Society to settle ex-slaves in West Africa, it celebrated the centennial of its independence in 1947. With this historical background, it has had extremely close relations, both diplomatic and economic, with the United States. Because of the country's strategic importance, American troops were stationed there in World War II. Its government is modeled on the American system and the Liberian dollar is at par with the American dollar.

During the past 30 years, Liberia has made remarkable economic progress, but even with outside help has been unable thus far to produce sufficient revenue to create much-needed educational and public health facilities. Illiteracy is still high among tribal groups in the interior but is steadily being reduced, and they have little share in the governing of the country which is largely in the hands of the 15,000 Americo-Liberians, descendants of the slaves who were freed on its shores. Revenue from the Firestone Rubber Company's plantation concessions has helped the government to escape from its chronic budget deficits. Further development of natural resources has, in some instances, been hindered by the sparse population of many parts of the interior which have only four or fewer persons per square mile.

GOVERNMENT. The government is modeled after that of the United States. The President and Vice President are popularly elected for the first time to a term of 8 years with succeeding terms of 4 years each. The 31-member House of Representatives is elected for 4 years, and the 10-member Senate for 6 years. Suffrage is universal to citizens of over 21 years of age who are of the Negro race and pay a minimum tax. A 1946 constitutional amendment provided for the seating of 13 chiefs in the House of Representatives—two from each county and one from each province in the hinterland. Liberia has an Armed Force of about 4,000.

SOCIAL AND ECONOMIC CONDITIONS. The English-speaking descendants of U.S. Negroes, known as Americo-Liberians, are the intellectual and ruling class. The aborigines, virtually all uncivilized, are divided into some 28 tribes speaking different dialects. Some are Moslems; others practice tribal religion. The Christian population includes Episcopalians, Methodists, Catholics, Baptists, and Presbyterians.

Chief exports in 1960 were rubber (66%), iron ore (20%), and diamonds (6%). Leading customers were the United States (74%), the Netherlands (5%), and West Germany (10%); leading suppliers, the United States (56%), West Germany (12%), and Britain (9%).

# Libya (Kingdom)

Area: 679,360 square miles.
Population (census 1958): 1,153,000 (Berber, with Arab admixture, 93%; Italian, 5%; Jewish, 2%).
Density per square mile: 1.7.
Ruler: King Idris I.
Prime Minister: Mohammed ben Othman.
Principal cities (census 1959): Tripoli, 172,200 (joint capital); Benghazi, 70,533 (joint capital).
Monetary unit: Libyan pound (£L).
Languages: Arabic, Italian.
Religions: Moslem (93%), Christian (5%), Jewish (2%).

## STATUS IN THE WORLD TODAY

The present government of Libya is comparatively friendly toward the United States, and under a 1954 agreement we maintain a large air base at Wheelus Field. More than one-quarter of the national income is derived in one form or another from the United States, and an American oil firm started commercial production from wells it had drilled early in 1959. The country, however, is the scene of considerable Soviet and Egyptian activity, and part of the population is impressed by Soviet offers to build roads, ports, and hospitals without political conditions attached. The western part of the country leans toward the West; the eastern part is more oriented toward the Middle East, with some pro-Nasser sentiment.

HISTORY AND GOVERNMENT. Libya, stretching along the northern coast of Africa between Tunisia and Egypt, was a part of the Turkish dominions from the sixteenth century until 1911. Following the outbreak of hostilities between Italy and Turkey in that year, Italian troops occupied Tripoli; Italian sovereignty was recognized in 1912 by the Treaty of Ouchy.

Libya was the scene of much desert fighting during World War II. After the fall of Tripoli on Jan. 23, 1943, it came under Allied administration. The U.N. General Assembly voted on Nov. 21, 1949, that Libya should become independent by 1952.

Following the adoption by the constituent assembly of a Constitution, the independence of the country was proclaimed by King Idris I on Dec. 24, 1951.

Under the Constitution, Libya is a hereditary monarchy with a federal form of government. Tripolitania, Cyrenaica, and the Fezzan are the constituent provinces. It has a bicameral Parliament consisting of a Senate of 24 members, half named by the King and half by the three provincial legislatures, and a House of Representatives elected on the basis of 1 deputy for every 20,000 inhabitants. Tripolitania has 35 members, Cyrenaica 15, and the Fezzan 5. The Cabinet, headed by the Prime Minister, is responsible to the federal Parliament.

The ruler, King Idris I, hereditary head of the powerful Senussi sect in Cyrenaica, was born in 1890.

SOCIAL AND ECONOMIC CONDITIONS. Tripolitania, with one-sixth the area, has 68 per cent of the population; Cyrenaica has 27 per cent and the Fezzan 5 per cent. About 75 per cent of the population is rural and about half of that is nomadic or semi-nomadic.

Animal husbandry is the basic economic activity, and there are considerable numbers of cattle, sheep, camels, and goats. Agriculture is possible only in the Mediterranean coastal region, where dates, olives, citrus fruit, wheat, and barley are grown, and in oases in the Fezzan and elsewhere; here the principal product is dates. Sponge and tunny fisheries are carried on off the coast.

Chief exports are peanuts, scrap iron, and esparto. In 1958, Italy was the leading customer (34%) and supplier (22.3%).

# Liechtenstein (Principality)

Area: 61 square miles.
Population (est. 1959): 16,274 (mostly German).
Density per square mile: 266.8.
Ruler: Prince Franz Joseph II.
Chief of Government: Alexander Frick.
Principal city (est. 1959): Vaduz, 3,277 (capital).
Monetary unit: Swiss franc.
Language: German.
Religion: Roman Catholic.

HISTORY AND GOVERNMENT. Tiny Liechtenstein lies on the east bank of the Rhine, just south of Lake Constance, between Austria and Switzerland. It abolished its army in 1868 and has managed to stay neutral and undamaged in all European wars since that date.

Founded in 1719, Liechtenstein became independent in 1866. Franz Joseph II, the reigning Prince, was born in 1906, and succeeded his great uncle, Franz I, in 1938. In 1943 he married Countess Gina Wilczek of Austria.

The Constitution of 1921 provided for a legislature, the *Landtag*, of 15 members elected by direct, universal suffrage. Liechtenstein adopted Swiss currency in 1921 and has been part of the Swiss Customs Union since 1924. Its foreign trade statistics are included in those of Switzerland, which also administers the country's telegraph and postal service.

Wheat, wine, and fruit are the chief products. There are small manufactures of cotton, leather, and pottery.

Liechtenstein's area includes low valley land and upland peaks—Falkais at 8,401 feet, and Naafkopf, 8,432 feet. The chief mineral product is marble.

# Lithuania

Area: 25,174 square miles.
Population (1959): 2,713,000 (1940: Lithuanian, 81% [1950: 55%]; German, 4%; Polish, 3%; Russian, 2%; others, 10%).
Density per square mile: 107.5.
Principal cities (1959): Vilnius (Wilno), 235,000 (capital); Kaunas, 214,000 (river port).
Language: Lithuanian.
Religions: Roman Catholic, 80%; Lutheran, 5.5%; others, 14.5%.

HISTORY AND GOVERNMENT. Southernmost of the three Baltic states, Lithuania in the middle ages was a grand duchy joined to Poland through royal marriage. Poles and Lithuanians merged forces to defeat the Teutonic Knights of Germany at Tannenberg in 1410 and extended their power far into Russian territory. In 1795, however, following the third partition of Poland, Lithuania fell into Russian hands and did not gain its independence until 1918, toward the end of World War I.

The republic was occupied by the U.S.S.R. in 1939 and annexed outright the following year. From 1940 to 1944 it was occupied by German troops and then was retaken by the Soviet Union. Western countries, including the United States, have not recognized the Russian annexation.

# Luxembourg (Grand Duchy)

Area: 998 square miles.
Population (est. 1959): 324,000 (Luxembourgian, French, German).
Density per square mile: 324.3.
Ruler: Grand Duchess Charlotte.
Premier: Pierre Werner.
Principal city (est. 1958): Luxembourg, 70,158 (capital, iron and steel).
Monetary unit: Luxembourg franc.
Languages: Luxembourgian, French, German.
Religion: Mainly Roman Catholic.

### STATUS IN THE WORLD TODAY

Luxembourg, traditionally neutral, is firmly committed to Free Europe. Although its military strength is negligible, it signed the North Atlantic Pact in 1949, a year after it abolished its unarmed neutrality and made military service compulsory. With Belgium and the Netherlands, it is a member of the Benelux Customs

Union, one of the five great trading areas of the world. Its foreign policy has been traditionally friendly to the United States.

HISTORY AND GOVERNMENT. Sigefroi, Count of Ardennes, an offspring of Charlemagne, was Luxembourg's first sovereign ruler. In 1060 the country came under the rule of the House of Luxembourg. From the 15th to the 18th centuries, Spain and Austria held it in turn. The Congress of Vienna in 1815 made it a Grand Duchy and gave it to William I, King of the Netherlands. In 1839 the Treaty of London ceded the western part of Luxembourg to Belgium. Luxembourg's legislature consists of an Upper Chamber appointed by the sovereign and of a Chamber of Deputies of 52 members elected for 6 years. Half the Chamber of Deputies is elected every 3 years.

ECONOMIC CONDITIONS. Although the soil is not very fertile, agriculture is prosperous. Principal crops are potatoes, oats, wheat, rye, and grapes.

The mining and metallurgical industries, based on iron ore found in the south, are the most important.

By a customs union between Belgium and Luxembourg which came into force on May 1, 1922, to last for 50 years, customs frontiers between the two countries were abolished. On Jan. 1, 1948, an economic union with Belgium and the Netherlands (Benelux) came into existence. Luxembourg's foreign-trade figures are included in those of Belgium and no separate statistics are available; exports consist chiefly of iron and steel products.

Luxembourg's prosperity depends largely on its large iron ore deposits.

# Mexico (Republic)
## (Estados Unidos Mexicanos)

Area: 759,178 square miles.
Population (1960 preliminary census): 34,625,903 (mestizo, 55%; Indian, 29%; white, 15%; others, 1%).
Density per square mile: 45.6.
President: Adolfo López Mateos.
Principal cities (est. 1959): Mexico City, 4,700,000 (capital); Guadalajara, 589,973 (manufacturing); Monterrey, 563,547 (metallic industries); Puebla, 309,115 (cotton textiles); Mérida, 198,970 (sisal); San Luis Potosi, 194,895 (mineral smelting).
Monetary unit: Peso.
Languages (1940): Spanish, 96.4%; Indian, 3.6%.
Religion: Predominantly Roman Cath.

## STATUS IN THE WORLD TODAY

Mexico has had one of the most stable governments in Latin America in the last two decades, and democratic institutions have become stronger. Three successive presidential elections were held in 1948, 1952 and 1958 without any major incident or attempt to overthrow the government, despite the fact that the elections were "managed" by the strongly entrenched government party, Partido Revolucionario Institucional. But freedom of speech, press, and thought are generally respected.

The country has made great social, economic, and political advances since its modern revolution began in 1910. Mexico's educational system and social-service institutions have expanded rapidly, particularly in the last 20 years. The agrarian reform, virtually completed under the 1934–40 administration of President Lazaro Cardenas, created a large group of small farmers, many with personal title to their lands, others members of "ejidos" or cooperative farms. The growth of this class meant creation of a much larger internal market for manufactured goods and paved the way for industrialization. Extensive foreign investment, particularly from the United States, has aided this industrialization. Automobile assembly plants, electrical-products factories, and clothing-manufacturing plants are among the new foreign-financed establishments. Previous existing industries such as steel and textiles have been expanded.

HISTORY. Mexico's early history is shrouded in mystery. At least two civilized races—the Mayas and later the Toltecs—preceded the wealthy Aztec empire, conquered in 1519–21 by the Spanish under Hernando Cortez. Spain ruled for the next 300 years until 1810 (the date was Sept. 16 and is now celebrated as Independence Day), when the Mexicans first revolted. They continued the struggle and finally won independence in 1821.

Turbulent years followed. From 1821 to 1877, there were two Emperors, several dictators and enough Presidents and provisional executives to make a new government on the average of every nine months. Mexico lost Texas (1836), and after defeat in the war with the United States (1846–48) it lost the area comprising the present states of California, Nevada, and Utah, most of Arizona and New Mexico, and parts of Wyoming and Colorado.

In 1855 the Indian patriot Benito Juárez began a series of liberal reforms, including the disestablishment of the Catholic Church, which had acquired vast property. A subsequent civil war was interrupted by the French invasion of Mexico (1861), the crowning of Maximilian of Austria as Emperor (1864), and then his overthrow and execution by forces under Juárez, who again became President in 1867.

The years after the fall of the dictator Porfirio Díaz (1877–80 and 1884–1911) were marked by bloody political-military strife and trouble with the U.S. culminating in the punitive expedition into northern Mexico (1916–17) in unsuccessful pursuit of the bandit-politician Pancho Villa. There was a continuous succession of various presidents and of internal strife until 1917, when a new congress was elected and a liberal constitution adopted. Since a brief period of civil war in 1920, Mexico has enjoyed a period of gradual agricultural, political and social reforms. Relations with the United States were again disturbed in 1938 when all foreign oil wells were expropriated. Agreement on compensation was finally reached in 1941.

GOVERNMENT. The President, popularly elected for six years and ineligible to succeed himself, governs with a Cabinet of ministers. The Federal Congress has two houses—the 162-member Chamber of Deputies, elected for three years (one for each 150,000 population) and the 60-member Senate, elected for six years. All married male citizens at least 18, and all single male citizens at least 21 are eligible to vote. Women received the right to vote in 1953.

Each of the 29 states has considerable autonomy, with a popularly elected Governor, legislature and local judiciary. The President appoints the Governors of the two Federal territories, and the governing body of the Federal District.

ECONOMIC CONDITIONS. *Agriculture.* Primitive agricultural methods are steadily giving way to modern practices. More than 17,000,000 acres are under cultivation. The Yucatán peninsula, at the southern end of the Gulf of Mexico, raises more than half of the world supply of sisal hemp.

Stockraising is important on non-arable land. Mexico's inventory of livestock in 1960 included an estimated 21,000,000 cattle, 5,400,000 sheep, and 8,700,000 hogs.

*Industry.* The leading industrial products are cotton cloth and thread, beer, sugar, iron, and steel.

Chief exports in 1959 were cotton (26%), coffee (18%), lead (5%), copper (4%), and zinc (5%). The U.S. took 57% of the exports and supplied 72% of the imports. Other leading customers were Japan, Britain, and West Germany. Leading imports included machinery, vehicles and iron and steel products.

NATURAL FEATURES AND RESOURCES. Mexico is a great, high plateau, open to the north, with mountain chains on east and west and with ocean-front lowlands lying outside of them. It has two big spears—the peninsula of Lower California, which is mountainous, and the Yucatán peninsula, which is mostly a low plain. The eastern mountains are marked by high volcanoes. *Minerals.* Mexico is one of the richest mineral countries in the world. It outranks all other countries in silver production. Other minerals are gold, lead, copper, zinc, antimony, tin, coal, and iron ore.

Most of the Mexican mining properties are foreign-owned, and the industry is declining in relative importance. The oilfields, lying along the east coast, were seized by the government in 1938, but later the foreign owners were indemnified.

*Forests.* Mexico's forests are of considerable importance; they include pine, oak, fir, mahogany, red and white cedar, and primavera. Resins, turpentine, and vegetable wax are also produced. Yucatán produces nearly all of the world's chicle, the juice of the sapodilla tree, used as the base of chewing gum.

## Monaco (Principality)

**Area: 0.606 square mile (375 acres).**
**Population (est. 1957): 21,000.**
**Density per square mile: 34,653.5.**
**Ruler: Prince Rainier III.**
**Principal and only cities (census 1951):** Monaco, 1,860; La Condamine, 9,858; Monte Carlo, 8,484.
**Monetary unit: French franc.**
**Language: French.**
**Religion: Roman Catholic.**

### STATUS IN THE WORLD TODAY

This world-famous gambling resort has been undergoing a domestic political crisis. In February, 1958, the National Council of Monaco passed unanimously a motion calling for constitutional reforms. Prince Rainier rejected the motion and declared that he would not tolerate attempts to curtail his powers. This warning was translated into action on January 29, 1959, when the Prince suspended the Constitution of 1911, dissolved the National Council and banned all public meetings. The move took place following a special session of the National Council which ended without voting the principality's budget. Prince Rainier has promised reforms of his own.

The special significance attached to the birth of descendants to Prince Rainier stems from a clause in the Treaty of July 17, 1919, between France and Monaco stipulating that in the event of vacancy of the Crown, the Monegasque territory would become an autonomous state under a French protectorate. In this eventuality, the Monegasques would have to forego their privilege of not paying taxes.

HISTORY AND GOVERNMENT. A tiny, hilly wedge driven into the French Mediterranean coast nine miles east of Nice, Monaco is a little land of pleasure with a tourist business that runs as high as 1,500,000 visitors a year. Monaco had popular gaming tables as early as 1856. Five years later, a 50-year concession to operate the games was granted to François Blanc, of Bad Homburg. This concession passed into the hands of a private company in 1898.

The Phoenicians, and after them the Greeks, had a temple on the Monacan headland honoring Hercules. From *Monoikos*, the Greek surname for this mythological strong man, the principality took its name. After being independent for 800 years, Monaco was annexed to France in 1793 by the French Revolutionists and was placed under Sardinia's protection in 1815. In 1861, it went under French guardianship but continued to be an independent country.

Prince Albert of Monaco gave the principality a Constitution in 1911, creating a National Council of eighteen members popularly elected for four years. The government is under a ministry, acting on the Prince's authority. The ruler, Prince Rainier III, born May 31, 1923, succeeded his grandfather, Louis II, on the latter's death, May 9, 1949. Rainier was married April 19, 1956, to Grace Kelly, U.S. actress. A daughter, Princess Caroline Louise Marguerite, was born Jan. 23, 1957, and a son, Prince Albert Louis Pierre on March 14, 1958.

# Mongolian People's Republic (Outer Mongolia)

Area: 591,121 square miles.
Population (est. 1959): 909,600 (Mongol, except for about 100,000 Russians and 50,000 Chinese).
Density per square mile: 1.5.
Chairman of Presidium: Zh. Sambu.
Prime Minister: Y. Tse Den-bal.
Principal city (est. 1960): Ulan Bator, 170,000 (capital).
Monetary unit: Tugherik.
Languages: Mongolian, Russian.
Religion: Lama-Buddhist.

### STATUS IN THE WORLD TODAY

The Mongolian People's Republic is a buffer state between China and Russia. It has been a Soviet satellite since 1924, although the Communists have insisted that it is a sovereign state and have tried, unsuccessfully, to obtain U.N. membership for it. Closed off from the outside world for many years, it now offers the shortest rail route between Moscow and Peiping, and its capital, Ulan Bator, is a stop on the Moscow-Peiping air line. In 1958 it signed its first economic aid pact with Red China and is now receiving assistance from that country as well as from the U.S.S.R.

HISTORY AND GOVERNMENT. The Mongolian People's Republic, known also as Outer Mongolia, is a Russian satellite that measures more than twice the area of Texas. It contains the original homeland of the historic Mongols, whose power reached its zenith during the thirteenth century under Kublai Khan. The area accepted Manchu rule in 1689, but after the Chinese Revolution of 1911 and the fall of the Manchus in 1912, the northern Mongol princes expelled the Chinese officials and declared independence under the Khutukhtu or "Living Buddha." In 1921, Soviet troops entered the country and facilitated the establishment of a republic by Mongolian revolutionaries in 1924 after the death of the last Living Buddha. China, meanwhile, continued to claim Outer Mongolia but was unable to back the claim with any strength. Under the Chinese-Russian Treaty of 1945, China agreed to give up Outer Mongolia, which, after a rigged plebiscite, became nominally independent.

The government of the republic is strikingly similar to the Soviet system. The Great Hural or Huruldan (parliament) is elected by universal suffrage, meets at least once in three years and picks 30 members to act as an executive committee —the Little Hural—which in turn selects a presidium of seven members as an interim body. A Cabinet of ten ministers appointed by the Little Hural governs the country.

ECONOMIC CONDITIONS. The country is largely pastoral. There are few areas suitable for crop growing, but some millet, rye, and wheat are produced. Most of the people are essentially nomadic or semi-nomadic; flocks and herds remain the chief source of wealth.

There are a few industrial enterprises. All land, natural resources, factories, mines, hay-making stations and public utilities are nationalized.

Foreign trade, a state monopoly, is carried on mainly with the Soviet Union, but also with Communist China. The leading exports are livestock, wool, hides, animal hair, meats, and furs.

NATURAL FEATURES AND RESOURCES. The productive regions of Outer Mongolia —a tableland ranging from 3,000 to 5,000 feet in elevation—are in the north, which is well drained by numerous rivers, including the Kerulen, Tola, Orkhon, and Selenga.

Reserves of 500,000,000 tons of coal are said to exist in the Nalaikha field near Ulan Bator; coal production in 1959 was 790,000 metric tons. Some gold is mined.

Deposits of antimony, copper, iron ore, lead, graphite, mercury, sulfur, and silver exist.

# Morocco (Kingdom)

## (Maroc)

**Area:** 171,305 square miles.
**Population (1960 provisional census):** 11,598,070.
**Density per square mile:** 61.3.
**Ruler:** King Hassan II.
**Prime Minister:** King Hassan II.
**Principal cities (census 1960):** Casablanca, 960,812 (chief seaport); Marrakesh, 241,900 (trading center); Rabat, 224,901 (French administrative center); Fez, 215,-812 (commercial center); Tetuán, 101,155 (Spanish administrative center).
**Monetary unit:** Dirham.
**Languages:** Arabic, French, Spanish.
**Religions:** Chiefly Moslem.

### STATUS IN THE WORLD TODAY

Morocco has proclaimed a policy of "nondependence," or neutrality, in world affairs, but the trend is actually to the left. The new kingdom permitted the Soviet Union to establish an embassy in Rabat in 1958, received arms from Czechoslovakia, and, after a visit from the Iraqi Foreign Minister, joined the Arab League. It has demanded the evacuation of all foreign troops from its soil, including the network of American bomber bases which was established in 1950 under an agreement with France. The United States has agreed in principle to turn the bases over to Morocco to strengthen the hands of the moderates against the extremists, but no date has been set for any evacuation. Spending by personnel at these bases is estimated to contribute some $30 million annually to the Moroccan economy, and in addition the country has received in aid from the United States $20 million in 1957, $30 million in 1958, and $40 million in 1959. It still has a trade deficit of about $70 million. Politically, the country is experiencing some unrest due to the split of the Istiqlal (Independence) party into two warring factions, right-wing and left-wing. A split between the King and the left-wing government resulted in his taking the premiership nine days before the first nation-wide elections scheduled for May 29, 1960. He said the new phase would lead to a constitutional monarchy based on democratic principles, and promised a constitution by 1962.

---

**HISTORY.** Morocco, about the size of California, is just south of Spain across the Strait of Gibraltar and looks out on the Atlantic from the northwest shoulder of Africa. It was once the home of the Berbers, who helped the Arabs invade Spain in A.D. 711 and then revolted against them and gradually won control of large areas of Spain for a time after 739.

The country was ruled successively by various native dynasties and maintained regular commercial relations with Europe, even during the 17th and 18th centuries when it was the headquarters of the famous Salli pirates. In the 19th century, clashes with the French and Spanish became frequent. Finally, in 1904, France and Spain divided Morocco into zones of French and Spanish influence, and these were established as protectorates in 1912.

Meanwhile, Morocco had become the object of big-power rivalry, which almost led to a European war in 1905 when Germany attempted to gain a foothold in the rich mineral country. By terms of the Algeciras Conference (1906), Morocco was internationalized economically and France's privileges were limited. War again seemed imminent in 1911, when Germany dispatched a warship to Agadir in an evident attempt to intimidate France. Again the dispute was settled, however, and this time Germany recognized France's right to establish a protectorate over Morocco.

The Tangier Statute, concluded by Britain, France and Spain in 1923, created an international zone at the port of Tangier, permanently neutralized and demilitarized. In World War II, Spain occupied the zone, ostensibly to ensure order, but was forced to withdraw in 1945.

Sultan Mohammed V was deposed by the French in Aug., 1953, and replaced by his uncle, but nationalist agitation forced his return in Nov., 1955. On his death, Feb. 26, 1961, his son, Hassan, became King.

France recognized the independence and sovereignty of Morocco on March 2, 1956. Spain followed on April 7, 1956. The Tangier international zone was abolished by a declaration signed Oct. 29, 1956. Morocco was admitted to the U.N. Nov. 12, 1956.

**GOVERNMENT.** In May, 1958 King Mohammed V promulgated a royal charter providing for the establishment of a Deliberative Assembly which shares with the King the exercise of legislative power. The charter also stresses the principle of individual and collective responsibility of Cabinet Ministers to the monarch, and provides for elections for rural and municipal councils which, in turn, elect representatives to the Deliberative Assembly.

**ECONOMIC CONDITIONS.** The natives are Berbers, roughly divided by customs and way of life into three groups—the Riff group along the coast, the central, or Berber, group in the mid-Atlas Mountains, and the southern, or Cleuh, in the high Atlas and the Sus. There is a large Jewish population. Most of the Europeans live in the cities.

Morocco is essentially agricultural. Corn,

beans, peas, hemp, wheat, barley, sorghum, citrus fruits, olives, and dates also are raised. In 1955 there were 15,400,000 sheep and 2,466,000 cattle.

In the former Spanish zone, agriculture is largely undeveloped but it has potential importance. Barley, wheat, maize and sorghum crops are the most important.

Manufacturing industries introduced by Europeans, mostly small, produce chemicals, flour, leather, stone, beverages and textiles. Native industries include carpet weaving and making Turkish slippers.

In 1958 chief exports were phosphate, barley, olive oil, and citrus fruit. France took 50 per cent of the exports and supplied 44 per cent of the imports, which included sugar, vehicles, petroleum products, cotton cloth, and tea. A large proportion of the trade was carried on with Spain. Major exports are iron ore, fish, and grain; imports include flour, sugar, tea, wine, and textiles.

Casablanca, which handles 80 per cent of the French zone trade, has perhaps the world's largest artificial port.

Exploitation of French Morocco's almost inexhaustible deposits of phosphate is a state monopoly. Other major minerals are coal, cobalt, iron ore, manganese ore, molybdenum, tin, zinc, and lead. Iron ore is the chief mineral of the Spanish zone; others are antimony and manganese.

NATURAL FEATURES. On the Atlantic coast there is a fertile plain; the Mediterranean coast is mountainous, making most of the Spanish zone a rugged area. The Atlas Mountains, running northeastward from the south to the Algerian frontier, average 11,000 feet in elevation.

# Nepal (Kingdom)

Area: 54,362 square miles.
Population (estimated 1959): 9,044,000 (Gurkha [predominant], Magar, Gurung, Bhotia [Tibetan], Newar).
Density per square mile: 111.2.
Ruler: Mahendra Bir Bikram.
Prime Minister: B. P. Koirala.
Principal city and capital: Katmandu (estimated population, 108,800).
Monetary unit: Nepalese rupee.
Languages: Parbatia, Gubhajius, Tibetan.
Religions: Hinduist, Buddhist.

## STATUS IN THE WORLD TODAY

Nepal, dependent as it is upon other nations for access to the rest of the world, follows the neutralist foreign policy of India, which is committed by treaty to go to Nepal's defense should it be attacked from any quarter. Formerly known as the "forbidden kingdom," which few foreigners could enter, the country has now gone so far in the other direction as to open a tourist bureau. Although concerned and sad over the Communist Chinese occupation of Tibet, Nepal follows the Indian policy of trying to maintain friendly relations with Red China because of its geographical position.

The country is getting economic assistance from the United States, India, Red China, and the U.S.S.R. The U.S. is also developing the nation's nine airports.

The Nepalese do not particularly like their dependence on India, but, except through China, they have no other access to the outside world. And Nehru, although yielding without any measurable opposition to Peiping's occupation of Tibet, has stated that India's true borders are the Himalaya Mountains on the north of Nepal, and that India was "not going to tolerate any person coming over that barrier."

HISTORY AND GOVERNMENT. A landlocked country about the size of Iowa, lying between the Republic of India and Tibet, Nepal contains Mt. Everest, the tallest measured mountain in the world.

The Gurkhas invaded Nepal from India in 1768 and conquered it. A commercial treaty was signed with Britain in 1792, and in 1816, after more than a year's hostilities, the Nepalese agreed to allow British residents to live in Katmandu, the capital. In 1923 Britain recognized the absolute independence of Nepal. King Tribhubana was deposed on Nov. 7, 1950, but was returned to the throne with Indian assistance on Feb. 15, 1951. On his death Mar. 13, 1955, his son Mahendra became ruler. Nepal was admitted to the U.N. in 1955.

The new Constitution promulgated by King Mahendra in February, 1959, provides for a constitutional monarchy with a bicameral parliament and a Cabinet responsible to the Lower House. The Upper House has 36 members, half of whom are elected by the Lower House and the other half appointed by the King. The Lower House has 109 members elected under Nepal's first electoral law, dated June 3, 1958. Candidates must be 25 years of age, and all Nepalese of 21 years and over are granted voting rights. In the elections held in February–April, 1959, the Nepali Congress Party, indentified with the revolutionary movement of 1950, won 74 seats in the Lower House. On May 27, 1959 the new cabinet was sworn in with B. P. Koirala, President of the Nepali Congress Party, as Premier. But in December, 1961, the King dismissed the Premier and dissolved the parliamentary government.

ECONOMIC CONDITIONS. Cultivated and

irrigated where possible, the main valley of Nepal grows rice, wheat, pulse, fruits, vegetables, spices, sugar cane, and potatoes. A few sheep and cattle are grazed. Manufacturing is limited to native handicraft, but jute and textile mills are being established. Trade with India and Pakistan passes through frontier stations; there are two mountain trade routes to Tibet.

Main exports include hides, skins, opium, gums, resins, dyes, jute, wheat, pulse, rice, spices, and timber. Two railroads enter Nepal for short distances—one from Raxaul, India, to Amlekhganj, the other from Jayauagar to Bijulpura.

NATURAL FEATURES AND RESOURCES. Along its southern border, Nepal has a strip of level land which is partly forested, partly cultivated. North of that is the slope of the Himalayan Range, including Mt. Everest (29,028 ft.), which was climbed for the first time in 1953, and many peaks higher than 20,000 feet. Mineral resources, nearly all unexploited, include lignite, copper, zinc, lead, sulfur, marble, and iron. Southern Nepal has valuable forests which yield gum, timber, resin, and dye. Hemp plants grow wild.

# Netherlands (Kingdom)
## (Koninkrijk der Nederlanden)

**Area:** 12,529 square miles.*
**Population (est. 1960):** 11,480,000 (practically all Dutch).
**Density per square mile:** 916.3.
**Sovereign:** Queen Juliana.
**Prime Minister:** Jan Aduard de Quay.
**Principal cities (est. 1960):** Amsterdam, 869,602 (capital, financial center); Rotterdam, 729,852 (chief port); The Hague, 606,-110 (seat of government); Utrecht, 254,186 (railway center); Haarlem, 169,215 (tulip center); Eindhoven, 166,032 (industrial center).
**Monetary unit:** Guilder.
**Language:** Dutch.
**Religions (census 1947):** Roman Catholic, 38.5%; Dutch Reformed, 31.0%; other Protestant, 13.3%; Jewish, 0.2%; others and no creed, 17.0%.

* Excluding waterways and bodies of water larger than 185 acres.

## STATUS IN THE WORLD TODAY

The foreign policy of the Netherlands is overwhelmingly in line with the Atlantic Pact, and the country is one of the firmest friends of the United States in Europe or in the world. It occupies a position in the world economy far out of proportion to its size as a transshipment point for trade both to and from the continent. It was the recipient of American aid after both World Wars.

The Netherlands lost most of its colonial empire in 1949, when its East Indies possessions achieved independence. It is still engaged in a dispute with its former colony over the ownership of West New Guinea (see *Indonesia*). In the Western hemisphere it owns a number of islands comprising the Netherlands West Indies, as well as Surinam (also known as Dutch Guiana) on the South American continent.

## MAJOR POLITICAL PARTIES

Roman Catholic People's party (49 seats in Second Chamber), led by Premier J. E. de Quay; Labor party (48 seats), led by J. J. A. Berger.

HISTORY AND GOVERNMENT. Julius Caesar found the low-lying Netherlands inhabited by Germanic tribes, the Nervii, Frisii, and Batavi. The Batavi on the Roman frontier did not submit to Rome's rule until 13 B.C., and then only as allies. A part of Charlemagne's empire in the eighth and ninth centuries A.D., the area later passed into the hands of Burgundy and the Austrian Hapsburgs, and finally in the sixteenth century came under Spanish rule. When Philip II of Spain suppressed political liberties and the growing Protestant movement in the Netherlands, a revolt led by William of Orange broke out in 1568. Under the Union of Utrecht in 1579, the seven northern provinces became the Republic of the United Netherlands.

The Dutch East India Company was established in 1602, and by the end of the seventeenth century Holland was one of the great sea and colonial powers of Europe.

The nation's independence was not completely established until after the Thirty Years' War, after which the country's rise as a commercial and maritime power began. In 1814 all the provinces of Holland and Belgium were merged into one kingdom, but in 1830 the southern provinces broke away to form the Kingdom of Belgium. A liberal constitution was adopted by the Netherlands in 1848. In spite of its neutrality in World War II the Netherlands was invaded by the Nazis in May, 1940, and the East Indies were later taken by the Japanese. The nation was liberated in May, 1945. In 1948, after a reign of fifty years, Queen Wilhelmina resigned and was succeeded by her daughter Juliana.

The Netherlands is a constitutional monarchy with a bicameral legislature. The Parliament consists of an Upper Chamber of 50 members elected for 6 years by representative bodies of the provinces, and of a Lower Chamber of 150 members elected by popular vote for 4 years. The Upper Chamber cannot introduce or amend bills, only approve or reject them. Members of Parliament are not eligible for Cabinet posts.

RULER. Queen Juliana, who was born April 30, 1909, was married on Jan. 7, 1937, to Prince Bernhard of Lippe-Biesterfeld (born in 1911). They have four daughters: Beatrix, heiress apparent (born Jan. 31, 1938); Irene (born 1939); Margriet Francisca (born 1943); and Maria Christina (born 1947).

ECONOMIC CONDITIONS. *Agriculture* Dutch farms are characteristically small, with only a few larger than 250 acres. Dairying is more important than crop growing; production of cheese milk, butter and eggs is under state control.

In 1959 there were 3,393,000 cattle, 2,586,000 hogs, 518,000 sheep, and 195,000 horses. Large quantities of vegetables and fruits are raised for export.

Almost as important as the dairy industry is the raising of tulip, hyacinth, and other flower bulbs in the area around Haarlem.

*Industry.* The Netherlands is a highly industrialized nation, utilizing both overseas raw materials and domestic agricultural products. Leading industries are textiles, clothing, shipbuilding, shoes, food, and building materials.

The Netherlands ranks high among the world's shipbuilding nations; also pig iron and steel are important. Amsterdam is one of the world's diamond-cutting centers.

*Trade.* Principal customers in 1959 were West Germany (22%), Belgium (15%), Britain (11%), and the U.S. and Canada (7%). Leading suppliers were West Germany (21%), Belgium (18%), other EPU/EF countries (13%), the U.S. and Canada (12%), and Britain (8%). The chief exports were petroleum and coal-tar products, dairy products and eggs, electrical machinery and apparatus, and fabrics and clothing. Leading imports were machinery, iron and steel and manufactures, petroleum and products, cereals and flour, and wood and manufactures.

*Communications.* The Dutch merchant marine is the seventh largest fleet in the world. An extensive network of rivers expanded by many canals has led to extensive development of inland shipping.

NATURAL FEATURES AND RESOURCES. Part of the great plain of north and west Europe, the Netherlands has maximum dimensions of 190 by 160 miles and is low and flat except in Limburg in the southeast, where some hills rise to 300 feet. About half the country's area is below sea level, making the famous Dutch dikes a requisite to the use of much land. Reclamation of land from the sea through dikes has continued through recent times.

All drainage reaches the North Sea, and the principal rivers—Rhine, Maas (Meuse), and Schelde—have their sources outside the country. The Rhine is the most heavily used waterway in Europe.

Netherlands minerals are few. The only important ones are coal, crude petroleum, and salt. There also are peat swamps and about 600,000 acres of forest.

## NETHERLANDS OVERSEAS TERRITORIES

**NETHERLANDS ANTILLES — Status:** Part of the United Kingdom of the Netherlands.
Area: 394 square miles.
Population (est. 1960): 196,116.
Capital: Willemstad (est. 1956: 46,899).
Governor: A. B. Speekenbrink.
Prime Minister: Ephraim Jonckheer.
Foreign trade (1959), exports, 1,342,000,-000 florins; imports, 1,464,000,000 florins. Chief export: petroleum products (87%).
Agricultural products: aloes, beans, corn. Manufactures: refined petroleum, straw hats.
Mineral products: lime phosphate, salt.

This comprises two groups of Caribbean islands 500 miles apart; one, about 40 miles off the Venezuelan coast, consists of Curaçao (173 sq. mi.), Bonaire (95 sq. mi.), and Aruba (69 sq. mi.); the other, lying to the northeast, consists of 3 small islands with a total area of 29 square miles. The Dutch acquired the island of Curaçao from Spain in 1634.

The Governor is assisted by a local Legislature and Cabinet. The area has complete autonomy in domestic affairs.

The economy of the Netherlands Antilles is based almost entirely on the refining at Curaçao and Aruba of crude petroleum, which comes chiefly from the adjacent Maracaibo fields in Venezuela.

**SURINAM (Dutch Guiana)—Status:** Part of the United Kingdom of the Netherlands.
Area: 55,143 square miles.
Population (est. 1959): 255,000.*
Capital: Paramaribo (pop. 1958: 105,400).
Governor: J. van Tilburg.
Prime Minister: S. D. Emanuels.
Foreign trade (1958): exports, 75,988,000 florins (78% to the U.S.); imports, 84,897,-000 florins (32% from the U.S.). Chief export, bauxite (80%).
Agricultural products: rice (1958: 85,049 metric tons), sugar, coffee.
Minerals (1959): bauxite, 3,430,000 metric tons; gold, 5,800 troy oz.
Forest products: balata (1958: 110 metric tons), timber.
* Including aborigines, numbering about 26,000.

Surinam lies in northeastern South America between British and French Guiana. It was received by the Dutch from England at the Peace of Breda (1667) in exchange for New York and at that time included British Guiana, which was seized by England in 1803 and formally ceded to her after the Napoleonic Wars.

The Governor of Surinam (appointed by the Crown) is assisted by a local Legislature and Cabinet, which have sole responsibility in domestic affairs.

Mining is the most important activity, and only about 65,000 acres are devoted to agriculture. The largest bauxite mines are owned by Aluminum Company of America subsidiaries.

From its settled coastal plain, Surinam runs back to a virtually unexplored mountain and jungle area.

**NETHERLANDS NEW GUINEA—Status:** Part of the United Kingdom of the Netherlands.
    Area: 160,618 square miles.
    Population (est. 1959): 715,661.
    Capital: Hollandia (pop. 1958: 16,335).
    Governor: Dr. P. J. Platteel.
    Agricultural products: sago, coconuts, sugar cane, sweet potatoes.
    Minerals: petroleum, nickel, chrome.

The western part of New Guinea, second largest island of the world, with smaller adjacent islands, forms part of the kingdom of the Netherlands. The area remained Dutch upon the transfer of sovereignty in Indonesia in Dec., 1949, with the understanding that its status would be determined within one year by negotiation between the Netherlands and Indonesia. Subsequent negotiations did not lead to any agreement.

Dutch influence dates back to the activities of the Dutch East India Company in the 17th century.

The Papuans are the dominant stock; there are also Melanesian and Negrito elements. Commerce and industry are almost unknown, except for oil production, and life is primitive, with head-hunting and cannibalism not unknown even today.

---

# Nicaragua (Republic)
## (República de Nicaragua)
    Area: 57,143 square miles.*
    Population (est. 1959): 1,450,349 (1943: mestizo, 69%; white, 17%; Negro, 9%; Indian, 5%).
    Density per square mile (land only): 25.4.
    President: Luis Somoza Debayle.
    Principal cities (est. 1959): Managua, 198,939 (capital); León, 48,541 (trading center); Granada, 31,648 (trading center); Chinandega, 18,667 (sugar).
    Monetary unit: Córdoba.
    Language: Spanish.
    Religion: Roman Catholic.
    * Including inland water area of 3,475 square miles.

---

**STATUS IN THE WORLD TODAY**

Nicaragua has been under the control of a military dictatorship since 1936, first under General Anastasio Somoza, who seized power that year, and since his assassination in 1956 under his son, Luis. Nicaragua is one of the targets of a group of revolutionists reported to have the encouragement of two recently liberated nations, Cuba and Venezuela. Under the Somozas, the country has experienced considerable economic development in which the family has participated and from which it has benefited. Agriculture has been diversified, a network of roads has been constructed and manufacturing has begun to appear in several cities.

---

HISTORY. Nicaragua, which established independence in 1838, was first visited by the Spaniards in 1522. The chief of the country's leading Indian tribe at that time was called Nicaragua, from whom the nation derived its name. A United States naval force intervened in 1909 after two American citizens had been executed, and a few U.S. Marines were kept in the country from 1912 to 1925. The Bryan-Chamorro Treaty of 1916 gave the United States an option on a canal route through Nicaragua, and naval bases. Disorder after the 1924 elections brought in U.S. Marines again, but they were withdrawn after the U.S.-supervised elections of 1928.

GOVERNMENT. The Constitution of 1950 provides for a President popularly elected for six years, and a two-house Congress— a 42-member Chamber of Deputies and a 16-member Senate—both elected for six years. Former Presidents of the republic automatically become Senators.

ECONOMIC CONDITIONS. More than half of Nicaragua is jungle-covered; agriculture, the leading industry, utilizes only 10 per cent of the total land.

Chief exports in 1959 were coffee (19%), cotton (41%), and gold (10%). Leading customers were the U.S. (24%), West Germany (14%), Japan (22%), and the Netherlands (7%); leading suppliers were the U.S. (41%), West Germany (7%), and the Netherlands Antilles (6%).

NATURAL FEATURES AND RESOURCES. Largest but most sparsely populated of the Central American nations, Nicaragua is mountainous in the west, with fertile valleys. A plateau slopes eastward toward the Caribbean.

Two big lakes—Nicaragua, about 100 miles long, and Managua, about 38 miles long—are connected by the Tipitapa River. The Pacific coast is bald and rocky; the Caribbean coast, swampy and indented, is aptly called the "Mosquito Coast."

Gold and silver are the most important minerals. One-third wooded, Nicaragua produces mahogany, rosewood, cedar, rubber, and ipecac root.

# Norway (Kingdom)
## (Norge)

Area: 125,065 square miles.
Population (est. 1960): 3,583,800 (Norwegian, 98.7%; Swedish, .8%; others, .5%).
Density per square mile: 28.7.
Sovereign: King Olaf V.
Prime Minister: Einar Gerhardsen.
Principal cities (est. 1958): Oslo, 461,591 (capital, chief port); (census 1950) Bergen, 114,711 (seaport, shipbuilding); Trondheim, 58,915 (seaport, timber, fish); Stavanger, 52,848 (seaport, fisheries).
Monetary unit: Krone.
Language: Norwegian.
Religions: Evangelical Lutheran (state), 96.8%; others, 3.2%.

### STATUS IN THE WORLD TODAY

Norway's foreign policy is strongly pro-Western and pro-American. Although its military strength is not great (army, navy, and air force are small), its strategic location and its firm adherence to NATO give it important significance in the cold war. For this reason it has been one of the targets of vituperative Moscow propaganda, having had a common frontier with the U.S.S.R. since the Russians took the Petsamo area from Finland in 1941.

### MAJOR POLITICAL PARTIES

Labor party (74 seats in Parliament-*Storting*) led by Prime Minister Einar Gerhardsen; Conservative party (29 seats), led by Alv Kjos.

HISTORY AND GOVERNMENT. Norwegians, like the Danes and Swedes, are of Teutonic origin. The Norsemen, also known as Vikings, ravaged the coasts of northwestern Europe from the eighth to the eleventh century.

In 1815, Norway, contrary to her wishes, fell under the control of Sweden. The union of Norway, inhabited by fishermen, sailors, merchants, and peasants, and Sweden, an aristocratic country of large estates and tenant farmers, was not a happy one, but it lasted for nearly a century. In 1905 the Norwegian parliament arranged a peaceful separation and invited a Danish prince to the Norwegian throne—King Haakon VII. A treaty with Sweden provided that all disputes were to be settled by arbitration and that no fortifications be erected on the common frontier. Since the separation the two countries have lived amicably as neighbors.

When World War I broke out, Norway joined with Sweden and Denmark in a decision to remain neutral and to co-operate in the joint interest of the three countries. In World War II Norway was invaded by the Germans on April 9, 1940. She resisted for two months before the Nazis took over complete control. King Haakon and his government fled to London, where they established a government-in-exile. Major Vidkun Quisling, who collaborated with the Nazis, was executed by the Norwegians in October, 1945.

Norway is a constitutional hereditary monarchy. Executive power is vested in the King together with a Cabinet, or Council of State, consisting of a Prime Minister and at least seven other members. The *Storting*, or Parliament, is composed of 150 members elected by the people under proportional representation. The *Storting* discusses and votes on political and financial questions, but divides itself into two sections (*Lagting* and *Odelsting*) to discuss and pass on legislative matters. The King cannot dissolve the *Storting* before the expiration of its term. There is universal suffrage, male and female, for all citizens over twenty-three. In 1913 Norway had the distinction of being the first independent nation to establish woman suffrage.

RULER. Olaf V, born July 2, 1903, only son of Haakon VII and Princess Maud (1869–1938), third daughter of Edward VII of England, succeeded to the throne on the death of his father Sept. 20, 1957. He married Princess Märtha of Sweden (1901–1954) on March 21, 1929. Their children are Princess Ragnhild Alexandria (born 1930), Princess Astrid (born 1932), and Prince Harald (born 1937).

ECONOMIC CONDITIONS. Land suitable for cultivation, estimated at less than 5 per cent of the total area, consists of strips in the deep narrow valleys and around fiords and lakes. Foodstuff production is insufficient to meet domestic needs. Leading crops, with 1959 production in metric tons, are wheat, 28,000; barley, 331,000; oats, 103,000; potatoes, 1,202,000 (1958); hay and fodder. The country is more adapted to stock raising than to crop growing; in 1958 there were 1,126,000 cattle, 1,809,000 sheep, 459,270 hogs, and 110,000 goats.

Raw materials produced in Norway form the basis of most of the manufactures. Leading industries are food, machinery, metals, wood, paper, and electro-chemicals.

In 1959 the leading customers were Britain (20%), West Germany (15%), Sweden (10%), and the U.S. and Canada (9%). Leading suppliers were Britain (13%), West Germany (20%), Sweden (16%), and the U. S. and Canada (11%). Chief exports were base metals (25%), fish and fish preparations (13%), pulp and waste paper (9%), and paper and manufactures (10%).

The normally adverse trade balance is

offset to some extent by invisible exports, particularly the earnings of the large merchant marine.

NATURAL FEATURES AND RESOURCES. Nearly 70 per cent of Norway is uninhabitable and covered by mountains, glaciers, moors, and rivers. The hundreds of deep fiords that cut into Norway's coast line give it an over-all ocean front of more than 12,000 miles. Islands off the coast, numbering almost 150,000, form a breakwater and make a safe coastal shipping channel.

Mineral resources are extensive, but coal deposits are entirely lacking except in Spitsbergen. Important minerals are iron ore, aluminum, pyrite ore, zinc, copper ore, molybdenum ore, tungsten, antimony ore, tin, and silver.

Cheap electric power, produced mainly by hydroelectric plants, makes possible the extraction of nitrogen from the air and manufacture of potassium nitrate, an important fertilizer.

The forests, largely in the south and southeast, are one of the chief natural resources. About 25% of the total area is covered with forests, of which 70% is pine.

Fishing is one of the principal industries, engaging as many as 100,000 persons.

# Panamá (Republic)
## (República de Panamá)

**Area:** 28,753 square miles.
**Population (est. 1960):** 1,053,000 (1940: mestizo, 65.34%; Negro, 13.31%; white, 11.07%; Indian, 9.53%; others, .75%).
**Density per square mile:** 36.6.
**President:** Roberto Chiari.
**Principal cities (est. 1958):** Panamá City, 238,980 (capital and chief port); Colón, 64,430 (chief Caribbean port); Ciudad David, 14,847 (bananas).
**Monetary unit:** Balboa.
**Language:** Spanish (official).
**Religion:** Roman Catholic, 93%; Protestant, 6%; others, 1%.

## STATUS IN THE WORLD TODAY

The importance of the Republic of Panamá, a pro-Western democracy, lies in the Panama Canal, which has become a convenient target of the country's extreme nationalists. Encouraged by Nasser's example, a few of them would like to nationalize the international waterway. Others want the United States to give Panamá 50% of the gross receipts from the operation of the canal. The government itself is protesting against alleged discrimination in the hiring of Panamanians in the Canal Zone and against sales in United States government-owned stores in the zone, a profitable business which it feels should go to its own re-

tailers. An Act of the Panamanian Congress extending territorial waters from three to twelve miles, which might force ships approaching and leaving the canal to pass through Panamá's jurisdiction, is a further cause of dispute, not only with the United States, but also with other nations.

In April, 1960, President Eisenhower put into effect a nine-point program, including improved housing and pay raises for Panamanian workers in the Canal Zone and an expanded training schedule for them. Politically, Panamá has experienced a series of minor upheavals in the past few years, and the landing of a group of less than 90 insurgents from Cuba was enough to cause a mild case of hysteria and an appeal for help to the Organization of American States. Economically, revenues from canal tolls are of decreasing importance, and the country is beginning to exploit natural resources which have not been touched since independence was achieved. A steel mill has been built, a manganese mine has been opened, and farm land is being extended to help provide food for a population which just reaches one million but which is expected to double in ten years.

## MAJOR POLITICAL PARTIES

Union Nacional de Oposición (18 seats in Congress), led by President Roberto Chiari; Coalición Patriótica Nacional (16 seats), led by Dr. Ricardo Arias.

HISTORY. Visited by Columbus in 1502 on his fourth voyage and explored by Balboa in 1513, Panamá was the principal transshipment point for Spanish treasure and supplies to and from South and Central America in colonial days. In 1821, when Central America revolted against Spain, Panamá joined Colombia, which already had declared its independence. For the next 82 years, Panamá attempted unsuccessfully to break away from Colombia. After U.S. proposals for canal rights over the narrow isthmus had been rejected by Colombia, Panamá proclaimed its independence with U.S. backing in 1903.

For canal rights in perpetuity, the United States paid Panamá $10,000,000, and agreed to pay $250,000 each year, increased to $430,000 after devaluation of the U.S. dollar in 1933 and to $1,930,000 under a revised treaty signed Jan. 25, 1955. In exchange, the United States got the Canal Zone, a ten-mile-wide strip across the isthmus and a considerable degree of influence in Panamá's affairs.

GOVERNMENT. The President is elected by direct popular vote for 4 years and may not succeed himself. There are also 2 Vice-Presidents elected for 4 years. The legislature consists of a unicameral National Assembly of 53 members elected by direct popular vote for 4 years. Panamá has universal suffrage.

ECONOMIC CONDITIONS. About five-eighths of the nation is unoccupied. A fourth of the population is in Colón and in Panamá City, the oldest white settlement on the Pacific coast of the Americas. In the cities, the lower classes are Negro and Negroid, descendants of British West Indian laborers on the canal.

Bananas are the main agricultural crop. Chief exports in 1959 were bananas (67%) and fresh shrimp (15%). The United States was the leading customer (73%) and supplier (93%).

The Panama Canal is the country's biggest economic asset. The main railway is the U.S. Government-owned Panamá Railroad, 47.64 miles long, bridging the isthmus from Panamá City to Colón. In recent years many foreign ships have been registered in Panamá to escape high labor costs and governmental regulations in other nations.

NATURAL FEATURES. Panamá is roughly the size of South Carolina. At the narrowest and lowest point, the canal bisects the country. Outlying islands number about 630 in the Caribbean, 116 in the Pacific.

# Paraguay (Republic)
## (República del Paraguay)

Area: 157,047 square miles.
Population (est. 1960): 1,760,000 (1950: mestizo, 94.9%; white, 3.0%; Indian, 2.1%).
Density per square mile: 11.2.
President: Gen. Alfredo Stroessner.
Principal cities (census 1950): Asunción, 201,340 (capital); Villarrica, 14,680 (sugar, tobacco); Concepción, 14,640 (port, Paraguay river); Encarnación, 13,321 (rail terminus).
Monetary unit: Guaraní.
Languages: Spanish (official), Guaraní.
Religion: Roman Catholic (official).

## STATUS IN THE WORLD TODAY

Paraguay has recently been the scene of considerable political unrest, possibly because the success of revolutionists in Cuba and Venezuela has revived hopes of opposition leaders, both inside the country and in exile. Although Gen. Alfredo Stroessner, the president, said in April, 1959, that he would send Congress a series of bills providing for gradual restoration of constitutional government, and later that month lifted the state of siege, a modified form of martial law, under which the country had been ruled since 1947. In May he dissolved the Chamber of Deputies, restored the stage of siege, and arrested scores of political leaders, some of them in the ruling Colorado party which, with the army, supports the government.

Despite the political unrest, the country enjoys economic stability and the government has instituted a certain amount of social and economic reform, such as giving small farmers land under an agrarian reform program, enacting social security legislation, extending collective bargaining, and encouraging a moderate degree of industrialization. The country remains, however, a predominantly agricultural and grazing nation.

HISTORY AND GOVERNMENT. In 1526 and again in 1529, Sebastian Cabot explored Paraguay when he sailed up the Paraná and Paraguay Rivers. From 1608 until their expulsion from the Spanish dominions in 1767, the Jesuits maintained an extensive establishment in the south and east of Paraguay. In 1811 Paraguay revolted against Spanish rule and became a nominal republic under two Consuls.

Actually Paraguay was governed by three dictators during the first 60 years of independence. The third, Francisco Lopez, declared war on both Brazil and Argentina in 1864–65, a conflict in which the male population was almost wiped out. A new constitution in 1870, designed to prevent dictatorships and internal strife, failed to do so, and not until 1912 did a period of comparative economic and political stability begin. The dispute between Paraguay and Boliva over the Chaco territory led to war in 1932 and was finally settled by the 1935 Buenos Aires peace conference, which gave most of the Chaco to Paraguay.

The Paraguayans are a homogeneous blend of Spanish, Portuguese, and Italian, with considerable Guaraní Indian blood. There are almost no Negroes; the 35,000 to 50,000 uncivilized Indians live mainly in the Chaco. The country is 90 per cent bilingual, with Guarani dominating over Spanish (the official language) in rural areas.

The President is elected by popular vote for 5 years. Paraguay has a Congress also elected by popular vote and a Council of State whose members are nominated by the Government. The Cabinet is appointed by the President and holds all effective power, merely informing the Congress and Council of State of its decisions.

ECONOMIC CONDITIONS. A well-favored land, Paraguay is predominantly a cattle country, keeping about 4,095,000 head. The soil is fertile and the climate suitable for subtropical crops. The chief cash crop is cotton.

Chief exports in 1959 were timber (13%), meat and products (31%), quebracho extract (11%), and cotton (7%). Principal customers and suppliers in 1959 were Argentina, the United States, and Germany.

NATURAL FEATURES AND RESOURCES. Eastern Paraguay, between the Paraná and Paraguay Rivers, is upland country with the thickest population settled on the grassy slope that inclines toward the Paraguay River. The greater part of the Chaco region, to the west, is covered with marshes, lagoons, dense forests, and jungles.

Forest resources are considerable, especially in the Chaco. Quebracho—the "Axe-breaker," a wood so heavy that it will not float—is the principal commercial tree. The wood has many uses, from paving blocks to ox-cart wheels. Quebracho tannic extract is the chief product.

# Peru (Republic)
## (República del Peru)

Area: 496,223 square miles.
Population (est. 1960): 10,827,000 (white and mestizo, 53%; Indian, 46%; Asiatic, Negro and others, 1%).
Density per square mile: 21.8.
President: Manuel Prado y Ugarteche.
Principal cities (est. 1958): Lima, 1,186,-212 (capital); Callao, 129,365 (port of Lima); Arequipa, 121,806 (commercial center); Cuzco, 68,483 (ancient Incan capital); Trujillo, 60,427 (mining).
Monetary unit: Sol.
Languages: Spanish, Quéchua, Aymará (Indian).
Religion: Roman Catholic.

## STATUS IN THE WORLD TODAY

Peru, where until recently military dictatorship was virtually endemic, has been undergoing an experiment in democracy which may completely transform the country's social structure. Traditionally ruled by an alliance of the commercial and rural aristocracy and the army, the country's political status quo has been challenged by the Aprista party, which arose from a student movement for university reform and social change. Although the Apristas showed they were the country's majority party, the party was declared illegal for many years. But the oppressiveness of the dictatorship, and general world developments, convinced an important segment of the economic aristocracy that the changes advocated by the Apristas were bound to come sooner or later and it would be better to have them come in a democratic manner through an Aprista regime than violently, as in neighboring Bolivia. This group's candidate for president, Manuel Prado, won in 1956 with the support of the Apristas, and immediately fulfilled his campaign promise to legalize the party. Since then he has presided over an uneasy regime which has guaranteed civil liberties but has been beset by serious economic and social problems.

## MAJOR POLITICAL PARTIES

Movimiento Democrática Pradista (57 seats in Chamber of Deputies), led by President Manuel Prado; Movimiento Lavalle (42 seats), led by Dr. Hernando de Lavalle; Partido Democrata Cristiano (40 seats), led by Dr. Luis Bedoya Reyes.

HISTORY. Peru, once part of the great Incan empire and later the major viceroyalty of Spanish South America, is more than three times the size of California. It was conquered in 1531–33 by Francisco Pizarro. On July 28, 1821, Peru proclaimed its independence, but the Spanish were not finally defeated until the Battle of Ayacucho on Dec. 9, 1824. For a hundred years thereafter the Peruvian course was rough. Revolutions were frequent, and a new war was fought with Spain in 1864–66. The dispute with Chile over Tacna and Arica was not finally settled until 1929.

GOVERNMENT. Under the 1933 Constitution, Peru elects by popular vote every six years a President, two Vice-Presidents and a bicameral Congress—a Senate of 52 members and a Chamber of 183 members. The President is ineligible to succeed himself. The Cabinet, headed by the Prime Minister, is presidentially appointed.

Most Peruvians are of mixed Spanish and Indian blood. The Indians come from three main stocks—Quéchua, Aymará (Colla), and Chuncho. There is a relatively large Asiatic population.

ECONOMIC CONDITIONS. Land under cultivation is estimated at only slightly more than 10 per cent of the total area, with more than 80 per cent of the population being dependent upon agriculture. About one-eighth of the cultivated area in the irrigated coastal valleys of the central region is devoted to cotton, the most important crop. Stock raising supplies most of the country's meat needs, as well as wool, hides, and skins for export. Llamas, used as beasts of burden, and vicuñas and alpacas, noted for their wool, are native to Peru. Livestock estimates in Dec., 1958, showed 3,176,000 cattle, 14,017,-000 sheep; (1957) 1,364,000 hogs, and 2,877,-200 alpacas and llamas.

Chief exports in 1959 were cotton (22%), fish and fish preparations (15%), sugar (12%), copper (8%), and lead (7%). Chief suppliers were the United States (41%), West Germany (12%), and Britain (7%);

chief customers, the United States (34%), Britain (10%), and Chile (10%). Principal Peruvian imports are machinery and motor vehicles, foodstuffs (especially wheat), iron and steel manufactures, electrical goods, and chemicals.

NATURAL FEATURES AND RESOURCES. The Andes Mountains divide Peru into three sharply differentiated zones. To the west is the coastline, much of it arid, extending for 50 to 100 miles inland.

The mountain area, with peaks over 20,000 feet high, lofty plateaus and deep valleys, lies centrally. Beyond the mountains to the east is the heavily forested slope leading to the Amazonian plains.

Peru has vast mineral resources. It ranks fifth in world silver production and mines about 25 per cent of the world's vanadium. But mining is second to agriculture, and nearly all of it is in the hands of foreign capital. Petroleum and copper are the most important, with the latter controlled by the American-owned Cerro de Pasco Corporation, which also accounts for much of the gold and silver output.

An important industry on the outlying islands is the gathering of guano (bird excrement), a valuable fertilizer.

# The Philippines (Republic)

**Area:** 115,707 square miles.
**Population** (est. 1960): 27,473,000 (Filipino, except [1948] 121,702 Chinese, 6,955 Americans, 1,886 Spanish and 3,319 others).
**Density per square mile:** 237.4.
**President:** Carlos P. Garcia.
**Principal cities** (est. 1959): Manila, 1,205,340 (seat of government, chief port); (est. 1952) Cebu, 205,201 (seaport); Quezon City, 159,730 (legal, future capital); Basilan, 141,640 (lumber); Bacolod, 126,-200 (sugar); Zamboanga, 124,710 (seaport).
**Monetary unit:** Peso.
**Languages:** English, Tagalog, Visayan, Spanish, Ilocano, Bicol.
**Religions** (census 1948): Roman Catholic, 82.9%; Aglipayan (Independent Philippine Catholic), 7.6%; Moslem, 4.1%; Protestant, 2.3%; others, 3.1%.

## STATUS IN THE WORLD TODAY

The foreign policy of the Philippines is pro-Western and anti-Communist, the new republic being a member of the Southeast Asia Treaty Organization. Emerging as an independent state after centuries of Spanish and American rule, the Philippine people have chosen to build a democratic society in close alliance with the United States. Militarily, the islands have relied for external defense on the United States, which secured the leasehold of a number of bases when independence was granted. In 1951 a mutual-defense pact was signed.

The most pressing problems facing the young republic are economic. They result largely from two causes: the great destruction wrought during World War II and the gradual imposition of tariffs on Filipino goods entering the American market. As long as the islands were administered by the United States, Filipino goods entered duty-free. Since the grant of commonwealth status to the islands in 1935, however, it has been United States policy gradually to end this preferential tariff treatment. Consequently, Filipino exports have been sharply reduced. Efforts are being made to offset this by stimulating the domestic production of commodities formerly imported and by diversification of agriculture. But import needs continue high and capital for domestic economic development is short. The United States has given substantial aid, the latest being an additional $125 million loan, but the solution to the quest for economic independence is not yet in sight.

## MAJOR POLITICAL PARTIES

Nacionalista party (83 seats in House of Representatives), led by President Carlos P. Garcia; Liberal party (19 seats), led by Diosdado Macapagal.

HISTORY AND GOVERNMENT. Fernando Magellan, the Portuguese navigator in the service of Spain, discovered the Philippines on March 16, 1521, and then 21 years later a Spanish exploration party named the group of islands in honor of Prince Philip, later Philip II of Spain. Spain retained possession of the islands for the next 350 years.

The Philippines were ceded to the United States in 1899 by the Treaty of Paris after the Spanish-American War. Meanwhile the Filipinos, led by Emilio Aguinaldo, had declared their independence. They continued guerrilla warfare against U.S. troops until the capture of Aguinaldo in March, 1901. By July, 1902, peace was established except among the Moros.

The first U.S. civilian Governor-General was William Howard Taft (1901–04). The Jones Law (1916) provided for the establishment of a Philippine Legislature composed of an elective Senate and House of Representatives. The Tydings-McDuffie Act (1934) provided for complete Philippine independence in 1946. Under a Constitution approved by the people of the Philippines May 14, 1935, the Commonwealth of the Philippines was inaugurated on Nov. 15 under the presidency of Manuel Quezon y Molina, who was re-elected in 1941.

The Philippines were invaded by Japanese troops on Dec. 8, 1941 (Philippine time), and after the fall of Bataan and Corregidor, President Quezon and his government fled to Washington, D.C. U.S. forces led by Gen. Douglas MacArthur re-invaded the islands in Oct., 1944, and after the liberation of Manila (Feb., 1945), Sergio Osmeña, who had succeeded to the presidency on the death of Quezon (Aug. 1, 1944), re-established the government.

Brig. Gen. Manuel A. Roxas y Acuña, who defeated Osmeña in the elections of April, 1946, became first head of the new independent republic. He died April 15, 1948, and was succeeded by the Vice-President, Elpidio Quirino. The latter was re-elected on Nov. 8, 1949, but lost a second bid for re-election to Ramón Magsaysay, who took office on Dec. 30, 1953. On his death in a plane crash March 17, 1957, Magsaysay was succeeded by Vice-President Carlos P. Garcia.

ECONOMIC CONDITIONS. *Agriculture and Industry.* Agriculture is the chief industry. Average size of the farms is ten acres, but there are many large plantations. Rice (palay) is the staple native food cereal, but production is insufficient to meet home consumption. The Philippines normally produce about half the world copra supply and a large proportion of the abacá (Manila hemp) supply; they are also a leading source of sugar and sugar products, normally the chief export. Other crops include sisal, kapok, cotton, corn, tobacco, coffee, rubber cacao, citrus fruits, and bananas. Livestock on March 31, 1959, included 3,596,000 water buffalo, the farmers' all-purpose animal, 836,080 cattle, 214,140 horses, and 5,765,370 hogs.

There are no large industrial establishments and activity is limited primarily to the processing of agricultural and forest products, such as sugar cane, coconuts, tobacco, abacá, and timber. Preparation of fine embroideries is an important industry.

In 1959, the chief exports were copra and other coconut products (39%), sugar (22%), wood (11%), and abacá (8%). Leading customers were the United States (about 50%), and Japan (20%); leading suppliers, the United States, Japan, and Indonesia. Leading imports were machinery and vehicles, cotton and manufactures, iron and steel, and petroleum and products.

NATURAL FEATURES AND RESOURCES. The Philippines are an archipelago of approximately 7,083 islands lying about 500 miles off the southeast coast of Asia. The northernmost island, Y'Ami, is sixty-five miles from Formosa, while the southernmost, Saluag, is thirty miles east of Borneo. Only 466 of the islands have an area of more than one square mile, and only 2,441 have names. The largest islands are Luzon in the north (40,814 sq. mi.),

Mindanao in the south (36,537 sq. mi.), Samar (5,124 sq. mi.), Negros (4,903 sq. mi.), and Palawan (4,550 sq. mi.).

*Minerals, Forests and Fisheries.* The Philippines possess large but relatively undeveloped mineral resources. Most important are gold, silver, iron ore, copper ore, chromite, manganese ore, lead, and zinc.

# Poland (People's Republic)
## (Polska Rzeczpospolita Ludowa)

Area: 120,359 square miles.
Population (est. 1959): 29,480,000.
Density per square mile: 244.9.
Chairman of State Council: Aleksander Zawadski.
Premier: Josef Cyrankiewicz.
Principal cities (est. 1959): Warsaw, 1,095,400 (capital); Lódz, 697,000 (industrial center); Wroclaw (Breslau), 414,600 (former German industrial center); Kraków, 462,500 (commercial center); Poznan, 394,800 (farm products).
Monetary unit: Zloty.
Language: Polish (more than 90%).
Religions: Roman Catholic, Jewish, Protestant.

### STATUS IN THE WORLD TODAY

Poland is the most unusual of Soviet satellites in that it has managed, despite Russian criticism, to substitute its own brand of communism for the Moscow variety and yet avoid the military intervention which Hungary suffered and the violent propaganda attacks which assailed Yugoslavia. Poland remains a dictatorship ruled by a single party, but it is a more benevolent dictatorship than in any other Communist-run country. Wladyslaw Gomulka rose to power in 1956 in a bloodless revolution because the Polish people supported his policy of national self-determination, democratic political reforms, and restoration of the health of the political economy. There has been some retreat from the extreme positions of freedom won by the people in 1956, but the fact that the people can still grumble at the tops of their voices clearly distinguishes them from their less fortunate neighbors.

Because of its geographical position, Poland cannot be entirely free of Soviet domination. Russian troops are stationed there to maintain the supply lines to the occupation forces in East Germany. And Poland's present frontiers have been created unilaterally by the Soviet Union and are not recognized by the Western powers. Consequently, Poland, having been forced to cede territory in the east to Russia, can look only to Russia to help it keep the German territory it received in return in the West. Having been partitioned and oppressed so often by both countries, the Poles dislike or hate the Germans and Russians in about equal proportion.

In its foreign relations the Polish government has little leeway in making independent decisions. The most the regime has been able to accomplish is to arrange small, short-term loans with the United States. Economically, it needs larger, long-term assistance. The former Stalinist policy of concentrating on heavy industry meant home construction and agriculture were starved for funds. Insufficient mechanical improvement in agriculture, coupled with forced collectivization resulted in a drop in farm production. Compulsory exports, until 1953, of coal, Poland's chief marketable material, to Russia at 1/12 of world prices robbed the country of possibilities of profitable trade and accumulation of convertible currency. Since 1956 the government has been trying to alleviate the worst of economic evils. Nonproductive, wasteful projects have been scrapped. Poland is no longer exploited in its export of coal and other items to Russia. Collectivization has been stopped and most of the existing collective farms disbanded. But the problems of economic rehabilitation are still staggering.

---

HISTORY. Little of certainty is known about Polish history before the eleventh century, when King Boleslaus I (the Brave) ruled over Bohemia, Saxony, and Moravia. Mongol invasions in 1241 and 1259 were repelled. Meanwhile, the Teutonic Knights were erecting in Prussia a state which included part of Poland and barred the latter's access to the Baltic. The Knights were defeated by Wladislaus II at Tannenberg in 1410 and became Polish vassals, and Poland regained a Baltic shoreline.

Poland reached the peak of its power between the fourteenth and sixteenth centuries. Poles scored military successes against the Russians and Turks. In 1683, King John Sobieski turned back the Turkish tide near Vienna.

These successes did not halt the process of decline which resulted from the lack of strong central authority, and Prussia, Russia, and Austria were able to carry out a first partition of the country in 1772, a second in 1792 and a third in 1795–96. For more than a century thereafter, there was no Polish state, but the Poles never ceased their efforts to regain their independence. World War I found them fighting unhappily on both sides.

The independence of Poland was formally proclaimed in November, 1918, and Marshal Josef Pilsudski was made Chief of State. In 1919, Ignace Paderewski, the famous pianist and patriot, became the first Premier. Russia attacked Poland in 1920 but the Poles, under Marshal Pilsudski and aided by the French, defeated the invaders. On May 12, 1926, Marshal Pilsudski seized complete power in a coup d'etat and ruled the country dictatorially until his death on May 12, 1935, when he was succeeded as commander of the army by Marshal Edward Smigly-Rydz.

Despite a 10-year nonaggression pact signed with Germany in 1934, Hitler attacked Poland on Sept. 1, 1939. Russian troops invaded from the east Sept. 17, 1939, and on Sept. 28 a German-Russian agreement was signed dividing Poland between Russia and Germany. W. Raczkiewicz formed a government-in-exile in France with Gen. Wladyslaw Sikorski as Premier; this government moved to London after France's defeat in 1940.

All of Poland was occupied by Germany after the Nazi attack on the Soviet Union in June, 1941. On July 30, 1941, Poland concluded an agreement with the U.S.S.R. voiding all German-Soviet agreements effected after Sept. 1, 1939.

The legal Polish government soon fell out with the Russians, however, and in July, 1944, a Communist-dominated Polish Committee of National Liberation received Soviet recognition. Moving to Lublin after that city's liberation, it proclaimed itself the Provisional Government of Poland on Dec. 31, 1944. Some former members of the Polish Government in London joined with the Lublin government to form the Polish Government of National Unity on June 28, 1945. Great Britain and the United States recognized this government on July 5, 1945.

On Aug. 2, 1945, in Berlin, Prime Minister Attlee, President Truman and Generalissimo Stalin established a new *de facto* western frontier for Poland, along the rivers Oder and Lausitzer Neisse, pending a final peace treaty. On Aug. 16 the Soviet Union and Poland signed a treaty delimiting the Soviet-Polish frontier. Under these agreements Poland was shifted westward. In the east it lost 69,860 square miles with 10,772,000 inhabitants; in the west it gained (subject to final peace-conference approval) 38,986 square miles with a prewar population of 8,621,000.

GOVERNMENT AND DEFENSE. The 1952 Constitution is based on that of the U.S.S.R. The supreme organ of state authority is the Sejm, composed of 425 members elected for four years by all citizens over 18.

ECONOMIC CONDITIONS. *Agriculture.* Poland remains essentially an agricultural country: the areas now under *de facto* Polish administration in the west accounted for 25% of Germany's pre-war food production. Farm lands lost to the Soviet Union were considerably larger in area than those gained from Germany.

*Industry.* Industrial facilities, although severely damaged during World War II, were not greatly affected by territorial concessions to the U.S.S.R., with the exception of the Lwów area. On the other hand, important German industrial areas, especially Silesia and the city of Stettin, are located in the territories under *de facto* Polish administration. As a result, postwar Poland has a much larger industrial potential. Almost all industries have been nationalized or placed under state control, and a planned economy has been introduced as part of the government's drive to make Poland an industrial nation.

*Trade.* Foreign trade is largely conducted by government bodies under the terms of numerous trade agreements with other nations. Major exports in 1954 were coal and coke, other raw materials, and semi-manufactures and agricultural products (mainly bacon and ham). Major imports were machinery, textiles, chemicals, and mineral products.

NATURAL FEATURES AND RESOURCES. Most of Poland is a plain with no natural boundaries except the Carpathian Mountains on the south and the Oder and Neisse Rivers on the west.

The acquisition of large coal deposits in German Silesia, combined with much larger reserves in the southwestern region, makes Poland one of the world's leading coal producers. Iron ore deposits are located in the Kielce and Radom districts and in German Silesia (metal content 34%). Zinc and lead ores are located chiefly in Upper Silesia and the voivodships of Kielce and Kraków. Pre-war Poland's principal oil-producing areas, Boryslaw-Drohobycz, are in the territory ceded to the Soviet Union; Among other deposits, Poland possesses copper, sulfur, chalk, clay, kaolin, marble, and granite.

# Portugal (Republic)
## (República Portuguesa)

Area: 35,599 square miles.
Population (est. 1960): 9,124,000 practically all Portuguese).
Density per square mile: 256.2.
President: Americo Deus R. Tomaz.
Premier: António de Oliveira Salazar.
Principal cities (census 1950): Lisbon, 790,434 (capital, seaport); Oporto, 284,842 (seaport, port wine); Setúbal, 44,235 (seaport; sardines); Coimbra, 42,640 (university); Funchal in Madeira Islands, 37,215 (Madeira wine).
Monetary unit: Escudo.
Language: Portuguese.
Religion: Roman Catholic.

## STATUS IN THE WORLD TODAY

Portugal, long an ally of Great Britain, is on the side of the free world in the current cold war and is a member of the North Atlantic Treaty Organization, which it joined in April, 1949. Situated in a vitally important geographical area on the Western periphery of Europe, the country is a kind of fixed aircraft carrier. Although there has been criticism about the logic and wisdom of including Portugal, a dictatorship, among the nations of Free Europe in NATO, it is said that support for the policy of containment of communism must be sought wherever it can be found. Defenders of the regime—as in other dictatorships—say that while it is admittedly opposed to democratic and liberal ideas, it has brought economic and political stability to Portugal. The opposition candidate for the Presidency in the elections of June, 1958, Lt. Gen. Humberto Delgado, deemed it necessary, after being stripped of his military titles, to seek refuge in the Brazilian embassy and then go into exile.

HISTORY AND GOVERNMENT. Portugal was a part of Spain until it won its independence in the middle of the twelfth century. King John I (1385–1433) unified his country at the expense of the Castilians and the Moors of Morocco. The expansion of Portugal was brilliantly coordinated by John's son, Prince Henry, surnamed the Navigator. In 1488 Bartholomew Diaz reached the Cape of Good Hope, proving that the Far East was accessible by sea. In 1498 Vasco da Gama reached the western coast of India. By the middle of the sixteenth century the Portuguese Empire included West and East Africa, Brazil, Persia, Indo-China, and Malaya.

In 1581 Philip II of Spain invaded Portugal and held her captive for 60 years. There followed a catastrophic decline of Portuguese commerce. Courageous and shrewd explorers, the Portuguese proved to be inefficient and corrupt colonizers. By the time the Portuguese dynasty was restored in 1640, Dutch, English, and French competitors began to seize the lion's share of the world's colonies and commerce. Portugal retained Angola and Mozambique in Africa and Brazil (until 1822), but her place as an imperial power was lost forever.

In the first half of the nineteenth century Portugal's political history was distinguished by dynasty quarrels and factional strife. The corrupt King Carlos, who ascended the throne in 1889, made João Franco the Premier with dictatorial power in 1906. In 1908 Carlos and his heir were shot dead on the streets of Lisbon. The new king, Manuel II, was driven from the throne in the Revolution of 1910. Portugal was proclaimed a republic with a system modeled upon that of France.

Traditionally friendly to Great Britain, Portugal entered World War I on the Allies' side, and Portuguese troops fought on the Western Front and in Africa. In 1926 a revolution drove out the President, and six years later the Salazar dictatorship began.

Dr. António de Oliveira Salazar, founder of the National Union in 1930, has been Premier and dictator of Portugal since 1932. The constitution, adopted by plebiscite in 1933, and amended in June, 1959, provides for a President chosen for a term of 7 years by an electoral college made up of members of the National Assembly and the Corporative Chamber and of representatives from each metropolitan district and overseas province. The National Assembly has 130 members elected by popular vote for 4 years and the Corporative Chamber represents various economic and social groups in the nation. The Premier is appointed by the President but neither the Premier nor his Cabinet are responsible to the National Assembly.

ECONOMIC CONDITIONS. Portugal's corporate state has a planned economy in which each producing unit regulates itself in the interest of the nation. Corporate units have been established in agriculture, industry, and finance.

Sixty per cent of Portugal's people are engaged in agriculture. Although wheat is the leading crop, it is insufficient to meet domestic needs, and grain must be imported. One of the world's leading winemakers, Portugal produces two famous kinds—Port in the vicinity of Oporto, and Madeira in the islands of the same name. In olive-oil production, Portugal usually ranks third in the world.

Leading crops are wheat, barley, and oats.

In 1959 the principal customers were continental EPU dependencies (30%), continental EPU countries (18%), Angola (18%), Britain (11%) and U.S. and Canada (11%); chief suppliers, continental EPU countries (47%), continental EPU dependencies (18%), Britain (13%) and U.S. and Canada (7%). The chief exports were cork (16%), wine (9%), and fish (14%), mainly sardines.

NATURAL FEATURES AND RESOURCES. Portugal is crossed by many small rivers, and also by three large ones which rise in Spain, flow into the Atlantic, and divide the country into three geographic areas. The Minho (Miño in Spain) River, part of the northern boundary, cuts through a mountainous area that extends south to the vicinity of the Douro (Duero) River. South of the Douro the mountains slope to the plains about the Tagus (Tejo) River. The remaining division is the southern one of Alentejo.

The Azores, stretching over a distance of 400 miles in the Atlantic, consist of nine islands divided into three groups, with total area of 888 square miles. The nearest continental land is Cape da Roca, Portugal, which lies 800 miles to the east. The Azores are an important station on Atlantic air routes, and both Britain and the United States established air bases there during World War II. Madeira, consisting of two inhabited islands, Madeira and Porto Santo, and two groups of uninhabited islands, lies in the Atlantic about 535 miles southwest of Lisbon.

Mineral resources have not been fully developed, but wolfram, coal, iron ore, copper, manganese, iron pyrites, lead, tin, and other ores are found.

Portugal is one of the world's leading producers of cork.

The fishing industry is a basic part of the national economy. Of special importance is the sardine industry centered at Setúbal.

---

### PORTUGUESE OVERSEAS TERRITORIES

|  | Area, sq. mi. | Population, est. 1959 |
|---|---|---|
| **AFRICA** | | |
| Angola | 481,352 | 4,550,000 |
| Cape Verde Islands | 1,557 | 195,000 |
| Mozambique | 302,329 | 6,310,000 |
| Portuguese Guinea | 13,948 | 565,000 |
| São Tomé and Principe | 372 | 64,000 |
| **ASIA** | | |
| Macao | 6 | 215,000 |
| Portuguese India | 1,619 | 649,000* |
| Timor | 5,763 | 496,000 |

* Estimated 1955.

The status of the Portuguese overseas territories is fixed by the Colonial Act of July, 1930, included in the Constitution approved March 19, 1933, and revised in 1951. Each territory has a Governor or Governor General, appointed by the Council of Ministers for an initial four-year term and responsible to the Minister of Overseas Territories at Lisbon. Each territory has financial and administrative autonomy.

ANGOLA (Portuguese West Africa)—
Status: Overseas territory.
Capital: Loanda (pop. 1955: 189,590).
Governor General: Dr. Alvaro Rodrigues da Silva Tavares.
Chief exports: coffee, diamonds, fish meal.
Agricultural exports (1958): coffee, 81,000 metric tons; sisal, cotton, sugar, maize, palm kernels and oil, peanuts, rice.

Minerals: diamonds (1958: 1,001,000 carats), lignite, copper.
Forest products: beeswax, timber.
Manufactures: sugar, palm oil, whale oil, fish oil.

Angola stretches along the west African coast for about 1,000 miles from Belgian Congo to the Cunene River. Outside of a coastal plain varying in width from thirty to 100 miles, the area is part of the great African plateau. The Angola coast and the Congo River were explored by the Portuguese in 1482–85, and Loanda was founded in 1576. A revolt in northeast Angola in 1961 accented the outmoded colonial methods of Portugal's dictatorship.

Angola is primarily an agricultural country. Its varied altitude enables it to produce both tropical and temperate crops. Excellent grazing land exists in many parts of the colony. The chief ports are Loanda and Lobito. The great majority of the population are of Bantu-Negro stock, mixed in the Congo district with pure Negro.

CAPE VERDE ISLANDS—Status: Overseas territory.
Capital (1950 census): Praia (population 3,573).
Governor: Maj. Silvino Silvéaio Marques.
Foreign trade (1959): exports, 319,600,-000 escudos; imports, 378,900,000 escudos. Chief exports: ships stores, preserved fish.
Agricultural products: coffee, millet, castor oil, oranges, hides.

This group of 14 volcanic islands lying off the west African coast was discovered in 1456 by the Venetian captain Alvise Cadamosto, in the service of Prince Henry the Navigator. The island of São Vicente is an important fueling station on the South American route. The vast majority of the inhabitants are mulattoes and Negroes—descendants of slaves brought to the islands from Africa by early settlers. Public slavery was abolished in 1854, and private slavery in 1876.

MOZAMBIQUE (Portuguese East Africa) —Status: Overseas territory.
Capital: Lourenço Marques (population 93,265).
Governor General: Cmdr. Pedro Correia de Barros.
Foreign trade (1958): exports, 2,028,-000,000 escudos; imports, 3,305,000,000 escudos. Chief exports: cotton, sugar, copra, sisal, cashew nuts.
Agricultural exports (1959): cotton, 45,-000 metric tons; sugar, 114,108 tons; copra, 37,639 tons; (1956) sisal, 27,940 tons; cashew nuts, 37,974 tons; tea, 6,276 tons.
Minerals: gold, coal, graphite, mica.
Forest products: mangrove bark, timber.

Mozambique, stretching for about 1,430 miles along Africa's southeast coast, was discovered by Vasco da Gama in 1498, although the Arabs had penetrated into the area as early as the 10th century A.D. It was first colonized in 1505, and by 1510 the Portuguese were masters of all the former Arab sultanates on the east African coast. The boundaries with British Central and South Africa were delimited in 1891, and with Tanganyika Territory in 1886 and 1890.

Agriculture is the chief industry. There are many large plantations, some of which are partially mechanized.

Ninety-nine per cent of the inhabitants are native Africans of the Bantu Tribes. The chief ports are Lourenço Marques and Beira, which is also the port for Rhodesia.

PORTUGUESE GUINEA—Status: Overseas territory.
Capital: Bissau (population 18,309).
Governor: Cmdr. António Augusto Peixoto Correia.
Foreign trade (1957): exports, 187,355,005 escudos; imports, 231,580,869 escudos. Chief exports: peanuts (53%), coconuts.
Agricultural products: peanuts, coconuts, copra, rice, palm oil.
Forest products: timber, wax, rubber.

This area, lying on the west African coast and almost surrounded by French West Africa, was discovered in 1446 by the Portuguese Nuno Tristão and was separated from the colony of the Cape Verde Islands in 1879. It consists of a low-lying coastal region and 60 islands off the coast. The country is undeveloped economically, and most of the natives are farmers. There are no railways, but navigable rivers totaling over 1,000 miles are important trade arteries.

SÃO TOMÉ AND PRINCIPE—Status: Overseas territory.
Capital: São Tomé (population 2,605).
Governor: Dr. Manuel Marques Abrantes do Amaral.
Foreign trade (1958): exports, 231,492,430 escudos; imports, 128,119,632 escudos. Chief exports: cacao (70%), copra (11%), coconuts, coffee.
Agricultural products: cacao, coffee, coconuts, copra, palm oil.

These volcanic islands, lying in the Gulf of Guinea about 150–175 miles off the west African coast, were discovered by the Portuguese in 1471. Most of the early inhabitants were convicts and Jews from Portugal and slaves from Brazil and the mainland, but the bulk of the present inhabitants are Negro contract laborers from the mainland and Cape Verde, engaged to work cacao plantations.

MACAO—Status: Overseas territory.
Capital: Macao (population 166,544).
Governor: Joaquim Marques Esparteiro.
Chief exports: fish, cement, preserves.
Manufactures: cement, preserves, firecrackers, vegetable oils, metal products.

Macao comprises the peninsula of Macao and the two small islands of Taipa and Colôane on the South China coast, about 35 miles from Hong Kong. Established by the Portuguese in 1557, it is the oldest European outpost in the China trade, but Portugal's sovereign rights to the port were not recognized by China until 1887, and its boundaries are still not delimited. The port has been eclipsed in importance by Hong Kong, but it is still a busy distribution center and also has an important fishing industry employing over 40,000 people. It is notorious for its opium trade and gambling houses. Most of the population is Chinese.

**PORTUGUESE INDIA—Status:** Metropolitan province.

Capital: Panjim (Nova Gôa) (population 31,950).

Governor General: Brig. Manuel Antonio Vassalo E Silva.

Foreign trade (1958): exports, 536,842,308 rupias* (mostly to Japan); imports, 874,-318,602 rupias. Chief exports: iron ore (71%), manganese ore (25%), cashew nuts.

Agricultural products: cashew nuts, coconuts, spices.

Minerals (exports 1957): iron ore, 1,739,-000 metric tons; manganese ore, 60,000 tons.

* 1 rupia = 5.97 escudos.

The area consists of Gôa and three islands on the Malabar coast of India; Damão and the territories of Dadará and Nagar-Aveli, on the Gulf of Cambay; and Diu, with the continental territories of Gocola and Simbor, on the coast of Gujarat. Gôa, captured in 1510 by the Portuguese, later became capital of the whole Portuguese empire in the east. The native population is largely Hindu. The Indian government has repeatedly pressed for the end of Portuguese rule here and as a result Indian-Portuguese relations have been very strained in the last few years.

**TIMOR—Status:** Overseas territory.

Capital: Dili (population 3,321).

Governor: Maj. Filipe Themudo Barata.

Foreign trade (1958): exports, 50,100,000 escudos (mostly to the Netherlands); imports, 74,900,000 escudos (mostly from Portugal). Chief exports: coffee, rubber.

Agricultural exports are: coffee, rubber, copra.

Forest products: sandalwood, wax.

Portuguese Timor consists of the eastern half of the island of Timor in the Malay Archipelago, with the territory of Ambeno and two neighboring islands. It was first settled by the Portuguese early in the sixteenth century. In 1859 the island was divided between Portugal and the Netherlands later boundary adjustments were made in 1904. Fishing and copra manufacture are important; trade is mostly in the hands of Chinese, Malayans, and Arabs.

Timor was occupied by Dutch and Australian troops in Dec., 1941, and by the Japanese in Feb., 1942.

# Rumania (People's Republic)
## (Republica Populara Româna)

Area: 91,699 square miles.

Population (census 1959): 18,256,000 (1948: Rumanian, 85.7%; Magyar, 9.4%; German, 2.2%; Jews, 0.9%; others [Turkish, Ruthenian, Bulgarian, Gypsy, Ukrainian] 1.8%).

Density per square mile: 199.1.

Chairman of Presidium: Ion Gheorghe Maurer.

Premier: Chivu Stoica.

Principal cities (est. 1959): Bucharest, 1,291,351 (capital); Cluj, 162,419 (Transylvanian industrial center); Timisoara, 148,-176 (western commercial center); Stalin (Brasov), 127,829 (industrial center); Ploesti, 123,937 (oil).

Monetary unit: Leu.

Languages: Rumanian, Hungarian, German, Turkish.

Religions (est. 1947): Eastern Orthodox, 81%; Greek Catholic, 9%; Roman Catholic, 7%; others, 3%.

## STATUS IN THE WORLD TODAY

Rumania, formerly one of the most anti-Communist of all East European countries, is today outwardly one of the most docile of the Soviet satellites. Although the U.S.S.R. has absorbed the long-disputed region of Bessarabia, it has restored Rumanian sovereignty over Transylvania, which was taken from Hungary after World War I but then reapportioned between the contending states by Hitler in 1940. The policies of the Communist party have been relatively cautious and, although not easy to bear, have fallen far short of the massive attempt at large-scale social transformation undertaken in Hungary and have also lacked the vicious terroristic character of Communist rule practised in that neighboring country.

One reason for the cautious policies may be the relatively small number of Rumanian Communists—they counted fewer than 500 adherents in 1944. This has meant the absence of a cadre of well-trained party members to fill government jobs and may well be the reason that the party leadership has been far less affected by purges and show trials than any other satellite Communist party. Rumania's strategic position is another reason why the U.S.S.R. is interested in keeping the peace there. It controls a long navigable stretch as well as the mouth of the Danube, and its oil deposits near Ploesti make it an important source of supply of a commodity not otherwise abundant in that part of the world.

Concessions from the Russians in the form of economic assistance have helped to alleviate a number of chronic economic difficulties. If Rumania is not a shining example of Communist achievements and displays far less militancy in imitating and supporting the Soviet Union than East Germany or Czechoslovakia, it is not a hotbed of troubles either. It is an island of relative tranquillity in an otherwise agitated part of the Soviet empire.

---

**HISTORY AND GOVERNMENT.** Most of Rumania was the Roman province of Dacia from about A.D. 100 to 275. From the sixth to the twelfth centuries, wave after wave of barbarian conquerors—Vlachs, Bulgars, and others—passed over the area. It became a kingdom in 1881.

The gains of World War I, making Rumania the largest Balkan state, included Bessarabia, Transylvania, and Bukovina. The Banat, a Hungarian area, was divided with Yugoslavia.

In 1926 Crown Prince Carol renounced his rights to the throne, and when King Ferdinand died on July 20, 1927, Carol's son, Michael (Mihai) became King under a regency. However, Carol returned from exile in 1930, was crowned King Carol II, and gradually became a powerful political force in the country. On Feb. 10, 1938, he abolished the democratic constitution of 1923. On June 21, 1940, the country was reorganized along Fascist lines, and the Fascist Iron Guard became the nucleus of the new totalitarian party. On June 27, the Soviet Union occupied Bessarabia and northern Bukovina. By the Axis-dictated Vienna Award of 1940, two-fifths of Transylvania went to Hungary, after which the King dissolved Parliament and granted the new Premier, Ion Antonescu, full power. Carol then abdicated and went into exile. Rumania subsequently signed the Axis Pact on Nov. 23, 1940, and the following June joined in Germany's attack on the U.S.S.R., reoccupying Bessarabia. Following the invasion of Rumania by the Red Army in Aug. 1944, King Michael led a coup d'etat which ousted the Antonescu government. An armistice with the U.S.S.R. was signed Sept. 12 in Moscow.

Elections held Nov. 19, 1946, resulted in a victory for the Communist-dominated government bloc. Michael abdicated on Dec. 30, 1947, and thereafter the nation was declared a "people's republic."

**ECONOMIC CONDITIONS.** Rumania is predominantly agricultural, with about 80 per cent of the population engaged on the soil. In wheat, rye and other grains, it is one of the richest countries of southeastern Europe. The largest acreage is usually devoted to corn and wheat. Other crops are flax, hemp, fruit, vegetables, potatoes, sugar beets, sunflower seeds, tobacco, and grapes. Stock raising is also important. In 1958, a 226-mile pipeline connecting Rumanian natural-gas fields with Hungarian centers was opened.

Agrarian reform measures effected in 1945 provided for the distribution of estates over 50 hectares (123.6 acres) in lots of 12½ hectares to each peasant.

Industrialization made considerable progress under a 5-year plan covering the years 1951–55, which emphasized the iron, steel, metal, machinery, and other heavy industries. The Soviet half-share in Soviet-Rumanian joint companies, which control the major industries, was sold to Rumania in 1954. Industries directly connected with agriculture, such as flour milling, distilling, and brewing, are still of basic importance. Probably the most important industries are food processing, textiles, metals, chemicals, wood, and paper. All but small business enterprises are nationalized.

Foreign trade is under complete government control. Principal exports are petroleum products, cereals and cereal products, wood and wood products. Leading imports are iron and manufactures, machinery and motors, vegetable fibers and products.

**NATURAL FEATURES AND RESOURCES.** The Carpathian Mountains divide Rumania's upper half from north to south and connect near the center of the country with the Transylvanian Alps, running east and west.

North and west of these ranges lies the Transylvanian plateau, and to the south and east are the plains of Moldavia and Walachia. In its last 190 miles, the Danube River flows through Rumania only. It enters the Black Sea in northern Dobruja, just south of the border of the Soviet Union.

By far the most valuable of Rumanian minerals is oil, produced chiefly in the Ploesti region about 35 miles north of Bucharest. Oil production amounted to 11,438,000 metric tons in 1959.

Natural gas from Transylvania is the second most important mineral. Other important minerals are iron ore, lignite, copper, gold, and silver. Uranium deposits have been reported.

---

## El Salvador (Republic)
### (República de El Salvador)

Area: 7,722 square miles.
Population (est. 1960): 2,613,000.
(mestizo, 78%; Indian, 11%; white, 11%).
Density per square mile: 338.4.
President: José Maria Lemus.
Principal cities (est. 1959): San Salvador, 221,708 (capital); Santa Ana, 67,-

255 (coffee); San Miguel, 32,204 (coffee, henequén).

Monetary unit: Colón.
Language: Spanish.
Religion: Roman Catholic.

## STATUS IN THE WORLD TODAY

El Salvador, the smallest of the 21 American republics, is a democracy which has enjoyed relative political and economic stability during the past ten years. Although most of the land is held by a few score wealthy families and cultivated by very poor workers, the country has been undergoing a moderate social revolution with a program of irrigation and the settlement of small farmers on reclaimed land, enactment of labor and social security legislation, and the growth of a labor movement. It is also one of the most densely populated countries in this hemisphere and has started new roads to open up unexploited land along the Pacific coast to relieve the population pressure elsewhere.

For the past 20 years or so, El Salvador has had a balanced budget and a favorable balance of trade, although the latter has been growing smaller with the fall of coffee prices on the world market. The government now has a 10-year, $156-million development program to diversify agriculture and build schools, homes, and light industry. A new tariff law was enacted in 1958 to encourage domestic manufacturing, and in recent years more than a hundred industrial plants have been established as power facilities have been expanded.

HISTORY AND GOVERNMENT. Pedro de Alvarado, a lieutenant of Cortez, conquered El Salvador in 1525. El Salvador struck out as an independent republic in 1839 after the dissolution of the Central American Union. Its history was that of Central America during the early period and its independent career for several decades was marked by numerous revolutions and wars against other Central American countries.

In Jan., 1931, the first free election in 20 years brought in Arturo Araujo as President. He was overthrown before the year was over. General Maximiliano Hernández Martínez, his successor, remained in power until May, 1944, when a general strike forced his resignation. The next regime, also militarist-led, lasted only five months, and was succeeded March 1, 1945, by a regime headed by Salvador Castañeda Castro, who was ousted Dec. 14, 1948, by a revolutionary junta. Major Oscar Osorio, one of the junta's members, was named President in the March, 1950, elections. Col. José Maria Lemus was elected to succeed him in the March 1956 elections.

The Constitution provides for a President, popularly elected for six years and ineligible to succeed himself, and a unicameral legislature elected by universal popular vote for two years.

Mestizos (mixed white and Indian) are the predominant racial group. There are no tribal Indians.

ECONOMIC CONDITIONS. El Salvador is one of the most intensively cultivated countries in Latin America. Coffee, which accounts for 64% of the total exports, is controlled in volume by a commission of officials and planters. Cotton is second in importance. In January, 1959, El Salvador followed Guatemala and Nicaragua in ratifying the Multilateral Treaty of Central American Free Trade and Economic Integration.

El Salvador's largest national enterprise, the Lempa river hydroelectric project, began partial operation in 1953.

NATURAL FEATURES AND RESOURCES. Most of El Salvador is a fertile volcanic plateau about 2,000 feet high. There are several volcanoes, some still active, and many lovely crater lakes. It is the only Central American country without an Atlantic coastline.

Gold, silver, coal, copper, iron, zinc, mercury, and sulfur are the nation's chief minerals.

Forest resources, much smaller than in other Central American states, include dyewood, mahogany, cedar, and walnut. El Salvador is a leading source of balsam.

# San Marino (Republic)

Area: 23.6 square miles.
Population (est. 1959): 15,000 (mostly Italian).
Density per square mile: 635.6.
Executive: two Regents selected every six months by the Grand Council.
Principal town: San Marino (est. pop. 2,000) (capital).
Monetary unit: Lira.
Language: Italian.
Religion: Roman Catholic.

HISTORY AND GOVERNMENT. San Marino, the oldest and smallest republic in the world, is one-tenth the size of New York City. It is entirely surrounded by Italy, in the Apennines near Rimini. According to tradition, San Marino was founded about A.D. 350 and had good luck for centuries in staying out of the interminable wars and feuds on the Italian peninsula.

San Marino hires its police and judges from Italy. It no longer confers titles for a consideration, but it does derive much revenue from the exporting of its postage stamps, which are changed often to keep philatelists buying. Other exports are barley, wine, and cattle, as well as building stone from Mount Titano.

Executive power is exercised by Regents, two of whom are appointed every six months from the popularly elected Grand Council. In April, 1959, the Grand Council decided to grant women the vote.

## Saudi Arabia (Kingdom)

Area: c. 617,762 square miles.
Population (est. 1956): 6,036,000.
Density per square mile: c. 9.8.
King: Saud ibn Abd al Aziz al Saud.
Principal cities (est. 1956): Mecca, 200,-000 (joint capital, religious center); Jidda, 160,000 (chief port); Riyadh, 150,000 (joint capital).
Monetary unit: Riyal.
Language: Arabic.
Religion: Moslem.

### STATUS IN THE WORLD TODAY

Saudi Arabia, which receives most of its income in oil royalties from an American corporation and which has given the United States the right to maintain a large air base at Dhahran, has not followed the lead of some of its sister Arab states in accepting any sort of assistance from the Soviet Union. It is maintaining a policy of neutrality in the Arab world, although in 1957 it protested against Egypt's meddling in the internal affairs of other states and in turn was accused by Nasser of trying to prevent the union of Egypt and Syria and of plotting to assassinate him.

The huge income from oil has led to the beginnings, however small, of a social revolution in this feudal kingdom and has placed the emphasis on internal rather than foreign policy problems. Ninety per cent of its inhabitants receive no benefit from the oil riches, and almost nothing has been spent for public health, education, and other social services. A middle class, which never existed before, is springing up as a result of the oil industry and may bring about social change. In the feudal hierarchy itself there is one faction which wants to continue the old free-spending ways for the benefit of the rulers, while another believes that country should have some measure of financial stability and some modernization of governmental machinery. A financial crisis led to a palace revolution in March, 1958, and Crown Prince Faisal, the King's brother and leader of the latter group, took control of the government. However, he resigned on Dec. 21, 1960. The King took over on Jan. 5, 1961. He appointed himself head of a new 7-member Supreme Planning Council empowered to carry out an economic development program.

HISTORY AND GOVERNMENT. The kingdom of Saudi Arabia, which occupies most of the Arabian peninsula, is almost entirely the creation of King Ibn Saud (1882–1953). Its earlier history is that of Arabia. Descendant of earlier Wahhabi rulers, Ibn Saud seized the emirate of Riyadh in 1902, and set himself up as leader of the Arab nationalist movement. The united kingdom of Saudi Arabia was one of the original members of the U.N. and joined the Arab League in 1945. King Ibn Saud died Nov. 9, 1953, and was succeeded by Saud (born 1902), the eldest to survive of his many sons.

Saudi Arabia is a nearly absolute monarchy. A Council of Ministers headed by the Prime Minister was formed in Oct., 1953. Hejaz and Nejd are under separate administrations. Tribal organizations are influential. There is a small army. There are no political parties.

The majority of the inhabitants are Bedouin—nomads following their flocks over the desert. The population is predominantly Sunni Moslem, and the religious law of Islam is the common law of the land. Mecca and Medina are the leading religious centers of Islam and the annual influx of pilgrims to those cities is the most important commercial activity outside the oil industry.

Saudi Arabia's desert climate restricts agriculture to the highlands of Asir and scattered oases. Dates are the staple crop; grain, fruits, and vegetables are also grown. Camels, sheep, and goats are raised and some animal products, such as hides, wool and ghee (clarified butter), are exported.

Oil, discovered in 1938 in the province of al-Hasa along the Persian Gulf, is produced by the U.S.-owned Arabian American Oil Co. (Aramco). The main production centers are in Ghawar, Abqaiq, Safaniya, Dammam, Qatif, and Khursaniya. Production has skyrocketed since World War II. The company's expenditures and payroll are important invisible exports, and oil revenues have greatly strengthened the financial position of the kingdom, which receives one-half the company's profits. The oilfields are connected by pipe line with the port of Sidon, Lebanon. Oil output in 1960 was 60,860,423 metric tons.

## Siam. See Thailand

## Somalia (Republic)

Area: 246,202 square miles.
Population (est. 1960): 1,900,000.

Density per square mile: c. 7.7.
President: Aden Abdullah Osman.
Premier: Abdi Rashid Shermake.
Principal cities (1958 est.): Mogadishu, 87,000 (capital); Hargeisa (30,000 in hot season, 40,000 in cold season).
Monetary unit: Somalo.
Language: Somali.
Religion: Moslem.

### STATUS IN THE WORLD TODAY

Somalia became an independent republic on July 1, 1960, through the union of two former colonies, British Somaliland and Italian Somaliland. Its population, the Somalis, are Hamites or Cushites, who probably originally came from Arabia. They are mostly nomads. A poor country with no natural resources, its exports comprise bananas, hides and skins. It is estimated by the World Bank that Somalia will need $6 million a year of outside help to keep going. Italy, which administered part of the country as a United Nations trusteeship for 10 years, has promised $3.6 million and is expected to continue its subsidy for Somali bananas. The United States has granted $5 million in aid since 1954.

Because of sentiment for the creation of a Greater Somalia involving union with the Somalis in Ethiopia, Kenya and French Somaliland, as well as unsettled boundary disputes between the new nation and Ethiopia, Somalia's foreign policy is viewed with suspicion in Addis Ababa. There is also the religious difference which separates the Christians in Ethiopia and the Moslems in Somalia and the problem of Ethiopia's only outlet to the sea—the railroad linking it with Djibouti in French Somaliland.

HISTORY AND GOVERNMENT. British troops first came to Somaliland in 1884 to protect British interests there, and gradually a number of protectorates were established. From 1901–1920 much of the interior was inaccessible because of a holy war which did not end until the fanatic Somali mullah who led it died. The Italian protectorate was established in 1889 and was under British military administration from 1941–1949. Italy took over the U.N. trusteeship in 1950.

The National Assembly which met July 1, 1960, consisted of the 88 members of the Somalia (Italian) legislature and the 33 members of the British Somaliland legislature. They elected a President, who will serve until national elections can be held in Somalia.

Chief exports are bananas, hides and cotton.

# South Africa, Republic of

Area: 472,359 square miles.*
Population (est. 1960): 14,929,000 (European, 20.9%; Bantu, 66.9%; mixed, 9.2%; Asiatic, 3.0%).
Density per square mile: 31.9.
President: Charles R. Swart.
Prime Minister: Hendrik Frensch Verwoerd.
Principal cities (est. 1959): Johannesburg, 1,052,600 (gold, industrial center); Capetown, 729,200 (seat of legislature, seaport); Durban, 634,400 (seaport); Pretoria, 343,300 (seat of administration); Port Elizabeth, 247,900 (seaport).
Monetary unit: South African pound (£SA).
Languages: English, Afrikaans.
Religions (European pop., 1946): Dutch Reformed Churches, 55%; Anglican Church, 19%; Methodist, 6%; Presbyterian, 5%; Roman Catholic, 5%; others 10%.

* Excluding South-West Africa.

### STATUS IN THE WORLD TODAY

Although the Republic of South Africa is definitely anti-Communist, the dominant policy of apartheid of the ruling Nationalist Party, which has been in power since 1948, is one which is opposed by many nations within the Free World. The Nationalists also sought, unsuccessfully, to maintain South Africa's neutrality in World War II in 1939, and since coming to power have fought for the formation of a republic and white supremacy. Increasing opposition by other Commonwealth members with large nonwhite populations to the Union's apartheid policy led to the Union's withdrawal from the Commonwealth in 1961.

In its ultimate form, the policy of apartheid is envisaged as total separation of the races by removing the Bantu from those areas presently occupied by Europeans. They would be forced to live in reserved areas which would be under African forms of local government. These areas would be industrialized gradually so that there would be no need to leave the area for work. It is, of course, universally acknowledged that complete separation is not possible in the foreseeable future, but this is the ultimate goal toward which the racial policy is directed, and a number of legislative acts to enforce certain aspects of apartheid have been promulgated in the past ten years. Increasingly repressive measures affecting the Negro population in 1959 and 1960 led to wide-spread strikes and demonstrations. The climax was an assassination attempt by a white settler which seriously wounded Prime Minister Verwoerd and resulted in a declaration of a "state of emergency."

The rise of a mining industry—with the discovery of gold and diamonds—transformed the traditional agricultural economy of South Africa, and since World War I the economic focus has been shifting to the cities and the industries growing up around them. Manufacturing now contributes the largest share of the Union's income. Over 50 per cent of the raw materials used in industry are produced within the Republic. Economic expansion has created a need for new capital resources and since World War II over $2 billion of foreign capital—chiefly British and European—has flowed into South Africa. If the Republic is to continue its growth both in the manufacturing and in the processing of raw materials, there would appear to be little alternative to employing and training more African workers, since the skilled-labor supply in some industries is already short. It remains to be seen how this need can be reconciled with the goals of apartheid.

## MAJOR POLITICAL PARTIES

National party (102 seats in House of Assembly), led by Prime Minister H. F. Verwoerd; United party (41 seats), led by Sir de Villiers Graaf.

HISTORY AND GOVERNMENT. Dutch settlers first came to South Africa in 1652. By the beginning of the eighteenth century, nearly 2,000 settlers were established. Although the colony was made up of Europeans from various countries, it assumed a thoroughly Dutch character.

In consequence of the Napoleonic wars Britain gained control over the Cape Colony in 1814 and within seven years 5,000 British settlers had taken up residence. The British administration freed the slaves upon whom many Boer farmers depended for labor and sought to establish equality of rights for the colored population, who worked in the main for Boer landowners. By the mid-nineteenth century the final form of the Union was emerging; settlers were scattered on the northern side of the Vaal and Orange rivers. In 1877, the British annexed the Transvaal territory, and although it was relinquished again in 1881, the act created bitter resentment among the Dutch settlers. The conflict between the imperialism of England and the republicanism of the Boer colonies culminated in the Jameson Raid, which was the opening gun of the bitter Anglo-Boer war (1899–1900).

The two years of war paved the way for the creation of the Union of South Africa, but it left behind a bitterness which lasts until today. The Union in its final form came into existence in 1910 by the South Africa Act. Though a Republic now, the form remains unchanged. At its head is the Republic Government, and within each of the four provinces (Cape, Transvaal, Orange Free State, and Natal) there are provincial parliaments. The dual nature of the Republic is illustrated by the fact that there are two capitals (Cape Town and Pretoria), two official languages (English and Afrikaans), two flags, and two national anthems. The Republic Parliament is made up of the House of Assembly, consisting of 163 members, and a Senate of eighty-nine members. House members hold their seats for 5 years and senators for 10 years unless Parliament is dissolved before the end of their terms.

ECONOMIC CONDITIONS. South Africa is predominantly a pastoral country, with less than 15 per cent of its area considered arable. Sheep and cattle raising are the principal occupations, especially in the high veldt. In 1957 there were 37,462,000 sheep, 12,042,000 cattle, and 665,000 hogs.

Climate and differences in terrain combine to give a great variety of agricultural products. The staple crop is maize, grown widely. In southwest Cape Province, products of the Mediterranean type predominate, while in the coastal belt of Natal and in northern Transvaal subtropical crops, especially sugar, are grown.

Food, beverages and tobacco, and metal products are leading products. As a result of the need for armaments a wartime iron and steel industry was established, and cement, chemical, textile, and auto assembly plants were expanded.

Chief exports in 1959 (besides gold) were wool (12%) and diamonds (9%). Main customers (1957) were Britain (30%), other sterling area (20%), and the United States and Canada (10%); leading suppliers, Britain (31%), the United States and Canada (21%), Germany (10%), other EPU countries (13%). Principal imports included textiles, farm and industrial machinery, motor vehicles, and petroleum products.

NATURAL FEATURES AND RESOURCES. The Republic has a high interior plateau, or veldt, nearly half of which averages 4,000 feet in elevation. There are no important mountain ranges, although the Great Escarpment, separating the veldt from the coastal plain, rises to over 10,000 feet. The principal river is the Orange, rising in Basutoland and flowing westward for 1,300 miles to the Atlantic.

Extensive mineral resources account for the economic prosperity. The Republic is the world's leading gold producer. Diamond production is now surpassed in importance by coal. Uranium, gypsum, tin, and tungsten also are mined.

The whaling industry, centered at Durban on the east coast, produces considerable amounts of whale oil. The Republic has extensive fishery resources along the 1,500 miles of coast line.

**SOUTH-WEST AFRICA—Status: Mandate.**
Administrator: Daniel du P. Viljoen.
Capital: Windhoek (population 36,000).
Agricultural products: hides and skins, butter, corn, wheat.
Minerals: diamonds, vanadium concentrates, tungsten, lead, tin, iron ore, copper.

The mandate, bounded on the north by Angola, and on the east by Bechuanaland and the Union of South Africa, was discovered by the Portuguese explorer Diaz in the late 15th century. It is for the most part a portion of the high plateau of South Africa with a general elevation of from 3,000 to 4,000 feet. It became a German colony in 1884 but was conquered by South African forces in 1915, becoming a Union mandate by the terms of the Treaty of Versailles. The Union of South Africa's application for incorporation of the territory into the Union was rejected by the United Nations assembly on Dec. 14, 1946, and the Union was invited to prepare a trusteeship agreement instead. By a law passed in April, 1949, however, the territory was brought into much closer association with the Union—including representation in the Union Parliament.

The country in general is better suited to grazing than to the raising of crops because of the light rainfall. The karakul sheep industry is well developed.

---

# Spain (Nominal Monarchy)
## (España)

Area: 194,396 square miles.
Population (est. 1960): 30,128,000 (Spanish, Basque, Catalan).
Density per square mile: 155.0.
Chief of State: Francisco Franco y Bahamonde.
Principal cities (est. 1960): Madrid, 1,-966,070 (capital); Barcelona, 1,503,062 (chief port; textiles); Valencia, 571,452 (silk, oranges); Seville, 450,213 (wines, iron ore); Saragossa, 291,181 (rail center); Málaga, 318,102 (seaport).
Languages: Spanish, Basque, Catalan.
Religion: Roman Catholic.

---

### STATUS IN THE WORLD TODAY

Although Spain is a dictatorship, its foreign policy is so dominated by one outstanding characteristic—unalterable opposition to communism—that it has become an ally of the United States in the cold war and is the site of important American naval and air bases. Because of Spain's favorable location in Western Europe, this is regarded by Western leaders as necessary strategy. Defenders of the policy that includes Spain as a military, but not ideological, ally point out that the choice of partners must be made on a realistic basis, as in the case of the Western democracies fighting with the U.S.S.R.

against Nazi Germany. Critics claim that the cold war is essentially an ideological struggle between nations supporting and opposing the central idea of freedom, and that to include a dictatorship among the "free" nations weakens the meaning of such terms as "Free Europe" and the "Free World." In 1946, the U.N. General Assembly moved that Spain be debarred from membership in the U.N. "until a new and acceptable government is formed." But nine years later, with the strong support of the Latin-American countries and the Arab League, the Assembly reversed its position and admitted Spain to membership.

Spain, predominantly agricultural, still finds it difficult to maintain a balance between production and consumption of foodstuffs. Although she has important mineral resources and raw materials, she has remained backward industrially and is faced with chronic financial difficulties. Since 1945 there has been progressive economic deterioration, the cost of living has risen stupendously and the gap between rich and poor widened. American financial aid in return for the lease of military bases has relieved to some extent what is basically a weak economic system. Despite this weakness, Franco maintains his regime because of his firm control of the Spanish army and, through the Falange, the totalitarian party, of police, secret police and trade unions. He is strongly supported by industrialists and financiers as well as by all Spaniards who fear communism and especially another civil war.

In the summer of 1959, Spain was finally admitted to the Organization for European Economic Cooperation (OEEC).

---

HISTORY AND GOVERNMENT. Spain, originally inhabited by Celts, Iberians, and Basques, became a part of the Roman Empire in 201 B.C., when it was conquered by Scipio Africanus. In A.D. 412 the barbarian Visigothic leader, Ataulf, crossed the Pyrenees and ruled Spain, first in the name of the Roman emperor and then independently. In A.D. 711 the Moslems under Tariq entered Spain from Africa and within a few years completed the subjugation of the country. In 732 the Franks, led by Charles Martel, defeated the Moslems at Tours, thus preventing the further expansion of Islam in southern Europe. Internal dissension of Spanish Islam invited a steady Christian conquest from the north.

Aragon and Castile became the most important Spanish states from the thirteenth to the fifteenth century, in time absorbing all the other peoples of Spain. Aragon and Castile were consolidated by the marriage of Ferdinand II and Isabella I. The last Moslem stronghold, Granada, was captured in January, 1492, the same year in which Columbus, under the sponsorship of Isabella, discovered America. With Moslem control ended, Roman Catholicism was established as the official state religion. The Jews (1492) and the Moslems (1502) were expelled from Spain at the cost of incalculable suffering and loss of life.

In the era of exploration, discovery, and colonization Spain won tremendous wealth and a vast colonial empire. The conquest of Peru by Pizarro (1533) and of Mexico by Cortes (1519) brought great prosperity to the motherland. The Spanish Hapsburg monarchy, through a series of wars, diplomatic negotiations, and marriages, became for a time one of the most powerful in the world.

In 1588 Philip II sent his Invincible Armada to invade England, but its destruction cost Spain her supremacy on the seas and paved the way for England's colonization of America. Spain then sank rapidly to the status of a second-rate power and never again played a major role in European politics.

In World War I Spain maintained a position of neutrality. In 1923 General Miguel Primo de Rivera became dictator. In 1930 Alfonso XIII revoked the dictatorship, but a strong antimonarchist and republican movement led to his abdication in 1931. The new Constitution declared Spain a workers' republic, broke up the large estates, separated church and state, and secularized the schools. The 1936 elections returned a strong Popular Front majority, with Manuel Azaña as President.

But political chaos persisted. On July 18, 1936, a conservative army officer in Morocco, Francisco Franco, led a mutiny against the government. The terrible civil war that followed lasted for three years and cost the lives of nearly a million men. It was, in effect, a dress rehearsal for World War II. Franco was aided by Fascist Italy and Nazi Germany, while Soviet Russia helped the Loyalist side. Several hundred leftist Americans served in the Abraham Lincoln brigade on the side of the republic. The war came to an end when Franco took Madrid on March 28, 1939.

Franco (b. Dec. 14, 1892) is *Caudillo* (leader), Chief of State, Prime Minister, and head of the Falange Party. He pushes the Falange into the foreground or background at will, depending upon political expediency. He appoints the cabinet. The *Cortés*, or parliament, established in July, 1942, may formulate legislation, but it must be satisfactory to the dictator.

In a referendum held July 6, 1947, the Spanish people approved a Franco-drafted succession law declaring Spain a monarchy again. Franco, however, is to continue as Chief of State, and upon his death or incapacity the government and a Council of the Realm constituted by the law are to nominate as King "that person of royal blood who is most qualified by right," subject to the approval of the *Cortés*. The law reserves to Franco the right to nominate his own successor, subject also to the *Cortés* approval by two-thirds vote. Franco is said to favor young Juan Carlos, the son of Don Juan, pretender to the Spanish throne.

ECONOMIC CONDITIONS. Livestock included in 1955, 3,011,000 cattle, 16,312,000 sheep, and 5,980,000 hogs. Wool production in 1959 was 14,900 metric tons, greasy basis.

Leading customers in 1959 included Britain, West Germany, the United States, and France; leading suppliers, the United States, France, Britain, and West Germany. Leading exports in 1959 were iron ore (40%), oranges (11%), and wine (11%). Principal imports were raw cotton, chemical products (especially fertilizer), petroleum, and vehicles.

*Industry.* The textile industry, concentrated in Catalonia, leads all others. The paper and chemical industries are also important, as well as pig iron and steel.

NATURAL FEATURES AND RESOURCES. Spain, less than 10 miles from Africa at the closest point, and separated from France by the Pyrenees, is generally a broad plateau sloping to south and east and crossed by a series of mountain ranges and river valleys.

*Minerals.* Spain's mineral wealth, second to agriculture in the national economy, yields millions of tons of ore, including coal, lignite, iron ore (metal content 50%), potash ore, lead ore, zinc ore, and mercury. Spain also produces copper, gold, magnesite, sulfur, tungsten, phosphates, silver, and, reportedly, uranium.

*Forests and Fisheries.* Spanish forests yield lumber, pine resins, cork, and esparto. Some 100,000 persons work in the fishing, canning, and related industries.

OUTLYING ISLANDS. Off Spain's east coast in the Mediterranean are the Balearic Islands, which total 1,936 square miles. The largest is Majorca. Sixty miles west of Africa are the Canary Islands.

---

### SPANISH COLONIAL POSSESSIONS

| Country | Area, sq. mi. | Population, est. 1960 |
|---|---|---|
| Morocco | | |
| Ifni | 579 | 52,000 |
| Ceuta, Melilla, Alhucemas, Chafarinas and Peñon de Velez | 82 | 146,000 |
| Spanish Sahara | 102,703 | 25,000 |
| Spanish Guinea | 10,831 | 216,000 |

# Sudan, The (Republic)

**Area:** 967,501 square miles.
**Population (census 1960):** 11,615,000.
**Density per square mile:** 12.0.
**President:** Ibrahim Abboud.
**Prime minister:** Ibrahim Abboud.
**Principal cities (census 1956):** Omdurman, 113,551 (commercial center); Khartoum, 93,103 (capital); El Obeid, 52,382 (gum arabic); Wad Medani, 48,131 (cotton, livestock); Port Sudan, 47,650 (chief port).
**Monetary unit:** Sudanese pound.
**Languages:** English, Arabic, Nilotic and Negro tribal dialects.
**Religions:** Moslem (Sunni), pagan, Christian.

---

## STATUS IN THE WORLD TODAY

The Sudan is a new republic where a military coup has ended parliamentary rule because of political and economic instability. Yet the army itself is divided, with the senior officers pro-Western and anti-Egyptian and the junior officers more nationalistic or leftist. But having finally achieved their independence, the Sudanese are determined to maintain it, so that their policy of neutrality extends not only to the West and to Soviet Russia but also to Nasser's Egypt. They are, however, cracking down on local Communists.

Having been ruled jointly by the British and the Egyptians for so long, the Sudan has no desire to become an Egyptian colony again, although there is considerable pro-Nasser sentiment in the northern, Moslem part of the country. Its present difficulties with Egypt stem from the use and diversion of the waters of the Nile River through the construction of the High Dam at Aswan. No agreement has yet been reached between the two countries on this project, which will flood some Sudanese territory. The Sudan controls the Upper Nile and, like Egypt, depends upon the Nile waters for its crops.

The Sudan's economic difficulties result mainly from its dependence on one export crop—cotton—and its failure to sell the 1956–57 crop and the subsequent pile-up of succeeding crops. It has been living on its reserve of consumer goods and, with a government deficit, has no funds for development. Early in 1959 it received $30 million in aid from the U.S. and $14 million from Britain. For some time it has rejected loans from the U.S.S.R. because it would have to spend the proceeds in the Communist bloc.

---

**HISTORY.** The early history of the Sudan (known as the Anglo-Egyptian Sudan between 1898 and 1955) is connected with that of Nubia, where a powerful local kingdom was formed in Roman times with its capital at Dongola. After conversion to Christianity in the sixth century A.D., it joined with Ethiopia and resisted Mohammedanization until the fourteenth century. Thereafter the area was broken up into many small states until 1820–22, when it was conquered by Mohammed Ali, Pasha of Egypt. Egyptian forces were evacuated during the Mahdist revolt (1881–98), but the Sudan was reconquered by the Anglo-Egyptian expeditions of 1896–98 and in 1899 became an Anglo-Egyptian condominium, which was reaffirmed by the Anglo-Egyptian treaty of 1936.

Egypt and Britain agreed in Feb., 1953, to grant self-government to the Sudan under an appointed Governor-General. Under the self-government statute of March 31, 1953, an all-Sudanese Parliament was elected in Nov.-Dec., 1953, and an all-Sudanese government was formed, headed by Ismail el-Azhari as Prime Minister. Under the agreement the Sudanese people were to determine their political status at the end of three years following the elections, but in Dec., 1955, the Parliament declared the independence of the Sudan, which, with the approval of Britain and Egypt, was proclaimed on Jan. 1, 1956. El-Azhari was replaced as Prime Minister by Abdullah Khalil on July 5. On March 20, 1958, the newly elected House of Representatives selected Abdullah Khalil to continue as Premier, but in November, 1958, he was ousted by Lt. Gen. Ibrahim Abboud, Commander-in-Chief of the Sudanese Army, who seized control, dissolved Parliament and suspended the Constitution.

**GOVERNMENT.** The government is administered by the Prime Minister and his Cabinet. A bicameral Parliament has a Senate of 50 members and a House of Representatives of 97 elected members.

**ECONOMIC CONDITIONS.** The northern part of the country is peopled by Arabic-speaking Moslems, while in the backward south Negroid pagan tribes predominate.

Long-staple cotton, the chief export crop, is grown under irrigation in the Kassala and Tokar areas of the north and in narrow strips along the main Nile. Durra, peanuts, corn, and oilseeds are grown elsewhere. Livestock raising is the occupation of most of the population.

Leading exports in 1959 were cotton (61%), gum arabic (8%), cottonseed, and peanuts. Leading customers were Britain (27%), India (11%), and Egypt (16%); leading suppliers, Britain (26%), India (10%), and Egypt (5%).

**NATURAL FEATURES AND RESOURCES.** About one-fourth the size of Europe, the Sudan extends from north to south about 1,200 miles and west to east about 1,000 miles. The northern region is a continuation of the Libyan Desert. The southern region is fertile, abundantly watered and, in places, heavily forested. It is traversed from north to south by the Nile, all of whose great tributaries are partly or entirely within its borders. The highest elevation is a mountain range parallel to the Red Sea, with heights of 4,000 to over 7,000 feet.

Salt is produced at Port Sudan, and gold deposits are worked at Gebeit, near the Red Sea. Most of the world's gum arabic comes from the semiarid Kordofan area of the west. The southern forests are rich in fibers and tannins.

# Sweden (Kingdom)

## (Sverige)

Area: 173,623 square miles.
Population (est. 1960): 7,471,345 (practically all Swedish).
Density per square mile: 43.0.
Sovereign: King Gustavus VI Adolphus.
Prime Minister: Tage Fritiof Erlander.
Principal cities (est. 1960): Stockholm, 807,909 (capital); Göteborg, 400,814 (chief port, shipbuilding); Malmö, 225,660 (seaport); (est. 1956) Norrköping, 89,226 (textiles); Hälsingborg, 74,947 (seaport).
Monetary unit: Krona.
Language: Swedish.
Religions: Swedish Lutheran, 99%; others, 1%.

### STATUS IN THE WORLD TODAY

Sweden, a traditionally neutral nation, has adopted a policy of neutrality in the cold war, although there is no doubt that public opinion favors the free world as against a Communist dictatorship. Invited to join the Atlantic pact in 1949, she declined but has taken drastic steps to maintain her neutrality. Military service is compulsory from the ages of 18 to 47. The army consists of about 600,000 men in addition to a Home Guard of 100,000. The air force, with modern jets built in Sweden and including at least 50 combat squadrons and 1,200 planes, is the fourth largest in the world. Sweden is also one of the most advanced countries in the world in the construction of atom-bomb-proof military and civilian shelters.

### MAJOR POLITICAL PARTIES

Social Democratic Labor party (114 seats in lower chamber), led by Premier Tage Erlander; Liberal party (40 seats), led by B. Ohlin; Conservative party (39 seats), led by J. Hjalmarson.

## HISTORY AND GOVERNMENT.

The earliest historical mention of Sweden is found in Tacitus' *Germania,* where reference is made to the powerful king and strong fleet of the Suiones. Toward the end of the tenth century Olaf Sköttkonung established a Christian stronghold in Sweden. The initial union with Norway came in 1397. In 1520 the Danish King, Christian II, conquered Sweden and in the "Stockholm Blood-Bath" put leading Swedish personalities to death. Gustavus Vasa (1523–1560) broke away from Denmark and fashioned the modern Swedish state.

Sweden played a leading role in the second phase (1630–1635) of the Thirty Years' War (1618–1648). By the Treaty of Westphalia (1648), Sweden obtained western Pomerania and some neighboring territory on the Baltic. In 1700 a coalition of Russia, Poland, and Denmark united against Sweden and by the Peace of Nystad (1721) forced her to relinquish Livonia, Ingria, Estonia, and parts of Finland.

From the Napoleonic wars Sweden emerged with the gain of Norway from Denmark and with a new royal dynasty stemming from Marshal Bernadotte of France, who became King Charles XIV (1818–1844). The artificial union between Sweden and Norway led to an unhappy feud. It was finally dissolved in 1905. Sweden maintained a position of neutrality in both World Wars.

Sweden is a constitutional monarchy. The king holds executive and judicial authority together with the Council of State, headed by the Prime Minister. The *Riksdag* consists of a First Chamber with 150 members elected by provincial and municipal councils and holding office for eight years, and a Second Chamber of 231 members popularly elected for four years. Men and women over 21 vote.

SOVEREIGN. Gustavus VI Adolphus, born Nov. 11, 1882, married (1) 1905, Princess Margaret Victoria (1882–1920); (2) 1923, Princess Louise Mountbatten (born 1889). To his first marriage was born Prince Gustavus Adolphus (born Apr. 22, 1906, killed in air crash Jan. 26, 1947), who was married in 1932 to Sibylla, Princess of Saxe-Coburg-Gotha; their offspring include a son, Carl Gustavus, the heir apparent, born April 30, 1946, and four daughters. Gustavus VI became King Oct. 30, 1950, on the death of his father, Gustavus V, who had reigned since 1907.

ECONOMIC CONDITIONS. *Agriculture.* Milk, butter, meat, grain, potatoes, and sugar beets are products of the broad fertile plains of the south; the north is limited to cattle raising and dairy farming.

The 1959 livestock estimates showed 229,000 horses, 2,580,000 cattle, 146,000 sheep, and 2,041,000 hogs.

*Industry.* The highly specialized machine industry produces separators, motors, electrical machines and apparatus, agricultural machinery, ball bearings, telephone equipment, and harbor works.

There are also large woolen, glass, and porcelain industries. Shipyards build for Swedish and foreign fleets. Timber and woodworking industries are extensive.

*Trade.* Leading exports in 1959 were wood pulp (14%), paper (10%), machinery and apparatus (13%), timber (9%), and iron ore (7%). Leading customers were Britain (15%), West Germany (15%), and U.S. and Canada (9%), and Norway (8%). Leading suppliers were West Germany (23%), Britain (14%), the United States and Canada (11%), and Norway (4%). The principal imports included machinery, petroleum and products, textiles and clothing, and automobiles.

NATURAL FEATURES AND RESOURCES. Sweden slopes eastward and southward from its peak elevation in the Kjölen mountains along the Norwegian border. In the north are mountains and many lakes. To the south and east are central lowlands, and south of them are fertile areas of forest, valley, and plain. Along Sweden's rocky coast, chopped up by bays and inlets, are many islands, the largest of which are Gotland and Oland.

*Minerals.* Sweden's iron ore deposits (metal content 60%) are among the world's richest. Those in central Sweden produce principally for domestic use, while the ones in Lapland to the north are worked largely for export, with much of the output being shipped through the Norwegian port of Narvik. Other major minerals are copper, gold, lead, arsenic ore, manganese ore, and silver. Coal production (270,000 tons in 1959) is comparatively small; imports of several million tons a year are therefore necessary.

*Forests and Fisheries.* About 60 per cent of Sweden is forested, mostly conifers, and there are vast forest products industries in the north. Sweden supplies a large percentage of the world's mechanical and chemical pulp.

# Switzerland (Republic)
## (Schweiz-Suisse-Svizzera)

**Area:** 15,941 square miles.
**Population** (est. 1960): 5,298,000 (Swiss, 91.2%; German, 3.6%; Italian, 3.1%; French, .9%; others, 1.2%—figures by place of birth).
**Density per square mile:** 332.4.
**President** (1961): Fredrich Wahlen.*

\* The vice-president ordinarily becomes president the next year. Vice-president in 1961: Paul Chaudet.

**Principal cities** (est. Dec. 1959); Zürich, 436,700 (textiles, banking); Basel, 206,200 (rail center, Rhine port); Geneva, 173,200; Bern, 164,900 (federal capital).
**Monetary unit:** Swiss franc.
**Languages:** German, 71.9%; French, 20.4%; Italian, 6.0%; Romansch, 1.1%; others, .6%.
**Religions:** Protestant, 57%; Roman Catholic, 41%; Jewish, .4%; other religions, 1.6%.

## STATUS IN THE WORLD TODAY

In Switzerland, the classic home of neutrality, the foreign policy is carefully neutral in the cold war, even though Swiss traditions have long reflected the best of Western democratic development. Because of this traditional policy, Geneva was chosen after World War I as the seat of the League of Nations, and the country still constitutes the headquarters of a number of international organizations and is a great center for all sorts of international meetings and humanitarian associations. It has always shown great sympathy for foreigners in distress and has been a haven for political refugees, from Hungarian patriots of 1848 to those fleeing from Nazi Germany, Fascist Italy, and the Iron Curtain countries. Switzerland has entered into no military alliances and is not a member of the United Nations, although it has joined several international agencies of the U.N. Relations with the United States have always been cordial and friendly, despite friction over such matters as American tariffs on Swiss watches and watch works.

## MAJOR POLITICAL PARTIES

Radical-Democratic party (51 seats in National Council), led by E. Dietschi; Socialist party (51 seats), led by Walter Bringolf; Conservative party (47 seats), led by Dr. Ettore Tenchio.

HISTORY AND GOVERNMENT. Called Helvetia in ancient times, Switzerland in the Middle Ages was a federation of fiefs of the Holy Roman Empire. Fashioned around the nucleus of three German forest districts of Schwyz, Uri, and Nidwalden, the Swiss Confederation slowly added new cantons. In 1648 the Treaty of Westphalia gave Switzerland her independence from the Holy Roman Empire. French revolutionary troops occupied Switzerland in 1798 and named it the Helvetic Republic, but Napoleon in 1803 restored its federal government. At this time, and again in 1815, the French- and Italian-speaking peoples of Switzerland were raised to political equality.

In 1815 the Congress of Vienna neutralized and recognized the independence of Switzerland. In the revolutionary period of 1848 the Catholic cantons seceded and organized a separate union called the *Sonderbund*. In 1848 the new Swiss constitution established a union modeled upon that of the United States. The Federal Constitution of 1874 established a strong central government while still maintaining large powers of local control in each canton.

The Swiss Confederation consists of 22 sovereign cantons, each of which has a veto power over federal legislation by referendum. Federal authority is vested in a bicameral legislature. The *Ständerat,* or State Council, consists of 44 members, two from each canton. The lower house, the *Nationalrat,* or National Council, has 196 members, one for each 24,000 of the population, elected for four-year terms. Executive authority is lodged in a board called the *Bundesrat,* or Federal Council, of seven members chosen by parliament. The Federal Council elects the President, who serves for a term of one year and is ordinarily succeeded by the Vice-President. The Federal Government regulates matters of war, peace, treaties, railroads, postal service, and the national mint. Each canton reserves for itself important local powers.

ECONOMIC CONDITIONS. In 1959 the leading customers were West Germany (17%), the United States and Canada (13%), Italy (8%), France (7%), and Britain (6%). Leading suppliers were West Germany (29%), the United States and Canada (12%), Italy (12%), France (11%), and Britain (7%). Leading exports were machinery, clocks and watches, chemicals and drugs, and textiles and clothing. Switzerland has a world-wide reputation for its highly skilled work in the manufacture of precision instruments, especially watches.

The Rhine, navigable from Basel to the North Sea, is the principal inland waterway. Railways built over rugged terrain, entailing construction of many bridges and tunnels, total about 4,900 miles, mostly electrified.

NATURAL FEATURES: Most of Switzerland comprises a mountainous plateau bordered by the great bulk of the Alps on the south and by the Jura Mountains on the northwest. About a fourth of the total area of Switzerland is covered by scenic mountains and glaciers.

The country's largest lakes, Geneva, Constance (Boden See), and Maggiore, straddle the French, German-Austrian, and Italian borders, respectively.

# Syria

## (as-Souriya)

Area: 71,228 square miles.
Population (est. 1959): 4,539,000 (Arab, Armenian, Kurdish, Turkish, French).
Density per square mile: 63.7.
Premier: Mamoun Kuzbari.
Principal cities (est. 1957): Damascus, 475,399 (capital); Aleppo, 466,026 (northern trading center); (est. 1954) Homs, 152,077 (farming, silk); Hama, 107,859 (Bedouin trading center).
Monetary unit: Syrian pound (£S).
Languages: Arabic, Aramaic, French.
Religions (est. 1954): Moslem, 86.3%; Christian, 12.8%; Jewish, 1%; others, .1%.

---

### STATUS IN THE WORLD TODAY

Syria, for the time being, is pro-Arab, but anti-Nasser. Egyptianization of the Syrian army and nationalization of banks and socialization of industry led to a revolt against the 3-year-old United Arab Republic and the re-emergence of Syria as an independent nation instead of a virtual colony of Egypt. The end of the U.A.R. was a definite setback for Nasser's ideas of running a Pan-Arabic Empire.

---

HISTORY. Ancient Syria was conquered by Egypt about 1500 B.C., and after that by Hebrews, Phoenicians, Assyrians, Chaldeans, Persians, and Greeks. From 64 B.C. until the Arab conquest in A.D. 636, it was part of the Roman Empire except during brief periods. The Arabs made it a trade center for their whole empire, but it suffered severely from the Mongol invasion in 1260 and fell to the Ottoman Turks in 1516. Syria remained a Turkish province until World War I.

A secret Anglo-French pact of 1916 put Syria in the French zone of influence. The League of Nations gave France a mandate over Syria after World War I, but the French were forced to put down several nationalist uprisings. In 1930, France recognized Syria as an independent republic, but still subject to the mandate. After nationalist demonstrations in 1939, the French High Commissioner suspended the Syrian Constitution. In 1941, British and Free French forces invaded Syria to eliminate Vichy control. During the rest of World War II, Syria was an Allied base. Again in 1945, nationalist demonstrations broke into actual fighting, and British troops had to restore order. Syrian forces met a series of reverses while participating in the Arab invasion of Palestine in 1948. After Mar. 30, 1949, when the government was overthrown by Husni Zayim, there were several army coups d'etat. That of Nov. 29, 1951, was engineered by Col. Adib

Shishakly. Elected President in July, 1953, Shishakly was ousted on Feb. 25, 1954, by the army, which named Hachem Bey el-Attassi President. On Aug. 18, 1955, Shukri al-Kuwatly was elected President. In February, 1958, with the formation of the United Arab Republic through the union of Egypt and Syria, Gamal Abdel Nasser became President of the new Republic and Kuwatly, who had been instrumental in the Egyptian-Syrian negotiations, retired from public office.

ECONOMIC CONDITIONS. Agriculture and animal breeding are the main industries. Only half the land is arable, and only a third is actually cultivated. Most crops require irrigation. Leading crops include sorghum, olives, cotton, wheat, barley, grapes, lentils, and tobacco. Stock raising is important among the nomads.

Leading exports in 1959 were raw cotton (48%), wheat (11%), and wool (9%). Principal customers were Lebanon (15%), France (16%), and Italy 10%); leading suppliers Britain (9%), the U.S. and Canada (8%), France (9%), and West Germany (13%).

NATURAL FEATURES. Coastal Syria is a narrow plain. Back of that is a range of coastal mountains, and still farther inland is a steppe area. In the east is the Syrian Desert, and in the southeast next to Jordan is the Jebel Druze Range.

---

# Thailand (Siam) (Kingdom)
## (Muang Thai)

Area: 198,456 square miles.
Population (est. 1960): 22,718,000 (1937: Thai, 90%*; Chinese, 3.4%; Indian and Malayan, 3.4%; others, 3.2%).
Density per square mile: 114.5.
Ruler: King Bhumibol Adulyadej.
Prime Minister: Sarit Thanarat.
Principal cities (est. 1957): Bangkok, 1,204,894 (capital, chief port); (census 1947) Khon Kaen, 153,934 (trading center); Buriram, 129,000 (farming); Thonburi, 118,682 (market center).
Monetary unit: Baht.
Languages: Thai (Siamese), Chinese.
Religions (census 1947): Buddhist, 95%; Moslem, 4%; others, 1%.

* Including about 2,500,000 of Chinese descent born in Siam.

---

## STATUS IN THE WORLD TODAY

Although Thailand sided with the Axis during World War II and thereby avoided the devastation of modern warfare, it has pursued a consistently pro-Western course since 1945. With Pakistan and the Philippines, it is one of the three Asian members of the Southeast Asia Treaty Organization. Nevertheless, it has grown apprehensive over its proximity to Red China (there is also a minority of 3 million Chinese in Thailand), and in the last few years has shown unmistakable signs of its readiness to seek an accommodation with Peiping if ever this should become advisable. Thailand has received grants and credits from the United States but none from the Communist bloc thus far.

Since the abolition of the absolute monarchy in 1932, the country has been plagued by political instability, with a constant struggle for power among individuals and factions of a new middle-class oligarchy of young officers and civilian intellectuals. Nevertheless, significant progress has been made in the establishment of democratic institutions. For more than a quarter century Thailand has had a parliament in which elected representatives have discussed public questions and often subjected government policy to searching criticism, even if the cabinet has not yet been brought under parliamentary control. Civil liberties have never been wholly suppressed; Bangkok in particular has a lively and often outspoken press.

---

HISTORY AND GOVERNMENT. The Siamese first began moving down into their present homeland from the Asiatic continent in the sixth century A.D., and by the end of the thirteenth century ruled most of the western portion. During the next 400 years, the Siamese fought sporadically with the Cambodians to the east and the Burmese to the west. The British obtained recognition of paramount interest in Siam in 1824, and in 1896 an Anglo-French accord guaranteed Siamese independence.

A coup on June 24, 1932, changed the absolute monarchy into a representative government with universal suffrage. After five hours of token resistance on Dec. 8, 1941, Siam yielded to Japanese occupation and became one of the springboards in World War II for the Japanese campaign against Malaya. After the fall of its pro-Japanese puppet government in July, 1944, Siam pursued a policy of passive resistance against the Japanese, and on Aug. 16, 1945, after the Japanese surrender, Siam repudiated the declarations of war it had made against Britain and the U.S. in 1942.

By a treaty signed with Britain and India Jan. 1, 1946, Siam renounced all wartime acquisitions of Malayan territory and agreed that no canal linking the Gulf of Siam with the Indian Ocean would be cut across Siamese territory without British concurrence.

In October, 1958, Thanarat, who was Supreme Commander of the armed forces, seized power in a bloodless coup. He proclaimed martial law, dissolved the National Assembly and the Council of Ministers, abrogated the Constitution of 1932, and banned all political parties. On January 28, 1959, the King proclaimed an Interim Constitution and on February 4, 1959, he appointed a 240-member Constituent Assembly to draft a permanent Constitution. The Constituent Assembly, which included 181 members of the armed forces, immediately appointed Thanarat Premier.

RULER. King Bhumibol Adulyadej, who was born Dec. 5, 1927, second son of Prince Mahidol of Songkhla, succeeded to the throne on June 9, 1946, when his brother, King Ananda Mahidol, died of a gunshot wound. He was married on April 28, 1950, to Princess Kitiyakara; their son, Vajiralongkorn, born July 28, 1952, is heir apparent.

ECONOMIC CONDITIONS. Almost 90 per cent of the population work at agriculture. Rice is the principal crop, the staple food and the leading export. It is the basis of Thailand's whole economy and the key to its prosperity. Next most important is rubber. Other products include coconuts, corn, tobacco, cotton, sesame, sugar cane, and soybeans. Livestock, poor in quality and quantity, is used mainly for hauling. Manufacturing is of little importance. Domestic business is largely controlled by Chinese.

Chief exports in 1959 were rice (34%), rubber (31%), and tin (6%). Leading customers were Malaya and Singapore, the United States, and Japan; leading suppliers, Japan, the United States, and Hong Kong.

NATURAL FEATURES AND RESOURCES. Thailand, about three-fourths the size of Texas, supports most of its population in the central alluvial plain, which is drained by the Chaupaya River and tributaries. There are small deposits of many important minerals and some precious stones. Only tin, gold, tungsten, and salt are in commercial production.

Almost 70 per cent of Thailand's total land area is forested. Teak, the main forest product, covers over one-third of this area, chiefly in the northern hill country.

**Languages:** Evhé (south), Haoussa (north), French, and other dialects.
**Religions:** Animist, Christian, Mohammedan.

---

### STATUS IN THE WORLD TODAY

Togo, which became independent on April 27, 1960, leans to the West but does not want to be drawn into the cold war. Its present government believes in a union of African states which leaves each member independent but which puts the smaller nations on an equal footing with the larger ones. Premier Olympio has let it be known that he will rely on the West for guidance and friendship and will continue to depend on France for financial aid and protective troops.

---

HISTORY AND GOVERNMENT. Brazilians were the first traders to settle in Togo. Established as a German colony (Togoland) in 1884, the area was split between the British and the French as League of Nations mandates after World War I and subsequently administered as United Nations trusteeships. The British portion voted for incorporation with Ghana and is now part of that country.

Relations between Ghana and Togo have been deteriorating because Togolanders fear Ghana's alleged "expansionist aims." Part of the trouble lies in the artificial boundaries of the two countries, with Ewe tribesmen settled on both sides of the frontier. The southern half of Togo is populated principally by the Ewe and Mina tribes; in the north the population is descended largely from Hamitic tribes. A number of political refugees from Ghana have also fled to Togo.

ECONOMIC CONDITIONS. Agriculture and grazing are the chief industries, with coffee, cacao, palm kernels and oil, cotton and copra the principal exports. Togo also produces dyewoods and oil palms and some iron ore. Exports (1959) amounted to 4,348,000,000 fr. C.F.A. (3,580,500,000 to France); imports, 3,755,000,000 (1,554,000,000 from France).

NATURAL FEATURES. The coastline, only 32 miles long, is low, sandy and without harbors. The Togo hills traverse the central section.

## Togo (Republic)

**Area:** 22,008 square miles.
**Population:** 1,642,000 (1,284 non-African).
**Density per square mile:** 74.6.
**Premier:** Sylvanus Olympio.
**Principal cities:** Lomé, 66,762 (capital).
**Monetary unit:** Franc C.F.A. (Communauté Française de l'Atlantique).*

* One franc C.F.A. = 0.02 new Fr. fr.

## Tunisia (Republic)

**Area:** 48,332 square miles.
**Population** (est. 1960): 3,965,000. (1946, by place of birth: Tunisian, 89.9%; French, 4.5%; Italian, 2.6%; others, 3%).
**Density per square mile:** 82.0.
**President:** Habib Bourguiba.
**Principal cities** (est. 1960): Tunis, 695,000 (capital); Sfax, 65,000 (phosphate

port); Sousse, 48,000 (seaport); Bizerte, 44,000 (seaport and naval base).

Monetary unit: Tunisian franc.
Languages: Arabic, French, Italian.
Religion: Predominantly Moslem.

## STATUS IN THE WORLD TODAY

The government of President Bourguiba, although anti-French, has been pro-Western in its foreign policy and, in general, anti-Nasser. In October, 1958, Tunisia broke off diplomatic relations with Egypt over interference in Tunisian affairs and an alleged plot to assassinate Bourguiba. But relations were resumed three years later when hostilities broke out briefly in Bizerte between French and Tunisian troops following native demonstrations against the French naval base there. It is the most Western-minded of the countries of North Africa and would like to liquidate its special economic and financial ties with France and be integrated economically with the Western world. It has received arms from the United States after refusing Soviet offers of aid and receives about $30 million a year in aid, a sum roughly equal to one-quarter of its budget.

Tunisia's relations with France have rapidly deteriorated because of the rebellion in Algeria. The rebel Algerian "government" is situated in Tunis, and there have been numerous instances of French troops chasing rebels on Tunisian territory under the doctrine of "hot pursuit." The Bourguiba regime was further irritated by devaluation of the French franc in December, 1958, by the alleged maintenance of a "spy ring" by a group of French civil servants in the postal and telegraph administration, and has claimed that parts of the French Sahara actually belong to Tunisia. French troops have been withdrawn except at the naval base of Bizerte, and Tunisia is pressing for their evacuation. More than half the 180,000 French who lived in Tunisia in 1956 have returned to France.

---

HISTORY AND GOVERNMENT. Tunisia was settled by the Phoenicians and Carthaginians in ancient times. Except for an interval of Vandal conquest in A.D. 439–533, it was part of the Roman Empire until the Arab conquest of 648–69. Then it was ruled by various Arab and Berber dynasties until the Turks took it in 1570–74. The founder of the present dynasty, Hussein ben'Ali, was proclaimed sovereign by the occupation troops in 1705 and later succeeded in making the office hereditary, although subject to nominal Turkish sovereignty.

Throughout much of its history, Tunisia was essentially a pirate state, preying on Mediterranean shipping. In modern times, Italy became the foremost economic power in the area, but after French troops occupied the country in 1881, the Bey signed a treaty acknowledging a French protectorate.

Following the Allied landings in North Africa in 1942, Tunisia became a battleground, with the Axis forces pinched between the British 8th Army advancing from Libya and the U. S., British and French forces from Algeria. The Axis units surrendered in May, 1943, and Tunisia was turned over to the Free French government of General de Gaulle.

Nationalist agitation forced France to grant internal autonomy to Tunisia in June, 1955, and to recognize Tunisian independence and sovereignty in March, 1956. Tunisia was admitted to the U. N. Nov. 12, 1956. The Constituent Assembly deposed the Bey on July 25, 1957, declared Tunisia a republic and elected Habib Bourguiba as the first President.

The executive power is vested by the Constitution in the President, who is elected for 5 years and may be re-elected for two additional terms. Legislative power is vested in a National Assembly elected by universal suffrage, but neither the President nor his Cabinet are responsible to the Assembly.

ECONOMIC CONDITIONS. Agriculture is the chief industry. Over a quarter of the arable land is in wheat. Other important crops are barley, oats, corn, sorghum, beans, and peas. The Cape Bon region is largely devoted to citrus fruits, the southern oases to dates. In 1957 there were 3,026,000 sheep, 544,000 cattle, (1954) 1,853,000 goats, and 202,000 camels.

Leading industries include flour milling, oil refining, lead smelting, and distilling. Native industries include the spinning and weaving of wool, and the making of pottery and leather goods.

Tunisia, Algeria, and France are under a single customs union for a number of products.

Leading exports in 1958 were phosphates, wheat, wine, cement, iron ore, and olive oil. France took 62% of the exports and supplied 71% of the imports.

NATURAL FEATURES AND RESOURCES. Tunisia, at the northermost bulge of Africa, thrusts out toward Sicily to mark the division between the eastern and western Mediterranean. It is mountainous in the north, covered by plains in the east, and projects southward to the Sahara area.

Tunisia's extremely rich deposits of phosphates are mined principally in the Gafsa and Kef regions. The iron ore is of good quality (55% metal content). Other minerals are lead, zinc, mercury, manganese, copper, and salt.

# Turkey (Republic)
## (Türkiye Cümhuriyeti)

**Area:** 301,381 square miles.
**Population** (1960 census): 27,802,224 (Turkish, 94%; Greek, 2.2%; Bulgarian, 1.4%; Yugoslavian, .9%; others, 1.5%).*
**Density per square mile:** 92.2.
**President:** Lt. Gen. Cemal Gursel.
**Premier:** Post now vacant.
**Principal cities** (census 1960): Istanbul, 1,719,922 (chief port, commercial center); Ankara, 646,151 (capital); Smyrna (Izmir), 370,923 (seaport); Adana, 230,024 (agricultural center); Bursa, 153,939 (silk, carpets); Eskisehir, 153,190 (trading center).
**Monetary unit:** Turkish pound (£T).
**Languages:** Turkish, Greek, Bulgarian.
**Religions:** Moslem, 99%; others, 1%.

* 1935 by place of birth.

## STATUS IN THE WORLD TODAY

Turkey, formerly labeled the "sick man of Europe," has achieved the transformation from Eastern empire to Western nation envisaged for it by Kemal Atatürk, and in the process has become one of the staunchest Western allies and a member of NATO. As a target for centuries of Muscovite imperialist expansion—whether Czarist or Communist—its people are naturally anti-Russian. It has a tough, 500,-000-man army, mechanized with American equipment, and has agreed to accept bases for Western guided missiles and rockets. Its relations with Greece, the nation with which it constitutes the southern flank of NATO, have improved since solution of the Cyprus problem. It is a member of the Central Treaty Organization (CENTO), the northern-tier alliance against Soviet aggression, and with Greece and Yugoslavia is a partner in the Balkan pact. In time of war it is in a position to close the Dardanelles to Soviet warships. During the Korean conflict, it sent a brigade to fight with the U.N. forces.

Economically, Turkey has been weakened by inflation, in part a by-product of too-rapid industrialization, with most factories dependent upon imported materials. In the fall of 1958 it received a $359 million credit from the United States and Europe to assist its economic recovery program. With exports lower than had been expected, exporters are now receiving government subsidies. Twenty-one companies, most of them American, are searching for oil.

These economic difficulties led to criticism of the government of Premier Menderes, who responded by suppressing freedom of the press, arresting opposition deputies and taking other unconstitutional and undemocratic measures. Repeated student demonstrations against the repressive measures finally led to Army intervention

in the spring of 1960 when Army officers seized power. A new Constitution proclaiming the Second Turkish Republic was adopted in July, 1961, with elections scheduled for Oct. 15.

---

HISTORY AND GOVERNMENT. The Ottoman Turks first appeared in the early thirteenth century A.D. Under the leadership of their Sultans, they gradually spread their hegemony over most of the Near East and the Balkans, capturing Constantinople in 1453 and storming the gates of Vienna in the seventeenth century. At the height of its power, the empire stretched from the Persian Gulf to the frontiers of Poland and from the shores of the Caspian Sea to Oran in Algeria.

The defeat of the Turkish navy at Lepanto in 1571 by the Holy League and of Turkish forces besieging Vienna in 1683 portended the decline of Ottoman power, reducing Turkey to the status of a pawn in Europe's political maneuvers. Russia moved into the Balkans in the eighteenth century and made herself official protector of the Balkan Christians. Fear of a Russian drive on Constantinople prompted England and France to declare war on Russia, and the Crimean War (1853–56) followed. As a result of the Russo-Turkish war (1877–78), Bulgaria became practically independent, and Rumania and Serbia threw off their nominal allegiance to the sultan. Further defeats were suffered by Turkey in a war with Italy (1911–12) and in the Balkan Wars (1912–13). Meanwhile, a revolt led by the Young Turks, an organization of youthful liberals, had forced the abdication of Sultan Abdul-Hamid in 1909 and established a constitutional regime.

On Aug. 2, 1914, at the outbreak of World War I, a secret alliance was signed between Germany and Turkey, whose army was advised by a German military mission, and in September the Allies declared war on Turkey. Turkish forces successfully defended the strategic Dardanelles, but British forces seized Palestine, Mesopotamia, and Syria; and the Hejaz revolted. By 1918 Allied forces held the territory along the Dardanelles and the Bosporus, and later Greek forces occupied Smyrna.

In 1919 the new Nationalist party, headed by Mustafa Kemal, was organized to resist the Allied occupation, and in 1920 a National Assembly elected Mustafa Kemal President of both the Assembly and the government. Under his leadership, the Nationalist government was recognized by foreign powers, the Greeks were driven out of Smyrna, and other Allied forces were withdrawn. The present Turkish boundaries (with the exception of Alexandretta, ceded to Turkey by France in 1939) were fixed by the Treaty of Lausanne (1923) and later negotiations. The caliphate and sultanate were separated and the sultanate abolished on Oct. 1, 1922. On Oct. 29, 1923, Turkey formally became a republic with Mustafa Kemal, who took the name of Kemal Atatürk, as its first President. The caliphate was abolished on March 3, 1924, and Atatürk proceeded to carry out an extensive program of reform, modernization, and industrialization.

The Montreux Convention (1936) gave Turkey sole responsibility for the defense of the Dardanelles.

General Ismet Inönü was elected to succeed Kemal Atatürk on the latter's death in 1938 and was re-elected in 1939, 1943, and 1946, but was defeated in 1950 and succeeded by Celâl Bayar. On Oct. 19, 1939, a mutual assistance pact was concluded with Britain and France. Turkey followed a neutral course during most of World War II, but on Feb. 23, 1945, she declared war on Germany and Japan, but took no active part in the conflict. After the abrogation of the Soviet-Turkish non-aggression pact in March, 1945, Turkey was subjected to Soviet pressure for a share in the control of the Dardanelles. To assist Turkey in effecting modernization necessary for the preservation of its national integrity, the United States in 1947 agreed to advance $100,000,000, all of which was to be used for the armed forces or to a lesser extent for economic projects directly related to Turkish defense. Turkey also received aid under the European Recovery Program. It became a full member of NATO in 1952.

ECONOMIC CONDITIONS. *Agriculture and Industry.* Agriculture is the principal economic activity, engaging about 65 per cent of the population. Only about 20 per cent of the land is under cultivation, but the government has made great efforts to modernize and improve farming. The most important cash crop is tobacco. Cotton is grown in the south of Asia Minor, while figs come exclusively from the Smyrna region. Grain crops include wheat and barley. Turkey is a leading exporter of olive oil; the Brusa region and the Ionian coast are the principal areas of cultivation. Opium poppies are grown in the Smyrna, Malatia, and Tokat regions.

Turkey is rich in livestock. The most important animal is the goat, of which there were 21,045,000 in Dec., 1953, including the valuable Angora, which thrives on the uplands of the plateau. There were also (Dec., 1959) 30,823,000 sheep, 12,484,000 cattle, and 1,333,000 horses. Wool production in 1959 was 22,900 metric tons, greasy basis.

Staple industries have been established in iron, steel, textiles, paper, glass, sugar, and cement. A large proportion of the factories are government-operated. Istanbul is the major industrial area.

Principal customers in 1959 were the United States and Canada (18%), Germany (22%), EPU countries (16%), and Britain (10%). Leading suppliers were the United States and Canada (22%), West Germany (19%), Britain (12%), and other EPU countries (17%). Chief exports were tobacco (26%), hazelnuts (12%), cotton (15%), and chrome (9%); leading imports were machinery, iron, steel, fuel, and oil.

NATURAL FEATURES AND RESOURCES. Turkey is divided into two natural areas by the historic waterway formed by the Dardanelles, the Sea of Marmara, and the Bosporus.

Turkey in Europe comprises an area about equal to the state of Massachusetts. It is hilly country drained by the Maritsa River and its tributaries. Almost all the population is concentrated in and near the two important towns, Istanbul (Constantinople) and Edirne (Adrianople). Turkey in Asia, or Anatolia, about the size of Texas, is roughly a rectangle in shape with its short sides on the east and west. Its center is a treeless plateau rimmed by mountains.

*Minerals and Forests.* Turkey's rich mineral resources are still comparatively unexploited. Deposits of copper are found in the large field at Arghana, near the Iraq-Syrian frontier. Turkey is also relatively rich in coal, with large deposits in the Eregli region on the Pontic coast some 150 miles from Istanbul. A virtual world monopoly is enjoyed in meerschaum, found in the Eskisehir district. Other important minerals include chromite, petroleum, manganese ore, iron ore (metal content 65%), emery, and antimony.

# Union of Soviet Socialist Republics

Area: 8,649,821 square miles.
Population (est. 1960): 214,400,000 (1939: Great Russian, 58.4%; Ukrainian, 16.6%; Byelorussian, 3.1%; Uzbek, 2.9%; Tartar, 2.5%; Kazakh, 1.8%; Armenian, Azerbaijani, Georgian, each 1.3%; more than 100 others, 10.8%).
Density per square mile: 24.8.
Chairman of Presidium of Supreme Council: Leonid I. Brezhnev.
Premier: N. S. Khrushchev.
Principal cities (census 1959): Moscow, 5,032,000 (capital); Leningrad, 2,888,000 (industrial center, shipbuilding); Kiev, 1,102,000 (industrial center, Ukraine); Kharkov, 930,000 (iron and steel, coal); Gorki, 942,000 (industrial, transportation center); Tashkent, 911,000 (textiles, tobacco); Kuybyshev, 806,000 (industrial center, Volga port); Novosibirsk, 887,000 (Siberian industrial center); Sverdlovsk, 777,-

000 (Ural industrial center); Tbilisi, 694,-000 (building materials, tobacco); Stalino, 701,000 (coal, metallurgy).

**Monetary unit:** Ruble.

**Languages:** See Population, above.

**Religions:** Russian Orthodox (predominant), Moslem, Roman Catholic, Jewish, Lutheran.

---

## STATUS IN THE WORLD TODAY

As one of the two super-powers, the Union of Soviet Socialist Republics has only one cardinal foreign policy: the creation of Communist governments in other nations of the world, whether by force or otherwise, all of them subservient to the dictates of Moscow. All its energies are bent toward this principal end; after more than forty years of Communist rule, the Russian worker still awaits the proletariat paradise promised him. Raising his low standard of living must be subordinated to the task of industrialization and the heavy burden imposed on the economy by military expenditures—estimated at some 15 per cent of the annual commitment of resources.

During World War II, this expansion of the Communist empire was accomplished by conquest and subversion and resulted in the creation of the belt of satellite states in Eastern Europe and the gradual assumption of power by the Reds in China. Now, with the specter of the end of all civilization in any atomic war, the Soviet formula calls for freezing the status quo in Europe, where Moscow feels that her "security" demands control of neighboring countries, and peaceful penetration of the "underdeveloped" countries by using economic, diplomatic, and propaganda methods.

Moscow views the "colonial and semi-colonial" nations as the area of greatest opportunity for the present. It poses as the major defender of peace and national sovereignty, as the protector of the small and recently colonial states in their common hostility to "Western imperialism" and to capitalism, and as a model of growth of a previously backward country. Yet, paradoxically, while pretending to assist these nations against "imperialism," the U.S.S.R. itself is as imperialistic as, if not more so, than the tsarist regime it replaced. Its policy of imperialistic penetration of the nations which it—temporarily—assists is camouflaged by a skillful propaganda campaign for peace and coexistence. But its intentions are to take control of these states and to eliminate whatever free democratic institutions exist, even as they have done in such Eastern European countries as Latvia, Lithuania, Estonia, Hungary, Rumania, and Czechoslovakia. If peaceful penetration is not enough, it helps its partner, Red China, support small "civil wars" which can be kept from turning into

a major war, or even military assistance on a larger and more open scale, as in Korea. But its primary method now is to undertake to construct industrial and social enterprises ranging from steel mills and dams to hospitals and stadiums and by stepping up mutually beneficial trade, although the benefits often flow only in the direction of Moscow.

Foreign policy in the Soviet sense is not limited to diplomacy. In addition to conventional international contacts through ambassadors and ministers, Moscow uses the international network of Communist parties and so-called front organizations as means of pressure and vehicles for the expansion of the Soviet orbit throughout the world.

Probably the greatest lasting accomplishment of the past forty years is the forced economic growth of the Soviet Union from a relatively backward state to a leader in many branches of economy, second only to the United States. In this giant effort the major emphasis has been on expansion of heavy industry, armaments, and machine tools, and a strikingly small proportion of the resources invested has gone into services and consumer goods. Although the worker theoretically owns all these means of production, he has benefited little from them. One careful study put the Soviet worker's real wages in 1950 at one-sixth of the American worker's. There has been some improvement since then, but nothing so striking as the giant strides made during the same years in the production of iron and steel, the extraction of iron and coal, or the harnessing of electric and nuclear power.

Agriculture still remains the principal headache of the production bosses in the Kremlin. Collectivization has not solved the problem of food, and the forced deliveries demanded of the collective farms have had to be eased as an incentive to greater production. For a time the population grew faster than the food supply, and more and more people were leaving the farms for the cities. While the Soviet Union is still agricultural—55 per cent of the population remains rural—it may find it easier to export raw materials and industrial products in return for food than to produce enough sustenance for its own population.

The U.S.S.R. is in fact a country of contradictions, with strengths as well as weaknesses, some of which are difficult to detect and estimate because of restrictions on the flow of information imposed by the Soviet regime. But a definition of tsarist Russia indicates that in some respects little has changed in the last fifty years: a multinational empire marked by a strong central government, a theory of the right and duty of the state to guide the destinies of its subjects, and the absence of free political life.

---

HISTORY. The history of Russia begins with the perhaps legendary figure of the Viking, Rurik, who according to tradition came to Russia in A.D. 862 and founded the first Russian dynasty in Novgorod. The various tribes were united by the spread of Christianity in the 10th and 11th centuries; Vladimir "the Saint" was converted in 988. During the 11th century the grand dukes of Kiev held such centralizing power as existed. In 1240 Kiev was destroyed by the Mongols, and the Russian territory was split into numerous smaller dukedoms, out of which three large centers emerged—Galicia, Moscow and Novgorod. The early dukes of Moscow extended their dominions through their office of tribute collector for the Mongols.

In the late 15th century, Ivan III, the reigning duke, acquired the rival kingdoms of Novgorod and Tver and threw off the Mongol yoke. Ivan IV, the Terrible (1533–84), first Muscovite duke to assume the title of Tsar, is considered to have founded the Russian State. He crushed the power of rival princes and boyars (great landowners), but Russia remained largely medieval until the reign of Peter the Great (1682–1725), grandson of the first Romanov Tsar, Michael (1613–45). Peter made extensive reforms aimed at westernization, and through his defeat of Charles XII of Sweden at the Battle of Poltava (1709), he extended Russia's boundaries to the west. Catherine the Great (1762–96) continued Peter's westernization program and also expanded Russian territory, acquiring the Crimea and part of Poland. During the reign of Alexander I (1801–25), Napoleon's attempt to subdue Russia was defeated (1812–13), and new territory was gained, including Finland (1809) and Bessarabia (1812). Alexander was the originator of the Holy Alliance, which crushed for a time Europe's rising liberal movement.

Alexander II (1855–81), pushed Russia's borders to the Pacific and into central Asia. Serfdom was abolished in 1861, but heavy restrictions were imposed on the emancipated class. Revolutionary strikes following Russia's defeat in the war with Japan forced Nicholas II (1894–1917) to grant a representative national body (Duma), elected by narrowly limited suffrage. It met for the first time in 1906. Nicholas continued in his reactionary course, however, and the overwhelmingly liberal Duma had little or no influence in the government.

World War I demonstrated the corruptness and inefficiency of the tsarist regime, although the call of patriotism held the poorly equipped army together for a time. Disorders broke out in Petrograd (now Leningrad) in March, 1917, and, following the winning over of the Petrograd garrison, the revolution was in full swing. Nicholas was forced to abdicate and was later killed by the revolutionists. A provisional government was formed, composed of both conservative and radical elements. This government, under the successive premierships of Prince Lvov and Alexander Kerensky, a Menshevik or moderate socialist, soon lost ground to the radical or Bolshevik wing of the Socialist Democratic Labor party. Finally, on Nov. 7, 1917, came the Second Revolution, engineered by Nikolai Lenin and Leon Trotsky. The humiliating Treaty of Brest-Litovsk (March 3, 1918) concluded the war with Germany, but civil war and intervention by foreign powers prevented the new Communist government from gaining control of all Russia until 1920. A brief war with Poland occurred in 1920, but it resulted in Russian defeat.

Soviet foreign policy—first featured by friendship with Germany and antagonism toward England and France and then, after Hitler's rise to power in 1933, by participation in the League of Nations and an anti-Fascist program—took another abrupt turn on Aug. 24, 1939, with the signing of a Soviet-German nonaggression pact. Territory seized from Poland (Sept. 1939) became part of the Ukrainian and Byelorussian S.S.R.'s; that secured from Finland at the conclusion of the Finnish war of 1939–40, part of the Karelian S.S.R. set up March 31, 1940; that secured from Rumania (Bessarabia and northern Bukovina), part of the Moldavian S.S.R. set up Aug. 2, 1940; and finally the formerly independent states of Estonia, Latvia, and Lithuania, occupied in June 1940, were absorbed into the U.S.S.R. as the 14th, 15th, and 16th Soviet Republics. The latter annexations have not been recognized by the United States, Britain, and the majority of other nations.

Immediately following their attack (June 22, 1941), the Germans seized approximately 500,000 square miles of Soviet territory, but Soviet forces resisted stubbornly, aided by increasing amounts of matériel from the United States and Britain. The great Soviet counteroffensive in the Stalingrad area (Nov., 1942–Feb., 1943) marked the turning point. Soviet troops gradually pushed the Nazis back and unleashed their final great offensive on Jan. 12, 1945. The nonaggression pact with Japan (1941) was denounced in April, 1945, and, following the declaration of war on Japan (Aug. 8, 1945), Soviet Far Eastern forces quickly occupied Manchuria, Karafuto, and the Kuriles.

Postwar territorial acquisitions include

the Carpatho-Ukraine (12,617 sq. mi.) obtained from Czechoslovakia June 29, 1945, incorporated into the Ukrainian S.S.R.; the Republic of Tannu Tuva in central Asia (64,000 sq. mi.), incorporated early in 1945 into the R.S.F.S.R.; Karafuto or southern Sakhalin (13,935 sq. mi.) and the Kurile Islands (3,944 sq. mi.), occupied by Soviet troops in Aug., 1945, and incorporated into the R.S.F.S.R.; the northern part of eastern Prussia (about 7,000 sq. mi.), placed under *de facto* Soviet administration at the Potsdam Conference and incorporated into R.S.F.S.R.; the Petsamo district of Finland, obtained *de jure* under the 1947 treaty and incorporated into the R.S.F.S.R.; and Poland east of the Curzon Line (69,860 sq. mi.), under terms of the Soviet-Polish treaty of Aug. 16, 1945, incorporated into the Ukrainian and Byelorussian S.S.R.'s.

COMMUNIST PARTY. Real power resides in the Communist party of the Soviet Union (CPSU), recognized by the constitution as the vanguard of the masses and endowed with authority which has permitted it to emerge victorious from every real or potential challenge in the past forty years. Khrushchev's victory, like Stalin's a generation earlier, is the victory of the party machine, and Moscow openly states that the role of the party will continue to increase, while "administrative and repressive" functions (state bureaucracy, army, and police) will "lose their former role" in the Soviet state.

The Bolshevik party has grown from a membership of some 300,000 in 1918 and 1,900,000 in 1938 (after extensive purges), to nearly 8,000,000 today. It is still a select group, thoroughly screened and subject to special obligations but also special privileges. As a group, it is the defender of the revolutionary order, a model for all to emulate and the holder of political monopoly. While state, economic, and other institutions may be decentralized and reorganized time and again, the party has retained—and, it is safe to say, will retain—its highly centralized, disciplined character as a matter of principle and of expediency.

The party organization has spawned almost half a million cells ("primary party organizations"), which exist in virtually all factories, farms, and government offices. Operating as essential "transmission belts," they are responsible to district (county) committees, which in turn are under the direction of regional (provincial) committees, with the lower officials in each instance named or approved from above. The higher strata are represented by party organizations on the level of each Union Republic and finally, at the top, the All-Union leadership.

Formally, infrequent Party Congresses are supreme in determining strategy and electing the Central Committee, which is the most powerful single body in the country. It is composed of about 150 members and "candidate" members picked to "guide the entire work of the party" and "direct the work of Soviet organs." Under Stalin the Central Committee atrophied and became as much of a fiction as did other institutions; under Malenkov it continued this ineffective existence. Khrushchev, on the other hand, appears to have "packed" it and restored it as a key instrument of government.

The importance of the Central Committee is enhanced by the fact that it directs a variety of staff departments, such as the "Agitprop" (responsible for "agitation and propaganda"), the Military Department (in charge of political control and indoctrination in the armed forces), the Foreign Department (which, since the dissolution of the Communist International in 1943, is responsible for contacts with Communist parties abroad) and the so-called Cadre Department (which has the crucial say-so on personnel selection and promotion). In addition it supervises the tens of thousands of party schools throughout the country.

The Central Committee meets in plenary session only about two or three times a year. In the interim, much of the actual work is carried on (in addition to the staff departments just described) by its Secretariat and the party Presidium (until 1952 known as the Politburo). The role of the Secretariat is suggested by the fact that Stalin was Secretary-General of the party during his rise to power, and Nikita

## Republics of the U.S.S.R.

| Republic and capital | Area sq. mi. | Population census, 1959 (thousands) |
|---|---|---|
| Russian S.F.S.R. (Moscow) | 6,593,391* | 117,494 |
| Ukraine (Kiev) | 232,046 | 41,893 |
| Kazakhstan (Alma Alta) | 1,064,092 | 1,520 |
| Byelorussia (Minsk) | 80,154 | 1,196 |
| Uzbekistan (Tashkent) | 158,069 | 8,113 |
| Georgia (Tbilisi) | 26,872 | 4,049 |
| Azerbaijan (Baku) | 33,475 | 3,700 |
| Lithuania† (Vilnius) | 25,174 | 2,713 |
| Moldavia (Chisinau) | 13,012 | 2,880 |
| Latvia† (Riga) | 24,595 | 2,094 |
| Kirghizia (Frunze) | 76,641 | 2,063 |
| Tadzhikistan (Stalinabad) | 55,019 | 1,982 |
| Armenia (Erivan) | 11,506 | 1,786 |
| Turkmenistan (Ashkhabad) | 188,417 | 9,301 |
| Estonia† (Tallinn) | 17,413 | 8,060 |

* Including the Karelo-Finnish S.S.R., incorporated into the R.S.F.S.R. in July 1956. † Discussed under World History in alphabetical position.

Khrushchev, too, used the similar post of First Secretary of the party (which he gained in September, 1953) as the springboard to dictatorship.

DEFENSE. The land, air, and sea forces are under control of the Defense Ministry. Military service is compulsory; the initial training period varies from two to five years. The armed forces, which were estimated to have reached a peak of more than 15,000,000 men in 1945, numbered between 4,350,000 and 4,600,000 men in 1956, and were believed to have been reduced to approximately 3,400,000 by 1957. The strength of the army, including MVD and MGN troops (secret police organizations with paramilitary formations), was between 2,800,000 and 3,200,000 in 1956. The air force had between 750,000 and 800,000 men and 20,000 planes, including advanced models of jet fighters and bombers. The navy had between 600,000 and 750,000 men.

Information about the Red fleet is as vague as that about the army and air force. In Dec., 1956, it was believed to have three battleships, thirty-two cruisers, 150 destroyers, 250 frigates and escort vessels, 475 submarines, and many coastal and river craft, patrol vessels, minesweepers, and various other small ancillary craft. Naval construction was emphasized in postwar five-year plans.

ECONOMIC CONDITIONS. *Agriculture.* Formerly an agricultural country, the Soviet Union has grown since about 1920 into an industrial-agricultural power, with agriculture making great advances at the same time.

The Union's diverse climate permits the growing of the most varied crops.

The progress of the livestock industry during the fifth five-year plan was particularly disappointing.

*Industry.* Almost all industry in the Soviet Union is carried on by organizations owned or controlled by the state. Industrialization of the country has been a major objective of its leaders. Completion of the first two five-year plans (1928–32, 1933–37) and of most of the third (1937–42) saw a great increase in the volume and versatility of Soviet industry.

The large-scale evacuation of plants to the East and the construction of new plants there during World War II, coupled with the eastward orientation of industry prior to the war, has shifted the balance to newly developed regions in Central Asia and Siberia from the Moscow-Leningrad area and the Ukraine. The new regions are now the center of Soviet industrial power, accounting for almost all magnesium and aluminum production, and more than 60 per cent of the pig iron and steel production. The production of consumers' goods

continues to be subordinate to the production of heavy capital equipment.

Large increases in production were reported under the fourth and fifth five-year plans and further increases were projected under the sixth five-year plan.

*Foreign Trade.* Soviet foreign trade is a state monopoly, and foreign goods are purchased in accordance with an over-all plan conducted under the supervision of the Foreign Trade Ministry.

No complete trade statistics have been issued since 1938.

According to official reports, the main exports in 1958 were machines and equipment (18.5%); metals, cotton, grain, and petroleum and products; chief imports, machines and equipment (24.5%); foodstuffs (14.9%); and consumer goods (14.4%). In 1959, 73.6% of the imports were from Communist countries.

NATURAL FEATURES AND RESOURCES. The U.S.S.R. is the largest unbroken political unit in the world, occupying more than one-seventh of the land surface of the globe. The greater part of its territory is a vast plain stretching from eastern Europe to the Pacific Ocean. This plain, relieved only occasionally by low mountain ranges (notably the Urals), consists of three zones running east and west: (1) the frozen marshy tundra of the Arctic; (2) the more temperate forest belt; and (3) the steppes or prairies to the south, which in southern Soviet Asia become sandy deserts. The topography is more varied in the South, particularly in the Caucasus between the Caspian and Black Seas, and in the Tien-Pamir mountain system bordering Afghanistan, Sinkiang, and Mongolia. Mountains (Stanovoi and Kolyma) and great rivers (Amur, Yenisei, Lena) also break up the sweep of the plain in Siberia.

*Minerals.* The U.S.S.R. is probably the richest country in the world in mineral resources, containing deposits of almost every known mineral. It ranks among the top producing nations in coal, chromite, iron ore, petroleum, gold, copper, manganese, and other products. The richest mineral region is that of the Ural Mountains, which lacks only good coking coal.

*Forests.* With a forested area of about 2,500,000,000 acres, the U.S.S.R. possesses a large proportion of the world's timber reserves. Most of the forested area is in Siberia, but there are also valuable stands in the Caucasus. Plans were made late in 1948 for the planting of huge forest belts 60 to 90 mi. wide in the southern steppes to protect fertile food-producing areas from the dry winds of the central Asian and Caspian deserts.

*Fisheries and Furs.* The rivers, lakes, and surrounding seas (except the Black

Sea) are rich in fish. The acquisition of former Japanese fisheries in Karafuto and the Kuriles greatly increased output of the Far-Eastern fish industry. Trapping is an important secondary industry, especially in eastern Siberia.

## UNITED ARAB REPUBLIC. See Egypt, Syria

## UNITED ARAB STATES. See Yemen

# Uruguay (Republic)
## (República Oriental del Uruguay)

Area: 72,172 square miles.
Population (est. 1958): 2,800,000 (1950: white, 89.1%; others, 10.9%).
Density per square mile: 38.8.
President of National Council: Eduardo Victor Haedo
Principal cities (est. 1959): Montevideo, 810,969 (capital); Mercedes, 44,900 (farming center); Salto, 44,900 (cattle raising); Paysandú, 44,000 (meat packing).
Monetary unit: Peso.
Language: Spanish.
Religion: Roman Catholic.

### STATUS IN THE WORLD TODAY

Uruguay, unlike its neighbors, has been one of the consistently democratic nations of South America. But like its neighbors, it is now faced with an economic crisis. For many years a grazing nation, it began to industrialize itself as a result of the depression and World War II. The new industries produced goods at high costs, which required high tariffs to protect them. Now one-third of the country's population is engaged in industry. Government employment has expanded to the point where another one-third works for the government. Excessively early retirement ages and other exaggerated provisions of the social security system, one of the first of its kind, have made it onerously costly. There is also a great deal of discontent with the plural executive system, whereby a nine-member National Council replaced the office of president. It now has six majority and three minority members.

HISTORY AND GOVERNMENT. Juan Diaz de Solis, a Spaniard, discovered Uruguay in 1516, but the Portuguese were first to settle it when they founded Colonia in 1680. After a long struggle, Spain wrested the country from Portugal in 1778. Uruguay revolted against Spain in 1811, only to be conquered in 1816–20 by the Portuguese from Brazil. Independence was reasserted

with Argentine help in 1825, and the republic was set up in 1830.

Independence, however, did not restore order, and a revolt in 1836 touched off nearly fifty years of factional strife with occasional armed intervention from Argentina and Brazil. Since 1900 there has been marked social and economic progress, a development which was interrupted by the 1929 depression and resultant unrest.

Under the 1934 Constitution, as amended in 1951, the executive power is exercised by a National Council of nine members, six of the majority and three of the minority party, appointed for a term of four years by the Senate and Chamber of Deputies meeting in joint session. The Presidency is rotated annually among members of the majority party in the Council. Members of the Senate and of the Chamber of Deputies are elected by popular vote for four years. A special tribunal of five members appointed by Congress arbitrates administrative disputes between the National Council and Congress.

ECONOMIC CONDITIONS. Cattle, sheep, meat, and wool dominate the Uruguayan economy. With nearly 80 per cent of its grassy land devoted to grazing, in 1959 there were 21,300,000 sheep and 6,900,000 cattle. Wool production in 1959 was 98,000 metric tons, clean. With only about 5 per cent of the land cultivated, a third of this grows wheat, the chief crop (1957–58: 596,-000 metric tons).

Uruguay slaughters more than two million head of cattle and sheep a year, and meat processing is the largest manufacturing industry. There are many modern plants for chilling or freezing meat and plants for liquid extract of beef.

In value, wool was the chief export (35%) in 1959, followed by meat (19%) and hides (10%). Chief customers were the Netherlands (10%), the United States (19%), Brazil (18%), Britain (9%), and the U.S.S.R. (9%); leading suppliers, the United States (21%), Brazil (11%), Venezuela (26%), and West Germany (6%). Leading imports included machinery, cotton, vehicles, fuels and lubricants, textiles, and sugar.

NATURAL FEATURES. Uruguay, a low, rolling plain in the south and a low plateau in the north, has a 120-mile Atlantic shore line, a 235-mile frontage on the Río de la Plata, and 270 miles on the Uruguay River, its western boundary.

# Vatican City State
## (Stato della Città del Vaticano)

Area: 108.8 acres.
Population (est. 1958): 1,000 (Italian, 85%; Swiss and others, 15%).

Ruler: The Supreme Pontiff.
Monetary unit: Lira.
Languages: Latin, Italian.
Religion: Roman Catholic.

The Vatican City State, sovereign and independent, is situated on the Vatican hill on the right bank of the Tiber in northwest Rome. The area has been intimately associated with the history of the Roman Catholic Church since the time of the martyrdom of St. Peter. From it the Pope exercised temporal sway for many centuries over a large part of central Italy; in 1859 the Papal States comprised an area of some 17,000 sq. mi. During the struggle for Italian unification, from 1860 to 1870, most of this area became part of Italy.

By an Italian law of May 13, 1871, the temporal power of the Pope was abrogated, and the territory of the Papacy was confined to the Vatican and Lateran palaces and the Villa of Castel Gandolfo. The Popes consistently refused to recognize this arrangement, and by the Lateran Treaty of Feb. 11, 1929, between the Vatican and the Kingdom of Italy, the exclusive dominion and sovereign jurisdiction of the Holy See over the city of the Vatican was again recognized, thus restoring the Pope's temporal authority over the area. Accompanying the treaty were conventions regulating the position of the Catholic Church in Italy and providing for reimbursement to the Vatican in final settlement of the claims of the Holy See against Italy for the loss of temporal power in 1870–71.

The Supreme Pontiff Pius XII (Eugenio Pacelli), died Oct. 9, 1958. He was born at Rome, March 2, 1876, proclaimed Cardinal in 1929, and elected Pope on March 2, 1939. He was crowned on March 12, 1939. He was succeeded on October 28, 1958, by Cardinal Angelo Giuseppe Roncalli, who became Pope John XXIII.

The Pope has full legal, executive, and judicial powers. Executive power over the area is in the hands of a Governor appointed by the Pope.

The College of Cardinals is the Pope's chief advisory body, and upon his death the cardinals elect his successor for life. The cardinals themselves are created for life by the Pope.

The central administration of the Roman Catholic Church throughout the world is carried on in the Vatican by twelve congregations, three tribunals, and four offices. In its diplomatic relations with foreign countries, the Vatican is represented by the Papal Secretary of State.

The Vatican has its own railway station, postal facilities, coinage, newspaper, radio, and television system. In addition to the Vatican itself, which includes St. Peter's Square, extraterritorial rights are enjoyed in thirteen buildings in the city of Rome outside Vatican City.

---

# Venezuela (Republic)
## (República de Venezuela)

Area: 352,143 square miles.
Population (est. 1960): 6,709,000* (mestizo, 65%; white, 20%; Negro, 8%; Indian, 7%).
Density per square mile: 19.1.*
President: Romulo Betancourt.
Principal cities (est. 1959): Caracas, 711,673 (capital); Maracaibo, 345,141 (oil); Barquisimeto, 153,916 (sugar, coffee, mining); Valencia, 121,913 (farming center).
Monetary unit: Bolívar.
Language: Spanish.
Religion: Roman Catholic.
* Excludes tribal Indians.

---

### STATUS IN THE WORLD TODAY

Venezuela, having overthrown the brutal and corrupt Perez Jimenez dictatorship in January, 1958, is now preoccupied with re-establishing democratic government. Governed by military dictators virtually since independence, it now has a popularly elected President and Congress. On the economic front, it is trying to diversify its economy and reduce its dependence on oil, which provides 95 per cent of its foreign exchange. It has put into execution an emergency economic plan of public works to absorb most of the 100,000 unemployed left by the Perez Jimenez regime. At the same time its Development Corporation has begun to extend loans to industries such as textiles, which need new equipment in order to improve efficiency and productivity; to bolster some of the weaker elements of the nation's economy; and to plan for a broader economy, less subject to the vagaries of the oil business.

---

HISTORY AND GOVERNMENT. Venezuela, a third larger than Texas, is the world's second greatest producer of oil, outranked only by the United States. Simón Bolívar, who led the liberation of much of the continent from Spain, was born in Caracas.

Columbus discovered Venezuela on his third voyage in 1498. A subsequent Spanish explorer gave the country its name, meaning "Little Venice." There were no important settlements until Caracas was founded in 1567. With Bolívar taking part, Venezuela was one of the first South American colonies to revolt against Spain in 1810, but it was not until 1821 that independence was won. Federated at first with Colombia and Ecuador, the country set up a republic in 1830, and then sank for many decades into a condition of revolt, dictatorship, and corruption.

Venezuela has a bicameral Congress, the 40 members of the Senate and the 160 members of the Chamber of Deputies being elected by direct popular vote to four-year terms. The President is elected for five years and Romulo Betancourt, leader of the Democratic Action Party, was elected to that office on December 7, 1958.

ECONOMIC CONDITIONS. Agricultural production has failed to keep pace with the food needs of the rapidly increasing population. The principal crop is coffee, grown on 60,000 plantations on the slopes of the coastal mountains. Stock raising, which is centered east of Lake Maracaibo, and on the llanos, is important.

There are few industries, the most important being woodworking, cotton textiles, and tobacco products. Electric power is plentiful. In 1958, 950,764,000 bbl. of crude petroleum were produced. Venezuela's first steel plant is under construction.

Oil, most of which is found on the shore of Lake Maracaibo, is the dominant factor in the economy. It accounts for 90% of exports and gives the country a big foreign trade balance and a treasury surplus.

In 1959 the United States supplied over 57 per cent of imports, which included for the most part machinery and equipment, metals and manufactures, foodstuffs, beverages, and textiles. In addition to petroleum and products (90%), chief exports in 1959 were iron ore, coffee, and cacao. Most of the crude oil goes to the United States via the islands of Curaçao and Aruba, refining centers in the West Indies.

NATURAL FEATURES AND RESOURCES. Mountain systems break Venezuela into four distinct areas: (1) the Maracaibo lowlands; (2) the mountainous region in the north and northwest; (3) the Orinoco basin, with the llanos (vast grass-covered plains) on its northern border and great forest areas in the south and southeast; (4) the Guiana highland, south of the Orinoco, accounting for nearly half the national territory. About 80 per cent of Venezuela is drained by the Orinoco and its 400 tributaries.

Oil production in 1959 was 1,033,000,000 barrels. Venezuela has gold mines in the region southwest of the Orinoco delta. A subsidiary of Bethlehem Steel Corp. began the mining of iron ore in the El Pao area south of the Orinoco river in 1950, while a U. S. Steel Corp. subsidiary is exploiting a rich "iron mountain" south of Ciudad Bolívar on the Orinoco.

# Vietnam, Democratic Republic of (North)

**Area:** 59,934 square miles.
**Population (est. 1958):** 15,280,000.

Density per square mile: 254.9.
President: Ho Chi-minh.
Premier: Pham Van-dong.
Principal cities (est. 1960): Hanoi, 643,-000 (capital); Haiphong, 170,000 (chief port).
Monetary unit: Dong.
Languages: Annamese, Chinese, French.
Religions: Buddhist, Christian.

## STATUS IN THE WORLD TODAY

North Vietnam, a satellite of both Moscow and Peiping, is ruled by the ruthless dictatorship of the Communist Viet Minh, who defeated the French in the Indo-China War. Its severity has caused 850,000 to flee to the south and led to at least one fairly widespread peasant revolt in the fall of 1956. But Viet Minh rule has not been seriously jeopardized, and according to creditable reports its army has been doubled to about 350,000 effectives in violation of the Geneva Agreements and armed with massive support from the Communist bloc.

Favored by possession of most of Indo-China's mineral wealth and almost all of its modest pre-Geneva industrial plant, it has been able to make more economic progress than South Vietnam. It has also received large-scale economic aid from the Soviet bloc, said to total nearly $100 million, and because of its resources has been making progress in industrialization.

HISTORY AND GOVERNMENT. The Democratic Republic of Vietnam comprises the northern part of the former state of Viêt-Nam and includes all of the former state of Tongking and the northern part of Annam. It is no longer a part of the French Union. The government of the republic is organized along typical Communist lines. The decision taken at Geneva in July, 1954, to re-unite North and South Vietnam in July, 1956, was thwarted by the policies of Ngo Dinh Diem, President of the Republic of South Vietnam.

In February, 1959, Communist China and North Vietnam signed an agreement under which North Vietnam was to receive $168,-775,000 in economic aid, and the following month the Soviet Union announced that it would give North Vietnam substantial economic and technical aid to build industrial installations.

The economy is based on agriculture and mining. The chief crop is rice, grown chiefly in the Red River delta and supplying in most years the requirements of the population. Other crops are maize, arrowroot, sugar cane, tea, coffee, tobacco, and sweet potatoes. Industry is not highly developed. There are important coal mines in the Quangyen basin near Haiphong. Tin, limestone, and gold also are produced.

A railway runs south from Hanoi along the coast and in the north connects through Langson with the railway network of Communist China.

# Vietnam, Republic of (South)

Area: 75,290 square miles.
Population (est. 1959): 13,960,000.
Density per square mile: 184.1.
President: Ngo Dinh Diem.
Principal cities (est. 1958): Saïgon-Cholon, 1,219,500 (capital, chief port); Tourane, 100,978 (port, naval base); Hué, 113,280 (rice; sawmills).
Monetary unit: Piastre.*
Languages: Annamese, French.
Religions: Buddhist, Christian.
* 1 piastre = 10 French metropolitan francs.

### STATUS IN THE WORLD TODAY

South Vietnam, which was not expected to survive for long after the Geneva Agreements which ended the savage Indo-China War, has survived and even flourished with a militantly anti-Communist policy and no nonsense about "neutralism." Three main factors account for this: (1) the courageous leadership of Ngo Dinh Diem, who contained and reduced to manageable proportions the threat of the Communist underground, and thereby established conditions of genuine security throughout his territory; (2) the massive political and material support of the United States, including the protection afforded by the Manila Pact (September, 1954) and assistance in receiving and integrating more than 850,000 refugees from the north into the life and economy of the country; and (3) the Communist decision, in line with the dictates of international strategy, to refrain from overt aggression or concerted efforts at subversion.

Economically, a land reform program has been instituted, land reclamation has proceeded apace and there have been important advances in the "infrastructure" (transportation, communications, technical training, etc.) of South Vietnam's underdeveloped economy. A modest beginning has been made in industrialization. American aid continues at high levels, averaging well over $200 million annually, not including military hard goods. On the negative side of the ledger, there has been little relaxation of the authoritarianism and repressiveness that have characterized Diem's government from the beginning. Most civil liberties remain rigidly circumscribed, and functioning democracy remains more an ideal than a reality.

HISTORY AND GOVERNMENT. The young republic of Vietnam comprises the southern part of the former state of Viêt-Nam and includes all of the former state of Cochin-China and the southern part of Annam.

A presidential-type constitution was promulgated on October 26, 1956, and general elections for South Vietnam's first National Assembly of 123 members represented a victory for President Diem's supporters. The constitution provides for a strong executive, and the President, who is elected for a term of five years, has veto power over all the bills that are passed by the Assembly.

According to the Geneva Agreements of July, 1954, which ended the Indo-China war, North and South Vietnam were to be reunified through elections in 1956. But President Diem flouted the provisions of the Geneva Agreements on the ground that the French and not his government had been a signatory to them. The U.S.S.R. has vetoed the admission of South Vietnam into the United Nations.

About 90 per cent of the people derive their livelihood from agriculture, most being employed in growing rice and rubber. The Mékong delta is one of the leading rice-exporting areas in the world. Production in 1958 included rice, 3,915,000 metric tons; rubber, 69,700 tons. Other crops are tea, coffee, maize, tobacco, kapok, and pepper. Water buffalo are used chiefly for draft purposes.

Factories, which are centered in Saïgon-Cholon, are small. They process goods for local consumption, as well as agricultural and forest products for export. Most important of the factories are the rice mills and the sawmills.

In 1959 the chief export was rubber. Leading customers were France, the United States, and Cambodia; the leading suppliers were the United States, Japan, and France.

Mineral resources are limited. Coal is most important; some deposits of phosphates and gold exist.

# Yemen (Kingdom)

Area: c. 75,290 square miles.
Population (est. 1959): 4,500,000.
Density per square mile: c. 59.8.
King: Ahmad ibn Yahya Hamid ed-Din.
Premier: Ahmad ibn Yahya Hamid ed-Din.
Principal cities (est.): Sana, 60,000 (capital); Hodeida, 30,000 (chief port); Taiz, 12,000 (seat of government).
Monetary unit: Riyal.
Language: Arabic.
Religion: Moslem.

## STATUS IN THE WORLD TODAY

Yemen, a backward little country which until recently was closed to foreigners, has lately been following the foreign policy of Nasser's Egypt. It has not joined his United Arab Republic but has become federated with it in what is called the United Arab States. When Nasser worked closely with the U.S.S.R., Yemen did too, receiving shipments of arms as well as a military mission and assistance from Red China. When Nasser turned against Communists inside Arab countries, Yemeni mobs displayed hostility toward the Soviets and Chinese. When an acute famine threatened early in 1959, however, Yemen received emergency shipments of wheat from the United States. It has also been carrying on intermittent minor warfare with the British along the undefined borders of the Aden protectorate, where it claims that some of the sheikdoms under British protection are actually part of Yemen.

HISTORY AND GOVERNMENT. The history of Yemen dates back to the Minaean kingdom (1,200–650 B.C.). It accepted Islam in 628 A.D., and in the tenth century came under the control of the Rassite dynasty of the Zaidi sect, which still rules. The Turks occupied the area from 1538 to 1630 and from 1849 to 1918. Its sovereign status was confirmed by treaties signed with Saudi Arabia and Britain in 1934.

Yemen is an absolute monarchy. The present ruler came to the throne in 1948, after insurgents murdered his father. The Imam (ruler) of Yemen is both the religious and temporal leader of the country and traces his ancestry to Ali, son-in-law of the Prophet Mohammed. Yemen has no parliament or political parties.

Unlike most of Arabia, the Yemeni highlands are well adapted to agriculture; they produce grain, fruit, vegetables, and Mocha coffee. Stock raising flourishes, particularly in the lowlands. Exports include coffee and hides.

# Yugoslavia (Republic)

## (Federativna Narodna Republika Jugoslavija)

**Area:** 98,766 square miles.
**Population** (est. 1960): 18,655,000 (1953: Serbian, 41.7%; Croat, 23.5%; Slovene, 8.8%; Macedonian, 5.3%; Albanian, 4.4%; others, 16.3%).
**Density per square mile:** 188.9.
**President:** Josip Broz (Tito).
**Principal cities** (census 1953): Belgrade (Beograd), 470,172 (capital); Zagreb, 350,-829 (Croat commercial center); Ljubljana, 138,981 (Slovenian industrial center); Sarajevo, 136,283 (Bosnian manufacturing center); Skopje, 122,143 (capital, Macedonia); Subotica, 115,402 (wheat).
**Monetary unit:** Dinar.
**Languages:** Serbo-Croat, Slovene, Macedonian (all official).
**Religions** (est. 1952): Greek Orthodox, 49.6%; Roman Catholic, 36.8%; Moslem, 12.5%; others, 1.1%.

## STATUS IN THE WORLD TODAY

Yugoslavia is every bit as much a Communist dictatorship as any of the Soviet satellites—a one-party state in which monopoly of power is exercised by a handful of men—but it differs from the satellites in one important respect: it has rebelled against the doctrine that Moscow, and Moscow alone, is the true fountainhead of all Communist ideology and has developed its own brand of home-grown communism. As a consequence it has come under heavy propaganda fire from all other Communist countries, including China, for its alleged ideological heresies which impaired the unity of the entire socialist camp. It has in its own way inflicted an embarrassing psychological defeat on the Kremlin by showing the satellites that there is a way to communism which does not demand blind obeisance to Moscow. Tito's independent stand was made possible by a number of factors: Soviet troops were not on Yugoslav soil; a territorial buffer existed between Yugoslavia and the U.S.S.R.; Tito was installed in full command of his country sooner than any other Communist in Eastern Europe and achieved his goals without Soviet assistance. Yugoslavia's expulsion from the Cominform came in 1948 over disagreements with Stalin over purely internal Communist matters. Stalin wanted to infiltrate Tito's party and subordinate it and its policies to direct dictation from Moscow. In 1955, Khrushchev and Bulganin traveled to Belgrade to try to heal the breach, blaming it on the discredited Stalinist policies. But a lasting reconciliation could not be effected.

Tito's present policy is one of studied neutrality. He advocates peace and opposes military blocs, and has entertained and visited with like-minded leaders of Arab and Asian nations, such as Nehru, Nasser, and other lesser potentates. His attitude toward the West can best be described as one of aloof appreciation of services rendered. There is no doubt that he owes his survival after the break with Russia to adequate and timely Western assistance. The United States alone provided him with a total of about $1.5 billion in aid, half economic and half military, while the Soviet Union has proposed postponing for five years promised economic credits valued at $285 million. But in return for vital support from the West Tito has not made any formal commitments for diplomatic, economic, or military cooperation with the West. In the United Nations he has voted with or against the Soviet bloc as warranted by the occasion.

---

HISTORY AND GOVERNMENT. Yugoslavia, fronting on the Adriatic Sea opposite Italy, was formed in 1919 out of some of Europe's oldest trouble spots in the Balkans. After a brief and unstable history of twenty-five years, it emerged from World War II as a Russian satellite.

The 1919 components of Yugoslavia were the old kingdoms of Serbia and Montenegro, and the following: Bosnia-Herzegovina, formerly administered jointly by Austria and Hungary; Croatia-Slavonia, which had had limited autonomy under Hungary; and Slovenia and Dalmatia, formerly administered by Austria.

Alexander I, son of King Peter of Serbia, became the first king of the new country on Aug. 16, 1921. His reign was a rocky one because the Croats, under Dr. Stephen Radić, unceasingly sought autonomy. Finally, a Croat assassinated Alexander in Marseilles, France, in 1934, and since his son Peter was a minor, a regency was set up under Prince Paul, the new King's uncle.

After pursuing an increasingly pro-Axis policy under the regent, Yugoslavia signed the Axis Pact on March 25, 1941; this caused the overthrow of the government two days later. On April 6 the country was invaded by the Nazis and was speedily occupied. While the King and government fled to the Near East and later to London, Yugoslavia was divided into German, Italian, Hungarian, and Bulgarian occupation zones.

Inside Yugoslavia, the Axis occupation was fought by two guerrilla armies—the Chetniks under Draža Mihajlović, who supported the monarchy; and the Partisans under Marshal Tito (Josip Broz), who leaned toward Russia. These two groups fought not only the Germans, but also each other. In November, 1943, Tito established an Executive National Committee of Liberation to act as a provisional government, thus repudiating King Peter.

In the elections of Nov. 11, 1945, Tito's forces won overwhelmingly, partly because the monarchist factions boycotted the balloting. Convening on Nov. 29, the new Assembly abolished the monarchy and set up the Federal People's Republic of Yugoslavia. Tito was Prime Minister, and his government won recognition from Britain and the United States.

The Tito government embarked upon an internal policy of ruthless oppression and elimination of opposition factions, including the summary trial and execution of Mikhailovic in 1946.

Soviet support enabled the nation to secure most of Italian Istria under the 1947 peace treaty, but efforts to secure sovereignty over the key port of Trieste were unsuccessful. Zone B of the former free territory of Trieste was, however, transferred to Yugoslavia in Oct., 1954.

Tito was elected President under the new Constitution on Jan. 14, 1953.

Yugoslavia is a federal republic composed of six units—Serbia (which includes the autonomous province of Vojvodina and the autonomous region of Kosovo-Metohija), Croatia, Slovenia, Bosnia-Herzegovina, Macedonia, and Montenegro. Actual administration is carried on by five State Secretaries responsible to an Executive Council. Control of the country remains with the Yugoslav Communist Party.

ECONOMIC CONDITIONS. Agriculture occupies about 80 per cent of the population. The principal crops are corn, wheat, sugar beets, hemp, hops, opium (in Macedonia), and tobacco (chiefly in Macedonia and Herzegovina). Excellent wines are produced in Dalmatia and Herzegovina and along the Danube.

In 1959 there were 5,038,000 cattle, 11,247,000 sheep, and 5,656,000 hogs.

Manufactures are limited for the most part to consumers' goods. Legislation passed Dec. 5, 1946, nationalized all private economic enterprises, public works and industries in forty-two branches of the national economy, including mining, metallurgy, and all industries which process natural products.

Leading customers in 1959 were West Germany (9%), Italy (12%), and the U.S.S.R. (10%); leading suppliers, the United States and Canada (20%), the U.S.S.R. (8%), West Germany (14%), and other EPU countries (14%). Chief exports in 1958 were copper, sawn timber, and livestock.

NATURAL FEATURES AND RESOURCES. About half of Yugoslavia is mountainous. In the north, the Dinaric Alps rise abruptly from the sea and progress eastward as a barren limestone plateau called the Karst. Montenegro is a jumbled mass of mountains, containing also some grassy slopes and fertile river valleys. Southern Serbia, too, is mountainous. A rich plain in the north and northeast, drained by the Danube, is the most fertile area of the country. The Danube and tributaries—the Drava, Sava, and Morava—in the northeast are the principal rivers.

Yugoslavia is the Balkans' principal mineral producer.

# SPORTS ORGANIZATIONS AND INFORMATION BUREAUS

AMATEUR ATHLETIC UNION OF THE U. S. 233 Broadway, New York 7, N. Y.

AMATEUR FENCERS LEAGUE OF AMERICA. 310 E. 49th St., New York 17, N. Y.

AMATEUR HOCKEY ASSN. OF THE U. S. Madison Square Garden, 307 W. 49th St., New York 19, N. Y.

AMATEUR SKATING UNION OF THE U. S. 512 Physicians and Surgeons Bldg., Minneapolis 2, Minn.

AMATEUR SOFTBALL ASSN. OF AMERICA. Suite 401, 11 Hill St., Newark 2, N. J.

AMATEUR TRAPSHOOTING ASSN. OF AMERICA. Vandalia, Ohio

AMERICAN AMATEUR BASEBALL CONGRESS. Box 44, Battle Creek, Mich.

AMERICAN BADMINTON ASSN. 905 So. Los Robles Ave., Pasadena, Calif.

AMERICAN BOWLING CONGRESS. 1572 E. Capitol Drive, Milwaukee 11, Wis.

AMERICAN CANOE ASSN., 15 Beacon Ave., New Haven, Conn.

AMERICAN FOOTBALL LEAGUE. 1111 Southland Center, Dallas 1, Tex.

AMERICAN HOCKEY LEAGUE. Box 190, Hempstead, N. Y.

AMERICAN HORSE SHOWS ASSN. 40 E. 54th St., New York 22, N. Y.

AMERICAN KENNEL CLUB. 221 Park Ave. So., New York 3, N. Y.

AMERICAN LAWN BOWLING ASSN. 3630-D Carmona Ave., Los Angeles 16, Calif.

AMERICAN LEAGUE (Baseball). 520 Boylston St., Boston 16, Mass.

AMERICAN MOTORCYCLE ASSOCIATION. 5030 No. High St., Columbus 8, Ohio

AMERICAN POWER BOAT ASSN. 2534 St. Aubin Ave., Detroit 7, Mich.

AMERICAN RACING DRIVERS CLUB (midget auto racing). 319 W. 48th St., New York 36, N. Y.

AMERICAN ROQUE LEAGUE, 5439 Vanderbilt Ave., Dallas 6, Texas.

AMERICAN WATER SKI ASSN. 7th St. & Ave. G, S.W., Winter Haven, Fla.

BASEBALL COMMISSIONER FORD C. FRICK. 30 Rockefeller Plaza, New York 20, N. Y.

BILLIARD CONGRESS OF AMERICA. 915 Edison Bldg., Toledo, Ohio.

BOWLING PROPRIETORS' ASSN. OF AMERICA. 111 S. Washington St., Park Ridge, Ill.

EASTERN COLLEGE ATHLETIC CONFERENCE. Hotel Manhattan, 8th Ave. & 45th St., New York 36, N.Y.

ELIAS BASEBALL BUREAU, 11 West 42d St., New York 36.

FIELD HOCKEY ASSN. OF AMERICA, 30 Wall St., New York 5, N. Y.

FISH AND WILDLIFE SERVICE. Dept. of the Interior, Washington 25, D. C.

GREATER NEW YORK RACING ASSN. SERVICE BUREAU, 300 Park Ave., New York 22, N. Y.

INTERNATL. AMATEUR ATHLETIC FEDERATION. Halton House, 23 Holborn, London, E. C. 1, England.

INTERNATIONAL GAME FISH ASSN. Alfred I. duPont Bldg., Miami 32, Fla.

THE JOCKEY CLUB, 300 Park Ave., New York 22, N. Y.

LITTLE LEAGUE BASEBALL. Williamsport, Pa.

NATL. ARCHERY ASSN. OF THE U. S. 20-A Yale Ave., Buffalo 26, N. Y.

NATL. ASSN. OF AMATEUR OARSMEN. 119 Heller Parkway, Newark 4, N. J.

NATL. ASSN. OF ANGLING AND CASTING CLUBS. P. O. Box 51, Nashville 2, Tenn.

NATL. ASSN. OF PROFESSIONAL BASEBALL LEAGUES (Minors). 720 E. Broad St., Columbus 15, Ohio

NATL. ASSN. OF STATE RACING COMMISSIONERS. Box 156, Lexington, Ky.

NATL. BASEBALL CONGRESS. Wichita 1, Kan.

NATL. BASKETBALL ASSN. Empire State Bldg., N. Y. 1

NATL. BOXING ASSN. 402 No. Syracuse St., Hagerstown, Ind.

NATL. COLLEGIATE ATHLETIC ASSN. 206 Fairfax Bldg., Kansas City 5, Mo.

NATL. DUCK PIN BOWLING CONGRESS. 1420 New York Ave., N.W., Washington 5, D. C.

NATL. FIELD ARCHERY ASSN., Rt. 2, Box 514, Redlands, Calif.

NATL. FOOTBALL LEAGUE. One Rockefeller Plaza, New York 20, N. Y.

NATL. HOCKEY LEAGUE. Sun Life Bldg., Montreal, Quebec.

NATL. HORSESHOE PITCHERS ASSN. 341 Polk St., Gary, Ind.

NATL. LEAGUE SERVICE BUREAU (Baseball). Carew Tower, Cincinnati 2, Ohio

NATL. RIFLE ASSN. OF AMERICA. 1600 Rhode Island Ave., Washington 6, D. C.

NATL. SKEET SHOOTING ASSN. 3409 Oak Lawn Ave., Dallas 19, Texas.

NATL. SKI ASSN. 1130-16th St., Denver 2, Colo.

NEW YORK STATE ATHLETIC COMMISSION (Boxing). 226 W. 47th St., New York 36, N. Y.

NORTH AMERICAN YACHT RACING UNION. 37 West 44th St., New York 36, N. Y.

PROFESSIONAL GOLFERS' ASSN. OF AMERICA. Box 277, Dunedin, Fla.

PROFESSIONAL HORSEMEN'S ASSN. 716 Madison Ave., New York City.

RODEO COWBOYS ASSN., 1744 Champa St., Denver 2, Colo

ROLLER SKATING RINK OPERATORS ASSN. OF AMERICA. 625 W. Seven Mile Rd., Detroit 3, Mich.

THOROUGHBRED RACING ASSNS. OF THE U. S. 220 East 42d St., New York 17, N. Y.

U. S. AMATEUR ROLLER SKATING ASSN. 120 West 42d St., New York 18, N. Y.

U. S. CHESS FEDERATION. 80 E. 11th St., New York 3, N. Y.

U. S. FIGURE SKATING ASSN. Rm. 517, 30 Huntington Ave., Boston 16, Mass.

U. S. GOLF ASSN. 40 E. 38th St., New York 16, N. Y.

U. S. HANDBALL ASSN. 505 No. Michigan Ave., Chicago 11.

U. S. LAWN TENNIS ASSN. 120 Broadway, New York 5, N. Y.

U. S. OLYMPIC ASSN. Olympic House, 57 Park Ave., New York 16, N. Y.

U. S. POLO ASSN. 250 Park Ave., New York 17, N. Y.

U. S. PROFESSIONAL LAWN TENNIS ASSN., 37 Wall St., New York 5, N. Y.

U. S. SOCCER FOOTBALL ASSN. 320 Fifth Ave., New York 1.

U. S. SQUASH RACQUETS ASSN. 1201 Genesee Bldg., Buffalo 2, N. Y.

U. S. TABLE TENNIS ASSN. 210 Saturn Drive, North Star, R.F.D. 3, Newark, Del.

U. S. TROTTING ASSN. P.O. Box 2058, Main Post Office, Columbus 16, Ohio

U. S. VOLLEYBALL ASSN. Rm. 1705, 291 Broadway, New York 7, N. Y.

WESTERN HOCKEY LEAGUE. Grosvenor House, 500 Wall St., Seattle 1, Wash.

WOMAN'S INTERNATIONAL BOWLING CONGRESS. 1225 Dublin Rd., Columbus 8, Ohio.

# SPORTS

> For 1961 sports champions and records, see special section beginning on Page 857.

## BASEBALL

THE POPULAR TRADITION that baseball was invented by Abner Doubleday at Cooperstown, N. Y., in 1839, has been enshrined in the Hall of Fame and National Museum of Baseball erected in that town, but research has proved that a game called "Base Ball" was played in this country and England before 1839. However, the first team baseball as we know it was played at the Elysian Fields, Hoboken, N. J., on June 19, 1846, between the Knickerbockers and the New York Nine. There was a gradual growth of baseball and an improvement of equipment and playing skill in the next fifty years. Soldiers returning home from the Civil War spread over the country the game they had learned to play in camp.

Historians have it that the first pitcher to throw a curve was William A. (Candy) Cummings in 1867. The Cincinnati Red Stockings were the first all-professional team and in 1869 they played 64 games without a loss. The standard ball of the same size and weight, still the rule, was adopted in 1872. The first catcher's mask was worn in 1875. The National League was organized in 1876. The first chest protector was donned in 1885. The three-strike rule was put on the books in 1887 and the four-ball ticket to first base came in 1889. The pitching distance, formerly shorter, was lengthened to 60 feet 6 inches in 1893 and the rules have been only slightly modified since that time.

The American League, under the vigorous leadership of B. B. Johnson, blossomed forth as a major league in 1901. Judge Kenesaw Mountain Landis, by action of the two major leagues, became Commissioner of Baseball in 1921 and, upon his death (1944), Albert B. Chandler, former United States Senator from Kentucky, was elected to that office (1945). Chandler failed to obtain a new contract, and he was succeeded by Ford C. Frick (1951), the National League president.

---

### PROFESSIONAL BASEBALL GOVERNMENT
#### NATIONAL LEAGUE—AMERICAN LEAGUE—NATIONAL ASSOCIATION

Ford C. Frick, Commissioner
Charles M. Segar, Secretary-Treasurer
30 Rockefeller Plaza, New York 20, N. Y.

#### NATIONAL LEAGUE

Warren C. Giles
President-Treasurer
Office: 2601 Carew Tower,
Cincinnati 2, Ohio
Service Bureau: Dave Grote, Manager

#### AMERICAN LEAGUE

Joseph E. Cronin
President-Secretary-Treasurer
Office: 520 Boylston St.,
Boston 16, Mass.
Public Relations: Joseph W. McKenney, Director

#### NATIONAL ASSOCIATION

George M. Trautman
President-Treasurer
Carl Lundquist
Director of Public Relations
720 East Broad St., Columbus 15, Ohio

775

# Baseball Statistics

*Source: The Little Red Book of Baseball*, published by The Elias Baseball Bureau, New York City.

## Record of World Series Games

Figures in parentheses indicate number of victories for each club. Pitchers named are winner and loser, respectively.

### 1903—BOSTON A. L. (5) vs. PITTSBURGH N. L. (3)

Managers—Jimmy Collins, Boston; Fred Clarke, Pittsburgh

| | | | | | |
|---|---|---|---|---|---|
| Oct. 1—Pittsburgh (Phillippe) | 7 | Boston (Young) | 3 | At Boston |
| Oct. 2—Boston (Dinneen) | 3 | Pittsburgh (Leever) | 0 | At Boston |
| Oct. 3—Pittsburgh (Phillippe) | 4 | Boston (Hughes) | 2 | At Boston |
| Oct. 6—Pittsburgh (Phillippe) | 5 | Boston (Dinneen) | 4 | At Pittsburgh |
| Oct. 7—Boston (Young) | 11 | Pittsburgh (Kennedy) | 2 | At Pittsburgh |
| Oct. 8—Boston (Dinneen) | 6 | Pittsburgh (Leever) | 3 | At Pittsburgh |
| Oct. 10—Boston (Young) | 7 | Pittsburgh (Phillippe) | 3 | At Pittsburgh |
| Oct. 13—Boston (Dinneen) | 3 | Pittsburgh (Phillippe) | 0 | At Boston |

### 1904—No Series

### 1905—NEW YORK N. L. (4) vs. PHILADELPHIA A. L. (1)

Managers—John J. McGraw, New York; Connie Mack, Philadelphia.

| | | | | | |
|---|---|---|---|---|---|
| Oct. 9—New York (Mathewson) | 3 | Philadelphia (Plank) | 0 | At Philadelphia |
| Oct. 10—Philadelphia (Bender) | 3 | New York (McGinnity) | 0 | At New York |
| Oct. 12—New York (Mathewson) | 9 | Philadelphia (Coakley) | 0 | At Philadelphia |
| Oct. 13—New York (McGinnity) | 1 | Philadelphia (Plank) | 0 | At New York |
| Oct. 14—New York (Mathewson) | 2 | Philadelphia (Bender) | 0 | At New York |

### 1906—CHICAGO A. L. (4) vs. CHICAGO N. L. (2)

Managers—Fielder Jones, Chicago A. L.; Frank L. Chance, Chicago N. L.

| | | | | | |
|---|---|---|---|---|---|
| Oct. 9—Chicago A (Altrock) | 2 | Chicago N (Brown) | 1 | At West Side Park |
| Oct. 10—Chicago N (Reulbach) | 7 | Chicago A (White) | 1 | At Comiskey Park |
| Oct. 11—Chicago A (Walsh) | 3 | Chicago N (Pfiester) | 0 | At West Side Park |
| Oct. 12—Chicago N (Brown) | 1 | Chicago A (Altrock) | 0 | At Comiskey Park |
| Oct. 13—Chicago A (Walsh) | 8 | Chicago N (Pfiester) | 6 | At West Side Park |
| Oct. 14—Chicago A (White) | 8 | Chicago N (Brown) | 3 | At Comiskey Park |

### 1907—CHICAGO N. L. (4) vs. DETROIT A. L. (0)

Managers—Frank L. Chance, Chicago; Hugh Jennings, Detroit.

| | | | | | |
|---|---|---|---|---|---|
| Oct. 8—Chicago (tie) | 3 | Detroit (tie) | 3 | At Chicago (12 inn.) |
| Oct. 9—Chicago (Pfiester) | 3 | Detroit (Mullin) | 1 | At Chicago |
| Oct. 10—Chicago (Reulbach) | 5 | Detroit (Siever) | 1 | At Chicago |
| Oct. 11—Chicago (Overall) | 6 | Detroit (Donovan) | 1 | At Detroit |
| Oct. 12—Chicago (Brown) | 2 | Detroit (Mullin) | 0 | At Detroit |

### 1908—CHICAGO N. L. (4) vs. DETROIT A. L. (1)

Managers—Frank L. Chance, Chicago; Hugh Jennings, Detroit.

| | | | | | |
|---|---|---|---|---|---|
| Oct. 10—Chicago (Brown) | 10 | Detroit (Summers) | 6 | At Detroit |
| Oct. 11—Chicago (Overall) | 6 | Detroit (Donovan) | 1 | At Chicago |
| Oct. 12—Detroit (Mullin) | 8 | Chicago (Pfiester) | 3 | At Chicago |
| Oct. 13—Chicago (Brown) | 3 | Detroit (Summers) | 0 | At Detroit |
| Oct. 14—Chicago (Overall) | 2 | Detroit (Donovan) | 0 | At Detroit |

### 1909—PITTSBURGH N. L. (4) vs. DETROIT A. L. (3)

Managers—Fred Clarke, Pittsburgh; Hugh Jennings, Detroit.

| | | | | | |
|---|---|---|---|---|---|
| Oct. 8—Pittsburgh (Adams) | 4 | Detroit (Mullin) | 1 | At Pittsburgh |
| Oct. 9—Detroit (Donovan) | 7 | Pittsburgh (Camnitz) | 2 | At Pittsburgh |
| Oct. 11—Pittsburgh (Maddox) | 8 | Detroit (Summers) | 6 | At Detroit |
| Oct. 12—Detroit (Mullin) | 5 | Pittsburgh (Leifield) | 0 | At Detroit |
| Oct. 13—Pittsburgh (Adams) | 8 | Detroit (Summers) | 4 | At Pittsburgh |
| Oct. 14—Detroit (Mullin) | 5 | Pittsburgh (Willis) | 4 | At Detroit |
| Oct. 16—Pittsburgh (Adams) | 8 | Detroit (Donovan) | 0 | At Detroit |

### 1910—PHILADELPHIA A. L. (4) vs. CHICAGO N. L. (1)

Managers—Connie Mack, Philadelphia; Frank L. Chance, Chicago.

| | | | | |
|---|---|---|---|---|
| Oct. 17—Philadelphia (Bender) | 4 | Chicago (Overall) | 1 | At Philadelphia |
| Oct. 18—Philadelphia (Coombs) | 9 | Chicago (Brown) | 3 | At Philadelphia |
| Oct. 20—Philadelphia (Coombs) | 12 | Chicago (McIntire) | 5 | At Chicago |
| Oct. 22—Chicago (Brown) | 4 | Philadelphia (Bender) | 3 | At Chicago (10 inn.) |
| Oct. 23—Philadelphia (Coombs) | 7 | Chicago (Brown) | 2 | At Chicago |

### 1911—PHILADELPHIA A. L. (4) vs. NEW YORK N. L. (2)

Managers—Connie Mack, Philadelphia; John J. McGraw, New York.

| | | | | |
|---|---|---|---|---|
| Oct. 14—New York (Mathewson) | 2 | Philadelphia (Bender) | 1 | At New York |
| Oct. 16—Philadelphia (Plank) | 3 | New York (Marquard) | 1 | At Philadelphia |
| Oct. 17—Philadelphia (Coombs) | 3 | New York (Mathewson) | 2 | At New York (11 inn.) |
| Oct. 24—Philadelphia (Bender) | 4 | New York (Mathewson) | 2 | At Philadelphia |
| Oct. 25—New York (Crandall) | 4 | Philadelphia (Plank) | 3 | At New York (10 inn.) |
| Oct. 26—Philadelphia (Bender) | 13 | New York (Ames) | 2 | At Philadelphia |

### 1912—BOSTON A. L. (4) vs. NEW YORK N. L. (3)

Managers—J. Garland Stahl, Boston; John J. McGraw, New York.

| | | | | |
|---|---|---|---|---|
| Oct. 8—Boston (Wood) | 4 | New York (Tesreau) | 3 | At New York |
| Oct. 9—Boston (tie) | 6 | New York (tie) | 6 | At Boston (11 inn.) |
| Oct. 10—New York (Marquard) | 2 | Boston (O'Brien) | 1 | At Boston |
| Oct. 11—Boston (Wood) | 3 | New York (Tesreau) | 1 | At New York |
| Oct. 12—Boston (Bedient) | 2 | New York (Mathewson) | 1 | At Boston |
| Oct. 14—New York (Marquard) | 5 | Boston (O'Brien) | 2 | At New York |
| Oct. 15—New York (Tesreau) | 11 | Boston (Wood) | 4 | At Boston |
| Oct. 16—Boston (Wood) | 3 | New York (Mathewson) | 2 | At Boston (10 inn.) |

### 1913—PHILADELPHIA A. L. (4) vs. NEW YORK N. L. (1)

Managers—Connie Mack, Philadelphia; John J. McGraw, New York.

| | | | | |
|---|---|---|---|---|
| Oct. 7—Philadelphia (Bender) | 6 | New York (Marquard) | 4 | At New York |
| Oct. 8—New York (Mathewson) | 3 | Philadelphia (Plank) | 0 | At Philadelphia (10 inn.) |
| Oct. 9—Philadelphia (Bush) | 8 | New York (Tesreau) | 2 | At New York |
| Oct. 10—Philadelphia (Bender) | 6 | New York (Demaree) | 5 | At Philadelphia |
| Oct. 11—Philadelphia (Plank) | 3 | New York (Mathewson) | 1 | At New York |

### 1914—BOSTON N. L. (4) vs. PHILADELPHIA A. L. (0)

Managers—George T. Stallings, Boston; Connie Mack, Philadelphia.

| | | | | |
|---|---|---|---|---|
| Oct. 9—Boston (Rudolph) | 7 | Philadelphia (Bender) | 1 | At Philadelphia |
| Oct. 10—Boston (James) | 1 | Philadelphia (Plank) | 0 | At Philadelphia |
| Oct. 12—Boston (James) | 5 | Philadelphia (Bush) | 4 | At Boston (12 inn.) |
| Oct. 13—Boston (Rudolph) | 3 | Philadelphia (Shawkey) | 1 | At Boston |

### 1915—BOSTON A. L. (4) vs. PHILADELPHIA N. L. (1)

Managers—William Carrigan, Boston; Patrick J. Moran, Philadelphia.

| | | | | |
|---|---|---|---|---|
| Oct. 8—Philadelphia (Alexander) | 3 | Boston (Shore) | 1 | At Philadelphia |
| Oct. 9—Boston (Foster) | 2 | Philadelphia (Mayer) | 1 | At Philadelphia |
| Oct. 11—Boston (Leonard) | 2 | Philadelphia (Alexander) | 1 | At Boston |
| Oct. 12—Boston (Shore) | 2 | Philadelphia (Chalmers) | 1 | At Boston |
| Oct. 13—Boston (Foster) | 5 | Philadelphia (Rixey) | 4 | At Philadelphia |

### 1916—BOSTON A. L. (4) vs. BROOKLYN N. L. (1)

Managers—William Carrigan, Boston; Wilbert J. Robinson, Brooklyn.

| | | | | |
|---|---|---|---|---|
| Oct. 7—Boston (Shore) | 6 | Brooklyn (Marquard) | 5 | At Boston |
| Oct. 9—Boston (Ruth) | 2 | Brooklyn (Smith) | 1 | At Boston (14 inn.) |
| Oct. 10—Brooklyn (Coombs) | 4 | Boston (Mays) | 3 | At Brooklyn |
| Oct. 11—Boston (Leonard) | 6 | Brooklyn (Marquard) | 2 | At Brooklyn |
| Oct. 12—Boston (Shore) | 4 | Brooklyn (Pfeffer) | 1 | At Boston |

### 1917—CHICAGO A. L. (4) NEW YORK N. L. (2)

Managers—Clarence H. Rowland, Chicago; John J. McGraw, New York.

| | | | | |
|---|---|---|---|---|
| Oct. 6—Chicago (Cicotte) | 2 | New York (Sallee) | 1 | At Chicago |
| Oct. 7—Chicago (Faber) | 7 | New York (Anderson) | 2 | At Chicago |
| Oct. 10—New York (Benton) | 2 | Chicago (Cicotte) | 0 | At New York |
| Oct. 11—New York (Schupp) | 5 | Chicago (Faber) | 0 | At New York |
| Oct. 13—Chicago (Faber) | 8 | New York (Sallee) | 5 | At Chicago |
| Oct. 15—Chicago (Faber) | 4 | New York (Benton) | 2 | At New York |

## 1918—BOSTON A. L. (4) vs. CHICAGO N. L. (2)

Managers—Ed Barrow, Boston; Fred Mitchell, Chicago.

| | | | | |
|---|---|---|---|---|
| Sept. 5—Boston (Ruth) | 1 | Chicago (Vaughn) | 0 | At Chicago |
| Sept. 6—Chicago (Tyler) | 3 | Boston (Bush) | 1 | At Chicago |
| Sept. 7—Boston (Mays) | 2 | Chicago (Vaughn) | 1 | At Chicago |
| Sept. 9—Boston (Ruth) | 3 | Chicago (Douglas) | 2 | At Boston |
| Sept. 10—Chicago (Vaughn) | 3 | Boston (Jones) | 0 | At Boston |
| Sept. 11—Boston (Mays) | 2 | Chicago (Tyler) | 1 | At Boston |

## 1919—CINCINNATI N. L. (5) vs. CHICAGO A. L. (3)

Managers—Patrick J. Moran, Cincinnati; William Gleason, Chicago.

| | | | | |
|---|---|---|---|---|
| Oct. 1—Cincinnati (Ruether) | 9 | Chicago (Cicotte) | 1 | At Cincinnati |
| Oct. 2—Cincinnati (Sallee) | 4 | Chicago (Williams) | 2 | At Cincinnati |
| Oct. 3—Chicago (Kerr) | 3 | Cincinnati (Fisher) | 0 | At Chicago |
| Oct. 4—Cincinnati (Ring) | 2 | Chicago (Cicotte) | 0 | At Chicago |
| Oct. 6—Cincinnati (Eller) | 5 | Chicago (Williams) | 0 | At Chicago |
| Oct. 7—Chicago (Kerr) | 5 | Cincinnati (Ring) | 4 | At Cincinnati |
| Oct. 8—Chicago (Cicotte) | 4 | Cincinnati (Sallee) | 1 | At Cincinnati |
| Oct. 9—Cincinnati (Eller) | 10 | Chicago (Williams) | 5 | At Chicago (10 inn.) |

## 1920—CLEVELAND A. L. (5) vs. BROOKLYN N. L. (2)

Managers—Tris Speaker, Cleveland; Wilbert J. Robinson Brooklyn.

| | | | | |
|---|---|---|---|---|
| Oct. 5—Cleveland (Coveleskie) | 3 | Brooklyn (Marquard) | 1 | At Brooklyn |
| Oct. 6—Brooklyn (Grimes) | 3 | Cleveland (Bagby) | 0 | At Brooklyn |
| Oct. 7—Brooklyn (Smith) | 2 | Cleveland (Caldwell) | 1 | At Brooklyn |
| Oct. 9—Cleveland (Coveleskie) | 5 | Brooklyn (Cadore) | 1 | At Cleveland |
| Oct. 10—Cleveland (Bagby) | 8 | Brooklyn (Grimes) | 1 | At Cleveland |
| Oct. 11—Cleveland (Mails) | 1 | Brooklyn (Smith) | 0 | At Cleveland |
| Oct. 12—Cleveland (Coveleskie) | 3 | Brooklyn (Grimes) | 0 | At Cleveland |

## 1921—NEW YORK N. L. (5) vs. NEW YORK A. L. (3)

Managers—John J. McGraw, New York N. L.; Miller J. Huggins, New York A. L.

| | | | | |
|---|---|---|---|---|
| Oct. 5—New York A (Mays) | 3 | New York N (Nehf) | 0 | At Polo Grounds |
| Oct. 6—New York A (Hoyt) | 3 | New York N (Douglas) | 0 | At Polo Grounds |
| Oct. 7—New York N (Barnes) | 13 | New York A (Quinn) | 5 | At Polo Grounds |
| Oct. 9—New York N (Douglas) | 4 | New York A (Mays) | 2 | At Polo Grounds |
| Oct. 10—New York A (Hoyt) | 3 | New York N (Nehf) | 1 | At Polo Grounds |
| Oct. 11—New York N (Barnes) | 8 | New York A (Shawkey) | 5 | At Polo Grounds |
| Oct. 12—New York N (Douglas) | 2 | New York A (Mays) | 1 | At Polo Grounds |
| Oct. 13—New York N (Nehf) | 1 | New York A (Hoyt) | 0 | At Polo Grounds |

## 1922—NEW YORK N. L. (4) vs. NEW YORK A. L. (0)

Managers—John J. McGraw, New York N. L.; Miller J. Huggins, New York A. L.

| | | | | |
|---|---|---|---|---|
| Oct. 4—New York N (Ryan) | 3 | New York A (Bush) | 2 | At Polo Grounds |
| Oct. 5—New York N (tie) | 3 | New York A (tie) | 3 | At Polo Grounds (10 inn.) |
| Oct. 6—New York N (Scott) | 3 | New York A (Hoyt) | 0 | At Polo Grounds |
| Oct. 7—New York N (McQuillan) | 4 | New York A (Mays) | 3 | At Polo Grounds |
| Oct. 8—New York N (Nehf) | 5 | New York A (Bush) | 3 | At Polo Grounds |

## 1923—NEW YORK A. L. (4) vs. NEW YORK N. L. (2)

Managers—Miller J. Huggins, New York A. L.; John J. McGraw, New York N. L.

| | | | | |
|---|---|---|---|---|
| Oct. 10—New York N (Ryan) | 5 | New York A (Bush) | 4 | At Yankee Stadium |
| Oct. 11—New York A (Pennock) | 4 | New York N (McQuillan) | 2 | At Polo Grounds |
| Oct. 12—New York N (Nehf) | 1 | New York A (Jones) | 0 | At Yankee Stadium |
| Oct. 13—New York A (Shawkey) | 8 | New York N (Scott) | 4 | At Polo Grounds |
| Oct. 14—New York A (Bush) | 8 | New York N (Bentley) | 1 | At Yankee Stadium |
| Oct. 15—New York A (Pennock) | 6 | New York N (Nehf) | 4 | At Polo Grounds |

## 1924—WASHINGTON A. L. (4) vs. NEW YORK N. L. (3)

Managers—Stanley R. Harris, Washington; John J. McGraw, New York.

| | | | | |
|---|---|---|---|---|
| Oct. 4—New York (Nehf) | 4 | Washington (Johnson) | 3 | At Washington (12 inn ) |
| Oct. 5—Washington (Zachary) | 4 | New York (Bentley) | 3 | At Washington |
| Oct 6—New York (McQuillan) | 6 | Washington (Marberry) | 4 | At New York |
| Oct. 7—Washington (Mogridge) | 7 | New York (Barnes) | 4 | At New York |
| Oct. 8—New York (Bentley) | 6 | Washington (Johnson) | 2 | At New York |
| Oct. 9—Washington (Zachary) | 2 | New York (Nehf) | 1 | At Washington |
| Oct. 10—Washington (Johnson) | 4 | New York (Bentley) | 3 | At Washington (12 inn.) |

### 1925—PITTSBURGH N. L. (4) vs. WASHINGTON A. L. (3)

Managers—William B. McKechnie, Pittsburgh; Stanley R. Harris, Washington.

| | | | | |
|---|---|---|---|---|
| Oct. 7—Washington (Johnson) | 4 | Pittsburgh (Meadows) | 1 | At Pittsburgh |
| Oct. 8—Pittsburgh (Aldridge) | 3 | Washington (Coveleskie) | 2 | At Pittsburgh |
| Oct. 10—Washington (Ferguson) | 4 | Pittsburgh (Kremer) | 3 | At Washington |
| Oct. 11—Washington (Johnson) | 4 | Pittsburgh (Yde) | 0 | At Washington |
| Oct. 12—Pittsburgh (Aldridge) | 6 | Washington (Coveleskie) | 3 | At Washington |
| Oct. 13—Pittsburgh (Kremer) | 3 | Washington (Ferguson) | 2 | At Pittsburgh |
| Oct. 15—Pittsburgh (Kremer) | 9 | Washington (Johnson) | 7 | At Pittsburgh |

### 1926—ST. LOUIS N. L. (4) vs. NEW YORK A. L. (3)

Managers—Rogers Hornsby, St. Louis; Miller J. Huggins, New York.

| | | | | |
|---|---|---|---|---|
| Oct. 2—New York (Pennock) | 2 | St. Louis (Sherdel) | 1 | At New York |
| Oct. 3—St. Louis (Alexander) | 6 | New York (Shocker) | 2 | At New York |
| Oct. 5—St. Louis (Haines) | 4 | New York (Ruether) | 0 | At St. Louis |
| Oct. 6—New York (Hoyt) | 10 | St. Louis (Reinhart) | 5 | At St. Louis |
| Oct. 7—New York (Pennock) | 3 | St. Louis (Sherdel) | 2 | At St. Louis (10 inn.) |
| Oct. 9—St. Louis (Alexander) | 10 | New York (Shawkey) | 2 | At New York |
| Oct. 10—St. Louis (Haines) | 3 | New York (Hoyt) | 2 | At New York |

### 1927—NEW YORK A. L. (4) vs. PITTSBURGH N. L. (0)

Managers—Miller J. Huggins, New York; Donie Bush, Pittsburgh.

| | | | | |
|---|---|---|---|---|
| Oct. 5—New York (Hoyt) | 5 | Pittsburgh (Kremer) | 4 | At Pittsburgh |
| Oct. 6—New York (Pipgras) | 6 | Pittsburgh (Aldridge) | 2 | At Pittsburgh |
| Oct. 7—New York (Pennock) | 8 | Pittsburgh (Meadows) | 1 | At New York |
| Oct. 8—New York (Moore) | 4 | Pittsburgh (Miljus) | 3 | At New York |

### 1928—NEW YORK A. L. (4) vs. ST. LOUIS N. L. (0)

Managers—Miller J. Huggins, New York; William B. McKechnie, St. Louis

| | | | | |
|---|---|---|---|---|
| Oct. 4—New York (Hoyt) | 4 | St. Louis (Sherdel) | 1 | At New York |
| Oct. 5—New York (Pipgras) | 9 | St. Louis (Alexander) | 3 | At New York |
| Oct. 7—New York (Zachary) | 7 | St. Louis (Haines) | 3 | At St. Louis |
| Oct. 9—New York (Hoyt) | 7 | St. Louis (Sherdel) | 3 | At St. Louis |

### 1929—PHILADELPHIA A. L. (4) vs. CHICAGO N. L. (1)

Managers—Connie Mack, Philadelphia; Joseph V. McCarthy, Chicago.

| | | | | |
|---|---|---|---|---|
| Oct. 8—Philadelphia (Ehmke) | 3 | Chicago (Root) | 1 | At Chicago |
| Oct. 9—Philadelphia (Earnshaw) | 9 | Chicago (Malone) | 3 | At Chicago |
| Oct. 11—Chicago (Bush) | 3 | Philadelphia (Earnshaw) | 1 | At Philadelphia |
| Oct. 12—Philadelphia (Rommel) | 10 | Chicago (Blake) | 8 | At Philadelphia |
| Oct. 14—Philadelphia (Walberg) | 3 | Chicago (Malone) | 2 | At Philadelphia |

### 1930—PHILADELPHIA A. L. (4) vs. ST. LOUIS N. L. (2)

Managers—Connie Mack, Philadelphia; Gabby Street, St. Louis.

| | | | | |
|---|---|---|---|---|
| Oct. 1—Philadelphia (Grove) | 5 | St. Louis (Grimes) | 2 | At Philadelphia |
| Oct. 2—Philadelphia (Earnshaw) | 6 | St. Louis (Rhem) | 1 | At Philadelphia |
| Oct. 4—St. Louis (Hallahan) | 5 | Philadelphia (Walberg) | 0 | At St. Louis |
| Oct. 5—St. Louis (Haines) | 3 | Philadelphia (Grove) | 1 | At St. Louis |
| Oct. 6—Philadelphia (Grove) | 2 | St. Louis (Grimes) | 0 | At St. Louis |
| Oct. 8—Philadelphia (Earnshaw) | 8 | St. Louis (Hallahan) | 1 | At Philadelphia |

### 1931—ST. LOUIS N. L. (4) vs. PHILADELPHIA A. L. (3)

Managers—Gabby Street, St. Louis; Connie Mack, Philadelphia.

| | | | | |
|---|---|---|---|---|
| Oct. 1—Philadelphia (Grove) | 6 | St. Louis (Derringer) | 2 | At St. Louis |
| Oct. 2—St. Louis (Hallahan) | 2 | Philadelphia (Earnshaw) | 0 | At St. Louis |
| Oct. 5—St. Louis (Grimes) | 5 | Philadelphia (Grove) | 2 | At Philadelphia |
| Oct. 6—Philadelphia (Earnshaw) | 3 | St. Louis (Johnson) | 0 | At Philadelphia |
| Oct. 7—St. Louis (Hallahan) | 5 | Philadelphia (Hoyt) | 1 | At Philadelphia |
| Oct. 9—Philadelphia (Grove) | 8 | St. Louis (Derringer) | 1 | At St. Louis |
| Oct. 10—St. Louis (Grimes) | 4 | Philadelphia (Earnshaw) | 2 | At St. Louis |

### 1932—NEW YORK A. L. (4) vs. CHICAGO N. L. (0)

Managers—Joseph V. McCarthy, New York; Charles J. Grimm, Chicago.

| | | | | |
|---|---|---|---|---|
| Sept. 28—New York (Ruffing) | 12 | Chicago (Bush) | 6 | At New York |
| Sept. 29—New York (Gomez) | 5 | Chicago (Warneke) | 2 | At New York |
| Oct. 1—New York (Pipgras) | 7 | Chicago (Root) | 5 | At Chicago |
| Oct. 2—New York (Moore) | 13 | Chicago (May) | 6 | At Chicago |

## 1933—NEW YORK N. L. (4) vs. WASHINGTON A. L. (1)

Managers—William H. Terry, New York; Joseph E. Cronin, Washington.

| | | | | |
|---|---|---|---|---|
| Oct. 3—New York (Hubbell) | 4 | Washington (Stewart) | 2 | At New York |
| Oct. 4—New York (Schumacher) | 6 | Washington (Crowder) | 1 | At New York |
| Oct. 5—Washington (Whitehill) | 4 | New York (Fitzsimmons) | 0 | At Washington |
| Oct. 6—New York (Hubbell) | 2 | Washington (Weaver) | 1 | At Washington (11 inn.) |
| Oct. 7—New York (Luque) | 4 | Washington (Russell) | 3 | At Washington (10 inn.) |

## 1934—ST. LOUIS N. L. (4) vs. DETROIT A. L. (3)

Managers—Frank F. Frisch, St. Louis; Gordon S. Cochrane, Detroit.

| | | | | |
|---|---|---|---|---|
| Oct. 3—St. Louis (J. Dean) | 8 | Detroit (Crowder) | 3 | At Detroit |
| Oct. 4—Detroit (Rowe) | 3 | St. Louis (W. Walker) | 2 | At Detroit (12 inn.) |
| Oct. 5—St. Louis (P. Dean) | 4 | Detroit (Bridges) | 1 | At St. Louis |
| Oct. 6—Detroit (Auker) | 10 | St. Louis (W. Walker) | 4 | At St. Louis |
| Oct. 7—Detroit (Bridges) | 3 | St. Louis (J. Dean) | 1 | At St. Louis |
| Oct. 8—St. Louis (P. Dean) | 4 | Detroit (Rowe) | 3 | At Detroit |
| Oct. 9—St. Louis (J. Dean) | 11 | Detroit (Auker) | 0 | At Detroit |

## 1935—DETROIT A. L. (4) vs. CHICAGO N. L. (2)

Managers—Gordon S. Cochrane, Detroit; Charles J. Grimm, Chicago.

| | | | | |
|---|---|---|---|---|
| Oct. 2—Chicago (Warneke) | 3 | Detroit (Rowe) | 0 | At Detroit |
| Oct. 3—Detroit (Bridges) | 8 | Chicago (Root) | 3 | At Detroit |
| Oct. 4—Detroit (Rowe) | 6 | Chicago (French) | 5 | At Chicago (11 inn.) |
| Oct. 5—Detroit (Crowder) | 2 | Chicago (Carleton) | 1 | At Chicago |
| Oct. 6—Chicago (Warneke) | 3 | Detroit (Rowe) | 1 | At Chicago |
| Oct. 7—Detroit (Bridges) | 4 | Chicago (French) | 3 | At Detroit |

## 1936—NEW YORK A. L. (4) vs. NEW YORK N. L. (2)

Managers—Joseph V. McCarthy, New York A. L.; William H. Terry, New York N. L.

| | | | | |
|---|---|---|---|---|
| Sept. 30—New York N (Hubbell) | 6 | New York A (Ruffing) | 1 | At Polo Grounds |
| Oct. 2—New York A (Gomez) | 18 | New York N (Schumacher) | 4 | At Polo Grounds |
| Oct. 3—New York A (Hadley) | 2 | New York N (Fitzsimmons) | 1 | At Yankee Stadium |
| Oct. 4—New York A (Pearson) | 5 | New York N (Hubbell) | 2 | At Yankee Stadium |
| Oct. 5—New York N (Schumacher) | 5 | New York A (Malone) | 4 | At Yankee Stadium (10 inn.) |
| Oct. 6—New York A (Gomez) | 13 | New York N (Fitzsimmons) | 5 | At Polo Grounds |

## 1937—NEW YORK A. L. (4) vs. NEW YORK N. L. (1)

Managers—Joseph V. McCarthy, New York A. L.; William H. Terry, New York N. L.

| | | | | |
|---|---|---|---|---|
| Oct. 6—New York A (Gomez) | 8 | New York N (Hubbell) | 1 | At Yankee Stadium |
| Oct. 7—New York A (Ruffing) | 8 | New Nork N (Melton) | 1 | At Yankee Stadium |
| Oct. 8—New York A (Pearson) | 5 | New York N (Schumacher) | 1 | At Polo Grounds |
| Oct. 9—New York N (Hubbell) | 7 | New York A (Hadley) | 3 | At Polo Grounds |
| Oct. 10—New York A (Gomez) | 4 | New York N (Melton) | 2 | At Polo Grounds |

## 1938—NEW YORK A. L. (4) vs. CHICAGO N. L. (0)

Managers—Joseph V. McCarthy, New York; Gabby Hartnett, Chicago.

| | | | | |
|---|---|---|---|---|
| Oct. 5—New York (Ruffing) | 3 | Chicago (Lee) | 1 | At Chicago |
| Oct. 6—New York (Gomez) | 6 | Chicago (Dean) | 3 | At Chicago |
| Oct. 8—New York (Pearson) | 5 | Chicago (Bryant) | 2 | At New York |
| Oct. 9—New York (Ruffing) | 8 | Chicago (Lee) | 3 | At New York |

## 1939—NEW YORK A. L. (4) vs. CINCINNATI N. L. (0)

Managers—Joseph V. McCarthy, New York; William B. McKechnie, Cincinnati.

| | | | | |
|---|---|---|---|---|
| Oct. 4—New York (Ruffing) | 2 | Cincinnati (Derringer) | 1 | At New York |
| Oct. 5—New York (Pearson) | 4 | Cincinnati (Walters) | 0 | At New York |
| Oct. 7—New York (Hadley) | 7 | Cincinnati (Thompson) | 3 | At Cincinnati |
| Oct. 8—New York (Murphy) | 7 | Cincinnati (Walters) | 4 | At Cincinnati (10 inn.) |

## 1940—CINCINNATI N. L. (4) vs. DETROIT A. L. (3)

Managers—William B. McKechnie, Cincinnati; Del Baker, Detroit.

| | | | | |
|---|---|---|---|---|
| Oct. 2—Detroit (Newsom) | 7 | Cincinnati (Derringer) | 2 | At Cincinnati |
| Oct. 3—Cincinnati (Walters) | 5 | Detroit (Rowe) | 3 | At Cincinnati |
| Oct. 4—Detroit (Bridges) | 7 | Cincinnati (Turner) | 4 | At Detroit |
| Oct. 5—Cincinnati (Derringer) | 5 | Detroit (Trout) | 2 | At Detroit |
| Oct. 6—Detroit (Newsom) | 8 | Cincinnati (Thompson) | 0 | At Detroit |
| Oct. 7—Cincinnati (Walters) | 4 | Detroit (Rowe) | 0 | At Cincinnati |
| Oct. 8—Cincinnati (Derringer) | 2 | Detroit (Newsom) | 1 | At Cincinnati |

## 1941—NEW YORK A. L. (4) vs. BROOKLYN N. L. (1)

Managers—Joseph V. McCarthy, New York; Leo E. Durocher, Brooklyn.

| | | | | |
|---|---|---|---|---|
| Oct. 1—New York (Ruffing) | 3 | Brooklyn (Davis) | 2 | At New York |
| Oct. 2—Brooklyn (Wyatt) | 3 | New York (Chandler) | 2 | At New York |
| Oct. 4—New York (Russo) | 2 | Brooklyn (Casey) | 1 | At Brooklyn |
| Oct. 5—New York (Murphy) | 7 | Brooklyn (Casey) | 4 | At Brooklyn |
| Oct. 6—New York (Bonham) | 3 | Brooklyn (Wyatt) | 1 | At Brooklyn |

## 1942—ST. LOUIS N. L. (4) vs. NEW YORK A. L. (1)

Managers—William Southworth, St. Louis; Joseph V. McCarthy, New York.

| | | | | |
|---|---|---|---|---|
| Sept. 30—New York (Ruffing) | 7 | St. Louis (M. Cooper) | 4 | At St. Louis |
| Oct.  1—St. Louis (Beazley) | 4 | New York (Bonham) | 3 | At St. Louis |
| Oct.  3—St. Louis (White) | 2 | New York (Chandler) | 0 | At New York |
| Oct.  4—St. Louis (Lanier) | 9 | New York (Donald) | 6 | At New York |
| Oct.  5—St. Louis (Beazley) | 4 | New York (Ruffing) | 2 | At New York |

## 1943—NEW YORK A. L. (4) vs. ST. LOUIS N. L. (1)

Managers—Joseph V. McCarthy, New York; William Southworth, St. Louis.

| | | | | |
|---|---|---|---|---|
| Oct.  5—New York (Chandler) | 4 | St. Louis (Lanier) | 2 | At New York |
| Oct.  6—St. Louis (M. Cooper) | 4 | New York (Bonham) | 3 | At New York |
| Oct.  7—New York (Borowy) | 6 | St. Louis (Brazle) | 2 | At New York |
| Oct. 10—New York (Russo) | 2 | St. Louis (Brecheen) | 1 | At St. Louis |
| Oct. 11—New York (Chandler) | 2 | St. Louis (M. Cooper) | 0 | At St. Louis |

## 1944—ST. LOUIS N. L. (4) vs. ST. LOUIS A. L. (2)

Managers—William Southworth, St. Louis N. L.; Luke Sewell, St. Louis A. L.

| | | | | |
|---|---|---|---|---|
| Oct.  4—St. Louis A (Galehouse) | 2 | St. Louis N (M. Cooper) | 1 | At Sportsman's Park |
| Oct.  5—St. Louis A (Donnelly) | 3 | St. Louis N (Muncrief) | 2 | At Sportsman's Pk. (11 inn.) |
| Oct.  6—St. Louis A (Kramer) | 6 | St. Louis N (Wilks) | 2 | At Sportsman's Park |
| Oct.  7—St. Louis N (Brecheen) | 5 | St. Louis A (Jakucki) | 1 | At Sportsman's Park |
| Oct.  8—St. Louis N (M. Cooper) | 2 | St. Louis A (Galehouse) | 0 | At Sportsman's Park |
| Oct.  9—St. Louis N (Lanier) | 3 | St. Louis A (Potter) | 1 | At Sportsman's Park |

## 1945—DETROIT A. L. (4) vs. CHICAGO N. L. (3)

Managers—Steve O'Neill, Detroit; Charles J. Grimm, Chicago.

| | | | | |
|---|---|---|---|---|
| Oct.  3—Chicago (Borowy) | 9 | Detroit (Newhouser) | 0 | At Detroit |
| Oct.  4—Detroit (Trucks) | 4 | Chicago (Wyse) | 1 | At Detroit |
| Oct.  5—Chicago (Passeau) | 3 | Detroit (Overmire) | 0 | At Detroit |
| Oct.  6—Detroit (Trout) | 4 | Chicago (Prim) | 1 | At Chicago |
| Oct.  7—Detroit (Newhouser) | 8 | Chicago (Borowy) | 4 | At Chicago |
| Oct.  8—Chicago (Borowy) | 8 | Detroit (Trout) | 7 | At Chicago (12 inn.) |
| Oct. 10—Detroit (Newhouser) | 9 | Chicago (Borowy) | 3 | At Chicago |

## 1946—ST. LOUIS N. L. (4) vs. BOSTON A. L. (3)

Managers—Eddie Dyer, St. Louis; Joseph E. Cronin, Boston.

| | | | | |
|---|---|---|---|---|
| Oct.  6—Boston (Johnson) | 3 | St. Louis (Pollet) | 2 | At St. Louis (10 inn.) |
| Oct.  7—St. Louis (Brecheen) | 3 | Boston (Harris) | 0 | At St. Louis |
| Oct.  9—Boston (Ferriss) | 4 | St. Louis (Dickson) | 0 | At Boston |
| Oct. 10—St. Louis (Munger) | 12 | Boston (Hughson) | 3 | At Boston |
| Oct. 11—Boston (Dobson) | 6 | St. Louis (Brazle) | 3 | At Boston |
| Oct. 13—St. Louis (Brecheen) | 4 | Boston (Harris) | 1 | At St. Louis |
| Oct. 15—St. Louis (Brecheen) | 4 | Boston (Klinger) | 3 | At St. Louis |

## 1947—NEW YORK A. L. (4) vs. BROOKLYN N. L. (3)

Managers—Stanley R. Harris, New York; Burton E. Shotton, Brooklyn.

| | | | | |
|---|---|---|---|---|
| Sept. 30—New York (Shea) | 5 | Brooklyn (Branca) | 3 | At New York |
| Oct.  1—New York (Reynolds) | 10 | Brooklyn (Lombardi) | 3 | At New York |
| Oct.  2—Brooklyn (Casey) | 9 | New York (Newsom) | 8 | At Brooklyn |
| Oct.  3—Brooklyn (Casey) | 3 | New York (Bevens) | 2 | At Brooklyn |
| Oct.  4—New York (Shea) | 2 | Brooklyn (Barney) | 1 | At Brooklyn |
| Oct.  5—Brooklyn (Branca) | 8 | New York (Page) | 6 | At New York |
| Oct.  6—New York (Page) | 5 | Brooklyn (Gregg) | 2 | At New York |

## 1948—CLEVELAND A. L. (4) vs. BOSTON N. L. (2)

Managers—Lou Boudreau, Cleveland; William Southworth, Boston.

| | | | | |
|---|---|---|---|---|
| Oct.  6—Boston (Sain) | 1 | Cleveland (Feller) | 0 | At Boston |
| Oct.  7—Cleveland (Lemon) | 4 | Boston (Spahn) | 1 | At Boston |
| Oct.  8—Cleveland (Bearden) | 2 | Boston (Bickford) | 0 | At Cleveland |
| Oct.  9—Cleveland (Gromek) | 2 | Boston (Sain) | 1 | At Cleveland |
| Oct. 10—Boston (Spahn) | 11 | Cleveland (Feller) | 5 | At Cleveland |
| Oct. 11—Cleveland (Lemon) | 4 | Boston (Voiselle) | 3 | At Boston |

## 1949—NEW YORK A. L. (4) vs. BROOKLYN N. L. (1)
### Managers—Casey Stengel, New York; Burton E. Shotton, Brooklyn.

| | | | | |
|---|---|---|---|---|
| Oct. 5—New York (Reynolds) | 1 | Brooklyn (Newcombe) | 0 | At New York |
| Oct. 6—Brooklyn (Roe) | 1 | New York (Raschi) | 0 | At New York |
| Oct. 7—New York (Page) | 4 | Brooklyn (Branca) | 3 | At Brooklyn |
| Oct. 8—New York (Lopat) | 6 | Brooklyn (Newcombe) | 4 | At Brooklyn |
| Oct. 9—New York (Raschi) | 10 | Brooklyn (Barney) | 6 | At Brooklyn |

## 1950—NEW YORK A. L. (4) vs. PHILADELPHIA N. L. (0)
### Managers—Casey Stengel, New York; Edwin M. Sawyer, Philadelphia.

| | | | | |
|---|---|---|---|---|
| Oct. 4—New York (Raschi) | 1 | Philadelphia (Konstanty) | 0 | At Philadelphia |
| Oct. 5—New York (Reynolds) | 2 | Philadelphia (Roberts) | 1 | At Philadelphia (10 inn.) |
| Oct. 6—New York (Ferrick) | 3 | Philadelphia (Meyer) | 2 | At New York |
| Oct. 7—New York (Ford) | 5 | Philadelphia (Miller) | 2 | At New York |

## 1951—NEW YORK A. L. (4) vs. NEW YORK N. L. (2)
### Managers—Casey Stengel, New York A. L.; Leo E. Durocher, New York N. L.

| | | | | |
|---|---|---|---|---|
| Oct. 4—New York N (Koslo) | 5 | New York A (Reynolds) | 1 | At Yankee Stadium |
| Oct. 5—New York A (Lopat) | 3 | New York N (Jansen) | 1 | At Yankee Stadium |
| Oct. 6—New York N (Hearn) | 6 | New York A (Raschi) | 2 | At Polo Grounds |
| Oct. 8—New York A (Reynolds) | 6 | New York N (Maglie) | 2 | At Polo Grounds |
| Oct. 9—New York A (Lopat) | 13 | New York N (Jansen) | 1 | At Polo Ground |
| Oct. 10—New York A (Raschi) | 4 | New York N (Koslo) | 3 | At Yankee Stadium |

## 1952—NEW YORK A. L. (4) vs. BROOKLYN N. L. (3)
### Managers—Casey Stengel, New York; Charles W. Dressen, Brooklyn.

| | | | | |
|---|---|---|---|---|
| Oct. 1—Brooklyn (Black) | 4 | New York (Reynolds) | 2 | At Brooklyn |
| Oct. 2—New York (Raschi) | 7 | Brooklyn (Erskine) | 1 | At Brooklyn |
| Oct. 3—Brooklyn (Roe) | 5 | New York (Lopat) | 3 | At New York |
| Oct. 4—New York (Reynolds) | 2 | Brooklyn (Black) | 0 | At New York |
| Oct. 5—Brooklyn (Erskine) | 6 | New York (Sain) | 5 | At New York (12 inn.) |
| Oct. 6—New York (Raschi) | 3 | Brooklyn (Loes) | 2 | At Brooklyn |
| Oct. 7—New York (Reynolds) | 4 | Brooklyn (Black) | 2 | At Brooklyn |

## 1953—NEW YORK A. L. (4) vs. BROOKLYN N. L. (2)
### Managers—Casey Stengel, New York; Charles W. Dressen, Brooklyn.

| | | | | |
|---|---|---|---|---|
| Sept. 30—New York (Sain) | 9 | Brooklyn (Labine) | 5 | At New York |
| Oct. 1—New York (Lopat) | 4 | Brooklyn (Roe) | 2 | At New York |
| Oct. 2—Brooklyn (Erskine) | 3 | New York (Raschi) | 2 | At Brooklyn |
| Oct. 3—Brooklyn (Loes) | 7 | New York (Ford) | 3 | At Brooklyn |
| Oct. 4—New York (McDonald) | 11 | Brooklyn (Podres) | 7 | At Brooklyn |
| Oct. 5—New York (Reynolds) | 4 | Brooklyn (Labine) | 3 | At New York |

## 1954—NEW YORK N. L. (4) vs. CLEVELAND A. L. (0)
### Managers—Leo E. Durocher, New York; Al Lopez, Cleveland.

| | | | | |
|---|---|---|---|---|
| Sept. 29—New York (Grissom) | 5 | Cleveland (Lemon) | 2 | At New York |
| Sept. 30—New York (Antonelli) | 3 | Cleveland (Wynn) | 1 | At New York |
| Oct. 1—New York (Gomez) | 6 | Cleveland (Garcia) | 2 | At Cleveland |
| Oct. 2—New York (Liddle) | 7 | Cleveland (Lemon) | 4 | At Cleveland |

## 1955—BROOKLYN N. L. (4) vs. NEW YORK A. L. (3)
### Managers—Walter Alston, Brooklyn; Casey Stengel, New York.

| | | | | |
|---|---|---|---|---|
| Sept. 28—New York (Ford) | 6 | Brooklyn (Newcombe) | 5 | At New York |
| Sept. 29—New York (Byrne) | 4 | Brooklyn (Loes) | 2 | At New York |
| Sept. 30—Brooklyn (Podres) | 8 | New York (Turley) | 3 | At Brooklyn |
| Oct. 1—Brooklyn (Labine) | 8 | New York (Larsen) | 5 | At Brooklyn |
| Oct. 2—Brooklyn (Craig) | 5 | New York (Grim) | 3 | At Brooklyn |
| Oct. 3—New York (Ford) | 5 | Brooklyn (Spooner) | 1 | At New York |
| Oct. 4—Brooklyn (Podres) | 2 | New York (Byrne) | 0 | At New York |

## 1956—NEW YORK A. L. (4) vs. BROOKLYN N. L. (3)
### Managers—Casey Stengel, New York; Walter Alston, Brooklyn.

| | | | | |
|---|---|---|---|---|
| Oct. 3—Brooklyn (Maglie) | 6 | New York (Ford) | 3 | At Brooklyn |
| Oct. 5—Brooklyn (Bessent) | 13 | New York (Morgan) | 8 | At Brooklyn |
| Oct. 6—New York (Ford) | 5 | Brooklyn (Craig) | 3 | At New York |
| Oct. 7—New York (Sturdivant) | 6 | Brooklyn (Erskine) | 2 | At New York |
| Oct. 8—New York (Larsen) | 2 | Brooklyn (Maglie) | 0 | At New York |
| Oct. 9—Brooklyn (Labine) | 1 | New York (Turley) | 0 | At Brooklyn (10 inn.) |
| Oct. 10—New York (Kucks) | 9 | Brooklyn (Newcombe) | 0 | At Brooklyn |

## 1957—MILWAUKEE N. L. (4) vs. NEW YORK A. L. (3)
### Managers—Fred Haney, Milwaukee; Casey Stengel, New York.

| | | | | |
|---|---|---|---|---|
| Oct. 2—New York (Ford) | 3 | Milwaukee (Spahn) | 1 | At New York |
| Oct. 3—Milwaukee (Burdette) | 4 | New York (Shantz) | 2 | At New York |
| Oct. 5—New York (Larsen) | 12 | Milwaukee (Buhl) | 3 | At Milwaukee |
| Oct. 6—Milwaukee (Spahn) | 7 | New York (Grim) | 5 | At Milwaukee (10 inn.) |
| Oct. 7—Milwaukee (Burdette) | 1 | New York (Ford) | 0 | At Milwaukee |
| Oct. 9—New York (Turley) | 3 | Milwaukee (Johnson) | 2 | At New York |
| Oct. 10—Milwaukee (Burdette) | 5 | New York (Larsen) | 0 | At New York |

## 1958—NEW YORK A. L. (4) vs. MILWAUKEE N. L. (3)
### Managers—Casey Stengel, New York; Fred Haney, Milwaukee.

| | | | | |
|---|---|---|---|---|
| Oct. 1—Milwaukee (Spahn) | 4 | New York (Duren) | 3 | At Milwaukee (10 inn.) |
| Oct. 2—Milwaukee (Burdette) | 13 | New York (Turley) | 5 | At Milwaukee |
| Oct. 4—New York (Larsen) | 4 | Milwaukee (Rush) | 0 | At New York |
| Oct. 5—Milwaukee (Spahn) | 3 | New York (Ford) | 0 | At New York |
| Oct. 6—New York (Turley) | 7 | Milwaukee (Burdette) | 0 | At New York |
| Oct. 8—New York (Duren) | 4 | Milwaukee (Spahn) | 3 | At Milwaukee (10 inn.) |
| Oct. 9—New York (Turley) | 6 | Milwaukee (Burdette) | 2 | At Milwaukee |

## 1959—LOS ANGELES N. L. (4) vs. CHICAGO A. L. (2)
### Managers—Walter Alston, Los Angeles; Al Lopez, Chicago.

| | | | | |
|---|---|---|---|---|
| Oct. 1—Chicago (Wynn) | 11 | Los Angeles (Craig) | 0 | At Chicago |
| Oct. 2—Los Angeles (Podres) | 4 | Chicago (Shaw) | 3 | At Chicago |
| Oct. 4—Los Angeles (Drysdale) | 3 | Chicago (Donovan) | 1 | At Los Angeles |
| Oct. 5—Los Angeles (Sherry) | 5 | Chicago (Staley) | 4 | At Los Angeles |
| Oct. 6—Chicago (Shaw) | 1 | Los Angeles (Koufax) | 0 | At Los Angeles |
| Oct. 8—Los Angeles (Sherry) | 9 | Chicago (Wynn) | 3 | At Chicago |

## 1960—PITTSBURGH N. L. (4) vs. NEW YORK A. L. (3)
### Managers—Danny Murtaugh, Pittsburgh; Casey Stengel, New York.

| | | | | |
|---|---|---|---|---|
| Oct. 5—Pittsburgh (Law) | 6 | New York (Ditmar) | 4 | At Pittsburgh |
| Oct. 6—New York (Turley) | 16 | Pittsburgh (Friend) | 3 | At Pittsburgh |
| Oct. 8—New York (Ford) | 10 | Pittsburgh (Mizell) | 0 | At New York |
| Oct. 9—Pittsburgh (Law) | 3 | New York (Terry) | 2 | At New York |
| Oct. 10—Pittsburgh (Haddix) | 5 | New York (Ditmar) | 2 | At New York |
| Oct. 12—New York (Ford) | 12 | Pittsburgh (Friend) | 0 | At Pittsburgh |
| Oct. 13—Pittsburgh (Haddix) | 10 | New York (Terry) | 9 | At Pittsburgh |

(For 1961 World Series see index)

## World Series Club Standing (Through 1960)

| | Series | Won | Lost | Pct. | | Series | Won | Lost | Pct. |
|---|---|---|---|---|---|---|---|---|---|
| Los Angeles (N) | 1 | 1 | 0 | 1.000 | Washington (A) | 3 | 1 | 2 | .333 |
| Boston (A) | 6 | 5 | 1 | .833 | Detroit (A) | 7 | 2 | 5 | .286 |
| New York (A) | 25 | 18 | 7 | .720 | Chicago (N) | 10 | 2 | 8 | .200 |
| St. Louis (N) | 9 | 6 | 3 | .667 | Brooklyn (N) | 9 | 1 | 8 | .111 |
| Cincinnati (N) | 3 | 2 | 1 | .667 | St. Louis (A) | 1 | 0 | 1 | .000 |
| Cleveland (A) | 3 | 2 | 1 | .667 | Philadelphia (N) | 2 | 0 | 2 | .000 |
| Philadelphia (A) | 8 | 5 | 3 | .625 | | | | | |
| Pittsburgh (N) | 5 | 3 | 2 | .600 | | | | | |
| Milwaukee (N) | 2 | 1 | 1 | .500 | | | | | |
| Boston (N) | 2 | 1 | 1 | .500 | | RECAPITULATION | | | |
| Chicago (A) | 4 | 2 | 2 | .500 | | | | | Won |
| New York (N) | 14 | 5 | 9 | .357 | American League | | | | 35 |
| | | | | | National League | | | | 22 |

## MAJOR LEAGUE FRANCHISE SHIFTS AND ADDITIONS

1953—Boston Braves (N. L.) became Milwaukee Braves. Home attendance, last season in Boston (1952), 281,278; first season in Milwaukee (1953), 1,826,397.

1954—St. Louis Browns (A. L.) became Baltimore Orioles. Home attendance, last season in St. Louis (1953), 297,238; first season in Baltimore (1954), 1,060,910.

1955—Philadelphia Athletics (A. L.) became Kansas City Athletics. Home attendance, last season in Philadelphia (1954), 627,100; first season in Kansas City (1955), 1,393,054.

1958—New York Giants (N. L.) became San Francisco Giants. Home attendance, last season in New York (1957), 653,923; first season in San Francisco (1958), 1,272,625.

1958—Brooklyn Dodgers (N. L.) became Los Angeles Dodgers. Home attendance, last season in Brooklyn (1957), 1,028,258; first season in Los Angeles (1958), 1,845,556.

1961—Washington Senators (A. L.) became Minnesota Twins. Home attendance, last season in Washington (1960), 743,404; first season in Minneapolis-St. Paul (1961), 1,256,722.

1961—Los Angeles enfranchised by the American League. Home attendance, first season (1961), 603,510.

1961—Washington Senators enfranchised by the American League (a new team, replacing the former Washington club, whose franchise was moved to Minneapolis-St. Paul). Home attendance, first season, 597,287.

## MAJOR LEAGUE STATISTICS
**lf—Left-field foul line; cf—center-field; rf—right-field foul line.  (2)—Indicates double-header.**

### American League

| Club, nickname and grounds | lf | cf | rf | Seating capacity | Record attendance* | Visiting club | Date |
|---|---|---|---|---|---|---|---|
| Baltimore Orioles—Memorial Stadium | 309 | 410 | 309 | 49,375 | 46,796 | New York (2) | May 16, 1954 |
| Boston Red Sox—Fenway Park | 315 | 420 | 302 | 33,357 | 41,766 | New York (2) | Aug. 12, 1934 |
| Chicago White Sox—Comiskey Park | 352 | 415 | 352 | 46,550 | 54,215 | New York (2) | July 19, 1953 |
| Cleveland Indians—Municipal Stadium | 320 | 410 | 320 | 73,811 | 84,587 | New York (2) | Sept. 12, 1954 |
| Detroit Tigers—Tiger Stadium | 340 | 440 | 325 | 52,904 | 58,369 | New York (2) | July 20, 1947 |
| Kansas City Athletics—Municipal Stadium | 360 | 421 | 353 | 31,241 | 34,065 | New York | Aug. 27, 1961 |
| Los Angeles Angels—Wrigley Field | 340 | 412 | 339 | 20,457 | 19,930 | New York | Aug. 22, 1961 |
| Minnesota Twins—Metropolitan Stadium | 330 | 412 | 330 | 30,022 | 41,357 | New York | Aug. 30, 1961 |
| New York Yankees—Yankee Stadium | 301 | 461 | 296 | 70,000 | 81,841 | Boston (2) | May 30, 1938 |
| Washington Senators—Griffith Stadium‡ | 388 | 438 | 320 | 28,669 | 35,563 | New York (2) | July  4, 1936 |

### National League†

| Club | lf | cf | rf | Seating capacity | Record attendance* | Visiting club | Date |
|---|---|---|---|---|---|---|---|
| Chicago Cubs—Wrigley Field | 355 | 400 | 353 | 36,755 | 46,965 | Pittsburgh (2) | May 31, 1948 |
| Cincinnati Reds—Crosley Field | 328 | 387 | 366 | 30,322 | 36,961 | Pittsburgh (2) | Apr. 27, 1947 |
| Los Angeles Dodgers—Memorial Coliseum‡ | 251 | 420 | 300 | 92,500 | 78,672 | San Francisco | Apr. 18, 1958 |
| Milwaukee Braves—County Stadium | 320 | 402 | 315 | 43,826 | 48,642 | Philadelphia | Sept. 27, 1959 |
| Philadelphia Phillies—Connie Mack Stadium | 334 | 447 | 329 | 33,608 | 40,720 | Brooklyn (2) | May 11, 1947 |
| Pittsburgh Pirates—Forbes Field | 365 | 457 | 300 | 35,000 | 44,932 | Brooklyn | Sept. 23, 1956 |
| St. Louis Cardinals—Busch Stadium | 351 | 426 | 310 | 30,500 | 45,770 | Chicago (2) | July 12, 1931 |
| San Francisco Giants—Candlestick Park | 335 | 410 | 335 | 42,500 | 42,269 | St. Louis | Apr. 12, 1960 |

* Regular season.   † Additional teams in 1962: Houston Colts, New York Mets.   ‡ Park used in 1961.

## MAJOR LEAGUE ALL-STAR GAME
### A.L.—American League.   N.L.—National League.

| Year | Date | Winning league and manager | Runs | Losing league and manager | Runs | Winning pitcher | Losing pitcher | Site | Paid attendance |
|---|---|---|---|---|---|---|---|---|---|
| 1933 | July 6 | A.L. (Mack) | 4 | N.L. (McGraw) | 2 | Gomez | Hallahan | Chicago A.L. | 47,595 |
| 1934 | July 10 | A.L. (Cronin) | 9 | N.L. (Terry) | 7 | Harder | Mungo | New York N.L. | 48,363 |
| 1935 | July 8 | A.L. (Cochrane) | 4 | N.L. (Frisch) | 1 | Gomez | Walker | Cleveland A.L. | 69,831 |
| 1936 | July 7 | N.L. (Grimm) | 4 | A.L. (McCarthy) | 3 | J. Dean | Grove | Boston N.L. | 25,556 |
| 1937 | July 7 | A.L. (McCarthy) | 8 | N.L. (Terry) | 3 | Gomez | J. Dean | Washington A.L. | 31,391 |
| 1938 | July 6 | N.L. (Terry) | 4 | A.L. (McCarthy) | 1 | Vander Meer | Gomez | Cincinnati N.L. | 27,067 |
| 1939 | July 11 | A.L. (McCarthy) | 3 | N.L. (Hartnett) | 1 | Bridges | Lee | New York A.L. | 62,892 |
| 1940 | July 9 | N.L. (McKechnie) | 4 | A.L. (Cronin) | 0 | Derringer | Ruffing | St. Louis N.L. | 32,373 |
| 1941 | July 8 | A.L. (Baker) | 7 | N.L. (McKechnie) | 5 | E. Smith | Passeau | Detroit A.L. | 54,674 |
| 1942 | July 6 | A.L. (McCarthy) | 3 | N.L. (Durocher) | 1 | Chandler | Cooper | New York N.L. | 34,178 |
| 1943 | July 13* | A.L. (McCarthy) | 5 | N.L. (Southworth) | 3 | Leonard | Cooper | Philadelphia A.L. | 31,938 |
| 1944 | July 11* | N.L. (Southworth) | 7 | A.L. (McCarthy) | 1 | Raffensberger | Hughson | Pittsburgh N.L. | 29,589 |
| 1945 | No game. | | | | | | | | |
| 1946 | July 9 | A.L. (O'Neill) | 12 | N.L. (Grimm) | 0 | Feller | Passeau | Boston A.L. | 34,906 |
| 1947 | July 8 | A.L. (Cronin) | 2 | N.L. (Dyer) | 1 | Shea | Sain | Chicago N.L. | 41,123 |
| 1948 | July 13 | A.L. (Harris) | 5 | N.L. (Durocher) | 2 | Raschi | Schmitz | St. Louis A.L. | 34,009 |
| 1949 | July 12 | A.L. (Boudreau) | 11 | N.L. (Southworth) | 7 | Trucks | Newcombe | Brooklyn N.L. | 32,577 |
| 1950 | July 11 | N.L. (Shotton) | 4 | A.L. (Stengel) | 3a | Blackwell | Gray | Chicago A.L. | 46,127 |
| 1951 | July 10 | N.L. (Sawyer) | 8 | A.L. (Stengel) | 3 | Maglie | Lopat | Detroit A.L. | 52,075 |
| 1952 | July 8 | N.L. (Durocher) | 3 | A.L. (Stengel) | 2b | Rush | Lemon | Philadelphia N.L. | 32,785 |
| 1953 | July 14 | N.L. (Dressen) | 5 | A.L. (Stengel) | 1 | Spahn | Reynolds | Cincinnati N.L. | 30,846 |
| 1954 | July 13 | A.L. (Stengel) | 11 | N.L. (Alston) | 9 | Stone | Conley | Cleveland A.L. | 68,751 |
| 1955 | July 12 | N.L. (Durocher) | 6 | A.L. (Lopez) | 5c | Conley | Sullivan | Milwaukee N.L. | 45,643 |
| 1956 | July 10 | N.L. (Alston) | 7 | A.L. (Stengel) | 3 | Friend | Pierce | Washington A.L. | 28,843 |
| 1957 | July 9 | A.L. (Stengel) | 6 | N.L. (Alston) | 5 | Bunning | Simmons | St. Louis N.L. | 30,693 |
| 1958 | July 8 | A.L. (Stengel) | 4 | N.L. (Haney) | 3 | Wynn | Friend | Baltimore A.L. | 48,829 |
| 1959† | July 7 | N.L. (Haney) | 5 | A.L. (Stengel) | 4 | Antonelli | Ford | Pittsburgh N.L. | 35,277 |
|  | Aug. 3 | A.L. (Stengel) | 5 | N.L. (Haney) | 3 | Walker | Drysdale | Los Angeles N.L. | 55,105 |
| 1960† | July 11 | N.L. (Alston) | 5 | A.L. (Lopez) | 3 | Friend | Monbouquette | Kansas City A.L. | 30,619 |
|  | July 13 | N.L. (Alston) | 6 | A.L. (Lopez) | 0 | Law | Ford | New York A.L. | 38,362 |

* Night game.   † Two games in 1959, 1960.   aFourteen innings.   bFive innings, rain.   cTwelve innings.

## MAJOR LEAGUE ATTENDANCE RECORDS

Single game—78,672, San Francisco at Los Angeles (N. L.), Apr. 18, 1958.

Doubleheader—84,587, New York at Cleveland (A. L.), Sept. 12, 1954.

Night—78,382, Chicago at Cleveland (A. L.), Aug. 20, 1948.

Season, home—2,620,627, Cleveland (A. L.), 1948.

Season, road—1,915,490, New York (A. L.), 1961 (81 games); 1,871,545, New York (A. L.), 1949 (77 games).

Season, league—11,150,099, American League, 1948.

World Series, single game—92,706, Chicago (A. L.) at Los Angeles (N. L.), Oct. 6, 1959.

World Series, all games (6)—420,784, Chicago (A. L.) and Los Angeles (N. L.), 1959.

# Major League Individual All-Time Records

Highest Batting Average—.438, Hugh Duffy, Boston N. L., 1894. (Since 1900—.424, Rogers Hornsby, St. Louis N. L., 1924).

Most Years Led League in Batting—12, Ty Cobb, Detroit A. L., 1907-15, 1917-19.

Most Years Batted .300 or Better—23, Ty Cobb, Detroit A. L., 1906-26, Philadelphia A. L., 1927-28.

Most hits—4,191, Ty Cobb, Detroit A. L., 1905-26, Philadelphia, 1927-28.

Most Hits, Season—257, George Sisler, St. Louis A. L., 1920.

Most Hits, Game (9 innings)—7, Wilbert Robinson, Baltimore N. L., 6 singles, 1 double, 1892. (Since 1900—6, by many.)

Most Hits, Game (extra innings)—9, John Burnett, Cleveland A. L., 18 innings, 7 singles, 2 doubles, 1932.

Most Hits in Succession—12, Mike Higgins, Boston A. L., in four games, 1938; Walt Dropo, Detroit A. L., in three games, 1952.

Most Consecutive Games Batted Safely—56, Joe DiMaggio, New York A. L., 1941.

Most Runs—2,244, Ty Cobb, Detroit A. L., 1905-26, Philadelphia 1927-28.

Most Runs, Season—196, William Hamilton, Philadelphia N. L., 1894. (Since 1900—177, Babe Ruth, New York A. L., 1921).

Most Runs, Game—7, Guy Hecker, Louisville A. A., 1886. (Since 1900—6, by many.)

Most Runs Batted In—2,209, Babe Ruth, Boston A. L., 1914-19, New York A. L., 1920-34, Boston N. L., 1935.

Most Runs Batted In, Season—190, Hack Wilson, Chicago N. L., 1930.

Most Runs Batted In, Game—12, Jim Bottomley, St. Louis N. L., 1924.

Most Home Runs—714, Babe Ruth, Boston A. L., 1915-19, New York A. L., 1920-34, Boston N. L., 1935.

Most Home Runs, Season—61, Roger Maris, New York A. L., 1961 (162 games); 60, Babe Ruth, New York A. L., 1927 (154 games).

Most Home Runs, Game—4, Robert Lowe, Boston N. L.,

1894; Ed Delahanty, Philadelphia N. L., 1896; Lou Gehrig, New York A. L., 1932; Chuck Klein, Philadelphia N. L., 1936; Pat Seerey, Chicago A. L., 1948; Gil Hodges, Brooklyn N. L., 1950; Joe Adcock, Milwaukee N. L., 1954; Rocky Colavito, Cleveland A. L., 1959; Willie Mays, San Francisco N. L., 1961.

Most Home Runs with Bases Filled—23, Lou Gehrig, New York A. L., 1927-38.

Most 2-Base Hits—793, Tris Speaker, Boston A. L., 1907-15, Cleveland A. L., 1916-26, Washington A. L., 1927, Philadelphia A. L., 1928.

Most 2-Base Hits, Season—67, Earl Webb, Boston A. L., 1931.

Most 2-Base Hits, Game—4, by many.

Most 3-Base Hits—312, Sam Crawford, Cincinnati N. L., 1899-1902, Detroit A. L., 1903-17.

Most 3-Base Hits, Season—36, Owen Wilson, Pittsburgh N. L., 1912.

Most 3-Base Hits, Game—4, George Strief, Philadelphia A. A., 1885; William Joyce, New York N. L., 1897. (Since 1900—3, by many.)

Most Games Played—3,033, Ty Cobb, Detroit A. L., 1905-26, Philadelphia A. L., 1927-28.

Most Consecutive Games Played—2,130, Lou Gehrig, New York A. L., 1925-39.

Most Bases on Balls—2,056, Babe Ruth, Boston A. L., 1915-19; New York A. L., 1920-34, Boston N. L., 1935.

Most Bases on Balls, Season—170, Babe Ruth, New York A. L., 1923.

Most Bases on Balls, Game—6, Walter Wilmot, Chicago N. L., 1891; Jimmy Foxx, Boston A. L., 1938.

Most Strikeouts—1,330, Babe Ruth, Boston A. L., 1914-19, New York A. L., 1920-34, Boston N. L., 1935.

Most Strikeouts, Season—138, Jim Lemon, Washington A. L., 1956.

Most Strikeouts, Game (9 innings)—5, by many.

Most Strikeouts, Game (extra innings)—6, Carl Weilman, St. Louis A. L., 15 innings, 1913; Don Hoak, Chicago N. L., 17 innings, 1956.

## PITCHING

Most Games Won—511, Cy Young, Cleveland N. L., 1890-98, St. Louis N. L., 1899-1900, Boston A. L., 1901-08, Cleveland A. L., 1909-11, Boston N. L., 1911.

Most Games Won, Season—60, Charles Radbourne, Providence N. L., 1884. (Since 1900—41, Jack Chesbro, New York A. L., 1904.)

Most Consecutive Games Won—24, Carl Hubbell, New York N. L., 1936 (16) and 1937 (8).

Most Consecutive Games Won, Season—19, Timothy Keefe, New York N. L., 1888; Rube Marquard, New York N. L., 1912.

Most Years Won 20 or More Games—16, Cy Young, Cleveland N. L., 1891-98, St. Louis N. L., 1899-1900, Boston A. L., 1901-04, 1907-08.

Most Shutouts—113, Walter Johnson, Washington A. L., 1907-27.

Most shutouts, season—16, George Bradley, St. Louis N. L., 1876; Grover Alexander, Philadelphia N. L., 1916.

Most Consecutive Shutouts—5, Harris White, Chicago A. L., 1904.

Most Consecutive Scoreless Innings—56, Walter Johnson, Washington A. L., 1913.

Most Strikeouts—3,508, Walter Johnson, Washington A. L. 1907-27.

Most Strikeouts, Season—505, Matthew Kilroy, Baltimore A. A., 1886. (Since 1900—348, Bob Feller, Cleveland A. L., 1946.)

Most Strikeouts, Game—19, Charles McSweeney, Providence N. L., 1884, 9 innings; Hugh Daly, Chicago U. A., 1884, 9 innings. (Since 1900—18, John Coombs, Philadelphia A. L., 1906, 24 innings; John Coombs, Philadelphia A. L., 1910, 16 innings; Bob Feller, Cleveland A. L., 1938, 9 innings; Warren Spahn, Boston N. L., 1952, 15 innings; Sandy Koufax, Los Angeles N. L., 1959, 9 innings.)

Most Consecutive Strikeouts—9, Michael Welch, New York N. L., 1884. (Since 1900—8, Max Surkont, Milwaukee N. L., 1953.)

Most Games Season—75, William White, Cincinnati N. L., 1879. (Since 1900—74, Jim Konstanty, Philadelphia N. L., 1950.)

Most Complete Games, Season—74, William White, Cincinnati N. L., 1879. (Since 1900—48, Jack Chesbro, New York A. L., 1904.)

## LIFETIME WORLD SERIES RECORDS

Most hits—71, Yogi Berra, New York A. L., 1947, 1949-53, 1955-58, 1960-61.

Most runs—41, Yogi Berra, New York A. L., 1947, 1949-53, 1955-58, 1960-61.

Most runs batted in—39, Yogi Berra, New York A. L., 1947, 1949-53, 1955-58, 1960-61.

Most home runs—15, Babe Ruth, Boston A. L., 1915-16, 1918, New York A. L., 1921-23, 1926-28, 1932.

Most bases on balls—33, Babe Ruth, Boston A. L., 1915-16, 1918, New York A. L., 1921-23, 1926-28, 1932.

Most strikeouts—36, Mickey Mantle, New York A. L., 1951-53, 1955-58, 1960.

Most times, member of winning team—9, Joe DiMaggio, New York A. L., 1936-39, 1941, 1947, 1949-51; Yogi Berra, New York A. L., 1947, 1949-53, 1956, 1958, 1961.

# National League Pennant Winners

| Year | Club | Manager | Won | Lost | Pct. | Year | Club | Manager | Won | Lost | Pct. |
|------|------|---------|-----|------|------|------|------|---------|-----|------|------|
| 1876 | Chicago | Albert G. Spalding | 52 | 14 | .788 | 1919* | Cincinnati | Patrick J. Moran | 96 | 44 | .686 |
| 1877 | Boston | Harry Wright | 31 | 17 | .646 | 1920 | Brooklyn | Wilbert Robinson | 93 | 61 | .604 |
| 1878 | Boston | Harry Wright | 41 | 19 | .683 | 1921* | New York | John J. McGraw | 94 | 59 | .614 |
| 1879 | Providence | George Wright | 55 | 23 | .705 | 1922* | New York | John J. McGraw | 93 | 61 | .604 |
| 1880 | Chicago | Adrian C. Anson | 67 | 17 | .798 | 1923 | New York | John J. McGraw | 95 | 58 | .621 |
| 1881 | Chicago | Adrian C. Anson | 56 | 28 | .667 | 1924 | New York | John J. McGraw | 93 | 60 | .608 |
| 1882 | Chicago | Adrian C. Anson | 55 | 29 | .655 | 1925* | Pittsburgh | William B. McKechnie | 95 | 58 | .621 |
| 1883 | Boston | John F. Morrill | 63 | 35 | .643 | 1926* | St. Louis | Rogers Hornsby | 89 | 65 | .578 |
| 1884 | Providence | Frank C. Bancroft | 84 | 28 | .750 | 1927 | Pittsburgh | Donie Bush | 94 | 60 | .610 |
| 1885 | Chicago | Adrian C. Anson | 87 | 25 | .777 | 1928 | St. Louis | William B. McKechnie | 95 | 59 | .617 |
| 1886 | Chicago | Adrian C. Anson | 90 | 34 | .726 | 1929 | Chicago | Joseph V. McCarthy | 98 | 54 | .647 |
| 1887 | Detroit | W. H. Watkins | 79 | 45 | .637 | 1930 | St. Louis | Gabby Street | 92 | 62 | .595 |
| 1888 | New York | James J. Mutrie | 84 | 47 | .641 | 1931* | St. Louis | Gabby Street | 101 | 53 | .656 |
| 1889 | New York | James J. Mutrie | 83 | 43 | .659 | 1932 | Chicago | Charles J. Grimm | 90 | 64 | .584 |
| 1890 | Brooklyn | William H. McGunnigle | 86 | 43 | .667 | 1933* | New York | William H. Terry | 91 | 61 | .599 |
| 1891 | Boston | Frank G. Selee | 87 | 51 | .630 | 1934* | St. Louis | Frank F. Frisch | 95 | 58 | .621 |
| 1892 | Boston | Frank G. Selee | 102 | 48 | .680 | 1935 | Chicago | Charles J. Grimm | 100 | 54 | .649 |
| 1893 | Boston | Frank G. Selee | 86 | 43 | .667 | 1936 | New York | William H. Terry | 92 | 62 | .597 |
| 1894 | Baltimore | Edward H. Hanlon | 89 | 39 | .695 | 1937 | New York | William H. Terry | 95 | 57 | .625 |
| 1895 | Baltimore | Edward H. Hanlon | 87 | 43 | .669 | 1938 | Chicago | Gabby Hartnett | 89 | 63 | .586 |
| 1896 | Baltimore | Edward H. Hanlon | 90 | 39 | .698 | 1939 | Cincinnati | William B. McKechnie | 97 | 57 | .630 |
| 1897 | Boston | Frank G. Selee | 93 | 39 | .705 | 1940* | Cincinnati | William B. McKechnie | 100 | 53 | .654 |
| 1898 | Boston | Frank G. Selee | 102 | 47 | .685 | 1941 | Brooklyn | Leo E. Durocher | 100 | 54 | .649 |
| 1899 | Brooklyn | Edward H. Hanlon | 88 | 42 | .677 | 1942* | St. Louis | William H. Southworth | 106 | 48 | .688 |
| 1900 | Brooklyn | Edward H. Hanlon | 82 | 54 | .603 | 1943 | St. Louis | William H. Southworth | 105 | 49 | .682 |
| 1901 | Pittsburgh | Fred C. Clarke | 90 | 49 | .647 | 1944* | St. Louis | William H. Southworth | 105 | 49 | .682 |
| 1902 | Pittsburgh | Fred C. Clarke | 103 | 36 | .741 | 1945 | Chicago | Charles J. Grimm | 98 | 56 | .636 |
| 1903 | Pittsburgh | Fred C. Clarke | 91 | 49 | .650 | 1946* | St. Louis | Edwin H. Dyer | 98 | 58 | .628 |
| 1904† | New York | John J. McGraw | 106 | 47 | .693 | 1947 | Brooklyn | Burton E. Shotton | 94 | 60 | .610 |
| 1905* | New York | John J. McGraw | 105 | 48 | .686 | 1948 | Boston | William H. Southworth | 91 | 62 | .595 |
| 1906 | Chicago | Frank L. Chance | 116 | 36 | .763 | 1949 | Brooklyn | Burton E. Shotton | 97 | 57 | .630 |
| 1907* | Chicago | Frank L. Chance | 107 | 45 | .704 | 1950 | Philadelphia | Edwin M. Sawyer | 91 | 63 | .591 |
| 1908* | Chicago | Frank L. Chance | 99 | 55 | .643 | 1951 | New York | Leo E. Durocher | 98 | 59 | .624 |
| 1909* | Pittsburgh | Fred C. Clarke | 110 | 42 | .724 | 1952 | Brooklyn | Charles W. Dressen | 96 | 57 | .627 |
| 1910 | Chicago | Frank L. Chance | 104 | 50 | .675 | 1953 | Brooklyn | Charles W. Dressen | 105 | 49 | .682 |
| 1911 | New York | John J. McGraw | 99 | 54 | .647 | 1954* | New York | Leo E. Durocher | 97 | 57 | .630 |
| 1912 | New Yrok | John J. McGraw | 103 | 48 | .682 | 1955* | Brooklyn | Walter Alston | 98 | 55 | .641 |
| 1913 | New York | John J. McGraw | 101 | 51 | .664 | 1956 | Brooklyn | Walter Alston | 93 | 61 | .604 |
| 1914* | Boston | George T. Stallings | 94 | 59 | .614 | 1957* | Milwaukee | Fred Haney | 95 | 59 | .617 |
| 1915 | Philadelphia | Patrick J. Moran | 90 | 62 | .592 | 1958 | Milwaukee | Fred Haney | 92 | 62 | .597 |
| 1916 | Brooklyn | Wilbert Robinson | 94 | 60 | .610 | 1959* | Los Angeles | Walter Alston | 88 | 68 | .564 |
| 1917 | New York | John J. McGraw | 98 | 56 | .636 | 1960* | Pittsburgh | Danny Murtaugh | 95 | 59 | .617 |
| 1918 | Chicago | Fred L. Mitchell | 84 | 45 | .651 |  |  |  |  |  |  |

* World Series winner.  † No World Series.

## MOST VALUABLE PLAYERS

(Baseball Writers Association selections)

### American League

1931 Lefty Grove, Philadelphia
1932–33 Jimmy Foxx, Philadelphia
1934 Mickey Cochrane, Detroit
1935 Hank Greenberg, Detroit
1936 Lou Gehrig, New York
1937 Charley Gehringer, Detroit
1938 Jimmy Foxx, Boston
1939 Joe DiMaggio, New York
1940 Hank Greenberg, Detroit
1941 Joe DiMaggio, New York
1942 Joe Gordon, New.York
1943 Spurgeon Chandler, New York
1944–45 Hal Newhouser, Detroit
1946 Ted Williams, Boston
1947 Joe DiMaggio, New York
1948 Lou Boudreau, Cleveland
1949 Ted Williams Boston
1950 Phil Rizzuto, New York

1951 Yogi Berra, New York
1952 Bobby Shantz, Philadelphia
1953 Al Rosen, Cleveland
1954–55 Yogi Berra, New York
1956–57 Mickey Mantle, New York
1958 Jackie Jensen, Boston
1959 Nellie Fox, Chicago
1960 Roger Maris, New York

### National League

1931 Frank Frisch, St. Louis
1932 Chuck Klein, Philadelphia
1933 Carl Hubbell, New York
1934 Dizzy Dean, St. Louis
1935 Gabby Hartnett, Chicago
1936 Carl Hubbell, New York
1937 Joe Medwick, St. Louis
1938 Ernie Lombardi, Cincinnati
1939 Bucky Walters, Cincinnati
1940 Frank McCormick, Cincinnati

1941 Dolph Camilli, Brooklyn
1942 Mort Cooper, St. Louis
1943 Stan Musial, St. Louis
1944 Marty Marion, St. Louis,
1945 Phil Cavarretta, Chicago
1946 Stan Musial, St. Louis
1947 Bob Elliott, Boston
1948 Stan Musial, St. Louis
1949 Jackie Robinson, Brooklyn
1950 Jim Konstanty, Philadelphia
1951 Roy Campanella, Brooklyn
1952 Hank Sauer, Chicago
1953 Roy Campanella, Brooklyn
1954 Willie Mays, New York
1955 Roy Campanella, Brooklyn
1956 Don Newcombe, Brooklyn
1957 Henry Aaron, Milwaukee
1958–59 Ernie Banks, Chicago
1960 Dick Groat, Pittsburgh

# American League Pennant Winners

| Year | Club | Manager | Won | Lost | Pct. | Year | Club | Manager | Won | Lost | Pct. |
|---|---|---|---|---|---|---|---|---|---|---|---|
| 901 | Chicago | Clark C. Griffith | 83 | 53 | .610 | 1931 | Philadelphia | Connie Mack | 107 | 45 | .704 |
| 902 | Philadelphia | Connie Mack | 83 | 53 | .610 | 1932* | New York | Joseph V. McCarthy | 107 | 47 | .695 |
| 903* | Boston | Jimmy Collins | 91 | 47 | .659 | 1933 | Washington | Joseph E. Cronin | 99 | 53 | .651 |
| 904† | Boston | Jimmy Collins | 95 | 59 | .617 | 1934 | Detroit | Gordon S. Cochrane | 101 | 53 | .656 |
| 905 | Philadelphia | Connie Mack | 92 | 56 | .622 | 1935* | Detroit | Gordon S. Cochrane | 93 | 58 | .616 |
| 906* | Chicago | Fielder A. Jones | 93 | 58 | .616 | 1936* | New York | Joseph V. McCarthy | 102 | 51 | .667 |
| 907 | Detroit | Hugh A. Jennings | 92 | 58 | .613 | 1937* | New York | Joseph V. McCarthy | 102 | 52 | .662 |
| 908 | Detroit | Hugh A. Jennings | 90 | 63 | .588 | 1938* | New York | Joseph V. McCarthy | 99 | 53 | .651 |
| 909 | Detroit | Hugh A. Jennings | 98 | 54 | .645 | 1939* | New York | Joseph V. McCarthy | 106 | 45 | .702 |
| 910* | Philadelphia | Connie Mack | 102 | 48 | .680 | 1940 | Detroit | Delmar D. Baker | 90 | 64 | .584 |
| 911* | Philadelphia | Connie Mack | 101 | 50 | .669 | 1941* | New York | Joseph V. McCarthy | 101 | 53 | .656 |
| 912* | Boston | J. Garland Stahl | 105 | 47 | .691 | 1942 | New York | Joseph V. McCarthy | 103 | 51 | .669 |
| 913* | Philadelphia | Connie Mack | 96 | 57 | .627 | 1943* | New York | Joseph V. McCarthy | 98 | 56 | .636 |
| 914 | Philadelphia | Connie Mack | 99 | 53 | .651 | 1944 | St. Louis | Luke Sewell | 89 | 65 | .578 |
| 915* | Boston | William F. Carrigan | 101 | 50 | .669 | 1945* | Detroit | Steve O'Neill | 88 | 65 | .575 |
| 916* | Boston | William F. Carrigan | 91 | 63 | .591 | 1946 | Boston | Joseph E. Cronin | 104 | 50 | .675 |
| 917* | Chicago | Clarence H. Rowland | 100 | 54 | .649 | 1947* | New York | Stanley R. Harris | 97 | 57 | .630 |
| 918* | Boston | Ed Barrow | 75 | 51 | .595 | 1948* | Cleveland | Lou Boudreau | 97 | 58 | .626 |
| 919 | Chicago | William Gleason | 88 | 52 | .629 | 1949* | New York | Casey Stengel | 97 | 57 | .630 |
| 920* | Cleveland | Tris E. Speaker | 98 | 56 | .636 | 1950* | New York | Casey Stengel | 98 | 56 | .636 |
| 921 | New York | Miller J. Huggins | 98 | 55 | .641 | 1951* | New York | Casey Stengel | 98 | 56 | .636 |
| 922 | New York | Miller J. Huggins | 94 | 60 | .610 | 1952* | New York | Casey Stengel | 95 | 59 | .617 |
| 923* | New York | Miller J. Huggins | 98 | 54 | .645 | 1953* | New York | Casey Stengel | 99 | 52 | .656 |
| 924* | Washington | Stanley R. Harris | 92 | 62 | .597 | 1954 | Cleveland | Al Lopez | 111 | 43 | .721 |
| 925 | Washington | Stanley R. Harris | 96 | 55 | .636 | 1955 | New York | Casey Stengel | 96 | 58 | .623 |
| 926 | New York | Miller J. Huggins | 91 | 63 | .591 | 1956* | New York | Casey Stengel | 97 | 57 | .630 |
| 927* | New York | Miller J. Huggins | 110 | 44 | .714 | 1957 | New York | Casey Stengel | 98 | 56 | .636 |
| 928* | New York | Miller J. Huggins | 101 | 53 | .656 | 1958* | New York | Casey Stengel | 92 | 62 | .597 |
| 929* | Philadelphia | Connie Mack | 104 | 46 | .693 | 1959 | Chicago | Al Lopez | 94 | 60 | .610 |
| 930* | Philadelphia | Connie Mack | 102 | 52 | .662 | 1960 | New York | Casey Stengel | 97 | 57 | .630 |

\* World Series winner.  † No World Series.

## NATIONAL BASEBALL HALL OF FAME
### Cooperstown, N. Y.

| Member | Elected | Member | Elected | Member | Elected |
|---|---|---|---|---|---|
| Alexander, Grover Cleveland | 1938 | Duffy, Hugh | 1945 | McGinnity, Joseph Jerome | 1946 |
| Anson, Adrian (Cap) | 1939 | Evers, John Joseph | 1946 | McGraw, John Joseph | 1937 |
| Baker, J. Frank (Home Run) | 1955 | Ewing, William B. (Buck) | 1939 | Nichols, Charles A. (Kid) | 1949 |
| Barrow, Edward Grant | 1953 | Foxx, James Emory | 1951 | O'Rourke, James H. | 1945 |
| Bender, Charles Albert (Chief) | 1953 | Frisch, Frank F. | 1947 | Ott, Melvin Thomas | 1951 |
| Bresnahan, Roger Philip | 1945 | Gehrig, Henry Louis | 1939 | Pennock, Herbert J. | 1948 |
| Brouthers, Dan | 1945 | Gehringer, Charles L. | 1949 | Plank, Edward S. | 1946 |
| Brown, Mordecai (Three-Finger) | 1949 | Greenberg, Henry Benjamin | 1956 | Radbourne, Charles | 1939 |
| Bulkeley, Morgan G. | 1937 | Griffith, Clark C. | 1946 | Robinson, Wilbert | 1945 |
| Burkett, Jesse C. | 1946 | Grove, Robert Moses (Lefty) | 1947 | Ruth, George Herman (Babe) | 1936 |
| Carey, Max George | 1961 | Hamilton, William Robert | 1961 | Schalk, Raymond | 1955 |
| Cartwright, Alexander Joy | 1938 | Hartnett, Charles L. (Gabby) | 1955 | Simmons, Aloysius Harry | 1953 |
| Chadwick, Henry | 1938 | Heilmann, Harry E. | 1952 | Sisler, George Harold | 1939 |
| Chance, Frank LeRoy | 1946 | Hornsby, Rogers | 1942 | Spalding, Albert Goodwill | 1939 |
| Chesbro, John Dwight | 1946 | Hubbell, Carl Owen | 1947 | Speaker, Tristram E. | 1937 |
| Clarke, Fred C. | 1945 | Jennings, Hughie | 1945 | Terry, William H. | 1954 |
| Cobb, Tyrus Raymond | 1936 | Johnson, Byron Bancroft | 1937 | Tinkers, Joseph B. | 1946 |
| Cochrane, Gordon (Mickey) | 1947 | Johnson, Walter Perry | 1936 | Traynor, Harold J. (Pie) | 1948 |
| Collins, Edward Trowbridge | 1939 | Keeler, Willie | 1939 | Vance, Arthur C. (Dazzy) | 1955 |
| Collins, James J. | 1945 | Kelly, Michael J. (King) | 1945 | Waddell, George E. (Rube) | 1946 |
| Comiskey, Charles Albert | 1939 | Klem, William Joseph | 1953 | Wagner, John P. (Honus) | 1936 |
| Connolly, Thomas H. | 1953 | Lajoie, Napoleon | 1937 | Wallace, Roderick John | 1953 |
| Crawford, Samuel E. | 1957 | Landis, Kenesaw Mountain | 1944 | Walsh, Edward A. | 1946 |
| Cronin, Joseph Edward | 1956 | Lyons, Theodore Amar | 1955 | Waner, Paul G. | 1952 |
| Cummings, William Arthur | 1939 | Mack, Connie | 1937 | Wheat, Zachary Davis | 1959 |
| Dean, Jay Hanna (Dizzy) | 1953 | Maranville, Walter J. (Rabbit) | 1954 | Wright, George | 1937 |
| Delahanty, Edward J. | 1945 | Mathewson, Christopher | 1936 | Wright, Harry | 1953 |
| Dickey, William M. | 1954 | McCarthy, Joseph V. | 1957 | Young, Denton T. (Cy) | 1937 |
| DiMaggio, Joseph Paul | 1955 | McCarthy, Thomas F. | 1946 | | |

## CY YOUNG AWARD
### "The Major League Pitcher of the Year"
(Baseball Writers Association selections)

| | | |
|---|---|---|
| 956 Don Newcombe, Brooklyn N. L. | 1958 Bob Turley, New York A. L. | 1960 Vernon Law, Pittsburgh N.L. |
| 957 Warren Spahn, Milwaukee N. L. | 1959 Early Wynn, Chicago A. L. | |

## National League Batting Champions

| Year | | Avg. | Year | | Avg. | Year | | Avg |
|---|---|---|---|---|---|---|---|---|
| 1876 | Roscoe Barnes, Chi | .404 | 1904 | Honus Wagner, Pitts | .349 | 1933 | Chuck Klein, Phila | .36 |
| 1877 | Jim White, Bost | .385 | 1905 | Cy Seymour, Cin | .377 | 1934 | Paul Waner, Pitts | .36 |
| 1878 | Abner Dalrymple, Mil | .356 | 1906 | Honus Wagner, Pitts | .339 | 1935 | Arky Vaughan, Pitts | .38 |
| 1879 | Cap Anson, Chi | .407 | 1907 | Honus Wagner, Pitts | .350 | 1936 | Paul Waner, Pitts | .37 |
| 1880 | George Gore, Chi | .365 | 1908 | Honus Wagner, Pitts | .354 | 1937 | Joe Medwick, St. L | .37 |
| 1881 | Cap Anson, Chi | .399 | 1909 | Honus Wagner, Pitts | .339 | 1938 | Ernie Lombardi, Cin | .34 |
| 1882 | Dan Brouthers, Buff | .367 | 1910 | Sherwood Magee, Phila | .331 | 1939 | John Mize, St. L | .34 |
| 1883 | Dan Brouthers, Buff | .371 | 1911 | Honus Wagner, Pitts | .334 | 1940 | Debs Garms, Pitts | .35 |
| 1884 | James O'Rourke, Buff | .350 | 1912 | Henry Zimmerman, Chi | .372 | 1941 | Pete Reiser, Bklyn | .34 |
| 1885 | Roger Connor, N. Y | .371 | 1913 | Jake Daubert, Bklyn | .350 | 1942 | Ernie Lombardi, Bost | .33 |
| 1886 | King Kelly, Chi | .388 | 1914 | Jake Daubert, Bklyn | .329 | 1943 | Stan Musial, St. L | .35 |
| 1887 | Cap Anson, Chi | .421 | 1915 | Larry Doyle, N. Y | .320 | 1944 | Dixie Walker, Bklyn | .35 |
| 1888 | Cap Anson, Chi | .343 | 1916 | Hal Chase, Cin | .339 | 1945 | Phil Cavaretta, Chi | .35 |
| 1889 | Dan Brouthers, Bost | .373 | 1917 | Edd Roush, Cin | .341 | 1946 | Stan Musial, St. L | .36 |
| 1890 | John Glasscock, N. Y | .336 | 1918 | Zach Wheat, Bklyn | .335 | 1947 | Harry Walker, St. L.-Phila. | .36 |
| 1891 | Wm. Hamilton, Phila | .338 | 1919 | Edd Roush, Cin | .321 | 1948 | Stan Musial, St. L | .37 |
| 1892 | Dan Brouthers, Bklyn., and | | 1920 | Rogers Hornsby, St. L | .370 | 1949 | Jackie Robinson, Bklyn | .34 |
| | Clarence Childs, Cleve | .335 | 1921 | Rogers Hornsby, St. L | .397 | 1950 | Stan Musial, St. L | .34 |
| 1893 | Hugh Duffy, Bost | .378 | 1922 | Rogers Hornsby, St. L | .401 | 1951 | Stan Musial, St. L | .35 |
| 1894 | Hugh Duffy, Bost | .438 | 1923 | Rogers Hornsby, St. L | .384 | 1952 | Stan Musial, St. L | .33 |
| 1895 | Jesse Burkett, Cleve | .423 | 1924 | Rogers Hornsby, St. L | .424 | 1953 | Carl Furillo, Bklyn | .34 |
| 1896 | Jesse Burkett, Cleve | .410 | 1925 | Rogers Hornsby, St. L | .403 | 1954 | Willie Mays, N. Y | .34 |
| 1897 | Willie Keeler, Balt | .432 | 1926 | Gene Hargrave, Cin | .353 | 1955 | Richie Ashburn, Phila | .33 |
| 1898 | Willie Keeler, Balt | .379 | 1927 | Paul Waner, Pitts | .380 | 1956 | Henry Aaron, Mil | .32 |
| 1899 | Ed Delahanty, Phila | .408 | 1928 | Rogers Hornsby, Bost | .387 | 1957 | Stan Musial, St. L | .35 |
| 1900 | Honus Wagner, Pitts | .381 | 1929 | Lefty O'Doul, Phila | .398 | 1958 | Richie Ashburn, Phila | .35 |
| 1901 | Jesse Burkett, St. L | .382 | 1930 | Bill Terry, N. Y | .401 | 1959 | Henry Aaron, Mil | .35 |
| 1902 | Clarence Beaumont, Pitts | .357 | 1931 | Chick Hafey, St. L | .349 | 1960 | Dick Groat, Pitts | .32 |
| 1903 | Honus Wagner, Pitts | .355 | 1932 | Lefty O'Doul, Bklyn | .368 | | | |

## National League Home Run Champions

| Year | | No. | Year | | No. | Year | | No |
|---|---|---|---|---|---|---|---|---|
| 1876 | George Hall, Phila. Athletics | 5 | 1904 | Harry Lumley, Bklyn | 9 | | Mel Ott, N. Y | 3 |
| 1877 | George Shaffer, Louisville | 3 | 1905 | Fred Odwell, Cin | 9 | 1933 | Chuck Klein, Phila | 2 |
| 1878 | Paul Hines, Providence | 4 | 1906 | Tim Jordan, Bklyn | 12 | 1934 | Mel Ott, N. Y., and | |
| 1879 | Charles Jones, Bost | 9 | 1907 | David Brain, Bost | 10 | | Rip Collins, St. L | 3 |
| 1880 | James O'Rourke, Bost. and | | 1908 | Tim Jordan, Bklyn | 12 | 1935 | Wally Berger, Bost | 3 |
| | Harry Stovey, Worcester | 6 | 1909 | John Murray, N. Y | 7 | 1936 | Mel Ott, N. Y | 3 |
| 1881 | Dan Brouthers, Buffalo | 8 | 1910 | Fred Beck, Bost., and | | 1937 | Mel Ott, N. Y., and | |
| 1882 | George Wood, Det | 7 | | Frank Schulte, Chi | 10 | | Joe Medwick, St. L | 3 |
| 1883 | William Ewing, N. Y | 10 | 1911 | Frank Schulte, Chi | 21 | 1938 | Mel Ott, N. Y | 3 |
| 1884 | Ed Williamson, Chi | 27 | 1912 | Henry Zimmerman, Chi | 14 | 1939 | John Mize, St. L | 2 |
| 1885 | Abner Dalrymple, Chi | 11 | 1913 | Cliff Cravath, Phila | 19 | 1940 | John Mize, St. L | 4 |
| 1886 | Arthur Richardson, Det | 11 | 1914 | Cliff Cravath, Phila | 19 | 1941 | Dolph Camilli, Bklyn | 3 |
| 1887 | Roger Connor, N. Y., and | | 1915 | Cliff Cravath, Phila | 24 | 1942 | Mel Ott, N. Y | 3 |
| | Wm. O'Brien, Wash | 17 | 1916 | Davis Robertson, N. Y., and | | 1943 | Bill Nicholson, Chi | 2 |
| 1888 | Roger Connor, N. Y | 14 | | Fred Williams, Chi | 12 | 1944 | Bill Nicholson, Chi | 3 |
| 1889 | Sam Thompson, Phila | 20 | 1917 | Davis Robertson, N. Y., and | | 1945 | Tommy Holmes, Bost | 2 |
| 1890 | Tom Burns, Bklyn., and | | | Cliff Cravath, Phila | 12 | 1946 | Ralph Kiner, Pitts | 2 |
| | Mike Tiernan, N. Y | 13 | 1918 | Cliff Cravath, Phila | 8 | 1947 | Ralph Kiner, Pitts., and | |
| 1891 | Harry Stovey, Bost., and | | 1919 | Cliff Cravath, Phila | 12 | | John Mize, N. Y | 5 |
| | Mike Tiernan, N. Y | 16 | 1920 | Cy Williams, Phila | 15 | 1948 | Ralph Kiner, Pitts., and | |
| 1892 | Jim Holliday, Cin | 13 | 1921 | George Kelly, N. Y | 23 | | John Mize, N. Y | 4 |
| 1893 | Ed Delahanty, Phila | 19 | 1922 | Rogers Hornsby, St. L | 42 | 1949 | Ralph Kiner, Pitts | 5 |
| 1894 | Hugh Duffy, Bost., and | | 1923 | Cy Williams, Phila | 41 | 1950 | Ralph Kiner, Pitts | 4 |
| | Robert Lowe, Bost | 18 | 1924 | Jacques Fournier, Bklyn | 27 | 1951 | Ralph Kiner, Pitts | 4 |
| 1895 | Bill Joyce, Wash | 17 | 1925 | Rogers Hornsby, St. L | 39 | 1952 | Ralph Kiner, Pitts., and | |
| 1896 | Ed Delahanty, Phila., and | | 1926 | Hack Wilson, Chi | 21 | | Hank Sauer, Chi | 3 |
| | Sam Thompson, Phila | 13 | 1927 | Hack Wilson, Chi., and | | 1953 | Ed Mathews, Mil | 4 |
| 1897 | Nap Lajoie, Phila | 10 | | Cy Williams, Phila | 30 | 1954 | Ted Kluszewski, Cin | 4 |
| 1898 | James Collins, Bost | 14 | 1928 | Hack Wilson, Chi., and | | 1955 | Willie Mays, N. Y | 5 |
| 1899 | John Freeman, Wash | 25 | | Jim Bottomley, St. L | 31 | 1956 | Duke Snider, Bklyn | 4 |
| 1900 | Herman Long, Bost | 12 | 1929 | Chuck Klein, Phila | 43 | 1957 | Henry Aaron, Mil | 4 |
| 1901 | Sam Crawford, Cin | 16 | 1930 | Hack Wilson, Chi | 56 | 1958 | Ernie Banks, Chi | 4 |
| 1902 | Tom Leach, Pitts | 6 | 1931 | Chuck Klein, Phila | 31 | 1959 | Ed Mathews, Mil | 4 |
| 1903 | James Sheckard, Bklyn | 9 | 1932 | Chuck Klein, Phila., and | | 1960 | Ernie Banks, Chi | 4 |

(See Index for 1961 Champions)

## American League Batting Champions

| Year | | Avg. | Year | | Avg. | Year | | Avg. |
|---|---|---|---|---|---|---|---|---|
| 1901 | Nap Lajoie, Phila | .422 | 1921 | Harry Heilmann, Det | .394 | 1941 | Ted Williams, Bost | .406 |
| 1902 | Ed Delahanty, Wash | .376 | 1922 | George Sisler, St. L | .420 | 1942 | Ted Williams, Bost | .356 |
| 1903 | Nap Lajoie, Cleve | .355 | 1923 | Harry Heilmann, Det | .403 | 1943 | Luke Appling, Chi | .328 |
| 1904 | Nap Lajoie, Cleve | .381 | 1924 | Babe Ruth, N. Y. | .378 | 1944 | Lou Boudreau, Cleve | .327 |
| 1905 | Elmer Flick, Cleve | .306 | 1925 | Harry Heilmann, Det | .393 | 1945 | George Sternweiss, N. Y. | .309 |
| 1906 | George Stone, St. L | .358 | 1926 | Heinie Manush, Det | .378 | 1946 | Mickey Vernon, Wash | .353 |
| 1907 | Ty Cobb, Det | .350 | 1927 | Harry Heilmann, Det | .398 | 1947 | Ted Williams, Bost | .343 |
| 1908 | Ty Cobb, Det | .324 | 1928 | Goose Goslin, Wash | .379 | 1948 | Ted Williams, Bost | .369 |
| 1909 | Ty Cobb, Det | .377 | 1929 | Lew Fonseca, Cleve | .369 | 1949 | George Kell, Det | .343 |
| 1910 | Ty Cobb, Det | .385 | 1930 | Al Simmons, Phila | .381 | 1950 | Billy Goodman, Bost | .354 |
| 1911 | Ty Cobb, Det | .420 | 1931 | Al Simmons, Phila | .390 | 1951 | Ferris Fain, Phila | .344 |
| 1912 | Ty Cobb, Det | .410 | 1932 | Dale Alexander, Det.-Bost | .367 | 1952 | Ferris Fain, Phila | .327 |
| 1913 | Ty Cobb, Det | .390 | 1933 | Jimmy Foxx, Phila | .356 | 1953 | Mickey Vernon, Wash | .337 |
| 1914 | Ty Cobb, Det | .368 | 1934 | Lou Gehrig, N. Y. | .363 | 1954 | Bobby Avila, Cleve | .341 |
| 1915 | Ty Cobb, Det | .369 | 1935 | Buddy Myer, Wash | .349 | 1955 | Al Kaline, Det. | .340 |
| 1916 | Tris Speaker, Cleve | .386 | 1936 | Luke Appling, Chi. | .388 | 1956 | Mickey Mantle, N. Y. | .353 |
| 1917 | Ty Cobb, Det | .383 | 1937 | Charles Gehringer, Det | .371 | 1957 | Ted Williams, Bost. | .388 |
| 1918 | Ty Cobb, Det | .382 | 1938 | Jimmy Foxx, Bost | .349 | 1958 | Ted Williams, Bost. | .328 |
| 1919 | Ty Cobb, Det | .384 | 1939 | Joe DiMaggio, N. Y. | .381 | 1959 | Harvey Kuenn, Det. | .353 |
| 1920 | George Sisler, St. L | .407 | 1940 | Joe DiMaggio, N. Y. | .352 | 1960 | Pete Runnels, Bost. | .320 |

## American League Home Run Champions

| Year | | No. | Year | | No. | Year | | No. |
|---|---|---|---|---|---|---|---|---|
| 1901 | Nap Lajoie, Phila | 13 | 1921 | Babe Ruth, N. Y. | 59 | 1941 | Ted Williams, Bost. | 37 |
| 1902 | Ralph Seybold, Phila | 16 | 1922 | Ken Williams, St. L | 39 | 1942 | Ted Williams, Bost. | 36 |
| 1903 | Buck Freeman, Bost | 13 | 1923 | Babe Ruth, N. Y. | 41 | 1943 | Rudy York, Det. | 34 |
| 1904 | Harry Davis, Phila | 10 | 1924 | Babe Ruth, N. Y. | 46 | 1944 | Nick Etten, N. Y. | 22 |
| 1905 | Harry Davis, Phila | 8 | 1925 | Bob Meusel, N. Y. | 33 | 1945 | Vern Stephens, St. L. | 24 |
| 1906 | Harry Davis, Phila | 12 | 1926 | Babe Ruth, N. Y. | 47 | 1946 | Hank Greenberg, Det. | 44 |
| 1907 | Harry Davis, Phila | 8 | 1927 | Babe Ruth, N. Y. | 60 | 1947 | Ted Williams, Bost. | 32 |
| 1908 | Sam Crawford, Det | 7 | 1928 | Babe Ruth, N. Y. | 54 | 1948 | Joe DiMaggio, N. Y. | 39 |
| 1909 | Ty Cobb, Det | 9 | 1929 | Babe Ruth, N. Y. | 46 | 1949 | Ted Williams, Bost. | 43 |
| 1910 | J. Garland Stahl, Bost | 10 | 1930 | Babe Ruth, N. Y. | 49 | 1950 | Al Rosen, Cleve. | 37 |
| 1911 | Franklin Baker, Phila | 9 | 1931 | Babe Ruth, N. Y., and | | 1951 | Gus Zernial, Chi.-Phila. | 33 |
| 1912 | Franklin Baker, Phila | 10 | | Lou Gehrig, N. Y. | 46 | 1952 | Larry Doby, Cleve. | 32 |
| 1913 | Franklin Baker, Phila | 12 | 1932 | Jimmy Foxx, Phila. | 58 | 1953 | Al Rosen, Cleve. | 43 |
| 1914 | Franklin Baker, Phila., and | | 1933 | Jimmy Foxx, Phila. | 48 | 1954 | Larry Doby, Cleve. | 32 |
| | Sam Crawford, Det. | 8 | 1934 | Lou Gehrig, N. Y. | 49 | 1955 | Mickey Mantle, N. Y. | 37 |
| 1915 | Robert Roth, Chi.-Cleve. | 7 | 1935 | Jimmy Foxx, Phila., and | | 1956 | Mickey Mantle, N. Y. | 52 |
| 1916 | Wally Pipp, N. Y. | 12 | | Hank Greenberg, Det. | 36 | 1957 | Roy Sievers, Wash. | 42 |
| 1917 | Wally Pipp, N. Y. | 9 | 1936 | Lou Gehrig, N. Y. | 49 | 1958 | Mickey Mantle, N. Y. | 42 |
| 1918 | Babe Ruth, Bost., and | | 1937 | Joe DiMaggio, N. Y. | 46 | 1959 | Rocky Colavito, Cleve., and | |
| | Clarence Walker, Phila. | 11 | 1938 | Hank Greenberg, Det. | 58 | | Harmon Killebrew, Wash. | 42 |
| 1919 | Babe Ruth, Bost. | 29 | 1939 | Jimmy Foxx, Phila. | 35 | 1960 | Mickey Mantle, N. Y. | 40 |
| 1920 | Babe Ruth, N. Y. | 54 | 1940 | Hank Greenberg, Det. | 41 | | | |

## BABE RUTH'S MAJOR LEAGUE HOME RUN RECORD

### Regular Season

| Year | Club | No. |
|---|---|---|
| 1914 | Boston (A) | 0 |
| 1915 | Boston (A) | 4 |
| 1916 | Boston (A) | 3 |
| 1917 | Boston (A) | 2 |
| 1918 | Boston (A) | 11 |
| 1919 | Boston (A) | 29 |
| 1920 | New York (A) | 54 |
| 1921 | New York (A) | 59 |
| 1922 | New York (A) | 35 |
| 1923 | New York (A) | 41 |
| 1924 | New York (A) | 46 |
| 1925 | New York (A) | 25 |
| 1926 | New York (A) | 47 |
| 1927 | New York (A) | 60 |
| 1928 | New York (A) | 54 |
| 1929 | New York (A) | 46 |
| 1930 | New York (A) | 49 |
| 1931 | New York (A) | 46 |
| 1932 | New York (A) | 41 |
| 1933 | New York (A) | 34 |
| 1934 | New York (A) | 22 |
| 1935 | Boston (N) | 6 |

### World Series

| Year | Club | No. |
|---|---|---|
| 1915 | Boston (A) | 0 |
| 1916 | Boston (A) | 0 |
| 1918 | Boston (A) | 0 |
| 1921 | New York (A) | 1 |
| 1922 | New York (A) | 0 |
| 1923 | New York (A) | 3 |
| 1926 | New York (A) | 4 |
| 1927 | New York (A) | 2 |
| 1928 | New York (A) | 3 |
| 1932 | New York (A) | 2 |

### All-Star Game

| Year | Club | No. |
|---|---|---|
| 1933 | American | 1 |
| 1934 | American | 0 |

### Totals

| | |
|---|---|
| Regular season | 714 |
| World Series | 15 |
| All-Star | 1 |

## TED WILLIAMS' MAJOR LEAGUE BATTING RECORD
### (All games with Boston Red Sox)

| | g | r | h | hr | rbi | avg | | g | r | h | hr | rbi | avg | | g | r | h | hr | rbi | avg |
|---|---|---|---|---|---|---|---|---|---|---|---|---|---|---|---|---|---|---|---|---|
| 1939.. | 149 | 131 | 185 | 31 | 145* | .327 | 1949.. | 155 | 150* | 194 | 43* | 159† | .343 | 1956.. | 136 | 71 | 138 | 24 | 82 | .345 |
| 1940.. | 144 | 134* | 193 | 23 | 113 | .344 | 1950.. | 89 | 82 | 106 | 28 | 97 | .317 | 1957.. | 132 | 96 | 163 | 38 | 87 | .388* |
| 1941.. | 143 | 135* | 185 | 37* | 120 | .406* | 1951.. | 148 | 109 | 169 | 30 | 126 | .318 | 1958.. | 129 | 81 | 135 | 26 | 85 | .328* |
| 1942.. | 150 | 141* | 186 | 36* | 137* | .356* | 1952.. | 6 | 2 | 4 | 1 | 3 | .400 | 1959.. | 103 | 32 | 69 | 10 | 43 | .254 |
| 1943–45... In military service | | | | | | | 1953.. | 37 | 17 | 37 | 13 | 34 | .407 | 1960.. | 113 | 56 | 98 | 29 | 72 | .316 |
| 1946.. | 150 | 142* | 176 | 38 | 123 | .342 | 1954.. | 117 | 93 | 133 | 29 | 89 | .345 | | | | | | | |
| 1947.. | 156 | 125* | 181 | 32* | 114* | .343* | 1955.. | 98 | 77 | 114 | 28 | 83 | .356 | Totals | 2292 | 1798 | 2654 | 521 | 1839 | .344 |
| 1948.. | 137 | 124 | 188 | 25 | 127 | .369* | * Led league. | | | | | | | † Tied for league lead. | | | | | | |

## JUNIOR WORLD SERIES
### International League vs. American Association
#### No series 1905, 1908-16, 1918-19, 1935.

| Year | Winner | Games W | L | Loser | Year | Winner | Games W | L | Loser |
|------|--------|---------|---|-------|------|--------|---------|---|-------|
| 1904 | Buffalo (IL) | 2 | 1 | St. Paul | 1939 | Louisville (AA) | 4 | 3 | Rochester |
| 1906* | Buffalo (IL) | 3 | 2 | Columbus | 1940 | Newark (IL) | 4 | 2 | Louisville |
| 1907 | Toronto (IL) | 4 | 1 | Columbus | 1941 | Columbus (AA) | 4 | 2 | Montreal |
| 1917 | Indianapolis (AA) | 4 | 1 | Toronto | 1942 | Columbus (AA) | 4 | 1 | Syracuse |
| 1920 | Baltimore (IL) | 5 | 1 | St. Paul | 1943 | Columbus (AA) | 4 | 1 | Syracuse |
| 1921 | Louisville (AA) | 5 | 3 | Baltimore | 1944 | Baltimore (IL) | 4 | 2 | Louisville |
| 1922 | Baltimore (IL) | 5 | 2 | St. Paul | 1945 | Louisville (AA) | 4 | 2 | Newark |
| 1923 | Kansas City (AA) | 5 | 4 | Baltimore | 1946 | Montreal (IL) | 4 | 2 | Louisville |
| 1924* | St. Paul (AA) | 5 | 4 | Baltimore | 1947 | Milwaukee (AA) | 4 | 3 | Syracuse |
| 1925 | Baltimore (IL) | 5 | 3 | Louisville | 1948 | Montreal (IL) | 4 | 1 | St. Paul |
| 1926 | Toronto (IL) | 5 | 0 | Louisville | 1949 | Indianapolis (AA) | 4 | 2 | Montreal |
| 1927 | Toledo (AA) | 5 | 1 | Buffalo | 1950 | Columbus (AA) | 4 | 1 | Baltimore |
| 1928* | Indianapolis (AA) | 5 | 1 | Rochester | 1951 | Milwaukee (AA) | 4 | 2 | Montreal |
| 1929 | Kansas City (AA) | 5 | 4 | Rochester | 1952 | Rochester (IL) | 4 | 3 | Kansas City |
| 1930 | Rochester (IL) | 5 | 3 | Louisville | 1953 | Montreal (IL) | 4 | 1 | Kansas City |
| 1931 | Rochester (IL) | 5 | 3 | St. Paul | 1954 | Louisville (AA) | 4 | 2 | Syracuse |
| 1932 | Newark (IL) | 4 | 2 | Minneapolis | 1955 | Minneapolis (AA) | 4 | 3 | Rochester |
| 1933 | Columbus (AA) | 5 | 3 | Buffalo | 1956 | Rochester (IL) | 4 | 0 | Rochester |
| 1934 | Columbus (AA) | 5 | 4 | Toronto | 1957 | Denver (AA) | 4 | 1 | Buffalo |
| 1936 | Milwaukee (AA) | 4 | 1 | Buffalo | 1958 | Minneapolis (AA) | 4 | 0 | Montreal |
| 1937 | Newark (IL) | 4 | 3 | Columbus | 1959 | Havana (IL) | 4 | 3 | Minneapolis |
| 1938 | Kansas City (AA) | 4 | 3 | Newark | 1960 | Louisville (AA) | 4 | 2 | Toronto |

\* Played tie game.

---

## Larsen's Perfect Game in '56 World Series

Don Larsen of the New York Yankees pitched the first no-run no-hit game in World Series history in 1956 and hurled a perfect game in so doing. Facing the Brooklyn Dodgers at the Yankee Stadium in the fifth game of the series on Oct. 8 Larsen retired 27 batters in a row. The righthander made only 97 pitches. The Yankees won, 2 to 0. The attendance was 64,519. The box score:

| BROOKLYN (N) | ab | r | h | po | a | e |
|--------------|----|---|---|----|----|----|
| Gilliam, 2b | 3 | 0 | 0 | 2 | 0 | 0 |
| Reese, ss | 3 | 0 | 0 | 4 | 2 | 0 |
| Snider, cf | 3 | 0 | 0 | 1 | 0 | 0 |
| Robinson, 3b | 3 | 0 | 0 | 2 | 4 | 0 |
| Hodges, 1b | 3 | 0 | 0 | 5 | 1 | 0 |
| Amoros, lf | 3 | 0 | 0 | 3 | 0 | 0 |
| Furillo, rf | 3 | 0 | 0 | 0 | 0 | 0 |
| Campanella, c | 3 | 0 | 0 | 7 | 2 | 0 |
| Maglie, p | 2 | 0 | 0 | 0 | 1 | 0 |
| aMitchell | 1 | 0 | 0 | 0 | 0 | 0 |
| Totals | 27 | 0 | 0 | 24 | 10 | 0 |

| NEW YORK (A) | ab | r | h | po | a | |
|--------------|----|---|---|----|----|----|
| Bauer, rf | 4 | 0 | 1 | 4 | 0 | |
| Collins, 1b | 4 | 0 | 1 | 7 | 0 | |
| Mantle, cf | 3 | 1 | 1 | 4 | 0 | |
| Berra, c | 3 | 0 | 0 | 7 | 0 | |
| Slaughter, lf | 2 | 0 | 0 | 1 | 0 | |
| Martin, 2b | 3 | 0 | 1 | 3 | 4 | |
| McDougald, ss | 2 | 0 | 0 | 0 | 2 | |
| Carey, 3b | 3 | 1 | 1 | 1 | 1 | |
| Larsen, p | 2 | 0 | 0 | 0 | 1 | |
| Totals | 26 | 2 | 5 | 27 | 8 | |

aCalled out on strikes for Maglie in 9th.

| | | | | | | | | | |
|---|---|---|---|---|---|---|---|---|---|
| Brooklyn | 0 0 0 | 0 0 0 | 0 0 0 — 0 |
| New York | 0 0 0 | 1 0 1 | 0 0 x — 2 |

Runs batted in—Mantle, Bauer. Home run—Mantle. Sacrifice—Larsen. Double plays—Reese and Hodges; Hodges, Campanella, Robinson, Campanella and Robinson. Left on bases—Brooklyn 0, New York 3. Bases on balls—Off Maglie 2 (Slaughter, McDougald). Struck out—By Larsen 7 (Gilliam, Reese, Hodges, Campanella, Snider, Gilliam, Mitchell), Maglie 5 (Martin, Collins 2, Larsen, Bauer). Runs and earned runs—Off Larsen 0–0, Maglie 2–2. Umpires—Pinelli (N), plate; Soar (A), first base; Boggess (N), second base; Napp (A), third base; Gorman (N), left field; Runge (A), right field. Time of game—2:06.

---

## Longest Game in the Majors

A 26-inning tie between the Brooklyn Dodgers and the Boston Braves of the National League on May 1, 1920, was the longest game in major league history. Played at Braves Field, Boston, the game was called because of darkness with the score 1–1. Brooklyn scored its run in the fourth inning and Boston matched it in the fifth. Both starting pitchers, Leon Cadore of Brooklyn and Joe Oeschger were still in the game at the end, 3 hours and 50 minutes after it had begun. Cadore allowed 15 hits, Oeschger 9. Cadore struck out 7 walked 5; Oeschger fanned 7, walked 4.

## National Baseball Congress Champions
### (Non-Pro)

| | | |
|---|---|---|
| 1935 Bismarck (N. D.) Corwin-Churchill | 1944 Sherman Field (Kans.) Flyers | 1953 Fort Leonard Wood (Mo.) Hilltop-pers |
| 1936 Duncan (Okla.) Halliburtons | 1945 Enid (Okla.) Army Air Field | |
| 1937 Enid (Okla.) Eason Oilers | 1946 St. Joseph (Mich.) Auscos | 1954 Wichita (Kan.) Boeing Bombers |
| 1938 Buford (Ga.) Bona Allens | 1947 Ft. Wayne (Ind.) General Electrics | 1955 Wichita (Kan.) Boeing Bombets |
| 1939 Duncan (Okla.) Halliburtons | 1948 Ft. Wayne (Ind.) General Electrics | 1956 Ft. Wayne (Ind.) Dairymen |
| 1940 Enid (Okla.) Champlins | 1949 Ft. Wayne (Ind.) General Electrics | 1957 Sinton (Tex.) Plymouth Oilers |
| 1941 Enid (Okla.) Champlins | 1950 Ft. Wayne (Ind.) Capeharts | 1958 Drain (Ore.) Black Sox |
| 1942 Wichita (Kan.) Boeing Bombers | 1951 Sinton (Tex.) Plymouth Oilers | 1959 Houston (Tex.) Fed-Marts |
| 1943 Camp Wheeler (Ga.) Spokes | 1952 Fort Meyer (Va.) Colonials | 1960 Grand Rapids (Mich.) Sullivans |

## National Collegiate A.A. Champions

| | | |
|---|---|---|
| 1947 California | 1952 Holy Cross | 1957 California |
| 1948 Southern California | 1953 Michigan | 1958 Southern California |
| 1949 Texas | 1954 Missouri | 1959 Oklahoma State |
| 1950 Texas | 1955 Wake Forest | 1960 Minnesota |
| 1951 Oklahoma | 1956 Minnesota | |

## Little League World Series

| | | |
|---|---|---|
| 1947 Williamsport, Pa. | 1952 Norwalk, Conn. | 1957 Monterrey, Mexico |
| 1948 Lock Haven, Pa. | 1953 Birmingham, Ala. | 1958 Monterrey, Mexico |
| 1949 Hammonton, N. J. | 1954 Schenectady, N. Y. | 1959 Hamtramck, Mich. |
| 1950 Houston, Tex. | 1955 Morrisville, Pa. | 1960 Levittown, Pa. |
| 1951 Stamford, Conn. | 1956 Roswell, N. M. | |

## American Legion Junior Champions

| | |
|---|---|
| 1926 Cook Post, Yonkers, N. Y. | 1943 Richfield Post, Minneapolis |
| 1927 No tournament | 1944 Bentley Post, Cincinnati |
| 1928 Oakland (Calif.) Post | 1945 Hoyle Post, Shelby, N. C. |
| 1929 South Buffalo Post, Buffalo, N. Y. | 1946 Crescent City Post, New Orleans |
| 1930 Baltimore & Ohio Railroad Post, Baltimore | 1947 Bentley Post, Cincinnati |
| 1931 South Side Post, So. Chicago, Ill. | 1948 Trenton (N. J.) Post |
| 1932 Callender Post, New Orleans | 1949-50 Erwin Post, Oakland, Calif. |
| 1933 National Post, Chicago | 1951 Crenshaw Post, Los Angeles |
| 1934 Fort Cumberland Post, Cumberland, Md. | 1952 Bentley Post, Cincinnati |
| 1935 Gaston Post, Gastonia, N. C. | 1953 Wheeler Post, Yakima, Wash. |
| 1936 Spartanburg (S. C.) Post | 1954 Downtown Post, San Diego, Calif. |
| 1937 East Lynn (Mass.) Post | 1955 Postal Employees Post, Cincinnati |
| 1938 San Diego (Calif.) Post | 1956 Stockholm Post, St. Louis |
| 1939 Omaha (Neb.) Post | 1957-58 Bentley Post, Cincinnati |
| 1940 Hill Post, Albemarle, N. C. | 1959 Edison Post, Detroit |
| 1941 San Diego (Calif.) Post | 1960 Crescent City Post, New Orleans |
| 1942 Sunrise Post, Los Angeles | |

---

# SOFTBALL

*Source:* Amateur Softball Association.

## World Amateur Champions

### MEN

| | |
|---|---|
| 1933 | J. L. Gillis, Chicago |
| 1934 | Ke-Nash-A's, Kenosha, Wis. |
| 1935 | Crimson Coaches, Toledo, Ohio |
| 1936 | Kodak Park, Rochester, N. Y. |
| 1937 | Briggs Mfg. Co., Detroit |
| 1938 | Pohlers, Cincinnati |
| 1939 | Carr's, Covington, Ky. |
| 1940 | Kodak Park, Rochester, N. Y. |
| 1941 | Bendix Brakes, South Bend, Ind. |
| 1942 | Deep Rock Oilers, Tulsa, Okla. |
| 1943-44 | Hammer Field, Fresno, Calif. |
| 1945-47 | Zollners, Ft. Wayne, Ind. |
| 1948 | Briggs Beautyware, Detroit |
| 1949 | Tip Top Tailors, Toronto, Ont. |
| 1950 | Clearwater (Fla.) Bombers |
| 1951 | Dow Chemical Co., Midland, Mich. |
| 1952-53 | Briggs Beautyware, Detroit |
| 1954 | Clearwater (Fla.) Bombers |
| 1955 | Raybestos Cardinals, Stratford, Conn. |
| 1956-57 | Clearwater (Fla.) Bombers |

| | |
|---|---|
| 1958 | Raybestos Cardinals, Stratford, Conn. |
| 1959 | Sealmasters, Aurora, Ill. |
| 1960 | Clearwater (Fla.) Bombers |

### WOMEN

| | |
|---|---|
| 1933 | Great Northerns, Chicago |
| 1934 | Hart Motors, Chicago |
| 1935 | Bloomer Girls, Cleveland |
| 1936-37 | National Mfg. Co., Cleveland |
| 1938-39 | J. J. Kreig's, Alameda, Calif. |
| 1940 | Arizona Ramblers, Phoenix, Ariz. |
| 1941 | Higgins, Midgets, Tulsa, Okla. |
| 1942-43 | Jax Maids, New Orleans |
| 1944 | Lind & Pomeroy, Portland, Ore. |
| 1945-47 | Jax Maids, New Orleans |
| 1948-49 | Arizona Ramblers, Phoenix |
| 1950-52 | Orange (Calif.) Lionettes |
| 1953 | Betsy Ross Rockets, Fresno, Calif. |
| 1954 | Leach Motors Rockets, Fresno, Calif. |
| 1955-56 | Orange (Calif.) Lionettes |
| 1957 | Hacienda Rockets, Fresno, Calif. |
| 1958-60 | Raybestos Brakettes, Stratford, Conn. |

# FOOTBALL

THE PASTIME of kicking a ball around goes back beyond the limits of recorded history. Ancient savage tribes played football of a primitive kind. There was a ball-kicking game played by Athenians and Spartans and Corinthians 2500 years ago and the Greeks had a name for it: *Episkuros.* The Romans had a somewhat similar game called *Harpastum* and are supposed to have carried the game with them when they invaded the British Isles in the First Century, B.C.

Undoubtedly the game known in the United States as Football traces directly to the English game of Rugby, though the modifications have been many and rather sweeping in some directions. There was informal football on our college lawns well over a century ago and an annual Freshman-Sophomore series of "scrimmages" began at Yale in 1840. But the first formal intercollegiate football game in this country was the Princeton-Rutgers contest at New Brunswick, N. J., on Nov. 6, 1869, with Rutgers winning by 6 goals to 4.

In those old days games were played with twenty-five, twenty, fifteen or eleven men on a side by mutual agreement. In 1880 there was a football convention at which Walter Camp of Yale persuaded the delegates to agree to a rule calling for eleven players on a side. In 1882 there was adopted the rule requiring the offensive team to make 5 yards in three downs or surrender the ball to its opponents. The game grew so rough that it was attacked as brutal by many critics and some colleges abandoned the sport. Conditions were so bad in 1906 that President Theodore Roosevelt, an enthusiast for all sports, called a meeting of Yale, Harvard, and Princeton representatives at the White House in the hope of reforming and improving the game. The outcome was that the game, with the forward pass introduced and some other modifications of the rules inserted, became faster and cleaner and gradually grew to the tremendous popularity it enjoys today.

Professional football, now firmly established, is an outgrowth of intercollegiate football. The first professional game was played in 1895 at Latrobe, Pa. The National Football League was founded in 1921. The All-America Conference went into action in 1946. At the end of the 1949 season the two major play-for-pay circuits merged, retaining the name of the older league. In 1960, a rival circuit, the American Football League, began operations.

## Famous Series Records
### Army-Navy

| Year | A | N | Year | A | N | Year | A | N | Year | A | N | Year | A | N | Year | A | N |
|---|---|---|---|---|---|---|---|---|---|---|---|---|---|---|---|---|---|
| 1880 | 0 | 24 | 1906 | 0 | 10 | 1919 | 0 | 6 | 1931 | 17 | 7 | 1941 | 6 | 14 | 1951 | 7 | 42 |
| 1891 | 32 | 16 | 1907 | 0 | 6 | 1920 | 0 | 7 | 1932 | 20 | 0 | 1942 | 0 | 14 | 1952 | 0 | 7 |
| 1892 | 4 | 12 | 1908 | 6 | 4 | 1921 | 0 | 7 | 1933 | 12 | 7 | 1943 | 0 | 13 | 1953 | 20 | 7 |
| 1893 | 4 | 6 | 1910 | 0 | 3 | 1922 | 17 | 14 | 1934 | 0 | 3 | 1944 | 23 | 7 | 1954 | 20 | 27 |
| 1899 | 17 | 5 | 1911 | 0 | 3 | 1923 | 0 | 0 | 1935 | 28 | 6 | 1945 | 32 | 13 | 1955 | 14 | 6 |
| 1900 | 7 | 11 | 1912 | 0 | 6 | 1924 | 12 | 0 | 1936 | 0 | 7 | 1946 | 21 | 18 | 1956 | 7 | 7 |
| 1901 | 11 | 5 | 1913 | 22 | 9 | 1925 | 10 | 3 | 1937 | 6 | 0 | 1947 | 21 | 0 | 1957 | 0 | 14 |
| 1902 | 22 | 8 | 1914 | 20 | 0 | 1926 | 21 | 21 | 1938 | 14 | 7 | 1948 | 21 | 21 | 1958 | 22 | 6 |
| 1903 | 40 | 5 | 1915 | 14 | 0 | 1927 | 14 | 9 | 1939 | 0 | 10 | 1949 | 38 | 0 | 1959 | 12 | 43 |
| 1904 | 11 | 0 | 1916 | 15 | 7 | 1930 | 6 | 0 | 1940 | 0 | 14 | 1950 | 2 | 14 | 1960 | 12 | 17 |
| 1905 | 6 | 6 | | | | | | | | | | | | | | | |

### Army-Notre Dame

| Year | A | ND | Year | A | ND | Year | A | ND | Year | A | ND | Year | A | ND | Year | A | ND |
|---|---|---|---|---|---|---|---|---|---|---|---|---|---|---|---|---|---|
| 1913 | 13 | 35 | 1920 | 17 | 27 | 1926 | 0 | 7 | 1932 | 0 | 21 | 1938 | 7 | 19 | 1944 | 59 | 0 |
| 1914 | 20 | 7 | 1921 | 0 | 28 | 1927 | 18 | 0 | 1933 | 12 | 13 | 1939 | 0 | 14 | 1945 | 48 | 0 |
| 1915 | 0 | 7 | 1922 | 0 | 0 | 1928 | 6 | 12 | 1934 | 6 | 12 | 1940 | 0 | 7 | 1946 | 0 | 0 |
| 1916 | 30 | 10 | 1923 | 0 | 13 | 1929 | 0 | 7 | 1935 | 6 | 6 | 1941 | 0 | 0 | 1947 | 7 | 27 |
| 1917 | 2 | 7 | 1924 | 7 | 13 | 1930 | 6 | 7 | 1936 | 6 | 20 | 1942 | 0 | 13 | 1957 | 21 | 23 |
| 1919 | 9 | 12 | 1925 | 27 | 0 | 1931 | 12 | 0 | 1937 | 0 | 7 | 1943 | 0 | 26 | 1958 | 14 | 2 |

### Harvard-Yale

| Year | H | Y | Year | H | Y | Year | H | Y | Year | H | Y | Year | H | Y | Year | H | Y |
|---|---|---|---|---|---|---|---|---|---|---|---|---|---|---|---|---|---|
| 1875 | 4g | 0g | 1891 | 0 | 10 | 1906 | 0 | 6 | 1921 | 10 | 3 | 1934 | 0 | 14 | 1949 | 6 | 29 |
| 1876 | 0g | 1g | 1892 | 0 | 6 | 1907 | 0 | 12 | 1922 | 10 | 3 | 1935 | 7 | 14 | 1950 | 6 | 14 |
| 1878 | 0g | 1g | 1893 | 0 | 6 | 1908 | 4 | 0 | 1923 | 0 | 13 | 1936 | 13 | 14 | 1951 | 21 | 21 |
| 1879 | 0g | 0g | 1894 | 4 | 12 | 1909 | 0 | 8 | 1924 | 6 | 19 | 1937 | 13 | 6 | 1952 | 14 | 41 |
| 1880 | 0g | 1g | 1897 | 0 | 0 | 1910 | 0 | 0 | 1925 | 0 | 0 | 1938 | 7 | 0 | 1953 | 13 | 0 |
| 1881 | 0g | 1g | 1898 | 17 | 0 | 1911 | 0 | 0 | 1926 | 7 | 12 | 1939 | 7 | 20 | 1954 | 13 | 9 |
| 1882 | 0g | 1g | 1899 | 0 | 0 | 1912 | 20 | 0 | 1927 | 0 | 14 | 1940 | 28 | 0 | 1955 | 7 | 21 |
| 1883 | 2 | 23 | 1900 | 0 | 28 | 1913 | 15 | 5 | 1928 | 17 | 0 | 1941 | 14 | 0 | 1956 | 14 | 42 |
| 1884 | 0 | 52 | 1901 | 22 | 0 | 1914 | 36 | 0 | 1929 | 10 | 6 | 1942 | 3 | 7 | 1957 | 0 | 54 |
| 1886 | 4 | 29 | 1902 | 0 | 23 | 1915 | 41 | 0 | 1930 | 13 | 0 | 1945 | 0 | 28 | 1958 | 28 | 0 |
| 1887 | 8 | 17 | 1903 | 0 | 16 | 1916 | 3 | 6 | 1931 | 0 | 3 | 1946 | 14 | 27 | 1959 | 35 | 6 |
| 1889 | 0 | 6 | 1904 | 0 | 12 | 1919 | 10 | 3 | 1932 | 0 | 19 | 1947 | 21 | 31 | 1960 | 6 | 39 |
| 1890 | 12 | 6 | 1905 | 0 | 6 | 1920 | 9 | 0 | 1933 | 19 | 6 | 1948 | 20 | 7 | | | |

# NATIONAL COLLEGE FOOTBALL CHAMPIONS

The "National Collegiate A. A. Football Guide" recognizes as unofficial national champion the team selected each year by press association polls. Where The Associated Press poll (of writers) does not agree with the United Press International poll (of coaches), the guide lists both teams selected. Prior to the press polls, the Rissman and Knute Rockne trophies, symbolic of the national title, were awarded annually from 1924 to 1936.

| | | | | | | | |
|---|---|---|---|---|---|---|---|
| 1924 | Notre Dame | 1934 | Minnesota | 1944 | Army | 1954 | Ohio State and |
| 1925 | Dartmouth | 1935 | So. Methodist | 1945 | Army | | U. C. L. A. |
| 1926 | Stanford | 1936 | Minnesota | 1946 | Notre Dame | 1955 | Oklahoma |
| 1927 | Illinois | 1937 | Pittsburgh | 1947 | Notre Dame | 1956 | Oklahoma |
| 1928 | So. California | 1938 | Texas Christian | 1948 | Michigan | 1957 | Auburn and Ohio |
| 1929 | Notre Dame | 1939 | Texas A & M | 1949 | Notre Dame | | State |
| 1930 | Notre Dame | 1940 | Minnesota | 1950 | Oklahoma | 1958 | Louisiana State |
| 1931 | So. California | 1941 | Minnesota | 1951 | Tennessee | 1959 | Syracuse |
| 1932 | Michigan | 1942 | Ohio State | 1952 | Michigan State | 1960 | Minnesota |
| 1933 | Michigan | 1943 | Notre Dame | 1953 | Maryland | | |

# RECORD OF ANNUAL POSTSEASON FOOTBALL GAMES

## Rose Bowl
(At Pasadena, Calif.)

- 1902 Michigan 49, Stanford 0
- 1916 Washington State 14, Brown 0
- 1917 Oregon 14, Pennsylvania 0
- 1918 Mare Island Marines 19, Camp Lewis 7
- 1919 Great Lakes 17, Mare Island Marines 0
- 1920 Harvard 7, Oregon 6
- 1921 California 28, Ohio State 0
- 1922 Washington and Jefferson 0, California 0
- 1923 So. California 14, Penn State 3
- 1924 Navy 14, Washington 14
- 1925 Notre Dame 27, Stanford 10
- 1926 Alabama 20, Washington 19
- 1927 Alabama 7, Stanford 7
- 1928 Stanford 7, Pittsburgh 6
- 1929 Georgia Tech 8, California 7
- 1930 So. California 47, Pittsburgh 14
- 1931 Alabama 24, Washington State 0
- 1932 So. California 21, Tulane 12
- 1933 So. California 35, Pittsburgh 0
- 1934 Columbia 7, Stanford 0
- 1935 Alabama 29, Stanford 13
- 1936 Stanford 7, S.M.U. 0
- 1937 Pittsburgh 21, Washington 0
- 1938 California 13, Alabama 0
- 1939 So California 7, Duke 3
- 1940 So. California 14, Tennessee 0
- 1941 Stanford 21, Nebraska 13
- 1942 Oregon State 20, Duke 16*
- 1943 Georgia 9, U. C. L. A. 0
- 1944 So. California 29, Washington 0
- 1945 So. California 25, Tennessee 0
- 1946 Alabama 34, So. California 14
- 1947 Illinois 45, U. C. L. A. 14
- 1948 Michigan 49, So. California 0
- 1949 Northwestern 20, California 14
- 1950 Ohio State 17, California 14
- 1951 Michigan 14, California 6
- 1952 Illinois 40, Stanford 7
- 1953 So. California 7, Wisconsin 0
- 1954 Michigan State 28, U. C. L. A. 20
- 1955 Ohio State 20, So. California 7
- 1956 Michigan State 17, U. C. L. A. 14
- 1957 Iowa 35, Oregon State 19
- 1958 Ohio State 10, Oregon 7
- 1959 Iowa 38, California 12
- 1960 Washington 44, Wisconsin 8
- 1961 Washington 17, Minnesota 7

\* Played at Durham, N. C.

## Sugar Bowl
(At New Orleans)

- 1935 Tulane 20, Temple 14
- 1936 Texas Christian 3, Louisiana State 2
- 1937 Santa Clara 21, Louisiana State 14
- 1938 Santa Clara 6, Louisiana State 0
- 1939 Texas Christian 15, Carnegie Tech 7
- 1940 Texas A & M 14, Tulane 13
- 1941 Boston College 19, Tennessee 13
- 1942 Fordham 2, Missouri 0
- 1943 Tennessee 14, Tulsa 7
- 1944 Georgia Tech 20, Tulsa 18
- 1945 Duke 29 Alabama 26
- 1946 Oklahoma A & M 33, St. Mary's (Calif.) 13
- 1947 Georgia 20, North Carolina 10
- 1948 Texas 27, Alabama 7
- 1949 Oklahoma 14, North Carolina 6
- 1950 Oklahoma 35, Louisiana State 0
- 1951 Kentucky 13, Oklahoma 7
- 1952 Maryland 28, Tennessee 13
- 1953 Georgia Tech 24, Mississippi 7
- 1954 Georgia Tech 42, West Virginia 19
- 1955 Navy 21, Mississippi 0
- 1956 Georgia Tech 7, Pittsburgh 0
- 1957 Baylor 13, Tennessee 7
- 1958 Mississippi 39, Texas 7
- 1959 Louisiana State 7, Clemson 0
- 1960 Mississippi 21, Louisiana State 0
- 1961 Mississippi 14, Rice 6

## Cotton Bowl
(At Dallas)

- 1937 Texas Christian 16, Marquette 6
- 1938 Rice 28, Colorado 14
- 1939 St. Mary's (Calif.) 20, Texas Tech 13
- 1940 Clemson 6, Boston College 3
- 1941 Texas A & M 13, Fordham 12
- 1942 Alabama 29, Texas A & M 21
- 1943 Texas 14, Georgia Tech 7
- 1944 Randolph Field 7, Texas 7
- 1945 Oklahoma A & M 34, Texas Christian 0
- 1946 Texas 40, Missouri 27

- 1947 Louisiana State 0, Arkansas 0
- 1948 Southern Methodist 13, Penn State 13
- 1949 Southern Methodist 21, Oregon 13
- 1950 Rice 27, North Carolina 13
- 1951 Tennessee 20, Texas 14
- 1952 Kentucky 20, Texas Christian 7
- 1953 Texas 16, Tennessee 0
- 1954 Rice 28, Alabama 6
- 1955 Georgia Tech 14, Arkansas 6
- 1956 Mississippi 14, Texas Christian 13
- 1957 Texas Christian 28, Syracuse 27
- 1958 Navy 20, Rice 7
- 1959 Air Force 0, Texas Christian 0
- 1960 Syracuse 23, Texas 14
- 1961 Duke 7, Arkansas 6

## Orange Bowl
(At Miami)

- 1933 Miami 7, Manhattan 0
- 1934 Duquesne 33, Miami 7
- 1935 Bucknell 26, Miami 0
- 1936 Catholic 20, Mississippi 19
- 1937 Duquesne 13, Mississippi State 12
- 1938 Alabama Poly. 6, Michigan State 0
- 1939 Tennessee 17, Oklahoma 0
- 1940 Georgia Tech 21, Missouri 7
- 1941 Mississippi State 14, Georgetown 7
- 1942 Georgia 40, Texas Christian 26
- 1943 Alabama 37, Boston College 21
- 1944 Louisiana State 19, Texas A&M 14
- 1945 Tulsa 26, Georgia Tech 12
- 1946 Miami 13, Holy Cross 6
- 1947 Rice 8, Tennessee 0
- 1948 Georgia Tech 20, Kansas 14
- 1949 Texas 41, Georgia 28
- 1950 Santa Clara 21, Kentucky 13
- 1951 Clemson 15, Miami 14
- 1952 Georgia Tech 17, Baylor 14
- 1953 Alabama 61, Syracuse 6
- 1954 Oklahoma 7, Maryland 0
- 1955 Duke 36, Nebraska 7
- 1956 Oklahoma 20, Maryland 6
- 1957 Colorado 27, Clemson 21
- 1958 Oklahoma 48, Duke 21
- 1959 Oklahoma 21, Syracuse 6
- 1960 Georgia 14, Missouri 0
- 1961 Missouri 21, Navy 14

# PROFESSIONAL FOOTBALL
## National League Champions

| Year | League Champion | W | L | T | Year | League Champion | W | L | T |
|------|-----------------|---|---|---|------|-----------------|---|---|---|
| 1921 | Chicago Bears (Staley's) | 10 | 1 | 1 | 1927 | New York Giants | 11 | 1 | 1 |
| 1922 | Canton Bulldogs | 10 | 0 | 2 | 1928 | Providence Steamrollers | 8 | 1 | 2 |
| 1923 | Canton Bulldogs | 11 | 0 | 1 | 1929 | Green Bay Packers | 12 | 0 | 1 |
| 1924 | Cleveland Indians | 7 | 1 | 1 | 1930 | Green Bay Packers | 10 | 3 | 1 |
| 1925 | Chicago Cardinals | 11 | 2 | 1 | 1931 | Green Bay Packers | 12 | 2 | 0 |
| 1926 | Frankford Yellow Jackets | 14 | 1 | 1 | 1932 | Chicago Bears | 7 | 1 | 6 |

| Year | Eastern Conference Winners (W–L–T) | Western Conference Winners (W–L–T) | League champion, playoff result |
|------|------------------------------------|------------------------------------|---------------------------------|
| 1933 | New York Giants (11–3–0) | Chicago Bears (10–2–1) | Chicago Bears 23, New York 21 |
| 1934 | New York Giants (8–5–0) | Chicago Bears (13–0–0) | New York 30, Chicago Bears 13 |
| 1935 | New York Giants (9–3–0) | Detroit Lions (7–3–2) | Detroit 26, New York 7 |
| 1936 | Boston Redskins (7–5–0) | Green Bay Packers (10–1–1) | Green Bay 21, Boston 6 |
| 1937 | Washington Redskins (8–3–0) | Chicago Bears (9–1–1) | Washington 28, Chicago Bears 21 |
| 1938 | New York Giants (8–2–1) | Green Bay Packers (8–3–0) | New York 23, Green Bay 17 |
| 1939 | New York Giants (9–1–1) | Green Bay Packers (9–2–0) | Green Bay 27, New York 0 |
| 1940 | Washington Redskins (9–2–0) | Chicago Bears (8–3–0) | Chicago Bears 73, Washington 0 |
| 1941 | New York Giants (8–3–0) | Chicago Bears (10–1–1)† | Chicago Bears 37, New York 9 |
| 1942 | Washington Redskins (10–1–1) | Chicago Bears (11–0–0) | Washington 14, Chicago Bears 6 |
| 1943 | Washington Redskins (6–3–1)† | Chicago Bears (8–1–1) | Chicago Bears 41, Washington 21 |
| 1944 | New York Giants (8–1–1) | Green Bay Packers (8–2–0) | Green Bay 14, New York 7 |
| 1945 | Washington Redskins (8–2–0) | Cleveland Rams (9–1–0) | Cleveland 15, Washington 14 |
| 1946 | New York Giants (7–3–1) | Chicago Bears (8–2–1) | Chicago Bears 24, New York 14 |
| 1947 | Philadelphia Eagles (8–4–0)† | Chicago Cardinals (9–3–0) | Chicago Cardinals 28, Philadelphia 21 |
| 1948 | Philadelphia Eagles (9–2–1) | Chicago Cardinals (11–1–0) | Philadelphia 7, Chicago Cardinals 0 |
| 1949 | Philadelphia Eagles (11–1–0) | Los Angeles Rams (8–2–2) | Philadelphia 14, Los Angeles 0 |
| 1950* | Cleveland Browns (10–2–0)† | Los Angeles Rams (9–3–0)† | Cleveland 30, Los Angeles 28 |
| 1951* | Cleveland Browns (11–1–0) | Los Angeles Rams (8–4–0) | Los Angeles 24, Cleveland 17 |
| 1952* | Cleveland Browns (8–4–0) | Detroit Lions (9–3–0)† | Detroit 17, Cleveland 7n |
| 1953 | Cleveland Browns (11–1–0) | Detroit Lions (10–2–0) | Detroit 17, Cleveland 16 |
| 1954 | Cleveland Browns (9–3–0) | Detroit Lions (9–2–1) | Cleveland 56, Detroit 10 |
| 1955 | Cleveland Browns (9–2–1) | Los Angeles Rams (8–3–1) | Cleveland 38, Los Angeles 14 |
| 1956 | New York Giants (8–3–1) | Chicago Bears (9–2–1) | New York 47, Chicago Bears 7 |
| 1957 | Cleveland Browns (9–2–1) | Detroit Lions (8–4–0)† | Detroit 59, Cleveland 14 |
| 1958 | New York Giants (9–3–0)† | Baltimore Colts (9–3–0) | Baltimore 23, New York 17‡ |
| 1959 | New York Giants (10–2–0) | Baltimore Colts (9–3–0) | Baltimore 31, New York 16 |
| 1960 | Philadelphia Eagles (10–2–0) | Green Bay Packers (8–4–0) | Philadelphia 17, Green Bay 13 |

* League was divided into American and National Conferences, 1950–52.   † Won divisional playoff.   ‡ Won at 8:15 of sudden death overtime period.

## American League Champions

| Year | Eastern Division winners (W–L–T) | Western Division winners (W–L–T) | League champion, playoff result |
|------|----------------------------------|----------------------------------|---------------------------------|
| 1960 | Houston Oilers (10–4–0) | Los Angeles Chargers (10–4–0) | Houston 24, Los Angeles 16 |

## Canadian Champions (Grey Cup)
(Since 1921, first year of the East–West playoff)

| | | | |
|---|---|---|---|
| 1921 | Toronto Argos | 1941 | Winnipeg Blue Bombers |
| 1922 | Queens University | 1942 | Toronto R. C. A. F. Hurricanes |
| 1923 | Queens University | 1943 | Hamilton Wildcats |
| 1924 | Queens University | 1944 | St. Hyacinthe-Donnaconna |
| 1925 | Ottawa Rough Riders | 1945 | Toronto Argonauts |
| 1926 | Ottawa Rough Riders | 1946 | Toronto Argonauts |
| 1927 | Toronto Balmy Beach | 1947 | Toronto Argonauts |
| 1928 | Hamilton Tigers | 1948 | Calgary Stampeders |
| 1929 | Hamilton Tigers | 1949 | Montreal Alouettes |
| 1930 | Toronto Balmy Beach | 1950 | Toronto Argonauts |
| 1931 | Montreal A. A. A. | 1951 | Ottawa Rough Riders |
| 1932 | Hamilton Tigers | 1952 | Toronto Argonauts |
| 1933 | Toronto Argonauts | 1953 | Hamilton Tiger-Cats |
| 1934 | Sarnia Imperials | 1954 | Edmonton Eskimos |
| 1935 | Winnipeg Blue Bombers | 1955 | Edmonton Eskimos |
| 1936 | Sarnia Imperials | 1956 | Edmonton Eskimos |
| 1937 | Toronto Argonauts | 1957 | Hamilton Tiger-Cats |
| 1938 | Toronto Argonauts | 1958 | Winnipeg Blue Bombers |
| 1939 | Winnipeg Blue Bombers | 1959 | Winnipeg Blue Bombers |
| 1940 | Ottawa Rough Riders | 1960 | Ottawa Rough Riders |

# GOLF

IT MAY BE that golf originated in Holland—historians believe it did—but certainly Scotland fostered the game and is famous for it. In fact, in 1457 the Scottish Parliament, disturbed because football and golf had lured young Scots from the more soldierly exercise of archery, passed an ordinance that "futeball and golf be utterly cryit doun and nocht usit." James I and Charles I of the royal line of Stuarts were golf enthusiasts, whereby the game came to be known as "the royal and ancient game of golf."

The golf balls used in the early games were leather covered and stuffed with feathers. Clubs of all kinds were fashioned by hand to suit individual players. The great step in spreading the game came with the change from the feather ball to the gutta-percha ball about 1850, and in 1860 formal competition began with the establishment of an annual tournament for the British open championship. There are records of "golf clubs" in the United States as far back as colonial days but no proof of actual play before John Reid and some friends laid out six holes on the Reid lawn in Yonkers, N. Y., in 1888 and played there with the golf balls and clubs brought over from Scotland by Robert Lockhart. This group then formed the St. Andrews Golf Club of Yonkers, and golf was established in this country.

However, it remained a rather sedate and almost aristocratic pastime until a 20-year-old ex-caddy, Francis Ouimet of Boston, defeated two great British professionals, Harry Vardon and Ted Ray, in the United States Open championship at Brookline, Mass., in 1913. This feat put the game and Francis Ouimet on the front pages of the newspapers and stirred a wave of enthusiasm for the sport. The greatest feat so far in golf history was that of Robert Tyre Jones, Jr. of Atlanta, Ga., in winning the British Open, the British Amateur, the U. S. Open and the U. S. Amateur titles in one year, 1930.

## Golf Statistics
*Source:* United States Golf Association.

### UNITED STATES OPEN CHAMPIONS

| Year | Winner | Score | Where played | Year | Winner | Score | Where played |
|------|--------|-------|--------------|------|--------|-------|--------------|
| 1895 | Horace Rawlins | 173 | Newport | 1927 | Tommy Armour (a) | 301 | Oakmont |
| 1896 | James Foulis | 152 | Shinnecock Hills | 1928 | Johnny Farrell (a) | 294 | Olympia Fields |
| 1897 | Joe Lloyd | 162 | Chicago | 1929 | R. T. Jones, Jr.(a,b) | 294 | Winged Foot |
| 1898* | Fred Herd | 328 | Myopia | 1930 | R. T. Jones, Jr.(b) | 287 | Interlachen |
| 1899 | Willie Smith | 315 | Baltimore | 1931 | Billy Burke (a) | 292 | Inverness |
| 1900 | Harry Vardon | 313 | Chicago | 1932 | Gene Sarazen | 286 | Fresh Meadow |
| 1901 | Willie Anderson (a) | 331 | Myopia | 1933 | John Goodman (b) | 287 | North Shore |
| 1902 | L. Auchterlonie | 307 | Garden City | 1934 | Olin Dutra | 293 | Merion |
| 1903 | Willie Anderson (a) | 307 | Baltusrol | 1935 | Sam Parks, Jr. | 299 | Oakmont |
| 1904 | Willie Anderson | 303 | Glen View | 1936 | Tony Manero | 282 | Baltusrol |
| 1905 | Willie Anderson | 314 | Myopia | 1937 | Ralph Guldahl | 281 | Oakland Hills |
| 1906 | Alex Smith | 295 | Onwentsia | 1938 | Ralph Guldahl | 284 | Cherry Hills |
| 1907 | Alex Ross | 302 | Philadelphia | 1939 | Byron Nelson (a) | 284 | Philadelphia |
| 1908 | Fred McLeod (a) | 322 | Myopia | 1940 | W. Lawson Little, Jr.(a) | 287 | Canterbury |
| 1909 | George Sargent | 290 | Englewood | 1941 | Craig Wood | 284 | Colonial |
| 1910 | Alex Smith (a) | 298 | Philadelphia | 1942-45 | No tournaments‡ | | |
| 1911 | J. J. McDermott (a) | 307 | Chicago | 1946 | Lloyd Mangrum (a) | 284 | Canterbury |
| 1912 | J. J. McDermott | 294 | Buffalo | 1947 | Lew Worsham (a) | 282 | St. Louis |
| 1913 | Francis Ouimet (a,b) | 304 | Brookline | 1948 | Ben Hogan | 276 | Riviera |
| 1914 | Walter Hagen | 290 | Midlothian | 1949 | Cary Middlecoff | 286 | Medinah |
| 1915 | Jerome D. Travers (b) | 297 | Baltusrol | 1950 | Ben Hogan (a) | 287 | Merion |
| 1916 | Charles Evans, Jr.(b) | 286 | Minikahda | 1951 | Ben Hogan | 287 | Oakland Hills |
| 1917-18 | No tournaments† | | | 1952 | Julius Boros | 281 | Northwood |
| 1919 | Walter Hagen (a) | 301 | Brae Burn | 1953 | Ben Hogan | 283 | Oakmont |
| 1920 | Edward Ray | 295 | Inverness | 1954 | Ed Furgol | 284 | Baltusrol |
| 1921 | James M. Barnes | 289 | Columbia | 1955 | Jack Fleck (a) | 287 | Olympic |
| 1922 | Gene Sarazen | 288 | Skokie | 1956 | Cary Middlecoff | 281 | Oak Hill |
| 1923 | R. T. Jones, Jr.(a,b) | 296 | Inwood | 1957 | Dick Mayer (a) | 298 | Inverness |
| 1924 | Cyril Walker | 297 | Oakland Hills | 1958 | Tommy Bolt | 283 | Southern Hills |
| 1925 | W. Macfarlane (a) | 291 | Worcester | 1959 | Bill Casper, Jr. | 282 | Winged Foot |
| 1926 | R. T. Jones, Jr. | 293 | Scioto | 1960 | Arnold Palmer | 280 | Cherry Hills |

(a) Winner in playoff. (b) Amateur. * In 1898 competition was extended to 72 holes. † In 1917, Jock Hutchison, with a 292, won an Open Patriotic Tournament for the benefit of the American Red Cross at Whitemarsh Valley Country Club. ‡ In 1942, Ben Hogan, with a 271, won a Hale American National Open Tournament for the benefit of the Navy Relief Society and USO at Ridgemoor Country Club.

## UNITED STATES AMATEUR CHAMPIONS

| Year | Winner | Year | Winner | Year | Winner |
|------|--------|------|--------|------|--------|
| 1895 | Charles B. Macdonald | 1915 | Robert A. Gardner | 1937 | John Goodman |
| 1896 | H. J. Whigham | 1916 | Charles Evans, Jr. | 1938 | Willie Turnesa |
| 1897 | H. J. Whigham | 1919 | S. D. Herron | 1939 | Marvin H. Ward |
| 1898 | Findlay S. Douglas | 1920 | Charles Evans, Jr. | 1940 | R. D. Chapman |
| 1899 | H. M. Harriman | 1921 | Jesse P. Guilford | 1941 | Marvin H. Ward |
| 1900 | Walter J. Travis | 1922 | Jess W. Sweetser | 1946 | Ted Bishop |
| 1901 | Walter J. Travis | 1923 | Max R. Marston | 1947 | Robert Riegel |
| 1902 | Louis N. James | 1924 | R. T. Jones, Jr. | 1948 | Willie Turnesa |
| 1903 | Walter J. Travis | 1925 | R. T. Jones, Jr. | 1949 | Charles Coe |
| 1904 | H. Chandler Egan | 1926 | George Von Elm | 1950 | Sam Urzetta |
| 1905 | H. Chandler Egan | 1927 | R. T. Jones, Jr. | 1951 | Billy Maxwell |
| 1906 | Eben M. Byers | 1928 | R. T. Jones, Jr. | 1952 | Jack Westland |
| 1907 | Jerome D. Travers | 1929 | H. R. Johnston | 1953 | Gene Littler |
| 1908 | Jerome D. Travers | 1930 | R. T. Jones, Jr. | 1954 | Arnold Palmer |
| 1909 | Robert A. Gardner | 1931 | Francis Ouimet | 1955 | Harvie Ward |
| 1910 | W. C. Fownes, Jr. | 1932 | C. R. Somerville | 1956 | Harvie Ward |
| 1911 | Harold H. Hilton | 1933 | G. T. Dunlap, Jr. | 1957 | Hillman Robbins |
| 1912 | Jerome D. Travers | 1934 | W. Lawson Little, Jr. | 1958 | Charles Coe |
| 1913 | Jerome D. Travers | 1935 | W. Lawson Little, Jr. | 1959 | Jack Nicklaus |
| 1914 | Francis Ouimet | 1936 | John W. Fischer | 1960 | Deane Beman |

## UNITED STATES P. G. A. CHAMPIONS

| Year | Winner | Year | Winner | Year | Winner | |
|------|--------|------|--------|------|--------|---|
| 1916 | Jim Barnes | 1933 | Gene Sarazen | 1949 | Sam Snead | |
| 1919 | Jim Barnes | 1934 | Paul Runyan | 1950 | Chandler Harper | |
| 1920 | Jock Hutchison | 1935 | Johnny Revolta | 1951 | Sam Snead | |
| 1921 | Walter Hagen | 1936 | Denny Shute | 1952 | Jim Turnesa | |
| 1922 | Gene Sarazen | 1937 | Denny Shute | 1953 | Walter Burkemo | |
| 1923 | Gene Sarazen | 1938 | Paul Runyan | 1954 | Chick Harbert | |
| 1924 | Walter Hagen | 1939 | Henry Picard | 1955 | Doug Ford | |
| 1925 | Walter Hagen | 1940 | Byron Nelson | 1956 | Jack Burke, Jr. | |
| 1926 | Walter Hagen | 1941 | Victor Ghezzi | 1957 | Lionel Hebert | |
| 1927 | Walter Hagen | 1942 | Sam Snead | 1958* | Dow Finsterwald | 276 |
| 1928 | Leo Diegel | 1944 | Bob Hamilton | 1959 | Bob Rosburg | 277 |
| 1929 | Leo Diegel | 1945 | Byron Nelson | 1960 | Jay Hebert | 281 |
| 1930 | Tommy Armour | 1946 | Ben Hogan | | | |
| 1931 | Tom Creavy | 1947 | Jim Ferrier | | * Match play prior to 1958. | |
| 1932 | Olin Dutra | 1948 | Ben Hogan | | | |

## UNITED STATES WOMEN'S OPEN CHAMPIONS

| Year | Winner | | Year | Winner | | Year | Winner | |
|------|--------|---|------|--------|---|------|--------|---|
| 1946 | Patty Berg (match play) | — | 1951 | Betsy Rawls | 293 | 1956 | Mrs. Katherine Cornelius (a). | 302 |
| 1947 | Betty Jameson | 295 | 1952 | Louise Suggs | 284 | 1957 | Betsy Rawls | 299 |
| 1948 | Mrs. Mildred D. Zaharias | 300 | 1953 | Betsy Rawls (a) | 302 | 1958 | Mickey Wright | 290 |
| 1949 | Louise Suggs | 291 | 1954 | Mrs. Mildred D. Zaharias | 291 | 1959 | Mickey Wright | 287 |
| 1950 | Mrs. Mildred D. Zaharias | 291 | 1955 | Fay Crocker | 299 | 1960 | Betsy Rawls | 291 |

(a) Winner in playoff.

## UNITED STATES WOMEN'S AMATEUR CHAMPIONS

| Year | Winner | Year | Winner | Year | Winner |
|------|--------|------|--------|------|--------|
| 1895 | Mrs. C. S. Brown | 1915 | Mrs. C. H. Vanderbeck | 1937 | Mrs. J. A. Page, Jr. |
| 1896 | Beatrix Hoyt | 1916 | Alexa Stirling | 1938 | Patty Berg |
| 1897 | Beatrix Hoyt | 1919 | Alexa Stirling | 1939 | Betty Jameson |
| 1898 | Beatrix Hoyt | 1920 | Alexa Stirling | 1940 | Betty Jameson |
| 1899 | Ruth Underhill | 1921 | Marion Hollins | 1941 | Mrs. Frank Newell |
| 1900 | Frances C. Griscom | 1922 | Glenna Collett | 1946 | Mrs. M. D. Zaharias |
| 1901 | Genevieve Hecker | 1923 | Edith Cummings | 1947 | Louise Suggs |
| 1902 | Genevieve Hecker | 1924 | Mrs. D. C. Hurd | 1948 | Grace Lenczyk |
| 1903 | Bessie Anthony | 1925 | Glenna Collett | 1949 | Mrs. D. G. Porter |
| 1904 | G. M. Bishop | 1926 | Mrs. G. H. Stetson | 1950 | Beverly Hanson |
| 1905 | Pauline Mackay | 1927 | Mrs. M. B. Horn | 1951 | Dorothy Kirby |
| 1906 | Harriot S. Curtis | 1928 | Glenna Collett | 1952 | Mrs. Jacqueline Pung |
| 1907 | Margaret Curtis | 1929 | Glenna Collett | 1953 | Mary Lena Faulk |
| 1908 | K. C. Harley | 1930 | Glenna Collett | 1954 | Barbara Romack |
| 1909 | D. I. Campbell | 1931 | Helen Hicks | 1955 | Patricia Lesser |
| 1910 | D. I. Campbell | 1932 | Virginia Van Wie | 1956 | Marlene Stewart |
| 1911 | Margaret Curtis | 1933 | Virginia Van Wie | 1957 | JoAnne Gunderson |
| 1912 | Margaret Curtis | 1934 | Virginia Van Wie | 1958 | Anne Quast |
| 1913 | Gladys Ravenscroft | 1935 | Mrs. E. H. Vare, Jr. | 1959 | Barbara McIntire |
| 1914 | Mrs. H. A. Jackson | 1936 | Pamela Barton | 1960 | JoAnne Gunderson |

(See Index for 1961 Champions)

# BRITISH OPEN CHAMPIONS

| Year | Winner | Score | Year | Winner | Score | Year | Winner | Score |
|---|---|---|---|---|---|---|---|---|
| 1860 | W. Park | 174 | 1891 | Hugh Kirkaldy | 166 | 1926 | R. T. Jones, Jr. | 291 |
| 1861 | Tom Morris, Sr. | 163 | 1892* | H. H. Hilton | 305 | 1927 | R. T. Jones, Jr. | 285 |
| 1862 | Tom Morris, Sr. | 163 | 1893 | W. Auchterlonie | 322 | 1928 | Walter Hagen | 292 |
| 1863 | W. Park | 168 | 1894 | J. H. Taylor | 326 | 1929 | Walter Hagen | 292 |
| 1864 | Tom Morris, Sr. | 167 | 1895 | J. H. Taylor | 322 | 1930 | R. T. Jones, Jr. | 291 |
| 1865 | A. L. Strath | 162 | 1896 | Harry Vardon (a) | 316 | 1931 | T. D. Armour | 296 |
| 1866 | W. Park | 169 | 1897 | H. H. Hilton | 314 | 1932 | G. Sarazen | 283 |
| 1867 | Tom Morris, Sr. | 170 | 1898 | Harry Vardon | 307 | 1933 | D. Shute (a) | 292 |
| 1868 | Tom Morris, Jr. | 170 | 1899 | Harry Vardon | 310 | 1934 | T. H. Cotton | 283 |
| 1869 | Tom Morris, Jr. | 154 | 1900 | J. H. Taylor | 309 | 1935 | A. Perry | 283 |
| 1870 | Tom Morris, Jr. | 149 | 1901 | James Braid | 309 | 1936 | A. H. Padgham | 287 |
| 1872 | Tom Morris, Jr. | 166 | 1902 | Alex Herd | 307 | 1937 | T. H. Cotton | 290 |
| 1873 | Tom Kidd | 179 | 1903 | Harry Vardon | 300 | 1938 | R. A. Whitcombe | 295 |
| 1874 | Mungo Park | 159 | 1904 | Jack White | 296 | 1939 | R. Burton | 290 |
| 1875 | Willie Park | 166 | 1905 | James Braid | 318 | 1946 | Sam Snead | 290 |
| 1876 | Bob Martin | 176 | 1906 | James Braid | 300 | 1947 | Fred Daly | 293 |
| 1877 | Jamie Anderson | 160 | 1907 | Arnaud Massy | 312 | 1948 | Henry Cotton | 284 |
| 1878 | Jamie Anderson | 157 | 1908 | James Braid | 291 | 1949 | Bobby Locke (a) | 283 |
| 1879 | Jamie Anderson | 170 | 1909 | J. H. Taylor | 295 | 1950 | Bobby Locke | 279 |
| 1880 | Bob Ferguson | 162 | 1910 | James Braid | 299 | 1951 | Max Faulkner | 285 |
| 1881 | Bob Ferguson | 170 | 1911 | Harry Vardon (a) | 303 | 1952 | Bobby Locke | 287 |
| 1882 | Bob Ferguson | 171 | 1912 | E. Ray | 295 | 1953 | Ben Hogan | 282 |
| 1883 | W. L. Fernie (a) | 159 | 1913 | J. H. Taylor | 304 | 1954 | Peter Thomson | 283 |
| 1884 | Jack Simpson | 160 | 1914 | Harry Vardon | 306 | 1955 | Peter Thomson | 281 |
| 1885 | Bob Martin | 171 | 1920 | George Duncan | 303 | 1956 | Peter Thomson | 286 |
| 1886 | D. L. Brown | 157 | 1921 | Jock Hutchison (a) | 296 | 1957 | Bobby Locke | 279 |
| 1887 | W. Park, Jr. | 161 | 1922 | Walter Hagen | 300 | 1958 | Peter Thomson (a) | 278 |
| 1888 | Jack Burns | 171 | 1923 | A. G. Havers | 295 | 1959 | Gary Player | 284 |
| 1889 | W. Park, Jr.(a) | 155 | 1924 | Walter Hagen | 301 | 1960 | Kel Nagle | 278 |
| 1890 | John Ball | 164 | 1925 | Jim Barnes | 300 | | | |

(a) Winner in playoff.   * In 1892 competition was extended to 72 holes.

# BRITISH AMATEUR CHAMPIONS

| Year | Winner | Year | Winner | Year | Winner |
|---|---|---|---|---|---|
| 1885 | A. F. MacFie | 1907 | John Ball | 1934 | W Lawson Little, Jr. |
| 1886 | H. G. Hutchinson | 1908 | E. A. Lassen | 1935 | W. Lawson Little, Jr. |
| 1887 | H. G. Hutchinson | 1909 | R. Maxwell | 1936 | H. Thomson |
| 1888 | John Ball | 1910 | John Ball | 1937 | R. Sweeny, Jr. |
| 1889 | J. E. Laidlay | 1911 | H. H. Hilton | 1938 | C. R. Yates |
| 1890 | John Ball | 1912 | John Ball | 1939 | A. Kyle |
| 1891 | J. E. Laidlay | 1913 | H. H. Hilton | 1946 | J. Bruen |
| 1892 | John Ball | 1914 | J. L. C. Jenkins | 1947 | Willie Turnesa |
| 1893 | Peter L. Anderson | 1920 | Cyril J. H. Tolley | 1948 | Frank Stranahan |
| 1894 | John Ball | 1921 | W. I. Hunter | 1949 | Max McCready |
| 1895 | L. M. B. Melville | 1922 | E. W. E. Holderness | 1950 | Frank Stranahan |
| 1896 | F. G. Tait | 1923 | R. H. Wethered | 1951 | Richard D. Chapman |
| 1897 | A. J. T. Allan | 1924 | E. W. E. Holderness | 1952 | Harvie Ward |
| 1898 | F. G. Tait | 1925 | Robert Harris | 1953 | Joe Carr |
| 1899 | John Ball | 1926 | Jess W. Sweetser | 1954 | Doug Bachli |
| 1900 | H. H. Hilton | 1927 | Dr. W. Tweddell | 1955 | Lt. Joe Conrad |
| 1901 | H. H. Hilton | 1928 | T. P. Perkins | 1956 | John Beharrell |
| 1902 | C. Hutchings | 1929 | C. J. H. Tolley | 1957 | Reid Jack |
| 1903 | R. Maxwell | 1930 | R. T. Jones, Jr. | 1958 | Joe Carr |
| 1904 | W. J. Travis | 1931 | E. Martin Smith | 1959 | Deane Beman |
| 1905 | A. G. Barry | 1932 | J. De Forest | 1960 | Joe Carr |
| 1906 | James Robb | 1933 | Hon. M. Scott | | |

# THE MASTERS TOURNAMENT WINNERS
### Augusta National Golf Club, Augusta, Ga.

| Year | Winner | Score | Year | Winner | Score | Year | Winner | Score |
|---|---|---|---|---|---|---|---|---|
| 1934 | Horton Smith | 284 | 1943–45 | No tournaments | | 1953 | Ben Hogan | 274 |
| 1935 | Gene Sarazen (a) | 282 | 1946 | Herman Keiser | 282 | 1954 | Sam Snead (a) | 289 |
| 1936 | Horton Smith | 285 | 1947 | Jimmy Demaret | 281 | 1955 | Cary Middlecoff | 279 |
| 1937 | Byron Nelson | 283 | 1948 | Claude Harmon | 279 | 1956 | Jack Burke | 289 |
| 1938 | Henry Picard | 285 | 1949 | Sam Snead | 282 | 1957 | Doug Ford | 283 |
| 1939 | Ralph Guldahl | 279 | 1950 | Jimmy Demaret | 283 | 1958 | Arnold Palmer | 284 |
| 1940 | Jimmy Demaret | 280 | 1951 | Ben Hogan | 280 | 1959 | Art Wall, Jr. | 284 |
| 1941 | Craig Wood | 280 | 1952 | Sam Snead | 286 | 1960 | Arnold Palmer | 282 |
| 1942 | Byron Nelson (a) | 280 | | | | | | |

(a) Winner in playoff.

# INTERNATIONAL TEAM MATCHES

## Walker Cup Record

### MEN (AMATEUR)

| Year | | Where played |
|---|---|---|
| 1922 | United States 8, Great Britain 4... | Southampton |
| 1923 | United States 6, Great Britain 5... | St. Andrews |
| 1924 | United States 9, Great Britain 3... | Garden City G. C. |
| 1926 | United States 6, Great Britain 5... | St. Andrews |
| 1928 | United States 11, Great Britain 1... | Wheaton, Ill. |
| 1930 | United States 10, Great Britain 2... | Royal St. George's |
| 1932 | United States 8, Great Britain 1... | Brookline, Mass. |
| 1934 | United States 9, Great Britain 2... | St. Andrews |
| 1936 | United States 9, Great Britain 0... | Pine Valley G. C., |
| 1938 | Great Britain 7, United States 4... | St. Andrews |
| 1947 | United States 8, Great Britain 4... | St. Andrews |
| 1949 | United States 10, Great Britain 2... | Winged Foot |
| 1951 | United States 6, Great Britain 3... | Southport |
| 1953 | United States 9, Great Britain 3... | Kittansett |
| 1955 | United States 9, Great Britain 2... | St. Andrews |
| 1957 | United States 8, Great Britain 3... | Minikahda |
| 1959 | United States 9, Great Britain 3... | Muirfield |

## World Amateur Championship

| Year | (MEN) | |
|---|---|---|
| 1958 | Australia (a)............................... | 918 |
| 1960 | United States............................... | 834 |

(a) Winner in playoff.

## Ryder Cup Record

### MEN (PROFESSIONAL)

| Year | | Where played |
|---|---|---|
| 1927 | United States 9½, Great Britain 2½.. | Worcester C. C. |
| 1929 | Great Britain 7, United States 5..... | Moortown, Eng. |
| 1931 | United States 9, Great Britain 3..... | Scioto C. C. |
| 1933 | Great Britain 6½, United States 5½.. | Southport, Eng. |
| 1935 | United States 9, Great Britain 3.... | Ridgewood C. C. |
| 1937 | United States 8, Great Britain 4..... | Southport, Eng. |
| 1947 | United States 11, Great Britain 1.... | Portland, Oreg. |
| 1949 | United States 7, Great Britain 5..... | Ganton, Eng. |
| 1951 | United States 9½, Great Britain 2½.. | Pinehurst, N. C. |
| 1953 | United States 6½, Great Britain 5½.. | Wentworth |
| 1955 | United States 8, Great Britain 4..... | Palm Springs |
| 1957 | Great Britain 7, United States 4..... | Worksop, Eng. |
| 1959 | United States 8½, Great Britain 3½.. | Palm Desert |

## Curtis Cup Record

### WOMEN AMATEUR

| Year | | Where played |
|---|---|---|
| 1932 | United States 5½, Great Britain 3½.. | Wentworth, Eng. |
| 1934 | United States 6½, Great Britain 2½.. | Chevy Chase |
| 1936 | United States 4½, Great Britain 4½.. | Gleneagles |
| 1938 | United States 5½, Great Britain 3½.. | Essex C. C. |
| 1948 | United States 6½, Great Britain 2½.. | Birkdale |
| 1950 | United States 7½, Great Britain 1½.. | Buffalo |
| 1952 | Great Britain 5, United States 4..... | Muirfield |
| 1954 | United States 6, Great Britain 3..... | Merion |
| 1956 | Great Britain 5, United States 4...... | Sandwich |
| 1958 | Great Britain 4½, United States 4½.. | Brae Burn |

# NATIONAL COLLEGIATE CHAMPIONSHIPS

**Conducted by United States Golf Association, 1897-1938; by National Collegiate A. A., since 1939.**

| Year | Individual | Team | Year | Individual | Team |
|---|---|---|---|---|---|
| 1897 | Louis P. Bayard, Jr., Princeton...... | Yale | 1930 | George T. Dunlap, Jr., Princeton...... | Princeton |
| 1898* | John Reid, Jr., Yale................. | Harvard | 1931 | George T. Dunlap, Jr., Princeton..... | Yale |
| | James F. Curtis, Harvard............. | Yale | 1932 | John W. Fischer, Jr., Michigan....... | Yale |
| 1899 | Percy Pyne, 2d, Princeton........... | Harvard | 1933 | Walter Emery, Oklahoma............. | Yale |
| 1900 | No tournament | | 1934 | Charles R. Yates, Georgia Tech....... | Michigan |
| 1901 | H. Lindsley, Harvard................. | Harvard | 1935 | Ed White, U. of Texas............... | Michigan |
| 1902* | Charles Hitchcock, Jr., Yale......... | Yale | 1936 | Charles Kocsis, Michigan............. | Yale |
| | H. Chandler Egan, Harvard........... | Harvard | 1937 | Fred Haas, Jr., L. S. U............... | Princeton |
| 1903 | F. O. Reinhart, Princeton............ | Harvard | 1938 | John P. Burke, Georgetown........... | Stanford |
| 1904 | A. L. White, Harvard................ | Harvard | 1939 | Vincent D'Antoni, Tulane............ | Stanford |
| 1905 | Robert Abbott, Yale................. | Yale | 1940 | F. Dixon Brooke, Virginia............ | { Princeton, L. S. U. |
| 1906 | W. E. Clow, Jr., Yale................ | Yale | | | |
| 1907 | Ellis Knowles, Yale.................. | Yale | 1941 | Earl Stewart, L. S. U............... | Stanford |
| 1908 | H. H. Wilder, Harvard............... | Yale | 1942 | Frank Tatum, Jr., Stanford.......... | { Stanford, L. S. U. |
| 1909 | Albert Seckel, Princeton............. | Yale | | | |
| 1910 | Robert E. Hunter, Yale.............. | Yale | 1943 | Wallace Ulrich, Carleton............ | Yale |
| 1911 | George C. Stanley, Yale............. | Yale | 1944 | Louis Lick, Minnesota............... | Notre Dame |
| 1912 | F. C. Davison, Harvard.............. | Yale | 1945 | John Lorms, Ohio State............. | Ohio State |
| 1913 | Nathaniel Wheeler, Yale............. | Yale | 1946 | George Hamer, Georgia.............. | Stanford |
| 1914 | Edward P. Allis, 3d, Harvard........ | Princeton | 1947 | Dave Barclay, Michigan............. | L. S. U. |
| 1915 | Francis R. Blossom, Yale............ | Yale | 1948 | Bobby Harris, San Jose St........... | San Jose St. |
| 1916 | J. W. Hubbell, Harvard.............. | Princeton | 1949 | Harvie Ward, North Carolina........ | No. Tex. St. |
| 1917–18 | No tournaments | | 1950 | Fred Wampler, Purdue.............. | No. Tex. St. |
| 1919 | A. L. Walker, Jr., Columbia.......... | Princeton | 1951 | Tom Nieporte, Ohio State........... | No. Tex. St. |
| 1920 | Jess W. Sweetser, Yale.............. | Princeton | 1952 | Jim Vickers, Oklahoma............. | No. Tex. St. |
| 1921 | J. Simpson Dean, Princeton.......... | Dartmouth | 1953 | Earl Moeller, Okla. A. & M.......... | Stanford |
| 1922 | Pollack Boyd, Dartmouth............ | Princeton | 1954 | Hillman Robbins, Jr., Memphis St..... | S. M. U. |
| 1923 | Dexter Cummings, Yael.............. | Princeton | 1955 | Joe Campbell, Purdue.............. | L. S. U. |
| 1924 | Dexter Cummings, Yael.............. | Yale | 1956 | Rick Jones, Ohio State............. | Houston |
| 1925 | G. Fred Lamprecht, Tulane.......... | Yale | 1957 | Rex Baxter, Houston............... | Houston |
| 1926 | G. Fred Lamprecht, Tulane.......... | Yale | 1958 | Phil Rodgers, Houston.............. | So. California |
| 1927 | Watts Gunn, Georgia Tech........... | Princeton | 1959 | Richard Crawford, Houston.......... | Houston |
| 1928 | M. J. McCarthy, Jr., Georgetown...... | Princeton | 1960 | Richard Crawford, Houston.......... | Houston |
| 1929 | Tom Aycock, Yale................... | Princeton | | * Two tournaments, in spring and fall. | |

# LAWN TENNIS

LAWN TENNIS is a comparatively modern modification of the ancient game of court tennis. Major Walter Clopton Wingfield thought that something like court tennis might be played outdoors on lawns and in December, 1873, at Nantclwyd, Wales, he introduced his new game under the name of *Sphairistike* at a lawn party. The game was a success and spread rapidly, but the name was a total failure and almost immediately disappeared when all the players and spectators began to refer to the new game as "lawn tennis." In the early part of 1874 a young lady named Mary Ewing Outerbridge returned from Bermuda to New York, bringing with her the implements and necessary equipment of the new game that she had obtained from a British Army supply store in Bermuda. Miss Outerbridge and friends played the first game of lawn tennis in the United States on the grounds of the Staten Island Cricket and Baseball Club in the spring of 1874.

For a few years the new game went along in haphazard fashion under varying rules. Tennis balls were of no standard size or texture. The nets were set at different heights up to 5 feet on the side and 4 feet in the middle. Some courts were marked out in hour-glass shape, narrow in the middle and wide at both ends. But about 1880 standard measurements for the court and standard equipment within definite limits became the rule. In 1881 the United States Lawn Tennis Association was formed and conducted the first national championship at Newport, R. I. The international matches for the Davis Cup began with a series between the British and United States players on the courts of the Longwood Cricket Club, Chestnut Hill, Mass., in 1900, with the home players winning.

## DAVIS CUP CHALLENGE ROUND RESULTS
### MEN

No matches in 1901, 1910, 1915–18, and 1940–45.

| Year | Result | Where played |
|------|--------|--------------|
| 1900 | United States 5, British Isles 0 | Chestnut Hill |
| 1902 | United States 3, British Isles 2 | Brooklyn |
| 1903 | British Isles 4, United States 1 | Chestnut Hill |
| 1904 | British Isles 5, Belgium 0 | Wimbledon |
| 1905 | British Isles 5, United States 0 | Wimbledon |
| 1906 | British Isles 5, United States 0 | Wimbledon |
| 1907 | Australasia 3, British Isles 2 | Wimbledon |
| 1908 | Australasia 3, United States 2 | Melbourne |
| 1909 | Australasia 5, United States 0 | Sydney |
| 1911 | Australasia 5, United States 0 | Christchurch |
| 1912 | British Isles 3, Australasia 2 | Melbourne |
| 1913 | United States 3, British Isles 2 | Wimbledon |
| 1914 | Australasia 3, United States 2 | Forest Hills |
| 1919 | Australasia 4, British Isles 1 | Sydney |
| 1920 | United States 5, Australasia 0 | Auckland |
| 1921 | United States 5, Japan 0 | Forest Hills |
| 1922 | United States 4, Australasia 1 | Forest Hills |
| 1923 | United States 4, Australasia 1 | Forest Hills |
| 1924 | United States 5, Australasia 0 | Philadelphia |
| 1925 | United States 5, France 0 | Philadelphia |
| 1926 | United States 4, France 1 | Philadelphia |
| 1927 | France 3, United States 2 | Philadelphia |
| 1928 | France 4, United States 1 | Paris |
| 1929 | France 3, United States 2 | Paris |
| 1930 | France 4, United States 1 | Paris |
| 1931 | France 3, Great Britain 2 | Paris |
| 1932 | France 3, United States 2 | Paris |
| 1933 | Great Britain 3, France 2 | Paris |
| 1934 | Great Britain 4, United States 1 | Wimbledon |
| 1935 | Great Britain 5, United States 0 | Wimbledon |
| 1936 | Great Britain 3, Australia 2 | Wimbledon |
| 1937 | United States 4, Great Britain 1 | Wimbledon |
| 1938 | United States 3, Australia 2 | Philadelphia |
| 1939 | Australia 3, United States 2 | Haverford |
| 1946 | United States 5, Australia 0 | Melbourne |
| 1947 | United States 4, Australia 1 | Forest Hills |
| 1948 | United States 5, Australia 0 | Forest Hills |
| 1949 | United States 4, Australia 1 | Forest Hills |
| 1950 | Australia 4, United States 1 | Forest Hills |
| 1951 | Australia 3, United States 2 | Sydney |
| 1952 | Australia 4, United States 1 | Adelaide |
| 1953 | Australia 3, United States 2 | Melbourne |
| 1954 | United States 3, Australia 2 | Sydney |
| 1955 | Australia 5, United States 0 | Forest Hills |
| 1956 | Australia 5, United States 0 | Adelaide |
| 1957 | Australia 3, United States 2 | Melbourne |
| 1958 | United States 3, Australia 2 | Brisbane |
| 1959 | Australia 3, United States 2 | Forest Hills |
| 1960 | Australia 4, Italy 1 | Sydney |

## WIGHTMAN CUP RECORD
### WOMEN

| Year | Result | Where played |
|------|--------|--------------|
| 1923 | United States 7, England 0 | Forest Hills |
| 1924 | England 6, United States 1 | Wimbledon |
| 1925 | England 4, United States 3 | Forest Hills |
| 1926 | United States 4, England 3 | Wimbledon |
| 1927 | United States 5, England 2 | Forest Hills |
| 1928 | England 4, United States 3 | Wimbledon |
| 1929 | United States 4, England 3 | Forest Hills |
| 1930 | England 4, United States 3 | Wimbledon |
| 1931 | United States 5, England 2 | Forest Hills |
| 1932 | United States 4, England 3 | Wimbledon |
| 1933 | United States 4, England 3 | Forest Hills |
| 1934 | United States 5, England 2 | Wimbledon |
| 1935 | United States 4, England 3 | Forest Hills |
| 1936 | United States 4, England 3 | Wimbledon |
| 1937 | United States 6, England 1 | Forest Hills |
| 1938 | United States 5, England 2 | Wimbledon |
| 1939 | United States 5, England 2 | Forest Hills |
| 1946 | United States 7, England 0 | Wimbledon |
| 1947 | United States 7, England 0 | Forest Hills |
| 1948 | United States 6, England 1 | Wimbledon |
| 1949 | United States 7, England 0 | Haverford |
| 1950 | United States 7, England 0 | Wimbledon |
| 1951 | United States 6, England 1 | Longwood |
| 1952 | United States 7, England 0 | Wimbledon |
| 1953 | United States 7, England 0 | Rye, N. Y. |
| 1954 | United States 6, England 0 | Wimbledon |
| 1955 | United States 6, England 1 | Rye, N. Y. |
| 1956 | United States 5, England 2 | Wimbledon |
| 1957 | United States 6, England 1 | Sewickley, Pa. |
| 1958 | England 4, United States 3 | Wimbledon |
| 1959 | United States 4, England 3 | Sewickley, Pa. |
| 1960 | England 4, United States 3 | Wimbledon |

# UNITED STATES CHAMPIONS

## Men's Singles

| | | | |
|---|---|---|---|
| 1881-87—Richard D. Sears | 1906—William J. Clothier | 1930—John H. Doeg | 1944-45—Frank Parker |
| 1888-89—Henry Slocum, Jr. | 1907-11—William A. Larned | 1931-32—H. E. Vines, Jr. | 1946-47—Jack Kramer |
| 1890-92—Oliver S. Campbell | 1912-13—M. E. McLoughlin* | 1933-34—Fred J. Perry | 1948-49—Richard Gonzales |
| 1893-94—Robert D. Wrenn | 1914—R. N. Williams II | 1935—Wilmer L. Allison | 1950—Arthur Larsen |
| 1895—Fred H. Hovey | 1915—William Johnston | 1936—Fred J. Perry | 1951-52—Frank Sedgman |
| 1896-97—Robert D. Wrenn | 1916—R. N. Williams II | 1937-38—J. Donald Budge | 1953—Tony Trabert |
| 1898-1900—Malcolm D. | 1917-18—R. Lindley Murray† | 1939—Robert L. Riggs | 1954—E. Victor Seixas, Jr. |
| Whitman | 1919—William Johnston | 1940—Donald McNeill | 1955—Tony Trabert |
| 1901-02—William A. Larned | 1920-25—William T. Tilden II | 1941—Robert L. Riggs | 1956—Ken Rosewall |
| 1903—Hugh L. Doherty | 1926-27—Jean Rene Lacoste | 1942—Frederick R. Schroeder | 1957—Mal Anderson |
| 1904—Holcombe Ward | 1928—Henri Cochet | 1943—Joseph Hunt | 1958—Ashley Cooper |
| 1905—Beals C. Wright | 1929—William T. Tilden II | | 1959-60—Neale Fraser |

* Challenge round abandoned in 1912. + Patriotic tournament in 1917.

## Men's Doubles

| | | |
|---|---|---|
| 1881—C. M. Clark-F. W. Taylor | 1918—W. T. Tilden II-Vincent Richards† | 1942—Gardnar Mulloy-W. F. Talbert |
| 1882-84—R. D. Sears-James Dwight | 1919—N. E. Brookes-G. L. Patterson | 1943—Jack Kramer-F. A. Parker |
| 1885—R. D. Sears-J. S. Clark | 1920—William Johnston-C. J. Griffin | 1944—Don McNeill-Robert Falkenburg |
| 1886-87—R. D. Sears-James Dwight | 1921-22—W. T. Tilden II-Vincent | 1945—Gardnar Mulloy-W. F. Talbert |
| 1888—O. S. Campbell-V. G. Hall | Richards | 1946—Gardnar Mulloy-W. F. Talbert |
| 1889—H. W. Slocum, Jr.-H. A. Taylor | 1923—W. T. Tilden II-B. I. C. Norton | 1947—Jack Kramer-F. R. Schroeder |
| 1890—V. G. Hall-Clarence Hobart | 1924—H. O. Kinsey-R. G. Kinsey | 1948—Gardnar Mulloy-W. F. Talbert |
| 1891-92—O. S. Campbell-R. P. Hunting- | 1925-26—Vincent Richards-R. N. Wil- | 1949—John Bromwich-William Sidwell |
| ton | liams II | 1950—John Bromwich-Frank Sedgman |
| 1893-94—Clarence Hobart-F. H. Hovey | 1927—W. T. Tilden II-F. T. Hunter | 1951—Frank Sedgman-Ken McGregor |
| 1895—M. G. Chace-R. D. Wrenn | 1928—G. M. Lott, Jr.-V. F. Hennessey | 1952—E. Victor Seixas, Jr.-Mervyn Rose |
| 1896—C. B. Neel-S. R. Neel | 1929-30—G. M. Lott, Jr.-J. H. Doeg | 1953—Mervyn Rose-Rex Hartwig |
| 1897-98—L. E. Ware-G. P. Sneldon, Jr. | 1931—W. L. Allison-John Van Ryn | 1954—E. Victor Seixas, Jr.-Tony Trabert |
| 1899-1901—Holcombe Ward-D. F. Davis | 1932—E. H. Vines, Jr.-Keith Gledhill | 1955—Kosei Kamo-Atsushi Miyagi |
| 1902-03—R. F. Doherty-H. L. Doherty | 1933-34—G. M. Lott, Jr.-L. R. Stoefen | 1956—Lewis Hoad-Ken Rosewall |
| 1904-1906—Holcombe Ward-B. C. Wright | 1935—W. L. Allison-John Van Ryn | 1957—Ashley Cooper-Neale Fraser |
| 1907-10—H. H. Hackett-F. B. Alexander | 1936—J. D. Budge-C. G. Mako | 1958—Ham Richardson-Alex Olmedo |
| 1911—R. D. Little-G. F. Touchard | 1937—Baron G. von Cramm-H. Henkel | 1959-60—Neale Fraser-Roy Emerson |
| 1912-14—M. E. McLoughlin-T. C. Bundy | 1938—J. D. Budge-C. G. Mako | |
| 1915-16—William Johnston-C. J. Griffin | 1939—A. K. Quist-J. E. Bromwich | |
| 1917—F. B. Alexander-H. A. Throckmor- | 1940-41—Jack Kramer-F. R. Schroeder | * Patriotic tournament in 1917. |
| ton* | | † Challenge round abandoned in 1918. |

## Women's Singles

| | | | |
|---|---|---|---|
| 1887—Ellen F. Hansell | 1901—Elisabeth H. Moore | 1915-18—Molla Bjurstedt*† | 1937—Anita Lizana |
| 1888-89—Bertha L. Town- | 1902—Marion Jones | 1919—Mrs. G. W. Wightman | 1938-40—Alice Marble |
| send | 1903—Elisabeth H. Moore | 1920-22—Mrs. Molla B. | 1941—Mrs. Sarah P. Cooke |
| 1890—Ellen C. Roosevelt | 1904—May G. Sutton | Mallory | 1946—Pauline M. Betz |
| 1891-92—Mabel E. Cahill | 1905—Elisabeth H. Moore | 1923-25—Helen N. Wills | 1947—A. Louise Brough |
| 1893—Aline M. Terry | 1906—Helen Homans | 1926—Mrs. Molla B. Mallory | 1948-50—Mrs. M. O. du Pont |
| 1894—Helen R. Helwig | 1907—Evelyn Sears | 1927-29—Helen N. Wills | 1951-52—Maureen Connolly |
| 1895—Juliette P. Atkinson | 1908—Mrs. Maud Bargar- | 1930—Betty Nuthall | 1954-55—Doris Hart |
| 1896—Elisabeth H. Moore | Wallach | 1931—Mrs. Helen W. Moody | 1956—Shirley Fry |
| 1897-98—Juliette P. Atkinson | 1909-11—Hazel V. Hotchkiss | 1932-35—Helen Jacobs | 1957-58—Althea Gibson |
| 1899—Marion Jones | 1912-14—Mary K. Browne | 1936—Alice Marble | 1959—Maria Bueno |
| 1900—Myrtle McAteer | | | 1960—Darlene Hard |

* Louise Hammond won patriotic tournament in 1917.
† Challenge round abandoned in 1918.

## Women's Doubles

| | |
|---|---|
| 1890—Ellen C. Roosevelt-Grace W. Roosevelt | 1905—Helen Homans-Carrie B. Neely |
| 1891—Mabel E. Cahill-Mrs. W. F. Morgan | 1906—Mrs. L. S. Coe-Mrs. D. S. Platt |
| 1892—Mabel E. Cahill-A. M. McKinley | 1907—Marie Weimer-Carrie B. Neely |
| 1893—Aline M. Terry-Hattie Butler | 1908—Evelyn Sears-Margaret Curtis |
| 1894-95—Helen R. Helwig-J. P. Atkinson | 1909-10—Hazel V. Hotchkiss-Edith E. Rotch |
| 1896—E. H. Moore-J. P. Atkinson | 1911—Hazel V. Hotchkiss-Eleonora Sears |
| 1897-98—J. P. Atkinson-Kathleen Atkinson | 1912—Dorothy Green-Mary K. Browne |
| 1899—Jane W. Craven-Myrtle McAteer | 1913-14—Mary K. Browne-Mrs. R. H. Williams |
| 1900—Edith Parker-Hallie Champlin | 1915—Mrs. G. W. Wightman-Eleonora Sears |
| 1901—J. P. Atkinson-Myrtle McAteer | 1916-17—Molla Bjurstedt-Eleonora Sears |
| 1902—J. P. Atkinson-Marion Jones | 1918-20—Marion Zinderstein-Eleanor Goss |
| 1903—E. H. Moore-Carrie B. Neely | 1921—Mary K. Browne-Mrs. R. H. Williams |
| 1904—May G. Sutton-Miriam Hall | 1922—Mrs. J. B. Jessup-Helen N. Wills |

1923—Kathleen McKane-Mrs. B. C. Covell
1924—Mrs. G. W. Wightman-Helen N. Wills
1925—Mary K. Browne-Helen N. Wills
1926—Elizabeth Ryan-Eleanor Goss`
1927—Mrs. L. A. Godfree-Ermyntrude Harvey
1928—Mrs. G. W. Wightman-Helen N. Wills
1929—Mrs. Phoebe Watson-Mrs. L. R. C. Michell
1930—Betty Nuthall-Sarah Palfrey
1931—Betty Nuthall-Mrs. E. B. Wittingstall
1932—Helen Jacobs-Sarah Palfrey
1933—Betty Nuthall-Freda James

1934—Helen Jacobs-Sarah Palfrey
1935—Helen Jacobs-Mrs. S. P. Fabyan
1936—Mrs. M. G. Van Ryn-Carolin Babcock
1937-40—Mrs. S. P. Fabyan-Alice Marble
1941—Mrs. S. P. Cooke-Margaret Osborne
1942-47—A. Louise Brough-Margaret Osborne
1948-50—A. Louise Brough-Mrs. Margaret O. du Pont
1951-54—Doris Hart-Shirley Fry
1955-57—A. Louise Brough-Mrs. Margaret O. du Pont
1958-59—Darlene Hard-Jeanne Arth
1960—Darlene Hard-Maria Bueno

## BRITISH (WIMBLEDON) CHAMPIONS

### Men's Singles

1877—S. W. Gore
1878—P. F. Hadow
1879-80—J. T. Hartley
1881-86—W. Renshaw
1887—H. F. Lawford
1888—E. Renshaw
1889—W. Renshaw
1890—W. J. Hamilton
1891-92—W. Baddeley
1893-94—J. Pim
1895—W. Baddeley
1896—H. S. Mahony
1897-1900—R. F. Doherty

1901—A. W. Gore
1902-06—H. L. Doherty
1907—N. E. Brookes
1908-09—A. W. Gore
1910-13—A. F. Wilding
1914—N. E. Brookes
1919—G. L. Patterson
1920-21—W. T. Tilden II
1922—G. L. Patterson
1923—W. M. Johnston
1924—J. Borotra
1925—R. Lacoste

1926—J. Borotra
1927—H. Cochet
1928—R. Lacoste
1929—H. Cochet
1930—W. T. Tilden II
1931—S. B. Wood
1932—H. E. Vines, Jr.
1933—J. H. Crawford
1934-36—F. J. Perry
1937-38—J. D. Budge
1939—R. L. Riggs
1946—Yvon Petra

1947—John A. Kramer
1948—R. Falkenburg
1949—F. R. Schroeder
1950—Budge Patty
1951—Richard Savitt
1952—Frank Sedgman
1953—E. Victor Seixas
1954—Jaroslav Drobny
1955—Tony Trabert
1956-57—Lewis Hoad
1958—Ashley Cooper
1959—Alex Olmedo
1960—Neale Fraser

### Men's Doubles

1879—L. R. Erskine-H. F. Lawford
1880-81—W. Renshaw-E. Renshaw
1882—J. T. Hartley-R. T. Richardson
1883—C. W. Grinstead-C. E. Welldon
1884-86—W. Renshaw-E. Renshaw
1887—P. Bowes-Lyon-H. W. W. Wilber-force
1888-89—W. Renshaw-E. Renshaw
1890—J. L. Pim-F. O. Stoker
1891—W. Baddeley-H. Baddeley
1892—H. S. Barrow-E. W. Lewis
1893—J. L. Pim-F. O. Stoker
1894-96—W. Baddeley-H. Baddeley
1897-1901—R. F. Doherty-H. L. Doherty
1902—S. H. Smith-F. L. Riseley
1903-05—R. F. Doherty-H. L. Doherty
1906—S. H. Smith-F. L. Riseley
1907—N. E. Brookes-A. F. Wilding
1908—A. F. Wilding-M. J. G. Ritchie

1909—A. W. Gore-H. R. Barrett
1910—A. F. Wilding-M. J. G. Ritchie
1911—M. Decugis-A. H. Gobert
1912-13—H. R. Barrett-C. P. Dixon
1914—N. E. Brookes-A. F. Wilding
1919—R. V. Thomas-P. O'Hara Wood
1920—R. N. Williams II-C. S. Garland
1921—R. Lycett-M. Woosnam
1922—R. Lycett-J. O. Anderson
1923—R. Lycett-L. A. Godfree
1924—V. Richards-F. T. Hunter
1925—J. Borotra-R. Lacoste
1926—H. Cochet-J. Brugnon
1927—W. T. Tilden II-F. T. Hunter
1928—H. Cochet-J. Brugnon
1929-30—W. Allison-J. Van Ryn
1931—G. M. Lott-J. Van Ryn
1932-33—J. Borotra-J. Brugnon

1934—G. M. Lott-L. R. Stoefen
1935—J. H. Crawford-A. K. Quist
1936—C. R. D. Tuckey-G. P. Hughes
1937-38—J. D. Budge-C. Gene Mako
1939—R. L. Riggs-E. T. Cooke
1946—J. A. Kramer-Tom Brown
1947—J. A. Kramer-R. Falkenburg
1948—J. Bromwich-F. Sedgman
1949—F. Parker-R. Gonzales
1950—J. Bromwich-A. Quist
1951-52—F. Sedgman-K. McGregor
1953—K. Rosewall-L. Hoad
1954—R. Hartwig-M. Rose
1955—R. Hartwig-L. Hoad
1956—L. Hoad-K. Rosewall
1957—G. Mulloy-B. Patty
1958—Sven Davidson-Ulf Schmidt
1959—Roy Emerson-Neale Fraser
1960—Dennis Ralston-Rafael Osuna

### Women's Singles

1884-85—M. Watson
1886—Miss Bingley
1887-88—L. Dod
1889—Mrs. Hillyard
1890—L. Rice
1891-93—L. Dod
1894—Mrs. Hillyard
1895-96—C. Cooper
1897—Mrs. Hillyard
1898—C. Cooper
1899-1900—Mrs. Hillyard
1901—Mrs. Sterry

1902—M. E. Robb
1903-04—D. K. Douglas
1905—M. Sutton
1906—D. K. Douglas
1907—M. Sutton
1908—Mrs. Sterry
1909—D. Boothby
1910-11—Mrs. L. Chambers
1912—Mrs. Larcombe
1913-14—Mrs. L. Chambers
1919-23—Mlle. Lenglen

1924—K. McKane
1925—Mlle. Lenglen
1926—Mrs. Godfree
1927-29—Helen Wills
1930—Mrs. F. S. Moody
1931—Frl. C. Aussen
1932-33—Mrs. F. S. Moody
1934—D. E. Round
1935—Mrs. F. S. Moody
1936—Helen Jacobs
1937—D. E. Round

1938—Mrs. F. S. Moody
1939—Alice Marble
1946—Pauline M. Betz
1947—Margaret Osborne
1948-50—A. Louise Brough
1951—Doris Hart
1952-54—M. Connolly
1955—A. Louise Brough
1956—Shirley Fry
1957-58—Althea Gibson
1959-60—Maria Bueno

### Women's Doubles

1913—Mrs. McNair-Miss Boothby
1914—E. Ryan-A. M. Morton
1919-23—Mlle. Lenglen-E. Ryan
1924—Mrs. Wightman-Helen Wills
1925—Mlle. Lenglen-E. Ryan
1926—E. Ryan-M. K. Browne
1927—E. Ryan-Helen Wills
1928—Mrs. H. Watson-P. Saunders
1929—Mrs. H. Watson-Mrs. Michell
1930—E. Ryan-Mrs. F. S. Moody

1931—Mrs. Shepherd-Barron-Mrs. Mudford King
1932—Mlle. D. Metaxa-Mlle. J. Sigart
1933-34—E. Ryan-Mme. Mathieu
1935-36—K. E. Stammers-F. James
1937—Mme. S. Mathieu-A. M. Yorka
1938-39—A. Marble-Mrs. S. P. Fabyan
1946—A. L. Brough-M. Osborne
1947—Doris Hart-Mrs. Pat Todd

1948-50—A. L. Brough-Mrs. M. O. du Pont
1951-53—Doris Hart-Shirley Fry
1954—A. L. Brough-Mrs. M. O. du Pont
1955—Angela Mortimer-Ann Shilcock
1956—Althea Gibson-Angela Buxton
1957—Althea Gibson-Darlene Hard
1958—Althea Gibson-Maria Bueno
1959—Darlene Hard-Jeanne Arth
1960—Darlene Hard-Maria Bueno

# THE OLYMPIC GAMES

**(W)—Site of Winter Games. (S)—Site of Summer Games.**

| | | | |
|---|---|---|---|
| 1896—Athens | 1924—Paris (S) | 1936—Berlin (S) | 1956—Melbourne (S) |
| 1900—Paris | 1928—St. Moritz (W) | 1948—St. Moritz (W) | 1960—Squaw Valley, |
| 1904—St. Louis | 1928—Amsterdam (S) | 1948—London (S) | Calif. (W) |
| 1906—Athens | | 1952—Oslo (W) | 1960—Rome (S) |
| 1908—London | 1932—Lake Placid (W) | 1952—Helsinki (S) | 1964—Innsbruck, |
| 1912—Stockholm | 1932—Los Angeles (S) | 1956—Cortina d'Am- | Austria (W) |
| 1920—Antwerp | 1936—Garmisch-Parten- | pezzo, Italy (W) | 1964—Tokyo (S) |
| 1924—Chamonix (W) | kirchen (W) | | |

THE first Olympic Games of which there is record occurred in 776 B.C. and consisted of one event, a great foot race of about 200 yards held on a plain by the River Alpheus (now the Ruphia) just outside the little town of Olympia in Greece. It was from that date that the Greeks began to keep their calendar by "Olympiads," the four-year spans between the celebrations of the famous games. There was a religious as well as an athletic significance to the ancient games and the shrines, temples and sacred fires within the Olympic enclosure were the scenes of worship all through the year whereas the Olympic Games, at the height of their popularity, never lasted more than five days and were held only once every four years.

The competition was entirely amateur at the start and the only prizes were laurel wreaths. Only free Greek citizens were allowed to compete and they had to undergo a strict training course that lasted ten months. But civic rivalry led to trickery and professionalism and the games became degraded after some centuries. When Rome conquered Greece, the Roman emperors turned the Olympic Games from patriotic, religious and athletic festivals into carnivals and circuses. They dragged on malodorously until they were finally halted by decree of Emperor Theodosius I of Rome in A.D. 394.

The modern Olympic Games, which started in Athens in 1896, are the result of the devotion of a French educator, Baron Pierre de Coubertin, to the idea that, since boys and athletics have gone together down the ages, education and athletics might well go hand-in-hand toward a better international understanding. He planned a revival of the ancient Olympic Games on a world-wide basis and succeeded in getting nine nations to send athletes to the first of the modern games in 1896. Since then more than 35,000 athletes representing about 60 nations have competed in the games.

Interrupted for the second time by war, the modern Olympic Games were resumed at London in 1948.

# OLYMPIC GAMES CHAMPIONS, 1896–1960
## TRACK AND FIELD—MEN

### 60-Meter Run

| | | |
|---|---|---|
| 1900 | Alvin Kraenzlein, United States | 7s. |
| 1904 | Archie Hahn, United States | 7s. |

### 100-Meter Run

| | | |
|---|---|---|
| 1896 | Thomas Burke, United States | 12s. |
| 1900 | F. W. Jarvis, United States | 10.8s. |
| 1904 | Archie Hahn, United States | 11s. |
| 1906 | Archie Hahn, United States | 11.2s. |
| 1908 | Reginald Walker, South Africa | 10.8s. |
| 1912 | Ralph Craig, United States | 10.8s. |
| 1920 | Charles Paddock, United States | 10.8s. |
| 1924 | Harold Abrahams, Great Britain | 10.6s. |
| 1928 | Percy Williams, Canada | 10.8s. |
| 1932 | Eddie Tolan, United States | 10.3s. |
| 1936 | Jesse Owens, United States | 10.3s.* |
| 1948 | Harrison Dillard, United States | 10.3s. |
| 1952 | Lindy Remigino, United States | 10.4s. |
| 1956 | Bobby Morrow, United States | 10.5s. |
| 1960 | Armin Hary, Germany | 10.2s. |

\* Wind assisted

### 200-Meter Run

| | | |
|---|---|---|
| 1900 | J. W. B. Tewksbury, United States | 22.2s. |
| 1904 | Archie Hahn, United States | 21.6s. |
| 1908 | Robert Kerr, Canada | 22.4.s |
| 1912 | Ralph Craig, United States | 21.7s. |
| 1920 | Allan Woodring, United States | 22s. |
| 1924 | Jackson Scholz, United States | 21.6s. |
| 1928 | Percy Williams, Canada | 21.8s. |
| 1932 | Eddie Tolan, United States | 21.2s. |
| 1936 | Jesse Owens, United States | 20.7s. |
| 1948 | Melvin E. Patton, United States | 21.1s. |
| 1952 | Andrew Stanfield, United States | 20.7s. |
| 1956 | Bobby Morrow, United States | 20.6s. |
| 1960 | Livio Berruti, Italy | 20.5s. |

### 400-Meter Run

| | | |
|---|---|---|
| 1896 | Thomas Burke, United States | 54.2. |
| 1900 | Maxey Long, United States | 49.4. |
| 1904 | Harry Hillman, United States | 49.2. |
| 1906 | Paul Pilgrim, United States | 53.2. |
| 1908 | Wyndham Halswelle, Great Britain (walkover) | 50s. |
| 1912 | Charles Reidpath, United States | 48.2s. |
| 1920 | Bevil Rudd, South Africa | 49.6s. |
| 1924 | Eric Liddell, Great Britain | 47.6s. |
| 1928 | Ray Barbuti, United States | 47.8s. |
| 1932 | William Carr, United States | 46.2s. |
| 1936 | Archie Williams, United States | 46.5s. |
| 1948 | Arthur Wint, Jamaica, B.W.I. | 46.2s. |
| 1952 | George Rhoden, Jamaica, B. W. I. | 45.9s. |
| 1956 | Charles Jenkins, United States | 46.7s. |
| 1960 | Otis Davis, United States | 44.9s. |

## 800-Meter Run

| | | |
|---|---|---|
| 96 | Edwin Flack, Great Britain | 2m.11s. |
| 00 | Alfred Tysoe, Great Britain | 2m.1.4s. |
| 04 | James Lightbody, United States | 1m.56s. |
| 06 | Paul Pilgrim, United States | 2m.1.2s. |
| 08 | Mel Sheppard, United States | 1m.52.8s. |
| 12 | Ted Meredith, United States | 1m.51.9s. |
| 20 | Albert Hill, Great Britain | 1m.53.4s. |
| 24 | Douglas Lowe, Great Britain | 1m.52.4s. |
| 28 | Douglas Lowe, Great Britain | 1m.51.8s. |
| 32 | Thomas Hampson, Great Britain | 1m.49.8s. |
| 36 | John Woodruff, United States | 1m.52.9s. |
| 48 | Malvin Whitfield, United States | 1m.49.2s. |
| 52 | Malvin Whitfield, United States | 1m.49.2s. |
| 56 | Tom Courtney, United States | 1m.47.7s. |
| 60 | Peter Snell, New Zealand | 1m.46.3s. |

## 1,500-Meter Run

| | | |
|---|---|---|
| 96 | Edwin Flack, Great Britain | 4m.33.2s. |
| 00 | Charles Bennett, Great Britain | 4m.6s. |
| 04 | James Lightbody, United States | 4m.5.4s. |
| 06 | James Lightbody, United States | 4m.12s. |
| 08 | Mel Sheppard, United States | 4m.3.4s. |
| 12 | Arnold Jackson, Great Britain | 3m.56.8s. |
| 20 | Albert Hill, Great Britain | 4m.1.8s. |
| 24 | Paavo Nurmi, Finland | 3m.53.6s. |
| 28 | Harry Larva, Finland | 3m.53.2s. |
| 32 | Luigi Beccali, Italy | 3m.51.2s. |
| 36 | Jack Lovelock, New Zealand | 3m.47.8s. |
| 48 | Henri Eriksson, Sweden | 3m.49.8s. |
| 52 | Joseph Barthel, Luxemburg | 3m.45.2s. |
| 56 | Ron Delany, Ireland | 3m.41.2s. |
| 60 | Herb Elliott, Australia | 3m.35.6s. |

## 5,000-Meter Run

| | | |
|---|---|---|
| 12 | Hannes Kolehmainen, Finland | 14m.36.6s. |
| 20 | Joseph Guillemot, France | 14m.55.6s. |
| 24 | Paavo Nurmi, Finland | 14m.31.2s. |
| 28 | Willie Ritola, Finland | 14m.38s. |
| 32 | Lauri Lehtinen, Finland | 14m.30s. |
| 36 | Gunnar Hockert, Finland | 14m.22.2s. |
| 48 | Gaston Reiff, Belgium | 14m.17.6s. |
| 52 | Emil Zatopek, Czechoslovakia | 14m.6.6s. |
| 56 | Vladimir Kuts, U.S.S.R. | 13m.39.6s. |
| 60 | Murray Halberg, New Zealand | 13m.43.4s. |

## 5-Mile Run

| | | |
|---|---|---|
| 06 | H. Hawtrey, Great Britain | 26m.26.2s. |
| 08 | Emil Voigt, Great Britain | 25m.11.2s. |

## 10,000-Meter Run

| | | |
|---|---|---|
| 12 | Hannes Kolehmainen, Finland | 31m.20.8s. |
| 20 | Paavo Nurmi, Finland | 31m.45.8s. |
| 24 | Willie Ritola, Finland | 30m.23.2s. |
| 28 | Paavo Nurmi, Finland | 30m.18.8s. |
| 32 | Janusz Kusocinski, Poland | 30m.11.4s. |
| 36 | Ilmari Salminen, Finland | 30m.15.4s. |
| 48 | Emil Zatopek, Czechoslovakia | 29m.59.6s. |
| 52 | Emil Zatopek, Czechoslovakia | 29m.17s. |
| 56 | Vladimir Kuts, U.S.S.R. | 28m.45.6s. |
| 60 | Peter Bolotnikov, U.S.S.R. | 28m.32.2s. |

## Marathon

| | | |
|---|---|---|
| 96 | Spiridon Loues, Greece | 2h.55m.20s. |
| 00 | Michel Teato, France | 2h.59m. |
| 04 | Thomas Hicks, United States | 3h.28m.53s. |
| 06 | W. J. Sherring, Canada | 2h.51m.23.6s. |
| 08 | John J. Hayes, United States | 2h.55m.18.4s. |
| 12 | Kenneth McArthur, South Africa | 2h.36m.54.8s. |
| 20 | Hannes Kolehmainen, Finland | 2h.32m.35.8s. |
| 24 | A. O. Stenroos, Finland | 2h.41m.22.6s. |
| 28 | A. B. El Ouafi, France | 2h.32m.57s. |
| 32 | Juan Zabala, Argentina | 2h.31m.36s. |

| | | |
|---|---|---|
| 1936 | Kitei Son, Japan | 2h.29m.19.2s. |
| 1948 | Delfo Cabrera, Argentina | 2h.34m.51.6s. |
| 1952 | Emil Zatopek, Czechoslovakia | 2h.23m.3.2s. |
| 1956 | Alain Mimoun, France | 2h.25m. |
| 1960 | Abebe Bikila, Ethiopia | 2h.15m.16.2s. |

## 110-Meter Hurdles

| | | |
|---|---|---|
| 1896 | Thomas Curtis, United States | 17.6s. |
| 1900 | Alvin Kraenzlein, United States | 15.4s. |
| 1904 | Frederick Schule, United States | 16s. |
| 1906 | R. G. Leavitt, United States | 16.2s. |
| 1908 | Forest Smithson, United States | 15s. |
| 1912 | Frederick Kelly, United States | 15.1s. |
| 1920 | E. J. Thomson, Canada | 14.8s. |
| 1924 | Daniel Kinsey, United States | 15s. |
| 1928 | Sydney Atkinson, South Africa | 14.8s. |
| 1932 | George Saling, United States | 14.6s. |
| 1936 | Forrest Towns, United States | 14.2s. |
| 1948 | William Porter, United States | 13.9s. |
| 1952 | Harrison Dillard, United States | 13.7s. |
| 1956 | Lee Calhoun, United States | 13.5s. |
| 1960 | Lee Calhoun, United States | 13.8s. |

## 200-Meter Hurdles

| | | |
|---|---|---|
| 1900 | Alvin Kraenzlein, United States | 25.4s. |
| 1904 | Harry Hillman, United States | 24.6s. |

## 400-Meter Hurdles

| | | |
|---|---|---|
| 1900 | J. W. B. Tewksbury, United States | 57.6s. |
| 1904 | Harry Hillman, United States | 53s. |
| 1908 | Charles Bacon, United States | 55s. |
| 1920 | Frank Loomis, United States | 54s. |
| 1924 | F. Morgan Taylor, United States | 52.6s. |
| 1928 | Lord David Burghley, Great Britain | 53.4s. |
| 1932 | Robert Tisdall, Ireland | 51.8s.* |
| 1936 | Glenn Hardin, United States | 52.4s. |
| 1948 | Roy Cochran, United States | 51.1s. |
| 1952 | Charles Moore, United States | 50.8s. |
| 1956 | Glenn Davis, United States | 50.1s. |
| 1960 | Glenn Davis, United States | 49.3s. |

* Record not allowed.

## 2,500-Meter Steeplechase

| | | |
|---|---|---|
| 1900 | George Orton, United States | 7m.34s. |
| 1904 | James Lightbody, United States | 7m.39.6s. |

## 3,000-Meter Steeplechase

| | | |
|---|---|---|
| 1920 | Percy Hodge, Great Britain | 10m.2.4s. |
| 1924 | Willie Ritola, Finland | 9m.33.6s. |
| 1928 | Toivo Loukola, Finland | 9m.21.8s. |
| 1932 | Volmari Iso-Hollo, Finland | 10m.33.4s.* |
| 1936 | Volmari Iso-Hollo, Finland | 9m.3.8s. |
| 1948 | Thure Sjoestrand, Sweden | 9m.4.6s. |
| 1952 | Horace Ashenfelter, United States | 8m.45.4s. |
| 1956 | Chris Brasher, Great Britain | 8m.41.2s. |
| 1960 | Zdzislaw Krzyskowiak, Poland | 8m.34.2s. |

* About 3,450 meters—extra lap by error.

## 3,200-Meter Steeplechase

| | | |
|---|---|---|
| 1908 | A. Russell, Great Britain | 10m.47.8s. |

## 4,000-Meter Steeplechase

| | | |
|---|---|---|
| 1900 | John Rimmer, Great Britain | 12m.58.4s. |

## 8,000-Meter Cross-Country

| | | |
|---|---|---|
| 1912 | Hannes Kolehmainen, Finland | 45m.11.6s. |

## 10,000-Meter Cross-Country

| | | |
|---|---|---|
| 1920 | Paavo Nurmi, Finland | 27m.15s. |
| 1924 | Paavo Nurmi, Finland | 32m.54.8s. |

## Cross-Country Team Races

| | | Pts. |
|---|---|---|
| 1912 | Sweden (8,000 meters) | 10 |
| 1920 | Finland (10,000 meters) | 10 |
| 1924 | Finland (10,000 meters) | 11 |

### Team Race

| | | Pts. |
|---|---|---|
| 1900 | Great Britain (5,000 meters) | 26 |
| 1904 | United States (4 miles) | 27 |
| 1908 | Great Britain (3 miles) | 6 |
| 1912 | United States (3,000 meters) | 9 |
| 1920 | United States (3,000 meters) | 10 |
| 1924 | Finland (3,000 meters) | 9 |

### 1,500-Meter Walk

| | | |
|---|---|---|
| 1906 | George V. Bonhag, United States | 7m.12.6s. |

### 3,000-Meter Walk

| | | |
|---|---|---|
| 1920 | Ugo Frigerio, Italy | 13m.14.2s. |

### 3,500-Meter Walk

| | | |
|---|---|---|
| 1908 | George Larner, Great Britain | 14m.55s. |

### 10,000-Meter Walk

| | | |
|---|---|---|
| 1912 | George Goulding, Canada | 46m.28.4s. |
| 1920 | Ugo Frigerio, Italy | 48m.6.2s. |
| 1924 | Ugo Frigerio, Italy | 47m.49s. |
| 1948 | John Mikaelsson, Sweden | 45m.13.2s. |
| 1952 | John Mikaelsson, Sweden | 45m.2.8s. |

### 10-Mile Walk

| | | |
|---|---|---|
| 1908 | George Larner, Great Britain | 1h.15m.57.4s. |

### 20,000-Meter Walk

| | | |
|---|---|---|
| 1956 | Leonid Spirin, U.S.S.R. | 1h.31m.27s. |
| 1960 | Vladimir Golubnichy, U.S.S.R. | 1h.34m.07.2s. |

### 50,000-Meter Walk

| | | |
|---|---|---|
| 1932 | Thomas W. Green, Great Britain | 4h.50m.10s. |
| 1936 | Harold Whitlock, Great Britain | 4h.30m.41.4s. |
| 1948 | John Ljunggren, Sweden | 4h.41m.52s. |
| 1952 | Giuseppe Bordoni, Italy | 4h.28m.7.8s. |
| 1956 | Norman Read, New Zealand | 4h.30m.42.8s. |
| 1960 | Donald Thompson, Great Britain | 4h.25m.30s. |

### 400-Meter Relay (4 x 100)

| | | |
|---|---|---|
| 1912 | Great Britain | 42.4s. |
| 1920 | United States | 42.2s. |
| 1924 | United States | 41s. |
| 1928 | United States | 41s. |
| 1932 | United States | 40s. |
| 1936 | United States | 39.8s. |
| 1948 | United States | 40.6s. |
| 1952 | United States | 40.1s. |
| 1956 | United States | 39.5s. |
| 1960 | Germany | 39.5s. |

### 1,600-Meter Relay (200-200-400-800)

| | | |
|---|---|---|
| 1908 | United States | 3m.27.2s. |

### 1,600-Meter Relay (4 x 400)

| | | |
|---|---|---|
| 1912 | United States | 3m.16.6s. |
| 1920 | Great Britain | 3m.22.2s. |
| 1924 | United States | 3m.16s. |
| 1928 | United States | 3m.14.2s. |
| 1932 | United States | 3m.8.2s. |
| 1936 | Great Britain | 3m.9s. |
| 1948 | United States | 3m.10.4s. |
| 1952 | Jamaica, B. W. I. | 3m.3.9s. |
| 1956 | United States | 3m.4.8s. |
| 1960 | United States | 3m.02.2s. |

### Pole Vault

| | | |
|---|---|---|
| 1896 | William Hoyt, United States | 10 ft. 9¾ in. |
| 1900 | Irving Baxter, United States | 10 ft. 9.9 in. |
| 1904 | Charles Dvorak, United States | 11 ft. 6 in. |
| 1906 | Fernand Gouder, France | 11 ft. 6 in. |
| 1908 | A. C. Gilbert, United States, and Edward Cook, United States (tie) | 12 ft. 2 in. |
| 1912 | Harry Babcock, United States | 12 ft. 11½ in. |
| 1920 | Frank Foss, United States | 13 ft. 5 in. |
| 1924 | Lee Barnes, United States | 12 ft. 11½ in. |
| 1928 | Sabin W. Carr, United States | 13 ft. 9⅜ i |
| 1932 | William Miller, United States | 14 ft. 1⅞ i. |
| 1936 | Earle Meadows, United States | 14 ft. 3¼ i |
| 1948 | Guinn Smith, United States | 14 ft. 1¼ i |
| 1952 | Robert Richards, United States | 14 ft. 11.14 |
| 1956 | Robert Richards, United States | 14 ft. 11½ |
| 1960 | Don Bragg, United States | 15 ft. 5⅛ i |

### Standing High Jump

| | | |
|---|---|---|
| 1900 | Ray Ewry, United States | 5 ft. 5 in. |
| 1904 | Ray Ewry, United States | 4 ft. 11 in. |
| 1906 | Ray Ewry, United States | 5 ft. 1⅝ in |
| 1908 | Ray Ewry, United States | 5 ft. 2 in. |
| 1912 | Platt Adams, United States | 5 ft. 4⅛ in |

### Running High Jump

| | | |
|---|---|---|
| 1896 | Ellery Clark, United States | 5 ft. 11¼ i |
| 1900 | Irving Baxter, United States | 6 ft. 2⅘ in |
| 1904 | Samuel Jones, United States | 5 ft. 11 in. |
| 1906 | Con Leahy, Ireland | 5 ft. 9⅞ in |
| 1908 | Harry Porter, United States | 6 ft. 3 in. |
| 1912 | Alma Richards, United States | 6 ft. 4 in. |
| 1920 | Richard Landon, United States | 6 ft. 4¼ in |
| 1924 | Harold Osborn, United States | 6 ft. 5 15/16 |
| 1928 | Robert W. King, United States | 6 ft. 4⅜ in |
| 1932 | Duncan McNaughton, Canada | 6 ft. 5⅝ in |
| 1936 | Cornelius Johnson, United States | 6 ft. 7 15/16 |
| 1948 | John Winter, Australia | 6 ft. 6 in. |
| 1952 | Walter Davis, United States | 6 ft. 8.32 in |
| 1956 | Charles Dumas, United States | 6 ft. 11¼ in |
| 1960 | Robert Shavlakadze, U.S.S.R. | 7 ft. 1 in. |

### Standing Broad Jump

| | | |
|---|---|---|
| 1900 | Ray Ewry, United States | 10 ft. 6⅖ in |
| 1904 | Ray Ewry, United States | 11 ft. 4⅞ i |
| 1906 | Ray Ewry, United States | 10 ft. 10 in. |
| 1908 | Ray Ewry, United States | 10 ft. 11¼ |
| 1912 | Constantin Tsicilitiras Greece | 11 ft. ¼ in |

### Running Broad Jump

| | | |
|---|---|---|
| 1896 | Ellery Clark, United States | 20 ft. 9¾ i |
| 1900 | Alvin Kraenzlein, United States | 23 ft. 6⅞ i |
| 1904 | Myer Prinstein, United States | 24 ft. 1 in. |
| 1906 | Myer Prinstein, United States | 23 ft. 7½ i |
| 1908 | Frank Irons, United States | 24 ft. 6½ i |
| 1912 | Albert Gutterson, United States | 24 ft. 11¼ |
| 1920 | Wm. Pettersson, Sweden | 23 ft. 5½ in |
| 1924 | DeHart Hubbard, United States | 24 ft. 5⅛ i |
| 1928 | Edward B. Hamm, United States | 25 ft. 4¾ i |
| 1932 | Edward Gordon, United States | 25 ft. ¾ in. |
| 1936 | Jesse Owens, United States | 26 ft. 5 5/16 |
| 1948 | Willie Steele, United States | 25 ft. 8 in. |
| 1952 | Jerome Biffle, United States | 24 ft. 10.03 |
| 1956 | Gregory Bell, United States | 25 ft. 8¼ in |
| 1960 | Ralph Boston, United States | 26 ft. 7¾ in |

### Standing Hop, Step and Jump

| | | |
|---|---|---|
| 1900 | Ray Ewry, United States | 34 ft. 8½ in |
| 1904 | Ray Ewry United States | 34 ft. 7¼ in |

### Running Hop, Step and Jump

| | | |
|---|---|---|
| 1896 | James B. Connolly, United States | 45 ft. |
| 1900 | Myer Prinstein, United States | 47 ft. 4¼ in. |
| 1904 | Myer Prinstein, United States | 47 ft. |
| 1906 | P. G. O'Connor, Ireland | 46 ft. 2 in. |
| 1908 | Timothy Ahearne, Great Britain | 48 ft. 11¼ in. |
| 1912 | Gustaf Lindblom, Sweden | 48 ft. 5⅛ in. |
| 1920 | Vilho Tuulos, Finland | 47 ft. 6⅞ in. |
| 1924 | Archie Winter, Australia | 50 ft. 11⅛ in. |
| 1928 | Mikio Oda, Japan | 49 ft. 10 13/16 |
| 1932 | Chuhei Nambu, Japan | 51 ft. 7 in. |
| 1936 | Naoto Tajima, Japan | 52 ft. 5⅞ in. |
| 1948 | Arne Ahman, Sweden | 50 ft. 6¼ in. |
| 1952 | Adhemar da Silva, Brazil | 53 ft. 2.59 in. |
| 1956 | Adhemar da Silva, Brazil | 53 ft. 7½ in. |
| 1960 | Jozef Schmidt, Poland | 55 ft. 1¾ in. |

### 16-Lb. Shot Put

| | | |
|---|---|---|
| 96 | Robert Garrett, United States | 36 ft. 2 in. |
| 00 | Richard Sheldon, United States | 46 ft. 3⅛ in. |
| 04 | Ralph Rose, United States | 48 ft. 7 in. |
| 06 | Martin Sheridan, United States | 40 ft. 4⅘ in. |
| 08 | Ralph Rose, United States | 46 ft. 7½ in. |
| 12 | Pat McDonald, United States | 50 ft. 4 in. |
| 20 | Ville Porhola, Finland | 48 ft. 7⅛ in. |
| 24 | Clarence Houser, United States | 49 ft. 2½ in. |
| 28 | John Kuck, United States | 52 ft. 11/16 in. |
| 32 | Leo Sexton, United States | 52 ft. 6 3/16 in. |
| 36 | Hans Woellke, Germany | 53 ft. 1¾ in. |
| 48 | Wilbur Thompson, United States | 56 ft. 2 in. |
| 52 | Parry O'Brien, United States | 57 ft. 1.43 in. |
| 56 | Parry O'Brien, United States | 60 ft. 11 in. |
| 60 | Bill Nieder, United States | 64 ft. 6¾ in. |

### 16-Lb. Shot Put (Both Hands)

| | | |
|---|---|---|
| 12 | Ralph Rose, United States | 90 ft. 5⅜ in. |

### 16-Lb. Hammer Throw

| | | |
|---|---|---|
| 00 | John Flanagan, United States | 167 ft. 4 in. |
| 04 | John Flanagan, United States | 168 ft. 1 in. |
| 08 | John Flanagan, United States | 170 ft. 4¼ in. |
| 12 | Matt McGrath, United States | 177 ft. 7 in. |
| 20 | Pat Ryan, United States | 173 ft. 5⅝ in. |
| 24 | Fred Tootell, United States | 174 ft. 10¼ in. |
| 28 | Patrick O'Callaghan, Ireland | 168 ft. 7½ in. |
| 32 | Patrick O'Callaghan, Ireland | 176 ft. 11⅛ in. |
| 36 | Karl Hein, Germany | 185 ft. 4 in. |
| 48 | Imre Nemeth, Hungary | 183 ft. 11½ in. |
| 52 | Jozsef Csermak, Hungary | 197 ft. 11.67 in. |
| 56 | Harold Connolly, United States | 207 ft. 2¾ in. |
| 60 | Vasily Rudenkov, (v,) U.S.S.R. | 220 ft. 1⅝ in. |

### 56-Lb. Weight Throw

| | | |
|---|---|---|
| 04 | Etienne Desmarteau, Canada | 34 ft. 4 in. |
| 20 | Pat McDonald, United States | 36 ft. 11⅝ in. |

### Discus Throw

| | | |
|---|---|---|
| 96 | Robert Garrett, United States | 95 ft. 7½ in. |
| 00 | Rudolf Bauer, Hungary | 118 ft. 2.9 in. |
| 04 | Martin Sheridan, United States | 128 ft. 10½ in. |
| 06 | Martin Sheridan, United States | 136 ft. ⅓ in. |
| 08 | Martin Sheridan, United States | 134 ft. 2 in. |
| 12 | Armas Taipale, Finland | 148 ft. 3.9 in. |
| 20 | Elmer Niklander, Finland | 146 ft. 7 in. |
| 24 | Clarence Houser, United States | 151 ft. 5¼ in. |
| 28 | Clarence Houser, United States | 155 ft. 2⅘ in. |
| 32 | John Anderson, United States | 162 ft. 4⅞ in. |
| 36 | Ken Carpenter, United States | 165 ft. 7⅜ in. |
| 48 | Adolfo Consolini, Italy | 173 ft. 2 in. |
| 52 | Simeon Iness, United States | 180 ft. 6.85 in. |
| 56 | Al Oerter, United States | 184 ft. 10½ in. |
| 60 | Al Oerter, United States | 194 ft. 2 in. |

### Discus Throw—Greek Style

| | | |
|---|---|---|
| 06 | Werner Jaervinen, Finland | 115 ft. 4 in. |
| 08 | Martin Sheridan, United States | 124 ft. 8 in. |

### Discus Throw (Both Hands)

| | | |
|---|---|---|
| 12 | Armas Taipale, Finland | 271 ft. 10⅛ in. |

### Javelin Throw

| | | |
|---|---|---|
| 06 | Eric Lemming, Sweden | 175 ft. 6 in. |
| 08 | Eric Lemming, Sweden | 179 ft. 10½ in. |
| 12 | Eric Lemming, Sweden | 198 ft. 11¼ in. |
| 20 | Jonni Myyra, Finland | 215 ft. 9¾ in. |
| 24 | Jonni Myyra, Finland | 206 ft. 6¾ in. |
| 28 | Eric Lundquist, Sweden | 218 ft. 6⅛ in. |
| 32 | Matti Jarvinen, Finland | 238 ft. 7 in. |
| 1936 | Gerhard Stoeck, Germany | 235 ft. 8 5/16 in. |
| 1948 | Kaj Rautavaara, Finland | 228 ft. 10½ in. |
| 1952 | Cy Young, United States | 242 ft. 0.79 in. |
| 1956 | Egil Danielsen, Norway | 281 ft. 2¼ in. |
| 1960 | Viktor Tsibulenko, U.S.S.R. | 277 ft. 8⅜ in. |

### Javelin Throw—Free Style

| | | |
|---|---|---|
| 1908 | Eric Lemming, Sweden | 178 ft. 7½ in. |

### Javelin Throw (Both Hands)

| | | |
|---|---|---|
| 1912 | Julius Saaristo, Finland | 358 ft. 11½ in. |

### Throwing the Stone (14 lbs.)

| | | |
|---|---|---|
| 1906 | Nicolas Georgantas, Greece | 65 ft. 4 1/5 in. |

### Tug of War

| | | | |
|---|---|---|---|
| 1904 | United States | 1912 | Sweden |
| 1906 | Germany | 1920 | Great Britain |
| 1908 | Great Britain | | |

### All-Around

| | | |
|---|---|---|
| 1904 | Thomas Kiely, Great Britain | 6,036 pts. |

### Pentathlon

| | | |
|---|---|---|
| 1906 | H. Mellander, Sweden | 24 pts. |
| 1912 | Ferdinand Bie, Norway | 21 pts. |
| 1920 | Eero Lehtonen, Finland | 14 pts. |
| 1924 | Eero Lehtonen, Finland | 16 pts. |

### Decathlon

| | | |
|---|---|---|
| 1912 | Hugo Wieslander, Sweden | 7,724.495 pts. |
| 1920 | Helge Lovland, Norway | 6,804.35 pts. |
| 1924 | Harold Osborn, United States | 7,710.775 pts. |
| 1928 | Paavo Yrjola, Finland | 8,053.29 pts. |
| 1932 | James Bausch, United States | 8,462.23 pts. |
| 1936 | Glenn Morris, United States | 7,900 pts.* |
| 1948 | Robert B. Mathias, United States | 7,139 pts. |
| 1952 | Robert B. Mathias, United States | 7,887 pts.† |
| 1956 | Milton Campbell, United States | 7,937 pts. |
| 1960 | Rafer Johnson, United States | 8,392 pts. |

* Point system revised. † Revised again.

## TRACK AND FIELD—WOMEN

### 100-Meter Run

| | | |
|---|---|---|
| 1928 | Elizabeth Robinson, United States | 12.2s. |
| 1932 | Stella Walsh, Poland | 11.9s. |
| 1936 | Helen Stephens, United States | 11.5s. |
| 1948 | Fanny Blankers-Koen, Holland | 11.9s. |
| 1952 | Marjorie Jackson, Australia | 11.5s. |
| 1956 | Betty Cuthbert, Australia | 11.5s. |
| 1960 | Wilma Rudolph, United States | 11s. |

### 200-Meter Run

| | | |
|---|---|---|
| 1948 | Fanny Blankers-Koen, Holland | 24.4s. |
| 1952 | Marjorie Jackson, Australia | 23.7s. |
| 1956 | Betty Cuthbert, Australia | 23.4s. |
| 1960 | Wilma Rudolph, United States | 24s. |

### 800-Meter Run

| | | |
|---|---|---|
| 1928 | Lina Radke, Germany | 2m.16.8s. |
| 1960 | Ljudmila Shevcova, U.S.S.R. | 2m.4.3s. |

### 80-Meter Hurdles

| | | |
|---|---|---|
| 1932 | Mildred Didrikson, United States | 11.7s. |
| 1936 | Trebisonda Valla, Italy | 11.7s. |
| 1948 | Fanny Blankers-Koen, Holland | 11.2s. |
| 1952 | Shirley S. de la Hunty, Australia | 10.9s. |
| 1956 | Shirley S. de la Hunty, Australia | 10.7s. |
| 1960 | Irina Press, U.S.S.R. | 10.8s. |

### 400-Meter Relay

| | | |
|---|---|---|
| 1928 | Canada | 48.4s. |
| 1932 | United States | 47s. |
| 1936 | United States | 46.9s. |
| 1948 | Holland | 47.5s. |
| 1952 | United States | 45.9s. |
| 1956 | Australia | 44.5s. |
| 1960 | United States | 44.5s. |

### Running High Jump

| | | |
|---|---|---|
| 1928 | Ethel Catherwood, Canada | 5 ft. 3 in. |
| 1932 | Jean Shiley, United States | 5 ft. 5¼ in. |
| 1936 | Ibolya Csak, Hungary | 5 ft. 3 in. |
| 1948 | Alice Coachman, United States | 5 ft. 6⅛ in. |
| 1952 | Ester Brand, South Africa | 5 ft. 5.75 in. |
| 1956 | Mildred McDaniel, United States | 5 ft. 9¼ in. |
| 1960 | Iolanda Balas, Rumania | 6 ft. ¾ in. |

### Running Broad Jump

| | | |
|---|---|---|
| 1948 | Olga Gyarmati, Hungary | 18 ft. 8¼ in. |
| 1952 | Yvette Williams, New Zealand | 20 ft. 5.66 in. |
| 1956 | Elzbieta Krzesinska, Poland | 20 ft. 10 in. |
| 1960 | Vera Krepkina, U.S.S.R. | 20 ft. 10¾ in. |

### Discus Throw

| | | |
|---|---|---|
| 1928 | Helena Konopacka, Poland | 129 ft. 11⅞ in. |
| 1932 | Lillian Copeland, United States | 133 ft. 2 in. |
| 1936 | Gisela Mauermayer, Germany | 156 ft. 3³⁄₁₆ in. |
| 1948 | Micheline Ostermeyer, France | 137 ft. 6½ in. |
| 1952 | Nina Romaschkova, U.S.S.R. | 168 ft. 8.5 in. |
| 1956 | Olga Fikotova, Czechoslovakia | 176 ft. 1½ in. |
| 1960 | Nina Ponomareva, U.S.S.R. | 180 ft. 8¼ in. |

### Javelin Throw

| | | |
|---|---|---|
| 1932 | Mildred Didrikson, United States | 143 ft. 4 in. |
| 1936 | Tilly Fleischer, Germany | 148 ft. 2¾ in. |
| 1948 | Herma Bauma, Austria | 149 ft. 6 in. |
| 1952 | Dana Zatopek, Czechoslovakia | 165 ft. 7.05 in. |
| 1956 | Inessa Janzeme, U.S.S.R. | 176 ft. 8½ in. |
| 1960 | Elvira Ozolina, U.S.S.R. | 183 ft. 8 in. |

### Shot Put

| | | |
|---|---|---|
| 1948 | Micheline Ostermeyer, France | 45 ft. 1½ in. |
| 1952 | Galina Zybina, U.S.S.R. | 50 ft. 2.58 in. |
| 1956 | Tamara Tishkyevich, U.S.S.R. | 54 ft. 5 in. |
| 1960 | Tamara Press, U.S.S.R. | 56 ft. 9⅞ in. |

## SWIMMING—MEN

### 50 Yards

| | | |
|---|---|---|
| 1904 | Zoltan de Halmay, Hungary | 28s. |

### 100 Meters

| | | |
|---|---|---|
| 1896 | Alfred Hajos, Hungary | 1m.22.2s. |
| 1904 | Zoltan de Halmay, Hungary | 1m.2.8s.* |
| 1906 | Charles Daniels, United States | 1m.13s. |
| 1908 | Charles Daniels, United States | 1m.5.6s. |
| 1912 | Duke P. Kahanamoku, United States | 1m.3.4s. |
| 1920 | Duke P. Kahanamoku, United States | 1m.1.4s. |
| 1924 | John Weissmuller, United States | 59s. |
| 1928 | John Weissmuller, United States | 58.6s. |
| 1932 | Yasuji Miyazaki, Japan | 58.2s. |
| 1936 | Ferenc Csik, Hungary | 57.6s |
| 1948 | Walter Ris, United States | 57.3s. |
| 1952 | Clarke Scholes, United States | 57.4s. |
| 1956 | Jon Henricks, Australia | 55.4s. |
| 1960 | John Devitt, Australia | 55.2s. |

* 100 yards.

### 200 Meters

| | | |
|---|---|---|
| 1900 | Frederick Lane, Australia | 2m.25.2s. |
| 1904 | Charles Daniels, United States | 2m.44.2s.* |

* 220 yards.

### 400 Meters

| | | |
|---|---|---|
| 1896 | Paul Neumann, Austria | 8m.12.6s.* |
| 1904 | Charles Daniels, United States | 6m.16.2s.† |
| 1906 | Otto Sheff, Austria | 6m.23.8s |
| 1908 | Henry Taylor, Great Britain | 5m.36.8s |
| 1912 | George Hodgson, Canada | 5m.24.4 |
| 1920 | Norman Ross, United States | 5m.26.8s |
| 1924 | John Weissmuller, United States | 5m.4.2s. |
| 1928 | Albert Zorilla, Argentina | 5m.1.6s. |
| 1932 | Clarence Crabbe, United States | 4m.48.4 |
| 1936 | Jack Medica, United States | 4m.44.5 |
| 1948 | William Smith, United States | 4m.41s. |
| 1952 | Jean Boiteux, France | 4m.30.7 |
| 1956 | Murray Rose, Australia | 4m.27.3 |
| 1960 | Murray Rose, Australia | 4m.18.3s |

* 500 meters. † 440 yards.

### 880 Yards

| | | |
|---|---|---|
| 1904 | Emil Rausch, Germany | 13m.11.4s |

### 1,000 Meters

| | | |
|---|---|---|
| 1900 | John Jarvis, Great Britain | 13m.40.2 |

### 1,200 Meters

| | | |
|---|---|---|
| 1896 | Alfred Hajos, Hungary | 18m.22.2s |

### 1,500 Meters

| | | |
|---|---|---|
| 1904 | Emil Rausch, Germany | 27m.18.2s |
| 1906 | Henry Taylor, Great Britain | 28m.28s.† |
| 1908 | Henry Taylor, Great Britain | 22m.48.4 |
| 1912 | George Hodgson, Canada | 22m. |
| 1920 | Norman Ross, United States | 22m.23.2 |
| 1924 | Andrew Charlton, Australia | 20m.6.6s. |
| 1928 | Arne Borg, Sweden | 19m.51.8 |
| 1932 | Kusuo Kitamura, Japan | 19m.12.4 |
| 1936 | Noboru Terada, Japan | 19m.13.7 |
| 1948 | James McLane, United States | 19m.18.5 |
| 1952 | Ford Konno, United States | 18m.30s. |
| 1956 | Murray Rose, Australia | 17m.58.9 |
| 1960 | John Konrads, Australia | 17m.19.6 |

* One mile. † 1,600 meters.

### 4,000 Meters

| | | |
|---|---|---|
| 1900 | John Jarvis, Great Britain | 58m.24s. |

### Relays

| | | |
|---|---|---|
| 1900 | Germany (200 meters, 5 men) | 32 pts. |
| 1904 | United States (200 yards) | 2m.4.6s. |
| 1906 | Hungary (1,000 meters) | 16m.52.4s |

### 800-Meter Relay

| | | |
|---|---|---|
| 1908 | Great Britain | 10m.55.6s |
| 1912 | Australasia | 10m.11.6s |
| 1920 | United States | 10m.4.4s |
| 1924 | United States | 9m.53.4s |
| 1928 | United States | 9m.36.2s |
| 1932 | Japan | 8m.58.4s |
| 1936 | Japan | 8m.51.5s |
| 1948 | United States | 8m.46s. |
| 1952 | United States | 8m.31.1s |
| 1956 | Australia | 8m.23.6s |
| 1960 | United States | 8m.10.2s |

### 100-Meter Backstroke

| | | |
|---|---|---|
| 1900 | Ernst Hoppenberg, Germany | 2m.47s.* |
| 1904 | Walter Brack, Germany | 1m.16.8s |
| 1908 | Arno Bieberstein, Germany | 1m.24.6s |
| 1912 | Harry Hebner, United States | 1m.21.2s |
| 1920 | Warren Kealoha, United States | 1m.15.2s |
| 1924 | Warren Kealoha, United States | 1m.13.2s |
| 1928 | George Kojac, United States | 1m.8.2s |
| 1932 | Masaji Kiyokawa, Japan | 1m.8.6s. |
| 1936 | Adolph Kiefer, United States | 1m.5.9s. |
| 1948 | Allen Stack, United States | 1m.6.4s. |
| 1952 | Yoshinobu Oyakawa, United States | 1m.5.4s. |
| 1956 | David Thiele, Australia | 1m.2.2s. |
| 1960 | David Thiele, Australia | 1m.1.9s. |

* 200 meters. † 100 yards.

## 200-Meter Butterfly

| | | |
|---|---|---|
| 1956 | Bill Yorzyk, United States | 2m.19.3s. |
| 1960 | Mike Troy, United States | 2m.12.8s. |

## 200-Meter Breast Stroke

| | | |
|---|---|---|
| 1908 | Frederick Holman, Great Britain | 3m.9.2s. |
| 1912 | Walter Bathe, Germany | 3m.1.8s. |
| 1920 | Haken Malmroth, Sweden | 3m.4.4s. |
| 1924 | Robert Skelton, United States | 2m.56.6s. |
| 1928 | Yoshiyuki Tsuruta, Japan | 2m.48.8s. |
| 1932 | Yoshiyuki Tsuruta, Japan | 2m.45.4s. |
| 1936 | Tetsuo Hamuro, Japan | 2m.42.5s. |
| 1948 | Joseph Verdeur, United States | 2m.39.3s. |
| 1952 | John Davies, Australia | 2m.34.4s. |
| 1956 | Masura Furukawa, Japan | 2m.34.7s. |
| 1960 | Bill Mulliken, United States | 2m.37.4s. |

## 400-Meter Breast Stroke

| | | |
|---|---|---|
| 1904 | Georg Zacharias, Germany | 7m.23.6s.* |
| 1912 | Walter Bathe, Germany | 6m.29.6s. |
| 1920 | Haken Malmroth, Sweden | 6m.31.8s. |

*\* 440 yards.*

## 400-Meter Medley Relay

| | | |
|---|---|---|
| 1960 | United States | 4m.5.4s. |

## 60-Meter Underwater

| | | |
|---|---|---|
| 1900 | de Vaudeville, France | 1m.53.4s. |

## 200-Meter Obstacle

| | | |
|---|---|---|
| 1900 | Frederick Lane, Australia | 2m.38.4s. |

## Springboard Dive

| | | Points |
|---|---|---|
| 1908 | Albert Zuerner, Germany | 85.5 |
| 1912 | Paul Guenther, Germany | 79.23 |
| 1920 | Louis Kuehn, United States | 10 |
| 1924 | Albert White, United States | 696.4 |
| 1928 | Pete Desjardins, United States | 185.04 |
| 1932 | Michael Galitzen, United States | 161.38 |
| 1936 | Richard Degener, United States | 163.57 |
| 1948 | Bruce Harlan, United States | 163.64 |
| 1952 | David Browning, United States | 205.29 |
| 1956 | Robert Clotworthy, United States | 159.56 |
| 1960 | Gary Tobian, United States | 170.00 |

## High Dive

| | | Points |
|---|---|---|
| 1904 | G. E. Sheldon, United States | 12.75 |
| 1906 | Gottlob Walz, Germany | 156 |
| 1908 | Hjalmar Johansson, Sweden | 83.75 |
| 1912 | Erik Adlerz, Sweden | 73.94 |
| 1920 | Clarence Pinkston, United States | 7 |
| 1924 | Albert White, United States | 487.3 |
| 1928 | Pete Desjardins, United States | 98.74 |
| 1932 | Harold Smith, United States | 124.80 |
| 1936 | Marshall Wayne, United States | 113.58 |
| 1948 | Samuel Lee, United States | 130.05 |
| 1952 | Samuel Lee, United States | 156.28 |
| 1956 | Joaquin Capilla, Mexico | 152.44 |
| 1960 | Bob Webster, United States | 91.28 |

## Plain High Dive

| | | Points |
|---|---|---|
| 1912 | Erik Adlerz, Sweden | 40 |
| 1920 | Arvid Wallman, Sweden | 7 |
| 1924 | Richard Eve, Australia | 160 |

## Plunge for Distance

| | | |
|---|---|---|
| 1904 | W. E. Dickey, United States | 62 ft. 6 in. |

# WATER POLO

| | | | |
|---|---|---|---|
| 1900 | Great Britain | 1932 | Hungary |
| 1904 | United States | 1936 | Hungary |
| 1908 | Great Britain | 1948 | Italy |
| 1912 | Great Britain | 1952 | Hungary |
| 1920 | Great Britain | 1956 | Hungary |
| 1924 | France | 1960 | Italy |
| 1928 | Germany | | |

# SWIMMING—WOMEN
## 100 Meters

| | | |
|---|---|---|
| 1912 | Fanny Durack, Australia | 1m.22.2s. |
| 1920 | Ethelda Bleibtrey, United States | 1m.13.6s. |
| 1924 | Ethel Lackie, United States | 1m.12.4s. |
| 1928 | Albina Osipowich, United States | 1m.11s. |
| 1932 | Helene Madison, United States | 1m.6.8s. |
| 1936 | Hendrika Mastenbroek, Holland | 1m.5.9s. |
| 1948 | Greta Andersen, Denmark | 1m.6.3s. |
| 1952 | Katalin Szoke, Hungary | 1m.6.8s. |
| 1956 | Dawn Fraser, Australia | 1m.2s. |
| 1960 | Dawn Fraser, Australia | 1m.1.2s. |

## 400 Meters

| | | |
|---|---|---|
| 1920 | Ethelda Bleibtrey, United States | 4m.34s.* |
| 1924 | Martha Norelius, United States | 6m.2.2s. |
| 1928 | Martha Norelius, United States | 5m.42.8s. |
| 1932 | Helene Madison, United States | 5m.28.5s. |
| 1936 | Hendrika Mastenbroek, Holland | 5m.26.4s. |
| 1948 | Ann Curtis, United States | 5m.17.8s. |
| 1952 | Valerie Gyenge, Hungary | 5m.12.1s. |
| 1956 | Lorraine Crapp, Australia | 4m.54.6s. |
| 1960 | Chris von Saltza, United States | 4m.50.6s. |

*\* 300 meters.*

## 400-Meter Relay

| | | |
|---|---|---|
| 1912 | Great Britain | 5m.52.8s. |
| 1920 | United States | 5m.11.6s. |
| 1924 | United States | 4m.58.8s. |
| 1928 | United States | 4m.47 6s. |
| 1932 | United States | 4m.38s. |
| 1936 | Holland | 4m.36s. |
| 1948 | United States | 4m.29.2s. |
| 1952 | Hungary | 4m.24.4s. |
| 1956 | Australia | 4m.17.1s. |
| 1960 | United States | 4m.8.9s. |

## 100-Meter Backstroke

| | | |
|---|---|---|
| 1924 | Sybil Bauer, United States | 1m.23.2s. |
| 1928 | Marie Braun, Holland | 1m.22s. |
| 1932 | Eleanor Holm, United States | 1m.19.4s. |
| 1936 | Dina Senff, Holland | 1m.18.9s. |
| 1948 | Karen Harup, Denmark | 1m.14.4s. |
| 1952 | Joan Harrison, South Africa | 1m.14.3s. |
| 1956 | Judy Grinham, Great Britain | 1m.12.9s. |
| 1960 | Lynn Burke, United States | 1m.9.3s. |

## 100-Meter Butterfly

| | | |
|---|---|---|
| 1956 | Shelley Mann, United States | 1m.11s. |
| 1960 | Carolyn Schuler, United States | 1m.9.5s. |

## 200-Meter Breast Stroke

| | | |
|---|---|---|
| 1924 | Lucy Morton, Great Britain | 3m.33.2s. |
| 1928 | Hilde Schrader, Germany | 3m.12.6s. |
| 1932 | Clare Dennis, Australia | 3m.6.3s. |
| 1936 | Hideko Maehata, Japan | 3m.3 6s. |
| 1948 | Nel van Vliet, Holland | 2m.57.2s. |
| 1952 | Eva Szekely, Hungary | 2m.51.7s. |
| 1956 | Ursala Happe, Germany | 2m.53.1s. |
| 1960 | Anita Lonsbrough, Great Britain | 2m.49.5s. |

## 400-Meter Medley Relay

| | | |
|---|---|---|
| 1960 | United States | 4m.41.1s. |

### Springboard Dive

| | | Points |
|---|---|---|
| 1920 | Aileen Riggin, United States | 9 |
| 1924 | Elizabeth Becker, United States | 474.5 |
| 1928 | Helen Meany, United States | 78.62 |
| 1932 | Georgia Coleman, United States | 87.52 |
| 1936 | Marjorie Gestring, United States | 89.27 |
| 1948 | Victoria M. Draves, United States | 108.74 |
| 1952 | Mrs. Patricia McCormick, United States | 147.30 |
| 1956 | Mrs. Patricia McCormick, United States | 142.36 |
| 1960 | Ingrid Kramer, Germany | 155.81 |

### High Dive

| | | Points |
|---|---|---|
| 1912 | Greta Johansson, Sweden | 39.9 |
| 1920 | Stefani Fryland, Denmark | 6 |
| 1924 | Caroline Smith, United States | 166 |
| 1928 | Elizabeth B. Pinkston, United States | 31.60 |
| 1932 | Dorothy Poynton, United States | 40.26 |
| 1936 | Mrs. Dorothy Poynton Hill, United States | 33.93 |
| 1948 | Victoria M. Draves, United States | 68.87 |
| 1952 | Mrs. Patricia McCormick, United States | 79.37 |
| 1956 | Mrs. Patricia McCormick, United States | 84.85 |
| 1960 | Ingrid Kramer, Germany | 91.28 |

## BASKETBALL

| 1904 | United States | 1952 | United States |
|---|---|---|---|
| 1936 | United States | 1956 | United States |
| 1948 | United States | 1960 | United States |

## BOXING

### Flyweight

| 1904 | George V. Finnegan, United States |
|---|---|
| 1920 | Frank De Genaro, United States |
| 1924 | Fidel La Barba, United States |
| 1928 | Anton Kocsis, Hungary |
| 1932 | Stephen Enekes, Hungary |
| 1936 | Willi Kaiser, Germany |
| 1948 | Pascual Perez, Argentina |
| 1952 | Nate Brooks, United States |
| 1956 | Terence Spinks, Great Britain |
| 1960 | Gyula Torok, Hungary |

### Bantamweight

| 1904 | O. L. Kirk, United States |
|---|---|
| 1908 | H. Thomas, Great Britain |
| 1920 | Clarence Walker, South Africa |
| 1924 | William Smith, South Africa |
| 1928 | Vittorio Tamagnini, Italy |
| 1932 | Horace Gwynne, Canada |
| 1936 | Ulderico Sergo, Italy |
| 1948 | Tibor Csik, Hungary |
| 1952 | Pentti Hamalainen, Finland |
| 1956 | Wolfgang Behrendt, Germany |
| 1960 | Oleg Grigoryev, U.S.S.R. |

### Featherweight

| 1904 | O. L. Kirk, United States |
|---|---|
| 1908 | R. K. Gunn, Great Britain |
| 1920 | Paul Fritsch, France |
| 1924 | Jackie Fields, United States |
| 1928 | L. Van Klaveren, Holland |
| 1932 | Carmelo A. Robledo, Argentina |
| 1936 | Oscar Casanovas, Argentina |
| 1948 | Ernesto Formenti, Italy |
| 1952 | Jan Zachara, Czechoslovakia |
| 1956 | Vladimir Safronov, U.S.S.R. |
| 1960 | Francesco Musso, Italy |

### Lightweight

| 1904 | H. J. Spanger, United States |
|---|---|
| 1908 | F. Grace, Great Britain |
| 1920 | Samuel Mosberg, United States |
| 1924 | Harold Nielsen, Denmark |
| 1928 | Carlo Orlandi, Italy |
| 1932 | Lawrence Stevens, South Africa |
| 1936 | Imre Harangi, Hungary |
| 1948 | Gerry Dreyer, South Africa |
| 1952 | Aureliano Bolognesi, Italy |
| 1956 | Richard McTaggart, Great Britain |
| 1960 | Kazimierz Pazdzior, Poland |

### Light Welterweight

| 1952 | Charles Adkins, United States |
|---|---|
| 1956 | Vladimir Enguibarian, U.S.S.R. |
| 1960 | Bonhumil Nemecek, Czechoslovakia |

### Welterweight

| 1904 | Al Young, United States |
|---|---|
| 1920 | T. Schneider, Canada |
| 1924 | Jean Delarge, Belgium |
| 1928 | Edward Morgan, New Zealand |
| 1932 | Edward Flynn, United States |
| 1936 | Sten Suvio, Finland |
| 1948 | Julius Torma, Czechoslovakia |
| 1952 | Zygmunt Chycha, Poland |
| 1956 | Necolae Linca, Rumania |
| 1960 | Giovanni Benvenuti, Italy |

### Light Middleweight

| 1952 | Laszlo Papp, Hungary |
|---|---|
| 1956 | Laszlo Papp, Hungary |
| 1960 | Wilbert McClure, United States |

### Middleweight

| 1904 | Charles Mayer, United States |
|---|---|
| 1908 | John Douglas, Great Britain |
| 1920 | Harry Mallin, Great Britain |
| 1924 | Harry Mallin, Great Britain |
| 1928 | Pietro Toscani, Italy |
| 1932 | Carmen Barth, United States |
| 1936 | Jean Despeaux, France |
| 1948 | Laszlo Papp, Hungary |
| 1952 | Floyd Patterson, United States |
| 1956 | Guenadii Chatkov, U.S.S.R. |
| 1960 | Eddie Crook, United States |

### Light Heavyweight

| 1920 | Edward Eagan, United States |
|---|---|
| 1924 | Harry Mitchell, Great Britain |
| 1928 | Victorio Avendano, Argentina |
| 1932 | David E. Carstens, South Africa |
| 1936 | Roger Michlot, France |
| 1948 | George Hunter, South Africa |
| 1952 | Norvel Lee, United States |
| 1956 | James Boyd, United States |
| 1960 | Cassius Clay, United States |

### Heavyweight

| 1904 | Sam Berger, United States |
|---|---|
| 1908 | A. L. Oldham, Great Britain |
| 1920 | R. Rawson, Great Britain |
| 1924 | Otto von Porat, Norway |
| 1928 | A. Rodriguez Jurado, Argentina |
| 1932 | Santiago A. Lovell, Argentina |
| 1936 | Herbert Runge, Germany |
| 1948 | Rafael Iglesias, Argentina |
| 1952 | Edward Sanders, United States |
| 1956 | Peter Rademacher, United States |
| 1960 | Francesco de Piccoli, Italy |

## FIGURE SKATING
### Men

| | | Points |
|---|---|---|
| 1908 | Ulrich Salchow, Sweden | 377.3 |
| 1920 | Gillis Grafstrom, Sweden | 405.5 |
| 1924 | Gillis Grafstrom, Sweden | 367.89 |
| 1928 | Gillis Grafstrom, Sweden | 385.77 |
| 1932 | Karl Schaefer, Austria | 371.1 |
| 1936 | Karl Schaefer, Austria | 422.7 |
| 1948 | Richard Button, United States | 191.177 |
| 1952 | Richard Button, United States | 192.256 |
| 1956 | Hayes Alan Jenkins, United States | 166.4 |
| 1960 | David Jenkins, United States | 1440.2 |

### Women

| | | |
|---|---|---|
| 1908 | Mrs. Madge Syers, Great Britain | 252.5 |
| 1920 | Magda Mauroy, Sweden | 182.7 |
| 1924 | Mrs. Herma Szabo-Planck, Austria | 299.17 |
| 1928 | Sonja Henie, Norway | 350.3 |
| 1932 | Sonja Henie, Norway | 328.94 |
| 1936 | Sonja Henie, Norway | 424.5 |
| 1948 | Barbara Ann Scott, Canada | 163.077 |
| 1952 | Jeannette Altwegg, Great Britain | 161.756 |
| 1956 | Tenley Albright, United States | 169.6 |
| 1960 | Carol Heiss, United States | 1490.1 |

### Pairs

| | | |
|---|---|---|
| 1908 | Alma Huber-Heinrich Burger, Germany | 11.2 |
| 1920 | Ludovika and Walter Jacobsson, Finland | 11.5 |
| 1924 | Helene Englemann-Alfred Berger, Austria | 10.64 |
| 1928 | Andree Joly-Pierre Brunet, France | 11.2 |
| 1932 | Andree and Pierre Brunet, France | 10.95 |
| 1936 | Maxie Herber-Ernst Baier, Germany | 11.5 |
| 1948 | Micheline Lannoy-Pierre Baughniet, Belgium | 11.227 |
| 1952 | Ria and Paul Falk, Germany | 11.4 |
| 1956 | Elisabeth Schwarz-Kurt Oppelt, Austria | 11.31 |
| 1960 | Barbara Wagner-Robert Paul, Canada | 80.4 |

### Special Figures

| | | |
|---|---|---|
| 1908 | Nikolai Panin, Russia | 43.8 |

## ICE HOCKEY

| | | | |
|---|---|---|---|
| 1920 | Canada | 1948 | Canada |
| 1924 | Canada | 1952 | Canada |
| 1928 | Canada | 1956 | U.S.S.R. |
| 1932 | Canada | 1960 | United States |
| 1936 | Great Britain | | |

## SPEED SKATING
### 500 Meters

| | | |
|---|---|---|
| 1924 | Charles Jewtraw, United States | 44s. |
| 1928 | Clas Thunberg, Finland, and Bernt Evensen, Norway (tie) | 43.4s. |
| 1932 | John Shea, United States | 43.4s. |
| 1936 | Ivar Ballangrud, Norway | 43.4s. |
| 1948 | Finn Helgesen, Norway | 43.1s. |
| 1952 | Ken Henry, United States | 43.2s. |
| 1956 | Evgeny Grishin, U.S.S.R. | 40.2s. |
| 1960 | Evgeny Grishin, U.S.S.R. | 40.2s. |

### 1,500 Meters

| | | |
|---|---|---|
| 1924 | Clas Thunberg, Finland | 2m. 20.8s. |
| 1928 | Clas Thunberg, Finland | 2m. 21.1s. |
| 1932 | John Shea, United States | 2m. 57.5s. |
| 1936 | Charles Mathisen, Norway | 2m. 19.2s. |
| 1948 | Sverre Farstad, Norway | 2m. 17.6s. |
| 1952 | Hjalmar Andersen, Norway | 2m. 20.4s. |
| 1956 | Evgeny Grishin, U.S.S.R., and Yuri Mikhailov, U.S.S.R. (tie) | 2m. 8.6s. |
| 1960 | Roald Edgar Aas, Norway, and Evgeny Grishin, U.S.S.R. (tie) | 2m.10.4s. |

### 5,000 Meters

| | | |
|---|---|---|
| 1924 | Clas Thunberg, Finland | 8m. 39s. |
| 1928 | Ivar Ballangrud, Norway | 8m. 50.5s. |
| 1932 | Irving Jaffee, United States | 9m. 40.8s. |
| 1936 | Ivar Ballangrud, Norway | 8m. 19.6s. |
| 1948 | Reidar Liakley, Norway | 8m. 29.4s. |
| 1952 | Hjalmar Andersen, Norway | 8m. 10.6s. |
| 1956 | Boris Shilkov, U.S.S.R. | 7m. 48.7s. |
| 1960 | Viktor Kosichkin, U.S.S.R. | 7m. 51.3s. |

### 10,000 Meters

| | | |
|---|---|---|
| 1924 | Julien Skutnabb, Finland | 18m. 4.8s. |
| 1928 | No decision, thawing of ice* | |
| 1932 | Irving Jaffee, United States | 19m. 13.6s. |
| 1936 | Ivar Ballangrud, Norway | 17m 24.3s. |
| 1948 | Ake Seyffarth, Sweden | 17m. 26.3s. |
| 1952 | Hjalmar Andersen, Norway | 16m. 45.8s. |
| 1956 | Sigvard Ericsson, Sweden | 16m. 35.9s. |
| 1960 | Knut Johannesen, Norway | 15m. 46.6s. |

* Irving Jaffee, United States, had best time, 18.36.5.

### Combined

| | | |
|---|---|---|
| 1924 | Clas Thunberg, Finland | 5.5 pts. |

## SPEED SKATING—WOMEN
### 500 Meters

| | | |
|---|---|---|
| 1960 | Helga Haase, Germany | 45.9s. |

### 1,000 Meters

| | | |
|---|---|---|
| 1960 | Klara Guseva, U.S.S.R. | 1m.34.1s. |

### 1,500 Meters

| | | |
|---|---|---|
| 1960 | Lidija Skoblikova, U.S.S.R. | 2m.25.2s. |

### 3,000 Meters

| | | |
|---|---|---|
| 1960 | Lidija Skoblikova, U.S.S.R. | 5m.14.3s. |

## 1960 OLYMPICS
## GOLD MEDAL DISTRIBUTION

| | Summer | Winter | Total |
|---|---|---|---|
| U.S.S.R. | 43* | 7† | 50 |
| United States | 34 | 3 | 37 |
| Germany | 12 | 4 | 16 |
| Italy | 13 | 0 | 13 |
| Australia | 8 | 0 | 8 |
| Turkey | 7 | 0 | 7 |
| Hungary | 6 | 0 | 6 |
| Japan | 4* | 0 | 4 |
| Norway | 1 | 3† | 4 |
| Poland | 4 | 0 | 4 |
| Sweden | 1 | 3 | 4 |
| Czechoslovakia | 3 | 0 | 3 |
| Finland | 1* | 2 | 3 |
| Rumania | 3 | 0 | 3 |
| Switzerland | 1 | 2 | 3 |
| Austria | 1 | 1 | 2 |
| Canada | 0 | 2 | 2 |
| Denmark | 2 | 0 | 2 |
| Great Britain | 2 | 0 | 2 |
| New Zealand | 2 | 0 | 2 |
| Bulgaria | 1 | 0 | 1 |
| Ethiopia | 1 | 0 | 1 |
| France | 0 | 1 | 1 |
| Greece | 1 | 0 | 1 |
| Pakistan | 1 | 0 | 1 |
| Yugoslavia | 1 | 0 | 1 |

* Finland and U.S.S.R. tied for first place in side horse (gymnastics); Japan and U.S.S.R. tied for first in long horse (gymnastics).

† Norway and U.S.S.R. tied for first in 1,500 meters (speed skating).

# OTHER 1960 OLYMPIC CHAMPIONS

## CANOEING

### KAYAK

1,000-m. singles—Erik Hansen, Denmark
1,000-m. tandem—Gert Fredricsson-Sven Sjodelius, Sweden
2,000-m. relay—Germany (Dieter Krause, Gunther Perleberg, Paul Lange, Friedhelm Wentzke)
Women's 500-m. singles—Antonina Seredina, U.S.S.R.
Women's 500-m. tandem—Maria Shubina-Antonina Seredina, U.S.S.R.

### CANADIAN

1,000-m. singles—Gianos Parti, Hungary
1,000-m. tandem—Sergey Marerenko-Leonid Geyshter, U.S.S.R.

## CYCLING

1,000-m. sprint—Sante Gaiordoni, Italy
1,000-m. time trial—Sante Gaiordoni, Italy
2,000-m. tandem—Giuseppe Beghetto-Sergio Bianchetto, Italy
4,000-m. team pursuit—Italy
Road race (17.5 kilo.)—Viktor Kapitonov, U.S.S.R.
Team road race (100 kilo.)—Italy

## EQUESTRIAN

3-day event—Lawrence Morgan, Australia
3-day event, team—Australia
Jumping—Raimondo d'Inzeo, Italy
Jumping, team—Germany
Dressage—Sergei Filatov, U.S.S.R.

## FENCING

Foil—Viktor Zdanovich, U.S.S.R. ......... Team—U.S.S.R.
Epee—Giuseppe Delfino, Italy ............ Team—Italy
Saber—Rudolph Karpati, Hungary ....... Team—Hungary
Women's foil—Adelheid Schmid, Germany. Team—U.S.S.R.

## GYMNASTICS

All-around—Boris Shakhlin, U.S.S.R.
Free standing—Nobuyuki Aihara, Japan
Long horse—Takashi Ono, Japan, and Boris Shakhlin, U.S.S.R. (tie)
Side horse—Eugen Ekman, Finland, and Boris Shakhlin, U.S.S.R. (tie)
Parallel bars—Boris Shakhlin, U.S.S.R.
Horizontal bar—Takashi Ono, Japan
Flying rings—Albert Asarian, U.S.S.R.
Team—Japan

### WOMEN

All-around—Larisa Latynina, U.S.S.R.
Free standing—Larisa Latynina, U.S.S.R.
Long horse—Margarita Nikolaeva, U.S.S.R.
Balance beam—Eva Bosakova, Czechoslovakia
Uneven parallel bars—Polina Astakhova, U.S.S.R.
Team—U.S.S.R.

## MODERN PENTATHLON

Individual—Ferenc Nemeth, Hungary
Team—Hungary

## ROWING

Single sculls—Vyacheslav Ivanov, U.S.S.R.
Double sculls—Vaclav Kozak-Pavel Schmidt, Czechoslovakia
Pairs—Valentin Boreiko-Oleg Golovanov, U.S.S.R.
Pairs with coxswain—Bernhard Knubel-Heinz Renneberg and Klaus Zerta, Germany
Fours—United States (Lake Washington R. C., Seattle—Art Ayrault, Ted Nash, Dick Wailes, John Sayre)
Fours with coxswain—Germany
Eights—Germany

## SHOOTING

Free rifle—Hubert Hamerer, Austria
Free pistol—Alexei Gustchin, U.S.S.R.
Trapshooting—Ion Dumitrescu, Rumania
Smallbore rifle, prone—Peter Kohnke, Germany
Smallbore rifle, three-position—Viktor Shanburkin, U.S.S.R.
Rapid-fire pistol—Bill McMillan, United States

## SKIING

Slalom—Ernst Hinterseer, Austria
Giant slalom—Roger Staub, Switzerland
Downhill—Jean Vuarnet, France
Jumping—Helmut Recknagel, Germany
Nordic combined—Georg Thoma, Germany
Biathlon—Klas Lestander, Sweden
15,000-m. cross-country—Hakon Brusveen, Norway
30,000-m. cross-country—Sixten Jernberg, Sweden
50,000-m. cross-country—Kalevi Hamalainen, Finland
40,000-m. cross-country relay—Finland (Alatalo Toimo, Eoro Mantyrants, Vaino Huhtala, Voikka Hakulinen)

### WOMEN

Slalom—Anne Heggtveit, Canada
Giant slalom—Yvonne Ruegg, Switzerland
Downhill—Heidi Bibl, Germany
10,000-m. cross-country—Marija Gusakova, U.S.S.R.
15,000-m. cross-country relay—Sweden (Irma Hohansson, Britt Strandberg, Sonja Ruthstrom)

## WEIGHTLIFTING

Bantamweight—Charles Vinci, United States
Featherweight—Yevgeni Minaev, U.S.S.R.
Lightweight—Viktor Bushuev, U.S.S.R.
Middleweight—Alexander Kurynov, U.S.S.R.
Light heavyweight—Ireneusz Palinski, Poland
Middle heavyweight—Arkadi Vorbiev, U.S.S.R.
Heavyweight—Yuri Vlasov, U.S.S.R.

## WRESTLING

### FREE STYLE

Flyweight—Ahmet Bilek, Turkey
Bantamweight—Terry McCann, United States
Featherweight—Mustafa Dagistanli, Turkey
Lightweight—Shelby Wilson, United States
Welterweight—Doug Blubaugh, United States
Middleweight—Hasan Gungor, Turkey
Light heavyweight—Ismet Atli, Turkey
Heavyweight—Wilfried Dietrich, Germany

### GRECO-ROMAN

Flyweight—Dumitru Pirvulescu, Rumania
Bantamweight—Oleg Karavaev, U.S.S.R.
Featherweight—Muzahir Sille, Turkey
Lightweight—Avtandil Koridze, U.S.S.R.
Welterweight—Mithat Bayrak, Turkey
Middleweight—Dimitrio Dobrev, Bulgaria
Light heavyweight—Teufik Kis, Turkey
Heavyweight—Ivan Bogdan, U.S.S.R.

## YACHTING

5.5 meter—George O'Day, United States
Star—Timir Pinegin, U.S.S.R.
Dragon—Crown Prince Constantine, Greece
Flying Dutchman—Peder Lunde, Norway
Finn monotype—Paul Elvstrom, Denmark

## OTHER TEAM SPORTS

Field hockey—Pakistan
Soccer—Yugoslavia

# 1959 PAN-AMERICAN GAMES CHAMPIONS

### BOXING

112-lb.—Miguel Botta, Argentina
119-lb.—Waldo Claudiano, Brazil
125-lb.—Carlos Aro, Argentina
132-lb.—Abel Laudonio, Argentina
140-lb.—Vincent Shomo, U. S.
147-lb.—Alfredo Cornejo, Chile
156-lb.—Wilbert McClure, U. S.
165-lb.—Abroa de Souza, Brazil
178-lb.—Amos Johnson, U. S.
Heavyweight—Allen Hudson, U. S.

### CYCLING

1,000-m. sprint—Juan Canto, Argentina
1,000-m. time trial—Anezio Argentao, Brazil
Road race—Ricardo Senn, Argentina
Road race, team—Argentina

### EQUESTRIAN

Dressage—Trish Galvin, U. S.
Dressage, team—Chile
3-day event—Michael Page, U. S.
3-day event, team—Canada
Jumping, team—United States

### FENCING

Foil—Harold Goldsmith, U. S.
Foil, team—United States
Epee—Roland Wommack, U. S.
Epee, team—United States
Saber—Allan Kwartler, U. S.
Saber, team—United States
Women—Maria Roldan, Mexico

### GYMNASTICS

All-around—John Beckner, U. S.
All-around, team—United States
Long horse—John Beckner, U. S.
Parallel bars—John Beckner, U. S.
Calisthenics—Abe Grossfeld, U. S.
Horizontal bar—Abe Grossfeld, U. S.
Still Rings—Abe Grossfeld, U. S., Jamile Ashmore, U. S. (tie)
Side horse—Gregor Weiss, U. S.
Tumbling—Harold Holmes, U. S.
Indian clubs—Francisco Alvarez, Mexico
Trampoline—Ron Munn, U. S.
Rope climb—Garvin Smith, U. S.

#### WOMEN

All-around—Ernestine Russell, Canada
All-around, team—United States
Side horse—Ernestine Russell, Canada
Balance beam—Ernestine Russell, Canada
Uneven parallel bars—Ernestine Russell, Canada
Calisthenics—Theresa Montefusco, U. S.

### MODERN PENTATHLON

Individual—Wensceslau Malta, Brazil
Team—United States

### ROWING

Eights—United States
Fours—United States
Fours with coxswain—United States
Pairs—U. S. (Robert Rogers, Ted Frost)
Pairs with coxswain—Uruguay (Gustavo Perez, Luis Aguiar, Raul Torrieri)
Doubles—U. S. (Jack Kelly, Jr., Bill Knecht)
Singles—Harry Parker, U. S.

### SHOOTING

English match—Arthur Cook, U. S.
English match, team—United States
Skeet—Gilberto Navarro, Chile
Skeet, team—United States
Free pistol—Nelson Lincoln, U. S.
Free pistol, team—United States
Center-fire pistol—Aubrey Smith, U. S.
Center-fire pistol, team—United States
Smallbore pistol, rapid fire—David Cartes, U. S.
Smallbore pistol, rapid fire, team—U. S.

### SMALLBORE RIFLE

Overall—Daniel Puckel, U. S.
Overall, team—United States
Prone—Gerald Ouelette, Canada
Prone, team—Canada
Kneeling—James Carter, U. S.
Kneeling, team—United States
Standing—James Carter, U. S.
Standing, team—United States

### FREE RIFLE

Overall—Daniel Puckel, U. S.
Overall, team—United States
Prone—Daniel Puckel, U. S.
Kneeling—Daniel Puckel, U. S.
Standing—Daniel Puckel, U. S.

### FREE RIFLE, RAPID FIRE

Overall—Daniel Puckel, U. S.
Overall, team—United States
Prone—Tommy Pool, U. S.
Kneeling—Daniel Puckel, U. S.

### SWIMMING

100-m. free—Jeff Farrell, U. S.
400-m. free—George Breen, U. S.
1,500-m. free—Alan Somers, U. S.
100-m. back—Frank McKinney, U. S.
200-m. breast—Bill Mullikan, U. S.
200-m. butterfly—Dave Gillanders, U. S.
800-m. freestyle relay—United States
400-m. medley relay—United States
3-m. springboard dive—Gary Tobian, U. S.
Platform dive—Alvaro Gaxiola, U. S.

#### WOMEN

100-m. free—Chris von Saltza, U. S.
200-m. free—Chris von Saltza, U. S.
400-m. free—Chris von Saltza, U. S.
100-m. back—Carin Cone, U. S.
200-m. breast—Ann Warner, U. S.
100-m. butterfly—Becky Collins, U. S.
400-m. freestyle relay—United States
400-m. medley relay—United States
Springboard dive—Paula Myers Pope, U. S.
Platform dive—Paula Myers Pope, U. S.

### TENNIS

Singles—Luis Ayala, Chile
Doubles—Gustavo and Antonio Palafox, Mexico
Women's singles—Althea Gibson, U. S.
Women's doubles—Yola Ramirez-Rosa Maria Reyes, Mexico
Mixed doubles—Yola Ramirez-Gustavo Ramirez, Mexico

### TRACK AND FIELD

100 m.—Ray Norton, U. S.
200 m.—Ray Norton, U. S.
400 m.—George Kerr, West Indies
800 m.—Tom Murphy, U. S.
1,500 m.—Dyrol Burleson, U. S.
5,000 m.—Bill Dellinger, U. S.
10,000 m.—Osvaldo Suarez, Argentina
Marathon—John J. Kelley, U. S.
3,000-m. stplchse.—Phil Coleman, U. S.
110-m. high hurdles—Hayes Jones, U. S.
400-m. hurdles—Josh Culbreath, U. S.
400-m. relay—United States
1,600-m. relay—West Indies
High jump—Charles Dumas, U. S.
Broad jump—Irvin Roberson, U. S.
Hop, step & jump—A. F. da Silva, Brazil
Pole vault—Don Bragg, U. S.
Shot put—Parry O'Brien, U. S.
Discus—Al Oerter, U. S.
Javelin—Buster Quist, U. S.
Hammer—Al Hall, U. S.
Decathlon—Dave Edstrom, U. S.

#### WOMEN

60 m.—Isabelle Daniels, U. S.
100 m.—Lucinda Williams, U. S.
200 m.—Lucinda Williams, U. S.
80-m. hurdles—Bertha Diaz, Cuba
400-m. relay—United States
High jump—Ann Flynn, U. S.
Broad jump—Anna Smith, U. S.
Shot put—Earlene Brown, U. S.
Discus—Earlene Brown, U. S.
Javelin—Marlene Ahrens, Chile

### WEIGHTLIFTING

123-lb.—Chuck Vinci, U. S.
132-lb.—Isaac Berger, U. S.
148-lb.—Juan Torres, Cuba
165-lb.—Tommy Kono, U. S.
181-lb.—Jim George, U. S.
198-lb.—Clyde Emrich, U. S.
Heavyweight—Dave Ashman, U. S.

### WRESTLING

114.5-lb.—Dick Wilson, U. S.
125.5-lb.—Dave Auble, U. S.
136.5-lb.—Lou Giani, U. S.
147.5-lb.—Jim Burke, U. S.
160.5-lb.—Doug Blubaugh, U. S.
174.5-lb.—Jim Ferguson, U. S.
191-lb.—Frank Rosenmayr, U. S.
Heavyweight—Dale Lewis, U. S.

### YACHTING

Dragon—Jorge Salas, Argentina
Finn monotype—Kenneth Albury, Bahamas
5.5-meter—George O'Day, U. S.
Flying Dutchman—Harry Sindle, U. S.
Lightning—E. Schmidt, Brazil
Snipe—Antonio Moraes, Brazil
Star—Durwood Knowles, Bahamas

### OTHER TEAM SPORTS

Baseball—Venezuela
Basketball—United States
Basketball, women—United States
Soccer—Argentina
Volleyball—United States
Volleyball, women—Brazil
Water Polo—United States

# ICE HOCKEY

ICE HOCKEY, by birth and upbringing a Canadian game, is an offshoot of field hockey. Some historians state that the first ice hockey game was played in Montreal in December, 1879, between two teams composed almost exclusively of McGill University students, but others assert that Kingston, Ont., or Halifax, N. S., were scenes of earlier hockey games. In the Montreal game of 1879 there were fifteen players on a side and they used an assortment of crude sticks to keep the puck in motion. Early rules allowed nine men on a side but the number was reduced to seven in 1886 and finally reduced to six, the standard of today.

The first governing body of the sport was the Amateur Hockey Association of Canada, organized in 1887. In the winter of 1894–95 a group of college students from the United States visited Canada, saw hockey played, became enthused over the game and introduced it as a winter sport when they returned home. This was the start of hockey in the United States. The first professional league was the International Hockey League that operated, strangely enough, not in Canada but in northern Michigan in 1904–06 and included as players such famous stars as Cyclone Taylor and Hod Stuart, later included in the Hockey Hall of Fame.

Until 1910, professionals and amateurs were allowed to play together on "mixed teams," but this arrangement ended with the formation of the first "big league," the National Hockey Association, in eastern Canada in 1910. The Pacific Coast League, to provide professional hockey in the West, was organized in 1911 with Seattle (and later other American cities) included in the circuit. The National Hockey League replaced the National Hockey Association in 1917. Boston, in 1924, was the first American city to join that circuit. The Stanley Cup, top trophy of hockey, was competed for by "mixed teams" from 1894 to 1910, thereafter by professionals.

## Professional Statistics
### STANLEY CUP WINNERS
**Emblematic of world professional championship.**

| | | | |
|---|---|---|---|
| 1894—Montreal A. A. A | 1910—Montreal Wanderers | 1927—Ottawa Senators | 1944—Montreal Canadiens |
| 1895—Montreal Victorias | 1911—Ottawa Senators | 1928—N. Y. Rangers | 1945—Toronto Maple Leafs |
| 1896—Winnipeg Victorias | 1912—Quebec Bulldogs | 1929—Boston Bruins | 1946—Montreal Canadiens |
| 1897—Montreal Victorias | 1913—Quebec Bulldogs | 1930—Montreal Canadiens | 1947—Toronto Maple Leafs |
| 1898—Montreal Victorias | 1914—Toronto | 1931—Montreal Canadiens | 1948—Toronto Maple Leafs |
| 1899—Montreal Victorias | 1915—Vancouver Millionaires | 1932—Toronto Maple Leafs | 1949—Toronto Maple Leafs |
| 1900—Montreal Shamrocks | 1916—Montreal Canadiens | 1933—N. Y. Rangers | 1950—Detroit Red Wings |
| 1901—Winnipeg Victorias | 1917—Seattle Metropolitans | 1934—Chicago Black Hawks | 1951—Toronto Maple Leafs |
| 1902—Montreal A. A. A. | 1918—Toronto Arenas | 1935—Montreal Maroons | 1952—Detroit Red Wings |
| 1903—Ottawa Silver Seven | 1919—Series unfinished† | 1936—Detroit Red Wings | 1953—Montreal Canadiens |
| 1904—Ottawa Silver Seven | 1920—Ottawa Senators | 1937—Detroit Red Wings | 1954—Detroit Red Wings |
| 1905—Ottawa Silver Seven | 1921—Ottawa Senators | 1938—Chicago Black Hawks | 1955—Detroit Red Wings |
| 1906—Montreal Wanderers | 1922—Toronto St. Patricks | 1939—Boston Bruins | 1956—Montreal Canadiens |
| 1907—Kenora Thistles | 1923—Ottawa Senators | 1940—N. Y. Rangers | 1957—Montreal Canadiens |
| 1907—Mont. Wanderers* | 1924—Montreal Canadiens | 1941—Boston Bruins | 1958—Montreal Canadiens |
| 1908—Montreal Wanderers | 1925—Victoria Cougars | 1942—Toronto Maple Leafs | 1959—Montreal Canadiens |
| 1909—Ottawa Senators | 1926—Montreal Maroons | 1943—Detroit Red Wings | 1960—Montreal Canadiens |

* March.

† The Montreal Canadiens and Seattle, P.C.H.L. champions, had played five games at Seattle, Wash., when an Influenza epidemic (which took the life of Joe Hall of the Canadiens) caused the Department of Health to stop the series. Each team won two games, with one contest ending in a tie.

### MOST VALUABLE PLAYER
#### The Hart Trophy
**Awarded annually to the player voted most valuable to his team in the regular N. H. L. season.**

| | | | |
|---|---|---|---|
| 1924 | Frank Nighbor, Ottawa | 1943 | Bill Cowley, Boston |
| 1925 | Billy Burch, Hamilton | 1944 | Babe Pratt, Toronto |
| 1926 | Nels Stewart, Montreal Maroons | 1945 | Elmer Lach, Montreal Canadiens |
| 1927 | Herb Gardiner, Montreal Canadiens | 1946 | Max Bentley, Chicago |
| 1928 | Howie Morenz, Montreal Canadiens | 1947 | Maurice Richard, Montreal Canadiens |
| 1929 | Roy Worters, New York Americans | 1948 | Buddy O'Connor, New York Rangers |
| 1930 | Nels Stewart, Montreal Maroons | 1949 | Sid Abel, Detroit |
| 1931–32 | Howie Morenz, Montreal Canadiens | 1950 | Chuck Rayner, New York Rangers |
| 1933 | Eddie Shore, Boston | 1951 | Milt Schmidt, Boston |
| 1934 | Aurel Joliat, Montreal Canadiens | 1952-53 | Gordon Howe, Detroit |
| 1935–36 | Eddie Shore, Boston | 1954 | Al Rollins, Chicago |
| 1937 | Babe Siebert, Montreal Canadiens | 1955 | Ted Kennedy, Toronto |
| 1938 | Eddie Shore, Boston | 1956 | Jean Beliveau, Montreal Canadiens |
| 1939 | Toe Blake, Montreal Canadiens | 1957-58 | Gordon Howe, Detroit |
| 1940 | Ebbie Goodfellow, Detroit | 1959 | Andy Bathgate, New York Rangers |
| 1941 | Bill Cowley, Boston | 1960 | Gordon Howe, Detroit |
| 1942 | Tom Anderson, New York Americans | | |

# BASKETBALL

BASKETBALL may be unique in sports. It is one game concerning which it is safe to state when, where and how it originated. In the winter of 1891–92, Dr. James Naismith, an instructor in the Y.M.C.A. Training College (now Springfield College) at Springfield, Mass., deliberately invented the game of basketball in order to provide indoor exercise and competition for the students between the closing of the football season and the opening of the baseball season. He affixed peach baskets overhead on the walls at opposite ends of the gymnasium and, with an association (soccer) football, organized teams to play his new game in which the purpose was to toss the ball into one basket and prevent, as far as possible, the opponents from tossing the ball into the other basket. Fundamentally, the game is the same today, though there have been improvements in equipment and changes in rules.

Because Dr. Naismith had eighteen available players when he invented the game, the first rule was: "There shall be nine players on each side." Later the number of players became optional, depending upon the size of the available court, but the five-player standard was adopted when the game spread over the country. United States soldiers introduced the game in Europe in World War I and, being taken up by foreign nations, it soon became a world-wide sport.

## National Collegiate A. A. Champions

| | |
|---|---|
| 1939—Oregon | 1950—C.C.N.Y. |
| 1940—Indiana | 1951—Kentucky |
| 1941—Wisconsin | 1952—Kansas |
| 1942—Stanford | 1953—Indiana |
| 1943—Wyoming | 1954—La Salle |
| 1944—Utah | 1955—San Francisco |
| 1945—Oklahoma A & M | 1956—San Francisco |
| 1946—Oklahoma A & M | 1957—North Carolina |
| 1947—Holy Cross | 1958—Kentucky |
| 1948—Kentucky | 1959—California |
| 1949—Kentucky | 1960—Ohio State |

## National Invitation Champions (NIT)
### (Madison Square Garden Tourney)

| | |
|---|---|
| 1938—Temple | 1950—C.C.N.Y. |
| 1939—Long Island U. | 1951—Brigham Young |
| 1940—Colorado | 1952—La Salle (Phila.) |
| 1941—Long Island U. | 1953—Seton Hall |
| 1942—West Virginia | 1954—Holy Cross |
| 1943—St. John's (Bklyn.) | 1955—Duquesne |
| 1944—St. John's (Bklyn.) | 1956—Louisville |
| 1945—DePaul | 1957—Bradley |
| 1946—Kentucky | 1958—Xavier (Cincinnati) |
| 1947—Utah | 1959—St. John's (Bklyn.) |
| 1948—St. Louis | 1960—Bradley |
| 1949—San Francisco | |

## National A. A. U. Champions

| | |
|---|---|
| 1897—23d St. Y.M.C.A., New York | 1935—So. Kansas Stage Lines, Kansas City |
| 1909–1900—Knickerbocker A. C., New York | 1936—Globe Refiners, McPherson, Kan. |
| 1901—Ravenswood Y.M.C.A., Chicago | 1937—Denver (Colo.) Safeways |
| 1904—Buffalo (N. Y.) Y.M.C.A. | 1938—Healey Motors, Kansas City |
| 1910—Portage, Wis. National Guard | 1939—Denver (Colo.) Nuggets |
| 1913–14—Cornell (Armour Playground), Chicago | 1940—Phillips Oilers, Bartlesville, Okla. |
| 1915—San Francisco Olympic Club | 1941—20th Century-Fox, Hollywood, Calif. |
| 1916—University of Utah | 1942—American Legion, Denver, Colo. |
| 1917—Illinois A. C. | 1943–48—Phillips Oilers, Bartlesville, Okla. |
| 1919—Los Angeles A. C. | 1949—Oakland (Calif.) Bittners |
| 1920—New York University | 1950—Phillips Oilers, Bartlesville, Okla. |
| 1921—Kansas City A. C. | 1951—Stewart Chevrolets, San Francisco |
| 1922—Lowe and Campbell, Kansas City | 1952–54—Peoria (Ill.) Cats |
| 1923—Kansas City A. C. | |
| 1924—Butler University | 1955—Phillips Oilers, Bartlesville, Okla. |
| 1925—Washburn College | 1956—Buchan Bakers, Seattle |
| 1926–27—Hillyards, St. Joseph, Mo. | 1957—U. S. Air Force |
| 1928–29—Cook Paint Co., Kansas City | 1958—Peoria (Ill.) Cats |
| 1930–32—Henry Clothiers, Wichita, Kan. | 1959—Wichita (Kan.) Vickers |
| 1933–34—Diamond DX Oilers, Tulsa, Okla. | 1960—Peoria (Ill.) Cats |

## Professional Champions

The National Basketball Association (N.B.A.) was created in 1949 by a merger of the National Basketball League and the Basketball Association of America. Champions follow:

### National League

| | |
|---|---|
| 1938—Goodyears | 1944—Fort Wayne |
| 1939—Firestones | 1945—Fort Wayne |
| 1940—Firestones | 1946—Rochester |
| 1941—Oshkosh | 1947—Chicago |
| 1942—Oshkosh | 1948—Minneapolis |
| 1943—Fort Wayne | 1949—Anderson |

### Association of America

| | |
|---|---|
| 1947—Philadelphia | 1949—Minneapolis |
| 1948—Baltimore | |

### National Association (NBA)

| | |
|---|---|
| 1950—Minneapolis | 1956—Philadelphia |
| 1951—Rochester | 1957—Boston |
| 1952—Minneapolis | 1958—St. Louis |
| 1953—Minneapolis | 1959—Boston |
| 1954—Minneapolis | 1960—Boston |
| 1955—Syracuse | |

# ATHLETES OF THE YEAR

The Associated Press annually polls outstanding sportswriters and broadcasters throughout the nation to select the outstanding male and female athletes of the year.

## MALE

| Year | Athlete | Sport |
|------|---------|-------|
| 1931 | Pepper Martin | Baseball |
| 1932 | Gene Sarazen | Golf |
| 1933 | Carl Hubbell | Baseball |
| 1934 | Dizzy Dean | Baseball |
| 1935 | Joe Louis | Boxing |
| 1936 | Jesse Owens | Track and field |
| 1937–38 | Don Budge | Tennis |
| 1939 | Nile Kinnick | Football |
| 1940 | Tommy Harmon | Football |
| 1941 | Joe DiMaggio | Baseball |
| 1942 | Frank Sinkwich | Football |
| 1943 | Gunder Hagg | Track and field |
| 1944–45 | Byron Nelson | Golf |
| 1946 | Glenn Davis | Football |
| 1947 | Johnny Lujack | Football |
| 1948 | Lou Boudreau | Baseball |
| 1949 | Leon Hart | Football |
| 1950 | Jim Konstanty | Baseball |
| 1951 | Dick Kazmaier | Football |
| 1952 | Bob Mathias | Track and field |
| 1953 | Ben Hogan | Golf |
| 1954 | Willie Mays | Baseball |
| 1955 | Howard (Hopalong) Cassady | Football |
| 1956 | Mickey Mantle | Baseball |
| 1957 | Ted Williams | Baseball |
| 1958 | Herb Elliott | Track and field |
| 1959 | Ingemar Johansson | Boxing |
| 1960 | Rafer Johnson | Track and field |

## FEMALE

| Year | Athlete | Sport |
|------|---------|-------|
| 1931 | Helene Madison | Swimming |
| 1932 | Mildred (Babe) Didrikson | Track and field |
| 1933 | Helen Jacobs | Tennis |
| 1934 | Virginia Van Wie | Golf |
| 1935 | Helen Wills Moody | Tennis |
| 1936 | Helen Stephens | Track and field |
| 1937 | Katherine Rawls | Swimming |
| 1938 | Patty Berg | Golf |
| 1939–40 | Alice Marble | Tennis |
| 1941 | Betty Hicks Newell | Golf |
| 1942 | Gloria Callen | Swimming |
| 1943 | Patty Berg | Golf |
| 1944 | Ann Curtis | Swimming |
| 1945–47 | Mildred (Babe) Didrikson Zaharias | Golf |
| 1948 | Fanny Blankers-Koen | Track and field |
| 1949 | Marlene Bauer | Golf |
| 1950 | Mildred (Babe) Didrikson Zaharias | Golf |
| 1951–53 | Maureen Connolly | Tennis |
| 1954 | Mildred (Babe) Didrikson Zaharias | Golf |
| 1955 | Patty Berg | Golf |
| 1956 | Patricia McCormick | Diving |
| 1957–58 | Althea Gibson | Tennis |
| 1959 | Maria Bueno | Tennis |
| 1960 | Wilma Rudolph | Track and field |

## SULLIVAN AWARD WINNERS

The James E. Sullivan Memorial Award is given annually to the amateur athlete voted by sports leaders as having done the most to advance sportsmanship.

| Year | Athlete | Sport |
|------|---------|-------|
| 1930 | Robert T. Jones, Jr. | Golf |
| 1931 | Bernard E. Berlinger | Track and field |
| 1932 | James A. Bausch | Track and field |
| 1933 | Glenn Cunningham | Track and field |
| 1934 | William R. Bonthron | Track and field |
| 1935 | W. Lawson Little, Jr. | Golf |
| 1936 | Glenn Morris | Track and field |
| 1937 | J. Donald Budge | Tennis |
| 1938 | Donald R. Lash | Track and field |
| 1939 | Joseph W. Burk | Rowing |
| 1940 | J. Gregory Rice | Track and field |
| 1941 | Leslie MacMitchell | Track and field |
| 1942 | Cornelius Warmerdam | Track and field |
| 1943 | Gilbert L. Dodds | Track and field |
| 1944 | Ann Curtis | Swimming |
| 1945 | Felix (Doc) Blanchard | Football |
| 1946 | Y. Arnold Tucker | Football |
| 1947 | John B. Kelly, Jr. | Rowing |
| 1948 | Robert B. Mathias | Track and field |
| 1949 | Richard T. Button | Figure skating |
| 1950 | Fred Wilt | Track and field |
| 1951 | Robert E. Richards | Track and field |
| 1952 | Horace Ashenfelter | Track and field |
| 1953 | Major Sammy Lee | Diving |
| 1954 | Malvin Whitfield | Track and field |
| 1955 | Harrison Dillard | Track and field |
| 1956 | Patricia McCormick | Diving |
| 1957 | Bobby Morrow | Track and field |
| 1958 | Glenn Davis | Track and field |
| 1959 | Parry O'Brien | Track and field |
| 1960 | Rafer Johnson | Track and field |

## HICKOK AWARD WINNERS

The richest award in sports is the $10,000 S. Rae Hickok Belt, which annually goes to the professional athlete of the year, as selected in a poll of sportswriters and sportscasters throughout the country.

| | | |
|------|---------|-------|
| 1950 | Phil Rizzuto | Baseball |
| 1951 | Allie Reynolds | Baseball |
| 1952 | Rocky Marciano | Boxing |
| 1953 | Ben Hogan | Golf |
| 1954 | Willie Mays | Baseball |
| 1955 | Otto Graham | Football |
| 1956 | Mickey Mantle | Baseball |
| 1957 | Carmen Basilio | Boxing |
| 1958 | Bob Turley | Baseball |
| 1959 | Ingemar Johansson | Boxing |
| 1960 | Arnold Palmer | Golf |

## TOP ATHLETES OF A HALF-CENTURY

In 1950 The Associated Press polled the nation's sports experts on the "greats" in various fields during the past half-century. The list of winners:

Male athlete—Jim Thorpe.
Female athlete—Mildred D. Zaharias.
Baseball player—Babe Ruth.
Football player—Jim Thorpe.
Fighter—Jack Dempsey.
Basketball player—George Mikan.
Track performer—Jesse Owens.
Golfer—Bobby Jones.
Tennis player—Bill Tilden.
Swimmer—Johnny Weissmuller.
Race horse—Man o' War.

# ROWING

ROWING goes back so far in history that there is no possibility of tracing it to any particular aboriginal source. The oldest rowing race still on the calendar is the "Doggett's Coat and Badge" contest among professional watermen of the Thames (England) that began in 1715. The first Oxford-Cambridge race was held at Henley in 1829. Competitive rowing in the United States began with matches between boats rowed by professional oarsmen of the New York water front. They were oarsmen who rowed the small boats that plied as ferries from Manhattan Island to Brooklyn and return, or who rowed salesmen down the harbor to meet ships arriving from Europe. Since the first salesman to meet an incoming ship had some advantage over his rivals, there was keen competition in the bidding for fast boats and the best oarsmen. This gave rise to match races for a purse or a side bet on many occasions. The first of such races was held in June, 1811, in four-oared gigs.

Amateur boat clubs sprang up in the United States between 1820 and 1830 and seven students of Yale joined together to purchase a four-oared lap-streak gig in 1843. The first Harvard-Yale race was held Aug. 3, 1852, on Lake Winnepesaukee, N. H. The first time an American college crew went abroad was in 1869 when Harvard challenged Oxford and was defeated on the Thames. There were early college rowing races on Lake Quinsigamond, near Worcester, Mass., and on Saratoga Lake, N. Y., but the Intercollegiate Rowing Association, in 1895, settled on the Hudson, at Poughkeepsie, as the setting for the annual "Poughkeepsie Regatta." In 1950 the I.R.A. shifted its classic to Marietta, Ohio, and in 1952 it was moved to Syracuse, N. Y. The National Association of Amateur Oarsmen, organized in 1872, has conducted annual championship regattas since that time. The first rowing races were held with lapstreak gigs but shells came into general favor about a century ago. The outrigger was invented in 1830 by Clasper, an Englishman. Yale used the sliding seat in 1870.

## Rowing Statistics

*Source:* From *American Rowing*, Copyright by Robert F. Kelley; courtesy of G. P. Putnam's Sons.

### Yale-Harvard Varsity Race Record

**Rowed at Centre Harbor, N. H., in 1852; Springfield, Mass., in 1855, 1872–73, 1876–77; Worcester, Mass., 1859 to 1870; Saratoga Lake, N. Y., 1874–75; New London, Conn., 1878 to 1895, 1898 to 1916, 1919 to 1941, and since 1947; triangular race at Poughkeepsie, N. Y., in 1897 with Cornell victor in 20:34; Derby, Conn., in 1918, 1942, and Boston, Mass., in 1946. Course was 2 miles in 1852; 3 miles from 1855 to 1875, and 4 miles thereafter.**

| Year | Winner | Time | Year | Winner | Time | Year | Winner | Time |
|---|---|---|---|---|---|---|---|---|
| 1852 | Harvard | [1] | 1893 | Yale | 25:01½ | 1927 | Harvard | 22:35⅕ |
| 1855 | Harvard | 22:00 | 1894 | Yale | 23:45½ | 1928 | Yale | 20:21⅗ |
| 1859 | Harvard | 19:18 | 1895 | Yale | 21:30 | 1929 | Yale | 21:20 |
| 1860 | Harvard | 18:53 | 1897 | Yale | 20:44 | 1930 | Yale | 20:09⅖ |
| 1864 | Yale | 19:01 | 1898 | Yale | 24:02 | 1931 | Harvard | 22:21 |
| 1865 | Yale | 18:42½ | 1899 | Harvard | 20:52½ | 1932 | Harvard | 21:29 |
| 1866 | Harvard | 18:43¼ | 1900 | Yale | 21:12⅘ | 1933 | Harvard | 22:46⅗ |
| 1867 | Harvard | 18:12¾ | 1901 | Yale | 23:37 | 1934 | Yale | 19:51⅘ |
| 1868 | Harvard | 17:48½ | 1902 | Yale | 20:20 | 1935 | Yale | 20:19 |
| 1869 | Harvard | 18:02 | 1903 | Yale | 20:19⅘ | 1936 | Harvard | 20:19 |
| 1870 | Harvard | 20:30[2] | 1904 | Yale | 21:40½ | 1937 | Harvard | 20:02 |
| 1872 | Harvard | 16:57 | 1905 | Yale | 22:33½ | 1938 | Harvard | 20:20 |
| 1873 | Yale | 16:59 | 1906 | Harvard | 23:02 | 1939 | Harvard | 20:48⅖ |
| 1874[3] | Harvard | 16:56 | 1907 | Yale | 21:10 | 1940 | Harvard | 21:38 |
| 1875 | Harvard | 17:05 | 1908[4] | Harvard | 24:10 | 1941 | Harvard | 20:40 |
| 1876 | Yale | 22:02 | 1909 | Harvard | 21:50 | 1942[7] | Harvard | 10:09⅗ |
| 1877 | Harvard | 24:36 | 1910 | Harvard | 20:46½ | 1946[8] | Harvard | 9:18 |
| 1878 | Harvard | 20:44¾ | 1911 | Harvard | 22:44 | 1947 | Harvard | 20:40 |
| 1879 | Harvard | 22:15 | 1912 | Harvard | 21:43½ | 1948 | Harvard | 19:21⅖ |
| 1880 | Yale | 24:27 | 1913 | Harvard | 21:42 | 1949 | Yale | 19:52⅘ |
| 1881 | Yale | 22:13 | 1914 | Yale | 21:16 | 1950 | Harvard | 21:36⅖ |
| 1882 | Harvard | 20:47½ | 1915 | Yale | 20:52 | 1951 | Harvard | 21:26 |
| 1883 | Harvard | 25:46½ | 1916 | Harvard | 20:02 | 1952 | Yale | 22:49 |
| 1884 | Yale | 20:31 | 1918[5] | Harvard | 10:58 | 1953 | Harvard | 20:09 |
| 1885 | Harvard | 25:15½ | 1919[6] | Yale | 21:42⅕ | 1954 | Yale | 21:58⅖ |
| 1886 | Yale | 20:42 | 1920 | Harvard | 23:11 | 1955 | Yale | 20:05 |
| 1887 | Yale | 22:56 | 1921 | Yale | 20:41 | 1956 | Yale | 19:26 |
| 1888 | Yale | 20:10 | 1922 | Yale | 21:53 | 1957 | Yale | 20:35 |
| 1889 | Yale | 21:30 | 1923 | Yale | 22:10 | 1958 | Yale | 22:39 |
| 1890 | Yale | 21:29 | 1924 | Yale | 21:58⅗ | 1959 | Harvard | 19:52 |
| 1891 | Harvard | 21:23 | 1925 | Yale | 20:26 | 1960 | Harvard | 19:41 |
| 1892 | Yale | 20:48 | 1926 | Yale | 20:14⅖ | | | |

[1] Harvard won by 3 to 4 lengths. [2] Yale ran into Harvard at turn and was disqualified. [3] Yale did not finish, being disabled in collision. [4] Yale stroke taken from shell near 3-mile mark. [5] Race was informal; rowed at 2 miles on Housatonic. [6] Course was 110 feet less than 4 miles. [7] Rowed at 2 miles. [8] Rowed at 1¾ miles.

# INTERCOLLEGIATE ROWING ASSOCIATION REGATTA
## (Varsity eight-oared shells)

Rowed at 4 miles, Poughkeepsie, N. Y., 1895-97, 1899-1916, 1925-32, 1934-41. Rowed at 3 miles, Saratoga, N. Y., 1898; Poughkeepsie, 1921-24, 1947-49; Syracuse, N. Y., since 1952. Rowed at 2 miles, Ithaca, N. Y., 1920; Marietta, Ohio, 1950-51. Racing suspended 1917-19, 1933, 1942-46.

| Year | Time | First | Second | Third | Fourth | Fifth | Sixth |
|------|------|-------|--------|-------|--------|-------|-------|
| 1895 | 21:25 | Columbia | Cornell | Pennsylvania | | | |
| 1896 | 19:59 | Cornell | Harvard | Pennsylvania | Columbia | | |
| 1897 | 20:47 4/5 | Cornell | Columbia | Pennsylvania | | | |
| 1898 | 15:51 1/2 | Pennsylvania | Cornell | Wisconsin | Columbia | | |
| 1899 | 20:04 | Pennsylvania | Wisconsin | Cornell | Columbia | | |
| 1900 | 19:44 3/5 | Pennsylvania | Wisconsin | Cornell | Columbia | Georgetown | |
| 1901 | 18:53 1/5 | Cornell | Columbia | Wisconsin | Georgetown | Syracuse | Pennsylvania |
| 1902 | 19:05 3 5 | Cornell | Wisconsin | Columbia | Pennsylvania | Syracuse | Georgetown |
| 1903 | 18:57 | Cornell | Georgetown | Wisconsin | Pennsylvania | Syracuse | Columbia |
| 1904 | 20:22 3/5 | Syracuse | Cornell | Pennsylvania | Columbia | Georgetown | Wisconsin |
| 1905 | 20:29 | Cornell | Syracuse | Georgetown | Columbia | Pennsylvania | Wisconsin |
| 1906 | 19:36 4/5 | Cornell | Pennsylvania | Syracuse | Wisconsin | Columbia | Georgetown |
| 1907 | 20:02 2 5 | Cornell | Columbia | Navy | Pennsylvania | Wisconsin | Georgetown |
| 1908 | 19:24 1/5 | Syracuse | Columbia | Cornell | Pennsylvania | Wisconsin | |
| 1909 | 19:02 | Cornell | Columbia | Syracuse | Wisconsin | Pennsylvania | |
| 1910 | 20:42 1/5 | Cornell | Pennsylvania | Columbia | Syracuse | Wisconsin | |
| 1911 | 20:10 4/5 | Cornell | Columbia | Pennsylvania | Wisconsin | Syracuse | |
| 1912 | 19:31 2/5 | Cornell | Wisconsin | Columbia | Syracuse | Pennsylvania | Stanford |
| 1913 | 19:28 3/5 | Syracuse | Cornell | Washington | Wisconsin | Columbia | Pennsylvania |
| 1914 | 19:37 4/5 | Columbia | Pennsylvania | Cornell | Syracuse | Washington | Wisconsin |
| 1915 | 19:36 3/5 | Cornell | Stanford | Syracuse | Columbia | Pennsylvania | |
| 1916 | 20:15 2/5 | Syracuse | Cornell | Columbia | Pennsylvania | | |
| 1920 | 11:02 3 5 | Syracuse | Cornell | Columbia | Pennsylvania | | |
| 1921 | 14:07 | Navy | California | Cornell | Pennsylvania | Syracuse | Columbia |
| 1922* | 13:33 3/5 | Navy | Washington | Syracuse | Cornell | Columbia | Pennsylvania |
| 1923 | 14:03 1 5 | Washington | Navy | Columbia | Syracuse | Cornell | Pennsylvania |
| 1924 | 15:02 | Washington | Wisconsin | Cornell | Pennsylvania | Syracuse | Columbia |
| 1925 | 19:24 4/5 | Navy | Washington | Wisconsin | Pennsylvania | Cornell | Syracuse |
| 1926 | 19:28 3/5 | Washington | Navy | Syracuse | Pennsylvania | Columbia | California |
| 1927 | 20:57 | Columbia | Washington | California | Navy | Cornell | Syracuse |
| 1928 | 18:35 4/5 | California | Columbia | Washington | Cornell | Navy | Syracuse |
| 1929 | 22:58 | Columbia | Washington | Pennsylvania | Navy | Wisconsin | |
| 1930 | 21:42 | Cornell | Syracuse | M.I.T. | California | Columbia | Washington |
| 1931 | 18:54 1/5 | Navy | Cornell | Washington | California | Syracuse | Pennsylvania |
| 1932 | 19:55 | California | Cornell | Washington | Navy | Syracuse | Columbia |
| 1934 | 19:44 | California | Washington | Navy | Cornell | Pennsylvania | Syracuse |
| 1935 | 18:52 | California | Cornell | Washington | Navy | Syracuse | Pennsylvania |
| 1936 | 19:09 3 5 | Washington | California | Navy | Columbia | Cornell | Pennsylvania |
| 1937 | 18:33 3/5 | Washington | Navy | Cornell | Syracuse | California | Columbia |
| 1938 | 18:19 | Navy | California | Washington | Columbia | Wisconsin | Cornell |
| 1939† | 18:12 3/5 | California | Washington | Navy | Cornell | Syracuse | Wisconsin |
| 1940 | 22:42 | Washington | Cornell | Syracuse | Navy | California | Columbia |
| 1941 | 18:53 3/10 | Washington | California | Cornell | Syracuse | Princeton | Wisconsin |
| 1947 | 13:59 1/5 | Navy | Cornell | Washington | California | Princeton | Syracuse |
| 1948 | 14:06 2/5 | Washington | California | Navy | Cornell | M.I.T. | Princeton |
| 1949 | 14:42 3/5 | California | Washington | Cornell | Navy | Princeton | Pennsylvania |
| 1950 | 8:07.5 | Washington | California | Wisconsin | Stanford | M.I.T. | Columbia |
| 1951 | 7:50.5 | Wisconsin | Washington | Princeton | California | Pennsylvania | M.I.T. |
| 1952 | 15:08.1 | Navy | Princeton | Cornell | Wisconsin | California | Columbia |
| 1953 | 15:29.6 | Navy | Cornell | Washington | Wisconsin | Columbia | California |
| 1954 | 16:04.4 | ‡Navy | Cornell | Washington | Wisconsin | California | Columbia |
| 1955 | 15:49.9 | Cornell | Pennsylvania | Navy | Washington | Stanford | California |
| 1956 | 16:22.4 | Cornell | Navy | Wisconsin | Washington | Stanford | Pennsylvania |
| 1957 | 15:26.6 | Cornell | Penn | Stanford | Princeton | Syracuse | Navy |
| 1958 | 17:12.1 | Cornell | Navy | Syracuse | Princeton | California | Pennsylvania |
| 1959 | 18:01.7 | Wisconsin | Syracuse | Navy | California | Washington | Cornell |
| 1960 | 15:57 | California | Navy | Washington | Brown | Tie: Cornell and Pennsylvania | |

\* Record for three miles. † Record for four miles. ‡ Disqualified.

SEVENTH—1925, Columbia; 1926, Wisconsin; 1927, Pennsylvania; 1928, Pennsylvania; 1930, Pennsylvania; 1931, Columbia; 1932, Pennsylvania; 1934, Columbia; 1935, Columbia; 1936, Syracuse; 1937, Wisconsin; 1938, Syracuse; 1939, Columbia; 1940, Wisconsin; 1941, Rutgers; 1947, Wisconsin; 1948, Pennsylvania; 1949, Wisconsin; 1950, Cornell; 1951, Stanford; 1952, Washington; 1953, Pennsylvania; 1954, Pennsylvania; 1955, Boston U.; 1956, Princeton; 1957, Dartmouth; 1958, Dartmouth; 1959, Dartmouth; 1960, Dartmouth and Rutgers (tie).

EIGHTH—1926, Cornell; 1930, Wisconsin; 1931, Wisconsin; 1932, M.I.T.; 1940, Princeton; 1941, M.I.T.; 1947, M.I.T.; 1948, Wisconsin; 1949, Columbia; 1950, Pennsylvania; 1951, Cornell; 1952, Stanford; 1953, Princeton; 1954, Boston U.; 1955, Princeton; 1956, Syracuse; 1957, M.I.T.; 1958, Wisconsin; 1959, Pennsylvania; 1960, Dartmouth and Rutgers (tie).

NINTH—1931, M.I.T.; 1941, Columbia; 1947, Pennsylvania; 1948, Syracuse; 1949, Syracuse; 1950, Princeton; 1951, Syracuse; 1952, Pennsylvania; 1953, Syracuse; 1954, Princeton; 1955, Wisconsin; 1956, M.I.T.; 1957, Wisconsin; 1958, M.I.T.; 1959, Princeton; 1960, Syracuse.

# BOWLING

THE GAME OF bowling that is the favorite sport of millions of "keglers" in the United States is an indoor development of the more ancient outdoor game that survives as lawn bowling. The outdoor game is prehistoric in origin and probably goes back to Primitive Man and round stones that were rolled at some target. It is believed that a game something like nine-pins was popular among the Dutch, Swiss and Germans as long ago as A.D. 1200 at which time the game was played outdoors with an alley consisting of a single plank 12 to 18 inches wide along which was rolled a ball toward three rows of three pins each placed at the far end of the alley. When the first indoor alleys were built and how the game was modified from time to time are matters of dispute. Much of the confusion arises from a lack of certainty as to which game is meant, "bowls" or "bowling," one with a "jack" and the other with "pins," in historical passages.

It is supposed that the early settlers of New Amsterdam (New York City) being Dutch, they brought their two bowling games with them. About a century ago the game of nine-pins was flourishing in the United States but so corrupted by gambling on matches that it was barred by law in New York and Connecticut. Since the law specifically barred "nine-pins," it was eventually evaded by adding another pin and thus legally making it a new game. The genius who thought up that simple method of outwitting the law and putting a popular game in motion once more remained modestly anonymous. With the increase in the number of pins, the old diamond formation of nine-pins was abandoned for the triangle set-up of ten-pins that remains the rule to this day. Various organizations were formed to make rules for bowling and supervise competition in the United States but none was successful until the American Bowling Congress, organized Sept. 9, 1895, became the ruling body.

## American Bowling Congress Tournament Records

*Source:* Ed Marcou, American Bowling Congress.

| Type of record | Holder and home city | Score | Year |
|---|---|---|---|
| High team total | Pfeiffer Beer, Detroit | 3243 | 1959 |
| High team game | Falstaff Beer, San Antonio, Texas | 1226 | 1958 |
| High doubles total | Steve Nagy–John Klares, Cleveland | 1453 | 1952 |
| High doubles game | John Gworek–Henry Kmidowski, Buffalo | 544 | 1946 |
| High singles total | Lee Jouglard, Detroit | 775 | 1951 |
| High all events total | Ed Lubanski, Detroit | 2116 | 1959 |
| High 3 games in any event | Lee Jouglard, Detroit | 775 | 1951 |

## AMERICAN BOWLING CONGRESS CHAMPIONS

### SINGLES

| Year | | Score | Year | | Score |
|---|---|---|---|---|---|
| 1901 | Frank Brill, Chicago | 648 | 1930 | Larry Shotwell, Covington, Ky. | 774 |
| 1902 | Fred Strong, Chicago | 649 | 1931 | Walter Lachowski, Erie, Pa. | 712 |
| 1903 | Dan A. Jones, Milwaukee | 683 | 1932 | Otto Nitschke, Cleveland | 731 |
| 1904 | Martin Kern, St. Louis | 647 | 1933 | Earl Hewitt, Erie, Pa. | 724 |
| 1905 | C. M. Anderson, St. Paul, Minn. | 651 | 1934 | Jerry Vidro, Grand Rapids, Mich. | 721 |
| 1906 | Frank J. Favour, Oshkosh, Wis. | 669 | 1935 | Don Brokaw, Canton, Ohio | 733 |
| 1907 | M. T. Levey, Indianapolis | *624 | 1936 | Charles Warren, Springfield, Ill. | 735 |
| 1908 | Archie Wengler, Chicago | 699 | 1937 | Gene Gagliardi, Mt. Vernon, N. Y. | 749 |
| 1909 | Larry Sutton, Rochester, N. Y. | *691 | 1938 | Knute Anderson, Moline, Ill. | 746 |
| 1910 | Thomas Haley, Detroit | 705 | 1939 | Jim Danek, Forest Park, Ill. | 730 |
| 1911 | James Blouin, Chicago | 681 | 1940 | Ray Brown, Terre Haute, Ind. | 742 |
| 1912 | Larry Sutton, Rochester, N. Y. | 679 | 1941 | Fred Ruff, Belleville, Ill. | 745 |
| 1913 | F. Peterson, Columbus, Ohio | 693 | 1942 | John Stanley, Cleveland | 756 |
| 1914 | William Miller, Detroit | 675 | 1946 | Lee Rollick, Los Angeles | 737 |
| 1915 | Wallace Pierce, Pueblo, Colo. | 711 | 1947 | Junie McMahon, Chicago | 740 |
| 1916 | Sam Schliman, Toronto | *685 | 1948 | Lincoln Protich, Akron, Ohio | 721 |
| 1917 | Otto Kallusch, Rochester, N. Y. | 698 | 1949 | Bernard Rusche, St. Bernard, Ohio | 716 |
| 1918 | C. Styles, Detroit | 702 | 1950 | Everett Leins, Aurora, Ill. | 757 |
| 1919 | Harry Cavan, Pittsburgh | 718 | 1951 | Lee Jouglard, Detroit | 775 |
| 1920 | Joe Shaw, Chicago | 713 | 1952 | Al Sharkey, Chicago | 758 |
| 1921 | F. Smith, Detroit | 702 | 1953 | Frank Santore, Long Island City, N. Y. | 749 |
| 1922 | Walter Lundgren, Chicago | 729 | 1954 | Tony Sparando, Rego Park, N. Y. | 723 |
| 1923 | Carl Baumgartner, Cincinnati | 724 | 1955 | Eddie Gerzine, Milwaukee | 733 |
| 1924 | Harry E. Snyders, Pittsburgh | 740 | 1956 | George Wade, Steubenville, Ohio | 744 |
| 1925 | Al Green, Chicago | 706 | 1957 | Bob Allen, Yonkers, N. Y. | 729 |
| 1926 | Ed Votal, Braddock, Pa. | 731 | 1958 | Ed Shay, Chester, Pa. | 733 |
| 1927 | William Eggers, Chicago | 706 | 1959 | Ed Lubanski, Detroit | 764 |
| 1928 | Henry Summers, St. Louis | 705 | 1960 | Paul Kulbaga, Cleveland | 726 |
| 1929 | Adolphe Unke, Milwaukee | 728 | * Won roll-off. | | |

## American Bowling Congress Champions (cont.)
### ALL-EVENTS

| Year | | Score | | | Year |
|------|-------------------------------|------|---|-------------------------------|------|
| 1901 | Frank Brill, Chicago | 1736 | 1929 | Otto Stein, Jr., St. Louis | 1974 |
| 1902 | John Koster, New York | 1841 | 1930 | George Morrison, Chicago | 1985 |
| 1903 | Fred Strong, Chicago | 1896 | 1931 | Michael Mauser, Youngstown, Ohio | 1966 |
| 1904 | Martin Kern, St. Louis | 1804 | 1932 | Hugh Stewart, Cincinnati | 1980 |
| 1905 | Jack G. Reilly, Chicago | 1791 | 1933 | Gilbert Zunker, Milwaukee | 2060 |
| 1906 | J. T. Peacock, Indianapolis | 1794 | 1934 | Walt Reppenhagen, Detroit | 1972 |
| 1907 | H. C. Ellis, Grand Rapids, Mich. | 1775 | 1935 | Ora Mayer, San Francisco | 2022 |
| 1908 | Russell Crable, E. Liverpool, Ohio | 1924 | 1936 | John Murphy, Indianapolis | 2006 |
| 1909 | James Blouin, Chicago | 1885 | 1937 | Max Stein, Belleville, Ill. | 2070 |
| 1910 | Thomas Haley, Detroit | 1961 | 1938 | Don Beatty, Jackson, Mich. | 1978 |
| 1911 | Jimmy Smith, Buffalo, N. Y. | 1919 | 1939 | Joe Wilman, Chicago | 2028 |
| 1912 | Phil Sutton, Louisville, Ky. | 1843 | 1940 | Fred Fisher, Buffalo, N. Y. | 2001 |
| 1913 | Ed Hermann, Cleveland | 1972 | 1941 | Harold Kelly, South Bend, Ind. | 2013 |
| 1914 | William Miller, Detroit | 1897 | 1942 | Stan Moskal, Saginaw, Mich. | 1973 |
| 1915 | Matty E. Faetz, Chicago | 1876 | 1946 | Joe Wilman, Chicago | 2054 |
| 1916 | Frank Thoma, Chicago | 1919 | 1947 | Junie McMahon, Chicago | 1965 |
| 1917 | H. Miller, Detroit | 1945 | 1948 | Ned Day, West Allis, Wis. | 1979 |
| 1918 | Harry Steers, Chicago | 1959 | 1949 | John Small, Chicago | 1941 |
| 1919 | Mort Lindsey, New Haven, Conn. | 1933 | 1950 | Frank Santore, Long Island City, N. Y. | 1981 |
| 1920 | Jimmy Smith, Milwaukee | 1915 | 1951 | Tony Lindeman, Detroit | 2005 |
| 1921 | Art Schieman, Rochester, N. Y. | 1909 | 1952 | Steve Nagy, Cleveland | 2065 |
| 1922 | Barney Spinella, Brooklyn, N. Y. | 1999 | 1953 | Frank Santore, Long Island City, N. Y. | 1994 |
| 1923 | William J. Knox, Philadelphia | 2019 | 1954 | Brad Lewis, Ashland, Ohio | 1985 |
| 1924 | A. F. Weber, Elizabeth, N. J. | 1975 | 1955 | Fred Bujack, Detroit | 1993 |
| 1925 | Clarence Long, Buffalo, N. Y. | 1977 | 1956 | Bill Lillard, Chicago | 2018 |
| 1926 | Harry Gerloski, Detroit | 1981 | 1957 | Jim Spalding, Louisville, Ky. | 2088 |
| 1927 | Barney Spinella, Brooklyn, N. Y. | 2014 | 1958 | Al Faragalli, Paterson, N. J. | 20 3 |
| 1928 | Phil Wolff, Chicago | 1937 | 1959 | Ed Lubanski, Detroit | 2116 |
|      |                                |      | 1960 | Vince Lucci, Trenton, N. J. | 1985 |

## NATIONAL MATCH GAME CHAMPIONS
**Tournaments Conducted by Bowling Proprietors Association of America**
*Source:* George Burton, Public Relations Director, BPAA
### SINGLES

| | | | |
|---------|----------------------------|---------|----------------------------|
| 1941–42 | John Crimmins, Detroit | 1951–52 | Junie McMahon, Fair Lawn, N. J. |
| 1942–43 | Connie Schwoegler, Madison, Wis. | 1952–53 | Don Carter, St. Louis |
| 1943–44 | Ned Day, Milwaukee | 1953–54 | Don Carter, St. Louis |
| 1944–45 | Buddy Bomar, Chicago | 1954–55 | Steve Nagy, Cleveland |
| 1945–46 | Joe Wilman, Chicago | 1955–56 | Bill Lillard, Chicago |
| 1946–47 | Andy Varipapa, Hempstead, N. Y. | 1956–57 | Don Carter, St. Louis |
| 1947–48 | Andy Varipapa, Hempstead, N. Y. | 1957–58 | Don Carter  St. Louis |
| 1948–49 | Connie Schwoegler, Madison, Wis. | 1958–59 | Billy Welu, St. Louis |
| 1949–50 | Junie McMahon, Fair Lawn, N. J. | 1959–60 | Harry Smith, St. Louis |
| 1950–51 | Dick Hoover, Akron, Ohio | | |

## WOMEN'S INTERNATIONAL BOWLING CONGRESS CHAMPIONS
*Source:* Eleanor Debus, Director of Public Relations, WIBC
### SINGLES

| Year | | Score | Year | | Score |
|------|-------------------------------|------|------|-------------------------------|------|
| 1918 | Mrs. F. Steib, Detroit | 537 | 1938 | Mrs. Rose Warner, Waukegan, Ill. | 622 |
| 1919 | Mrs. R. Littlefield, Newark, N. J. | 594 | 1939 | Helen Hengstler, Detroit | 626 |
| 1920 | Mrs. T. Humphreys, St. Louis | 559 | 1940 | Mrs. Sally Twyford, Aurora, Ill. | 626 |
| 1921 | Mrs. Emma Jaeger, Toledo, Ohio | 579 | 1941 | Nancy Huff, Los Angeles | 662 |
| 1922 | Mrs. Emma Jaeger, Toledo, Ohio | 603 | 1942 | Tillie Taylor, Newark, N. J. | 659 |
| 1923 | Mrs. Emma Jaeger, Toledo, Ohio | 594 | 1946 | Val Mikiel, Detroit | 682 |
| 1924 | Alice Keeny, Indianapolis | 593 | 1947 | Agnes Junker, Indianapolis | 650 |
| 1925 | Mrs. E. Reich, Chicago | 622 | 1948 | Shirlee Wernecke, Chicago | 696 |
| 1926 | Mrs. L. Weismann, Indianapolis | 579 | 1949 | Mrs. Clara Mataya, St. Louis | 658 |
| 1927 | Mrs. F. Ehrhart, Akron, Ohio | 577 | 1950 | Cleo Stallkamp, Newport, Ky. | 669 |
| 1928 | Anita Rump, Ft. Wayne, Ind. | 622 | 1951 | Ida Simpson, Buffalo, N. Y. | 639 |
| 1929 | Mrs. Agnes Higgins, Chicago | 637 | 1952 | Lorene Craig, Kansas City, Mo. | 672 |
| 1930 | Anita Rump, Ft. Wayne, Ind. | 613 | 1953 | Marge Baginski, Berwyn, Ill. | 637 |
| 1931 | Mrs. Myrtle Schulte, St. Louis | 650 | 1954 | Helen Martin, Peoria, Ill. | 668 |
| 1932 | Audrey McVay, Kansas City, Mo. | 668 | 1955 | Nellie Vella, Rockford, Ill. | 695 |
| 1933 | Mrs. Sally Twyford, Aurora, Ill. | 628 | 1956 | Lucille Noe, Columbus, Ohio | 708 |
| 1934 | Marie Clemensen, Chicago | 712 | 1957 | Eleanor Towles, Peoria, Ill. | 664 |
| 1935 | Marie Warmbier, Chicago | 652 | 1958 | Ruth Hertel, Lexington, Tenn. | 622 |
| 1936 | Mrs. Ella Burmeister, Madison, Wis. | 612 | 1959 | Mrs. Mae Ploegman Bolt, Chicago | 664 |
| 1937 | Mrs. Anna Gottstine, Buffalo, N. Y. | 647 | 1960 | Marge McDaniels, Mt. View, Calif. | 649 |

## Women's International Bowling Congress Champions (cont.)

### ALL-EVENTS

| Year | | Score | Year | | Score |
|------|--|-------|------|--|-------|
| 1918 | Mrs. Emma Jaeger, Toledo, Ohio | 1552 | 1938 | Dorothy Burmeister, Chicago | 1843 |
| 1919 | Mrs. B. Husk, Newark, N. J. | 1580 | 1939 | Ruth Troy, Dayton, Ohio | 1724 |
| 1920 | Mrs. M. Leibrich, Chicago | 1606 | 1940 | Mrs. Tess Morris, Chicago | 1777 |
| 1921 | Mrs. Emma Jaeger, Toledo, Ohio | 1557 | 1941 | Mrs. Sally Twyford, Aurora, Ill. | 1799 |
| 1922 | Mrs. R. Abraham, Milwaukee | 1659 | 1942 | Nina Van Camp, Chicago | 1888 |
| 1923 | Deane Zapf, Toledo, Ohio | 1582 | 1946 | Catherine Fellmeth, Chicago | 1835 |
| 1924 | Mrs. Rose Steger, Chicago | 1647 | 1947 | Marge Dardeen, Cincinnati | 1826 |
| 1925 | Mrs. Grayce Garwood, Cleveland | 1703 | 1948 | Virgie Hupfer, Burlington, Iowa | 1850 |
| 1926 | Mrs. E. Lackey, Ft. Wayne, Ind. | 1641 | 1949 | Cecelia Winandy, Chicago | 1840 |
| 1927 | Mrs. Grayce Garwood, Cleveland | 1644 | 1950 | Marion Ladewig, Grand Rapids, Mich. | 1796 |
| 1928 | Mrs. Emma Jaeger, Toledo, Ohio | 1713 | 1951 | LaVerne Haverley, Los Angeles | 1788 |
| 1929 | Mrs. Emma Jaeger, Toledo, Ohio | 1700 | 1952 | Virginia Turner, Gardena, Calif. | 1854 |
| 1930 | Mrs. Selva Twyford, Chicago | 1727 | 1953 | Doris Knechtges, Detroit | 1886 |
| 1931 | Mrs. Myrtle Schulte, St. Louis | 1742 | 1954 | Anne Johnson, Hazleton, Pa. | 1880 |
| 1932 | Marie Warmbier, Chicago | 1807 | 1955 | Marion Ladewig, Grand Rapids, Mich. | 1890 |
| 1933 | Mrs. Sally Twyford, Aurora, Ill. | 1765 | 1956 | Doris Knechtges, Detroit | 1867 |
| 1934 | Mrs. Esther Ryan, Milwaukee | 1763 | 1957 | Anita Cantaline, Detroit | 1859 |
| 1935 | Marie Warmbier, Chicago | 1911 | 1958 | Mae Ploegman, Chicago | 1828 |
| 1936 | Mrs. Ella Burmeister, Madison, Wis. | 1683 | 1959 | Pat McBride, Grand Rapids, Mich. | 1927 |
| 1937 | Mrs. Louise Stockdale, Detroit | 1761 | 1960 | Judy Roberts, Angola, N. Y. | 1836 |

# DUCK PINS

*Source:* A. L. Ebersole, Executive Secretary, National Duck Pin Bowling Congress.

## WORLD RECORDS

### MEN

| Type of Record | Holder and home city | Score | Year |
|----------------|---------------------|-------|------|
| Game, singles | Ted Pitera, Fall River, Mass. | 240 | 1960 |
| 3-game set, singles | Arthur Lemke, Lowell, Mass. | 542 | 1943 |
| Game, doubles | Truman Cowart–Billy Allen, Atlanta, Ga. | 360 | 1954 |
| 3-game set, doubles | Mike Avon–Paul Jarmon, Washington, D. C. | 929 | 1952 |
| Game, team | Winchester–Packard, Washington, D. C. | 797 | 1948 |
| 3-game set, team | National Premium Beer, Baltimore | 2135 | 1955 |

### WOMEN

| Type of Record | Holder and home city | Score | Year |
|----------------|---------------------|-------|------|
| Game, singles | Vivian Walsh, Washington, D. C. | 232 | 1954 |
| 3-game set, singles | Dorothy Hull, Danbury, Conn. | 506 | 1961 |
| Game, doubles | Hazel Wells–Ruby Hovanic, Bridgeport, Conn. | 338 | 1949 |
| 3-game set, doubles | Nancy Moissonnier–Dinna Moissonnier, Danbury, Conn. | 837 | 1961 |
| Game, team | Fulford's Colony Radio–TV, Washington, D. C. | 749 | 1959 |
| 3-game set, team | Star Laundry, Norwalk, Conn. | 1965 | 1951 |

## National Duck Pin Bowling Congress Tournament Champions

### SINGLES

| Year | | Score | Year | | Score |
|------|--|-------|------|--|-------|
| 1928 | Albert Fischer, Washington, D. C. | 403 | 1946 | Charles Kebart, New Haven, Conn. | 471 |
| 1929 | Howard Campbell, Washington, D. C., and Jack Whalen, Washington D. C. | 430 | 1947 | Winny Guerke, Baltimore | 445 |
| 1930 | Jack Otto, Torrington, Conn. | 432 | 1948 | Mike Dziadik, Derby, Conn. | 466 |
| 1931 | Jack Whalen, Washington, D. C. | 435 | 1949 | John Catino, Stamford, Conn. | 480 |
| 1932 | William Arnold, Annapolis, Md. | 428 | 1950 | Hal Tucker, Baltimore | 487 |
| 1933 | Howard Furlong, Hartford, Conn. | 440 | 1951 | Steve Witowski, Cromwell, Conn., and Tom Stirling, New Haven, Conn. | 457 |
| 1934 | Nick Tronsky, Willimantic, Conn. | 453 | 1952 | Frank Hanley, Shelton, Conn. | 452 |
| 1935 | John Bianchi, New Haven, Conn. | 458 | 1953 | Al Rush, Baltimore | 457 |
| 1936 | Carl Frisk, New Britain, Conn. | 445 | 1954 | Vince Della, Baltimore | 443 |
| 1937 | William E. Powell, Roanoke, Va. | 439 | 1955 | Walter Surowiecki, Meriden, Conn., and James Parker, Attleboro, Mass. | 445 |
| 1938 | Astor Clarke, Washington, D. C., and Bob Liberto, Baltimore | 448 | 1956 | Al Burrell, Atlanta, Ga. | 430 |
| 1939 | Nick Tronsky, Willimantic, Conn. | 447 | 1957 | Pat Crescenzi, Washington, D. C. | 441 |
| 1940 | Eddie Johnson, New Haven, Conn. | 482 | 1958 | Francis Toolin, Fall River, Mass. | 456 |
| 1941 | Julian Easterday, Annapolis, Md. | 459 | 1959 | Hilmar Sperschneider, Baltimore | 473 |
| 1942 | Bill Krauss, Roslyn, Va. | 456 | 1960 | Tony Dela Rocco, Hamden, Conn. | 485 |
| 1943–45 | No tournaments. | | | | |

(See Index for 1961 Champions)

# POLO

POLO originated "somewhere east of Suez" but exactly where never has been determined. There is pictorial proof that it was played many centuries ago in Persia, Japan, China and Tibet, but it reached England by way of a border tribe in India known as the Manipuri. British army officers in India, about 1860, found the Manipuri playing polo and learned the game from them. The fact that the Manipuri used small native horses—they had no others—was the reason for the early height limit (14 hands) on polo mounts, from which arose the custom of calling them "polo ponies," which was abandoned in 1919.

In 1869 some officers of the 10th Hussars, returning from India, introduced the game in England and informal games were played with as many as eight players on a side. Formal competition at Hurlingham, the great shrine of the game, began in 1876 with five players on a side, which

number was cut to four in 1882. In 1884 an outstanding English player by the name of John Watson invented the backhand stroke and much improved the tactics of the game.

James Gordon Bennett, Jr., noted American newspaper owner and editor, saw polo at Hurlingham in 1875, brought the implements to this country, had a carload of cow ponies sent up from Texas and promoted a game that was played indoors at the Dickel Riding Academy at Fifth Avenue and 39th Street, New York City, in 1876. Polo moved outdoors to the Jerome Park race course and other suitable places soon after. One field on which it was played, at Fifth Avenue and 110th Street, was taken over by the New York baseball team in the National League and that is why the field on which the "Giants" played ball, although there had been two changes in site, still is called "the Polo Grounds."

## INTERNATIONAL MATCHES

### Great Britain vs. United States

| Year | Winner | Site |
|---|---|---|
| 1886 | Great Britain | Newport, R. I. |
| 1902 | Great Britain | Hurlingham |
| 1909 | United States | Hurlingham |
| 1911 | United States | Meadow Brook |
| 1913 | United States | Meadow Brook |
| 1914 | Great Britain | Meadow Brook |
| 1921 | United States | Hurlingham |
| 1924 | United States | Meadow Brook |
| 1927 | United States | Meadow Brook |

| Year | Winner | Site |
|---|---|---|
| 1930 | United States | Meadow Brook |
| 1936 | United States | Hurlingham |
| 1939 | United States | Meadow Brook |

### Argentina vs. United States

| Year | Winner | Site |
|---|---|---|
| 1928 | United States | Meadow Brook |
| 1932 | United States | Buenos Aires |
| 1936 | Argentina | Meadow Brook |
| 1950 | Argentina | Buenos Aires |

## NATIONAL OPEN CHAMPIONS

Not held from 1905 to 1909, inclusive; 1911, 1915, 1917, 1918, and from 1942 to 1945, inclusive.

#### 1904—WANDERERS
1—C. R. Snowden
2—J. E. Cowdin
3—J. M. Waterbury, Jr.
Back—L. Waterbury

#### 1910—RANELAGH
1—R. N Grenfell
2—F. Grenfell
3—Earl of Rocksavage
Back—F. A. Gill

#### 1912—COOPERSTOWN
1—F. S. von Stade
2—C. C Rumsey
3—C. P. Beadleston
Back—M. Stevenson

#### 1913—COOPERSTOWN
1—F. S. von Stade
2—C. C. Rumsey
3—C. P. Beadleston
Back—M. Stevenson

#### 1914—MEADOW BROOK
1—N. L. Tilney
2—J. W. Webb
3—W. G. Loew
Back—H. Phipps

#### 1916—MEADOW BROOK
1—H. Phipps
2—C. C. Rumsey
3—W. G. Loew
Back—D. Milburn

#### 1919—MEADOW BROOK
1—F. H. Prince, Jr.
2—J. W. Webb
3—F. S. von Stade
Back—D. Milburn

#### 1920—MEADOW BROOK
1—F. S. von Stade
2—J. W. Webb
3—R. E. Strawbridge, Jr.
Back—D. Milburn

#### 1921—GREAT NECK
1—L. E. Stoddard
2—R. Wanamaker, II
3—J. W. Webb
Back—R. E. Strawbridge, Jr.

#### 1922—ARGENTINE
1—J. B. Miles
2—J. D. Nelson
3—D. B. Miles
Back—L. L. Lacey

#### 1923—MEADOW BROOK
1—R. Belmont
2—T. Hitchcock, Jr.
3—R. E. Strawbridge, Jr.
Back—D. Milburn

#### 1924—MIDWICK
1—E. G. Miller
2—E. L. Pedley
3—A. P. Perkins
Back—C. F. Burke

#### 1925—ORANGE COUNTY
1—W. A. Harriman
2—J. W. Webb
3—M. Stevenson
Back—J. C. Cowdin

#### 1926—HURRICANES
1—S. Sanford
2—E. L. Pedley
3—Capt. C. T. I. Roark
Back—R. E. Strawbridge, Jr.

#### 1927—SANDS POINT
1—W. A. Harriman
2—T. Hitchcock, Jr.
3—J. C. Cowdin
Back—L. E. Stoddard

#### 1928—MEADOW BROOK
1—C. V. Whitney
2—W. F. C. Guest
3—J. B. Miles
Back—M. Stevenson

#### 1929—HURRICANES
1—S. Sanford
2—Capt. C. T. I. Roark
3—J. W. Webb
Back—R. E. Strawbridge, Jr.

#### 1930—HURRICANES
1—S. Sanford
2—E. L. Pedley
3—Capt. C. T. I. Roark
Back—R. E. Strawbridge, Jr.

#### 1931—SANTA PAULA
1—A. Gazzotti
2—José Reynal
3—Juan Reynal
Back—M. Andrada

#### 1932—TEMPLETON
1—M. G. Phipps
2—W. F. C. Guest
3—S. B. Iglehart
Back—R. R. Guest

## National Open Polo Champions (Cont.)

**1933—AURORA**
1—S. H. Knox
2—J. P. Mills
3—E. T. Gerry
Back—E. J. Boeseke, Jr.

**1934—TEMPLETON**
1—M. G. Phipps
2—W. F. C. Guest
3—S. B. Iglehart
Back—R. R. Guest

**1935—GREENTREE**
1—G. H. Bostwick
2—T. Hitchcock, Jr.
3—G. Balding
Back—J. H. Whitney

**1936—GREENTREE**
1—G. H. Bostwick
2—G. Balding
3—T. Hitchcock, Jr.
Back—J. H. Whitney

**1937—OLD WESTBURY**
1—M. G. Phipps
2—Cecil Smith
3—S. B. Iglehart
Back—C. V. Whitney

**1938—OLD WESTBURY**
1—M. G. Phipps
2—Cecil Smith
3—S. B. Iglehart
Back—C V. Whitney

**1939—BOSTWICK FIELD**
1—G. H. Bostwick
2—R. L. Gerry, Jr.
3—E. T. Gerry
Back—E. H. Tyrrell-Martin

**1940—AKNUSTI**
1—G. S. Smith
2—R. L. Gerry, Jr.
3—E. T. Gerry
Back—A. L. Corey, Jr.

**1941—GULF STREAM**
1—J. H. A. Phipps
2—M. G. Phipps
3—C. S. von Stade
Back—A. L. Corey, Jr.

**1946—HERRADURA**
1—Gabriel Gracida
2—Guillermo Gracida
3—Alejandro Gracida
Back—José Gracida

**1947—OLD WESTBURY**
1—P. Silvero
2—C. C. Combs
3—S. B. Iglehart
Back—G. Oliver

**1948—HURRICANES**
1—L. Sheerin
2—P. Perkins
3—Cecil Smith
Back—S. Sanford

**1949—HURRICANES**
1—L. Sheerin
2—R Cavanaugh
3—Cecil Smith
Back—S. Sanford

**1950—BOSTWICK FIELD**
1—G. H. Bostwick
2—George Oliver
3—A. L. Corey, Jr.
Back—D. Milburn, Jr.

**1951—MILWAUKEE**
1—Pedro Silvero
2—Peter Perkins
3—George Oliver
Back—Bob Uihlein

**1952—BEVERLY HILLS**
1—Bob Fletcher
2—Tony Veen
3—Robert Skene
Back—Carlton Beal

**1953—MEADOW BROOK**
1—Henry Lewis, III
2—Philip Iglehart
3—A. L. Corey, Jr.
Back—G. H. Bostwick

**1954—M. BROOK CCC**
1—A. D. Beveridge
2—Paul Barry
3—A. L. Corey, Jr.
Back—G. H. Bostwick

**1955—DETROIT CCC**
1—A. D. Beveridge
2—William Linfoot
3—Paul Barry
Back—Harold Barry

**1956—BRANDYWINE**
1—Raworth Williams
2—Ray Harrington
3—Clarence Combs
Back—William Mayer

**1957—DETROIT CCC**
1—A. D. Beveridge
2—Robert Beveridge
3—George Oliver
Back—Harold Barry

**1958—DALLAS A. C.**
1—Rayworth Williams
2—William Linfoot
3—Robert Skene
Back—Luis Ramos

**1959—CIRCLE F, DALLAS**
1—Delmar Carroll
2—Ray Harrington
3—William Mayer
Back—Russell Firestone

**1960—OAK BROOK CCC**
1—A. D. Beveridge
2—Wayne Brown
3—Cecil Smith
Back—Harold Barry

---

## CHESS
*Source: American Chess Bulletin of New York.*

### World Champions

| | |
|---|---|
| 1851–58 | Adolph Anderssen, Germany |
| 1858–62 | Paul Morphy, New Orleans, La. |
| 1862–66 | Adolph Anderssen, Germany |
| 1866–94 | William Steinitz, Austria |
| 1894–1921 | Emanuel Lasker, Germany |
| 1921–27 | Jose R. Capablanca, Cuba |
| 1927–35 | Alexander A. Alekhine, U.S.S.R. |
| 1935–37 | Dr. Max Euwe, Netherlands |
| 1937–46 | Alexander A. Alekhine, U.S.S.R.* |
| 1948–57 | Mikhail Botvinnik, U.S.S.R. |
| 1957–58 | Vassily Smyslov, U.S.S.R. |
| 1958–60 | Mikhail Botvinnik, U.S.S.R. |
| 1960–61 | Mikhail Tal, U.S.S.R. |

\* Alekhine, a French citizen, died while champion.

### United States Champions

| | |
|---|---|
| 1852–62 | Paul Morphy, New Orleans, La. |
| 1871–87 | George H. Mackenzie, New York |
| 1887–92 | Max Judd, St. Louis, Mo. |
| 1892–94 | Simon Lipschuetz, New York |
| 1894 | Jackson W. Showalter, Georgetown, Ky. |
| 1894 | Albert B. Hodges, Staten Island, N. Y.* |
| 1894–97 | Jackson W. Showalter, Georgetown, Ky. |
| 1897–1906 | Harry Nelson Pillsbury, Boston, Mass. |
| 1906–09 | Jackson W. Showalter, Georgetown, Ky. |
| 1909–36 | Frank J. Marshall, New York |
| 1936–44 | Samuel Reshevsky, New York† |
| 1944–46 | Arnold S. Denker, New York |
| 1946 | Samuel Reshevsky, Boston |
| 1948 | Herman Steiner, Los Angeles |
| 1951 | Larry Evans, New York |
| 1954–57 | Arthur Bisguier, New York |
| 1958–60 | Bobby Fischer, Brooklyn, N. Y. |

\* Retired after winning return match with Showalter.
† In 1942, Isaac I. Kashdan of New York was co-champion for a while because of a tie with Reshevsky in that year's tournament. Reshevsky won the play-off.

---

## RODEO
*Source: Gene Lamb, Editor, Rodeo Sports News, Denver, Colo.*

### Rodeo Cowboys' Association, All-Around Cowboy

1947—Todd Whatley, Hugo, Okla.
1948—Gerald Roberts, Strong City, Kan.
1949—Jim Shoulders, Henryetta, Okla.
1950—Bill Linderman, Walla Walla, Wash.
1951—Casey Tibbs, Ft. Pierre, S. D.
1952—Harry Tompkins, Dublin, Tex.
1953—Bill Linderman, Walla Walla, Wash.

1954—Buck Rutherford, Lenapah, Okla.
1955—Casey Tibbs, Ft. Pierre, S. D.
1956—Jim Shoulders, Henryetta, Okla.
1957—Jim Shoulders Henryetta, Okla.
1958—Jim Shoulders, Henryetta, Okla.
1959—Jim Shoulders, Henryetta, Okla.
1960—Harry Tompkins, Dublin, Tex.

# SQUASH RACQUETS
## National Champions

| | | | | | | |
|---|---|---|---|---|---|---|
| 1907–08 | John A. Miskey | 1936–38 | Germain G. Glidden | 1930 | Hazel Hotchkiss Wightman |
| 1909 | W. L. Freeland | 1939 | Donald Strachan | 1931 | Ruth Hall Banks |
| 1910 | John A. Miskey | 1940 | A. Willing Patterson | 1932 | Mrs. William F. Howe, Jr. |
| 1911 | F. S. White | 1941–42 | Charles W. Brinton | 1933 | Susan Noel |
| 1912 | Constantine Hutchins | 1943–45 | No tournaments | 1934 | Mrs. William F. Howe, Jr. |
| 1913 | Mortimer L. Newhall | 1946–47 | Charles W. Brinton | 1935 | Margot Lumb |
| 1914 | Constantine Hutchins | 1948 | Stanley W. Pearson, Jr. | 1936–37 | Anne Page |
| 1915–17 | Stanley W. Pearson | 1949 | Hunter H. Lott, Jr. | 1938 | Cecile Bowes |
| 1918–19 | No tournaments | 1950–51 | Edward Hahn | 1939 | Anne Page |
| 1920 | Charles C. Peabody | 1952 | Harry Conlon | 1940–41 | Cecile Bowes |
| 1921–23 | Stanley W. Pearson | 1953 | Ernie Howard | 1942–46 | No competition |
| 1924 | Gerald Robarts | 1954 | G. Diehl Mateer, Jr. | 1947 | Anne Page Homer |
| 1925–26 | W. Palmer Dixon | 1955 | Henri Salaun | 1948 | Cecile Bowes |
| 1927 | Myles P. Baker | 1956 | G. Diehl Mateer, Jr. | 1949 | Janet Morgan |
| 1928 | Herbert N. Rawlins, Jr. | 1957–58 | Henri Salaun | 1950 | Elizabeth Howe |
| 1929 | J. Lawrence Pool | 1959 | Ben Heckscher | 1951 | Jane Austin |
| 1930 | Herbert N. Rawlins, Jr. | 1960 | G. Diehl Mateer, Jr | 1952–53 | Margaret Howe |
| 1931 | J. Lawrence Pool | | | 1954 | Lois Dilks |
| 1932–33 | Beekman Pool | | **WOMEN** | 1955 | Janet Morgan |
| 1934 | Neil J. Sullivan | 1928 | Eleonora Sears | 1956–59 | Mrs. Pepper Constable, Jr. |
| 1935 | Donald Strachan | 1929 | Mrs. William F. Howe, Jr. | 1960 | Margaret Varner |

# SQUASH TENNIS
## National Champions

| | | | | | | |
|---|---|---|---|---|---|---|
| 1911–12 | Alfred Stillman | 1923 | R. Earl Fink | 1946 | Frank R. Hanson |
| 1913 | George Whitney | 1924 | Fillmore Van S. Hyde | 1947 | Frederick B. Ryan, Jr. |
| 1914 | Alfred Stillman | 1925 | William Rand, Jr. | 1948–50 | H. Robert Reeve |
| 1915–17 | Eric S. Winston | 1926 | Fillmore Van S. Hyde | 1951 | J. T. P. Sullivan |
| 1918 | Fillmore Van S. Hyde | 1927–29 | Rowland B. Haines | 1952 | H. Robert Reeve |
| 1919 | John W. Appel, Jr. | 1930–40 | Harry F. Wolf | 1953 | Howard J. Rose |
| 1920 | Auguste J. Cordier | 1941 | Joseph J. Lordi | 1954–56 | H. Robert Reeve |
| 1921 | Fillmore Van S. Hyde | 1942 | H. Robert Reeve | 1957–59 | J. Lenox Porter |
| 1922 | Thomas R. Coward | 1943–45 | No tournaments | 1960 | James Prigoff |

# RACQUETS
## National Champions

| | | | | | | |
|---|---|---|---|---|---|---|
| 1890–91 | B. Spalding de Garmendia | 1909 | H. F. McCormick | 1934 | E. M. Edwards |
| 1892 | J. S. Tooker | 1910 | Quincy A. Shaw, Jr. | 1935 | H. D. Sheldon |
| 1893–94 | B. Spalding de Garmendia | 1911–12 | Reginald Fincke | 1936 | E. M. Edwards |
| 1895 | J. S. Tooker | 1913–14 | Lawrence Waterbury | 1937–39 | Robert Grant, III |
| 1896–97 | B. Spalding de Garmendia | 1915 | C. C. Pell | 1940 | Warren Ingersoll, III |
| 1898 | F. F. Rolland | 1916 | S. G. Mortimer | 1941 | Robert Grant, III |
| 1899 | Quincy A. Shaw, Jr. | 1917 | C. C. Pell | 1942–45 | No tournaments |
| 1900 | Eustace H. Miles | 1918–19 | No tournaments | 1946 | Robert Grant, III |
| 1901 | Quincy A. Shaw, Jr. | 1920–22 | C. C. Pell | 1947 | J. Richards Leonard |
| 1902 | Clarence H. Mackay | 1923 | S. G. Mortimer | 1948–51 | Robert Grant, III |
| 1903 | Payne Whitney | 1924–25 | C. C. Pell | 1952 | S. W. Pearson, III |
| 1904 | George H. Brooke | 1926 | S. G. Mortimer | 1953 | Robert Grant, III |
| 1905 | Lawrence Waterbury | 1927–28 | C. C. Pell | 1954–56 | Geoffrey W. T. Atkins |
| 1906 | Percy D. Haughton | 1929 | H. D. Sheldon | 1957 | Charles Pearson |
| 1907 | Reginald Fincke | 1930 | S. G. Mortimer | 1958 | Clarence C. Pell, Jr. |
| 1908 | Quincy A. Shaw, Jr. | 1931–33 | C. C. Pell | 1959–60 | Geoffrey W. T. Atkins |

# COURT TENNIS
## National Champions

| | | | | | | |
|---|---|---|---|---|---|---|
| 1892 | Richard D. Sears | 1920–25 | Jay Gould | 1940 | James H. Van Alen |
| 1893 | Fiske Warren | 1926 | C. Suydam Cutting | 1941 | Alastair B. Martin |
| 1894–95 | B. Spalding de Garmendia | 1927 | George Huband | 1942–45 | No tournaments |
| 1896 | Lawrence M. Stockton | 1928–29 | Hewitt Morgan | 1946 | Robert Grant, III |
| 1897 | George R. Fearing, Jr. | 1930 | Lord Aberdare | 1947 | E. M. Beals, Jr. |
| 1898–99 | Lawrence M. Stockton | 1931–32 | William C. Wright | 1948–49 | Ogden Phipps |
| 1900 | Eustace H. Miles | 1933 | James H. Van Alen | 1950–56 | Alastair B. Martin |
| 1901–04 | Joshua Crane | 1934–37 | Ogden Phipps | 1957–58 | Northrup Knox |
| 1905 | Charles E. Sands | 1938 | James H. Van Alen | 1959 | James Bostwick |
| 1906–17 | Jay Gould | 1939 | Ogden Phipps | 1960 | Northrup Knox |
| 1918–19 | No tournaments | | | | |

# BADMINTON

## National Champions

| | | | | | | |
|---|---|---|---|---|---|---|
| 1937–38 | Walter Kramer | 1955 | Joseph Alston | 1940 | Evelyn Boldrick |
| 1939–42 | David Freeman | 1956–57 | Finn Kobbero | 1941 | Thelma Kingsbury |
| 1943–46 | No competition | 1958 | Jim Poole | 1942 | Evelyn Boldrick |
| 1947–48 | David Freeman | 1959–60 | Tan Joe Hok | 1943–46 | No competition |
| 1949–50 | Marten Mendez | | | 1947–53 | Ethel Marshall |
| 1951 | Joseph Alston | | **WOMEN** | 1954 | Judith Devlin |
| 1952 | Marten Mendez | | | 1955 | Margaret Varner |
| 1953 | David Freeman | 1937–38 | Mrs. Del Barkhuff | 1956–60 | Judith Devlin |
| 1954 | Eddy Choong | 1939 | Mary Whittemore | | |

# TABLE TENNIS

## National Champions

| | | | | | | |
|---|---|---|---|---|---|---|
| 1931 | Marcus Schussheim | 1945–49 | Richard Miles | 1935 | Ruth Hughes Aarons |
| 1932 | Coleman Clark* | 1950 | John Leach | 1936 | Ruth Hughes Aarons† |
| | Marcus Schussheim* | 1951 | Richard Miles | 1937 | Ruth Hughes Aarons‡ |
| 1933 | James M. Jacobson* | 1952 | Louis Pagliaro | 1938–39 | Emily Fuller |
| | Sidney Heitner* | 1953–55 | Richard Miles | 1940–44 | Sally Green |
| 1934 | James McClure* | 1956 | Erwin Klein | 1945 | Davida Hawthorn |
| | Sol Schiff* | 1957 | Bernard Bukiet | 1946 | Bernice Charney |
| 1935 | Abe Berenbaum | 1958 | Martin Reisman | 1947 | Leah Thall |
| 1936 | Viktor Barna† | 1959 | Bob Gusikoff | 1948 | Peggy McLean |
| | Sol Schiff‡ | 1960 | Martin Reisman | 1949 | Leah Thall Neuberger |
| 1937 | Laszlo Bellak† | | | 1950 | Reba Kirson Monness |
| 1938 | Laszlo Bellak | | **WOMEN** | 1951–53 | Leah Thall Neuberger |
| 1939 | James McClure | 1933 | Jessie Purves* | 1954 | Mildred Shahian |
| 1940–42 | Louis Pagliaro | | Fanny Pockrose* | 1955–57 | Leah Thall Neuberger |
| 1943 | William Holzrichter | 1934 | Ruth Hughes Aarons* | 1958–59 | Susie Hoshi |
| 1944 | John Somael | | Iris Little* | 1960 | Sharon Acton |

* Co-champions. At the time there were two national associations, each with its own champion.   † Open championships.   ‡ Closed championships.

# LACROSSE

## National Intercollegiate Champions

*Source:* United States Intercollegiate Lacrosse Association.

| | | | | | |
|---|---|---|---|---|---|
| 1881–82 | Harvard | 1914 | Cornell, Lehigh | 1939–40 | Maryland |
| 1883 | Yale | 1915 | Harvard, Johns Hopkins | 1941 | Johns Hopkins |
| 1884–85 | Princeton | 1916 | Cornell, Lehigh | 1942 | Princeton |
| 1886–90 | Records not available | 1917 | Stevens Tech, Lehigh | 1943 | Navy |
| 1891 | Johns Hopkins | 1918 | Stevens Tech | 1944 | Army |
| 1892–97 | Records not available | 1919 | Stevens Tech, Johns Hopkins | 1945 | Army, Navy |
| 1898–1900 | Johns Hopkins | 1920 | Syracuse, Lehigh | 1946 | Navy |
| 1901 | Records not available | 1921 | Lehigh | 1947–48 | Johns Hopkins |
| 1902 | Johns Hopkins | 1922 | Syracuse | 1949 | Johns Hopkins, Navy |
| 1903 | Records not available | 1923 | Johns Hopkins | 1950 | Johns Hopkins |
| 1904 | Swarthmore | 1924–25 | Syracuse | 1951 | Army, Princeton |
| 1905 | Columbia, Cornell, Harvard, Swarthmore | 1926–27 | Johns Hopkins | 1952 | Virginia, R.P.I. |
| | | 1928 | Johns Hopkins, Maryland, Navy, Rutgers | 1953 | Princeton |
| 1906–07 | Cornell, Johns Hopkins | | | 1954 | Navy |
| 1908 | Harvard, Johns Hopkins | 1929 | Navy, Union | 1955–56 | Maryland |
| 1909 | Harvard, Columbia, Johns Hopkins | 1930–31 | St. John's (Md.) | 1957 | Johns Hopkins |
| | | 1932–35 | No champions | 1958 | Army |
| 1910 | Harvard, Swarthmore | 1936 | Maryland | 1959 | Army, Johns Hopkins, Maryland |
| 1911 | Harvard, Johns Hopkins | 1937 | Maryland, Princeton | | |
| 1912 | Harvard | 1938 | Navy | 1960 | Navy |
| 1913 | Harvard, Johns Hopkins | | | | |

### North-South Game Record

| | | | |
|---|---|---|---|
| 1940—North 6, South 5 | 1947—North 15, South 3 | 1952—South 15, North 7 | 1957—North 14, South 10 |
| 1941—South 7, North 6 | 1948—North 11, South 6 | 1953—South 12, North 9 | 1958—South 26, North 6 |
| 1942—North 6, South 3 | 1949—South 11, North 6 | 1954—North 13, South 11 | 1959—South 10, North 9 |
| 1943—South 9, North 5 | 1950—North 12, South 8 | 1955—South 12, North 11 | 1960—South 13, North 12 |
| 1946—North 14, South 14 | 1951—North 12, South 11 | 1956—South 20, North 10 | |

# MOTORBOATING

Since the source of power—the internal combustion engine—is the same in the motorboat as it is in the automobile, the history of motorboat racing parallels that of auto racing. There was a sporting risk in driving the early power boats. As soon as they began to show a degree of dependability, there came the informal rivalries of the rivers and lakes. These led to the formal contests of speed and endurance over marked courses under the control of the American Power Boat Association. The races were severe tests of all parts of power boats and what was learned in the annual Gold Cup competition, which started in 1904, caused a great improvement in the designing of engines and hulls. The development of the outboard motor opened up another branch of power boat competition of wide popularity.

## Motorboating Statistics

### GOLD CUP WINNERS

Beginning with 1922 the race for the American Power Boat Association Gold Cup was open only to displacement boats of over 25 feet in length and powered with motors of not more than 625 inches piston displacement. In 1946 the rules were liberalized to encourage the entry of smaller, less expensive craft. Boats now are required to be between 25 and 40 feet in length, with horsepower unlimited.

| Year | Winner and owner | Best heat m.p.h. | Year | Winner and owner | Best heat m.p.h. |
|------|------------------|------------------|------|------------------|------------------|
| 1904 | STANDARD, C. C. Riotte | 23.6 | 1931 | HOTSY TOTSY, V. Kliesrath–R. Hoyt | 54.92 |
| 1904 | VINGT-ET-UN II, W. Sharpe Kilmer | 25.3 | 1932 | DELPHINE IV, Horace E. Dodge | 59.21 |
| 1905 | CHIP, J. Wainwright | 15.9 | 1933 | EL LAGARTO, G. Reis | 60.866 |
| 1906 | CHIP II, J. Wainwright | 20.6 | 1934 | EL LAGARTO, G. Reis | 58.06 |
| 1907 | CHIP II, J. Wainwright | 20.8 | 1935 | EL LAGARTO, G. Reis | 57.582 |
| 1908 | DIXIE II, E. J. Schroeder | 30.9 | 1936 | IMPSHI, Horace E. Dodge | 47.120 |
| 1909 | DIXIE II, E. J. Schroeder | 32.9 | 1937 | NOTRE DAME, Herbert Mendelson | 68.645 |
| 1910 | DIXIE III, F. K. Burnham | 33.6 | 1938 | ALAGI, Theo Rossi | 66.08 |
| 1911 | MIT II, J. H. Hayden | 36.1 | 1939 | MY SIN, Z. G. Simmons Jr. | 67.05 |
| 1912 | P. D. Q. II, Alfred G. Miles | 44.5 | 1940 | HOTSY TOTSY III, Sidney Allen | 51.316 |
| 1913 | ANKLE DEEP, C. S. Mankowski | 50.49 | 1941 | MY SIN, Z. G. Simmons Jr. | 52.509 |
| 1914 | BABY SPEED DEMON II, Paula Blackton | 48.5 | 1946 | TEMPO VI, Guy Lombardo | 70.878 |
| 1915 | MISS DETROIT, Miss Detroit P. B. A. | 49.7 | 1947 | MISS PEPSI V, Dossin Brothers | 57.02 |
| 1916 | MISS MINNEAPOLIS, Miss Minneapolis B. A. | 48.5 | 1948 | MISS GREAT LAKES, Albin Fallon | 56.982 |
| 1917 | MISS DETROIT II, Gar Wood | 56.5 | 1949 | MY SWEETIE, E. Gregory–E. Schoenherr | 78.645 |
| 1918 | MISS DETROIT III, Detroit Yachtsmen | 52.1 | 1950 | SLO-MO-SHUN IV, Stanley S. Sayres | 80.892 |
| 1919 | MISS DETROIT III, Gar Wood | 56.3 | 1951 | SLO-MO-SHUN V, Stanley S. Sayres | 91.766 |
| 1920 | MISS AMERICA, Gar Wood | 70.0 | 1952 | SLO-MO-SHUN IV, Stanley S. Sayres | 84.355 |
| 1921 | MISS AMERICA, Gar Wood | 56.5 | 1953 | SLO-MO-SHUN IV, Stanley S. Sayres | 95.268 |
| 1922 | PACKARD-CHRISCRAFT, J. G. Vincent | 40.6 | 1954 | SLO-MO-SHUN V, Stanley S. Sayres | 99.784 |
| 1923 | PACKARD-CHRISCRAFT, J. G. Vincent | 44.4 | 1955 | GALE V, Joseph Schoenith | 100.954 |
| 1924 | BABY BOOTLEGGER, Caleb Bragg | 46.4 | 1956 | MISS THRIFTWAY, Willard Rhodes | 100.906 |
| 1925 | BABY BOOTLEGGER, Caleb Bragg | 48.4 | 1957 | MISS THRIFTWAY, Willard Rhodes | 104.016 |
| 1926 | GREENWICH FOLLY, G. H. Townsend | 49.22 | 1958 | HAWAII KAI, Edgar Kaiser | 108.739 |
| 1927 | GREENWICH FOLLY, G. H. Townsend | 50.99 | 1959 | MAVERICK, William T. Waggoner, Jr. | 106.278 |
| 1929 | IMP, R. F. Hoyt | 50.489 | 1960 | No contest. | |
| 1930 | HOTSY TOTSY, V. Kliesrath | 56.05 | | | |

### HARMSWORTH TROPHY WINNERS

| Year | Boat and Country | Speed* | Year | Boat and Country | Speed* |
|------|------------------|--------|------|------------------|--------|
| 1903 | NAPIER I, France | 19.53 | 1921 | MISS AMERICA II, United States | 59.75 |
| 1904 | TREFLE-A-QUATRE, England | 26.63 | 1926 | MISS AMERICA V, United States | 61.118 |
| 1905 | NAPIER II, England | 26.03 | 1928 | MISS AMERICA VII, United States | 59.325 |
| 1906 | YARROW-NAPIER, England | 15.48 | 1929 | MISS AMERICA VIII, United States | 75.287 |
| 1907 | DIXIE I, United States | 31.78 | 1930 | MISS AMERICA IX, United States | 77.233 |
| 1908 | DIXIE II, United States | 31.347 | 1931 | MISS AMERICA VIII, United States | 85.861 |
| 1910 | DIXIE III, United States | 36.04 | 1932 | MISS AMERICA X, United States | 78.489 |
| 1911 | DIXIE IV, United States | 40.28 | 1933 | MISS AMERICA X, United States | 86.939 |
| 1912 | †MAPLE LEAF IV, England | 43.18 | 1949 | SKIP-A-LONG, United States | 94.285 |
| 1913 | MAPLE LEAF IV, England | 57.45 | 1950 | SLO-MO-SHUN IV, United States | 100.680 |
| 1920 | MISS AMERICA I, United States | 61.51 | 1956 | SHANTY I, United States | 94.772 |
| | | | 1959 | MISS SUPERTEST III, Canada | 99.786 |
| | | | 1960 | MISS SUPERTEST III, Canada | 115.972 |

\* In statute miles per hour.
† First of hydroplanes to win, predecessors being all displacement craft.

# YACHTING

JASON sailed in search of the Golden Fleece. Cleopatra (according to Shakespeare) had a royal barge with purple sails. Columbus had three sailing ships when he crossed the Atlantic westward in 1492. But who the first sailor was and where he launched his primitive craft nobody ever will know. The word "yacht" is of Dutch origin and the first "yacht race" of record in the English language was a sailing contest from Greenwich to Gravesend and return in 1662 between a Dutch yacht designed and, at some part of the race, sailed by Charles II of England. The royal yacht won the contest.

The first yacht club was organized at Cork, Ireland, in 1720 under the name of the Cork Harbour Water Club, later changed to the Royal Cork Yacht Club. The Royal Yacht Squadron was organized at Cowes in 1812 and the name changed to the Royal Yacht Club in 1820. The New York Yacht Club was organized aboard the Stevens schooner "Gimcrack" on July 30, 1844, and a clubhouse erected at Elysian Fields, Hoboken, N. J., the following year.

From that time until the Civil War races were held over courses starting from the water off the yacht club promontory. One course was to the Sandy Hook Lightship and return.

In 1850 the celebrated "America" was built by a group of New York yachtsmen and sent abroad to compete at Cowes. In a race around the Isle of Wight, with a special cup as a prize, the "America" defeated fourteen English boats and brought back the trophy that has been raced for as "The America's Cup" in many international yacht races since that time.

## AMERICA'S CUP RECORD

First race in 1851 around Isle of Wight, Cowes, England. First defense and all others through 1920 held 30 miles off New York Bay. Races from 1930 through 1937 held 30 miles off Newport, R. I.

Conducted as one race only in 1851 and 1870; best four-of-seven basis, 1871; best two-of-three, 1876-1887; best three-of-five, 1893-1901; best four-of-seven, 1930-1937. Figures in parentheses indicate number of races won.

| Year | Winner and owner | Loser and owner |
|------|------------------|-----------------|
| 1851 | AMERICA (1), John C. Stevens, U. S. | *AURORA, T. Le Marchant, England |
| 1870 | MAGIC (1), Franklin Osgood, U. S. | †CAMBRIA, James Ashbury, England |
| 1871 | ‡COLUMBIA (2), Franklin Osgood, U. S. | LIVONIA (1), James Ashbury, England |
|      | SAPPHO (2), William P. Douglas, U. S. | |
| 1876 | MADELEINE (2), John S. Dickerson, U. S. | COUNTESS OF DUFFERIN, Chas. Gifford, Canada |
| 1881 | MISCHIEF (2), J. R. Busk, U. S. | ATALANTA, Alexander Cuthbert, Canada |
| 1885 | PURITAN (2), J. M. Forbes-Gen. Charles Paine, U. S. | GENESTA, Sir Richard Sutton, England |
| 1886 | MAYFLOWER (2), Gen. Charles Paine, U. S. | GALATEA, Lt. William Henn, England |
| 1887 | VOLUNTEER (2), Gen. Charles Paine, U. S. | THISTLE, James Bell et al, Scotland |
| 1893 | VIGILANT (3), C. Oliver Iselin et al, U. S. | VALKYRIE II, Lord Dunraven, England |
| 1895 | DEFENDER (3), C. O. Iselin-W. K. Vanderbilt-E. D. Morgan, U. S. | VALKYRIE III, Lord Dunraven-Lord Lonsdale-Lord Wolverton, England |
| 1899 | COLUMBIA (3), J. P. Morgan-C. O. Iselin, U. S. | SHAMROCK I, Sir Thomas Lipton, Ireland |
| 1901 | COLUMBIA (3), Edwin D. Morgan, U. S. | SHAMROCK II, Sir Thomas Lipton, Ireland |
| 1903 | RELIANCE (3), Cornelius Vanderbilt et al, U. S. | SHAMROCK III, Sir Thomas Lipton, Ireland |
| 1920 | RESOLUTE (3), Henry Walters et al, U. S. | SHAMROCK IV (2), Sir Thomas Lipton, Ireland |
| 1930 | ENTERPRISE (4), Harold S. Vanderbilt et al, U. S. | SHAMROCK V, Sir Thomas Lipton, Ireland |
| 1934 | RAINBOW (4), Harold S. Vanderbilt, U. S. | ENDEAVOUR (2), T. O. M. Sopwith, England |
| 1937 | RANGER (4), Harold S. Vanderbilt, U. S. | ENDEAVOUR II, T. O. M. Sopwith, England |
| 1958 | COLUMBIA (4), Henry Sears et al, U. S. | SCEPTRE, Hugh Goodson et al, England |

* Fourteen British yachts started against America; Aurora finished second. † Cambria sailed against 23 U. S. yachts and finished tenth. ‡ Columbia was disabled in the third race, after winning the first two; Sappho substituted and won the fourth and fifth.

# CASTING

## National Fly and Bait Casting Records

*Source:* Paul N. Jones, Executive Secretary, American Casting Association

### COMBINED EVENTS

| | |
|---|---|
| All distance—Jon Tarantino, San Francisco | 3,406 ft. |
| Distance baits—William J. Lovely, St. Louis | 2,367 ft. |
| Distance flies—R. L. Hetzel, Kansas City | 1,163 ft. |
| All accuracy—Casper Rigamer, New Orleans | 396 pts. |
| Accuracy baits—Casper Rigamer, New Orleans | 198 pts. |
| Accuracy flies—Don Meyer, Burbank, Calif.; Fred Mathis, San Francisco; Charles Sutphin, Indianapolis, and Steve Aleshi, Kansas City | 200 pts. |

### SINGLE EVENTS—DISTANCE

| | ft. |
|---|---|
| Trout fly (average)—Jack Crossfield, San Francisco | 186⅔ |
| Trout fly (long cast)—Jon Tarantino, San Francisco | 201 |
| Salmon fly (average)—R. L. Hetzel, Kansas City | 213 |
| Salmon fly (long cast)—Jon Tarantino, San Francisco | 227 |
| ⅜-oz. bait (average)—Richard Ward, Washington, D. C. | 368 |
| ⅜-oz. bait (long cast)—Richard War, Washington, D. C. | 386 |
| ⅝-oz. bait (average)—Charles Schall, St. Louis | 443 |
| ⅝-oz. bait (long cast)—Jon Tarantino, San Francisco | 453 |

### SINGLE EVENTS—AVERAGE

| | pts. |
|---|---|
| Dry fly—Held by 10 casters | 100 |
| Wet fly—Held by 69 casters | 100 |
| ⅜-oz. bait—Charles Sutphin, Indianapolis, and William True, Minneapolis | 100 |
| ⅝-oz. bait—Joe A. Halbleib, Louisville, Ky.; Frank Halper, Chicago, and Don Allen, Smithville, Mo. | 100 |

# AUTO RACING

THE FIRST automobiles on the road were erratic in action and driving them or even riding in them was considered a trifle risky, hence it became the sporting thing to do. Experimental excursions in crude cars gave rise to rivalry in speed over the rough roads of the Gay Nineties and this eventually led to formal contests, the first of which was a road race from Paris to Rouen in 1894, with 26 cars showing up at the starting line. Formal competition in the United States started with a road race in the Chicago district on Thanksgiving Day, 1895, and the winner, J. F. Duryea, covered the road distance of 54.36 miles at the astonishing average of 7.5 miles per hour!

Around 1900 Paris became the hub of road racing in Europe and each year there were raucous, dusty and dangerous races from Paris to Berlin, to Vienna, to Madrid and other cities on the Continent. Accidents were so numerous to drivers and spectators that, after a gory group of mishaps in the forepart of the Paris–Madrid race of 1903, the contest was halted at Bordeaux by public authorities and all road racing was brought under control. Other kinds of auto racing were exposed to view. Some contests, including 24-hour races for stock models, were held on circular or oval tracks originally built for horse racing. Finally came the special racing strips for autos, including such famous autodromes as Brooklands in England and the Indianapolis Speedway in the United States.

As a test of engine and chassis under severe conditions and great strain, auto racing rendered invaluable assistance in the development of the motor car of today.

## National Champions

*Source:* United States Auto Club

| | | | |
|---|---|---|---|
| 1902 Harry Harkness | 1919 Howard Wilcox | 1938 Floyd Roberts | **STOCK CAR** |
| 1903 Barney Oldfield | 1920–21 Thomas Milton | 1939 Wilbur Shaw | 1950 Jay Frank |
| 1904 George Heath | 1922 James Murphy | 1940–41 Rex Mays | 1951 Rodger Ward |
| 1905 Victor Hemery | 1923 Eddie Hearne | 1946–48 Ted Horn | 1952 Marshall Teague |
| 1906 Joe Tracy | 1924 James Murphy | 1949 Johnnie Parsons | 1953 Frank Mundy |
| 1907 Eddie Bald | 1925 Peter DePaolo | 1950 Henry Banks | 1954 Marshall Teague |
| 1908 Louis Strang | 1926 Harry Hartz | 1951 Tony Bettenhausen | 1955 Frank Mundy |
| 1909 George Robertson | 1927 Peter DePaolo | 1952 Chuck Stevenson | 1956 Johnny Mantz |
| 1910 Ray Harroun | 1928–29 Louis Meyer | 1953 Sam Hanks | 1957 Jerry Unser |
| 1911 Ralph Mulford | 1930 Billy Arnold | 1954 Jimmy Bryan | 1958–59 Fred Lorenzen |
| 1912 Ralph DePalma | 1931 Louis Schneider | 1955 Bob Sweikert | 1960 Norm Nelson |
| 1913 Earl Cooper | 1932 Bob Carey | 1956–57 Jimmy Bryan | |
| 1914 Ralph DePalma | 1933 Louis Meyer | 1958 Tony Bettenhausen | **ROAD RACING** |
| 1915 Earl Cooper | 1934 Bill Cummings | 1959 Rodger Ward | 1958 Dan Gurney |
| 1916 Dario Resta | 1935 Kelly Petillo | 1960 A. J. Foyt | 1959 August Pabst |
| 1917 Earl Cooper | 1936 Mauri Rose | | 1960 Carroll Shelby |
| 1918 Ralph Mulford | 1937 Wilbur Shaw | | |

## History of the One-Mile Speed Mark

The first recorded effort for one mile was made in 1898 by Chasseloup-Laubat, driving a Jentaud, in France. His average was 39.24 m.p.h. This was increased to 65.79 in 1899 by Jenatzy, also in France. The first man to travel better than 100 m.p.h. was Rigolly, in 1904, at 103.56 m.p.h., followed by Baras, with 104.53 in the same year. The first over 200 m.p.h. was Major H. O. D. Segrave, who drove a Sunbeam at 203.79 in 1927 at Daytona, Florida.

In 1947 John Cobb of London became the first person to travel more than 400 m.p.h. on land. The Englishman accomplished the feat on Sept. 16 at Bonneville, Utah, while raising the world mile record to 394.196 m.p.h. and the world kilometer (.62137 of a mile) mark to 393.825 m.p.h.

Cobb's fastest mile was covered in 8.93 seconds and his average speed was 9.1325 seconds. The Briton drove at the rate of 385.645 m.p.h. for the mile and 388.019 for the kilometer on the southward run, then increased his pace to 403.135 m.p.h. and 399.808, respectively, on the northward sprint, the best times ever recorded.

Those who held the world record since it was held to 300 m.p.h. follow (all at Bonneville):

| Date | Driver | Car | Average |
|---|---|---|---|
| Sept. 3, 1935 | Sir Malcolm Campbell | Bluebird Special | 301.1292 |
| Nov. 19, 1937 | Capt. G. E. T. Eyston | Thunderbolt #1 | 311.42 |
| Aug. 27, 1938 | Capt. G. E. T. Eyston | Thunderbolt #1 | 345.5 |
| Sept. 15, 1938 | John Cobb | Railton | 350.2 |
| Sept. 16, 1938 | Capt. G. E. T. Eyston | Thunderbolt #1 | 357.5 |
| Aug. 23, 1939 | John Cobb | Railton Red Lion | 368.9 |
| Sept. 16, 1947 | John Cobb | Railton-Mobil Special | 394.196 |

## Indianapolis Motor Speedway Winners
### (500-mile race)

| Year | Winner | Car | Second | Time | m.p.h |
|------|--------|-----|--------|------|-------|
| 1911 | Ray Harroun | Marmon | Mulford | 6:42:08 | 74.59 |
| 1912 | Joe Dawson | National | Tetzloff | 6:21:06 | 78.72 |
| 1913 | Jules Goux | Peugeot | Wishart | 6:35:05 | 75.93 |
| 1914 | Rene Thomas | Delage | Duray | 6:03:45 | 82.47 |
| 1915 | Ralph DePalma | Mercedes | Resta | 5:33:55 | 89.84 |
| 1916* | Dario Resta | Peugeot | De Aleve | 3:34:17 | 84.00 |
| 1917–18 | No races | | | | |
| 1919 | Howard Wilcox | Peugeot | Hearne | 5:40:42 | 88.05 |
| 1920 | Gaston Chevrolet | Monroe | Thomas | 5:38:32 | 88.62 |
| 1921 | Tommy Milton | Frontenac | Sarles | 5:34:44 | 89.62 |
| 1922 | Jimmy Murphy | Murphy Special | Hartz | 5:17:30 | 94.48 |
| 1923 | Tommy Milton | H. C. S. Special | Hartz | 5:29:50 | 90.95 |
| 1924 | L. L. Corum–Joe Boyer | Dusenberg Special | Cooper | 5:05:23 | 98.23 |
| 1925 | Peter DePaolo | Dusenberg Special | Lewis | 4:56:39 | 101.13 |
| 1926† | Frank Lockhart | Miller Special | Hartz | 4:10:14 | 95.904 |
| 1927 | George Souders | Dusenberg Special | Devore | 5:07:33 | 97.54 |
| 1928 | Louis Meyer | Miller Special | Moore | 5:01:33 | 99.48 |
| 1929 | Ray Keech | Simplex Special | Meyer | 5:07:25 | 97.58 |
| 1930 | Billy Arnold | Miller-Hartz Special | Cantlon | 4:58:39 | 100.448 |
| 1931 | Louis Schneider | Bowes Special | Frame | 5:10:28 | 96.629 |
| 1932 | Fred Frame | Miller-Hartz Special | Wilcox | 4:48:03.79 | 104.144 |
| 1933 | Louis Meyer | Tydol Special | Shaw | 4:48:00.75 | 104.162 |
| 1934 | Bill Cummings | Boyle Products Special | Rose | 4:46:05.20 | 104.863 |
| 1935 | Kelly Petillo | Gilmore Special | Shaw | 4:42:22.71 | 106.240 |
| 1936 | Louis Meyer | Ring Free Special | Horn | 4:35:03.39 | 109.069 |
| 1937 | Wilbur Shaw | Shaw-Gilmore Special | Hepburn | 4:24:07.80 | 113.580 |
| 1938 | Floyd Roberts | Burd Piston Ring Special | Shaw | 4:15:58.40 | 117.200 |
| 1939 | Wilbur Shaw | Boyle Special | Snyder | 4:20:47.39 | 115.035 |
| 1940 | Wilbur Shaw | Boyle Special | Mays | 4:22:31.17 | 114.277 |
| 1941 | Floyd Davis–Mauri Rose | Noc-Out Hose Clamp Special | Mays | 4:20:36.24 | 115.117 |
| 1942–45 | No races | | | | |
| 1946 | George Robson | Thorne Eng. Special | Jackson | 4:21:26.71 | 114.820 |
| 1947 | Mauri Rose | Blue Crown Special | Holland | 4:17:52.17 | 116.338 |
| 1948 | Mauri Rose | Blue Crown Special | Holland | 4:10:23.33 | 119.814 |
| 1949 | Bill Holland | Blue Crown Special | Parsons | 4:07:15.97 | 121.327 |
| 1950‡ | Johnnie Parsons | Wynn's Fiction Proof Spl. | Holland | 2:46:55.97 | 124.002 |
| 1951 | Lee Wallard | Belanger Special | Nazaruk | 3:57:38.05 | 126.244 |
| 1952 | Troy Ruttman | Agajanian Special | Rathmann | 3:52:41.88 | 128.922 |
| 1953 | Bill Vukovich | Fuel Injection Spl. | Cross | 3:53:01.69 | 128.740 |
| 1954 | Bill Vukovich | Fuel Injection Spl. | Bryan | 3:49:17.27 | 130.840 |
| 1955 | Bob Sweikert | John Zink Special | Bettenhausen | 3:53:59.53 | 128.209 |
| 1956 | Pat Flaherty | John Zink Special | Hanks | 3:53:28.84 | 128.490 |
| 1957 | Sam Hanks | Belond Exhaust Special | Rathmann | 3:41:14.25 | 135.601 |
| 1958 | Jimmy Bryan | Belond A-P Special | Amick | 3:44:13.80 | 133.791 |
| 1959 | Rodger Ward | Leader Card 500 Rdstr. | Rathmann | 3:40:49.20 | 135.857 |
| 1960 | Jim Rathmann | Ken-Paul Special | Ward | 3:36:11.36 | 138.767 |

\* 300 miles.   † Race ended at 400 miles owing to heavy rain.   ‡ Race ended at 345 miles because of rain.

# CYCLING
## NATIONAL AMATEUR CHAMPIONS

| Year | Winner | Year | Winner |
|------|--------|------|--------|
| 1921 | Arthur Nieminsky, New York | 1940 | Furman Kugler, New Jersey |
| 1922 | Carl Hambacher, Jew Jersey | 1941 | Marvin Thomson, Illinois |
| 1923 | Charles Barclay, California | 1945 | Ted Smith, New York |
| 1924 | Charlie Winter, New York | 1946 | Don Hester, California |
| 1925–26 | Edward Merkner, Illinois | 1947–48 | Ted Smith, New York |
| 1927 | Jimmy Walthour, Jr., New York | 1949 | James Lauf, Maryland |
| 1928 | R. J. Connor, District of Columbia | 1950 | Robert Pfarr, Wisconsin |
| 1929 | Sergio Matteini, New York | 1951 | Gus Gatto, California |
| 1930 | Bobby Thomas, Wisconsin | 1952 | Steve Hromjak, Ohio |
| 1935 | Cecil Hursey, Georgia | 1953 | Ronald Rhoads, California |
| 1936 | Jackie Simes, New Jersey | 1954–58 | Jack Disney, California |
| 1937 | Charles Bergna, New Jersey | 1959–60 | James Rossi, Illinois |
| 1939 | Martin Deras, California | | |

# BILLIARDS

APPARENTLY nobody knows where billiards originated. Some trace the game back to ancient Greece or early Egyptian days; others insist it originated in France or England in medieval times. Shakespeare must have believed the Egyptian tale, because in *Antony and Cleopatra* he has Cleopatra saying: "Let's to billiards; come, Charmian." There is an illustration of Louis XIV of France playing billiards in 1694 and using a shovel-shaped stick to set the "cue ball" in motion, from which it is evident that the pointed cue was a later development.

Certainly the game was popular in England and on the Continent in the seven-teenth and eighteenth centuries and early settlers in North America are supposed to have introduced the game here. How to apply "English" to a billiard ball was discovered by Jack Carr, an Englishman, in 1820. A Frenchman named Mingaud is credited with having invented the "draw" shot at about the same time and also to have devised leather tips for wooden cues. Championship competition, amateur and professional, is a modern development in billiards. The first formal professional tournament held in the United States took place in New York in 1863 with eight players competing. The first three-cushion tournament was held in St. Louis in 1878.

## Billiards Statistics

*Source:* John Canelli, Secretary, The Billiard Congress of America.

### World Three-Cushion Champions

| | | | | | | | |
|---|---|---|---|---|---|---|---|
| 1878 | Leon Magnus | 1911 | Alfredo DeOro | 1917-18 | Alfredo DeOro | 1931 | Arthur Thurnblad |
| 1899 | W. H. Catton | 1912 | Joe Carney | 1918-19 | Augie Kieckhefer | 1932 | Augie Kieckhefer |
| 1900 | Eugene Carter | 1912 | John Horgan | 1919 | Alfredo DeOro | 1933 | Welker Cochran |
| 1900 | Lloyd Jevne | 1913-14 | Alfredo DeOro | 1919 | R. L. Cannafax | 1934 | John Layton |
| 1907 | Harry P. Cline | 1915 | George Moore | 1920 | John Layton | 1935 | Welker Cochran |
| 1908 | John Daly | 1915 | William H. Huey | 1921 | Augie Kieckhefer | 1936 | Willie Hoppe |
| 1908 | Thomas Hueston | 1916 | Alfredo DeOro | 1921-23 | John Layton | 1937-38 | Welker Cochran |
| 1908-09 | Alfredo DeOro | 1916 | Charles Ellis | 1923 | Tiff Denton | 1939 | Joe Chamaco |
| 1910 | Fred Eames | 1916 | Charles McCourt | 1924-25 | R. L. Cannafax | 1940-44 | Willie Hoppe |
| 1910 | Alfredo DeOro | 1916 | Hugh Heal | 1926-27 | Otto Reiselt | 1944-45 | Welker Cochran |
| 1910 | John Daly | 1916 | George Moore | 1927 | Augie Kieckhefer | 1947-52 | Willie Hoppe |
| 1910 | Thomas Hueston | 1917 | Charles McCourt | 1928 | Otto Reiselt | 1953 | Ray Kilgore |
| 1911 | John Daly | 1917 | R. L. Cannafax | 1928-30 | John Layton | 1954-60 | No tournament |

### World Pocket Billiard Champions

| | | | | | | | |
|---|---|---|---|---|---|---|---|
| 1878-80 | Cyrille Dion | 1899-1900 | Alfredo DeOro | 1912 | R. J. Ralph | 1936 | James Caras |
| 1881 | Gottlieb Wahlstrom | 1901 | Frank Sherman | 1913 | Alfredo DeOro | 1937 | Ralph Greenleaf |
| 1882-83 | Albert Frey | 1901 | Alfredo DeOro | 1913-15 | Bennie Allen | 1938-39 | James Caras |
| 1884 | J. L. Malone | 1902 | William Clearwater | 1916 | Emmet Blankenship | 1940 | Andrew Ponzi |
| 1886-87 | Alfred Frey | 1902 | Grant Eby | 1916 | John Layton | 1941 | Willie Mosconi |
| 1887 | J. L. Malone (f) | 1903-04 | Alfredo DeOro | 1916-18 | Frank Taberski | 1941 | Erwin Rudolph |
| 1887-88 | Alfredo DeOro | 1905 | Jerome Keogh (f) | 1919-24 | Ralph Greenleaf | 1942 | Irving Crane |
| 1888 | Frank Powers | 1905 | Alfredo DeOro | 1925 | Frank Taberski | 1942 | Willie Mosconi |
| 1889 | Albert Frey | 1905 | Thomas Hueston (f) | 1926 | Ralph Greenleaf | 1943 | Andrew Ponzi |
| 1889 | Alfredo DeOro | 1906 | Thomas Hueston | 1926 | Erwin Rudolph | 1943-45 | Willie Mosconi |
| 1890 | H. Manning | 1906 | John Horgan | 1926 | Thomas Hueston | 1946 | Irving Crane |
| 1891 | Frank Powers (f) | 1906 | Jerome Keogh | 1927 | Frank Taberski | 1946-48 | Willie Mosconi |
| 1892-94 | Alfredo DeOro | 1907-08 | Thomas Hueston | 1927-28 | Ralph Greenleaf | 1949 | James Caras |
| 1895 | William Clearwater | 1908 | Frank Sherman | 1928 | Frank Taberski | 1950-53 | Willie Mosconi |
| 1895 | Alfredo DeOro | 1908 | Alfredo DeOro | 1929 | Ralph Greenleaf | 1954 | No tournament |
| 1896 | Frank Stewart (f) | 1909 | Charles Weston | 1929 | Frank Taberski | 1955 | Irving Crane |
| 1897 | Grant Eby | 1909 | John Kling | 1930 | Erwin Rudolph | 1955 | Willie Mosconi |
| 1897 | Jerome Keogh | 1910 | Thomas Hueston | 1930-32 | Ralph Greenleaf | 1956-60 | No tournament |
| 1898 | William Clearwater | 1910 | Jerome Keogh | 1933-34 | Erwin Rudolph | | |
| 1898 | Jerome Keogh | 1910-12 | Alfredo DeOro | 1935 | Andrew Ponzi | | (f) Forfeit. |

### National Amateur Three-Cushion Champions

Since 1945, tournament has been limited to athletic clubs and identified as the national amateur invitational three-cushion billiard championship.

| | | | | | | | |
|---|---|---|---|---|---|---|---|
| 1910 | Pierre Maupome | 1925-26 | Dr. A. J. Harris | 1930 | R. B. Harper | 1946 | Edward Lee |
| 1911 | Charles Morin | 1927 | Robert M. Lord | 1931 | Frank Flemming | 1946-48 | Robert M. Lord |
| 1919 | Arthur Newman | 1927 | Dr. L. P. Macklin | 1931-35 | Edward Lee | 1948 | C. T. Vandenovert† |
| 1920 | W. B. Huey | 1928 | J. N. Bozeman | 1936 | Edward Lee* | 1948-53 | Edward Lee |
| 1921 | Earl Lookabaugh | 1929 | Charles Jordan | 1937 | A. Primeau | 1954 | Lee Lerner |
| 1922 | Frank Flemming | 1929 | Max Shimon | 1938 | Gene Deardorff | 1955 | No tournament |
| 1923 | Robert M. Lord | 1930 | Joseph Hall | 1939-40 | Gene Deardorff | 1956 | Edward Lee |
| 1924 | Frank Flemming | 1930 | Max Shimon | 1945-46 | C. T. Vandenover | 1957 | Stanhope Adams |
| | | | | | | 1958-60 | Edward Lee |

* World champion.       † Match.

# BOXING

WHETHER it be called pugilism, prize fighting or boxing, there is no tracing "the Sweet Science" to any definite source. Tales of rivals exchanging blows for fun, fame or money go back to earliest recorded history and classical legend. There was a mixture of boxing and wrestling called the "pancratium" in the ancient Olympic Games and in such contests the rivals belabored one another with hands fortified with heavy leather wrappings that were sometimes studded with metal. More than one Olympic competitor lost his life at this brutal exercise.

There was little law or order in pugilism until Jack Broughton, one of the early champions of England, drew up a set of rules for the game in 1743. Broughton, called "the father of English boxing," also is credited with having invented boxing gloves. However, these gloves—or "mufflers" as they were called—were used only in teaching "the manly art of self-defense" or in training bouts. All professional championship fights were contested with "bare knuckles" until 1892, when John L. Sullivan lost the heavyweight championship of the world to James J. Corbett in New Orleans in a bout in which both contestants wore regulation gloves.

The Broughton rules were superseded by the London Prize Ring Rules of 1838. The 8th Marquis of Queensberry, with the help of John G. Chambers, put forward the "Queensberry Rules" in 1866, a code that called for gloved contests. Amateurs took quickly to the Queensberry Rules, the professionals slowly.

There is no official international set of rules for boxing even today. Amateur organizations set rules for amateurs in different countries and professional rules set by boxing commissions vary even in different sections of the United States, but the variations are for the most part minor. A prize fighter doesn't have to change his style greatly to ply his trade anywhere in the world.

## Boxing Statistics

Source: Nat Fleischer's All-Time Record Book and Encyclopedia of Boxing, published and copyrighted by The Ring Book Shop, Inc., Madison Square Garden, New York, N. Y.

### Boxing's Biggest Gates

WF—Won on foul;     ND—No decision.     (1st)—First bout.     (2d)—Second bout;     (3d)—Third bout.

| Date | Winner; weight     Loser, weight | Rounds | Site | Receipts | Attendance. |
|---|---|---|---|---|---|
| Sept. 22, 1927 | Tunney (189½)-Dempsey (192½) (2d).. | 10 | Soldier Field, Chicago........... | $2,658,660 | 104,943 |
| June 19, 1946 | Louis (207)-Conn (187) (2d).......... | KO 8 | Yankee Stadium, New York.... | 1,925,564 | 45,266 |
| Sept. 23, 1926 | Tunney (189½)-Dempsey (190) (1st).... | 10 | Sesquicentennial Stdm., Phila.... | 1,895,733 | 120,757 |
| July  2, 1921 | Dempsey (188)-Carpentier (172)........ | KO 4 | Boyle's 30 Acres, Jersey City..... | 1,789,238 | 80,000 |
| Sept. 14, 1923 | Dempsey (192½)-Firpo (216½)......... | KO 2 | Polo Grounds, New York........ | 1,188,603 | 82,000 |
| July 21, 1927 | Dempsey (194½)-Sharkey (196)....... | KO 7 | Yankee Stadium, New York.... | 1,083,530 | 75,000 |
| June 22, 1938 | Louis (198¾)-Schmeling (193) (2d)..... | KO 1 | Yankee Stadium, New York.... | 1,015,012 | 70,000 |
| Sept. 24, 1935 | Louis (199¼)-Max Baer (210½)........ | KO 4 | Yankee Stadium, New York.... | 1,000,832 | 88,150 |
| Sept. 21, 1955 | Marciano (188¼)-Moore (188)........ | KO 9 | Yankee Stadium, New York.... | 948,117 | 61,574 |
| June 25, 1948 | Louis (213½)-Walcott (194¾) (2d)...... | KO 11 | Yankee Stadium, New York.... | 841,739 | 42,667 |
| June 20, 1960 | Patterson (190)-Johansson (194¾) (2d). | KO 5 | Polo Grounds, New York........ | 824,891 | 31,892 |
| Sept. 12, 1951 | Robinson (157½)-Turpin (159) (2d)..... | KO 10 | Polo Grounds, New York........ | 767,626 | 61,370 |
| June 12, 1930 | Schmeling (188)-Sharkey (197) (1st).... | WF 4 | Yankee Stadium, New York.... | 749,935 | 79,222 |
| June 22, 1937 | Louis (197¼)-Braddock (197).......... | KO 8 | Comiskey Park, Chicago....... | 715,470 | 45,500 |
| July 26, 1928 | Tunney (192)-Heeney (203½)........ | KO 11 | Yankee Stadium, New York.... | 691,014 | 45,890 |
| Sept. 29, 1941 | Louis (202¼)-Nova (202½)............ | KO 6 | Polo Grounds, New York........ | 583,711 | 56,549 |
| Sept. 23, 1957 | Basilio (153½)-Robinson (160) (1st).... | 15 | Yankee Stadium, New York.... | 556,467 | 38,072 |
| June 19, 1936 | Schmeling (192)-Louis (198) (1st)..... | KO 12 | Yankee Stadium, New York.... | 547,541 | 42,088 |
| June 17, 1954 | Marciano (187½)-Charles (185½) (1st). | 15 | Yankee Stadium, New York.... | 543,092 | 47,585 |
| Sept. 11, 1924 | Wills (217)-Firpo (224½)............. | ND 12 | Boyle's 30 Acres, Jersey City..... | 509,135 | 70,000 |
| Sept. 23, 1952 | Marciano (184)-Walcott (196).......... | KO 13 | Municipal Stdm., Phila......... | 504,645 | 40,379 |
| May  13, 1961 | Patterson (194¾)-Johansson (206½) (3d) | KO 6 | Convention Hall, Miami Beach, Fla. | 502,000 | 15,532 |
| June 26, 1959 | Johansson (196)-Patterson (182) (1st).. | KO 3 | Yankee Stadium, New York...... | 469,650 | 18,215 |
| July 16, 1926 | Delaney (166½)-Berlenbach (174¼) (3d) | 15 | Ebbets Field, Brooklyn.......... | 461,789 | 49,186 |
| July 23, 1923 | Leonard (134)-Tendler (133½) (2d)..... | 15 | Yankee Stadium, New York.... | 452,648 | 58,519 |
| July  4, 1919 | Dempsey (187)-Willard (245)........... | KO 3 | Toledo, Ohio................... | 452,224 | 19,650 |
| June 18, 1941 | Louis (199½)-Conn (174) (1st)........ | KO 13 | Polo Grounds, New York........ | 451,743 | 60,071 |
| Sept. 24, 1953 | Marciano (185)-LaStarza (184¾) (2d). | KO 11 | Polo Grounds, New York........ | 435,817 | 44,562 |
| June 21, 1932 | Sharkey (205)-Schmeling (188) (2d).... | 15 | Long Island City Bowl, N. Y... | 432,465 | 61,863 |
| June 14, 1934 | Max Baer (209½)-Carnera (263¼).... | KO 11 | Long Island City Bowl, N. Y. | 428,000 | 56,000 |
| July 16, 1947 | Graziano (154¼)-Zale (159) (2d)...... | KO 6 | Chicago Stadium............... | 422,918 | 18,547 |
| June 25, 1952 | Maxim (173)-Robinson (157½)......... | KO 14 | Yankee Stadium, New York.... | 421,615 | 47,983 |
| Feb. 27, 1929 | Sharkey (192)-Stribling (182).......... | 10 | Flamingo Park, Miami Beach, Fla.. | 405,000 | 40,000 |
| July 12, 1923 | Firpo (214)-Willard (242)............. | KO 8 | Boyle's 30 Acres, Jersey City..... | 390,837 | 80,000 |
| May  12, 1923 | { Firpo (212)-McAuliffe (200)......... | KO 3 | } Yankee Stadium, New York...... | 385,040 | 31,000 |
|  | { Willard (245)-Floyd Johnson (195).... | KO 11 | | | |
| June 27, 1929 | Schmeling (187)- Uzcudun (192½) (1st). | 15 | Yankee Stadium, New York.... | 378,902 | 65,000 |
| July 27, 1922 | Leonard (134¹⁵⁄₁₆)-Tendler (134¾) (1st). | ND 12 | Boyle's 30 Acres, Jersey City..... | 367,862 | 54,685 |
| Sept. 17, 1954 | Marciano (187)-Charles (192½) (2d).... | KO 8 | Yankee Stadium, New York...... | 352,654 | 34,330 |

# HISTORY OF WORLD HEAVYWEIGHT CHAMPIONSHIP FIGHTS

## (Bouts in which a new champion was crowned)

| Date | Where held | Winner, weight, age | Loser, weight, age | Rounds | Referee |
|---|---|---|---|---|---|
| Sept. 7, 1892 | New Orleans, La. .... | James J. Corbett, 178 (26)... | John L. Sullivan, 212 (33).. | 21 | Prof. John Duffy |
| Mar. 17, 1897 | Carson City, Nev.... | Bob Fitzsimmons, 167 (34) .. | James J. Corbett, 183 (30).. | KO 14 | George Siler |
| June 9, 1899 | Coney Island, N. Y. .(a)James J. Jeffries, 206 (24).. | Bob Fitzsimmons, 167 (37). | KO 11 | George Siler |
| Feb. 23, 1906 | Los Angeles........(b)Tommy Burns, 180 (24).... | Marvin Hart, 188 (29)...... | 20 | James J. Jeffries |
| Dec. 26, 1908 | Sydney, N. S. W.... | Jack Johnson, 196 (30)...... | Tommy Burns, 176 (27).... | KO 14 | Hugh McIntosh |
| April 5, 1915 | Havana, Cuba........ | Jess Willard, 230 (31)...... | Jack Johnson, 205½ (37) .. | KO 26 | Jack Welch |
| July 4, 1919 | Toledo, Ohio....... | Jack Dempsey, 187 (24).... | Jess Willard, 245 (35)...... | KO 3 | Ollie Pecord |
| Sept. 23, 1926 | Philadelphia.......(c)Gene Tunney, 189½ (28)... | Jack Dempsey, 190 (31).... | 10 | Pop Reilly |
| June 12, 1930 | New York.......... | Max Schmeling, 188 (24)... | Jack Sharkey, 197 (27).... | WF 4 | Jim Crowley |
| June 21, 1932 | Long Island City.... | Jack Sharkey, 205 (29)...... | Max Schmeling, 188 (26)... | 15 | Gunboat Smith |
| June 29, 1933 | Long Island City.... | Primo Carnera, 260½ (26)... | Jack Sharkey, 201 (30).... | KO 6 | Arthur Donovan |
| June 14, 1934 | Long Island City.... | Max Baer, 209½ (25)...... | Primo Carnera, 263¼ (27).. | KO 11 | Arthur Donovan |
| June 13, 1935 | Long Island City.... | Jim Braddock, 193¾ (29) .. | Max Baer, 209½ (26) ..... | 15 | Jack McAvoy |
| June 22, 1937 | Chicago............ | Joe Louis, 197¼ (23)...... | Jim Braddock, 197 (31).... | KO 8 | Tommy Thomas |
| June 22, 1949 | Chicago..........(d)Ezzard Charles, 181¾ (27).. | Joe Walcott, 195½ (35).... | 15 | Davey Miller |
| Sept. 27, 1950 | New York..........(e)Ezzard Charles, 184½ (29).. | Joe Louis, 218 (36)........ | 15 | Mark Conn |
| July 18, 1951 | Pittsburgh.......... | Joe Walcott, 194 (37)...... | Ezzard Charles, 182 (30).. | KO 7 | Buck McTiernan |
| Sept. 23, 1952 | Philadelphia.......(f)Rocky Marciano, 184 (28) .. | Joe Walcott, 196 (38)...... | KO 13 | Charley Daggert |
| Nov. 30, 1956 | Chicago............ | Floyd Patterson, 182¼ (21).. | Archie Moore, 187¾ (39) .. | KO 5 | Frank Sikora |
| June 26, 1959 | New York.......... | Ingemar Johansson, 196 (26) | Floyd Patterson, 182 (24) .. | KO 3 | Ruby Goldstein |
| June 20, 1960 | New York.......... | Floyd Patterson, 190 (25)... | Ingemar Johansson, 193¾ (27) | KO 5 | Arthur Mercante |

(a) Jeffries retired as champion in March 1905. He named Marvin Hart and Jack Root as leading contenders and agreed to referee their fight in Reno, Nev., on July 3, 1905, with the stipulation that he would term the winner the champion. Hart, 190 (28), knocked out Root, 171 (29), in the 12th round. (b) Burns claimed the title after defeating Hart. (c) Tunney retired as champion after defeating Tom Heeney on July 26, 1928. (d) After Louis announced his retirement as champion on March 1, 1949, Charles won recognition from the National Boxing Association as champion by defeating Walcott. (e) Charles gained undisputed recognition as champion by defeating Louis, who came out of retirement. (f) Retired as champion April 27, 1956.

# BARE KNUCKLE HEAVYWEIGHT CHAMPIONS, 1719–1892

1719—Jim Figg
1734—George Taylor
1740—Jack Broughton
1750—Jack Slack
1760—Bill Stevens
1761—George Meggs
1765—Bill Darts
1777—Harry Sellers
1780—Jack Harris
1785—Tom (Jackling) Johnson
1790—Big Ben Brain
1792—Daniel Mendoza
1795—John Jackson (retired)
1802—Jem Belcher
1805—Henry Pearce (Game Chicken)
1808—John Gully (declined title)
1809—Tom Cribb received belt, not transferable, and cup
1824—Tom Spring received four cups; resigned title.
1825—Jem Ward received belt, not transferable.
1838—James (Deaf) Burke claimed title.
1839—William Thompson (Bendigo) beat Burke; claimed championship; received belt from Jem Ward.
1841—Nick Ward (Jem's brother) beat Ben Caunt, Feb. 2. In return match Caunt beat Nick Ward and received belt by subscription. It was transferable.
1845—Thompson beat Caunt and got belt.
1850—Bill Perry (The Tipton Slasher), after fight with Paddock, claimed title.
1851—Harry Broome won title from Perry.
1853—Perry claimed title when Broome forfeited £200 to him in a match; retired from ring on Aug. 13.
1857—Tom Sayers beat Perry for £200 a side and new belt.
1860—Sayers retired after 42-round draw with John C. Heenan (The Benicia Boy), leaving old belt open for competition.

1860—Sam Hurst (The Stalybridge Infant) beat Paddock and received belt.
1861—Jem Mace beat Hurst.
1862—Mace beat Tom King for £200 a side and the belt.
1862—King beat Mace and claimed belt. Subsequently gave it up. Declined to meet Mace again. Mace claimed belt.
1863—King beat Heenan for £1,000 a side.
1865—Joe Wormald beat Andrew Marsden for £200 a side and belt, which had been claimed by both. Belt was given to Wormald, who forfeited £120 to Mace.
1866—Mace and Joe Goss fought draw with £200 a side and belt at stake.
1867—Wormald received £200 forfeit from Ned O'Baldwin and claimed belt when O'Baldwin failed to appear at starting place.
1867—Mace and O'Baldwin drew; £200 a side; title and belt in abeyance.
1869—Mike McCoole defeated Tom Allen and claimed American championship.
1870—Mace claimed world title by knocking out Allen in 10 rounds.
1873—Mace retired and Allen claimed title of world champion by defeating McCoole.
1876—Allen fought Joe Goss, ranked next to Mace in England. Allen was disqualified in the 27th round for fouling and Goss was recognized as world champion under London Prize Ring Rules.
1880—Paddy Ryan knocked out Goss in the 87th round on May 30, near Colliers Station, W. Va., and became the first American to hold the undisputed world's bare knuckle championship.
1882—John L. Sullivan knocked out Ryan in the 9th round at Mississippi City, Miss., on Feb. 7 and became the last bare knuckle champion.
1889—Sullivan defeated Jake Kilrain in the last bare knuckle championship fight. The bout, on July 8 at Richburg, Miss., went 75 rounds.

# OTHER WORLD BOXING TITLEHOLDERS

## LIGHT HEAVYWEIGHT CHAMPIONS

| | |
|---|---|
| 1903 | —Jack Root, George Gardner |
| 1903–05 | —Bob Fitzsimmons |
| 1905–12 | —Philadelphia Jack O'Brien (r) |
| 1912–16 | —Jack Dillon |
| 1916–20 | —Battling Levinsky |
| 1920–22 | —Georges Carpentier |
| 1923 | —Battling Siki |
| 1923–25 | —Mike McTigue |
| 1925–26 | —Paul Berlenbach |
| 1926–27 | —Jack Delaney (a) |
| 1927 | —Mike McTigue |
| 1927–29 | —Tommy Loughran (a) |
| 1930 | —Jimmy Slattery |
| 1930–34 | —Maxie Rosenbloom |
| 1934–35 | —Bob Olin |
| 1935–39 | —John Henry Lewis (a) |
| 1939 | —Melio Bettina |
| 1939–41 | —Billy Conn (a) |
| 1941 | —Anton Christoforidis (NBA) |
| 1941–48 | —Gus Lesnevich |
| 1948–50 | —Freddie Mills |
| 1950–52 | —Joey Maxim |
| 1952 | —Archie Moore (x) |
| 1961 | —Harold Johnson (NBA) |

(a)Abandoned title. (r)Retired. (x)NBA withdrew
recognition in 1961.

## MIDDLEWEIGHT CHAMPIONS

| | |
|---|---|
| 1867–72 | —Tom Chandler |
| 1872–81 | —George Rooke |
| 1881–82 | —Mike Donovan (r) |
| 1884–91 | —Jack (Nonpareil) Dempsey |
| 1891–97 | —Bob Fitzsimmons (a) |
| 1908 | —Stanley Ketchel, Billy Papke |
| 1908–10 | —Stanley Ketchel (d) |
| 1913 | —Frank Klaus |
| 1913–14 | —George Chip |
| 1914–17 | —Al McCoy |
| 1917–20 | —Mike O'Dowd |
| 1920–23 | —Johnny Wilson |
| 1923–26 | —Harry Greb |
| 1926 | —Tiger Flowers |
| 1926–31 | —Mickey Walker (a) |

1931–41—The National Boxing Association and the New York
State Athletic Commission were divided on title
holders throughout these years. The following were
regarded as champions by one body or the other
in this period: Gorilla Jones, Ben Jeby, Marcel Thil,
Lou Brouillard, Vince Dundee, Teddy Yarosz, Babe
Risko, Freddy Steele, Al Hostak, Solly Krieger,
Fred Apostoli, Ceferino Garcia, Ken Overlin, Billy
Soose, Tony Zale.

| | |
|---|---|
| 1941–47 | —Tony Zale |
| 1947–48 | —Rocky Graziano |
| 1948 | —Tony Zale |
| 1948–49 | —Marcel Cerdan |
| 1949–51 | —Jake La Motta |
| 1951 | —Ray Robinson, Randy Turpin |
| 1951–52 | —Ray Robinson (r) |
| 1953–55 | —Carl Olson |
| 1955–57 | —Ray Robinson |
| 1957 | —Gene Fullmer, Ray Robinson |
| 1957–58 | —Carmen Basilio |
| 1958–60 | —Ray Robinson (x) |
| 1960–61 | —Paul Pender (y) |
| 1959 | —Gene Fullmer (NBA) |
| 1961 | —Terry Downes (y) |

(a)Abandoned title. (d)Died. (r)Retired. (x)NBA
withdrew recognition in 1959; recognized thereafter
only by New York and Massachusetts. (y)Recognized
by New York and Massachusetts only.

## WELTERWEIGHT CHAMPIONS

| | |
|---|---|
| 1892–94 | —Mysterious Billy Smith |
| 1894–96 | —Tommy Ryan |
| 1896 | —Kid McCoy (a) |
| 1896–1900 | —Mysterious Billy Smith |
| 1900 | —Rube Ferns |
| 1900–01 | —Matty Matthews |
| 1901 | —Rube Ferns |
| 1901–04 | —Joe Walcott |
| 1904 | —Dixie Kid (a) |
| 1904–06 | —Joe Walcott |
| 1906–07 | —Honey Mellody |
| 1907 | —Mike (Twin) Sullivan (a) |
| 1915–19 | —Ted Lewis |
| 1919–22 | —Jack Britton |
| 1922–26 | —Mickey Walker |
| 1926–27 | —Pete Latzo |
| 1927–29 | —Joe Dundee |
| 1929–30 | —Jackie Fields |
| 1930 | —Young Jack Thompson |
| 1930–31 | —Tommy Freeman |
| 1931 | —Young Jack Thompson |
| 1931–32 | —Lou Brouillard |
| 1932–33 | —Jackie Fields |
| 1933 | —Young Corbett 3d |
| 1933–34 | —Jimmy McLarnin |
| 1934 | —Barney Ross |
| 1934–35 | —Jimmy McLarnin |
| 1935–38 | —Barney Ross |
| 1938–40 | —Henry Armstrong |
| 1940–41 | —Fritzie Zivic |
| 1941–46 | —Freddie Cochrane |
| 1946 | —Marty Servo (r) |
| 1946–51 | —Ray Robinson (a) |
| 1951 | —Johnny Bratton (NBA) |
| 1951–54 | —Kid Gavilan |
| 1954–55 | —Johnny Saxton |
| 1955 | —Tony DeMarco |
| 1955–56 | —Carmen Basilio |
| 1956 | —Johnny Saxton |
| 1956–57 | —Carmen Basilio (a) |
| 1958 | —Virgil Akins |
| 1958–60 | —Don Jordan |
| 1960–61 | —Benny (Kid) Paret |
| 1961 | —Emile Griffith |
| 1961 | —Benny (Kid) Paret |

(a)Abandoned title. (r)Retired.

## Famous Firsts in Boxing

**First to regain heavyweight championship:** Floyd Patterson, by a knockout victory over Ingemar Johansson, at the Polo Grounds, New York, June 20, 1960.

**First set of boxing rules and first set of boxing gloves:** Made by Jack Broughton, 1743.

**First glove fight:** Between two English boxers, at Aix-la-Chapelle, France, October 8, 1818.

**First million-dollar gate:** Jack Dempsey *vs.* Georges Carpentier at Boyle's Thirty Acres, Jersey City, N. J., July 2, 1921 ($1,789,238).

**First round-by-round fight broadcast:** Dempsey *vs.* Carpentier, 1921, J. Andrew White announcer.

**First fight on television (publicly screened):** Eric Boon *vs.* Arthur Danahar, Harringay Arena, London, England, February 23, 1939.

## LIGHTWEIGHT CHAMPIONS

1885–96—Jack McAuliffe*
1896–99—Kid Lavigne
1899–02—Frank Erne
1902–08—Joe Gans
1908–10—Battling Nelson
1910–12—Ad Wolgast
1912–14—Willie Ritchie
1914–17—Freddy Welsh
1917–25—Benny Leonard (r)
1925   —Jimmy Goodrich
1925–26—Rocky Kansas
1926–30—Sammy Mandell
1930   —Al Singer
1930–33—Tony Canzoneri
1933–35—Barney Ross (a)
1935–36—Tony Canzoneri
1936–38—Lou Ambers
1938–39—Henry Armstrong
1939–40—Lou Ambers
1940–41—Lew Jenkins
1941–42—Sammy Angott (r)
1943–47—The National Boxing Association and the New York State Athletic Commission recognized different champions in these years. Title holders, according to the N. Y. Commission, were Beau Jack and Bob Montgomery and, according to the NBA, Sammy Angott, who made a comeback, Juan Zurita and Ike Williams. Williams defeated Montgomery in 1947 to provide a universal champion.
1947–51—Ike Williams
1951–52—James Carter
1952   —Lauro Salas
1952–54—James Carter
1954   —Paddy DeMarco
1954–55—James Carter
1955–56—Wallace Smith
1956   —Joe Brown

* McAuliffe was champion of America, but never held the world crown, his battle for the world title with Jem Carney of England in 1887 resulting in a 74-round draw. (a) Abandoned title. (r) Retired.

## FEATHERWEIGHT CHAMPIONS

1889   —Dal Hawkins (a)
1890   —Billy Murphy
1892–1900—George Dixon
1900–01—Terry McGovern
1901   —Young Corbett (a)
1901–12—Abe Attell
1912–23—Johnny Kilbane
1923   —Eugene Criqui
1923–25—Johnny Dundee (a)
1925–27—Louis (Kid) Kaplan (a)
1927–28—Benny Bass
1928   —Tony Canzoneri
1928–29—Andre Routis
1929–32—Battling Battalino (a)
1932   —Tommy Paul (NBA); Kid Chocolate (N. Y. Comm.).
1933–36—Freddie Miller
1936–37—Petey Sarron
1937–38—Henry Armstrong (a)
1938–40—Joey Archibald
1940–41—Harry Jeffra, Joey Archibald
1941–42—Chalky Wright
1942–48—Willie Pep
1948–49—Sandy Saddler
1949–50—Willie Pep
1950–57—Sandy Saddler (r)
1957–59—Kid Bassey
1959   —Davey Moore

(a) Abandoned title. (r) Retired.

## BANTAMWEIGHT CHAMPIONS

1890–92—George Dixon (a)
1894–99—Jimmy Barry (r)
1899–1900—Terry McGovern (a)
1901   —Harry Harris (a)
1902–03—Harry Forbes
1903–04—Frankie Neil
1904   —Joe Bowker (a)
1905–07—Jimmy Walsh (a)
1910–14—Johnny Coulon
1914–17—Kid Williams
1917–20—Pete Herman
1920–21—Joe Lynch
1921   —Pete Herman
1921–22—Johnny Buff
1922–24—Joe Lynch
1924   —Abe Goldstein
1924–25—Eddie (Cannonball) Martin
1925   —Charlie (Phil) Rosenberg (d)
1927–28—Bud Taylor (NBA) (a)
1929–35—Al Brown
1935–36—Baltazar Sangchili
1936   —Tony Marino
1936–37—Sixto Escobar
1937–38—Harry Jeffra
1938–40—Sixto Escobar (r)
1940–42—Lou Salica
1942–47—Manuel Ortiz
1947   —Harold Dade
1947–50—Manuel Ortiz
1950–52—Vic Toweel
1952–54—Jimmy Carruthers (r)
1954–56—Robert Cohen
1956–57—Mario D'Agata
1956   —Raul Macias (NBA)
1957–59—Alphonse Halimi
1959–60—Jose Becerra (r)
1960–61—Alphonse Halimi (x)
1961   —Eder Jofre (NBA)
1961   —Johnny Caldwell (x)

(a) Abandoned title. (d) Deprived of title when unable to make weight for championship bout. (r) Retired. (x) Recognized by Europe as champion.

## FLYWEIGHT CHAMPIONS

1916–23—Jimmy Wilde
1923–25—Pancho Villa (d)
1925   —Frankie Genaro
1925–27—Fidel La Barba (r)
1927–31—The NBA and the New York Commission recognized different champions in these years. Claimants at various times were Corporal Izzy Schwartz, Frankie Genaro, Emile Spider Pladner, Midget Wolgast and Young Perez.
1932–35—Jackie Brown
1935–38—Benny Lynch (a)
1939   —Peter Kane (a)
1943–47—Jackie Paterson (d)
1947–50—Rinty Monaghan (r)
1950   —Terry Allen
1950–52—Dado Marino
1952–54—Yoshio Shirai
1954–60 Pascual Perez
1960   —Pone Kingpetch

(a) Abandoned title. (d) Died. (r) Retired.

## PROFESSIONAL WEIGHT LIMITS

| | lbs. |
|---|---|
| Flyweight | 112 |
| Bantamweight | 118 |
| Featherweight | 126 |
| Lightweight | 135 |
| Welterweight | 147 |
| Middleweight | 160 |
| Light heavyweight | 175 |
| Heavyweight | over 175 |

# ICE (FIGURE) SKATING

## World Champions

| | | | | | |
|---|---|---|---|---|---|
| 1896 | Gilbert Fuchs, Germany | 1929 | Gillis Grafstrom, Sweden | 1915–21 | No competition |
| 1897 | Gustav Hugel, Austria | 1930–36 | Karl Schafer, Austria | 1922–26 | Mrs. Szabo Plank, Austria |
| 1898 | H. Grenander, Sweden | 1937–38 | Felix Kaspar, Austria | 1927–36 | Sonja Henie, Norway |
| 1899–1900 | Gustav Hugel, Austria | 1939 | Graham Sharp, England | 1937 | Cecilia Colledge, England |
| 1901–05 | Ulrich Salchow, Sweden | 1940–46 | No competition | 1938–39 | Megan Taylor, England |
| 1906 | Gilbert Fuchs, Germany | 1947 | Hans Gerschweiler, Switzerland | 1940–46 | No competition |
| 1907–11 | Ulrich Salchow, Sweden | 1948–52 | Richard Button, United States | 1947–48 | Barbara Ann Scott, Canada |
| 1912–13 | Fritz Kachler, Austria | 1953–56 | Hayes Jenkins, United States | 1949–50 | Aja Vrzanova, Czechoslovakia |
| 1914 | Gosta Sandahl, Sweden | 1957–59 | David Jenkins, United States | 1951 | Jeannette Altwegg, England |
| 1915–21 | No competition | 1960 | Alain Giletti, France | 1952 | Jacqueline du Bief, France |
| 1922 | Gillis Grafstrom, Sweden | | | 1953 | Tenley Albright, United States |
| 1923 | Fritz Kachler, Austria | | **WOMEN** | 1954 | Gundi Busch, Germany |
| 1924 | Gillis Grafstrom, Sweden | 1906–07 | Madge Syers, England | 1955 | Tenley Albright, United States |
| 1925–28 | Willi Boeckl, Austria | 1908–11 | Lily Kronberger, Hungary | 1956–60 | Carol Heiss, United States |
| | | 1912–14 | Meray Horvath, Hungary | | |

## National Champions

| | | | | | |
|---|---|---|---|---|---|
| 1914 | Norman Scott | 1943 | Arthur Vaughn, Jr. | 1921–24 | Mrs. Theresa Weld Blanchard |
| 1915–17 | No competition | 1944–45 | No competition | 1925–27 | Beatrix Loughran |
| 1918 | Nathaniel Niles | 1946–52 | Richard Button | 1928–33 | Maribel Vinson |
| 1919 | No competition | 1953–56 | Hayes Jenkins | 1934 | Suzanne Davis |
| 1920–24 | Sherwin Badger | 1957–60 | David Jenkins | 1935–37 | Maribel Vinson |
| 1925 | Nathaniel Niles | | | 1938–40 | Joan Tozzer |
| 1926 | C. I. Christenson | | | 1941 | Jane Vaughn |
| 1927 | Nathaniel Niles | | **WOMEN** | 1942 | Mrs. Jane Vaughn Sullivan |
| 1928–34 | Roger Turner | 1914 | Theresa Weld | 1943–48 | Gretchen Merrill |
| 1935–39 | Robin Lee | 1915–17 | No competition | 1949–50 | Yvonne Sherman |
| 1940–41 | Eugene Turner | 1918 | Mrs. R. S. Beresford | 1951 | Sonya Klopfer |
| 1942 | Bobby Specht | 1919 | No competition | 1952–56 | Tenley Albright |
| | | 1920 | Theresa Weld | 1957–60 | Carol Heiss |

## Joe Louis' Title Fights

| | | | | | |
|---|---|---|---|---|---|
| June 22, 1937* | Jim Braddock, Chicago | KO 8 | Feb. 17, 1941 | Gus Dorazio, Philadelphia | KO 2 |
| Aug. 30, 1937 | Tommy Farr, Yankee Stad. | W 15 | Mar. 21, 1941 | Abe Simon, Detroit | KO 13 |
| Feb. 23, 1938 | Nathan Mann, Mad. Sq. Garden | KO 3 | Apr. 8, 1941 | Tony Musto, St. Louis | KO 9 |
| Apr. 1, 1938 | Harry Thomas, Chicago | KO 5 | May 23, 1941 | Buddy Baer, Washington, D. C. | W disq. 7 |
| June 22, 1938 | Max Schmeling, Yankee Stad. | KO 1 | June 18, 1941 | Billy Conn, Polo Grounds | KO 13 |
| Jan. 25, 1939 | John Henry Lewis, Mad. Sq. Garden | KO 1 | Sept. 29, 1941 | Lou Nova, Polo Grounds | KO 6 |
| Apr. 17, 1939 | Jack Roper, Los Angeles | KO 1 | Jan. 9, 1942 | Buddy Baer, Mad. Sq. Garden | KO 1 |
| June 28, 1939 | Tony Galento, Yankee Stad. | KO 4 | Mar. 27, 1942 | Abe Simon, Mad. Sq. Garden | KO 6 |
| Sept. 20, 1939 | Bob Pastor, Detroit | KO 11 | June 19, 1946 | Billy Conn, Yankee Stad. | KO 8 |
| Feb. 9, 1940 | Arturo Godoy, Mad. Sq. Garden | W 15 | Sept. 18, 1946 | Tami Mauriello, Yankee Stad. | KO 1 |
| Mar. 29, 1940 | Johnny Paychek, Mad. Sq. Garden | KO 2 | Dec. 5, 1947 | Joe Walcott, Mad. Sq. Garden | W 15 |
| June 20, 1940 | Arturo Godoy, Yankee Stad. | KO 8 | June 25, 1948 | Joe Walcott, Yankee Stad. | KO 11 |
| Dec. 16, 1940 | Al McCoy, Boston | KO 6 | Sept. 27, 1950† | Ezzard Charles, Yankee Stad. | L 15 |
| Jan. 31, 1941 | Red Burman, Mad. Sq. Garden | KO 5 | | | |

\* Won title.  † After announcing retirement as champion on Mar. 1, 1949, Louis returned to boxing and sought to regain title in bout with Charles.

## Marciano Was Unbeaten as a Pro

Rocky Marciano, heavyweight boxing champion of the world and winner of each of his 49 fights as a professional, announced his retirement from the ring on April 27, 1956. He is the only heavyweight champion ever to retire without losing a professional fight or even boxing to a draw.

Marciano won the title on Sept. 23, 1952, in Philadelphia, by knocking out Joe Walcott in the 13th round. He defended his crown six times. His gross purses for his 49 professional bouts have been estimated at $2,000,000.

Marciano was born in Brockton, Mass., on Sept. 1, 1924.

Of his 49 victories, the retired champion scored 43 by knockouts, more than half of them within three rounds.

These were Marciano's championship fights:

| | | |
|---|---|---|
| Sept. 23, 1952* | Joe Walcott, Philadelphia | KO 13 |
| May 15, 1953 | Joe Walcott, Chicago | KO 1 |
| Sept. 24, 1953 | Roland LaStarza, Polo Grounds | KO 11 |
| June 17, 1954 | Ezzard Charles, Yankee Stad. | W 15 |
| Sept. 17, 1954 | Ezzard Charles, Yankee Stad. | KO 8 |
| May 16, 1955 | Don Cockell, San Francisco | KO 9 |
| Sept. 21, 1955 | Archie Moore, Yankee Stad. | KO 9 |

\* Won title.

# ICE (SPEED) SKATING

## World Records

*Source:* International Skating Union (I.S.U.).

| Event | Record | Recordholder and country | Where made | Date |
|---|---|---|---|---|
| 500 meters.... | 0:40.2.......... | Evgeny Grishin, U.S.S.R........ | Lake Misurina, Italy.......... | Jan. 22, 1956 |
| | 0:40.2.......... | Evgeny Grishin, U.S.S.R........ | Lake Misurina, Italy.......... | Jan. 28, 1956 |
| 1,000 meters.... | 1:22.8.......... | Evgeny Grishin, U.S.S.R........ | Alma Ata, U.S.S.R........... | Jan. 12, 1955 |
| 1,500 meters.... | 2:06.3.......... | Juhani Jarvinen, Finland....... | Squaw Valley, Calif........... | Mar. 1, 1959 |
| 3,000 meters.... | 4:40.2.......... | Anton Huiskes, Holland........ | Davos, Switzerland........... | Jan. 24, 1953 |
| 5,000 meters.... | 7:45.6.......... | Boris Shilkov, U.S.S.R........ | Alma Ata, U.S.S.R........... | Jan. 9, 1955 |
| 10,000 meters.... | 15:46.6.......... | Knut Johannesen, Norway...... | Squaw Valley, Calif........... | Feb. 27, 1960 |
| All-around....... | 184.638 pts....... | Dimitry Sakunenko, U.S.S.R...... | Alma Ata, U.S.S.R........... | Jan. 9–10, 1955 |

### WOMEN

| | | | | |
|---|---|---|---|---|
| 500 meters.... | 0:45.6.......... | Tamara Rylova, U.S.S.R........ | Alma Ata, U.S.S.R........... | Jan. 11, 1955 |
| 1,000 meters.... | 1:33.4.......... | Tamara Rylova, U.S.S.R........ | Alma Ata, U.S.S.R........... | Jan. 12, 1955 |
| 1,500 meters.... | 2:25.2.......... | Lidija Skoblikova, U.S.S.R....... | Squaw Valley, Calif........... | Feb. 21, 1960 |
| 3,000 meters.... | 5:13.8.......... | Rimma Zhukowa, U.S.S.R....... | Alma Ata, U.S.S.R........... | Jan. 23, 1953 |
| 5,000 meters.... | 9:01.6.......... | Rimma Zhukowa, U.S.S.R....... | Alma Ata, U.S.S.R........... | Jan. 24, 1953 |
| All-around....... | 196.416 pts....... | Tamara Rylova, U.S.S.R........ | Alma Ata, U.S.S.R........... | Jan. 20–21, 1960 |

## National Outdoor Champions

| | | |
|---|---|---|
| 1891–92 Joseph Donoghue | 1933 Melvin Johnson | 1929 Loretta Neitzel |
| 1893–95 John Johnson | 1934 James Webster | 1930 Leila Potter* |
| 1896–97 John Nilsson | 1935–37 Marvin Swanson | 1931 Elsie Muller |
| 1898–99 No competition | 1938 Vic Ronchetti | 1932 Helen Bina |
| 1900 Leroy See | 1939 Ken Bartholomew | 1933 Kit Klein |
| 1901–07 Morris Wood | 1940 Leo Freisinger | 1934 Dorothy Franey |
| 1908–10 Edmund Lamy | 1941–42 Ken Bartholomew | 1935 Kit Klein |
| 1911–14 Robert McLean | 1943–45 No competition | 1936 Dorothy Franey |
| 1915 Russell Wheeler* | 1946 Robert Fitzgerald | 1937 Maddy Horn |
| 1916 Hary Cody | 1947 Ken Bartholomew | 1938 Mary Dolan |
| 1917 Arthur Staff | 1948 George Fisher | 1939–40 Maddy Horn |
| 1918–19 No competition | 1949 Ray Blum | 1941–42 Carmalita Landry |
| 1920 Roy McWhirter | 1950–56 Ken Bartholomew | 1943–46 No competition |
| 1921 Charles Jewtraw | 1957 Ken Bartholomew, Bobby | 1947 Betty Mitchell |
| 1922 Roy McWhirter | Snyder (tie) | 1948 Betty Mitchell, Lorraine Sabbe |
| 1923 Harry Kaskey | 1958 Gene Sandvig | 1949 Lorraine Sabbe |
| 1924 Charles Gorman* | 1959–60 Ken Bartholomew | 1950 Janice Christopherson |
| 1925 Francis Allen | | 1951 Barbara Marchetti, |
| 1926 O'Neill Farrell* | ### WOMEN | Gwendolyn DuBois |
| 1927 No competition | 1921–23 Gladys Robinson* | 1952 Barbara Marchetti |
| 1928 Lloyd Guenther | 1924–25 Rose Johnson* | 1953–56 Pat Gibson |
| 1929 Allen Potts | 1926 Lois Littlejohn | 1957 Mary Maland |
| 1930 Jack Shea | 1927 No competition | 1958–59 Jeanne Omelenchuk |
| 1931 Frank Stack† | 1928 Elsie Muller | 1960 Mary Novak |
| 1932 James Webster | | |

\* International champion.   † North American Champion.

# CURLING

## National Champions

1957 Hibbing, Minn. (Harold Lauber, skip; Louis Lauber, Peter Beasy, Matt Brklich)

1958 Detroit (C. Douglas Fisk, skip; Mike Slyziuk, Ernest Slyziuk, V. Merritt Knowlson)

1959 Hibbing, Minn. (Frank Kleffman, skip; Dick Brown, Terry Kleffman, Nick Jerulle)

1960 Grafton, N. D. (Orvil Gilleshammer, skip; Glenn Gilleshammer, Wilmer Collette, Don LaBonte)

## U. S. Figure Skaters Perish in Crash; World Meet Off

Eighteen United States figure skaters, on their way to the world championships in Prague, were among 73 persons killed when a Sabena Airlines jet crashed near Brussels on Feb. 15, 1961. The dead included six skaters who less than three weeks earlier had won the four major U. S. titles. They were Bradley Lord and Laurence Owen, the men's and women's champions; Dudley Richards and Maribel Owen, the pairs champions, and Larry Pierce and Diane Sherbloom, the dance champions. Mrs. Maribel Vinson Owen, mother of Laurence and Maribel, also died in the crash. She was the national figure skating champion from 1928 to 1933 and from 1935 to 1937.

The 1961 world championship tournament was cancelled because of the tragedy.

# Standard Measurements in Sports

## BASEBALL

Home plate to pitcher's box—**60 feet 6 inches.**

Plate to second base—127 feet 3⅜ inches.

Distance from base to base (home plate included)—90 feet.

Size of bases—15 inches by 15 inches.

Pitcher's plate—24 inches by 6 inches.

Batter's box—6 feet by 4 feet.

Home plate—17 inches by 17 inches, cut to a point at rear.

Home plate to backstop—Not less than 60 feet (recommended).

Weight of ball—Not less than 5 ounces nor more than 5¼ ounces.

Circumference of ball—Not less than 9 inches nor more than 9¼ inches.

Bat—Must be round, not over 2¾ inches in diameter at thickest part, nor more than 42 inches in length, and of hardwood in one piece or laminated.

## FOOTBALL

Length of field—120 yards.*

Width of field—53⅓ yards (160 feet).

Height of goal posts—20 feet.

Height of crossbar—10 feet.

Width of goal posts—23 feet 4 inches, inside to inside, and not more than 24 feet, outside to outside.

Length of ball—11 to 11.25 inches (long axis).

Circumference of ball—21.25 to 21.50 inches (middle); 28 to 28.5 inches (long axis).

* Includes 10 yards of end zone on either side.

## LAWN TENNIS

Size of court—Rectangle 78 feet long and 27 feet wide (singles); 78 feet long and 36 feet wide (doubles).

Height of net—3 feet in center, gradually rising to reach 3-foot 6-inch posts at each side of court.

Ball—Shall be more than 2½ inches and less than 2⅝ inches in diameter and weigh more than 2 ounces and less than 2 1/16 ounces.

Service line—21 feet from net.

## ICE HOCKEY

Size of rink—200 feet long by 85 feet wide (desired size).

Size of goal—6 feet wide by 4 feet in height.

Puck—1 inch thick and 3 inches in diameter; made of vulcanized rubber; weight —six ounces (unofficial).

Length of stick—Not more than 53 inches from heel to end of shaft nor 14¾ inches from heel to end of blade. Blade should not exceed 3 inches in height, except goalkeeper's stick, which shall not exceed 3½ inches in height except at the heel, where it must not exceed 4½ inches.

## BOWLING

Lane dimensions—Overall length 62 feet 10 3/16 inches, measuring from foul line to pit (not including tail plank), with ½ inch tolerance permitted. Foul line to No. 1 pinspot 60 feet, with ½ inch tolerance permitted. Lane width, not less than 41 inches, nor more than 42. Approach, not less than 15 feet. Gutters, not less than 9 inches nor more than 9½ inches wide.

Ball—Circumference, not more than 27 inches. Weight, 10 pounds minimum, 16 pounds maximum. Balance, tolerance of 3 ounces between top finger hole side and bottom. One ounce tolerance between right and left sides. One ounce tolerance between front and back sides.

## GOLF

Weight of ball—Not greater than 1.620 ounces.

Size of ball—Not less than 1.680 inches in diameter.

Velocity of ball—Not greater than 250 feet per second when tested on U.S.G.A. apparatus, with 2 per cent tolerance.

Hole—Shall be 4¼ inches in diameter and at least 4 inches deep.

Clubs—Fourteen is the maximum number permitted.

## BASKETBALL

### (National Collegiate A. A. Rules)

Playing court—94 feet long by 50 feet wide (maximum dimensions).

Baskets—Rings 18 inches in inside diameter, with white cord nets, 15 to 18 inches in length. Each ring is made of metal and is not more than ⅝ of an inch in diameter.

Height of basket ring—10 feet.

Weight of ball—Not less than 20 ounces nor more than 22.

Circumference of ball—No greater than 30 inches and not less than 29½.

Free-throw line—15 feet from the face of the backboard.

## BOXING

Size of ring—Professional matches take place in an area not less than 18 nor more than 20 feet square. It is enclosed by three covered ropes, each not less than one inch in diameter. The floor has a 2-inch padding that extends at least 6 inches beyond the roped area in the case of elevated rings.

Gloves—In professional fights, 8-ounce gloves generally are used, except in title contests, where 6-ounce gloves are the custom. A.A.U., 8 ounces up to welterweight, 10 ounces in heavier divisions.

# FENCING

*Source:* Amateur Fencers League of America.

## National Champions

### FOIL

| | |
|---|---|
| 1892 | W. Scott-O'Connor |
| 1893 | William Heintz |
| 1894 | Charles Bothner |
| 1895 | Albertson Van Zo Post |
| 1896 | G. Kavanaugh |
| 1897 | Charles Bothner |
| 1898 | No competition |
| 1899 | G. Kavanaugh |
| 1900 | F. Townsend |
| 1901 | Charles Tatham |
| 1902 | J. P. Parker |
| 1903 | F. Townsend |
| 1904-05 | Charles Bothner |
| 1906 | S. D. Breckinridge |
| 1907 | C. Waldbott |
| 1908 | W. L. Bowman |
| 1909 | O. A. Dickinson |
| 1910 | G. K. Bainbridge |
| 1911 | George Breed |
| 1912 | Sherman Hall |
| 1913 | P. J. Meylan |
| 1914 | S. D. Breckinridge |
| 1915 | O. A. Dickinson |
| 1916 | A. E. Sauer |
| 1917 | Sherman Hall |
| 1918 | No competition |
| 1919-20 | Sherman Hall |
| 1921 | F. W. Honeycutt |
| 1922 | H. M. Raynor |
| 1923 | R. Peroy |
| 1924 | Leo Nunes |
| 1925-28 | George Calnan |
| 1929 | Joseph Levis |
| 1930-31 | George Calnan |
| 1932-33 | Joseph Levis |
| 1934 | Hugh Alessandroni |
| 1935 | Joseph Levis |
| 1936 | Hugh Alessandroni |
| 1937 | Joseph Levis |
| 1938 | Dernell Every |
| 1939 | Norman Lewis |
| 1940 | Dernell Every |
| 1941 | Dean Cetrulo |
| 1942-43 | Warren Dow |
| 1944 | Alfred Snyder |
| 1945 | Dernell Every |
| 1946 | Jose de Capriles |
| 1947 | Dean Cetrulo |
| 1948 | Nathaniel Lubell |
| 1949 | Daniel Bukantz |
| 1950-51 | Silvio Giolito |
| 1952-53 | Daniel Bukantz |
| 1954 | Joseph Levis |
| 1955 | Albert Axelrod |
| 1956 | Sewall Shurtz |
| 1957 | Daniel Bukantz |
| 1958 | Albert Axelrod |
| 1959 | Joseph Paletta |
| 1960 | Albert Axelrod |

### EPEE

| | |
|---|---|
| 1892 | Barnard O'Connor |
| 1893 | Graeme Hammond |
| 1894 | R. O. Haubold |
| 1895 | Charles Bothner |
| 1896 | Albertson Van Zo Post |
| 1897 | Charles Bothner |
| 1898 | No competition |
| 1899 | M. Diaz |
| 1900 | W. D. Lyon |
| 1901-03 | Charles Tatham |
| 1904 | Charles Bothner |
| 1905 | W. Scott-O'Connor |
| 1906 | W. Grebe |
| 1907 | W. D. Lyon |
| 1908 | Paul Benzenberg |
| 1909-10 | A. de la Poer |
| 1911 | George Breed |
| 1912 | Albertson Van Zo Post |
| 1913 | A. E. Sauer |
| 1914 | F. W. Allen |
| 1915 | J. A. MacLaughlin |
| 1916 | William Russell |
| 1917 | Leo Nunes |
| 1918 | No competition |
| 1919 | William Russell |
| 1920 | R. W. Dutcher |
| 1921 | C. R. McPherson |
| 1922 | Leo Nunes |
| 1923 | George Calnan |
| 1924 | Leo Nunes |
| 1925 | William Russell |
| 1926 | Leo Nunes |
| 1927 | Harold Van Buskirk |
| 1928 | Leo Nunes |
| 1929 | F. S. Righeimer |
| 1930 | M. Pasche |
| 1931 | Miguel de Capriles |
| 1932 | Leo Nunes |
| 1933-34 | Gustave Heiss |
| 1935 | Thomas Sands |
| 1936 | Gustave Heiss |
| 1937 | Thomas Sands |
| 1938 | Jose de Capriles |
| 1939 | Loyal Tingley |
| 1940 | Fred Seibert |
| 1941 | Gustave Heiss |
| 1942 | Henrique Santos |
| 1943 | Robert Driscoll |
| 1944 | Miguel de Capriles |
| 1945 | Max Gilman |
| 1946 | Charles Wolfe |
| 1947 | James Strauch |
| 1948-50 | Norman Lewis |
| 1951 | Jose de Capriles |
| 1952 | Abelardo Menendez |
| 1953 | Donald Thompson |
| 1954 | Sewall Shurtz |
| 1955-56 | Abram Cohen |
| 1957-58 | Richard Berry |
| 1959 | Henry Kolowrat |
| 1960 | David Micahnik |

### SABER

| | |
|---|---|
| 1892 | R. O. Haubold |
| 1893-94 | Graeme Hammond |
| 1895-97 | Charles Bothner |
| 1898 | No competition |
| 1899 | G. Kavanaugh |
| 1900 | J. L. Ervin |
| 1901-03 | Albertson Van Zo Post |
| 1904 | A. G. Anderson |
| 1905 | K. B. Johnson |
| 1906-07 | A. G. Anderson |
| 1908 | G. W. Postgate |
| 1909 | A. E. Sauer |
| 1910 | J. T. Shaw |
| 1911 | A. G. Anderson |
| 1912 | C. A. Bill |
| 1913 | A. G. Anderson |
| 1914 | W. Von Blejenburgh |
| 1915-16 | Sherman Hall |
| 1917 | Arthur Lyon |
| 1918 | No competition |
| 1919 | Arthur Lyon |
| 1920 | Sherman Hall |
| 1921 | C. R. McPherson |
| 1922 | Leo Nunes |
| 1923 | L. M. Schoonmaker |
| 1924 | J. F. Gignoux |
| 1925 | Joseph Vince |
| 1926 | Leo Nunes |
| 1927-28 | Nickolas Muray |
| 1929 | Leo Nunes |
| 1930 | Norman Armitage |
| 1931-33 | John Huffman |
| 1934-36 | Norman Armitage |
| 1937-38 | John Huffman |
| 1939-43 | Norman Armitage |
| 1944 | Tibor Nyias |
| 1945 | Norman Armitage |
| 1946 | Tibor Nyilas |
| 1947 | James Flynn |
| 1948 | Dean Cetrulo |
| 1949 | Umberto Martino |
| 1950-53 | Tibor Nyilas |
| 1954 | George Worth |
| 1955 | Richard Dyer |
| 1956 | Tibor Nyilas |
| 1957-58 | Daniel Magay |
| 1959 | Tomas Orley |
| 1960 | Eugene Hamori |

### WOMEN'S FOIL

| | |
|---|---|
| 1912 | A. Baylis |
| 1913 | Mrs. W. H. Dewar |
| 1914 | M. Stimson |
| 1915 | Jessie Pyle |
| 1916 | Mrs. C. H. Voorhees |
| 1917 | Florence Walton |
| 1918-19 | No competition |
| 1920-23 | Adeline Gehrig |
| 1924 | Mrs. C. H. Hopper |
| 1925-26 | Mrs. Florence Schoonmaker |
| 1927 | S. Stern |
| 1928 | Marion Lloyd |
| 1929 | Mrs. Florence Schoonmaker |
| 1930 | Mrs. Harold Van Buskirk |
| 1931 | Marion Lloyd |
| 1932-33 | Dorothy Locke |
| 1934-35 | Helene Mayer |
| 1936 | Mrs. Joanne de Tuscan |
| 1937-39 | Helene Mayer |
| 1940 | Helena Mrockowska |
| 1941-42 | Helene Mayer |
| 1943 | Helena Mroczkowska |
| 1944 | Madaline Dalton |
| 1945 | Maria Cerra |
| 1946 | Helene Mayer |
| 1947-48 | Mrs. Helena Mroczkowska Dow |
| 1949 | Polly Craus |
| 1950-51 | Janice Lee York |
| 1952 | Mrs. Maxine Mitchell |
| 1953 | Paula Sweeney |
| 1954-55 | Mrs. Maxine Mitchell |
| 1956-57 | Mrs. Janice Lee Romary |
| 1958 | Mrs. Maxine Mitchell |
| 1959 | Maria del Pilar Roldan |
| 1960 | Mrs. Janice Lee Romary |

# SOCCER
*Source:* Flannery News Bureau of New York.

## National Challenge Cup
### Emblematic of U. S. Championship
(Senior amateur and professional elevens)

1914 Brooklyn (N. Y.) Field Club
1915–16 Bethlehem (Pa.) Steel Co. F. C.
1917 Fall River (Mass.) Rovers
1918–19 Bethlehem (Pa.) Steel Co. F. C.
1920 Ben Miller F. C., St. Louis, Mo.
1921 Robins Dry Dock F. C., Brooklyn, N. Y.
1922 Scullin Steel F. C., St. Louis, Mo.
1923 Paterson (N. J.) F. C.
1924 Fall River (Mass.) F. C.
1925 Shawsheen S. C., Andover, Mass.
1926 Bethlehem (Pa.) Steel Co. F. C.
1927 Fall River (Mass.) F. C.
1928 New York Nationals S. C.
1929 Hakoah All-Stars, New York
1930–31 Fall River (Mass.) F. C.
1932 New Bedford (Mass.) F. C.
1933–34 Stix, Baer & Fuller F. C., St. Louis, Mo.
1935 Central Breweries S. C., St. Louis, Mo.
1936 First German American S. C., Philadelphia
1937 New York Americans S. C.
1938 Sparta A. B. A., Chicago, Ill.
1939 St. Mary's Celtic S. C., New York
1940 No official champion*
1941 Pawtucket (R. I.) F. C.
1942 Gallatin S. C., Pittsburgh
1943–44 Brooklyn (N. Y.) Hispano S. C.
1945 Brookhattan S. C., New York
1946 Vikings, Chicago
1947 Ponta Delgada F. C., Fall River, Mass.
1948 Joe Simpkins S. C., St. Louis, Mo.
1949 Morgan (Pa.) S. C.
1950 Joe Simpkins S. C., St Louis, Mo.
1951 German-Hungarian S. C., New York
1952 Harmarville (Pa.) S. C.
1953 Chicago Falcons
1954 New York Americans
1955 Eintracht S. C., New York
1956 Harmarville (Pa.) Hurricanes
1957 Kutis, St. Louis
1958 Los Angeles Kickers
1959 McIlwaine Canvasbaks, San Pedro, Calif.
1960 Ukrainian Nationals, Philadelphia

* Finalists: Baltimore (Md.) S. C. and Sparta A. B. A. Chicago, Ill.

## National Amateur Challenge Cup

1923 No official champion*
1924 Fleisher Yarn F. C., Philadelphia
1925 Toledo (Ohio) F. C.
1926 Defenders F. C., New Bedford, Mass.
1927 Heidelberg (Pa.) F. C.
1928 No official champion†
1929 Heidelberg (Pa.) F. C.
1930 Raffies F. C., Fall River, Mass.
1931 Goodyear F. C., Akron, Ohio
1932 Shamrock S. C., Cleveland, Ohio
1933 German American S. C., Philadelphia
1934 German American S. C., Philadelphia
1935 W. W. Riehl S. C., Castle Shannon, Pa.
1936 First German S. C., Brooklyn, N. Y.
1937 Highlander F. C., Trenton, N. J.
1938 Ponta Delgada F. C., Fall River, Mass.
1939 St. Michael's A. C., Fall River, Mass.
1940 Morgan-Strasser S. C., Morgan, Pa.
1941 Fall River (Mass.) S. C.
1942 Fall River (Mass.) S. C.
1943 Morgan-Strasser S. C., Morgan, Pa.
1944 Eintracht S. C., New York
1945 Eintracht S. C., New York
1946 Ponta Delgada F. C., Fall River, Mass.
1947 Ponta Delgada F. C., Fall River, Mass.
1948 Ponta Delgada F. C., Fall River, Mass.
1949 Elizabeth (N. J.) Sport Club
1950 Ponta Delgada F. C., Fall River, Mass.
1951 German-Hungarian S. C., New York
1952 St. Louis Raiders
1953 Ponta Delgada, Fall River, Mass.
1954 Beadling (Pa.) S. C.
1955 Heidelberg (Pa.) Tornadoes
1956 Kutis, St. Louis
1957 Kutis, St. Louis
1958 Kutis, St. Louis
1959 Kutis, St. Louis
1960 Kutis, St. Louis

* Medals to semifinalists: Fleisher Yarn F. C., Philadelphia; Roxbury (Mass.) F. C.; Jeannette (Pa.) F. C.; Swedish American A. A., Chicago, Ill. † Finalists: Powers-Hudson-Essex F. C., Fall River, Mass.; and Swedish American A. C., Detroit, Mich.

## National Collegiate Champions

1959 St. Louis

1960 St. Louis

# BOBSLEDDING
## National Records
Made at Mt. Van Hoevenberg slide, Lake Placid, N. Y., the only bobsled run in America

### Mile Course
(Times in minutes and seconds)

2-man (single heat)—Eugenio Monti–Sergio Siorpaes, Italy (Feb. 12, 1961).......................... 1:09.22
2-man (4 heats)—Eugenio Monti–Sergio Siorpaes, Italy (Feb. 12, 1961)........................ 4:42.67
4-man (single heat)—Stan Benham, driver; Pat Martin; Charles Pandolph; John Helmer, brake, Sno Birds of Lake Placid (Feb. 22, 1957)........ 1:08.88
4-man (4 heats)—Eugenio Monti, Italy, driver; Pat Martin, Massena, N. Y.; Gary Sheffield, Lake Placid, N. Y.; Charles Pandolph, Saranac Lake, N. Y., brake (Feb. 21, 1960).................... 4:38.66

### Half-Mile Course

2-man (single heat)—Stan Benham–Charles Pandolph, Lake Placid B. C. (Jan. 15, 1961)......... 0:38.03
2-man (4 heats)—Fred Fortune–John Young, Lake Placid B. C. (Jan. 3, 1959)..................... 2:36.76
4-man (single heat)—James Bickford, driver; Pat Buckley; Lucien Miron; William Dupree, brake, Saranac Lake B. C. (Jan. 27, 1946)..................... 0:37.08
4-man (4 heats)—James Bickford, driver; Pat Buckley; Lucien Miron; William Dupree, brake, Saranac Lake B. C. (Jan. 27, 1946)..................... 2:29.07

# DOG SHOWS
## Westminster Kennel Club Exhibition

| Year | Best in show | Breed | Owner |
|------|--------------|-------|-------|
| 1907–09 | Ch. Warren Remedy | Fox terrier, smooth | Winthrop Rutherfurd |
| 1910 | Ch. Sabine Rarebit | Fox terrier, smooth | Sabine Kennels |
| 1911 | Ch. Tickle Em Jock | Scottish terrier | A. Albright, Jr. |
| 1912 | Ch. Kenmore Sorceress | Airedale terrier | William P. Wolcott |
| 1913 | Ch. Strathway Prince Albert | Bulldog | Alex H. Stewart |
| 1914 | Ch. Brentwood Hero | Old English sheep dog | Mrs. Tyler Morse |
| 1915–16 | Ch. Matford Vic | Fox terrier, wire | George W. Quintard |
| 1917 | Ch. Conejo Wycollar Boy | Fox terrier, wire | Mrs. Roy A. Rainey |
| 1918 | Ch. Haymarket Faultless | Bull terrier | R. H. Elliot |
| 1919 | Ch. Briergate Bright Beauty | Airedale terrier | G. L. L. Davis |
| 1920 | Ch. Conejo Wycollar Boy | Fox terrier, wire | Mrs. Roy A. Rainey |
| 1921 | Ch. Midkiff Seductive | Cocker spaniel | William T. Payne |
| 1922 | Ch. Boxwood Barkentine | Airedale terrier | Frederic C. Hood |
| 1924 | Ch. Barberryhill Bootlegger | Sealyham terrier | Bayard Warren |
| 1925 | Ch. Governor Moscow | Pointer | Robert F. Maloney |
| 1926 | Ch. Signal Circuit | Fox terrier, wire | Halleston Kennels |
| 1927 | Ch. Pinegrade Perfection | Sealyham terrier | Frederic C. Brown |
| 1928 | Ch. Talavera Margaret | Fox terrier, wire | R. M. Lewis |
| 1929 | Land Loyalty of Bellhaven | Collie | Mrs. Florence B. Ilch |
| 1930–31 | Ch. Pendley Calling of Blarney | Fox terrier, wire | John G. Bates |
| 1932 | Ch. Nancolleth Markable | Pointer | Giralda Farms |
| 1933 | Ch. Warland Protector of Shelterock | Airedale terrier | S. M. Stewart |
| 1934 | Ch. Flornell Spicy Bit of Halleston | Fox terrier, wire | Halleston Kennels |
| 1935 | Ch. Nunsoe Duc de la Terrace of Blakeen | Poodle | Blakeen Kennels |
| 1936 | Ch. St. Margaret Magnificent of Clairedale | Sealyham terrier | Clairedale Kennels |
| 1937 | Ch. Flornell Spicy Piece of Halleston | Fox terrier, wire | Halleston Kennels |
| 1938 | Daro of Maridor | English setter | Maridor Kennels |
| 1939 | Ferry v. Rauhfelsen of Giralda | Doberman pinscher | Giralda Farms |
| 1940–41 | Ch. My Own Brucie | Cocker spaniel | H. E. Mellenthin |
| 1942 | Ch. Wolvey Pattern Edgerstoune | West Highland terrier | Mrs. John G. Winant |
| 1943 | Ch. Pitter Patter of Piperscroft | Miniature poodle | Mrs. P. H. B. Frelinghuysen |
| 1944 | Ch. Flornell Rare-Bit of Twin Ponds | Welsh terrier | Mrs. Edward P. Alker |
| 1945 | Shieling's Signature | Scottish terrier | Mr. and Mrs. T. H. Snethen |
| 1946 | Ch. Hetherington Model Rhythm | Fox terrier, wire | Mr. and Mrs. T. H. Carruthers III |
| 1947 | Ch. Warlord of Mazelaine | Boxer | Mr. and Mrs. R. C. Kettles, Jr. |
| 1948 | Ch. Rock Ridge Night Rocket | Bedlington terrier | Mr. and Mrs. W. A. Rockefeller |
| 1949 | Mazelaine's Zazarac Brandy | Boxer | Mr. and Mrs. John P. Wagner |
| 1950 | Ch. Walsing Winning Trick of Edgerstoune | Scottish terrier | Mrs. John G. Winant |
| 1951 | Ch. Bang Away of Sirrah Crest | Boxer | Dr. and Mrs. R. C. Harris |
| 1952–53 | Ch. Rancho Dobe's Storm | Doberman pinscher | Mr. and Mrs. Len Carey |
| 1954 | Ch. Carmor's Rise and Shine | Cocker Spaniel | Mrs. Carl E. Morgan |
| 1955 | Ch. Kippax Fearnought | Bulldog | Dr. John A. Saylor |
| 1956 | Ch. Wilber White Swan | Toy poodle | Bertha Smith |
| 1957 | Ch. Shirkhan of Grandeur | Afghan | Sunny Shay-Dorothy Chenade |
| 1958 | Ch. Puttencove Promise | Standard poodle | Mr. and Mrs. George Putnam |
| 1959 | Ch. Fontclair Festoon | Miniature Poodle | Clarence Dillon |
| 1960 | Ch. Chik T'Sun of Caversham | Pekingese | Mr. and Mrs. C. C. Venable |

# SKI JUMPING
## National Records

*Source:* Harold A. Grinden, Historian, National Ski Association of America, Duluth, Minn.

| Year | Made by and place | Feet |
|------|-------------------|------|
| 1904 | T. Walters, Ishpeming, Mich. | 82 |
| 1905 | Julius Kulstad, Ishpeming, Mich. | 97½ |
| 1907 | Ole Feiring, Duluth, Minn. | 112 |
| 1907 | Ole Mangseth, Red Wing, Minn. | 114 |
| 1908 | John Evenson, Duluth, Minn. | 116 |
| 1908 | John Mangseth, Duluth, Minn. | 117 |
| 1908 | John Evenson, Ishpeming, Mich. | 122 |
| 1909 | Ole Larson, Eau Claire, Wis. | 131 |
| 1910 | Oscar Gunderson, Chippewa Falls, Wis. | 138 |
| 1910 | August Nordby, Ishpeming, Mich. | 140 |
| 1911 | Anders Haugen, Ironwood, Mich. | 152 |
| 1913 | Ragnar Omtvedt, Ironwood, Mich. | 154–158–169 |
| 1916 | Ragnar Omtvedt, Steamboat Springs, Colo. | 192½ |
| 1917 | Henry Hall, Steamboat Springs, Colo. | 203 |
| 1919 | Anders Haugen, Dillon, Colo. | 213 |
| 1919 | Lars Haugen, Steamboat Springs, Colo. | 214 |
| 1920 | Anders Haugen, Dillon, Colo. | 214 |
| 1932 | Glen Armstrong, Salt Lake City | 224 |
| 1934 | John Elvrum, Big Pines, Calif. | 240 |
| 1937 | Alf Engen, Salt Lake City, Utah | 244.42 |
| 1939 | Alf Engen, Big Pines, Calif. | 251 |
| 1939 | Bob Roecker, Iron Mountain, Mich. | 257 |
| 1941 | Torger Tokle, Leavenworth, Wash. | 273 |
| 1941 | Torger Tokle, Olympian Hill, Hyak, Wash. | 288 |
| 1942 | Torger Tokle, Iron Mountain, Mich. | 289 |
| 1949 | Sverre Kongsgaard, Hyak, Wash. | 290 |
| 1949 | Joe Perrault, Iron Mountain, Mich. | 297 |
| 1950 | Art Devlin, Steamboat Springs, Colo. | 307 |
| 1951 | Ansten Samuelstuen, Steamboat Springs, Colo. | 316 |
| 1959 | Jim Brennan, Iron Mountain, Mich. | 316 |

# TRACK AND FIELD

RUNNING, jumping, hurdling and throwing weights—track and field sports, in other words—are as natural to boys and young men as eating, drinking and breathing. Unorganized competition in this form of sport goes back beyond the Cave Man era. Organized competition begins with the first recorded Olympic Games in Greece, 776 B. C., when Coroebus of Elis won the only event on the program, a race of approximately 200 yards. The Olympic Games, with an ever-widening program of events, continued until "the glory that was Greece" had faded and "the grandeur that was Rome" was tarnished, and finally were abolished by decree of Emperor Theodosius I of Rome in A. D. 394. The Tailteann Games of Ireland are supposed to have antedated the first Olympic Games by some centuries, but we have no records of the specific events and winners thereof.

Professional contests of speed and strength were popular at all times and in many lands, but the widespread competition of amateur athletes in track and field

sports is a comparatively modern development. The first organized amateur athletic meet of record was sponsored by the Royal Military Academy at Woolwich, England, in 1849. Oxford and Cambridge track and field rivalry began in 1864 and the English amateur championships were established in 1866. In the United States such organizations as the New York Athletic Club and the Olympic Club of San Francisco conducted track and field meets in the 1870's, and a few colleges joined to sponsor a meet in 1874. The success of the college meet led to the formation of the Intercollegiate Association of Amateur Athletes of America and the holding of an annual set of championship games beginning in 1876.

Many athletic clubs joined the National Association of Amateur Athletes of America, formed in 1879, but dissension broke up this organization and the Amateur Athletic Union, organized in 1888, has been the ruling body in American amateur athletics since that time.

## Track and Field Statistics

### MEN'S WORLD RECORDS

Recognized by the International Amateur Athletic Federation as of Oct. 1, 1961

#### RUNNING

| Event | Record | Holder | Home country | Where made | Date |
|---|---|---|---|---|---|
| 100 yd | 9.2 s | Frank Budd | United States | New York | June 24, 1961 |
| 220 yd | 20 s | David Sime | United States | Sanger, Calif. | June 9, 1956 |
| 440 yd | 45.7 s | Glenn Davis | United States | Berkeley, Calif. | June 14, 1958 |
| 880 yd | 1 m. 46.8 s | Tom Courtney | United States | Los Angeles | May 24, 1957 |
| 1 mi | 3 m. 54.4 s | Herb Elliott | Australia | Dublin | Aug. 6, 1958 |
| 2 mi | 8 m. 32 s | Albert Thomas | Australia | Dublin | Aug. 7, 1958 |
| 3 mi | 13 m. 10.8 s | Albert Thomas | Australia | Dublin | July 9, 1958 |
| 6 mi | 27 m. 43.8 s | Sandor Iharos | Hungary | Budapest | July 15, 1956 |
| 10 mi | 48 m. 12 s | Emil Zatopek | Czechoslovakia | Boleslav, Czech. | Sept. 29, 1951 |
| 15 mi | 1 h. 14 m. 1 s | Emil Zatopek | Czechoslovakia | Celakovice, Czech. | Oct. 29, 1955 |
| 1 hr | 12 mi. 810 yd | Emil Zatopek | Czechoslovakia | Boleslav, Czech. | Sept. 29, 1951 |

#### RUNNING—METRIC DISTANCES

| Event | Record | Holder | Home country | Where made | Date |
|---|---|---|---|---|---|
| 100 meters | 10 s | Armin Hary | Germany | Zurich, Switzerland | June 21, 1960 |
| | | Harry Jerome | Canada | Saskatoon, Canada | July 15, 1960 |
| 200 m | 20 s | David Sime | United States | Sanger, Calif. | June 9, 1956 |
| 400 m | 44.9 s | Otis Davis | United States | Rome | Sept. 6, 1960 |
| | | Carl Kaufmann | Germany | Rome | Sept. 6, 1960 |
| 800 m | 1 m. 45.7 s | Roger Moens | Belgium | Oslo | Aug. 3, 1955 |
| 1,000 m | 2 m. 16.7 s | Siegfried Valentin | Germany | Potsdam, Germany | July 19, 1960 |
| 1,500 m | 3 m. 35.6 s | Herb Elliott | Australia | Rome | Sept. 6, 1960 |
| 2,000 m | 5 m. 2.2 s | Istvan Rozsavoigyi | Hungary | Budapest | Oct. 2, 1955 |
| 3,000 m | 7 m. 52.8 s | Gordon Pirie | Great Britain | Malmo, Sweden | Sept. 4, 1956 |
| 5,000 m | 13 m. 35 s | Vladimir Kuts | U.S.S.R. | Rome | Oct. 13, 1957 |
| 10,000 m | 28 m. 18.8 s | Peter Bolotnikov | U.S.S.R. | Kiev, U.S.S.R. | Oct. 15, 1960 |
| 20,000 m | 59 m. 51.6 s | Emil Zatopek | Czechoslovakia | Boleslav, Czech. | Sept. 29, 1951 |
| 25,000 m | 1 h. 16 m. 36.4 s | Emil Zatopek | Czechoslovakia | Celakovice, Czech. | Oct. 29, 1955 |
| 30,000 m | 1 h. 35 m. 1 s | Albert Ivanov | U.S.S.R. | Moscow | June 6, 1957 |
| 1 hr | 20,052 meters 40 cm | Emil Zatopek | Czechoslovakia | Boleslav, Czech. | Sept. 29, 1951 |
| 3,000 m. steeplechase | 8 m. 31.4 s | Zdzislaw Krzyskowiak | Poland | Tula, U.S.S.R. | June 26, 1960 |

## WALKING

| Event | Record | Holder | Home country | Where made | Date |
|---|---|---|---|---|---|
| 2 mi. | 12 m. 45 s. | Werner Hardmo | Sweden | Malmo, Sweden | Sept. 1, 1945 |
| 5 mi. | 34 m. 32.8 s. | J. Dolezal | Czechoslovakia | Manchester, Eng. | Oct. 15, 1955 |
| 7 mi. | 48 m. 15.2 s. | Werner Hardmo | Sweden | Kumla, Sweden | Sept. 9, 1945 |
| 10 mi. | 1 h. 10 m. 45.8 s. | J. Dolezal | Czechoslovakia | Boleslav, Czech. | April 30, 1954 |
| 20 mi. | 2 h. 31 m. 33 s. | Anatoli Vedjakov | U.S.S.R. | Moscow | Aug. 23, 1958 |
| 30 mi. | 4 h. 7 m. 11 s. | S. Lobastov | U.S.S.R. | Moscow | Aug. 23, 1958 |
| 1 hr. | 8 mi. 1025 yd. | John Mikaelsson | Sweden | Stockholm | Sept. 1, 1945 |
| 2 hr. | 16 mi. 743 yd. | Anatoli Egorov | U.S.S.R. | Leningrad | July 15, 1959 |

## WALKING—METRIC DISTANCES

| Event | Record | Holder | Home country | Where made | Date |
|---|---|---|---|---|---|
| 3,000 m. | 11 m. 51.8 s. | Werner Hardmo | Sweden | Malmo | Sept. 1, 1945 |
| 5,000 m. | 20 m. 26.8 s. | Werner Hardmo | Sweden | Kumla | July 31, 1945 |
| 10,000 m. | 42 m. 18.3 s. | Grigory Panichkin | U.S.S.R. | Stalinabad | May 7, 1958 |
| 15,000 m. | 1 h. 5 m. 18 s. | Leonid Spirin | U.S.S.R. | Dnepropetrovsk | Sept. 24, 1957 |
| 20,000 m. | 1 h. 27 m. 5 s. | Vladimir Golubnichy | U.S.S.R. | Simferopol, U.S.S.R. | Sept. 23, 1958 |
| 30,000 m. | 2 h. 17 m. 16.8 s. | Anatoli Egorov | U.S.S.R. | Leningrad | July 15, 1959 |
| 50,000 m. | 4 h. 16 m. 8.6 s. | S. Lobastov | U.S.S.R. | Moscow | Aug. 23, 1958 |
| 1 hr. | 13,812 m. | John Mikaelsson | Sweden | Stockholm | Sept. 1, 1945 |
| 2 hr. | 26,249 m. | Anatoli Egorov | U.S.S.R. | Leningrad | July 15, 1959 |

## HURDLES (10 hurdles)

| Event | Record | Holder | Home country | Where made | Date |
|---|---|---|---|---|---|
| 120 yd. | 13.2 s. | Martin Lauer | Germany | Zurich, Switzerland | July 7, 1959 |
| | | Lee Calhoun | United States | Berne, Switzerland | Aug. 21, 1960 |
| 220 yd. | 21.9 s. | Don Styron | United States | Baton Rouge, La. | April 2, 1960 |
| 440 yd. | 49.7 s. | Gerhardus Potgieter | South Africa | Cardiff, Wales | July 22, 1958 |
| 110 m. | 13.2 s. | Martin Lauer | Germany | Zurich, Switzerland | July 7, 1959 |
| | | Lee Calhoun | United States | Berne, Switzerland | Aug. 21, 1960 |
| 200 m. | 21.9 s. | Don Styron | United States | Baton Rouge, La. | April 2, 1960 |
| 400 m. | 49.2 s. | Glenn Davis | United States | Budapest | Aug. 6, 1958 |

## RELAY RACES

| Event | Record | Holder | Home country | Where made | Date |
|---|---|---|---|---|---|
| 440 yd. (4 x 110) | 39.6 s. | University of Texas | United States | Modesto, Calif. | May 30, 1959 |
| | | (Wally Wilson, Eddie Southern, Hollis Gainey, Ralph Alspaugh) | | | |
| 880 yd. (4 x 220) | 1 m. 22.6 s. | Abilene Christian | United States | Modesto, Calif. | May 31, 1958 |
| | | (Bill Woodhouse, Jim Segrist, George Peterson, Bobby Morrow) | | | |
| 1 mi. (4 x 440 yd.) | 3 m. 5.6 s. | National Team | United States | Walnut, Calif. | Aug. 12, 1960 |
| | | (Eddie Southern, Earl Young, Otis Davis, Jack Yerman) | | | |
| 2 mi. (4 x 880 yd.) | 7 m. 19.4 s. | National Team | United States | London | Sept. 14, 1960 |
| | | (Ernie Cunliffe, Tom Murphy, Jack Yerman, Jerry Siebert) | | | |
| 4 mi. (4 x 1 mi.) | 16 m. 25.2 s. | National Team | Hungary | Budapest | Sept. 29, 1959 |
| | | (Lajos Kovacs, Bela Szekeres, Sandhor Iharos, Istvan Rozsavolgyi) | | | |

## RELAY RACES—METRIC DISTANCES

| Event | Record | Holder | Home country | Where made | Date |
|---|---|---|---|---|---|
| 400 m. (4 x 100) | 39.5 s. | National Team | United States | Melbourne | Dec. 1, 1956 |
| | | (T. Baker, L. King, T. Murchison, R. Morrow) | | | |
| | | National Team | Germany | Cologne | Aug. 29, 1958 |
| | | (M. Steinbach, M. Lauer, H. Futterer, M. Germar) | | | |
| | | National Team | Germany | Rome | Sept. 7, 1960 |
| | | (Bernd Cullmann, Armin Hary, Walter Mahlendorf, Martin Lauer) | | | |
| | | National Team | Germany | Rome | Sept. 8, 1960 |
| | | (Bernd Cullmann, Armin Hary, Walter Mahlendorf, Martin Lauer) | | | |
| 800 m. (4 x 200) | 1 m. 22.6 s. | Abilene Christian | United States | Modesto, Calif. | May 31, 1958 |
| | | (Bill Woodhouse, Jim Segrist, George Peterson, Bobby Morrow) | | | |
| 1,600 m. (4 x 400) | 3 m. 2.2 s. | National Team | United States | Rome | Sept. 8, 1960 |
| | | (Jack Yerman, Earl Young, Glenn Davis, Otis Davis) | | | |
| 3,200 m. (4 x 800) | 7 m. 15.8 s. | National Team | Belgium | Brussels | Aug. 8, 1956 |
| | | (A. Bailleux, A. Langenus, E. Leva, R. Moens) | | | |
| 6,000 m. (4 x 1,500) | 15 m. 11.4 s. | National Team | East Germany | Poznan, Poland | Aug. 9, 1958 |
| | | (S. Herman, K. Richtzenhain, H. Reinnagel, S. Valentin) | | | |

## DECATHLON

| Points | | Holder | Home country | Where made | Date |
|---|---|---|---|---|---|
| 8,683 | | Rafer Johnson | United States | Eugene, Ore. | July 8–9, 1960 |

## FIELD EVENTS

| Event | Record | Holder | Home country | Where made | Date |
|---|---|---|---|---|---|
| High jump | 7 ft. 3¾ in. | John Thomas | United States | Palo Alto, Calif. | July 1, 1960 |
| Broad jump | 26 ft. 11¼ in. | Ralph Boston | United States | Walnut, Calif. | Aug. 12, 1960 |
| Hop, step & jump | 55 ft. 10¼ in. | Jozef Schmidt | Poland | Olsztyn, Poland | Aug. 5, 1960 |
| Pole vault | 15 ft. 9¼ in. | Don Bragg | United States | Palo Alto, Calif. | July 2, 1960 |
| Shot put | 65 ft. 10 in. | Bill Nieder | United States | Walnut, Calif. | Aug. 12, 1960 |
| Discus throw | 196 ft. 6½ in. | { Edmund Piatkowski | Poland | Warsaw | June 14, 1959 |
| | | Rink Babka | United States | Walnut, Calif. | Aug. 12, 1960 |
| Javelin throw | 282 ft. 3½ in. | Al Cantello | United States | Compton, Calif. | June 5, 1959 |
| Hammer throw | 230 ft. 9 in. | Harold Connolly | United States | Walnut, Calif. | Aug. 12, 1960 |

# WOMEN'S WORLD RECORDS
## RUNNING

| Event | Record | Holder | Home country | Where made | Date |
|---|---|---|---|---|---|
| 100 yd. | 10.3 s. | Marlene Mathews | Australia | Sydney | Mar. 20, 1958 |
| 220 yd. | 23.2 s. | Betty Cuthbert | Australia | Hobart, Australia | Mar. 7, 1960 |
| 440 yd. | 53.7 s. | Maria Itkina | U.S.S.R. | Krasnodar, U.S.S.R. | Sept. 12, 1959 |
| 880 yd. | 2 m. 6.1 s. | Joy Jordan | Great Britain | Welwyn, England | Sept. 24, 1960 |
| 60 m. | 7.2 s. | Betty Cuthbert | Australia | Sydney | Feb. 27, 1960 |
| 100 m. | 11.3 s. | { Shirley de la Hunty | Australia | Warsaw | Aug. 4, 1955 |
| | | Vera Krepkina | U.S.S.R. | Kiev, U.S.S.R. | Sept. 13, 1958 |
| | | Wilma Rudolph | United States | Rome | Sept. 2, 1960 |
| 200 m. | 22.9 s. | Wilma Rudolph | United States | Corpus Christi, Tex. | July 9, 1960 |
| 400 m. | 53.4 s. | Maria Itkina | U.S.S.R. | Krasnodar, U.S.S.R. | Sept. 12, 1959 |
| 800 m. | 2 m. 4.3 s. | { Ljudmila Shevcova | U.S.S.R. | Moscow | July 3, 1960 |
| | | Ljudmila Shevcova | U.S.S.R. | Rome | Sept. 7, 1960 |

### RELAY RACES

| | | | | | |
|---|---|---|---|---|---|
| 440 yd. (4 x 110) | 45.3 s. | National Team | Gr. Brit. & No. Ire. | Cardiff, Wales | July 26, 1958 |
| | | (H. Young, J. Paul, D. Hyman, V. Weston) | | | |
| 880 yd. (4 x 220) | 1 m. 36 s. | National Team | Germany | Leipzig | July 26, 1958 |
| | | (Hannelore Sadau, Gisela Birkemeyer, Barbara Mayer, Christa Studnick) | | | |
| 1½ mi. (3 x 880 yds.) | 6 m. 36.2 s. | National Team | Hungary | Tata | July 21, 1954 |
| | | (A. Bacskai, A. Oros, A. Kazi) | | | |
| 400 m. (4 x 100) | 44.4 s. | National Team | United States | Rome | Sept. 7, 1960 |
| | | (Martha Hudson, Lucinda Williams, Barbara Jones, Wilma Rudolph) | | | |
| 800 m. (4 x 200) | 1 m. 36 s. | National Team | Germany | Leipzig | July 26, 1958 |
| | | (Hannelore Sadau, Gisela Birkemeyer, Barbara Mayer, Christa Studnick) | | | |
| 2,400 m. (3 x 800) | 6 m. 27.4 s. | National Team | U.S.S.R. | Kiev, U.S.S.R. | Sept. 9, 1958 |
| | | (Lyubov Yanvareva, Dora Kozlova, Ljudmila Shevcova) | | | |

### HURDLES

| | | | | | |
|---|---|---|---|---|---|
| 80 m. | 10.5 s. | Gisela Birkemeyer | Germany | Leipzig, Germany | July 24, 1960 |

### FIELD EVENTS

| | | | | | |
|---|---|---|---|---|---|
| High jump | 6 ft. 1 in. | Iolanda Balas | U.S.S.R. | Bucharest, Rumania | July 10, 1960 |
| Broad jump | 20 ft. 11¾ in. | Hildrun Claus | Germany | Erfurt, Germany | Aug. 7, 1960 |
| Shot put | 58 ft. 4 in. | Tamara Press | U.S.S.R. | Moscow | Aug. 13, 1960 |
| Discus throw | 187 ft. 6 in. | Tamara Press | U.S.S.R. | Rome | Sept. 12, 1960 |
| Javelin throw | 195 ft. 4½ in. | Elvira Ozolina | U.S.S.R. | Bucharest, Rumania | June 4, 1960 |

### PENTATHLON

| Points | Holder | Home country | Where made | Date |
|---|---|---|---|---|
| 4,972 | Irina Press | U.S.S.R. | Kiev, U.S.S.R. | Oct. 17–18, 1960 |

# WEIGHTLIFTING
## National A. A. U. Heavyweight Champions

| | | Lbs. | | | Lbs. | | | Lbs. |
|---|---|---|---|---|---|---|---|---|
| 1928 | Tom Tyler | 760 | 1939 | Steve Stanko | 895 | 1950 | John Davis | 1010 |
| 1929 | William Rohrer | 1045 | 1940 | Steve Stanko | 950½ | 1951 | John Davis | 1062 |
| 1930 | Albert Manger | 1001 | 1941 | Jonn Davis | 1009¾ | 1952 | John Davis | 1002½ |
| 1931 | William Rohrer | 784½ | 1942 | John Davis | 905 | 1953 | John Davis | 990 |
| 1932 | Albert Manger | 704 | 1943 | John Davis | 940 | 1954 | Norbert Schemansky | 1050 |
| 1933 | John Mallo | 760½ | 1944 | Frank Schofro | 850 | 1955 | Paul Anderson | 1145 |
| 1934 | William Good | 1210 | 1945 | H. G. Curtis | 855 | 1956 | Paul Anderson | 1175 |
| 1935 | William Good | 1205 | 1946 | John Davis | 916 | 1957 | Dave Ashman | 955 |
| 1936 | John Grimek | 786½ | 1947 | John Davis | 900 | 1958 | Dave Ashman | 1000 |
| 1937 | David Mayor | 835 | 1948 | John Davis | 1025 | 1959 | Dave Ashman | 1040 |
| 1938 | Steve Stanko | 850 | 1949 | Norbert Schemansky | 885 | 1960 | Jim Bradford | 1085 |

# HISTORY OF THE RECORD FOR THE MILE RUN

| Time | Athlete | Country | Year | Where Made |
|---|---|---|---|---|
| 4:56.0 | Charles Lawes | England | 1864 | England |
| 4:36.5 | Richard Webster | England | 1865 | England |
| 4:29.0 | William Chinnery | England | 1868 | England |
| 4:28.8 | W. C. Gibbs | England | 1868 | England |
| 4:26.0 | Walter Slade | England | 1874 | England |
| 4:24.5 | Walter Slade | England | 1875 | London, England |
| 4:23.2 | Walter George | England | 1880 | London, England |
| 4:21.4 | Walter George | England | 1882 | London, England |
| 4:19.4 | Walter George | England | 1882 | London, England |
| 4:18.4 | Walter George | England | 1884 | Birmingham, England |
| 4:18.2 | Fred Bacon | Scotland | 1894 | Edinburgh, Scotland |
| 4:17.0 | Fred Bacon | Scotland | 1895 | London, England |
| 4:15.6 | Thomas Conneff | United States | 1895 | Travers Island, N. Y. |
| 4:15.4 | John Paul Jones | United States | 1911 | Cambridge, Mass. |
| 4:14.4 | John Paul Jones | United States | 1913 | Cambridge, Mass. |
| 4:12.6 | Norman Taber | United States | 1915 | Cambridge, Mass. |
| 4:10.4 | Paavo Nurmi | Finland | 1923 | Stockholm, Sweden |
| 4:09.2 | Jules Ladoumegue | France | 1931 | Paris, France |
| 4:07.6 | Jack Lovelock | New Zealand | 1933 | Princeton, N. J. |
| 4:06.8 | Glenn Cunningham | United States | 1934 | Princeton, N. J. |
| 4:06.4 | Sydney Wooderson | England | 1937 | London, England |
| 4:06.2 | Gunder Hagg | Sweden | 1942 | Göteborg, Sweden |
| 4:06.2 | Arne Andersson | Sweden | 1942 | Stockholm, Sweden |
| 4:04.6 | Gunder Hägg | Sweden | 1942 | Stockholm, Sweden |
| 4:02.6 | Arne Andersson | Sweden | 1943 | Göteborg, Sweden |
| 4:01.6 | Arne Andersson | Sweden | 1944 | Malmö, Sweden |
| 4:01.4 | Gunder Hägg | Sweden | 1945 | Malmö, Sweden |
| 3:59.4 | Roger Bannister | England | 1954 | Oxford, England |
| 3:58.0 | John Landy | Australia | 1954 | Turku, Finland |
| 3:57.2 | Derek Ibbotson | England | 1957 | London, England |
| 3:54.5 | Herb Elliott | Australia | 1958 | Dublin, Ireland |

## WORLD'S FASTEST MILES

Until May 6, 1954, the day Roger Bannister of England ran the mile in 3 minutes 59.4 seconds, many observers clung to the belief it was impossible for man to dip below four minutes.

The progress man has made since is best illustrated by the performance of Albert Thomas, an Australian, four years after Bannister's epic feat. Competing in Dublin, Ireland, on Aug. 6, 1958, Thomas went by the finish line in 3:58.6, four-fifths of a second faster than Bannister's clocking, and netted no more than a dismal fifth place in the race! It was in this race that Herb Elliott, Thomas' countryman, shattered the world record with a time of 3:54.5.

By the end of August, 1961, the mile had been run under four minutes a total of 69 times by 26 men. Led by Elliott, who had 17 such performances, five Australian runners had accounted for 31 of these efforts. Seven miles under four minutes had been recorded by United States athletes. Don Bowden of California did 3:58.7 on June 1, 1957. Dyrol Burleson of Oregon and Jim Beatty of North Carolina followed with three such performances each.

| Time | Athlete | Country | Date | Where Made |
|---|---|---|---|---|
| 3:54.5 | Herb Elliott | Australia | Aug. 6, 1958 | Dublin, Ireland |
| 3:55.4 | Herb Elliott | Australia | Sept. 3, 1958 | London, England |
| 3:55.9a | Merv Lincoln | Australia | Aug. 6, 1958 | Dublin, Ireland |
| 3:56.5 | Siegfried Valentin | Germany | May 28, 1959 | Frankfurt, Germany |
| 3:57.0 | Herb Elliott | Australia | Sept. 23, 1960 | Dublin, Ireland |
| 3:57.2 | Derek Ibbotson | England | July 19, 1957 | London, England |
| 3:57.5b | Ron Delany | Ireland | Aug. 6, 1958 | Dublin, Ireland |
| 3:57.5c | Murray Halberg | New Zealand | Aug. 6, 1958 | Dublin, Ireland |
| 3:57.6 | Dyrol Burleson | United States | May 24, 1961 | Eugene, Ore. |
| 3:57.8 | Herb Elliott | Australia | May 16, 1958 | Los Angeles, Calif. |
| 3:57.9 | Herb Elliott | Australia | June 21, 1958 | Bakersfield, Calif. |
| 3:58.0 | John Landy | Australia | June 21, 1954 | Turku, Finland |
| 3:58.0 | Herb Elliott | Australia | Aug. 29, 1958 | Malmö, Sweden |
| 3:58.0 | Jim Beatty | United States | May 28, 1960 | Modesto, Calif. |
| 3:58.1 | Herb Elliott | Australia | June 6, 1958 | Compton, Calif. |
| 3:58.4 | Derek Ibbotson | England | June 15, 1957 | Glasgow, Scotland |
| 3:58.5 | Dan Waern | Sweden | Sept. 4, 1957 | Malmö, Sweden |
| 3:58.5a | Merv Lincoln | Australia | June 21, 1958 | Bakersfield, Calif. |

aFinished second.  bFinished third.  cFinished fourth.

# WORLD ALL-TACKLE FISHING RECORDS

## Caught with Rod and Reel in Salt Water

*Source:* International Game Fish Association.

| Species | Lb., oz. | Length | Girth | Where caught | Year | Angler |
|---|---|---|---|---|---|---|
| Albacore | 69 | 42″ | 32½″ | St. Helena | 1956 | P. Allen |
| Amberjack | 120—8 | 62″ | 40″ | Kona, Hawaii | 1955 | C. W. McAlpin |
| Barracuda | 103—4 | 66″ | 31¼″ | West End, Bahamas | 1932 | C. E. Benet |
| Bass, Calif. Black Sea | 514 | 86″ | 82″ | San Clemente, Calif. | 1955 | J. Patterson |
| Bass, Calif. White Sea | 83—12 | 65½″ | 34″ | Baja California, Mex. | 1953 | L. C. Baumgardner |
| Bass, Channel | 83 | 52″ | 29″ | Cape Charles, Va. | 1949 | Zack Waters, Jr. |
| Bass, Sea | 8 | 22″ | 19″ | Nantucket Sound, Mass. | 1951 | H. R. Rider |
| Bass, Giant Sea | 551 | 100″ | .... | Galveston Bay, Texas | 1937 | G. Pangarakis |
| Bass, Striped | 73 | 60″ | 30½″ | Vineyard Sound, Mass. | 1913 | C. B. Church |
| Blackfish (Tautog) | 21—6 | 31½″ | 23½″ | Cape May, N. J. | 1954 | R. N. Sheafer |
| Bluefish | 24—3 | 41″ | 22″ | San Miguel, Azores | 1953 | M. da Silva Veloso |
| Bonito, Oceanic | 39—15 | 39″ | 28″ | Walker Cay, Bahamas | 1952 | F. Drowley |
| Cobia | 102 | 70″ | 34″ | Cape Charles, Va. | 1938 | J. E. Stansbury |
| Cod | 74—4 | 66″ | 43″ | Boothbay Harbor, Me. | 1960 | James J. Duggan |
| Dolphin | 76 | 63″ | .... | Acapulco, Mexico | 1957 | R. G. Stotsbery |
| Drum, Black | 94—4 | 51½″ | 42″ | Cape Charles, Va. | 1957 | James L. Johnson |
| Flounder, Summer | 21—4 | 36½″ | 35″ | Martencillo, Chile | 1959 | D. V. Serrano |
| Kingfish | 81 | 71½″ | 29¼″ | Karachi, Pakistan | 1960 | George E. Rusinak |
| Marlin, Black | 1560 | 174″ | 81″ | Cabo Blanco, Peru | 1953 | A. C. Glassel, Jr. |
| Marlin, Blue | 780 | 156¾″ | 66″ | San Juan, P. R. | 1959 | Eric Widdowson |
| Marlin, Pacific Blue | 1003 | 168″ | 80″ | Kona, Hawaii | 1960 | Jim Schultz |
| Marlin, Silver | 911 | 160″ | 76″ | Kona, Hawaii | 1957 | Dale Scott |
| Marlin, Striped | 692 | 161″ | .... | Balboa, California | 1931 | A. Hamann |
| Marlin, White | 161 | 104″ | 33″ | Miami, Florida | 1938 | L. F. Hooper |
| Pollack | 42 | 52″ | 39″ | Scituate, Mass | 1960 | Francis C. Ward |
| Roosterfish | 114 | 64″ | 33″ | La Paz, Mexico | 1960 | Abe Sackheim |
| Sailfish, Atlantic | 141 | 101″ | .... | Ivory Coast, Africa | 1961 | Tony Burnand |
| Sailfish, Pacific | 221 | 129″ | .... | Santa Cruz Is., Galapagos Is. | 1947 | C. W. Stewart |
| Sawfish | 890—8 | 193″ | 92″ | Fort Amador, Canal Zone | 1960 | Jack Wagner |
| Shark, Mako | 1000 | 144″ | .... | Mayor Island, N. Z. | 1943 | B. D. H. Ross |
| Shark, Porbeagle | 366—8 | 100″ | 46″ | Montauk, N. Y. | 1960 | D. P. Walker |
| Shark, Thresher | 922 | .... | .... | Bay of Islands, N. Z. | 1937 | W. W. Dowding |
| Shark, Tiger | 1422 | 163″ | 95″ | Cape Moreton, Australia | 1958 | J. H. Robinson |
| Shark, White | 2664 | 202″ | 114″ | South Australia | 1959 | Alfred Dean |
| Snook (Robalo) | 50—8 | 55″ | .... | Gatun Spillway, Canal Zone | 1944 | J. W. Anderson |
| Swordfish | 1182 | 179¼″ | 78″ | Iquique, Chile | 1953 | L. E. Marron |
| Tarpon | 283 | 86 3/5″ | .... | Lake Maracaibo, Venezuela | 1956 | M. Salazar |
| Tuna, Allison (Yellowfin) | 266—8 | 82½″ | 49½″ | Kona, Hawaii | 1959 | Brooks Kelley |
| Tuna, Atlantic Big-Eyed | 295 | 78½″ | 40″ | San Miguel, Azores | 1960 | Arsenio Cordeiro |
| Tuna, Blackfin | 44—8 | 41½″ | 28½″ | Capetown, South Africa | 1957 | G. B. Mercorio |
| Tuna, Bluefin | 977 | 116″ | 94½″ | St. Ann Bay, Nova Scotia | 1950 | D. McI. Hodgson |
| Tuna, Pacific Big-Eyed | 435 | 93″ | 63½″ | Cabo Blanco, Peru | 1957 | R. V. A. Lee |
| Weakfish | 17—8 | 46″ | 19″ | Mullica River, N. J. | 1944 | A. Weisbecker, Jr. |
| Weakfish, Spotted | 15—3 | 34½″ | 20½″ | Fort Pierce, Fla. | 1949 | C. W. Hubbard |
| Yellowtail | 105—12½ | 65″ | 40″ | Bahia de Topolobampo, Mexico | 1955 | M. A. Yant |

## Caught with Rod and Reel in Fresh Water

*Source:* Mary Ball, *Field & Stream.*

| Species | Lb., oz. | Length | Girth | Where caught | Year | Angler |
|---|---|---|---|---|---|---|
| Black Bass, Largemouth | 22—4 | 32½″ | 28½″ | Montgomery Lake, Ga. | 1932 | George W. Perry |
| Black Bass, Smallmouth | 11—15 | 27″ | 21⅔″ | Dale Hollow Lake, Ky. | 1955 | David L. Hayes |
| Bluegill (Sunfish) | 4—12 | 15″ | 18¼″ | Ketona Lake, Ala. | 1950 | T. S. Hudson |
| Carp | 55—5 | 42″ | 31″ | Clearwater Lake, Minn. | 1952 | Frank J. Ledwein |
| Catfish, Channel | 57 | 44.2″ | 32.8″ | Santee Cooper Res., S. C. | 1960 | C. B. Dennis |
| Dolly Varden | 32 | 40½″ | 29¾″ | Lake Pend Oreille, Idaho | 1949 | N. L. Higgins |
| Muskellunge | 69—15 | 64½″ | 31¾″ | St. Lawrence River, N. Y. | 1957 | Arthur Lawton |
| Perch, White | 4—12 | 19½″ | 13″ | Messalonskee Lake, Maine | 1949 | Mrs. Earl Small |
| Perch, Yellow | 4—3½ | .... | .... | Bordentown, New Jersey | 1865 | Dr. C. C. Abbot |
| Pickerel, Eastern chain | 9—6 | 31″ | 14″ | Homerville, Ga. | 1961 | Baxley McQuaig, Jr. |
| Pike, Northern | 46—2 | 52½″ | 25″ | Sacandaga Reservoir, N. Y. | 1940 | Peter Dubuc |
| Salmon, Atlantic | 79—2 | .... | .... | Tanaelv, Norway | 1928 | Henrik Henriksen |
| Salmon, Chinook | 92 | 58½″ | 36″ | Skeena River, B. C. | 1959 | Heinz Wichmann |
| Salmon, Landlocked | 22—8 | 36″ | .... | Sebago Lake, Maine | 1907 | Edward Blakely |
| Salmon, Silver | 31 | .... | .... | Cowichan Bay, B. C. | 1947 | Mrs. Lee Hallberg |
| Trout, Brook | 14—8 | 31½″ | 11½″ | Nipigon River, Ontario | 1916 | Dr. W. J. Cook |
| Trout, Brown | 39—8 | .... | .... | Loch Awe, Scotland | 1866 | W. Muir |
| Trout, Lake | 63—2 | 51½″ | 32¾″ | Lake Superior | 1952 | Hubert Hammers |
| Trout, Rainbow or Steelhead | 37 | 40½″ | 28″ | Lake Pend Oreille, Idaho | 1947 | Wes Hamlet |
| Walleye | 25 | 41″ | 29″ | Cedar Bluff, Tenn. | 1960 | Mabry Harper |

# SWIMMING

THERE IS THE ancient tale of Leander of Abydos swimming the Hellespont nightly to call on Helen of Sestos, but nobody kept the time on his trips. However, Lord Byron swam one leg of the old Leander course, Sestos to Abydos, on May 3, 1810, in 1 hour 10 minutes. The famous British poet was a noted swimmer and once, in an endurance trial at Venice, was in the water for 4 hours 10 minutes. Distance swimming was the early type of competition. Captain Matthew Webb achieved fame by being the first to swim the English Channel—Dover to Calais—in August, 1875, in 21 hours 45 minutes. Many other swimmers, men and women, have conquered the Channel since that time. Gertrude Ederle, of New York City, was the first woman to accomplish the feat. Miss Ederle swam the Channel Aug. 6, 1926, in 14 hours 34 minutes, breaking the existing record at that time. Since then the record has been lowered by a number of men and women.

Regular competition at short as well as long distances and indoor as well as outdoor came with the development of such organizations as the Amateur Athletic Union and the building of indoor and outdoor swimming pools. Swimming has been on the Olympic program since the start of the modern Olympic Games at Athens in 1896.

## WORLD RECORDS

In a move to end confusion over world records, the International Amateur Swimming Federation (F.I.N.A.) began in 1957 to recognize only those marks which are made in 50-meter or 55-yard pools. As of May 1, 1957, all previously recognized records established in pools of other lengths were wiped out. Some of these were replaced when F.I.N.A. certified new records later in 1957 and again in following years. The record list which follows was approved by the federation on Sept. 3, 1960, upon the conclusion of the Olympic swimming program in Rome.

### Men

#### FREE STYLE

| Distance | Record | Holder | Country | Where Made | Date |
|---|---|---|---|---|---|
| 100 meters | 0:54.6 | John Devitt | Australia | Brisbane | Jan. 28, 1957 |
| 110 yards | 0:55.1 | John Devitt | Australia | Sydney | Feb. 7, 1959 |
| 200 meters | 2:01.5 | Tsuyoshi Yamanaka | Japan | Osaka, Japan | July 26, 1959 |
| 220 yards | 2:01.6 | Jon Konrads | Australia | Sydney | Feb. 20, 1960 |
| 400 meters | 4:15.9 | Jon Konrads | Australia | Sydney | Feb. 23, 1960 |
| 440 yards | 4:15.9 | Jon Konrads | Australia | Sydney | Feb. 23, 1960 |
| 800 meters | 8:59.6 | Jon Konrads | Australia | Sydney | Jan. 10, 1959 |
| 800 yards | 8:59.6 | Jon Konrads | Australia | Sydney | Jan. 10, 1959 |
| 1,500 meters | 17:11.0 | Jon Konrads | Australia | Sydney | Feb. 27, 1960 |
| 1,650 yards | 17:11.0 | Jon Konrads | Australia | Sydney | Feb. 27, 1960 |

#### BREASTSTROKE

| 100 meters | 1:11.5 | W. Minaschkin | U.S.S.R. | Leipzig, Germany | Sept. 15, 1957 |
|---|---|---|---|---|---|
| 110 yards | 1:12.4 | Terry Gathercole | Australia | Townsville, Australia | June 28, 1958 |
| 200 meters | 2:36.5 | Terry Gathercole | Australia | Townsville, Australia | June 28, 1958 |
| 220 yards | 2:36.5 | Terry Gathercole | Australia | Townsville, Australia | June 28, 1958 |

#### BUTTERFLY

| 100 meters | 0:58.7 | Lance Larson | United States | Toledo | July 24, 1960 |
|---|---|---|---|---|---|
| 100 yards | 1:00.5 | Lance Larson | United States | Culver City, Calif. | July 8, 1960 |
| 200 meters | 2:12.8 | Mike Troy | United States | Rome | Sept. 2, 1960 |
| 220 yards | 2:17.5 | Neville Hayes | Australia | Townsville, Australia | Aug. 6, 1960 |

#### BACKSTROKE

| 100 meters | 1:01.5 | John Monckton | Australia | Melbourne | Feb. 15, 1958 |
|---|---|---|---|---|---|
| 110 yards | 1:01.5 | John Monckton | Australia | Melbourne | Feb. 15, 1958 |
| 200 meters | 2:16.0 | Tom Stock | United States | Toledo | July 24, 1960 |
| 220 yards | 2:18.4 | John Monckton | Australia | Melbourne | Feb. 18, 1958 |

#### INDIVIDUAL MEDLEY

| 400 meters | 5:04.5 | Dennis Rounsavelle | United States | Toledo | July 24, 1960 |
|---|---|---|---|---|---|
| 440 yards | 5:08.8 | Ian Black | Great Britain | Cardiff | June 6, 1959 |

## FREE STYLE RELAYS

| Distance | Record | Holder | Country | Where Made | Date |
|---|---|---|---|---|---|
| 400 meters | 3:44.4 | National Team | United States | Tokyo | July 21, 1959 |
| | | (Elton Follett, Lance Larson, Jeff Farrell, Joe Alkire) | | | |
| 440 yards | 3:45.7 | National Team | Australia | Townsville, Australia | Aug. 2, 1960 |
| | | (Geoffrey Shipton, John Devitt, Jon Henricks, Dave Dickson) | | | |
| 800 meters | 8:10.2 | National Team | United States | Rome | Sept. 1, 1960 |
| | | (George Harrison, Dick Blick, Mike Troy, Jeff Farrell) | | | |
| 880 yards | 8:16.6 | National Team | Australia | Townsville, Australia | Aug. 6, 1960 |
| | | (Jon Henricks, Dave Dickson, Jon Konrads, Murray Rose) | | | |

## MEDLEY RELAYS
### (Back, Breast, Butterfly, Free Style)

| Distance | Record | Holder | Country | Where Made | Date |
|---|---|---|---|---|---|
| 400 meters | 4:05.4 | National Team | United States | Rome | Sept. 1, 1960 |
| | | (Frank McKinney, Paul Hait, Lance Larson, Jeff Farrell) | | | |
| 440 yards | 4:14.2 | National Team | Australia | Cardiff | July 25, 1958 |
| | | (John Monckton, Terry Gathercole, Brian Wilkinson, John Devitt) | | | |

# Women
## FREE STYLE

| Distance | Record | Holder | Country | Where Made | Date |
|---|---|---|---|---|---|
| 100 meters | 1:00.2 | Dawn Fraser | Australia | Sydney | Feb. 23, 1960 |
| 110 yards | 1:00.2 | Dawn Fraser | Australia | Sydney | Feb. 23, 1960 |
| 200 meters | 2:11.6 | Dawn Fraser | Australia | Sydney | Feb. 27, 1960 |
| 220 yards | 2:11.6 | Dawn Fraser | Australia | Sydney | Feb. 27, 1960 |
| 400 meters | 4:44.5 | Chris von Saltza | United States | Detroit | Aug. 5, 1960 |
| 440 yards | 4:45.4 | Ilsa Konrads | Australia | Sydney | Jan. 9, 1960 |
| 800 meters | 9:55.6 | Jane Cederqvist | Sweden | Uppsala, Sweden | Aug. 17, 1960 |
| 880 yards | 10:11.4 | Ilsa Konrads | Australia | Hobart, Australia | Feb. 19, 1959 |
| 1,500 meters | 19:25.7 | Ilsa Konrads | Australia | Sydney | Jan. 14, 1959 |
| 1,650 yards | 19:25.7 | Ilsa Konrads | Australia | Sydney | Jan. 14, 1959 |

## BREASTSTROKE

| Distance | Record | Holder | Country | Where Made | Date |
|---|---|---|---|---|---|
| 100 meters | 1:19.0 | U. Kuper | Germany | Leipzig, Germany | July 14, 1960 |
| 110 yards | 1:21.2 | Rosemary Lassig | Australia | Bundaberg, Australia | Jan. 7, 1960 |
| 200 meters | 2:49.5 | Anita Lonsbrough | Great Britain | Rome | Aug. 27, 1960 |
| 220 yards | 2:52.5 | Ada den Haan | Netherlands | Blackpool | May 18, 1957 |

## BUTTERFLY

| Distance | Record | Holder | Country | Where Made | Date |
|---|---|---|---|---|---|
| 100 meters | 1:09.1 | Nancy Ramey | United States | Chicago | Sept. 2, 1959 |
| 110 yards | 1:10.8 | Dawn Fraser | Australia | Sydney | Feb. 23, 1960 |
| 200 meters | 2:34.4 | Marianne Heemskirk | Netherlands | Leipzig, Germany | June 12, 1960 |
| 220 yards | 2:37.0 | Becky Collins | United States | Redding, Calif. | July 19, 1959 |

## BACKSTROKE

| Distance | Record | Holder | Country | Where Made | Date |
|---|---|---|---|---|---|
| 100 meters | 1:09.2 | Lynn Burke | United States | Detroit | Aug. 5, 1960 |
| 110 yards | 1:11.9 | Judy Grinham | Great Britain | Cardiff | July 23, 1958 |
| 200 meters | 2:33.3 | Satoko Tanaka | Japan | Tokyo | July 23, 1960 |
| 220 yards | 2:37.2 | Marilyn Wilson | Australia | Townsville, Australia | Aug. 4, 1960 |

## INDIVIDUAL MEDLEY

| Distance | Record | Holder | Country | Where Made | Date |
|---|---|---|---|---|---|
| 400 meters | 5:36.5 | Donna de Varona | United States | Indianapolis | July 15, 1960 |
| 440 yards | 5:40.2 | Sylvia Ruuska | United States | Redding, Calif. | July 17, 1959 |

## FREE STYLE RELAYS

| Distance | Record | Holder | Country | Where Made | Date |
|---|---|---|---|---|---|
| 400 meters | 4:08.9 | National Team | United States | Rome | Sept. 3, 1960 |
| | | (Joan Spillane, Shirley Stobs, Carolyn Wood, Chris von Saltza) | | | |
| 440 yards | 4:16.2 | National Team | Australia | Townsville, Australia | Aug. 6, 1960 |
| | | (Dawn Fraser, Alva Colquhoun, Ilsa Konrads, Lorraine Crapp) | | | |

## MEDLEY RELAYS
### (Back, Breast, Butterfly, Free Style)

| Distance | Record | Holder | Country | Where Made | Date |
|---|---|---|---|---|---|
| 400 meters | 4:41.1 | National Team | United States | Rome | Sept. 2, 1960 |
| | | (Lynn Burke, Patty Kempner, Carolyn Schuler, Chris von Saltza) | | | |
| 440 yards | 4:50.2 | National Team | Australia | Townsville, Australia | Aug. 4, 1960 |
| | | (Gerry Beckett, Rosemary Lassig, Janice Andrew, Dawn Fraser) | | | |

## Olympic Emblem Protected by Law

Federal law forbids the use of the Olympic emblem or the words, "Olympic" and "Olympiad" for business or advertising purposes or for theatrical or athletic performances to any persons, corporations, or associations other than the United States Olympic Association, its subordinate organizations, and its employees and officers.

# COLLEGE COLORS AND NICKNAMES

Air Force—Silver-Blue; Falcons
Akron—Blue-Gold; Zips
Alabama—Crimson-White; Crimson Tide
Alfred—Purple-Gold; Saxons
Amherst—Purple-White; Lord Jeffs
Arizona—Crimson-Blue; Wildcats
Arizona State (Tempe)—Maroon-Gold; Sun Devils
Arkansas—Cardinal-White; Razorbacks
Army—Black-Gold-Gray; Cadets
Auburn—Orange-Blue; Tigers
Baylor—Green-Gold; Bears
Boston Coll.—Maroon-Gold; Eagles
Boston U.—Scarlet-White; Terriers
Bowdoin—White; Polar Bears
Bowling Green—Brown-Orange; Falcons
Bradley—Cardinal-White; Braves
Brigham Young—Blue-White; Cougars
Brooklyn—Maroon-Gold; Kingsmen
Brown—Brown-White; Bruins
Bucknell—Orange-Blue; Bisons
Buffalo—Blue-White; Bulls
Butler—Blue-White; Bulldogs
California—Blue-Gold; Golden Bears
Canisius—Blue-Gold; Griffins
Carnegie Tech—Tartan Plaid; Tartans
Catholic—Red-Black; Cardinals
Centre—Gold-White; Colonels
Chicago—Maroon; Maroons
Cincinnati—Red-Black; Bearcats
Citadel—Blue-White; Bulldogs
City Coll. of N. Y.—Lavender; Beavers
Clemson—Purple-Orange; Tigers
Coast Guard—Blue-White; Cadets
Colgate—Maroon; Red Raiders
Coll. of Pacific—Orange-Black; Tigers
Colorado—Silver-Gold; Buffaloes
Columbia—Blue-White; Lions
Connecticut—Blue-White; Huskies, Uconns
Cornell—Carnelian-White; Big Red
Creighton—White-Blue; Blue Jays
Dartmouth—Green; Indians
Davidson—Red-Black; Wildcats
Dayton—Red-Blue; Flyers
Delaware—Blue-Gold; Blue Hens
Denver—Red-Gold; Pioneers
DePaul—Scarlet-Blue; Blue Demons
Detroit—Cardinal-White; Titans
Drake—White-Blue; Bulldogs
Duke—Blue-White; Blue Devils
Duquesne—Red-Blue; Dukes
Florida—Orange-Blue; Gators
Franklin & Marshall—Blue-White; Diplomats
Fordham—Maroon; Rams
Furman—Purple-White; Purple Hurricane
Georgetown—Blue-Gray; Hoyas
George Washington—Buff-Blue; Colonials
Georgia—Red-Black; Bulldogs
Georgia Tech—White-Gold; Yellow Jackets
Gonzaga—Blue-White; Bulldogs
Hamilton—Buff-Blue; Continentals
Hampden-Sydney—Garnet-Gray; Tigers
Hardin-Simmons—Purple-Gold; Cowboys
Harvard—Crimson; The Crimson
Hobart—Orange-Purple; Statesmen

Holy Cross—Purple; Crusaders
Houston—Scarlet-White; Cougars
Howard—Blue-White; Bisons
Idaho—Silver-Gold; Vandals
Illinois—Orange-Blue; Illini
Indiana—Cream-Crimson; Hoosiers
Iowa—Gold-Black; Hawkeyes
Iowa State—Cardinal-Gold; Cyclones
Johns Hopkins—Blue-Black; Blue Jays
Kansas—Crimson-Blue; Jayhawkers
Kansas State—Purple-White; Wildcats
Kentucky—Blue-White; Wildcats
Knox—Purple-Gold; Siwashers
Lafayette—Maroon-White; Leopards
La Salle—Blue-Gold; Explorers
Lehigh—Brown-White; Engineers
Louisiana State—Purple-Gold; Tigers
Louisville—Cardinal-Black; Cardinals
Loyola (Ill.)—Maroon-Gold; Ramblers
Maine—Blue-White; Black Bears
Manhattan—Green-White; Jaspers
Marquette—Blue-Gold; Warriors
Maryland—Red-White; Terrapins
Massachusetts—Maroon-White; Redmen
Merchant Marine—Blue-Gray; Mariners
Miami (Fla.)—Orange-Green-White; Hurricanes
Miami (Ohio)—Red-White; Redskins
Michigan—Maize-Blue; Wolverines
Michigan State—Green-White; Spartans
Middlebury—Blue-White; Panthers
Minnesota—Maroon-Gold; Gophers
Mississippi—Red-Blue; Rebels
Mississippi State—Maroon-White; Maroons
Missouri—Black-Gold; Tigers
M.I.T.—Cardinal-Gray; Beavers
Montana—Copper-Silver-Gold; Grizzlies
Navy—Blue-Gold; Midshipmen
Nebraska—Scarlet-Cream; Cornhuskers
Nevada—Silver-Blue; Wolfpack
New Hampshire—Blue-White; Wildcats
New Mexico—Cherry-Silver; Lobos
New York U.—Violet; Violets
Niagara—Purple-White; Purple Eagles
North Carolina—Blue-White; Tar Heels
North Carolina State—Scarlet-White; Wolfpack
North Dakota—Green-White; Sioux
Northeastern—Red-Black; Huskies
Northwestern—Purple-White; Wildcats
Notre Dame—Blue-Gold; Fighting Irish
Occidental—Orange-Black; Bengals
Ohio State—Scarlet-Gray; Buckeyes
Ohio U.—Green-White; Bobcats
Oklahoma—Red-White; Sooners
Oklahoma State—Orange-Black; Cowboys
Omaha—Red-Black; Indians
Oregon—Yellow-Green; Webfoots
Oregon State—Orange-Black; Beavers
Penn State—Blue-White; Nittany Lions
Pennsylvania—Red-Blue; Quakers
Pittsburgh—Blue-Gold; Panthers
Princeton—Orange-Black; Tigers
Providence—Black-White; Friars
Purdue—Gold-Black; Boilermakers
Rhode Island—Blue-White; Rams
Rice—Blue-Gray; Owls

Richmond—Red-Blue; Spiders
Rochester—Yellow; Yellowjackets
Rollins—Blue-Gold; Tars
R.P.I.—Cherry-White; Engineers
Rutgers—Scarlet; The Scarlet
St. Francis (N. Y.)—Red-Blue; Terriers
St. John's (N. Y.)—Red-White; Redmen
St. Joseph's (Pa.)—Crimson-Gray; Hawks
St. Lawrence—Scarlet-Brown; Larries
St. Louis—Blue-White; Billikens
St. Mary's (Calif.)—Red-Blue; Galloping Gaels
San Francisco—Green-Gold; Dons
San Jose State—Gold-White; Spartans
Santa Clara—Cardinal-White; Broncos
Seattle—Maroon-White; Chieftains
Seton Hall—Blue-White; Pirates
Sewanee—Purple-White; Tigers
South Carolina—Garnet-Black; Gamecocks
South Dakota—Scarlet-White; Coyotes
So. California—Cardinal-Gold; Trojans
So. Methodist—Red-Blue; Mustangs
Springfield—Maroon-White; Maroons
Stanford—Cardinal-White; Indians
Swarthmore—Garnet; Little Quakers
Syracuse—Orange; Orangemen
Temple—Cherry-White; Owls
Tennessee—Orange-White; Vols
Texas—Orange-White; Longhorns
Texas A. & M.—Maroon-White; Aggies
Texas Christian—Purple-White; Horned Frogs
Texas Tech—Scarlet-Black; Red Raiders
Toledo—Blue-Gold; Rockets
Tufts—Blue-Brown; Jumbos
Tulane—Green-Blue; Green Wave
Tulsa—Crimson-Blue-Gold; Golden Hurricane
Tuskegee—Gold-Crimson; Golden Tigers
U.C.L.A.—Blue-Gold; Bruins
Utah—Crimson-White; Utes
Utah State—Blue-White; Aggies
Vanderbilt—Gold-Black; Commodores
Vermont—Green-Gold; Catamounts
Villanova—Blue-White; Wildcats
Virginia—Blue-Orange; Cavaliers
V.M.I.—Red-White-Yellow; Keydets
V.P.I.—Orange-Maroon; Gobblers
Wake Forest—Gold-Black; Demon Deacons
Washington & Lee—Blue-White; Generals
Washington (Mo.)—Myrtle-Maroon; Bears
Washington (Wash.)—Purple-Gold; Huskies
Washington State—Crimson-Gray; Cougars
Wayne State—Green-Gold; Tartars
Wesleyan—Cardinal-Black; Cardinals
Western Reserve—Red-White; Red Cats
W. Virginia—Gold-Blue; Mountaineers
Wichita—Black-Gold; Wheatshockers
William & Mary—Green-Gold-Silver; Indians
Williams—Royal Purple; Ephmen
Wisconsin—Cardinal; Badgers
Wyoming—Brown-Gold; Cowboys
Yale—Blue; Bulldogs, Elis

# HORSE RACING

ANCIENT DRAWINGS on stone and bone prove that horse racing is at least 3000 years old, but Thoroughbred Racing is a modern development. Practically every thoroughbred in training today traces its registered ancestry back to one or more of three sires that arrived in England about 1728 from the Near East and became known, from the names of their owners, as the Byerly Turk, the Darley Arabian and the Godolphin Arabian. The Jockey Club (English) was founded at Newmarket in 1750 or 1751 and became the custodian of the Stud Book as well as the court of last resort in deciding turf affairs.

There was horse racing in this country before the Revolution, but the great lift to the breeding industry came with the importation in 1798, by Col. John Hoomes of Virginia, of Diomed, winner of the Epsom Derby of 1780. Diomed's lineal descendants included such famous stars of the American turf as American Eclipse and Lexington. From 1800 to the time of the Civil War there were race courses and breeding establishments plentifully scattered through Virginia, North Carolina, South Carolina, Tennessee, Kentucky, and Louisiana. In fact, thoroughbred racing was largely a Southern sport and that was one reason why the Confederacy had such excellent cavalry in the Civil War. A century ago crack horses were matched in four-mile races that were run in heats, best two out of three!

The oldest stake event in North America is the Queen's Plate, a Canadian fixture that was first run in the Province of Quebec in 1836. The oldest stake event in the United States is The Travers, which was first run at Saratoga in 1864. The gambling that goes with horse racing and trickery by jockeys, trainers, owners, and track officials caused attacks on the sport by reformers and a demand among horse racing enthusiasts for an honest and effective control of some kind, but nothing of lasting value to racing came of this until the formation of The Jockey Club in 1894. The Jockey Club, composed of about sixty members chosen from the aristocracy of the turf, was all-powerful in racing regulation until the State Racing Commissions came into being as a result of mutuel betting and the great revenues that came with the tax on the "daily handle."

## Horse Racing Statistics

Statistics relative to thoroughbred racing in this publication are reproduced from the *American Racing Manual*, by special permission of the copyright owners, TRIANGLE PUBLICATIONS, INC. Reproduction prohibited.

## HISTORY OF THE AMERICAN TRIPLE CROWN

### BELMONT STAKES

**Belmont Park; 3-year-olds; 1½ miles.**

**Run at Jerome Park prior to 1890; run at Morris Park from 1890 to 1905. Distance 1⅝ miles prior to 1874; reduced to 1½ miles, 1874; reduced to 1¼ miles, 1890; changed to 1⅛ miles, 1893; increased to 1¼ miles, 1895; increased to 1⅜ miles, 1896; changed to 1¼ miles in 1904 and 1905; increased to 1½ miles, 1926.**

| Year | Winner | Jockey | Wt. | Win val. |
|---|---|---|---|---|
| 1867 | Ruthless | J. Gilpatrick | 107 | $ 1,850 |
| 1868 | General Duke | R. Swim | 110 | 2,800 |
| 1869 | Fenian | C. Miller | 110 | 3,350 |
| 1870 | Kingfisher | W. Dick | 110 | 3,750 |
| 1871 | Harry Bassett | W. Miller | 110 | 5,450 |
| 1872 | Joe Daniels | J. Rowe | 110 | 4,500 |
| 1873 | Springbok | J. Rowe | 110 | 5,200 |
| 1874 | Saxon | G. Bardee | 110 | 4,200 |
| 1875 | Calvin | R. Swim | 110 | 4,450 |
| 1876 | Algerine | W. Donohue | 110 | 3,700 |
| 1877 | Cloverbrook | C. Holloway | 110 | 5,200 |
| 1878 | Duke of Magenta | L. Hughes | 118 | 3,850 |
| 1879 | Spendthrift | S. Evans | 118 | 4,250 |
| 1880 | Grenada | L. Hughes | 118 | 2,800 |
| 1881 | Saunterer | T. Costello | 118 | 3,000 |
| 1882 | Forester | J. McLaughlin | 118 | 2,600 |
| 1883 | George Kinney | J. McLaughlin | 118 | 3,070 |
| 1884 | Panique | J. McLaughlin | 118 | 3,150 |
| 1885 | Tyrant | P. Duffy | 118 | 2,710 |
| 1886 | Inspector B. | J. McLaughlin | 118 | 2,720 |
| 1887 | Hanover | J. McLaughlin | 118 | 2,900 |
| 1888 | Sir Dixon | J. McLaughlin | 118 | 3,440 |
| 1889 | Eric | W. Hayward | 118 | 4,960 |
| 1890 | Burlington | S. Barnes | 118 | 8,560 |
| 1891 | Foxford | E. Garrison | 118½ | 5,070 |
| 1892 | Patron | W. Hayward | 122 | 6,610 |
| 1893 | Comanche | W. Simms | 117 | 5,310 |
| 1894 | Henry of Navarre | W. Simms | 117 | 6,680 |
| 1895 | Belmar | F. Taral | 119 | 2,700 |
| 1896 | Hastings | H. Griffin | 122 | 3,025 |
| 1897 | Scottish Chieftain | J. Scherrer | 115 | 3,550 |
| 1898 | Bowling Brook | F. Littlefield | 122 | 7,810 |
| 1899 | Jean Bereaud | R. Clawson | 122 | 9,445 |
| 1900 | Ildrim | N. Turner | 126 | 14,790 |
| 1901 | Commando | H. Spencer | 126 | 11,595 |
| 1902 | Masterman | J. Bullman | 126 | 13,220 |
| 1903 | Africander | J. Bullman | 126 | 12,285 |
| 1904 | Delhi | G. Odom | 126 | 11,575 |
| 1905 | Tanya | E. Hildebrand | 121 | 17,240 |
| 1906 | Burgomaster | L. Lyne | 126 | 22,700 |
| 1907 | Peter Pan | G. Mountain | 126 | 22,765 |
| 1908 | Colin | J. Notter | 126 | 22,765 |
| 1909 | Joe Madden | E. Dugan | 126 | 24,550 |
| 1910 | Sweep | J. Butwell | 126 | 9,700 |
| 1913 | Prince Eugene | R. Troxler | 109 | 2,825 |
| 1914 | Luke McLuke | M. Buxton | 126 | 3,025 |
| 1915 | The Finn | G. Byrne | 126 | 1,825 |
| 1916 | Friar Rock | E. Haynes | 126 | 4,100 |
| 1917 | Hourless | J. Butwell | 126 | 5,800 |
| 1918 | Johren | F. Robinson | 126 | 8,950 |
| 1919 | Sir Barton | J. Loftus | 126 | 11,950 |
| 1920 | Man o' War | C. Kummer | 126 | 7,950 |
| 1921 | Grey Lag | E. Sande | 126 | 8,650 |
| 1922 | Pillory | C. H. Miller | 126 | 39,200 |
| 1923 | Zev | E. Sande | 126 | 38,000 |
| 1924 | Mad Play | E. Sande | 126 | 42,880 |
| 1925 | American Flag | A. Johnson | 126 | 38,500 |
| 1926 | Crusader | A. Johnson | 126 | 48,550 |
| 1927 | Chance Shot | E. Sande | 126 | 60,910 |

## Belmont Stakes (Cont.)

| Year | Winner | Jockey | Wt. | Win val. | Year | Winner | Jockey | Wt. | Win val. |
|---|---|---|---|---|---|---|---|---|---|
| 1928 | Vito | C. Kummer | 126 | 63,430 | 1944 | Bounding Home | G. L. Smith | 126 | 55,000 |
| 1929 | Blue Larkspur | M. Garner | 126 | 59,650 | 1945 | Pavot | E. Arcaro | 126 | 52,675 |
| 1930 | Gallant Fox | E. Sande | 126 | 66,040 | 1946 | Assault | W. Mehrtens | 126 | 75,400 |
| 1931 | Twenty Grand | C. Kurtsinger | 126 | 58,770 | 1947 | Phalanx | R. Donoso | 126 | 78,900 |
| 1932 | Faireno | T. Malley | 126 | 55,120 | 1948 | Citation | E. Arcaro | 126 | 77,700 |
| 1933 | Hurryoff | M. Garner | 126 | 49,490 | 1949 | Capot | T. Atkinson | 126 | 60,900 |
| 1934 | Peace Chance | W. D. Wright | 126 | 43,410 | 1950 | Middleground | W. Boland | 126 | 61,350 |
| 1935 | Omaha | W. Saunders | 126 | 35,480 | 1951 | Counterpoint | D. Gorman | 126 | 82,000 |
| 1936 | Granville | J. Stout | 126 | 29,800 | 1952 | One Count | E. Arcaro | 126 | 82,400 |
| 1937 | War Admiral | C. Kurtsinger | 126 | 38,020 | 1953 | Native Dancer | E. Guerin | 126 | 82,500 |
| 1938 | Pasteurized | J. Stout | 126 | 34,530 | 1954 | High Gun | E. Guerin | 126 | 89,000 |
| 1939 | Johnstown | J. Stout | 126 | 37,020 | 1955 | Nashua | E. Arcaro | 126 | 83,700 |
| 1940 | Bimelech | F. A. Smith | 126 | 35,030 | 1956 | Needles | D. Erb | 126 | 83,600 |
| 1941 | Whirlaway | E. Arcaro | 126 | 39,770 | 1957 | Gallant Man | W. Shoemaker | 126 | 77,300 |
| 1942 | Shut Out | E. Arcaro | 126 | 44,520 | 1958 | Cavan | P. Anderson | 126 | 73,440 |
| 1943 | Count Fleet | J. Longden | 126 | 35,340 | 1959 | Sword Dancer | W. Shoemaker | 126 | 93,525 |
|  |  |  |  |  | 1960 | Celtic Ash | W. Hartack | 126 | 96,785 |

# KENTUCKY DERBY
### Churchill Downs; 3-year-olds; 1¼ miles.

| Year | Winner | Jockey | Wt. | Win val. | Year | Winner | Jockey | Wt. | Win val. |
|---|---|---|---|---|---|---|---|---|---|
| 1875 | Aristides | O. Lewis | 100 | $2,850 | 1917 | Omar Khayyam | C. Borel | 117 | 16,600 |
| 1876 | Vagrant | R. Swim | 97 | 2,950 | 1918 | Exterminator | W. Knapp | 114 | 14,700 |
| 1877 | Baden Baden | W. Walker | 100 | 3,300 | 1919 | Sir Barton | J. Loftus | 112½ | 20,825 |
| 1878 | Day Star | J. Carter | 100 | 4,050 | 1920 | Paul Jones | T. Rice | 126 | 30,375 |
| 1879 | Lord Murphy | C. Schauer | 100 | 3,550 | 1921 | Behave Yourself | C. Thompson | 126 | 38,450 |
| 1880 | Fonso | G. Lewis | 105 | 3,800 | 1922 | Morvich | A. Johnson | 126 | 46,775 |
| 1881 | Hindoo | J. McLaughlin | 105 | 4,410 | 1923 | Zev | E. Sande | 126 | 53,600 |
| 1882 | Apollo | B. Hurd | 102 | 4,560 | 1924 | Black Gold | J. D. Mooney | 126 | 52,775 |
| 1883 | Leonatus | W. Donohue | 105 | 3,760 | 1925 | Flying Ebony | E. Sande | 126 | 52,950 |
| 1884 | Buchanan | I. Murphy | 110 | 3,990 | 1926 | Bubbling Over | A. Johnson | 126 | 50,075 |
| 1885 | Joe Cotton | E. Henderson | 110 | 4,630 | 1927 | Whiskery | L. McAtee | 126 | 51,000 |
| 1886 | Ben Ali | P. Duffy | 118 | 4,890 | 1928 | Reigh Count | C. Lang | 126 | 55,375 |
| 1887 | Montrose | I. Lewis | 118 | 4,200 | 1929 | Clyde Van Dusen | L. McAtee | 126 | 53,950 |
| 1888 | Macbeth II | G. Covington | 115 | 4,740 | 1930 | Gallant Fox | E. Sande | 126 | 50,725 |
| 1889 | Spokane | T. Kiley | 118 | 4,970 | 1931 | Twenty Grand | C. Kurtsinger | 126 | 48,725 |
| 1890 | Riley | I. Murphy | 118 | 5,460 | 1932 | Burgoo King | E. James | 126 | 52,350 |
| 1891 | Kingman | I. Murphy | 122 | 4,680 | 1933 | Brokers Tip | D. Meade | 126 | 48,925 |
| 1892 | Azra | A. Clayton | 122 | 4,230 | 1934 | Cavalcade | M. Garner | 126 | 28,175 |
| 1893 | Lookout | E. Kunze | 122 | 4,090 | 1935 | Omaha | W. Saunders | 126 | 39,525 |
| 1894 | Chant | F. Goodale | 122 | 4,020 | 1936 | Bold Venture | I. Hanford | 126 | 37,725 |
| 1895 | Halma | J. Perkins | 122 | 2,970 | 1937 | War Admiral | C. Kurtsinger | 126 | 52,050 |
| 1896 | Ben Brush | W. Simms | 117 | 4,850 | 1938 | Lawrin | E. Arcaro | 126 | 47,050 |
| 1897 | Typhoon II | F. Garner | 117 | 4,850 | 1939 | Johnstown | J. Stout | 126 | 46,350 |
| 1898 | Plaudit | W. Simms | 117 | 4,850 | 1940 | Gallahadion | C. Bierman | 126 | 60,150 |
| 1899 | Manuel | F. Taral | 117 | 4,850 | 1941 | Whirlaway | E. Arcaro | 126 | 61,275 |
| 1900 | Lieut. Gibson | J. Boland | 117 | 4,850 | 1942 | Shut Out | W. D. Wright | 126 | 64,225 |
| 1901 | His Eminence | J. Winkfield | 117 | 4,850 | 1943 | Count Fleet | J. Longden | 126 | 60,725 |
| 1902 | Alan-a-Dale | J. Winkfield | 117 | 4,850 | 1944 | Pensive | C. McCreary | 126 | 64,675 |
| 1903 | Judge Himes | H. Booker | 117 | 4,850 | 1945 | Hoop Jr. | E. Arcaro | 126 | 64,850 |
| 1904 | Elwood | F. Prior | 117 | 4,850 | 1946 | Assault | W. Mehrtens | 126 | 96,400 |
| 1905 | Agile | J. Martin | 122 | 4,850 | 1947 | Jet Pilot | E. Guerin | 126 | 92,160 |
| 1906 | Sir Huon | R. Troxler | 117 | 4,850 | 1948 | Citation | E. Arcaro | 126 | 83,400 |
| 1907 | Pink Star | A. Minder | 117 | 4,850 | 1949 | Ponder | S. Brooks | 126 | 91,600 |
| 1908 | Stone Street | A. Pickens | 117 | 4,850 | 1950 | Middleground | W. Boland | 126 | 92,650 |
| 1909 | Wintergreen | V. Powers | 117 | 4,850 | 1951 | Count Turf | C. McCreary | 126 | 98,050 |
| 1910 | Donau | F. Herbert | 117 | 4,850 | 1952 | Hill Gail | E. Arcaro | 126 | 96,300 |
| 1911 | Meridian | G. Archibald | 117 | 4,850 | 1953 | Dark Star | H. Moreno | 126 | 90,050 |
| 1912 | Worth | C. H. Shilling | 117 | 4,850 | 1954 | Determine | R. York | 126 | 102,050 |
| 1913 | Donerail | R. Goose | 117 | 5,475 | 1955 | Swaps | W. Shoemaker | 126 | 108,400 |
| 1914 | Old Rosebud | J. McCabe | 114 | 9,125 | 1956 | Needles | D. Erb | 126 | 123,450 |
| 1915 | Regret | J. Notter | 112 | 11,450 | 1957 | Iron Liege | W. Hartack | 126 | 107,950 |
| 1916 | George Smith | J. Loftus | 117 | 9,750 | 1958 | Tim Tam | I. Valenzuela | 126 | 116,400 |
|  |  |  |  |  | 1959 | Tomy Lee | W. Shoemaker | 126 | 119,650 |
|  |  |  |  |  | 1960 | Venetian Way | W. Hartack | 126 | 114 850 |

## "TRIPLE CROWN" WINNERS IN THE UNITED STATES
### (Kentucky Derby, Preakness and Belmont Stakes)

| Year | Horse | Owner | Year | Horse | Owner |
|---|---|---|---|---|---|
| 1919 | Sir Barton | J. K. L. Ross | 1941 | Whirlaway | Warren Wright |
| 1930 | Gallant Fox | William Woodward | 1943 | Count Fleet | Mrs. John Hertz |
| 1935 | Omaha | William Woodward | 1946 | Assault | Robert J. Kleberg |
| 1937 | War Admiral | Samuel D. Riddle | 1948 | Citation | Warren Wright |

## PREAKNESS STAKES
### Pimlico; 3-year-olds; 1 3/16 miles.

| Year | Winner | Jockey | Wt. | Win val. |
|---|---|---|---|---|
| 1873 | Survivor | G. Barbee | 110 | .... |
| 1874 | Culpepper | M. Donohue | 110 | .... |
| 1875 | Tom Ochiltree | L. Hughes | 110 | .... |
| 1876 | Shirley | G. Barbee | 110 | .... |
| 1877 | Cloverbrook | C. Holloway | 110 | .... |
| 1878 | Duke of Magenta | C. Holloway | 110 | .... |
| 1879 | Harold | W Hughes | 110 | $2,550 |
| 1880 | Grenada | W. Hughes | 110 | 2,000 |
| 1881 | Saunterer | W. Costello | 110 | 1,950 |
| 1882 | Vanguard | W. Costello | 110 | 1,250 |
| 1883 | Jacobus | G. Barbee | 110 | 1,635 |
| 1884 | Knight of Ellerslie | S. H. Fisher | 110 | 1,905 |
| 1885 | Tecumseh | J. McLaughlin | 118 | 2,160 |
| 1886 | The Bard | S. H. Fisher | 118 | 2,050 |
| 1887 | Dunboyne | W. Donohue | 118 | 1,675 |
| 1888 | Refund | F. Littlefield | 118 | 1,185 |
| 1889 | Buddhist | H. Anderson | 118 | 1,130 |
| 1894 | Assignee | F. Taral | 122 | 1,830 |
| 1895 | Belmar | F. Taral | 115 | 1,350 |
| 1896 | Margrave | H. Griffin | 115 | 1,350 |
| 1897 | Paul Kauvar | Thorpe | 108 | 1,420 |
| 1898 | Sly Fox | W. Simms | 120 | 1,450 |
| 1899 | Half Time | R. Clawson | 104 | 1,580 |
| 1900 | Hindus | H. Spencer | 106 | 1,900 |
| 1901 | The Parader | Landry | 118 | 1,605 |
| 1902 | Old England | L. Jackson | 115 | 2,240 |
| 1903 | Flocarline | W. Gannon | 113 | 1,875 |
| 1904 | Bryn Mawr | E. Hildebrand | 108 | 2,355 |
| 1905 | Cairngorm | W. Davis | 114 | 2,145 |
| 1906 | Whimsical | W. Miller | 108 | 2,355 |
| 1907 | Don Enrique | G. Mountain | 107 | 2,260 |
| 1908 | Royal Tourist | E. Dugan | 112 | 2,455 |
| 1909 | Effendi | W. Doyle | 116 | 3,225 |
| 1910 | Layminster | R. Estep | 84 | 3,300 |
| 1911 | Watervale | E. Dugan | 112 | 2,700 |
| 1912 | Colonel Holloway | C. Turner | 107 | 1,450 |
| 1913 | Buskin | J. Butwell | 117 | 1,670 |
| 1914 | Holiday | A. Schuttinger | 108 | 1,355 |
| 1915 | Rhine Maiden | D. Hoffman | 104 | 1,275 |
| 1916 | Damrosch | L. McAtee | 115 | 1,380 |
| 1917 | Kalitan | E. Haynes | 116 | 4,800 |
| 1918* | War Cloud | J. Loftus | 117 | 12,250 |
| 1918 | Jack Hare Jr. | C. Peak | 115 | 11,250 |
| 1919 | Sir Barton | J. Loftus | 126 | 24,500 |
| 1920 | Man o' War | C. Kummer | 126 | 23,000 |
| 1921 | Broomspun | F. Coltiletti | 114 | 43,000 |
| 1922 | Pillory | L. Morris | 114 | 51,000 |
| 1923 | Vigil | B. Marinelli | 114 | 52,000 |
| 1924 | Nellie Morse | J. Merimee | 121 | 54,000 |
| 1925 | Coventry | C. Kummer | 126 | 52,700 |
| 1926 | Display | J. Maiben | 126 | 53,625 |
| 1927 | Bostonian | A. Abel | 126 | 53,100 |
| 1928 | Victorian | R. Workman | 126 | 60,000 |
| 1929 | Dr. Freeland | L. Schaefer | 126 | 52,325 |
| 1930 | Gallant Fox | E. Sande | 126 | 51,925 |
| 1931 | Mate | G. Ellis | 126 | 48,225 |
| 1932 | Burgoo King | E. James | 126 | 50,375 |
| 1933 | Head Play | C. Kurtsinger | 126 | 26,850 |
| 1934 | High Quest | R. Jones | 126 | 25,175 |
| 1935 | Omaha | W. Saunders | 126 | 25,325 |
| 1936 | Bold Venture | G. Woolf | 126 | 27,325 |
| 1937 | War Admiral | C. Kurtsinger | 126 | 45,600 |
| 1938 | Dauber | M. Peters | 126 | 51,857 |
| 1939 | Challedon | G. Seabo | 126 | 53,710 |
| 1940 | Bimelech | F. A. Smith | 126 | 53,230 |
| 1941 | Whirlaway | E. Arcaro | 126 | 49,365 |
| 1942 | Alsab | B. James | 126 | 58,175 |
| 1943 | Count Fleet | J. Longden | 126 | 43,190 |
| 1944 | Pensive | C. McCreary | 126 | 60,075 |
| 1945 | Polynesian | W. D. Wright | 126 | 66,170 |
| 1946 | Assault | W. Mehrtens | 126 | 96,620 |
| 1947 | Faultless | D. Dodson | 126 | 98,005 |
| 1948 | Citation | E. Arcaro | 126 | 91,870 |
| 1949 | Capot | T. Atkinson | 126 | 79,985 |
| 1950 | Hill Prince | E. Arcaro | 126 | 56,115 |
| 1951 | Bold | E. Arcaro | 126 | 83,110 |
| 1952 | Blue Man | C. McCreary | 126 | 86,135 |
| 1953 | Native Dancer | E. Guerin | 126 | 65,200 |
| 1954 | Hasty Road | J. Adams | 126 | 91,600 |
| 1955 | Nashua | E. Arcaro | 126 | 67,550 |
| 1956 | Fabius | W. Hartack | 126 | 84,250 |
| 1957 | Bold Ruler | E. Arcaro | 126 | 65,250 |
| 1958 | Tim Tam | I. Valenzuela | 126 | 97,900 |
| 1959 | Royal Orbit | W. Harmatz | 126 | 136,200 |
| 1960 | Bally Ache | R. Ussery | 126 | 121,000 |

\* Race run in two divisions in 1918.

## WINNERS OF OTHER TRADITIONAL STAKES
### AMERICAN DERBY
#### Washington Park; 3-year-olds; 1 1/8 miles.

| Year | Winner |
|---|---|
| 1884 | Modesty |
| 1885 | Volante |
| 1886 | Silver Cloud |
| 1887 | C. H. Todd |
| 1888 | Emperor of Norfolk |
| 1889 | Spokane |
| 1890 | Uncle Bob |
| 1891 | Strathmeath |
| 1892 | Carlsbad |
| 1893 | Boundless |
| 1894 | Rey el S'ta A'ta |
| 1898 | Pink Coat |
| 1900 | Sidney Lucas |
| 1901 | Robert Waddell |
| 1902 | Wyeth |
| 1903 | The Picket |
| 1904 | Highball |
| 1916 | Dodge |
| 1926 | Boot to Boot |
| 1927 | Hydromel |
| 1928 | Toro |
| 1929 | Windy City |
| 1930 | Reveille Boy |
| 1931 | Mate |
| 1932 | Gusto |
| 1933 | Mr. Khayyam |
| 1934 | Cavalcade |
| 1935 | Black Helen |
| 1937 | Dawn Play |
| 1940 | Mioland |
| 1941 | Whirlaway |
| 1942 | Alsab |
| 1943 | Askmenow |
| 1944 | By Jimminy |
| 1945 | Fighting Step |
| 1946 | Eternal Reward |
| 1947 | Fervent |
| 1948 | Citation |
| 1949 | Ponder |
| 1950 | Hill Prince |
| 1951 | Hall of Fame |
| 1952 | Mark-Ye-Well |
| 1953 | Native Dancer |
| 1954 | Errard King |
| 1955 | Swaps |
| 1956 | Swoon's Son |
| 1957 | Round Table |
| 1958 | Nadir |
| 1959 | Dunce |
| 1960 | T. V. Lark |

### When Is a Horse a Horse?

Terms by which a horse is known in racing, as explained by John I. Day of the Thoroughbred Racing Associations: A *foal* is a young horse of either sex and while unweaned is known as a *suckling*. When separated from his *dam*, or maternal parent, he is a *weanling* until Jan. 1 following his birth, when he becomes a *yearling*. He may be a *colt*, if male, and remain so (unless he becomes a *gelding*, or unsexed) until he is 5 years old; or, if female, a *filly* until 5. From 5 on, they are *horses* or *mares* and when they become parents, *sires* or *dams*.

## ARLINGTON CLASSIC
### Arlington Park; 3-year-olds; 1 mile.

| Year | Winner | Year | Winner | Year | Winner | Year | Winner |
|---|---|---|---|---|---|---|---|
| 1929 | Blue Larkspur | 1937 | Flying Scot | 1945 | Pot o' Luck | 1953 | Native Dancer |
| 1930 | Gallant Fox | 1938 | Nedayr | 1946 | The Dude | 1954 | Errard King |
| 1931 | Mate | 1939 | Challedon | 1947 | But Why Not | 1955 | Nashua |
| 1932 | Gusto | 1940 | Sirocco | 1948 | Papa Redbird | 1956 | Swoon's Son |
| 1933 | Inlander | 1941 | Attention | 1949 | Ponder | 1957 | Clem |
| 1934 | Cavalcade | 1942 | Shut Out | 1950 | Greek Song | 1958 | A Dragon Killer |
| 1935 | Omaha | 1943 | Slide Rule | 1951 | Hall of Fame | 1959 | Dunce |
| 1936 | Granville | 1944 | Twilight Tear | 1952 | Mark-Ye-Well | 1960 | T. V. Lark |

## ARLINGTON FUTURITY
### Arlington Park; 2-year-olds; ¾ mile.

| Year | Winner | Year | Winner | Year | Winner | Year | Winner |
|---|---|---|---|---|---|---|---|
| 1927 | Misstep | 1938 | Thingumabob | 1946 | Cosmic Bomb | 1954 | Royal Note |
| 1928 | Double Heart | 1939 | Andy K | 1947 | Piet | 1955 | Swoon's Son |
| 1932 | Ladysman | 1940 | Swain | 1948 | Mr. Busher | 1956 | Greek Game |
| 1933 | Far Star | 1941 | Sun Again | 1949 | Wisconsin Boy | 1957 | Leather Button |
| 1934 | Toro Nancy | 1942 | Occupation | 1950 | To Market | 1958 | Restless Wing |
| 1935 | Grand Slam | 1943 | Jezrahel | 1951 | Hill Gail | 1959 | T. V. Lark |
| 1936 | Case Ace | 1944 | Free for All | 1952 | Mr. Good | 1960 | Pappa's All |
| 1937* | Tiger | 1945 | Spy Song | 1953 | Hasty Road | | * Dead heat. |
| | Teddy's Comet | | | | | | |

## EPSOM DERBY
### Epsom Downs, England; 3-year-olds; 1 mile, 885 yards.

| Year | Winner | Year | Winner | Year | Winner | Year | Winner |
|---|---|---|---|---|---|---|---|
| 1780 | Diomed | 1822 | Moses | 1864 | Blair Athol | 1905 | Cicero |
| 1781 | Y. Eclipse | 1823 | Emilius | 1865 | Gladiateur | 1906 | Spearmint |
| 1782 | Assassin | 1824 | Cedric | 1866 | Lord Lyon | 1907 | Orby† |
| 1783 | Saltram | 1825 | Middleton | 1867 | Hermit | 1908 | Signorinetta |
| 1784 | Sergeant | 1826 | Lap Dog | 1868 | Blue Gown | 1909 | Minoru |
| 1785 | Aimwell | 1827 | Mameluke | 1869 | Pretender | 1910 | Lemberg |
| 1786 | Noble | 1828 | Cadland | 1870 | Kingcraft | 1911 | Sunstar |
| 1787 | Sir P. Teazle | 1829 | Frederick | 1871 | Favonius | 1912 | Tagalie |
| 1788 | Sir Thomas | 1830 | Priam | 1872 | Cremorne | 1913 | Aboyeur |
| 1789 | Skyscraper | 1831 | Spaniel | 1873 | Doncaster | 1914 | Durbar II† |
| 1790 | Rhadamanthus | 1832 | St. Giles | 1874 | Geo. Frederick | 1915 | Pommern |
| 1791 | Eager | 1833 | Dangerous | 1875 | Calopin | 1916 | Fifinella |
| 1792 | John Bull | 1834 | Plenipotentiary | 1876 | Kisber | 1917 | Gay Crusader |
| 1793 | Waxy | 1835 | Mundig | 1877 | Silbio | 1918 | Gainsborough |
| 1794 | Daedalus | 1836 | Bay Middleton | 1878 | Sefton | 1919 | Grand Parade |
| 1795 | Spread Eagle | 1837 | Phosphorus | 1879 | Sir Bevvs | 1920 | Spion Kop |
| 1796 | Didelot | 1838 | Amato | 1880 | Bend Or | 1921 | Humorist |
| 1797 | Colt by Fidget | 1839 | Bloomsbury | 1881 | Iroquois† | 1922 | Captain Cuttle |
| 1798 | Sir Harry | 1840 | Little Wonder | 1882 | Shotover | 1923 | Papyrus |
| 1799 | Archduke | 1841 | Coronation | 1883 | St. Blaise | 1924 | Sansovino |
| 1800 | Champion | 1842 | Attila | 1884* | St. Gatien | 1925 | Manna |
| 1801 | Eleanor | 1843 | Cotherstone | | Harvester | 1926 | Coronach |
| 1802 | Tyrant | 1844 | Orlando | 1885 | Melton | 1927 | Call Boy |
| 1803 | Ditto | 1845 | Merry Monarch | 1886 | Ormonde | 1928 | Felstead |
| 1804 | Hannibal | 1846 | Pyrrhus the First | 1887 | Mer. Hampton | 1929 | Trigo |
| 1805 | Card. Beaufort | 1847 | Cossack | 1888 | Ayrshire | 1930 | Blenheim |
| 1806 | Paris | 1848 | Surplice | 1889 | Donovan | 1931 | Cameronian |
| 1807 | Election | 1849 | T. Flying Dutchman | 1890 | Sanfoin | 1932 | April the Fifth |
| 1808 | Pan | 1850 | Voltigeur | 1891 | Common | 1933 | Hyperion |
| 1809 | Pope | 1851 | Teddington | 1892 | Sir Hugo | 1934 | Windsor Lad |
| 1810 | Whalebone | 1852 | Dan. O'Rourke | 1893 | Isinglass | 1935 | Bahram |
| 1811 | Phantom | 1853 | W. Australian | 1894 | Ladas | 1936 | Mahmoud |
| 1812 | Octavius | 1854 | Andover | 1895 | Sir Visto | 1937 | Mid-Day Sun |
| 1813 | Smolensko | 1855 | Wild Dayrell | 1896 | Persimmon | 1938 | Bois Roussel |
| 1814 | Blucher | 1856 | Ellinton | 1897 | Galtee More | 1939 | Blue Peter |
| 1815 | Whisker | 1857 | Blink Bonny | 1898 | Jeddah | 1940 | Pont l'Eveque |
| 1816 | Prince Leopold | 1858 | Beadsman | 1899 | Flying Fox | 1941 | Owen Tudor |
| 1817 | Azor | 1859 | Musjid | 1900 | Diamond Jubilee | 1942 | Watling Street |
| 1818 | Sam | 1860 | Thormanby | 1901 | Volodyovski† | 1943 | Straight Lead |
| 1819 | Tiresias | 1861 | Kettledrum | 1902 | Ard Patrick | *1944 | Ocean Swell |
| 1820 | Sailor | 1862 | Caractacus | 1903 | Rock Sand | 1945 | Dante |
| 1821 | Gustavus | 1863 | Macaroni | 1904 | St. Amant | 1946 | Airborne |

## Epsom Derby (Cont.)

| | | | | | | | |
|---|---|---|---|---|---|---|---|
| 1947 | Pearl Diver | 1951 | Arctic Prince | 1955 | Phil Drake | 1958 | Hard Ridden |
| 1948 | My Love | 1952 | Tulyar | 1956 | Lavadin | 1959 | Parthia |
| 1949 | Nimbus | 1953 | Pinza | 1957 | Crepello | 1960 | St. Paddy |
| 1950 | Galcador | 1954 | Never Say Die† | | * Dead heat. | † American bred or owned. | |

## FUTURITY STAKES

### Aqueduct; 2-year-olds; 6½ furlongs.

| Year | Winner | Year | Winner | Year | Winner | Year | Winner |
|---|---|---|---|---|---|---|---|
| 1888 | Proctor Knott | 1906 | Electioneer | 1925 | Pompey | 1943 | Occupy |
| 1889 | Chaos | 1907 | Colin | 1926 | Scapa Flow | 1944 | Pavot |
| 1890 | Potomac | 1908 | Maskette | 1927 | Anita Peabody | 1945 | Star Pilot |
| 1891 | His Highness | 1909 | Sweep | 1928 | High Strung | 1946 | First Flight |
| 1892 | Morello | 1910 | Novelty | 1929 | Whichone | 1947 | Citation |
| 1893 | Domino | 1913 | Pennant | 1930 | Jamestown | 1948 | Blue Peter |
| 1894 | The Butterflies | 1914 | Trojan | 1931 | Top Flight | 1949 | Guillotine |
| 1895 | Requital | 1915 | Thunderer | 1932 | Kerry Patch | 1950 | Battlefield |
| 1896 | Ogden | 1916 | Campfire | 1933 | Singing Wood | 1951 | Tom Fool |
| 1897 | L'Alouette | 1917 | Papp | 1934 | Chance Sun | 1952 | Native Dancer |
| 1898 | Martimas | 1918 | Dunboyne | 1935 | Tintagel | 1953 | Porterhouse |
| 1899 | Charcornac | 1919 | Man o' War | 1936 | Pompoon | 1954 | Nashua |
| 1900 | Ballyhoo Bey | 1920 | Step Lightly | 1937 | Menow | 1955 | Nail |
| 1901 | Yankee | 1921 | Bunting | 1938 | Porter's Mite | 1956 | Bold Ruler |
| 1902 | Savable | 1922 | Sally's Alley | 1939 | Bimelech | 1957 | Jester |
| 1903 | Hamburg Belle | 1923 | St. James | 1940 | Our Boots | 1958 | Intentionally |
| 1904 | Artful | 1924 | Mother Goose | 1941 | Some Chance | 1959 | Weatherwise |
| 1905 | Ormondale | | | 1942 | Occupation | 1960 | Little Tumbler |

## GRAND NATIONAL STEEPLECHASE

### Liverpool, England; 6-year-olds and over; 4 miles, 856 yards (Aintree Course).

| Year | Winner | Year | Winner | Year | Winner | Year | Winner |
|---|---|---|---|---|---|---|---|
| 1839 | Lottery | 1869 | The Colonel | 1898 | Drogheda | 1928 | Tipperary Tim |
| 1840 | Jerry | 1870 | The Colonel | 1899 | Manifesto | 1929 | Gregalach |
| 1841 | Charity | 1871 | The Lamb | 1900 | Ambush II | 1930 | Shaun Goilin |
| 1842 | Gaylad | 1872 | Casse Tete | 1901 | Grudon | 1931 | Grakle |
| 1843 | Vanguard | 1873 | Disturbance | 1902 | Shannon Lass | 1932 | Forbra |
| 1844 | Pioneer | 1874 | Reugny | 1903 | Drumcree | 1933 | Kellsboro Jack† |
| 1845 | Cure All | 1875 | Pathfinder | 1904 | Moifaa | 1934 | Golden Miller |
| 1846 | Pioneer | 1876 | Regal | 1905 | Kirkland | 1935 | Reynoldstown |
| 1847 | Matthew | 1877 | Austerlitz | 1906 | Ascetic's Silver | 1936 | Reynoldstown |
| 1848 | Chandler | 1878 | Shifnal | 1907 | Eremon | 1937 | Royal Mail |
| 1849 | Peter Simple | 1879 | The Liberator | 1908 | Rubio† | 1938 | Battleship† |
| 1850 | Abd el Kader | 1880 | Empress | 1909 | Lutteur III | 1939 | Workman |
| 1851 | Abd el Kader | 1881 | Woodbrook | 1910 | Jenkinstown | 1940 | Bogskar |
| 1852 | Miss Mowbray | 1882 | Seaman | 1911 | Glenside | 1946 | Lovely Cottage |
| 1853 | Peter Simple | 1883 | Zoedone | 1912 | Jerry M | 1947 | Caughoo |
| 1854 | Bourton | 1884 | Voluptuary | 1913 | Covertcoat | 1948 | Sheila's Cottage |
| 1855 | Wanderer | 1885 | Roquefort | 1914 | Sunloch | 1949 | Russian Hero |
| 1856 | Freetrader | 1886 | Old Joe | 1915 | Ally Sloper | 1950 | Freebooter |
| 1857 | Emigrant | 1887 | Gamecock | 1916* | Bermouth | 1951 | Nickel Coin |
| 1858 | Little Charley | 1888 | Playfair | 1917* | Ballymacad | 1952 | Teal |
| 1859 | Half Caste | 1889 | Frigate | 1918* | Poethlyn | 1953 | Early Mist |
| 1860 | Anatis | 1890 | Ilex | 1919* | Poethlyn | 1954 | Royal Tan |
| 1861 | Jealousy | 1891 | Come Away | 1920 | Troytown | 1955 | Quare Times |
| 1862 | Huntsman | 1892 | Father O'Flynn | 1921 | Shaun Spadah | 1956 | E. S. B. |
| 1863 | Emblem | 1893 | Cloister | 1922 | Music Hall | 1957 | Sundew |
| 1864 | Emblematic | 1894 | Why Not | 1923 | Sgt. Murphy† | 1958 | Mr. What |
| 1865 | Alcibiade | 1895 | W. M. f. Borneo | 1924 | Master Rob't | 1959 | Oxo |
| 1866 | Salamander | 1896 | The Soarer | 1925 | Double Chance | 1960 | Merryman II |
| 1867 | Cortolvin | 1897 | Manifesto | 1926 | Jack Horner† | | * Substitute race. |
| 1868 | The Lamb | | | 1927 | Sprig | | † American bred or owned. |

## HOLLYWOOD GOLD CUP

### Hollywood Park; 3-year-olds and over; 1¼ miles.

| Year | Winner, age | Year | Winner, age | Year | Winner, age | Year | Winner, age |
|---|---|---|---|---|---|---|---|
| 1938 | Seabiscuit (5) | 1945 | Challenge Me (4) | 1950 | Noor (5) | 1955 | Rejected (5) |
| 1939 | Kayak II (4) | 1946 | Triplicate (5) | 1951 | Citation (6) | 1956 | Swaps (4) |
| 1940 | Challedon (4) | 1947 | Cover Up (4) | 1952 | Two Lea (6) | 1957 | Round Table (3) |
| 1941 | Big Pebble (5) | 1948 | Shannon II (7) | 1953 | Royal Serenade (5) | 1958 | Gallant Man (4) |
| 1944 | Happy Issue (4) | 1949 | Solidarity (4) | 1954 | Correspondent (4) | 1959 | Hillsdale (4) |
| | | | | | | 1960 | Dotted Swiss (4) |

## SANTA ANITA DERBY
### Santa Anita Park; 3-year-olds; 1⅛ miles.

| Year | Winner | Year | Winner | Year | Winner | Year | Winner |
|------|--------|------|--------|------|--------|------|--------|
| 1935 | Gille | 1941 | Porter's Cap | 1950 | Your Host | 1956 | Terrang |
| 1936 | He Did | 1945 | Bymeabond | 1951 | Rough'n Tumble | 1957 | Sir William |
| 1937 | Fairy Hill | 1946 | Knockdown | 1952 | Hill Gail | 1958 | Silky Sullivan |
| 1938 | Stagehand | 1947 | On Trust | 1953 | Chanlea | 1959 | Silver Spoon |
| 1939 | Ciencia | 1948 | Salmagundi | 1954 | Determine | 1960 | Tompion |
| 1940 | Sweepida | 1949 | Old Rockport | 1955 | Swaps | | |

## SANTA ANITA HANDICAP
### Santa Anita Park; 3-year-olds and over; 1¼ miles.

| Year | Winner, age | Year | Winner | Year | Winner | Year | Winner |
|------|-------------|------|--------|------|--------|------|--------|
| 1935 | Azucar (7) | 1940 | Seabiscuit (7) | 1949 | Vulcan's Forge (4) | 1955 | Poona II (4) |
| 1936 | Top Row (5) | 1941 | Bay View (4) | 1950 | Noor (5) | 1956 | Bobby Brocato (5) |
| 1937 | Rosemont (5) | 1945 | Thumbs Up (6) | 1951 | Moonrush (5) | 1957 | Corn Husker (4) |
| 1938 | Stagehand (3) | 1946 | War Knight (6) | 1952 | Miche (7) | 1958 | Round Table (4) |
| 1939 | Kayak II (4) | 1947 | Olhaverry (8) | 1953 | Mark-Ye-Well (4) | 1959 | Terrang (6) |
| | | 1948 | Talon (6) | 1954 | Rejected (4) | 1960 | Linmold (4) |

## TRAVERS STAKES
### Saratoga; 3-year-olds; 1¼ miles.

| Year | Winner | Year | Winner | Year | Winner | Year | Winner |
|------|--------|------|--------|------|--------|------|--------|
| 1864 | Kentucky | 1887 | Carey | 1916 | Spur | 1938 | Thanksgiving |
| 1865 | Maiden | 1888 | Sir Dixon | 1917 | Omar Khayyam | 1939 | Eight Thirty |
| 1866 | Merrill | 1889 | Long Dance | 1918 | Sun Briar | 1940 | Fenelon |
| 1867 | Ruthless | 1890 | Sir John | 1919 | Hannibal | 1941 | Whirlaway |
| 1868 | The Banshee | 1891 | Vallera | 1920 | Man o' War | 1942 | Shut Out |
| 1869 | Glenelg | 1892 | Azra | 1921 | Sporting Blood | 1943 | Eurasian |
| 1870 | Kingfisher | 1893 | Stowaway | 1922 | Little Chief | 1944 | By Jimminy |
| 1871 | Harry Bassett | 1894 | Henry of Navarre | 1923 | Wilderness | 1945 | Adonis |
| 1872 | Joe Daniels | 1895 | Liza | 1924 | Sun Flag | 1946 | Natchez |
| 1873 | Tom Bowling | 1897 | Rensselaer | 1925 | Dangerous | 1947 | Young Peter |
| 1874 | Attila | 1901 | Blues | 1926 | Mars | 1948 | Ace Admiral |
| 1875 | D'Artagnan | 1902 | Hermis | 1927 | Brown Bud | 1949 | Arise |
| 1876 | Sultana | 1903 | Ada Nay | 1928 | Petee-Wrack | 1950 | Lights Up |
| 1877 | Baden Baden | 1904 | Broomstick | 1929 | Beacon Hill | 1951 | Battlefield |
| 1878 | Duke of Magenta | 1905 | Dandelion | 1930 | Jim Dandy | 1952 | One Count |
| 1879 | Falsetto | 1906 | Gallavant | 1931 | Twenty Grand | 1953 | Native Dancer |
| 1880 | Grenada | 1907 | Frank Gill | 1932 | War Hero | 1954 | Fisherman |
| 1881 | Hindoo | 1908 | Dorante | 1933 | Inlander | 1955 | Thinking Cap |
| 1882 | Carley B | 1909 | Hilarious | 1934 | Observant | 1956 | Oh Johnny |
| 1883 | Barnes | 1910 | Dalmatian | 1935 | Gold Foam | 1957 | Gallant Man |
| 1884 | Rataplan | 1913 | Rock View | 1936 | Granville | 1958 | Piano Jim |
| 1885 | Bersan | 1914 | Roamer | 1937 | Burning Star | 1959 | Sword Dancer |
| 1886 | Inspector B | 1915 | Lady Rotha | | | 1960 | Tompion |

## WASHINGTON, D. C., INTERNATIONAL
### Laurel; 3-year-olds and over; about 1½ miles.

| Year | Winner | Year | Winner | Year | Winner | Year | Winner |
|------|--------|------|--------|------|--------|------|--------|
| 1952 | Wilwyn (4) | 1954 | Fisherman (3) | 1956 | Master Boing (3) | 1958 | Sailor's Guide (6) |
| 1953 | Worden II (4) | 1955 | El Chama (4) | 1957 | Mahan (6) | 1959 | Bald Eagle (4) |
| | | | | | | 1960 | Bald Eagle (5) |

## WASHINGTON PARK FUTURITY
### Washington Park; 2-year-olds; 3/4 mile.

| Year | Winner | Year | Winner | Year | Winner | Year | Winner |
|------|--------|------|--------|------|--------|------|--------|
| 1937 | Tiger | 1945 | Revoked | 1950 | To Market | 1955 | Swoon's Son |
| 1940 | Porter's Cap | 1946 | Education | 1951 | Oh Leo | 1956 | Greek Game |
| 1941 | Alsab | 1947 | Bewitch | 1952 | Mr. Paradise | 1957 | Jewel's Reward |
| 1942 | Occupation | 1948 | Model Cadet | 1953 | Hasty Road | 1958 | Restless Wing |
| 1943 | Occupy | 1949 | Curtice | 1954 | Georgian | 1959 | Venetian Way |
| 1944 | Free for All | | | | | 1960 | Crozier |

## WIDENER HANDICAP
### Hialeah Park; 3-year-olds and over; 1¼ miles.

| Year | Winner, age | Year | Winner, age | Year | Winner, age | Year | Winner, age |
|------|-------------|------|-------------|------|-------------|------|-------------|
| 1936 | Mantagna (4) | 1942 | The Rhymer (4) | 1950 | Royal Governor (6) | 1955 | Hasty Road (4) |
| 1937 | Columbiana (4) | 1944 | Four Freedoms (4) | 1951 | Sunglow (4) | 1956 | Nashua (4) |
| 1938 | War Admiral (4) | 1946 | Armed (5) | 1952 | Spartan Valor (4) | 1957 | Bardstown (5) |
| 1939 | Bull Lea (4) | 1947 | Armed (6) | 1953 | Oil Capitol (6) | 1958 | Oligarchy (4) |
| 1940 | Many Stings (5) | 1948 | El Mono (4) | 1954 | Landlocked (4) | 1959 | Bardstown (7) |
| 1941 | Big Pebble (5) | 1949 | Coaltown (4) | | | 1960 | Bald Eagle (5) |

## WORLD RECORDS

| Distance | Horse, age, weight, track and location | Date | Time |
|---|---|---|---|
| ¼ | Big Racket, 4, 111, Hipodromo de las Americas, Mexico City, Mexico | February 5, 1945 | :20⅘ |
| 2½ f. | Pichirilo, 2, 117, Hipodromo de las Americas, Mexico City, Mexico | March 25, 1954 | :26⅗ |
| ⅜ | Atoka, 6, 105, Butte, Mont. | September 7, 1906 | :33½ |
| 3½ f. | Joe Blair, 5, 115, Juarez, Mexico | February 5, 1916 | :39 |
| | Deep Sun, 7, 120, Shenandoah Downs, Charlestown, W. Va. | July 11, 1959 | :39 |
| ½ | Beau Madison, 2, 120, Turf Paradise, Phoenix, Ariz. | March 30, 1957 | :45 |
| 4½ f. | Roman Sentinel, 2, 117, Turf Paradise, Phoenix, Ariz. | April 3, 1951 | :51 |
| ⅝ | Bettyanbull, 5, 120, Turf Paradise, Phoenix, Ariz. | February 8, 1959 | :56⅖ |
| 5½ f. | Porterhouse, 6, 125, Hollywood Park, Inglewood, Calif. | June 13, 1957 | 1:02⅖ |
| 5¾ f. | Fighting Fox, 4, 126, Empire City, Yonkers, N. Y. | July 8, 1939 | 1:07⅖ |
| | Doublrab, 4, 130, Empire City, Yonkers, N. Y. | July 18, 1942 | 1:07⅖ |
| ¾ | *Gelding by Blink-Broken Tendril, 3, 123, Brighton, England | August 6, 1929 | 1:06⅕ |
| | Dumpty Humpty, 4, 115, Golden Gate Fields, Albany, Calif. | November 2, 1957 | 1:08 |
| 6½ f. | Tyhawk, 4, 117, Turf Paradise, Phoenix, Ariz. | February 8, 1959 | 1:14⅘ |
| | Golden Notes, 5, 124, Hawthorne, Cicero, Ill. | September 19, 1959 | 1:14⅘ |
| | Little Tytus, 4, 116, Hawthorne, Cicero, Ill. | September 17, 1960 | 1:14⅘ |
| ⅞ | El Drag, 4, 115, Hollywood Park, Inglewood, Calif. | May 21, 1955 | 1:20 |
| 1 mi. | Swaps, 4, 128, Hollywood Park, Inglewood, Calif. | June 9, 1956 | 1:33⅕ |
| | Intentionally, 3, 121, Washington Park, Homewood, Ill. | June 27, 1959 | 1:33⅕ |
| 1 mi. 70 yd. | Mark Antony, 4, 115, Rockingham Park, Salem, N. H. | September 6, 1958 | 1:39⅕ |
| 1 1/16 | Swaps, 4, 130, Hollywood Park, Inglewood, Calif. | June 23, 1956 | 1:39 |
| 1⅛ | Bug Brush, 4, 113, Santa Anita Park, Arcadia, Calif. | February 14, 1959 | 1:46⅖ |
| 1 3/16 | Fleet Bird, 4, 123, Golden Gate Fields, Albany, Calif. | October 24, 1953 | 1:52⅗ |
| 1¼ | Noor, 5, 127, Golden Gate Fields, Albany, Calif. | June 24, 1950 | 1:58⅕ |
| 1⅜ | Man o' War, 3, 126, Belmont Park, Elmont, N. Y. | June 12, 1920 | 2:14⅕ |
| 1½ | The Bastard, 3, 124, Newmarket, England | October 18, 1929 | 2:23 |
| 1 mi. 4½ f. | Mistucky, 9, 113, River Downs, Cincinnati, Ohio | June 26, 1946 | 2:41⅖ |
| 1⅝ | Swaps, 4, 130, Hollywood Park, Inglewood, Calif. | July 25, 1956 | 2:38⅕ |
| 1 mi. 5½ f. | Distribute, 9, 109, River Downs, Cincinnati, Ohio | September 7, 1940 | 2:51⅗ |
| 1¾ | Noor, 5, 117, Santa Anita Park, Arcadia, Calif. | March 4, 1950 | 2:52⅘ |
| 1⅞ | Pharawell, 5, 119, Gulfstream Park, Hallandale, Fla. | April 8, 1947 | 3:13⅘ |
| 2 | Polazel, 3, 142, Salisbury, England | July 8, 1924 | 3:15 |
| 2 mi. 40 yd. | Winning Mark, 4, 107, Thistle Down Park, Cleveland, Ohio | July 20, 1940 | 3:29⅖ |
| 2 mi. 70 yd. | Filisteo, 7, 116, Pimlico, Baltimore, Md. | October 30, 1941 | 3:30⅘ |
| 2 1/16 | Midafternoon, 4, 126, Jamaica, Jamaica, N. Y. | November 15, 1956 | 3:29⅗ |
| 2⅛ | Ceinturion, 5, 119, Newbury, England | September 29, 1923 | 3:35 |
| 2 3/16 | Santiago, 5, 112, Narragansett Park, Pawtucket, R. I. | September 27, 1941 | 3:51⅕ |
| 2¼ | Dakota, 4, 116, Lingfield, England | May 27, 1927 | 3:37⅗ |
| 2⅜ | Wiki Jack, 4, 97, Tijuana, Mexico | February 8, 1925 | 4:15 |
| 2½ | Miss Grillo, 6, 118, Pimlico, Baltimore, Md. | November 12, 1948 | 4:14⅗ |
| 2⅝ | Worthman, 5, 101, Tijuana, Mexico | February 22, 1925 | 4:51⅖ |
| 2¾ | Shot Put, 4, 126, Washington Park, Homewood, Ill. | August 14, 1940 | 4:48⅘ |
| 2⅞ | Bosh, 5, 100, Tijuana, Mexico | March 8, 1925 | 5:23 |
| 3 | Farragut, 5, 113, Agua Caliente, Mexico | March 9, 1941 | 5:15 |
| 3⅜ | Winning Mark, 4, 104, Washington Park, Homewood, Ill. | August 21, 1940 | 6:13 |
| 4 | Sotemia, 5, 119, Churchill Downs, Louisville, Ky. | October 7, 1912 | 7:10⅘ |

* 3/4 mile course at Brighton is started on a hill and is down grade to within one-third of a mile of the finish.

## Straight Course

| | | | |
|---|---|---|---|
| ¼ | Red Jones, 7, 126, Cranwood Race Course, Warrensville Heights, Ohio | October 21, 1958 | :21⅕ |
| ⅜ | King Rhymer, 2, 118, Santa Anita Park, Arcadia, Calif. | February 27, 1947 | :32 |
| ½ | Gloaming, 6, 127, Trentham, Wellington, New Zealand | January 12, 1921 | :45 |
| 4½ f. | The Pimpernel, 2, 118, Belmont Park, Elmont, N. Y. | May 17, 1951 | :49⅘ |
| | Reneged, 2, 118, Belmont Park, Elmont, N. Y. | June 7, 1955 | :49⅘ |
| ⅝ | Devineress, 3, 103, Epsom Downs, Epsom, England | June 2, 1933 | :54⅗ |
| 5½ f. | Delegate, 7, 113, Belmont Park, Elmont, N. Y. | October 10, 1951 | 1:01⅗ |
| ¾ | Vestment, 2, 115, Belmont Park, Elmont, N. Y. | October 15, 1954 | 1:07⅘ |
| 6½ f. | Porter's Mite, 2, 119, Belmont Park, Elmont, N. Y. | September 17, 1938 | 1:14⅖ |
| | Native Dancer, 2, 122, Belmont Park, Elmont, N. Y | September 27, 1952 | 1:14⅖ |
| ⅞ | First Edition, 4, 126, Hurst Park, Hampton Court, England | May 25, 1926 | 1:20 |
| 1 | Mopsus, 3, 105, Brighton, England | June 22, 1939 | 1:32 |
| 1¼ | Banquet, 3, 108, Monmouth Park, N. J. | July 17, 1890 | 2:03¾ |

### Record Betting Day at a Race Track

The greatest amount of money ever wagered on a single horse racing program was bet on the nine-race card presented at Aqueduct on Memorial Day in 1960. A crowd of 70,992 fed $5,560,628 into the mutuel machines. The previous record was $5,016,745 at Belmont Park on Sept. 22, 1945, bet by 49,614 persons.

## LEADING JOCKEYS SINCE 1936

| Year | Jockey | Mounts | Winners | Unplaced | Pct. |
|------|--------|--------|---------|----------|------|
| 1936 | B. James | 1,106 | 245 | 505 | .22 |
| 1937 | J. Adams | 1,265 | 260 | 642 | .21 |
| 1938 | J. Longden | 1,150 | 236 | 575 | .21 |
| 1939 | D. Meade | 1,284 | 255 | 628 | .20 |
| 1940 | E. Dew | 1,377 | 287 | 709 | .21 |
| 1941 | D. Meade | 1,164 | 210 | 611 | .18 |
| 1942 | J. Adams | 1,120 | 245 | 540 | .22 |
| 1943 | J. Adams | 1,069 | 228 | 511 | .21 |
| 1944 | T. Atkinson | 1,539 | 287 | 808 | .19 |
| 1945 | J. D. Jessop | 1,085 | 290 | 445 | .27 |
| 1946 | T. Atkinson | 1,377 | 233 | 758 | .17 |
| 1947 | J. Longden | 1,327 | 316 | 566 | .24 |
| 1948 | J. Longden | 1,197 | 319 | 494 | .27 |
| 1949 | G. Glisson | 1,347 | 270 | 679 | .20 |
| 1950 | W. Shoemaker | 1,640 | 388 | 756 | .24 |
| 1950 | J. Culmone | 1,676 | 388 | 787 | .23 |
| 1951 | C. Burr | 1,162 | 310 | 585 | .24 |
| 1952 | A. DeSpirito | 1,482 | 390 | 633 | .26 |
| 1953 | W. Shoemaker | 1,683 | 485 | 686 | .29 |
| 1954 | W. Shoemaker | 1,251 | 380 | 508 | .30 |
| 1955 | W. Hartack | 1,702 | 417 | 772 | .25 |
| 1956 | W. Hartack | 1,387 | 347 | 604 | .25 |
| 1957 | W. Hartack | 1,238 | 341 | 511 | .25 |
| 1958 | W. Shoemaker | 1,133 | 300 | 511 | .26 |
| 1959 | W. Shoemaker | 1,285 | 347 | 549 | .27 |
| 1960 | W. Hartack | 1,402 | 307 | 658 | .22 |

## LEADING TRAINERS SINCE 1936
### (Winners saddled)

| Year | Name | Winners | Earnings |
|------|------|---------|----------|
| 1936 | H. Jacobs | 177 | 155,789 |
| 1937 | H. Jacobs | 134 | 142,474 |
| 1938 | H. Jacobs | 109 | 116,609 |
| 1939 | H. Jacobs | 106 | 100,907 |
| 1940 | D. Womeldorff | 108 | 112,137 |
| 1941 | H. Jacobs | 123 | 165,964 |
| 1942 | H. Jacobs | 133 | 186,371 |
| 1943 | H. Jacobs | 128 | 210,775 |
| 1944 | H. Jacobs | 117 | 306,821 |
| 1945 | S. Lipiec | 127 | 238,361 |
| 1946 | W. Molter | 122 | 329,725 |
| 1947 | W. Molter | 155 | 833,970 |
| 1948 | W. Molter | 184 | 1,015,547 |
| 1949 | W. Molter | 129 | 696,184 |
| 1949 | W. H. Bishop | 129 | 236,131 |
| 1950 | R. H. McDaniel | 156 | 441,590 |
| 1951 | R. H. McDaniel | 164 | 539,204 |
| 1952 | R. H. McDaniel | 168 | 573,837 |
| 1953 | R. H. McDaniel | 211 | 751,957 |
| 1954 | R. H. McDaniel | 206 | 834,390 |
| 1955 | F. H. Merrill, Jr. | 154 | 298,794 |
| 1956 | V. R. Wright | 177 | 532,344 |
| 1957 | V. R. Wright | 192 | 527,271 |
| 1958 | F. H. Merrill, Jr. | 171 | 320,827 |
| 1959 | V. R. Wright | 172 | 534,319 |
| 1960 | F. H. Merrill, Jr. | 143 | 344,459 |

## LEADING MONEY-WINNING OWNERS

| Year | Name | Amount |
|------|------|--------|
| 1936 | Milky Way Farm Stable | 206,450 |
| 1937 | Mrs. Charles S. Howard | 214,559 |
| 1938 | H. Maxwell Howard | 226,495 |
| 1939 | Belair Stud | 284,250 |
| 1940 | Charles S. Howard | 334,120 |
| 1941 | Calumet Farm | 475,091 |
| 1942 | Greentree Stable | 414,432 |
| 1943 | Calumet Farm | 267,915 |
| 1944 | Calumet Farm | 601,660 |
| 1945 | Maine Chance Farm | 589,170 |
| 1946 | Calumet Farm | 564,095 |
| 1947 | Calumet Farm | 1,402,436 |
| 1948 | Calumet Farm | 1,269,710 |
| 1949 | Calumet Farm | 1,128,942 |
| 1950 | Brookmeade Stable | 651,399 |
| 1951 | Greentree Stable | 637,242 |
| 1952 | Calumet Farm | 1,283,197 |
| 1953 | A. G. Vanderbilt | 987,306 |
| 1954 | King Ranch | 837,615 |
| 1955 | Hasty House Farm | 832,879 |
| 1956 | Calumet Farm | 1,057,383 |
| 1957 | Calumet Farm | 1,150,910 |
| 1958 | Calumet Farm | 946,262 |
| 1959 | Cain Hoy Stable | 742,081 |
| 1960 | C. V. Whitney | 1,039,091 |

## TOP MONEY-WINNING HORSES

| Year | Horse and age | Starts | 1st | Amount |
|------|---------------|--------|-----|--------|
| 1936 | Granville (3) | 11 | 7 | 110,295 |
| 1937 | Seabiscuit (4) | 15 | 11 | 168,580 |
| 1938 | Stagehand (3) | 15 | 8 | 189,710 |
| 1939 | Challedon (3) | 15 | 9 | 184,535 |
| 1940 | Bimelech (3) | 7 | 4 | 110,005 |
| 1941 | Whirlaway (3) | 20 | 13 | 272,386 |
| 1942 | Shut Out (3) | 12 | 8 | 238,872 |
| 1943 | Count Fleet (3) | 6 | 6 | 174,055 |
| 1944 | Pavot (2) | 8 | 8 | 179,040 |
| 1945 | Busher (3) | 13 | 10 | 273,735 |
| 1946 | Assault (3) | 15 | 8 | 424,195 |
| 1947 | Armed (6) | 17 | 11 | 376,325 |
| 1948 | Citation (3) | 20 | 19 | 709,470 |
| 1949 | Ponder (3) | 21 | 9 | 321,825 |
| 1950 | Noor (5) | 12 | 7 | 346,940 |
| 1951 | Counterpoint (3) | 15 | 7 | 250,525 |
| 1952 | Crafty Admiral (4) | 16 | 9 | 277,225 |
| 1953 | Native Dancer (3) | 10 | 9 | 513,425 |
| 1954 | Determine (3) | 15 | 10 | 328,700 |
| 1955 | Nashua (3) | 12 | 10 | 752,550 |
| 1956 | Needles (3) | 8 | 4 | 440,850 |
| 1957 | Round Table (3) | 22 | 15 | 600,285 |
| 1958 | Round Table (4) | 20 | 14 | 662,780 |
| 1959 | Sword Dancer (3) | 13 | 8 | 537,004 |
| 1960 | Bally Ache (3) | 15 | 10 | 455,045 |

## Round Table Racing's Biggest Money Winner

When Round Table was retired from racing late in 1959, the 5-year-old had earned $1,749,869, the highest on record for any horse. Round Table, owned by Travis Kerr of Oklahoma City, had been in 66 races. He won 43 of these starts, placed second 8 times and third 5 times.

Horses which led the money-winning list before Round Table:

| | Starts | 1st | 2d | 3d | Earnings |
|---|--------|-----|----|----|----------|
| Nashua | 30 | 22 | 4 | 1 | $1,288,565 |
| Citation | 45 | 32 | 10 | 2 | 1,085,670 |
| Stymie | 131 | 35 | 33 | 28 | 918,485 |
| Armed | 81 | 41 | 20 | 10 | 817,475 |
| Assault | 42 | 18 | 6 | 7 | 675,470 |
| Whirlaway | 60 | 32 | 15 | 9 | 561,161 |
| Seabiscuit | 89 | 33 | 15 | 13 | 437,730 |
| Sun Beau | 74 | 33 | 12 | 10 | 376,744 |

# HARNESS RACING

OLIVER WENDELL HOLMES, the famous Autocrat of the Breakfast Table, wrote that the running horse was a gambling toy but the trotting horse was useful and, furthermore, "horse-racing is not a republican institution; horse-trotting is." Oliver Wendell Holmes was a born and bred New Englander and New England was the nursery of the harness racing sport in America. Pacers and trotters were matters of local pride and prejudice in Colonial New England and, shortly after the Revolution, the Messenger and Justin Morgan strains produced many winners in harness racing "matches" along the turnpikes of New York, Connecticut, Rhode Island, Massachusetts, Vermont, and New Hampshire.

There was English thoroughbred blood in Messenger and Justin Morgan and, many years later, it was blended in Rysdyk's Hambletonian, foaled in 1849. Hambletonian was not particularly fast under harness but his descendants have had almost a monopoly of prizes, titles, and records in the harness racing game. Hambletonian was purchased as a foal with its dam for a total of $124 by William Rysdyk of Goshen, N. Y., and made a modest fortune for the purchaser.

Trotters and pacers often were raced under saddle in the old days and, in fact, the custom still survives in some places in Europe. Dexter, the great trotter that lowered the mile record from 2:19¾ to 2:17¼ in 1867, was said to handle just as well under saddle as when pulling a sulky. But as sulkies were lightened in weight and improved in design, trotting under saddle became less common and finally faded out in this country.

## WORLD RECORDS

### Established in a Race or Against Time at One Mile

*Source:* Larry Evans, Publicity Director, United States Trotting Association.

#### TROTTING ON MILE TRACK

|  | Record | Holder | Driver | Where Made | Year |
|---|---|---|---|---|---|
| All age | 1:55 1/4 | Greyhound | Sep Palin | Lexington, Ky. | 1938 |
| Yearling | 2:15 1/5 | Rilda Rose | Ike Bailey | Lexington, Ky. | 1955 |
| 2-year-old | 1:58 3/5(r) | Impish | Frank Ervin | Lexington, Ky. | 1961 |
| 3-year-old | 1:58 | Titan Hanover | Harry Pownall | Du Quoin, Ill. | 1945 |
|  | 1:58 | Emily's Pride | Flick Nipe | Lexington, Ky. | 1958 |
|  | 1:58 | Yankee Lass | Frank Ervin | Lexington, Ky. | 1958 |
|  | 1:58 | Expresson | Frank Ervin | Lexington, Ky. | 1959 |
| 4-year-old | 1:57 1/4(r) | Greyhound | Sep Palin | Springfield, Ill. | 1936 |
|  | 1:57 1/4 | Spencer Scott | Fred Egan | Lexington, Ky. | 1941 |

#### TROTTING ON HALF-MILE TRACK

|  | Record | Holder | Driver | Where Made | Year |
|---|---|---|---|---|---|
| All age | 1:59 3/4 | Greyhound | Sep Palin | Goshen, N. Y. | 1937 |
| Yearling | 2:21 1/2 | U. Forbes | H. C. Moody | Louisville, Ky. | 1913 |
| 2-year-old | 2:03 1/2(r) | Titan Hanover | Harry Pownall | Delaware, Ohio | 1944 |
| 3-year-old | 2:00 3/5 | Caleb | John Simpson | Delaware, Ohio | 1961 |
| 4-year-old | 2:00 1/5(r) | Galophone | W. Robert Walker | Westbury, N. Y. | 1956 |

#### PACING ON MILE TRACK

|  | Record | Holder | Driver | Where Made | Year |
|---|---|---|---|---|---|
| All age | 1:54 3/5 | Adios Butler | Paige West | Lexington, Ky. | 1960 |
| Yearling | 2:14 3/4 | Royal Lady 2nd | O. M. Powell | Indianapolis | 1939 |
| 2-year-old | 1:57(r) | Bullet Hanover | John Simpson | Indianapolis | 1959 |
| 3-year-old | 1:55 3/5 | Bullet Hanover | John Simpson | Lexington, Ky. | 1960 |
| 4-year-old | 1:54 3/5 | Adios Butler | Paige West | Lexington, Ky. | 1960 |

#### PACING ON HALF-MILE TRACK

|  | Record | Holder | Driver | Where Made | Year |
|---|---|---|---|---|---|
| All age | 1:55 3/5 | Adios Butler | Edward Cobb | Delaware, Ohio | 1961 |
| Yearling | 2:15 2/5 | F. E. Scott | E. Cunningham | Montreal, Que. | 1959 |
| 2-year-old | 2:00 4/5(r) | Muncy Hanover | Earle Avery | Delaware, Ohio | 1959 |
| 3-year-old | 1:58 3/5(r) | Muncy Hanover | Earle Avery | Delaware, Ohio | 1960 |
|  | 1:58 3/5(r) | Bullet Handover | John Simpson | Delaware, Ohio | 1960 |
| 4-year-old | 1:57 4/5(r) | Bye Bye Bird | Clint Hodgins | Westbury, N. Y. | 1959 |

(r) Record made in race.

### Betting Record for Pari-Mutuel Harness Racing

Records for betting and for attendance at a pari-mutuel harness racing track were established at Roosevelt Raceway, Westbury, N. Y., on Aug. 20, 1960. A crowd of 54,861 wagered $2,730,113 on the nine-race program that evening. The previous betting record of $2,692,585 had been set at the same track on Nov. 30, 1959. The previous attendance record was 50,336, set at Roosevelt Raceway in 1957.

# HISTORY OF TRADITIONAL HARNESS RACING STAKES
## The Hambletonian
**Three-year-old trotters. One mile. Raced at Syracuse, N. Y., 1926, 1928; at Lexington, Ky., 1927, 1929 at Goshen, N. Y., 1930-42, 1944-56; at Yonkers, N. Y., 1943; at Du Quoin, Ill., since 1957.**

| Year | Winner | Driver | Best time | Total purse |
|---|---|---|---|---|
| 1926 | Guy McKinney | Nat Ray | 2:04 3/4 | $ 73,451.32 |
| 1927 | Isola's Worthy | Marvin Childs | 2:03 3/4 | 54,194.44 |
| 1928 | Spencer | W. H. Leese | 2:02 1/2 | 66,226.25 |
| 1929 | Walter Dear | Walter Cox | 2:02 3/4 | 60,309.60 |
| 1930 | Hanover's Bertha | Tom Berry | 2:03 | 56,859.84 |
| 1931 | Calumet Butler | Dick McMahon | 2:03 1/4 | 50,921.39 |
| 1932 | The Marchioness | Will Caton | (a)2:01 1/4 | 49,489.26 |
| 1933 | Mary Reynolds | Ben White | 2:03 3/4 | 40,459.88 |
| 1934 | Lord Jim | H. M. Parshall | 2:02 3/4 | 25,845.44 |
| 1935 | Greyhound | Sep Palin | 2:02 1/4 | 33,221.43 |
| 1936 | Rosalind | Ben White | 2:01 3/4 | 35,643.83 |
| 1937 | Shirley Hanover | Henry Thomas | 2:01 1/4 | 37,912.58 |
| 1938 | McLin Hanover | Henry Thomas | 2:02 1/4 | 37,962.37 |
| 1939 | Peter Astra | H. M. Parshall | 2:04 1/4 | 40,502.46 |
| 1940 | Spencer Scott | Fred Egan | 2:02 | 43,658.45 |
| 1941 | Bill Gallon | Lee Smith | 2:05 | 38,729.86 |
| 1942 | The Ambassador | Ben White | 2:04 | 38,954.38 |
| 1943 | Volo Song | Ben White | (b)2:02 1/2 | 42,298.03 |
| 1944 | Yankee Maid | Henry Thomas | 2:04 | 33,577.12 |
| 1945 | Titan Hanover | Harry Pownall | 2:04 | 50,196.96 |
| 1946 | Chestertown | Tom Berry | 2:02 1/2 | 50,995.57 |
| 1947 | Hoot Mon | Sep Palin | 2:00 | 46,267.93 |
| 1948 | Demon Hanover | Harrison Hoyt | 2:02 | 59,941.18 |
| 1949 | Miss Tilly | Fred Egan | 2:01 2/5 | 69,791.08 |
| 1950 | Lusty Song | Del Miller | 2:02 | 75,209.12 |
| 1951 | Mainliner | Guy Crippen | 2:02 3/5 | 95,263.93 |
| 1952 | Sharp Note | Bi Shively | 2:02 3/5 | 87,637.55 |
| 1953 | Helicopter | Harry Harvey | (c)2:01 3/5 | 117,117.98 |
| 1954 | Newport Dream | Del Cameron | 2:02 4/5 | 106,830.68 |
| 1955 | Scott Frost | Joe O'Brien | 2:00 3/5 | 86,863.32 |
| 1956 | The Intruder | Ned Bower | 2:01 2/5 | 100,603.99 |
| 1957 | Hickory Smoke | John Simpson | 2:01 | 111,126.25 |
| 1958 | Emily's Pride | Flick Nipe | 1:59 4/5 | 106,719.24 |
| 1959 | Diller Hanover | Frank Ervin | 2:01 | 125,283.98 |
| 1960 | Blaze Hanover | Joe O'Brien | (d)1:59 3/5 | 144,590.14 |

(a) By Hollyrood Dennis.  (b) By Worthy Boy and by Volo Song.  (c) By Morse Hanover.  (d) By Quick Song and by Hoot Frost.

## Little Brown Jug
**Three-year-old pacers. Raced at Delaware County Fair Grounds, Delaware, Ohio.**

| Year | Winner | Driver | Best time | Total Purse |
|---|---|---|---|---|
| 1946 | Ensign Hanover | Wayne Smart | (a)2:02 3/4 | $35,358.65 |
| 1947 | Forbes Chief | Del Cameron | 2:05 | 38,200.00 |
| 1948 | Knight Dream | Frank Safford | 2:07 1/5 | 47,528.58 |
| 1949 | Good Time | Frank Ervin | 2:03 2/5 | 58,281.30 |
| 1950 | Dudley Hanover | Del Miller | 2:02 3/5 | 56,525.47 |
| 1951 | Tar Heel | Del Cameron | 2:00 | 66,280.55 |
| 1952 | Meadow Rice | Wayne Smart | 2:01 3/5 | 60,463.35 |
| 1953 | Keystoner | Frank Ervin | (b)2:02 3/5 | 54,972.21 |
| 1954 | Adios Harry | Morris MacDonald | (c)2:01 2/5 | 69,332.06 |
| 1955 | Quick Chief | Bill Haughton | (d)2:02 | 66,608.83 |
| 1956 | Noble Adios | John Simpson | 2:00 4/5 | 52,666.05 |
| 1957 | Torpid | John Simpson | 2:00 4/5 | 73,528.15 |
| 1958 | Shadow Wave | Joe O'Brien | 2:01 | 65,252.94 |
| 1959 | Adios Butler | Clint Hodgins | 1:59 2/5 | 76,582.00 |
| 1960 | Bullet Hanover | John Simpson | (e)1:58 3/5 | 66,510.89 |

(a) By Royal Chief.  (b) By Newport Chief.  (c) By Phantom Lady.  (d) By Dottie's Pick.  (e) By Bullet Hanover and Muncy Hanover.

# HARNESS RACING RECORDS FOR THE MILE

| TROTTERS | | | PACERS | | |
|---|---|---|---|---|---|
| Time | Trotter, age, driver | Year | Time | Pacer, age, driver | Year |
| 1:57¾ | Peter Manning, 5, T. W. Murphy | 1921 | 1:56¼ | Dan Patch, 7, M. E. McHenry | 1903 |
| 1:57 | Peter Manning, 6, T. W. Murphy | 1922 | 1:56 | Dan Patch, 8, H. C. Hersey | 1904 |
| 1:56¾ | Peter Manning, 6, T. W. Murphy | 1922 | 1:55¼ | Dan Patch, 9, H. C. Hersey | 1905 |
| 1:56¾ | Greyhound, 5, Sep Palin | 1937 | 1:55 | Billy Direct, 4, Vic Fleming | 1938 |
| 1:56 | Greyhound, 5, Sep Palin | 1937 | 1:55 | Adios Harry, 4, Luther Lyons | 1955 |
| 1:55¼ | Greyhound, 6, Sep Palin | 1938 | 1:54⅗ | Adios Butler, 4, Paige West | 1960 |

# 1961 CHAMPIONS AND RECORDS

## BASKETBALL

### NATIONAL COLLEGIATE A.A. CHAMPIONSHIP

(At Kansas City)

| CINCINNATI (70)* | g | fa-f | pf | pts | OHIO STATE (65) | g | fa-f | pf | pts |
|---|---|---|---|---|---|---|---|---|---|
| Wiesenhahn | 8 | 1-1 | 3 | 17 | Havlicek | 1 | 2-2 | 2 | 4 |
| Thacker | 7 | 4-1 | 0 | 15 | Hoyt | 3 | 1-1 | 3 | 7 |
| Hogue | 3 | 6-3 | 3 | 9 | Lucas | 10 | 7-7 | 4 | 27 |
| Yates | 4 | 5-5 | 3 | 13 | Nowell | 3 | 3-3 | 1 | 9 |
| Bouldin | 7 | 3-2 | 4 | 16 | Siegfried | 6 | 3-2 | 2 | 14 |
| Sizer | 0 | 0-0 | 0 | 0 | Knight | 1 | 0-0 | 1 | 2 |
| Heidotting | 0 | 0-0 | 0 | 0 | Gearhart | 1 | 0-0 | 1 | 2 |
| Totals | 29 | 19-12 | 13 | 70 | Totals | 25 | 16-15 | 14 | 65 |

* One overtime period.

Half-time score—Ohio State 39, Cincinnati 39. Regulation time score—Ohio State 61, Cincinnati 61.

### NATIONAL INVITATION TOURNAMENT FINAL

(At New York)

| PROVIDENCE (62) | g | fa-f | pf | pts | ST. LOUIS (59) | g | fa-f | pf | pts |
|---|---|---|---|---|---|---|---|---|---|
| Zalucki | 7 | 3-3 | 1 | 17 | Reid | 3 | 2-2 | 3 | 8 |
| Moynahan | 3 | 0-0 | 1 | 6 | Harris | 0 | 0-0 | 0 | 0 |
| Flynn | 3 | 2-2 | 0 | 8 | Hartweger | 0 | 0-0 | 1 | 0 |
| Hadnot | 6 | 9-6 | 4 | 18 | W. Nordmann | 5 | 7-6 | 3 | 16 |
| Ernst | 2 | 0-0 | 2 | 4 | Book | 2 | 1-1 | 3 | 5 |
| Egan | 4 | 2-1 | 0 | 9 | Luechtfeld | 0 | 0-0 | 0 | 0 |
| Totals | 25 | 16-12 | 8 | 62 | Kieffer | 9 | 0-0 | 1 | 18 |
| | | | | | Mankowski | 6 | 0-0 | 1 | 12 |
| | | | | | Latinovich | 0 | 0-0 | 0 | 0 |
| | | | | | Totals | 25 | 10-9 | 12 | 59 |

Half-time score—Providence 35, St. Louis 31.

### OTHER CHAMPIONS

N. C. A. A. College Division—Wittenberg
National Basketball League—Cleveland Pipers
National Association (N. A. I. A.)—Grambling
National Junior College—Pueblo, Colo.
Ivy League—Princeton
Atlantic Coast—Wake Forest
Southern—George Washington
Big Ten—Ohio State
Southeastern—Mississippi State
Big Eight—Kansas State
Skyline—Utah
Big Five—Southern California
Yankee—Rhode Island
Missouri Valley—Cincinnati
Border—Arizona State
Middle Atlantic—St. Joseph's
Rocky Mountain—Colorado College
Ohio Valley—Morehead
Southwest—Texas Tech
Mid-American—Ohio U.
West Coast—Loyola, L. A.

### WOMEN

National A. A. U.—Wayland Baptist College, Plainview, Tex.

### ALL-AMERICA SELECTIONS

(Associated Press poll)

| FIRST TEAM | SECOND TEAM |
|---|---|
| Jerry Lucas, Ohio State | Walt Bellamy, Indiana |
| Tom Stith, St. Bonaventure | Tony Jackson, St. John's |
| Terry Dischinger, Purdue | Frank Burgess, Gonzaga |
| Roger Kaiser, Georgia Tech | Bill McGill, Utah |
| Chet Walker, Bradley | Doug Moe, North Carolina |

### NATIONAL A.A.U. CHAMPIONSHIP

(At Denver)

| CLEVELAND PIPERS (107) | g | fa-f | pf | pts | DENVER TRUCKERS (96) | g | fa-f | pf | pts |
|---|---|---|---|---|---|---|---|---|---|
| Adams | 11 | 6-6 | 2 | 28 | Walker | 8 | 11-9 | 3 | 25 |
| Swartz | 6 | 7-7 | 4 | 19 | Mangham | 6 | 0-0 | 5 | 12 |
| Sharrar | 5 | 9-6 | 5 | 16 | Moran | 10 | 3-3 | 4 | 23 |
| Taylor | 6 | 4-3 | 3 | 15 | Belmont | 2 | 2-2 | 3 | 6 |
| Barnhill | 7 | 8-7 | 2 | 21 | Lane | 7 | 4-4 | 4 | 18 |
| McCollom | 2 | 7-4 | 1 | 8 | Olson | 3 | 2-0 | 5 | 6 |
| Hamilton | 0 | 0-0 | 0 | 0 | Salz | 3 | 0-0 | 4 | 6 |
| Totals | 37 | 41-33 | 17 | 107 | Totals | 39 | 22-18 | 28 | 96 |

Half-time score—Denver 47, Cleveland 43.

### COLLEGIATE RANKINGS

(Associated Press poll)

| Team | 1st place votes | Pts. |
|---|---|---|
| 1—Ohio State | 36 | 360 |
| 2—Cincinnati | 0 | 313 |
| 3—St. Bonaventure | 0 | 250 |
| 4—Kansas State | 0 | 204 |
| 5—North Carolina | 0 | 173 |
| 6—Bradley | 0 | 132 |
| 7—Southern California | 0 | 102 |
| 8—Iowa | 0 | 95 |
| 9—West Virginia | 0 | 66 |
| 10—Duke | 0 | 64 |

## BOBSLEDDING

Source: Lucien Miron, Adirondack Bobsled Club

### World Championships

(At Lake Placid, N. Y.)

2-man—Eugenio Monti–Sergio Siorpaes, Italy ...... 4:42.67
4-man—Eugenio Monti, driver; Furio Nordio; Benito
Rigoni; Sergio Siorpaes, brake .................. 2:18.40
brake (2 heats only) ............................ 2:18.40

### National A. A. U. Championships

(At Lake Placid, N. Y.)

2-man—William Dodge-Stephen Phillips, Adirondack
(N. Y.) B. C. .................................... 4:53.83
4-man.—Larry McKillip, driver; Mike Baumgartner;
Neil Rogers; Jim Lamy, brake, Saranac Lake
(N. Y.) B. C. .................................... 4:42.08

## CURLING

Source: L. T. Kreutzig, *North American Curling News.* South Milwaukee, Wis.

### Champions

World—Canada (Edmonton, Alta.) (Hector Gervais, skip; Ray Werner, Vic Raymer, Wally Ursuliak)
United States—Seattle (Frank Crealock, skip; Ken Sherwood, John Jamieson, Bud McCarthy)
Women's United States—The Country Club, Brookline, Mass. (Peggy Patterson, skip; Katie Cutler, North Lincoln, Kinty Morss)
Canadian—Edmonton, Alta. (Hector Gervais, skip; Ron Anton, Ray Werner, Wally Ursuliak)

### Alaskan Wins Dog Sled Title

Leo Kriska of Koyukuk, Alaska, won the 75-mile world sled dog championship at Anchorage in 1961. Kriska's team of dogs had an elapsed time of 5 hours 52 minutes 10 seconds for three 25-mile heats.

# PROFESSIONAL BASKETBALL
## NATIONAL BASKETBALL ASSOCIATION
*Source:* Haskell Cohen, Publicity Director, National Basketball Association.

## REGULAR SEASON

### Final Standing of the Clubs

#### EASTERN DIVISION

| | W | L | Pct. | Scoring avg. For | Agst. |
|---|---|---|---|---|---|
| Boston Celtics | 57 | 22 | .721 | 119.7 | 114.1 |
| Philadelphia Warriors | 46 | 33 | .582 | 121.0 | 120.0 |
| Syracuse Nationals | 38 | 41 | .481 | 121.3 | 119.2 |
| New York Knickerbockers | 21 | 58 | .266 | 113.6 | 120.1 |

#### WESTERN DIVISION

| | W | L | Pct. | Scoring avg. For | Agst. |
|---|---|---|---|---|---|
| St. Louis Hawks | 51 | 28 | .645 | 118.7 | 115.2 |
| Los Angeles Lakers | 36 | 43 | .456 | 114.0 | 114.1 |
| Detroit Pistons | 34 | 45 | .430 | 118.6 | 121.0 |
| Cincinnati Royals | 33 | 46 | .418 | 117.9 | 121.3 |

### Leading Scorers

| | GP | FG | FT | Pts. | Avg. |
|---|---|---|---|---|---|
| Wilt Chamberlain, Phila. | 79 | 1251 | 531 | 3033 | 38.3 |
| Elgin Baylor, Los Angeles | 73 | 931 | 676 | 2538 | 34.8 |
| Oscar Robertson, Cincinnati | 71 | 756 | 653 | 2165 | 30.5 |
| Bob Pettit, St. Louis | 76 | 769 | 582 | 2120 | 27.9 |
| Jack Twyman, Cincinnati | 79 | 796 | 405 | 1997 | 25.3 |
| Dolph Schayes, Syracuse | 79 | 594 | 680 | 1868 | 23.6 |
| Willie Naulls, New York | 79 | 737 | 372 | 1846 | 23.4 |
| Paul Arizin, Philadelphia | 79 | 650 | 532 | 1832 | 23.2 |
| Bailey Howell, Detroit | 78 | 607 | 601 | 1815 | 23.3 |
| Gene Shue, Detroit | 78 | 650 | 465 | 1765 | 22.6 |
| Richie Guerin, New York | 79 | 612 | 496 | 1720 | 21.8 |
| Cliff Hagan, St. Louis | 78 | 661 | 383 | 1705 | 21.8 |
| Tom Heinsohn, Boston | 74 | 627 | 325 | 1579 | 21.3 |
| Hal Greer, Syracuse | 79 | 623 | 305 | 1551 | 19.6 |
| Clyde Lovellette, St. Louis | 67 | 599 | 273 | 1471 | 21.8 |
| Jerry West, Los Angeles | 79 | 529 | 331 | 1389 | 17.6 |
| Bob Cousy, Boston | 76 | 513 | 352 | 1378 | 18.1 |
| Bill Russell, Boston | 78 | 532 | 258 | 1322 | 16.9 |
| Richard Barnett, Syracuse | 78 | 540 | 240 | 1320 | 16.9 |
| Frank Ramsey, Boston | 79 | 448 | 295 | 1191 | 15.1 |
| Sam Jones, Boston | 78 | 474 | 210 | 1158 | 14.8 |
| Rudy LaRusso, Los Angeles | 79 | 416 | 323 | 1155 | 14.6 |
| Wayne Embry, Cincinnati | 79 | 458 | 221 | 1137 | 14.4 |
| Dick Garmaker, New York | 71 | 415 | 275 | 1102 | 15.6 |
| David Gambee, Syracuse | 79 | 397 | 291 | 1085 | 13.7 |
| Larry Costello, Syracuse | 75 | 407 | 270 | 1084 | 14.4 |
| John Kerr, Syracuse | 79 | 419 | 218 | 1056 | 13.4 |
| Don Ohl, Detroit | 79 | 427 | 200 | 1054 | 13.3 |
| Tom Gola, Philadelphia | 74 | 420 | 210 | 1050 | 14.2 |
| Guy Rodgers, Philadelphia | 78 | 397 | 206 | 1000 | 12.8 |
| Arlen Bockhorn, Cincinnati | 79 | 420 | 152 | 992 | 12.5 |
| Bill Sharman, Boston | 60 | 383 | 210 | 976 | 16.3 |
| Phil Jordon, Cinn.-N.Y. | 79 | 360 | 208 | 928 | 11.7 |
| George Lee, Detroit | 74 | 310 | 276 | 896 | 12.0 |
| Len Wilkens, St. Louis | 75 | 335 | 220 | 890 | 11.9 |
| Bob Ferry, Detroit | 79 | 350 | 189 | 889 | 11.2 |
| Rod Hundley, Los Angeles | 79 | 323 | 223 | 869 | 11.0 |
| Walt Dukes, Detroit | 73 | 286 | 281 | 853 | 11.7 |

### Individual Leaders

Points—Wilt Chamberlain, Philadelphia . . . . . . . . . . . . . 3033
Scoring average—Wilt Chamberlain, Philadelphia . . . . . . 38.3
Field goals—Wilt Chamberlain, Philadelphia . . . . . . 1251
Field goal percentage—Wilt Chamberlain, Philadelphia  505
Free throws scored—Dolph Schayes, Syracuse . . . . . . . . 680
Free throws scored, percentage—Bill Sharman, Boston 921
Rebounds—Wilt Chamberlain, Philadelphia . . . . . . . . . . 2149
Rebounds per game—Wilt Chamberlain, Philadelphia . . 27.2
Assists—Oscar Robertson, Cincinnati . . . . . . . . . . . . . . . 690
Assists per game—Oscar Robertson, Cincinnati . . . . . . . 9.7
Personal fouls—Paul Arizin, Philadelphia . . . . . . . . . . . 335
Most points, one game—Elgin Baylor, Los Angeles . . . . . 71

### Official All-N.B.A. Selections

| FIRST TEAM | SECOND TEAM |
|---|---|
| Bob Pettit, St. Louis | Dolph Schayes, Syracuse |
| Elgin Baylor, Los Angeles | Tom Heinsohn, Boston |
| Wilt Chamberlain, Philadelphia | Bill Russell, Boston |
| Bob Cousy, Boston | Larry Costello, Syracuse |
| Oscar Robertson, Cincinnati | Gene Shue, Detroit |

## PLAYOFFS

### Eastern Division

Semi-final—Syracuse defeated Philadelphia, 3 games to 0

Final—Boston defeated Syracuse, 4 games to 1

\*March 19—Boston 128, Syracuse 115
March 21—Syracuse 115, Boston 98
\*March 23—Boston 133, Syracuse 110
March 25—Boston 120, Syracuse 107
\*March 26—Boston 123, Syracuse 101
  \* At Boston.

### Western Division

Semi-final—Los Angeles defeated Detroit, 3 games to 2

Final—St. Louis defeated Los Angeles, 4 games to 3

\*March 21—Los Angeles 122, St. Louis 118
\*March 22—St. Louis 121, Los Angeles 106
March 24—Los Angeles 118, St. Louis 112
March 25—St. Louis 118, Los Angeles 117
\*March 27—Los Angeles 121, St. Louis 112
March 29—St. Louis 114, Los Angeles 113 (OT)
\*April 1—St. Louis 105, Los Angeles 103
  \* At St. Louis.

### Championship Series

Boston defeated St. Louis, 4 games to 1

\*April 2—Boston 129, St. Louis 95
\*April 5—Boston 116, St. Louis 108
April 8—St. Louis 124, Boston 120
April 9—Boston 119, St. Louis 104
\*April 10—Boston 121, St. Louis 112
  \* At Boston.

### Leading Scorers

| | GP | FG | FT | Pts. | Avg. |
|---|---|---|---|---|---|
| Elgin Baylor, Los Angeles | 12 | 170 | 117 | 457 | 38.1 |
| Bob Pettit, St. Louis | 12 | 117 | 109 | 353 | 29.4 |
| Jerry West, Los Angeles | 12 | 99 | 77 | 275 | 22.9 |
| Cliff Hagan, St. Louis | 12 | 104 | 56 | 264 | 22.0 |
| Tom Heinsohn, Boston | 10 | 82 | 33 | 197 | 19.7 |
| Bill Russell, Boston | 10 | 73 | 45 | 191 | 19.1 |
| Frank Ramsey, Boston | 10 | 55 | 61 | 171 | 17.1 |
| Len Wilkens, St. Louis | 12 | 63 | 44 | 170 | 14.2 |
| Bill Sharman, Boston | 10 | 68 | 32 | 168 | 16.8 |
| Bob Cousy, Boston | 10 | 67 | 167 | 16.7 | |
| Dolph Schayes, Syracuse | 8 | 51 | 63 | 165 | 20.6 |

### Individual Leaders

Points—Elgin Baylor, Los Angeles . . . . . . . . . . . . . . . . . . 457
Scoring average—Elgin Baylor, Los Angeles . . . . . . . . . . 38.1
Field goals—Elgin Baylor, Los Angeles . . . . . . . . . . . . . . 170
Field goal percentage—Bill Sharman, Boston . . . . . . . . . .511
Free throws scored—Elgin Baylor, Los Angeles . . . . . . . . 117
Free throws scored, percentage—Dolph Schayes,
  Syracuse . . . . . . . . . . . . . . . . . . . . . . . . . . . . . . . . . . . .900
Rebounds—Bill Russell, Boston . . . . . . . . . . . . . . . . . . . . 299
Rebounds per games—Bill Russell, Boston . . . . . . . . . . . 29.9
Assists—Bob Cousy, Boston . . . . . . . . . . . . . . . . . . . . . . . 99
Assists per game—Bob Cousy, Boston . . . . . . . . . . . . . . . 9.9
Personal fouls—Ray Felix, Los Angeles . . . . . . . . . . . . . . 52
Most points, one game—Elgin Baylor, Los Angeles . . . . . 49

### Western All-Stars Win N.B.A. Game

The West won the 11th annual National Basketball Association All-Star Game in 1961, defeating the East, 153-131, in Syracuse on Jan. 17.

# ICE HOCKEY
Source: Stan Fischler, *New York Journal-American*

## National Hockey League

### REGULAR SEASON

#### Final Standing of the Clubs

| | W | L | T | Goals For | Agst. | Pts. |
|---|---|---|---|---|---|---|
| Montreal Canadiens..... | 41 | 19 | 10 | 254 | 188 | 92 |
| Toronto Maple Leafs.... | 39 | 19 | 12 | 234 | 176 | 90 |
| Chicago Black Hawks... | 29 | 24 | 17 | 198 | 180 | 75 |
| Detroit Red Wings...... | 25 | 29 | 16 | 195 | 215 | 66 |
| New York Rangers...... | 22 | 38 | 10 | 204 | 248 | 54 |
| Boston Bruins.......... | 15 | 42 | 13 | 176 | 254 | 43 |

#### Leading Scorers

| | GP | G | A | Pts. | PIM |
|---|---|---|---|---|---|
| Bernie Geoffrion, Montreal .. | 64 | 50 | 45 | 95 | 29 |
| Jean Beliveau, Montreal..... | 69 | 32 | 58 | 90 | 57 |
| Frank Mahovlich, Toronto... | 70 | 48 | 36 | 84 | 131 |
| Andy Bathgate, New York... | 70 | 29 | 48 | 77 | 22 |
| Gordie Howe, Detroit....... | 64 | 23 | 49 | 72 | 30 |
| Norman Ullman, Detroit..... | 70 | 28 | 42 | 70 | 34 |
| Red Kelly, Toronto......... | 64 | 20 | 50 | 70 | 12 |
| Dickie Moore, Montreal..... | 57 | 35 | 34 | 69 | 62 |
| Henri Richard, Montreal..... | 70 | 24 | 44 | 68 | 91 |
| Alex Delvecchio, Detroit..... | 70 | 27 | 35 | 62 | 26 |
| Bill Hay, Chicago........... | 69 | 11 | 48 | 59 | 45 |
| Bob Nevin, Toronto......... | 68 | 21 | 37 | 58 | 13 |
| Bobby Hull, Chicago........ | 70 | 31 | 25 | 56 | 43 |
| Andy Hebenton, New York.. | 70 | 26 | 28 | 54 | 10 |
| Camille Henry, New York.... | 53 | 28 | 25 | 53 | 8 |
| Stan Mikita, Chicago........ | 66 | 19 | 34 | 53 | 100 |
| Vic Stasiuk, Bost.-Det....... | 69 | 15 | 38 | 53 | 51 |
| Bert Olmstead, Toronto..... | 67 | 18 | 34 | 52 | 84 |
| Marcel Bonin, Montreal..... | 65 | 16 | 35 | 51 | 45 |
| Jerry Toppazzini, Boston.... | 67 | 15 | 35 | 50 | 35 |
| Don McKenney, Boston...... | 68 | 26 | 23 | 49 | 22 |
| Murray Balfour, Chicago..... | 70 | 21 | 27 | 48 | 123 |
| Dean Prentice, New York.... | 56 | 20 | 25 | 45 | 17 |
| Dave Keon, Toronto........ | 70 | 20 | 25 | 45 | 6 |
| Bill Hicke, Montreal........ | 69 | 18 | 27 | 45 | 31 |
| Ken Wharram, Chicago...... | 64 | 16 | 29 | 45 | 12 |
| Charlie Burns, Boston....... | 62 | 15 | 26 | 41 | 16 |
| Ron Murphy, Chicago....... | 70 | 21 | 19 | 40 | 30 |
| George Sullivan, New York.. | 70 | 9 | 31 | 40 | 66 |
| John Bucyk, Boston........ | 70 | 19 | 20 | 39 | 48 |
| Murray Oliver, Det.-Bost.... | 70 | 17 | 22 | 39 | 16 |
| Billy Harris, Toronto........ | 66 | 12 | 27 | 39 | 30 |
| Doug Harvey, Montreal..... | 58 | 6 | 33 | 39 | 48 |
| Eric Nesterenko, Chicago.... | 68 | 19 | 19 | 38 | 125 |
| Al Johnson, Detroit........ | 70 | 16 | 21 | 37 | 14 |
| Bill Gadsby, New York...... | 65 | 9 | 26 | 35 | 49 |
| Pierre Pilote, Chicago....... | 70 | 6 | 29 | 35 | 165 |
| Earl Ingarfield, New York.... | 66 | 13 | 21 | 34 | 18 |
| Tod Sloan, Chicago......... | 67 | 11 | 23 | 34 | 48 |
| Allan Stanley, Toronto...... | 68 | 9 | 25 | 34 | 42 |
| Pete Goegan, Detroit....... | 67 | 5 | 29 | 34 | 78 |
| Ab McDonald, Chicago...... | 61 | 17 | 16 | 33 | 22 |
| Dick Duff, Toronto......... | 67 | 16 | 17 | 33 | 54 |
| George Armstrong, Toronto.. | 47 | 14 | 19 | 33 | 21 |
| Doug Mohns, Boston....... | 65 | 12 | 21 | 33 | 63 |
| Ralph Backstrom, Montreal.. | 69 | 12 | 20 | 32 | 44 |
| Ed Litzenberger, Chicago.... | 62 | 10 | 22 | 32 | 14 |
| Ed Shack, N.Y.-Tor....... | 67 | 15 | 16 | 31 | 107 |
| Don Marshall, Montreal..... | 70 | 14 | 17 | 31 | 8 |
| Jean-Guy Talbot, Montreal.. | 70 | 5 | 26 | 31 | 143 |
| Bronco Horvath, Boston..... | 47 | 15 | 15 | 30 | 15 |
| Brian Cullen, New York..... | 42 | 11 | 19 | 30 | 6 |
| Leo LaBine, Bost.-Det....... | 64 | 9 | 21 | 30 | 66 |

#### Official All-N.H.L. Selections

| FIRST TEAM | Pos. | SECOND TEAM |
|---|---|---|
| Johnny Bower, Tor. | G | Glenn Hall, Chi. |
| Doug Harvey, Mont. | D | Allan Stanley, Tor. |
| Marcel Pronovost, Det. | D | Pierre Pilote, Chi. |
| Jean Beliveau, Mont. | C | Henri Richard, Mont. |
| Bernie Geoffrion, Mont. | R.W. | Gordie Howe, Det. |
| Frank Mahovlich, Tor. | L.W. | Dickie Moore, Mont. |

#### Trophy Winners

Hart (most valuable player)—Bernie Geoffrion, Montreal
Ross (leading scorer)—Bernie Geoffrion, Montreal
Lady Byng (sportsmanship)—Red Kelly, Toronto
Calder (leading rookie)—Dave Keon, Toronto
Vezina (leading goalie)—Johnny Bower, Toronto
Norris (best defenseman)—Doug Harvey, Montreal

### STANLEY CUP PLAYOFFS

#### Preliminary Series

Chicago defeated Montreal, 4 games to 2.

March 21—Montreal 6, Chicago 2
March 23—Chicago 4, Montreal 3
*March 26—Chicago 2, Montreal 1 (52:12 ovt.)
*March 28—Montreal 5, Chicago 2
April 1—Chicago 3, Montreal 0
*April 4—Chicago 3, Montreal 0
* At Chicago.

Detroit defeated Toronto, 4 games to 1.

March 22—Toronto 3, Detroit 2 (24:51 ovt.)
March 25—Detroit 4, Toronto 2
*March 26—Detroit 2, Toronto 0
*March 28—Detroit 4, Toronto 1
April 1—Detroit 3, Toronto 2
* At Detroit.

#### Championship Series

Chicago won the Stanley Cup, defeating Detroit, 4 games to 2.

*April 6—Chicago 3, Detroit 2
April 8—Detroit 3, Chicago 1
*April 10—Chicago 3, Detroit 1
April 12—Detroit 2, Chicago 1
*April 14—Chicago 6, Detroit 3
April 16—Chicago 5, Detroit 1
* At Chicago.

#### Leading Scorers

| | GP | G | A | Pts. | PIM |
|---|---|---|---|---|---|
| Gordie Howe, Detroit........ | 11 | 4 | 11 | 15 | 10 |
| Pierre Pilote, Chicago........ | 12 | 3 | 12 | 15 | 8 |
| Bobby Hull, Chicago......... | 12 | 4 | 10 | 14 | 4 |
| Stan Mikita, Chicago........ | 12 | 6 | 5 | 11 | 21 |
| Murray Balfour, Chicago..... | 11 | 5 | 5 | 10 | 14 |
| Alex Delvecchio, Detroit..... | 11 | 4 | 5 | 9 | 0 |
| Ken Wharram, Chicago...... | 12 | 3 | 5 | 8 | 12 |
| Vic Stasiuk, Detroit......... | 11 | 2 | 5 | 7 | 4 |
| Bill Hay, Chicago........... | 12 | 2 | 5 | 7 | 20 |
| Phil Goyette, Montreal...... | 6 | 3 | 3 | 6 | 0 |
| Henri Richard, Montreal..... | 6 | 2 | 4 | 6 | 22 |
| Leo LaBine, Detroit......... | 11 | 3 | 2 | 5 | 4 |
| Marcel Pronovost, Detroit.... | 9 | 2 | 3 | 5 | 0 |
| Val Fonteyne, Detroit....... | 11 | 3 | 2 | 5 | 0 |
| Eric Nesterenko, Chicago.... | 11 | 2 | 3 | 5 | 6 |
| Jean Beliveau, Montreal..... | 6 | 0 | 5 | 5 | 0 |
| Dickie Moore, Montreal..... | 6 | 3 | 1 | 4 | 4 |
| Howie Young, Detroit....... | 11 | 2 | 2 | 4 | 30 |
| Gilles Tremblay, Montreal.... | 6 | 1 | 3 | 4 | 0 |
| Ed Litzenberger, Chicago.... | 10 | 1 | 3 | 4 | 2 |
| Claude Provost, Montreal.... | 6 | 1 | 3 | 4 | 4 |

# HANDBALL

## U.S.H.A. Championships—Four-Wall
(At Denver)

Singles—John Sloan, Chicago
Doubles—John Sloan, Chicago–Vic Hershkowitz, Brooklyn
Master's doubles (40 years and over)—Frank Coyle–Gus Lewis, Chicago

## A.A.U.-Y.M.C.A.—Four-Wall
(At Akron, Ohio)

Singles—Oscar Obert, New York A.C.
Doubles—Oscar and Ruby Obert, New York A.C.

## A.A.U.—One-Wall
(At Brooklyn)

Singles—Steve Sandler, Hebrew Educational Society, Brooklyn
Doubles—Oscar and Ruby Obert, New York A.C.

## Minor League Hockey
### AMERICAN LEAGUE
#### Final Standing of the Clubs

|  | W | L | T | Goals For | Agst. | Pts. |
|---|---|---|---|---|---|---|
| *Springfield | 49 | 22 | 1 | 345 | 205 | 99 |
| Hershey | 36 | 32 | 4 | 218 | 210 | 78 |
| Cleveland | 36 | 35 | 1 | 231 | 234 | 73 |
| Buffalo | 35 | 34 | 3 | 259 | 261 | 73 |
| Rochester | 32 | 36 | 4 | 259 | 245 | 68 |
| Quebec | 30 | 39 | 3 | 217 | 268 | 63 |
| Providence | 26 | 46 | 0 | 225 | 331 | 52 |

* Won playoffs.

### WESTERN LEAGUE
#### Final Standing of the Clubs

|  | W | L | T | Goals For | Agst. | Pts. |
|---|---|---|---|---|---|---|
| Calgary | 44 | 22 | 4 | 300 | 215 | 92 |
| *Portland | 38 | 23 | 9 | 242 | 192 | 85 |
| Vancouver | 38 | 29 | 3 | 208 | 191 | 79 |
| Seattle | 37 | 28 | 5 | 262 | 222 | 79 |
| Spokane | 33 | 34 | 3 | 247 | 258 | 69 |
| Victoria | 27 | 41 | 2 | 220 | 267 | 56 |
| Edmonton | 27 | 43 | 0 | 229 | 295 | 54 |
| Winnipeg | 21 | 45 | 4 | 191 | 259 | 46 |

* Won playoffs.

### EASTERN PROFESSIONAL LEAGUE
#### Final Standings of the Clubs

|  | W | L | T | Goals For | Agst. | Pts. |
|---|---|---|---|---|---|---|
| *Hull–Ottawa | 41 | 20 | 9 | 268 | 187 | 91 |
| Sault Ste. Marie | 32 | 29 | 9 | 236 | 234 | 73 |
| Kitchener–Waterloo | 31 | 28 | 11 | 220 | 215 | 73 |
| Kingston | 29 | 33 | 8 | 259 | 269 | 66 |
| Sudbury | 28 | 33 | 9 | 236 | 257 | 65 |
| Montreal | 19 | 37 | 14 | 167 | 224 | 52 |

* Won playoffs

---

# ROLLER SKATING

### A. R. S. A. Championships
*Source:* U. S. Amateur Roller Skating Association.

(At Detroit)

Singles—George Auble, Bayonne, N. J.
Women's singles—Dawn Brown, Trenton, N. J.
Dance—Jay and Janet Slaughter, Chicago
Mixed pairs—Paul Zukowski–Dianne Ludwig, Elizabeth, N. J.
Women's pairs—Dawn Brown–Eunice Prokop, Trenton, N. J.
Fours—Lee Brown–Sandra Speicher–Lyndell Edgington–Renee Aulberry, Marion, Ind.
Speed—David Kieft, Grand Haven, Mich.
Women's speed—Judy Armer, Reading, Pa.

### Rink Operators Championships
*Source:* Roller Skating Rink Operators Association.

(At Fort Worth, Tex.)

Singles—William Madigan, Pasadena, Calif.
Women's singles—Beverly Bowers, Canada
Dance—Jack Greer–Linda Jo Baker, Atlanta
Esquire dance—Lawrence Andrews–Marie Andrews, Lakemore, Ohio
Pairs—Doug Eley–Judy Nance, Long Beach, Calif.
Fours—Louis Parker–Sylvia Ritchie–David Schafer–Sue Welch, Pontiac, Mich.
Figures—Philip Sukel, Oak Lawn, Ill.
Women's figures—Linda Jo Baker, Atlanta
Speed—Eddie Perales, Gardena, Calif.
Women's speed—Mary Merrell, Santa Ana, Calif.

---

## Amateur Hockey
### WORLD CHAMPIONSHIPS
(At Geneva, Switzerland)
#### Final Standing of the Clubs

|  | W | L | T | Goals For | Agst. | Pts. |
|---|---|---|---|---|---|---|
| *Canada | 6 | 0 | 1 | 45 | 11 | 13 |
| Czechoslovakia | 6 | 0 | 1 | 33 | 9 | 13 |
| U.S.S.R. | 5 | 2 | 0 | 51 | 20 | 10 |
| Sweden | 4 | 3 | 0 | 33 | 27 | 8 |
| East Germany | 2 | 5 | 0 | 21 | 33 | 4 |
| United States | 1 | 5 | 1 | 24 | 43 | 3 |
| Finland | 1 | 5 | 1 | 19 | 43 | 3 |
| West Germany | 0 | 5 | 2 | 10 | 45 | 2 |

* Although Canada and Czechoslovakia were tied in the final standings, Canada was proclaimed champion for having scored more goals.

### EASTERN LEAGUE
#### NORTHERN DIVISION

|  | W | L | T | Goals For | Agst. | Pts. |
|---|---|---|---|---|---|---|
| New Haven | 38 | 25 | 1 | 278 | 221 | 77 |
| Clinton | 30 | 32 | 2 | 267 | 228 | 62 |
| Jersey | 24 | 39 | 1 | 210 | 254 | 49 |
| New York | 18 | 45 | 1 | 196 | 293 | 37 |

#### SOUTHERN DIVISION

|  | W | L | T | Goals For | Agst. | Pts. |
|---|---|---|---|---|---|---|
| Greensboro | 40 | 22 | 2 | 339 | 257 | 82 |
| *Johnstown | 40 | 22 | 2 | 273 | 215 | 82 |
| Philadelphia | 32 | 28 | 4 | 227 | 278 | 68 |
| Charlotte | 25 | 34 | 5 | 221 | 265 | 55 |

* Won playoffs.

### INTERNATIONAL LEAGUE
#### EASTERN DIVISION

|  | W | L | T | Goals For | Agst. | Pts. |
|---|---|---|---|---|---|---|
| Toledo | 36 | 33 | 1 | 274 | 260 | 71 |
| Fort Wayne | 31 | 35 | 3 | 304 | 265 | 65 |
| Muskegon | 25 | 41 | 4 | 243 | 319 | 54 |
| Indianapolis | 20 | 46 | 4 | 217 | 313 | 44 |

#### WESTERN DIVISION

|  | W | L | T | Goals For | Agst. | Pts. |
|---|---|---|---|---|---|---|
| Minneapolis | 50 | 20 | 2 | 323 | 229 | 102 |
| *St. Paul | 46 | 22 | 4 | 309 | 233 | 96 |
| Omaha | 35 | 32 | 3 | 254 | 235 | 73 |
| †Milwaukee | 1 | 15 | 1 | 45 | 115 | 3 |

* Won playoffs. † Suspended operations.

### OTHER CHAMPIONS

National Collegiate—Denver
National senior—Estes H. C., Rockland, Mass.
National junior—Conley H. C., West Roxbury, Mass.
National midget—Thompson–Cain H. C., Detroit
National bantam—Shell Warriors H. C., Sault Ste. Marie, Mich.
Canadian senior (Allan Cup)—Galt, Ont.
Canadian junior (Memorial Cup)—St. Michael's College, Toronto

---

# ROQUE

### American Roque League Champions
First division—Wayne Stephens, Lubbock, Tex.
Second division—Curley Maynard, Eastland, Tex.
Yoursey Trophy—Ivy Huddleston, Lubbock, Tex.
William Cup—J. C. Roberts, San Jose, Calif.
Benedict Cup—Robert Gollehon, Littlefield, Tex.

# ICE (SPEED) SKATING

*Source:* Ken Hall, American Skating Union Statistician

## World Championships

(At Goteborg, Sweden)

Champion—Henk van der Grift, Netherlands... 189.213 pts.
500 m.—Evgeny Grishin, U.S.S.R. ................. 0:41.7
1,500 m.—Henk van der Grift, Netherlands ........ 2:17.8
5,000 m.—Ivar Nilsson, Sweden ................... 7:58.0
10,000 m.—Viktor Kosichkin, U.S.S.R. ........... 16:35.9

### WOMEN

(At Tonsberg, Norway)

Champion—Valentina Stenina, U.S.S.R. ........ 202.533 pts.
500 m.—Valentina Stenina, U.S.S.R. .............. 0:48.1
1,000 m.—Valentina Stenina, U.S.S.R. ............ 1:37.8
1,500 m.—Valentina Stenina, U.S.S.R. ............ 2:33.3
3,000 m.—Inga Voronina, U.S.S.R. ............... 5:23.4

## North American Outdoor

(At Lake Placid, N. Y.)

Champion—Arnold Uhrlass, Yonkers, N.Y. ......... 24 pts.
220 yds.—Tom Augustitus, Detroit ................ 0:19.1
440 yds.—Tom Augustitus, Detroit ................ 0:36.1
880 yds.—Arnold Uhrlass, Yonkers, N. Y. ......... 1:17.2
¾-mi.—Floyd Bedbury, St. Paul, Minn. ......... 2:06.3
Mile—Arnold Uhrlass, Yonkers, N. Y. ............ 2:53.3
2-mi.—Arnold Uhrlass, Yonkers, N. Y. ........... 5:51.8
5-mi.—Arnold Uhrlass, Yonkers, N. Y. .......... 14:49.9
Intermediate—Tom Gray, St. Paul, Minn. ......... 21 pts.
Junior—Jack Walters, Brighton, Mass., and Roger
Capon, Champaign, Ill. ................... 13 pts.
Juvenile—John Wurster, Bellston Spa, N. Y. ....... 13 pts.

### WOMEN

Champion—Jean Ashworth, Wilmington, Mass. ...... 23 pts.
220 yds.—Jean Ashworth, Wilmington, Mass. ....... 0:21.5
440 yds.—Jean Ashworth, Wilmington, Mass. ....... 0:40.6
880 yds.—Jean Ashworth, Wilmington, Mass. ....... 1:34.2
¾-mi.—Jean Ashworth, Wilmington, Mass. ....... 2:32.6
Mile—Gail Purdy, Glens Falls, N. Y. .............. 3:12.3
Intermediate—Beverly Gorton, St. Paul, Minn. ...... 15 pts.
Junior—Mary Meyers, St. Paul, Minn. ............ 13 pts.
Juvenile—Michele Greene, Saratoga Springs, N. Y... 13 pts.

## North American Indoor

(At Buffalo, N. Y.)

Champion—Terry McDermott, Essexville, Mich. ..... 14 pts.
440 yds.—Terry McDermott, Essexville, Mich. ....... 0:40.1
880 yds.—Terry McDermott, Essexville, Mich. ....... 1:22.9
¾-mi.—Tom Augustitus, Detroit ................. 2:08.9
Mile—Bob McCarthy, Queens Village, N. Y. ....... 2:51.2
2-mi.—Bob McCarthy, Queens Village, N. Y. ....... 6:06.5
Intermediate—Bob Fenn, Flushing, N. Y. .......... 20 pts.
Junior—Jack Walters, Brighton, Mass. ............ 10 pts.
Juvenile—Ray Novak, Lombard, Ill. ............... 13 pts.

### WOMEN

Champion—Jean Ashworth, Wilmington, Mass. ...... 15 pts.
440 yds.—Mary Novak, Lombard, Ill. .............. 0:45.5
880 yds.—Jean Ashworth, Wilmington, Mass. ....... 1:38.5
¾-mi.—Jean Ashworth, Wilmington, Mass. ....... 2:14.7
Mile—Jean Ashworth, Wilmington, Mass. .......... 3:08.1
Intermediate—Edith Johnson, Buffalo, N. Y. ....... 15 pts.
Junior—Janice Smith, Rochester, N. Y. ........... 10 pts.
Juvenile—Jeanne Walters, Brighton, Mass. ........ 11 pts.

---

## Waldo Gains Barrel-Jumping Crown

Jim Waldo of Portland, Ore., dethroned Leo LeBel of Flushing, L.I. as the world barrel-jumping champion in the 1961 competition at the Grossinger (N.Y.) Country Club. Waldo cleared 16 barrels for a distance of 25 feet 11½ inches.

## United States Outdoor

(At St. Paul, Minn.)

Champion—Ed Rudolph, Chicago .................. 15 pts.
220 yds.—Terry McDermott, Essexville, Mich. ...... 0:17.8
440 yds.—Ken Bartholomew, Minneapolis ......... 0:38.1
880 yds.—Andy Korenak, West Allis, Wis. .......... 1:13.3
¾-mi.—Arnold Uhrlass, Yonkers, N. Y. .......... 2:20.5
Mile—Ed Rudolph, Chicago ...................... 2:40.2
2-mi.—Floyd Bedbury, St. Paul, Minn. ........... 6:20.2
5-mi.—Arnold Uhrlass, Yonkers, N. Y. .......... 15:42.2
Intermediate—Tom Gray, St. Paul, Minn. .......... 19 pts.
Junior—Jack Walters, Brighton, Mass. ............ 13 pts.
Juvenile—Bob Christianson, Minneapolis .......... 10 pts.

### WOMEN

Champion—Jean Ashworth, Wilmington, Mass. ...... 23 pts.
220 yds.—Jean Ashworth, Wilmington, Mass. ....... 0:21.2
440 yds.—Mary Novak, Lombard, Ill. .............. 0:43.1
880 yds.—Jean Ashworth, Wilmington, Mass. ....... 1:38.4
¾-mi.—Jean Ashworth, Wilmington, Mass. ....... 2:33.9
Mile—Jean Ashworth, Wilmington, Mass. .......... 3:07.0
Intermediate—Karen Kaper, Chicago .............. 11 pts.
Junior—Kay Dickey, Minneapolis ................. 10 pts.
Juvenile—Vicki Gutgesell, West Allis, Wis. ......... 7 pts.

## United States Indoor

(At West Allis, Wis.)

Champion—Keith Meyer, Chicago, and Bob McCarthy,
Queens Village, N. Y. ....................... 14 pts.
440 yds.—Keith Meyer, Chicago ................. 0:41.6
880 yds.—Bob McCarthy, Queens Village, N. Y. ..... 1:22.6
¾-mi.—Bob McCarthy, Queens Village, N. Y. ....... 2:10.0
Mile—Brian Schmitzer, Chicago .................. 2:53.4
2-mi.—Ed Rudolph, Chicago ..................... 6:26.3
Intermediate—Bob Fenn, Flushing, N. Y. .......... .20 pts.
Junior—Terry Evans, Chicago .................... 10 pts.
Juvenile—Pete Cefalu, West Allis, Wis. ........... 11 pts.

### WOMEN

Champion—Mary Novak, Lombard, Ill. ............ 16 pts.
440 yds.—Mary Novak, Lombard, Ill. .............. 0:46.5
880 yds.—Mary Novak, Lombard, Ill. .............. 1:33.2
¾-mi.—Darlene Sechanic, Boston ............... 2:24.0
Mile—Darlene Sechanic, Boston .................. 3:13.6
Intermediate—Loretta Chapman, Pontiac, Mich. ..... 9 pts.
Junior—Kathy Sullivan, Cheboygan, Mich. ......... 11 pts.
Juvenile—Linda Schubert, West Allis, Wis. ......... 11 pts.

# FIGURE SKATING

## North American Championships

(At Philadelphia)

Men—Donald Jackson, Canada
Women—Laurence Owen, Winchester, Mass.
Pairs—Otto and Maria Jelinek, Canada
Dance—William McLachlin-Virginia Thompson, Canada

## United States Championships

(At Colorado Springs)

Men—Bradley Lord, Boston
Women—Laurence Owen, Winchester, Mass.
Pairs—Dudley Richards, Boston–Maribel Owen, Winchester, Mass.
Gold dance—Larry Pierce, Indianapolis–Diane Sherbloom, Los Angeles
Silver dance—Ralph Owen–Rosemary McEvoy, Brooklyn, N. Y.
Junior—Monty Hoyt, Denver
Women's junior—Lorraine Hanlon, Boston
Junior pairs—Ronald and Vivian Joseph, Chicago
Novice—Peter Meyer, Buffalo, N. Y.
Women's novice—Albertina Noyes, Boston

# TRACK AND FIELD
## National A. A. U. Championships

### Men's Indoor
(At New York)

60 yds.—Frank Budd, Villanova.................... 0:06.1
60-yd. high hurdles—Hayes Jones, Ypsilanti, Mich... 0:07.0
600 yds.—Eddie Southern, U. S. Air Force.......... 1:11.9
1,000 yds.—Ernie Cunliffe, Paio Alto, Calif....... 2:08.0
Mile—Jim Beatty, Santa Clara (Calif.) Youth Village 4:09.3
3 miles—Bruce Kidd, East York T. C., Toronto..... 13:47.0
1,060-yd. medley relay—N. Y. Pioneer Club (Cal
  Barnes, Ron Basil, Doyle Whittaker, Emil Dufau) 1:56.1
Mile relay—Morgan State (Lou Smith, Tom Anderson,
  Lee Martin, Lawson Smart)..................... 3:16.3
2-mile relay—Holy Cross (John O'Connor, Jay Bowers,
  Tom Noering, Charles Buchta).................. 7:39.8
High jump—Valery Brumel, U.S.S.R. ...... 7 ft. 2 in.
Broad jump—Ralph Boston, Tennessee State.. 26 ft. 6¼ in.
Pole vault—Don Bragg, Delaware Valley A. A.,
  Philadelphia. ............................. 15 ft. 3 in.
Shot put—Parry O'Brien, Los Angeles........ 61 ft. 3 in
35-lb. weight—Bob Backus, New York A. C.... 66 ft. 6 in
Team—New York A. C. ........................ 16 pts

### Women's Indoor
(At Columbus, Ohio)

50 yds.—Willye White, Daley Youth Foundation,
  Chicago.................................... 0:06.0
70-yd. hurdles—JoAnn Terry, Tennessee State..... 0:09.5
100 yds.—Wilma Rudolph, Tennessee State........ 0:10.8
220 yds.—Vivian Brown, Tennessee State.......... 0:25.2
440 yds.—Lillian Greene, Colorado State......... 1:00.4
880 yds.—Helen Shipley, Liberty A. C., Lexington,
  Mass...................................... 2:21.6
440-yd. relay—Daley Youth Foundation, Chicago
  (Willye White, Doris May, Ernestine Pollards,
  Lacey O'Neal) ............................. 0:48.8
880-yd. medley relay—Ohio T. C. (Melissa Long, Sue
  Knott, Pat Watkins, Wanda Fuller)............. 1:53.1
High jump—Rose Robinson, Chicago.......... 5 ft. 4 in.
Standing broad jump—Sandra Smith, Daley
  Youth Foundation, Chicago............... 8 ft. 11 in.
Shot put—Cynthia Wyatt, Williamsville, N. Y... 39 ft. 11 in.
Basketball throw—Jean Hofbauer, Chicago
  O'Haliaren Club.........................102 ft. 5½ in
Team—Daley Youth Foundation, Chicago.......... 38 pts

### Women's Outdoor
(At Gary, Ind.)

100-yds.—Wilma Rudolph, Tennessee State........ 0:10.8
200 yds.—Lacey O'Neal, Chicago.................. 0:25.0
440 yds.—Jackie Peterson, Police A. L., New York... 0:59.5
880 yds.—Billie Pat Daniels, San Mateo (Calif.) Girls
  A. A..................................... 2:19.2
440-yd. relay—Daley Youth Foundation, Chicago
  (Willye White, Lacey O'Neal, Doris May, Ernestine
  Pollards).................................. 0:47.0
880-yd. relay—San Mateo (Calif.) Girls A. A. (Billie
  Pat Daniels, Jackie Mack, Nancy Duensing, Benetta
  Johnson).................................. 1:49.0
80-m. hurdles—Cherrie Parrish, Laurel T. C., San
  Francisco.................................. 0:11.5
High jump—Liz Josefson, Spartan A. C., Los
  Angeles.................................... 5 ft. 1 in.
Broad Jump—Willye White, Daley Youth
  Foundation, Chicago................... 19 ft. 11½ in.
Shot put—Earlene Brown, Spartan A. C., Los
  Angeles.................................. 47 ft. 8½ in.
Discus—Earlene Brown, Spartan A. C., Los
  Angeles.................................. 149 ft. 4½ in.
Javelin—Fran Davenport, Vista, Calif........ 137 ft. 8 in.
Team—Daley Youth Foundation, Chicago.... 88 pts.

### Men's Outdoor
(At New York)

100 yds.—Frank Budd, Villanova................. 0:09.2
220 yds.—Paul Drayton, Villanova............... 0:21.0
440 yds.—Otis Davis, Emerald Empire A. A., Eugene,
  Ore....................................... 0:46.1
880 yds.—Jim Dupree, Southern Illinois Salukis.... 1:48.5
Mile—Dyrol Burleson, Emerald Empire A. A., Eugene
  Ore....................................... 4:04.9
3 miles—Laszlo Tabori, Santa Clara (Calif.) Youth
  Village.................................... 13:50.0
6 miles—John Gutknecht, Chapel Hill, N. C........ 28:52.6
3,000-m. steeplechase—Charles Jones, Fort Lee, Va. 8:48.0
2-mile walk—Ron Zinn, U. S. Military Academy..... 14:46.8
120-yd. high hurdles—Hayes Jones, Pontiac, Mich... 0:13.6
220-yd. low hurdles—Don Styron, Southern Illinois
  Salukis................................... 0:23.2
440-yard hurdles—Cliff Cushman, Grand Forks (N. D.)
  A. C...................................... 0:50.9
High jump—Bob Avant, Southern California
  Striders.................................. 7 ft.
Broad jump—Ralph Boston, Tennessee State 26 ft. 11¼ in.
Hop, step and jump—Bill Sharpe, Philadel-
  phia Pioneer Club...................... 52 ft. 4¾ in.
Pole vault—Ron Morris, Southern California
  Striders.................................. 15 ft. 8 in.
Shot put—Dallas Long, Southern California
  Striders.................................. 62 ft. 2 in.
Discus—Jay Silvester, Santa Clara (Calif.)
  Youth Village........................... 195 ft. 8 in.
Javelin—John Fromm, Washington A. C.,
  Seattle.................................. 249 ft. 11½ in.
Hammer—Harold Connolly, Southern Cali-
  fornia Striders.......................... 213 ft. 6½ in.
Team—Southern California Striders........ 120 pts.

### Other Outdoor

Decathlon—Paul Herman, Westmont College.... 7,142 pts.
Pentathlon—Bill Toomey, U. of Colorado........ 3,484 pts.
All-around—Bill Urban, New York A. C....... 7,483 pts.
15,000 m.—George Foulds, Pittsburgh......... 49:39.3
20,000 m.—Peter McArdle, New York A. C........ 1:03:43.0
30,000 m.—Peter McArdle, New York A. C....... 1:45:44.5
Marathon—John Kelley, Boston A. A......... 2:26:53.4
1-hour—Peter McArdle, New York A. C.... 11 mi. 1,077 yds.
3,000-m. team—Central Jersey T. C. (Attila Matray,
  John Portee, Carmen Lunetta)................ 13 pts.

### RELAYS

440-yd.—Tarrytown (N. Y.) S. S. C. (Les Prinz, Al
  Washington, Walker Beverly, Mel Blanheim).... 0:41.5
Mile—East York T. C., Toronto (Bud Scott, Doug
  Gilbert, George Shepard, Bill Crothers)........ 3:13.8
2½-mi. medley—East York T. C., Toronto (Bill
  Crothers, Bob Patterson, Jim Snider, Bruce Kidd) 10:03.1

### WALKING

10,000 m.—Ron Zinn, U. S. Military Academy..... 49:34.0
15,000 m.—Ron Zinn, U. S. Military Academy.... 1:15:03.0
20,000 m.—Ron Zinn, U. S. Military Academy... 1:41:51.0
25,000 m.—Ron Laird, N. Y. Pioneer Club....... 2:11:36.0
35,000 m.—Ron Laird, N. Y. Pioneer Club....... 3:28:05.0
40,000 m.—Ron Laird, N. Y. Pioneer Club....... 3:48:05.0
50,000 m.—John Allen, Buffalo, N. Y............ 4:38:19.6

### Finn Captures Boston Marathon

Eino Oksanen of Helsinki, Finland, won
the Boston Marathon in 1961, defeating
John Kelley of the Boston A.A. by 25 yards.
Oksanen's time for the 26-mile, 385-yard
course was 2 hours 23 minutes 29 seconds.

# Track and Field (Cont.)

## NATIONAL COLLEGIATE A.A.

(At Philadelphia)

| | |
|---|---|
| 100 yds.—Frank Budd, Villanova | 0:09.4 |
| 220 yds.—Frank Budd, Villanova | 0:20.8 |
| 440 yds.—Adolph Plummer, New Mexico | 0:46.2 |
| 880 yds.—John Bork, Western Michigan | 1:48.3 |
| Mile—Dyrol Burleson, Oregon | 4:00.5 |
| 3 miles—Pat Clohessy, Houston | 13:47.7 |
| 3,000-m. steeplechase—John Lawler, Abilene Christian | 9:01.1 |
| 120-yd. high hurdles—Jerry Tarr, Oregon | 0:13.9 |
| 440-yd. hurdles—Dixon Farmer, Occidental | 0:50.8 |
| High jump—John Thomas, Boston University | 7 ft. 2 in. |
| Broad jump—Don Meyers, Colorado | 25 ft. |
| Hop, step and jump—Luther Hayes, Southern California | 51 ft. 2¼ in. |
| Pole vault—George Davies, Oklahoma State; Dick Gear, San Jose State, and Jim Brewer, Southern California (tie) | 15 ft. 4 in. |
| Shot put—Dallas Long, Southern California | 63 ft. 3½ in. |
| Discus—Glen Passey, Utah State | 176 ft. 8 in. |
| Javelin—Chuck Wilkinson, Redlands | 247 ft. 8½ in. |
| Hammer—Tom Pagani, California Poly | 194 ft. 10½ in. |
| Team—Southern California | 65 pts. |

## INDOOR MILE WINNERS

| | |
|---|---|
| All-Eastern, Baltimore—Ed Moran, New York A. C. | 4:08.8 |
| Massachusetts K. of C.—Charles Jones, U. S. Army | 4:07.8 |
| Oregon Invitational, Portland—Jim Beatty, Santa Clara (Calif.) Youth Village | 4:07.4 |
| Los Angeles Invitation—Jim Beatty, Santa Clara (Calif.) Youth Village | 4:06.4 |
| International Meet of Champions, Winnipeg—Bruce Kidd, East York T. C., Toronto | 4:12.1 |
| Boston A. A. (Hunter)—Istvan Rozsavolgyi, Hungary | 4:06.8 |
| Washington Star—Ed Moran, New York A. C. | 4:11.5 |
| Millrose (Wanamaker)—Istvan Rozsavolgyi, Hungary | 4:06.0 |
| Will Rogers Games, Fort Worth—John Cooper, No. Texas State | 4:18.9 |
| Philadelphia Inquirer—Istvan Rozsavolgyi, Hungary | 4:05.4 |
| Los Angeles Times—Istvan Rozsavolgyi, Hungary | 4:07.0 |
| New York A. C. (Baxter)—Istvan Rozsavolgyi, Hungary | 4:04.0 |
| Mason-Dixon, Louisville—Ernie Cunliffe, Palo Alto, Calif. | 4:09.9 |
| National Interscholastic—John Camien, Sewanhaka H. S., Floral Park, N.Y. | 4:23.1 |
| National A. A. U.—Jim Beatty, Santa Clara (Calif.) Youth Village | 4:09.3 |
| Central Collegiate—Dick Pond, Western Michigan | 4:10.2 |
| New York K. of C. (Columbian)—Istvan Rozsavolgyi, Hungary | 4:01.8 |
| Far West Classic, Portland, Ore.—Dyrol Burleson, Oregon | 4:03.8 |
| Heptagonal—Bob Mack, Yale | 4:16.5 |
| Metropolitan College—Jimmy Brown, New York University | 4:17.4 |
| Big Ten—Ergas Leps, Michigan | 4:15.8 |
| Big Eight—Bill Dotson, Kansas | 4:08.9 |
| Chicago Relays (Bankers)—Istvan Rozsavolgyi, Hungary | 4:04.7 |
| I. C. 4-A—Steve Paranya, Wesleyan | 4:15.6 |
| Milwaukee Journal—Jim Greele, Emerald Empire A. A., Eugene, Ore. | 4:03.6 |
| Cleveland K. of C.—Tom O'Hara, Loyola, Chicago | 4:08.8 |
| Canadian Championship, Winnipeg—Jim Irons, Toronto Olympic Club | 4:13.4 |
| Highlander, Hamilton, Ont.—Jimmy Brown, New York University | 4:19.0 |

## INTERCOLLEGIATE A.A.A.A. (IC4A)

### Indoor

(At New York)

| | |
|---|---|
| 60 yds.—Frank Budd, Villanova | 0:06.1 |
| 60-yd. high hurdles—Leon Pras, Villanova | 0:07.4 |
| 600 yds.—Jim Stack, Yale | 1:10.6 |
| 1,000 yds.—Tom Carroll, Yale | 2:10.7 |
| Mile—Steve Paranya, Wesleyan | 4:15.6 |
| 2 miles—Bob Mack, Yale | 9:08.6 |
| Mile relay—Princeton (William Walpole, Whitney Azoy John Gardner, Dick Edmunds) | 3:20.2 |
| 2-mile relay—Holy Cross (John O'Connor, Jay Bowers, Tom Noering, Charles Buchta) | 7:43.5 |
| High jump—John Thomas, Boston University | 6 ft. 6 in. |
| Broad jump—Robert O'Brien, Manhattan | 24 ft. |
| Pole vault—John Murray, Cornell | 14 ft. 6 in. |
| Shot put—William Joe, Villanova | 54 ft. 6¼ in. |
| 35-lb. weight—Henry Jud Sage, Navy | 63 ft. 4¼ in. |
| Team—Yale | 30 pts. |

### Outdoor

(At New York)

| | |
|---|---|
| 100 yds.—Frank Budd, Villanova | 0:09.6 |
| 220 yds.—Frank Budd, Villanova | 0:21.4 |
| 440 yds.—Dick Edmunds, Princeton | 0:48.1 |
| 880 yds.—Jon Dante, Villanova | 1:55.5 |
| Mile—Steve Paranya, Wesleyan | 4:15.9 |
| 3 miles—Bob Lowe, Brown | 14:11.8 |
| 3,000-m. steeplechase—Pat Traynor, Villanova | 9:25.3 |
| 120-yd. high hurdles—Bill Johnson, Maryland | 0:14.8 |
| 440-yd. hurdles—Jay Luck, Yale | 0:53.1 |
| Mile relay—Fordham (Peter Weiss, Tom Kenny, Doug Tynan, Frank Tomeo) | 3:18.5 |
| High jump—John Thomas, Boston University | 6 ft. 5 in. |
| Broad jump—Calvin Glass, St. John's | 23 ft. 5¼ in. |
| Hop, step and jump—Winston Cooper, St. John's | 48 ft. 9 in. |
| Pole vault—John Murray, Cornell, and John Belitza, Maryland (tie) | 14 ft. |
| Shot put—William Joe, Villanova | 54 ft. ½ in. |
| Discus—Edward Kohler, Fordham, and Michael Pyle, Yale (tie) | 158 ft. 10 in. |
| Javelin—Nick Kovalakides, Maryland | 222 ft. 4 in. |
| Hammer—Stanley Doten, Harvard | 189 ft. 10 in. |
| Team—Villanova | 46 pts. |

---

# ARCHERY

## World Championships

(At Oslo, Norway)

| | Pts. |
|---|---|
| Men—Joseph Thornton, Tahlequah, Okla. | 2,310 |
| Women—Nancy Vonderheide, Cincinnati | 2,173 |
| Men's team—United States (Joseph Thornton, Tahlequah, Okla.; Clayton Sherman, Madison, Wis.; William Bednar, Hartville, Ohio) | 6,600 |
| Women's team—United States (Nancy Vonderheide, Cincinnati; Grace Frye, Toledo, Ohio; Victoria Cook, Minneapolis) | 6,276 |

## National Field Archery Championships

(At Hot Springs, Ark.)

| | |
|---|---|
| Freestyle—Robert Kadlec, Rochester, Minn. | 2,950 |
| Instinctive—Lon Stanton, Lake Ozark, Mo. | 2,744 |
| Heavy tackle—Russell Hawes, Philomont, Va. | 2,461 |

### WOMEN

| | |
|---|---|
| Freestyle—Ann Clark, Cincinnati | 2,710 |
| Instinctive—Theressa Carter, San Francisco | 1,991 |
| Heavy tackle—Anna Van Dolson, Vallejo, Calif. | 1,637 |

# INTERCOLLEGIATE CONFERENCE TEAM CHAMPIONS
## National Collegiate Athletic Association (N. C. A. A.)

Baseball—Southern California
Basketball—Cincinnati (university division); Wittenberg (college division)
Fencing—New York University
Golf—Purdue
Gymnastics—Penn State
Ice hockey—Denver
Skiing—Denver
Swimming—Michigan
Tennis—U.C.L.A.
Track and field—Southern California
Wrestling—Oklahoma State

### ATLANTIC COAST
Baseball—Duke
Basketball—Wake Forest
Golf—Duke
Lacrosse—Maryland
Swimming—Maryland, North Carolina and North Carolina State (tie)
Tennis—North Carolina
Track and field—Maryland (indoors and outdoors)
Wrestling—Maryland

### BIG EIGHT
Baseball—Oklahoma State
Basketball—Kansas State
Golf—Oklahoma State
Swimming—Oklahoma
Tennis—Oklahoma State
Swimming—Oklahoma
Track—Kansas (indoors); Oklahoma (outdoors)
Wrestling—Oklahoma State

### BIG FIVE
Baseball (California Intercollegiate Association)—Southern California
Basketball—Southern California
Golf—Washington
Gymnastics—California
Rowing (Western Sprint Regatta)—Washington
Swimming—Southern California
Tennis—U. C. L. A.
Track and field—Southern California
Water polo—California

### BIG TEN
Baseball—Michigan
Basketball—Ohio State
Fencing—Illinois
Golf—Ohio State
Gymnastics—Michigan
Ice hockey—Michigan
Swimming—Indiana
Tennis—Michigan
Track and field—Michigan (indoors and outdoors)
Wrestling—Michigan State

### BORDER
Baseball—Arizona
Basketball—Arizona State and New Mexico State (tie)
Golf—Arizona State
Rifle—Arizona
Tennis—Arizona
Track and field—Arizona

### EASTERN COLLEGE
Eastern Baseball League—Navy
Metropolitan Baseball League—St. John's
Tri-State Basketball League—Fairfield
E. C. A. C. Basketball Trophy (major college)—St. Bonaventure

E. C. A. C. Basketball Cup (small college)—Williams
Intercollegiate Fencing Association—New York University
Eastern Golf Association—Princeton
Eastern Gymnastic League—Navy
Eastern Association of Rowing Colleges—Navy
Eastern Swimming League—Navy and Yale (tie)
Eastern Tennis Association—Princeton
Heptagonal Games Association, track and field—Yale (indoors and outdoors)
Metropolitan Track and Field Association—Manhattan (indoors and outdoors)
Eastern Wrestling Association—Lehigh

### IVY LEAGUE
Basketball—Princeton
Fencing—Columbia
Ice hockey—Harvard
Lacrosse—Princeton
Squash—Yale
Wrestling—Columbia

### MASON-DIXON
Baseball—Baltimore
Basketball—Mount St. Mary's
Golf—Randolph-Macon
Tennis—Johns Hopkins
Track and field—American
Swimming—Loyola
Wrestling—Baltimore

### MID-AMERICAN
Baseball—Western Michigan
Basketball—Ohio U.
Golf—Ohio U.
Swimming—Ohio U.
Tennis—Western Michigan
Track and field—Western Michigan
Wrestling—Miami

### MIDDLE ATLANTIC STATES
Baseball—Delaware
Basketball—Albright (college division)
Fencing—Stevens Tech
Golf—Bucknell
Swimming—West Chester State
Tennis—Lehigh
Track and field—St. Joseph's (university division); West Chester State (college division)
Wrestling—Wilkes

### MOUNTAIN STATES
Baseball—Wyoming (Eastern division); Brigham Young (Western division)
Basketball—Utah and Colorado State (tie)
Golf—New Mexico
Swimming—Denver
Tennis—Utah
Track and field—Brigham Young
Wrestling—Wyoming and Colorado State (tie)

### N.A.I.A.
Baseball—East Carolina
Basketball—Grambling
Golf—Lamar Tech
Swimming—North Central, Ill.
Tennis—Pan American
Track and field—Texas Southern
Wrestling—Lock Haven State

### NATIONAL JR. COLLEGE
Baseball—Wilmington, N. C.
Basketball—Pueblo, Colo.
Golf—Odessa, Tex.
Rifle—Cameron State, Lawton, Okla.
Swimming—Bay City, Mich.
Tennis—Pratt, Kan.
Track and field—Howard County, Big Spring, Tex.
Wrestling—Lamar, Colo.

### SOUTHEASTERN
Baseball—Louisiana State
Basketball—Mississippi State
Golf—Georgia
Swimming—Florida
Tennis—Florida
Track and field—Auburn

### SOUTHERN
Baseball—West Virginia
Basketball—George Washington
Golf—Virginia Tech
Rifle—The Citadel
Swimming—V. M. I.
Tennis—The Citadel
Track and field—Furman (indoors); The Citadel (outdoors)
Wrestling—Virginia Tech

### SOUTHWEST
Baseball—Texas
Basketball—Texas Tech
Golf—Texas Tech (individual); Texas A. & M. (team)
Swimming—Southern Methodist
Tennis—Texas
Track and field—Texas

### YANKEE
Baseball—Connecticut
Basketball—Rhode Island
Golf—Massachusetts
Rifle—Maine
Track and field—Maine

### OTHER CHAMPIONS
Intercollegiate Rowing Association—California
National intercollegiate weightlifting—Maryland
National intercollegiate polo—Cornell
U. S. Intercollegiate Lacrosse Association—Army and Navy (tie)

# SWIMMING
## National A. A. U. Championships

### Men's Indoor
(At New Haven, Conn.)

| | |
|---|---|
| 100-yd. free—Steve Clark, Los Altos, Calif.......... | 0:46.8 |
| 220-yd. free—Steve Clark, Los Altos, Calif......... | 2:00.0 |
| 440-yd. free—Murray Rose, Southern California | 4:18.2 |
| 1,500-m. free—Murray Rose, Southern California.... | 17:43.7 |
| 100-yd. back—Charles Bittick, Southern California.. | 0:53.4 |
| 220-yd. back—Charles Bittick, Southern California.. | 2:07.7 |
| 100-yd. breast—Chet Jastremski, Bloomington, Ind.. | 0:59.6 |
| 220-yd. breast—Chet Jastremski, Bloomington, Ind.. | 2:26.7 |
| 100-yd. butterfly—Frank Legacki, Ann Arbor, Mich.. | 0:51.9 |
| 220-yd. butterfly—Mike Troy, Bloomington, Ind..... | 2:10.9 |
| 200-yd. medley—Ted Stickles, Bloomington, Ind..... | 2:02.1 |
| 400-yd. medley—Charles Bittick, Southern California | 4:23.7 |
| 400-yd. freestyle relay—New Haven (Conn.) S. C. (Michael Austin, James Loofbourrow, David Tyler, Gary Ball).................................... | 3:15.9 |
| 400-yd. medley relay—North Carolina A. C. (Thompson Mann, Peter Fogarsy, Ed Spencer, Harry Bloom) | 3:39.9 |
| 1-m. dive—Lou Vitucci, Hollywood, Fla..... | 505.95 pts. |
| 3-m. dive—Ron O'Brien, Station WBNS, Columbus, Ohio.................................. | 529.55 pts. |
| Team—Southern California..................... | 74 pts. |

### Men's Outdoor
(At Los Angeles)

| | |
|---|---|
| 100-m. free—Steve Clark, Santa Clara (Calif.) S. C... | 0:54.4 |
| 200-m. free—Tsuyoshi Yamanaka, Japan........... | 2:00.4 |
| 400-m. free—Tsuyoshi Yamanaka, Japan........... | 4:17.5 |
| 1,500-m. free—Roy Saari, El Segundo (Calif.) S. C... | 17:29.8 |
| 100-m. back—Bob Bennett, Kristensen S. S., North Hollywood, Calif.............................. | 1:01.3 |
| 200-m. back—Tom Stock, Indianapolis A. C........ | 2:11.5 |
| 100-m. breast—Chet Jastremski, Indianapolis A. C... | 1:07.5 |
| 200-m. breast—Chet Jastremski, Indianapolis A. C... | 2:29.6 |
| 100-m. butterfly—Fred Schmidt, New Trier S. C., Winnetka, Ill................................. | 0:58.6 |
| 200-m. butterfly—Carl Robie, Vesper Boat Club, Philadelphia............................... | 2:12.6 |
| 200-m. medley—Ted Stickles, Indianapolis A. C..... | 2:15.9 |
| 400-m. medley—Ted Stickles, Indianapolis A. C..... | 4:55.6 |
| 400-m. medley relay—Indianapolis A. C. (Tom Stock, Chet Jastremski, Lary Schulhof, Pete Sintz)...... | 4:03.0 |
| 800-m. freestyle relay—Indianapolis A. C. (Alan Somers, Dick Allen, Mike Troy, Pete Sintz)...... | 8:17.9 |
| 3-m. dive—John Vogel, Lafayette, Ind.......... | 485.51 pts. |
| Platform dive—Don Harper, Station WBNS, Columbus, Ohio............................... | 483.40 pts. |
| Team—Indianapolis A. C..................... | 125½ pts. |

### NATIONAL COLLEGIATE A.A.
(At Seattle)

| | |
|---|---|
| 50-yd. free—Frank Legacki, Michigan............. | 0:21.4 |
| 100-yd. free—Steve Jackman, Minnesota........... | 0:48.5 |
| 220-yd. free—Murray Rose, Southern California..... | 2:00.6 |
| 440-yd. free—Murray Rose, Southern California..... | 4:17.9 |
| 1,500-m. free—Murray Rose, Southern California.... | 17:21.8 |
| 100-yd. back—Charles Bittick, Southern California.. | 0:53.9 |
| 200-yd. back—Charles Bittick, Southern California.. | 1:57.1 |
| 100-yd. breast—Dick Nelson, Michigan........... | 1:02.1 |
| 200-yd. breast—Ron Clark, Michigan............. | 2:13.4 |
| 100-yd. butterfly—Dave Gillanders, Michigan....... | 0:52.9 |
| 200-yd. butterfly—Dave Gillanders, Michigan....... | 1:58.6 |
| 200-yd. medley—John Kelso, Denver............. | 2:02.9 |
| 400-yd. freestyle relay—Harvard (Alan Engelberg, William Zentgraf, Robert Kaufmann, Bruce Hunter) | 3:18.3 |
| 400-yd. medley relay—Ohio State (L. B. Shaefer, Tom Kovacs, Artie Wolfe, John Plain)............... | 3:40.3 |
| 1-m. dive—Curt Genders, Florida State.......... | 459.4 pts. |
| 3-m. dive—Lou Vitucci, Ohio State............. | 491.65 pts. |
| Team—Michigan............................ | 85 pts. |

### Women's Indoor
(At Miami, Fla.)

| | |
|---|---|
| 100-yd. free—Chris von Saltza, Santa Clara (Calif.) S. C.......................................... | 0:55.8 |
| 250-yd. free—Chris von Saltza, Santa Clara (Calif.) S. C.......................................... | 2:39.0 |
| 500-yd. free—Chris von Saltza, Santa Clara (Calif.) S. C.......................................... | 5:34.5 |
| 100-yd. back—Nina Harmar, Vesper Boat Club, Philadelphia............................... | 1:04.2 |
| 200-yd. back—Chris von Saltza, Santa Clara (Calif.) S. C.......................................... | 2:19.9 |
| 100-yd. breast—Jean Ann Bellakamp, Indianapolis A. C.......................................... | 1:12.9 |
| 250-yd. breast—Susan Rogers, Ann Arbor (Mich.) S. C.......................................... | 3:19.7 |
| 100-yd. butterfly—Kathy Ellis, Indianapolis A. C.... | 1:01.7 |
| 200-yd. butterfly—Becky Collins, Indianapolis...... | 2:18.4 |
| 200-yd. medley—Donna de Varona, Berkeley (Calif.) Y. M. C. A................................. | 2:19.3 |
| 400-yd. medley—Becky Collins, Indianapolis....... | 4:55.5 |
| 400-yd. freestyle relay—Multnomah A. C., Portland, Ore. (Joan Matich, Noel Gabie, Nancy Kanaby, Carolyn Wood)............................. | 3:51.6 |
| 400-yd. medley relay—Multnomah A. C. Portland, Ore. (Noel Gabie, Jackie Danielson, Nancy Kanaby, Carolyn Wood)............................. | 4:20.0 |
| 1-m. dive—Joel Lenzi, Southern Illinois.......... | 454.7 pts. |
| 3-m. dive—Joel Lenzi, Southern Illinois.......... | 450.3 pts. |
| Team—Multnomah A. C., Portland, Ore......... | 57½ pts. |

### Women's Outdoor
(At Philadelphia)

| | |
|---|---|
| 100-m. free—Robyn Johnson, Northern Virginia A. C., Arlington, Va................................ | 1:03.2 |
| 200-m. free—Carolyn House, Los Angeles A. C...... | 2:18.9 |
| 400-m. free—Carolyn House, Los Angeles A. C...... | 4:52.3 |
| 1,500-m. free—Carolyn House, Los Angeles A. C..... | 19:46.3 |
| 100-m. back—Nina Harmer, Vesper Boat Club, Philadelphia............................... | 1:11.0 |
| 200-m. back—Nina Harmer, Vesper Boat Club, Philadelphia............................... | 2:35.0 |
| 100-m. breast—Dale Barnhard, Congressional C. C., Washington, D. C............................ | 1:22.6 |
| 200-m. breast—Jean Dellakamp, Indianapolis A. C.. | 2:56.7 |
| 100-m. butterfly—Susan Doerr, Vesper Boat Club, Philadelphia............................... | 1:08.2 |
| 200-m. butterfly—Becky Collins, Indianapolis...... | 2:32.8 |
| 200-m. medley—Donna de Varona, LaFayette, Calif.. | 2:35.0 |
| 400-m. medley—Donna de Varona, LaFayette, Calif.. | 5:34.5 |
| 400-m. freestyle relay—Vesper Boat Club, Philadelphia (Susan Doerr, Nina Harmer, Martha Randall, Lyn Hopkins)............................. | 4:17.0 |
| 400-m. medley relay—Vesper Boat Club, Philadelphia (Nina Harmer, Barbara Cesneau, Susan Doerr, Lyn Hopkins)............................. | 4:50.3 |
| 3-m. dive—Joel Lenzi, Fort Lauderdale, Fla...... | 453.80 pts. |
| Platform dive—Barbara McAlister, Los Angeles A. C.......................................... | 288.5 pts. |
| Team—Vesper Boat Club, Philadelphia......... | 75½ pts. |

### Long Distance

| | |
|---|---|
| Men (4 mi.)—Murray Rose, Southern California... | 1:25:14.5 |
| Women (3 mi.)—Patsy Harrower, Indianapolis A. C. | 1:12:28.0 |

### Yale Swim Streak Ends at 201

A one point defeat, 48 to 47, administered by Navy on Feb. 4, 1961, ended a streak of 201 dual meet victories scored by the Yale swimming team over a period of 16 years. The last previous loss was to Army in 1945.

# SKIING

*Source:* Harold A. Grinden, Historian, National Ski Association.

## United States Championships

### ALPINE

#### (At Pinkham Notch, N. H.)

Slalom—Rod Hebron, Canada...................... 2:00.8
Giant slalom—Gordon Eaton, Littleton, N. H......... 3:56.9
Downhill—cancelled
Combined—Rod Hebron, Canada................. 2.38 pts.

### WOMEN

Slalom—Linda Meyer, Mammoth Mountain, Calif..... 1:26.3
Giant slalom—Nancy Holland, Canada............. 4:02.2
Downhill—cancelled
Combined—Nancy Greene, Canada.............. 6.56 pts.

### JUMPING

#### (At Brattleboro, Vt.)

Senior—Ansten Samuelstuen, Steamboat Springs,
  Colo........................................... 224.7 pts.
Junior—Clyde Brodt, Minneapolis............... 204.9 pts.
Veterans—Phil Dunham, Brattleboro, Vt......... 185.5 pts.

### OTHER EVENTS

15-kilo. cross-country, class A—Robert Gray, Colorado University................................. 1:06.54
15-kilo. cross-country, class B—Jimmy Mattson,
  Western State College......................... 1:11.34
30-kilo. cross-country—Larry Damon, Burlington, Vt. 2:04.31

### National Collegiate A. A.

#### (At Middlebury, Vt.)

Slalom—Wallace (Bud) Werner, Colorado.......... 1:35.2
Downhill—Gordon Eaton, Middlebury.............. 1:15.3
Alpine combine—Wallace (Bud) Werner, Colorado 99.67 pts.
Jumping—Cris Selbeck, Denver.................. 226.3 pts.
Cross-country—Charles Akers, Maine........... 1:09:17.0
Nordic combined—John Bower, Middlebury......194.12 pts.
Skeimeister—Art Bookstrom, Dartmouth........366.24 pts.

### TEAM

|  | Pts. |
|---|---|
| Champion—Denver | 376.19 |
| Slalom—Denver | 94.75 |
| Downhill—Middlebury | 97.61 |
| Jumping—Denver | 89.88 |
| Cross-country—Denver | 94.30 |

# SYNCHRONIZED SWIMMING

## Women's National A. A. U. Championships

### INDOORS

#### (At San Francisco)

Solo—Papsie Georgian, Athens A. C., Oakland, Calif.
Stunt—Papsie Georgian, Athens A. C., Oakland, Calif.
Duet—Louella Sommers-Phyllis Firman, Merionettes, San
  Francisco
Team—Merionettes, San Francisco (Margaret Durbrow,
  Phyllis Firman, Sharon Hood, Louella Sommers, Claire
  Vida)

### OUTDOORS

#### (At Union, N. J.)

Solo—Papsie Georgian, Athens A. C., Oakland, Calif.
Duet—Barbara Burke-Joanne Schaack, University A. C., Los
  Angeles
Team—Merionettes, San Francisco (Margaret Durbrow,
  Phyllis Firman, Sharon Hood, Louella Sommers, Claire
  Vida)

# BOWLING

## American Bowling Congress Tournament

### (At Detroit)

#### REGULAR DIVISION

Singles—Lyle Spooner, St. Cloud, Minn............. 726
Doubles—Joseph Macaluso-Eugene Hering, Irvington,
  N. J......................................... 1,342
All-events—Luke Karen, Detroit.................. 1,960
Team—Meyerland Builders, Houston................ 3,134

#### CLASSIC DIVISION

Singles—Earl Johnson, Chicago.................... 733
Doubles—Don Ellis-Joe Kristof, Northbrook, Ill....... 1,331
All-events—Bob Brayman, Detroit................. 1,963
Team—Brentwood Bowl, San Francisco............. 5,983

## Bowling Proprietors' Association of America Champions

Singles (all-star)—Bill Tucker, Rock Hill, Mo.... 318.49 pts.
Women's singles (all-star)—Phyllis Notaro, Brant,
  N. Y........................................ 144.13 pts.
Team—Falstaff Beer, St. Louis................ 80.039 pts.
Women's team—Falstaff Beer, Chicago........ 11,181 pins
Doubles—Ray Bluth-Dick Weber, St. Louis...... 14,170 pins
Women's doubles—Helen Duval-Nobu Asami,
  Richmond, Calif............................. 6,306 pins
Duckpin (all-star)—Dave Volk, Baltimore...... 163.04 pts.
Women's duckpin (all-star)—Frances Wilson,
  Washington, D. C............................ 72.14 pts.
Team handicap—Machinist 830-Western Lanes,
  Louisville, Ky.............................. 9,570 pins
Junior scratch—Dick Ernst, Indianapolis........ 27.12 pts.
Junior handicap—Dennis Jennison, Boise, Ida... 27.10 pts.
Girls junior handicap—Kit Kinkle, Grand Rapids,
  Mich...................................... 27.14 pts.

## Women's International Bowling Congress

### (At Fort Wayne, Ind.)

Singles—Elaine Newton, Park Forest, Ill.......... 661
Doubles—Georgiena Eakins-Betty Long, Youngstown,
  Ohio....................................... 1,239
All-events—Evelyn Teal, Miami, Fla.............. 1,848
Team, Division No. 1—Allgauer Restaurant, Chicago .. 2,919
Team, Division No. 2—Santelli Lumber Company,
  Lyons, N. Y................................ 2,478
Queens tournament—Janet Harman,
  Los Angeles....................... 6 wins, 0 losses

# DUCK PINS

## National Duck Pin Bowling Congress

### (At Warwick, R. I.)

Singles—Robert Goss, New London, Conn........... 463
Doubles—William Stalcup-Pat Crescenzi, Washington,
  D. C....................................... 875
Team—Airway Major, Warwick, R. I............ 2,083
All-events—Fosco Fatorini, Washington, D. C....... 1,293
Women's singles—Jessie Falls, Gastonia, N. C......... 458
Women's doubles—Nancy Moissonnier-Donna Mois-
  sonnier, Danbury, Conn....................... 837
Women's team—Coppola Ford, Bridgeport, Conn..... 1,876
Women's all-events—Jessie Falls, Gastonia, N C...... 1,210
Mixed doubles—Dan Riccio-Gloria Darchik, Bridgeport,
  Conn...................................... 831

# WATER POLO

## National A. A. U. Champions

Indoors—Lynwood S. C., Los Angeles
Outdoors—New York A. C.
Women's indoors—Ann Arbor (Mich.) S. C.

# GOLF

## U. S. Open Championship

(At Oakland Hills C. C., Birmingham, Mich.)

Gene Littler, Singing Hills, Calif.... 73 68 72 68—281
Bob Goalby, Crystal River, Fla..... 70 72 69 71—282
Doug Sanders, Ojai, Calif........... 72 67 71 72—282
*Jack Nicklaus, Columbus, Ohio..... 75 69 70 70—284
Mike Souchak, Grossinger, N. Y .... 73 70 68 73—284
Doug Ford, Tuckahoe, N. Y.......... 72 69 71 74—286
Eric Monti, Los Angeles............ 74 67 72 73—286
Dow Finsterwald, Tequesta, Fla..... 72 71 71 72—286
Jacky Cupit, Longview, Tex......... 72 72 67 76—287
Gardner Dickinson, Jr., Tequesta, Fla. 72 69 71 75—287
Gary Player, South Africa.......... 75 72 69 71—287
Al Geiberger, Santa Barbara, Calif... 71 70 73 74—288
*Deane Beman, Bethesda, Md........ 74 72 72 70—288
Dave Douglas, St. Louis............ 72 72 75 70—289
Ben Hogan, Fort Worth, Tex........ 71 72 73 73—289
Arnold Palmer, Latrobe, Pa......... 74 75 70 70—289

* Amateur.

Leaders—at 18 holes: Bobby Brue (69), Tommy Bolt and Bob Goalby (70); at 36: Bob Rosburg and Sanders (139), Ford, Geiberger, Monti, Littler, Brue and Dickinson (141); at 54: Sanders (210), Cupit, Souchak and Goalby (211).

## Other Champions

| | |
|---|---|
| British Open—Arnold Palmer, Latrobe, Pa.......... | 284 |
| French Open—Kel Nagle, Australia.............. | 271 |
| National P. G. A.—Jerry Barber, Los Angeles........ | *277 |
| Masters—Gary Player, South Africa................. | 280 |
| Canadian Open—Jacky Cupit, Longview, Tex....... | 270 |
| Canadian P. G. A.—Stan Leonard, Canada......... | †203 |
| Eastern Open—Doug Sanders, Ojai, Calif........... | 275 |
| Western Open—Arnold Palmer, Latrobe, Pa........ | 271 |
| World Senior—Paul Runyon, La Jolla, Calif....(match play) | |
| P. G. A. Senior—Paul Runyon, La Jolla, Calif........ | 278 |
| Canada Cup—Sam Snead, White Sulphur Springs, W. Va.......... | 272 |

* Defeated Don January, Dallas, 67–68, in 18 hole playoff. † 54 holes.

## Other P. G. A. Winners

| | |
|---|---|
| Los Angeles Open—Bob Goalby, Crystal River, Fla..... | 275 |
| San Diego Open—Arnold Palmer, Latrobe, Pa........(a)275 | |
| Bing Crosby National—Bob Rosburg, Palo Alto, Calif. . | 282 |
| San Francisco Open—Gary Player, South Africa...... | 272 |
| Palm Springs Classic (90 holes)—Billy Maxwell, Dallas | 345 |
| Phoenix Open—Arnold Palmer, Latrobe, Pa..........(a)270 | |
| Panama Open—Pete Cooper, Lakeland, Fla........... | 273 |
| Tucson Open—Dave Hill, Jackson, Mich..............(a)269 | |
| Baton Rouge Open—Arnold Palmer, Latrobe, Pa...... | 266 |
| Maracaibo Open—Don Whitt, Borrego Springs, Calif... | 283 |
| Caracas Open—Don Whitt, Borrego Springs, Calif..... | 272 |
| Greater New Orleans Open—Doug Sanders, Ojai, Calif. | 272 |
| Puerto Rico Open—Billy Maxwell, Dallas............. | 273 |
| Pensacola Open—Tommy Bolt, Crystal River, Fla...... | 275 |
| St. Petersburg Open—Bob Goalby, Crystal River, Fla. . | 261 |
| Sunshine Open—Gary Player, South Africa........... | 273 |
| Jamaica Open—Jim Ferree, Crystal River, Fla....... | 275 |
| Azalea Open (54 holes)—Jerry Barber, Los Angeles...(a)213 | |
| Greater Greensboro Open—Mike Souchak, Grossinger, N. Y.......... | 276 |
| Houston Classic—Jay Hebert, Lafayette, La..........(a)276 | |
| Texas Open—Arnold Palmer, Latrobe, Pa........... | 270 |
| Waco Turner Open—Butch Baird, Galveston, Tex...... | 281 |
| Tournament of Champions—Sam Snead, White Sulphur Springs, W. Va.................... | 273 |
| Colonial National—Doug Sanders, Ojai, Calif........ | 281 |
| Hot Springs Open—Doug Sanders, Ojai, Calif......... | 273 |
| Sam Snead Festival—Sam Snead, White Sulphur Springs, W. Va............. | 266 |
| "500" Festival Open—Doug Ford, Tuckahoe, N. Y.....(a)273 | |
| Memphis Open—Cary Middlecoff, Memphis........... | 266 |
| Buick Open—Jack Burke, Jr., Kiamesha Lake, N. Y. ..(a)284 | |
| St. Paul Open—Don January, Dallas................. | 269 |
| Milwaukee Open—Bruce Crampton, Australia........ | 272 |
| Insurance City Open—Billy Maxwell, Dallas........(a)271 | |
| Carling Open—Gay Brewer, Jr., Crystal River, Fla..... | 277 |

| | |
|---|---|
| American Classic—Jay Hebert, Lafayette, La.........(a)278 | |
| Dallas Open—Earl Stewart, Jr , Dallas............... | 278 |
| Denver Open—Dave Hill, Dallas.................... | 263 |
| Greater Seattle Open—Dave Marr, Sun City, Ariz....(a)265 | |
| Portland Open—Billy Casper, Jr., Apple Valley, Calif.. | 273 |
| Bakersfield Open—Jack Fleck, Los Angeles.........(a)276 | |
| Ontario Open—Eric Monti, Los Angeles............(a)277 | |

(a) Won in playoff.

## Amateur

U. S.—Jack Nicklaus, Columbus, Ohio (defeated Dudley Wysong, McKinney, Tex , in final, 8 and 6)

British—Michael Bonallack, England (defeated James Walker, Scotland, in final, 6 and 4)

French—Jacques Moerman, Belgium (defeated William Pierce, England, in final, 1 up)

Canadian—Gary Cowan, Canada

Eastern—Deane Beman, Bethesda, Md.

Western—Jack Nicklaus, Columbus, Ohio

Southern—Billy Joe Patton, Morganton, N. C.

North and South—Bill Hyndman, Huntington Valley, Pa.

Trans-Mississippi—Herb Durham, Dallas

Colonial invitation—Dick Crawford, Jacksonville, Ark.

World Senior—Howard Creel, Colorado Springs, Colo.

National Collegiate A. A.—Jack Nicklaus, Ohio State

U. S. public links—Dick Sikes, Springdale, Ark.

U. S. senior—Dexter Daniels, Winter Haven, Fla.

U. S. junior—Charles McDowell, Virginia Beach, Va.

U. S. pee wee—John La Ponzina, Miami Shores, Fla.

## WOMEN

### U. S. Open Championship

(At Baltusrol G. C., Springfield, N. J.)

Mickey Wright, San Diego, Calif...... 72 80 69 72—293
Betsy Rawls, Spartanburg, S. C...... 74 76 73 76—299
Ruth Jessen, Seattle, Wash......... 75 73 77 75—300
Louise Suggs, Atlanta, Ga.......... 78 74 76 73—301
Marilynn Smith, French Lick, Ind..... 77 74 77 75—303
JoAnn Prentice, Birmingham, Ala.... 72 76 80 76—304
Barbara Romack, Sacramento, Calif.. 77 77 78 74—306
*Marlene Stewart Streit, Canada..... 74 77 77 78—306
Mary Lena Faulk, Sea Island, Ga..... 78 77 80 73—308
Shirley Englehorn, Spokane, Wash... 80 73 78 77—308
*Mrs. Philip Cudone, Bloomfield, N. J.. 77 76 75 80—308

* Amateur.

### Other Champions

| | |
|---|---|
| National P. G. A.—Mickey Wright, San Diego..... | 287 |
| Canadian Open—Judy Darling, Canada........(match play) | |
| Titleholders—Mickey Wright, San Diego, Calif..... | 299 |
| Triangle Round Robin—Mary Lena Faulk, Sea Island, Ga.................... | 35 pts. |
| Eastern Open—Mary Lena Faulk, Sea Island, Ga.... | *214 |
| Western Open—Mary Lena Faulk, Sea Island, Ga.... | 290 |
| Babe Zaharias Open—Mary Lena Faulk, Sea Island, Ga.................... | *211 |
| American Ladies Open—Judy Kimball, Sioux City, Ia. | 295 |

* 54 holes.

### Amateur

U. S.—Anne Quast Decker, Seattle (defeated Phyllis Preuss, Pompano Beach, Calif , in final, 14 and 13)

British—Marley Spearman, England (defeated Diane Robb, England, in final, 7 and 6)

Eastern—Marge Burns, Greensboro, N. C.

Western—Anne Quast Decker, Seattle

Southern—Polly Riley, Fort Worth, Tex.

North and South—Barbara McIntire, Lake Park, Fla.

Trans-Mississippi—JoAnne Gunderson, Kirkland, Wash.

National intercollegiate—Judy Hoetmer, Washington

U. S. junior—Mary Lowell, Hayward, Calif.

U. S. pee wee—Roberta Albers, Tampa, Fla.

### TEAM

Ryder Cup—United States 14½, Great Britlan 9½

Walker Cup—United States 11, Great Britain 1

Canada Cup—United States

National Collegiate—Purdue

U. S. public links—Honolulu

## TABLE TENNIS

*Source:* Peter W. Roberts, National Chairman, History Committee, U. S. Table Tennis Association.

### World Championships

(At Peking, China)

Singles—Chuang Tse-Tung, Communist China
Doubles—Nobuyo Hoshino-Koji Kimura, Japan
Women's singles—Chiu Chung-Hui, Communist China
Women's doubles—Maria Alexandru-Georgeta Pitica, Rumania
Mixed doubles—Ichiro Ogimura-Kimizo Matsuzaki, Japan
Men's team (Swaythling Cup)—Communist China
Women's team (Corbillon Cup)—Japan

### United States Championships

(At Detroit)

Singles—Erwin Klein, Los Angeles
Doubles—Bernard Bukiet, Germany–Bob Fields, New York
Women's singles—Leah Thall Neuberger, New York
Women's doubles—Sharon Acton, Wilmington, Calif.–Valleri Smith, Los Angeles
Mixed doubles—Bob Gusikoff, New York–Sharon Acton, Wilmington, Calif.
Junior singles—Clark Goldstein, Washington, D. C.
Junior women's singles—Barbara Chaimson, Beverly, Md.
Boys' singles—Richard Jackson, Hope Valley, R. I.
Girls' singles—Joy Foster, Jamaica, W. I.
Senior singles—Max Marinko, Canada
Senior doubles—Tibor Hazi, White Plains, N Y –James Verta, Kensington, Md.
Esquire singles (men 50 years and over)—Cecil Woodworth, Denver

## BADMINTON

*Source:* Hans Rogind, Publicity Chairman, American Badminton Association.

### United States Championships

(At Long Beach, Calif.)

Singles—Jim Poole, San Diego, Calif.
Doubles—Joe Alston–Wynn Rogers, Pasadena, Calif.
Women's singles—Judith Devlin Hashman, England
Women's doubles—Judith Devlin Hashman–Susan Devlin Peard, England
Mixed doubles—Wynn Rogers, Pasadena, Calif.–Judith Devlin Hashman, England

### All-England

(At Wembley)

Singles—Erland Kops, Denmark
Doubles—Finn Kobbero–Jorgen Hansen, Denmark
Women's singles—Judith Devlin Hashman, England
Women's doubles—Judith Devlin Hashman–Susan Devlin Peard, England
Mixed doubles—Finn Kobbero–Kirsten Thorndahl, Denmark

## LACROSSE

*Source:* Jack Kelly, Editor, *The Lacrosse Newsletter*, Bay Shore, N. Y.

### National Champions

Intercollegiate—Army and Navy (tie)
Open—Baltimore L. C.
North-South game—South 12, North 9, at Annapolis, Md.

### All-America Selections

FIRST TEAM—Goal: Howard Krongard, Princeton. Defense: Neal Reich, Navy; Mike Byrne, Johns Hopkins; Richard Buckner, Army. Midfield: Clayton Beardmore, Maryland; Sam Wilder, Army; Alphonse Kelz, Baltimore. Attack: Jerry Schmidt, Johns Hopkins; Thomas Mitchell, Navy; Henry Peterson, Virginia

## SQUASH RACQUETS

### National Champions

Open—Roshan Khan, Pakistan
Amateur—Henri Salaun, Boston
Doubles—G. Diehl Mateer, Jr.–John Hentz, Philadelphia
Veterans—Calvin MacCracken, Englewood, N. J.
Team—Pacific Coast
Intercollegiate—Steve Vehslage, Princeton
Intercollegiate team—Yale
Women's singles—Margaret Varner, Wilmington, Del.
Women's doubles—Mrs. Nathan Stauffer–Mrs. John Bottger, Cynwyd, Pa.

## RACQUETS

U. S. open—David Norman, Canada
U. S. amateur—David Norman, Canada
U. S. amateur doubles—R. L. O. Bridgman–John Clench, England
Tuxedo Gold Racquet—James Bostwick, Old Westbury, N. Y.

## COURT TENNIS

U. S. open—James Bostwick, Old Westbury, N. Y.
U. S. amateur—Northrup Knox, Buffalo, N. Y.
U. S. open doubles—James and George Bostwick, Old Westbury, N. Y.
U. S. amateur doubles—Northrup and Seymour Knox, Buffalo, N. Y.
Tuxedo Gold Racquet—James Bostwick, Old Westbury, N. Y.

## AUTO RACING

### Winners of Major Races

Indianapolis 500—A. J. Foyt, Houston (Bowes Special), 139.130 mph.
Sebring, Fla., 12-hour endurance race (sports cars)—Phil Hill, Santa Monica, Calif.–Olivier Gendebein, Belgium (Ferrari), 1,081.60 miles, 90.133 mph.
Monaco Grand Prix, 196 miles—Stirling Moss, Great Britain (Lotus Climax), 70.66 mph.
Dutch Grand Prix, 195 miles—Wolfgang von Trips, Germany (Ferrari), 95.13 mph.
1,000 kilometers, Nurburgring, Germany (sports cars)—Masten Gregory, Kansas City–Lucky Casner, Miami, Fla, (Maserati), 79.2 mph.
Le Mans (France) 24-hour endurance race (sports cars)—Phil Hill, Santa Monica, Calif.–Olivier Gendebein, Belgium (Ferrari), 2,779.95 miles, 115.4 mph.
Belgian Grand Prix, 264 miles—Phil Hill, Santa Monica, Calif. (Ferrari), 128.0 mph.
French Grand Prix, 268 miles—Giancarlo Baghetti, Italy (Ferrari), 119.79 mph.
British Grand Prix, 225 miles—Wolfgang von Trips, Germany (Ferrari), 83.91 mph.
Grand Prix of Germany and Europe, 212.4 miles—Stirling Moss, Great Britain (Lotus), 92.28 mph.
Vanderbilt Cup, Bridgehampton, N. Y., 72.25 miles (Formula Junior)—Peter Ryan, Canada, 87.95 mph.
Southern 500, Darlington, S C (stock cars)—Nelson Stacy, Mason County, Ky. (Ford), 117.802 mph.
Grand Prix of Italy, 267 miles—Phil Hill, Santa Monica, Calif. (Ferrari), 103.2 mph.
Road America 500, Elkhart Lake, Wis. (sports cars)—Walter Hansgen, Westfield, N. J.–Augie Pabst, Milwaukee (Maserati), 82.29 mph.
Grand Prix of the United States, Watkins Glen, N. Y., 230 miles—Innis Ireland, Scotland (Lotus), 103.22 mph.

# TENNIS

## United States Championships

(At Forest Hills, N. Y., and Brookline, Mass.)

Singles—Roy Emerson, Australia (defeated Rod Laver, Australia, in final, 7-5, 6-3, 6-2)

Doubles—Chuck McKinley, St. Louis-Dennis Ralston, Bakersfield, Calif.

Women's singles—Darlene Hard, Montebello, Calif. (defeated Ann Haydon, Great Britain, in final, 6-3, 6-4)

Women's doubles—Darlene Hard, Montebello, Calif.-Lesley Turner, Australia

Mixed doubles—Bob Mark-Margaret Smith, Australia

## England

(At Wimbledon)

Singles—Rod Laver, Australia (defeated Chuck McKinley, St. Louis, in final, 6-3, 6-1, 6-4)

Doubles—Neale Fraser-Roy Emerson, Australia

Women's singles—Angela Mortimer, Great Britain (defeated Christine Truman, Great Britain, in final, 4-6, 6-4, 7-5)

Women's doubles—Karen Hantze, Chula Vista, Calif.-Billie Jean Moffitt, Long Beach, Calif.

Mixed doubles—Fred Stolle-Lesley Turner, Australia

## France

(At Paris)

Singles—Manuel Santana, Spain (defeated Nicola Pietrangeli, Italy, in final, 4-6, 6-1, 3-6, 6-0, 6-2)

Doubles—Rod Laver-Roy Emerson, Australia

Women's singles—Ann Haydon, Great Britain (defeated Yola Ramirez, Mexico, in final, 6-2, 6-1)

Women's doubles—Sandra Reynolds-Renee Schuurman, South Africa

Mixed doubles—Rod Laver, Australia-Darlene Hard, Montebello, Calif.

## Australia

(At Melbourne)

Singles—Roy Emerson, Australia (defeated Rod Laver, Australia, in final, 1-6, 6-3, 7-5, 6-4)

Doubles—Bob Mark-Rod Laver, Australia

Women's singles—Margaret Smith, Australia (defeated Jan Lehane, Australia, in final, 6-1, 6-4)

Women's doubles—Mary Smith-Mary Reitano, Australia

Mixed doubles—Bob Hewitt-Jan Lehane, Australia

## U. S. Clay Court Championships

(At Chicago and Bethesda, Md.)

Singles—Bernard Bartzen, Dallas

Doubles—Chuck McKinley, St. Louis-Dennis Ralston, Bakersfield, Calif.

Women's singles—Edda Buding, Germany

Women's doubles—Justina Bricka-Carole Hanks, St. Louis

Senior singles—Bryan Grant, Atlanta

Senior doubles—Bryan Grant-Larry Shippey, Atlanta

Father-and-son—Hugh Lynch, Jr.-Hugh Lynch 3d, Washington, D. C.

## U. S. Indoor Championships

(At New York and Brookline, Mass.)

Singles—Dick Savitt, New York

Doubles—Chris Crawford, Piedmont, Calif.-Ron Holmberg, Brooklyn, N. Y.

Women's singles—Janet Hopps, Seattle

Women's doubles—Janet Hopps, Seattle-Kay Hubbell, Conway, N. H.

Mixed doubles—Bud Collins, Boston-Janet Hopps, Seattle

Senior singles—Chauncey Depew Steele, Jr., Cambridge, Mass.

Senior doubles—Reginald Weir, New York-George Ball, Woodhaven, N. Y.

## Other United States Champions

National Collegiate singles—Allen Fox, U. C. L. A.

National Collegiate doubles—Rafael Osuna-Ramsey Earnhart, Southern California

Interscholastic singles—Arthur Ashe, Sumner H. S., St. Louis

Interscholastic doubles—Mickey Shad-Jackie Cooper, Xavier H. S., Louisville, Ky.

Senior singles—Gardnar Mulloy, Miami, Fla

Senior doubles—Cliff Sutter, Greenwich, Conn.-Ernie Sutter, New Orleans

Junior singles—Charles Pasarell, Puerto Rico

Junior doubles—Clark Graebner, Lakewood, Ohio-Charles Pasarell, Puerto Rico

Boys singles—William Harris, West Palm Beach, Fla.

Boys doubles—Jeff Brown, Carmichael, Calif.-Leon Penero, Stockton, Calif.

Boys singles (13 and under)—Hughby Curry, Orlando, Fla.

Boys doubles (13 and under)—Hughby Curry, Orlando, Fla.-Zan Guerry, Chattanooga

Boys singles (11 and under)—Dickie Stockton, San Rafael, Calif.

Boys doubles (11 and under)—Dickie Stockton, San Rafael, Calif.-Richard Bohrnstedt, Redlands, Calif.

Father-and-son—H. W. and William Bond, La Jolla, Calif.

### WOMEN

College girls, singles—Terry Ann Fretz, Occidental

College girls, doubles—Terry Ann Fretz, Occidental-Mary Sherar, Yakima Valley J. C.

Senior singles—Kay Hubbell, Conway, N. H.

Senior doubles—Marjorie Buck, Manchester, Mass.-Kay McKean, Hamilton, Mass.

Girls singles (18 and under)—Victoria Palmer, Phoenix, Ariz.

Girls doubles (18 and under)—Victoria Palmer, Phoenix, Ariz.-Judy Alvarez, Ybor City, Fla.

Girls singles (15 and under)—Jane Albert, Pebble Beach, Calif.

Girls doubles (15 and under)—Jane Albert, Pebble Beach, Calif.-Jean Danilovich, Jackson, Calif.

Girls singles (13 and under)—Peaches Bartkowicz, Hamtramck, Mich.

Girls doubles (13 and under)—Paulette Verzin, La Mesa, Calif.-Patsy Rippy, Shawnee, Okla.

Girls singles (11 and under)—Sheryl Smith, North Miami Beach, Fla.

Girls doubles (11 and under)—Sheryl Smith, North Miami Beach, Fla.-Ann Roberts, Coral Gables, Fla.

### Team

Wightman Cup (women)—United States defeated England, 6 to 1, at Chicago

National Collegiate A. A.—U. C. L. A.

# MODERN PENTATHLON

## World Championship

(At Moscow)

| | Pts. |
|---|---|
| Individual—Igor Novikov, U.S.S.R. | 5,217 |
| Team—U.S.S.R. | 15,220 |

## National Championship

(At San Antonio, Tex.)

Individual—Lt. Alan Jackson, U. S. Army .......... 4,732.24

# VOLLEYBALL

## U. S. Volleyball Assn. Championships

(At Duluth, Minn.)

Open—Hollywood (Calif.) Y.M.C.A. Stars

Intercollegiate—Santa Monica City College

Women—Long Beach (Calif.) Breakers

## RIFLE AND PISTOL SHOOTING

*Source:* Paul B. Cardinal, National Rifle Association.

### National Championships

Pistol—Sgt. 1/c William B. Blankenship, Jr., U. S. Army....... 2,631–119
Smallbore rifle, prone (.22 cal.)—Airman 3/c Victor L. Auer, U. S. Air Force....... 4,784–359
Smallbore rifle, four-position (.22 cal.)—1st Lt. Tommy G. Pool, U. S. Army....... 1,567–079
M1 service rifle—Sgt. Charles D. Davis, U. S. Army 640–051
Civilian M1 service rifle—Jacob Svela, Portland, Ore....... 631–050
Bolt rifle—Jay G. Harris, Susanville, Calif....... 642–057

#### WOMEN

Pistol—Lucille Chambliss, Winter Haven, Fla....... 2,509–081
Smallbore rifle, prone—Janet S. Friddell, Toledo, Ohio....... 4,776–302
Smallbore rifle, four-position—Jilann O. Brunett, Grand Rapids, Mich....... 1,546–067
M1 service rifle—WAC Barbara J. Hile, U. S. Army 618–028
Bolt rifle—Martha R. Ventres, Stamford, Conn....... 623–044

### National Trophy Matches

Pistol—PO 1/c Stanford H. Hulstrom, U. S. Coast Guard....... 293–13
Team pistol—U. S. Army Blue....... 1,132–035
Rifle—Sgt. 1/c Alfred B. Falcon, U. S. Army....... 248–25
Team rifle—U. S. Army Blue....... 1,472–130

### Indoor

Smallbore rifle (.22 cal.)—Bobbie Johnson....... 795
College smallbore rifle—Bruce A. Meredith, West Virginia U....... 299
Team smallbore rifle—U. S. Army Blue....... 1,581
College team smallbore rifle—West Virginia U....... 1,164
Pistol—M/Sgt. Richard M. Stineman, U. S. Army....... 886
College pistol—Richard B. O'Keefe, U. S. Coast Guard Academy....... 287
Team pistol—Ford Ord, Calif....... 1,167
College team pistol—U. S. Military Academy....... 1,120

## TRAPSHOOTING

### Grand American Tournament

(At Vandalia, Ohio)

#### GRAND AMERICAN HANDICAP

Men—Steve Barringer, Russell, Kan....... 99
Women—Sharon Ann Kingen, McCordsville, Ind....... *96
Junior—Douglas Holman, Defiance, Ohio....... 97
Subjunior—Roland Rabb, Belleville, Ill....... *95
Professional—R. J. Tobin, Canada....... 92

#### OTHER EVENTS

Double targets—Joe Hiestand, Hillsboro, Ohio....... 98
Clay targets—Tony Biagi, Highland Park, Ill....... *200
Preliminary handicap—Elbert Lesley, Reading, Ohio... 100
Overall—John Sternberger, Englewood, Ohio....... 976

* Won title in shoot-off.

### National Amateur Championships

(At Pelham Manor, N. Y.)

Singles—Ralph Bevis, Bennington, Vt....... *196
Women—Mary Christopher, Bristol, Pa....... *182
Handicap—William Rheaume, Worcester, Mass....... 96
Doubles—Nick Egan, New York....... 91
Senior—Ben Higginson, Newburgh, N. Y....... 189
Junior—Danny O'Neill, Allentown, Pa....... 178
Family—C. J. and R. B. McArthur, Colmar, Pa....... 378
Overall—Lou Hidu, Fairfield, Conn....... 445

* Won title in shoot-off.

## CASTING

*Source:* Paul N. Jones, Executive Secretary, American Casting Association.

### United States Championships

(At Long Beach, Calif.)

All-around—Jon Tarantino, San Francisco

#### DISTANCE—COMBINED

| | ft. |
|---|---|
| All distance—Jon Tarantino, San Francisco | 3,349 |
| Baits—Jon Tarantino, San Francisco | 2,211 |
| Flies—R. L. Hetzel, Kansas City | 1,163 |

#### ACCURACY—COMBINED

| | pts. |
|---|---|
| All accuracy—Steve Aleshi, Kansas City | 387 |
| Baits—Charles Sutphin, Indianapolis | 191 |
| Flies—Steve Aleshi, Kansas City | 200 |

#### DISTANCE—SINGLE

| | avg. | long cast |
|---|---|---|
| Trout fly—Jon Tarantino, San Francisco | 180⅓ | 186 |
| Salmon fly—R. L. Hetzel, Kansas City | 213 | 217 |
| ⅜-oz. bait—Jon Tarantino, San Francisco | 345⅓ | 350 |
| ⅝-oz. bait—Ed Lanser, St. Louis | 394⅔ | 400 |

#### ACCURACY—SINGLE

| | pts. |
|---|---|
| Dry fly—Steve Aleshi, Kansas City | 100 |
| Wet fly—Ed A. Thomas, Los Angeles | 100 |
| ⅜-oz. bait—Bill True, Minneapolis | 95 |
| ⅝-oz. bait—Charles Sutphin, Indianapolis | 98 |

## SPEARFISHING

### National Championships

(At Newport, R. I.)

| | Pts. |
|---|---|
| Men—Long Beach (Calif.) Neptunes (Terry Lentz, Bob Weaver, Jim Baldwin) | 215.12 |
| Women—Connecticut Council of Diving Clubs (Marilyn Snyder, Shirley Johnson) | 27.14 |

## SKEET SHOOTING

### N. S. S. A. World Championships

(At Reno, Nev.)

All-around—Peter W. Candy, Los Angeles....... 546 x 550
12 gauge—William Hay Rogers, Atherton, Calif.... 250 x 250
20 gauge—Andy Laird, Stockton, Calif....... 100 x 100
28 gauge—Lt. James R. Clark, Ft. Benning, Ga.... 100 x 100
.410 gauge—Robert Shuley, Roselle, Ill....... 99 x 100

#### WOMEN

All-around—Lucretia Thomas, Dallas....... 535 x 550
12 gauge—Lucretia Thomas, Dallas....... 246 x 250
20 gauge—Lucretia Thomas, Dallas....... 99 x 100
28 gauge—Kathleen Wells Fitchett, Baltimore..... 100 x 100
.410 gauge—Katheleen McGinn, Houston....... 94 x 100

## DOG SHOWS

### Best in Show

Westminster Kennel Club (New York)—Ch. Cappoquin Little Sister, toy poodle, owned by Florence Michelson, Fort Lauderdale, Fla.

International Kennel Club (Chicago)—Ch. Conifer's Lance, Irish setter, owned by Frank and Katherine Wheatley, Allen Park, Mich.

Eastern Dog Club (Boston)—Ch. Pixietown Serenade of Hadleigh, Pomeranian, owned by Mrs. Ruth H. Bellick, Janson, Mass., and Lady Conyers, Bermuda

# HORSE RACING

### The Triple Crown
(Jockeys in parentheses)

KENTUCKY DERBY, Churchill Downs, Louisville, Ky., May 6, $125,000 added, 3 year olds, 126 pounds, 1¼ miles—1, Carry Back (Sellers); 2, Crozier (Baeza); 3, Bass Clef (Baldwin); 4, Dr. Miller (Shoemaker); 5, Sherluck (Arcaro); 6, Globemaster (Rotz); 7, Four-and-Twenty (Longden); 8, Flutterby (Moreno); 9, Loyal Son (Hansman); 10, On His Metal (Dodson); 11, Light Talk (Nono); 12, Ambiopoise (Ussery); 13, Ronnie's Ace (Maese); 14, Dearborn (Phelps); 15, Jay Fox (Gilligan).

Time—2:04. Mutuels—Carry Back, $7.00, 4.20, 3.20; Crozier, $4.60, 4.20; Bass Clef, $5.60. Winner owned by Mrs. Jack Price. Winner's purse, $120,500. Margin of victory, ¾ length. (Bass Clef, Ronnie's Ace, Jay Fox, mutuel field; Four-and-Twenty, Flutterby, Alberta Ranches entry.)

PREAKNESS STAKES, Pimlico, Baltimore, May 20, $150,000 added, 3 year olds, 126 pounds, 1 3/16 miles—1, Carry Back (Sellers); 2, Globemaster (Rotz); 3, Crozier (Baeza); 4, Dr. Miller (Hinojosa); 5, Sherluck (Boulmetis); 6, Hitting Away (Ussery); 7, Nashua Blue (Thornburg); 8, Orleans Doge (Hettinger); 9, Crimson Fury (Carstens).

Time—1:57 3/5. Mutuels—Carry Back, $4.00, 3.20, 2.20; Globemaster, $8.00, 3.40; Crozier, $2.40. Winner owned by Mrs. Jack Price. Winner's purse, $126,200. Margin of victory, ¾ length.

BELMONT STAKES, Belmont Park, Elmont, N. Y., June 3, $125,000 added, 3 year olds, 126 pounds, 1½ miles—1, Sherluck (Baeza); 2, Globemaster (Rotz); 3, Guadalcanal (M. Ycaza); 4, Ambiopoise (Ussery); 5, Dr. Miller (Hinojosa); 6, Hitting Away (Woodhouse); 7, Carry Back (Sellers), 8, Bal Musette (Leonard); 9, Flutterby (Longden).

Time—2:29 1/5. Mutuels—Sherluck, $132.10, 50.20, 18.00; Globemaster, $15.30, 9.00; Guadalcanal, $7.90. Winner owned by Jacob Sher. Winner's purse, $104,900. Margin of victory, 2¼ lengths.

### Foreign Races

Epsom Darby (England)—Psidium (Poincelet), winner's purse, $96,734

Grand National Steeplechase (England)—Nicolaus Silver (Beasley), winner's purse, $51,156

Queen's Plate (Canada)—Blue Light (Dittfach), winner's purse, $46,475

### Other Major U. S. Stakes Winners
(Winner's Purse $50,000 or More)

| | |
|---|---:|
| American Derby—Beau Prince (S. Brooks) | $ 71,400 |
| Arlington Classic—Globemaster (Rotz) | 72,900 |
| Arlington Futurity—Ridan (Hartack) | 127,050 |
| Beldame Hcp.—Airmans Guide (H. Grant) | 62,400 |
| Brooklyn Hcp.—Kelso (Arcaro) | 73,320 |
| Californian Stakes—First Balcony (E. Burns) | 67,700 |
| Champagne Stakes—Donut King (M. Ycaza) | 146,800 |
| Coaching Club American Oaks—Bowl of Flowers (Arcaro) | 75,806 |
| Cowdin Stakes—Jaipur (Arcaro) | 52,438 |
| Delaware Hcp.—Airmans Guide (H. Grant) | 104,687 |
| Del Mar Futurity—Weldy (York) | 62,390 |
| Dwyer Hcp.—Hitting Away (Woodhouse) | 54,340 |
| Flamingo Stakes—Carry Back (Sellers) | 84,370 |
| Florida Derby—Carry Back (Sellers) | 75,100 |
| Frizette Stakes—Cicada (Shoemaker) | 83,575 |
| Futurity Stakes—Cyane (M. Ycaza) | 85,650 |
| Grey Lag Hcp.—Mail Order (L. Adams) | 56,420 |
| Gulfstream Park Hcp.—Tudor Way (Hartack) | 74,000 |
| Hawthorne Gold Cup—T. V. Lark (Longden) | 78,250 |
| Hialeah Turf Cup Stakes—Wolfram (Rotz) | 62,400 |
| Hollywood Derby—Four-and-Twenty (Longden) | 77,900 |
| Hollywood Gold Cup—Prince Blessed (Longden) | 102,100 |
| Hollywood Juvenile Championship—Rattle Dancer (Yanez) | 102,800 |

| | |
|---|---:|
| Hopeful Stakes—Jaipur (Arcaro) | 76,228 |
| Jersey Derby—Ambiopoise (Ussery) | 80,600 |
| John B. Campbell Hcp.—Conestoga (Gilbert) | 76,992 |
| Man o' War Hcp.—Wise Ship (Gustines) | 65,000 |
| Matron Stakes—Cicada (Shoemaker) | 61,028 |
| Metropolitan Hcp.—Kelso (Arcaro) | 74,100 |
| Monmouth Hcp.—Don Poggio (Boulmetis) | 72,995 |
| Mother Goose Stakes—Funloving (Ussery) | 56,793 |
| San Juan Capistrano Hcp.—Don't Alibi (Shoemaker) | 68,100 |
| Santa Anita Derby—Four-and-Twenty (Longden) | 100,000 |
| Santa Anita Hcp.—Prove It (Shoemaker) | 100,000 |
| Santa Anita Maturity—Prove It (Shoemaker) | 93,370 |
| Sapling Stakes—Sir Gaylord (I. Valenzuela) | 74,046 |
| Sorority Stakes—Batter Up (Woodhouse) | 60,000 |
| Spinaway Stakes—Cicada (I. Valenzuela) | 52,455 |
| Suburban Hcp.—Kelso (Arcaro) | 72,735 |
| Sunset Hcp.—Whodunit (M. Ycaza) | 52,800 |
| Travers Stakes—Beau Prince (S. Brooks) | 54,210 |
| United Nations Hcp.—Oink (Gilligan) | 65,000 |
| Washington Park Futurity—Ridan (Hartack) | 128,250 |
| Washington Park Hcp.—Chief of Chiefs (C. Meaux) | 72,900 |
| Widener Hcp.—Yorky (Sellers) | 81,770 |
| Wood Memorial Stakes—Globemaster (Rotz) | 56,062 |
| Woodward Stakes—Kelso (Arcaro) | 71,240 |
| World's Playground Stakes—Green Ticket (Guerin) | 92,062 |

# HARNESS RACING

THE HAMBLETONIAN, Du Quoin, Ill., Aug. 30, 3-year-old trotters, one mile. 1st heat—1, Harlan Dean; 2, Matastar; 3, Caleb. Time—1:58 2/5. 2d heat—1, Harlan Dean; 2, Caleb; 3, Spectator. Time—1:59. Final placings—1, Harlan Dean; 2, Caleb; 3, Matatstar. Winner, Harlan Dean, driven by Jimmy Arthur, owned by Keystone Stables, Meadow Lands, Pa. Total purse—$131,573.01. Winner's purse—$77,364.93.

LITTLE BROWN JUG, Delaware, Ohio, Sept. 21, 3-year-old pacers, one mile. 1st heat—1, Lang Hanover; 2, Adiosand; 3, Hogan Hanover. Time—2:01. 2d heat—1, Way Wave; 2, Henry T. Adios; 3, Al Sam. Time—2:01 2/5. 3d heat—1, Henry T. Adios; 2, Way Wave; 3, Lang Hanover. Time—1:58 4/5. 4th heat—1, Henry T. Adios; 2, Lang Hanover; 2, Way Wave. Time—2:05. Final placings—1, Henry T. Adios; 2, Way Wave; 3, Lang Hanover. Winner, Henry T. Adios, driven by Stanley Dancer, owned by Dr. and Mrs. Nicholas Derrico, Pelham Manor, N. Y. Total purse—$70,069.14. Winner's purse—$21,721.44.

# MOTORCYCLING
*Source:* L. A. Kuchler, American Motorcycle Association

### National Champions
(100 miles and over, road races; others, track)

| | |
|---|---:|
| Grand national champion—Carroll Resweber, Cedarburg, Wis. | 62 pts. |
| 5 miles—Carroll Resweber, Cedarburg, Wis. | 4:33.90 |
| 8 miles—Neil Keen Pasadena, Calif. | 8:12.79 |
| 10 miles—Carroll Resweber, Cedarburg, Wis. | 9:16.30 |
| 15 miles—Dick Mann, El Sobrante, Calif. | 14:03.56 |
| 25 miles—Joe Leonard, San Jose, Calif. | 17:36.75 |
| 50 miles—Carroll Resweber, Cedarburg, Wis. | 33:54.41 |
| 100 miles—Joe Leonard, San Jose, Calif. | 1:40:53.13 |
| 150 miles—Carroll Resweber, Cedarburg, Wis. | 1:49:17.79 |
| 200 miles—Roger Reiman, Kewanee, Ill. | 2:53:17.51 |
| 45 cu. in. TT, 7 miles—Bart Markel, Flint, Mich. | 7:17.38 |
| 45 cu. in. TT, 7 miles—Joe Leonard, San Jose, Calif. | 7:18.42 |

# CYCLING

### United States Championships
Men—James Rossi, Chicago
Women—Edith Johnson, Buffalo
Junior—Allen Grieco, Hackensack, N. J.

# ROWING

*Source:* William J. Harahan III, Public Relations Officer, National Association of Amateur Oarsmen; Editor, *Rowing News and Rowing Guide.*

## Intercollegiate Rowing Association

(At Syracuse, N. Y.)

Varsity (3 miles)—1, California, 16:49.2; 2, Cornell, 16:50.6; 3, M. I. T., 17:02.9; 4, Washington, 17:16.8; 5, Pennsylvania, 17:20.6; 6, Navy, 17:22.1; 7, Brown, 17:22.2; 8, Wisconsin, 17:30.2; 9, Syracuse, 17:36.8; 10, Princeton, 17:41.0; 11, Dartmouth, 17:44.1; 12, Rutgers, 17:47.1; 13, Columbia, 17:51.6.

| | |
|---|---|
| Junior varsity (3 miles)—Cornell | 17:12.7 |
| Freshman (2 miles)—Washington | 10:51.6 |

## Other Intercollegiate Regattas

| | |
|---|---|
| Adams Cup (1¾ miles)—Navy | 9:42.0 |
| Blackwell Cup (2 miles)—Yale | 11:55.8 |
| Carnegie Cup (1¾ miles)—Cornell | 8:53.6 |
| Childs Cup (1 5/16 miles)—Pennsylvania | 6:09.2 |
| Compton Cup (1¾ miles)—Harvard | 10:19.6 |
| Dad Vail Trophy (2,000 meters)—Brown | 6:19.5 |
| Eastern Association championship (2,000 meters)—Navy | 6:01.5 |
| Goes Trophy—Navy* | |
| Harvard–Yale (4 miles)—Harvard | 22:00.0 |
| Oxford–Cambridge (4¼ miles)—Cambridge | 19:22.0 |
| Packard Cup (3 miles)—Syracuse | 9:48.4 |
| Washington–California (2¾ miles)—California | 14:00.0 |
| Western intercollegiate championship (2,000 meters)—Washington | 6:32.2 |

* Race cancelled because of weather. Trophy awarded on outcome of Eastern championship race.

## United States Championships

(At Philadelphia)

(2,000 meters, except dashes)

| | |
|---|---|
| Single sculls—Seymour Cromwell, Riverside B. C., Cambridge, Mass. | rowover |
| Double sculls—William Flint–Ted Nash, Lake Washington R. C., Seattle | 6:35.1 |
| Pairs—Edward Ferry–Conn Findlay, Stanford Crew Assn., Palo Alto, Calif. | 6:58.3 |
| Pairs with coxswain—Edward Ferry–Conn Findlay, Stanford Crew Assn., Palo Alto, Calif. | 7:47.0 |
| Fours—Lake Washington R. C., Seattle | 6:28.3 |
| Fours with coxswain—Lake Washington R. C., Seattle | 7:07.8 |
| Eights—Lake Washington R. C., Seattle | 5:57.4 |
| ¼-mi. dash—Seymour Cromwell, Riverside B. C., Cambridge, Mass. | 1:12.4 |
| Association singles—Seymour Cromwell, Riverside B. C., Cambridge, Mass. | 7:15.0 |
| Quadruple sculls—Vesper B. C., Philadelphia | 6:35.2 |
| Intermediate eights—Undine Barge Club, Philadelphia | 6:23.9 |
| 150-lb. ¼-mi. dash—James Barker, Undine Barge Club, Philadelphia | 1:16.4 |
| 150-lb. singles—John Welchli, Detroit B. C. | 7:17.4 |
| 150-lb. doubles—George Kuhn–William Walker, Detroit B. C. | 6:51.1 |
| 150-lb. quadruple sculls—Undine Barge Club, Philadelphia | 6:51.8 |
| 150-lb. fours with coxswain—Detroit B. C. | 6:53.5 |
| 150-lb. eights—St. Catherines (Ont.) R. C. | 6:04.5 |
| Team (Barnes Trophy)—Detroit B. C. | 95½ pts. |

## British Royal Henley

(At Henley-on-Thames, England—1 5/16 miles)

| | |
|---|---|
| Grand Challenge Cup (eights)—U.S.S.R. Central Sports Club (Navy) | 6:43 |
| Thames Challenge Cup (lightweight eights)—U. of London | 7:03 |
| Diamond sculls (singles)—Stuart MacKenzie, Australia | 8:34 |

# FENCING

*Source:* Jose R. de Capriles, Editor, *American Fencing*

## World Championships

(At Turin, Italy)

| | Individual | Team |
|---|---|---|
| Foil | Richard Parulski, Poland | U.S.S.R. |
| Epee | Jack Guittet, France | U.S.S.R. |
| Saber | Iakov Rylskii, U.S.S.R. | Poland |
| Women | Heidi Schmid, Germany | U.S.S.R. |
| Overall | | U.S.S.R. |

## United States Championships

(At Los Angeles)

Foil—Lawrence Anastasi, Salle Csiszar, Philadelphia
Epee—Lt. Robert Beck, U. S. Navy
Saber—Daniel Magay, Pannonia A. C., San Francisco
Women—Janice Lee Romary, Los Angeles Fencing Academy

### TEAM

Foil—New York A. C. (Silvio Giolito, John Mooney, Edwin Richards, Ralph Spinella)
Epee—New York A. C. (Michael Alexander, Regis King, Jay Powell, Ralph Spinella)
Saber—Pannonia A. C., San Francisco (Jack Baker, Gerard Biagini, Daniel Magay, Alex Orban)
Three-weapon—Salle Csiszar, Philadelphia (Martin Davis, David Micahnik, Larry Anastasi, Eugene Hamori)
Women—Salle Santelli, New York (Ann Drungis, Sophronia Pierce, Betty Santelli, Evelyn Terhune)
Overall (Martini & Rossi Trophy)—New York A. C. (50 pts.)

## National Collegiate A. A.

(At Princeton, N. J.)

Foil—Herb Cohen, New York University
Epee—Jerry Halpern, New York University
Saber—Israel Colon, New York University
Team—New York University (79 pts.)

## Intercollegiate Fencing Association

(At Bronx, N. Y.)

Foil—Herb Cohen, New York University
Epee—Jerry Halpern, New York University
Saber—Alan Schwartz, Columbia

### TEAM

Three-weapon—New York University
Foil—New York University
Epee—New York University
Saber—New York University and Columbia

# CANOEING

*Source:* William J. Rhodes, American Canoe Association

## National Canoe Racing Championships

(At Washington, D. C.)

Canoe singles—Frank B. Havens, Washington (D. C.) C. C.
Canoe tandem—Walter Haase–Roger Van de Muelebroecke, Potomac B. C., Washington, D. C.
Canoe fours—Tom Palmby–Lee Stitzenberger–Andy Weigandt–Dennis Van Valkenburg, Washington (D. C.) C. C.
Kayak singles—Donald L. Dodge, Niles (Mich.) C. C.
Kayak tandem—Russell Dermond–Mike Pagkos, Yonkers (N. Y.) C. C.
Kayak fours—Donald L. Dodge–F. Albert–Gert Grigoleit–J. Huber, Niles (Mich.) C. C.
Women's kayak singles—Glorianne Perrier, Washington (D. C.) C. C.
Women's kayak tandem—Nell Fisher–Glorianne Perrier, Washington (D. C.) C. C.
Team—Washington (D. C.) C. C.

# BOXING
## World Championship Fights in 1961

| Date | Title at stake | Defender | Challenger | Winner | Round(s) | Where held |
|------|---------------|----------|-----------|--------|----------|-----------|
| Jan. 14 | *Middleweight | Paul Pender | Terry Downes | Pender | KO 7 | Boston |
| Feb. 7 | †Light Heavyweight | Harold Johnson | Jesse Bowdry | Johnson | KO 9 | Miami Beach |
| Mar. 4 | ‡Middleweight | Gene Fullmer | Ray Robinson | Fullmer | 15 | Las Vegas |
| Mar. 13 | Heavyweight | Floyd Patterson | Ingemar Johansson | Patterson | KO 6 | Miami Beach |
| Mar. 19 | Jr. Lightweight | Flash Elorde | Joey Lopes | Elorde | 15 | Manila |
| Mar. 25 | ‡Bantamweight | Eder Jofre | Piero Rollo | Jofre | KO 9 | Rio de Janeiro |
| Apr. 1 | Welterweight | Benny (Kid) Paret | Emile Griffith | Griffith | KO 13 | Miami Beach |
| Apr. 8 | Featherweight | Davey Moore | Danny Valdez | Moore | KO 1 | Los Angeles |
| Apr. 19 | Lightweight | Joe Brown | Dave Charnley | Brown | 15 | London |
| Apr. 22 | *Middleweight | Paul Pender | Carmen Basilio | Pender | 15 | Boston |
| Apr. 24 | ‡Light Heavyweight | Harold Johnson | Von Clay | Johnson | KO 2 | Philadelphia |
| May 10 | Jr. Welterweight | Diulio Loi | Carlos Ortiz | Loi | 15 | Milan |
| May 30 | xBantamweight | Johnny Caldwell | Alphonse Halimi | Caldwell | KO 8 | London |
| June 3 | Welterweight | Emile Griffith | Gaspar Ortega | Griffith | KO 12 | Los Angeles |
| June 10 | Light Heavyweight | Archie Moore | Giulio Rinaldi | Moore | 15 | New York |
| June 27 | Flyweight | Pone Kingpetch | Mitsunori Seki | Pone | 15 | Tokyo |
| July 11 | *Middleweight | Paul Pender | Terry Downes | Downes | KO 9 | London |
| Aug. 5 | ‡Middleweight | Gene Fullmer | Florentino Fernandez | Fullmer | 15 | Ogden, Utah |
| Aug. 19 | ‡Bantamweight | Eder Jofre | Ramon Arias | Jofre | KO 7 | Caracas |
| Aug. 29 | ‡Light Heavyweight | Harold Johnson | Eddie Cotton | Johnson | 15 | Seattle |
| Sept. 30 | Welterweight | Emile Griffith | Benny (Kid) Paret | Paret | 15 | New York |

\* Recognized by New York, Massachusetts and Europe.  † Fought for vacant National Boxing Association light heavyweight title, after N. B. A. withdrew recognition from Archie Moore as champion.  ‡ N. B. A.  x Recognized by Europe as champion.

## AMATEUR BOXING
### National A. A. U. Championships
(At Pocatello, Idaho)

112-lb.—Peter Gonzales, Portland, Ore.
119-lb.—John Howard, Portland, Ore.
125-lb.—Ralph Ungricht, Provo, Utah
132-lb.—Woody Marcus, Pocatello, Idaho
139-lb.—James Caldwell, Shawano, Wis.
147-lb.—Phil Baldwin, Muskegon, Mich.
156-lb.—Bobby Pasquale, Tacoma, Wash.
165-lb.—Leotis Martin, Toledo, Ohio
178-lb.—Bobby Christopherson, Madison, Wis.
Heavyweight—Rudy Davis, Philadelphia

## WEIGHTLIFTING
### National A. A. U. Championships
(At Santa Monica, Calif.)

| | Press | Snatch | Clean and Jerk | Total |
|---|---|---|---|---|
| 123-lb.—Charles Vinci, Cleveland | 240 | 225 | 275— | 740 |
| 132-lb.—Isaac Berger, York, Pa. | 250 | 230 | 310— | 790 |
| 148-lb.—Paul Goldberg, Philadelphia | 230 | 225 | 290— | 745 |
| 165-lb.—Frank Spellman, Los Angeles | 260 | 230 | 310— | 800 |
| 181-lb.—Tommy Kono, Honolulu | 310 | 290 | 380— | 980 |
| 198-lb.—Bill March, York, Pa. | 310 | 280 | 360— | 950 |
| Heavyweight—Jim Bradford, Washington, D. C. | 380 | 315 | 375— | 1,070 |

## JUDO
### National A. A. U. Championships
(At San Jose, Calif.)

140-lb.—Sumikichi Nozaki, Gardena, Calif.
160-lb.—Toshiyuki Seino, U. S. Air Force
180-lb.—Ben Campbell, San Jose, Calif.
Heavyweight—George Harris, U. S. Air Force
Grand champion—George Harris, U. S. Air Force
Team—U. S. Air Force (15 pts.)

## WRESTLING
### National A. A. U. Championships
(At Toledo, Ohio)
#### FREE STYLE

114.5-lb.—Dick Wilson, University of Toledo
125.5-lb.—Usaku Imaizumi, Japan
136.5-lb.—Lee Allen, Multnomah A. C., Portland, Ore.
147.5-lb.—Mike Rodriquez, University of Michigan
160.5-lb.—Steve Friedman, New York A. C.
174-lb.—Russ Camilleri, San Francisco Olympic Club
191-lb.—Dan Brand, San Francisco
Heavyweight—Dale Lewis, University of Oklahoma
Team—San Francisco Olympic Club (44 pts.)

#### GRECO-ROMAN

114.5-lb.—Dick Wilson, University of Toledo
125.5-lb.—Joe Gomez, San Francisco Olympic Club
136.5-lb.—Lee Allen, Multnomah A. C., Portland, Ore.
147.5-lb.—Fritz Boger, Chicago Y. M. C. A.
160.5-lb.—Julius Beno, San Francisco Olympic Club
174-lb.—Russ Camilleri, San Francisco Olympic Club
191-lb.—Zoltan Pentek, New York A. C.
Heavyweight—Pat Lovell, San Francisco
Team—San Francisco Olympic Club (71 pts.)

### National Collegiate A. A.
(At Corvallis, Ore.)

115-lb.—Elliott Simons, Lock Haven State
123-lb.—Duwane Miller, Oklahoma
130-lb.—Larry Lauchle, Pittsburgh
137-lb.—Norman Young, Michigan State
147-lb.—Larry Hayes, Iowa State
157-lb.—Phil Kinyon, Oklahoma State
167-lb.—Don Conway, Oregon State
177-lb.—Bob Johnson, Oklahoma State
191-lb.—Len Lordino, Colorado State College
Heavyweight—Dale Lewis, Oklahoma
Team—Oklahoma State (82 pts.)

### Adams Regains U. S. Billiards Title
Stanhope Adams of Chicago regained the national amateur three-cushion billiard championship in 1961.

# YACHTING

## Ocean and Distance Racing

St. Petersburg to Fort Lauderdale (403 miles)—Pipe Dream, Walter Colquitt, Greenwich, Conn.

Miami to Nassau (184 miles)—Paper Tiger, John Powell, St. Petersburg, Fla.

Miami to Montego Bay (807 miles)—Escapada, Baldwin M. Baldwin, Pasadena, Calif.

Annapolis to Newport (468 miles)—Reindeer, Newbold Smith, Philadelphia

Los Angeles to Tahiti (3,571 miles)—Athens, James Willhite, San Francisco

Transpacific (Los Angeles to Honolulu, 2,225 miles)—Nam Sang, A. B. Robb, Jr., Newport Harbor, Calif.

Marblehead to Halifax (360 miles)—Robin Too II, Ted Hood, Marblehead, Mass.

Chicago to Mackinac (333 miles)—Blue Horizon, Dick Kaup, Chicago

## Champions

North American sailing (Mallory Cup)—Harry Melges, Jr., Lake Geneva, Wis.

Junior North American sailing (Sears Cup)—Steven Wales, Marblehead, Mass.

Women's North American sailing (Adams Cup)—Timothea Schneider, Oyster Bay, N. Y.

North American intercollegiate dinghy (Morss Trophy)—M. I. T.

National interscholastic sailing—Loomis School

North American midget sailing—Steve Bedell, Bellport, N. Y.

## Class Champions

Atlantic, national—Briggs Cunningham, Green Farms, Conn.

Comet, international—Norman Freeman, Ithaca, N. Y.

Cougar catamaran, national—Comdr. Edward Cotter, U. S. Coast Guard

Dragon, North American—Walter Swindeman, Toledo, Ohio

Duster, national—Charles Stadler, Union Lake, Pa.

Finn monotype, national—Glen Foster, Oyster Bay, N. Y.

Finn, North American—Fred E. Miller, Jr., Newport Harbor, Calif.

5-0-5, North American—Logan Goar, Houston

5.5 meter, world—Louis Noverraz, Switzerland

5.5 meter, national—Ernest Fay, Houston

Flying Dutchman, North American—Harry Sindle, Toms River N. J.

Flying Scot, national—Kevin O'Reilly, Detroit

14-foot dinghy, national—Peter Eising, Seattle

Highlander, international—Allen Bower, Mentor Harbor, Ohio

International one design, world—Fred Olsen, Norway

Jet 14, international—John Applegate, Beachwood, N. J.

Jollyboat, North American—Dink Vail, Fishing Bay, Va.

Lightning, world—Tom Allen, Buffalo, N. Y.

Luders 16, international—Buddy Friedrichs, New Orleans

Morth, world—Ronald Patterson, Collingswood, N. J.

One-Ten, international—Albert A. Frost, Jr., San Diego

Pelican, national—Ronald Swanson, Dunedin, Fla.

Penguin, international—Otto Scherer, Jr., Grosse Pointe, Mich.

Raven, national—Al Bortolotti, Detroit

Rhode bantam, national—Jeff Robertson, Ithaca, N. Y.

Snipe, world—Axel Schmidt, Brazil

Snipe, national—Harry Levinson, Indianapolis

Star, world—Bill Buchan, Seattle

Star, North American—Dick Stearns, Northfield, Ill.

Thistle, national—Ed Walsh, Camden, N. J.

Tigercat, national—Walter Crump, Milford, Conn.

Two-Ten, international—Robert M. Sides, Marblehead, Mass.

Windmill, international—Homer Luzier, Sarasota, Fla.

Wood Pussy, national—Robert Blair, Cold Spring Harbor, N. Y.

Y-flyer, national—Randall Swan, Charleston, S. C.

# MOTORBOATING

## Major Trophy Winners

Gold Cup—Miss Century 21, driven by Bill Muncey, Seattle

Harmsworth Trophy—Miss Supertest III, driven by James Thompson, Canada

Detroit Memorial Trophy—Gale V, driven by Bill Cantrell, Detroit

Diamond Cup—Miss Century 21, driven by Bill Muncey, Seattle

Seafair Trophy—Miss Bardahl, driven by Ron Musson, Akron, Ohio

Gold Coast Marathon—Skylark, driven by Bob Seever, South Miami, Fla.

Silver Cup—Canceled after second heat, in which Bob Hayward, Canada, driving Miss Supertest III, was killed

President's Cup—Miss Century 21, driven by Bill Muncey, Seattle

# WATER SKIING

*Source:* American Water Ski Association

## World Championships

(At Long Beach, Calif.)

| | |
|---|--:|
| Champion—Bruno Zaccardi, Italy | 2,667 pts. |
| Slalom—James Jackson, Delray Beach, Fla. | 46 pts. |
| Tricks—Jean Marie Muller, France | 3,397 pts. |
| Jumping—Larry Penacho, San Diego | 150 ft. |

### WOMEN

| | |
|---|--:|
| Champion—Sylvie Hulsemann, Luxembourg | 2,911 pts. |
| Slalom—Janelle Kirtley, Birmingham, Ala. | 38 pts. |
| Tricks—Sylvie Hulsemann, Luxembourg | 2,554 pts. |
| Jumping—Renata Hansluwka, Austria | 83 ft. |

## United States Championships

(At Austin, Tex.)

| | |
|---|--:|
| Champion—Mike Ambsry, Orange, Calif. | 2,745 pts. |
| Slalom—James Jackson, Delray Beach, Fla. | 38 pts. |
| Tricks—Charles Stearns, Bellflower, Calif. | 3,215 pts. |
| Jumping—James Jackson, Delray Beach, Fla. | 134 ft. |

### WOMEN

| | |
|---|--:|
| Champion—Janelle Kirtley, Birmingham, Ala. | 2,726 pts. |
| Slalom—Jenny Hodges, Birmingham, Ala. | 53 pts. |
| Tricks—Janelle Kirtley, Birmingham, Ala. | 2,530 pts. |
| Jumping—Barbara Cooper, Lakeland, Fla. | 91 ft. |

# SOCCER

*Source:* Flannery News Bureau, New York.

## Major U. S. Winners

National Challenge Cup—Ukrainian Nationals, Philadelphia

National Amateur Cup—Kutis, St. Louis

National Junior Cup—Hakoah A. C., San Francisco

International League—Dukla, Czechoslovakia

American League—Ukrainian Nationals, Philadelphia

## Foreign

Europe Cup—Benfica, Lisbon

British Championship—England

English Football Cup—Tottenham

English League—Tottenham

Scottish League—Glasgow Rangers

Scottish Cup—Dumfermline

---

## Milwaukee Wins National Polo Title

The Milwaukee Polo Club won the national open championship in 1961. The winning foursome consisted of Guillermo Gracida, Julio Muller, George Oliver and Robert Uihlein.

# MAJOR LEAGUE BASEBALL RECORDS FOR 1961

## American League
### Final Standing of the Clubs

| | New York | Detroit | Baltimore | Chicago | Cleveland | Boston | Minnesota | Los Angeles | Kansas City | Washington | Won | Lost | Percentage | Games Behind |
|---|---|---|---|---|---|---|---|---|---|---|---|---|---|---|
| N. Y. | — | 10 | 9 | 12 | 14 | 13 | 14 | 12 | 14 | 11 | 109 | 53 | .673 | — |
| Det. | 8 | — | 9 | 12 | 12 | 10 | 11 | 14 | 12 | 13 | 101 | 61 | .623 | 8 |
| Balt. | 9 | 9 | — | 11 | 9 | 11 | 11 | 8 | 13 | 14 | 95 | 67 | .586 | 14 |
| Chi. | 6 | 6 | 7 | — | 12 | 9 | 9 | 10 | 14 | 13 | 86 | 76 | .531 | 23 |
| Cleve. | 4 | 6 | 9 | 6 | — | 13 | 10 | 10 | 8 | 12 | 78 | 83 | .484 | 30½ |
| Bost. | 5 | 8 | 7 | 9 | 5 | — | 11 | 11 | 10 | 10 | 76 | 86 | .469 | 33 |
| Minn. | 4 | 7 | 7 | 9 | 8 | 7 | — | 9 | 11 | 8 | 70 | 90 | .438 | 38 |
| L. A. | 6 | 4 | 10 | 8 | 8 | 7 | 8 | — | 9 | 10 | 70 | 91 | .435 | 38½ |
| K. C. | 4 | 6 | 5 | 4 | 9 | 8 | 7 | 9 | — | 9 | 61 | 100 | .379 | 47½ |
| Wash. | 7 | 5 | 4 | 5 | 6 | 8 | 9 | 8 | 9 | — | 61 | 100 | .379 | 47½ |

## National League
### Final Standing of the Clubs

| | Cincinnati | Los Angeles | San Francisco | Milwaukee | St. Louis | Pittsburgh | Chicago | Philadelphia | Won | Lost | Percentage | Games Behind |
|---|---|---|---|---|---|---|---|---|---|---|---|---|
| Cincinnati | — | 12 | 12 | 15 | 14 | 11 | 10 | 19 | 93 | 61 | .604 | — |
| Los Angeles | 10 | — | 10 | 12 | 12 | 13 | 15 | 17 | 89 | 65 | .578 | 4 |
| San Francisco | 10 | 12 | — | 11 | 9 | 12 | 17 | 14 | 85 | 69 | .552 | 8 |
| Milwaukee | 7 | 10 | 11 | — | 14 | 12 | 13 | 16 | 83 | 71 | .539 | 10 |
| St. Louis | 8 | 10 | 13 | 8 | — | 13 | 15 | 13 | 80 | 74 | .519 | 13 |
| Pittsburgh | 11 | 9 | 10 | 10 | 9 | — | 11 | 15 | 75 | 79 | .487 | 18 |
| Chicago | 12 | 7 | 5 | 9 | 7 | 11 | — | 13 | 64 | 90 | .416 | 29 |
| Philadelphia | 3 | 5 | 8 | 6 | 9 | 7 | 9 | — | 47 | 107 | .305 | 46 |

### THE LEADERS

| | |
|---|---|
| Batting—Norman Cash, Detroit | .361 |
| Home runs—Roger Maris, New York | 61 |
| Runs batted in—Roger Maris, New York | 142 |
| Runs—Roger Maris, New York | 132 |
| Hits—Norman Cash, Detroit | 193 |
| Doubles—Al Kaline, Detroit | 41 |
| Triples—Jake Wood, Detroit | 14 |
| Stolen bases—Luis Aparicio, Chicago | 53 |

### PITCHING

| | |
|---|---|
| Victories—Whitey Ford, New York | 25 |
| Percentage—Whitey Ford, New York (25–4) | .862 |
| Earned run average—Dick Donovan, Washington | 2.40 |
| Strikeouts—Camilo Pascual, Minnesota | 221 |

### THE LEADERS

| | |
|---|---|
| Batting—Roberto Clemente, Pittsburgh | .351 |
| Home runs—Orlando Cepeda, San Francisco | 46 |
| Runs batted in—Orlando Cepeda, San Francisco | 142 |
| Runs—Willie Mays, San Francisco | 129 |
| Hits—Vada Pinson, Cincinnati | 208 |
| Doubles—Henry Aaron, Milwaukee | 39 |
| Triples—George Altman, Chicago | 12 |
| Stolen bases—Maury Wills, Los Angeles | 35 |

### PITCHING

| | |
|---|---|
| Victories—Warren Spahn, Milwaukee, and Joey Jay, Cincinnati | 21 |
| Percentage—Johnny Podres, Los Angeles (18–5) | .783 |
| Earned run average—Warren Spahn, Milwaukee | 3.01 |
| Strikeouts—Sandy Koufax, Los Angeles | 269 |

## ROGER MARIS HITS 61 HOMERS IN '61

Roger Maris, 27-year-old New York Yankees outfielder, hit 61 home runs in the 1961 American League season to surpass Babe Ruth's 1927 record feat of 60 homers in a season. The 61st Maris homer came in his team's 162d and final game.

Because Ruth's 60 were achieved in a 154-game season, Baseball Commissioner Ford Frick had ruled in mid-season that to erase Ruth's record, a player would have to do so within 154 games, the number played before the American League expanded to ten teams in 1961. Thus Ruth's mark continues on the books, along with that set by Maris. At 154 games, Maris had 59 home runs.

Major league players who have hit the most home runs in one season:

| | | |
|---|---|---|
| 61 | Roger Maris, New York (A) | 1961 |
| 60 | Babe Ruth, New York (A) | 1927 |
| 59 | Babe Ruth, New York (A) | 1921 |
| 58 | Jimmy Foxx, Philadelphia (A) | 1932 |
| 58 | Hank Greenberg, Detroit (A) | 1938 |
| 56 | Hack Wilson, Chicago (N) | 1930 |
| 54 | Babe Ruth, New York (A) | 1920 |
| 54 | Babe Ruth, New York (A) | 1928 |
| 54 | Ralph Kiner, Pittsburgh (N) | 1949 |
| 54 | Mickey Mantle, New York (A) | 1961 |

| | | |
|---|---|---|
| 52 | Mickey Mantle, New York (A) | 1956 |
| 51 | Ralph Kiner, Pittsburgh (N) | 1947 |
| 51 | John Mize, New York (N) | 1947 |
| 51 | Willie Mays, New York (N) | 1955 |
| 50 | Jimmy Foxx, Boston (A) | 1938 |
| 49 | Babe Ruth, New York (A) | 1930 |
| 49 | Lou Gehrig, New York (A) | 1934 |
| 49 | Lou Gehrig, New York (A) | 1936 |
| 49 | Ted Kluszewski, Cincinnati (N) | 1954 |

### Ruth Tops All-Time Homer List

The 61 home runs Roger Maris hit in 1961 gave him a lifetime major league total of 158. Babe Ruth continues to lead the list in this category, with 714. These are the players who hit 300 or more homers in the majors, through 1961:

| | | | |
|---|---|---|---|
| Babe Ruth | 714 | Joe DiMaggio | 361 |
| Jimmy Foxx | 534 | Gil Hodges | 361 |
| Ted Williams | 521 | John Mize | 359 |
| Mel Ott | 511 | Yogi Berra | 340 |
| Lou Gehrig | 493 | Hank Greenberg | 331 |
| Stan Musial | 444 | Willie Mays | 319 |
| Duke Snider | 384 | Al Simmons | 307 |
| Mickey Mantle | 374 | Rogers Hornsby | 302 |
| Ed Mathews | 370 | Chuck Klein | 300 |
| Ralph Kiner | 369 | | |

# Batting Averages

(Unofficial—200 at bats or more)

## American League

| | g | ab | r | h | hr | rbi | avg. |
|---|---|---|---|---|---|---|---|
| Cash, Detroit | 159 | 535 | 119 | 193 | 41 | 132 | .361 |
| Howard, New York | 129 | 446 | 64 | 155 | 21 | 78 | .348 |
| Kaline, Detroit | 153 | 586 | 116 | 190 | 19 | 82 | .324 |
| Piersall, Cleveland | 121 | 484 | 81 | 156 | 6 | 40 | .322 |
| Mantle, New York | 153 | 514 | 131 | 163 | 54 | 128 | .317 |
| Runnels, Boston | 143 | 360 | 49 | 114 | 3 | 38 | .317 |
| Woodling, Washington | 110 | 342 | 39 | 107 | 10 | 57 | .313 |
| Robinson, Chicago | 132 | 432 | 69 | 134 | 11 | 60 | .310 |
| Blanchard, New York | 93 | 243 | 38 | 74 | 21 | 54 | .305 |
| Gentile, Baltimore | 148 | 486 | 96 | 147 | 46 | 141 | .302 |
| Battey, Minnesota | 133 | 460 | 70 | 139 | 17 | 55 | .302 |
| Francona, Cleveland | 155 | 592 | 87 | 178 | 16 | 85 | .301 |
| Romano, Cleveland | 142 | 509 | 76 | 152 | 21 | 80 | .299 |
| Brandt, Baltimore | 138 | 516 | 93 | 153 | 16 | 72 | .297 |
| Siebern, Kansas City | 153 | 561 | 68 | 166 | 18 | 98 | .296 |
| Sievers, Chicago | 141 | 491 | 76 | 145 | 27 | 92 | .295 |
| Johnson, Washington | 61 | 224 | 27 | 66 | 6 | 29 | .295 |
| Lumpe, Kansas City | 148 | 568 | 81 | 167 | 3 | 54 | .294 |
| Snyder, Baltimore | 115 | 312 | 46 | 91 | 1 | 13 | .292 |
| Herzog, Baltimore | 81 | 323 | 39 | 94 | 5 | 35 | .291 |
| Colavito, Detroit | 163 | 583 | 129 | 169 | 45 | 140 | .290 |
| Nixon, Boston | 87 | 242 | 24 | 70 | 1 | 19 | .289 |
| Killebrew, Minnesota | 150 | 541 | 94 | 156 | 46 | 122 | .288 |
| Pearson, Los Angeles | 144 | 427 | 92 | 123 | 7 | 41 | .288 |
| B. Robinson, Baltimore | 163 | 668 | 89 | 192 | 7 | 61 | .287 |
| Green, Minnesota | 156 | 660 | 92 | 171 | 9 | 50 | .285 |
| L. Thomas, N.Y.-L.A. | 132 | 452 | 77 | 129 | 24 | 70 | .285 |
| Landis, Chicago | 140 | 535 | 87 | 151 | 21 | 83 | .282 |
| Lollar, Chicago | 118 | 337 | 38 | 95 | 7 | 41 | .282 |
| Howser, Kansas City | 158 | 612 | 108 | 171 | 3 | 45 | .280 |
| Minoso, Chicago | 152 | 540 | 91 | 151 | 14 | 82 | .280 |
| Versalles, Minnesota | 129 | 511 | 65 | 143 | 7 | 53 | .280 |
| Wagner, Los Angeles | 132 | 453 | 74 | 127 | 28 | 78 | .280 |
| Green, Washington | 110 | 364 | 52 | 102 | 18 | 62 | .280 |
| Bilko, Los Angeles | 114 | 294 | 49 | 82 | 20 | 59 | .279 |
| Smith, Chicago | 147 | 532 | 88 | 148 | 28 | 92 | .278 |
| Causey, Kansas City | 104 | 311 | 37 | 86 | 8 | 49 | .277 |
| Kubek, New York | 153 | 617 | 84 | 170 | 8 | 46 | .276 |
| Temple, Cleveland | 129 | 518 | 72 | 143 | 3 | 59 | .276 |
| G. Thomas, Det.-L.A. | 96 | 288 | 41 | 79 | 13 | 59 | .274 |
| Aparicio, Chicago | 156 | 625 | 90 | 170 | 6 | 45 | .272 |
| Berra, New York | 119 | 395 | 62 | 107 | 22 | 61 | .271 |
| Carreon, Chicago | 78 | 229 | 32 | 62 | 4 | 27 | .271 |
| Boros, Detroit | 116 | 396 | 51 | 107 | 5 | 62 | .270 |
| King, Washington | 109 | 263 | 43 | 71 | 11 | 46 | .270 |
| Maris, New York | 161 | 590 | 132 | 159 | 61 | 142 | .269 |
| Power, Cleveland | 147 | 563 | 64 | 151 | 5 | 63 | .268 |
| Skowron, New York | 150 | 561 | 77 | 150 | 28 | 89 | .267 |
| Held, Cleveland | 146 | 509 | 67 | 136 | 23 | 78 | .267 |
| Malzone, Boston | 151 | 590 | 74 | 157 | 14 | 87 | .266 |
| Yastrzemski, Boston | 148 | 583 | 72 | 155 | 11 | 80 | .266 |
| Averill, Los Angeles | 115 | 323 | 55 | 86 | 21 | 59 | .266 |
| Brown, Detroit | 93 | 308 | 32 | 82 | 16 | 45 | .266 |
| E. Robinson, Baltimore | 96 | 222 | 37 | 59 | 8 | 30 | .266 |
| Phillips, Cleveland | 143 | 566 | 64 | 144 | 18 | 72 | .264 |
| Adair, Baltimore | 133 | 386 | 42 | 102 | 9 | 37 | .264 |
| Jensen, Boston | 137 | 498 | 64 | 131 | 13 | 66 | .263 |
| Buddin, Boston | 115 | 339 | 58 | 89 | 6 | 41 | .263 |
| Hardy, Boston | 85 | 281 | 46 | 74 | 3 | 37 | .263 |
| Richardson, New York | 162 | 662 | 80 | 172 | 3 | 49 | .261 |
| O'Connell, Washington | 138 | 493 | 61 | 128 | 1 | 36 | .260 |
| Hinton, Washington | 106 | 339 | 51 | 88 | 6 | 35 | .260 |
| Wertz, Bost.-Det. | 107 | 323 | 33 | 84 | 11 | 60 | .260 |
| Green, Boston | 88 | 219 | 33 | 57 | 6 | 27 | .260 |
| Schilling, Boston | 158 | 646 | 87 | 167 | 5 | 62 | .259 |
| Kirkland, Cleveland | 148 | 525 | 84 | 136 | 27 | 95 | .259 |
| Wood, Detroit | 162 | 663 | 96 | 171 | 11 | 69 | .258 |
| Lemon, Minnesota | 129 | 423 | 57 | 109 | 14 | 53 | .258 |
| Bruton, Detroit | 160 | 596 | 100 | 153 | 17 | 63 | .257 |
| McAuliffe, Detroit | 80 | 285 | 35 | 73 | 6 | 33 | .256 |
| Carey, K.C.-Chi. | 95 | 266 | 41 | 68 | 3 | 25 | .256 |
| Hunt, Los Angeles | 149 | 479 | 70 | 122 | 25 | 84 | .255 |
| Posada, Kansas City | 116 | 344 | 37 | 87 | 7 | 53 | .253 |
| Fox, Chicago | 159 | 606 | 67 | 152 | 2 | 51 | .251 |
| Tasby, Washington | 141 | 494 | 54 | 124 | 17 | 63 | .251 |
| Koppe, Los Angeles | 91 | 338 | 46 | 85 | 5 | 41 | .251 |
| Tuttle, K.C.-Minn. | 138 | 454 | 53 | 113 | 5 | 46 | .249 |
| Keough, Washington | 135 | 390 | 56 | 97 | 9 | 35 | .249 |
| Long, Washington | 123 | 377 | 52 | 94 | 17 | 49 | .249 |
| Hansen, Baltimore | 155 | 533 | 51 | 132 | 12 | 61 | .248 |
| Fernandez, Detroit | 133 | 435 | 41 | 108 | 3 | 40 | .248 |
| Martin, Minnesota | 108 | 374 | 44 | 92 | 6 | 36 | .246 |
| Allison, Minnesota | 159 | 566 | 83 | 136 | 29 | 104 | .245 |
| Triandos, Baltimore | 115 | 397 | 35 | 97 | 17 | 63 | .244 |
| Kluszewski, Los Angeles | 107 | 263 | 32 | 64 | 15 | 40 | .243 |
| Pignatano, Kansas City | 92 | 243 | 31 | 59 | 4 | 22 | .243 |
| Pagliaroni, Boston | 120 | 376 | 50 | 91 | 16 | 58 | .242 |
| Sullivan, Kansas City | 117 | 331 | 42 | 80 | 6 | 40 | .242 |
| Bridges, Los Angeles | 84 | 229 | 20 | 55 | 2 | 15 | .240 |
| Cottier, Det.-Wash. | 111 | 344 | 40 | 81 | 2 | 34 | .235 |
| Geiger, Boston | 140 | 499 | 82 | 116 | 18 | 64 | .232 |
| Del Greco, Kansas City | 74 | 239 | 34 | 55 | 5 | 21 | .230 |
| Martin, Chicago | 110 | 275 | 26 | 63 | 5 | 32 | .229 |
| Klaus, Washington | 91 | 251 | 26 | 57 | 7 | 30 | .227 |
| Bertoia, Minn.-K.C.-Det. | 98 | 270 | 35 | 61 | 2 | 25 | .226 |
| Throneberry, K.C.-Bost. | 96 | 226 | 26 | 51 | 11 | 35 | .226 |
| Boyer, New York | 148 | 503 | 61 | 113 | 11 | 55 | .225 |
| Gardner, Minn.-N.Y. | 86 | 253 | 24 | 57 | 2 | 13 | .225 |
| Aspromonte, L.A.-Cleve. | 88 | 308 | 34 | 69 | 2 | 19 | .224 |
| Roarke, Detroit | 86 | 229 | 21 | 51 | 2 | 22 | .223 |
| Lopez, New York | 93 | 243 | 27 | 54 | 3 | 22 | .222 |
| Johnson, N.Y.-K.C. | 96 | 301 | 32 | 63 | 8 | 44 | .209 |
| Breeding, Baltimore | 90 | 244 | 32 | 51 | 1 | 16 | .209 |
| Williams, Baltimore | 103 | 310 | 37 | 64 | 8 | 24 | .206 |
| Stephens, Balt.-K.C. | 94 | 241 | 26 | 49 | 4 | 28 | .203 |
| Veal, Washington | 69 | 218 | 21 | 44 | 0 | 8 | .202 |
| Yost, Los Angeles | 76 | 213 | 29 | 43 | 3 | 15 | .202 |
| Daley, Washington | 71 | 203 | 12 | 39 | 2 | 17 | .192 |

## National League

| | g | ab | r | h | hr | rbi | avg. |
|---|---|---|---|---|---|---|---|
| Clemente, Pittsburgh | 144 | 572 | 100 | 201 | 23 | 89 | .351 |
| Pinson, Cincinnati | 154 | 607 | 101 | 208 | 16 | 87 | .343 |
| Boyer, St. Louis | 153 | 589 | 109 | 194 | 24 | 95 | .329 |
| Moon, Los Angeles | 134 | 463 | 79 | 152 | 17 | 87 | .328 |
| Aaron, Milwaukee | 155 | 603 | 115 | 197 | 34 | 120 | .327 |
| Robinson, Cincinnati | 153 | 545 | 117 | 176 | 37 | 124 | .323 |
| Flood, St. Louis | 132 | 335 | 53 | 108 | 2 | 21 | .322 |
| Fairly, Los Angeles | 111 | 245 | 42 | 79 | 10 | 48 | .322 |
| Lynch, Cincinnati | 91 | 181 | 33 | 57 | 13 | 50 | .315 |
| Cepeda, San Francisco | 152 | 585 | 105 | 182 | 46 | 142 | .311 |
| M. Alou, San Francisco | 81 | 200 | 38 | 62 | 6 | 24 | .310 |
| Mays, San Francisco | 154 | 572 | 129 | 176 | 40 | 123 | .308 |
| Mathews, Milwaukee | 152 | 572 | 103 | 175 | 32 | 91 | .306 |
| Altman, Chicago | 138 | 518 | 77 | 157 | 27 | 96 | .303 |
| Burgess, Pittsburgh | 100 | 323 | 37 | 98 | 12 | 52 | .303 |
| Stuart, Pittsburgh | 138 | 532 | 83 | 160 | 35 | 117 | .301 |
| Hoak, Pittsburgh | 145 | 503 | 72 | 150 | 12 | 61 | .298 |
| Howard, Los Angeles | 92 | 267 | 36 | 79 | 15 | 45 | .296 |
| Snider, Los Angeles | 85 | 233 | 35 | 69 | 16 | 56 | .296 |
| Post, Cincinnati | 99 | 282 | 44 | 83 | 20 | 57 | .294 |
| F. Alou, San Francisco | 132 | 415 | 59 | 120 | 18 | 53 | .289 |
| Musial, St. Louis | 123 | 372 | 46 | 107 | 15 | 70 | .288 |
| Coleman, Cincinnati | 150 | 520 | 63 | 149 | 26 | 87 | .287 |
| White, St. Louis | 153 | 591 | 89 | 169 | 20 | 90 | .286 |
| Cunningham, St. Louis | 113 | 322 | 60 | 92 | 7 | 40 | .286 |
| Adcock, Milwaukee | 152 | 562 | 77 | 160 | 35 | 108 | .285 |
| Santo, Chicago | 154 | 578 | 83 | 164 | 23 | 83 | .284 |
| Wills, Los Angeles | 148 | 613 | 105 | 173 | 1 | 31 | .282 |
| Thomas, Chi.-Mil. | 139 | 473 | 65 | 133 | 27 | 73 | .281 |
| Walls, Philadelphia | 91 | 261 | 32 | 73 | 8 | 30 | .280 |
| Javier, St. Louis | 113 | 445 | 58 | 124 | 2 | 41 | .279 |
| Williams, Chicago | 146 | 529 | 75 | 147 | 25 | 86 | .278 |
| Banks, Chicago | 138 | 511 | 75 | 142 | 29 | 79 | .278 |
| T. Davis, Los Angeles | 132 | 460 | 60 | 128 | 15 | 58 | .278 |
| Davenport, San Francisco | 137 | 436 | 65 | 121 | 12 | 65 | .278 |
| Torre, Milwaukee | 113 | 406 | 40 | 113 | 10 | 42 | .278 |
| Freese, Cincinnati | 152 | 575 | 78 | 159 | 26 | 87 | .277 |
| Gonzalez, Philadelphia | 126 | 426 | 58 | 118 | 12 | 59 | .277 |
| Groat, Pittsburgh | 148 | 596 | 71 | 164 | 6 | 55 | .275 |
| Bertell, Chicago | 92 | 267 | 20 | 73 | 2 | 33 | .273 |
| Kasko, Cincinnati | 146 | 469 | 64 | 127 | 2 | 27 | .271 |
| Maye, Milwaukee | 110 | 373 | 68 | 101 | 14 | 41 | .271 |
| McCovey, San Francisco | 106 | 328 | 59 | 89 | 17 | 50 | .271 |
| Skinner, Pittsburgh | 119 | 381 | 61 | 102 | 3 | 42 | .268 |
| Callison, Philadelphia | 138 | 455 | 74 | 121 | 9 | 47 | .266 |
| Larker, Los Angeles | 97 | 282 | 29 | 75 | 5 | 38 | .266 |
| Rodgers, Chicago | 73 | 214 | 27 | 57 | 6 | 23 | .266 |
| Mazeroski, Pittsburgh | 152 | 558 | 71 | 148 | 13 | 59 | .265 |
| Kuenn, San Francisco | 131 | 471 | 60 | 125 | 5 | 46 | .265 |
| Bolling, Minnesota | 148 | 585 | 86 | 153 | 15 | 56 | .262 |
| Virdon, Pittsburgh | 146 | 599 | 81 | 156 | 9 | 58 | .260 |
| Ashburn, Chicago | 109 | 305 | 49 | 79 | 0 | 19 | .259 |
| Herrera, Philadelphia | 126 | 400 | 56 | 103 | 13 | 51 | .258 |
| Amaro, Philadelphia | 135 | 381 | 34 | 98 | 1 | 32 | .257 |
| Amalfitano, San Francisco | 109 | 384 | 64 | 98 | 2 | 23 | .255 |
| James, St. Louis | 108 | 349 | 43 | 89 | 4 | 44 | .255 |
| Heist, Chicago | 109 | 321 | 49 | 82 | 7 | 37 | .255 |
| Bell, Cincinnati | 103 | 235 | 27 | 60 | 3 | 33 | .255 |
| W. Davis, Los Angeles | 128 | 339 | 57 | 86 | 12 | 45 | .254 |
| Pagan, San Francisco | 134 | 434 | 38 | 110 | 5 | 46 | .253 |
| Zimmer, Chicago | 128 | 477 | 57 | 120 | 13 | 40 | .252 |
| Demeter, L.A.-Phil. | 121 | 411 | 57 | 103 | 21 | 70 | .251 |
| Roseboro, Los Angeles | 128 | 394 | 59 | 99 | 18 | 59 | .251 |
| Taylor, Philadelphia | 106 | 400 | 47 | 100 | 2 | 27 | .250 |
| C. Smith, L.A.-Phil. | 113 | 435 | 47 | 108 | 11 | 50 | .248 |
| Bouchee, Chicago | 112 | 319 | 49 | 79 | 12 | 38 | .248 |
| Spencer, St. L.-S.F. | 97 | 319 | 46 | 79 | 12 | 48 | .248 |
| Bailey, San. S.F. | 120 | 383 | 43 | 94 | 13 | 53 | .245 |
| Gilliam, Los Angeles | 144 | 439 | 74 | 107 | 4 | 32 | .244 |
| Kindall, Chicago | 96 | 310 | 37 | 75 | 9 | 44 | .242 |
| Hodges, Los Angeles | 109 | 215 | 25 | 52 | 8 | 32 | .242 |
| Hiller, San Francisco | 70 | 240 | 38 | 57 | 2 | 12 | .238 |
| Taylor, Chicago | 89 | 235 | 26 | 56 | 3 | 29 | .238 |
| Neal, Los Angeles | 108 | 341 | 40 | 80 | 10 | 48 | .235 |
| Malkmus, Philadelphia | 121 | 342 | 39 | 79 | 7 | 31 | .231 |
| Blasingame, S.F.-Cinn. | 126 | 451 | 60 | 100 | 1 | 21 | .222 |
| McMillan, Milwaukee | 154 | 505 | 42 | 111 | 7 | 49 | .220 |
| Dalrymple, Philadelphia | 129 | 378 | 23 | 83 | 5 | 42 | .220 |
| Lillis, L.A.-S.F. | 105 | 239 | 24 | 51 | 0 | 12 | .213 |
| Zimmerman, Cincinnati | 76 | 205 | 8 | 42 | 0 | 10 | .205 |

# Pitching Records
(Unofficial—10 or more decisions)

## American League

| | g | ip | h | bb | so | w | l | era |
|---|---|---|---|---|---|---|---|---|
| Hoeft, Baltimore | 35 | 138 | 106 | 55 | 100 | 7 | 4 | 2.02 |
| Arroyo, New York | 65 | 119 | 83 | 49 | 86 | 15 | 5 | 2.19 |
| Wilhelm, Baltimore | 51 | 110 | 89 | 41 | 85 | 9 | 7 | 2.29 |
| Morgan, Los Angeles | 59 | 92 | 74 | 17 | 39 | 8 | 2 | 2.35 |
| Donovan, Washington | 23 | 169 | 138 | 35 | 61 | 10 | 10 | 2.40 |
| Stafford, New York | 36 | 195 | 188 | 59 | 102 | 14 | 9 | 2.68 |
| Mossi, Detroit | 59 | 101 | 85 | 25 | 51 | 7 | 8 | 2.76 |
| Lown, Chicago | 35 | 240 | 237 | 47 | 137 | 15 | 7 | 2.96 |
| Pappas, Baltimore | 26 | 178 | 134 | 77 | 88 | 13 | 9 | 3.03 |
| Pizarro, Chicago | 39 | 195 | 164 | 89 | 188 | 14 | 7 | 3.05 |
| Hall, Baltimore | 29 | 122 | 102 | 30 | 91 | 7 | 5 | 3.10 |
| Terry, New York | 31 | 189 | 162 | 42 | 87 | 16 | 3 | 3.14 |
| Brown, Baltimore | 27 | 167 | 153 | 33 | 61 | 10 | 6 | 3.18 |
| Bunning, Detroit | 38 | 268 | 232 | 71 | 193 | 17 | 11 | 3.19 |
| Ford, New York | 39 | 283 | 242 | 17 | 209 | 25 | 4 | 3.21 |
| Lary, Detroit | 36 | 275 | 252 | 67 | 147 | 23 | 9 | 3.24 |
| Archer, Kansas City | 39 | 205 | 204 | 62 | 104 | 9 | 15 | 3.25 |
| Daniels, Washington | 32 | 212 | 184 | 80 | 107 | 12 | 11 | 3.27 |
| Schwall, Boston | 25 | 179 | 167 | 110 | 90 | 15 | 7 | 3.27 |
| Funke, Cleveland | 56 | 92 | 79 | 31 | 64 | 11 | 11 | 3.33 |
| Barber, Baltimore | 37 | 248 | 194 | 130 | 149 | 18 | 12 | 3.34 |
| Monbouquette, Boston | 32 | 236 | 233 | 100 | 161 | 14 | 14 | 3.39 |
| Coates, New York | 43 | 141 | 128 | 53 | 80 | 11 | 5 | 3.45 |
| Pascual, Minnesota | 35 | 252 | 205 | 100 | 221 | 15 | 16 | 3.46 |
| Wynn, Chicago | 17 | 110 | 88 | 47 | 64 | 8 | 2 | 3.52 |
| Sheldon, New York | 35 | 163 | 149 | 55 | 84 | 11 | 5 | 3.59 |
| Kralick, Minnesota | 33 | 242 | 257 | 64 | 136 | 13 | 11 | 3.61 |
| McBride, Los Angeles | 38 | 242 | 227 | 102 | 179 | 12 | 15 | 3.64 |
| Fowler, Los Angeles | 53 | 89 | 68 | 29 | 77 | 5 | 8 | 3.64 |
| Estrada, Baltimore | 33 | 212 | 159 | 132 | 160 | 15 | 9 | 3.69 |
| Pierce, Chicago | 39 | 182 | 190 | 54 | 106 | 10 | 9 | 3.76 |
| Bowsfield, Los Angeles | 41 | 157 | 154 | 63 | 87 | 11 | 8 | 3.78 |
| Grant, Cleveland | 35 | 245 | 207 | 109 | 146 | 15 | 9 | 3.86 |
| McLain, Washington | 33 | 212 | 220 | 48 | 76 | 8 | 18 | 3.86 |
| Kaat, Minnesota | 36 | 201 | 188 | 82 | 122 | 9 | 17 | 3.90 |
| Fisher, Baltimore | 36 | 196 | 205 | 75 | 117 | 10 | 13 | 3.90 |
| Foytack, Detroit | 32 | 170 | 152 | 56 | 87 | 11 | 10 | 3.92 |
| Ramos, Minnesota | 42 | 264 | 265 | 80 | 172 | 11 | 20 | 3.95 |
| Kutyna, Minnesota | 50 | 143 | 147 | 48 | 64 | 6 | 3 | 3.97 |
| Latman, Cleveland | 45 | 177 | 163 | 54 | 109 | 13 | 5 | 4.02 |
| Hawkins, Cleveland | 30 | 133 | 139 | 59 | 51 | 7 | 9 | 4.06 |
| Bell, Cleveland | 34 | 228 | 214 | 100 | 163 | 12 | 16 | 4.11 |
| Kline, L. A.-Det. | 36 | 161 | 172 | 61 | 97 | 8 | 9 | 4.14 |
| Larsen, K. C.-Chi. | 33 | 89 | 85 | 40 | 66 | 8 | 2 | 4.15 |
| Donohue, Det.-L. A. | 52 | 121 | 116 | 65 | 100 | 5 | 7 | 4.17 |
| Shaw, Chi.-K. C. | 40 | 222 | 246 | 76 | 91 | 12 | 14 | 4.18 |
| Sisler, Washington | 45 | 60 | 55 | 48 | 29 | 2 | 8 | 4.20 |
| Grba, Los Angeles | 40 | 212 | 197 | 114 | 106 | 11 | 13 | 4.25 |
| Daley, K. C.-N. Y. | 39 | 193 | 211 | 73 | 120 | 12 | 17 | 4.29 |
| McLish, Chicago | 31 | 163 | 178 | 48 | 83 | 10 | 13 | 4.36 |
| Hobaugh, Washington | 26 | 126 | 141 | 64 | 67 | 7 | 9 | 4.43 |
| Burnside, Washington | 33 | 113 | 106 | 52 | 54 | 4 | 9 | 4.54 |
| Herbert, K. C.-Chi. | 34 | 221 | 245 | 68 | 115 | 12 | 14 | 4.60 |
| Bass, Kansas City | 40 | 171 | 164 | 82 | 74 | 11 | 11 | 4.68 |
| Rakow, Kansas City | 45 | 125 | 132 | 47 | 82 | 2 | 8 | 4.68 |
| Fornieles, Boston | 57 | 119 | 121 | 64 | 70 | 9 | 8 | 4.69 |
| Perry, Cleveland | 35 | 224 | 237 | 87 | 90 | 10 | 17 | 4.74 |
| Walker, Kansas City | 36 | 168 | 161 | 97 | 55 | 8 | 14 | 4.82 |
| Gabler, Washington | 29 | 93 | 104 | 37 | 33 | 3 | 8 | 4.84 |
| Conley, Boston | 33 | 200 | 229 | 67 | 116 | 11 | 14 | 4.86 |
| Delock, Boston | 28 | 156 | 185 | 52 | 82 | 6 | 9 | 4.90 |
| Ditmar, N. Y.-K. C. | 32 | 108 | 119 | 37 | 42 | 2 | 8 | 5.17 |
| Duren, N. Y.-L. A. | 44 | 104 | 89 | 79 | 110 | 6 | 13 | 5.19 |
| Regan, Detroit | 32 | 120 | 134 | 41 | 46 | 10 | 7 | 5.25 |
| Nuxhall, Kansas City | 37 | 128 | 135 | 65 | 82 | 5 | 8 | 5.34 |
| Baumann, Chicago | 53 | 188 | 249 | 59 | 75 | 10 | 13 | 5.60 |
| Muffett, Boston | 38 | 113 | 129 | 36 | 50 | 3 | 11 | 5.65 |
| Moeller, Los Angeles | 33 | 113 | 122 | 83 | 87 | 4 | 8 | 5.81 |

## National League

| | g | ip | h | bb | so | w | l | era |
|---|---|---|---|---|---|---|---|---|
| Perranoski, Los Angeles | 53 | 92 | 82 | 41 | 56 | 7 | 5 | 2.64 |
| Miller, San Francisco | 63 | 122 | 95 | 37 | 86 | 14 | 5 | 2.66 |
| McMahon, Milwaukee | 53 | 92 | 84 | 50 | 54 | 6 | 4 | 2.84 |
| Schultz, Chicago | 41 | 67 | 57 | 25 | 57 | 7 | 6 | 2.96 |
| Spahn, Milwaukee | 38 | 263 | 236 | 64 | 115 | 21 | 13 | 3.01 |
| Brosnan, Cincinnati | 53 | 80 | 77 | 18 | 39 | 10 | 4 | 3.04 |
| O'Toole, Cincinnati | 39 | 253 | 229 | 93 | 178 | 19 | 9 | 3.09 |
| Simmons, St. Louis | 30 | 196 | 203 | 64 | 99 | 9 | 10 | 3.12 |
| McCormick, San Fran. | 35 | 250 | 234 | 75 | 163 | 13 | 16 | 3.20 |
| Gibson, St. Louis | 35 | 211 | 186 | 119 | 166 | 13 | 12 | 3.24 |
| Gibbon, Pittsburgh | 30 | 195 | 185 | 57 | 145 | 13 | 10 | 3.32 |
| Koufax, Los Angeles | 42 | 256 | 212 | 96 | 269 | 18 | 13 | 3.52 |
| Jay, Cincinnati | 34 | 247 | 217 | 92 | 157 | 21 | 10 | 3.53 |
| O'Dell, San Francisco | 46 | 130 | 132 | 32 | 109 | 7 | 5 | 3.60 |
| Drysdale, Los Angeles | 40 | 244 | 236 | 83 | 181 | 13 | 10 | 3.69 |
| Sadecki, St. Louis | 31 | 223 | 196 | 102 | 114 | 14 | 10 | 3.71 |
| Purkey, Cincinnati | 36 | 246 | 245 | 51 | 116 | 16 | 12 | 3.73 |
| Podres, Los Angeles | 32 | 183 | 192 | 51 | 124 | 18 | 5 | 3.74 |
| Jackson, St. Louis | 33 | 211 | 203 | 56 | 113 | 14 | 11 | 3.75 |
| Ferrarese, Philadelphia | 42 | 139 | 120 | 68 | 88 | 5 | 12 | 3.76 |
| Cardwell, Chicago | 39 | 259 | 243 | 89 | 155 | 15 | 14 | 3.82 |
| Face, Pittsburgh | 62 | 92 | 94 | 10 | 56 | 6 | 12 | 3.82 |
| Willey, Milwaukee | 35 | 160 | 147 | 64 | 91 | 6 | 12 | 3.83 |
| Friend, Pittsburgh | 41 | 236 | 271 | 44 | 107 | 14 | 19 | 3.85 |
| Ellsworth, Chicago | 37 | 187 | 213 | 48 | 91 | 10 | 11 | 3.85 |
| Marichal, San Francisco | 29 | 185 | 182 | 48 | 124 | 13 | 10 | 3.89 |
| Hendley, Milwaukee | 19 | 97 | 96 | 40 | 43 | 5 | 7 | 3.90 |
| Williams, Los Angeles | 41 | 235 | 213 | 108 | 204 | 15 | 12 | 3.91 |
| Burdette, Milwaukee | 40 | 274 | 295 | 33 | 92 | 18 | 11 | 3.97 |
| Hunt, Cincinnati | 29 | 136 | 130 | 66 | 73 | 9 | 10 | 3.97 |
| Nottebart, Milwaukee | 38 | 126 | 117 | 48 | 64 | 6 | 7 | 4.07 |
| Haddix, Pittsburgh | 29 | 156 | 159 | 41 | 100 | 10 | 6 | 4.10 |
| Broglio, St. Louis | 37 | 175 | 166 | 75 | 113 | 9 | 12 | 4.11 |
| Buhl, Milwaukee | 32 | 188 | 180 | 98 | 77 | 9 | 10 | 4.12 |
| Mahaffey, Philadelphia | 36 | 219 | 205 | 70 | 160 | 11 | 19 | 4.15 |
| Sanford, San Francisco | 38 | 217 | 201 | 87 | 112 | 13 | 9 | 4.23 |
| Loes, San Francisco | 26 | 115 | 114 | 39 | 53 | 6 | 5 | 4.23 |
| Hobbie, Chicago | 36 | 199 | 207 | 54 | 103 | 7 | 13 | 4.25 |
| Anderson, Chicago | 57 | 152 | 162 | 56 | 95 | 7 | 10 | 4.26 |
| Francis, Pittsburgh | 23 | 103 | 110 | 47 | 53 | 2 | 8 | 4.28 |
| Sullivan, Philadelphia | 49 | 159 | 161 | 53 | 114 | 3 | 16 | 4.30 |
| Maloney, Cincinnati | 27 | 95 | 86 | 59 | 57 | 6 | 7 | 4.36 |
| Owens, Philadelphia | 20 | 107 | 119 | 32 | 39 | 5 | 10 | 4.46 |
| Buzhardt, Philadelphia | 41 | 202 | 200 | 65 | 91 | 6 | 18 | 4.50 |
| Jones, San Francisco | 37 | 128 | 135 | 57 | 105 | 8 | 8 | 4.50 |
| McDaniel, St. Louis | 55 | 94 | 117 | 31 | 66 | 10 | 6 | 4.88 |
| Curtis, Chicago | 31 | 180 | 220 | 61 | 57 | 10 | 13 | 4.90 |
| Mizell, Pittsburgh | 25 | 100 | 120 | 32 | 35 | 7 | 10 | 5.04 |
| Farrell, Phil.-L. A. | 25 | 99 | 119 | 47 | 90 | 8 | 7 | 5.18 |
| Elston, Chicago | 68 | 93 | 108 | 44 | 69 | 6 | 7 | 5.61 |
| Roberts, Philadelphia | 26 | 117 | 154 | 23 | 54 | 1 | 10 | 5.85 |
| Short, Philadelphia | 39 | 127 | 157 | 71 | 77 | 6 | 12 | 5.95 |
| Craig, Los Angeles | 42 | 113 | 130 | 62 | 63 | 5 | 6 | 6.13 |

## 1961 Major League All-Star Games

Two major league All-Star games were played in 1961, and for the first time in 31 such contests, the second of these classics ended in a tie.

The first game, played in San Francisco on July 11, resulted in a 5-4 victory for the National League in ten innings. A single by Roberto Clemente drove across the winning run in a game marked by seven errors. Rain halted the second clash on July 31 in Boston. The teams were tied, 1-1, at the end of nine innings.

### First Game, at San Francisco, July 11

| | | | | | | | | | | | R | H | E |
|---|---|---|---|---|---|---|---|---|---|---|---|---|---|
| American... | 0 | 0 | 0 | 0 | 0 | 1 | 0 | 0 | 2 | 1— | 4 | 4 | 2 |
| National.... | 0 | 1 | 0 | 1 | 0 | 0 | 0 | 1 | 0 | 2— | 5 | 11 | 5 |

Batteries—Ford, Lary (4), Donovan (4), Bunning (6), Fornieles (8), Wilhelm (8) and Romano, Berra, Howard; Spahn, Purkey (4), McCormick (6), Face (9), Koufax (9), Miller (9) and Burgess. HR—Killebrew, Altman. WP—Miller. LP—Wilhelm. Time of game—2:53. Attendance—44,115. Net receipts—$259,230.81. Managers, AL—Paul Richards, NL—Danny Murtagh.

### Second Game, at Boston, July 31

| | | | | | | | | | R | H | E |
|---|---|---|---|---|---|---|---|---|---|---|---|
| National..... | 0 | 0 | 0 | 0 | 0 | 1 | 0 | 0— | 1 | 5 | 1 |
| American.... | 1 | 0 | 0 | 0 | 0 | 0 | 1 | 4 | 0 | | |

Game called, rain. Batteries—Purkey, Mahaffey (3), Koufax (5), Miller (7) and Burgess, Rossboro; Bunning, Schwall (4), Pascual (7) and Romano, Howard. HR—Colavito. Time of game—2:27. Attendance—31,851. Net receipts—$172,298.19. Managers, NL—Murtagh, AL—Richards.

## Spahn Hurls Lone No-Hitter

Warren Spahn of Milwaukee pitched the only no-hit game in the majors in 1961. The 40-year-old southpaw defeated the San Francisco Giants in Milwaukee on April 28, 1 to 0. Only two men reached base—both on walks—and both were eliminated by double plays.

On Aug. 11, Spahn achieved the 300th victory of his big league career, becoming the third lefthander ever to do so. He finished the season with a career total of 309 victories.

# 1961 WORLD SERIES

## New York Yankees (A.L.) defeated Cincinnati Reds (N.L.), 4 games to 1

### 1st Game—at New York, Wed., Oct. 4

**CINCINNATI (N)**

| | ab | r | h | rbi |
|---|---|---|---|---|
| Blasingame,2b | 3 | 0 | 0 | 0 |
| dLynch | 1 | 0 | 0 | 0 |
| Kasko, ss | 4 | 0 | 1 | 0 |
| Pinson, cf | 4 | 0 | 0 | 0 |
| Robinson, lf | 2 | 0 | 0 | 0 |
| Post, rf | 3 | 0 | 1 | 0 |
| Freese, 3b | 3 | 0 | 0 | 0 |
| Coleman, 1b | 2 | 0 | 0 | 0 |
| D. Johnson, c | 2 | 0 | 0 | 0 |
| aCardenas | 1 | 0 | 0 | 0 |
| Zimmerman,c | 0 | 0 | 0 | 0 |
| O'Toole, p | 2 | 0 | 0 | 0 |
| bGernert | 1 | 0 | 0 | 0 |
| Brosnan, p | 0 | 0 | 0 | 0 |
| Totals | 29 | 0 | 2 | 0 |

**NEW YORK (A)**

| | ab | r | h | rbi |
|---|---|---|---|---|
| Richardson,2b | 4 | 0 | 3 | 0 |
| Kubek, ss | 3 | 0 | 0 | 0 |
| Maris, cf, rf | 4 | 0 | 0 | 0 |
| Howard, c | 4 | 1 | 1 | 1 |
| Skowron, 1b | 3 | 1 | 1 | 1 |
| Berra, lf | 2 | 0 | 0 | 0 |
| Lopez, rf | 2 | 0 | 0 | 0 |
| cBlanchard | 1 | 0 | 0 | 0 |
| Reed, cf | 0 | 0 | 0 | 0 |
| Boyer, 3b | 3 | 0 | 1 | 0 |
| Ford, p | 3 | 0 | 0 | 0 |
| Totals | 29 | 2 | 6 | 2 |

aStruck out for D. Johnson in 8th inning. bGrounded out for O'Toole in 8th. cPopped out for Lopez in 8th. dPopped out for Blasingame in 9th.

| Cincinnati | 0 0 0 | 0 0 0 | 0 0 0—0 |
|---|---|---|---|
| New York | 0 0 0 | 1 0 1 | 0 0 x—2 |

E—None. HR—Howard, Skowron. DP—Johnson-Kasko-Coleman. LOB—Cincinnati 3, New York 8. BB, off—O'Toole 4 (Kubek, Skowron, Berra, Lopez). SO, by—O'Toole 2 (Maris, Skowron), Brosnan 1 (Skowron), Ford 6 (Blasingame 2, Robinson 2, O'Toole, Cardenas). H, off—O'Toole 6 in 7 innings, Brosnan 0 in 1, Ford 2 in 9. R & ER, off—O'Toole 2-2. WP—Ford. LP—O'Toole.

Umpires—Runge (A), plate; Conlan (N), 1b; Umont (A), 2b; Donatelli (N), 3b; Crawford (N), lf; Stewart (A), rf. Time—2:11. Paid attendance—62,397. Net receipts—$419,430.83.

### 2d Game—at New York, Thur., Oct. 5

**CINCINNATI (N)**

| | ab | r | h | rbi |
|---|---|---|---|---|
| Chacon, 2b | 4 | 1 | 1 | 0 |
| Kasko, ss | 5 | 0 | 1 | 0 |
| Pinson, cf | 5 | 0 | 1 | 0 |
| Robinson, lf | 4 | 2 | 0 | 0 |
| Coleman, 1b | 5 | 1 | 2 | 2 |
| Post, rf | 4 | 2 | 2 | 0 |
| Freese, 3b | 2 | 0 | 0 | 0 |
| Edwards, c | 4 | 0 | 2 | 2 |
| Jay, p | 4 | 0 | 0 | 0 |
| Totals | 37 | 6 | 9 | 4 |

**NEW YORK (A)**

| | ab | r | h | rbi |
|---|---|---|---|---|
| Richardson,2b | 4 | 0 | 1 | 0 |
| Kubek, ss | 4 | 0 | 1 | 0 |
| Maris, cf | 3 | 1 | 0 | 0 |
| Berra, lf | 4 | 1 | 2 | 2 |
| Blanchard, rf | 4 | 0 | 0 | 0 |
| Howard, c | 3 | 0 | 0 | 0 |
| Skowron, 1b | 3 | 0 | 0 | 0 |
| Boyer, 3b | 2 | 0 | 0 | 0 |
| Terry, p | 2 | 0 | 0 | 0 |
| aLopez | 0 | 0 | 0 | 0 |
| Arroyo, p | 0 | 0 | 0 | 0 |
| bGardner | 1 | 0 | 0 | 0 |
| Totals | 30 | 2 | 4 | 2 |

aWalked for Terry in 7th inning. bLined out for Arroyo in 9th.

| Cincinnati | 0 0 0 | 2 1 1 | 0 2 0—6 |
|---|---|---|---|
| New York | 0 0 0 | 2 0 0 | 0 0 0—2 |

E—Boyer, Arroyo, Berra. 2B—Post, Edwards, Pinson. HR—Coleman, Berra. DP—Chacon-Kasko-Coleman 2. LOB—Cincinnati 8, New York 7. BB, off—Jay 6 (Skowron, Maris, Howard, Boyer 2, Lopez), Terry 2 (Chacon, Freese), Arroyo 2 (Robinson, Freese). SO, by—Jay 6 (Kubek 2, Maris 2, Skowron 2), Terry 7 (Kasko 2, Freese, Post, Pinson, Coleman, Jay), Arroyo 1 (Jay). H, off—Jay 4 in 9 innings, Terry 6 in 7, Arroyo 3 in 2. R & ER, off—Jay 2-2, Terry 2-4, Arroyo 1-2. PB—Howard. WP—Jay. LP—Terry.

Umpires—Conlan (N), plate; Umont (A), 1b; Donatelli (N), 2b; Runge (A), 3b; Crawford (N), lf; Stewart (A), rf. Time—2:43. Paid attendance—63,083. Net receipts—$420,027.39.

### 3d Game—at Cincinnati, Sat., Oct. 7

**NEW YORK (A)**

| | ab | r | h | rbi |
|---|---|---|---|---|
| Richardson,2b | 4 | 0 | 1 | 0 |
| Kubek, ss | 4 | 1 | 1 | 0 |
| Maris, rf | 4 | 1 | 1 | 1 |
| Mantle, cf | 4 | 0 | 0 | 0 |
| Reed, cf | 0 | 0 | 0 | 0 |
| Berra, lf | 3 | 0 | 1 | 0 |
| Howard, c | 4 | 0 | 1 | 0 |
| Skowron, 1b | 3 | 0 | 0 | 0 |
| Boyer, 3b | 3 | 0 | 0 | 0 |
| Stafford, p | 2 | 0 | 0 | 0 |
| Daley, p | 0 | 0 | 0 | 0 |
| cBlanchard | 1 | 1 | 1 | 1 |
| Arroyo, p | 0 | 0 | 0 | 0 |
| Totals | 32 | 3 | 6 | 3 |

**CINCINNATI (N)**

| | ab | r | h | rbi |
|---|---|---|---|---|
| Chacon, 2b | 3 | 1 | 1 | 0 |
| aLynch | 0 | 0 | 0 | 0 |
| bBlasingame,2b | 0 | 0 | 0 | 0 |
| fBell | 1 | 0 | 0 | 0 |
| Kasko, ss | 4 | 0 | 2 | 1 |
| Pinson, cf | 4 | 0 | 1 | 0 |
| Robinson, rf | 4 | 0 | 1 | 1 |
| Coleman, 1b | 4 | 0 | 0 | 0 |
| Post, lf | 4 | 0 | 0 | 0 |
| Freese, 3b | 3 | 0 | 0 | 0 |
| Edwards, c | 3 | 1 | 1 | 0 |
| dCardenas | 1 | 0 | 1 | 0 |
| Purkey, p | 3 | 0 | 0 | 0 |
| eGernert | 1 | 0 | 0 | 0 |
| Totals | 35 | 2 | 8 | 2 |

aDrew intentional walk for Chacon in 7th inning. bRan for Lynch in 7th. cHit homer for Daley in 8th. dDoubled for Edwards in 9th. eGrounded out for Purkey in 9th. fGrounded out for Blasingame in 9th.

| New York | 0 0 0 | 0 0 0 | 1 1 1—3 |
|---|---|---|---|
| Cincinnati | 0 0 1 | 0 0 1 | 0 0 0—2 |

E—Stafford. 2B—Robinson, Howard, Edwards, Cardenas. HR—Blanchard, Maris. SB—Richardson. LOB—New York 3, Cincinnati 8. BB, off—Purkey 1 (Berra), Stafford 2 (Freese, Lynch). SO, by—Purkey 3 (Berra, Mantle 2), Stafford 5 (Chacon, Robinson, Purkey 3), Arroyo 2 (Robinson, Freese). H, off—Purkey 6 in 9 innings, Stafford 7 in 6 2/3, Daley 0 in 1/3, Arroyo 1 in 2. R & ER, off—Purkey 2-3, Stafford 2-2. WP—Arroyo. LP—Purkey.

Umpires—Umont (A), plate; Donatelli (N), 1b; Runge (A), 2b; Conlan (N), 3b; Crawford (N), lf; Stewart (A), rf. Time—2:15. Paid attendance—32,589. Net receipts—$213,533.91.

### 4th Game—at Cincinnati, Sun., Oct. 8

**NEW YORK (A)**

| | ab | r | h | rbi |
|---|---|---|---|---|
| Richardson,2b | 5 | 1 | 3 | 0 |
| Kubek, ss | 5 | 0 | 1 | 0 |
| Maris, rf, cf | 3 | 2 | 0 | 0 |
| Mantle, cf | 2 | 0 | 1 | 0 |
| aLopez, rf | 3 | 1 | 1 | 2 |
| Howard, c | 4 | 1 | 1 | 0 |
| Berra, lf | 2 | 1 | 0 | 0 |
| Skowron, 1b | 3 | 0 | 3 | 1 |
| Boyer, 3b | 4 | 0 | 1 | 2 |
| Ford, p | 2 | 0 | 0 | 0 |
| Coates, p | 1 | 0 | 0 | 0 |
| Totals | 34 | 7 | 11 | 6 |

**CINCINNATI (N)**

| | ab | r | h | rbi |
|---|---|---|---|---|
| Chacon, 2b | 4 | 0 | 1 | 0 |
| Kasko, ss | 4 | 0 | 1 | 0 |
| Pinson, cf | 4 | 0 | 0 | 0 |
| Robinson, rf | 4 | 0 | 1 | 0 |
| Post, lf | 4 | 0 | 1 | 0 |
| Freese, 3b | 4 | 0 | 0 | 0 |
| Coleman, 1b | 4 | 0 | 0 | 0 |
| D. Johnson, c | 2 | 0 | 2 | 0 |
| cBell | 1 | 0 | 0 | 0 |
| Zimmerman,c | 0 | 0 | 0 | 0 |
| O'Toole, p | 1 | 0 | 0 | 0 |
| bGernert | 1 | 0 | 0 | 0 |
| Brosnan, p | 0 | 0 | 0 | 0 |
| dLynch | 1 | 0 | 0 | 0 |
| Henry, p | 0 | 0 | 0 | 0 |
| Totals | 31 | 0 | 5 | 0 |

aRan for Mantle in 4th inning. bHit into force play for O'Toole in 5th. dGrounded out for D. Johnson in 7th. dStruck out for Brosnan in 8th.

| New York | 0 0 0 | 1 1 2 | 3 0 0—7 |
|---|---|---|---|
| Cincinnati | 0 0 0 | 0 0 0 | 0 0 0—0 |

E—Pinson. 2B—Richardson, Howard, Boyer. DP—Kasko-Chacon-Coleman, Kubek-Richardson-Skowron, Freese-Chacon-Coleman, Coleman (unassisted). LOB—New York 6, Cincinnati 7. BB, off—O'Toole 3 (Skowron, Maris, Ford), Brosnan 3 (Berra 2, Maris), Coates 1 (Robinson). Struck out, by—O'Toole 2 (Kubek, Howard), Brosnan 3 (Lopez, Howard, Coates), Henry 2 (Kubek, Maris), Ford 1 (Chacon), Coates 2 (Lynch, Freese). H, off—O'Toole 5 in 5 innings, Brosnan 6 in 3, Henry 0 in 1, Ford 4 in 5 (faced 1 batter in 6th), Coates 1 in 4. R & ER, off—O'Toole 2-2, Brosnan 5-5. HP, by Ford 1 (Robinson), Coates 1 (Robinson). Wild pitch—Brosnan. WP—Ford. LP—O'Toole.

Umpires—Donatelli (N), plate; Runge (A), 1b; Conlan (N), 2b; Umont (A), 3b; Crawford (N), lf; Stewart (A), rf. Time—2:27. Paid attendance—32,589. Net receipts—$213,533.91.

## Ford Erases Ruth Pitching Mark

A pitching record for consecutive scoreless innings in World Series play, established by Babe Ruth, was shattered by Whitey Ford of the New York Yankees in 1961. Ruth, then with the Boston Red Sox, pitched 29⅔ innings of scoreless baseball in the 1916 and 1918 series. Ford reached 32 scoreless innings before retiring after five innings of the fourth game with Cincinnati on Oct. 8, 1961. His streak included two games in 1960 and the first game in 1961.

## 5th Game—at Cincinnati, Mon., Oct. 9

| NEW YORK (A) | ab | r | h | rbi |  | CINCINNATI (N) | ab | r | h | rbi |
|---|---|---|---|---|---|---|---|---|---|---|
| Richardson,2b | 6 | 1 | 1 | 0 |  | Blasingame,2b | 4 | 1 | 1 | 0 |
| Kubek, ss | 6 | 2 | 2 | 0 |  | eChacon | 1 | 0 | 0 | 0 |
| Maris, cf, rf | 5 | 0 | 1 | 1 |  | Kasko, ss | 5 | 1 | 2 | 0 |
| Blanchard, rf | 4 | 3 | 3 | 2 |  | Pinson, cf | 5 | 0 | 1 | 0 |
| Reed, cf | 0 | 0 | 0 | 0 |  | Robinson, rf | 4 | 1 | 2 | 3 |
| Howard, c | 5 | 3 | 2 | 0 |  | Coleman, 1b | 4 | 1 | 1 | 0 |
| Skowron, 1b | 5 | 2 | 2 | 3 |  | Post, lf | 3 | 1 | 2 | 2 |
| Lopez, lf | 4 | 2 | 2 | 5 |  | Freese, 3b | 4 | 0 | 1 | 0 |
| Boyer, 3b | 3 | 0 | 2 | 1 |  | Edwards, c | 4 | 0 | 1 | 0 |
| Terry, p | 1 | 0 | 0 | 0 |  | Jay, p | 0 | 0 | 0 | 0 |
| Daley, p | 1 | 0 | 0 | 1 |  | Maloney, p | 0 | 0 | 0 | 0 |
|  |  |  |  |  |  | K. Johnson, p | 0 | 0 | 0 | 0 |
| Totals | 40 | 13 | 15 | 13 |  | aBell | 1 | 0 | 0 | 0 |
|  |  |  |  |  |  | Henry, p | 0 | 0 | 0 | 0 |
|  |  |  |  |  |  | Jones, p | 0 | 0 | 0 | 0 |
|  |  |  |  |  |  | bGernert | 1 | 0 | 0 | 0 |
|  |  |  |  |  |  | Purkey, p | 0 | 0 | 0 | 0 |
|  |  |  |  |  |  | cCardenas | 1 | 0 | 0 | 0 |
|  |  |  |  |  |  | Brosnan, p | 0 | 0 | 0 | 0 |
|  |  |  |  |  |  | dLynch | 1 | 0 | 0 | 0 |
|  |  |  |  |  |  | Hunt, p | 0 | 0 | 0 | 0 |
|  |  |  |  |  |  | Totals | 38 | 5 | 11 | 5 |

aFouled out for K. Johnson in 2d inning. bCalled out on strikes for Jones in 4th. cFlied out for Purkey in 6th. dGrounded out for Brosnan in 8th. eGrounded out for Blasingame in 9th.

| | | | | | | | | |
|---|---|---|---|---|---|---|---|---|
| New York | 5 1 0 | 5 0 2 | 0 0 0—13 |
| Cincinnati | 0 0 3 | 0 2 0 | 0 0 0— 5 |

E—Coleman, Daley, Kasko, Purkey. 2B—Howard, Boyer, Maris, Freese, Blanchard, Robinson. 3B—Lopez. HR—Blanchard, Robinson, Lopez, Post. S—Terry, Lopez, Daley. SF—Daley. LOB—New York 10, Cincinnati 7. BB, off—Maloney 1 (Blanchard), Henry 2 (Boyer, Howard), Purkey 2 (Blanchard, Boyer), Hunt 1 (Maris). SO, by—Maloney 1 (Terry), Henry 1 (Lopez), Purkey 2 (Maris, Skowron), Brosnan 1 (Maris), Hunt 1 (Howard), Daley 3 (Gernert, Freese, Blasingame). H, off—Jay 4 in 2/3 innings, Maloney 4 in 2/3, K. Johnson 0 in 2/3, Henry 4 in 1 1/3, Jones 0 in 2/3, Purkey 0 in 2/3, Brosnan 3 in 2, Hunt 0 in 1, Terry 6 in 2 1/3, Daley 5 in 6 2/3. R & ER, off—Jay 4-4, Maloney 2-2, Henry 5-5, Purkey 2-0, Terry 3-3, Daley 2-0. HP, by—Daley 1 (Post). Wild pitch—Brosnan. WP—Daley. LP—Jay. Umpires—Runge (A), plate; Conlan (N), 1b; Umont (A), 2b; Donatelli (N), 3b; Crawford (N), lf; Stewart (A), rf. Time—3:05. Paid attendance—32,589. Net receipts—$213,533.91.

## World Series Batting Records

### CINCINNATI

| | g | ab | r | h | 2b | 3b | hr | rbi | bb | so | avg |
|---|---|---|---|---|---|---|---|---|---|---|---|
| *Chacon, 2b | 4 | 12 | 2 | 3 | 0 | 0 | 0 | 0 | 1 | 2 | .250 |
| *Lynch | 4 | 3 | 0 | 0 | 0 | 0 | 0 | 0 | 1 | 1 | .000 |
| †Blasingame, 2b | 3 | 7 | 1 | 1 | 0 | 0 | 0 | 0 | 0 | 3 | .143 |
| *Bell | 3 | 3 | 0 | 0 | 0 | 0 | 0 | 0 | 0 | 0 | .000 |
| Kasko, ss | 5 | 22 | 1 | 7 | 0 | 0 | 0 | 1 | 0 | 2 | .318 |
| Pinson, cf | 5 | 22 | 0 | 2 | 1 | 0 | 0 | 0 | 0 | 3 | .091 |
| Robinson, lf, rf | 5 | 15 | 3 | 3 | 2 | 0 | 1 | 4 | 3 | 4 | .200 |
| Post, rf, lf | 5 | 18 | 3 | 6 | 1 | 0 | 1 | 2 | 0 | 1 | .333 |
| Freese, 3b | 5 | 16 | 0 | 1 | 1 | 0 | 0 | 3 | 4 | .063 |
| Coleman, 1b | 5 | 20 | 2 | 5 | 0 | 0 | 1 | 2 | 0 | 1 | .250 |
| D. Johnson, c | 2 | 4 | 0 | 2 | 0 | 0 | 0 | 0 | 0 | 0 | .500 |
| *Cardenas | 3 | 3 | 0 | 1 | 1 | 0 | 0 | 0 | 0 | 1 | .333 |
| Zimmerman, c | 2 | 0 | 0 | 0 | 0 | 0 | 0 | 0 | 0 | 0 | .000 |
| Edwards, c | 3 | 11 | 1 | 4 | 2 | 0 | 0 | 2 | 0 | 0 | .364 |
| O'Toole, p | 2 | 3 | 0 | 0 | 0 | 0 | 0 | 0 | 0 | 1 | .000 |
| *Gernert | 4 | 4 | 0 | 0 | 0 | 0 | 0 | 0 | 0 | 1 | .000 |
| Brosnan, p | 3 | 2 | 0 | 0 | 0 | 0 | 0 | 0 | 0 | 1 | .000 |
| Jay, p | 2 | 4 | 0 | 0 | 0 | 0 | 0 | 0 | 0 | 2 | .000 |
| Purkey, p | 2 | 3 | 0 | 0 | 0 | 0 | 0 | 0 | 0 | 3 | .000 |
| Henry, p | 2 | 0 | 0 | 0 | 0 | 0 | 0 | 0 | 0 | 0 | .000 |
| Maloney, p | 1 | 0 | 0 | 0 | 0 | 0 | 0 | 0 | 0 | 0 | .000 |
| K. Johnson, p | 1 | 0 | 0 | 0 | 0 | 0 | 0 | 0 | 0 | 0 | .000 |
| Jones, p | 1 | 0 | 0 | 0 | 0 | 0 | 0 | 0 | 0 | 0 | .000 |
| Hunt, p | 1 | 0 | 0 | 0 | 0 | 0 | 0 | 0 | 0 | 0 | .000 |
| Totals | 5 | 170 | 13 | 35 | 8 | 0 | 3 | 11 | 8 | 27 | .206 |

### NEW YORK

| | g | ab | r | h | 2b | 3b | hr | rbi | bb | so | avg |
|---|---|---|---|---|---|---|---|---|---|---|---|
| Richardson, 2b | 5 | 23 | 2 | 9 | 1 | 0 | 0 | 0 | 0 | 3 | .391 |
| Kubek, ss | 5 | 22 | 3 | 5 | 0 | 0 | 1 | 1 | 4 | .227 |
| Maris, cf, rf | 5 | 19 | 4 | 2 | 1 | 0 | 1 | 2 | 4 | 6 | .105 |
| Mantle, cf | 2 | 6 | 0 | 1 | 0 | 0 | 0 | 0 | 0 | 2 | .167 |
| Howard, c | 5 | 20 | 5 | 5 | 3 | 0 | 1 | 1 | 2 | .250 |
| Skowron, 1b | 5 | 17 | 3 | 6 | 0 | 1 | 5 | 3 | 4 | .353 |
| Berra, lf | 4 | 11 | 2 | 3 | 0 | 1 | 3 | 5 | 1 | .273 |
| †Lopez, rf, lf | 4 | 9 | 3 | 3 | 0 | 1 | 1 | 7 | 2 | 3 | .333 |
| *Blanchard, rf | 4 | 10 | 4 | 4 | 1 | 0 | 2 | 3 | 2 | 0 | .400 |
| Reed, cf | 4 | 0 | 0 | 0 | 0 | 0 | 0 | 0 | 0 | 0 | .000 |
| Boyer, 3b | 5 | 15 | 0 | 4 | 2 | 0 | 0 | 3 | 4 | 0 | .267 |
| Ford, p | 2 | 5 | 1 | 0 | 0 | 0 | 0 | 0 | 0 | 0 | .000 |
| Terry, p | 2 | 3 | 0 | 0 | 0 | 0 | 0 | 0 | 0 | 1 | .000 |
| Arroyo, p | 2 | 0 | 0 | 0 | 0 | 0 | 0 | 0 | 0 | 0 | .000 |
| *Gardner | 1 | 1 | 0 | 0 | 0 | 0 | 0 | 0 | 0 | 0 | .000 |
| Stafford, p | 1 | 2 | 0 | 0 | 0 | 0 | 0 | 0 | 0 | 0 | .000 |
| Daley, p | 1 | 1 | 0 | 0 | 0 | 0 | 0 | 1 | 0 | 0 | .000 |
| Coates, p | 1 | 1 | 0 | 0 | 0 | 0 | 0 | 0 | 0 | 1 | .000 |
| Totals | 5 | 165 | 27 | 42 | 8 | 1 | 7 | 26 | 24 | 25 | .255 |

\* Pinch hitter.  † Pinch runner.

# GYMNASTICS

## National A. A. U. Championships
### (At Dallas)

| | |
|---|---|
| All-around—Nobuyuki Aihara, Japan | 114.85 |
| Floor exercises—Nobuyuki Aihara, Japan | 19.600 |
| Long horse—Takashi Mitsukuri, Japan | 19.275 |
| Side horse—Shuji Tsurumi, Japan | 19.275 |
| Parallel bars—Nobuyuki Aihara, Japan | 19.425 |
| Horizontal bar—Takashi Mitsukuri, Japan | 19.600 |
| Still rings—Nobuyuki Aihara, Japan | 19.600 |
| Tumbling—Harold Holmes, Urbana, Ill. | 19.300 |
| Rebound Tumbling—Tom Osterland, Ann Arbor, Mich. | 18.900 |
| Flying rings—Tom Darling, East Lansing, Mich. | 18.550 |
| Rope climb—Robert Winter, Tarrytown (N. Y.) Spiked Shoe Club | 3.9 sec. |
| Team—Southern Illinois Salukis | 43⅓ pts. |

### WOMEN

| | |
|---|---|
| All-around—Kazuko Kadowaki, Japan | 73.866 |
| Floor exercises—Muriel Grossfeld, Indianapolis | 19.034 |
| Side horse vault—Kazuko Kadowaki, Japan | 18.599 |
| Balance beam—Kazuko Kadowaki, Japan | 18.833 |
| Uneven parallel bars—Doris Fuchs, Rochester, N. Y. | 19.217 |
| Tumbling—Barbara Galleher, Dallas A. C. | 18.850 |
| Rebound tumbling—Barbara Galleher, Dallas A. C. | 18.850 |

### National Collegiate A. A.
#### (At Champaign, Ill.)

All-around—Greg Weiss, Penn State
Free exercises—Bob Lynn, Southern California
Rope climb—Paul Davis, California
Side Horse—Jim Fairchild, California
Horizontal bar—Bruce Klaus, Southern Illinois
Rebound tumbling—Tom Gompf, Ohio State
Parallel bars—Jeff Cardinelli, Springfield, Mass., and Fred Tijirina, Southern Illinois
Flying rings—Frank Snay, Navy
Still rings—Fred Orlofsky, Southern Illinois
Tumbling—Jack Ryder, Florida State
Team—Penn State (88½ pts.)

# LAWN BOWLING

*Source:* W. G. (Bill) Hay, Honorary President, American Lawn Bowling Association.

## National Open Championships

Singles—R. L. Fullerton, Canada
Doubles—J. H. Davis-Charles Brereton, Canada
Rinks—Hugh McGuigan-William Deakin-James Law-J. S. Muir, Canada

## Champion of Champions Tournament

Singles—James Candelet, Pawtucket, R. I.
Doubles—George Dunn-Albert Presutti, Niagara Falls, N. Y.

# HORSESHOE PITCHING
## Major Champions

World—Harold Reno, Sabina, Ohio
National A. A. U.—Roger Ehlers, St. Charles, Ill.
National A. A. U. doubles—Roger Ehlers, St. Charles, Ill.-Jack Stout, Melrose Park, Ill.

# MINOR LEAGUE BASEBALL

## JUNIOR WORLD SERIES

Buffalo (International League) defeated Louisville (American Association), 4 games to 0

## PAN-AMERICAN ASSN. PLAYOFFS

San Antonio (Texas League) defeated Vera Cruz (Mexican League), 4 games to 2

## CLASS AAA

### American Association

#### FINAL STANDING OF THE CLUBS

|              | W  | L  | Pct. |            | W  | L  | Pct. |
|--------------|----|----|------|------------|----|----|------|
| Indianapolis | 86 | 64 | .773 | Houston    | 73 | 77 | .487 |
| Louisville   | 80 | 70 | .533 | Dallas-Ft. W. | 72 | 77 | .483 |
| Denver       | 75 | 73 | .507 | Omaha      | 62 | 87 | .416 |

#### THE LEADERS

| | |
|---|---|
| BA—Don Wert, Denver | .328 |
| HR—Cliff Cook, Indianapolis | 32 |
| RBI—Cliff Cook, Indianapolis | 119 |
| Pitching, victories—Don Rudolph, Indianapolis | 18 |
| Pitching, ERA—Federico Olivo, Louisville | 2.66 |
| Pitching, strikeouts—Charlie Spell, Omaha | 164 |

#### FINAL PLAYOFFS

Louisville defeated Houston, 4 games to 2

### International League

#### FINAL STANDING OF THE CLUBS

|            | W  | L  | Pct. |             | W  | L  | Pct. |
|------------|----|----|------|-------------|----|----|------|
| Columbus   | 92 | 62 | .597 | Toronto     | 76 | 79 | .490 |
| Charleston | 88 | 66 | .571 | Richmond    | 71 | 83 | .461 |
| Buffalo    | 85 | 67 | .559 | Jersey City | 70 | 82 | .461 |
| Rochester  | 77 | 78 | .497 | Syracuse    | 56 | 98 | .364 |

#### THE LEADERS

| | |
|---|---|
| BA—Ted Savage, Buffalo | .325 |
| HR—John Powell, Rochester | 32 |
| RBI—Frank Leja, Syracuse | 98 |
| Pitching, victories—Ray Washburn, Charleston | 16 |
| Pitching, ERA—Ray Washburn, Charleston | 2.31 |
| Pitching, strikeouts—Bobby Veale, Columbus | 210 |

#### FINAL PLAYOFFS

Buffalo defeated Rochester, 4 games to 1

### Pacific Coast League

#### FINAL STANDING OF THE CLUBS

|            | W  | L  | Pct. |                | W  | L  | Pct. |
|------------|----|----|------|----------------|----|----|------|
| Tacoma     | 97 | 57 | .630 | Portland       | 71 | 83 | .461 |
| Vancouver  | 87 | 67 | .565 | Hawaii         | 68 | 86 | .442 |
| Seattle    | 86 | 68 | .558 | Spokane        | 68 | 86 | .442 |
| San Diego  | 72 | 82 | .468 | Salt Lake City | 67 | 87 | .435 |

#### THE LEADERS

| | |
|---|---|
| BA—Carlos Bernier, Hawaii | .351 |
| HR—Gene Oliver, Portland | 36 |
| RBI—Harry Simpson, San Diego | 105 |
| Pitching, victories—Gaylord Perry, Tacoma, and Ron Herbel, Tacoma | 16 |
| Pitching, ERA—Ron Piche, Vancouver | 2.26 |
| Pitching, strikeouts—Sam McDowell, Salt Lake City | 156 |

## CLASS AA

| League and champion | Playoff winner |
|---|---|
| Mexican—Vera Cruz | No playoffs |
| Southern Assn.—Chattanooga | No playoffs |
| Texas—Amarillo | San Antonio |

## CLASS A

| League and champion | Playoff winner |
|---|---|
| Eastern—Springfield | No playoffs |
| South Atlantic—Asheville | No playoffs |

### CLASS B

| | |
|---|---|
| Carolina—Wilson (both halves) | No playoffs |
| Northwest—Lewiston (1st half), Yakima (2d half) | Lewiston |
| Three-I—Topeka | No playoffs |

### CLASS C

| | |
|---|---|
| California—Reno (both halves) | No playoffs |
| Mexican Center—Aquascalientes | No playoffs |
| Northern—Duluth-Superior | Aberdeen |
| Pioneer—Boise (1st half), Great Falls (2d half) | Great Falls |

### CLASS D

| | |
|---|---|
| Alabama-Florida—Selma (both halves) | No playoffs |
| Appalachian—Middlesboro | No playoffs |
| Florida State—Tampa (1st half), Sarasota (2d half) | Tampa |
| Midwest—Waterloo (1st half), Quincy (2d half) | Quincy |
| New York-Penn—Geneva | Olean |
| Sophomore—Hobbs (1st half), Albuquerque (2d half) | Hobbs |
| Western Carolina—Statesville (1st half), Salisbury (2d half) | Shelby |

### Other Baseball Champions

National Baseball Congress—Ponchatoula (La.) Athletics
National Collegiate A. A.—Southern California
National Junior College—Wilmington, N. C.
American Legion Junior—Luke-Greenway Post, Phoenix, Ariz.
Little League—El Cajon, Calif.
Little League, Senior Div.—Natrona Heights, Pa.
Hearst Sandlot Classic—New York City Stars
Babe Ruth League—San Carlos, Calif.
Connie Mack World Series—Culver City, Calif.
All-America Amateur Assn., Limited Div.—New Orleans
Pony League World Series—Hamtramck, Mich.
Colt League—Joliet, Ill.
V.F.W. Teeners—Gastonia, N. C.
National Amateur Federation, Junior—Detroit

# SOFTBALL

## World Champions

(Amateur Softball Association)

Men—Aurora (Ill.) Sealmasters
Women—Whittier (Calif.) Gold Sox
Men's slow pitch—Hamilton Tailors, Cincinnati
Women's slow pitch—Dairy Cottage, Covington, Ky.

# CHESS

*Source: American Chess Bulletin, New York.*

## World Champions

Men—Mikhail Botvinnik, U.S.S.R.
Women—Elizabeth Bykova, U.S.S.R.
Junior—Bruno Parma, Yugoslavia
Students team—U.S.S.R.

## United States Champions

Men—Bobby Fischer, Brooklyn
Women—Lisa Lane, New York
Open—Pal Benko, New York
Open speed—Robert Byrne, Indianapolis
Amateur—Edgar T. McCormick, East Orange, N. J.
Junior—Robin Ault, Cranford, N. J.

# INDEX

We have endeavored to prepare the INDEX for easy use by professional researchers and the average Mr. and Mrs. Public. This goal presents many difficulties and we honestly hope we have succeeded. Where we have failed we would appreciate your help. If you cannot find anything quickly and you think it's our fault, kindly send suggestions and criticisms to:

THE INFORMATION PLEASE ALMANAC
444 Madison Avenue
New York 22, N. Y.

## CONTINUATION OF ADDENDA FROM PAGE 7

## UNITED NATIONS (page 608)

The 16th General Assembly continued to admit new members. Sierra Leone was admitted as the 100th member on Sept. 27, and the total membership reached 101 after the dissolution of the United Arab Republic. Syria and Egypt are now individual members of the U.N. Syria was restored to full membership on Oct. 13; the 4-man delegation is headed by Ambassador Farid Chachloui.

An effort has been made to persuade Nationalist China not to veto the application of Outer Mongolia for U.N. membership. If Nationalist China does not veto Outer Mongolia's application, it is likely that Mauritania will be admitted, which will increase the membership to 103.

## U.S.S.R. (page 763)

On Oct. 17, 4,799 delegates representing 9,716,000 Communists filed into a new marble palace for the 22nd Communist Party Congress, the first regular such gathering since February, 1956. They heard Premier Nikita Khrushchev on foreign policy and on domestic economic goals.

In the foreign policy field, he announced that the U.S.S.R. would detonate a 50-megaton bomb, equal to 50 million tons of TNT, on Oct. 31. He made no changes in his demands on West Berlin and an East German peace treaty, although he did say he would not insist on signing the treaty before the end of the year "if the Western powers show readiness to settle the German problem." He praised Cuba and castigated the Communist leaders of Albania and Yugoslavia.

For the Russians themselves, Mr. Khrushchev promised them by 1980: rent-free modern housing, the world's shortest working day, longer paid vacations and expanded free medical care. As far as production was concerned, he boasted that by 1980 the U.S.S.R. would be the world's greatest industrial power with steel production at an annual level of 250 million tons (currently 65 million tons) and agricultural production multiplied three and one-half times.

## WEATHER AND CLIMATE (page 203)

Hurricane Carla hit the Texas and Louisiana coasts on Sept. 11–12, 1962. The land station with the highest recorded wind speed was Port Lavaca, Tex. —173 mph. The hurricane devastated Texas and Louisiana Gulf Coast cities from Corpus Christi, Tex., to Cameron, La., with 15-foot tides and 15 inches of rain. The slow movement of the storm and adequate warnings prevented much loss of life.

Deaths from Hurricane Carla totaled 40. The damage caused by the storm was estimated at $200 million.

(Continued on next page)

## SPACE AGE NEWS (page 52)

The United States drew bitter criticism from leading astronomers in this country and England for sending into orbit (Oct. 21) a *Midas* satellite designed to release a band of 350 million tiny copper needles around the world, 2,000 miles up. The scientists feared examination of the Universe would be hampered by the needle cloud. The United States hoped the aerial copper band would form a reflector for greatly improved world radio communication. The needle experiment had no direct connection with project *Midas*. This satellite was used because it had the available space to carry the needles and was capable of going into the orbit necessary for the experiment.

## GERMAN FEDERAL REPUBLIC (page 700)

Chancellor Konrad Adenauer of West Germany agreed to resign in the summer of 1963 if the Parliament now renews his term as Chancellor. This was part of the price he paid for a tentative agreement with the Free Democratic Party (Oct. 22) to participate in a coalition government. The Free Democrats also demanded the dismissal of Heinrich von Brentano as Foreign Minister, charging that he is too pliant to the wishes of the Western powers.

**October 23**—The Soviet Union was reported to have conducted the 22nd and 23rd nuclear explosions. One was the largest man-made explosion in history—a force equal to about 30 million tons or more of TNT. The other explosion was beneath the water—the first Soviet underwater explosion to be announced.

**October 23**—There was an indication of a possible rift between Premier Chou En-lai and Premier Khrushchev over Soviet denunciations of Albania. Speculation of the rift was heightened when Premier Chou left Moscow unexpectedly (for Peiping?) where he was attending the 22nd Congress of the Soviet Communist Party.

**October 23**—The Nobel Peace Prize for 1960 was awarded to Zulu Chief Albert Luthuli of South Africa, foe of the apartheid, now living in exile.

Address all Correspondence to
INFORMATION PLEASE ALMANAC
*444 Madison Ave., New York 22, N. Y.*

## DATE DUE

|  |  |  |  |
|--|--|--|--|
|  |  |  |  |
|  |  |  |  |
|  |  |  |  |
|  |  |  |  |
|  |  |  |  |
|  |  |  |  |
|  |  |  |  |
|  |  |  |  |
|  |  |  |  |
|  |  |  |  |
|  |  |  |  |
|  |  |  |  |
|  |  |  |  |
|  |  |  |  |
|  |  |  |  |
|  |  |  |  |

GAYLORD      PRINTED IN U.S.A.